GUIDE TO THE MANUSCRIPT COLLECTIONS

in the

DUKE UNIVERSITY LIBRARY

# Guide to the Cataloged Collections
in the
# Manuscript Department of the William R. Perkins Library
# Duke University

Editors:
Richard C. Davis
Linda Angle Miller

Associate Editors:
Harry W. McKown, Jr.
Erma Paden Whittington

Clio Books
Santa Barbara, California
Oxford, England

Copyright © 1980 by Duke University

All rights reserved including the right to reproduce in whole or in part without the written permission of the publishers.

Both research and publication of this guide have been assisted by grants from the National Endowment for the Humanities.

**Library of Congress Cataloging in Publication Data**

Duke University, Durham, N.C. Library.
   Guide to the manuscript collections in the Duke University Library.

   Includes index.
   1. Manuscripts--North Carolina--Durham--Catalogs.
2. Duke University, Durham, N.C. Library--Catalogs.
I. Davis, Richard C., 1939-   II. Miller, Linda Angle.   III. Title.
Z6621.D87D84   1980      016.091'09756563     79-28688
ISBN 0-87436-299-7

American Bibliographical Center--Clio Press
2040 Alameda Padre Serra, Box 4397
Santa Barbara, California 93103

Clio Press, Ltd.
Woodside House, Hinksey Hill
Oxford OX1, 5BE, England

Manufactured in the United States of America

*To
Dr. Mattie U. Russell,
Curator of Manuscripts,
for her dedication and service to
Duke University
since 1948*

TABLE OF CONTENTS

|  | Page Number |
|---|---|
| Introduction | ix |
| COLLECTIONS | 1 |
| INDEX | 651 |

# Introduction

Since 1894, with the assistance of the Trinity College Historical Society and the George Washington Flowers Fund, the libraries of Duke University and its predecessor, Trinity College, have collected manuscripts of historical interest. The first guide to these manuscripts was compiled during the period 1939-1943 with the assistance of the Historical Records Survey. Published in 1947 by Duke University Press, this <u>Guide to the Manuscript Collections in the Duke University Library</u>, prepared by Nannie M. Tilley and Noma Lee Goodwin, described 1,896 collections of two or more items each. Cataloged manuscripts then totaled 1,000,000 items and 3,000 volumes. During the next three decades the cataloged holdings of the Manuscript Department increased more than 450 percent and at the present time exceed 4,500,000 items and 15,200 volumes. Described herein are 6,000 collections ranging in size from one to 442,000 items and extending in time from the fourteenth century to the present.

The essential character of the holdings of the Manuscript Department has not changed since the first catalog was published in 1947. The George Washington Flowers Fund continues to be the most important contributor of new collections, and the southeastern United States is still the focus of the holdings. Collections date mostly from the later 1700s and the nineteenth century, but the proportion of sources for the twentieth century has increased. Holdings are especially strong in such fields as the antebellum South, the Civil War and Reconstruction, Afro-American history, slavery and the abolition movement in the United States, religion, education, politics, social history, business and economic history, labor and socialism in the United States, and Southern literature. In addition, a concerted effort was made to collect manuscripts on the history of Great Britain and the British Empire, an endeavor begun by the late Professor William B. Hamilton and now supported by the Hamilton Fund. British manuscripts exceed 50,000 items and greatly enhance the international scope of the source material.

This guide describes only the cataloged holdings of the Manuscript Department of Perkins Library. Other manuscripts at Duke University are found in the Rare Book Room of Perkins Library, the Duke University Archives, and in the Medical Center Library's Josiah Trent Collection of the History of Medicine. Many of the descriptions in the Tilley-Goodwin guide have been revised; some have been entirely rewritten. In other cases, the sketches appearing in this guide are unchanged from those in the old one. Some 985 of the larger collections are listed in the National Union Catalog of Manuscript Collections, but in almost every case, these collections are described more thoroughly in the present volume.

Microfilm of material held elsewhere is not included in this guide. Only that microfilm supplemental to manuscript collections at Duke is noted. Photocopies on paper are described as other manuscripts and noted as copies.

Manuscripts at Duke are cataloged under a system devised in the early years of the department and continued with modifications to the present time. There are four principal alphabetical card files: the main entry file, the autograph file, the subject file, and the geographical file. The main entry file consists of a title card for each collection, followed by a detailed sketch of the contents. In the case of some of the larger collections, the sketch on cards has been abandoned in favor of inventories in booklet form. The autograph file lists all letters and other manuscripts written or signed by persons prominent enough to be identified in standard biographical reference works. The subject file records references to notable persons, organizations, institutions, events, places, topics, and objects mentioned in significant detail in the collections. The geographical file lists all collections according to their principal place of interest, usually giving one location for each collection.

This guide, compiled between September, 1977, and November, 1979, is based on the main entry file. The form of titles and the sequence of entries follow the forms and the sequence established in that file. As in the Tilley-Goodwin volume, whenever the inclusive dates of a collection might be misleading, the dates of the period covered by the bulk of the manuscripts are given in parenthesis. The user should also be aware that the place names given in title lines represent the residences or other localities with which the subject of the collection is particularly identified, and not necessarily the geographical focus of the material in the collection. Limitations of various types apply to the use of some materials. Such collections are described as "restricted." Information on the nature of specific restrictions may be obtained from the Curator of Manuscripts.

The Index provides access to the descriptions in the guide. The user will find pertinent collections identified in the index under specific subject headings and under names of towns, cities, counties, states, countries, and other broad geographical regions. Subject headings are subdivided geographically and place entries are subdivided by subject. Thus a collection pertaining to agriculture in North Carolina is found in the index under "AGRICULTURE--North Carolina" and also under "NORTH CAROLINA--Agriculture." Where it was not practical to make such subdivisions, cross-references were made from place to subject. Under "SOUTH CAROLINA--Civil War," for example, there is a cross-reference to see "CIVIL WAR--South Carolina." The index includes all personal names mentioned in the descriptive entries in the body of the guide. There are numerous cross-references between related subjects. One should note that the index is based on the descriptions written for the guide and cannot match in thoroughness and detail the subject, name, and geographical card files in the Manuscript Department. Consequently, the researcher should also consult the card catalog or inquire about its contents.

Two grants from the National Endowment for the Humanities supported the compilation of this guide and its publication. A substantial grant for the continuation of the editorial function was received from the Mary Duke Biddle Foundation. Additional funding from the Duke University Library ensured completion of the project. Many related expenses were subsumed in the operating budget of the Manuscript Department.

In addition to the persons credited on the title page, numerous staff members of Perkins Library were associated with the work on this guide. Connie R. Dunlap, university librarian, initiated the Manuscript Department's search for grants and assisted with the arrangements for additional funding in the later stages of the project. Mattie U. Russell, curator of manuscripts, provided advice and moral support and gave the staff the latitude to function effectively. William R. Erwin, Jr., assistant curator for cataloging, who had general oversight of the project, obtained the initial funding and aided with many details. Sandra Dillahunt, chief typist, and Eugenia Hatley prepared the camera-ready copy. Cathy Reiland, Bill Slayton, Darleen Johnson, Patricia Dumphy, Kenneth Bauzon, Noma Fishe, John Harding, William Randolph, Kathleen Stokes, Kathleen Sharp, and Steve Fox filed the thousands of cards for the index. Kenneth Berger and Linda Sowers proofread the text. Kenneth Barnes proofread the index and expertly performed many other tasks necessary for the completion of the project.

## Collections

1. WILLIAM B. ABBOTT PAPERS, 1862-1864. 10 items. Frederick County, Va.

   Papers of a well-to-do farmer including several documents relating to the evaluation of damage done to his property by C.S.A. troops in 1862 and receipts for hay purchased by the C.S.A in August, 1864.

2. ABBOTT & COMPANY PAPERS, 1856-1871. 66 items. Philadelphia, Pa.

   Miscellaneous letters concerning scales sold by Abbott & Company.

3. ERNEST L. ABEL PAPERS, (1925-1928) 1952. 550 items and 8 vols. West Palm Beach (Palm Beach County), Fla.

   Correspondence and printed material of Ernest L. Abel, postal union organizer and official. Correspondence deals with organizing efforts and charters, finances and the per capita tax, disaster relief for Post Office employees by the Red Cross after a hurricane, conventions, and legislation. Printed material consists of programs for various Florida postal organizations' conventions, 1927-1947, including the Florida State Convention of the National Association of Letter Carriers and National Federation of Post Office Clerks, the Florida Postal Groups, the Joint Convention of Florida Postal Organizations, the Florida Federation of Post Office Clerks, and the Florida State Convention of the National Federation of Post Office Clerks.

4. LASCELLES ABERCROMBIE PAPERS. 1 item.

   Letter to "Ivy" from Abercrombie (1881-1938), English poet and critic, concerning injuries Abercrombie received in an accident. Transcribed from his _Emblems of Love_ (1912).

5. JAMES ABERCROMBY, FIRST BARON DUNFERMLINE, PAPERS, 1840-1851. 20 items. County Midlothian, Scotland.

   Letters to James Loch, member of Parliament, including comments on political affairs in Britain and Ireland, with references to the Corn Laws, landlord-tenant relationships, the political activities of Robert Peel, _Trinity_ v. _Baliol_, effects of universal suffrage in America, ecclesiastical affairs in Scotland, the Poor Laws, Lord Carlisle's health, Lord John Russell's Reform Bill, Daniel O'Connell, currency and banking regulations, the conditions of labor, the report of the Railroad Commission of the Board of Trade, and reminiscences of William Pitt.

6. THOMAS E. ABERNATHY PAPERS, 1800-1857. 8 items. Pulaski (Giles County), Tenn.

   Miscellaneous bills, receipts, and business letters, including mention of cotton prices in Tennessee, 1847, and charges for dental treatment, 1853 and 1855.

7. DANIEL ABERNETHY PAPERS, 1862-1865. 19 items. [Dinwiddie County?] Va.

   Letters of Daniel Abernethy, a Confederate soldier, to his wife and father, containing gossip and comments on desertion and scarcity of food, and references, in 1864, to the probability of overtures of peace to the North by North Carolina.

8. M.A. ABERNETHY LEDGER, 1886-1903. 1 vol. (435 pp.) Statesville (Iredell County), N.C.

   General mercantile accounts.

9. [ABERNETHY AND COMPANY?] LEDGER, 1866-1879. 1 vol. (183 pp.) Newton (Catawba County), N.C.

   Mercantile accounts.

10. ABERNETHY LIBRARY OF AMERICAN LITERATURE PAPERS, 1836-1898. 63 items.

    Typed copies of letters of Thomas Willis White, Paul Hamilton Hayne, Lafcadio Hearn, DuBose Heyward, Richard Malcolm Johnston, John Pendleton Kennedy, William Gilmore Simms, and Alice French (pseud. Octave Thanet). The originals are the property of the Abernethy Library of Middlebury College, Middlebury, Vermont. The White letters contain occasional references to Edgar Allan Poe [partially published: Arthur Hobson Quinn, _Edgar Allan Poe: A Critical Biography_ (New York, 1941)]. The Hayne letters are addressed to Julia Caroline (Ripley) Dorr and contain comments on her poetry and on contemporary writers. Hearn's letters were written from Japan to his publishers. The letters of Simms and Alice French contain literary comment, but those of Heyward, Johnston, and Kennedy are largely notes of thanks or requests for addresses.

11. W. ABNEY LEDGER, 1861-1863. 1 vol. (27 pp.)

    Mercantile accounts.

12. JAMES ABSTON DAYBOOK, 1823. 1 vol. Waterloo Mills, Va.

    Fragmentary mercantile accounts; only a few of the entries contain detailed statements.

13. HENRY J. ACKER PAPERS, 1864. 3 items. Wisconsin.

    A printed pamphlet entitled Gulf Spy, which includes a fanciful story of spying on Confederate fortifications at Mobile, Alabama, and an essay about the presidential election of 1864; the manuscript from which the pamphlet was printed; and a photocopy from the National Archives of Acker's service record with the 23rd Wisconsin Infantry.

14. SIR THOMAS DYKE ACLAND, ELEVENTH BARONET, PAPERS, 1859-1898. 61 items. London, England.

    Chiefly letters to Acland from his son, Sir Arthur Herbert Dyke Acland, 13th Baronet, discussing education, labor, agriculture, the cooperationists, and other political and governmental affairs. There are frequent references to the personal and political life of Acland's elder son, Sir Charles Thomas Dyke Acland, 12th Baronet. Several letters, 1869-1870, relate to Arthur Acland's student days at Christ Church College, Oxford.

15. JAMES MAKITTRICK ADAIR PAPERS, 1797. 1 item. England.

    Letter to Richard and William Lee about Adair's financial affairs, the war, economic conditions, the government, and the public spirit in Scotland.

16. SIR ROBERT ADAIR PAPERS, 1785-1830. 3 items. London, England.

    Letter, 1785, seeking information on William Pitt's legislative proposals for Irish commerce; and letters, 1830, seeking appointment to the embassy at Vienna and discussing Adair's embassy there in 1806-1808.

17. WILLIAM H.P. ADAIR PAPERS, 1836-1858. 11 vols. Greenville (Meriwether County), Ga.

    Chiefly tavern accounts relating to the sale of liquor; also mercantile accounts, 1 vol., 1836, and the journal of a tailor shop, 1 vol., 1852.

18. WILLIAM P. ADAIR PAPERS, 1860-1862. 5 items. Barnesville (Lamar County), Ga.

    Letters from Confederate Army camps in Barnesville, Georgia, and Cumberland Gap, Tennessee.

19. ALFRED ADAMS PAPERS, 1862-1864. 5 items. Sugar Grove (Watauga County), N.C.

    Photocopies of Civil War letters from Adams' son, G.F. Adams, and B.C. McBride, both members of the 1st North Carolina Cavalry stationed near Richmond. Topics include McBride's recovery from a head wound in Winder Hospital, scouting on the Potomac, camp life, and the scarcity of food and clothing.

20. CRAWFORD C. ADAMS PAPERS, 1867-1885. 15 items and 3 vols. Washington, D.C.

    Clippings relating to Adams' career as U.S. deputy marshal in Louisville, Kentucky, and in administrative and special agent positions with the Departments of the Interior and the Treasury, and as a member of various fraternal organizations. The cases he investigated included pension frauds, smuggling, and timber frauds in Calcasieu Parish, Louisiana. There are also poems; copies of letters describing a tour of Britain and Europe in 1875 and commenting on labor reform in England, politics in Virginia and Kentucky, the Ku Klux Klan, and anti-Catholic sentiment; and a volume of pen and ink drawings.

21. HENRY L. ADAMS PAPERS, 1842. 6 items. Wilmington (New Hanover County), N.C.

    Affidavits concerning damage done to the brig Frothingham on a voyage from Wilmington to Martinique and the loss of the cargo of lumber and naval stores.

22. HERBERT BAXTER ADAMS PAPERS, (1891-1902) 1913. 52 items. Baltimore, Md.

    Photostatic copies of letters of Herbert B. Adams (1850-1901), historian and one of the organizers of the American Historical Association in 1884, consisting chiefly of communications from Stephen Beauregard Weeks and John Spencer Bassett concerning the organization of the History Department at Trinity College, Durham, North Carolina, the quarrel between Weeks and John Franklin Crowell, president of Trinity College, the Trinity College Historical Society, the advanced study of William Kenneth Boyd, and current political problems in North Carolina. Included also are a few letters from W.T. Laprade to Professor John Martin Vincent concerning a graduate thesis in history. The originals are in the Adams correspondence at Johns Hopkins University.

23. JOHN P. ADAMS PAPERS, 1846, 1851. 2 items. Baltimore, Md.

    Letters concerning a Baltimore and Florida railroad and the export of coffee from Caracas, Venezuela.

24. MARGARET CRAWFORD ADAMS PAPERS, 1901. 1 item. Congaree (Richland County), S.C.

A letter from Charles Henry Simonton, formerly a captain of the Washington Artillery of Charleston, South Carolina, describing the firing of the first shot at Fort Sumter.

25. OLIVER C. ADAMS PAPERS, 1839-1896. 22 items. North Canton (Hartford County), Conn.

Miscellaneous letters including descriptions of settlement and crops in Perry County, Illinois, 1844; mining in Sierra County, California, 1856; tobacco planting in Connecticut, 1863; and several letters of Union soldiers describing camp life in Greenfield, Massachusetts, and Banks's campaign to open the Mississippi in 1863.

26. SARAH (EVE) ADAMS DIARY, 1813-1814. 1 vol. (52 pp.) Richmond County, Ga.

Relates to the Eve family and includes many references to Christ Presbyterian Church, Augusta, Georgia. Accompanied by an identification list of persons mentioned in the will of Oswell Eve, father of Sarah (Eve) Adams.

27. STERLING ADAMS LEDGER, 1852-1871. 1 vol. (130 pp.) Stokes County, N.C.

Merchant and planter.

28. THOMAS ADAMS ACCOUNT BOOKS, 1768-1808. 2 vols. Augusta County, Va.

Accounts, chiefly of tobacco to be sold for Virginia planters and goods to be purchased in London, of Thomas Adams, a member of the Virginia House of Burgesses and of the Continental Congress and a tobacco factor and merchant, showing prices, shipping charges, and a record of the sale of Adams's estate. One item among a number of commissions to be executed in London was for Thomas Jefferson.

29. THOMAS ADAMS PAPERS, 1814-1818. 4 items. Albemarle and Fluvanna Counties, Va.

Letters by members of the Adams family discussing personal and business matters; camp life, diseases, substitutions and discharges during the War of 1812; alleged crimes by Negroes; and the purchase of slaves.

30. W.G. ADAMS ACCOUNT BOOK, 1851-1863. 1 vol. [Virginia?]

A physician's record of services rendered and fees received.

31. WADE HILL ADAMS PAPERS, 1901-1922. 6 items. New York, N.Y.

Included is a letter, 1901, of John C. Kilgo, president of Trinity College, discussing his legal affairs; and a letter of Mrs. Joseph E. Cockrell to her daughter, Mrs. Jane (Cockrell) Adams, commenting on the 19th general conference of the Methodist Episcopal Church, South; J.C. Kilgo's illness; and the selection of a new president for Southern Methodist University.

32. WILLIAM ADAMS PAPERS, 1832-1887. 74 items. Goochland County, Va.

Business papers, probably of a small-scale planter, including promissory notes, tax and other receipts, bills, and one letter from the commission firm of William R. Pugh of Richmond, Virginia, concerning tobacco prices.

33. WILLIAM C. ADAMS DIARY, 1829-1830, 1857-1863. 1 vol. (360 pp.) Albemarle County, Va.

The journal of a prosperous Virginia planter, describing wheat production, use of guano and plaster, osage orange trees, the sickness and death of his wife, and activities of his children, including the illness of Harriet Adams, evidently tuberculosis; the education of William Poultney Adams, his experiences in the Confederate Army, wedding, and activities in the slave patrol. There are many references to personal finances, slaves, travel by carriage, arrival and departure of packet boats, cases tried as justice of the peace, secession, rumors of military activities, and Methodist and other church services. There is a lengthy account of a trip with Harriet to a general conference of the Methodist Church at Nashville, Tennessee, and return through Chicago, Niagara, Albany, New York City, Philadelphia, Baltimore, and Washington, D.C. There are references to hiring of Adams' slaves and inventories of his property for taxation.

34. ADAMS FAMILY PAPERS, 1785-1914. 9 items. Quincy (Norfolk County), Mass.

Miscellaneous items associated with the family, including a letter of John Adams to John Jay reporting his reception at the Court of St. James; land grants and other papers signed by John Quincy Adams; and letters to Charles Francis Adams, Jr., signed by James Calloway, Thomas Leonard Livermore, and William Henry Schofield.

35. ADAMS AND SMITH ACCOUNT BOOK, 1860-1862. 1 vol. (34 pp.) Lexington (Davidson County), N.C.

Records purchases of cloth and sales of salt.

36. CHARLES BOWYER ADDERLEY, FIRST BARON NORTON, PAPERS, 1876. 1 item. London, England.

Letter from William Schaw Lindsay explaining a series of articles which culminated in publication of Manning the Royal Navy and Mercantile Marine (1877).

37. JOHN ADGER PAPERS, 1839, 1852. 2 items. Charleston, S.C.

Letters concerning renewals of subscriptions to the Presbyterian of Philadelphia, Pennsylvania.

38. APPHIA C. ADKINS PAPERS, 1847-1849. 3 items. Cumberland Court House (Cumberland County), Va.

Family correspondence.

39. GEORGE HAWARD ADSHEAD PAPERS, 1880-1900. 13 items. Pendleton, Lancashire, England.

Included are letters from William Gee describing censorship of the press in Russia; Frederick Armitage relating to his travels in Naples, Egypt, and Greece; Arthur Patchett Martin commenting on his writings; and Isabella Petrie-Mills concerning her biography of her husband, John Mills, From Tinder-Box to the "Larger" Light. There is also a manuscript by Richard Wright Procter, "The Manchester Ophelia," that was published in his The Memorials of Bygone Manchester.

40. ADVERTISING COLLECTION, 19th-20th Centuries. 4,500 items and 2 vols.

Printed booklets, leaflets, broadsides and trade cards relating to the promotion and sale of various products and services, chiefly in the United States. The United States section of this collection is arranged by subject; foreign material is arranged by countries.

41. AFRICA PAPERS, 1781-1958. 16 items.

Several items relate to church affairs, including letters of Samuel A. Crowther describing Christian missions in southern Nigeria and the havoc caused by slave traders, 1852; John Wilson mentioning disorders in South Africa; Joseph Williams describing missionary work in southern Tanganyika, 1882; Zakaria Kizito Kisingiri describing his mother's funeral in Uganda, 1912; John William Colenso, Bishop of Natal, noting the uncertainty of his career, 1864; and T. Durant Philip on missionary work in Cape Colony, 1849. There is a picture of Paulus Moort, rector of Trinity Episcopal Church in Monrovia, Liberia. Other material includes a letter of N. Abcarius about a plot against the Mahdi of Sudan, 1885; the complaint of a minor official in Cairo against British inactivity in the Sudan, 1889; and two items pertaining to the visit of George V to Port Said, 1911. There is a small volume of economic statistics on the Cape Colony, 1781-1803, 38 pp.; a letter of Arthur D. Cushing describing looting during the Boer War, 1901; engravings of two maps showing the course of the Nile and Niger rivers, 1821; and the typescript of an article by Cyril Sofer on race in South Africa, 1958.

42. JOHN AGG PAPERS, 1797-1846. 209 items and 1 vol. Washington, D.C.

Papers of an English-born writer and Washington political reporter containing legal papers of family members; early romantic prose writings, a short play, and verse; a description of Washington, D.C., in fictional format, 1836; clippings of Agg's political satire from the Washington Republican; a fragment of his history of the United States Congress published in 1837; biographical data on political leaders; clippings from the United States Gazette, December, 1828-December, 1829, and January-March, 1841, containing Agg's day-by-day accounts of events in Congress and Washington; his reports on Congress for the New York Commercial Advertiser; and a portrait of Alexander Hamilton, ca. 1797, by an Irish artist.

43. FRANCES (WALKER) YATES AGLIONBY PAPERS, 1821-1933. 1,013 items. Charles Town (Jefferson County), W. Va.

Family letters kept by Frances Aglionby until 1902 and thereafter by her daughter Jeannette. Included is a genealogy of the Aglionby and Yates family. Early letters describe travel and various localities in Virginia and West Virginia; the Virginia Female Institute at Staunton, crops, slaves, neighbors and relatives. Family letters between England and America after 1854 emphasize crops, dogs, cattle, poultry, politics, Charles Yates's inheritance and his adoption of the Aglionby name, London society and manners, the court of Napoleon III, Virginia politics, travels in England and Ireland, English country life, British and European politics, English opinion on slavery and abolition, Civil War hardships, aid for Confederate prisoners, the effect of the war on English cotton mill workers, imprisonment of Charles Yates Aglionby and John Yates Beall and the execution of the latter, hardships during Reconstruction, and the importation of Irish labor. The letters from 1867 to 1933 of Frank K. Yates Aglionby, eldest son of Charles and Frances, start with his transatlantic voyage and describe English manners, customs, and politics; life at Oxford University and as a clergyman in the Church of England; the Oxford Movement in the church; travels in England, Ireland, and Europe with frequent mention of the condition of the poor; English missionary work in Africa; news coverage of the Franco-Prussian War; revivals and evangelism; friendship with William Cabell Rives III; the Alabama claims; English opinion of American politics; British Imperialism; and transatlantic steamship travel. Letters of Jeanette Aglionby describe travel to Philadelphia and Mount Desert, Maine, in 1881 and to London and Europe in 1890, including comments on English choirs and sermons. There are also clippings dealing with Church of England procedures and family events, and pictures of family members.

44. WILLIAM G. AGNEW AND J.S. AGNEW PAPERS, 1861-1864. 62 items. Alpine (Chattooga County), Ga.

Letters of two Confederate soldiers, probably brothers, to their relatives in Georgia. Letters of William Agnew, who served in the first battle of Bull Run and in the Peninsula campaign, deal with military affairs, sickness, camp conditions, rumors, former neighbors in the army, and requests for food and clothing. J.S. Agnew's letters, written from Chickamauga, Tennessee, and Camp Foster, Georgia, are concerned with personal and military matters.

45. EGLANTINE AGOURS PAPERS, 1856-1889. 22 items. Stanton (Haywood County), Tenn.

Letters written to Eglantine Agours (or Agurs) by her relatives in Tennessee, Texas, and South Carolina, containing chiefly family news, but with some reference to secession, civilian and military life in the South, conscription, the battle of Shiloh, the 12th Regiment of Tennessee Volunteers, and Reconstruction in South Carolina.

46. OSCAR AICHEL PAPERS, 1861-1863. 6 items. Charleston, S.C.

Wartime letters written in German script. Aichel apparently was a grocer.

47. HENRY HINCHLIFF AINLEY PAPERS, [1904?]. 1 item. London, England.

Letter from Robert South, dramatist, to Ainley, British actor-manager, regarding a work by South.

48. ALABAMA. DALLAS COUNTY. CHANCERY COURT DOCKET, 1856-1863. 1 vol. Selma (Dallas County), Ala.

49. JAMES LUSK ALCORN PAPERS, 1871. 1 item. Coahoma County, Miss.

Letter ordering volumes from a bookseller.

50. WILLIAM ALDERMAN PAPERS, 1853-1864. 5 items. Cumberland County, N.C.

Three legal documents relating to the purchase of slaves; receipt for taxes paid the Confederate States Tax Office; letter from William Vink of Ellicott City, Maryland, describing his plans for the manufacture of paper from palmetto wood.

51. ADAM LEOPOLD ALEXANDER PAPERS, 1785 (1803-1889) 1909. 361 items. Washington (Wilkes County), Ga.

Family correspondence of Adam Leopold Alexander (1803-1882), planter and businessman with interests in banking, railroads, and mercantile firms. Included are letters from Yale University, New Haven, Connecticut; the University of Virginia, Charlottesville; schools of Washington, Georgia; New England secondary schools, 1830-1840, 1850; letters concerning Civil War and Reconstruction; and miscellaneous deeds and other papers.

52. BETTIE ALEXANDER PAPERS, 1860-1863. 9 items. Monroe County, W. Va.

Personal letters from Bettie Alexander, apparently a schoolgirl, to her sister in Fincastle, Virginia. Frequent mention is made of sick, wounded, or killed Confederate soldiers, runaway Negroes, and Federal troops.

53. EDWARD PORTER ALEXANDER PAPERS, 1863-1905. 4 items. Georgetown (Georgetown County), S.C.

Letter inquiring about Confederate losses in Virginia; list of the artillery of the Army of Northern Virginia; letter declining to attend a reunion of Confederate veterans, 1905.

54. ETHEL ALEXANDER PAPERS, 1962. 2 items. New York, N.Y.

Letter from Alexander T. Case discussing the production of his play, "A Soldier and Mr. Lincoln," and enclosing a copy of an unused prologue.

55. HENRY M. ALEXANDER SCRAPBOOK, 1857-1860. 1 vol. (180 pp.) New York, N.Y.

List of bondholders, correspondence, reports of earnings, clippings, notes, and other documents concerning the financial affairs of the Steubenville and Indiana Rail Road.

56. JAMES H. ALEXANDER DIARY, 1862. 1 vol. (51 pp.) Centreville (Fairfax County), Va.

Diary kept while James H. Alexander was in a Confederate camp near Centreville. It contains intimate details of life in the Confederate Army, including a description of the company dispute with Colonel William Nelson Pendleton about building a church and attending services, and references to Northern newspapers.

57. MILLER ALEXANDER PAPERS, 1850-1900. 211 items. Saint Louis, Mo.; Miss.; and Ky.

Letters of 1850-1860 are to Reuben Alexander of Marrow Bone, Cumber County, Kentucky, and are largely from H. Craft, land agent, relating to land sales in Mississippi. Letters after 1864 are personal and family correspondence of Miller Alexander, a tobacco buyer and general merchant, who may have been the son of Reuben. The letters concern tobacco culture and marketing in Kentucky and Missouri, and also mention the state of education in Missouri; religious conditions, frequently using Biblical language even in discussing commercial affairs; travels in Arkansas, Kentucky, Missouri, Idaho, Mississippi, Texas, Ohio, Utah, and Washington Territory, with reference to the economy and religion. There are frequent references to national politics and political leaders and to race relations.

58.  ROBERT P. ALEXANDER NOTES, 1856-1857. 1 vol. Charlottesville (Albemarle County), Va.

Robert P. Alexander's notes on physiology and surgery taken from lectures delivered by Dr. James Lawrence Cabell at the University of Virginia.

59.  S. CALDWELL ALEXANDER PAPERS, 1850. 1 vol. North Carolina.

Essays, generally short expositions of traditional theological and philosophical positions, written by Alexander as a student at the Columbia Theological Seminary, a Presbyterian institution in Columbia, South Carolina.

60.  ALEXANDER AND O'NEILL PAPERS, 1867. 21 items and 1 vol. Charleston, S.C.

Alexander and O'Neill was a firm dealing in wholesale and retail hay, grain, etc., in Charleston. The owners were H.F. Alexander and J.J.A. O'Neill. The ledger contains accounts for April to August, 1867. It was later used as a scrapbook for recipes. There is also a business card of Alexander and O'Neill and a number of handwritten recipes.

61.  ALEXANDER FAMILY PAPERS, 1778-1810. 7 items. Burke and Lincoln Counties, N.C.

Land deeds.

62.  ALEXANDER FAMILY PAPERS, 1795-1870. 36 items. Campbell County, Va.

Mostly legal documents signed by Robert, John, John D., and William K. Alexander as clerks of the Campbell County, Virginia, Superior Court. Subjects include land claims, deeds, the settlement of estates, and other legal affairs, and bills and receipts for court costs.

63.  GEORGE BENTON ALFORD PAPERS, 1847-1925. 24 items. Holly Springs (Wake County), N.C.

Business and personal letters, bills and receipts of the president of the Holly Springs Land and Improvement Company; papers about North Carolina Baptist ministers; ordination certificate, 1847, for the Rev. Johnson Olive, probably the father-in-law of George Benton Alford; and his certificate of membership, 1884, in the North Carolina Baptist Ministers' Life Assn. There is also material on Alford's son, Green Haywood Alford.

64.  WILLIAM ROUNSEVILLE ALGER PAPERS, 1847. 1 item. Boston, Mass.

Note by Alger, clergyman and author, to a Mr. Winsor.

65.  JEAN-ADOLPHE ALHAIZA PAPERS, 1870-1916. 287 items. Paris, France.

Papers of a French socialist editor, author, and associate of Charles Fourier. Included is the manuscript, 1150 pp., of Dictionnaire de Sociologie Phalanstérienne: Guide des Oeuvres Complètes de Charles Fourier, by Édouard Silberling (Paris: 1911). There is also a biographical and bibliographical file of French and foreign socialists, which serves as a partial author index for the periodicals La Phalange and La Reforme Industrielle. Among the more important French associationists listed are Victor Prosper Considérant, Alexandre-François Baudet-Dulary, César Daly, François Marie Charles Fourier, Mme. Gatti de Gammond, Marc-Amédée Gramier, Victor-Antoine Hennequin, Just Muiron, Charles Pellarin, Hippolyte Renaud, Mme. Clarisse Vigoureux, and Édouard Silberling. The Germans, F.L. Goertner and C.F. Grieb, are noted as involved in an associative colony in Texas in the 1830's. Great Britain is represented by Hughes Doherty. Americans include Albert Brisbane, Horace Greeley, and Parke Godwin.

66.  C. TACITUS ALLEN MEMOIRS, 1893-1919. 1 vol. (169 pp.) Lunenburg County, Va.

Reminiscences of Allen's Civil War experiences, first in the 20th Regiment, Virginia Volunteers, including an account of the battle of Rich Mountain; the subsequent retreat; disbandment of Allen's unit and organization of Co. F, 2nd Regiment, Virginia Artillery; defense of Richmond; loss of Fort Harrison and battle of Sayler's Creek; and Allen's capture and imprisonment in the Old Capitol Prison in Washington and later on Johnson's Island, Lake Erie. Included is a roster of the officers and men serving in Allen's company and a 1893 Memorial Day address on "The Confederate Soldier in History." Glued inside the back cover is a 1919 poem on the United Daughters of the Confederacy.

67.  CHARLES HARRIS ALLEN PAPERS, 1893-1902. 7 items. London, England.

Six letters, 1893-1902, from Lord Cromer review the work of the Home for Freed Women Slaves in Cairo, Egypt, the progress of the campaign against slavery in the Sudan, and Allen's career as secretary of the British and Foreign Anti-Slavery Society. One letter from Lord Curzon, 1897, criticizes statements by Allen and Joseph A. Pease concerning the government's policy about slavery on Zanzibar.

68. DAVID B. ALLEN PAPERS, 1844-1847. 2 items. Oxford (Granville County), N.C.

A legal paper concerns a court judgment against Allen and others, 1844, and a letter concerns legal and financial affairs, 1847.

69. DWIGHT ALLEN PAPERS, 1863. 2 items. Geneva (Walworth County), Wis.

Letters of a Union soldier discussing camp life, discipline, casualties, Confederate and Union generals, and statements by Confederate deserters concerning demoralization in the Army of Tennessee.

70. ETHAN ALPHONSO ALLEN LETTER BOOK, 1818-1835. 1 vol. Norfolk, Va.

Copies of letters of Ethan A. Allen (1789-1855), son of Ethan Allen of Revolutionary War fame, graduate of the U.S. Military Academy, West Point, New York, and captain in the U.S. Army. Generally routine in nature, the letters are largely concerned with recruiting service for the 2nd Battalion of Artillery in Virginia and Maryland, reports to auditors and other officials of the U.S. Treasury Department, and efforts to obtain his portion of military bounty land due his father. Included also are copies of letters received by Allen; a description of the fort at Craney Island, Norfolk County, Virginia, in 1820; a letter to President James Monroe protesting the omission of his name from the rolls of the U.S. Army; a draft of Allen's will; and business correspondence with the firm of Aldis and Davis.

71. JAMES ALLEN DAYBOOKS, 1838-1843. 4 vols. Grafton County, N.H.

Record of sales of general merchandise.

72. JAMES LANE ALLEN PAPERS, 1889-1911. 56 items. Cincinnati, Ohio.

Ten letters and a telegram from Allen to Joseph Marshall Stoddard, editor of Lippincott's Magazine, concerning Allen's Kentucky writings and their publication; a letter from Allen to Charles Burr Todd regarding a proposed Society of American Authors; clippings concerning Allen, printed copies of some of his writings, and articles on the country about which he wrote; and letters, chiefly 1888-1889, to Richard Watson Gilder and Robert Underwood Johnson, editors of The Century, about Allen's writings for that magazine. Topics include Allen's plans to collect his articles in book form, 1888; an outline for a historical novel of Kentucky life, 1889; plans for lectures on the literature of the New South, 1890; and the effect on Allen's work of his poor eyesight, caused by typhoid fever, 1889.

73. JAMES WALKINSHAW ALLEN NOTEBOOK, 1848-1864. 1 vol. Mount Prospect (Bedford County), Va.

Notebook of James W. Allen (d. 1862), a student at Virginia Military Institute, Lexington, and later colonel in the 2nd Virginia Infantry, C.S.A., containing collections of poems and quotations. Included also is a comment on the life and death of J.W. Allen, signed by J.N. Allen.

74. JOHN ALLEN PAPERS, 1814-1881. 24 items. Fincastle (Botetourt County), Va.

Business and personal correspondence, including letters from Chapman Johnson and Richard L.T. Beale concerning land purchases and the settlement of a court case. One letter from Polly Allen Caldwell describes winter in New Orleans, 1837, and Revolutionary War pension claims. A letter of 1845 provides a description of Memphis, Tennessee.

75. JOHN ALLEN PAPERS, 1853-1884. 1 vol. Hunsucker's Store (Montgomery County), N.C.

Account book, 1853-1884, including copies of letters by Allen, early 1880s, and miscellaneous notes, among them militia records, 1860-1861.

76. JOHN ALLEN PAPERS, 1864 (1870-1879) 1885. 39 items. Franklin County, N.C.

Personal and business letters of John Allen, Confederate soldier, teacher, and civil engineer. The collection relates chiefly to the Civil War, teaching, college life, and financial difficulties during Reconstruction. Included also are a report card of James Parker, of the Oxford (N.C.) High School, giving a description of the courses offered; and four letters from relatives and friends in Texas and Missouri.

77. OSCAR H. ALLEN PAPERS, 1898-1899. 3 items. Nebraska.

Letters from Allen in Army camps at Jacksonville, Florida, and Havana, Cuba, to Florence Lytle of Jacksonville, commenting on life in the 3rd Nebraska Infantry and on the death of a friend, Jonas H. Lien, 1st South Dakota Infantry, killed in the Philippines.

78. R. ALFRED ALLEN PAPERS, 1864-1866. 1 vol. New London (Huron County), Ohio.

Diary of Allen's service as hospital steward with the 22nd New York Cavalry, 1864-1865, with brief entries describing the battle of the Wilderness, Jubal Early's Valley campaign, and the siege of Petersburg; personal financial accounts; and weekly reports on the regimental sick. There is also reference to Allen's postwar return to Ohio.

79.    RICHARD ALLEN DAYBOOK AND ACCOUNT BOOK, 1839-1874. 2 vols. Keysville (Charlotte County), Va.

Records of a small country merchant.

80.    W.A. ALLEN LEDGERS, 1872-1879. 2 vols. Opossum Trot (Anson County), N.C.

Records of sales of general merchandise.

81.    WELD NOBLE ALLEN PAPERS, 1852-1873. 25 items. Maine.

Documents relating to Allen's naval career, including his appointment to Annapolis, orders to him as commander of the sloop of war Oneida in the West Indies, 1863, and with the Western Gulf Blockading Squadron in command of the Oneida and later the gunboat New London, 1863-1864; Allen's report of the capture of the schooner Raton del Nilo; orders to serve on naval general courts-martial on the Portsmouth, 1863, in Boston, 1869, and in New York, 1872; and an account of Allen's command of a shore detachment in the attack on Fort Fisher at the mouth of the Cape Fear River, North Carolina, during which he was wounded, December, 1864-January, 1865.

82.    WILLIAM C. ALLEN PAPERS, 1857-1866. 7 items. Haywood County, Tenn.

Included is Allen's will dividing his eight slaves between his wife and nephew. Most of the other items refer to John Allen of Edgefield District, South Carolina, revealing his exemption from conscription because of physical disability in 1863; wartime scarcity; and high prices. A letter, 1866, of H. Allen, a sharecropper tenant in Holly Springs, Mississippi, deals with his family's losses during a typhoid epidemic in the preceding year.

83.    ALLEN-ANGIER FAMILY PAPERS, 1843-1971. 1,749 items and 8 vols. Durham, N.C., and Washington, D.C.

Papers kept by Zalene Allen Angier include correspondence, 1936-1969, largely letters from her brother George Venable Allen (1903-1970), diplomat, official of the Tobacco Institute, and trustee of Duke University. Allen's letters describe his diplomatic career and personal matters, including foreign relations and social life in Greece, Egypt, and Iran in the 1930s and 1940s; the royal family of Iran; the Potsdam Conference; and customs of Saudi Arabia. Letters of the 1950s mention celebrities Allen met, such as Yehudi Menuhin and Aristotle Onassis; and relations of the U.S. with India and of Russia with Yugoslavia. Letters of Allen's wife Katherine Martin Allen reflect diplomatic social life. Clippings relate to Allen's career as diplomat and as director of the United States Information Agency, to his family, and to his death. Miscellaneous papers include invitations; White House dinner menus; press releases; a report, February 9, 1932, on Japanese-Chinese relations; articles by Allen; and other printed materials. There are photographs of Allen and many acquaintances, including Marshall Tito, Mohammed Reza Pahlavi, Jawaharlal Nehru, Amjad Ali, Abba Eban, Wellington Koo, Dwight D. Eisenhower, John Foster Dulles, and William Fulbright. Papers, 1945-1970, kept by George and Katherine Allen include letters from Eisenhower and Dulles about Allen's shift from the State Department to the USIA; a report on the political situation in Iran, January 21, 1948; correspondence on Egyptian-U.S. relations in the 1950s and the Henry A. Byroade scandal, the Cold War, the cigarette smoking and health controversy, and on Allen's speeches. Enclosed with a letter from Allen of May 10, 1970, is a petition against slavery by the Baptist Church of Augusta, Maine, dated August 17, 1843. There are files of speeches and related correspondence on Russia, propaganda, the space race, foreign policy, peace, the tobacco industry, India, Iran, UNESCO, and other topics. There is material on the Dulles and Eisenhower oral history projects and on various honors and awards received by Allen. Two scrapbooks contain clippings about Allen's career and family photographs. There is also a photocopy of his book-length manuscript reminiscence of experiences as Ambassador to Iran in the 1940s and 1950s; a letter from Josephus Daniels, 1940, commenting on Allen's review of Daniels' book, Tar Heel Editor; and a tape recording of Allen's address, 1967, to the Tobaccoland Kiwanis Club on the United States in the world.

84.    SAMUEL AUSTIN ALLIBONE PAPERS, 1856. 1 item. Philadelphia, Pa.

Letter from Allibone, lexicographer and librarian, to an unidentified manuscript dealer concerning the purchase of a manuscript Bible, Biblia Latina.

85.    ELIZABETH BEATTY (JOHNSTON) ALLISON PAPERS, 1866-1969. 16 items. Turnersburg (Iredell County), N.C.

Letters written by Harriet N. (Espey) Vance, wife of Zebulon Baird Vance, and others of her family to Mrs. Allison. The correspondence deals with family and personal affairs and has little information about Vance's public life. A letter by Marianna Long, Vance's great granddaughter, identifies members of her family and comments on the disposition of other papers left at the Vance estate.

86.    MARTIN O. ALLISON AND JOHN ALLISON PAPERS, 1777-1846. 8 items. Chenango County, N.Y.

Letters from Francis Armstrong, Florida, New York [?]; John Barbour, Wilkes, Ohio; David and Ann Armstrong, Milton, New York [?]; and others concerning such topics as securing a minister for Florida, crops, hard times, Locofocos, migration to Texas, price of wheat in New York State, and other matters.

87. WILLIAM H. ALLISON PAPERS, 1851-1860. 8 items. Richmond, Va.

Chiefly letters to William H. Allison from his mother, written while he was a student at Richmond.

88. JOSEPH ALLRED PAPERS, 1819-1864. 37 items. Randolph County, N.C.

Business and personal correspondence of Joseph Allred; land deed of Mahlon Allred; list of subscribers for building a church at New Union [?].

89. BENJAMIN ALLSTON PAPERS, 1856-1878. 13 items. Charleston, S.C.

Military and personal correspondence of Benjamin Allston (1833-1900), Confederate officer and Protestant Episcopal minister, and some executive correspondence of Robert Francis Withers Allston (1801-1864), including three letters relative to an engineering project in progress on the Savannah River in 1858. Included also are several letters to "Ben" Allston from another minister, W.B.W. Howe, all mentioning the desirability of reserving a portion of church auditoriums for Negro worshipers, and personal letters from feminine correspondents.

90. PHILLIP ALLWOOD COMMONPLACE AND LETTER BOOK, 1793-1804. 1 vol. (504 pp.) Wandsworth, Surrey, England.

Records of many literary and scientific matters investigated by Allwood, an English clergyman educated at Cambridge University. Several letters related to the review in the British Critic of his Literary Antiquities of Greece (London: 1799).

91. LEONARD ALMAN PAPERS, 1862-1864. 18 items. North Carolina.

Letters to Alman's wife, Caroline, written by Alman's comrades, chiefly Dan. P. Boger, describing experiences with the 7th North Carolina Volunteers and imprisonment, probably at Camp Lookout, Maryland. There are accounts of several battles in Virginia, including a skirmish at Orange Court House, 1862.

92. JOHN ALMON PAPERS, 1769 (1771-1772). 48 items. London, England.

Almon (1735-1805) was a bookseller and political pamphleteer. The collection includes letters from John Calcraft (1726-1772) and drafts of notes for Almon's replies. The principal topics include the politics of the King's ministers and their opposition, and the politics of contending factions in the city of London. Frequently mentioned are Almon's trial, 1770, for publishing Junius' "Letter to the King"; the Portsmouth fire, 1771; revenues in Ireland and England; the health of the Princess of Wales; continental diplomacy and military affairs, especially as regards the fates of Poland and Turkey and the prospects of war; the stock market decline; and Spanish activity in the West Indies. Persons mentioned prominently include John Burgoyne, Edmund Burke, Lord Chatham, Jeremiah Dyson, the Duke of Grafton, John Horne, Henry Luttrell, Lord Mansfield, William Nash, Lord North, Lord Rockingham, John Sawbridge, Lord Shelburne, Lord Temple, Lord Townshend, and John Wilkes.

93. A.D. ALMOND PAPERS, 1865-1866. 5 items. Charlottesville (Albemarle County), Va.

Merchants' bills to A.D. Almond and A.T. Almond.

94. J.W. ALSTON PAPERS, 1918. 1 item. France.

Army orders.

95. WILLIAM ALSTON PAPERS, 1861-1885. 3 items. Henderson (Vance County), N.C.

One letter describing a Civil War camp, and two accounts from William Alston's store.

96. ALUMINUM COMPANY OF CANADA, LIMITED, PAPERS, 1915-1968. 4 items and 3 vols. Montreal, Canada.

Four published brochures and two albums of photographs with a forward and summary of company history by T.L. Brock. The albums concern James Buchanan Duke's visits to the Saguenay region of Canada, 1915, and to Quebec, 1925. The collection concerns Duke's role in the development of the hydroelectric resources of the Lake St. John and Saguenay River system of central Quebec, his formation of the Quebec Development Company, and agreement with Arthur Vining Davis to form the Aluminum Company of Canada, Ltd.

97. JOHN AMBLER PAPERS, 1788-1864. 26 items. Richmond, Va.

Personal and business correspondence of Ambler (1762-1836), a planter. Two letters from William Tucker of Amherst County, Virginia, concern agriculture; one from Robert Ambler to Beverly Ambler relates to army life during the Civil War; and one from Chapman Johnson to Ambler concerns the Norton estate, to which Mrs. Ambler was one of the heirs. There are also business and other personal items including the draft of a play and an essay on the importance of study.

98. PHILIP ST. GEORGE AMBLER PAPERS, 1856-1879. 6 items. Washington (Rappahannock County), Va.

Correspondents include Conway Robinson, Robert C. Stanard, and John Ambler.

99.  AMBLER-BROWN FAMILY PAPERS, 1780-1865. 4 items. Charles Town (Jefferson County), W. Va.; Fauquier County, Va.

Typescripts of documents largely relating to the genealogy of several related families of Westmoreland and Fauquier counties, Virginia, and Jefferson County, West Virginia; the early history of Richmond, Williamsburg, Yorktown, and Alexandria, Virginia, and Washington, D.C.; and sidelights on outstanding figures of the Revolution and the early Republic. The diary of Lucy Johnson Ambler of Fauquier County, 1862-1863, 17 pp., comments on major Civil War battles, civilian morale and hardships, and depredations by Union troops. Copies of family letters, 1780-1823, largely between Betsy (Ambler) Garrington, Ann (Ambler) Fisher, Mildred (Smith) Dudley, and Frances Cairnes, refer to Virginia events and the history of the Ambler, Jacquelin, Marshall, Burwell, and Washington families; social life and religion of the Revolutionary War era; hardships caused by British military activities in the Virginia Tidewater, the impact of French troops on social life, the parentage of Lewis Warrington, the Mount Vernon household of George and Martha Washington, and the early city of Washington. There are also several memoirs of the marriage of John Marshall and Mary Willis (Ambler) Marshall. A memoir of Governor Thomas Brown of Florida, "Account of the Lineage of the Brown Family," 1865, 170 pp., beginning with the emigration from England of Edwin (or Edward) Brown in 1608, describes the social life, customs, and politics of Virginia up to the Civil War. There are references to the Templemen, Washington, Collins and related families, tobacco planting, the Revolutionary War, the invention of post office boxes, education, gambling, economic effects of the War of 1812, Virginia militia during that war, transatlantic travel in 1820, and settlement in Jefferson, Westmoreland, Berkeley, and Fauquier counties, Charles Town and Harpers Ferry. A photocopy of a letter by Elizabeth (Brown) Douglas of Key West, Florida, ca. 1850, describes the captured slave ship Mohawk and conditions on board.

100.  AMERICAN COLONIZATION SOCIETY PAPERS, 1851. 2 items. Jefferson County, Miss.

Power of attorney from John S. Chambliss to Captain David Bone of Natchez relating to his claim for services rendered the society; and supporting affidavit of J.E. Calhoun of Claiborne County.

101.  AMERICAN FEDERATION OF HOSIERY WORKERS PAPERS, 1941. 2 vols. Philadelphia, Pa.

Mimeographed briefs pertaining to wages. One was prepared by the American Federation of Hosiery Workers (Independent) and presented to the Hosiery Industry Committee under the provisions of the Fair Labor Standards Act. The other brief was presented to the Seamless Hosiery Industry Committee by the National Association of Hosiery Manufacturers, Inc.

102.  AMERICAN LITERATURE PAPERS, 1927-1966. 3,494 items. Durham, N.C.

Records of American Literature, a quarterly journal of literary history, criticism, and bibliography published since 1929 by Duke University Press with the cooperation of the American Literature Group of the Modern Language Association. Included are minutes of the group, 1931-1937, 1941, 1944; reports of standing committees, 1941-1942, 1945-1947, 1950; reports of literary meetings of the group, 1930-1941; the charter for American Literature; annual reports of the journal, 1929-1930, 1933, 1935-1947; correspondence, 1926-1954, of chairmen of the editorial board Jay Broadus Hubbell, Clarence Gohdes, and Arlin Turner chiefly with editors, advisers, and reviewers. Topics include organization, planning, and operation of the journal; editorial policies; nomination of editors and members of the advisory editorial board; subscriptions; reviews and reviewers; other editorial matters; program planning for annual meetings of the group; special project plans; bibliographies; committee reports. The major portion of the collection consists of correspondence with Roy Prentice Basler, 1931-1953, 42 items; Walter Blair, 1929-1966, 94 items; Edward Scullery Bradley, 1926-1965, 243 items; William Braswell, 1929-1966, 61 items; William B. Cairnes, 1928-1932, 99 items; Killis Campbell, 1927-1936, 109 items; Oscar Cargill, 1933-1964, 36 items; Harry Hayden Clark, 1927-1957, 140 items; Oral Sumner Coad, 1929-1954, 41 items; Harold Milton Ellis, 1928-1943, 45 items; Norman Foerster, 1927-1953, 118 items; James David Hart, 1942-1954, 38 items; Emory Holloway, 1930-1952, 73 items; Howard Mumford Jones, 1928-1954, 108 items; Ernest Erwin Leisy, 1927-1955, 184 items; Thomas Ollive Mabbott 1928-1964, 146 items; Tremaine McDowell, 1928-1955, 100 items; Kenneth Ballard Murdock, 1927-1956, 279 items; Gregory Lansing Paine, 1928-1950, 150 items; Fred Lewis Pattee, 1928-1948, 102 items; Henry August Pochmann, 1929-1954, 62 items; Ralph Leslie Rusk, 232 items; Robert Ernest Spiller, 1927-1952, 302 items; Arlin Turner, 1935-1951, 26 items; Warren Austin, 1930-1951, 73 items; and Stanley Thomas Williams, 1927-1954, 252 items.

103.  AMERICAN WRITERS PAPERS, 1814-1969. 167 items and 1 vol.

Miscellaneous letters of American authors, editors, and other literary figures, primarily relating to literary topics. There are also a few drafts, poems, and other manuscripts, and clippings. Writers include Charles Francis Adams, Jr., W. Hervey Allen, Jr., J.D. Anders, Susan B. Anthony, Irving Addison Bacheller, J.H.A. Bone, Mary Louise Booth, Arthur Brisbane, S.P. Brockwell, William Crary Brownell, William Cullen Bryant, Frances (Hodgson) Burnett, H. Witter Bynner, Henry Colburn, F. Marion Crawford,

John Ross Dix, Mortimer Drummond, Augustine Joseph Hickey Duganne, James Thomas Fields, Francis Fontaine, Mary Wilkins Freeman, Hamlin Garland, Caroline Gilman, Edward Everett Hale, James Hale, John Judson Hamilton, William Harden, Robert Lewis Harrison, Gerhart Hauptmann, Julian Hawthorne, George W. Humphreys, Alexander Johnston, Mary Johnston, George Kennan, B.A. Konkle, H.E. Krehbiel, William John Lawrence, Henry Charles Lea, Anna Leonowens, Henry Cabot Lodge, Samuel Longfellow, Abbott Lawrence Lowell, Hamilton Wright Mabie, Mary McCarthy, William McFee, John Bach McMaster, Robert Whitehead McNeely, Margaret (Mitchell) Marsh, James Brander Matthews, Henry Louis Mencken, Richard Kendall Munkittrick, Charles E. Norton, Fitz-James O'Brien, John Williamson Palmer, Bliss Perry, William Lyon Phelps, Parker Pillsbury, Josiah Quincy, Allen Raymond, Louis Rhead, Dominique Rouquette, Charles Monroe Sheldon, Robert E. Sherwood, William Lukens Shoemaker, Katherine Drayton Mayrant Simons, Francis Hopkinson Smith, Arthur Stedman, George Sumner, John Reuben Thompson, Frederick Tuckerman, Henry T. Tuckerman, Louis Untermeyer, Gertrude de Vingut, Carolyn Wells, John H. White, Ella (Wheeler) Wilcox, and others. The anonymous manuscript volume, unbound, discusses various versions and editions of Shakespeare's *Hamlet*, as well as editors, critics, and plagiarists.

104. ELECTA E. (RAY) AMES AND FORDYCE W. AMES PAPERS, 1849-1931. 246 items. DeRuyter (Madison County), N.Y.

Largely letters from the Ames's son, Frank, and from Electa Ames's sister, Jane C. (Ray) Warren, and Jane's husband, Jared W. Warren. The Warrens, of Rutherford County, Tennessee, discuss schools and teaching there, and in one letter of August 27, 1863, describe the treatment of slaves, Civil War conditions in Tennessee, and a battle which took place on or near their property. Two letters are from Electa Ames's brother, J. M. Ray, a Union soldier.

105. FISHER AMES PAPERS, 1790, 1801. 2 items. Dedham (Norfolk County), Mass.

A letter, 1790, from Federalist leader Ames to U.S. Judge John Lowell of Massachusetts concerns legislation to prevent frauds in the payment of North Carolina veterans of the Revolutionary War, and reviews the character of John Jay. A letter, 1801, to Benjamin Bourne evaluates an unidentified applicant for an editorial position with a Federalist paper.

106. JAMES TYLER AMES PAPERS, 1865. 2 items. Chicopee (Hampden County), Mass.

Letters, November 2 and 18, 1865, from W.M. Mitchell in Milledgeville and in Dougherty County, Georgia, seeking to interest Ames, a munitions manufacturer, in investments in cotton plantation land.

107. JESSIE (DANIEL) AMES PAPERS, 1902-1946. 1 item. Tryon (Polk County), N.C.

Photocopy of a history, or possibly preparatory notes for a work on the founding of the Woman's Division of the Commission on Interracial Cooperation in 1920 and a brief summary of its activities up to 1940. Included is a narrative, minutes, speeches, and reports. Jessie Ames, general field secretary of the commission, added marginal comments in 1946.

108. JACOB AMICK AND [JOHN AMICK?] PAPERS, 1813-1873. 2 vols. Randolph County, N.C.

A tenor book and account book, 1813-1854, 73 pp., contains rules of harmony, notes for sacred songs, and a few farming accounts; accompanied by a ledger, 1854-1867, 66 pp.

109. AMNESTY OATHS OF EX-CONFEDERATES, 1862-1867. 18 items.

110. RICHARD AMOS PAPERS, 1850 (1858-1869) 1893. 108 items. Ayresville (Stokes County), N.C.

Family letters, most of which were written before the Civil War from Shelby County, Indiana, where one of the Amos brothers had settled.

111. KARL JOACHIM ANDERSEN PAPERS, 1882-1899. 46 items. Copenhagen, Denmark.

Letters, in the English, French, and German languages, from conductors and musicians in Western Europe, Russia, and America, to Andersen, a Danish flautist. Correspondents include Paul Taffanel, 1883-1895, 11 items; G. Dumon, 1888, 2 items; Johann Heinrich Wilhelm Barge, 1882-1888, 8 items; W. Bukovsky, 1894, 1 item; Albert Fransella, 1890-1896, 3 items; Moritz Fürstenau, 1883-1888, 4 items; R. Kukula, 1887-1890, 6 items; Oskar Köhler, 1889, 2 items; Wilhelm Popp, 1887, 1 item; Robert E. Steel, 1899, 1 item; Richard Unger, 1891, 1 item; Theodor Winkler, 1883-1896, 3 items; F. Waterstraat, 1882-1888, 3 items.

112. ADEN ANDERSON PAPERS, 1842-1854. 5 items. Frederick County, Md.

Land deeds.

113. ALBERT ANDERSON PAPERS, 1909. 6 items. Raleigh (Wake County), N.C.

Business letters to James M. Templeton, Jr.

114. CHARLES M. ANDERSON PAPERS, 1852-1893. 1 item and 1 vol. Mount Solon (Augusta County), Va.

A tailor's account book, probably kept

by Anderson, with entries to 1873 (largely 1852-1858); also a receipt, 1893.

115. EDWARD C. ANDERSON PAPERS, 1861-1863. 7 items. Savannah, Ga.

Two letters of Anderson, Confederate agent in France and England, to his family concern Union arms purchases and European support for the South; one letter, 1862, describes the plight of a Northerner in Savannah and economic conditions in that city.

116. EDWIN ALEXANDER ANDERSON, JR., PAPERS, 1915-1918. 13 items and 1 vol. Wilmington (New Hanover County), N.C.

Papers relating to Anderson's duty at the Naval War College, 1915-1916, include material on the logistics and battle tactics of submarine warfare. Relating to his service as commander of the American Patrol detachment in the Caribbean, 1917-1918, is the typescript of a war diary describing fleet operations, political affairs in Guatemala and Honduras, and the relations between the two countries.

117. FRANCIS THOMAS ANDERSON PAPERS, 1828 (1850-1858) 1915. 443 items. Fincastle (Botetourt County), Va.

This collection concerns also the activities of Joseph Reid Anderson (1813-1892). Included are business papers pertaining to mining operations and Francis Thomas Anderson's Cloverdale Furnace, a part of the Tredegar Iron Works; miscellaneous letters and papers concerning the sale of slaves, collection of debts, rental of property, teaching, and school tuition. Included also are a charge for the ministry of A.B. McCorkle; two summonses; and a printed plea, March 4, 1846, addressed to Anderson, seeking funds to help the widow and children of John Hampden Pleasants, "recently killed in a duel."

118. GEORGE ANDERSON PAPERS, 1870-1885. 24 items. Glasgow, Lanarkshire, Scotland.

Letters addressed to Anderson, a British politician, relating to such topics as army reform, 1870; Gladstone's refusal to go to Glasgow, 1871; burials legislation, 1878; Gladstone's political plans, farmers and prices, and the Scottish Church, 1879; Mecca and Portugal, 1881-1883; government expenses, 1883; and electoral procedure, 1884.

119. JAMES ANDERSON PAPERS, 1782. 1 item. Monkshill, Aberdeenshire, Scotland.

Anderson's refutation of the charge that he had plagiarized Josiah Tucker's Cui Bono, July 4, 1782.

120. JAMES M. ANDERSON PAPERS, 1935. 1 item. (22 pp.) Tuscaloosa, Ala.

Mimeographed copy of a speech by James A. Anderson before the Tuscaloosa Kiwanis Club on Union General James H. Wilson's raid into central Alabama, 1865.

121. RICHARD HERON ANDERSON PAPERS, 1864. 1 item. Savannah, Ga.

Manuscript extract from Confederate General Anderson's account of the operations of the I Corps of the Army of Northern Virginia after Longstreet was disabled until Spotsylvania Court House.

122. V.V. ANDERSON PAPERS, 1820 (1847-1890) 1921. 873 items and 8 vols. Calahaln (Davie County), N.C.

Personal, business, and political correspondence, accounts, legal papers, diaries, and bills and receipts of members of the Anderson family of Davie County. Records of C.J. Anderson, storekeeper and census enumerator for western North Carolina, 1880 and 1890 censuses, include instructions on liquor manufacturing and marketing and on the counting of persons. Records of Charles Anderson, justice of the peace of Davie County, include material on court cases, estate settlements, and state and local politics, 1872-1891. There are deeds and contracts relating to land acquisition by the family; teaching certificates and teachers' records; and letters relating to religion, camp meetings, temperance, slave purchases, and the treatment of slaves. Civil War letters of A.A. Anderson and A.J. Anderson relate to service in Ewell's division and describe training camps, clothing, equipment, discipline, sickness, minor engagements in Virginia, the effects of conscription, and hospital conditions. There are materials on civilian commodity prices, the collection of back pay of deceased soldiers, and poems about the war. Postwar letters relate to farming, livestock diseases, bee keeping, and tobacco. There are some postmaster's records from Calahaln, 1889-1899. Printed materials include local newspapers, forms, political broadsides, and agricultural pamphlets. The volumes include a brief pocket diary, 1913; a teacher's roll, 1891-1892; a ledger of Anderson and Brothers, 1868 (1868-1870) 1877; a ledger of C. and G.J. Anderson and Company, 1854-1858; and an account book of C. Anderson and Brother, 1858-1861.

123. Z.W. ANDERSON BAND BOOK, 1865. 1 vol. (108 pp.) Wilkes County, Ga.

A hand-written book of tunes used in the Confederate Army. Anderson served with the 37th Georgia Regiment. Included are notes on the surrender of Joseph E. Johnston's army.

124. ANDREAS MICHAEL ANDREADĒS PAPERS, 1933. 1 item. Athens, Greece.

Letter relating to Andreadēs' presentation to a professor Scott of a copy of his book, Philippe Snowden: L'homme et sa politique financière (Paris: 1930).

125. BENJAMIN ANDREW PAPERS, 1783, 1786. 2 items. Liberty County, Ga.

Promissory note to James Dunwody, and a petition from John McLean to the Chief Justice of Georgia for the collection of a debt.

126. BENJAMIN WHITFIELD ANDREWS PAPERS, 1848-1885. 5 items. Logan's Store and Patten's Home (Rutherford County), N.C.

Business and personal letters; subjects include mining in Arkansas, 1857, and commodity prices, South Carolina, 1885.

127. CHARLES H. ANDREWS PAPERS, 1846 (1874-1882) 1885. 75 items. Madison (Morgan County), Ga.

Letters of Andrews and his wife to their son, Louis H., 16 items, describe the life of small farmers raising cotton, cane, and other crops. Letters, 30 items, from Confederate veterans provide information for Andrew's projected history of the 3rd Georgia Regiment. Among the correspondents are John F. Jones, Reuben B. Nisbet, Joseph E. Johnston, and Jubal A. Early. Miscellaneous material, 29 items, includes letters from John McIntosh Kell, Adjutant General of Georgia, to C.H. Andrews and Son regarding insurance on the insane asylum at Milledgeville; and an incomplete manuscript history of the 3rd Regiment by J.W. Lindsey and Andrews.

128. CHARLES WESLEY ANDREWS PAPERS, 1808-1901. 3,643 items and 1 vol. Shepherdstown (Jefferson County), W. Va.

Family and other letters and documents relating to the Page, Meade, Lee, and Custis families of Virginia; the Robinson and Mines families of Maryland; and the Andrews family of New England; their movement westward from the tidewater following the Revolution; social life; the War of 1812; the treatment of slaves; manumission and colonization; plantation houses; doctrine of the Protestant Episcopal Church; travel in Europe, the Near East, and Africa; business activities and travel in the Middle West; and the Civil War. There are many letters by Ann Randolph (Meade) Page; her daughter Sarah Walker (Page) Andrews; Sarah's husband Charles Wesley Andrews; Matthew and Ann Randolph (Meade) Page; Mary (Randolph) Meade; Anna (Robinson) Andrews; and their relatives. There are also letters, 1839-1840, from Liberia by Robert M. and John M. Page, former slaves.

Letters of Bishop William Meade relate to the revival of the Protestant Episcopal Church in Virginia after 1815. The influence of the Oxford Movement in the U.S. and the resulting church division is shown in correspondence of C.W. Andrews from 1845 to his death in 1875. There are many letters and papers on religious matters by Andrews's parishioners while he was pastor at Shepherdstown, West Virginia. Much material, especially correspondence with Charles Pettit McIlvaine, relates to the effect of the Civil War on the church. Other prominent clergymen included in the collection are William Sparrow, James May, and John Seeley Stone. There are account books for religious tracts, the Evangelical Knowledge Society, and the Episcopal Church at Shepherdstown. A series of travel letters, 1841-1842, from C.W. Andrews to his wife and to the editors of the <u>Episcopal Recorder</u> (Philadelphia), review the state of religion in England, France, Italy, Greece, Egypt, Syria, and Africa, describing Bechuanas and Kaffirs in South Africa and missionary work in Sierra Leone. Included are details of buildings, monuments, antiquities, and scenery.

There are letters, 1851-1890, relating to the flour milling business of James Yeatman and George Robinson in Saint Louis, Missouri; letters from Matthew Page Andrews I describing his travels on the midwestern prairies in the 1850s, Indians, the Kansas constitutional struggle, land speculation and settlement. His love letters to Anna Robinson, later his wife, comment on his legal education and career.

M.P. Andrews's letters also describe secessionist sentiment, employment in the C.S.A. treasury, events in Richmond during the Civil War, and experiences in the 3rd Virginia Regiment in 1864-1865. His correspondence and that of C.W. Andrews and Charles McIlvaine describe the Civil War along the Potomac, the battles of Manassas and Antietam, details of military activity, office seekers in Richmond, newspaper reporting of the war, prices and shortages, censorship, treatment of Confederate wounded, and life under Federal occupation. Postwar family letters include many from C.W. Andrews II and Matthew Page Andrews II containing descriptions of school life and Virginia colleges during the 1880s.

Also in the collection are vestry minutes of the Zion Protestant Episcopal Church of Charles Town, West Virginia, 1816-1820; legal documents; passports; poems; sermons; C.W. Andrews's diary at Middlebury College, Vermont, 1826; clippings; account books; personal journals, diaries, and notebooks of family members, particularly of C.W. Andrews; scrapbooks; a register of the African Missionary Society, 1820; a subscription book, 1830, concerning the outfitting of freed slaves sent to Liberia; the Civil War diary, 1864-1865, of M.P. Andrews I; and a commonplace book of Mary Meade, 1832-1833. There is a key to families and places.

129. EVERETT C. ANDREWS PAPERS, 1859-1888. 18 items. New Haven, Conn.

Business papers; military orders; pension papers.

130. GEORGE ANDREWS PAPERS, 1802. 1 item. Dover (Strafford County), N.H.

Letter to George Andrews from [William?] Andrews describing his experiences moving to the Mississippi territory and local economic conditions in Natchez, Mississippi.

131. JAMES O. ANDREWS PAPERS, 1859-1861. 8 items. Chappell Hill (Washington County), Tex.

Personal and business letters addressed to William Harris of Williamston, North Carolina.

132. WILLIAM B.G. ANDREWS PAPERS, 1862 (1863-1865) 1870. 27 items. Pittsylvania County, Va.

Personal letters from a Confederate soldier to his father, Thomas A. Andrews, and a poem by Ellen Easley. Topics include the death of a female slave; religion and preaching; marriages; commodity prices in Virginia; casualties; prisoners; the sieges of Suffolk, 1863, and Petersburg, 1865; the battles of Nashville, 1864, Gordonsville, 1864, and Sayler's Creek, 1865; Confederate government; sickness; conscription; election of officers in the 10th Battalion of Virginia Heavy Artillery; Confederate and Union generals; rumors about the Confederate peace commissioners, 1865; and rumors about Lee's call for the use of Negro troops.

133. LIDA (DUKE) ANGIER PAPERS, 1948. 1 item. Durham, N.C.

A biographical sketch of Mrs. Angier by her daughter, Carlotta Gilmore (Angier) Satterfield, discussing the family, the Duke Memorial Church, and philanthropy.

134. MALBOURNE A. ANGIER PAPERS, 1895-1899. 3 vols. Durham, N.C.

Malbourne A. Angier was a grocer and local political officeholder who served as mayor of Durham and county commissioner. He was the father-in-law of Benjamin N. Duke. This collection comprises two ledgers and a daybook of the M.A. Angier Co., a grocery business principally owned by Benjamin N. Duke. Other owners included Angier, James T. Stagg, Thomas J. Walker, and W.T. O'Brien.

135. GEORGE ANGLE PAPERS, 1862-1872. 81 items. Logan (Hocking County), Ohio.

Letters of an officer of the 90th Regiment of Ohio Infantry Volunteers, 1862-1863, discussing the Civil War in Kentucky and Tennessee, camp life, casualties, furloughs, health, hospitals, pickets, supplies, and the capture by Confederates of a train near Nashville. There are also letters by Angle's wife, Sarah, and daughter, Ella.

136. FLORENCE WINTER ANKENEY PAPERS, 1897-1927. 132 items and 3 vols. Hagerstown (Washington County), Md.

Miscellaneous correspondence, business, and legal papers, and patent medicine advertisements. Three ledgers, 1841-1893, contain accounts of a general store started by Samuel and Henry Troup and continued by John C. Ankeney.

137. GABRIELE D'ANNUNZIO PAPERS, 1930. 1 item. Gardone, Italy.

Photocopy of a report on Lt. Romano Manzutto written by d'Annunzio while he was general of the Division of Aeronautics.

138. ANONYMOUS ACCOUNT BOOKS, 1793-1884. 19 vols.

Merchants' account books or unidentified account books from Augusta, Georgia, April 1796; Elkhorn, Pennsylvania, 1818-1871; Woodville, [Virginia?], 1819-1821; New Market, Virginia, 1823; [Lincoln County, Georgia?], 1831-1839; Davidson County, North Carolina, 1835-1839; Newton, North Carolina, 1866-1880; [Panola, Mississippi?], 1883-1884; and Virginia, 1838-1839. Physicians' account books from South Carolina, 1824-1831, and [Davidson County, North Carolina?], 1835-1839. Tobacco factor's account book from Virginia, 1821-1823.

139. ANONYMOUS ALBUM, 1871. 1 vol.

Photographs of European scenes, prominent Europeans, and works of art.

140. ANONYMOUS ALBUMS. 2 vols. Washington.

Photographs taken along the Columbia and Kettle rivers.

141. ANONYMOUS BOOK OF POETRY. 1 vol.

142. ANONYMOUS COMMONPLACE BOOK, ca. 1830. 1 vol.

Poems and clippings of a religious character.

143. ANONYMOUS DAYBOOK, 1769-1770. 1 vol. (176 pp.) Louisa County, Va.

This daybook contains the records of what appears to have been a general store which operated either in the town of Louisa or in surrounding Louisa County, Virginia. The book contains the names of many of the inhabitants of the county and lists purchases, specifying quantities and prices. The last twenty-four pages of the daybook were used as a scrapbook, probably by Henrietta B. Hill, in the 1830s.

144. ANONYMOUS DAYBOOK, 1789-1790. 1 vol. (500 pp.) Prince William County, Va.

Shipments of tobacco are recorded from warehouses at Dumfries, Aquia, Boydshole, Colchester, Machodoc, and Quantico; the largest accounts are for the firm of Smith, Huie, Alexander and Company whose trade included consignments to Rotterdam in the Netherlands. A large general account for Timothy Brundige, merchant of Dumfries, is dated September 25, 1789. James Reid's accounts are also prominent, especially relative to the ship *Molly*.

145. ANONYMOUS DAYBOOK, 1828-1833. 1 vol. (68 pp.) [Virginia?]

A merchant's record of customers, commodities, and commodity prices.

146. ANONYMOUS DAYBOOK AND LEDGER, 1851-1855. 2 vols. Wardensville (Hardy County), W. Va.

Records of a tannery or other dealer in hides and leather. Among the accounts are those of William S. Downs of Port Republic, Virginia.

147. ANONYMOUS DAYBOOKS, 1881-1901, 1920-1924. 10 vols. Abernethy, N.C.

Largely merchants' records.

148. ANONYMOUS DAYBOOKS, 1792 (1820-1860) 1873. 11 vols.

Records of businesses in Georgia, North Carolina, Virginia, and Massachusetts.

149. ANONYMOUS DIARY, 1865-1868. 1 vol. (296 pp.) Baltimore, Md.

The diary concerns family matters, public celebrations, and a storm in August, 1867, which is further described by a clipping from the Baltimore *Sun*.

150. ANONYMOUS DIARY, 1831. 1 vol. (61 pp.)

The author of this diary records the events occurring August 20, 1831, the first day of a trip from Boston to Albany, New York. He describes a journey from Boston to Providence by stagecoach and then into Long Island Sound on a steamboat. He reports the conversations of three South Carolinians traveling with him on such subjects as the tariff, nullification, secession, slavery, salaries for clergymen, and prostitution. He describes Providence and Newport, Rhode Island, and gives a detailed account of the accommodations of his ship, the *Boston*. Anecdotes about Washington Allston, the painter, and Thomas Cooper, the educator, are also recorded.

151. ANONYMOUS DIARY, 1838. 1 vol. (50 pp.) Natchez (Adams County), Miss.

Account of a trip by steamboat from Natchez to Houston, Texas.

152. ANONYMOUS DIARY, 1843-1844. 1 vol. Accomac County, Va., and Atkinson (Rockingham County), N.H.

This diary of a twenty-seven-year-old schoolteacher from New England, probably Atkinson, New Hampshire, records experiences and impressions in Accomac County, Virginia. Most of the entries concern his observations of the South and Southerners, and his opinions on such subjects as slavery, religion, and politics. He describes a meeting with Congressman Henry Alexander Wise. This volume was formerly cataloged as the diary of A. T. Allen.

153. ANONYMOUS DIARY, 1854-1855. 1 vol. (164 pp.) England.

Diary of a young Englishman's experiences on British transport ships carrying men and equipment to the Crimean War. Vessels included were the *Palmerston*, the *Pyrenees*, and the *Mary Ann*. Ports visited were Malta, Constantinople, Varna, Eupatoria, Sevastopol, Balaklava, and Genoa. There is comment on naval and military activities, two ship lists, and a number of colored drawings of ships, military personnel, and others.

154. ANONYMOUS DIARY, 1861-1863. 1 vol. (62 pp.) Gordonsville (Orange County), Va.

Diary of a Virginia woman which is concerned with local events of the Civil War. There is frequent mention of the activities of Confederate General Thomas Jonathan Jackson, whose troops often passed through the town going between Richmond and Charlottesville, and reflections on civilian life and economic conditions in the Confederacy.

155. ANONYMOUS DIARY, 1861-[1865?]. 2 vols. Brock's Gap (Rockingham County), Va.

In 1861 the author of this diary traveled from Virginia to Texas to Tennessee, commenting at some length on people and places, and particularly on secessionist sentiment. The second volume contains Confederate Army memoranda centering around the 7th Virginia Regiment, Cavalry. Among the many places described in some detail are Charlottesville, Virginia; Holly Springs, Mississippi; New Orleans, Louisiana; Paris, Texas; and Grand Junction, Tennessee. There is a detailed description of the steamboat trip from New Orleans to Shreveport, and mention of Francis H. Hill, formerly of Virginia.

156. ANONYMOUS DIARY, 1868. 1 vol. Bethania (Forsyth County), N.C.

This diary appears to have been kept by a woman who was a member of a large farm family. The brief entries are concerned with the details of farm life, such as baking, washing, cleaning house, visiting neighbors, going to church, and attending funerals and baptismal ceremonies.

157. ANONYMOUS DIARY, 1878. 1 vol.

This diary covers the period from April 6, 1878, to November 9, 1878, and describes the pilgrimage of an American lady to the museums and royal palaces of Europe. She toured through England, France, Germany, Sweden, Norway, and Russia. Among many other things, she reports on seeing Henry Irving in a play in London, visiting the Exposition Universelle in Paris, and meeting General and Mrs. Ulysses Simpson Grant in Norway.

158. ANONYMOUS DIARY, 1820. 1 vol. Savannah (Chatham County), Ga.

A travel journal by a Savannah physician on a trip from Savannah to Greenville, South Carolina, containing road directions and comments on accommodations prices, and social customs. The journal also contains accounts of patients.

159. ANONYMOUS HOUSEWIFE'S SCRAPBOOK AND DAYBOOK, ca. 1877 and 1839-1840. 1 vol. (172 pp.) Hedgesville (Berkeley County), W. Va.

160. ANONYMOUS JOURNAL, 1849-1850. 1 vol. (110 pp.) Columbia Furnace (Shenandoah County), Va.

Accounts for a general store which traded with the operators of the Columbia iron furnace and with the owners of other furnaces in the area.

161. ANONYMOUS JOURNAL, 1853-1854. 1 vol. (396 pp.) Hagerstown (Washington County), Md.

Records of a general merchant.

162. ANONYMOUS JOURNAL, 1861-1865. 3 items. Newtown (Fairfield County), Conn.

A journal kept by one of the officers of the steamer George Leary from April, 1864, to January, 1865. The journal describes transporting troops, wounded, and prisoners primarily between Fortress Monroe, Virginia, and the James River; contrabands to Philadelphia, New York, and Boston; and Confederate prisoners to Hilton Head, South Carolina, to be exchanged for Union prisoners. Accompanying the journal is a picture of Captain Robert B. Benson and a bill, 1861, for Benson's share of the insurance on the ship Sultana and her cargo.

163. ANONYMOUS LEDGER, 1861-1866. 1 vol. Selma (Dallas County), Ala.

The record book of C. L. Ewing as superintendent of the Southern Railway Company, 1899-1901, is incorporated into this ledger.

164. ANONYMOUS LEDGER, 1767-1776. 1 vol. (482 pp.) New Bern (Craven County), N.C.

Merchant's record book with accounts for many local people. The ledger shows trade with Philadephia in pitch, tar, turpentine, staves, grain, and other foodstuffs.

165. ANONYMOUS LEDGER, 1794-1800. 105 ff. (unbound). Perquimans County, N.C.

Merchant's ledger listing a wide range of manufactured and agricultural commodities with their prices. One of the larger accounts is for Exum Newby.

166. ANONMYOUS LEDGER, 1806-1816. 193 ff. Elkton (Cecil County), Md.

Account book of a tavern keeper. The ledger records taxes, investments in bank stock, and numerous references to stagecoach operations and tavern expenses.

167. ANONYMOUS LEDGER, 1831-1838. 141 pp. Lawrenceville (Gwinnett County), Ga.

Apparently the account book of a physician, itemizing visits, medicines, and prices.

168. ANONYMOUS LEDGER AND SCRAPBOOK, 1848-1864, 1885-1896. 521 pp. Augusta (Richmond County), Ga.

Ledger of a physician giving accounts for services and medicines. It was later used as a scrapbook for clippings on Confederate history and personalities and topics of interest to women.

169. ANONYMOUS LEDGERS, 1817-1869, 1878-1931. 22 vols.

Merchants' records, personal accounts, and unidentified.

170. ANONYMOUS LEGAL NOTEBOOK, [before 1865]. 93 pp. Virginia.

171. ANONYMOUS LEGAL NOTEBOOK. 60 pp. North Carolina.

Legal notes based on decisions made in North Carolina cases.

172. ANONYMOUS LOGBOOK, 1767-1768. 1 vol. New England.

This logbook records four commercial voyages among the English colonies in North American and the West Indies and also to England, involving the ships Joannah and Grizzel, with detailed references to cargo, destination, and customers, especially in connection with a voyage to North Carolina.

173. ANONYMOUS MEDICAL NOTEBOOK, 1834-1836. 1 vol.

Student notebook on lectures given by John Patten Emmet at the University of Virginia and lectures given by George Bacon Wood at the University of Pennsylvania, all of which were concerned with pharmacy.

174. ANONYMOUS MEDICAL NOTEBOOK, 1850-1851. 1 vol. (173 pp.) Würzburg, Bavaria, Germany.

Describes diseases and prescriptions and contains notes evidently on the lectures of Drs. Wilhelm Rapp (1794-1868) and Maximilian Adolph Langenbeck (1818-1877).

175. ANONYMOUS MERCHANT'S ACCOUNT, 1765. 1 item. Alexandria, Va.

One sheet listing credit customers including Jacob Hite, Thomas Monroe, and George Washington.

176. ANONYMOUS NOTEBOOK, 1799-1895. 1 vol. Digby (Digby County), Nova Scotia.

One section of this volume records the sale of goods salvaged from the wrecked ship Culloden. The other section contains the records of the Sissiboo Baptist Church and a note on Negro Baptists in Nova Scotia.

177. ANONYMOUS NOVEL, 18th century. 1 item and 1 vol. England.

Copy of a novel (280 pp.) by a woman, possibly from Hampshire.

178. ANONYMOUS NOVEL: "A LITTLE PICTURE." 6 vols.

A sentimental novel with the setting in France and Germany during and after the Franco-Prussian War. The plot concerns romance between individuals of enemy nations.

179. ANONYMOUS PAPERS, 17th century. 1 vol. England.

Volume of sermons of an unidentified clergyman, presumably an Anglican.

180. ANONYMOUS PHOTOGRAPH ALBUM, early 1900s. 1 vol.

Photographs from travel on the ocean and in Virginia; North Carolina; Washington, D.C.; and Niagara Falls, New York.

181. ANONYMOUS PHYSICIANS' BOOK OF TREATMENTS AND REMEDIES, 1630. 1 vol. (660 pp.) Germany.

182. ANONYMOUS POEM: "EDWIN AND LAURA." 4 vols. [Virginia?].

Rough draft and revised copy of a narrative poem, "Edwin and Laura," evidently written by a Virginian after 1825. There are descriptions of places in Virginia and critical observations on local customs. Topics include therapeutic springs in the western part of the state; popular writers and magazines; and the University of Virginia, its expensive operation, its faculty, and the hiring of foreigners for the faculty. A supplement describes mercenary Richmond merchants and lazy members of the legislature. Included also is a poem on drinking.

183. ANONYMOUS SCRAPBOOK, 1864-1890. 14 items and 1 vol. Martin County, N.C.

Clippings, for the most part on economic and political subjects, concerned with both state and national affairs.

184. ANONYMOUS SCRAPBOOK AND LADY'S LEDGER, 1868-1872, 1836-1840. 1 vol. (570 pp.)

Scrapbook of newspaper clippings.

185. ANONYMOUS SCRAPBOOK, 1898. 1 vol. (308 pp.) Worcester (Worcester County), Mass.

Clippings and pictures about several Massachusetts regiments which served in Cuba in the Spanish-American War. Primary focus is on the 2nd Massachusetts Regiment.

186. ANONYMOUS SONGBOOK, 1861-1862. 1 vol.

Confederate songs.

187. ANONYMOUS TOBACCO BOOK, 1823. 1 vol. Richmond, Va.

188. ANONYMOUS. ZANGA'S LINES FROM THE REVENGE. 26 pp.

The lines of the revengeful Moor, Zanga, from Edward Young's tragedy, The Revenge (1721), with cues from the roles of other characters.

189. CHARLES V. ANSON PAPERS, 1886. 1 item. London, England.

Invitation from Sultan Abdallah of the Comoro Islands to Commander Charles V. Anson to discuss a treaty for the abolition of slavery in the islands.

190. THOMAS ANSON, FIRST VISCOUNT ANSON PAPERS, 1773-1799. 47 items. Shugborough Hall, Staffordshire, England.

Forty-seven bills and receipts of Thomas Anson, First Viscount Anson (1767-1818), Sir George Anson (1769-1849), and their father, George Anson (d. 1789).

191. ANSON COUNTY, N.C., TAX LISTS, 1903-1906. 4 vols.

Volumes list taxpayers alphabetically, with Negro and white accounts differentiated, amounts owed and amounts paid recorded, and county, state, school, and road taxes entered in separate columns.

192. ANSON COUNTY, N.C., PUBLIC SCHOOL COMMITTEE, DISTRICT NO. 23 FOR WHITE RACE REGISTER, 1896-1897. 1 vol.

Register of public school.

193. KENT APPERSON DAYBOOKS, 1819-1860. 2 vols. Blacksburg (Montgomery County), Va.

Accounts of the sale of general merchandise.

194. RICHARD APPERSON PAPERS [ca. 1800]. 2 items. Petersburg (Dinwiddie County), Va.

Papers of Richard Apperson, a Revolutionary soldier, concerning a duel with a Dr. Holmes.

195. DILMUS J. APPLEBERRY PAPERS, 1810 (1850-1896) 1901. 1,750 items. Fluvanna County, Va.

Business, family, and legal correspondence of a plantation owner, largely composed of accounts, bills, invoices, indentures, and land surveys. Letters, some of a business nature, comprise about 5 percent of the collection. Correspondents whose names appear most often are Pettit and Leake, a legal firm of Goochland Court House; Atlantic and Virginia Fertilizing Company of Richmond, Virginia; and Dilmus Appleberry's nephew, Thomas A. Bledsoe.

196. NATHAN APPLETON PAPERS, 1850-1899. 143 items. Boston, Mass.

Correspondence of a businessman allied to the publishing firm of Appleton and Co. His interests included politics, international commerce and banking, foreign affairs, art and artists, humanitarian movements, and the Grand Army of the Republic. There are several letters concerning the difficulties of organizing Civil War troops and the experiences of Northern soldiers in the South. Appleton's continuing interest in international fairs and expositions is shown in a number of letters, including his correspondence on the Paris Exposition, for which he served as commissioner. Appleton received letters in the 1870s from Anson Burlingame, Charles B. Norton, and Francis W. Rice, among others, on the prospects for a Central American interoceanic canal, and there are many letters on various international business affairs from people such as Henry S. Gillig, Charles Bowles, and Charles B. Norton. Appleton's long-term interest in the Grand Army of the Republic is reflected in his correspondence with John Palmer, a commander-in-chief of the Grand Army of the Republic, and a number of prominent generals.

197. PRASCA ARBORÉ & CO., 1759-1760. 9 items. Cadiz, Spain.

These documents, written in French, concern the voyage of the brigantine _Les Bons Amis_, which was stopped by both English and French corsairs as it returned with a cargo of sugar from Saint Domingue to Cadiz. The papers include a list of the cargo brought from Europe and a report on the voyage written by the captain.

198. LESLIE O. ARBOUIN PAPERS, 1899. 1 item. Cartagena, Colombia.

Photocopy of a diary kept while on a river boat trip up the Magdalena River in Colombia. Contains detailed descriptions of the people, towns, and wildlife Arbouin encountered.

199. CHARLES ARBUTHNOT PAPERS, 1804-1807. 5 items. London, England.

Letters from Arbuthnot to the Foreign Office written while Arbuthnot was ambassador extraordinary at Constantinople. In the letters he discussed the financial arrangements and burdens of his embassy.

200. JOSEPH ARCH PAPERS, 1873, 1883. 2 items. Barford, Warwickshire, England.

A facsimile letter from Arch appealing on behalf of the National Agricultural Union and a letter stating Arch's opinion on financial compensation for members of the House of Commons.

201. ARCHBISHOP OF TRIER CANONICAL AND CIVIL LAW BOOK, 1700s. 1 vol. (171 pp.) Trier, Prussia (Germany).

202. JOHN ARCHDALE PAPERS, 1694-1705. 77 items. London, England, and Charleston, S.C.

Photostatic copies of original papers in the British Museum, pertaining to the Province of Carolina, most of which fall within the administration, 1694-1696, of Governor John Archdale (1642-1717), and include many of his letters. The collection concerns the enticing of German colonists into the province; the establishment of the Church of England; dissension in the Carolinas; living conditions in the colonies; religious dissension in regard to qualifications for office-holding and representation in the assembly; freedom of religion; rights and privileges of aliens; mistreatment of the Indians; and sales of land. Included are a speech by Governor John Archdale to the assembly and various commissions; a description of North Carolina and St. Augustine, Florida; a marriage license for a member of the Archdale family; petitions in behalf of the French settlers; patent grants; maps of the Charleston, South Carolina, settlement and of the eastern North Carolina seaboard; and a copy of Culpeper's draft of the Ashley River.

203. FLETCHER HARRIS ARCHER PAPERS AND NOTEBOOKS, 1804 (1847-1885) 1900. 984 items and 15 vols. Petersburg (Dinwiddie County), Va.

Correspondence of Fletcher H. Archer (b. ca. 1817), lawyer and soldier, including letters written from Mexico during the Mexican War; Civil War papers concerning Archer's service in the 5th Virginia Infantry Brigade, among which are letters, morning reports, subsistence returns, diaries, and scrapbooks of Archer's poems; letters covering economic and legal phrases or Reconstruction; account books of Archer's legal business; sermons, three account books and various legal and financial papers of his father, Allin LeRoy Archer (b. 1783), a Methodist minister.

204.  WILLIAM M. ARCHER PAPERS, 1861-1862. 9 items. Richmond, Va.

Letters and papers relating to Confederate army life in Alabama and Virginia. Units mentioned specifically are the 2nd Regiment of Alabama Volunteers and the 13th Regiment of Alabama Volunteers.

205.  WILLIAM SEGAR ARCHER LETTERS, 1823-1847. 4 items. Amelia County, Va.

Letters of a lawyer, U.S. representative, and U.S. senator. One item comments on the political situation in 1846 and criticizes Polk's administration.

206.  J. W. AREHEART PAPERS, 1862, 1865. 2 items. South Carolina.

Letter and a schedule dealing with the value of Confederate and state currency in 1862 and 1865.

207.  WILLIAM H. AREHART DIARIES, 1863-1865. 3 vols. Harrison County, W. Va.

Civil War diary of William Arehart, Confederate soldier of Company H, 12th Regiment, Virginia Cavalry, describing his war activities and camp life.

208.  ARITHMETICS, 1761-1853. 27 vols.

Numerous volumes kept by pupils, according to general practice, containing rules and illustrative examples of various arithmetical processes, extending in general from simple addition to arithmetical progressions. The twenty-six arithmetics, as follows, were sometimes part of a collection but more often are separate items. David Barger, 1841, Botetourt County, Virginia; Nelson Bost, 1850, Olive Branch, North Carolina; Ann Eliza Brown, n.d., n.p.; George Pinckney Clay, 1853, Catawba County, North Carolina; William Cowan, 1795, n.p.; Alexander Cuningham, n.d., Petersburg, Virginia; Michael Doub, 1809, Stokes County, North Carolina; William Ellett, 1761, North Carolina; John Ferguson, 1805, Mecklenburg County, North Carolina; H. O. Flagg, n.d., n.p.; Laurence Hatcher, 1835, n.p.; Silas Henton, 1812, n.p.; P. D. Holland, 1815-1819, Franklin County, Virginia; Mark R. Laffoon, 1808, Surry County, North Carolina; Thomas Latta, 1807, n.p.; William Law, 1807, Darlington, South Carolina; Miles S. Lowrance 1845, Taylorsville, North Carolina; John Matlock, 1837, Caswell County, North Carolina; Hartwell Motley, 1837, n.p.; Allen W. Pegram, 1834, 1841, Guilford County, North Carolina, 2 vols.; James Reeves, 1828, n.p.; Abraham Rickerson, 1803 [Georgia?]; Samuel V. Smaw, n.d., Washington, North Carolina; John Spinks, 1832, n.p.; Ann Stevens, n.d., n.p.; John Teague, 1832, Davidson County, North Carolina; Samuel Vines, 1829, Washington, North Carolina; and Squire Meadows, 1827-1828, Person County, North Carolina.

209.  J. C. ARMENTROUT LEDGER, 1881-1923. 1 vol. (115 pp.) Stuarts' Draft (Augusta County), Va.

Mercantile accounts.

210.  THOMAS ARMENTROUT LEDGER, 1829-1859. 1 vol. (178 pp.) South River (Augusta County), Va.

Miller's account.

211.  JOSEPH S. ARMFIELD PAPERS, 1883-1886. 3 items. Jamestown (Guilford County), N.C.

Letters to a gunsmith relating to family affairs and an order for making a gun.

212.  WALKER KEITH ARMISTEAD PAPERS, 1824-1827. 1 vol. Upperville (Loudoun County), Va.

Letter book containing the incoming and outgoing correspondence of the commanding colonel of the 3rd Regiment of Artillery, United States Army. The letters deal mainly with routine military matters such as courts-martial, supplies, recruitment, and reports. Among the correspondents are Samuel Cooper, John Adams Dix, Thomas Sidney Jesup, and Roger Jones.

213.  JOHN ARMSTRONG PAPERS, 1827-1880. 26 items. Greensburg (Westmoreland County), Pa.

Legal papers concerned with the settlement of estates and debts. Includes a letter, 1848, from General C. P. Markle stating that his father would not consider becoming a candidate for governor and a letter, 1842, concerning the settlement of George Remaly's estate.

214.  THOMAS R. ARMSTRONG LETTERS. 1813-1833. 6 items. Stokes County, N.C.

Letters concerning land claims, speculations, and litigation in Tennessee; and a benefit lottery for Oxford (N.C.) Academy.

215.  WILLIAM G. ARMSTRONG PAPERS, 1848-1882. 292 items. Columbia (Tyrrell County), N.C.

Letters of a merchant whose business consisted largely of the sale of shingles and lumber. Letters are also concerned with borrowing money from the Bank of the Cape Fear. Some family letters are included, and there is a land deed from Thomas Armstrong to

Bennett Armstrong of Tyrrell County.

216. VIRGINIA H. ARNETT PAPERS, 1863. 3 items. Rehoboth (Wilkes County), Ga.

Letters from two Confederate soldiers, Robert T. Cullars and George W. Normans, describing campaigning in Virginia, particularly under General George B. Hood.

217. SIR EDWIN ARNOLD PAPERS, 1870-1903. 136 items. London, England.

Correspondence of a British poet and journalist, for the most part of a very general nature but indicative of his associations and acquaintances. The correspondence includes a series of letters, 1895-1901, from Takaaki Kato, the Japanese ambassador in London; Sir George Birdwood's recommendation for the European colonization of Northern Burma, 1886; U.S. Ambassador Thomas F. Bayard's comments on Anglo-American relations, 1896; H. Dharmapala's letter, 1896, about the restoration of Buddh Gaya; Joseph Chamberlain's response to the government's critics during the Boer War, 1900; John Mason Cook's reaction to his first trip to Japan, 1893; and various inquiries and responses to articles Arnold had done for the Daily Telegraph.

218. JOHN ARNOLD PAPERS, 1851-1894. 300 items and 14 vols. New Braunfels (Comal County), Tex.

Correspondence, financial records, and account books, generally written in German, of a general goods merchant, including prices for many commodities, principally alcoholic beverages and foodstuffs. With these papers is a diary of a train trip from Texas to Nashville, Tennessee, which appears to be connected with a Whitsett family. There is also an undated map of the route in Atascosa County of the Chicago, St. Louis, and Texas Air Line Railroad.

219. RICHARD ARNOLD PAPERS, 1859 (1861-1865) 1867. 140 items. Charleston, S.C.

Business papers of Richard Arnold, who operated a blacksmith shop. The numerous itemized accounts reveal the trend of prices during the Civil War period. Statements of fees show that Arnold's children attended Miss Edmond's School in Charleston and Spartanburg Female College, both in South Carolina.

220. RICHARD DENNIS ARNOLD PAPERS, 1832-1875. 27 items and 4 vols. Savannah, Ga.

Papers of a physician, including a diary, scrapbook, receipt book, and account book. The papers are almost entirely business and professional correspondence. Filed with the papers is Arnold's diary for the years 1832-1838, which reflects his experience as a young physician in Savannah, and describes various aspects of the city's social life. The diary contains a lengthy account of a duel and describes a visit by General Winfield Scott. The indexed scrapbook is made up almost entirely of newspaper clippings on a variety of subjects such as local and national politics, railroads and taxation, health and medicine, opera and drama, and Civil War subjects. The receipt book shows both household and medical expenditures for 1848-1859, and the account book contains the records of estates for which Arnold was an administrator.

221. SALLIE E. (UMSTOTT) ARNOLD PAPERS, 1864-1871. 21 items. New Creek (Mineral County), W. Va.

This collection is comprised, for the most part, of letters written to Sallie Arnold between 1864 and 1866 by Union soldiers and friends. The correspondence is personal, but there is a description of a train trip from McConnellsburg, Pennsylvania, to Peoria City, Illinois, in 1866, and a description of a Dunkard camp meeting, also in 1866.

222. ARNOLD AND COOLEY LEDGER, 1854-1855. 1 vol. (651 pp.) Wadesboro (Anson County), N.C.

Merchant's account book.

223. ANDREW ARTHUR PAPERS, 1904-1951. 13 items and 6 vols. Orrville (Dallas County), Ala.

The individual items in this collection concern Arthur's family and farm. The volumes are financial records and membership lists of St. Paul's African Methodist Episcopal Church, 4 vols., and minute books of a lodge and a benevolence society, 2 vols.

224. CHESTER A. ARTHUR PAPERS, 1913-1962. 1,516 items and 301 vols. Richmond, Va.

Papers of Chester A. Arthur, sign painter and labor union official of Virginia, include information on labor legislation; wages; strikes; employment; labor newspapers; the American Federation of Labor; the Brotherhood of Painters, Decorators, and Paperhangers of America; the Sign and Pictorial Painters Local Union, especially during the period 1943-1953 when Arthur served as financial secretary; the poll tax; and Virginia gubernatorial, local, and presidential elections of 1945, 1947, and 1952. Correspondents include William Green, Harry F. Byrd, and William Z. Foster. In addition to correspondence, there is a substantial volume of labor publications.

225. KARL EVERETT ASHBURN PAPERS, 1948-1965. 24 items. New Orleans, La.

This collection consists of invitations for political functions, two letters, Christmas greeting cards, a 1965 Baylor University commencement program, and newspaper clippings relating to President John F. Kennedy's visit to Texas in 1963 and his assassination.

226. TURNER W. ASHBY PAPERS, 1869. 2 items. Alexandria (Arlington County), Va.

Business letters dealing with Ashby's bankruptcy.

227. SAMUEL A'COURT ASHE PAPERS, 1856 (1858-1888) 1950. 96 items. Raleigh (Wake County), N.C.

Letters from Alfred Thayer Mahan (1840-1914), naval officer and historian, to Samuel A'Court Ashe (1840-1938), Confederate veteran, author, and editor. The earlier letters portray the developing characters of the young men, both educated at the U.S. Naval Academy, Annapolis, Maryland, and the writers comment on naval affairs. Included also are photographs of both as young men. [Partially published: Rosa Pendleton Chiles (ed.), Letters of Alfred Thayer Mahan to Samuel A'Court Ashe, 1858-59 (Duke University Library Bulletin, No. 4, Durham, N.C., 1931).] In addition, the collection contains a biographical sketch of Mahan prepared by Ashe in 1930 and several letters concerning the Samuel A. Ashe Chapter of the Children of the Confederacy, Wadesboro, North Carolina.

228. RICHARD ASHHURST PAPERS, 1827-1857. 11 items. Philadelphia, Pa.

Correspondence of a wholesale merchant, relating to orders, collection of debts, and sales.

229. ANTHONY ASHLEY-COOPER, SEVENTH EARL OF SHAFTESBURY, PAPERS, 1822-1882. 31 items. London, England.

Personal and business letters of Lord Shaftesbury, including four items pertaining to his father, Cropley Ashley-Cooper, Sixth Earl of Shaftesbury. The collection also contains a letter from the Reverend James Loutit to Henry Austin Bruce, Home Secretary, about the economic plight of the population of the Shetland Islands.

230. CHARLES ASHLIN PAPERS, 1848-1852. 8 items. Columbus, Ohio.

Letters of a physician describing a trip from Richmond to Columbus in 1848 and discussing Locofocoism in Columbus, cholera epidemics, and family affairs.

231. GEORGE ASHMAN PAPERS, 1781-1784. 11 items. Bedford County, Pa.

Business letters of a Revolutionary lieutenant of militia dealing with the problems of raising troops, securing money for their payment, and obtaining adequate military equipment and food supplies.

232. JOHN W. ASHMEAD PAPERS, 1854. 3 items. Philadelphia, Pa.

Three letters from William Meade Addison, United States district attorney for Maryland, to Ashmead, United States district attorney for Pennsylvania, claiming jurisdiction in the case of the mutiny on the Garmany.

233. HERBERT HENRY ASQUITH, FIRST EARL OF OXFORD AND ASQUITH, PAPERS, 1912-1939. 16 items. London, England.

Largely political correspondence including letters from King George V on Britain's policy toward the First Balkan War, 1912; Winston Churchill's resignation from the War Council, 1915; Lord Askwith on the coal strike of 1921; Herbert Gladstone commenting on Asquith's speech on W. E. Gladstone and discussing the future of the Liberal Party, 1922; Lady Frances Balfour speculating about the election of 1922; Ramsay Macdonald on unpreparedness and the worries of his situation, 1935; Austen Chamberlain reacting to the government's handling of the Hoare-Laval Pact, 1935; King George VI praising Neville Chamberlain and expressing doubt that the war would come, 1938; and the Archbishop of Canterbury on Franklin D. Roosevelt's peace appeal to Hitler and Mussolini, 1939.

234. WILLIAM S. ATKINS ACCOUNT BOOK, 1852-1865. 1 vol. Hernando (De Soto County), Miss.

Account book of a Mississippi wagoner.

235. ALEXANDER S. ATKINSON PAPERS, 1789-1909. 27 items. St. Mary's (Camden County), Ga.

Papers representing three generations of the Atkinson family, including correspondence of Dr. Burwell Atkinson, cotton planter, giving details of cotton marketing and prices, 1831-1842; of Alexander S. Atkinson, dealing with his law practice and the execution of claims, 1843-1845; and of Judge Samuel C. Atkinson, 1909.

236. ATLANTA AND RICHMOND AIR LINE RAILWAY COMPANY LETTER BOOK, 1871-1872. 1 vol. (232 pp.) Richmond, Va.

Business letters to A. S. Buford (1826-1911), president of the Atlanta and Richmond Air Line Railway Company, generally from the secretary of the company, Larkin Smith, and the banking firm of Lancaster

Brown & Co., New York. Smith wrote of notes due, stock sold, and curatives for Buford's perennial invalidism. Letters of Lancaster Brown & Co. were usually concerned with notes.

237.  ATLANTIC AND NORTH CAROLINA RAILROAD RECORDS, 1884-1931. 2 vols. North Carolina.

Minute book of the board of directors, 1884-1931, and a stock transfer book, 1897-1922.

238.  ATLANTIC AND WESTERN RAILWAY COMPANY PAPERS, 1905-1968. 41,600 items and 214 vols. Sanford (Lee County), N.C.

Office files, comprising the bulk of the collection, provide information on the economic life of the area served by the Atlantic and Western between Sanford and Lillington in Lee and Harnett counties, particularly on the production of lumber and agricultural goods, and show the effect of World Wars I and II on the operation of the road, especially in the negotiations with the U.S. Railroad Administration, 1918-1928. There are correspondence, printed material, advertisements, and pictures of railway equipment, supplies, and rolling stock, including many drawings and specifications for locomotives, both steam and diesel, and for gasoline-powered railroad motor cars used after 1917. The Edwards Railway Motor Car Company of Sanford is frequently mentioned. A large amount of material concerns the Association of American Railroads; the American Short Line Railroad Association, including an incomplete series of its Weekly Information Bulletin, 1933-1952; the North Carolina Railroad Association; the Southern Short Line Railroad Conference; the Eastern North Carolina Traffic Club; the Short Line Railroad Association of North Carolina; and the North Carolina Short Line Railroad Association. There are also minutes, 2 vols., for the meetings of the board of directors and the stockholders, 1912-1944, 1961, 1965-1966; financial records including ledgers, cashbooks, and journals; annual reports, 1914, 1916-1921, 1925, 1927-1928; reports to the Interstate Commerce Commission, 1913-1926, 1928-1956; and reports to the North Carolina Utilities Commission, 1934-1953, 1956-1959.

239.  MARTHA ATWATER PAPERS, 1879-1883. 10 items. Sparta (Hancock County), Ga.

Personal correspondence of Martha Atwater with nieces and nephews.

240.  W. AND G. T. AUGUSTIN DAYBOOK AND LEDGER, 1841-1845. 2 vols. Lawrenceville (Brunswick County), Va.

Accounts of a general mercantile firm.

241.  JAMES M. AUGUSTUS PAPERS, 1864, 1875. 2 items. [Ohio?].

Personal letters from son to mother.

242.  ALBERTA AULICK PAPERS, 1834-1887. 24 items. Winchester (Frederick County), Va.

Letters, for the most part from brother to sister, dealing with family matters. Two letters, 1834 and 1859, were written by an uncle, John H. Aulick, an officer in the U.S. Navy; one deals with appointments to the United States Naval Academy in 1834.

243.  ELLEN AUMACK PAPERS, 1864-1865. 9 items. Port Richmond (Wapello County), Iowa.

This collection consists primarily of letters from a soldier in the 2nd Iowa Regiment concerning his service in Tennessee and in Sherman's campaign in North Carolina. Places mentioned include Goldsboro and Raleigh, North Carolina.

244.  EIN AUSFLUG NACH NORDDEUTSCHLAND UND IN DIE NORDSEE IM JAHRE 1842, 1842. 1 vol. (251 pp.) Germany.

Translation of title: A trip to North Germany and in the North Sea, 1842.

245.  BENJAMIN AUSTIN AND HENRY REID PAPERS, 1756 (1790-1820) 1879. 625 items. Burke County, N.C.

Correspondence and other papers of Austin and Reid, justices of the peace and farmers, consisting of legal papers, court records, tax lists, militia rosters, election lists and returns. There are personal letters from relatives in Georgia, Kentucky, and Indiana. Topics include blacksmithing, farming, abolitionist sentiment in Indiana, and Burke County politics.

246.  LORING AUSTIN PAPERS, 1818-1819. 21 items. Boston, Mass.

Official and personal correspondence of the superintendent of the recruiting service of the United States Army, 8th Regiment. Included are weekly reports on enlistments, desertions, supplies, and bounties from a recruiter in Providence, Rhode Island, and letters concerning appropriations, the appointment of Dr. Thaddeus Hubbard, and relations with fellow officers.

247.  JOSEPH B. AUSTIN PAPERS, 1858. 1 item. Chicago, Ill.

A facsimile business letter extolling farm land in Illinois being offered for sale by the Illinois Central Railroad Company.

248.  ISAAC THOMAS AVERY, SR., PAPERS, 1899. 1 item. Morganton (Burke County), N.C.

Letter to Avery from James Marion Baker, then serving as assistant librarian of the United States Senate.

249. TRUEMAN G. AVERY PAPERS, 1868. 5 items and 1 vol. Buffalo (Erie County), N.Y.

Diary of a trip made by Avery and his wife by steamboat, railroad, and stagecoach from New Orleans to Washington, D.C. He describes the cities of Mobile, Montgomery, Macon, Savannah, Jacksonville (Fla.), Charleston, Wilmington, Richmond, and Washington, among others. Avery had political conversations with Mayor Gustavus Horton of Mobile and Governor Robert M. Patton of Alabama; attended church services of Negro Methodists in Mobile and Charleston; and saw Negroes in the Catholic cathedral at Mobile.

250. ERNEST AXON PAPERS, 1939. 1 item. Buxton, Derbyshire, England.

Letter from the assistant curator of the Carmarthenshire Antiquarian Society concerning George Eyre Evans and the rarity of complete sets of *Antiquarian Notes*.

251. H. G. AYER DIARY, 1862. 1 vol. (160 pp.) Manchester (Hillsborough County), N.H.

Diary of a trooper in the 1st New Hampshire Regiment, Cavalry, describing life in camp and service in the field. Ayer was stationed at Pawtucket, Rhode Island; near Washington, D.C.; and at various places in Virginia. There is a brief mention of the battle of Shiloh and the death of General Albert S. Johnston and comments on the battle of Cedar Mountain, the second battle of Manassas, and the battle of Fredericksburg.

252. PATRICK HENRY AYLETT PAPERS, 1851-1914. 22 items. Richmond, Va.

This is a collection of legal papers, letters, and manuscript articles, primarily built around the lives and careers of Aylett and his son-in-law, William Lawrence Royall, and focusing on the Civil War. Several items concern the capture of Royall by Union troops in March, 1865.

253. ALBERT AYLOR PAPERS, 1840 (1871-1916) 1933. 176 items and 4 vols. Madison County, Va.

Personal and business correspondence and papers of the Aylor family. The first part of the collection, 1840 to 1882, contains material on the manufacture of chairs and accounts of land sales and transfers in Virginia, and includes references to the religious revival in Virginia in 1840 and the depression of 1875. Papers for 1893-1933 are for the most part personal and contain many photographs. There are several pictures of roads and bridges in Virginia, including two showing Robinson's River in the flood of 1912. Among the volumes is a catalog for Wilson College, Chambersburg, Pennsylvania, for 1903-1904.

254. ROMEYN BECK AYRES PAPERS, 1864-1912. 4 items.

Miscellaneous letters, one from Ayres to General George Gordon Meade acknowledging his appointment as a major general and three to Mrs. Ayres from John M. Schofield and Daniel E. Sickles.

255. THOMAS W. BABB PAPERS, 1890. 13 items and 1 vol. Plymouth (Washington County), N.C.

Accusations and evidence against Thomas W. Babb, Baptist minister, charging him with misconduct and misappropriation of funds. Mentioned in the correspondence are Columbus Durham, D. E. Riddick, and R. T. Vann.

256. ORVILLE ELIAS BABCOCK PAPERS, 1871. 2 items. Washington, D.C.

Letter from Babcock, U.S. Army officer, aide-de-camp and private secretary to U.S. Grant, to H. A. Spaulding concerning personal business matters. Letter from Joseph Hayne Rainey to Babcock concerning a list of men attending a convention in South Carolina.

257. NATHAN LYNN BACHMAN SCRAPBOOKS, 1933-1934. 2 vols. Chattanooga (Hamilton County), Tenn. and Washington, D.C.

258. JOHN BACKHOUSE PAPERS, 1740-1956. 4,473 items and 7 vols. London, England.

Business and personal correspondence of the Backhouse family, principally, of John Backhouse (1784-1845), merchant and British Under Secretary of State for Foreign Affairs. Material for the 18th century and as late as the 1840s reflects the family's mercantile operations, including efforts to collect pre-Revolutionary debts in America. There is considerable correspondence during the first decade of the 1800s from Backhouse's associates in mercantile firms at Amsterdam and Hamburg. A series of 128 letters, 1805-1842, from Jacques Augustin Galiffe, historian and genealogist of Geneva, Switzerland, includes vivid descriptions of Italy and its cultural life. Relating to George Canning are personal, political, and administrative papers, 1812-1827, which document Canning's relationship with Backhouse, the authorship of a pamphlet published against Canning in 1818, his appointment and resignation as Governor General of India, the extent of his patronage in that office and at the Board of Control for India, problems with his son (William Pitt Canning), and other matters. There is a detailed commentary by Backhouse upon the formation of the cabinet in 1827. Family correspondence, which dominates the papers after the 1820s, contains numerous references to the Foreign Office and occasionally to relations with particular countries, notably Circassia, France, Greece, Russia, Turkey, and the United States. Letters and diaries of Backhouse's son, George, and his wife include references to the slave trade and describe their life at Havana while he was commissary judge there. There are numerous letters from Backhouse's son, John, from Canton and Amoy, China, while he served at the consulate (ca. 1843-1855), and papers of the Jeudwines and the Sheppards. Topics include art, literature, music, and education. There are clippings, drawings, photographs, engravings, autographs, invitations, calling cards, wax seals, valentines, and genealogical materials. In the collection is a more extensive description, a selective list of correspondents and an index of persons, places and subjects.

259. ELECTUS BACKUS PAPERS, 1860. 1 item. Detroit, Mich.

Letter recording the activities of Electus Backus, Sr., in the War of 1812.

260. A. S. BACON PAPERS, 1864-1898. 8 items. Baltimore, Md.

Business letters and papers.

261. AUGUSTUS OCTAVIUS BACON PAPERS, 1886-1914. 5 items. Macon (Bibb County), Ga.

Letters of Bacon, U.S. Senator from Georgia. One deals with Georgia politics in 1886. There is printed material on the funeral service for Bacon in 1914 in the U.S. Senate Chamber.

262. HERBERT T. BACON PAPERS, 1820 (1824-1846) 1859. 10 items. Nottoway County, Va.

Correspondence of Herbert T. Bacon, of his family, and of the Gregory family, concerning amusements and courtships. One letter, May 14, 1846, analyzes the progress of the Mexican War.

263. GEORGE EDMUND BADGER PAPERS, 1799-1861. 23 items and 2 vols. Raleigh (Wake County), and New Bern (Craven County), N.C.

Personal and business letters from George E. Badger (1795-1866), U.S. Senator, 1846-1855, and Secretary of the Navy, 1841. Most letters are to Thomas Mandeville Carlisle concerning family and business matters, especially a disagreement between the Postmaster General and the railroads. A letter to R. B. Temple refers to Zachary Taylor's election. One commonplace book by Badger contains miscellaneous material, legal notes, a 1785 address by Joseph Brown Ladd, and several brief essays. It mentions New Bern Academy. A commonplace book of Frances L. Badger includes original poems by her, and copies of two sermons.

264. WILLIAM BADHAM, JR., PAPERS, 1817 (1962-1870) 1897. 799 items and 12 vols. Edenton (Chowan County), N.C.

Principally family and business correspondence and papers of William Badham, Jr. (b. 1835), North Carolina lawyer, merchant, and Confederate soldier, and a few political letters to William Badham, Sr., from Thomas Bragg, M. E. Manly, John W. Moore, Kenneth Rayner, George Reade, and others. The Civil War letters, written from near Petersburg, Virginia, and Smith Island, at the mouth of the Cape Fear River in North Carolina, contain price quotations on blockade goods, descriptions of army life on Smith Island, and comments on peace advocates in the Confederacy. Much of the correspondence consists of love letters from Badham to his wife, Louisa (Jones) Badham. Also included are miscellaneous papers, probably connected with Badham's legal practice; the business papers of his father-in-law, John M. Jones; and several letters from J. C. Badham, representative from Chowan County in the North Carolina House of Commons in 1854, 1856, and 1858, referring to political maneuverings in the Assembly. Twelve volumes contain Badham's dry goods accounts, ca. 1859-1876; a teacher's register kept by Louisa Badham; and accounts of a sale of the furniture of John Jones.

265. ARTHUR PENDLETON BAGBY PAPERS, 1842. 1 item. Monroe County, Ala.

Letter from Benjamin Fitzpatrick to Bagby, U. S. Senator from Alabama, requesting a naval appointment for a friend.

266. BENNETTE M. BAGBY PAPERS, 1830 (1860-1894) 1920. 910 items. Powhatan County, Va.

Correspondence of the Bagby and Flippin families, planters, soldiers, and educators, especially the papers of Bennette M. Bagby, and family letters of his second wife, Louisa B. (Flippin) Bagby. Letters from Bagby's sons and nieces of his second wife are numerous. The letters deal chiefly with the period of secession, Civil War, and Reconstruction, revealing the economic plight of the South; hardships from disease, especially the yellow fever epidemic in Louisiana; camp life; educational conditions; and the attempts of the South at readjustment after the Civil War. Many of the family letters are written from Kentucky, Louisiana, Mississippi, Missouri, Texas, and various parts of Virginia. Included are college letters from Randolph-Macon College, Boydton, Virginia, and letters which discuss the systems of education in Louisiana, Mississippi, Texas, and Virginia, and describe the hardships of the public schoolteacher.

267. GEORGE WILLIAM BAGBY PAPERS, 1861-1863. 3 items. Virginia.

A letter from R. B. Rhett, Jr., expressing hope that Bagby will reestablish his connection with the Mercury, and attacking the military policy of Jefferson Davis; a letter from an unidentified friend in Lynchburg, Virginia, dealing with personal and local matters; and a letter from Edward S. Joynes concerning the circulation of a brief biography of Dr. Harrison, a University of Virginia professor.

268. JOHN BAGFORD PAPERS, 1708. 1 item. London, England.

Letter from Thomas Hearne, historical antiquary, to Bagford, British book and pamphlet collector, concerning their mutual library interests.

269. TILMON F. BAGGARLY PAPERS, 1860-1879. 125 items. Iredell County, N.C.

Chiefly correspondence between Baggarly, farmer, mechanic, and Confederate soldier, and his wife, Nancy. Baggarly's letters discuss the war, camp life, diseases, and deserters. Nancy's letters reflect the hardships faced by soldiers' wives.

270. NICHOLAS BAGGS PAPERS, 1917-1918. 3 items. Abington (Montgomery County), Pa.

A letter from Baggs to Henry Pickney McCain, Adjutant General of the United States; McCain's reply; and a letter from John McElroy, editor of the National Tribune, to Baggs, concerning Civil War statistics.

271. DOCTON WARREN BAGLEY DIARY, 1856-1864. 1 vol. (358 pp.) Williamston (Martin County), N.C.

Diary, 1861-1864, of D. W. Bagley (1801-1878), treasurer of the Martin County Volunteer Company of the Confederate Army, giving detailed accounts of military events in eastern North Carolina and the activities of the company. One section contains clippings related to the Civil War. Also included are thirty-seven pages of records, 1856-1860, of the Roanoke Steamboat Company.

272. EDWARD F. BAGLEY PAPERS, 1861. 2 items. Georgia.

Two letters from Edward F. Bagley (d. 1861), Confederate major general, to his sister on his resignation from the U.S. Army and on conditions at Fort Pulaski, Georgia.

273. JOSEPH E. BAILEY PAPERS, 1876-1905. 35 items. Whitakers (Nash County), N.C., and Hays County, Tex.

Family correspondence of a planter in the vicinity of Whitakers who lived for a while in Texas. Topics include personal matters and farm management.

274. JOSIAH WILLIAM BAILEY PAPERS, 1833 (1930-1946) 1967. ca. 422,400 items and 10 vols. Raleigh (Wake County), N.C., and Washington, D.C.

The papers of Josiah W. Bailey (1873-1946), editor, attorney, and U.S. Senator, 1930-1946, consist largely of correspondence and supporting printed material, although there are also financial records, clippings, volumes, broadsides, pictures, and memorabilia. They depict Bailey's family, personal, religious, and professional life, and reflect his wide range of interests in state and national issues. The Personal Series includes family and personal correspondence and memorabilia; information relating to the Baptist Church in North Carolina, Baptist publications, especially the Biblical Recorder, and church-affiliated institutions such as Wake Forest, Mars Hill College, and Chowan College; manuscript notes, drafts and corrections, typescripts, and printed copies of Bailey's writings, addresses, statements; financial papers; and invitations and engagements. The Legal Series, ca. 1900-1940, consists of correspondence relating to Bailey's practice and the legal profession, and a sample of case files from Bailey's law office. The Pre-Senatorial Series is generally devoted to issues concerning North Carolina, especially agriculture, politics, economic conditions, election reform, railroads and ports, roads, temperance, the development of public education, racial issues, and woman suffrage. There is considerable information on Bailey's 1924 gubernatorial campaign, the presidential campaign of 1928, the 1930 Senate race, and the Democratic Party. In the Senatorial Series, 1931-1946, material pertaining to national affairs predominates, although Bailey's strong interest in North Carolina remains evident. The series consists of correspondence from constituents ranging from semi-literate farmers to heads of industry; letters to and from public officials; notes of Bailey's speeches and copies of statements; and related printed material. Topics include agriculture, trade and commerce, foreign policy, the Depression, economic concerns, judicial affairs, labor and management, military affairs, national defense, North Carolina and national politics, opposition to the New Deal, the Democratic Party, prohibition, and relief. Volumes include financial records; the yearbooks of several Raleigh women's clubs; marriage booklet of Christopher Thomas Bailey, Jr., Bailey's brother, and Mary Himbish; list of wedding gifts, probably of Josiah and Edith (Pou) Bailey; and a book of embroidery patterns, 1860. An inventory describes the collection in detail.

275. LETITIA M. BAILEY AUTOGRAPH ALBUM, 1860-1862. 1 vol. (125 pp.) Charlottesville (Albemarle County), Va.

Autograph album of Letitia M. Bailey.

276. THEODORUS BAILEY PAPERS, 1869. 1 item. Washington, D.C.

Letter from Bailey, Rear Admiral, to his nephew, T. Bailey Myers, about Admiral Farragut's retraction of his criticism of Bailey's leadership in the battle of Mobile in 1864.

277. WILLIAM HENRY BAILEY, SR., PAPERS, 1843-1901. 24 items. N.C. and Houston, Tex.

Miscellaneous papers of Bailey (1831-1909), lawyer and author. The bulk of the papers concerns legal problems in connection with silver mines near Lexington, N.C., owned by Fred H. Stith. Included are Stith's descriptions of his holdings, especially the Bonanza Silver Mine. Several letters comment upon the ability of various North Carolina lawyers. One item consists of a list of home remedies. Correspondents include Bailey, Kemp Plummer Battle, Johnson D. McCall, and Levi M. Scott.

278. CHARLES WALLACE ALEXANDER NAPIER ROSS COCHRANE-BAILLIE, SECOND BARON LAMINGTON, PAPERS, 1903-1908. 52 items and 3 vols. Lamington, Lanarkshire, Scotland, and London, England.

Papers of Lord Lamington, relating to his governorship of Bombay, India. Letters and administrative notes concern budget surpluses and recommendations for local use; development of a program for inoculation against the plague; administrative and diplomatic matters in India; the system of presidency governments versus centralization; and relations between Hindus and Muslims, Europeans and Indians. Correspondents include George Nathaniel Curzon, First Marquis Curzon of Kedleston; Gilbert John Elliot-Murray-Kynynmound, Fourth Earl of Minto; Sir Shahu Chhatrapati, Maharaja of Kolhapur; Horatio Herbert Kitchener, First Earl Kitchener of Khartoum; and John Morley, Viscount Morley of Blackburn. Volumes consist of two letter books with a separate index. The first contains 165 regular and detailed dispatches from the governor to the secretary of state for India and seventy-two dispatches to the viceroy of India. The second includes twenty-two letters from other prominent persons. The handwritten indexes refer to various persons and topics as administration, agriculture, the army, commerce, the courts, education, public finance, industry, journalism, public health, social life and customs, the British protectorate of Aden, and transportation, especially railroads.

279. WILLIAM T. BAIN PAPERS, 1850-1865. 89 items. Raleigh (Wake County), N.C.

Principally the family letters of William Bain, his wife, and children to his daughter, Mollie (Bain) Bitting of Germantown, North Carolina, concerning Bain's Masonic interests, difficulties with his unruly slaves, "Black Republicanism" of the North, a speech made in Raleigh by Stephen A. Douglas in 1860, hopes for a strong Confederacy, and meetings of the legislature. Also included are a letter from a friend of Mrs. Bitting in Petersburg, Virginia, describing the new public buildings there, and a letter to Lewis Bitting from a friend in Georgia telling of his drugstore business.

280. SIR EDWARD BAINES PAPERS, 1832-1880. 29 items. Leeds, Yorkshire, England.

Political correspondence of Baines (1800-1890), journalist, economist, and member of the House of Commons, 1859-1874. Letters from Thomas Babington Macaulay concern Macaulay's political career, Belgian independence from the Netherlands, the ministry's legislative plans concerning the East India Company and the abolition of slavery, and other political matters. Letters from William Ewart Gladstone discuss his proposed national budget in 1860 calling for a reduction of duties on various commodities, measures to change the franchise laws; and other political topics. Other letters refer to Baines' defeat in 1874, Gladstone's victory in 1880, the granting of a knighthood to Baines, and political concerns of the Liberals.

281. CHAMBERS BAIRD, SR., AND CHAMBERS BAIRD, JR., PAPERS, 1817-1933. 2,255 items. Ripley (Brown County), Ohio.

Papers of Chambers Baird, Sr. (b. 1811), lawyer, politician, and paymaster in the U. S. Army, 1863-1866, and Chambers Baird, Jr. (b. 1860), lawyer and politician, consist of correspondence, 1821-1933; legal papers, 1817-1920; financial records, 1841-1919; and some printed material. Most of the correspondence before 1885 pertains to the elder Baird and his law practice; his duties as paymaster; and cases concerning soldiers' bounties, claims, and pensions. Early correspondence is routine and refers to collecting debts, land sales in Ohio and elsewhere, financial matters, the insurance business, and plans for the construction of a railroad in southern Ohio. Civil War papers concern the Union Party and the recruitment of troops. Letters about soldiers' claims begin in April, 1863, and comprise the bulk of the correspondence during 1866-1885. Correspondence of 1886-1933 is chiefly that of Chambers Baird, Jr., concerning his business and legal affairs, travels, and literary interests. There is correspondence (1895-1903) with Nelson W. Evans, a Portsmouth, Ohio, attorney and amateur historian.

Legal papers include deeds, wills, promissory notes, and documents relative to civil suits, largely from Brown County, Ohio; material relating to soldiers' discharges, claims, and bounties, 1863-1880; courts-martial records, 1863; and paymaster's records, 1863-1866. The financial papers consist of some of Baird's accounts, records of transportation furnished to soldiers, and distribution rolls showing Baird's disbursement of funds. Printed material concerns soldiers' bounties and pension claims.

282. ROBERT BAIRD PAPERS, 1832 (1856-1871) 1873. 1,425 items. Manchester (Henrico County), Va.

Business papers of Robert Baird and his partner, Peter Small, concerning an iron foundry for the production of water wheels, circular saws, spindles, castings, gate fixtures, etc. Papers reflect the changes in foundry operations under James D. Craig, who managed the business from Baird's death (ca. 1866) until taken over by Baird's son, James S. Baird, 1872.

283. DANIEL BAKER PAPERS, 1839-1858. 18 items. Winchester (Frederick County), Va.

Business letters of Daniel Baker, a journeyman carpenter, commenting on labor conditions in the 1850s; and family letters from relatives in Kentucky, Missouri, and Ohio.

284. ELEANOR J. W. BAKER PAPERS, 1848-1895. 1 item and 1 vol. Boston, Mass.

Letter, 30 pp., of Eleanor Baker (d. 1891), written to Anna Gurney (1797-1857), English scholar and author, describing travels in the South in 1848. Beginning at Baltimore, Maryland, she traveled to Washington, D.C.; Alexandria, Fredericksburg, and Richmond, Virginia; Wilmington, North Carolina; Charleston, South Carolina; Savannah, Macon, Barnesville, and Columbus, Georgia; Montgomery and Mobile, Alabama; and New Orleans, Louisiana. Included are descriptions of the various cities visited; speeches by Henry Clay and Daniel Webster; travel by railroad, steamboat, and stagecoach; slavery and abolitionism; cotton and rice plantations; and attitudes of Southerners toward the North. The volume, _Address at the Funeral of Mrs. Eleanor J. W. Baker of Dorchester_, by Rev. Theodore T. Munger, 1895 (Boston: 1895), 19 pp., also included eulogies by others.

285. HENRY BAKER PAPERS, 1862. 5 items. Newton (Baker County), Ga.

Letters from Henry Baker, private in Longstreet's Corps of the Confederate Army, to his wife. The letters are concerned chiefly with inquiries about home conditions.

286. HENRY DUNSTER BAKER PAPERS, 1794-1953. 272 items and 8 vols. Durham, N.C.

Papers of Henry D. Baker (1873-1939), U.S. consular official and newspaper editor and publisher, contain correspondence, clippings, genealogy, printed material, pictures, and volumes. The bulk of the papers before 1900 refer to the Griffiths, Speir, Willis and Austin families of England and Australia, related through Baker's wife, Gwyneth Griffiths. They concern family matters, and the service of Charles Ralph Griffiths (1790-1850) as British vice consul and consul at Buenos Aires, 1823-1846. Material after 1900 relates to the consular career of Henry Baker in Tasmania, 1907-1911, Bombay, 1913-1914, and Trinidad, 1916-1927; Baker's service as commercial attaché at Petrograd, Russia; and his opposition to trade with Russia, 1930-1931. Tasmanian Scrapbook, 1907-1911, includes clippings, photographs, and pictures relating to Tasmania, Australia, New Zealand, and the islands of the Bass Straits. Scrapbook, 1911-1933, contains pamphlets, articles, speeches, pictures, clippings and letters concerning relations with Russia during World War I and in 1930-1931, and Baker's activities in the United States, Trinidad, Tasmania, India, and New Zealand. There are also printed copies of books by Baker and by Charles H. Baker; family photographs and copies of portraits, especially from the Griffiths family; photographs of Trinidad and Baker's trip to Persia, 1916; and photographs of "Erryd," Victorian home of the Griffiths in Wales. Printed material consists of speeches, articles and pamphlets by and about Baker. The clippings, 1910-1951, include articles by and about Baker and items about the countries in which he served. An extensive genealogical folder contains information about the Baker and Dunster families of America and the Griffiths, Speir, Willis, Hart, and Blondeau families of England and Australia.

287. ISAAC BAKER PAPERS, 1848-1858. 28 items. Winchester (Frederick County), Va.

Papers of Isaac Baker, Lutheran minister, consist of his correspondence with Mary C. Dosh of Strasburg, Virginia; Dosh family correspondence; quarterly reports of Angerona Seminary, including curriculum; and some legal papers.

288. JAMES H. BAKER PAPERS, 1863-1865. 30 items. Surry County, N.C.

Letters from James H. Baker (d. 1865), Confederate soldier, describing his experiences in active service at Weldon, North Carolina, in 1864, and his stay in the General Hospital in Richmond, Virginia, which he entered October, 1864.

289. JOHN BAKER PAPERS, 1761-1785. 5 items. Savannah, Ga.

Legal documents consisting of a land survey, land grants, a legal case, a power of attorney, and a certificate of citizenship for Thomas Graves of Georgia.

290. [JOHN BAKER?] ACCOUNT BOOK, 1821-1849. 1 vol. (179 pp.) Perquimans County, N.C.

Plantation accounts.

291. N. C. BAKER AND H. C. BAKER PAPERS, 1822, 1900. 2 items. Winchester (Frederick County), Va.

Memorandum book, 1822, of N. C. Baker describing his travels to Philadelphia, New York and New Haven. Discussed were religious concerns, shipping, hunting, an election, a circus, tomatoes, books and a fire. A letter by H. C. Baker, 1900, mentions works on the assassination of Abraham Lincoln.

292. THOMAS J. BAKER PAPERS, 1861-1892. 362 items. Hagerstown (Washington County), Md.

Business and personal correspondence, personal bills and receipts of Thomas J. Baker, boat captain on the Chesapeake and Ohio Canal.

293. HAROLD LYMAN BALDWIN PAPERS, 1913-1966. 26 items. New York, N.Y.

Personal correspondence of Harold L. Baldwin, brother of Alice Mary Baldwin, first dean of the Woman's College of Duke University. Included are letters from poet Marianne Moore, commenting on Baldwin's poetry. Also included are seven photographs of Baldwin family members.

294. ARTHUR JAMES BALFOUR, FIRST EARL OF BALFOUR, PAPERS, 1882-1908. 2 items and 1 vol. London, England.

A letter from Lord Balfour (1848-1930), Prime Minister of England, 1902-1905, to George Wyndham, Chief Secretary for Ireland, discussing political matters; and a letter by Balfour, published in the Conservative and Unionist, noting the meeting of the National Union and stressing unity. An album, 1882-1893, contains routine letters from Aretas Akers-Douglas, Joseph Chamberlain, the Duke of Argyll, Lord Salisbury, the Duke of Devonshire, Balfour, Hugh Arnold-Forster, Alfred Lyttelton, Sir William H. Dyke, Lord Randolph Churchill, Lord Ritchie, and William E. Gladstone. There is some mention of Irish affairs.

295. JOHN BALL, SR., AND JOHN BALL, JR., PAPERS AND ACCOUNT BOOKS, 1773 (1803-1833) 1892. 3,211 items and 26 vols. Charleston, S.C.

Personal and business correspondence, papers, and account books of John Ball, Sr. (1760-1817), wealthy rice planter of Charleston, South Carolina, and of his son, John Ball, Jr. (1782-1834). The business papers of the collection are chiefly concerned with the rice industry in the Charleston area, 1791-1833, and include receipts, bills, accounts, lists of slaves, descriptions of rice crops, and purchase of horses; and numerous letters from John Slater, a London commission merchant. Included also are accounts kept by John Ball, Jr., as guardian of his half brothers and sisters and administrator of his father's estate. The bulk of the letters after 1826 are from the younger children of John Ball, Sr., and Martha Caroline (Swinton) Ball (later the wife of Louis Augustin Thomas Taveau): Alwyn, Hugh Swinton, and Elias Octavus. Many of the letters were written from Partridge's Military Academy of Norwich, Vermont, and Middletown, Connecticut, and reflect the attitudes of the younger moneyed class of the early nineteenth century. Among the correspondents are John Ewing Calhoun, William Drayton, Alexander Garden, Francis Huger, and the Laurens, Rutledge, Taveau, and other South Carolina families.

296. JOHN BALL MANUSCRIPT, 1909. 1 vol. (98 pp.) Charleston, S.C.

Typed copy of "Chronicles of Comingtee Plantation."

297. KEATING SIMONS BALL PLANTATION BOOK, 1850-1859, 1866. 1 vol. Comingtee (Berkeley County), S.C.

Comingtee Plantation accounts of Keating S. Ball, a rice planter, giving lists of food and supplies furnished the slaves; and, for 1866, articles of agreement with various freedmen.

298. MOLLIE BALL AUTOGRAPH ALBUM, 1854. 1 vol. (50 pp.) "Windsor Shades," New Kent County, Va.

Album of poems and prose from Mollie Ball's friends; one reference to Hanover Academy, Hanover County, Virginia, indicates that she was a student there.

299. THOMAS C. BALL PAPERS, 1882 (1884-1906) 1920. 47 items. Richmond (Madison County), Ky.

Correspondence of Thomas C. Ball, a merchant of Richmond and Stanford, chiefly from relatives in Missouri and Texas, describing social life and customs.

300. WILLIAM WATTS BALL PAPERS, 1805-1952. 28,214 items and 133 vols. Charleston, S.C.

Personal, financial, and professional correspondence of W. W. Ball (1868-1952), newspaper editor. A substantial portion of the papers consists of family correspondence containing information on school and college life; Hollywood in the 1930s and 1940s; social life and customs in Laurens, Charleston, and Columbia, South Carolina; and England, the Italian battlefront, and a journey across the Atlantic during World War II. Ball's financial papers, scattered throughout the collection, generally relate to real estate investments, stock holdings in textile mills, and the depression as it affected his financial situation. A major part of the correspondence pertains to state and national politics. Letters discuss Tillmanism and Bleasism; the state primary system and election reform; state and national elections; opposition to the New Deal and the formation of the Southern Democratic Party; and other local, state, and national issues. Material on race relations begins as early as 1916, but is particularly abundant from the 1930s on. Involved with the issue of states' rights versus federal control, the "Negro problem" includes the anti-lynching movement, enfranchisement and control of the Negro vote, racial unrest, segregation, and other matters. The papers reveal Ball's interest in education, especially the development of schools of journalism, the expansion of the state-supported college system, the University of South Carolina, and the South Carolina School for the Deaf, Dumb, and Blind. Other papers relate to Ball's editorship of various newspapers, principally The State and the News and Courier, and to his publishing efforts. There is also material on the textile industry in South Carolina, labor unrest and unionization, prohibition, woman suffrage, the depression, World Wars I and II, recollections by Ball and others of social life, customs and politics during the 1870s through the 1890s, the economic and industrial development of South Carolina, genealogy of the Watts and Ball families, and drafts and copies of speeches and editorials. Correspondents include editors, publishers, educators, politicians, financiers, and industrialists, principally from South Carolina, although some national figures are found. There are photographs, 1890-1940, of Ball and his associates. Volumes include family account books, 1911-1942; a memorandum book, 1901; scrapbooks, 1893-1951; a digest of the military service of Frank Parker, 1894-1945; and Ball's diary, 1916-1952.

301. BALLARD'S VALLEY PLANTATION PAPERS, 1766 (1786-1848) 1873. 235 items and 9 vols. St. Mary's Parish, Jamaica.

Financial papers and account books of Ballard's Valley Plantation, detailing the number and condition of slaves or apprentices and stock, purchases of goods, accounts payable, size of crops, and sales of sugar, rum, and cattle. Letters after 1837 also discuss crop conditions, the repeal of the Corn Laws, trouble with the freed Negroes in 1838, and the importation of Chinese labor in 1846.

302. SARAH E. R. BALLOWE ALBUM AND NOTEBOOK, 1848-1874. 2 vols. Fluvanna County, Va.

Autograph album, 1848-1854, containing poetry and prose from friends, and a chemistry notebook, 1874; included also are poems and copies of letters, 1851.

303. JAMES M. BALTHROPE PAPERS, 1854-1865. 11 items. Palmyra (Marion County), Mo.

Personal letters of James Balthrope, a teacher, to William Engle describing life in northern Missouri.

304. IRA LEO BAMBERGER PAPERS, 1884. 3 items.

Letters from George Becker and C. M. Evarts concerning legal cases.

305. GEORGE BANCROFT PAPERS, 1845-1885. 22 items. New York, N.Y.

Typed transcripts of fifteen letters to David L. Swain, president of the University of North Carolina, relating to the history of the state. The originals are at the University of North Carolina. Topics include the Regulators, Loyalists, Mecklenburg Declaration, Governors William Tryon and Alexander Martin, and Hermon Husband and Edmund Fanning. Original items include a letter to C. C. Jones on the employment of women and children in Germany and a note, 1885, of thanks for Jones's article on Richard H. Wilde; a letter from H. C. Van Schaack regarding the publication of his pamphlet on Henry Cruger; and notes relating to appointments by Bancroft as Secretary of the Navy, and to payment from publishers.

306. BANDINEL FAMILY PAPERS, (1763-1906) 1940. 403 items and 6 vols. England.

Records of a family formerly resident on Jersey in the Channel Islands. Most of the manuscripts during 1763-1815 concern Rev. Robert Hunter, an Anglican clergyman, and his family. Among topics discussed are the University of Glasgow, Hunter's students, the Church of England, and the Church of Scotland. Writers include John and William Anderson describing British activity in India; William Hunter and other former students; and Alexander Kennedy, an army surgeon at Hyderabad. Correspondence of Hunter's son-in-law, James Bandinel (1783-1848), contains personal letters to his wife and material relating to his work as a clerk in the Foreign Office, including the suppression of the slave trade and other African affairs, such as the explorations of John Davidson. Among topics occasionally mentioned are the daughter of the Earl and Countess of Rosebery; Queen Caroline, wife of George II; the Thames Tunnel; the life of Bandinel's son at Wadham College, Oxford; and social life on Lord Nugent's estate. There is a volume containing poems and Bandinel's translation of Spanish ballads by the Marqués de Santillana; and genealogical information about the Hunter family. Papers of Bandinel's son, the Rev. James Bandinel (1814-1893), relate largely to his clerical career, the Oxford Movement, his writings, and include correspondence with William Palmer, Henry E. Napier, Alfred R. Symonds, A. P. Stanley, and Rev. Robert Montgomery. There is a volume with a sermon and some poetry. Papers of Rev. Bandinel's son, James Julius Frederick Bandinel (b. 1815), include scattered items relating to service as a consular official at Newchwang, Manchuria, and pertain to the Sino-Japanese War, the Boxer Rebellion, and the Russo-Japanese War. The collection also includes materials of the related Le Mesurier family of Guernsey in the Channel Islands, including a diary, 1794, of Thomas Le Mesurier recording travels in Germany, Denmark, and Sweden; and scattered Le Mesurier letters of the early 19th century.

307. BANK OF BERKELEY IN VIRGINIA DAYBOOK, 1857-1858. 1 vol. (446 pp.) Martinsburg (Berkeley County), W. Va.

308. BANK OF BLACKSBURG DAYBOOK, 1892. 1 vol. (150 pp.) Blacksburg (Montgomery County), Va.

309. BANK OF CAPE FEAR RECORDS, 1835-1870. 71 vols. Washington (Beaufort County), N.C.

Balances from deposit ledger, 1836-1842; bill book, 1846-1855; collection book, 1855-1859; collection tickler, 1849-1855; daybook, 1843-1850; deposit book, 1849-1856; deposit ledgers, 1842-1854; discount ledgers, 1836-1862; general ledgers, 1836-1859; letter books, 1836-1870; minutes of board of directors, 1835-1857; offering books, 1836-1860; state of the bank, 1836-1868; and tellers' books, 1836-1860.

310. BANK OF CASWELL PAPERS, 1905-1912. 4 vols. Milton (Caswell County), N.C.

Daily balance book, 1910-1912; Register of drafts drawn on National Park Bank of New York, 1905-1907; letterpress books, 1907-1908, 1911-1912.

311. BANK OF THE STATE OF GEORGIA PAPERS, 1817-1869. 404 items. Savannah, Ga.

Deeds, indentures, and other legal and business papers, including powers of attorney from leading men and business firms of Georgia, references to transfers of the bank's stock, and land records. Some papers contain comments on the Panic of 1837 and the importance of cotton in restoring the Southern economy.

312. BANK OF THE VALLEY LEDGERS, 1852-1860. 2 vols. Romney (Hampshire County), W. Va.

313. JOHN BANKS PAPERS, 1784. 1 item. Charleston, S.C.

Letter from Henry Bromfield, Jr., of London commenting on the heavy demands from America for British goods.

314. NATHANIEL PRENTICE BANKS PAPERS, 1850-1880. 109 items. Waltham (Middlesex County), Mass.

The bulk of this collection, 90 items, concerns Banks's military career as commander of the Department of Annapolis during 1861. Topics include secessionist sentiment in Maryland, the arrest of political prisoners, Union leadership in Washington, and the status of Roman Catholics; and Banks's subsequent operations in the Shenandoah Valley. These papers appear to be a portion of the files captured by General Thomas Jonathan Jackson near Winchester, Virginia, in May, 1862, and are thus related to the selection of letters printed in Secret Correspondence Illustrating the Conditions of Affairs in Maryland, published by Southern sympathizers at Baltimore, 1863. A photocopy of this pamphlet is included with the collection. The collection also contains scattered items relating to Banks's political career; his operations on the Mississippi, 1863; the exchange of prisoners; and his postwar publications. Among the correspondents are Montgomery Blair, Benjamin F. Butler, Charles Carroll Fulton, and George Brinton McClellan.

315. JOSEPH BANNER PAPERS, 1832-1843. 4 items. Germanton (Stokes County), N.C.

Letters concerning the postal service. Joseph Banner carried the mail from Germanton to Salem. Included is one letter from Augustine H. Shepard, a member of Congress from North Carolina.

316. WILLIAM H. BANTA DIARY, 1862. 1 vol. (76 pp.) New York, N.Y.

Diary of William H. Banta, a Federal soldier who served in the campaign in eastern North Carolina; mention is made of Norfolk, Virginia, and the Virginia.

317. BAPTIST FEMALE COLLEGE PAPERS, 1881-1888. 3 items and 1 vol. Lexington (Lafayette County), Mo.

Includes a ledger with student's accounts.

318. BAPTIST (PRIMITIVE) MISCELLANEOUS PAPERS, 1909. 5 items. Mabank (Kaufman County), Tex., and Greenville (Pitt County), N.C.

Letters relating to doctrine and religious experiences; writers are J. C. Denton, S. Hassell, E. R. Robinson, Henry B. Tucker, and K. L. Hardee.

319. BAPTISTS. NORTH CAROLINA. ROBESON UNION CONSTITUTION AND MINUTES, 1884-1891. 1 vol. (112 pp.)

320. BAPTISTS. NORTH CAROLINA. STATE CONVENTION REGISTER OF ASSOCIATIONS, 1868. 1 vol. (28 pp.)

List of churches and ministers of the following associations: Central, Raleigh, Tar River, Rocky River, Pamlico, Yadkin, Flat River, Brown Creek, Cedar Creek, Beulah, Cape Fear, and Eastern.

321. FRANÇOIS BARBÉ-MARBOIS, MARQUIS DE BARBÉ-MARBOIS, PAPERS, 1786. 1 item. Paris, France.

Letter, June 29, 1786, possibly to the Chevalier de Brun, written from Port-au-Prince, Saint Domingue (now Haiti), where Barbé-Marbois served as intendant, concerning contraband and commercial relations between the French West Indies and the United States.

322. JAMES BARBOUR PAPERS, 1812-1855. 9 items. Orange County, Va.

Papers of a governor of Virginia, U.S. Senator, and U.S. Secretary of War, including references to Indian affairs, the Richmond fire in 1811, a proposed canal between the Potomac and Rappahannock rivers, commissions of 1812-1815, and pension payments in 1827.

323. JOHN N. BARBOUR PAPERS, 1832-1881. 62 items. Boston, Mass.

Letters and documents dealing with the activities of the partnership of Barbour and his cousin, John W. Sullivan. Most of the documents of 1832-1834 and a few later items relate to trade and finance. Places mentioned include Maine; Massachusetts; New Hampshire; Dubuque, Iowa; Italy; and South America. There is material concerning the ships and their captains, the cargoes, prices, insurance, rates of exchange, quality of goods, and economic conditions affecting commerce. W. S. Fitzwilliam is mentioned as the agent between Sullivan and Barbour and the branches of Gower and Co. in London, Trieste, and Genoa. Products shipped include cotton, wool, hides, rags, fruits, fish, oil, coffee, sugar, shellac, gum, honey, nuts, silk, indigo, rice, wheat, Indian corn, rye, oats, beans, barley, steel, wax, camels hair, ginger, hemp, senna, Persian berries, cocoa, dyes, brimstone, and wood. Beginning in 1837 most of the papers concerned copper claims in the Lake Superior region. There is some mention of Sullivan's interest in the American Land Company, Alabama Land Company, and Mississippi Land Company. Participating in the copper claims were Sullivan's brother-in-law, John Adams Dix of New York; Benjamin Franklin Butler; Thomas Perkins; and other prominent political leaders and public officials. There is also reference to the estate of Seth Adams, 1880-1881. Principal correspondents in the collection are Isaac Adams, John N. Bolles, Henry Leavitt Ellsworth, W. S. Fitzwilliam, S. W. Higgins, Bela Hubbard, John M. Stockton, and John W. Sullivan.

324. SAMUEL M. BARCLAY PAPERS, 1824-1851. Bedford (Bedford County), Pa.

Largely papers of the law firm of Murdock and Barclay, ca. 1831-1840, with several references to Pennsylvania and national politics.

325. GRAHAM ARTHUR BARDEN PAPERS, 1933 (1935-1960). 264,615 items. New Bern (Craven County), N.C.

The collection consists largely of the office files of a U.S. Representative from eastern North Carolina. There is a small amount of material during 1933-1934 relating to Barden's work in the state general assembly and his first Congressional campaign, but his Congressional files, 1935-1960, are comprehensive and contain correspondence, public statements, drafts of speeches, legal briefs, and reports, including printed bills and documents relating to the collection, often with Barden's marginal comments and corrections. There is also printed material in information files and clippings and photographs of Seymour Johnson Air Force Base and of Goldsboro, North Carolina. The collection pertains heavily to Barden's work on behalf of projects affecting his district and to his work as member and chairman of the House Committee on Education and Labor. Major issues include federal aid to education, labor-management relations, labor standards, and minimum wage legislation. Among correspondents are other committee members, legislators, government officials, educators, labor leaders, businessmen, and prominent North Carolinians. Constituent mail concerns projects, employment prospects, veterans' benefits, and other issues immediately affecting Barden's largely rural district, such as agriculture, fishing, lumbering, preliminary processing of tobacco, and furniture manufacturing. There are records concerning the establishment of several military installations, including Seymour Johnson Air Force Base and Camp Lejeune Marine Base. An inventory of the collection is available in the library.

326. THOMAS GEORGE BARING, FIRST EARL OF NORTHBROOK, PAPERS, 1870-1904. 29 items. London, England.

Included is correspondence relating to Baring's direction of the Admiralty Office as First Lord, 1880-1885, largely concerning personnel and administrative organization. Among writers are William Gladstone; Stephen Edward Spring-Rice; William Codrington; Edward Seymour, Twelfth Duke of Somerset; and Thomas Brassey. Letters relating to British politics about 1900 include several from Sir Edward Grey giving opinions of leading politicians and one from Sayaji Rao Gaekwar III, Maharaja of Baroda. There are also extracts from letters, 1879-1880, of Sir Neville Bowles Chamberlain, Commander-in-Chief of the Madras Army, criticizing British policies that led to the Second Afghan War and commenting on finances in India. There is correspondence relating to the Royal Geographical Society, 1879-1880, and some miscellaneous letters.

327. JOHN E. BARKER PAPERS, ca. 1852-1873.
5 items. Cincinnati, Ohio.

Personal letters.

328. SAMUEL BARKER PAPERS, 1848-1876.
23 items. Thorntown (Boone County), Ind.

Family correspondence between settlers in Indiana and relatives in Randolph County, North Carolina, describing crops, opportunities in the West, commodity prices, and personal matters. Some items mention the Woody family which moved from Guilford County, North Carolina, to Boone County, Indiana. Also included are papers relating to the James Sluder family of Ashe County, North Carolina, and La Grange, Randolph County. Among the writers is Levi Cox of Randolph County.

329. SIMEON BARKER PAPERS, 1882-1883.
9 items. New Salem (Randolph County). N.C.

Personal and business letters. Topics include the illness of Barker's wife; New Garden Academy, New Garden, North Carolina; and a publication of the Society of Friends.

330. PETER BARKSDALE PAPERS, 1783-1895.
448 items. Halifax County, Va.

Letters, 1780s-1790s, of William and Randolph Barksdale, merchants of Petersburg, Virginia, and Peter Barksdale, farmer of Halifax County, Virginia, concern the purchase of slaves and other commerce in Petersburg, and tobacco culture in Halifax County. Later correspondence is of Cornelia (Barksdale) Wimbish and her husband, John W. Quarles, merchant of Jackson and Memphis, Tennessee; of Edward Barksdale while at the University of Virginia and Jefferson Medical College; and of other members of the family. Topics include the hiring out of slaves; travel by stage and steamboat; the stabbing of Senator Ephriam Hubbard Foster of Tennessee, 1841; cholera in New Orleans and Memphis, 1849; yellow fever in Norfolk and Richmond, 1850; student life at the University of Virginia; the Sons of Temperance; local politics in Virginia and Tennessee; collection of debts; the Dan River Baptist Association, 1846; tailoring; commissions for Elisha Barksdale in the Virginia State Cavalry, 1819 and 1829; and the schooling of the Barksdale children.

331. BARKSDALE-HANNAH FAMILY PAPERS, 1811-1870. 30 items. Charlotte County, Va.

Letters of the children of Grief Barksdale (1774-1850), merchant and planter of Rough Creek, Charlotte County, Virginia, including Charlotte (1813-1886), Claiborne (1820-1883), Nancy (1829-1904), and Susan (1832-1863); and business and personal correspondence of Charlotte's husband, Samuel Hannah (1796-1859), of Charleston, Kanawha County; Charlotte County; and Lynchburg. Topics include business conditions and interests, especially relating to tobacco; slave hiring in Richmond, 1827; schooling of the Barksdale children; and conditions in Arkansas, 1870. Two letters from Hannah's agent in Liverpool, England, 1828-1829, concern British import duties.

332. SIR GEORGE HILARO BARLOW, FIRST BARONET, PAPERS, 1802-1847.
52 items. Farnham, Surrey, England.

Memoranda, correspondence, and copies of correspondence, largely relating to Barlow's petition for a peerage and documenting his service as a British administrator in India. Topics include the establishment of a legal code for Bengal, the conclusion of the Mahratta War in 1805, the Madras Army mutiny of 1809, and Barlow's struggles with his opponents on the East India Company's Court of Governors, which led to his recall in 1812. There is also correspondence, 1844-1845, provoked by the publication of Edward Thornton's History of the British Empire in India. Several miscellaneous manuscripts concern British politics, in part on the Isle of Wight.

333. JOHN BARNARD PAPERS, 1862-1863.
2 items. Deerfield (Franklin County), Mass.

Letters from a private in the Union Army concerning sickness among troops near Baton Rouge, Louisiana, 1862, and giving a graphic description of the Battle of Port Hudson, Louisiana, 1863.

334. JOHN GROSS BARNARD PAPERS, 1864-1865.
2 items. Washington, D.C.

Manuscript copy of documents exchanged between Barnard, chief engineer on Grant's staff, and Major General Burnside, July 3-August 6, 1864, relative to mining operations under the Confederate defenses at Petersburg, Virginia, and the battle of the Crater on July 30; and an extract from a letter by Barnard to his wife, April 2, 1865, reporting on the last days of the siege of Petersburg.

335. GEORGE BARNBY COMMONPLACE BOOK, 1746.
1 vol. (48 pp.) England.

Transcriptions of songs prevalent in the 1740s.

336. JOHN W. BARNES PAPERS, 1862-1863.
10 items. Kentucky.

Letters from John W. Barnes, a private in the Confederate Army, concerning defense of Vicksburg in 1863, camp life, rations, crops, and the shooting of deserters.

337. RICHARD BARNES PAPERS, 1752 (1758-1787) 1796. 29 items. Culpeper County, Va.

Legal depositions in the case of Jonathan Beckwith and Younger Helsick v. John Alexander and Gerald Hoose over the estate of Richard Barnes, their father-in-law.

338. WILLIAM SPEIGHT BARNES PAPERS, 1924-1971. 3 items. Tucson (Pima County), Ariz.

A telegram from Barnes, president of the men's association at Trinity College, to James B. Duke expressing gratification for Duke's endowment and pledging their support to the development of the university.

339. GODFREY BARNSLEY PAPERS, 1824 (1840-1861) 1873. 3,667 items and 1 vol. Savannah, Ga.

Letters to Godfrey Barnsley (1805-1872), Savannah agent for general import and export brokers of Liverpool, England, from his children; correspondence among the children; detailed lists comprised of accounts with physicians, invoices, prices of building materials for "Woodlands" (Barnsley's estate), records of sales and imports of cotton, bills, and receipts. There are letters from three of the Barnsley sons who attended the preparatory school of Charles Green at Jamaica Plain, Massachusetts; and letters from Barnsley's three daughters at Montpelier Female Institute, near Macon, Georgia. Much of the material concerns Harold Barnsley, who traveled over New England and other northern sections of the United States, in China, and on the seas; references to the Civil War, in which several of the sons served, and to depredations suffered by the family. Beginning in 1867 there are several letters from two of Barnsley's sons, George, a physician, and Lucien, both of whom went to South America with an emigrant group under the leadership of one McMullen. They shortly severed connections with this group, however. George followed his profession, while Lucien engaged in a number of enterprises, operating in turn a rice mill, apothecary's shop, brick manufactory, and gold mine. Most of this work was at Iguape, Sao Paulo Province, and near Rio de Janeiro, Brazil. The letters contain descriptions of the natives, the countryside, and political, social and economic conditions of the country. The collection also contains a ledger, 1828-1844. Throughout much of the papers there are references to spiritualism, seances, and mediums.

340. L. A. BARR DAYBOOK, 1855-1858. 1 vol. Frederick County, Md.

Daybook of a farmer at "Piedmont" or "Piedmonte," apparently in Frederick County. There are explanatory comments on farm operations and accounts with laborers.

341. JAMES F. BARRETT PAPERS, 1942-1943. 48 items. Atlanta, Ga.

Correspondence and printed material of James F. Barrett, staff assistant on the War Savings Staff, Atlanta, Georgia, principally concerning the United Brotherhood of Carpenters and Joiners of America (AFL) and the furniture industry of North Carolina, but also including letters relating to labor support for the War Bond Campaign and the Payroll Deduction Plan, reports and other material relating to the National War Labor Board cases involving the Carpenters and Joiners and various furniture companies, and two addresses by Joe Boyd, representative of the Carpenters and Joiners.

342. SIR ROBERT BARRIE PAPERS, 1765-1953. 733 items and 2 vols. Swarthdale, Lancashire, England.

The papers relate to Admiral Barrie's career in the Vancouver expedition, 1791-1795; the French Revolutionary and Napoleonic Wars; the War of 1812; and his service as naval commissioner in Canada, 1819-1834. Included is a small group of material relating to the 31st Regiment of Foot in Florida and Britain during the 1760s and 1770s when the Admiral's father, Dr. Robert Barrie, was surgeon's mate. A selective subject index is filed with the collection.

343. N. A. BARRIER PAPERS, 1861-1864. 4 items. Roanoke Island, N.C.

Civil War letters of Confederate soldiers, including a brief description of the Battle of Drewry's Bluff.

344. W. A. BARRIER ACCOUNT BOOKS, 1860-1862, 1887, 1893-1897. 3 vols. Lexington (Davidson County), N.C.

345. GEORGE WILLIAM BARRINGTON, SEVENTH VISCOUNT BARRINGTON, PAPERS, 1619 (1822-1901). 464 items. Beckett, Berkshire, England.

Correspondence of the 1820s-1850s centers upon Henry Frederick Francis Adair Barrington (1808-1882), uncle of the Seventh Viscount. Letters of 1829 concern the death of George, Fifth Viscount Barrington, in Italy. There are reports, 1839-1840, by Henry Barrington on political and economic conditions in Greece and on antiquities there. Correspondence for the 1840s and 1850s records the political and economic life of Cape Colony. Correspondence, memoranda, miscellaneous documents, notes, clippings of George William, Seventh Viscount Barrington (1824-1886), from the 1860s to the 1880s concern a wide range of political and foreign affairs topics, such as parliamentary reform, elections, the House of Lords, and relations with Russia and Turkey. Letters, 1900-1901, from Barrington's grandson, Lawrence William Palk, Third Baron Haldon, relate his experience with the Imperial Yeomanry during the Boer War. There are four portraits of members of the Palk family and eight of Disraeli, whom the Seventh Viscount served as secretary. Included with the collection is a selective index of persons and topics.

346. SHUTE BARRINGTON PAPERS, 1803-1818.
5 items. Durham, Durham County,
England.

Letters of Shute Barrington, Bishop of Durham, to Thomas Layton and Richard Burn, concerning appointments and routine ecclesiastical business.

347. SAMUEL BARRON II PAPERS, 1836.
1 item. "Malvern," near Loretto
(Essex County), Va.

A routine business letter of Barron, U.S. naval officer.

348. JAMES H. BARROW PAPERS, 1864. 3 items. Orange County, Va.

Letters from James H. Barrow, private in the 61st Virginia Regiment, C.S.A., chiefly concerning his illness and convalescence in the Chimborazo Hospital, Richmond, Virginia.

349. MIDDLETON POPE BARROW PAPERS, 1877, 1887. 2 items. Athens (Clarke County), Ga.

Correspondence of Middleton P. Barrow (1839-1903), staff officer to Howell Cobb during the Civil War. Later a lawyer, he completed the term of Benjamin Harvey Hill in the U.S. Senate. One letter concerns the interests of a divorced woman with certain investments; the other, the Richmond and Danville Railroad.

350. WILLIAM TAYLOR BARRY PAPERS, 1829, 1830. 2 items. Washington, D.C.

Correspondence of William T. Barry (1785-1835), lawyer and postmaster general, 1829-1835. The letters concern Commodore David Porter and changes in the form of the new postal guide.

351. ELLEN BARTLETT PAPERS, 1856-1888.
519 items. Broad Brook (Hartford County), Conn.

Letters to Bartlett concerning the schools and colleges of Connecticut and Illinois, the education of women, teachers and their salaries, and social life and customs.

352. SIR ELLIS ASHMEAD BARTLETT PAPERS, 1891. 1 item. London, England.

A letter of solicitation for England, Conservative weekly penny newspaper published by Bartlett.

353. HARRIET F. BARTLETT PAPERS, 1899.
4 items. Colorado Springs
(El Paso County), Colo.

Letters from Mrs. Bartlett concerning the estrangement between herself and her husband, her objections to a divorce, and personal financial matters.

354. LEVI BARTLETT PAPERS, (1809-1824) 1853. 35 items. Kingston (Rockingham County), N.H.

Correspondence of a physician and local politician containing information on the American Antiquarian Society, local academies, politics, medicine, phrenology, and business affairs. There are also drafts of several letters on theology to the editor of the Universalist Magazine. One of the correspondents was Josiah Butler, U.S. congressman from New Hampshire, 1817-1823.

355. CLARISSA HARLOWE BARTON PAPERS, 1868-1883. 5 items and 1 vol. Washington, D.C.

The pocket diary, September-December, 1869, of European travels of Clara Barton, nurse and founder of the American Red Cross, referring principally to Geneva, Switzerland, and Corsica, and to prices and living conditions there. There are references to Clarence Horton Upton, U.S. consul in Geneva; Sir Edwin Arnold, editor of the London Daily Telegraph; and to Thomasina M. A. E. Campbell, author. Also included are two calling cards of Miss Barton, clippings, and a letter to H. W. Clark, 1868, referring to her lecture schedule.

356. GERTRUDE WILLIAMSON (BAKER) BARTON PAPERS, 1878-1921. 129 items. Winchester (Frederick County), Va.

Mrs. Barton's letters concern local and state work for the Protestant Episcopal Church. Letters from her husband, Robert Thomas Barton, Sr. (1842-1917) refer to his career as a Virginia lawyer as well as to personal matters; his letters of 1916 mention the service of R. T. Barton, Jr., in the National Guard on the Mexican border. Other writers include Mason Gaither Ambler on political and financial affairs in West Virginia; Robert Nicholson Scott Baker on life in the U.S. Naval Academy and in the navy; Bishop Robert Atkinson Gibson on missionary work; and Marie Elizabeth (Jeffries) Hobart on the performance of one of her plays.

357. JESSIE BARTON AND JOHN R. MULVANY PAPERS, 1805-1903. 65 items and 1 vol. St. Clairsville (Belmont County), and Zanesville (Muskingum County), Ohio.

Largely letters concerning politics and legislative processes in Pennsylvania, the extent of Southern support for Calhoun's doctrines, Ohio Democratic politics, the Bank of the United States, campaigns during the Mexican War, and life in California during the gold rush. Authors include A. R. McIlvain, John C. Calhoun, Benjamin Tappan, Duff Green, R. H. Miller, William P. Simpson, and P. H. Mulvany. There are also clippings, land records, and other materials.

358. SAMUEL R. BARTON PAPERS, 1841-1924. 69 items. North Oxford (Worcester County), Mass.

Records concerning Stephen Barton's business at Bartonsville, North Carolina, manufacturing and selling plough handles and other lumber products, and Barton's legal problems, his trade between the lines during the Civil War, and his arrest and imprisonment at Norfolk, Virginia, by Union troops. Included is a narrative written to O. L. Mann giving an account of Barton's experiences. Papers after 1865 concern the attempt of Samuel R. Barton, son and heir of Stephen Barton, to recover damages for the burning of his father's property by the 3rd New York Cavalry in April, 1865; the part played by Clara Barton in securing the release from prison of her brother, Stephen; and the trial of Union officers responsible for Stephen's arrest. Correspondents include E. Benton Fremont, Orrin L. Mann, John R. Kirby, Franklin W. Kilpatrick, Ellen Spencer Mussey, and Horace T. Sanders.

359. SETH MAXWELL BARTON PAPERS, 1862. 5 items. Fredericksburg (Spotsylvania County), Va.

Orders given under command of Confederate general Barton, 1862, to Col. C. J. Philips of the 52nd Georgia Regiment. Topics include depredations on private property and straggling; guards and pickets; personnel matters.

360. WILLIAM BASDEN PAPERS, 1764 (1787-1829) 1859. 6 items. Onslow County, N.C.

Papers concerning transfer of land by the Basden family and the renting of turpentine forest land; and the will of Erasmus H. Coston.

361. WILLIAM MALONE BASKERVILL PAPERS, 1886-1901. 38 items. Nashville (Davidson County), Tenn.

Letters to William M. Baskervill (1850-1899), author and professor of English at Vanderbilt University, Nashville, Tennessee, from Albert Hansen, Joel Chandler Harris, Clifford Anderson Lanier, Mary (Day) Lanier, and Thomas Nelson Page, in answer to his request for material on their lives and works for his current writings, and concerning invitations to speak on various occasions.

362. JOHN W. BASKERVILLE LEDGER, 1830-1837. 1 vol. Boydton (Mecklenburg County), Va.

Accounts of a merchant.

363. WILLIAM BASKERVILLE PAPERS, 1799-1884. 101 items. "Lombardy Grove," Mecklenburg County, Va.

Correspondence and papers of William Baskerville, a planter. The earlier letters discuss crops and the curing of tobacco; many of the letters for 1802-1804 concern the education of his son, Charles, and of John R. Lucas, a student at the University of Edinburgh, Scotland. Among the items of interest are: letters from Lucas recounting Great Britain's preparation for war during the Napoleonic period; brief allusion to Colonel William Byrd's "Westover"; fluctuations of wheat prices; effect of approaching Civil War on price levels; Confederate action near Romney, Virginia, under General T. J. Jackson's command; and lists of commodity prices.

364. FREDERICK THOMAS BASON PAPERS, 1928-1957. 53 items. London, England.

Correspondence, largely with British literary figures, of a London author and bookseller. Among writers are Leonard Russell, Michael Sadleir, John Betjeman, John Connell, Stephen Graham, Francis Brett Young, Marie Adelaide (Belloc) Lowndes, Walter John De La Mare, John Cowper Powys, and Naomi Jacob. A complete list of writers is filed with the collection.

365. VICTOR H. BASSETT PAPERS, 1789 (1915-1938). 762 items. Savannah, Ga.

Papers collected by a physician and librarian of the Georgia Medical Society relating to public health in Georgia, Georgia physicians, midwives, smallpox inoculation, University of Pennsylvania medical instruction in the early 19th Century, Federal Emergency Relief Administration employment for nurses, and Works Progress Administration malaria control projects. Included are letters, reports, extracts, articles, charts, lists, genealogical data on the McAllister and White families of Pennsylvania and the Le Conte and Habersham families of Georgia, and a journal of J. J. Waring and Joseph Fred. Waring in London, Dublin, and Paris, 1853-1855. Writers of correspondence include William Gibbons, Horace Senter, David Ramsey, John C. Warren, John Le Conte, and T. F. Abercrombie.

366. SIR EDWARD BATES, FIRST BARONET, PAPERS, 1875. 1 item. Gyrn Castle, Flintshire, Wales.

Letter from Sir Stafford Northcote, supporting Bates against criticism by Samuel Plimsoll.

367. HERBERT ERNEST BATES PAPERS, 1930-1968. 6 items. Ashford, Kent, England.

Letters from Bates (1905-1974) discussing literary matters.

368. JOHN A. BATES PAPERS, 1896.  1 item. New Bedford (Bristol County), Mass.

Reminiscences of a soldier in the 2nd Massachusetts Infantry and the 3rd Massachusetts Cavalry regiments during the Civil War. Bate's observations relate to the year 1864 and describe a smallpox epidemic in New Orleans; Washington, D.C., and the Shenandoah Valley, including the battle of Winchester.

369. THOMAS BATES PAPERS, 1811-1820. 95 items.  Gainsborough, Lincolnshire, England.

Largely business and personal letters of a dealer in coffee, tea, and chocolate, with information on commodity prices and finance in England in 1819; the War of 1812; Unitarian religion; anti-Catholic prejudice; William Marriott's appointment to Columbia College, N.Y.; the bones of Thomas Paine brought to England by William Cobbett; and the publication of Paine's works in England in 1819.  Correspondents include B. Wright, J. De Camp, and David Kidd.

370. HENRY BATHURST PAPERS, 1822, 1823. 2 items.  Norwich, Norfolk, England.

A letter to George Glover, Archdeacon of Sudbury, from the Bishop of Norwich commenting on the prospects of legislation concerning the Catholic question; and a personal letter concerning family matters.

371. GEORGE MAGRUDER BATTEY PAPERS, 1940. 4 items.  Washington, D.C.

Genealogical materials concerning the Battey family and a letter of Robert Battey of Rome, Georgia.

372. LOUIS NARCISSE BAUDRY DES LOZIÈRES PAPERS, (1770-1825) 1876. 91 items.  Paris, France.

Diplomas and certificates relating to the education, career, and memberships of this French lawyer, soldier, traveler, and writer; passports; residence papers; certificates of citizenship; military records; and other legal documents and honors.

373. BAUGH & SONS COMPANY PAPERS, 1905-1932.  101 items. Philadelphia, Penn.

Photographs and advertisements for a producer and distributor of phosphate fertilizer and agricultural chemicals based in Philadelphia and in Norfolk, Virginia, and connected with the Baugh Chemical Co. in Baltimore and Ohio.  Topics include offices, factories, products, personnel, and crops.  Farm scenes are from New Jersey, Pennsylvania, and North Carolina.

374. JOHN BAUSERMAN ACCOUNTS, 1838-1841. 6 vols.  Hawkinstown (Shenandoah County), Va.

Daybooks and ledger.

375. THOMAS BAXTER PAPERS, 1825-1871. 106 items and 1 vol. Petersburg (Dinwiddie County), Va.

Business and family letters of a commission merchant and businessman, containing information on an uncooperative slave; secession in Virginia; the response to secession in Connecticut; civilian life during the Civil War; descriptions of Confederate fortifications at Norfolk, Virginia, 1861, and Winton, North Carolina, 1862; comment on traitors in northeastern North Carolina; use of buildings in Greensboro, North Carolina for hospitals, 1864; war conditions in Plaquemines Parish, Louisiana; Radical Republicans during Reconstruction; freedmen; and the Virginia Military Institute. Clippings, 14 items, are of sayings and couplets, many of them by Samuel H. Marks of Petersburg.  There is a commonplace book, 1820s-1830s, and a letter from George Wythe Randolph.

376. FRANCES COURTENAY BAYLOR PAPERS, 1898. 1 item.  Winchester (Frederick County), Va.

Letter to Joseph Marshall Stoddart concerning literary matters.

377. ELBERT W. BAYNES PAPERS, 1834 (1843-1864) 1879.  75 items. Jasper County, Ga.

Business correspondence of a tannery including notes from patrons sending for tanning the skins of cattle, horses, and occasionally of dogs and cats; information on prices for the hiring of slaves, for cotton, and general merchandise; on Baynes's debts and other legal problems; and on conditions during Reconstruction.  Postwar letters include a young girl's impressions of Houston, Texas.  Correspondents include Isaac A. Hibler, Richard R. Roby, and Baynes's daughter, Tucker.

378. SELINA E. BAYNES AUTOGRAPH ALBUM, 1858-1879.  1 vol. (36 pp.) Bushy Fork (Person County), N.C.

Typical album kept by a young girl.

379. HARVEY R. BEACH PAPERS, 1861-1869. 8 items.  Milford (New Haven County), Conn.

Personal and business correspondence of Harvey R. and Henry Beach, carriage manufacturers, concerning the collection of claims at New Orleans, Louisiana; conditions of the carriage business; and settlement of an estate.

380. EDWARD BEALE DIARY, 1817-1818.
1 vol. Manchester, England.

Personal diary of Edward Beale, apparently an American in England for study or treatment for lameness under one Dr. Taylor. The diary, in code, is chiefly concerned with Beale and Honor Green's questionable romance, with occasional references to his man, Horace, and the treatment of Negroes in Charleston [S.C.?].

381. JAMES BEALE PAPERS, 1864-1865.
5 items. Richmond, Va.

Receipts for goods purchased by a physician.

382. RICHARD LEE TURBERVILLE BEALE PAPERS, 1848-1862. 3 items. Westmoreland County, Va.

Letters from Richard L. T. Beale (1819-1893), a Virginia lawyer and congressman, one, 1848, asking for a congressional report, and the other, 1862, to his wife, describing his experiences in the Confederate Army.

383. JOSEPH S. BEALL PAPERS, 1861-1863.
3 items. Kingston (Plymouth County), Mass.

Letters from Federal soldiers to Joseph S. Beall, asking him to persuade citizens to supply revolvers to volunteers, commenting on the Kingston Company stationed in Virginia, and describing the Banks Expedition at Baton Rouge, Louisiana.

384. THOMAS BEALL ACCOUNT BOOK, 1784-1793.
1 vol. Washington, D.C.

Accounts of a general merchant in Georgetown.

385. UPTON BEALL PAPERS, 1809-1810.
4 items. Washington, D.C.

Letters concerning a lawsuit in which Francis Scott Key was counsel for John Norwood, and the importation and purchase of salt by the firm of Stewart and Beall.

386. GEORGE W. BEAMAN PAPERS, 1863-1865.
5 items. Vermont.

Official papers of George W. Beaman, a native of Vermont, while assistant paymaster on the S.S. *Union*, a store ship stationed off Key West, Florida.

387. BEAR CREEK PRIMITIVE BAPTIST CHURCH RECORDS, 1858-1917. Lenoir County, N.C.

Church minutes for 1858-1917 and lists of members for 1858-1904.

388. ALONZO G. BEARDSLEY PAPERS, 1787 (1861-1863) 1897. 1,596 items and 1 vol. Auburn (Cayuga County), N.Y.

This collection, largely the correspondence of the law firm of Theodore Medad Pomeroy, William Allen, and Alonzo G. Beardsley, also contains the papers of several combinations of lawyers who preceded this firm. The early papers, beginning about 1800, center on John Porter, judge, state senator, and law partner of New York Governor Enos Thompson Throop. In about 1840 the Porter letters merge into those of William Allen, and for the next fifteen years the correspondence reflects Allen's legal practice and depicts life in Auburn, New York. The letters of Alonzo Beardsley begin about 1842, but it is not until 1855 that he and Allen become partners. During the 1850s the papers also include the letters of Samuel Blatchford, a New York City attorney. For the most part, papers during 1840-1860 concern business and legal practice in New York state and throughout the northeastern United States. For the Civil War period there are the 1860s papers of Theodore M. Pomeroy from Cayuga County, New York, a U.S. representative. Topics include appointments and promotions; aid to wounded soldiers; defenses on the Great Lakes; the organization of the 5th, 111th, and 138th New York regiments; the Conscription Act of 1863 and its enforcement; and civilian morale and the activities of Southern sympathizers, especially in 1863. Pomeroy's correspondence also concerns patronage, party organization and rivalry, and service to constituents. From 1865 to 1870 there is much family correspondence, particularly letters to Nellie Bisby of Attica, New York. Between 1865 and 1868 many papers appear from Dodge and Stevenson Manufacturing Company, makers of reapers and mowers. After 1870 letters of Alonzo Beardsley relate to miscellaneous subjects, such as gold mining in North Carolina and Alabama, 1872; the Oswego Starch Company; and N. M. Osborne & Company, makers of harvesting machines. Numerous legal papers and documents reflect all phases of the Osborne firm's work. There is a large amount of related printed matter. The collection also included genealogical material on the Van Dorn, Peterson, and Quick families of New York.

389. ELIE BEATTY PAPERS, 1826-1851.
42 items. Hagerstown (Washington County), Md.

Business correspondence of a bank cashier.

390. G. H. BEATTY PAPERS, 1861-1862.
8 items. Lisbon (Sampson County), N.C.

Letters from a Confederate soldier to his mother and to another member of his family, and a list of articles owned by the Lisbon Ladies Aid Society; accounts of company movements and army life at Forts Caswell and

Fisher, North Carolina, as well as the area around Gordonsville, Virginia.

391. ELIZABETH H. BEAUCHAMP PAPERS, 1844 (1863-1869) 1919. 34 items. Davie County, N.C.

Business and personal correspondence of Elizabeth H. Beauchamp, widow of John Beauchamp, concerning land owned by her and by her son, Joel. Included also are love letters from Washington Green.

392. SIR FRANCIS BEAUFORT PAPERS, 1796-1802. 1 vol. London, England.

Account book listing the personal and professional expenses and items of income of Lt. Beatty aboard H.M.S. *Phaeton*. Beatty's share of the prize money from captured ships is included.

393. BEAUFORT COLLEGE TRUSTEES JOURNAL, 1795-1868. 1 item and 1 vol. Beaufort (Beaufort County), S.C.

Typed copy of the minutes of the proceedings of the college trustees. Some questions confronting them were the handling of legacies, changes in buildings, replacing members of the faculty, and student discipline. Among the trustees were Edward Barnwell, John Barnwell, John Bull, John Alexander Cuthbert, Henry Middleton Fuller, William J. Grayson, Henry Holcombe, and John Allen Stuart, short biographies of whom are filed with the journal. There is also a letter of 1816, from Joseph Emerson Worcester, who was a candidate for a teaching position at the college.

394. BEAUFORT COUNTY, N.C., SCHOOL DISTRICT NO. 65 REGISTER, 1887-1895. 1 vol. (64 pp.)

395. PIERRE GUSTAVE TOUTANT BEAUREGARD PAPERS, 1844-1893. 475 items. New Orleans, La.

Letters and papers of P. G. T. Beauregard (1818-1893), Confederate brigadier general, president of the New Orleans, Jackson and Mississippi Railway, and adjutant general of Louisiana. The collection includes an 1847 memorandum on the fortification of Jalapa, Mexico; Special Order No. 14 from General Robert Patterson, May 3, 1847, transferring Lt. Beauregard from the volunteers to the United States Engineers; a letter to Jefferson Davis from Beauregard offering his services to the Confederacy; letters to Jefferson Davis and Samuel Cooper immediately after the first battle of Manassas in 1861; telegrams, 1861-1862, from Generals Robert S. Ripley, Sterling Martin Wood, Sterling Price, and James E. Slaughter on troop movements and supplies in Mississippi; a letter from Beauregard to Thomas Jordan on Robert E. Lee's 1862 campaign against McClellan on the Peninsula; a list of telegrams sent and received in February and April, 1862, concerning Fort Pillow; a report from Albert S. Johnston to Judah Benjamin on the military situation in the West in February 1862, after the fall of Fort Henry; shorthand notes of a conference in 1863 with Jefferson Davis, Joseph E. Johnston, and G. W. Smith to plan Johnston's Vicksburg campaign; a letter in 1864 from Daniel H. Hill warning Beauregard of Grant's threat to Petersburg, Virginia; a series of telegrams from General William J. Hardee concerned with operations in South Carolina and Georgia in 1865; and telegrams from 1865 on the movement of troops and supplies in Georgia and Alabama. The papers for the years after the Civil War deal with such subjects as Louisiana politics, railroad building in Louisiana and Mexico, various business ventures, and questions about the war, particularly Beauregard's part in it. They include a letter in 1866 from Beauregard to Robert E. Lee on Reconstruction; a letter from Beauregard to Frederick A. Porcher in 1876 concerning some documents discovered in Salisbury, North Carolina, which Beauregard identified as pertaining to the defense of Charleston, South Carolina; and a letter to Isham G. Harris in 1880 on the Shiloh campaign. There is a clipping describing Beauregard's funeral in 1893.

396. BEAVER CREEK AND BLUFF COTTON MILLS RECORDS, 1878-1908. 3 vols. Fayetteville (Cumberland County), N.C.

Stock ledgers, journal, and other records of a cotton mill.

397. JESSE BECK PAPERS, 1790-1844. 90 items. Amherst County, Va.

This collection consists, for the most part, of personal and family correspondence, legal papers, bills, receipts, and other business papers. Many records relate to transactions in land and slaves and accounts with local merchants.

398. JOHN CREPPS WICKLIFFE BECKHAM PAPERS, 1904. 1 item. Louisville (Jefferson County), Ky.

Letter from Beckham, governor of Kentucky, to a county chairman of the Democratic party recommending two Negro campaign workers.

399. WILLIAM M. BECKHAM ACCOUNT BOOK, 1836-1867. 1 vol. (144 pp.) Alexander County, N.C.

Mercantile and farm accounts.

400. SIR GEORGE BECKWITH PAPERS, 1809-1819. 5 items. London, England.

Letters dealing with Beckwith's conquest of Martinique in 1809. Also, one letter in 1819 explaining the changes in army policy necessitating Beckwith's retirement as commander in Ireland.

401. JOHN BECKWITH PAPERS, 1810-1882.
51 items. Petersburg, Va.

Business correspondence of John Beckwith (1785-1870), a physician, concerning antidyspeptic and antibilious pills, which he made and advertised by testimonials from many prominent men, especially from North Carolina. The set contains a few personal letters, including one from Mrs. George Edmund Badger. Correspondents are chiefly from North Carolina. Included also are receipts and bills.

402. JOHN WATRUS BECKWITH PAPERS, 1877.
1 item. Marietta (Cobb County), Ga.

Letter from the Episcopal Bishop of Georgia concerning stock in the Georgia Central Railroad.

403. WILLIAM F. BEDELL PAPERS, 1863-1876.
11 items. Madison (Dane County), Wis.

Correspondence of a soldier in the Union Army commenting on camp life in Virginia and Kentucky and describing Chicago, Illinois, in 1864.

404. BEDINGER-DANDRIDGE FAMILY PAPERS, 1763-1957. 12,997 items and 191 vols. Shepherdstown (Jefferson County), W. Va.

The correspondence and papers of five generations of families from Virginia, West Virginia, Kentucky, Ohio, and New York. The primary portion of the collection is made up of the personal and family papers of Caroline Danske (Bedinger) Dandridge (1854-1914), a writer and horticulturalist. From 1866 to her marriage in 1877, Danske Dandridge's correspondence is concerned with social life in Virginia and Washington, D.C., and with family matters. Her literary correspondence begins in the early 1880s and continues until the year of her death. Correspondents include John Esten Cooke, Edmund C. Stedman, Oliver Wendell Holmes, John Greenleaf Whittier, and Thomas W. Higginson. There are sustained exchanges of letters with William Hayes Ward, editor of The Brooklyn Independent which published much of her work; with the poet Lizette Woodworth Reese of Baltimore; and Margaretta Lippincott. Material on gardening begins to appear in the papers for the 1890s and includes a large number of letters and eleven notebooks. Danske Dandridge's family correspondence continues with her sister, Mrs. J. F. B. (Mary Bedinger) Mitchell, and her brother, Henry Bedinger IV, as well as with her numerous cousins. The correspondence of Adam Stephen Dandridge (1844-1924) reflects his career in the West Virginia House of Representatives and his business as a seller of farm machinery. Correspondence and papers of Serena Katherine (Violet) Dandridge, daughter of Danske and Adam Stephen Dandridge, bear on her career as an illustrator for the zoologist, Hubert Lyman Clark, and reflect her interest in woman suffrage and the Swedenborgian Church. There are also twelve volumes of her writings in manuscript. The correspondence and papers of Danske Dandridge's father, Henry Bedinger III, include letters on literary subjects from Thomas Willis White, Philip Pendleton Cooke, and Nathaniel Beverley Tucker; papers from his years as a member of the United States House of Representatives from 1845-1849; records of his service, 1853-1858, first as consul and then as minister of the United States in Sweden and in particular his negotiation of a treaty with Sweden in 1857; and his notebooks containing poems and comments on social life in Virginia. Letters of Caroline B. (Lawrence) Bedinger, mother of Danske Dandridge, to her husband's family in the South and her relatives in New York, concern her experience as a young woman in Washington, D.C., and Virginia; her stay in Copenhagen; the Civil War experiences of her husband's family and her own; family life; and the education of her children. The collection contains a large number of transcripts made by Danske Dandridge from originals in the possession of various branches of her family, including the Swearingens, Shepherds, Morgans, Rutherfords, Worthingtons, Washingtons, Kings, Brownes, and Lawrences for the period from the American Revolution to the Civil War. There are also copies of letters and documents from the Lyman C. Draper manuscripts at the University of Wisconsin. Essentially, they are the papers of three brothers, George Michael Bedinger (1756-1843), Henry Bedinger II (1753-1843), and Daniel Bedinger (1761-1818), and their descendents and connections. Among the many subjects discussed are Indian warfare and conditions on the Virginia frontier; descriptions of the events of the Revolution; trading in salt and fur; experiences of Americans held prisoner by the British during the Revolution; flour milling in the Potomac valley; trade and transport of farm commodities; travel on the Mississippi to New Orleans, 1811-1812; James Rumsey and the development of the steamboat; the settling of Kentucky and Ohio; descriptions of Washington, D.C., Philadelphia, and Baltimore at various times from 1800-1860; antebellum social life, South and North; and extensive comments on politics through 1860, particularly on the opposition to Federalism and the early Democratic-Republican Party.

405. ALFONSO DE LA CUEVA, MARQUÉS DE BEDMAR PAPERS, 1620. 1 vol. Spain.

Book entitled "Relatione della Republica di Venetia fatta alla Maesta del Re Cattolico Filippo III di Spagna per il suo Ambasciatore Don Alonso dalla Cueva Residente ordinario in Venetia l'anno 1620." It is a political, economic, topographical, military, and social account of the Venetian state attributed to Bedmar, who was Spanish ambassador to Venice during 1607-ca. 1618.

406. CATHARINE ESTHER BEECHER PAPERS, 1856. 1 item. Litchfield (Litchfield County), Conn.

Letter from a Mrs. Brainerd describing a trip to the western United States.

407. HENRY WARD BEECHER PAPERS, 1878. 4 items. Brooklyn, N.Y.

Miscellaneous items concerning Beecher.

408. JAMES CHAPLIN BEECHER PAPERS, 1865-1866. 2 items and 1 vol. Elmira (Chemung County), N.Y.

One volume consisting of a journal of Beecher's activities in Charleston, South Carolina, overseeing the transition of the freedmen from slave to wage earner, and a memorandum book containing summaries of complaints brought to him by the freedmen. Also, two letters stating his general view of how freedmen should be treated.

409. P. T. BEEMAN PAPERS, 1845-1879. 8 vols. Lanesboro (Anson County), N.C.

Business records, some of which belonged to a physician.

410. THOMAS STIRLING BEGBIE PAPERS, 1863-1871. 7 items. London, England.

Description of the organization and activities of the Albion Trading Company, a group of blockade runners in the American Civil War. Ships mentioned include the _Lady Stirling_, the _Talisman_, the _Calypso_, and the _Hope_.

411. CATHERINE P. (WILMER) BEIDELMAN PAPERS, 1830 (1862-1874) 1905. 30 items. Philadelphia, Pa.

Personal correspondence of the Beidelman and Wilmer families. The letters concern the marriage of Mary Wilmer to the Reverend John Nicholson of Rahway, New Jersey; John Wilmer's voyage around Cape Horn to Chile during the 1830's; the marriage of Catherine P. Wilmer to David Beidelman; the Civil War experiences of Wilmer and Daniel Beidelman, Jr., members of the 19th Regiment, Pennsylvania Volunteers; and the destitution of the people of southern Maryland and northern Virginia during the Civil War.

412. GRANVILLE W. BELCHER PAPERS, 1861-1865. 11 items. Henry County, Va.

Personal letters which reflect events in the Civil War such as the second battle of Manassas and the battle of Gettysburg.

413. JAMES BELCHER PAPERS, 1782. 2 items. Savannah, Ga.

Documents concerning the reimbursement of James Belcher, a Loyalist, for losses sustained when the British evacuated Savannah. Included also is one document signed by General Anthony Wayne.

414. WILLIAM W. BELCHER PAPERS, 1857-1859. 9 items. Abbeville District, S.C.

Miscellaneous business and legal papers.

415. WILLIAM WORTH BELKNAP, 1852-1875. 34 items. Washington, D.C.

Correspondence of William W. Belknap (1829-1890), Iowa legislator, Federal officer in the Civil War, and secretary of war under President Grant, concerning contested elections; the Ku Klux Klan; appointments to the United States Military Academy, West Point, New York; political appointments; stationing troops in Alabama in 1872; President Grant's desire to hold an election in Georgia in 1870; and settlement of war claims against the Navy, 1875.

416. ABRAHAM BELL & SONS PAPERS, 1834-1854. 239 items. New York, N.Y.

Business correspondence including letters concerning the importation of Irish linens through a firm headed by James C. Bell.

417. ALFRED W. BELL PAPERS, 1848 (1862-1864) 1896. 285 items. Franklin (Macon County), N.C.

Personal correspondence of a mountain family, interesting for information on social and economic conditions in the extreme western section of North Carolina during the Civil War period. The personal letters of Alfred W. Bell, who organized a troop of Confederate volunteers in 1861 with himself as captain, relate his war experiences. The postwar letters show his endeavor to re-establish himself in the dental profession.

418. E. J. BELL INVENTORY, 1868. 1 vol. [Danville (Pittsylvania County), Va.?]

Inventory of the estate of a merchant in bankruptcy by D. W. McKinney, U.S. marshal.

419. EBENEZER BELL PAPERS, 1833-1857. 23 items. Hyde County, N.C.

Family correspondence of a group of small farmers in eastern North Carolina with comments on crops.

420. J. J. BELL DIARY, 1861. 1 vol. (62 pp.) North Carolina.

Diary of J. J. Bell, 8th Regiment, North Carolina State Troops, a Confederate soldier, describing life at Camp Macon, North Carolina.

421. JAMES MARTIN BELL PAPERS, 1768-1870.
13,557 items and 47 vols.
Hollidaysburg (Blair County), Pa.

Correspondence, business papers, and legal papers of a lawyer, ironmaster, banker, and politician. Papers on the iron industry, 1830-1870, deal with financing, acquisition of raw materials, labor, processing, and distribution. Bell opened his first bank in 1848, and his correspondence and financial papers reveal day-to-day banking practice; the strains on the national financial system in the antebellum period and the attempts of bankers to achieve some degree of stability; the dynamics of banking expansion; the creation of a national bank in Huntingdon, Pennsylvania, under the Currency Act of 1863; and the promotion of the United States government's 5-20 loan in central Pennsylvania in 1863. An extensive correspondence on local, state, and national politics includes material on the Anti-Masonic Party in the 1830s; the Whig Party, 1830-1840; the Republican Party in the 1850s; Pennsylvania's Buckshot War, 1838-1839; the debate in 1840 over the resumption of specie payment in Pennsylvania; the maneuvering behind the creation of Blair County, Pennsylvania, from Huntingdon County in 1846; and the political climate of Pennsylvania in the secession crisis. Legal papers reflect Bell's expertise in Pennsylvania land law, and include mortgages, court judgements, and records of the collection of notes and the administration of estates and wills. Letters from Dewitt Clinton concern the Juniata River Canal; lengthy correspondence with J. Edgar Thompson relates to the Pennsylvania Railroad; and other letters deal with the sale of the Main Line of the Pennsylvania State Improvements System. There is material on the Pennsylvania state school system; the development of telegraph service; and addictive use of laudanum; mobilization for the Civil War; the effect of the war on the banking and business system of the North; and local reaction to Confederate operations in Pennsylvania. Printed matter deals with such subjects as temperance, road and bridge building, abolitionism, schools, public works, and politics. The volumes include account books of iron companies, notebooks, bank books, household accounts, and a journal kept by Bell when he was a member of the Pennsylvania Senate Committee on Internal Improvements, 1839.

422. MADISON BELL PAPERS, 1877. 2 items. Atlanta, Ga.

Letters of a Georgia Republican requesting an appointment as U.S. marshal.

423. MAJOR BELL PAPERS, 1853-1864.
11 items. Elizabeth City (Pasquotank County), N.C.

Business letters with information on the prices of goods; and letters from Christian Bell, a student at Chowan Female College at Murfreesboro, North Carolina, commenting on student interests, college life, and a Negro insurrection of 1854.

424. THOMAS A. BELL PAPERS, 1861-1863.
4 items. Virginia.

Personal letters, almost illiterate, from Thomas A. Bell, a Confederate soldier, to his sister, Fannie.

425. HENRY (HEINRICH HAUER) BELLAMANN PAPERS, 1915-1931. 22 items and 2 vols. New York, N.Y., and Columbia (Richland County), S.C.

This collection contains material on the development of Bellamann's interest in Dante and includes his translation of a portion of the Divine Comedy.

426. WILLIAM BELLAMY PAPERS, 1815 (1843-1869) 1888. 100 items. Enfield (Halifax County), N.C.

Family and business correspondence and papers of William Bellamy, evidently a planter, and Joseph Bellamy, a lawyer, including land-sale contracts, Methodist Conference resolutions concerning separation from Northern Methodists in 1844, receipts for professional fees, legal papers, records of prices of farm produce, and a few Civil War letters.

427. WILLIAM BELLAMY JOURNAL, 1870-1876.
1 vol. (179 pp.) Rehoboth (Bristol County), Mass.

The journal of a sea captain and farmer which records routine activities and transactions relating to the farm. The first half of this volume is the journal and letter book of Edwin Fairfield Forbes and is entered under his name.

428. JOHN BELLE PAPERS, 1793. 1 item. Lexington (Fayette County), Ky.

A sight draft signed by a member of the Quartermaster Department, United States Army.

429. HENRY WHITNEY BELLOWS, 1844.
1 item. New York, N.Y.

Letter from Dexter Clapp commenting on the Unitarian Church in the South.

430. J. T. BELLUNE DIARY, 1861-1862.
1 vol. (110 pp.) Hamburg (Aiken County), S.C.

Farm diary giving weather conditions, amounts of wood sold, and comments on planting.

431. WILLIAM CHRISTIE BENET PAPERS, 1923.
2 items. Abbeville (Abbeville County), S.C.

Letters concerning the drafting in

1894 of a memorial to be presented to Congress by South Carolina, protesting the extension of the power of the Federal courts.

432.  PARK BENJAMIN PAPERS, 1838.  1 item.  Boston, Mass.

Letter to music critic John Sullivan Dwight.

433.  EDWARD BENNER PAPERS, 1870.  3 items.  Richmond, Va.

Business letters, mostly concerned with the Jefferson Insurance Company.

434.  BENNET ORDER BOOK, 1861.  1 vol. (26 pp.)  Harman (Washington County), Ohio.

Special and general orders concerning troops guarding the Marietta and Cincinnati Railroad.

435.  BRYANT BENNETT PAPERS, 1767 (1840-1875) 1902.  775 items and 5 vols.  Williamston (Martin County), N.C.

Correspondence and papers of Bryant Bennett, merchant and planter, and of his family.  Included are mercantile accounts of the firms of Bennett and Hyman in Williamston and of Bennett and Price in Hamilton (both places in Martin County), school letters from a normal school in Oxford, North Carolina, deeds, promissory notes, receipts for land sold for taxes, plantation account books containing household and farm accounts, lists of slaves and supplies issued to them, business records dealing with the marketing of cotton at Norfolk, Virginia, agricultural treatises by one S. W. Outterbridge of Martin County, and letters to Bennett after he had moved to Plymouth, North Carolina, in 1869.

436.  FRANCES N. BENNETT PAPERS, 1857-1858.  21 items.  Orange County, N.C.

Personal letters describing social life, amusements, and religious affairs in the country.

437.  JAMES GORDON BENNETT PAPERS, 1861-1862.  1 vol.  New York, N.Y.

Logbook of the United States revenue cutter _Henrietta_, operating off the eastern coast of the United States.

438.  R. NELSON BENNETT PAPERS, 1874-1879.  7 items.  Putney (Windham County), Vt.

Personal letters.

439.  CHARLES BENNITT PAPERS, 1872-1904.  23 items.  Durham, N.C.

Personal letters dealing with family matters.  Additional Bennitt papers are on microfilm at Duke University.

440.  JAMES BENNITT PAPERS, 1820-1962.  153 items and 6 vols.  Orange and Durham Counties, N.C.

Personal, business, and legal papers of a farmer, including the muster roll for a company of the Hillsborough regiment of militia (1845-1860); also material concerning the restoration of the Bennitt house, where General William T. Sherman received the surrender of General Joseph E. Johnston in 1865.

441.  EDWARD FREDERICK BENSON PAPERS, 1920.  1 item.  London, England.

Letter from Alfred Charles William Hamsworth, First Viscount Northcliffe, stating that his newspapers would support a movement for the restoration of Rheims Cathedral.

442.  GODFREY RATHBONE BENSON, FIRST BARON CHARNWOOD, PAPERS, 1906.  1 item.  London, England.

Letter from Herbert Asquith.

443.  BENSON FAMILY PAPERS, 1810-1813.  9 items.  Philadelphia, Pa.

Letters from Thomas Benson of Kentucky and Ohio to his mother, sister Catherine, and brother John in Philadelphia.  Included is a description of the siege of Fort Meigs on the Maumee River in Ohio during the War of 1812.

444.  BENSON-THOMPSON FAMILY PAPERS, 1803 (1820-1860) 1936.  856 items and 8 vols.  Marion (Perry County), Ala.

Personal correspondence and business papers of the Benson, Thompson, and Moore families who migrated from Greenville County and Spartanburg County, South Carolina, to Alabama.  Correspondence between the groups in South Carolina and Alabama is concerned for the most part with family matters.  However, political events are occasionally discussed, and a number of letters, 1836-1840, deal with the Alabama militia.  The collection includes letters reflecting conditions in Alabama during the Civil War; several items on medical education at the University of Louisiana (Tulane University), 1866-1868; and records of the Marion (Alabama) Grange, No. 95, 1873-1876.

445.  SIR SAMUEL BENTHAM PAPERS, 1799.  1 item.  London, England.

Letter from Earl Spencer, First Lord of the Admiralty, on naval matters.

446.  WILLIAM CAVENDISH BENTINCK PAPERS, 1808 (1814-1833) 1848.  29 items.  London, England.

Mostly business and personal letters to Lieutenant Colonel Kenah; six items are by Lord William George Frederick Cavendish Bentinck.

447. WILLIAM HENRY CAVENDISH-BENTINCK, THIRD DUKE OF PORTLAND, PAPERS, 1783-1808. 15 items. London, England.

Miscellaneous letters, for the most part concerned with domestic politics and foreign affairs.

448. B. G. BENTLEY PAPERS, 1830-1836. 6 items. Williamston (Martin County), N.C.

Personal correspondence of B. G. Bentley, a merchant recently from Scotland, with Catherine Thompson, a widow in Scotland.

449. EDMUND CLERIHEW BENTLEY PAPERS, 1897-1920s. 5 items. London, England.

Four letters from John Buchan, First Baron Tweedsmuir, concern student life at Oxford. There is also a partial letter by Bentley concerning his writing.

450. WILLIAM BENTLEY PAPERS, ca. 1804. 1 item. Salem (Essex County), Mass.

An undated fragmentary letter from Benjamin Crowninshield III, a student in the College of William and Mary.

451. HORACE BENTON PAPERS, 1849-1864. 14 items. Cleveland (Cuyahoga County), Ohio.

Personal letters dealing with religious and family matters.

452. LORD CHARLES WILLIAM DE LA POER BERESFORD, FIRST BARON BERESFORD, PAPERS, 1879-1918. 40 items. London, England.

Correspondence of a British naval officer and politician concerning navy administration, strength and mobilization policy, maneuvers, personnel reform, technology, Beresford's commands, elections and politics, British leadership, and the prospects of the Empire. Writers include naval officers, political leaders, and royal personages, such as John A. Fisher; Kaiser Wilhelm II; Herbert Bismarck; Lord Wolseley; Louis Mountbatten; Lord Goschen; George, Prince of Wales; Carl Meyer; and Sir George Stuart White.

453. WILLIAM BERESFORD PAPERS, 1844-1882. 182 items. London, England.

Letters to Beresford, British politician, mostly concerning politics, relating to his brief term as Secretary at War, 1852, and to a legal case against him, 1853-1854.

454. CARTER BURWELL BERKELEY PAPERS, 1801 (1813-1816) 1856. 6 items. Urbanna (Middlesex County), Va.

Business correspondence of Carter B. Berkeley, Virginia politician, concerning tobacco shipments and finances, and brief comments on the War of 1812.

455. SIR GEORGE HENRY FREDERICK BERKELEY PAPERS, 1849-1850. 3 items. Richmond, Surrey, England.

Letters to Berkeley, British commander-in-chief at Madras, probably from General Sir George Brown, concerning military activity and personnel.

456. WILLIAM N. BERKELEY PAPERS, 1771 (1795-1810) 1878. 35 items. Hanover County, Va.

Letters chiefly to William N. Berkeley from N. Atkinson, the overseer of Berkeley's "Goose Pond" plantation, describing in detail crops, marketing of livestock, and weather conditions. There are also an account of tobacco sent by Robert Beverly to England in 1771, physician's accounts for 1791-1799, and two poems by Edmund Berkeley.

457. MARGARETTA C. (VAN METRE) BERLIN PAPERS, 1819-1868. 29 items. White Post (Clarke County), Va.

Letters chiefly relating to family matters; writers include Mary (Van Metre) Tharp of Ohio and George W. Berlin of White Post.

458. JOEL A. BERLY ACCOUNT BOOKS, 1856-1888. 13 vols. Pomaria (Newberry County), S.C.

Accounts, 12 vols., and a formula book.

459. [E. L. BERNARD?] ACCOUNTS, 1815-1857. 5 vols. New Orleans, La.

Records in the French language of a New Orleans commission merchant.

460. GEORGE S. BERNARD PAPERS, 1816-1912. 34 items and 3 vols. Petersburg (Dinwiddie County), Va.

Papers related to the Civil War interests of a Confederate veteran, writer, and lawyer. One letter and three postcards are responses to Bernard's inquiries concerning persons who served in the conflict. Scrapbooks and loose clippings concern the Ashley family, William M. Tweed, local matters in Petersburg, and war subjects, especially as related to Bernard's service in the 12th Virginia Infantry. There are excerpts from a diary of Bernard's war experience of 1862 with added comments. Battles described include Seven Pines, Malvern Hill, Second Manassas, Crampton's Gap, Chancellorsville, Sewell's Point, French's Field, and Frazier's

Farm. A copy of Bernard's book, War Talks of Confederate Veterans, is included with the collection. There are also two pictures-- the gunboat Mendota at Deep Bottom, James River; and the Chesterfield Bridge over the North Anna River.

461. THOMAS J. BERREY PAPERS, 1885-1916. 230 items and 9 vols. Luray (Page County), Va.

Correspondence from insurance companies which Berrey served as agent relates to insurance on buildings and livestock. Letters from Henry Marvin Wharton concern the affairs of Luray College and the Whosoever Farm, 1895-1898 and 1900. Letters from William Coleman Bitting refer to his Baptist church in New York City and to politics. Papers relating to the Page Courier of which Berrey was an editor concern advertising policy and a controversy between coeditor Andrew Broaddus and S. J. Richey over the bankrupt Valley Land and Improvement Company headed by D. F. Kagey. Miscellaneous correspondence, financial papers, and ledgers also concern the Courier. There is a minute book, 1899-1901, of the Philalethian Literary Society of Luray College; a record book, 1889-1891, on scholarship and deportment at Luray Female Institute; and a grade book, 1890-1900, for students at Luray College.

462. JOHN BERRIDGE PAPERS, 1773. 1 item. Everton, Bedfordshire, England.

A letter from Berridge, an Anglican divine, to his cousin, a Mrs. Leach, commenting on his health, family matters, and his religious views.

463. JOHN MACPHERSON BERRIEN, SR., PAPERS, 1820-1852. 9 items. Savannah, Ga.

Letters by Berrien, U. S. senator and politician, containing some comment on national politics.

464. CHARLES BERRY PAPERS, 1842-1867. 13 items. Front Royal (Warren County), Va.

Largely letters from Berry, while a Confederate soldier, to his family. There are also family letters, 1842, from Eliza M. Griggs of Charles Town, West Virginia, probably the mother of Charles Berry.

465. JOHN BERRY PAPERS, 1755-1885. 41 items and 1 vol. Hillsborough (Orange County), N.C.

Papers of a North Carolina builder and architect, including records relating to land and letters containing references to the Civil War, its effect on the cattle industry of Texas, and information on the genealogy of the Vincent family of Lamar, Texas, and of the Berry family.

466. JOHN BERRY AND THOMAS L. BERRY PAPERS, 1833-1838. 5 items. Baltimore, Md.

Bills of lading for shipments of fire brick to John W. Willis, Richmond, Virginia.

467. WILLIAM BERRY DAYBOOK, 1836-1858. 1 vol. (339 pp.) Berry Ferry (Clarke County), Va.

468. HENRY BESANCON DIARY, 1862-1864. 3 vols. Geneseo (Livingston County), N.Y.

Diary of a musician assigned to the 104th Regiment of New York Volunteers relating movements of his unit in Virginia and referring to service as a nurse in divisional hospitals. Included is a list of expenditures giving wartime prices.

469. GEORGE BESORE PAPERS, 1822-1866. 105 items. Waynesboro (Franklin County), Pa.

Bills, receipts, orders, invoices, license, promissory notes, and business letters of a general merchant.

470. B. W. BEST PAPERS, 1865. 1 item. Greene County, N.C.

Pardon issued by Andrew Johnson.

471. MARY MATILDA BETHAM PAPERS, 1840. 2 items. Westmorland County, England.

Biographical and genealogical notes concerning Mary Betham's father, William Betham (1749-1839), English clergyman and antiquarian.

472. RICHARD BETHELL, FIRST BARON WESTBURY, PAPERS, 1853-1894. 43 items. London, England.

Letters of Bethell and his family, including Bethell's explanation to his children of his resignation as Lord Chancellor of Great Britain, 1865; letters from political figures, including Ulrich John de Burgh, First Marquis of Clanricarde, and Henry George Grey, Third Earl Grey, concerning disestablishment of the Church of Ireland, 1869; letters on various parliamentary topics of the 1870s, including legislation regarding copyright, legal procedures, and foreign affairs; and two letters of John Griffiths, Keeper of the Archives at Oxford, concerning a bust and tablet memorializing Bethell. There are also letters to Eleanor Margaret (Tennant) Bethell, Baroness Westbury, from the English authors, Lady Elizabeth (Rigby) Eastlake, and Frances Minto (Dickinson) Elliott.

473. R. H. BEVANDAG PAPERS, 1917. 1 item. Providence (Providence County), R.I.

Letter from H. E. Counsell, Oxford, England, concerning the effect of World War I on Oxford, the losses at the Somme, and prospects of peace.

474. JAMES T. BEVELY PAPERS, 1861-1862. 4 items. Sydnorsville (Franklin County), Va.

Letters of a Confederate soldier describing enlistments and army life.

475. HENRY BEVERIGE DIARY, 1864. 1 vol. (100 pp.) New Market (Shenandoah County), Va.

Diary of a hospital steward in the 25th Virginia Regiment, C.S.A., describing camp life, executions of deserters, and duties of an army surgeon.

476. ROBERT BEVERLEY PAPERS, 1815. 1 item. Essex County, Va.

Letter from Lucy (Beverley) Randolph mentioning financial misfortunes.

477. RICHARD BIBB PAPERS, 1803. 1 item. Fredericksburg (Spotsylvania County), Va.

A letter, apparently from James Madison, Union Courthouse, South Carolina, commenting on the conditions of his employment by the clerk of the district court, the unhealthful conditions in Charleston each summer, and commodity and land prices.

478. THOMAS BIBB PAPERS, 1823-1892. 180 items. Huntsville (Madison County), Ala., and Thibodeaux (Lafourche Parish), La.

Papers of the governor of Alabama consisting of mortgages on land and slaves near Thibodeaux, deeds to lots in New Orleans, receipts, notes, lists of slaves, other land papers relating to holdings in Louisiana and Arkansas, and the management of Bibb's estate after his death.

479. BIBB COUNTY ACADEMY PAPERS, 1838-1859. 9 items. Macon (Bibb County), Ga.

Financial reports of the trustees of this public school, including a proposal to abandon the female academy as economically unwise and concentrate on support of a college.

480. ALEXANDER BIDDLE PAPERS, 1776-1911. 574 items. Philadelphia, Pa.

Largely papers of various members of the Biddle family, including letters, bills, receipts, invoices, estate inventories, and land grants. Topics include merchandise imported from Liverpool, Birmingham, and Sheffield; charges for brokerage, drayage, insurance, and commissions; St. John's School, Sing Sing, New York; land in Missouri, Indiana, Illinois, and Pennsylvania; and charities. Biddles represented in the collection include A. W., Alexander, Annie, Arthur, Charles, Clement, Jr., E. R., George W., J. Wilmer, James W., Julia W., L. A., Lynford, Marion, Mary D., Mary L. C., Sarah, Thomas, Thomas A., and W. R. There are also papers of John Horn, Jr., the estate of Ralph Peters, Mark Willcox, and Henry J. Williams.

481. ANTHONY JOSEPH DREXEL BIDDLE, JR., CHECK STUBS, 1919. 1 vol. (4 pp.) New York, N.Y.

482. JAMES WILLIAMS BIDDLE LEDGER, 1869-1871. 1 vol. (236 pp.) Fort Barnwell (Craven County), N.C.

General mercantile accounts.

483. MARY (DUKE) BIDDLE CHECK STUBS, 1915-1918. 1 vol. (313 pp.) New York, N.Y.

484. SAMUEL SIMPSON BIDDLE PAPERS, 1764-1895. 3,586 items and 11 vols. New Bern (Craven County), N.C.

Business and personal correspondence of four generations of members of the Simpson and Biddle families, principally those of John Simpson (1728-1788), locally a prominent Revolutionary figure, his son Samuel, and his great-grandson Samuel Simpson Biddle (1811-1872), both families being prominent in local affairs. The early letters, including several from John Simpson's brother in Boston, are largely concerned with business, including deeds, Simpson's property in Boston, and shipment of goods. One letter, in 1790, indicates that Simpson was associated in business with Dr. Hugh Williamson in Fayetteville, North Carolina. Other correspondence is concerned with probable purchase of land from John Haywood; one contract, 1810, with a tenant on Simpson's land; agricultural and business interests of Samuel Simpson Biddle in the 1840's and 1850's; the education of Samuel Simpson Biddle at the University of North Carolina, Chapel Hill; and the education of several of his children at various schools in North Carolina, including Wake Forest College, Louisburg Academy, Chowan Female College, Oxford Female College, and a school at Warrenton.

William P. Biddle, father of Samuel Simpson Biddle, was a Baptist minister, who associated with his father-in-law in farming and business. Many letters of other ministers are included, with considerable information on activities of the Baptist Church in the area of Fort Barnwell and New Bern. There are also minutes of Neuse (Baptist) Association, November 4, 1843, and of a conference meeting of the Baptist Church of Christ at Harriett's Chapel, September, 1853.

A large proportion of the letters refer to the Civil War, S. S. Biddle, Jr., and James W. Biddle having enlisted in the Confederate Army in 1861. These letters contain descriptions of campaigns, troop movements, camp life, and epidemics among soldiers and civilians. References are also made to naval conflicts along the coast, Federal prisoners, execution of deserters and of Southern traitors, fortifications at James Island, South

Carolina, various generals, including P. G. T. Beauregard and Wade Hampton, and the confiscation of Southern property by Federal forces. There are also comments on the comparative merits of Z. B. Vance and W. W. Holden as governors.

There are many notes, deeds, and wills, and numerous letters from two of Samuel Biddle's daughters, Mary and Rosa, and from a son, B. F. Biddle, at Wake Forest College, and lists of names and valuations of slaves left by Samuel Simpson and William P. Biddle to their children. There are eleven account books, five small stud books, and a large number of bills and receipts concerned with the mercantile and farming interests of the Simpsons and Biddles. Among the correspondents are John D. Bellamy, William Gaston, John Haywood, Thomas Meredith, and John Stanly.

485. SIR GEORGE BIDDLECOMBE MEMOIR, 1823-1872. 1 vol. (368 pp.) Portsea, Hampshire, England.

An account of Biddlecombe's experiences as a British naval officer, including a visit to the grave of Napoleon Bonaparte on St. Helena in 1824; participation in the Burmese War, 1825; the activities of Doña Apolinaria, a spy for Simón Bolívar; Biddlecombe's naval surveys in various parts of the world; the Crimean War; meetings with royalty; and his being knighted by Queen Victoria.

486. ASA BIGGS PAPERS, 1827-1886. 161 items and 1 vol. Williamston (Martin County), N.C., and Norfolk (Norfolk County), Va.

Pre-Civil War letters refer to a mercantile firm in which the Biggs family had an interest. Two letters are from Cushing Biggs Hassell. Wartime correspondence includes letters, concentrated in 1864-1865, of two sons, Henry A. and William Biggs, describing service in the 17th North Carolina Regiment and Manley's Battery near Petersburg and Wilmington. There is no material in this collection concerning Biggs's political career. His letters to his wife are personal in nature. There is a brief diary begun by Biggs's daughter, possibly Della, in 1855 during a visit to Washington, which largely records household duties and financial accounts.

487. ANNIE CECELIA (BULMER) BILL PAPERS, 1924-1943. 8 items. Boston, Mass.

Personal letters, some relating to Christian Science.

488. J. T. BILLENSTEIN MEMOIR. 1 vol. (228 pp.)

Narrative, written in the form of a journal, of the service of the U.S.S. Brooklyn, 1862-1863, in operations against New Orleans. Includes transcripts of official correspondence and orders.

489. DAVID BILLMYER PAPERS, 1832-1906. 998 items. Shepherdstown (Jefferson County), W. Va.

Family letters and papers largely relating to personal matters. Included are letters of the related Shepherd family. Letters of Henry E. Unseld describe New Orleans during 1854-1855, with reference to theatre, social life, the Irish uprising, Know-Nothings, and yellow fever epidemics; experiences in the Nicaraguan War of 1856; and travels in Warrensburg, Missouri, and in Illinois, 1858-1859. Letters of David Billmyer, member of the House of Delegates, 1867-1868, discuss the permanent location of the state capital and his businesses--a dry goods store in Shepherdstown and a grain boat on the Potomac River. Letters from William H. and Sallie Billmyer concern West Virginia Agricultural College, Morgantown, and Hagerstown Female Seminary, Hagerstown, Maryland, 1868-1869. Several letters from relatives recount military events in Virginia, 1861. There are many references to religion and temperance.

490. EDWARD F. BIRCKHEAD PAPERS, 1842-1895. 237 items. Earleyville, Va.

Papers of a physician and farmer; included are references to prices and shipment of corn, meal, plaster, wheat, flour, and tobacco; and bills for medical services. Letters from James S. Hamm describe social life and customs of Gainesville, Alabama, during the 1840s and comment on the murder of Dr. Sidney S. Perry by Col. John A. Winston. One letter of 1850 from Philadelphia describes medical study, abolitionist sentiment, and a Jenny Lind concert. There are accounts of a committee to dispense aid to indigent families of soldiers during the Civil War; letters from Birckhead's daughter Millie concerning schooling at the Piedmont Female Academy; and accounts of the estates of Nehemiah Birckhead and William P. Wilkerson.

491. BIRMINGHAM POLITICAL UNION PAPERS, 1831. 1 item. Birmingham, Warwickshire, England.

Draft committee report on organization of the Union.

492. JAMES BISLAND PAPERS, 1822-1835. 15 items. Natchez (Adams County), Miss.

Deeds for slaves purchased from Peter and William Bisland.

493. EDWARD BISHOP PAPERS, 1864. 1 item. Athens (Clarke County), Ga.

Letter of a Confederate recruit stationed at Griffin, Georgia, describing camp life.

494. G. EDWARD BISHOP PAPERS, 1861.
2 items. Rhode Island.

Letter, accompanied by a map of northern Virginia, by a musician in the 4th Rhode Island Volunteer Regiment describing the movement to Washington, D.C., and conditions in camp there; and a letter describing the capture of Fort Macon, North Carolina, and conditions around Beaufort.

495. SARAH E. BISHOP PAPERS, 1871-1878.
2 items. Clement (Sampson County), N.C.

Family letters.

496. WILLIAM T. BISHOP PAPERS, 1818-1863.
72 items. Hummelstown (Dauphin County), Pa.

Family and business letters, largely to Bishop or his father, Charles Bishop of Manchester, Pennsylvania; and letters from Slater T. Walker to William Bishop's wife, Caroline (Walker) Bishop. Letters of the 1830s when William and Caroline Bishop lived in Louisville, Kentucky, and Manchester, Pennsylvania, concern the sale of a slave, illness, cholera, and business affairs. Papers of the 1840s relate to Walker's dry goods business in Hummelstown, to Bishop's court contest with the Savings Bank of Baltimore, and to the Sons of Temperance, which Bishop apparently served as a lecturer. Letters of the later 1840s concern his employment as a justice of the peace and debt collector and conflicts over the Walker family property. Among the correspondents are Carrie Bishop, John C. Bucher, Henry A. Muhlenberg, and J. W. Oliver.

497. LEONARD BISSELL PAPERS, 1842.
2 items. Madison (Morgan County), Ga.

Letters from cotton factors of Augusta, Georgia, describing the cotton market, prices, and futures.

498. TITUS BISSELL LETTERS, 1854-1865.
15 items. Charleston, S.C.

Letters, largely from Titus Bissell to his mother, discussing family affairs; two items describe the siege of Charleston during the Civil War and the part played by Titus's sons Tite and Neddy.

499. ROBERT BISSET PAPERS, 1769-1799.
6 items. London, England.

Correspondence of a British army officer concerning military affairs. Places mentioned include St. Augustine, Florida, 1769. Persons include Sir William Fawcett, William Pitt, and the Duke of York.

500. B. LEWIS BITTING PAPERS, (1858-1864) 1886. 19 items. Rural Hall (Forsyth County), N.C.

Family correspondence largely concerning gossip, but mentioning the progress of the Civil War and an organization known as the "Heroes of America," July 17, 1864, and material from 1877-1878 on the sale of manufactured tobacco in South Carolina.

501. JOHN DANIEL BIVENS PAPERS, 1817 (1840-1925) 1939. 1,584 items and 26 vols. Ravenel (Dorchester County), S.C.

Mercantile accounts and family and business correspondence of John D. Bivens (1863-1921), merchant, trial justice in Collins Township, county commissioner, state legislator, and presidential elector. The collection consists chiefly of family correspondence and legal papers, revealing many facts concerning political problems and methods in South Carolina, 1885-1915, and account books of a country merchant dealing in cotton. Included are letters concerning Bivens's attending Sheridan Classical School in Orangeburg, South Carolina; cards from Coleman L. Blease, governor of South Carolina; letters concerning Bivens's son, John Lucas Bivens, who attended Clemson College, South Carolina; account books of D. T. Bivens of Ridgeville, South Carolina; school trustees' record, Delman's School House, Collins Township; household accounts; farm accounts; and a criminal trial docket, 1909-1922, of George W. Elsey, a justice of the peace preceding Bivens.

502. HARRIET MATILDA BLACK PAPERS, 1860 (1862-1864) 1889. 78 items. Pomaria (Newberry County), S.C.

Letters to Harriet Matilda Black from her brothers and cousins in the Confederate Army. There are references to the "Beef Club," evidently a co-operative food venture among the soldiers, and the canal built for the siege of Vicksburg.

503. HARVEY BLACK LEDGERS, 1865-1893.
2 vols. Blacksburg (Montgomery County), Va.

Physician's accounts.

504. FRANCIS BLACKBURNE PAPERS, 1849.
1 item. Dublin, Ireland.

Letter from Edward B. Sugden commenting on his recent book, politics and judiciary in Ireland and England, and poor relief.

505. VALENTINE BLACKER LETTER BOOK, 1798-1813. 1 vol. (349 pp.) Madras, India.

Letters of an officer of the Madras Army in the service of the East India Company; also included are a few letters from his uncle, General Sir Barry Close. Topics include the India careers of Blacker and Close, military campaigns and expeditions, and observations on the countryside and the life and customs of southern India. Filed with the letter book is a descriptive calendar.

506. CHARLES MINOR BLACKFORD, SR., AND THOMAS JELLIS KIRKPATRICK PAPERS, 1848-1870. 8 items. Lynchburg (Campbell County), Va.

Miscellaneous material concerning a law firm.

507. JOHN STUART BLACKIE PAPERS, 1892. 1 item. Edinburgh, Scotland.

Letter from the Earl of Fife expressing his opinion about the undesirability of large landed estates.

508. HOMER BLACKMON PAPERS, 1862-1864. 4 items. Point Jefferson (Morehouse Parish), La.

Letters from J. A. Dunn, overseer of Blackmon's plantation near Point Jefferson, about the building of a cotton gin, illness among the slaves, Civil War refugee life at Walnut Hill, Arkansas, and the behavior of slaves under French occupation.

509. R. BLACKNALL AND SON PRESCRIPTION BOOK, 1901-1903. 1 vol. Durham, N.C.

Druggist's prescription book.

510. J. WILLIAM BLACKSHEAR PAPERS, 1846-1865. 50 items. Macon (Bibb County), Ga.

Chiefly war letters of J. William Blackshear, Confederate soldier, fiancé and ultimately the husband of Marian Baber, who was the daughter of Ambrose Baber; and of George D. Smith, Confederate soldier and cousin of the Babers. The letters include descriptions of the fall of Port Royal, South Carolina, 1861, and graphic descriptions of army life and activities on St. Simon's Island, Georgia. Other correspondents wrote of efforts of "Yankees" in 1865 to get teachers for Negro schools in Savannah, impressions of Texas, high cost of living, styles in women's clothes, poor mail service, and depredations of Sherman's soldiers.

511. EDWARD L. BLACKWELL PAPERS, 1869-1879. 2 vols. Fairfield (Hyde County), N.C.

Records of a general merchant at Fairfield, with detailed entries of transactions. Payments by customers are identified by cash, goods, labor, and other services. Negro customers are identified in both ledgers; the smaller volume, 1869-1871, was kept entirely for Negro customers. It also contains the accounts, 1873-1879, of Jones Spencer, administrator of Blackwell's estate. Included is an account of sales of the perishable property of the estate, June 2, 1873, which amounts to a partial inventory of the store.

512. ELIZABETH BLACKWELL PAPERS, 1838, 1847. 2 items. Warrenton (Fauquier County), Va.

A personal letter from Elizabeth Blackwell's daughter, Betsy, and her son-in-law, J. H. (Edmunds?); and a letter concerning interest on a loan.

513. WILLIAM THOMAS BLACKWELL PAPERS, 1883-1889. 93 items and 30 vols. Durham, N.C.

Business records of a tobacco manufacturer, tobacco merchant, and banker, including the records of the Bank of Durham. Correspondents include N. A. Ramsey reporting on mica-bearing lands of the University of North Carolina in the western part of the state and V. Ballard regarding accounts due the Bank of Durham.

514. DAVID K. BLACKWOOD PAPERS, 1851 (1852-1856) 1881. 16 items. Chapel Hill (Orange County), N.C.

Personal correspondence of David K. Blackwood with his brothers, J., James J., and M. J. Blackwood.

515. FREDERICK TEMPLE HAMILTON-TEMPLE-BLACKWOOD, FIRST MARQUIS OF DUFFERIN AND AVA, PAPERS, 1870 (1886-1888) 1895. 35 items. "Clandeboye," County Down, Northern Ireland.

Letters relating to Lord Dufferin's term as governor-general of India, chiefly addressed to Dufferin's advisor, Sir Andrew Richard Scoble, and concerning appointments to office and requests for advice. Included is a pamphlet giving Dufferin's reply, 1877, to charges against his appointment of Sir Charles Umpherston Aitchison to his council. There is also comment by Dufferin, 1872, on John Bright's clauses added to the Irish Land Act, permitting government loans to support tenant purchases of lands. There are a few letters by Lady Dufferin and by Sir Henry Blackwood, First Baronet.

516. SIR HENRY BLACKWOOD, FIRST BARONET, PAPERS, 1810-1827. 3 items. London, England.

Letters, 1827, to an attorney, Julius Hutchinson, concerning the collection of debts from a Mr. De Bruyn; and a letter of commendation, 1810, from Admiral Sir Charles Cotton.

517. BLADEN COUNTY, N.C., ENTRY TAKER'S BOOK, 1778-1796. 1 vol. (600 pp.) North Carolina.

Contemporary copy of an entry taker's book of land grants describing location of each tract.

518. CYNTHIA BLAIR AND MILDRED BLAIR PAPERS, (1852-1859) 1892. 79 items. Randolph County, N.C.

Correspondence of two young girls with relatives and friends in Randolph County and the surrounding area, with references to the social life of the pre-war period. A few letters from the spring of 1861 show the anticipation of the outbreak of hostilities. Correspondents include Nancy and Elizabeth Royall, R. R. Tomlinson, Elizabeth and William S. McGee, E. I. Julian, A. H. Ardella, Delphina Brown, Alson Kine, Betty Elder, Mary M. Miller (a cousin in Iowa), and Rachael Mendenhall.

519. FRANCIS PRESTON BLAIR PAPERS, 1831-1867. 35 items. Washington, D.C.

Letters addressed to Blair, relating to Democratic politics, especially to the extent of support for Andrew Jackson, and to Blair's private business affairs. Writers include Benjamin F. Linton, W. H. Hardwick, R. C. Hancock, George C. Skipworth, J. W. McKee, Cassius M. Clay, Francis Scott Key, George Mifflin Dallas.

520. W. A. BLAIR PAPERS, 1835-1842. 10 items. Peoria (Peoria County), Ill.

Personal letters concerning W. A. Blair's changes of fortune as he moved from Portsmouth, Virginia, to Peoria and thence to St. Louis, Missouri.

521. RALPH ROYD BLAKELY PAPERS, 1918-1957. 304 items. Clinton (Laurens County), S.C.

Papers relating to Blakely's efforts to qualify for disability compensation based on illness suffered as a soldier in World War I; and correspondence relating to political patronage and the Republican Party in South Carolina. Included are materials related to the efforts of J. Yandell Blakely to be appointed a U.S. district attorney in South Carolina, and R. R. Blakely's efforts to become postmaster. There is also material relating to several minor offices in the state party held by J. Y. and R. R. Blakely. Included are printed materials circulated by Republicans in opposition to policies of the Democratic administration.

522. N. L. BLAKEMORE PAPERS, 1849-1869. 4 items. Page County, Va.

Letters of N. L. Blakemore, connected with the Shenandoah Iron Works, concerning business conditions and prices.

523. ANGUS R. BLAKEY PAPERS, 1820 (1840-1865) 1888. 653 items. Madison and Albemarle counties, Va.

Personal and business papers of a Virginia attorney, including some papers of his various partners, Francis H. Hill, Oscar Reierson, William Oswald Fry, and James Blakey. Topics frequently discussed include temperance; purchases and prices of slaves; politics, political leaders, events, and appointments to office; Revolutionary War pensions and bounty lands; the Mexican War; insurance; legal affairs; the secessionist spirit in Virginia; the state secession convention and Blakey's role as a delegate; preparations in the South for military activity; religion; land; hiring out of slaves and their use in the iron and coal industries of Virginia during the war; commodity prices and speculation in the Confederacy; avoidance of conscription; salt mining and trade; the encouragement of white immigration to Virginia after the war; the faculty of the University of Virginia and other colleges; Blakey's participation in the management of the Insurance Company of America; and conventions of former Confederates. Among the writers of letters are A. D. Almond, Joseph Reid Anderson and Co., James Barbour, John Brown Barbour, John Strode Barbour, Sr., T. C. Blakey, William Brown, James Lawrence Cabell, Francis Edward Garland Carr, Edward N. Covell, Nathan P. Dodge, William L. Early, Joseph T. Field, G. D. Gray, John Thomas Harris, D. J. Hartsook, William Wirt Henry, Samuel H. Jeter, James Lawson Kemper, J. L. Kent, Margaret F. C. Lewis, Richard McIlwaine, Jeremiah Morton, T. M. Niven, S. H. Parrott, William H. Richardson, John Rutherfoord, W. P. Strother, John W. Taylor, Robert H. Turner, Charles Scott Venable, James W. Walker, H. N. Wallace, Henry Alexander Wise.

524. AUSTIN BLALOCK PAPERS, 1863-1864. 3 items. Person County, N.C.

Letters of a private in the 35th North Carolina Regiment describing camp life near Richmond, Virginia, and in Martin County, North Carolina.

525. TILMON BLALOCK PAPERS, 1825-1861. 33 items. Yancey County, N.C.

Papers of Tilmon Blalock, a farmer, lieutenant colonel in the North Carolina Militia, and captain in the Mexican War. The papers consist of military reports, records of army supplies received, applications for pensions, and Blalock's will.

526. LOUIS BLANC PAPERS, 1850. 1 item. Paris, France.

Manuscript of an article, "La Situation," by Blanc, French socialist and politician, attacking the restrictive French election law of 1850 and apparently intended for publication in Le Nouveau Monde, but suppressed by intimidation of the printer.

527. CHARLES W. BLANCHARD PAPERS, 1930. 1 item. New Bern (Craven County), N.C.

Correspondence with J. M. Templeton relating to the founding of the Cary School.

528. EDWARD LITT LAMAN BLANCHARD PAPERS, 1886. 1 item. London, England.

Letter to H. Plowman, June 9, 1886.

529. WILLIAM BLANDING JOURNAL, 1828. 2 items and 1 vol. Camden (Kershaw County), S.C.

Journal of a trip to Asheville, North Carolina, with descriptions of gold mines in North and South Carolina; comments on politics in the U.S. and South Carolina; and two hand drawn maps of iron works at Catawba Springs, North Carolina and Chesterfield, South Carolina.

530. ELIZABETH J. (HOLMES) BLANKS PAPERS, 1832-1888. 112 items and 1 vol. Fayetteville (Cumberland County), N.C.

Family and business correspondence of the Blanks family, planters and lawyers, who moved from North Carolina to Mississippi, and, failing in business undertakings there, returned to North Carolina. The letters concern settlement of the estate of one of the Blanks and give information on prices and general economic conditions, on the history of the Holmes and Blanks families, and on the activities of William Blanks, Jr., who joined the New York firm of J. T. Murray & Company in 1866. Many of the letters, written by the women of the family, are filled with personal affairs, religious discussions, prophecy, and stories of hardships and anxiety attending the Civil War. A notebook contains information on the McLaurin and MacMurphy families.

531. JAMES BLANTON PAPERS, 1808-1897. 859 items. Cumberland County, Va.

Largely bills and receipts relating to Blanton's ante-bellum tobacco commission business, Farmville, Virginia, and some records of farming and carriage manufacturing in Cumberland County. A letter, 1848, from Blanton's son, Philip Southall Blanton, describes his studies at Jefferson Medical College, Philadelphia, including the theft of the body of a Negro woman, found to have been buried alive. There are also papers of Walker B. Blanton, principally drafts of articles concerning the Patrons of Husbandry, and of James M. Blanton, Virginia state commissioner of agriculture in the 1880s. A few letters of Confederate soldiers in the 18th Virginia Regiment of Volunteers in North Carolina and Virginia mention smallpox in camp near Tarboro, North Carolina, 1864, and comment on morale near the end of the war.

532. JAMES L. B. BLAUVELT PAPERS, 1862-1867. 5 items. New Brunswick (Middlesex County), N.J.

Personal correspondence of James L. B. Blauvelt, an officer in the U.S. Navy, concerning Civil War activities around Pensacola Bay, Florida; Mobile Bay, Alabama; and Vicksburg, Mississippi.

533. F. A. BLECKLEY PAPERS, (1862-1865) 1880. 44 items. Chatham County, N.C.

Personal letters from F. A. Bleckley, a private in the Confederate Army, and from his brother, William L. Bleckley. One letter, January 23, 1865, concerns a proposed armistice.

534. SYLVESTER BLECKLEY PAPERS, 1875, 1881. 2 items. Anderson (Anderson County), S.C.

Personal letters from Sylvester Bleckley, a general merchant, to his uncle, Charles Bleckley, in Catawba County, North Carolina.

535. JOHN BLIGH, FOURTH EARL OF DARNLEY, PAPERS, 1738-1858. 99 items. "Cobham Hall," Gravesend, Kent, England.

Letters and printed material of Bligh and members of his family. Topics include the Act of Union; political activities of Daniel O'Connell and Catholic emancipation; elections to the House of Commons; Irish elections and criticism of the government's Irish policy; English politics and appointments to the ministry; trade with Russia, Sweden, and Denmark in iron; rises in the price of coal; rises in the price of food; and genealogy. Writers of letters include members of the royalty, the peerage, and political leaders. Letters, 1830, of Prince Leopold (later King of Belgium) discuss his refusal to accept the crown of Greece. There is a 1796 account of naval engagements with the French off the Irish coast.

536. CHARLES GEORGE BLOMFIELD PAPERS, 1854-1865. 2 items and 2 vols. Tellicherry, Madras, India.

Papers of a British officer in the Madras Army and superintendent of police in Malabar, 1857-1867. Included is a record book of the Malabar Police Corps containing a brief historical account, 1854-1860, up to the incorporation into the Mofussel Police. Also in the collection are Blomfield's official diaries, 1864 and July-December, 1865, with details of crime, investigations, and judicial proceedings, and marginal comments by the inspector general, Lewis Hankin.

537. CHARLES JAMES BLOMFIELD PAPERS, 1835-1861. 13 items. London, England.

Chiefly miscellaneous letters addressed to Blomfield, Bishop of London, and to his wife, Dorothy Kent Blomfield. Writers include Sir Robert Peel and other prominent persons; among topics mentioned are relief of the destitute, ecclesiastical matters, and appointments.

538. AMELIA (JENKS) BLOOMER PAPERS, 1895. 1 item. Council Bluffs (Pottawattamie County), Iowa.

Clipping of an article that appeared in a Columbus, Ohio, newspaper shortly after Mrs. Bloomer's death. It gives a brief account of this woman best known for the mode of dress which she adopted and to which her name has been given.

539. H. P. BLOUNT PAPERS, 1881-1919. 42 items.

Personal letters, including a description, 1881, of living conditions and child labor in Atlanta, Mrs. Blount's singing abilities, Blount's election to the Georgia Historical Society, and the admission of his daughter to the Athens State Normal College, 1908.

540. JOHN GRAY BLOUNT PAPERS, 1780-1826. 27 items. Washington (Beaufort County), N.C.

Business letters to Blount, merchant, shipper, planter, and politician. Topics include proceedings of the state legislature, the building of a courthouse in Beaufort County, appointments of two magistrates, Blount's business, and land deeds and indentures.

541. WILLIE BLOUNT PAPERS, 1809, 1810. 2 items. Knoxville (Knox County), Tenn.

Letters from Willie Blount (1768-1835), Tennessee legislator and governor, dealing with the removal of Indians from Tennessee.

542. BLOUNT FAMILY GENEALOGY. 1 item.

Photocopy of the family tree of the descendents of Robert Taft of Scotland (fl. 1202).

543. MARY A. BLUDWORTH PAPERS, 1862-1913. 37 items. York (York County), S.C.

Family letters dealing with social life and customs in South Carolina; the temperance movement; Civil War battles including the Peninsular Campaign and Chancellorsville; the Rollins family; and a Confederate veterans' organization called the Immortal 600.

544. EDMUND BLUM PAPERS, 1841-1876. 13 items and 2 vols. Salem (Forsyth County), N.C.

Business correspondence of Blum, a coppersmith employed by John D. Brown of Salisbury, North Carolina. Included is Blum's report as secretary-treasurer of Shady Mount Sunday School, giving a brief history of the school; a letter of 1838 from John C. Blum; and daybooks, 1844-1852, 1857-1864.

545. ELIZABETH F. BLYTH PAPERS, 1819-1834. 23 items. Georgetown (Georgetown County), S.C.

Letters from commission merchants handling the sale of rice.

546. JAMES LOCKE BOARDMAN PAPERS, 1844 (1858-1874) 1881. 25 items. Greensboro (Hale County), Ala.

Letters of James L. Boardman, 5th Alabama Regiment, C.S.A., of his brother, Henry Boardman, 62nd Alabama Regiment, C.S.A., and their father, Volney Boardman (b. 1810). The father's letters concern the education of his daughter, Margaret. The sons' letters describe camp life, supplies, campaigns, the Harper's Ferry and Winchester Railroad, and the Ku Klux Klan.

547. JOHN B. BOBBITT PAPERS, 1886-1888. 36 items. Raleigh (Wake County), and Goldsboro (Wayne County), N.C.

Papers of John B. Bobbitt, Methodist minister, concerning the collection of pledges for the Trinity College Endowment Fund, and the publication of The Methodist Advance and The Christian Educator and Trinity Endowment.

548. JOHN A. BOGART PAPERS, 1838. 1 item. New York, N.Y.

Routine letter from Mahlon Dickerson (1770-1853), U.S. senator from New Jersey, to Bogart, collector of the customs in New York.

549. WILLIAM ROBERTSON BOGGS PAPERS, 1855-1857. 7 items. Troy (Rensselaer County), N.Y.

Papers of William R. Boggs, officer in the armies of the U.S.A. and the C.S.A., include family letters, two calling cards, an invitation, and a note on the death of William R. Boggs, Jr.

550. THADDEUS S. BOINEST PAPERS, 1849-1871. 26 items. Pomaria (Newberry County), S.C.

Business correspondence of Thaddeus S. Boinest, Lutheran minister and president of the Immigration Society of Newberry, South Carolina, chiefly on matters connected with the Immigration Society.

551. WILLIAM P. BOISSEAU PAPERS, 1866-1871. 11 items. Dinwiddie County, Va.

Personal letters from William P. Boisseau to his father with occasional references to crops and the weather.

552. EDWARD WILLIAM BOK PAPERS, 1894-1923. 4 items. Merion (Montgomery County), Pa.

Papers of Edward W. Bok (1863-1930), author and editor, include three letters from cartoonist William Allen Rogers concerning drawings he had made for Bok's use, and a letter of thanks to Samuel Griffin Wingfield for his comments on Bok's books.

553. GEORGE HENRY BOKER PAPERS, 1859-1869. 7 items. Philadelphia, Pa.

Letters from George H. Boker (1823-1890), writer and diplomat, to Charles Warren Stoddard, criticizing Stoddard's poetical works. [Published: Jay B. Hubbell, "George Henry Boker, Paul Hamilton Hayne, and Charles Warren Stoddard: Some Unpublished Letters," American Literature, V (May, 1933), 146-165.]

554. JOHN A. BOLIN PAPERS, 1862-1864. 5 items. Auburn (Lee County), Ala.

Letters of John A. Bolin, 17th Regiment, Alabama Volunteers, C.S.A., to his wife, Mary J. Bolin, describing camp life and military activities.

555. JOSEPH CLAUDE MARIE BOLLERY PAPERS, 1928-1945. 7 items. La Rochelle, France.

Letters of Bollery (b. 1890), editor of Cahiers Léon Bloy, to Guido Colucci concerning calligraphy done by Colucci and watercolor illustrations done by his brother, Gio Colucci, for La Boue from Bloy's Sueur de Sang; and a copy of the minutes of the meeting establishing the Amis de Léon Bloy.

556. A. J. BOLLING PAPERS, 1849-1889. 15 items and 1 vol. Oak Ridge (Guilford County), N.C.

The volume contains a ledger, 1870-1889, 251 pp., for Bolling's general store in northwestern Guilford County. Many pages are missing from the ledger; the first 94 pages are the ledger, 1849-1852, of Samuel Dwiggins from his general store near Guilford, in west-central Guilford County. Loose items include envelopes and invoices, some of them from J. L. King, manufacturer of plug, twist, and navy tobacco at Greensboro, North Carolina.

557. RICHARD M. BOLLING PAPERS, 1843-1909. 18 items. Richmond and Norfolk (Norfolk County), Va.

Chiefly the business papers of Captain Richard M. Bolling, Engineer in Charge of Survey of the Seaboard Airline Railway Company. Included are three postcards and some genealogical information.

558. WILLIAM BOLLING PAPERS, 1724 (1776-1859) 1883. 877 items. Goochland County, Va.

The papers and correspondence of William Bolling (1789-1849), planter, cavalry commander in the War of 1812, sheriff, and descendant of Pocahontas, include information concerning Bolling's farming operations; prices of wheat and tobacco; flour milling industry in Richmond; slaves; the Randolph, Robertson, and Meade families and their plantations; David Meade's removal to Kentucky in 1796; Albemarle Agricultural Society; William Bolling's services in the War of 1812 in the vicinity of Norfolk, Virginia; John Braidwood, an Englishman who taught deaf-mutes; Bremo Seminary (Fluvanna County, Virginia); University of Virginia, Charlottesville, including description of Thomas Jefferson; Oxford Iron Works in Campbell County, Virginia; and travel to Rome and Switzerland. Among the correspondents are Mary Bolling, Thomas Bolling, John Braidwood, John Hartwell Cocke, David Meade, Anne (Meade) Randolph, David Meade Randolph, Richard Randolph, Bolling Robertson, and John Robertson. [One letter of David Meade is published. See Bayrd Still (ed.), "The Westward Migration of a Planter Pioneer in 1796," William and Mary College Quarterly, 2d Ser., XXI, 318-343.]

559. JOHN BOLTON PAPERS, 1836. 1 item. New York, N.Y.

Routine business letter, with copy of another enclosed, from Baring Brothers and Company, London, to John Bolton, agent for the Planters Bank in New York.

560. FERDINAND F. BOLTZ PAPERS, 1864-1865. 1 vol. Indiana.

Combination daybook, memorandum book and diary of Boltz, 88th Regiment, Indiana Volunteers, containing brief accounts of his regiment; Sherman's march through Georgia; the siege of Savannah; and the march through the Carolinas ending at Richmond, Virginia.

561. EDWARD EARLE BOMAR PAPERS, 1757 (1880-1938) 1942. 556 items and 18 vols. Spartanburg (Spartanburg County), S.C.

Personal and professional papers of E. E. Bomar (b. 1861), Baptist minister, and his father, John E. Bomar (1827-1899), lawyer and politician. The correspondence of John Bomar includes family letters; papers dealing with legal cases; letters discussing politics, including a letter from Daniel W. Wallace, U.S. representative from South Carolina (1848-1853), commenting on the political issue of slavery and predicting the Civil War; and material relating to Bomar's service as trustee of Limestone College, Converse College, the Kennedy Free Library, Spartanburg Female Seminary, and Spartanburg Male Academy. The major portion of the E. E. Bomar correspondence consists of family letters which discuss family matters, the life and growth of missions in Japan, 1938, and political events in Manila, 1931-1935. Other papers concern the work of the Foreign Mission Board of the Southern Baptist Convention, 1900-1906; leading Baptists and religious figures, including a discussion of a revival in Charleston led by Dwight L. Moody; and the pastorates of the churches he served. Miscellaneous papers and volumes include notebooks on law and seminary lectures, memorandum books, ca. 1878-1882, sermon notes, various church calendars and histories, clippings on religious matters, bills and receipts, and genealogical information.

562. BOMPIANI PAPERS, 1844. 1 item. Preston, Lancashire, England.

Letter from Professor Bompiani to an English nobleman attempting to identify a figure depicted in the tiling of the latter's dining room.

563. OCTAVIUS BOND PAPERS, 1797-1811. 28 items. England.

Papers of a British army officer, 4th Regiment, Native Infantry, include Bond's appointments and commissions from cadet to captain, copies of letters concerning claims of his regiment against the East India Company for prize money from the Mysore War, and a log recording voyages to India, 1797, and from India to England, 1810.

564. THOMAS M. BONDURANT PAPERS, 1834 (1856-1891). 18 items. Richmond, Va.

Business and political correspondence of Thomas M. Bondurant, Virginia politician, containing comments on the Liverpool tobacco market and the Jacksonian financial policy.

565. MILLEDGE LUKE BONHAM PAPERS, 1861-1864. 10 items. Columbia (Richland County), S.C.

Papers of Milledge L. Bonham (1813-1890), governor of South Carolina (1863-1865), including letters from William Johnston, president of the Charlotte and South Carolina Railroad, which concern the shipment of cotton to Wilmington, North Carolina, for running the blockade; receipts for expenditures from the contingent fund; a note on balloon experiments conducted for the Union Army; letters discussing army regulations, the first battle of Manassas, and the site of a projected military prison; and a petition from citizens of the Marlborough District objecting to an Executive Council order to obstruct the Pee Dee River and calling all white males into active military service.

566. ELI WHITNEY BONNEY PAPERS, 1805-1914. 596 items. Camden (Kershaw County), S.C.

Personal and business papers of E. W. Bonney (1810-1868), merchant. Prior to 1830, the papers are of the Lee family, related through Bonney's wife, Rebecca (Lee) Bonney (1811-1877). Lee records consist of the correspondence of Francis S. Lee with Charleston cotton factors and with friends at the Virginia Springs; and deeds and estate papers. Other ante-bellum materials include mercantile records; letters from Northern friends commenting on the Smithson funds, Daniel Webster, slavery and secession; letters from sons at academies near Asheville, North Carolina, and Winnsboro and Columbia, South Carolina, describing discipline, curriculum, and student life; and a diary remarking on religious, social and mercantile affairs. Civil War letters, chiefly from sons Usher Parsons and Charles Levett Bonney, describe secession; the war in Virginia, Florida, and Mississippi, especially the siege of Pensacola, First Manassas, the Seven Days Battles, and the siege of Petersburg; and life in Richmond. Correspondence after the war reveals efforts of the family to reestablish themselves; and discusses confiscation of cotton and other property, the credit system, prices, politics, Negroes, and Reconstruction in Louisiana, Mississippi, Alabama, Florida, and Texas.

567. LETTIE BONNIFIELD PAPERS, 1861-1885. 17 items. St. George, Va.

Letters of Sergeant Andrew Donaldson Stewart, 25th Regiment, Ohio Volunteers, to Lettie Bonnifield describing the movement of his own and other Union regiments, predominately in northern Virginia.

568. JOHN BONSACK PAPERS, 1786 (1816-1908) 1929. 2,000 items and 34 vols. Bonsack (Roanoke County), Va.

Personal and business correspondence, and accounts and genealogical records of the Bonsack and Plaine families, connected by marriage. Included are school and college letters from Emory and Henry College, Virginia, 1851; Calvert College, New Windsor, Maryland, 1851-1852; State Normal School, Millersville, Pennsylvania, 1881; Roanoke College, Salem, Virginia, 1882; and Eastman Business College, Poughkeepsie, New York, 1883. Included also are letters concerning woolen factories in Good Intent, Virginia, 1862, and at Bonsack, Virginia, during the 1880s; references to David H. Plaine's work as a churchman, teacher, and a politician in and around Roanoke, Virginia; accounts of Jacob Bonsack (1819-1889), as a merchant in Good Intent, Virginia; and accounts of Harry E. Plaine as a hardware dealer in Broken Bow, Nebraska, during the 1880s. About fifty letters, 1786-1851, are written in German to two John Bonsacks, father (1760-1795) and son (1781-1859), Included are several religious tracts, memorandum books, study notes, and short diaries. The diaries contain accounts of a trip in 1856 from Randolph County, Virginia, to Madison, Wisconsin; travels in the vicinity of Carlisle, Pennsylvania, and a record kept by D. H. Plaine in 1857.

569. GEORGE BOOKER PAPERS, 1850-1862. 43 items. Hampton (Elizabeth City County), Va.

Letters to George Booker (1816 [?]-1878) from M. R. H. Garnett, R. M. T. Hunter, and Henry A. Wise, relating principally to politics. Included are discussions of Garnett's race for a seat in the House of

Representatives, the Kansas-Nebraska Act, the 1856 presidential election, abolitionism, states' rights, and secession.

570. ROBERT BOOLE PAPERS, 1675. 1 item. Bideford, Devonshire, England.

Indenture between Robert Boole and John Champlin, merchants of Bideford.

571. HIRAM CASSEL BOONE PAPERS, 1820-1832. 4 items. Brandenburg (Meade County), Ky.

Letters from Congressmen Jonathan Jennings, Ratliff Boon, and John Tipton to H. C. Boone (b. 1789) concerning Boone's claim against the government, and one letter referring to Boone's wedding.

572. TURIN BRADFORD BOONE DIARIES, 1911-1912. 2 vols. Washington, D.C.

Typewritten diaries of Boone, member of the staff of Morgan Shuster, Treasurer General of Persia, titled "Persian Diary, 1911-1912" and "Around the World." The second, in part an abridgement of the first, describes a trip in the Eastern Mediterranean and Europe. He discusses Persian finances and foreign policy, politics, religions, art and architecture, and places he visited. Persons mentioned include Sherwood Eddy and Mohamet V (1844-1918), Sultan of Turkey.

573. CHARLES H. BOOTH PAPERS, 1852-1886. 12 items. Kalamazoo (Kalamazoo County), Mich.

Personal and business letters of a real estate and insurance agent, mentioning travel in Europe and discussing railroads.

574. EDWIN T. BOOTON PAPERS, 1828-1907. 1,286 items and 17 vols. Luray (Page County), Va.

Business and legal papers of E. T. Booton, attorney, mayor and county judge, concerning his early journalistic efforts as Page County's reporter for the Richmond newspapers; local and state politics; the Baptist Church and the Y.M.C.A. in Luray; his duties as mayor of Luray and his appointment as county judge; business and industrial expansion in Luray; and the development of Luray College, and the Whosoever Farm and Orphanage. Legal papers concern the collection of debts or rent and the settlement of estates. Volumes include letterpress books, notebooks, and the account books of W. E. Lauck, J. E. Shenk, and his father, John G. Booton, pertaining to his medical practice.

575. ANSON BORCHART PAPERS, 1864-1879. 436 items. Savannah, Ga.

Chiefly bills and receipts of a bakery. Included are several deeds.

576. MARTIN BORCKHOLDER ACCOUNTS AND ARITHMETIC BOOK, 1798-1832. 1 vol. (78 pp.) Rockingham County, Va.

Records of contributions for a church building in Rockingham County, and a student's copy of an arithmetic book.

577. BORLAND FAMILY PAPERS, 1806-1867. 8 items. New Orleans, La.

Papers of three generations of the Borland family, Thomas, Euclid, and Euclid, Jr. Included are documents pertaining to payment of a matron at the hospital at Fort Johnson; letters from Euclid Borland, a doctor in the U. S. Navy, discussing his service on the John Adams, cholera, Italy and Marseilles; an account of the record of Euclid, Jr. in the 6th Virginia Infantry Regiment, C. S. A., and the passport of Euclid, Jr.

578. GEORGE HENRY BORROW MANUSCRIPT, [ca. 1856]. 1 item. Oulton Broad, England.

Cancelled passage of The Romany Rye.

579. JACKSON L. BOST PAPERS, 1849 (1855-1866) 1905. 564 items and 2 vols. Olive Branch (Union County), N.C.

Personal and business papers of Jackson L. Bost (b. 1832), physician and major in the Confederate Army. Included are family letters; several letters concerning his war activities; bills and receipts; account books of his medical practice containing a record of visits and fees; and a ciphering book of Nelson Bost.

580. THE BOSTON VIGILANCE COMMITTEE ACCOUNT BOOK, 1850-1861. 1 vol. (83 pp.) Boston, Mass.

Treasurer's account book.

581. ALEXANDER ROBINSON BOTELER PAPERS, 1776 (1836-1889) 1898. 1,682 items and 4 vols. Shepherdstown (Jefferson County), W. Va.

Correspondence of Alexander R. Boteler's father, Dr. Henry Boteler, for 1776-1837; family letters of Alexander R. Boteler (1815-1892), Virginia political leader, congressman, and Civil War soldier, with sidelights on his career at Princeton College, Princeton, New Jersey, his courtship of Helen Macomb Stockton, whom he later married, his altercations with Charles J. Faulkner, and "Yankee" depredations at his home, "Fountain Rock," during the Civil War; political correspondence, 1855-1870, relating to the election of 1860 and the Constitutional Union Party; letters concerning Boteler's travels about the country in 1882-1884 while a member of the U.S. tariff commission; correspondence concerning claims of James Rumsey as inventor of the first steamboat; and legal and personal papers of Helen (Stockton)

Boteler's father, Ebenezer S. Stockton, and grandfather, Robert Stockton. Volumes include Boteler's diary, 1845, relative to his farming activities; a scrapbook on the election of 1848; a scrapbook containing clippings, letters, and pictures devoted principally to the activities and interests of Boteler; and a scrapbook containing clippings, letters, and pictures concerning the Pendleton, Digges, and Pope families, especially the life of Dudley Digges Pendleton who married Helen Stockton Boteler. Among the correspondents are A. R. Boteler, Lewis Cass, Samuel Cooper, John B. Floyd, S. B. French, Wade Hampton, T. J. Jackson, Andrew Johnson, R. E. Lee, John Letcher, W. P. Miles, John Page, Thomas N. Page, Rembrandt Peale, W. N. Pendleton, W. C. Rives, Alexander Robinson, W. H. Seward, J. E. B. Stuart, Jacob Thompson, J. R. Thompson, Dabney C. Wirt.

582. JAMES BOTTELEY AND CHARLES HART PAPERS, 1865-1950. 1 vol. (73 pp.) Birmingham, England.

Autograph book containing the signatures of prominent English Methodists, and letters from notable Englishmen including Charles Darwin, Thomas Huxley, John Tyndall, and Robert William Dale.

583. GORDON BOTTOMLEY PAPERS, 1936. 1 item. Carnforth, Lancashire, England.

Letter from Bottomley describing a journey he and his wife took, and discussing his book, The Acts of Saint Peter, a Cathedral Festival Play.

584. LAWSON BOTTS PAPERS, 1861-1862. 2 items. Winchester (Frederick County), Va.

A letter from Lt. Col. Lawson Botts, 2nd Virginia Infantry, C.S.A., mentioning troop movements in Virginia and the destruction of "Dam No. 5" near Winchester; and a letter containing family news from a female member of the Botts family.

585. WILLIAM C. BOUCK PAPERS, 1842-1845. 6 items. Schoharie County, N.Y.

Letters to William C. Bouck, governor of New York, 1842-1844, requesting appointments to collectorships on the Erie Canal.

586. JEAN BOULIGNY PAPERS, 1700s. 1 vol. Spain.

Photostatic copy of "Plan para el establisimiento general en España del comercio activo," in which Bouligny discusses the importance of commerce to Spain and proposes the establishment of Consulados or courts of commerce to encourage and regulate trade and settle disputes. Included is a detailed plan for the functioning and placement of the Consulados. Original held in the Archivo Historico Nacional.

587. RICHARD SOUTHWELL BOURKE, SIXTH EARL OF MAYO, PAPERS, 1869. 1 item. Palmerston House, County Kildare, Ireland.

Statement by Lord Bourke (1822-1872), Viceroy and Governor General in India, 1869-1872, concerning his policy toward Afghanistan.

588. SYLVANUS BOURNE PAPERS, 1799-1815. 12 items. Amsterdam, Netherlands.

Letters of Sylvanus Bourne, U.S. consul to the Netherlands, concerning salaries and consular responsibilities, diplomatic affairs in Europe, American commercial relations with combatant countries, a case before the state supreme court of Pennsylvania, and the availability of rooms for rent in the District of Columbia.

589. JOHN MALACHI BOWDEN PAPERS, 1861-1865. 1 item. Meriwether County, Ga.

Typescript (23 pp.) of Bowden's "Some of my Experiences as a Confederate soldier, in the Camp and on the battlefield, in the Army of Northern Virginia," describing his service in the 2nd Georgia Regiment until his capture, his prison experiences at Point Lookout, Maryland, and his return home.

590. NATHANIEL FLEMING BOWE PAPERS, 1836-1875. 115 items. Magnolia (Henrico County), Va.

Chiefly family letters of Bowe, his children, and their cousins. Also included are letters from Confederate soldiers, business papers relative to the sale of cotton and the purchase of slaves, and documents concerning the protection of Bowe's property at the end of the Civil War and amnesty oaths taken by Bowe and his son-in-law, J. Boyd.

591. MORTON BOWEN PAPERS, 1853. 1 item. Franklin County, Mo.

Document appointing Thomas W. Graves of Caswell County, North Carolina, as attorney.

592. REUBEN DEAN BOWEN PAPERS, 1857-1938. 26,672 items and 11 vols. Paris (Lamar County), Tex.

Chiefly the business papers of R. D. Bowen (1859-1939), consisting of correspondence, clippings, pamphlets, and printed material and volumes. A major portion of the collection concerns agriculture, especially cotton; Bowen's efforts to increase the uses for cotton; cotton storage; railroad freight rates; taxation of cotton and woolen mills; shipment of cotton to Europe during World War I; the Agricultural Adjustment Act; price fixing of farm products; and the problems of the farmers. Many of the papers are related to national and local agricultural organizations, including the Farmers' Educational and Co-operative Union of America,

Alabama Cotton Growers Association, South Texas Cotton Growers Association, National Grange, Farm Bureau, Farmers' Union, Texas Grain Dealers Association, Milk Producers Association, National Cooperative Milk Producers' Federation, and National Boll Weevil Control Association. Letters also deal with World War I, United States involvement, and post-war policies toward Germany; prohibition; anti-trust legislation; the Ku Klux Klan; food and drug legislation; labor unrest and unionization and politics, especially Warren Harding, Senators E. D. Smith and Ben Tillman, and the 1930 senatorial campaign in Louisiana. Volumes include account books, 1923, bankbooks, 1915-1929, the baby book of Bowen's daughter Adelaide Marie (b. 1896), and Adelaide's diaries, 1918-1921.

593. WILLIAM HORTON BOWER PAPERS, 1870-1888. 260 items. Lenoir (Caldwell County), N.C.

The papers of William H. Bower, lawyer and U.S. congressman from North Carolina, 1893-1895, relate chiefly to personal and family matters, with some references to North Carolina politics and education. Also included are several letters from people who had migrated to Texas, California, and Oregon, and a broadside, "Davenport Female College Must Be Rebuilt."

594. GEORGE BOWERS PAPERS, 1822-1865. 99 items. Berkeley County, W. Va.

Receipts, bills, indentures, promissory notes and summonses of a schoolteacher.

595. GEORGE MEADE BOWERS ALBUMS AND SCRAPBOOK, 1898-1917. 3 vols. Martinsburg (Berkeley County), W. Va.

Volumes of George M. Bowers (1863-1925), U.S. congressman from West Virginia, 1916-1923. Included are a scrapbook, 1898-1914; an album, 1916, containing congratulatory telegrams sent upon Bowers' election to Congress; and an album, ca. 1917, containing photographs of a Congressional Party in Hawaii.

596. ROBERT BOWIE PAPERS, 1811-1812. 4 items. "Mattaponi," Prince George County, Md.

The papers of Robert Bowie (1750-1818), governor of Maryland, consist of three recommendations for appointments and a commission.

597. EDGAR ALFRED BOWRING JOURNAL, 1841-1842, 1844-1850, 1852-1857. 14 vols. London, England.

Journal of Edgar A. Bowring (1826-1911), civil servant with the Board of Trade. Detailed accounts include comments on Parliamentary sessions with discussions of the business conducted and analyses of votes taken; his work with the Board of Trade, containing information on Lords Clarendon and Granville; cabinet and Privy Council meetings; the Anti-Corn Law League; the work of Prince Albert and the Royal Commission concerning the Exhibition of 1851; the Crimean War; the activities and letters of his family, especially his father, Sir John Bowring, governor of Hong Kong; China policy; articles he wrote anonymously or under a false name defending the Royal Commission and his father's China policy; the Irish situation; daily weather observations; social and cultural events; and a yearly accounting of his personal expenses.

598. SIR JOHN BOWRING PAPERS, 1833 (1849-1859) 1904. 65 items. Larkbear, Devonshire, England.

Principally family correspondence of Sir John Bowring (1792-1872), diplomat in China, governor of Hong Kong, and member of Parliament. Letters, primarily concerning Sir John's career in China, discuss British policy, commercial treaty negotiations at the Taku Forts, war at Canton in 1857, the customs duties dispute at Shanghai, the government of Hong Kong, and missionaries. Also included are references to the Portuguese colony of Macao, Sir John's travels to Java, prominent Englishmen in the Orient, contemporary politics in England, and reflections on his earlier political career.

599. CALVERT BOWYER PAPERS, 1738. 1 item. Westmill, Hertfordshire, England.

A lease of property by Bowyer to John Wright.

600. ALFRED BOYD PAPERS, 1831-1865. 10 items. Boydton (Mecklenburg County), Va.

Miscellaneous letters and papers including the registration certificate of a free mulatto girl of Northumberland County, Virginia.

601. ALSTON BOYD PAPERS, 1825-1836. 5 items and 2 vols. Lawrenceville (Gwinnett County), Ga.

Ledger, 1829-1831, of a general merchant, itemizing goods and prices, and a letter book, 1825-1832, relating to the purchase of merchandise for the store and the sale of local cotton.

602. ARCHIBALD H. BOYD PAPERS, 1841 (1848-1869) 1897. 46 items. Lenox Castle (Rockingham County), N.C.

Business correspondence of Archibald H. Boyd and of his son, James E. Boyd. Included are the letters of a slave trader, Samuel R. Browning, reporting on the health of the slaves, the condition of the market, and his transactions; Civil War letters from James E. Boyd describing living conditions and military activities in the area around Richmond and Petersburg, Virginia; and letters of James Boyd concerning state politics, his position as U.S. Attorney for the Western District, and his stockholdings in the Marine and River Phosphate Company of Charleston, South Carolina, and the Merchants and Manufacturers Association of Greensboro, North Carolina.

603. HOGMIRE L. BOYD MEMORANDUM BOOK, 1834-1855. 1 vol. (98 pp.) [Jefferson County, W. Va.?]

604. JOHN BOYD PAPERS, 1783-1794. 61 items. Richmond, Va.

Business letters dealing with the settlement of bonds and debts; pages from a journal, 1783; miscellaneous poems, some of which were written by John Boyd, a Richmond broker; pages from a journal containing accounts of the settlement of the estate of Robert Boyd, 1786; and an inventory.

605. JOSEPH FULTON BOYD PAPERS, 1861-1869. 12,356 items and 16 vols. Ky., Tenn., N.C., Ala., and Ga.

Quartermaster Corps records of the Army of the Ohio, especially the 2nd division and the 23rd Corps. Included are records of supplies, containing lists of tools, food prices, and supplies captured from the Confederates; and monthly and quarterly reports, 1861-1863. Forage records consist of vouchers, receipts, requisitions, reports and monthly statements. Financial papers concern payments to military personnel. Records of transportation include receipts, requisitions, and vouchers for horses, wagons, services, and equipment; and reports, among them a list, 1864, of the number of men, officers, and horses in the Army of the Ohio. Steamship papers, 1865, record transportation of men, horses, and equipment, and the condition of lighthouses. There are individual and consolidated reports on civilian labor. Other papers relate to the secret service, 1861-1865. Personnel papers contain battlefield orders, 1864-1865, orders for the Freedmen's Bureau, court-martial reports, and reports of the army, 1864-1865. Papers of the U.S. Military Railroad in North Carolina, comprise reports on men and equipment carried, accidents and thefts, and property sales; and correspondence concerning friction between military and railroad officials, problems with the Negro troops, and the shipment of cotton and resin. Reports on civilian purchases cover all supplies other than forage and horses. There are also extra duty reports; strength reports, chiefly those of the 11th Maine, 52nd Pennsylvania, 47th, 56th and 100th New York, and 104th Pennsylvania Volunteers; routine correspondence, primarily letters which accompanied reports; miscellaneous papers, generally concerned with Negroes, the conversion of schools into hospitals, and other concerns of the quartermaster; and general orders and circulars. Volumes include account books, 1861-1864; forage records, 1861-1862; military telegrams, 1864-1866; and an abstract and letter book, 1861-1869.

606. R. F. BOYD & COMPANY PAPERS, 1886-1895. 1 vol. Greensboro (Guilford County), N.C.

Purchase book of company selling boots, shoes, trunks, etc.

607. ROBERT BOYD PAPERS, 1861-1871. 86 items. Abbeville County, S.C.

Letters from Robert Boyd's sons, Andrew, Daniel, John T., R. P., and William, and his son-in-law, Fenton Hall, all in the Confederate Army. Topics include camp life, hardships of war, discipline, the heavy toll of measles and pneumonia, and life as a prisoner of war.

608. WIER BOYD PAPERS, 1856 (1861-1862) 1886. 67 items. Dahlonega (Lumpkin County), Ga.

Correspondence of Wier Boyd, legislator and colonel in the Confederate Army, 52nd Regiment, Georgia Volunteers. Subjects include army life, the appointment of officers, family matters, agricultural conditions, a tax to provide funds for the families of soldiers, the educational system, and smallpox.

609. WILLIAM E. BOYD PAPERS, 1854. 14 items. Cahaba (Dallas County), Ala.

Papers relating to a dispute between William E. Boyd and Thomas J. Mackey, the latter having been accused of swindling several firms in or near Cambridge, Massachusetts. Included are three letters of C. C. Jones, Jr., relative to Mackey's activities.

610. WILLIAM KENT BOYLE PAPERS, 1861-1889. 478 items. Bladensburg (Prince Georges County), Md.

Principally the sermons of a Methodist minister, written mainly in the 1870s, with some exegetical notes attached. Included also are some legal and financial papers, correspondence, and book reviews and testimonial letters concerning a new hymnbook.

611. ELIZA HALL (BALL) GORDON BOYLES PAPERS, 1823-1881. 173 items. Fayetteville (Lincoln County), Tenn.

Letters to Eliza H. Gordon Boyles from her brothers, George H. and Robert H. Ball; from her son, John R. Boyles, concerning the Mexican War, his journey to California, and gold mining and life in California; from her son, George B. Boyles, relating to the study of law and life in the Confederate Army; and from other Confederate soldiers, concerning politics and political figures, camp life, and military activities. Also included are references to cholera epidemics and education.

612. MARY ANN BOYLES PAPERS, 1861-1918.
90 items. Stokes County, N.C.

Civil War letters of the eight Boyles brothers, six of whom died from undernourishment, exposure, and wounds, concerning war conditions, camp life in North Carolina and Virginia, lack of clothes, execution of deserters, the food supply at home; and a photograph of Mary Ann Boyles in 1918.

613. BOYTE FAMILY PAPERS, 1962-1967.
108 items. Durham, N.C.

Papers of Harry Chatten Boyte and his wife, Sara Margaret Evans, while undergraduates at Duke University, relating to their activities. Papers concern the Vietnamese conflict, resistance to conscription, race relations, union organization of textile workers and the non-academic employees of Duke University, the presidential election of 1964, the Students for a Democratic Society, and the Southern Student Organizing Committee.

614. J. E. BRADBURN PAPERS, 1861-1862.
2 items. Little River, N.C.

Letters to Confederate soldiers concerning food prices, speculation in cotton and horses, and politics.

615. SAMUEL BRADBURY PAPERS, 1863-1865.
16 items. Conn.

Chiefly letters from Andrew Jackson Crossley, who served with the U.S. Engineers of the Army of the Potomac, describing the work of the engineers, military activities, camp life, and Negro troops.

616. THOMAS BRADFORD PAPERS, 1789-1901.
212 items. Philadelphia, Pa.

Papers of Thomas Bradford (1745-1838), a printer, concern county prisons in Pennsylvania and a program of religious instruction for inmates; cholera epidemics in Philadelphia and elsewhere; slaughter and devastation from the Napoleonic Wars, and Andrew Jackson's administration. Also included are the papers of Thomas R. Peters, paymaster of the 1st Regiment of Pennsylvania Volunteers in the Civil War. Among the correspondents are Caleb Cushing, Peter Hagner, and William B. Sprague.

617. AMY MORRIS BRADLEY PAPERS, 1806-1921.
138 items and 14 vols. Wilmington (New Hanover County), N.C.

Correspondence, clippings, and financial papers of Amy Morris Bradley (1823-1904), educator. Letters in the 1850s concern her stay in Costa Rica, and William Walker and the Filibuster War in Nicaragua. Civil War letters reflect Bradley's duties as a nurse. Other letters deal with her educational work in establishing free schools for poor white children, the advanced classes later becoming the Tileston Normal School. Volumes include diaries and letter books, ca. 1844-1871, containing letters to relatives and friends, poetry, and entries about her daily life; a record book, 1862-1865, of her work with the U.S. Sanitary Commission; account books, 1866-1895, for the Wilmington Mission and Tileston Normal School; a record book and scrapbook, 1882-1891, for the Tileston School; and a record book of the Soldiers' Memorial Society and the American Unitarian Association, 1867.

618. [ELISHA BRADLEY?] DIARY, 1818-1822.
1 vol. Connecticut.

Description of a journey by steamboat and sailing vessel from Augusta, Georgia, to New York, including miscellaneous accounts.

619. GEORGE Y. BRADLEY LETTERS, 1845-1868. 6 items. Powhatan County, Va.

Correspondence of George Y. Bradley, merchant, concerning the poverty and unsettled conditions during 1867-1868, and difficulties with Negro servants in 1868.

620. JONAS A. BRADSHAW PAPERS, 1855-1864.
60 items. Alexander County, N.C.

Family correspondence of Jonas A. Bradshaw, a private in the Confederate service, touching upon campaigns, camp life, and war weariness, but limited mainly to reports on his health and his desire to be at home.

621. JAMES BRADY PAPERS, 1850-1865.
6 items. Randolph County, N.C.

Papers of James Brady, a soldier in the Confederate Army, concerning the estate of John A. Craven, of which he was executor in 1850; and his services in the Civil War.

622. MARY BRADY PAPERS, 1848-1869.
6 items. Jackson (Butts County), Ga.

Letters to Mary Brady from her sons who had migrated to or traveled in Louisiana, Texas, and Mexico. Two letters fall in the Confederate period.

623. BRAXTON BRAGG PAPERS, 1847-1869.
43 items. Warrenton (Warren County), N.C., and Thibodeaux Parish, La.

Correspondence of Braxton Bragg (1817-1876), Confederate general, chiefly concerning military affairs. Correspondents include Jefferson Davis, Patrick Cleburne, Samuel Cooper, and James A. Seddon.

624. THOMAS BRAGG PAPERS, 1842-1871.
44 items. Raleigh (Wake County), N.C.

Political and legal correspondence of Thomas Bragg (1810-1872), North Carolina lawyer, governor, and attorney general of the Confederate States of America. Much of the material concerns the controversy over the sale of property belonging to the Portsmouth and Roanoke Railroad Company.

625. WILLIAM BRAGG PAPERS, 1765-1781. 8 items and 2 vols. Whitehaven, England, and Petersburg (Dinwiddie County), Va.

Papers and a letter book of William Bragg, a merchant, concern trade with Indians and hunters for deerskins and the shipping of skins and tobacco to England. A diary records sermons, religious commentaries, and hymns.

626. ROBERT BRAGGE PAPERS, 1770s. 1 vol. London, England.

Manuscript entitled "Doctor Robert Bragge and his Lady, their Journey to Bath, perform'd in the year 1770," published as *The Journey of Dr. Robert Bongout and his Lady to Bath performed in the year 177-*, a satire in verse on Dr. Robert Bragge, with a portrait (London: J. Dodsley, 1778). Included as a frontispiece for the manuscript, dated 1886, is a drawing of Dr. Bragge by E. Evans.

627. THOMAS E. BRAMLETTE PAPERS, 1863. 1 item. Frankfort (Franklin County), Ky.

Thanksgiving Proclamation of Bramlette, governor of Kentucky, on October 17, 1863.

628. Edward B. Branch Papers, 1861-1862. 1 vol. Petersburg (Dinwiddie County), Va.

Letterpress book of Edward Branch concerns his business career as an insurance agent and his connections with S. G. Branch and Brother; and his service in the Quartermaster Corps of the Confederate Army. The latter papers, November, 1861-March, 1862, relate principally to the shipment of supplies for the Southern troops, and are for the most part routine.

629. JOHN P. BRANCH ACCOUNT BOOK, 1848. 1 vol. Petersburg (Dinwiddie County), Va.

Wood and drayage accounts.

630. MARY COOK BRANCH DIARY, 1886. 1 vol. (8 pp.) Richmond, Va.

Personal diary, including comments on sermons and a trip to Williamsburg, Virginia.

631. BRANCH FAMILY PAPERS, 1778-1889. 801 items and 13 vols. Enfield (Halifax County), N.C.

The papers of John Branch (1782-1863), governor of North Carolina, U.S. senator, and secretary of the navy, and of his nephews, Joseph Branch, lawyer, and Lawrence O'Bryan Branch (1820-1863), lawyer and brigadier general in the Confederate Army, concern political appointments in 1829-1830; land speculation, chiefly in Leon County, Florida; the legal practices of Joseph and Lawrence O'Bryan Branch in Florida and North Carolina; and Whig politics and Union sentiment in North Carolina. Volumes include a scrapbook and daybook, a letter book, two notebooks on public questions, and a list of political constituents supporting Lawrence O'Bryan Branch; account books of his wife, Nancy (Blount) Branch; and details of the affairs of Governor Branch in his last years.

632. G. M. BRAUNE NOTEBOOKS, 1892. 3 vols. [Germany?]

Three student mathematics notebooks, written in German.

633. WILLIAM HUGGINS BRAWLEY PAPERS, 1893. 5 items. Charleston, S.C.

A letter to Brawley, U.S. representative, from J. Henry Toole, a Negro of Rock Hill, South Carolina, seeking a position. There are three letters of recommendation. There are also papers concerning the claim of Charles P. Petit for an increase in pension.

634. CARTER BRAXTON PAPERS, 1821-1890. 41 items and 2 vols. Hanover County, Va.

Accounts of a Virginia planter.

635. JOHN CABELL BRECKINRIDGE PAPERS, 1860-1871. 7 items. Lexington (Fayette County), Ky.

Letters and a telegram to John C. Breckinridge (1821-1875), vice president of the United States, 1857-1861, and a major general in the Confederate Army, from A. Dudley Mann, William P. Johnston, William Emmett Simms and others, concerning the presidential elections of 1860 and 1864, and military affairs.

636. SAMUEL LIVINGSTON BREESE PAPERS, 1823-1878. 5 items and 4 vols. Middletown (Middlesex County), Conn., and New York, N.Y.

Papers of Samuel L. Breese, a commander in the U.S. Navy, include drafts of letters written by Breese, a journal, two letter books, and an order book. The journal contains accounts of a cruise in the Mediterranean on the U.S.S. *Lexington*, 1827-1828, including descriptions of foreign and commercial relations with Greece and Turkey; a cruise in the western Mediterranean on the U.S.S. *Cumberland* and the U.S.S. *Columbia*, 1843-1845, including a description of the bombardment of Tangiers; and a cruise in the Gulf of Mexico on the U.S.S. *Albany*, 1846-1847, including a detailed account of naval operations in the Mexican War. The letter books, 1837-1853 and 1855-1858, discuss routine naval matters; the activities of the various ships commanded by Breese, especially in Vera Cruz, the fishing grounds off Newfoundland and Labrador, the Mediterranean, the Great Lakes, and during the Mexican War; and Breese's activities as military governor of

Tuspan. The order book, 1875-1878, contains night orders issued by Breese aboard the U.S.S. *Ossipee*.

637. GEORGE WILLIAM BRENT PAPERS, 1862-1881. 138 items. Augusta (Richmond County), Ga., and Montgomery (Montgomery County), Ala.

Military dispatches, official correspondence, and reports of George W. Brent, colonel in the Confederate Army, and assistant adjutant general of the Military District of the West. The papers concern the affairs of the Georgia Railroad and the disorganization in Mississippi during the last months of the Confederacy. Included are detailed accounts of subsistence stores, railroad equipment, troop movement, ordnance depots, and supplies after Sherman's march. A letter from Leonidas Polk explains why he disobeyed orders. Other correspondents include Simon B. Buckner, John F. Branch, Howell Cobb, B. D. Fry, Duff C. Green, E. H. Harris, and J. R. Waddy.

638. RICHARD BRENT PAPERS, 1769-1802. 3 items. Loudoun County, Va.

Legal documents of Richard Brent (1757-1814), Virginia politician, including a statement concerning a roadway survey, 1775; and a letter requesting proof of citizenship for a man impressed on a British warship, 1802.

639. HULDAH ANNIE (FAIN) BRIANT PAPERS, 1846 (1861-1865) 1888. 118 items. Santa Luca (Gilmer County), Ga.

Legal correspondence of Ebenezer Fain and war correspondence of his daughter, Huldah A. (Fain) Briant, chiefly from M. C. Briant, whom she married in 1864. Included also are letters from other members of the family. The letters contain accounts of the Battle of Manassas, 1861; enthusiasm for the Confederacy in Texas; impressment of a local Jew's merchandise for the army by women; and refugee families from Georgia.

640. JOSEPH BRICKELL PAPERS, 1810-1829. 5 items. Fort Barnwell (Craven County), N.C.

Inventory and sales accounts of a merchant.

641. JOHN LUTHER BRIDGERS, JR., PAPERS, 1860 (1873-1877) 1894. 727 items and 4 vols. Tarboro (Edgecombe County), N.C.

Papers of John L. Bridgers, Jr. (b. 1850), attorney. Letters from his half brother, Robert R. Bridgers (1819-1888), concern family matters; cotton prices and the cotton market; Peruvian guano and other fertilizers; subscriptions to the Wilmington and Weldon Railroad, of which R. R. Bridgers was president; request of O. C. Marsh of the Yale College Museum for fossils from the marl beds of North Carolina; the estate of Henry T. Clark, R. R. Bridgers' father-in-law; the incarceration of Preston L. Bridgers, son of R. R. Bridgers, and T. W. Strange at Waynesville, North Carolina, for the alleged murder of one Murray; and a lawsuit between R. R. Bridgers and John R. McDaniel. Other papers consist of bills of lading for cotton sold by New York factors, and bills for guano. Volumes include a journal and expense accounts, 1867-1894; a letter book, 1876-1877; and letterpress copybooks, 1873-1875. The journal, 1867-1868, was kept while John Bridgers was at military school in Lexington, Virginia.

642. CHARLES E. BRIDGES PAPERS, 1862-1868. 96 items. Montgomery (Montgomery County), Ala.

Business and personal correspondence of Charles E. Bridges pertains to family matters; employment at John D. Gray's rolling mills, an iron-producing concern in Montgomery, and the difficulties in obtaining coke; post-war hardships faced by Bridges' mother, sister, and brother in Georgia; fear of uprisings and violence by freedmen; rental of the stores and warehouses owned by Bridges' sister, Ann Stephenson; and Bridges' employment with Howard Tully and Company, cotton factors and commission merchants.

643. ROBERT BRIDGES PAPERS, 1868-1928. 100 items. Hancock (Washington County), Md.

Business and family papers, including receipts; correspondence of Bridges' children, mentioning Mary Baldwin College, Hampden-Sydney College, Saddlers, Bryan & Stratten Business School, St. Hildas' Hall, and Princeton; and letters concerning a patient.

644. "A BRIEF NARRATION OF THE PRESENT ESTATE OF THE BILBAO TRADE ETC.," [1650?]. 34 pp. England.

Manuscript, original or copy, of a published work concerning the decline of English trade with Bilbao, Spain, since 1640, and remedies to restore a flourishing trade. It consists of two parts linked by a petition from thirty-four Bilbao traders to the Council of Trade.

645. ALPHEUS BRIGGS PAPERS, 1698-1930. 1 item. North Carolina.

Typescript of "A history of North Carolina yearly meeting (from the beginning until 1930) and education in North Carolina yearly meeting," by Briggs. It concerns the Society of Friends.

646. CLAY STONE BRIGGS PAPERS, 1919. 32 items. Galveston, Tex.

Papers of Clay Stone Briggs (1876-1933), U.S. representative from Texas, 1919-1933, concerning his first year in office. Material pertains to problems following World War I, the national banking system, the national budget, and Democratic politics in 1918. Correspondents include J. S. Williams, R. S. Brookings, Homer Cummings, Julius Barnes, Tom Connally, H. J. Drane, and S. O. Bland.

647. GEORGE BRIGGS PAPERS, 1837-1908. 164 items. Hurdle Mills (Person County), N.C.

Family letters of George Briggs, farmer and Confederate soldier, concerning family matters; prices of farm products and slaves in North Carolina, Alabama, Kentucky, and Texas; the hardships of a soldier in the Civil War, including a description of a hospital scene; social and religious activities, 1870-1900; and the experiences of John Buggs, a nephew of George, and a Baptist minister.

648. JAMES WILSON BRIGHT PAPERS, 1894 (1897-1905) 1920. 42 items. Baltimore, Md.

Letters to James W. Bright (1852-1926), philologist and professor at the Johns Hopkins University, Baltimore, Maryland, from friends and colleagues, concerning literary and other professional matters. Among the correspondents are Joseph Carhart, Alexander Green, R. H. Hudnal, C. N. Lagley, Lord Northbrook, John Phelps, Charles H. Ross, W. H. Schofield, Edward S. Sheldon, Reed Smith, and Robert Stein.

649. JOHN BRIGHT PAPERS, 1840-1888. 44 items. Rochdale, Lancashire, England.

Papers of John Bright (1811-1889), British statesman, concern the Corn Laws, free trade, Home Rule in Ireland, the Liberal Party, the Crimean War, suffrage and the use of the ballot, land reform in Ireland, capital punishment, and several routine matters.

650. RICHARD BRIGHT PAPERS, 1820. 1 item. Bristol, Gloucestershire, England.

Letter from Richard Hart Davis, M. P. for Bristol, to Richard Bright (1745-1840), merchant, explaining his refusal to present to Queen Caroline an address from a meeting of which Bright was chairman.

651. KENNETH MILLIKAN BRIM STAMP BOOK, 1861-1864. 1 vol. Greensboro (Guilford County), N.C.

Postage stamps, covers, engraved stationery with patriotic designs, homemade envelopes, all relating to the postal service of the Confederacy, 1861-1864.

652. HERMAN BRIMMER PAPERS, 1786. 1 item. Boston, Mass.

Business letter from John B. Lohier to Herman Brimmer, merchant, mentioning mercantile affairs, commodity prices, and business in Washington, North Carolina.

653. WILLIAM BRISBANE RECEIPT BOOK, 1790-1838. 1 vol. Greenville (Greenville County), S.C.

Receipt book containing mainly small routine business receipts, with occasional references to slaves and the settlement of an estate.

654. THOMAS D. BRISLEY PAPERS, 1863. 31 items. Cooper (Washington County), Me.

The letters of Private Thomas D. Brisley of the 6th Maine Volunteers principally concerning crop conditions at home, with some references to his military activities and the reorganization of the Union Army.

655. BRITISH-AMERICAN TOBACCO COMPANY, LTD., PAPERS, 1842-1929. 5 items and 367 vols. Petersburg (Dinwiddie County), Va.

Records of the British-American Tobacco Company and its subsidiaries, David Dunlop, T.C. Williams Company, Cameron & Cameron, Export Leaf Tobacco Company, Bland Tobacco Company, and William Cameron & Brother. Included are records of the Petersburg branch of British-American and a combined accounting of British-American, T.C. Williams and David Dunlop. There are records of production and sales, cost sheets, payroll and time records, shipping books, storage records, stock books, and weekly and monthly reports. For David Dunlop and Cameron & Cameron there are records dating prior to their mergers with British-American in 1903. David Dunlop records, beginning in 1824, are ledgers, journals, letter books, payroll records, bills of exchange, and invoice and shipping books. Six of these volumes are available only on microfilm. Records of Cameron & Cameron, 1892-1904, include letterpress books, inventories, sales books, and trial balances. An extensive guide is with the collection.

656. BRITISH MUSEUM ADDITIONAL MANUSCRIPT 14,538, ca. 10th century. 1 item. London, England.

Photocopy of folios from "Treatise Against Heresies, and Other Theological Works" containing an early Syriac manuscript of the Odes and Psalms of Solomon.

657. JAMES G. BROACH PAPERS, 1861-1863. 5 items. [Caswell County, N.C.?]

Civil War correspondence, containing a request for money for a furlough and references to conditions of crops at home.

658. WILLIAM GILLES BROADFOOT PAPERS, 1943-1944. 18 items. Wilmington (New Hanover County), N.C.

Correspondence relating to organization of a shipping company at Morehead City and Wilmington and contracts with the War Shipping Administration.

659. WILLIAM L. BROADDUS PAPERS, 1850-1899. 277 items. Macomb (McDonough County), Ill.

Chiefly letters from Broaddus, a Union officer during the Civil War, to his wife, Martha. The few antebellum items relate to activities in Macomb, especially the administration of the estate of Thomas D. Hayden. Wartime letters average two or three a week, and describe Broaddus' activities with the 16th Regiment of Illinois Infantry in camps in Illinois and Missouri and campaigns at Island No. 10 and Corinth; and, later with the 78th Regiment of Illinois Infantry Volunteers in Kentucky and Tennessee. There are frequent comments on such topics as evaluations of other officers and generals; the Knights of the Golden Circle; and the hanging of Confederate spies. Places mentioned include Franklin, Shelbyville, and Chattanooga, Tennessee. There are letters from Col. Carter Van Vleck and Lt. W. D. Ruddle and resolutions adopted by officers of the 78th concerning Broaddus' death at the battle of Chickamauga. Postwar letters concern Mrs. Broaddus' pension.

660. A. BROCKENBROUGH AND FLOYD W. WILLIAMS PAPERS, 1850 (1870-1900). ca. 250 items. Cape Charles (Northampton County), Va., and Baltimore, Md.

Letters, bills, and receipts largely concerning the Chesapeake Agricultural Fair Association, truck farming on the Eastern Shore, and the estate of Floyd W. Williams. Brockenbrough was executor of Williams' estate.

661. JOHN C. BRODNAX PAPERS, 1830 (1856-1919) 1929. 1,389 items. Greensboro (Guilford County), N.C.

Family correspondence of three generations centering chiefly around John G. Brodnax (1829-1907), Confederate surgeon and practicing physician. Letters from 1857 to 1867, generally from Lynchburg, Virginia, refer to the sale of slaves and, during the war years, are concerned with the question of fleeing or remaining to face the advancing Federals. Included also are Brodnax's appointment as assistant surgeon general of the North Carolina Hospital at Petersburg, Virginia, and his oath of allegiance to the United States. Other items pertaining to Dr. Brodnax are letters to his wife, beginning in 1881, while she visited her relatives in summer; a speech against railroad taxation in 1879; a group of petitions in 1877 requesting that Brodnax be made superintendent of the North Carolina State Insane Asylum; and an undated article on optical surgery. Included also is genealogical material as well as other materials connected with the activities of Brodnax's wife in the Daughters of the American Revolution and the United Daughters of the Confederacy.

A number of letters were written from schools and colleges attended by members of the family, including Salem Female Academy, Salem, North Carolina, and St. Mary's College, Raleigh, North Carolina, during 1912; N. I. Smith's School in Leaksville during 1879 and 1880; Bingham School in Orange County during 1883; Bingham School in Asheville, and Old Point Comfort College, Virginia, after 1909. Included also are letters from Mrs. Barr, an aunt of Mrs. Brodnax, and her children from 1877 to 1884 while traveling in Europe and studying music in Germany.

There are letters from Mary (Brodnax) Glenn and her family while in Mexico, where her husband worked for a railroad company, a mining firm, and as secretary to the American consul general; letters of this period are filled with references to conditions in Mexico, especially concerning political upheavals around 1910. Included also are papers relative to the settlement of the estate of John Brodnax, Jr., after 1909, and a group of sermons delivered by James Kerr Burch, a Presbyterian minister and father-in-law of Dr. John G. Brodnax.

662. SAMUEL HOUSTON BRODNAX PAPERS, 1862 (1870-1932). 918 items. Walnut Grove (Walton County), Ga.

Letters, 35 items, between Joel Brodnax and his father, Samuel (1810-1880), concern business, farming, and the employment of freedmen in Georgia; three items refer to a battle in Florida in 1864 and comment on Confederate currency; two letters mention state politics. The collection largely relates to Samuel H. Brodnax, brother of Joel, a cotton farmer and banker in central Georgia. Topics include the schooling of his children at Middle Georgia Military and Agricultural College, North Georgia Agricultural School, and the University of Georgia; the school board at Walnut Grove; Brodnax's term in the Georgia legislature; Freemasonry; and genealogy. The political correspondence, 1890-1891, relates to Brodnax's candidacy for the legislature, patronage, and requests for endorsement of other political candidates. There are allusions to temperance and Negro voting.

663. WILLIAM ST. JOHN FREMANTLE BRODRICK, FIRST EARL of MIDLETON, PAPERS, 1890-1933. 1 item and 1 vol. Peper Harow Park, Surrey, England.

A volume of letters, 1890-1933, addressed to Lord Midleton, British statesman, and to Lady Midleton, probably compiled for their autograph value, but containing comment on military and political affairs, foreign relations, and colonial policy, with frequent mention of affairs in Egypt and India. Writers include Arthur William Patrick Albert, Duke of Connaught and Strathearn; Herbert Henry Asquith, First Earl of Oxford and Asquith; Arthur Balfour; Sir Redvers Henry Buller; Sir William Francis Butler; George, Duke of Cambridge; Sir Henry Campbell-Bannerman; Randall Davidson, Archbishop of

Canterbury; Joseph Chamberlain; Austen Chamberlain; Sir Evelyn Baring, Earl of Cromer; George Nathaniel Curzon, Marquis Curzon of Kedleston; Lord Grey of Fallodon; Horatio Herbert Kitchener, First Earl of Kitchener; Sir Frank Lascelles; John Morley, Viscount Morley of Blackburn; Archibald Philip Primrose, Earl of Rosebery; and Garnet Joseph Wolseley.

664. WILLIAM BROGDEN PAPERS, 1832 (1861-1865) 1868. 174 items. "Roe Down," Prince Georges and Queen Annes Counties, Md.

Civil War letters of Arthur and Harry Brogden to their parents and sisters give an account of Confederate operations in Mississippi and Tennessee and imprisonment at Fort Delaware. Arthur Brogden, chief surgeon in William H. Jackson's calvary division, describes Hood's Tennessee campaign in November and December, 1864. There is also antebellum family correspondence and poetry; material on the related Lemmon family of Baltimore; and Arthur Brogden's notebook, 1859, of remedies and drugs.

665. WILLIAM BROGDEN, JR., ACCOUNTS, 1768-1824. 5 vols. Annapolis (Anne Arundel County), Md.

Accounts of the estate of Rev. William Brogden; mercantile accounts; accounts of Capt. Judson Coolidge; references to a branch store at Pigg's Point.

666. CHARLTON P. BROOKE DIARY, 1886-1887. 1 vol. Bingham School, Orange County, N.C.

A student's diary, containing several pages of autographs, lists of school faculty and officers, items concerning life at the Bingham School, and comments on the "poor whites" of the region.

667. ROBERT BROOKE PAPERS, 1795, 1796. 2 items. Richmond, Va.

A land grant, 1795, and a letter, 1796, to Robert Brooke (1751-1799), governor of Virginia, from Governor John H. Stone of Maryland, proposing an interchange of copies of laws among all the states of the Union.

668. STEPHENS BROOKE PAPERS, 1784-1794. 5 items. Pitt County, N.C.

Business letters concerning notes of indebtedness.

669. IVESON L. BROOKES PAPERS, 1784-1888. 709 items and 11 vols. Hamburg (Aiken County), S.C.

Correspondence of a Baptist preacher and landholder in South Carolina and Georgia and his family and descendents. Topics include the management of cotton plantations; tariff and the nullification controversy; transportation conditions; banking; missionary work among slaves; student life in Washington, D.C., and a student's view of ante-bellum politics; diseases, health, and remedies; Baptist doctrine and doctrinal disputes; religious revivals; the impact of the Civil War on civilian life; the work of aid societies; destruction of Rome, Georgia, by Union troops; and wartime economic problems; mining near Potosi, Missouri; race relations in marriage and religion; politics in South Carolina in 1877; Columbian College in Washington, D.C.; Brookes' family genealogy; and his sermon notes.

670. ABBIE M. BROOKS DIARY, 1872-1876. 1 vol. (280 pp.) Atlanta, Ga.

Diary of a semi-invalid, concerning travel in Florida, boarding in Georgia, and everyday happenings in a small Georgia town.

671. EDWARD J. BROOKS PAPERS, 1866-1886. 8 items. Lenoir County, N.C.

Legal documents of Edward J. Brooks, justice of the peace and school committeeman, including his commission in the militia, his oath of office, and complaints. Included also is a long letter from John C. Scarborough, superintendent of North Carolina schools.

672. FRANCIS BROOKS PAPERS, 1773 (1833-1835) 1839. 22 items. Greenville (Pitt County), N.C.

Letters to Francis Brooks from friends and relatives in Tennessee, Indiana, and Georgia, concerning farm produce prices and family and personal matters.

673. THOMAS COOKE BROOKS PAPERS, 1877. 2 vols. Roxboro (Person County), N.C.

Notes on lectures in chemistry courses at the University of North Carolina.

674. ULYSSES R. BROOKS PAPERS, 1861 (1902-1908) 1911. 86 items. Columbia (Richland County), S.C.

Approximately one half of the collection consists of Civil War letters, some written by Ulysses R. Brooks (1846-1917), Confederate soldier, lawyer, and newspaper columnist; and others to him from W. T. Brooker, M. C. Butler, J. W. DuBose, and Richard I. Morris, all Confederate veterans. Butler's letters contain Civil War reminiscences used by Brooks in his articles, many of which also appear in the collection as clippings.

675. BENJAMIN W. BROOKSHIRE AND M. BENSON LASSITER PAPERS, 1852 (1860-1890) 1931. 644 items and 7 vols. Pekin (Montgomery County), N.C.

Correspondence and other personal, business, and land papers of a physician of Gray's Cross Roads in Randolph County and of

Pekin and Mt. Gilead in Montgomery County. There is some information on lands in Indian Territory during the 1890s and farm life in North Carolina during the early 1900s. The volumes include ledgers and other accounts, and a prescription book, which also contains a list of voters in Cheek's Creek Township, 1890. A few letters to Brookshire's son, Charles E. Brookshire, refer to education at the Bingham School in Orange County and Oakdale Academy in Oakdale, North Carolina, in the 1880s.

676. JOSEPH BROTHERTON PAPERS, 1838, 1846. 2 items. Manchester, Lancashire, England.

Letter from John Benjamin Smith, 1838, concerning Thomas Clarkson and taxes; and a letter from Elkanah Armitage, 1846, concerning repeal of the corn laws.

677. WILLIAM H. BROTHERTON PAPERS, 1803 (1861-1870) 1910. 137 items. Lincoln County, N.C.; and Tenn.

Correspondence of William H. and James Brotherton, during and immediately after the Civil War. About sixty of the letters are from William H. Brotherton, a private in the Confederate Army, and were written from the vicinity of Richmond, Fredericksburg, and Orange Court House, Virginia; they concern camp life and field activities during the Civil War, desertions from the Confederate ranks, and prisoners. The remainder of the letters are from James Brotherton, who had moved from North Carolina to East Tennessee, and concern distilling whiskey and brandy, and Ku Klux Klan activities near Lynchburg, Tennessee, in 1868. There are also miscellaneous indentures and other business papers.

678. HENRY PETER BROUGHAM, FIRST BARON BROUGHAM AND VAUX, PAPERS, 1799-1957. 38 items. London, England.

Personal letters and political correspondence of Brougham, British statesman, chiefly comment on legislation and governmental policies. Included is Robert Southey's opinion, 1831, on governmental encouragement of literary work, and comments by Lord Clarendon on domestic and foreign affairs, 1846-1855, and on Irish policy.

679. A. BROUSEAU & CO. PAPERS, 1864-1866. 22 items. New Orleans, La.

Bills and receipts of a carpet firm; and an insurance policy covering merchandise, sugar, and molasses in warehouses.

680. ALFRED BROWER PAPERS, (1840-1842) 1863. 4 items. Randolph County, N.C.

Papers concerning the sale and transfer of slaves between Thomas Goldston, Sarah (Goldston) Brower, Alfred Brower, and Frances Myrick.

681. ADAM K. BROWN PAPERS, 1862-1865. 11 items. Guernsey County, Ohio.

Letters from Adam K. Brown, a corporal in Company I, 80th Ohio Volunteer Infantry, U.S. Army, to his parents, describing camp life in the Federal Army and captured Confederate soldiers in five different Southern states.

682. ALEXANDER BROWN PAPERS, 1814 (1861-1863) 1878. 70 items. "Glenmore," Nelson County, Va.

Largely personal and family correspondence, including some material referring to business affairs, crops, weather, typhoid fever, yellow fever, smallpox, prices, salt distribution during the Civil War, politics and newspapers, military events, care of wounded Confederates, Richmond life in wartime, army life, religion, local and family gossip.

683. ANN ELIZA BROWN MANUSCRIPT, [early 1800s?]. 1 vol.

Manuscript of an arithmetic.

684. AUGUST W. BROWN PAPERS, 1849-1850. 3 items. [Lunenburg (Worcester County), Mass.?]

Personal letters to Brown's brother.

685. BEDFORD BROWN PAPERS, 1830-1906. 67 items. Caswell County, N.C.

Political letters from Francis P. Blair, Sr., John Henry Boner, L. I. Brown, James Buchanan, James Fenimore Cooper, George W. Dallas, Weldon N. Edwards, Martin Van Buren, Aaron Ward, Philo White, and Levi Woodbury. Topics include national political issues and politicians from the Jackson era through Reconstruction, Pennsylvania politics during the 1830s-1850s, and North Carolina politics during the 1870s. Also in the collection are Bedford Brown's pardon signed by Andrew Johnson, and miscellaneous personal and family documents.

686. BETTIE R. BROWN PAPERS, 1863. 2 items. Sparta (Hancock County), Ga.

Letters from Bettie R. Brown to a friend in the Confederate Army; one letter describes an elaborate wedding in wartime Charleston, South Carolina.

687. CHARLES BROWN PAPERS, 1803-1874. 22 items. Albemarle County, Va.

Subjects include business and personal affairs; "Traveller's Rest," Buckingham County, Virginia; vaccinations; Freemasonry; Confederate cavalry operations in 1863 and depredations committed by troops.

688.   CHARLES H. BROWN PAPERS, 1863-1876. 24 items. South Norwalk (Fairfield County), Conn.

Business papers, chiefly bills and receipts, and Charles H. Brown's discharge from the U.S. Army.

689.   CHARLES S. BROWN PAPERS, 1864-1865. 30 items. Flint (Genesee County), Mich.

Letters of a clerk in the 21st Michigan Volunteer Infantry describing the march from Chattanooga, Tennessee, by Dalton, Atlanta, Milledgeville, and Augusta to Savannah, Georgia, in 1864, and across South Carolina to Raleigh, North Carolina; camp life; chaplains; foraging; the burning of Atlanta; destruction of property; the hanging of a Confederate; the battle of Bentonville, North Carolina; the reaction in Sherman's Army to the news of Lee's surrender and the death of Lincoln.

690.   CHARLES W. BROWN PAPERS, 1912. 5 items. Philomont (Loudoun County), Va.

One letter from Thomas McAdory Owen soliciting Brown's support for the candidacy of Oscar W. Underwood for the presidential nomination of the Democratic Party, and four publications of the Underwood National Campaign Committee.

691.   FRANK CLYDE BROWN PAPERS, 1912-1974. ca. 54,000 items, 230 records, 60 wax cylinders, and ca. 50 aluminum discs. Durham, N.C.

Records collected by Brown as secretary of the North Carolina Folklore Society, 1913-1943, largely relating to folklore in the state but containing a small amount of material from other parts of the U.S. and Canada. There are indexed correspondence; fragmentary transcripts; photographs; the draft of a talk; a typed bibliography of folklore; a handwritten index to the Journal of American Folklore, 1880-1916; field notes relating to the recordings; a biographical sketch; 24 boxes of transcripts ranging from pencilled notes on scrap paper to typescripts, including a few drawings, photographs, and samples of quilting and lace; and 35 boxes of articles, student papers, and printed items. Papers of the general editors who succeeded Brown, Newman Ivey White and Paull Franklin Baum, contain drafts of portions of the published work; progress reports to the society; published reviews; memoranda concerning the participation of Duke University and Duke University Press; general correspondence; papers relating to foundation grants, publication, and the employment of clerical staff; correspondence between editors and associate editors; and typescripts prepared for publication. Papers of the several associate editors include typescripts and drafts relating to particular types of material, such as ballads, songs, games, rhymes, superstitions, musical scores, riddles, legends, proverbs, and folk speech. Records of Charles Bond include his preliminary analysis of the collection done in 1970-1971; a tabulation of unpublished items; correspondence with the Archive of Folksong of the Library of Congress; notes on the contents of the collection; and tape copies of recordings of previously unpublished material. Also in the collection are the original wax cylinders and aluminum discs, and 78 rpm records made from these by the Library of Congress Archive of Folksong. Much of the material was published as The Frank C. Brown Collection of North Carolina Folklore, 7 vols., 1952-1964.

692.   GEORGE HUBBARD BROWN PAPERS, 1757 (1850-1878) 1933. 815 items and 2 vols. Washington (Beaufort County), N.C.

Indentures, deeds, wills, receipts, and other papers, including a few letters relating to Brown's law practice; a bankbook of Alex C. Stanly of New Bern; and a memorandum book. Correspondents include John H. Small.

693.   GEORGE M. BROWN PAPERS, 1829 (1834-1881). 191 items. Cartersville (Cumberland County), Va.

Correspondence of George M. Brown, country doctor and farmer, concerning development of Mexico, Florida, Texas, and California; John Brown's raid, 1859; effects of Civil War on noncombatants; commodity prices during and after the Civil War; Reconstruction; and his views on slavery, Negroes in politics, "Yankees," the Virginia debt, temperance in drink, and treatment of tuberculosis.

694.   GEORGE W. BROWN PAPERS, 1869-1871. 4 items. Grafton (Taylor County), W. Va.

Letters from Arthur I. Boreman (1823-1896), governor of West Virginia and U.S. senator, to George W. Brown, who was a U.S. revenue collector, regarding appointment of Brown's subordinates.

695.   GEORGE WILLIAM BROWN PAPERS, 1874. 1 item. Baltimore, Md.

Letter of introduction to John B. Brewer, Rockville, Maryland.

696.   J. R. BROWN PAPERS, 1864-1865. 4 items. Calhoun [Ga.?]

Letters from J. R. Brown, private in the Confederate Army, concerning current rumors as to the end of the war, desertions to the Union forces, and the limited rations in 1865.

697. JOHN A. BROWN PAPERS, 1864. 39 items. Yorkville (York County), S.C.

Business correspondence of the Yorkville agent for the Bank of Chester (Chester, South Carolina).

698. JOHN R. BROWN PAPERS, 1854 (1856-1861) 1905. 212 items and 21 vols. Earpsborough (Edgecombe County), N.C.

Mercantile records of Brown's firm, earlier known as Fowler and Clements, which purchased merchandise in Petersburg and Baltimore; account books, daybooks, and ledgers; and register of public school district no. 11 of Johnston County, 1901-1905.

699. JOHN W. BROWN PAPERS, 1822, 1836. 2 items. Buncombe County, N.C.

Letters to William Forster, Mifflin County, Pennsylvania, 1822, discussing farmland management; and letter to Andrew L. Buchanan, also of Mifflin County, 1836. Brown was a U.S. representative from Pennsylvania in the 1820s and a resident of North Carolina after 1827.

700. JOSEPH EMERSON BROWN PAPERS, 1859-1889. 35 items. Canton (Cherokee County), Ga.

Letters of Joseph E. Brown (1821-1894), governor of Georgia and U.S. senator, dealing with the disposal of the stores received from the Augusta Arsenal, 1861, and with the defeat of the Federal forces near Cedar Keys, Florida, 1865. Letter of T. R. R. Cobb recommending an appointee for attorney general of Georgia; letter of an English adventurer in the Confederate Army regarding politics in Georgia; letter of C. G. Memminger regarding finances of the Confederacy; letter of J. H. Reagan regarding exemption of a postmaster in Georgia; a long letter complaining of horse stealing by Wheeler's cavalry and General Joseph Wheeler's answer to the charge; letters from 1860-1861 concerning arms for the Columbus Guards, training of artillerymen, extradition of a criminal from South Carolina, the state secession convention, and raising the Georgia militia; a letter of 1862 regarding conscription; and a letter, 1865, to Brown proposing the use of slaves as soldiers. Other letters are from Brown in later life.

701. MARY BROWN PAPERS, 1862-1865. 16 items. Hamilton (Madison County), N.Y.

Letters from William Henry Brown, a Union soldier with the Army of the Potomac, describing life at the Odd Fellows Hall Hospital, Washington, D.C.; temperance meetings there; the U.S. Army General Hospital in Baltimore; service on the U.S.S. Union at Key West, Florida; and a storm experienced by the U.S.S. Memphis. Subjects mentioned include the 61st Regiment of New York Infantry Volunteers, camp life and casualties and Confederate prisoners.

702. NEILL BROWN PAPERS, 1792 (1811-1867). 45 items. Philadelphus (Robeson County), N.C.

Correspondence of Neill Brown, a North Carolina Presbyterian minister, commenting on the heavy emigration from the state in the first part of the nineteenth century and the early settlement of Tennessee; correspondence of Hugh and Duncan Brown and John Gillespie, Neill Brown's son-in-law; and a paper, apparently written by a slave to Brown, reproaching him for turning his back on the Negroes and preaching to the whites.

703. OBADIAH BROWN PAPERS, 1799-1899. 78 items. Van Buren County, Mich.

Miscellaneous letters and business papers, including several letters from Union soldiers stationed near Poolesville, Maryland, 1863.

704. THOMAS W. BROWN, JR., PAPERS, 1862. 7 items. Wilmington (New Hanover County), N.C.

Letters from an officer of Company A (German Volunteers), 18th Regiment, North Carolina Infantry (State Troops), describing life in Union prisons at Fort Columbus, Governor's Island, New York, and at Johnson's Island, Sandusky, Ohio, and expressing hope for a prisoner exchange.

705. WILLIAM BROWN LEDGER, 1776-1791. 1 vol. (26 ff.) Bath (Beaufort County), N.C.

Accounts for a tavern, ferry, and port charges, at Bath, 1776-1791; and farm accounts of the Thomas D. and Samuel V. Smaw family near Washington, North Carolina, 1820s-1840s. Tavern accounts include those of Thomas Respass, Sr., and Thomas Respass, Jr.

706. WILLIAM GARROTT BROWN PAPERS, 1891-1927. 1,011 items and 2 vols. Marion (Perry County), Ala., and Cambridge (Middlesex County), Mass.

Personal and professional correspondence and literary notes of William Garrott Brown (1868-1913), historian and essayist. Included also are letters to John Spencer Bassett giving biographical information on Brown; Brown's diploma from Harvard; and a copy of his will. The letters center around Brown's literary work and friends; the efforts of so-called Southern liberals to make the Republican party respectable in the South; the attempts of liberals of the nation to halt the imperialistic policies of Theodore Roosevelt by supporting Woodrow Wilson; and maneuvering behind the passing of the Aldrich monetary bill, which formed the basis of the Federal

Reserve System. Included are many letters from editors of Harper's Weekly and the Youth's Companion. Among the correspondents are: Charles Francis Adams, Edwin A. Alderman, Frederic Bancroft, J. S. Bassett, Gamaliel Bradford, William Garrott Brown (including some copies), W. L. Courtney (of the English Fortnightly Review), William A. Dunning, William Preston Few, W. W. Finley, Walter L. Fleming, Richard W. Gilder, Carter Glass, Edmund W. Gosse, Gilliam Grissom, Norman Hapgood, T. P. Harrison, Harper and Brothers, A. B. Hart, Hamilton Holt, A. E. Holton, E. M. House, D. F. Houston, J. F. Jameson, J. N. Larned, Henry Cabot Lodge, Hamilton W. Mabie, S. W. McCall, A. C. McLaughlin, Shailer Mathews, John M. Morehead, John T. Morgan, David A. Munro, S. N. D. North, Charles E. Norton, Walter Hines Page, Bliss Perry, Herbert Putnam, James Ford Rhodes, Theodore Roosevelt, D. C. Roper, H. E. Scudder, Ellery Sedgwick, Thomas Settle, James T. Shotwell, H. L. Stimson, Moorfield Storey, F. W. Taussig, William R. Thayer, Frank B. Tracy, Oscar W. Underwood, Booker T. Washington, and Woodrow Wilson (copies). Additional papers include copies of Brown's letters collected by Bruce Clayton while writing his dissertation. They are in part reproduced from the Charles William Eliot Papers, Harvard University Library, and relate to Brown's career, the Harvard Guide to American History, Southern feelings toward Harvard and Massachusetts, and race relations. Other Brown letters reproduced by Clayton from the Edward Mandell House Papers, Yale University Library, concern Woodrow Wilson's presidential campaign, 1912.

707. WILLIAM R. BROWN PAPERS, 1857-1884. 3 items. Hamilton (Martin County), N.C.

Letters concerning shares of stock which William R. Brown held in the Southern Pacific Railroad Company, 1857, and a letter of sympathy after he had lost his property, 1884.

708. WILLIAM WASHINGTON BROWN PAPERS, 1861-1863. 17 items. Georgia.

Letters from William W. Brown, a Confederate volunteer from Georgia, written from a camp in Virginia to his mother, Vashti Brown, concerning army life and personal matters.

709. BROWN AND IVES PAPERS, 1803. 1 item. Providence, R.I.

Letter to D. & I. (or J.) Moses of Boston concerning land scrip in Georgia and Mississippi.

710. BROWN FAMILY PAPERS, 1862. 5 items. Virginia.

Letters of Jesse, Austin, and Bardin Brown, Confederate soldiers, to their family, revealing low morale among Southern troops.

711. G. L. P. BROWNE PAPERS, 1854-1855. 2 items. Ringwood (Halifax County), N.C.

Personal letters from G. L. P. Browne, a Methodist minister, to Thomas G. Lowe, also a Methodist minister of Halifax County.

712. THOMAS BROWNE PAPERS, 1751. 1 vol. London, England.

Survey of the estate of John Bouverie (d. 1750) with descriptions of land, buildings, timber, and other features of each farm, town house, and shop; names and rental status of tenants; and observations on economic conditions. Browne (1708?-1780) was a British heraldic official and land surveyor.

713. AMOS G. BROWNING PAPERS, 1860-1913. 21 items and 1 vol. Maysville (Mason County), Ky.

Clippings, some bound in a scrapbook, largely concerning the opening phase of the Civil War, including accounts of the first battle of Bull Run and Democratic views of the Lincoln administration. These clippings were taken from newspapers published in Ohio, Kentucky, and Missouri.

714. HUGH CONWAY BROWNING PAPERS, 1767-1968. 177 items. Hillsborough (Orange County), N.C.

Records of related Orange County families, with genealogies of the Browning and Few families and copies of letters of the Holden and Lockhart families. Included are Civil War letters written by Levi Young Lockhart and his brothers to their mother, Emeline (Dortch) Lockhart, and their sister, Eleanor Anne Lockhart, while serving in the 27th North Carolina Infantry and the 19th North Carolina Regiment (2nd Cavalry). Their letters dwell on food, clothing, sickness, casualties, and troop movements, particularly fighting in Virginia near the end of the war. Many letters are from Kinston following the Union capture of New Bern, North Carolina, in 1862. There is also correspondence, 1964-1968, between John A. Holden of La Place, Louisiana, and Browning concerning the Holden genealogy, including the parentage and activities of North Carolina Governor William Woods Holden and a number of the Holden family wills.

715. ORVILLE HICKMAN BROWNING PAPERS, 1866, 1869. 2 items. Quincy (Adams County), Ill.

Letters relating to Browning's term as U.S. secretary of the interior. One item from Joseph H. Bradley, Sr., is a recommendation for Henry A. Klopfer; the second, from Browning to M. D. Phillips, mentions the Illinois Agricultural Society as a source of information on the resources of that state.

716. WILLIAM GANNAWAY BROWNLOW PAPERS, 1862-1866. 4 items. Knoxville (Knox County), Tenn.

Two letters concern arrangements for lectures in the North while Brownlow was a fugitive from Tennessee during the early years of the Civil War. Two letters were written as Reconstruction governor of Tennessee, 1865-1866; one of them, to chief justice of the U.S. Supreme Court Salmon Portland Chase, comments on the prospects of the 14th Amendment.

717. RICHARD BROWNRIGG LEDGER, 1757-1759. 1 vol. (360 pp.) Edenton (Chowan County), N.C.

Merchant's ledger including itemized accounts for barter.

718. [OZE REED BROYLES ?] PAPERS, 1794-1873. 23 items. Anderson (Anderson District), S.C.

Included are a dissenting church certificate issued in County Antrim, Ireland, 1794, to Neal and Mary Gageby; land deeds and indentures from Washington County, Tennessee, and Anderson District, South Carolina, containing the names of such early residents as Montgomery, Henly, Johnston, Williams, Palmer, Livingston, Reese, Harris, Earle, and Lawrence; letter of Governor Joseph E. Brown of Georgia to Broyles, 1863, reviewing Confederate economic problems, conscription, provisioning of troops, and aid to soldiers' families; addresses by Broyles on the Second Bank of the United States, the Sub-Treasury Bill, slavery, the Wilmot Proviso, agriculture and railroad construction; and a document concerning the financial affairs of Broyles and Thomas McCartha, 1846.

719. BENJAMIN BRUBAKER PAPERS, 1844-1861. 3 items. Roanoke County, Va.

A family letter of 1844, and two documents of the Confederate government appropriating property of Jacob Brubaker, a resident of Indiana.

720. MATTHEW JOSEPH BRUCCOLI PAPERS, 1972-1973. 43 items. Columbia (Richland County), S.C.

The papers of Matthew Bruccoli (b. 1937), professor of English at the University of South Carolina, comprise manuscript copies of contributions to The Chief Glory of Every People, and correspondence between Bruccoli and the contributors. The contributions include chapters by James Grossman on James Fenimore Cooper, Marston LaFrance on Stephen Crane, Sidney Hook on John Dewey, Eleanor Tilton on Ralph Waldo Emerson, Arlin Turner on Nathaniel Hawthorne, Clayton Eichelberger on William Dean Howells, William Hedges on Washington Irving, Jay Leyda on Herman Melville, Thomas McHaney on William Gilmore Simms, Joel Porte on Henry David Thoreau, James Cox on Mark Twain, and James Miller on Walt Whitman.

721. CHARLES KEY BRUCE PAPERS, 1839-1847. 22 items. Cumberland (Allegany County), Md.

Correspondence of a Baltimore and Ohio Railroad civil engineer, dealing with the construction of the railroad between Harpers Ferry, West Virginia, and Cumberland, Maryland.

722. PHILIP ALEXANDER BRUCE PAPERS, 1894. 3 items. Charlottesville (Albemarle County), Va.

Papers of Philip Alexander Bruce (1856-1933), author and editor of the Virginia Magazine of History and Biography, relating to a critical review of Barons of the Potomack and Rappahannock by Moncure Daniel Conway (1832-1907) which appeared in the magazine. Included are a letter from Conway replying in detail to the review; a clipping of the letter published in the Richmond Times; and a draft of Bruce's response, addressed to the editor of the Richmond Times.

723. HENRY M. BRUNS COMMONPLACE BOOK, 1853-1888. 1 vol. (271 pp.) South Carolina.

Quotations and other information of interest to Bruns, with citations to sources. Included are a report by Mayor William A. Courtenay on the funds of the College of Charleston, 1881, and lists of aged residents of Charleston in 1887 and 1888 with birth dates and notations concerning deaths.

724. BRUNSWICK LAND COMPANY ARTICLES OF AGREEMENT, 1836. 1 vol. (18 pp.) Lawrenceville (Brunswick County), Va.

Articles of agreement for selling, trading, and speculating in lands in Texas, signed by James H. Gholson, Thomas S. Gholson, John D. Kirby, William Kirby, Henry Lewis, R. Kidder Meade, A. T. B. Merritt, and William H. E. Merritt.

725. BRUNSWICK AND WESTERN RAILROAD COMPANY REPORTS, 1888-1894. 135 vols. Brunswick (Glynn County), Ga.

Incomplete annual, semiannual, quarterly, and monthly financial reports showing earnings of a line absorbed in 1901 by the Savannah and Western Railroad and later by the Atlantic Coast Line Railroad.

726. MARY E. BRUSH PAPERS, 1841-1844. 9 items. Huntington (Suffolk County), N.Y.

Letters to Mary Brush's sister and cousin describing family affairs, Methodist meetings, the Huntington temperance society, and Fourth of July celebrations.

727. JAMES L. BRYAN ACCOUNT BOOK, 1856-1857. 1 vol. (10 pp.) [Raleigh (Wake County), N.C. ?]

Records of the settlement of Bryan's estate.

728. MATTHEW BRYAN PAPERS, 1847-1852. 23 items. Augusta County, Va.

Business letter to Bryan, relating to the manufacturing and sale of plows, shoes, and iron in Virginia.

729. WILLIAM JENNINGS BRYAN PAPERS, 1903. 1 item. Lincoln (Lancaster County), Neb.

Letter to Susan L. Avery thanking her for some articles she had sent The Commoner.

730. BRYAN FAMILY PAPERS, 1717-1956. 2,942 items and 39 vols. New Bern (Craven County), N.C.

This collection consists of the papers of John Herritage Bryan (1798-1870); of the family of James West Bryan (1805-1864); and of related families of Virginia and North Carolina. Papers contain letters from James West Bryan relating to family, business, and political topics, including evaluations of public support for John Herritage Bryan as U.S. Representative from North Carolina, 1825-1829; William Biddle Shepard giving opinions of Andrew Jackson, comments on the Webster-Hayne debate, and seeking advice on Shepard's gubernatorial candidacy, 1850; William Alexander Graham describing the abolitionists and the compromises of the Fillmore administration. There are also letters of Henry Ravenscroft Bryan, the son of John Herritage Bryan, concerning family and routine business, Post-Civil War politics in North Carolina, criticism of the military government, and two letters, 1873, from his brother J. H. Bryan, discussing conditions in Brazil. John Herritage Bryan's legal papers largely relate to land in Craven County, Wake County, and Raleigh, and to the purchase and sale of slaves; there are also wills, pardons signed by Andrew Johnson, contracts with former slaves relating to sharecropping, and material concerning the Atlantic and North Carolina Railroad. Miscellaneous papers include speeches, documents, bills and receipts, writings of Henry Ravenscroft Bryan, a paper describing a geological field trip under the direction of Elisha Mitchell at the University of North Carolina, 1855, and two sketches of the life of John Herritage Bryan by a son, William S. Bryan.

Papers of the family of James West Bryan contain material relating to the Washingtons of Kinston, North Carolina, the Shepards of Beaufort and New Bern, and the Donnells of New Bern and Raleigh. Included are letters of Richard Dobbs Spaight II, describing social life of New Bern and economic growth following steamboat connections with Norfolk; letters concerning state government in North Carolina, 1828-1837, reflecting the role of the Whig Party, the Reform convention of 1835, and the organization of a new general assembly; descriptions of office seeking in Washington, D.C., the purchase of merchandise in New York and business conditions there, and the panic of 1837. Papers of the Donnell family contain letters from John Robert Donnell to his daughter Mary (Donnell) Shepard relating to New Orleans investments of the 1850s; overseer's reports on a plantation at Lake Comfort, Hyde County, North Carolina, 1862-1864; and letters describing the life of refugees fleeing Union occupation of the North Carolina coast. Papers of James Augustus Bryan (1839-1923), James West Bryan's son, contain material on the collection of money for a Raleigh monument to Lawrence O'Bryan Branch, 1863; correspondence with Mary (Shepard) Bryan; correspondence with New York and Baltimore firms concerning the lumber business of the Tuscarora Steam and Grist Mills, Craven County, from the 1860s and 1870s; and correspondence concerning banking interests in New Bern. There are also deeds, indentures, and other documents for land along the Neuse and Trent Rivers in Craven County, 1717-1876; household and business receipts; shipping papers for lumber, accounts of lumber sales, other receipts, and bankbooks for the Tuscarora and the Lake Mills; shipment papers for freight on the Atlantic and North Carolina Railroad; and financial papers of the Donnell family in Hyde County, North Carolina after 1855 and Englewood, New Jersey, after 1868. A diary kept after 1834 by George T. Olmsted describes the social life of Princeton, New Jersey, but relates largely to the operation of the Delaware and Raritan Canal, and includes frequent references to Robert Field Stockton. There is a cookbook started for Annis (Boudinot) Stockton on the occasion of her marriage, 1762, to Richard Stockton, and added to by subsequent generations until late in the 19th century. The volume also includes a section on household remedies. Some of the earlier recipes were published in Eliza Leslie, Seventy-Five Receipts (Philadelphia: 1828).

Additional papers largely concern land transactions and genealogy of the Bryan and Donnell heirs of Richard Dobbs Spaight (1758-1802) and include a few personal papers of family members in Virginia and North Carolina. There is also a series of financial, legal, and miscellaneous items including genealogies of the Bryan and Washington families and records of Charles S. Bryan and his relatives.

A table of families is at the beginning of the collection.

731. JOHN EMORY BRYANT PAPERS, 1851-1907. 1,818 items and 40 vols. Union (Lincoln County), Me.; and Georgia.

Correspondence, published writings, and other papers relating to Bryant's Civil War service with the 8th Maine Volunteers, his activities as agent of the Freedmen's Bureau, leader of the Negro Republicans in Georgia, and his interest in temperance and the Methodist Church. Miscellaneous legal and financial papers and account books relate to his business ventures. His journal kept in youth, 3 vols., incomplete, gives glimpses of life in Maine and at Maine Wesleyan Seminary in Kent's Hill. The journal, 2 vols., 1866, 1876, kept by his wife, Emma, includes a description of the personnel of the Freedmen's Bureau in Augusta, Georgia. An autobiographical sketch by Bryant's daughter, Alice (Bryant) Zeller, gives much information on the life of her parents. Several letter books relate to Reconstruction Georgia. Correspondence, 1 vol., 1876-1878, of Bryant and Volney Spalding includes material on the elections of 1876; Bryant's fight with the Savannah collector of revenue, James Atkins; the founding of the Georgia Republican; and the 1877 state constitution. A letter book 1888-1890 relates to Bryant's business ventures in New York. The letter book and scrapbook, 1875-1879, of William Anderson Pledger, Negro editor of Georgia, includes autobiographical notes. Three Confederate Army letter books include official correspondence of the headquarters of Gen. Raleigh Edward Colston's brigade at Fort Bartow, Georgia, 1864; official correspondence, 1863-1864, of Camp Cooper, Macon, Georgia, and Camp Randolph, Decatur, Georgia, both centers for the instruction of conscripts; and correspondence, 1863-1864, of the commandant of conscription at Macon and Griffith, Georgia. Bryant and Christopher C. Richardson, an officer of the 12th Marine Volunteers, used these captured volumes for their own records, including lists of Confederates taking amnesty oaths; memoranda of their postwar law partnership in Augusta; minutes of the Republican Club in Augusta, 1868; Bryant's letters, 1865, for the Freedmen's Bureau at Augusta; letters of Gen. Rufus Saxton, commander of the Freedmen's Bureau, 1865; and clippings from the Loyal Georgian, 1866. Other scrapbooks include letters and papers of Bryant's service with the 8th Maine Volunteers in South Carolina, 1 vol., 1861-1864; clippings of Georgia newspapers illustrating Reconstruction life, especially Negro life, 3 vols., 1868-1894; and material after 1887, 8 vols., concerning Emma Bryant and Alice (Bryant) Zeller; Grant Memorial University, Athens, Tennessee; temperance; and the position of women. Account books, 1873-1899, reflect Bryant's business ventures and include a register, 1873-1875, of the staff of the Savannah Customs House with their contributions to the Republican Party. There are also loose clippings, including many on the work of the Methodist Church in education in the South after 1876. Also included in the collection are photocopies of related broadsides and pamphlets. Major correspondents include Henry McNeal Turner.

732. SAMUEL S. BRYANT SCRAPBOOK, 1832-1836. 1 vol. Norfolk (Norfolk County), Va.

A collection of sentimental and religious poems, many of which were written by Samuel Bryant, a Methodist minister.

733. WILLIAM CULLEN BRYANT PAPERS, 1839-1895. 34 items. New York, N.Y.

Miscellaneous letters by Bryant, largely concerning literary matters, travel, and personal affairs; signed and dated copies of several of his poems; and a letter from Johannes Adam Oertel regarding illustrations to accompany one poem.

734. SAMUEL BRYARLY PAPERS, 1787-1884. 662 items and 4 vols. White Post (Clarke County), Va.

Family correspondence of the Bryarly brothers, Virginia planters, relating to agricultural conditions in Virginia and to general conditions in Mississippi, Ohio, and Tennessee, where several of the Bryarly sons had moved. Material for 1850-1860 consists of claims and promissory notes dealing with settlement of Samuel Bryarly's (d. 1850) accounts; material for 1860-1884 consists of personal letters, bills, and summonses of Richard Bryarly. Included also for 1813-1863 are plantation account books, and a scrapbook, of Richard and Rowland Bryarly.

735. JAMES BRYCE, VISCOUNT BRYCE, PAPERS, 1886-1900. 4 items. London, England.

Miscellaneous letters from Bryce commenting on the Irish Home Rule Bill, 1886; the defeat of Harry Smith, Liberal M.P. from Falkirk, 1895; the extreme High Church faction of the Church of England, 1899; and the efforts of Ernest Parke to publish an inexpensive edition of Shakespeare.

736. JAMES BRYDGES, THIRD DUKE OF CHANDOS, PAPERS, 1759. 1 item. London, England.

Letter discussing an election contest in Hampshire where Henry Bilson-Legge opposed Sir Simeon Stuart, Third Baronet.

737. JOSEPH RALEIGH BRYSON PAPERS, 1946. 3 items. Greenville (Greenville County), S.C.; and Washington, D.C.

Correspondence between Bryson, U.S. representative from South Carolina, and St. George Leakin Sioussat of the Library of Congress, analyzing an undated note by Edward George Earle Lytton Bulwer (1803-1873), which is apparently an order for tobacco.

738. PETER BUCHAN PAPERS, 1835. 1 item. Peterhead, Aberdeenshire, Scotland.

Letter to Messrs. Roake and Varty, London booksellers, concerning possible publication of a book by Buchan on British politics and a collection of Scottish ballads.

739. CLAUDIUS BUCHANAN PAPERS, 1807. 1 item. Broxbourne, Hertfordshire, England.

Letter to a Rev. Dr. Kohlhof from Buchanan, a chaplain in Bengal, concerning the translation of the New Testament into the Malayalam language.

740.  HUGH BUCHANAN PAPERS, 1835 (1850-1860) 1861. 24 items. Newnan (Coweta County), Ga.

Business papers, usually letters requesting legal aid from Hugh Buchanan (1823-1890), lawyer, member of the Georgia legislature, 1855, 1857, and member of U.S. Congress, 1881-1885; and two personal letters from members of the family.

741.  JAMES BUCHANAN PAPERS, 1838-1860. 12 items. Lancaster (Lancaster County), Pa.

Largely letters from various political leaders urging the appointment of constituents to office while Buchanan was president; and one land grant signed by Buchanan.

742.  JOHN BUCHANAN PAPERS, 1826-1827. 3 items. Annapolis (Anne Arundel County), Md.

Report of John Buchanan's son, Thomas, a student at Dickinson College, Carlisle, Pennsylvania, and an estimate of a year's expense at the college; notification that Dickinson College would confer on Buchanan the honorary degree of Doctor of Laws; and a letter concerning the transfer of his son to a school in Georgetown.

743.  THOMAS E. BUCHANAN PAPERS, 1711 (1833-1858) 1952. 648 items. Williamsport (Washington County), Md.

Largely family correspondence of John Buchanan, Thomas E. Buchanan, Nancy Buchanan, Phillip Dandridge, S.P. Dandridge, Sarah Dandridge, Dabney Carr Harrison, Peyton Harrison, Nannie D. Thomas, and other members of the Thomas family. Also, cancelled checks, wills, deeds, and a scrapbook of the Buchanan, Dandridge, and Thomas families. Subjects of the letters include plantation life and management in Virginia and Maryland; slavery and slave insurrections; schools and colleges and school and college life in Virginia, New Jersey, and Massachusetts; social life and customs in Maryland and Virginia; the Presbyterian church in Virginia; the Whig party in Massachusetts; and opposition to secession in Virginia. Among correspondents are Charles E. Dudley, Charles J. Faulkner, Sr., Robert M. T. Hunter, William Lucas, Isaac McKim, Henry Taylor, Henry St. George Tucker, and Beverley Tucker.

744.  DANIEL BUCK PAPERS, 1849-1900. 385 items. Spring Garden (York County) and Philadelphia, Pa.

Business papers of a cabinetmaker and lumber dealer including correspondence, deeds, bills, receipts, and promissory notes.

745.  SAMUEL D. BUCK PAPERS, ca. 1890. 1 item. Winchester (Frederick County), Va.

Reminiscences of Buck's Civil War career as an officer in the 13th Virginia Volunteer Infantry, 1861-1865, describing campaigns under Jackson and Early, with details of troop movements, the conduct of generals, battles, and camp life.

746.  JOHN BUCKHOUT PAPERS, 1853-1858. 3 items.

Records of business transactions between the Buckhout and Hatfield families, including receipts and a promissory note.

747.  WILLIAM BUCKLAND PAPERS, 1840, 1848. 2 items. London, England.

Letter, 1840, of Sir Richard Owen, concerning Buckland's work as a geologist; and a letter from Joseph Phillimore, 1848, written to Buckland as dean of Westminister, asking if records revealed whether John, Baron Hervey, and his brother Henry had been students at Westminister School in the 1700s.

748.  E. G. BUCKLES DIARY, 1866-1867. 2 vols. Berkeley County, West Virginia.

Diary of a physician describing his family, patients, medicine, road conditions, and Negroes. Meetings of Negro radicals are mentioned.

749.  EDWIN G. BUCKLES COMMONPLACE BOOK, 1841-1848. 1 vol. (111 pp.) Rose Hill (Jefferson County), West Virginia.

750.  JOSEPH BUCKMINISTER RECEIPT, 1782. 1 item. Boston, Mass.

Receipt signed by Buckminister (1751-1812).

751.  SIMON BOLIVAR BUCKNER PAPERS, 1863-1914. 6 items. Munfordville (Hart County), Ky.

Miscellaneous letters, chiefly personal, of the Confederate lieutenant general and 1896 National Democratic candidate for vice president. One item, 1863, deals with intelligence of Union troop movements in Kentucky.

752.  DAVID BUEL PAPERS, 1811-1814. 19 items. Troy (Rensselaer County), N.Y.

Letters of courtship to Harriet Hillhouse of Montville, Connecticut, with comments on health, religion, the War of 1812, and on William Samuel Johnson, member of the U.S. Constitutional Convention.

753.  JOHN BUFORD PAPERS, 1804 (1854-1857) 1898.  604 items.  Bedford County, Va.

Family and business letters, bills, receipts, and other papers mentioning commodity prices in Virginia; clothes; hiring of slaves; procuring labor, especially slaves, supplies, and legislative appropriations for railroad construction in Virginia; feeding of railroad construction workers; state politics; health; land in Virginia and in Missouri; ties for railroad construction; and naval stores in North Carolina.

754.  CATHERINE JANE (McGEACHY) BUIE PAPERS, 1819 (1861-1865) 1899.  636 items.  Robeson County, N.C.

Personal correspondence of a North Carolina family, giving a Confederate private soldier's view of the Civil War, descriptions of the march through Pennsylvania, 1863, and the battle of Fort Fisher, North Carolina, 1865.  Letters of women of the family reveal hardships from scarcity of small necessities during the war and fear of freed Negroes. Included are letters from friends and relatives at Trinity and Davidson colleges in North Carolina and Wofford College, Spartanburg, South Carolina, commenting upon student interests and reactions to political trends; sidelights on a small school in Bladen County, where Catherine McGeachy taught during the Civil War; and letters concerning Reconstruction.  Catherine McGeachy, who married Duncan A. Buie in 1866, was later postmistress at Buie (Robeson County), North Carolina.

755.  JOHN BUIE PAPERS, 1853 (1861-1864).  24 items.  Tippah County, Miss.

Letters of John Buie, a Confederate soldier, to his father, John C. Buie, of Moore County, North Carolina, including comment on campaigns in Mississippi and Tennessee, and Bragg's raid into Kentucky, 1862.

756.  MARY ANN S. M. BUIE LETTERS, 1842-1871.  26 items.  Cumberland County, N.C.

Family letters, with comment on the prices at which slaves were sold and hired, 1849; numerous references to deaths of Confederate soldiers; and comment on Reconstruction.

757.  HENRY BUIST PAPERS, 1868, 1871.  2 items.  Charleston, S.C.

Buist's appointment, signed by Governor Robert Kingston Scott, 1869, to a commercial convention in Memphis; and a letter, 1871, to Gen. Rush C. Hawkins concerning a lawsuit arising out of Civil War blockade running.

758.  WILLIAM BULL PAPERS, 1770, 1774.  2 items.  Charleston, S.C.

Petition of James Coachman to be appointed guardian of a mulatto child, who was given her freedom by the will of Jonathan Drake, and a proclamation of Bull as lieutenant governor and commander in chief of South Carolina.

759.  ARCHIBALD BULLOCH PAPERS, 1776-1829.  7 items.  Savannah, Ga.

Letters and commissions, 3 items, 1776-1777, signed by Archibald Bulloch, governor of Georgia; and three business letters, ca. 1811, of Archibald S. Bulloch, collector of the Port of Savannah.

760.  BARSHA BULLOCK PAPERS, 1840-1888.  96 items.  Enfield (Halifax County), N.C.

Family letters chiefly relating to personal subjects.  There are a few references to the Civil War in North Carolina and Virginia, and to Thomas D. Bullock, 5th Regiment of North Carolina Infantry Volunteers.

761.  JOHN BULLOCK PAPERS, 1784-1920.  Williamsboro (Vance County), N.C.

Papers of several generations of a family of southern Virginia and central North Carolina, including correspondence of John and William H. Bullock, a second John Bullock and his wife, Susan M. (Cobb) Bullock, their daughter-in-law, Judith (Watkins) Bullock, and her daughter Rebecca (Bullock) Fuller and other children and grandchildren.  The names of related families appear frequently, such as Goode, Farrar, Taylor, Boyd, Hamilton, and Pearson.  There are also many letters to Sallie (Tarry) Harrison.  Topics include farming; silkworm culture, 1839; University of North Carolina faculty and student disputes, 1858; secessionist sentiment in Granville County; Walter Bullock's Civil War service in North Carolina and Virginia; the Presbyterian and Episcopal churches; the Spanish-American War; and genealogy.  The diaries of Susan M. (Cobb) Bullock include one small volume recording her visit to the mountains of Tennessee and North Carolina, 1848, and a daily journal, 1869-1871, kept in one of her husband's account books.

762.  WILLIAM HENRY LYTTON EARLE BULWER, BARON DALLING AND BULWER, PAPERS, 1850-1853.  23 items.  Washington, D.C.

Personal and diplomatic correspondence of Sir Henry Lytton Bulwer (1801-1872), author and British minister to the United States, containing comments on the political situation in the United States during debates on the Compromise of 1850, the presidential election of 1852, slavery, and the colonization of Negroes.

763. JABEZ BUNTING PAPERS, 1836. 1 item. London, England.

A letter to Bunting, Methodist minister, from George Grey, under secretary for the colonies, concerning the use by the Wesleyan Missionary Society of a parliamentary grant for the establishment of Negro schools in the British West Indies, and noting the views of Lord Glenelg, Colonial Secretary.

764. ELIZABETH BUNTYN PAPERS, 1862-1865. 43 items.

Letters from Morgan and Frank Buntyn and J. M. Matthews, soldiers in the Confederate Army. One item, 1864, relates to the surrender of Savannah.

765. STEPHEN GANO BURBRIDGE PAPERS, 1863-1864. 1,365 items. Kentucky.

Military telegrams which passed through the office of Major General S. G. Burbridge, U.S. Army, concerning troop movements, the civil administration of Kentucky, Morgan's raid into Kentucky, and other facets of military life; and a map showing the location of the 10th Division, 13th Artillery Corps at the siege of Vicksburg.

766. USHER LLOYD BURDICK PAPERS, 1937. 7 items. Washington, D.C.

Correspondence of Usher L. Burdick (b. 1879), governor of North Dakota and member of U.S. Congress, concerning the origin and nature of a two-dollar note issued by the Bank of Mecklenburg, Charlotte, North Carolina, in 1874.

767. HIRAM BURGESS ACCOUNT BOOK, 1853-1874. 1 vol. (84 pp.) Grant County, W. Va.

Accounts of a distiller and farmer relating to sales of whiskey and to work by agricultural laborers.

768. MARTHA J. (TRIST) BURKE PAPERS, 1887. 1 item. Alexandria (Arlington County), Va.

Letter from Martha J. Burke to Jesse C. Green describing the manuscripts she is sending him. The manuscripts are letters and copies of letters from Thomas Jefferson and James Madison to members of her family.

769. THOMAS BURKE PAPERS, 1776, 1782. 2 items. Hillsborough (Orange County), N.C.

A letter from Thomas Burke (ca. 1747-1783) to Richard Henry Lee concerning the movement of Virginia Tories, and a letter from Burke, probably to Edmund Pendleton, complaining of the neglect he has suffered at the hands of the governor of North Carolina.

770. THOMAS T. BURKE PAPERS, 1863-1917. 17 items. Chatham County, N.C.

Personal correspondence of the Burke family, and the Collins and Freeman families of Ross County, Ohio. The letters contain information on smallpox in Chatham County, commodity prices in Chatham and Ross counties, and the life of a Confederate soldier at Charleston, South Carolina.

771. H. L. BURKETT PAPERS AND DIARY, 1862-1872. 8 items. Waynesboro (Wayne County), Tenn.

Papers and diary of H. L. Burkett, planter and slaveholder. The diary covers 1862 and contains comments on the weather, crops, Union forces, Confederate forces, military operations near the Tennessee River, and personal affairs. Included also is a broadside, 1872, announcing that Burkett would speak on Waynesboro "fifty years ago."

772. LINGURN SKIDMORE BURKHEAD SERMON BOOK, 1852-1865. 1 vol. Plymouth (Washington County), N.C.

Copies of sermons of Lingurn S. Burkhead (1824-1887), a Methodist minister of Plymouth and Wilmington, North Carolina.

773. ANSON BURLINGAME PAPERS, 1859. 1 item. Boston, Mass.

Letter to Anson Burlingame (1820-1870), diplomat and congressman, from Hardie Hogan Helper, brother of Hinton Rowan Helper, concerning his financial problems and his imprisonment resulting from his distribution of his brother's work on slavery.

774. SIR RICHARD BURN PAPERS, 1926-1935. 4 items. Oxford, Oxfordshire, England.

Papers of Burn (1871-1947) of the Indian Civil Service, concerning the Tenancy Acts and the Congress Party. Correspondents include Gokul Chand and Sir Sita Ram.

775. ANNIE BURNMAN AUTOGRAPH ALBUM, 1871-1872. 1 vol. (35 pp.) Memphis, Tenn.

Autograph album of a student in the State Female College, Memphis, Tennessee.

776. AUGUSTA A. BURNHAM AND ELETHINE BURNHAM PAPERS, 1841-1854. 34 items. Lowell and Littleton (Middlesex County), Mass.

Family correspondence containing information on Lowell Institute, the mills, and rural life in New Hampshire.

777. H. B. BURNHAM DOCKET BOOKS AND INDEX, 1864-1870. 2 vols. Richmond, Va.

Docket book rendered almost illegible

by its use as a scrapbook, and an index to a letter book, both apparently kept by the U.S. Military Police.

778. ARCHIBALD W. BURNS JOURNAL, 1846-1847. 1 vol. (30 pp.) New Jersey.

Journal describing visit of Archibald W. Burns to Mexico during the Mexican War. References are made to Major General Winfield Scott, General Zachary Taylor, army headquarters at Camargo, and the battle at Monterey.

779. WILLIAM HENRY BURR PAPERS, 1897. 1 item. Washington, D.C.

Letter from William Henry Burr, American author, to James B. Elliott discussing Thomas Paine.

780. GEORGE BURRINGTON PAPERS, 1723-1732. 4 items. London, England.

Papers of George Burrington (ca. 1680-1759), colonial governor of North Carolina, include two sets of instructions from the Lords Proprietors concerning enforcement of the laws relating to trade and navigation, and two letters from Burrington discussing the political situation in North Carolina, public sentiment regarding quit-rents and the acquisition of land, and his friends on the Board of Trade.

781. BENJAMIN BURROUGHS PAPERS, 1809-1847. 9 items. Savannah, Ga.

Letters and papers of Benjamin Burroughs, a Georgia planter, concerning the sale of horses, furniture, tools, livestock, and slaves; and improvements at Cold Spring Plantation. Included also is a letter, 1847, from Theodore S. Fay in Berlin, commenting on his travels in Europe.

782. DAVID BURROUGHS PAPERS, 1814-1818. 5 items. Phelps (Ontario County), N.Y.

Business papers concerning bonds for debts, apprenticeship papers, and a land deed.

783. JOHN BURROUGHS PAPERS. 4 items. West Park (Ulster County), N.Y.

Papers of John Burroughs (1837-1921), naturalist and author, include an autograph copy of notes for "The Friendly Rocks"; a letter to Mary Hoyt Freligh concerning his friend William Vanamee; the poem, "Waiting"; and a photograph of Burroughs.

784. JOHN BURROUGHS ACCOUNT BOOK, 1855-1885. 1 vol. Jefferson County, Ark.

Accounts of the estates of six persons for whom John Burroughs appears to have been administrator.

785. RICHARD D. BURROUGHS PAPERS, 1807-1889. 2,144 items. Upper Marlborough (Prince Georges County), Md.

Personal and business papers of Richard D. Burroughs, tavern keeper and planter, and of his son, John William Burroughs, planter. The bulk of the collection consists of personal, household, and agricultural accounts, statements and letters from commission merchants in Baltimore and Georgetown, especially Thompson and Spalding. Other papers concern Richard Burroughs' administration of the estate of his aunt, Judith Davis; John's education in Georgetown College, Georgetown, D.C., and the College of St. James, Hagerstown, Md., 1843-1848; and Richard's stay at the springs in Virginia for his health, 1850s.

786. VALERIA G. BURROUGHS ALBUM AND COMMONPLACE BOOKS, 1830-1872. 3 vols. Savannah, Ga.

An album containing copies of poems; a commonplace book, 1831-1841, with poems, religious comments and references to family deaths; and a commonplace book, 1844-1872, including the minutes, correspondence and the constitution of the Female Seamen's Friend Society of Savannah, Ga., 1844-1861, and household accounts, lists, and recipes, 1866-1872.

787. WILLIAM BERRIEN BURROUGHS PAPERS, 1872-1938. 440 items. Brunswick (Glynn County), Ga.

Papers of William B. Burroughs, genealogist, local historian and rice planter, comprise letters, receipts, bills, accounts, and clippings, including information on early Georgia history, and the Berrien, Burroughs, Stewart, and Milledge families of Georgia.

788. ELIZABETH BURROW PAPERS, 1842-1928. 38 items and 1 vol. Thomasville (Davidson County), N.C.

Miscellaneous papers of Elizabeth Burrow include letters from her husband, Henry Burrow, during the Civil War, an advertising booklet published by the Ford Motor Company, 1912, obituaries of several Thomasville citizens, and a copy of The Chairmaker, June, 1924.

789. H. LANSING BURROWS COMMONPLACE BOOK, 1856-1865. 1 vol. (99 pp.) Richmond, Va.

Manuscript copies of the Weekly Herald of Richmond, edited by H. Lansing Burrows, 1856-1857. Superimposed upon many pages are clippings about Richmond, 1863-1865.

790. JAMES A. BURROWS PAPERS, 1861-1869. 40 items. North Carolina.

Personal letters from James A. Burrows, a Confederate soldier, to his brother, Frank Burrows.

791. ARMISTEAD BURT PAPERS, 1759-1933. 5,675 items. Abbeville (Abbeville County), S.C.

Political and legal correspondence of Armistead Burt (1802-1883), South Carolina planter and member of U.S. Congress. The political correspondence deals largely with the policies of John C. Calhoun and the question of secession. After 1860 the material relates chiefly to Burt's law practice, especially to the management of estates of Confederate soldiers, and the Calhoun estate. Other matters referred to include the political corruption and economic conditions in postwar South Carolina. Among the correspondents are Armistead Burt, Pierce M. Butler, Henry Toole Clark, Thomas Green Clemson, T. L. Deveaux, James H. Hammond, A. P. Hayne, Reverdy Johnson, Hugh S. Legaré, Augustus B. Longstreet, W. N. Meriwether, James L. Petigru, Francis W. Pickens, Robert Barnwell Rhett, Richard Rush, Waddy Thompson, and Louis T. Wigfall.

792. A. M. BURTON JOURNALS, 1815-1842. 4 vols. Beattie's Ford (Lincoln County), N.C.

Journals and daybooks of a general merchant and postmaster.

793. COLUMBIA Y. BURTON PAPERS, 1864-1865. 6 items. Frederick (Frederick County), Md.

Letters to his cousin, James T. Bland, a prisoner of war in Elmira, New York.

794. JAMES H. BURTON PAPERS, 1872-1894. 6 items and 1 vol. Leeds, England, and Middleburg (Loudoun County), Va.

Letterpress book and letters of James H. Burton, engineer, inventor, and farmer, dealing with business matters. Much of the early correspondence concerns Burton's attempts to secure remuneration from either the British or American governments, or from private manufacturers in both countries, for their use of his process of manufacturing steel gun barrels. Included are references to labor conditions in England and the business affairs of various English and American armament companies--Remington & Sons, the Winchester Repeating Arms Company, Greenwood & Batley, National Arms & Ammunition, and the Providence Tool Company. The bulk of the material after 1873 deals with Burton's farm business including orders for supplies, receipts, sales of stock and produce, and sales and purchases of land in Virginia, West Virginia, and Georgia.

795. ROBERT BURTON PAPERS, (1771-1838) 1925. 102 items and 1 vol. Granville County, N.C.

Business papers and records of Robert Burton (1747-1825), Revolutionary soldier and lawyer, and his son, Horace A. Burton. Robert Burton was apparently also a wholesale commission merchant having connections with leaders of the Transylvania Land Company. The account book contains records of patrons, among whom were Leonard Henley Bullock, Hutchins Burton, John Burton, Charles Rust Eaton, Benjamin Hawkins, Richard and Samuel Henderson, Thomas Lanier, Archibald Leonard, General Stephen Moore, the Reverend Henry Patillo, Bromfield Ridley, and Judge John Williams.
Among the papers are references to the Transylvania Land Company; letters of Robert Houston and John Rhea of Knoxville, Tennessee, regarding the purchase of land from Richard Henderson's estate; and copies of court records of Madison County, Kentucky, regarding Henderson's property there. After 1830 the collection centers around business and personal correspondence of Horace A. Burton, son of Robert Burton, including a number of papers concerning John and William Ragland and their heirs. Several letters, after 1880, are concerned with genealogy. Among the correspondents are William A. Graham, T. T. Hicks, Frank Nash, John Rhea, and Lewis Williams.

796. ROBERT OSWALD BURTON PAPERS, 1861-1864. 9 items. Halifax County, N.C.

Letters to Rev. R. O. Burton (1811-1891), a Methodist minister, relating to church affairs, business matters, the Civil War, and the education of his son, Andrew Joyner Burton (b. 1848), at Belmont, North Carolina, and at the University of North Carolina, Chapel Hill. Included is an itemized account of Andrew's expenses at the University, 1863.

797. JOSHUA BURTZ PAPERS, 1844-1866. 3 items. Cherokee County, Ga.

Business papers of planter Joshua Burtz, including an agreement with freedman William Parks for land and supplies furnished to Parks as a tenant farmer.

798. LEWIS BURWELL PAPERS, 1802-1891. 8 items. Dayton (Marengo County), Ala.

Family correspondence.

799. LUCY (COLE) BURWELL PAPERS, 1751-1905. 1,077 items and 2 vols. Manson (Warren County), N.C.

Family and personal correspondence of Lucy (Cole) Burwell reflecting the social life of an agrarian family for four generations, and including letters of Henry, Lewis A., Lucy, Mary, Spotswood, and William Burwell; and two autograph letters of W. F. Tillett; an account book for the mercantile business of

Lewis A. Burwell, 1807-1808, Mecklenburg County, Virginia, and for the mercantile firm of White and Burwell, 1866-1868.

800. WILLIAM M. BURWELL PAPERS, 1864. 2 items. Liberty [(Bedford County), Va.?]

Brief and nearly illegible notes concerning a knitting machine.

801. WILLIAM H. BUSBEY PAPERS, 1861-1864. 15 items. Wilmington (Clinton County), Ohio.

Personal letters of William H. Busbey, a soldier in the 1st Regiment, Kentucky Volunteers, U.S.A., concerning politics in Ohio, including the gubernatorial race in 1863 of Clement Vallandigham against John Brough; the Freemasons; crime in Ohio; the life of a soldier; and military activities in Tennessee.

802. BUSIC'S STORE DAYBOOK, 1854-1855. 1 vol. (579 pp.) Brandon (Rankin County), Miss.

Accounts of a general mercantile business.

803. BENJAMIN FRANKLIN BUTLER PAPERS, 1864-1893. 4 items. Lowell (Middlesex County), Mass.

Papers of Benjamin F. Butler (1818-1893), Massachusetts legislator, Federal general, U.S. congressman, and governor of Massachusetts, pertain largely to his financial affairs. Several letters refer to the dismissal of an officer. Included are references to organized labor, the eight-hour law, and Butler's attitude toward the Negro.

804. CHARLES BUTLER PAPERS, 1767 (1815-1845) 1885. 81 items. Craven County, N.C.

Tax receipts, indentures and land grants of the Butler family.

805. EDWARD GEORGE WASHINGTON BUTLER PAPERS, 1821-1888. 140 items. Iberville (Iberville Parish), La.

Correspondence of E. G. W. Butler (1800-1888), planter and U.S. Army officer, dealing with military affairs, the Mexican War, the Civil War, slavery, Lincoln's election, politics and government, railroads, Southern social life and customs, Reconstruction, and contemporary European affairs. Among the correspondents are Caroline (Deslonde) Beauregard, Braxton Bragg, James Buchanan, Jefferson Davis, Alexander Duncan, Edmund P. Gaines, Andrew Jackson, J. E. Johnston, Mary Ann Randolph (Custis) Lee, Robert E. Lee, Eleanor Parke (Custis) Lewis, Leonidas Polk, John Slidell, and Martin Van Buren.

806. ISAAC BUTLER AND LELAND W. BUTLER PAPERS, 1818 (1830-1886) 1916. 1,631 items. Caroline County, Va.

Personal and business correspondence and business papers of the Butler family, Virginia planters and teachers. The early letters are from Isaac Butler's stepchildren, most of them being from James Childs and Emily (Childs) Ballard of Jackson County, Florida. Another section of material relates to the settlement of the estate of Isaac Butler (died at Loda, Illinois, 1857), for which Leland W. Butler was executor. The remainder consists of a long correspondence between Isaac's oldest son, Thomas, and his uncle, Leland, up to 1883; and family letters from relatives in Illinois, New York, and Ohio, describing social and economic conditions.

807. LOUISA BUTLER PAPERS, 1847 (1861-1865) 1874. 32 items. Stone Mountain (DeKalb County), Ga.

Family correspondence of the Butler family consisting of three brothers, all in the Confederate Army, and of two sisters. The letters reflect Civil War conditions, poverty of Reconstruction days and conditions around Palatka, Florida, where Dr. R. S. Butler settled after the war.

808. MARVIN BENJAMIN BUTLER PAPERS, 1861-1864. 21 items. Salem Center (Steuben County), Ind.

Personal correspondence between Marvin B. Butler, soldier in the 44th Indiana Infantry Volunteers and state legislator, and his future wife, Harriet M. Fuller, concerning camp life; military activities, especially the battle of Stone's River, Buell's pursuit of Bragg in 1862, and the Vicksburg campaign; his illness and subsequent discharge; and life on the home front.

809. NICHOLAS MURRAY BUTLER PAPERS, 1905. 1 item. New York, N.Y.

Letter from Nicholas Murray Butler (1862-1947), president of Columbia University, 1901-1945, to Sadler (perhaps Sir Michael Ernest Sadler, British educator) discussing his conversations with Kaiser Wilhelm II.

810. PIERCE BUTLER PAPERS, 1791-1814. 4 items. (Beaufort County), S.C.

Three letters of Pierce Butler (1744-1822), U.S. congressman, concerning legal matters and the payment of a mortgage; and a bill of exchange signed over to him in 1791.

811. ROBERT BUTLER LEDGER, 1832-1851. 1 vol. (200 pp.) Smithfield (Isle of Wight County), Va.

Personal accounts of Robert Butler, apparently a physician, including rental accounts.

812. WILLIAM BUTLER PAPERS, 1750, 1756. 2 items. Great Ogeechee District, Ga.

A land grant, and a plat for 200 acres of pine land.

813. ALBERT I. BUTNER PAPERS, 1820 (1870-1896) 1907. 66 items. Stokes and Forsyth counties, N.C.

Personal and business papers of Albert I. Butner, superintendent of schools in Forsyth County, consist of personal letters, including one of 1855 describing a balloon ascension at Salem, North Carolina; correspondence relating to education in North Carolina and school affairs in Forsyth County; rough minutes of the Forsyth County Board of Education, 1890-1895; and a temporary school register for Bethania Public School, 1904-1905. Correspondents include John Franklin Heitman and J. W. Giles.

814. ELIZA BUTTON PAPERS, 1864-1865. 13 items. Waterford (Saratoga County), N.Y.

Letters from Myron Adams, Jr., member of the U.S. Signal Corps, to Eliza concerning religion, education, and his plans to study law, with scattered references to military activities.

815. SIR THOMAS FOWELL BUXTON, FIRST BARONET, PAPERS, 1826. 1 item. London, England.

Letter from William Wilberforce to Sir Thomas Fowell Buxton, First Baronet (1786-1845), concerning Lord Grenville's suggestions for the abolition of slavery in the colonies, and personal matters.

816. GEORGE STEVENS BYNG, SECOND EARL OF STRAFFORD, PAPERS, 1837, 1847. 2 items. London, England.

Broadside copy of a letter from Lord Strafford (1806-1886), member of Parliament, to Thomas Arber supporting the parliamentary candidacy of George DeLacy Evans and John Temple Leader; and a letter from Lord Hardinge, governor general of India, concerning the size of the Indian army and the use of corporal punishment.

817. BENJAMIN FRANKLIN BYNUM PAPERS, 1806-1909. 299 items and 2 vols. Germanton (Stokes County), N.C.

Business and personal correspondence of the Bynum family includes letters between Hampton Bynum and John M. De Saussure concerning the claim of Bynum against an estate of which De Saussure was administrator, and several deeds of Bynum; reports and communications from schools attended by the Bynums, including Winston Male Academy, Kernersville Academy, Bingham School and Trinity College; letters from tenant farmers; letters from William Preston Bynum (b. 1861), and from R. S. Bynum who practiced law in Waxahachie, Texas, during the late 1870s; and letters from B. F. Bynum, Jr., to his father concerning the sale of plug tobacco in South Carolina and Georgia, 1871-1878, including references to prices, brokers' fees, evasions of revenue tax, and the difficulties of selling manufactured tobacco. Volumes include a commonplace book, 1874-1884, of W. P. Bynum containing diary entries for 1884, reminiscences, and lectures and comments on philosophical, scientific, and religious topics; and a scrapbook, 1875-1909, of W. P. Bynum II, containing clippings, addresses, and a biographical sketch of W. P. Bynum.

818. HARRY FLOOD BYRD PAPERS, 1928. 3 items. Richmond, Va.

Letter from Harry F. Byrd (1887-1966), governor of Virginia and U. S. senator, to Charles T. Lassiter, and Lassiter's reply, concerning the proposed amendments to the Virginia constitution and methods of publicizing them; and an invitation to a farewell dinner for Commander Richard Evelyn Byrd.

819. WILLIAM BYRD PAPERS, 1717-1757. 3 items. (180 pp.) Charles City County, Va.

Typed copies of correspondence and papers, 1720-1757, of William Byrd of Westover (1674-1744), colonial Virginia statesman, including notes, deeds, land grants, petitions, and other business papers from originals in the Brock collection, Huntington Library, San Marino, California (17 typescript pages); a photostat (162 pages) of his Secret History of the Dividing Line, 1728; and a letter from Byrd in London, 1717/1718, giving an account of his activities, particularly in regard to the Courts of Oyer and Terminer while agent for the Virginia Council of State.

820. WILLIAM BYRNES DIARY, 1863. 1 vol. Pennsylvania.

Diary of Lieutenant William Byrnes, 95th Regiment, Pennsylvania Volunteers, which describes campaigns at Chancellorsville, Gettysburg, and Rappahannock Station, as well as various picket actions and skirmishes. He discusses camp life, casualties, deserters, discipline, foraging, and prisoners, and mentions U.S. Generals Joseph J. Bartlett, George G. Meade, John Sedgwick, and Horatio G. Wright.

821. GEORGE GORDON NOEL-BYRON, SIXTH BARON BYRON, PAPERS, 1816-1817. 1 item. London, England.

Manuscript copy of a poem written by Lord Byron (1788-1824) to Thomas Moore which differs slightly from the version published in The Works of Lord Byron.

822. CHARLES H. CABANISS PAPERS, 1802 (1830-1877). 78 items. Halifax Courthouse (Halifax County), Va.

Family and business correspondence of Charles H. Cabaniss as sheriff of Halifax County and as a tobacco dealer; of William Cabaniss and other members of the Cabaniss family; and of Philip Howerton (b. 1800), deputy sheriff under Cabaniss.

823. ELBRIDGE G. CABANISS PAPERS, 1872-1903. 85 items. Savannah, Ga.

Business and family correspondence of Elbridge G. Cabaniss, particularly with his brother H. H. Cabaniss, manager of the Atlanta Journal, and J. W. Cabaniss, a Macon banker, centering on Georgia in the 1870s. Included are receipts of the American Legion of Honor.

824. CABELL FAMILY PAPERS, 1755-1909. 91 items and 5 vols. Virginia.

Miscellaneous papers of the descendants of Nicholas Cabell of "Liberty Hall," Nelson County, Virginia. Included are land grants; financial and legal papers of George Cabell, Jr., son of Nicholas; official papers of William H. Cabell (1772-1853), governor of Virginia, also a son of Nicholas; bills and receipts; letter of 1848 from Carter P. Johnson to James Lawrence Cabell (1813-1889), surgeon, and son of George, Jr., concerning education in Virginia; letters of William Daniel Cabell with copies of letters from Robert E. Lee, concerning Norwood High School and the erection of a chapel in honor of Lee; letters of Henry Coalter Cabell (1820-1889), son of William H., and his son, James Alston Cabell, pertaining to the administration of the estate of Jane (Alston) Cabell, Henry's wife; and letters of Brigadier General William Lewis Cabell (1827-1911), C.S.A., and Lieutenant General, Trans-Mississippi Department, United Confederate Veterans, concerning the growth of the department, his years as department commander, 1890-1907, and several veterans' reunions. Volumes include the chemistry notebook, 1883-1884, of Julian Mayo Cabell (b. 1860), son of Henry, while at the University of Virginia; and the records, 1861-1865, of a general hospital in Charlottesville, Virginia, directed by James Lawrence Cabell, including accounts, a list of patients, an invoice of medicines, and a letterpress book.

825. ELEAZAR CABLE PAPERS, 1866-1872. 4 items.

Two letters from Timothy Murphy concerning family matters, crops, the building of a road, and the Freehold Railroad; a letter from John Coffing pertaining to a lawsuit against the Housatonic Railroad; and a tax notice.

826. GEORGE WASHINGTON CABLE PAPERS, 1879-1922. 57 items. Northampton (Hampshire County), Mass., and New Orleans, La.

Papers of a George Washington Cable (1844-1925), novelist, relate chiefly to personal and routine matters. Included are several letters to Robert Underwood Johnson containing references to Cable's literary career; an engraving by Timothy Cole of the painting of Cable by Abbott Handerson Thayer, with Cable's signature attached; and an incomplete manuscript of a story.

827. ARTEMUS S. CADDELL PAPERS, 1838-1864. 84 items. Moore County, N.C.

Personal correspondence of A. S. Caddell, teacher and private in the 26th North Carolina Regiment, C.S.A., containing information on family, social, and religious life during the war, and desertion and draft evasion. Included are Caddell's contracts with the Moore County common schools, 1855-1862.

828. THOMAS CADELL, SR., AND THOMAS CADELL, JR., PAPERS, 1775-1832. 87 items. London, England.

Business and financial papers of Thomas Cadell, Sr. (1742-1802), and Thomas Cadell, Jr. (1773-1836), booksellers and publishers. The bulk of the correspondence pertains to Cadell's publication of the History and Antiquities of the Tower of London, by John Whitcomb Bayley (London: 1812 and 1821). Among other publications discussed are Joseph Warton's edition of The Works of Alexander Pope (London: 1797) and two works by Thomas Somerville, History of Great Britain During the Reign of Queen Anne (London: 1798) and Observations on a Passage in the Preface to Mr. Fox's Historical Work, Relative to the Character of Dr. Somerville as an Historian [1808?]. Included are correspondence with A. Strahan concerning Somerville's works and requests from Quintin Craufurd about certain publications.

829. CHARLES R. CADMAN PAPERS, 1918. 8 items. Toronto (Jefferson County), Ohio.

Family correspondence of Charles R. Cadman, U.S. Navy, describing life at Great Lakes Naval Station, his transfer to Philadelphia, and opinion on the duration of the war.

830. JOHN CADWALADER PAPERS, 1771, 1785. 2 items. "Bennett's Regulation," Kent County, Md.

Will of General John Cadwalader (1742-1786), and a bill for taxes due from the estate.

831. EMMA L. CAIN PAPERS, 1861-1869. 63 items. Olin (Iredell County) and Clarksville (Dare County), N.C.

Personal letters from Confederate soldiers in camps in Virginia and North Carolina, and from schoolmates.

832. PATRICK H. CAIN PAPERS, 1783-1940. 2,903 items and 1 vol. Mocksville and Settle (Davie County), N.C.

Personal, legal, business, and financial papers of the Cain family. Included are letters describing life and social customs in Georgia, 1824-1827; school life at girls' academies, 1843-1856, at Normal College (later Trinity College), 1855-1856, at a seminary, 1869, and at the University of North Carolina, 1871-1880; western migration and western lands; business methods; prices of products and services, the value of slaves, and wages and tenancy of freedmen; the life of Confederate soldiers, including accounts of military activities, especially First Manassas and Gettysburg, and comments on conditions in the army and on officers, Jefferson Davis, and Abraham Lincoln. Legal papers consist of land grants, deeds, mortgages, arrests and summonses for debts, promissory notes, and material relating to the administration of various estates. There are broadsides concerning Jonathan Worth and W. W. Holden. Financial records consist of tax receipts; accounts, 1889-1895, kept in advertising booklets; and a ledger containing patient accounts, 1906-1925, belonging to Dr. John M. Cain. Correspondents include George Burgess Anderson, Francis Asbury, Samuel Ashe, Kemp P. Battle, John Joseph Bruner, D. R. Bruton, Lyman Copeland Draper, David Moffatt Furches, Will H. Hayes, William Hill, Hamilton C. Jones, Leonidas Polk, Zebulon Vance, and Jonathan Worth.

833. JOHN S. CAIRNS PAPERS, 1896. 1 item. Weaverville (Buncombe County), N.C.

A list of birds observed in western North Carolina by Cairns.

834. WILLIAM CALDER PAPERS, 1861-1865. 2 items and 2 vols. Wilmington (New Hanover County), N.C.

Diaries of William Calder, Confederate soldier, concerning Hillsborough Academy, secession in Hillsboro and Raleigh, training at Garysburg, North Carolina, and Richmond, Virginia, and the final campaign against Sherman's army in North Carolina; and papers dealing with a leave of absence for William's brother, Robert.

835. DAVID FRANK CALDWELL PAPERS, 1851-1897. 22 items. Greensboro (Guilford County), N.C.

Letters from prominent North Carolina officials concerning internal affairs. A letter of 1864 reports on the trials of deserters and the shortage of rations.

836. ELIZA F. CALDWELL PAPERS, 1860-1874. 20 items. Santa Rosa (Sonoma County), Calif.

Personal letters of Eliza F. Caldwell from family and friends in Mississippi. Several letters during the Civil War describe prison conditions at Johnson's Island, Ohio. Letters in 1866 discuss social and economic conditions in Mississippi, and continuing secessionist influence as well as the possibility of renewed conflict with Union sympathizers.

837. JOHN CALDWELL PAPERS, 1857-1870. 6 items. North Carolina.

Letters to John Caldwell, a music teacher, concerning prospective students; letters from the Gaddy family in Arkansas describing crops, economic conditions, railroad construction, and religious activities; and letters from an itinerant minister on the Arkansas-Louisiana-Texas border concerning frontier conditions and religious matters.

838. TOD ROBINSON CALDWELL PAPERS, 1839-1874. 177 items. Morganton (Burke County), N.C.

Family, business, and political correspondence of Tod R. Caldwell (1818-1874), lieutenant governor, 1868-1871, and governor of North Carolina, 1871-1874, including material on Reconstruction in the state.

839. W. S. CALDWELL PAPERS, 1864. 2 items. Shelbyville (Shelby County), Ky.

Petitions of W. S. Caldwell, a merchant, concerning the revocation of his business license by officials of the Federal Army.

840. CATHERINE ANN CALHOUN PAPERS, 1847-1854. 4 items. Stewartsville (Richmond County), N.C.

Family letters to Catherine A. Calhoun, including references to horse-powered cotton gins in Louisiana, 1847, and farm prices, 1851.

841. [JAMES EDWARD CALHOUN?] LOGBOOK, 1817-1829. 1 vol. (248 pp.)

Logbook covering the cruises of the U.S.S. Congress in the West Indies and South America, 1817, and in South America, 1817-1818; the U.S.S. Constitution from the United States to Gibraltar, 1824; the U.S.S. Actress from Gibraltar to the United States, 1824-1825; the U.S.S. Macedonian in South America, 1826-1827; and the U.S.S. Boston in South America, 1827-1829. Included are reports on the weather, location and course, and descriptions of places visited.

842. JOHN CALDWELL CALHOUN PAPERS, 1765-1902. 382 items. Abbeville (Abbeville County), S.C.

The papers of the Calhoun family, comprised of family letters and documents. Letters discuss business, personal and family affairs; social life and customs; national and state politics; Indian affairs; slavery; and the government and constitution of the Confederate States of America. Documents, mainly 1771-1875, include bills, receipts, wills, estate papers, summonses, plantation accounts, and legal papers. Also the papers of John C. Calhoun (1782-1850), dealing with personal, family, business, and political affairs. Letters concern family matters; national and state politics; the Nullification Crisis; the presidential campaigns of 1840, 1844, and 1848; abolitionism and slavery; states' rights; major political figures; the Mexican War; tariffs; the Second Bank of the United States; railroads; agriculture; and Calhoun's service as Secretary of War, including material on Florida, the Creek and Cherokee Indians, and the Army.

843. WILLIAM LOWNDES CALHOUN PAPERS, 1892-1901. 8 items. Atlanta, Ga.

Letters of William L. Calhoun (1837-1908), public official and lieutenant colonel of the Fourth Battalion, Georgia Volunteers, include letters from John McIntosh Kell, adjutant general of Georgia, concerning routine battalion matters; and letters from Stephen D. Lee to Calhoun concerning their mutual involvement with the Confederate Veterans Association and the Confederate Soldiers' Home at Atlanta.

844. WILLIAM PATRICK CALHOUN PAPERS, (1903), 1912. 16 items. Edgefield (Edgefield County), S.C.

Letters of William Patrick Calhoun (b. 1851), attorney and nephew of John C. Calhoun, chiefly concern the controversy as to whether the last Confederate Cabinet meeting was held in Abbeville, South Carolina, or Washington, Georgia. Principal political figures are discussed. Also a letter of 1912 pertaining to the gubernatorial election in South Carolina.

845. CALHOUN DEBATING SOCIETY MINUTES, 1857-1858. 1 vol. (40 pp.) Plaquemines (Iberville Parish), La.

Constitution, bylaws, list of members, and minutes, including debates on historical and political questions.

846. NICHOLAS CALLAN SCRAPBOOK AND DIARY, 1860-1868. 2 vols. Washington, D.C.

The diary of Nicholas Callan, apparently a lawyer, covers the period 1860, 1867-1868, and concerns his law practice, state of the weather, politics, the unsettled condition of the country both before and after the Civil War, religion, and various government issues. The scrapbook contains various newspaper clippings concerning current political issues, especially the inauguration of President Ulysses S. Grant, 1869. The scrapbook, made from a book of records of the militia of the District of Columbia, contains a few readable pages of these militia records.

847. ELIZA CALLAWAY PAPERS, 1819-1825. 4 items. Virginia.

Bills and receipts of Eliza Callaway.

848. PHILIP POWELL CALVERT PAPERS, 1911-1933. 78 items. Philadelphia, Pa.

Letters to Philip P. Calvert, editor of the Entomological News, concerning articles for that journal, editorial policy, nomenclature in entomology, rules and suggestions for contributions to the journal, and the character of Fordyce Grinnell, Jr.

849. SAMUEL CALVIN PAPERS, 1792 (1838-1883) 1929. 2,757 items and 4 vols. Hollidaysburg (Blair County), Pa.

Personal, business, political, and legal papers of Samuel Calvin (1811-1890), lawyer and U.S. congressman, 1849-1851. Included are letters concerning local and state Whig politics, especially, 1846-1851; letters, reports and maps dealing with the Rico Reduction and Mining Company of Rico, Colorado; correspondence relating to national politics, especially the tariff and currency questions, slavery, and the Compromise of 1850; letters and notices regarding transportation in Pennsylvania by railroad, canals and roads; letters from Iowa concerning westward expansion, roads to the West and land prices; business correspondence, 1856, and two ledgers and a daybook, 1849-1857, of the Alleghany Forge and the Rebecca Furnace Company of Hollidaysburg; letters discussing real estate in Washington, D.C.; a ledger, 1835-1840, and a daybook, 1840-1845, of the Brookland Furnace, McVeytown, Pennsylvania; bills and receipts; and legal documents. Miscellaneous items include a detailed letter describing a cholera epidemic in Philadelphia, 1793; single issues of several newspapers; political circulars; and the constitution and minutes of the Old Warrior and Clay Club of Hollidaysburg, 1844.

850. CHURCHILL CALDON CAMBRELENG PAPERS, 1832, 1835. 2 items. Huntington (Suffolk County), N.Y.

Letter from Joel Roberts Poinsett to Churchill C. Cambreleng, U.S. congressman and chairman of the House Foreign Affairs Committee, concerning financial matters; and a letter from William C. Rives discussing the French Claims Controversy as expressed in Andrew Jackson's annual message to Congress.

851. GIDEON D. CAMDEN PAPERS, 1834-1888. 37 items. Clarksburg (Harrison County), W. Va.

Business, personal, and legal papers of Judge Gideon D. Camden, including a letter of 1887 describing the Loomis National Library Association.

852. WILLIAM S. CAMDEN PAPERS, 1861-1863. 4 items. Temperance (Nelson County), Va.

Personal letters of Camden, probably a Confederate soldier.

853. CAMDEN AND CHARLESTON STEAMBOAT COMPANY DAYBOOK, 1836-1889. 1 vol. (276 pp.) Kershaw County and Charleston County, S.C.

Financial accounts of a steamboat company.

854. KATE CAMENGA PAPERS, 1862-1865. 25 items. South Brookfield (Madison County), N.Y.

Letters to Kate Camenga from a soldier in the 7th New York Battery, 10th Corps, U.S.A., concerning military activities around Richmond, 1864-1865, and from Diedrich F. Camenga at the U.S. Army General Hospital at Point Lookout, Maryland, describing the food, Negro soldiers, weather, nuns as nurses, and the search for John Wilkes Booth.

855. C. W. CAMMACK PAPERS, 1854-1890. 3 items. New Orleans, La.

A letter from W. S. Slaughter; a biographical sketch of Robert Cammack, farmer, and a soldier in the War of 1812, and father of C. W. Cammack; and an obituary of Robert Cammack.

856. SAMUEL CAMP PAPERS, 1861-1894. 78 items. Great Barrington (Berkshire County), Mass.

Business papers of Samuel Camp, physician during the Civil War, concerning recruitment, purchases of substitutes, physical examinations, and medical prescriptions.

857. ANNA B. CAMPBELL PAPERS, 1815 (1861-1865). 50 items. South Londonderry (Windham County), Vt.

Principally the letters of Private Henry L. Campbell, 2nd Regiment, U.S. Sharpshooters, to his mother, Anna B. Campbell, concerning his activities.

858. CHARLES CAMPBELL PAPERS, 1617-1895. 1,313 items and 5 vols. Petersburg (Dinwiddie County), Va.

Copies of historical documents and letters, and personal papers of Charles Campbell (1807-1876), historian, editor, and antiquarian. Included are original letters from St. George Tucker, Lewis Cass, Pierre Soule, Edward Everett, Beverley Randolph, Andrew Jackson, Robert Beverley, and others, as well as copies of letters from Richard Henry Lee, Arthur Lee, Theodorick Bland, Jr., Captain John Smith, John Randolph of Roanoke, John Adams, Powhatan Ellis, Patrick Henry, John Jay, and others. The papers also contain rough drafts and preliminary notes for Campbell's publications, a number of manuscript poems, and a transcription of the minute book of the city council of Richmond, Virginia, 1782-1795. The volumes contain personal accounts, records of Anderson Academy, Petersburg, Virginia, of which Campbell was principal, and historical notes.

859. SIR COLIN CAMPBELL, FIRST BARON CLYDE, PAPERS, 1818. 1 item. Glasgow, Lanarkshire, Scotland.

Letter from Sir Colin Campbell, First Baron Clyde (1792-1863), field marshal, to John McLean concerning the end of a tour of duty with the 60th Royal Americans; the unit's commander, John Forster Fitzgerald; and personal matters.

860. DANIEL K. CAMPBELL PAPERS, 1858-1865. 13 items. Cumberland County, N.C.

Personal letters to Daniel K. Campbell, a soldier stationed at Camp Leventhrop, Halifax County, North Carolina, and at various places in Virginia.

861. DAVID A. CAMPBELL PAPERS, 1851. 1 item. Jonesville (Lee County), Va.

Letter from David A. Campbell to his son, accused of murder in Alabama, concerning the crime, and criticizing Judge Benjamin Estil of the fifteenth judicial district of Virginia.

862. LORD FREDERICK CAMPBELL PAPERS, 1772. 1 item. Coombe Bank, Kent, England.

Personal letter from Sir Robert Murray Keith, army officer and diplomat, to Lord Frederick Campbell (1729-1816), member of Parliament and Lord Clerk Register of Scotland.

863. GEORGE DOUGLAS CAMPBELL, EIGHTH DUKE OF ARGYLL, PAPERS, ca. 1863-1874. 7 items. London, England.

Letters of George, Eighth Duke of Argyll (1823-1900), British statesman, concerning the drafting of a code of laws for India, the use of a narrow gauge railroad system in India, Indian revenue, Anglo-American and Anglo-Confederate relations, and charges against Britain relating to the Confederate raiders Alabama and Florida. Correspondents include John Romilly, Robert Francis Fairlie, Sir Charles E. Trevelyan, and Charles Sumner.

864. SIR HUGH PURVES-HUME-CAMPBELL, SEVENTH BARONET, PAPERS, 1839-1884. 59 items. London, England.

Letters written to Sir Hugh Hume Campbell (b. 1812) and his second wife, Juliana Rebecca (Fuller) Hume Campbell, are mainly replies to social invitations. Several letters concern Lady Campbell's book, Prayer, published in 1884. Correspondents include literary figures and titled persons of society.

865. JAMES LYLE CAMPBELL PAPERS, 1781-1920. 788 items. Gerrardstown (Berkeley County), W. Va.

Correspondence and legal and business papers of the Campbell and related Lyle, McKeowen, Henshaw, Burns, and Tabb families, centering around the career of James Lyle Campbell (ca. 1810-1875), farmer and attorney, but also covering that of his father, James Campbell, and of his son, James W. Campbell, (ca. 1840-ca. 1910). The bulk of the collection consists of legal papers, receipts, bills, land deeds and indentures, wills, estate and executors' papers, and court orders and opinions. Family correspondence comments on life in Berkeley County, Virginia; farming in Virginia and Missouri; commodity prices and cattle in Missouri; Kansas and the "border ruffians"; railroads; politics, especially the Know-Nothing Party; and Confederate sentiment.

866. JAMES MACNABB CAMPBELL PAPERS, 1892. 1 item. Bombay, India.

Letter from James MacNabb Campbell, Indian official and compiler of the Bombay Gazetteer, discussing the Scythian invasions and rule of India in the second to the fifth centuries, A.D.

867. JOHN CAMPBELL PAPERS, 1795-1814. 11 items. Edinburgh, Scotland.

Letters to John Campbell (1766-1840), Scottish philanthropist, concerning arrangements for taking a group of African children from Sierra Leone to Britain for education; missionaries; Campbell's religious work and the support of the Cameronian Presbyterians; and family affairs of Thomas Babington. Correspondents include William Wilberforce, Zachary Macaulay, Thomas Babington, Charles Grant, and Henry Thornton.

868. SIR JOHN NICHOLL ROBERT CAMPBELL, SECOND BARONET, PAPERS, 1814 (1824-1839) 1841. 260 items. Carrick Buoy, Ballyshannon, County Donegal, Ireland.

Papers of Sir John Nicholl Robert Campbell (1799-1870), army officer and diplomat in the East India Company, concerning Campbell's service as second assistant and as envoy to Persia. Correspondence, memoranda, and documents detail the problems of divided authority among the British Foreign Office, the East India Company, and the Supreme Government in India; efforts to stabilize the Persian government and to minimize Russian influence; diplomatic relations with Persia under envoys Sir Henry Willock, Sir John Macdonald Kinneir, Sir John Campbell, Sir Henry Ellis, and Sir John McNeill; the conflict between Willock and Campbell to succeed Kinneir; British military aid to the Shah of Persia; charges brought against Sir John's official conduct; and relations between Persia and Turkey. Correspondents include Abbas Mirza; James Brant; William Blunt; Lord William Cavendish Bentinck; Sir Henry Ellis; Francis Farrant; Sir Robert Grant; Edward Law, First Earl of Ellenborough; Sir John Macdonald Kinneir; Sir John Malcolm; Sir John McNeill; George Swinton; George Willock; Sir Henry Willock; W. H. Wyburd; and William Harry Vane, First Duke of Cleveland.

869. ROBERT CAMPBELL ACCOUNT BOOK, 1779-1781. 1 vol. (200 pp.) Beaufort (Beaufort County), S.C.

Financial records of a British officer during the American Revolution.

870. THOMAS CAMPBELL PAPERS, 1824-1826. 26 items. Philadelphia, Pa.

Papers of Thomas Campbell, a merchant, principally relating to the indebtedness of the firm of I. and F. Gorin. The papers concern the collection of debts, the purchase and shipment of supplies, and a creditor firm, John Gill, Jr., & Co. Also, a partnership agreement between Campbell, and Joseph P. Brown and John M. Shirley, concerning the operation of a store in Russellville, Kentucky.

871. ZOÉ JANE CAMPBELL PAPERS, 1855-1898. 152 items. New Orleans, La.

Principally family letters to Zóe Jane Campbell during the Civil War concerning Confederate Army matters such as troop movements, immorality among the soldiers, complaints against officers, soldiers' pay, and health conditions. There is considerable information on the U.S. military prisons at Elmira, New York, and at Belleville, Louisiana. Also included is material on social life and customs in New York and Washington, D.C., and on the internal disorders in northern Mexico in the late 1850s.

872. CAMPBELL FAMILY PAPERS, 1731-1969. 8,334 items and 37 vols. Abingdon (Washington County), Va.

Family, business, and political correspondence of David Campbell (1779-1859), governor of Virginia, 1837-1840, lieutenant colonel in the War of 1812, major general in the state militia west of Blue Ridge mountains; and of William Bowen Campbell (1807-1867), governor of Tennessee, 1847-1848, and member of U.S. Congress, 1837-1843, 1865-1866; and of their families, friends, and political associates.

David Campbell (1779-1859), a deist and devotee to the reforms of the American Revolution, left a set of remarkable papers concerned with many activities, including education, politics, wars, religion, household economy, methods of travel, slavery, secession, commission business, settlement of the old Southwest, legal practice, and general mercantile pursuits. Included also are many letters concerned with the War of 1812, in which he served as major and lieutenant colonel of infantry, with information bearing on quarrels among officers, inefficiency of military organization, courts-martial, lack of patriotism, and promotion of officers over their seniors.

From 1814 until 1837, while David Campbell was political leader of western Virginia, his papers reflect his career, throwing light on state politics, state militia, affairs of the office of clerk of court, which position he held, many intimate details of the Virginia Assembly, in which he served, 1820-1824, and accounts of various journeys made to Philadelphia when buying goods for his mercantile establishment in Abingdon. Campbell's papers for 1837-1840 contain material on the common schools, the panic of 1837, establishment of the Virginia Military Institute, Lexington, and the state asylum for the deaf, dumb, and blind. After 1840 his papers refer to his activities as school commissioner, as trustee of an academy and of Emory and Henry College, Washington County, Virginia, as justice of the peace, and as a planter.

In letters to his wife, his nieces, and his nephews are many references to Thomas Mann Randolph, Winfield Scott, the bank and sub-treasury of the Jackson-Van Buren era, disapproval of emotion in religion, concern for the plight of the free Negro, and interest in historical works and literature. Included also are accounts of various Revolutionary battles in which his forebears took part, of the early history of the Abingdon vicinity, and of religious denominations.

Letters, 1785-1811, to David Campbell include those of his uncle, Arthur Campbell (1742-1811), famous Indian fighter and Revolutionary patriot, containing treatises on democratic government; comments on thought of French philosophers of the eighteenth century; reminiscences of the Revolution; and comments on European affairs, especially the rise of despotism under Napoleon. Other letters to David Campbell include many from William C. Rives during the most active period of Campbell's leadership in Virginia politics. Letters to Maria Hamilton (Campbell) Campbell (1783-1859), wife of Governor David Campbell, from her father, Judge David Campbell (1753-1832), contain information on the early settlement of eastern Tennessee, government and politics of the young state, and information on Archibald Roane, his brother-in-law and an early governor of Tennessee.

Letters of John Campbell (1789-186?), member of the executive council of the governor of Virginia, member of the state constitutional convention of Alabama, 1819, treasurer of the United States, and brother of Governor David Campbell, contain information on student life at Princeton College, Princeton, New Jersey, prominent men and events in Richmond, 1810-1817 and 1819-1829, War of 1812, John Taylor of Caroline, Virginia penitentiary, Spencer Roane, states' rights, Lafayette's visit, Jacksonian campaign of 1824-1828, Virginia constitutional convention of 1829, Richmond Theatre fire of 1811, Andrew Jackson as president, Peggy O'Neale affair, storage of specie in 1837, rise of the Whig party, Washington gossip, and Washington bureaucracy. In the letters of Arthur Campbell (1791-1868), brother of Governor David Campbell and government clerk in Washington, 1831-1851, are accounts of mercantile pursuits in Tennessee; Andrew Jackson; Thomas Ritchie; and Washington gossip.

Letters of James Campbell (1794-1848), lawyer and member of Tennessee legislature, contain accounts of his college life and studies at Greenville, Tennessee, law practice in Tennessee, settlement of Alabama, Tennessee legislation, literary and historical works, the theater in Nashville, and dramatic literature of his day.

Letters and papers of Governor William Bowen Campbell, nephew of Governor David Campbell, contain accounts of his legal training in the law school of Henry St. George Tucker at Winchester, Virginia; law practice in Tennessee; services as circuit judge; activities in Creek and Seminole wars, 1836; small-scale farming operations; mercantile establishment in Carthage, Tennessee; firm of Perkins, Campbell, and Company, commission merchants in New Orleans; banking business as president of the Bank of Middle Tennessee at Lebanon; Mexican War; activities of the Whig party in Tennessee; career as governor; plans to prevent secession; bitter local fighting of the Civil War; and his career as a Unionist during and after the war, including his disappointment in methods of Reconstruction by Congress while he was a member of that body in 1865-1866.

Of the many letters by women, those of Virginia Tabitha Jane (Campbell) Shelton, niece and adopted daughter of Governor David Campbell, contain valuable information on social events in Richmond while her uncle was governor; household economy; dress; slavery; methods of travel; literary works; conditions of Union University, Murfreesboro, Tennessee, Brownsville Female Academy, Brownsville, Tennessee, and West Tennessee College, Jacksonville, Tennessee, where her husband, William Shelton, taught; political campaigns; slavery; and a variety of items important in the social history of the period. Included in the collection also are the letters of Adine Turner, remarkable for their literary excellence and sparkling wit. Numerous letters from relatives in Arkansas reveal much information connected with the early history of that state. Letters of the McClung family of East Tennessee contain information on the

settlement, growth, and Civil War in that area.
Also included are papers for several related families, including the Owens, Montgomerys, Kelleys, and Newnans. Papers, 1811-1831, concern the estate of Hugh Montgomery, and a Moravian tract on that land. Letters in the 1830s include several from Daniel Newnan, U.S. congressman from Georgia, dealing with Andrew Jackson, Sam Houston, and political corruption. Letters of the Owen family, originally of North Carolina, deal with Daniel Grant, a Methodist minister of Georgia, 1788-1796, his opposition to the Baptists, and the disturbance of his conscience by the question of owning slaves; the Great Revival of 1800 as described by Thomas Owen; and medical education in Philadelphia of John Owen, 1810-1812, and of his sons, Benjamin Rush Owen (1813-1849) and John Owen (1825-1889). Papers of David C. Kelley include letters concerning his education in medical school at the University of Nashville, 1850s, and his service as missionary in China, along with his wife, Amanda (Harris) Kelley, 1855; several writings by him, including "A New Philosophical Discovery"; legal papers; and family correspondence with his second wife, Mary Owen (Campbell) Kelley, 1870s and 1880s, and his son, David C. Kelley, Jr., 1890s and early twentieth century.

Genealogical material includes two notebook tablets containing copies of North Carolina and Tennessee wills, deeds, marriage records, and other documents pertaining to the Wherry, Bowen, Montgomery, Newnan, Campbell, and Kelley families. There are religious writings, poetry, leaflets, booklets, and clippings. Volumes are chiefly account books of Governor William B. Campbell. Also included are a daily journal kept by David Campbell while governor of Virginia, a volume containing copies of his wife's letters to him, 1812-1825, a short diary kept by William B. Campbell during the Mexican War, a diary of John D. Owen, and a photograph album containing pictures of members of the Campbell, Kelley, Pilcher, Owen, and Lambuth families.

Among the correspondents are Joseph Anderson, William S. Archer, Alexander Barry, Thomas Barrow, John Bell, William Blount, Willie Blount, O. H. Browning, William G. Brownlow, B. F. Butler, Joseph C. Cabell, A. Campbell, David Campbell, William B. Campbell, William P. A. Campbell, Newton Cannon, Mathew Carey, George Christian, Henry Clay, Thomas Claiborne, I. A. Coles, Edmund Cooper, J. J. Crittenden, Claude Crozet, Jefferson Davis, L. C. Draper, J. H. Eaton, Benjamin Estill, Emerson Etheridge, M. Fillmore, S. M. Fite, William H. Foote, E. H. Foster, Joseph Gales, Horatio Gates, M. P. Gentry, William A. Graham, Felix Grundy, A. P. Hayne, G. F. Holmes, George W. Hopkins, Andrew Jackson, Cave Johnson, Charles C. Johnston, William B. Lewis, L. McLane, Bishop James Madison, A. J. Marchbanks, P. Mayo, R. J. Meigs, William Munford, P. N. Nicholas, A. O. P. Nicholson, Thomas Parker, John M. Patton, Balie Peyton, Timothy Pickering, Franklin Pierce, J. R. Poinsett, James Knox Polk, William C. Preston, J. A. Quitman, J. G. M. Ramsey, T. J. Randolph, T. M. Randolph, William C. Rives, Thomas Ritchie, A. Roane, Wyndham Robertson, Theodore Roosevelt, Edmund Ruffin, Benjamin Rush, John Rutherfoord, Winfield Scott, Alexander Smith, William B. Sprague, A. Stevenson, Jordan Stokes, W. B. Stokes, A. H. H. Stuart, Johnston Taylor, Zachary Taylor, Waddy Thompson, H. St. G. Tucker, Martin Van Buren, J. W. C. Watson, Daniel Webster, Gideon Welles, H. L. White, J. S. Yerger, and F. K. Zollicoffer.

873. JOSÉ DEL CAMPILLO Y COSÍO PAPERS, 1731-1743. 2 vols. Spain.

Bound, handwritten manuscript of <u>Nuevo sistema de Govierno Económico para la America</u> . . . , written in 1743 but not published until 1789; and a letter book containing the correspondence of José del Campillo with Don José Patiño, Spanish Prime Minister, and with the Duque de Montemar, General of the Italian Expedition, concerning the Spanish military expeditions in Italy in the early 1730s.

874. WILLIAM BEALL CANDLER ACCOUNT BOOK, 1878. 1 vol. Villa Rica (Carroll and Douglas counties), Ga.

Account book of a general merchant.

875. CANE CREEK FACTORY MINUTE BOOK, 1837-1857. 1 vol. Cane Creek, N.C.

Records of a cotton mill.

876. DUNCAN S. CANNADY PAPERS, 1845-1865. 9 items and 1 vol. New Light (Wake County), N.C.

Business papers of D. S. Cannady, general merchant and cotton factor.

877. CHARLES JOHN CANNING, EARL CANNING PAPERS, 1842-1862. 4 items. London, England.

A manuscript minute entitled "Services of Civil Officers and others during the Mutiny and Rebellion" concerns the mutiny of the Bengal Army in 1857-1858. Miscellaneous letters including two written while Canning was under secretary of state for foreign affairs (1841-1846).

878. GEORGE CANNING PAPERS, 1797-1827. 17 items. London, England.

Miscellaneous items concerning Canning's official and personal business, including a letter to Lord Bexley, April 11, 1827, pertaining to Canning's formation of a government and an unsigned memorandum of July 23, 1797, recording a consultation with Canning about British attempts to negotiate an end to the French war.

879. JAMES CANNON, JR., PAPERS, 1869-1955. 12,046 items and 10 vols. Richmond, Va., and Washington, D.C.

Methodist clergyman, journalist, and leader in the prohibition movement. Diaries, correspondence, reports, minutes, journals, articles, legal papers, pamphlets, obituaries, and other papers. Main interest centers in the material reflecting Cannon's part in the presidential campaign of 1928; the coverage is mainly for 1921-1937. Much material relates to Cannon's activities in the Anti-saloon League of America, the Anti-Saloon League of Virginia, the Board of Temperance and Social Service of the Methodist Episcopal Church, South, the World League Against Alcoholism, the General Conference and the Virginia quarterly conferences of the Methodist Episcopal Church, South, Methodist missionary enterprises, and world conferences of temperance groups. Other papers pertain to his leadership in the effort to unify the northern and southern branches of the Methodist Church, the Senate investigation of his expenditures in the anti-Smith campaign of 1928, his participation in a lawsuit against Randolph-Macon College, and his leadership in establishing the Lake Junaluska (N.C.) assembly grounds of the Methodist Church. Lesser groups of earlier papers relate to the founding and operation of Blackstone College for Girls, which Cannon headed (1894-1918) and his editorial work with the Baltimore and Richmond Christian Advocate and its predecessor, the Southern Methodist Recorder. Correspondents include Harry F. Byrd, Carter Glass, Josephus Daniels, Cordell Hull, Herbert Hoover, Frank Knox, William G. McAdoo, H. L. Mencken, Collins Denny, Gerald P. Nye, Warren A. Candler, Charles Evans Hughes, John R. Mott, Edwin D. Mouzon, Claude A. Swanson, Woodrow Wilson, Charles C. Carlin, Charles Curtis, Walter F. George, Andrew Mellon, Robert F. Wagner, William Hodges Mann, and G. W. Ochs-Oakes.

880. CANTERBURY CLUB MINUTES, 1896-1898. 1 vol. Durham, N.C.

Minute book of a literary club of Durham with a record of programs.

881. JOHN CANTEY PAPERS, 1848-1863. 11 items. Camden (Kershaw County), S.C.

Personal and business correspondence of John Cantey, Confederate soldier. One letter from John Cantey to J. L. Manning concerns bank notes and endorsements; another letter, 1860, describes the spirit of the people and business conditions in Memphis, Tennessee, at the outbreak of the Civil War; and the remaining letters are to his wife and concern plantation affairs, runaway slaves, troop movements, procuring and making salt, and scarcity of food during the Civil War.

882. HENRY CAPEN PAPERS, 1856-1924. 273 items. Bloomington (McLean County), Ill.

Letters to friends and relatives advising on financial conditions, particularly in 1873 and 1876, and specific advice on mortgages, loans, stock purchases, and leases. There are numerous references to religious matters and several financial pledges to the New School Presbyterian Church.

883. ELLISON CAPERS PAPERS, 1860 (1861-1865) 1906. 167 items. Columbia (Richland County), and Charleston, S.C.

Letters and papers of a Confederate general who became a clergyman in the Protestant Episcopal Church and, eventually, Episcopal Bishop of South Carolina. The collection consists, for the most part, of Civil War letters from Capers to his wife dealing with war and religion, including descriptions of the events leading up to the surrender of Fort Sumter in Charleston, 1860-1861; the defense of Charleston in 1863; the Chattanooga campaign, September 1863; and the Atlanta campaign of 1864. Several postwar letters deal with the Atlanta and Chattanooga campaigns and there are scattered references to Capers' career in the church. A few maps or sketches of troop movements accompany the letters and there is a brief diary for August-December, 1861.

884. HARRIETTE CAPERTON PAPERS, 1856-1865. 1 vol. "Elmwood," Union (Monroe County), W. Va.

Autograph album of a student at Virginia Female Institute in Staunton, Virginia.

885. CAPITOLI DELLA COMPAGNIA DELL ALMA CROCE DI LUCCA, 1591. 1 vol. (75 pp.) Italy.

Rules of the company of the Almighty Cross of Lucca, an organization of artisans under the auspices of the Roman Catholic Church.

886. EDWARD CARDWELL, FIRST VISCOUNT CARDWELL, PAPERS. 1854, 1871. 2 items. London, England.

Miscellaneous political correspondence.

887. SIR BENJAMIN HALLOWELL CAREW PAPERS, 1794-1831. 55 items. Beddington Park, Surrey, England.

Miscellaneous aspects of Carew's career in the Royal navy, primarily during his service in the wars with France, 1794-1814, and his time as commander-in-chief on the Irish coast, 1816-1818.

888. SIR REGINALD POLE-CAREW PAPERS, 1895-1898. 22 items. Antony, County Cornwall, England.

Letters to a British army officer from prominent contemporary figures including Sir Frederick Sleigh Roberts, First Earl Roberts; Sir George Stuart White; and Sir John James Hood Gordon. Correspondence concerns Indian military and political affairs for the most part, particularly campaigns on the northwest frontier and the application of Pole-Carew for military office in India.

889. HENRY CHARLES CAREY PAPERS, 1860-1874. 4 items. Philadelphia, Pa.

Miscellaneous letters concerned, for the most part, with Carey's writings and speeches.

890. MATHEW CAREY PAPERS, 1802. 1 item. Philadelphia, Pa.

Letter from Joseph Priestley concerning two works that he was submitting for publication.

891. JAMES MANDEVILLE CARLISLE PAPERS, 1836-1872. 66 items. Washington, D.C.

Private and legal correspondence of James M. Carlisle (1814-1877), a prominent Washington lawyer and counsel for Jefferson Davis, referring to land claims in Mexico and the claims of war-impoverished Southerners.

892. THOMAS CARLYLE PAPERS, 1809-1927. 92 items. London, England. Restricted.

Miscellaneous correspondence, papers, and clippings. Literary correspondence includes expressions of opinion about a number of authors and books; Carlyle's opinion on the formation of an authors' society; letters to his secretary, Henry Larkin, about details of editing; discussion of drama; and letters concerned with the publication of his work and the work of others. There are also a number of personal letters from Carlyle or his wife; fragments of Carlyle's notes and manuscripts for _History of Friedrich II of Prussia Called Frederick the Great_ and _Critical and Miscellaneous Essays_; and a volume of clippings on Carlyle's life and work compiled by his biographer, David Alec Wilson.

893. MARGARET CAROLINE (STOCKTON) CARMICHAEL PAPERS, 1859-1871. 130 items. Statesville (Iredell County), N.C.

The bulk of the collection consists of letters to Margaret Stockton from William W. Carmichael of Abilene, Kansas, before their marriage in May, 1870. Included also are six Civil War letters, and letters from school friends whom Margaret Stockton knew at Concord Female College, Statesville, North Carolina.

894. THOMAS PETTERS CARNES PAPERS, 1794-1795. 4 items. Milledgeville (Baldwin County), Ga.

Personal correspondence of Thomas P. Carnes (1762-1820), lawyer, legislator, judge, and member of U.S. Congress, 1793-1795. The letters, written by Carnes while attending Congress, include comments on the affairs of the nation, Barbary pirates, John Jay's mission to London, and the attempt of the United States to maintain prestige among European powers.

895. CAROLINA MILITARY INSTITUTE PAPERS, 1875-1876. 1 vol. (90 pp.) Charlotte (Mecklenburg County), N.C.

Minutes of the Cadet Polytechnic Society.

896. SIR JOSEPH PHILIPPE RENÉ ADOLPHE CARON PAPERS, 1892-1893. 196 items. Ottawa, Ontario, Canada.

Clippings, mostly editorials, concerning charges that Caron had used government funds to support Conservative Party candidates in the elections of 1887.

897. CAROTHERS COAL COMPANY PAPERS, 1936-1941. 81 items and 4 vols. Selma (Dallas County), Ala.

Bills and receipts of the Carothers Coal Company and other firms, including the Katzenburg Coal Company. The collection also includes two daybooks and two ledgers.

898. JULIAN SHAKESPEARE CARR PAPERS, 1885-1976. 12 items and 1 vol. Durham (Durham County), N.C.

Two routine letters of a tobacco and textile manufacturer and civic leader. The collection also contains clippings and photographs pertaining to the Carr family and homes; a farm journal (1910-1911) with directives from Carr to his manager, B. S. Skinner; and samples of chewing and twist tobacco and handmade cigarettes produced in the 1880s at Blackwell's Durham Tobacco Company.

899. MARIA (GRAHAM) CARR PAPERS, 1892. 1 item. Harrisonburg (Rockingham County), Va.

Manuscript copy of "My Recollections of Rocktown now known as Harrisonburg from 1817-1820" includes comments on celebrations, religious activities, schools, and anecdotes about local residents.

900. MARY M. CARR DIARY, 1860-1865. 1 vol. (154 pp.) Bastrop (Morehouse Parish), La.

Concerned with day-to-day life on a cotton plantation and the relationship of the Carrs with their neighbors and friends.

901. OBED WILLIAM CARR PAPERS, 1855-1885. 22 items. Trinity College (Randolph County), N.C.

Papers relating to the leave of absence of Obed W. Carr (b. 1833) from Trinity College, where he was professor of Greek, for Confederate service, and his resignation from the army because of ill health. Two items concern the financial affairs of Trinity College. Included also is a typewritten copy of Carr's journal, with scattered entries covering 1855-1878, although the greater part relates to the Civil War.

902. VIRGINIA (SPENCER) CARR PAPERS, 1867-1977. 4,000 items. Columbus (Muscogee County), Ga.

Correspondence, notes, clippings, and other materials gathered by Professor Carr during her research for and the writing of her biography of Carson McCullers, The Lonely Hunter (Garden City, N.Y.: Doubleday, 1975). The collection contains four groups of papers. Alphabetical files, 1867-1976, 10 boxes, consist of correspondence of Virginia Carr with McCullers' literary, musical, and theatrical colleagues and friends, both famous and ordinary. These letters also reflect the relations between Carr and the McCullers family and the executors of Carson McCullers' estate, and with the publishers of the biography. Persons represented include Elizabeth Ames, W. H. Auden, Leonard Bernstein, Paul Bowles, John Ciardi, David Diamond, Granville Hicks, John Huston, Jordan Massee, Louis Untermeyer, Eudora Welty, Tennessee Williams, and many others. Truman Capote is mentioned frequently.
Research material files, 1907-1976, 3 boxes, arranged alphabetically, include clippings, articles, reviews, copies of correspondence, and notes on McCullers' life and career, with copies of some letters from the alphabetical or family files. There is also a detailed chronology of McCullers' life; genealogical data about the McCullers, Smith, Waters, and Gachet families; interview notes; acknowledgments for assistance during research and writing; and letters received in response to the book.
The McCullers family correspondence files, 1933-1967, 1 box, contain copies of letters by Carson (Smith) McCullers, her husband James Reeves McCullers, and her mother Marguerite (Waters) Smith; most of the items are from Carson to David Leo Diamond, 1940s, and to John Huston, 1966-1967.
The draft files, 1969-1975, 2 boxes, contain a copy of Virginia Carr's doctoral dissertation on McCullers (Florida State University, 1969); notes for the dissertation; galley and foundry proofs for The Lonely Hunter; and portions of the manuscript for the book, edited with marginalia by David Diamond, Leo Lerman, Eleanor (Clark) Warren, and others.

903. SNOAD B. CARRAWAY PAPERS, 1857-1864. 8 items. Kinston (Lenoir County), N.C.

Business letters of Snoad B. Carraway, Lenoir County planter, pertaining to the sale of cotton on the New York market; and his will.

904. JOHN WARREN CARRIGAN PAPERS, 1817-1901. 318 items and 2 vols. Cabarrus County, N.C.

Family correspondence covering rather completely the lives of the eleven children (Andrew Noel, Catherine, Cornelia, John Warren, Margaret Rebecca, Martha Matilda, Mary, Nancy Elizabeth, Samuel K., Sarah, and William Adams) of James Carrigan (1788-1843), planter, showing especially the struggles and achievements of the seven children by his first wife who were orphaned by his death. The letters were written from Alabama, Arkansas, North Carolina, South Carolina, and Texas, from members of the family variously engaged in farming, medicine, textile work (cotton mills), mercantile business, and teaching. Included also are a few letters from Andrew Noel Carrigan, dealing with his service in the Confederate Army, and a daybook of Samuel K. Carrigan and a ledger of William Adams Carrigan.

905. ISAAC HOWELL CARRINGTON PAPERS, 1842-1945. 1,537 items. Richmond, Va.

Correspondence and papers of a lawyer and Confederate officer. Letters include Carrington's personal and official correspondence while he was serving as provost marshal of Richmond, Virginia, from 1863-1865, and refer to problems of supply and discipline, camp life, reports of troop movements and engagements, routine orders, and Confederate and Virginia politics. The papers also relate to Carrington's law practice with Robert Ould from 1865 to 1881 and contain the autograph collection of his son, Seddon Carrington, and his daughter, Mary Coles Carrington.

906. WILLIAM A. CARRINGTON PAPERS, 1863-1864. 14 items. Richmond, Va.

Correspondence and papers of William A. Carrington, a physician and medical director (with the Army of Northern Virginia?), dealing with transfers of medical officers, complaints and comments on existing arrangements, contracts with physicians, and other matters concerning medicine and surgery during the Civil War.

907. WILLIAM FONTAINE CARRINGTON PAPERS, 1809 (1862-1867). 19 items. Cole's Ferry (Charlotte County), Va.

Letters of William F. Carrington, U.S. and later Confederate Navy surgeon, containing opinions on secession in Virginia, and an inventory of medicine on board the Confederate States ram Baltic.

908. JEAN DE CARRO PAPERS, 1805-1841.
1 item. Carlsbad, Czechoslovakia.

Letter pertaining to the introduction of vaccination into Ceylon.

909. CHARLES CARROLL PAPERS, 1847.
2 items. Doughoregan Manor (Howard County), Md.

Letters concerning livestock, written by Charles Carroll (1801-1862), agriculturist of Maryland, to Colonel Josiah Ware, of Jefferson County, West Virginia.

910. THOMAS CARROLL AND [M. I.?] MONTGOMERY ACCOUNT BOOK AND INVENTORY, 1847-1859. 2 vols. Ridgeway (Warren County), N.C.

Business records of Ridgeway merchants.

911. SAMUEL T. CARROW PAPERS, 1866-1877.
2 vols. Beaufort County, N.C.

A ledger, 1866-1869, contains accounts of Carrow's store at Washington, North Carolina, which apparently ceased operation about 1868. Payments are recorded by cash, goods, and labor. A ledger, 1868-1877, primarily relates to Carrow's sizeable farm, but also includes entries for his employment as sheriff, 1868-1871, accounts for overseers of roads, 1868-1869, and taxes collected, 1870. The farm accounts reveal labor performed in exchange for merchandise, including work done by tenants. There are also charges for use of Carrow's cotton gin and press.

912. ALEXANDER CARSON PAPERS, 1760-1858.
5 items. Orange County, N.C.

Grant for land on the Eno River in 1760 signed by Lord Granville, and land deeds in Orange and Alexander counties.

913. JAMES H. CARSON ORDER BOOK, 1861.
1 vol. (166 pp.) Winchester (Frederick County), Va.

Orders pertaining chiefly to routine matters issued by Brigadier General James H. Carson to the 16th Brigade, Virginia Militia, from July to September, 1861.

914. WILLIAM H. CARSTARPHEN LEDGERS, 1875-1884. 3 vols. Williamston (Martin County), N.C.

Merchant's record books.

915. JEDEDIAH CARTER PAPERS, 1863-1864.
10 items. Danville (Pittsylvania County), Va.

Personal letters from "Jed" Carter, Confederate soldier, stationed at Charles City Court House, Virginia, to his wife, Susan; one letter, 1864, from his mother, reports that he is a captive at Fort Norfolk, Virginia.

916. MILTON CARTER PAPERS, 1860-1864.
5 items. Mountain Grove (Smith County), Tex.

Family correspondence of Milton Carter, private in the Confederate Army, stationed near Dalton, Georgia.

917. ROBERT CARTER PAPERS, 1772-1794.
2 items and 18 vols. "Nomini Hall," Westmoreland County, Va.

Letter books and memorandum books of Robert Carter (1728-1804), Virginia planter and iron manufacturer, concerning colonial plantation life, slavery, manumission, the iron industry, religious theory, tobacco cultivation in Virginia, etc. Included in the material are copies of letters from Robert Carter to Charles Carroll, Benjamin Day, William Ebzer, Thomas Fairfax, William Grayson, Patrick Henry, Ludwell Lee, Richard Lee, Peyton Randolph, George Tuberville, John Tuberville, and George Wythe; and letters to Carter from Alexander Campbell, Christopher Collins, Thomas Jones, Richard Lee, George Newman, John Overall, and Simon Triplett. Typewritten copies are included with the original manuscripts.

918. ROBERT WORMELEY CARTER PAPERS, 1813-1850. 16 items. "Sabine Hall," Richmond County, Va.

Miscellaneous correspondence of a planter.

919. VALLIE BURGESS CARTER PAPERS, 1852-1944. 300 items and 2 vols. Gerrardstown (Berkeley County), W. Va.

Family correspondence, papers, and two ledgers (1852-1860, 1861-1884) of James P. Carter, a physician.

920. WILLIAM CARTER PAPERS, 1840-1886.
438 items. Defiance (Defiance County), Ohio.

This collection is made up for the most part of routine legal correspondence and papers from the 1840s. There are occasional references to Ohio politics.

921. WILLIAM S. CARTER PAPERS, 1830-1922.
571 items and 7 vols. Fairfield (Hyde County), N.C.

Business letters, legal documents, bills, receipts, and account books of a farmer and businessman.

922. JOHN CARTWRIGHT PAPERS, 1796-1824.
14 items. London, England.

Letters from Cartwright and members of his family on the agitation for parliamentary reform, the relationship between parliamentary reform and a potential French invasion (1796), and routine business and personal matters.

923. ELI WASHINGTON CARUTHERS PAPERS, 1821-1862. 252 items. North Carolina.

Sermons of Eli W. Caruthers (1793-1865), a Presbyterian minister; and an unpublished antislavery manuscript,"American Slavery and the Immediate Duty of the Slaveholders," written by Caruthers at the request of his friends.

924. WILLIAM ALEXANDER CARUTHERS PAPERS, 1808-1935. 38 items. Lexington (Rockbridge County), Va. and Savannah, Ga.

Photocopies of miscellaneous personal and literary correspondence and clippings.

925. GEORGE WASHINGTON CARVER PAPERS, 1928. 1 item. Tuskegee (Macon County), Ala.

Letter from Carver discussing two students and religion.

926. ALICE CARY PAPERS, 1870. 2 items. New York, N.Y.

A small picture and a four-line poem.

927. MONIMIA FAIRFAX CARY PAPERS, 1861. 1 item. Culpeper Court House (Culpeper County), Va.

Letter inquiring about the need for nurses in the hospital at Richmond, Virginia.

928. [CARY CREDIT UNION BANK?] RECORDS, 1914-1915. 1 vol. (135 pp.) Cary (Wake County), N.C.

Mutilated volume containing savings accounts of members.

929. SAMUEL F. CASE PAPERS, 1861-1865. 29 items. Fulton (Oswego County), N.Y.

Personal and financial correspondence of Case and his wife. Most of the letters came to Case as president and cashier of the Citizen's National Bank of Fulton; however, they reflect many of the events of the Civil War and contain information on the 110th, 147th, and 184th New York Regiments.

930. M. B. CASEY PAPERS, 1846-1884. 8 items. Rockford (Coosa County), Ala.

Family correspondence of M. B. Casey, a farmer.

931. SILAS CASEY PAPERS, 1862. 4 items. Washington, D.C.

Routine orders and instructions relating to Casey's Division, U.S. Army.

932. LEWIS CASS PAPERS, 1823-1858. 7 items. Detroit, Mich.

Miscellaneous letters and papers including a request for information on the Sioux Indians; payments to be made to the Cherokee Indians, 1832; and a letter from James Buchanan concerning the ratification of a treaty with Peru, 1858.

933. PAUL CASSARD NOTEBOOK, 1914. 1 vol. (95 pp.)

934. MARTIN CASWELL PAPERS, 1765-1775. 6 items. Dobbs County (now Lenoir and Greene counties), N.C.

Court summonses and warrants for arrest signed by Martin Caswell as clerk of the Dobbs County Court of Pleas and Quarter Sessions.

935. RICHARD CASWELL PAPERS, 1777-1790. 16 items. Fayetteville (Cumberland County), N.C.

Letters and papers concerned with military affairs, the militia, Loyalists, legislative business, and Indian affairs.

936. JOHN H. CATHCART PAPERS, 1865-1869. 1 vol. Winnsboro (Fairfield County), S.C.

Journal of a substantial general merchant.

937. CATHOLIC CHURCH PAPERS, 1653. 1 item. Vatican City

Latin manuscript giving the views of Dr. Hennebes on the idea of grace during the Jansenist controversy.

938. CATHOLIC CHURCH OF THE HOLY TRINITY OF AUGUSTA (GA.) MINUTES AND ACCOUNTS, 1835-1848. 1 vol. (82 pp.) Augusta (Richmond County), Ga.

Minutes of meetings of the congregation relative to rebuilding the church; and operating expense accounts, 1838-1848.

939. CATHOLIC CHURCH. CONGREGAZIONE DELL' IMMUNITA ECCLESIASTICA PAPERS, 19th century. 1 vol. Vatican City.

Scrapbook containing manuscripts, printed pamphlets, and circulars relating to the history and functions of the Sagra Congregazione Dell' Immunità Ecclesiastica.

940. G. WASHINGTON CATLETT PAPERS, 1835-1868. 4 items. Port Royal (Caroline County), Va.

Miscellaneous personal letters and one bill.

941. HENRY CATLIN PAPERS, 1861-1868. 86 items. Harwinton (Litchfield County), Conn.

Letters of a soldier in the 19th Connecticut Regiment, for the most part concerned with weather conditions, health, camp life, the draft, and enlistment.

942. CARRIE (LANE) CHAPMAN CATT PAPERS, 1928. 1 item. New York, N.Y.

Letter stating that Mrs. Catt will not be able to address the senior class of the North Carolina College for Women (now the University of North Carolina at Greensboro).

943. JAMES H. CAUSTEN SCRAPBOOK, 1816-1870. 1 vol. (552 pp.) Washington, D.C.

This collection relates to the life-long work of James H. Causten representing American citizens who sought compensation for losses of ships and cargoes to France in the 1790s. The volume contains circular letters to the claimants, 1822-1870, the texts of bills in Congress, 1829-1863, and various petitions, memorials, and pamphlets relating to the claims.

944. SPENCER COMPTON CAVENDISH, EIGHTH DUKE OF DEVONSHIRE, PAPERS, 1874. 1 item. London, England.

Facsimile letter to Charles Gilpin explaining plans to establish a West End Liberal Club.

945. WILLIAM CAVENDISH, FIFTH DUKE OF DEVONSHIRE, PAPERS. 6 items. London, England.

Letter, engraving, poems, and a design of a portion of a residence for Georgiana (Spencer) Cavendish, Duchess of Devonshire, and for Elizabeth (Hervey) Foster Cavendish, Duchess of Devonshire, the first and second wives respectively of William Cavendish, Fifth Duke of Devonshire.

946. MADISON JULIUS CAWEIN PAPERS, 1892-1914. 5 items. Louisville (Jefferson County), Ky.

Miscellaneous letters and two clippings of The Sun from 1910 carrying poems by Cawein and others.

947. CAZENOVE AND COMPANY PAPERS, 1860-1868. 3 items and 1 vol. Alexandria (Arlington County), Va.

Letterpress book of commission merchants, a list of the firm's debtors in October, 1865, and a form letter sent to them.

948. JUAN MARIA CEBALLOS PAPERS, 1854-1857. 184 items. New York, N.Y.

Letters in English and Spanish concerned with the business of an import-export house including orders, acknowledgements of orders, and receipt of shipments from New York, Boston, London, Paris, Buenos Aires, Havana, and Tampico.

949. HUGH RICHARD HEATHCOTE CECIL, FIRST BARON QUICKSWOOD, PAPERS, 1902. 1 item. London, England.

Letter written by Cecil concerning the Education Act of 1902.

950. CENTRAL RAILROAD AND BANKING COMPANY OF GEORGIA PAPERS, 1866-1894. 7 vols. Savannah, Ga.

This collection consists of six volumes of banking ledgers, 1866, 1869, 1874, 1879, 1887, and 1870-1894, and one volume of railroad records showing agents' accounts in Georgia and Alabama, 1891.

951. MANUEL CEVALLOS ESCALERA PAPERS, 1820-1833. 40 items. Canta, Peru.

Original documents and copies relating to the military career of a lieutenant colonel of militia and subdelegate of the province of Canta.

952. CEYLON PAPERS, 1946. 1 vol.

Scrapbook of clippings from a special issue of The Times of Ceylon marking the centenary of the newspaper and the sesqui-centennial of British rule on the island. Deals with the history of Ceylon and the island's agricultural, commercial, and economic conditions.

953. GEORGE ALBERT CHACE PAPERS, 1862-1890. 7 items and 1 vol. Lakeville (Plymouth County), Mass.

Letters of a soldier in the 3rd Massachusetts Volunteer Militia describing eight months of service in North Carolina in 1862-1863. A diary covers approximately the same period.

954. MARY JANE (COOK) CHADICK DIARY, 1862-1865. 1 vol. Huntsville (Madison County), Ala.

Typed copy of diary of Mary Chadick, wife of William Davidson Chadick, describing Federal raids on and occupation of Huntsville; and commenting on local people and trouble with slaves occasioned by the presence of Federal troops.

955. DAVID CHADWICK PAPERS, 1859. 1 item. London, England.

Letter from Robert Lowe responding to Chadwick's pamphlet Parliamentary Representation.

956. WASHINGTON SANDFORD CHAFFIN PAPERS, 1841-1916. 108 items and 23 vols. Lumberton (Robeson County), N.C.

Personal correspondence, sermon notes, diaries, and bills of Washington S. Chaffin (1815-1895), a North Carolina Methodist minister and circuit rider; and a letter from Chaffin's son, Robert, concerning his entrance into the Confederate Army, in addition to several to his mother, including one which gives a detailed description of Jacksonville, Florida, in 1900. The collection includes information on Reconstruction, the Freedmen's Bureau in Robeson County, "Yankee" depredations in Lumberton and Fayetteville, and the behavior of the newly freed Negroes, as well as religious introspection and notes on various Methodist conferences and an unsigned will. The diaries cover the years 1845-1887.

957. ALEXANDER CHALMERS PAPERS, 1826. 1 item. London, England.

Letter from Michael Bland commenting on a book by Nicholas Carlisle entitled Collections for a History of the . . . Family of Bland (1826).

958. JOHN ARMSTRONG CHALONER PAPERS, 1862-1932. 6,472 items and 1 vol. Cobham (Albemarle County), Va.

Business and personal correspondence, legal briefs, literary manuscripts, and miscellaneous papers of John Armstrong Chaloner or Chanler (1862-1935), eccentric millionaire and great-grandson of John Jacob Astor. The letters, about half the collection, are concerned with attempts to have himself declared sane after a brief internment in Bloomingdale Asylum at White Plains, New York, by his family because of his excessive interest in spiritualism; efforts to obtain possession of his estate; verdicts from psychologists concerning his mental condition; the fostering of motion pictures for rural areas; the circulation of some of his poems on European politics prior to 1914; and congratulations to Chaloner on obtaining a favorable verdict regarding his sanity in the U.S. Supreme Court. His literary manuscripts are generally confined to treatises on the lunacy laws of various states. The briefs and legal notes are concerned with trials and appeals against the state of New York, and against the Washington Post for slander. Included also are canceled checks; telegrams; invitations and clippings, the latter largely confined to the career of his divorced wife, Amélie Rives (1863-1945), who later married Prince Pierre Troubetzkoy, and to the comment caused by the popular phrase coined by Chaloner: "Who's looney now?" Among the correspondents are Philip Alexander Bruce, Richard Evelyn Byrd, J. H. Choate, Walter Duranty, A. C. Gordon, Joseph Jastrow, Claude Kitchin, Lee Slater Overman, and W. L. Phelps.

959. DANIEL HENRY CHAMBERLAIN PAPERS, 1874-1877. 3 items. Columbia (Richland County), S.C.

Letters to Charles Nordhoff on politics, a political appointment, and personal matters.

960. G. HOPE (SUMMERELL) CHAMBERLAIN PAPERS, 1821-1946. 3,397 items and 21 vols. Raleigh (Wake County), and Chapel Hill (Orange County), N.C.

Correspondence and papers of an author, artist, house counselor, and civic worker. The letters from 1921-1946 concern family matters for the most part but also reflect Chamberlain's career as an author of local history and her work at Duke University as the house counselor of Pegram House. Scattered older letters include a letter from Herbert J. Hagermand of the American Embassy at Saint Petersburg, 1889; letters on the Russo-Japanese War, 1905; and letters from John Spencer Bassett, 1903. The other items in the collection include genealogical material on the Chamberlains; material on the Caraleigh Phosphate and Fertilizer Works; clippings of articles about Chamberlain and her books; drafts of some of her writings; copy of a journal of a trip to Europe in 1792-1793; diary of Chamberlain's trip to Europe in 1929; and personal diaries, 1923-April, 1926, and 1943.

961. JOSHUA LAWRENCE CHAMBERLAIN PAPERS, 1905. 1 item. Brunswick (Cumberland County), Me.

Letter from Adelbert Ames concerning proposed legislation in Congress relating to Civil War veterans.

962. WILLIAM CHAMBERLAYNE GENERAL ORDER BOOK, 1814. 1 vol. (125 pp.) Richmond, Va.

Military orders issued to the brigade of General William Chamberlayne (1764-1836), Revolutionary soldier, member of Virginia House of Delegates, brigadier general in the Virginia militia, and sportsman, from Camp Fairfield, near Richmond, Virginia, during the War of 1812.

963. ALFRED OTIS CHAMBERLIN PAPERS, 1862-1865. 111 items. Cambridge (Middlesex County), Mass.

Letters from a soldier in the 23rd Massachusetts Regiment. For the most part the correspondence is personal, occasionally describing camp life or events in the war. Chamberlin spent most of his time in eastern North Carolina but he was in Virginia for the winter of 1863-1864.

964. A. T. CHAMBERS PAPERS, 1860. 1 item. New Braunfels (Comal County), Tex.

Letter concerning transfer of land.

965. BENMAMIN W. CHAMBERS ACCOUNT BOOKS, 1846-1855. 8 vols. Camden (Kershaw County), S.C.

General accounts of Benjamin W. Chambers, a cotton factor of Camden.

966. HENRY ALEXANDER CHAMBERS PAPERS, 1863-1865. 27 items. Chattanooga (Hamilton County), Tenn.

Personal letters to Chambers and Laura Lenoir describing life in North Carolina during the Civil War.

967. JAMES S. CHAMBERS PAPERS, 1796 (1833-1850) 1918. 55 items. Charlotte (Mecklenburg County), N.C.

Family correspondence of a minister dealing with health, economic conditions, social matters, and, especially, religion and church life.

968. JENNIE CHAMBERS PAPERS, 1838-1936. 1,818 items and 8 vols. Harpers Ferry, W. Va.

Letters and papers of the Chambers family and the Castle family. The bulk of the collection deals with the Chambers and pertains, in general, to the social life of the period from the viewpoint of a moderately well-to-do small town family. Includes letters from Union soldiers who boarded with the Chambers during the Civil War. There is a commonplace book, 1873, and daybooks, 1880-1886, 1888.

969. SIDNEY C. CHAMBERS PAPERS, 1924. 13 items. Durham, N.C.

Letters of S. C. Chambers (b. 1878), Durham city attorney, pertaining to the elimination of the grade crossing on Chapel Hill Street, Durham, North Carolina.

970. CHAMBERS-MACDONALD FAMILY PAPERS, 1827-1842. 7 items. Exeter, Devonshire, England.

Letters of several civil and military officials in India primarily concerned with family matters and military duties. One letter deals with missionary work.

971. CHAMBERSBURG AND BEDFORD TURNPIKE COMPANY PAPERS, 1835. 4 items. Pennsylvania.

Legal papers of the company.

972. SYDNEY S. CHAMPION PAPERS, 1838-1907. 108 items. Champion Hill (Hinds County), Miss.

Typescript copies of letters between Champion and his wife, Matilda Montgomery Champion, for the most part dealing with the Civil War. Champion's letters describe service with the 28th Mississippi Cavalry in the defense of Vicksburg, 1862-1863, and campaigns in Georgia and under John Bell Hood in Tennessee, 1864-1865.

973. GEORGE CHAMPLIN AND CHRISTOPHER CHAMPLIN PAPERS, 1775. 1 item. Newport (Newport County), R.I.

A report to merchants in the slave trade on the market at Grenada, Windward Islands.

974. I. EDGAR CHANCELLOR PAPERS, 1878-1882. 6 items. Charlottesville (Albemarle County), Va.

Correspondence concerning the settlement of a debt and the payment of a premium to the Globe Mutual Life Insurance Company.

975. RANSOM A. [CHANCY?] PAPERS, 1746-1957. 122 items. Pitt County, N.C.

Miscellaneous items pertaining to a land dispute. Includes deeds and indentures concerning the land in question and copies of the testimony given in the trial that resulted from the dispute.

976. DANIEL CHANDLER PAPERS, 1827-1854. 2 items. Mobile (Mobile County), Ala.

Letters of a lawyer. Includes a lengthy letter on legal training.

977. WILLIAM ELLERY CHANNING PAPERS, 1835-1846. 4 items. Boston, Mass.

A letter concerning money for a charitable purpose, and sermon notes of William Ellery Channing (1780-1842), Unitarian minister. One of the sermons points out some of the evils attending slavery.

978. EDWIN HUBBELL CHAPIN PAPERS, 1845, 1854. 2 items. New York, N.Y.

Correspondence of Edwin H. Chapin (1814-1880), orator, author, and minister, concerning acceptance of a pastorate of a church in New York City, and a promise to give a lecture. He was a Universalist minister in Charleston, South Carolina, in 1845.

979. JOSEPH CHAPLIN AND JOSEPH C. HAYS PAPERS, 1741-1891. 460 items. Sharpsburg (Washington County), Md.

Bills, contracts, court decrees, promissory notes, business letters, deeds of Washington County, and other legal and business papers.

980. ELIZABETH A. CHAPMAN PAPERS, 1848. 1 item. New London (New London County), Conn.

Letter from a sister describing an epidemic in Natchez, Mississippi.

981. JOHN CHAPMAN PAPERS, 1851-1867. 14 items. London, England.

Correspondence with Edward Lombe concerned with the beginning of Chapman's career as editor of the *Westminster Review*. The letters deal with Lombe's ideas on reform and various publishing projects in which he was interested as well as the editorship of the journal. Additional letters deal with articles for the *Westminster Review* and the Crimean War.

982. THOMAS CHAPMAN PAPERS, 1819-1851. 5 items. Craven County, N.C.

One personal letter and legal papers including several indentures.

983. THOMAS CHAPMAN PAPERS, 1852 (1855-1860) 1870. 52 items. Midway (Bullock County), Ala.

Personal letters concerned with clerking in Midway, travelling in the early 1850s, teaching in Tennessee, and life under Reconstruction.

984. WILLIAM CHAPMAN ACCOUNT BOOKS, 1800-1821. 3 vols. Charles County, Md.

Records of a country merchant.

985. FRED DAVIS CHAPPELL PAPERS, 1954-1969. 257 items and 26 vols. Greensboro (Guilford County), N.C.

Correspondence concerning the publication of Chappell's writings and his work on the faculty of the English Department of the University of North Carolina at Greensboro. The collection also contains drafts of Chappell's prose and poetry, for the most part kept in notebooks.

986. LEROY CHAPPELL PAPERS, 1853-1867. 15 items. Kinston (Lenoir County), N.C.

Personal and professional correspondence of a physician.

987. CHARLESTON COTTON EXCHANGE PAPERS, 1880-1952. 718 items and 11 vols. Charleston, S.C.

The papers of the Exchange include minutes of meetings of the Board of Directors in 1884; financial statements, 1896-1898, 1929-1930; letter of invitation to prospective members, 1910; and groups of reports on the cotton market at Charleston, 1936-1944, 1948-1950. The volumes contain statistics on the shipping of cotton and other goods at Charleston, 1880-1905; cotton receipts at ports in the United States, 1899-1906; price quotations from several markets in naval stores, 1881-1886; and the finances of the Exchange, 1888-1938.

988. CHARLESTON DEMOCRATIC CONVENTION PAPERS, 1860. 172 items. Charleston, S.C.

Includes minutes; resolutions; committee reports; ballots; letters by the delegations from Louisiana, Mississippi, Arkansas, Florida, South Carolina, and Texas upon their withdrawal from the convention; a letter from the Massachusetts delegation protesting the exclusion of Benjamin F. Hallett; and newspaper clippings.

989. CHARLESTON, S.C., DISTRICT COURT RECORD, 1816-1823. 1 vol.

Record of cases tried in the Charleston District Court.

990. CHARLOTTESVILLE, VA., WOOLEN MILLS SAMPLE BOOK. 1 vol. (17 pp.)

This volume contains samples of woolen cloth and illustrations of the military uniforms manufactured from that cloth by Brown and Co. of Philadelphia.

991. ROBERT MILLEGE CHARLTON PAPERS, 1844-1851. 3 items and 1 vol. Savannah, Ga.

Scrapbook containing Charlton's poems, a sermon in his handwriting, and letters discussing the sermon.

992. HARVEY CHASE AND OLIVER CHASE PAPERS, (1825-1835) 1857. 264 items. Fall River (Bristol County), Mass.

Business papers of the Troy Cotton and Wool Manufactory at Fall River, concerning the sale of cotton.

993. SAMUEL CHASE PAPERS, 1838. 1 item. Ottawa (La Salle County), Ill.

Letter concerning the contributions of the Diocese of Illinois to the funds of the General Convention of the Protestant Episcopal Church.

994. SAMUEL CHASE PAPERS, 1787-1816. 16 items. Baltimore, Md.

Miscellaneous letters, bills, and legal papers of Chase and his son, Samuel Chase, Jr.

995. SETH CHASE PAPERS, 1840. 2 items. Andover (Essex County), Mass.

Letters from family members in the west.

996. CHATHAM COUNTY, GA., RECORDS, 1875-1883. 1 vol. (287 pp.) Savannah, Ga.

Records of county commissioners, including amounts paid for various expenses.

997. CHATHAM TOWN COMPANY MINUTES, 1819-1823. 1 vol. Cheraw (Chesterfield County), S.C.

Records of land sales, building, and general improvements of the Chatham Town Company (Chatham Town later became Cheraw, S.C.).

998. GENES V. CHAVERS DAYBOOK, 1855-1863. 1 vol. (220 pp.) Wadesboro (Anson County), N.C.

Records of a blacksmith.

999. JAMES A. CHEATHAM AND R. J. MOORE PAPERS, 1803-1867. 1,628 items. Ridgeway (Warren County), N.C.

Itemized accounts of purchases made by James A. Cheatham and R. J. Moore, general merchants; and promissory notes and business letters, showing trend of prices in the 1880s and during the first two years of the Civil War.

1000. RICHARD CHEATHAM PAPERS, 1874-1875. 1 vol. Charlottesville (Albemarle County), Va.

Notebook for the course in political economy taught by Noah Knowles Davis at the University of Virginia. Includes a roster of the class.

1001. JOHN CHEESBOROUGH PAPERS, 1804 (1866-1910) 1914. 105 items. Biltmore (Buncombe County), N.C.

Correspondence concerned, for the most part, with a dispute over the title to several islands in the Florida Keys. There are also items dealing with Cheesborough's land in Tennessee; court cases in Laurens District, South Carolina, 1804-1807; Cheesborough's career as a teacher in the Philippine Islands; Edmund R. Cheesborough and the operation of the commission form of government in Galveston, Texas; and the establishing of a United States Government weather station in 1872 on the summit of Mount Mitchell, North Carolina.

1002. JOHN CHEESMENT-SEVERN PAPERS, 1818. 1 item. "The Hall," Penybont, Radnorshire, Wales.

Letter from Lord Stanhope discussing relations with France, Louis XVIII, and the reasons why Allied troops should not be withdrawn.

1003. WILLIAM D. CHEEVER PAPERS, 1813-1864. 103 items. New York, N.Y.

This collection contains mainly abstracts of provisions, receipts, and other papers relating to supplies for the United States Army and the New York State Militia during the War of 1812. One item, February 1, 1864, concerns Colonel Henry A. V. Post of the 2nd Regiment of New York Sharpshooters (Infantry Volunteers).

1004. GISBOURN J. CHERRY PAPERS, 1838-1839. 3 vols. Washington County, N.C.

Books of advanced mathematical problems, many of which relate to surveying and are in the categories of plane and solid geometry.

1005. LUNCEFORD R. CHERRY PAPERS, 1836-1865. 25 items. Edgecombe County, N.C.

Family correspondence between relatives in North Carolina and Texas, 1839-1845. Also letters from a soldier in the 15th Regiment of North Carolina State Troops dealing with conditions in North Carolina and Virginia and the battles of Fredericksburg, Gettysburg, and Fort Sumter.

1006. ROBERT GREGG CHERRY PAPERS, 1914-1946. 7 items. Gastonia (Gaston County), N.C.

Miscellaneous correspondence and papers, for the most part related to Cherry's political career. Includes a lengthy mimeographed copy of a manuscript describing a woman's experiences with psychic visions.

1007. CHESAPEAKE AND DELAWARE CANAL COMPANY MEMORANDUM BOOK, 1827-1828. 1 vol. (81 pp.) Annapolis (Anne Arundel County), Md.

Volume containing mostly records of payments for excavations of earth.

1008. CHESAPEAKE AND OHIO CANAL COMPANY PAPERS, 1891-1923. 102 items and 7 vols. Williamsport (Washington County), Md.

Papers include business correspondence; records of daily business at Williamsport, Maryland; and daily reports of boats and cargoes clearing Williamsport from March 30 to April 28, 1911. Volumes, bearing various dates from 1891 to 1923, include daybooks, returns of manifests, records of waybills, and return of waybills.

1009. CHESHIRE, SULLIVAN & CANADAY, INC., PAPERS, 1912 (1930-1949). ca. 38,000 items. Charleston, S.C.

Papers of a firm of cotton merchants and exporters consisting of alphabetically arranged files of correspondence, invoices, and other records of financial transactions. The papers outline the structure and extent of the company's domestic and foreign operations, recording its dealings with agents, cotton merchants, textile mills, the New York Cotton Exchange, insurance companies, banks, agencies of the federal government and of South Carolina, commission merchants, shipping companies, railroads, and others. Business included the purchase, consignment, storage, compressing, and sale of cotton, and also hedging in the speculative market of cotton futures.

1010.   FRANCIS RAWDON CHESNEY PAPERS, ca. 1831-1833. 1 item. Mourne, County Down, Northern Ireland.

Undated and unsigned manuscript entitled "Observations on Persia as an Ally, and the Cheapest as well as Most Important Frontier Line of Our Indian Empire." It is a detailed analysis of Persia with recommendations for British foreign policy in that region.

1011.   ALEXANDER CHESNUT PAPERS, 1861-1864. 12 items. De Kalb County, Ga.

Family correspondence of Alexander Chesnut, a planter, largely concerned with crops and the war.

1012.   JAMES CHESNUT, JR., PAPERS, 1779-1872. 112 items. Camden (Kershaw County), S.C.

Business and family correspondence and military papers of a South Carolina politician and Confederate officer including letters to his children in school; papers dealing with the sale of a plantation, the marketing of cotton, and the settlement of debts; a petition seeking apprehension of persons guilty of arousing discontent among slaves; a description of the fortifications around Charleston, South Carolina; letters concerning disaffection in Tennessee in 1862; and a copy of a printed letter from Chesnut concerning the investigation of fraud in the government of South Carolina in 1871.

1013.   JAMES CHESSIER DAYBOOK, 1873. 1 vol. Martinsville (Henry County), Va.

Daybook of James Chessier, merchant.

1014.   FREDERICK WILLIAM CHESSON PAPERS, 1858-1905. 167 items. London, England.

Correspondence primarily concerns the humanitarian efforts of Chesson and his friends in the interest of native peoples in territories in Europe, Asia, and Africa. There is comment on Turkey, Greece, Bulgaria, and the Armenians in 1878-1880; the Afghan War, 1878-1881; Indian affairs, 1882 and 1884; Sierra Leone, 1858; South Africa and adjacent areas, 1872-1884; and scattered references to slavery and the slave trade in various parts of the world. There is also material relating to domestic British politics in this period. The principal correspondents are Sir George Campbell; William Edward Forster; Arthur Hobhouse, First Baron Hobhouse; Walter Henry James, Second Baron Northbourne; John Laird Mair Lawrence, First Baron Lawrence; Edmond George Petty-Fitzmaurice, First Baron Fitzmaurice; Sir John George Shaw-Lefevre; J. W. Welborne; and John Morley.

1015.   WILLIAM L. CHESSON PAPERS, 1783 (1806-1869) 1894. 1,346 items and 6 vols. Plymouth (Washington County), N.C.

Business and personal papers and correspondence of William L. Chesson, clerk of the court of Washington County; of four of his brothers and two sisters, the material of the early years being largely confined to legal papers of William L. Chesson. Many papers are concerned with John B. Chesson's wholesale fish house of Armistead and Chesson; with the correspondence of Andrew Chesson and Joshua Swift, a member of the North Carolina General Assembly, including an election in 1836 and strife in the Assembly between Whigs and supporters of Martin Van Buren. The collection includes a letter, 1865, to the chief of police in Beaufort, North Carolina, from the Freedmen's Bureau in Washington, North Carolina, demanding arrest of a person who had failed to answer charges; a letter, 1878, which refers to a shipload of Negroes and whites on their way to the Republican convention at Edenton; and comments about legislation regarding fishing in North Carolina waters. The volumes contain the business records of a blacksmith and the mercantile firms of Hodges and Chesson, and Chesson and Ross, and others.

1016.   LANGDON CHEVES PAPERS, 1807-1860. 6 items. Charleston, S.C.

Correspondence of Langdon Cheves (1776-1857), lawyer, member of U.S. Congress, and director of the Second U.S. Bank, concerning immigration from the West Indies in 1807 and banking; and his son's request for arms for the Palmetto Hussars in December, 1860.

1017.   RACHEL SUSAN (BEE) CHEVES PAPERS, 1846 (1861-1884) 1911. 215 items and 2 vols. Savannah, Ga.

The collection consists, for the most part, of personal and family correspondence dealing with day-to-day life and reflecting events of the Civil War and Reconstruction, including a description of the burning of Columbia, South Carolina. The correspondence, 1848-1868, of John Richardson Cheves, concerns work on the defenses of Charleston, South Carolina; service as a physician in the Confederate Army; and attempts to regain his property after the war. There are a number of letters from Joseph Cheves Haskell reflecting his experiences in the Civil War, including camp life, aftermath of the battle of Gettysburg, and the campaigns around Chattanooga and Knoxville in 1863. The collection also contains several items on the Marshall family of Charleston, South Carolina, including report cards from the High School of Charleston, 1856-1860; an account of the earthquake of 1886 in Charleston; and two memoranda books of Alexander W. Marshall, Jr., sergeant major in the 2nd South Carolina Artillery, which contain personal notes, maps, and forage records from the Civil War.

1018. ROBERT SMITH CHEW PAPERS, 1812. 12 items. Fredericksburg (Spotsylvania County), Va.

Summonses before the Corporation Court of Fredericksburg.

1019. CHICORA MINING AND MANUFACTURING COMPANY RECORDS, 1870-1872. 1 vol. (47 pp.) Charleston, S.C.

Minutes of the organization of the corporation and subsequently of the board of directors. The firm was organized to mine phosphates, earths, marls, rocks, and minerals and to manufacture chemicals, acids, and fertilizers.

1020. NANNIE CHILDRESS PAPERS, 1849 (1862-1863) 1944. 10 items. Airy Hill (Powhatan County), Va.

Personal and family correspondence. Includes letters concerning the California gold rush of 1849.

1021. GEORGE WILLIAM CHILDS PAPERS, 1861, 1885. 2 items. Philadelphia, Pa.

A letter concerning an application for a job on Childs' Public Ledger and offering Childs a collection of pamphlets on the telegraph in the South; and a letter giving the British attitude toward the Civil War in the United States.

1022. DABNEY CHILES PAPERS, 1812-1837. 4 items. Caroline County, Va.

The will of Reuben Goodwin for 1812, and of Dabney Chiles for 1815; and papers in litigation over Chiles's will.

1023. ROBERT HALL CHILTON PAPERS, 1863-1864. 4 items. Westmoreland County, Va.

Military correspondence of Robert H. Chilton (1816-1879), brigadier general in the Confederate Army.

1024. ROBERT W. CHILTON, JR., PAPERS, 1808 (1897-1901). 270 items. Washington, D.C.

The collection is made up for the most part of the correspondence of the chief of the United States Consular Bureau and concerns the operations and problems of the consular service, 1897-1901. The papers include a few personal items about Chilton's marriage, work, and health; applications for positions in various consulates; letters describing problems in the service such as housing, salary levels, and political interference; correspondence concerning United States commerce and foreign relations; and a few items on domestic politics. Other items in the collection include a letter by Mary Lamb with a postscript by Charles Lamb, 1808; detailed lists of commodity prices for a number of years between 1808 and 1883 from Washington, D.C., Baltimore, and other cities; and a lengthy report on improved agricultural practices.

1025. CHINESE NEWS SERVICE PAPERS, 1944-1947. 370 items. New York, N.Y.

Mimeographed news releases of the Chinese News Service, an official agency of the Chinese government.

1026. BOLLING R. CHINN ACCOUNTS AND PLANTATION RECORDS, 1843-1893. 6 vols. Cypress Hall, Baton Rouge, La.

Records and accounts of Bolling R. Chinn, planter, slaveowner, and merchant, including plantation records, 1843-1872; account book, 1857-1870; ledger, 1866-1886; time book, 1871-1872; and daybook, 1873-1893.

1027. WILLIAM HENRY CHIPPENDALE PAPERS, 1853-1864. 5 items. London, England.

Letters written to William H. Chippendale (1801-1888), an actor, pertaining to professional matters.

1028. ALEXANDER ROBERT CHISOLM PAPERS, 1861. 1 item. Charleston, S.C.

Typed copy of journal for the period before and during the bombardment of Fort Sumter.

1029. THOMAS HOLLEY CHIVERS PAPERS, 1833-1859. 635 items. Washington (Wilkes County), Ga.

Literary correspondence and works of Thomas H. Chivers (1809-1858), Georgia poet, including letters to editors, publishing houses, and critics; several letters concerning similarity in the works of Chivers and Edgar Allan Poe and the question of plagiarism; clippings of his published poems and reviews of his writings; and unpublished manuscripts of his works, which make up the bulk of the collection. Among the correspondents are Ossian Euclid Dodge, Moses Dow, John S. Dwight, Edwin Forrest, John Gierlow, Henry Beck Hirst, Jennie Lind, Charles R. Rode, and James M. Smith.

1030. B. CHRISTIAN PAPERS, 1862. 1 item. Richmond, Va.

Letter concerning the appointment of a postmaster; the progress of the war; and the spirit of the officials in Richmond.

1031. JOHN BEVERLY CHRISTIAN PAPERS, 1829 (1852-1900) 1904. 519 items and 3 vols. Uniontown (Perry County), Ala.

Correspondence of the related Christian and Storrs families about personal and family matters. Volumes contain the notes of a law student at the University of Alabama, Tuscaloosa, 1879-1880; minutes of an agricultural fair, 1880-1884; and minutes of lodge meetings, 1897-1898.

1032. M. E. CHRISTIAN PAPERS, 1879. 1 item. Baltimore, Md.

Personal letter discussing religion.

1033. WILLIAM WALTER CHRISTIAN PAPERS, 1855-1862. 168 items. Christiansburg (Roanoke County), Va.

Correspondence of William W. Christian, Confederate soldier. One letter, 1859, from his mother, Mary Ann Christian, describes excitement evidently aroused by John Brown's raid; many of the other letters are to his fianceé, Carrie Harmon, and describe the confusion and conditions of the first Confederate military camp in northern Virginia, and his stay in a hospital in Lynchburg.

1034. WILLIE CHUNN PAPERS, 1861-1884. 75 items. Manassas (Tattnall County), Ga.

Civil War letters between a Confederate Army officer and his wife.

1035. CHURCH OF ENGLAND. DIOCESE OF WINCHESTER, PAPERS, 1705. 1 vol. (43 pp.) Hampshire, England.

These items form part of the response to "An Inquiry Concerning the Present State of the Churches in Hampshire." They are questionnaires addressed to the priests of parish churches and chapels concerning organization and financing. Not all of the churches of Hampshire are represented, and not all of the questionnaires are complete.

1036. FRANK C. CHURCHILL PAPERS, 1906-1909. 14 items and 1 vol. Washington, D.C.

Letters and papers relating for the most part to the taking of a census of the eastern band of the Cherokee Indians in 1907-1908. Includes a one volume census roll and two unbound partial rolls.

1037. JOHN WESLEY CHURCHILL PAPERS, 1889. 1 item. Andover (Essex County), Mass.

Letter concerning the poetry of John Townsend Trowbridge.

1038. WILLIAM CHURCHILL PAPERS, 1811-1851. 4 items. Greene County, N.C.

Two letters to William Churchill from a brother in the Mississippi Territory, commenting on farming conditions, the purchase of cattle, and the Creek War of 1813-1814 in Alabama; and two letters from a son who was a soldier in the Mexican War and later a resident of Boston, Massachusetts.

1039. SAMUEL T. CILLEY PAPERS, 1855-1892. 132 items. Fairfax (Franklin County), Vt.

Miscellaneous letters of Cilley and various members of his family concerning the Civil War and other subjects.

1040. LEWIS JACOB CIST PAPERS, 1841-1867. 10 items. Cincinnati, Ohio.

Correspondence related to the collection of autographs.

1041. CITIZENS NATIONAL BANK PAPERS, 1903-1942. 20 items and 80 vols. Durham, N.C. Restricted.

Records of the Citizens National Bank and its predecessor, the Morehead Banking Company. The Morehead Bank is represented by a checks and deposits book, a collection register, and a cashier's letterpress book, all dating from 1903-1905. The records of Citizens National Bank include daily balance books, 1907-1919; bank journals, 1905-1919; subsidiary account books, especially for the 1920s and 1930s; cashier's letterpress books, 1905-1911, with partial runs for 1913 and 1915; and a small group of unbound correspondence, 1907-1908, 1918.

1042. HORATIO CLAGETT LEDGER, 1815-1823. 1 vol. (628 pp.) [Brunswick?] (Washington County), Md.

1043. THOMAS CLAGETT PAPERS, 1847-1848. 3 items. Upper Marlboro (Prince George's County), Md.

Business papers.

1044. F. CLAIBORNE PLANTATION BOOK, 1853-1854. 1 vol.

1045. HAMILTON CABELL CLAIBORNE MUSIC NOTEBOOK. 1 vol. (10 pp.) Richmond, Va.

Music notes and staff.

1046. [JOHN F.?] CLAIBORNE AND [W. L.?] JETER ACCOUNT BOOKS, 1853-1860. 3 vols. Danville (Pittsylvania County), Va.

Daybook, ledger, and account book of the firm of Claiborne and Jeter, merchants of Danville.

1047.  JOHN FRANCIS HAMTRAMCK CLAIBORNE PAPERS, 1858. 1 item and 1 reel microfilm. Natchez (Adams County), Miss.

Letter concerning the burning of a dwelling near Claiborne's residence; microfilm of Claiborne's diaries and reminiscences, 1820s-1840s, in the Library of Congress.

1048.  WILLIAM CHARLES COLES CLAIBORNE PAPERS, 1803. 2 items. Mississippi Territory.

Letter from Claiborne, governor of Mississippi Territory, to the territorial legislature announcing the signature of two bills and a photocopy of a proclamation from Claiborne stating that the province of Louisiana had passed under the control of the United States.

1049.  CLAIRE [CLARA MARY JANE] CLAIRMONT DIARIES, 1814-1826. 7 vols. Europe. Restricted.

Photostatic copies of a diary and reminiscenses of Claire (Clara Mary Jane) Clairmont, giving descriptions of France, Switzerland, Italy, and the Rhine Valley as she saw them when accompanying Percy Bysshe Shelly and Mary Godwin on their elopement; accounts of her daily activities, including readings (with frequent quotations and comments), her social calls, and her philosophic musings; descriptions of her life as governess in a family of Moscow, Russia; and reminiscences of her youth. Frequent allusions to the Shelleys and Byron are usually of an indirect and impersonal nature. References to grief at being separated from her daughter, Allegra, are numerous. There is no material for the years 1815-1817 and 1822-1824.

1050.  WILLIAM KEATING CLARE PAPERS, 1863. 39 items. Elizabeth (Union County), N.J.

Letters of a Civil War soldier, originally from Ireland, who served in the 9th New York State Militia. His letters describe camp life and the battle of Gettysburg.

1051.  C. P. CLARK DIARY, 1847-1863. 1 vol. Hartford County, Conn.

Diary of a farmer with almost daily one-line entries concerning farm activities.

1052.  CHRISTOPHER HENDERSON CLARK PAPERS, 1810-1824. 4 items. Bedford County, Va.

Business papers.

1053.  COURTNEY J. CLARK PAPERS, 1841-1874. 2 vols. Jacksonville, Ala.

Notes taken by C. J. Clark of Selma, Alabama, as a medical student at Louisville Medical Institute, Louisville, Kentucky, and later as a practicing surgeon in the Confederate Army.

1054.  CYNTHIA A. W. CLARK PAPERS, 1898-1909. 1,307 items. Northhampton (Hampshire County), Mass.

Personal and family correspondence of Cynthia A. W. Clark, and almost unintelligible letters of her son, Arthur Wilson Clark, who was mentally deranged and often signed himself "Napoleon Bonaparte." The early letters contain a few scattered references to the Spanish-American War.

1055.  EDWIN CLARK PAPERS, 1789 (1878-1918) 1930. 3,518 items and 118 vols. Weldon (Halifax County), N.C.

Apparently the complete records and business correspondence of a general merchant in Weldon. The collection includes also a letter from Washington and Lee University, Lexington, Virginia, where a son attended school, and a letter from an instructor at Oak Ridge Academy, Guilford County, North Carolina, 1917. There are also one hundred and fifteen daybooks, 1880-1918; two ledgers, 1878; and an index to the ledgers.

1056.  ENOCH CLARK PAPERS, 1852-1878. 55 items. Chatham County, N.C.

Correspondence concerning property; finances; desertion, and commodity prices in North Carolina during the Civil War and the operation of the salt works at Wilmington; experiences in Georgia during and after the Civil War; contracts with a former slave; and family affairs.

1057.  FRANCIS CLARK PAPERS, 1895. 1 item. London, England.

Letter from Queen Victoria concerning Clark's illness.

1058.  FREDERICK W. CLARK PAPERS, 1861-1889. 199 items. Northampton (Hampshire County), Mass.

Correspondence of a New England family concerning personal and business matters, the Civil War, and California. The letters of Frederick Clark, a soldier in the 10th Regiment of Massachusetts Volunteers, describe in some detail day-to-day life in camp near Washington, D.C., and campaigning with McClellan in Virginia, 1861-1862, while letters from other members of the family discuss activities at home. There are several letters from family members in California in the late 1870s describing economic conditions and attitudes toward the Chinese.

1059. HENRY CLARK PAPERS, 1809-1845. 632 items. Campbell County, Va.

This collection consists for the most part of the business letters, bills, receipts, and checks of a tobacco planter. There are also a few legal papers and personal letters. Includes a letter, 1831, from a member of the House of Delegates of Virginia concerning the discussions of slavery in the legislature following the Nat Turner insurrection.

1060. HENRY SELBY CLARK PAPERS, 1842-1888. 28 items. Greenville (Pitt County), N.C.

Miscellaneous business and personal correspondence, including a description of a trip in the Ohio and Mississippi valleys in 1842 and a letter of the Reconstruction period assessing the future prospects of the South.

1061. HENRY TOOLE CLARK PAPERS, 1757-1885. 1,343 items. Tarboro (Edgecombe County), N.C.

The collection is made up chiefly of the bills, receipts, accounts, indentures, and other business and legal papers of a planter with holdings in North Carolina, Tennessee, and Alabama. There is correspondence concerning social life in Washington, D.C. in 1829-1830; affairs in Alabama in 1842; and Clark's political career, especially with his tenure as governor of North Carolina, 1861-1862. The official and political correspondence includes patronage letters; requests for military appointments; discussions of North Carolina's part in the Civil War; and a confidential letter to the Secretary of War concerning the weakening of the Confederate Army through desertion.

1062. JAMES BEAUCHAMP CLARK PAPERS, 1897-1917. 4 items. Bowling Green (Pike County), Mo.

Three addresses delivered by Clark in the United States House of Representatives and one letter.

1063. JAMES M. CLARK PAPERS, 1863-1864. 3 items.

Personal letters of an officer on the ironclad U.S.S. *Sangamon*.

1064. JOSEPH D. CLARK PAPERS, 1963. 1 item. Raleigh (Wake County), N.C.

"Fifty Years of the North Carolina Folklore Society," a paper presented at the annual meeting of the society, December 6, 1963.

1065. M.H. CLARK AND H.D. FAULKNER LETTER BOOK, 1859-1860. 1 vol. (876 pp.) New York, N.Y.

Business letters of Clark and Faulkner. Many pertain to bonds, loans, and taxes.

1066. SAMUEL B. CLARK PAPERS, 1764-1890. 174 items and 3 vols. Brothersville (Richmond County), Ga.

Correspondence of the Clark family and related families in Virginia and Georgia. The early letters from Virginia deal with family matters, social life, farming, commerce, politics, and the Revolution. Anderson family letters refer to religion and include letters of a soldier in the War of 1812 describing the American blockade of the British in Alexandria, Virginia, and life at Camp Mitchell near Richmond. The papers of the Clarks in Georgia begin in 1840 and concern social life, land transactions, and life at Emory College at Oxford, Georgia. There are several Civil War letters from various branches of the family, one of which concerns the construction of the C.S.S. *Virginia*.

1067. THEOPHILUS CLARK PAPERS, 1834-1836. 3 items. Tinmouth (Rutland County), Vt.

Three letters from Caleb Smith Ives, an Episcopal clergyman, giving his impression of Alabama and describing his work there.

1068. WALTER CLARK, SR., PAPERS, 1895-1903. 4 items. Raleigh (Wake County), N.C.

Three articles prepared for the *University Magazine* of the University of North Carolina entitled "Counties in North Carolina that have Disappeared," "North Carolina in War," and "North Carolina Troops in South America," which concerns the Cartagena expedition to Venezuela, 1740. Also a letter to Funk and Wagnalls Co. concerning a book they had published.

1069. WILLIAM W. CLARK PAPERS, 1848-1864. 22 items. Athens (Clarke County), Ga.

Miscellaneous items including several telegrams and letters relating to Clark's service in the Confederate Congress.

1070. ADAM CLARKE PAPERS, 1739 (1783-1851) 1875. 301 items. Great Britain.

Letters of Adam Clarke to his wife and children and later correspondence among the family concerning the publication of Clarke's biography. The collection covers Clarke's career as a minister and contains material on the development of the Wesleyan Methodist Church; the ministries of John Wesley, Thomas Coke, George Whitefield; the British reaction to the French Revolution; missionary work in Palestine and the Shetland Islands; and the effects of the industrialization in England.

1071. ALFRED ALEXANDER CLARKE PAPERS, 1848-1899. 61 items. "Close Hall," Wells, Somersetshire, England.

Drawings and engravings of buildings and scenes, churches and country houses, for the most part in Somersetshire.

1072. ALICE (JUDAH) CLARKE PAPERS, 1895.
1 vol. Vincennes (Knox County), Ind.

A history of the family of Joseph McCorkle, Revolutionary War veteran, pioneer, farmer, slaveholder, and abolitionist.

1073. GEORGE W. CLARKE PAPERS, 1852-1866.
35 items. Locust Dale (Madison County), Va.

Letters and papers concerned with farm business, particularly with the sale of farm products.

1074. JAMES FREEMAN CLARKE PAPERS, 1833-1905. 44 items. Boston, Mass.

Miscellaneous collection of items concerning the career of a Unitarian minister, founder of the Church of the Disciples in Boston.

1075. JAMES T. CLARKE PAPERS, 1848-1878.
18 items. Mount Solon (Augusta County), Va.

Personal correspondence of a physician concerning such subjects as politics, medicine, and internal improvements in Virginia.

1076. JOSEPH E. CLARKE PAPERS, 1865.
1 item. Gloucester (Camden County), N.J.

Letter from Clarke's son in the Union Army, stationed in Keokuk, Iowa.

1077. LEWIS CLARKE PAPERS, 1847 (1860-1872) 1876. 246 items. Rocky Springs (Claiborne County), Miss.

Records of a plantation store.

1078. MARY H. CLARKE PAPERS, 1844-1848.
4 items. Columbus (Muscogee County), Ga.

Personal correspondence with parents in Lumpkin, Georgia, and friends at Mercer University.

1079. SIR STANLEY DE ASTEL CALVERT CLARKE PAPERS, 1846-1913. 91 items. London, England.

Correspondence of an official of the royal household of Great Britain. Most of the letters are either by or about members of the royal family and they are primarily personal or social with only occasional references to political matters.

1080. CLARKE'S STATION BAPTIST CHURCH MINUTES, 1821-1832. 1 vol. Wilkes County, Ga.

Includes rules of decorum and lists of members.

1081. THOMAS CLARKSON PAPERS, 1807-1846.
18 items. "Playford Hall," near Ipswich, Suffolk, England.

Miscellaneous collection of letters to and from Clarkson and clippings about his death. For the most part these items are concerned with the abolition of slavery in the British Empire, in the French overseas possessions, and in the United States.

1082. THOMAS W. CLAWSON PAPERS, ca. 1942-1944. Wilmington (New Hanover County), N.C.

Chiefly material concerning the Wilmington, N.C., race riot of 1898, as described by Colonel Thomas W. Clawson (1854-ca. 1942), city editor of the Wilmington Messenger and editor of the Wilmington Star, 1902-1924. Included are an article entitled "The Wilmington Race Riot of 1898: Recollections and Memories," written by Clawson ca. 1942, and "Exhibit A," consisting of a copy of a controversal editorial in the Wilmington Record on August 18, 1898; and copies of other pertinent papers.

1083. CASSIUS MARCELLUS CLAY PAPERS, 1851-1875. 5 items. Lexington (Fayette County), Ky.

Four letters, 1851-1856, from Cassius Marcellus Clay (1810-1903), editor and abolitionist, to Edmund Quincy concerning personal affairs, politics, and problems encountered by Clay for publicly stating his anti-slavery views; and a letter, 1875, to W. Scott Smith asking his support for the vice-presidential nomination of the Democratic Party.

1084. CLEMENT CLAIBORNE CLAY PAPERS, 1811 (1821-1915) 1925. 8,543 items and 25 vols. Huntsville (Madison County), Ala.

Personal, business, and political correspondence, accounts, diaries, memoranda, college notes, scrapbooks, and clippings of Clement Claiborne Clay (1816-1882), lawyer, U.S. senator, Confederate diplomat, and planter; of his father, Clement Comer Clay (1789-1866), lawyer, planter, U.S. congressman and senator, and governor of Alabama; of his mother, Susanna Claiborne (Withers) Clay (1798-1866); of his wife, Virginia Caroline (Tunstall) Clay (1825-1915), who wrote A Bell of the Fifties: Memoirs of Mrs. Clay, of Alabama, covering Social and Political Life in Washington and the South, 1853-1866: Put into Narrative Form by Ada Sterling (New York: Doubleday, 1904); and of his brothers, Hugh Lawson Clay and John Withers Clay, and of their wives.

Letters deal with family matters, including education of the elder Clay's three sons at the University of Alabama, Tuscaloosa, and the University of Virginia, Charlottesville; management of two or more cotton plantations and approximately fifty slaves; civic affairs in Huntsville; state politics, 1819-1860; Democratic and Whig party alignments, rivalries, and disputes; presidential elections, especially in 1844, 1852, and 1856; Clement Comer Clay's governorship, 1835-1837; the Creek War, 1836; the panic of 1837; Clement Claiborne Clay's election as a Democrat to the U.S. Senate in 1853 and his re-election in 1857. Other political matters referred to include the Compromise of 1850; Kansas-Nebraska difficulty; break with Stephen A. Douglas; Democratic Convention of 1860; secession; and organization of the Confederate government. Personal letters refer to social life in Alabama and in Washington, D.C.; visits to springs and health resorts; and Clement Claiborne Clay's travels for his health through Florida, 1851, and later to Arkansas and Minnesota.

Subjects of the Civil War years include Clement Claiborne Clay's political activities in the Confederate States Senate; his relations with Jefferson Davis; Federal raids on and occupation of Huntsville, consequent disruption of civilian life, and demoralization of slaves; J. W. Clay's publication of the Huntsville *Democrat* in various towns; Clay's defeat in the election of 1863 for the Confederate Senate; his and other agents' work in Canada, assisting in the return of escaped Confederate prisoners to Confederate territory; plots of a general revolt in the Northwestern states designed to join these states to the Confederacy; the Democratic Convention of 1864; Horace Greeley's efforts for peace, 1864; plans and execution of the Confederate raid on St. Albans, Vermont, 1864; Clay's return from Canada; and the final days of the Confederacy.

Material relating to the aftermath of the Civil War concerns accusations against Clay for complicity in Lincoln's assassination, Clay's surrender to Federal authorities, his imprisonment at Fortress Monroe, Virginia, and the efforts of Virginia (Tunstall) Clay to obtain her husband's release. Papers for the period 1866-1915 generally pertain to personal matters, principally Clay's poverty, his attempts to retrieve his confiscated property, the settlement of his father's estate, efforts to re-establish farming operations, and his years in the insurance business, 1871-1873, with Jefferson Davis; and Virginia (Tunstall) Clay's dissatisfaction with a restricted social life, her tour of Europe, 1884-1885, and her efforts in later years to operate the plantation. There are occasional references to political affairs.

The volumes consist of an executor's book of the estate of C. C. Clay, Sr., 1866-1869; letter books, 1864-1865; letterpress copy covering insurance business; memorandum books, 1853-1864, containing a mailing list of constituents and other notations; notebook, 1835-1841, containing college lecture notes; receipt books; legal fee book, 1814-1815; scrapbooks, ca. 1848-1903, one of which contains plantation accounts, 1870-1873, and minutes of the Madison County Bible Society, 1820-1830; and the diaries and scrapbooks, 1859-1905, of Virginia (Tunstall) Clay.

Correspondents include Jeremiah S. Black, E. C. Bullock, C. C. Clay, Sr., C. C. Clay, Jr., David Clopton [Virginia (Tunstall) Clay's second husband], W. W. Corcoran, J. L. M. Curry, Jefferson Davis, Varina Davis, Benjamin Fitzpatrick, U. S. Grant, Andrew Johnson, L. Q. C. Lamar, Clifford Anderson Lanier, Sidney Lanier, Stephen R. Mallory, Nelson A. Miles, James K. Polk, John H. Reagan, R. B. Rhett, E. S. Shorter, Leroy P. Walker, Louis T. Wigfall, and William L. Yancey.

1085. GEORGE PINKNEY CLAY COPYBOOK, 1853. 1 vol. (120 pp.) Catawba County, N.C.

A practice book of handwriting, and arithmetic problems.

1086. HENRY CLAY PAPERS, 1802-1852. 137 items. Lexington (Fayette County), Ky.

Correspondence of Henry Clay (1777-1852), Kentucky statesman, dealing with the U.S. Bank, public finance, Missouri Compromise, cabinet appointments in 1817, possibility of the purchase of Texas by the United States in 1825, the panic of 1819, tariff, Nullification, and the Whig Party. There is also evidence of Clay's desire to be president, especially in 1844. Other topics referred to are his private debts; horse breeding; various lawsuits; sale and purchase of lands; appointments to the U.S. Military Academy, West Point, New York, and to political offices; introduction of English cattle into the Western country; long discussion of Kentucky bluegrass; and his refusal to free three of his slaves. There are several letters of Clay's daughter, Anna B. (Clay) Erwin, commenting on family and personal matters and to some extent on Washington society.

1087. JOHN CLAY PAPERS, 1821-1873. 37 items and 1 vol. Preston, Lancashire, England.

Correspondence and an album of letters of John Clay (1796-1858), Anglican clergyman and British prison reformer, and his son, Walter Lowe Clay, also an Anglican clergyman, principally concerning crime and prisons. Correspondents discuss the causes and prevention of crime, the methods to be used in prisons and reformatories, appropriate parliamentary legislation, alcoholic consumption, the condition of the industrial and agricultural working classes, and the roles of the church and secular and religious education. Among the correspondents are Charles Adderly, Lord Brooke, Mary Carpenter, William Shove Chalk, the Bishop of Chester, Sir Smith Child, George Combe, Emily Davies, Augustus De Morgan, George Dixon, Lord Ebrington, Lord Ingestre, John Just, Lord Lifford, John Malcolm Forbes Ludlow, Lord Lyttelton, Eliza Meteyard, John Stuart Mill, Professor Mittermaier, Ogle William Moore, John Somerset Pakington, John Wilson-Patten, John Richardson Porter, Samuel Redgrave, James Harrison Rigg, Charles Savile Roundell, Lord Sandon, Robert A. Slaney, William Cooke Taylor, Georg Varrentrapp, and Sir John Eardley-Wilmot.

1088. JOSEPH CLAY, SR., PAPERS, 1767-1800.
8 items and 1 vol. Savannah, Ga.

Legal and business papers of Joseph Clay, Sr. (1741-1805), merchant, Revolutionary officer, and member of Continental Congress. The volume contains depositions made before Clay, as senior assistant judge of Chatham County, Georgia, by several mariners from the brigantine Bachelor, commanded by Robert Etherington, concerning charges that the brigantine was supplying aid to British troops at Charleston, South Carolina.

1089. CLAYTON AND ERWIN PAPERS, 1860.
2 items. Napoleon (Desha County), Ark.

Correspondence of the law firm of Clayton and Erwin concerning a debt owed Alexander Craig of Richmond, Virginia, by Solon B. Jones.

1090. GEORGE ROOTES CLAYTON PAPERS, (1801-1829) 1884. 35 items. Louisville (Jefferson County), and Milledgeville (Baldwin County), Ga.

Personal papers of George Rootes Clayton (1779-1840), state legislator and public official, concerning family matters; the health of Major General James Jackson; the University of Georgia; a duel between William H. Crawford and Peter L. Van Allen; an accounting, 1806, of the gold, silver, United States stocks, and the funds known as the Yazoo deposit in the Georgia treasury; internal improvements; the estate of George Clayton; and the sale of cotton, land, and slaves.

1091. MARTHA HARPER CLAYTON PAPERS, 1846-1884. 39 items. Greensboro (Greene County), Ga.

Letters to Martha Harper Clayton from friends and from Confederate soldiers describing social matters, the battle of Chickamauga, and trials of deserters. Also included are letters between Robert T. Clayton in Bluefields, Nicaragua, and W. R. Grace and Co. of New York discussing the price of rubber; a letter from Robert T. Clayton concerning the Republican Party in Georgia; and information on the Clayton family.

1092. W. C. CLAYTON PAPERS, 1860-1862.
4 items. Richmond, Va.

Personal correspondence of W. C. Clayton while a student at Centre College, Danville, Kentucky, while in a Richmond hospital, and while in the Confederate Army stationed at Centreville and Richmond, in Virginia, with comments on food, weather, friends, and homesickness.

1093. CLAYTON-BROWN-LEFTWICH-PAPERS, 1802-1826. 277 items and 1 vol. Lynchburg (Campbell County), Va.

Principally the business papers of three firms: Brown, Leftwich, and Co.; Leftwich and Clayton; and Brown and Clayton; containing bills, receipts, and mercantile accounts. Correspondence concerns social life and customs in Virginia; purchases and sales of slaves in Virginia; and commodity, particularly tobacco, prices and sales in Richmond, New York, Great Britain, and the Netherlands. A memorandum book, 1816-1818, contains financial accounts for Brown, Leftwich, and Co.

1094. JOHN CLEEK PAPERS, 1829-1863.
15 items. Bath County, Va.

Correspondence of the Cleek and related Bradley and Brown families dealing with family matters, Hot and Warm Springs, a visit of P. T. Barnum's show to Staunton, Virginia, and the battle of Gettysburg.

1095. JAMES J. CLEER PAPERS, 1864-1865.
2 items.

Letters of a Union sailor on the U.S.S. Maratanza near Wilmington, North Carolina, describing attacks on Fort Fisher.

1096. WILLIAM F. CLEGG PAPERS, 1871-1872.
1 vol. Chatham County, N.C.

A classbook for the Trent and Deep River circuits of the Methodist Episcopal Church, South, served by Rev. William F. Clegg (1827-1875). The circuits include Chatham, Moore, and Carteret counties.

1097. CYRIL CONISTON CLEMENS PAPERS, 1930-1961. 96 items. Webster Groves (Saint Louis County), Mo.

Principally letters from George Santayana (1863-1952), poet, novelist, and philosopher, to Cyril Clemens, editor of the Mark Twain Quarterly and cousin of Samuel Clemens. Santayana discusses personal matters, his own writings and the progress of his work, the writings of others about his life and philosophy, and the work of other literary figures. Attached to many letters are clippings about Santayana's works, which Santayana was returning to Clemens, along with his marginal comments. Also included are the manuscript and galley proof of Santayana's article, "Tom Sawyer and Don Quixote"; a reprint, "Brief History of My Opinion," a chapter from Contemporary American Philosophy, Personal Statements, edited by George P. Adams and William P. Montague; a proof of Clemens's article, "An American Philosopher in Exile, George Santayana"; and a typed copy of his booklet, George Santayana: An American in Exile. The latter two items contain corrections by Santayana.

1098. JEREMIAH CLEMENS PAPERS, 1853. 1 item. Huntsville (Madison County), Ala.

Letter of Jeremiah Clemens (1814-1865), soldier, novelist, and senator, concerning the application of Henry Myers for a pursership in the Navy.

1099. SAMUEL LANGHORNE CLEMENS PAPERS, 1903-1910. 3 items. Hannibal (Marion County), Mo. Restricted.

Copy of a letter from Samuel Clemens (1835-1910), author, to the publisher Munro about a literary matter; a copy of Mark Twain's Seventieth Birthday: Souvenir of Its Celebration (Harper and Brothers, 1905); and an obituary of Clemens from an unidentified publication.

1100. JOHN MARSHALL CLEMENT PAPERS, 1830-1872. 24 items. Mocksville (Davie County), N.C.

Family, school, and legal correspondence of John M. Clement (1825-1886), lawyer and member of the North Carolina state legislature. School letters are from De Witt C. Clement, while at Clegg's College, near Mocksville, North Carolina, to John M. Clement while attending college at Gettysburg, Pennsylvania, and to Clement's sister while at Edgeworth Female Academy, Greensboro, North Carolina. Included also are a letter discussing the presidential election of 1840, letters and a speech on the political activities of the Whigs and Democrats in North Carolina; a letter from Merryhill, North Carolina, concerning the Civil War; and an essay on card playing.

1101. THOMAS GREEN CLEMSON PAPERS, 1848-1870. 4 items. "Fort Hill," Oconee County, S.C.

Papers of Thomas G. Clemson (1807-1888), South Carolina educator, diplomat, and son-in-law of John C. Calhoun. Included are an agreement between Clemson and his overseer Reuben H. Reynolds, 1848; a financial statement, 1849; a letter of introduction, 1865, for James Edward Calhoun to Max Van den Bergh, vice-consul of the United States at Antwerp, in which Clemson comments upon the effects of emancipation on the labor supply in the South; and a letter, 1870, from Anna Maria (Calhoun) Clemson concerning her family's estate.

1102. ANDREW CLENDENING DAYBOOK AND LEDGER, 1852-1864. 1 vol. (18 pp.) [Winchester?] (Frederick County), Va.

Mercantile accounts.

1103. STEPHEN GROVER CLEVELAND PAPERS, 1885-1904. 6 items. New York, N.Y.

Three routine letters written by Grover Cleveland (1837-1908), president of the United States; a letter of recommendation; and invitations to the inaugural balls in 1885 and 1893.

1104. CLEVELAND COTTON MILL ACCOUNTS, 1888-1896. 3 vols. Lawndale (Cleveland County), N.C.

Cotton house records of a cotton mill.

1105. JACOB B. CLICK PAPERS, 1861-1867. 30 items. Dayton (Rockingham County), Va.

Family letters of Private Jacob B. Click, C.S.A., discussing personal affairs and the war. Included are references to the 5th Regiment, Virginia Cavalry, and the 10th Virginia Regiment, C.S.A.; military engagements, especially the first battle of Bull Run, the Peninsular Campaign, and the battles of Fredericksburg, Kelly's Ford, Gettysburg, and Chancellorsville; prisoners; camp life; sickness and scarcity of food; morale; and various Confederate and Union officers.

1106. NATHAN CLIFFORD PAPERS, 1843. 1 item. Washington, D.C. and Cornish (York County), Me.

Letter from Nathan Clifford (1803-1881), U.S. congressman, 1839-1843, and associate justice of the U.S. Supreme Court, 1858-1881, to J. H. Hedges concerning the residence of Joshua A. Lowell, late congressman from Maine.

1107. JOHN L. CLIFTON PAPERS, 1784 (1830-1889) 1916. 4,714 items and 11 vols. Clinton (Sampson County) and Faison (Duplin County), N.C.

Correspondence, legal papers, bills and receipts of John L. Clifton, businessman, clergyman, and possibly attorney, are principally concerned with the administration of numerous estates: William G. Alford, Thomas Bennett, Henry Britt, Joshua Craddock, Nanny Darden, Humphrey Flowers, Fred Herring, Allen King, Bryant King, Elizabeth McPhail, Jesse Oates, Lewis Pipkin, Benjamin Revel, Josiah B. Stevens, Needham Stevens, and Joseph Strickland. Included in the estates papers are contracts for hiring slaves, deeds for the sale of slaves, land deeds, several wills and marriage licenses, lists of commodity prices, and price lists published by commission merchants in New York, 1883 and 1886. Family correspondence consists of letters from Clifton's sons, H. J. and F. A., while serving in the Confederate Army in South Carolina and Virginia. They describe the battle of Fort Sumter, officers' pay and costs of supplies, fortifications at Georgetown and Wilmington, a retreat from Fredericksburg to Richmond, and the siege of Charleston. Miscellaneous items include an ordination certificate of John L. Clifton in the Free Will Baptist Church, 1835; papers dealing with the suit of John L. Clifton v. Francis Westbrook and John Atkinson; and powers of attorney. Volumes include a ledger, 1842-1861, of John L. Clifton; a daybook, 1837-1838, of William S. Clinton; daybook, 1852-1857, of James A. Tillman, a physician; and student copybooks.

1108. JACOB CLINGMAN AND COMPANY LETTER BOOK AND ACCOUNTS, 1816-1829. 1 vol. (79 pp.) Huntsville (Surry County), N.C.

1109. THOMAS LANIER CLINGMAN PAPERS, 1833-1885. 8 items and 3 vols. Asheville (Buncombe County), N.C.

Papers of Thomas L. Clingman (1812-1897), U.S. Congressman and senator, and Confederate brigadier general, include letters, 1859-1880, to his neice, Jane A. Puryear, concerning his activity in public life, a projected trip to Europe in 1859, and family matters; a letter from Clingman recommending the appointment of Bushrod W. Vick to a consulship; and a letter, 1863, to Clingman concerning desertion in his brigade during his absence. The volumes consist of three of his brigade order books, 1862-1864, containing orders and letters, 276 items, concerning Confederate military activity around Camp Whiting, North Carolina; and a notebook, 1833, evidently prepared by Clingman while studying law.

1110. HENRY PELHAM FIENNES PELHAM-CLINTON, FOURTH DUKE OF NEWCASTLE, PAPERS, 1847. 1 item. London, England.

Letter from Lord George Bentinck to the Duke of Newcastle (1785-1851), author and politician, analyzing the recent parliamentary election in which Edward Cardwell defeated Lord John Manners.

1111. CLIONIAN DEBATING SOCIETY PROCEEDINGS, 1851-1858. 1 vol. Charleston, S.C.

A record of meetings and final dissolution of the Clionian Debating Society.

1112. JOSEPH CLISBY RECEIPT BOOK, 1857-1862. 1 vol. Macon (Bibb County), Ga.

Receipt book for printing the *Christian Index*.

1113. EDWARD CLODD PAPERS, 1883-1894. 15 items. London, England.

Papers of Edward Clodd (1840-1930), British banker and author, principally concern the Society of Authors and its chairman, Sir Walter Besant. Included are several personal letters. Correspondents include Ada Bayly, Sir Walter Besant, Edward Clodd, Moncure Conway, Dean Frederic W. Farrar, David Edward Hughes, Sir Edwin Ray Lankester, Clement Shorter, and Hesba Stretton.

1114. CHARLES MATHEW CLODE PAPERS, 1862-1882. 28 items. London, England.

Correspondence of Charles Mathew Clode (1818-1893), solicitor and legal secretary at the War Office, and author, pertains to the Militia Act of 1852 and other military statutes; the merits of the local militia, the volunteer forces, and compulsory service; and the manufacture of Armstrong guns for customers other than the War Department.

1115. JOHN CLOPTON PAPERS, 1629 (1775-1897) 1915. 11,890 items and 26 vols. New Kent County, and Manchester (Chesterfield County), Va.

Family correspondence and miscellaneous papers of four generations of the Clopton family and three generations of the Wallace family. The papers from 1629 to 1732 are genealogical records. Papers of John Clopton (1756-1816), Virginia legislator and U.S. Representative, 1795-1799, 1801-1816, contain comments on the Revolutionary War, the Continental Congress, Jay's Treaty, the Alien and Sedition Acts, politics in the Jeffersonian Republican Party, the Embargo Act, American relations with France, and the fear of a slave insurrection. Letters to a son, John Bacon Clopton (b. 1785), Virginia judge, pertain to the operation of a plantation in New Kent County. Correspondence of Charles Montriou Wallace, Sr. (1825-1910), Richmond merchant, includes accounts of an overland journey to California, 1849, and subsequent residence there; Confederate trade with Nassau and England; Reconstruction in the South; the writer's early life in Richmond; politics in Richmond and Virginia; travels in England, Scotland, and the South; literary pursuits, especially book collection, and other matters. Also of interest are letters of William Manson Wallace, Jr., describing life in the U.S. Navy, 1845; letters of Jefferson Wallace (1823-1864) describing a journey to California by way of Panama, and from St. George, Bermuda, concerning a secret mission for the Confederate government; Civil War letters from William Izard Clopton, and others from his mother, Maria (Foster) Clopton, wife of John B. Clopton; letters from the Crenshaw commission firm in Richmond concerning wartime and postwar business conditions; letters of Jefferson Wallace (b. 1864), concerning the publishing, fertilizer, and insurance businesses; letters of Adelaide Clopton, a teacher who was a granddaughter of John Clopton, relating to the Chesapeake Female College; and letters from Wallace relatives in Scotland and England. Volumes include financial record books, 1861-1865, of Adelaide Clopton, containing lists of students, tuition accounts, and the minutes and the constitution of the Keecoughton Literary Society at Chesapeake Female College; housekeeping accounts, ca. 1857-1885; a poetry scrapbook, and an essay on "Knitting in Virginia as a Fine Art," 1898-1899, by Joyce Wilkinson (Clopton) Wallace; legal case book, 1820, of John B. Clopton; lists of books belonging to Charles M. Wallace, Sr.; diaries and journals, 1865-1910, of Charles M. Wallace, including accounts of his travels in England, Scotland, and the American South; the record book of the Black Creek Temperance Society of Hanover County, Virginia, 1830-1831; account books of Jefferson Wallace; and a daybook and ledger, 1860-1867, of William Wallace & Sons, grocers and liquor dealers.

1116. MARY E. CLOUD PAPERS, 1847-1884. 218 items. Front Royal (Warren County), Va.

Personal correspondence among the brothers and sisters of a minister's family and their relatives and friends. The letters are chiefly concerned with the personal relations of a family of extremely religious temperament. There are a few letters from Sara (Cloud) Gibbons and her husband, A. S. Gibbons, a teacher at the College of the Pacific, Stockton, California, and Ohio University, Athens. Civil War letters concern military activities in Virginia, Maryland, and Pennsylvania, camp life, and Johnson's Island prison.

1117. ANDREW CLOW PAPERS, 1785-1790. 58 items. Philadelphia, Pa.

Business papers chiefly from merchants in Charleston, South Carolina; Alexandria, Virginia; and Hagerstown, Maryland; concerning the shipment of goods, efforts to collect money, and trade conditions. Also included are bills of Andrew Clow & Co., and a letter describing activity of the British fleet around Philadelphia.

1118. MARY WILLING CLYMER AUTOGRAPH ALBUM, 1856-1861. 1 vol. (86 pp.) Washington, D.C.

Verses from friends to Mary Clymer.

1119. ALBERT A. COBB AND COMPANY PAPERS, 1863-1893. 12 items. Boston, Mass.

Routine business letters pertaining to Albert A. Cobb and Company and other insurance companies.

1120. EATON COBB PAPERS, 1825-1938. 163 items. Edgecombe County, N.C.

Principally the business papers of Eaton Cobb and others, including the Bowditches, the McNairs, and the Thigpens, comprised of bills, receipts, and IOUs, 1826-1897. Legal papers include land deeds. Miscellaneous items include a letter, 1834, concerning the purchase or hire of a slave so that she could live with her husband; a memorandum, 1847, listing payments to canal hands; and instructions on the use of the cotton gin.

1121. HOWELL COBB PAPERS, 1843-1868. 55 items. Athens (Clarke County), Ga.

Papers of Howell Cobb (1815-1868), lawyer, member of U.S. Congress, member of President James Buchanan's cabinet, Confederate major general, and governor of Georgia, concerning a tax system for Georgia; Whig and Democratic politics in Georgia; military activities, including a letter, 1863, from Robert Toombs about raising a regiment for home defense, and a letter, April, 1865, to Joseph E. Brown about sending troops to aid Alabama; disaffection with the Confederate government in Georgia; and his work in Congress and as Secretary of the Treasury. Also included are a letter, 1860, from his wife, Mary Ann (Lamar) Cobb, describing a state dinner and a party given at the White House for the Prince of Wales; and a memorial prepared by the Macon bar at Cobb's death.

1122. JOB COBB PAPERS, 1861-1862. 2 items. Tarboro (Edgecombe County), N.C.

Letters from Job Cobb, private in the Confederate Army, stationed first at Yorktown and later at Richmond, Virginia, during the Peninsular campaign. The letters mention rations, food prices, and his hatred of the enemy.

1123. THOMAS READE ROOTES COBB PAPERS, 1852-1862. 19 items. Cherry Hill (Jefferson County), Ga.

Civil War papers and routine political correspondence of T. R. R. Cobb (1823-1862), Georgia statesman and Confederate general, including vouchers of pay received by enlisted men and officers of Cobb's Georgia Legion, two letters regarding the death of Edward F. Bagley, 1861, and a letter to his wife from Fredericksburg, Virginia, discussing the war.

1124. WILLIAM COBBETT PAPERS, 1820, 1887. 2 items. London, England.

Letter from William Cobbett (1762-1835), British essayist, politician, and agriculturalist, appealing for funds to support his candidacy to Parliament; and a letter from his daughter, Susan, concerning the collection of sets of Cobbett's Weekly Political Register for libraries.

1125. JOHN F. COBBS DOCKET BOOK, 1868-1869. 1 vol. Danville (Pittsylvania County), Va.

Lists of bankrupts, and court docket for counties in the vicinity of Danville.

1126. RICHARD COBDEN PAPERS, 1840-1864. 42 items. Manchester, Lancashire, England.

Correspondence of Richard Cobden (1804-1865), Manchester industrialist, member of Parliament, and a founder of the National Anti-Corn Law League, principally relate to his opposition to the Corn Laws. Other topics of concern include the national budget, free trade, British-French relations, military and naval armament, the revolutions of 1848, the possibility of war with Russia over the Eastern Question, the extension of the franchise, popular education, and crime.

1127. ANN COBIA PAPERS, 1810-1869. 37 items and 1 vol. Charleston, S.C.

Business and legal papers of Sarah, Ann, and Mary Cobia. Volume contains an inventory, accounts, sales, and receipts of Ann Cobia's estate.

1128. ALBERT LUCIAN COBLE PAPERS, 1844 (1895-1900) 1929. 635 items and 1 vol. Statesville (Iredell County), N.C.

Principally the legal papers, letters, and documents, 1895-1900, of Judge Albert L. Coble (1855-1918), concerning his service as Superior Court Judge. Other papers include bills and receipts; letters discussing the Spanish-American War and World War I; letters, 1913, discussing trouble in the Episcopal parish at Statesville; letters, 1920s, pertaining to the work of Mrs. Coble in the North Carolina Federation of Women's Clubs; and several items, 1920s, concerning the Republican Party in North Carolina, including a plan of organization, 1922. The volume contains the minutes of the Alpha Book Club, of which Mrs. Coble was a member.

1129. A. JACKSON COCHRAN PAPERS, 1844-1883. 19 items. Greenbrier County, W. Va.

Papers of A. Jackson Cochran and other members of the Cochran family comprised of sheriff's summonses and personal letters.

1130. GEORGE COCHRAN PAPERS, 1830-1832. 35 items. Franklin County, Pa.

Legal papers of George Cochran, constable of Washington township, Pennsylvania.

1131. JOHN LEWIS COCHRAN PAPERS, 1861-1870. 6 items. Charlottesville (Albemarle County), Va.

Business papers of John Lewis Cochran, editor, lawyer, captain in the Confederate Army, and judge.

1132. GEORGE COCKBURN PAPERS, 1899-1900. 2 items. London, England.

Letters of Colonel George Cockburn (1856-1925) chronicle the siege of Ladysmith, Natal, by the Boers.

1133. JOHN HARTWELL COCKE PAPERS, 1825-1872. 11 items. Surry County, Va.

Business letters of John Hartwell Cocke (1780-1866), planter, agricultural reformer, and brigadier general in the War of 1812, concerning the purchase of land in Perry County, Alabama, the weather, crop conditions, prices, and the health of slaves. Other items include letters to Dr. Cary Charles Cocke, son of J. H. Cocke; a report on the progress of a younger John Hartwell Cocke at the University of Virginia, Charlottesville; and the will and accompanying documents of Philip St. George Cocke, son of J. H. Cocke.

1134. RICHARD IVANHOE COCKE PAPERS, 1824-1864. 93 items. Fluvanna County, Va.

Promissory notes, accounts, and other business papers of Richard I. Cocke (b. 1820), planter.

1135. WILLIAM A. COCKEFAIR PAPERS, 1861-1862. 1 vol. Indiana.

Diary of William A. Cockefair, 15th Regiment, Indiana Volunteers, concerning the military activities of his regiment in Virginia, Kentucky, Tennessee, Mississippi, and Alabama.

1136. FRANCIS MARION COCKRELL PAPERS, 1861-1895. 12 items. Warrensburg (Johnson County), Mo.

Routine correspondence of Francis M. Cockrell (1834-1915) while serving in the U.S. Senate. Some biographical material is also included.

1137. MONROE FULKERSON COCKRELL PAPERS, 1859-1972. 627 items and 4 vols. Evanston (Cook County), Ill.

The papers of Monroe Fulkerson Cockrell, a Chicago banker, consist of his notes and correspondence concerning historical research, copies of his essays, and material he had privately printed. The bulk of the material pertains to various issues of Civil War history, including the activities of General George E. Pickett at the battle of Gettysburg; the furniture in the William McLean house at Appomattox, Virginia; the location of the graves of several military leaders; the siege of Vicksburg; the battle of Corinth, Mississippi; and the route taken by the members of the Confederate cabinet as they fled Richmond in 1865. Included are a copy of a letter, 1862, from General A. P. Hill discussing the activities of Confederate and Union troops, and the building of the Manassas Junction-Centerville Confederate Military Railroad; a copy of a letter, 1864, describing General William T. Sherman's expedition, and war conditions in Mississippi; and a letter, 1865, describing General Nathan Bedford Forrest. Other items of interest are letters from Shirley Seifert relating to her book Destiny in Dallas; notes and correspondence concerning the rumor that General Erwin J. E. Rommel was sent to the United States by Adolph Hitler to study the strategy of various Civil War battles; a typed manuscript, "The Flavor of Life in Small Towns," containing jokes and anecdotes exchanged between Cockrell and John R. Smith of Martinsville, Virginia; a bound volume, "Gathered Flowers," consisting of correspondence between Cockrell and his Georgia friends; and volumes IX-XVI of Cockrell's magazine <u>After Sundown</u>, which contain Cockrell's journal describing a trip in 1955 from Evanston to the southeastern United States, a copy of a letter describing early life in Washington, Georgia, and letters from William Allen White, John W. Davis, and Katherine Anne Porter.

1138. SARAH (HORTON) COCKRELL PAPERS, 1861-1871. 64 items. Dallas (Dallas County), Tex.

Principally Civil War letters of Colonel George W. Guess (1829-1868), of the 31st Regiment, Texas Volunteer Cavalry, "Spright's Brigade," to Sarah (Horton) Cockrell (1819-1892), from various camps in Texas, Arkansas, and Louisiana. Included are descriptions of camp life, the health of soldiers, discharges, military activities, especially the battle of Oak Hill, Confederate and Union officers, the capture of Martin D. Hunt who had preached against conscription, the seizure of Guess's cotton by Federal troops, and accusations that Guess was trading with the Federals. Also included are several letters from other Confederate soldiers, Confederate receipts, an account, 1868, of the property of Sarah Cockrell which she alleged was taken by Federal troops, and letters, 1871, describing the behavior of Negro policemen and the arrival of Negro troops in Groesbeck, Texas.

1139. JOHN SOMERS COCKS, FIRST EARL SOMERS, PAPERS, 1785. 1 item. London, England.

Letter from John Russell, later Sixth Duke of Bedford, to Lord Somers (1760-1841), member of the House of Commons, 1782-1806, concerning legislative measures for Ireland, parliamentary reform, and personal matters.

1140. WILLIAM FREDERICK CODY PAPERS, 1916. 2 items. Cody (Park County), Wyo.

Letter of William Frederick Cody (1846-1917), best known as "Buffalo Bill," U.S. government scout and guide, and Nebraska legislator, to Brother Miner concerning a visit of seventy-five "Brothers" of the National Home of Bedford, Virginia, to Cody; and an itinerary card for "Buffalo Bill (Himself) and the 101 Ranch Shows Combined."

1141. COE-LANCKSTER GENEALOGY, 14th-18th centuries. 1 item. Suffolk County, England.

Genealogy of the Coe, also spelled Coo, and Lanckster families.

1142. T. J. COFFEY NOTEBOOK. 1 vol. (162 pp.) Hollidaysburg (Blair County), Pa.

Notes on <u>The First Part of the Institutes of the Laws of England</u> (Coke upon Littleton).

1143. ROBERT BARRY COFFIN PAPERS, 1855. 1 item. New York, N.Y.

Letter from author Frederick Swartwout Cozzens to Robert Barry Coffin, editor of <u>Home Journal</u> and <u>The Table</u>, acknowledging receipt of a check, and declining an invitation.

1144. JAMES O. COGHILL PAPERS, 1843 (1861-1864) 1894. 88 items. Henderson (Vance County), N.C.

Principally the Civil War letters of the four sons of Captain James O. Coghill, all members of the 13th North Carolina Volunteers (after May, 1862, the 23rd North Carolina Regiment), describing military activities in Virginia, Maryland, and Pennsylvania; sickness in the army; and aid to the soldiers of the 23rd Regiment from their families in North Carolina. Included are frequent references to other members of the 23rd Regiment.

1145. ALONZO B. COHEN PAPERS, 1860-1865. 32 items. Carrollton (Pickens County), Ala.

Civil War letters describing camp life and the battles at Manassas.

1146. SOLOMON COHEN PAPERS, 1863-1864. 13 items. Savannah, Ga.

Official letters to Solomon Cohen, Confederate postmaster at Savannah, from the Post Office Department in Richmond discussing routine matters such as appointments, routes, and delays in delivery.

1147. JOHN COLBORNE, FIRST BARON SEATON, PAPERS, 1819-1854. 53 items. Lyneham Park, Devonshire, England.

Principally letters to John Colborne, First Baron Seaton (1778-1863), British general and colonial official, from Generals Sir George Thomas Napier and Sir William Francis Patrick Napier pertaining to the Peninsular War. Letters include detailed discussions of plans for Sir William's book on the war, sources to be used, specific battles and campaigns, and British and French generals. There are also references to the education and early military careers of the sons of Sir George and Sir William and to the career of Sir Charles James Napier, a brother. Scattered letters concern Canada, Guernsey Island, the Ionian Islands, South Africa, South Australia, and British and French politics.

1148. WEBSTER J. COLBURN PAPERS, 1889.
1 item.  Wisconsin.

Letter to Webster J. Colburn, a major in the U.S. Army during the Civil War, from Montgomery Cunningham Meigs concerning the twentieth annual reunion of the Army of the Cumberland.

1149. ROBERT COLBY PAPERS, 1856-1899.
11 items.  New York.

Bills and receipts of Robert Colby, and a copy of The Christian Arbitrator and Peace Record of February, 1889.

1150. ARTHUR VANCE COLE PAPERS, 1912-1976.
594 items and 7 vols.  Durham, N.C.

Letters, miscellaneous papers, clippings, printed material and pictures of Arthur Vance Cole (1880-1976) pertain to his activities as a union organizer for the Tobacco Workers International Union (T. W. I. U.), 1919-1920; his involvement with the Durham County Republicans, especially 1926-1936, including material on local, state, and national campaigns; his position as U.S. Commissioner of the Eastern District of North Carolina, ca. 1935-1945; and his membership in the Masons, ca. 1937-1974.  The volumes include a dues book and memorandum books concerning his work for the T. W. I. U.; volumes concerning the Durham County Republicans, containing names, addresses, and telephone numbers of the Executive Committee and local candidates in the election of 1928, correspondence from the state office concerning the campaign of 1930, and rough minutes of the Executive Committee meetings in 1934 and 1936; and a Record of Proceedings in Criminal Cases, 1935-1945, recording cases heard before Cole and in Durham.

1151. JESSE W. COLE PAPERS, 1867-1871.
9 vols.  Orange County, N.C.

Account books for a general store, including daybooks, ledgers, and inventory lists.

1152. JOHN NELSON COLE PAPERS, 1873-1948.
7 items and 1 vol.  Raleigh (Wake County), N.C.

Personal letters of the Reverend Doctor John Nelson Cole, of the Methodist Episcopal Church, South; a tract on Baptism in a Nutshell (1891) by Rev. Dr. Charles Taylor; and a scrapbook, 1892-1898, containing newspaper and magazine clippings, many written by Cole, criticizing Baptist practices and Presbyterian doctrine, items discussing Greensboro (N.C.) Female College and the prospect of establishing a Methodist female college in Raleigh, and other miscellaneous papers.

1153. ANN (RANEY) THOMAS COLEMAN PAPERS, 1846-1892.  78 items.  Pointe Coupee Parish, La. and Port Lavaca (Calhoun County), Tex.

Personal and family letters of Ann (Raney) Thomas Coleman; and a typescript (333 pp.) of her personal reminiscences describing her early life at Whitehaven, Cumberland County, England; the immigration of her family to the United States; and her subsequent life in Louisiana and Texas.  Included are accounts of her marriage to a wealthy landowner, their efforts to open a plantation in Louisiana, her second marriage and later divorce, and her efforts to support herself.  She also discusses agriculture, social life in Louisiana and Texas, the Mexican War, and slavery.

1154. HAWES H. COLEMAN PAPERS, 1806 (1845-1895) 1921.  87 items and 2 vols.  Arkadelphia (Clark County), Ark.

Correspondence of the Coleman family, including accounts of social life and customs in Arkansas during and after the Civil War; the establishment of Ouachita College in Arkadelphia; the introduction of the telegraph in Arkansas; pensions to Confederate veterans; the labor situation during Reconstruction; and Negroes during Reconstruction.  Diaries contain records of financial transactions in the pre-war era; accounts of several military actions and the confiscation of property by Federal and Confederate troops; records of farm life in Arkansas; cotton prices during Reconstruction; and recipes and medical prescriptions.

1155. LAURENCE VAIL COLEMAN PAPERS, 1927.
1 item.  Washington, D.C.

Letter from zoologist Roy Chapman Andrews in China to Laurence Vail Coleman, museum expert, concerning the destruction of Chinese antiquities, the "robber generals," and the embargo on the exportation of museum specimens.

1156. LINDSEY COLEMAN PAPERS, 1845 (1863-1864) 1871.  29 items.  Amherst County, Va.

Letters of the Coleman family principally concerning the sale of agricultural products to the Confederate government.

1157. COLERAIN BAPTIST CHURCH RECORDS, 1821-1909.  7 items and 3 vols.  Colerain (Bertie County), N.C.

Church minutes, 1829-1904, containing membership lists, rules, the covenant, financial records, obituaries, and historical statements; a history of the church; a letter of dismissal; and other miscellaneous papers.

1158. JAMES DUKE COLERIDGE PAPERS, 1853.
1 item. Thorverton, Devonshire, England.

Letter from James Duke Coleridge (1788-1857), British divine, concerning the parliamentary by-election of William E. Gladstone over Dudley Perceval.

1159. SAMUEL TAYLOR COLERIDGE PAPERS, 1795-1808. 1 item and 1 vol. England.

Memorandum book of Samuel Taylor Coleridge (1772-1834), British literary figure, containing several of his poems, some varying from the printed versions; and a letter from Coleridge to William Allen (1770-1843) mentioning work he was doing for Thomas Clarkson.

1160. EMILIE S. COLES PAPERS, 1880-1923. 54 items. Scotch Plains (Union County), N.J.

Correspondence of Emilie S. Coles, largely from editors concerning her writings which were published in newspapers and magazines. Also included are personal letters from Mary J. Porter and others.

1161. WALTER COLES PAPERS, 1850-1869. 6 items. Pittsylvania County, Va.

Correspondence of Walter Coles, probably a planter, include a letter from Thomas Stanhope Bocock, U.S. representative from Virginia, 1847-1861; a printed letter from Bocock advertising the Weekly Washington (D.C.) Union; a letter from Thomas Hamlet Averett, U.S. representative from Virginia, 1849-1853, concerning the Democratic nomination to the House desired by both himself and Bocock; a letter pertaining to the estate of R. T. Coles; and a letter discussing the sale of Coles's tobacco.

1162. SCHUYLER COLFAX PAPERS, 1866, 1868. 2 items. South Bend (Saint Joseph County), Ind.

A political letter from Schuyler Colfax (1823-1885), vice-president of the United States, concerning the scheduling of a caucus; and a clipping, 1868, assessing Colfax's ability to serve as vice-president.

1163. A COLLECTION OF MANUSCRIPT POETRY, 17th and 18th centuries. 1 vol. England.

Primarily copies of 17th century English poetry, including poems by George Herbert, William Strode, Charles Sedley, and William Davenant, written in what may have been the commonplace book of Robert Clarke; also poetry of the 18th century written in a different handwriting. The volume is described in English Language Notes, X (March, 1973), 201-208.

1164. CUTHBERT COLLINGWOOD, FIRST BARON COLLINGWOOD PAPERS, 1807-1809. 3 items. Newcastle-upon-Tyne, Northumberland County, England.

Two letters of Admiral Collingwood of the British Navy, commander of the Mediterranean fleet, to Captain Mansfield of H.M.S. Minotaur mentioning his weariness of war, ship construction, and Mansfield's support off Sardinia; and a letter from Sir Robert Adair, British diplomat in Turkey, concerning the diplomatic relations of Britain, Russia, and Austria with Turkey.

1165. JOSIAH COLLINS PAPERS, 1819-1850. 3 items. Edenton (Chowan County), N.C.

The will of Josiah Collins and two personal letters.

1166. MICHAEL COLLINS PAPERS, 1826-1861. 5 items. Warrenton (Warren County), N.C.

Correspondence of Michael Collins, North Carolina planter, including a letter from his son at Wake Forest College, North Carolina, in 1845, with a list of school supplies and prices; and an undated letter to a local newspaper on the evils of allowing slaves to come into town on Sunday to sell produce in exchange for whiskey.

1167. THOMAS HIGHTOWER COLLINS PAPERS, 1950-1976. 30,956 items. Chapel Hill (Orange County), N.C. Restricted.

Papers of journalist Thomas Hightower Collins representing his work as author of newspaper columns, books, and pamphlets on old-age retirement. The collection contains copies of his publications, including Golden Years: How to Prepare to Retire; "Inquiring About Retiring"; several editions of The Golden Years; and clippings and transcripts of columns--"The Golden Years," 1950-1966, and "The Senior Forum," 1956-1963. There are also letters and printed material related to Collins's columns; press releases, 1951-1965; correspondence, mainly comprised of letters from readers, with scattered letters from friends, relatives, newspaper editors, and General Features Corporation, 1951-1976; and writings and addresses, 1967-1968, some descriptive of life in Chapel Hill.

1168. WILLIAM F. COLLINS NOTEBOOK, 1826. 1 vol. (134 pp.) Middletown (Middlesex County), Conn.

Notebook kept by Collins while a student at the American Literary, Scientific, and Military Academy containing letters, obituaries, poems or songs, and eulogies; and notes of lectures given by Alden Partridge on fortifications, artillery, gunnery, attack, defence, and tactics.

1169. COLLINS MANUFACTURING COMPANY PAPERS, 1833-1853. 154 items. Hartford (Hartford County), Conn.

Business correspondence of a company manufacturing axes and heavy cutlery, with wholesalers in New York, Boston, Philadelphia, Baltimore, and New Orleans, and with iron and steel manufacturers in New York, Philadelphia, and Baltimore.

1170. ALFRED HOLT COLQUITT PAPERS, [1846?] 1889. 6 items. Troup County, Ga.

Papers of Alfred Holt Colquitt (1824-1894), U.S. congressman and senator, Confederate major general, and governor of Georgia, and of his father, Walter Terry Colquitt (1799-1855), U.S. congressman, including a letter by Walter T. Colquitt concerning politics and the upcoming presidential election, and a letter of Alfred H. Colquitt to C. C. Jones, Jr., discussing his address on the New South.

1171. WILLIAM NEYLE COLQUITT PAPERS, 1901 (1911-1915) 1923. 1,043 items. Savannah, Ga.

Correspondence of William Neyle Colquitt, lawyer, newspaper reporter and publisher, and politician, concerning the pre-convention campaigns of Judson Harmon and Oscar W. Underwood for the 1912 presidential nomination; recommendations of Colquitt for several federal positions; and the raising of funds for and erecting of a monument at Midway, Georgia, to the memory of Generals James Screven and Daniel Stewart. There is also correspondence dealing with automobile races in Savannah in 1911 and 1912. Correspondents include prominent national and state politicians.

1172. COLUMBIA CITY CENTRAL LABOR UNION PAPERS, 1929-1939. 1 vol. Columbia (Richland County), S.C.

A ledger listing credits and debits of the various unions affiliated with the City Central Labor Union (AFL), including the City Federation of Traders, the Brotherhood of Railroad Carmen of America, No. 300, and the Carpenters and Joiners, No. 1778.

1173. WILLIAM COMBE PAPERS, 1813-ca. 1823. 1 vol. (21 pp., 18 illus.) London, England.

Manuscript volume entitled "Oxford University" contains seventeen color plates and one black and white plate depicting the academic costumes of the University, with accompanying explanatory text. The plates were published by Rudolph Ackermann in _A History of the University of Oxford, Its Colleges, Halls, and Public Buildings_ (London: 1814), for which William Combe (1741-1823), British author, supplied the text. The text in the manuscript may be a copy of Combe's work.

1174. NATHANIEL COMER PAPERS, 1840-1860. 21 items. County Line (Davie County), N.C.

Family letters of Nathaniel and Catherine Comer from relatives in Pettis County, Missouri, concerning family matters, the condition and prices of crops, the Mexican War, and journeys by Russell G. Comer to Sante Fe and Salt Lake City.

1175. JOSHUA COMFORT AND MERRIT COMFORT PAPERS, 1862-1865. 70 items. Ithaca (Tompkins County), N.Y.

Civil War letters from Joshua and Merrit Comfort, New York State Volunteers, to their parents, concerning the battles of Missionary Ridge, Tennessee, and Fredericksburg, Virginia; military conscription; drafting of Maryland Negroes; the siege of Petersburg; Sherman's march; living conditions among the Federal troops; desertions; pay; furloughs; and military duties.

1176. COMMENCEMENT ADDRESS. 1 vol. 27 pp.

An address on the subject of the education of women, probably from the antebellum period.

1177. SAMUEL WILSON COMPTON PAPERS, 1840-1925. 1 item and 14 vols. Manchester (Adams County), Ohio.

Reminiscences and autobiography of Samuel Wilson Compton (b. 1833), farmer, soldier, peddler, and teacher, describing his early life in Manchester; student days at Miami University and Lebanon Normal School; farming in Ohio; his maternal grandfather, Israel Donelson; his Civil War experiences with the 12th Ohio Volunteer Infantry, especially at Antietam, Lynchburg, and South Mountain; and his travels in Iowa, Indiana, Wisconsin, Minnesota, Michigan, and Illinois.

1178. W. S. COMSTOCK AND CO. PAPERS, 1849-1851. 7 items. Montgomery, Ala.

Letters to P. L. Coley, New England manufacturer of shoes, containing orders and complaints about shipments, and references to commodity and land prices in Alabama.

1179. CONFEDERATE LEAGUE SUBSCRIPTION BOOK, 1862-1870. 1 vol. West Baton Rouge, La.

Record of donations to the Confederacy, usually in the form of sugar, cotton, molasses, or wood. The volume also contains a few records of Bolling R. Chinn's plantation, Cypress Hall, 1868-1870. Chinn probably kept the records for the Confederate League.

1180. CONFEDERATE STATES OF AMERICA. CONGRESS. PAPERS, 1861-1865. 98 items and 2 vols.

Original enrolled statutes, 96 items, bearing the signatures of the presiding officers of the House of Representatives and the Senate and the approval of President Jefferson Davis. Ninety of these items belong to the 2d sess., Second Confederate Congress (Nov. 7, 1864-Mar. 18, 1865). These acts have been published in Laws and Joint Resolutions of the Last Session of the Confederate Congress, edited by Charles W. Ramsdell (Durham: Duke University Press, 1941). Also in the collection is the official register of the acts of the Confederate Congress, 1861-1865, 1 vol., giving title and dates of passage and approval of acts of both the provisional (incomplete) and permanent congresses. There are typescript copies of the acts and the register. There is also a register of bills and joint resolutions of the Confederate House of Representatives, 1864, 1 vol. (14 pp.), showing dates of actions taken, passage, and approval. Miscellaneous papers are a petition, 1863, from an unidentified planter of Coahoma County, Mississippi, describing conditions in the delta after the fall of Vicksburg, and a letter, 1865, to William P. Miles, member of Congress, seeking an appointment.

1181. CONFEDERATE STATES OF AMERICA. EXECUTIVE DEPARTMENTS. PAPERS, 1861-1865. 467 items.

Papers relating to the Department of Justice, 1861-1865, deal primarily with legal proceedings, including the defense of Stephen W. Crawford of Georgia, 1861; an explanation offered the French consul in New York of why a French citizen may no longer do business at Camp Benjamin, 1862; several court-martial proceedings, 1863; a circular regarding punishment for the destruction of a church, 1864; charges against Major E. S. Burford, II Cavalry Corps; and charges against Union sympathizers turned over to the 45th Virginia Regiment. Papers relating to the Navy Department, 1861-1865, 16 items, include applications for leave; a promotion notification; a report, 1865, concerning plunder of stores; letters, 1862-1863, 3 items, concerning the captured schooner Willet S. Robbins; a report from the C.S.S. Gov. Moore; quartermaster's reports for the C.S.S. Virginia (No. 2), 1864, 2 items; report of the gunboat Sentinel, 1862, 1 item, at Roanoke Island; and vouchers, 1863-1864, 14 items, for travel, maintenance of steamers, and supplies at Shreveport, Louisiana. Papers relating to the Post Office Department, 1861-1865, 10 items, are largely reports from postmasters in Smith Bridge (Robeson County) and Harrington, North Carolina; Landon District, Abbeville, and Woodlawn (Edgefield County), South Carolina; and Austinville, Wythe County, Virginia; also a letter, 1863, regarding military exemption of postal contractors and administrative procedures regarding postage stamps. Papers of the State Department, 1861, 1 item, consist of a letter from C. J. N. Raynor providing a cipher for an agent in New York. Papers of the Treasury Department include accounts with the Confederate government in Camden County, North Carolina, 1864-1865, 1 vol., 15 pp.; auditors' office papers, 1861-1865, 8 items, containing claims of relatives of deceased soldiers, claims for an abandoned horse, and requisitions for money; papers of the office of the Secretary, 1861-1865, 23 items and 1 vol., containing checks, receipts, orders, and letters concerning treasury certificates and bonds, taxes and government indebtedness to railroads, and conscription orders. There are also receipts of tax in kind collected in the 7th Congressional District, Virginia, 1863-1864, 2 vols.; estimates and assessments of tax in kind, 1863-1865, 245 items and 10 vols., for Upson County, Georgia, and Mecklenburg, Albemarle, Amherst, Buckingham, Nelson, and Fluvanna counties, Virginia; and warrants, 1863-1865, 13 items, issued to Confederate agents abroad (Colin J. McRae, Ambrose Dudley Mann, and John Slidell), to Columbus Upson as governor of Arizona Territory, to Judah P. Benjamin, Secretary of State, for payment to the "Secret Service," and for payment of large sums to deputies in preparation for the evacuation of Richmond. There are also records of several branches of the War Department, as follows. Papers of the Adjutant and Inspector General's Office, 1861-1865, 82 items, are primarily orders signed by John Withers. Papers, 1864-1865, 4 items, of the Bureau of Conscription, largely concern furloughs and absent soldiers. Papers of the Bureau of Ordnance, 1862-1863, 5 items, are routine. Papers of the Engineer Bureau, 1862-1865, 7 items, contain checks, and letters concerning construction of a bridge at Demopolis and rails for the repair of railroads in Georgia. Papers of the Office of Inspector of Field Transportation, 1864-1865, 10 items, contain complaints about the impressment of horses and mules, reports on the inspection of roads, and the use of government wagons for private freight. Papers of the Office of Secretary, 1861-1863, 26 items, concern foreign trade and the effects of the blockade, transfer of U.S. property to the Confederate government, commissions in the Confederate Army, and passport forms. Papers of the Quartermaster General's Office, 1861-1865, 23 items, are orders, requisitions, letters, circulars, an indenture, and transportation passes for soldiers. Papers of the Subsistance Department, 1862-1865, 8 items, are mostly estimates of funds needed for various periods for [Charles C.] Crews' Brigade, the 12th Texas Cavalry, 17th Texas Cavalry, and the 7th North Carolina Regiment.

1182. CONFEDERATE STATES OF AMERICA. ARMY. MISCELLANY, MAPS, 1861-1865. 9 items.

Included are maps of Fort Pulaski; Garlington, Mississippi; roads between Columbus and Tuscaloosa; and the Wilmington-Fort Fisher area in December, 1864, signed by

John O'C. Barclay, U.S. Navy, showing the placement of the Union fleet.

1183. CONFEDERATE STATES OF AMERICA. ARMY. MISCELLANY, OFFICERS' AND SOLDIERS' LETTERS, 1861-1865. 492 items.

Letters from Confederate personnel which are unrelated to other collections, largely commenting on camp life, food, health, weather, homesickness, military campaigns and battles, prisoners and prison life, and prices. One letter of 1876 by Lewis E. Harvie, former president of the Richmond, Danville, and Piedmont railroads, defends the railroad's role in supplying the defense of Richmond.

1184. CONFEDERATE STATES OF AMERICA. ARMY. MISCELLANY. PRISON PAPERS, 1861-1865, 26 items and 1 vol.

Letters, a diary, and oaths of allegiance from Confederate prisoners at Old Capitol Prison, Washington, D.C.; Camp Chase, Columbus, Ohio; Palmyra, Missouri; Point Lookout, Maryland; Fort Delaware in Delaware Bay; Fort McHenry; Johnson's Island, Sandusky Bay, Ohio; and Rock Island in the Mississippi River between Rock Island, Illinois, and Davenport, Iowa. There are also receipts for property of Union prisoners in Andersonville, Georgia, and a guard report from Castle Pinckney, Charleston, South Carolina.

1185. CONFEDERATE STATES OF AMERICA. ARMY. TYPES OF RECORDS. 2,853 items.

Abstracts of dispatches received, North Carolina, 1864-1865, 1 vol. (510 pp.); applications for transfer, 1863-1864, 4 items; discharge certificates, 1861-1865, 26 items, including attached receipts for discharge pay; commissary papers, 1861-1865, 78 items; commissions and enlistment papers, 1861-1864, 12 items; exemption papers, 1862-1864, 12 items; field returns, 1861-1864, 12 items, showing organization and strength for armies and departments; order book, 1 vol. (62 pp.) of Victor J. B. Girardy, adjutant general at Augusta Arsenal, Georgia; records relating to hospitals, including an account of the expenditures for Chimborazo Hospital, Richmond, 1863-1865, 1 vol.; letterpress book of James Lawrence Cabell, superintendent of Charlottesville, Virginia, hospital, 1 vol., 1861-1862; miscellaneous hospital records, 1861-1865, 45 items; routine papers of the Surgeon General's Office, Richmond, 1861-1865, 12 items; papers of hospitals in North Carolina, 1862-1865, 10 items; of McPhersonville Hospital, South Carolina, 1862-1864, 4 items; and of hospitals in Virginia, 64 items and 5 vols.; impressment papers, 1863-1865, 10 vols., concerning the taking of cattle, horses, and slaves for work on fortifications and public works; morning reports, 1862-1865, 35 items, of various regiments, brigades, and battalions; ordnance reports and requisitions, 1861-1865, 47 items; payrolls, 1862-1865, 11 items, including muster rolls, receipts for pay received, and lists of pay and clothing for various individuals and units; provision returns and requisitions, 1861-1865, 30 items; quartermasters' papers, 1862-1865, 1,429 items and 1 vol., including records of John Jenkins, Motte A. Pringle (Charleston, South Carolina), Hamilton J. Stone (Anderson's Division, Army of Northern Virginia), and Fleming A. Saunders (pay vouchers for various Virginia regiments); quartermasters' accounts, 1863-1864, 1 vol. (156 pp.), for Mississippi and Alabama; reports on clothing, 1864-1865, 16 items, relating to the 34th Georgia Regiment and the 29th Alabama Regiment; reports of men present and absent, 1861-1865, 48 items, for various Arkansas, Georgia, Kentucky, Tennessee, and Texas regiments; reports on transportation, 1862-1865, 33 items, include information of transportation facilities in various units and reports of the arrival and departure of troops at Augusta, Georgia, 1865.

1186. CONFEDERATE STATES OF AMERICA. ARMY UNITS. 300 items and 1 vol.

Papers, 1861-1865, 71 items, of the Army of Mississippi relate to ordnance, supply, medicine, scouting, furloughs, signals, casualties, paroled federal prisoners, organization, transportation, and cotton. Persons mentioned include N.A. Birge, Adolph Dies, William Joseph Hardee, Albert Sidney Johnston, and Thomas Jordan. There are references to Mississippi cavalry, the 17th and 18th Louisiana Volunteer Regiments, Daniel Ruggles' Division, the Partisan Rangers, and the Washington (Louisiana) Artillery. Battles mentioned include Farmington, Mississippi, 1862, and Shiloh. Papers of the Army of Northern Virginia, 1862-1865, 25 items and 1 vol., are mainly miscellaneous orders. For the Army of Tennessee, 16 items and 1 vol., 1862-1865, there are miscellaneous orders and letters relating to furloughs, military life, supplies, organization of the artillery; also a dispatch book, including many dispatches, November and December, 1864, from John B. Hood to Beauregard, concerning the battle of Franklin and Union cavalry raids at Greenville and Pollard, Alabama. For the Department of Richmond, 1864, 2 items, there are conscription notices. Papers of the Department of South Carolina and Georgia, 1862-1865, 59 items, are largely orders of John C. Pemberton concerning surgeons, officers and their commands, discharges, publication of orders, the form of reports, courts-martial, supplies, and Beauregard's commands and inspections; there is also a memorandum on the condition of the fortifications on Sullivan's Island, April 6, 1864, by Roswell S. Ripley. For the District of the Gulf there is an order signed by Gen. Dabney H. Maury, 1864, concerning a detail for special duty. Relating to the Florida 8th Regiment of Volunteers are muster rolls, 1864, 9 items. For Georgia State Troops there are general orders for the 2nd Brigade and other units, 1861-1865, 31 items and 2 vols. Miscellaneous letters, reports, and orders concern various regiments of Louisiana, 1861-1863, 19 items and 1 volume. Records of North Carolina State Troops, 1861-1865, 36 items and 4 vols., concern the 2nd, 4th, 11th, 12th, 13th, 25th, 27th, 37th, and 66th Regiments, and contain letters, general orders, muster rolls, payrolls, requisitions for supplies, orders for movements, courts-martial, lists of veterans, lists of medical exemptions from duty, and a history of the 13th Regiment by H. C. Wall. For South Carolina State Troops, 1861-1864, 14 items and 1 vol., there are receipts for supplies and pay, letters, courts-martial papers, and an agreement of Lancaster District citizens to form a company of home guards which became Company A of the 9th South Carolina Infantry. Relating to Tennessee State Troops are rolls, 1 vol., 1861-1862, of the 3rd Regiment. For Virginia State Troops, 1861-1865, 2 items, there are lists of soldiers. For Wheeler's Cavalry Corps there are reports, 1865, 18 items, of Thomas Harrison's Brigade, Dibrell's Brigade, Iverson's Division, 11th Texas Cavalry, and 3rd Arkansas Cavalry, concerning transportation, ordnance, extra-duty rolls, medical and sanitary conditions, supplies, and lists of men.

1187.   CONFEDERATE STATES OF AMERICA. MISCELLANY, 1861-1865, 238 items and 3 vols.

Autographs, some clipped, of Confederate officers and leaders; permits; poems; Civil War slogans and cacheted envelopes; and a volume of notes on C.S.A. War Department documents concerning blockade-running.

1188.   CONFEDERATE STATES OF AMERICA. NAVY. PAPERS, 1863. 1 item.

Poem by "Clea" in memory of Midshipman E. H. Edwards, who died of typhoid fever in Mobile, 1863.

1189.   CONFEDERATE STATES OF AMERICA, PAPERS RELATING TO STATE GOVERNMENTS, 1861-1865, 324 items.

For Georgia there are bonds for state or county officers, 1864-1865, 6 items; oaths of office, 1863-1865, 60 items; tallies of votes cast by soldiers in state and regimental elections, 1862-1865, 42 items, of the 2nd, 5th, 13th, 32nd, 37th, and 46th Regiments of Georgia Volunteers; and 6th Regiment of Georgia State Guards; 51st Regiment of Georgia Militia; 2nd Georgia Battalion of Sharp Shooters; and the 6th Georgia Cavalry; also tax receipts, 1861-1865, 59 items; militia accounts and expenditures, 1861-1865, 47 items, concerning the Spalding Grays [2nd Independent Battalion, Georgia Infantry], Stark's Volunteers [13th Georgia Infantry], Ringgold Rangers [13th Georgia Infantry?], Hunter Guards [30th Georgia Infantry], Bartow's Artillery [22nd Battalion Georgia Siege Artillery?], Byer's Volunteers, and Gray's Infantry; military records, 1861-1864, 11 items, largely lists of men subject to enrollment in 431st District, Spalding County, and Clay County. Relating to North Carolina are miscellaneous papers of the state Adjutant General's Office, 1861-1865, 6 items; tax returns, 1863-1864, 4 items. For South Carolina there are papers of the Ordnance Office, 1861-1862, 73 items, mainly orders, receipts, and ordnance requisitions related to supplies for forts in Charleston harbour; Treasury Department papers, 1860-1861, 5 items, of a miscellaneous character; and an ordinance of the state legislature, 1862, enabling those in military service to vote. Relating to Virginia are papers of miscellaneous agencies, 1861-1864, 6 items, and income tax returns of Wythe County, 1864, 6 items.

1190.   CONFEDERATE STATES OF AMERICA. RECORDS OF STATE AGENCIES. COURT RECORDS, PAMLICO DISTRICT, GOLDSBORO, N.C., 1850 (1861-1865) 1915. 3,233 items.

Records of the Confederate courts of Pamlico District concern the sequestration of alien property in eastern North Carolina, generally debts due northern businesses, chiefly in New York and Philadelphia, by Southern firms and individuals; and prize ships captured from the North. Included are references to the North Carolina property of Adele (Cutts) Douglas, widow of Stephen A. Douglas. Papers relating to poor relief and claims, 1861-1865, 478 items and 1 vol., Jones County, Georgia, and Craven, Martin, and Warren counties, North Carolina, largely relate to aid for soldiers' families. There are a few papers of the U.S. District Court prior to 1861 and after 1865.

1191.   CONFEDERATE VETERAN PAPERS, 1786-1933. 620 items. Nashville (Davidson County), Tenn.

Correspondence, unpublished articles, and other material written for a periodical published between 1893 and 1932. Included are memoirs and other accounts of military campaigns and battles, lists of servicemen, biographies of statesmen and soldiers, military prison records, transcripts of original reports and orders, poems, lists of soldiers buried in various Confederate cemeteries, and papers relating to the design of the Confederate flag, the participation of women in the Civil War, the Reconstruction period, and the Ku Klux Klan.

1192.   CONGRESS OF INDUSTRIAL ORGANIZATIONS. INDUSTRIAL UNION COUNCILS. NORTH CAROLINA PAPERS, 1953-1954. 64 items. Charlotte (Mecklenburg County), N.C.

Correspondence of Haywood D. "Red" Lisk, president of the North Carolina State Industrial Union Council, and of J. R. Graham, C.I.O. representative for the Council, concerning political action, financial matters, and meetings; and other miscellaneous items, including applications for affiliation.

1193. CONGRESS OF INDUSTRIAL ORGANIZATIONS. INDUSTRIAL UNION COUNCILS. TENNESSEE PAPERS, 1938-1953.
1,777 items. Nashville (Davidson County), Tenn.

Correspondence of various officers of the Tennessee State Industrial Union Council, including Paul R. Christopher, S. Matthew Lynch, and Harold S. Marthenke; of John Brophy, Director of the Industrial Union Councils; and of various organizations and labor unions such as the National Farmers' Union, the Office for Emergency Management, the Bureau of National Affairs, the United Furniture Workers of America, and the Knoxville War Housing Committee concerning matters affecting the Tennessee State Industrial Union Council and its members.

1194. CONGRESS OF INDUSTRIAL ORGANIZATIONS. INDUSTRIAL UNION COUNCILS. VIRGINIA PAPERS, 1928-1957.
6,698 items and 49 vols. Richmond, Va.

The papers of the Virginia State Industrial Union Council consist of correspondence, leaflets, flyers, pamphlets, serials and other printed material. The correspondence is principally that of Charles C. Webber, president of the Virginia Council. The papers relate to various labor unions, including the Oil Workers International Union, the United Public Workers of America, and the telephone unions; labor organizations such as the American Labor Research Institute, Inc., the Highlander Folk School, and the Southern School for Workers; issues such as segregation and discrimination, the poll tax, child labor, industrial safety, and anti-union legislation; religious groups including the Federal Council of the Churches of Christ in America, the National Study Conference on the Church and Economic Life, and the Virginia Council of Churches, Inc.; labor-related organizations including the Virginia Child Labor Committee, the U.S. Department of Labor, the Wage Stabilization Board, and the Office of Price Administration; and the Progressive Citizens for America. There are also serials such as Labor Letter and The National Reporter, as well as material for conventions of the national C.I.O. and the Virginia State Industrial Union Council.

1195. CONGRESS OF INDUSTRIAL ORGANIZATIONS. ORGANIZING COMMITTEE. NORTH CAROLINA PAPERS, 1909-1957.
29,824 items and 52 vols. Charlotte (Mecklenburg County), N.C.

Correspondence, leaflets, bulletins, pamphlets, fliers, reports, radio scripts, clippings, serials, and other printed material relating principally to the campaign of the Organizing Committee of the Congress of Industrial Organizations (C.I.O.) to unionize unorganized workers in North Carolina, 1946-1953. The correspondence is chiefly that of William J. Smith (b. 1902), North Carolina director for the C.I.O. Organizing Committee, 1946-1950, and of Franz E. Daniel, North Carolina director, 1950-1953. Material pertaining to the United Furniture Workers of America (U.F.W.A.) includes correspondence of U.F.W.A. state and national officials, material concerning the companies the U.F.W.A. was trying to organize, information on the High Point (North Carolina) Organizing Committee, and a Wage Stabilization Guide prepared by the U.F.W.A. Papers relating to the Textile Workers Union of America (T.W.U.A.) include material on the various mills and manufacturing companies the T.W.U.A. was attempting to organize; grievances against Marshall Field and Company, Manufacturing Division, heard by an arbitration board; an article by Frank T. de Vyver entitled "Union Fratricide: The Textile Workers' Split"; strikes in textile mills; the organizing drive in the Cabarrus County area of North Carolina, particularly the campaign directed at the Cannon Mills Company, Concord; North Carolina legislators; medical care in North Carolina; the labor laws in North Carolina; the National Labor Relations Board; and the Federal Communications Commission. Membership records list members of unions at various companies in the state, as well as initiation fees paid. Serials include The CIO Round-Up, the Textile Bulletin, and The Department Store Organizer.

1196. CONGRESS OF INDUSTRIAL ORGANIZATIONS. ORGANIZING COMMITTEE. SOUTH CAROLINA PAPERS, 1946-1953.
12,592 items and 20 vols. Spartanburg (Spartanburg County) and Columbia (Richland County), S.C.

Papers of the South Carolina Organizing Committee of the Congress of Industrial Organizations (C.I.O.) principally relate to efforts to organize workers in the textile industries of the piedmont region of South Carolina. Correspondence is chiefly that of Franz E. Daniel, South Carolina director of the C.I.O. Organizing Committee, 1946-1950, and South Carolina state director of the Textile Workers Union of America (T.W.U.A.), 1946-1949, and of Lloyd P. Vaughan, South Carolina director of the C.I.O. Organizing Committee, 1950-1953, with union officials of the C.I.O. the Organizing Committee, and the T.W.U.A. There are also references to the Amalgamated Clothing Workers of America, the International Woodworkers of America, the United Furniture Workers of America, the Food, Tobacco, Agricultural and Allied Workers Union of America, the Communications Workers of America, and the Retail, Wholesale and Department Store Union; and material on labor-related groups such as the American Arbitration Association, the Labor Press Association, Inc., and the National Religion and Labor Foundation. Scattered papers concern issues such as atomic energy, the Ku Klux Klan, and anti-union propaganda, and groups not directly connected with labor, including the Southern Conference for Human Welfare, the American Cancer Society, the Fellowship of Southern Churchmen, and the Cooperative Broadcasting Association. Also included are press releases, pamphlets, financial papers, clippings, and reports. Serials include <u>UPA</u> <u>Adviser</u> (United Paperworkers of America), <u>U.D.A. Congressional Newsletter</u> (Union for Democratic Action), and <u>Cavil-cade</u> (Labor Press Associated, Inc.).

1197. CONGRESS OF INDUSTRIAL ORGANIZATIONS. ORGANIZING COMMITTEE. TENNESSEE PAPERS, 1940-1953. 70,923 items and 147 vols. Knoxville (Knox County), Tenn.

Papers of the Tennessee Organizing Committee of the Congress of Industrial Organizations (C.I.O.) pertain to the activities of the committee in organizing workers primarily in the textile and steel industries. The correspondence is chiefly that of Paul Revere Christopher (1910-1974), director of the C.I.O. in Tennessee, 1940-1955, but also includes that of Maurice R. Allen, director of the C.I.O. Organizing Committee in Tennessee, whose major responsibility was with the United Gas, Coke, and Chemical Workers of America, and of Bethel T. Judd, a C.I.O. field representative. Correspondents include national and state union officials as well as political leaders. Material on the Textile Workers Union of America (T.W.U.A.) includes information on the organizing efforts at the Standard-Coosa-Thatcher Company, Chattanooga, Tennessee; correspondence of Joseph R. White, vice-president and director of the Tennessee T.W.U.A., and of Herbert S. Williams, Alabama director of the T.W.U.A.; the files of Joel B. Leighton, a national representative and then an international representative of the T.W.U.A.; union membership cards for the employees of Standard-Coosa-Thatcher Company, Gluck Brothers, Inc., Tennessee Furniture Industries, Inc., and Morrison Turning Company; contact cards for workers in the Standard-Coosa-Thatcher Company; and dues records for Chattanooga and the contiguous northwest Georgia area. Among the other unions on which there is information are the United Steelworkers of America; the United Furniture Workers of America; the United Gas, Coke, and Chemical Workers of America; the Amalgamated Clothing Workers of America; the United Automobile, Aircraft, and Agricultural Implement Workers of America; the American Newspaper Guild; the Food, Tobacco, Agricultural, and Allied Workers Union of America; the International Woodworkers of America; the International Union of Mine, Mill, and Smelter Workers; the United Mine Workers of America; the United Cannery, Agriculture, Packing and Allied Workers of America; and the International Union of Electrical, Radio, and Machine Workers. There are records of the organizing committees of the government and civic employees, insurance and allied workers, plant guards, telephone workers, utility workers, optical and instrument workers, steelworkers, and paper workers. Material on the national C.I.O. includes topics such as legislative issues, the department of education and research, various conferences, a directory, the National C.I.O. War Relief Committee, and the National C.I.O. Community Services Committee. There is information on various labor and labor-related organizations including the Joint Labor Legislative Committee; the Labor Institute of America; the Southern School for Workers, Inc.; the Highlander Folk School; the United Labor Conference; the American Arbitration Association; and the American Labor Education Service, Inc. Among the government agencies with which the organizing committee had to deal are the National Labor Relations Board, the Office of Price Administration, the Treasury Department, the U.S. Department of Labor, the National Wage Stabilization Board, and the National War Labor Board. There is also material on various political groups such as the Americans for Democratic Action, the Good Government Group, and the Committee for Constitutional Government; religious groups, including the National Religion and Labor Conference, the Federal Council of the Churches of Christ in America, and the National Conference of Christians and Jews, Inc.; health and charitable organizations such as the American Red Cross and the community chest; and others such as the Southern Conference Educational Fund and the American Veterans Committee. Various state groups are represented in the papers including the Tennessee State Planning Commission, the Tennessee Committee for Justice in Columbia, the Joint Labor Legislative Council, and the National Housing Agency. There is also material on several Tennessee governmental agencies including the Department of Employment Security, the Department of Labor, the Department of Public Welfare, and the General Assembly. Papers refer to such issues as strikes and arbitration, workmen's compensation, health programs, legislation, and cases before the National Labor Relations Board. Also included are press releases, radio programs and scripts, leaflets and fliers, and financial papers. Membership records, by company, represent many Tennessee unions. There are also records in card form of applications for membership in the International Woodworkers of America section for the Empire Furniture Company, membership cards in the United Packinghouse Workers of America section for the East Tennessee Packing Company, and the C.I.O. Organizing Committee contact cards for the Peerless Woolen Mills. Serials include <u>The CIO News</u>, <u>Joint Labor Legislative Bulletin</u>, <u>The National Reporter</u>, <u>Tennessee Industrial Planning Newsletter</u>, and <u>Labor Information Bulletin</u>.

1198. CONGRESS OF INDUSTRIAL ORGANIZATIONS. ORGANIZING COMMITTEE. VIRGINIA PAPERS, 1941-1953. 14,703 items and 49 vols. Richmond, Va.

Papers of the Virginia Organizing Committee of the Congress of Industrial Organizations (C.I.O.) relating to the activities of the Committee in organizing workers in various industries in Virginia. The correspondence is principally that of Ernest Byron Pugh, regional director for the Virginia C.I.O. and Virginia director for the

C.I.O. Organizing Committee, and of Theodore Dennis du Cuennois, assistant state director of the C.I.O. Organizing Committee in Virginia, with various union officials and political leaders. There is information on many unions including the Food, Tobacco, Agricultural and Allied Workers Union of America; the International Union of Electrical, Radio, and Machine Workers, and its predecessor the United Electrical, Radio, and Machine Workers of America; the Oil Workers International Union; the Textile Workers Union of America; the United Automobile, Aircraft, and Agricultural Implement Workers of America, with material on local unions; the United Cannery, Agricultural, Packing, and Allied Workers of America; the United Gas, Coke, and Chemical Workers of America; the United Mine Workers of America; the United Paperworkers of America; the United Shoe Workers of America; and the United Steelworkers of America. There are also records of the organizing committees for the Distillery Workers, Government and Civic Employees, the Insurance and Allied Workers, the Telephone Workers, the United Construction Workers, and the Steel Workers. There is material on labor-related groups such as the Southern School for Workers, the United Labor Legislative Committee, and the Virginia United Labor Committee. Various state and local agencies represented include the Richmond Chamber of Commerce, the Virginia State Chamber of Commerce, the Richmond Citizens Association, Inc., and the General Assembly. Among the governmental agencies are the Wage Stabilization Board, various bureaus and divisions of the U.S. Department of Labor, and the Virginia Department of Labor and Industry. Other groups on which there is information include the Southern Regional Council, Inc.; the Safety Advisory Council; and the Mid-Century White House Conference on Children and Youth. Various issues covered in the papers are a telephone strike in 1950; cost of living statistics; discrimination; portal-to-portal pay; C.I.O. councils, conventions, and conferences; national health insurance; communism; the Democratic National Committee; and gubernatorial candidates. Also included are press releases, radio scripts, charter applications, leaflets, fliers, resolutions, and <u>UPA Advisor</u> (United Paperworkers of America).

1199. CONGRESS OF INDUSTRIAL ORGANIZATIONS. POLITICAL ACTION COMMITTEE. NORTH CAROLINA PAPERS, 1944-1954. 2,142 items and 9 vols. Charlotte (Mecklenburg County), N.C.

The papers of the North Carolina Political Action Committee (P.A.C.) of the Congress of Industrial Organizations (C.I.O.) relating to the activities of the committee in promoting the C.I.O. viewpoint on political issues and in advocating registration and voting in local and national elections. These papers are the files of Earl Lafayette Sandefur (1899-1951) who in 1947 was the acting executive director and then executive director and secretary-treasurer of the North Carolina Political Action Committee. There is correspondence with various union officials and political leaders. Among the unions on which there is information are the Amalgamated Clothing Workers of America; the American Federation of Hosiery Workers; the Communications Workers of America, including the Telephone Workers Organizing Committee; the Industrial Union of Marine and Shipbuilding Workers of America; the Retail, Wholesale, and Department Store Union; the Textile Workers Union of America; and the United Steelworkers of America. There is also material on various topics, such as the Taft-Hartley Act, constitutions, and the national office; and on organizations such as the North Carolina Recreation Commission, the State Industrial Union Councils, and the United Labor Political Committee for North Carolina. Other types of materials contained in the collection are fliers; leaflets; financial records of the North Carolina State C.I.O. Political Action Committee; releases of the National Labor Relations Board, 1951-1952; and the questionnaires employed by the committee in a canvass of members of the General Assembly in 1951 to ascertain from each legislator the profession, the number of terms served, and the desire to return to the General Assembly.

1200. CONGRESS OF INDUSTRIAL ORGANIZATIONS. POLITICAL ACTION COMMITTEE. TENNESSEE PAPERS, 1943-1952. 387 items and 1 vol. Nashville (Davidson County), Tenn.

Papers of the Tennessee Political Action Committee of the Congress of Industrial Organizations (C.I.O.) relate to the activities of the Committee in procuring and disseminating information concerning political issues, promoting the C.I.O. viewpoint on issues affecting its welfare, and maintaining an accounting of elections and the voting records of Tennessee officials. These papers are from the files of Paul Revere Christopher (1910-1974), C.I.O. director for Tennessee, 1940-1955; of James E. Payne, chairman of the Chattanooga Area Political Action Committee and a field representative in Chattanooga; and of Bethel T. Judd, C.I.O. field representative in Chattanooga and a member of the State Central Committee and the executive committee of the Tennessee State C.I.O. Political Action Committee. Correspondence, primarily with union officials and political leaders, concerns the activities of the Chattanooga, the Tennessee state, and the national C.I.O. Political Action Committees. There are also minutes of several meetings of the Tennessee State Political Action Committee; various editions of its rules of operation; and the rules of operation for the Chattanooga Area C.I.O. Political Action Committee. Pamphlets and leaflets published by the National C.I.O. Political Action Committee concern issues such as elections, voting, political action, wages, housing, legislation, voter registration, and finances. A volume consisting of mimeographed sheets pertains to political education institutes and the national C.I.O. Political Action Committee.

1201. CONGRESS OF INDUSTRIAL ORGANIZATIONS. POLITICAL ACTION COMMITTEE. VIRGINIA PAPERS, 1944-1953. 428 items and 4 vols. Richmond, Va.

Papers relating to the activities of the Virginia Political Action Committee (P.A.C.) of the Congress of Industrial Organizations (C.I.O.) include correspondence, reports, petitions, releases, financial statements, program statements, and pamphlets. The correspondence is primarily that of Charles C. Webber, president and director of the Virginia C.I.O. Political Action Committee and president of the Virginia State Industrial Union Council with various union officials and political leaders. Included is correspondence from the Tidewater C.I.O. Political Action Committee. The papers concern such topics as the Taft-Hartley Act; the International Union of Electrical, Radio, and Machine Workers; radio programs by labor unions; elections and political campaigns in Virginia and on the national level. There are also membership report forms for the Virginia State C.I.O. Political Action Committee.

1202. CONGRESS OF INDUSTRIAL ORGANIZATIONS. PUBLICITY DEPARTMENT. NORTH CAROLINA PAPERS, 1946-1953. 2,797 items and 2 vols. Charlotte (Mecklenburg County), N.C.

Papers of the North Carolina Publicity Department of the Congress of Industrial Organizations (C.I.O.) relating to its function of informing C.I.O. members and the general public about the activities of the C.I.O. and affiliated unions, and countering anti-union and anti-labor propaganda. Included are the correspondence of national publicity department directors Len De Caux, Allan L. Swim, and Henry C. Fleisher, and of North Carolina publicity department directors, William W. Weiss, E. Paul Harding, and L. Edward Lashman, Jr.; press and news releases; mimeographed bulletins and fliers; material concerning radio and various radio stations, including radio scripts; pamphlets; speeches; serials; and clippings principally from the Charlotte News and the Charlotte Observer, but from other North Carolina newspapers as well. There is information on various unions such as the Amalgamated Clothing Workers of America; the American Newspaper Guild; the Communications Workers of America; the Textile Workers Union of America; the United Furniture Workers of America; the United Steelworkers of America; the United Stone and Allied Products Workers of America; and the United Transport Service Employees. Among the organizations and governmental agencies covered in these papers are the Labor Press Association, Inc.; the Office of Price Stabilization; the President's Health Needs of Nation Commission; the Southern Regional Council, Inc.; the U.S. Department of Labor; and the United Merchants and Manufacturers, Inc. The papers concern issues affecting labor including living costs, wages, prices, labor laws, taxes, anti-union pressures, strikes, the Fair Labor Standards Act, and the movement in the South to organize workers in various industries. The serials consist of CIO News of North Carolina, CIO Round-Up, Carolina CIO Bulletin, North Carolina Staff Bulletin, and Why Not?

1203. BENJAMIN CONLEY PAPERS, 1876-1887. 84 items. Atlanta, Ga.

Family and business papers of Conley, governor of Georgia. Subjects include cotton prices in Georgia; the depression of 1877; yellow fever, diphtheria, smallpox, and typhus; politics; floods; land; patronage; the presidential election of 1884. Correspondents include G. B. Chamberlin and Joseph Bryan Cumming.

1204. W. T. CONN PAPERS, 1861-1862. 3 items. Milledgeville (Baldwin County), Ga.

Typed copies of letters from W. T. Conn, a Confederate lieutenant, concerning the battle of Manassas, 1861, camp life, forced marches, religious opinions, care of the wounded in Richmond, and family matters.

1205. CONNECTICUT BUREAU OF VITAL STATISTICS, RECORDS, 1884-1897. 1 vol.

Abstracts of records of births, marriages, and deaths in Branford, Bethel, New Haven, North Canaan, Plymouth, Redding, Roxbury, Salisbury, Sharon, Sprague, Stonington, Thomaston, Voluntown, Waterford, Wolcott, and Woodbridge.

1206. JAMES CONNER PAPERS, 1864. 2 items. Charleston, S.C.

Transcripts of letters by Confederate General Conner to his mother, describing his life in Richmond.

1207. PHINEAS SANBORN CONNER PAPERS, 1865. 1 item. Cincinnati, Ohio.

A letter to Conner, assistant surgeon of the United States, concerning the effects of a soldier who had died in a hospital, and, on the reverse, a draft of Conner's reply.

1208. CHARLES MAGILL CONRAD PAPERS, 1848, 1852. 2 items. Washington, D.C.

Correspondence of Charles M. Conrad (1804-1878), lawyer, member of U.S. Congress, and secretary of war under President Millard Fillmore, relating to his addressing a Whig meeting and to pension matters.

1209. ISAAC CONRAD INVENTORY OF ESTATE, 1849-1850. 1 vol. (76 pp.) Forsyth County, N.C.

Inventory of estate of Isaac Conrad and complaint in Forsyth County Court of Equity concerning George F. Wilson and Jacob Conrad, administrators for the estate.

1210. JOSEPH CONRAD PAPERS, 1897-1965. 195 items and 7 vols. Bishopsbourne, Kent, England.

Letters by Conrad to Sir Sidney Colvin and his wife, Lady Frances, and to Henry Arthur Jones and his daughter, Jennie Doris Arthur (Jones) Thorne, discussing literary and personal matters, and letters by Conrad concerning literary and business subjects to his publisher T. Fisher Unwin and to David S. Meldrum, an advisor to Wm. Blackwood & Sons. There is comment on current events such as the career of Admiral J. R. Jellicoe and the activities of Conrad's son, Borys, in France during World War I, as well as on Conrad's writings, and the works of other authors. Frequently mentioned are Henry James and John Galsworthy. These letters have been published in part in W. M. Blackburn, ed., Joseph Conrad: Letters to William Blackburn and David S. Meldrum (Durham: 1958). There are also manuscripts by Conrad; letters from Conrad's uncle, Tadeusz Bobrowski, 1869-1893; an album of photographs, 1860-1890, of Conrad's Polish relatives, partly unidentified; and scrapbooks, 6 vols., compiled by Conrad's wife, Jessie (George) Conrad, with clippings on the writer's visit to the United States in 1923; obituaries and tributes following Conrad's death, 1924; copies of his last letters and an unfinished book manuscript; reviews of A Handbook of Cookery for a Small House, by Jessie Conrad; the manuscript of Joseph Conrad as I Knew Him (1926), by Jessie Conrad; reviews of Joseph Conrad: Life and Letters (1927), by G. Jean-Aubrey; articles on the Conrad memorial at Bishopsbourne; and reviews of Joseph Conrad and His Circle, by Jessie Conrad. There are also loose clippings and photocopies of other clippings concerning Conrad and his work.

1211. WILLIAM G. CONRAD PAPERS, 1884-1902. 94 items. "Montana Hall," White Post (Clarke County), Va.

Family letters, some mentioning Conrad's business interests in New York, Montana, and Canada, which in part concerned railroad contracts. Conrad held positions with I. G. Baker and Company, Fort Benton, Montana Territory; Conrad Brothers, Bankers, Great Falls, Montana; and the Northwestern National Bank, Great Falls.

1212. ARCHIBALD CONSTABLE PAPERS, 1801. 2 items. Edinburgh, Scotland.

Letters from Philippe D'Auvergne, Prince de Bouillon, commander of British naval forces at Jersey, to Constable, bookseller and publisher of Edinburgh. The letters concern book orders and discuss the sources of D'Auvergne's library.

1213. G. S. CONVERSE PAPERS, 1847-1851. 14 items. New Haven (New Haven County), Conn.

Two letters to Converse and 12 speeches written by him as a student in Yale University.

1214. FRANCIS SEYMOUR CONWAY, FIRST MARQUIS OF HERTFORD, PAPERS, 1766. 1 item. London, England.

Letter from Conway, lord lieutenant of Ireland, 1765-1766, and lord chamberlain, 1766-1782, commenting on government interference in the borough of Oxford. The addressee was Richard Hamond.

1215. MONCURE DANIEL CONWAY PAPERS, 1856-1907. 13 items. New York, N.Y.

Miscellaneous personal and business letters of a Virginia abolitionist, Unitarian minister, and author. Topics are chiefly literary matters, Conway's writings, and his difficulties with his Washington, D.C., congregation because of his abolitionism. One letter is by William T. Head of England.

1216. CHARLES E. COOK PAPERS, 1863-1864. 5 items. Boston, Mass.

Papers concerned with insurance on cargoes lost to Confederate commerce raiders.

1217. ED. F. COOK LETTER BOOK, 1912-1914. 1 vol. (88 pp.) Nashville (Davidson County), Tenn.

Typed copies of letters and excerpts of letters on missionary activities.

1218. SIR EDWARD TYAS COOK PAPERS, 1902. 1 item. London, England.

Letter from Cook to Miss Helen Pelham Dale relative to his editing the complete works of John Ruskin.

1219. FLAVIUS JOSEPHUS COOK PAPERS, 1847-1916. 814 items and 12 vols. Boston, Mass. and Ticonderoga (Essex County), N.Y.

Correspondence, scrapbooks, biographical material, notes, lectures, literary manuscripts, sermons, drafts, poems, hymns, speeches, printed matter, and clippings. Most material dates from 1859-1901, and covers Cook's career as lecturer on current topics, science, religion, theology, ethics, temperance, prohibition, and other subjects. Manuscripts of Cook's Preludes, the Monday lectures delivered at the Tremont Temple, Boston, and addresses before students at colleges and seminaries. Some papers reflect the theological controversies of the late 19th century, and the disputes over the relation of evolution and other scientific subjects to traditional religion. Includes a summary of Cook's life and work, 1874-1884, an account of Nathaniel S. Shaler's views on Darwin's theories, and a largely complete unpublished biography of Cook by his wife. Among the correspondents are ministers, professors, and heads of colleges and universities.

1220. HORATIO R. COOK MEMORANDUM BOOK, 1842-1888. 1 vol. (114 pp.) Beech Island (Aiken County), S.C.

Memorandum book of a physician and planter, containing notes on diseases, prescriptions, remedies, geology, agriculture, and Reconstruction politics including a discussion of the Hamburg, South Carolina, riots.

1221. MARY JANE COOK PAPERS, 1855. 2 items. Marysville (Yuba County), Calif.

Personal correspondence from Mrs. Mary Jane Cook to her mother.

1222. ORCHARD COOK PAPERS, 1807. 1 item. Wiscasset (Lincoln County), Me.

Letter written while Cook was a member of the United States House of Representatives from Massachusetts discussing the Massachusetts judiciary, Congress, foreign relations, and Dr. Charles Jarvis.

1223. SALLY COOK PAPERS, 1839-1879. 4 items. Rutland (Meigs County), Ohio.

Correspondence concerned with family affairs and local news.

1224. THOMAS COOK PAPERS, 1759-1792. 22 items. Granville County, N.C.

Collection contains a description of Cook's land in 1778, several land deeds from Granville County belonging to Cook, and a number of routine bills and receipts.

1225. EDWARD WILLIAM COOKE PAPERS, 1855-1878. 9 items. London, England.

Miscellaneous letters to Cooke concerned, for the most part, with his painting. Three letters are from the artist, Edward Lear; and one letter from Thomas Sopwith discusses the authenticity of the painting, "The Blue Boy."

1226. GEORGE A. COOKE PAPERS, 1878-1879. 4 items. Philadelphia, Pa.

Love letters from Cooke to his fiancée.

1227. JOHN ESTEN COOKE PAPERS, 1840-1896. 289 items and 7 vols. Millwood (Clarke County), Va.

Professional and personal correspondence and literary notes of John Esten Cooke and of his brother, Philip Pendleton Cooke, including manuscript copies of published works. Centering around John Esten Cooke are letters from boyhood friends, a few Civil War letters, many business and critical letters from his publishers and literary friends during the 1870s and 1880s, five small volumes of war notes [partially published: see J. B. Hubbell (ed.), "The War Diary of John Esten Cooke," Journal of Southern History, VII (Nov. 1941), 526-540]; holograph manuscript of Surry of Eagle's Nest; an article, "On the Road to Despotism"; a manuscript, "A Legend of Turkey Buzzard Hollow"; a copy of an article entitled "The Virginia Declaration of Independence" [published in the Magazine of American History, vol. XI, no. 5 (May, 1884)]; and an appreciation of Philip Pendleton Cooke. Concerning Philip Pendleton Cooke there is a group of letters from him to his father [partially published: see David K. Jackson, "Philip Pendleton Cooke: Virginia Gentleman, Lawyer, Hunter, and Poet," in American Studies in Honor of William Kenneth Boyd, ed. David K. Jackson (Durham, N.C., 1940), and John D. Allen, Philip Pendleton Cooke (Chapel Hill, N.C., 1942)].

Among the correspondents are W. H. Appleton, George W. Bagby, Alexander R. Boteler, W. H. Browne, O. B. Burie, M. B. T. Clark, J. E. Cooke, Philip Pendleton Cooke, W. De Hass, M. Schele De Vere, H. K. Douglas, E. A. Duyckinck, G. C. Eggleston, William Evelyn, Wade Hampton, J. W. Harper, H. B. Hirst, J. B. Jones, J. P. Kennedy, C. C. Lee, W. H. Lee, B. W. Leigh, A. H. Sands, W. G. Simms, David Strother, and Beverly Tucker.

1228. ROBERT BRUCE COOKE PAPERS, 1928-1973. 2 items and 1 vol. Durham, N.C.

Volume of wage statistics, 1928-1965, including job classifications and wage rates for six textile mills owned by Erwin Mills, Inc.

1229. DENNIS COOLEY PAPERS, 1820-1853. 20 items. Washington (Macomb County), Michigan.

Letters to Cooley from his brother, Henry Cooley, of Monticello, Georgia, complaining of the general agricultural decline of the region; from H. P. Sartwell of Penn Yan, New York, discussing various drugs and other medical matters; and a number of letters discussing plants.

1230. OLIVER S. COOLIDGE PAPERS, 1861-1864. 43 items. Cambridge, Mass.

Civil War letters of a soldier who served in the 24th Massachusetts Regiment, 1861-1862, and in the enlisted bodyguard of

General Ambrose E. Burnside, 1862-1864. The letters contain some description of action at Roanoke Island, North Carolina; New Bern, North Carolina; and Fredericksburg, Virginia; but for the most part they describe army life and the places Coolidge visited. Coolidge often refers to his marital difficulties and to a former problem with alcoholism. The collection also contains routine military papers relating to pay, leaves, and discharge.

1231. JAMES ROWE COOMBS RECOLLECTIONS, 1867-1868. 1 vol. Twiggs County, Ga.

Typed copy of "Recollections of a Twiggs County Planter," by James R. Coombs (b. 1820), including accounts of his infancy in North Carolina, removal to Georgia in 1825, schooling, frontier Methodist camp meetings, slaves, agriculture in Georgia, George P. Cooper (his early schoolmaster), early settlers of Twiggs County, production of cotton, frontier merchants, and local politics, all generally prior to 1840.

1232. CHARLES LEE COON PAPERS, 1752-1927. 518 items and 1 vol. Wilson (Wilson County), N.C.

Papers collected by Coon relating to his history of German settlers in North Carolina. They include clippings, especially obituary notices and genealogical articles; lists of names; copies of records of the New Jerusalem Church in Davie County, North Carolina, Daniels Church in Lincoln County, and Zion's Church; material on David Henkel and the Lutheran Church in North Carolina in the early nineteenth century; and correspondence related to Coon's research.

1233. ALBERT D. COOPER PAPERS, 1888-1891. 1 vol. Asheville (Buncombe County), N.C.

Journal of a general merchant.

1234. JAMES COOPER PAPERS, 1850-1854. 3 items. Washington, D.C.

Letter on national politics and the question of slavery in the territories written by Cooper when he was United States senator from Pennsylvania; letter giving Cooper's opinion on a fugitive slave bill; and biographical sketch of Cooper.

1235. JOHN SNIDER COOPER PAPERS, 1863-1865. 2 vols. Mount Gilead (Morrow County), Ohio.

Diary of John Cooper who served in the 7th Ohio Regiment, the U.S. Engineers, the 8th U.S. Regiment (Colored), and the 107th Ohio Regiment. Includes a description of Cooper's work with the U.S. Engineers in Virginia and Maryland, 1863; entries concerning the movement of his company and camp life; and comments on the last months of the war when he was stationed in South Carolina. There are few descriptions of military engagements, and Fredericksburg is the only battle discussed in detail.

1236. SAMUEL COOPER PAPERS, 1718-1798. 324 items. Boston, Mass.

The items forming this collection are photocopies of papers and letters held principally in the New York Public Library and the Henry E. Huntington Library. The collection contains a number of Cooper's sermons and a portion of his correspondence, almost exclusively from the period of the Revolutionary War, including exchanges of letters with Samuel Adams, Benjamin Franklin, Arthur Lee, John Hancock, and several prominent Frenchmen interested in the American cause. Miscellaneous items include a proclamation from Count d'Estaing urging Frenchmen in the new American states to support the Revolution, 1778, and an essay encouraging the Canadian colonies to join the Revolution, [1780?]. Copies of Cooper's diary cover portions of 1764, 1769, 1775, and 1776.

1237. WILLIAM COOPER PAPERS, 1802-1814. 11 items. Rowan County, N.C.

The collection is made up mainly of the receipts of William and Samuel Cooper.

1238. COOPER & HAINES PAPERS, 1895-1898. 1 vol. Capon Bridge (Hampshire County), W. Va.

Daybook of a firm of general merchants.

1239. SIR ARTHUR STOCKDALE COPE PAPERS, 1889-1893. 9 items. Treniffle, near Launceston, Cornwall, England.

Letters dealing mainly with appointments to see Cope.

1240. HENRY COPENHAVER PAPERS, 1839-1865. 15 items. Marion (Smyth County), Va.

Papers of a farmer, for the most part from the period of the Civil War, pertaining to Confederate taxes on and requisitions for Copenhaver's crops and livestock.

1241. DANIEL DENISON COPP PAPERS, 1839-1856. 3 items and 1 vol. Savannah, Georgia.

Family correspondence of Daniel D. Copp, including a letter from Belton A. Copp concerning the division of his mother's estate, apparently in Groton, Connecticut; and a letter from George A. Copp in Lowndes County, Mississippi. Also included is a commonplace book containing essays, stories, and poetry by Mary E. Copp and diary entries from August, 1854, to May, 1856.

1242. FRANCIS PORTEUS CORBIN PAPERS, 1662-1885. 719 items. Philadelphia, Pa.

Letters and papers of Francis P. Corbin and his family, particularly his father-in-law, James Hamilton. The earliest group of items pertains to the Corbin family in Virginia in the 17th and 18th centuries and includes land grants and property lists. The business papers of James Hamilton and James Hamilton Couper, who were merchants in Georgia and South Carolina, run from 1759 to 1818. The business papers after 1818 are those of James Hamilton who established a mercantile business of his own in Philadelphia. The papers of Francis Porteus Corbin begin in 1828, the year in which he became a resident of Paris, France. They include reports on crops, prices, and conditions of slaves and land from Corbin's sugar plantation in Louisiana; correspondence about the breeding, racing, and sale of horses; material on the settlement of James Hamilton's estate; letters concerning Corbin's investments in stocks and bonds; and reports on the management of the rice plantation "Hopetown" in Georgia from James Hamilton Couper in the 1850s and from his son after the Civil War. There is also material on European reaction to the Civil War, the activities of Confederate commissioner John Slidell in France, and the trip of Corbin's son, Richard Washington Corbin, through the federal blockade to serve in the Confederate army.

1243. WILLIAM WILSON CORCORAN PAPERS, 1838-1887. 59 items. Washington, D.C.

Personal letters from W. W. Corcoran to Nannie W. Tunstall, a cousin of Governor James L. Kemper of Virginia.

1244. CORINTH BENEVOLENT SEWING SOCIETY CONSTITUTION AND MINUTES, 1857-1858. 1 vol. (12 pp.) Fluvanna County, Va.

Constitution, and minutes of three meetings of the society.

1245. CORNELIUS AND CO. PAPERS, 1848. 4 items. Baltimore, Md.

Papers concerning styles, orders, and sales of chandeliers and candelabra.

1246. SARAH CORNELL PAPERS, 1858-1869. 65 items. Dickersonville (Niagara County), N.Y.

Personal letters from soldiers in the 23rd New York Battery. Includes brief mention of military action around New Bern and Kinston, North Carolina.

1247. CORPENING FAMILY PAPERS, 1780-1922. 992 items. Burke and Caldwell Counties, N.C.

The greatest part of this collection is made up of business papers, commercial papers, and legal papers, including deeds and wills. There is a varied and miscellaneous correspondence among several generations of the family from 1838 through the late 19th century. The correspondence includes reports on conditions in California from 1886 through 1905; descriptions of the looting of Murphy, North Carolina, in 1863; an account of a debate in the 40th North Carolina Regiment on the advisability of using Negro soldiers, 1865; and a roll of students from Amherst Academy, Cora, North Carolina, 1898.

1248. F. J. CORTINA DIARY, 1919-1920. 3 vols. Florida and Georgia.

Diary containing data on violations of the 18th Amendment.

1249. THOMAS CORWIN PAPERS, 1861. 1 item. Lebanon (Warren County), Ohio.

Letter from Corwin, then minister to Mexico, concerning mail service between Mexico and the United States.

1250. DABNEY COSBY, JR., PAPERS, 1844-1856. 10 items. Halifax Court House (Halifax County), Va.

Miscellaneous correspondence which includes business letters; a letter to Dabney from his father commenting on the activities of the North Carolina legislature in 1851; and three letters from Dabney while a student at Washington College and the University of Virginia, 1854-1856.

1251. WILLIAM C. COSENS RECEIPT BOOK, 1862-1871. 1 vol. (132 pp.) Savannah, Ga.

Cash receipts for goods, showing high prices prevalent during the Civil War.

1252. ERASMUS H. COSTON PAPERS, 1744 (1854-1869) 1939. 966 items and 1 vol. Palo Alto (Onslow County), N.C.

Papers and correspondence of a farmer, teacher, county registrar of deeds, and postmaster for both the United States and the Confederate States. The collection contains business and legal papers including deeds, wills, items dealing with the administration of estates, Confederate bonds, material on the slave trade, information about prices for farm commodities and consumer goods, and data on farming operatings in general and cotton farming in particular. The collection also includes letters pertaining to the University of North Carolina and Trinity College, items on the operation of the post office system, material concerning

Methodism in North Carolina, Civil War letters, and a daybook, 1860-1864. The post-Civil War papers for the most part concern the Freeman family.

1253. EDMUND COTTLE PAPERS, 1862-1863. 18 items. Randolph (Norfolk County), Mass.

Letters of a soldier in the 4th Massachusetts Regiment describing life in camp; moving with the Nathaniel Banks Expedition by sea to Louisiana, 1863; and service in Louisiana.

1254. J. W. T. COUCH LEDGER, 1894. 1 vol. (56 pp.) Siler City (Chatham County), N.C.

1255. JOHN COUCH PAPERS, 1843-1940. 80 items. Orange County, N.C.

Letters between a soldier in the 66th North Carolina Regiment and his wife discussing camp life and military engagements in eastern North Carolina and Virginia. There are items of Shields family correspondence from the period before the Civil War and letters between Couch and his daughter dealing with personal matters and business after 1865.

1256. WILLIAM A. COUCH PAPERS, 1783-1920. 855 items and 2 vols. Orange and Durham Counties, N.C.

Papers and correspondence of several generations of the Couch family and related families, containing a large number of legal papers. Includes information on business connections and agricultural practices; papers dealing with local and school affairs and a school census, 1868; a will, 1801, giving a detailed listing of personal property, landholdings, and slaves; and papers concerning the 66th North Carolina Regiment in the Civil War. One volume concerns the administration of an estate; the other is a printed copy of the constitution of the Farmers' State Alliance of North Carolina, 1889.

1257. WILLIAM H. COUCHMAN ACCOUNT BOOK, 1852-1892. 1 vol. (70 pp.) Van Clevesville (Berkeley County), W. Va.

1258. COUNCIL OF SOUTHERN UNIVERSITIES, INC., PAPERS, 1952-1963. 5 items and 5 vols. Chapel Hill (Orange County), N.C. Restricted.

Papers include the charter of the Council, the application of the Council for tax exemption, and correspondence concerning the application for tax exemption. The volumes contain the agenda and minutes of the Council, 1952-1963, and the agenda and minutes of the Southern Fellowships Fund, 1954-1962.

1259. MARY A. (HORTON) COUNCILL PAPERS, 1862-1864. 13 items. Boone (Watauga County), N.C.

Letters from soldiers in the 37th North Carolina Regiment and the 58th North Carolina Regiment concerning camp life, military actions, and army discipline in eastern North Carolina and Tennessee.

1260. COURTNEY-OLIVER FAMILY PAPERS, 1863-1919. 109 items. London, England.

Letters to Leonard Henry Courtney, First Baron Courtney; John Mortimer Courtney; William Prideaux Courtney; and Louise d'Este (Courtney) Oliver and her husband, Richard Oliver, concerning political and administrative matters in Britain, New Zealand, and Canada. There is also mention of the writings of William Courtney.

1261. F. R. COUSINS PAPERS, 1836-1850. 5 items. Pittsylvania County, Va.

Business letters and bills.

1262. DAVID COVERSTONE PAPERS, 1779-1899. 72 items. Mine Run Furnace (Shenandoah County), Va.

Papers and correspondence of a farmer concerning business matters, the settlement of an estate in the 1870s, and reports from relatives who had gone to settle in Arkansas and Texas.

1263. JOHN COVINGTON PAPERS, 1805-1875. 19 items. Culpeper County, Va.

Miscellaneous collection of legal papers, business letters, and lists of current prices.

1264. COVINGTON AND MACON RAIL ROAD COMPANY MINUTES, 1885-1888. 1 vol. (116 pp.) Georgia.

1265. JAMES B. COWAN ACCOUNT BOOK, 1872-1873. 1 item. Selma (Dallas County), Ala.

Unbound account book of a physician.

1266. JOHN COWAN ACCOUNT BOOK AND DIARY, 1844. 1 vol.

Brief diary and personal accounts kept by John Cowan.

1267. JOSEPH COWAN MEMORANDUM BOOK, 1813-1814. 1 vol. Staunton (Augusta County), Va.

Fee book of Joseph Cowan, apparently a lawyer.

1268. NANCY H. COWAN PAPERS, 1830-1904. 112 items. Covington (Newton County), Ga.

Personal papers and correspondence of Nancy H. Cowan, concerned with the Chester District of South Carolina and the vicinity of Covington, Georgia, before the Civil War, and with letters from soldiers of limited education during the war period. Early letters bear on the collection of debts due John Cowan, husband of Nancy Cowan, in the Chester District, and the poverty of relatives in the same section. Letters from five of Nancy Cowan's sons, Confederate soldiers, tell of marches in Kentucky and South Carolina, fighting around Vicksburg, details of camp life, desertions, and scarcity of food and soap. Included also are bylaws of the Lewisville Rifle Company, pardons, amnesty oaths, and a post-bellum labor contract.

1269. WILLIAM COWAN PAPERS, 1795-1804. 6 items and 1 vol. Rowan County, N.C.

Collection consists of Cowan's arithmetic book, 1795, and several miscellaneous financial papers.

1270. COWAN FAMILY PAPERS, 1765-1939. 1 item. Orange County, N.C.

Family record of marriages, births, and deaths.

1271. WINIFRED A. COWAND PAPERS, 1861-1884. 105 items. Holly Grove (Bertie County), N.C.

Personal letters of the family of Starkey Cowand, consisting chiefly of letters from Joseph J. Cowand to his cousin, Winifred A., daughter of Starkey Cowand. Included also are letters from suitors and from her sisters. Those of Joseph J. Cowand, a Confederate soldier, contain references to hardships and homesickness. Included also are folksongs and bits of doggerel popular with the members of his company, usually located near Petersburg, Virginia, and in eastern North Carolina.

1272. ROBERT E. COWART PAPERS, 1908-1924. 9 items. Dallas, Tex.

Letters from Thomas Taylor Munford on the battle of Five Forks and a letter on the presidential election of 1924.

1273. JOSEPH COWEN PAPERS, 1881, 1885. 2 items. Newcastle-upon-Tyne, Northumberland, England.

Political letters, including a list of Cowen's speaking engagements in the election of 1885.

1274. LEOPOLD COPELAND PARKER COWPER PAPERS, 1864. 1 item. Portsmouth (Norfolk County) and Alexandria (Alexandria County), Va.

Letter reporting local and family news.

1275. MARY OCTAVINE (THOMPSON) COWPER PAPERS, 1903-1968. 3,158 items and 30 vols. Durham, N.C.

Letters and papers of a sociologist and social worker whose interests included woman suffrage; working conditions in North Carolina generally and especially in the textile industry; juvenile delinquency and the creation of juvenile courts; and the formation of child care centers. The collection contains personal correspondence, 1903-1966, including letters on training camp life in World War I and descriptions of France in the years after the Second World War; correspondence and papers on the woman suffrage movement, 1914-1930, particularly on Cowper's work as executive secretary of the North Carolina League of Women Voters in 1924; letters on the investigation of working conditions in the textile mills of North Carolina and on the attempts to secure protective legislation for women and children; printed matter, including reports and newspaper clippings on investigations of working conditions and other work of the League of Women Voters; Cowper's published and unpublished writings including the notes for several of her articles; and material on a controversy between milk producers and consumers in Durham, North Carolina, 1948-1949. There are also letters and papers on the creation and operation of child care centers in Durham, including a correspondence file, 1938-1964; reports and board minutes of the Durham Nursery School, 1938-1962; the legal papers of the Durham Nursery School, 1943-1958, and its financial papers, 1938-1965; and case histories, clippings, and other items concerned with the school's activities.

1276. E. B. COX PAPERS, 1862, 1864. 2 items. Mississippi.

Letters of a private in the Confederate Army, commenting on camp life, military campaigns, and personal affairs. One letter is from Tullahoma, Tennessee, and the other is from Ward's Station, Georgia.

1277. JONATHAN ELWOOD COX PAPERS, 1889-1928. Ca. 46,000 items and 57 vols. High Point (Guilford County), N.C.

The business papers and correspondence, 1900-1921, deal primarily with the production of shuttle and bobbin stock for the textile industry, but there is also extensive correspondence relating to Cox's other business interests, his community and civic activities, and his interest in Republican Party politics. The volumes, 1889-1928, consist of journals, daybooks, trial balance books, inventory records, order books, ledgers, and other business records.

1278. TALTON L. L. COX PAPERS, 1858-1918. 108 items. Franklinville, Gladesborough, New Market, and Randleman (Randolph County), N.C.

For the most part business papers and letters relating to distilleries and the United States Internal Revenue Service in North Carolina. There are also a number of personal letters and a series of soldiers' letters from the Civil War. Miscellaneous items include teacher's certificates, income tax blanks for 1871, printed instructions to assessors of the income tax, and reports and a circular from the United States Department of Agriculture.

1279. THOMAS E. COX PAPERS, 1835-1853. 8 items. Richmond, Va.

Personal letters written by and to Thomas E. Cox, a student at the College of William and Mary, Williamsburg, Virginia, 1835-1836, and later a physician in Richmond.

1280. COX FAMILY GENEALOGY, 1941. 40 pp. Wayne County, N.C.

Typed copy.

1281. COX, KENDALL, AND COMPANY PAPERS, 1860-1880. 2 vols. Wilmington (New Hanover County), N.C.

Letterpress book, 1861-1862, and daybook, 1860-1861, of a mercantile concern dealing in such products as cotton, corn, liquor, salt, fish, coffee, and molasses. The letterpress book contains references to the blockade of Wilmington and the threat of attack by General Burnside. The latter part of the letterpress book contains business accounts of a merchant in Albany, New York, 1879-1880.

1282. DAVID LUCIUS CRAFT PAPERS, 1853-1874. 110 items. Brownsville (Fayette County), Pa.

Letters from David L. Craft, chiefly to his sister, Carrie, describing battles and sections of the country through which he passed while serving as sergeant and lieutenant in the signal corps of the Federal Army in General Ambrose E. Burnside's Coast Division, notably areas around Washington, D.C., Annapolis, Maryland, and eastern North Carolina. There are also letters concerning Craft's service with the United States Army, 1867-1874, in posts at Charleston, South Carolina, and in the West. Included are comments on oaths of allegiance taken in the spring of 1862 by citizens of New Bern, North Carolina; extortionate prices of merchandise in that town; an expedition to Port Royal, South Carolina; the superiority of Confederate generals and soldiers to the Federals; a Confederate ram's playing havoc with Federal ships in Pamlico Sound during April, 1864; his opinion as to the feeling of the soldiers toward the presidential candidates in 1864; hardships of travel in the West; army life at posts in the Indian Territory and Kansas; and descriptions of Indians.

1283. JOHN A. CRAIG PAPERS, 1849 (1854-1858) 1896. 89 items. Shippensburg (Cumberland County), Pa.

The papers in this collection are almost entirely receipts from Philadelphia nurseries for ornamental shrubs and trees. The letters include a description of the state of agriculture and the prevalence of cholera in Virginia, 1849; comment on Presbyterian missionary work in Iowa in the 1850s and 1860s; and correspondence from friends in California, 1853-1856.

1284. LOCKE CRAIG PAPERS, 1865-1924. 125 items and 1 vol. Asheville (Buncombe County), N.C.

Personal correspondence and papers of Locke Craig (1860-1924), North Carolina legislator, 1898-1903, and governor, 1913-1917. Included are letters from his mother; recommendations from professors at the University of North Carolina, Chapel Hill; letters of Craig to his sons, Carlyle and Arthur, at the United States Naval Academy, Annapolis, Maryland, and one letter from Carlyle Craig giving an account of his voyage to the Azores, including the island of Fayal, and other places; copies of many of Locke Craig's political and religious speeches, including one on Masonry; and one chemistry notebook kept by Craig at the University of North Carolina. Among the correspondents are J. W. Bailey, Kemp P. Battle, H. G. Connor, A. W. Mangum, W. J. Peele, J. C. Pritchard, Woodrow Wilson, F. D. Winston, and G. T. Winston.

1285. MARY E. CRAIG PAPERS, 1853-1881. 56 items. Hillsborough (Orange County), N.C.

Family correspondence of Mary E. Craig and of her sister and brothers, all teachers, the brothers also being Confederate soldiers. Included also is a letter of W. H. Strayhorn, Confederate soldier, on the futility of war; and family correspondence after the war.

1286. PORTER CRAIG PAPERS, 1862-1863. 3 items. Ohio.

Civil War letters from Camp John Sherman, Washington, D.C., and a camp near Clarksville, Tennessee.

1287. PEARL MARY TERESA (RICHARDS) CRAIGIE PAPERS, 1896. 2 items. London, England.

Miscellaneous letters concerned with her literary career.

1288. W. G. CRANCH DIARY, 1825.
1 vol. (38 pp.)

Shorthand diary, evidently of a lawyer.

1289. W. IRVING CRANDALL PAPERS, 1858-1892. 43 items. Green Bay (Brown County), Wis., and Chattanooga (Hamilton County), Tenn.

Miscellaneous letters dealing with the presidential election of 1860, the Japanese Embassy, the iron industry in Tennessee, and Brazilian agriculture, social life, and customs.

1290. W. H. CRANE RECEIPT BOOK, 1857-1864. 1 vol. (28 pp.) Savannah, Ga.

Record of cash receipts.

1291. TILMAN CRANFORD PAPERS, 1822-1877. 1,064 items. Rowan County, N.C.

Papers of Tilman Cranford, constable and deputy sheriff of Rowan County, relative to the case of W. A. Houck v. J. J. Albright, and promissory notes, contracts, executor's bonds, bills, receipts, deeds of trust, tax in kind estimates, summonses, and warrants evidently in Cranford's hands because of his office.

1292. BARTLETT Y. CRAVEN PAPERS, 1844-1868. 9 items and 1 vol.

Receipts, 1844-1868, and a daybook, 1853-1862.

1293. JOHN A. CRAVEN ACCOUNT BOOK, 1856-1871. 1 vol. (88 pp.)

Merchant's account book.

1294. THOMAS TINGEY CRAVEN PAPERS, 1861. 1 vol.

Copies of Craven's official correspondence, July 1, 1861-December 2, 1861, as commander of the Potomac River Flotilla, United States Navy.

1295. ABEL H. CRAWFORD PAPERS, 1863-1865. 1 vol. Cotton Valley (Macon County), Ala.

Typed copies of the letters of a soldier in the 61st Alabama Regiment. The letters concern the Wilderness campaign, the defense of Petersburg, the battle of Cedar Creek, all in 1864, and the final months of the war in Virginia. The papers contain one letter from Crawford's slave, Jim Crawford, who was his servant in the army, and copies of the muster rolls of the 45th and 61st Alabama Regiments.

1296. GEORGE WALKER CRAWFORD PAPERS, 1782 (1837-1847). 27 items. Milledgeville (Baldwin County), Ga.

Miscellaneous items concerning political and legal matters, including letters to Crawford about the militia; the document signed by Zachary Taylor appointing Crawford secretary of war; testimony of Luke Mann regarding the plundering of his house, 1782; petition to the president and council in Augusta protesting a grant of land to a group of Virginians [1784]; a manuscript copy of a report, 1794, of a committee of the Georgia House of Representatives concerning sale of western lands of the state; and a letter concerning the filling of a public office.

1297. JOEL CRAWFORD PAPERS, 1839. 1 item. Sparta (Hancock County), Ga.

Letter from Crawford giving information on the construction of the Western and Atlantic Railroad.

1298. MARTHA (FOSTER) CRAWFORD DIARIES, 1846-1881. 7 vols. Clinton (Greene County), Ala., and Shanghai, China.

Diaries of Martha (Foster) Crawford (1830-1893), the wife of Tarleton Perry Crawford, as a young woman in Alabama, 1846-1851; and later as a Baptist missionary to China. Topics include conditions in Shanghai from 1852 to 1864 and afterwards at Tengchow, Shantung, and her reactions to the Civil War in the United States. Her diary shows the impact of the American Protestant missionary on China with a day-by-day record of the lives of the two missionaries. The Shanghai period covers the Taiping rebellion and reveals the hope that the rebellion might furnish a means for converting the Empire to Christianity. Included also are several printed pamphlets and an original manuscript history of missions in China.

1299. SAMUEL WYLIE CRAWFORD PAPERS, 1861-1870. 4 items. Montgomery (Montgomery County), Ala.

Letter from John Titcomb Sprague, 1861, commenting on Fort Sumter and its commander, Robert Anderson; orders from Crawford, 1870, as commander of United States troops in Alabama instructing officers on the policing of the polls during the coming election; and a letter from the sheriff of Montgomery, 1870, concerning threat of a riot.

1300. SARAH ANN (GAYLE) CRAWFORD PAPERS, 1826-1926. 39 items and 1 vol. Mobile (Mobile County), Ala.

Correspondence representing several generations of the Crawford and Gayle families and a notebook kept by William B. Crawford while a medical student in France, 1832-1833, under the surgeon Guillaume Dupuytren, containing notes on Dupuytren's lectures and operations.

1301. WILLIAM CRAWFORD PAPERS, 1864. 3 items. Beith, Scotland.

Correspondence concerning Crawford's interest in the British tobacco trade during the American Civil War, including information on blockade running, supplies, and prices.

1302. WILLIAM HARRIS CRAWFORD PAPERS, 1790 (1842-1862) 1867. 126 items. Woodlawn, near Crawford (Oglethorpe County), Ga.

A miscellaneous collection of papers and letters reflecting Crawford's interest in domestic American politics and international relations. The items concerned with foreign affairs include letters from 1805 on the claims of United States citizens against Denmark; letters, 1813-1814, from Secretary of State James Monroe, to Crawford as minister to France on the state of the American legation in Paris, the situation resulting from the deposal of Napoleon I, and the establishing of peace negotiations with Great Britain; correspondence on United States-Brazilian relations and an analysis of French politics, both 1815; letters on the Adams-Onis treaty, 1817; several letters concerning relations between Sweden and Denmark, 1818; and a description of the situation of France in 1820 under Bourbon rule. There is material on the routine business of Crawford's various offices including papers concerning the military academy, 1815; a document presenting the case of underpaid government clerks, 1815; receipts signed by Crawford as secretary of the treasury, 1816; Crawford's analysis of the coinage of the United States, 1818; and a letter to Crawford in 1820 concerning land speculation in Louisiana. The political items in the collection include Crawford's opinion on the authority of Georgia courts and his interpretation of the Constitution, 1815; a description of Tennessee politics, 1821; an analysis of New England politics and an attack on John Quincy Adams, ca. 1824; letters on the election of 1828; and several letters dealing with Andrew Jackson, Jacksonian politics, and the tariff issue.

1303. JOHN HARVIE CREECY PAPERS, 1949. 2 items. Richmond, Va.

Genealogy of the Harvie family.

1304. EDWARD CRENSHAW PAPERS, 1861-1864. 17 items. Greenville (Butler County), Ala.

Letters concerning Crenshaw's service in the Confederate army, including information on the organization of various military units in Alabama and Virginia.

1305. LEROY A. CRENSHAW PAPERS, 1849. 1 item. Richmond, Va.

Letter concerning transfer of land.

1306. JAMES A. CREWES PAPERS, 1857-1891. 70 items. Oxford (Granville County), N.C.

Miscellaneous business papers, legal papers, and personal correspondence.

1307. JACOB CRISCOE PAPERS, 1850, 1852. 2 items. Ashboro (Randolph County), N.C.

Personal letters.

1308. JOHN JORDAN CRITTENDEN PAPERS, 1786-1932. 1,055 items and 3 vols. Frankfort (Franklin County), Ky.

Family and political correspondence of John J. Crittenden (1787-1863), Kentucky statesman and governor, and letters pertaining to the publication of the Life of John J. Crittenden (Philadelphia: 1871) by his daughter, Ann Mary Butler (Crittenden) Coleman. There are also two scrapbooks, a letter book, and speeches of Crittenden; family correspondence and papers of Mrs. Coleman including her will and the will of her husband; Civil War letters from her children; letters concerning Chapman Coleman's career in the U.S. foreign service; a copy of Crittenden's will; and copies of the Crittenden-Coleman genealogy. In addition to the published correspondence are letters from Thomas Hart Benton, James Buchanan, William Butler, Henry Clay, Millard Fillmore, Andrew Jackson, James Madison, John Marshall, James Monroe, Franklin Pierce, Winfield Scott, William H. Seward, Alexander H. Stephens, Benjamin Taylor, Zachary Taylor, John Tyler, and Daniel Webster.

1309. THOMAS THEODORE CRITTENDEN PAPERS, 1819. 1 item. Lexington (Fayette County), Ky.

Letter concerning the purchase of bank notes.

1310. [WALTER OKE CROGGON?] ALBUM, 1832-1874. 1 vol. (148 pp.) Ireland.

Album of drawings, prints, and autographs of several British Methodist clergymen.

1311. JOHN WILSON CROKER PAPERS, 1793-1861. 2,874 items. London, England.

Papers of an essayist, politician, and secretary of the admiralty dealing for the most part with political matters; naval affairs, particularly operations in the Napoleonic Wars and the War of 1812; parliamentary reform; the Conservative Party; the British Constitution; governmental finance; the Corn Laws and the Peelites; politics, law, government, religion, and economic conditions in Ireland; French politics, government, and relations between

Great Britain and France; conditions in Canada; and the Church of England. Also includes comment on the important political events and personalities of his time. There are detailed subject and name indexes for this collection.

1312. ALICE CROMSON PAPERS, 1871-1887. 27 items. Locust Level (Stanly County), N.C.

Personal letters from friends and relatives, reflecting home and community life.

1313. CRONLY FAMILY PAPERS, 1806-1944. 1,962 items and 66 vols. Wilmington (New Hanover County), N.C.

Letters and papers of various members of the Cronly family and their Beatty, Dickson, and McLaurin relatives in Laurinburg, Wadesboro, Wilmington, and other North Carolina cities concerning family and social affairs and business interests. Includes letters on the financial troubles of the Wilmington, Charlotte, and Rutherford Railroad Company, 1870-1871; legal papers of the railroad; and minutes of the board of directors. There are also letters, legal and financial papers, account books, and a letterpress book from the early 1860s to the late 1890s for Cronly and Morris, real estate dealers and public auctioneers; correspondence on Democratic Party politics in Wilmington, 1918; letters from a soldier in the 2nd North Carolina Regiment during the Spanish-American War, 1898; the unpublished writings of Jane M. Cronly including a novel and several short stories on social life, religious attitudes, and racial attitudes in Wilmington, North Carolina, in the late 19th century; and fragments of diaries kept by Jane Cronly and her mother during the Civil War. The collection includes two memoirs of family experiences during the Civil War, particularly in Wilmington; several miscellaneous volumes including two on the Wilmington race riot, 1898; and a number of unidentified photographs, probably of the Cronly family.

1314. JOHN CRONMILLER PAPERS, 1846-1853. 5 items. Savage (Howard County), Md.

Personal letters.

1315. WILLIAM HENRY CROOK PAPERS, 1879. 1 item. Washington, D.C.

Letter from the Librarian of Congress to Crook concerning books which President Rutherford B. Hayes wished to borrow.

1316. R. N. CROOKS PAPERS, 1876-1880. 10 items. Harrellsville (Hertford County), N.C.

Personal letters of a Methodist minister and his daughter devoted largely to local news and the church.

1317. SARAH CROSBY PAPERS, 1760-1804. 2 items and 1 vol. Leeds, Yorkshire, England. Restricted.

Letter book and two letters of the first woman preacher authorized by John Wesley. The letter book (1760-1774) is mainly outgoing correspondence on religion, particularly Methodism. There are memoranda, copies of letters between John Wesley and Mary Bosanquet; and extracts from the diary of Jane Cooper. The two loose items are letters from John Wesley and Mary (Bosanquet) Fletcher.

1318. JAMES F. CROSS PAPERS, 1887-1898. 1 item and 1 vol. Great Cacapon (Morgan County), W. Va.

Docket kept by Cross as justice of the peace for the Cacapon district, 1887-1898, primarily 1887-1893; and a letter of 1897 addressed to him.

1319. THOMAS CROSS PAPERS, 1846-1861. 4 items. Montgomery County, Tenn.

A list of slaves belonging to the estate of George Cross; receipts for slaves; and a letter, 1861, commenting on the raising of troops at the beginning of the Civil War and divided sentiment in Tennessee over secession.

1320. JOHN HENRY VERINDER CROWE PAPERS, 1917-1942. 10 items. Caversham, Berkshire, England.

The collection consists mainly of letters to Crowe from Jan Christian Smuts concerning Smuts's East African campaign of 1917-1918 and Crowe's history of that campaign. Letters of 1941 and 1942 also comment on World War II.

1321. BENJAMIN WILLIAMS CROWNINSHIELD PAPERS, 1815-1816. 2 items. Boston, Mass.

Letters discussing appointments in the United States Navy.

1322. E. A. CRUDUP DIARY, 1857-1860, 1867-1872. 2 vols. Franklin County, N.C.

Plantation diaries, containing accounts of expenses incident to keeping slaves; local news; and accounts of crop conditions.

1323. W. J. CRUMPLER DIARY AND ACCOUNT BOOK, 1875. 1 vol. (146 pp.) Pantego (Beaufort County), N.C.

Agricultural diary and accounts kept in a notebook prepared by the Patrons of Husbandry, containing some printed matter relative to that organization.

1324. E. W. CRUTCHFIELD PAPERS, 1886-1889. 27 items. Kent's Store (Fluvanna County), Va.

Business and personal correspondence.

1325. HENRY M. CRYDENWISE PAPERS, 1861-1867. 43 items. Otsego County, N.Y.

Letters describe Crydenwise's life as a soldier in the 90th New York Regiment in Florida and South Carolina; subsequent service as an officer in the 96th United States Regiment (Colored); and employment as an overseer on a large plantation near Vicksburg, Mississippi.

1326. JOHN CULBERSON AND SAMUEL J. CULBERSON PAPERS, 1839-1864. 24 items. Mudlick Post Office (Chatham County), N.C.

Correspondence, including personal narratives of the Civil War.

1327. J. M. CULBERTSON PAPERS, 1862-1865. 17 items. Laurens District, S.C.

Correspondence of Culbertson and his son serving in the Confederate Army. Gives an account of the capture of Roanoke Island, North Carolina, 1862, and mentions the burning of Elizabeth City, North Carolina.

1328. WILLIAM CULBERTSON PAPERS, 1862-1863. 37 items. Ohio.

Letters of a soldier who enlisted in the 38th Ohio Regiment and later served in the 1st Battalion Pioneer Brigade, Army of the Cumberland, describing army life and giving an account of the battle of Murfreesboro, 1863.

1329. THOMAS CULBRETH PAPERS, 1832-1835. 5 items. Denton (Caroline County), Md.

Routine correspondence concerned with Culbreth's office as Clerk of the Maryland Executive Council. Includes a letter from United States Senator Henry Goldsborough on the principles of the Whig Party, 1834.

1330. SHELBY MOORE CULLOM PAPERS, 1910. 1 item. Springfield (Sangamon County), Ill.

Personal letter.

1331. J. P. CULP PAPERS, 1864-1865. 3 items. Cabarrus County, N.C.

Personal letters of a soldier in the 20th North Carolina Regiment.

1332. CUMBERLAND VALLEY MUTUAL PROTECTION CO. PAPERS, 1856-1872. 1,628 items. Carlisle (Cumberland County), Pa.

Papers consist of letters from policyholders, and the letters and accounts of insurance agents and agencies concern the routine business of selling insurance and settling claims. Letters in 1870 and 1872 describe the organization and financing of the Peoples' Savings Bank of Monongahela City, Pennsylvania, and the Monongahela City Fire and Life Insurance Company. There are numerous letters from disappointed customers.

1333. ALFRED CUMMING PAPERS, 1792 (1850-1860) 1889. 751 items and 9 vols. Augusta (Richmond County), Ga., and Utah.

Family and political correspondence of William Clay Cumming; Thomas Cumming; and Alfred Cumming (1802-1873), participant in the "Mormon War," 1857-1861, with material on Mormon history and frontier and pioneer life.

Letters of William Clay Cumming, brother of Alfred Cumming, 1805-1818, contain mention of books read and studied at Princeton College, Princeton, New Jersey, in 1805; description of studies, living arrangements, and teachers in the Litchfield Law School, operated at Litchfield, Connecticut, by Tapping Reeve; accounts of violent opposition to Federalism in New England; description of climate and countryside around Litchfield; participation of William Clay Cumming's brother, Joseph, in disturbances at Princeton College, 1807; his activities in the War of 1812 as commander of a company in Florida, campaigns in New York as a colonel, criticisms of officers, a dispute with General George Izard, adoption of a system of discipline for the infantry; description of a trip in 1815 from New York to New Orleans with accounts of Louisville, Lexington, and the Mammoth Cave in Kentucky, Asheville, North Carolina, Nashville, Tennessee, Baton Rouge and New Orleans, Louisiana; a few comments on Brazil and Uruguay, which he visited in 1816; and mention of John McDonogh.

A series of letters by Elizabeth Wells (Randall) Cumming to members of her family describes the arduous trip to Utah, scenery, frontier conditions, and Indian troubles. The collection includes hints of discrepancies in Cumming's account with the U.S. government while territorial governor. Included also are nine volumes: journal of an expedition to the Blackfoot Indians with notes and instructions, 1855; two letter books and official proceedings of a commission to hold council with Blackfoot and other Indian tribes, 1855; two letterpress copybooks, 1857-1861, 1859-1860, containing copies of letters to government officials, and to James Buchanan, Lewis Cass, Howell Cobb, John B. Floyd, A. S. Johnston, and Brigham Young; and four scrapbooks containing newspaper clippings and broadsides. Among the correspondents are W. W. Bibb, J. S. Black,

James Buchanan, Lewis Cass, Alfred Cumming, J. B. Floyd, Albert Sidney Johnston, William Medill, B. F. Perry, Franklin Pierce, Alexander H. Stephens, G. M. Troup, and Brigham Young.

1334. JOHN CUMMING PAPERS, 1861-1865. 93 items. South Carolina.

Letters of a soldier in the 5th South Carolina Cavalry from South Carolina and Virginia contain information on managing the home farm and on the bombardment of Battery Wagner, the hardships of camp life, and the destruction caused by Union raiders, 1864.

1335. RICHARD J. CUNDIFF AND WILLIAM N. REESE PAPERS, 1836-1872. 15 items. Franklin County, Va.

Personal letters containing comments on the panic of 1837 and on slavery.

1336. ALEXANDER CUNINGHAM PAPERS, 1740 (1825-1859) 1918. 6,327 items and 44 vols. Petersburg (Dinwiddie County), Va. and Cunningham's Store (Person County), N.C.

Business records and some personal correspondence of four generations of the Cuningham family, consisting of Robert Cuningham (d. ca. 1788); Alexander Cuningham (d. ca. 1850), and his brother, Richard M. Cuningham; the latter's son, John Wilson Cuningham (1820-1887); and Richard M. Cuningham's grandson, John Somerville Cuningham (1861-1922), merchants and planters. The early papers center around the mercantile interests of Alexander and Richard M. Cuningham in Petersburg, and the former's planting interests in Person County, North Carolina. Records also reflect Richard M. Cuningham's dealings in cotton with James and William Trahern. Included are records of the flourishing business in Petersburg with papers showing extensive transactions in a commission business of cotton and tobacco and large planting interests, including copies of contracts with overseers and tenants; and letters to John Garner, partner of Richard M. Cuningham and manager of the firm's business in Person County and in Alabama during the 1820s and possibly later. The collection also contains a few family letters in 1818; letters from Alexander Cuningham, Jr., while a student at the University of North Carolina, Chapel Hill, 1845-1846, and from another son while at Leasburg Academy, Caswell County, North Carolina; and bills for merchandise bought by John W. Cuningham, 1850-1859. Papers of John Somerville Cuningham concern his work as a field agent for the Bureau of Crop Estimates of the U.S. Department of Agriculture, politics in North Carolina, activities of the League to Enforce Peace, 1916, and personal and family matters. Among the volumes are copybooks, cotton storage records, daybooks, invoices, cashbooks, orders, ledgers, letter books, bills, memoranda, salt and flour accounts, and plantation books. Among the correspondents are C. B. Aycock, R. H. Battle, A. L. Brooks, Tod R. Caldwell, F. L. Fuller, J. B. Grimes, W. W. Kitchin, B. R. Lacy, C. D. McIver, S. F. Mordecai, J. M. Morehead, J. E. Pogue, F. M. Simmons, and C. A. Swanson.

1337. ANN PAMELA CUNNINGHAM PAPERS, 1857-1874. 17 items. Laurens (Laurens County), S.C.

Letters relating to the collection of money for the Mount Vernon Ladies Association of the Union.

1338. WILLIAM H. CUNNINGHAM COPYBOOK, 1835. 1 vol. Virginia.

A schoolboy's copybook of mottoes.

1339. CURRENCY COLLECTION, 1754-1944. ca. 3,271 items.

A miscellaneous collection of pieces of money, negotiable paper, and instruments of debt from the United States, foreign countries, and private corporations. Includes currency issued at various times by the government of the United States and by or in the states or colonies of Alabama, Arkansas, Connecticut, Delaware, Florida, Georgia, Indiana, Kentucky, Louisiana, Maine, Maryland, Massachusetts, Michigan, Mississippi, Missouri, Nebraska, New Hampshire, New Jersey, New York, North Carolina, Ohio, Pennsylvania, South Carolina, Tennessee, Texas, Utah, Vermont, Virginia, and the District of Columbia, including many state bank notes. Also contains currency or bonds from Argentina, Austria-Hungary, Belgium, Canada, China, Cuba, France, Germany, Great Britain, Haiti, Hungary, Italy, Japan, Mexico, and Russia. There are Confederate bonds, depository receipts, and currency issued by the government of the Confederate States and by or in the states of Alabama, Georgia, North Carolina, and South Carolina. Also includes a small number of bonds issued by local government in the United States and by private corporations. The collection contains a copper plate for printing five dollar bills in North Carolina in 1776.

1340. JABEZ LAMAR MONROE CURRY PAPERS, 1854 (1882-1903) 1931. 736 items and 4 vols. Richmond, Va.

The major part of the collection is the correspondence of J. L. M. Curry with his son, Manly Bowie Curry, mainly in the years 1884-1903. The correspondence is personal, for the most part, but there are occasional references to Curry's career in education. The collection also contains two letter books covering a portion of the time Curry served as United States minister to Spain (1885-1888) which have extensive observations on Spain, its rulers, customs, and environment; a few items of correspondence with relatives; newspaper clippings; photographs of the Curry family and of the Philippines; and a typewritten journal kept by Manly Lamar Curry while serving with the United States Marine Corps in Nicaragua, 1930-1931.

1341. MARGARET CURRY PAPERS, 1813-1891. 43 items. Fair Grove (Davidson County), N.C.

Personal correspondence.

1342. GEORGE WILLIAM CURTIS PAPERS, 1884, 1888. 2 items. New York, N.Y.

Miscellaneous letters, one of which concerns an article written by Curtis.

1343. GEORGE NATHANIEL CURZON, FIRST MARQUIS CURZON OF KEDLESTON, PAPERS, 1895-1925. 36 items. Hackwood, Hampshire, England.

Letters concerned, for the most part, with Curzon's activities in gathering paintings and sculpture for Victoria Memorial Hall in Calcutta, India.

1344. CUSHING FAMILY PAPERS, 1743-1911. 966 items and 5 vols. Scituate (Plymouth County), Mass.

Correspondence in this collection is mainly for the years 1848-1887 and is made up of the personal and family letters of Mary Jacobs Cushing, Olive Cushing, John Cushing, and Nathaniel Grafton Cushing. The correspondence contains family news; a few letters on the Civil War service of John Cushing concerning army life and pay; information about John Cushing's later attempts to establish farms in Iowa and Nebraska; and a series of letters, 1872-1873, from Taylor Z. Thistle, a freedman studying at Nashville Normal and Collegiate Theological Institute, Nashville, Tennessee. Legal papers include bills of sale, land plats, leases, and a copy of the division of the estate of John Cushing, 1798. Miscellaneous items include remedies for various diseases and a printed copy of the constitution of a temperance society. Among the volumes are an account book for staple groceries and a personal account book for 1852. There are numerous bills and receipts; a statement of wages for a schoolmaster, 1806-1807; and records of shipbuilding expenses, 1810-1819.

1345. CHARLOTTE SAUNDERS CUSHMAN PAPERS, 1 item. Boston, Mass.

Social note from Frances Anne Kemble.

1346. SALLIE C. CUSTER PAPERS, 1855, 1876. 2 items. Decatur (Macon County), Ill.

Personal correspondence.

1347. SETH JOHN CUTHBERT PAPERS, 1780-1788. 4 items. Augusta (Richmond County), Ga.

Correspondence of a major in the commissary division of the Georgia Militia concerning supplies in Augusta and the removal of the treasury from Savannah to Augusta.

1348. FREDERICK CUTLER AND SARAH (MONROE) CUTLER PAPERS, 1863-1864. 11 items. Boxford (Essex County), Mass.

Letters from soldiers in the 47th Massachusetts Regiment, describing garrison duty in New Orleans, 1863, and commenting on the Negro troops of the 4th Louisiana Regiment (Colored).

1349. EDWIN A. CUTTER PAPERS, 1862-1863. 35 items. Newburyport (Essex County), Mass.

Letters of a soldier in the 48th Massachusetts Regiment concerning the siege of Port Hudson, Louisiana. Included are descriptions of life at Camp Wenham, Massachusetts; New Orleans and Baton Rouge; camp life in Louisiana; the attack on Port Hudson and reaction to the news of the fall of Vicksburg.

1350. CHISWELL DABNEY, JR., PAPERS, 1791-1886. 753 items and 8 vols. Lynchburg (Campbell County), Va.

Business papers of Chiswell Dabney, Jr. (d. 1865), attorney, and of his son, George William Dabney, consisting of legal papers and documents, including the will of Chiswell Dabney, Jr., merchants' letters, invoices, bills, and receipts.

1351. ROBERT LEWIS DABNEY PAPERS, 1838, 1847. 2 items. Thompson's Cross Roads (Louisa County), Va.

A letter from Moses Drury Hoge, Presbyterian minister, to R. L. Dabney concerning Hoge's education, Randolph-Macon College, President John Tyler, and social customs in North Carolina; and a letter from William Henry Ruffner, also a Presbyterian minister, discussing courses and lectures at Princeton Theological Seminary, the biblical scholarship of Jacob J. Janeway, and the temperance leaders John B. Gough and Lucian Minor.

1352. JOHN ADOLPHUS BERNARD DAHLGREN PAPERS, 1848 (1864-1870). 32 items. Philadelphia, Pa.

Family letters of Admiral Dahlgren (1809-1870). Civil War letters from his sister, Patty (Dahlgren) Read, describe hardships suffered, depredations of Confederate and Union soldiers, the "Ironsides Affair," and several senators and officers. A letter from Dahlgren to Captain Johnston B. Creighton orders that Negroes be allowed to move freely about Georgetown, South Carolina. Letters,

1867, from Eva Dahlgren to her father describe her travels in Europe, especially Italy.

1353. DAISY HOSIERY MILLS PAPERS, 1913-1922. 7 vols. Burlington (Alamance County), N.C.

Records of the Daisy Hosiery Mills, manufacturers of men's and women's cotton and mercerized seamless hosiery, include ledgers, journals, trial balances, a voucher register, and a sales journal. Later records appear under May McEwen Kaiser, the name taken after consolidation.

1354. B. J. DALBY ACCOUNT BOOKS, 1855-1858. 3 vols. Virginia.

Account books containing inventories of slaves, livestock, and farming implements; and records of plowing, planting, cultivating, and harvesting on a Virginia plantation.

1355. MARY (BRAND) DALL PAPERS, 1846-1889. 331 items. Lexington (Fayette County), Ky., and Baltimore, Md.

Family letters between the Brands and Dalls, principally concerning family matters and social life. Several letters deal with the commission mercantile business in Baltimore and New York, and travel conditions in Texas, California, and the east.

1356. JAMES L. DALLAM PAPERS, 1858-1869. 20 items. Paducah (McCracken County), Ky.

Personal correspondence of James L. Dallam, cashier, Commercial Bank of Kentucky, to his wife, including mention of camp meetings.

1357. CHARLES ANDERSON DANA PAPERS, 1865, 1885. 2 items. New York, N.Y.

A letter from Edward Cantrell asking assistance in securing his release from Johnson's Island prison; and a letter from Charles A. Dana to Frank A. Burr describing his mission to the Department of the Mississippi in 1863 to make a financial report, his engagement in the cotton trade, and the problems between the cotton trade and military operations.

1358. JOHN DANDRIDGE ACCOUNT BOOKS, 1764-1830. 2 vols. Worcester, England.

Account books of John Dandridge, attorney, and adjutant in the British army while in South Carolina, Georgia, and Florida during the Revolutionary War, and in Dublin, Ireland, and various English barracks. Included are records of miscellaneous expenses of his own and of others, including Captain King's Carolina Rangers.

1359. JOHN B. DANFORTH PAPERS, 1854-1864. 1 vol. Richmond, Va.

Letterpress copybook of personal, business, and military correspondence of John B. Danforth, Confederate soldier and member of the firm of Danforth and Brushwood, Richmond commission merchants. The collection contains copies of letters to his friends and business associates, including Andrew Stevenson of Albemarle County, Virginia, and Colonel John Rutherfoord, merchant and governor of Virginia. Included also are letters of a religious nature to friends and ministers; letters answering notes of sympathy upon his first wife's death; and a long series of letters to General William H. Richardson, adjutant general of Virginia, to Governor John Letcher, and other officials, while Danforth served as colonel of the 1st Virginia Militia with the duty of safeguarding the city of Richmond, 1863-1864. The letters to General Richardson are concerned with reluctance of Danforth's men to stand guard, recommendations for courts-martial, requests for uniforms and supplies, and failure to call young government officials for their share of guard duty.

1360. BEVERLEY DANIEL PAPERS, 1814. 1 item. Raleigh (Wake County), N.C.

Circular letter to Beverley Daniel, marshal of North Carolina, from the office of the commissary general of prisoners, Washington, D.C., discussing U.S. and British prisoners of war during the War of 1812.

1361. HARRIET BAILY (BULLOCK) DANIEL PAPERS, 1753 (1857-1933) 1957. 207 items and 1 vol. Oxford (Granville County), N.C.

Principally the personal correspondence of Harriet B. Daniel (1849-1934) with family and friends in Arkansas and Tennessee. Of interest are Civil War letters from Samuel Venable Daniel concerning coastal defenses at Hatteras Island and the Federal blockade, and the battles of Cold Harbor and Petersburg; material concerning the University of North Carolina at Chapel Hill, including a printed letter from President David Lowry Swain describing a new state statute prohibiting certain student activities; letters describing Presbyterian and Methodist church history in Arkansas in the 1850s; and a letter telling of a convention of the Young Women's Christian Association in 1922. There is also a copy of the original land grant for Tranquility Plantation made in 1753. Printed material includes a tourist guide to Arkansas and a book of "Arkansas Facts" from the 1920s; <u>A Brief Sketch of the History of the Protestant Episcopal Church in the Missionary District of Western Texas</u>; and the Bicentennial Anniversary Program of the Nut Bush Presbyterian Church, Townsville, North Carolina, 1957. Pictures include photographs of reunions of Confederate veterans in San Marcos, Texas, and Granville County, North Carolina. A photograph album of Lucy E.

Daniel (b. 1884), daughter of Samuel Venable Daniel, of San Marcos, Texas, portrays family and friends. There is also some genealogical information.

1362. J. H. DANIEL PAPERS, 1850-1856. 2 items. Conetoe (Edgecombe County), N.C.

Personal letters of J. H. Daniel discussing religion, family matters, crops and commodity prices, and a journey in Pennsylvania.

1363. JOHN REEVES JONES DANIEL PAPERS, 1841, 1856. 2 items. Halifax (Halifax County), N.C.

Letters from J. R. J. Daniel (1802-1868), lawyer, member of General Assembly, 1823-1834, attorney general of North Carolina, 1834-1841, and member of U.S. Congress, 1841-1853. Included are a letter, 1841, to Secretary of the Navy George Edmund Badger, concerning Jerome B. Zollicoffer's application for entrance to the U.S. Naval Academy; and a letter, 1856, to John Cook Rives, concerning the sale of a land warrant.

1364. JOHN WARWICK DANIEL PAPERS, 1849 (1876-1909) 1910. 488 items. Lynchburg (Campbell County), Va.

Correspondence of John W. Daniel (1842-1910), U.S. congressman, 1885-1887, and senator, 1887-1910. Many letters from ex-officers of the Confederate Army discuss battles and leaders of the Civil War, especially the battles of Gettysburg, Chancellorsville, Spotsylvania, and Bentonville, the Valley Campaign, and Generals Robert E. Lee and Jubal A. Early. Other topics of primary interest are politics during Reconstruction, various presidential campaigns, Virginia politics, United States expansion, foreign policy with Spain and Cuba, and the Spanish-American War. Correspondents consist of prominent politicians and ex-officers of the Confederate Army, including Charles F. Adams, Charles B. Aycock, Judah P. Benjamin, Richard P. Bland, William Jennings Bryan, Matthew C. Butler, John W. Daniel, Jefferson Davis, Jubal A. Early, Henry D. Flood, Carter Glass, Ulysses S. Grant, Stephen P. Halsey, Wade Hampton III, Winfield S. Hancock, George F. Hoar, Joseph E. Johnston, Philander C. Knox, L. Q. C. Lamar, Fitzhugh Lee, William Mahone, Justin S. Morrill, John S. Mosby, Richard Olney, Lee S. Overman, Boies Penrose, Thomas C. Platt, Matthew S. Quay, Theodore Roosevelt, Elihu Root, Adlai E. Stevenson, Benjamin Tillman, Daniel W. Voorhees, Henry Watterson, and others.

1365. WILLIAM C. DANIELL PAPERS, 1859-1864. 36 items. Savannah, Ga.

Legal papers of William C. Daniell, Confederate receiver of alien property for southern Georgia, pertaining chiefly to answers to questionnaires sent by the Confederate court on alien property held by southern business agents, including Gazaway B. Lamar and Robert Habersham.

1366. HENRY DANIELS PAPERS, 1865. 1 vol. (68 pp.) Lawrenceville (Brunswick County), Va.

Records of the Freedmen's Bureau, including lists of Negroes and former slaves who worked at the Government Farm and who drew rations from the government. Included also are contracts between Negro laborers and white employers and warnings from Henry Daniels to the white men who had failed to fulfil their contracts.

1367. JOSEPHUS DANIELS PAPERS, 1913-1935. 219 items and 40 vols. Raleigh (Wake County), N.C. and Washington, D.C.

Papers of Josephus Daniels (1862-1948), U.S. secretary of the navy, 1913-1921, U.S. ambassador to Mexico, 1933-1942, and editor of the Raleigh (N.C.) News and Observer. The collection comprises addresses made by Daniels on a variety of subjects; correspondence, including a letter, 1917, to Philip G. Straus concerning the condition of the U.S. Navy; thirty-four letterpress volumes of correspondence, 1915-1921, and two letterpress volumes of telegrams, 1916-1920, primarily concerned with affairs of the Department of the Navy, but also containing comments about personal and political matters; and four volumes of press books, 1913-1918, containing press releases and bulletins.

1368. THOMAS COWPER DANIELS PAPERS, (1889-1894) 1933. 2 vols. New Bern (Craven County), and Durham, N.C.

Volumes of a member of the Trinity College class of 1891, comprised of Daniels' senior thesis, "Should the U.S. Government Control the Railroads?" and a scrapbook containing clippings about athletics at Trinity College, where Daniels was a member of the football and track teams.

1369. JACOB S. DANNER LEDGERS, 1833-1869. 6 vols. Middleburg (Loudoun County), Va.

Mercantile accounts of a general store.

1370. ABSALOM F. DANTZLER PAPERS, 1840-1878. 287 items. Jasper County, Miss.

Principally letters between Absalom F. Dantzler (d. 1862) and his wife, Susan (Millsaps) Dantzler, while he was in the Mississippi legislature, 1859-1862, and in the Confederate Army, 1862. Letters discuss the workings of the legislature during secession and the first year of the war, the Know-Nothing Party, immigration, camp life, sickness, the battles of Iuka and Corinth,

Mississippi, home and family matters, and the activities of Negroes in the community. Early papers include letters from Dantzler in California, 1849-1850, family letters of Susan Millsaps, and addresses given by Dantzler, especially while attending Centenary College in Louisiana.

1371. LEWIS DANTZLER THESIS, 1835. 1 vol. (32 pp.) Saint Matthews (Calhoun County), S.C.

"An Inaugural Dissertation on Malaria," M.D., Medical College of South Carolina, 1835. Included are several pages of notes on acids.

1372. DANVILLE BANK CHECK STUBS, 1859. 1 vol. Danville (Pittsylvania County), Va.

1373. ARTHUR JOHNSON DANYELL SCRAPBOOK, 1862-1864. 1 vol. (104 pp.) England.

Scrapbook of Lieutenant Arthur Johnson Danyell, 31st Regiment, of the British army in China, containing a map of a journey through China and accounts of Tientsin, the Great Wall, Peking, and the coast; a description of the Taku forts; a portion of an account of an expedition to survey the terrain around Shanghai; and a passport.

1374. U. DART, SR., RECORDS, 1838-1869. 1 vol. (146 pp.) Brunswick (Glynn County), Ga.

Tax assessments, 1838-1845; extracts from ordinances passed by the City Council, 1838-1842; copies of land grants issued by the King of England for lots in Brunswick; extracts from the proceedings of the Colonial Council of Georgia, 1764-1772; a plan of the town of Brunswick; and a list of Tories in Georgia whose property was confiscated during the Revolution.

1375. JANE ELIZABETH DASHER PAPERS, 1803-1863. 32 items. Effingham County, Ga.

Miscellaneous family papers, comprising those of Christian Dasher, tax collector and sheriff of Effingham County, including commissions of office, tax forms, and family land deeds; bills and receipts, several concerning medical treatment of slaves; and records concerning the estate of C. Dasher, father of Jane Elizabeth Dasher.

1376. HELEN J. (THOMPSON) SAWYER DAUGHERTY PAPERS, 1849-1892. 174 items. Edenton (Chowan County), N.C.

Principally the correspondence between Helen Daugherty (d. 1877) and her relatives and friends, discussing personal matters, Federal forces in Edenton, freedmen in North Carolina, the early days of Reconstruction, and Mrs. Daugherty's conversion to Catholicism. Letters after 1877 concern the care of her children, Louisa Cleveland Sawyer and Willie Daugherty, and the career of her second husband, Beverly W. Daugherty, an Episcopal priest. Included are several sermons.

1377. LOUISE DAUGHERTY PAPERS, 1925. 5 items. Washington, D.C.

Routine business letters to Louise Daugherty of the Louise Flower Shop.

1378. FANNY ELIZABETH (VINING) GILL DAVENPORT PAPERS, 1866. 1 item. London, England, and New York, N.Y.

Personal letter from actress Sidney Frances (Cowell) Bateman (1823-1881) to actress Fanny Davenport (1829-1891).

1379. HENRY B. DAVENPORT NOTEBOOK, 1851. 1 vol. Charlottesville (Albemarle County), Va.

Notes on Spanish and French literature made by Henry B. Davenport, a student at the University of Virginia. Included also are notes on surveying by S. H. Gardner and E. C. Davenport, made while attending an academy in Charles Town, West Virginia, in 1881.

1380. IRA DAVENPORT PAPERS, 1828-1842. 7 items. Hornellsville (Steuben County), N.Y.

Letters of Ira Davenport pertaining to real estate in New York.

1381. EPHRAIM DAVIDSON BANK BOOK, 1825-1828. 1 vol. (70 pp.) Iredell County, N.C.

Records of deposits made by Ephraim Davidson in the State Bank of North Carolina, Salisbury, North Carolina.

1382. GEORGE F. DAVIDSON PAPERS, 1748-1887. 1,660 items and 14 vols. Iredell County, N.C.

Personal correspondence, legal papers, account books, and diaries of the Davidson family. The correspondence includes a letter concerning the land and timber around Covington, Newton County, Georgia, 1824; one giving terms for renting land and hiring Negroes, 1838; another describing life in Mississippi in 1863, Federal raids, the Negroes, and the condition of the Confederacy; and others, 1882, telling of the work in China of John W. Davis, a missionary of undetermined denomination, and contrasting the Chinese and missionary methods of teaching. Included also are twelve account books and diaries of George F. Davidson, Iredell County planter and lawyer, showing expenditures, receipts, and daily activity on his plantation; and two account books concerning the settlement of the estate of Rufus Reid.

1383. JAMES DAVIDSON RECORD BOOK, 1825-1860. 1 vol. Petersburg (Dinwiddie County), Va.

Record of inquests by James Davidson while coroner of Petersburg.

1384. JAMES D. DAVIDSON PAPERS, 1829 (1836-1859) 1878. 318 items. Lexington (Rockbridge County), Va.

Legal, business, and personal papers of James D. Davidson, an attorney, pertaining to clients and court cases, estates, personal debts, agriculture, commodity prices, genealogy, business, banking, and politics. Several Civil War letters give accounts of military operations, hardships, the salt supply in the Confederate States, casualties and horses. A letter of 1857 mentions Frederick Cousins, a Negro physician.

1385. JAMES WOOD DAVIDSON PAPERS, 1856-1893. 3 items. Winnsboro (Fairfield County), S.C.

Typed copies of letters of James Wood Davidson (1829-1905), author and journalist, to A. B. Wardlaw, discussing activities at South Carolina College, new members of the faculty, and Davidson's personal work; and a letter to George A. Wauchope containing information on Davidson's Living Writers of the South, and his proposed "Dictionary of Southern Authors."

1386. JOHN DAVIDSON PAPERS, 1781-1794. 5 items. Annapolis (Anne Arundel County), Md.

Financial papers of a merchant.

1387. WILLIAM LEE DAVIDSON PAPERS, 1792-1794. 3 items. Davidson's Creek (Iredell County?), N.C.

Papers dealing with claims of the heirs of William Lee Davidson (1746-1781), brigadier general of the militia of the Salisbury District of North Carolina, against the U.S. Treasury and the State of North Carolina for compensation after his death during the Revolutionary War.

1388. FREDERICK WILLIAM DAVIE ACCOUNT BOOKS, 1850-1871. 3 vols. Charleston, S.C.

Records of the estate of Frederick William Davie, kept by his wife, Mary F. Fraser Davie, as administratrix, 1850-1871; accounts of Davie's estate with James Adger & Co., commission merchants engaged in buying cotton, 1850-1851; and accounts of household and personal expenses.

1389. WILLIAM RICHARDSON DAVIE PAPERS, 1782-1799. 4 items. Halifax (Halifax County), N.C.

Papers of William Richardson Davie (1756-1820), lawyer, Revolutionary soldier, and governor of North Carolina, include a letter from DeBretigney concerning Davie's marriage; a land grant; a letter from William Polk concerning the Blount Conspiracy to invade Florida and Louisiana; and a letter from James Holderness of Rockingham County, North Carolina, concerning a legal matter involving W. Ricks.

1390. C. A. DAVIES AND COMPANY RECORDS, 1875-1882. 1 vol. (583 pp.) Ogdensburg (Saint Lawrence County), N.Y.

Records of the C. A. Davies and Company, hardware dealers, include a business journal, 1875-1877, and accounts for the estate of C. A. Davies, 1878-1882.

1391. M. D. DAVIES DIARY, 1850-1856. 1 vol. (375 pp.) Alabama.

1392. A. B. DAVIS AND CO. PAPERS, 1860-1880. 83 items and 2 vols. Philadelphia, Pa.

Business papers of a manufacturer of scales, including orders, testimonial letters, a letter book, 1859-1860, and a daybook, 1861-1862.

1393. AMANDA DAVIS PAPERS, 1812-1861. 30 items. Boykins Depot (Southampton County), Va.

Personal and family letters of Amanda Davis, including a Civil War letter from Camp Cook, Virginia, and an account book.

1394. B. P. DAVIS AND BROTHER LEDGER, 1875-1880. 1 vol. (145 pp.) Arcola (Warren County), N.C.

Mercantile accounts.

1395. CHARLES W. DAVIS PAPERS, 1845-1855. 8 items. Baltimore, Md.

Family and business correspondence, including a letter from Charles W. Ross at Princeton to his grandfather, describing an altercation between students and town authorities.

1396. DOLPHIN A. DAVIS AND JOHN A. MATTHEWS PAPERS, 1820 (1827-1829). 31 items. Fayetteville (Cumberland County), N.C.

Business correspondence of cotton brokers at Fayetteville, North Carolina, and Cheraw, South Carolina, with merchants of South Carolina and New York. Included is information on prices and business methods.

1397.  E. A. DAVIS PAPERS, 1861-1865.
10 items. Decatur (DeKalb County), Ga.

Correspondence commenting on crops, prices, food, horses, camp life, and sickness among Confederate soldiers during the Civil War; and the raising of peaches in Georgia.

1398.  FREDERIC L. DAVIS TYPESCRIPT.
1 vol. (258 pp.)

Typescript of a novel, apparently unpublished, by Davis entitled "Harry Marshall of Virginia."

1399.  GEORGE DAVIS PAPERS, 1857, 1874.
2 items. Wilmington (New Hanover), N.C.

Letter from George Davis discussing the Mecklenburg Declaration and a letter from John Newland Maffitt discussing the leadership of Captain James M. Cook as a Confederate naval officer.

1400.  GEORGE T. M. DAVIS PAPERS, 1840-1841. 3 items. Alton (Madison County), Ill.

Letter to George T. M. Davis, a lawyer, concerning Democratic-Whig rivalry in Illinois, and two letters dealing with routine legal matters.

1401.  ISAAC DAVIS PAPERS, 1782 (1790-1828) 1878. 611 items. Stanardsville (Orange County), Va.

Correspondence of Isaac Davis, Jr., and of his son, Thomas Davis, concerning land in Kentucky; Indian wars and war with Great Britain, 1790-1828; lawsuit of Thomas Davis against Robert Wickliffe; election of James Barbour to the Virginia House of Delegates; Thomas Davis's plantation and purchase of horses; politics; and William Smith, governor of Virginia. Among the correspondents are Robert H. Banks, James Barbour, Isaac Davis, Jr., Thomas Davis, William Fitzhugh Gordon, Enoch Smith, and Robert Wickliffe.

1402.  JASPER DAVIS PAPERS, 1834-1868.
169 items. Halifax County, Va.

Principally personal and student letters of the brothers and sisters of Jasper Davis, from Salem College, Baptist Seminary at Richmond, and Yale, discussing social life and customs, religion, temperance, visits to White Sulphur Springs, West Virginia and the Independent Order of Odd Fellows. Several Civil War letters concern Union sentiment in Virginia, 1860, the battle of Fair Oaks, Virginia, and the defense of Richmond, 1864.

1403.  JEFFERSON DAVIS PAPERS, 1841-1938.
706 items. Beauvoir (Harrison County), Miss.

Personal and official correspondence of Jefferson Davis (1808-1889), U.S. senator, U.S. secretary of war, and president of the Confederate States of America. Ante-bellum letters refer to the Whig Party, the Democratic Party, the Kansas question, slavery controversy, abolitionists, the Mormons, and Davis's election to the U.S. Senate, 1857. The bulk of the material, covering the Civil War period, relates to secession; formation of the Confederacy; efforts to bring about the secession of Maryland; purchase of munitions in the North and in Europe; civil and military appointments; activities of the Confederate Navy; Unionist sentiment in East Tennessee; military operations, including the defenses of the Mississippi River, Norfolk (Virginia), Chattanooga (Tennessee), Charleston (South Carolina), Vicksburg (Mississippi), Mobile (Alabama), and Atlanta (Georgia); blockade running; conscription; exemptions from military service; Federal occupation of New Orleans; war profiteering; difficulties between the states and the Confederate government; the attitude of France and Great Britain toward the Confederacy; the killing of General Earl Van Dorn; destruction of cotton and other property on Davis's Mississippi plantation; taxation; desertions; conditions in the Trans-Mississippi Department and in Alabama; Sherman's March to the Sea; Confederate secret service; the question of raising Negro troops; the French expedition to Mexico; conditions during the final days of the Confederacy; and the retreat of Confederate Government from Richmond, April, 1865.

Post-bellum letters, chiefly personal, refer to Davis's imprisonment and release, including a manuscript of "Lines on Jefferson Davis while a prisoner at Fortress Monroe"; his activities in the insurance business; his poor health; reminiscences of the Civil War; controversies with former Confederate officers; a proposed canal across Florida; and biographies of Jefferson Davis. Included are a clipping of his funeral, and a letter from his wife, Varina (Howell) Davis, explaining the scarcity of authentic Jefferson Davis autographs.

Among the correspondents are J. P. Benjamin, M. L. Bonham, Braxton Bragg, J. C. Breckenridge, Joseph E. Brown, James Chesnut, Jr., Caleb Cushing, Jubal A. Early, N. B. Forrest, W. Hampton, B. N. Harrison, G. A. Henry, H. V. Johnson, J. E. Johnston, John Letcher, James Longstreet, S. R. Mallory, J. M. Mason, C. G. Memminger, J. H. Morgan, J. J. Pettus, F. W. Pickens, L. Polk, G. W. Randolph, J. H. Reagan, J. A. Seddon, E. Kirby Smith, William Smith, Pierre Soulé, Z. B. Vance, T. H. Watts, and D. L. Yulee.

1404.  JOHN DAVIS PAPERS, 1841. 1 item. Worcester (Worcester County), Mass.

Letter from John Davis, governor of Massachusetts, to General Dearborn regarding the British colonial system.

1405. JOHN DAVIS, JR., PAPERS, 1846-1865. 14 items. Lexington (Lafayette County), Mo.

Personal letters of John Davis, Jr. (1770-1865), merchant, in which he discusses in detail a trip from Baltimore, Maryland, to Lexington, Missouri, 1858; family matters; and conditions in Missouri.

1406. JOSEPH DAVIS PAPERS, 1859-1861. 45 items. Leonardtown (Saint Mary's County), Md.

Personal letters from Davis to his fiancée, Rosaltha Burnell.

1407. JULIA ROXIE DAVIS PAPERS, 1817-1898. 208 items. Westminister (Guilford County), N.C.

Personal correspondence of Julia Davis, a Quaker, concerning domestic life, quilting parties, yearly meetings, crops, recipes and patterns, and New Garden Seminary. Included are letters from a brother-in-law, Frank Davis, while a student and librarian at Haverford College, Haverford, Pennsylvania, and while studying in Germany.

1408. LOIS (WRIGHT) RICHARDSON DAVIS PAPERS, 1851-1881. 543 items. Lowell (Middlesex County), Mass.

Personal letters of Lois (Wright) Richardson Davis chiefly with her children by her first husband, Luther Richardson. Letters from daughters Louensa (1831-1877) and Ellen A. (b. ca. 1835), who moved to Mobile, Alabama, in the late 1850s and whose husbands joined the Confederate militia, record the reactions of newly transplanted Northerners to the South before and during the outbreak of the Civil War. Letters from sons, Charles Henry (b. 1843) and Luther L. (1841-1864), both in the 26th Regiment of Massachusetts Volunteer Infantry, discuss army life, duties in Louisiana and Virginia, and several military engagements. Letters from Eunice, whose second husband was William S. Connolly, a black sea captain and shipowner of Grand Cayman Island, describe life there. Also included are receipts, clippings, legal forms, and pictures.

1409. MARY (MILLER) DAVIS PAPERS, (1849-1878) 1906. 99 items. Richmond, Va.

Chiefly letters between Mary Miller and her mother, Elizabeth H. Miller, while the former was attending a school for girls at Edge Hill, Virginia, pertaining to family matters, prices, and requests for foodstuffs. Letters from William and Dudlee Miller, brothers of Mary, describe poverty in North Carolina, and a lecture to a group of southern Negroes concerning their civil rights.

1410. MARY P. DAVIS PAPERS, 1861-1864. 18 items. Patrick Springs (Patrick County), Va.

Chiefly personal letters of Mary P. Davis and her cousin, Benjamin A. Davis, a Confederate soldier, concerning family matters, business affairs, salt works in Virginia, taxes, commodity and land prices, the hiring and the sale of slaves, army life, troop movements and military engagements, casualties, deserters, substitutes, food supply, and depredations inflicted by the Union Army.

1411. MATTHEW S. DAVIS, JR., PAPERS, 1859-1905. 17 items. Louisburg (Franklin County), N.C.

Personal and business papers of Matthew S. Davis, Jr. (1830-1906), president of Louisburg College, Louisburg, North Carolina, including references to student life at Roanoke Male Academy, Hamilton, North Carolina, Louisburg Female College and Trinity College.

1412. MYRA DAVIS PAPERS, 1877 (1903-1910) 1934. 32 items. El Oro and Guanajuato, Mexico.

Correspondence of Myra Davis with her family in Colorado, Missouri, and North Carolina. Among the letters are descriptions of the Mexican countryside, 1905; social customs in Mexico, 1906; and the anti-American demonstration, 1911.

1413. NANCY T. DAVIS PAPERS, 1827-1845. 3 items. Morgan County, Ga.

Family letters to Nancy T. Davis from her brothers, reflecting the family's religious interests.

1414. S. D. DAVIS ACCOUNT BOOK, 1855-1890. 1 vol. (473 pp.) Vienna (Forsyth County), N.C.

Accounts of S. D. Davis, a country physician.

1415. SAMUEL DAVIS PAPERS, 1794-1819. 788 items. Portsmouth (Norfolk County), Va.

Bills, accounts, receipts, etc., of Samuel Davis, master of various trading vessels, pertaining to labor of sailors, and prices of food and of commercial products.

1416. SOLOMON DAVIS ACCOUNT BOOK, 1812-1826. 1 vol. (380 pp.) Montgomery County, Md.

Plantation records.

1417. W. G. DAVIS PAPERS, 1880-1908. 24 items. Ophir (Montgomery County), N.C.

Legal papers and items concerning road work in lieu of payment of taxes. Davis was chairman of the board of supervisors of Ophir Township, and justice of the peace.

1418. WILLIAM WATTS HART DAVIS PAPERS, 1861-1869. 227 items. Doylestown (Bucks County), Pa.

Mainly orders concerning the 104th Pennsylvania Regiment, which after January, 1863, was part of the Union forces occupying the sea islands of South Carolina. Included are orders restricting the sale of liquor to soldiers and letters concerning drunkenness. Other orders, circulars, and correspondence deal with camp regulations, discipline, and proper attire. There are an engraving of Davis and clippings, some concerning Davis's later historical writings. A letter of September 21, 1869, from Alfred Howe Terry comments on Davis's history of his regiment.

1419. MARY F. DAVIDSON PAPERS, 1860-1865. 23 items. [North Carolina?]

Letters from Confederate soldiers, mostly in the 28th Regiment of North Carolina Infantry, describing army life and illnesses; a battle at Cape Hatteras, 1861; the shooting of a Negro who was trying to burn the bridge; Fort Fisher and Wilmington.

1420. E. D. DAVISSON ACCOUNT BOOK, 1844-1860. 1 vol. (96 pp.) Loudoun County, Va.

Accounts for groceries and general merchandise purchased from various merchants around Hillsborough. Clippings have been pasted over several of the accounts.

1421. FREDERICK AUGUSTUS DAVISSON NOTEBOOK, 1830. 1 vol. Loudoun County, Va.

Notes taken in the medical school of Transylvania College, Lexington, Kentucky, in the classes of Drs. Cooke, Caldwell, Short, and others.

1422. ANDREW H. H. DAWSON PAPERS, 1856, 1866. 3 items. New York, N.Y., and Savannah, Ga.

Letters from Thomas L. Snead and George N. Lester, former Confederate congressman, in response to Dawson's requests for their autographs; and a letter, 1856, by Dawson, possibly to T. R. R. Cobb, concerning politics, speeches by R. A. Toombs and A. H. Stephens, and Millard Fillmore's chances for the presidency.

1423. EDGAR G. DAWSON PAPERS, 1845-1889. 60 items. Baltimore, Md.

Personal and business letters; bills, and receipts, including a labor agreement, 1870, with Negroes in Barbour County, Alabama; personal letters by Eva Eve Jones, 1882; references to politics, Peruvian guano, personal debts in Georgia, cotton, and St. Mark's School in Southborough, Massachusetts; and two minor items concerning Dawson's Confederate army career.

1424. FRANCIS WARRINGTON DAWSON PAPERS, 1386 (1859-1950) 1963. 7,846 items and 69 vols. Charleston, S.C., and Versailles, France.

The collection comprises the papers of Francis Warrington ("Frank") Dawson (1840-1889), whose original name was Austin John Reeks; his wife, Sarah Ida Fowler (Morgan) Dawson; and of their son, Francis Warrington Dawson II, known as Warrington Dawson (1878-1962). The papers are primarily literary in character, with many editorials, newspaper writings, short stories, novels, articles, and scrapbooks, diaries, and reminiscences, but also many letters. Papers of the senior Dawson contain three scrapbooks of clippings, letters, etc., which Dawson had arranged as a sort of biography of himself; loose letters and papers, primarily correspondence with his wife; two letterpress volumes with his replies to many of the letters in the scrapbooks and in the loose papers. Morgan family correspondence beginning in 1859 describes the social life and customs in Baton Rouge and New Orleans, Louisiana; in Paris, France; and the death of Henry Waller Morgan in a duel in 1861. Letters of Thomas Gibbes Morgan, Sr., describe Confederate mobilization in 1861. Correspondence of Frank Dawson and members of the Morgan family describe Dawson's passage on the blockade runner Nashville, his career as ordnance officer in Longstreet's corps and later in Fitzhugh Lee's cavalry corps; the destruction of homes in Louisiana by the war and Butler's conduct in New Orleans; the battle of Fredericksburg; imprisonment at Fort Delaware; refugee life at Macon, Mississippi; cavalry operations; the causes of Confederate defeat; a duel of Henry Rives Pollard, editor of the Richmond Examiner; politics and journalism in Reconstruction South Carolina; the editorial policies of Dawson's paper, the Charleston News and Courier; accusations of bribery, fraud, and libel; the courtship of Dawson and Sarah (Morgan) Dawson; Dawson's refusal of a challenge to a duel by Martin Witherspoon Gary; the army bill, 1879; the Tilden-Hayes disputed election, 1876; the redemption of South Carolina; Morgan family genealogy; travel in Italy and Europe in the 1880s; education in South Carolina; state-supported colleges and the Citadel; the Charleston earthquake, 1866; Dawson's alleged remarks about Grover Cleveland reported in the New York World, 1886; labor and labor organizations; the tariff; court procedures in South Carolina;

Confederate veterans' organizations; Democratic Party affairs; Dawson's debts; his murder; and the settlement of his estate. Among Dawson's frequent correspondents are Daniel Henry Chamberlain, Edward B. Dickinson, Samuel Dibble, Fitzhugh Lee, Robert Baker Pegram, Henry A. M. Smith, Hugh Smith Thompson, Benjamin Ryan Tillman, Giddings Whitney, and Benjamin H. Wilson.

There is also correspondence of Sarah Dawson and Warrington Dawson, newsman, novelist, editor, special assistant to the American Embassy in Paris, and director of French research for Colonial Williamsburg. This material gives glimpses of French life, 1900-1950, and information on the families of Joseph Conrad and Theodore Roosevelt. Regular letters of Sarah Dawson to Eunice (Martin) Dunkin (Mrs. William Huger Dunkin) and to her sister, Mrs. Lavina (Morgan) Drum of Bethesda, Maryland, comment on French and Washington, D.C., social life and customs. Dawson's writings as Paris correspondent of the United Press Associations of America after 1900 are in clippings in the scrapbooks. They reflect French and world affairs. Topics treated in correspondence include Theodore Roosevelt's safari; Roosevelt's opinions; press relations for the Roosevelt party in Africa; Roosevelt's reviews of Dawson's books; Dawson's lectures and writings; Conrad's writings; other literary matters; John Powell's career as a concert pianist; seances and mediums; the Taft administration; Roosevelt and race relations; the Negro in Liberia, Nigeria, Haiti, and the U.S.; Roosevelt's political career; the Fresh Air Art Society of London; the organization of the press bureau in the U.S. embassy in Paris; and the work of the Foreign Department of the Committee on Public Information.

Embassy memoranda by Dawson cover the Central Powers; the Supreme War Council meetings; French labor; the liberated regions of France; the Young Men's Christian Association; reaction to U.S. requisition of Dutch shipping; the Rhine frontier; allied land transportation; French government bureaus, personnel, politics, and administration; economic affairs; and finance in the Far East. Postwar diplomatic memoranda by Dawson, 1946-1958, 3 vols., concern French economic conditions, labor, communism, atomic warfare, politics, French leaders including Charles de Gaulle, Indochina, and the U.S.S.R.

Letters also cover German reparations; relief work in Austria and the Near East; details of embassy staff work; George Harvey's mission to Europe, 1921; the Washington Disarmament Conference; French finance and politics; war debts; international finance; Coueism; French socialism; a crisis in the publication of the Charleston News and Courier, 1927; the boy scout movement; the Conrad family after Joseph's death; Theodore Roosevelt; U.S. investment in the U.S.S.R.; the restoration of Colonial Williamsburg, Virginia; the French dead at Yorktown; research in French sources on Rochambeau's army; reports to Harold Shurtleff, in charge of the research department of Colonial Williamsburg; the research of Peter Stuyvesant Barry on his grandfather, Frank Dawson; personal and family matters; Dawson's health; restoration of the Lee mansion, "Stratford"; the Great Depression in the United States and in France; the genealogy of the Chambrun family; the role of Lafayette in Florida land settlement; the Compañía Arrendataria del Monopolio de Petroleos, a Spanish firm in which the French Petroleum Company held an interest; the war records of Theodore Roosevelt's sons; and autograph collecting for the Schroeder Foundation, Webster Groves, Missouri. Major correspondents of Warrington Dawson include Ethel (Dawson) Barry, Phyllis (Windsor-Clive) Benton, Jessie Conrad, Joseph Conrad, Annie Cothran, Alice Dukes, Camille Flammarion, Clarence Payne Franklin, A. H. Frazier, Hugh Gibson, Alice Stopford Green, Yves Guyot, Mary Goodwin, William Archer Rutheroord Godwin, Herman Hagedorn, Ralph Tracy Hale, Constance (Cary) Harrison, Leland Harrison, Elizabeth Hayes, Henriette Joffre, James Kerney, Grace King, Rudyard Kipling, Georges Ladoux, William Loeb, Jr., Samuel Frank Logan, Andrew W. Miller, C. V. Miller, Francois Millet, L. D. Morel, James Morris Morgan, Frederick Palmer, John Powell, Auguste Rodin, the Duke and Duchess de Rohan, Edith Roosevelt, Nicholas Roosevelt, Theodore Roosevelt, Max Savelle, H. L. Schroeder, George Sharp, Hallie (Clough) Sharp, Philip Simms, George E. Smith, Vance Thompson, and Robert William Vail.

A group of transcripts of diplomatic dispatches of Comte Louis Barbe Charles Sérurier, French minister in Washington, to Talleyrand, Oct., 1812-June, 1813, describe the opening phrases of the War of 1812, United States opinion concerning France, the divorce proceedings of Elizabeth (Patterson) Bonaparte, interviews with Secretary of State James Monroe, Joel Barlow's negotiations for a commercial treaty with France, embargo, non-importation, and impressment; Republican and Federalist activities; and affairs in New Granada (Columbia). A later series of dispatches from the French minister in Washington, Alphonse J. Y. Pageot, 1835-1848, relates to American spoliation claims against France, American public opinion, analyses of nullification, the Bank of the United States crisis, abolition, and other aspects of American politics. Dispatches of 1841-1843 from Madrid contain information on Spanish affairs, and the guardianship and marriage of the Spanish queen. Later dispatches from Washington concern commercial relations between France and the United States; annexation of Texas and Oregon; the Mexican War and the question of slavery in the territories and its implications for disunion; and the war's effect on French commerce.

Among bills, receipts, and legal papers are materials of J. M. Morgan and the DeSaussure-Trenholm family, financial papers of the Charleston News and Courier, and records of the settlement of the estate of Frank Dawson.

There are manuscripts of writings by Sarah Dawson; manuscripts, fragments, lectures by Warrington Dawson and Theodore Roosevelt; a log and a diary of Roosevelt's African trip; Roosevelt's notes on the policy of his administration in regard to Negroes; extracts from letters and speeches which the former president supplied for use in connection with Dawson's book, Opportunity and Theodore Roosevelt; manuscripts of the book; essays and drafts by Jessie Conrad, Auguste Rodin, Vance Thompson, and Georges Ladoux, reflecting on Dawson's friendships and literary collaborations; and other manuscripts dealing with psychical research. There are also manuscripts, research instructions, notes, page proofs, and other papers resulting from Dawson's research for Colonial Williamsburg, and from his novels and short stories; genealogical papers of the Morgan family and related Gibbes, Fowler, Waller, Hunt, Bunyan, and Baynton families, including a chart of the Reeks family of England; and notes for Dawson's lectures on art, France, Charleston, the Negro in America, Joseph Conrad, and Theodore Roosevelt.

Bound volumes include Frank Dawson's scrapbooks, 1875-1888, 3 vols., relating to his editorship of the Charleston News and Courier and to Democratic politics, and contain editorials, and other newspaper clippings relating to Dawson, letters from his friends, and speeches. There is information on Dawson's opinions concerning the economic theories of Henry George and letters from George. There are also letterpress books, 2 vols., 1870s-1887, largely containing political correspondence. Miscellaneous volumes hold Dawson's plays, poems, clippings, and copies of letters from Mary Haxall. Business records include an address book; cashbook, 1886-1888; ledger, 1867-1872; notebook on the finances of the News and Courier; a private ledger, 1867-1887; and miscellaneous financial notebooks.

For Sarah Dawson there are scrapbooks, 1853-1882, 3 vols., with clippings, her letters to the News and Courier, and accounts of the death of Frank Dawson and tributes to him. Sarah Dawson's manuscript diaries, 1862-1866, 6 vols. (largely published 1913), also include notes from ca. 1896-1906. There are notebooks of Sarah explaining her husband's death, a manuscript by Warrington Dawson commenting on the same subject, and biographical accounts of Frank Dawson and other family members. Other notebooks of Sarah Dawson, 4 vols., 1898-1908, concern her life, travel, and psychical phenomena.

There are diaries of Warrington Dawson, 1898, 1914-1918, 1930-1931, 1934-1945, 4 vols., and of Ethel Dawson, 1888-1891, 1 vol. Warrington's reminiscences of World War I deal with the French intelligence service and attributes the origin of his illness and that of Woodrow Wilson to German biological warfare. A second reminiscence concerns his work for the American Embassy in the 1930s and his life in Paris under German occupation, and has information on the dietary work of B. Lytton-Bernard (Bernard Trappachuh). A third reminiscence gives a mystical interpretation of world events, 1932-1945. Warrington Dawson also left scrapbooks, 1884-1952, 4 vols., preserving many of his newspaper writings.

Dawson's collection of French manuscripts and autographs, 1386-1830, relates to his interest in genealogy and concern the de Béthune, de Créqui, Chevalier, and related families, and include a few parchments concerning Maximilien de Béthune, Duc de Sully, and Henry IV, King of France.

The collection includes a number of photographs of Joseph and Jessie Conrad, Warrington Dawson, Sarah Dawson, Ethel (Dawson) Barry, Herbert Barry, Frank Dawson, Daniel H. Chamberlain (Reconstruction governor of South Carolina), François Millet, Woodrow Wilson, Archibald Forbes, Lord Windsor, the Château de Josselin (signed by the Duke and Duchess de Rohan), historical monuments and their inscriptions in Virginia, and Warrington Dawson's Versailles apartment.

There is also microfilm, 1 reel, of published and unpublished works by and about Warrington Dawson and Joseph Conrad, filmed from the originals at the Ralph Foster Museum, The School of the Ozarks, Point Lookout, Missouri.

1425. NATHANIEL HENRY RHODES DAWSON PAPERS, 1861-1862. 25 items. Selma (Dallas County), Ala.

Civil War correspondence of Nathaniel H. R. Dawson (1829-1895), Alabama legislator and captain in the Confederate Army, relative to early campaigns in Virginia.

1426. RICHARD WILLIAM DAWSON PAPERS, 1966. 1 item. Uniontown (Fayette County), Pa.

Genealogy. The library also holds microfilm, 1 reel, of Dawson's papers, 1863-1865, 9 items and 4 vols., filmed from originals in the possession of Mary Wallace Dawson, Uniontown, Pennsylvania. This collection concerns the 85th Pennsylvania Volunteers near New Bern, North Carolina, and during the siege of Charleston, the siege of Petersburg, and the attack on Fort Fisher.

1427. WILLIAM CROSBY DAWSON RECEIPT BOOK, 1822-1845. 1 vol. (325 pp.) Greensborough (Green County), Ga.

Receipt book of W. C. Dawson (1798-1856), Georgia politician and United States senator.

1428. SAMUEL DEAL PAPERS, 1831-1893. 55 items. China Grove (Rowan County), N.C.

Family correspondence concerning social life, customs, and farming in Iredell County, North Carolina, and Grant County, Kansas.

1429. MILES B. DEAN PAPERS, 1931-1936. 26 items. Hayfield (Frederick County), Va., and Philadelphia, Pa.

Articles and letters concerning state relief, national and local politics and political leaders, and the centralization of government under the New Deal.

1430. W. B. DEAN LETTER BOOK, 1863-1864. 1 vol. Folly Island (Charleston County), S.C.

Copies of letters written by Federal officers encamped on Folly Island, where W. B. Dean, a lieutenant in the United States Army, was stationed.

1431. CHARLES DEANE PAPERS, 1779-1886. 6 items. Boston, Mass.

A deed for land in Suffolk County, Massachusetts, 1779; correspondence with Samuel Foster Haven concerning The Records of the Company of the Massachusetts Bay; and letters to C. C. Jones concerning Jones's writings.

1432. JULIA DEANE PAPERS, 1863-1864. 29 items. Goldsboro (Wayne County), N.C.

Letters to Julia Deane from Confederate soldiers commenting on their activities in the field, the defense of Richmond in 1864, and prospects of peace. Most of the letters are from William A. Peacock.

1433. HENRY ALEXANDER SCAMMELL DEARBORN PAPERS, 1802-1848. 12 items. Boston, Mass.

Correspondence of a Massachusetts politician relating to national and state politics, nullification, and internal improvements, especially canals and railroads in the Boston area and in Pennsylvania. Authors of letters include Henry Dearborn (1751-1829), Joseph Gardner Swift, and Gerald Ralston.

1434. JOHN J. DEARING PAPERS, 1820-1899. 183 items. Covington (Newton County), Ga.

Business and family correspondence of a doctor. Topics include the estate of William Dearing in southwest Georgia and Mississippi; the slave trade; the Civil War; and Southern Masonic Female College. Included are tax receipts, promissory notes, a patriotic speech, a court brief for a lawsuit, wills, deeds, grants, and insurance policies. Writers of letters include Albin P. Dearing of Athens, Georgia; Mrs. J. G. Kennedy; Howell Cobb; and George W. Randolph.

1435. ST. CLAIR DEARING PAPERS, 1864. 2 items. Georgia.

Set of playing cards made by Colonel Dearing and a daguerreotype of Dearing and two other officers.

1436. WASHINGTON DEARMONT PAPERS, 1787 (1851-1930) 1944. 5,223 items and 64 vols. Clarke County, Va.

Routine family and business correspondence of a farmer, some of it relating to Dearmont's position as a salt agent. A few Civil War letters contain orders preparatory to the march on Harpers Ferry and letters concerning the procurement of salt and horses. Later correspondence concerns Mamie Dearmont and relates in part to politics. There are also business papers of George Weaver, a merchant at White Post. Most of the collection consists of routine legal and financial papers and account books; also school compositions, clippings, and miscellaneous printed material. There are account books of Greenbury W. Weaver, 1851-1856; the White Post Post Office; G. C. Hamil; and William Berry of Clarke County. One volume contains ledgers of G. C. Hamill and of Washington Dearmont.

1437. NOAH DEATON PAPERS, 1863-1864. 4 items. Caledonia (Moore County), N.C.

Letters to relatives from a soldier in the 26th North Carolina Regiment describing the battle of Gettysburg; prison life at Point Lookout, Maryland; and mentioning the health and fortunes of various other soldiers.

1438. DAVID D. DEBERRY AND JOHN T. McKINNON PAPERS, 1760 (1850-1869) 1918. 1,517 items and 8 vols. Montgomery County, N.C.

Letters and other papers of Deberry, a land surveyor, and of John T. McKinnon who managed Deberry's affairs during his military service. Included are deeds; receipts; bills; promissory notes; surveying records; certificates of discharge to soldiers employed by the Yadkin Manufacturing Co.; estate papers of John Deberry; Georgia and Alabama lottery broadsides; a report to the general assembly from the Presbytery of Fayetteville, North Carolina, 1876; tax in kind reports; and bankruptcy papers. Letters mention a raid in 1857 against the Seminoles in Florida; settlement around Maumelle, Arkansas, 1859; Deberry's army pay; and commodity speculation in 1862. There are also daybooks of David D. DeBerry and John T. McKinnon, and a souvenir booklet for a convention of Masons at Baltimore, 1887.

1439. JAMES DUNWOODY BROWNSON DEBOW PAPERS, 1779-1915. 1,615 items and 3 vols. New Orleans, La.

Business and personal papers of an editor and agricultural and commercial reformer, including copies of historical documents apparently collected by DeBow in connection with his statistical work for the state of Louisiana and the U.S. Census Bureau; a diary, 1836-1842; essays written while a student at College of Charleston, 1840-1843; two temperance lectures delivered during a tour of New England, 1844; letters from Maunsell White concerning White's backing of DeBow's Review; correspondence with the Review's agents and subscribers; the journal's bills and accounts; records, including correspondence with Christopher Gustavus Memminger and George Alfred Trenholm, relating to the Confederacy's cotton and produce loan; post-war letters concerning proposed railroads between the South and the West, especially the Tennessee and Pacific Railroad; letters to DeBow's wife, Martha E. (Johns) DeBow, from her girlhood friends and from DeBow; and DeBow's history of the Civil War, written for his children. Other correspondents include Charles Gayarré, George Fitzhugh, Edmund Ruffin, William Gilmore Simms, Charles E. Fenner, Freeman Hunt, John W. Daniel, Eugene F. Falconnet, Charles Frederick Holmes, John McRae, Oliver Otis Howard, Reverdy Johnson, Robert E. Barnwell, and William W. Boyce. There is a scrapbook, 1 vol., containing accounts of Civil War campaigns collected by DeBow.

1440. WILLIAM GERARD DE BRAHM PAPERS, 1755-1790. 7 items. Savannah, Ga.

Photostatic copy of a view and profile of a lighthouse to be erected in East Florida; estimate of materials and expenses for the project, 1761; papers relating to land surveys in St. John's Parish, 1760-1761; and an order for tea, 1759.

1441. CHARLES MANNING FORCE DEEMS PAPERS, 1855-1891. 3 items. New York, N.Y.

Letters, 1881, 1891, about Cornelius Vanderbilt's philanthropy, Deems's publications, and the American Institute of Christian Philosophy; and a printed flyer advertising Deems's The Annals of Southern Methodism for 1855 and 1856.

1442. CARLOS G. DE GARMENDIA PAPERS, (1866-1868) 1894, 1917-1919. 382 items. Baltimore, Md.

Business correspondence and charter parties of a shipping and commission merchant and importer of wines, liquors, and cigars, from Havana and Matanzas, Cuba. Papers after 1917 are those of C. M. De Garmendia, manager of the Flag Signal Instruction Company of Tuscarora, Maryland.

1443. HENRY DEHUFF PAPERS, 1790-1894. 218 items. Lebanon (Lebanon County), Pa.

Legal papers including material relating to DeHuff's guardianship of the children of George Heilman and of Eliza Seltzer; and records pertaining to lawsuits. Names mentioned include Lydia and Sarah Bowman, Margaret DeHuff, Rudolph Eisenhower, Jacob K. Sidle, and Charles S. Franz.

1444. F. C. DELAMAR PAPERS, 1861. 1 item.

Manuscript map of the Manassas battlefield.

1445. JOHN THADEUS DELANE PAPERS, 1861. 1 item. London, England.

A draft of a letter from an unidentified Southerner in Washington, D.C., to Delane as editor of the London Times discussing the political crisis in the United States in 1861.

1446. HORACE FRANKLIN DE LANO PAPERS, 1846-1854. 910 items. Shrewsbury (Monmouth County), N.J., and Texas.

Largely routine records connected with De Lano's post as quartermaster officer at Fort Mason, Texas, 1851-1852, and relating to supplies, equipment, and food. There are a few personal and business letters from G. P. Knapp of New Jersey; from De Lano's brothers, Fred and Martin; from a Dr. [Joel?] Martin, post physician at Fort Martin Scott, Texas; and from a number of fellow West Point graduates.

1447. PATRICK H. DELPHANE PAPERS, 1869-1874. 37 items. Kinsley Mills (Fauquier County?), Va.

Business papers of a corn and wheat dealer and miller.

1448. S. C. DE LARCOHEAULION PAPERS, 1865-1871. 8 items. "Black Point," Saint Mary's (Camden County), Ga.

Papers relating to the title to lands of Black Point plantation and their sale.

1449. T. C. DE LEON LETTERS, 1892, 1899. 2 items. Mobile, Ala.

Two letters by De Leon, Southern author and playwright, discussing writing and publishing.

1450. FRANCOIS CHARLES DELÉRY POETRY, 1839-1894. 1 vol. New Orleans, La.

Handwritten poems, written 1839-1879, by Deléry, a physician, and transcribed by Marie Reynes. The volume is signed by Edgar Deléry, son of the author. In the French language.

1451. ULRIC ALBERT DELETTRE PAPERS, 1846-1887. 11 items. Horry District, S.C.

Largely documents relating to the ownership of land. Included are a few letters, some by M. N. DeLettre, discussing family affairs.

1452. WILLIAM M. DE LONG PAPERS, 1863. 3 items. Chattanooga (Hamilton County), Tenn.

Letters of a Federal soldier describing a camp in Somerville, West Virginia, and the battle of Chickamauga.

1453. J. WILLIAM DEMBY PAPERS, 1864-1865. 2 vols. Little Rock (Pulaski County), Ark.

Typed copies of two works published by Demby: "History of the Third Missouri Cavalry," by A. W. M. Petty, 111 pp. (1865), and "The War in Arkansas," by Demby, 64 pp. (1864).

1454. RAYMOND DEMERE PAPERS, 1754-1755. 4 items. Frederica (Glynn County), Ga.

Legal papers in a review of the case of Caleb Davis v. Raymond Demere as heard before Noble Jones, justice of the general court, over the forcible detention of one of Davis's ships in 1747, including Demere's petition and depositions of witnesses: Thomas Goldsmith, James Penny, and William Abbott.

1455. ELIZABETH JANE DEMING PAPERS, 1834-1835. 1 vol. Pittsfield (Berkshire County), Mass.

Autograph album containing poems expressing friendship for Miss Deming.

1456. WILLIAM JOSEPH DENISON PAPERS, 1833. 1 item. London, England.

A letter from Denison, banker and politician, concerning the payment of election expenses.

1457. THOMAS DENMAN, FIRST BARON DENMAN, PAPERS, 1825-1874. 10 items. Middleton, Lancashire, England.

Miscellaneous personal and political letters concerning the Reform Bill, 1831, and other subjects. Authors include Denman; Thomas, Second Baron Denman; and Lord Althorp.

1458. B. A. DENMARK PAPERS, 1860-1878. 5 items. Athens (Clarke County), Ga.

Philosophical musings of I. I. Flournoy and a letter from Henry B. Thompkins introducing Denmark to Josephus Camp.

1459. SAMUEL B. DENNEY PAPERS, 1818 (1838-1841) 1842. 37 items. Nelson County, Va.

Business papers, including references to Samuel [?] Garland and Christopher T. Estes.

1460. JOHN E. DENNIS PAPERS, 1847-1848. 2 items. Bishopville (Lee County), S.C.

Letters from W. H. Dennis of Richmond, Virginia, to his brother, John E. Dennis, mentioning education, slavery and slave prices, tobacco, cotton prices and crops, and politics.

1461. J. DE PALMA PAPERS, 1863-1864. 31 items. Columbia (Richland County), S.C.

Legal papers of Union prisoners in the Confederate States Military Prison, Columbia, South Carolina, appointing De Palma as their attorney to collect the amount due them from the United States Army. The money so secured was to be used to repay loans extended by De Palma.

1462. TUNIS DE PEW PAPERS, 1860-1931. 24 items. Nyack (Rockland County), N.Y.

Letters; checks; bills; receipts; and a telegram to De Pew, a nurseryman or florist.

1463. ROZA (SOLOMON) DE PONTE JOURNAL, 1882, 1886. 1 vol. (44 pp.) England, Scotland, France, and Switzerland.

Journal of tours by Mrs. De Ponte, a Southern actress. Included are photographs.

1464. MARY LOUISA AMELIA (BOOZER) BEECHER, COUNTESS DE POURTALÈS-GORGIER, PAPERS, (1878-1908) 1959. 17 items. Florence, Italy.

Photocopies of letters and clippings; there are descriptions of Hong Kong; Galle (Point De Galle), Ceylon; Java; and the volcanic eruption of Krakatoa, 1883.

1465. THOMAS DE QUINCEY MANUSCRIPT, 1 vol. (25 pp.)

Typed copy of "Some Thoughts on Biography," by Thomas De Quincey. Incomplete.

1466. GEORGE WYMBERLEY JONES DE RENNE PAPERS, 1782-1916. 43 items. Savannah, Ga.

Two items concern Dr. George Jones, father of G. W. Jones, later known as De Renne. These items are an affidavit concerning his imprisonment by the British and a receipt for the sale of a slave. There are some papers of the Central Bank of Georgia bearing the names of Solomon Cohen, Tomlinson Fort, and I. K. Tefft. Letters to De Renne concern the Buchanan administration, the president's nephew Cole Baker, politics and politicians of the era, railroad building in Georgia and South Carolina, the coming of the Civil War, Reconstruction, and Negro suffrage. Writers include F. Dainese, Thomas F. Drayton, James H. Hammond, H. I. McIntyre, James P. Screven, and John Screven.

1467. WILLIAM LORD DE ROSSET PAPERS, 1820-1898. 239 items and 1 vol. Wilmington (New Hanover County), N.C.

Chiefly family correspondence and a few legal and financial papers, miscellany, including some genealogy, and a daybook, 1861. There are letters, 1820-1826, by Catherine Fullerton De Rosset including a few to her son, Armand John De Rosset II. Most of the collection relates to her grandson, William Lord De Rosset, and concerns the death of his first wife in 1861, his courtship and marriage to Elizabeth Simpson Nash of Hillsborough, North Carolina, 1863; the death of his son, Armand John, in 1874; and a trip to England, 1874.

1468. HENRY WILLIAM DE SAUSSURE AND WILMOT GIBBES DE SAUSSURE PAPERS, 1788-1916. 131 items and 3 vols. Charleston, S.C.

Correspondence and papers of Henry William De Saussure (1763-1839), Revolutionary soldier, South Carolina legislator, 1790-1807, director of the United States Mint, 1795, and judge of the chancery court in South Carolina, 1808-1833; and of his grandson, Wilmot Gibbes De Saussure (1822-1886), South Carolina legislator and Confederate Army officer. Among the earlier letters are comments on the establishment and early years of South Carolina College (now the University of South Carolina), Columbia, and the Mexican War. The Civil War correspondence concerns North Carolina's attitude toward secession, 1861; the gloomy outlook of the Confederacy, 1862; the plight of the poor in Charleston; the siege of Savannah, 1863; Federal raids, 1865; hospital funds; and W. G. De Saussure's trip from Charleston to Aiken, South Carolina, 1865. The post-bellum material includes information on the political phases of Reconstruction in the South; an interview between Henry A. De Saussure and Carl Schurz; occupation of Charleston houses by Federal officers; disbanding of Negro troops; effect of the contested election in South Carolina, 1877; and the Charleston earthquake, August 31, 1886. Included also are three docket books, 1832-1867, of cases tried in the Court of Equity of the Charleston District; documents concerning real estate transfers; and genealogical records of the Bacot, Burden, De Saussure, Gourdin, Hamilton, Huger, Mood, Pringle, and Swinton families. There are other materials relating to the Huguenot settlers in South Carolina, including a copy of a manuscript narrative by Thomas Gaillard.

Among the correspondents and persons mentioned are P. G. T. Beauregard, Henry Alexander De Saussure, John M. De Saussure, Adam T. Millican, Benjamin Silliman, and Henry D.A. Ward.

1469. ROBERT AND WILLIAM DE SCHWEINITZ PAPERS, 1862. 5 items. Salem (Forsyth County), N.C.

Papers of Robert William de Schweinitz (1819-1901), prominent Moravian and principal of the Salem Female Academy, 1853-1866, containing printed forms explaining the increase in the cost of tuition and board, from June to December, 1862, at Salem Academy. There are also two letters on the same subject.

1470. JOSEPH DESHA PAPERS, 1825. 1 item. Frankfort (Franklin County), Ky.

Commission as captain in the 33rd Kentucky Militia Regiment for Augustus Frederick, signed by Joseph Desha, governor of Kentucky.

1471. [PIERRE-JEAN DE SMET?] NOTES, 1871. 1 vol. (13 pp.) Near St. Louis, Mo.

Photocopies of a manuscript translating religious terms into Indian dialects.

1472. ROBERT MARION DEVEAUX PAPERS, 1758-1894. 350 items. Stateburg (Sumter County), S.C.

Personal and business correspondence of the Singleton, Deveaux, and Moore families, prominent planters of South Carolina, including letters of J. K. Paulding, Richard Singleton, and Abraham Van Buren. The Singleton papers consist chiefly of military records, plats, and indentures of Captain Matthew Singleton of St. Mark's Parish, with a few letters from Richard Singleton to his daughters. The Deveaux portion of the collection consists mainly of plantation records with a few letters from Deveaux's children at school. The Moore papers are personal and legal. Included also is one volume containing accounts of the estate of V. M. Deveaux, of Miss Marion S. Deveaux, and plantation records for "The Ruins" and the Oakley and Pinckney plantations.

1473. AUBREY THOMAS DE VERE PAPERS, 1872, 1877. 2 items. London, England.

Letters to Derwent Coleridge concerning De Vere's poems, some of which refer to Derwent's father, S. T. Coleridge.

1474.   GEORGE H. DEVEREUX PAPERS,
        1849 (1850) 1852.  36 items.
        Boston, Mass.

Reports by Devereux, adjutant general of the Massachusetts militia, to Governor George Nixon Briggs and correspondence between Devereux and General Eleazar Stone. Included are statistical data on personnel, arms, and equipment; evaluation of the encampment of 1850 and the reforms instituted in 1849; and recommendations for further improvement.

1475.   DEVEREUX FAMILY PAPERS, 1776
        (1839-1900) 1936.  454 items and
        4 vols.  Raleigh (Wake County),
        N.C.

Largely concerned with personal and family affairs; the chief correspondents in the collection are Thomas Pollock Devereux (1793-1869), his sister-in-law Sarah Elizabeth Devereux, his son John Devereux (1819-1893), daughter-in-law Margaret (Mordecai) Devereux (1824-1910), and Robert L. Maitland of New York, a business associate. A few letters relate to the Civil War careers of John Devereux, chief quartermaster of North Carolina, and his son, Thomas Pollock Devereux, and describe camp life. Postwar papers concern land sales, lawsuits over estates, and involvement in the French spoliation claims. There are also comments on slaves and manumission, Dare County, lumbering, the Lane and Mordecai families, cranberry culture, and land surveys. There are financial and legal papers, writings of Margaret Devereux, clippings, and genealogical material; a family reminiscence by Margaret Devereux; a recipe book; a composition book of Annie Lane Devereux; a personal and professional ledger, 1821-1839, of Thomas Pollock Devereux; and a plantation account book, 1842-1863, of John Devereux, relating to Barrow, Montrose, and Runiroi plantations and giving extensive lists of slaves with names, dates of birth, purchase, or death; and other notations.

1476.   JAMES H. DEVOTIE PAPERS,
        1839-1925.  286 items and 3 vols.
        Columbus (Muscogee County), Ga.

Letters of the children of James H. DeVotie, Baptist minister of Alabama and Georgia. Included are references to DeVotie's churches at Marion, Alabama; Gainesville, Alabama; La Grange, Georgia; Columbus, Georgia; and Griffin, Georgia. Most of the collection consists of letters from Jefferson Howard DeVotie (who also wrote his name Howard Jefferson DeVotie), describing his education at Furman University, Greenville, South Carolina; Mercer University, Penfield, Georgia; Jefferson Medical College, Philadelphia; and the Medical Department of the University of Louisiana. DeVotie describes his service as surgeon with the 17th Georgia Infantry Regiment and the 7th South Carolina Artillery Battalion during the Civil War; he discusses the capture of New Orleans by Union troops, the hospital work of James Lawrence Cabell, the condition of the Confederate wounded, the condition of the 2nd Georgia Infantry after the battle of Sharpsburg; and the defense of Charleston, South Carolina, 1863. There are a few letters of Jefferson Howard DeVotie's brother, Jewett Gindrat DeVotie; letters of his sister, Elizabeth Annie DeVotie describing student life at Judson Female Institute, Marion, Alabama; and letters of two presidents of Judson, Milo Parker Jewett and Archibald J. Battle. The collection includes a scrapbook of business and social cards, railroad tickets, and social invitations and programs, largely from Columbus, Georgia, and other places during the 1850s and 1860s; an account book; records of James H. DeVotie's expenses and collections while traveling as financial secretary of the Southern Baptist Convention, 1856; and some correspondence and personal accounts of one of his sons, 1862-1863.

1477.   DEWITT FAMILY PAPERS, 1863-1866.
        9 items.  New York, N.Y.

Topics of these miscellaneous letters include the use of substitutes in the draft in New York; conditions around Shell Mound, Tennessee, after occupation by Union troops; the occupation of Charleston, South Carolina, by Negro troops; and a school for Negroes run by Union troops on Sullivan's Island. Writers of these letters are Julian F. DeWitt and other members of the DeWitt family; and James G. Foster.

1478.   NATHANIEL BARKSDALE DIAL PAPERS,
        1915 (1923-1935).  2,662 items.
        Laurens (Laurens County), S.C.,
        and Washington, D.C.

Political and business papers of a United States senator from South Carolina, 1919-1925, and an industrial promoter. Dial's senatorial papers concern routine patronage and service to constituents; his opposition to a soldiers' bonus bill; an amendment to the law governing contracts for cotton futures; power development at Muscle Shoals, Alabama; his opposition to the child labor law; enforcement of Prohibition; a plan to use seized alien property to finance American agricultural exports; economy in government; the attempt to establish a national park in the Appalachian mountains; and Dial's unsuccessful fight for renomination in 1924. Dial's business interests include the Reedy River Power Company; the Sullivan Power Company; Laurens Cotton Mills; the Laurens Glass Works; the development of cutover land near McBee, South Carolina; the promotion of various inventions; the attempt to develop a clay bed in Georgia; mines in Nevada and North Carolina; the Eastern Public Service Company (a bus line); and a health resort in Sweetsprings, West Virginia. Printed material includes a copy of a hearing before a committee of the United States House of Representatives on regulating cotton exchanges, 1930, and a typescript of a committee hearing on Dial's bill to finance American agricultural exports with seized alien property.

1479. ORANGE J. DIBBLE PAPERS, 1841-1885. 66 items and 9 vols. Erie County, N.Y.

Business papers of a tanning company. Volumes include ledgers, 1848-1876, and journals, 1854-1858, 1860, 1862.

1480. SAMUEL DIBBLE PAPERS, 1779 (1855-1900) 1910. 1,672 items. Orangeburg (Orangeburg County), S.C.

Primarily the legal and business papers of a lawyer and legislator. The material before 1850 is made up entirely of legal papers including land surveys, titles, and transfers. The papers after 1850 include a few business papers of David A. Rice, a retail clothing merchant; items from the period of the Civil War dealing with taxes, requisitions, and assessments; material dealing with the activities of the South Carolina Land Commission, 1869-1872, including papers from a legislative committee which investigated the commission in 1877; legal papers dealing with phosphate mining, 1870s; material on Dibble's work for the Democratic Party in the elections of 1880 and 1892; items concerning education including lists showing the number of South Carolina students by counties in colleges and universities outside of the state and in the state in 1879; and scattered papers dealing with the Branchville and Bowman Railroad and the Enterprise Cotton Mills in the 1890s. Miscellaneous items include surveyor's notebooks, printed legal cases, speeches of United States congressmen, business notebooks, and printed material pertaining to the activities of the United Confederate Veterans.

1481. JAMES DICK AND STEWART COMPANY LETTER BOOK, 1773-1781. 1 vol. (448 pp.) Annapolis (Anne Arundel County), Md.

Letter book of a mercantile firm trading in agricultural products and manufactured goods with England, Spain, Portugal, the Madeira Islands, and the West Indies. The correspondence is primarily business, giving detailed marketing information on the goods in which the firm dealt and discussing economic conditions before and during the Revolution. The letters reflect the coming of the Revolution, particularly in the description of the burning of a company ship, the Peggy Stewart, and its cargo of tea in 1774 and in the opposing loyalist and patriot sympathies of the two partners.

1482. ROBERT PAINE DICK PAPERS, 1855-1895. 10 items. Greensboro (Guilford County), N.C.

Lectures and speeches on Hebrew poetry and history, Biblical heroes, Sunday schools, and temperance. Also two letters one of which concerns the Confederate dividends of the North Carolina Railroad Company.

1483. HIDER D. DICKENS PAPERS, 1856-1877. 15 items. North Carolina.

Letters of a Confederate soldier imprisoned at Elmira, New York, and a few family letters, including two from a student at Greensboro (North Carolina) Female College, 1876-1877.

1484. ASBURY DICKENS PAPERS, 1832-1855. 3 items. Washington, D.C.

Letters of Asbury Dickens (1780-1861), secretary of the United States Senate, to Matthew Carey regarding census figures and a circular concerned with the distribution of the works of John Adams. Included also is a personal letter from Archibald Dixon.

1485. GEORGE W. DICKENSON PAPERS, 1786 (1815-1892) 1919. 721 items and 7 vols. Henry County, Va.

Business and family papers including bills, receipts, and notes; notebooks dealing with the theory and practice of surveying; Civil War letters and muster rolls of Company F, 57th Virginia Regiment, 1861; and a letter, 1874, concerning the organization of local Granges.

1486. JOHN DICKENSON LETTER BOOK, 1835-1843. 1 vol. Danville (Pittsylvania County), Va.

Business letters of a general merchant concerning orders for goods in Richmond and transportation of the goods.

1487. JOHN DICKEY PAPERS, 1784-1786. 1 vol. Iredell County, N.C.

Daybook for a mercantile store in Charles County, Maryland, 1784; in St. Marys County, Maryland, 1785; and in Rowan County, North Carolina, 1785-1786. The store seems to have been owned by John Dickey, a resident of Iredell County in 1790. William Cowan of western Rowan County may have been a partner.

1488. ANNA ELIZABETH DICKINSON PAPERS, 1866-1871. 3 items. Philadelphia, Pa.

Letters concerning speaking engagements and the publication of articles.

1489. JOSEPH DICKINSON PAPERS, 1848-1858. 4 items. Richmond, Va.

Correspondence of the slave-trading firm, Dickinson and Hall, concerning the slave market and prices for Negroes.

1490. JOSEPH DICKINSON AND WASHINGTON DICKINSON PAPERS, 1822-1868. 23 items. Franklin County, Va.

Miscellaneous letters concerning travels to Missouri and Mobile, Alabama, and slave trading in Alabama in 1854.

1491. MATTHEW DICKINSON PAPERS, 1791-1813. 65 items. Louisburg (Franklin County), N.C.

Letters and papers of Matthew Dickinson (d. ca. 1809), head of Franklin Academy, Louisburg, North Carolina, and lawyer. The items of the collection concern personal affairs. They are mostly accounts and records of money borrowed and loaned. There is a price list from a Raleigh book-dealer, 1806.

1492. SAMUEL DICKINSON AND DAVID BLACK PAPERS, 1801. 18 items. Edenton (Chowan County), N.C., and Norfolk (Norfolk County), Va.

Letters concerning marketing of shingles; cost of boat construction at Norfolk, Virginia; lumber for the West Indian market; and payments to the legatees of Robert Smith of Edenton, North Carolina.

1493. THOMAS DICKINSON PAPERS, 1780-1781. 1 vol. St. Eustatius, West Indies.

Ledger of a commission merchant on St. Eustatius. Also used as a ledger by Allen Grist in Washington, North Carolina, 1813-1816.

1494. JEANNIE A. DICKSON PAPERS, 1857 (1865-1886) 1905. 37 items. New Orleans, La.

Letters and papers of Jeannie A. Dickson, writer and daughter of Samuel Henry Dickson, Charleston, South Carolina, and New Orleans, Louisiana, physician and author. The bulk of the collection consists of letters and poems of Paul Hamilton Hayne, George Herbert Sass, and John R. Thompson. Hayne's letters include his opinion of Northern magazines, views on politics, literary production of contemporary Southern writers, and the condition of Georgia after the Civil War. Material connected with Sass is largely poetry, most of which was later published. Thompson's letters include comments on current literary productions and criticisms of Jeannie Dickson's work. One letter is from John Russell.
Mentioned in the collection are: Henry Dickson Bruns, John Bruns, [George] Washington Cable, James Wood Davidson, Charles E. A. Gayarré, Gervais Robinson, William Gilmore Simms, Frances C. (Fisher) Tiernan's <u>Valerie Aylmer</u>, and the works of Richard D. Blackmore, Charles Reade, and Sir Walter Scott.

1495. JOSEPH DICKSON NOTES, 1817. 1 vol. Virginia.

Instructions for measuring the cubic contents of vessels.

1496. ANTHONY DIGGES PAPERS, 1783-1799. 5 items. Washington (Beaufort County), N.C.

Pages from the account book of Digges, a sea captain plying the coast of North Carolina; an agreement for the sale of a schooner; and letters to Digges concerning maritime affairs.

1497. HENRY DILD ESTATE ACCOUNTS, 1913. 1 vol. (4 pp.) Uniontown (Perry County), Ala.

Administrator's accounts of the estate of Henry Dild.

1498. HUBERT DILGER PAPERS, 1862-1863. 64 items. Franklin (Southampton County), Va.

Papers of the captain of the Mountain Howitzer Battery, 1st Virginia Artillery, concerning the transfer of troops and supplies to his command.

1499. SIR CHARLES WENTWORTH DILKE, SECOND BARONET PAPERS, 1875-1904. 23 items. London, England.

Correspondence of an English politician including short notes to Sir Guy Douglas Arthur Fleetwood Wilson; routine political correspondence; letters to the editor of the <u>Daily Graphic</u> commenting on the relative military strength of the great powers, 1890, and stating his reaction to recent parliamentary elections, 1892; and a letter, 1891, giving his opinion on the occupation of Egypt.

1500. JAMES F. DILLARD PAPERS, 1861-1865. 5 items. Washington (Wilkes County), Ga.

Family letters of a Confederate soldier describing a trip from Georgia to Richmond, Virginia, via Charleston, South Carolina, 1861, and explaining removal of camp sites from Fredericksburg, Virginia, because of general poverty and poor soil of the area.

1501. JOHN JAMES DILLARD PAPERS, 1822-1870. 41 items. Elk Furnace (Nelson County), Va.

Letters and papers of the Dillard family consisting of a few items of political correspondence including a letter on the presidential election of 1840; letters from the Civil War describing campaigns in Virginia; family correspondence discussing the law, anesthetics, the Democratic Party, Negro servants, and a description of Philadelphia;

and financial papers relating to the purchase and shipping of gunpowder from Connecticut by Alfred Woodroof.

1502. CHARLES KNAPP DILLAWAY PAPERS, 1809-1858. 3 items. Roxbury (Suffolk County), Mass.

Letters concerning the American Antiquarian Society.

1503. FRANK DILLON PAPERS, 1852-1854. 12 items. London, England.

Letters to Dillon and his wife, Josephine Dillon, mainly from Giuseppe Mazzini concerned with personal matters but occasionally commenting on politics.

1504. SIR WILLIAM HENRY DILLON PAPERS, 1819-1855. 141 items. London, England.

Letters to Dillon from a number of naval officers concerning, for the most part, personal and professional matters, including a number of letters, 1835-1836, discussing a British legion then fighting in the civil war in Spain.

1505. JOSEPH SHERMAN DILTZ PAPERS, 1862-1886. 166 items. Urbana (Champaign County), Ohio.

Correspondence of a private in the 66th Ohio Regiment consisting largely of letters to his wife, Mary (Milledge) Diltz, and giving much information on social, political, and economic trends of that period. The collection contains information on Federal activities in Maryland, Virginia, Tennessee, and Alabama; battle of Missionary Ridge, 1863, battle of Cedar Mountain, 1862, and other Civil War battles; condition of food and living quarters and morale of soldiers in Federal camps; execution of deserters; appearance of battlefields and hospitals after battles; Jefferson Davis and Colonel Charles Candy; Copperheads; Confederate military prisons; the Ohio gubernatorial election of 1863, in which Clement L. Vallandigham was candidate; assassination of Abraham Lincoln and the false rumor of the assassination of William H. Seward; and commodity and land prices, wage rates, and crop fluctuations, notably of wheat in Iowa. Among the correspondents are Catherine, Joseph S., and Thomas Diltz.

1506. JOHN BULL SMITH DIMITRY PAPERS, 1850 (1857-1887) 1910. 580 items. Jackson (Hinds County), Miss.

Letters of John B. S. Dimitry (1835-1901), Confederate soldier, author, chief clerk in the Confederate Post Office Department, and professor of languages at Montgomery Female College, Christiansburg, Virginia; and of his relatives by marriage, the Stuart and Mayes families of Mississippi. The papers connected with Dimitry consist of one letter from his father, Alexander Dimitry; two letters from John H. Reagan, one giving a résumé of the condition of the country in 1866 and the other recommending Dimitry for a position; a letter of John B. S. Dimitry, 1865, analyzing the state of the Confederacy after the adjournment of the last Confederate Congress; and letters of Dimitry and his wife, Adelaide (Stuart) Dimitry, describing their stay in South America with accounts of the ocean voyage, Jamaica, Barranquilla, Bogotá, Colombia, a trip through the Andes, the climate, political and economic factors, educational facilities, the inhabitants of areas in which they traveled, and plans for future literary works. Correspondence connected with the Stuart family centers around Colonel Oscar J. E. Stuart, father of Adelaide (Stuart) Dimitry; her three brothers, only one of whom survived service in the Confederate Army; and her sister, Annie Elizabeth Stuart, who married Robert Burns Mayes, a lawyer and probate judge. Correspondence concerned with the three Stuart brothers relates to life and work at the University of Mississippi, Oxford, prior to 1861; lukewarm patriotism of Virginians around Lynchburg; cost of uniforms and equipment; scarcity of ammunition and of other supplies; anticipated military action at Manassas in 1861; beauty of the Virginia countryside; Pratt's Hospital near Lynchburg; military action in Virginia at Manassas, Bethel Church, Dranesville, Leesburg, all in 1861, and Fredericksburg, 1862; and references to desertion, morale, censorship, theatrical productions given by the troops, and camp life in general. Letters of Adelaide Stuart during the Civil War refer to her work in the Columbia (S.C.) branch of the Confederate treasury. After 1865 correspondence relates to the legal practice of Colonel Oscar J. E. Stuart, political conditions in Mississippi especially during Reconstruction, growth of the Patrons of Husbandry, financial reverses, and mathematical studies of R. B. Mayes. Included also are literary works of R. B. Mayes, generally on theological subjects. Many of the letters of the Stuart brothers are typed copies.

1507. CHARLES AUGUSTUS ROPES DIMON PAPERS, 1864-1878. 19 items. Mobile, Ala.

Military papers and correspondence describing the operations of the U.S.S. Currituck, 1864; discussion of the activities of the 86th United States Regiment (Colored), 1867; and an order of General John Pope removing the mayor and chief of police of Mobile, Alabama, for failure to maintain order, 1867. Also several papers relating to fugitives from justice.

1508. THOMAS DIMSDALE, FIRST BARON DIMSDALE, PAPERS, 1776. 1 item. Essendon, Hertfordshire, England.

Letter of attorney from Dimsdale and his brother in relation to a question of property.

1509. GEORGE H. DINGES PAPERS, 1852-1874. 1 vol. Mt. Crawford (Rockingham County), Va.

Cash accounts related to a sadler's business; notes made by a medical student; and the financial records of a doctor.

1510. EDGAR DINSMORE PAPERS, 1864-1865. 4 items. Connecticut.

Letters from Edgar Dinsmore, a Negro soldier in the 54th Massachusetts Regiment, to Carrie Drayton, Brooklyn, New York, commenting on campaign activities, an anticipated early Union victory, and the assassination of Abraham Lincoln [Published: Richard B. Harwell (ed.), "Edgar Dinsmore Letters," Journal of Negro History, XXV (July, 1940), 363-371.]

1511. ROBERT DINWIDDIE PAPERS, 1753-1756. 3 items. Williamsburg (James City County), Va.

Letter from George Washington, 1753, discussing Indian affairs in Virginia; document registering the appointment of judges for the trial of a slave accused of a felony, 1754; and a land grant, 1766.

1512. DISMAL SWAMP LAND COMPANY PAPERS, 1763 (1830-1871) 1879. 4,328 items and 8 vols. Suffolk (Nansemond County), Va.

Business papers of the Dismal Swamp Land Company with a list of original partners including George Washington; and the subdivision of shares during the prosperous years of the company when sale of cypress shingles and staves yielded large profits. Records include accounts of low profits in the 1780s and in the panic of 1837, labor problems during early years, trespassers, transportation problems, and difficulties experienced by the executive agent in arranging a satisfactory time for annual meetings of stockholders. Included also are monthly accounts of work and production, contemporary copies of wills of practically all stockholders, and frequent lists of stockholders. Among later stockholders were David and Richard K. Meade, the college of William and Mary, Williamsburg, and members of many leading families of Virginia. Among the volumes are check stubs, 1840-1863; accounts, letter books, and shingle records, 1795-1843; and bankbooks, 1837-1853. The correspondence consists largely of letters to and from the presidents and executive agents; and a few letters from Thomas Walker, an original stockholder.

1513. R. T. DISMUKES NOTEBOOK, 1838-1839. 1 vol. Mocksville (Davie County), N.C.

Notebook of a medical student entitled "Notes on Benjamin W. Dudley, Professor of Anatomy and Surgery in the Medical Department of Transylvania University, Lexington, Ky."

1514. DOROTHEA LYNDE DIX PAPERS, 1865-1887. 5 items. Trenton (Mercer County), N.J.

Miscellaneous letters.

1515. JOHN ADAMS DIX PAPERS, 1820-1865. 8 items. New York, N.Y.

Letters to Dix from his brother, Roger Sherman Dix, describing the battle of Buena Vista. Letters written by John Adams Dix include an account of the activities of General Jacob Brown, commander of the Northern Division of the United States Army, 1820, and a letter from the period when Dix was secretary of state in New York.

1516. MORGAN DIX PAPERS, 1868. 1 item. Poughkeepsie (Dutchess County), New York.

Letter of introduction from Samuel F. B. Morse.

1517. COLUMBUS H. DIXON PAPERS, 1863-1864. 2 items. Shelby (Cleveland County), N.C.

Personal letters of a soldier in the 49th North Carolina Regiment.

1518. EVELYN MILUS DIXON SCRAPBOOK, 1894-1956. 1 vol. England.

Volume of autographs and sketches containing, for the most part, the signatures of leading British Methodists of the nineteenth and twentieth centuries and a number of missionaries.

1519. HENRY TURNER DIXON PAPERS, 1862. 1 item. Washington, D.C.

Letter to the Paymaster General of the United States Army from Dixon demanding a court of inquiry to investigate an accusation that had been brought against him.

1520. MUMFORD H. DIXON DIARY, 1864. 1 vol. (14 pp.) Vicksburg (Warren County), Miss.

Diary of a captain in the 3rd Regiment of Govan's Brigade, Cleburne's Division, Army of Tennessee, describing the opposition to Sherman in the Atlanta campaign. Mentions the fight at New Hope Church; the death of General Leonidas Polk; the battle of Atlanta; and the battle of Franklin, Tennessee.

1521. THOMAS DIXON PAPERS, 1892-1959. 231 items and 5 vols. Raleigh (Wake County), N.C.

Correspondence, papers, and writings of Thomas Dixon. Correspondence contains material on the Mt. Mitchell Association of

Arts and Sciences, apparently having to do with land development, 1927-1928; the publication of Dixon's last novel, The Flaming Sword, 1939-1940; and letters relating to the religious beliefs of Dixon's second wife, Madelyn (Donovan) Dixon. There is a miscellaneous group of financial papers and a number of legal papers concerning copyrights and contracts with companies producing Dixon's plays. Writings include bound holograph drafts of The Sins of the Father and The Sun Virgin; proofs of The One Woman, pasted and bound; typed drafts of Dixon's plays; the first unrevised sketch of Dixon's dramatic adaptation of The Clansman; and a scenario for the filmed version of Birth of a Nation.

1522. WILLIAM MACNEILLE DIXON PAPERS, 1896. 1 item. Worthing, Sussex, England.

Letter from Rowland Prothero requesting an article from Dixon on George Meredith for the Quarterly Review.

1523. WINSOR DIXON PAPERS, 1770-1888. 201 items and 1 vol. Greene County, N.C.

The collection contains deeds and promissory notes concerning land transfers in Dobbs and Glasgow counties, North Carolina, for the most part involving John Holliday and the Holliday family; Winsor Dixon's journal, begun in 1823 when he was a schoolteacher; and papers pertaining to Dixon's purchase of slaves, teaching activities, the Free Will Baptist Church, the Disciples of Christ, prices for agricultural commodities, Dixon's will, and an inventory of his goods at the time of his death. The collection also contains the papers of the Lyon family of Edgecombe County, North Carolina, including letters from a member of the Edgecombe Guards stationed in Raleigh, North Carolina, 1861, describing camp life and letters concerning the scarcity of money and general hard times in the South, 1868. Also one volume of records of Dixon's guardianship of minors, 1848-1855.

1524. S. D. DOAR PAPERS, 1848 (1859-1865). 8 items. Charleston, S.C.

Correspondence of a rice planter on hiring slaves, erecting irrigation machinery, shipping rice during the Civil War, and the evacuation of Charleston in 1865.

1525. JAMES COCHRAN DOBBIN PAPERS, 1821-1856. 16 items. Fayetteville (Cumberland County), N.C.

Papers and letters including a power of attorney from John Moore Dobbin to John R. Buie to act in a slave sale; a legal comment on inheritance laws; letters from David Lowry Swain and Peter Force concerning the collection of documents on the history of North Carolina; and routine correspondence from Dobbin's term as secretary of the navy.

1526. HENRY AUSTIN DOBSON PAPERS, 1911. 2 items. London, England.

Autograph and proof sheet of a poem written in honor of King George V by Dobson.

1527. OLIVER HART DOCKERY PAPERS, 1868-1869. 2 items. Richmond County, N.C.

Routine correspondence related to Dockery's service as a United States congressman, including a letter, 1868, containing biographical information on Dockery.

1528. WILLIAM EDWARD DODD PAPERS, 1939. 1 item. Chicago (Cook County), Ill.

Reply to a letter from President Roosevelt explaining that sickness had prevented Dodd from attending several meetings.

1529. DAVID DODGE PAPERS, 1803-1806. 2 vols. Dunstable (Hillsborough County), N.H.

A ledger and a daybook and ledger containing accounts for purchases of lumber, shingles, building supplies, tools, and cordwood; fees for cutting wood; sales of rum and other liquor, tobacco, cheese, and general merchandise; and fees for labor. Many of the accounts relate to Fletcher and Hall, Robert Fletcher, and Fletcher & Kendall.

1530. MARY ELIZABETH (MAPES) DODGE PAPERS. 1 item. New York, N.Y.

A note referring to a caricature of William E. Gladstone in Punch and other subjects.

1531. JAMES DODSON PAPERS, 1816-1875. 89 items. Hawkins County, Tenn.

Business papers of a dealer in builders' supplies and materials, showing price levels. Included also are a few legal documents and surveyors' plats.

1532. SARAH ANN (RICE) DOGAN PAPERS, 1821-1835. 5 items. Columbia (Richland County), S.C.

Personal letters.

1533. JONATHAN PRENTISS DOLLIVER PAPERS, 1909. 2 items. Fort Dodge (Webster County), Iowa.

Correspondence referring to a contemplated commencement address at Trinity College, Durham, North Carolina, and Dolliver's cancellation of the engagement.

1534. WILLIAM BODHAM DONNE PAPERS, 1853-1854. 2 items. London, England.

Routine letters by Donne.

1535. CLEMENT DORSEY PAPERS, [1814?]. 1 item. "Summerseat," near Laurel Grove (St. Mary's County), Md.

Letter to the governor of Maryland from Dorsey regarding the arming of state soldiers.

1536. LEWIS DOSTER AND SONS PAPERS, 1862-1863. 371 items. Bethlehem (Northampton County), Pa.

Financial papers relating to the estate of Lewis Doster and to the purchase of equipment for his woolen manufacturing mill, Moravian Woolen Mills, which comprised a large portion of his estate.

1537. CHARLES C. DOTEN PAPERS, 1861. 40 items. Plymouth (Plymouth County), Mass.

Letters to a captain of the 3rd Massachusetts Regiment from friends at home, describing the enthusiasm of the early days of the Civil War in a northern town.

1538. WILLIAM CLARK DOUB PAPERS, 1778 (1820-1869) 1899. 334 items and 4 vols. Forsyth and Stokes Counties, N.C.

Personal, family, and professional correspondence and papers of various members of the Doub family, particularly Peter Doub, Michael Doub, and William Clark Doub. Items in the collection for the early years are mainly land deeds and indentures. The letters and papers for the years 1820-1870 are for the most part those of Peter and Michael Doub and include personal and business letters; legal papers; letters concerning Joseph C. Doub's service in the Confederate Army; comments on teachers and teaching in North Carolina; papers on religious subjects, pertaining mainly to the Methodist Church, such as sermons, essays, religious musical scores, church rules and membership lists, and Sunday school lists. A few items are in German script. The collection also contains Peter Doub's sketch, 1867, on Methodism in North Carolina from 1832 to 1840, stressing the church's educational achievements and describing the origins of several Methodist schools; an English translation of Aeschylus's Prometheus Vinctus by Robert Potter and an English translation of Books I, II, and III of Homer's Odyssey; William Clark Doub's Index Rerum; and a preacher's journal, 1826-1856, which belonged to Michael Doub.

1539. DOUBLE SHOALS COTTON MILL DAYBOOK, 1875-1879. 1 vol. Cleveland County, N.C.

Records of a cotton mill.

1540. ULYSSES DOUBLEDAY PAPERS, 1862. 1 item. New York, New York.

A letter by Ulysses Doubleday (1824-1893), major of the 4th New York Artillery, to F. W. Ballard, describing the difficulty of securing appointments to the staff of his brother, General Abner Doubleday. The writer criticizes a lack of leadership in the army and praises Lincoln's responsiveness to emancipation influence.

1541. DOUGHTY FAMILY PAPERS, 1665-1686, 1743-1748. 1 vol. (130 pp.) Hanworth, Norfolk, England.

Notes and memoranda, 1665-1686, including a letter, a copy of a charge to a grand jury, remedies, proverbs, poems, Biblical quotations, financial records; and a diary concerning family matters, 1743-1748, entered by various members of the Doughty family in the blank pages of a printed almanac, Riders British Merlin (1665).

1542. ELEANOR (HALL) DOUGLAS PAPERS, 1798-1845. 25 items. Staunton (Augusta County), Va.

Correspondence reflecting social and economic conditions and referring specifically to the purchase of farmland, weaving and spinning, and family matters.

1543. HENRY KYD DOUGLAS PAPERS, (1861-1866) 1949. 32 items. Washington County, Md.

Civil War letters from Henry Kyd Douglas to Helen Macomb Boteler describing in detail military movements and camp life, including the battle of Cross Keys, 1862; the battle of Port Republic, Virginia, 1862; and the battle of Fredericksburg, 1862. Several of the letters were written from the prison on Johnson's Island, near Sandusky, Ohio.

1544. STEPHEN ARNOLD DOUGLAS PAPERS, 1848-1861. 4 items. Washington, D.C.

Miscellaneous items, including a letter from Douglas to a delegate to the Democratic Party conventions at Charleston, South Carolina, and Baltimore, Maryland, 1860, giving his views on the preservation of the Union.

1545. SYLVESTER DOUGLAS, FIRST BARON OF GLENBERVIE, PAPERS, 1794-1795. 1 item. London, England.

Douglas's draft memorandum concerning his retirement from the legal profession, his appointment as chief secretary to the Lord Lieutenant of Ireland, his claims to that office and that of Secretary of State for Ireland, and the settlement by which he would enter Parliament and become Surveyor of the Woods, a commissioner of the Treasury, and a commissioner for Indian affairs.

1546. FREDERICK DOUGLASS PAPERS, 1875-1880. 2 items. Washington, D.C.

A Douglass autograph and a letter of Douglass to Pinckney Benton Stewart Pinchback, 1875, mentioning a meeting to be held as a preliminary to the Republican National Convention of 1876.

1547. JAMES WALTER DOUGLASS PAPERS, 1800-1897. 725 items. Fayetteville (Cumberland County), N.C.

Family and clerical correspondence of James Walter Douglass, a North Carolina Presbyterian minister, including letters from his wife, Frances Ann (Richardson) Taylor Douglass, to her son, Henry P. Taylor, while a student at Princeton College, Princeton, New Jersey. The letters to Henry P. Taylor from his mother contain frequent parental admonitions; letters of J. W. Douglass relate chiefly to religious and church matters.

1548. WILLIAM BOONE DOUGLAS, SR., PAPERS, 1809 (1860-1940) 1948. 1,873 items and 11 vols. Corydon (Harrison County), Ind.

Lawyer, engineer, and surveyor. Correspondence, memorandum books, daybooks, notebooks on the Pueblo Indians, and other papers of Douglass and of various members of the Boone and Douglass families, especially of his father, Benjamin P. Douglass, Indiana State representative, and his son, William Boone Douglas, Jr., an official of the United States consular service. The letters pertain to the Kansas-Nebraska question, the passing of the first overland mail from California through Cassville, Mo., in 1858, elections to be held in Indiana in 1860, Douglass's surveying activities, establishment of a national park of the cliff cities of New Mexico, the securing of power from Boulder Dam, and other matters. Civil War letters from both Union and Confederate soldiers are included; also an emancipation document for some slaves in Indiana Territory, designs submitted to the Patent Office, a biographical sketch of Douglass, and genealogical data on the Boone and related families.

1549. DOUGLAS AND BROTHERS PAPERS, 1849. 7 items. Thompsonville (Hartford County), Conn.

Business correspondence, including specifications and orders, of a shipbuilding firm.

1550. STEPHEN DOUTHIT PAPERS, 1851-1854. 1 vol. Salem (Forsyth County), N.C.

Daybook of a blacksmith shop.

1551. JOHN FREEMAN EDWARD DOVASTON PAPERS, 1864-1866. 3 items and 1 vol. West Felton, Shropshire, England.

Volume contains three essays, "Memoir of Sir Christopher Wren with a list of his Principal Works"; "Ancient Christmas Customs"; and "Self-made Men." Also a poem, epitaphs, and an envelope.

1552. JOHN FREEMAN MILWARD DOVASTON PAPERS, 1808-1813. 19 items. West Felton, Shropshire, England.

Collection includes literary correspondence with John Hamilton Reynolds and Charlotte Cox Reynolds and love letters from A. Maria Williams.

1553. JAMES DOVE PAPERS, 1814-1864. 106 items. Darlington District, S.C., and Greene County, Miss.

Letters and papers of the Dove family, dealing with economic conditions in Mississippi, 1820-1840; plantation life in Mississippi and South Carolina; and sidelights on various business enterprises in which James Dove was interested, including the management of a plantation and the settlement of several estates.

1554. NEAL DOW PAPERS, 1896. 1 item. Portland (Cumberland County), Me.

Letter concerning the "Maine Law" and temperance reform.

1555. A. J. DOWD PAPERS, 1864-1865. 5 items. [Raleigh (Wake County), N.C.?]

Family correspondence of a Confederate soldier.

1556. SAMUEL SMITH DOWNEY PAPERS, 1762 (1800-1900) 1965. 3,276 items and 3 vols. Granville County, N.C.

The early portion of this collection is made up of the papers of Ephraim Macquillen, a merchant of Richmond, Virginia, containing letters, bills, and receipts from business firms in New York, Philadelphia, and Boston to which he sold flour and tobacco and from which he bought supplies. The papers of Samuel S. Downey--which also contain papers of James Webb Alexander, John Granville Smith, Thomas Downey, and James Downey--concern Samuel S. Downey's administration of the estate of John G. Smith and the many suits involving the estate; management of plantations in Mississippi and North Carolina including correspondence and legal papers dealing with hiring slaves to build a railroad from Natchez to Jackson, Mississippi, in the 1830s; letters from factors in Richmond, Virginia, concerning Downey's tobacco; and the Civil War letters of Downey's sons, for the most part describing the effects of the war on civilians. The collection also contains land deeds and legal papers from Granville County, North Carolina; a diary of a trip by boat from Nashville to New Orleans and back, 1827; various wills including those of John G. Smith, James Downey, and Samuel S. Downey; printed matter on a number of subjects including Shiloh Sabbath School, temperance, Caldwell Institute in Greensboro, North Carolina, various pieces of farm and household machinery, the Harrison family in America, and several insurance policies; material on the history of Grassy Creek Presbyterian Church in Granville County; and letters relating to the Southern Temperance Convention in Fayetteville, North Carolina, 1835. Volumes include a ledger of John G. Smith, 1798-1803, which contains a daybook of Ann A. Davis, 1887-1901, and a ledger of Samuel S. Downey, 1828-1874.

1557.  SAMUEL DOWNING PAPERS, 1814-1889. 139 items. Lancaster (Lancaster County), Va.

Miscellaneous personal and business papers of the Downing family. Letters discuss migration to Missouri; Republicans; freedmen; and a tornado in Liberty County, Texas, 1876.

1558.  ROBERT DOWNMAN ACCOUNT BOOK, 1802-1846. 1 vol. (78 pp.) Petersburg (Dinwiddie County), Va.

Lists of slaves belonging to various owners with their ages and dates of birth; list of birth dates for the children of a free woman; lists relating to appraisal and sales of estates; accounts relating to guardianships; recipes for bread and French biscuits. Members of the Hood and Downman families are mentioned.

1559.  WILLIAM S. DOWNS DAYBOOKS AND LEDGERS, 1853-1903. 7 vols. Port Republic (Rockingham County), Va.

Records of a tannery and saddlery.

1560.  D. W. DOWTIN PAPERS, 1862-1865. 11 items. Greenwood County, S.C.

Letters of a Confederate soldier to his mother and sister largely relating to camp life.

1561.  SIR FRANCIS DRAKE PAPERS, 1595-1596. 1 item.

Photocopy of Drake's will and codicil.

1562.  WILLIAM DRAYTON PAPERS, 1815-1833. 13 items. Charleston, S.C.

Routine political correspondence of William Drayton, chiefly concerning appointments and the estate of John Drayton.

1563.  FERDINAND JULIUS DREER, SR., PAPERS, 1867. 1 item. Philadelphia, Pa.

Letter to Dreer from John C. Hamilton asking to see his collection of papers of prominent Americans.

1564.  DRENAN FAMILY PAPERS, 1862-1865. 59 items. Morrisville (Lamoille County), Vt.

Letters by Union soldiers from Vermont who were stationed in Washington, D.C., Virginia, and Maryland during the Civil War. Correspondence concerns camp life, United States Army hospitals, particularly the general hospitals at Harpers Ferry and Fort Schuyler, and the battle of Culpeper Court House, 1862.

1565.  CHARLES DRESSER PAPERS, 1830-1836. 5 items. Halifax Court House (Halifax County), Va.

Correspondence of a Protestant Episcopal minister and educator with officials of the Virginia Bible Society, the American Tract Society, and the Southern Churchman.

1566.  WILLIAM DREW PAPERS, 1858-1885. 13 items. Jefferson County, W. Va.

Personal correspondence of the Drew family.

1567.  AMOS S. DREWRY AND COMPANY RECORDS, 1854-1861. 2 vols. Lawrenceville (Brunswick County), Va.

Cashbooks, 1854-1857, and ledgers, 1854-1861, of the operator of an inn and tavern. Also contains accounts for a similar business, Nicholson and Company, which begin in 1858.

1568.  GEORGE COKE DROMGOOLE AND RICHARD B. ROBINSON PAPERS, 1767-1974. 4,555 items and 9 vols. Lawrenceville (Brunswick County), Va.

Papers of George Coke Dromgoole, Edward Dromgoole, and other members of the Dromgoole family, including the papers of Richard B. Robinson, George C. Dromgoole's nephew by marriage. The papers of George C. Dromgoole concern family, business, and political matters and include a large number of letters dealing with plantation work and the management of slaves; items on the Democratic Party before the Civil War; and letters from Edward Dromgoole when he was a student at the University of North Carolina at Chapel Hill. The papers of Richard B.

Robinson include correspondence, business papers, and a daybook, 1848-1868. The papers of Edward Dromgoole deal largely with legal and business matters and contain plantation records; receipts for the tobacco tithe of 1864; a contract with a freedman; accounts of cotton sales; a number of letters from tenants after the Civil War discussing in great detail the problems of farm management; and letters from a student at Virginia Military Institute in the 1870s. The collection contains legal records from Brunswick County, Virginia, including justice of the peace, county, and circuit court minutes, orders, summonses, warrants, and depositions. The volumes include daybooks, plantation books, an account book dealing with the estate of Thomas Dromgoole, and a notebook describing Edward Dromgoole's home and containing genealogical material on the Dromgoole family.

1569. HENRY HOME DRUMMOND PAPERS, 1826. 1 item. Blair Drummond, Perthshire, Scotland.

Letter which originally accompanied a memorial from a group of shipowners on the subject of free trade. The contents of the memorial are summarized in the letter.

1570. JOSEPH A. DRUMMOND PAPERS, 1861-1863. 32 items. James Island, S.C.

Letters of a Confederate soldier describing military activities around Charleston, South Carolina, and discussing his family and events at home.

1571. THOMAS WORTLEY DRURY PAPERS, 1904. 2 items. London, England.

Letters to Drury, a member of the Royal Commission on Ecclesiastical Discipline, dealing with church matters.

1572. EGBERT DU BOIS PAPERS, 1860 (1866-1891) 1901. 523 items. Bluffton (Beaufort County), S.C.

Family and business letters of Du Bois, who moved from New York after the Civil War to plant cotton in South Carolina. The collection includes the Civil War letters of William O. Rahn to his wife describing military life; correspondence with merchants in New York and cotton factors and commission merchants in Charleston, South Carolina; and letters from a son describing his work as a lawyer in Albany, New York.

1573. JOEL H. DUBOSE PAPERS, 1895-1928. 2 items. Atlanta (Fulton County), Ga.

Letters to DuBose from Allen Daniel Candler and Hoke Smith.

1574. JOSEPH VILLARS DUBREUIL PAPERS, 1760-1850. 45 items and 1 vol. Tchoupetoulas (Orleans Parish), La., and French West Indies.

Papers of Joseph Villars Dubreuil, a French monarchist, lieutenant colonel of the French Army, who was stationed in Santo Domingo during part of the French Revolution and who later became the founder of a wealthy cane- and cotton-planting family of Louisiana. The collection includes family and business papers and documents of a public nature concerning Louisiana including petitions, proposed laws, census returns, treasury reports, and copies of legislative speeches bearing on the relation of the Territory of Louisiana to the Federal government of the United States. Included also is one volume containing bits of French verse. The papers are in French.

1575. HENRY A. DUC, SR., AND HENRY A. DUC, JR., PAPERS, 1840-1909. 248 items. Charleston, S.C.

Business and family correspondence of H. A. Duc and his son, H. A. Duc, Jr., tinsmiths, including many invoices, 1840-1859, from a New York dealer in uncut tin and sheet iron; descriptions of latest tin-working machinery in New York in 1870; information on young Duc's inventions (marine engine and elastic fluid engine); personal letters from widely dispersed relatives concerning Nebraska sod houses, 1874; St. Augustine, Florida, and orange crops, 1878; student life at the United States Naval Academy, Annapolis, Maryland, and activities on the U.S.S. Charleston; and prices charged by one Saunders, a painter of miniatures. Included also are one letter of R. W. Gibbes and an undated manuscript entitled "Literature in Charleston." The volume is Duc's ledger, 1843-1856.

1576. SIR EDMUND FREDERICK DU CANE PAPERS, 1891. 1 item. London, England.

Letter from Du Cane commenting on the increase in the number of young offenders committed to reformatory and industrial schools in Great Britain.

1577. EDWARD BISHOP DUDLEY, SR., PAPERS, 1838-1846. 3 items. Wilmington (New Hanover County), N.C.

Papers include a land grant from Dudley to Neill Munn of Montgomery County, North Carolina, and a letter to the sheriff of Pasquotank County, North Carolina, granting a stay of execution, 1838.

1578. JOHN W. DUDLEY PAPERS, 1816 (1852-1861) 1867. 22 items. Cincinnati, Ohio.

Miscellaneous family letters between Dudley and his immediate family in Ohio to other members of his family in Virginia. There are occasional comments on politics and business conditions.

1579. JOHN D. DUFFIELD PAPERS, 1836-1892. 3 vols. Welsh Run (Franklin County), Pa.

Two physicians's account books, 1836-1858, and one account book later used as a scrapbook for miscellaneous items.

1580. CHARLES DUFFY PAPERS, 1840 (1858-1859) 1888. 17 items. Catherine Lake (Onslow County), N.C.

Political correspondence of Charles Duffy, New Bern, North Carolina, druggist, one letter of which describes the campaign of the Whig Party in the election of 1840; other letters pertain to the education of Duffy's sons, Charles and Lawrence, who were in a West Point preparatory school in New York City, ca. 1858.

1581. FREDERICK A. DUGAS PAPERS, 1825-1848. 15 items and 1 vol. Edgefield District, S.C.

Deeds, mercantile accounts, and personal letters of a French-American family. Several of the letters are in French. Included also is a record of visits, charges, and payments kept in diary form in 1854 by Louis Alexander Dugas (1806-1884), a prominent physician of Augusta, Georgia.

1582. ANTOINE CHARLES DU HOUX, BARON DE VIOMÉNIL, PAPERS, 1782. 4 items. Versailles, France.

Printed materials: facsimile of a letter, 1782; portraits of the French commanders at the surrender of Cornwallis by John Trumbull and the Baron de Vioménil; and maps of the Baron's travels in America.

1583. ANGIER BUCHANAN DUKE CHECK STUBS, 1914-1918. 8 vols. New York, N.Y.

1584. BENJAMIN NEWTON DUKE PAPERS, 1834-1941. 36,406 items and 96 vols. Durham, N.C.

Personal, business, financial and legal papers of Benjamin N. Duke (1855-1929), tobacco manufacturer, industrialist, and philanthropist. The collection contains important materials on the tobacco, textile and electric power industries, including W. Duke, Sons and Company, the American Tobacco Company, Erwin Mills, Mayo Mills, Durham Electric Lighting Company, the Spray Water Power and Land Company, the Dallas Cable Railroad, and the Durham Fertilizer Company. The building of Trinity College in Durham is described in correspondence with presidents John Franklin Crowell, John Carlisle Kilgo, and William Preston Few, Trinity College treasurers, faculty, and students; financial reports; resolutions; and photographs. There is also material on other beneficiaries of Duke's philanthropy including North Carolina College, Kittrell College, Louisburg College, Wofford College, Lincoln Memorial University, Lincoln Hospital, the Salvation Army, the Durham Y.W.C.A., and the Belleau Wood Memorial Association. Financial papers consist of receipts, notes, lists of dividends and interest, investments, gifts, tax statements, and the financial papers of his wife, Sarah Pearson (Angier) Duke. Legal papers are chiefly deeds and plats of land, 1834-1928, of B. N. Duke's real estate in Durham. Personal papers include baptismal records of his children; biographical material; and correspondence and photographs pertaining to Duke's family and his homes, "The Terrace," later "Four Acres," in Durham; Duke's Farm near University Station, North Carolina; his Florida home; and his home at Irvington on the Hudson. There is some material on the gubernatorial race between Julian Shakespeare Carr and Daniel Lindsay Russell. Volumes include albums, 1923, containing birthday greetings and photographs of Trinity College; check stubs, 1901-1918; a daybook, 1899-1901, of B. N. and J. B. Duke; invoice books, 1892-1898; a ledger, 1899-1901; letter books, 1892-1924; minute book, 1907-1908, and stock certificate book, 1907, of the Alaska Dredging and Power Company; record books, 1905-1906, and scrapbook, 1905, of the Solomon River Hydraulic Mining Company; records of stocks, bonds, and dividends, 1892-1918; photographs of Duke Farms; and a scrapbook, 1929, "In Memoriam."

1585. JAMES BUCHANAN DUKE PAPERS, 1764 (1917-1928) 1940. 7,460 items and 25 vols. New York, N.Y.

Personal, legal, business and financial papers of James B. Duke (1856-1925), tobacco manufacturer, industrialist, and philanthropist. The major portion of the collection relates to the settlement of the part of Duke's estate which he left to the descendants of his aunts and uncles. Included are letters between the many claimants and the executors of the estate; genealogical records of the Duke family, consisting of typescripts of census returns, marriage bonds, wills, land deeds, tax records, and court minutes; the research notes of Charles Caldwell on the Duke family; claims and affidavits of the claimants; a copy of James B. Duke's will; and court transcripts of the suit of a number of the claimants against the executors of the Duke estate. Other legal papers concern the conveyance of the property of W. Duke, Sons and Company to the American Tobacco Company, and trial papers in the case of John R. Miller v. American Tobacco Company. There is some business correspondence related to W. Duke, Sons and Company and the American

Tobacco Company, as well as some personal correspondence pertaining to his early years. The collection also contains an original copy of the indenture establishing the Duke Endowment, and correspondence regarding aid to Trinity College. Miscellaneous papers include clippings; articles; a reminiscent sketch of James B. Duke by George Garland Allen; a reel of motion picture film of James B. Duke; photographs of the Dukes and Duke Farms, Somerville, New Jersey; two memorial volumes from the Duke Endowment and one from the Board of Trustees of Furman University after James B. Duke's death; and memorabilia.

1586. W. DUKE, SONS & CO., PAPERS, 1876-1904. 3 boxes and 3 vols. Durham, N.C.

Premiums, booklets, and other advertising devices used by tobacco manufacturers. The majority are those of W. Duke, Sons & Co., but also included are premiums of Kinney Brothers, New York and Richmond; William S. Kimball and Co., Rochester, New York; Goodwin and Co., New York; Allen and Ginter, Richmond; Lone Jack Cigarette Co., Lynchburg, Virginia; S. F. Hesse and Co.; and Marburg Bros., Baltimore, Maryland.

1587. WALTER PATTERSON DUKE PAPERS, 1840-1884. 210 items. Hadensville (Goochland County), Va.

Personal and business correspondence of the Duke family, containing letters from William B. Duke near Caledonia, Virginia; from J. E. Duke of Tennessee; Napoleon Duke of New York State; and Walter Patterson Duke of Arkansas and later of Texas, where these three had removed after the Civil War. All were engaged in farming, and the bulk of the material deals with conditions of crops and prices of cotton and corn. Two letters describe the purpose and activities of the Ku Klux Klan in Tennessee, and other letters refer to a general store and an agency for the Southern Fertilizing Company in Goochland County, operated by Walter P. Duke after his return to the county, ca. 1871. Among the correspondence are many letters of W. H. Gilham, of the Southern Fertilizing Company of Richmond, Virginia, for which company Walter P. Duke served as agent.

1588. WASHINGTON DUKE PAPERS, 1676-1968. 2,637 items and 7 vols. Durham, N.C.

Personal, business, and financial papers of Washington Duke (1820-1905), tobacco manufacturer and philanthropist. Business and financial papers related to tobacco and textiles include correspondence dealing with business transactions and profits; and financial records of W. Duke, Sons & Co., including ledgers, 1873-1877 and 1893-1905, and a warehouse account book containing records of shipping and purchases of leaf tobacco, 1876-1884. Other financial records are comprised of correspondence pertaining to Duke's generosity toward relatives; educational institutions such as Louisburg College, Kittrell College, Rutherford College, and Trinity College; the Methodist Episcopal Church, South; and various orphanages. A journal and a cashbook, 1893-1905, record gifts to family members, other individuals, and various institutions, as well as dividends from investments. Other materials include Duke family genealogy; a family Bible; photographs of the Duke Homestead; correspondence, brochures, and addresses and other memorabilia from the dedication of the Duke Homestead.

1589. THE DUKE ENDOWMENT PAPERS, 1856-1970. Ca. 92,000 items, 181 vols., and 28 phonotapes. New York, N.Y. Restricted.

Papers of The Duke Endowment include personal financial records and a few legal items and correspondence of James Buchanan Duke; correspondence, legal papers, and financial papers relative to the settlement of James Buchanan Duke's estate; financial records of the Buchanan Investment Corporation and of Duke Farms; financial records relating to the operation of The Endowment; and records of the Duke Divinity School concerning rural church building and maintenance, 1926-1941. Reports include annual reports of the orphan section, 10 vols., 1927-1939; annual reports of the hospital section, 3 vols., 1928, 1932, 1933; annual reports of The Endowment, 4 vols., 1963, 1973, 1974; and yearbooks of The Endowment, 31 vols., 1924-1957. Financial records of the Duke Construction Company, 1927-1930, concern construction of Duke University. There are also memorials of The Endowment and the Duke Power Company concerning James B. Duke and Edward Carrington Marshall; tapes and transcripts of a series of interviews conducted by Frank W. Rounds, Jr., with friends and associates of James B. Duke; photographs of members of the Duke family, James B. Duke's associates, and the interviewees; and printed material relating to James B. Duke.

1590. A. J. DULA PAPERS, 1908. 1 item. (14 pp.) Caldwell County, N.C.

Reminiscences of the history of Company A, 22nd Regiment, North Carolina Volunteers, narrated by Private A. J. Dula. He describes various battles, including the Peninsular Campaign, the Seven Days battle, the capture of Harper's Ferry, the battles of Fredericksburg, Chancellorsville, and Gettysburg, and the defense of Richmond; camp life and the unhealthful conditions; casualties; his injury and recuperation; his capture and parole; and the speech of Governor Vance at Orange Court House, Virginia. Included is a list, compiled in 1865, of the men in Company A, noting injuries received, discharges, desertions, etc.

1591. M. M. DULL PAPERS, 1852 (1870-1890) 1904. 84 items. Spottswood (Augusta County), Va.

Papers of M. M. Dull consist of letters concerning personal and business affairs, commodity prices, social life and customs, and weather and crops; and bills and receipts. Also included are references to a religious revival, Negroes, the arrival of a threshing machine, physicians and hospitals, and travels to Niagara Falls, Saint Louis, Detroit, Omaha, and Atlanta.

1592. ALEXANDER DUNBAR PAPERS, 1868. 1 item. Waco (McLennan County), Tex.

Letter from Dunbar to Robert Bonnor (Robert Bonner, editor of the New York Ledger?), describing Texas and its people.

1593. BLANTON DUNCAN PAPERS, 1866-1876. 6 items. Chattanooga (Hamilton County), Tenn.

Letters of Blanton Duncan, a Confederate enthusiast, dealing chiefly with the proposed visit of James G. Blaine to New Orleans in 1866.

1594. CHARLES B. DUNCAN ACCOUNT BOOK, 1860-1861. 1 vol. Lynchburg (Campbell County), Va.

Account book of a Lynchburg merchant.

1595. ENNIS DUNCAN, JR., DIARY, 1814-1815. 1 vol. (65 pp.) Kentucky.

Mimeographed copy of the diary of Ennis Duncan, Jr., an orderly sergeant and provost marshal in the 16th Regiment, Kentucky Militia Detached, describing the itinerary of the unit into Canada and thereafter, during the War of 1812. Also included are descriptions of problems among the officers, ill-trained and ill-disciplined troops, camp life, sickness and deaths, desertion, the French and the Indians, gambling, stealing, opium and whiskey.

1596. WILLIAM E. DUNCAN LETTER BOOK, 1862. 1 vol. (211 pp.) Dublin Depot (Pulaski County), Va.

Letter book of Captain William E. Duncan, an adjutant quartermaster in the Confederate Army, containing copies of letters concerned with obtaining and transporting supplies for the army, principally the 45th Virginia Regiment, but also the 8th Virginia Cavalry and several unspecified units. Included is a letter describing the fighting at Lewisburg, West Virginia.

1597. WILLIAM P. S. DUNCAN PAPERS, 1847-1868. 7 items. New Orleans, La.

Two letters from General Johnson Kelly Duncan, C.S.A., to his brother, William P. S. Duncan, advising him on a vocation, and discussing a promotion in the army; a broadside entitled The Late General Duncan, C.S.A., containing general orders of notification of Duncan's death and an obituary notice; and personal letters from J. K. Duncan's wife, Mary, to W. P. S. Duncan's wife, Rose. All are photostatic copies.

1598. HENRY DUNDAS, FIRST VISCOUNT MELVILLE, PAPERS, 1779-1813. 469 items and 1 vol. London, England.

Correspondence and documents of Henry Dundas, First Viscount Melville (1742-1811), Secretary of State for War, 1794-1801, and First Lord of the Admiralty, 1804-1805, concerning the defenses of England and Scotland; recruitment and other matters related to the militia, volunteers, fencibles, and the regular army; the strength and disposition of British troops, principally land forces, on the continent and in the colonies; military operations on the continent; domestic Secret Service operations as well as intelligence about foreign naval operations; the activities of the French royalists in the Vendée; military affairs in India, Egypt, and Ireland; parliamentary elections and other political matters in Scotland; Scottish emigration to America; Catholic emancipation in Ireland; and domestic and foreign policy.

1599. ROBERT SAUNDERS DUNDAS, SECOND VISCOUNT MELVILLE, PAPERS, 1811-1849, 213 items. London, England.

Papers of Robert Saunders Dundas, Second Viscount Melville (1771-1851), British statesman and First Lord of the Admiralty, 1812-1827, principally concern his duties at the Admiralty. Much of the correspondence is with Sir Thomas Byam Martin, comptroller of the Navy, 1816-1831, and deals with Martin's duties on the Spanish and Dutch coasts in the war with France; the annual naval budget; and construction and maintenance of the British fleet. Other correspondence relates to defenses along the United States-Canadian border; negotiations for the purchase of timber in Austria; the dockyards; the Cape of Good Hope; relations with Brazil and Portugal; relations with Algiers; the purchase of steam engines for a number of small warships; poor relief in Ireland; and military, naval and diplomatic operations in the Mediterranean Sea, 1815.

1600. JOHN DUNDORE PAPERS, 1839-1854. 5 items and 1 vol. Port Republic (Rockingham County), Va.

Business letters to Captain John Dundore, discussing land and the settlement of estates in Virginia; and a daybook, 1849-1858, for the tannery of the firm of Dundore and Eddins, 1849-1852, and its successor, John Dundore, 1852-1858.

1601. ADAM L. DUNLOP AND DANIEL RIFE PAPERS, 1802-1875. 378 items. Staunton (Augusta County), Va.

Personal correspondence of two families united by the marriage of Elizabeth Dunlop and Daniel Rife (often spelled Reiff), centering around settlement of the West and the Civil War. The bulk of the letters are concerned with the West, including travel to that section, hog raising and farming in Indiana, high wages in Illinois, and family affairs in Staunton and in the West, all before 1860. Among the Civil War letters, chiefly from William A. Dunlop, a Confederate soldier, are comments on the battle of Manassas, 1861, courts-martial, desertions, various combats, Stonewall Jackson, camp life, and prisoners. Adam L. Dunlop's letters came from Madison, Missouri, after his removal to the West, while members of the Rife family wrote from various sections of the West, chiefly to Daniel Rife, who remained in Augusta County. Several of the early letters are in German.

1602. JOHN D. DUNN PAPERS, 1801-1917. 202 items and 4 vols. Bentonville Township (Johnston County), N.C.

Papers of John D. Dunn (b. ca. 1827), comprised of family and business correspondence, accounts, receipts, and legal papers, relate to Dunn's life in Alabama and North Carolina. Letters discuss family matters, crops and prices, overseers and treatment of slaves, the gubernatorial election of 1860 and secession in North Carolina, camp life and illness during the Civil War, life in the prison barracks at Elmira Prison Camp, New York, and steamboats in Alabama. Volumes include a receipt book, 1853-1858, of a steamboat company at Mobile, Alabama, containing records of the wages of the crews; an account book, 1850s, of A. B. Drake of Drake's Landing, Alabama; an account book containing entries for persons at landings along the Alabama River; and a payroll book, 1855-1859, of a number of steamboats operating in Alabama.

1603. ROBERT DUNN PAPERS, 1860. 1 item. London, England.

Announcement of Herbert Spencer's forthcoming A System of Philosophy to Robert Dunn (1799-1877), British surgeon in an effort to obtain subscribers.

1604. NANCY DUNNAGAN PAPERS, 1846-1880. 26 items. Orange County, N.C.

Letters to Nancy Dunnagan from her children and grandchildren in Union and Webster counties, Kentucky, discussing family matters and farming. Included are estate papers of Timothy Dunnagan, her husband.

1605. MRS. EDWARD DUNNING PAPERS, 1844-1863. 5 items.

Correspondence of the Dunning family, commenting on slavery, social life before and during the Civil War, and the town of Williamsburg, Virginia, in 1851.

1606. RICHARD G. M. DUNOVANT PAPERS, 1861. 145 items. Charleston, S.C.

Official papers of Brigadier General Richard G. M. Dunovant, C.S.A., relating to the defense of Charleston Harbor, South Carolina, and to the preparations made by Confederate Army forces in anticipation of the attack on Fort Sumter. The majority of the papers concern the fortification, provisioning, and garrisoning of the forts and batteries, and include construction reports, requisitions and reports concerning ordnance supplies, and lists of officers and men.

1607. WILLIAM B. DUPREE PAPERS, 1895. 3 items. New York, N.Y.

Letters from former Civil War generals, John M. Schofield, Alexander P. Stewart, and Oliver O. Howard, to William B. Dupree in answer to the question, "What do you consider your greatest achievement as a general in the Civil War?"

1608. ELIZA ANN DUPUY PAPERS, 1867-1880. 52 items. Flemingsburg (Fleming County), Ky.

Literary correspondence of Eliza Ann Dupuy (1814-1881), author, with Robert Bonner, editor of the New York Ledger, concerning the publication of her stories. The letters include comments on Bonner's race horses, the trial of Henry Ward Beecher, and biographical information on Eliza Ann Dupuy and Bonner. Included also is one letter from T. B. Peterson.

1609. C. DURAND PAPERS, 1842-1851. 3 items. New York, N.Y.

Two routine business letters by G. B. Cummins of Savannah, Georgia, to C. Durand, a merchant of Goodhue and Company; and a letter by Cummins concerning the prelude to the Revolution of 1848 in France, cotton prices on the Liverpool market, and the United States presidential campaign of 1848.

1610. JOHN B. DURFEE PAPERS, 1861-1865. 115 items. Newport, R.I.

Civil War letters of the four Durfee brothers, John B. and Benjamin of the 9th Regiment, Rhode Island Volunteers; A. Y., stationed off Pensacola, Florida, aboard the *Mississippi*; and William H., Jr., of the 5th Regiment, Rhode Island Volunteers, and a prisoner at the military prison at Charleston, South Carolina.

1611. DURHAM COTTON MANUFACTURING COMPANY, 1910-1934. 34,236 items and 66 vols. Durham, N.C.

Business papers of the Durham Cotton Manufacturing Company, producers of various types of cotton cloth, containing information on prices of raw and manufactured cotton; export of cotton cloth; types of cloth manufactured; types of machinery used; operating expenses; wages, salaries, and benefits; and stockholders, dividends and distribution of excess profits. Also included are invoices of goods sold by the brokerage firm of Joshua L. Baily & Co. of Philadelphia, 1912-1916, and 1921-1926; monthly accounts of Joshua L. Baily & Co., 1915-1934; invoices for goods shipped directly from the factory, 1931-1934; and cancelled checks, 1915-1927. Volumes include check stubs, 1914-1933; letterpress copybooks of correspondence, 1910 and 1923-1930; letterpress copybooks of invoices, 1918-1931; and receipt books, 1932-1933.

1612. DURHAM HOSIERY MILLS PAPERS, 1887-1962. 5,427 items and 50 vols. Durham, N.C.

Business papers of the Durham Hosiery Company and its successor, the Durham Hosiery Mills, comprise correspondence, bills, broadsides, time books, letter books, records, inventories, journals, vouchers, check stubs, ledgers, and stock certificates. The bulk of the correspondence pertains to the Durham Hosiery Company while George M. Graham served as secretary and treasurer from its organization in 1895 until 1897. Letters deal with machinery bought from Northern firms, newly organized textile mills in the South, the installation and repair of machinery, and the sale of hosiery. Also included are two letters, 1919 and 1920, concerning the organization of the personnel department; and a financial statement of 1962. Volumes of the Durham Hosiery Company consist of an account book, 1896; check stubs, 1895-1899; cashbooks, 1869; check express book from the Indelible Dye Works of Philadelphia, 1896-1897; inventories, 1898; a ledger, 1897-1898; a journal, 1895-1897; letter books, 1895-1897; dye house records, 1897-1898; records of stock certificates, 1895-1897; and time books, 1896-1898. Volumes pertaining to the Durham Hosiery Mills include ledgers, journals, and voucher registers from the following plants: Mill No. 3 at High Point, 1906-1922; Mill No. 4 at Carrboro, 1909-1922; Mill No. 6 at Durham, 1914-1921; and Mill No. 7 at Carrboro, 1913-1922.

1613. W. J. HUGH DURHAM PAPERS, 1859. 1 item. Orange County, N.C.

Personal letter from W. J. H. Durham, a student at Jefferson Medical College in Philadelphia, to his brother concerning family matters.

1614. ZACHARY TAYLOR DURHAM PAPERS, 1869-1876. 11 items. Savannah, Ga.

Personal correspondence of Z. T. Durham with Brantley A. Denmark and Arthur Howell of Savannah, Georgia, reflecting the difficulties of Reconstruction, and including a letter describing Southern feelings about the Fourth of July. A letter, 1872, by Durham, describes Texas, and a letter, 1874, from John Snyder in San Francisco, describes that city and other parts of the west.

1615. ETIENNE DUTILH AND JOHN GOTTFRIED WACHSMUTH PAPERS, 1771 (1788-1804) 1923. 323 items. Philadelphia, Pa.

Principally business correspondence, bills, receipts, invoices, orders, letters of exchange, manifests of ships' cargoes, notes and accounts of Etienne Dutilh and J. G. Wachsmuth, merchants engaged in the West Indian and European trade. There are several papers of Stephen Dutilh, a Philadelphia merchant, and two letters relating to the capture of one of his ships by a French privateer. Also included are papers concerning legal cases in which the firm was plaintiff, letters pertaining to trade difficulties with France and Great Britain, and several price lists.

1616. JOSEPH DUVALL PAPERS, 1845-1908. 6 vols. Baltimore, Md.

Records of a merchant, including account books, 1878-1885 and 1904-1908; a cashbook, 1870-1873; a daybook, 1871-1873; a journal, 1870-1885; and a ledger containing a cobbler's accounts, 1845-1879.

1617. W. D. F. DUVALL DIARY, [1862?]. 1 vol. (22 pp.) Melrose (Rockingham County), Va.

Diary of a Confederate soldier, giving an account of camp life, September 15-19; a march to Culpeper Court House; a camp on Freeman's Hill; and the burned bridge at Rapidan Station, all in Virginia.

1618. RICHARD M. DWYER PAPERS, 1881-1906. 66 items. Sperryville (Rappahannock County), Va., and North Hampton (Clarke County), Ohio.

Personal letters to Richard M. Dwyer, discussing family news, the weather, crops, sickness, deaths, gossip, and weddings.

1619. NATHAN G. DYE PAPERS, 1851 (1862-1865) 1899. 367 items and 2 vols. Monmouth (Jackson County), Iowa.

Letters and diaries of Nathan G. Dye, principally while serving with the 24th Iowa Volunteers, describing military activities in Mississippi, Louisiana, Georgia, North Carolina and Virginia, camp life, food, disease, and rumors. Papers between 1872 and 1899 deal chiefly with Dye's efforts to obtain a pension.

1620. WILLIAM T. DYER PAPERS, 1840. 1 item. Fayette (Howard County), Mo.

Letter of recommendation for Colonel Birch of Missouri for a governmental post in Washington by William T. Dyer, chairman of the Tippecanoe Club of Howard County.

1621. EAGLE TAVERN REGISTER, 1843-1844. 1 vol. (66 pp.) Watkinsville (Oconee County), Ga.

Also includes poems and records of a schoolteacher.

1622. EDWARD EARLE PAPERS, 1840. 1 item. Philadelphia, Pa.

Letter of Earle trying to identify Michel Ney, Marshal of France, as one Michael Rudolph, Revolutionary War veteran of Elkton, Maryland.

1623. RALPH E. W. EARLE PAPERS, 1833. 7 items. Washington, D.C.

Miscellaneous notes to Earle, a portraitist, concerning Washington society during the Jackson administration and a printed pen-and-ink sketch (self-portrait?) of Earle.

1624. JUBAL ANDERSON EARLY PAPERS, 1846-1889. 20 items. Virginia.

Miscellaneous letters and papers including a few items of routine military correspondence from the Civil War; comments on Reconstruction; mention of the problems confronting the Southern Historical Society of which Early was the president; items dealing with railroad building; Early's criticism of biographical sketches of himself; and a photocopy of the will which Early made in 1867.

1625. PETER C. EARNHARDT PAPERS, 1862-1863. 1 vol. [Fond du Lac County?], Wis.

Diary of a soldier, probably a member of the 3rd Wisconsin Regiment, containing a daily record of the routine activities of military life.

1626. JAMES S. EASLEY AND WILLIAM W. WILLINGHAM LETTER BOOKS, 1853-1855. 2 vols. Halifax (Halifax County), Va.

Business letters to the firm of James S. Easley and William W. Willingham from land agents in Illinois and, more particularly, in Iowa.

1627. PYRANT EASLEY PAPERS, 1816-1824. 7 items and 1 vol. [Virginia?]

Items dealing with the disposition of slaves belonging to the estate of Pyrant Easley.

1628. JAMES W. EAST PAPERS, 1869-1870. 2 items. Lexington (Rockbridge County), Va.

Business notes.

1629. EAST INDIA COMPANY. INDIA. MADRAS PRESIDENCY. EXTRACTS FROM RECORDS, 1755-1775. 1 vol. (84 pp.) Madras, India.

Volume entitled "Extracts from the East India Company's Records, at Madras, Relative to the Conduct of the Nabob Walau Jau, 1755," concerning the political and financial relationship of Mohammed Ali, Nabob of Arcot, with the officials of the Madras Presidency.

1630. EAST TENNESSEE LAND COMPANY PAPERS, 1893-1894. 5 items. Harriman (Roane County), Tenn.

Circulars sent out to stockholders relating to the reorganization of the company.

1631. BRANNER EASTERLY PAPERS, 1854-1888. 61 items. Carbondale (Jackson County), Ill.

Letters of Easterly and various members of his family concerning the problems of managing the farm while Easterly was in the United States Army during the Civil War; Northern and Southern views of Reconstruction; and family matters.

1632. SIR JOHN EASTHOPE, FIRST BARONET, PAPERS, 1809 (1834-1847) 498 items. London, England.

Letters and papers of Sir John Easthope, financier, Whig politician, and owner of the semi-official newspaper, The Morning Chronicle, commenting on many of the important political issues of the day and illustrating the relationship between the press and British politics. The collection includes a number of letters reflecting Easthope's interest in Spain and Portugal and his promotion of railroads in those countries; a series of letters by Henry, Lord Brougham, 1834-1861, containing discussions of Whig politics and comments on education, church-state relations, French politics and Anglo-French relations, the Crimean War, the Corn Laws, and various political figures; a series of letters between Easthope and the Earl of Durham, 1834-1840, concerning mainly British relations with Russia and Durham's work in Canada; letters from Lord John Russell, 1836-1846, concerned for the most part with national political issues but also containing comments on the Webster-Ashburton Treaty and Canadian affairs; letters from Daniel O'Connell in 1836, 1837, and 1840 concern political patronage; a series of letters by Lord Palmerston during 1836-1848 are about foreign affairs; and a short series from Richard Cobden relate to industrial and agricultural distress in England. Other correspondents include George Edward Anson; the Duke of Essex; Edward J. Stanley, Second Baron Stanley of Alderley; Sir Thomas Wilde; Lord Methuen; the Earl of Clarendon; and Lord Shaftesbury.

1633. BENJAMIN EATON LETTER BOOK, 1805. 1 vol. (42 pp.) Boston, Mass.

Letters from Benjamin Eaton while in Liverpool to his employer, Peter Wainwright, apparently a tobacco dealer in Boston.

1634. HENRY JAMES EATON PAPERS, 1 vol. Concord (Merrimack County), N.H.

Genealogy of the Eaton family.

1635. JOHN HENRY EATON PAPERS, 1829-1830. 2 items. Washington, D.C.

Routine letters to Eaton as United States secretary of war, making recommendations for appointments.

1636. WALTER PRICHARD EATON PAPERS, 1933-1934. 3 items. Sheffield (Berkshire County), Mass.

Three articles: "Wildflower Gardens of Old New England," an article on Thoreau, and an unfinished article, "American Drama vs. Literature."

1637. WILLIAM EATON PAPERS, 1831. 1 item. Washington, D.C.

Letter from Eaton to John Thorne, presumably about the War of 1812.

1638. VALERIUS EBERT PAPERS, 1861. 1 item. Frederick (Frederick County), Md.

Letter discontinuing a subscription to the Home Journal because of its abolitionist proclivities.

1639. WILLIAM KEARNEY EBORN PAPERS, 1835-1912. 4 vols. Martin County, N.C.

One volume concerning legal procedures and issues and two volumes of sermons, sermon notes, and biblical quotations with commentaries by Eborn.

1640. GEORGE EDEN, FIRST EARL OF AUCKLAND, PAPERS, 1847. 2 items. London, England.

Letter from Lord Palmerston, Foreign Secretary, to Auckland, First Lord of the Admiralty, suggesting that the idea of offering the Pacific naval command to Sir Charles Napier was undesirable.

1641. WILLIAM EDEN, FIRST BARON AUCKLAND, PAPERS, 1772-1804. 25 items. London, England.

Letters from Auckland, British Ambassador Extraordinary at the Hague, 1793, reporting on the progress of the coalition against France (copied from originals in the Public Record Office, London). Also included is a letter from William Pitt, 1787, concerning the East India Convention, and several other letters from various persons, dealing for the most part with foreign affairs.

1642. LACY THOMAS EDENS PAPERS, 1935. 1 vol. (36 pp.) Durham, N.C.

"A Brief History of Centenary M. E. Church, South, N.C. Conference, 1935."

1643. EDGEMONT COMMUNITY CENTER PAPERS, 1943. 1 vol. (29 pp.) Durham, N.C.

"Report of the Fact Finding Committee and Durham Council of Social Agencies, 1943, March 24."

1644. KATE EDMOND PAPERS, 1835 (1881-1883) 1886. 25 items. Selma (Dallas County), Ala.

This collection is made up for the most part of letters written to Kate Edmond by Carrie McCord who went with her family to Brazil in 1881 to join her father, a physician there. The letters discuss Brazilian social life and customs; cities of Bahia and Rio de Janeiro; floods and landslides in Campos; smallpox in that city in 1882 and 1883; and the visit of the Emperor and Empress to celebrate bringing electricity there.

1645. STERLING F. EDMONDS PAPERS, 1838-1850. 70 items. Selma (Dallas County), Ala.

The collection is made up of receipts, accounts for the yearly hiring of slaves, and papers relating to lawsuits, for the most part involving the financial situation of Sterling Edmonds.

1646. HENRY EDMONDSON PAPERS, 1822-1849. 12 items. Fotheringay (Montgomery County), Va.

Family and business correspondence of a Virginia justice of the peace.

1647. THOMAS EDMONDSON AND ISAAC EDMONDSON PAPERS, 1783 (1800-1820) 1874. 68 items. Baltimore, Md.

Business papers of merchants dealing in woolen and cotton cloth, some of which was imported from England. Also includes the business transactions of Dr. Thomas Edmondson in the 1840s and a few family letters.

1648. WILLIAM EDMONDSON PAPERS, 1742-1860. 26 items. Idle, Yorkshire, England.

Collection contains a group of documents, 1742-1842, on poor relief at Idle and other places nearby, including papers dealing with the construction and operation of a workhouse at Idle. Also correspondence and papers, 1833-1838, concerning the agitation of woolen manufacturers for repeal of the Factory Acts including a printed draft of a bill, a list of persons who signed a mill owners' petition, and correspondence with Lord Morpeth, the Earl of Harewood, Earl Fitzwilliam, Edward Baines, and William Rookes Crompton Stansfield about the campaign in Parliament.

1649. NINIAN EDMONSTON PAPERS, 1835-1864. 12 items. Waynesville (Haywood County), N.C.

Family letters of the Edmonstons, who migrated from the vicinity of Waynesville, North Carolina, to Dubois County, Indiana, and to Vandalia, Illinois; and Civil War letters of Benjamin and Basil B. Edmonston, sons of Ninian Edmonston, who had remained in North Carolina and joined the Confederate forces.

1650. SIR HERBERT BENJAMIN EDWARDES PAPERS, 1852. 1 item. London, England.

Letter from Edwardes concerning his book, A Year on the Punjab Frontier, and including comment on the war in Burma.

1651. AUGUSTUS F. EDWARDS PAPERS, 1846-1860. 4 items. Darlington (Darlington County), S.C.

Personal letters of a lawyer of Darlington, South Carolina, and one letter from his sister, a student at the Misses Bates' School in Charleston, South Carolina.

1652. CHARITY EDWARDS PAPERS, 1816 (1839-1879). 11 items. Greene County, N.C.

Personal letters from Salem, North Carolina, where Charity Edwards was in school, and from Columbus, Mississippi, where she later lived.

1653. FREDERICK COMMINS EDWARDS PAPERS, 1883-1945. 213 items and 79 vols. DeLand (Volusia County), Fla.

The principal part of this collection is made up of the journals kept by Frederick C. Edwards between 1884 and 1945 reflecting Edwards's career as an Episcopal minister and his study of psychical phenomena, especially life after death. They contain letters, sermons, nature essays, book orders, and some clippings and financial records with numerous entries for 1933-1935 commenting on Franklin Roosevelt, the New Deal, and the effects of the Depression on the people Edwards saw and knew; and a considerable amount of material concerning Edwards's interest in spiritualism and psychical research, including mention of sittings with various mediums and a few transcriptions of these sittings. The unbound letters are those of Edwards's son, Frederick Trevenen Edwards, describing his experiences in World War I. There is a typed copy of these letters emended by Edwards, and they were published in 1954 by Elizabeth Satterthwait. The collection also contains assorted volumes and notebooks including Trevenen Edwards's poetry and prose and Frederick Edwards's nature poems.

1654. GEORGE T. EDWARDS PAPERS, 1852. 1 item. Russellville (Logan County), Ky.

Letter to Edwards in which the writer discusses his debts and poverty, his prospects for obtaining a government loan, and the illness of Henry Clay.

1655. HARRY P. EDWARDS PAPERS, 1870-1977. 293 items. New Bern (Craven County), N.C.

Papers of a railroad executive on short-line railroads in North Carolina, Florida, and Alabama and a designer and manufacturer of gasoline powered railway passenger cars. The collection is made up of photographs, clippings, printed matter, and a small number of letters relating to Edwards's career with the Atlantic and Western Railroad, the Atlanta and St. Andrews Bay Railroad, the Atlantic and East Carolina Railroad, and the Edwards Railway Motor Car Company. The photographs are mainly of personnel, rolling stock, and engines of the various companies, and printed material includes catalogs, circulars, statistics, and maps.

1656. JOHN EDWARDS, SR., PAPERS, 1811-1877. 8 items. Lincoln County, N.C.

Collection consists principally of deeds and indentures for land in North Carolina.

1657. LEVI EDWARDS PAPERS, 1830 (1860-1874) 1889. 53 items. Onslow County, N.C.

Miscellaneous correspondence.

1658. R. P. EDWARDS ACCOUNT BOOK, 1852-1875. 1 vol. (106 pp.) Catawba (Catawba County), N.C.

Sawmill accounts.

1659. WELDON NATHANIEL EDWARDS PAPERS, 1800-1870. 21 items. Ridgeway (Warren County), N.C.

Scattered correspondence and papers of Edwards concerning his entrance into politics, the Civil War, Reconstruction, and the Democratic Party.

1660. WILLIAM GREY EGERTON PAPERS, (1888-1917) 1966. 12 items and 22 vols. Macon (Warren County), N.C.

Records for a general store operated by two generations of the Egerton family. The collection contains a daybook for the store at Macon, North Carolina, 1888-1889; an incomplete series of daybooks and ledgers for the Macon store, 1904-1912; two ledgers of William G. Egerton, 1910-1917; an account book for a cotton gin, 1906-1913; and miscellaneous letters and papers including the reminiscences of Mary Egerton (Thornton) Lawrence, 1966, concerning the store.

1661. ROBERT LAWRENCE EICHELBERGER PAPERS, 1910-1962. 19,007 items and 173 vols. Asheville (Buncombe County), N.C.

Letters and papers of an officer in the United States Army who served in the Siberian Expedition, 1918-1920, held high command during World War II, and had direct command of United States occupation forces in Japan. The collection contains a small general correspondence series, 1872-1941, including a set of letters written while Eichelberger was a student at the United States Military Academy, 1905; official and professional correspondence, 1922-1929, and 1942-1949, made up of a portion of the letters to and from Eichelberger in his various military posts; a personal correspondence series containing letters to his wife, family, and friends, 1942-1949, including letters from a number of Japanese concerning Eichelberger's part in the occupation, 1948; a personal and official correspondence series, 1950-1962; letters between Eichelberger and his literary agent, 1946; material dealing with military intelligence in the Philippine Department, 1920-1921; letters concerning the review board of the Asheville Chamber of Commerce, 1955-1958; and papers concerning Eichelberger's work on the North Carolina Ports Authority, 1957-1960. The collection also contains Eichelberger's personal military service records; papers, 1918-1924, from the Siberian Expedition, including letters, reports, miscellaneous papers, and maps, dealing for the most part with military intelligence, and intelligence summaries covering the years 1918-1920; a large number of papers from the Second World War includes histories of the Americal Division and the 32nd Infantry Division; reports on the activation of the 77th Division, 1942; reports on operations which Eichelberger commanded, including Buna-Sanananda, 1942-1943, Hollandia, 1944, Biak, 1944, Leyte-Samar, 1944, Mindoro-Marinduque, 1944, Panay-Negros and Cebu, 1945, Palawan, Zamboanga, and Jolo, 1945, and papers relating to planning for the invasion of Japan; training directives and field orders for the Eighth Army, 1944-1945; and maps of the Philippine Islands. There are many items relating to the occupation of Japan including reports on the economy, education, and public health and welfare; army monthly summaries; and summations of military activities and non-military activities. The collection contains Eichelberger's diaries, 1918-1961; dictated memoranda on many aspects of his career, either typed or in shorthand; speeches and statements, 1930-1961; press releases and clippings; scrapbooks; and memorabilia. There are 25 photograph albums depicting Eichelberger's career and a large number of unmounted photographs; copies of various editions of the United States Military Academy yearbook, The Howitzer; a history of the 8th Army; several films from the period of the occupation of Japan showing Eichelberger's residence, military reviews, and Japanese customs; and recordings of interviews with Eichelberger in 1945, 1949, and 1952, and addresses by Eichelberger in 1946, 1947, 1948, and other years.

1662. ALBERT EINSTEIN PAPERS, ca. 1948. 1 item. Princeton (Mercer County), N.J.

Letter of Einstein written as chairman of the Emergency Committee of Atomic Scientists.

1663. JAMES ADAMS EKIN PAPERS, 1862-1883. 48 items and 4 vols. Pittsburgh (Allegheny County), Pa.

Letters concerning Ekin's service in the Quartermaster Corps of the Union Army in the Civil War; scattered items relating to a bill before the United States Senate in 1882 requiring Army officers to retire at age sixty-two; and telegrams concerning the shooting of President Garfield.

1664. SAMUEL ELBERT PAPERS, 1769-1788. 42 items and 1 vol. Savannah, Georgia.

Personal and legal papers including land deeds; certificates for land bounties; an inventory of the estate of Peter Stedler, 1772; and a letter from Leonard Marbury, 1779, discussing the British defeat at Bryan Creek Bridge, Georgia. Also an account book kept by Elbert from 1776 to 1788 which includes accounts of the 2nd Battalion of the State of Georgia, 1776-1777, plantation records, and Elbert's personal accounts.

1665. JOHN ADAMS ELDER PAPERS, 1837-1910. 127 items. Fredericksburg (Spotsylvania County), Va.

Letters to John Adams Elder from John Minor, a Fredericksburg patron, commenting in detail on the sketches which Elder sent back from Düsseldorf, Germany, where he was studying drawing; Civil War letters to Maggie Elder from Confederate soldiers; correspondence with William Wilson Corcoran concerning Elder's commission to paint portraits of Thomas J. Jackson and Robert E. Lee, 1875-1876; official reports of the battle of the Little Big Horn and letters relative to Elder's painting "Custer's Last Charge," 1876-1877; letters from publishers in connection with the reproduction of Elder's works; and correspondence with Caspar Buberl about the creation of the bronze monument, "Appomattox."

1666. JOHN D. ELDER ACCOUNT BOOKS, 1848-1860. 3 vols. Fredericksburg (Spotsylvania County), Va.

Records of a bootmaker.

1667. AUGUSTUS CHRISTIAN GEORGE ELHOLM PAPERS, 1793-1794. 11 items. Washington (Wilkes County), Ga.

Letters of Elholm, apparently adjutant general of militia, dealing with rations, arms, and the problems of frontier defense.

1668. CHARLES WILLIAM ELIOT PAPERS, 1884-1910. 3 items. Cambridge (Middlesex County), Mass.

Miscellaneous correspondence.

1669. BENEVOLENT AND PROTECTIVE ORDER OF ELKS, DURHAM, NORTH CAROLINA, LODGE 568, PAPERS, 1900-1912. 3 vols. Durham, N.C.

Contains question books, 1900-1905, 1905-1912, including the names, ages, and occupations of local residents, and a time dimit book, 1903-1911, containing forms for permission to resign in good standing.

1670. ALFRED WASHINGTON ELLET PAPERS, 1759-1870. 135 items and 1 vol. Bunker Hill (Macoupin County), Ill.

Early papers include an indenture and a record of the marriage ceremony of Hannah Erwin and Israel Israel. The major portion of the collection is made up of the letters of Mary Ellet to her sons Alfred Ellet and Edward Carpenter Ellet, for the most part concerning family matters and local business. Also contains correspondence concerning the management of a plantation in Mississippi after the Civil War, and sketches of the lives and military careers of Charles Ellet, Jr., and Alfred W. Ellet including an account of Charles Ellet's work in the development of the steam ram and descriptions of the action of the ram fleet in several important battles of the Civil War. There is one volume of genealogical material on the Lloyd and Carpenter families.

1671. WILLIAM ELLETT ARITHMETIC, 1761. 1 vol. [King William County?], Va.

Book of problems and rules.

1672. L. S. ELLINGTON PAPERS, 1866-1868. 2 items. Griffin (Spalding County), Ga.

Letters of a Radical Republican during Reconstruction in Georgia. Describes activities of the Ku Klux Klan.

1673. N. DANE ELLINGWOOD PAPERS, 1838-1843. 14 items. New York, N.Y.

Routine business items.

1674. GILBERT ELLIOT, FIRST EARL OF MINTO, PAPERS, 1793-1807. 3 items. Minto House, Roxburghshire, Scotland.

Miscellaneous letters including a long letter, 1793, explaining the British withdrawal from Toulon.

1675. SIR HENRY MIERS ELLIOT PAPERS, 1827-1858. 73 items. Calcutta, India.

Letters, 1840-1853, from Elliot to his son who was attending several preparatory schools in England, containing comments on the Winchester School and Elliot's reflections on his own student days there. Papers dealing with Indian affairs include documents about Elliot's education for Indian service, 1827-1828; items concerning his appointments and assignments; papers pertaining to revenue department operations, 1834-1835; and varied material dealing with Indian administration.

1676. BENJAMIN ELLIOTT, SR., ADDRESSES, 1813-1861. 1 vol. (150 pp.) Charleston, S.C.

Addresses by Benjamin Elliott, Sr., before the Literary and Philosophical Society of Charleston, South Carolina, 1815, and for the 4th of July, 1817. Also, one or two addresses by his son, Benjamin Elliott, Jr.

1677. BENJAMIN P. ELLIOTT PAPERS, 1805-1886. 179 items. New Salem (Randolph County), N.C.

Letters covering a complete generation of the Elliott family and relating to the founding of Trinity College (now Duke University); Braxton Craven's publication, the Southern Index; gold mining in North Carolina; the Civil War; Reconstruction; economic growth of North Carolina; and state politics.

1678. JOHN ELLIOTT PAPERS, 1821. 1 item. Washington, D.C.

A letter from Elliott, United States senator from Georgia, discussing a bill on Indian affairs.

1679. STEPHEN ELLIOTT PAPERS, 1808-1863. 115 items. Hertford (Perquimans County), N.C.

Family and business papers of a merchant in Norfolk, Virginia.

1680. THOMAS J. ELLIOTT PAPERS, 1862-1864. 38 items. Chesterfield County, Va.

Family and Civil War letters of a Confederate soldier, giving brief accounts of the battles of Second Manassas, Drewry's Bluff, and Harper's Ferry, all in 1862.

1681. THOMAS P. ELLIOTT PAPERS, 1834-1872. 15 items. Northampton County, N.C.

Personal letters of Thomas P. Elliott, with descriptions of a train ride in 1834, a trip to the Middle West, and school life at Westtown School, near Philadelphia, Pennsylvania.

1682. THOMAS RHETT SMITH ELLIOTT PAPERS, 1785-1891. 108 items. Beaufort (Beaufort County), and Charleston, S.C.

Family correspondence of a rice planter and operator of several plantations before and after the Civil War in the Beaufort and Charleston areas, revealing attitudes and problems of Southerners during and after the Civil War. Included also are deeds, 1785 and 1802, recording the transfer of land in South Carolina to William Skirving, and letters of Guerard and William Heyward while prisoners on Johnson's Island, Ohio.

1683. H. ELLIS PAPERS, 1861. 1 item. Palmyra (Marion County), Mo.

Letter showing sentiment in Palmyra, Missouri, at the outbreak of the Civil War.

1684. HENRY ELLIS PAPERS, 1757-1760. 8 items. Savannah, Ga.

Routine documents signed by Ellis as governor of Georgia.

1685. JAMES E. ELLIS PAPERS, 1935. 3 items. Santa Maria, Rio Grande do Sul, Brazil.

Letter from Ellis, executive secretary of the Methodist Church of Brazil, containing information about his church.

1686. JEREMIAH B. ELLIS PAPERS, 1844-1888. 103 items and 1 vol. Fulton (Davie County), N.C.

Business papers of Ellis and other members of the Ellis family, including a ledger from a general store, 1852-1888, and a school record from Shady Grove, North Carolina, 1844, giving pupils, attendance, and some grades.

1687. JOHN WILLIS ELLIS PAPERS, 1852-1860. 3 items. Raleigh (Wake County), N.C.

The collection includes a letter from Ellis, Governor of North Carolina, to John Letcher, Governor of Virginia, concerning a proposal to resurvey the Virginia-North Carolina border and a letter concerning a plan to divert all Southern trade to the port of Baltimore, Maryland.

1688. LEMUEL ELLIS PAPERS, 1852-1889. 55 items and 2 vols. Chatham County, N.C.

Letters and business papers of a general merchant and justice of the peace containing correspondence with brothers in Fayetteville, North Carolina, and Darlington, South Carolina, in the 1850s; ledgers of a general store, 1857-1863; court records, warrants, orders, and case accounts in the 1870s and 1880.

1689. ROBERT WILLIAM ELLISTON PAPERS, 1815. 1 item. London, England.

Personal letter to Robert W. Elliston's wife, Elizabeth (Rundall) Elliston.

1690. HENRY LEAVITT ELLSWORTH PAPERS, 1843. 1 item. Washington, D.C.

A true copy of the patent office record of a patent on cooking stoves.

1691. ELMORE INSURANCE COMPANY CASHBOOK, 1860-1867. 1 vol. (402 pp.) Charleston, S.C.

Cashbook of a fire and marine insurance company, of which W. M. Martin was president and Joseph Whilden secretary.

1692. GEORGE W. ELSEY PAPERS, 1909-1922. 1 vol. (52 pp.) Ravenel, S.C.

Criminal docket of a justice of the peace.

1693. RICHARD ELWARD PAPERS, 1845-1860. 21 items and 2 vols. Natchez (Adams County), Miss.

Daybook of a printer, stationer, bookbinder, and bookseller, 1845-1847; subscription book, 1848-1852, for Elward's newspaper, the Mississippi Free Trader, including business letters and receipts concerning the newspaper and records relating to Elward's duties as postmaster of Natchez.

1694. FREDERICK DAVID ELY PAPERS, 1857-1887. 4 items. Boston, Mass.

Personal and business letters.

1695. ELY AND WALKER DRY GOODS COMPANY PAPERS, 1883-1960. 31 items and 14 vols. Saint Louis, Mo.

Records of a firm of textile manufacturers and distributors, containing financial statements, 1884-1953; minutes of the meetings of the stockholders and of the board of directors, 1883-1954; general ledgers, 1906-1920, 1938-1953, 1959-1960; factory ledgers, 1931-1959; capital assets and depreciation book, 1959-1960; and documents concerning federal tax matters, 1918-1926.

1696. DAVID EMANUEL PAPERS, 1786, 1805. 2 items. Burke County, Ga.

A receipt for rations for a small company of troops, 1786, and an affidavit of 1805 describing an encounter between Tories and Continental troops near James Butler's plantation in lower Georgia in 1780.

1697. J. MILTON EMERSON JOURNAL, 1841-1842. 1 vol. (127 pp.) Belhaven (Accomack County), Va.

Journal of a teacher who went from New Hampshire to Virginia, by way of New York City and Philadelphia, to take a position at Matchapungo Academy. Contains descriptions of his trip south by water and rail; social customs and religious life on the Eastern Shore of Virginia; treatment of slaves; and the appearance of villages in Virginia. Also describes a visit to Washington, D.C., in 1842 including a view of John Quincy Adams in the House of Representatives and a visit with President Tyler.

1698. RALPH WALDO EMERSON PAPERS, 1844-1877. 13 items. Concord (Middlesex County), Mass.

Miscellaneous items including two original poems, "No Fate Save the Victim's Fault Is Low," 1877, and "To the Humble-bee."

1699. EDWIN EMERY PAPERS, 1862-1875. 36 items. Sanford (York County), Me., and Southbridge and Whitinsville (Worcester County), Mass.

Letters of Emery while he was a soldier in the Union Army and later as a teacher. Includes information on camp life, especially on the moral and religious attitudes of the soldiers; the battle of Spotsylvania Court House; and school curricula, discipline, and teaching methods.

1700. JOSE R. EMERY PAPERS, 1862, 1864. 2 items. Charleston, S.C.

Letters describing life in Charleston while the city was under seige.

1701. ARTHUR EMMERSON PAPERS, 1793-1906. 318 items and 2 vols. Portsmouth (Norfolk County), Va.

Personal and business papers of Arthur Emmerson and his family concerning the sale of timber to the U.S. Navy, 1830s; the administration of schools in Franklin County, North Carolina; the operations of the Confederate commissary department in western Virginia; and life in Portsmouth, Virginia, during the occupation by Federal troops, 1864. Also contains a volume concerning Trinity Episcopal Church in Portsmouth; and a volume of John Emmerson's business records from the 1860s.

1702. WILLIAM HELMSLEY EMORY PAPERS, 1847-1851. 2 items. Washington, D.C.

Correspondence, including a letter, 1851, from Charles C. Perry discussing a scientific project he was undertaking with J. L. R. Agassiz, Asa Gray, and Joseph LeConte.

1703. EMORY COLLEGE PAPERS, 1839-1849. 4 items. Oxford (Newton County), Ga.

Letters expressing appreciation for having been invited to become honorary members of the Few Society of Emory College.

1704. SUSAN W. EMPIE PAPERS, 1855. 2 items. Richmond, Va.

Personal letters from Adam Empie.

1705.  WILLIAM R. ENECKS PAPERS,
       1800-1865.  6 items.
       Screven County, Ga.

Letters and papers of a cotton farmer concerning the cotton and slave market in Savannah; the wounding of his son in the battle of Atlanta; and contracts with freedmen for farming, 1865.

1706.  ADOLPH ENENKL PAPERS, 1885.
       3 items and 1 vol.  Austria.

A journal of artillery school exercises.

1707.  FLORA D. ENGLAND PAPERS,
       1955-1956.  3 items.
       Marion (Perry County), Ala.

Typescripts of three genealogies prepared by Flora England on the Gayle family and other families in Perry County and central Alabama.

1708.  SAMUEL ENGLE RECEIPTS,
       1823-1833.  7 items.  Jefferson County, West Virginia.

Receipts and accounts signed or made out to Samuel Engle, landowner and planter.

1709.  WILLIAM ENGLES PAPERS, 1853-1883.
       12 items.  Harpers Ferry
       (Jefferson County), W. Va.

Correspondence and papers of a lumber dealer concerning militia, settlement of debts, and the Union occupation of Beaufort, South Carolina.

1710.  ENTERPRISE STREET RAILROAD COMPANY
       MINUTES, 1888-1890.  1 vol.
       (51 pp.)  Savannah, Ga.

Copies of act of incorporation, minutes, and clippings of the Enterprise Street Railroad Company.

1711.  JOSEPH ENTLER PAPERS, 1823-1878.
       130 items and 5 vols.
       Shepherdstown (Jefferson County), W. Va.

Invoices, bills, receipts, ledgers and daybooks of a grocer and general merchant. Includes correspondence from Confederate prisoners at Union prisons at Point Lookout, Maryland, and at Fort Delaware, Delaware.

1712.  EPISCOPAL CHURCH FEMALE MITE SOCIETY
       CONSTITUTION, 1823-1882.  1 vol.
       (88 pp.) Leesburg (Loudoun County), Va.

Constitution of a mite society in a Protestant Episcopal Church and a list of contributors.

1713.  MISS J. C. R. EPPES NOTEBOOK,
       ca. 1880.  1 vol. (500 pp.)
       Orlando, Fla.

Contains notes on Florida and many law notes of a member of the Eppes family, probably early 19th century.

1714.  JOHN WAYLES EPPES PAPERS,
       1807-1819.  15 items.
       "Millbrook," Buckingham County, Va.

Personal letters from John Wayles Eppes (1773-1823), nephew and son-in-law of Thomas Jefferson, member of Virginia House of Delegates, 1801-1803, member of United States Congress, 1803-1811, 1813-1817, and United States senator, 1817-1819, chiefly to Francis Eppes (b. 1801), his son by his first wife, Maria (Jefferson) Eppes (1778-1804), written while he was in preparatory school near Lynchburg and at the University of Virginia, Charlottesville.  Parental letters discuss the development of character and the value of the study of history.  In the set are two letters, November, 1814, from John Wayles Eppes to Alexander James Dallas, secretary of the treasury, in which Eppes expresses his fears that national credit and confidence might be impaired by a statement that "national credit no longer existed" which Dallas had made before a congressional committee on the Bank question.  Included also is a deed, 1817, from John Wayles Eppes to Thomas Jefferson Randolph.

1715.  J. D. EPPS DIARY, 1886.
       1 vol. (190 pp.)  Woodruff
       (Spartanburg County), S.C.

Diary of a storekeeper dealing with local news.

1716.  DAVID STEUART ERSKINE, ELEVENTH
       EARL OF BUCHAN, PAPERS,
       1780-1806.  2 items.  Dryburgh, Berwickshire, Scotland.

Exchange with the Fourth Earl of Selkirk concerning the method of selecting Scottish representative peers.

1717.  THOMAS ERSKINE, FIRST BARON
       ERSKINE, PAPERS, 1806.  2 items.
       London, England.

Miscellaneous letters related to Erskine's service as Lord Chancellor.

1718.  JAMES R. ERVIN, SR., PAPERS,
       1850-1864.  3 items.
       Warm Springs (Bath County), Va.

Two letters from Ervin's son while he was a student at the Virginia Military Institute, 1850-1851, and one while he was a prisoner of war at Johnson's Island, Sandusky, Ohio, 1864.

1719. ERWIN MILLS RECORDS, 1907, 1916. 1 vol. (697 pp.) Durham, N.C.

Inventories of the Cooleemee (North Carolina) Plant.

1720. THOMAS P. ESKRIDGE AND JOHN B. ESKRIDGE PAPERS, 1853-1861. 5 items and 1 vol. Staunton (Augusta County), Va.

Ledger, 1854, of an apothecary, and scattered receipts.

1721. HENRI ESTIENNE MANUSCRIPT, 1575. 1 vol. (72 pp.)

Italian translation of Discovrs merveillevx de la vie, actions & déportemens de Catherine de Medicis. . . (1574). The authorship of this work is uncertain, but it has been attributed to Estienne.

1722. ESTRAY PAPERS, 1901-1918. 34 items. Noxubee County, Miss.

County ranger's official record of strayed cattle.

1723. ESTRAY BOOK AND WOLF SCALP CERTIFICATES, 1848. 1 vol. McHenry County, Ill.

Justices' and constables' records of strayed cattle and bounties paid for wolf scalps.

1724. MARY SUE ETHRIDGE PAPERS, 1889-1900. 37 items. Sunbury (Gates County), N.C.

Family correspondence with occasional references to local politics, social life and customs, and religion.

1725. EUPHRADIAN ACADEMY RECORD BOOK, 1824-1836. 1 vol. Rockingham (Richmond County), N.C.

Regulations of the Euphradian Academy, record of board meetings, commencement accounts, and other information.

1726. JAMES BIDDLE EUSTIS PAPERS, 1865-1886. 8 items. New Orleans, La.

Chiefly dispatches from James B. Eustis while he was serving as assistant adjutant general on General Joseph E. Johnston's staff. They are concerned with the difficulties of obtaining supplies and transportation in the Confederate Army during the last months of the war, including the feasibility of transferring rails from one railroad line to another.

1727. CLEMENT ANSELM EVANS PAPERS, 1880-1911. 3 items. Atlanta, Ga.

Letters of Evans, former Confederate general and commander-in-chief of the United Confederate Veterans concerning business and a United Confederate Veterans reunion.

1728. ELIZA CAROLINE (WASHINGTON) EVANS PAPERS, 1842-1874. 15 items. Goldsboro (Wayne County), N.C.

The collection is made up of family correspondence, including a letter, 1842, commenting on economic conditions and describing a ball in Washington, D.C., and a temperance meeting; a letter, 1842, describing a lecture by James Pollard Espy and commenting at length on his meteorological theories.

1729. GEORGE K. EVANS PAPERS, 1862-1863. 5 items. Farmville (Prince Edward County), Va.

Letters from a Confederate private describing his picket duties, other camp activities, and expressing concern regarding his farming operations.

1730. HARRIET L. (SCOLLAY) EVANS MEMORANDUM BOOK, 1864-1899. 1 vol. (240 pp.) Middleway (Jefferson County), W. Va.

This notebook was originally the property of John Joseph Hickey and came into the possession of Harriet Evans who copied into it excerpts from various writers and notes on domestic matters. Includes an account of the burning of Harriet Evans's home by a Union soldier, 1864.

1731. JOHN B. EVANS PAPERS, 1862-1865. 97 items. Butts County, Ga.

Correspondence of a lieutenant in the 53d Georgia Regiment, describing in detail his experiences in the army and commenting on the epidemic of measles in 1862. Included also are letters from Evans's wife giving accounts of conditions at home.

1732. JOSEPH R. EVANS PAPERS, 1822-1835. 11 items. Philadelphia, Pa.

Letters to a merchant and shipper concerning the shipment of turpentine and lumber from New York and Boston.

1733. THOMAS EVANS PAPERS, ca. 1827. 4 items. Philadelphia, Pa.

A letter, ca. 1827, to Thomas Evans, a Philadelphia druggist and prominent Quaker minister and editor, copies of scattered entries from the minutes of Morning Meetings of the Society of Friends in London, 1692-1709, concerning the reading and publication of works by Stephen Crisp, Thomas Ellwood,

George Fox, William Penn, and George Whitehead. Among those who attended the meetings and assisted with the readings were Thomas Lower, Charles Marshall, William Mead, Ambrose Rigg, John Tomkins, and Joseph Wyeth.

1734. WILLIAM MAXWELL EVARTS PAPERS, 1878-1882. 4 items. Washington, D.C.

Letters to Evarts as United States secretary of state dealing with routine official and personal business, including a letter, 1880, requesting Evarts to expedite negotiations of the International Copyright Treaty signed by numerous prominent American writers.

1735. SALLIE EVE DIARY, 1772-1773. 1 vol. (32 pp.) Philadelphia, Pa.

Comments in the diary of a young girl on the weather, family matters, and excursions to nearby places.

1736. RICHARD EVERARD PAPERS, 1727. 1 item. Edenton (Chowan County), N.C.

Letter of Everard, the last proprietary governor of North Carolina, to Thomas Amory, prominent Boston merchant, discussing Indian troubles and ordering sugar and window glass.

1737. EDWARD EVERETT PAPERS, 1842-1861. 5 items. Boston, Mass.

Routine correspondence including a letter, 1860, to a Mrs. Eve in Augusta, Georgia, reflecting his interest in the preservation of Mount Vernon and a letter, 1860, discussing his recent publication, The Mount Vernon Papers.

1738. LILLIE (MOORE) EVERETT PAPERS, 1890-1948. 275 items and 15 vols. Rockingham (Richmond County), N.C.

Correspondence and papers of Lillie (Moore) Everett concerning the history of various religious groups in Richmond County, especially Methodists. The correspondence, 1924-1942, contains information on various ministers, churches, and local history. There is a copy of Everett's "Methodism in Richmond County and Rockingham, 1786-1941," in which she discusses John Wesley and other early leaders of Methodism; camp meetings; the Pee Dee and Piedmont circuits; the Woman's Missionary Society; and Negro Methodism. There is a miscellaneous collection of clippings and a number of volumes containing Everett's notes on Methodism and church history and material relating to the Woman's Missionary Society.

1739. PATIENCE EVERETT PAPERS, 1861-1864. 6 items. Haynesville, Ga.

Correspondence concerning the scarcity of food during the Civil War and Andersonville Military Prison.

1740. BENJAMIN STODDERT EWELL AND RICHARD STODDERT EWELL PAPERS, 1862-1865. 13 items and 1 vol. Richmond, Va.

Personal and Civil War correspondence of Benjamin Stoddert Ewell (1810-1894), including a letter to the Richmond Whig in vindication of the burning of Richmond by his brother in 1865. The papers of Richard Stoddert Ewell (1817-1872), general in the Confederate Army, include a letter concerning the defenses of Richmond in 1864; a voucher for rations for his staff; a letter, 1862, from Thomas J. Jackson to Ewell commenting on the battle of Cedar Mountain; a note, 1863, concerning the beginning of the retreat of the Army of Northern Virginia from Carlisle, Pennsylvania, toward Gettysburg, Pennsylvania; and a letter book giving an interesting account of the maneuvers of the Army of Northern Virginia, especially the attacks on the north side of the James River, September 29, 1864.

1741. JOHN S. EWELL PAPERS, 1861. 5 items. Oakland (Colorado County), Tex.

Letters giving details of a journey made by John S. Ewell and his nine slaves from Lynchburg, Virginia, to New Orleans, Louisiana, with comments on the latter city; included also are lengthy comments on land, crops, and prices in Texas, where Ewell arrived in February, 1861.

1742. ANDREW EWING PAPERS, 1850. 1 item. Washington, D.C.

Letter from Ewing, member of Congress from Tennessee, describing in detail the political maneuverings in the House and Senate over the Compromise of 1850.

1743. THOMAS EWING, SR., PAPERS, 1833-1849. 3 items. Lancaster (Fairfield County), Ohio.

Miscellaneous correspondence, including a letter, 1849, to Robert H. Williamson concerning the construction of an addition to the Patent Office building.

1744. M. L. F. DIARY, 1840-1841. 1 vol. Somerville (Culpeper County), Va.

Diary of M. L. F., who may have been a Presbyterian minister.

1745. JOHN CHRISTOPHER FABER PAPERS, 1836-1857. 6 items. Spartanburg (Spartanburg County), S.C.

Personal correspondence of John C. Faber, a physician, containing information on social customs and economic conditions of plantation owners and businessmen. Included are references to the Seminole War; difficulties between the United States and France, 1836; cotton crops, 1849; and prices for land and slaves in Charleston, 1857.

1746. C. [WILLIAM?] FACKLER PAPERS, 1861-1863. 5 items. Huntsville (Madison County), Ala.

Typed copies of letters of the Fackler family, principally discussing personal matters. Included are letters by C. W. Fackler, a Confederate soldier in Tennessee, containing comments on Generals Braxton Bragg, Nathan B. Forrest, and Joseph E. Johnston.

1747. EDWIN MILTON FAIRCHILD PAPERS, 1866-1922. 122 items. Baltimore, Md.

Papers of Edwin Milton Fairchild (1865-1939), American educationist, and of his wife, Mary Salome (Cutler) Fairchild (1855-1921), library lecturer. The majority of the letters, 1897-1915, concern the creation and work of the National Institute for Moral Education, and were either by or to Milton Fairchild and Bernard Nadal Baker, a Baltimore businessman interested in moral education. Correspondents include magazine publishers, college presidents, school principals, educational societies, and patrons of the Institute. The papers of Mary Fairchild include her high school compositions, 1866-1870; notes of congratulations on her wedding, 1897; and letters from librarians in New York and Massachusetts.

1748. WILLIAM TURNER FAIRCLOTH PAPERS, 1841-1887. 10 items and 2 vols. Goldsboro (Wayne County), N.C.

College orations, class notes, legal papers, and accounts of William Faircloth (1829-1900), a North Carolina jurist, educated at Wake Forest College. Included also is a diary of a journey made in 1853 from Macon, North Carolina, to New England, describing the country traversed, the Crystal Palace, and P. T. Barnum's show in New York.

1749. FRANKLIN WILLIAM FAIREY PAPERS, 1837 (1862-1865) 1880. 22 items and 6 vols. Branchville (Orangeburg County), S.C.

Papers of F. W. Fairey, planter and operator of a grist mill, including receipts for payment of monetary taxes to the Confederate government, a notice concerning impressment of surplus farm products, and a petition for his exemption from military service in order to operate the mill. The account books and ledgers relate to farming, milling, the sawmill business, and magistrate's court.

1750. THOMAS FAIRFAX, SIXTH LORD FAIRFAX OF CAMERON, PAPERS, 1748, 1766. 2 items. Northern Neck, Va.

Deeds signed by the sixth Lord Fairfax of Cameron (1693-1781), proprietor of the Northern Neck of Virginia.

1751. SOLOMON WESLEY FAISON PAPERS, 1855-1863. 14 items. Clinton (Sampson County), N.C.

Papers of Solomon Wesley Faison, corporal in the 36th North Carolina Regiment, containing letters from friends at school, 1850s, including a letter, 1856, referring to Wake Forest College; Civil War letters discussing relatives fighting in the Army of Northern Virginia; and a poem, "To the Sampson County Volunteers."

1752. FAISON FAMILY PAPERS, 1719-1857. 22 items. Sampson County, N.C.

Deeds to land acquired by members of the Faison family in Sampson (formerly Duplin County), North Carolina, and Burlington County, New Jersey. Former owners included George Bell, Jr., James Thompson, William Thompson, members of the Watkins (Wadkins) family, and Elias Faison Shaw.

1753. THOMAS FALCONER PAPERS, 1835-1853. 17 items. London, England.

Letters of Thomas Falconer (1805-1882), British country court judge, concerning municipal elections at Bath, Chartist agitation, legal cases, the Bath Grammar School, and personal and family matters.

1754. JOHN FANE, TENTH EARL OF WESTMORLAND, PAPERS, 1777. 2 items. "Apethorpe House," Northamptonshire, England.

Letter from John Charles Villiers to John Fane, Tenth Earl of Westmorland (1759-1841), British official, outlining a reading program for studying French history.

1755. JOHN FANE, ELEVENTH EARL OF WESTMORLAND, PAPERS, 1837-1876. 22 items. London, England.

Papers of John Fane, Eleventh Earl of Westmorland (1784-1859), British army officer and diplomat, concerning diplomatic appointments, the recognition of Louis Napoleon as ruler of France, the government of Austria, the Eastern Question, economic, social and political change in Britain, and personal matters. Correspondents include Lord Aberdeen, Lord Clarendon, Julian Henry Charles Fane, Lord Malmesbury, Lord Palmerston, and Lord Stratford de Redcliffe.

1756. EDMUND FANNING PAPERS, 1796-1808. 11 items. Prince Edward Island, Canada.

Papers of Edmund Fanning (1737-1818), American loyalist, governor of Nova Scotia and of Prince Edward Island, and general in the British Army, pertaining to accounts and vouchers for the garrison of Prince Edward Island Fencibles. Included are references to the Board of Commissioners for Auditing Public Accounts, and personal financial sacrifices during his term of office.

1757. WILLIAM P. FARISH DAYBOOK, 1829-1835. 1 vol. (128 pp.) Albemarle County, Va.

Planting and harvesting records and expenses of a wheat farmer. Included are some poetry and memoranda.

1758. BELMONT MERCER FARLEY PAPERS, 1787-1965. 19,722 items and 44 vols. Washington, D.C.

Professional and personal papers of Belmont Mercer Farley (1891-    ), American educator. Professional papers concern academic freedom, educational television, reading and illiteracy, rural education, attacks on textbooks, federal aid to education, school construction, and strikes. Also discussed are the Ford Foundation, communism, peace and war, the military, and the atomic bomb. There is material related to the National Education Association, of which Farley was Assistant Director of the Division of Publications and later Director of Press and Radio Relations; and a public relations handbook for the schools with which Farley was involved. Also included are Farley's articles and addresses, scripts for the radio program "Our American Schools," 1935-1936, a draft of Our American Public Schools, and a copy of his dissertation. Other material pertains to conventions of various organizations that Farley attended, such as the County and Rural Area Superintendents, the National Association of Public School Adult Educators, and the Association for Higher Education. Personal correspondence consists principally of family letters, with information on public education in Missouri and California, and material on the family genealogy.

1759. FARMER'S ACCOUNT BOOK, 1880-1881. 1 vol. (33 pp.)

Anonymous records kept by a farmer including records of monetary advances made to tenants, and memoranda.

1760. FARMERS' AND EXCHANGE BANK OF CHARLESTON PAPERS, 1860. 1 vol. Charleston, S.C.

Daily record of deposits, withdrawals and charges against depositors, including a daily total of the bank's funds.

1761. FARMERS BANK OF VIRGINIA CHECK STUBS, 1858-1860. 1 vol. Danville (Pittsylvania County), Va.

Drafts and credits, with names of many account holders.

1762. ISAAC T. FARNSWORTH PAPERS, 1827-1841. 19 items. Natchez (Adams County), Miss.

Principally family letters of Isaac T. Farnsworth, businessman and plantation agent, concerning family matters, with references to slavery, trade, Natchez, commodity prices, mosquitoes, yellow fever, Andrew Jackson, the Mississippi flood of 1828, Jackson's war on the Bank of the United States, the fire of 1836 in Natchez, and the panic of 1837.

1763. OREN E. FARR PAPERS, 1859-1892. 74 items. Mill Village (Sullivan County), N.H.

Chiefly the Civil War letters of Oren E. Farr, 16th New Hampshire Volunteers, U.S.A., describing camp life, military duties and engagements in Louisiana, the exchange of prisoners, prices in New Orleans and New York City, health conditions, Fort Buchanan, slaves joining the Union lines, and attempts to raise a sunken boat. The remaining letters are family correspondence.

1764. JACOB FARRABOUGH AND AARON FARRABOUGH PAPERS, (1765-1816) 1878. 32 items. Baltimore County, Md., and Granville County, N.C.

Receipts, promissory notes, and mercantile accounts of Jacob Farrabough of Baltimore County, Maryland, and of Aaron Farrabough, who owned land in Granville County, North Carolina.

1765. FREDERIC WILLIAM FARRAR PAPERS, 1885-1886. 2 items. Canterbury, Kent, England.

Letter (19 pp.) from Cyril Lytton Farrar to Frederic William Farrar (1831-1903), British clergyman and dean of Canterbury, 1893-1903, discussing the political condition of England, the character of the Liberals, and the destruction of the Constitution; and a letter from Martin Farquhar Tupper concerning the contributions of the nonconformists in charitable work for the poor.

1766. MARY FARRAR PAPERS, 1916-1919. 25 items. Dorchester (Norfolk County), Mass.

Principally letters to Mary Farrar from Jennie (Stone) Abrams, concerning personal affairs, Alan Seeger's "I Have a Rendezvous with Death," the Red Cross, the Russian Revolution, World War I, and the return of the Jews to Palestine.

1767. THOMAS J. FARRAR PAPERS, 1856-1894. 28 items. Fluvanna County, Va.

Personal letters of Thomas J. Farrar, assistant principal of Cove Academy, Covesville, Virginia, and Maria L. Megginson, who married about 1868.

1768. EMMA J. FASOLD PAPERS, 1871-1920. 286 items. Sunbury (Northumberland County), Pa.

Personal and family papers of Emma J. Fasold concerning family affairs; a trip to Germany, 1894; Chicago, 1880-1881; Carthage College, Chicago, Illinois, where her brother Philip M. taught, and where her brother-in-law Edward Fry Bartholomew was president, 1884-1888; and Augustana College and Theological Seminary, where E. F. Bartholomew also taught. Miscellaneous papers include cards, invitations, and announcements; financial papers; legal papers; and printed programs.

1769. CHARLES JAMES FAULKNER, SR., PAPERS, 1815-1883. 371 items and 1 vol. Berkeley County, W. Va.

Papers of Charles James Faulkner, Sr. (1806-1884), lawyer, congressman, minister to France, and Confederate soldier, principally concerning political and legal matters. Included are letters discussing the bill to renew the Bank of the United States; the nullification crisis; the presidential election of 1856; Faulkner's duties as minister to France, 1859-1861; his arrest by the Secretary of War and subsequent exchange as a political hostage; West Virginia politics, 1880s; claims of the Baptist Church of Charles Town, West Virginia, against the U. S. government for material used while the church was a U.S. hospital; a report on agriculture in New York, 1838; clippings on slavery; notes and records of the West Virginia Constitutional Convention of 1872; and legal papers pertaining to his law practice.

1770. CHARLES JAMES FAULKNER, JR., PAPERS, 1876-1897. 144 items and 1 vol. Martinsburg (Berkeley County), W. Va.

Predominantly telegrams and letters of condolence to Charles James Faulkner, Jr. (1847-1929), U.S. senator, upon the death of his wife, Sallie (Winn) Faulkner, 1891. Also included are a letter, 1878, from Faulkner to his wife; a program, 1879, of a concert for the benefit of the Martinsburg Light Artillery; and lecture notes, 1866-1867, from the law class of John B. Minor at the University of Virginia.

1771. WILLIAM CUTHBERT FAULKNER PAPERS, 1936-1967. 20 items and 1 vol. Oxford (Lafayette County), Miss.

This collection consists of photocopies of letters between James W. Webb, professor of English at the University of Mississippi, and Arlin Turner, English professor at Duke University, discussing funds for a portrait of Faulkner, and an article on Faulkner in the *Saturday Evening Post*; clippings of articles on Faulkner and of photographs of Faulkner, his family and friends; *Mid-South, the Commercial Appeal Magazine* (April 4, 1965), containing an article on Faulkner; the *Oxford Eagle* (April 22, 1965), a William Faulkner souvenir edition; a photocopy of a program of the Southern Literary Festival held by the University of Mississippi in Faulkner's honor; and *The Falkner Feuds* by Thomas Felix Hickerson (Chapel Hill: 1964).

1772. THOMAS P. FAVROT PAPERS, 1815. 3 items. Camp Mandeville (Saint Tammany Parish), La.

Military orders sent to Thomas P. Favrot, Acting Assistant Adjutant General in the U.S. Army during the War of 1812.

1773. ENOCH FAW DIARY, 1851-1857. 1 vol. (26 pp.) Randolph County, N.C.

Typescript of the diary of Enoch Faw (b. 1835), while attending Normal College, 1851-1856, and while reading law under General A. J. Hansell in Marietta, Georgia, 1856-1857. The diary contains comments on courses and books, expenses, social events, religion, the weather, girl friends, and genealogical data.

1774. HENRY FAWCETT PAPERS, 1864. 1 item. Cambridge, Cambridgeshire, England.

Letter of Henry Fawcett (1833-1884), British statesman and professor of political economy at Cambridge, to the editor of *The Financial Reformer* protesting its statements on his speech concerning taxation.

1775. JOHN NICHOLAS FAZAKERLEY PAPERS, 1809-1851. 70 items. "Burwood Park," Surrey, England.

Principally political correspondence of John Nicholas Fazakerley (1787-1852), British statesman. Among the topics discussed are the war with France; various ministerial changes and their effects on British politics; Catholic Emancipation; the Irish political situation; paper currency; British foreign policy toward Greece and Portugal, 1829; parliamentary reform, 1830-1831; Belgian independence; bastardy laws, 1832; politics in France, 1832; the offer to Fazakerley of the governorship of Canada and the embassy at Brussels, 1835; the Poor Laws, 1837; and the

Corn Laws, 1839. Also included are personal notes and descriptions of travel in Spain; Genoa, Italy; and Geneva, Switzerland.

1776. FEDERAL RESERVE BANK OF ATLANTA RECORDS, 1917-1945. 938 items. Atlanta, Ga.

Materials pertaining to the home front during both world wars. World War I items include posters, cartoons, and anti-German propaganda sheets urging Americans to buy savings bonds. World War II materials consist of ration books and coupons, advertisements for savings bonds, data on Atlanta during the war, clippings and articles on various industries such as rubber, sugar, and shipbuilding, and clippings and government documents on wages and hours.

1777. ABNER FEIMSTER PAPERS, 1799-1873. 6 items and 3 vols. Liberty (Iredell County), N.C.

Routine business, personal and legal papers of a general merchant. Included are two daybooks and a ledger.

1778. PHILIP RICARD FENDALL PAPERS, 1658-1962. 624 items. Alexandria (Arlington County), Va. and Washington, D.C.

Letters and copies of letters of Philip Ricard Fendall (1795-1868), attorney, concerning Whig politics, the reorganization of the National Journal, the writing of a life of Madison, book collecting, the Anti-Masonic Party, the Washington National Monument Society, Columbian College, and Princeton University. Personal letters are generally from his uncle, Richard Bland Lee, and his cousin, Richard Henry Lee, as well as other members of the Lee family. Letters of 1892 discuss the work of the American Colonization Society. Correspondence and documents, 1658-1962, refer to the Fendall family.

1779. E. D. FENNELL PAPERS, 1849-1864. 9 items. Darien (McIntosh County), Ga.

Civil War letters of a Confederate soldier commenting on camp life, food shortages, desertions, elections among the soldiers, and prices of horses, hogs and corn.

1780. [A. W. FENTON?] PAPERS, ca. 1893-1894. 1 item. (82 pp.)

Typed manuscript of a state-by-state account of the secession crisis, entitled "A Retrospect. How the States of the Federal Union, North and South, met the Crisis of 1861," written from a pro-Northern point of view.

1781. JOHN FERGUSON ARITHMETIC MANUSCRIPT, 1805. 1 vol. Mecklenburg County, N.C.

Arithmetic tables, formulas and problems.

1782. SAMUEL WRAGG FERGUSON PAPERS, 1863-1948. 12 items and 1 vol. Greenville (Greenville County), Miss.

Military dispatches of Brigadier General Samuel Wragg Ferguson (1834-1917), C.S.A., concerning troop movements and supplies; and a manuscript (155 pp.) entitled "Memoirs of Samuel Wragg Ferguson," telling of his early life, his years as a cadet at the U.S. Military Academy, his career in the U.S. Army in Kansas and Utah, 1857-1861, and his Civil War experiences.

1783. FERGUSON FAMILY PAPERS, 1874-1900. 5 items and 1 vol. Wake County, N.C.

An account book containing ledger and journal entries, 1874-1875, for a general store and commission business under several owners, and the "Rules and Regulations of Mt. Pleasant Masonic School" in the Kelvin Grove community and some tuition accounts, 1877; photographs of Anderson Ferguson and his family; letters; and the will of Betty Ann Ferguson.

1784. SARAH ELIZA FERREBEE AND AMANDA E. (FERREBEE) WELCH PAPERS, 1832-1921. 143 items. Hampshire County and Mineral County, W. Va.

Family letters of Sarah Eliza Ferrebee (d. 1866), a schoolteacher, and Amanda E. (Ferrebee) Welch, probably her sister, containing some information on the prices of agricultural products. Included are invitations and announcements, poetry, legal papers, financial papers, an agreement by Lucretia (Coffin) Mott to teach in a common school, and a program listing the Confederate veterans of Hampshire County who were given Crosses of Honor by the United Daughters of the Confederacy.

1785. WILLIAM FERREL PAPERS, 1857-1899. 208 items. Washington, D.C.

Papers of William Ferrel (1819-1891), American meteorologist, concerning his career with the Coast and Geodetic Survey and the Signal Office. Included are letters from eminent American and European scientists concerning meteorological subjects; copies of Ferrel's writings and publications; photographs of an eclipse of the sun, 1860, and of several scientists; an account of Bethany College, Lancaster, Pennsylvania, Ferrel's alma mater; and bills and receipts.

1786.  FERRIDAY FAMILY PAPERS,
       1864-1896. 1 vol. Adams and
       Claiborne Counties, Miss., and
       Easton (Northampton County), Pa.

   A daybook, 1864-1867, containing the accounts of various members of the Ferriday family, including accounts of a plantation at or near Natchez, Mississippi, land in Iowa and Wisconsin, investments, and personal expenses; and agricultural accounts, 1895-1896, of Pendleton Ferriday, containing accounts for laborers or tenants.

1787.  WILLIAM PITT FESSENDEN PAPERS,
       1862-1869. 12 items.
       Portland (Cumberland County), Me.

   Letters to William Pitt Fessenden (1806-1869), lawyer, politician, U.S. senator, and financier, concerning political matters and foreign affairs. Letters relate to the Negro suffrage provision in the Virginia Constitution of 1868; Fessenden's vote during impeachment proceedings against Andrew Johnson; the "Copperheads" in Vermont and Maine; U.S. relations with Belgium, Greece, and Turkey; and King Leopold I.

1788.  LEVI A. FESTERMAN PAPERS, 1861.
       1 item. Rowan County, N.C.

   Letter of a Confederate soldier describing the first battle of Manassas and the casualties there.

1789.  WILLIAM FEW PAPERS, 1779-1809.
       17 items. New York and Georgia.

   Letters of William Few (1748-1828), statesman, Revolutionary soldier, and banker, concerning the Creek Indians in Georgia, the location of the national capital, and routine business matters; letters from Benjamin Few concerning militia activities during the Revolutionary War and the Creeks; and a summons, an indenture, and a bill of sale for seventy slaves, of Ignatius Few.

1790.  JOHN FICKLEN PAPERS, 1844-1849.
       12 items. Falmouth (Stafford
       County), Va.

   Personal letters of John Ficklen to his future wife, Sally A. Slaughter, including a description of a journey from Fredericksburg, Virginia, to Halifax.

1791.  JOHN W. FIELD PAPERS, 1824
       (1829-1923) 1933. 504 items.
       Chincoteague (Accomack County),
       Va.

   Correspondence and legal papers of the allied Field and McMaster families, including letters from William S. McMaster to his sister, Elizabeth Ann, describing the Ohio region, 1820s; letters from L. H. K. McMaster to Elizabeth describing Missouri, 1835-1840; typewritten record of the court martial of Dr. John Fields; legal documents concerning the ownership of land on Chincoteague and Assoteague Islands by John W. and Samuel M. Field, 1870s; papers on litigation concerning oyster-planting rights to lands off Assoteague Island, early 1900s; letters of John S. McMaster (1859-1924) concerning family history, the Eastern Shore, and Francis Makemie, founder of the Presbyterian Church in America, 1900-1920; and clippings on Virginia and Maryland genealogy, political figures, and fruit and vegetable culture. Manuscript volumes consist of a legal notebook, an account book, a composition book, and memoranda.

1792.  FIELD-MUSGRAVE FAMILY PAPERS,
       1739-1966. 2,168 items and
       15 vols. Stockbridge
       (Berkshire County), Mass., and
       East Grinstead, Sussex, England.

   Professional and personal papers of Sir Anthony Musgrave (1828-1888), British colonial official; of his wife, Jeanie Lucinda (Field) Musgrave (1833-1920); and of her father, David Dudley Field (1805-1894), lawyer and law reformer. Papers of David Dudley Field concern his early life; his education at Stockbridge Academy and at Williams College, including bills and receipts, and correspondence about student life and professors; religion, especially the rise of the Unitarian Church; his early career in New York; law reform; the compilation of civil, penal, and criminal codes for New York, and as a model for other states; international law, including maritime law and admiralty courts; the reform of municipal government; the Association for the Reform and Codification of the Law of Nations, 1870s; the Institut de Droit International; the laying of the Atlantic Cable, 1866; and the Hague Peace Conference, 1899. Personal correspondence includes letters, 1830s, with the Hopkins family, Mark, Harry, and his future wife, Jane Lucinda; and letters, 1870-1894, with the Musgrave family. Also in the collection are clippings pertaining to the Field and Hopkins families; some legal papers; diaries, 1875-1894, of David Dudley Field; "Recollections of My Early Life, Written in the Spring of 1832," by Field; his commonplace book, 1824-1827; his "Autobiography," 1805-1836; a journal, 1831-1835, containing comments on his studies and reading; a journal, 1836, principally concerning the fatal illness of his wife; journals, 1836-1837 and 1851, describing his travels in Europe; volume of Jane Lucinda (Hopkins) Field containing recollections of her youth, written in 1832, and a journal, 1833-1835, Poetical Extracts of Jane Lucinda (Hopkins) Field; Personal Recollections of David Dudley Field written in 1892; and correspondence, 1898, relating to a biography of Field written by his brother, Henry Martyn Field.

   Sir Anthony Musgrave's papers, correspondence, dispatches, and writings pertain principally to the administration of various colonial governments, particularly Jamaica. Jamaican materials, 1877-1883, concern the case of Pulido v. Musgrave, colonial rule, the immigration of laborers to Jamaica, the membership of the Legislative Council, the reorganization of the judicial system, colonial defense, customs, commercial relations with the United States and Canada, and Cuban revolutionaries in Jamaica. Other papers pertain to the administration of St. Vincent, 1861-1864; Newfoundland, 1864-1869, especially concerning the Newfoundland fisheries; British Columbia, 1869-1872; Natal, 1872, including information on native policy, education and marriage, the constitution, and relations between Natal, the Transvaal, and the Zulus; South Australia, 1873; and Queensland, 1883-1888. There are letters concerning Sir Anthony's writings on political economy, 1870s, as well as pamphlets of his works; correspondence, 1887, concerning the formation of the Westminster Review Company and the publication of the Westminster Review; a Private Letter Book, 1868-1878, containing confidential letters to other officials and personal correspondence; a scrapbook, 1874-1881, with reviews of his writings, and information on the social, economic, and political affairs of Jamaica and South Australia; and a Memorial Scrapbook, 1868-1908, comprised of pictures, clippings, telegrams and letters concerning the death of Sir Anthony.

Lady Musgrave's papers include personal correspondence; letters, 1890-1901, with Samuel Walker Griffith concerning Australia, including information on the federation of Australia, the Australian constitution, labor unrest, the separation movement, and his work as chief justice of Queensland and of Australia; letters, 1910-1911, dealing with Anglican mission work among miners and loggers in British Columbia; "Notes for My Sons," containing biographical information about herself and her relatives; and a scrapbook, 1810-1913, of letters from prominent persons. Other materials include correspondence, 1918-1920, of Mark Hopkins III concerning the work of the Red Cross in France; letters, 1886-1891, from Dudley Field Musgrave (1873-1895), son of Sir Anthony, describing life as a naval cadet and his service in the Mediterranean; correspondence and printed material pertaining to railroads, especially the Berkshire Street Railway Company of Stockbridge; pictures of the Field and Musgrave family members; and genealogical material on the Field, Musgrave, Hopkins, Byam, Sergeant, Dyett, and Abbott families.

1793. WILLIAM H. FIELDING PAPERS, 1860-1865. 10 items. South Carolina.

Papers of a farmer and Confederate soldier including letters referring to the war in South Carolina and Virginia, the testing of a Negro's loyalty to the South, a measles epidemic, and conditions at Summerville and Sullivan's Island, South Carolina; and a list of men serving in "Beat Company, No. 2, 42nd Regiment, First Battalion."

1794. OBADIAH FIELDS PAPERS, 1784 (1820-1827) 1855. 19 items. Rockingham County, N.C.

Letters and papers of a slave trader, with data on slave prices and the territory of Obadiah Field's trade.

1795. JOHN FIFER PAPERS, 1862-1865. 27 items. Muncie (Delaware County), Ind.

Personal letters of a Union soldier in the 84th Indiana Infantry Regiment to his wife, containing references to troop movements principally in Tennessee.

1796. MILLARD FILLMORE PAPERS, 1848-1851. 4 items. Buffalo (Erie County), N.Y.

Papers of Millard Fillmore (1800-1874), president of the United States, including a land grant, a pardon, a letter from Horace Webster (1794-1871) concerning the financial affairs of Geneva College, Geneva, New York, and a letter to the Rev. Dr. John Chase Lord (1805-1877) pertaining to Lord's sermon, Higher Law and the Fugitive Slave Bill (1851).

1797. FINCASTLE & LEWISBURG AND CHRISTIANSBURG & NATURAL BRIDGE MAIL-STAGES PAPERS, 1834. 49 items. Virginia.

Waybills for the two stage lines recording the names of passengers, points of departure and destination, fares, names of drivers or other agents, and baggage and other items transported.

1798. ALEXANDER T. FINDLEY, JOSEPH R. FINDLEY, AND WILLIAM M. FINDLEY PAPERS, 1826 (1861-1865) 1879. 162 items. Altoona (Blair County), Pa.

Chiefly the Civil War letters of three brothers in the Union Army from northern camps near Altoona and elsewhere, and from camps in South Carolina, containing comments on conditions in the army; military campaigns; the lack of wisdom in freeing Negroes; Negro regiments in the U.S. Army; yellow fever epidemic; anticipation of an attempt by the C.S.S. Atlanta (formerly the steamer Fingal) to break the blockade of Savannah; destruction of Southern homes by Confederates; failure of ministers in Missouri to take the oath of loyalty, 1865; and methods of obtaining commissions in the army. Other letters concern the Huntingdon County Temperance Society; the presidential election of 1840; Joseph R. Findley's business in Saint Louis and a trip to Europe; and travels in the West by William M., Thomas F., and J. Woods Findley, including comments on moral standards and problems between whites and the Chinese in San Francisco.

1799. JAMES J. FINDLEY PAPERS, 1864-1865. 9 items. Milledgeville (Baldwin County), Ga.

Principally orders and sub-vouchers of Colonel James J. Findley, in command of the 1st Regiment of Georgia State Cavalry, C.S.A.

1800. JOHN FINLEY PAPERS, 1810-1861. 2 vols. Wilkesboro (Wilkes County), N.C.

Papers of Major John Finley (1778-1865), merchant, comprised of a ledger, 1831-1861, containing accounts of a store in Wilkesboro of the firm owned by Finley and his uncle, Colonel William P. Waugh; and a ledger, 1810-1812, of a store at Rockford, in Surry County, with references to William P. Waugh.

1801. WILLIAM A. J. FINNEY PAPERS, 1849-1876. 86 items. Museville (Pittsylvania County), Va.

Business, Civil War, and political correspondence of a member of a firm of slave traders, giving a detailed picture of methods of conducting and financing the slave trade, with accounts of purchases in Virginia and sales in the markets of New Orleans, Louisiana, and Mobile and Montgomery, Alabama. Included are notices regarding the slave market in Richmond. Civil War letters show that many members of the Finney family were in the Confederate Army. There are references to Finney's attempts to raise a company, his hiring of a substitute, the battle of Big Bethel, the maintenance of the Danville Railroad, and appeals for food. Letters of the 1870s pertain to Finney's political activities in Virginia.

1802. HAMILTON FISH PAPERS, 1850-1873. 4 items. Washington, D.C., and New York, N.Y.

Routine letters and thank-you notes of Hamilton Fish (1808-1893), U.S. statesman.

1803. ALBERT KENRICK FISHER JOURNAL, 1886. 2 items. Washington, D.C.

Manuscript and typescript journals of a trip made by Albert Kenrick Fisher (1856-1948), ornithologist, to investigate rice cultivation areas and bird life in South Carolina, Georgia, Florida, Alabama, and Louisiana. Included are lists of birds, animals, and plants; descriptions of the methods of rice cultivation on various plantations; and descriptions of experiments with rice as a forage crop.

1804. AMORY FISHER PAPERS, 1822-1855. 19 items. Tuscaloosa (Tuscaloosa County), Ala.

Letters of Amory Fisher who made and sold cotton gins and spinning machines, written to his brother, Leonard, in Bangor, Maine. The letters describe living conditions in Alabama and visits to relatives in Tennessee.

1805. BENJAMIN FRANKLIN FISHER PAPERS, (1865-1866) 1914. 18 items and 1 vol. Valley Forge (Chester County), Pa., and Washington, D.C. Restricted.

Personal, business, and military letters of Benjamin Franklin Fisher (ca. 1835-1916), lawyer and U.S. Army officer. Business letters concern collection and payment of debts. Military correspondence relates to his unsuccessful attempt to keep his position as Chief Signal Officer, and to his efforts to procure promotions and better positions for the men under his command. Personal and political letters discuss the Democratic and Republican parties, the Radical Republicans, the Thirteenth Amendment to the U.S. Constitution, the agreement between Generals William T. Sherman and Joseph E. Johnston, the Wilderness battlefield, and Negro suffrage.

1806. JANE FISHER PAPERS, 1858-1904. 67 items. Sherrill's Ford (Catawba County), N.C.

Civil War letters from Confederate soldiers to Lavinia, Mandy, and Jane Fisher, principally concerning personal matters but also containing information on deserters in both armies, a measles epidemic, movements of troops in Virginia and North Carolina, a Confederate attack on a Union railroad near Kinston, North Carolina, and the battle of Richmond, 1862. Postwar correspondence is mainly to Jane Fisher from the Rev. L. M. Berry concerning the Baptist churches he served in Illinois, Iowa, and Missouri, the towns in which he lived, and commodity prices in Illinois; and from his son, A. Moore Berry, a Saint Louis, Missouri, attorney.

1807. LINDLEY FISHER PAPERS, 1848-1849. 4 items. Philadelphia, Pa.

Business papers, one concerning Francis Bach and Co.

1808. CLINTON BOWEN FISK PAPERS, 1863, 1889. 2 items. New York, N.Y.

Letter from Clinton Bowen Fisk (1828-1890), U.S. Army officer and official in the Freedmen's Bureau, to General Leonard Fulton Ross concerning the position of his brigade; and a personal letter to Irene E. Gilbert, a former associate at Fisk University.

1809. R. S. FITCH PAPERS, 1862.
5 items. Fleming County, Ky.

Letters from R. S. Fitch, a private in the Federal Army, chiefly to Margaret Shanklin, describing his army experiences and commenting on camp life.

1810. EDMUND B. FITZGERALD COPYBOOK, 1863. 1 vol. (20 pp.) Lynchburg (Campbell County), Va.

Copybook with cover made from the Lynchburg Virginian for September 11, 1863.

1811. JOHN FITZGERALD PAPERS, 1817-1902. 74 items. Nottoway County, Va.

Business and personal correspondence of John Fitzgerald, plantation owner, merchant, and apparently a school executive of Nottoway County. Included are references to tobacco sold, insurance, and a trip in 1870 by rail and steam from Virginia to Moscow, Kentucky, by way of Cincinnati. There are also a number of applications for teaching positions at Oak Grove Academy, Nottoway County.

1812. ELIZABETH D. FITZHUGH PAPERS, 1829-1861. 22 items. Fredericksburg (Spotsylvania County), Va.

Personal letters containing some genealogical information.

1813. HENRY FITZHUGH PAPERS, 1746-1789. 3 items and 2 vols. "Bedford," Stafford County, Va.

Letter book, 1746-1774, and ledger, 1747-1789, of Henry Fitzhugh (1723-1783), tobacco planter, concerning the production of tobacco from its planting to its sale by factors in London. Included also are household and plantation store accounts; invoices; and information on social life and customs in Virginia, the purchase of land, and the care and management of slaves.

1814. PHILIP A. FITZHUGH AND WILLIAM BULLITT FITZHUGH PAPERS, 1821 (1880-1920) 1939. 226 items. Eastville and Machipongo (Northampton County), Va.

Principally family letters of Philip A. Fitzhugh, a physician, and William Bullitt Fitzhugh, sergeant at arms of the Virginia House of Delegates in 1938. Included are an account of Philip A. Fitzhugh for the college tuition of his two daughters; Civil War poetry; Daughters of the American Revolution essays; papers relating to the Virginia Colonial Dames; a copy of the Amateur Times (Eastville, Virginia: December, 1885); and advertisements for medical supplies.

1815. SIR ALMERIC WILLIAM FITZROY PAPERS, 1896-1926. 73 items. London, England.

Papers of Sir Almeric William FitzRoy (1851-1935) principally concerning his years as clerk of the Privy Council, 1898-1923. The papers relate to education in England, and in London, and university expansion; reform of the London government; the Fashoda Crisis of 1898; the accession of Edward VII; the cabinet crisis of 1903; and other political matters. Correspondents include Arthur Balfour, Lord Balfour of Burleigh, Sir Arthur Bigge, Lord Davey, the Duke of Devonshire, Lord Goschen, Richard Burdon Haldane, Lord Halsbury, Sir William Harcourt, Lord James of Hereford, Lord Morley of Blackburn, Lord Rosebery, Lord Salisbury, Frederick Temple, the Archbishop of Canterbury, and Beatrice Webb.

1816. THOMAS FITZSIMONS PAPERS, 1808. 1 item. Philadelphia, Pa.

Letter from Thomas Fitzsimons (1741-1811), merchant and statesman, in his capacity as chairman of the board of trustees of the University of Pennsylvania to Benjamin Williams, president of the trustees of the University of North Carolina, concerning admissions policies.

1817. GEORGE A. FLAGG PAPERS, 1860 (1862-1866) 1883. 5,120 items. Harpers Ferry (Jefferson County), W. Va.

Letters, military telegrams, and papers of Captain George A. Flagg, Assistant Quartermaster of the Army of the Potomac, U.S.A., pertaining to supplies and logistics in Maryland and West Virginia. Letters and telegrams include requisitions for supplies, recommendations, requests from civilians for payment or inquiries for the sale of goods, letters concerning remuneration for property damage, and correspondence relating to the impressment of Negro laborers. There are also circulars dealing with quartermaster regulations, daily record sheets of supplies, account sheets of Flagg's activities, receipt rolls of hired men, and reports on the means of transportation and animals at Harpers Ferry.

1818. H. O. FLAGG NOTEBOOK, [ca. 1854-1855]. 1 vol. (112 pp.) [Georgia, and Hawkins County, Tenn.?]

Entries contain arithmetic problems, rules for solving equations and other mathematical formulas, verses, form for making out bail bonds, forms of declarations for land warrants, surveying rules, definitions of Latin phrases used in law, and a list of letters received and answered.

1819. HENRY G. FLAGG PAPERS,
1862-1895. 23 items.
Whitesburg (Hamblen County),
Tenn.

Muster and payrolls, clothing and ordnance accounts of the 4th Regiment of Tennessee Volunteer Infantry and the 1st Tennessee Cavalry, U.S.A., in which Henry G. Flagg was an officer. Also a letter of Flagg's to the U.S. Congress concerning pensions; and papers pertaining to war claims.

1820. DANIEL J. FLANDERS PAPERS,
1863-1865. 51 items.
Buxton (York County), Maine.

Personal letters of Captain David J. Flanders, commanding officer of the 6th Company of New Hampshire Heavy Artillery, discussing camp life, U.S. Sanitary Commission field hospitals and physicians, food and clothing, pillaging, the siege of Petersburg, the surrender of Robert E. Lee and the Army of Northern Virginia, and Confederate prisons.

1821. FLAT CREEK TOWNSHIP RECORDS,
1871-1886. 1 vol. (280 pp.)
Mecklenburg County, Va.

Local government records comprised of the Flat Creek Township Board's Minutes, 1871-1875, containing material on roads, poor relief, taxation, and an election for a public school tax; a list of hands eligible for road work; a list of delinquent township levies, 1871-1872; the treasurer and collector's financial statement, 1873; court records, 1878-1882; Masonic minutes; and the accounts of W. H. C. Walker.

1822. REBECCA J. FLEETWOOD PAPERS,
1864-1871. 13 items.
Hertford (Perquimans County),
N.C.

Personal letters, two of which were written from Chowan Female College, Murfreesboro, North Carolina.

1823. ANNA FLEMING PAPERS, 1859.
3 items. Charlotte
(Mecklenburg County), N.C.

Report cards of a student at Charlotte Female Institute, Charlotte, North Carolina.

1824. GEORGE FLEMING PAPERS, 1866-1870.
5 items. Hanover County, Va.

Deeds and indentures relating to the transfer of land and the payment of debts.

1825. JAMES L. FLEMING PAPERS,
1891. 8 items.

Letters to James Fleming, corresponding secretary for the Confederate Survivors' Association, accepting or declining invitations to a reunion of this group. Included are letters from John Bratton, Joseph Brent, Winfield S. Featherston, Johnson Hagood, James Henry Law, A. L. Long, N. Miller, Thomas Taylor Munford, and F. A. Sharp.

1826. M. B. FLEMING PAPERS, 1848-1862.
27 items. Dutchville
(Granville County), N.C.

Correspondence of the Fleming family, including comments on a smallpox epidemic, 1848; Whig politics in North Carolina, 1850; and the military situation after the first battle of Manassas, 1861.

1827. LUCY MUSE (WALTON) FLETCHER PAPERS,
1816-1968. 38 items and 10 vols.
Broadway (Rockingham County), Va.

Papers of Lucy Muse (Walton) Fletcher (1822-1908) include family letters, chiefly between her parents, Lucinda (Muse) Walton and William Claiborne Walton; clippings containing biographical information; a poem eulogizing William C. Walton by Lydia Sigourney; genealogical information; pictures of the William C. Walton and the Patterson Fletcher families; and the reminiscences and diaries of Lucy Fletcher. The reminiscences, 1829-1852, recall her childhood in Alexandria, Virginia, her education at the School of Catharine Beecher in Hartford, Connecticut, social life in Virginia, travels to New England and Washington, D.C., her marriage to the Reverend Patterson Fletcher (1815-1892), and life as a minister's wife. Her diaries, 1852-1870, describe various places in which they lived; the Civil War years, including civilian hardships, the care of the sick and wounded, the fall of Richmond, and Negro soldiers and freedmen; Presbyterian Church affairs; and economic difficulties after the war.

1828. WILLIAM HENRY HARRISON FLICK
PAPERS, 1792 (1845-1888) 1894.
1,794 items and 1 vol.
Martinsburg (Berkeley County),
W. Va.

Personal and political papers of William Henry Harrison Flick (ca. 1847-1894), lawyer and politician. Political papers relate to the Republican Party in West Virginia; the elections of 1870, 1886, and 1888; the Flick Amendment abolishing the test oaths as a basis for West Virginia citizenship; the taking of the tenth U.S. Census in West Virginia; Democratic Party methods; the Republican-Greenback-Labor Party ticket in the campaign of 1880; and Flick's career as U.S. district attorney for West Virginia, beginning in 1881. Family letters describe life in Nebraska in the 1870s and 1880s, a visit to Berkeley Springs, and student life at Wilson College, Chambersburg, Pennsylvania, 1885-1886. Also included are a brief diary, 1882, by Flick, bills and receipts, household and mercantile accounts, papers of the Wiltshire family, legal papers, and papers concerning the Masons and the Grand Army of the Republic.

1829. W. H. FLINN PAPERS,
1862-1863. 7 items. Georgia.

Letters to W. H. Flinn, evidently a merchant, concerning the wholesale purchase of goods, including one letter bearing on the scarcity of textile goods for private consumption produced by the "Augusta Factory" after the factory was restricted to the manufacture of "shirting and sheeting" for the Confederate government.

1830. EDWARD FLOOD PAPERS, 1864-1889.
24 items. New Orleans, La.

Correspondence and military papers of Captain Edward Flood, commander of the Pioneer Corps of Early's Division, Army of Northern Virginia, C.S.A., relating to the rebuilding of bridges around Lexington and Staunton, Virginia, 1864-1865, and his application for Superintendent of Improvements for New Orleans, 1888.

1831. ANNE (PUTNEY) FLORA PAPERS,
1939. 1 item. (43 pp.) Durham, N.C.

Typescript of an article "State Police: Connecticut, Pennsylvania, New York and New Jersey," written by a graduate student at Duke University.

1832. WILLIAM WALTON FLOURNOY PAPERS,
1857-1934. 11 items. De Funiak Springs (Walton County), Fla.

Papers of William Walton Flournoy (b. 1874) are principally concerned with Flournoy family genealogy. Included is a copy of a sermon, 1857, delivered at the funeral of Richard W. Flournoy by Dr. T. V. Moore, entitled "The Christian Lawyer."

1833. MARK D. FLOWERS PAPERS, 1864.
13 items. Memphis (Shelby County), Tenn.

Special and general orders of Captain Mark D. Flowers, assistant adjutant general of the 1st Brigade, Enrolled Militia, District of Memphis, dealing with local duties and organization.

1834. FLOWERS OF THE HOLY LAND.
1 vol.

Pressed flowers and their identifying names.

1835. JOHN FLOYD PAPERS, 1767-1822.
4 items. Camden County, Ga.

Papers of John Floyd (1769-1839) concern land and timber.

1836. JOHN BUCHANAN FLOYD PAPERS,
1830-1862. 263 items. Abingdon (Washington County), Va.

Military papers of John Buchanan Floyd (1806-1863), governor of Virginia, statesman and Confederate soldier. Principally routine, the papers relate to his Civil War campaigns in western Virginia, and to the situation at Fort Donelson. Letters of 1861 generally reflect enthusiasm for the war.

1837. JAMES FLYNN PAPERS, 1914.
1 vol. (221 pp.) Pocahontas County, W. Va.

"Notes on Deeds and Titles to Lobelia Lands, Pocahontas County, West Virginia," of which James Flynn was a trustee, containing a list of the lots, and a resume of their legal and financial status.

1838. OWEN R. FLYNN PAPERS,
1865-1867. 212 items. Suffolk (Nansemond County), Va.

Chiefly bills for all types of general merchandise, including cotton, pork and peas.

1839. FOGG BROTHERS CO. PAPERS,
1848-1851. 157 items. Boston, Mass.

Business letters to Fogg Brothers Co., commission merchants, concerning prices of silk, lace, and fringes; trade with China; and orders for shipments to firms in New York and New Jersey.

1840. EDWARD FOLLETT DIARY, 1864-1865.
1 vol. Bellevue (Eaton County), Mich.

Record of Follett's service with the 28th Michigan Volunteer Infantry, Nov., 1864-May, 1865, in Kentucky, Tennessee, Ohio, Virginia, and Washington, D.C.; in a hospital in Virginia or Washington, D.C.; at Fortress Monroe; and in North Carolina. A note at the end of the diary explains that Follett became ill and died on May 18, 1865.

1841. MONTGOMERY M. FOLSOM PAPERS,
1892-1899. 17 items. Atlanta, Ga.

Photographs, poems, and prose articles, and obituaries of Folsom clipped from the Atlanta Journal.

1842. WILLIAM WINSTON FONTAINE PAPERS,
1899-1945. 8 items and 1 vol. Austin (Travis County), Texas.

Clippings and a commonplace book relating to the genealogy of several Virginia families, including the Ayletts, Byrds, Catos, Cleburnes, Creightons, Fontaines, Kidders, Lewises, Massies, Meads, Popes, Telfairs, Wests, and Woodsons. There is also information on Mary Ann (Phillips) Wills, Robert L. Penn, Virginia land patents of the 17th-18th centuries, and American literature and history.

1843. JAMES FOORD JOURNAL, 1804. 1 vol. Milton (Norfolk County), Mass.

Journal kept during a trip to Frankfort, Kentucky, to clear land titles confused by claims of squatters, French and Indian War veterans, and grantees of the Transylvania Company. Partly published in Bayrd Still, ed., "To the West on Business in 1804," *Pennsylvania Magazine of History and Biography*, 64 (January, 1904), 1-21.

1844. HENRY STUART FOOTE PAPERS, 1876. 1 item. Washington, D.C.

A letter to Rev. C. K. Marshall.

1845. JOHN B. FOOTE PAPERS, 1862-1865. 86 items. Utica (Oneida County), N.Y.

Letters of a Union soldier of the 117th New York Volunteers to his family, from his entry into service until his discharge. Topics include training around Washington, D.C., service at Suffolk, Virginia, and Folly Island, South Carolina; the sieges of Charleston, Petersburg, and Richmond; the capture of Fort Fisher; convalescence in hospitals near Wilmington and New Bern, North Carolina; camp life; confiscation of Southern property; conscription of Negroes; desertion; disease; health conditions; furloughs; morale; morals; prisoners; rumors; and transportation. There are a few letters from a cousin, Daniel P. Sanford, also a Union soldier, from New Bern and Carolina City, North Carolina, relating to camp life and slow pay.

1846. ALFRED FORBES ACCOUNT BOOKS, 1858-1871. 4 vols. Greenville (Pitt County), N.C.

Daybook and account books of a Greenville merchant.

1847. EDWIN FAIRFIELD FORBES PAPERS, 1861-1865. 1 vol. (161 pp.) East Dixmont (Penobscot County), Maine.

Journal and letter book recording Forbes' life on the Andaman Islands in the Indian Ocean as a member of the Indian Naval Brigade. The second half of the volume is the journal, 1870-1876, of William Bellamy, a farmer and sea captain of Rehoboth, Massachusetts.

1848. PETER FORCE PAPERS, 1825-1856. 6 items. Washington, D.C.

Miscellaneous letters, including one from Thomas Loraine McKenney, Aug. 15, 1825, concerning John C. Calhoun's role in passage of a treaty between the Creek Indians and the state of Georgia; a letter of introduction from George Perkins Marsh, September 5, 1849, on behalf of James Meacham, his successor as representative from Vermont; letters from David Lowry Swain, March 29, 1854, and August 14, 1856, sending Force writings on North Carolina history; and a letter from James Cochran Dobbin, U.S. secretary of the navy, May 31, 1856, concerning a suggestion made by Swain.

1849. A. C. FORD PAPERS, 1833-1859. 4 items. Eaton (Preble County), Ohio.

Miscellaneous items, in part concerning land in Nebraska and Ohio.

1850. HENRY FORD PAPERS, 1862-1864. 6 items. Marshfield (Plymouth County), Mass.

Civil War letters from John M. Ford, an enlisted man in the 37th Regiment of Massachusetts Volunteers to his brother, Henry Ford, relating to the war in Virginia and Washington, D.C.

1851. VINCENT FORD AUTOGRAPH BOOK, 1862-1879. 1 vol. (46 pp.) Brooklyn (Kings County), N.Y.

Autographs, largely of congressmen.

1852. FOREST HISTORY SOCIETY, INC., INTERVIEWS, 1959. 2 items. Santa Cruz, Calif.

Transcripts of interviews with E. L. Demmon and with Elis Olsson and Reuben B. Robertson on the development of the pulp and paper industry in the southeastern United States and the conservation of forest resources. Mentioned are the Chesapeake Corporation, West Point, Virginia; the Champion Paper and Fiber Company; and the U.S. Forest Service Southeastern Forest Experiment Station.

1853. GEORGE HOKE FORNEY PAPERS, 1862-1864. 7 items. Jacksonville (Calhoun County), Ala.

Photocopies of Civil War letters by a lieutenant colonel in Loring's Division of the Confederate Army, describing the Vicksburg campaign, John C. Pemberton, William W. Loring, the battle of Baker's Creek, and morals of the soldiers.

1854. NATHAN BEDFORD FORREST PAPERS, 1862-1866. 393 items. Memphis (Shelby County), Tenn.

Copies of orders and communications addressed to army surgeons connected with Forrest's cavalry corps. Subjects include transportation, appointments, and hospitals. One item is a letter from Forrest to President Andrew Johnson repledging his loyalty.

1855.   JOHN FORSYTH PAPERS,
        1790-1840.  12 items.  Augusta
        (Richmond County), Ga.

   Correspondence relating to Forsyth's service as governor of Georgia, minister to Spain, and secretary of state.

1856.   JOHN A. FORSYTH PAPERS, 1818-1864.
        44 items.  Statesville
        (Iredell County), N.C.

   Letters and accounts of John A. and Henderson Forsyth, merchants.  There are accounts of Charleston wholesalers; a letter, 1837, from Thomas Reid, who describes Aberdeen, Scotland, and comments on the Reform Bill of 1832; letters of R.S. Gracy on slave trading; and letters of R.H. Carson on medical practice in Demopolis, Alabama.  Many letters relate to buying and selling slaves.

1857.   SIR THOMAS DOUGLAS FORSYTH
        PAPERS, 1869, 1875.  2 items.
        London, England.

   A letter, 1869, from Lord Mayo on Forsyth's negotiation of a boundary dispute between India and Afghanistan and commenting on Anglo-Russian relations; and a letter, 1875, from Evelyn Baring, secretary to Lord Northbrook, Viceroy of India, explaining that George Allen's Pioneer article did not represent the government's view of Forsyth's mission to settle the status of the Karenni States in Burma.

1858.   HENDERSON FORSYTHE DAYBOOKS,
        1834-1850.  2 vols.
        Statesville (Iredell County), N.C.

   General mercantile accounts.

1859.   DAVID FORT PAPERS, 1864.
        3 items.  Virginia.

   Personal letters from David Fort, a Confederate soldier stationed near Orange Court House, Virginia, to his family.

1860.   WASHINGTON FOSDICK PAPERS, 1865.
        1 item.

   A letter, Aug. 8, 1865, to Taber & Co., discussing whaling expeditions, cartographic errors, and encounters with the C.S.S. Shenandoah.

1861.   ALFRED M. FOSTER AND JOHN A. FOSTER
        PAPERS, 1801-1919.  683 items and
        4 vols.  Wilkes County, N.C.

   Invoices and business papers of Alfred M. Foster, merchant, 1801-1866; the Civil War diary of John A. Foster, 1864-1865; reminiscence by him of part of his service from 1862 in the 52nd Regiment of North Carolina Infantry, including descriptions of the battle of the Wilderness, rations, and camp life; papers relating to his administration of the family estate in North Carolina after 1866; and letters from family members in the vicinity of Van Zandt County, Texas.  A few letters indicate John A. Foster was a distillery inspector for the U.S. government.  Texas letters include idealistic descriptions from G. E. Gray, a brother-in-law.  There are also account books, 1837-1839, 1865, 3 vols., and a daybook, 1853-1867, 1 vol., of Alfred M. and John A. Foster.

1862.   ELLEN FOSTER AND SUSAN FOSTER
        PAPERS, 1843.  3 items.  Baltimore, Md.

   Personal correspondence, mentioning a benefit party given for the sufferers of Fall River, a tea, and a comic opera, La Fille du Regiment.

1863.   JOHN FOSTER RECEIPT BOOK,
        1795-1801.  1 vol.  (223 pp.)
        Richmond, Va.

   Receipts of a merchant selling oats, hemp, brandy, tobacco, ships' cables, and cordage.  The volume mentions Foster's two sons, Gandy and Henry.

1864.   KATE D. FOSTER DIARY, 1863-1872.
        1 item and 1 vol.  (40 pp.)
        Adams County, Mississippi.

   Diary of the daughter of James Foster, plantation owner of Madison Parish, Louisiana.  About two-thirds of the entries date from the latter half of 1863 and concern the Civil War and Miss Foster's opinions about the righteousness of the Southern cause and the effect of the war on her home and on local Negroes.  Postwar entries concern personal matters.  The diary's inside covers are pasted with clippings of pro-Southern patriotic poetry.  There is also a typescript of the entire text.

1865.   LAFAYETTE SABINE FOSTER PAPERS,
        1860-1869.  20 items.  Norwich
        (New London County), Conn., and
        Washington, D.C.

   Letters from Foster, U.S. senator from Connecticut, to his niece, Mrs. William L. Gaylord of Fitzwilliam, New Hampshire, and his sister, Mrs. F. W. Hyde of Norwich, Connecticut.  The letters are personal in nature, describing a visit of the Japanese embassy in 1860, the confusion after the first battle of Bull Run, and the behavior of Congress while counting the electoral vote of 1869.

1866.   MARTHA LYMAN FOSTER PAPERS,
        1864.  2 items.  Washington, D.C.

   Letters from two congressmen sending Martha Lyman Foster their photographs.

1867. THOMAS GARDNER FOSTER PAPERS, 1863. 1 item. Columbus [?] (Muscogee County), Ga.

A personal letter to Foster, son of Thomas Flournoy Foster, congressman from Georgia, from a cousin in Braxton Bragg's Army of Tennessee.

1868. WILLIAM N. FOSTER PAPERS, 1862-1863. 2 items and 1 vol. Ohio.

Foster's commission as lieutenant colonel in the 110th Regiment of Ohio Volunteer Infantry; his discharge; and a diary, Jan. 1 through June 13, 1863, largely kept in camp near Winchester, Virginia.

1869. ANTHONY FOTHERGILL PAPERS, ca. 1750s. 1 vol. Ravenstonedale, Westmoreland, England.

A manuscript treatise attacking the doctrine of original sin, especially as it was advocated by the Methodists. A note on the title page, May 28, 1763, by William Fothergill, son and executor of the estate of Anthony, authorizes Edward Walton to have the manuscript printed.

1870. ISAAC H. FOUST DAYBOOKS AND LEDGER, 1852-1861. 6 vols. Reed Creek and Deep River (Randolph County), N.C.

1871. JOSEPH S. FOWLER PAPERS, 1779-1870. 2,406 items and 4 vols. Fairfield (Fairfield County), Conn., and Craven County, N.C.

Included are records, 1779-1809, of a mercantile business run by Stephen Fowler, Fairfield, Connecticut, and after 1805 of Trenton, Jones County, North Carolina, which engaged in trade between New York and North Carolina. Stephen's son Joseph about 1820 engaged in export of lumber, naval stores, tobacco, grain, and blackeyed peas from North Carolina to Bermuda; and later in costal trade from New Bern to New York. There is also correspondence relating to his duties as U.S. deputy marshal, Pamlico District, North Carolina, 1831-1860. Family correspondence predominates between 1840 and 1860. For the Civil War years there are many letters from Joseph S. Fowler, Jr., written largely from the Confederate Commissary Office, Kinston, North Carolina. The collection also includes diplomas; a ledger of Joseph S. Fowler, (1817-1834), 1836, 1866, 1 vol.; financial and legal papers, 1800-1860; broadsides concerning state policies; the logbook of Absalom Fulford kept on the Neuse River lightship, 1845-1849, recording weather and the passage of ships; certificates for jurors, U.S. District Court, New Bern, 1839-1858; business letters addressed to DeWitt C. Fowler and Brother at Bay River, 1860-1868, a general store and liquor dealer; and a few items relating to North Carolina schools. Among correspondents in the collection are Silvester Brown, Benjamin Q. Tucker, Absalom Fulford, and Wesley Jones.

1872. SIR ROBERT NICHOLAS FOWLER, FIRST BARONET, PAPERS, 1885. 2 items. London, England.

Letters from James Lowther, Conservative member of Parliament, concerning politics.

1873. ASA G. FOWLKES PAPERS, 1845-1861. 1 vol. Petersburg (Dinwiddie County), Va.

An account book kept by Fowlkes for a tobacco factory operated in partnership with James W. Smithey, 1845-1849, including a profit and loss statement, 1848-1849; accounts, 1849-1850, for the administration of Fowlkes's estate, including several pages on the hiring of slaves, with names of slaves, owners, and employers, including McEnery & McCulloch, David Dunlop, and other tobacco manufacturers of Petersburg. There is also a legal opinion of William Green concerning the estate of James M. McCulloch which involves the disposition of slaves belonging to the partnership of McEnery & McCulloch; and an account of the estate of John Crostick.

1874. GUSTAVUS VASA FOX PAPERS, 1863. 1 item. Washington, D.C.

A telegram to John Ericsson ordering the discontinuation of experiments with an unnamed vessel as that ship was wanted off Charleston.

1875. HENRY RICHARD VASSALL FOX, THIRD BARON HOLLAND, PAPERS, 1806 (1836-1837) 1852. 195 items. London, England.

Letters, 1809, 20 items, from the Third Baron Holland (1773-1840) and Elizabeth (Vassall) Fox, Baroness Holland, to Admiral John Purvis, were written on a visit to Spain and largely concern passage to England for persons, goods, or correspondence, or social arrangements. There is some comment on troop movements. One letter of 1839 expresses the hope that Protestant dissenters will support the suspension of the constitution of Jamaica as the legislature there opposes efforts to emancipate Negroes. Letters, 1836-1837, 167 items, from Lord Granville Leveson-Gower, First Earl Granville, British ambassador in Paris, and from Lady Granville, chronicle the politics and personalities of the ministries in Paris and London, Louis Philippe, and the Carlist War in Spain. A letter, 1852, from Caroline, Duchesse d'Aumale, daughter-in-law of Louis Philippe, to Baroness Holland discusses the Duc d'Aumale and other members of the family. Included are transcriptions by Holland's son, Henry Edward, Fourth Baron Holland, of his correspondence, 1850, with Lord John Russell and Sir Robert Adair concerning the publication of Holland's Foreign Reminiscences. There are also some miscellaneous letters of Holland.

1876. HIMER FOX PAPERS, 1844-1875. 1 vol. Columbia Township (Randolph County), N.C.

An account book, with most of the entries representing the 1850s and 1860s to about 1867, relating chiefly to the operation of a sawmill and containing numerous accounts for laborers. The sawmill, referred to sometimes as Fox and Craven and sometimes as H. Fox & Co., was operated for a time in partnership with John A. Craven.

1877. JOHN FOX PAPERS, 1784 (1825-1892). 2,139 items. Lexington (Lexington County), S.C.

Family and business papers of John Fox, and of his business associate, William L. Miller. Topics mentioned include the settlement of various estates; the militia; South Carolina College, the University of Virginia, and other South Carolina colleges and schools; railroads; the behavior of slaves; buying and selling of slaves; business agreements between Fox, Miller, and others; cotton production; local politics; tax lists; Know-Nothings; the visit of the Japanese embassy to New York in 1860; the visit of the Great Eastern; secession; living conditions in Richmond during the Civil War; use of cotton by factories around Baltimore; participation of Negroes in politics; jury lists; also bills, receipts, daybooks and account books, 17 vols., of John Fox and of Fox and Miller. Many postwar letters deal with Fox's debts caused by loss of his property and slaves; letters of John Fox's brother, Washington Fox, concern the operation of a sawmill owned by another brother, Daniel, in Wilcox County, Alabama, and the drabness of his bachelor existence. Daniel was elected an Alabama state representative in 1853; his letters comment on Benjamin Fitzpatrick, C. C. Clay, Jr., internal improvements, and public schools. The collection contains genealogical data. Also represented are Lemuel Boozer, Isaiah Caughman, Henry C. Geiger, Elijah Gautt, William and Henry Leroy Hendrix, Jacob Meetze, A. J. Norris, W. E. Sawyer, and Thomas Shelton.

1878. JOHN WILLIAM FOX, JR., PAPERS, 1890-1897, 1901. 40 items. Big Stone Gap (Wise County), Va.

Letters of a novelist and short story writer to his publishers, Harper & Brothers and The Century. Letters of 1890-1896 are to Richard Watson Gilder and Robert Underwood Johnson of The Century and concern the publication of Fox's story, "A Cumberland Vendetta." Letters of 1897 are to Harper & Brothers and concern two of Fox's books, Hell-fer-Sartain and The Kentuckians. A letter of 1901, from Fox to an unidentified person named Ellen, refers to borrowing some of her ideas for Fox's forthcoming book Bluegrass and Rhododendron.

1879. WILLIAM JOHNSON FOX PAPERS, 1836. 1 item. London, England.

A letter from Robert Nicoll submitting poetry for publication in Fox's magazine, The Monthly Repository.

1880. ANATOLE FRANCE PAPERS, 1901-1932. 18 items and 2 vols. France.

Clippings by and about France and his writings and the sale of his art collection and other effects.

1881. A. B. FRANK DIARY, 1865. 1 vol. (82 pp.) [Setez?] (Lancaster County), Pennsylvania.

Diary kept by A. B. Frank, evidently a Federal soldier, from January 1 to September 17, 1865, regarding weather conditions, camp routine, and General Cadwallader Colden Washburn's coming from Memphis, Tennessee, and reviewing the cavalry.

1882. ALEXANDER FRANK PAPERS, 1858-1878. 82 items. Cedar Bush (Davidson County), N.C.

Correspondence of three North Carolina families, the Headricks (Hedricks), Bosses, and Franks, who settled in Illinois, Missouri, Indiana, and Kentucky, regarding life on the new farmlands as compared with their previous life in North Carolina. One letter from G. W. Frank describes his course of instruction at a North Carolina school, and another from Alexander Frank to his wife, Susanna, is concerned with desertions from the Confederate Army. Letters of George W. and Jesse M. Frank describe the movements of the 48th North Carolina Infantry in the Petersburg area, with comments on food, religion, and camp life; miscellaneous other Civil War letters of the Franks and their cousins, the Leonards, mention skirmishes in Virginia, food, the battles of Spotsylvania Court House and of North Anna Creek.

1883. NELSON FRANK PAPERS, 1908-1961. 290 items. New York, N.Y.

Papers collected by the labor columnist for the New York News World-Telegram and Sun generally concerning the American Federation of Labor and the Congress of Industrial Organizations and affiliated unions, Communism in the labor movement, labor welfare, the careers of Philip Murray and Walter Philip Reuther, and the United Steel Workers of America strike, 1952. These materials include press releases, newsletters, circulars, radio scripts, and processed reports.

1884. BENJAMIN FRANKLIN PAPERS, 1757-1841. 7 items. Philadelphia, Pa.

Transcript of a letter from Franklin to John Langdon, president of New Hampshire, protesting, on behalf of the Abolition Society of Pennsylvania, against importation of slaves on New Hampshire vessels; photocopy of a letter of 1782 (original in the library of the University of Pennsylvania) from Richard Prince of Newington Green, England, introducing two young men, one traveling on the continent for pleasure, the other a migrant to America, and expressing hope for an early end to the war between England and the colonies; and a printed announcement concerning the printing press at which Benjamin Franklin worked as journeyman, with several attached affidavits concerning the authenticity of the press.

1885. H. L. FRANKLIN LETTERS, 1861-1862. 15 items. Vermont.

Letters of a soldier stationed at Camp Griffin, Virginia, to his mother. They deal primarily with food sent from home and with loneliness.

1886. JAMES C. FRANKLIN PAPERS, 1862-1864. 17 items. Pittsylvania County, Va.

Correspondence of a Confederate soldier discussing the Pratt hospital in Lynchburg and the Chimborazo in Richmond; supplies, food, sickness, furlough, desertions, casualties; absence without leave; Confederate generals; and the battle at Richmond.

1887. MARY G. FRANKLIN PAPERS, 1842-1855. 2 vols. Cherokee County, Ga.

An account book, 1847-1855, apparently kept by Mrs. Franklin, a widow, concerning a gold mine, sawmill, farm, water-powered mill, and coal and slate mining begun by her on a 40-acre lot on the Etowah River which she won in the gold lottery of 1832. Included are entries for work by hired hands and slaves in these operations and the adjunct shop and stamper. Work by both men and women is recorded. An account book, 1842-1843, of Mrs. Franklin's son, Bedney L. Franklin, is largely a cashbook of expenditures, both business and personal, and includes accounts for hired workers, a list of slaves, and accounts of profits from the mine in January-April, 1843. This volume was later used by Ophelia Yearby of Athens, Georgia, who copied into it two letters she wrote to the (Atlanta) <u>Sunny</u> <u>South</u>. Mrs. Franklin's holdings became the Franklin & McDonald Mining and Manufacturing Co. after 1882.

1888. WILLIAM TEMPLE FRANKLIN PAPERS, 1809. 1 item. Paris, France.

Letter of George Fox of Philadelphia to Franklin, a resident of Paris and grandson of Benjamin Franklin, introducing George Emlen, also of Philadelphia.

1889. FREDERICK FRASER PAPERS, 1740-1924. 23 items and 1 vol. Beaufort (Beaufort County), S.C.

Papers of a cotton planter of the South Carolina low country containing material on commercial problems during the War of 1812; fragmentary records on the cotton factorage business of Fraser and Thompson; information on cotton sales for Frederick Fraser by his nephew Joseph August Winthrop in Charleston; references to sea-island cotton and to a large Russian contract for cloth; a letter from Iredell Jones, a cousin, concerning his trial as a member of the Ku Klux Klan, 1872. A scrapbook (152 pp.) contains miscellaneous material on the De Saussure and many other South Carolina families and on social life in the state and the Civil War. Included are portraits, poems, letters, copies of tombstone engravings, invitations, material about patriotic societies and ancestors, and newspaper clippings. There are letters from Henry De Saussure Fraser, a C.S.A. surgeon in Virginia; he comments on life as a Union prisoner, 1863-1864, in Fort McHenry and Old Capitol Prison and hopes of escape; military activities and anticipation of British intervention; and depredations of the Army of the Potomac. He also describes the Charleston earthquake, 1886. The scrapbook also contains material on Mr. and Mrs. Edgar Warner Mills in the Far East and on their memberships in patriotic societies. Also in the scrapbook is a small volume of De Saussure family genealogy. Other persons mentioned in the collection include Thomas Boone Fraser, Sr., Daniel De Saussure (1735-1798), and Henry William De Saussure (1763-1839).

1890. JAMES FRASER PAPERS, 1779-1789. 1 vol. Halifax, Nova Scotia, Canada.

Copies of deeds, affidavits, a bill of sale for Negroes, inventories of real and personal property, and a catalog of books of the property of a Presbyterian clergyman of Hillsborough, North Carolina, who fled as a Loyalist to New Brunswick and later to Halifax during the American Revolution. Fraser's Hillsborough estate, "Hartford," was used by Cornwallis as British headquarters in Hillsborough and later occupied and, according to Fraser, damaged by American troops.

1891. MARY (DE SAUSSURE) FRASER PAPERS, 1780-1886. 395 items and 4 vols. Charleston, S.C.

Correspondence, business papers, and account books of three generations of the Fraser family of Charleston. Included in the collection are a few records concerning William R. Davie, prominent Federalist, governor of North Carolina, and one of the founders of the University of North Carolina, Chapel Hill; bills and receipts made to Mary (Fraser) Davie, second wife of Frederick William Davie, which constitute more than half the collection; and a letter to Alexander Fraser from Charles Lorimer of Shooter's Hill, Kent, England, concerning property in South Carolina. The greater part of the collection consists of correspondence of Mary (De Saussure) Fraser (1772-1853), wife of Frederick Fraser (1762-1816), including letters from her son, Frederick Grimké Fraser, in Beaufort, South Carolina, dealing with life around Beaufort, 1831-1841, family affairs, farming operations, political matters, clothing and equipment for slaves, and religious revivals held by one Walker; letters from her daughter, Mary (Fraser) Daniel, while touring Europe in 1844; family letters from Edward McCrady (1833-1903), South Carolina soldier and historian; a letter from Charles Fraser, the artist, to his mother; and papers regarding William Davie's career as peace commissioner to France in 1799. Included also is an early nineteenth-century memorandum entitled "Amount Expenses of a Journey from Charleston to the Virginia Hot and Sulphur Springs and back to Charleston via Philadelphia." Among the other correspondents are Timothy Bloodworth, Sarah (Jones) Davie, and John Rust Eaton. Included also is an account book, 1850-1851, of the estate of Frederick William Davie with James Adger and Company, apparently commission merchants engaged in cotton buying; and records kept by Mary F. (Fraser) Davie as administratrix of her husband's estate and accounts of household and personal expenditures. Included also are one hundred and five clippings.

1892. MARY JANE FRASER NOTEBOOK, 1842. 1 vol. (66 pp.) Charleston, S.C.

Notes on "The Church Universal" in the form of questions and answers.

1893. JOSEPH FRAVEL LEDGER, 1874-1904. 1 vol. (438 pp.) Woodstock (Shenandoah County), Va.

Ledger of a manufacturer of furniture, doors, blinds, sashes, and other wooden articles. Until 1881 the business was a partnership between Joseph and his brother David Fravel. Accounts are most abundant for the 1880s and 1890s and include prices of the firm's products.

1894. RICHARD BEVERLY FRAYSER PAPERS, 1841-1885. 16 items and 1 vol. Appomattox County, Va.

Most of the papers are copies of public prayers; articles, some submitted for newspaper publication; and public addresses, among them one given on the occasion of President Grant's burial and one in opposition to the secession of Virginia. Included are advertisements and broadsides for Washington Academy, Amelia County, Virginia, and Blue Ridge Academy, Bedford County, Virginia. There is also a printed order, 1861, directing the organization of the police and courts in Patrick County and the administration of oaths of allegiance to the Confederacy.

1895. E. W. FRAZIER PAPERS, 1860-1879. 8 items. Bush Hill (Randolph County), N.C.

Genealogical material.

1896. STEPHEN FRAZIER PAPERS, 1852-1871. 79 items. Alexander and Catawba counties, N.C.

Letters of a Confederate soldier in the 45th North Carolina Regiment stationed in Virginia; near Goldsboro, North Carolina; and Kinston, North Carolina. There are also letters to Stephen Frazier's wife Mary Elizabeth (Fulp) Frazier from her sisters and her husband, discussing family affairs and the war.

1897. [ELI FREEMAN?] LEDGER, 1855-1858. 1 vol. (128 pp.) Wadesboro (Anson County), N.C.

A ledger of a firm that repaired and maintained carriages and buggies.

1898. FREEMASONS. FAYETTEVILLE (CUMBERLAND COUNTY), N.C. PHOENIX LODGE, NO. 8. PAPERS, 1793-1854. 4 items.

Articles of agreement, 1798, leasing part of Mason's Hall to Fayetteville Academy; a contract for construction work on a lodge, 1793.

1899. FREEMASONS. WILMINGTON (NEW HANOVER COUNTY), N.C. LODGE NO. 319. PAPERS, 1794-1910. 39 items.

Accounts; brief history of Masonry in the United States and in North Carolina; and biographical sketches of some of the grand masters of the lodge, including Richard Caswell, George Patterson, Louis Henry De Rossett, John Lucas Cantwell, William A. Cumming, Thomas B. Carr, Edward Wilson Manning, William P. Oldham, Alexander and Rudolph E. Heide, and John D. Bellamy.

1900. JOHN CHARLES FRÉMONT PAPERS, 1856. 1 item. Monterey (Monterey County), Calif.

A letter to Henry Stephens Randall, agriculturalist and historian, advising that some books mailed by Randall had not been received.

1901. SAMUEL GIBBS FRENCH PAPERS, 1848-1904. 18 items. Woodbury (Gloucester County), N.J.

Requisitions for army supplies during the Mexican War; pay accounts, 1848; orders to and for French, an officer during the Mexican War and afterward, and in the Confederate Army during the Civil War. Two letters of 1894 indicate that French was then living in New Jersey.

1902. THEODORE FRENCH LEDGER AND DAYBOOK, 1820-1824. 2 vols. Boston, Mass., and Concord (Merrimac County), N.H.

1903. SOCIETY OF FRIENDS. CHELMSFORD, ENGLAND. MINUTES, 1868-1884. 1 vol. (376 pp.)

Bible class minutes, 1868-1870, and Young Women Friends' Christian Union minutes, 1876-1884.

1904. SOCIETY OF FRIENDS. DUTCHMAN CREEK (DAVIE COUNTY), N.C., PREPARATIVE MEETING. PAPERS, 1894-1902. 1 item and 1 vol.

Minutes; list of members; reports to the East Bend Monthly Meeting, Yadkin County; blank form for statistical report.

1905. HENRY ELIAS FRIES PAPERS, 1869 (1874-1877) 1884. 30 items. Salem (Forsyth County), N.C.

Letters from Henry E. Fries (b. 1857), interested in the development of electricity, to his mother while he was a student at Davidson College, North Carolina. The collection gives some information on Davidson College in the middle 1870's and concerns Fries's studies, his professors, his friends, and general activities of student life. Included is a catalog of the products of the woolen, cotton, and flour mills owned by F. & H. Fries, Salem, North Carolina, containing some cloth samples.

1906. JACOB FRIEZE SERMONS. 1 vol. (222 pp.) Rhode Island.

Included are notes on a sermon by Wilbur Fisk, a Methodist Episcopal minister, and sermons by Frieze, Universalist minister in Rhode Island and in Wilmington, North Carolina, with critical comments on Methodists and Presbyterians.

1907. CHARLES S. FROST PAPERS, 1873-1913. 216 items. Watkins (Schuyler County), N.Y.

Largely business letters from manufacturing companies and wholesale dealers to Frost, proprietor of a general merchandise store and the Glen Park Hotel, Watkins, New York. Included are printed lists of wholesale and retail prices. There are also a letter, 1899, from Frost's son Glen of the New York legislature, mentioning race relations; and a letter, 1899, of Benjamin B. Odell, chairman of the Republican state committee, concerning politics.

1908. DANIEL A. FROST JOURNALS, 1808-1837. 6 vols. Wilmington (New Hanover County), N.C.; New York, and Poughkeepsie (Dutchess County), N.Y.

Business affairs and social and religious activities of a merchant in Wilmington, later a merchant and boardinghouse keeper in New York City and a farmer at Poughkeepsie. There is information on social life and customs; camp meetings; fortification of Brooklyn during the War of 1812; Presbyterian church in New York; and elections there in the 1830s.

1909. MILTON FROST LETTERS, 1838-1882. 22 items. Baltimore, Md.

Letters of a minister, filled with religious exhortations. Correspondents include his brother William Frost describing living conditions in Texas, and his sister Rebecca, writing from Greensboro Female College, 1847.

1910. JAMES ANTHONY FROUDE PAPERS, 1861-1890. 16 items. London, England.

Miscellaneous letters and social notes from Froude, British historian. Many items are of uncertain date. The collection includes letters to Edwin De Leon, American diplomat, concerning sectionalism in the United States; to Fanny Kingsley, widow of the British author Charles Kingsley; to Lady Augusta Stanley, wife of Arthur Penrhyn Stanley, Dean of Westminster, discussing Froude's writings; to General John Jarvis Bisset on the government of South Africa, 1877; a statement against having a literary authority in England comparable to the French Academy; and letters discussing Froude's discovery of William Thomas's sixteenth century work, "The Pilgrim," and plans for its publication; to Robert Spence Watson about a lecture appointment at Newcastle, 1866; to poet John Westland Marston, 1877; and to American publisher Charles Scribner concerning international copyright, 1879.

1911. SIR JOSEPH FULLER PAPERS, 1819-1841. 35 items. London, England.

Personal, social, and military letters to General Fuller, his wife, Mary (Floyd) Fuller, and daughter Juliana Rebecca Fuller. Correspondents include Baron Knesebeck; the Earl of Munster; General Charles D'Orsay; Sir Robert Peel, Second Baronet; the Countess of Pembroke; Sir Robert Smirke; Lord Walpole; and the Duke of Wellington. A letter, Dec. 5, 1838, of General Viscount Rowland Hill proposes to relieve Fuller of the presidency of the board of general officers and to nominate General Sir J. C. Dalbiac to replace him.

1912. SOLON L. FULLER PAPERS, 1861-1863. 48 items. Georgia.

Correspondence of a Confederate soldier and his family portraying some of the economic and health problems of a Southern farm family during the Civil War.

1913. STEPHEN FULLER PAPERS, 1702 (1786-1796). 42 items and 2 vols. London, England.

Scrapbooks of press copies of letters, manuscript tables, clippings and pages from newspapers, and letters collected by the colonial agent for Jamaica, 1763-1794, representing that colony in London. There are many letters to well-known inventors and doctors relating to scientific advances; letters on trade and legislation affecting Jamaica; on the government and politics of England and Jamaica; the anti-slavery movement; tables of customs statistics and import and export lists; letters to George Rose and William Pitt concerning a proposed marine insurance agency and the abolition of vice admiralty courts; slave insurrections in the Spanish West Indies, 1790s; sugar rebates; elimination of competition from other colonies like Sierra Leone; the right of Jamaica to trade with America during war and hurricane crises; protective tariffs and suppression of smuggling which injured Jamaica's rum industry; a statue of George Brydges, Lord Rodney, which Fuller purchased for Jamaica from sculptor John Bacon; planting of breadfruit in the West Indies; the Freeport Act; statistics on population, proportioned by race; the regency crisis of George III; naval preparations for war with Spain during the Nootka Sound Controversy, 1790; the foreign imbroglios of William Pitt; war with France, 1793; and the politics resulting in Fuller's loss of the agency. There are also letters of congratulation to him for a job well done. Loose materials include pages from account books and letters relating to topics similar to those above, and editorials. Clippings concerning the slave trade are scattered throughout the collection. Important correspondents to Fuller are William Blake, Joseph Maria Chacon, Henry Dundas, George Augustus Eliott, William Wyndham Grenville, Charles Jenkinson, Charles Lennox, William Pitt the Younger, and Howard Thomas.

1914. WILLIAMSON WHITEHEAD FULLER PAPERS, 1922-1935. 2 items and 2 vols. Briarcliffe Manor (Westchester County), N.Y.

Material written by Fuller, who was general counsel for the American Tobacco Company, includes a letter to a nephew eulogizing James B. Duke, 1925; an epitaph for Archibald Henderson Boyden, 1930, and a small handmade volume of light verse written for his daughter, Janet, and dated 1922-1932. Most of the poems in this volume have been published in By-Paths, a collection of occasional writings of Williamson W. Fuller (1926). There is also a printed memorial address to Fuller delivered by Justice Junius Parker before the Supreme Court of North Carolina, 1935, including remarks of Chief Justice Stacy accepting a portrait of Fuller for the court chambers.

1915. FULLER-THOMAS FAMILY PAPERS, 1810-1904. 1,322 items. Louisburg (Franklin County) and Wilmington (New Hanover County), N.C.

Personal and business papers of Jones Fuller (1808-1870), a cotton broker, merchant, and Methodist minister of Mobile, Alabama, and Louisburg, North Carolina; his son Edwin Wiley Fuller (1847-1876), a writer and poet; William George Thomas (d. ca. 1889), a physician of Wilmington; and their relatives.

1916. DAVID FULLERTON PAPERS, 1787-1920. 218 items. Greencastle (Franklin County), Pa.

Papers of Fullerton (1772-1843), major during the War of 1812; U.S. representative from Pennsylvania, 1819-1820; and Pennsylvania state senator, 1827-1839; and papers of the Ervin, Gordon, and Snively families. Topics include Fullerton's business interests, the Franklin Rail Road Company, of which he was treasurer; the settlement of estates in Pennsylvania; and the state supreme court. A few papers deal with the Civil War.

1917. JOSEPH SCOTT FULLERTON PAPERS, 1864. 4 items. Cleveland (Bradley County), Tenn.

An order from Fullerton as assistant adjutant general, Fourth Army Corps, to Col. Edward M. McCook; and clippings.

1918.  SALLIE M. H. FULTON PAPERS,
       1848-1865.  42 items.
       Baltimore, Md.

Correspondence of a Baltimore belle, including personal letters from her young friends in Charles Town, West Virginia, and in York, Pennsylvania, with comments on social life and customs.  One of the York letters tells of the Confederate invasion and compliments the orderly conduct of the soldiers; another speaks of the numbers of young men leaving for the army.

1919.  WINSTON FULTON LEDGER,
       1851-1855.  1 vol. (531 pp.)
       Danbury (Stokes County), N.C.

Ledger of a general merchant.

1920.  ANDREW FUNKHOUSER PAPERS,
       1786 (1836-1908) 1941.
       1,968 items and 13 vols.  Mount Jackson (Shenandoah County), Va.

Family letters and business papers of the Funkhouser family, and, after 1910, of the Miller family.  Most of the papers prior to 1830 are deeds for land in Philadelphia and Virginia.  There are two land patents, one signed by Edmund Randolph, governor of Virginia, to Peter Hoshaur, 1788, and one signed by Joseph Johnson, governor of Virginia, to Andrew Funkhouser, 1851.  From the 1830s there are numerous letters from relatives in Virginia, Ohio, Missouri, Indiana, and Wisconsin describing the move westward, religion, railroads, economic conditions, land speculation, opposition to slavery, commerce, Indians, army forts, legal affairs, stock raising, farming, sickness and health, and the Mormon problem in Missouri.  Many of these letters are from Funkhouser's son-in-law, John Kerr, a lawyer and speculator.  There are also several wills and estate papers.  Civil War letters include items from R. H. Simpson with directions for his home farm and statements about Walker's and Archer's brigades on Funkhouser's land and the amount of wood they used.  There is an account book mentioning Confederate Army purchases; papers relating to a claim against the United States for farm buildings, equipment and products burned or seized by order of General Sheridan; and tax in kind estimates and receipts.  A diary of Rev. G. H. Snapp of the United Brethren in Christ Church, a brother-in-law of Andrew's son, Casper, discusses his circuit, revivals, conferences, and chaplains in the army; there are also many letters to Snapp down to 1900.  Other letters are from commission merchants in Winchester, Baltimore, Alexandria, and Washington both before and after the Civil War; price current bulletins from Washington, 1890s; and other business letters.  Most of the letters after 1880 are from the children of Casper Funkhouser.  There is a related genealogical and biographical sketch.  These letters describe Shenandoah Seminary, Dayton, Virginia, 1880-1882; Bonebrake Theological Seminary, Dayton, Ohio; teaching at various places in Ohio, Maryland, Virginia, and New Jersey in the 1880s and 1890s; and family affairs.  Papers concerning the family of Edward J. Miller include tax receipts, wheat allotment applications, and condolences on Miller's death.  Printed materials with the collection relate to teaching, insurance, an 1899 civil service examination, and standing orders for a mental hospital.  Other business papers include tax receipts for Andrew Funkhouser, 1830-1886; tax receipts on Missouri land, 1850-1880; notes, receipts, and bills.  Numerous letters refer to the temperance movement in the United Brethren Church and to Andrew Funkhouser's work as a trustee.  In the 1880s there are business papers of the Shenandoah Valley Assembly.  Bound volumes include the roll of shareholders and minutes of the meetings of the Shenandoah Valley Assembly, daybooks, 1847-1861, and a ledger, 1836-1843, of Andrew Funkhouser, a list of the personal property of Jacob R. Funkhouser, 1856, and daybooks of John Bauserman, a merchant of Hawkinstown, Shenandoah County, Virginia.

1921.  JOSEPH FUQUA PAPERS, 1853.
       1 item.  New Canton (Buckingham County), Va.

A letter from Frederick W. Bass about legal affairs.

1922.  SAMUEL FUQUA ACCOUNT BOOK,
       1835-1866.  1 vol.  Charlotte County, Va.

Account book of Samuel Fuqua, agent for Richard Gaines.  The volume contains records of household expenses, labor, settlement of estates, etc.; and a written agreement between a Virginia planter and his slaves regarding their continued service after emancipation.

1923.  MCDONALD FURMAN PAPERS,
       1883-1903.  36 items and
       1 vol.  Privateer (Sumter District), S.C.

Family and business correspondence of McDonald Furman (1863-1904), lecturer, student of local history, and member of the South Carolina Historical Society, largely from his aunt "Ann" and from Mrs. D. Eli Dunlap, a teacher in the Presbyterian Mission School established for the Catawba Indians in York County, South Carolina.  Included are political comments and references to Clemson College, South Carolina, and Richard Furman's writings.  Also, among the undated material, are a biographical sketch of Richard Furman and a long genealogical chart showing the connections of the Furman family.

Included also is an unusual account book for Cornhill Plantation in Sumter District, apparently kept by John Blount Miller from its beginning in 1827 until about 1860, when it was evidently taken over by his son-in-law, Dr. John H. Furman.  The book contains a note that Dr. John H. Furman (d. 1902) and Susan Miller went to Cornhill Plantation on November 20, 1859. The plantation book includes many different types of records kept by Miller: receipts; expenditures; marriages, births, and deaths of slaves; weekly rations and clothing issued to his slaves; domestic animals on the plantation; corn, cotton, and other crops produced; illnesses, deaths, and visits of members of the family; lands owned and inventories of tools; rules for governing slaves; accounts of unusual weather; and lists of keys. In the latter portion of the account book, kept by John H. Furman, there are many records of contracts with freedmen, and accounts of money and goods advanced to them. A letter of James L. Furman, 1891, relates to the publication of his history of Louisiana.

1924. HENRY SANDERSON FURNISS, FIRST BARON SANDERSON, PAPERS, 1930. 1 item. London, England.

A letter from Sanderson commenting upon leaving his post at Oxford University and assuming his duties in the House of Lords.

1925. FANNIE (BENNETT) GADDY PAPERS, 1864-1880. 72 items. Polkton (Anson County), N.C.

Personal and love letters of Fannie Bennett from her cousin and later husband, Risden B. Gaddy, including letter describing a knightly tournament and a gander pulling held by Rufus Barringer's cavalry brigade.

1926. JAMES GADSDEN PAPERS, 1777-1856. 32 items. Charleston, S.C.

Papers of the family of Gadsden (1788-1858), Florida planter, member of legislative council of Florida Territory, and minister to Mexico in 1853. Included are references to British strategy during the Revolutionary War and the defenses of Charleston, 1777; an inventory and the marriage contract of Philip Gadsden Edwards and Anna Margaret Edwards; a letter, 1836, concerning abolitionist publications; a letter, 1842, to Paymaster General Nathan Towson, concerning claims for supplies furnished the Florida Militia; and photostats of diplomatic correspondence largely from Percy W. Doyle and W. G. Lettsom to the Earl of Clarendon, British Secretary of Foreign Affairs, pertaining to United States-Mexican relations, discussing the Gadsden Purchase, Santa Anna, and conditions and rumors in Mexico.

1927. GEORGE GAGE PAPERS, 1864-1903. 2 items and 4 vols. Beaufort (Beaufort County), S.C.

Three letter books of George Gage and the journal of his wife, Sarah Marshall (Ely) Gage. A letter book, 1873-1876, concerns Gage's positions as collector of customs and superintendent of lights, including references to trade at Beaufort and Port Royal, the South Carolina Free School Fund, and teachers' salaries and attendance statistics of black and white children at St. Helena's and St. Luke's parishes. A letter book, 1884-1890, deals principally with Gage's business operating a sawmill, but also contains information on South Carolina politics, particularly the local government in Beaufort, and letters to Clara Barton, president of the American Red Cross. A letter book, 1894-1903, pertains chiefly to family matters, with references to construction carried on by the United States government in the Beaufort harbor. The journal, 1864-1866, of Sarah Gage contains the minutes of the Freedmen's and Home Relief Association of Lambertville, New Jersey, and accounts of her travels from Philadelphia to Beaufort and her work as a teacher in the Negro schools. Included are comments on her social life, the work of the Freedmen's bureau, and the status of the Negro.

1928. WILLIAM M. GAGE AND JOHN R. PERRY PAPERS, 1856 (1882-1915). 1,603 items. Saratoga Springs (Saratoga County), N.Y.

Letters, bills, and receipts pertaining to the operation of the United States Hotel, Saratoga Springs, operated by William M. Gage and John R. Perry. Included are bills and receipts, 1880s, addressed to Janwin and Gillis, operators of the Troy House, Troy, New York.

1929. PETER CORDES GAILLARD PAPERS, 1858. 1 item. Charleston, S.C.

Letter to H. M. Haig in Paris, France, concerning business matters and a monument to be erected in memory of John C. Calhoun.

1930. EDMUND PENDLETON GAINES PAPERS, 1815-1857. 3 items. New Orleans, La.

Chiefly a report of 1838 from General Edmund Pendleton Gaines (1777-1849) concerning national defense, emphasizing the importance of railroads, and criticizing reliance on defense works and fortifications. Included is a discussion of the system he proposed in his Canals and Turnpike Roads (1826), and the constitutional justification for his plan.

1931. EDWIN LEWIS GAINES COMMONPLACE BOOK, 1899-1911. 1 vol. (30 pp.) "Locust Hill," Culpeper (Culpeper County), Va.

Correspondence, accounts, and records of a farm near Culpeper, Virginia.

1932.  J. M. GAINES BOOKS, 1866-1914. 31 vols. Washington County, Md.

Ledgers, 1873-1911, daybooks, 1868-1889, account books, 1866-1871 and 1882-1898, diary, 1866-1867, a cashbook, 1869-1876, a physician's waiting list, 1870-1878, and a farm book, 1907-1914.

1933.  JAMES S. GAINES PAPERS, 1823 (1836-1876). 12 items. Sullivan County, Tenn.

Letters to James S. Gaines and his wife, Letitia Gaines, from family and business associates, with interesting comments on the sale of a slave in 1845, on a camp meeting, and on a yellow fever epidemic in Alabama in 1854.

1934.  ORA B. GAINES PAPERS, 1862. 2 items. Massachusetts.

Personal letters from Ora B. Gaines, a member of Company E, 46th Regiment, Massachusetts Volunteers, stationed near New Bern, North Carolina, during the winter of 1862, concerning the weather, food, and army life.

1935.  JAMES GAIRDNER PAPERS, 1771-1816. 84 items. Charleston, S.C.

Letters and accounts of a Charleston merchant dealing in lumber, rum, tar, and wine, with firms in England, France, and the British West Indies. Included are references to difficulties of commerce during the Napoleonic period.

1936.  ELLA GAITHER PAPERS, 1881-1891. 24 items. Mocksville (Davie County), N.C.

Personal and family letters.

1937.  JOSEPH GALES PAPERS, 1814-1869. 6 items and 1 vol. Washington, D.C.

Business papers of Joseph Gales (1786-1860), publisher, and his wife, Sarah Juliana Maria (Lee) Gales. Included are mercantile and household accounts, 1814-1816; letters pertaining to a mineral lease on land owned by Sarah Gales; and a ledger of Gales & Seaton, publishers of the National Intelligencer, the Annals of Congress, the Register of Debates in Congress, and the American State Papers, containing accounts, 1825-1854, and a list of bad debts extending back to 1815, with figures and explanatory notes.

1938.  CHARLES GALLAGHER PAPERS, 1885-1888. 11 items. New York, N.Y.

Papers of Charles Gallagher include a letter of application, 1885, discussing his Civil War service as purveyor to General Benjamin F. Butler and as adviser to L. C. Baker in tracing the assassin of Abraham Lincoln; and statements, Congressional bills, and other papers relating to Gallagher's claims for relief for the loss of his schooner Nimrod during the Civil War.

1939.  GALLAHER FAMILY PAPERS, 1800-1924. 2,037 items and 7 vols. Charles Town (Jefferson County), W. Va.

Principally the personal correspondence of the Gallaher and related Wilson families. Included are letters of Alpheus Waters Wilson (1834-1916), a Methodist bishop in Baltimore, and of Augusta Virginia Wilson, a Methodist missionary and school-teacher, describing her activities on a Creek reservation in the Indian Territory, 1887-1890, and at Chihuahua and Guadalajara, Mexico, 1890-1898. There are receipts, ca. 1820-1880, for advertisements and subscriptions to the Virginia Free Press, published by the Gallahers, copies of advertisements, and scattered letters referring to the newspaper business, as well as some legal papers, printed material, and other miscellaneous papers.

1940.  ARTHUR R. GALLIMORE PAPERS, ca. 1933. 2 items. Canton, China.

A reprint of an article written for The New East by Arthur R. Gallimore, member of the South China Mission of the Southern Baptist Convention, entitled "The New Work of the South China Mission among the Hakkas in Wai Chow"; and a Christmas card containing a photograph of Gallimore.

1941.  SIR ALEXANDER TILLOCH GALT PAPERS, 1883. 1 item. Seaforth, Quebec, Canada.

Letter to Sir Alexander Tilloch Galt, Canadian government official, concerning financial matters.

1942.  ROBERT GALT NOTEBOOKS, 1858-1860. 3 vols. Fluvanna County, Va.

Notes taken by Robert Galt on medical and chemistry lectures at the University of Pennsylvania, Philadelphia.

1943.  WILLIAM GALT, JR., PAPERS, 1812 (1816-1835) 1941. 102 items. Richmond, Va.

Personal and business correspondence and clippings of William Galt, Jr., concerning his removal from Scotland to America to work in the countinghouse of William Galt, Sr., a distant relative; his imminent trip to Richmond; politics in America; the people and customs of Virginia; the will of William Galt, Sr.; and references in the letters of John and Mary Allan, cousins of William Galt, Jr., to Edgar Allan Poe, foster child of John Allan. Among the correspondents are John Allan, Mary Allan, Allan Fowlds, Margaret Galt, Thomas Galt, William Galt, Sr., John Miller, and Nicholas Walsh.

1944. GANDY FAMILY PAPERS,
1848-1868. 18 items.
Darlington (Darlington County), S.C.

Fragmentary correspondence of a South Carolina planter; an account sheet showing the expenses of a daughter at Salem Female Academy, Salem, North Carolina, 1862; and a letter concerning details of executing the law to impress slaves for labor on Confederate fortifications.

1945. JAMES R. GARBER PAPERS,
1861, 1864. 2 items.
Selma (Dallas County), Ala.

Family letters of a Confederate soldier concerning the purchase of land by a member of the Garber family, and the treatment of horses in the regiment during his absence.

1946. ANN HENSHAW GARDINER PAPERS,
1753-1970. 3,518 items,
77 vols. and 1 tape.
Martinsburg (Berkeley County), W. Va.

Personal, legal, and financial correspondence, clippings, pamphlets, broadsides, and volumes of Ann Henshaw Gardiner, a nursing school teacher. The papers contain information on genealogy, especially the Henshaw, Snodgrass and Gardiner families, as well as some on the related Anderson, Verdier, Turner, Evans, McConnell, Pendleton, Robinson, and Rawlings families; the history of Berkeley County; the flour milling businesses of the Henshaw and of the Snodgrass families; slaves, including lists of slaves and their ages, and material pertaining to runaways; the passage of the woman suffrage amendment; politics in Berkeley County, and in Washington, D.C.; and the beginnings of the nursing program at Duke University Hospital, Durham, North Carolina. Financial papers include bills and receipts, loans, and household and business accounts of Levi Henshaw (1769-1843) and Levi Henshaw (1815-1896), and of Robert Verdier Snodgrass (1792-1861). Legal papers concern the settlement of numerous estates; judicial positions, such as justice of the peace and clerk of court, held by various members of the Henshaw and Snodgrass families, including material on schools, roads, runaway slaves, the hiring of servants, and the mail; the acquisition of land, including deeds, survey plats, and land office records; and the militia, including class rolls, rosters, and officers' lists. Volumes include an Age Book, 1821-1861, of the Snodgrass family and their slaves; daybooks and farm books, 1803-1840s; postal card albums; an autograph album; albums and manuscript histories of the first ten years of the Duke University School of Nursing, including pictures, programs, invitations, clippings, letters, poems, and pamphlets; and scrapbooks. There is also a cassette tape of an address by Ann Gardiner at the fortieth anniversary banquet of the Alumni Association of the Nursing School of the Duke Medical Center, April 10, 1970.

1947. AMANDA E. (EDNEY) GARDNER PAPERS,
1833-1892. 89 items.
Cahaba (Dallas County), Ala.

Personal and family letters of Amanda E. (Edney) Gardner containing comments on social life and customs in the antebellum South, the descriptions of the Florida countryside with references to the danger from Indians and to the climate, and the education at Presbyterian Female Collegiate Institute, Talladega, Alabama, of her daughter, Elizabeth A. Gardner, 1854-1855. Civil War letters from her son, John A. Gardner, a Confederate soldier, describe a military skirmish, the first battle of Manassas, camp life, illness, the election of regimental officers, wages, and conscription.

1948. CAROLINE GARDNER PAPERS,
1857-1864. 36 items.
Randolph County, N.C.

Civil War letters to Caroline Gardner from Thomas J. Gardner, 2nd Regiment, North Carolina Cavalry, and from Marshall Moffitt, describing camp life, military skirmishes, prisoners, and a speech by Governor Vance, 1864. Also included are papers of the Kivett family of Missouri containing descriptions of Texas County, Missouri, and camp life during the war.

1949. HERBERT COULSTOUN GARDNER, FIRST BARON BURGHCLERE OF WALDEN, PAPERS, 1914-1915. 2 items.
London, England.

Personal letter of Herbert Coulstoun Gardner, First Baron Burghclere of Walden, (1846-1921), to Edmund William Gosse; and a poem by Gardner entitled "After-Math" (The Times [London], November 27, 1914).

1950. JOHN L. GARDNER PAPERS,
1868-1869. 28 items.
New Bern (Craven County), N.C.

Personal and business letters and shipping invoices addressed to John L. Gardner, a shipping agent of New Bern. Letters mention commodity prices in North Carolina. Invoices list merchandise shipped from New York City to New Bern.

1951. PARIS CLEVELAND GARDNER PAPERS,
1834-1976. 3,156 items. Shelby (Cleveland County), N.C.

Personal, legal, and professional papers of Paris Cleveland Gardner (1887-1974), attorney, and staff member of the Federal

Trade Commission. Correspondence, 1919-1940, pertains largely to Gardner's financial concerns, but also contains information on conditions in Oklahoma, ca. 1916-1924, North Carolina state politics, 1920s and 1930s, state and national elections, 1920s and 1930s, the state election laws, 1926-1927, and Workmen's Compensation Laws, 1920s. Legal papers comprise documents, 1926-1932, relating to his parents' estates and to his repeated candidacy for solicitor; and files, 1834-1932, for his private legal practice, containing records of a lawsuit between a sharecropper and his landlord, of the harrassment of a member of the International Workers of the World, of the investigation of the title to an oil field near Beaumont, Texas, and of the Shelby Building and Loan Association. The Federal Trade Commission files reflect Gardner's position as attorney-examiner investigating deceptive advertising practice and contain complaints about misleading or false advertising, and papers dealing with investigative procedures and techniques, including interviews and scientific testing of claims about products by the Bureau of Standards. Printed material, 1918-1935, clippings, 1918-1936, and miscellany, 1926-1948, principally concern North Carolina politics.

1952. LOUIS GARESCHÉ PAPERS, 1849-1925. 85 items. Washington, D.C.

Correspondence of Louis Garesché with French families whose forebears had settled in the West Indies, concerning his family history; with his sisters, who aspired to become nuns; and from Catholic priests and church officials in praise of his father, Colonel Julius Peter Garesché (1821-1862), soldier and founder of the Society of St. Vincent de Paul.

1953. JAMES ABRAM GARFIELD PAPERS, 1880-1882. 6 items. Cleveland (Cuyahoga County), Ohio.

Papers of James A. Garfield (1831-1881), president of the United States, include two letters of recommendation for office seekers; an invitation to Garfield's inaugural ball; a facsimile of a letter from Garfield to Marshall Jewell, chairman of the Republican National Committee, denouncing as a forgery the Morey letter concerning Chinese immigration; an announcement of a memorial service in Garfield's honor; and a certificate of the Garfield National Masonic Memorial Association of Washington, D.C.

1954. ADDISON GARLAND PAPERS, 1835-1862. 7 items. Washington, D.C.

Military papers of an officer in the U.S. Marine Corps, including three letters notifying him of promotions and a membership certificate of the U.S. Naval Lyceum.

1955. JAMES GARLAND PAPERS, 1798 (1804-1873) 1881. 215 items. Lynchburg (Campbell County), Va.

Papers of James Garland (1791 or 1792-1885), lawyer, judge, legislator, and public official, comprise business letters, mercantile accounts, bills and receipts, and legal correspondence, accounts and papers. Included is some information on Richard Newton Hewitt, M.D., and the Hewitt family, and elections in 1869 and 1873.

1956. JAMES GARLAND ACCOUNT BOOKS, 1817-1840. 4 vols. Danville (Pittsylvania County), Va.

Account books of a Danville lawyer.

1957. THOMAS GARLAND PAPERS, 1805 (1829-1870) 1911. 944 items. "Buck Island," Albemarle County, Va.

Personal and business correspondence of Thomas Garland, including letters from James Maury Garland giving analyses of the prices of staple products, especially tobacco; and letters concerning agriculture, styles in women's dress during the first half of the nineteenth century, antagonism toward slavery, and interest in state politics.

1958. BENJAMIN A. GARLINGER, SR., PAPERS, 1819-1895. 24 items. Hagerstown (Washington County), Md.

Business and personal letters and legal documents, including land deeds, relating to Benjamin A. Garlinger, Sr.

1959. JOHN GARNER PAPERS, 1825-1828. 26 items. Cunningham's Store (Person County), N.C.

Business letters.

1960. SAMUEL GARNER AND CO. ACCOUNT BOOK, 1869-1873. 1 vol. (31 pp.) [Winston, N.C.?]

Stagecoach fares received by S. B. Spainhower for Samuel Garner and Co.

1961. JACK H. GARNET PAPERS, 1895. 3 items. New York, N.Y.

Love letters between Jack H. Garnet and his girlfriend, Edith R.

1962. JAMES MERCER GARNETT PAPERS, 1733-1923. 153 items and 4 vols. Aldie (Loudoun County), Va.

The papers of the Garnett family include personal and business letters of James Mercer Garnett (1770-1843), educator, legislator, and agriculturalist; letters from Henry St. George Tucker commenting on the administrations of Jefferson and Madison and on American foreign policy; family correspondence between Ann Garnett and her brother, Theodore Stanford Garnett, a college student; letters from James Mercer Garnett (1840-1916) while studying in Germany, 1869-1870, describing his travels and experiences; a chronicle of service in the Confederate Army of James Mercer Garnett (1840-1916), giving accounts of several major battles and skirmishes, privations of the army life, individual characteristics of various officers, anecdotes, and newspaper clippings of Civil War developments; and family correspondence, 1890-1916, concerning genealogical questions.

1963.   ROBERT SELDEN GARNETT, JR., PAPERS, 1853. 1 item.

A letter from Robert Seldon Garnett, Jr. (1819-1861), brigadier general in the Confederate Army, concerning useless supplies.

1964.   J. P. GARRICK LEDGER, 1871-1874. 1 vol. (205 pp.) Pickens (Pickens County), S.C.

Mercantile accounts.

1965.   JAMES P. GARRICK ACCOUNT BOOKS, 1875-1890. 2 vols. Richland County, S.C.

Accounts of a plantation store.

1966.   J. P. GARRIS PAPERS, 1886. 2 items. Statesville (Iredell County), N.C.

Personal letters to J. P. Garris, including a letter from a bootlegger serving a prison sentence in Statesville.

1967.   WILLIAM A. GARRISON PAPERS, 1863. 4 items. Indiana.

Letters from William A. Garrison, a private in the Federal Army under the command of General Robert Huston Milroy and stationed in western Virginia, to his wife, concerning his provost guard duty, rations, General Milroy, and army life.

1968.   WILLIAM LLOYD GARRISON PAPERS, 1860, 1876. 2 items. Roxbury (Suffolk County), Mass.

Personal letters to William Lloyd Garrison (1805-1879), abolitionist and reformer, from Hinton Rowan Helper and Aaron Macy Powell.

1969.   HENRY GARST AND JOHN GARST PAPERS, 1830-1867. 155 items and 4 vols. Roanoke County, Va.

Business and personal correspondence of Henry and John Garst, operators of two sawmills and a flour mill, and probably brothers. John Garst's papers, largely personal, cover the years 1830-1849. Among the Henry Garst papers is a petition from citizens of Roanoke County to James A. Seddon, Confederate secretary of war, requesting that Henry Garst be exempted from military duty in order to operate his flour mill; a certificate excusing Henry Garst from military duty for sixty days in order to serve as miller in Roanoke County; tax in kind assessments; notice of the impressment of his mill to furnish Confederate supplies; rationing slips given to civilians to get flour and meal from Garst's mill; and three volumes of records for Henry Garst's flour mill and one for his sawmill.

1970.   ALFRED EDWARD GARWOOD PAPERS, 1860s-1882. 1 vol. Newport, Monmouthshire, England.

Draft of chapters 17-45 of Forty Years of an Engineer's Life at Home and Abroad, With Notes By the Way (Newport, Monmouthshire: 1903) by Alfred Edward Garwood, British mechanical engineer. These chapters describe his years in Russia working for various railway lines, 1860s-1877, and in Egypt as head of the Locomotive, Carriage, and Wagon Departments of the Egyptian Government Railways, 1877-1882.

1971.   ELIZA GARY CONTEST BOOK. 1 vol. (65 pp.) Abbeville (Abbeville County), S.C.

Record of contestants and number of "coupons" from each, as well as contributors and amount of donation.

1972.   MARTIN WITHERSPOON GARY PAPERS, 1855-1879. 10 items. Edgefield County, S.C.

Papers of Martin Witherspoon Gary, lawyer and Confederate brigadier general, include documents, 1876, protesting election irregularities in Edgefield County by Republican and Negro voters; a letter, 1877, to the editors of the Augusta Chronicle and Constitutionalist explaining his opposition to the acceptance by Southern Democrats of appointments from President Rutherford B. Hayes; and a letter, 1879, to the editor of the Abbeville Medium opposing the election of Wade Hampton to the U.S. Senate.

1973.   W. B. GASKINS DIARY, 1861-1862. 1 vol. Dorchester (Suffolk County), Mass.

Diary of a Federal soldier, describing skirmishes with the "rebels," food of soldiers, etc. The diary was found on the battlefield of Perryville, Kentucky, 1863.

1974.   FLORIAN LEOPOLD GASSMAN PAPERS, 18th century. 3 items. Vienna, Austria.

Unpublished musical scores for string trio comprised of twelve fugues each, composed by Florian Leopold Gassman (1729-1774), Bohemian conductor and composer. Manuscripts containing these same fugues are also cataloged in Warren Kirkendale, Fuge und Fugato in der Kammermusik des Rokoko und der Klassik (Tutzing: 1966).

1975.   WILLIAM GASTON PAPERS, 1814.
        1 item. New Bern
        (Craven County), N.C.

Letter of recommendation from William Gaston (1778-1844), jurist and member of Congress, 1813-1815, to Secretary of the Navy William Jones.

1976.   SIR WILLIAM FORBES GATACRE PAPERS, 1898. 1 item. Hazel Mill, Stroud, Gloucestershire, England.

Letter of Sir William Forbes Gatacre (1843-1906), major general of the British Army, describing the battle in the Sudan that resulted in the capture of Omdurman, and the Mahdi's tomb, of which there is a drawing.

1977.   ADDISON W. GATES PAPERS,
        1814-1905. 163 items and 1 vol.
        Macedon (Wayne County), N.Y.

Personal, business, and political correspondence of Addison W. Gates, attorney and state legislator. Included are letters, 1881, from factions in the Republican Party concerning the election of successors to Roscoe Conkling and Thomas Collier Platt; clippings pertaining to the gubernatorial campaign of 1894; routine requests for appointments; and speeches, notes, and scattered comments on various issues and politicians. A notebook contains quotations and comments, with a few political references.

1978.   GATHORNE GATHORNE-HARDY,
        FIRST EARL OF CRANBROOK,
        PAPERS, 1867-1892. 17 items.
        London, England.

Political letters of Sir Gathorne Gathorne-Hardy (1814-1906), British political official, concerning army appropriations, the granting of booty to the army, the education of the children of Roman Catholic soldiers, a Parliamentary committee to study the capitation rate, and other routine matters.

1979.   RICHARD JORDAN GATLING PAPERS,
        1880, 1898. 2 items.
        Hartford (Hartford County), Conn.

Personal letters of Richard J. Gatling (1818-1903), developer of the revolving machine gun, including information about himself and a new gun being manufactured.

1980.   MATTHEW GAULT PAPERS, 1842-1867.
        42 items. Hookset (Merrimack
        County), N.H.

Personal correspondence of members of the Gault family containing comments on cotton planting, emigration to Texas, abolitionism, secession, the policies of Lincoln toward the South, the government of the Confederate States of America, army life during the Civil War, freedmen and the Freedmen's Bureau, the scarcity of labor, the Radical Republicans, politics in Texas, and President Andrew Johnson's Peace Proclamation.

1981.   ELBERT H. GAY ACCOUNTS,
        1841-1845. 2 vols.
        Augusta (Richmond County), Ga.

Accounts of Elbert H. Gay as administrator for the estate of Samuel Howard.

1982.   CHARLES ÉTIENNE ARTHUR GAYARRÉ
        PAPERS, 1882-1895. 14 items.
        New Orleans, La.

Letters of Charles E. A. Gayarré (1805-1895), author, to John Dimitry including comment on the reception of his own lecture on the French Revolution; to C. C. Jones acknowledging the receipt of several addresses and his article on Wilde; to Colonel J. F. H. Claiborne commenting on the publication of Claiborne's History of Mississippi; to George T. Heath concerning the publishers of Gayarré's History of Louisiana; and other routine letters.

1983.   WILLIAM GAYLORD PAPERS,
        1861-1865. 24 items.
        Fitzwilliam (Cheshire County), N.H.

Family correspondence of the Gaylord family including accounts of local political controversies; letters of army life and descriptions of the countryside in Virginia and Maryland from John D. Gaylord, a Federal soldier of Company D, 21st Connecticut Volunteers; one letter from his brother, James, also a Federal soldier, from Hampton Hospital (Va.?); letter of instructions to Juliette Gaylord, a member of the New England Women's Auxiliary Association of the U.S. Sanitary Commission; and letters from William Gaylord, a minister, one in particular describing a visit to his brother, James, in the 1st Connecticut Cavalry on the Rapidan River in Virginia.

1984.   NOAH L. GEBBART, SR., AND
        EMMANUEL MARTIN GEBBART PAPERS,
        1844 (1855-1864) 1900. 116 items
        and 1 vol. Ottumwa (Wapello
        County), Iowa, and California.

Letters to Noah L. Gebbart, Sr., who was engaged in mining lead and quartz in California, concerning his life there; letters from some of his Masonic brothers telling of his murder; letters relating to the Knights of the Golden Circle in Iowa; and Civil War letters of E. Martin Gebbart, soldier in the 15th Regiment of Iowa Volunteers, describing his military activities at Shiloh, Vicksburg, and Atlanta, food and amusements in the army, Negro troops, deserters, and foraging and destruction by the Union Army. Included is a memorandum book and journal, 1863-1865, giving an account of his trip with Sherman's army from Vicksburg to Meridian and back.

1985.   JAMES T. GEE PAPERS,
        1837-1864. 10 items.
        Selma (Dallas County), Ala.

Family and Civil War correspondence of James T. Gee, a surgeon in the Confederate Army, and letters of Gee's father containing comments on the panic of 1837 and the election of 1840 and 1844.

1986.   GEE FAMILY PAPERS, 1816-1850.
        38 items. Wilcox County, Ala., and Halifax County, N.C.

Business and legal correspondence of Sterling, Nevill, Charles, and Joseph Gee relating chiefly to Alabama plantation life and the settlement of a large estate; and a few letters bearing on land speculation.

1987.   GENNETT LUMBER COMPANY PAPERS,
        1832 (1920-1945) 1954.
        16,000 items and 20 vols.
        Asheville (Buncombe County), N.C.

Correspondence, business records, and contracts and other legal papers pertaining to the activities of the Gennett Lumber Company.

1988.   JOHN JOSEPH GENTRY PAPERS,
        1816-1908. 14 items.
        Spartanburg (Spartanburg County), S.C.

Land deeds and agreements contracted by the Gentry and Camp families of Spartanburg and Laurens counties, South Carolina.

1989.   GEOGRAPHY MANUSCRIPT, 1812.

Geography manuscript of Theresia Mantz.

1990.   FURNIAFUL GEORGE PAPERS,
        1861-1877. 41 items. Doctor Town (Wayne County), Ga.

Family letters of five brothers, Asa, David, Furniaful, George, and John, Confederate soldiers, telling of living conditions in the army and of military activities in Georgia and Mississippi. Included also is a bit of folk poetry.

1991.   GEORGE III, KING OF GREAT BRITAIN, PAPERS, 1773-1806. 3 items.
        London, England.

Papers of George III (1738-1820), King of Great Britain, include a warrant to the treasury commissioners, a letter of George III concerning the sale of some of the horses in the royal stables, and a facsimile of the "Olive Branch Petition."

1992.   STEFAN GEORGE PAPERS, 1939-1941.
        7 items. Restricted.

Translations, 1939-1941, into English by Carol North Valhope and Ernst Morwitz of the works of German poet Stefan George (1868-1933), comprised of "The Books of Eclogues and Eulogies . . . ," "Hymns, Pilgrimages, Algabal," "The Kingdom Come," "The Seventh Ring," "The Star of the Covenant," "The Tapestry of Life and The Songs of Dream and of Death with a Prelude," and "The Year of the Soul."

1993.   GEORGIA PAPERS, 1727-1947.
        3,403 items.

Miscellaneous papers pertaining to Georgia comprised of the Georgia Colony Papers, 1727-1776, the Georgia Revolutionary Papers, 1776-1783, the Georgia State Papers, 1783-1947, Georgia Legal Records, and Georgia Militia Records. The Colony Papers consist of correspondence, accounts, indentures, land grants, deeds, plats, and petitions relative to the early history of the colony, its government, the trustees of the colony, colonial defense, and James Oglethorpe. The Revolutionary Papers contain accounts of payment to militia, claims for property used by Continental troops, accounts for services to prisoners of war, and material pertaining to Loyalists. The State Papers are comprised of correspondence, financial papers, legal papers, and political documents concerning the proceedings of the executive council, 1786; the settlement of debts owed by Georgia merchants to British merchants; social life and customs in Georgia; legal matters; financial difficulties during Reconstruction; the history of Georgia, including the Yazoo land fraud, the War of 1812, and Eastern Florida; the Civil War, including soldiers' letters, receipts, writs of habeas corpus, and papers concerning confiscated property, substitutes, loss of life, and medical supplies; the Atlantic and Gulf Railroad, 1870s; Baptist and Methodist church affairs; and the U.S. Census of 1880. Miscellaneous Legal Papers include Inferior and Superior Court records, summonses, writs, petitions, papers of administration, estates records, land deeds and sales, land surveys, commissions of office signed by Georgia governors, and scattered county court records, especially of Chatham, Richmond, and Franklin counties. Other papers refer to the Cherokee Indian Land Lottery, 1847, the settlement of German Lutherans in Georgia, the establishment of a public school system, and slavery including materials on sales, purchases, and slave patrols. Confederate legal papers refer to crimes, jail sentences, tax and road levies, minors in the service of the C.S.A., property, and exemptions. Militia Records are those of Clarke County, 1811-1827, and of Chatham County, the 1st Volunteer Regiment of Georgia.

1994. GEORGIA. BANKS COUNTY ACCOUNT BOOK, 1877. 1 vol. (74 pp.)

Probably a tax receiver's book.

1995. GEORGIA. BIBB COUNTY SUPERIOR COURT DOCKET, 1842-1845. 1 vol. (51 pp.)

Docket of the Superior Court of Bibb County, also containing some records of the Inferior Court.

1996. GEORGIA. CHATHAM COUNTY PAPERS, 1816. 1 item.

Hand-drawn and hand-painted map of "Cedar Grove," the plantation of A. Abraham, showing the location of the plantation, how the land was utilized, and drawings of the residence, two outbuildings, and the surrounding trees.

1997. GEORGIA. FRANKLIN COUNTY PAPERS, 1790-1881. 750 items.

Principally legal papers of Franklin County, consisting of land deeds and grants, warrants, promissory notes, accounts, receipts, tax in kind assessments, surveyors' plats, and documents pertaining to the administration of estates. Also included are personal business correspondence, and information on land and commodity prices.

1998. GEORGIA. GREENE COUNTY PAPERS, 1785-1900. 488 items and 89 vols.

Legal records and papers of Greene County Courts, comprised of an administrator's estate book, 1815-1825, for the estate of Isaac Harrison Watts; registration books, 1806, 1825, and 1829, for Georgia land lotteries; Superior Court records, including appearance dockets, 1792-1818, 1827-1832, and 1846-1857, judgment dockets, 1803-1805 and 1812-1818, bar docket, 1811-1814, execution docket, 1882-1889, minute books, 1792-1806, and record books, 1801-1809; Inferior Court records, including appearance dockets, 1791-1794 and 1800-1810, judgment docket, 1792-1797, minute book, 1790-1791, record books, 1800-1809, estray books, 1799-1809 and 1822-1835, list of licenses granted for retailing liquor, 1820-1829, and constable's bond book, 1848-1864; judgment docket of a Justice Court, 1809; Land Court records, including judgment dockets, 1791-1795, and a minute book, 1794-1798; land conveyance record books, 1785-1810; tax record books, 1788-1837 and 1854-1859; and tax execution docket, 1889-1890. Supplementing these volumes are papers consisting principally of summonses, subpoenas, affidavits, appeals, warrants, executive orders, inventories of estates, bills and receipts, two wills, interrogatories to be used for exhibits in obtaining affidavits, and the documents of clerks of the Superior Court and judges of various Greene County courts.

1999. GEORGIA. MERIWETHER COUNTY LOTTERY BOOKS, 1832. 2 vols.

Names of persons entitled to draw in a gold lottery and in a land lottery in Georgia.

2000. GEORGIA. RICHMOND COUNTY. SUPERIOR, INFERIOR, AND COUNTY COURTS, 1853-1868. 1 vol. (102 pp.) Augusta, Ga.

Account book for writs returnable by the sheriff and other officers to the Superior and Inferior courts of Richmond County, 1853-1868.

2001. GEORGIA. SAVANNAH COURT RECORDS, 1869-1881. 1 vol. (236 pp.)

Sentence book.

2002. GEORGIA. SUPERIOR COURT. SLAVE IMPORTATION REGISTER, 1820-1821. 1 vol. Richmond County, Ga.

A record of testimony at the clerk's office of the Richmond Superior Court by slaveowners who swore that the slaves listed were imported solely for service and labor. Slaves are described by name, age, and sometimes occupation and physical characteristics.

2003. GEORGIA. WILKES COUNTY COURT PAPERS, 1779-1845. 275 items. Washington (Wilkes County), Ga.

Records of cases tried before Inferior and Superior courts of Wilkes County, including assault and battery, trespass vi et armis, damage, cost, and debts.

2004. GEORGIA AIRLINE RAILROAD COMPANY ACCOUNT BOOK, 1858-1864. 1 vol. Georgia.

Account book of the Georgia Airline Railroad Company, showing the stocks and stockholders, 1858, and salt prices in the Confederate States of America, 1864.

2005. GEORGIA HISTORICAL SOCIETY PAPERS, 1808-1889. 15 items. Savannah, Ga.

Letters concerning business transactions of the society, including a letter from Charles C. Jones, Jr., accepting an invitation to speak and a resolution of thanks to him; a letter relative to the formation of a Ladies Literary and Art Society; a memorial to the Georgia legislature containing a brief history of the society; a letter by Governor Henry D. McDaniel on the fiftieth anniversary of the society; and clippings giving accounts of the society's activities.

2006.   UNIVERSITY OF GEORGIA PAPERS,
        1800-1856.  5 items.  Athens
        (Clarke County), Ga.

   A letter, 1800, from President Moses Waddel, to George Jones concerning the scholastic progress of Jones's son, and Columbia County; a letter, 1823, from Waddel to William Noble recommending John H. Gray for a teaching position; deeds, 1855 and 1856, for land sold by the university; and a list of university presidents, 1802-1829.

2007.   WILLIAM GERHARDT PAPERS,
        1832-1909.  35 items.
        Martinsburg (Berkeley County),
        W. Va.

   Papers of William Gerhardt, teacher and clergyman, include several teaching contracts, programs for Examination Day exercises and a schedule for classes at Western Carolina Male Academy, 1855-1857, a list of contributors to a German church in the United States, some genealogical information, and several letters in German.

2008.   GEORGE SACKVILLE GERMAIN, FIRST
        VISCOUNT SACKVILLE, PAPERS,
        1779.  2 items.  London, England.

   Letter to George Sackville Germain, First Viscount Sackville (1716-1785), as British secretary of state for the colonies, from Sir Henry Clinton, then commander of the British forces in the United States, discussing the unsuccessful siege of Savannah by French and American forces, the loss of the British warship Experiment, and the reinforcement of the Bermuda garrison.  Accompanying the letter is a list of enclosures, which are not included in the collection.

2009.   GERMAN SCRAPBOOKS ON THE IMPERIAL
        FAMILY, 1888-1898.  41 items and
        2 vols.  Germany.

   Scrapbooks pertaining largely to the death and funeral of Kaiser Wilhelm I in 1888.  Loose clippings concern the death of Kaiserin Augusta, wife of Wilhelm I, in 1890, the centenary of the birth of Wilhelm I in 1897, and other matters.

2010.   GERMAN-AMERICAN MUTUAL LOAN AND
        BUILDING ASSOCIATION PAPERS,
        1886-1893.  23 items.
        Savannah, Ga.

   Cancelled stock certificates in the German-American Loan and Building Association.

2011.   GERMANY POSTERS.  25 items.

   Posters containing examples of Nazi Realism, primarily of medieval and World War I subjects.  Included are World War II campaign maps and a print of Adolph Hitler.

2012.   CHARLES GEROCK PAPERS, 1832-1877.
        32 items.  Palo Alto (Onslow
        County), N.C.

   Principally lawyers' letters, 1862-1877, to Charles Gerock concerning the case of the State of Mississippi v. N. G. Nye, in which Gerock brought suit against Nye for a considerable sum of money, and two petitions, 1832, from former Continental Army soldiers for military pensions.

2013.   LOUIS GERSTMAN PAPERS,
        1874-1897.  21 vols.  Selma
        (Dallas County), Ala.

   Letter books and a policy memorandum book of an insurance agent, as representative at various times for the Protection Life Insurance Company of Chicago, the Royal Canadian Insurance Company, the Amazon Insurance Company, the Royal Insurance Company of Liverpool, and the London and Lancashire Fire Insurance Company of Liverpool, and as an independent agent.

2014.   THOMAS SAUNDERS GHOLSON PAPERS,
        1818-1860.  48 items.  Petersburg
        (Dinwiddie County), Va.

   Papers of Thomas Saunders Gholson (1808-1868), jurist and statesman, are largely those of his law firm relating to local cases, some of which pertain to the hiring and purchase of slaves.

2015.   PIETRO GIANNONE PAPERS,
        18th Century.  1 vol.
        Naples, Italy.

   Manuscript volume, presumably a copy, of Giannone's "Trattato de' Rimedj contro le Scommuniche invalide... Luglio 1723," in which he responded to his excommunication from the Roman Catholic Church and to the prohibition of his book, Istoria civile del Regno de Napoli.

2016.   GORDON BUTCHER GIBBENS PAPERS,
        1884-1904.  564 items.
        Parkersburg (Wood County), W. Va.

   Letters and papers of a printer, engraver, dealer in paper goods and Republican politician.  The collection is made up for the most part of letters written to Gibbens between the years 1892 and 1900 concerning West Virginia politics and the Republican party.  Gibbens served as a middle man between the state leaders of the Republican party and local party workers.  The correspondence concerns patronage, party strategy, and party intrigues and includes letters relating to the election of 1894 when Gibbens managed the successful congressional campaign of Warren Miller; the election of 1896 during which Gibbens worked for Republican candidates on all levels; and Gibbens' unsuccessful attempt after the victory of 1896 to secure from the party the rewards which he felt his efforts merited.

2017.   EDMUND A. GIBBES PAPERS,
        1862-1869.  4 items.
        Charleston, S.C.

Scattered personal correspondence concerning family affairs and the sale of slaves of a wealthy Charleston physician engaged in some undefined occupation during the Civil War, probably blockade running.

2018.   JAMES S. GIBBES PAPERS,
        1855-1860.  4 items.
        Charleston, S.C.

Personal and business letters of a Charleston, South Carolina, merchant concerning the state of the cotton market in Charleston and Savannah, Georgia, and visits to New York.

2019.   JOHN GIBBONS PAPERS,
        1758-1814.  670 items and 1 vol.
        Charleston, S.C., and
        Savannah, Ga.

The major part of this collection is made up of correspondence and papers of John Gibbons, Jr., and his family. The papers deal with Gibbons's business as a merchant and with the various offices which he held. Included are correspondence and accounts with the largest commercial firms in Charleston, South Carolina, and Savannah, Georgia; Gibbons's papers as vendue master in Charleston until 1790 and in Savannah after 1791, with records of the settlement of estates and the sale of slaves; material relating to the various public positions held by Gibbons in Georgia during the 1790s, such as treasurer of the state and paymaster of the militia; many papers relating to the lengthy settlement of the estate of Captain John Carman after 1778 and the estate of John Benfield, Gibbons's father-in-law; and a number of items from the Revolution, including material about shipping, the sale of prizes, and Gibbons's experience as a British prisoner of war in Charleston. There are several scattered papers dealing with land sales in Georgia in the late eighteenth and early nineteenth centuries and a receipt book, 1761-1773, for the firm of Liston, Benfield, and Jones of Charleston, South Carolina.

2020.   WILLIAM GIBBONS, JR.,
        1728-1803.  807 items and 1 vol.
        "Sharon," near Savannah, Ga.

Correspondence of a wealthy rice planter and justice of the peace, William Gibbons, Jr., and his family, including his father, William Gibbons, Sr., and his uncle, Joseph Gibbons. The papers of William Gibbons, Sr., and Joseph Gibbons begin in the 1750s and describe life on some of the early large plantations in Georgia. They include promissory notes, bills, and receipts for household necessities, house building, plantation equipment, and medical care; notes on the price of rice over a number of years; material on the management of plantations and especially on the proper use of overseers and the problems of absentee ownership; and continuing comments on the purchase, management, and sale of slaves. The letters and papers of William Gibbons, Jr., provide more material on plantation life and the management of slaves and land and also contain bills and receipts for goods sold to American troops during the Revolution; notes on horse breeding and racing; correspondence on the cost of schooling at Princeton College in 1786; papers relating to the purchase of former Indian lands in Georgia; and a miscellaneous expense journal of William Gibbons, Jr., 1771-178-.

2021.   WILLIAM KELLY GIBBS PAPERS,
        1867-1871.  18 items.
        Smith Grove (Davie County),
        N.C.

Lecture notes of a student at Trinity College (North Carolina), including samples of his poetry and prose.

2022.   CHRISTIANA M. GIBSON SCRAPBOOK,
        1834-1886.  1 vol.  (78 pp.)
        Edinburgh, Scotland.

A scrapbook of autograph letters and autographs.

2023.   HAMILTON L. GIBSON PAPERS,
        1846-1865.  19 itmes.
        Newton (Frederick County), Va.

Business correspondence of a wagonmaker of Newton, Virginia, giving information on that industry, with technical terms, specifications, and prices.

2024.   JAMES W. GIBSON PAPERS,
        1860-1862.  9 items.
        Newton (Catawba County), N.C.

Miscellaneous Civil War letters of Gibson and others.

2025.   RANDALL LEE GIBSON PAPERS,
        1883-1887.  4 items.
        New Orleans, La.

Routine personal and social correspondence.

2026.   SIR ROBERT GIFFEN PAPERS,
        1876.  1 item.  London, England.

Letter to Giffen from Henry Labouchere, liberal politician and journalist, soliciting an article for Truth, a newspaper he was starting.

2027.   LYMAN D. GILBERT PAPERS,
        1793-1890.  354 items.
        Harrisburg (Dauphin County), Pa.

Correspondence and papers, 1870-1890, of Lyman Gilbert, deputy attorney general of Pennsylvania, containing a number of letters from Samuel E. Dimmock, state attorney general, concerning legal business the internal affairs of the attorney general's office, and cases in which the state was involved. Gilbert's personal and professional correspondence concerns the settlement of estates; various charities; railroads and corporations, including a letter on a case against John D. Rockefeller; Marcus Albert Reno, 1880; and politics. The collection also contains letters, 1833-1854, to John C. Kunkel, a member of the senate of Pennsylvania, concerning legislation relating to transportation and social issues; correspondence and papers, 1857-1859, of Henry Gilbert, a merchant of Harrisburg, Pennsylvania, including orders for merchandise, bills and receipts, and business letters; papers, 1872, of John B. McPherson, a lawyer in Harrisburg, concerning settlement of estates and property matters; and miscellaneous items, including the report of Edward Thomas, rector of Trinity Church, Edisto, South Carolina, for the years 1833-1854, listing baptisms, marriages, and communicants.

2028. SHEPHERD D. GILBERT ALBUM, 1883-1886. 1 vol. (22 pp.) Salem (Essex County), Mass.

Photographs of scenes in western North Carolina along the French Broad, Oconaluftee, and Tuckasegee rivers and elsewhere in that area.

2029. SIR WALTER RALEIGH GILBERT, FIRST BARONET, PAPERS, 1850-1851. 14 items. London, England.

Twelve letters to Gilbert from Lord Dalhousie, Governor General of India, and drafts of two of Gilbert's replies. Letters concern military matters and promotions for Gilbert and for his son-in-law, Captain Richard Shubrick.

2030. JOHN M. GILCHRIST PAPERS, 1840. 5 items. Charleston, S.C.

Letters describing plantations in South Carolina being offered to Gilchrist for sale.

2031. ANDREW S. GILE PAPERS, 1862. 10 items. Haverhill (Essex County), Mass.

Personal letters from a soldier in the 35th Massachusetts Regiment, describing camp life, training, and troop movements.

2032. MARY ZILPHA GILES PAPERS, 1846-1942. 132 items. Greenwood (Abbeville County), S.C.

Letters and papers of Mary Z. Giles concerning her education at Trinity College in Randolph County, North Carolina, in the 1870s, which was done at home with members of the faculty as tutors; her experience as a schoolteacher; and a trip abroad with her sister Persis. The collection includes receipts for tuition at Trinity College; a charter, 1889, for the Giles sisters and their mother to conduct Greenwood Female College in Greenwood, South Carolina; and letters from missionaries in India, China, and Guatemala.

2033. JACOB GILES PAPERS, 1889-1890. 11 items. Richmond Furnace (Franklin County), Pa.

Business papers.

2034. WILLIAM BRANCH GILES PAPERS, 1826-1830. 5 items. Amelia County, Va.

Miscellaneous letters and papers, including three documents signed by Giles as governor of Virginia.

2035. LIZZIE (INGERSOLL) GILL PAPERS, 1831-1881. 162 items. "Spring Brook," near Poughkeepsie (Dutchess County), N.Y.

Primarily the social and family correspondence of Lizzie Gill and members of her family including descriptions of social life in Savannah and Rome, Georgia, and in Fall River, Massachusetts, and a description of Abraham and Mary Todd Lincoln as they passed through Poughkeepsie, New York, on their way to Washington for Lincoln's first inaugural.

2036. GILL FAMILY PAPERS, 1851-1875. 30 items. Pleasant Grove (Alamance County), N.C.

Letters from members of the Gill family dealing for the most part with personal affairs and family business. Contains accounts of the experiences of a girl at High Point Female Seminary, North Carolina, in 1860, including a description of Hinton Rowan Helper burning books on the seminary grounds; letters from a soldier in the 33rd North Carolina Regiment during the Civil War; and letters from a soldier in the 42nd North Carolina Regiment, 1862-1864.

2037. GROVES GILLES PAPERS, 1771-1774. 2 items. Madras, India.

Folios 56-78 of an unbound diary of March 1-April 2, 1774, written by an Englishman attached to the court of Mohammed Ali Khan, Nabob of Arcot. Gilles, who has been tentatively identified as the diarist, provides a daily commentary on his relations with the military, naval, and civil officials of the Madras Presidency, and the Nabob and his court and family. Also includes a four page manuscript entitled "Advice from the Maharatta Camp 4th Dec., 1771, left with the Nabob by the Gov." concerning the activities of the Mahrattas and news about the Nabob's subjection of Tanjore.

2038. GEORGE LEWIS GILLESPIE PAPERS, 1897. 1 vol. (47 pp.) Tennessee.

Documents relating to the awarding of the Congressional Medal of Honor to George Lewis Gillespie for gallantry in action near Bethesda Church, Virginia, 1864.

2039. SARAH, JONATHAN, P. W., AND MARIA GILLETT PAPERS, 1843-1873. 6 items. Canaan (Litchfield County), Conn.

Family letters.

2040. WILLIAM H. GILLILAND PAPERS, 1836-1868. 366 items and 2 vols. Charleston, S.C.

Family and business correspondence of William H. Gilliland, cotton factor and merchant of Charleston, consisting of letters addressed to him from John P. and Caroline Burke of Wilcox County, Alabama, for whose estate he acted as trustee. The letters portray the ever-recurring "hard luck" of the unsuccessful planter. Included also are account books showing charitable donations, 1860-1861, and receipts and disbursements of the Hampton Social Club, 1868.

2041. GILLINGHAM-STITH FAMILY PAPERS, 1836-1932. 4,072 items and 2 vols. Davidson County, N.C.

Letters and papers of Alberta Bassett (Stith) Jones Gillingham and of her brother Fred H. Stith pertaining, for the most part, to the operation of gold, silver, copper, sulphur, and zinc mines in the Cid district of Davidson County, North Carolina. Also includes many legal papers relating to quarrels between Alberta Gillingham and Fred Stith over ownership of their father's share of the Ward Gold Mine in Davidson County; material relating to the North Carolina Children's Home Society; items pertaining to Alberta Gillingham's musical compositions; a series of letters between Alberta Gillingham and William H. Bailey, Sr., a lawyer of Charlotte, North Carolina; and material concerning Furnifold M. Simmons's campaign for re-election to the United States Senate in 1930.

2042. DANIEL COIT GILMAN PAPERS, 1887-1907. 4 items. Baltimore, Md.

Letters of Daniel Coit Gilman (1831-1908), president of the University of California, Berkeley, 1872-1875, and of the Johns Hopkins University, Baltimore, Maryland, 1875-1902, referring to literary and personal matters.

2043. JOHN TAYLOR GILMAN PAPERS, 1808. 1 item. Exeter (Rockingham County), N.H.

Letter commenting on politics and social life in Exeter, New Hampshire, and Portland, Maine.

2044. NATHANIEL GILMAN PAPERS, 1830-1895. 8 items. Exeter (Rockingham County), N.H.

Personal letters to and from Nathaniel Gilman and members of his family. Includes mention of studies at Harvard University, 1853, and the Massachusetts state constitutional convention, 1853.

2045. SAMUEL GILMAN PAPERS, 1850-1854. 4 items. Charleston, S.C.

Three personal letters of Samuel Gilman and a holograph manuscript of a poem by Caroline (Howard) Gilman, entitled, "To Miss S. Waring, On her seeing me paint the hearth in my Husband's Study."

2046. WILLIAM C. GILMAN PAPERS, 1909. 1 item. Norwich (New London County), Conn.

Letter from Gilman to his cousin, Arthur Gilman, concerning William Gilman's book, A Memoir of Daniel Wadsworth Coit of Norwich, Connecticut.

2047. FRANCIS WALKER GILMER NOTEBOOK AND JOURNAL, 1815-1822. 1 vol. Virginia.

Notebook of Francis W. Gilmer (1790-1826), Virginia lawyer and educator, including genealogical notes; scattered references to Thomas Jefferson; unrelated historical allusions; a Cherokee-English vocabulary; and notes on a journey from Virginia to Georgia, including comments on Southern plants and animals. [Partially published: R. B. Davis (ed.), "An Early Virginia Scientist's Botanical Observations in the South," Virginia Journal of Science, III (May, 1942), 132-139.]

2048. GEORGE N. GILMER PAPERS, 1879-1883. 1 item. [N.C.?]

Observations on the Negro, some of which were directed to the North Carolina Christian Advocate.

2049. GEORGE ROCKINGHAM GILMER PAPERS, 1838. 2 items. Milledgeville (Baldwin County), Ga.

Two letters from Gilmer as governor of Georgia, including a letter, 1838, to Joseph Wheeler concerning the enforcement of the Treaty of New Echota, which had been made with the Cherokee tribe in 1835.

2050. JULIANA (PAISLEY) GILMER DIARY, 1840-1850. 1 item. Greensboro (Guilford County), N.C.

A personal diary concerned with family matters. Includes a description of a political demonstration in Greensboro, North Carolina, in 1840, led by a General Edney; a temperance meeting; and the mustering of volunteers for service in the Mexican War in Greensboro, 1847.

2051. THOMAS W. GILMER NOTEBOOKS, 1817-1870. 10 vols. Fredericksburg (Spotsylvania County), Va.

Lecture notes given by Thomas W. Gilmer at Union Theological Seminary, Hampden-Sidney College, Prince Edward County, Virginia, 1859-1869, and sermon notes from his later years as a Presbyterian minister in Virginia. One volume, originally an account book of the firm A. and F. Minor, contains Confederate music pasted on the first pages and history notes in a handwriting similar to Gilmer's.

2052. ROBERT GILMOR PAPERS, 1838-1841. 2 items and 1 vol. Baltimore, Md.

Two letters to Edward D. Ingraham discussing Gilmor's autograph collection and a catalog of that collection, 1832.

2053. MARION FOSTER GILMORE PAPERS, 1910. 1 item. Louisville (Jefferson County), Ky.

Letter of Marion Foster Gilmore to the literary editor of The Banner, Nashville, Tennessee, asking for publicity for her volume of poems, Virginia: A Tragedy and Other Poems.

2054. CHARLES GILPIN PAPERS, 1832-1875. 239 items. London, England.

Letters to Charles Gilpin, publisher and reform member of Parliament, for the most part from 19th century British reformers, concerned with social and political subjects.

2055. ANTONIO DE GIMBERNAT Y ARBÓS PAPERS, 1790. 1 vol. Madrid, Spain.

Volume contains the grant of nobility to Gimbernat y Arbós by King Carlos IV.

2056. PAOLO GIORGI PAPERS, 1930-1934. 8 items. Rome, Italy.

Manuscript and typescript poems of Giorgi and a note from him to Guido Mazzoni.

2057. ANDRÉ GIRODIE PAPERS, ca. 1910. 14 items. Paris, France.

Notes and clippings by Girodie.

2058. MARIA (JAMES) REVELEY GISBORNE DIARY, 1820. 1 vol. (143 pp.) London, England.

Diary (photostatic copy of original in the British Museum) of Mrs. Maria (James) Reveley Gisborne, May 2 to September 26, 1820, including an account of a journey from Italy and a short stay in London. The diary opens with an account of the journey from Leghorn, Italy, to London, with comments on the hardships of travel and on the Italian and French landscapes and national temperaments.
Beginning with the entry of June 11, comments revolve around Maria (James) Reveley Gisborne's social acquaintances, generally prominent literary figures. Included are references to the William Godwin family, their relations with Percy Bysshe Shelley, and their opinion of his attitude and works; a description of Samuel Taylor Coleridge and a report of his remarks on Washington Allston's return to America as a result of his wife's prejudice against England; allusions to Coleridge's wish to translate Goethe's Faust, his interest in the works of Pedro Calderón de la Barca, and his attitude toward Shelley and William Godwin; an account of John Keats's illness at the home of Leigh Hunt, and of the preparation by Hunt of an article defending Shelley against the attacks of William Gifford, editor of the Quarterly Review; and references to William Godwin's opinions of Lord Byron's works, of Sir Joshua Reynolds and other artists, of William Wordsworth's works, and of Mathilda, a novel by an unidentified feminine friend of Maria (James) Reveley Gisborne. Included also is an account given by Arnaud Descolles, traveling companion of the Gisbornes, of the shipwreck and death of the family of one Colonel Egerton; and a portion of the journal kept by John Gisborne at Leghorn, Itay, from October to November 6, 1827, including a description of the actual scene of Shelley's "Ode to a Skylark."

2059. MORDECAI GIST PAPERS, 1782, 1791. 2 items. Baltimore County, Md., and Charleston, S.C.

Letter to Gist from Captain James Smith of the Maryland artillery concerning his promotion and a letter from Gist to Richard Hampton relating to the purchase of indents.

2060. WILLIAM EWART GLADSTONE, 1841-1904. 52 items. London, England.

Miscellaneous collection of the letters and papers of William Ewart Gladstone, including a few items by Catherine (Glynne) Gladstone, Steven Edward Gladstone, and

Herbert John Gladstone. Correspondence concerns politics, colonial government, church matters, and appointments. Printed material includes clippings, for the most part on the life of William E. Gladstone, and a broadside, 1874, of one of Gladstone's speeches.

2061. LOUISA B. GLAIZE AUTOGRAPH ALBUM, 1855-1861. 1 vol. (114 pp.) Virginia.

Album of poems and autographs.

2062. ELLEN ANDERSON GHOLSON GLASGOW PAPERS, (1901) 1976. 5 items. Richmond, Va.

Letters to Henry Troth concerning photographs he submitted for use in Ellen Glasgow's book, Voice, and for her personal collection; and one page from the Ellen Glasgow Newsletter concerning literary rights to her manuscripts, 1965.

2063. GLASGOW (BARREN COUNTY) KENTUCKY, SURVEY, [1863?]. 1 vol. (85 pp.)

Surveyor's notebook with plat of the town of Glasgow and plats of roads in the vicinity, with bearings and distances, and notations concerning foliage, geographical features, elevations, structures, and land use, and names of residents or property owners; a list of "reliable union men"; and a list of equipment "turned over," Oct. 1, 1863, including shovels, wheelbarrows, etc. The flyleaf bears the names S. H. Cottle, Simeon Cottle, and Samuel A. Smith.

2064. JOSEPH GLASS PAPERS, 1804-1824. 9 items. Frederick County, Va.

Family, professional, and business correspondence of a Presbyterian minister including a letter, 1818, describing the trip of a large family from Virginia to Kentucky by wagon.

2065. ROBERT HENRY GLASS PAPERS, 1863. 2 items. Lynchburg (Campbell County), Va.

A business letter, 1863, by Robert Henry Glass and G. W. Hardwicke and an undated memorandum of a legal matter pertaining to Elizabeth Glass.

2066. ALBERT GLEAVES PAPERS, 1924. 1 item. Yonkers (Westchester County), N.Y.

Letter from P. F. Harrington to Albert Gleaves, both retired officers of the United States Navy, discussing the career of Stephen B. Luce.

2067. GEORGE ROBERT GLEIG PAPERS, 1864-1869. 7 items. London, England.

Collection consists for the most part of letters to Gleig involving routine personal and business matters.

2068. TYRE GLEN PAPERS, 1820-1889. 1,261 items and 2 vols. Surry County, N.C.

The papers of Tyre Glen (d. 1875), slave trader, general merchant, planter, and postmaster. They contain, in addition to copious information on slave trading in the 1830s and 1840s, references to Glen's Union sympathies and claims for horses confiscated by the U.S. Army; farming; exemptions from the Confederate Army; a mutilated circular concerning regulations of the Confederate Navy School at Richmond, Virginia; Richmond (Va.) Female Institute, and Basil Manly, Jr.; St. Mary's College at Raleigh, North Carolina; and the Baptist Church in North Carolina. Two volumes include accounts of slaves, mercantile interests, and general expenses.

2069. ELIZABETH F. GLENN PAPERS, 1818-1874. 61 items. Union County, N.C.

Letters and papers of Elizabeth Glenn and her family, for the most part concerned with personal and family matters. Contains a number of letters from soldiers in the Confederate Army including descriptions of training in eastern North Carolina, 1861-1862, and action in Virginia, 1862-1863; medical treatment and hospital life; and a vivid account of a battlefield death.

2070. MARGARET GLOCKLER ALBUM, 1899-1934. 1 vol. Minneapolis, Minn.

A postage stamp album.

2071. GLOUCESTERSHIRE, ENGLAND, POLL BOOK, 1714, 1734. 1 vol.

Record of the official results of the parliamentary election for Gloucestershire on May 8, 1734, including, for comparison, the results of a similar election in 1714.

2072. JOSIAH GLOVER DISTILLER'S BOOK, 1886-1893. 1 vol. Earpsborough (Johnston County), N.C.

Records of a distillery.

2073. ISABELLA DALLAS GLYN PAPERS, 1871. 2 items.

Routine correspondence of an actress.

2074. RICHMOND GOBBLE PAPERS, 1864-1865. 5 items. Lexington (Davidson County), N.C.

Personal and business papers, including a certificate about the registration of Confederate bonds, a Confederate order for wheat and flour, and an oath of allegiance to the United States, 1865.

2075. ALLEN H. GODBEY PAPERS,
1931-1942. 6 items.
Duke University, Durham,
North Carolina.

Letters and circulars prepared by Dr. Allen H. Godbey concerning his dispute with President William Preston Few and the School of Religion at Duke University.

2076. C. O. GODFREY AND
THOMAS WARDELL PAPERS,
1868-1875. 5 items.
Hannibal (Marion County), Mo.

Letters of partners in a coal mining firm, concerning a disagreement about a contract from the Union Pacific Railroad Company for mining its coal.

2077. GODMAN DIARY, 1820-1823.
1 vol. Park Hatch, Surrey,
England.

Diary kept by a sister of Joseph Godman (1791-1874) describing trips to Paris and the chateau country of France. Includes comments on John Wilson Croker and Theodore Edward Hook, who were among the diarist's traveling companions.

2078. JOHN GODWIN PAPERS,
1855-1859. 8 items.
Sampson County, N.C.

Correspondence between John Godwin and his brother, who had moved to Texas, commenting on the high prices of 1857.

2079. JOHANN WOLFGANG VON GOETHE
PAPERS, ca. 1805. 1 item.
Germany.

Routine letter from Goethe, as prime minister of the Duchy of Sachsen-Weimar, to Christian Gottlab von Voight, one of his cabinet.

2080. DANIEL LEWIS GOLD PAPERS,
1806-1865. 59 items.
Lawrenceville (Lawrence
County), Ill.

Letters and papers of Daniel Lewis Gold, his father, Daniel L. Gold, and other members of his family. Includes letters of Emiline (Gold) Spindle mentioning cholera and yellow fever epidemics in Tennessee; letters to the elder Gold from Bishop Norval Wilson concerning camp meetings and other religious activities around Winchester, Virginia, in the 1840s and letters from Richard C. L. Moncure concerning the settlement of the Julian-Wiatt estate, 1846; and letters of Daniel Lewis Gold concerning his new home in Lawrenceville, Illinois.

2081. LOUIS GOLD PAPERS,
1930-1934. 14 items and
1 vol. Brooklyn, N.Y.

Letters from Henry Louis Mencken to Louis Gold concerning articles that Gold was writing for the American Mercury. The volume is a collection of articles done for the American Mercury by Gold under his own name and under the pseudonym Lewis G. Arrowsmith, for the most part concerned with medical practice in New York and during World War I.

2082. MARY WASHINGTON GOLD PAPERS,
1900-1943. 20 items.
Berryville (Clarke County), Va.

Mainly personal, political, and business letters addressed either to Thomas D. Gold, a Virginia state senator, or to his daughter, Mary Washington Gold. Correspondents include Ray Stannard Baker, William Jennings Bryan, Harry Flood Byrd, Sr., and Carter Glass, Sr.

2083. LOUIS P. GOLDBERG PAPERS,
1929-1957. 839 items.
New York, N.Y.

Letters and papers of Louis P. Goldberg, lawyer and leader in the socialist movement in the United States. Contains essentially the files of the Social Democratic Federation including minutes, press releases, and resolutions; a report, 1935, on the "Yankee Stadium Affair"; and material related to the division between the Social Democratic Federation and the Socialist Party and Goldberg's attempt to bring the two groups together. Also contains papers from Goldberg's tenure as councilman in New York City, 1941-1956; letters relating to a trip to Israel, 1951; addresses, lectures, and notes on such subjects as law, socialism, social democracy, New York City affairs, politics, and civil rights; and printed matter including pamphlets, leaflets, and clippings.

2084. EDMUND LEE GOLDSBOROUGH PAPERS,
1901-1903. 37 items and 1 vol.
Shepherdstown (Jefferson County),
W. Va.

Material relating to field trips made by Edmund Lee Goldsborough as a staff member of the United States Fish Commission, later the United States Bureau of Fisheries. A trip to Hawaii, 1901, is represented by snapshots showing Barton Warren Evermann, David Starr Jordan, William Harris Ashmead, John N. Cobb, Albertus Hutchinson Baldwin, and Charles Bradford Hudson. Diary of an Alaska trip, 1903, describes field trips in southeastern Alaska and a visit to Metlakhtla in the Annette Islands.

2085. LOUIS MALESHERBES GOLDSBOROUGH PAPERS, 1827-1877. 523 items and 1 vol. Washington, D.C.

Family and official correspondence of Louis M. Goldsborough (1805-1877), superintendent of the U.S. Naval Academy, Annapolis, Maryland, and rear admiral in the U.S. Navy. The personal correspondence contains two letters of William Wirt, whose daughter, Elizabeth Gamble Wirt, married Goldsborough. In 1831 there are letters of courtship from Goldsborough to his future wife. The remainder of the personal correspondence, with the exception of a few letters from Catherine Wirt relative to the death of William Wirt and two long diary-like letters, 1835, relaying gossip of families of Richmond, Virginia, is between Goldsborough and his wife generally concerning family matters. Several of Goldsborough's letters were written from Mexican waters, and one in particular gives a vivid and full description of the battle of Tuxpan in 1847. Goldsborough's letters during the Civil War period refer to the Mason-Slidell affair, Federal gunboats on the James River, the Confederate ironclad Virginia, and Secretary of War E. M. Stanton's interference with the armies of Generals George B. McClellan and Irvin McDowell to the supposed disadvantage of Federal war efforts. Letters from Goldsborough, while he was in command of the European Squadron, 1865-1869, contain a description of Castle Miramar in Trieste, Italy, and the Empress Carlota, who lived there at the time. Among other personal letters are several from members of the Robinson family, relatives of Elizabeth Gamble (Wirt) Goldsborough, including some describing war conditions in Williamsburg and Norfolk, Virginia.

The bulk of the collection consists of routine correspondnece in connection with Goldsborough's naval career, including copies of calculations from the Bureau of Ordnance, sailing instructions, reports of itineraries of vessels, lists of foods, reports of engineers, copies of directions signed by Secretary of the Navy Gideon Welles, and letters of introduction. Official papers are most numerous while Goldsborough commanded the European Squadron. Included also is a large hand-drawn map, 1877, of the Castle Hayne Vineyard Company Plantation of New Hanover County, North Carolina, showing many details including swamps, streams, and abandoned rice fields. One letter book, 1859-1861, contains the official correspondence of Goldsborough as captain of the U.S. Frigate Congress. Material relating to the investigating commission of the Navy headed by Goldsborough, set up to try charges against Benjamin F. Isherwood, includes a copy of extracts from reports of Isherwood in 1867 and 1868; letter, 1869, from David D. Porter to Isaac Newton; and a statement of the comparative weights of the U.S.S. Wyoming and the U.S.S. Monongahela.

2086. AMBROSE ELLIOTT GONZALES PAPERS, 1908, 1924. 2 items. Columbia (Richland County), S.C.

Letter, 1908, to Gonzales from Matthew C. Butler commenting on an article on William T. Sherman's campaign in South Carolina which had recently appeared in Gonzales's papers, The State, and a letter, 1924, from Gonzales to William Adger Law discussing Gonzales's memoirs.

2087. INDEPENDENT ORDER OF GOOD TEMPLARS. GRAND LODGE OF NORTH CAROLINA. HEALTH SEAT LODGE, NO. 40 PAPERS, 1876-1879. 16 items and 2 vols. Henderson (Vance County), N.C.

Collection contains copies of ceremonial services; commissions of I. W. Kittrell as lodge deputy, 1878, 1879, and a letter from the grand worthy secretary that accompanied one of the commissions; a blank copy of a credential for a representative to the state convention; a Proposition Book with entries for proposed members, 1876-1878; and the constitution, by-laws, and roll book of the lodge. A diary and set of farm accounts, 1884-1885, are included in the constitution, by-laws, and roll book.

2088. INDEPENDENT ORDER OF GOOD TEMPLARS. GRAND LODGE OF NORTH CAROLINA. NEW HOPE LODGE, NO. 296 PAPERS, 1881-1889. 5 items and 1 vol. Catawba (Catawba County), N.C.

Collection contains a card of ceremonial odes; loose manuscripts, including minutes, 1888, and reports, at least one of which is 1889; and a volume of minutes, 1881-1889.

2089. GAYLORD G. GOODELL PAPERS, 1837-1874. 73 items. Volney (Oswego County), N.Y.

Family correspondence discussing Indian outrages in the territories, local food prices, carpetbagger activities in Virginia, experiences in Texas during the revolution against Mexico, and family matters.

2090. JESSE B. GOODIN PAPERS, 1829-1903. 183 items. Wake County, N.C.

Collection contains receipts, summonses, promissory notes, and occasional accounts of Jesse B. Goodin and letters from his sons who served in the 30th North Carolina Regiment and the 1st North Carolina Regiment, Junior Reserves. The letters give some description of camp life in eastern North Carolina and in the vicinity of Caroline County, Virginia, and descriptions of treatment in hospitals in Richmond, Virginia, and Lynchburg, Virginia.

2091.   ZEPHANIAH W. GOODING PAPERS,
        1833-1872.  113 items.
        Bristol (Ontario County), N.Y.

   Letters and papers of Zephaniah W. Gooding and his family and a short series of letters from the family of Gooding's wife, Martha (Jones) Gooding.  The bulk of the letters concern Gooding's service in the 85th New York Regiment, 1861-1864, and contain descriptions of camp life as well as descriptions of skirmishes on the Potomac; the U.S.S. Monitor and the C.S.S. Virginia, 1862; the battlefield scene after the battle of Williamsburg, 1864; the battle of Fair Oaks, Virginia, 1862; and action in North Carolina, 1862-1864, at Kinston, Whitehall, Goldsboro, and Roanoke Island.  Letters, 1871-1872, concern the movement of the Gooding and Jones families to the western United States and include comments on economic conditions, land prices, and other factors influencing the decision to move; the teaching profession; and the presidential election of 1872.

2092.   ISAAC E. GOODRICH PAPERS,
        1856-1894.  45 items.
        Clinton (Kennebec County), Me.

   The major part of this collection is composed of the Civil War letters of William Morey of the 2nd Maine Regiment commenting on camp life and military routine and describing the first battle of Bull Run and the battle of Mill Springs, Kentucky.  Also contains a letter, 1864, commenting on Indian troubles on the plains and a description, 1856, of the gold country of California, the process of gold mining, and life in the mining camps.

2093.   JOHN ZACHEUS GOODRICH PAPERS,
        1863.  1 item.  Stockbridge
        (Berkshire County), Mass.

   A copy of a letter, 1863, from Hinton Rowan Helper (1829-1909), U.S. consul in Buenos Aires, to Goodrich, former U.S. representative from Massachusetts and then collector of customs, Boston, concerning exchange rates of Argentine currency.

2094.   GEORGE A. GORDON PAPERS,
        (1850-1860) 1866.  77 items.
        Charleston, S.C.

   Letters of George A. Gordon's sisters, Cad and Lydia, and Gordon's letters to his girl friend Krilla commenting on social life in Charleston, South Carolina; yellow fever; and policy of the Mercury, which Gordon helped edit; and the docking of a slave ship in Charleston.

2095.   JAMES H. GORDON ACCOUNT BOOK,
        1883-1885.  1 vol.
        [Port Gibson (Claiborne
        County), Miss.?]

   Accounts of a general merchant, with inventories for the years 1883, 1885, giving prices, quantities, and descriptions of the merchandise.

2096.   JOHN BROWN GORDON PAPERS,
        1872 (1877-1899) 1949.  16 items.
        Atlanta, Ga.

   Letters of John Brown Gordon, major general in the Confederate Army and United States senator, to Charles Colcock Jones, Jr., concerning the Confederate Survivors' Association and the centennial of Washington's inauguration; letter, 1882, to Major Temple, chief engineer of the Louisville and Nashville Railroad discussing the idea of planting a colony of New Englanders in a county in Georgia through which the railroad passed; and routine letters dealing with business, politics, and veterans' affairs.

2097.   JOHN CAMPBELL GORDON, FIRST MARQUIS
        OF ABERDEEN AND TEMAIR, PAPERS,
        1888.  1 item.  London, England.

   Letter to W. Waithman Caddell concerning imperial federation.

2098.   WILLIAM GORDON, SEVENTEENTH EARL
        OF SUTHERLAND, PAPERS, 1745-1747.
        5 items.  Dunrobin Castle,
        County Sutherland, Scotland.

   Copies of papers relating to William Gordon's attempt to receive compensation for the money he had spent in opposing the rebellion led by Charles Edward, the Young Pretender, 1745-1746, including a statement of his case, an account of the expenses, and copies of related correspondence with Henry Pelham.

2099.   CHARLES ALEXANDER GORE PAPERS,
        1830-1894.  115 items.
        London, England.

   The collection contains a variety of political letters from many governmental leaders on divers topics and a few items of personal correspondence.  One group of letters focuses on the cabinet crisis of December, 1845.

2100.   HENRY W. GORHAM PAPERS,
        1857-1863.  55 items.
        Brooklyn, N.Y.

   Personal and family correspondence of Henry W. Gorham, who served in the 13th New York Regiment during the Civil War.  The letters describe camp life to some extent, but have little to say about the war.

2101.   JOHN C. GORHAM DIARY,
        1815-1853.  1 vol.  (14 pp.)
        [Halifax County, N.C.]

   Sporadic entries in the diary of John C. Gorham, concerning farm products and timber shipped on the Tuscarora, a local trading schooner.

2102. SIR EDMUND WILLIAM GOSSE PAPERS, 1857-1958. 318 items. London, England.

Papers pertaining to Gosse's biography, The Life of Algernon Charles Swinburne, containing correspondence with many persons who had known the poet, including authors, professors, Swinburne's relatives and friends, former schoolmates in Eton College and Oxford University, and other contemporaries. Only a portion of the material in these letters was incorporated into the biography. There are also a number of letters to Gosse from other authors dealing for the most part with literary matters, including letters, 1879-1914, from Robert Bridges; letters, ca. 1888-1921, from George Moore; letters, 1885-1915, from Henry James; and letters, 1872-1891, from Henrik Ibsen. The Ibsen letters are in Norwegian, and some of the Moore and James letters are copies. The collection also contains notes on Swinburne's life and writing by Gosse; memorabilia on Swinburne and his work by several people; copies of some of Swinburne's poems; and printed material and facsimiles mainly of Swinburne's writing, but also of several reviews of his work.

2103. WILLIAM MURRAY GOSSIP PAPERS, 1904-1925. 1 vol. Inverness, Scotland.

A scrapbook containing clippings, letters, documents, and memorabilia concerning William Murray Gossip and his father James Alexander Gossip, Gossip family genealogy, cycling and camping, World War I, and events in Inverness and its environs.

2104. CHARLES L. GOULD PAPERS, 1862-1863. 3 items. Brattleboro (Windham County), Vt.

Correspondence between a Union soldier and his family in Vermont. Included also is a bit of verse, possibly original.

2105. JOHN H. GOULD PAPERS, 1860. 3 items. Baltimore, Md.

Letters from Harrison Gould of the Richmond Dispatch to his brother, John H. Gould of the Baltimore Sun discussing the presidential election of 1860 and the position of Republicans in Richmond, Virginia.

2106. JOHN MEAD GOULD PAPERS, 1841-1943. 3,300 items and 287 vols. Portland (Cumberland County), Me.

Correspondence and papers of John Mead Gould concerning his experience in the Civil War, his activities in veterans' organizations, and his work as historian of the 1st-10th-29th Maine Regiment. The correspondence in the collection relates in part to Gould's service in the 1st Maine Regiment and its successors, the 10th Maine Regiment and the 29th Maine Regiment and contains descriptions of the situation in Washington, D.C., 1861; guard duty on the Baltimore and Ohio Railroad at Relay, Maryland, 1861-1862; the battle of Winchester, 1862; the battle of Cedar Mountain, 1862; two fragments from field notes on the Maryland campaign and the battle of Antietam, 1862; the Red River expedition, 1864; operations in the Shenandoah Valley, 1864; and occupation duty in Darlington, South Carolina, 1865. There is family correspondence, especially for 1864; correspondence relating to Gould's attempt to establish a lumber business in South Carolina, 1866-1867; correspondence with other veterans after the war concerning Gould's history of the three regiments, validating pension claims, and veterans' organizations; correspondence of Adelthia Twitchell and Amelia Jenkins Twitchell, who went from Maine to teach freedmen in Beaufort, South Carolina, 1864-1865; and letters relating to the early career of the zoologist, Edward Sylvester Morse. Legal papers in the collection include commissions, discharges, furloughs, pensions, and papers from the superior provost court, Darlington, South Carolina, 1865-1866. Rolls and reports of the 1st-10th-29th Maine Regiment, 1861-1869, form the official papers of those units and concern supplies, finances, furloughs and other service records. The records of sixty-five consecutive reunions of the 1st-10th-29th Regiment veterans, 1869-1933, include lists of personnel, minutes, and obituaries. The collection also contains notebooks with biographical data on veterans; memorandum diaries of John M. Gould, 1854-1874; diary of Levi Johnson while he was with the 29th Regiment in South Carolina, 1865; the diary of Amelia Jenkins (Twitchell) Gould, 1860, 1862, 1863, 1864-1865; the diary of Samuel McClellan Gould, a Presbyterian minister, 1841-1845, 1890-1895; and diaries of excursions to Antietam, Cedar Mountain, and other battlefields of the Civil War, 1884-1912. There are clippings, broadsides, and pamphlets pertaining to battles and casualties, veterans' affairs, and politics and numerous pictures of the men of the 1st-10th-29th Regiment in the war and at various reunions.

2107. ROBERT NEWMAN GOURDIN PAPERS, 1789-1926. 459 items and 3 vols. Charleston, S.C.

Papers and correspondence of Robert Newman Gourdin and members of his family concerning business and personal matters. Business correspondence and papers relate to the firm of Gourdin, Matthieson and Company, commission merchants and dealers in rice, sea island cotton, and wine, and pertain to Robert N. Gourdin's promotion of railroads. Other items in the collection concern national politics, 1844; duels in South Carolina, 1853 and 1856; runaway slaves in 1861; the situation at Fort Sumter, 1861; the siege of Charleston during the Civil War; life in Cheraw and Florence, South Carolina, in the

Civil War; economic conditions in Charleston, 1861-1865; Reconstruction; and St. Michael's, St. Philip's, and other Charleston churches. Also letters from Alfred Huger containing comments on political matters and the Benton-Foote feud. Volumes are a geography of Chatham County, Georgia, and an account book, 1849-1862, belonging to Robert N. Gourdin, relating mainly to estates.

2108. GRABUR SILK MILLS, INC., PAPERS, 1934-1948. 60 items and 34 vols. Burlington (Alamance County), N.C.

Records of a silk-throwing firm owned by McEwen Knitting Co. and May Hosiery Mills, which after 1940 merged to form May-McEwen-Kaiser. The collection consists of financial statements, arranged chronologically, which include balance sheets and profit-and-loss statements, and occasionally other types of statements, most frequently unit cost analyses, profit and loss by lot clearance or completed billings, and departmental manufacturing expenses; account books including ledgers, journals, cash receipt journals, cash disbursement journals, trial balances, each of which covers most of the period 1935-1948, and less extensive series of other accounts, mostly for purchasing, production, and sales. There are also miscellaneous reports.

2109. JOHN PATRICK GRACE PAPERS, 1902-1940. 12,077 items and 3 vols. Charleston, S.C. Restricted.

Correspondence of a Charleston attorney, editor, and politician relating to his career, including such topics as corruption in local elections, 1911-1920; the founding of and the editorial politics of the Charleston American; Wilson's neutrality policy and U.S. entry into World War I; state, national, and world politics in the 1920s and 1930s, including comments on Adolph Hitler; speculation in Florida real estate; and losses in the depression. Correspondents include William W. Ball, Ibra C. Blackwood, James F. Byrnes, Hamilton Fish, Jr., Olin D. Johnston, W. Turner Logan, Pat McCarran, Thomas Gordon McLeod, James E. Murray, George W. Norris, James A. Reed, John Gardiner Richards, Ellison D. Smith, Eugene Talmadge, and Millard E. Tydings. Legal papers relate to the business of the Charleston American, the Chesapeake Bay Bridge Co., and many cases handled by Grace, including the trial of O. B. Limehouse, a sheriff accused of farming prisoners out in peonage and in sending obscene matter through the mail. Other records include bills and receipts, and scrapbooks, 3 vols., 1923, 1927, 1931-1935, of newspaper clippings.

2110. GRACE EPISCOPAL CHURCH. CHARLESTON, S.C. PAPERS, 1855. 1 item.

List of tunes sung at Grace Church.

2111. GRACE EPISCOPAL CHURCH PARISH PAPERS. 1 item. Morganton (Burke County), N.C.

Historical sketch by Col. W. S. Pearson of mission work.

2112. WILLIAM BENJAMIN GRACIE PAPERS, 1916. 1 item. New York, N.Y.

Letter from William B. Gracie, an officer in the U.S. Army, from Camp Eagle Pass, Texas, discussing the fear of attack by Francisco "Pancho" Villa, the questionable loyalty of the Mexicans, the possibility of U.S. troops crossing into Mexico, and the weather and living conditions in the area.

2113. ROBERT S. GRACY PAPERS, 1828-1848. 8 items. Iredell County, N.C., and Montgomery County, Ala.

Papers concerning business affairs of the Gracy family and the settlement of the estate of Robert S. Gracy by his brother Mercer; subjects mentioned are slaves and prices of slaves. Correspondents include Isaac Jarratt, a slave trader of Huntsville, North Carolina.

2114. W. EDWIN GRADY PAPERS, 1889-1916. 20 items. Savannah, Ga.

Business papers of a realtor and insurance man.

2115. EMMA GRAHAM PAPERS, 1859-1891. 15 items. Cheraw (Chesterfield County), S.C.

Social letters from relatives.

2116. HUGH GRAHAM DAYBOOKS, 1803-1851. 5 vols. Tazewell (Claiborne County), Tenn.

Merchant's account, 1803-1804, and daybook, 1808-1814, from Bent Creek, [Tennessee?], and daybooks, 1818-1820, 1833-1834, and 1839-1851, from Tazewell.

2117. JAMES GRAHAM PAPERS, 1831-1850. 13 items. Salisbury (Rowan County), N.C.

Correspondence between Graham and a brother-in-law, Joseph W. Rogers of Cabarrus County, largely concerning their family; mention is made of the execution of a slave for murder. A letter from John W. B. Houston, a nephew of Graham, from Fort Washataw, Arkansas, 1847, concerns the Mexican War and opportunities for capital in Arkansas; one from Marshall, Texas, 1850, relates to slave trading and praises the Chickasaw Indians with whom he is doing business.

2118.  JOHN GRAHAM PAPERS, 1773-1776. 2 items. Savannah, Ga.

List of accounts of Graham with John Sommerville in Savannah, 1773, and a letter concerning the sale of horses, 1776. Graham later served as lieutenant governor of Georgia, 1779-1782.

2119.  WILLIAM GRAHAM DIARY, July 19-Nov. 17, 1864. 16 pp. Georgia and Illinois.

Typescript copy of the diary kept by a sergeant in the 53rd Illinois Volunteer Infantry during the Atlanta campaign and after.

2120.  WILLIAM GRAHAM PAPERS, 1783-1885. 1,113 items and 12 vols. Lexington (Rockbridge County), Va.

Records of three generations of a family of Scots-Irish Presbyterians. Correspondence of Reverend William Graham (1746-1799), who moved from Pennsylvania to Lexington, Virginia, about 1776 and was one of the founders of Liberty Hall Academy (later Washington and Lee University) refers largely to his investment in land on the Ohio River near Marietta after 1796, and his lawsuit claiming he had been cheated. The bulk of the collection comprises the correspondence of William's brother, Edward Graham, a lawyer and professor at Washington College. There are many letters between Edward's wife, Margaret (Alexander) Graham, and her children. Represented are William A., Archibald A., Nancy, Elizabeth, and Edward, Jr. Included is correspondence of Edward Graham with Edmund Ruffin concerning scientific experimentation and many letters concerning the patent application of William A. Graham, an inventor, for his fire extinguisher. There is also correspondence of Dr. John Graham and Beverly Tucker Lacy, grandsons of Edward Graham. Account books of Archibald Graham of Lexington, 1840-1880, 7 vols., include one volume (6 pp.) on the administration of Edward Graham's estate and the guardianship of Martha and Elizabeth Lyle. Account books, 2 vols., of Edward, Sr., contain judgments and court actions, 1801-1811, and accounts of Washington College, Lexington, 1831-1836. A commonplace book, 1820, may relate to Edward Graham. There is a genealogy of the Alexander and Graham families by John A. Graham.

2121.  WILLIAM ALEXANDER GRAHAM PAPERS, 1841-1896. 58 items. Hillsborough (Orange County) and Lincoln County, N.C.

Letters to Graham as governor of North Carolina, 1844-1848, and U.S. secretary of the navy, 1850-1852, seeking appointments and commissions; letters of Graham's son, William A. Graham, Jr., relating to his education, his service in the 2nd North Carolina Cavalry (later 19th North Carolina Volunteers) during the Civil War in eastern North Carolina, where he described agricultural practices, Pembroke, and the Cabarrus family; and in Virginia, at Norfolk and in an action between Smithfield and Blackwater Bridge, 1863; and later in the adjutant general's office. There is also information on the status of Negroes in the postwar South, and comment on the family's business producing and selling corn, wheat, and cotton and operation of a sawmill, grist mill, a charcoal furnace, and the working of gold, iron, and copper deposits.

2122.  WILLIAM GRAHAM AND SIMPSON COMPANY PAPERS, 1774-1786. 12 items. [Savannah, Ga.?]

Accounts with London merchants for imports of clothing, oil and pigments, hatchets, Indian trade guns, and other goods; and account of cash paid for lumber rafts.

2123.  THE GRAND COUNCIL, TEMPERANCE REFORM. RECORD BOOK, 1873-1879. 1 vol. (161 pp.). Van Buren (Crawford County); Greenwood (Sebastian County); and Ozark (Franklin County), Arkansas.

Minutes and constitutions.

2124.  GEORGE W. GRANT PAPERS, 1861-1892. 82 items. Reading (Berks County), Pa.

Chiefly letters from George W. Grant, an officer with the 88th Regiment, Pennsylvania Volunteers, to his father, James A. Grant, and sister, Mary Jane Grant, in Reading, Pennsylvania, with information on Union Army camp life, furloughs, pay, promotions, army surgeons, Fredericksburg after the battle, the first day of Gettysburg, and prison life at Libby Prison (Richmond, Virginia), Camp Oglethorpe (Macon, Georgia), Roper Hospital (Charleston, South Carolina), and the Confederate Military Prison (Columbia, South Carolina). There are also diaries kept by Grant covering portions of his imprisonment and an account of his last days at Macon and transfer to Charleston with a description of the Union siege of Charleston, 1864. There are also two poems by Union prisoners and a few bills and receipts.

2125.  ULYSSES SIMPSON GRANT PAPERS, 1868-1874. 12 items. Washington, D.C.

Letters of recommendation for office seekers during Grant's presidency of the U.S.; a letter from Peter Dox, U.S. representative from Alabama, concerning a proposed Atlantic-Mississippi canal, 1872;

reminiscences of a sergeant in the 5th U.S. Cavalry about serving as a member of the bodyguard for Grant and Lincoln during their meeting at Petersburg, April 3, 1865; letters concerning minor legislation; and miscellaneous materials.

2126.  SIR WILLIAM GRANT PAPERS,
       1788-1836.  51 items.
       London, England.

Chiefly letters to Grant, (1752-1832), British politician and member of parliament, from prominent political leaders, churchmen, jurists, members of the royal family, and others, formerly bound in a scrapbook by J. J. Frobisher of Dawlish, Devonshire.  Relating to miscellaneous political, administrative, and literary matters are letters from John Abercrombie, 1836; Charles Alexandre de Calonne, [1801?]; Henry Dundas, 1798; Lord Eldon, 1817; George III; Reginald Heber, 1822; Henry Mackenzie, 1805; the Duke of Northumberland, 1806; Spencer Perceval, 1810; Henry Phillpotts, Bishop of Exeter, 1831; William Pitt the Younger, 1799, 1804; and William Van Mildert, Bishop of Durham, 1831.

2127.  WILLIAM CHARLES GRANT PAPERS,
       1868.  1 item.  "Hillersdon
       House," Cullompton, Devonshire,
       England.

Letter to Grant (1817-1877) from Sir Stafford Northcote, secretary of state for India, explaining his position on disestablishment of the Church of Ireland.

2128.  WILLIAM G. GRANT PAPERS,
       1847, 1851.  2 items.
       Cleveland, Ohio.

Routine business letters.

2129.  GRANT COUNTY SUNDAY SCHOOL
       ASSOCIATION RECORDS, 1887-1889.
       6 items.  Grant County, W. Va.

Minutes, November, 1887, to November, 1888; constitution; reports on printed forms of member churches including South Mill Creek and Elkhorn Baptist churches, Medley Methodist, and Union, Corner, and Fall's Creek churches.

2130.  JOHN WILLIAM GRANTHAM PAPERS,
       1822 (1866-1873) 1924.
       1,946 items and 6 vols.
       Middleway (Jefferson County),
       W. Va.

Letters, 10 items, concerning the political career of Grantham, a member of the West Virginia legislature, 1872-1881; a petition, 1872, against removal of the capital from Charleston to Wheeling; business papers of a country store run by Grantham and James W. League, 1850-1890; papers concerning Grantham's agency for the Arlington Mutual Life Insurance Co., of Charlottesville, Virginia, 1870s; family letters; and a circular letter, 1871, from Hudson Wood & Co., purchasing agents in New York, offering Grantham a chance to join in a counterfeiting scheme.  Bound volumes include check stubs, 1856-1858, 1 vol.; daybooks, 1850, 1854-1860, 2 vols., one partly used as a scrapbook; House bills of the West Virginia legislature, 1872-1873, 2 vols.; memorandum books of Grantham's mercantile business, 1871-1875, 1879-1887, 7 vols.

2131.  WILLIAM CLARK GRASTY AND
       JOHN P. RISON PAPERS,
       1788 (1800-1869) 1876.
       8,001 items and 118 vols.
       Pittsylvania County, Va.

Business records of three generations of merchants of Green Hill, Stony Hill, Mount Airy, and Danville, all in Pittsylvania County, Virginia, centering around the Grasty and Rison families.  With the exception of ledgers and daybooks, there is little information concerning the senior partner, Samuel Pannill of Green Hill, in the firm of Grasty and Pannill, save that he felt he had been treated unfairly by Philip L. Grasty.  Most of the unbound material in the early part of the collection concerns the activities of Philip L. Grasty (d. 1827) at Stony Hill, where he carried on a diversified type of merchandising largely based on the barter system.  In 1806 Grasty moved his store to Mount Airy; from then until 1827 the papers reveal the type of drugs, hardware, books, and dry goods in general demand; the barter system so common at the time; and the diversified type of business, including in addition to his general store, the operation of a tavern, a plantation, a blacksmith shop, a simplified type of banking, and the keeping of a post office.  There are also countless orders on Grasty for goods to be delivered to the bearer, often a slave, and many receipts, mortgages, and notes covering a wide area around Pittsylvania County.

2132.  CHARLES GRATIOT, JR.,
       ANDREW TALCOTT, AND
       RENE EDWARD DE RUSSEY PAPERS,
       1817-1861.  18 items.
       Fortress Monroe and Old Point
       Comfort (Hampton County), Va.

Letters to engineers at Fortress Monroe and Old Point Comfort relative to the construction of lighters, the supplying of construction materials for fortifications, and other matters.

2133.  JOHN GRATTAN PAPERS, 1790-1800.
       3 items.  London, England.

Two letters, 1790, from Grattan, formerly adjutant and quartermaster general in India, seeking a promotion; and a letter of his widow, Lucia Grattan, sister of Henry Cary, Eighth Viscount Falkland, appealing to the East India Company for a pension.

2134. JOHN J. GRAVATT PAPERS, 1864.
1 item. Richmond, Va.

A report, November 16, 1864, by Assistant Surgeon S. P. Christian on a trip to North Carolina to entrain a group of sick and wounded soldiers, addressed to John J. Gravatt, medical officer in charge at General Hospital No. 9 in Richmond.

2135. JAMES T. GRAVES ACCOUNT BOOKS, 1848-1871. 2 vols. Stantonsburg (Wilson County), N.C.

Physician's accounts.

2136. WILLIAM GRAVES PAPERS, 1837-1868. 21 items. Bedford County, Va.

Business letters.

2137. D. W. GRAY PAPERS, 1849. 1 item. Buena Vista, Mexico.

Letter from a Texas Ranger concerning marauding Comanches in northern Mexico.

2138. EDWIN GRAY PAPERS, 1808. 2 items. Washington, D.C.

Letter of Gray, U.S. representative from Virginia, objecting to a printed notice by Senator Stephen Row Bradley calling for nominating candidates for president and vice president of the United States by members of Congress.

2139. FRANCIS CALLEY GRAY DIARY, 1811-1815. 1 vol. Boston, Mass.

Diary kept by Gray (1790-1856) on a journey across Europe while returning from service as unpaid secretary to the U.S. legation in St. Petersburg. It describes travel conditions in Russia; the conditions of the peasants in Russia, Estonia, and Prussia; libraries, palaces, art galleries, scientific cabinets, and churches in Berlin; and has a brief account of his trip across England to Liverpool. That portion of the diary after Dec., 1814, which describes a trip to Monticello, has been published as Thomas Jefferson in 1814, edited by Henry S. Rowe and T. Jefferson Collidge, Jr.

2140. MRS. HIRAM GRAY PAPERS, 1858-1865. 4 items. Cheraw (Chesterfield County), S.C.

Included are a letter from Gen. William J. Hardee to Gen. Sherman asking the protection of Mrs. Gray, a Northerner, during the Union occupation; a reply by Sherman; and an order that the Gray family not be molested.

2141. JAMES S. GRAY PAPERS, 1854-1886. 28 items. Washington, D.C.

Largely miscellaneous items dealing with family matters and local politics in Virginia; a few by J. Ambler Smith of Richmond comment on the Tilden-Hayes election; a letter of Edward Gray, 1881, concerns purchase rates of Confederate bonds by brokers.

2142. RICHARD L. GRAY ACCOUNTS, 1849-1859. 3 vols. Winchester (Frederick County), Va.

Records of a cigar manufacturer whose operations were on a small scale.

2143. JOHN BRECKENRIDGE GRAYSON PAPERS, 1847-1853. 9 items. Gaines' Mill (Hanover County), Va.

Papers of an officer in the U.S. Army and later in the Confederate Army, largely checks and receipts for supplies during the Mexican War. One letter of 1853 concerns the purchase of a farm.

2144. WILLIAM JOHN GRAYSON PAPERS, 1832, 1834. 2 items. Beaufort (Beaufort County), S.C.

An appointment for Grayson as commissioner in equity for the Beaufort District, South Carolina, 1832, and a letter from Grayson while a member of Congress in 1834 giving fatherly advice to his son, William John, Jr., in school in Charleston.

2145. HENRY SYDNEY GRAZEBROOK PAPERS, 1885. 2 items. London, England.

Two letters to Grazebrook (1836-1896) from Rev. Thomas Proctor Wadley concerning Grazebrook's book, The Heraldry of Worcestershire.

2146. GREAT BRITAIN PAPERS (LITERARY), 1707-1948. 240 items. Great Britain.

Miscellaneous collection of letters, poems, and clippings which relate to various British writers, poets, dramatists, and historians, some of them containing details of biographical interest and discussions of literary subjects. Included are a volume of anonymous verse, ca. 1800-1807; an appeal of Allan McLeod for subsistence during his imprisonment, 1802; letters, 1806-1807, 2 items, of Dennis O'Bryan (1755-1832) concerning Charles James Fox and a proposed biography of Fox; a letter, 1822, of William Kitchiner concerning the publication of national songs of England; a letter, 1825, of Horatio Smith (1779-1849) to Cyrus Redding (1785-1870), about writing for Redding's journal, the New Monthly Magazine; a letter, 1831, by Sidney (Owenson) Morgan discussing her dispute with her former publisher, Henry Colburn; a letter, [1832?], by Robert Keeley (1793-1869) praising a play by James Sheridan

Knowles; an account, 1832, of the death of Hannah (Spurr) Kilham, a missionary in Africa; a letter of Louisa Stuart concerning the works and personal life of John Gibson Lockhart; a plea by Elizabeth (Barrett) Browning for pardon of Victor Hugo, 1857; a letter of Samuel Goldwin, 1859, discusses William Ewart Gladstone and his reelection problems; a letter [1863?] of Louise de la Ramée to J. T. March concerning payment from William Tinsley, publisher, for Granville de Vigue (published 1863) and mentioning comments on the book by Charles Edward Mudie; Benjamin Leopold Farjeon to William Tinsley describing the completion of Bread and Cheese and Kisses (published 1874); letters (1881, 4 items) of John Morley to Armine T. Kent relating to publication in Fortnightly Review of Kent's article, "Leigh Hunt as a Poet"; letters, 1892-1905, 5 items, of William Thomas Stead to Charles Frederic Moberly Bell commenting upon the election of 1892, and the ministerial status of the Earl of Rosebery; a letter, 1897, of Oswald Crawford to Harper and Brothers concerning the publication of a work by Violet Hunt; translations by Joseph Dacre Carlyle (1759-1804) of nine Arabic poems which were printed in Epiphanius Wilson, ed., Arabian Literature (London: 1900); a letter of George Macaulay Trevelyan thanking Francis Albert Rollo Russell for allowing use of Lord John Russell's diary; a letter, 1910, of Leopold James Maxse to Henry Brereton Marriott Watson concerning publication of articles in the National Review and the Observer; letters, 1920-1921, 2 items, of Frank Harris, editor of Pearson's Magazine, commenting on an attempt by Alfred Bruce Douglas, son of the Eighth Marquis of Queensbury, to suppress a book by George Moore for indecency, on the sons of Oscar Wilde, and on Wilde's authorship of The Portrait of Mr. W. H.; a letter, 1926, by Max Beerbohm commenting on caricatures by David Low; a letter of Clare Leighton, 1929, to Frank Ernest Hill, editor of Longmans, Green and Co., concerning her wood engravings for illustrations; a letter of Stanley Naylor to Sydney Carroll written in search of work ghostwriting autobiographies for illustrious persons. Among others represented in the collection by miscellaneous letters, poems, articles, and fragments are Hannah Bott; Edward George Earle Lytton Bulwer-Lytton, First Baron Lytton; Rosina Doyle (Wheeler) Bulwer-Lytton, Baroness Lytton; William Chambers; Herbert Edwin Clarke; Katherine Cooper; Agnes Mary Frances (Robinson) Duclaux; Maria Edgeworth; John Foster (1770-1843); Simon Forman; Abraham Hayward; Felicia Dorothea (Browne) Hemans; Harold Joseph Laski; Andrew Millar; Robert Montgomery; George Augustus Moore; William Orme; Olivia (Wilmot) Serres (1772-1834); Philip Nicholas Shuttleworth (1782-1842), Bishop of Chichester; Samuel Smiles; Andrew James Symington; Scott Titchfield; Theodosia Trollope.

2147. GREAT BRITAIN PAPERS (MILITARY AND NAVAL), 1730-1914. 1,079 items and 1 vol. Great Britain.

A chronological file contains miscellaneous orders, commissions, and letters, including a letter of William Amherst, 1775; a letter, 1866, of General Sir John Fox Burgoyne evaluating the economic prospects of the United States and the "imperialistic" temper of its government; a letter, 1801, of Lord Colville reporting the seizure of American and Danish vessels; a letter of Sir Thomas Fraser (b. 1840); eleven items, 1822-1846, of Thomas Graham, Baron Lynedoch; a letter, 1830, of Rowland Hill, First Viscount Hill; letters, 2 items, 1782, of General Alexander Leslie, reporting from Charleston, South Carolina, and discussing the military conditions in the Southern colonies; a letter from General Charles O'Hara, 1781, from camp near Wilmington, North Carolina, describing the campaigns and the condition of his brigade following the battle of Guilford Courthouse; and a commission of James Reynell. An anonymous volume, 25 pp., late 18th-early 19th centuries, contains exercises and field regulations for infantry. There is also a large amount of routine official correspondence and reports of the quartermaster general's office, requesting routes for military travel within Great Britain, concerning commissary supplies and related matters, and reporting on the quartering of units; and there are routine correspondence and reports of the paymaster general consisting of directives from the treasury, cost estimates, and forms for disbursement of funds.

2148. GREAT BRITAIN PAPERS (MISCELLANEOUS), 1670-1968. 275 items and 1 vol.

Included are an 18th century copy of a report of the Board of Trade and Plantations, December 12, 1719, to George I, relating to prohibition of export of wool from Great Britain and Ireland, prohibition of the import of calico cloth, and encouragement of the silk trade; a letter of Thomas Hicks, 1756, to John Warburton, concerning Hicks's family arms; a letter, 1798, of Peter Cavallier concerning his military service; letters, 1809, to Richard Sharp relating to financial speculation and the U.S. embargo; a letter of Simon Gray, 1815, discussing his new book on population, The Happiness of States; a letter, 1830, of John Buckland describing cultivation of hops in Kent; a letter, 1831, of Sir William Gell discussing archeological investigations in Italy; a letter of Sir Hugh Percy, Third Duke of Northumberland, 1840, soliciting support for his candidacy for the chancellorship of Cambridge University; a letter from Henry Edward Manning, 1851, affirming his belief in the doctrinal supremacy of the Catholic Church; a manuscript and letter, 1860, of Thomas Gutherie (1803-1873) relating to a temperance article by him; a letter by William Foster-Vesey-Fitzgerald, 1866, on Christianity in the

Orient, especially India; a letter of Lord Sidney Godolphin Osborne, 1867, about problems of voting in conclaves of bishops; a letter of James Spencer Northcote, 1869, concerning the sale and distribution of his book on the Roman catacombs; a letter of introduction for Joseph Henry to J. H. Pulman, librarian of the House of Lords, 1870, by J. C. Webster; a letter, 1871, by Octavia Hill on the work of the Charity Organization Society; a letter, 1874, by Mary Carpenter, philanthropist, protesting remarks of James Fraser, Bishop of Manchester, about Carpenter's religious interests; an apprenticeship contract for a shipwright, 1877; letters of Charles William Fowler, 1882, describing missionary work in Sarawak among the Land Dyaks; a letter of Thomas John Barnardo, 1888, on his charitable efforts among destitute children in London; a letter of George William Kitchin, Dean of Winchester, 1889, concerning publications of the Hampshire Record Society; a letter of Arnold Henry Savage Landor, 1900, describing entry of the allies into Peking at the end of the Boxer Rebellion; and a letter, 1902, of Alexander Henry Craufurd (1843-1917) to Hugh Black concerning their writings on religious subjects. Among undated items are a rough sketch by David Roberts; notes by Richard Pares on Lewis B. Namier's *England in the Age of the American Revolution*; a letter of Joseph Mallord William Turner, landscape painter, to William Finden, engraver, concerning two drawings; a letter of Alexander James Beresford-Hope to Charles Forbes René de Montalembert, concerning Montalembert's historical writing, and cabinet politics; and a political note of G. Lathom Browne to Benjamin Disraeli. Among the many well-known persons represented in the collection are Sir William Martin Conway; Charles Hayes; Thomas Holliday; Henry Edward, Cardinal Manning; William Markham, Archbishop of York; and Sir Edwin Henry Landseer. Other topics on which there is some discussion include construction work on the Mersey and Irwell Canal, 1772; the work of Thomas Falconer in behalf of the Church of England, 1836; the health of Edward VII, 1898; and genealogy.

2149. GREAT BRITAIN PAPERS (POLITICAL), 1717-1944. 179 items.

Letters from many leading British political figures touching upon the main themes of the eighteenth and nineteenth centuries, the Irish question, rural education, the Napoleonic Wars, the bombardment of Canton, and Balkan affairs, Chartist and Corn Law agitation, abolition of slavery, Poor Laws, political alliances, and democracy. A copy of a letter of Alexander Robertson, Thirteenth Baronet, 1716, to John Erskine, Sixth Earl of Mar, relates to their exile in France as Jacobites; an order upon the treasury, 1730, concerns payments to Thomas Pelham, secretary to the British embassy at Paris; a letter of Charles James Fox, 1783, concerns politics and appointments; a letter of the Duke of Richmond, 1783, objects to the timing of peace negotiations with the Americans and explains his withdrawal from the cabinet; a letter of George Rose, secretary to the treasury, concerns Pitt's decision on the terms of the Loyalty Loan; a letter of Charles Cornwallis, 1802, to Castlereagh concerns Castlereagh's joining the cabinet; a letter of William Henry Vane, First Duke of Cleveland, 1807, criticizes the ministry of the Duke of Portland and Spencer Perceval; a letter of William Windham, 1808, seeks counsel in opposition to the military policy of Castlereagh; a letter of George Tierney, 1809, concerns prospects for defeating the ministry of Spencer Perceval; a letter of Lord Talbot, 1817, to Henry Addington, Viscount Sidmouth, comments upon riots by the laboring classes; a letter by Lord Lyndhurst, 1826, concerns election campaigns for Parliament; letters of Henry Pelham Fiennes Pelham-Clinton, Duke of Newcastle, to Sir Charles Wetherell, 1830, 1831, concern elections; a letter of Benjamin Wiffen relates to the abolition of slavery, 1832; a letter of John Wood, 1832, is about politics in Dorsetshire; a letter of the Earl of Ripon, 1834, concerns restrictions against Dissenters; a letter of Earl Fitzwilliam, 1842, relates to the Corn Laws; a letter of the Fifteenth Earl of Derby, 1852, seeks the adherence of Thomas Musgrave, Archbishop of York, to a royal commission on the problems of religious worship and education; a letter of William Edward Forster to Alexander Ireland, 1853, about Lancashire strikes and conditions among the working classes; a letter of 1857 to Apsley Pellatt mentions Richard Cobden's motion of censure against the government for the bombardment of Canton; a letter of Thomas Cooper to John Alfred Langford, author of books on Birmingham, Staffordshire, etc., 1857, seeks wage statistics on behalf of the general board of health, Whitehall; a letter of Samuel Morley, 1859, discusses Lord John Russell's proposal for parliamentary reform; a letter of Charles Pelham Villiers, 1860, complains of difficulties in administering the Poor Laws; a letter of Sir William Cavendish, Seventh Duke of Devonshire, 1866, mentions a bill to remove restrictions on dissenters at Oxford and Cambridge universities; a letter of the Marquess of Dufferin, 1867, is about the failure of the legal tender bill in the United States; a letter of Thomas Walsh, Irish landowner, 1870, denounces the Irish Land Act; a letter of Henry Fawcett to Robert Smith Bartlett, 1873, relates his opposition to legislation prohibiting work by married women; a letter of Joseph Chamberlain to Frederick Braby concerns politics, 1877; a letter of Herbert Gladstone, 1880, explains the actions of his father, the prime minister, in blocking Austrian ambitions in the Balkans; letters of George Douglas Campbell, 1880, 1885, oppose government interference in contracts of landlords with their tenants; a letter of the Eighth Duke of Devonshire, Secretary of State for India, 1880, expresses regret about Fawcett's speech against Edward Stanhope; a letter of John Wodehouse, First Earl of Kimberley, 1882, describes the selection of Anglican bishops for Sierra Leone; a letter of the Third

Marquis of Salisbury to the First Marquis of Abergavenny, 1883, accepts the presidency of the Constitutional Club; a letter of Charles Bradlaugh of the National Reformer to James Macaulay, 1884, concerns revealed religion; a letter, 1884, of William Edward Forster concerns politics; letters, 1884 and 1897, of Joseph Chamberlain concern politics; a letter, 1886, of Sir Alfred Milner, First Viscount Milner, to Thomas Spring-Rice, Second Baron Monteagle of Brandon, praises the Salisbury ministry; a letter of John Elliot Burnes, a Labor M.P., 1895, concerns the democratization of British government and society; a letter, 1904, from the Eighth Duke of Devonshire to Freeman Freeman-Thomas concerns candidates for Parliament; a letter of Joseph Chamberlain, 1906, relates to Sir Theodore Vivian Samuel Angier's entry into politics on behalf of tariff reform; a letter of Sir Francis Dyke Acland, 1914, speculates on the behavior of Italy as a member of the Triple Alliance; a letter of Richard Haldane, 1916, deals with criticism he has received; a letter of James Bryce, Viscount Bryce, 1916, to the Lord Mayor refers to the American Relief Fund and to refugees. Others represented in the collection are Sir James Graham; Thomas Hodgson; the Duchess of York and Albany (1817); Stearne Ball Miller; William IV; and Edward VII.

2150.   GREAT BRITAIN.   CONSULATE,
        SAVANNAH, GA., PAPERS,
        1816 (1824-1867) 1875.
        488 items.

The papers consist mainly of routine correspondence from the British consul general in Washington and the Foreign Office in London to British consuls in Savannah, and of letters from citizens of Great Britain residing in the U.S. who were seeking the assistance of their home government. Most of the latter feared they would be conscripted into Confederate service. Several items concern the mistreatment of Negro seamen who were British subjects.

2151.   GREAT BRITAIN.   COURT OF
        BANKRUPTCY PAPERS,
        1764-1772.   1 vol.
        London, England.

Account of fees received for John Yorke (1728-1801), fourth son of the First Earl of Hardwicke, and the patentee for making out commissions of bankruptcy. His deputy, F. A. Hindley, received the fees until 1766 and possibly thereafter.

2152.   GREAT BRITAIN.   PARLIAMENT.
        HOUSE OF COMMONS PAPERS,
        1628.   1 item.   London, England.

Fragment of a manuscript volume containing transcripts of speeches by members of a committee of the House of Commons during a conference with representatives of the House of Lords held to induce the Lords to join in the Petition of Right, 1628. Included are speeches and resolutions by Sir Dudley Digges, Sir Edward Littleton, John Shelden, Sir Edward Coke, and also remonstrances to the King against the Duke of Buckingham and on the subject of the bill for tonnage and poundage. Much of the material has been published in Cobbett, Parliamentary History of England, vol. II.

2153.   GREAT BRITAIN.   PARLIAMENT.
        HOUSE OF LORDS PAPERS,
        1 vol.   London, England.

Manuscript volume entitled "Remembrances--for Order and Decency to be kept, in the Upper House of Parliament, by the Lords when His Majesty is not there, leaving the Solemnity belonging to his Majesty's coming to be marshalled by those Lords to whom it more properly appertans."

2154.   GREAT BRITAIN.   PRIVY SEAL
        OFFICE PAPERS, 1695-1830.
        71 items.   London, England.

Dockets, 1794-1830, abstracting proposed letters-patent, largely concerning civil, colonial, and ecclesiastical appointments, royal pardons, grants of baronetcies, appointments of various administrative commissions, the charter of the London Institution, and warrants for the payment of funds to the army and navy. There is also correspondence between the Privy Seal Office and other governmental bodies, usually the Treasury Office. These letters concern requests for information about the number of employees and their salaries and other sources of income from official duties. A few items relate to the Signet Office.

2155.   GREAT BRITAIN.   SOUTHERN DEPARTMENT.
        DIPLOMATIC DISPATCHES.   SPAIN.
        1717-1732.   2 vols.   London,
        England.

Diplomatic correspondence between the Secretariat of the Southern Department responsible for foreign relations with Southern Europe and colonial affairs, and British envoys in Spain. Most of the dispatches are for the years 1717 and 1731; a few are for 1720 and 1726. There is a descriptive calendar. Dispatches of 1717 by George Bubb, later George Bubb Dodington, Lord Melcombe, envoy to Spain concern regulation of trade between the two countries; the conflict between Spain and Austria in Italy; the quarrel between Spain and Portugal over the implementation of the terms of the treaty of Utrecht; and the status of a group of Irish, Catholic, and Jacobite traders claiming dual Spanish and English citizenship. Part of these documents has been published in Lloyd Sanders, Patron and Place-Hunter: A Study of George Bubb Dodington, Lord Melcombe (New York: 1919). There are also letters, 1717, 1720, and 1726, from Bubb's successor, William Stanhope, First Earl of Harrington. They describe Spanish military preparations and the kidnapping of Johan Willem Ripperda from his refuge in Stanhope's house. Dispatches of 1731-1732, when Sir Benjamin Keene was English minister to Spain are largely instructions of Thomas Pelham-Holles, First Duke of Newcastle-under-Lyme, Secretary of State for the Southern Department, and relate to the crisis in Italy over the succession to the Duchy of Parma and to commercial relations and Spanish depredations against English commerce, including the incident of Jenkins' Ear.

2156. GREAT BRITAIN. SOUTHERN DEPARTMENT. DIPLOMATIC DISPATCHES. SPAIN. 1738. 1 vol. London, England.

Documents on the diplomatic relations of Britain and Spain prior to the outbreak of the war of Jenkins' Ear and to the seizure of English vessels in the West Indies. Included are a general history, dated January, 1738, of Anglo-Spanish treaties since the wars of Henry VIII and their application to the West Indies trade; copies of correspondence between London and Madrid, 1737-1738; and documents of 1727 relating to the Spanish siege of Gibraltar, largely concerning legal aspects of fighting in the absence of a declaration of war.

2157. GREAT BRITAIN. TREASURY. PAPERS, 1822-1825. 32 items. London, England.

Receipts and legal documents relating to payment of pensions to foreign nationals, most of whom were Frenchmen.

2158. GREAT BRITAIN. TREASURY. PATRONAGE RECORD BOOK, 1770-1782. 1 vol. London, England.

List of recommendations by influential Englishmen to appointments and commissions in various revenue divisions of the treasury providing a detailed view of the structure of a governmental office dealing with revenue collection.

2159. GREAT BRITAIN. VICE CONSULATE. WILMINGTON, N.C. PAPERS. 1872-1922. 3 vols.

Register of British ships entering the port, 1873-1922, with detailed information about each vessel; register of consular acts, 1872-1882, itemizing fees; and public instruments of protest and declaration, 1889-1890. The vice consuls were Alexander Sprunt and later his son James Sprunt, owners of the cotton exporting firm of Alexander Sprunt & Son, Inc.

2160. HORACE GREELEY PAPERS, 1852, 1869. 2 items. New York, N.Y.

Letter from Horace Greeley (1811-1872), newspaper editor and reformer, concerning Greeley's assistance on a work about an unnamed woman writer that the addressee has in progress; and a letter dealing with a dispute involving coal miners.

2161. ADELINE ELLERY (BURR) DAVIS GREEN PAPERS, 1796-1956. 1,545 items and 6 vols. Fayetteville (Cumberland County), N.C.

Papers of Adeline E. (Burr) Davis Green (1843-1931) include letters, 1851-1853, from James M. Burr, brother of Adeline (Burr) Davis Green, to his wife describing his life in California searching for gold; James Burr's journal entitled "Journal of a Cruise to California and the Diggins"; Civil War letters from her second husband and cousin, Wharton Jackson Green (1831-1910), later agriculturist and U.S. congressman, while a prisoner-of-war at Johnson's Island, Ohio; letters, 1882-1885, from her first husband, David Davis (1815-1886), jurist and U. S. senator, describing daily proceedings in the senate, social functions in Washington, D.C., and notable persons; letters from friends of Davis concerning personal and political matters; letters, 1906-1928, from Jessica Randolph Smith and others pertaining to the Daughters of the Confederacy; and letters, 1911-1931, from James Henry Rice, Jr. (1868-1935), ornithologist, naturalist, editor, and literary figure, discussing politics, conservation, South Carolina culture, world affairs, especially relative to Germany and Russia, his rice plantations, and the League of Nations.

2162. C. H. GREEN PAPERS, 1860-1861. 3 items. Front Royal (Warren County), Va.

Personal letters to C. H. Green from relatives in Hannibal, Missouri.

2163. C. R. GREEN LEGAL NOTES, 1875. 2 vols.

Letterpress copies of legal notes on corporations and on statute of limitations.

2164. DUFF GREEN PAPERS, 1865-1872. 3 items. Dalton (Whitfield County), Ga.

Papers of Duff Green (1791-1875), editor and industrial promoter, include a prospectus of The Daily Laborer, which Green planned to publish; a letter to his grandson explaining his failure to publish The Daily Laborer and describing his plans for national and state banking systems, a national currency, and a system to bring education within the reach of all; and a deposition concerning property in Vicksburg, Mississippi.

2165. DUFF GREEN PAPERS, 1817 (1822-1875) 1894. 1,795 items and 160 vols. Falmouth (Stafford County), Va.

Business records of Duff Green (d. ca. 1854), merchant and manufacturer, of his son, McDuff, and of their partners and successors in a business dealing in various types of produce, including wheat, flour, textile products, general merchandise, etc. The firm operated under various names, including Duff Green, Duff Green and Son, the son apparently being William J. Green (d. ca. 1871), Green and Lane, and Green and Scott.

Unbound papers consist principally of business and a few personal letters. Bound volumes comprise records of the Bellemont and Eagle flour mills and other flour mills, and relate to the inspection of flour; cotton factories, generally branches of the Falmouth Manufacturing Company, owned and operated by the Greens, Scotts, and Lanes; a large general mercantile establishment; and dividends accruing to the various partners. There are full accounts of the operation of the Elm Cotton Factory, where Osnaburg, sail duck, bagging, wagon tents, etc. were manufactured as early as 1842. Mercantile ledgers and daybooks show the sale of various types of farm supplies, such as Osnaburg, ground plaster, flour, clover seed, and sundries. Unbound volumes include daybooks; ledgers; account books; records of cotton purchased, wood hauled, cloth shipped, flour sent by boat, and wheat hauled; cashbooks; memoranda; baling books; wool-carding books; time books; records of production, cash sales, wages, and expenses; letter books; invoices; notes and bills; and receiving and delivery books.

The records equally concern flour milling, general merchandise, and textile manufacture. There are also volumes of George J. Lightner and of John M. O'Bannon, who apparently had business connections with Duff Green. The records reflect the gradual emergence of Fredericksburg as a business center and the consequent decline of Falmouth.

2166. J. H. GREEN PAPERS, 1864. 4 items. Vicksburg (Warren County), Miss.

Bills and a permit to J. H. Green from the St. Louis surveyor of customs to ship goods into belligerent territory.

2167. JAMES GREEN PAPERS, 1778-1824. 7 items. New Bern (Craven County), N.C.

Fragmentary mercantile accounts.

2168. MARK GREEN PAPERS, 1855-1856. 12 items. England.

Letters from Mark Green, a sharpshooter in the British army and acting corporal of the 1st Battalion Rifle Brigade, describing the seige of Sevastopol, Russia; life in the trenches; battles; hospitalization in Scutari, Turkey; his return to his regiment; and conditions in the camp and in Sevastopol.

2169. MOSES GREEN PAPERS, 1814-1815. 5 items. Charles City Court House (Charles City County), Va.

Morning reports and forage and provision returns of Captain A. Stevenson's company of artillery of 2nd Elite Corps of the Virginia militia commanded by Colonel Moses Green, in the service of the U.S. Army; and regimental orders issued by Green.

2170. RICHARD L. GREEN PAPERS, 1802-1803. 32 items.

The papers of the manager or administrator of the New Bank Estate, listing wages paid to a number of employees, and to white and black laborers. Drayage, wheelbarrows, and sawyers are noted.

2171. THOMAS GREEN CLASS BOOK, 1865-1871. 1 vol. (72 pp.) Harpers Ferry (Jefferson County), W. Va.

A class book of a Methodist Episcopal Church.

2172. TIMOTHY GREEN AND TIMOTHY R. GREEN PAPERS, 1789-1840. 75 items. New York, N.Y.

Papers of Timothy Green, merchant and attorney, and Timothy R. Green, attorney, include business papers concerning timber for ships, cotton, and a marble quarry; deeds; records of judgment obtained in the Supreme Court in (DeWitt) Clinton v. Green; letters concerning patents; legal papers dealing with debts, estates, mortgages, and land sales; and personal correspondence.

2173. W. B. GREEN PAPERS, 1852-1853. 2 items. Petersburg (Dinwiddie County), Va.

Letters concerning legal matters from W. B. Green to the law firm of Smith and Herndon in Eutaw, Alabama.

2174. W. T. GREEN PAPERS, 1861-1862. 4 items. Alpine (Chattooga County), Ga.

Family correspondence of W. T. Green, a Confederate soldier stationed with his cousin, Henry, at Yorktown, Virginia.

2175. WILLIAM MERCER GREEN PAPERS, 1864-1885. 5 items. Sewanee (Franklin County), Tenn.

Personal correspondence of The Right Reverend William Mercer Green (1798-1887), the first Protestant Episcopal Bishop of Mississippi and a founder of the University of the South in Sewanee.

2176. GREEN & RYLAND PAPERS, 1874-1877. 2 vols. Petersburg (Dinwiddie County), Va.

A journal and a cashbook of Lucius Green and A. G. Ryland, grocers and commission merchants handling cotton, tobacco, wheat, corn, flour, and other produce, and agents for Farmers' Friend Fertilizer.

2177. GREEN LINE RAIL ROAD CAR ASSOCIATION MINUTE BOOK, 1870-1879. 1 vol. (82 pp.) Atlanta, Ga.

Minutes of the Executive Committee of the Green Line Rail Road Car Association.

2178. DAVID GREENE PAPERS, 1861-1862. 3 items. Talbotton (Talbot County), Ga.

Personal correspondence between David Greene, a Confederate soldier, and his sister, Ginnie, discussing health conditions in the army, casualties in the battle of Dranesville, 1861, and matters at home.

2179. NATHANAEL GREENE PAPERS, 1778-1786. 199 items. "Mulberry Grove" (Chatham County), Ga.

Papers of Nathanael Greene (1742-1786), Revolutionary War general, include reports, requisitions, and correspondence pertaining to the quartermaster department of the Continental Army while Greene was quartermaster general, 1778-1780; papers concerning the war in South Carolina and Georgia during Greene's term as commander of the troops in the Southern states, 1780-1783, covering matters such as the battles at Ninety Six, South Carolina, and Augusta, Georgia, conflicts between civilian and military authorities, problems over the relationship of the militia, the state troops and the Continental Army, supplies, and the sustaining of the military effort after the surrender at Yorktown; and papers, 1783-1786, pertaining to Greene's business affairs and to the relationship of Georgia to the British and Spanish inhabitants of Florida.

2180. ROSE (O'NEAL) GREENHOW PAPERS, (1860-1864) 1952. 10 items. Richmond, Va.

Civil War letters from Rose (O'Neal) Greenhow (d. 1864), agent and spy in the Confederate service to Alexander Robinson Boteler and Jefferson Davis reporting on the progress of her work. Included are comments on the defenses and bombardment of Charleston, South Carolina, in July, 1863; the fall of Vicksburg, 1863; her mission to Europe, including interviews with Napoleon III and Nicholas Patrick Stephen, Cardinal Wiseman; a conversation with Frank Vizetelly; the question of recognition of the Confederate States of America by France and Spain; and the position of James Murray Mason. A clipping, 1952, from the New Hanover Record & Advertiser, Wilmington, North Carolina, concerns the honored dead in the Oakdale Cemetery in Wilmington, among whom is Rose Greenhow.

2181. HORATIO GREENOUGH PAPERS, 1839. 1 item. Florence, Italy.

Copy of a letter of Horatio Greenough (1805-1852), sculptor, to George W. Greene, American consul at Rome, 1837-1845, mentioning two other sculptors, Shobal Vail Clevenger and Thomas Crawford.

2182. GREENVILLE FIRST BAPTIST CHURCH PAPERS, 1909-1911. 3 items. Greenville (Greenville County), S.C.

Sixth and seventh annual reports and an undated chart of financial statistics of the Greenville First Baptist Church.

2183. GREENVILLE LADIES' ASSOCIATION MINUTES, 1861-1865. 1 vol. Greenville (Greenville County), S.C.

Typed copies of portions of the minutes of the Greenville Ladies' Association, an organization to aid Confederate soldiers.

2184. ALFRED BURTON GREENWOOD PAPERS, 1861. 1 item. Bentonville (Benton County), Ark.

Letter of Alfred Burton Greenwood, lawyer, former U.S. congressman, and Commissioner of Indian Affairs, and later Confederate representative, concerning secession, the neutrality of the Indians on the Arkansas border, and personal financial affairs in Washington, D.C.

2185. MAXCY GREGG PAPERS, 1861. 1 item. Columbia (Richland County), S.C.

Letter from Captain J. M. Gladberry to Maxcy Gregg (1814-1862), colonel of the 1st South Carolina Volunteers, requesting arms and ammunition.

2186. WILLIAM GREGG, JR., PAPERS, 1863. 1 item. Graniteville (Aiken County), S.C.

Letter from James B. Campbell to William Gregg, founder of the Graniteville Company and pioneer cotton manufacturer in South Carolina, concerning legal affairs.

2187. WILLIAM L. GREGG PAPERS, 1861-1862. 2 items. South Carolina.

Letters written by William L. Gregg, Confederate soldier, from South Island, South Carolina, and Camp Hager, Virginia, to his father, reflecting dissatisfaction with camp life, daily activities in camp, and his strong religious feelings.

2188. EDWIN CLARKE GREGORY PAPERS, 1877-1948. 3,699 items. Salisbury (Rowan County), N.C.

Papers of Edwin Clarke Gregory (1875-1948), lawyer, politician, farmer, and speculator, of his father-in-law, Lee Slater Overman (1854-1930), U.S. senator, 1902-1930, and of his son, E. C. Gregory, Jr., attorney. Included are routine political correspondence of Lee S. Overman, especially concerning his 1902 campaign; constituent mail pertaining to the treatment of German spies, 1917-1918, and to Overman's defense of North Carolina against bribery accusations by Alabama Senator J. Thomas Heflin; correspondence dealing with Gregory's interest in gold mining in North Carolina; political correspondence covering Gregory's years as state senator and his interests in agriculture, dependents, the blind, and public libraries; the correspondence of Margaret (Overman) Gregory concerning the state organization of the Robert E. Lee Foundation, and the American Red Cross; and the legal correspondence of E. C. Gregory, Jr.

2189. MARY GREGORY PAPERS, 1859-1862. 4 items. Granville County, N.C.

Family letters from G. T. Biven [?] containing references to local politics and to the selection of a terminal for an extension of the Roanoke Valley Railroad; and Civil War letters describing the hardships of camp life, and the election of officers for a military company.

2190. RICHARD GREGORY PAPERS, 1828-1844. 4 items. Virginia.

Documents pertaining to the administration of the estate of Elizabeth Gregory, wife of Richard Gregory.

2191. RICHARD HENRY GREGORY PAPERS, 1905-1910. 23 items and 4 vols. Tarboro (Edgecombe County), N.C.

Diaries and photographs of Richard Henry Gregory's journeys to and in China, probably for the British-American Tobacco Company. A memorandum book contains routine entries about his trip from Rocky Mount, North Carolina, to New York, San Francisco, Honolulu, Japan, and Shanghai, China. A diary describes places visited in China, Chinese customs, the growing and processing of tobacco, farms and crops, styles of houses, temples and shrines, and economic conditions. There are photographs of sights along the Hankow-Peking Railroad, the Han River, the raising and processing of tobacco, and the British-American Tobacco Company cigarette factory, probably located at or near Hankow.

2192. WILLIAM H. GREGORY PAPERS, 1857-1923. 344 items and 10 vols. Stovall (Granville County), N.C.

Papers of William H. Gregory while at the University of Virginia, 1859-1860, in the Confederate service, 1864-1865, and in the mercantile and publishing businesses in Oxford during the 1870s and 1880s, containing information on tobacco culture, social life and customs, amusements, education, the Civil War, and genealogy. Included are lists of students at Belmont Academy, 1859, in Granville County and at the Oxford Classical and Grammar School, 1859-1860. The volumes are brief diaries for scattered years, 1873-1903.

2193. JOHN GREIG PAPERS, 1846-1847. 6 items. Canandaigua (Ontario County), N.Y.

Principally the letters of Robert Wilson, a merchant in Liverpool, England, to John Greig (1779-1858), lawyer, banker, educator, and Congressman, discussing the grain trade, the Anglo-American dispute over Oregon, the Mexican War, and politics in England, including Lord John Russell, Sir Robert Peel, and the repeal of the Corn Laws.

2194. JOHN FREDERICK GREIN AND PHILIP JACOB GREIN PAPERS, 1731. 1 vol. (305 pp.) Trier, Germany.

"Various Legal Documents Which Could be Useful Not Only to an Apostolic Notary but Also to an Imperial Notary," compiled by John Frederick Grein and Philip Jacob Grein.

2195. GRENOBLE (GÉNÉRALITÉ) RECORDS, 1702-1762. 1 vol. Grenoble, France.

Lists of religious fugitives, presumably Huguenots, their property, and receipts and expenditures associated with the management of their properties, 1761-1762; records from the dispatch of tax funds to officials in Paris, 1757-1762; and tax records from the Élection de Gap, 1702-1720.

2196. GRENOBLE. COMPAGNIE DES PÉNITENTS BLANCS DE NOTRE DAME DU CONFALON ET DE LA MISÉRICORDE RECORDS, 1682-1791. 3 vols. Grenoble, France.

Records of the Confraternity of White Penitents include two volumes of minutes and records of the admission of new members. There are a few printed items contained in the volumes, including the Règlement pour la Confrérie des Pénitens érigée en cette Ville de Grenoble, sous le Vocable de Notre-Dame du Confalon, concernant les fonctions de la

<u>Miséricorde</u> <u>qu'ils</u> <u>désirent</u> <u>exercer</u> <u>pour</u> <u>la</u> <u>plus</u> <u>grande</u> <u>gloire</u> <u>de</u> <u>Dieu</u>.

2197. GRENOBLE. MONASTÈRE DE SAINTE CLAIRE RECORDS, 1500-1794. 2 vols. Grenoble, France.

Records of the Monastery of Sainte Claire at Grenoble include an inventory of the monastery's official documents and records; an alphabetical index of benefactors and debtors; the "Premier Registre" containing copies and extracts of endowments, 1500-1609; a list of revenues and dates on which they were to be paid; and the "Second Registre" containing a list of endowments from the early 1600s.

2198. GEORGE NUGENT-GRENVILLE, BARON NUGENT, PAPERS, 1833-1843. 2 items. Lilies, Buckinghamshire, England.

Letters of George Nugent-Grenville, Baron Nugent (1788-1850), British author and statesman, concerning sources for a study on capital punishment, and legal and financial matters.

2199. GEORGE NUGENT-TEMPLE-GRENVILLE, FIRST MARQUIS OF BUCKINGHAM, PAPERS, 1781-1797. 5 items. London, England.

Correspondence of George Nugent-Temple-Grenville, First Marquis of Buckingham (1753-1813), British statesman, concerning operation of the exchequer, politics in Ireland, a sacred pillar from pagan times, and the militia under his command.

2200. THOMAS GRENVILLE PAPERS, 1801-1854. 14 items. London, England.

Letters of Thomas Grenville (1755-1846), British politician and book collector, discussing taxes, book collecting, the disposition of his library upon his death, and military and naval affairs pertaining to his position as First Lord of the Admiralty; and a printed genealogy of the Grenville family, and an obituary notice. The library also holds microfilm of Grenville material from the British Museum.

2201. WILLIAM WYNDHAM GRENVILLE, BARON GRENVILLE, PAPERS, 1801-1828. 13 itmes. London, England.

Correspondence of William Wyndham Grenville, Baron Grenville (1759-1834), British statesman, concerning his campaign for the chancellorship of the University of Oxford; several honorary degrees; the formation of a new cabinet,1809; and other matters.

2202. MRS. THOMAS BAXTER GRESHAM PAPERS, 1895-1913. 2 vols. Baltimore, Md.

Minutes, 1895-1899, of the Baltimore Chapter No. 8 of the United Daughters of the Confederacy; and a list of manuscripts and mementos of the Confederacy owned by Mrs. Gresham.

2203. WILLIAM GRESLEY PAPERS, 1839-1859. 4 items. Boyne Hill, Berkshire, England.

Correspondence of William Gresley (1801-1876), British divine, with Edward Churton discussing the planning and editing of a series of religious and social tales entitled <u>The</u> <u>Englishman's</u> <u>Library</u>, contributors to the publication, a draft of the prospectus, and Gresley's book, <u>The</u> <u>Ordinance</u> <u>of</u> <u>Confession</u>.

2204. WILLIAM C. GRIDLEY PAPERS, 1870-1871. 5 items. West Candor (Tioga County), N.Y.

Business papers of a woolen manufacturer.

2205. J. W. GRIFFIN PAPERS, 1862-1863. 7 items. Selma (Dallas County), Ala.

Personal letters of J. W. Griffin, Confederate soldier, farmer, and minister, commenting on his work in the Confederate hospitals near Richmond, Virginia, and wartime hardships.

2206. WINGFIELD GRIFFIN NOTES, 1871-1872. 1 vol. Charlottesville (Albemarle County), Va.

Lecture notes from law classes at the University of Virginia.

2207. A. J. GRIFFITH ACCOUNT BOOK, 1867. 1 vol. Danville (Pittsylvania County), Va.

Accounts of a general merchant.

2208. ROBERT EGLESFIELD GRIFFITH PAPERS, 1827-1828. 2 items. Philadelphia, Pa.

Correspondence of Robert E. Griffith (1789-1850), a Philadelphia physician and medical instructor at the University of Virginia, Charlottesville, referring to Western lands and financial matters.

2209. ELIZA M. (FRAME) GRIGGS PAPERS, 1831-1884. 2 vols. Charles Town (Jefferson County), W. Va.

Ledger and commonplace book of Eliza Griggs, wife of Lee Griggs (1790-1831), a Charles Town physician.

2210. JOHN BERKLEY GRIMBALL PAPERS, 1727 (1840-1900) 1930. 1,605 items and 5 vols. Charleston, S.C.

Papers of John Berkley Grimball (1800-1893), South Carolina planter, and of his family; and papers of Mrs. Elias VanderHorst and other members of the VanderHorst family. Papers of the Grimball family include correspondence pertaining to social life and customs of the planter class, cotton, secession, the Civil War, slavery, slave revolts during the war, and financial hardships during Reconstruction. Civil War letters from Grimball's sons in the Confederate Army--William H., Arthur, Berkley, and Lewis M. (a surgeon)--describe military activities and life in the army. Letters from Grimball's son, John, in the Confederate Navy, describe naval affairs and engagements, a journey to Australia, and surrender to the British in Liverpool. There is also correspondence pertaining to and copies of pardons; family letters, 1831-1832, from Miss H. M. Wilcocks of Philadelphia to her niece, Mrs. John Berkley Grimball; postwar letters from John Grimball in Britain, France, Mexico, and, after 1870, New York, concerning his fear of returning to the United States, livestock and land prices in Mexico, relations between Mexico and France, political conditions in Mexico, the colonization of Americans in Mexico, and his legal practice in New York; wills; papers dealing with the estate of John Berkley Grimball; a memorandum book recording shares, bonds, and dividends; an account book, 1861-1865, of John Berkley Grimball with the Bank of South Carolina; a receipt book, 1895-1899, of Berkley Grimball recording servants' wages, newspaper clippings; a letter and daybook, 1891-1894, of Berkley Grimball; and genealogy of the Grimball family, 568-1893. Papers of the VanderHorsts consist principally of letters from S. Rutherford of New York to her sister, Mrs. Elias VanderHorst of Charleston, a receipt book of the VanderHorst family, and other scattered papers.

2211. JOHN A. GRIMBELL PAPERS, 1828-1835. 3 items. Jackson (Hinds County), Miss.

Letters to Grimbell, secretary of state for Mississippi, from Abram M. Scott, John A. Quitman, and Charles Lynch, soliciting political support and seeking information on the schedules of the circuit courts.

2212. BRYAN GRIMES PAPERS, 1864. 1 item. Grimesland (Pitt County), N.C.

Letter from Bryan Grimes (1828-1880), commanding officer of the 4th Regiment of North Carolina State Troops, to Colonel W. H. Taylor, dealing with punishment for deserters.

2213. JAMES GRIMES DAYBOOK, 1840-1880. 1 vol. (121 pp.) Branchville (Orangeburg County), S.C.

Daybook of a general merchant.

2214. SARAH GRIMES PAPERS, 1893-1912. 2 vols. Washington County, Md.

Ledger, 1893-1902, and a farm book, 1902-1912.

2215. THOMAS WINGFIELD GRIMES, JR., PAPERS, 1860-1862. 6 items. Columbus (Muscogee County), Ga.

Letters of Thomas Wingfield Grimes, Jr. (1844-1905), member of U.S. Congress, 1887-1891, written while he was a student at Emory College, Oxford, Georgia, and the University of Georgia, Athens.

2216. THOMAS W. GRIMES PAPERS, 1824-1831. 40 items. Greensborough (Greene County), Ga.

Business and routine correspondence of Thomas W. Grimes, postmaster and merchant of Greensborough, Georgia, including information on the shipment of goods from Augusta, Georgia, and the hiring of a Negro from Farish Carter. A letter from Grimes's brother describes a trip from Georgia to Washington, D.C.

2217. WILLIAM HENRY GRIMES PAPERS, 1845-1884. 24 items. Sharpsburg (Washington County), Md.

Personal correspondence of William Henry Grimes concerning his unsuccessful courtship with Sallie Seymour, prices of commodities and buggies, conditions in Mexico, 1847, and secession.

2218. GRIMKÉ FAMILY PAPERS, 1782-1868. 13 items. Charleston, S.C.

Papers of John Faucheraud Grimké (1752-1819), Continental soldier and South Carolina jurist; of his son, Thomas Smith Grimké (1786-1834); and of his grandson Edward Montague Grimké (1832-1895). Included are references to supplies for the Continental Army, ratification of the peace treaty between the United States and Great Britain, the activities of the North Carolina Assembly, the affairs of the Broad River Company, epistemology, and financial and personal matters. Also included are letters concerning the estates of John F. Grimké's father and of Thomas Roper, husband of Mary Smith (Grimké) Roper.

2219. GRINDLAY AND COMPANY SCRAPBOOK, 1861-1876. 1 vol. (406 pp.) London, England.

Scrapbook containing clippings, pamphlets and manuscripts relating to the British Army in India. They are primarily orders and regulations all about facets of the livelihood of military personnel from recruitment to retirement, compiled by Grindlay and Company, agents for military personnel in the Indian service, and owned by Robert Melville Grindlay (1786-1877).

2220. EUGENE GRISSOM RECORDS, 1875-1887. 4 vols. Raleigh (Wake County), N.C.

Register of admissions and scrapbooks of the North Carolina State Hospital for the Insane, of which Eugene Grissom (1831-1902), physician and psychiatrist, was superintendent.

2221. WILLIAM LEE GRISSOM PAPERS, 1892-1910. 559 items. Greensboro (Guilford County), N.C.

Correspondence and papers of William L. Grissom (1857-1912), a Methodist minister. Included in the collection are letters from subscribers to the North Carolina Christian Advocate, which Grissom edited; school compositions of the Grissom children; bank statements and canceled checks; and a letter from John Franklin Crowell. Included also are cashbooks, notebooks, memoranda of Grissom, and seven volumes of the diary of Thomas Mann (1769-1830), Methodist minister, covering the years 1805-1808, 1810-1814, 1816, 1828, 1829-1830, and concerning Mann's work as a circuit rider, collected by Grissom for his works on the history of the Methodist Church in North Carolina. There are also notes and sketches for these works.

2222. JAMES REDDING GRIST AND RICHARD GRIST PAPERS, (1791-1874) 1920. 3,263 items and 6 vols. Washington (Beaufort County), N.C.

Business correspondence of James Redding Grist (d. 1874), dealer in lumber and naval stores; of his uncle, Richard Grist, operator of a general store and exporter of naval stores; and of his father, Allen Grist, operator of a general store. Early papers, 1791-1817, are those of John Kennedy, who preceded Allen Grist as sheriff of Beaufort County, and comprise personal correspondence, bills and receipts, financial accounts, and official papers, including a list of taxables for Longacre, 1815, and Washington, 1816, districts of Beaufort County. After 1827 business letters, accounts, prices current, and cargo manifests relate to Richard Grist, the operation of his general store, and the exportation of naval stores, barrel staves, peas, corn, pork, and lard to an agent in the West Indies in return for sugar, rum, etc. After 1834 the correspondence concerns Richard Grist's export business in New Bern, North Carolina, and the turpentine and lumber business of James Redding Grist near Wilmington, North Carolina. Included is information on the methods of obtaining turpentine and rosin and the prices of each, the hiring and purchase of slaves, and coastwise trade. Postwar letters deal with the efforts of James Redding Grist to revive his trade in naval stores. Also included are letters from members of the families of George M. Bonner, Bryan Grimes, and John G. Blount, relatives of the Grists; and letters of Henry Toole Clark concerning business matters between 1834 and 1842.

2223. EDWARD GRISWOLD, CHARLES GRISWOLD, AND JOEL GRISWOLD PAPERS, 1862-1865. 44 items. Guilford (New Haven County), Conn.

Letters of three brothers serving in the Union Army describing camp life, activities in South Carolina, Virginia, and Florida, the siege of Charleston Harbor, 1863, the siege of Petersburg, 1864, the 1864 presidential election, food supplies, paid substitutes in the army, the desertion of Confederate soldiers to the Union lines, the capture of the Confederate ironclad Fingal, Lee's surrender, and the assassination of Lincoln.

2224. WILLIAM MCCRILLIS GRISWOLD PAPERS, 1896-1897. 29 items. Cambridge (Middlesex County), Mass.

Letters from Nicholas Murray Butler, William Torrey Harris, Lovick Pierce, and Irwin Shepard to William McCrillis Griswold (1853-1899) concerning an index which Griswold prepared for the National Educational Association's Proceedings.

2225. DANIEL WEBSTER GROH PAPERS, 1823 (1856-1898) 1950. 528 items. Breathedsville (Washington County), Md.

Principally correspondence of Daniel Webster Groh and his brother, both travelling salesmen, discussing their work and commenting on President Andrew Johnson and his politics, a coal strike in 1877, the election of 1884, farming and teaching in Illinois, and food prices in New York. Material concerning Groh's book The Tariff Nut Shell, including drafts of letters to the editor and notations of main points in his argument, reflects his interest in free trade, the ideas of Henry George, proposed changes in the electoral system, prohibition, freethinking, and criticism of religion. Scattered items include a description of the systems and treatment of scarlet fever in the 1850s; letters to postmasters seeking their help in selling territory in their counties; interest rates on a loan in Kentucky; a political circular for James G. Blaine; a pamphlet on the tariff by Blaine and others; a draft of a constitution for the Massachusetts Single Tax League in 1890; the Constitution of Agnostic Moralists;

an advertisement for the Freethinkers Magazine; and an issue of the Cooperative Commonwealth from Dallas, Texas, November, 1894.

2226. FRANCIS GROSE PAPERS, 1783.
1 item. London, England.

Letter of Francis Grose (1758?-1814), British soldier and colonial administrator, concerning the debts and estates of his father, Francis Grose (1731-1791), antiquary and draftsman; and the reply of D. Croasdille.

2227. JOHN GROSE PAPERS, 1826.
1 vol. Bloomfield House, near Bath, Somersetshire, England.

Compilation of poetry, much of which appears to be original, related to such subjects as courtship, marriage, and the virtues of womanhood; extracts copied from various printed works; and miscellaneous notations on subjects of interest to Grose.

2228. NICOLAI FREDERIK SEVERIN GRUNDTVIG PAPERS, 1862.
2 items. Aasen, Denmark.

Sermon of Nicolai Frederik Severin Grundtvig (1783-1872), Danish author, hymn writer, pastor, and bishop of the Evangelical Lutheran Church; and a picture of him from a newspaper.

2229. JOHN W. GUERRANT PAPERS, 1803-1868. 11 items and 1 vol. Pittsylvania County, Va.

Business letters and accounts of John W. Guerrant, a general merchant who operated a flour mill and a sawmill in Pittsylvania County and a mercantile business in various places in Virginia.

2230. JACOB HENRY GUEST JOURNALS AND LEDGERS, 1860-1869. 4 vols. Ogdensburg (St. Lawrence County), N.Y.

Itemized accounts probably of a mercantile business. Loose items include a map of the Gate House Lot of the Heuvelton and Canton Falls Plank Road as surveyed in 1851.

2231. ROMEO HOLLAND GUEST PAPERS, 1953 (1955-1960) 1964. 410 items. Greensboro (Guilford County), N.C.

Copies of the papers of Romeo H. Guest, businessman and industrialist, and originator of the idea of the Research Triangle Park, North Carolina, concerning the development of the Research Triangle.

2232. LAWRENCE J. GUILMARTIN AND JOHN FLANNERY PAPERS, (1867-1892) 1912. 30,156 items. Savannah, Ga.

Business papers of L. J. Guilmartin & Co., 1867-1877, and after 1877, of John Flannery and Co., cotton factors, commission merchants, and agents for several manufacturing concerns. Correspondence, principally with merchants and farmers in Georgia and Florida, concerns the purchase and sale of cotton, and to a lesser extent, other commodities, loans on crops, prices of cotton and other commodities, a government tax on cotton, 1867, and speculation in cotton. Also included are bills and receipts, deeds for land sold in Florida and Georgia, copies of insurance policies, and the report of a suit, 1860s, brought against L. J. Guilmartin & Co. Scattered letters refer to Negroes and Reconstruction, bankruptcy laws in Georgia, and trading through the Grange.

2233. I. A. GUNN LEDGER, 1812-1814. 2 vols. Prospect Hill (Fairfax County), Va.

Estate ledger and journal of I. A. Gunn, a general merchant and planter.

2234. JULES GUTHRIDGE PAPERS, 1903-1909. 8 items. Washington, D.C.

Invitations and other social items of Mr. and Mrs. Jules Guthridge.

2235. JOHN BRANDON GUTHRIE PAPERS, 1863. 1 item. Murfreesboro (Rutherford County), Tenn.

Letter of Lieutenant John B. Guthrie (d. 1900), of the 1st Kentucky Infantry, describing the battle of Stones River, Tennessee.

2236. ROBERT GUYTON AND JAMES B. HEASLET PAPERS, 1862-1865. 193 items. Perrysville (Allegheny County), Pa.

Letters of Robert Guyton and his uncle, James B. Heaslet, both serving with the 139th Regiment of Pennsylvania Volunteers, concerning the battles of 2nd Manassas, Fredericksburg, Spotsylvania Court House, and Cold Harbor, the aftermath of battle, the siege of Petersburg, foraging for food, desertion in the Union and Confederate armies, the U.S. Sanitary Commission, religious services in the camps, rumors, and Lee's surrender. Included are a tract of the American Tract Society and a sketch of the battle lines at Fredericksburg.

2237.  WALTER GWYNN PAPERS, 1860-1861. 18 items. Fort Moultrie (Charleston County), S.C.

Correspondence of Walter Gwynn, Confederate captain of engineers in charge of improving defenses of Fort Moultrie, concerning labor and requisitions for materials and for ordnance supplies.

2238.  HABERSHAM FAMILY PAPERS, 1750-1860. 51 items. Savannah, Ga.

Miscellaneous legal documents and correspondence relating primarily to the business affairs of James Habersham and his sons, James Habersham, Jr., John Habersham, and Joseph Habersham. Numerous legal papers concerning the early history of Georgia include material on the settlement of the estate of William Gibbons, Sr., 1787, and the estate of James Habersham, Sr., 1795-1804. Business papers concern the first and second Bank of the United States in Savannah and the silk industry in Georgia, 1751. The collection also contains a list of the members of the Evening Club and Golf Club of Savannah, 1810-1815.

2239.  JAMES GORDON HACKETT PAPERS, 1788-1952. 196 items. North Wilkesboro (Wilkes County), N.C.

The early letters in this collection are those of Caroline Louisa (Gordon) Hackett, mother of James Gordon Hackett, with various members of her family including a sister who had settled in Cherokee County, Alabama, and James Byron Gordon, later a general in the Confederate Army. Later letters are to Mary (Grimes) Hackett, wife of James Gordon Hackett concerning family matters and the service of a nephew in Europe in World War II. The collection also contains a speech, 1940, by Hackett introducing Clyde R. Hoey, miscellaneous clippings, and genealogical material on the Hackett, Grimes, Gordon, and Herndon families.

2240.  JOHN C. HACKETT PAPERS, 1849 (1862-1888) 1896. 149 items. Guilford Court House (Guilford County), N.C.

Letters of the related Hackett, Barton, Fields, Swain, and Kirkman families, for the most part dealing with family matters and reporting on conditions in the western territories and states. Civil War letters from a soldier in the 45th North Carolina Regiment and other soldiers concerning food, sickness, desertion, prices, 'fraternization among Federal and Confederate pickets, and the use of observation balloons by the Federal troops at Fredericksburg. Postwar letters from Indiana and Illinois mention commodity prices and wages.

2241.  ROBERT J. HACKLEY PAPERS, (1873-1877) 1892. 22 items. Brunswick County, Va.

Letters of Robert J. Hackley, an engineer on various ships of the Pacific Mail Steamship Company, describing his journeys and activities from San Francisco to Yokohama, Japan, Shanghai, China, and other ports; and commenting on missionary efforts in Japan, and on family matters.

2242.  JOSEPH HACKNEY AND COMPANY LEDGER, 1815-1823. 1 vol. (224 pp.) Warren County, Pa.

Ledger of a merchant.

2243.  M. T. HADERMAN PAPERS, 1864-1865. 5 items. Pennsylvania.

Letters of a soldier in the 3rd United States Infantry Division at the siege of Petersburg, Virginia. He discusses camp life, picket duty, and building forts and entrenchments, and he describes the Federal attack on Petersburg on April 2, 1865.

2244.  MARY E. HADLY PAPERS, 1860-1868. 17 items. Williamston (Martin County), N.C.

Personal correspondence.

2245.  SIR WILLIAM HENRY HADOW PAPERS, 1916. 1 item. Sheffield, Yorkshire, England.

Letter to Hadow from Lord Haldane concerning a political movement in Wales.

2246.  HERMANN ANTON CONRAD HAGEDORN PAPERS, 1856-1926. 407 items and 1 vol. New York, N.Y.; Niederwalluf and Göttingen, Germany.

Family and business correspondence of a German-American businessman. The collection contains many letters from Hermann A. C. Hagedorn's mother and sisters in German script. Business papers in German and English concern stock purchases, Hagedorn's financial problems, and other business matters. Miscellaneous items include a wedding invitation and a notice in German to the members of the German Society of the city of New York.

2247.  ROBERT G. HAILE PAPERS, 1861-1864. 7 items. Essex County, Va.

Letters from a Confederate soldier to his wife.

2248.  HIRAM HAINES PAPERS, 1826-1838. 78 items and 1 vol. Petersburg (Dinwiddie County), Va.

Personal letters of Hiram Haines to his wife. Those for the years 1826-1828 give interesting descriptions of travel, of conditions in Orange, Caswell, and Person counties, and Hillsboro and Raleigh, North Carolina, and of life, manners, and customs of the time. Included also is a notebook with genealogical information on the Haines family and poetry of Hiram Haines.

2249.   H. S. HALBERT PAPERS, 1884.
        3 items. Crawford, Miss.

Letters concerning Indian culture, especially the Creek, Shawnee, and Choctaw tribes; and plans to excavate possible mounds.

2250.   JOHN W. HALBERTON PAPERS,
        1856-1860. 98 items.
        Canandaigua (Ontario
        County), N.Y.

Business and personal letters of John W. Halberton, including letters from his son who was working as a clerk in New York City to learn about business and letters from Halberton's associates, debtors, and his attorney discussing Halberton's business affairs and describing the panic of 1857.

2251.   HALCYON LITERARY CLUB PAPERS,
        1912-1968. 55 items.
        Durham, N.C.

Miscellaneous items relating to the Halcyon Literary Club including a file of the programs of the club, 1919-1968, complete except for the years 1957-1958 and 1961-1962.

2252.   JOHN A. HALDERMAN PAPERS,
        1857-1889. 28 items.
        Washington, D.C.

Miscellaneous personal correspondence, primarily from the 1880s while Halderman was in the diplomatic service of the United States.

2253.   EDWARD JOSEPH HALE PAPERS,
        1862-1863. 1 vol.
        Fayetteville (Cumberland
        County), N.C.

Roster kept by Edward J. Hale as adjutant of the 56th North Carolina Regiment, containing the names of the commissioned officers of the regiment, the commissioned officers of the Staunton Hill Artillery of Virginia, a calendar, August-October, 1862, showing leaves and assignments of officers, and a record of the movements of the 56th Regiment.

2254.   CHARLES HALL PAPERS, 1803.
        1 item. Tavistock,
        Devonshire, England.

Letter to Hall from Thomas Belsham concerning the publication of a book Hall had written, probably his Effects of Civilization on the People in European States (1805).

2255.   DANIEL KIRKE HALL PAPERS,
        1862-1865. 70 items.
        Pittsford (Rutland County), Vt.

Papers relate to Daniel K. Hall's military career as an enlisted soldier and an officer in the 12th Vermont Regiment and as a captain and commissary of subsistence in the United States Army. Contains permits to travel, passes, and orders and many items concerning the Subsistence Department including special and general orders pertaining to instructions for rations of food and related supplies.

2256.   EDWARD HALL AND THOMAS H. HALL
        PAPERS, 1795, 1820. 2 items.
        Tarboro (Edgecombe County), N.C.

Letter to Edward Hall from William R. Davie, concerning a legal case, [1795?], and a letter from Thomas H. Hall, member of the United States Congress, to the North Carolina land office concerning the issue of a land warrant, 1820.

2257.   HENRY C. HALL PAPERS, 1861-1864.
        18 items and 1 vol.
        Danbury (Fairfield County), Conn.

Letters from Henry C. Hall, captain in the 8th Connecticut Volunteers, to his family, containing comments on Civil War campaigns and battles in North Carolina and Virginia, conscription, Negro regiments, army life, and equipment and supplies.

2258.   JAMES FREDERICK HALL LETTER
        BOOK, 1862-1864. 1 vol.
        Tarrytown (Westchester
        County), N.Y.

Contains the letters of James F. Hall in his capacity as lieutenant colonel of the 1st New York Regiment, Engineers, and provost marshal general of the Department of the South. The letters deal with routine military matters and also discuss construction work undertaken by Hall's regiment, the utility of providing rations for Southerners of questionable loyalty, an internal dispute in Hall's regiment, and the case of a British subject accused of blockade running.

2259.   JOHN HALL JOURNAL,
        1828-1830. 1 vol. (212 pp.)
        England.

Journal of John Hall, master of the Duke of Kent, on a commercial voyage to the Pacific coast of the Americas. Entries mainly concern sailing conditions, including readings of temperature and barometric pressure, comments on the speed and rigging of the ship, and notations of the ship's position. There are occasional comments on trade and passengers.

2260.  JOSEPH W. HALL PAPERS, 1856-1866. 28 items. Salisbury (Rowan County), N.C.

Miscellaneous letters, for the most part from the Civil War, including a copy of the appointment of J. W. Hall as surgeon in the Confederate prison at Salisbury, North Carolina; letters relating to the purchase of Confederate bonds; tax in kind blanks, 1865; and a letter, 1862, reporting strong Union sentiment in Knoxville, Tennessee.

2261.  LIBBIE HALL PAPERS, 1861-1863. 5 items. Steuben County, N.Y.

Miscellaneous letters concerning the Civil War.

2262.  LYMAN HALL PAPERS, 1783-1793. 4 items. Savannah, Ga.

Papers include a land bounty certificate; a copy of the will of Mary (Osborne) Hall; a warrant, 1784, relating to damages owed to Lyman Hall; and an extract from a speech given by Lyman Hall in the Georgia House of Assembly, 1783.

2263.  SAMUEL CARTER HALL PAPERS, 1829, 1853. 2 items. London, England.

Letter, 1853, from James Emerson Tennent concerning an exhibition of wood engravings and a letter, 1829, from John Malcolm concerning an article for Samuel C. Hall's periodical, The Amulet.

2264.  THOMAS L. HALL PAPERS, 1839-1850. 8 items. Florence (Pike County), Ill.

Letters to Thomas L. Hall from his brother, J. W. Hall, a physician in St. Louis, Missouri, commenting for the most part on family matters, but with occasional mention of politics and economic conditions.

2265.  THOMAS WILLIAM HALL PAPERS, 1809-1894. 124 items and 1 vol. Baltimore, Md.

Letters of Thomas W. Hall, Baltimore stockbroker, concerning investments in mid-western railroads, particularly the Marietta and Cincinnati Railroad. Early papers are those of John Wood, a merchant of Baltimore, including a description of the first gas lights in the city, 1817, and legal papers of Joshua and Thomas Gilpin relating to their business, the Delaware Brandywine Paper Mills. The collection also contains papers of William Maxwell Wood, including the manuscript of his book, Fankwei, describing his voyage to the Far East, 1855-[1858?], as ship's doctor aboard the U.S.S. San Jacinto and giving an account of the Second Opium War; and a journal chiefly concerned with William M. Wood's career in the Civil War as fleet surgeon of the North Atlantic blockade and inspector of hospitals in North Carolina, 1863. He describes a visit by President Lincoln to the U.S.S. Minnesota, 1862.

2266.  TOWNSEND MONCKTON HALL PAPERS, 1770-1898. 10 items and 1 vol. Dublin, Ireland.

Manuscript memoirs of Townsend Monckton Hall, for the most part concerning his military career including the winter campaign of 1794-1795 in the Netherlands; the capture of Saint Lucia in the West Indies, 1796; the Irish rebellion and projected French invasion of 1798; the Egyptian campaign of 1801; and service in India as military secretary and first aide-de-camp to the commander-in-chief at Madras, Sir John Francis Caradoc (Cradock), 1804-1805; and as paymaster of the Hyderabad Subsidiary Force, 1805-1807. Hall's memoirs also contain an account of the events leading to the return of Napoleon to France in 1814 and a description of Napoleon reviewing his troops in Paris, 1814.

2267.  WILLIAM HENRY HALL PAPERS, 1736-1862. 1,013 items and 7 vols. West River (Anne Arundel County), Md.

Correspondence and papers of several generations of tobacco planters containing information on tobacco cultivation and the tobacco trade, including a detailed discussion of plantation management in an overseer's contract, 1764, and papers illustrating the shift from tobacco to lumber and wheat after 1800; comments on politics and government in Maryland, 1778; a description of the life of an American seaman impressed into the British navy, 1796; letters, 1810-1813, discussing cotton planting in South Carolina; and an account of a plot for an insurrection of slaves in Marlboro District, South Carolina, 1810. Volumes include account books of John Hall, William Henry Hall, and others 1765-1788, 1792-1902, 6 vols., and an exercise book, 1850-1853, which belonged to Harriet Hall.

2268.  WILLIAM HUNT HALL PAPERS, 1862-1880. 12 items. New York, N.Y.

Photocopies of papers relating, for the most part to William H. Hall's service in the Confederate Army, including his commission, orders, parole, and pardon.

2269.  HALL FAMILY PAPERS, 1869-1965. Wilmington (New Hanover County), N.C.

Collection contains correspondence between Maggie T. (Sprunt) Hall and her daughters, Jessica Dalziel Hall and Susan Eliza Hall, dealing with family matters, Wellesley College, and women's work in the Presbyterian Church, particularly the Women's Foreign Missionary Society. Also copies of letters from Presbyterian missionaries in various parts of the world, 1949-1965, sent to Jessica D. Hall, Susan E. Hall, and

Jane Hall by the Missionary Correspondence Department of the Board of World Missions of the Presbyterian Church in the United States, including letters from Ecuador, Brazil, Mexico, Korea, Japan, Africa, China, and Formosa. Miscellaneous items in the collection include greetings and reports from missionaries, a picture of Madame and General Chiang Kai-shek, and a student handbook of Wellesley College, 1901.

2270.  HENRY WAGER HALLECK PAPERS, 1861-1865. 3 items. New York, N.Y.

Correspondence of Henry Wager Halleck, Federal major general, concerning the break between friends on opposite sides in 1861, rumors of the mental derangement of General William T. Sherman, and a letter, 1863, from General George Gordon Meade giving his reasons for not attacking the Confederate Army on the Rapidan in September, 1863.

2271.  THOMAS LLOYD HALSEY PAPERS, 1818-1821. 2 items. Providence (Providence County), R.I.

Agreement, 1818, between Thomas L. Halsey, American consul in Buenos Aires, 1812-1819, and Frederick Thiesen concerning Halsey's participation in privateering operations against Spain and other matters and a letter, 1821, from Halsey describing conditions in Argentina.

2272.  LOUIS HAMBURGER PAPERS, 1857-ca. 1900. 53 items. Waynmanville (Upson County), Ga.

Correspondence of Louis Hamburger concerning personal and family matters and his career, first as a dealer in millinery goods and after the Civil War as a commission merchant and textile manufacturer in partnership with George P. Swift. Collection also contains two grade reports from Wesleyan Female College, Macon, Georgia, and a photograph.

2273.  WILLIAM JAMES HAMERSLEY PAPERS, 1839-1879. 648 items. Hartford (Hartford County), Conn.

Papers of William James Hamersley, a retail book, stationery, office equipment, and paint merchant, are mainly bills and receipts for household and business matters, containing information about book prices in the mid-19th century. Papers of William J. Hamersley's son, William Hamersley, a lawyer and judge, contain correspondence on business matters concerning stocks and bonds, insurance, and real estate, including land sales and titles in Iowa, Illinois, West Virginia, and Virginia; letters on politics, including comments on Samuel J. Tilden and the presidential election of 1876, and on John Sherman, secretary of the treasury; and correspondence concerning legal cases including those handled by Hamersley as state's attorney of Connecticut. Legal papers include deeds, a memorandum, and a power of attorney.

2274.  G. C. HAMILL LEDGER, 1850-1854. 1 vol. (201 pp.) White Post (Clarke County), Va.

Accounts of sales of general merchandise and foodstuffs arranged by name of customer. In same volume with ledger of Washington Dearmont.

2275.  GEORGE ASHMAN HAMILL PAPERS, 1840-1871. 62 items. Bedford (Bedford County), Pa., and Martinsburg (Berkeley County), W. Va.

Bills and receipts of George A. Hamill, a physician, and letters to him from his brother, William Cromwell Hamill, dealing for the most part with family and personal matters.

2276.  ALEXANDER HAMILTON PAPERS, 1780, 1791. 2 items. New York, N.Y.

Letter, 1780, from Hamilton to Elizabeth Schuyler concerning the Benedict Arnold affair and the death of Major John André, and a letter, 1791, to Alisha Thomas and James Taylor, treasury agents for North Carolina, enquiring whether North Carolina had ever issued its own certificates of indebtedness in lieu of those of the United States.

2277.  H. C. HAMILTON AND COMPANY ACCOUNT BOOK, 1839-1842. 1 vol. (185 pp.) Beattie's Ford (Lincoln County), N.C.

Account book of a general mercantile store containing invoice records, 1839-1842, and three annual inventories, 1840-1842, itemizing the stock.

2278.  JAMES HAMILTON, JR., PAPERS, 1823-1882. 12 items. Charleston, S.C.

Routine business and political correspondence of James Hamilton, Jr., concerning political appointments and several of the enterprises in which he was engaged.

2279.  JOHN ANDREW HAMILTON, FIRST VISCOUNT SUMNER, PAPERS, 1917. 1 item. London, England.

Letter from Lord Bryce concerning the draft of a memorandum he was preparing for the British government outlining the structure of the future League of Nations.

2280. MARMADUKE HAMILTON PAPERS, 1806 (1842-1895) 1950. 204 items and 16 vols. Savannah, Ga.

Miscellaneous letters and papers of Marmaduke Hamilton and members of his family relating primarily to Hamilton's business as dry goods and commission merchant and to politics. The collection contains legal papers including deeds of sale for slaves; indentures for the sale of property; deeds for property owned by Marmaduke Hamilton and his partners; and land grants and deeds to Everard Hamilton, George R. Clayton, and J. R. Hayes. Correspondence includes a letter from Marmaduke Hamilton to Alexander H. Stephens, 1882, concerning an appointment to the Georgia Railroad Commission; an unsigned draft of a letter to Thomas A. Edison on the construction of an artificial ear; and a letter to Marmaduke Hamilton notifying him of his appointment as a deputy collector of internal revenue in Georgia. Miscellaneous material includes invitations; orders, 1863, from General Q. A. Gillmore to Colonel Israel Garrard of the 7th Ohio Regiment, Cavalry; phrenological analysis of Marmaduke Hamilton; and handbills for a local election, 1885. Volumes consist of letter books of John F. Hamilton and Marmaduke Hamilton; a brief diary and a combination copy and daybook of John F. Hamilton; daybooks and ledgers; and a record book of Everhard Hamilton's slaves.

2281. PAUL HAMILTON PAPERS, 1806, 1811. 2 items. Saint Paul's Parish, S.C.

Papers of Paul Hamilton, South Carolina governor and secretary of the navy, consist of a land grant, 1806, and a request for a naval appointment, 1811.

2282. WILLIAM BASKERVILLE HAMILTON PAPERS, 1700s-1972. 45,000 items and 200 vols. Durham, N.C.

Papers of William B. Hamilton, professor of history at Duke University, Durham, North Carolina, specialist in the history of Mississippi and in the history of Great Britain in the 18th and 19th centuries, and editor of the South Atlantic Quarterly, 1956-1972. The collection contains personal papers, Duke University papers, and research material for publications on Mississippi history and British history. Personal papers include letters and papers dealing with family matters; correspondence with Eudora Welty, Hubert Creekmore, and Nash Kerr Burger and other writers from Mississippi; correspondence with historians and educators; correspondence with professional organizations and learned societies; material dealing with University of Mississippi, the Mississippi Historical Society, and the Mississippi Department of Archives and History; miscellaneous printed items; family photographs pertaining to the history of Mississippi and Great Britain; copies of Hamilton's reviews, speeches, and writings; and material relating to various trips. Duke University papers contain correspondence, reports, notes on committee activity concerning many areas of university life, including material relating to the Department of History; a large number of items concerning the reorganization and strengthening of the faculty and the creation of the University Council, later the Academic Council; papers on the establishment of Duke Historical Publications; files relating to library development; papers from the Committee on Commonwealth Studies; and material concerning the South Atlantic Quarterly. The collection also contains notes, transcripts, and photographic copies of documents relating to Hamilton's historical research. Mississippi research material concerns, for the most part, the territorial period, 1798-1817, and includes copies of a number of judicial records from Adams County; notes; and microfilm and photographic copies of many types of documents. The Grenville research material contains extensive notes and photographic and microfilm copies of many documents relating to a projected but unwritten biography of William Wyndham Grenville, First Baron Grenville. Mansfield research material is made up primarily of notes for a biography of William Murray, First Earl of Mansfield. Australia and New Zealand research material includes information on politics in New Zealand, 1870-1900, and notes on sources of manuscripts and newspapers in Australian libraries. There is a small quantity of notes on the presentments of grand juries in the United States, 18th century-20th century.

2283. WILLIAM H. A. HAMILTON PAPERS, 1875. 4 items. Hagerstown (Washington County), Md.

Business letters to William H. A. Hamilton.

2284. HAMILTON TOWNSHIP TAX LISTS, 1877-1879. 1 vol. Martin County, N.C.

Tax lists of Hamilton township.

2285. HANNIBAL HAMLIN PAPERS, 1862-1970. 4 items. Bangor (Penobscot County), Me.

Letter, 1866, from Hannibal Hamlin to A. Smythe, collector of the Port of New York, asking assistance for a friend and a blotter said to have been used in correcting the Emancipation Proclamation.

2286. JOHN HENRY HAMM PAPERS, 1864-1875. 18 items. Greensboro (Guilford County), N.C.

Letters to Hamm from members of his family concerning personal and family matters.

2287.	NATHANIEL A. HAMMER PAPERS, 1827-1880.  28 items. Guilford County, N.C.

Receipts and other business papers of Nathaniel A. Hammer, overseer of roads in Guilford County, North Carolina.

2288.	J. B. N. HAMMET PAPERS, 1840s-1850s.  4 items and 2 vols.  Sumter County, S.C.

A volume of handwritten copies of forms to be used for legal documents; legal and financial documents concerning Hammet's practice of law; and a volume of his client's accounts, 1846-1851.  Among the clients represented is E. H. Mellichamp.

2289.	WILLIAM HAMMET AND BENJAMIN HAMMET PAPERS, 1789-1865.  45 items and 1 vol.  Charleston, S.C.

Correspondence of Methodist ministers of Charleston, South Carolina, and the Bermudas, dealing with a schism in the Methodist Church (ca. 1791), and the confessions of Benjamin Hammet's slave, Bacchus, concerning the threatened slave uprising in Charleston, 1822; and documents relating to the Savannah-Charleston stage line.

2290.	JAMES HENRY HAMMOND PAPERS, 1835-1875.  21 items. Newberry District, S.C.

Letters of James H. Hammond (1807-1864), lawyer, member of U.S. Congress, 1835-1836, governor of South Carolina, 1842-1844, and U.S. senator, 1857-1860.  Included are a letter to R. H. Wilde concerning the purchase of a slave and hiring an overseer; and one to F. W. Pickens giving his theory of government.  Other letters, to William B. Hodgson, are concerned with the state of the nation, crops, prices of slaves, real estate, Hodgson's literary efforts, and religion.  The collection also contains letters written to James H. Hammond's son Claudius Marcellus Hammond from members of his family commenting on the Civil War and Reconstruction.

2291.	MARCUS CLAUDIUS MARCELLUS HAMMOND PAPERS, 1873-1874. 4 items.  Beech Island (Aiken County), S.C.

Letters to Hammond from William Pinckney Starke discussing his impressions of Urbana University, Urbana, Ohio; politics in Ohio and elections of 1874; and racial attitudes in Ohio.

2292.	OLIVER T. HAMMOND PAPERS, 1837.  2 items. Norwich (Chenango County), N.Y.

Letters from Oliver T. Hammond, principal of the Union Seminary at Norwich, to John F. Hubbard, concerning the advantages of Yale University as an educational institution.

2293.	SAMUEL HAMMOND PAPERS, 1782-1801.  4 items. Savannah, Ga.

Miscellaneous items by Hammond, including a promissory note and a letter concerning an estate.

2294.	SAMUEL HAMMOND PAPERS, 1796-1897.  93 items. Asheboro (Randolph County), N.C.

The collection is made up mainly of letters to Samuel Hammond from his brothers in the western part of the United States concerning the settlement of the estate of their father, Ezra Hammond, and commenting on commodity prices in Indiana, Iowa, Texas, and Kansas; Republican politics in Indiana, 1876, and presidential elections in 1876, 1880, and 1884; and labor unrest in Indiana, 1876.  The collection also contains two copies of Ezra Hammond's will, 1875, and indentures for land in Randolph county.

2295.	THOMAS HAMMOND PAPERS, 1751 (1820-1879) 1914.  3,507 items. Libertytown, Md.

The collection consists of the legal, business, and personal papers of various members of the Hammond family.  The earliest items are records of grants and other transfers of land to Nathan Hammond and Vachel Hammond during the second half of the 18th century.  The papers of Thomas Hammond are mainly the records of his service as administrator of estates or as guardian of orphans, but they also include land surveys, deeds, mortgages, bills, bonds, indentures, promissory notes, reports from farm overseers, agreements with tenants, and receipts for taxes, household bills, and slave purchases. The papers of Dawson V. Hammond, brother of Thomas Hammond, concern the administration of the estate of Thomas Hammond and the administration of several other estates.

2296.	SIR ANDREW SNAPE HAMOND, FIRST BARONET, PAPERS, 1783-1862.  230 items and 1 vol.  Lynn, Norfolk, England.

Letters and papers of Sir Andrew Snape Hamond and his son, Admiral Sir Graham Eden Hamond.  Papers, 1795-1803, of Sir Andrew S. Hamond are from his tenure as comptroller of the Royal Navy and, for the most part, concern the importation of naval stores from northern Europe.  The papers, 1799-1806, of Graham Eden Hamond are letters to his parents describing his experience as commander of the British warships <u>Champion</u>, <u>Blanche</u>, <u>Plantagenet</u>, and <u>Lively</u> at Cuxhaven, Germany; in the blockade of Valetta, Malta, 1800; the blockade of the Danish and Swedish coasts and the attack on Copenhagen, 1801; in service off the coasts of France and Spain, 1801; and at Gibraltar, Malta, Naples, and Messina, 1805-1806.  Papers, 1824-1862, are mainly the incoming correspondence of

Graham D. Hamond concerning naval discipline, 1824; a report on smallpox vaccine, 1825; a series of letters from George Charles Blake, in command of H.M.S. Pearl on the Irish station, 1828-1832; report of Lieutenant Arthur Grant of H.M.S. Fisgard on a navigational expedition around the tip of South America, 1845; a discussion of the problems of manning the navy in emergencies and the advisability of impressment, 1848-1854; and numerous letters concerning promotions and pensions.

2297. CALEB HAMPTON PAPERS, 1846-1880. 265 items. China Grove (Rowan County), N.C.

The collection consists, for the most part, of letters from John Hampton and David Hampton to their uncle, Caleb Hampton and other members of their family describing their experiences, 1861-1865, while they were in the Confederate Army. They discuss fraternization between Northern and Southern soldiers and daily life during the siege of Petersburg, Virginia. The letters of Caleb Hampton describe local political disturbances and reflect a general war-weariness.

2298. E. D. HAMPTON PAPERS, (1857-1875) 1895. 32 items. Lexington (Davidson County), N.C.

Miscellaneous papers of E. D. Hampton, sheriff of Davidson county, including a letter, 1857, from Philip T. Hay, a student at the University of North Carolina, concerning one of his slaves who was in the Davidson county jail; letter, 1860, commenting on the presidential election; letters concerning land and business matters; and a handbill, 1868, advocating disenfranchisement of the Negro in North Carolina.

2299. FRANK ARMFIELD HAMPTON PAPERS, 1918-1953. 236 items and 25 vols. Greensboro (Guilford County), N.C., and Washington, D.C.

Letters and papers of Frank A. Hampton, trial examiner, later senior attorney with the Federal Power Commission, concerning personal, business, and political matters. Letters of William G. McAdoo, Jr., to Hampton discuss national politics and local politics in California, New York, and North Carolina; the 18th Amendment; Alfred E. Smith and the Democratic convention of 1924; and prospects for the Democratic convention of 1928. A few letters, 1936, discuss a proposed biography of Furnifold McLendel Simmons by J. Fred Rippy, and several letters, 1951, relate to Hampton's recommendation that the Virginia Electric Company be allowed to build a hydroelectric power plant at Roanoke Rapids, North Carolina. Volumes in the collection include two scrapbooks of material dealing with the political career of Furnifold M. Simmons, Frank A. Hampton, and political affairs, 1918-1928; and notebooks containing reports of hearings of the Federal Power Commission and procedural matters concerning the commission. Clippings relate mainly to Furnifold M. Simmons, including his political campaign against Josiah William Bailey, 1930; presidential campaigns of 1920, 1924, and 1928; and North Carolina politics in the 1920s.

2300. WADE HAMPTON PAPERS, 1791-1934. 45 items. Columbia (Richland County), S.C.

Correspondence of Wade Hampton (1818-1902), South Carolina statesman, dealing with the breeding of horses, 1840s; secession; the sale of slaves; Hampton's Legion in the Civil War, including a list of the German volunteers serving in the Legion; Reconstruction; Negro suffrage; the depression of land values; the Ku Klux Klan; and the role of Thomas Mackey in the campaign of 1876 which restored control of South Carolina to the Democratic Party. Included also is a letter of Hampton's grandfather, Wade Hampton (1752-1835), concerning an Indian expedition; and a letter, 1796, from Nathan Stark to John Hampton, brother of Wade Hampton (1752-1835), discussing the election of United States senators and representatives from South Carolina.

2301. JOHN FRANCIS HAMTRAMCK, JR., PAPERS, 1757-1862. 2,622 items and 8 vols. Shepherdstown (Jefferson County), W. Va.

Family and business correspondence of John Francis Hamtramck, Jr. (1798-1858), graduate of U.S. Military Academy, West Point, New York, U.S. Indian agent for the Osage Indians, colonel in the Mexican War, and planter. The collection may be divided as follows: letters of Hamtramck's father, Colonel John Francis Hamtramck (also spelled Hamtranck); papers of Walter Selby, Shepherdstown merchant and father of John F. Hamtramck, Jr.'s, second and third wives; a few letters to and from Mary Williams, evidently John F. Hamtramck, Jr.'s, first wife, written while she was in school at St. Joseph's Academy, near Emmittsburg, Maryland; a letter from Mary R. Hamtramck to her father, John F. Hamtramck, Jr., while attending school at the Ladies' Academy of the Visitation, Georgetown, D.C., in 1834; letters of William Clark to Indian agents; papers concerned with the Osage Indians while Hamtramck was agent; family and business letters of Jesse Burgess Thomas; and papers relating to the Mexican War. Volumes include an order book, 1847-1848, of the United States Army in the Mexican War containing orders issued by Colonel John F. Hamtramck, Jr., Brigadier General John Ellis Wool, Major General Zachary Taylor, and a few orders from the War Department in Washington; a blotter of money transactions made by John F. Hamtramck in St. Louis, 1827-1830; a ledger, 1833-1837, and a journal, 1833-1835, from the mercantile firm John F. Hamtramck; inventory of the possessions of John F. Hamtramck, Jr., 1831;

and an autograph album of Sarah E. (Selby) Hamtramck.

2302.   AMMON G. HANCOCK PAPERS, 1846 (1847-1855) 1888. 345 items.  Lynchburg (Campbell County), Va.

Business papers of Ammon G. Hancock (d. 1888), tobacco dealer.  The letters to Hancock are generally from tobacco manufacturers and exporters of Richmond, with accounts of the Richmond tobacco market and orders for tobacco.  Included also are similar letters from dealers and manufacturers in New York City, Petersburg, Virginia, and New Orleans, Louisiana; and orders from the long-established English firm of John K. Gilliat and Company of London.

2303.   ASENATH ELLEN (COX) HANCOCK PAPERS, 1880-1936.  450 items.  Asheboro (Randolph County), N.C.

Family correspondence and miscellaneous legal and financial papers, invitations, printed material, and advertising material.

2304.   JOHN HANCOCK AND TORRY HANCOCK PAPERS, 1774-1838.  9 items. Boston, Mass.

Letter, 1774, from Captain James Scott to Colonel John Hancock, reporting the safe arrival of the ship Hayley and commenting on reaction to the Boston Tea Party in London; letter, 1779, from William Lee to John Hancock concerning his movements and his plans for defending New York City and discussing the treatment of Tories in the area.  Also receipts for pew rent, postage, bridge tolls, and taxes.

2305.   O. VICTOR HANCOCK PAPERS, 1861-1863.  11 items. Chesterfield County, Va.

Letters of O. Victor Hancock to his father concerning his job and tobacco prices in Richmond and, later, his experiences in the Civil War, including letters from Manassas, Camp Ewell, and Leesburg describing trench graves, camp life, and sickness among the soldiers.

2306.   WINFIELD SCOTT HANCOCK PAPERS, 1863-1885.  24 items.  Montgomery County, Pa.

Copies of letters from George Gordon Meade to Winfield Scott Hancock explaining why he did not engage Robert E. Lee's Confederate forces in the early fall of 1863 and announcing the promotion of Hancock and others, 1864; correspondence regarding the part played by the 56th Pennsylvania Regiment at the battle of the Wilderness; and a series of letters from Hancock to Philippe Albert d'Orleans, Comte de Paris, concerning Civil War materials.

2307.   GEORGE HANDLEY PAPERS, 1783-1788.  8 items. Augusta (Richmond County), Ga.

Letters and papers of George Handley, soldier in the American Revolution and governor of Georgia, concerning routine military matters; letter from General Elijah Clark, 1788, requesting state troops for Franklin County, Georgia, to protect people while gathering their crops; and extracts from the minutes of meetings of the Executive Council of Georgia, 1785.

2308.   FRANK A. HANDY DIARY, 1862-1865. 7 vols.  Piqua (Miami County), Ohio.

Diaries kept by Frank A. Handy, a lieutenant in Company C, 94th Ohio Volunteer Infantry.  The diaries give accounts of the celebration held in Nashville, Tennessee, over the capture of Atlanta; an interview with General W. S. Rosecrans; a trip to Washington; attempts to gain a higher commission; business transactions of the company; and social life, customs, and outstanding plantations near Nashville.

2309.   N. B. HANDY COMPANY DAYBOOK, 1842-1844.  1 vol.  (454 pp.) Lynchburg (Campbell County), Va.

Accounts for general merchandise and groceries.

2310.   HARRISON H. HANES PAPERS, 1861-1862.  26 items.  Davie County, N.C.

Letters of a soldier in the 4th North Carolina Regiment concerning camp life in North Carolina and Virginia.

2311.   CONSTANT C. HANKS PAPERS, 1861-1865.  53 items. Hunter (Green County), N.Y.

Letters of a soldier in the 20th New York Regiment to his family containing long descriptions of camp life; discussions of religious feelings among soldiers and the work of army chaplains, particularly Methodists; descriptions of the treatment of wounded and sick soldiers and accounts of Hanks's visits to hospitals in or near Washington, D.C.; numerous comments on contrabands and a long essay, 1864, on slavery, contrabands, and Negroes; a description of the aftermath of the second battle of Bull Run, 1862; note of an inspection tour by Dorothea Lynde Dix, 1863; a general description of the battle of Chancellorsville, 1863; and comments on the work of the Sanitary Commission and on Negro and Indian troops, 1864.

2312.   CORNELIUS R. HANLEITER DIARY, 1861-1863.  4 vols.  Savannah, Ga.

Typed copies of the diaries of an officer of the Joe Thompson Artillery (Georgia) operating in the vicinity of Savannah, Georgia, describing troop movements; the condition, purchase, and maintenance of ordnance stores; army discipline; daily camp routine; sickness among the soldiers; the activities of Federal blockading vessels; and the operation of a small salt works.

2313. MARCUS ALONZO HANNA PAPERS, 1902. 2 items. Cleveland (Cuyahoga County), Ohio.

Letters by Marcus Alonzo Hanna dealing with the selection of a picture of William McKinley for a volume of memorial addresses.

2314. HANNER FAMILY PAPERS, 1814-1872. 20 items. Guilford County, N.C.

Correspondence among members of the Hanner family concerning family matters, agricultural productivity, migration to the western United States, and land and commodity prices.

2315. JACK HANNIBAL PAPERS, 1878. 1 item. Tuscaloosa (Tucaloosa County), Ala.

Letter from Jack Hannibal, a freedman, to his former owner.

2316. HENRY S. HANNNIS AND COMPANY SALES BOOK, 1870-1872. 1 vol. (678 pp.) Hannisville (Berkeley County), W. Va.

Sales book of Henry S. Hannis and Company, flour millers and distillers, and the sales records, 1879-1881, of Alexander Parks, Jr., a flour miller.

2317. AUGUSTIN HARRIS HANSELL PAPERS, 1862, 1889. 2 items. Thomasville (Thomas County), Ga.

Letter, 1862, of Augustin Harris Hansell concerning Confederate recruitment and local defense in Georgia and a letter, 1889, of Hansell responding to a request for an autograph.

2318. WILLIAM RICHARD HANSFORD PAPERS, 1839 (1850-1874) 1878. 50 items. Portsmouth (Norfolk County), Va.

Personal correspondence of William R. Hansford, a Confederate soldier, including comments on the yellow fever epidemic in Portsmouth in 1855, and the robbery and assault of a white girl by Negroes in Mobile in 1864.

2319. ALEXANDER CONTEE HANSON PAPERS, 1785, 1805. 2 items. Annapolis (Anne Arundel County), Md.

Official papers of Hanson as Chancellor of Maryland.

2320. JOHN W. HARBISON PAPERS, 1854-1874. 54 items. Marshall County, W. Va.

The collection is made up mainly of the Civil War letters of John W. Harbison of the 12th West Virginia Regiment concerned with campaigns in western Virginia.

2321. GEORGE WILLIAM RICHARD HARCOURT PAPERS, 1749 (1801-1807) 1823. 61 items. Ankerwycke Park, Buckinghamshire, England.

Letters and papers of George William Richard Harcourt consisting primarily of letters to Harcourt from his superior while he was commandant of Vellore, India, concerning the mutiny of July 10, 1806, and its aftermath. Correspondents include Sir John Francis Caradoc and John Munro. The letters deal with the causes of the mutiny, the officers who suppressed it, the reliability and recruitment of native forces, and the problem of dealing with local leaders who may have been involved in the mutiny. There are items concerning Harcourt's military operations in Cuttack, India, during the Mahratta War, 1803-1805, and two letters relating to his estate in the Virgin Islands.

2322. SIR WILLIAM GEORGE GRANVILLE VENABLES VERNON-HARCOURT PAPERS, 1875-1899. 4 items. London, England.

Papers of William George Granville Venables Vernon-Harcourt, barrister and leader of the Liberal Party, including a letter, 1894, discussing a legal matter and voting rights; a letter, 1897, to Sir Robert Giffen concerning foreign trade and trade with the colonies; and a letter, 1899, discussing the Transvaal.

2323. [JAMES H. HARDAWAY?] JOURNAL, 1813-1818. 1 vol. (507 pp.) Pleasant Grove (Lunenburg County), Va.

Accounts of a dealer in general merchandise.

2324. EDWARD HARDCASTLE PAPERS, 1883-1950. 10 items. London, England.

Letters to Edward Hardcastle, British Conservative politician, including letters, 1883, from Lord Randolph Churchill commenting on a bill concerning the Indian judiciary and criticizing Conservative Party organizations; letters, 1883, 1886, from Arthur Balfour on party matters; and letters from Lord Salisbury on the Affirmation (Oaths) Bill, 1883; the situation in Egypt and South Africa, 1884; and a reply to charges of an intrigue with the Irish, 1885.

2325.   WILLIAM JOSEPH HARDEE PAPERS,
        1863-1871.  7 items.
        Selma (Dallas County), Ala.

Correspondence and papers of William Joseph Hardee (1815-1873), Confederate brigadier general.  Included are a letter, 1863, written from Tullahoma, Tennessee, to Lieutenant Colonel George W. Brent, giving a full account of the Confederate maneuvers after the campaign in Kentucky; a receipt given Major Norman B. Smith for a mule; a memorandum, 1864, by Hardee concerning troop movements near Savannah; a letter, 1865, to Hardee from General Joseph Wheeler about Confederate and Union troop movements in South Carolina; and a business letter, 1871, to John L. Bridgers, of Tarboro, North Carolina.

2326.   EDWARD HARDEN PAPERS, 1772-1971.
        2,504 items and 27 vols.
        Athens (Clarke County), Ga.

Political, family, and business papers of Edward Harden (1784-1849), planter and politician; of his second wife, Mary Ann Elizabeth (Randolph) Harden (1794-1874); of their son, Edward Randolph Harden (1815-1884), telegraph operator and lawyer; of their daughter, Mary Elizabeth Greenhill Harden (1811-1887); and of Edward Randolph Harden's children.  Papers of Edward Harden include a diary with information concerning the operation of "Silk Hope," a rice plantation near Savannah, with inventory of equipment and work done during 1827; lists of slaves; references to "Mulberry Grove" and "Oak Grove" plantations; courtship letters to Mary Ann Elizabeth Randolph, who became his second wife in 1810; letters to his wife about farm work to be done in his absence; letters of Peter Randolph, father-in-law of Harden; letters to his wife while in the Georgia legislature in 1825; and letters and papers pertaining to his duties as counsel for the Cherokee Indians, U.S. marshal in Georgia, 1843, and collector of the port of Savannah, 1844.  Letters, 1846-1847, from Washington, D.C., while Harden served as Indian Commissioner, concern Washington social life and customs, office seekers, bureaucracy, James K. Polk and Sarah (Childress) Polk, and Dolly (Payne) Todd Madison.  Also included are letters from Howell Cobb, concerning his efforts to obtain political offices for Harden; land grants; commissions; passports; hotel bills; letters of introduction for a tour of Europe made by the Harden family in 1819; legal papers consisting chiefly of depositions, letters, and notes pertaining to Harden's law practice; letters relative to the course of study and tuition fees of Harden's daughter, Mary, while at the Latouche School in Savannah; letters connected with the activities of the Georgia Historical Society; and information regarding Thomas Spalding of Sapelo Island.  Other papers consist of an account by Harden of his appointment to and removal from the collectorship of the port of Savannah; receipts; a few account books and diaries; deeds, letters of dismissal, and other papers pertaining to the Mars Hill Baptist Church; and references to various residents of Athens, Georgia, where Harden conducted a law school after 1830.

Letters of Mary Ann Elizabeth (Randolph) Harden are to her husband; to her daughter, Mary Elizabeth Greenhill Harden, while the latter attended school in Savannah; and to her son, Edward Randolph Harden, while he attended the University of Georgia, Athens, 1829-1830.  Papers, 1849-1860, chiefly concern her efforts to get land warrants for her husband's services in the War of 1812, and papers, 1865-1874, deal with her attempts to obtain a pension on the same grounds.

Letters, 1854-1856, of Edward Randolph Harden describe his duties as judge of the first court in the territory of Nebraska and conditions there.  Letters, 1859-ca. 1870, of Edward Randolph Harden, of his daughter Anna, and of other children of Mary Ann Elizabeth (Randolph) Harden, reflect the poverty of the family and conditions of the time.  Civil War letters of Edward Randolph Harden describe the activities of the army while he served as an officer of the Georgia state troops, civilian life, and commodity prices.  Postwar letters concern his removal from Rome to Cuthbert and later to Quitman, all in Georgia; and his desultory practice of law supplemented by storekeeping and, in 1870, by work as a census enumerator.  There are also letters of the related Jackson family, including correspondence between Asbury Hull Jackson and his family describing his service in the 44th Georgia Regiment, the fighting around Richmond in 1862, and the battles of Antietam, Chancellorsville, Gettysburg, the Wilderness, and Spotsylvania.  Clippings concern the formation of the 3rd, 4th, 6th, 10th, and 16th Georgia Regiments in the early days of the war.

Among the letters to Mary Elizabeth Greenhill Harden is a proposal of marriage from John Howard Payne, author of "Home Sweet Home!" whom she met when he visited Georgia in the interest of the Cherokee Indians.  According to tradition her father refused to allow the match.  The collection also contains other proposals, all of which she refused; and her diary, 1853-1883.

Throughout the collection are frequent letters from Henrietta Jane (Harden) Wayne, daughter of Edward Harden by his first marriage and wife of James Moore Wayne's nephew.  Her letters give detailed accounts of life in Savannah and the people there, including mention of James Moore Wayne (1790-1867).

Among the correspondents are John Macpherson Berrien, Sr., Benjamin Harris Brewster, Joseph Emerson Brown, Howell Cobb, William Crosby Dawson, Hugh Anderson Haralson, Benjamin Harvey Hill, Amos Kendall, John Henry Lumpkin, John Howard Payne, Richard Rush, Thomas Jefferson Rusk, Thomas Spalding, William Henry Stiles, Israel Keech Tefft, George Michael Troup, James Moore Wayne, and Lewis Williams.

2327. EDWARD JENKINS HARDEN PAPERS, 1840-1885. 99 items. Savannah, Ga.

Letters, 1840-1859, of Matilda A. Harden, mother of Edward Jenkins Harden, dealing for the most part with financial matters; papers dealing with the settlement of the estate of Matilda A. Harden; and letters involving the estate of Mary E. Demeré.

2328. SARAH P. HARDEN PAPERS, 1868-1879. 9 items. Henry County, Ind.

Family correspondence of Sarah P. Harden, John Harden, Mary Harden, and Ann Harden to their aunt and uncle, Sarah and John Hackett, in one of the Carolinas.

2329. WILLIAM G. HARDESTY LEDGER, 1845-1857. 1 vol. (139 pp.) Clear Brook [Frederick County?], Va.

Volume of business accounts, a part of which has been used as a scrapbook.

2330. WILLIAM D. HARDIN PAPERS, 1838 (1870-1900) 1946. 894 items and 11 vols. Fentriss and Pleasant Garden (Guilford County), N.C.

The collection contains business and personal letters, bills, and receipts of William D. Hardin and family, and William Henry Ragan, dealing for the most part with local affairs, including legal matters, retail merchandising, education, religion, politics, Masonry, flour milling, and farming. Volumes include four registers for common school districts in Guilford County, North Carolina, 1879-1895; school notebooks; minute book of Pleasant Garden Farmers' Alliance, No. 2195, of Guilford County; and a poll book, 1924, for Fentriss Precinct, Guilford County.

2331. EZEKIAH HARDING AND JOHN HARDING PAPERS, 1852-1868. 41 items. Clover Depot (Halifax County), Va.

Business letters of the mercantile firm of E. and J. Harding and of its branch firms at Danville, Pleasant Grove (Lunenburg County), and Moore's Ordinary, all in Virginia. Included are invoices for liquor, a few dealers' circulars, and one letter of a Confederate soldier, dated January 17, 1865, mentioning scarcity of food, low morale among the soldiers, and their hope for the immediate fall of Fort Fisher and the end of the war.

2332. A. J. HARDY AND WILLIAM B. KING LETTER BOOK, 1834-1843. 1 vol. Turner's Cross Roads (Bertie County), N.C.

Copies of business letters of Hardy and King, general merchants of eastern North Carolina.

2333. HAYWOOD HARDY AND W. D. HARDY PAPERS, 1862. 2 items. Martinsburg (Berkeley County), W. Va.

Letters of Confederate soldiers to their father. One letter concerns the battle of Sharpsburg, and the other discusses feelings about reenlistment.

2334. THOMAS HARDY PAPERS, 1904-1929. 3 items. Dorsetshire, England.

A letter from Thomas Hardy (1840-1928) to Edward Clodd, commenting on the first days of World War I; proof sheets of Hardy's drama, The Dynasts, with his notes on the work; and a letter, 1904, from Edmund Gosse on the death of the poet, Adela Florence (Cory) Nicholson (Laurence Hope).

2335. WILLIAM E. HARDY PAPERS, 1783-1894. 64 items. Maybinton (Newberry District), S.C.

Letters and papers of William E. Hardy, including indentures: personal letters; an account book; bills; Civil War letters written from camps around Richmond and Petersburg, Virginia; business letters; and contracts with freedmen.

2336. ROBERT W. HARGADINE PAPERS, 1867-1869. 13 items. Philadelphia, Pa.

Letters and papers of Robert W. Hargadine containing rough notes of a thesis at the University of Pennsylvania for the degree of doctor of medicine, 1867; personal letters from William M. Nickerson, assistant surgeon on the U.S.S. Pensacola; letters from Annie L. Hargadine describing a European tour, 1869; and Hargadine's appointment as a resident physician at St. Mary's Hospital, Philadelphia, Pennsylvania.

2337. J. H. HARGRAVE ACCOUNT BOOKS, 1852-1892. 15 vols. Pittsylvania County, Va.

Accounts of J. H. Hargrave (1822-1891), a general merchant and manufacturer of chewing tobacco.

2338. ELIZABETH R. HARGROVE PAPERS, 1817-1892. 220 items. Townsville (Vance County), N.C.

Letters and papers of Elizabeth R. Hargrove, for the most part concerned with family matters and local events. Includes letters from nephews attending college at Wake Forest College and the University of North Carolina.

2339. ISRAEL W. HARGROVE PAPERS, 1839-1867. 9 items. Granville County, N.C.

The collection includes documents relating to the pardon of Israel W. Hargrove after the Civil War, land deeds, and Hargrove's will, 1867.

2340. MARCELLUS M. HARGROVE PAPERS,
1884-1910. 13 items and
16 vols. Luray (Page County),
Va.

Diaries, 1893-1908, of Marcellus M. G. Hargrove concerned with his work as a teacher in various schools in Virginia, particularly the Luray College for Young Ladies. The collection also contains an address book, a college roll, and miscellaneous papers.

2341. JAMES HARLAN PAPERS,
1865. 1 item.
Washington, D.C.

Letter to James Harlan, secretary of the interior of the United States, from John A. Strother, a planter in the Mississippi delta, suggesting that unemployed freedmen from Virginia be sent to repair the levees on the lower Mississippi.

2342. THOMAS J. HARLEY PAPERS,
1824-1911. 277 items and
2 vols. Hedgesville
(Berkeley County), W. Va.

Bills, receipts, and legal papers of Thomas J. Harley and of the McCue, Speck, and Hedges families, including wills, deeds, papers relative to the settlement of estates, and rent contracts for land. Volumes consist of a ledger, 1855-1856, which belonged to James Denny of Mountain View, Virginia, and a scrapbook of poems.

2343. WILLIAM W. HARLLEE PAPERS,
1862. 9 items. Marion
(Marion County), S.C.

Applications for military appointments to William W. Harllee, South Carolina legislator, lieutenant-governor, and brigadier general in the Confederate Army; and a letter discussing a project to establish a farm for raising medicinal products.

2344. VIRGINIA HARLOW PAPERS,
1941-1942. 9 items.
Duke University, Durham, N.C.

Letters concerning possible sources of the letters of Thomas Sergeant Perry.

2345. GEORGE W. HARMON PAPERS,
1842-1846. 2 items.
Granville, [Pa.?]

Correspondence regarding a judgement against J. F. Esty.

2346. HARMONY COUNCIL TEMPERANCE
REFORM RECORD BOOK,
1875-1879. 1 vol.
(159 pp.) Van Buren
(Crawford County), Ark.

Minutes of meetings.

2347. HARMONY HOLINESS CHURCH MINUTES,
1910-1943. 1 vol. (296 pp.)
Harmony (Iredell County), N.C.

Includes treasurer's record.

2348. [THOMAS BIGGS HARNED?] PAPERS.
3 items. Camden (Camden
County), N.J.

Two essays on Walt Whitman's literary contributions and personal life and a note to the recipient of the essays. The author of the essays is thought to be Thomas Biggs Harned, Whitman's literary executor.

2349. BENJAMIN J. HARPER PAPERS,
1848, 1861. 2 items.
Preston, Miss.

A letter, 1848, from Mary T. Harper, concerning family matters, cotton crops, plantation life in Mississippi, and the presidential campaign of 1848; and a letter, 1861, from Benjamin J. Harper, a Confederate soldier.

2350. FRANCIS HARPER PAPERS,
1846-1854. 8 items.
New Bern (Craven County), N.C.

Papers of the estate of Francis Harper, referring to the renting of turpentine forest lands and the hiring of Negroes.

2351. JULIA A. (THORNE) HARPER PAPERS,
1909. 1 item. New York, N.Y.

Personal note of the wife of James Harper, founder of Harper and Brothers, presenting to one De Bost a copy of Woodrow Wilson's biography of George Washington.

2352. ROBERT GOODLOE HARPER PAPERS,
1818-1821. 4 items.
Baltimore, Md.

The collection contains a letter, 1818, from Robert Hills concerning construction projects in Baltimore, Maryland; a letter, 1821, from the Italian sculptor, Raimondo Trentanove concerning a bust of George Washington; and two business letters.

2353. COSTEN JORDAN HARRELL PAPERS,
1969. 1 item. Decatur
(De Kalb County), Ga.

Copy of a sermon, "God is our home," delivered June 29, 1969, Philadelphia Methodist Church in Sunbury, Gates County, North Carolina, by retired Bishop Harrell.

2354. ELIAS B. HARRINGTON PAPERS,
1819-1869. 104 items.
Fayetteville (Cumberland
County), N.C.

Business papers including bills, promissory notes, deeds, other legal documents, and many summonses to appear in court for nonpayment of debts.

2355. G. W. HARRINGTON LEDGER, 1830-1831. 1 vol. (318 pp.) Gallatin (Copiah County), Miss.

General mercantile accounts.

2356. ISAAC HARRINGTON DAYBOOK, 1847-1862. 1 vol. (241 pp.) Grafton Centre (Grafton County), N.H.

Records of a shoe shop.

2357. JOHN MCLEAN HARRINGTON PAPERS, 1760-1901. 967 items and 4 vols. Harnett County, N.C.

Correspondence of John McLean Harrington (1839-1887), teacher, surveyor, clerk, and sheriff of Harnett County in 1865, and of his father, James Stephens Harrington (1806-1888), member of the North Carolina state legislature in 1858 and 1870. Letters contain information on "Archie Black's Academy" at Haywood in Chatham County, North Carolina; public-school teaching; activities of the Republican Party in North Carolina during post-bellum years; family activities; Edgeworth Female Academy in Greensboro during 1859; and the Civil War. Included also are receipts; legal documents; a manuscript dated May 9, 1855, on "Northern Laborers," defending Northern laborers from aspersions probably cast on them by Southerners; a diary kept by John McLean Harrington while teaching school in 1860; minutes of the Pine Forest Debating Society; and weather reports for 1869-1870 and 1879-1882. Among additional papers are manuscript newspapers published by Harrington, the Weekly News and The Times; clippings; and letters to Allene Ramage regarding J. M. Harrington. The collection includes information on politics in North Carolina, 1860-1861.

2358. S. C. HARRINGTON PAPERS, 1856. 2 items. Lawrence (Douglas County), Kan.

Letters introducing a certain Clayton, who had been wounded in the capture of "the Southern ruffian, Titus," to S. C. Harrington's friends and relatives in the East.

2359. BENJAMIN FRANKLIN HARRIS PAPERS, 1861-1865. 12 items. Oxford (Granville County), N.C.

Letters from merchants or textile manufacturers in North Carolina during the Civil War, concerning business transactions and market conditions during the war and after.

2360. BENJAMIN JAMES HARRIS PAPERS, 1778 (1811-1813) 1883. 399 items. Richmond, Va.

Agreements for the hire of slaves; business letters from various merchants and commission firms, accompanied by accounts and relating to the state of the cotton and tobacco markets. There are frequent allusions to the effect of the War of 1812 and the Napoleonic campaigns on these markets. Letters for late 1813 mention the valuation of gold imports from foreign countries and the acceptability of currency from the various states. Firms represented in the collection include Jona Meigs of Savannah, Georgia; T. & R. Gwathmey of Lynchburg, Virginia; Edw. S. Waddey of Norfolk, Virginia; Wm. H. Imlay & Co. of Hartford, Connecticut; Stevens & Athearn of Boston, Massachusetts; Strong & Havens of New York; Thomas Richardson of Fayetteville, North Carolina; Blair Burwell of Augusta, Georgia; N. & D. Talcott of New York; and Fox and Richardson of Richmond. There also are Civil War letters from Maurice and Daniel E. Temple to their sister, Eliza Temple, with references to life in Pettit's Battery [1st Regiment New York Light Artillery?].

2361. CHARLES J. HARRIS PAPERS, 1863-1865. 57 items. Willett (Cortland County), N.Y.

Letters from Charles J. Harris, a private in the Federal Army stationed in Virginia, Florida, and South Carolina, commenting on conditions in the South, his reaction to Copperhead activities, and his bitterness against John Wilkes Booth after Lincoln's death.

2362. CHARLES J. HARRIS PAPERS, 1850 (1854-1870) 1913. 369 items. Macon (Bibb County), Ga.

Personal correspondence of Charles J. Harris (1834-1892), lawyer, Georgia legislator, and colonel in the Confederate Army, and of his wife, Mary C. (Wiley) Harris. The earlier portion of the collection consists of Mary C. (Wiley) Harris's bills, school reports, and letters while she was a student at a school conducted by the Misses Gill in Philadelphia, Pennsylvania. One letter, 1885, from Miss Gill comments on the literature of the period.

2363. DAVID BULLOCK HARRIS PAPERS, 1789-1894. 5,067 items and 9 vols. Fredericshall (Louisa County), Va.

Business and personal correspondence of David B. Harris (1814-1864), tobacco exporter and Confederate general; and of his father, wife, and children. David B. Harris's father, Frederick Harris, while in the Virginia House of Delegates, wrote letters to his wife and later to David B. Harris. Otherwise the papers reflect the career of David B. Harris, many being concerned with the U.S. Military Academy, West Point, New York, while Harris was a student, 1829-1833. Included also are many letters relating to Harris's tobacco business in Virginia and Kentucky; and to the Civil War, with military papers and maps. There are also many letters to Harris's widow, usually from her children; many receipts and account books relating to the tobacco business; prices current; statements of J. K. Gilliat and Company, tobacco importers in London; letter of N.W. Harris, brother of David B., concerning the tobacco business; letters from William T. Barrett, brother-in-law and partner of Harris in Kentucky; and letters concerning Harris's successful venture in trading with Brazil, exchanging flour for coffee. Among the correspondents are P. G. T. Beauregard, D. H. Mahan, and Sylvanus Thayer. Added material includes an account book, 1845-1857, listing prices of slaves; personal and business correspondence and financial and legal papers, including items addressed to Miss Chattie C. McNeill, St. Paul's, North Carolina; settlement of estates of D. C. Overton, Martha Overton, and D. B. Harris; Harris's tobacco business; and the sale of slaves.

2364.  MRS. E. L. HARRIS PAPERS,
       1873-1894.  150 items.
       Slabe (Goochland County), Va.

Mrs. Harris was a book agent for Harper and Brothers and most of the correspondence is from the subscription book department of Harper and Brothers. There is some information on the sale of Alfred Roman's <u>Military Operations of General Beauregard in the War between the States</u> (1884) and the effect of Beauregard's connection with the Louisiana lotteries.

2365.  E. M. HARRIS PAPERS,
       1862-1864.  10 items.
       Cartersville (Bartow County), Ga.

Business correspondence of E. M. Harris, a trader dealing in yarn, leather, and other items; and a letter from his sister-in-law, Adaline A. Hollingsworth, concerning family matters, local news, prices, and provisions.

2366.  ELIZABETH A. F. HARRIS DIARY,
       1866.  1 vol.  (174 pp.)
       New Orleans, La.

Diary kept by a Southern woman on a trip to Canada where whe met with many unreconstructed Confederates, including Jubal A. Early; included are accounts of her trip north through Saint Louis, Chicago, and Detroit, and her return by New York.

2367.  ELIZABETH BALDWIN (WILEY) HARRIS PAPERS, 1858 (1862-1893) 1958.
       10 items and 6 vols.
       Sparta (Hancock County), Ga.

Six volumes and several fragments of the diary of the mistress of a substantial plantation. There is also a genealogy and a few letters.

2368.  FISHER SANFORD HARRIS PAPERS,
       1889-1966.  203 items and
       4 vols.  Salt Lake City, Utah.

Correspondence concerning Utah state politics of the 1890s; the campaign by Harris (1865-1909) for the U.S. Senate; the lynching of a Negro in Colorado in 1900; publicity efforts on behalf of tourism in the western United States; and the See America First League. Speeches relate to political topics of the same period. Clippings describe Harris's death and burial and his political and promotional career. Some material relates to the role of the Morman Church in state politics.

2369.  FREDERICK A. HARRIS PAPERS,
       1817-1844.  126 items.
       New London (Campbell County), Va.

Family and business correspondence of a farmer of Campbell County, Virginia, including letters from his brothers William, of Huntsville, Alabama, and Salem (Franklin County), Tennessee; and Hannibal, of Jude's Ferry, Powhatan County, Virginia. The letters describe farming; the effects of the panic of 1819 on farmers of Virginia; the production of corn, wheat, and tobacco; an unsuccessful mercantile venture by Hannibal Harris; the work of slaves and the hiring of slaves; poverty and debts; and migration to the frontier.

2370.  HENRY ST. GEORGE HARRIS PAPERS,
       1823 (1850-1879) 1887.  143 items.
       Diana Mills (Buckingham County), Va.

Business and personal letters mentioning crops; commodity prices; salt works; land sales; social life and customs; schools and teachers; religion and preachers; national politics; personal debts; politics and government in Virginia, Mississippi, and Texas; marriage prospects for young ladies in San Francisco; a slave insurrection; newspapers and gossip; life and hardships in the South during the Civil War and Reconstruction; battles in Virginia; slave behavior during the war; and freedmen after the war. Writers include Cornelia Boaz; Richard C. Glenn; William E. Glenn; Ada A., D. M., Evalina M., Henry S. G., Mary W., and William Harris; and Stanley Reynolds.

2371.  ISHAM GREEN HARRIS LETTERS,
       1861-1891.  4 items.
       Nashville (Davidson County), Tenn.

Correspondence of Isham G. Harris (1818-1897), Tennessee senator, 1847-1848, member of U.S. Congress, 1849-1851, Tennessee governor, 1857-1861, and U.S. senator, 1877-1897. Included in the collection are a letter, 1861, from John H. Savage, volunteering to organize Tennessee for Confederate support; a letter from A. S. Curry, Trenton, Tennessee, applying for the directorship of a bank there; and a letter, 1891, from Harris to Ben W. Austin, concerning a letter of General Albert Sidney Johnston.

2372. IVERSON LOUIS HARRIS PAPERS, 1827-1878. 28 items. Milledgeville (Baldwin County), Ga.

Papers of a Georgia judge. There is legal correspondence of the firm of Hansell & Harris, attorneys, from the 1820s; and family letters from the Hansell, Hall, and Harris families thereafter. Topics include the Civil War, relief work by the ladies of Milledgeville, and Sherman's march through the town. Included are letters of Joseph E. Brown, Civil War governor of Georgia, written during the late 1860s.

2373. JAMES HARRIS PAPERS, 1813-1852. 7 items. Diana Mills (Buckingham County), Va.

Letters of a tobacco planter concerning prices and marketing conditions at Richmond, Virginia.

2374. JOEL CHANDLER HARRIS PAPERS, 1870-1909. 15 items. Atlanta (Fulton County), Ga.

Letters of Joel Chandler Harris (1848-1908), author and humorist, to Georgia (Harrison) Starke and Nora-Belle Starke, sister and niece respectively of James P. Harrison, editor of the Monroe Advertiser of Forsyth, Georgia, and onetime employer of Harris. The letters give accounts of the vicissitudes of Harris's career as a newspaperman and contain occasional comment on his own literary works and those of his contemporaries. In one letter he mentions that his verses "To Nora Bell" have been pronounced "very fine" by Paul Hayne. Several earlier letters, of an introspective cast, give the author's own account of his character and personality. Included also is a letter of application, probably to Stilson Hutchins of the Washington (Georgia) Post, and a note to Miss Jeannette Gilder concerning his "Plough-Hands' Song." [Partially published: Julia C. Harris, Life and Letters of Joel Chandler Harris (New York, 1918).]

2375. JOHN D. HARRIS PAPERS, 1861-1865. 6 items. North Carolina.

Letters of a Confederate soldier, one written from the field.

2376. JOHN Y. HARRIS PAPERS, 1831-1901. 81 items. Dinwiddie County, Va.

Business papers of an attorney and his law partner, A. M. Organ; one item, 1875, concerns work on township roads and timber for a plank road. There are also letters by Harris's brother-in-law, J. M. Dennis, relating to Reconstruction economic and political conditions in the cotton belt, especially in South Carolina.

2377. JOSIAH HARRIS PAPERS, 1872. 5 items. Thomasville (Davidson County), N.C.

Letters and accounts to Josiah Harris, a dealer in barrel staves, from the firm of Peters [Petus?] and Reed which handled his staves.

2378. LEVI HARRIS PAPERS, 1840-1870. 52 items. Charlotte Court House (Charlotte County), Va.

Letters from relatives living in various parts of Virginia, chiefly Buckingham County, concerning family news of farmers.

2379. RENCHER NICHOLAS HARRIS PAPERS, 1857 (1926-1965). 2,085 items and 27 vols. Durham, N.C.

Papers of Rencher Nicholas Harris (1900-1965), a leading Negro executive of Durham, North Carolina, who held positions with the Banker's Fire Insurance Company of Durham and related firms, and in the National Negro Business League, the Durham city council, the Durham school board, and civic organizations. Included are files on his career in Durham city and county politics in the 1950s and 1960s, especially as concerns race relations and minority rights and other problems of city government, such as airports, assessments, budgets, fire protection, recreation, and parking meters. There are a substantial number of appraisal reports on real estate in the Durham area and files on the Durham committee on human relations, the Lincoln Hospital, and the local chapter of the National Association for the Advancement of Colored People, and on property acquisitions of North Carolina College. Included in addition to correspondence are clippings, snapshots, deeds, contracts, other legal papers, speeches, and the Harris family album, containing letters back as far as 1857, photographs, and clippings. Among the correspondents is Carla (Myerson) Eugster.

2380. [RICHARD HARRIS?] ACCOUNT BOOK, 1864-1876. 1 vol. (68 pp.) [Powhatan County, Va.?]

Personal expenditures of a planter, including records of income from wheat crops and sums of money advanced to freedmen working for him.

2381. THOMAS W. HARRIS PAPERS, 1800 (1833-1860) 1887. 204 items. Halifax County, N.C.

Bills and receipts concerning the sale of cotton, tobacco, and wheat by commission merchants of Petersburg, Virginia; and promissory notes.

2382. HARRIS CHAIR COMPANY JOURNAL, 1908-1912. 1 vol. Millboro (Randolph County), N.C.

Journal of a small manufacturing firm. It did business with the Worth Manufacturing Company; among its officers was T. D. Harris.

2383. BENJAMIN HARRISON PAPERS, 1780-1785. 5 items. Charles City County, Va.

Letters of Benjamin Harrison (1726-1791), governor of Virginia, 1781-1784, relating to the importation of salt, 1783; the commission to regulate navigation on the Potomac River, 1785; a land grant to Robert Cunningham, 1782; and two typed copies of the will of Harrison.

2384. BENJAMIN HARRISON PAPERS, 1888-1889. 3 items. Indianapolis, Ind.

A brief note, 1888, by Benjamin Harrison (1833-1901), to Charles Emory of Carthage, Jasper County, Missouri, concerning Harrison's unit in the Civil War, the 70th Regiment of Indiana Infantry; a printed copy of Harrison's inaugural address as president of the United States; and a printed souvenir distributed at Harrison's inaugural ball, 1889.

2385. CHARLES L. HARRISON PAPERS, 1834-1845. 7 items. Jackson County, Tex.

Titles and deeds to land in Jackson and Liberty counties, Texas, several of which are in Spanish. Charles L. Harrison was one of the early American settlers in Texas.

2386. EDWIN HARRISON PAPERS, 1788-1928. 495 items. St. Louis, Mo.

Correspondence, bills, receipts, and other papers of James Harrison (b. 1803), businessman of Fayette and later of St. Louis, Missouri, concerning his trade down the Mississippi River with New Orleans and with Chihuahua, Mexico; mining in Saint François County, Missouri; and the Iron Mountain Railroad. Also included are correspondence and other papers of James's son, Edwin Harrison (1836-1904), relating to his multitude of business and philanthropic interests; the latter include the Missouri Historical Society, Washington University, and the American Association for the Advancement of Science. There are also some letters from personal friends and copies of poems.

2387. GEORGE B. HARRISON PAPERS, 1821-1924. 13,419 items and 79 vols. Boyce (Clarke County), Va.

Correspondence between George B. Harrison and his brother and sisters, Henry, Maria, and Agnes, relatives of the prominent Harrison family of Virginia. There are about a dozen letters concerning the filibustering expedition to Cuba, 1869-1870; an unsuccessful lumber and sawmill business in West Virginia; farming and the price of land in Florida, 1880s; the attempt of the city of Canaveral, Florida, to seek federal construction of a seawall to protect its harbor; and law practice in Richmond in the 1870s and 1880s, and later in Boyce. There is some genealogy, many cancelled checks, bills, receipts, legal papers, clippings, and advertisements. Included are volumes used as daybooks by the Jefferson Insurance Company, 1860-1869, and daybooks by George B. Harrison.

2388. GEORGE PAUL HARRISON PAPERS, 1863, 1889. 2 items. Savannah, Ga.

One letter from George Paul Harrison (1841-1922), soldier and politician, to Governor Joseph E. Brown concerning an illegal distillery in the Savannah River swamp; and one from Harrison to C. C. Jones, Jr., regarding the latter's address to the Augusta (Georgia) Confederate Survivors' Association.

2389. HENRY HARRISON PAPERS, 1842-1860. 16 items. Berkeley County, W. Va.

Letters chiefly concerning the settlement of Henry Harrison's estate, including the sale of furniture and slaves; one Negro woman was to be freed and sent to Liberia.

2390. HENRY SYDNOR HARRISON PAPERS, 1894-1958. 1,162 items and 1 vol. New York, N.Y.

Correspondence, clippings, and miscellaneous papers relating the career of Henry Sydnor Harrison (1880-1930) as newspaperman and novelist; there are letters, 1916, from H. L. Mencken enlisting support for a protest against the suppression of Theodore Dreiser's novel, The Genius; letters and poems of James Branch Cabell in part concerning his affection for Harrison's sister; many appreciative letters from readers of Harrison's novels and articles; and clippings of poetry and reviews.

2391. JAMES H. HARRISON PAPERS, 1855-1864. 9 items. Caswell County, N.C.

Personal letters, some of which were written while James H. Harrison was a Confederate soldier.

2392. JAMES P. HARRISON ACCOUNT BOOKS, 1829-1867. 16 vols. Oak Grove (Brunswick County), Va.

General mercantile accounts, including ledgers, 1829-1867, daybooks, 1844-1867, accounts of an auction sale, 1854, and accounts of an estate, 1854-1856. The firms represented are J. & P. Harrison and P. Harrison & Co.

2393. JAMES THOMAS HARRISON PAPERS, 1865. 1 item. Columbus (Lowndes County), Miss.

A letter from Harrison (1811-1879), an ex-Confederate congressman, to his wife telling her that he will not be permitted to take his seat in the U.S. House of Representatives after having been elected upon the return of Mississippi to the Union.

2394. JESSE HARRISON PAPERS, 1856-1880. 77 items. New Bern (Craven County), N.C.

Civil War letters written by a "buffalo" (a coastal dweller in North Carolina who sympathized with the Federal forces) behind the Federal lines at Washington, North Carolina, and letters written after the war describing the financial difficulties of the Harrison family.

2395. JOHN W. HARRISON DIARY, 1861. 1 vol. (124 pp.) Clarksburg (Harrison County), W. Va.

Diary of John W. Harrison, a Confederate soldier, describing the routine of camp life.

2396. WILLIAM F. HARRISON PAPERS, 1852 (1861-1862) 1872. 27 items. Goochland County, Va.

Civil War letters from Harrison to his wife describing fighting in western Virginia under Generals Garnett and Loring and in the Shenandoah Valley under Jackson; training and discipline; health and sanitary conditions in camps; hardships of army life; furloughs and enlistments. Harrison was an officer in the 23rd Regiment of Virginia Volunteers. Two letters of 1871-1872 concern railroad construction in West Virginia.

2397. HARRISON FAMILY PAPERS, 1773-1878. 51 items. Berkeley County, W. Va.

Plats and indentures for land in Berkeley County purchased by Samuel Harrison after 1773; construction contracts for his son, James Harrison; genealogical information on the Harrison family; and bills and receipts relevant to the settlement of the estates left by the Harrisons.

2398. ROBERT PRESTON HARRISS PAPERS, 1927-1975. 3,569 items and 160 vols. Baltimore, Md.

Correspondence, writings, clippings, tearsheets, printed material, pictures, miscellany, and tape recordings of a Baltimore novelist and newspaperman. There are many very brief notes to Harriss and his wife by Henry Louis Mencken, his wife Sara (Haardt) Mencken, and brother August Mencken. There are also letters from George Bernard Shaw concerning Harriss's unsuccessful attempt to interview him in 1931; from John J. Pershing concerning the assassination of French President Doumer in 1932; and from Ezra Pound on the poet Emanuel Carnevali, economic theory, and journalism, politics, and culture in America, 1933. Attached memoranda by Harriss explain his meetings with Shaw and Pershing. The collection includes letters from friends of Harris, notes and writings concerning his attendance at international conferences and events, travel essays, drafts for reviews, and drafts of articles. There are a typescript by Sara Mayfield of Exiles from Paradise (1971); photographs of Harriss and of the Fayetteville, North Carolina, vicinity, the Duke University campus, and protest demonstrations in Durham in 1963 and on the Duke campus in 1969; appointment calendars, 1972-1975; memorandum books of Harriss's trip to the West Indies Conference, 1944, and attendance at the official opening of Brasília, 1960; a run of Menckeniana, 1962-1965, a quarterly journal published by the Enoch Pratt Library; pamphlets on Mencken; cassettes of a tape recording of Harriss by Theo Lippmann regarding H. L. Mencken; a run of the Baltimore literary, art, and theater journal, Gardens, Houses, and People, 1947-1957, which Harriss edited; engravings by Don Swann; other works of art; and many magazines, portions of newspapers, and clippings containing Harriss's writings, especially relating to culture and the arts.

2399. THOMAS WHITMEL HARRISS PAPERS, 1795 (1828-1873) 1891. 303 items. Littleton (Halifax County), N.C.

Family and business correspondence of Thomas W. Harriss (1795-1870), a tobacco planter, including letters to members of the family in Tennessee and Mississippi, and correspondence, 1870-1891, of Harriss's son, Thomas. Included in the collection are an inventory of the property of Elias Harriss; accounts giving prices of cotton, tobacco, and various small commodities; and letters concerning the University of North Carolina (Chapel Hill), commission merchants in North Carolina and Virginia, treatment of slaves in Mississippi, the Panacea Springs in Halifax County, Andrew Jackson, erection of the "Philanthropic Hall" at the University of North Carolina in 1837, the Warrenton Temperance Association in 1842, a dinner honoring John C. Calhoun in 1842, Randolph-Macon College (Boydton, Virginia) and Dr. Charles F. Deems (1854?), the Pioneer Agricultural Club in Halifax County in 1882, and Harriss's nomination for the house in the North Carolina legislature. Among the correspondents are Lawrence O'B. Branch, I. Harriss, Thomas W. Harriss, William H. Harriss, and Edmund Ruffin.

2400. ALBERT BUSHNELL HART PAPERS,
1890-1924. 108 items.
Cambridge (Middlesex County),
Mass.

Correspondence, clippings, and pamphlets of Albert Bushnell Hart (1854-1943), professor and historian of Harvard University. The collection may be divided into three distinct parts: letters and pamphlets, 1890-1892, concerned with the writing and publishing of Fugitive Slaves (Cambridge, 1891), written by Marion Gleason McDougall under the direction of Hart, with financial assistance from Anna Boynton Thompson; letters and clippings concerned with the inaccuracies of a speech delivered by Julian S. Carr of Durham, North Carolina, at Washington and Lee University, Lexington, Virginia, June 3, 1916; and correspondence, 1919-1924, concerned with an academic debate between Hart and Lyon Gardiner Tyler of the College of William and Mary, Williamsburg, Virginia, on the founding of the United States and on various aspects of the Civil War. There are also letters from Walter Hines Page concerning articles to be written by Hart for magazines which Page edited. Among the pamphlets and clippings are Dr. Lyon G. Tyler's pamphlet, Virginia First; circulars advertising the book Fugitive Slaves; an American History Leaflet of November, 1893, edited by Hart and concerned with "Ordinances of Secession"; "The African Riddle," an article by Hart printed in the Saturday Evening Post, October 28, 1905; and articles on the size of the Confederate Army. Among the correspondents are Henry Nichols Blake, Ginn and Company, Albert Bushnell Hart, Marion Gleason McDougall, Mildred Lewis Rutherford, Anna Boynton Thompson, and Lyon Gardiner Tyler.

2401. HENRY GEORGE HART PAPERS,
1841-1858. 14 items.
London, England.

Letters from British army officers contributing additions or corrections to Hart's Army List.

2402. OLIVER HART DIARY, 1723-1780.
1 item. Charleston, S.C.

Mimeographed copy of the diary of the pastor of the Baptist Church in Charleston, 1750-1780, prepared by the South Carolina Baptist Historical Society. Included is information on the history of the church in Charleston and on the occupation of Charleston by British forces, 1780. Notes accompanying the diary by Loulie Latimer Owen provide biographical information on Hart. A portion of the diary was printed in the Charleston Year Book, 1896.

2403. WILLIAM HART LETTER BOOK,
1809-1816. 1 vol.
Paramaribo, Surinam.

Correspondence of the colonial commissary on the West Indian island of Saint Lucia and later in Surinam under British occupation. The letters primarily concern trade between Surinam; Saint Lucia; Barbados; Cork and Belfast, Ireland; Liverpool, England; and other places in the West Indies and America.

2404. MATTHEW HARTLEY PAPERS,
1872. 1 item. [London, England?]

Letter by Hartley, evidently a clerk in Parliament.

2405. JEFFERSON HARTMAN PAPERS.
1863-1865. 13 items.
Shamokin Dam (Snyder County), Pa.

Correspondence of two Union Army soldiers during the Civil War describing life in the army, concern for home affairs, and the effect of Lincoln's assassination. Samuel P. Hartman, brother of Jefferson, was in the 49th Regiment of Pennsylvania Volunteers, and was stationed at Petersburg, Virginia.

2406. JOHN H. HARTMAN PAPERS,
1823 (1850-1865). 62 items.
Rowan County, N.C.

Personal letters from John Hartman, a Confederate soldier, to his wife.

2407. CHARLES FREDERIC HARTT PAPERS,
1859-1906. 459 items.
New York, Massachusetts, and Brazil.

An essay by Hartt on music; letters to Louis Agassiz from a scientific expedition to Brazil, 1865; letters of a carpetbagger's Southern wife in Augusta, Georgia; Hartt's certificate of membership in the American Ethnological Society; letters to Hartt's fiancee and wife Lucy C. (Lynde) Hartt; letters of condolence to Mrs. Hartt on her husband's death; correspondence between Hartt and John C. Branner while serving on the Geological Commission of Brazil; correspondence between Mrs. Hartt and the trustees of Buffalo Female Academy which she served as principal; letters of Rollin Lynde Hartt to his mother describing student life at Williams College; letters from Mrs. Hartt and her daughter Mary Bronson Hartt while travelling abroad; the will and papers concerning the estate of Charles R. Lynde, brother of Mrs. Hartt; letters of Rollin Hartt describing ministerial work in Leverett, Massachusetts, and ministerial work and race relations in Helena, Montana, 1890s. There are also letters from Fred T. Aldridge, George W. Cable, Mary C. Cook, Fred P. Forster, Jessie Clark (Knight) Hartt, Charles R. Lynde, and Richard K. Noye.

2408. EDWARD L. HARTZ PAPERS,
1861-1867. 392 items.
Pottsville (Schuylkill County), Pa.

Papers of a U.S. Army officer including letters, 1861, concerning the opening military actions of the Civil War in Texas; letters, 1864, relating to an expedition to return dissatisfied Negroes from Haiti to the United States; telegrams, 1864, received by Hartz as assistant quartermaster at Chattanooga concerning supply problems and railroad transportation in support of Sherman's army; and letters, 1864-1866, reflecting Hartz's successful attempt to be reinstated in the army following his discharge in 1864 for drunkenness.

2409. GEORGE BRINTON MCCLELLAN HARVEY PAPERS, 1878-1909. 84 items. Deal (Monmouth County), N.J.

Editorial correspondence of the North American Review which Harvey edited. The letters largely relate to the submission of manuscripts for publication. Authors include Marie Wiert, Elizabeth (Washburn) Wright, L. R. Wilfley, and Robert De Courcy Ward.

2410. GLEN HARVEY PAPERS, 1809 (1851-1894) 1948. 207 items. Charleston, S.C.

Largely letters from relatives in England to Glen and Rosa Harvey and from Harvey to his wife in Walhalla, South Carolina, while he was working for a manufacturing house in Charleston; topics mentioned include the lightning strike on St. Michael's Church in Charleston, 1866; the burning of the Crystal Palace, 1867; the labor supply in Australia; and the outbreak of the Franco-Prussian War and its effect on iron and cotton stocks in London. There are also papers of 1828 concerning the purchase of cloth from Russell Wheeler of North Stonington, Connecticut, by John Andrews, agent of the Richmond Manufacturing Co. of Providence, for shipment to Africa; a letter of Mary Sutton, 1844, describing missionary work in Cuttack, India; letters from the Gilman family of Exeter, Massachusetts, describing life there, 1853; and letters of Henry Morton Dunham, New England organist, and his wife.

2411. JAMES E. HARVEY PAPERS, 1800s. 2 vols. Washington, D.C.

Albums with small portraits, photographs, copies of paintings, and sketches from the 16th-19th centuries of prominent persons of the United States, Portugal, Great Britain, France, Russia, China, and Germany; also depicted are historic buildings.

2412. JONATHAN HARVEY PAPERS, 1803-1816. 4 items. Baltimore, Md.

Business correspondence of a Baltimore merchant with a Philadelphia bank and a New York mercantile house.

2413. WILLIAM CLIFTON HARVEY PAPERS, 1859-1867. 5 items. [Petersburg (Dinwiddie County), Va.?]

A letter, memorandum book, copybook, and two diaries relating to service in the 43rd Virginia Volunteer Regiment.

2414. M. A. HARVIN ACCOUNT BOOK, 1921-1928. 1 vol. (28 pp.) Charleston, S.C.

Accounts relating to investments, possibly of estate funds.

2415. WILLIAM J. HARWOOD AND W. B. ROSE PAPERS, 1871. 1 item. Richmond, Va.

Copy of an agreement concerning transfer of land in Henrico County, Virginia.

2416. JOHN CHEVES HASKELL MEMOIRS, 1903. 1 item. Abbeville (Abbeville County), S.C.

Typescript copy of the Civil War memoirs of a Confederate officer and political figure describing Charleston before the fall of Fort Sumter; Confederate leaders; the battles of Ball's Bluff, Seven Pines, Brandy Station, Gettysburg, Bristoe Station, the Wilderness, and Cold Harbor; actions around New Bern and Washington, North Carolina; the siege of Petersburg and the battle of the Crater; analysis of why the Southerners lost at Gettysburg; conditions in Richmond; General Custer's saddle and his spurs; the surrender at Appomattox; and his last interview with Lee.

2417. WILLIAM O. HASKELL PAPERS, 1855-1888. 388 items. Boston, Mass.

Family letters of Haskell, Boston manufacturer of school furniture and later a farmer in Mason, New Hampshire, and his children and his brothers and sisters. Topics include business, taxes, payment of bills, mortgages, prices, and orders; some letters concern the renting and selling of Blake House in East Lebanon, New Hampshire. Letters from John Brent, 1881-1882, describe the development of Florida. There is a Haskell family tree and about 25 letters concerning genealogy. There are also a few legal papers and miscellaneous items.

2418. JOHN W. HASKINS PAPERS, 1856 (1866-1876). 17 items. Buckingham County, Va.

Personal correspondence of a Virginia family, with brief references to agricultural and educational conditions immediately after the Civil War.

2419. CUSHING BIGGS HASSELL PAPERS, 1814-1926. 256 items and 3 vols. Williamston (Martin County), N.C.

A miscellaneous group of correspondence and other material relating principally to Cushing Biggs Hassell (1808-1880) and his son Sylvester Hassell; the mercantile business of Cushing in Williamston; Sylvester's search for a teaching position in 1868; the reorganization of the University of North Carolina, 1875; the state constitutional convention of 1875; the sale of land for settlement of an estate; and legal matters. Among the correspondents are Kemp Plummer Battle, Asa Biggs, Ezra Cornell, William Ruffin Cox, Braxton Craven, and Pleasant Daniel Gold. There are deeds and indentures from Surry and Yadkin counties; and references to purchases by Isaac Jarratt and members of the Puryear family.

2420. ELIZA HASTINGS PAPERS, 1860-1887. 33 items. North Carolina.

Personal letters of Eliza, James A., and Thomas W. Hastings, including a few Confederate soldier's letters.

2421. FRANCIS RAWDON-HASTINGS, FIRST MARQUIS OF HASTINGS AND SECOND EARL OF MOIRA, PAPERS, 1806-1822. 14 items and 1 vol. London, England.

The volume is the first part, 1813-1814, of Hastings's private journal, 1813-1818. It was in large part published as The Private Journal of the Marquess of Hastings, edited by his daughter, the Marchioness of Bute (London: 1858), and is largely a review of Hastings's ideas about British policy in India and detailed descriptions of his travels there. Among the unpublished portions are a description of his voyage from Portsmouth to India, a visit to Mauritius, and numerous omissions from daily entries in India. There are frequent variations between the published journal and the manuscript in spelling and capitalization. There is a calendar filed with the journal. There are also a few miscellaneous items of personal and political correspondence, including letters, 1818, to Earl Mountcashell concerning patronage in India and to Leicester Stanhope and Admiral Sir Henry Blackwood on the political and military situation in India. A letter to Dr. [George?] Holcombe states a desire to leave India. A letter, 1815, from William Frederick, Second Duke of Gloucester and Edinburgh, relates the death at Waterloo of Hastings Brudenell Forbes, Hastings's nephew.

2422. WARREN HASTINGS PAPERS, 1781-1818. 4 items. Daylesford, Worcestershire, England.

Letters of the governor general of India; included are references to relations between the Madras Presidency and Mohammed Ali, Nabob of Arcot and ruler of the Carnatic.

2423. PHILO HATCH PAPERS, 1835-1836. 2 items. Barrington (Yates County), N.Y.

Deeds between Hatch and Joseph Barthalomew.

2424. LAURENCE HATCHER ARITHMETIC, 1835. 1 vol.

Incomplete.

2425. ORIE LATHAM HATCHER PAPERS, 1916. 1 item. Richmond, Va.

Miss Hatcher was a prominent Southern woman educator. This letter from Ellis Paxson Oberholtzer congratulates her on her Shakespeare pageant.

2426. WILLIAM HAYNIE HATCHETT PAPERS, 1828 (1836-1849) 1852. 69 items. Lunenburg (Lunenburg County), Va.

Letters from Hatchett (b. 1817) as a student at the University of Virginia, Charlottesville, 1835, and other general correspondence, including letters from Peter Stokes, Alabama slave dealer, giving prices of slaves, 1845-1846; and from Henry Stokes as a student at the University of Virginia, 1839, giving accounts of professors, especially of Gessner Harrison and George Tucker. There is also a family genealogy.

2427. HATCHETT FAMILY PAPERS, 1767-1965. 320 items. Caswell County, N.C., and Prince Edward County, Va.

Papers of three generations of farmers, centering around William Russell Hatchett (1794-1878), Allen Lillious Hatchett (1838-1919), and William Henry Hatchett (1860-ca. 1950). Included are correspondence from relatives throughout the South chiefly concerning weather and prices as they affect crops. There are some accounts of civilian life during the Civil War and a few items relating to Trinity College, 1878-1879. There is a fragmentary and incomplete genealogy.

2428. THOMAS D. HATHAWAY PAPERS, 1842. 1 item. Edenton (Chowan County), N.C.

Letter of T. A. Jordan, Gatesville, North Carolina, concerning the reception given Baptist ministers in that town.

2429. T. C. HAUSER AND GEORGE F. WILSON RECORDS, 1840-1857. 5 vols. Yadkinville and Doweltown (Yadkin County), N.C.

Merchants' ledger and daybooks.

2430. JOHAN HAVAAS PAPERS, 1920. 1 item. Granvin, Norway.

Letter from Johannes Lid, botanist, to Johan Havaas, lichenologist, concerning the identification of a plant specimen and research on plant groups and moss flora in the western part of Norway.

2431. JOHN A. HAVEN PAPERS, 1821-1823. 29 items. Boston, Mass.

Business letters to W. F. and B. Salter, merchants in Fayetteville, North Carolina, concerning Boston prices.

2432. BENJAMIN HAWKINS PAPERS, 1798. 1 item. Roberta (Crawford County), Ga.

Letter from Hawkins (1754-1816), who was then Indian agent for all tribes South of the Ohio River, requesting powder and lead from the United States factor, Edward Price.

2433. ELIJAH T. D. HAWKINS PAPERS, 1861-1864. 6 items. [Georgia?]

Letters from Elijah T. D. Hawkins, Confederate soldier of the 46th Georgia Volunteers, to his family. One letter, July 23, 1864, mentions a Confederate victory in the Atlanta campaign the day previous, in which General William H. T. Walker was killed and General States Rights Gist and Tillman Hawkins, Elijah's brother, were wounded.

2434. JOHN HAWKINS PAPERS, 1858-1861. 9 items. Ithaca (Tompkins County), N.Y.

Business correspondence to Hawkins, discussing prices of corn, oats, and horses.

2435. MARMADUKE J. HAWKINS PAPERS, 1856 (1884-1905). 43 items. Ridgeway (Warren County), N.C.

Business and political correspondence of Marmaduke Hawkins (1850-1920), North Carolina lawyer and local politician. Among the correspondents are Walter Clark and F. M. Simmons.

2436. BYRON M. HAWKS PAPERS, 1846-1899. 23 items. Monroe County, N.Y.

Letters concerning Hawks's student life at Dartmouth, 1846-1848; teaching in an academy at South Yarmouth, Massachusetts, 1848; problems of establishing a law practice on the frontier in Fond du Lac (Wisconsin or Minnesota?) and personal and family matters. Most of the collection comprises checks and bills relating to Rochester, New York.

2437. FRANCIS LISTER HAWKS PAPERS, 1810, 1827. 2 items. New Bern (Craven County), N.C.

Letters of Francis L. Hawks (1798-1866), lawyer, Protestant Episcopal minister, editor, and historian, and of his father, Francis Hawks, one concerning the printing of the younger Hawks's work on the North Carolina Supreme Court and the other from Hawks's father, collector of the port of New Bern, describing a suspicious vessel in 1810.

2438. WILLIAM E. HAWKS PAPERS, 1861-1868. 20 items. New York, N.Y.

Bills of Hawks and of William E. Hawks, Jr., officers of the Soda Springs Land and Cattle Company.

2439. PETER W. HAWTHORNE PAPERS, 1843-1861. 4 items. Lunenburg County, Va.

Letters from Hawthorne's sister and from a business associate, Nathaniel Reise.

2440. JOHN MILTON HAY PAPERS, 1900. 1 item. Washington, D.C.

Note by Hay (1838-1905) acknowledging a letter from B. F. Brown.

2441. WILLIAM HAY PAPERS, 1786-1807. 5 items. Franklin County, Ga.

Deeds and surveyor's plat of several tracts of land sold by William Hay.

2442. HARRY HAYDEN PAPERS, 1942. 1 item. Wilmington (New Hanover County), N.C.

Typescript of a revision of "The Story of the Wilmington Rebellion," a portion of a projected larger work, "Hell, Heaven, or Home," intended as a white supremacist tract on American history. <u>The Story of the Wilmington Rebellion</u> was originally published at Wilmington in 1936 (32 pp.)

2443. HORACE EDWIN HAYDEN PAPERS, 1877. 1 item. Wilkes-Barre (Luzerne County), Pa.

A letter from John Jay (1817-1894) thanking Hayden (1837-1917) for corrections to a speech Jay had delivered.

2444. ALEXANDER L. HAYES PAPERS, 1850. 2 items. Lancaster (Lancaster County), Pa.

Letters of a Lancaster attorney to his client about usury, jurors, and Judge Ellis Lewis.

2445. KIFFIN R. HAYES PAPERS, 1944. 3 items. Paris, France.

War poems.

2446. RUTHERFORD BIRCHARD HAYES PAPERS, 1877-1881. 9 items. Fremont (Sandusky County), Ohio.

Letters to Hayes, U.S. president, recommending various persons for appointment for office. One letter of the Rev. Dr. James Freeman Clarke, a Unitarian minister of Boston, concerns General H. S. Huidekoper. Other writers are John Tyler Morgan, Benjamin Franklin Perry, John Lee Chapman, and William Wade Dudley. A letter from John Sherman concerns a bill for the relief of William H. Thompson, a collector of internal revenue in North Carolina. There is also one brief note of introduction from Hayes for a friend.

2447. LUTHER HAYMOND, THOMAS HAYMOND, AND WILLIAM HAYMOND PAPERS, (1784-1849) 1899. 135 items. Clarksburg (Harrison County), W. Va.

Family and business correspondence relating chiefly to speculation in Western lands.

2448. ARTHUR PERONNEAU HAYNE PAPERS, 1838-1859. 3 items. Charleston, S.C.

One letter from Arthur P. Hayne (1790-1867), soldier, lawyer, and U.S. senator, to Robert J. Walker contains some information on the presidential campaign of 1844; one from Mitchell King, gives the qualifications of a good English grammar; the third, from Hayne to Thomas Aspinwall, U.S. consul in London, 1838, concerns the prospects for fire insurance companies in Charleston.

2449. PAUL HAMILTON HAYNE PAPERS, 1815-1944. 4,615 items and 58 vols. Charleston, S.C., and Columbia County, Ga.

Correspondence, papers, notes, clippings, and works of Paul Hamilton Hayne (1830-1886), Southern poet and editor of Russell's Magazine; of his wife, Mary Middleton (Michel) Hayne; and of his son, William Hamilton Hayne (1856-1929). During Hayne's early years, many letters and copies of letters are from him to his wife, to Richard Henry Stoddard, to John Esten Cooke, and to many others. Hayne's letters cover a variety of subjects including, before the Civil War, comments on abolition in Boston, a trip to Boston in 1854, literature in the South, lecture tours, Bostonians and Southerners, plans for Russell's Magazine, secession, Bayard Taylor, Theodore Parker, W. G. Simms, E. B. Browning, Henry Timrod, T. B. Aldrich, J. R. Thompson, D. F. Jamison, and various other events and people, the latter often literary figures. During the war period his letters mention the attack on Charleston, the Federal blockade, possibility of recognition of the Confederate States of America by France and England, Northern and Southern military leaders, Negro uprisings, and Southern periodicals. From 1865 until his death, Hayne's letters cover a variety of subjects, although in general they deal with literary criticism, publishers, and authors, including practically every Southern writer of importance at the time, Northern writers, and English authors. There are also letters from many of these authors to Hayne with criticism of various literary works. Hayne's letters contain frequent uncomplimentary references to Walt Whitman and William Dean Howells, evidences of Hayne's friendship with John G. Whittier, references to Alfred, Lord Tennyson, A. T. Bledsoe, Charles Reade, Charles Dickens, Edgar Allen Poe, Henry Wadsworth Longfellow, and a host of others. Along political lines there is mention of the Freedmen's Bureau, greenback currency, Reconstruction, Negroes, "Yankeeisation" of the South, general political and economic conditions during the Reconstruction period, Southern indifference to literature, and letters of encouragement to younger writers. The correspondence furnishes a vast store of information on the activity of Southern literary figures, their poverty, the newspapers and periodicals of the North and South, and a growing affiliation between Southern writers and Northern publishers, especially in Hayne's case. Other topics include Eugene Lemoine Didier's life of Poe; the Southern Review; the John C. Calhoun Monument Association; Robert Y. Hayne; temperance; voting by Negro clergy in South Carolina Episcopal church conferences; and various Southern universities. There are also comments on trips to the North made by Hayne after 1865. Ten of Hayne's diaries, 1864-1885, consist largely of notations of letters received and answered; and four scrapbooks, and numerous clippings, often contain literary comment. Included also are many of Hayne's literary works, chiefly those already published.

Among the first papers of the collection are family letters from Hayne's father, also Paul Hamilton Hayne, an officer in the U.S. Navy, and letters concerning the early death of Hayne's father. During the same period there are letters to Robert Y. Hayne relative to family affairs, tariff, Nullification, the Palmetto Flag, John C. Calhoun, and the generally disturbed period of the early 1830s and 1850s. Included also are many letters from various literary figures to Mary Middleton (Michel) Hayne after the death of her husband, and likewise copies of her letters to literary figures, generally with reference to Hayne's career. Nineteen diaries and literary notebooks, and numerous clippings of Hayne's son, William Hamilton Hayne, include titles of and payments received for articles and poems of the son, comments on business relations with publishers, newspaper notices of his literary works, criticisms of readings and plays, numerous references to his father, domestic sidelights, and notes on life in Charleston, South Carolina. Two undated letters by Elizabeth Drew (Barstow) Stoddard (1823-1902) to William Winter discuss Hayne's cousin Jane McElheney, better known by her stage name, Ada Clare. There is correspondence, 1943-1944, 6 items, between Robert F. Metzdorf, curator of the R. B. Adam collection at the Rush Rhees Library at the University of Rochester, and Jay B. Hubbell and Nannie M. Tilley regarding a scrapbook of Hayne which Metzdorf had found in the Rhees Library.

Among the correspondents are the following: Henry Abbey, Oscar Fay Adams, Henry Mills Alden, Alfred Aldrich, Alfred Proctor Aldrich, Charles Aldrich, Willis Boyd Allen, Isaac W. Avery, John Kendrick Bangs, Waitman T. W. Barbe, Joseph Walker Barnwell, Charlotte F. Bates, Archibald John Battle, Charles Joseph Bayne, P. G. T. Beauregard, James Berry Bensel, Richard Doddridge Blackmore, Willis H. Bocock, Edward William Bok, G. H. Booker, Mary Louise Booth, Eugene Cunningham Branson, Herbert H. Brown, William Hand Browne, Edward Livermore Burlingame, Hezekiah Butterworth, George Henry Calvert, Esther Bernon Carpenter, Fred Hayden Carruth, Edward Ross Champlin, Essie B. Cheesborough, Kate Upson Clark, Richard H. Clark, Jennie Thornley Clarke, Charles Jones Colcock, Jr., Charles Washington Coleman, Jr., Thomas Stephens Collier, Wilkie Collins, John Esten Cooke, William Wilson Corcoran, John Blaisdell Corliss, Dinah Maria (Mulock) Craik, Forrest Crissey, Sumner Archibald Cunningham, Richard Henry Dana, Jefferson Davis, Charles Force Deems, Edward Denham, Eugene Lemoine Didier, Mary B. Dodge, Mary Elizabeth Mapes Dodge, Julia Caroline (Ripley) Dorr, John Thomas Duffield, Harry Stillwell Edwards, Hugo Erichsen, Clarence Fairfield, Edgar Fawcett, Frances Christine Fisher, Henry Lynden Flash, Henry Allen Ford, Thomas B. Ford, Frank Foxcroft, Daniel Frohman, Rose W. Fry, McDonald Furman, W. D. Gaillard, Charles Etienne Arthur Gayarré, Thomas R. Gibson, Jeannette Leonard Gilder, Basil Lanneau Gildersleeve, Lawrence Gilman, John Brown Gordon, William Thomas Hale, H. G. C. Hallock, Henry Elliott Harman, Joseph Wesley Harper, Jr., Julian LaRose Harris, Carter Henry Harrison, Jr., Caskie Harrison, James Albert Harrison, Julian Hawthorne, Mary M. M. Hayne, Robert Young Hayne, William Hamilton Hayne, Atticus G. Haywood, Thomas Wentworth Higginson, Maxwell Hill, Carl Holliday, Oliver Wendell Holmes, Hamilton Holt, James Barron Hope, Charles William Hubner, Alfred Huger, Gaillard Hunt, Benjamin Franklin Hutchinson, Andrew Jackson, Florence Barclay Jackson, Henry Rootes Jackson, John G. James, Theodore Dehon Jervey, Charles Colcock Jones, Jr., Elizabeth Jordan, Charles William Kent, Annie (Chambers) Bradford Ketchum, Edward Smith King, Norman Goree Kittrell, Richard Wilson Knott, Cornelius Kollock, Clifford Anderson Lanier, Henry Wysham Lanier, Sidney Lanier, Hugh Swinton Legaré, Ludwig Lewisohn, Andrew Adgate Lipscomb, Henry W. Longfellow, Daniel Lathrop, Newell Lovejoy, Hamilton Wright Mabie, Justin McCarthy, James Thompson McCleary, Annie (Russell) Marble, Donald Robert Perry Marquis, Wightman Fletcher Melton, Middleton Michel, Richard Fraser Michel, Edwin Mims, William Henry Milburn, Will Seymour Monroe, John Torrey Morse, Jr., Harrison Smith Morris, Montrose Jonas Moses, Charles Wells Moulton, John Albert Murphy, Margaret M. Osgood, Thomas Nelson Page, Walter Hines Page, Franklin Verzelius Newton Painter, Benjamin Morgan Palmer, Samuel Minturn Peck, John Herbert Phillips, John James Piatt, Joseph Daniel Pope, Francis Peyre Porcher, Thomas Edward Potterton, Harriet Waters Preston, Margaret (Junkin) Preston, Charles Todd Quintard, Marion Calhoun Legaré Reeves, Charles Francis Richardson, Annie Simms Roach, Edward Payson Roe, Charles Hunter Ross, Dante Gabriel Rossetti, Adelaide Louise Rouse, Francis S. Saltus, Clinton Scollard, Whitmarsh Benjamin Seabrook, John Conrad Seegers, Jr., J. F. Simmons, William Gilmore Simms, James Marion Sims, Orlando Jay Smith, M. A. Snowden, Yates Snowden, Henry Martin Soper, Caroline (Abbot) Stanley, Frank Lebby Stanton, Arthur Stedman, Edmund Clarence Stedman, Alexander H. Stephens, Frank Lincoln Stevens, Henry Jerome Stockard, Elizabeth Drew (Barstow) Stoddard, Richard Henry Stoddard, Frederick Abbott Stokes, Algernon Charles Swinburne, James Maurice Thompson, John Reuben Thompson, Waddy Thompson, Jr., Henry Timrod, Richard Handfield Titherington, William Peterfield Trent, Alexander Troy, Henry Clay Trumbull, Eleanor Tully, Richard Walton Tully, Hanford D. D. Twiggs, Moses Coit Tyler, James Albert Waldron, Anna Lydia Ward, William Haynes Ward, Charles Dudley Warner, Thomas Edward Watson, George Armstrong Wauchope, John Langdon Weber, William Lander Weber, Edwin Percy Whipple, Louise Clark Whitelock, John Greenleaf Whittier, Frances Elizabeth Caroline Willard, Walter Williams, Richard Hooker Wilmer, Gilbert Lord Wilson, James Ridout Winchester, Owen Wister, and Constance Fenimore Woolson.

The fifteen letters of Constance Fenimore Woolson have been published in Jay B. Hubbell, "Some New Letters of Constance Fenimore Woolson," <u>New England Quarterly</u>, XIV (1941), 715-735. See also Jay B. Hubbell (ed.), <u>The Last Years of Henry Timrod, 1864-1867: Including Letters of Timrod to Paul Hamilton Hayne and Letters about Timrod by William Gilmore Simms, John R. Thompson, John Greenleaf Whittier, and Others. With Four Uncollected Prose Pieces. Drawn Chiefly from the Paul Hamilton Hayne Collection in the Duke University Library</u> (Durham, N.C., 1941);

Charles R. Anderson, "Charles Gayarré and Paul Hayne: The Last Literary Cavaliers," in *American Studies in Honor of William Kenneth Boyd*, ed. David K. Jackson (Durham, N.C.: 1940); and O. M. McKeithan, ed., *Selected Letters: John Garland James to Paul Hamilton Hayne and Mary Middleton Hayne* (Austin, Texas: 1946). The Calvert letters have been published in part by Ida Gertrude Everson, *George Henry Calvert: American Literary Pioneer* (New York, 1944).

There are also microfilm copies of typed copies, 1868-1880, of Hayne's letters to Sidney Lanier (Johns Hopkins University); letters, 1859-1878, from Hayne to Bayard Taylor (Cornell University); letters, 1860-1880, from Hayne to Henry W. Longfellow and R. H. Dana; and Hayne's letters and manuscripts, 1869-1884 (Huntington Library).

2450. ROBERT YOUNG HAYNE PAPERS, 1822-1839. 4 items. Charleston, S.C.

Miscellaneous business and political letters to Hayne (1791-1839), attorney, U.S. senator, and South Carolina governor.

2451. WILLIAM HAMILTON HAYNE PAPERS, 1877-1917. 297 items and 20 vols. Augusta (Richmond County), Ga.

Papers of Hayne (1856-1929), American poet and author. Correspondence, 1894-1913, consists of business letters to Hayne; some discuss his father, Paul Hamilton Hayne. There are manuscripts, typescripts, printed copies, clippings, and sheet music of Hayne's poems and articles, and notes on the publication of his poems, biographical material, and other papers. Diaries, 1877-1878, describe social life and customs in Charleston. A literary ledger, 1882-1895, lists titles and publication information on Hayne's writings and payments received. There is also a notebook, 1877; literary notebooks, 1887-1916, which resemble diaries, and include copies of correspondence relating to the publication of Hayne's works with many references to leading literary figures; and two scrapbooks of clippings.

2452. FRANK W. HAYNES PAPERS, 1903-1907. 61 items. Hamptonville (Yadkin County), N.C.

Letters from clients to Haynes, an attorney.

2453. JOSEPH N. HAYNES PAPERS, 1862-1891. 53 items. Dover (Strafford County), N.H.

Civil War letters of a soldier in the 10th New Hampshire Regiment describing training and campaigns in Virginia and Maryland; hardships and bad food; the battle of Fredericksburg; Newport News, Norfolk, and Yorktown; refugee Negroes; picket duty; Bermuda Hundred; and Chafin's farm.

2454. BERTRAND E. HAYS LETTER BOOK, 1836-1839. 1 vol. [Pattonsburg (Botetourt County), Va.?]

A volume containing copies of personal letters and accounts of miscellaneous expenditures in business activities.

2455. JOHN WILLIS HAYS PAPERS, 1814-1901. 5,426 items. Oxford (Granville County), N.C.

Correspondence and legal papers of John W. Hays (1834-1901), a prominent Oxford lawyer, including many deeds which came into his hands through his law practice, and many letters from clients concerning details of business. Many notes, bonds, indentures, and accounts are also included.

2456. JAMES WOOD HAYWARD PAPERS, 1833-1886. 220 items. Boxborough (Middlesex County), Mass.

Business papers of Stetson & Avery, a shipping firm of New Orleans, concerning Boston clients, Griggs and Wilde, 1830s; papers concerning town meetings and elections kept by Hayward as town marshal, 1836; shipping accounts of milk of the Farmers' Butter and Cheese Co. of West Acton, Massachusetts, 1860s; and a family record kept by Hayward's son, Charles Sumner Hayward.

2457. FRANCIS HAYWOOD PAPERS, 1848-1899. 10 items. Edge Lane Hall, Lancashire, England.

Letters, 1848-1849, responding to Haywood's revised translation of Kant's *Critique of Pure Reason* (1848); writers include Augustus DeMorgan, George Henry Lewes, John Hulbert Glover, William Whewell, and William Kent, most of whom comment upon Kant and their own philosophical studies. Several miscellaneous items include a memoir by Haywood's daughter, Lucy Franklin, "People I have Known," published anonymously in the *Cornhill Magazine* (Sept., 1899).

2458. JOHN HAYWOOD AND EDMUND BURKE HAYWOOD PAPERS, 1800-1865. 24 items. Raleigh (Wake County), N.C.

The first part of the collection consists of letters regarding a shortage of state funds charged to John Haywood (1755-1827), treasurer of North Carolina, and the interest of Willis Alston in determining the shortage. The latter part of the collection is composed of official letters of Edmund Burke Haywood (1825-1894), son of John Haywood and Confederate surgeon and director of government hospitals in Raleigh, North Carolina, and gives much information on medical administration during the Civil War. Among the correspondents are E. Burke Haywood, George W. Haywood, John Haywood, Thomas Ruffin, and Edward Warren.

2459.  CLEMMENCE G. HAYWORTH PAPERS, 1867-1877. 4 items. Randolph County, N.C.

A letter, 1867, appointing Clemmence G. Hayworth an election official in Randolph County, North Carolina; letters from J. E. Hayworth in Hendrix County, Indiana, describing conditions there and remarking on the effect of the railroad strike of 1877; and a tax evaluation list for 1868.

2460.  LEIGHTON WILSON HAZLEHURST PAPERS, 1793-1885. 124 items. Bethel (Glynn County), Ga.

Personal letters of Jane E. Johnston to her niece, Mary Jane (McNish) Hazlehurst from Savannah and Bethel, Georgia, and "The Hermitage" plantation near Savannah. There is information on the Burroughs, Hazlehurst, and other families and their marriages. The letters mention politics, with references to Daniel Webster's visit to Savannah, 1847, and secession; real estate; church affairs; "Yamassee" plantation; diseases; slavery and a runaway; and social life and customs in Georgia.

2461.  FRANKLIN HARVEY HEAD PAPERS. 1 item. New York.

A typed copy of Head's pamphlet, Studies in Early American History: A Notable Lawsuit (Chicago: privately printed, [1898]), giving a fictional story about a lawsuit between Frederick Law Olmsted and members of the Astor family over Captain Kidd's fortune.

2462.  ISAAC BROOKS HEADEN PAPERS, 1848-1855. 1 vol. Chatham County, N.C.

Physician's account book containing information on a number of patients residing in Chatham County, medicine prescribed, medical treatment of slaves, and the estate of G. S. Fields, for which one of the Headens served as administrator.

2463.  AUGUSTUS HEALY AND JEANETTE (REID) HEALY PAPERS, 1920-1922. 151 items and 4 vols. Chicago, Ill.

Diaries kept by Jeannette (Reid) Healy describing their two and a half year honeymoon tour of Japan, Korea, China, the Philippines, Hong Kong, French Indo-China, Thailand, Singapore, India, and Africa, principally describing the tourist sights and places they visited. Included are 150 pictures and a clipping from their three-month safari in Kenya.

2464.  COLUMBUS HEARD PAPERS, 1855-1878. 18 items. Greensboro (Greene County), Ga.

Letters to Columbus Heard, jurist, concerning personal and legal matters, and the difficult years of Reconstruction.

2465.  LAFCADIO HEARN PAPERS, 1890. 1 item. New York.

Letter from Lafcadio Hearn (1850-1904), author, to Charles E. A. Gayarré (1805-1895), New Orleans historian, concerning the publication of Gayarré's "Southern Question."

2466.  HARTWELL P. HEATH PAPERS, 1820-1895. 42 items. Petersburg (Dinwiddie County), Va.

Letters dealing with business of the law firm of Heath and Mason at Petersburg; letters of Roscoe B. and J. H. Heath to their uncle, Francis E. Rives; bills and receipts; and an indenture of Francis E. Rives.

2467.  ROBERT R. HEATH PAPERS, 1816-1874. 1,061 items. Edenton (Chowan County), N.C.

Papers of Robert R. Heath, lawyer and jurist, comprise legal and business correspondence, bills, receipts, and other legal papers. Included is a letter from his daughter, Laura (Sister Angela) while a novitiate at St. Joseph's Seminary.

2468.  WILLIAM HEATH AND JOSEPH CURTIS PAPERS, 1725-1864. 18 items. Roxbury (Suffolk County), Mass.

Papers of William Heath, general in the Continental Army during the American Revolution, and of Joseph Curtis, large landowner in Roxbury, related by marriage. Heath papers include a record of water rights obtained by William Heath's father or grandfather, copy of a letter to Heath by George Washington discussing U.S. relations with France, copy of Heath's will, and items relating to property owned by Heath's daughter, Sarah (Heath) Gardner. Curtis papers are concerned mainly with the disposition of his estate, including two land indentures and his will.

2469.  BENJAMIN SHERWOOD HEDRICK PAPERS, 1848-1893. 6,033 items and 4 vols. Chapel Hill (Orange County), N.C., and Washington, D.C.

Personal, political, and official papers of Benjamin Sherwood Hedrick (1827-1886), professor of chemistry at the University of North Carolina, Chapel Hill, 1854-1856, and examiner in the Patent Office, Washington, D.C., 1861-1886. Early papers are concerned with personal matters, especially the courtship of his future wife, Mary Ellen Thompson, his work and colleagues at the Nautical Almanac Office, woman's rights, news of the social life in Chapel Hill and the faculty of the University of North Carolina, and his plans for a school of science at the university. Papers, 1856, include correspondence and faculty minutes pertaining to Hedrick's dismissal from the university for his outspoken views on slavery and his support of John C. Frémont. Subsequent letters concern speaking engagements and offers for jobs, tension between the North and the South, the commercial crisis of 1857, the Know-Nothings, Republican politics, antislavery, secessionists versus unionists in North Carolina, and military preparations, especially in the Washington, D.C. area. Civil War letters pertain to military engagements and activities, resistance to conscription, officers, refugees, Lincoln's policies and the government's stand on the issue of slavery, prisoners of war, the emigration of North Carolinians to Indiana, Negro troops in the Union Army, the assassination of Lincoln, and the surrender of Johnston. Postwar letters relate to North Carolina politics, Hedrick's efforts to get North Carolina back into the Union, the economic and social changes and hardships during Reconstruction, and affairs at the university. Topics discussed include the gubernatorial campaign between W. W. Holden and Jonathan Worth and the aftermath of Worth's election, poverty and destruction in North Carolina, the writing and ratification of a new state constitution, Negro suffrage, the 14th Amendment, the Test Oath, the confiscation of property, freedmen and the Freedmen's Bureau, education for Negroes, the proposed Black Code, repudiation of the state debt, the Heroes of America, the Ku Klux Klan, the occupation of North Carolina by Federal troops, the celebration of the 4th of July, problems between the Internal Revenue Service and distilleries, delegates to the National Union Convention in Philadelphia, 1866, conditions at the university, and financial matters including investments in bonds and gold, and greenbacks. The patent papers, relating to Hedrick's various positions in the Division of Chemistry and Metallurgy of the Patent Office, consist of correspondence pertaining to inventions, reports on disputed patent cases, decisions on applications, summonses to and testimony in federal court hearings on patent cases, patent drawings, and statements of patent claims by inventors. Printed materials include advertisements, commencement announcements and other items related to educational institutions, broadsides concerning ante-bellum matters, Reconstruction pamphlets, items pertaining to various clubs and organizations, clippings concerning politics, and other items. Bills and receipts cover four decades of business transactions, beginning with Hedrick's college days. There are also drafts of political speeches and newspaper articles, school papers, and genealogical items. The volumes consist of three memorandum books and a daybook.

2470. CHARLES A. HEDRICK PAPERS, 1877-1885. 48 items. Macksville (Pendleton County), W. Va.

Papers of Charles A. Hedrick consist of personal and business letters and postcards, bills and receipts, and mercantile accounts.

2471. SIR ARTHUR HELPS PAPERS, ca. 1853-1874. 61 items. London, England.

Letters to Sir Arthur Helps (1813-1875), clerk of the Privy Council and author, from James Anthony Froude (1818-1894), historian and author, discussing Sir Arthur's works, his own literary efforts, his editorship of Fraser's Magazine, 1860-1874, and British politics, including foreign policy, British leaders, Ireland, and British colonial policy; and letters from politicians, authors, and ministers on similar topics. Correspondents include Sir Edwin Arnold, John Thadeus Delane, Frederic Harrison, Sir Arthur Helps, Benjamin Jowett, Leopold George Duncan Albert, the Duke of Albany, Robert Lowe, Sir Theodore Martin, John Frederick Denison Maurice, Sir John Everett Millais, Richard Monckton Milnes, Sir Henry Frederick Ponsonby, Henry Reeve, Lord John Russell, Odo Russell, Samuel Smiles, Herbert Spencer, Lord Stanley, Sir Henry Taylor, Tom Taylor, Martin Farquhar Tupper, and Victoria, Crown Princess of Prussia.

2472. SOLOMON HELSABECK PAPERS, 1899-1970. 3 items. King (Stokes County), N.C.

Circular letter advertising Trinity Park High School, Durham, North Carolina; a form for names of prospective students; and a letter of gift stating the origin of these papers.

2473. HEMPHILL FAMILY PAPERS, 1784 (1831-1929) 1958. 12,150 items and 28 vols. Due West (Abbeville County) and Charleston, S.C.

Papers of Reverend John Hemphill (1761-1832), minister in the Associate Reformed Presbyterian Church; of James Calvin Hemphill (1850-1927), journalist; of Robert Reid Hemphill (1840-1908), editor and state senator; and of other members of the Hemphill family. Early letters and sermons relate to the Associate Reformed Presbyterian Church in South Carolina. Other important matters include slavery, African Colonization Society, missionaries to Liberia, temperance, politics, affairs at South Carolina College, Columbia, the activities in Texas of John Hemphill (son of Reverend John Hemphill), the Civil War, war activities of women, the South Carolina constitutional convention, the bankruptcy of South Carolina, the Ku Klux Klan, and freedmen as laborers. The bulk of the papers from the 1870s on are of James Calvin Hemphill. Topics of concern include South Carolina politics, various presidential campaigns, Benjamin Tillman and Cole Blease, the publishing activities of James Calvin Hemphill, the colonization of Negroes in Africa, the murder of Francis W. Dawson I, editor of the Charleston (South Carolina) News and Courier, the Woman's Christian Temperance Union, the Silver Question, the Charleston earthquake of 1886, woman suffrage proposal of 1892, railroads, the South Carolina Inter-State and West Indian Exposition, William McKinley and imperialism, the establishment of a school of journalism at Columbia University, race relations in the Mississippi delta, 1905, the experience of William L. Hemphill as an engineer in the tin mines of Bolivia, "yellow journalism," World War I, the League to Enforce Peace, and prominent political and journalistic figures of the time. Volumes of James Calvin Hemphill consist of daybooks, 1880-1897; letter books, 1894-1903; and scrapbooks, 1887-1916, of newspaper clippings. For Robert Reid Hemphill there are a commonplace book; a daybook, 1876-1882; a legal case book, 1866-1880; a scrapbook, 1873-1892; and a teacher's record.

2474. A. C. HENDERSON ACCOUNT BOOKS, 1856-1868. 6 vols. Yanceyville (Caswell County), N.C.

Cashier's and teller's account books of the Bank of Yanceyville.

2475. ARCHIBALD ERSKINE HENDERSON PAPERS, 1841-1917. 221 items. Williamsboro (Granville County), N.C.

Family and Civil War correspondence of Archibald E. Henderson (b. 1843) on life in the Confederate Army and conditions in the South during Reconstruction. Included is an account of the Kick and Stephens affairs in Caswell County, North Carolina.

2476. DAVID HENRY HENDERSON PAPERS, 1951. 5 items. Charlotte (Mecklenburg County), N.C.

Papers of David Henry Henderson (b. 1914), lawyer and state legislator, dealing with the redistricting of the state senatorial districts and reapportioning the state House of Representatives. Included are the report of the House committee of which Henderson was vice-chairman, and maps of the current and recommended districts.

2477. JOHN HENDERSON PAPERS, 1791. 1 item. Pacolet (Spartanburg County), S.C.

Letter from Henry Bailey to John Henderson describing the recent visit of George Washington to Charleston, South Carolina.

2478. MARY HENDERSON PAPERS, 1851. 1 item. Hedgesville (Berkeley County), W. Va.

Personal letter of Alexander Dunkin to his sister, Mrs. Mary Henderson.

2479. SAMUEL HENDERSON PAPERS, 1864. 1 item. New York.

Copy of a diary of a Union soldier while a prisoner at Andersonville, Georgia, and Florence, South Carolina, in which he comments on living conditions, food rations, attempted escapes, and fellow prisoners, including men from the 14th Regiment of New York Heavy Artillery.

2480. W. F. HENDERSON PAPERS, 1865. 9 items. Charlotte (Mecklenburg County), N.C.

Letters and documents concerning an equity case involving the purchase of cotton, submitted to the military authorities because of the lack of adequate civilian facilities.

2481. WILLIAM F. HENDERSON NOTEBOOKS, 1860-1884. 2 vols. Chapel Hill (Orange County), N.C.

Medical notebooks, one of which was written over a daybook.

2482. EUGENE RUSSELL HENDRIX PAPERS, 1764-1914. 164 items. Kansas City (Jackson County), Mo.

Papers of Eugene Russell Hendrix (1847-1927), bishop of the Methodist Episcopal Church, South, and antiquarian, are comprised of letters from presidents of the British Wesleyan Conference, from Methodist bishops in America, including both the Northern and Southern branches after 1845, from other notable Methodists, and from other prominent figures. The letters concern Methodism in America, prominent Methodists, the split of the church over the issue of slavery, ministry to Negroes, relations between Northern and Southern Methodists, and episcopal and routine matters.

2483. GEORGE W. HENDRIX PAPERS, 1808 (1826-1885) 1910. 74 items. Elkville (Wilkes County), N.C.

Papers of George W. Hendrix, justice of the peace and landowner, concerning the conveyance of properties in Wilkes County and his duties as justice of the peace; of James Kelley Hendrix, surveyor, pertaining to the surveying of land whose ownership was disputed; and of William B. Hendrix, Confederate soldier, describing camp life. Also included are several lists of taxables in Wilkes County.

2484. CHARLES HENDRY ACCOUNT BOOK, 1856-1866. 1 vol. (22 pp.) Westminister (Carroll County), Md.

Account book of Charles Hendry. Several pages are covered over with clippings of household hints.

2485. HENKEL FAMILY PAPERS, 1812-1953. 165 items. New Market (Shenandoah County), Va.

Papers of members of the Henkel family, most of whom were Lutheran ministers, are comprised of notes for sermons, articles, and lectures; account books; several Civil War letters; materials concerning the Lutheran

Publishing House in New Market operated by Solomon Henkel (1777-1847) and Ambrose Henkel (1786-1870), including correspondence, orders for printed goods and advertising space, bills and receipts, and pamphlets on book reviews; and family letters from relatives in North Carolina and Tennessee. The majority of the notes and account books are in German.

2486. DAVID HENLEY PAPERS, 1791-1800. 50 items. Washington, D.C., and Tennessee.

Correspondence and papers of David Henley (1748-1823), officer in the Revolutionary Army, commissioner of Indian affairs in Tennessee, and clerk in the War Department, dealing with treaties, agreements, and relations between the whites and the Choctaw and Creek Indians, including the exchange of prisoners, reparations for murders, inroads by whites and Indians, and compensation for stolen horses; establishment of post roads from Tennessee to the South Carolina border and to Natchez, Mississippi; establishment of a trading post at Muscle Shoals, Alabama; and establishment of the Indian Treaty Line from the Kentucky Trace to the Gaps of the Cumberland and along Campbell's line to the Clinch River, and the difficulties of the commissioners in deciding on this line. Among the correspondents are William Blount, Benjamin Hawkins, David Henley, William McCleish, James McHenry, Samuel Mitchell, and James Robertson.

2487. FRANCIS W. HENRY PAPERS, 1867-1868. 3 items. Byhalia (Marshall County), Miss.

Letters from Francis W. Henry, collector for B. E. Wofford and J. Frank Wofford, concerning the collection of private debts during Reconstruction.

2488. GUSTAVUS ADOLPHUS HENRY, JR., PAPERS, 1861-1865. 3 items. Clarksville (Montgomery County), Tenn.

Confederate military dispatches of Gustavus A. Henry, assistant adjutant general, commenting on troop movements and the conditions of roads in South Carolina in 1865.

2489. ISAAC HENRY PAPERS, 1794 (1811-1828) 1841. 59 items. Centerville (Prince William County), Va.

Family, professional, and business correspondence of Isaac Henry as U.S. Navy surgeon and later as a Virginia planter. Included is a letter, 1814, from his father, Hugh Henry, describing the fortifications around Philadelphia.

2490. J. L. HENRY PAPERS, 1862-1864. 4 items. Virginia.

Civil War letters of a Confederate soldier discussing personal affairs, various Union and Confederate generals and units, Union prisoners, Confederate and Union casualties, desertions, and troop movements and engagements, including campaigns in Maryland and Pennsylvania, the sieges of Vicksburg and Richmond, and the battle of Cedar Run, 1862.

2491. JACOB HENRY PAPERS, 1806-1839. 6 items and 1 vol. Carteret County, N.C., and Charleston, S.C.

Papers of Jacob Henry, merchant and member of the North Carolina legislature and later a Charleston merchant, include a notice of his candidacy to the North Carolina legislature, a personal letter, and a pamphlet of miscellaneous information. The volume is a daybook and memorandum book, and contains testimony on his losses in a fire, 1838.

2492. JAMES VERNOR HENRY PAPERS, 1833-1834. 2 items. Lancaster (Lancaster County), Pa.

Records of the contested will of Benjamin Vernor, of which James V. Henry was the beneficiary.

2493. JEREMIAH HENRY AND BYRON V. HENRY PAPERS, 1832-1912. 154 items and 2 vols. Lilesville (Anson County) and Wake Forest (Wake County), N.C.

Personal, family, and business correspondence of Jeremiah Henry, farmer and school commissioner, and of Byron V. Henry, a younger member of the family, while a student at Wake Forest College. Letters centering around the elder Henry relate to farming and obtaining teachers for the local school. Included are two letters, 1833-1834, from his brother, Isom, giving accounts of farm life in Greene County, Alabama, and similar letters from friends recently settled in Tennessee, Louisiana, and other parts of Alabama. There are several Civil War letters, including a discussion of the siege of Petersburg. Letters, 1873-1874, are to Byron V. Henry while a student at Wake Forest College, and a letter, 1878, describes the buildings and student organizations at the college. There are letters, 1882-1885, from members of the Carrol family, parents of Jeremiah Henry's wife, from Thomasville, Georgia; letters, 1880s and 1890s, from cousins describing their social life; and letters of T. B. Henry containing references to the Grange and the temperance movement. Several papers pertain to the Valley Mutual Life Association of Virginia. Legal papers include land deeds and estates papers. A printed item deals with the Denver (North Carolina) Seminary. The volumes are ledgers.

2494. JOSEPH HENRY PAPERS, 1837-1874. 10 items. Washington, D.C.

Miscellaneous papers of Joseph Henry (1797-1878), first director of the Smithsonian Institution, including several letters pertaining to the administration of the Smithsonian.

2495.   PATRICK HENRY PAPERS, 1777-1897.
        11 items.  Hanover County, Va.

        Papers of Patrick Henry (1736-1799), Virginia statesman, include commissions; land grants; a letter from David Mason discussing the progress of his march to South Carolina and the men and supplies under his command; a circular letter to the members of the court of Pittsylvania County, Virginia, concerning the administration of taxes and pensions in Virginia; a printed letter from Henry listing the duties of a lieutenant in raising and provisioning his troops; a clipping comparing Henry and Thomas Jefferson; and a clipping, 1897, describing Henry's burial place and relics of Henry that were owned by his grandson, William Wirt Henry.

2496.   PATRICK HENRY PAPERS,
        1925-1929.  4 items.
        Brandon (Rankin County), Miss.

        Personal letters to Patrick Henry (1843-1930) from Alfred E. Smith, John Sharp Williams, and H. D. Whitfield containing scattered comments on the activities of the Democratic Party.

2497.   ROBERT R. HENRY PAPERS,
        1822-1847.  71 items.
        Savannah, Ga.

        Correspondence of Robert R. Henry, merchant, concerning irregularities in the revenue service as administered by the collector of the port of St. Mary's, Georgia, and Henry's desire for the position; accusations against Martin Van Buren, New York Governor Enos Throop, and Inspector General of Potash and Pearlashes George Seamen for political favoritism and fraud; needed changes in inspection laws; and the estate of Benjamin Vernor of Lancaster, Pennsylvania, including much biographical and genealogical material.

2498.   [SAMUEL HENRY AND THOMAS M. DARNALL?] LEDGER, 1817-1819.  1 vol. (214 pp.)
        Harrisonburg (Rockingham County), Va.

        Mercantile accounts.

2499.   HENRY CLAY SOCIETY RECORD BOOK,
        1845-1847.  1 vol. (131 pp.)
        Staunton (Augusta County), Va.

        Constitution, by-laws, and minutes of the Henry Clay Society.

2500.   CHARLES HENSHAW PAPERS,
        1861-1862.  14 items.  Buffalo (Erie County), N.Y.

        Letters from a captain in the 100th Regiment of New York Volunteer Infantry, stationed at Camp Morgan and near Yorktown, Virginia, to his mother and sisters describing army life.

2501.   SILAS HENTON MANUSCRIPT,
        1812.  1 vol.

        Arithmetic problems and answers.

2502.   JOHN HERBERT AND FRANCIS C. HERBERT PAPERS, 1832-1833.
        9 items.  Richmond, Va.

        Letters of the Herbert family concerning efforts to collect from the federal government the claims of their father, Thomas Herbert, Revolutionary naval captain, for half pay for life.

2503.   EDWARD THOMAS HERIOT PAPERS,
        1852-1854.  3 items.
        Georgetown (Georgetown County), S.C.

        Letters of Edward Thomas Heriot, a large planter and slaveowner, describing his trip to Great Britain, his voyage across the Atlantic to New York, his railroad trip to South Carolina, personal affairs, and his various estates and slaves.  Also included is a defense of slavery and a criticism of abolition, Harriet Beecher Stowe, and Fredrika Bremer.

2504.   JOHN HERR PAPERS, 1862-1867.
        72 items.  Donnelsville (Clark County), Ohio.

        Letters of John Herr, a corporal in the 94th Regiment, Ohio Volunteer Infantry, describing troop movements across Georgia mountains in 1863, commodity prices, Confederate evacuation of breastworks at Resaca (Georgia), voting for Abraham Lincoln for president, the desire to devastate South Carolina in retaliation for having initiated hostilities, the burning of Atlanta, and the march from Savannah, Georgia, to Fayetteville, North Carolina.  Herr criticized his "treasonous" family for showing sympathy for the Confederacy.  Also included are references to financial affairs in Ohio.

2505.   HERTZLER FAMILY PAPERS, 1820 (1880-1910) 1920.  ca. 600 items.  Lancaster County, Pa.

        Family and business papers of John, Jacob, and Edward Hertzler, merchants in the wholesale grain and flour business, including correspondence, shipping invoices, and orders from grain, dairy feed, sacking, grinding machinery and flour companies.  The firm was John Hertzler & Sons, 1860-1900.

2506.   WILLIAM HETH PAPERS, 1795-1799.
        15 items.  Bermuda Hundred (Charles City County), Va.

        Papers of William Heth (1735-1808), collector for Bermuda Hundred, Virginia, including circulars issued to collectors, instructions regarding sea letters and passports, regulations for arming merchant vessels, comments on recapture of American vessels from the French and strained relations with France, and a list of vessels registered and licensed in 1797.

2507. H. HETSLER PAPERS, 1861. 2 items. Germantown (Montgomery County), Ohio.

Letters of an Ohio soldier describing hardships of army life.

2508. JOSEPH HEWES PAPERS, 1779. 1 item. Lazy Hill, N.C.

Letter from John Campbell to Joseph Hewes (1730-1779), merchant and delegate to the Continental Congress, describing the public attitude in North Carolina, general distress and inflation, coinage weights and values, and the need for a mint.

2509. FAYETTE HEWITT PAPERS, 1894. 2 items. Frankfort (Franklin County), Ky.

A letter of Fayette Hewitt (1831-1909), Confederate Army officer, to Thomas D. Osborne concerning the return of bodies of soldiers killed in various battles, including Chickamauga; and a picture and biographical sketch of Hewitt.

2510. RICHARD NEWTON HEWITT PAPERS, 1836 (1861) 1873. 84 items. "Otter Oaks," Campbell County, Va.

Principally the Civil War correspondence of Richard Newton Hewitt, a Confederate Army physician, containing comments on personal affairs, the difficulties of army life, prices of salt and supplies, the first battle of Manassas, the blockade of Southern ports, prisoners, picket duty, troop movements, food, clothing, sickness, hospitals, a measles epidemic, music, and various Confederate and Union officers and leaders. Other personal correspondence refers to commodity prices, slaves, religion, weather and crops, the settlement of estates, the University of Virginia and its students and social life, and railroads.

2511. JOHN C. HEYER AND COMPANY DAYBOOK, 1858-1860. 1 vol. (452 pp.) Wilmington (New Hanover County), N.C.

Daybook of the general mercantile business of John C. Heyer and William A. Heyer. Included are a few irregular accounts, 1860-1861 and 1867.

2512. T. D. HEYWARD PAPERS, 1886-1888. 3 items. South Island (Georgetown County), S.C.

Two letters from Selma Heyward to her husband, T. D. Heyward, in Savannah, Georgia, describing earthquakes in South Carolina; and a special order issued by the Savannah Volunteer Guards ordering the holding of elections.

2513. ALMA [HIBBARD?] JOURNAL, 1854-1855. 1 vol. (120 pp.) "Mountain View" (Clarke County), Va.

Journal of a Northern teacher who lived and worked in the home of Bishop William Meade in western Virginia. The journal contains comments on the Meade household; social life, customs, pecularities of speech in the area; and slavery.

2514. ANDREW HICKENLOOPER, JR., PAPERS, 1885. 2 items. Cincinnati, Ohio.

Letter, 1885, to Andrew Hickenlooper, Jr., from Schuyler Hamilton concerning the Society of the Army of the Tennessee.

2515. JOHN JOSEPH HICKEY MEMORANDUM BOOK, 1837-1876. 1 vol. (259 pp.) Jefferson County, W. Va., and Perryville (Perry County), Mo.

Memorandum book of John Joseph Hickey, an attorney in Jefferson County, Virginia, and Perryville, Missouri, containing notes on local people and events; legal activities at various courts; and a political meeting of followers of Martin Van Buren in Jefferson County, 1839. The volume also contains merchant's accounts from the 1870s; a letter book; docket books; and miscellanea from Virginia and Missouri.

2516. PAUL ROBINSON HICKOK PAPERS, 1925. 1 item. Binghamton (Broome County), N.Y.

Letter from Walter Lowrie Fisher to Paul Robinson Hickok discussing the character of President William Howard Taft.

2517. EDWARD BRODNAX HICKS AND DAVID S. HICKS PAPERS, 1800 (1836-1894) 1913. 3,503 items and 13 vols. Lawrenceville (Brunswick County), Va.

Business, personal, and legal correspondence of Edward B. Hicks (d. 1858), lawyer and planter, and of his son, David S. Hicks, lawyer, planter, and land agent. Papers of Edward B. Hicks include jockey club dues, records connected with his duties as sheriff in 1821 and possibly later, and with Hicks' position as superintendent of schools in Brunswick County in 1847. Included also is an extensive series of letters and papers relating to the operation, in partnership with John W. Paup, of a plantation at Red River, Arkansas, in 1837 and later. Letters also show that Hicks engaged in the business of selling slaves at New Orleans, Louisiana, during 1852. Other interesting letters are from Lewis Taylor on the War of 1812 and another, in 1817, relative to disturbances at Princeton College, Princeton, New Jersey, caused by refusal of professors to accept state bank notes.

Centering around David S. Hicks after

1858, the papers are largely legal documents, notes, and correspondence concerned with his law practice and the administration of the estate of Edward R. Hicks. The most continuous series among these legal papers is a set of letters from Leigh R. Page, a Richmond attorney. Papers also pertain to the efforts of Hicks and one Turnbull to sell lands in Brunswick County to Northerners. Included also are records of Hicks's activities as judge of Brunswick County, as dealer in Texas lands, and as an organizer of the Atlantic and Danville Railroad. One letter, June 30, 1866, from D. J. Claiborne, Jr., concerns Southern Negro congressmen. Fifteen letters from General Thomas Ewing are concerned with the Atlantic and Danville Railroad. The volumes, generally mercantile records, evidently came into the collection as a result of Hicks's legal practice and duties as sheriff.

2518. THOMAS HICKS PAPERS, 1859. 1 item. Trenton Falls (Oneida County), N.Y.

Letter to Thomas Hicks from G. W. Van Derlip concerning possible revisions to a portrait which Hicks had completed.

2519. HICKS, JONES & MALLORY PAPERS, 1864-1866. 37 items. Lawrenceville (Brunswick County), Va.

Business papers, bills, and receipts of the Hicks, Jones, and Mallory Shoe Shop.

2520. JOSEPH HIERHOLZER LETTER BOOK, 1859-1863. 1 vol. (240 pp.) Richmond, Va.

A merchant's letterpress copybook concerning the prices of hides, transportation facilities, and the Civil War.

2521. HENRY MUHLENBERG HIESTER AND MARCIA C. M. HIESTER PAPERS, 1830 (1872-1919) 1928. 3,946 items and 32 vols. "Millmont," Mercersburg (Franklin County), Pa.

Letters and papers of Henry Muhlenberg Hiester and Maria C. M. Hiester for the most part concerned with personal matters and routine family business. The collection contains invitations, calling cards, copies of fire insurance policies, printed matter concerning the Western North Carolina Mining and Improvement Company and the Marconi Wireless Telegraph Company of America, copies of wills, and financial papers such as bills and receipts. The correspondence includes a series of personal and family letters of Joseph M. Hiester and letters to Maria Hiester from H. W. Freedley concerning his service in the 3rd United States Regiment in the Civil War. Volumes are memorandum books of Henry Muhlenberg Hiester and Maria C. M. Hiester, one of which contains genealogical information on the Hiester family; notes of a student at Princeton University on lectures in mathematics and psychology, 1872, law, 1874-1876, and a music notebook, ca. 1821; a journal of a European tour, 1855; and a number of account books and daybooks mainly 1830-1870, containing records for Millmont Mills, Millmont Farm, Montgomery Mills, Hiester and Hain, and Hiester and Shippen, millers.

2522. THOMAS WENTWORTH HIGGINSON PAPERS, 1868-1906. 59 items. Cambridge (Middlesex County), Mass.

Miscellaneous correspondence of Thomas Wentworth Higginson on literary and personal matters. The collection includes "The Nonsense of It. Short Answers to Common Objections against Woman Suffrage," by Higginson.

2523. SILAS HIGHBY PAPERS, 1855. 2 items. Oneida County, N.Y.

Letters from Orra Garvin to Silas Highby and his wife dealing with personal and family matters.

2524. WILLIAM A. HIGHTOWER PAPERS, 1849-1864. 26 items. Halifax County, Va.

Letters of William A. Hightower while a student at Randolph-Macon College, Boydton, Virginia, 1859-1860, and while a Confederate soldier. Most of the letters concern his college life; his Civil War letters concern various skirmishes under Stonewall Jackson's command.

2525. KARL EMIL HILDEBRAND PAPERS, 1936. 1 vol. Stockholm, Sweden.

A typed copy, in German, of Afrika, kolonimakter och infödda folk (Africa, Colonial Powers and Native Peoples) published in 1936 and written by Karl Emil Hildebrand.

2526. ADAMS SHERMAN HILL PAPERS, 1859-1864. 75 items. Cambridge (Middlesex County), Mass.

Letters of Adams Sherman Hill concerned primarily with his work as a reporter for the New York Tribune and, after 1863, with the Chicago Daily Tribune. The collection contains material relating to his job in the home office of the Tribune and letters pertaining to his experience as a Washington correspondent for the newspaper during the Civil War. The letters include instructions from Charles Anderson Dana and Sydney Howard Gay of the Tribune staff in New York to Hill in Washington; letters to Hill from his sources in the government and military; correspondence with Whitelaw Reid of the Cincinnati Gazette concerning Hill's supply of articles for that paper; and letters from Joseph Medill, Horace White, and Henry Villard discussing Hill's articles for the Chicago Daily Tribune.

2527.  AMBROSE POWELL HILL PAPERS,
       1856, 1862.  1 item.
       Washington, D.C.

Letter, 1856, from Ambrose Powell Hill, later a general in the Confederate Army, to Carrie Redfield discussing personal matters and comments, 1862, written on the letter by Redfield.

2528.  BENJAMIN HILL ACCOUNT BOOK,
       1773-1802.  1 vol.
       [Granville County, N.C.]

Accounts of Benjamin Hill (d. 1802), a planter, who raised corn and tobacco and bred horses. Included is a list of dates of birth of Hill's children.

2529.  DANIEL HARVEY HILL PAPERS,
       1860-1889.  14 items.
       Charlotte (Mecklenburg County), N.C.

Miscellaneous letters and papers of Daniel Harvey Hill including scattered items pertaining to his service in the Confederate Army; a letter to C. C. Jones, Jr., concerning their love for the Confederacy; and material relating to Hill's work as editor of The Land We Love.

2530.  DANIEL S. HILL PAPERS, 1796-1891.
       243 items and 2 vols.
       Louisburg (Franklin County), N.C.

Family and political correspondence of Daniel S. Hill, a leader in organizing the Friends of Temperance, concerning the Whig party, secession, the Civil War, Reconstruction, temperance, cotton sales, and the United States Patent Office; and letters from friends and relatives attending Jefferson Medical College, Philadelphia, and Louisburg Academy. The collection also contains legal and financial papers relating to Hill and two account books.

2531.  FRANCIS H. HILL PAPERS,
       1860, 1861.  2 items.  Madison
       (Madison County), Va.

Letter, 1860, to Francis H. Hill from William Green discussing legal affairs; and a letter, 1861, by Hill concerning legal affairs, local and national politics, and secession.

2532.  HIRAM HILL AND OTIS G. HILL
       PAPERS, 1831-1937.  800 items.
       Williamsburg (Hampshire County), Mass.

Letters of the brothers, Hiram Hill and Otis G. Hill, concern the management of their dairy farms; their joint investments in midwestern real estate, eastern banks, and midwestern railroads; and Otis G. Hill's service in the Massachusetts state legislature, 1857. Correspondence of the children of Otis G. Hill include letters from students at Wilbraham Academy and schools in New Haven, Connecticut. The collection also contains legal papers including deeds, wills, contracts, and a document relative to a suit for divorce; and printed matter, including an official program of the International Congress of Freethinkers, 1893, and a series of letters written by an unidentified traveler in Japan, 1887.

2533.  J. A. HILL PAPERS, 1865-1880.
       13 items.  Albany (Dougherty County), Ga.

Letters pertaining to the Macon and Western Railroad.

2534.  J. D. HILL PAPERS, 1862.
       2 items.  Virginia.

Letters from J. D. Hill, a Confederate soldier, to his brother, William, describing financial matters and army life around Richmond and Centreville in 1862.

2535.  JAMES HILL COMMONPLACE BOOK,
       1804.  1 vol.  Franklin County, Ga.

Commonplace book of James Hill, a minister, probably Methodist, containing Biblical quotations and original poetry of Hill.

2536.  JAMES DAVIDSON HILL PAPERS,
       1861-1864.  15 items.  Alabama, Georgia, Mississippi, and Louisiana.

Miscellaneous letters and papers relating to James Davidson Hill's service as an officer in the Confederate Army. The collection includes orders, reports on supplies and enemy troop movements, letters recommending Hill for promotion, and a letter, 1864, from a Louisiana planter to Admiral David Dixon Porter of the United States Navy seeking compensation for goods confiscated by Federal soldiers.

2537.  JOEL EDGAR HILL PAPERS, 1872
       (1889-1903) 1910.  267 items.
       Stokes County, N.C.

Family and personal correspondence of Joel Edgar Hill, mail clerk and schoolteacher, generally from his father, brothers, sisters, and women friends. Most interesting are the letters of Hill's father during 1877 while Joel Hill lived in Washington, D.C., suggesting that he see Z. B. Vance or Matt W. Ransom about a government position. Included also are many letters of Jesse Walling, of Washington, with comments on Julia Marlowe and Joseph Jefferson. The letters of Hill's brother, W. Lee Hill, reflect the career of the latter in medical school in Baltimore, Maryland, and as a physician in Cranberry, Lexington, and Stokes County, all in North Carolina.

2538. JOSEPH B. HILL PAPERS,
1812-1872. 3 items.
Muscogee County, Ga.

A letter and two legal papers.

2539. N. HILL PAPERS, 1862-1863.
3 items. York County, S.C.

Personal letters from N. Hill, Confederate soldier, to his wife; and a letter from Fannie Nicholson, a student at Greensboro Female College, Greensboro, North Carolina.

2540. NATHAN H. HILL PAPERS,
1865-1867. 31 items.
Lincolnton (Lincoln County), N.C.

Letters mainly to Nathan H. Hill concerning his work teaching freedmen in Lincolnton, North Carolina, including letters from Albion W. Tourgée.

2541. RICHARD HILL LETTER BOOK,
1743. 1 vol. (89 pp.)
Charleston, S.C.

Letter book of Richard Hill, a Charleston, South Carolina, merchant, kept on a trip to England. Correspondence is with English merchants, ship's captains, bankers, and others connected with the South Carolina trade; concerning the colony of Georgia, the West Indian trade, commodity prices in English markets, and reports of the discovery of a silver mine in the Cherokee country 300 miles from Charleston.

2542. ROWLAND HILL PAPERS,
1824-1827. 1 item.
London, England.

A manuscript entitled "Purchasing the Freedom of and Giving a Christian Education to Negro Slave Children," written by Samuel Starbuck in 1824 and sent by him to Rowland Hill in 1827.

2543. WILLIAM HILL PAPERS, 1859, 1865.
2 items. Abbeville (Abbeville County), S.C.

Photocopies of letters of William Hill of Abbeville, South Carolina, to his brother, David Hill, in Ireland, describing the typical Irish-American, a projected tour of Ireland by his son, and conditions in Abbeville, 1865.

2544. WILMER W. HILL PAPERS, 1854-1929.
72 items. Johnson, Vt., and Minneapolis, Minn.

Letters, broadsides, clippings, receipts, and a report card of a teacher who taught at Bell Institute, Underhill Flats, Vermont, and in Minneapolis, Minnesota.

2545. HENRY WASHINGTON HILLIARD PAPERS,
1843-1886. 5 items. Atlanta, Ga.

Miscellaneous correspondence of Henry Washington Hilliard, U.S. representative from Alabama, Confederate general, and attorney, including a letter, 1860, to Harper and Brothers expressing optimism about Alabama's chances of remaining in the Union; a letter, 1868, to Chief Justice Salmon P. Chase referring to hearings on the proposed trial of Jefferson Davis and mentioning the visit of Kate (Chase) Sprague and Governor William Sprague of Rhode Island to Augusta, Georgia; and responses to autograph collectors.

2546. JOSEPH HILLIARD ACCOUNT BOOK,
1827-1832. 1 vol.

Daybook of a general merchant.

2547. PAUL HERMAN HILLIARD PAPERS,
1862-1910. 54 items. Stonington (New London County), Conn.

Letters of Paul Herman Hilliard, a soldier in the 21st Connecticut Regiment, describing army life and commenting on fighting in Virginia, 1862, and execution of a deserter, 1864. Later material concerns Hilliard's work in the adjutant general's office in Hartford, Connecticut; his job as postmaster in Westerly, Rhode Island; and his attempts to get an army pension.

2548. SARAH CATHERINE HIMES PAPERS,
1867 (1871-1890). 16 items.
Russell County, Ala.

Personal letters of Sarah Catherine Himes to her uncle in Waynesville, North Carolina, containing a few references to crops, prices, Reconstruction, politics, and labor conditions.

2549. OSCAR B. HINCKLEY DIARY,
1863-1865. 3 vols.
New York, N.Y.

Diary of Oscar B. Hinckley, a Federal soldier, consisting chiefly of observations on the weather but mentioning a trip to New Bern, North Carolina, Camp Currituck Canal, and daily army activities.

2550. RAYMOND W. HINES TIME BOOKS,
1910-1911. 3 vols. Richmond, Va.

Construction work-time books of a Richmond contractor.

2551. WILLIAM HINES PAPERS,
1781-1836. 7 items. Virginia.

Letters to William and Samuel B. Hines, pertaining to privateering, relations of the United States with England, the embargo, New England's opposition to the War of 1812, and the election of 1836. Among the correspondents are Richard Blow, Thomas Gholson, Edwin Gray, John Hamilton, and John Young Mason.

2552. JOHN B. HINKSON PAPERS, 1856-1905. 210 items. Delaware County, Pa.

Letters and papers of John B. Hinkson contain letters from his parents while he was a student at LaFayette College, Easton, Pennsylvania, discussing family affairs, community news, and money matters. Hinkson's mother describes a visit to Philadelphia and the penitentiary there, and there are letters to Hinkson commenting on the situation in Kansas, 1858, and a letter, 1859, from Henry Ward Beecher recommending the services of a Dr. Mann. The correspondence, 1859-1860, between Hinkson and H. DeHaven Manley, a midshipman at the United States Naval Academy, Annapolis, Maryland, contains descriptions of student life, classwork, and events and personalities at their respective schools. Manley comments on the Maryland legislature meeting in Annapolis; mentions William Chauvenet, astronomer and mathematician then at the Naval Academy; and describes the visit of Edward Maynard to the Academy in 1860 to demonstrate his rifle. Hinkson describes a near riot at LaFayette in 1859, and there are many comments in the letters on politics and events of the day. After 1862 the collection contains the routine papers of Hinkson's law practice in Media, Pennsylvania.

2553. HINSDALE FAMILY PAPERS, 1712-1973. 2,502 items and 55 vols. Raleigh (Wake County), N.C.

Letters and papers of several generations of the Hinsdale family. Papers of John Wetmore Hinsdale (1843-1921), lawyer and businessman, contain letters and a diary, 1860-1864, concerning his education at a boarding school in Yonkers, New York, and at the University of North Carolina, 1858-1861; his service in the Confederate Army as aide-de-camp to his uncle, General Theophilus Hunter Holmes, and adjutant to General James Johnston Pettigrew and General William Dorsey Pender, including descriptions of troop movements, comments on many Confederate officers, and accounts of the battle of Seven Pines, the Seven Days' battle, and the battle of Helena; the effects of the Civil War on Southerners at home; and events during Reconstruction. There is a notebook kept by John W. Hinsdale in law school at Columbia University; letterpress books, 1886-1892, 25 vols., relating to his career as an attorney in Raleigh, North Carolina, specializing in insurance, corporation, and railroad law, including several letterpress books which deal with the business of the Carolina Brownstone Company; and a bound volume containing orders, circulars, and letters from the Confederate War Department to General Theophilus H. Holmes, 1863-1865. There are also a volume of claim records, 1889-1890, and a collection book, 1870-1876, both concerning Hinsdale's legal practice, and a ledger, 1873-1875, from the Diamond Cotton Chopper and Cultivator Company of Fayetteville, North Carolina, containing accounts for customers and agents, many of which are annotated with remarks about the individual's occupation, character, reliability, and financial circumstances. The papers of Ellen (Devereux) Hinsdale, wife of John W. Hinsdale, contain material pertaining to the General Pettigrew Chapter of the United Daughters of the Confederacy; the Daughters of the American Revolution; and the Ladies' Hospital Aid Association of Rex Hospital, Raleigh, North Carolina, including minute books for that organization, 1896-1902. Papers of the children of John W. Hinsdale and Ellen D. Hinsdale contain the courtship letters, 1903-1904, of Elizabeth Christophers Hinsdale and Jack Metauer Winfree, a physician and instructor at the Medical College of Virginia, including comments by Winfree on his work; courtship letters, 1908, of Annie Devereux Hinsdale and Harold Vincent Joslin; and letters concerning World War I, including an account of Ellen D. Hinsdale's decision to join the American Red Cross in France and descriptions of working conditions in a war industry. The papers, 1930-1935, of John W. Hinsdale, Jr., pertain mainly to his political career as a state senator from Wake County, North Carolina, and as a candidate for governor of North Carolina, 1932, and contain material reflecting his interest in changing the state tax structure, organizing the North Carolina State Board of Health and the North Carolina Board of Examiners, and establishing state control over maintenance of country roads. The collection contains a series of legal papers, 1712-1926, and a series of financial papers, 1864-1961. Miscellaneous items include clippings of Civil War reminiscences, weddings and deaths, and the legal career of John W. Hinsdale, Sr.; a map of Raleigh, 1847; family photographs and family writings; genealogical material on the Hinsdale, Devereux, Lane, and Pollock families of North Carolina, the Livingston and Bayard families of New York, and the Johnson and Edwards families of Connecticut; and a volume containing diary entries; memoranda, and accounts of an anonymous person from Hertford in Perquimans County, North Carolina, 1755.

2554. MEBANE HINSHAW PAPERS, 1851-1901. 66 items. Randleman (Randolph County), N.C.

Papers of Mebane Hinshaw contain correspondence with cousins in Kansas regarding the settlement of a family estate and letters to his wife while he was serving in the 6th North Carolina Regiment during the Civil War describing the punishment inflicted by the Confederate Army on Quakers who would not fight and commenting on the low morale in the army in 1865. Letters of J. W. Hinshaw, son of Mebane Hinshaw, describe labor conditions and agricultural practices in the states of Missouri, Kansas, Colorado, and Texas through which he passed as traveling salesman for a tree and plant nursery.

2555.  THOMAS HINSHAW PAPERS,
       1848-1923.  28 items and 8 vols.
       Randolph County, N.C.

Papers contain an account, 1863, by Thomas Hinshaw of his difficulties as a Quaker who was drafted into the Confederate army but refused to bear arms including a description of his punishment by the 52nd North Carolina Regiment and his capture, treatment, and subsequent release by Union forces. The collection also contains material relating to the Society of Friends, including two printed letters from the Yearly Meetings in London, 1848 and 1851; and eight ledgers from Hinshaw's mercantile firm, 1875-1900.

2556.  WILLIAM G. HINSON PAPERS,
       1770-1913.  37 items.
       Charleston, S.C.

The collection contains legal papers, 1770-1913, mainly wills and deeds, relating to William G. Hinson's landholdings on James Island, South Carolina; a few items of personal correspondence, 1884-1899; and letters and clippings concerning the parentage of Abraham Lincoln.

2557.  ERNST HINTZE PAPERS, 1942-1943.
       2 items.  Karlsruhe, Germany.

The collection contains a printed communication, 1942, to the German officer corps from the German Armed Forces High Command and a postcard, 1943, to Ernst Hintze from a friend in the German army.

2558.  HISTORIA Y CONQUISTA DE TUNIZ,
       [16th century].  1 vol.  (204 pp.)
       Tunis, Tunisia.

Typed copy of a manuscript from the Biblioteca Nacional in Madrid, Spain. In Spanish. There is a typed explanatory preface in French, and list of chapter titles in English.

2559.  CORNELIUS BALDWIN HITE, JR.,
       PAPERS, 1711 (1855-1889) 1918.
       2,342 items and 2 vols.
       Winchester (Frederick County), Va.

The collection contains report sheets for Cornelius B. Hite, Jr., from several schools in Virginia, 1855-1860; letters from the period of the Civil War, for the most part dealing with the impact of the war on civilians in western Virginia; a large amount of material showing the effect of Reconstruction on Cornelius B. Hite, Jr., and his relatives, including descriptions of economic distress, politics, and the migration of many Virginians to the western United States. There are letters describing social life and community health in Winchester, Virginia, in the 1870s; conditions at Shenandoah Valley Academy, 1868; and a long trip to Texas, 1875-1876. Letters, 1890-1895, are to Elizabeth Augusta (Smith) Hite, mother of Cornelius Baldwin Hite, Jr., from her sisters and grandchildren. The collection contains legal papers of the Christman, Fravel, and Branson families from 1797; a 19th century copy of excerpts from a journal kept by Ann Butler (Brayne) Spotswood, 1709-1711; and legal papers and letters of the Gales family, 1824-1865. Miscellaneous items include 6 volumes of songs, poetry, and scrapbooks; bills and receipts; clippings; printed matter; and an account book, 1838-1841, and a ledger, 1839-1841, of Cornelius Baldwin Hite, Sr.

2560.  E. B. HITT PAPERS, 1863.
       3 items.  Augusta (Richmond County), Ga.

Business letters concerning the purchase of property.

2561.  ROBERT BRUCE HOADLEY PAPERS,
       1861-1866.  12 items.
       Comanche (Clinton County), Iowa.

Letters of a soldier in the 26th Iowa Regiment describing his service at the siege of Vicksburg and with the army of General William T. Sherman in Georgia and South Carolina.

2562.  JOHN T. HOAK PAPERS, 1913.  2 items.
       Cleveland (Cuyahoga County), Ohio.

Two eye-witness accounts of the capture and imprisonment of Jefferson Davis.

2563.  EBENEZER ROCKWOOD HOAR PAPERS,
       1869.  1 item.  Concord (Middlesex County), Mass.

Letter to Ebenezer R. Hoar, attorney general of the United States, from Secretary of the Treasury George Sewall Boutwell, concerning laws designed to prevent the spread of disease from foreign countries among cattle in the United States.

2564.  ELIZABETH HOAR PAPERS, 1844.
       2 items.  Concord (Middlesex County), Mass.

Manuscript and typescript record of Elizabeth Hoar's trip to Charleston, South Carolina, with her father, Samuel Hoar, who had been employed by the governor of Massachusetts to test the constitutionality of certain laws of South Carolina under which many Negro citizens of Massachusetts, seamen on vessels trading at ports in South Carolina, were seized, imprisoned, and sometimes sold as slaves.

2565.  ROBERT HOBART, FOURTH EARL
       OF BUCKINGHAMSHIRE, PAPERS,
       1815.  1 item.  London, England.

A report from Charles Webb LeBas, dean of the East India College, to Robert Hobart on a student rebellion at the school.

2566.  JAMES OLIN HOBBS, SR., AND
       JAMES OLIN HOBBS, JR., PAPERS,
       1806-1916.  641 items and
       14 vols.  Covington
       (Alleghany County), Va.

Correspondence, mercantile records, account books, bills and receipts, and voting-registration certificates of Hobbs, his son, James Olin Hobbs, Jr., businessmen of Alleghany and Augusta counties, Virginia, and the Hobbs family.  Subjects include economic conditions (1835-1875) of western Virginia, the temperance movement in Virginia, and conditions in the Methodist Episcopal Church, South, during the early Reconstruction period.

2567.  THOMAS HOBBS PAPERS, 1867-1869.
       18 items.  Petersburg
       (Dinwiddie County), Va.

Accounts from Hurt, Todd, & Gee for mackerel, whiskey, and miscellaneous articles and accounts of tobacco sales in Dinwiddie County, Virginia.

2568.  WILBUR HOBBY PAPERS, 1956-1968.
       10,000 items.  Durham, N.C.
       Restricted.

Papers of Wilbur Hobby, Durham labor leader, as southeast area director of the Committee on Political Education of the AFL-CIO.  The collection includes material from Georgia, Kentucky, North Carolina, Virginia, Florida, and South Carolina on voting records, issue positions, activities of Congressmen and other political officials, elections statistics, reports of state labor conferences, memoranda on unionization in various industries, reports of the state directors of the Committee on Political Education, and state labor publications.

2569.  J. A. HOBSON ACCOUNT BOOK,
       1869-1874.  1 vol.
       Danville (Pittsylvania
       County), Va.

Account book of a general merchant.

2570.  HIMELIUS M. HOCKETT PAPERS,
       1851-1898.  7 items and 1 vol.
       Center (Randolph County), N.C.

Papers of Himelius M. Hockett, including miscellaneous bills and receipts; a practice writing tablet of Susannah Hockett; and a personal daybook of expenditures, 1855-1898.

2571.  SAMUEL HODGDON PAPERS, 1794.
       6 items.  Philadelphia, Pa.

Letters to Hodgdon, colonel in the Pennsylvania militia, from Clement Biddle, quartermaster of Pennsylvania, concerning supplies for the troops engaged in suppressing the Whiskey Rebellion.

2572.  J. D. HODGES PAPERS, 1884-1887.
       14 items.  Davie County, N.C.

Correspondence of J. D. Hodges, professor of Greek and modern languages at Trinity College, Randolph County, North Carolina, and teacher in the public schools, with James T. LeGrand, lawyer of Rockingham, North Carolina, concerning business matters and Hodges's desire for an appointment at the University of North Carolina.

2573.  JOHN D. HODGES PAPERS, 1875-1878.
       2 items.  Monroe (Union
       County), N.C.

Ledger for the Monroe High School, Monroe, North Carolina, 1875-1878, and one undated list of cotton production.

2574.  ELIZA S. HODGSON PAPERS,
       1858-1866.  15 items.
       Illinois.

Personal and family letters.

2575.  DAISY M. L. HODGSON AND
       MINNIE A. B. HODGSON AUTOGRAPH
       ALBUMS, 1877-1894.
       2 vols.  New Orleans, La.

Autographs of various eminent people.

2576.  MINNIE A. B. HODGSON PAPERS,
       1875-1899.  6 items.  New Orleans,
       La.

Miscellaneous items including a manuscript article by John C. Potts, 1875; a letter of Thomas R. Markham, 1879; and several clippings.

2577.  WILLIAM HODGSON DAYBOOK,
       1807-1809.  1 vol. (73 pp.)
       Virginia.

Includes entries for Bushrod Washington, Benjamin Harrison, Carter Beverley, and John Stuart.

2578.  WILLIAM BROWN HODGSON PAPERS,
       1817-1871.  55 items.
       Savannah, Ga.

Correspondence of William B. Hodgson (1801-1871), author, linguist, and diplomat.  The bulk of the correspondence was written from Algiers to Peter Force, J. Q. Adams, and John McLean by Hodgson during 1826-1828, while chargé d'affaires at Algiers, and is concerned with relations between Algeria, England, and France, with emphasis on tactlessness of French and English consuls, and description of the country.  Other letters to Hodgson deal with accounts of tribes in the Sahara Desert; the discovery of fossils near Savannah; a cholera epidemic among slaves in 1849; and accounts of Hodgson's travels in Italy during 1850-1851.  There are letters from James Hamilton Couper on scientific studies; letters on appointments to foreign service posts; and letters on national politics and foreign relations. Ten of the letters are photostatic copies.

2579. JOHN W. HODNETT PAPERS, 1861-1863. 6 items. Meriwether County, Ga.

Letters of John W. Hodnett, Confederate soldier, to his brother, sister, and father, with comments on the hardships of war and the various battles and campaigns in which he was engaged.

2580. MARGARET (HOLFORD) HODSON PAPERS, 1821. 1 item. Dawlish, Devonshire, England.

Letter, presumably to Margaret (Holford) Hodson, from Henrietta Maria Bowdler, discussing the literary work of Joanna Baillie, mutual acquaintance, and personal and family matters.

2581. CLYDE ROARK HOEY PAPERS, 1943 (1944-1954). 167,220 items. Washington, D.C., and Shelby (Cleveland County), N.C.

Office files created during the term of Hoey (1877-1954) as U.S. senator, 1944-1954, including correspondence, typed and printed material, clippings, and photographs. There are separate series of correspondence, arranged alphabetically by year, and alphabetical subjects. Both series contain similar material. Constituent mail forms the bulk of the correspondence, often urging support or opposition to particular legislation, such as universal military training, grain exports to India, tax measures, North Carolina projects including power dams, defense plants, and appropriations to local interest groups. There are also requests for assistance in obtaining employment or promotions, changing military status, and obtaining visas; requests for publications; letters of commendation; and publicity about individual constituents. Correspondence concerning legislation or commenting upon world or domestic affairs comes from all parts of the country, with some letters, frequently brief transmittal notes or personal greetings, from senators and representatives. There are a few letters involving the Hoey family, particularly correspondence between Hoey and his son-in-law Dan M. Paul. Speeches and miscellaneous items are included in the subject file. There is an inventory to the collection.

2582. JOSEPH HOFF MEMORANDUM BOOK, 1853-1854. 1 vol. Bertie County, N.C.

Accounts of the estate of Joseph Hoff.

2583. DAVID HOFFMAN PAPERS, 1850. 1 item. New York, N.Y.

Letter to David Hoffman from Robert Walsh, consul general of the United States in Paris, concerning Hoffman's essay on the formation of a British and American land and emigration company.

2584. THOMAS P. HOGE PAPERS, 1863-1864. 3 items. Halifax County, Va.

A letter from Thomas P. Hoge concerning his efforts to have his plantation overseer exempted from military service in 1863; a family letter from his sons, Whit and Moses, Confederate privates, 1863; and a letter from his wife, Mary C. Hoge, revealing her anxiety for the safety of her sons, 1864.

2585. HOGG AND CAMPBELL DAYBOOK, 1772-1773. 1 vol. (250 pp.) Wilmington (New Hanover County), N.C.

Accounts of a mercantile firm.

2586. HOGG AND CLAYTON LETTER BOOK AND ACCOUNTS, 1762-1771. 1 vol. Charleston, S.C., and Wilmington (New Hanover County), N.C.

Letters written by a Charleston mercantile firm, concerning shipments and receipts of goods, and sales accounts with many references to naval stores.

2587. JOHN W. HOLBERTON PAPERS, 1856-1860. 98 items. Canandaigua (Ontario County), N.Y.

Letters to John W. Holberton, for the most part concerned with business and personal matters including letters reporting the failure of brokerage and banking firms in New York, 1857; letters on Democratic Party politics, 1857; and a letter from William H. Powell, an artist, advocating that the United States government employ American artists rather than foreigners such as Horace Vernet.

2588. WILLIAM H. HOLDEN PAPERS, 1788-1914. 387 items. Orange County, N.C.

The collection contains tax receipts and notes of the Holden family and family correspondence, for the most part addressed to Kittie Holden, daughter of William H. Holden, from various relatives in North Carolina and Tennessee. Early letters, 1788-1840, are those of John Holden. Also includes school advertisements for the Holly Springs Female Institute in Mississippi, 1859, and the State Female College near Memphis, Tennessee, 1874.

2589. WILLIAM WOODS HOLDEN PAPERS, 1841-1929. 773 items and 15 vols. Raleigh (Wake County), N.C.

The papers of William Woods Holden (1818-1892), journalist, provisional governor of North Carolina, 1865-1868, and governor of North Carolina, 1868-1870, concern the administration of an estate, 1843-1850, the family of Holden's first wife, Ann Augusta (Young) Holden; the education of Holden's daughter, Laura Holden, at Salem Academy, Salem, North Carolina, 1858-1859; the convention of the Democratic Party at Charleston, South Carolina, and the presidential campaign of Stephen A. Douglas, 1860; Holden's duties as provisional governor; Ku Klux Klan activities in 1870 and problems of Reconstruction; the impeachment of Holden in 1871; Holden's attempts to find employment in Washington, D.C., 1871; Holden's defense of his administration in the press during the 1870s; the suit of Josiah Turner against Holden which ended in 1894; evaluations of Holden's political career by William Kenneth Boyd and J. G. de Roulhac Hamilton; and the defense of Holden by his daughters after his death. The collection contains printed matter dealing with Holden's political career, North Carolina history, the Methodist Church, and the Turner-Holden case. There are copies of many of Holden's poems; copies of some of his proclamations as governor; a copy of Holden's memoirs in his daughter's hand and a typed copy by William K. Boyd; copies of a number of Holden's editorials; a copy of his history of journalism in North Carolina; and a number of clippings from North Carolina, papers dealing with Holden and his career. Volumes include the scrapbook of Holden's second wife, Louisa Virginia (Harrison) Holden, containing clippings of romantic poetry pasted in the ledger of a Raleigh, North Carolina merchant, ca. 1820-1830; scrapbooks of other members of the Holden family, including William W. Holden's scrapbook, 1880, containing clippings on the history of North Carolina and the history of Raleigh, 1835-1860; letterpress book of William W. Holden while he was postmaster at Raleigh; and a ledger, 1858-1864, containing accounts for printing and advertising furnished by the Raleigh Standard.

2590. T. E. HOLDING & COMPANY PAPERS, 1904-1907. 1 vol. Wake Forest (Wake County), N.C.

Ledger of a firm of druggists.

2591. WILLIAM C. HOLGATE PAPERS, 1798-1911. 1,605 items. Defiance (Defiance County), Ohio.

Papers, 1798-1852, of William C. Holgate and his father Curtis Holgate contain business and legal correspondence concerning Curtis Holgate's investments in New York railroad stock and lands in Ohio; William C. Holgate's interest in the growth of Defiance, Ohio, where he settled in 1836, including the development of canals, roads, and schools, 1840-1848, and the creation of Defiance County, 1845; economic conditions in Ohio and Mississippi; the abolition and temperance movements; the Presbyterian and Methodist churches; and the national election of 1840. Correspondence, 1872-1911, of Fannie Maud (Holgate) Harley contains references to birth control, abortions, a smallpox epidemic, life in various women's academies, and routine family matters.

2592. HOLL PAPERS, 1888. 6 vols. [Germany?]

Notes on theology taken in German by Holl, a candidate for a theological degree, on courses taught by Professors Weizäcker, Weiss, Schurer, Schmidt, and Schaeffer, probably at the University of Tübingen in Germany.

2593. ASA HOLLAND PAPERS, 1836-1876. 32 items. Hale's Ford (Franklin County), Va.

The collection consists of routine forms and correspondence relating to Asa Holland's position as postmaster of Hale's Ford, Virginia; letters from Jubal A. Early concerning financial matters; and papers relating to the Rocky Mount Turnpike and the Sons of Temperance.

2594. JOHN HOLLAND PAPERS, 1793-1806. 3 items. Chatham County, Ga.

Papers and an account book concerning a debt owed to John Holland by Zachariah Cox, a Philadelphia merchant.

2595. JOHN W. HOLLAND PAPERS, 1859-1876. 20 items. Lexington (Davidson County), N.C.

Correspondence among members of a family in North Carolina, Virginia, the Midwest and the Southwest. The letters describe the trip west; prices in western states; and the political and racial situation in Abbeville County, South Carolina, 1876.

2596. TURNER W. HOLLEY PAPERS, 1784 (1836-1864) 1885. 165 items. Chester County, S.C.

Deeds to South Carolina plantations, 1784-1840, and family and Civil War correspondence of Turner W. Holley, who served in the 17th South Carolina Regiment and in 1st South Carolina Regiment, Cavalry, in South Carolina and in Virginia. Holley was stationed with troops defending Charleston, South Carolina; fought in the Richmond, Virginia, area; and took part in the Gettysburg campaign.

2597. FREDERICK WILLIAM MACKEY HOLLIDAY PAPERS, 1846 (1862-1895) 1899. 2,174 items and 20 vols. Winchester (Frederick County), Va.

The papers of Frederick William Mackey Holliday contain letters from Holliday while a student at Yale University, 1846; papers relating to the 33rd Virginia Regiment, which Holliday raised and commanded during the Civil War; letters concerning the International Exhibition held in Philadelphia in 1876, at which Holliday served as a commissioner from Virginia; and letters and papers relating to Holliday's election as governor of Virginia in 1877 and letters from his term as governor, for the most part dealing with routine political and administrative matters. Printed material includes <u>The Struggles, Perils and Hopes of the Negroes in the United States</u>, a pamphlet by Reverend C. Clifton Penick; a typed copy, "The Virginia Debt in Politics," by William L. Royall, published in 1897 as <u>History of the Virginia Debt Controversy</u>; and broadsides, campaign literature, and other political material. Volumes include 10 scrapbooks of clippings; letter books of Holliday as a student at Yale and the University of Virginia, 1845-1849, and as governor of Virginia, 1878-1879; and 4 record books concerning Holliday's legal work.

2598. HORATIO NELSON HOLLIFIELD PAPERS, 1861-1864. 51 items. Sandersville (Washington County), Ga.

Letters and papers concerning Horatio Hollifield's Confederate cavalry in Georgia and duties as army surgeon at Newport, Florida, including his reports for the Confederate hospital at Newport.

2599. JOHN HOLLINGSWORTH PAPERS, 1807 (1831-1852) 1880. 32 items. Edgefield District, S.C.

Bills of sale for slaves sold by John Hollingsworth (d. 1833) and a contract between D. F. Hollingsworth and his overseer. Included also are papers concerned with the settlement of Hollingsworth's estate.

2600. JOSEPH P. HOLLINGSWORTH LEDGER, 1815-1822. 1 vol. (187 pp.) [Union Mills (Fluvanna County), Va.?]

Sales of flour, wheat, and rye.

2601. MARY HOLLINGSWORTH JOURNAL, 1860. 1 vol. (125 pp.) Winchester (Frederick County), Va.

Diary of Mary Hollingsworth on a trip from Harpers Ferry, West Virginia, to Cincinnati, Ohio, containing descriptions of the Ohio Reform School Farm, the Shaker village near Lebanon, Ohio, and the scenery and people she saw.

2602. SETH HOLLISTER PAPERS, 1860-1865. 16 items. Washington (Litchfield County), Conn.

Letters to Seth Hollister from his cousins in the 8th Connecticut Regiment during the Civil War and from other soldiers describing the training center at Annapolis, Maryland; camp life in Virginia and North Carolina; and New Bern, North Carolina.

2603. HOLLY GROVE BAPTIST CHURCH MINUTES, 1822-1910. 2 vols. Bertie County, N.C.

Includes lists of members, contributions, and miscellaneous items.

2604. FREDERIC BLACKMAR MUMFORD HOLLYDAY PAPERS, 1842-1969. Durham, N.C.

Miscellaneous letters of the Kennedy, Mumford, Hewlett, and Mann families, mainly from Michigan, containing some references to state political matters and the Civil War. Letters and papers of Willoughby O'Donoughue, surgeon of the 1st Michigan Regiment, Engineers and Mechanics, contain enlistment and discharge papers, mustering-out lists, and papers concerning the Grand Army of the Republic. Papers of Frederic Blackmar Mumford, dean of the University of Missouri College of Agriculture, contain family letters, clippings, pictures, legal papers, diplomas and special awards, a diary, 1945, and a scrapbook tracing Mumford's career, 1917-1938.

2605. JAMES HOLLYDAY PAPERS, 1768-1786. 25 items. Chestertown (Kent County), Md.

Papers relating to a legal dispute between James Chalmers and George Rome involving land confiscated by the state of Maryland during the American Revolution.

2606. JOSEPH GEORGE EPHRIAM HOLMAN PAPERS, 1853-1974. 9 items and 3 vols. Preble County, Ohio.

The collection contains diaries of Joseph George Ephriam Holman, kept while he was working on the construction of the Fort Wayne and Southern Rail Road, 1853-1854; mining gold in Colorado, 1862-1863; and farming in Preble County, Ohio. Other items relate mainly to the Holman family, including a Bible record of Joseph G. E. Holman's family and an account of the capture of George Holman, grandfather of Joseph G. E. Holman, by Simon Girty and Indians.

2607. ABIEL HOLMES PAPERS, 1820. 1 item. Cambridge (Middlesex County), Mass.

Letter of Abiel Holmes, a minister in the Congregational Church, acknowledging a gift from his former parishoners to the American Education Society.

2608. ALEXANDER HOLMES PAPERS, 1861-1865. 163 items. Boston, Mass.

Letters and papers of Alexander H. Holmes, president of the Old Colony and Fall River Railroad, relate largely to business matters. There are also many letters to his son, J. H. Holmes, who was traveling extensively in Europe.

2609. DAVID HOLMES PAPERS, 1802-1826. 5 items. Washington (Adams County), Miss.

Correspondence of David Holmes, governor of the Mississippi Territory and later governor of the state of Mississippi, concerning the early settlement of the territory, the territorial militia, and his election as governor in 1826 and subsequent resignation.

2610. EMMA EDWARDS HOLMES DIARIES, 1861-1862. 2 vols. Charleston, S.C.

Diaries kept by Emma E. Holmes giving a detailed account of the Charleston fire in 1861 and of Civil War activities, including local gossip, marriages, flirtations, the purchase of a rapid-fire gun by the city of Charleston, and the election of officers by the Palmetto Guard.

2611. GABRIEL HOLMES PAPERS, 1822. 1 item. Raleigh (Wake County), N.C.

A form letter from Gabriel Holmes, governor of North Carolina, to Allen Trimble, acting governor of Ohio.

2612. GEORGE FREDERICK HOLMES PAPERS, 1767-1960. 521 items and 65 vols. Charlottesville (Albemarle County), Va.

Correspondence, notes, diaries, and literary works of George Frederick Holmes (1820-1897), scholar, educator, author; and correspondence of William Howard Perkinson (1861-1898), educator and son-in-law of Holmes; and of Joseph Henry Herndon Holmes (1794-1831) and Mary Ann (Pemberton) Holmes (1790-ca. 1862), father and mother of George Frederick Holmes.

The papers of Joseph Henry Herndon Holmes, barrister of Demerara, British Guiana, consist of treatises on contracts and exchange of money, fragments of poetry, poems, his will, and pictures. Among the papers of Mary Ann (Pemberton) Holmes are the following: a brief record of her life in Demerara with interesting comments on the people and the country, family history and genealogy, personal letters, epitaphs, and verses of Stephen Pemberton written while attending Oriel College, Oxford, England.

The papers of George Frederick Holmes are chiefly concerned with family affairs, including financial troubles, and accounts from his wife, Eliza Lavalette (Floyd) Holmes, of the unsatisfactory performance of Negro servants; accounts of Holmes's connection with educational institutions, notably Richmond College, Virginia, College of William and Mary, Williamsburg, Virginia, the University of Mississippi, Oxford, and the University of Virginia, Charlottesville. The correspondence throws considerable light on dissensions in the Board of Visitors at the College of William and Mary in 1848. The collection consists of Holmes's correspondence with leading literary figures and educators of the South; notes and works on almost every phase of philology, grammar, history, political science, and economics; notes for lectures; articles and manuscripts for books and periodicals; lists of students; examination questions; and diaries which cover a great part of the period from 1856 to 1891. The collection includes a letter book, 1834-1874, containing contemporary copies of letters, in Holmes's hand, of many notable figures, among whom are E. E. Bellinger, Auguste Comte, J. D. B. DeBow, Thos. R. Dew, R. T. W. Duke, Wm. H. Ellet, Geo. Fitzhugh, John B. Floyd, Wm. Harper, R. R. Howison, R. W. Hughes, D. F. Jamison, Wm. S. Lewis, Francis Lieber, P. N. Lynch, Jno. McClintock, Cornelius Mathews, W. E. Martin, B. B. Minor, W. G. Minor, T. V. Moore, J. D. Munford, Edw. Nicholson, Wm. Ogilby, Cotesworth Pinckney, J. D. Pope, Wm. C. Preston, Jas. Ryder, W. G. Simms, R. W. Singleton, A. G. Summer, Jno. R. Thompson, Jas. H. Thornwell, Samuel Tyler, and D. K. Whitaker.

Papers of William Howard Perkinson are confined to a few records of his work as professor of Latin and Greek at the University of Virginia, a few business papers, and records of the administration of the estate of George Frederick Holmes. Some of Perkinson's letters to his wife give glimpses of the management of the university and of his work. M. Schele De Vere and W. Gordon McCabe, as well as a number of scholars in England, were among Perkinson's correspondents.

2613. ISAAC EDWARD HOLMES PAPERS, 1787-1859. 13 items. Charleston, S.C.

Legal papers, ca. 1787, of John Bee Holmes, father of Isaac E. Holmes, concerning a case involving John Young; and correspondence of Isaac E. Holmes, as a member of the United States Congress, consisting chiefly of requests and recommendations for political appointments.

2614. MARCELLA FAYETTE HOLMES CLASS NOTES, 1 vol. (53 pp.) Double Cabins (Henry County), Ga.

Notes taken in a Latin class.

2615. MATTHEW HOLMES AND JOHN A. HOLMES PAPERS, 1855-1856. 8 items. [Londonderry, Pa.?]

Receipts for money paid by the town of Londonderry to Matthew and John A. Holmes.

2616. NICKELS J. HOLMES PAPERS, 1834 (1842-1888) 1927. 917 items and 1 vol. Laurens (Laurens County), S.C.

Family correspondence and legal papers of Nickels J. Holmes, school principal, commissioner of elections, and Presbyterian minister. The collection concerns Holmes's education at the University of Edinburgh, Scotland, the westward movement after the Civil War, social activities of younger people, religion, education, Reconstruction, service as an associate justice on a circuit court, Joseph E. Holmes's attitude toward the South and the Negro problem, and agricultural practices at Cornell University, Ithaca, New York, including ensilage and the construction of silos. Included is a volume of lecture notes on moral philosophy.

2617. THEOPHILUS HUNTER HOLMES PAPERS, 1861-1867. 732 items. Sampson County, N.C.

Military correspondence and papers of Theophilus H. Holmes (1804-1880), general in the Confederate Army, concerning the Trans-Mississippi Department, 1863, and the North Carolina Reserves, 1864-1865. Included are papers of J. W. Hinsdale, written from Virginia, while under the command of Holmes, who was his uncle; petitions from women asking for protection of lives and property; material on the battle of Helena, Arkansas, 1863; and requests for reserves to be sent into active service, and equally urgent requests for their services in agriculture. There are letters from Generals Joseph E. Johnston and J. G. Martin, and from John Shepherd, written while he was traveling in France, Austria, and Germany in 1867. Military telegrams to Holmes as head of the North Carolina State Reserve, 1864-1865, concern troop movements and skirmishes; the effort to protect Plymouth, North Carolina; the Confederate ram, Albemarle; Sherman's invasion of the state; and the final days of the war.

2618. ALLEN HOLT AND J. HOLT DAYBOOK, 1859-1862. 1 vol. (600 pp.) Cane Creek (Alamance County), N.C.

Accounts of general merchants and postmaster's records.

2619. HAMILTON BOWEN HOLT PAPERS, 1904. 1 item. New York, N.Y.

Letter to Hamilton B. Holt, editor of the Independent, from John Sharp Williams concerning the operations of the stock market and financial institutions in New York.

2620. HINES HOLT PAPERS, 1829, 1857. 2 items. Columbus (Muscogee County), Ga.

Papers of Hines Holt, lawyer, member of the United States Congress, and Confederate congressman, containing one certificate and a letter of advice to his son.

2621. JOHN HOLT AND WILLIAM HOLT ACCOUNT BOOK, 1842-1844. 1 vol. (54 pp.) Halifax County, Va.

Store book of a general mercantile firm.

2622. MICHAEL WILLIAM HOLT NOTES, 1836-1837. 1 vol. (184 pp.) Orange County, N.C.

Notes on lectures taken by Michael W. Holt while at a medical school in Philadelphia, Pennsylvania.

2623. HOLT FAMILY GENEALOGY, 1635-1951. 1 vol. (137 pp.)

Descendants of Nicholas Holt who migrated to Massachusetts from England, 1635, and related families.

2624. A. HOLTON LEDGER, 1846-1883. 1 vol. (186 pp.) Ramseur (Randolph County), N.C.

Accounts of a physician, including two items regarding the settlement of an estate, 1891.

2625. ETHEL HOLTZCLAW PAPERS, 1846-1889. 3 items. Greenville County, S.C.

Deeds to lands in Greenville County, South Carolina.

2626. GEORGE JACOB HOLYOAKE PAPERS, 1873 (1874-1894) 1931. 357 items. London, England.

Papers of George Jacob Holyoake, author and social reformer, contain clippings and letters to his friend, William H. Duignan, including Holyoake's definition of secularism, 1874; a report of correspondence with Wendell Phillips and Robert Ingersoll, 1875; material concerning Holyoake's financial situation, 1875; letters concerning an attempt to acquire a pension, 1881; clippings relating to Holyoake's American trip, 1882; and letters concerned with Irish Home Rule and clippings on the Home Rule fight in Parliament, 1893.

2627. PERCY J. HOME PAPERS, 1936-1948. 15 items. London, England.

Letters and manuscripts sent by Nelson Springer to Percy J. Home, artist and writer for The Sphere, an illustrated magazine published in London. Springer describes the towns of Edenton, North Carolina, Tarpon Springs, Florida, and El Paso, Texas; the presidential campaigns and the candidates of 1936 and 1948; postwar economic conditions in Great Britain and the United States; various American newspapers; and the first cyclotron.

2628.  J. H. HONEYCUTT ACCOUNT BOOK, 1847-1862. 1 vol. (340 pp.) [Cabarrus County, N.C.?]

Blacksmith accounts.

2629.  ROBERT W. HONNOLL PAPERS, 1862. 4 items. Polk County, Tenn.

Letters from Robert W. Honnoll, Confederate lieutenant in the 23rd Regiment, Tennessee Volunteers, stationed at Corinth, Mississippi, concerning camp life and family matters, and commenting on prospects for peace and opposition to Lincoln in the North.

2630.  JOHN BELL HOOD PAPERS, 1862-1865. 6 items. Nashville (Davidson County), Tenn.

Miscellaneous papers of John Bell Hood (1831-1879), lieutenant general in the Confederate Army, include a letter, 1864, from Hood to General Joseph Wheeler asking his cooperation in a charge about to be made; a report to Secretary of War James A. Seddon concerning an engagement at Franklin, Tennessee; an order pertaining to furloughs; a letter to Hood containing an order for Cheatham's Corps; a pass; and biographical information.

2631.  JOHN C. HOOD PAPERS, 1848-1866. 57 items. Near Smithfield (Johnston County), N. C.

Papers of John C. Hood consist of his papers as assistant quartermaster of Meadow Township, Johnston County, in charge of official aid to families of Confederate soldiers, with names of committee members, money paid out for relief, names of soldiers' families and corn and meat supplies held by each; and Civil War letters from B. R. Hood, serving in the Camp Guards and in the 24th North Carolina Regiment, and from David W. Hood, in the 67th North Carolina Regiment, describing camp life and food, the second battle of Manassas and other engagements and skirmishes, and the possibility of hiring a substitute.

2632.  THOMAS HOOD PAPERS, 1828, 1844. 2 items. London, England.

Personal letters of Thomas Hood (1799-1845), British poet, to Robert Balmanno and Frederick Oldfield Ward.

2633.  JOHN HOOK PAPERS, 1737 (1770-1848) 1889. 7,389 items and 103 vols. Hale's Ford (Franklin County), Va.

Letters, papers, and mercantile records of John Hook (1745-1808), wealthy Scottish merchant and Tory; of the mercantile firm of Bowker Preston, Hook's son-in-law, and Smithson H. Davis at Goose Creek, Bedford County, Virginia; and of a similar firm of Asa, Smithson H., and Alexander G. Holland and John D. Booth at Halesford and Germantown, both in Franklin County, the Holland family apparently being connected with the Hook family by marriage.

The records of John Hook are comprised of daybooks, ledgers, letter books, and memoranda of the mercantile firm of Ross and Hook at New London, Campbell County Virginia, 1771-1784, of branch stores at Bedford Court House and Falling River in Bedford County, and of John Hook's mercantile establishment in Hale's Ford from 1784 to 1808. These records reflect the nature of goods in common use, the volume of trade, the large trade in iron, the manufacture of plantation tools at Hook's blacksmith shop, and the operation of his distillery. Concerning the mercantile operations are various memoranda and notes kept by Hook relative to debts due him, places of abode of the debtors, and the type of security for the debts; schedule of court days in the various counties of Virginia; inventories of goods; and letters relative to the operation of his business. Many of the records reveal information on the operation of Hook's valuable plantations, two in Franklin County and one in Montgomery County; much concerning the purchase, prizing and shipment of tobacco, usually on the barter basis; and information on large-scale purchase of Revolutionary land warrants with long lists of land owned by Hook.

A great proportion of Hook's papers relate to sequestration proceedings brought against him by David Ross, his partner in business from 1771 until after the Revolution. Concerning the suit are numerous depositions, explanations, histories of the operation of the firm, letters, inventories, lists of questions to be asked of his lawyers (Edmund Randolph and Philip Norborne Nicholas) and witnesses, copies of letters and documents, and petitions to the Court for various concessions. There are many papers and letters relative to Hook's efforts to recover from Congressman George Hancock a slave whom his enemies claimed to have been a free Negro kidnapped and held in slavery. Included are long lists of slaves; many papers concerning Hook's determination to serve as administrator of the estate of an Englishman, Jeffrey Gresley, who had owed Hook a large sum; many papers concerning the suit of sequestration after Hook's death; papers dealing with the administration of Hook's estate; numerous depositions and other papers relative to the disposition of the estate of Henry Hook, son of John Hook; and letters discussing the Revolutionary War, fugitive slaves, and prominent political figures.

Included also are papers concerning Hook's troubles with the Bedford County Committee of Safety, and two letter books. The papers connected with the Committee of Safety consist of a summons, a rough draft of Hook's reply, his discharge from jail, his oath of allegiance, and others of a similar nature, all bearing on an accusation that Hook had disseminated pamphlets antagonistic to the American cause. The letter books, 1763-1784, contain much information on mercantile pursuits in colonial Virginia, Hook's partnerships, analyses of trade opportunities at various locations, and information on several Scottish merchants prominent in colonial Virginia and their connections in Scotland. Included also is much information concerning David Ross and his connections with Hook before the Hook-Ross suit was started. Among the letters is information on Hook's family life, his wife, his children, his father and his father's family in Scotland, and his brothers in Jamaica.

Records centering around Bowker Preston and Smithson H. Davis pertain to the operation of mercantile establishments at Goose Creek and Falling River in Bedford County from 1813 until about 1830, with letters between the partners concerning goods purchased in Philadelphia, Pennsylvania, New York City, and Richmond and Lynchburg, Virginia; the purchase, prizing, and sale of tobacco; and the disastrous effects of the panic of 1819. There are also inventories of goods, including one in 1819 which contains the titles of many books and different types and styles of merchandise in common use; ledgers, daybooks, and other mercantile records; and personal letters to Preston after the dissolution of the firm.

Records pertaining to the Holland family are, with the exception of a constable's records kept by Asa Holland while an officer of Franklin County, confined to correspondence, ledgers, account books, and daybooks for the mercantile firms of Asa and Smithson H. Holland and John D. Booth.

Included also are manuscript arithmetic books kept by Robert Hook, Peter D. Holland, and John Hook, Jr., and numerous volumes containing accounts of the Ross-Hook lawsuit. Scattered through the papers and memoranda are various recipes for the cure of rheumatism, an affliction of both Hook and Preston. Among the correspondence are a few perfunctory letters from James Innes, H. H. Leavitt, B. W. Leigh, P. N. Nicholas, and Edmund Randolph. Included also are numerous documents signed by W. W. Hening and copies of Hook's letters and legal documents concerning the Ross-Hook suit.

2634.   L. C. HOOK PAPERS, 1888-1909.
        6 items. Hook's Mills
        (Hampshire County), W. Va.

Personal and business letters to L. C. Hook, including a letter from Charles W. Swisher, secretary of state of West Virginia and Republican gubernatorial candidate, enclosing a political broadside by Governor W. M. O. Dawson in his behalf.

2635.   ROBERT W. HOOKE PAPERS, (1861-1862)
        1877. 75 items. Winchester
        (Frederick County), Va.

Civil War correspondence of Colonel William W. Hooke, serving in the Virginia Militia, and of his sons, Robert W., in the 1st Regiment, Virginia Cavalry, and William Franklin, in the 4th Virginia Militia and the 2nd Virginia Regiment, describing camp life and health conditions, hardships during the war, casualties and desertion, commodity shortages, and military engagements and leaders.

2636.   EDWARD HOOKER PAPERS, 1806-1815.
        17 items. Farmington
        (Hartford County), Conn.

Family letters of Edward Hooker describing the slave trade in South Carolina, several trips made in that state, his life in Cambridge (South Carolina), where he was president of the college there, his position at South Carolina College, Columbia, trouble with the British, and the British frigate Leopard; and letters of John Hooker, Edward's brother, and a lawyer in Columbia (South Carolina), describing an earthquake, 1812, his first dose of castor oil, a trip to Catawba Springs (North Carolina), the attitude of the inhabitants of Columbia toward the War of 1812, and religious fervor in the town.

2637.   JOHN HOOMES PAPERS, (1780-1800) 1810.
        98 items. Bowling Green
        (Caroline County), Va.

Records and accounts of the brig Mars and correspondence of John Hoomes (d. 1805), Virginia tobacco merchant, with London merchants to whom he sold tobacco and from whom he bought dry goods; and letters dealing with Hoomes's purchase of horses from England. The collection relates to the price and quality of Virginia tobacco, general conditions of the market, difficulties of transportation, relations between English and American merchants, effects of European war on the markets, and the interest of Virginians in horse breeding during the eighteenth century.

2638.   AURELIA HOOPER PAPERS, 1851-1873.
        29 items. Yanceyville
        (Caswell County), N.C.

Primarily Civil War letters from Private George Leitz, 17th Virginia Regiment, C.S.A., to Aurelia Hooper, including a description of the gunboat Neuse under construction near Kinston by the state of North Carolina. A letter, 1871, refers to property lost in the Chicago Fire. Also included is a pledge signed by those interested in forming a volunteer rifle company.

2639.   JOHN WALTER HOOPER PAPERS, 1850-1872.
        7 items. Baltimore, Md.

Personal letters.

2640.   LUCY HAMILTON (JONES) HOOPER PAPERS.
        1 item. Philadelphia, Pa., and
        Paris, France.

Letter from Lucy Hamilton (Jones)

Hooper (1835-1893), editor and journalist, concerning her plan to publish a compilation of selected writings of American poets.

2641. M. S. HOOPER JOURNAL, 1840-1842, 1 vol. (132 pp.) [Medford?] (Middlesex County), Mass.

Journal of a businessman, in partnership with his father, W. A. Hooper, engaged in refining sugar and shipping cargoes to the Far East and England. The journal is largely concerned with shipping, principally to the Orient, and reports about the Opium War in China.

2642. WILLIAM HOOPER PAPERS, 1867. 4 items. Wilson (Wilson County), N.C.

Letters from William Hooper, who with his brothers, J. D. and Thomas C. Hooper, and R. F. Hunt, comprised the faculty of the Wilson Female Seminary, to Maria J. Beattie, a graduate of Edgeworth Seminary, Greensboro, North Carolina, concerning her qualifications for teaching in the Wilson Female Seminary; and a personal letter dealing with a family matter.

2643. EDWARD HOOVER PAPERS, 1886-1897. 30 items. Pleasant Hall (Franklin County), Pa.

Letters of Edward Hoover giving detailed accounts of farm life, farming methods, prices of crops, and church activities, including revivals, love feasts, and preaching.

2644. HERBERT CLARK HOOVER PAPERS, 1929. 1 item. West Branch (Cedar County), Iowa.

A letter of Herbert Hoover (1874-1964), president of the United States, paying tribute to Harvey C. Couch who was being honored by citizens in Arkansas.

2645. EDWIN G. HOPE PAPERS, 1863-1906. 7 items. Louisa County, Va.

Letters concerning the pensioning of a wounded Civil War veteran.

2646. DANIEL C. HOPKINS PAPERS, 1823-1870. 42 items. Edgecombe County, N.C.

Miscellaneous bills, receipts, indentures, and warrants, several of which deal with the hiring and wage scale of slaves.

2647. EDWARD HOPKINS PAPERS, 1841. 1 item. Darien (McIntosh County), Ga.

Letter of Roger Lawson Gamble, U.S. representative from Georgia, 1833-1835 and 1841-1843, discussing rumors of the split in the president's cabinet and the effect it had had on holding up all appointments.

2648. HENRY H. HOPKINS PAPERS, 1862-1865. 14 items. Virginia.

Civil War letters of Henry H. Hopkins, serving in the U.S. Army and stationed at Alexandria, Virginia, and eventually chaplain of the 120th Regiment of New York Volunteers, to Mary Ames and Winona C. Ames discussing the conversion of Fairfax Seminary into a convalescent camp, the surrender of Harpers Ferry, the New York draft riots, the battle of Cold Harbor, the siege of Petersburg, family matters, and the building of a chapel.

2649. O. C. HOPKINS ACCOUNT BOOK, 1866. 1 vol. (72 pp.)

Detailed accounts of supplies sold and used on Hopkins's plantation.

2650. MRS. O. K. HOPKINS PAPERS, 1945. 2 items. Durham, N.C.

Letter to Mrs. O. K. Hopkins, former missionary to Cuba, from Sergeant Eleanor L. Bruster in New Guinea about missions there; and a letter from Ensign E. E. Newson from Okinawa concerning premature celebrations taking place there when peace rumors were started.

2651. WILLIAM H. HORAH PAPERS, 1832-1847. 6 items. Salisbury (Rowan County), N.C.

Routine business letters to William H. Horah, agent for the State Bank of North Carolina to 1834 and for the Bank of Cape Fear, 1834-1863, dealing with the transfer of bills of exchange and other matters.

2652. JOHN HORN LEDGER, 1875-1886. 1 vol. (742 pp.) Capon Bridge (Hampshire County), W. Va.

Mercantile accounts.

2653. THOMAS HARTWELL HORNE PAPERS, 1856. 1 item. London, England.

Letter of Thomas Hartwell Horne (1780-1862), British Biblical scholar, bibliographer, and polemic, concerning criticism of the tenth edition of his Introduction to the Critical Study and Knowledge of the Holy Scriptures (1856), which included a work by Dr. Samuel Davidson entitled The Text of the Old Testament Considered.

2654. JAMES H. HORNER PAPERS, 1811-1876. 76 items. Oxford (Granville County), N.C.

Chiefly the Civil War letters of Captain James H. Horner, 13th Regiment and later the 23rd Regiment of North Carolina Volunteers, describing the first battle of Manassas, picket duty, camp life, the scarcity of commissioned officers, and an army chaplain. Scattered letters before and after the war refer to family matters and his position as a schoolteacher in Oxford.

2655.     HUGH G. HORTON PAPERS, 1939-1953. 11 items. Williamston (Martin County), N. C.

Principally correspondence between Hugh G. Horton, North Carolina state legislator, and Joseph Isaac Byrum, Sr., a poet, concerning a legal case in which Horton had represented Byrum. Also included are a copy of the Democratic Party platform, 1942, and a letter urging Horton's support of a bill in the state senate.

2656.     MARY J. HORTON PAPERS, 1880-1882. 1 vol.

Card album and scrapbook containing greeting cards and appliqués, including cards for Christmas, the New Year, Easter, and Valentine's Day.

2657.     WILLIS HORTON PAPERS, 1803-1910. 174 items. Wake County, N. C.

Correspondence of the Horton and Clark families and business papers of Willis Horton, a lawyer. One letter gives a description of activities at the siege of Petersburg in 1864; another, from a Federal soldier, describes his fighting in eastern South Carolina and Federal preparations at Yorktown, Virginia, in 1864.

2658.     EDMUND HOSKINS PAPERS, 1815-1819. 15 items. Edenton (Chowan County), N. C.

Business correspondence of a merchant including account sheets and two letters dealing with privateering during the War of 1812.

2659.     GEORGE HOSLER PAPERS, 1846, 1851. 2 items. Rockingham County, Va.

Business letters addressed to George Hosler.

2660.     MICHAEL HOUSER PAPERS, 1825-1869. 24 items. Stokes and Forsyth Counties, N. C.

Tax receipts, 1825-1839, land indentures, and bills and receipts of Michael Houser.

2661.     CHRISTOPHER HOUSTON PAPERS, ca. 1955. 1 vol. (180 pp.) Houstonville (Iredell County), N. C., and Columbia (Maury County), Tenn.

Typed copy of "The Life and Letters of Christopher Houston" edited and compiled by Gertrude Dixon Enfield, containing a sketch of Houston's life (1744-1837) and family correspondence. Letters discuss personal and business affairs, crops and the weather, the War of 1812, commodity prices in Tennessee, slavery and an insurrection in Mississippi, religion and the Presbyterian Church, education, Andrew Jackson, the Indians, the Missouri controversy, nullification, and cholera in Tennessee.

2662.     GEORGE SMITH HOUSTON PAPERS, 1831-1899. 475 items. Athens (Limestone County), Ala.

Political correspondence of George S. Houston (1811-1879), member of U.S. Congress, senator, and governor of Alabama, dealing with Alabama politics, especially 1845-1850; letters showing Houston's interest in Texas lands; routine letters of congratulations upon his election and of condolence upon his death and the deaths of other members of his family; and clippings. Correspondents include J. A. S. Acklen, O. H. Bynum, Reuben Chapman, C. C. Clay, Jr., C. C. Clay, Sr., Jeremiah Clemens, Jefferson Davis, M. C. Gallaway, G. S. Houston, David Hubbard, J. S. Kennedy, J. L. Martin, A. C. Matthews, F. G. Norman, E. A. O'Neal, William S. Parrott, and J. E. Saunders.

2663.     PLACEBO HOUSTON PAPERS, 1790-1861. 25 items. Houstonville (Iredell County), N. C.

Personal and family correspondence of Placebo Houston, a captain in the North Carolina rangers, 1777-1780, with relatives in Alabama, Mississippi, and Missouri, describing the climate and crops, social life and customs, prices of slaves and land, religion, and daily life. Included are several wills.

2664.     SAMUEL HOUSTON PAPERS, 1825-[1832?] 3 items. Nashville (Davidson County), Tenn.

Papers of Samuel Houston (1793-1863), general in the War of 1812, member of U.S. Congress, 1823-1825, governor of Tennessee, 1827-1829, president of Texas, and U.S. senator, 1846-1859, include a letter to John Taylor concerning Houston's trip toward Marlboro, South Carolina; and a land grant issued while governor of Tennessee.

2665.     WILLIAM CHURCHILL HOUSTON PAPERS, 1779. 1 item. Princeton (Mercer County), N.J.

Letter from W. C. Houston (1746-1788), professor of mathematics and natural philosophy at the College of New Jersey, to James Ewing about raising troops, supplies, and money for the Revolutionary forces.

2666.     JOHN HOUSTOUN PAPERS, 1773-1793. 18 items. Savannah, Ga.

Papers of John Houstoun (1744-1796), governor of Georgia and jurist, include an order for the defense of Richmond County; a letter, 1784, from John Habersham discussing negotiations with Indian representatives concerning land purchases, and an incident between Georgia residents and Indians; a statement of dissent from the Boundary Commission concerning the boundary dispute between South Carolina and Georgia; a petition to adjourn court to allow jurors to put down an Indian attack; and miscellaneous land grants, indentures, and summonses.

2667. WILL HOUSTOUN PAPERS, 1731. 2 items. England.

Copy of a letter from ship's surgeon Houstoun from Vera Cruz, Mexico, describing the wreck of the Snow Assiento, requesting transfer to another ship, and commenting on the collection of plants; and a photoprint of Houstoun's signature.

2668. HENRY HOWARD PAPERS, 1858-1859. 2 items. Floyd (Floyd County), Va.

Business letters to Henry Howard from S. R. Aldridge concerning personal debts.

2669. JOHN EAGER HOWARD PAPERS, 1789-1829. 7 items and 1 vol. "Belvedere" (Baltimore County), Md.

Official papers of John Eager Howard (1752-1827), governor of Maryland; and a notebook kept by his son, William Howard (1793-1834), while a pupil of the phrenologist Franz Josef Gall (1758-1828), and afterwards as a civil engineer, containing biographical comments on Gall, phrenological theories, and a sketch of the ramparts of a fort.

2670. JOHN H. HOWARD PAPERS, 1848-1880. 86 items and 1 vol. Grahamville (Beaufort County), S. C.

Miscellaneous papers of John H. Howard include letters concerning the sale and the care of slaves, papers related to the administration of the estate of Mrs. A. M. Lawrence of Marietta, Georgia, receipts for pew rent and Episcopal publications, and legal papers. A daybook, 1851-1864, records slave lists, supplies, cattle, remedies, blacksmith work, pew rents, and work for the C.S.A. Army as captain of the Beaufort District Troop of cavalry, listing supplies, repairs, and tents.

2671. TAZEWELL M. HOWARD PAPERS, 1855-1865. 15 items. Campbellton (Fulton County), Ga.

Letters of Tazewell M. Howard, physician, to a younger brother who was a medical student in Philadelphia, Pennsylvania, containing brief references to the Know-Nothing Party, secession, and a rumor that Governor Henry A. Wise of Virginia had been murdered by abolitionists; and Civil War letters of Dr. T. H. Howard and H. L. Honnell from Georgia, Kentucky and Mississippi.

2672. EDWARD T. HOWE PAPERS, 1874-1878. 6 items. New York, N. Y.

Letters concerning a lighthouse in New York City.

2673. HENRY HOWE PAPERS, ca. 1844. 1 vol. (29 pp.) [Richmond?], Va.

Salesman's prospectus of Howe's Historical Collections of Virginia, with a partial list of subscribers; and notes on "Analysis of Notions and Thoughts" and English grammar.

2674. LUTHER HOWE ACCOUNTS OF ESTATE, 1836. 1 vol. (13 pp.) New Orleans, La.

Bill of sale by the heirs of Luther Howe for his land, slaves, and a brick plant which he had operated in partnership with François Xavier Martin.

2675. ROBERT HOWE PAPERS, 1777-1778. 2 items. Brunswick County, N. C.

Letters from Robert Howe (1732-1786), planter and general in the Continental Army, discussing Samuel Elbert's attempt to invade Florida, conditions in Georgia and South Carolina, his proposal for an expedition to East Florida, the arrival of British ships near Savannah, and the poor condition of American defenses at Savannah.

2676. SAMUEL GRIDLEY HOWE PAPERS, 1868. 1 item. Boston, Mass.

Note of Samuel Gridley Howe, physician, reformer, and husband of Julia Ward Howe, written on the reverse side of a fragment of a letter probably written by his wife.

2677. SOLOMON HOWE PAPERS, 1819-1838. 47 items. New Salem (Franklin County), Mass.

Family correspondence of Solomon Howe and his wife, Mary Howe, and their children. Included are letters, 1819, from Jedediah Howe, concerning his stereotype foundry in New York City; letters, 1819-1821, from Milton Howe, who conducted a school in Richmond County, Virginia, giving some description of the country and his impressions of the people; letters from Celia Babbett, describing a journey to Orangeville, New York, and customs in western New York; and miscellaneous letters concerning New Englanders' reactions to the South, the depression following the panic of 1819, crops, commodity prices, and family matters.

2678. DAVID HOWELL PAPERS, 1829-1847. 15 items. Charles Town (Jefferson County), W. Va.

Correspondence between David Howell and his wife Hannah, and Howell's father's family in Clark County, Ohio, discussing family matters with references to commodity prices, a smallpox epidemic in Wheeling, Virginia, (now West Virginia) and Pittsburgh, Pennsylvania, 1829; the burning of Bushrod Washington's house; the death of President William Henry Harrison; and an abolitionist debate in Ohio.

2679. JOSHUA B. HOWELL PAPERS, 1862-1864. 13 items. South Carolina and Virginia.

Miscellaneous papers of Colonel Joshua B. Howell (d. 1864), 85th Pennsylvania Regiment, U.S.A., include ordnance, morning, and quartermaster reports; special orders concerning Howell's commands at Hilton Head, South Carolina, and Gloucester Point, Virginia; letter from Howell discussing a battle near Franklin, Virginia; letter from General Alfred Howe Terry to Katherine W. Howell concerning her husband's injuries and promotion to brigadier general; and letters requesting passes for Benjamin P. Howell, in order that he could recover his brother's body.

2680. PHILIP H. HOWERTON PAPERS, 1817-1879. 828 items. "Oakland" (Halifax County), Va.

Business letters pertaining to the Halifax County tobacco firm in which Philip Howerton was interested first with William Cabaniss and later with his son, William Matthew Howerton; personal letters to Judith and Eliza Howerton while they were students in St. Mary's College, Raleigh, North Carolina; letters from W. M. Howerton while a student at the University of North Carolina, Chapel Hill; and letters relative to the sale of the Clark threshing machine, the office of sheriff which Howerton held, and general labor conditions after the Civil War.

2681. WALTER M. HOWLAND AND GEORGE S. TILTON PAPERS, 1852-1871. 85 items. Massachusetts.

Letters of Walter M. Howland, serving in the quartermaster branch of the Union Army, and of George S. Tilton, 1st Massachusetts Cavalry, describing camp life, sickness, hospitals and nurses, picket duty, furloughs, religion, a prison camp near Chicago, newspaper criticism of military maneuvers, and military engagements, including a guerilla raid on a train, cavalry attack on Confederate artillery near Culpeper, Virginia, the devastation of Sulphur Springs, Virginia, and a Confederate attack causing the evacuation of a Union camp from Johnsonville to Nashville, Tennessee. Scattered letters refer to the presidential campaign of 1852, spring races at Louisville, Kentucky, 1865, and the Chicago Fire, 1871.

2682. THOMAS C. HOYT AND ISAIAH F. HOYT PAPERS, 1844-1909. 90 items. Beverly (Essex County), Mass.

The papers of Thomas C. Hoyt, captain of the barque Arthur, include letters to his family describing his voyages to Africa, 1847; papers dealing with the pepper trade off the coast of Sumatra, including letters from George Gardner, owner of the Arthur, containing instructions on routes to Sumatra, prices to pay for raw pepper, and the disposal of pepper on the European market, financial papers including letters of credit from European financial houses and invoices of the content of the cargo carried to Sumatra for trade, and letters from captains of other pepper ships, commenting on the pepper crop and prospects for purchasing peppers in different localities; and papers dealing with the New England Shoe and Leather Association, of which his nephew, Charles Hoyt was president. Papers of Isaiah F. Hoyt are principally concerned with his efforts to obtain money owed him for his service in the Union Army, in the 32nd Massachusetts Volunteers. Scattered references concern his business affairs as secretary of the Union Flax Mills in Chicago and as deputy collector of Internal Revenue for the First District of Illinois. Also included are correspondence of Josephine Hoyt, wife of Isaiah F. Hoyt, with a real estate dealer concerning the disposal of some property, and several letters by Isaiah's sons, Charles and Arthur, pertaining to the New England Shoe and Leather Association.

2683. EDMUND WILCOX HUBARD PAPERS, 1858. 2 items. Farmville (Prince Edward County), Va.

Papers of Edmund W. Hubard (1806-1878), planter and member of U. S. Congress, 1841-1847, referring to the appointment of a manager of the public schools and to physicians practicing in Richmond.

2684. EPAPHRODITUS E. HUBBARD PAPERS, 1842-1906. 119 items. Haddam and Higganum (Middlesex County), Conn.

Miscellaneous papers of Epaphroditus E. Hubbard include insurance policies; indentures; Democratic ticket for officers of Haddam, 1867; manual of homeopathy; personal letters; broadsides; receipts; and a handbill by Edwin Hubbard for use in soliciting money for the writing of a history of the Hubbard family.

2685. JOEL HUBBARD PAPERS, 1811-1855. 30 items. Republican Grove (Halifax County), Va.

Letter to Joel Hubbard, Baptist minister, from Eli Ball concerning the work of the General Association of Virginia in gathering information about Baptist churches in the state; a personal letter from Hubbard's cousin, Jesse E. Adams; and letters concerning financial matters and the repayment of money which Hubbard had loaned.

2686.   WADE H. HUBBARD PAPERS, 1864-1865.
        20 items.  Wilmington
        (New Hanover County), N.C.

Civil War correspondence of Wade H. Hubbard, a private in the Confederate Army stationed near Wilmington, North Carolina, showing his attitude toward the war, describing the battle of Fort Fisher, 1865, and discussing farm conditions at home.

2687.   A. HUBBELL AND E. CURRAN PAPERS,
        1838-1845.  5 items.  New York.

Business correspondence and promissory notes of Hubbell and Curran.

2688.   HORATIO HUBBELL PAPERS, 1840-1864.
        13 items.  Philadelphia, Pa.

Miscellaneous papers of Horatio Hubbell, lawyer, including letters from Samuel F. B. Morse regarding Hubbell's claim to priority in the suggestion of a trans-Atlantic telegraph cable.

2689.   JAY BROADUS HUBBELL PAPERS,
        1905-1977.  3,473 items.  Durham, N. C.

The papers of Jay Broadus Hubbell, professor emeritus of American Literature at Duke University, include correspondence, unpublished manuscripts, reprints, pictures, and clippings.  Correspondents include former students, colleagues, and prominent authors of the early 20th Century, among them Robert Frost, Ellen Glasgow, Carl Sandburg, Allen Tate, and John Hall Wheelock. The unpublished manuscripts record the development of American Literature as an academic discipline separate from English Literature.  The collection also includes reviews and letters pertaining to Hubbell's own writings and reprints of articles inscribed to Hubbell by former students and colleagues.

2690.   WALTER HUBBELL PAPERS, 1838.
        1 item.  Canandaigua
        (Ontario County), N.Y.

Letter from Walter Hubbell to his wife describing his trip to Detroit through Lake Ontario and Lake Erie.

2691.   BEN HUBERT PAPERS, 1812-1878.
        43 items.  Bryan (Brazos County), Texas.

Papers of Ben Hubert, 6th Regiment, Louisiana Volunteers, C.S.A., are principally love letters written during the Civil War to his future wife, Letitia Bailey.  There are scattered references to a fight on the Potomac, 1861; the fall of New Orleans, 1862; a request to Letitia Bailey to make a "Battle Flag"; the town of Bryan, Texas; and a reunion there of Hood's Brigade, 1876.  Also included is some correspondence of Ben Hubert's sisters.

2692.   SALLIE DONELSON HUBERT PAPERS,
        1850-1895.  20 items.  Barnett
        (Warren County), Ga.

Letters from Richard M. Johnston, head of the Pen Lucy School for Boys in Waverly, Maryland, to his cousin, Sallie D. Hubert, discussing family matters, his conversion and that of his six youngest children to Catholicism, arrangements for publishing a cookbook that Sallie Hubert had written, and family history.  There is also a circular of the Pen Lucy School, a program of lectures to be given by Johnston at the Convent of Notre Dame in Maryland, 1879, and a petition to raise money for John C. Calhoun in 1850.

2693.   GEORGE N. HUCKINS PAPERS, 1858-1861.
        1 vol.  (63 pp.) Berea
        (Cuyahoga County), Ohio.

Diary of George N. Huckins (b. 1838), a Methodist minister, while a student at Baldwin University in Berea, and while serving several churches in northern Ohio. Short, introspective entries generally relate to his doubts about his qualifications as a minister and to his matrimonial prospects, with brief references to his school activities and studies, John Brown, James Buchanan, the election of Lincoln and the beginning of the Civil War, and slavery.

2694.   CHARLES HUDSON PAPERS, 1876.  1 item.
        Lexington (Middlesex County), Mass.

Personal letter of Charles Hudson (1795-1881), politician and author.

2695.   ALFRED HUGER PAPERS, 1853-1863.
        3 vols.  Charleston, S. C.

Letterpress books of Alfred Huger (1788-1872), Charleston planter, attorney and postmaster, containing discussions and comments on personal and family matters, religion, especially the doctrine of miracles and church matters, duels, slavery, free Negroes, yellow fever epidemics, restrictions against Negro seamen visiting Charleston, treatment of slaves and of free Negroes, the banking crisis of 1857, filibustering in Latin America, railroads, suffrage, South Carolina politics, nullification, secession, the Charleston fire of 1861, the battle of Port Royal, South Carolina (1861), diplomatic recognition of the Confederate States of America, Confederate naval operations in Louisiana and off the Carolina coast, Confederate politics and government, the Sequestration Act, the siege of Charleston (1863), and Confederate relations with Great Britain.

2696. BENJAMIN HUGER PAPERS, 1783-1862. 16 items. Charleston, S. C.

Principally the correspondence of Benjamin Huger (1806-1877), an artillery expert, dealing with the manufacture of ammunition by Joseph Reid Anderson and Dr. Carmichael for Fortress Monroe and the armory at Harpers Ferry, Virginia, 1850-1851. Also included are a letter of 1803 from Daniel Huger, secretary of state, to the South Carolina legislature requesting an appropriation for the repair of the building where the records were kept; an indenture, 1824; a letter from John P. Martin discussing the problems of the mail and stage service; and letter, 1862, of Huger to Josiah Tattnall concerning military and naval operations in Virginia.

2697. OSSIAN HUGGINS PAPERS, 1868-1876. 7 items. Summerville (Chattooga County), Ga.

Personal letters from Ossian Huggins while a student at Washington College with comments on courses offered, requirements for obtaining degrees, and Robert E. Lee as president of the College. Included are two letters of a later period.

2698. JOHN HUGHES PAPERS, 1782-1823. 5 items. Burke County, N. C.

Land deeds.

2699. NICHOLAS COLLIN HUGHES PAPERS, 1886-1893. 6 items. Chocowinity (Beaufort County), N. C.

Letters from Collier Cobb, Thomas Egleston, and Samuel Hart to Nicholas C. Hughes, Episcopal minister, criticising his work, Genesis and Geology; and a personal letter from his brother, John Hughes.

2700. ROBERT W. HUGHES PAPERS, 1875-1881. 4 items. Norfolk, Va.

Recommendations for political appointments for the eastern part of Virginia from Robert W. Hughes (b. 1821), U. S. judge for that district, Confederate soldier, and candidate for governor of Virginia, 1873.

2701. VICTOR HUGO PAPERS. 1 item. Paris, France.

Facsimile of a holograph manuscript, probably a poem, by Victor Hugo.

2702. THOMAS ABRAM HUGUENIN AUTOBIOGRAPHY, ca. 1890. 1 vol. (41 pp.) Charleston, S. C.

Autobiography of Thomas A. Huguenin, major in the Confederate Army, with emphasis on the evacuation of Battery Wagner.

2703. HUIE, REID AND COMPANY PAPERS, (1782-1793) 1930. 37 items. Dumfries (Prince William County), Va.

Typed or photostatic copies of correspondence between the agents for the trading firms of Huie, Reid and Company, Dumfries; and Smith, Huie, Alexander and Company, Glasgow, Scotland. Topics include the tobacco markets in England and on the continent; demand, prices, and political influence on economic conditions. A letter, 1930, and an essay entitled "Old Letters from Dumfries, Va." by Bessie W. Gahn describe the economic and historical setting in which Huie, Reid and Company operated.

2704. DAVID WATTS HULINGS PAPERS, 1819-1863. 32 items. Lewistown (Mifflin County), Pa.

Personal and business papers of David Watts Huling, attorney, include family letters, indentures, contracts, legal papers concerning suits over deeds and damage suits against turnpike companies, bills, invoices and receipts.

2705. CHARLES H. HULL PAPERS, 1903. 3 items. Ithaca (Tompkins County), N. Y.

Letters from Charles H. Hull, professor at Cornell University, Ithaca, to W. H. Glasson, professor at Trinity College, Durham, North Carolina, concerning the resignation of John Spencer Bassett.

2706. ALEXANDER VON HUMBOLDT PAPERS, 1849. 1 item. Berlin, Germany.

Letter from Alexander von Humboldt (1769-1859), German naturalist and traveler.

2707. DAVID HUME PAPERS, 1760-1776. 18 items. Edinburgh, Scotland.

Photostatic copies of papers of David Hume (1711-1776), Scotch philosopher and historian, concerning the quarrel between Hume and Jean Jacques Rousseau over a pension for the latter, and commenting on the publication of the Clarendon Papers and on Sir James Dalrymple and Edward Gibbon.

2708. JOSEPH HUME PAPERS, 1813-1853. 38 items. "Burnley Hall," County Norfolk, England.

Correspondence of Joseph Hume (1777-1855), British politician and liberal reformer, discussing Hume's election to Parliament; taxes, including tax stamps for books and papers, county rates, and property taxes; military matters, especially Hume's desire for economy and retrenchment in the army and an end to naval and military sinecures; the policies of Sir James Brooke, Raja of Sarawak, Borneo; the criminal laws and the removal of convicts from the country; reform politics and the election of reform candidates; Hume's motion against Orange Societies; and policies of the Colonial Office, including a request of the Hudson's Bay Company for a monopoly over Vancouver Island, and the colonization of western Canada.

2709. ROBERT HUME PAPERS, 1869-1871. 5 items. Charleston, S. C.

Legal and financial papers, tax receipts, and receipts for physician's bills.

2710. E. J. HUMPHRIES PAPERS, 1861-1869. 3 items. Milledgeville (Baldwin County), Ga.

Letters, 1861, of E. J. Humphries, a member of the Governor's Horse Guards, while at Camp Davis, Lynchburg, Virginia; a letter, 1869, from an Augusta, Georgia, commission merchant to Humphries.

2711. ALBERT HUMRICKHOUSE PAPERS, 1809-1920. 390 items and 3 vols. Shepherdstown (Jefferson County), W. Va.

Business and family correspondence of Albert Humrickhouse (d. 1864), Shepherdstown postmaster, constable, and merchant, principally concerning his duties as postmaster, the settlement of the estate of John Weis, and mercantile matters. Also included are Jefferson County deeds and summonses. Several letters refer to Locofocoism in Maryland, 1844, and the Total Abstinence Society of Shepherdstown, 1845. There are a daybook, 1823-1824, and a ledger, 1833-1834, of Samuel Humrickhouse. A mercantile ledger, 1813-1821, of Albert Humrickhouse has many pages covered with clippings from the latter half of the 19th century.

2712. CHARLES ANTHONY HUNDLEY PAPERS, 1841-1921. 2,436 items. Charlotte County and Denniston (Halifax County), Va.

Papers of Charles A. Hundley (d. 1863), planter, commission agent and lawyer; of his father, Elisha Hundley (d. 1879), planter and land speculator; and of Daniel W. Owen, related by marriage, a planter, businessman, and member of the Virginia House of Delegates. Included are personal letters and school compositions of Charles A. Hundley while a student at Emory and Henry College; letters, 1849-1850, related to a California expedition organized by Elisha Hundley; correspondence, 1850-1852, between Charles A. Hundley and his future wife, Fanny Edmunds; correspondence, 1853-1861, of Elisha Hundley pertaining to mid-western land firms, and to the operation of his tobacco farm by Charles; correspondence after 1863 dealing with the estate of Charles A. Hundley and with the raising of his children, Eddy and Nannie; correspondence of Nannie Hundley while attending the Augusta Female Seminary, Staunton, Virginia; correspondence after 1879 concerning the estate of Elisha Hundley; letters after 1914 from the political associates and constituents of Daniel W. Owen concerning legislative issues; letters from D. B. Owen, Daniel Owen's son, concerning the management of the latter's farm, "Hyco Hill Stock Farm"; and letters from business firms in which Daniel Owen owned stock. Scattered letters refer to the Salem Female Institute, 1857; the Atlantic Cable, 1858; the need for higher education for women, 1914; a committee to aid women and children in warring Europe, 1914; the Owen Memorial Fund for the building erected in Kwangju, Korea, 1914; the education of D. W. Owen's son, F. C. Owen, at Hampden-Sydney Institute, Farmville, Virginia, 1916-1917; and the fighting in France, 1918.

2713. ELLEN HUNDLEY POEMS, 1852. 1 vol. (26 pp.) Henrico County, Va.

Original poetry composed by Ellen Hundley for her children. Included is the beginning of a diary covering December 1-3, 1852.

2714. NATHAN G. HUNT PAPERS, 1838-1890. 163 items and 1 vol. Huntsville (Yadkin County), N. C.

Papers of Nathan G. Hunt, merchant, include antebellum correspondence of young girls describing their household tasks, schooling, and their boyfriends; letters from Marmaduke D. Kimbraugh while a medical student at the University of Pennsylvania and during his early years as a physician; and letters from relatives in the Idaho territory describing farming conditions, prices, intermarriage with the Indians, and conversion to Christianity; and a ledger, 1852-1867, of Nathan Hunt.

2715. PLEASANT HUNT PAPERS, 1866. 1 item. Pleasant Garden, N. C.

Personal letter to Pleasant Hunt from his niece in Salem, Iowa.

2716. SAMUEL G. HUNT PAPERS, 1777-1863. 21 items. Forestville (Wake County), N. C.

Principally the Civil War correspondence between Samuel G. Hunt, a Confederate soldier, and his wife describing camp life and conditions at home. Included are land deeds, 1777-1842, in Granville County, North Carolina.

2717. WASHINGTON HUNT PAPERS, 1850. 1 item. Lockport (Niagara County), N. Y.

Letter to Washington Hunt (1811-1867), comptroller of New York and later governor, concerning a claim for a pension for the widow of a Continental Army officer.

2718. WILLIAM HOLMAN HUNT PAPERS, 1853-1891. 6 items. London England.

Letters to William Holman Hunt

(1827-1910), British painter, from poet Coventry Kersey Dighton Patmore discussing an attack upon the Royal Academy for its refusal to exhibit two pictures by John Brett, Hunt's painting, and other matters.

2719. HUNT & SMITH PAPERS, 1809.
1 item. Huntston, _____.

Receipt from Coles Creek Cotton Gin to Jacob Cable of Huntston.

2720. CHARLES N. HUNTER PAPERS, 1818-1931.
2,944 items and 18 vols.
Raleigh (Wake County), N. C.

Personal and professional papers of Charles N. Hunter (ca. 1851-1931), Negro educator and editor, include correspondence and other material on the problems of the Negro after the Civil War, Negro education, race relations, temperance, and family matters and personal finances. Scrapbooks contain clippings and other items concerning race relations and social, political, and economic affairs pertaining to the Negro. Correspondents include prominent national and state politicians and editors.

2721. J. C. HUNTER & CO. PAPERS, 1884-1888.
2 vols. Union (Union County), S. C.

Daybook and ledger of a general mercantile firm owned by J. C. Hunter, E. R. Wallace, and James H. Maxwell.

2722. JAMES HUNTER PAPERS, 1864-1865.
4 items. Augusta (Richmond County), Ga.

Confederate army orders concerning the defense of Savannah, signed by James Hunter for the acting adjutant general.

2723. ROBERT MERCER TALIAFERRO HUNTER PAPERS, 1836. 1 item. Richmond, Va.

Letter from Robert Mercer Taliaferro Hunter (1809-1887), lawyer and statesman, to C. G. Griswold concerning a proposal relative to banking and compromise resolutions on the abolition question.

2724. WILLIAM W. HUNTER PAPERS, 1864-1865.
105 items. Savannah, Ga.

Letters to William W. Hunter, Confederate naval commander, from Sidney Smith Lee, captain in charge of the Office of Orders and Detail, C.S.A. Navy Department, from John M. Brooke, commander in charge of the Office of Ordnance and Hydrography, C.S.A. Navy Department, and from other naval officers regarding ships, supplies, watchwords, men absent without leave and deserters, courts-martial, the laying of torpedoes in the harbor of Savannah, and other naval matters, with numerous references to various Confederate ships.

2725. HUNTER FAMILY PAPERS, 1844, 1847.
2 items. Pennsylvania.

Letter from Andrew H. Hunter (1804-1888), lawyer and Whig politician, to William Beale; and a letter to General Andrew Hunter, Marshal of the District of Columbia, from a clerk who considered himself underpaid.

2726. DANIEL HUNTINGTON PAPERS, 1862-1881.
3 items. New York, N.Y.

Letters to Daniel Huntington (1816-1906), painter, from J. Strickler Jenkins concerning Jenkins's portrait, from John Bigelow pertaining to a portrait of Samuel J. Tilden, and from Philip Henry Sheridan discussing Sheridan's portrait.

2727. ELIJAH HUNTLEY PAPERS, 1864-1877.
27 items. Deep Creek (Anson County), N. C.

Personal correspondence of Elijah Huntley, farmer, including letters from a friend at Pine Bluff, Arkansas, describing the countryside, inhabitants, and agricultural and economic conditions; a letter of similar nature concerning Houston County, Georgia; and papers relating to the estate of Lewis Griggs for which Huntley was administrator.

2728. CHARLES H. HUNTON PAPERS, 1815-1896.
425 items. Buckland (Prince William County), Va.

Business letters of Charles H. Hunton, connected with the Fauquier and Alexandria Turnpike Company; partial record of a toll-gate keeper, 1844-1845; letters from Hunton to his son, Henry, a student at the College of William and Mary, Williamsburg, Virginia, 1855-1858, and Henry Hunton's student letters with comments on expenses, traveling, tuition, school living conditions, the curriculum, and the personality of the professors, among whom are Benjamin S. Ewell, Silas Totten, and Thomas T. L. Snead; letters pertaining to Henry Hunton's marriage to Mary P. Carter, of Westmoreland County; letters from Philadelphia, Pennsylvania, where Henry Hunton later studied art, with comments on his teacher, James Reid Lambdin; letters from Charles Hunton, which show opposition to secession and his antipathy toward such events as John Brown's Raid; and postwar letters by the younger sisters of Henry and Mary P. (Carter) Hunton, concerning social and home life during Reconstruction.

2729. EPPA HUNTON PAPERS, 1875-1905.
12 items. Warrenton (Fauquier County), Va.

Business letters of Eppa Hunton (1822-1908), brigadier general in the Confederate Army, concerning his legal practice in Washington, D. C.; personal letters commenting on Confederate veterans' reunions;

a letter of recommendation; and a calling card with a note by Hunton.

2730. ELIAS HURLEY PAPERS, 1866-1885. 22 items. Mount Gilead (Montgomery County), N. C.

Personal and business correspondence of Elias Hurley, with mention of railroads, politics, and land claims in North Carolina.

2731. WILLIAM MINOR HURST PAPERS, 1829-1850. 17 items. Harrisburg (Dauphin County), Pa.

Personal correspondence of William Minor Hurst, who worked in the office of the auditor general of Pennsylvania, including letters from a young woman to whom he was paying court.

2732. HURT FAMILY PAPERS, 1860-1925. 16 items. Halifax and Pittsylvania Counties, Va.

Miscellaneous papers of the Hurt family, especially brothers Henry Hays Hurt and John Linn Hurt, both state political leaders. Included are letters discussing state politics, legal papers concerning the appointment of members of the Hurt family to various official positions in local government; a financial statement, 1899, for Chatham, Virginia, of which W. B. Hurt was mayor; and a newspaper clipping about W. H. F. Lee.

2733. HERMANN HUSING PAPERS, 1859. 9 items. Bremen, Germany.

Papers dealing with the collision of the U.S.S. _Mississippi_ with the barque _Diana_, whose captain was Hermann Husing. Papers concern the accident, damages, and claims.

2734. JOHN HUSKE AND JAMES HOGG AND COMPANY LEDGER, 1783-1789. 1 vol. Fayetteville (Cumberland County), N. C.

Financial records.

2735. WILLIAM HUSKISSON PAPERS, 1794. 2 items. London, England.

Letters from Philippe D'Auvergne, Prince de Bouillon, to William Huskisson (1770-1830), British statesman, concerning communications with French royalists, a plot against the King, and the illness of Sir Evan Nepean.

2736. DAVID HUTCHESON PAPERS, 1885-1899. 9 items. Washington, D. C.

Principally personal letters to David Hutcheson (b. 1834), librarian and member of the staff of the Library of Congress, from Daniel F. Frazer, chemist of Glasgow, Scotland, and father of social anthropologist Sir James George Frazer.

The letters discuss personal matters; the writing, publication, and sale of _The Story of the Making of Buchanan Street_; James Frazer's works on a translation of Pausanias, his articles for the _Encyclopaedia Britannica_, and his _The Golden Bough_; and British economy and politics.

2737. JAMES HUTCHESON PAPERS, 1811-ca. 1868. 1 vol. Richmond, Va.

Receipt book, 1811-1813, recording payments for freight and storage on commodities bought in various places in Virginia; and a statement, ca. 1868, about the circumstances in the election of a new pastor at the Bethel Presbyterian Church, Greenville, Virginia.

2738. JOHN HUTCHESON MANUSCRIPT, 1705. 1 vol. (616 pp.) Armagh, County Armagh, Northern Ireland.

Manuscript of "A Brief Explication of the Shorter Catechisme with Practicall Inferences from the Doctrines Thereof."

2739. JAMES HILL HUTCHINS POEMS, 1834-1881. 1 vol. (94 ff.) Austin (Travis County), Tex.

Original poetry by James Hill Hutchins including "My Native Town" concerning New Bern, North Carolina, poetry dating from the Civil War, poetry about historic events in Texas, and other topics. Explanatory notes are often included with the text.

2740. NATHAN LOUIS HUTCHINS, SR., AND NATHAN LOUIS HUTCHINS, JR., PAPERS, 1815 (1830-1869) 1906. 630 items and 1 vol. Lawrenceville (Gwinnett County), Ga.

Papers of Nathan Louis Hutchins, Sr. (1799-1870), and Nathan Louis Hutchins, Jr. (1835-1905), both Georgia lawyers, judges and legislators, are comprised chiefly of letters from clients and fellow attorneys concerning cases in progress. Also included are the business papers of James Austin, family and business letters, and correspondence concerning political campaigns. A letter-book, 1854-1856, contains correspondence pertaining to an estate administered by Nathan L. Hutchins, Sr.

2741. [HUTCHISON ?] AND TOWNSHEND ACCOUNT BOOK, 1827-1829. 1 vol. Middleburg [Ga.?]

Accounts of one Hutchison and Townshend McVeigh, general merchants.

2742. FREDERICK HUTH AND COMPANY PAPERS, 1810-1850. 166 items. London, England.

Business correspondence of the mercantile firm of Frederick Huth and Company including letters from Spain, France, Germany, Argentina, the Philippines, and the United States, concerning shipments of tobacco, fish, wool, tallow, flax, black pepper, cocoa, cinnamon, wheat, and sugar. Also discussed are the economic and political conditions in the various countries which might affect their shipping business.

2743. RICHARD HUTSON PAPERS, 1776. 2 items. Charleston, S. C.

Copies of letters of Richard Hutson (1748-1795), lawyer and Revolutionary patriot, describing the arrival of the British fleet at the Charleston bar, the British attack, the bombardment of Sullivan's Island, the American defense, and the repulse of the British troops.

2744. ROBERT G. HUTSON PAPERS, 1769 (1813-1887) 1909. 115 items. Pine Grove (Union County), S. C.

Principally the personal correspondence of Robert G. Hutson (d. 1864), a Confederate soldier, with scattered comments on military and economic affairs. Early papers are South Carolina deeds. Other letters concern Robert Hutson's death, and opinion on General Johnson Hagood's order to charge at Petersburg, June 28, 1864.

2745. WILLIAM H. HYATT PAPERS, 1850-1872. 43 items. Norwalk (Fairfield County), Conn.

Letters from William H. Hyatt, who served in the quartermaster corps of the Federal army, to his mother, commenting on the possible ending of the war; a letter, 1865, mentioning prison camps; letters concerning the Gifford Hyatt family of Washington, North Carolina; and miscellaneous material consisting of high school themes and clippings.

2746. JOHN HYDE PAPERS, 1891-1898. 5 items. Washington, D. C.

Correspondence of John Hyde, statistician, official in the Department of Agriculture, and editor of the National Geographic, concerning statistical reports on agriculture, banking, etc.

2747. MCKENZIE HOOKS HYMAN PAPERS, 1954-1962. 14 items. Cordele (Crisp County), Ga.

Copy of a letter from McKenzie Hooks Hyman (1923-1963), author, commenting on his years as a student at Duke University, Durham, North Carolina, and his novel No Time for Sergeants; and clippings pertaining to his literary career.

2748. WILLIAM IDLER PAPERS, 1868-1877. 3 items. Philadelphia, Pa.

Letters to William Idler concerning the claim of Jacob Idler against the government of Venezuela; and a letter of recommendation.

2749. M. C. IJAMES PAPERS, 1872-1926. 18 items and 2 vols. Mocksville (Davie County), N. C.

An account book, 1886-1924, containing the accounts of M. C. Ijames, a physician, for his patients, 1886-1905; his account with the Bank of Davie, 1916-1924; a list of property sold by S. W. Little, a physician; Little's farm accounts, 1893-1901; and Ijames's accounts as executor of Little's estate. An account book of the Ijames family, 1851-1925, containing accounts of the firm of Anderson and Ijames, 1851-1853, and of its successor, G. J. Anderson and Company, 1851-1854; daybook entries for a surveyor, 1917-1925; mercantile and other miscellaneous accounts, 1909-1924; and several entries for the 1850s. Items include letters of S. W. Little, a list of voters for 1926 in the North Calahaln Township of Davie County, a campaign letter, 1924, from Baxter Durham concerning his reelection as state auditor of North Carolina, and miscellaneous papers of M. C. Ijames.

2750. STONEHEWER EDWARD ILLINGWORTH JOURNAL AND LETTER BOOK, 1871-1872. 1 vol. (260 pp.) Borough Court, Winchfield, Hampshire, England.

Journal and letter book of Stonehewer E. Illingworth (1842-1910), a director of the St. John del Rey Mining Company, Ltd., describing his travels in the Brazilian provinces of Rio Grande do Sul and Minas Gerais, the gas lighting of three major cities in Rio Grande do Sul inaugurated by Messrs. Upward and Illingworth as contractors for the San Pedro Brazilian Gas Company, Ltd., and his inspections of the gold mines of the St. John del Rey Mining Company at Morro Velho and of other gold and diamond mines.

2751. THOMAS ILLINGWORTH DIARY, 1755-1759. 1 vol. Silsden and Yeadon, Yorkshire, England. Restricted.

Diary of Thomas Illingworth during his years as a teacher in Yeadon, principally devoted to his spiritual life but also with references to the early Methodist movement in Yorkshire, theological issues of early Methodism, disputes between the Methodist societies and the Church of England parishes, the relationship of the Methodists to the Moravians, George Whitefield's Calvinistic theology, discipline problems in his school, and subject matter and classroom methods.

2752. ILLINOIS. ADAMS COUNTY SCHOOL DISTRICT NO. 1. DIRECTORS MINUTE BOOK, 1855-1871. 1 vol. (240 pp.)

Minute book of the directors of School District No. 1, Range No. 1, south of Range 5 West.

2753.  THOMAS S. IMBORDEN MANUSCRIPT, 1934. 16 pp. Bricks (Halifax County), N. C.

History of the Brick School, a school for Negroes, whose benefactress was Mrs. Joseph Keasby Brewster-Brick of New York, written by its principal, T. S. Imborden, educator, describing the development and improvement of the school.

2754.  IMMORTALITÉ AND FLYING FISH LOGBOOKS, 1872-1876. 1 vol. (204 pp.)

Journal and logbook of two ships of the British navy, the Immortalité on cruise in the Caribbean, the Mediterranean and the Atlantic, and the Flying Fish on patrol off Madagascar for the suppression of the slave trade.

2755.  HENRY ALEXANDER INCE PAPERS, 1842-1848. 2 vols. London, England.

Letter books of Henry Alexander Ince, confidential employee of the London commercial house of Palmer, Mackillop, Dent & Co., concerning his journey to the United States in order to examine investments and to settle claims against individual and business debtors that had defaulted. The letter books contain correspondence to and from his employers in England and to and from his legal and financial advisers and the debtors in America. The investments and claims involved banks, including the Union Bank of Florida, Tallahassee, the North American Trust and Banking Company of New York, the Bank of Darien, Georgia, the Bank of Louisiana, and Charleston, South Carolina, banks; midwestern canals; the New York and Erie Railroad; real estate in Lockport and New York City, New York; and plantations in Florida. The correspondence also discusses economic conditions in England and the United States; the problems of British investors; and the grain, cotton, and money markets in the United States and England.

2756.  INDIA PAPERS, 1737-1947. 45 items.

Miscellaneous items relating to the history of India, especially during the period of British rule, including a manuscript (12 pp.), 1798, by John Baird discussing a plan for increasing the opium trade in India; letters, 1799-1800, from Sir James Henry Craig, commander of a British division in Bengal, concerning the military situation in India; letters, 1801-1802, from John Chamier, chief secretary to the Madras government, pertaining to his desire for a seat on the Madras Council and future reforms; manuscripts, 1796-1805, discussing various aspects of the import and export trade between India and America, recording statistics and noting products involved; a map, 1820, of portions of Nagpur and Rewa provinces; letter, 1849, from Thomas Boaz requesting funds for a college to train Indian clergymen; a list, 1849, of goods purchased for Boston, Massachusetts, merchants; letter, 1866, from Henry R. E. Wellesley, Madras 1st Light Cavalry, describing his duties and the climate in India, hunting trips, British politics, and the sepoy army; letter, 1867, from Francis Napier, Tenth Baron Napier, governor of Madras, concerning the structure of the Indian government and his desire for a strong central government; letter, 1879, from General Frederick Sleigh Roberts, First Earl Roberts, discussing parts of his campaign in Afghanistan; letter, 1880, from Sir William Milbourne James criticizing British military ventures into Afghanistan; letter, 1882, from General Frederick Sleigh Roberts objecting to British policy of abandoning Kandahar and expressing fear of a Russian advance; letter, 1883, from John Wodehouse, First Earl of Kimberley, secretary of state for India, concerning the Rajputana railway and the Egyptian telegraph; letters, 1886, from Sir Herbert Hope Risley discussing his work on a census glossary and on marriage customs in Bengal; letter, 1893, from Sir Henry Mortimer Durand, foreign secretary in India, discussing his book, Helen Trevelyan; letter, 1902, from Sir Evelyn Baring, First Earl of Cromer, pertaining to plans for the Indian railway; letter, 1915, from Sir Stephen George Sale reviewing the legal basis for viceroyalty in India; letter, 1930, from Sir William Malcolm Hailey criticizing English newspapers for using India as an issue against the Labour Party and discussing the Indian Congress Party; and a letter, 1947, from Chakravarti Rajagopalachari, governor of West Bengal, discussing some of the changes in India since independence.

2757.  INDIAN SPRINGS BAPTIST CHURCH PAPERS. 1 item. Indian Springs (Butts County), Ga.

Typed historical sketch of the Indian Springs Baptist Church established in 1825.

2758.  RUFUS INGALLS PAPERS, 1862-1865. 5 items. New York, N. Y.

Routine business letters pertaining to the Quartermaster Department of the Army of the Potomac, of which Rufus Ingalls was chief quartermaster.

2759.  WILLIAM RALPH INGE PAPERS. 1 item. Brightwell Manor, Wallingford, Berkshire, England.

Letter, written between 1911 and 1934, from William Ralph Inge (1860-1954), Anglican clergyman and author, inviting the addressee to join the "Brotherhood," a dining club whose other members are named.

2760.  CHARLES JARED INGERSOLL PAPERS, 1846. 1 item. Philadelphia, Pa.

Letter from Samuel A. Douglass

to Charles Jared Ingersoll, U. S. Congressman, requesting aid in obtaining a commission and discussing public attitude toward the Mexican War.

2761. SAMUEL DELUCENNA INGHAM PAPERS, 1829-1830. 9 items. Washington, D. C.

Routine correspondence of Samuel Delucenna Ingham while U.S. secretary of the treasury.

2762. E. B. INGRAM PAPERS, 1895-1896. 1 vol. Society Hill (Darlington County), S. C.

Journal of E. B. Ingram, employee of a general merchandise store, containing business records, and Ingram's comments on local affairs, the weather, business activity at the store, the arrival of drummers, and the preaching of Negro girl.

2763. JOHN INGRAM PAPERS, 1852-1863. 12 items. Forsyth County, N. C.

Correspondence between a Confederate soldier and his wife discussing camp life, desertion, conditions at home, crops, and lack of money.

2764. JOHN H. INGRAM PAPERS, 1878-1905. 12 items. London, England.

Letters written to John H. Ingram (1849-1916), an English literary figure, from scholars in Berlin, Leipzig, Budapest, and Paris, concerning Ingram's works and his interest in Edgar Allan Poe. They contain comment especially upon Poe's influence on French literature.

2765. INN REGISTER AND ACCOUNT BOOK, 1832-1835. 1 vol. (131 pp.) North Carolina.

Register of guests and grocery accounts of a small inn.

2766. *INTENDED* LOGBOOK, 1862. 1 vol. (86 pp.) London, England.

Logbook of the *Intended* recording primarily routine matters about its journey from London to Nassau and America, including weather, course, speed, and location. Also described is the seizure of the ship as a war prize and the sailing of the ship to Philadelphia by the prize crew.

2767. INTERNATIONAL BROTHERHOOD OF ELECTRICAL WORKERS, LOCAL UNION NO. 382, PAPERS, 1903-1950. 1,206 items and 25 vols. Columbia (Richland County), S. C.

Records of the International Brotherhood of Electrical Workers, Local Union No. 382 (AFL) include correspondence of the financial secretary, the recording secretary, business agent, and officials of the international union discussing job openings, financial matters such as fees, dues and wages, union cards, and legislation; agreements and contracts usually between Local 382 and the electrical contractors of Columbia; electrical examinations; applications for membership; traveling cards; a receipt book containing receipts for dues, salaries, hall rent, and benefits; a dues book, 1905-1910; executive board minutes, 1931-1950; and minutes, 1903-1928, of the general meetings of Local 382.

2768. INTERNATIONAL BROTHERHOOD OF ELECTRICAL WORKERS, LOCAL UNION NO. 776, PAPERS, 1938-1953. 39 items and 15 vols. Charleston, S.C.

Records of the International Brotherhood of Electrical Workers, Local Union No. 776 (AFL), include correspondence concerning the Charleston Building and Construction Trades Council, the Charleston Shipbuilding and Drydock Company, and business affairs of Local 776; agreements of Local 776 with various companies; a report of a conference between the Charleston Shipbuilding and Drydock Company and several union organizations; a "Joint Petition to Wage Stabilization Board" presented by Local 776 and the West Virginia Pulp and Paper Company; the proceedings of the 1946 and of the 1948 conventions of the International Brotherhood of Electrical Workers; pamphlets of agreements, 1946-1952, involving Local 776, the Charleston (South Carolina) Mill of the West Virginia Pulp and Paper Company, and the South Carolina Power Company; copies of minutes, 1944, for regular meetings and Executive Board meetings of Local 776; items pertaining to disputes and other matters involving the Charleston Building and Construction Trades Council; a typed copy of an address by James F. Barrett, publicity director in the South for the American Federation of Labor, entitled "Place of the American Federation of Labor in the Economics and Social Welfare of the South"; and minutes, 1939-1942, of meetings of Local 776.

2769. INTERNATIONAL LADIES' GARMENT WORKERS' UNION. UPPER SOUTH DEPARTMENT PAPERS, 1960. 1 item. Baltimore, Md.

A four-year contract of the International Ladies' Garment Workers' Union, Upper South Department (AFL), with the Marion (Virginia) Manufacturing Corporation, the Holston Manufacturing Corporation, the Abingdon Manufacturing Corporation, and the Harwood Manufacturing Corporation.

2770. INTERNATIONAL MOLDERS' UNION OF NORTH AMERICA, LOCAL UNION NO. 121, PAPERS, 1934-1937. 3 items and 1 vol. Radford (Montgomery County), Va.

Papers of the International Molders' Union of North America, Local Union No. 121, (AFL), consist of a pamphlet containing the constitution and rules of order of the International Molders' Union; a financier's report for the third quarter of 1937; and an invoice concerning non-journeymen stamps.

2771. INTERNATIONAL TYPOGRAPHICAL UNION, LOCAL UNION NO. 43, PAPERS, 1886-1953. 2,803 items and 183 vols. Charleston, S. C.

Papers of the International Typographical Union, Local Union No. 43, include correspondence, 1912-1948, primarily of the various persons who served as secretary-treasurer of Local 43, discussing arbitration, a ten per cent assessment on earnings of union members to promote the 44-hour week, wages, strike benefits and contributions, conventions, membership, dues, and traveling cards; information sent from the International Typographical Union; an incomplete run of _The Bulletin_, 1940-1953; the Chapel Chairman's Monthly Itemized Reports, 1936-1950; Monthly (Stamp) Reports, 1910-1939, containing copies of the reports sent by the financial secretary of the local union to the secretary-treasurer of the International Typographical Union, with stamp, financial, and membership statements; account books, 1913-1930, detailing individual collections of fines and assessments, expenditures, and receipts; Secretary's Monthly Itemized Reports, 1920-1936, recording the dues collected by the union; Secretary's Daily Cash Books, 1931-1949, containing daily receipts such as dues and other fees, as well as disbursements for salaries, rent, and postage; minute books, 1886-1911 and 1928-1938; applications for membership, 1923-1938, and for apprentice membership, 1932-1938; old age pension rolls, 1940-1945; _Fiftieth Anniversary, Charleston Typographical Union, No. 43_ (1936); and _22nd Session, The Virginia-Carolinas Typographical Conference_ (1942).

2772. INTERNATIONAL TYPOGRAPHICAL UNION, LOCAL UNION NO. 54, PAPERS, 1921-1945. 17 items and 3 vols. Raleigh (Wake County), N. C.

The papers of International Typographical Union, Local Union No. 54, consist of a pamphlet containing a record of the suit in 1921 of Marguerite McGinnis, et al. vs. the union; contracts; amendments; a set of resolutions adopted in 1944 in memory of Thomas L. Briggs, a member of the union; a letter from Howard T. Colvin, commissioner of conciliation, to Lawrence E. Nichols, president of Local 54, concerning wages and contracts; and minutes, 1925-1945.

2773. INTER-RACIAL RELATIONS MEETINGS PAPERS, 1934-1936. 4 items. Chapel Hill (Orange County), N. C., and Richmond, Va.

Programs of inter-racial relations meetings held in Raleigh and Winston-Salem, North Carolina, and Norfolk, Virginia, 1934-1936.

2774. INTRACOASTAL WATERWAY MAP, 1930. 1 item. North Carolina and South Carolina.

Survey map of the "Intracoastal Waterway Right-of-Way from Cape Fear River, N. C. to Little River, S. C." made by Lewis L. Merritt.

2775. SAM IRBY PAPERS, 1931-1932. 297 items. New Orleans, La.

Original manuscript of _Kidnapped by The Kingfish, By Sam Irby, the Victim_ (Laurel, Miss.: 1932), a book attacking Huey P. Long's political methods; several letters to the publisher regarding publication of the book; the revised manuscript; the galley proof; and some miscellaneous material including copy for and one issue of _The Louisiana Guardian_.

2776. JAMES IREDELL, SR., AND JAMES IREDELL, JR., PAPERS, 1724-1890. 1,046 items and 6 vols. Edenton (Chowan County), N. C.

Family, personal, political, public, and legal papers of James Iredell, Sr. (1751-1799), statesman and associate justice of the U.S. Supreme Court; of his wife, Hannah (Johnston) Iredell; and of their son, James Iredell, Jr. (1788-1853), governor of North Carolina, 1827, U.S. senator, 1828-1831, and attorney.

The papers of James Iredell, Sr., concern the Revolutionary War, state and national politics, his duties as Supreme Court justice, and family matters. Included are letters discussing independence versus loyalty to Great Britain; British colonial policy; the operation of the war, both militarily and politically; state financial difficulties; peace treaty with Great Britain; various political pamphlets published 1783-1784; North Carolina politics; formulation and ratification of the Constitution; Federalists versus Anti-Federalists in North Carolina; amendments to the Constitution; funding of the national debt and assumption of the state debt; cession of western lands to the Federal government; relations between Great Britain and the United States; the regulation of the slave trade; the establishment of the University of North Carolina; Iredell's duties as Supreme Court Justice and his assignment to the Southern circuit; U.S. negotiations with the Creek Indians; the Whiskey Rebellion; yellow fever epidemics in Philadelphia, 1793 and 1797-1798; the presidential campaign of 1796; and disunionist sentiment in Virginia, 1799. There is also correspondence from friends and relatives in England and Ireland, especially from his cousin Margaret Macartney giving accounts of her travels in England and Ireland in the 1770s, and from Henry Eustace McCulloh, a relative of Iredell and large landholder in North Carolina, concerning people and events in North Carolina, and on McCulloh's efforts to obtain titles to his North Carolina lands and the unfair character of the Confiscation Act.

Correspondence of James Iredell, Jr., concerns his education at the College of New Jersey, Princeton; his election to the governorship of North Carolina; requests for patronage and aid in obtaining appointments to the U.S. military and naval academies; defalcation of a Federal employee of Elizabeth City, North Carolina; public lands; Andrew Jackson's political standing in North Carolina; national and state politics; nullification; family matters; and Picot's school for young ladies in Philadelphia, Pennsylvania, where Iredell wished to send his daughter. Correspondence of Hannah (Johnston) Iredell includes letters from her brother, Samuel Johnston, concerning political and family matters, letters from P. Lowther describing the people and customs around Yorktown, Virginia, and letters from the Page family at Rosewell Plantation, Gloucester County, Va. Other papers include bills and receipts; legal notes and reports of James Iredell, Sr., and James Iredell, Jr.; land deeds and indentures; commissions of office; drafts of political pamphlets of James Iredell, Sr., including an address to George III giving reasons why Iredell and other British-born Americans feel compelled to renounce their allegiance to the crown, and a letter "To The Public" upholding the right of judicial review; genealogies of the Iredell, McCulloh and Macartney families; poetry; and diplomas from various University of North Carolina societies. Volumes are legal memoranda of James Iredell, Sr., while a Supreme Court justice containing his personal notes in cases argued; his customs book for the Port of Roanoke (Edenton, North Carolina), 1772-1776; Edenton Academy Schoolbook of James Iredell, Jr., 1802-1803; and the legal memoranda of James Iredell, Jr., as court reporter of the decisions of the Supreme Court of North Carolina, 1835-1837. Among the correspondents are John Branch, John C. Calhoun, Henry Clay, William Richardson Davie, William Johnson Dawson, Oliver Ellsworth, Robert Y. Hayne, John Haywood, William Hooper, John Jay, Samuel Johnston, Charles Lee, Henry Lee, Archibald Maclaine, Willie P. Mangum, John Marshall, John Motley Morehead, Timothy Pickering, Richard Dobbs Spaight, Zachary Taylor, John Tyler, and Hugh Williamson.

2777. OSCAR BROWN IRELAND PAPERS, 1861-1865. 116 items. New York, N. Y.

Civil War correspondence of Oscar Brown Ireland (1840-1915), actuary, consists of letters from Appleton Sturgis while serving on U.S. transport ships taking troops to Yorktown, Virginia, for the Peninsular Campaign, containing references to life in Washington, D. C., during the war and the activities of the Monitor and the Virginia, and while a clerk in the Ordnance Office of the Department of the Gulf in New Orleans, describing Federal occupation of the city, the attitudes of the civilians, the battle of Galveston, Texas, 1863, and the siege of Port Hudson, Louisiana, 1863; and the letters of Oscar Brown Ireland, serving as an officer in the Signal Corps, describing the movement of troops and supplies for the siege of Petersburg, Sheridan's Valley Campaign, camp life, troop morale, and his duties as a signal officer.

2778. JARED IRWIN PAPERS, 1783-1855. 15 items. Washington County, Ga.

Correspondence of Jared Irwin (1751-1818), member of the state legislature, and governor of Georgia, 1796-1797, includes a letter from Captain Webb justifying his action in a skirmish with the Indians; a letter to Governor George Mathews informing him of a new militia commander at Fort Twiggs; a letter from John Habersham submitting a treaty with the Creek Indians for his approval; a letter from Abraham Baldwin regarding the investigation of the conspiracy of William Blount; and several items referring to the sale, the transportation and the marriage of slaves.

2779. ALFRED IVERSON PAPERS, 1861. 1 item. Richmond, Va.

Letter to Alfred Iverson (1798-1873), Georgia jurist, congressman, and senator, concerning the confinement of a friend to a lunatic asylum.

2780. RALPH IZARD PAPERS, 1775-1821. 5 items. Charleston, S.C.

Papers of Ralph Izard (1742-1804), delegate to the Continental Congress, 1782-1783, and U.S. senator from South Carolina, 1789-1795, include a letter, 1775, from Izard to Arthur Lee describing affairs in the colonies and Sir James Wright, governor of Georgia; a letter concerning payment of a debt of his son, George Izard; and a testimonial letter of Governor William Moultrie and two certificates proving that Izard was a member of the South Carolina legislature at the time his property was sold during the American Revolution as British property.

2781. ANDREW JACKSON PAPERS, 1796 (1814-1843) 1907. 62 items. Nashville (Davidson County), Tenn.

Papers of Andrew Jackson (1767-1845), general in the U.S. Army and president of the United States, 1829-1837, chiefly concern military and Indian affairs. Letters discuss an engagement with the British at Mobile, Alabama, 1814; raids of the Creek and Seminole Indians; relations of the U.S. government with Indians in Alabama; the use of U.S. troops to remove intruders from Cherokee lands; affairs of the military department of the South when Jackson was in command, 1816; construction of a military road from Nashville to New Orleans, 1816; and military actions in the Seminole Wars, 1835-1842. Several letters discuss politics during and after Jackson's presidency, including a photostatic copy of a letter concerning relations between Jackson and John Rhea and the break with John C. Calhoun. A letter, 1907, from Attorney Shipp contains a copy of a letter from John McKee, U.S. agent for the Chickasaw Indians, 1812-1813, telling that the Choctaws will fight the Creeks, and a copy of an address by Jackson to the assembled Creek and Cherokee warriors, 1814. Clippings, 1812-1818, concern military actions against the British in Florida and Georgia during the War of 1812, fighting with the Creek, and Jackson's invasion of West Florida.

2782. ASA JACKSON SURVEY BOOKS, 1844-1856. 2 vols. Loudoun County, Va.

Records of land surveyed by Asa Jackson in and around Loudoun County, Virginia.

2783. ASA M. JACKSON PAPERS, 1877-1927. 32 items. Athens (Clarke County), Ga.

Invitations to local commencements and entertainments received by Judge Asa M. Jackson.

2784. SIR CHARLES JAMES JACKSON PAPERS, 1907. 5 items. London, England.

Letters of Sir Charles James Jackson, antiquarian, concerning his writing on English plate, communion plate, silver and goldsmiths, etc.

2785. EBENEZER JACKSON LETTER BOOKS, 1801-1820. 2 vols. Savannah, Ga.

Correspondence of Ebenezer Jackson, apparently secretary of the Tennessee Land Company, concerning the bush lands of Georgia ceded by the Indians; stock in the Tennessee Land Company, 1816; the climate of Savannah; the prospect of a compromise between Congress and claimants of Georgia lands, 1813; speculation in Sea Island cotton; cotton and rice prices; the War of 1812; and personal and family matters.

2786. EVIE HARDEN JACKSON JOURNAL, 1901-1902. 1 vol. (196 pp.) Austell (Cobb County) and Decatur (De Kalb County), Ga.

Journal of Evie Harden Jackson describing her visit to Austell, Georgia, and her life and activities as a music teacher at an Orphan's Home in Decatur, Georgia.

2787. HENRY ROOTES JACKSON PAPERS, 1860, 1874. 2 items. Savannah, Ga.

Letter from Oliver H. Prince to Henry Rootes Jackson (1820-1898) dealing with legal and family matters; and a letter from Jackson to Charles Jones, Jr., praising his book, The Siege of Savannah.

2788. JAMES JACKSON PAPERS, 1775-1843. 34 items. Savannah, Ga.

Personal, legal, political, and military papers of James Jackson (1757-1806), U.S. senator, 1793-1795 and 1801-1806, and governor of Georgia, 1798-1801. A number of letters are concerned with supplies for the militia, orders for troop movements, the duty of preventing a landing in Georgia of Negroes from the West Indies, and trouble with the Indians. Political correspondence includes Jackson's announcement in 1795 of his candidacy for the state legislature; a letter explaining his refusal to accept the governorship of Georgia in 1788; a copy of the Yazoo Land Act of 1795; a letter referring to attempts to connect Jackson with the sale of western lands, and the testimony of John Guthrie showing the means used in securing passage of the act; and a letter from Abraham Baldwin concerning negotiations to settle Georgia's western boundaries. Legal papers pertain to cases, and include a letter to Joseph Clay protesting the filing of a judgment against Jackson, and a letter commenting on William Few's supposed activities to exclude lawyers from Richmond County. Two letters from Jackson to Edward Langworthy relate to materials for a history of Georgia and contain comments on David Ramsay's history of South Carolina and the part played by Georgia in the Revolutionary War. Also included are bills for books and merchandise purchased in London in 1784 and a contract for hiring a slave, 1785.

2789. JAMES JACKSON PAPERS, 1861. 1 item. Athens (Clarke County), Ga.

Personal letter of James Jackson (1819-1887), jurist.

2790. JOSEPH FRANCIS AMBROSE JACKSON PAPERS, 1829-1944. 237 items. Philadelphia, Pa.

Papers of Joseph Francis Ambrose Jackson (1867-1946), editor, critic, and historian, include ca. 100 letters, 1914-1944, from Mary Elizabeth Phillips concerning her biography of Edgar Allan Poe entitled Poe, The Man (1926) principally pertaining to her research, to her efforts to find a publisher, and to a rival biography; letters from other Poe experts, including James Howard Whitty two facsimile letters of Edgar Allan Poe and a photograph of a portrait of the author; notes; programs; and bills. Other correspondents include Edward William Bok, Nathaniel Lord Britton, William Bayard Hale, Archibald Henderson, Fiske Kimball, Roger Lewis, Alden March, Arthur Hobson Quinn, George Henry Sargent, and William Wesley Young.

2791.   JOSEPHUS JACKSON PAPERS, 1857-1877. 36 items. Brandon (Rutland County), Vt.

Personal letters of Josephus Jackson, 12th Regiment of Vermont Volunteers, discussing personal matters, camp life, casualties and prisoners, troop movements, commodity prices, battles and skirmishes, and sickness, hospitals, vaccinations, and nurses.

2792.   THOMAS JONATHAN JACKSON PAPERS, 1855 (1861-1865) 1906. 4,723 items. Lexington (Rockbridge County), Va.

Personal and military papers and records of "Stonewall" Jackson (1824-1863), general in the Confederate Army. Jackson's official and personal correspondence includes requests for furloughs; vouchers; descriptions of military movements around Staunton, Virginia, in 1862; the payroll of Turner Ashby's cavalry company raised following John Brown's raid, 1859; a letter, 1855, to Jackson's aunt, Clementine Neal; two letters by Jackson's wife; a letter, 1861, from Jackson to Colonel James Walkinshaw Allen, requesting permission to allow the Jefferson County soldiers to march to Shepherdstown to vote; a letter to General P. G. T. Beauregard concerning captured property; a letter, 1862, to S. Bassett French pertaining to religious denominations opposed to war; references to enemy movements around Harpers Ferry; and appointments of men to office. Official records include the commissary records of Wells J. Hawks (1814-1873), major and chief commissary of subsistence to Generals Jackson, Ewell, and Early, and of William B. Warwick, major and commissary for General Fitzhugh Lee's Cavalry Division; the commissary records of John J. Halsey, captain and commissary of subsistence of the 6th Virginia Cavalry; and the quartermaster records of William Miller, captain and assistant quartermaster of the 7th Virginia Cavalry.

2793.   THOMAS P. JACKSON ACCOUNT BOOK, 1820-1826. 1 vol. (72 pp.) Travellers' Rest, S.C.

Accounts of Thomas P. Jackson, apparently a merchant and blacksmith, as well as a dealer in whiskey.

2794.   JACKSON-TROUT FAMILY PAPERS 1828-1929. 370 items and 4 vols. Front Royal (Warren County), Va.

Papers of the related Jackson, Trout, and Pagett families of Virginia include letters discussing family matters, flood of the Mississippi River, 1844, the Civil War, and the Morgantown (West Virginia) Female Academy; correspondence concerning politics in the 1880s, including letters from state and national politicians and the National Association of Democratic Clubs; papers related to the law practice of John R. Jackson and his son, Edward; papers dealing with the real estate and insurance agency of Wilber A. Trout; some genealogical notes; correspondence and miscellaneous materials on the Nifty Jiffy Corporation, a chain of grocery markets based in Atlanta and proposed for Virginia; and printed material including broadsides of the Democratic ticket in the election of 1888, a leaflet on St. Luke's Home for the Sick, Richmond, Virginia, and school reports of the Trout children. Volumes include poetry, ca. 1830, and a printed account of the trial of William Fitzgerald Trout for murder, 1936.

2795.   JACKSONVILLE, PENSACOLA & MOBILE RAILROAD COMPANY PAPERS, 1870. 1 vol. Tallahassee (Leon County), Fla.

Passenger report book of the Jacksonville, Pensacola & Mobile Railroad for traffic between Quincy and Jacksonville. Many pages are missing and others have been pasted over with clippings, usually short stories from newspapers or magazines.

2796.   JOHN JEREMIAH JACOB PAPERS, 1780-1813. 3 items. Cumberland (Allegany County), Md.

Papers of John Jacob include a letter by him from Hillsborough, North Carolina, describing a battle with the British during the Revolutionary War; and two documents signed by Bishop Francis Asbury, one proclaiming Jacob a deacon in the Methodist Episcopal Church and another proclaiming him an elder.

2797.   EDWARD B. JACOBS & NEWCOMEN PAPERS, 1841-1842. 6 items. Front Royal (Warren County), Va.

Business correspondence of Edward B. Jacobs & Newcomen, who were evidently flour merchants or owners of flour mills, concerning their business with C. D. Hinks & Co., flour merchants in Baltimore, Maryland, and with the Bank of the Valley in Virginia.

2798.   NEIL H. JACOBY PAPERS, 1932. 1 vol. (20 pp.) Chicago, Ill.

Typescript (carbon) of a study for the Social Science Research Committee, University of Chicago, on "The Estimation of Yields for State Tobacco Taxes."

2799. JAEGER DIARY, 1885-1894.
1 vol. (200 pp.) Rustburg (Campbell County), Va.

The diary of the wife of a minister, probably Episcopal, who founded an orphanage at Rustburg for Negro children.

2800. EMMA JAMES PAPERS, 1897-1899.
11 items. Walnut Cove (Stokes County), N. C.

Personal letters to Emma James, principally from members of her family, discussing family affairs, crops, diseases, and family finances. Included is a love letter from Winston, North Carolina.

2801. HENRY JAMES PAPERS, 1871-1897.
17 items. London, England.

Papers of Henry James (1843-1916), American-born novelist, include letters to various publishers concerning his work, a letter concerning a work by the Hon. Lady Grey-Egerton, letters answering dinner invitations, and a cancelled check from his publisher; and five letters of his father, Henry James, Sr., a lecturer and writer on religious, social, and literary topics, to the Reverend John T. Sargent concerning invitations to visit and to give lectures.

2802. JOSHUA JAMES PAPERS, 1863-1868.
9 items. New Carthage (Tensas Parish), La.

Correspondence of Joshua James, a Louisiana planter, with various members of the U.S. Army and Navy concerning damages and destruction to his property committed by Union troops, and a letter, 1868, to Robert J. Walker seeking legal advice in regard to his losses.

2803. WILLIAM A. JAMES PAPERS, 1864-1865.
4 items. North Carolina.

Personal letters of a Confederate soldier discussing Confederate troop movements, officers, deserters, the Confederate attempt to recapture New Bern, North Carolina, 1864, and the siege of Petersburg, 1864.

2804. JAMESTOWN (NORTH CAROLINA) BRANCH OF THE FARMERS' ALLIANCE MINUTES, 1888-1892. 1 vol. (106 pp.) Davie County, N. C.

2805. DAVID FLAVEL JAMISON PAPERS, 1842-1862. 12 items. Barnwell County, S. C.

Papers of David Flavel Jamison (1810-1864), planter, author, and politician, include letters referring to secession, the proposed attack on Fort Sumter, the future of the Confederacy, the relocation of mortar batteries on James Island, and the defense of Charleston; poetry written by Jamison, 1851; and routine material pertaining to Jamison's responsibilities as secretary of war for South Carolina.

2806. RICHARD E. JAQUES PAPERS, 1863-1865.
55 items. Charleston, S. C.

Personal correspondence between Private Richard E. Jaques, C.S.A., stationed at James Island, South Carolina, with his fiancée, L. A. Syme, principally discussing personal matters with references to camp life, the bombardment of Charleston, blockade runners, and the lack of necessities and luxuries among Confederate women.

2807. WILLIAM HENRY JAQUES PAPERS. 1896-1897. 12 items. Trenton (Mercer County), N. J.

Papers of William Henry Jaques (1848-1916) concerning the naval reserve of New Jersey which he commanded, 1895-1898, discussing the supply, finance, training, and administration of the naval reserve.

2808. JARRATT-PURYEAR FAMILY PAPERS, 1807 (1843-1879) 1918. 2,345 items and 4 vols. Surry and Yadkin Counties, N. C.

Papers of the related Jarratt, Puryear, Clingman, Poindexter and Cash families, and especially of Isaac A. Jarratt, soldier in the War of 1812, landholder, merchant, and distiller. The collection concerns family matters and local affairs; the education of Mary Jarratt at St. Mary's College, Raleigh, North Carolina; the education of Augustus Jarratt at the University of North Carolina, Chapel Hill, and conditions at the university preceding the Civil War; Isaac Jarratt's partnership with Tyre Glen in the slave trade between Alabama and North Carolina, 1830-1835; the Creek War of 1836; United States relations with Mexico, 1842; a survey of Wilson, North Carolina, 1851; frontier conditions in Texas; the Civil War, including troop movements in North Carolina and Virginia, conditions in the Confederate Army, conscription, lists of absentees, official orders for enrolling new age groups, conscription lists, casualty lists, payments to widows, and home conditions; freedmen, including letters from former slaves inquiring about relatives; Jarratt's efforts to get whiskey during the war; North Carolina politics after the war; whiskey taxes; conditions in California; a Texas counterfeit affair in which A. B. Clingman was unjustly suspected; the business affairs of the Jarratt family; the administration of the estates of Samuel L. Davis, William Doss, Sally Doss, and Polly Sapp by Isaac Jarratt and of the estate of Richard Clauselle Puryear (d. 1867) by Jarratt and by his son, Richard Clingman Puryear (b. 1848); and the law practice of Richard Clingman Puryear, including the collection of many claims, 1870-1900. Volumes include a plantation account book, 1834-1881, containing lists and prices of slaves bought and sold in 1834 and 1835; a plantation account book, 1866-1871, recording supplies and cash advanced to tenants; an administration book, 1845-1848, concerning the estate of Matthew A. Doss; and a ledger, 1869-1870, of Isaac A. Jarratt & Sanderford, a general mercantile firm, containing the records of the sale of whiskey.

2809.   JOHN M. JARRELL PAPERS, 1848-1884. 61 items. Yadkin County, N. C.

Letters from John M. Jarrell (d. ca. 1871) to his wife, Juliet (Kelly) Jarrell, describing conditions in Raysville, Indiana; letters to Mrs. Jarrell from her brother, W.D. Kelly, describing social, economic and political conditions in Malvern and Rockport, Arkansas, before and after the Civil War; and a letter from Rebecca A. Kelly concerning events in Huntsville, North Carolina, noting the purchase of the bodies of the Siamese twins, Chang and Eng, by Northern doctors.

2810.   THOMAS JORDAN JARVIS PAPERS, 1879-1891. 3 items. Greenville (Pitt County), N.C.

Letters from Thomas Jordan Jarvis (1836-1915), Confederate captain, North Carolina governor, 1879-1885, minister to Brazil, 1885-1889, and U.S. senator, replying to biographers who sought information on his career, and to a philatelist concerning several issues of stamps.

2811.   JOSEPH JASTROW PAPERS, 1875-1961. 995 items and 14 vols. Madison (Dane County), Wis.

Papers of Joseph Jastrow (1863-1944), psychologist, include correspondence of Jastrow and his wife, Rachel (Szold) Jastrow, with their families principally concerning family matters, but with references to affairs of the University of Wisconsin; Judaism in Baltimore, Maryland, and Madison, Wisconsin; and the Zionist movement; photographs of the Szold and Jastrow families; manuscripts of his lectures, speeches, prose and poetry; the galley proofs of several articles; a diary kept during a vacation in Spain; a scrapbook containing copies of his articles and book reviews; a compilation of his early writings; copies of his articles in pamphlet form; and newspaper clippings.

2812.   JOHN JAY PAPERS, 1765, 1789. 2 items. New York, N. Y.

Papers of John Jay (1745-1829), statesman and first chief justice of the U. S. Supreme Court, include a personal letter by Jay, 1765, and a letter of introduction to Jay for John Churchman, a scientist, 1789.

2813.   JOSEPH M. JAYNES PLANTATION ACCOUNT BOOKS, 1854-1860. 5 vols. Brandon (Rankin County), Miss.

Plantation accounts of Joseph M. Jaynes, giving daily records of cotton picked and inventories of sheep and hogs.

2814.   JOHN J. JEFCOAT PAPERS, 1850-1891. 178 items. Orangeburg (Orangeburg County), S. C.

Correspondence between a Confederate soldier and his wife describing troop movements, hardships of army life, and difficulties in managing the farm. The later letters concern Jefcoat's brother-in-law, Daniel P. Walker, a wagoner on a railroad construction job in east Tennessee.

2815.   THOMAS JEFFERSON PAPERS, 1776-1961. 16 items. Albemarle County, Va.

Papers of Thomas Jefferson (1743-1826), president of the United States, 1801-1809, include land grants, 1781, to John Felder and to James Prewit; letter, 1797, discussing in detail the activities of the first special session of Congress in June, 1797, prospects of the Republican Party, merits of various newspapers, and relations with France and England; letter, 1799, to Nicholas Meriwether Lewis concerning an exchange of land grants between himself and Lewis; letter, 1801, from William Scales to Jefferson seeking aid from the U.S. government in return for a new navigational method; copy of Jefferson's speech to the Indians, 1806; copy of an act supplementary to the Embargo Act; letter, 1807, to John Daly Burk, president of the Petersburg (Virginia) Company of Riflemen, expressing thanks to that organization for its offer of services to the government; facsimile of a letter, 1817, to Joseph C. Cabell discussing his ideas about elementary and college education; photostatic copies of two letters, including one describing the family and estate of Wilson Cary Nicholas; and copy of part of an article published in October, 1961, on facsimiles made in 1936 of a letter written in 1803 by Jefferson to one of his creditors.

2816.   THOMAS GEORGE WASHINGTON JEFFERSON PAPERS, 1861-1863. 34 items. Hartford (Hartford County), Conn.

Civil War letters of Thomas G. W. Jefferson, 25th Regiment of Connecticut Volunteers, describing sickness in his regiment, foraging, a Negro regiment, military activities, and public opinion concerning General Benjamin F. Butler.

2817.   JEFFERSON CITY BRIDGE AND TRANSIT COMPANY ALBUM, 1895-1896. 1 vol. (50 pp.) Jefferson City (Cole County), Mo.

Fifty photographs illustrating the construction of the Jefferson City Bridge over the Missouri River.

2818.   ROBERT J. JEFFORDS PAPERS, 1861-1864. 53 items. Charleston, S. C.

Military correspondence of Robert

J. Jeffords, colonel in 5th South Carolina Cavalry, C.S.A., pertaining to his relations and disputes with other officers, especially General P. G. T. Beauregard. The collection gives information on Beauregard's difficulties in and around Charleston.

2819.  AMELIA (HIGH) JEFFREYS PAPERS, 1801-1904.  1,080 items.  Raleigh (Wake County), N. C.

Papers of Amelia (High) Jeffreys (1813-1865), wife of Robert N. Jeffreys, Jr., include the business papers of Robert N. Jeffreys chiefly as guardian of the six orphan children of James and Winifred Newsome, including names and ages of the children, receipts for money issued them, bills for medical attention to their slaves, and contracts for hiring the slaves; papers of the children of Robert N. Jeffreys--Robert N., Jr., Jacob H., James G., and John O.--and of Josiah R. Jeffreys; the records of Amelia (High) Jeffreys as guardian of her daughter, Alvarado Ovando Jeffreys, including accounts of expenditures for clothing and tuition, and contracts for hiring slaves; the papers of William H. High, Amelia's brother, concerning her business affairs and local politics; postwar papers relating to the agricultural business of R. Walter Jeffreys including bills and receipts from Raleigh merchants and from Baltimore, Maryland, commission merchants, and two broadsides pertaining to election regulations; scattered personal letters; several papers of Lewis Pipkin; and records pertaining to tuition and scholarships at St. Mary's School, Raleigh, and at Salem Female Academy, Salem, North Carolina.

2820.  MRS. JAMES M. JEFFREYS PAPERS, 1823-1852.  5 items.  Red House (Caswell County), N.C.

Personal letters, two of which give accounts of trips to Washington, D. C., in 1823 and to New York in 1826.

2821.  JOHN O. JEFFREYS PAPERS, 1844-1855.  5 items.  Raleigh (Wake County), N. C.

Fragments of John Jeffreys's mercantile accounts and one letter written to two policemen concerning a prisoner.

2822.  LEONIDAS JEFFREYS PAPERS, 1835-1866.  21 items.  Wake County, N. C.

Personal letters, including several relative to Leonidas Jeffreys's experiences as a student at the University of Virginia, Charlottesville, 1845-1846, and a short itinerary of a trip through Virginia, Tennessee, Alabama, and South Carolina by Robert N. Jeffreys in 1835.

2823.  R. W. JEFFREYS BANKBOOK, 1875.  1 vol. (40 pp.) Raleigh (Wake County), N.C.

Bankbook of R. W. Jeffreys's account with the State National Bank, Raleigh, North Carolina.

2824.  WILLIAM JEFFREYS PAPERS, 1808-1874.  728 items.  Franklin County, N. C.

Business papers and correspondence of William Jeffreys (d. ca. 1860), farmer, including deeds, tax receipts, shop accounts, lists of lumber used, store accounts, legal papers from a justice of the peace in Wake County, 1811-1822, and business letters concerning plantation affairs.  Several papers are those of J. Robert Jeffreys, probably the son of William Jeffreys, including a list of men drafted into service from Buffalo District, January 27, 1862.

2825.  WILLIAM A. JEFFREYS ACCOUNT BOOK, 1868-1871.  1 vol. (110 pp.) Franklin County, N.C.

Mercantile accounts.

2826.  JOHN HEWITT JELLETT PAPERS, 1870.  1 item.  Dublin, Ireland.

Letter from the Duke of Manchester to John Hewitt Jellett (1817-1888), provost of Trinity College, Dublin, discussing an ecclesiastical convention to reorganize the Church of Ireland.

2827.  CHARLES JONES JENKINS PAPERS, 1814-1880.  15 items.  Augusta (Richmond County), Ga.

Papers of Charles Jones Jenkins (1805-1883), lawyer, Georgia legislator, supreme court justice and governor, regarding finances of the state of Georgia in 1866, Jenkins's removal from the office of governor and Federal control of the state, the history of Georgia, and the administration of several estates; land deeds; tax returns; and a personal letter to his future wife.

2828.  MRS. CHRISTOPHER C. JENKINS PAPERS, 1823-1858.  108 items.  Charleston, S. C.

Family correspondence of Mrs. Christopher C. Jenkins, consisting of letters from her husband while on a northern trip in 1823 escorting his nieces to Dr. Seidel's Academy near Bethlehem, Pennsylvania, and while visiting Philadelphia (Pennsylvania), Saratoga Springs (New York), and other northern places in 1826; letters from a married daughter living in Walterboro, South Carolina, discussing family matters and social life; and letters from her daughter, Maria, while a student at Montpelier Academy near Macon, Georgia, describing life at school and her studies.

2829. GERTRUDE JENKINS PAPERS, 1859-1908. 1 vol. (104 pp.) Williamsboro (Granville County) and Winston-Salem (Forsyth County), N. C.

Typed manuscript entitled "Endurin' the War," compiled by Gertrude Jenkins containing the reminiscences of Robert Alexander Jenkins, a Confederate soldier, describing his adventures leaving his northern school in Pittsburgh, Pennsylvania, in 1859, the raid on the arsenal at Harpers Ferry by John Brown, the battle of the C.S.S. Virginia with the U.S.S. Monitor, military engagements at Hanover Court House and Seven Pines (Virginia), the retreat of General Joseph E. Johnston through North Carolina, the last meeting of the C.S.A. government, and the final surrender at Bennett House, Durham, North Carolina; the narrative of Margaret Elizabeth Clewell, future wife of Robert A. Jenkins, describing the journey of young women from Salem Female Academy (Salem, North Carolina) to Fauquier County (Virginia) to nurse the sick of the 21st North Carolina Infantry, the hospital and care of the sick at Thoroughfair Gap, and the battlefield at Manassas; copies of the letters of Lieutenant Francis Christian Clewell, 1st Missouri Cavalry, describing the siege at Vicksburg, the military prison at Johnson's Island, Ohio, his exchange and the rejoining of his regiment, and his capture and imprisonment on Ship Island in the Gulf of Mexico; and a copy of an undated letter describing the occupation of Salem, North Carolina, by the 10th Ohio Volunteers.

2830. MARTHA I. JENKINS PAPERS, 1860-1917. 30 items. Warrenton (Warren County), N. C.

Personal letters to Martha I. Jenkins from friends and relatives concerning crops, prices, health, religion, and family matters. One letter, 1882, from a friend at the Presbyterian Eye and Ear Charitable Hospital in Baltimore, Maryland, describes an operation on her eye performed by opthalmologist, Dr. John Julian Chisolm, and the use of chloroform.

2831. MICAH JENKINS PAPERS, 1855-1879. 48 items. Edisto Island (Charleston County), S. C.

Chiefly personal and military correspondence of Micah Jenkins (1835-1864), brigadier general in the Confederate Army, containing accounts of campaigns and tactics, troop movements, courts-martial, camp life, the blockading of the Charleston (South Carolina) harbor, the first battle of Manassas, the battles of Fredericksburg and Chattanooga, politics in the promotion of officers, and the C.S.A. Congress. A letter, 1867, from Asbury Coward describes the difficulties in South Carolina during Reconstruction, commenting on crops, prices, education, and politics; and discusses King's Mountain Military School, Yorkville, South Carolina, which he and Jenkins had founded in 1855. Two letters, 1879, from M. I. Jenkins describe U.S. Army life in Colorado.

2832. WALKER JENKINS DIARY, 1861. 1 vol. Woodstock (Shenandoah County), Va.

Diary evidently kept by a merchant, with brief comments on the outbreak of the Civil War and descriptions of camp life and mercantile transactions.

2833. WILLIAM HORTON PEACE JENKINS PAPERS, 1845-1925. 2,417 items and 10 vols. Oxford (Granville County), N. C.

Papers of W. H. P. Jenkins consist principally of the records of the public schools of Granville County, North Carolina, 1881-1895, while Jenkins was superintendent of public instruction for the county. Jenkins's annual reports to the state superintendent contain statistics on teachers, including salary and race; schools, including the number of districts, the number of school buildings and number of terms, and the value of school property; pupils, by sex and race, and with comparison of numbers of school age children with numbers of pupils attending school; average and total attendance; teachers' institutes held and number of teachers attending, by race; textbooks; school board members; and funds. Accompanying work sheets provide a detailed breakdown by township and by district. A special questionnaire, 1885, concerns textbooks used, their quality and distribution. County treasurer's reports give data on the disbursement of school funds. The annual school census records the names of each family head, by race, and the number and sex of the children, as well as listing school houses and property values. Individual teachers' reports are requests for salary and include information on the teachers, numbers of pupils by sex, and average attendance record. Financial papers concern requisitions from schools for money for supplies and repairs.

Other papers include personal and family correspondence; legal papers consisting of summonses and warrants issued by justice of the peace E. J. Jenkins, 1878-1896; a clipping describing a teachers' institute held in Granville County and the role of educator Charles Duncan McIver; a notice to former students of North Carolina State Normal and Industrial College, Greensboro, North Carolina, of the decennial commencement, 1902; and a photograph of the "Class of 1914" at an unidentified school. Volumes include a docket book, 1878-1892, for a justice of the peace in Brassfield Township, Granville County, North Carolina; a record of accounts with tenants, 1886-1900; an account book, 1853-1882, recording accounts with employees; account books, 1857-1859, pertaining to the Mount Energy School, Granville County, and containing records of tuition and the sales of books and other supplies; an account book, 1854-1871, including records of the estate of Josiah Peace; an account book, 1845-1866, containing records for the collection of taxes in kind, 1864-1865; a memorandum book printed by Walton, Whann and Company, Wilmington, Delaware; an account book, 1883; and a ledger and cash book, 1916.

2834. JENKINS & FOSTER ACCOUNT BOOK, 1884-1885. 1 vol. (171 pp.) Fluvanna County, Va.

Records of a general mercantile business.

2835. CHARLES JENKINSON, FIRST EARL OF LIVERPOOL, PAPERS, 1792-1822. 9 items. London, England.

Papers of Charles Jenkinson, First Earl of Liverpool, include a copy of the minutes of a conference between Lord Liverpool and M. de Curt concerning relations of the French National Convention and Great Britain, 1792; a letter, 1796, discussing Lord Liverpool's actions regarding an honor which the Corporation of Liverpool was to grant him; a letter, 1804, from William Pitt discussing the change of offices made by Jenkinson after the change in ministry; letter, 1808, from William Morton Pitt agreeing to serve in a prison inquiry; an order, 1808, transferring prisoners from Newgate Prison; a letter, 1808, from Foreign Secretary George Canning concerning travelers to Heligoland on alien passports; and several routine letters pertaining to social invitations and recommendations.

2836. ROBERT BANKS JENKINSON, SECOND EARL OF LIVERPOOL, PAPERS, 1669-1900. 9 items and 1 vol. London, England.

Papers of Robert Banks Jenkinson, Second Earl of Liverpool (1770-1828), government official and member of Parliament, consist principally of a volume (114 ff.) entitled "Some Reminisences of the Past, 1900," which is a compilation of letters, reports, and documents chiefly from the first quarter of the nineteenth century. The volume contains several seventeenth century documents on manors, reports regarding British claims and interests in territories in the Mediterranean and Central America, and letters about the libel trials conducted by Attorney General Spencer Perceval, 1804; the Catholic Question, 1805 and 1826; military operations during the French Revolutionary and Napoleonic Wars; ministerial politics and governmental reform in Russia, and Russian relations with Great Britain and France, 1803; a defense of British naval strategy in the War of 1812; the affair of Queen Caroline, 1820; the controversy regarding the transferral of the Preventive Water Guard from the authority of the Treasury to that of Customs and Admiralty; agriculture in the 1820s; the illness of George IV, 1826; the parliamentary elections of 1826; the Corn Laws, 1826; routine matters such as appointments, recommendations and peerages; and memorabilia of Queen Victoria's Diamond Jubilee Procession. Letters of George Canning concern the revision of a parliamentary resolution and the management of the business by the House of Commons; letters of Lord Palmerston regard an appointment, the pension of army widows and a cure for ophthalmia; and letters, 1825, of Lord Chancellor Eldon concern a motion before the House of Commons about the arrears of cases before him. Among the correspondents are Gerrard Andrewes, Charles Arbuthnot, George Canning, Lord Chancellor Eldon, Henry Essex Edgeworth de Firmont, Sir Henry Halford, Richard Hurd, Lord Hutchinson, the Duke of Kent, Sir William Knighton, the Earl of Liverpool, Charles Long, Stephen Lushington, the Count de Marcoff, Viscount Melville, Lord Palmerston, Robert Peel, Spencer Perceval, Lord Ravensworth, Lord Redesdale, Olivia Serres, Lord Sidmouth, the Duke of Wellington, Count Alexandre Worontzov, Mikhail Worontzov, and Count Séméon Worontzov.

2837. WILLIAM JENKS PAPERS, 1811-1835. 4 items. Boston, Mass.

Letter, 1835, from Thomas Winthrop Coit discussing the English translation of the Bible published in 1560; a personal letter; and two financial papers.

2838. ANNIE (FOUCH ?) JENNINGS PAPERS, 1815-1929. 519 items and 2 vols. Brownsville (Washington County), Md.

Papers of Annie (Fouch?) Jennings include the business papers of Samuel Jennings I, David Fouch, and Samuel Jennings II, farmers and millers of wheat; land deeds and surveys; debts; tax listings; correspondence concerning family matters and social life in Maryland, Iowa, Illinois, and South Dakota; papers related to the English estate of William Jenners, Sunday School lessons of the 1870s, and genealogies of the Fouch and Jennings (or Jenners) families. Volumes include the account book, 1852-1853, of David Fouch [?] for milling flour, and a route book, 1882-1883, of Fred O'Bran.

2839. WILLIAM JERDAN PAPERS, 1837, 1847. 2 items. Kelso, Roxburghshire, Scotland.

Letters to William Jerdan (1782-1869), editor of the Literary Gazette, from Patrick Murphy (1782-1847), weather prophet, discussing the publication of his weather table in the Gazette and the weather for the next month, and from entomologist Frederick William Hope (1797-1862) referring to personal matters.

2840. EDWARD JERNINGHAM PAPERS, 1814. 1 item. London, England.

Letter from Alexandre Angélique, Duc de Talleyrand-Périgord, replying to a letter from Edward Jerningham (1774-1822), barrister-at-law, and commenting on the military and diplomatic situation prior to

Napoleon's abdication.

2841. AUGUSTUS JESSOPP PAPERS, 1882-1896. 9 items. Norwich, Norfolk, England.

Correspondence of Augustus Jessopp (1823-1914), British schoolmaster and historical writer specializing in medieval English ecclesiastical history, and William Stubbs, a bishop of the Church of England and historian, concerning research problems related to their publications and their interest in the medieval church.

2842. THOMAS SIDNEY JESUP PAPERS, 1787-1850. 99 items and 2 vols. Berkeley County, W. Va.

Military papers of Thomas Sidney Jesup (1788-1860), U.S. Army officer, quartermaster general of the army, 1818-1860, commander of the army in the Creek Nation, 1836, and commander of the army in Florida, 1836-1837. Correspondence and letter books relate to preparations for the Spanish attack on New Orleans, Spanish depredations on American shipping in the Gulf of Mexico, and a shortage of funds for supply and payroll, 1816; Jesup's duties as superintendent of recruiting for the 1st Regiment of Infantry, 1816-1817; his command of Federal, Georgia, and Alabama troops, military operations against hostile Creeks, relations with Creek allies, and Indian removal, 1836; his command of the army in Florida against the Seminoles, possible negotiations with the Indians, the battles of Withlacoochee River and Fort Miami, and relief for Negroes who voluntarily surrendered, 1836-1837; duties and problems as quartermaster during the Mexican War, military operations on the eastern coast of Mexico, the attack on Vera Cruz, and the campaign in northeastern Mexico; and the use of steamers in warfare. Also included are several papers of his father-in-law, William Croghan, concerning land in Kentucky granted for service in the American Revolution to Richard Barron, for whom Croghan was surveyor.

2843. GERALDINE ENDSOR JEWSBURY PAPERS, 1853. 1 item. Sevenoaks, Kent, England.

Personal letter from novelist Elizabeth Gaskell to Geraldine Endsor Jewsbury (1812-1880), British novelist.

2844. LEWIS JOEL PAPERS, 1861-1899. 22 items. London, England.

Papers of Lewis Joel, British consular official, are made up of official documents relating to Joel's assignments to various consular posts and commissions, mainly in Latin America, and a few personal letters.

2845. JOHN JOHNS, JR., PAPERS, 1769-1890. 77 items. Richmond, Va.

The papers of John Johns, Jr., contain letters from his father and mother in the 1840s and 1850s generally concerning religion and personal matters, and correspondence in the 1860s with various magazine and newspaper editors for whom Johns was writing, including Henry Rives Pollard of the Daily Richmond Examiner, Alfred Hudson Guernsey of Harper's Magazine, James Gordon Bennett of The (New York) Herald, and William Dallas Chesterman of the Richmond Dispatch.

2846. A. N. JOHNSON PAPERS, 1859-1861. 3 items. Fayetteville, N. C.

Miscellaneous letters to A. N. Johnson, including one from James Williams, a schoolteacher at Asbury Academy, Cary, North Carolina.

2847. ANDREW JOHNSON PAPERS, 1853-1926. 47 items. Washington, D. C.

Papers of Andrew Johnson, president of the United States, 1865-1869, include a letter, 1863, from Johnson as governor of Tennessee concerning a military trial; an appointment, a land grant, and a commission signed by Johnson; requests for pardons from former Confederates; a petition from the "freemen" of Savannah, Georgia, to the House of Representatives of the United States, objecting to the conduct of Johnson as president; and a letter from an official in the United States Patent Office concerning tea plants which were being sent to one of Johnson's constituents as part of an experiment in growing tea in the United States.

2848. AUSTIN JOHNSON PAPERS, 1829-1861. 9 items. Rupert (Bennington County), Va.

Papers showing Austin Johnson's ardent interest in the antislavery movement, including a formal statement of his opposition to the American Colonization Society, and addresses on capital punishment, domestic manufacturing, and slavery as a moral wrong. Included in letters are references to the Rupert (Vt.) Peace Society, the Bennington (Vt.) Journal, and personal affairs.

2849. BRADLEY TYLER JOHNSON PAPERS, 1851-1909. 922 items. Frederick (Frederick County), Md.

Civil War reminiscences, references to the Spanish-American War, correspondence, and personal accounts of Bradley Tyler Johnson (1829-1903), brigadier general in the Confederate Army, Maryland lawyer and politician, including letters from Henry Adams, James Cardinal Gibbons, Wade Hampton, Joseph E. Johnston, and Henry Cabot Lodge. There are also an incomplete diary of a trip as correspondent to Cuba during the Spanish-American War; a memoir of the 1st Maryland Regiment in 1863 by Johnson; a series of letters by Holmes Offley Paulding while he was on an expedition against the Sioux Indians, 1876; muster roll of Company B, 21st Virginia Regiment, 1861; and commissary records of a prison hospital.

2850. CHARLES B. JOHNSON PAPERS, 1861-1865. 10 items. Sherman (Grayson County), Tex.

Letters, reports, and accounts of Charles B. Johnson, a quartermaster's agent and contractor, concerning supplies for the Confederate Army and for various Indian tribes, including the Wichita, 1861-1862, the Osage, 1864, and the Seminole, 1865.

2851. CHARLES EARL JOHNSON PAPERS, 1845-1890. 138 items and 1 vol. Raleigh (Wake County), N. C.

The papers of Charles Earl Johnson, physician, president of the Medical Society of North Carolina, and surgeon general of North Carolina during the Civil War, contain routine family correspondence between Johnson and his father, Charles Earl Johnson, and his mother, Anne Williams (Taylor) Johnson; a letter, 1849, describing student life at the University of Pennsylvania Medical School; and a letter, 1864, from William Gilmore Simms to Theodore H. Hill discussing poetry. The collection also contains bills and receipts, 1870-1890; a memoir on the death of Charles Earl Johnson; and an unbound copy of his book, The Question of Insanity and Its Medico-Legal Relations (1869) with fragments of notes.

2852. CHARLES SPURGEON JOHNSON, SR., PAPERS, 1931. 1 item. Nashville (Davidson County), Tenn.

A typescript of "Historical Data on the Negro," by Charles Spurgeon Johnson, Sr., author, educator, and president of Fisk University in Nashville, Tennessee.

2853. EDWARD JOHNSON PAPERS, 1674-1784. 3 items. Cecil County, Md.

Land deeds, 1674, of Edward Johnson, and a copy, made in 1784, of Johnson's will which was dated 1697.

2854. ELLEN (COOPER) JOHNSON PAPERS, 1924. 1 item. Conway (Horry County), S.C.

The memoirs of Ellen (Cooper) Johnson describe growing up in Conway, South Carolina; early schooling in the area and attendance at Spartanburg Female Academy, Spartanburg, South Carolina; several raids by Confederate deserters on farms of her relatives; a speech by Wade Hampton at Conway during Reconstruction; religious revivals; and the history of her family and other prominent families in the area.

2855. ELLEN L. JOHNSON PAPERS, 1856-1889. 15 items. Forsyth County, N. C.

Personal and family correspondence referring to a disagreement over a land boundary, White Plain Academy at Chesterfield, South Carolina, religion and a camp meeting, migration to Arkansas and Texas, and the sale of harvesting machinery.

2856. GEORGE K. JOHNSON PAPERS, 1860-1861. 6 items. North Creek (Philips County), Ark.

Business and personal letters of a cotton merchant, mainly from Carroll, Hoyt and Company, New Orleans, Louisiana.

2857. GEORGE WESLEY JOHNSON PAPERS, 1829 (1831-1888) 1939. 2,620 items and 77 vols. Farmington (Davie County), N. C.

Business and family papers of George W. Johnson, postmaster, justice of the peace, general merchant, and farmer; of his brother and business partner, James M. Johnson; of George W. Johnson's son, Francis Marion Johnson; and of other members of the family. The collection contains letters to George W. Johnson from friends in Tennessee relative to agricultural and economic conditions there, 1838-1844; letters between George W. and James M. Johnson while one or the other bought goods in Philadelphia, Pennsylvania, before the Civil War; bills, accounts, receipts, orders, promissory notes, and letters of a business nature, including occasional reference to another brother of George W. Johnson, Hiram, who had a financial interest in the mercantile establishment; numerous letters from George W. Johnson, his wife, Martha Johnson, and friends, including one at Wake Forest College, North Carolina, to Francis Marion Johnson while the latter was a student at the University of North Carolina, Chapel Hill, 1855-1858; letters, 1858-1861, from another brother of George W. Johnson, J. H. Johnson, who was operating a store at East Bend in Yadkin County, North Carolina, as well as references to the debt of Olin High School, North Carolina, notices of meetings of "Mocksville Lodge No. 134," letters to Martha Johnson from her daughter, Jennie, while a student at Greensboro Female College, North Carolina, 1857-1859, prices of foods and general commodities, letters from Eagle Mills, Buffalo Paper Mills, and W. Turner's cotton mill at Turnersburg, North Carolina, and bills of lading for various commodities.

Material during the Civil War period is limited to a few letters in 1863 from W. G. Johnson (younger brother of George W. Johnson) near Kinston, North Carolina; tax in kind returns and a petition from Francis Marion Johnson asking for military exemption on the basis of operating a grist mill. Postwar material consists largely of mercantile records of the Farmington store showing that goods were purchased from wholesale firms in New York City; Philadelphia,

Pennsylvania; Richmond and Lynchburg, Virginia; Baltimore, Maryland; and Winston-Salem, Charlotte, Wilmington, and Salisbury, North Carolina.

Volumes consist of small notebooks, recording goods bought by George W. Johnson; daybooks; ledgers; postal records of the Farmington, North Carolina, post office, 1838-1856, including postage books, newspaper postage books, and receipt books for registered letters; blacksmith accounts; itinerary of a journey made by George W. Johnson, S. Taylor, and D. N. Reynolds through North Carolina and Tennessee in 1836; minutes of the Farmington Lodge No. 46 of the Independent Order of Odd Fellows; and the Davie County Division of the Sons of Temperance. Included also are a few business letters from Nathaniel Boyden and Son, and a letter to Francis M. Johnson from a friend in Norfolk, Virginia, describing a typhoid epidemic in 1855.

2858. HARRIET (MYERS) JOHNSON PAPERS, 1860-1865. 24 items. Michigan.

Letters to Harriet (Myers) Johnson from members of her family in the 11th Michigan Regiment and the 23rd Michigan Regiment describing camp life on the Potomac River and at Camp Morten, Bardstown, Kentucky; the occupation of Corinth, Mississippi, 1862; and the battle of Stones River, Tennessee.

2859. HENRY JOHNSON PAPERS, 1845. 1 item. Donaldsonville (Ascension Parish), La.

Letter of Henry Johnson, governor of Louisiana and later United States representative and United States senator from Louisiana.

2860. HERSCHEL VESPASIAN JOHNSON PAPERS, 1812-1880. 830 items and 31 vols. "Sandy Grove," Bartow (Jefferson County), Ga.

The papers of Herschel Vespasian Johnson, judge, governor of Georgia, United States senator from Georgia, and Confederate States senator from Georgia, consist of correspondence, 1835-1878, and letter books, 1849-1877, for the most part concentrating on the years 1865-1878. The correspondence contains a description of agricultural conditions in Alabama, 1835; letter from James Knox Polk, 1844, and William Hawkins Polk, 1846, on politics; letters on railroad construction, 1849; correspondence concerning Johnson's attempt to prevent a sectional split in the Democratic Party, 1856-1860; political correspondence with Alexander Hamilton Stephens beginning in 1860; accounts of the Democratic Party conventions in Charleston, South Carolina, and Baltimore, Md., 1860; letters concerning Johnson's campaign as Democratic candidate for vice-president of the United States, 1860; letters on the secession convention in Georgia; correspondence relating to Johnson's service in the Confederate government; letters on Reconstruction and numerous letters to his children and brothers depicting life in Georgia after the Civil War; correspondence relating to Johnson's postwar law practice and, especially, his attempt to test the constitutionality of a federal cotton tax; letters concerning Johnson's appointment as a Georgia circuit court judge, 1873; and miscellaneous letters, including items relating to a biography of Johnson written by Percy Scott Flippin. The collection also contains a manuscript autobiography of Johnson, 1867; 3 volumes of his speeches and essays; and a volume entitled "The Presidential Question Discussed," written by Johnson in 1840 to support the candidacy of Martin Van Buren to be president of the United States.

2861. HUGH W. JOHNSON PAPERS, 1810-1922. 135 items and 1 vol. Mud Lick (Chatham County), N. C.

Personal correspondence for the most part between Hugh W. Johnson and Emily (Pike) Johnson during their courtship, 1879-1884, containing references to New Garden Academy; prohibition and temperance; and conditions at the University of North Carolina, 1883. There are also letters on education in North Carolina, 1857; the settlement of the estate of Elizabeth Johnson, 1812; and the opening of a new academic year at Trinity College, 1902. Printed items include a clipping, 1902, from The Messenger of Siler City, North Carolina; a commencement program, 1882, from Mount Vernon Academy, Chatham County, North Carolina; and an undated tract by M. W. Knapp entitled Giant Alcohol. Volume contains accounts and personal entries of Moses E. D. Pike and entries for the number of hours he worked at various places, 1844-1866.

2862. J. R. JOHNSON AUTOGRAPH ALBUM, 1863-1864. 1 vol. Johnson's Island, Ohio.

Autographs of Confederate prisoners.

2863. JEFFERSON DEEMS JOHNSON, JR., PAPERS, 1915-1955. 1,820 items. Clinton (Sampson County), and Raleigh (Wake County), N. C.

The papers of Jefferson Deems Johnson, Jr., North Carolina politician and judge, consist of correspondence; legislative papers; drafts and notes for speeches; general papers on the United States senatorial campaign of 1948 in North Carolina; printed material and clippings about J. Melville Broughton; general papers, printed material, and clippings on the United States senatorial campaign of 1950 in North Carolina; and miscellaneous clippings and printed matter. Correspondence, 1928-1955, contains routine letters concerning Johnson's activities in the North Carolina Senate, 1937-1941;

correspondence relating to the campaign of J. Melville Broughton for the U.S. Senate in 1948, including memoranda, form letters, and lists of campaign workers; and letters dealing with the campaign of Frank Porter Graham for the United States Senate, 1950. Legislative papers, 1937-1941, contain petitions on local prohibition measures in Sampson County, North Carolina; material on tobacco production and market quotas; and drafts of revenue measures. Drafts and notes for Johnson's speeches, 1930-1946, deal mainly with religious and patriotic addresses, except for a few speeches in support of Franklin D. Roosevelt, 1944. Papers on the United States senatorial campaign of 1948 contain material on the Broughton organization which Johnson headed including lists of county managers; mailing lists; memos from Broughton to Johnson; notes on telephone conversations; press releases; drafts of some of Broughton's speeches; and election returns. Material on the campaign of Frank Porter Graham for the United States Senate, which Johnson also headed, includes lists of campaign workers; mailing lists; Graham's campaign schedule; memoranda; press releases; copies of radio addresses; notes on telephone conversations; election returns; and figures on contributions to Graham's campaign. Miscellaneous items include copies of speeches by J. Melville Broughton as governor of North Carolina, 1944; lists of managers and committees for Broughton's gubernatorial campaign, 1940; lists of delegates and their votes in the 1940 North Carolina Democratic Party convention; and lists of workers for Robert Gregg Cherry in the gubernatorial campaign of 1944.

2864. JOHN JOHNSON DIARY, 1864-1865. 1 vol. Charleston, S. C.

Diary of John Johnson describing his experiences as an engineering officer in the Confederate Army on the coast of South Carolina and in the withdrawal through South Carolina and North Carolina under the pressure of the Union Army of General William T. Sherman. Johnson made notes on a tour of the coastal defenses of South Carolina, various stages of the Confederate withdrawal, the battle of Averasboro, the battle of Bentonville, and the surrender negotiations between William T. Sherman and Joseph E. Johnston.

2865. JOHN O. JOHNSON PAPERS, 1856-1883. 35 items. Parsonfield (York County), Me.

Personal letters of John O. Johnson and others. In a letter, 1863, to his father, Johnson discusses politics, the war, deserters from the Union Army, and General Henry W. Halleck.

2866. JOSEPH TRAVIS JOHNSON PAPERS, 1889-1919. 26 items. Spartanburg, S.C., and Washington, D.C.

Photocopies of personal letters to Joseph Travis Johnson, congressman from South Carolina and federal judge of the Western Division of South Carolina, giving information on South Carolina politics and on the presidential election of 1916.

2867. NADIAH P. JOHNSON PAPERS, 1862-1864. 13 items. Fall River (Bristol County), Mass.

Letters from a 1st lieutenant in the Union Army to his aunt and uncle describing camp life, military activity, officer's pay, and hospital treatment, in Martinsburg, West Virginia, Harpers Ferry, West Virginia, and Charleston, South Carolina.

2868. REVERDY JOHNSON PAPERS, 1863-1871. 3 items. Baltimore, Md.

Letters to J. Andrew Jackson Creswell, W. Eubank, and Edward B. Wheeler.

2869. ROBERT CHARLES JOHNSON JOURNAL, 1792-1793. 1 item. New York, N. Y.

Typed copy of a diary kept by Robert Charles Johnson on a visit to Europe, containing description of a visit to Parliament in London, an account of interviews with Edmund Burke, and notes on a tour of France and Italy.

2870. ROBERT E. JOHNSON PAPERS, 1804-1866. 57 items. Raleigh (Wake County) and Warrenton (Warren County), N. C.

Papers of Robert E. Johnson, the Johnson family, and the family of Joseph Gales of Raleigh, North Carolina, concerning social life; Weston Gales's duties as editor of the Raleigh Register, 1824; the presidential election of 1824; the visit of General Lafayette to Fayetteville, North Carolina, 1825; and the naval career of Robert E. Johnson. Robert E. Johnson's papers contain letters, 1825-1826, while he was a student at Middletown Military Academy, Middletown, Connecticut; a letter, 1824, describing social life in Paris, France; and letters, 1828-1839, and an excerpt from a journal concerning naval cruises in the Pacific.

2871. ROBERT UNDERWOOD JOHNSON PAPERS, 1881-1929. 64 items. New York, N. Y.

Papers of Robert Underwood Johnson, made up for the most part of letters to him from prominent authors, publishers, educators, and diplomats, and concerning his editorship of the Century Magazine, and his ambassadorship to Italy. Correspondents include Henry M. Alden, Edward Porter Alexander, Arlo Bates, Don Carlos Buell, Frederick Douglass, Henry Theophilus Frick, John Finley, Mary Hallock Foote, Horace Howard Furness, John Work Garrett, Joseph B. Gilder, Roy Rolfe Gilson, Louise Stedman Gould, Arthur Twining Hadley, Charles Haldane, Myron Timothy Herrick,

David Jayne Hill, John Jay (1817-1894), Peter Augustus Jay, Joseph Jefferson, H. G. Leach, Ivy Ledbetter Lee, Charles Battell Loomis, Thomas Raynesford Lounsbury, George Brinton McClellan, Harriet Monroe, Merrill Moore, Meredith Nicholson, Henry Fairfield Osborn, William Lyon Phelps, Henry Codman Potter, George Haven Putnam, Henry P. Rogers, Thomas Lathrop Stedman, William James Stillman, John Ward Stimson, Ruth McEnery Stuart, Edith Matilda Thomas, Lewis Frank Tooker, Ridgely Torrence, Edward Waterman Townsend, Charles Dudley Warner, Henry White.

2872. THOMAS JOHNSON COMMONPLACE AND ACCOUNT BOOK, 1777. 1 vol. (20 pp.) [Md.?]

Agricultural accounts and quotations from Revolutionary constitutions probably kept by Thomas Johnson (1732-1818), member of Continental Congress, governor of Maryland, and associate justice of the United States Supreme Court.

2873. [W. T. JOHNSON?] ACCOUNT BOOK, 1825-1834. 1 vol. (75 pp.) Louisburg (Franklin County), N. C.

Account book belonging to one or more persons who operated a tavern.

2874. WILL H. JOHNSON PAPERS, 1916-1932. 12 items. Lexington (Davidson County), N. C.

Business and personal letters of Will H. Johnson and his family, including a letter, 1928, discussing the Baptist Orphanage in Thomasville, North Carolina.

2875. WILLIAM JOHNSON II, PAPERS, 1798. 3 items. Charleston, S. C.

Letters to William Johnson II, from John Faucheraud Grimké of Charleston, South Carolina, discussing Grimké's pamphlet, Instructions for Exercising Cannon and Mounting and Dismounting.

2876. WILLIAM RANSOM JOHNSON, SR., PAPERS, 1821-1870. 268 items. Petersburg (Dinwiddie County), Va.

A few business papers of William R. Johnson (1782-1849), North Carolina horse breeder and turfman, 1821-1843; but chiefly business papers of his son, William Ransom Johnson, Jr., 1843-1870, concerning plans for developing Texas lands, the administration of his father's estate, the collecting of internal revenue from tobacco manufacturers, and a letter from John Minor Botts.

2877. DON P. JOHNSTON, SR., PAPERS, 1929-1950. 220 items. Wake Forest (Wake County), N. C., and Okeechobee (Okeechobee County), Fla.

Business papers of Don P. Johnston, Sr., who was involved in banking and real estate enterprises in Florida and textile manufacturing in North Carolina, contain items, 1929-1935, related to the failure of the Peoples Bank of Okeechobee, Okeechobee, Florida; and records of the firm of Johnston and Company, sales agents for textile mills, including the correspondence, 1943-1950, of L. C. Milliken, a partner in the firm; trial balances, 1943-1945; and tax returns and papers, 1943-1950.

2878. ELOISE JOHNSTON PAPERS, 1940-1941. 7 items. Warm Springs (Bath County), Va.

Correspondence between Eloise Johnston and Louise L. Edelmann concerning Eloise Johnston's sister, the novelist Mary Johnston.

2879. JAMES A. JOHNSTON DAYBOOK, 1865. 1 vol. (11 pp.) Lynchburg (Campbell County), Va.

Record of the commissary stores issued and sold at Pratt Hospital in Lynchburg, Virginia.

2880. JOB JOHNSTON PAPERS, 1810 (1821-1852) 1863. 20 items. Fairfield County, S. C.

Correspondence of Job Johnston (1793-1862), chancellor of South Carolina College, 1830-1859, and later associate justice of the court of appeals in South Carolina. Included are letters referring to the building program of the Associate Reformed Presbyterian Church; a letter condemning an Associate Reformed Presbyterian member for communing with the Methodists and Johnston's defense of the accused; Johnston's address on the character of Cato the Younger delivered at the South Carolina College commencement, December 3, 1810, Columbia; a letter from Henry Summer (1809-1869), advocating establishment of a newspaper in Columbia for propagation of principles designed to solve the political problems of South Carolina, 1851; comments on horse racing; a record book of Johnston's slaves, giving dates of purchase, births, and deaths; a partial list of Johnston's law books; receipts for farm supplies; and a letter of E. E. Jackson, describing her work in a Confederate hospital near Charlottesville, Virginia.

2881. JOHN WARFIELD JOHNSTON PAPERS, 1778-1890. 416 items. Abingdon (Washington County), Va.

Papers of John Warfield Johnston, United States senator from Virginia, his wife, Nicketti (Floyd) Johnston, and other members of the Johnston, Preston, and Floyd families. The papers of John Warfield Johnston and Nicketti (Floyd) Johnston contain personal correspondence and letters from their children, including letters, 1886, from Joseph Beverly Johnston who was with the

Alaska Commercial Company in Ounalaska [Unalaska], Alaska. There are several manuscripts of John Warfield Johnston, including an autobiography; reminiscences of his senatorial career; short stories; and essays on the period of the American Revolution, the Republican Party, General Joseph Eggleston Johnston, and currency problems. The collection also contains the papers of Francis Smith Preston (1765-1835) and his sister, Letitia (Preston) Floyd concerning pioneer life, plantation management, politics in Virginia and the nation, and family and personal affairs; the papers of the children of John Floyd and Letitia (Preston) Floyd relating to family matters, Roman Catholicism, the experiences of George Rogers Clark Floyd as a territorial official in Wisconsin in the 1840s, and the early career of George Frederick Holmes, the husband of Eliza Lavalette Floyd; a letter, 1863, of Joseph Eggleston Johnston to his wife, Lydia (McLane) Johnston, justifying his actions in the Vicksburg campaign; and letters of John Warfield Johnston, father of John Warfield Johnston, and his wife, Louisa (Bowen) Johnston, including personal and family correspondence and a few letters to Johnston from John Peter Mettauer.

2882. JOSEPH EGGLESTON JOHNSTON PAPERS, 1855-1885. 40 items. Prince Edward County, Va.

Correspondence of Joseph E. Johnston (1807-1891), general in the Confederate Army, relating to the battle of Manassas, 1861; the conduct of General Braxton Bragg; operations in middle Tennessee in 1864; the problem of obtaining supplies for the Confederacy; the military situation in Mississippi, 1863; and low morale among people in South Carolina and Georgia in 1865. Included also are a letter from Johnston to Jefferson Davis, explaining the failure of the pursuit of the enemy after the battle of Manassas; a copy of General Order No. 18, issued at Greensboro, North Carolina, 1865; and postwar personal letters.

2883. RICHARD MALCOLM JOHNSTON PAPERS, 1886-1895. 25 items. Baltimore, Md.

The collection contains letters of Richard Malcolm Johnston to Robert Underwood Johnson of Century Magazine, concerning lectures or readings which Richard M. Johnston was going to make from his stories of middle Georgia; a letter from Johnston to James R. Randall, praising his journalistic style; and four letters, 1888-1895, from Johnston to his lecture agent, James Burton Pond, concerning Johnston's lecturing plans.

2884. ROBERT JOHNSTON PAPERS, 1783-1795. 1 vol. (72 pp.) Drogheda, County Louth, Ireland.

Accounts of a merchant on the east coast of Ireland revealing trade with Liverpool and other places in England and Ireland. A few entries note exports, predominently of linen, to Virginia. Several pages are missing from the volume; there is an index.

2885. ROBERT D. JOHNSTON PAPERS, 1864. 2 items. Virginia.

Letters of Robert D. Johnston, brigadier general in the Confederate Army, stating that the charges against Colonel H. E. Coleman were without foundation.

2886. WILLIAM L. JOHNSTON ACCOUNT BOOK, 1853-1858. 1 vol. (141 pp.)

Accounts of a physician.

2887. ZACHARIAH JOHNSTON AND THOMAS JOHNSTON PAPERS, 1717-1858. 626 items and 7 vols. Augusta County and Rockbridge County, Va.

Papers of Zachariah Johnston contain letters and documents of Zachariah and his father, William Johnston, dealing with land and legal problems, including several letters beginning in 1781 from Edmund Randolph, their attorney; a number of letters to Zachariah concerning his service in the Virginia legislature, including a letter, 1785, about the proposed act of religious freedom for Virginia; letters, 1789 and 1790, from George Mason on a dispute in Fairfax County over the location of the county seat; letters concerning the administration of Virginia's western lands; the will of Zachariah Johnston, 1800; and Zachariah Johnston's bills and receipts, 1748-1800. Volumes include a commonplace book begun in Ireland by William Johnston and continued in America by Zachariah, and a journal kept by Zachariah Johnston on a trip to Kentucky, 1794.

2888. A. H. JONES INVOICE BOOK, 1848-1849. 1 vol. (310 pp.) Noxubee County, Miss.

Invoice book for the successive firms of Jones and Smith (1844-1847) and A. H. Jones (1848-1849), dealers in dry goods and hardware. The accounts show the goods purchased, the suppliers, and the routes the goods traveled to Noxubee County. There are inventories for 1846 and 1848 and an undated earlier inventory.

2889. ARTHUR JONES PAPERS, 1795-1841. 13 items. Edenton (Chowan County), N. C.

The collection is made up mainly of the business papers of Arthur Jones relating to the shipment of herring, salt, cotton, and pork.

2890. BENJAMIN JONES PAPERS, 1840-1879. 11 items. Guilford County, N. C.

Personal letters, one of which

describes a trip on packet boats on the James and the Kanawha rivers in 1870, and another which describes the establishment of the insane asylums at Morganton and Wilmington, North Carolina, the latter for Negroes.

2891. CALVIN T. JONES ACCOUNT BOOK, 1851. 1 vol. (94 pp.)

Accounts of Calvin T. Jones, a blacksmith.

2892. CATHERINE ELLA JONES PAPERS, 1852-1863. 50 items. Washington, D. C., and Shanghai, China.

Letters of Catherine Ella Jones, a missionary to China.

2893. CHARLES COLCOCK JONES, JR., PAPERS, 1763-1926. 850 items and 67 vols. Savannah, Ga.

The letters and papers of Charles Colcock Jones, lawyer, Confederate soldier, and historian, form a miscellaneous collection containing items on the gathering of historical materials; letters from many famous literary and civic figures thanking Jones for copies of his books; material relating to various tribes of American Indians and to the development of the Indian policy of the United States; letters describing life in California in the mid-19th century and the hardships of the ocean voyage to California; material on the Civil War, including data on the numbers of men provided by various Union states, foreign born generals in the Union Army, the lack of preparedness in Virginia in 1861, relations with Joseph E. Johnston and Jefferson Davis (1861), Bragg's campaign in Kentucky, battles of Augusta and Columbia, Confederate operations on Morris Island (South Carolina, 1863), behavior of Negroes in a southern state in 1866, and the use of Negroes in constructing fortifications for the Confederacy; items pertaining to the 1st Regiment of Chatham County (Georgia) Militia during the American Revolution and after; and material concerning surveying a boundary line between Virginia and North Carolina, abolitionists, and Confederate veterans. Volumes include commonplace books; lecture notes on literature, natural philosophy, and physics; autograph albums; journals; scrapbooks; occasional addresses; records of Harvard Law School Moot Court; manuscript text of "History of the Church of God," by Jones's father, Charles Colcock Jones; manuscript of Jones's History of Georgia, published in 1883; and a long series of letter books containing copies of Jones's letters.

2894. CHARLES EDGEWORTH JONES PAPERS, 1815-1929. 499 items and 5 vols. Augusta (Richmond County), Ga.

The papers of Charles Edgeworth Jones contain correspondence related to his work as historian of the Confederate Survivors Association of Augusta, Georgia; letters from many prominent people acknowledging copies of articles which Jones had sent them; manuscript and printed copies of numerous articles by Jones on state and local history, the Civil War, and Confederate veterans; copies of Jones's poems; and records of the Confederate Survivors Association. Volumes include a scrapbook, 1815-1904, and a roster of the Confederate Survivors Association of Augusta, 1898-1909.

2895. [CHARLES R. JONES?] LEDGER, 1880-1882. 1 vol. (224 pp.) North Carolina.

Merchant's accounts, listing customers and their purchases, largely "sundries," including some debits for contributions to the Methodist Church. Payments by cash, work, wood, and lumber are indicated. An enclosed note from M. Hammond, 1885, indicates the residence of one customer as Bush Hill (now Archdale, Randolph County), North Carolina. There is also a list of people written to concerning prohibition, 1885.

2896. CHESTER JONES PAPERS, 1853-1888. 42 items. Vermont.

Correspondence of Chester Jones, his relatives, and friends, concerning the hiring of substitutes during the Civil War, smallpox cases and smallpox vaccinations, 1882, and teaching in Wisconsin.

2897. EDWIN LEE JONES PAPERS, 1946. 4 items. Charlotte (Mecklenburg County), N. C.

Letters written by Edwin Lee Jones while he was an official observer of the atomic bomb test in Bikini, Marshall Islands, July 1, 1946, describing the preparations for the test and the effects of the explosions on Bikini and Kwajalein atolls.

2898. ELECTUS W. JONES PAPERS, 1860-1863. 18 items. Chautauqua (Chautauqua County), N. Y.

Letters of Electus W. Jones and James G. Macomber, soldiers in the 120th New York Regiment and the 154th New York Regiment, respectively, during the Civil War. The letters describe army life in camps and forts around Washington, D. C.; the army's farewell to General George B. McClellan, 1862; the battle of Fredericksburg; the "Mud March," 1863; and Vicksburg, Mississippi, after its surrender.

2899. ERNEST CHARLES JONES PAPERS, 1844. 1 item. Manchester, Lancashire, England.

A letter to Ernest Charles Jones from F. Radziwill, who was to be godfather of Jones's son.

2900. FLETCHER JONES PAPERS, 1861-1864.
20 items. [Alabama?]

Personal letters from Fletcher Jones, a Confederate soldier, to his wife and correspondence of the Jones family regarding prices, crops, and family affairs.

2901. GEORGE NOBLE JONES PAPERS, 1786-1872.
31 items. Savannah, Ga.

Papers of George Noble Jones contain business letters concerning Jones's Florida plantations; letters of Robert Habersham, George N. Jones's business agent in Savannah, Georgia; plantation journals and reports of overseers in the 1850s; a letter from George N. Jones to his son on Reconstruction, 1867; and price lists of commodities on the Liverpool market, 1867. The papers of George Jones, grandfather of George Noble Jones, contain business letters concerning sea island cotton and letters from a student at Harvard University, 1806.

2902. GEORGE W. JONES PAPERS, 1832 (1862-1865). 34 items. Spring Garden (Pittsylvania County), Va.

Letters of George W. Jones, an officer in the 18th Virginia Regiment, to his wife concerning commodity prices in Richmond, Virginia; his tobacco crop and factory; and war news, including descriptions of the battle of Seven Pines, 1862; the Seven Days' battle, 1862; Stuart's raids around McClellan's army, 1862; the siege of Washington, North Carolina, 1863; the Gettysburg campaign; and Jones's life in military prison at Johnson's Island, Ohio, 1863-1865.

2903. HENRY A. JONES PAPERS, 1838-1849.
8 items. Augusta (Richmond County), Ga.

Letters of Henry A. Jones, a physician, mentioning his attending medical school in Augusta; his marriage in 1849; cotton planting, including a letter from his overseer; and his medical practice.

2904. ISAAC DASHIELL JONES PAPERS, 1841.
1 item. Washington, D. C.

Letter of Isaac Dashiell Jones from the United States House of Representatives concerning the tariff bill which had passed the House.

2905. J. F. JONES PAPERS, 1860-1865.
4 items. Iredell County, N. C.

Contracts to pay Jones for teaching letters, spelling, reading, writing, arithmetic, and grammar; directions for making brilliant white wash; and a love letter, 1865, from Jones to an unidentified girl.

2906. J. HOWARD JONES PAPERS, 1879-1888.
31 items. Thomasville (Davidson County), N. C.

Bills, receipts, and letters of J. Howard Jones, concerning business affairs and legal matters, including Jones's divorce. Also contains payrolls of the Rich Fork Copper Mine.

2907. J. W. JONES DIARY, 1859-1860.
1 vol. (176 pp.) Utica (Oneida County), N. Y.

Diary of the purser's clerk on the Mystic, which patrolled the African coast to capture slave-trading vessels. It includes a full description of St. Helena and Napoleon's old tomb.

2908. JEREMIAH T. JONES PAPERS, 1841-1878.
5 items and 5 vols. Chesterfield County, Va.

Largely financial records associated with Jeremiah T. Jones, an official or part owner of David Watkins & Co., a coal firm with mines near Midlothian, Chesterfield County, Virginia. A large account book, 1841-1853, includes special accounts for Jones, David Watkins, Howell D. Watkins, and Richard Davis, apparently owners or officers of the firm; a few accounts, 1849, for the Gowrie Mines in Chesterfield County; and entries for hired and slave labor, goods purchased or sold, coal, blacksmith work, expenses, and the shipment of coal by railroad in the 1840s. Smaller volumes contain figures and specifications for mine shafts and machinery, coal and slate deposits, accounts for food and clothing, blacksmithing, and coal shipments. One volume is a shoe and clothing account book, 1854-1857, and another, 1877-1878, which records the sale of food and clothing, may be the record of a company store. Loose papers include a list of workers, 1853, and the plan of a mine.

2909. JOHN JONES PAPERS, 1778-1870.
5 items. Griffin (Spalding County), Ga.

Miscellaneous letters and business accounts of the large importing firm of John Jones and Company of Georgia and South Carolina in the time of the American Revolution.

2910. JOHN JONES RECEIPT BOOKS, 1797-1820.
2 vols. Liberty County, Ga.

Cash receipts of John Jones, sheriff of Liberty County, Georgia.

2911. JOHN ROBERT JONES PAPERS, 1847-1851.
1 vol. Harrisonburg (Rockingham County), Va.

A scrapbook kept while John Robert Jones was a student at Virginia Military Institute.

2912. JOSEPH JONES PAPERS, 1824. 2 items. Milo (Yates County), N. Y.

Two deeds.

2913. JOSEPH JONES PAPERS, 1681 (1794-1842) 1895. 704 items. Petersburg (Dinwiddie County), Va.

Business and personal correspondence of Joseph Jones (1727-1805), a major general of the Virginia militia, and of his children and grandchildren, including deeds, militia records, general orders, military correspondence, letters regarding western lands, circulars from the Treasury Department, lists of licensed vessels, and miscellaneous papers pertaining to the port of Petersburg, of which Jones was collector. Among the correspondents are John Adams, W. H. Crawford, Albert Gallatin, Joseph Jones, Richard Bland Lee, James Madison, Timothy Pickering, John Randolph, and John Tyler.

2914. JOSEPH S. JONES DAYBOOK, 1875-1900. 6 items and 1 vol. Panther Creek (Yadkin County), N. C.

Accounts for the sale of general merchandise and foodstuffs, with names of customers and indication of means of payment by cash, labor, or produce. Six loose items inserted in the volume are correspondence, 1875-1876, concerning the appointment and work of J. S. Jones as an U.S. Internal Revenue gauger for distilled spirits; an undated application for appointment as a census supervisor; and a note listing local delegates elected to the county Republican convention, 1900.

2915. KATE JONES COPYBOOK, 1861. 1 vol. Bethania (Forsyth County), N. C.

School copybook containing essays and poems.

2916. KIMBROUGH JONES PAPERS, 1800 (1842-1869). 36 items. Wake County, N. C.

Family correspondence of Kimbrough Jones, politician and member of the North Carolina constitutional convention of 1835.

2917. LEWIS J. JONES PAPERS, 1862-1864. 7 items. Kentucky.

Letters from Lewis J. Jones, a soldier in the Union Army, to his wife, describing troop movements and the country through which he marched.

2918. LLOYD JONES PAPERS, 1862. 1 item. London, England.

Letter from John Malcolm Forbes Ludlow to Lloyd Jones concerning the American Civil War, British politics, Robert Buchanan, The Beehive, and censorship of Jones's newspaper articles.

2919. M. JONES ACCOUNT BOOK, 1856-1859. 1 vol. (82 pp.) Wilmington (New Hanover County), N. C.

Accounts of a turpentine and rosin business.

2920. MARTHA M. JONES PAPERS, 1840-1904. 113 items. Tuscaloosa County, Ala.

Letters to Martha M. Jones from various members of her family, particularly from her sister, Margaret C. Templeton, in Texas, describing the terrain, crops, customs, conditions during the Civil War, diseases, religious development, and educational facilities.

2921. MATTHIAS JONES PAPERS, 1836. 1 item. Ridge Spring (Saluda County), S.C.

An account of sales, including furniture, land, farm implements, livestock, and slaves.

2922. MERIWETHER JONES PAPERS, 1817-1921. 3,273 items and 15 vols. Richmond, Va.

The papers of Meriwether Jones, mining engineer and mine manager, mainly concern his business ventures and the mining and processing operations he managed in association with Ferral C. Dininny, Jr., of New York. Papers of the Alleghany Iron Company contain correspondence consisting of 7 letterpress books, 1892-1897, and unbound letters, 1896-1897, from Thomas Catesby Jones, brother of Meriwether Jones and manager of the company's furnace at Iron Gate, Virginia. These volumes concern the operations of the furnace, local and state politics, schools at Iron Gate, and contain letters to national and state legislators about taxation and the company's right to issue scrip. The Alleghany Iron Company's records also contain a daybook for the Iron Gate Furnace, 1892-1896; a book of chemical analyses, 1892-1896; and a volume of railroad transportation rates, 1892-1893. Papers of the Columbia Mining and Land Company consist of a copy of the company charter, 1891. Papers of F. C. Dininny, Jr., a mining concern, contain daily mine reports, 1895-1896, a letterpress book, 1893-1896; and a record of coal shipments, 1892-1897. The papers of Meriwether Jones, ca. 1900-1921, concern the James River Coal Corporation, including a time book, 1906-1916, for that company listing names, time worked, wages, and money deducted; the Old Dominion Tobacco Warehouse, 1914-1920; and the class of 1874, Virginia Military Institute.

2923. NOBLE WIMBERLY JONES PAPERS, 1766-1811. 16 items. Savannah, Ga.

Papers of Noble Wimberly Jones contain a letter from Jones to Benjamin Franklin lamenting the outbreak of hostilities near Boston, Massachusetts; letter concerning the hiring of slaves; certificate of the colony of Georgia, used as currency; act, 1778, of the House of Assembly of Georgia setting up a superior court system, signed by Jones as speaker; two statements relative to state funds; and papers concerning the estate of Noble W. Jones.

2924. OLIVER H. JONES PAPERS, 1832-1861. 253 items. Wilmington (New Hanover County), N. C.

Business letters and accounting records sent to Oliver H. Jones of New York City by R. W. Brown & Son, Potter & Parsley, and Neff & Jones, his marketing agents in Wilmington, North Carolina, show price figures and supply and demand fluctuations for such North Carolina imports as dairy products, flour, hay, beef, pork, and liquors and exports such as naval stores, beeswax, and rice.

2925. RICHARD JONES PAPERS, 1797-1878. 152 items and 9 vols. Lynchburg (Campbell County), Va.

The papers of Richard Jones contain an "English Classical Education" certificate, 1808; letters concerning Jones's work as a teacher; plantation accounts and doctor's bills for slaves; daybooks and records of fees and cases as coroner of Pittsylvania County, Virginia; and Jones family papers, including a land grant, 1797, deeds, and wills.

2926. ROBERT JONES, JR., AND WILLIE JONES PAPERS, 1759-1865. 22 items. Halifax County and Granville County, N. C.

Legal papers of Robert Jones, Jr., and his son Willie contain deeds, indentures, and documents involving the marriage settlement of Peter Jones of Halifax, 1757.

2927. ROBERT RANDOLPH JONES PAPERS, 1743-1951. 594 items and 1 vol. Petersburg (Dinwiddie County), Va.

The papers of Robert Randolph Jones concern his career as an educator, including letters of recommendation from many prominent Virginians; letters from Jones to his wife while he was superintendent of public schools in Petersburg, Virginia; and material concerning his work as superintendent of public schools in El Paso, Texas, 1914-1941. The collection also contains the papers of the Blackwell family of Lunenburg County, Virginia, and the related Hawthorn, Edmondson, Goodwin, and Cabaniss families. The letters, bills, receipts, and legal papers are primarily those of John Blackwell and concern his administration of a number of estates, flatboat life on the Red River, and education.

2928. ROGER JONES PAPERS, 1810-1849. 12 items and 1 vol. Washington, D. C.

Fragment of a letter book, 1810-1811, kept by Roger Jones while an officer in the United States Marine Corps aboard the U.S.S. John Adams concerning his efforts to obtain supplies, especially clothes, for the men under his command, and payroll matters. Also routine letters and orders of Jones as adjutant general in the United States Army.

2929. RUFUS HENRY JONES PAPERS, 1797-1919. 135 items and 1 vol. Wake County, N. C.

The papers of Rufus Henry Jones include items pertaining to his grandfather, father, and uncles and material on the Rencher and Merritt families of North Carolina. The papers concern land transactions; local politics; the study of law; a Methodist revival in Olin, North Carolina, 1859; and events of the Civil War described by relatives in Alabama, Mississippi, Arkansas, and North Carolina. Also contains a memorandum book, 1797-1854, of Henry Jones, containing references to a distillery and accounts for salt, beef, pork, and butter.

2930. SAMUEL T. JONES PAPERS, 1839-1902. 80 items and 2 vols. Columbia (Richland County), S. C.

The papers of Samuel T. Jones include items relating to his wife, Eugenia M. (Hart) Jones and at least one son, Benjamin Hart Jones. The papers are mainly concerned with Samuel T. Jones's career as a teacher and include letters and a fragment of a diary describing a trip, 1849, made by Jones to observe the school systems of the major eastern cities. There are also biographical sketches and papers on philosophical, ethical, and religious questions by Jones, some of which were written while he was a student at South Carolina College, Columbia, South Carolina. Volumes include an account book kept by Samuel T. Jones as a student and an account book kept by Benjamin Hart Jones during the Civil War and as a farmer in Alabama.

2931. SEABORN JONES, SR., PAPERS, 1761-1847. 177 items. Augusta (Richmond County), Ga.

Legal and personal correspondence and papers of Seaborn Jones, a Georgia lawyer. The collection is chiefly concerned with legal cases and suits in the courts of Georgia, including material, 1799-1801, on the patent for Eli Whitney's cotton gin. Included also are letters relating to a female educational society in Liberty County, Georgia, 1838; the siege of Savannah, 1779, activities of the American forces, and damage done to property by the British during the Revolutionary War. Among the correspondents are Thomas P. Carnes,

Joseph Clay, Wade Hampton, Robert Goodloe Harper, James Jackson, John McIntosh, Horatio Marbury, John Milledge, William W. Seaton, and George Walton.

2932. THOMAS JONES PAPERS, ca. 1816. 2 items. [Va. ?]

The collection contains two speeches by Thomas Jones; a Fourth of July address and a talk on education.

2933. THOMAS K. JONES PAPERS, 1754 (1787-1815) 1836. 56 items. Boston, Mass.

Business correspondence among various commission firms of Massachusetts, Virginia, and North Carolina, primarily Thomas K. Jones of Boston; Elias Parker of Petersburg, Virginia; and Laurason and Fowle of Alexandria, Virginia; but also including William Walter & Company of Boston; Josiah Faxon, John G. Ladd, and D. Sheldon, all of Alexandria; Wilson & Cunningham of Norfolk, Virginia; and A. Hattridge of Wilmington, North Carolina. The letters concern the details of shipping, the state of the market for various items of trade, and some discussion of ways of evading customs duties.

2934. THOMAS THWEATT JONES PAPERS, 1757-1976. 6,437 items and 61 vols. Durham, N. C.

The papers of Thomas Thweatt Jones contain correspondence, memoranda and reports, addresses and writings, printed material, volumes, pictures, legal papers, financial papers, genealogical material, and clippings, pertaining to his career as a physician in Durham, North Carolina; his interest in the subjects of alcoholism, care of the terminally ill, mental health, industrial medicine and occupational health, and the changing role of the general practitioner; and his family, including his father, Robert Randolph Jones, and his father-in-law, David Howard Scanlon. Correspondence contains scattered letters, 1830-1889, of the Jones family and the related Bolling and Randolph families; letters, 1889-1932, of Robert Randolph Jones, including letters from his years as a student at Hampden-Sydney College, 1889-1893, and correspondence, 1901-1932, with his wife and children, dealing primarily with family and personal matters, but occasionally relating to his work in public school systems in Virginia and Texas; and the letters of Thomas Thweatt Jones, 1932-1974, concerning mainly family and personal affairs, 1932-1947, and concerning Jones's career and professional interests, 1947-1974, including correspondence with such organizations as the American Medical Association, the North Carolina Medical Society, the North Carolina Mental Hygiene Society, the Durham Council on Alcoholism, and Alcoholics Anonymous; letters commenting on talks and published articles; and correspondence relating to Jones's attempt to found an alcoholic rehabilitation center in Durham, 1962-1965. The bulk of the memoranda and reports in the collection consist of a general file, containing material on Jones's service in the United States Army during World War II, the work of the North Carolina Medical Society and the American Academy of General Practice, and investigations done at the University of North Carolina, Chapel Hill, concerning the relationship between the press and the medical profession; memoranda and reports on alcoholism, 1953-1974, from various organizations in which Jones was active; and material, 1954-1974, relating to mental health, including the training of general practitioners in psychiatry and the activities of the North Carolina Mental Health Association and the North Carolina Neuropsychiatric Association. Smaller groups of memoranda and reports contain minutes, resolutions, and reports, 1956-1972, of the First Presbyterian Church of Durham; a few items from Watts Hospital in Durham, 1957-1972; and memoranda from Duke University Medical Center in Durham, 1964-1972. Addresses and writings include articles, speeches, and notes for speeches by Jones, 1952-1973, on alcoholism, agathanasia (death with dignity), heart attacks, the nervous woman, and the general practitioner. Other writings, 1875-1973, include "A Study of Scripture Teaching as to the Holy Spirit," 1875-1880, by John Blackwell; a biographical sketch, 1940, of Aline McKenzie by David Howard Scanlon; and writings by various experts on alcoholism. Printed material in the collection is almost entirely concerned with Thomas T. Jones's professional interests and contains items on death, geriatrics, industrial medicine, general practitioners, and family medicine; a large amount of material on alcoholism, including pamphlets, tracts, periodicals, and clipped articles; and items on mental health. Volumes in the collection include pamphlets, paperback books, and copies of journals and magazines dealing with topics of professional interest to Jones, similar to the topics covered in the printed material, and personal volumes, including the sermon of D. H. Scanlon on his retirement from the ministry, 1938; trip diaries of D. H. Scanlon, 1923, and Mary (Scanlon) Jones, 1926, describing Spain, Portugal, Greece, Turkey, Palestine, and Egypt; 2 volumes of the poems of Aline McKenzie and a scrapbook about her; the family Bible of Robert Randolph Jones; and Thomas T. Jones's personal appointment calendar, 1960. The large number of photographs in the collection are of Thomas T. Jones and his wife and children, the ancestors of Thomas T. Jones and Mary (Scanlon) Jones, and organizations with which Jones was connected. Legal papers, 1757-1974, contain a few wills, deeds and mortgages. Financial papers, 1818-1970, contain only a few items, including receipts and accounts of Jones's ancestors from the first half of the 19th century. Genealogical material, 1858-1973, concerns the Bolling, Blackwell, Randolph, Scanlon, Gruver, and Jones families.

Clippings, 1887-1976, deal for the most part with Jones's professional interests, but a few concern members of his family. Miscellany, 1901-1970, include questionnaires from a study of alcoholism in Durham and various invitations, certificates, and membership cards.

2935. THOMAS W. JONES PAPERS, 1816-1852. 20 items. Mecklenburg County and Brunswick County, Va.

Correspondence of Thomas W. Jones, a physician, his wife, Mary (Armistead) Jones, and his father, John Jones, a planter, concerning medical school in Philadelphia, social life and customs, family affairs, Protestant Episcopal Bishop John Stark Ravenscroft, and the Petersburg, Virginia, cotton market.

2936. WALTER JONES PAPERS, 1781-1880. 136 items and 1 vol. Washington, D. C.

Family correspondence of Walter Jones (1776-1861), lawyer and soldier, with an occasional letter to Walter Jones on legal business. The letters include several from a son, Thomas Walter, who served on the Bartlett Commission for establishing the boundary between Mexico and the United States, and the diary of Thomas Walter Jones, 1851-1852.

2937. WILLIAM JONES PAPERS, 1838-1865. 46 items. Augusta (Richmond County), Ga.

Receipted bills for merchandise, 1838-1842; miscellaneous petitions to courts in Wilkes County, Georgia; and other legal documents addressed to the sheriffs of Wilkes County.

2938. WILLIAM B. JONES ACCOUNT BOOKS, 1924-1931. 6 vols. Raleigh (Wake County), N. C.

Records of a law firm and a farm.

2939. WILLIAM H. JONES PAPERS, 1833 (1860-1865) 1888. 207 items. Amherst County, Va.

The correspondence of William H. Jones and his family is made up for the most part of letters dealing with Civil War, concerning Southern enthusiasm at the beginning of the war; commodity prices in Virginia; living conditions in the Confederacy and camp life in the Confederate Army; many skirmishes and battles; troop movements; and casualties.

2940. DANIEL W. JORDAN PAPERS, 1827 (1843-1875) 1913. 4,250 items and 8 vols. Camden (Kershaw County), S. C.

Family and business correspondence and accounts of Daniel W. Jordan (ca. 1790-1883), planter, slaveholder, and South Carolina legislator. The collection includes Jordan's bookkeeping diploma, 1827; references to the University of Alabama, Tuscaloosa, 1847; letters from Benjamin Blossom & Son and De Rossit & Brown, both of New York City, concerning Jordan's turpentine business; letters concerning slavery; receipts from Aldert Smedes, St. Mary's College, Raleigh, North Carolina, for tuition of Rowena Ralston, 1854, and Victoria Jordan, 1856; letters from "Sallie Vic" (Victoria Jordan), 1857-1858, and from Cora Jordan, 1860, while they attended a school in Charleston, South Carolina; letters from W. J. Bingham of W. J. Bingham & Sons' Select School, Oaks, Orange County, North Carolina, concerning Valentine Jordan's attendance, 1860-1861; letters concerning the deaths of Victoria (Jordan) Davie and her husband in the burning of the steamship Charmer, 1861; and letters concerning Jordan's cotton business relations with Lyon Brothers & Company of Baltimore, Maryland. The account books cover the period 1836-1877 and include lists of Negroes, ration accounts, and cotton-picking accounts. Among the correspondents are Joseph B. Bryan, H. G. Carrison, John S. Cheek, H. S. Ellenwood, William R. Harris, M. W. Ransom, John C. Tuttle, and William A. Tuttle.

2941. HENRY T. JORDAN AUTOGRAPH BOOK, 1863-1864. 1 vol. Roxboro (Person County), N. C.

Autographs of Henry T. Jordan's fellow Confederate prisoners at Johnson's Island, Ohio.

2942. JOHN JORDAN PAPERS, 1815-1845. 13 items and 2 vols. Woodstock (Shenandoah County), Va.

Business records of a tanner including a ledger, 1815-1824, and a tanyard book, 1826-1845. The tanyard book is a chronological listing of accounts with debits and credits on facing pages; most entries are for a few individuals including Henry S. Wunder and Jacob and Isaac R. Dinges, who were involved in the operation of the tanyard. There are also some accounts for hired labor.

2943. JOHN A. JORDAN PAPERS, 1853, 1865. 2 items. Richmond, Va.

Letter of John A. Jordan discussing events of the Civil War, the news in Richmond, Virginia, and the failure of the Hampton Roads Conference, and letter to a Colonel Jordan concerning the sale of a slave.

2944. THOMAS JORDAN PAPERS, 1861-1885. 239 items. Charleston, S. C.

Papers of Jordan, Confederate chief of staff under General P.G.T. Beauregard, concerning a quarrel on Beauregard's staff and routine military matters. Also contains reports to Beauregard concerning the defense of Charleston, South Carolina, and the surrounding area; military operations in Virginia; and a reconnaissance of the Tennessee River. There are a few items after 1865 concerning reminiscenses of the war by Jordan and Beauregard.

2945. JAMES YADKIN JOYNER PAPERS, 1943-1955. 3 items. LaGrange (Lenoir County), N. C.

James Y. Joyner's account of how he came to be appointed superintendent of public instruction in North Carolina in 1902 and items relating to this account.

2946. JOSHUA E. JOYNER PAPERS, 1863-1864. 5 items. Southampton County, Va.

Family letters from a Confederate private, with some mention of the battle of Gettysburg, 1863.

2947. TOBIAS JULIAN AND BOHAN JULIAN PAPERS, 1833-1861. 8 items. Randolph County, N. C.

Personal letters to Tobias and Bohan Julian.

2948. HORACE HOWARD JUSTIS DIARY, 1857-1859. 1 vol. (103 pp.) Des Moines College, West Point, Iowa.

Diary of Horace H. Justis, apparently from Cincinnati, Ohio, kept while a law student at Des Moines College and while a country schoolteacher in Mississippi.

2949. HENRY KAGEY PAPERS, 1769-1883. 706 items. Shenandoah County, Va.

Indentures, wills, bonds, accounts of settlements of estates, especially of William Smith, and a few mercantile accounts of Henry Kagey. Some of the documents are in German script. There are also personal letters, some from settlers in Ohio, which include religious musings, references to weather and crop conditions, and family and local news. Civil War letters include those of Caspar C. Henkel, surgeon of the 2nd Regiment of Virginia Militia describing health, quarters, and military actions near Winchester, Virginia, and Martinsburg, West Virginia; a contract for a substitute for David F. Kagey dated November 22, 1861; and love letters from Kagey date from 1863. Letters between Henkel and Kagey, 1863-1864, have information on medical training in Virginia, on the execution of deserters, on avoidance of the draft, and on the purchase of substitutes. There are also minutes of the Association for the Relief of Maimed Soldiers in New Market, February, 1864; reports on sick and wounded in the 25th, 42nd, and 48th Regiments of Virginia Infantry, July, 1864; and a fragment of Kagey's diary.

2950. HANS KARL KANDLBINDER PAPERS, 1956-1967. 10 items and 2 vols. Straubinger, Bavaria, Germany.

Typescript in German of the reminiscence in diary form written by a graduate student at Duke University in 1953-1954, with miscellaneous articles by Kandlbinder and correspondence with the Department of Alumni Affairs of Duke University.

2951. ROBERT GARLICK HILL KEAN PAPERS, 1870. 4 items. Lynchburg (Campbell County), Va.

Communications to Kean from the firm of Thomas Jellis Kirkpatrick and Charles Minor Blackford, Sr., and Edward Smith Brown, all attorneys of Lynchburg, concerning legal matters and mentioning Judge William Daniel, Jr., and his son John Warwick Daniel, also a Lynchburg attorney.

2952. HENRY C. KEARNEY PAPERS, 1827 (1868-1890) 1923. 36 items. Franklinton, (Franklin County), N.C.

Business correspondence of Henry C. Kearney, evidently a planter and minor businessman, concerning prices and containing a number of excise tax receipts for tobacco and brandy.

2953. JOHN KEBLE PAPERS, 1808-1859. 7 items. Hursley, Hampshire, England.

A few personal letters of John Keble, Sr. (d. 1835), and letters of his son, John Keble (1792-1866), Vicar of Hursley and a founder of the Oxford Movement in the Church of England, to Sir John Taylor Coleridge and others. Topics include resolutions presented at Winchester concerning the authority of the church in matters of faith; Keble's biography of Thomas Wilson, Bishop of Sodor and Man; and disturbances in London following an effort to revive ritual, 1859.

2954. JOSEPH KEEDING PAPERS, 1834. 2 items. New Albany and Orleans (Orange County), Ind.

Letters to his family from a debtor who had fled his home in Frederick County, Virginia, to reclaim his fortunes and reputation in the West, where he made his living as a schoolteacher, bookkeeper, and postmaster.

2955. ELISHA FORD KEEN PAPERS, 1832-1922. 7 items. "Cottage Hill," Pittsylvania County, Va.

Included are a list of lands sold for taxes in Franklin County, Virginia, 1832; receipt for the sale of slaves, 1860; letters describing the Civil War in Virginia, 1864; and a scroll, 1922, commemorating "Lady Astor Day," in honor of the nativity of Viscountess

Nancy Witcher (Langhorne) Shaw Astor, granddaughter of E. F. Keen.

2956. MARY KEESE PAPERS, 1844, 1848. 2 items. Augusta (Richmond County), Ga.

Personal letters containing a description of an explosion on a steamboat, probably on the Savannah River.

2957. ALEXANDER KEEVER PAPERS, 1861-1893. 71 items. Catawba County, N. C.

Family correspondence including several Civil War letters from camps in Virginia and North Carolina.

2958. JOSEPH WARREN KEIFER, SR., ORDER BOOK, 1862-1863. 1 vol. (8 pp.) Moorefield (Hardy County), West Virginia, and Winchester (Frederick County), Va.

General orders by Joseph Warren Keifer, Sr., colonel of the 110th Regiment, Ohio Infantry, issued as commander of Union troops in the vicinity of Moorefield, West Virginia, 1862, and as commander of the 2nd Brigade, Milroy's Division, near Winchester, Virginia, January and February, 1863. Topics include loyalty oaths to be taken by citizens in occupied Virginia, pillage by troops, discipline, food, marksmanship, drill, and awards in the 110th and 122nd Ohio Regiments.

2959. SYLVANUS KEITH AND CARY KEITH PAPERS, 1798-1880. 220 items. Bridgewater (Plymouth County), Mass., and Charleston, S. C.

Business papers of a merchant and shipper of Bridgewater who traded between Providence (Rhode Island), New York City, and Charleston (South Carolina), contain a partnership contract and letters between Sylvanus Keith and Seth Lathrop, his half brother, describing damage caused by hurricanes in Charleston, 1804-1810; documents relating to the ship Saluda; problems of debtors; and the effect on business of the strained relations of the United States and Britain, 1807-1808. There is also family correspondence of Cary Keith concerning social life and customs of Charleston, and letters from other relatives, including Sylvanus's daughter Carolina (Keith) Coy and niece Olive Keith. One letter, 1880, from Ida Tillson, describes an American mission school in Japan.

2960. LAURENCE MASSILLON KEITT PAPERS, 1855-1864. 146 items. Orangeburg District, S. C.

Correspondence of Laurence M. Keitt (1824-1864), lawyer, member of U. S. Congress, 1852-1861, and Confederate officer. The earlier letters are chiefly from Keitt to Susanna Sparks prior to their marriage; although personal, they contain some comment on politics, the American Party, and Washington, D.C., society. The Civil War letters refer to politics, battles, campaigns, military strategy, and deserters and mutiny among the troops in January, 1864. Keitt was in command of the forces on Sullivan's Island, South Carolina, 1862-1864. The last items are letters of condolence on Keitt's death in the battle of Cold Harbor, June, 1864.

2961. THOMAS ELLISON KEITT PAPERS, 1768-1945. 761 items and 8 vols. Clemson (Oconee County), S. C.

Papers of the related Wadlington, Bauskett, and Keitt families of Newberry County, South Carolina. Included are a genealogical chart; social and personal letters with some information on slave sales and purchases, cotton mills, smallpox, and Charleston; papers of Thomas Bauskett, a planter, and J. L. Keitt, a farmer, attorney, and state legislator; and Civil War letters of Ellison Summerfield Keitt, captain in the 20th Regiment of South Carolina Troops and later the 19th South Carolina Cavalry Battalion, including muster rolls, 1863, of Company M, 20th Regiment. Correspondents include James Wadlington, Thomas Wadlington, John Bauskett, Caroline (Wadlington) Keitt, Thomas W. Keitt, Thomas Ellison Keitt, Laurence Massillon Keitt, Harriet (Sondley) Wadlington, Ann (Bauskett) Wadlington, and William W. Boyce. Legal papers, 1770-1913, consist of indentures, wills, deeds, plats, summonses, and records of trial and judgment, and in part concern the work of Thomas Bauskett, attorney, and James Wadlington, judge. Financial papers, 1768-1902, include promissory notes, bills, and receipts, and small account books of Sarah Cates's children, 1819, and Thomas Bauskett, 1798. There is a ledger, 1758-1803, of Thomas Wadlington, Sr.; an inventory of the estate of James Wadlington, 1831-1850; mercantile account book, 1831-1879, of Ann (Bauskett) Wadlington; and account books, 4 vols., 1931-1939, of Mrs. Thomas Wadlington Keitt, including the wages paid agricultural laborers and amounts subscribed to the Methodist Church at Clemson. There are miscellaneous speeches, prayers, and writings, and printed material including pamphlets and clippings related to the Wadlington and Keitt families.

2962. SIR GEORGE WILLIAM KEKEWICH PAPERS, 1866 (1890-1902) 1920. 118 items. London, England.

Letters to Kekewich (1841-1921), secretary of the privy council's committee on education, the science and art department, and the board of education, concerning his work with educational administration and legislation. Many of the letters are from Lord Cranbrook and the Duke of Devonshire, lord presidents of the Privy Council, and Sir Arthur Herbert Dyke Acland and Sir John Eldon Gorst, vice presidents of the committee on education. They concern administration and personnel of elementary and secondary schools; and problems between Anglican and Catholic schools.

2963.  JOHN McINTOSH KELL PAPERS, 1785-1921. 4,268 items and 1 vol. Darien (McIntosh County), Ga.

Family correspondence of John M. Kell (1823-1900), U.S. naval officer, executive officer of C.S.S. Sumter and Alabama, and captain of the Confederate ironclad Richmond, consisting of letters from Kell to his mother, Marjory Spalding (Baillie) Kell; to his wife, Julia Blanche (Munroe) Kell; and a few to his sisters. Beginning with Kell's first absence from home after his receiving a midshipman's warrant in 1841, his letters cover the period of his service in the U.S. Navy and in the Confederate Navy. The letters include names of ships on which Kell served; accounts of cruises; references to social activities on board ship and on land, especially at the Warrington Navy Yard near Pensacola, Florida; references to Commodore Matthew C. Perry and methods for obtaining a treaty with Japan; a description of the funeral of Commodore Alexander James Dallas in the bay of Callao, Peru, and nearby Bonavista; the countryside in the vicinity of Cape Town, South Africa; descriptions of Montevideo, Uruguay, accounts of customs there and references to President Carlos Antonio Lopez of Paraguay in 1858; and many comments regarding naval duties and officers.

After 1860 Kell's letters are concerned with his resignation from the U.S. Navy and his duties with Confederate Navy. Included are references to the Warrington Navy Yard and its seizure by the state of Florida; Kell's prospective command of the C.S.S. Everglade; condition of the C.S.S. Savannah when he took command temporarily in 1861; running the blockade on C.S.S. Sumter from July 2, 1861, until June 17, 1862, and abandonment of the Sumter at Gibraltar as unfit for further service; his subsequent duties on board the C.S.S. Alabama under Captain Raphael Semmes and a graphic description of the capture of the Alabama's fifty-sixth prize near Cape Town, South Africa; a brief stay at Nassau, N. P., in the Bahama Islands; and several letters describing his duties as commander of the ironclad Richmond under Rear Admiral Raphael Semmes of the James River Squadron from January to March, 1865.

Among the personal and family matters, Kell's letters contain numerous references to agricultural conditions in Georgia; Sapelo Island off the coast of Georgia; his cousin Thomas Spalding and Spalding's son, Randolph, who married Kell's sister, Evy; his children; and his mother. Included also are an album, 1853-1855, and scrapbooks, 1863, 1904, of Julia Blanche (Munroe) Kell, [Partially published; John McIntosh Kell, Recollections of a Naval Life, Washington, 1900.]

The collection includes correspondence from the antebellum period down to the 1890s and business papers of Nathan Campbell Munroe of Macon, Georgia, his wife Tabitha Easter (Napier) Munroe, their daughter Julia Blanche (Munroe) Kell, wife of John McIntosh Kell, and other members of the Munroe and related families--the Hendley Varners, McDonoughs of Henry County, the Spaldings, McIntoshes, and Napiers. Topics include Georgia and national politics; the Bank of the United States ; railroad construction in Georgia; Christ Church Episcopal Parish in Macon; Montpelier Institute, a female seminary in Monroe County; Salem Female Academy, Salem, North Carolina; temperance; schooling at Montauban, France; the Bibb County Academy (the Macon Free School after 1858); the Macon Female Academy (now Wesleyan College), and other institutions; the duel between Thomas Butler King, U.S. representative from Georgia, and Charles Spalding following Spalding's accusation that King had gained election to Congress by misrepresenting his stand on the policies of Henry Clay and the Bank of the United States; relations between students and townsfolk at the University of Alabama in Tuscaloosa in the 1850s; riverboat transportation in Alabama; and the fight between the Monitor and Virginia described by Robert D. Minor, Confederate naval officer. There are also letters from Confederate naval officers William E. Evans and Robert T. Chapman, and from soldiers in the 10th Georgia Infantry, one describing the invasion of Pennsylvania just before Gettysburg. Correspondence of Richard F. Armstrong, Anna (Semmes) Bryan, and Arthur Sinclair concerns the publication of Sinclair's book, Two Years on the Alabama (1895), and the accuracy of the information in that work. There are other letters from former Confederates relating to their life since the war and a proposal for restoration of ex-Confederate naval officers to the U.S. Navy retired list.

Additional letters received by Julia Blanche (Munroe) Kell from school friends, family, her husband, his relatives, and her children, comment on such topics as religion, agriculture, the navy, China, South America, the Civil War, cotton and rice plantations, Negroes, Reconstruction, and medical remedies. There are also bills, receipts, genealogy, poems, and short stories related to Mrs. Kell. Other bills and receipts from the 1820s-1860s reveal the work in education of Nathan C. Munroe.

Volumes include general orders and general watch and quarter bills of the U.S. Frigate Savannah, 1843-1847; and logs kept by John McIntosh Kell as midshipman on the U.S.S. Falmouth, 1841-1843, and on the Savannah and the Shark, 1843-1847. There is an unpublished manuscript by Mrs. Kell, "The Life and Letters of John McIntosh Kell," written in 1908; and also a scrapbook of clippings about noted Confederate leaders, pasted in the journal of an unidentified commission merchant.

2964. JACOB KELLER DAYBOOK, 1854-1868. 1 vol. (30 pp.) Shenandoah County, Va.

Records of Jacob and Charlotte Keller, keepers of the poor house of Beckford Parish.

2965. WILLIAM KELLER PAPERS, 1881-1888. 3 items and 1 vol. Tom's Brook (Shenandoah County), Va.

Ledger containing records of Keller's work repairing and manufacturing wagons, buggies, sleighs, and farm implements. An undated manuscript contains directions and ingredients for coats of filling and stuffing on vehicle bodies.

2966. THOMAS F. KELLEY PAPERS, 1850 (1862-1864) 1866. 21 items. Campbell County, Va.

Personal correspondence of Thomas F. Kelley, Martha Sublett, and Samuel M. Sublet, concerning Virginia during the Civil War, commodity prices, military campaigns, the blockade and economic conditions, military life and health, conscription, medical examinations given to inductees, and presidential elections in the North and their implications for peace.

2967. SAMUEL KELLO PAPERS, 1813-1814. 4 items. Southampton County, Va.

Personal letters written during the War of 1812 concerning military service, the ownership and sale of a slave, and congratulations to Kello on his marriage.

2968. JOHN KELLOGG AND S. W. KELLOGG PAPERS, 1841-1851. 18 items. West Point (Orange County), New York.

Largely letters concerning the life of John Kellogg as a cadet at the United States Military Academy, 1846-1849.

2969. MINER KILBOURNE KELLOGG PAPERS, 1885. 2 items. Cleveland (Cuyahoga County), Ohio.

Two manuscripts by Kellogg, artist and author, describing his restoration of the "Virgin and Child" painted by Da Vinci, then owned by Liberty Emery Holden of Cleveland and since given to the Cleveland Museum of Art.

2970. JOHN N. KELLY PAPERS, 1769-1935. 540 items and 9 vols. Clarkton (Bladen County), N. C.

Papers of John N. Kelly of Bladen County; Ann Kelly, a relative; and Neill Kelly, a nephew, relating to the turpentine business in Georgia and Florida after the Civil War; student life at Columbian College (now George Washington University), 1851; slavery as a political issue; secession; Quakers as conscientious objectors; the loss of Fort Fisher and the blockade of Wilmington; the 36th Regiment of North Carolina Artillery Volunteers at Fort Fisher; and capture by Federal troops. Several retrospective letters deal with Fort Fisher. Reconstruction letters from Mississippi and North Carolina concern cotton, land, railroads, commodity prices, politics, and the Vernon (North Carolina) Female Academy; there are also lists of slaves' birth dates; lists of students, especially of students studying church music; a will; and antebellum militia bylaws. One letter, 1918, from J. C. Kelly concerns a soldier's desire for a temporary release to help with the crops.

2971. WILLIAMSON KELLY PAPERS, 1852-1882. 76 items. Lawrenceville (Brunswick County), Va.

Mostly mercantile accounts and letters about personal affairs and the Civil War in Virginia, especially from Williamson Kelly's brother, Lt. Alfred Kelly of the 21st Regiment of Virginia Infantry Volunteers, relating to Jackson's Shenandoah Valley campaigns and campaigns in Virginia and Maryland; equipment and clothing shortages and health conditions; and the battle of the Wilderness, 1864. There is a receipt for the sale of a slave, January, 1865.

2972. ROBERT KELTON PAPERS, 1837-1848. 6 items. Lancaster (Lancaster County), Pa.

Personal and family letters.

2973. JOHN MITCHELL KEMBLE PAPERS, 1829-1857. 49 items and 2 vols. London, England, and Hanover, Germany.

Notebooks, manuscripts, drafts, loose notes, and letters of Kemble (1807-1857), philologist and historian. One volume, 399 pp., contains two biographical sketches and copies of 174 letters, largely items omitted from Kemble's published work, State Papers and Correspondence Illustrative of the Social and Political State of Europe (London: 1857). The other volume, 199 pp., contains extracts from Latin and Norman-French records concerning regulations regarding money, weights, and measures. There are also drafts of part of Kemble's The Saxons in England (London: 1849) and other writings, some unpublished. Research notes relate to the topics of his historical inquiries. Letters are chiefly to his wife and to William B. Dunne who handled his affairs while Kemble was in Germany.

2974. LAURA C. KEMP PAPERS, 1859-1867. 62 items. Winchester (Frederick County), Va.

Personal correspondence between a schoolgirl at Cottage Hill College, Maryland, and her family, containing parental admonitions, family news, and local gossip.

2975. WILLIAM KEMP PAPERS, 1810-1822. 13 items. Shenandoah (now Page) County, Va.

Correspondence of William Kemp, a soldier in the War of 1812, with his wife, dealing with army life, and personal and domestic affairs. Two letters from his wife, Sarah, give detailed descriptions of events at home.

2976. SIR JOHN ARROW KEMPE PAPERS, 1866-1909. 135 items. London, England.

Kempe served as private secretary to Sir Stafford Northcote when Northcote was chancellor of the exchequer. Most of these letters are brief inquiries and instructions from Northcote to Kempe. Twenty-one items, 1906-1909, while Kempe was comptroller and auditor general, concern details of government finance; correspondents include Thomas Gibson Bowles and Sir Robert Williams.

2977. BENJAMIN FRANKLIN KEMPER AND BROTHERS, DAYBOOK AND INVENTORY, 1854. 1 vol. (171 pp.) Port Republic (Rockingham County), Va.

This daybook is the first half of a volume that also contains a daybook, 1862-1865, of the tannery of William S. Downs of Port Republic. The daybook entries are for general merchandise.

2978. FANNIE V. KEMPER PAPERS, 1848-1891. 124 items. Cross Keys, (Rockingham County), Va.

Letters from students at a girls' school in Staunton, Virginia, and from James N. Turner, a cousin of Fannie V. Kemper, while at the University of North Carolina, Chapel Hill, giving interesting details of student life in the 1850s. Included also are letters from Turner while acting as surveyor for the Western North Carolina Railroad, and letters from relatives who had moved to South Carolina and Georgia.

2979. MICHAEL J. KENAN PAPERS, 1814-1897. 40 items. Dallas County, Ala.

Miscellaneous correspondence and financial papers, primarily relating to Michael J. Kenan, sheriff of Dallas County in 1858 and 1861, his wife Anna B., and daughter Fannie, and to the settlement of Kenan's estate.

2980. THOMAS H. KENAN PAPERS, 1855 (1861-1877) 1892. 37 items. Milledgeville (Baldwin County), Ga.

Family correspondence of Thomas H. Kenan, physician. During the Civil War, Kenan served as aide-de-camp to General Wm. H. T. Walker, but the collection contains no war material of value. One letter to Kenan from a fellow physician describes graphically the symptoms attending a fatal case of scarlet fever.

2981. THOMAS STEPHEN KENAN PAPERS, 1885 (1911-1912). 8 items. Raleigh (Wake County), N. C.

Letters of condolence to Mrs. Kenan on the death of her husband, Thomas Stephen Kenan (1838-1912); and other miscellaneous personal papers. There are also muster rolls, 1862-1863, of Company A, 43rd North Carolina Regiment of Infantry, of which Kenan was colonel.

2982. AMOS KENDALL PAPERS, 1848. 1 item. Washington, D. C.

Letter from Sears Cook Walker seeking Kendall's aid in obtaining telegraphic communication with the Charleston Observatory.

2983. SETH H. KENDALL PAPERS, 1790-1932. 829 items and 16 vols. Boston, Mass.

Correspondence of the family of Seth H. Kendall, a Boston dentist, and the related families of Arthur Byrnes and G.S. Wemble. Letters from Seth's son, Edward D., to his parents concern his travels throughout the eastern and midwestern states as an organizer and salesman for the Manhattan Life Insurance Company and other life insurance companies in smaller cities.

2984. WILLIAM P. KENDALL ACCOUNT BOOKS, 1838-1867. 5 vols. Wadesboro (Anson County), N. C.

Daybook of mercantile accounts, 1838-1842, 1 vol., from Kendall's store at Cheraw, South Carolina; ledgers, 1850-1855, from Kendall's mercantile store at Wadesboro; a volume of miscellaneous accounts, 1860s, which contains the text of a speech, probably from the late 19th or early 20th Century, on the colonization of Negroes in Africa and their role in American civilization; and a volume of cash accounts, 1856-1859, including some accounts of estates administered by Kendall during the 1860s.

2985. JOHN PENDLETON KENNEDY PAPERS, 1822-1859. 8 items. Baltimore, Md.

Letters of Kennedy (1795-1870), author and attorney, commenting on legal cases, politics, and literary affairs, particularly his own writings. There are some reviews by Kennedy and one letter, 1856, by Martin Farquhar Tupper, an English author. The library also holds microfilm of Kennedy's journal, 1829-1839; his journal of travel in England and on the continent, 1856; and his letters to Elizabeth Gray, 1832-1840.

2986. SAMUEL KENNEDY PAPERS, 1804-1819. 12 items. Morgantown (Monongalia County), W. Va.

Letters relating to service at Norfolk in the summer of 1814 in the Monongalia Artillery Regiment of the Virginia Militia and describing the march to Norfolk. Included are Kennedy's commission as first lieutenant in the Virginia militia, 1804, and an indenture of Augusta County, Virginia, 1812, concerning a land sale by Charles Stuart and his wife.

2987. WILL KENNEDY PAPERS, 1862-1865. 6 items. Indiana.

Letters from Kennedy, a company clerk in the 52nd Regiment of Indiana Volunteers, to his sister, A. S. Kennedy, describing campaigns in Kentucky, Tennessee, Missouri, Mississippi, and Alabama; camp life; food; the countryside; and rumors.

2988. RICHARD P. KENNER PAPERS, 1862-1870. 17 items. Elizabeth City County, Va.

Receipts, permits, passes, requisitions, and licenses issued to Richard P. Kenner, a Confederate soldier.

2989. GEORGE W. KENNEY PAPERS, 1860-1865. 126 items. Harrisburg (Dauphin County), Pa.

Included are letters of George W. Kenney, a lieutenant in Company P of the 1st Regiment of California (Pennsylvania), afterwards called the 71st Pennsylvania Infantry, describing his training and his capture at Leesburg, Virginia, and imprisonment at Libby Prison, Richmond, where he commented on the plight of Union Colonel M. Corcoran, held by the Confederates as a hostage for the safety of privateers tried for piracy following the Enchantress affair. Subsequent letters concern Kenney's service in the Army of the Potomac during the Peninsular Campaign, his death there, and efforts to have his body returned to Pennsylvania.

2990. SAMUEL PIERCE KENNEY PAPERS, 1861-1864. 3 items. Georgia.

Family letters of Samuel P. Kenney, a Confederate cavalryman, telling of army life and giving an account of a plan of the soldiers in Longstreet's corps for obtaining horses.

2991. LYMAN WALTER VERE KENNON PAPERS, 1863-1917. 142 items and 1 vol. Rhode Island.

Kennon's letters to his wife, Anna Kennon; letters from his superior officers in the U.S. Army; and some printed materials and a scrapbook relating to his military career. There are a number of items relating to General George Crook, whom Kennon served as aide-de-camp, and his quarrel with General Alfred H. Terry over the circumstances of the capture of Geronimo; descriptions of the heat, insects, and life in the tropics during surveys for the Central American railroad, 1891-1892; the Civil War service of Henry Algernon DuPont, 1895-1896; military preparations in Florida during the Spanish-American War, the invasion of Cuba, and meetings between General John R. Brooke and Máximo Gómez concerning the use of U.S. funds supplied to the Cubans; and the occupation of the Philippines after 1899.

2992. JOHN E. KENT DAYBOOK, 1851-1853. 1 vol. (552 pp.) Blacksburg (Montgomery County), Va.

General merchandise sales.

2993. RICHARD KENT PAPERS, 1759. 2 items. Savannah, Ga.

Land grant of 1759 and accompanying certificate concerning town lot seven and farm lot nine, Eyles Tything, Heathcote Ward, Savannah.

2994. T. F. KENT PAPERS, 1859-1863. 14 items. London, England.

Letters 1859, 1862, of Sir John Taylor Coleridge concerning a commission on the administration of roads, which Kent apparently served as secretary, and letters after 1863 concerning organization of the Commission for Penal Servitude and Transportation, including many from the Third Earl Grey and Sir George Grey.

2995. KENTUCKY GENEALOGY, 1942. 1 vol. (88 pp.)

"Genealogies and Historical Recorder," vol. 2, compiled by Annie Walker Burns. Mimeographed list of vital statistics, military service records, etc.

2996. LLOYD KENYON, FIRST BARON KENYON, 1782. 1 item. London, England.

Kenyon's opinion, as attorney general, concerning the supply of naval vessels in the East Indies.

2997. MOSES WARREN KENYON PAPERS, 1849-1870. 19 items and 1 vol. St. George (Dorchester County), S. C.

Civil War letters of W. A. Kenyon, soldier in Company A, Infantry, Hampton's Legion (South Carolina volunteers), to his brother Moses Warren Kenyon with detailed accounts of troop movements and descriptions of various locales in Virginia, including the Peninsular Campaign and the battle of Williamsburg; the landing of Federal troops at Bennett's Point, South Carolina, 1861; and the battles of Lookout Mountain, Tennessee, and Chickamauga, where Kenyon was captured. Included is the morning report, 1 vol.,

Nov. 1864-April, 1865, of Company D, Palmetto Battalion, Light Artillery (3rd Battalion South Carolina Artillery).

2998. CHARLES HENRY BELLENDEN KER PAPERS, 1856-1868. 23 items. London, England.

Largely letters from Baron Cranworth, Lord Chancellor, concerning legal reform, especially land title legislation, and Lord Westbury's work as lord chancellor.

2999. JOHN BARRETT KERFOOT PAPERS, 1840-1856. 13 items. Pittsburgh (Allegheny County), Pa.

Letters written to Kerfoot, headmaster of St. James' Hall, later the College of St. James, Washington County, Maryland. Several letters from William A. Muhlenberg, largely personal, contain information about St. Paul's College on Long Island and comment on Philip Schaff's church history. The remaining letters are from various Protestant Episcopal educators. Correspondents include Russell Trevett, Libertus Van Bokkelen, William Edward Wyatt, James Lloyd Breck, and J. Mason Campbell.

3000. WILLIAM G. KERNER PAPERS, 1859-1863. 10 items. Kernersville (Forsyth County), N. C.

Miscellaneous items including the muster roll of the 121st Regiment of North Carolina Militia, Apr. 29, 1863.

3001. JOHN ROBERT KERNODLE, JR., PAPERS, 1963-1966. 42 items. Burlington (Alamance County), N. C.

Printed and mimeographed literature and a few letters concerning organizations with which Kernodle and his wife were affiliated as undergraduates at Duke University. Among the organizations represented are the Methodist Student Movement, the National Student Christian Federation, the United Campus Christian Fellowship, the National Council of Churches' Delta Ministry in Mississippi, the University Christian Movement, and religious groups at Duke University. Many items are devoted to the civil rights movement in the South.

3002. BESSIE M. C. KERR SCRAPBOOK, 1878-1879. 1 vol. (55 pp.) Shallow Ford (Yadkin County), N. C.

Clippings of poems, and recipes posted over a child's commonplace book.

3003. JANE P. KERR PAPERS, 1891-1899. 13 items. Concord (Cabarrus County) and Panther Creek, N. C.

Family letters, including one from Mrs. Kerr's uncle, Thomas L. Clingman, 1893, revealing his poor financial state, and several letters concerning lands and mineral rights left by Clingman and family attempts to redeem this property before it was sold for taxes.

3004. EDWARD KERSHNER PAPERS, 1861 (1863-1885) 1902. 375 items. Clearspring (Washington County), Md.

Papers of a surgeon in the U. S. Navy, including correspondence concerning his conduct and court-martial; orders; sick reports; inventories of medicines, hospital supplies, etc., on several vessels; hygiene regulations for tropical climates; smallpox vaccination reports; clippings, typed brief, and testimony in the court-martial of Kershner in 1895; and copies of bills in the U.S. Congress for reinstatement of Kershner. There are detailed reports on medical supplies and sickness among seamen on board the ships on which Kershner was stationed. There is also a report on yellow fever from Panama, 1888.

3005. FRANK B. KESSLER (KESLOR) PAPERS, 1868-1888. 156 items. Martinsburg (Berkeley County), W. Va.

Family letters of a railroad brakeman and his wife. Largely personal, the letters contain mention of racial violence in West Virginia, 1871; unemployment, 1876; and bills for coal, food, and rent.

3006. KEY FAMILY PAPERS, 1792-1856. 10 items. Maryland.

Two business letters, 1792, 1794, of Philip Key (1750-1820) to a Port Tobacco, Maryland, merchant named Blair; letters of Francis Scott Key (1780-1843) include letters to his family describing a trip through Western Pennsylvania, 1840-1841. There are also items relating to legal cases in which Key took part, and an undated transcription of a trial of runaway slaves. Letters of Philip Barton Key III (d. 1859) concern legal matters. His correspondents include Caleb Cushing and Elisha Whittlesey.

3007. HORACE KEYES PAPERS, 1863-1864. 7 items. Michigan.

Letters written by a soldier in the 25th Regiment of Michigan Infantry to his relatives discussing camp life, troop movements, rumors, picket duty, casualties, and army hospitals in Louisville, Kentucky, and Jeffersonville, Indiana.

3008. WILLIAM JUDAH KEYSER PAPERS, 1809-1940. 2,115 items and 24 vols. Milton (Santa Rosa County) and Pensacola (Escambia County), Fla.

Papers of Keyser (1821-1877) and members of his family concerning family matters and the management of Keyser, Judah, and Company, lumber exporters of Pensacola, Florida, which became Keyser and Company after William Swift Keyser assumed control about 1880. Early letters are from Milton, Florida, where W. J. Keyser operated before the Civil War, and concern cotton, cattle, and lumber. Under Keyser's son, the firm became one of the largest exporters of pine timber, shipping from Florida, Alabama, Mississippi, and Texas to New York, Liverpool, and elsewhere. Civil War papers concern the shipment of cattle for the Confederate Army. Some postwar letters deal with the New England relatives of Harriot (Swift) Keyser (Mrs. W. J. Keyser), and later the English relations of her daughter, Nell; others describe conditions under military occupation, the shipment of lumber, and social life in Florida and Virginia. Many business letters are from merchants in Pensacola, Havana, and New Orleans, and from the Pensacola law firm of C. L. Le Baron. Other topics in family letters include student life at the Charlier Institute for Young Gentlemen, New York, 1870; European travel; Sir William Dawson; missionary work in Turkey; the Spanish-American War; the poetry, other writings, and career of John Wallace Crawford; the Florida Chautauqua; politics; and the launching of the U.S.S. Pensacola, 1929. There is also correspondence between the W. S. Keyser Export Company of Pensacola and G. R. Crossley, New York exporter of pine and other commodities.

3009. JOHN G. KEYTON PAPERS, 1861-1864. 21 items. Rockingham County, Va.

Letters from John G. Keyton, a private in the Confederate Army, one letter containing comments on extreme hardships in 1864.

3010. MICHAEL KIDWILER PAPERS, 1814-1846. 32 items. Jefferson County, W. Va.

Receipts, bills, and other business papers of Michael Kidwiler (d. ca. 1834), a farmer; of his sons, Charles and Jacob Kidwiler; of his administrator, Richard Duffield; and of a justice of the peace, Joseph MacMurran.

3011. JOHN ZACHARIAH KIERNANDER PAPERS, 1781. 1 item. Calcutta, India.

A letter by Kiernander (1711-1799), a Danish missionary to Balthasar Burman, dated December 28, 1781, describing financial difficulties.

3012. JOHN RICHARDSON KILBY PAPERS, 1755 (1840-1889) 1919. 39,489 items and 19 vols. Suffolk (Nansemond County), Va.

Legal and miscellaneous papers of John Richardson Kilby (1819-1878) and of his son, Wilbur John Kilby (1850-1907), lawyers; and of members of the Riddick family. The great bulk of the papers is concerned with legal activities of the two Kilbys, including, during the 1840's, the case of Harriett Whitehead, whose mind had been impaired by the murder of all her family in the Nat Turner Insurrection, 1831. The legal papers are generally concerned with administration of estates, collection of bills, and adjustments of property. The wills and papers concerning trusteeships and chancery suits contain much genealogical and historical data for Nansemond County and vicinity. Among the estates extensively represented are those of Miles Dougherty, Robert Smith, Josiah Riddick, Andrew McAlister, and J. C. Langhorne. Included also are extensive lists of slaves. There are papers relating to claims of William B. Whitehead in the seizure by the Confederate government of the sloop Whisper for blockading. Included also are many letters and other records centering around local politics for Nansemond County, especially during the career of Wilbur John Kilby; references to free Negroes, one item listing school taxes assessed on free Negroes of St. Bride's, Portsmouth, and Elizabeth City parishes for 1845, and the will of Thomas Tartt bequeathing freedom to his slaves (the will was contested in 1856); references to work of the American Colonization Society including attempts in the 1850s to arouse interest among free Negroes in the Society, and one letter of a former slave, Randolph Kilby, who had been resettled in Liberia, giving in detail activities and conditions of Kilby's former slaves then in Liberia; and information relative to Richard H. Riddick, agent of the Albemarle Swamp Land Company and merchant at Pantego, North Carolina; letters of Riddick's wife, Missouri Riddick; and letters of a Confederate soldier to Anna Riddick relative to action around Fredericksburg, Va., and Shepherdstown, W. Va., and a description of Midway Hospital at Charlottesville, Virginia. Other information includes scattered correspondence concerning activities of the Whigs during the 1850s; references to activities of the Methodist Episcopal Church before the Civil War; an account of the cholera epidemic in Suffolk during 1849; two letters from a merchant of St. Louis, Missouri, describing effects of the panic of 1857 and the Pike's Peak gold rush of 1859; a letter describing deplorable conditions in Charleston, South Carolina, with swaggering and plundering Negro soldiers on every corner; and a series of letters in 1891 and 1899 relative to the Negro Reformatory Association of Virginia. There are also several volumes of daybooks and memorandum books and many printed broadsides concerning land sales in the Nansemond area.

3013. MRS. M. A. KILLINGSWORTH PAPERS, 1865. 3 items. Greenville (Pitt County), N. C.

Personal letters to Mrs. Killingsworth from acquaintances in Greenville and New Bern, North Carolina, retailing local gossip and mentioning the capture of a part of a company of Greenville militia by Federal soldiers.

3014. HENRY KILLION ACCOUNT BOOK, 1831-1833. 1 vol. (110 pp.) Lawrenceville (Brunswick County), Va.

Accounts of Henry Killion, apparently a tanner, showing purchases of hides and sales of leather.

3015. D. T. KIMBALL PAPERS, 1829-1848. 8 items. Ipswich (Essex County), Mass.

Family letters of an Ipswich minister.

3016. FRANKLIN G. KIMBALL PAPERS, 1830-1865. 6 items. Mobile, Ala.

Bills of sale and correspondence concerning the sale of slaves; also two amnesty oaths, 1865.

3017. GEORGE H. KIMBROUGH PAPERS, 1834-1858. 9 items. Springfield (Green County), and Kemper County, Miss.

Letters from friends and family members.

3018. KIMMELL HOUSE PAPERS, 1858-1861. 1 item. Washington, D.C.

Pages from the register of a lodging house or small hotel.

3019. CAMPBELL KING PAPERS, 1917-1933. 259 items and 1 vol. Flat Rock (Henderson County), N. C.

Papers of Campbell King, U.S. Army officer, include official communications concerning promotions, tranfers, military honors, and medals of King; general and special army orders, and military telegrams; descriptions of the 1st Infantry Division during World War I and of the employment of the Provisional Squadron of the 2nd U.S. Cavalry Division in the St. Mihiel offensive; army pamphlets; photographs of General King and other army officers; and a newspaper clipping scrapbook containing accounts of General King. Of interest are a letter from Secretary of the Interior Franklin Knight Lane requesting King's advice on an appropriation from Congress to develop farms for retired World War I servicemen, and King's reply; and letters from fellow officers upon King's retirement, 1933, including a note from Douglas MacArthur to King thanking him for his support.

3020. CARL HOWIE KING AND MARY (ESKRIDGE) KING PAPERS, 1918-1973. 3,993 items and 1 vol. Salisbury (Rowan County), N.C.

Papers of Carl Howie King (1898-1967), Methodist minister and executive secretary of the Board of Education of the Western North Carolina Conference, 1934-1967; and of Mary (Eskridge) King (1901-1973), active in affairs of the Methodist Episcopal Church, South, and president of the Women's Society of Christian Service of the Western North Carolina Conference, 1960-1964. The papers of Carl King consist principally of letters to Dr. King from people to whom he had sent copies of his pamphlet, Historical Highlights of the Educational Ministry. There are also a copy of the pamphlet; an essay written while he was a student at Trinity College, Durham, North Carolina, 1918; clippings concerning his years as a student at Yale; and concert and theater programs. The papers of Mary (Eskridge) King concern her activities in Methodist affairs on the local, regional, and national level, and as president of the Women's Society of Christian Service, and her service on the Board of Missions, on the Board of Christian Social Concerns, and on special committees dealing with extremism and church priorities. Correspondence, pamphlets, brochures, fly-leaves, and broadsides deal with Methodism and higher education in North Carolina; the Women's Society of Christian Service including local and national concerns, conferences, and administrative matters; the meeting of the North Carolina Council of Churches, 1968-1969; the Methodist Board of Hospitals, 1963-1964; the Interreligious Foundation for Community Organization, 1970-1972; Methodism and public affairs, including political conservatism and the John Birch Society, the Civil Rights movement, the Supreme Court decision on prayer in the public schools, and communism; affairs of the Western North Carolina Conference, including priority planning and the Guild-O-Gram; ecumenicalism, the National Council of Churches, and the World Council of Churches; the Board of Missions of the United Methodist Church, including conferences and foreign and domestic missionary activity; General Conference of the United Methodist Church, 1964 and 1972; Methodism and human rights and social concerns, including Civil Rights, the Black Manifesto, the Vietnam War, student unrest, etc.; National Convocation of Methodist Youth, 1959; Conference Schools of Christian Missions; the Regional School Committee; the United Methodist Development Fund; and Biblical studies and program planning.

3021. H. P. KING MEMORANDA, 1842-1843. 1 vol. (110 pp.) Quallatown (Jackson County), N. C.

Memoranda of H. P. King's household expenses, and of men working in his tanyard.

3022. HORATIO KING PAPERS, 1847-1897. 52 items. Washington, D.C.

Papers of Horatio King include King's testimony regarding the cost and operation of a press and concerning the Daily & Weekly Courier; letters from Charles Ledyard Norton and from Martha Joanna Reade (Nash) Lamb concerning articles written by King for the Magazine of American History, of which Lamb was editor; letters from Sir Julian Pauncefote and a draft of a letter from King to Pauncefote pertaining to a biographical study of Queen Victoria which King had prepared for publication; personal correspondence between King and Justin Smith Morrill generally relating to Morrill's birthday including printed copies of rhymes which King wrote in honor of Morrill; letters from Charles Cooper Nott and from John James Ingalls concerning an amendment to the Constitution to change the date of the presidential inauguration; personal correspondence and routine invitations; and a letter to King's son, Horatio Collins King, from Adelbert Ames concerning the text of a speech made by Ames on the fighting at Fort Fisher, North Carolina, during the Civil War.

3023. JOEL KING PAPERS, 1785-1868. 150 items. Louisburg (Franklin County), N. C.

Family and business correspondence, accounts, and receipts of a cotton planter.

3024. JOHN PENDLETON KING PAPERS, 1846-1875. 12 items. Augusta (Richmond County), Ga.

Correspondence and miscellaneous papers of John Pendleton King (1799-1888), lawyer, judge, U.S. senator, 1833-1837, and president of the Georgia Railroad and Banking Company and of the Atlanta and West Point Railroad, relate to the Georgia Railroad Company, including route schedules and government contracts for transportation of the mail.

3025. JOHNSON W. KING DIARY, 1844-1845. 1 vol. (122 pp.) Murphy (Cherokee County), N.C.

A personal diary kept by Johnson W. King, partner of Wm. H. Thomas, containing accounts of business transactions, farming, legal business, and duties as postmaster.

3026. JOSEPH KING, JR., DIARIES, 1849-1850. 2 vols. Baltimore, Md.

Diaries of Joseph King, Jr., concerning personal and family matters; his farm at Havre de Grace, Maryland; the Society of Friends, of which he was a member; migration to California; and his activities as a member of the board of trustees of a farm school, a house of refuge, and an orphanage.

3027. LEANDER KING PAPERS, 1866. 1 item. Wayne County, Ohio.

An affidavit by Leander King claiming compensation for his service in the U.S. Army in 1865 until the surrender of General Robert E. Lee.

3028. N. J. KING PROMISSORY NOTES, 1840-1859. 2 items. Raleigh (Wake County), N.C.

Promissory notes of N. J. King to the state of North Carolina for money borrowed for the survey of Cherokee land in 1838.

3029. PENDLETON KING PAPERS, 1876-1906. 196 items. Greensboro (Guilford County), N.C.

Correspondence of Pendleton King, government official, and of his wife, Helen (Ninde) King, concerning their studies in Europe before their marriage in 1879, Helen King's literary efforts, women's rights, abstinence and the temperance movement, the election of 1876, the theater, the churches of Henry Ward Beecher and Thomas D. Talmage, social life in Connecticut in 1880, the raising of their children, Helen and Rush, the Virginia elections in 1883, the presidential election of 1884, and King's appointment as American consul at Aix-la-Chapelle, Germany.

3030. RUFUS KING PAPERS, 1843-1850. 25 items. Cincinnati (Hamilton County), Ohio.

Letters of Thomas Worthington King, broker and commission merchant, to his brother, Rufus King (1817-1891), lawyer and dean of the faculty at the Cincinnati Law School, Cincinnati, Ohio, concerning personal and family matters, including a family dispute, business conditions in New Orleans, price and market fluctuations, and the Locofoco Party and the 1844 election.

3031. WILLIAM KING PAPERS, 1806-1809. 4 items. Abingdon (Washington County), Va.

Will of William King; letters of William Trigg, executor of the King estate; and an inventory of stock belonging to King and Lynn.

3032. WILLIAM RUFUS DEVANE KING PAPERS, 1827-1852. 2 items. Selma (Dallas County), Ala.

Letters of William Rufus Devane King (1786-1853), lawyer, U.S. senator, and vice-president of the U.S., to J. W. White discussing the charges of peculation against John C. Calhoun, the prospects for the reelection of John Randolph of Roanoke to Congress, and the administration of John Quincy Adams; and to John MacRae concerning personal matters and the campaign of Franklin Pierce for the presidency in 1852.

3033. WILLIS H. KING PAPERS, 1860-1865. 15 items. Chapel Hill (Orange County), N.C.

Correspondence of Willis H. King and his sons, Bellfield King and Whitfield D. King, all Confederate soldiers, 11th Regiment, North Carolina Infantry Volunteers, discussing army life, desertion, food, the illness of Willis King, and the death of Whitfield King.

3034. HENRY KINGMAN PAPERS, 1796-1876. 850 items. Pelham (Hampshire County), Mass.

Papers of Henry Kingman, teacher, landowner, and local official, include legal papers consisting of wills, deeds, indentures, affidavits, and warrants relating to cases heard before Kingman and others as justices of the peace for Hampshire County; bills and receipts concerning personal debts, legal fees, and the purchase or sale of farm products and merchandise; a petition of the voters of Pelham to the members of the state legislature asking that they refuse to seat David Abercrombie in the House of Representatives; papers pertaining to the militia companies in Hampshire County, chiefly attendance records at company musters; and personal correspondence with references to the social life in Andover, Massachusetts.

3035. KING'S MOUNTAIN RAILROAD COMPANY PAPERS, 1862-1865. 97 items. Yorkville (York County), S.C.

Records of the King's Mountain Railroad Company consisting of records of mail, freight, and passengers; yearly reports of the president and directors to the stockholders; and bills and receipts.

3036. WILLIAM BEATTY KINGSTON PAPERS, 1877-1894. 26 items. London, England.

Letters to William Beatty Kingston (1837-1900), British journalist, correspondent for the *Daily Telegraph* in London, and its editor, from Sir Edwin Henry Egerton, diplomat; from Henry De Worms, First Baron Pirbright, a member of Parliament; and from two Rumanian statesmen, Prince Ion Ghica and Demetrius Ghica, discussing the Russo-Turkish War in 1877, correspondents of the *Daily Telegraph*, political conditions in Russia and Rumania, British foreign affairs, and other matters.

3037. EDWARD WILKINSON KINSLEY PAPERS, 1862-1889. 109 items. Boston, Mass.

Correspondence of Edward Wilkinson Kinsley (b. 1829), businessman, principally concerning his activities in soliciting funds for societies aiding the freedmen, in lobbying for Congressional action to grant equal pay to Negro volunteers serving in the U.S. Army, and personally assisting former slaves. Correspondents discuss the issue of the payment to Negro troops; the service of various Negro troops during the Civil War, particularly the 55th Massachusetts Regiment during its service in South Carolina and Georgia, with mention of the 54th Massachusetts, and the 35th Regiments of U.S. Colored Troops; life in New Bern, North Carolina, during its occupation, skirmishes with Confederate troops, and efforts to educate and provide for the freed slaves; citizen reaction to having a Negro in charge of enforcing peace and emancipation in Orangeburg, South Carolina; and politics in the 1870s.

3038. JOHN HENDRICKS KINYOUN PAPERS, 1851-1898. 163 items. Yadkin County, N.C., and Centerview (Johnson County), Mo.

Personal correspondence of John Hendricks Kinyoun (1825-1903), physician and surgeon in the Confederate Army, includes a letter, 1851, from Kinyoun while a student at Columbian College, Washington, D.C., describing a meeting of the American Colonization Society; correspondence between Kinyoun and his wife, Elizabeth A. (Conrad) Kinyoun, during the Civil War discussing camp life, the health of the troops, supplies, food, his work in Winder Hospital, Richmond, Virginia, troop movements and military engagements especially of the 28th North Carolina Volunteers and the 66th North Carolina Infantry, and his views on the Confederacy and its cause; postwar letters written to the Kinyouns after they moved to Centerview, Missouri; and a folder of writings which includes a political speech, 1896, by Kinyoun criticizing the Cleveland administration and espousing the free silver doctrine.

3039. J. H. KIPPS LEDGER, 1897-1914. 1 vol. (217 pp.) Blacksburg (Montgomery County), Va.

Rental and mercantile accounts.

3040. JOHN H. KIRACOFE PAPERS, 1861-1871. 69 items. Rockingham County, Va.

Correspondence between the Kiracofe brothers in the Confederate Army and their families at home describing camp life and personal matters.

3041. EPHRAIM KIRBY PAPERS, 1763 (1780-1804) 1878. 2,899 items and 1 vol. Litchfield (Litchfield County), Conn.

The papers of Ephraim Kirby (1757-1804), Revolutionary soldier, lawyer, state legislator, and land speculator, consist of correspondence, broadsides, legal papers, bills and receipts pertaining to the Revolutionary War, early settlements west of the Alleghenies and Alabama, land speculation, internal improvements, and politics. Revolutionary War letters describe life in the Continental Army, morale, equipment and confusion in the quartermaster department, military engagements including the battle of Germantown and the surrender of Cornwallis, the conduct of General Oliver Wolcott, the beginnings of Ephraim Kirby's legal practice, and the purchase of law books. Political correspondence concerns the government of the United States under the Articles of Confederation, the ratification of the Constitution, foreign relations with Great Britain especially involving the British-held western posts and a commercial treaty, the Citizen Genet affair, James Madison's resolutions regarding trade and navigation, proposal to arm frigates against Algiers, Jay's Treaty, Whiskey Rebellion, the need for taxation for revenue, the presidential campaigns of 1796 and 1800, relations with France, Cherokee Indian affairs, the use of political patronage, Republican versus Federalist politics especially in Connecticut, Kirby's years as a Republican in the Connecticut state legislature, the repeal of the Judiciary Act of 1801, and American relations with Spain after the Louisiana Purchase. Other correspondence relates to Kirby's legal practice, especially the collection of debts and the publication and sale of his book <u>Reports of Cases Adjudged in the Superior Court and Court of Errors of the State of Connecticut from the Years 1785 to May, 1788</u>; lands claimed by both Pennsylvania and Connecticut; land speculation by Kirby and others in lands in Pennsylvania, New York, Vermont, and Georgia, and in the Western Reserve of which Kirby was a proprietor; early settlement of western lands; the Yazoo land fraud; the building of turnpikes, especially in Connecticut and Pennsylvania; the Connecticut militia in which Kirby was an officer; Kirby's duties as supervisor of the U.S. Revenue for Connecticut; routes and the operation of the U.S. Post Office; the collection of debts; the settlement of the estate of Reynold Marvin, with whom Kirby studied law; the Royal Arch Masons of the United States, of which Kirby was the first general grand high priest, including some material written in code; a description of Washington, D.C., 1802; Kirby's partnership in a slitting mill; the financial suit of William Hillhouse against Kirby and Jeremiah Mason; Kirby's report to Thomas Jefferson on the Mississippi Territory including a description of the lands east of the Pearl River, settlers, produce, trade conditions, Spanish settlements in West Florida and Mobile, Spanish military posts, and Indian tribes; a yellow fever epidemic in New Orleans, 1804; and the settlement of Ephraim Kirby's estate. A diary of Reynold Marvin Kirby, son of Ephraim Kirby, describes his life in the U.S. Army during the War of 1812 beginning when he entered the army in 1813 as a lieutenant in the 3rd U.S. Artillery and telling of his military engagements and duties.

3042. SAMUEL F. KIRBY ACCOUNT BOOK, 1785-1804. 1 vol. (68 pp.) [Petersburg (Dinwiddie County), Va.?]

Accounts of a tavern keeper, showing prices of meals, whiskey and brandy.

3043. WILLIAM KIRBY PAPERS, 1810-1888. 56 items. Clinton (Sampson County), N.C.

Papers of William Kirby include family correspondence; correspondence concerning the education of his daughter, Lillian, at the St. Joseph's School, Hickory, North Carolina, and letters from Lillian while attending school; business letters regarding the collection of rents and debts; receipts for payment of Confederate taxes; and letters concerning the administration of the estate of James B. Pigford of which Kirby was executor.

3044. KIRBY FAMILY PAPERS, 1831-1876. 13 items and 13 vols. Spartanburg (Spartanburg County), S.C.

Mercantile accounts, including ledgers, daybooks, cashbooks, and account books, for the firms of John T. Kirby, Kirby & Wilson, A. H. Kirby, and Kirby & Vernon; a ledger, 1856-1859, containing student accounts with the Spartanburg Female College, Spartanburg, South Carolina; a tax in kind account book, 1863-1865, and papers recording the agricultural products acquired from local residents, and goods taken for use by the Confederate Army; and the memorandum book, 1874-1876, of A. H. Kirby while serving as a county commissioner of Spartanburg County, including information about the construction and repair of bridges and roads, and drainage.

3045. JAMES B. KITCHEN PAPERS, 1797-1866. 26 items and 3 vols. Sussex County, Va.

Blacksmith accounts, 1797-1822, of James B. Kitchen; and miscellaneous bills and receipts of various people.

3046. HORATIO HERBERT KITCHENER, FIRST EARL KITCHENER, PAPERS, 1885. 2 items. London, England.

Papers of Horatio Herbert Kitchener, First Earl Kitchener (1850-1916), field marshal in the British Army, include a letter, 1885, concerning the Nile Expedition of 1884-1885; and a letter, dating probably from the 1900s, concerning the efforts of Butcher, Norton, and himself to get an unidentified bill passed by Parliament.

3047. SEYMOUR KITCHING PAPERS, 1871-1893. 19 items. Fort Supply, Okla. (Indian Territory)

Personal correspondence of Seymour Kitching, medical officer in the U.S. Army, including a few letters written from Fort Supply dealing with camp situations, letters from Kitching's wife in Virginia, and letters from his mother in London and Meriden, England.

3048. CHARLOTTE WILSON (POWE) KITTRELL PAPERS, 1902-1961. 55 items. Tryon (Polk County), N.C.

Papers of Charlotte Wilson (Powe) Kittrell, teacher, include two letters from Helen M. Eddy concerning bird calls and local dialects of the North Carolina mountains; a letter from Senator Strom Thurmond about nullification; a letter relating to the desegregation crisis of 1956; clippings pertaining to South Carolina political history, reminiscences and descriptions of Cheraw (South Carolina) racial segregation, relatives and family servants, bishops of the Episcopal Church, and the death of Wade Hampton; and a copy of a speech on segregation by Congressman L. Mendel Rivers in 1956.

3049. WILLIAM A. KLEINSCHMIDT PAPERS, 1888-1893. 4 items. St. Louis, Mo.

Papers of William A. Kleinschmidt consist of his diploma from Central Wesleyan College, Warrenton, Missouri, 1888; invitation to commencement, 1888; a copy of the program for the Ivy Planting at the college; and the marriage license of Kleinschmidt and Emma L. Schaberg.

3050. SIR EDWARD KNATCHBULL, NINTH BARONET, PAPERS, 1834. 1 item. London, England.

Letter from Charles Edward Poulett Thomson to Sir Edward Knatchbull, Ninth Baronet (1781-1849), discussing clandestine trade and the enforcement of the Corn Laws.

3051. ANNA P. KNIGHT PAPERS, 1858-1901. 86 items. Normal (McLean County), Ill.

Chiefly personal and family correspondence of Anna P. Knight, teacher, concerning personal matters, travel in California, teaching experiences, and the Chicago Columbian Exposition in 1893; and several business letters pertaining to commodity and land prices in Ohio, Indiana, and Illinois.

3052. B. F. KNIGHT PAPERS, 1840-1866. 23 items. Edgecombe County, N.C.

Correspondence of B. F. Knight, a Baptist minister, principally dealing with religious matters; and three Civil War letters.

3053. JOHN KNIGHT PAPERS, 1788-1891. 1,323 items and 16 vols. Natchez (Adams County), Miss., and Frederick (Frederick County) and Baltimore, Md.

Correspondence, legal papers, financial papers, diaries and printed material constitute the papers of John Knight (1806-1864), merchant, planter, and investor. Included are personal correspondence of Mary (McCleery) Knight with her sister Frances (McCleery) Beall; letters from Roger Brooke Taney to William Murdock Beall explaining his refusal of the vice-presidency and discussing his interest in the presidency; and correspondence between John Knight and Frances Zeruiah Susanna Beall during their courtship. Correspondence, 1830-1864, with friends and relatives, and with Enoch Pratt, a Baltimore banker in charge of Knight's finances, discusses the political conflict between Henry Clay and Andrew Jackson; economic conditions in the United States, especially concerning the cotton market; banking and bank failures; the panic of 1857; investment in cotton land in Mississippi, Louisiana, and Arkansas; the purchase and sale of slaves; the treatment and medical care of slaves; the operation of Knight's various plantations; piracy on the Mississippi River, 1841; cholera and yellow fever epidemics, 1832, 1833, 1837, and 1841; education at the Frederick Female Academy, Frederick, Maryland; financial conditions in the United States during the Civil War; U.S. relations with England during the war; the course of the Civil War, especially in Maryland; Knight's attempts at various cures for ill health, including water cures, hot springs, and baths; and the Knights' tours in Europe, 1850-1864. Bills and receipts generally concern Knight's business interests and travel expenses. Legal papers include land deeds, partnership papers, lists of slaves and papers related to their purchase and sale, and the wills of William M. Beall and John Knight. Printed materials consist of a genealogical chart, visiting cards, medical prescriptions, the constitution of the American Common School Society in 1838, clippings on finance, and travel materials. There are also school exercises, a copy of John Knight's paper of 1861 on the cotton question, a list of articles on Hyde Park Plantation, ca. 1845, and pictures of ships of the leading mail packet lines of the Trans-Atlantic Service, 1848-1864. Diaries, 1845-1865, of Frances (Beall) Knight describe in detail life in Natchez, Mississippi, and the several visits and journeys throughout all of Europe, as well as Egypt, Turkey, and Russia, made by the Knights, 1850-1864; diaries, 1852-1869, of Frances Beall Knight, daughter of John and Frances (Beall) Knight, also describe life in Europe, although in less detail; diaries, 1850-1855, of John Knight contain financial notes and hotel lists. Miscellaneous volumes center around Knight's financial transactions.

3054. JONATHAN KNIGHT PAPERS, 1826-1858. 35 items. East Bethlehem (Washington County), Pa.

Typed copies of a biographical sketch and letters of Jonathan Knight (1787-1858), surveyor, engineer, state legislator and U.S. congressman. Letters to family members discuss his work in Illinois on the National Road, his visit to England and France to study locomotives and railroads, his work on the Baltimore and Ohio Railroad, the presidential campaign of 1840, Whig and Democratic politics, slavery, the Quakers, commodity prices in Pennsylvania, railroad building in Iowa, his election to Congress, and the Brooks-Sumner affair.

3055. JAMES DAVIS KNOWLES PAPERS. 1 item. Providence, R.I.

Manuscript verses composed by Knowles (1798-1838), Baptist clergyman and teacher, supplemental to Thomas Gray's

Elegy Written in a Country Churchyard. With minor changes, the supplement was included as "Additional Stanzas" in the edition of Gray's work published in New York by Leavitt & Allen, [1852 ?].

3056. SIR JAMES THOMAS KNOWLES PAPERS, 1895. 1 item. London, England.

Letter (11 pp.) from Lord Roberts to Sir James Thomas Knowles (1831-1908), editor of the Nineteenth Century, criticizing articles by Henry Elsdale and Sir William Laird Clowes which advocate withdrawal of the British fleet from the Mediterranean, and discuss a scheme of imperial federation to strengthen the empire.

3057. ROBERT KNOX PAPERS, 1836. 1 item. Charlestown (Suffolk County), Mass.

Letter describing the weathering of a storm off the coast of Massachusetts in a sailing vessel.

3058. DAVID KOONCE AND GEORGE KOONCE PAPERS, 1844-1871. 11 vols. Harpers Ferry (Jefferson County), W. Va.

Mercantile accounts of a general store; tax lists and receipts; and court dockets.

3059. HENRY KOPMAN PAPERS, 1861-1865. 7 items. New Orleans, La.

Correspondence of a Confederate soldier concerning personal matters, camp life, and clothing, and predicting the course of the war.

3060. HENRY CLAY KREBS PAPERS, 1816 (1863-1868) 1934. 110 items. Winchester (Frederick County), Va.

Indentures apprenticing Henry C. Krebs's father, Isaac Krebs, to Benjamin Lefever to learn merchandising; indentures, 1828 and 1846, apprenticing boys to Isaac Krebs to learn shoemaking; personal correspondence of Henry Clay Krebs, Confederate soldier in the 13th Virginia Regiment, with Lizzie Beard of Harrisonburg, Virginia, whom he married in 1865; and letters of their children, William F. and Frank Harmon Krebs.

3061. WASHINGTON KROESEN LEDGER, 1842-1847. (91 pp.) Martinsburg (Berkeley County), W. Va.

Consignment records for general merchandise.

3062. KU KLUX KLAN PAPERS, 1870-1969. 38 items.

Miscellaneous papers relating to the Ku Klux Klan including legal documents, 1870, containing the testimony of former members of the Klan before the Supreme Court of North Carolina concerning Klan activities in the state, 1868-1870, especially in Alamance County, and describing the organization, rituals, rules, dress, signs, and crimes of the Ku Klux Klan, with references to similar organizations, the White Brotherhood and the Constitutional Union Guard, and to opposing groups, the Heroes of America and the Union League of America; a letter from a Klan member to Charles Sumner denouncing radical politicians; a purported copy of a commission of a Grand Counsellor of the Heroes of America; a reproduction of the serial The Imperial Night-Hawk, April 25, 1923; a letter, 1940, to Lamar Q. Bail, city editor of the Atlanta Constitution, regarding Frank Dudley's King Cobra; a typescript of a statement made by Imperial Wizard James R. Venable in 1966; a copy of the serial The Clansman, 1967; a selected bibliography of and an outline of the history of the Klan; and pamphlets and clippings concerning race relations in the United States in the twentieth century.

3063. GEORGE FREDERICK KUNZ PAPERS, 1885-1917. 43 items. New York, N.Y.

Correspondence of George Frederick Kunz (1856-1932), mineralogist, concerning gems, precious stones, and other minerals, principally in North Carolina, and a collection of Indian relics.

3064. A. KUYKENDALL LEDGER, 1823-1839. 1 vol. (426 pp.) Romney (Hampshire County), W. Va.

Accounts of a tanner for hides, skins, shoes, bridles, and other similar products.

3065. EUGENE LABICHE RECORD BOOK, 1869-1904. 1 vol. (34 pp.) Augusta (Richmond County), Ga.

Record book of Eugene Labiche, containing family records, extracts from Shakespeare's plays, some German translations, and estate records.

3066. LABOR MISCELLANY PAPERS, 1901-1970. 1,606 items and 171 vols.

Correspondence, fliers, bulletins, pamphlets, leaflets, broadsides, reports, agreements, convention proceedings, and serials comprise the miscellaneous papers related to labor and labor unions. Papers concern various topics including collective bargaining, jobs for women, strikes, labor policies, taxes, mediation, pay increases, presidential elections, pension plans, labor relations, civil rights, world affairs, workers' education, labor conferences and conventions, labor leaders, and labor schools and institutes. Included are reports, 1953-1957, in Spanish made by the Council of Labor Relations of Puerto Rico on a series of union cases; the Textile Workers Voice, 1949-1955, published by the textile section of the Carolina District of the Communist Party, U.S.A.; Fighter for Peace,

February, 1952, published by the student section of the Communist Party U.S.A.; printed material pertaining to the American Federation of Labor, the American Federation of Labor-Congress of Industrial Organizations, and the Congress of Industrial Organizations; and correspondence, 1951-1956, with various unions and union officials principally in the South concerning the establishment at Duke University, Durham, North Carolina, of a collection of materials recording growth and development of the Southern labor movement.

3067. HENRY LABOUCHERE, FIRST BARON TAUNTON, PAPERS, 1840, 1856. 2 items. London, England.

A letter, 1840, from Lord Palmerston to Henry Labouchere, First Baron Taunton (1798-1869), member of Parliament and governmental official, discussing diplomatic negotiations of Britain between Turkey and Mehemet Ali of Egypt, and the domestic ramifications of Palmerston's policies; and a letter, 1856, from the Duke of Cambridge commending the governor and legislature of the Cape Colony for their attitude toward the Foreign Legion settlers.

3068. WILLIAM A. LACKEY PAPERS, 1854 (1858-1860) 1876. 71 items and 1 vol. Rockbridge County, Va.

Papers of William A. Lackey and other members of the Lackey family contain personal and business letters, legal papers, and bills and receipts concerning the settlement of estates, business and personal affairs, and slaves. Also contains a memorandum book, 1859-1860, relating to the settlement of the estate of Thomas Lackey.

3069. SAMUEL W. LACKLAND AND FRANCIS LACKLAND PAPERS, 1790 (1820-1860) 1886. 1,641 items. Charles Town (Jefferson County), W. Va.

The papers of Samuel W. Lackland and his son, Francis Lackland, contain personal and business letters; legal papers, 1790-1883, including a copy, 1800, of a plea naming George Washington as a defendant in a case involving an estate and Washington's signed reply; and bills, receipts, and accounts relating to slave sales and purchases and commodity prices in Virginia. The collection includes the correspondence, 1856-1858, of Francis Lackland while he was principal assistant engineer on the 2nd division of the Blue Ridge Rail Road Company, in charge of a survey from Knoxville, Tennessee, to the North Carolina line, concerning financial matters; engineering, surveying, and construction problems; and politics.

3070. BENJAMIN RICE LACY PAPERS. 1846-1912. 109 items. Raleigh (Wake County), N.C.

Personal and business correspondence of a North Carolina family, prominent in religious, educational, and political circles, and copies of numerous speeches made before social and fraternal organizations by Benjamin Rice Lacy (1854-1929), member of the Brotherhood of Locomotive Engineers, commissioner of labor and printing, and treasurer of North Carolina.

3071. LADIES VOLUNTEER AID SOCIETY OF THE PINE HILLS MINUTES, 1861. 1 vol. (44 pp.) Chapel Hill (Ouachita Parish), La.

Minutes recording the organization and meetings of the Ladies Volunteer Aid Society of the Pine Hills, chartered by the Ladies Volunteer Aid Society of Monroe, to support two companies of soldiers from the area. In later entries the organization is called the Ladies Volunteer Aid Society of Chapel Hill.

3072. MARIE JOSEPH PAUL ROCH YVES GILBERT DU MOTIER, MARQUIS DE LAFAYETTE, PAPERS, 1825. 1 item. Paris, France.

Letter of Lafayette introducing Achille Murat, son of the former king of Naples, and a group of his friends.

3073. JEAN LAFFITE PAPERS, 1814-1815. 3 items. New Orleans, La.

Photocopies of a letter to Laffite from Lieutenant Colonel Edward Nicholls, commander of the British forces in the Floridas, offering him a captaincy in return for a cessation of hostilities towards Britain and her allies; a response by Lafitte to Captain Nicholas Lockyer saying that he was considering the proposal; and a letter from Andrew Jackson thanking him for his assistance at the battle of New Orleans.

3074. MARK R. LAFFOON ARITHMETIC BOOK, 1808. 1 vol. Surry County, N.C.

Volume of arithmetic problems and exercises.

3075. JOHN BASEL LAMAR PAPERS, 1822-1867. 8 items. Bibb County, Ga.

Correspondence of John B. Lamar concerning secession, the Civil War, and agriculture.

3076. LUCIUS QUINTUS CINCINNATUS LAMAR PAPERS, 1875, 1887. 2 items. Oxford (Lafayette County), Miss.

Letter of Lamar to Richard J. Hinton and a clipping announcing Lamar's second marriage.

3077. ALPHONSE MARIE LOUIS DE LAMARTINE PAPERS, 1836-1869. 6 items. Paris, France.

A facsimile of Lamartine's draft of the poem "Meditations Harmonies Poetiodes Jocelin," engravings of Lamartine, and engraving of Countess Marguerite (Power) Farmer Blessington, and three obituaries of Lamartine.

3078. H. MACK LAMB AND NANCY JANE LAMB PAPERS, 1885-1886. 13 items. Randolph County, N.C.

Letters to H. Mack Lamb and Nancy Jane Lamb from relatives in Stuart, Iowa, and letters to her parents from a girl living at Science Hill, Randolph County, N.C.

3079. WILLIAM LAMB PAPERS, 1893. 1 item. Norfolk (Norfolk County), Va.

Letter from Lamb to Edwin H. Brigham concerning Lamb's published accounts of the battles of Fort Fisher, North Carolina, in the Civil War, and his lecture on blockade running.

3080. WILLIAM LAMB, SECOND VISCOUNT MELBOURNE, PAPERS, 1816, 1831. 5 items. London, England.

Letters to Lord Melbourne concerning the Reform Bill of 1832, military pensioners in Ireland, and a proposal to establish a harbor of refuge for shipping at Mounts Bay, Cornwall. Two items, 1816, are personal letters from Lady Melbourne to Lady Shelley.

3081. NATHAN P. LAND PAPERS, 1849-1868. 6 items. Cassville (Bartow County), Ga.

Correspondence of Nathan P. Land, concerning political factions involved in his effort to be elected clerk of the Georgia senate, his real estate investments, provisions and stores of the Confederate Army, and family matters.

3082. JOHN LANDES PAPERS, 1828. 1 item. Greenville (Muhlenberg County), Ky.

Letter from D.C. Landes to his father, John Landes, commenting on the political division in Illinois between the partisans of John Quincy Adams and those of Andrew Jackson.

3083. NEWTON LANDON PAPERS, 1863-1928. 89 items. East Canton (Bradford County), Pa.

Letters of Newton Landon include letters to him while he was a soldier in the 15th New York Regiment of Engineers, during the Civil War.

3084. CHARLES S. LANDRAM LETTERPRESS BOOKS, 1901-1922. 5 vols. Luray (Page County), Va.

Business letters and letters involving the settlement of estates.

3085. JOHN C. LANE PAPERS, 1889-1896. 2 items. Youngstown (Mahoning County), Ohio.

Financial papers of John C. Lane.

3086. WILLIAM PRESTON LANE, JR., PAPERS, 1921-1943. 5,335 items. Hagerstown (Washington County), Md.

The political papers of William Preston Lane, businessman and Democratic politician, contain material on national politics, 1924-1942, concerning presidential elections, Democratic Party conventions, and domestic political issues; and state politics, 1924-1943, concerning local and state political figures, local elections, state legislation, and local Democratic Party business. There is also material in the period ca. 1920-ca. 1940 on county, state, and national legal associations; political and administrative affairs in Washington County government; local patronage; local banks, particularly their financial condition in the 1930s; the Washington County school board; and local aircraft companies, especially Fairchild Aviation in Hagerstown, Maryland.

3087. JOHN LANG PAPERS, 1813-1814. 1 vol. Ireland.

Diary of John Lang, a lieutenant of the British Army in the 19th Light Dragoons, recording his experiences in Canada during the War of 1812. Lang describes skirmishing along the Niagara River, 1813, and gives secondhand accounts of several other engagements, notably the battles of Chippewa and Lundy's Lane. Also contains descriptions of the St. Lawrence Valley, the north shore of Lake Ontario, and the cities of Quebec, Three Rivers, and Montreal, and observations on the inhabitants.

3088. JOHN DALLAS LANGSTON, JR., PAPERS, 1941-1970. 434 items. Durham, N.C.

The collection is made up for the most part of clippings of editorials from the Durham (N.C.) Sun written by John Dallas Langston during the time he was editor of the paper, 1966-1969.

3089. LILLIE LANGTRY PAPERS. 1 item. London, England.

Undated letter from Lillie Langtry, British actress, to the Countess of Aylesford.

3090. HOSEA LANIER AND W. B. LANIER PAPERS, 1831-1846. 10 items. Martin County, N.C.

Family correspondence between the Lanier family of North Carolina and their relatives in Tennessee, with descriptions of Tennessee.

3091. MARCELLUS V. LANIER PAPERS, 1829-1904. 42 items. Oxford (Granville County), N.C.

Letters and papers of Marcellus V. Lanier contain letters from his father and brothers concerning family matters and business affairs, deeds of property belonging to the Lanier family, and a copy of a speech by Marcellus V. Lanier.

3092. SIDNEY LANIER PAPERS, (1857-1881) 1942. 73 items. Baltimore, Md.

Typed and handwritten copies of letters by Sidney Lanier (1842-1881), Georgia poet and musician, including some written from Oglethorpe University, Milledgeville, Georgia; a few Civil War letters; letters pertaining to the writing of the cantata for the centennial celebration at Philadelphia, Pennsylvania, in 1876; correspondence regarding Lanier's lectures in Baltimore; and an autographed poem, "Rose Morals" [published by Jay B. Hubbell, "A Lanier Manuscript," Library Notes (Duke University), II (November, 1937), 2-3]. Included also is one original letter from Clifford A. Lanier to Edwin Mims concerning publication in the South Atlantic Quarterly of a poem, "Idealism," by the former and a letter to Mims from Dudley Buck, referring to correspondence from Sidney Lanier. The copies of the letters have been partially published [Charles R. Anderson et al. (eds). The Centennial Edition of the Writings of Sidney Lanier (10 vols., Baltimore, 1945)].

3093. GEORGE T. LANIGAN PAPERS, [1900?]. 1 vol. (36 pp.) St. Louis, Mo.

Booklet entitled "Something doing in the Orient," by George T. Lanigan, made up of typed copies of press cables reporting news from the Orient, each cable followed by doggerel verse.

3094. CHARLES LANMAN PAPERS, 1828-1869. 26 items. Washington, D.C.

The papers of Charles Lanman contain brief, biographical sketches of 12 congressmen from North Carolina, which were prepared for various editions of Lanman's Dictionary of the United States Congress, in 1859 and in the 1860s, including Joseph Carter Abbott, Thomas Lanier Clingman, William Davidson, John Adams Gilmer, David Heaton, James Madison Leach, David Settle Reid, Alfred Moore Scales, Henry Marchmore Shaw, Francis Edwin Shober, John Pool, and Warren Winslow. Other items in the collection concern the preparation of the Dictionary.

3095. NATE LANPHEUR PAPERS, 1862-1864. 27 items. Allegany County, N.Y.

The collection contains letters of Nate Lanpheur, a soldier in the 85th New York Regiment at Plymouth, North Carolina, 1863; a memoir, 1864, written by Lanpheur after his return from Confederate prison describing the siege and fall of Plymouth to Confederate troops in April, 1864; and scattered letters from Union soldiers serving in Virginia, 1862-1864.

3096. ROBERT LANSING PAPERS, 1910-1920. 3 vols. Washington, D.C.

The papers of Robert Lansing, attorney and secretary of state of the United States, contain typescript copy, with handwritten corrections, of a book by Lansing entitled "Principles of American Political Parties"; manuscript notes and a partial manuscript draft of an article on sovereignty; and typescripts of 21 addresses and articles, 1918-1920, in general concerning United States participation in World War I, the peace conference, and the postwar international order.

3097. GUSTAVE LANSON PAPERS, 1900-1927. 33 items. Paris, France.

Professional and personal letters and papers of Gustave Lanson.

3098. SAMUEL M. LANTZ AND J. P. RINKER DAYBOOKS AND LEDGERS, 1823-1875. 8 vols. Union Forge (Shenandoah County), Va.

Records of a firm which dealt in general merchandise and apparently operated a forge.

3099. PIETRO LANZILLI PAPERS, 1899-1901. 7 items. Guatemala.

Miscellaneous business and legal papers of Pietro Lanzilli, a merchant and manufacturer in Guatemala.

3100. WILLIAM LAPRADE ACCOUNT BOOKS, 1839-1885. 2 vols. Franklin County, Va.

Daybooks of William Laprade's gristmill.

3101. JOHN WHITFIELD LAPSLEY PAPERS, 1848-ca. 1900. 7 items. Selma (Dallas County), Ala.

The papers of John W. Lapsley contain an autograph draft, 1862, of an appeal by Lapsley to the president and congress of the Confederacy in behalf of railroad construction generally, and specifically for those lines leading out of Selma, Alabama; Lapsley's commission, 1883, in the Cave Spring Guards by the governor of Georgia;

and photographs of portraits of Lapsley, his wife, and his son.

3102. SAMUEL LARNED PAPERS, 1825. 1 item. Providence (Providence County), R.I.

Letter of Samuel Larned, secretary of the United States legation to Chile, describing Chile, the capital city, Santiago, and analyzing the political situation in that country.

3103. JOSEPH HART LARWILL PAPERS, 1835-1910. 20 items. Bucyrus (Crawford County), and Wooster (Wayne County), Ohio.

Letters and papers of Joseph Hart Larwill and his family concern land transactions; business matters; and politics.

3104. DANIEL WILLIAM LASSITER, FRANCIS RIVES LASSITER, AND CHARLES TROTTER LASSITER PAPERS, 1832 (1887-1910) 1927. 21,749 items and 3 vols. Philadelphia, Pa., and Petersburg (Dinwiddie County), Va.

Family, professional, and legal correspondence and papers of David William Lassiter (1827-1903), a Petersburg physician; and of his two sons, Francis Rives Lassiter (1866-1909), Boston attorney, Petersburg city attorney, member of U.S. Congress 1900-1909, and Charles Trotter Lassiter (b. 1870), member of Virginia House of Delegates, 1901-1904, and of the Virginia Senate, 1906-1912. Much of the material concerns the career of Francis Rives Lassiter as a politician and congressman. A large part of the correspondence is of a routine nature. Three volumes include a letter book of Francis Rives Lassiter, accounts of his estate administered by D. W. Lassiter, and an account book of D. W. Lassiter.

3105. GEORGE LATHAM LEDGER, 1832-1833. 1 vol. (284 pp.) Falmouth (Stafford County), Va.

Records of a general merchant.

3106. HENRY GREY LATHAM AUTOGRAPH BOOK, 1851-1855. 1 vol. (229 pp.) Lynchburg (Campbell County), Va.

Notes and signatures of students and professors at the University of Virginia.

3107. MINNA BYRD LATHROP JOURNAL, 1874-1875. 1 vol. (132 pp.)

Journal of a trip to London and Dover, England.

3108. LATHROP'S STOCK COMPANY PAPERS, 1892-1895. 23 items. Boston, Mass.

Collection of programs for the plays presented by the Lathrop's Stock Company in Boston, Massachusetts.

3109. GEORGE LATIMER PAPERS, 1859. 3 items. San Juan, Puerto Rico.

Letters from a New Englander named "Yankee Tom," apparently intended for publication, describing the seizure by Spanish authorities of a ship bringing 1,100 slaves into the Caribbean.

3110. S. H. LATIMER PAPERS, 1856-1861. 5 items. Montgomery County, Ga.

Personal letters of S. H. Latimer, a physician and member of the Georgia secession convention.

3111. JOSEPH W. LATTA MUSTER ROLL, 1862-1864. 11 items. North Carolina.

Muster records for Company A, 66th North Carolina Regiment.

3112. THOMAS LATTA ARITHMETIC BOOK, 1807. 1 vol.

Manuscript volume of arithmetic exercises and problems.

3113. JAMES S. LATTNER PAPERS, 1861-1863. 6 items. Franklin County, Ga.

Miscellaneous letters and papers relating to James S. Lattner's service in the Confederate Army and his position as judge of inferior court in Georgia.

3114. ISAAC LAUCK LEDGER, 1817-1819. 1 vol. (141 pp.) Martinsburg (Berkeley County), W. Va.

Unidentified accounts under the names of customers.

3115. JOSEPH B. LAUGHTON PAPERS, 1861-1862. 5 items. Brooklyn, N.Y.

Letters of a soldier in the 38th New York Regiment describing the movements and campaigns of the Army of the Potomac, especially during the battles of Yorktown, Williamsburg and Richmond in 1862.

3116. HENRY LAURENS PAPERS, 1777-1792. 3 items. Charleston, S.C.

Letter to Henry Laurens (1724-1792), Charleston merchant and planter and member of the Continental Congress, concerning the salary of his aide, Moses Young. Included also is a letter to Laurens from his son, John, in the Revolutionary Army, requesting books on military strategy, and a letter, 1781, to Henry Laurens from Thomas Burke, William Sharpe, and Samuel Johnston asking him to support their suggestion that the British navy and army be attacked from the seacoast of North Carolina.

3117. DUNCAN W. LAURIN PAPERS, 1851-1852. 4 items. Springfield (Richmond County), N.C.

Letters from Reverend J. Jones Smyth, a Presbyterian minister, to Duncan W. Laurin, concerning a school which Laurin wished to start.

3118. ELIE A. F. LAVALLETTE PAPERS, 1826 (1830-1860) 1928. 558 items and 10 vols. Virginia and Maryland.

Family and official correspondence and papers of Elie A. F. Lavallette (ca.1790-1862), rear admiral of the U.S. Navy. Largely confined to official papers, the collection contains a brief biography of Lavallette; correspondence, 1846-1847, bearing on Lavallette's administration as civil and military governor of Mazatlán, Mexico, which city he had captured; papers bearing on the capture of an American seaman in 1851 by Selim, king of the island of Johanna, while Lavallette served in the patrol of the African coast to suppress slave trade; and many routine reports from subordinates to Lavallette and correspondence with the Portuguese concerning customs duties while the Mediterranean fleet's headquarters were at Porto Praya in the Cape Verde Islands; and information on the "Jaffa Affair," in which several American citizens were murdered at Jaffa, Syria, by five Turks. Included also are letters of Lavallette to his wife, Mary Lavallette, and from his son, Stephen Decatur Lavallette, generally in the period, 1826-1848; papers on navigation by hydraulic methods; and a table of lighthouses on the island of Sicily, July 11, 1859. The ten volumes include a combination logbook and diary while on a South American cruise, 1820-1822; two journals, 1833-1835, containing weather observations, punishments administered to miscreant sailors, records of the sick, and amounts of supplies on board; four letter books, including letters of Lavallette to George Bancroft, A. B. Warford, Lewis Warrington in 1846, chiefly regarding friction between Lavallette and Warford, engineer at the Memphis Navy Yard; letters to Francisco de Leon, Francisco Vidal, and other members of the Mazatlán Junta; to William B. Shubrick and Thomas Ap Catesby Jones, 1847-1848; routine letters from Lavallette to Samuel Barrow, William A. Graham, John P. Kennedy, William B. Shubrick, Daniel Webster, and various naval officers; a general order book; and a logbook of the frigate Congress. Among the correspondents are J. C. Dobbin, W. H. Gardener, Jas. Glynn, Francis H. Gregory, Isaac Hull, E. A. F. Lavallette, Robt. H. Leese, Uriah P. Levy, J. M. McIntosh, S. P. Quackenbush, Jos. J. Roberts (president of Liberia), Vicente Rocafuerte, Isaac G. Strain, Isaac Toucey, Levi Woodbury, and M. B. Woolsey.

3119. ANDRIEN DE LA VIEUVILLE D'ORVILLE, COMTE DE VIGNACOURT, PAPERS, ca. 1724. 1 vol. Paris, France.

A work entitled "Country Amusements," which is an annoymous English translation of Les Amusements de la campagne ou le Défi Spirituel, Nouvelle Galante et Comique (Paris, 1724), by Adrien de La Vieuville D'Orville, Comte de Vignacourt.

3120. EDWARD LAW, FIRST BARON ELLENBOROUGH, PAPERS, 1812. 1 item. London, England.

Letter of Edward Law (1750-1818), Lord Chief Justice of England, giving his opinions on repeal of the Five Mile and Conventicle acts and on making concessions to the Dissenters.

3121. EDWARD LAW, FIRST EARL OF ELLENBOROUGH, PAPERS, 1831. 1 item. London, England.

Letter to Edward Law (1790-1871), from Sir Robert Peel discussing strategy for the opening of Parliament and the crisis over the Reform Bill.

3122. EVANDER McIVOR LAW PAPERS, 1887-1888. 11 items. Yorkville (York County), S.C.

Letters of Evander McIvor Law to Isaac R. Pennypacker, editor of The Weekly Press in Philadelphia, Pennsylvania, concerning papers which Law had written on the Seven Days' battle, the second battle of Manassas, the battles of Chickamauga and Chattanooga, and General Longstreet's Knoxville campaign.

3123. WILLIAM LAW PAPERS, 1761-1890. 1,843 items and 20 vols. Darlington (Darlington County), S.C.

Personal and business correspondence and papers of William Law (1792-1868), planter, merchant, and leader of the local militia; and of the DuBose family; and of Cyrus Bacot, with whom Law was connected by marriage. As captain of the Black Creek Militia, 1813-1820, Law's papers include muster rolls, accounts of courts-martial, lists of absentees with their excuses, and numerous orders. Law's plantation records are confined to frequent lists of slaves, accounts of cotton planted and produced, and weights of hogs killed. The bulk of the papers is concerned with Law's activities as a merchant in partnership with Daniel DuBose, including records of large amounts of cotton sold to Charleston commission merchants, of turpentine and bricks sold, and papers, bills, receipts, account books, daybooks, cashbooks, and ledgers. Included also are an account book of lumber sold by Law and Cyrus Bacot, and letters and papers showing Law's activities in the temperance movement and the Presbyterian Church. Personal letters, largely confined to the period after 1839, fall into three categories; letters of sympathy at the death of Law's wife in 1839; frequent letters from members of the Cooper and DuBose families; and letters from Law's brother, James Robert Law, who was often involved in financial difficulties. Letters from James Robert Law are concerned with planting operations in Sumter District, South Carolina, and, beginning with 1848, in Madison County, Florida.

Included also are a description of the Alabama River and its fertile lowlands by William I. DuBose written from Fort Claiborne, Monroe County, Mississippi, in 1815; accounts of a trip to Red Sulphur Springs as well as other springs in Virginia in 1835; a long account by James R. Law relative to a marl bed on his Sumter plantation, and Civil War letters from William Law's son revealing numerous incidents of camp life.

3124. WILLIAM AUGUSTUS LAW PAPERS, 1771 (1860-1927). 1,503 items. Darlington County, S.C.

The papers of William Augustus Law concern the Law family generally up until 1868 and contain the correspondence of William A. Law relating to the management of his plantation, 1868-1900, including correspondence with William K. Ryan, a factor in Charleston, South Carolina, and commission merchant Henry Cobia; items concerning prices and the cotton market; and letters relating to the purchase of agricultural equipment. Correspondence among William A. Law, his wife, Julia Law, and their children deal with family business and local news. The collection contains many bills and receipts, including some concerning Law's sister, Laura Zimmerman, and an account of Law's Civil War experiences, written in 1903.

3125. JOSEPH LAWLER PAPERS, 1820-1861. 65 items. Salem (Fauquier County), Va.

Letters of the Lawler family relating for the most part to the settlement of land in Kentucky and Indiana, and commenting on food and commodity prices, politics, and social and religious activities.

3126. HANNAH R. LAWRENCE PAPERS, 1861-1865. 12 items. Chatham County, N.C.

Letters to Hannah R. Lawrence from her Moffitt cousins in the Confederate Army. The letters concern camp life, personal matters, and the battle of the Wilderness. The Moffitts were in the 5th North Carolina Regiment, the 44th North Carolina Regiment, and the 46th North Carolina Regiment.

3127. LUTHER LAWRENCE AND JAMES LAWRENCE PAPERS, 1862-1865. 17 items. Maine.

Letters from soldiers mainly from the 11th Maine Regiment, concerning camp life, health, equipment, troop movements in Virginia, and campaigning in Florida and South Carolina.

3128. STRINGER LAWRENCE PAPERS, 1755. 1 vol. London, England.

Manuscript, signed, of "A Narrative of Affairs on the Coast of Coromandel from 1730-1754," by Stringer Lawrence, describing the struggle between the British and the French for India. This narrative was published as the first part of History of the War in India (London: 1759), compiled by Richard Owen Cambridge.

3129. W. P. LAWRY PAPERS, 1866. 1 item. Louisiana (Pike County), Mo.

Letter of W. P. Lawry to Mrs. Felton of Fairfax, Vermont, discussing personal matters and national politics, particularly criticizing the policies of President Andrew Johnson toward the South.

3130. ROBERT LAWSON PAPERS, 1776 (1781-1787) 1825. 40 items. Richmond, Va.

Correspondence and papers of Robert Lawson (d. 1805), brigadier general of the Virginia Militia during the American Revolution. The material chiefly concerns army movements and military promotions, with a few letters on family affairs. There are also an account book containing a record of money granted Lawson for raising troops, and later letters indicating that Lawson had moved to Kentucky, having also considered South Carolina. Included also are a letter of America (Lawson) Lewis to Lafayette in 1825 sending him some of her father's papers for brief examination, and routine letters of Thomas Jefferson while governor of Virginia. Among the correspondents are Jno. Beckley, S. Hardy, Thomas Jefferson, B. Lawson, R. Lawson, Richard Henry Lee, A. L. Lewis, J. P. G. Muhlenburg, T. Nelson, Frederick Wilhelm von Steuben, G. Weason, and O. H. Williams.

3131. ALEXANDER ROBERT LAWTON PAPERS, 1861-1872. 11 items. Savannah, Ga.

Letters of Alexander R. Lawton (1818-1896), lawyer and brigadier general in the Confederate Army, relating chiefly to Civil War military affairs.

3132. CHARLES LAYDEN PAPERS, 1855-1859. 6 items. Perquimans County, N.C.

Personal correspondence between Charles Layden and his two brothers, one in Indiana and the other in Liverpool, England.

3133. WARREN E. LAYDISE PAPERS, 1864-1865. 32 items. Seneca Falls (Seneca County), N.Y.

Letters of Warren E. Laydise, a soldier in the 9th New York Artillery Regiment within Maryland and Virginia, discuss camp life, casualties, food, prisoners of war, and the Petersburg campaign, 1864-1865.

3134. SAMUEL J. LAZENBY PAPERS, 1842-1880. 26 items. Camak (Warren County), Ga.

Letters to Samuel J. Lazenby concerning conditions in Sparta, Georgia, in 1870, comments on Reconstruction, and debts owed to Lazenby by P. H. Hill and Sterling G. Brinkley. Other letters are from college students whose education Lazenby financed.

3135. FRANCES C. LEA PAPERS, (1843-1860) 1879. 22 items. Philadelphia, Pa.

Family and personal letters, giving descriptions of Cincinnati, Ohio, in 1851 and at Jordan's Springs, Virginia, in 1854.

3136. JAMES H. C. LEACH PAPERS, 1745-1880. 271 items. Farmville (Prince Edward County), Va.

The papers of James H. C. Leach contain personal letters from his sons, James and Richard, his daughter, Sue, and other relatives, dealing with family matters and student life at Washington College, the medical school of the University of Maryland, and Hampden-Sydney College. Letters from the period of the Civil War concern the 21st Virginia Regiment, medicine in the Confederate Army, the battle of Fredericksburg, Confederate deserters, and the treatment of civilians by Union troops.

3137. SIR JOHN LEAKE PAPERS, 1704. 1 item. London, England.

Letter to John Leake from Charles Hedges, secretary of state for the Southern Department, relating news of enemy naval preparations during the War of the Spanish Succession.

3138. EDWARD LEAR PAPERS, 1850-1874. 3 items. London, England.

A letter from Edward Lear to Chichester Fortescue, Lord Carlingford, reporting Lear's conditional acceptance by the Royal Academy and poking fun at the Academy and signed, holograph copies of two poems by Lear, "The Duck and the Kangaroo," 1873, and "The Cummerbund," 1874.

3139. THOMAS P. LEATHERS PAPERS, 1891. 3 items.

Plans and description for a large river steamboat and an agreement to build the same for Captain Thomas P. Leathers.

3140. LEATHERS, LATTA AND COMPANY DAYBOOK, 1854-1855. 1 vol. South Lowell (Orange County), N.C.

Daybook of a general mercantile business operated by John B. Leathers and James Latta.

3141. WILLIAM THOMAS LEAVELL AND EDWARD ALLEN HITCHCOCK McDONALD PAPERS, 1831-1932. 5,136 items. Charles Town (Jefferson County), W. Va.

The collection is made up of the papers of William Thomas Leavell (1812-1899), Episcopal clergyman and farmer, and his son-in-law, Edward Allen Hitchcock McDonald (1832-1912), Confederate officer, attorney, and businessman. The papers of William Thomas Leavell contain correspondence with leaders of the Episcopal Church, including Bishop John Johns, Bishop G. W. Peterkin, Bishop A. M. Randolph, Bishop Charles Clayton Penick, and Bishop W. H. Meade concerning church business, doctrinal disputes within the church, and debates between the Episcopal Church and other Protestant denominations; family letters and papers which provide information on the salaries, duties, and home life of a minister; material pertaining to the economic and agricultural conditions in Leavell's parishes, including Westover (Virginia), Rappahannock and Madison (Virginia), Hedgesville (West Virginia), and Berkeley Springs (West Virginia) and genealogical material on many of his parishioners; letters of William T. Leavell while he was a student at Bristol College, Bristol, Pennsylvania, 1833-1836, and at Fairfax Institute, near Alexandria, Virginia, 1836-1837; letters of Leavell's brothers and sisters relating to farming in Spotsylvania County and Culpeper County, Virginia, in the years before 1850; correspondence between William T. Leavell's daughter, Anne Leavell and John M. Daniel in the 1870s, both before and after their marriage; and 93 of William T. Leavell's sermons. The papers of Edward Allen Hitchcock McDonald contain letters from Civil War veterans of McDonald's regiments, the 11th Virginia Cavalry and the 77th Virginia Militia, concerning battles and skirmishes in which they participated; a manuscript copy of McDonald's "The History of the Laurel Brigade," and letters, 1870-1890, pertaining to the Louisville Abstract and Loan Company and general business conditions in Louisville, Kentucky.

3142. ABNER JOHNSON LEAVENWORTH AND FREDERICK P. LEAVENWORTH PAPERS, 1812-1915. 1,826 items and 14 vols. Petersburg (Dinwiddie County), Va.

Sermons and religious correspondence and memorandum books of Abner Johnson Leavenworth (1803-1869), Presbyterian minister and educator, and of his son, Frederick. The collection contains material on the Leavenworth family genealogy, history, religious and missionary work and sermons; a tuition ledger for Van Buren (Ark.) Female Seminary, 1860-1862; and an autograph album, 1822. Included also are letters of the Civil War and Reconstruction periods and a journal describing the siege and fall of Petersburg as seen by a citizen of the town. Half the collection consists of sermons, although, during the ante-bellum years, there are many letters from theological students in Connecticut, Massachusetts, and New York. The volumes are autograph albums, memoranda, tuition ledgers, genealogical notes of both Abner Johnson and Frederick P. Leavenworth and a diary of Fredcrick P. Leavenworth for the years 1857-1865. Among the correspondents are Calvin Colton, Harrison Gray Otis Dwight, Jeremiah Evarts, Samuel Lee, Benjamin Palmer, and Noah Porter.

3143. HENRY LEAVENWORTH PAPERS, 1839-1848. 18 items. Burlington (Chittenden County), Vt.

Miscellaneous letters to Henry Leavenworth, concerning legal matters and the practice of the law.

3144. MAGGIE B. LECATO PAPERS, 1797-1874. 98 items and 2 vols. Locust Mount (Accomack County), Va.

The collection is made up for the most part of letters to Maggie B. LeCato from girlhood friends. Also contains a daybook, 1810-1823, of Read, Teackle & Company of Watchaprique, [Maryland?].

3145. W. ROBERT LECKIE PAPERS, 1768-1905. 1,872 items and 18 vols. Washington D.C.

Business papers, 1768-1840, of W. Robert Leckie (d. 1839), military engineer; and plantation records of William Hendrick (d. ca. 1859), planter of Mecklenburg County, Virginia, and son-in-law of Leckie. The papers of W. Robert Leckie, who was educated in Scotland, are concerned with construction of public buildings, canals, arsenals, aqueducts, fortifications, masonry of the Chesapeake and Ohio Canal, and surveying and building of walls in the District of Columbia. Included also are the records of a lawsuit between Leckie and James Couty; papers relative to experiments in the production of lime, cement, and bricks; nine letters from Isaac Roberdeau revealing practices of engineers of the period; and a 91 page report of the commissioners appointed by the president for planning the defense of the United States. This report, though undated, was probably made after the War of 1812 and includes extensive details relative to the problems of defense, including topography, waterways, roadways, population, distances, and probable expenses of constructing forts. Some of Leckie's papers reflect his efforts to obtain contracts for the construction of such buildings at the Augusta Arsenal. Among the volumes also are the following: memorandum book of John Leckie, associated with his father; accounts, 1828-1829, of engineering contracts and cement stone quarries at Shepherdstown, Virginia, Seneca [Maryland?], Baltimore, Maryland, and a point near the Monocacy River; and a memorandum book containg data for surveying water lines, leveling streets, and building aqueducts in Georgetown and Washington, D. C.

The papers of Hendrick and those of his wife, after his death, constitute a long record of the sales of plantation products and the purchase of supplies from commission merchants in Petersburg, Virginia, and the operation of a series of corn and grain farms. Hendrick's children wrote letters from Princeton University, Princeton, New Jersey, Virginia Military Institute, Virginia, Lexington, and various academies which they attended. Among the volumes are children's writing books, plantation account books, a memorandum book, and accounts of a mercantile firm. The Leckie and Hendrick papers overlap, the collection containing also some records of Hendrick's forbears.

3146. WILLIAM J. LEDBETTER PAPERS, 1820-1865. 13 items. Richmond County, N.C.

Personal letters to William J. Ledbetter from his relatives and friends, including a letter, 1865, discussing General William T. Sherman's invasion of North Carolina.

3147. DR. LEE PAPERS, 1863-1864. 4 items. Georgia.

Letters to an unidentified physician from a Confederate soldier, describing camp life in Virginia and the siege of Petersburg, Virginia.

3148. EDMUND JENNINGS LEE II, PAPERS, 1737-1912. 6,373 items and 11 vols. Shepherdstown (Jefferson County), W. Va.

The letters and papers of Edmund Jennings Lee II, concern the Lee family, the related Rutherford, Lucas, Dandridge, Rust, Washington, and Shepherd families, and Lee's law practice. The collection contains correspondence among the brothers Edmund Jennings Lee II, Charles Henry Lee, Richard Henry Lee, and Cassius Francis Lee pertaining for the most part to Edmund J. Lee's extensive legal practice; letters and papers relating to the settlement of the estate of Rezin Davis Shepherd in which Edmund J. Lee's children had an interest; letters concerning family matters; bills and receipts, primarily from Edmund J. Lee's legal practice and business interests; miscellaneous family writings; and family pictures. Correspondence from the period of the Civil War includes copies of letters from Edwin Grey Lee, son of Edmund J. Lee, describing his service in the Confederate Army and alluding to his later work with the Confederate secret service in Virginia and Canada. There are 8 volumes dealing with legal matters including notes on the law and financial ledgers; a ledger from the Virginia-Maryland Bridge Company, 1849-1851; a record book, 1818-1848, from the Shepherdstown and Winchester Turnpike Company; diaries of Henrietta (Bedinger) Lee, 1874-1877, Edwin Grey Lee, 1864-1865 and

1865, and Edmund Jennings Lee III, 1866; and a book of notes from a logic class taken by George Rust Bedinger at the University of Virginia, 1859, which was later used as a letter book and ledger.

3149.   FITZHUGH LEE PAPERS, 1865-1898. 19 items. Glasgow (Rockbridge County), Va.

Miscellaneous letters of Fitzhugh Lee and material related to Lee's career including commissary records from Lee's cavalry command, 1865; letter relating to the Spanish-American War; letter from Lee as governor of Virginia; and routine letters of recommendation.

3150.   HENRY LEE PAPERS, 1769-1825. 4 items. Washington, D.C.

Miscellaneous letters to Lee on political and personal matters, including a letter, 1825, from Benjamin Watkins Leigh, Sr., concerning the court-martial of Captain David Porter of the United States Navy.

3151.   JOHN FITZGERALD LEE PAPERS. 1 item. Washington, D.C., and Prince Georges County, Md.

Undated letter from John Fitzgerald Lee concerning a tax return for Mrs. Graham in 1864.

3152.   LUCY B. LEE PAPERS, 1862-1876. 8 items. Templeton (Worcester County), Mass.

Letters to Lucy B. Lee from her sons in the Union Army in Virginia and North Carolina.

3153.   PHILIP LUDWELL LEE LEDGER, 1743-1783. 1 vol. (66 pp.) Westmoreland County, Va.

Accounts of food, merchandise, equipment, and other supplies purchased for a plantation.

3154.   R. H. LEE PAPERS, 1862. 6 items. Mobile (Mobile County), Ala.

Letters of a Confederate soldier to his wife.

3155.   RANSON LEE PAPERS, 1841 (1849-1882) 1908. 214 items. Cockrum (De Soto County), Miss.

The collection contains letters to Ranson Lee and his family from relatives in North Carolina, concerning family matters, but giving some information on economic and social conditions and slavery during the Civil War; there are letters from Lee's sons in the Confederate Army; and letters from students at Mississippi Female College, Hernando, Mississippi, La Grange Female College, La Grange, Tennessee, and Crozer Seminary, Chester, Pennsylvania.

3156.   RICHARD BLAND LEE PAPERS, 1816-1818. 2 items. Washington, D.C.

Letters to Richard B. Lee from John Augustine Smith concerning business affairs and the settlement of the estate of Henry Lee.

3157.   ROBERT EDWARD LEE PAPERS, 1749-1939. 199 items and 5 vols. Arlington (Alexandria County), Va.

Family and military correspondence of Robert E. Lee (1807-1870), Confederate general in chief; and of his descendants; and a few letters of Francis Lightfoot Lee, Richard Henry Lee, Henry Lee, and Mary Ann Randolph (Custis) Lee. The letters deal with many phases of Robert E. Lee's life from his marriage in 1832 until his death, including family and personal affairs, especially in his letters to a cousin, Mrs. Anna M. Fitzhugh; settlement of the Custis estate; and improvements at Arlington. During the Civil War the correspondence consists of official and family letters, the former containing much information on military activities. The postwar letters reveal details of domestic arrangements following the family's removal to Lexington, Virginia. One volume contains 295 telegrams (collected and arranged by C. C. Jones, Jr., and published: D. S. Freeman, Lee's Dispatches, New York, 1915) sent by Lee from the field to Jefferson Davis and the Confederate War Department, many having been endorsed by James A. Seddon. These dispatches relate to troop movements, reports of the intelligence service, skirmishes, enemy activities, transportation of prisoners and wounded men, and other details of military operations. Included also are two scrapbooks of "Memorials to Lee"; a small notebook in R. E. Lee's hand, 1857-1860, containing amounts of meat purchased for the Arlington household; and a letterpress book of Robert E. Lee III, a lawyer of Washington, D.C.

3158.   SARAH (WALLIS) BOWDICH LEE PAPERS, 1820s. 2 items. England.

Untitled manuscript (439 pp.) by the British naturalist, Sarah (Wallis) Bowdich Lee, narrating the history of African exploration and attempting to provide a survey of European knowledge of Africa, ca. 1825.

3159.   STEPHEN DILL LEE PAPERS, 1902-1907. 5 items. Columbus (Lowndes County), Miss.

Letters of Stephen Dill Lee concerning personal matters and reminiscences of his service in the Confederate Army during the Civil War.

3160. LEE FAMILY PAPERS, 1780-1851. 229 items. "Needwood," near Petersville (Frederick County), Md.

Papers of the Lee family are made up for the most part of the letters and papers of John Lee, lawyer and Federalist politician, and his brother-in-law, Outerbridge Horsey, attorney general of Delaware and U.S. senator from Delaware, relating to their joint ownership of a sugar plantation in Thibodeauville, Louisiana, 1828-1834, including a number of items from the lawsuit which ended the partnership pertaining to the management of the plantation. Also contains a few papers of Thomas Sim Lee concerning his service as governor of Maryland, 1779-1783.

3161. DAVID LEECH PAPERS, 1808 (1822-1842) 1875. 42 items. York District, S.C.

Letters of David Leech and his family, for the most part concerned with migration to Mississippi, Alabama, and Ohio. Contains a letter, 1824, criticizing the doctrine of the New Light Presbyterians, and copies, 1854, of the prospectus of the Kansas Free State.

3162. HUGH SWINTON LEGARÉ PAPERS, 1837-1843. 7 items. Charleston, S.C.

Miscellaneous correspondence of Hugh Swinton Legaré, lawyer, editor, and politician, concerning politics, Legaré's legal practice, and the purchase of books for his library. Also contains a letter, 1838, from Joel Poinsett, secretary of war of the United States, pertaining to a treaty with the Sioux Indians, and a letter from the sculptor, John Stevens Cogdell, concerning his career.

3163. JAMES MATHEWES LEGARÉ PAPERS, 1844-1953. 30 items. Aiken (Aiken County), S.C.

Photostatic copies of letters of James Mathewes Legaré (1823-1859), poet and inventor, to Evert A. Duyckinck, Thomas Powell, and John R. Thompson, concerning respectively the Literary World, Living Authors of England, and the Southern Literary Messenger. References are made to Legaré's literary productions. Included also is a letter giving a very full description of his inventions called "Dual Air Engine" and "Plastic Cotton," and an allusion to financial stress incurred by these ventures. [Published: C. C. Davis, "Poet, Painter, and Inventor: Some Letters by James Mathewes Legaré," North Carolina Historical Review, XXI (July, 1944), 215-231.] Also a copy of Legaré's The New Aria: A Tale of Trial and Trust and two letters pertaining to it.

3164. KATE (WALPOLE) LEGARÉ PAPERS, 1811-1845 and 1883-1887. 3 items and 2 vols. Johns Island (Charleston County), S.C.

Personal diaries, 1883-1887, regarding friends, relatives, storms, and local events.

3165. THOMAS LEGARÉ PAPERS, 1811-1812. 10 items. Charleston, S.C.

Correspondence of Thomas Legaré (1766-1842) and James Legaré with Jedediah Morse relative to their sons' entrance to Yale College, New Haven, Connecticut, from which the two boys graduated in 1815.

3166. EMMA A. LEGG PAPERS, 1861-1864. 62 items. Auburn (Worcester County), Mass.

The collection contains the letters of Charles A. Legg, William Howard Legg, and Luther Legg, describing their service in the Union Army during the Civil War. The few letters of Luther Legg concern duty with the 51st Massachusetts Regiment at New Bern, North Carolina, and Beaufort, North Carolina, in 1862-1863, and the letters of William Howard Legg concern campaigning in Virginia with the 1st Massachusetts Cavalry, 1862. The letters of Charles A. Legg describe his brief service with the 3rd Battalion, Massachusetts Rifles, at Baltimore, 1861, and his career with the 1st Massachusetts Cavalry, 1862-1864, in South Carolina and Virginia.

3167. HAMPTON LeGRAND LEDGERS, 1825-1888. 9 vols. Richmond County, N.C.

Records of a general merchant and family accounts.

3168. JAMES T. LeGRAND NOTEBOOK, 1869. 1 vol. Trinity College (Randolph County), N.C.

Notes on mental science, taken by James T. LeGrand at Trinity College, Randolph County, North Carolina, in a course taught by Braxton Craven.

3169. BENJAMIN WATKINS LEIGH, SR., PAPERS, 1813-1853. 10 items. Richmond, Va.

Correspondence of Benjamin W. Leigh, Sr., concerning legal affairs; Leigh's stand, as United States senator, on the Bank of the United States, 1834; and fighting around Norfolk, Virginia, during the War of 1812.

3170. HENRY C. LEIGHTON DIARY, 1862-1863. 1 vol. (25 pp.) [Oskaloosa?] (Mahaska County), Iowa.

Diary of a soldier in the 33rd Iowa Regiment describing campaigning in Kentucky and down the Mississippi to Memphis, Tennessee.

3171. JOEL B. LEIGHTON PAPERS, 1942-1943. 293 items and 3 vols. Greensboro (Guilford County), N.C.

The files of Joel B. Leighton as national representative of the Textile Workers Union of America contain material on an election at Burlington Dyeing and Finishing Company, Inc., to determine union representation; items on Cone Mills and Burlington Mills; the executive council report for the second biennial convention of the Textile Workers Union of America, 1941; and correspondence with prominent Congress of Industrial Organizations officials and T. W. U. A. officials such as Emil Rieve, Lucy Randolph Mason, George Baldanzi, and Paul R. Christopher.

3172. EDWARD WILLIAM LEINBACH PAPERS, 1832 (1862-1865). 70 items. Salem (Forsyth County), N.C.

Family and Civil War correspondence of Edward W. Leinbach, a Confederate soldier and director of music at the Salem Female Academy, concerning life in the army and family affairs. Among the correspondents are Charles S. Chandler, and James Leinbach.

3173. FRANCOIS LE MARIE PAPERS, 1714, 1717. 2 items. Louisiana and Pensacola (Escambia County), Fla.

Memoir on Louisiana, 1717, and a letter written at Pensacola, Florida, 1714, describing Louisiana and Florida and the habits of different tribes of Indians.

3174. WILLIAM M. LEMEN PAPERS, 1849-1852. 8 items. Hedgesville (Berkeley County), W. Va.

Letters to William M. Lemen from his father and sisters while he was a student at Dickinson College in Carlisle, Pennsylvania, and while his sisters attended Mt. Nebo Seminary, Mt. Nebo, Pennsylvania.

3175. ELIZA A. LEMON PAPERS, 1861-1864. 8 items. Virginia.

Family letters, containing some information on the Civil War.

3176. THOMAS LENOIR PAPERS, 1771 (1838-1880) 1912. 1,977 items and 30 vols. Caldwell County, N.C.

Business and family letters of Colonel Thomas Lenoir (1780-1861), of his father, General William Lenoir (1751-1839), and especially of Colonel Thomas Lenoir's eight children. The earlier papers include legal documents, a stud book, and family letters. Those of John Norwood (1727-1802) contain comments during the late 1790s on the spread and reception of deism in North Carolina and on the political situation in France and England; and one letter of Lewis Williams is concerned with Joseph Seawell Jones's *A Defense of the Revolutionary History of the State of North Carolina* . . . (Boston and Raleigh, 1834). Other topics include Cherokee Indian murders of whites in Buncombe County, 1794; North Carolina cession of sites for coastal forts, 1794; North Carolina militia; commodity prices; land; overseers; the attitude of Tennessee electors toward Thomas Jefferson, 1804; plans to extinguish the claims of Indians to lands in Tennessee; the coming War of 1812; the attitude of North Carolina electors toward Madison, 1812; criticism of Jackson's stand on the *Worcester* v. *Georgia* decision; nullification in South Carolina; emigration to Missouri; David L. Swain; and the conduct of Sam Houston in 1840 on his way to woo Margaret M. Lea of Alabama.

The majority of the collection, connected directly with Colonel Thomas Lenoir, consists of family papers concerning chiefly the settlement of the William Lenoir estate; the activities of the former's brother, William Ballard Lenoir (1781-1855) in Lenoir, Roane County, Tennessee; and the former's sons, Rufus Theodore and Walter Waightstill Lenoir, who were students at the University of North Carolina, Chapel Hill. The most valuable letters are those concerning the livestock farming operations of Thomas Isaac Lenoir in Haywood County, North Carolina, before the Civil War.

There are but few Civil War letters. During the postwar period there are letters of Walter Waightstill Lenoir from Crab Orchard, probably in Haywood County, and Shulls Mills, Watauga County, North Carolina, containing references to North Carolina politics, including the role of W. W. Holden and the Methodist Episcopal Church, South, in North Carolina politics in 1866. There are also occasional treatises on diseases of cattle. Included in this collection are letters of the Gwynn family and of the Pickens family of South Carolina, both related to the Lenoirs by marriage; of Rufus Theodore Lenoir and his sons at the University of North Carolina; of Julia A. Oertel, wife of a Protestant Episcopal minister and artist who came from Bavaria, Germany, and settled in Caldwell County, North Carolina; of Rufus T. Lenoir, Jr., as a student at Davis Military School, Winston, North Carolina, in 1893; and of Sarah Joyce Lenoir; and memoranda of farming operations, 1878-1901. There is a genealogical table of the Lenoir family and a slave list.

The volumes contain mercantile records; personal diary of Walter Waightstill Lenoir (1823-1890), started while a student at the University of North Carolina, and concerned also with the death of his wife and his career as an attorney; lists of notes payable; survey records of William Lenoir; account books; and a diary of William Avery Lenoir, 1837-1852 (with gaps), which contains biographical information on Waightstill Avery and his family, a description of Henry Clay's plantation, the construction of turnpikes in North Carolina, and a planned railroad to

Tennessee. There are unbound pages from account books, receipts for dues paid the Protestant Episcopal Church, surveyor's field notes and plats made in 1885, legal papers of various types, French notes, deeds, warrants, and records of hearings before justices of the peace. Among the correspondents are W. J. Bingham, Calvin J. Cowles, Charles R. Deems, S. F. Patterson, and Lewis Williams.

3177. LENOIR HIGH SCHOOL PAPERS, 1946. 3 items. Lenoir (Caldwell County), N.C.

Pictures of Capt. Edward W. Faucette and his nephew Col. Henry Clay Dixon, schoolmaster at Finley High School, Lenoir, N.C., 1861-1881. Also a clipping.

3178. LENOIR (N.C.) HIGH SCHOOL BAND SCRAPBOOKS, 1927-1971. 57 vols. Lenoir (Caldwell County), N.C.

Photographs, clippings, programs, photocopies of correspondence.

3179. ROBERT LESLIE PAPERS, 1783 (1814-1872) 1934. 15,398 items. Petersburg (Dinwiddie County), Va.

Correspondence, accounts, invoices, statements, and legal papers of Leslie, a member of the mercantile firm of Leslie and Shepherd of Petersburg, Virginia, and an agent of the firm of John and James Dunlop of London. Included are papers of the Dunlops concerning their American business and property. There are many references to Scots doing business in the United States. The papers before 1819 largely concern the processing and sale of cotton, tobacco, rice, and western lands. Most of the papers after 1819 pertain to tobacco manufacture in the Richmond-Petersburg area. Other topics include Leslie's career, family, travels to England; the life of textile workers in Glasgow in the 1810s; Roslin plantation near Petersburg; the collection of debts; lands held by the Dunlops in Virginia, Missouri, Illinois, and elsewhere in the U.S.; the panic of 1837; slaveholding and attitudes toward slavery; mercantile prices and U.S.-British trade; and the maintenance of American property held by Englishmen. The later material includes correspondence and business records of Leslie's nephews, Robert L. Watson and John McGill, partners in the firm. Their papers include tobacco correspondence from Australia during the 1850s. Dating after 1880 are a few papers of McGill and Mahone, the latter probably connected by marriage. Frequent correspondents in the collection include John Laird and Son, of Georgetown, D.C.; John Bryan of Richmond; Canadian firms connected with the Dunlops; James Dunwoody Brownson DeBow; John Young Mason; John Rutherfoord; Hiram Moore Smith; and William Oliver Smith.

3180. GEORGE N. LESTER PAPERS, 1862, 1889. 2 items. Marietta (Cobb County), Ga.

Papers of George N. Lester (d. 1892), lawyer, superior court judge, Confederate soldier, and member of the second Confederate Congress, regarding the Kennesaw Infantry and an address by C. C. Jones, Jr.

3181. LOVELL A. LESURE PAPERS, 1863-1913. 19 items and 2 vols. Oakdale (Worcester County), Mass.

Civil War letters of a soldier in the 36th Regiment, Massachusetts Volunteers, to his wife; diaries, 1863-1864; and clippings. In civilian life Lesure manufactured wagons and carriages. The diaries concern army life in Tennessee; the letters describe homesickness, religious feelings, military life, and fighting around Petersburg, Virginia, 1865.

3182. JOHN LETCHER PAPERS, 1849-1897. 24 items. Lexington (Rockbridge County), Va.

Letcher was a member of the U.S. House of Representatives, 1851-1859, and governor of Virginia, 1860-1863. The papers contain commissions and miscellaneous letters, mostly concerning state politics.

3183. THE LEVANT COMPANY PAPERS, 1768 (1800-1870) 1902. 134 items and 3 vols. London, England.

Letters and documents relating to British trade with the Levant in the 19th century, the operations of the British trading company, and the relations of British officials and traders with Turkish citizens and government. Included are references to highwaymen, 1803; tariff rates in the Ottoman Empire, 1806; shipping; British administration of Corfu, 1817; the work of Lloyd's of London in insuring goods; the marriage of a company merchant to a Turkish citizen, 1824; the numbers of foreign ships in Constantinople; complaints about the behavior of Turkish officials; the status of British subjects in Turkish courts and prisons; and an investigation into a collision between a British steamship and a Turkish boat in which Ali Sahlib Pasha was killed, 1858. Correspondents represented in the collection are Robert Adair, V. N. Black, Henry L. Bulwer, Stratford Canning, John Cartwright, A. Carlton Comberbatch, Robert M. Comberbatch, F. H. Dyke, Bartholomew Frere, Edmund Hammond, Edmund Hornby, Robert Liston, H. Mandeville, William Meyer, Niven Moore, Isaac Morier, I. B. Paterson, M. B. Pisani, W. H. Richardson, Spencer Smith, Edward Henry Stanley, and Thomas Thornton.

3184. OCTAVIA (WALTON) LE VERT PAPERS, 1862-1866. 7 items. Mobile, Ala.

Social notes of an author and society personality; included are some personal letters from General P. G. T. Beauregard mentioning his sorrow at the death of his wife, and his postwar life as a railroad president.

3185. GRANVILLE GEORGE LEVESON-GOWER, SECOND EARL GRANVILLE, PAPERS, 1869. 3 items. London, England.

Letters from Prime Minister Gladstone to Granville, then colonial secretary, discussing plans for legislation which culminated in the Irish Land Act of 1870.

3186. HENRY LEWALLEN PAPERS, 1825-1881. 48 items. Asheboro (Randolph County), N.C.

Personal papers of a Methodist Protestant minister dealing with his mental health, book and stationery selling, preaching, and Rutherford College. Included are legal papers concerning the Presnall family.

3187. LEWARD COTTON MILLS, INC., PAPERS, 1881-1935. 41 items and 51 vols. Worthville (Randolph County), N.C.

Account books and miscellaneous records of a firm organized in 1923 and absorbed by Fieldcrest Mills, Inc., in 1965. The collection consists of an incomplete series of records of Leward Cotton Mills, Inc., 1923-1935; and of predecessor firms, the John M. Worth Manufacturing Company, 1881-1913 (called the Worth Manufacturing Company after 1889); Worth's Mill No. 1, 1893-1913; Mill No. 3, 1900-1912; the Worth Manufacturing Company Store, a general store, 1882-1885; Riverside Mills, Inc., 1913-1923; Central Manufacturing Company, 1885-1903; Engleworth Mills, 1894-1901; and the Worthville Store Company, a general store, 1916-1933. Record types include ledgers, subsidiary ledgers, profit and loss accounts, cash journals, inventories, stockholders' minutes, directors' minutes, financial statements, cashbook, shipping book, consignment books, invoice books, journals, order books, daybooks, articles of incorporation, bylaws, bills payable, record of production, payroll books, bonus payroll ledger, and miscellaneous letters and documents. Not all types of records are present for each firm. The collection is inventoried on cards.

3188. BURWELL BOYKIN LEWIS PAPERS, 1843-1894. 687 items. Tuscaloosa (Tuscaloosa County), Ala.

Family correspondence of Burwell Boykin Lewis (1838-1885) and of his wife's family, the Garlands. Although the correspondence pertains mainly to family affairs, there are references to the Civil War, Reconstruction, railroad frauds in Alabama, the administration of the University of Alabama, Tuscaloosa, Louise Lewis's stay in Paris, 1890-1892, as an art student, and the development of the coal and iron industry in Alabama. Aproximately one-third of the letters, between Lewis and his wife, are personal in nature. Among the correspondents are Landon Cabell Garland, Louise Lewis, and Lucinda Rose (Garland) Lewis.

3189. CLIVE STAPLES LEWIS PAPERS, 1942. 1 item. Cambridge, England.

A letter of C. S. Lewis (1898-1963), British scholar and author, written while a fellow and tutor of Magdalen College, Oxford, stating an argument for the existence of objective truth and objective good.

3190. DAVID JOHN LEWIS PAPERS, 1905-1949. 3,282 items and 12 vols. Cumberland (Allegany County), Md.

Papers of Lewis (1869-1952), lawyer and U.S. representative from Maryland, 1910-1916 and 1930-1939; member of the U.S. Tariff Commission, 1916-1925; and member of the National Mediation Board, 1939-1943. Included are recommendations for Lewis's appointment to the tariff commission as the choice of free trade interests, 1916; and letters, 1917-1925, relating to the collection of data on costs of production and productive capability in the United States. A later series of tariff letters, 1929-1930, include some from William Thomas Rawleigh, spice and extract manufacturer and free trader; other letters concern the Hawley-Smoot tariff of 1929 and deal with proposed rates for many types of products. Papers relating to the tariff, 1910-1950, largely reflect the period when Lewis was special consultant to the Rawleigh Tariff Bureau, 1925-1930, including notes, reports, statistics, Congressional prints, voting records of Congressmen, and memoranda. They concern proposed rates for many types of goods and contain information about the productive capacity of American industry and the cost of production. Scattered throughout the collection are miscellaneous letters concerning politics and Lewis's political career. Letters from the 1940s concern international relations and the Senate's treaty powers. There are also letters, legal documents, and other papers relating to a lawsuit against the Cumberland, Maryland, water department, 1925-1948. Some World War II letters from Lewis's Welsh relatives describe the hardships of life in Great Britain. After 1943 there are letters relating to spiritualism, especially concerning the work of such organizations as the Society for Psychical Research in London, the American Society for Psychical Research, New York; and the Duke University Parapsychology Laboratory. Printed materials accompanying the collection include Congressional reports, hearings, speeches, newspaper clippings, press releases, publications of the Rawleigh Tariff Bureau, and election campaign material. Scrapbooks, 12 vols., contain letters from prominent individuals, clippings concerning Lewis's career and his unsuccessful campaign for the U.S. Senate in 1938.

3191. DIXON HALL LEWIS PAPERS, 1838.
2 items. Montogomery, Ala.

Letters of Dixon H. Lewis (1802-1848), member of U.S. Congress, 1828-1840, and U.S. senator, 1840-1848, to David Hubbard of Alabama, asking for copies of speeches of Daniel Webster and urging Hubbard to tell the people to what extent members of Congress were bound to banks as stockholders or debtors.

3192. FREDERICK B. A. LEWIS PAPERS, 1861-1899. 1 vol. Watertown (Jefferson County), N.Y.

Letters concerning the career of a U.S. Navy medical officer, largely orders relating to service in New York, Philadelphia, Portugal, and at the U.S. Naval Academy, then in Newport, Rhode Island, for the duration of the Civil War. Writers of letters include Gideon Welles, David D. Porter, William Radford, and William K. Van Reypen.

3193. GEORGE W. LEWIS PAPERS, 1862.
4 items. Winchester (Frederick County), Va.

Business letters concerning the estate of Robert W. Carter, for which Lewis was executor, and claims against the estate of Francis B. Jones.

3194. JOHN FRANCIS LEWIS PAPERS, 1874-1894.
4 items. Lynnwood (Rockingham County), Va.

Correspondence of John Francis Lewis (1818-1895), Virginia politician interested in the Readjuster movement, consisting of replies to requests for autographs and a notice of change of address.

3195. JOHN W. LEWIS PAPERS, 1835-1861.
5 vols. North Carolina.

Papers of a Methodist Episcopal preacher and circuit rider, including sermons, circuit plans, a journal of his itinerary in Tar River Circuit, 1846, and classbooks listing members and contributions, including Negro members.

3196. MILO LEWIS PAPERS, 1801-1846.
50 items. Naugatuck (New Haven County), Conn.

Letters of Thomas Lewis, a minister and instructor in a local academy in Sunbury, Liberty County, Georgia, to his father, Samuel Lewis of Connecticut; also letters of James Morris concerning the return of Thomas' belongings to his family. Later letters concern Milo Lewis, a merchant who supplied peddlers in the South and shipped cotton to Connecticut; and Herbert C. Peabody, Lewis' agent in Mobile, Alabama. Also mentioned frequently are cotton factories in the South, national politics, and shipments of cheese to William H. Bunnell, Mobile commission merchant.

3197. WILLIAM LEWIS PAPERS, 1829-1833.
1 vol. Clinton County, Mo.

Minutes of the Temperance Society of The Fork (Clinton County), Missouri, including membership lists, and the constitution.

3198. WILLIAM DAVID LEWIS PAPERS, 1839.
10 items. Philadelphia, Pa.

Letters from R. M. Whitney to William David Lewis (1792-1881), private secretary to Henry Clay, 1814-1815, and for many years cashier of the Girard Bank in Philadelphia, Pennsylvania. The letters relate to the unsuccessful attempt to make Whitney president of the Commercial and Railroad Bank of Vicksburg, Mississippi, and contain material on banks in 1839.

3199. LEWIS FAMILY PAPERS, 1804-1891.
834 items and 6 vols. Hancock County, Ky.

Personal correspondence and business and legal papers of William Linton Lewis of Hancock County, Kentucky; his son Frederick D. Lewis; and other members of the Lewis family which migrated from Loudoun County, Virginia, to Kentucky about 1815. The correspondence is largely with Dunnington family and other relations in Charles County, Maryland, and in Loudoun County, up to 1850. Letters from W. L. Lewis are dated in Nelson, Breckinridge, and Hancock counties, Kentucky, and Perry and Harrison counties, Indiana. Topics include reference to the Disciples of Christ, 1835; medical studies at Transylvania University, Lexington, Kentucky, 1835-1836; the candidacy of John Hardin McHenry for Congress, 1839; organizational material, 1873-1874, and quarterly returns, 1874-1878, of Linton Lodge, No. 911, at Lewisport, Kentucky, of the Independent Order of Good Templars, Grand Lodge of Kentucky. There are letters of John C. Lewis, son of F. D. Lewis, describing dairying and sheepherding in Larimer County, Colorado, 1882, and letters of Kate (Lewis) Moorman, daughter of F. D. Lewis, from Hillsboro, Hill County, Texas, 1883-1889. Volumes include a daybook, 1847-1848, of Lewis and Keen, a mercantile store at Cloverport, Breckinridge County, containing an agreement between Lewis and A. H. Keen, inventory of goods, correspondence of John W. Johnson, and personal accounts of F. D. Lewis, 1858-1876. There are ledgers, a daybook, and promissory notes relating to Vincent Lewis' medical practice in Hancock County, Kentucky, 1872-1874. The collection also includes scattered letters and subscription lists relating to various Kentucky Baptist churches which were members of the Goshen Association, Salem Association, and North Bend Association. They relate to transfers of membership, salaries of ministers, and instructions of delegates from local churches to association meetings.

3200. LEWIS FAMILY PAPERS, 1802-1852. 71 items. Berryville (Clarke County), and "Woodlawn" (Fairfax County), Va.

Letters from Alexander Wood, overseer of Audley Farm, an estate in Battletown (now Berryville), to the owner, Lawrence Lewis (1767-1839), nephew of George Washington. Wood's letters give minute details of the products of the farm and their prices, and note the sale of slaves. Also in the collection are personal letters to Lawrence Lewis's son, Lorenzo Lewis.

3201. DAVID S. LIBBEY PAPERS, 1862-1865. 23 items. Sunkhaze (Penobscot County), Me.

Letters of a soldier in the 8th Maine Regiment of Volunteers, containing descriptions of army life; the battle of Fair Oaks, 1864; the march across North Carolina from Wilmington to Magnolia, 1865; and the town of Raleigh and the country surrounding it.

3202. LIBERTY HALL ACADEMY RECORDS, 1774-1803. 2 vols. Lexington (Rockbridge County), Va.

An account book, 1782-1789; and a copy of the minutes of the board of trustees.

3203. EVAN J. LIDE PAPERS, 1833-1887. 131 items and 13 vols. Darlington (Darlington County), S.C.

Family correspondence of Evan J. Lide, a South Carolina cotton buyer, including business correspondence; letters from Lide's son, who served in the Confederate Army, with comment on the Mason-Slidell affair; General T. J. Jackson's invasion of Maryland; and General George B. McClellan's movements around Richmond in 1862. Included also are account books, daybooks, and ledgers of a general merchant; one volume in concerned with the settlement of the estate of E. J. Lide.

3204. FRANCIS LIEBER PAPERS, 1834-1867. 6 items. Columbia (Richland County), S.C.; and New York, N.Y.

Miscellaneous letters by Lieber (1800-1872), educator and political scientist. One item describes an interview with President Millard Fillmore; the others chiefly concern Lieber's publications.

3205. JOHN LIGGAT AND ALEXANDER LIGGAT PAPERS, 1819-1864. 8 items. Lynchburg (Campbell County), Va.

Letters of genealogical interest, of members of the Liggat family, and a copy of resolutions of the Lynchburg city council, 1864, concerning payment of dividends by the Virginia and Tennessee Railroad.

3206. LILLINGTON OIL MILL COMPANY PAPERS, 1913-1923. 29 items and 2 vols. Lillington (Harnett County), N.C.

Records of a firm manufacturing cottonseed oil, hulls, meal, cotton linters, and soybean meal and oil. The volumes include an agreement to organize the business; a certificate of incorporation; bylaws; lists of stockholders; minutes of directors and stockholders, 1913-1922, and financial statements. Among the loose papers are reports of the president, financial statements, a tax report, correspondence, stockholder proxies, and duplicate minutes.

3207. ABRAHAM LINCOLN PAPERS, 1860-1965. 22 items. Springfield (Sangamon County), Ill.

Chiefly facsimiles of Lincoln letters; clippings; and other miscellany concerning Lincoln and his assassination. There are two original letters; one is to Lincoln from John Jordan Crittenden, James Streshly Jackson, and William Henry Wadsworth concerning an appointment for Elisha Warfield Tarlton, 1861; and a letter to Lincoln from Thomas E. Bramlette, governor of Kentucky, 1864, criticizing military rule in that state.

3208. ABRAHAM LINCOLN PAPERS, 1793-1800. 2 items. Worcester (Worcester County), Mass.

Business letters of a Worcester attorney.

3209. BENJAMIN LINCOLN PAPERS, 1778-1804. 13 items. Hingham (Plymouth County), Mass.

Papers, largely letters and reports to Lincoln, relating to his command of American troops in the Southern Department during the Revolutionary War. Writers include John Houstoun on the fall of Savannah, December 29, 1778; Andrew Williamson on funds for pay of the Georgia militia and a proposed truce in northern and central Georgia, April 9, 1779; Casimir Pulaski on British troop movements around Charleston, May 15, 1779; Lincoln on disposition of the spoils of war, Sept. 23, 1779; John Wereat on civil government in Georgia, August 18, 1779; Count d'Estaing on plans for the siege of Savannah, September 14, 1779; Lachlan McIntosh on political divisions among Georgia troops, December 11, 1779; Francis Marion on the military situation in Savannah, January 31, 1780; Andrew Williamson on Spanish activities at Pensacola and Mobile, 1780; and John Rutledge on the locations of troops defending South Carolina, April 25, 1780. There is one certificate, 1804, signed by Lincoln as collector of the Port of Boston. The library also holds microfilm, 13 reels and index, of Benjamin Lincoln papers owned by the Massachusetts Historical Society.

3210. LINCOLNTON FEMALE ACADEMY PAPERS, 1821-1908. 20 items and 2 vols. Lincolnton (Lincoln County), N.C.

Receipts, committee reports, rolls of trustees, committee reports, and minute books of the board of trustees, including lists of students examined before the board and occasional information on salaries of teachers.

3211. LINCOLNTON MINISTERIAL ASSOCIATION PAPERS, 1904-1936. 6 items and 1 vol. Lincoln County, N.C.

Minutes of the association meetings; topics include religious work and issues of social morality such as temperance, blue laws, and censorship of motion pictures.

3212. JOHN LIND SERMONS, ca. 1809-1824. 2 vols. Hagerstown (Washington County), Md.

3213. ROBERT C. S. LIND PAPERS, 1838-1839. 3 vols. Pittsburgh, Pa.

Included are a scrapbook of Hannah Smith Lind; a copybook of Robert C. S. Lind containing a sermon by Matthew Lind Fullerton and a letter and sermon by John Lind; and a family record book.

3214. HORACE B. LINDSEY PAPERS, 1949. 1 vol. (22 pp.) Durham, N.C.

Genealogy of the family of Thomas Lloyd (ca. 1736-1792) of Hillsborough, N.C.

3215. JACOB H. LINDSEY PAPERS, 1873-1886. 33 items. Bridgewater (Rockingham County), Va.

Correspondence of Jacob H. Lindsey, local Republican leader, and of his son, Stuart F. Lindsey. Among the correspondence are letters from Republican leaders of western Virginia relative to jobs and party organization. Letters to Stuart Lindsey indicate that he was an office seeker. Included also are circulars and broadsides relative to circulation of the National Republican, tariff rates, and the Tenth Census; rules of order and circulars of the Independent Order of Odd Fellows of Bridgewater; and a pollbook of Staunton, Virginia, for 1886. The collection contains one letter from William Mahone.

3216. MAJOR LINES PAPERS, 1813-1865. 11 items. New Haven, Conn.

Family letters of a New Haven man while resident in Charleston, South Carolina.

3217. LEWIS FIELDS LINN PAPERS, 1834 [?]. 1 item. Washington, D.C.

A letter by Linn, U.S. senator from Missouri, concerning a law case.

3218. KATE D. (CONANT) LINSLEY PAPERS, (1853-1888) 1928. 38 items. Thetford (Orange County), Vt.

Family letters containing references to a daguerreotyper in Thetford, 1853; home remedies; charades; a Vermont girl teaching Negro children in Beaufort, South Carolina, 1863; postal service; a Georgia man fleeing to the North to avoid conscription into the Confederate Army; a Negro woman who had fled the South coming from Washington, D.C., to do housework, 1869; and schoolgirl life in an academy in Thetford, Vermont, 1888.

3219. ROBERT O. LINSTER PAPERS, 1840 (1861-1899) 1907. 113 items. Statesville (Iredell County), N.C.

A few letters of Hugh Kelly, physician; letters of Robert O. Linster, a clerk in the 4th Regiment, North Carolina State Troops, during the Civil War; postwar love letters from Linster to the daughter of Hugh Kelly, Cornelia, (later Cornelia [Kelly] Linster); and papers of their son, Roy L., who used the surname Leinster, and who served in the 1st Regiment North Carolina Volunteer Infantry during the Spanish-American War and thereafter became a high ranking officer in the North Carolina National Guard. There are also several anonymous poems concerning the activities of the Woman's Christian Temperance Union.

3220. JOHN CHARLES LINTHICUM PAPERS, 1931. 2 items. Baltimore, Md.

Speeches by Linthicum, U.S. representative from Maryland, concerning Congressional recognition of Francis Scott Key's "The Star Spangled Banner" as the national anthem.

3221. E. BURTON LINVILLE PAPERS, 1842 (1863-1896) 1905. 238 items and 1 vol. Belew's Creek (Forsyth County), N.C.

Letters from Linville's brother, A. J. Linville, a schoolteacher at Fenn's Bridge, Georgia, concern the fear of conscription into the Confederate Army. His letters after 1865 concern medical studies at the University of Michigan and dwell on skating parties, current fashions in Ann Arbor, and commodity prices. After 1868 A. J.'s letters describe family and financial affairs of a medical practitioner at Freeport, Indiana. Letters of Aaron Y. Linville, E. B.'s son, were written while a medical student in New York City and relate impressions of Washington, D.C., 1886; the vote for Henry George in the New York mayoral election in 1886; and baseball, 1888. Papers of E. B. Linville as justice of the peace, 1871-1896, include summonses, affidavits, warrants, judgments, and complaints. There are also shoemaking accounts and two contracts for furnishing timber to the Cape Fear and Yadkin Valley Railway Company.

3222. RAPHAEL LION PAPERS, 1861-1899. 25 items. Utica (La Salle County), Ill.

Personal letters in the French language.

3223. CORNEILLE (ASHE) LITTLE PAPERS, 1922-1940. 272 items. Wadesboro (Anson County), N.C.

Family letters, including many from Mrs. Little's cousin, Miss Willie Ashe, and her brother, Samuel A'Court Ashe (1840-1938), Raleigh newspaperman, historian, and last surviving officer of the Confederate regular army. Some of Ashe's letters are to Mrs. J. H. Caudle of Wadesboro, North Carolina. The collection also includes an article, 1913, by Mary Grierson of Morrisville, North Carolina, on civilian life during the Civil War.

3224. HENRY ALEXANDER LITTLE PAPERS, 1890. 1 item. London, England.

Little (1837-1908) was a general in the British Army. This letter, from Major General Sir George Stuart White, concerns Multan pottery and military activities in Burma.

3225. LITTLE RIVER LUMBER COMPANY LEDGER, 1926-1929. 1 vol. Star (Montgomery County), N.C.

Monthly balances and accounts of a branch at Ellerbe, Richmond County.

3226. EDWARD JOHN LITTLETON, FIRST BARON HATHERTON, PAPERS, 1827. 1 item. Teddesley Park, Staffordshire, England.

Letter of Littleton (1791-1863), British politician, expressing his views on Catholic emancipation, the strategy of the Dissenters, and the repeal of the Test and Corporation Acts.

3227. E. LIVELLY PAPERS, 1857. 1 item. Scranton (Lackawanna County), Pa.

A letter of condolence on the death of a child, written to Matilda Miller.

3228. WILLIAM ROSCOE LIVERMORE PAPERS, 1854-1950. 92 items. Boston, Mass.

Letters and other papers concerning Livermore's publications on military subjects, his development of cartridge clips for use in rifles, infringements on his patents, and his career in the U.S. Army. Correspondents include Melville Bull, Curtis Guild, Jr., John Codman Ropes, John Patten Story, John McAllister Schofield, and John Moulder Wilson.

3229. JOSEPHINE E. LIVEZEY PAPERS, 1828 (1876-1896) 1913. 204 items. Baltimore, Md.

Family correspondence, including descriptions of travel and of resorts from Virginia to Maine; parties given by the Du Pont family in Wilmington, Delaware, 1886; the illness of Jane Addams, 1910; conversations of Bernard N. Baker (Josephine Livezey's brother-in-law) with William Howard Taft, Theodore Roosevelt, and Gifford Pinchot, 1910; and the mercantile business of John Ely in Attleboro, Pennsylvania, 1843.

3230. CHARLES LIVINGSTON PAPERS, 1812-1829. 9 items and 1 vol. Greenock, Scotland.

Papers and letter book of a Scottish shipowner engaged in trade of Greenock, Liverpool, and Belfast with Charleston, South Carolina, and Wilmington, North Carolina. Shipments to America include Irish and Scottish potatoes, salt, stoneware, and iron pipe. The ships also carried Irish immigrants. Cargoes on return voyages include turpentine and naval stores from North Carolina and sea island cotton from South Carolina, cane reeds, staves, rice, and tar. There is comment on insurance, wages in Charleston, trade conditions, the 1822 Navigation and Trade Acts of Great Britain, and port conditions at Wilmington, 1822.

3231. EDWARD LIVINGSTON PAPERS, 1828-1831. 3 items. Washington, D.C.

One letter to William P. Farrand of Harrisburg, Pennsylvania, 1828, concerns business ventures in Georgia and South Carolina, and land in North Carolina. Two letters, 1831, by Livingston while U.S. secretary of state, concern personal finances and complaints against the U.S. consul in Havana.

3232. JOHN LLOYD PAPERS, 1811, 1831. 2 items. Upperville (Fauquier County), Va.

A letter from Thomas H. Drew to John Lloyd, a Virginia merchant, concerning a property transaction, and a personal letter from Lloyd's wife, Anne.

3233. THOMAS LLOYD PAPERS, 1705-1962. 132 items. Hillsborough (Orange County), N.C.

Photocopies of wills, deeds, and other colonial, state and county records from Virginia and North Carolina; Bible records; and correspondence concerning Lloyd, his descendants, and related families.

3234. WILLIAM WATKISS LLOYD PAPERS, 1845. 1 item. London, England.

Letter accompanying a gift of Lloyd's essay, <u>Xanthian Marbles</u>, to Sir Charles Fellows.

3235. GEORGE G. LOBDELL PAPERS, 1858-1879. 28 items. Wilmington (New Castle County), Del.

Business letters from various railroad companies to Lobdell, Bush and Lobdell, and the Lobdell Car Wheel Company.

3236. JAMES LOCH PAPERS, 1851. 1 item. London, England.

Letter of William G. Hayter, Liberal whip and patronage secretary to the treasury, requesting the presence of Loch, member of Parliament for Wick, Cornwall, in the House of Commons on February 11, 1851, for a vote on Disraeli's motion for the relief of the owners and occupiers of land.

3237. WILLIAM F. LOFTIN PAPERS, 1834-1863. 17 items. Union Mills and Goldsboro (Wayne County), N. C.

Letters of Loftin to his mother, Ann B. Bryan, at Uniontown, Alabama, chiefly concerning civilian life in North Carolina during the Civil War, secession, rumors, refugees from New Bern, conscription, yellow fever, the battle of Kinston (December, 1862), depredations by Union soldiers, and the 63rd North Carolina Cavalry during the Gettysburg campaign. There is a deed for the sale of slaves, 1834, and a settlement of slaves among family members.

3238. LORD AUGUSTUS WILLIAM FREDERICK SPENCER LOFTUS PAPERS, 1858-1892. 15 items. London, England.

Papers of a British diplomat who served at Vienna, Munich, Berlin, and St. Petersburg in the 1860s and 1870s, and later as governor of New South Wales and Norfolk Island. Topics include Prussian politics, royalty, and statesmen; the constitutional crisis in Austria and Hungary; appointments in the British diplomatic service; Berlin's plans to counter any Orleanist movement in Spain; investment in the coal and iron industry of Russia; the Russo-Turkish War; an Afghan pretender; Russian society; Loftus's views on the relations of England with her colonies and the danger of American influence; Forsyth's mission to Sinkiang, China; the status of landlords in Ireland; and politics and personalities in Lima, Peru. Writers of letters include Sir William Barrington, Lord Bloomfield, Edward Robert Bulwer-Lytton, Alexander Alfred Dunlop, Robert Percy French, Lord Granville, Sir Lepel Henry Griffin, Lord Claud Hamilton, Loftus, Arthur Ordway, Lord Alfred Henry Paget, George Strachey, and Sir Edward Thornton.

3239. BERKELY LOGAN PAPERS, 1858-1872. 5 items. Leitersburg (Washington County), Md.

Letters from H. C. Logan in San Francisco to Berkely Logan advocating secession for the South and an Independent republic for the Pacific coast.

3240. JOHN ALEXANDER LOGAN PAPERS, 1878. 1 item. Chicago, Ill.

A letter by Logan, U.S. representative and senator from Illinois, to F. Moore.

3241. SOLOMON B. LOHR PAPERS, 1850-1884. 20 items and 2 vols. Davidson County, N.C.

Papers of a justice of the peace concerning debts and disputes, and account books of a general merchant.

3242. JOHN TAYLOE LOMAX PAPERS, 1854. 1 item. Fredericksburg (Spotsylvania County), Va.

Letter to T. H. Pollard, clerk of the Circuit Court, Hanover Court House, Virginia, outlining his opinion in the case of Thompson v. Dickinson and other cases pending.

3243. NANNIE LOMAX PAPERS, 1846-1848. 3 items. Chillicothe (Ross County), Ohio.

Personal letters from Nannie Lomax, a girl who had moved to Ohio, to her friend in Virginia, with exhortations that the friend be a more devout Catholic.

3244. ALEXANDER LONDON PAPERS, 1940. 1 item. Washington, D.C.

A letter from London, Royal Netherlands minister to the United States, to G. A. Nuermberger relating to acquisition of a Dutch government publication by Duke University Library.

3245. ANNE LONDON PAPERS, 1727. 1 item. Shaston St. Peter, Dorsetshire, England.

A bond of twenty-five pounds to Anne London from William and Charles Knott.

3246. ALEXANDER LONG MEMORANDUM BOOK, 1805-1832. 1 vol. [Virginia?]

A memorandum book with references to hiring slaves in Virginia and an opium remedy for diseases.

3247. AUGUSTUS WHITE LONG PAPERS, 1935-1936. 5 items. Brevard (Transylvania County), N.C.

Correspondence of Long, retired professor of English at Trinity College, the University of North Carolina, and Princeton, concerning the genealogy of the Long family of Orange County, North Carolina. There is also a memorandum by Delia White Woodward, Long's aunt, describing the occupation of

Chapel Hill by Federal troops during the Civil War in 1865.

3248. CHARLES ALEXANDER LONG AND LUCY MAIE (YORK) LONG PAPERS, 1892-1970. 8,269 items and 4 vols. Brazil; and Ardmore (Carter County), Okla.

Largely personal letters from friends and relatives and correspondence between the Longs while one or both of them were in Brazil on missionary work for the Methodist Church and with the Granberry Institute in Rio de Janeiro. Correspondents include Lucy Long's father, Davidson Victor York; H. C. Tucker; and American and Brazilian church officials. There are also pamphlets, magazines, and volumes dealing with missionary work, morality, and Brazilian history; banners and mementos of the Granberry Institute; placards and signs bearing moral slogans; diplomas; and blueprints relating to Long's senior thesis at the University of Oklahoma concerning deep wells in the southern great plains of the United States. A copy of the thesis is also in the collection. Some of the correspondence and most of the printed material are in the Portuguese language.

3249. CRAWFORD WILLIAMSON LONG PAPERS, 1849-1853. 3 items. Jefferson (Jackson County), Ga.

A booklet and clippings relating to Long's claim to be the discoverer of anesthesia.

3250. DAVID LONG PAPERS, 1868-1905. 571 items. Midway (Davidson County), N.C.

Official correspondence and a few personal letters of David Long, Midway postmaster. Included also are circular letters from various publishers and advertising companies.

3251. GEORGE LONG PAPERS, 1831-1879. 26 items. Poulton, Lancashire, England.

Letters of George Long (1800-1879), English scholar and editor, professor of ancient languages at the University of Virginia, Charlottesville, 1824-1831, and lecturer, to his friend, Henry Tutwiler, of Alabama. The first three, written in the 1830s, request articles for the _Quarterly Journal of Education_, and the remainder, written in the years 1873-1879, discuss the social and economic changes through which the South was passing. There are comments on the status of education for women in England, on similarities and dissimilarities of American and English life, and on Thomas Jefferson, James Madison, and James Monroe. [Partially published; Thomas Fitzhugh (ed.), _Letters of George Long_ (University of Virginia Library, Charlottesville, Va. 1917.]

3252. HUEY PIERCE LONG PAPERS, 1929-1940. 35 items. New Orleans, La.

Letters, circulars, and clippings concerning Long's career as governor of Louisiana, 1928-1931, and U.S. senator, 1931-1935, including correspondence about the "Share our Wealth Society of America." Correspondents include J. O. Fernandez, Gerald L. K. Smith, and Robert S. Maestri.

3253. JOHN LONG PAPERS, 1827-1856. 9 items. Clarksville (Montgomery County), Pa.

Personal letters including one item, 1850, describing life in the California gold fields.

3254. JOHN W. LONG PAPERS, 1834-1888. 18 items and 2 vols. Jefferson (Frederick County), Md.

Personal and business papers, including a bill of sale for property of the estate of Rebecca Branson, 1834; a petition, 1877, protesting actions of the radicals in Congress during the contest over the presidential election of 1876; a diary, 1886-1887, with descriptions of farm activities and the weather, including heavy snows; and a daybook, 1862-1888, containing accounts for farm products and some diary entries, including references to the 1876 presidential election.

3255. JOSEPH LONG PAPERS, (1820-1860) 1902. 209 items. Stephensburg (Frederick County), Va.

Letters to Long from friends and relatives who migrated from Virginia to Illinois, Indiana, Ohio, and Missouri. Topics include Long's landholdings in Adams County, Illinois; boat traffic on the Ohio, 1829; cholera in Ohio and Missouri, 1832-1833; the visit of Andrew Jackson and Black Hawk to Baltimore, 1833; prices of wheat and corn in the West; the effect of the demand of livestock in Oregon and California on prices in Missouri, 1853; prices of slaves and opposition of Missourians toward slavery; and the experiences of a slave who escaped to Canada, 1840. Letters from James H. Carson to Long concern the election of Robert M. T. Hunter over Governor William Smith as U. S. senator from Virginia, 1847. There are also a copy of the muster roll of Captain John Pitman's company, 1st Regiment, Virginia militia, 1814, and a few legal papers.

3256. NICHOLAS LONG PAPERS, 1750-1797. 5 items. Halifax (Halifax County), N.C.

A letter by Long as deputy quartermaster general, Continental Army, to James Hunter, Jr., 1778, concerning transportation and supply; and four deeds relating to land in Halifax County.

3257. WILLIAM R. LONG MULE COMPANY PAPERS, 1910-1913. 1 vol. Smithfield (Johnston County), N.C.

A ledger with several pieces of letterhead stationery and invoices in an envelope attached to the inside front cover, relating to a firm dealing in horses and mules.

3258. JAMES M. LONGACRE PAPERS, 1847-1861. 60 items. Philadelphia, Pa.

Personal and family letters to Longacre including descriptions of Wilmington, North Carolina, 1855, by Andrew Longacre; student life in Bethlehem (Pennsylvania) Seminary; and descriptions by Orleans Longacre of Civil War blockade duty on the U.S.S. Iroquois, the pursuit of the C.S.S. Sumter in the West Indies, and Martinique and the Virgin Islands.

3259. HENRY WADSWORTH LONGFELLOW PAPERS, 1859, 1874. 2 items. Cambridge (Middlesex County), Mass.

A letter from Edward Everett to Longfellow, November 15, 1859, concerns a reading by Mrs. Blunt under the auspices of the Mercantile Library Association; a letter by Longfellow, August 20, 1874, concerns arrangements for the first reading of the poem, "The Hanging of the Crane."

3260. RONALD STEWART LONGLEY PAPERS, 1944. 1 item. Wolfville, Nova Scotia, Canada.

A letter from Longley, professor of history at Arcadia University in Wolfville, to William Colgate, concerning the source of the portrait used as a frontispiece in Longley's biography of Sir Francis Hicks.

3661. AUGUSTUS BALDWIN LONGSTREET PAPERS, 1841-1859. 3 items. Augusta (Richmond County), Ga.

Letters from Longstreet to James B. Longacre of Philadelphia concerning plans for establishing a bank in Georgia; and a letter from Longstreet's nephew, James Longstreet, 1859, describing plans for the education of his children and the life of a U.S. Army officer in New Mexico Territory.

3262. JAMES LONGSTREET PAPERS, 1848-1904. 59 items. Gainesville (Hall County), Ga.

Letters largely relating to Reconstruction and the role of the Republican Party in the South, and commenting on campaigns and battles of the Civil War, including Chickamauga, Seven Pines, Chancellorsville, Gettysburg, and others. Most of the letters are by Longstreet to various persons, or are by Daniel Harvey Hill to Longstreet. Included is a letter, 1863, from General Roger Atkinson Pryor to Longstreet concerning plans to remove Pryor from his command; a letter, 1888, from Longstreet to Emily A. Park providing information on Loreta Janeta Velaques who served in the Confederate Army under the disguise of Lieutenant Harry Buford; and a letter, 1904, by General E. P. Alexander to Frederic Bancroft which discusses the generalship of Longstreet and Mrs. Longstreet's book, Lee and Longstreet at High Tide. There are also clippings. The library holds microfilm of other Longstreet letters which are in the possession of a private owner.

3263. M. D. W. LOOMIS PAPERS, 1861-1862. 3 items. Fairfax Court House (Fairfax County), Va.

Orders relating to the work of an assistant quartermaster with the XI Corps of the Union Army of the Potomac.

3264. CHARLES PHINEAS LORD PAPERS, 1816-1866. 81 items. North Berwick (York County), Me.

Letters of an officer with Massachusetts troops during the Civil War. While he was assigned to the 6th Massachusetts Regiment of Volunteers, Lord's letters describe the movement to Washington, 1861; attack by mobs in Baltimore; and the occupation of Baltimore during the election of June, 1861. While with 8th Massachusetts Volunteers, Lord described a hurricane off Cape Hatteras, 1861; military activity along the South Carolina Coast from Beaufort, Port Royal, and Hilton Head; disease, malaria, and yellow fever; the selling of supplies to troops by officers; picket duty; food; the bombardment of Fort Walker on Hilton Head; the attack on Fort Pulaski; the political appointment of officers and the election of officers; a religious group, the "Gideonites," who taught Negroes at Hilton Head; the fight between the U.S.S. Weehawken and the C.S.S. Atlanta; the attacks on Fort Wagner and Fort Sumter; hatred of Copperheads; the burning of Jacksonville, Florida, 1863; and Negroes as soldiers.

3265. CHESTER SANDERS LORD PAPERS, 1887-1931. 118 items. New York, N.Y.

Papers of Chester Sanders Lord (1850-1933), New York journalist and managing editor of the Sun (New York), consisting largely of letters concerning invitations to the Lotus Club, congratulations on various honors which Lord received, positions he held, the Sun, and reactions to Lord's speeches. Writers include Chauncy M. Depew, Martin H. Glynn, Lord Northcliffe, Will Irwin, S. S. McClure, Clarence H. Mackay, Frank A. Munsey, Adolph Ochs, Thomas Nelson Page, Nathan Straus, William Sulzer, Cornelius Vanderbilt, and Louis Wiley.

3266. GEORGE LORD PAPERS, 1832-1871. 19 items. Boston, Mass.

Letters of a Boston mercantile family. Four letters are by Daniel Denison Slade, physician and scientist, describing medical studies and student life at Harvard, 1845-1846. One item by a relative of Lord relates working conditions in the textile manufacturing town of Cohoes, New York, 1846.

3267. GEORGE HORACE LORIMER PAPERS, 1921. 2 items. Wyncote (Montgomery County), Pa.

Correspondence of Albert C. Ritchie, governor of Maryland, concerning the credentials of a Mr. O'Donnell, a journalist investigating prisons in Baltimore while claiming to represent the Saturday Evening Post, of which Lorimer (1868-1937) was editor.

3268. WILLIAM WING LORING PAPERS, 1861-1862. 39 items. Wilmington (New Hanover County), N.C.

Papers of William W. Loring (1818-1886), Florida legislator and brigadier general in the Confederate Army. The collection concerns the Confederate quartermaster and commissary departments and includes requests for furloughs and reports on the movement of troops, especially in Fayette County, Virginia (now West Virginia).

3269. BENSON JOHN LOSSING PAPERS, 1856-1889. 18 items. Dover Plains (Dutchess County), N.Y.

The papers of Lossing, author and historian, include a letter, 1856, from Samuel Adams Lee concerning his biography of Henry ("Light Horse Harry") Lee; a letter, 1858, from George Henry Moore, regarding the publication of Charles Lee's papers; a letter, 1865, from Captain William R. Woodin, 150th Regiment of New York Infantry Volunteers, describing Charleston after its capture by Union troops, and listing documents concerning secession taken from the vacant home of Robert Barnwell Rhett and sent to Lossing; correspondence, 1870s and 1880s, between Lossing and Charles Colcock Jones, concerning the writings and publications of both men; correspondence with Jones and John F. Pickett about the great seal of the Confederate States of America; and a handwritten draft of an article by Lossing, "Castilians in the Land of the Flowers," on Panfilo de Narváez's expedition to Florida in 1527.

3270. PIERRE LOTI PAPERS, 1912-1967. 5 items. Hendaye, France.

Letters of Pierre Loti (originally named Louis Marie Julien Viaud), a French author, to his servant Pierre Scoarnec giving instructions on minor matters; letters to Furman A. Bridgers from Scoarnec and André Lestable, a postal official, concerning possible sources of information about Loti; and a letter by Bridgers explaining the manuscripts described above.

3271. LOUIS XIII PAPERS, 1610. 1 item. Paris, France.

A document signed by Louis XIII, king of France, and confirmed by his mother as regent, in which the king grants 6,000 livres to the Cardinal de Souris to indemnify him for coming to Paris and assisting in the coronation of the queen at the command of Henry IV.

3272. LOUISBURG FEMALE AND MALE ACADEMIES PAPERS, 1815-1824, 1856-1870. 35 items. Louisburg (Franklin County), N.C.

Lists of students and fees at the female academy, 1815-1824, and a receipt for the salary of Ann Benedict, "principal instructress," 1824; and reports of the male academy, 1856-1870, signed by M. L. Davis, principal, listing students and giving attendance and grades.

3273. LOUISIANA PURCHASE PAPERS, 1803. 1 vol. (53 pp.)

Photostatic copies of papers concerning the firms of Francis Baring and Co. of London and Hope and Co. of Amsterdam, holders of the bonds issued to pay for the Louisiana Territory. Writers include Napoleon Bonaparte, Thomas Jefferson, Robert Livingston, James Monroe, Albert Gallatin, François Barbé Marbois, and Alexander Baring. The originals are in the Howard Memorial Library, New Orleans. Partly in the French language.

3274. LOUISIANA STATE BANK CHECK STUBS, 1859-1861. 1 vol. (116 pp.) New Orleans, La.

Also blank checks.

3275. LOUISIANA STATE FEDERATION OF POST OFFICE CLERKS PAPERS, 1952. 5 items. Shreveport (Cadd Parish), La.

Processed material, including instructions for delegates to a convention of the Louisiana State Federation in Alexandria, Louisiana; and newsletters of the state and national federations concerning that convention.

3276. MATHEW N. LOVE PAPERS, 1827 (1860-1865) 1868. 121 items. Henderson County, N.C.

Family correspondence of Mathew N. Love, successively lieutenant, captain, major, lieutenant colonel, and colonel in the 25th North Carolina Volunteers of the Confederate Army; and of his four brothers, John Wesley, George W., S. Ervin, and Robert C. Love, all soldiers in the Confederate Army. A few papers prior to 1861 consist of such items as a commission to Mathew N. Love as captain of the Clear Creek Company in the 8th Regiment of North Carolina Militia in 1853, two certificates of Love as a teacher in the public schools, several letters from friends, and a few letters from relatives in South Carolina and Tennessee, including comments on the Whig Party. One letter from Mathew N. Love in 1868 describes farming operations in the vicinity of Dardanelle, Arkansas, where he was cultivating cotton.

    The bulk of the collection consists of letters written by the Love brothers while serving in the Confederate Army. Apparently the five brothers survived the Civil War. The letters were written from eastern South Carolina, eastern North Carolina, and the vicinity of Richmond, Virginia. The correspondence contains comments relative to skirmishes, hard-fought battles, picket duty, food, methods of preparing food, deserters, terrain of the fighting, length of period of service in the army, health of Henderson County boys in the Regiment, religious services in camp, and prices of general commodities. One letter from the sheriff of Henderson County to Mathew N. Love, June 14, 1861, orders that all free Negroes of Love's company be brought to the county seat in order to have their "free papers" arranged. Among the war correspondence are letters from a cousin guarding a bridge in East Tennessee from "tories"; and letters from a girl cousin in Mississippi telling of war and war conditions in that state, especially after the fall of Vicksburg. Included also are a few copies of poems and songs, one poem having been composed in camp by a soldier upon parting with his friends "perhaps forever."

3277.    JULIA LORD (NOYES) LOVELAND PAPERS, 1855-1965. 31 items and 2 vols. Wilkes-Barre (Luzerne County), Pa.

    Included is a diary kept by Mrs. Loveland, 1855-1856, on trips through the South with her cousin, Caroline. The diary describes Richmond social life, religious services, clergymen, Negroes, and Negro religious activities; and the resort of Magnolia, Florida, and short trips from there to Saint Augustine, Palatka, and Hibernia. There are comments on John Adams Dix, Bishop Alonzo Potter, and members of the Trumbull family of Connecticut who visited Magnolia. There are also personal letters of Mrs. Loveland to her family, one letter describing hazards faced by an unescorted female on New York streetcars; mementos relating to the election of Henry Martyn Hoyt as governor of Pennsylvania, 1879; notes apparently made with the intention of editing the diary; genealogical information on the Noyes and Loveland families; and clippings relating to the two families, including obituaries, poems, and news articles.

3278.    ANN (HEATLY) REID LOVELL PAPERS, 1819-1850. 17 items. Orangeburg (Orangeburg County), S.C.

    Correspondence of Ann Lovell, an aunt of the wife of Langdon Cheves (1776-1857), and her relatives, with scattered information about Cheves and his plantations near Savannah, Georgia, and Pendleton, South Carolina; and epidemics of scarlet fever, 1833, and cholera, 1834. The letters largely concern business, personal, and family affairs. An undated memorandum concerns the monument erected by Mrs. Lovell to the memory of her first husband, William Reid, an officer in the American Revolution, and her children.

3279.    WILLIAM S. LOVELL JOURNAL, 1852. 1 vol. (169 pp.)

    Journal kept by a midshipman on board of the U.S. storeship *Relief*, January 8 to August 11, 1852, during a cruise out of New York delivering supplies to various naval vessels in the Atlantic Ocean.

3280.    CHARLES F. LOW PAPERS, 1861 (1864) 1892. 41 items. Jamaica Plain (Suffolk County), Mass.

    Family letters, largely of Low, a private in the 6th Regiment, Massachusetts Volunteer Infantry, July-October, 1864. Three miscellaneous items of 1861-1862 concern the Winthrop Guard of Jamaica Plain. Most of the collection concerns Low's war service in the Washington vicinity as a carpenter and guard for Confederate prisoners; the service of his brother, James A. Low, of the 7th Regiment of Ohio Volunteers, at Fort McHenry and Fort Marshall, Baltimore, who offers advice on joining the army; and from other family members who describe the war as seen from the civilian perspective and relate the patriotic fervor during the reelection of Lincoln in 1864. There are also clippings and a pamphlet concerning the sixteenth reunion of the 1st Maine Heavy Artillery, 1892.

3281.    THOMAS LOW PAPERS, 1861-1865. 4 items and 1 vol. Pekin (Niagara County), N.Y.

    Letters and a diary of a sergeant, later lieutenant, in the Rocket Battalion Artillery, later 23rd Independent Battery, New York Volunteers. The diary, 1861-1863, portrays daily life of a soldier, low morals of the troops, intemperance, rumors, disease, and monotony. Entries made in Washington, D.C., include descriptions of mud, Congressional sessions, lectures at the Smithsonian, some poems, and an account of Fairfax Court House, Virginia. The diary also describes rockets and target practice; the sea journey to North Carolina; the U.S.S. *Monitor* off Fortress Monroe, Virginia; camp life at New Bern; opinions about draft evaders who fled to Canada; the attacks on

Washington, North Carolina, April, 1863; and the recruitment of Negro troops for the U.S. Army. The correspondence with family members includes a letter written at the hospital on City Point, Virginia, shortly before Low's death; it describes the reaction of the wounded to the news of Lee's surrender and mentions a visit by Abraham Lincoln.

3282. WILLIAM HARRISON LOWDERMILK PAPERS, 1863-1870. 3 vols. Cumberland (Allegany County), Md.

Lowdermilk's journal, 1864, 2 vols., describes service with 6th Kentucky Infantry and at the headquarters of the IV Corps of the Army of the Cumberland under the pseudonym Harry Morton. Included is an account of the Franklin-Nashville campaign, December, 1864. An autograph album, 1 vol., contains signatures of officers of the IV Corps. These volumes were used in the claim of Lowdermilk's widow for the pension of Harry Morton.

3283. CHARLES RUSSELL LOWELL AND CHARLES HENRY DALTON LETTERPRESS BOOK, 1861. 1 vol. Washington, D.C., and Boston, Mass.

Letters from the official agents in Washington, D.C., for the governor of Massachusetts, May 16-November 23, 1861, a position held successively by Lowell and, after May 23, by Dalton. There are almost daily letters to John Albion Andrew, governor of Massachusetts; and less frequent letters to high federal officials. Topics include federal authorization for the formation of state regiments; dates of departure of troops for Washington; rations and equipment; appointment of surgeons; the care of sick and wounded; the sale of the Massachusetts ships Cambridge and Pembroke to the federal government; events in Washington; the coastal defenses of Massachusetts; and the color of uniforms.

3284. JAMES RUSSELL LOWELL PAPERS, 1855-1890. 51 items. "Elmwood," Cambridge (Middlesex County), Mass.

Letters by Lowell, commenting on his lectures, a trip to Europe, desire for the appointment of one Cutler to the Harvard faculty, the difficulty of writing a poem for a special occasion, qualifications of Tom Talbot, illness, a falsehood told on Phillips Brooks, Hoar's ability as a toastmaster, and regrets that invitations cannot be accepted. There are also poems by Lowell; a social note by his wife, Frances D. Lowell, to Mrs. T. M. Wheeler; a poem by his aunt, Anna Cabot Lowell, a parody on an ode by Southey; a leaflet of the American Copyright League of which Lowell was president; and two calling cards.

3285. LOWELL STORE DAYBOOKS, 1877-1881. 2 vols. Lowell (Gaston County), N.C.

Records of a general merchandise store known as the Pin Hook Store until October, 1878, Pin Hook being a local name for Woodlawn Mills and also the name of the railroad station at Lowell.

3286. SIR GEORGE RIVERS LOWNDES PAPERS, 1915-1934. 57 items. Ringwood, Hampshire, England.

Correspondence addressed to Lowndes that concerns a variety of political, administrative, and judicial matters in which he was involved as law member of the council of the governor general of India, 1915-1920. Topics include the High Courts of Judicature in Bombay and Madras, the judicial committee of the Privy Council, appointments to the governors council, the Privy Council, the high courts and other courts; policies concerning military rank held by Afghans and Nepalese; a libel suit over statements in Sir Valentine Chirol's book, Indian Unrest; the Winchester War Memorial Committee; the Indian legislature; politics and government finance in Bombay; and Lowndes' pension.

3287. WILLIAM LOWNDES AND THOMAS LOWNDES LETTERS, 1795-1846. 8 items. Charleston, S.C.

Correspondence of William Lowndes (1782-1822), South Carolina legislator, 1806-1810, and member of U.S. Congress, 1811-1822; and of his brother, Thomas Lowndes (1776-1843), South Carolina legislator, 1796-1800, and member of U.S. Congress, 1801-1805. The letters are chiefly personal and include a description of William Lowndes's death at sea. Among the correspondents are John Connel, Robert Wilson Gibbes, and Thomas and William Lowndes.

3288. ALEXANDER LOWRANCE AND JOHN LOWRANCE PAPERS, 1749-1796. 6 items and 1 vol. Rowan County, N.C.

Ledger of a tavern, 1749-1796, 157 pp., recording the sale of rum and other liquor, with entries for purchases by John Dickey of Iredell County and other residents of Rowan, Iredell, and nearby counties. Alexander Lowrance was probably an early owner of the tavern; John Lowrance seems to have been the owner in 1791. The loose items are financial and legal notes, two of them concerning John Lowrance.

3289. MILES S. LOWRANCE ARITHMETIC BOOK, 1845. 1 vol. (49 pp.) Taylorsville (Alexander County), N.C.

Manuscript.

3290. ALICE LOWREY PAPERS, 1890-1903. 121 items. Oak Ridge (Guilford County), N.C.

Letters from former students who boarded at the Lowrey family home while they attended Oak Ridge Institute. The letters largely describe social activities and courtship. There is some mention of Montgomery, Alabama, and yellow fever there in 1897; and of the election of 1896 in Randolph County.

3291. EDWARD LUCAS AND WILLIAM LUCAS LETTERS, 1821-1868. 138 items. Charles Town (Jefferson County), W. Va.

Legal, business, and personal correspondence of Edward Lucas (1780-1858), lawyer, merchant, and politician, and member of the Virginia House of Delegates, 1819-1822, 1830, 1831, and of U. S. Congress, 1833-1837. Included is correspondence of William Lucas (1800-1877), member of the Virginia House of Delegates, 1838-1839, and of U. S. Congress, 1839-1841, 1843-1845, and delegate to the Virginia constitutional convention, 1850-1851. The letters contain references to the removal of the Indians from Alabama in 1833, John C. Calhoun, Henry Clay, Andrew Jackson, nullification, removal of bank deposits, and routine political letters concerning requests for positions, pensions, public lands, and general accounts of congressional activity. Included also are letters of Daniel B. Lucas, son of William Lucas, written while a student at the University of Virginia, Charlottesville, 1850, with comments on his studies and professors.

3292. EDWARD VERRALL LUCAS PAPERS. 1 item. London, England.

Letter commenting on the poetry of one Jeffrey.

3293. LUCAS-ASHLEY FAMILY PAPERS, 1830-1909. 24 items. Charlottesville (Albemarle County), Va., and Madison (Madison County), Fla.

Papers of the Lucas and Ashley families of Virginia, South Carolina, and Florida include a document, 1830, transferring ownership of a female slave; report cards, 1858, for Villeboro Female Seminary in Virginia; and letters concerning personal and family affairs, the effects of the Civil War on civilian life, particularly in Charlottesville, Virginia, reports of the burning of Brandon and Jackson, Mississippi, by Union troops and the activities of soldiers in the 17th South Carolina Regiment, and a description of student life at Greenville Military Academy, Greenville, South Carolina, in 1880.

3294. JOHN LUFTBURROW PAPERS, 1768. 1 item. Charleston, S.C.

Apprenticeship contract with John Eastburn, shipwright of Charleston.

3295. ALICE (HOUSTON) LUIGGI PAPERS, 1866 (1948-1952). 1,514 items. New York, N.Y.

Material gathered by Mrs. Luiggi while writing her book, 65 Valiants (University of Florida Press: 1965), on American teachers in Argentina, 1870-1888. The bulk of the collection consists of letters of various sources about each of the teachers, and notes taken in interviews, and from other sources. There are copies of letters of the 1870s and 1880s by Domingo Faustino Sarmiento and Mary Tyler (Peabody) Mann. The collection is arranged alphabetically by names of teachers. There is information on kindergartens in Boston, Saint Louis, and Washington, D.C.; and the Armstrong, Atkinson, Eccleston, and Stearns families. There are a diary of Sarah Eccleston, 1883-1886; pictures of Mrs. Mann and Sarmiento; and photographs of busts of Horace Mann and Abraham Lincoln.

3296. GEORGE LUMPKIN PAPERS, 1848, 1853. 2 items. Hermon (St. Lawrence County), N.Y.

Personal letters from George Lumpkin to his sister, with a discussion of religion, crops, economic conditions, and some mention of his brother.

3297. WILSON LUMPKIN PAPERS, 1833-1862. 6 items. Athens (Clarke County), Ga.

A commission signed by Lumpkin as governor of Georgia; family letters; a letter from Lumpkin's nephew, John H. Lumpkin, U.S. representative, evaluating Democratic candidates for president in 1856; and a letter by Crawford W. Long declining an invitation to join a medical school faculty.

3298. DAVID P. LUPTON PAPERS, 1889-1898. 4 items. Winchester (Frederick County), Va.

Personal letters.

3299. RILEY LUTHER PAPERS, 1860 (1862-1864) 1904. 40 items. Why Not (Randolph County), N.C.

Correspondence between a Confederate soldier and his wife. Luther served in Virginia and spent some time in the guardhouse in Greensboro, North Carolina. One letter, 1904, concerns the election of members to the Charleston, South Carolina, country club.

3300. THOMAS LYNCH AND MARY (BINGHAM) LYNCH PAPERS, 1794-1895. 599 items and 1 vol. Mason Hall (Orange County), N.C.

Personal correspondence of the families of Thomas Lynch and of his wife, Mary (Bingham) Lynch. Included is material relative to Thomas Lynch, Presbyterian minister of the Orange Presbytery, 1794-1869; to his son, W. B. Lynch, who conducted an academy at High Point, North Carolina; and to Major Robert Bingham, head of Bingham School at Mebane, North Carolina. There is also a ledger (1 vol., 88 pp., 1860-1881) and some correspondence and other business papers of Lemuel Lynch, brother of Thomas and a silversmith and jeweler of Hillsborough, North Carolina. The itemized ledger entries record repair work on jewelry, timepieces, and other items owned by many local residents.

3301. MARY A. LYNDALL PAPERS, 1855-1873. 35 items. Smithfield (Johnston County), N.C.

Papers of Mary Lyndell and her relatives, the Watsons, Higdons, Lyndalls, and Accinellys. Topics include the estate of Thomas Lyndall and his Missouri bonds; family affairs; yellow fever in Portsmouth and Norfolk, Virginia, 1855; battles on the Peninsula, 1862; the quality of Confederate officers; movements of the 50th Regiment of North Carolina troops; the behavior of Sherman's men toward civilians; and women's styles, 1868. Many of the letters are by G.B. Watson and W.B. Lyndall.

3302. JAMES LYONS PAPERS, 1826-1876. 5 items. Richmond, Va.

Correspondence of James Lyons (b. 1801), Virginia legislator and Confederate congressman, concerning an appointment for the former superintendent of the insane hospital at Williamsburg, Virginia, and delegates to the Southern Commercial Convention of 1858; and commenting on proposed legislation to expedite court action.

3303. JAMES LYTCH DAYBOOK, 1880-1889. 1 vol. Scotland County, N.C.

Records of sales and shipments of a cotton planter, sold especially in North Carolina, South Carolina, and Georgia.

3304. WILLIAM HENRY LYTTELTON, FIRST BARON LYTTELTON, LETTER BOOK, 1763-1766. 1 vol. London, England.

Copies of outgoing personal letters of Lyttelton, governor of Jamaica. Governmental affairs are discussed at various times, especially in letters to Lovell Stanhope, secretary of state, and Stephen Fuller, colonial agent. Appointment of a new agent, and commercial and military events are noted. Letters to John Hume, storekeeper of ordnance in South Carolina, mention politics there and trade, especially the shipment of garden seeds. Letters to merchants and bankers in England concern the governor's household goods, furniture, clothes, and financial affairs.

3305. BERNARD LYTTON-BERNARD PAPERS, 1913 (1915-1916) 1960. 51 items. Guadalajara, Mexico.

Correspondence between Lytton-Bernard (earlier known as Bernhard Trappschuh), physical culturalist of London, Chicago, and Guadalajara, and Francis Warrington Dawson II, of Versailles, France. Topics include health, Dawson's writings, the Fresh Air Art Society, and their respective careers.

3306. MAUREEN (COBB) MABBOTT PAPERS, 1929-1971. 182 items. New York, N.Y.

Letters from actress Blanche Yurka to Maureen (Cobb) Mabbott and her husband, Thomas Ollive Mabbott, professor and authority on the works of Edgar Allan Poe, and to her sister, Rose Yurka, discussing plays and movies in which she appeared, her travels abroad, several noted playwrights and actors, and mutual friends.

3307. ROBERT C. MABRY PAPERS, 1805 (1885-1897) 1931. 529 items and 8 vols. Ridgeway (Warren County), N.C.

Papers of Robert C. Mabry, merchant and farmer, consist of family and business correspondence containing sidelights on social life and customs and economic conditions; insurance policies; indentures; and copies of wills. The bulk of the family correspondence is that of Helen Mabry while a student at Greensboro Female College, Greensboro, North Carolina, 1895-1896. Several letters from Alice U. Goodman, future wife of Robert C. Mabry, describe living and working conditions of a schoolteacher in Louisa County, Virginia. Also included are a cashbook, 1858-1884; ledgers for general merchandise, 1852-1865; an invoice book for goods purchased, 1893; and account books, 1858-1882, for the mercantile firm of Mabry and Read, one of which also contains scattered birth and marriage records.

3308. WILLIAM MILLER McALLISTER PAPERS, 1854-1870. 143 items. Covington (Alleghany County), Va.

Correspondence of William Miller McAllister, Confederate soldier and attorney, while he was attending Virginia Military Institute, Lexington, Virginia, during the Civil War; and after the war as an attorney. Letters discuss life at the Farm School, [Covington?], and at Virginia Military Institute; military engagements, the reputation of the Army of the West, and the religious state of dying soldiers; and the Northern attitude toward the South. Included is an insurance policy with the Piedmont Real Estate Insurance Company.

3309. WILLIAM STEPHENS MATTHEW McALLISTER PAPERS, 1785-1893. 14 items. Savannah, Ga.

Business and legal papers of the McAllister family include a sale paper of the Georgia Land Company; a grand jury judgment; a petition of the grand jury of Jefferson County requesting reforms in the voting laws and in the criminal code; the will and estate papers of Richard McAllister; a deed for the purchase of the land of Josiah Tattnall, a Loyalist; and personal letters and invitations.

3310. ELLEN McALPIN PAPERS, 1832 (1848-1895) 1905. 107 items. Savannah, Ga.

Principally family letters to Laura J. (Bulloch) Locke, wife of Joseph L. Locke, while the family was living in Grafenburg, Germany, and in Italy. While most of the letters are nearly illegible, one letter, 1856, describes life in Venice. There are also several letters from Savannah, Georgia, during the Civil War containing references to the progress of the war, and letters to Ellen McAlpin from her sister, Georgia, a schoolteacher in Saint Paul, Minnesota.

3311. JAMES WALLACE McALPIN PAPERS, 1853-1897. 178 items. Savannah, Ga.

Chiefly the letters of Maria Sophia (Champion) McAlpin to her husband, James Wallace McAlpin, a Georgia rice planter, and several letters to her father, Aaron Champion. Also included are a few letters from their sons, Henry and James McAlpin, several financial papers, a newspaper clipping about General Frederick Townsend, and a family tree for James and Maria McAlpin.

3312. MELCHOR RAFAEL DE MACANAZ MANUSCRIPT, [1722?]. 144 pp. Spain.

Copy of a political work ascribed to Melchor Rafael de Macanaz (1670-1760), Spanish statesman and author, entitled "Auxilios para bien governar una Monarquia." The work purports to date from 1722, but the date of the manuscript is uncertain as it is probably a copy. "Auxilios" was published by Don Antonio Valladares de Sotomayor in 1788 as part of his _Semanario Erudito_, and in 1789 as a separate volume.

3313. ARTHUR MacARTHUR LETTER BOOK, 1900. 1 vol. (514 pp.) Manila, Philippine Islands.

Typed copies of the official correspondence of Major General Arthur MacArthur (1845-1912), military governor of the Division of the Philippines, concerning the administration of the insular government and its transition from military to civilian government. Letters discuss commissary affairs, customs, internal revenue, currency, budgets, banking, judicial system, education, especially instruction in English, the Philippine Civil Service Board, sanitation, markets, bridges and highways, the reorganization of the auditing department, and the conflict of authority between MacArthur and William Howard Taft, head of the commission to restore civilian control.

3314. CHARLES E. MACARTHY PAPERS, 1878-1914. 11 items. Forsyth (Monroe County), Ga.

Chiefly letters of patent granted by the U.S. Patent Office to Macarthy, whose inventions included several pulley devices for improving horsepower, a cotton press, and railroad car couplings.

3315. GEORGE MACARTNEY, FIRST EARL MACARTNEY, PAPERS, 1779-1798. 158 items. London, England.

The papers of George Macartney, (1737-1806), British diplomat and colonial governor, are principally letters, 1781-1784, from Sir Edward Hughes, British naval commander-in-chief in Asia, while Macartney was governor and president of Madras, concerning naval operations against the Dutch and the French; military operations of Sir John Brathwaite and Eccles Nixon in southern India and of Sir Eyre Coote in northern India; accounts of sea battles; and peace settlements with Mahrattas in 1782, with the French in 1783, and with Mysore in 1784. Other correspondence relates to his duties as ambassador to China, 1792-1794, and as governor of the Cape of Good Hope, 1796-1798. Included are letters discussing prisoner exchange with the Americans at Martinique, 1779; revenue administration, 1781; the conflict between civil and military authority in Madras, 1783; missionary work in China, 1795; the East India Company factory at Canton and Macao, China, 1796; the Chinese viceroy at Canton and the embassy to China, 1796; the campaign of John Hudleston to become a director of the East India Company and the hostility of Henry Dundas, 1797; the refusal of the Court of Directors to grant the government an interest-free loan, 1797; war with France and the defense of Ireland, 1797; the proposed expedition against Manila, Philippines, 1797; the disposition of Tipu Sultan and his army in Mysore, 1797; the accession of Vizri Ali as Nabob of Oudh, and the possible attack on Hindustan by Zemaun Shah, 1797; war prizes, 1798; and the water and drainage system at Cape Town, 1798, and other routine and administrative matters. Also included are bills and receipts of Lord and Lady Macartney. Among the correspondents are Henry Baring, John Byron, Sir Alured Clarke, Sir James Henry Craig, William Fullarton, W. Greene, John Hudleston, Sir Edward Hughes, Sir Andrew Mitchell, Mr. Plumb, George Proctor, Sir George Leonard Staunton, and Willem Stephanus van Ryneveld.

3316. ZACHARY MACAULAY PAPERS, 1812.
1 item. London, England.

Letter from Zachary Macaulay (1768-1838), British philanthropist and figure in the movement to abolish the slave trade, to Captain Close recommending Robert Grant, a barrister who was "new in the cause," for Close's advocate, and noting a meeting that Grant and his brother Charles would attend.

3317. VARDRY ALEXANDER McBEE PAPERS, 1818-1857. 26 items. Lincolnton (Lincoln County), N.C.

Family letters to Vardry A. McBee discussing financial difficulties, how to make a carriage, railroad development in the Carolinas and Georgia, contracts let for a railroad into Greenville (South Carolina), road construction, a remedy for a cold, the admission of California as a free state, the construction of a steam sawmill, a runaway slave, sickness among slaves, arrangements for the care of several slaves, and the transfer of the management of a cotton factory and paper mill from Alexander McBee to Vardry McBee.

3318. ANDREW JAY McBRIDE PAPERS, 1861-1879. 94 items. Fayetteville (Fayette County) and Atlanta, Ga.

Letters of Andrew Jay McBride, a Confederate officer, to Mary Frances Johnson whom he married in 1864, mainly concerning personal matters and their courtship, but also describing the life of a soldier, conditions in Williamsburg, Virginia, during the war; military engagements, including the first battle of Manassas, the fighting at Hampton (Virginia) and Russellville (Tennessee), the assault on Fort London at Knoxville (Tennessee), the battle of the Wilderness, and the battle of Jonesboro (Georgia); Sherman's march through Georgia; the arming of Negroes for military service; and business ventures at the end of and after the war.

3319. JOHN McBRIDE PAPERS, 1845-1846.
3 items. Abbeville (Abbeville County), S.C.

Business letters of the mercantile firm of McBride and Posey concerning money borrowed and notes due.

3320. WILLIAM GORDON McCABE PAPERS, 1865-1917. 5 items. Petersburg (Dinwiddie County), Va.

Papers of William Gordon McCabe, schoolmaster and author, include a eulogistic poem by McCabe written in honor of General John Pegram after his death at the battle of Hatcher's Run during the Civil War; a letter, 1888, from Herbert Baxter Adams concerning McCabe's writings and a proposed legislative grant to the College of William and Mary, Williamsburg, Virginia; a note, 1916, from James Montgomery Beck; a letter, 1917, from William C. Whittle, a lieutenant on the C.S.S. Shenandoah, concerning pamphlets about the ship written by himself and by Cornelius E. Hunt, another crew member; and a genealogy of the McCabe family.

3321. ALEXANDER McCALL PAPERS, 1847-1851.
7 items. Nashville (Davidson County), Tenn.

Business letters from John Ramage to Dr. Alexander McCall dealing with salt sales, speculation, and transportation in Alabama; cotton prices and speculation; sales and purchases of slaves; and president Zachary Taylor.

3322. DUNCAN McCALL AND DUGAL McCALL PAPERS, 1832-1874. 2 items and 3 vols. Tensas County, La., and Claiborne County, Miss.

Plantation journals and accounts of a small Mississippi corn farmer, Dugal McCall, and of his son, Duncan, cotton planter and corn grower of Louisiana, recording daily activities, cotton picked by individual slaves, supplies issued to slaves, and lists of slaves. There are references to Oakland College (the site of Alcorn Agricultural and Mechanical College), close to Dugal McCall's farm; the nearby town of Rodney in Jefferson County; lumber hauled to the college; a boardinghouse; the behavior of the students; and Mr. Dimitry of the board of trustees. The main entries relate to personal matters and plantation affairs, including attendance at Methodist churches by Dugal in Claiborne and Jefferson counties, Mississippi, and attendance at Baptist churches by Duncan in both Louisiana and Mississippi; visits to and from friends; the weather; tasks performed by the slaves; brickmaking; purchases of supplies; the planting of fruit trees; the sale of agricultural products; the cultivation, ginning, and pressing of cotton; elections and voting on the Whig ticket; the sale of wood to captains of steamboats; trips to Natchez, Mississippi, by boat; and credit arrangements with a New Orleans commission merchant.

3323. HUGH McCALL PAPERS, 1802-1824.
9 items. Savannah, Ga.

Papers of Hugh McCall, Georgia historian, include the inspection roll of Captain Hugh McCall's Company; letters concerning McCall's duties as military storekeeper in Savannah, including one from Quartermaster General Thomas Sidney Jesup; letter from William Williams relative to published court reports; letter from McCall to Joseph Jones requesting historical data on Jones's family; letter from McCall to John Clark, governor of Georgia, concerning the imprisonment and trial of General Hopkins and his son; and a letter from Edmund Pendleton Gaines pertaining to the yellow fever epidemic in Savannah in 1820.

3324. REBECCA MARIAH (OXFORD) McCALL PAPERS, 1780-1934. 380 items and 1 vol. Gamewell (Caldwell County), N.C.

Papers of Rebecca Mariah (Oxford) McCall (b. 1833) consist of deeds, indentures and other legal papers; items concerning the settlement of an estate, possibly that of Rebecca McCall; financial papers; items relating to the Anderson family, especially Leland Anderson of Lenoir, North Carolina; letters from the brothers of Rebecca McCall, William C. Oxford, James Oxford, and Sion Harrington Oxford, during their military service with the Confederate Army; and a ledger of A. B. Oxford.

3325. JOHN MOORE McCALLA PAPERS, 1785-1917. 1,813 items and 40 vols. Lexington (Fayette County), Ky., and Washington, D.C.

Personal, business, financial, military, and legal correspondence and papers, pamphlets, journals, letter books, ledgers, and clippings comprise the papers of John Moore McCalla (b. 1793), lawyer, politician, and brigadier general of the Kentucky militia. Correspondence discusses personal matters; the presidential elections of 1844, 1848, and 1852; the gubernatorial campaign in Kentucky, 1844-1845, between William O. Butler and William Owsley; Henry Clay; the Whig and Democratic parties; Democratic political patronage; the Mexican War; the annexation of Texas and Oregon and its effects on foreign affairs; the activities of McCalla and others in the American Party; life in Michigan; the preservation of the Union; the inauguration of Abraham Lincoln and the coming of the Civil War; the military and political situation during the Civil War; various business ventures, including the litigation and disputes surrounding a portable gas patent and the development of a factory in Texas to manufacture meat biscuits; and claims against the U.S. government. Other papers relate to McCalla's duties as U.S. marshal for the District of Kentucky, ca. 1829-1841, and his service as 2nd auditor in the Treasury Department, 1845-1849, which involved the business of the U.S. Army during the Mexican War. Military papers include militia rosters, accounts, courts-martial papers, and correspondence and two articles written by McCalla concerning the performance of the Kentucky Volunteer Militia during the War of 1812. Legal papers consist of deeds, wills, claims, leases, contracts, indentures, and papers dealing with the settlement of estates and McCalla's legal practice. Clippings relate to politics, temperance, Presbyterianism in Lexington, Presbyterian clergymen, the Ladies' Union Benevolent Society, woman and child labor, and the Lexington Light Infantry. Other papers include the correspondence of McCalla's father, Dr. Andrew J. McCalla, including several letters discussing the treatment of mental patients and the Eastern Lunatic Asylum in Lexington, Kentucky, which Andrew McCalla helped found; the correspondence of Sally Page Andrews of Shepherdstown, West Virginia; the correspondence of John Moore McCalla, Jr., and his wife, Helen Varnum (Hill) McCalla, concerning family matters, travel, and the handling of several estates left to Helen McCalla; correspondence and business papers relating to the real estate holdings of the Hills and the Varnums; letters from several former McCalla slaves, who had colonized in Liberia, concerning conditions there, 1834-1836; an original poem by William O. Butler on the battle at River Raisin (Frenchtown), Michigan, in 1813; papers relating to a house built by Hornblower and Marshall for John and Helen McCalla in 1887; guardianship reports of Joseph B. Varnum, Jr., for his niece, Helen Hill; and bills and receipts.

Volumes include letter books, 1830-1868, containing the business and personal correspondence of John M. McCalla; ledgers containing newspaper clippings, financial accounts, weather reports, an index to cases in Congress in the 1850s, and an accounting of property rental and construction; a pamphlet, 1839, with an address given at the fiftieth anniversary of the Lexington Light Infantry; a notebook, 1844, of notes on the Bank of the United States, the Land Distribution Bill, the tariff, Henry Clay, the Texas question, and the Whig-controlled 27th Congress; account books and literary and art notebooks of Helen Louise Sargent; a volume containing family cookery, medical receipts, and household accounts in ante-bellum Washington, D.C.; a journal, 1860-1861, of Dr. John M. McCalla, Jr., as agent for the U. S. government in the return of Negroes captured from a slaver, describing his journey to Liberia, the political and social conditions there, and life in Washington, D.C., in 1861; ledgers to the estates left to Helen McCalla; and a gift book from the 1890s.

3326. WILLIAM H. McCANNON DAYBOOK, 1818-1821. 1 vol. (395 pp.) Westminster (Carroll County), Md.

Records of a general merchant.

3327. GEORGE A. McCARTER PAPERS, 1849-1862. 9 items. York County, S.C.

Family letters concerning personal matters and money, and three letters relating to the Civil War.

3328. JOHN GRAY McCARTER PAPERS, 1862-1866. 1 item and 1 vol. Milford (Worcester County), Mass.

Papers of John Gray McCarter, a carpenter, and a soldier in the 25th Regiment, Massachusetts Volunteer Infantry, consist of miscellaneous orders and correspondence related to his service in the commissary and the quartermaster's departments, and an application for a leave of absence.

3329. WILLIAM McCAULEY LEDGER, 1892-1906. 1 vol. (245 pp.) Beaver Creek District (Washington County), Md.

Ledger, 1892, of a business handling grain, cattle, sheep, and hogs; and accounts, 1895-1906, of general merchandise and farm records of William McCauley.

3330. HENRY KENT McCAY PAPERS, 1881-1885. 2 items. Atlanta, Ga.

Papers of Henry K. McCay (1820-1886), lawyer, Confederate soldier, member of the Georgia constitutional convention of 1868, and judge of the U.S. district court of northern Georgia, 1882-1886, concerning a visit to White Sulphur Springs, West Virginia, and a school for the blind in Philadelphia, Pennsylvania.

3331. ROBERT ANDERSON McCLELLAN PAPERS, 1861-1907. 41 items. Athens (Limestone County), Ala.

Chiefly the Civil War letters of Robert Anderson McClellan, 7th Regiment, Alabama Cavalry, to members of his family discussing civilian and military conditions in Alabama, Georgia, and Tennessee during the war; desertion; Union sentiment in Tennessee; the campaigns at Fort Donelson, Tennessee, and Raleigh, North Carolina; speculation in Georgia; and Abraham Lincoln and Braxton Bragg. Also included is an obituary notice of McClellan in 1898.

3332. ROBERT McCLELLAND PAPERS, 1855. 1 item. Detroit, Mich.

Copy of a letter from McClelland (1807-1880), lawyer, congressman, 1843-1849, governor of Michigan, 1851-1853, and secretary of the interior, 1853-1857, to Martin H. Johnson concerning fees for medical services rendered by Johnson while employed by the Department of the Interior.

3333. JACOB McCORD PAPERS, 1848-1861. 11 items. Winchester (Frederick County), Va.

Personal correspondence of a Virginia family, including two letters from friends or relatives in Iowa describing economic conditions there and prices of commodities.

3334. SAMUEL EUSEBIUS McCORKLE PAPERS, 1786-1789. 7 items. Thyatira (Rowan County), N.C.

Sermons by Samuel Eusebius McCorkle (1746-1811), Presbyterian minister at Thyatira Church, teacher at his classical school, Zion-Parnassus, and trustee of the University of North Carolina, including one entitled "The Anniversary of American Independence, July 24, 1786."

3335. CYRUS HALL McCORMICK PAPERS, 1855-1861. 8 items. Chicago, Ill.

Business correspondence pertaining to the sale of reapers invented by Cyrus McCormick (1809-1884); and a personal letter.

3336. McCORMICK & PRICE DAYBOOK, 1886-1899. 1 vol. (194 pp.) Berryville (Clarke County), Va.

Records of a general mercantile business.

3337. MOSES McCOWN PAPERS, 1839. 1 item. Orange County, N.C.

Survey of the land of Moses McCown, miller, on which Cole's Mill was located.

3338. JESSIE MARION (WALL) McCOY PAPERS, 1941-1943. 73 items. Randleman (Randolph County), N.C.

Letters to Jessie McCoy while in nurse's training at Duke University, from soldiers discussing training, camp life, entertainment for the troops, personal matters, Duke University, and football; and from her mother, Marion A. Wall, stationed in Ft. Des Moines, Iowa, while serving in the Women's Army Auxiliary Corps describing her duties and activities, and social life in Des Moines and Ft. Des Moines.

3339. WILLIAM E. McCOY PAPERS, 1849-1871. 21 items. Augusta (Richmond County), Ga.

Chiefly the letters of William E. McCoy, 1st Regiment, Georgia Volunteers, C.S.A., to his parents, Charles and Frances (Tutt) McCoy, discussing his duties; the hardships of army life; military maneuvers; morale; the reorganization of the Confederate Army; the purchase of supplies; life in Americus, Georgia; and the activities of the Furlow Masonic Female College. Two letters from Lieutenant Tom Tutt, 1st Regiment, Georgia Volunteers, describe the fighting in western Virginia at Laurel Mill and Carrick's Ford and the retreat of Confederate troops.

3340. EDWARD McCRADY, SR., PAPERS, 1861. 1 item. Charleston, S.C.

Letter from Edward McCrady, Jr. (1833-1903), lawyer, legislator and historian, to his father, Edward McCrady, Sr., lawyer and theologian, while serving in the 1st Regiment, South Carolina Volunteers, describing in detail the murder of one Axson by a Georgian named Davis, and the ramifications of the action.

3341. JAMES BENNETT McCREARY DIARY, 1862-1864. 1 vol. (75 pp.) Richmond (Madison County), Ky.

Typed copy of a war diary kept by James B. McCreary (1838-1918), governor of Kentucky, 1875-1878, and lieutenant colonel in the Confederate Army, giving an account of General John Hunt Morgan's raid, 1863, north of the Ohio River, and of life in Kentucky and Tennessee during the Civil War.

3342. NATHANIEL McCREARY PAPERS, 1863. 4 items. Dorchester (Norfolk County), Mass.

Letters from Nathaniel McCreary, a steel polisher, and soldier in the 42nd Massachusetts Regiment, U.S.A., while a prisoner of war in Houston, Texas, and New Orleans, Louisiana, describing the camp for paroled prisoners at Bayou Gentilly near New Orleans, rations, visits to New Orleans, and mail service.

3343. WILLIAM G. McCREARY PAPERS, 1864-1865. 10 items. Champaign County, Ohio.

Chiefly letters to William G. McCreary or his family from U.S. soldiers describing conditions in Atlanta, Georgia, after its capture by Union troops; Sherman's march through Georgia and the Carolinas; and the Patent Office and the Capitol in Washington, D.C.

3344. CARSON (SMITH) McCULLERS PAPERS. 1 item. Nyack (Rockland County), N.Y.

Typed, inscribed copy of a short story by Carson McCullers (1917-1967), author, entitled "A Tree. A Rock. A Cloud."

3345. JAMES M. McCULLOCH PAPERS, 1861-1865. 1 vol. Petersburg (Dinwiddie County), Va.

Ledger of a tobacco firm, probably McEnery & McCulloch, which manufactured chewing tobacco.

3346. JAMES W. McCULLOCH PAPERS, 1863. 2 items. Georgia.

Letters from James W. McCulloch, a Confederate soldier stationed near Fredericksburg, Virginia, concerning camp life, difficulties of a journey to camp after a furlough, and need for clothing.

3347. HENRY McCULLOH PAPERS, 1745-1763. 3 items and 3 vols. London, England.

The papers of Henry McCulloh (ca. 1700-ca. 1779) consist of a deed, 1745, granting land in North Carolina to McCulloh, with notes on the back relating to the payment of quitrents and forfeiture of the land some twenty years later; a copy of the proposed stamp duties on the American colonies as formulated by McCulloh; copies of minutes of a conference with McCulloh concerning the stamp duties; and three essays. One essay relates to his service from 1739 to 1745 as Inspector for Improving the Quit Rents for North and South Carolina, and contains general proposals and complaints concerning the inefficiency of colonial administration, and pleas for his salary. A Miscellaneous Essay with Respect to Our Great Boards, to the Exchequer and to America (1762) proposes and discusses various administrative reforms for the British government, including colonial administration. McCulloh discusses the theory and practice of the royal government and reviews its organization since the reign of Queen Elizabeth I in "A Treatise Endeavouring to Demonstrate That Let Who Will Be Entrusted with the Direction or Management of Our Publick Concerns, They Will Be Liable to an Infinite Number of Misstakes and Inadvertencies in the Whole of Their Conduct Unless They Restore the Ancient System of Our Publick Boards, On the Doing of Which the Dignity and Safety of This Crown and Kingdom, Seem in a Great Measure to Depend."

3348. GEORGE McCULLOUGH PAPERS, 1969. 2 items. New York, N.Y.

Letters from Lester G. Maddox, governor of Georgia, 1967-1971, and Walter E. Washington, mayor commissioner, 1967-1975, and mayor, 1975--, of Washington, D.C., in response to congratulatory letters from McCullough. Maddox commented on the political situation in Georgia concerning the state's budget.

3349. McCULLOUGH-HUTCHISON FAMILY PAPERS, 1823-1936. 147 items. Fairfield County, S.C.

Papers of the McCullough and Hutchison families include letters, 1820s-1850s, from relatives in Caugherty Lisbunny, and Ballymoney, Ireland, discussing agricultural conditions, currency matters, and religious conflict between Protestants and Catholics; letters, 1883-1900, from friends and relatives in Texas; and official papers, 1886-1889, including arrest warrants and other legal notices, relating to Robert Hutchison's duties as constable.

3350. WILLIAM McCUTCHEON PAPERS, 1807 (1820-1864) 1867. 26 items. Sumter District, S.C.

Papers relating to the affairs of the McCutcheon family and to the estate of William Wilden, of which William McCutcheon was executor. Included also is a fragmentary diary kept by a Miss Clarke of South Carolina during the Civil War while serving as a nurse in the Midway Hospital in Charlottesville, Virginia.

3351. JOHN A. McDADE PAPERS, 1831-1876. 216 items. Cedar Grove (Orange County), N.C.

Personal and business papers of John A. McDade, tobacco planter, include letters from friends and relatives discussing prices, crops, weather, politics, and health; letters from H. Lee McDade, son of John A. McDade, while serving in the Confederate Army, describing camp life, food, prices, disease, military operations, and his months as a prisoner of war at Point Lookout, Maryland; postwar correspondence and other papers relating to economic difficulties, including a notice of bankruptcy and a broadside concerning the sale of land; a notice of persons killed and wounded during the war; and a religious poem.

3352. W. T. McDADE AND COMPANY DAYBOOK, 1877. 1 vol. (339 pp.) Eatonton (Putnam County), Ga.

Accounts of W. T. McDade and Company, selling various kinds of liquor, "drinks," tobacco products, and foodstuffs.

3353. McDANIEL AND LEE PAPERS, 1823 (1840s) 1864. 667 items. Lynchburg (Campbell County), Va.

Business papers of the merchandising firm of McDaniel and Lee including letters discussing commodity prices in Virginia, bills, receipts, accounts, and other miscellaneous mercantile papers.

3354. PETER McDAVID PAPERS, 1861 (1862-1864) 1912. 21 items. Greenville (Greenville County), S.C.

Family correspondence and letters of Peter McDavid, a Confederate soldier, concerning military movements in Tennessee and Virginia and his enduring faith in the Confederacy.

3355. CHARLES JAMES McDONALD PAPERS, 1842, 1859. 2 items. Marietta (Cobb County), Ga.

Letter from Charles James McDonald, governor of Georgia, 1839-1843, and justice on the state supreme court, 1855-1859, to Dr. William H. Pritchard, discussing economic conditions in Georgia, the affairs of the Central Bank, and opposition in the interior of the state to control from Savannah and Augusta; and a letter from McDonald concerning a legal matter and his retirement from the court.

3356. FURMAN McDONALD PAPERS, 1883-1903. 34 items. Privateer (Sumter County), S.C.

Personal letters to Furman McDonald, lecturer and historian, from his aunt, "Ann," concerning personal matters, with references to political affairs, to Clemson College (Clemson, South Carolina), and to articles written by McDonald; business letters principally from Mrs. D. Eli Dunlap, a teacher, relating to the Presbyterian Mission School in Leslie, South Carolina, for the Catawba Indians; and a biographical sketch of Richard Furman.

3357. MARSHALL McDONALD PAPERS, 1777 (1819-1896) 1926. 5,088 items and 2 vols. Washington, D.C.

Papers of Marshall McDonald (b. 1835; also spelled MacDonald), ichthyologist, inventor, and teacher, include correspondence, 1820s, of his father, Angus William MacDonald, a fur trader and Indian fighter, relating to the St. Louis Missouri Fur Company of which Angus was a partner, and fur trading trips, containing descriptions of several Indian tribes including the Sioux and Arikaras; family correspondence, 1830s-1850s, of the Griggs and Berry families; Civil War correspondence and orders containing information on the war in Virginia, McDonald's activities at New Orleans (Louisiana) and Vicksburg (Mississippi), the first battle of Manassas, the Vicksburg campaign, and logistics and the transportation of supplies; Civil War military papers, chiefly 1862-1863, while McDonald was ordnance officer at Vicksburg for the Department of Mississippi and Eastern Louisiana, including invoices of ordnance and ordnance stores, requisitions, receipts, slave rolls, a report of enemy operations in West Virginia, 1864, and a list of free Negroes turned over to the engineers at Fort Anderson; postwar correspondence of the McCormick family, and correspondence between McDonald and Mary E. McCormick before and after their marriage, including references, 1866-1874, to Robert E. Lee and his family, and to life at Virginia Military Institute, Lexington, Virginia; correspondence, 1876-ca. 1895, relating to McDonald's service on various commissions pertaining to fish, including U.S. commissioner of fish and fisheries, discussing ideas for inventions of fish hatching devices, the distribution of young fish, the patented McDonald Fishway, the methods of fish culture in Europe and the United States and visits to various fisheries; correspondence and lists of members and dues paid, 1890-1894, of the National Society of the Daughters of the American Revolution of which Mary McDonald was treasurer general, 1890-1892; several items pertaining to the Sons of the American Revolution; lists, notes, writings, drawings, and printed material relating to fish; a volume containing notes on military tactics, supplies, and the organization of the 1st Army Corps of the Confederate Army; and a letterpress book, 1888-1892, containing McDonald's correspondence while U.S. Fish Commissioner.

3358. JOHN McDONOGH PAPERS, (1802-1851) 1950. 103 items. New Orleans, La.

Business and personal correspondence of John McDonogh (1799-1850), New Orleans merchant and philanthropist; and a newspaper article, 1950, on McDonogh's career.

3359. ANGUS DOUGAL McDOUGALL PAPERS, 1969. 1 vol. Durham, N.C.

Photocopies of pencil drawings by McDougall, officer at the Control Desk of Perkins Library, Duke University. Entitled "Impressions from a Desk," the drawings depict students, faculty and staff members, and visitors.

3360. SUSAN McDOWALL DIARY AND SCRAPBOOK, 1856-1880. 1 vol. (116 pp.) Camden (Kershaw County), S.C.

Diary of Susan McDowall (1840-1923) describing school and social life at Patapsco Institute, Ellicott's Mills, Maryland, in 1856; clippings of poems and biographical notes; and a note written after the death of her father, William Douglas McDowall (1808-1879).

3361. CHARLES McDOWELL PAPERS, 1782. 1 item. Quaker Meadows (Burke County), N.C.

Letter from General Charles McDowell (ca. 1743-1815) to Colonel Dixon containing an order to raise men, arms, horses, and supplies, and to rendezvous on the Catawba River for service.

3362. JAMES McDOWELL II PAPERS, 1767-1888. 756 items. Lexington (Rockbridge County), Va.

Personal, family, and business correspondence of James McDowell II (1795-1851), governor of Virginia, 1843-1846, and U.S. representative, 1846-1851, consists chiefly of correspondence from McDowell's plantation overseers relating to affairs of his various estates. There are also references to land speculation; bank matters; local financial affairs; and politics, especially in letters from his brother-in-law, Thomas Hart Benton. A few papers pertain to James McDowell I, colonel in the Virginia Militia, and to James McDowell III, M. D.

3363. KATHERINE SHERWOOD (BONNER) MacDOWELL PAPERS, 1877. 1 item. Galveston (Galveston County), Tex.

Letter from Sherwood Bonner (1849-1883), short story writer and novelist, to Daniel L. Milliken, editor of <u>Cottage Hearth Magazine</u>, discussing her daily life in Texas and her intention to write a new novel. The letter is published in "An Annotated and Indexed Edition of the Letters of Sherwood Bonner" by Jean Nosser Biglane.

3364. THOMAS DAVID SMITH McDOWELL PAPERS, 1798-1891. 276 items. Elizabethtown (Bladen County), N.C.

Personal and business correspondence and legal papers of Thomas D.S. McDowell (1823-1898), North Carolina legislator and Confederate congressman. Correspondence contains references to politics, and to affairs at the University of North Carolina and in Chapel Hill, North Carolina. Also included are deeds, land grants, wills, and records of land and timber transactions.

3365. WILLIAM McDOWELL ACCOUNT BOOK, 1834-1836. 1 vol. Virginia.

Account book of a business establishment, apparently a tavern, giving customers' accounts for board, etc.

3366. GEORGE McDUFFIE PAPERS, 1819-1870. 251 items. Abbeville (Abbeville County), S.C.

Personal, business, and political correspondence and papers of George McDuffie (ca. 1788-1851), lawyer, U.S. congressman, 1821-1834, governor of South Carolina, 1834-1836, and U.S. senator, 1842-1846. Included are correspondence discussing Nullification, states' rights, tariffs, the Whig Party, the Mexican War, John C. Calhoun, William H. Harrison, and Martin Van Buren; family accounts; indentures; and other records.

3367. MARY SINGLETON McDUFFIE PAPERS, 1849-1872. 41 items. Cherry Hill (Berkeley County), S.C.

Papers of Mary Singleton McDuffie (b. 1830), daughter of George McDuffie and wife of Wade Hampton, are chiefly correspondence with Armistead Burt concerning the management and settlement of her father's estate. Also included are correspondence discussing personal and family matters; genealogical material; and a portrait of Mary Singleton (McDuffie) Hampton.

3368. D. T. McEACHIN ACCOUNT BOOK, 1869-1877. 1 vol. Gold Hill (Davie County), N.C.

Accounts of D. T. McEachin, apparently a general merchant and blacksmith.

3369. S. A. McELWEE PAPERS, 1855. 4 items. Due West (Abbeville County), S.C.

Personal letters by S. A. McElwee while a student at Erskine College, Due West, South Carolina.

3370. ELIZA J. McEWEN PAPERS, 1862-1863. 5 items.

Civil War letters of A. D. McEwen, Confederate soldier, to his sister, Eliza J.

McEwen, while stationed at Fort Fisher, North Carolina, describing life at the fort, fishing, illness and death, prayer meetings, weather, and the activities of the blockaders and blockade runners.

3371.  ALLEN McFARLANE PAPERS, 1860-1867. 11 items. Chesterfield District, S.C.

Papers relating to the purchase of slaves, 1860, by Allen McFarlane, a South Carolina planter and president of the Cheraw and Coalfields Railroad Company; a letter, May, 1862, addressed to the Cheraw Presbyterian Church, asking for the bells of that church for a Confederate foundry; a requisition for slaves, February, 1865, for the defenses of South Carolina; and contracts between McFarlane and certain freedmen, 1866-1867.

3372.  JAMES McFARLANE PAPERS, 1892-1898. 6 items. Towanda (Bradford County), Pa.

Business papers.

3373.  ALEXANDER McFARLIN PAPERS, 1815-1821. 1 vol. Washington, D.C.

Commonplace book containing poetry and miscellaneous financial records.

3374.  McGAVOCK CONFEDERATE CEMETERY RECORD BOOK, 1864-1900. 84 pp. Franklin (Williamson County), Tenn.

Photocopy of the record book of the Confederate soldiers buried in McGavock's Confederate Cemetery after the battle of Franklin, Tennessee, on November 30, 1864. Also included are clippings on Colonel John McGavock.

3375.  WILLIAM McGAW AND JOHN McGAW PAPERS, 1773-1816. 12 items. Abbeville (Abbeville County), S.C.

Land indentures concerning members of the McGaw family.

3376.  LILY McGEE PAPERS, 1893-1894. 11 items. Van Buren (Crawford County), Ark.

Correspondence of Lily McGee related to a tableau to be presented at a convention of the United Confederate Veterans, in which Lily McGee was to represent her state. Included is a letter from Henry Clay Fairman to Albert Capers Guerry, requesting that Guerry paint portraits of the tableau cast for the International Exposition to be held in Atlanta, Georgia, in 1895.

3377.  McGEHEE-ROWLETT FAMILIES PAPERS, 1819-1847. 4 items. Halifax County, Va.

Correspondence of the McGehee and Rowlett families concerning religion, camp meetings, and the collection by Brother Perry of $50,000 for a religious institute to be established in Nashville, Tennessee.

3378.  CHARLES MACGILL PAPERS, 1786 (1830-1878) 1906. 1,038 items. Hagerstown (Washington County), Md.

Personal, business, political, and professional correspondence of Charles Macgill, Maryland surgeon and Confederate sympathizer, and of his family. Prior to the Civil War, the correspondence contains references to Macgill's political affiliations as a Van Buren elector in 1836; and numerous letters from Francis Thomas (1799-1876), member of the Maryland legislature and governor of Maryland, 1841-1843, relative to politics and to the marital scandal in which Thomas was involved. Included also are documents bearing Thomas's signature commissioning Macgill as lieutenant colonel and later as colonel of the Maryland militia; several letters to Charles Macgill from his brother, James, stationed on the U.S.S. Potomac, relative to naval activities at Vera Cruz in 1847; and letters and circulars of the 1850s relative to Macgill's standing in his profession and his position as a member of the standing committee of the Medical and Chirurgical Faculty of Maryland.

The correspondence, following Macgill's imprisonment, October 1, 1861, first at Fort Lafayette, New York, and later at Fort Warren, Boston, Massachusetts, for his Confederate sympathies, bears on the divided sympathies of Maryland as a border state. Included are the letters of Charles Macgill and of his wife containing comments on his impatience and his treatment while imprisoned (until November, 1862); imprisonment of his son, James, at different times; willful neglect of Confederate wounded; depredations against persons and property of Confederate sympathizers by Unionists; nursing sick and wounded Confederates by his wife, daughters, and nieces; high prices; agricultural activities; local gossip; and persons required to take the oath of allegiance, and indignities suffered by them upon refusal. Included also are letters from Francis Thomas relative to Macgill's refusal to take the oath of allegiance.

Warned not to return to Hagerstown in 1865, the family moved to Richmond Virginia, and Macgill entered into partnership with George Proctor Kane (1820-1878) in the Roanoke Tobacco Company of Danville, Virginia. Numerous letters and papers concerned with the venture, 1865-1869, throw light on tobacco prices, machinery for its manufacture, possibility of combining scrap tobacco with bone dust for fertilizer, and numerous business transactions of the firm. Papers during the 1870s are concerned with the trial of Macgill by the Richmond Academy of Medicine for a minor breach of professional ethics. After 1877 the collection contains recommendations from political figures for General James Macgill, son of Dr. Charles Macgill, to aid the former in obtaining the office of commissioner to mark the graves of Confederate soldiers.

3379.   JOHN D. McGILL PAPERS, 1834-1850. 59 items. Middlesex (King and Queen County), Va.

Personal and business papers of John D. McGill, attorney; and legal papers of McGill and Woodward which dissolved ca. 1846.

3380.   WILLIAM ARCHIBALD McGIRT PAPERS, 1912-1936. 47 items. Wilmington (New Hanover County), N.C.

Papers of William A. McGirt (b. 1883), N. C. state highway commissioner and president of the North Carolina Good Roads Association, chiefly pertaining to highways and the good roads movement in North Carolina. Many letters are routine. Also included are letters dealing with McGirt's efforts as president of the Woodrow Wilson Club of Wilmington in behalf of Wilson's campaigns in 1912 and 1916.

3381.   JOHN McGLASHAN PAPERS, 1816-1886. 50 items. Pictou, Nova Scotia, Canada, and Savannah, Ga.

Papers of John McGlashan concerning a dispute over a tract of land in Halifax County, Nova Scotia, purchased from William Frazer in 1816. Included are descriptions of Pictou and Nova Scotia in 1835 and 1871-1873.

3382.   JAMES McGOWAN PAPERS, 1859-1863. 17 items and 2 vols. Georgia.

Papers of James McGowan, serving with the 1st Regiment of Georgia Volunteers, also known as the Irish Jasper Greens, include bills; a summons to meeting and drill; a pass; a picture of a member of the Irish Jasper Greens; two roll books; and a hat of the Irish Jasper Greens.

3383.   SAMUEL McGOWAN PAPERS, 1910-1935. 228 items. Laurens (Laurens County), S.C.

Chiefly personal letters from Rear Admiral Samuel McGowan (1870-1934), paymaster of the U.S. Navy and head of the Navy Bureau of Supplies and Accounts during World War I, to Mrs. Beaufort W. Ball concerning the maintenance and enlargement of the Laurens cemetery, including minutes of the trustees, and rules and resolutions. Papers relating to McGowan's naval service include letters of recommendation and commendation from prominent officials; articles by McGowan on the prevention of war and the role of the United States in keeping world peace; statements dealing with South Carolina politics; papers pertaining to McGowan's service as chief highway commissioner, 1925-1926, concerning the building and maintenance of South Carolina highways; and several memorial addresses made by the Reverend Walter Carl Subke in honor of McGowan.

3384.   JAMES McHENRY PAPERS, 1797-1800. 59 items. New York, N.Y., and Baltimore, Md.

Correspondence of James McHenry (1753-1816), physician and secretary of war under George Washington and John Adams, consists of typewritten copies of letters from William Vans Murray, minister to the Netherlands, to McHenry dealing with relations between the United States and France; typewritten copies of letters from George Washington to McHenry concerning appointments; typewritten copies of letters from Alexander Hamilton to McHenry pertaining to western lands; correspondence between McHenry and William Barry Grove, U.S. representative from North Carolina, discussing politics and political unrest in North Carolina; and several routine letters concerning administrative matters. Many of the typewritten copies have been published in Bernard C. Steiner, The Life and Correspondence of James McHenry (Cleveland: 1907).

3385.   NICCOLO MACHIAVELLI PAPERS, 1531. 1 item. Florence, Italy.

Photocopy of "Discorsi de N. Machiavegli." The original is in the British Museum.

3386.   ALEXANDER McINNIS PAPERS, 1753-1853. 41 items and 5 vols. Orangeburg Court House (Orangeburg County), S.C.

Papers of Alexander McInnis, surveyor, principally relating to land surveys in North and South Carolina, including grants; plats; correspondence dealing with resurveys; and volumes concerning surveys, one of which contains a roster of Scotch Highlanders from Richmond County, North Carolina. Several letters from his sister discuss family matters, including part of the family who moved to "the west."

3387.   B. L. McINNIS RECORD BOOK, 1863-1864. 1 vol. (286 pp.) Virginia.

Records of forage, clothing, transportation, and other supplies. Some pages were used as a child's practice book for penmanship and vocabulary. Many pages blank.

3388.   JAMES SIMMONS McINTOSH PAPERS, 1833-1834. 13 items. Ft. Mitchell (Russell County), Ala.

Military correspondence of Brevet Major James Simmons McIntosh, Commanding Officer, 4th Regiment, U.S. Infantry, pertaining to the Creek Indians, the expulsion of intruders from Creek lands, and the conflict between civil and military authority.

3389.   LACHLAN McINTOSH PAPERS, 1763-1838. 24 items. Savannah, Ga.

Papers of Lachlan McIntosh (1725-1806), soldier and statesman, include a letter, 1776, from British officers on board the Henchenbrook concerning negotiations between the Americans and the British for the release of prisoners and ships; photocopy of a 1788 copy of a 1767 survey of Darien, Georgia; protest, 1782, concerning the loss of property in Savannah; letter to the governor relating to graft by surveyors; letter concerning runaway slaves; letters pertaining to the settlement of the estates of Robert Baillie and George Baillie; letter, 1813, discussing cotton culture in East Florida; and legal papers.

3390. THOMAS M. McINTOSH PAPERS, 1822-1895. 55 items. Thomasville (Thomas County), Ga.

Letters from Kate Crosland to friends in Georgia including a letter, 1864, discussing General William T. Sherman, a Negro insurrection in North Carolina, a lynching in South Carolina, slaves, and a smallpox outbreak in South Carolina; and the letters of Thomas M. McIntosh while studying at Atlanta Medical College, Atlanta, Georgia, 1873-1875, telling of professors, lectures on mental disease, and a debate among students and professors on the subject of the admission of women to medical schools. A letter fragment, ca. 1780s, describes travel in New York and the North.

3391. ARCHIBALD McINTYRE PAPERS, 1833-1866. 140 items. Albany (Albany County), N.Y.

Principally correspondence of Archibald McIntyre concerning attempts to sell gold mining property in North Carolina. Several letters give technical details concerning the mines, particularly the Phoenix and Reed Mines in Cabarrus County, and describe the property and prospects for finding gold there. There is also a copy of the charter to incorporate the North Carolina Manufacturing, Mining and Land Company. Other papers include a letter, 1842, discussing economic conditions and politics; personal letters; the will of Walter Monteith of New York; and military orders issued during the Civil War.

3392. BENJAMIN FRANKLIN McINTYRE DIARIES, 1862-1864. 3 vols. Keokuk (Lee County), Iowa.

Diary of B. F. McIntyre, officer in the 19th Iowa Volunteer Infantry, U.S.A., describing military engagements of the regiment during the Civil War, including the battles of Pea Ridge and Prairie Grove, Arkansas, and the siege and occupation of Vicksburg, Mississippi; relations between the officers and soldiers; the condition of Negroes in Union and Confederate territory; the utilization of Negro troops; duties at Fort Brown, Brownsville, Texas; political situation at Matamoras, Mexico; and social life and customs in Texas and Mexico.

3393. JOHN McIVER PAPERS, 1852-1868. 22 items. Moore County, N.C.

Correspondence of John McIver, physician of Moore County, containing letters on family matters written during the Civil War; letters on the political situation in North Carolina in 1863; descriptions of plantation life and hardships in Mississippi, where a brother, D. J. McIver, moved after the war; and letters relating to the settlement of the McIver estate in Moore County.

3394. LEONARD LEOPOLD MACKALL PAPERS, 1922. 7 items. Savannah, Ga.

Correspondence of Leopold Mackall (1879-1937), bibliographer and editor, with DuBose Heyward, Charles Hanson Towne and Basil Lanneau Gildersleeve concerning the sending of the most recent yearbook of the Poetry Society of South Carolina to Towne and Gildersleeve.

3395. CATHERINE McKAY AUTOGRAPH ALBUM, 1840-1841. 1 vol. (22 pp.) Salem (Forsyth County), N.C.

Autograph album kept by Catherine McKay, mother of Rosa (Bryan) Parrish, while the former was a student at Salem College.

3396. ELIZA ANNE (McQUEEN) MACKAY PAPERS, 1796 (1825-1847) 1876. 270 items and 2 vols. Savannah, Ga.

Correspondence and other papers of Eliza Anne (McQueen) Mackay (b. 1778), daughter of John McQueen and wife of Robert Mackay, referring to the Cherokee Indians; the price of slaves in Louisiana; student life at Yale College, New Haven, Connecticut; the Whig Party; the U.S. Army in the 1830s; remedies for various diseases; the travels of Robert Mackay in Europe, 1797-1799, including business correspondence and accounts for lodging and purchases; and the Berrien, Cowper, Elliott, Habersham, Huger, Pinckney, Screven, Stiles, and Tattnall families. Also included are religious poetry and prose by M. C. McQueen; a deed, 1831; a schedule for the settlement of the estate of Mrs. Mary Ann Stiles; and a tax book, 1832-1859, listing property of members of the Mackay, McQueen, Cowper, and Stiles families.

3397. GEORGE L. MacKAY SHORT STORIES. 4 items. Richmond, Va.

Typed copies of two of George L. MacKay's short stories entitled "On the War Path" and "Preacher Dan"; and form letters of rejection from Liberty and Collier's magazines.

3398. JOHN McKAY PAPERS, 1800 (1872-1879) 1890. 63 items. Shoe Heel (now Maxton) (Robeson County), N.C.

Accounts and correspondence relating to the business activities of John McKay, principally in naval stores and general merchandise. Accounts appear for the firm of McKay and McLean, the firm of McKay and Gilchrist, and for McKay separately.

3399. JOHN H. McKELPESH PAPERS, 1816-1817. 1 vol. (142 pp.) Baltimore, Md.

Notebook of John H. McKelpesh in Dr. Nathaniel Potter's class in the practice of physick at the University of Maryland, discussing yellow fever, the treatment of fevers and other diseases, visits to the hospital, and the theories of Drs. Benjamin Rush, Benjamin Smith Barton, and William Cullen.

3400. GEORGE W. McKENNEY PAPERS, 1865-1905. 46 items. Oldenplace (Dinwiddie County), Va.

Papers of George W. McKenney include personal and family correspondence, requests for loans, business correspondence, an insurance policy of the Farmers' Mutual Benefit Association of Virginia, and circulars pertaining to regulations and the operation of the U.S. Post Office.

3401. WILLIAM ROBERTSON McKENNEY PAPERS, 1865 (1880-1900) 1930. 4,440 items. Petersburg (Dinwiddie County), Va.

Business papers of William Robertson McKenney relating to his law practice, principally concerning the settlement of estates and the sale of real estate in Petersburg. Papers of the 1870s are for the firm of Jones and McKenney.

3402. ELIZABETH G. MacKENZIE PAPERS, 1896-1897. 13 items. Charleston, S.C.

Personal letters to a schoolteacher from friends and relatives.

3403. ALFRED AUGUSTUS McKETHAN PAPERS, 1860-1927. 513 items. Fayetteville (Cumberland County), N.C.

Correspondence and papers concerning Alfred Augustus McKethan's carriage and buggy manufacturing business in Fayetteville, 1852-1875, consisting chiefly of correspondence with New York and New Jersey varnish and iron firms, and orders for carriages and buggies; and letters from Alfred A. McKethan, son of Edwin Turner McKethan, while a midshipman in the U.S. Navy, while stationed in Honolulu, 1893-1895, and while cruising on the U.S. steamers *Alliance* and *Philadelphia*.

3404. DANIEL N. MACKEY PAPERS, 1864-1865. 5 items. Point Lookout (St. Marys County), Md.

Letters from Daniel N. Mackey, son of John T. Mackey of Dry Creek, South Carolina, and Confederate soldier, while a prisoner of war at Point Lookout, describing conditions in the prison. Included also is a letter from his father to Anna Chaise.

3405. THOMAS JEFFERSON McKIE PAPERS, 1825 (1868-1893) 1895. 796 items and 2 vols. Woodlawn (Edgefield County), S.C.

Papers of Thomas Jefferson McKie, physician and farmer, include correspondence discussing politics, Reconstruction, conditions of the freedmen and the Freedmen's Bureau, the Negro vote, efforts of whites to regain political control, the Hayes-Tilden presidential election, Wade Hampton's stand on the state debt, immigration to South Carolina, and other matters; lists of goods purchased by Thomas McKie in the 1820s; report and letters of J. M. McKie while at the Greenville (South Carolina) high school in 1873; letters to Thomas McKie from women applying for position as governess; correspondence concerning a land dispute with Benjamin Tillman and Dr. Meriwether; advertisements; an article by Thomas McKie; a presidential address to the South Carolina Medical Association; an account book, 1858-1879, of Thomas McKie's farm and home containing prices of cotton, food, books, household goods, guano, and clothing; and a letterpress book, 1869-1895, discussing teachers and teaching, the property dispute, and other business and personal matters.

3406. ISAAC McKIM PAPERS, 1812-1835. 5 items. Baltimore, Md.

Correspondence of Isaac McKim (1775-1838), merchant involved in importing and shipping, and U.S. congressman, discussing the debate in Congress on tariffs, 1824; the proper weight of canvas for sails for schooners; and other matters. Included is a letter of his uncle, Alexander McKim (1748-1832), U.S. congressman, to a constituent concerning a "privatering memorial" before Congress in 1812.

3407. WILLIAM McKINLEY PAPERS, 1896-1901. 6 items. Canton (Stark County), Ohio.

Miscellaneous papers relating to William McKinley (1843-1901), president of the United States, 1897-1901, consist of a letter from McKinley to James M. Moody, Waynesville, North Carolina; a Republican badge and a banner of the presidential campaign of 1896; a facsimile of a letter from John McCall after McKinley's death, praising him; a newspaper account of McKinley's assassination; and a President McKinley memorial bookmark.

3408. DAVID EDWARD McKINNE PAPERS, 1900. 6 items. Princeton (Johnston County), N.C.

Letters to David Edward McKinne (b. 1847), merchant and officer in the 71st Regiment, North Carolina Troops, C.S.A., from other former members of the 71st Regiment concerning his compilation of a historical sketch of the regiment. Included are the reminiscences of B. B. Raiford and William Fessenden Beasley. McKinne's account was published in Walter Clark, *Histories of the Several Regiments and Battalions from North Carolina* (1901).

3409. W. M. McKINNEY PAPERS, 1861-1863. 14 items. Virginia and Tennessee.

Letters of W. M. McKinney, 15th Regiment, Indiana Volunteers, U.S.A., to his cousin, Abby, describing skirmishes, camp life, the military government in Tennessee, and the popularity of Iuka, Mississippi, as a health resort.

3410. WILLIAM BERRY McKOY PAPERS, 1853-1916. 87 items and 16 vols. Wilmington (New Hanover County), N.C.

The papers of William Berry McKoy (b. 1852), lawyer, include an account book, 1875-1877, and ledgers, 1877-1880, of McKoy, his brother, Robert Hasell McKoy (b. 1855), his cousin, Thomas H. McKoy, Jr., and his mother, Mrs. F. E. McKoy, containing personal accounts as well as office accounts of the law partnership of Robert and Thomas McKoy. A letterpress book, 1879-1880, contains the business correspondence of John L. Boatwright and Thomas H. McKoy, Sr., grocers, including two letters to Senator Zebulon B. Vance regarding the need for federal legislation against the adulteration of food. Account books, 1853-1859, of Henry Bacon, Sr., William B. McKoy's father-in-law, contain personal and professional accounts and memoranda; many are related to the construction of the charter lines of the Illinois Central Railroad, with estimates, statistics, drawings and computations, and contracts for the cutting of lumber. A medical notebook of William Augustus Berry (1804-1875), physician and grandfather of William Berry McKoy, includes medical prescriptions for various diseases, as well as memoranda on liquor, whitewash, fertilizer, dental work, marble, horse medicine, crop planting, etc. Letters and typescripts, 1881-1883, from Francis Henry Bacon (1856-1940), McKoy's brother-in-law, while on an expedition to excavate the site of the ancient Greek city of Assos in Asia Minor, describe the archaeological work and the personnel, with several drawings and a color sketch. There are official records of the Masons, 1875-1913, particularly 1912-1913 when McKoy was the Grand Mason of the Grand Lodge of North Carolina, relating to the routine and charitable activities of the Masons. A letterpress book, 1889-1915, deals with William B. McKoy's legal business, including the North Carolina Agricultural and Mechanical College for the Colored Race, now North Carolina Agricultural and Technical State University, Greensboro (North Carolina), building and loan associations, New Hanover County and North Carolina politics and government, insurance laws and regulations, taxation, and prohibition. Also included are a voter registration book, 1896-1897, of Harnett Township, New Hanover County; a daybook, 1894, of a butcher establishment; a checkbook, 1889-1891; and two indices to a law library and an index to an unidentified legal work.

3411. JOHN MACKY PAPERS, ca. 1703-1704. 1 vol. (238 pp.) London, England.

Manuscript entitled "The Court and Kingdom of England" which is a variant copy of John Macky's "Characters of the Court of Great Britain," a portion of his *Memoirs of the Secret Services of John Macky, Esq.* (London: 1733), containing concise biographies of public men. There is marginalia of a later date.

3412. ISABELLA CRAIG McLANAHAN NOTEBOOK. 1 vol. (66 pp.) Franklin County, Pa.

World history notes.

3413. LOUIS McLANE PAPERS, 1830-1838. 7 items. Washington, D.C.

Papers of Louis McLane (1786-1857), member of U.S. Congress, 1817-1827, and U.S. senator, 1827-1829, minister to England; secretary of the treasury, 1831; secretary of state, 1833; and president of the Baltimore and Ohio Railroad, concerning routine business of the Treasury Department, the career of William Rufus King, an inquiry pertaining to iron and steel production, and the "present crisis" of 1832, probably nullification.

3414. ANNA B. McLAURIN PAPERS, 1841-1878. 48 items. Griffin (Spalding County), Ga.

Personal correspondence of Anna B. McLaurin, daughter of the Reverend Hugh McLaurin, and letters of condolence to her mother upon Anna's death.

3415. DUNCAN McLAURIN PAPERS, 1779 (1822-1872) 1922. 1,887 items and 1 vol. Richmond County, N.C.

Personal and political correspondence, legal papers, bills and receipts, and printed material comprise the papers of Duncan McLaurin (1787-1872), teacher, lawyer, state legislator, and farmer. Correspondence, including many letters from friends and relatives who migrated to Mississippi, discuss the removal of the Choctaw Indians; Indian wars in Georgia and Alabama; economic conditions, especially the panics of 1837 and 1857; the Bank of the United States; banks and currency; cotton production, markets, and prices; slavery, the sale of slaves, runaway slaves, and the fear of slave insurrections; the abolition movement; the annexation of California; land prices and speculation; the growth of religious denominations in Mississippi and Louisiana; the development of schools in Mississippi, Georgia, and North Carolina, and of Wake Forest Institute (Wake Forest, North

Carolina), and Union Seminary (Richmond, Virginia); the temperance movement; travel by rail, 1833; the development of roads and canals in North Carolina, 1840; telegraph lines; the postal service; damage to Natchez, Mississippi, by a tornado, 1840; the Mexican War; politics in North Carolina, South Carolina, Mississippi, Alabama, and Georgia; national politics, including presidential elections, 1832-1848; the Civil War, including camp life, economic conditions, food supplies, the hope for foreign intervention, morale, conscription and desertion, the blockade of Southern ports, the battles of Murfreesboro (Tennessee), Jackson (Mississippi), Port Royal Harbor (South Carolina), and Hanover Court House (Virginia), and the siege of Vicksburg (Mississippi); economic conditions and Reconstruction government in Mississippi; and difficulties with sharecroppers and debtors. Legal papers consist of deeds, contracts, wills, court orders, and, after 1850, papers pertaining to the wardship of his sister, Isabel Patterson, and her children after her mental breakdown. Miscellaneous printed items include an atlas, 1835, with a list of slaves at the end of the war on the flyleaf; a memorial to the North Carolina state legislature from the Society of Friends, 1832; a reply to President Jackson's proclamation on nullification; an advertisement of the poison springs at Mooresville, North Carolina; a report of the treasurer of the University of North Carolina to the trustees, 1839; a report of the Merchants Bank of New Bern, the Bank of the State of North Carolina, and the Bank of Cape Fear, 1838; price current bulletins, 1874; a North Carolina Republican campaign circular, 1873; two tracts opposing free silver; program of the Guilford County Baptist Sunday School Convention, Greensboro, North Carolina, 1891; and The Prison News, Raleigh, North Carolina, for March 1, 1932.

3416. LAUCHLIN W. McLAURIN PAPERS, 1817-1924. 454 items. Laurinburg (Scotland County), N.C.

Papers of Lauchlin W. McLaurin consist of reports and receipts relating to McLaurin's duties as a Confederate tax collector; business letters from his partner, "H. C. B.," concerning stock in hardware, paper, and envelopes; personal correspondence; letters from D. C. McIntyre describing Reconstruction in Alabama and the economic effects of emancipation; papers concerning prices of commodities, household articles and slaves; a bulletin, 1893, from the Jones Seminary for girls at All Healing Springs, North Carolina; land and slave deeds; summonses; the will of Nancy McLaurin; fire and life insurance policies; stock certificates from two North Carolina railroads; and other miscellaneous papers.

3417. LAFAYETTE McLAWS PAPERS, 1862-1895. 99 items and 2 vols. Savannah, Ga.

Papers of Lafayette McLaws (1821-1897), major general in the Confederate Army, include copies of reports, depositions, correspondence, and proceedings relating to neglect of duty charges brought against McLaws by General James Longstreet for failure to make proper preparations for an assault on Knoxville, Tennessee, during the siege of that city in 1863; correspondence and two volumes concerning the Atlantic and Mexican Gulf Canal Company of which McLaws was president; correspondence and portions of manuscripts pertaining to articles on various campaigns of the Civil War, including Longstreet's Tennessee campaign, the Peninsular campaign under General John Magruder, and the battles of Antietam and Gettysburg; and correspondence dealing with efforts of McLaws to secure a pension for services in the U.S. Army before 1861.

3418. CLARA VICTORIA (DARGAN) MACLEAN PAPERS, 1849-1920. 718 items and 21 vols. Columbia (Richland County), S.C.

The collection of Clara Victoria (Dargan) Maclean (1841-1923), generally known as Clara V. Dargan, teacher, writer of fiction and poetry, and wife of Joseph Adams Maclean, includes her personal diaries, 1860-1920; an autograph album, 1873; a book of rhymes and sketches, 1850-1864; two scrapbooks; a copy of Fenélon, 1888, containing her notes and comments; and personal correspondence and papers. The collection contains much information on Southern literature, the effect of the Civil War on literary effort and remuneration, and the genealogy of the Dargan and Strother families. Among the correspondents are John Henry Boner, Matthew Calbraith Butler, James Wood Davidson, James Nathan Ells, William Evelyn, Paul Hamilton Hayne, and Henry Timrod.

3419. JOHN D. McLENNAN PAPERS, 1836-1888. 6 items. Troup County, Ga.

Personal letters.

3420. A. McLOY AND J. W. RICE LEDGER, 1866-1869. 1 vol. (291 pp.) Charleston, S.C.

Mercantile accounts.

3421. FITZ HUGH McMASTER PAPERS, 1913-1921. 3 items. Columbia (Richland County), S.C.

Typed copies of addresses delivered at The Citadel commencement, Charleston, South Carolina, June, 1913; at the Bankers' Association at the Isle of Palms, June, 1914; and at the Kosmos Club at Columbia, South Carolina, October, 1921.

3422. ALEXANDER McMILLAN PAPERS, 1815-1893. 213 items. Lumberton (Robeson County), N.C.

Political correspondence, 1860-1861, of Alexander McMillan, North Carolina legislator, concerning the suspension of specie payment, union versus secession, length of service for Confederate volunteers, pay of soldiers, and the raising of an army in North Carolina; Civil War letters from McMillan's sons in the Confederate Army, discussing difficulties in obtaining supplies, the death of David McMillan from typhoid fever in a Confederate hospital, the capture of Daniel McMillan and his imprisonment at Point Lookout (Maryland), desertion, illness, camp life, the springs and hospital at Huguenot Springs (Virginia), and other war-related matters; and personal correspondence, including letters from friends in Texas and correspondence concerning a local scandal involving members of the McMillian family. Miscellaneous items include a document, 1834, recording the sale of a slave; a contract, 1866, of a freedman outlining his duties as a tenant farmer; and a romantic poem, 1868.

3423. ARCHIBALD McMILLAN PAPERS, 1816-1818. 9 items. Horse Shoe Swamp (Bladen County), N.C.

Personal correspondence written while McMillan was in England, including a discussion of the purchase of American stock.

3424. McMULLEN FAMILY PAPERS, 1783-1968. 10,015 items and 38 vols. Washington, D.C.

Family and business correspondence and invention papers of the McMullen family. The papers of John McMullen (1791-1870), inventor, consist of correspondence concerning family matters in Ireland; McMullen's efforts to assist relatives in gaining passage to the United States, the operation of his farm in Sinking Valley in Pennsylvania; a trip to England, 1850-1851, to sell his inventions; the invention of machines to knit stockings and fish nets; patents; the receipt of the Exhibitor's Medal for a machine shown at the Exhibition of the Works of All Nations at the Crystal Palace, London, England, in 1853 including a letter from President Millard Fillmore notifying him of the award; and an exhibition of a knitting machine at the New York Crystal Palace at the Exhibition of the Industry of All Nations in 1854. The papers of John Francis McMullen (1830-1900), son of John McMullen, and of his wife, Lavalette (Johnston) McMullen (d. 1941), daughter of John Warfield Johnston, senator from Virginia, include correspondence while John Francis McMullen attended St. Mary's College, Baltimore, Maryland; letters from William Hand Browne (1828-1912), editor and librarian, describing his travels in the South during the early years of the Civil War; personal and family correspondence with friends and relatives, including letters from Senator Johnston containing references to his political activities; letters from the Sisters of the Order of the Visitation of Holy Mary concerning the education of the McMullen daughters at various schools run by the order; letters of Jean de Hedonville describing cattle ranching in Montana, life on the Crow Indian Reservation, and a camping trip to Yellowstone National Park; correspondence relating to the settlement of the estate of John Warfield Johnston; and business correspondence concerning his father's inventions and cattle raising. Correspondence of the children of John Francis and Lavalette McMullen consists of letters of Mary McMullen, principally while a companion to Jane Agnes Riggs, daughter of George Washington Riggs, Washington banker, describing Riggs family history and their travels in Europe and the United States before World War I; letters to Mary from her cousin, novelist Mary Johnston (1870-1936); family letters of John Francis McMullen II (d. 1944), an engineer; letters of Benedict Dysart McMullen, writer, while serving with the American Red Cross in Europe during World War I; correspondence of Joseph Benjamin McMullen (d. 1965), inventor, concerning his many inventions, including aerial "drop" bombs during World War I, automobile accessories, kitchen utensils, household gadgets, and pressure and pull firing devices and collapsible vehicles during World War II; and papers relating to the settlement of a disputed legacy left Mary McMullen by Jane Riggs and correspondence concerning the sale of much of the inheritance. Also included are papers relating to the estates of the various members of the McMullen family; invention papers consisting of patents and descripttions of the work of John McMullen and Joseph B. McMullen; bills and receipts; lists of library books and Catholic publications purchased; manuscripts of William Hand Browne, John Bannister Tabb, Mary McMullen, and Dysart McMullen; and miscellaneous reports, certificates, and invitations from the many schools the McMullens attended. Volumes consist of various business books of John McMullen and John Francis McMullen; subscription for the Catholic Church of Sinking Valley, 1830s; volumes of Joseph B. McMullen concerning his inventions; notebooks of writings and clippings of Mary McMullen and Dysart McMullen; album of snapshots of their home, "Woodley," near Ellicott City, Maryland; and notebooks of Nicketti McMullen containing copies of old letters and data. There are also pictures of various members of the McMullen family and of homes at Wytheville, Thorn Springs, and Ellicott City.

3425. ANNABELLA McNAIR PAPERS, 1838-1842. 3 items. Cowper Hill (Robeson County), N.C.

Personal letters to Annabella McNair from her cousins, Neil McNair, a medical student in Philadelphia, Pennsylvania, in 1838; and Thomas G. McFarland, a businessman and farmer of Rossville, Georgia.

3426. JOHN McNAIR PAPERS,
1783 (1794-1824) 1832. 79 items. Statesburg (Sumter County), S.C.

The collection contains business and legal letters which deal especially with the settlement of the estate of John McNair.

3427. JOHN SMITH McNAUGHT DIARY, 1863-1865. 1 vol. Massachusetts.

Diary of a soldier in the 11th United States Regiment during the Civil War in various campaigns in Virginia. Entries concern Confederate prisoners and deserters, troop movements and camp life in the Army of the Potomac, and General J. E. B. Stuart's raid toward Alexandria, Virginia, in 1864.

3428. JOHN M. McNEEL PAPERS, 1862, 1864. 2 items. Georgia.

Letters from John M. McNeel, a Confederate private stationed in Alabama, mentioning camp life, forced marches, scarcity of food, and desertions.

3429. THOMAS C. McNEELY PAPERS, 1839-1861. 9 items. Salisbury (Rowan County), N.C.

Personal correspondence of Thomas C. McNeely, including references to Davidson College, Davidson, North Carolina; local politics; and life in the Confederate Army.

3430. THOMAS M. McNEELY PAPERS, 1831-1884. 12 items. Mocksville (Davie County), N.C.

Family letters and papers concerning the administration of the estate of John Knight.

3431. DUNCAN McNEILL PAPERS,
1794 (1836-1852) 1856. 75 items. Fayetteville (Cumberland County), N.C.

Business correspondence concerned with carriage manufacturing and the sale of furniture.

3432. HECTOR H. McNEILL PAPERS, 1835-1896. 110 items and 4 vols. Robeson County, N.C.

Correspondence of Hector H. McNeill, a Presbyterian minister. The collection includes letters from his sons, Thomas A. and Franklin McNeill, commenting on their Civil War activities, including life at Fort Fisher (North Carolina), rations, and moral conditions among the soldiers; letters from Franklin McNeill while at Davidson College, North Carolina; letters from J.W. Malloy, a student at Davidson College in 1861, giving detailed observations on professors and college life; and correspondence of Hector H. McNeill with his colleagues, dealing with religious problems and the Presbyterian Church, 1835-1861. Volumes concern business and religious matters, including one pertaining to the General Assembly (Presbyterian) of 1840 in Philadelphia.

3433. JOHN CHARLES McNEILL PAPERS, 1904-1941. 19 items. Charlotte (Mecklenburg County), N.C.

The collection contains a typed copy of a personal letter, 1907, from John Charles McNeill, poet, attorney, legislator, and journalist, to his aunt; writings on McNeill by Josiah William Bailey; and letters about McNeill written to Alice Morella Polk as a part of her research for a thesis on McNeill done at Duke University in 1941.

3434. JOHN H. McNEILL PAPERS, 1861-1884. 56 items and 2 vols. Lumberton (Robeson County), N.C.

The collection is made up for the most part of business and personal letters and other papers relating to John H. McNeill, including Civil War letters which contain information on the 4th North Carolina Regiment, the 7th North Carolina Regiment, camp life, and campaigning in North Carolina and Virginia. Other papers concern social life in North Carolina, the <u>Lumberton</u> (North Carolina) <u>Times</u>, settlement of estates in Mississippi, and the Buie and McRae families. Volumes include a teacher's roll book and a list of distillers.

3435. MARY MARGARET McNEILL PAPERS, 1861-1870. 60 items. St. Paul's (Robeson County), N.C.

Letters to Mary Margaret McNeill from Confederate soldiers at Fort Fisher and Fort Caswell in North Carolina and Charleston, South Carolina, concerning camp life; health, casualties; the Union blockade of Wilmington, North Carolina; military action on the North Carolina coast; a visit by Jefferson Davis to Fort Caswell, 1863; and an unsuccessful assault on Fort Sumter in 1863.

3436. NEILL McNEILL PAPERS,
1793 (1850-1865) 1899. 146 items. Robeson County, N.C.

Letters and papers of Neill McNeill, first lieutenant of the 43rd Regiment of North Carolina Militia, chairman of the board of common schools, and a justice of the peace. The correspondence concerns settlements in Alabama in 1847, Civil War activities around Richmond, Virginia, and agricultural conditions in Kemper County, Mississippi. Of interest are the papers, 1847-1855, of McNeill, giving information on pupils, subjects taught, and teachers' salaries. Included also are incomplete weather reports for Robeson County for 1856-1862, wills, indentures, property executions, and miscellaneous court records.

3437. ROBERT W. McNEILLY PAPERS, 1851-1883. 11 items. Cleveland County, N.C.

Family correspondence, a deed, a marriage license, and an amnesty oath of Robert W. McNeilly. Among the correspondents are Peter Buff and W. L. Saunders.

3438. ALEXANDER GALLATIN McNUTT PAPERS, 1836-1864. 8 items. Vicksburg (Warren County), Miss.

Papers of Alexander G. McNutt (1801-1848), lawyer and Mississippi senator and governor, including a letter on Mississippi land, a circular to probate courts, political clippings concerning his opposition to the payment of the state debt, and items pertaining to politics in Mississippi during the 1840s.

3439. NATHANIEL MACON PAPERS, 1798-1854. 37 items. Monroe (Warren County), N.C.

Papers of Nathaniel Macon (1758-1837), Revolutionary War figure and member of U.S. Congress, concern the settlement of claims from the Revolution; miscellaneous items from Macon's legislative career; the suggestion in 1824 that Macon replace William Crawford as the prospective Republican (Jeffersonian) Party presidential candidate; Macon's efforts to get material on the history of North Carolina; the death of John Randolph of Roanoke; and Macon's health in his last years. Included also are copies of three letters to Charles Tait regarding national politics in 1815, which have been published; William K. Boyd (ed.), "Letters of Nathaniel Macon to Judge Charles Tait," Trinity College Historical Society *Historical Papers*, Ser. 8 (1908-1909), pp. 3-5.

3440. ALEXANDER M. McPHEETERS, SR., PAPERS, 1861-1868. 79 items. Liberty (Bedford County), Va., and Raleigh (Wake County), N.C.

Papers of Alexander M. McPheeters, Sr., concern the Civil War, including descriptions of the battle of South Mills, 1862, and the Peninsular campaign, 1862; McPheeters's views of army life and his evaluation of various Confederate officers; and his opinions on Confederate Army reorganization. Letters to McPheeters from his business partner, Henry Ghiselin, report on general business conditions, the economic and military situation in Norfolk, Virginia, the effect of the Union blockade on commodity prices, and the difficulties of transportation. Other letters to McPheeters concern Virginia Military Institute, Lexington, Virginia, in 1861; the operation of railroads in Virginia during the war; the evacuation of Norfolk, Virginia, by Confederate forces, 1862; the Democratic (Conservative) State Convention in Raleigh, North Carolina, 1868; and a Republican demonstration and barbecue in Raleigh, 1868.

3441. JAMES BIRDSEYE McPHERSON PAPERS, 1863. 2 items. Sandusky County, Ohio.

Letters to James B. McPherson, general in the Union Army, from the quartermaster in Vicksburg concerning the issuance and branding of captured stock, and from Eugene Hill, a former Confederate traveling agent, concerning rams and gunboats being constructed by the Confederacy in Mobile, Alabama, for an attack on New Orleans.

3442. JOHN D. McPHERSON PAPERS, 1865-1877. 10 items. Washington, D.C.

Professional correspondence of John D. McPherson, Washington lawyer, concerning cases likely to be heard by the U.S. Supreme Court. One client requests compensation for Negroes lost during the Civil War, and another asks for a pardon and for restoration of his vessel, the *Trent*, formerly in the service of the Confederate States of America.

3443. JAMES McQUEEN PAPERS, 1839. 1 item. London, England.

A copy of a memorandum of James McQueen, British geographer, to Lord Glenelg, colonial secretary, containing McQueen's recommendations for British treaties with African chieftains and for the instructions to British agents in Africa. This memorandum is published in McQueen's *A Geographical Survey of Africa . . . To Which Is Prefixed, A Letter To Lord J. Russell, Regarding the Slave Trade, and the Improvement of Africa* (London: 1840).

3444. JOHN McQUEEN PAPERS, 1786. 3 items. [Savannah, Ga.?]

Photocopies of dinner invitations to John McQueen from D'Estaing and Lafayette and a request for information on the value and title of General Oglethorpe's possessions in North America.

3445. JOHN McQUEEN PAPERS, 1850-1859. 7 items. Bennettsville (Marlboro County), S. C.

Routine political correspondence of John McQueen (1804-1867), member of U.S. Congress, 1849-1860, and of the Confederate Congress, chiefly on appointments and recommendations for jobs. Also contains a clipping of a letter from McQueen to Lewis Tappan on slavery.

3446. SIR JOHN MACRA PAPERS, 1784-1847. 75 items. Ardintoul (County Ross and Cromarty), Scotland.

The collection contains the papers of Sir John Macra and members of his family, concerning Macra's service in India and Indian military affairs, 1784-1832, including letters, 1812-1826, from Lord Hastings, governor general of India; Macra's participation in military campaigns in Sweden and Spain, 1807-1812; and the activities of Macra's kin in India, Nepal, Scotland, and Canada.

3447.  HUGH MacRAE PAPERS, 1817-1943. 4,233 items and 37 vols. Wilmington (New Hanover County) and Fayetteville (Cumberland County), N.C.

From the ante-bellum period there are papers of MacRae's grandfather, Alexander MacRae, concerning the management of plantations in Florida and the second Seminole War; of Archibald MacRae, pertaining to his career in the United States Navy, including a voyage to the Azores and the Mediterranean Sea, 1838, observation of the British attack on Egyptian forces, 1840, participation in the Mexican War in California, voyage to Hawaii, 1847, and descriptions of political and social events in Chile while part of the United States Naval Expedition to the Southern Hemisphere, 1849-1852; of John Colin MacRae and Henry MacRae, relating to the construction and management of railroads in North Carolina and general construction and transportation development in Florida, Georgia, South Carolina, and Virginia, including correspondence concerning quarrels between the Wilmington and Manchester Railroad, headed by Alexander MacRae, and other North Carolina lines; and of John MacRae and Donald MacRae, concerning their general commission business in Wilmington, North Carolina, founded in 1849, the Endor Iron Works (McIver, North Carolina), begun in 1857, and the political activities of John MacRae in Wilmington.

Civil War papers reflecting army life are those of William MacRae, Robert Bruce MacRae, Henry MacRae, and Walter G. MacRae, all of whom served in the Confederate Army, for the most part in North Carolina and Virginia. Their letters describe numerous battles and skirmishes and depict camp life in the 1st, 5th, and 87th North Carolina Regiments and the 2nd North Carolina Regiment, Cavalry. Letters of Donald MacRae, John Colin MacRae, Roderick MacRae, and Alexander MacRae, Jr., concern conditions at home during the war and family business interests, including the sale of cotton, blockade running, operations of an iron works, manufacture of salt, an epidemic of yellow fever in Wilmington, speculation and economic dislocation at the end of the war, and the occupation of Wilmington by Union troops.

Papers for the years after the Civil War are primarily those of Donald MacRae and his son, Hugh MacRae. Papers of Donald MacRae concern the handling of family real estate; settlement of claims on property in Florida; the guano business, particularly the Navassa Guano Company; general business interests, including the development of Linville, North Carolina, as a resort by the Linville Improvement Company and the Western North Carolina Stage Coach Company; and power development, especially the Great Falls Water Power Mining and Iron Company. The papers after 1890 are increasingly those of Hugh MacRae and concern his business interests, including the Wilmington Street Railroad Company, the Consolidated Railways, Light and Power Company, the Central Carolina Power Company in South Carolina, the Tidewater Power Company, and the Investment Trust Company of Wilmington (North Carolina), and his interest in land development and land reclamation, including the formation of farm communities near Wilmington, the promotion of legislation designed to help tenant farmers acquire their own land and to encourage immigration, the creation of the Carolina Trucking Development Company and the Carolina Real Estate Trust Company, and MacRae's work with the National Economy League and the Southern Economic Council in the 1930s.

The collection contains bills and receipts from many of the businesses in which the MacRae family was interested and a number of volumes dealing with personal and business matters, including works on rural rehabilitation; a diary of Robert Bruce MacRae, 1865-1866; a volume of Hugh MacRae's experiment records, 1909; "Roll of the Wilmington Hibernian Society," 1866-1879; account books of Alexander MacRae; record book of Donald MacRae, Company K, 2nd North Carolina Regiment, in the Spanish-American War; letter book of Hugh MacRae, 1899-1900; and mercantile and shipping records for J. & D. MacRae of Wilmington, 1858-1860.

3448.  J. N. W. McRAE PAPERS, 1853, 1861. 2 items. Whiteville (Columbus County), N.C.

A personal letter, 1853, from Mary Ann G. McRae, and a letter, 1861, from a student at Brook Hill Institute, commenting briefly on local reaction to the disturbed national situation.

3449.  JOHN A. McRAE DAYBOOKS, 1854-1856. 2 vols. Caledonia (Moore County), N.C.

Records of a general merchant.

3450.  SHEPARD S. McREYNOLDS PAPERS, 1932-1939. 3 items. Russellville (Logan County), Ky.

The collection is made up for the most part of genealogical material on the McReynolds family, including a diary, 1823, of a trip by Benjamin McReynolds in Virginia and Kentucky.

3451.  JOHN JACKSON McSWAIN PAPERS, 1910-1941. 11,805 items and 15 vols. Greenville (Greenville County), S.C. Restricted.

The letters and papers of John Jackson McSwain, United States congressman from South Carolina, contain a small amount of correspondence dealing with his entrance into politics, for the most part concerning the presidential elections of 1912 and 1916, and a large volume of material, 1921-1936, from his years in the Congress. Among the subjects appearing in the letters and papers are the South Carolina senatorial campaigns of 1924 and 1930; prominent South Carolina politicians, including Nathaniel Barksdale Dial, Ellison DuRant Smith, and James Francis Byrnes; patronage problems; cotton farming and cotton manufacturing; The Citadel and the University of South Carolina; a trip to Denmark and Sweden to observe farming practices; prohibition; New Deal legislation and McSwain's changing relationship with President Franklin D. Roosevelt; data on World War I, including reports prepared by the Legislative Reference Service of the Library of Congress; material reflecting McSwain's special interest in national defense and military affairs, including letters and reports discussing military supplies, organization of the armed forces, the Reserve Officer Training Corps, and the encouragement of military aviation; and material concerning McSwain's quarrel with William Randolph Hearst. Correspondence after 1937 is largely that of Dixon D. Davis, postmaster of Greenville, South Carolina, and former secretary to McSwain. The collection also contains speeches, clippings, and campaign material related, for the most part, to the subjects covered in McSwain's political letters and papers.

3452. "THE MAD DOG," late 18th century. 14 items.

A paper card case, twelve hand drawn and colored cards, and manuscript instructions for playing a game called, "The Mad Dog Or: Take Care of Yourself."

3453. SIR THOMAS HERBERT MADDOCK PAPERS, 1843. 2 items. London, England.

Letters to Sir Thomas Herbert Maddock, British administrator in India, from James Thomason concerning administrative matters and the Sind War, and from Lord Ellenborough, governor general of India, on the possibility of strengthening British influence in Gwalior.

3454. WASHINGTON MADDUX ACCOUNTS, 1840-1862. 8 vols. Oak Forest (Lunenburg County), and Richmond, Va.

Records of a firm, or firms, apparently retailing general merchandise, under the names of Washington Maddux and Asa George Barnes, Inc., William H. Maddux and Co., and Maddux and Co.

3455. JAMES MADISON PAPERS, 1803-1830. 14 items. "Montpelier" (Orange County), Va., and Washington, D.C.

Routine letters of James Madison, one written while he was secretary of state, and letters from Julia Maria (Dickinson) Tayloe to Dorothea (Payne) Todd Madison, probably written after 1837.

3456. JAMES MADISON PAPERS, 1787-1808. 23 items. Williamsburg (James City County), Va.

Political correspondence of James Madison, president of the College of William and Mary, Williamsburg, Virginia, and bishop of the Protestant Episcopal Church in Virginia, with Henry Tazewell, for the most part concerning relations between the United States and France. Also contains resolutions drawn up in a meeting in James City County, Virginia, in 1797 relative to Franco-American relations and a letter to Madison from François Jean de Chastellux, French soldier and historian, commenting on the future of the United States.

3457. JOHN EUCLID MAGEE DIARY, 1861-1863. 1 vol. (117 pp.) Grenada (Grenada County), Miss.

Diary of John E. Magee, an officer in Stanford's Battery, describing camp life and military engagements in the western campaigns of the Civil War. The diary contains accounts of the battles of Shiloh, Perryville, and Stones River, all in 1862, and comments on various Confederate officers, particularly Braxton Bragg; discipline; army morale; and the hardships of soldiering.

3458. SARAH MAGILL PAPERS, 1836-1904. 50 items. Winchester (Frederick County), Va.

Correspondence of Sarah Magill with members of her immediate family and with cousins in the Bronaugh and Smith families. The letters, concerned for the most part with family business, mention the education of women and the Revolutionary War record of Charles Magill.

3459. THATCHER MAGOUN, SR., AND THATCHER MAGOUN, JR., PAPERS, 1854-1855. 14 items. Boston, Mass.

Business letters to Magoun and Son, a mercantile firm of Boston, Massachusetts, written from the Chincha Islands and Callao, Peru, by captains of the firm's ships concerning guano imports into the United States.

3460. PERKINS MAGRA PAPERS, 1768-1830. 155 items. London, England.

Letters and papers of Perkins Magra, British army officer, contain letters, 1768-1769, relating to his duties as commanding officer of Dover Castle; letters, 1782-1786 and 1804, from Lord George Henry Lennox and his daughter Mary Louisa, concerning personal matters and the military careers of the two men; papers, 1791-1804, from Magra's tenure as consul general at Tunis, relating to negotiations with the Bey of Tunis, service to stranded British subjects, and provisions for the British Mediterranean fleet; letters, 1808-1809, from

Admiral Sir George Cranfield Berkeley discussing the situation in Portugal; a few references to Magra's archeological interests, including a description of a visit to the ruins at Zaghwan in North Africa; and notes on Tunis, probably written while Magra was consul general.

3461. ANDREW GORDON MAGRATH PAPERS, 1839-1889. 5 items. Charleston, S.C.

Letters of Andrew Gordon Magrath, concerning personal and legal matters, and commenting on George Alfred Trenholm and the semicentennial celebration of the Georgia Historical Society.

3462. A[LLAN?] B[OWIE?] MAGRUDER PAPERS, 1861. Richmond, Va.

Letters of A. B. Magruder, concerning rent for a house.

3463. JOHN BANKHEAD MAGRUDER PAPERS, 1840, 1862. 1 item & 1 vol. Houston, Tex.

Letter, 1840, from Magruder discussing his financial affairs, and Magruder's report of his part in the Seven Days' battles, 1862.

3464. JOHN BOWIE MAGRUDER PAPERS, 1856-1865. 16 items. Albemarle County, Va.

Letters from John Bowie Magruder (1839-1863), as a student at the University of Virginia, Charlottesville, 1856-1859, and as a Confederate soldier, 1861-1863, and letters written by his family and relatives after his death in the battle of Gettysburg, July 3, 1863. The small collection is especially rich in Civil War material, with its description of modes of travel and inconveniences of camp life. An eighteen-page letter written from camp near Fredericksburg, Virginia, December 4, 1862, contains much information on "Yankee" depredations near Culpeper, Virginia, the second battle of Manassas, 1862, camp life, and Magruder's personal affairs. A letter from a cousin to Magruder's family informs them of his death; and other family letters describe Sheridan's raids and the frantic efforts of the Magruders to hide foodstuffs, cattle, and personal valuables from the invaders.

3465. JULIA MAGRUDER PAPERS, 1894-1905. 25 items. Concord (Cabarrus County), N.C.

Letters of Julia Magruder, American author, concerning the publication of her article, "The Princess Sonia," in the May, 1895, issue of The Century, and the publication of "Lancelot, Guinevere and Arthur" in the March, 1905, issue of The North American Review.

3466. SIMON J. MAGWOOD PAPERS, 1834, 1860. 2 items. Charleston, S.C.

Personal letters from an army officer at Fort Gibson, Arkansas, 1834, and from Simon J. Magwood's mother.

3467. WILLIAM MAHONE PAPERS, (1863-1865) 1890. 285 items. Petersburg (Dinwiddie County), Va.

The collection is made up for the most part of commissary papers from William Mahone's service in the Confederate Army during the Civil War.

3468. PIERCE MAHONY PAPERS, 1830. 1 item. Dublin, Ireland.

Letter to Pierce Mahony from Richard Lalor Sheil reporting on the elections in Waterford, Ireland.

3469. JAMES F. MAIDES PAPERS, 1862-1865. 6 items. Jones County, N.C.

Letters of James F. Maides, a private in the Confederate Army, describing actions around Richmond and Petersburg, Virginia, and showing his doubt as to Confederate success after 1863.

3470. JAMES PATRICK MAJOR PAPERS. 1 item. Austin (Travis County), Tex.

Letter from James Patrick Major to D. D. Williamson concerning a contract for road steamers.

3471. SIR JOHN MALCOLM PAPERS, 1831. 1 item. London, England.

Letter to Sir John Malcolm, British administrator and diplomat, from John Barker, British consul at Alexandria, Egypt, concerning plans for a steam navigation route to India by way of Egypt.

3472. MALET FAMILY PAPERS, 1832-1908. 6,186 items and 17 vols. London, England.

The papers in this collection are those of Sir Alexander Malet, 2nd Baronet (1800-1886), British diplomat; his wife, Mary Anne Dora (Spalding) Malet; and their sons, Sir Henry Charles Eden Malet, 3rd Baronet, and Sir Edward Baldwin Malet, 4th Baronet, (1837-1908). Sir Alexander Malet's letters to his mother chronicle his duty in Russia, 1824-1827; Portugal, 1833-1835; Holland, 1836-1843; and Austria and Germany, 1844-1845. Three letter books contain copies of 1,844 dispatches that he wrote to the Foreign Office while acting as envoy to the Germanic Confederation at Frankfort, 1852-1866. Bismarck, a friend of the family, was at Frankfort during 1851-1858, and conversations with him were reported in the correspondence. Letters, 1842-1877, to Mary Anne, Lady Malet, from Sophia Frederica Mathilda, queen of the

Netherlands, contain many details of Queen Sophia's personal life; extensive comment on the political and diplomatic affairs of England, France, Germany, Austria, Italy, and Russia, particularly England and France; analyses of European leaders, especially Napoleon III; and discussions of many of her friends and acquaintances in the aristocracy of Europe. Letters, 1850-1867, to Lady Malet from Lord Stanley contain observations on cabinets and parliamentary politics in the administrations of Lord John Russell, the Earl of Derby (Stanley's father), Lord Aberdeen, and Lord Palmerston; and comments on literature, the career of Napoleon III, the Crimean War, India, Irish members of Parliament, and the political and diplomatic situation in Germany. Letters, 1835-1839, to Lady Malet from Frances Eden describe life in India. Letters from Henry Charles Eden Malet to his parents give an account of his experiences as a soldier in the Crimean War, describing operations around Sevastopol and including many maps and sketches. Other letters on the Crimean War concern naval operations, Florence Nightingale, and the general condition of the British army and navy. The letters of Sir Edward Malet cover virtually his whole career. He was in Washington during the Civil War, in Paris during the Franco-Prussian War and Commune, in Constantinople at the conclusion of the Russo-Turkish War, and in Egypt as agent and consul-general during 1879-1885. He saw service in Peking, 1873; Athens, 1874; Rome, 1875-1876; Brussels, 1884; and Berlin, 1884-1895. One series of 1,644 letters, written to his parents, record all of his career except the last few years in Berlin. Incoming correspondence from politicians, diplomats, friends, and relatives number more than 2,200 items. One volume contains copies of Malet's dispatches from Egypt during 1881-1883. Printed matter is made up mainly of ceremonial items concerning the marriage of Princess Louise of Great Britain in 1891 and the visit of the emperor and empress of Germany for that occasion. The volume is an album of 44 sketches, battle plans, and watercolors of the siege of Sevastopol done by Henry Charles Eden Malet.

3473. JOHN FREDERICK MALLET PAPERS, 1853-1884. 1 vol. New Bern (Craven County), N.C.

Journal of John Frederick Mallet, farmer and itinerant Methodist minister.

3474. STEPHEN RUSSELL MALLORY PAPERS, 1861-1868. 3 items. Pensacola (Escambia County), Fla.

A photocopy of Stephen R. Mallory's will; a letter by Mallory, 1861, commenting on the death of a Dr. L'Engle; and a commission signed by Mallory as secretary of the navy of the Confederate States of America.

3475. HENRY W. MALLOY PAPERS, 1846-1899. 3 items. Laurinburg (Scotland County), N.C.

List of property sold from the estate of Alexander Malloy, a planter of Richmond County, North Carolina, 1846-1849; and contracts for tenant farmers in Richmond County, 1897 and 1899.

3476. ELLIS MALONE PAPERS, 1778-1927. 1,263 items. Louisburg (Franklin County), N.C.

Papers of Ellis Malone, North Carolina physician and farmer who had land holdings in several southern states, and his son James Ellis Malone, also a physician. Letters, 1778-1877, were written to Ellis Malone, primarily on business and family matters and contain discussions of economic conditions in North Carolina, Mississippi, Tennessee, and South Carolina. Similar letters after 1877 are to James Ellis Smith. Legal papers include deeds of sale for land, indentures, surveying records, insurance policies, and records of crop liens. Financial papers are made up of accounts with patients, records of the purchase of medical supplies, accounts of the hire and sale of slaves, tax receipts, and records of cotton sales. The collection also contains material on freemasonry in North Carolina; the Tar River Circuit of the Methodist Episcopal Church, South, 1849-1885; and a medical daybook, 1865-1868.

3477. SIR THOMAS MALORY PAPERS, 1470. 475 pp. Winchester, Hampshire, England.

Photocopy of a manuscript containing eight works by Sir Thomas Malory, the last of which was entitled "La Morte d'Arthure." The original manuscript is at the Fellows' Library, Winchester College, Winchester, England, and has been published in Eugene Vinaver, The Works of Sir Thomas Malory.

3478. GEORGE WILLIAM MANBY PAPERS, 1813. 1 item. London, England.

Letter to George William Manby, British inventor, from Samuel Whitbread, replying to Manby's request for assistance in having one of his publications translated into foreign languages.

3479. LEWIS M. MANEY PAPERS, 1862-1867. 7 items. Murfreesboro (Rutherford County), Tenn.

Photocopies of letters of appreciation to Mrs. Lewis M. Maney for her kindness in treating Colonel William W. Duffield of the 9th Michigan Regiment, Cavalry, after he was wounded in an attack on Murfreesboro, Tennessee, by Nathan Bedford Forrest, Confederate general, in 1862. Also a letter from Duffield's lieutenant-colonel, J.G. Parkhurst, regarding Maney's claims for cotton seized by the military authority.

3480. FERDINAND FRANZ MANGOLD CONSPECTUS. 308 pp.

Conspectus, in English, of Der Feldzug in Nord-Virginien im August 1862 by Ferdinand Franz Mangold (Hanover: 1881).

3481. ADDISON MANGUM LEDGER, 1871-1872. 1 vol. (274 pp.) Flat River (Durham County), N.C.

Ledger of a general mercantile firm.

3482. ADOLPHUS W. MANGUM PAPERS, 1849-1899. 61 items and 6 vols. Chapel Hill (Orange County), N.C.

Letters, poetry, essays, lectures, sermons, and business papers of Adolphus W. Mangum. Includes records of meetings of the board of trustees of Randolph-Macon College, Ashland, Virginia. Also five volumes on religion and one hymnal.

3483. WILLIE PERSON MANGUM PAPERS, 1763-1861. 142 items and 1 vol. Red Mountain (Durham County), N. C.

Letters to Willie P. Mangum (1792-1861), North Carolina judge, member of United States Congress, 1823-1826, and U. S. senator, 1830-1836, 1840-1853, from George E. Badger, John C. Calhoun, Henry Clay, W. C. Preston, and Daniel Webster, concerning state and national maneuvering of the Whig Party; legal papers, deeds, etc., revealing the Mangum ancestry; and a family Bible, containing a list of children born to one of Mangum's slaves.

3484. WYATT MANGUM PAPERS, 1839-1860. 6 items. Granville County, N.C.

Miscellaneous business and legal papers.

3485. LOUIS MANIGAULT PAPERS, 1776 (1840-1878) 1883. 2,038 items and 4 vols. Charleston, S.C.

Papers of Louis Manigault and the Manigault family contain a few letters of Joseph Manigault, loyalist living in England during the American Revolution, to his father in America describing his activities and the difficulties of his position; letters, 1802-1808, to Gabriel Manigault from the children of Ralph Izard, his father-in-law, commenting on a drought in Virginia, 1806, criticizing the people of the South Carolina up-country, 1808, and discussing the effect of the embargo on Charleston, 1809; and letters, 1808-1824, from Margaret (Izard) Manigault to her family concerning family affairs and describing the life of the upper class in Charleston, South Carolina, and Philadelphia, Pennsylvania. Personal and family papers of Charles Izard Manigault, 1820-1837, include letters from friends in the Far East and Africa describing a cholera epidemic in Mauritania in 1820 and a military expedition in Sumatra, Dutch East Indies, in 1821; a description of Boston and its foreign trade, 1818; comments on the effects of the panic of 1819 in Charleston and Philadelphia; a travel journal kept by one of Ralph I. Manigault's sisters on a trip through the northeastern United States and Canada in 1825; description of a cholera epidemic in Philadelphia in 1832; and a discussion of South Carolina College and its new president, Robert Woodard Barnwell, 1836, There are also correspondence of Louis Manigault as a student at Yale College, New Haven, Connecticut, in the 1840s, and letters throughout the ante-bellum period on the activities of Delta Beta Phi fraternity at Yale.

Letters and papers, 1837-1883, concern the management of a number of rice plantations owned by Louis Manigault and Charles Izard Manigault, particularly "Gowrie" plantation on Argyle Island, including slave lists, work schedules, business papers, instructions to overseers, records of provisions and care of slaves, lists of prices for rice, records for construction and maintenance of canals and fields, and correspondence on all phases of plantation work. There is also material reflecting the difficulty of working the plantations after the Civil War, particularly troubles with free labor.

Civil War letters pertain to family life; the Charleston fire of 1861; the effect of disunion on the market for rice and on the discipline of slaves; the imprisonment of a member of the Manigault family at Fort Delaware; and a letter, 1864, critical of conditions at Andersonville Prison, Georgia, and a map of the prison.

Louis Manigault's papers, 1878-1882, concern his work as secretary to the Belgian consulate in Charleston and contain a list of Belgian consuls in Charleston, 1834-1882, with biographical information for many of the men. Three of the volumes in the collection relate to Louis Manigault's management of "Gowrie" plantation, including a prescription book for slave medicines, 1852; a notebook on the preparation of land for rice planting, 1852; and a memorandum book, 1858. There is also an account book from Louis Manigault's days as a student at Yale College, 1845.

3486. MARY H. MANKIN PAPERS, 1843. 3 items. Baltimore, Md.

Three letters from W. A. Clendenin, a Baltimore physician, to Mary H. Mankin, daughter of commission merchant Isaiah Mankin, describing his love for her, his illness, and his business affairs.

3487. HEZEKIAH MANLEY PAPERS, 1826-1834. 71 items. Fluvanna County, Va.

Bills and receipts.

3488. CHARLES MANLY PAPERS, 1849-1853. 4 items. Raleigh (Wake County), N.C.

Routine correspondence of Charles Manly, governor of North Carolina, and a commission signed by him.

3489. CHARLES MANLY AND BASIL MANLY III PAPERS, 1873. 8 items. Georgetown (Scott county), Ky., and Staunton (Augusta County), Va.

Letters of Basil Manly, III (1825-1892), and Charles Manly (b. 1837), Baptist ministers and members of a prominent Virginia family, commenting on family matters and pastoral and educational affairs.

3490. HENRY MANLY PAPERS, 1823-1843. 6 items. Philadelphia, Pa.

Business letters of a printing firm, particularly letters concerning a trip to the South, 1839-1840, to secure printing contracts.

3491. ADELINE SUSAN MANN PAPERS, 1834. 1 item. Boston, Mass.

Love letter to Adeline Susan Mann from Edward Young.

3492. BENJAMIN PICKMAN MANN PAPERS, 1875-1886. 6 items. Cambridge (Middlesex County), Mass.

Business letters and legal papers of Benjamin Pickman Mann.

3493. CHARLES MANN PAPERS, 1864-1872. 1 vol. Missouri.

Letter book of Charles Mann, an officer of artillery in the Union Army, who served in the western theater during the Civil War, containing letters, 1864-1865, sent by Mann in his capacity as assistant chief of artillery, Department of the Mississippi, concerning assignment of men, tactics, promotions, drills, horses, and detached officers and soldiers. Also contains copies of poems.

3494. CHARLES MANN PAPERS. 1 item. Gloucester (Gloucester County), Va.

An undated letter by Charles Mann, an Episcopal minister, discussing a religious controversy in Virginia involving the Universalists, the Methodists, and the Baptists.

3495. HORACE MANN PAPERS, 1845-1848. 8 items. Boston, Mass.

Photostatic copies of letters to Horace Mann (1796-1859), prominent educator of Massachusetts, from R. B. Gooch, asking Mann's advice concerning the establishment of a system of public education in Virginia; from H. R. West, concerning the education of women in Mississippi; and from J. B. Newby, concerning normal schools for North Carolina. Included also are indentures granting freedom to slaves from their former masters, and one certificate of freedom issued to a Negro.

3496. JOHN ANDREW MANN PAPERS, 1861-1863. 32 items. Louisville (Jefferson County), Ky.

Letters of John A. Mann, a soldier in the Union Army, concerning campaigning in Kentucky and Tennessee, and his participation in the battles of Shiloh and Corinth. Some of the letters are in German.

3497. THOMAS MANN JOURNAL, 1805-1830. 7 vols. Amherst County, Va.

Journals of Thomas Mann, a circuit riding preacher in the Virginia Conference of the Methodist Episcopal Church, concerning his preaching and his journeys in Virginia and North Carolina. The journals cover all or parts of the years 1805-1808, 1810-1816, 1828-1830.

3498. CHARLES CECIL JOHN MANNERS, SIXTH DUKE OF RUTLAND, PAPERS, 1843-1856. 15 items. "Belvoir Castle," Leicestershire, England.

Letters of Charles Cecil John Manners concerning agriculture, labor, poor law and parish rates, and protection and free trade; and a letter of John James Robert Manners, later Seventh Duke of Rutland, concerning church matters and a monument for the poet, Robert Southey.

3499. NANCY L. MANNEY ALBUM, 1845-1853. 1 vol. (59 pp.) Beaufort (Carteret County), N.C.

Autograph album of a young girl, which includes a full page poem by Thomas P. Ricaud, a prominent minister.

3500. BENJAMIN W. MANNING PAPERS, 1847-1883. 4 items. Rockford (Coosa County), Ala.

Miscellaneous papers, including a letter, 1861, describing health conditions at Camp Governor Moore near Mobile, Alabama, where the 18th Alabama Regiment encamped.

3501. JOHN LAWRENCE MANNING PAPERS, 1778-1864. 23 items. Sumter (Sumter County), S.C.

Miscellaneous papers including letters from George Washington, Lafayette, Charles Cotesworth Pinckney, and P. G. T. Beauregard; a memorandum of articles taken by the British from John Chesnut during the American Revolution; a letter, 1854, to Manning from Lemuel Blake concerning a textbook on the United States Constitution; and a letter from Benjamin Harris Brewster of

Philadelphia discussing Democratic politics in Pennsylvania and the state delegation to the forthcoming Charleston convention.

3502. EDWIN R. MANSON PAPERS, 1863-1865. 16 items. Maine.

Letters from Edwin R. Manson of the 2nd Maine Regiment, Cavalry, describing Confederate casualties and prisoners, camp life in the Union Army, sickness, food, and troop movements in Virginia, Florida, and Louisiana.

3503. JAMES ALEXANDER MANSON PAPERS, 1897-1912. 19 items. London, England.

Seventeen letters, 1897-1906, to James Alexander Manson from Sir Arthur Thomas Quiller-Couch, concern writings by Quiller-Couch and manuscripts of other authors about which he was advising Manson, editor of Cassell and Company. There are also a signed, autograph manuscript and a revised proof of Quiller-Couch's "Foreword" to Parodies and Imitations, Old and New (London: 1912), edited by J. A. Stanley Adams and Bernard C. White.

3504. THERESIA MANTZ GEOGRAPHY, 1812. 1 vol.

Geography notes.

3505. HORATIO MARBURY PAPERS, 1799-1807. 6 items. Louisville (Jefferson County), Ga.

Miscellaneous letters and papers of Horatio Marbury, relating to his duties in several state positions in Georgia.

3506. JAMES CALVIN MARCOM DIARY, 1862-1863. 1 vol. (154 pp.) Raleigh (Wake County), N.C.

Diary of James Calvin Marcom describing his experiences at Camp Holmes near Raleigh, North Carolina, and in a fight at Kinston, North Carolina, in 1862. Entries in the diary concern camp life, especially the securing of supplies and provisions; training of troops; treatment of Union prisoners; and incidents of resistance to Confederate impressment.

3507. WILLIAM LEARNED MARCY PAPERS, 1845-1855. 7 items. Albany (Albany County), N.Y.

Letters of William L. Marcy (1786-1857), Troy, New York, lawyer, U.S. senator, New York governor, and secretary of state, concerning aid to a young man going to Wisconsin; the Oregon question; the appointment of a marshal in Raleigh, North Carolina; an infraction committed by George Bibb Crittenden, son of John J. Crittenden, as an army officer; and routine matters.

3508. MARIETTA AND NORTH GEORGIA RAILROAD COMPANY PAPERS, 1892. 2 items. Marietta (Cobb County), Ga.

An unsigned document establishing a trust to reorganize the Marietta and North Georgia Railroad Company and an undated statement of the railroad's reorganization.

3509. MARINE INSURANCE COMPANY MINUTES, 1798-1802. 1 vol. Alexandria (Arlington County), Va.

Fragmentary minutes of directors' meetings concerned with the election of officers, seal of the company, rules to be observed, lists of members present and absent, and duties of officers.

3510. FANNIE M. MARION PAPERS, 1859. 3 items. Greenville (Greenville County), S.C.

Personal letters to friends.

3511. FRANCIS MARION PAPERS, 1781. 1 item. Berkeley County, S.C.

Letter to Francis Marion from William Harden informing him of British and American military activity in South Carolina.

3512. ROBERT MARION PAPERS, 1790-1824. 70 items. Georgetown (Georgetown County), S.C.

Miscellaneous papers, including bills and receipts for the schooling of Miss V. Ashby; papers relating to the estate of Anthony Ashby; letter, 1808, describing Washington, D.C., and commenting on the political situation; letter, 1823, from Thomas Ruffin discussing the presidential aspirations of John Quincy Adams, Henry Clay, and William H. Crawford; and a letter from Carter Beverley to Robert S. Garnett, member of the the U.S. House of Representatives, dealing with the presidential election of 1824.

3513. MARION FOUNDRY AND MACHINE WORKS RECORD BOOK, 1906-1920. 3 items and 1 vol. Marion (Smyth County), Va.

Minutes of meetings of the stockholders of the Marion Foundry and Machine Works and a resolution, 1920, of the board of directors of the company.

3514. ALLAN BYRON MARKHAM, SR., MAPS, 1961, 1965. 2 items. North Carolina. Restricted.

Maps drawn by Allan Byron Markham showing the location of early land grants in western Wake County, North Carolina, 1740-1806; and in Durham County, North Carolina, 1750-1800.

3515. BENJAMIN MARKHAM PAPERS, 1836-1866. 21 items. Orange County, N.C.

Correspondence, including a few Civil War letters, showing methods used in escaping military service, and a letter, 1866, regarding the freedmen and labor contracts and expressing the intention of supporting the national government. The papers before 1861 consist largely of tax receipts.

3516. A. H. MARKLAND PAPERS, 1885-1887. 3 items. Washington, D.C.

Letters of Alexander Robinson Boteler to A. H. Markland concerning the movement for the acquisition of Santo Domingo, and a treaty with Hawaii providing a coaling station for the United States.

3517. LOUIS L. MARKS AUTOGRAPH BOOK, 1858. 1 vol. (119 pp.) Lexington (Rockbridge County), Va.

3518. S. MARKS AND COMPANY PAPERS, 1878-1886. 5 items. Roseburg (Douglas County), Ore.

Four business letters and a bill to S. Marks and Company, mentioning commodity prices in Oregon in the 1880s and routine business matters.

3519. S. S. MARRETT PAPERS, (1862-1863) 1883. 69 items. Clayton (Adams County), Ill.

The collection is made up for the most part of letters, 1862-1863, written by S. S. Marrett to his wife concerning his service in the 3rd Illinois Regiment, Cavalry, in Missouri, Arkansas, Louisiana, and Mississippi during the Civil War. He describes his activities as a scout, the difficulties of living off the land, condition of the Southern civilians whom he met, and life in camp.

3520. ISAAC MARSH PAPERS, 1862-1863. 79 items. Chariton (Lucas County), Iowa.

Letters of Isaac Marsh, a Union soldier in the 34th Iowa Regiment, to his wife concern camp life, maneuvers of the Union Army toward Vicksburg, Mississippi, and captured Confederate soldiers, including a group of Texas Rangers.

3521. JONATHAN MARSH LEDGER, 1803-1806. 1 vol. Bath (Beaufort County), N.C.

Ledger of a general merchant.

3522. LUCIUS B. MARSH PAPERS, 1861-1865. 6 items. Boston, Mass.

Miscellaneous papers of Lucius B. Marsh, a colonel in the 47th Massachusetts Regiment in Louisiana and a member of the firm of Marsh, Talbot, and Wilmarth Company which supplied uniforms to the Massachusetts militia in 1865.

3523. CHARLES KIMBALL MARSHALL PAPERS, 1878. 4 items. Vicksburg (Warren County), Miss.

Miscellaneous items, including a letter from Charles Kimball Marshall to D. M. Key, postmaster general of the United States, regarding the adoption by the Post Office Department of a double envelope and postal card which Marshall had evidently invented.

3524. EUGENE MARSHALL PAPERS, 1839-1962. 838 items and 35 vols. Minnesota.

Diaries, 1851-1905, and correspondence, 1847-1918, of a surveyor, farmer, banker and cavalryman during the Civil War and Sioux Wars, 1862-1865. The collection describes military experience in Kentucky, Tennessee, Alabama, and along the Missouri River Valley; towns and society in New England, the upper Middle West, Tennessee, and the Mississippi Valley; Texas on the eve of secession; the effect of the Civil War on middle Tennessee; the Red River carters; the development of Brockton, Massachusetts; religion; education; Negroes; Southern Unionists; women; immigrants; Indians; medicine; agriculture; and individuals including William T. Sherman, Horace Mann, and Ignatius Donnelly. There are also many letters from Marshall's sister in Brockton, Massachusetts, 1861-1910, concerning economic conditions, labor problems, the education and careers of women, medical education, nativism, and immigration and industrialization in Brockton.

3525. FRANCIS MARSHALL PAPERS, 1844. 1 item. Columbia (Richland County), S.C.

Letter regarding a deed of conveyance from W. L. Marshall to W. L. Clayton.

3526. JOHN MARSHALL PAPERS, 1816-1933. 3 items. Washington, D.C.

Letter, 1824, from John Marshall to Henry Jackson of Georgia concerning an estate. Also a letter, 1816, of John Marshall about his son's training.

3527. JOSEPH WARREN WALDO MARSHALL PAPERS, 1809-1930. 1,488 and 2 vols. Abbeville (Abbeville County), S.C.

Family correspondence and business papers of Joseph W. W. Marshall (1820-1904), physician of Abbeville, South Carolina, and of his family, especially a relative, Anne Eliza Marshall (b. 1845) of Greenville, South Carolina. Included are family letters, bills for medical supplies, and papers relative to an extensive business in real estate. The papers of Ann Eliza Marshall include numerous letters written while on a tour of Europe in the 1890s; family reminiscences with references to the founding of Barhamville

(S.C.) School for girls; the Ku Klux Klan; a journal with detailed accounts of the European tour; numerous genealogical accounts with especial emphasis on family connections of Pierce Butler; and a typed copy of the Constitution of the Woman's Foreign Missionary Union of the Enoree Presbytery.

3528. MATTHIAS MURRAY MARSHALL PAPERS, 1862-1865. 5 items. Chapel Hill (Orange County), N.C.

Letters to Matthias Murray Marshall from a former student in the Confederate Army commenting on the neglect of religion in the army, and personal letters to Marshall from Susan Wingfield.

3529. WILLIAM B. MARSHALL ACCOUNT BOOK, 1849-1899. 1 vol. (396 pp.) Aldie (Loudoun County), Va.

Accounts for repair and carpentry work and miscellaneous items including a record of the heirs of James Hixon of Loudoun County; a brief list of officers and men who served in the War of 1812; and the formula for a medical preparation of the late 1870s.

3530. MARSHALL AND PARKER ACCOUNT BOOKS, 1852-1855. 5 vols. Albemarle (Stanley County), N.C.

Daybooks and a ledger showing the sales accounts of a general mercantile firm.

3531. MARSHALL FAMILY PAPERS, 1852. 1 item. Laurens (Laurens County), S.C.

A letter by Mrs. R. H. Marshall to her grandsons describing plantation life near Laurens, details of slaves' work in corn shucking, and relations between masters and slaves.

3532. SAMUEL ARELL MARSTELLER PAPERS, 1783 (1820-1859) 1865. 239 items. Buckland (Prince William County), Va.

Business and personal correspondence of Samuel A. Marsteller (b. ca. 1795), planter, and of his father, P. G. Marsteller, evidently a merchant in Alexandria, Virginia, consisting of letters and deeds relative to land in the West; letters to Samuel A. Marsteller while a student at Dickinson College, Carlisle, Pennsylvania; letters to Marsteller from friends at Dickinson, especially one describing Federalist sentiment on the campus in 1813; letters of J. G. Bailey describing streams, soil, and wood in Kentucky and Missouri; several letters to Marsteller from his brother, Philip F. Marsteller, describing a celebration on July 4, 1826, in Charleston, South Carolina, and family and business activities in other years in Charleston; legal papers, business and personal letters, and bills of Samuel A. Marsteller after settling in Prince William County in 1828; a few letters of the Civil War period relating to the wounding of Marsteller's son, Le Claire A. Marsteller; and some of the latter's letters in 1861 while at Virginia Military Institute, Lexington, and in the vicinity of Harpers Ferry, West Virginia.

3533. BENJAMIN F. MARTIN PAPERS, 1862-1864. 10 items.

Letters from a Confederate soldier to his wife describing camp life and giving instructions for the operation of their farm.

3534. E. BARTON MARTIN PAPERS, 1856-1887. 228 items. Selma (Dallas County), Ala.

Letters of E. Barton Martin to his wife, Julia (Glascock) Martin, concern their courtship and Martin's experiences in Texas as a travelling salesman (one of the first to sell by sample) for the dry goods firm of P. J. Willis and Brothers of Galveston, Texas.

3535. JAMES R. MARTIN AND ROBERT WILSON PAPERS, 1861-1863. 19 items. Pickens District, S.C.

Civil War letters from privates in the Confederate Army.

3536. JOHN MARTIN PAPERS, 1782. 3 items. Augusta (Richmond County), Ga.

Letters to John Martin, governor of Georgia, from General Anthony Wayne discussing the need to reduce the number of deserters from regular and militia troops in Georgia and other military matters, and a letter from John Habersham concerning papers related to John Houstoun.

3537. JOHN K. MARTIN PAPERS, 1850-1880. 4 items. Richmond, Va.

Letters to Martin on political matters, including a pension bill, the election of Rutherford B. Hayes, Virginia politics, and a bill in the Virginia legislature concerning warrants on county land.

3538. JOHN SANFORD MARTIN PAPERS, 1917-1958. 8,586 items and 16 vols. Winston-Salem (Forsyth County), N.C.

The papers of John Sanford Martin, North Carolina newspaper editor and political figure, contain correspondence, 1912-1951, relating, for the most part, to Martin's long career as editor of the Journal and Sentinel, newspapers of Winston-Salem, North Carolina. Letters pertaining to national and state politics form an important part of this correspondence and concern the presidential election of 1928 and the split in the Democratic Party in North Carolina over the candidacy of Alfred E. Smith of New York; opposition to the state sales tax in North Carolina in the 1930s; Martin's leadership in the liberal wing of the Democratic Party in North Carolina and his attempts to bring the state party in line with the New Deal; state and national contests in the elections of 1936; an attempt by Martin and liberal Democrats to keep conservative Democrats from obtaining a federal license for a radio station in Winston-Salem; and pressures put on North Carolina Democrats to join the Dixiecrats in 1948. Papers, 1936-1937, deal with the purchase of the Piedmont Publishing Company, owner of the Journal and the Sentinel, by the Gordon Gray family of Winston-Salem, leaders of North Carolina's conservative Democrats; the decision to retain Martin as editor of the papers; and the establishment of a working relationship between Martin and Gordon Gray. Correspondence from the period of World War II concerns the debate over the entry of the United States into the war, politics in North Carolina during the war, activities at home, and discussions about American policy after the war, including a confidential transcript of an interview with President Harry S. Truman in 1945 on future relations with the Soviet Union and the United Nations. Letters, 1930s-1940s, provide information on economic and social problems in North Carolina from a number of committees on which Martin served. After 1940 there is much material on racial problems in Winston-Salem, and throughout North Carolina and the South. Material reflecting Martin's interest in the Baptist Church includes correspondence concerning various fund raising drives within the church, Wake Forest College and its relocation in Winston-Salem, Campbell College, North Carolina Baptist Hospital, and the purchase of the Biblical Recorder by the North Carolina State Baptist Convention, 1938-1939. Correspondence after 1932 reflects Martin's concern for the improvement of public primary and secondary education in North Carolina and letters, 1941-1957, concern Martin's service on the North Carolina State Board of Education. The collection also includes the minutes of the board of education, 1943-1953, and memoranda on school finance, legislation, integration, curricula, teacher certification and salary, textbooks, school lunches, and student loans. Printed material in the collection pertains to temperance, the R. J. Reynolds Tobacco Company, Wake Forest University, Baptists in North Carolina, politics in North Carolina and the United States, and societies of professional journalists. There are a large number of Martin's speeches and editorials covering all aspects of his career.

3539.  LUTHER MARTIN PAPERS, 1789-1810. 5 items. Baltimore, Md.

Miscellaneous correspondence of Luther Martin, delegate to the Constitutional Convention of 1787 and attorney general of Maryland, concerning debts owed to Maryland, newspaper statements about Martin, and his law practice.

3540.  MORGAN MARTIN PAPERS, 1822-1884. 34 items. Hamptonville (Yadkin County), N.C.

Tax receipts, indentures, and letters to Morgan Martin from relatives who had moved to Nodaway County, Missouri, in the 1840s reporting on family affairs, commodity prices in Missouri and Indiana, corn and grain farming, cattle raising, and the great demand for cattle in 1850 by those who wanted to drive them to California and Oregon. Letters in the 1870s are from relatives in Texas, Missouri, Kansas, and Indiana.

3541.  MYRA C. MARTIN PAPERS, 1858-1864. 10 items. Rock Mills (Randolph County), Ala.

Personal letters to Myra C. Martin, including letters from Confederate soldiers.

3542.  RAWLEY WHITE MARTIN PAPERS, (1851-1868) 1910. 88 items. Competition, now Chatham (Pittsylvania County) and Lynchburg (Campbell County), Va.

Miscellaneous personal letters of Rawley White Martin including love letters between him and Ellen Johnson and scattered letters from his period of service as a Confederate officer, concerning the Peninsular Campaign of 1861, Confederate Army hospitals, physicians, troop movements, and casualties.

3543.  ROWENA MARTIN ALBUM, 1853-1857. 1 vol. (44 pp.) Mocksville, (Davie County), N. C.

Autograph album.

3544.  SUE A. (RICHMOND) MARTIN PAPERS, 1854-1875. 20 items. Leasburg (Caswell County), N.C.

Mainly letters to Sue A. Martin from her mother, Martha A. Richmond, concerning personal affairs and family business. The letters contain occasional references to Reconstruction in North Carolina.

3545.  WARREN FREDERICK MARTIN PAPERS, 1917-1921. 306 items. Philadelphia, Pa., and Washington, D.C.

Miscellaneous papers of Warren Frederick Martin, lawyer and secretary to Senator Philander Chase Knox, containing bills and receipts, and correspondence concerning property Martin had leased; personal and legal business of Reed Knox and Joseph Knox; requests from various people for military assignments during World War I; the amount of property in the United States owned by citizens of the Central Powers; and the Smith bill for federal aid to education, 1918.

3546. WILLIAM A. MARTIN PAPERS, 1862-1864. 11 items. Anderson District, S.C.

Letters from William A. Martin to his wife, Rebecca E. Martin, concerning his service in the 22nd South Carolina Regiment in South Carolina, North Carolina, and Virginia.

3547. GEORGE JACOB MARTZ PAPERS, 1833-1867. 63 items. Harrisburg (Dauphin County), Pa.

Mainly bills and receipts of the Reverend George Jacob Martz.

3548. LUCILLE WRIGHT (MURCHISON) MARVIN PAPERS, 1913-1964. 3 items and 21 vols. Wilmington (New Hanover County), N.C.

Personal account books of Lucille Wright (Murchison) Marvin, including investment accounts, 1913-1926; account books, 1910-1954; and cash accounts, 1940-1954 and 1959.

3549. JUAN FRANCISCO MASDEU PAPERS, 1815. 1 vol. (ca. 130 pp.) Barcelona, Spain.

A transcript of an apparently unpublished work, "Monarquía Española" by Juan Francisco Masdeu, Jesuit and Spanish historian.

3550. ARMISTEAD THOMSON MASON PAPERS, 1813. 2 items. Leesburg (Loudoun County), Va.

Two muster rolls of the company of Captain Epas. Sydnor of the 5th Virginia Militia, engaged in the United States service during the War of 1812, sent to Colonel Armistead Thomson Mason.

3551. AUGUSTA S. MASON SCRAPBOOK, 1859-1860. 1 vol. (71 pp.) Portland (Cumberland County), Me.

Scrapbook of newspaper clippings and poetry.

3552. BESSIE N. MASON PAPERS, 1807 (1881-1944) 1948. 500 items. York (York County), S.C.

Letters and postcards to Bessie N. Mason, dealing for the most part with personal matters but with scattered references to Hampden-Sydney College and Hollins College in Virginia; Mitchell College in North Carolina; the Civil War in Georgia and Tennessee; Memphis, Tennessee, in the 1880s and Sam Jones's revivals in Memphis in 1893; the Arizona Territory in the 1890s; the battle of San Juan and the taking of Santiago, Cuba, 1898; and the Philippine Islands in the early 1900s. The collection also contains sermons, sermon outlines, cooking recipes, and bills and receipts.

3553. ELEANOR PRESTON MASON DAYBOOK, 1870-1876. 1 vol. (177 pp.) Chigwell, Essex, England.

House expense book for "The Marchins."

3554. HORATIO MASON PAPERS, 1808-1848. 1 vol. Toddy Pond, Swanville Township (Waldo County), Me.

Ledger for lumber mills owned by Horatio Mason.

3555. JAMES MASON PAPERS, 1847-1864. 5 items. Hawkinsville (Pulaski County), Ga.

Correspondence of James, Daniel H., and Benjamin F. Mason, apparently brothers, concerning gold on their father's land in 1858, James's service in the Confederate Army at Vicksburg in 1863, and Benjamin's illness in a hospital at Cuthbert, Georgia, in 1864.

3556. JAMES MURRAY MASON PAPERS, 1835-1865. 20 items. Winchester (Frederick County), Va.

Personal and business papers of James M. Mason (1798-1871), member of the United States Congress and Confederate commissioner to England and France, contain letters to A. J. Beresford-Hope in England concerning social engagements and events in the Civil War, letters of Mason to Philip Clayton Pendleton of Martinsburg, West Virginia, dealing with social matters and describing the disorganization of the U.S. House of Representatives and the paralysis of the government in 1860, and business correspondence.

3557. JOHN YOUNG MASON PAPERS, 1844-1849. 5 items. Richmond, Va.

Correspondence of John Young Mason, who was a member of the U.S. House of Representatives and held several political offices, containing a letter, 1849, from Simon Cameron recommending a contractor from Pennsylvania who was bidding on a project in Virginia; a letter to Mason from Willie P. Mangum and other prominent North Carolinians recommending James Abbott for a lieutenancy in the United States Navy; and letters written for Mason while he was secretary of the navy of the United States concerning the investigation of a ship alleged to be in the slave trade, 1844, and the transportation of Wilson Shannon to Mexico to assume his duties as ambassador, 1844.

3558. LUCY RANDOLPH MASON PAPERS, 1917-1954. 6,528 items and 4 vols. Richmond, Va., and Atlanta, Ga.

The papers of Lucy Randolph Mason, social reformer and southeastern public relations representative for the Congress of Industrial Organizations (C.I.O.).

Correspondence before 1937 pertains mainly to the Richmond League of Women Voters. During 1937-1954, correspondence concerns C.I.O. unions; strikes; wages, hours, and working conditions in various Southern industries; competition between the C.I.O. and the American Federation of Labor; the Highlander Folk School, Monteagle, Tennessee; Southern School for Workers, Richmond, Virginia; Southern Regional Council; Southern Conference Education Fund; the Political Action Committee of the C.I.O.; the administration of Franklin D. Roosevelt; penal reform; Georgia politics and government, especially the gubernatorial election of 1946; and the enlistment of churches for labor causes and opposition to racial prejudice. Papers contain speeches and notes for speeches given by Lucy Mason and several given by Henry Wallace. Also minutes, memoranda, and miscellany concerning union and philanthropic activities; printed matter, including publications of the C.I.O. Federal Council of Churches, Southern Regional Council, Southern Conference Education Fund, and National Religious and Labor Fund; and clippings relating to labor unions, Georgia politics, and the administrations of Franklin D. Roosevelt and Harry S. Truman.

3559.  MARY ELIZA MASON PAPERS, 1827-1838. 1 vol. Mattawoman (Charles County), Md.

Original poems written by Mary Eliza Mason and copies of poems by prominent writers of the period.

3560.  THOMSON FRANCIS MASON PAPERS, (1778-1884) 1886. 152 items. Alexandria (Arlington County), Va.

Letters and papers of Thomson Francis Mason (d. 1838), and of his father, Thomson Francis Mason (d. ca. 1820), and of the former's wife, Elizabeth (Price) Mason, and their children. The collection falls into four categories; papers showing the purchase of supplies from John Davis for Revolutionary soldiers from 1778 until 1781, evidently from the papers of Thomson F. Mason, (d. ca. 1820); letters and papers of Thomas F. Mason (d. 1838) relative to the settlement of his father's estate, legal matters, sale of land during the 1820s and 1830s, and in 1837 the lease of Mason's farm to Bailey Tyler with provision for "due rotation for the fallow crop" as well as the use of clover and plaster; letters of Elizabeth (Price) Mason to her children, especially Francis while at Princeton College, Princeton, New Jersey, and of friends and lawyers to her on business matters involving lawsuits over property; and, after 1850, letters to Francis Mason from his friends and sisters. The letters and papers centering around Elizabeth (Price) Mason contain many references to family affairs, farming operations, and the Loudoun County estate owned by her husband and Richard H. Henderson, with comments on the difficulties of travel between her home, "Culross," near Alexandria, Virginia, and "Eagle's Rest," in Loudoun County, Virginia. Included also are letters from James Barbour, John J. Crittenden, John K. Griffin, and Eleanor Parke (Custis) Lewis. One letter from Carry Mason, daughter of Elizabeth (Price) Mason, contains a reference to the superior character and ability of Robert E. Lee.

3561.  MASSACHUSETTS BOSTON OVERSEERS OF THE POOR PAPERS, 1826-1860. 13 items.

Routine items pertaining to the duties of the Overseers of the Poor of Boston, Massachusetts.

3562.  MASSACHUSETTS VOLUNTEER MILITIA AUTOGRAPH ALBUM, 1863. 1 vol. (118 pp.) New Bern (Craven County), N.C.

Autographs of Company F, Massachusetts Regiment, usually giving the height and home address of the signers and containing brief remarks about some of the signers.

3563.  LUCY C. MASSENBURG PAPERS, 1838-1916. 78 items. Louisburg (Franklin County), N.C.

Letters to Lucy C. Massenburg and her family from other family members and friends concerning personal matters and local news; recipes for making dyes; religion in general and religious practices in the Confederate Army; a yellow fever epidemic, 1867; temperance; and Negroes serving on a jury in North Carolina, 1868.

3564.  LUCIUS S. MASSEY SERMONS, 1922-1927. 5 vols. Red Springs (Robeson County), and Hertford (Perquimans County), N.C.

Sermons of a minister of the Methodist Episcopal Church, South.

3565.  JOHN W. MASSIE PAPERS, 1837 (1864-1868). 12 items. Westminster (Carroll County), Md.

Civil War letters of a Copperhead, relating to suspects, arrests, evasion of the draft law; and letters discussing possibilities of mercantile business in Texas.

3566.  WILLIAM MASSIE PAPERS, 1766-1890. 614 items. "Pharsalia," (Nelson County), Va.

Papers of William Massie (1795-1862), including some papers of his brother, Thomas (b. 1782), and of their father, Thomas Massie (d. 1834), all planters of Nelson County, and papers of William Massie's children and grandchildren. Among the papers are surveyors' plats of lands owned by the Massies; family letters; indentures; deeds; genealogical material; inventory of William

Massie's estate; architect's drawing for plantation buildings; a letter from a student of Hampden-Sydney College, Virginia, 1834; papers relating to the division of the elder Thomas Massie's estate; and a series of letters and other records of the Massie plantations including a diagram for crop rotation, plantation account books, a weather memorandum book for 1858-1860, and a book of orchard reports. The papers also contain business letters and bills from firms in Richmond and Lynchburg (Virginia), Baltimore (Maryland), and other cities listing prices for tobacco, wheat, corn, flour, and other commodities and discussing general economic and business conditions; a few letters dealing with William Massie's political career as a member of the Virginia House of Delegates, 1839-1840, and sheriff of Nelson County in the 1840s; Civil War material, including an incomplete letter, 1862, describing the battle of Shiloh, and items relating to the impressment of Massie property by the Confederacy; and an eyewitness account of the Chicago fire of 1871.

3567. LUCY MARIA (BUTLER) MASSY, BARONESS MASSY, PAPERS, 1828-1860. 34 items. Dublin, Ireland.

Letters, mainly in French, to Lucy Maria (Butler) Massy from her cousin, Anne Butler, describing a variety of persons, subjects, and events in the social and cultural life of Dublin, Ireland, including Mr. Glennon, a taxidermist who specialized in birds; an exhibition by Stephen Catterson Smith, a portrait painter; the Dublin Exposition of 1853; spiritualism and a seance by Mrs. W. R. Hayden, an American medium; the marriage of the Reverend James Rumsey to Elizabeth Medlycott; poetry by Julia Lees; Mr. Knapp, a teacher of navigation; a piano concert by a child prodigy, Arthur Napoleão; tax evasion and the new revenue law in Ireland, 1852; Susan Doyne and mining in County Wicklow; and the Parnell family. The collection also contains an incomplete, anonymous manuscript discussing the role of the mother in the family, written in response to statements in The Life, Character, and Remains of the Rev. Richard Cecil (London: 1811).

3568. CORNELIUS MASTEN PAPERS, 1797-1840. 29 items. Milo and Penn Yan (Yates County), N.Y.

The collection is made up mainly of indentures, deeds, legal papers, and business letters pertaining to Cornelius Masten's land transfers in New York; and a letter from John Martineau, 1824, concerning a proposed cotton factory near Huntsville, Alabama.

3569. MASTER BUILDERS' EXCHANGE OF PHILADELPHIA, PENNSYLVANIA, MINUTES, 1886-1891. 1 vol. (289 pp.) Philadelphia, Pa.

3570. THOMAS MASTERS PAPERS, 1801-1846. 24 items. New York, N. Y.

The collection contains official papers and letters of credit carried by Thomas Masters as supercargo on the brig Maria during a voyage to the Mediterranean 1801; a charge against the Maria drawn by Don Manuel de Medina y Jimenez, concerning an encounter with the Spanish corsair Felucca Esperanza; and letters concerning sugar cane planting and trade in the Danish West Indies, 1825, and a trip through the southern United States, 1840.

3571. ALEKSANDER MATEJKO PAPERS, 1966. 4 items. Warsaw, Poland.

Papers on economic and social conditions in Poland prepared by Dr. Aleksander Matejko of Warsaw, Poland, while he served as a visiting professor of sociology at the University of North Carolina at Chapel Hill, North Carolina.

3572. R. B. MATHESON PAPERS, 1862-1864. 5 items. Statesville (Iredell County), N.C.

Business letters and receipts, concerning the purchase of a buggy and harness and the shipment of supplies to Alexander County, North Carolina, for wives and mothers of soldiers.

3573. GEORGE MATHEWS PAPERS, 1786-1794. 22 items. Augusta (Richmond County), Ga.

Papers of George Mathews, member of the United States Congress, 1789-1791, and governor of Georgia, 1793-1796, contain a bond for trustees of an estate, giving some information on the administration of confiscated estates; appointment of Philip Milledge as tax collector for Chatham and Richland counties, Georgia; land grants; letter, 1794, from James Gunn, United States senator and from Georgia, concerning the danger of a war with Great Britain; bill for the hire of a slave; and a copy of a dissent by Governor George Mathews to an act of the Georgia legislature for disposing of unappropriated territory of that state, 1794.

3574. TANDY B. MATHEWS PAPERS, 1844-1889. 54 items. Warminster (Nelson County), Va.

Letters and business papers of Tandy B. Mathews, a carpenter and overseer of a lumber yard for the James River and Kanawha Canal Company, dealing with affairs of the canal and family matters.

3575. G. H. MATHEWSON PAPERS, 1932-1934. 8 items. Jackson (Butts County), Ga.

Papers of G. W. Mathewson include letters, 1934, dealing with gubernatorial campaign of Eugene Talmadge.

3576. JOHN MATLOCK ARITHMETIC BOOK [1850?]. 1 vol. Caswell County, N.C.

Manuscript volume of arithmetic problems and exercises.

3577. WILLIAM GEORGE MATON PAPERS, 1815. 1 item. London, England.

Letter to William George Maton, a London physician, from Thomas Hardwicke, discussing Hardwicke's connection with the Linnaean Society and his submission to the society of a drawing of a sawfish from the Ganges River.

3578. GEORGE MATTHEWS PAPERS, 1853-1864. 129 items. Boston, Mass.

The papers of George Matthews relate to his work as captain of the National Eagle, a sailing ship owned by Fisher and Company of Boston, Massachusetts, engaged in trading voyages to India and various ports in North and South America. Letters concern the difficulties of raising and retaining a crew; disease among the sailors; the various cargoes carried by the ship; repairs on the vessel; the Sepoy revolt in India, 1857; and the threat of Confederate privateers and commerce raiders.

3579. JAMES S. MATTHEWS ACCOUNT BOOK, 1902-1908. 1 vol. (388 pp.) [Baltimore, Md.?].

Accounts of a general merchant.

3580. J. B. MATTHEWSON PAPERS, 1840-1847. 7 items. Providence (Providence County), R.I.

Business letters mentioning the potato trade and potato prices.

3581. WILLIAM GEORGE MATTON PAPERS, 1859-1887. 4 items. High Point (Guilford County), N.C.

Papers of William George Matton, minister and presiding elder of the northern Methodist Episcopal Church in North Carolina, contain his memoirs, 1866-1883, concerning his decision to come to the South as a preacher; the work of the northern Methodists throughout North Carolina; relations with the Methodist Episcopal Church, South; relations between the white and black membership of the church; church sponsorship of schools, including Bennett College at Greensboro, North Carolina, and North Carolina Seminary at High Point, North Carolina; camp meetings; annual conferences in North Carolina and their presiding bishops; several general conferences of the church; temperance; and local churches throughout the state. The collection also contains a brief autobiographical statement written in 1887, which records Matton's church in New York City, 1859-1866, and summarizes his career in North Carolina, 1867-1887; and an incomplete speech or sermon.

3582. JAMES T. MATTOX DAYBOOK, 1880-1881. 1 vol. (67 pp.) Marshall (Fauquier County), Va.

Records of a blacksmith.

3583. MAUDE AND WRIGHT LETTERPRESS BOOK, 1865-1866. 1 vol. (994 pp.) Augusta (Richmond County), Ga.

Letters of a firm dealing primarily in cotton.

3584. BENJAMIN MAULSBERG LEDGER, 1840-1851. 1 vol. Leesburg (Loudoun County), Va.

Business ledger of a saddler, with a few livery accounts.

3585. DABNEY HERNDON MAURY PAPERS, 1875. 2 items. Richmond, Va.

Letter of Dabney Herndon Maury, Confederate general and organizer of the Southern Historical Society, to Colonel J. P. Nicholson concerning Maury's attempts to find a northern publisher for his articles on the Civil War; and a biographical questionnaire filled in by Maury.

3586. MATTHEW FONTAINE MAURY PAPERS, 1829-1871. 166 items. Lexington (Rockbridge County), Va.

Family and professional correspondence of Matthew F. Maury (1806-1873), famous hydrographer. Many of the letters are written from Mexico and from Virginia Military Institute, Lexington, and concern the publication of Maury's Physical Survey of Virginia. Many letters addressed to Matthew F. Maury were from his cousin, Rutson Maury, relative to family affairs. Included also are letters from Dabney Herndon Maury.

3587. RICHARD LAUNCELOT MAURY PAPERS, 1824 (1866-1889) 1908. 5,696 items and 35 vols. Richmond, Va.

Papers of Richard Launcelot Maury (1840-1907), his wife, Susan Gatewood (Crutchfield) Maury, and his son, Matthew Fontaine Maury III (b. 1863), and papers relating to many other members of the Maury family, including Richard L. Maury's father, Matthew Fontaine Maury (1806-1873). Correspondence contains letters, 1824, of Dabney M. Herndon and his family, especially his daughter, Ann Hull Herndon, who became the wife of Matthew F. Maury (1806-1873); correspondence, 1856, 1858, 1860, of Matthew F. Maury concerning his investments in land in Minnesota; a few letters and papers of Richard L. Maury, Matthew F. Maury, and John H. Maury from the period of the Civil War, mainly concerning Richard's service with the 24th Virginia Regiment and John's experiences in Mississippi; copies of letters, 1865, of Matthew F. Maury concerning the post of "Imperial Commissioner of Colonization" which he accepted from Maximilian, Emperor of Mexico; letters, 1865-1866, of Susan C. Maury describing her life in Mexico, where Richard L. Maury was serving as assistant to his father; correspondence, 1866-1868, of Richard L. Maury and Susan C. Maury describing Richard's attempts to find employment in Cuba and Nicaragua, and their life at Javali Mine, Nicaragua, which he managed, including letters from Lucy and Elie Maury in England and Rutson Maury in New York; correspondence, after 1869, of Richard L. Maury's law firm, Maury and Letcher, of Lexington, Virginia; letters, 1869-1873, of Matthew F. Maury and letters concerning his estate, 1873; letters, 1881-1885, from Matthew F. Maury III (b. 1863), as a student at the University of Virginia and at the Columbian University Law Department in Washington, D. C.; letters, 1886, of Matthew F. Maury III, while on a European tour; correspondence of the law firm of Richard L. Maury and Matthew F. Maury III; correspondence of Richard L. Maury with Civil War veterans concerning the battles in which he fought and letters pertaining to Confederate veterans' organizations; letters of Richard L. Maury relating to his Huguenot ancestors; and correspondence pertaining to the estate of Richard L. Maury, 1907. Legal papers contain land deeds of various members of the Maury family; Mexican land grants and legal papers; papers related to legal cases involving the Universal Life Insurance Company of New York and Eugenia M. Hodge v. Wheeling Lands; survey reports and maps; and the wills of Matthew F. Maury and Richard L. Maury. Financial papers include records of Maury and Letcher, 1869-1874; papers concerning the financial affairs of C. W. Maury and Company, New York stockbrokers Richard L. Maury, 1873-1907; and financial records of Matthew F. Maury. Collection also contains genealogical material on the Maury family and several related families and a history of the Maury family by Richard L. Maury; a number of Confederate bonds; school reports of Matthew F. Maury III; clippings, published speeches, and pamphlets, for the most part dealing with the Civil War, including Richard L. Maury's In Memoriam, a tribute to Matthew F. Maury; journal, 1886, of the European tour of Matthew F. Maury III; notebook of Matthew F. Maury III, on the sermons of Dr. Charles Minnigerode of St. Paul's Church, Richmond, Virginia; the journal of Richard L. Maury kept while on a trip to London, England, 1873; expense account for European trips taken by Richard L. Maury's family, 1890, 1892; Richard L. Maury's expense accounts, 1869-1907; diary of Richard L. Maury, 1866-1867; diary of Ann Maury, 1889; and a scrapbook of clippings, 1861-1865, mainly from the Richmond Enquirer and the Richmond Whig, concerning the Civil War.

3588.   JONATHAN MAXCY PAPERS, 1800.  1 item.
        Providence, R.I.

Letter from Jonathan Maxcy, president of Rhode Island College, to Jonathan Edwards, Jr., president of Union College, Schenectady, New York, recommending a person named Allen for a professorship in mathematics and natural philosophy.

3589.   VIRGIL MAXCY PAPERS, 1834-1838.
        6 items.  Charleston, S.C.

Financial papers of Virgil Maxcy, including an account of the public auction of a slave family in Charleston, South Carolina, in 1837.

3590.   SAMUEL BELL MAXEY PAPERS, 1878.
        1 item.  Paris (Lamar County), Tex.

Routine administrative letter of U. S. Senator Samuel Bell Maxey of Texas.

3591.   SARAH P. MAXWELL PAPERS, 1779, 1801.
        2 items.  Savannah, Ga.

Letters of Sarah P. Maxwell, concerning the seizure and return of thirty of her slaves by British troops, and giving recipes for home remedies.

3592.   SIR WILLIAM MAXWELL PAPERS,
        1915-1939.  29 items.  Aberdeen, Aberdeenshire, Scotland.

Letters to Sir William Maxwell, newspaper executive and member of the Unionist Party, concerning his activities in Unionist and Conservative party politics.

3593.   DAVID MAY PAPERS, 1839-1862.
        11 items.  Petersburg (Dinwiddie County), Va.

Papers of David May include a letter to a Southern woman in New York City, 1861; a letter, 1862, concerning the support of the family of a Confederate soldier; and letters concerning personal debts and the settlement of debts in Virginia.

3594.   JOHN FREDERICK MAY PAPERS, 1861.
        1 item.  Washington, D.C.

Letter from John Frederick May, a noted surgeon, to General Mansfield reporting that May had been refused a pass to inspect the entrenchments of the United States Army on the Potomac.

3595.   MAY McEWEN KAISER COMPANY, INC.,
        PAPERS, 1913-1948.  80 vols.
        Burlington (Alamance County), N.C.

The collection is made up primarily of a major series of account books of May McEwen Kaiser Company, Inc., and its predecessor, May Hosiery Mills, manufacturer of rayon, cotton, nylon, and silk hosiery. The volumes include balance sheets, 1927-1947; trial balances, 1913-1948; ledgers, 1913-1948; journals, 1915-1948; cashbooks, 1919-1948; voucher registers, 1918-1948; operating ledgers, 1935-1948; cost ledgers, 1935-1948; sales journals, 1918-1928; and sales summaries, 1945-1948. There are also stock registration books, 1927-1942, and stock transfer books, 1927-1941. Two volumes contain records for Daisy Hosiery Mills and May Hosiery Mills. For May Hosiery Mills there are accounts receivable, 1917-1921; trial balances, 1913-1918, 1921-1926; inventories, 1914-1918, 1921-1926; and outstanding customers' notes and acceptances, 1919-1922. For Daisy Hosiery Mills there are accounts receivable, 1917-1922; trial balances, 1921-1922; inventories, 1921-1922; and outstanding customers' notes and acceptances, 1919.

3596. EDWARD THOMAS MAY PAPERS, 1873-1882. 6 items. Washington (Beaufort County), N.C.

Material relating to Trinity College, Randolph County, North Carolina, including pictures of Trinity students, 1873-1874; Edward Thomas May's report card from Trinity, 1881-1882; a newspaper account of the Trinity commencement of 1882; and a notice of a lecture by Charles W. May on the Spanish-American War.

3597. W. W. MAYBERRY PAPERS, 1890-1893. 100 items. Laredo (Webb County), Tex.

Business correspondence of W. W. Mayberry, an agent of the Mexican National Railroad. Included also is a fragment of a short story probably written by a member of the family.

3598. BRANTZ MAYER PAPERS, 1634-1879. 42 items and 1 vol. Baltimore, Md.

Papers of Brantz Mayer, lawyer, historian, and author, contain a letter, 1768, from Bennet Allen, an 18th century Anglican clergyman, to Governor Sharpe of Maryland concerning a riot in Allen's parish; letter, 1787, pertaining to property left by Bennet Allen in America at the time of the American Revolution; letter, 1847, of the Duke of Wellington; letters from William Pinkney White in the 1870s revealing Mayer's interest in obtaining U. S. government publications for the Maryland Historical Society; correspondence, 1866, between Brantz Mayer and Ezra Abbot, librarian of Harvard University, concerning the charter of Maryland; legal papers, 1857-1860, of Brantz Mayer relating to disputes over land claims in Florida under the will of John McDonogh; transcript from a document in the British Museum, prepared for Mayer's publication of A Relation of Maryland, Reprinted from the London Edition of 1635 (New York: 1865); report, 1858, by John Henry Alexander on the location of sources for the history of Maryland; and the roster of committees of the city council of Baltimore, 1864. There are also a few items pertaining to the law practice of Charles F. Mayer, brother of Brantz Mayer; and a "lexiconbook" in Latin, Greek, and German kept by Christian Mayer, father of Brantz Mayer as a boy in Ulm, Germany, and manuscripts in French and German describing the trade of Ulm.

3599. MINOR C. MAYER PAPERS, 1876-1892. 5 items. Charlotte (Mecklenburg County), N.C.

Business papers of a grocer, and an itemized account for the construction of the home of Minor C. Mayer on Tryon Street in Charlotte, North Carolina.

3600. D. F. MAYHEW ACCOUNT BOOK, 1853-1881. 1 vol. (74 pp.) Iredell County, N.C.

Accounts of a general merchant.

3601. JAMES MEACHAM JOURNALS, 1788-1797. 8 vols. Virginia and North Carolina.

Daily records of James Meacham (1763-1820), of Sussex County, Virginia, an itinerant minister of the Virginia Methodist Episcopal Conference. The entries concern his travels as a circuit rider for the Roanoke, Hanover, and Portsmouth circuits, meetings held, general church matters and the question of slavery. [Published: W. K. Boyd (ed.), "A Journal and Travel of James Meacham, 1789-1797," Trinity College Historical Society Papers, Ser. 9 (1912), pp. 66-95; Ser. 10 (1914), pp. 87-102.]

3602. CURTIS G. MEADE LEDGER AND DAYBOOK, 1883-1928. 1 vol. (360 pp.) White Post (Clarke County), Va.

Unidentified ledger, also containing farm and household accounts.

3603. GEORGE MEADE PAPERS, 1888. 1 item. Philadelphia, Pa.

A letter to a Mr. Johnson from Meade (d. 1897), providing information about the Civil War career of General George Gordon Meade.

3604. ELIZABETH MEADOWS PAPERS, 1862. 2 items. Maxey (Oglethorpe County), Ga.

A letter to Mrs. Elizabeth Meadows from Sarah Street, inquiring about James Street and John Meadows, Confederate soldiers who had been reported missing; and a letter from J. H. Armstrong to Sophronia Meadows, describing Civil War activities around Chattanooga, Tennessee, 1862, and commenting on that section of the country.

3605. SQUIRE MEADOWS ARITHMETIC BOOK, 1827-1829. 1 vol. (166 pp.) Person County, N. C.

A manuscript volume of arithmetic problems and exercises. Also contains promissory notes and a justice of the peace summons.

3606. JAMES MEAGHER PAPERS, 1863-1867. 3 items. Jackson (Hinds County), Miss.

Papers of a British subject who lived in Jackson, Mississippi, during most of the Civil War, concerning the confiscation by Union troops of nearly two hundred bales of his cotton, and Meagher's attempt to collect damages.

3607. ADELAIDE SAVAGE MEARES, 1773-1955. 161 items and 7 vols. Wilmington (New Hanover County), N.C.

Papers of Adelaide Savage Meares are made up of miscellaneous family letters, documents, genealogical material, biographical sketches, and clippings. Correspondence includes a letter, 1803, from James A. Neal to his student, Ann Claypoole; letter of introduction, 1841, to President John Tyler for Frederick C. Hill; report of Walker Meares to the board of education of New Hanover County, North Carolina, 1885, on the condition of the public schools; letter, 1901, relating to Belgrade Institute, Maysville, North Carolina; letter, 1903, concerning a trip to Saratoga Springs, New York; letters, 1913 and 1916, describing the first public church wedding in Wilmington, North Carolina, in 1856; and letters, 1932, of Adelaide S. Meares relating to a European trip. Volumes in the collection include two books containing translations of Homer and Virgil, done by Joseph Hill Wright while a student at St. Timothy's Hall, near Baltimore, Maryland, 1849-1850; composition book of Adelaide S. Meares while a student at Tileston Institute, Wilmington, North Carolina, 1875-1877; account book, 1878-1880, for "Point Peter" plantation near Wilmington; two books of original and copied poems from the 1820s; and one book of poetry from the 1880s. The collection also contains clippings concerning Adelaide S. Meares's family and Wilmington; and genealogical and biographical sketches giving information on the Meares, Claypoole, and Hill families.

3608. MECKLENBURG COUNTY PUBLIC SCHOOL COMMITTEE, [CHARLOTTE?] DISTRICT FOR WHITE RACE, ca. 1880s. 1 vol. Charlotte (Mecklenburg County), N.C.

Register of common schools.

3609. MEDICAL LECTURE NOTEBOOK, 1834. 1 vol. (42 pp.) Philadelphia, Pa.

Class notes taken by an unidentified medical student at the University of Pennsylvania.

3610. WILLIAM W. MEECH PAPERS, 1862. 1 item and 1 vol. Burlington (Burlington County), N.J.

Register of letters written by William W. Meech, an army chaplain at the United States hospital, Newport News, Virginia, containing summaries of letters to the families of soldiers who died at the hospital, usually noting the cause of death and the circumstances of the soldier's last hours; letters to Meech's family and friends discussing his work; and letters to ministers and editors requesting newspapers, magazines, and books for the hospital.

3611. ALEXANDER BEAUFORT MEEK PAPERS, 1834 (1841-1865). 42 items and 5 vols. Tuscaloosa (Tuscaloosa County), and Mobile (Mobile County), Ala.

Correspondence, literary works, and diaries of Alexander Beaufort (apparently christened Alexander Black) Meek (1814-1865), newspaper editor and author; and of his brother, Samuel Mills Meek (b. 1830). The correspondence is largely confined to a few letters, 1848-1850, of Julia A. Mildred Harris with poems submitted by her to Meek for publication, including "Erin," "The Swiftness of Time," "Sacred to the Memory of Mrs. Amelisse Eslava," "New Year's Address for 1850," "Revenge," and "The World-Sick Man." Literary works of A. B. Meek include several poems, all apparently unpublished: "The Dream of the Dying Prophet"; "Air-Star-Spangled Banner"; "Proem! Prelude"; "The Pilgrims of Mt. Vernon"; and fragments of manuscripts. Included also are the holograph manuscripts of "To Egeria" and "The Nuptial Fête," published in Songs and Poems of the South (Mobile, 1857); and a lecture delivered before the Tuscaloosa Lyceum, "The Red Men of Alabama." There are also printed poems, largely carriers' addresses, and one holograph manuscript in two volumes of a published work, Red Eagle (New York: 1855, and Montgomery: 1914).

Of greater importance are two volumes of a diary kept by A. B. Meek in 1834 and 1836. The first volume, though largely devoted to descriptions of feminine charms, contains many items of interest, including a short autobiographical sketch; many descriptions of church services; references to one Dr. Harden, a former president of Jackson College, a manual labor school of Maury County, Tennessee; references to members of the Alabama legislature; comments on his study of law and his reading of current literature; many references to Pfister's Book Store in Tuscaloosa; a biographical account of John M. Robinson (d. 1829), author of The Savage, by Piomingo, a Headman and Warrior of the Muscogulgee Nation (Philadelphia: 1910); accounts of the Clintonian Debating Society and the Tuscaloosa Moot Court, organized by young lawyers; occasional poems; and an account of the observation of July 4, 1834. The diary kept in 1836 is devoted to the "Florida Expedition" against the Seminole Indians in 1836 with references to the steamboat trip from Tuscaloosa to Tampa Bay; a stop in Mobile and attending the theater there; Fort Pickens and its fortifications; skirmishes with the Seminoles; his first view of sea island cotton; foraging; the state of agriculture in Florida in 1836; unpalatable drinking water in Florida; the troops on the expedition; and the arrival of Generals Winfield Scott and Duncan L. Clinch. Included also is a list of the officers and men of Tuscaloosa and officers of the Alabama Regiment of Volunteers.

Among the several items connected with S. M. Meek is a diary, 1851-1855, recounting his travels from Tuscaloosa via Columbus, Mississippi, to the Choctaw Agency, Oktibbeha County, Mississippi, at which latter place he taught school, and including descriptions of weddings, political rallies at Starkville, Mississippi, a debating society, his reading of current literature, camp meetings, and the Masons, with frequent mention of Dr. Burt, brother of Armistead Burt, and frequent comments regarding girls. Included also are a long political letter from James S. Hamm in 1862 with an account of one Foote, probably Henry Stuart Foote; an address of Colonel S. M. Meek on the works of Robert Burns; and a scrapbook kept in 1865 relative to national politics.

3612. HELEN COLLINS MEGREW PAPERS. 1 item. Washington, D. C.

A manuscript sketch entitled "Historic Bit of Washington" by Helen Collins Megrew, which mentions George Washington, James Madison, and Dolly Madison, and contains a description of "The Octagon," the home of Colonel John Tayloe.

3613. CALVIN D. MEHAFFEY PAPERS, 1864-1866. 10 items. Marietta (Lancaster County), Pa.

Letters of Calvin D. Mehaffey, a staff officer in the Union Army, to his mother, concerning personal matters, the Union occupation of New Orleans, and garrison and staff life.

3614. RETURN JONATHAN MEIGS PAPERS, 1802, 1814. 2 items. Brownsville (Paulding County), Ga.

Letter, 1802, to Return Jonathan Meigs from William L. Lovely concerning opposition of the Cherokee Indians to the establishment of a certain garrison in their nation, and a business letter, 1814, of Return Jonathan Meigs, son of Return Jonathan Meigs, written while he was postmaster general of the United States.

3615. CHRISTOPHER GUSTAVUS MEMMINGER PAPERS, 1861-1878. 20 items. Charleston, S. C.

Correspondence of Christopher Gustavus Memminger, South Carolina legislator and secretary of the treasury of the Confederate States of America, concerning routine official and personal business, requests for appointment to office, measures to finance the Confederate government, the pay of Thompson Allan, commissioner of taxes of the Confederacy, and the staff requirements of the Confederate customhouse at Charleston, South Carolina, in 1861.

3616. MEMORANDUM BOOK, 1859-1862. 1 vol. (46 pp.)

Accounts of a wood dealer, possibly A. Coleman.

3617. HENRY LOUIS MENCKEN PAPERS, 1901-1971. 5,434 items. Baltimore, Md.

This collection, relating to the work of Henry Louis Mencken as a theater critic and reflecting his lifelong interest in the theater, contains clippings of reviews of European and American plays performed in the United States; articles on the works and lives of various playwrights, including Gabriele D'Annunzio, Gerhart Hauptmann, Sir Arthur Wing Pinero, Victorien Sardou, and George Bernard Shaw; articles on literary criticism; general articles on the theater in various countries, including Germany, Russia, Ireland, England, and the United States; and articles on social issues such as woman suffrage and censorship. The collection also contains a few pictures of playwrights, typed copies of columns on specific plays or the theater generally, and book orders.

3618. THOMAS CORWIN MENDENHALL PAPERS, 1884-1887. 4 items. Terre Haute (Marion County), Ind.

Business letters to Thomas Corwin Mendenhall including a letter, 1886, from John Alfred Brashear mentioning astronomy and a letter, 1887, from Charles Frederick Marvin mentioning the use of seismoscopes for studying earthquakes.

3619. HENRY L. MENEREE, JR., ACCOUNT BOOKS, 1865-1873. 13 vols. Sperryville (Rappahannock County), Va.

Daybooks, 1865-1873; inventory of merchandise, 1867-1868; and ledger, 1865-1866, of a general merchant.

3620. WILLIAM M. MENLOVE PAPERS, 1857-1866. 56 items. Charleston, S.C.

Business papers of William M. Menlove and his father, Edward Menlove, concerning the settlement of the estate of Jane Menlove of Allerton, Yorkshire, England, sister of Edward Menlove; the Great Western Insurance Company of New York; and the beginning of the Civil War.

3621. CALOHILL MENNIS PAPERS, 1816-1828. 10 items. Bedford County, Va.

Papers of Calohill Mennis, an attorney, concern the collection of debts and other legal matters.

3622. ROBERT MENZIES PAPERS, 1805-1812. 7 items. Rockingham Court House (Rockingham County), N.C.

Correspondence of Robert Menzies, lieutenant of militia, includes a letter, 1802, to Menzies reporting on desertion from the militia in the vicinity of Leaksville, North Carolina, and requesting protection for the town; and a letter of Menzies, 1806, mentioning a public whipping for harboring a runaway slave and possession of a stolen saddle.

3623. CHARLES FENTON MERCER PAPERS, 1814, 1830. 2 items. Richmond, Va.

Letter from John T. Brooke to Charles F. Mercer (1778-1858), lawyer, Virginia state legislator, 1810-1817, and U.S. congressman, 1817-1841, concerning public finance; and a letter from Mercer pertaining to a pension for a Revolutionary War veteran.

3624. GEORGE ANDERSON MERCER PAPERS, 1862-1863. 1 item and 1 vol. Savannah, Ga.

Scrapbook kept by George A. Mercer, a captain in the Confederate Army, containing newspaper clippings on Civil War events, including accounts of battles, gunboats destroyed, the attack on Charleston, the funeral of General Thomas Jonathan Jackson, and Federal rule in New Orleans; and an official letter congratulating Lieutenant George W. Williams and the battery at Genesis Point (Fort McAllister), Georgia, for their gallant conduct under attack by Union vessels in 1862.

3625. JESSE MERCER PAPERS, 1805. 2 items. Washington (Wilkes County), Ga.

Letters of Jesse Mercer (1769-1841), Baptist minister, editor of The Christian Index, and president of the Baptist state convention, to Nancy Anthony, probably a member of his congregation, concerning religion and marriage.

3626. JESSE MERCER PAPERS, 1837 (1840-1843) 1925. 35 items. Tarboro (Edgecombe County), N.C.

Chiefly letters from Robert R. Bridgers and John L. Bridgers to their cousin, Jesse Mercer, while they were students at the University of North Carolina, Chapel Hill, North Carolina, describing their life and activities. Also included are two letters from students at St. Mary's College, Raleigh, North Carolina; a letter from Alabama discussing the range of salaries of teachers and clerks, and prices of land and slaves; and copies of the wills of Andrew J. Cotton, James L. Cotton and Robert R. Bridgers.

3627. JOHN FRANCIS MERCER PAPERS, 1783, 1802. 2 items. "Cedar Park," Anne Arundel County, Md.

Letter to John Francis Mercer, Revolutionary soldier, U.S. congressman, and governor of Maryland, from George Weedon on establishing a peacetime military system; and a letter to Mercer discussing the state militia and its artillery ordnance.

3628. WILLIAM NEWTON MERCER PAPERS, 1864. 2 items. New Orleans, La.

Letters relating to Mercer (1792-1879?), a physician, planter, and banker. One item is a letter to C.H. Russel [Russell?] explaining Mercer's refusal to sign an oath of allegiance to the United States, his Unionist sentiments, his Mississippi plantations, and guerrilla activity near Natchez, Mississippi. The other item is a copy of a letter from Secretary of the Treasury Salmon P. Chase to Benjamin Franklin Flanders about Mercer's case.

3629. MERCHANTS AND MECHANICS LAND COMPANY PAPERS, 1873 (1892-1905) 1908. 1,444 items and 19 vols. Savannah, Ga.

Correspondence, ledgers, daybooks, bills, receipts, payrolls, contracts, check stubs, cancelled checks, report of the value of property owned, lists of stockholders, and other papers of the Merchants and Mechanics Land Company and of the Savannah and Isle of Hope Railroad Co. (later, the Savannah, Tybee, and Atlantic Railway Co.). Also included is the correspondence of Daniel Gugel Purse, president of both companies.

3630. GEORGE MEREDITH PAPERS, 1856-1907. 4 items. Dorking, Surrey, England.

Personal and business letters of George Meredith, British novelist, including a letter commenting on a volume containing articles on Madame de Lieven and her relations with Metternich and Guizot.

3631. JONATHAN MEREDITH PAPERS, 1819-1857. 11 items. Baltimore, Md.

Papers of Jonathan Meredith, lawyer and businessman, concerning the business affairs of Governor George Howard and Thomas Tennant, the claim of himself and Reverdy Johnson against the estate of Charles Carroll of Carrollton, and his oration delivered on the death of President William Henry Harrison.

3632. WILLIAM MORRIS MEREDITH PAPERS, 1859. 1 item. Washington, D.C.

Personal letter of W. M. Meredith, Pennsylvania lawyer, official, and secretary of the treasury.

3633. MERIAM-ADAMS FAMILY PAPERS, 1797-1945. 1,465 items. Barre (Worcester County), and Greenfield and Turners Falls (Franklin County), Mass.

Papers of the Meriam and Adams families focusing on Jotham Addison Meriam (1813-1887), teacher, highway surveyor, and dairy farmer; his daughter, Charlotte Eliza (Meriam) Adams (b. 1843); and his granddaughter, Elizabeth L. Adams. Correspondence before the Civil War is primarily with family members discussing personal matters and agriculture in various states, particularly in Massachusetts. Correspondence of Elizabeth L. Adams chiefly relates to her work with various charitable and religious organizations, including Near East Relief, The Golden Rule Foundation, the Porto Rico Child Feeding Committee, the China Famine Relief, the Mooseheart Home and School, the Federal Council of the Churches of Christ in America, the American Missionary Association, the Board for Christian Work in Santo Domingo, the General Committee on Army and Navy Chaplains, and the All-Russian Evangelical Christian Union. The collection also contains correspondence, programs, printed appeals, information on function and history, and pictures pertaining to the International Sunshine Society and its activities, including the Blind Babies Home and Kindergarten in New York City, and the proposed Pine Tree Sunshine Lodge for semi-invalids to be in Southern Pines, North Carolina. Other correspondence concerns Miss Adams's efforts to raise money by sending lists of names of public school teachers for use in advertising to businesses in exchange for payment of merchandise. Miscellaneous papers consist of Meriam family genealogy, invitations, and calling cards. Mortgage deeds, an assignment of mortgage, and promissory notes constitute the legal items. Printed material includes a copy of The Union Gospel News; two small songbooks, one dated 1895; and an appeal from the Golden Rule Foundation.

3634. JOSEPH W. MERRELL PAPERS, 1858-1861. 3 items. Moss Point (Jackson County), Miss.

Papers of Joseph W. Merrell, engineer at a sawmill and on steamboats, consist of two letters attesting to his character and competence, and a personal letter.

3635. RUTH M. MERRIAM DIARY, 1892. 1 vol. (53 pp.) Washington, D.C.

Diary of a young girl while quarantined because of scarlet fever.

3636. AUGUSTUS SUMMERFIELD MERRIMON PAPERS, 1873-1884. 5 items. Raleigh (Wake County), N.C.

Papers of Augustus Summerfield Merrimon (1830-1892), jurist and U. S. senator, concerning minor matters relating to his senatorial career, such as the procurement of government publications.

3637. BENJAMIN H. MERRITT PAPERS, 1856-1892. 22 items. Somers (Westchester County), N.Y.

Routine business and personal correspondence of Benjamin H. Merritt discussing economic conditions in Minnesota, the financial affairs of the Northern Pacific Railroad, the settlement of an estate in New York, patent laws in Canada, and the hiring of three Negro maids including their work contracts.

3638. JOHN MERRITT ACCOUNT BOOKS, 1807-1854. 2 vols. Granville County, N.C.

Merchant's account books, 1807-1814 and 1852-1854.

3639. JOHN W. MERRITT PAPERS, 1838-1886. 69 items. Guilford County, N.C.

Financial papers of John W. Merritt and members of his family, including items, 1840-1847, concerning the settlement of the estate of William C. Merritt.

3640. WALTER GORDON MERRITT PAPERS, 1915-1924. 1,371 items. New York, N.Y.

Papers of Walter Gordon Merritt (b. 1880), lawyer, concerning the case of the Pennsylvania Mining Company v. the United Mine Workers of America, in which the union was charged with conspiracy to hinder interstate commerce. Included is the correspondence of Merritt, chief attorney for the mining company, with James K. Gearhart, president of the company; Paul McKennon, an attorney also representing the mining company; W. A. Hardman, an investigator working for Merritt; James B. McDonough, serving in the company's interests; and Henry S. Drinker, Jr., a Philadelphia lawyer. The correspondence concerns the preparation of briefs, the securing of depositions and affidavits, the development of arguments, legal arrangements between the mining company and the attorneys, and the general prosecution of the case. Also included are depositions and motions connected with the case, and Legal Bulletins 1-11 of the American Federation of Labor, 1924.

3641. WILLIAM E. MERRITT PAPERS, 1864-1865. 4 items. Chicago, Ill.

Papers of William E. Merritt, 1st Illinois Artillery, U.S.A., consist of two letters to his wife discussing foraging by the troops, his refusal to reenlist, and his desire to return home; and a letter and a clipping referring to his death.

3642. WILLIAM H. E. MERRITT PAPERS, 1834-1889. 215 items. Lawrenceville (Brunswick County), Va.

Family and business correspondence and papers of William H. E. Merritt, Virginia legislator, 1866, and plantation owner. The correspondence concerns prices and sales of slaves; the intentions of a slave to buy her freedom, 1857; the removal of sick soldiers from the campus of the University of Virginia, Charlottesville, Virginia, 1861; life in the Confederate Army; the capture of Roanoke Island, North Carolina, by Union troops, 1862; the possibility of using slaves in the Confederate Army; criticism of President Jefferson Davis and his civil and military staff, and of the events of the time; prices of commodities and slaves in Mississippi before the war and conditions of the Negroes after the war; the cost and content of a young girl's education; soil erosion; a new fence law; labor conditions; and personal matters. Also included are family and plantation accounts and bills.

3643. JOHN L. MERTENS PAPERS, 1844-1853. 47 items. Petersburg (Dinwiddie County), Va.

Letters from John L. Mertens, tobacco manufacturer of Petersburg, to his son in New Orleans, Louisiana, containing information on tobacco prices, the problems of the selling the manufactured product, and labor in the plant at Petersburg.

3644. JEAN MESLIER TESTAMENT, 1729. 1 vol. (58 pp.) Paris, France.

Extracts from a biography of Jean Meslier, Catholic priest, with portions of his sermons.

3645. CHARLES THEOPHILUS METCALFE, FIRST BARON METCALFE, PAPERS, 1820. 1 item. London, England.

Letter from Sir John Malcolm to Charles Theophilus Metcalfe, First Baron Metcalfe (1785-1846), British colonial administrator, principally in India, but also governor of Jamaica and of Canada, discussing the possibility of war in the Sindh, the means of executing it, and the recommendations of James Tod, political agent in the western Rajput states.

3646. METHODIST CHURCH PAPERS, 1764-1969. ca. 4,700 items and 386 vols.

The Methodist Church Papers relate principally to the Methodist Episcopal Church, South. Although there are records from other states, the bulk of the papers are those from the region of the Western North Carolina Conference and of the North Carolina Conference. Scattered papers pertain to areas outside the South.

Among the papers are two original letters, a deed, and copies of letters of Francis Asbury; papers, 1858-1889, of William W. Bennett; a sermon, 1785, by Thomas Coke; papers of Erskin Pope; a funeral sermon, 1864, by Archibald A. McMannen; the appointment book, 1833-1848, of W. W. Albea covering his preaching circuits in North Carolina and Virginia; licenses; ministerial trials; sermons; class books; miscellaneous letters; programs; letters relating to the Duke Endowment Superannuate Fund; material on the development of Sunday schools in the nineteenth century; numerous historical sketches concerning Methodism, Methodist ministers, and Methodist churches; the minutes, 1848-1849, of the Wisconsin Annual Conference; and Catalogue and Price List of 1885 from the Methodist Publishing House, Nashville, Tennessee. Papers relating to the unification of the Methodist Church include addresses, 1911, before the Joint Committee on Methodist Federation, Chattanooga, Tennessee; Plan of Union, 1938, with work sheets of the judicial council of the Methodist Episcopal Church, South, original and final drafts, printed copy of the plan, and a picture of the General Conference in 1906; reports, 1929-1939, on the revision of the Methodist Hymnal, including a list of hymns by Charles Wesley; minutes, 1939, of the Joint Commission on Methodist Union, Jackson, Mississippi; and papers, 1939, of a test case on unification tried in Clarendon County, South Carolina.

The principal portion of the records of the Western North Carolina Conference are papers, 1909-1950, of the Board of Missions and Church Extension, and include applications for aid; correspondence concerning the applications, and the financial situation of various churches within the jurisdiction of the board; bank statements; cancelled checks; a bankbook, treasurer's records; minutes; and other papers. Other records of the conference are minute book, 1919-1939, of the board of finance; journal, 1902-1905, of the conference; and "Key to Map of the Western North Carolina Conference, Me[thodist] E[piscopal] Church, South," by John Carlisle Kilgo. The remainder of the records relate to specific districts, circuits, and churches, and a consist of the following: Asheville District quarterly conference minutes, 1912-1916; Charlotte District conference records, 1913-1914; papers of Lincolnton First Church of Gastonia and Shelby districts, including registers, 1909-1954, and quarterly conference minutes, 1902-1962; Greensboro District records including Alamance Circuit quarterly conference records, 1893-1908, Randolph Circuit church registers, 1902-1928, and quarterly conference minutes, 1893-1896, 1901-1915, and 1919-1930, Mount Airy District, West Davie Circuit quarterly conference records, 1922-1923; North Wilkesboro District, Jefferson Circuit church registers, 1893-1932, and quarterly conference record book, 1926-1929; Salisbury District records including quarterly conference minutes, 1895-1898, for Salisbury and Church Street Church; Shelby District records including district minutes, 1917-1927, Polkville Church conference minutes, 1897-1914, and quarterly conference minutes for Double Shoals and Polkville circuits, 1892-1895, Polkville Circuit, 1911-1927, and Shelby Station and Central Shelby, 1917-1920, and Statesville District records including quarterly conference minutes of presiding elder, 1894, Broad Street Church register, 1917-1924, Hopewell Church records, 1884-1895, Morganton Circuit church register, 1889-1902, and quarterly conference records, 1906-1910, 1919-1924, and 1928-1932.

Most significant among the papers of the North Carolina Conference are the journals, 1838-1913. Other records and papers include a clipping, 1837, concerning appointments of the 31st session of the annual conference; minutes, 1838-1847, of the relief society, which gave financial aid to ministers, their widows and children; account book, 1887; exam questions, 1895, for admission to the conference; conference statistics, 1886-1889 and 1894-1913; minute book, 1902-1919, of the Raleigh Advocate Publishing Company; annual report, 1908, to the North Carolina Conference Historical Society; minute book, 1911-1930, and ledger, 1910-1930, of the board of education; the Sunday school board annual reports, 1926-1931; the board of publication report, 1928-1929; papers relating to missions, including letters of 1821 concerning missionary work among the Creek Indians, letters of 1900-1908 dealing with missionary work in India, and the Board of Missions papers from 1927; minutes, 1848-1957, of the Board of Trustees; and North Carolina Conference Historical Directory by Joseph W. Watson and C. Franklin Grill (Raleigh: 1976), containing historical data about each church in the conference.

The remainder of the papers of the North Carolina Conference relate to specific districts, and to individual circuits and churches within the districts. For the Charlotte District there are quarterly conference minutes, 1860-1881, and a register, 1877-1886, of the Monroe, Matthews, and Clear Creek circuits. Records for the Danville District are quarterly conference minutes, 1844-1858, of the Caswell and Yanceyville circuits. Among the Durham District papers are district conference minutes, 1885-1912; quarterly conference minutes, 1912-1927; Bethany Church conference minutes, 1885-1886, and Sunday school records, 1891-1896; Burlington (Front Street) Church quarterly conference minutes, 1899-1906; quarterly conference minutes, 1897-1898, of Burlington, Graham, and Haw River circuits; Carr Church membership register, 1887-1897; Durham Circuit register, 1889-1925, and quarterly conference minutes, 1895-1898 and 1903-1934; Gregson Street Church membership register, 1908-1927; Leasburg Circuit quarterly conference minutes, 1885-1914 and 1923-1930; Leasburg Church conference minutes, 1885-1902; Union Church conference minutes, 1885-1904; Main Street Church quarterly conference minutes, 1890-1910, board of stewards' proceedings, 1891-1908, church assessments, 1900, and membership register, 1885-1907; Milton Circuit quarterly conference minutes, 1894-1901; Mt. Tirzah Circuit pastor's book, 1932-1933; Pittsboro Circuit quarterly conference minutes, 1926-1930, conference records, 1888-1894 and 1935-1943, church register, 1894-1901, and Sunday school conference record, 1918-1920; Woodsdale Circuit quarterly conference minutes, 1902-1908; and Yanceyville Circuit quarterly conference minutes, 1891-1902. Records of the Duke Memorial Church, also located within Durham District, include quarterly conference minutes, records, and reports, 1915-1941; minutes of the board of stewards, 1916-1923 and 1945-1956; Epworth League annual report, 1909, and record books, 1911-1912; membership register, 1885-1924; and the Women's Missionary Society papers, 1919-1933, minutes, 1917-1925, and 1934-1935, and roll books, 1912-1929. For the Elizabeth City District there are quarterly conference minutes for the district, 1911-1914 and 1919-1921, and for the following circuits: Camden, 1898-1909; Chowan, 1896-1897, with church records, 1914; Columbia, 1900-1903 and 1908-1911; Dare, 1896-1903; Gates, 1886-1911; Hatteras, 1896-1911; Hertford, 1874-1904; Kittrell's Church, 1898-1903; Kitty Hawk, 1896-1899 and 1904-1911; Moyock, 1907-1910; North Gates, 1895-1902; Pantego, 1896-1898; Pasquotank, 1896-1899 and 1903-1906; Perquimans, 1895-1918; Roanoke Island Station, 1896-1911; and South Camden, 1899-1902. Also for the Elizabeth City District are the Elizabeth City Church records, 1914 and 1919-1920, and the Hertford Church Sunday school record book, 1904-1905. Fayetteville District records consist of quarterly conference minutes, 1922-1923; Haw River quarterly conference minutes, 1854-1887; Pittsboro Circuit quarterly conference records and minutes, 1895-1934; Rockingham Circuit quarterly conference minutes, 1845-1869; Rockingham Station pastor's visiting and memorandum book, 1889-1890; and Mt. Olivet Church class book, 1854-1871. Among the records for the Greensboro District are the Chatham Circuit quarterly conference minutes, 1838-1841, baptismal records, 1833-1841, financial records, 1833-1837, and membership list, 1839; Forsyth Circuit preachers' class book and plan of the circuit, 1875-1876; Mt. Pleasant Church class book, 1857-1866; Franklinsville Circuit quarterly conference minutes, 1850-1862; Guilford Circuit quarterly conference minutes, 1832-1865; Pleasant Garden Circuit quarterly conference minutes, 1880-1883; Randolph Circuit quarterly conference minutes, 1875-1887, and papers, 1881-1889; Tabernacle and Union Church, Sunday school minute book, 1841-1854; South Guilford and Pleasant Garden circuits quarterly conference minutes, 1861-1883; Stokesburg Church class book, 1860-1877; Trinity College Circuit quarterly conference minutes, 1863; Yanceyville Circuit quarterly conference minutes, 1858-1872; and Haw River Circuit church book, 1841-1852. Included in the Hillsboro District records are district conference minutes, 1882-1884; church conference minutes of Bethany Church, 1884, of Leasburg Church, 1883-1884, and of Union Church, 1883-1884; and the quarterly conference minutes of the following: Franklinsville Circuit, 1865-1871; Franklinsville and Cedar Falls Station, 1872; Guilford Mission, 1867; Leasburg Circuit, 1883-1884; South Guilford Circuit, 1867-1872; and Yanceyville Circuit, 1872-1877. Records for the New Bern District are district conference records, 1893-1909; and the quarterly conference minutes, 1837-1844, for Newport and Trent circuits. Records for the Raleigh District are quarterly conference minutes, 1914-1915, and records, 1935-1939; Buckhorn Circuit records, 1870-1901; Cary Circuit quarterly conference minutes, 1912; Franklinsville Circuit quarterly conference minutes, 1849-1850; Henderson Station treasurer's book, 1888-1894; and Tar River Circuit plan and preacher's class book, 1846-1847. Rockingham District records include quarterly conference minutes, 1891-1893; quarterly conference minutes of presiding elder, 1914; and Singletary Church quarterly conference minutes, 1905-1920. For the Salisbury District there are district conference minutes, 1868-1875; Forsyth Circuit class book, 1851; and Iredell Circuit church records, 1834-1850 and 1894, and quarterly conference minutes, 1823-1873. Among the Shelby District records are district conference minutes, 1870-1876; Double Shoals Circuit quarterly conference records, 1884-1887; Gaston Circuit quarterly conference minutes, 1882-1889; Lincolnton Circuit quarterly conference minutes, 1869-1881; Brindletown Church class book, 1857-1872; Rock Spring Circuit quarterly conference minutes, 1868-1876, and records, 1877-1880, and church register, 1881-1895; and Stanley Creek Circuit quarterly conference minutes, 1890. Trinity College District records consist of district conference records, 1885-1890; and quarterly conference minutes of Franklinsville Circuit, 1862-1865, of Randolph Circuit, 1888-1892, and of South Guilford Circuit, 1863-1865. Warrenton District records are quarterly conference minutes, 1913-1915. For the Washington District there are district conference minutes, 1896-1910; quarterly conference minutes, 1907; quarterly conference minutes of presiding elder, 1907-1908; quarterly conference records of Columbia Circuit, 1892-1895, and of Hatteras Circuit, 1887-1890; and quarterly conference minutes of the following: Bath Circuit, 1849-1894, including church records, 1860-1902; Dare Circuit, 1892-1895; First Methodist Church, Washington, 1911-1913; Ocracoke and Hatteras Circuits, 1892-1895; Roanoke Island Station, 1892-1895; and Washington Station, 1891-1914, including church register, 1887-1893. Included in the Wilmington District records are district conference records, 1866-1897; Elizabeth Circuit quarterly conference minutes, 1875-1907; Singletary Church quarterly conference minutes, 1895-1905; Wilmington Church board of stewards' records, 1880-1888; and records of the Fifth Street Church consisting of church registers, 1851-1888, church conference minutes, 1903-1905, records, 1844-1870, and quarterly conference minutes, 1873-1904. District conference records, 1892-1894, relate to Wilson District. Miscellaneous papers include Bath Church records, 1860-1902, and recording steward's book, 1849-1891; church records of Bladen Circuit, 1922-1923, Camden Circuit (Mann's Harbor), 1919-1921, and Littleton Circuit, 1915-1916; Pittsylvania Circuit minutes, 1854-1856; and Hopewell Church (Randolph County) reports, 1955-1960.

There are also papers and records of other conferences. For the Alabama Conference there is a class book, 1851-1879, of the Pleasant Hill Society which also includes records of deaths, marriages, removals, transfers, and expulsions. Records of the Baltimore Conference (Independent) consist of quarterly conference minutes of the Rockingham District for Bridgewater Circuit, 1864-1865, and for Rockingham and Upper Rockingham circuits, 1863. Included in the Baltimore Conference are quarterly conference minutes, 1866-1874, of the Rockingham District, Bridgewater Circuit, with miscellaneous records, 1849-1908. Among the Georgia Conference records are Dahlonega Methodist Church book, 1861-1877; Carrolltown Mission minutes, 1830-1846; and Dahlonega and Jones Chapel Station papers, 1878. Board of Trustees records, 1809-1867, of the Methodist Meeting House comprise the Kentucky Conference records. In the Mississippi Conference records are the quarterly conference minutes, 1835-1877, of White Sand, Westville, and Mt. Carmel circuits; and a map, 1850s, of Holly Spring Circuit. For the Tennessee Conference there are minutes, 1880-1885, of the East Tennessee annual Conference, containing frequent mention of aid to freedmen; and a report on the publishing house, 1917. West Virginia Conference records are the Jefferson Circuit twentieth century thank offerings, 1899-1901.

Records of the South Carolina Conference are principally quarterly conference minutes for the following districts and circuits: Camden District, Montgomery Circuit, 1808, and Rocky River Circuit, 1807-1809; Catawba District, Lincolnton Circuit, 1863, and Rocky River Circuit, 1810-1819; Cheraw District, Wadesboro Circuit, 1845; Fayetteville District, Wadesboro Circuit, 1849; Lincolnton District, Lincolnton Circuit, 1828-1852 and 1860-1862; Shelby District, 1867-1870, Lincolnton Circuit, 1855-1859 and 1864-1869, and Lincolnton Station, 1864-1868; and Spartanburg District, Lincolnton Circuit, 1853-1854. There is also a steward's book, 1846-1873, of Marion District, Bennettsville Circuit.

Records for the Virginia Conference consist of conference minutes, 1806-1808; and minutes, 1902-1910, of the board of education. Danville District records are Chatham Circuit quarterly conference minutes, 1833-1838. For the Fredericksburg and Washington Districts there are Loudoun Circuit quarterly conference minutes, 1850-1858. Neuse District records consist of New River Circuit quarterly conference minutes, 1815-1823, and financial records, 1815-1817; and Trent Circuit quarterly conference minutes, 1824-1832.

In the New Bern District records there are New River Circuit financial records, 1805-1808; and Trent Circuit quarterly conference minutes, 1833-1836. Suffolk District records are conference minutes, 1872-1885, and 1892-1894; Currituck Circuit quarterly conference steward's book, 1858-1859; Gates Circuit church register, 1784-1840 and 1866-1877, and recording steward's book, 1817-1872; North Gates Circuit church register, 1884-1937; and Pasquotank Circuit general church record, 1854-1858. Also included are quarterly conference minutes for the following Suffolk District circuits: Camden, 1886-1897; Gates, 1872-1895; Hertford, 1892-1894; Kitty Hawk, 1887-1891; North Gates, 1889-1895 and 1907-1910; Pasquotank, 1883-1887 and 1891-1895; Perquimans, 1891-1894; and Roanoke Island and Dare Mission, 1888-1891. Records of Yadkin and Salisbury districts are Iredell Circuit quarterly conference minutes, 1823-1851.

Records of the North Carolina District of the former Methodist Protestant Church include Mt. Hermon Circuit class book, 1895-1898; and Winston Circuit quarterly conference minutes, 1890-1907, and class books, 1895-1904.

Other papers, not included in those described above, are the records, 1909-1952, of the American Mission in North Africa, 3738 items, and the papers, 1878-1959, of the Women's Missionary Society (later the Women's Society of Christian Service), 1,440 items and 741 volumes. Records of the American Mission in North Africa include correspondence of Edwin F. Frease, superintendent of the Methodist American Mission in North Africa, and of Joseph J. Cooksey and J. H. C. Purdon, the Mission's representatives in Tunis, with missionaries who served under the Methodist Board of Missions in North Africa; and contracts, bills, and receipts for the residences of various missionaries. Among the papers of the Women's Missionary Society are annual reports of the Women's Missionary Society, of the Foreign Women's Board, and of the Women's Missionary Council; conference reports; board of missions' missionary yearbooks; various journals; maps and descriptive literature of mission stations; committee and statistical reports; scrapbooks; pictures; memorabilia; some correspondence; and other papers.

3647.   E. S. METTS PAPERS, 1860-1864.
        6 items. [Alabama?]

Correspondence of E. S. Metts to her cousins, Alexander and Susan Tilghman, discussing personal matters; the Confederate attack on Santa Rosa Island, Pensacola Harbor, 1861; and the progress of the war. An unrelated letter, 1864, describes an attempt to recover some slaves.

3648.   GEORGE P. METZ PAPERS, 1860-1891.
        4 items and 6 vols. Pleasant Hill (Miami County), Ohio.

Papers of George P. Metz, an ambulance driver in the 99th Indiana Infantry, U.S.A., in the Civil War, include two letters from H. C. Williams probably his brother-in-law, describing life in Minnesota and telling of his enlistment in the Union Army; a letter fragment from Metz probably during the siege of Vicksburg, Mississippi; a volume of miscellaneous information including vital statistics and financial transactions; Metz's Civil War diaries; typescript of the diaries and the three letters; and a postcard telling of the reunion of the 99th Indiana. The diaries tell of wounded and the hospitals; agricultural observations; depredations by Union soldiers; food; weather; religious service; rumors; and minor accounts of the battles in which the 99th Indiana was involved, including the siege of Vicksburg, the Jackson (Mississippi) campaign, the battle of Chattanooga (Tennessee), the Atlanta (Georgia) campaign, and Sherman's march through Georgia and the Carolinas.

3649.   MEXICO. ARCHIVO GENERAL DE LA NACIÓN RECORDS, 1782-1821.
        205 items. Mexico City, Mexico.

Photocopies of documents relating to the Mexican Wars of Independence. The originals are in the Archivo General de la Nación, Mexico City, Mexico. A list of the documents is included in the collection.

3650.   MEXICO. ARCHIVO GENERAL DE LA NACIÓN RECORDS, 1551-1830. 5 items. Mexico City, Mexico.

Typewritten transcripts concerning the early history of the University of Mexico, from the following volumes located in Mexico, Archivo general de la nación: "Catedras y Claustros," 1553-1561, 1750-1760; "Diversas materias," 1560-1732; "Reales Cédulas," 1667; "Substituciones de Cátedras y lugares desde el año de 1724 hasta 1830." Among the titles are: "Lista de los colegios y seminarios de Mexico"; "Cédula real sobre la fundación del estudio, setiembre, 1551"; "Claustro pleno de esta real universidad de Mexico, abril 26 de 1714"; "De la fundacion de la insigne y real universidad de Mexico, noviembre 3, 1596"; "Donativo de la real universidad, octubre 27, 1704."

3651.   MEXICO PAPERS, 1927. 1 item. (61 pp.)

A report on oil lands held by foreigners in Mexico, entitled "Extensiones aproximidas de los adquirados . . . por las companias petroleras-extranjeras . . . . "

3652. HENRY MEYER ACCOUNTS, 1851-1861. 1 vol. (150 pp.) Charleston, S.C.

Arrears list of the German Artillery, a local military organization of Charleston, South Carolina.

3653. A. C. MEYERS PAPERS, 1862. 3 items. Germanton (Stokes County), N.C.

Personal correspondence of a Confederate soldier.

3654. THEODORE AUGUST MEYSENBURG JOURNAL, 1864. 1 vol. (34 pp.)

Notes apparently kept by Major Meysenburg, assistant adjutant-general of the District of Harpers Ferry under the command of General Franz Sigel, detailing positions of Union troops in the lower Shenandoah Valley on July 1, 1864, and their movements and actions during the opening phase of Jubal Early's Washington raid, until July 19 when Meysenburg accompanied Sigel to Baltimore. Included are a hand-drawn map of the Martinsburg-Hagerstown-Harpers Ferry area and loose diagrams illustrating standard tactics.

3655. ALONZO T. MIAL ACCOUNT BOOK, 1868-1871. 1 vol. (40 pp.) Wake County, N.C.

Account book of a merchant.

3656. J. L. MICHAUX PAPERS, 1879. 12 items. Greensboro (Guilford County), N.C.

Subscription bills for the Central Protestant.

3657. WILLIAM ENGLISH MICKLE, SR., PAPERS, 1849 (1900-1910) 1941. 430 items. Mobile, Ala.

Papers of William E. Mickle, Sr. (1846-1920), adjutant general of the United Confederate Veterans (U.C.V.), include photographic copies of his discharge from the Confederate Army in February, 1865, and a subsequent order of March 3, 1865, ordering him to post duty at Mobile. Correspondence of the Bolling family, 1870-1887, concerns an inherited tract of land in Texas, with references to railroads, cities, and other aspects of Texas life. Correspondence of the U.C.V. forms the bulk of the collection and concerns reunions, encampments, monuments, prison conditions during the war, personnel in the U.C.V., internal politics, lobbying in Washington, and the Confederate Mining Company. Papers of William E. Mickle, Jr., relate to the Spanish-American War when he served as quartermaster in the 2nd Alabama Infantry, U.S.V.; his futile attempt to secure a regular army commission; service in the Alabama National Guard after 1900; service in the home guard during World War I; and efforts to obtain a civil service appointment.

3658. MIDDLESEX, ENGLAND. RECORDS, 1802. 6 vols.

List of the freeholders of the County of Middlesex, apparently connected with the contested parliamentary election of 1802 between George Byng, Sir Francis Burdett, and George Boulton Mainwaring, with some notations concerning the new election in 1804 between Burdett and the son of Mainwaring.

3659. ARTHUR MIDDLETON PAPERS, 1800-1837. 1 item and 1 vol. Madrid, Spain, and Charleston County, S.C.

A copy of a letter, 1800, from Middleton's grandmother to her daughter commenting on social life and various individuals in Jamaica (original in the South Carolina Historical Society); and Middleton's diary kept while American chargé d'affaires in Madrid, describing the Carlist War in 1837. The diary has been published in the Southern Quarterly, vol. 7 (April and July, 1969).

3660. JAMES MIDDLETON PAPERS, 1882-1908. 39 items. Garner (Wake County), N.C.

Family letters of a seller of agricultural and domestic machinery in Rand's Mills and Garner, North Carolina. There are descriptions of the Georgia towns of Abbeville, 1894; Columbus, 1895; and Americus, 1899; comments on the Georgia gubernatorial election of 1894; and a description of gold mining at Anaconda, Colorado, 1901.

3661. JOHN MIDDLETON AND ROBERT MIDDLETON PAPERS, 1787-1835. 16 items. Elbert County, and Augusta (Richmond County), Ga.

Routine personal, business, and legal papers, including a commission for John Middleton as 2nd lieutenant in the state militia, 1815; a document concerning slave sales in Georgia, 1809; and references to land sales and the settlement of estates.

3662. THOMAS MIFFLIN PAPERS, 1784. 1 item. Annapolis (Anne Arundel County), Md.

A letter, 1784, from Mifflin, president of the Congress of the Confederation, to George Clinton, governor of New York, stating that garrisons for the northern and western posts cannot be provided until a quorum is present in Congress.

3663. WILEY MIKELL PAPERS, 1784-1886. 25 items. Bulloch County, Ga.

Papers relating to land titles and surveys of Mikell's plantation, including an inventory of his property when he took the oath of allegiance to the United States, 1865.

3664. WILLIAM JOSEPH MIKELL PAPERS, 1809. 3 items. Edisto Island (Berkeley County), S.C.

Papers relating to Mikell's estate, an Edisto Island plantation, including lists of slaves, their value, and who was to have them.

3665. HENRY MILES PAPERS, 1839-1868. 10 items. Monkton (Addison County), Vt.

Letters and documents of Henry Miles (1795-1885), a Quaker abolitionist, dealing with the Society of Friends, the antislavery movement, the free-produce movement, the Fugitive Slave Law, the personal liberty laws, the Free Produce Association of Western Vermont, the Freedmen's Aid Association, and the agitations of William Lloyd Garrison.

3666. JAMES WARLEY MILES PAPERS, 1838-1876. 115 items. Charleston, S.C.

Chiefly letters from Miles (1818-1875), a Protestant Episcopal minister in South Carolina, to Mrs. Thomas John Young, and kept by her. The letters largely concern theology and philosophy, etymology and grammar, with critical comments on the opponents of historical criticism of the Bible. There are references to Mrs. Young's brothers, Henry Gourdin and Robert Newman Gourdin; to Miles's catalog of his personal library, now housed at the College of Charleston where he taught and served as librarian; to his poetry and essays; and to the anonymous publication of some of his poems in Russell's Magazine, which had been arranged by Mrs. Young. The collection also contains some manuscripts of Miles's sermons and a few papers of Thomas John Young and his son, Louis Gourdin Young.

3667. JOSEPH A. MILES PAPERS, 1841-1862. 8 items. Marietta (Cobb County), Ga.

Personal correspondence of the family of Joseph A. Miles, a Confederate soldier, concerning crops, his family, and local news.

3668. THOMAS MILEY PAPERS, 1864-1866. 7 items. Castleman's Ferry (Clarke County), Va.

Personal correspondence of Thomas Miley, 6th Regiment of Virginia Cavalry; Caldwell G. Miley, 8th Regiment of Virginia Infantry; and Amos Miley.

3669. MILFORD BAPTIST CHURCH MINUTES, 1831-1868. 1 vol. (218 pp.) Greenville District, S.C.

Records of baptisms, membership, and services. Members included whites, slaves, and freedmen.

3670. JOHN STUART MILL PAPERS, 1839-1870. 6 items. London, England.

Letters by Mill (1806-1873), British philosopher, concerning such topics as the publication of his book on logic, 1842; his acquaintanceship with Charles Austin, candidate for a seat in Parliament; and invitations declined. A letter to Sir Henry Cole concerns Mill's plans to relinquish ownership of the London and Westminster Review.

3671. JOHN MILLEDGE, JR., PAPERS, 1755-1853. 40 items. Augusta (Richmond County), Ga.

Correspondence of Milledge (1757-1818), U.S. congressman and senator and governor of Georgia, deals largely with state and national politics, mentioning the election of Jefferson as president, amendments to the U.S. Constitution, government for the new Louisiana purchase, the impeachment of Samuel Chase and John Pickering, South Carolina and Georgia boundaries, land grants to Revolutionary War veterans, Jefferson's farming, yellow fever in South Carolina, the Oregon boundary dispute, and the Polk administration. Correspondents include Abraham Baldwin, Thomas Mann Randolph, James Burchell Richardson, Josiah Meigs, Henry Lee, Thomas Jefferson, Joseph Habersham, Augustin Smith Clayton, Thomas Rowse and Robert Augustus Toombs. There is also material relating to the settlement of the estate of Milledge's wife, Martha (Galphin) Milledge; land grants and other papers executed by Milledge as governor; and documents concerning the purchase of slaves.

3672. ANDREW J. MILLER PAPERS, 1831-1854. 20 items. Augusta (Richmond County), Ga.

Business papers, including material relating to lawsuits over the collection of debts; a physician's accounts; land sales; and the settlement of an estate in Georgia.

3673. ANN ELIZA (ASHE) MILLER PAPERS, 1860-1864. 17 items. Wilmington (New Hanover County), N.C.

Largely letters by Mrs. Miller, wife of James Miller, a physician in the Confederate Army, to her father-in-law while she was a refugee from Wilmington during the Civil War. One letter from Samuel A'Court Ashe, Mrs. Miller's cousin, discusses Ashe family genealogy.

3674. EDWARD C. MILLER PAPERS, 1863-1890. 177 items. Chesterfield County, Va., and New York, N.Y.

Letters of an architect and civil engineer relating to personal and business affairs, legal matters, love, suicide, travel in Germany, crops in Virginia, and national and Virginia state politics. Correspondents include B. A. Hancock, E. H. Flournoy,

Asa Gray, Hermann Luckhardt, Alfred R. Courtney, Henry G. Cannon, Edward C. Becker, George Thurber, and Ernest von Ninonberg.

3675. JAMES P. MILLER NOTES, 1811-1812. 1 vol. Philadelphia, Pa.

Notes taken by James P. Miller from the medical lectures of Benjamin Rush at the University of Pennsylvania.

3676. JOHN BLOUNT MILLER PAPERS, 1773-1856. 178 items. Sumterville (Sumter County), S.C.

Legal correspondence, bills of sale for slaves, papers concerning land transactions in the Sumter district, and other business papers of Miller (d. 1851), district commissioner in equity. Six items, 1840-1843, concern the Bethel Baptist Church. Correspondents include W. H. DeSaussure, C. C. Memminger, John B. O'Neall, R. Y. Hayne, and Thomas Sumter.

3677. JOHN D. MILLER PAPERS, 1830-1865. 6 items and 2 vols. Hillsborough (Orange County), N.C.

Papers of a small merchant and farmer near Hillsborough in Orange County include a manuscript arithmetic book, 1830, which shows that Miller was studying business arithmetic, probably in Hillsborough Academy; a commonplace book, 1845-1848, listing prices of commodities sold to various people of the county and noting Miller's marriage, July 25, 1847, to Martha M. Jackson; miscellaneous loose accounts, including one to Captain John Berry, 1858-1860; and a love poem dated 1846.

3678. JOHN L. MILLER DAYBOOK, 1849. 1 vol. (150 pp.) Strasburg (Shenandoah County), Va.

Sales of general merchandise.

3679. JOHN W. MILLER LEDGER, 1835-1839. 1 vol. (363 pp.) State Mills, Va.

Merchandise, sawmill and post office accounts.

3680. JOSEPH A. MILLER PAPERS, 1882 (1891-1905) 1943. 387 items and 1 vol. Nineveh (Warren County), Va.

Included are letters dealing with local interests of constituents while Miller represented Frederick County in the Virginia House of Delegates, referring to such topics as toll rates of the Valley Turnpike Company; correspondence of Joseph Miller's daughters, Shirley and Mabel, with friends and relatives, especially relating to Mabel's career as a penmanship teacher and exponent of the Palmer method in North Carolina; and a letterpress book containing business letters of R. L. Miller of Winchester, Virginia, 1889.

3681. MABEL M. MILLER AUTOGRAPH ALBUM, 1882-1889. 1 vol. (150 pp.) Somerville (Fauquier County), Va.

Autographs collected by a schoolgirl.

3682. STEPHEN DECATUR MILLER PAPERS, 1828-1834. 7 items. Stateburg (Sumter County), S.C.

Papers relating to Miller, South Carolina governor and U.S. senator, including a letter, 1830, from James A. Cocke, newspaper editor of Lancaster, South Carolina, concerning politics and journalism there; a draft of a letter, 1830, to the editor of an unnamed newspaper challenging the editor's federalist views; and receipts and notices concerning subscriptions to various papers.

3683. THOMAS MILLER DAYBOOK, 1849-1850. 1 vol. (140 pp.) Alexander County, N.C.

Accounts of a country merchant.

3684. WILLIAM MILLER PAPERS, 1837-1949. 21 items and 5 vols. London, England.

Material collected by Miller, scholar of Charles Dickens's works and author of a Dickens bibliography, including articles from British and American periodicals and newspapers recording the reception given Dickens by contemporary critics; several illustrated articles describing the locales used as settings for the novelist's works; reminiscences by Dickens's children and others who knew him; and articles containing letters by Dickens, Thomas Carlyle, William Makepeace Thackery, and others.

3685. WILLIAM A. MILLER PAPERS, 1923. 2 items. Lynchburg (Campbell County), Va.

Recollections of Lynchburg by William A. Miller; and a letter by his son, Wirt H. Miller, forwarding his father's recollections to Charles M. Guggenheimer.

3686. WILLIAM HENRY MILLER PAPERS, 1865. 1 item. Harrisburg (Dauphin County), Pa.

A letter from Paul Leidy, a former U.S. representative from Pennsylvania, to Miller, politician and journalist, cancelling a newspaper subscription and mentioning radical criticism of U.S. Grant for his leniency toward Lee.

3687. MILLER FAMILY PAPERS, 1785-1947. 161 items. Winchester (Frederick County), Va.

Legal papers, 1785, concerning the Clover and Cochran families of Frederick County; family, legal, and financial papers starting in 1808 concerning the family of John and Abraham Miller, George S. Miller, and George's brother, Lewis A. Miller, a medical student in Philadelphia in the 1840s and in 1852 a member of the Virginia legislature. Topics include the conviction of two slaves for the murder of their master. One letter, 1866, is from Robert E. Lee to Mrs. Godfrey Miller, declining an invitation. Papers, 1910-1930, concern the leasing of land in Oklahoma, oil speculation there, and the town of Preston.

3688. MILLER LAURENCE AND COMPANY LEDGER, 1848-1859. 1 vol. (110 pp.) Statesville (Iredell County), N.C.

Accounts receivable ledger of a firm in an unidentified business.

3689. CHARLES F. MILLS PAPERS, 1836-1872. 23 items and 2 vols. Savannah, Ga.

A letterpress book, 1852-1867; a cashbook, 1836-1846; and business and legal letters of Mills, who exported cotton from Savannah to northern cities and to Europe.

3690. ELIZABETH AMANDA MILLS PAPERS, 1820-1883. 92 items. Granite Hill (Iredell County), N.C.

Letters about family affairs and Confederate Army life between Elizabeth Mills and her brothers, Richard W., Charles Frank, and William Harrison Mills. There are remarks revealing the attitude of Southerners toward conscription and enlistment.

3691. MARY S. MILLS PAPERS, 1861-1865. 12 items. Beach Ridge (Niagara County), N.Y.

Letters to Mary S. Mills from Union soldiers stationed at forts in Maryland and around Washington, D.C. Writers include William B. Hutton, 5th New York Cavalry; W. B. Tallmers and [Delavern Vimslyke?], 8th New York Heavy Artillery; Lucas S. Childs; George F. Poole; and a cousin Oliver.

3692. ROBERT S. MILLS PAPERS, 1840-1867. 1 vol. Cedar Spring (Greene County?), Tenn.

Miscellaneous accounts kept by Mills at several locations in Tennessee and Virginia. Accounts from Blacksburg, Virginia, are for hauling coal and wood and other transactions, 1851-1852. Accounts of 1854-1856 concern farming and the hire of both free and slave labor. Invoices, 1867, pertain to mercantile goods for Messrs. Thornburgh and Hoskins. There are copies of letters, 1855, of rail officials concerning the selection of a route between Bean's Station and Paint Rock for the Cincinnati, Cumberland Gap, and Charleston Railroad; a letter of 1853 relating to a business dispute with Senator John Bell over investment in the boat Saladin; and a letter to James B. Harris, 1844, about the purchase of an unhealthy slave.

3693. ALFRED MILNER, FIRST VISCOUNT MILNER, PAPERS, 1886-1918. 15 items. London, England.

Milner (1854-1925), British statesman and administrator in South Africa, 1897-1905, and member of the cabinet, 1916-1919. His letters include a discussion of the campaign for Parliament, 1886; the land law for Ireland, 1887; a critique of his successor's policies toward the Boers, 1906; a defense of military conscription, 1915; a discussion of Lord Hugh Cecil's reprimand for criticizing the Royal Flying Corps, 1918; and personal notes.

3694. RICHARD MONCKTON MILNES, FIRST BARON HOUGHTON, PAPERS, 1854-1940. 35 items. London, England.

Papers of Milnes (1809-1885), British statesman, author, and literary patron. Included are "Prefatory Stanzas," from "Columbus and the Mayflower," and a letter transmitting them to Joseph Hunter and discussing the Rhodes family. The bulk of the collection comprises copies of personal letters to Milnes, 1873-1880, 27 items, and poems, 3 items, by Cincinnatus Hiner Miller, known as Joaquin Miller, made from originals then in the possession of the Milnes family. Miller's letters describe Italy and literary and public figures; some of them are printed, excerpted, or summarized in Modern Language Quarterly, vol. 3 (June, 1942), pp. 297-306. There are also a letter of transmittal accompanying these items from F. L. Kent to Clarence Gohdes, 1940; and a copy of a clipping concerning Miller.

3695. JOHN MILTON PAPERS, 1765-1816. 7 items. Louisville (Jefferson County), Ga.

Certificates bearing the signature of Milton as notary public and as secretary of state of Georgia. They relate to lands and estates. A letter, 1799, of William Stith concerns land grants to the University of Georgia.

3696. J. F. MINIS PAPERS, 1874-1920. 19 vols. Savannah, Ga.

Daybooks, ledgers, receipt book, contract book, and indexes to ledgers of J. F. Minis and Co., commission merchants and shipping agents of Savannah.

3697. MINNEQUA HISTORICAL SOCIETY BULLETINS, 1938-1940. 4 items. Pueblo, Colo.

Mimeographed bulletins concerning the history and folklore of the Old West.

3698. MICHAEL MINNICK PAPERS, 1861-1897. 21 items. Middletown (Henry County), Ind.

Correspondence of Minnick and his son, Andrew J. Minnick, concerning personal affairs and the Civil War.

3699. PETER CARR MINOR AND HUGH MINOR NOTEBOOKS, 1812-1860. 7 vols. Charlottesville (Albemarle County), Virginia.

Agricultural notebooks of Peter Minor (1783-1827), agricultural reformer and owner of Ridgeway Plantation in Albemarle County, Virginia, showing records of expenses, lists of tools and other items purchased, products sold, and memoranda of wheat produced, 1812-1816; plantation diary or agricultural notes, 1822-1823, containing entries relative to the production of tobacco, corn, wheat, hay, the use of plaster, the weather, operation of a grist mill, building fences, and numerous other activities; and a six-page leaflet memorandum of subscriptions obtained for John Stuart Skinner's American Farmer, 1822-1825, and two loose sheets of memoranda. Agricultural notebooks or diaries of his son, Hugh Minor (1807-1875), also of Ridgeway Plantation, cover the following years: 1828-1834, 1838-1839, 1842-1844, and a few entries for later years. These diaries are concerned with operations similar to those of his father except for a rather full description of Ridgeway Plantation and greater detail as to farming operations. The notes of both men contain much on methods of producing tobacco and on crop rotation in practice.

3700. WILLIAM B. MINOR NOTEBOOK, 1860-1870. 1 vol. University of Virginia, Charlottesville, Va.

Notes on versification, grammar, etc., taken by William B. Minor (d. 1861), as a student at the University of Virginia, 1860, and copies of poems on the Confederate cause written by members of Minor's family.

3701. FRANCIS MINOT PAPERS, 1852. 1 item. Boston, Mass.

A letter from Rufus Woodward of Worcester, Massachusetts, 1852, referring to the Harvard class of 1841.

3702. MISSISSIPPI. JUSTICE COURT (CHOCTAW COUNTY) DOCKET BOOK, 1848-1855. 1 vol.

Records of a court having jurisdiction over civil cases in which the amount in dispute did not exceed fifty dollars. S. S. Dunn was the justice of the peace. There are clippings relating to the election of 1876 and to local history pasted over some of the pages at the beginning of the volume.

3703. MISSOURI. MILITIA PAPERS, 1860-1865. 66 items.

Correspondence of Missouri governors Claiborne Fox Jackson, Hamilton Rowan Gamble, and Thomas C. Fletcher; and adjutants general George A. Parsons, Warwick Hough, and John B. Gray. Letters of December 1860, from Lieutenant Colonel John S. Bowen of the Southwest Battalion of Militia, Little Osage, Missouri, reflect efforts to secure the Kansas border from antislavery guerrillas. Letters, reports, and other documents of 1861 concern the enlistment and equipment of Union volunteer militia. Units mentioned are companies raised at Valley Forge Iron Works and American Iron Mountain Company in St. Francis and St. Louis counties, and Captain James Craig's Big River Company, 5th Regiment of Missouri Volunteer Militia. There are also records concerning the reorganization of militia units, 1863.

3704. DAVID BRYDIE MITCHELL PAPERS, 1804-1821. 4 items. Milledgeville (Baldwin County), Ga.

Papers relating to Mitchell, governor of Georgia, 1809-1813, 1815-1817. Included are a letter from Mitchell as attorney general to Governor John Milledge concerning local politics, including the Yazoo affair, 1804; a commission for Thomas H. Penn as notary public, 1812; a letter from Peter Deveaux of Savannah seeking to purchase some tracts of land; and an account of Mitchell's expenditures as agent of the Creek Indians, 1817-1821.

3705. DONALD GRANT MITCHELL PAPERS, 1858. 1 item. Edgewood [New Haven], Conn.

A personal letter by Mitchell (1822-1908), an author under the name Ik Marvel, to a Mr. Mann.

3706. GEORGE SINCLAIR MITCHELL PAPERS, 1928-1947. 2,124 items and 4 vols. Atlanta, Ga.

Largely newspaper clippings relating to the organization of labor unions in the South, especially Alabama and North Carolina, including a great deal of material concerning the incidents at Gastonia and Marion, North Carolina, 1929-1930. There are also notebooks, 4 vols., containing a report of a survey of the power structure of Georgia made by James Mackay and Calvin Kytle, 1947.

3707. JACOB DUCHÉ MITCHELL PAPERS, 1824-1860. 3 vols. Lynchburg (Campbell County), Va., and Princeton (Mercer County), N.J.

Two volumes of poetry by Reverend Mitchell of the Second Presbyterian Church of Lynchburg and his diary, 1860, which deals almost exclusively with his pastoral duties.

3708. JAMES A. MITCHELL PAPERS, 1836-1854. 8 items and 1 vol. Pittsylvania County, Va.

Legal correspondence of James A. Mitchell, an attorney; letters to John A. Mitchell of the same address; a letter, 1836, of James Bland to James A. Mitchell certifying receipt of a refund for a slave who had died soon after purchase; and an account book containing expenses of travelling with slaves from Virginia to Mississippi, the names of the slaves, and the prices received, 1834-1835.

3709. JOHN W. MITCHELL PAPERS, 1837-1843. 11 items. New York, N.Y.

Personal and business letters to John W. Mitchell; correspondents include Cornelius Van Rensselaer, members of the Genet and Vernon families, and others. One letter, 1837, notes the price received for a female slave in South Carolina.

3710. NINA CORNELIA MITCHELL PAPERS, 1854 (1910s-1920s) 1958. 4,021 items and 46 vols. Flushing (Long Island), N.Y., and Shepherdstown (Jefferson County), W. Va.

Largely family letters; genealogical material; Civil War papers of John Fulton Berrien Mitchell, Sr., an officer in the 2nd New York Volunteer Cavalry, 1862-1864, concerning ordnance and camp and garrison equipage; and letters concerning European travel in the 1870s; life in Columbia University during the early 1900s; life in France, Italy, and England and the United States during World War I; British Expeditionary Forces hospitals and nurses; treatment of wounded soldiers, especially the work among the blind of an organization called Le Phare de France; war work by women; postwar relief work; the Food for France Fund; life in Paris during the 1920s; and Sufism. Correspondents include John Fulton Berrien, Jr.; Henry Bedinger; Edward Bedinger Mitchell; Nina Cornelia (Mitchell) Wickham (the aunt of Nina Cornelia Mitchell); Gladys Elliott; Winifred Holt; and John Fulton Berrien Mitchell, Jr. There are also a few miscellaneous legal and financial papers and miscellaneous invitations, calling cards, school exercises by John Berrien Mitchell, Sr., at Columbia College, 1860-1861; report cards, 1890s, for Stephen H. Dandridge at Shepherd College; solicitations from charities; clippings; and diaries and miscellaneous writings by various family members, especially by Nina Cornelia Mitchell about her experiences, particularly in Europe. One diary, 1860, by Sarah P. (Berrien) Mitchell describes a trip to Lake Superior and the mines which she saw there. There are also photographs of family members and of their homes.

3711. WILLIAM MITCHELL PAPERS, 1809-1865. 12 items. Burke County, Ga.

Records of Mitchell's guardianship of Anna, William, and David Green.

3712. WINFIELD HENRI MIXON PAPERS, 1895-1932. 10 items and 7 vols. Selma (Dallas County), Ala.

Papers relating to an official of the African Methodist Episcopal Church, including miscellaneous items and clippings concerning mainly a conference of women in Nashville, 1895; Mixon's diary, 6 vols., covering scattered years from 1895 to 1915, an account of his travels and activities on behalf of the church and referring to the condition of various churches in his district and to routine matters related to his office; and scattered comments on Masonry and on Payne University in Selma. One volume records Mixon's church activities and includes a report to his bishop covering 1892-1895. This volume also contains a miscellaneous record of the financial affairs of a fraternal organization, kept by someone other than Mixon, with references to social conditions.

3713. ANDREW MOFFETT PAPERS, 1862-1875. 91 items and 1 vol. Charleston, S.C.

A collection of autographs, primarily of Confederate generals.

3714. HENRY M. MOFFITT PAPERS, 1847. 4 items. Washington, D.C.

Professional papers of an attorney.

3715. WILLIAM NASSAU MOLESWORTH PAPERS, 1860-1885. 19 items. Spotland, Lancashire, England.

Correspondence of Molesworth (1816-1890), British clergyman and historian, including letters from Richard Cobden, 1860-1865, concerning political and international affairs and Molesworth's writings; a letter of introduction for Molesworth, 1865, written by Alfred Kingston of the Public Record Office to Nicholas Hamilton of the British Museum where Molesworth wanted to see diplomatic correspondence from the reign of William III; letters of George Jacob Holyoake, 1874-1879, concerning Molesworth's History of England from 1830 and the dedication of Holyoake's History of the Equitable Pioneers; a letter by Molesworth to H. D. Nicoll, 1882, with autobiographical information; a letter of acknowledgment from Sir Edward Hamilton, 1882, concerning Molesworth's newest book; letters of John Bright, 1879-1885, relating to Molesworth's honorary degree from the University of Glasgow, the reaction of Christians to General Charles Gordon, and foreign policy; a letter of Sir Wilfrid Lawson, 1883, regarding his "local veto" and temperance bills before Parliament; a letter of Edward Bouverie Pusey concerning Arthur Perceval, the political aspects of the Oxford and Irvingite movements; and a letter from Lord Brougham explaining the dissolution of Parliament in 1831.

3716.   J. B. MOLYNEAUX PAPERS, 1913. 1 item. Cleveland (Cuyahoga County), Ohio.

A speech by Molyneaux reminiscing about the company he commanded during the Civil War in the 7th Regiment of the Ohio Infantry Volunteers.

3717.   BRIDGET MONAHAN PAPERS, 1848-1894. 124 items. Savannah, Ga.

Papers concerning the administration of the estate of Hugh Monahan, her husband; and their sons' work at Manhattan College, New York, 1871-1873.

3718.   MONBO COTTON MILL INVOICES, 1908-1918. 1 vol. Catawba (Catawba County), N.C.

General and monthly invoices.

3719.   ST. LEGER LANDON MONCURE PAPERS, 1851-1889. 59 items. Ruther Glen (Caroline County), Va.

Moncure (1834-1898) was a farmer and a clerk for the state auditor of Virginia. His papers are largely routine family and business correspondence, but include information describing Holston Springs, Virginia, a health resort, in 1860; conditions in Richmond, 1862; a preference for Negroes over whites as hired hands, 1878; and the prospects for entering politics in Texas, 1866, and in Virginia, 1878. Two items relate to instruction in Sunday schools, 1887-1888.

3720.   JAMES MONROE PAPERS, 1790-1846. 17 items. Albemarle County, Va.

Business letters, legal documents, a commission, and land grants signed by Monroe as president of the United States or governor of Virginia. One letter to Frances Taliaferro Brooke concerns the election of 1828. There is a photostatic copy of a reprieve for a slave sentenced to death for conspiracy and insurrection, signed by Monroe as governor, 1802.

3721.   JOHN MONROE PAPERS, 1775 (1850-1899) 1948. 3,217 items and 37 vols. Capon Bridge (Hampshire County), W. Va.

Records of three Virginia families, including that of Colonel Alexander Monroe, his son John Monroe, and John's sons James A. and J. Turner Monroe; the family of James Caudy; and the family of Joseph Kackley. Monroe family papers concern county and state politics; land; and personal property. There are tax records; daybooks relating to the sale of merchandise; and miscellaneous accounts, business, and legal papers. There is information on the Virginia secession convention, 1861, and the occupation of Romney, Virginia, by Union troops. The collection includes James Caudy's land and tax records for Hampshire County, ca. 1850 and 1860, including lists of slaves, livestock, and real and personal property; a list of voters and a list of persons liable for militia duty (114th Virginia Regiment); militia guard reports, 1861; and instructions issued to Caudy as a tax collector. Kackley family papers portray the movement westward to Kentucky, Indiana, and Colorado. There are also letters describing settlement in Colorado, 1887-1888; printed items relating to the Strasburg Land and Improvement Company, 1891-1893; tax records, 1882-1884; a book of household remedies and patent medicines, 1882-1883; and legal papers conveying land in Berkeley County, Virginia (now West Virginia), from Samuel Strode to Conrad Miller, 1775; and other documents of the Morgan, Millar [or Miller], and Taber families. Other correspondents include Henry Bedinger, John J. Cornwell, James Sloan Kuykendall, Jared Williams, and Joshua S. Zimmerman.

3722.   WILLIAM JOHN MONSON, FIRST VISCOUNT OXENBRIDGE, PAPERS, 1872-1876. 204 items. London, England.

Largely letters from Sir Edmund John Monson, First Baronet (1834-1909), then British consul general at Budapest, to his brother William John Monson (1829-1898), an officer of the royal household. Monson comments on politics in Hungary; British commerce and financial interests there; elections in Britain and the administrations of Gladstone and Disraeli; literary figures of his acquaintance including Lord Lytton (1831-1891), Charles James Lever (d. 1872), and Ámin Vámbéry; events at All Souls College, Oxford, and his unsuccessful effort to obtain an appointment there; a legal controversy over the Tichborne baronetcy and estate; and the visits to Budapest of the Prince of Wales and to Berlin by the Shah of Persia, 1873. Included are two letters, 1876, from William Richard Holmes, British consul in Bosnia, concerning the rebellion in Bosnia-Herzegovina and the resulting diplomatic incident. There are a few letters relating to Sir Leoline Jenkins (1623-1685), and an unidentified photograph that may be a picture of Sir Edmund Monson.

3723.   BASIL MONTAGU PAPERS, 1812. 1 item. London, England.

A personal letter from Samuel Henley, principal of the East India College, to Montagu (1770-1851), British legal writer.

3724. JOHN MONTAGU, FOURTH EARL OF SANDWICH, PAPERS, 1775. 1 item. "Hinchingbrook," Huntingdonshire, England.

A letter by Montagu (1718-1792), First Lord of the Admiralty, December 30, 1775, analyzing the military situation in America and blaming British losses on a refusal to use force rather than conciliatory measures.

3725. LORD ROBERT MONTAGU PAPERS, 1863. 1 item. London, England.

A letter from Montagu (1825-1902), member of Parliament, to C. E. Macqueen of Manchester, discussing taxation and the manner in which Parliament appropriated funds and the administration spent them.

3726. ANDREW JACKSON MONTAGUE PAPERS, ca. 1903-1906. 1 item. Richmond, Va.

A carbon copy, undated, of a petition addressed to Montague, governor of Virginia, 1902-1906, asking his pardon for a Negro who had been convicted of second degree murder.

3727. MONTAGUE FAMILY PAPERS, 1844-1864. 9 items. Granville County, N.C.

A letter, 1844, of James Y. Montague from Wake Forest College to his father, William, gives a detailed physical description of Henry Clay and discusses the tariff and taxation. Papers relating to A. B. Montague while serving with the 44th North Carolina Regiment in 1862-1864, include a pass and personal letters from relatives in the Allen family.

3728. JOHN MONTGOMERY, JR., PAPERS, 1809-1820. 5 items. Baltimore, Md.

Letters of Montgomery (1764-1828), who served as U.S. representative from Maryland, 1807-1811; attorney general of Maryland, 1811-1818; and mayor of Baltimore, 1820-1826. The letters concern a recommendation for a midshipman's appointment in the navy, the extradition to Pennsylvania of a man arrested in Maryland, 1813; and comments, 1813, to John Stoughton on the commercial situation in the War of 1812. A letter to Governor Samuel Sprigg concerns a legal case, 1820.

3729. SEABORN MONTGOMERY, JR., PAPERS, 1861-1865. 49 items. Georgia.

Letters by Seaborn Montgomery, Jr., to his parents and sister, Julia Montgomery, of Americus, Georgia, while he was a student at Collingsworth Institute, Talbotton, Georgia, 1861-1862; at the Georgia Military Institute in Marietta, 1863-1864; and in the Confederate Army, 1864-1865. His letters describe student life, the funerals of General Preston Smith and Captain Donnelson of Tennessee who fell at Ringgold, anxiety to participate in the war, problems with a Negro servant, troop movements in Georgia, desertion, destruction in Atlanta, use of convicts in the Confederate Army, and the hardships of army life.

3730. B. MOODY AND Y. M. MOODY PAPERS, 1861, 1864. 2 items. Virginia.

Letters from the Moodys, probably brothers, while in the Confederate Army, commenting on family matters, camp life, a party in Petersburg, and conditions and prices in Petersburg, 1864.

3731. JACOB P. MOOMAW PAPERS, 1861. 2 items. Bedford County, Va.

Letters of a Confederate private commenting on hardships of camp life, food, and lack of religion among soldiers.

3732. [A. MOORE?] NOTEBOOK, 1857. 1 vol. (74 pp.) Illinois.

Apparently accounts and a memoir by a supervisory employee of the Illinois Central Railroad concerning construction or maintenance. The accounts give the cost of material and labor. The memoir apparently was written in response to criticism. Work mentioned took place between Wapella and Dixon and on the Rock Island branch. There is technical information on the How [Howe?] truss bridge and the Bollman iron bridge.

3733. FRANCIS MOORE MANUSCRIPT. 1 vol. (233 pp.)

A manuscript by Moore, storekeeper for the trustees of the colony of Georgia, based on his journal. The manuscript, "A Voyage to Georgia, Begun the 15th of October, 1735," was published in London, 1744, and again as <u>Collections of the Georgia Historical Society</u>, Vol. 1, 1840. Appended to the manuscript is an anonymous and unpublished sketch of the life of James Edward Oglethorpe, 5 pp. Moore's account centers on the establishment of Frederica, Georgia, but includes information on other settlements in the colony, Indian relations, and an expedition against the Spanish in Florida.

3734. FRANK MOORE PAPERS, 1865-1866, 1871-1872. 187 items. New York, N.Y.

Papers of Horatio Franklin Moore (1828-1904), known as Frank Moore, editor and author of works on the Revolution and the Civil War, are primarily letters to him concerning his book, <u>Women of the War</u> (Chicago: 1866), an account of the service of Northern women during the Civil War. Most of those mentioned in the collection served as nurses or in related capacities. Letters are both from the women and from former patients. There are also letters, 1871-1872, by Moore, then in France, to his brother

George Henry Moore. These letters refer to French politics and government under Louis Adolphe Thiers, but chiefly discuss the works of early Americana which Moore collected in France for sale in New York. There is also some undated material, a few clippings, and miscellaneous writings.

3735. GEORGE HENRY MOORE PAPERS, 1860. 3 items. New York, N.Y.

Letters to Moore (1823-1892), librarian and historian, from Charles Carter Lee, Sr. (1798-1871), son of General Henry ("Light Horse Harry") Lee. The letters concern Moore's book, "Mr. Lee's Plan--March 29, 1777": The Treason of Charles Lee (New York: 1860), and Charles Carter Lee's manuscript defending Charles Lee (1731-1782), Revolutionary War general; the submission of that manuscript to the Virginia Historical Society; and the possibility of reading it before the New York Historical Society. Letters of General Charles Lee, which had once been among the papers of Henry Lee and had since disappeared, are mentioned.

3736. SIR GRAHAM MOORE PAPERS, 1812-1840. 5 items. Cobham, Surrey, England.

Correspondence of Moore (1764-1843), British admiral, including a letter, 1812, from him to Henry Kinsey concerning the status of Kinsey's son, an officer on the H. M. S. Chatham; letters, 1824, of Sir Charles James Napier concerning the acquisition of source material for his brother Sir William Francis Patrick Napier's History of the War in the Penisula (London: 1828-1840) and the controversy over Sir John Moore's role in that campaign; and a letter from Napier, 1840, concerning the Chartist disorders.

3737. SIR HENRY MOORE PAPERS, 1766. 1 item. New York.

Commission for Jabez Sargent as lieutenant, signed by Sir Henry Moore, Baronet (1713-1769), governor of New York.

3738. HENRY MOORE PAPERS, 1830. 1 item. London, England.

A letter from Alexander Knox (1757-1831) to John Wesley's assistant, Henry Moore (1751-1844), concerns Moore's writings, Knox's parents and their involvement in Methodism, Methodism in Londonderry, Wesley's role in Christianity, and Methodist ministers in Londonderry, including Thomas Williams, James Clough, and Mark Davis.

3739. J. AND W. MOORE [?] LEDGER, 1858-1862. 1 vol. (534 pp.) Greenville (Pitt County), N.C.

A detailed record of sales of general merchandise.

3740. J. HARRY MOORE AUTOGRAPH BOOK, 1867-1868. 1 vol. Hampden-Sydney (Prince Edward County), Va.

Messages addressed to Moore by fellow students in Union Theological Seminary and in Hampden-Sydney College. Some of the entries mention Chi Phi and Epsilon Phi Kappa Delta societies, and student life. There are two poems.

3741. JAMES OTIS MOORE PAPERS, 1850 (1864-1865) 1888. 241 items. Saco (York County), Me.

Letters, 214 items, chiefly between Moore (1822-1886) and his wife, Mary Elizabeth (Ross) Moore. Included are love letters written prior to their marriage and letters of 1858-1859 discussing the possibility of going to China as a missionary. Letters of 1864-1865 concern the Civil War services of Moore, a homeopathic physician, assigned at various times to the 22nd U.S. Colored Troops; the 3rd Division Hospital, 18th Army Corps; and the 1st U.S. Colored Troops. There are descriptions of living conditions of fugitive Negroes near Yorktown, Virginia; the use of opium; hospitals before Petersburg; the explosion of ammunition barges at City Point, August, 1864; the expeditions to Wilmington and Fort Fisher, North Carolina, 1865; evaluations of Benjamin F. Butler and other generals; entry into Richmond; Lincoln's funeral parade in Washington; the search for John Wilkes Booth; and service at Brownsville, Texas, in the summer of 1865. After the war the Moores moved to Haverhill, Massachusetts. There are a few letters from Moore to his daughter, Sarah Elizabeth, while she was a student at Wellesley College, 1876-1878. There are also poems, 20 items, by Mrs. Moore, and genealogical tables, 7 items, concerning Moore's ancestors, the Chadbournes of Berwick, Maine, and the Moores of Stratham, New Hampshire.

3742. JOHN MOORE PAPERS, 1803-1843. 38 items. Baltimore, Md.

Letters from Moore to his wife, Elizabeth S. (Stump) Moore, including love letters prior to their marriage in 1814 and letters concerning the War of 1812 near Baltimore and Chesapeake Bay. Topics include British General Robert Ross and American Commodores John Rogers, David Porter, and Oliver Hazard Perry; the bombardment of Fort McHenry; Admiral Sir George Cockburn; John Stuart Skinner; and the administrations of Jefferson and Madison. There are also personal and business letters concerning prices of commodities and land, debts, and imprisonment for debt.

3743. JOHN MOORE PAPERS, 1802. 2 items. Lincolnton (Lincoln County), N.C.

Two letters from Duncan Cameron to Moore about establishing Federalist newspapers to oppose the Jeffersonian parties. He discusses the journalistic venture of William Duane and Joseph Gales, Sr.

3744. SIR JOHN SAMUEL MOORE PAPERS, 1843-1892. 139 items. Alverstoke, Hampshire, England.

The papers of Moore (1831-1916), British naval officer, are primarily letters to his wife and official reports. They describe his service on the H.M.S. Salamander in 1862-1865 and the H.M.S. Pearl, 1866-1870, including church services and dramatic entertainments aboard ship, in Australia, Singapore, China, Japan, and elsewhere in the Far East, with visits to Madeira and Vancouver Island. Moore mentioned rebel activity in Japan, 1867-1869. There are certificates, appointments, and orders relating to Moore's rank and assignment to various ships and to his retirement; correspondence and documents of 1882 reporting on the British bombardment of Alexandria; a printed copy of Admiral Seymour's correspondence with the Admiralty in that year; and other records concerning the military and naval situation in Egypt and negotiations with the Pasha while Moore was Seymour's secretary. A letter, 1884, to Captain George Parsons describes life on Ascension Island. Two items concern the Royal Naval Exhibition, 1891-1892.

3745. JOHN T. MOORE PAPERS, 1861-1897. 126 items. Winston (Forsyth County), N.C.

Letters and papers of John T. Moore, regarding the tobacco industry around Winston during the 1870s and including information on the difficulties of selling manufactured tobacco, and tobacco prices; and references to "Dick" (R. J.) Reynolds. Included also are detailed letters from his brother, Charles E. Moore, regarding sheep raising in Colorado, Kansas, and New Mexico, and mentioning Indian raids, pre-empted lands, Mexican labor, and living conditions on the sheep ranches.

3746. JOHN WHEELER MOORE, SR., PAPERS, 1877-1901. 9 items. Powellsville (Hertford County), N.C.

Personal letters relating to Moore (1833-1906) and his family. A letter of Moore's uncle, J. H. Wheeler, concerns their mutual interest in the writing and publishing of history. A letter, 1877, from R. J. Gatling, inventor of the Gatling gun, concerns sources of information on his life for a book Moore was compiling on men born in Hertford County. There is also a letter from Supreme Court Justice W. N. H. Smith. The library holds a microfilm of the card index in the North Carolina Division of Archives and History, Raleigh, to Moore's Roster of North Carolina Troops in the War Between the States (Raleigh: 1882).

3747. MARY MOORE PAPERS, 1830-1864. 32 items. Yazoo County, Miss.

Business papers of Mary Moore and her husband Allen Moore (d. 1852), planters.

3748. MERRILL MOORE PAPERS, 1942. 1 item. Durham, N.C.

Moore (1903-1957) was a psychiatrist and poet. This item is "Only Through Books and Only Through Libraries: A Sonnet for the Duke University Library."

3749. N. B. MOORE JOURNAL, 1841-1870. 1 vol. Augusta (Richmond County), Ga.

Combination daybook, ledger, and journal kept by N. B. Moore, a planter, showing hands hired and hay sold.

3750. R. G. MOORE PAPERS, 1851. 1 item. Stanislaus River, Calif.

Letter describing life in the California gold fields.

3751. SID F. MOORE PAPERS, 1863-1870. 10 items and 1 vol. Hardin County, Ohio.

This collection includes a letter, 1864, by Thomas Shawn; muster rolls, 1864, for units of the 118th Ohio Volunteer Infantry, in which Moore served during the Civil War, rising from sergeant to captain; a certified copy of letters of guardianship for Joseph Zimmerman's grandchildren; pictures, including one of Moore's gravemarker in Hueston Cemetery near Forest, Ohio, and a photograph and an ambrotype of Moore; a price list for army supplies; clippings; and a diary, August 15, 1863-February 7, 1864, describing troop movements of the 118th regiment in Ohio, Kentucky, and Tennessee and the battle of Mossy Creek, Tennessee, December 29, 1863. Part or all of the diary may have been published in the Lima (Ohio?) News.

3752. STEPHEN MOORE PAPERS, 1761-1894. 71 items and 2 vols. "Mt. Tirzah," Person County, N.C.

Papers of Moore (1733-1799), a New York resident who had migrated to Canada with British troops during the French and Indian War and later settled in Orange County, now Person County, North Carolina; and papers of his family. Included are deeds and other material relating to lands in Orange, now Person, County from the 1770s and later; business letters, legal papers, and financial records of Stephen, his son Phillips Moore, and his grandson Stephen Moore, including material on the settlement of the estate of the first Stephen, and the will of his daughter, Ann Moore, 1852. Three items concern the medical treatment of one of Stephen's daughters by Benjamin Rush. There is an account book concerning Stephen Moore's business as an outfitter for ships in Quebec, 1767-1770, and the administration of his estate in North Carolina, 1799-1813. A daybook, 1845-1852, relates to the family mercantile business at "Mt. Tirzah." There is also a genealogical table and a biographical sketch of the family by John Alton Price of Durham.

3753.  THOMAS MOORE COMMONPLACE BOOK, 1804-1846. 1 vol. (460 pp.) Havana, Cuba.

Commonplace book kept by Thomas Moore, a Liverpool merchant, while in Havana. Included are maps of various West Indian islands, pictures of harbors, tables of measures and weights, tables of exchange, current prices of staples, insurance rates, an oath required of free men of the Russia Company in 1804, and the distances in nautical miles from London to the leading cities of the world.

3754.  THOMAS MOORE PAPERS, 1817-1871. 28 items. Baltimore, Md.

Personal letters to an Irish immigrant watchmaker from relatives and friends. Topics include social and economic conditions in Ireland; the unfitness of physicians in Orwigsburg, Pennsylvania, 1817; David Moore's travels in South Carolina and work there in the Society Hill Union Factory, a cotton and wool spinning mill; Dabney H. Maury's memories of the Mobile campaign, during the Civil War; German immigrants in Pennsylvania; and legal affairs.

3755.  W. S. MOORE PAPERS, 1862, 1863. 2 items. [Bardstown (Nelson County), Ky.?]

Letters from W. S. Moore, a Confederate soldier stationed at Fredericksburg, Virginia, mentioning skirmishes, picket duty, Northern newspapers, and family affairs.

3756.  WILLIAM HENRY MOORE PAPERS, [1875?]-1914. 90 items and 1 vol. Rockingham (Richmond County), N.C.

Manuscript sermons of a minister in the Methodist Episcopal Church, South.

3757.  MOORESVILLE MILLS PAPERS, 1893-1960. ca. 15,000 items and 290 vols. Mooresville (Iredell County), N.C.

Records of a firm established in 1893 as Mooresville Cotton Mills by J. E. Sherrill and others, and later becoming a manufacturer of cotton, wool, and synthetic fabrics, draperies, upholstery, toweling, and clothing. The firm was absorbed by Burlington Industries in 1955. Included is a "historical file" of printed and typed articles; selected documents, 1914-1935, containing financial data; and photographs of employees, offices, and aerial photographs of the plant. There are also some legal documents relating to the firm's charter, receivership, and bylaws.

There are extensive minutes, 1893-1955, 3 vols., of meetings of stockholders and the board of directors; minutes, 1936-1951, of the executive committee of the board of directors; audit reports, 1921-1954; and financial statements, 1932-1933, 1937-1955.

Stock records include common stock ledgers, 1893-1923, 5 vols.; a preferred stock ledger, 1917-1923; stock lists and miscellaneous records, 1897-1955; preferred stock certificates, 1917-1942; common stock certificates, 1893-1955; bonds for lost certificates, 1946-1955; broadsides for the issuance of preferred stock, 1923, and for a renewal, 1926. Appraisals of the corporation are dated 1935, 1946, and 1948. Account books include a journal and ledger, 1914-1916; cashbooks, 1905-1909, 2 vols.; cash journals, 1912-1913, 1921-1926, 3 vols.; check and deposit registers, 1948-1954, 3 vols.; cloth and towel inventories, 1936-1942, 1948-1949, 9 vols.; and a cost ledger, 1954. Unbound accounting records include inventories, 1933-1939, 1960-1962; local, state, and federal tax records, 1893-1956; and construction contracts and records, 1958-1960. There is also fragmentary correspondence, 1952-1955, for the towel division, the decorative fabrics division, the apparel fabrics division, and for William J. Fullerton who held various offices principally in merchandising and sales.

3758.  S. T. MOORMAN PAPERS, 1847-1848. 4 items. Charlottesville (Albemarle County), Va.

Bills for books and other reading matter from Richmond, Virginia, merchants to Moorman, a Methodist minister.

3759.  ALLEN MORAGNE PAPERS, 1766 (1873-1904) 1911. 83 items. Bordeaux (Abbeville County), S.C.

Genealogical chart of the Moragne family; land grant to Isaac Moragne for land in Abbeville District, South Carolina, 1829; papers relating to suits against Peter B. Moragne; bills and letters of Peter B. Moragne, most of the letters being from his son-in-law, John H. Brady, a farmer and schoolteacher in Hinds County, Mississippi, who mentions farming, the conduct of a country store, and a yellow fever epidemic; and letters and other papers of Allen Moragne and Mrs. S. W. Moragne of Bordeaux, including a description of Talladega, Alabama, in 1891.

3760.  GEORGE HENRY ROBERTS MORAN DIARY, 1878. 1 vol. (65 pp.) Arizona Territory.

Diary of a U.S. Army surgeon.

3761. JACOB MORDECAI PAPERS, (1784-1904) 1936. 2,474 items. Warrenton (Warren County), N.C., and Richmond, Va.

Personal correspondence and papers of Jacob Mordecai (1762-1838), educator and progenitor of a family long prominent in North Carolina and Virginia; and of his children and grandchildren. The majority of the letters are of a personal nature, but they include several important series of letters, as follows: copies of letters from Rachel (Mordecai) Lazarus (1788-1838) to Maria Edgeworth, beginning in 1816; of Ellen Mordecai (1790-1884) to her brother, Solomon Mordecai (1792-1869), while he was a medical student at Philadelphia, Pennsylvania, and later as a physician in Mobile, Alabama; of Ellen Mordecai, regarding her long tenure as a teacher in her father's school at Warrenton, North Carolina, and later as a governess in New York City, 1848-1852; of Caroline (Mordecai) Plunkett (1794-1862) and her husband, Achilles Plunkett (d. 1824), while they conducted a school at Warrenton, North Carolina, and of her later life as a teacher in Mobile; and of Alfred Mordecai (1804-1887) to members of his family while a student at the U. S. Military Academy, West Point, New York, 1819-1823. The correspondence contains frequent comment on literature of the day, and information on social life and customs in general, and especially in Warrenton and Richmond, and on life in Mobile, 1823-1860. Letters of Samuel Mordecai (1786-1865) refer in part to his writing of <u>Richmond in By-Gone Days</u> (Richmond: 1856), and to land in <u>Wisconsin</u> sold for taxes. Included also are Jacob Mordecai's ledger containing personal and school accounts, 1811-1818; Samuel Mordecai and Company's ledger, 1839-1865, Petersburg, Virginia; and Isabel R. Mordecai's journals, 1858-1861, Charleston, South Carolina. There is also a secretary's report of the Sick Soldiers Relief Society, Raleigh, North Carolina, October 1, 1861; a description by Marshall De Lancey Haywood of the Mordecai residence in Raleigh with related correspondence of Pattie Mordecai, 1936; correspondence of Emma Mordecai, daughter of Jacob, with relatives and friends, including Solomon Cohen, an attorney of Savannah, describing European travel, and with Sally Vaughn Norral, a former slave; and bills, receipts, and bank statements of various family members.

3762. EUGENE MOREHEAD PAPERS, 1879-1892. 276 items. Durham, N.C.

Business and personal correspondence of Morehead (1845-1889), banker of Durham and financial agent of tobacco firms. Among the correspondents are his wife Lucy while she was in Savannah, 1879, partly concerning the First Presbyterian Church of Durham; George Washington Watts, secretary and treasurer of W. Duke, Sons and Company, writing about business and house lots in Durham, 1879; and William M. Morgan, who reports on Morehead's bank while Morehead was absent in Asheville, New York, and Savannah. There is also correspondence concerning Morehead's quarrel with Washington Duke, 1886; the Durham Fertilizer Company; Durham schools of the 1880s; the need for capital in business expansion, especially in tobacco industry firms such as Blackwell's Durham Tobacco Company, Faucett and Company, and W. Duke, Sons and Company; and the formation of the Bank of Durham under William Thomas Blackwell. There are also condolences on the death of Morehead and bills and receipts of Lucy Lathrop from local stores. Other correspondents include J. Turner Morehead, James Dinwiddie, Washington Duke, Benjamin Duke, and James B. Duke, Julian S. Carr, Samuel T. Morgan, and Gerard Watts.

3763. JAMES TURNER MOREHEAD, JR., PAPERS, 1812-1939. 694 items. Greensboro (Guilford County), N.C.

Legal and family correspondence and papers of James Turner Morehead (1838-1919), colonel in the Confederate Army, North Carolina legislator, and prominent lawyer; and of a younger James T. Morehead. The papers chiefly concern the legal profession of Morehead, although there are a few family papers dating back to 1812. Included are indentures, wills, notes, receipts, writs, and other legal documents. The personal letters include a few from Julian Shakespeare Carr, Sr., Robert Paine Dick, and James T. Morehead, Jr.

3764. JOHN MOTLEY MOREHEAD PAPERS, 1842-1843. 4 items. Raleigh (Wake County), N.C.

Official correspondence of John Motley Morehead (1769-1866), governor of North Carolina, 1841-1844.

3765. WILLIAM MOREHEAD PAPERS, 1825-1898. 2,395 and 18 vols. Cumberland (Alleghany County), Md.

Business letters of a merchant of household furnishings. Topics include sales and purchases of goods, particularly stoves and water pumps; shipment of goods; borrowing of money; payment of promissory notes; etc. There are also advertisements, bills, receipts, account books, and other records.

3766. JOSEPH MORELAND PAPERS, 1846. 1 item. Cleveland (Bradley County), Tenn.

A letter to Nicklas Williams of Panther Creek, North Carolina, from Moreland, a former neighbor who had moved to Tennessee.

3767. ARTHUR A. MORGAN PAPERS, 1836. 3 items. Perry (Houston County), Ga.

Letters concerning the organization of a railroad company in Georgia, rental of the Arthur A. Morgan property, prospects for the "Union party" in 1836, and references to nullification.

3768.  EDWIN DENISON MORGAN PAPERS, 1861. 1 item. New York, N.Y.

A letter of Daniel Butterfield to Morgan, governor of New York concerning the oncoming war and the readiness of his regiment, the 12th New York Militia.

3769.  EDWIN WRIGHT MORGAN PAPERS, 1839-1850. 5 items. Philadelphia, Pa.

Routine papers concerning the service of Morgan (ca. 1823-1869) with the 2nd U.S. Artillery Regiment as recruiting officer.

3770.  HENRY MORGAN PAPERS, 1851-1859. 7 items. Wysox (Bradford County), Pa.

Business correspondence of Morgan, an attorney. One letter from an employee of the pension office, Washington, D.C., volunteers impressions of congressional activity, particularly the charges against Representative John Jamison Pearce of Pennsylvania of attempting to buy votes for Nathaniel P. Banks, and the popularity of Buchanan.

3771.  IRBY MORGAN PAPERS, 1861-1865. 11 items. Montgomery, Ala.

Correspondence of Irby Morgan, a Confederate soldier in the 51st Regiment of Alabama Cavalry Volunteers; S. D. Morgan, in Confederate Army ordnance; and General John Hunt Morgan. Topics include the merits of particular models of rifles and ammunition; the need for skilled ordnance workmen; and the proposed removal of machinery from the Harpers Ferry arsenal.

3772.  JAMES MORGAN DAYBOOK, 1847-1858. 1 vol. New Washington (Harris County), Tex.

Records of transactions in land, farming, hiring of slaves, cattle raising, and other business ventures in New Washington, a town now extinct but formerly located near Morgan's Point, and concerned with the development of the Houston area. Some of the transactions concern David Harris and Sidney Sherman.

3773.  JOHN MORGAN AND COMPANY LEDGER, 1838-1840. 1 vol. (408 pp.) Shenandoah County, Va.

Entries for various types of merchandise, commodities, and services.

3774.  JOHN TYLER MORGAN PAPERS, 1898-1899. 5 items. Selma (Dallas County), Ala.

Letters of John Tyler Morgan (1824-1907) while U.S. senator. The collection chiefly concerns an article he wrote for the North American Review on American intervention in Cuba and the Philippines.

3775.  THOMAS GIBBES MORGAN, SR., AND THOMAS GIBBES MORGAN, JR., PAPERS, 1776-1946. 44 items. Baton Rouge, La.

Copies of correspondence relating to the career of Colonel George Morgan, father of Thomas Gibbes Morgan, agent for Indian affairs in Pittsburgh, 1776, including letters of Lafayette and Washington concerning the Indian vocabulary compiled for the universal dictionary of all languages compiled for the Empress of Russia, 1786. Certificates relating to the career of Judge Thomas Gibbes Morgan, Sr. (1799-1861), date during 1823-1839. Papers of Thomas Gibbes Morgan, Jr. (d. 1864), relate to his Civil War career as an officer of the 7th Louisiana Volunteers (Sarsfield Rangers), and in other commands from the Trans-Mississippi Department to Antietam; his wounding and convalescence; the prospects of Louisiana after the fall of Vicksburg; and imprisonment in Old Capitol Prison, Washington, D.C., 1863-1864. A letter of Sarah Fowler Morgan describes life in New Orleans and the Confederate raider Charles ("Savez") Reed as he passed through the city as a prisoner. Mrs. Morgan also comments on her northern cousins. Letters of Gibbes Morgan tell of Johnson's Island Prison in Ohio. The collection includes a genealogical chart and data on homes of Morgan family members compiled by Thomas G. Morgan, Jr.'s son, Howell Morgan.

3776.  MORGAN-MALLOY COTTON MILLS PAPERS, 1869-1898. 23 vols. Laurel Hill (Scotland County), N.C.

Records of firms operated by Mark Morgan (1837-1916) and Charles Malloy, including daybooks of the company store, time books, cotton account books, cotton gin accounts, daybooks, store books, production books, and invoice books.

3777.  JUSTIN SMITH MORRILL PAPERS, 1844-1868. 16 items. Strafford (Orange County), Vt.

Correspondence and lecture notes of Morrill, U.S. representative and senator, dealing chiefly with his anti-slavery position.

3778.  CHARLES JEWETT MORRIS PAPERS, 1862-1863. 41 items. Bethany (New Haven County), Conn.

Civil War letters by a soldier in the 27th Regiment of Connecticut Infantry Volunteers. Morris comments on the leadership of Generals McClellan and Burnside; the fortifications of Washington; depredations; casualties at Fredericksburg; fraternization of Union and Confederate troops and the exchange of newspapers; food and health; Democratic Party politics; treatment of deserters; abolitionist control of the Republicans; Lincoln's appearance; capture at Chancellorsville and parole; Confederate generals Jackson and Lee and predictions of Confederate victory.

3779. GEORGE POPE MORRIS PAPERS, 1861. 1 item. New York, N.Y.

A letter to Morris, editor of the Home Journal, from Augusta Brown Garrett about poems by her brother.

3780. ROBERT MORRIS PAPERS, 1785-1795. 13 items. Philadelphia, Pa.

Correspondence, maps, and other papers of Robert Morris (1734-1806), Philadelphia financier, concerning the purchase of tobacco in North Carolina and the Yazoo land fraud in Georgia.

3781. STEPHEN BRENT MORRIS PAPERS, 1972-1975. 64 items. Columbia (Howard County), Md.

Papers concerning Masonic organizations in Durham, North Carolina, while Morris was a graduate student at Duke University. The collection comprises letters, programs, memoranda, and other documents and memoranda, including some statistics.

3782. THOMAS MORRIS COMMONPLACE BOOK, 1855-1873. 1 vol. (70 pp.) Carnesville (Franklin County), Ga.

Included are some Franklin County Inferior Court records, 1860-1864.

3783. WILLIAM MORRIS PAPERS, 1807-1922. 530 items and 3 vols. Nixonton (Pasquotank County), N.C.

Business, personal, and legal papers of William Morris, a local politician, including a few Civil War letters; letters from relatives who moved to Indiana in the 1860s; business letters from Norfolk merchants, 1859-1922; a volume of Civil War reminiscences; and an account book of Dr. Nathaniel Peabody and his wife, Elizabeth (Palmer) Peabody, of Salem, Massachusetts, concerning small sums for repairs, purchases and collection of rents. Among the subjects of the correspondence are a lottery in Delaware; a forthcoming novel of Virginius Dabney (1835-1894); teaching in Virginia; and religion. Correspondents include Patrick Henry Winston (b. 1820) and John Francis Heath (d. 1862), who wrote in defense of slavery and in opposition to immigration into the United States.

3784. J. S. MORRISON PAPERS, 1840-1845. 2 items. Bedford (Bedford County), Pa.

A letter to J. S. Morrison from an unidentified person in Mount Vernon, Ohio, commenting on the scarcity of money and conditions in Illinois and Missouri; and a letter from Morrison to William H. West of Philadelphia, regarding a loan.

3785. JAMES MORRISON PAPERS, 1818 (1820-1858) 1893. 46 items. Brownsburg (Rockbridge County), Va.

Family letters, and letters dealing with religious subjects addressed to James Morrison, a Presbyterian minister of Brownsburg. Included also are letters to Hallie N. Morrison, probably James Morrison's granddaughter, who was head of a school at Brownsburg.

3786. JOHN ROBERT MORRISON PAPERS, 1834. 1 item. Hong Kong.

A letter concerning missionary activities in Macao from Robert Morrison to his son, John Robert Morrison (1814-1843), colonial official. Francis, Lord Napier, and Lady Napier are mentioned.

3787. THOMAS MORRISON PAPERS, 1851-1887. 13 items and 1 vol. Iredell County, N.C.

An account book, 1851-1882, badly mutilated, containing mercantile and farm accounts; miscellaneous financial papers; receipts for subscriptions to the Landmark (Statesville, North Carolina); bills showing wages; a promissory note; and a request for leave of absence from the 7th Regiment of North Carolina Troops, 1865.

3788. BEVERLY PRESTON MORRISS PAPERS, 1814 (1848-1947). 1,904 items and 3 vols. Amherst County, Va.

Letters of Morriss, a physician, describe life as a medical student in Philadelphia and Washington in 1848 and the national election of that year. Civil War letters relate to Morriss' medical practice and operation of a farm and tannery in Amherst County, Virginia; the army service of his two nephews, one of whom was Charles Watts; the sale of C.S.A. bonds; Milroy's campaign in the Shenandoah Valley; camp life, prices, morale and discipline; the Bedford County militia; conscription and clothing of recruits; the Vicksburg Campaign and conditions there; rising physicians' fees; Sheridan's Valley Campaign; life in the trenches at Petersburg; the hiring of slaves; and rumors. Postwar correspondence concerns Morriss' routine professional and family activities. A few letters concern the Oakland Female Home School, Nelson County, 1873. Papers relating to Morriss' daughters, Loula and Jessie, concern Southwest Virginia Institute, teaching, and family matters, There are three account books for the Civil War period and miscellaneous items, including 1,036 bills and receipts.

3789. CLARA J. (JOHNSON) MORROW PAPERS, 1856-1936. 160 items. Allegheny City (Allegheny County), Pa.

Family correspondence of Johnson and Morrow relatives, including primarily Clara J.

(Johnson) Morrow, her brother Henry J. Johnson, her husband James Elmer Morrow, and their son Jay Johnson Morrow. There are descriptions of Cumberland, Maryland, during the Civil War; postwar army life in Mobile, Alabama, and at Mt. Vernon Arsenal; and teaching during the 1860s and 1870s. Correspondence of Henry J. Johnson, national guard officer, editor of the Cumberland Daily News, and postmaster of Cumberland, contains letters from many politicians and veterans, including E. T. Noyes, R. S. Matthews, James G. Blaine, Milton G. Urner, Winfield S. Hancock, John Alexander Logan, William Hamilton Gibson, and William Woods Averell. Letters of Brigadier General Jay Johnson Morrow follow his career in the U.S. Army Corps of Engineers from West Point to the Philippines in 1902, where he describes an earthquake on Mindanao; Washington, D.C., where he served as engineering commissioner; and France during World War I. There are printed announcements of graduations and other social events, and clippings of newspaper stories about members of the family.

3790.  JAMES MORROW PAPERS, 1840-1847. 4 items. Willington (Abbeville County), S.C.

Letters of Morrow (1820-1865), botanist and explorer, concerning life at Davidson College as a student and at South Carolina College. Two items are from Morrow's parents offering advice and admonitions.

3791.  JEDIDIAH MORSE PAPERS, 1811-1812. 3 items. Charlestown (Suffolk County), Mass.

Morse (1761-1826) was a clergyman and geographer. A letter from Thaddeus Osgood describes Thomas Jefferson's interest in his proposed missionary work; Samuel Swift describes books, his career in bookselling, and debts; and James E. B. Finley discusses qualifications of [Martin Luther?] Hurlbut for the post of principal of Beaufort (South Carolina) College.

3792.  FREDERICK S. MOSBY PAPERS, 1863. 1 item. Manchester (Chesterfield County), Va.

Photocopy of a letter from Fortune Mosby to his brother, Captain Frederick S. Mosby, describing smallpox in Manchester, Virginia; health conditions among Confederate troops; morale in the Confederacy; and confidence in the leadership of Robert E. Lee.

3793.  JOHN SINGLETON MOSBY PAPERS, 1862-1932. 69 items. Warrenton (Fauquier County), Va.

Papers of John Singleton Mosby (1833-1916), lawyer and Confederate ranger commanding "Mosby's Partisan Rangers," (43rd Battalion of Virginia Cavalry after 1863), of his military activities in the winter of 1862-1863; an explanation of his reprisal execution of seven Union prisoners of war; list of Federal prisoners paroled on the order of Colonel Mosby; and a fragmentary volume of invoices over which is written a fictional account of a wedding in the Northern Neck of Virginia, known during the war as "Mosby's Confederacy," reflecting the hardships faced by civilians. Correspondence, 1880s-1890s, is concerned with Mosby's writings on his military activities, including his book Mosby's War Reminiscences and Stuart's Cavalry Campaigns (Boston: 1887), newspaper sketches, and a proposed complete account of his activities during the war; a detailed refutation of criticisms of James Ewell Brown Stuart's raid at Gettysburg, Pennsylvania, in a pamphlet written by Thomas Lafayette Rosser; a series of articles by James Longstreet published in Belford's Monthly and The Century, 1891-1892; other Civil War histories being written during the 1880s and 1890s; and comments on wages and working conditions on the Southern Pacific Railroad during the 1890s. Correspondence, 1904-1913, relates to Mosby's membership in the Republican Party and his reasons for joining that organization; political patronage; publication of magazine and newspaper articles on the Civil War; Mosby's work as assistant attorney in the U.S. Department of Justice; and two letters by a Confederate soldier relating his part in the battle of Gettysburg. Included is a letter, 1904, from President Theodore Roosevelt discussing his administration's relationship to the South.

3794.  ARTHUR T. MOSELEY AND WILLIAM P. MOSELEY PAPERS, 1756 (1801-1896) 1907. 1,022 items and 11 vols. Buckingham County, Va.

Letters and papers of Arthur Moseley and of his son, William P. Moseley, containing mostly business records and accounts. The family was interested in tobacco growing, plantation economy in general, Revolutionary War bounty lands, and mining ventures. The collection contains many accounts and receipts showing purchases for the family and lists of drugs purchased by Dr. William P. Moseley. Included also are cashbooks, account books, memoranda, bankbooks, a book of tax receipts for 1852 and 1882, and a record of taxes assessed, 1791-1795.

3795.  FRANKLIN J. MOSES PAPERS, 1839-1857. 9 items. Sumter (Sumter County), S.C.

Bills of sale for slaves purchased by Franklin J. Moses (1838-1906), journalist and governor of South Carolina, 1872-1874.

3796.  JOSEPH WINN MOSES PAPERS, 1876-1877. 5 items. Montgomery (Montgomery County), Ala.

Papers of Joseph Winn Moses, containing a letter from Paul Hamilton Hayne and newspaper clippings of three of Hayne's poems. Included also is a general order from headquarters of the Alabama Militia in 1876.

3797.   MONTROSE JONAS MOSES PAPERS, 1789-1960. 22,079 items and 409 vols. New York, N.Y.

Papers of Montrose Jonas Moses (1878-1933), drama critic, journalist, and author of works on American and European drama and on children's literature, principally relating to his career. Correspondence pertains to his work as a reader for Thomas Y. Crowell Company and for Little, Brown and Company; his activities as liason between Little, Brown and Company and several authors under contract to prepare works for publication; his participation in the affairs of the Authors Club of New York and the Drama League of America, both at the national and local levels; and his own literary projects. Beginning in 1915, there are carbon copies of outgoing correspondence. Notebooks, clippings, research notes, drafts, some correspondence, and other papers relate to Margaret Anglin, Sir James Matthew Barrie, Phillip Barry, Ethel Barrymore, Sarah Bernhardt, Billie Burke, Heinrich Conreid, Owen Davis, John Drinkwater, Edwin Forrest, James A. Herne, Henrik Ibsen, Sir Rabindranath Tagore, and other playwrights and actors prominent in the 19th and early 20th centuries; American and British drama; children's literature; baseball; the entertainment of troops at U.S. Army camps during World War I; the costs of medical care; and the development of regional or "little" theaters. Scrapbooks contain the majority of his articles clipped from the journals and newspapers in which they appeared. Other papers include lectures and speeches; copies of works by other writers; financial papers consisting chiefly of royalty statements from publishers recording the sales of Moses's books; transcripts of Moses's weekly radio programs broadcast from 1930 to 1934 on the National Broadcasting Company network and on a local New York station; photographs of prominent actors and authors and of scenes from various plays; pictures of camp life in the U.S. Army during World War I; theater programs; scrapbooks of clippings from playbills of the last quarter of the 19th century; scrapbook with clippings concerning Sarah Bernhardt; scrapbook of items relating to Thomas Jonathan Jackson, compiled by Jackson's wife; and Moses's copy of The Tales of Mother Goose (Boston: 1903) with marginalia and annotations written by Moses. Correspondents include Winthrop Ames, Margaret Anglin, David Belasco, Henry Adams Bellows, May Friend Bennett, William Frederick Bigelow, Abbie Farwell Brown, Richard Eugene Burton, Royal Jenkins Davis, William Crowell Edgar, John Erskine, William Clyde Fitch, Daniel Frohman, Hamlin Garland, Norman Bel Geddes, Harley Granville Granville-Barker, Hilary Abner Herbert, Hamilton Holt, Roland Holt, Henry Arthur Jones, Charles Rann Kennedy, Frederick Koch, Percy MacKaye, James Brander Matthews, Edith Wynne Matthison, Langdon Elwyn Mitchell, Arthur Huntington Nason, Eugene Gladstone O'Neill, Charles Fulton Oursler, William Lyon Phelps, Elmer Rice, Charles William Taussig, Augustus Thomas, Carl Van Doren, Eugene Walter, Kate Douglas (Smith) Wiggin, Percival Wilde, and Stark Young.

3798.   CHARLES MOSS PAPERS, 1792-1810. 35 items. Oxford, Oxfordshire, England.

Letters to Charles Moss (1763-1811), bishop of Oxford, concerning the election of William Wyndham Grenville, Baron Grenville, as chancellor of the University of Oxford; a commencement ceremony at the University of Oxford; and the ecclesiastical career of Bishop Moss. Correspondents are Anne (Pitt) Grenville, Lord Grenville, and William Wickham. Also included are three documents relating to the appointment of Charles Moss as bishop of Oxford in 1807.

3799.   HARTWELL MOTLEY ARITHMETIC NOTEBOOK, 1837. 1 vol.

Practice arithmetic problems, and some genealogical information in a notebook kept by Hartwell Motley (b. 1801).

3800.   A. B. MOTTE ORDER BOOK, 1800-1801. 1 vol. (22 pp.) Charleston, S.C.

Copies of general orders of the Federal artillery company of Charleston kept by A. B. Motte, orderly sergeant. These orders are copies of documents signed by Langdon Cheves and James Duncan, captains. They are generally routine in nature, calling for courts-martial, musters, reviews, parades, and reports; but one order, May 8, 1801, calls for the firing of a salute "as Vice President Burr passes Fort Mechanic."

3801.   JACOB RHETT MOTTE PAPERS, 1743 (1835-1857) 1902. 305 items and 4 vols. Charleston, S.C.

Miscellaneous papers of Jacob Rhett Motte (1811-1868), Charleston physician, planter, and surgeon in the U.S. Army, 1836-1844, and in the Confederate Army, contain business correspondence; bills and accounts, including records of the furniture and household articles purchased by Motte and his wife, Mary Maham (Haig) Motte, after their marriage in 1845; records of books purchased; papers concerning Motte's service in the U.S. Army with troops in Creek and Cherokee territory, fighting the Seminoles, and removing the Winnebago Indians, including letters regarding medical supplies and regulations for the medical branch of the Army; letters, 1830s, with references to South Carolinians who had fought during the sieges of Charleston and Savannah during the Revolutionary War and affairs of St. Philip's Church in Charleston; references to slavery problems and financial reverses on Motte's farm, and to prices of horses, carriages, farming implements, and clothing; post-Civil War letters reflecting economic hardships; agreement, 1785, between Abraham Motte and Henry Kennan to establish a commission and factorage business in Charleston; extracts from the will of Charlotte Broughton; essays written by J. R. Motte as an adolescent; tax in kind report by Motte made in 1865; an account book, 1838-1842, relating to the settlement of Issac Motte's estate; will of Mary Motte and account book, 1842-1845, concerning the settlement of her estate; and plantation book, 1846-1871, giving a record of purchases, deaths, and births of slaves, provisions issued, and work assigned them.

3802. WILLIAM MOULTRIE PAPERS, 1781-1787. 2 items. Charleston, S.C.

Papers of William Moultrie (1730-1805), Revolutionary soldier, statesman, and governor of South Carolina, including a surveyor's plat and land grant conveying land to A. Young and T. Mitchell; and a letter from Moultrie to "the Master of the American Flag of Truce now in the harbour of Charleston," requesting passage for two American officers.

3803. MOUNT CLIO ACADEMY LEDGER, 1819-1835. 1 vol. (48 pp.) Robeson County, N.C.

Tuition accounts.

3804. MOUNT PLEASANT MISSIONARY SOCIETY RECORD BOOK, 1881-1883. 1 vol. (46 pp.) [Frederick County, Md.?]

Record of members and dues paid.

3805. STEPHEN MOYLAN PAPERS, 1805. 1 item. Philadelphia, Pa.

Letter from Albert Gallatin to Stephen Moylan (1737-1811), Revolutionary soldier and agent in Pennsylvania for the payment of invalid pensions, concerning a remittance from the U.S. Treasury for payment.

3806. THACKER MUIRE AND THOMAS S. DOUGLAS MUIRE PAPERS, 1824-1885. 24 items. Walkerton (King and Queen County), Va.

Family papers of Thacker Muire and of his son, Thomas S. Douglas Muire, including land deed of Anne Temple; will of Henry Timberlake; letters from Bethany College, Wellsburg, Virginia; personal correspondence; and an item of Democratic Party literature, 1885.

3807. PETER M. MULL PAPERS, 1862-ca. 1900. 8 items. Catawba County, N.C.

Papers of Peter M. Mull, captain in the 55th North Carolina Regiment of State Troops, C.S.A., including typed list of officers and privates of Company F; typed copy of order, 1863, from General Robert E. Lee concerning the conduct of Confederate troops in Union territory; order, 1865, giving Mull a furlough for disability; photograph of Mull and his brothers, John M. Mull and Ezra Mull, upon their enlistment; and photographs of reunions of Company F.

3808. GEORGE HENRY MÜLLER PAPERS, 1798-1852. 8 vols. Beaver (Beaver County), Pa.

Diaries and memoirs of George Henry Müller, a German immigrant of 1808, pertaining to his family, his life and travels, and his coffee-growing and mercantile business in Cuba. His "Reminiscences," written to his son William in 1833, include descriptions of his early youth and apprenticeship in Germany and London and his later life in America; the genealogy of the Müller family, 1476-1833; an account of his being shipwrecked off South Carolina and his trip by stage from Charleston, South Carolina, to Baltimore, Maryland; and contain rich historical data of the United States, 1812-1817. Included also are notes on religion and philosophy, weather reports in Beaver, Pennsylvania, 1850-1852, and data on the lives of English poets. Several volumes are in German script.

3809. MUNFORD-ELLIS FAMILY PAPERS, 1777 (1830-1900) 1942. 12,501 items and 21 vols. Richmond (Henrico County), and Lynchburg (Campbell County), Va.

Family, personal, and business papers of three generations of the Munford and the Ellis families of Virginia, connected by the marriage of George Wythe Munford and Elizabeth Throwgood Ellis in 1838. The papers contain information on politics, literary efforts, social life and customs, economic conditions, and military questions principally in nineteenth century Virginia.
Letters and papers of the Munford family center around William Munford (1775-1825) of the first generation, George Wythe Munford (1803-1882) of the second generation, and the children of George Wythe Munford, notably Thomas Taylor Munford (1831-1918), Sallie Radford (Munford) Talbott (1841-1930), Lucy Munford and Fannie Ellis Munford.
The letters of William Munford (1775-1825) are concerned with some details relative to the management of his plantation in Mecklenburg County, Virginia, by an overseer, his legal practice in the early 1800s in southside Virginia, accounts of his election to the governor's council in 1805, and political questions confronting the council. The collection also contains letters concerning possible publication by Thomas Willis White of a novel written by Ursula Anna (Munford) Byrd, sister of William Munford. Letters of friends and relatives and members of the first generation of Munfords are also included.
Volumes are an account book, 1799-1873; and a miscellany, 1790-1814, containing poems of William Munford, a list

of the books in his library, and a list of subscribers to the Munford and William W. Hening *Reports of Cases argued and determined in the Supreme court of appeals of Virginia*. Chief of the literary works are two poems, "The Richmond Cavalcade" (1798), and its sequel, "The Richmond Feast" (1799), in Hudibrastic verse aimed at the political maneuvers of the Federalists. Also included are original poems by John Blair, Thomas Bolling Robertson, Anna (Munford) Byrd, St. George Tucker, and Mrs. John Page of Rosewell concerning social matters; and other poems by Munford, some of which were later published in the Richmond (Virginia) *Enquirer*.

George Wythe Munford (1803-1882), named for the mentor of his father, was clerk of the Virginia House of Delegates, an office which he held until the end of the Civil War, when he attempted farming until forced by reverses to secure a clerkship in the U.S. Census Bureau. Correspondence concerns the Mexican War, including letters from Admiral William Radford aboard the U.S.S. *Warren* blockading the Mexican coast at Mazatlán; Virginia Military Institute, Lexington, Virginia, 1845; Virginia politics, including letters from Henry Alexander Wise while governor; the people and countryside around Lynchburg, Virginia, where he went for recuperation during the summer; his gubernatorial campaign in Virginia, 1863; the fall of Richmond, April, 1865, and his flight to western Virginia, including descriptions of his reactions and those of his relatives, and the uncertainty of the future; his application for a pardon and the response of President Andrew Johnson; detailed accounts in letters to his son, Thomas, of his struggles, work, and the labor system relating to his farming attempts in Gloucester County, Virginia, 1866-1873; his work in preparing a Virginia code of laws, 1873; the Readjuster Movement, which resulted in his removal from office as a clerk in the House of Delegates to which he had returned after farming; his experiences as clerk in the census office in Washington, 1880-1882; the Southern Historical Society, of which he was secretary; and people and social life and customs in Virginia, Maryland, and Washington, D. C., including letters from his daughters while employed as governesses. Included also are notes, correspondence, and the original manuscript of his *The Two Parsons* (Richmond: 1884), published after his death, as well as correspondence about the two ministers, John Buchanan and John Blair. A poems and account book, 1821-1837, contains poetry by George Wythe Munford, including "The Gander Pull or James City Games," and sentimental poems, some written to his relatives; poetic letters; and a cashbook. Other volumes include an inventory of his household furniture purchased in 1834; and account books, 1835-1865.

A large portion of the collection relates to Thomas Taylor Munford (1831-1918), planter, brigadier general in the cavalry of the Confederate Army, and lecturer on Confederate military history. Correspondence pertains to the difficulties of farming; the Civil War, including the shortage of rations, typhoid and diphtheria on the plantation, charges brought against Munford by General Thomas Lafayette Rosser, and the fate of the Confederacy, with copies of letters and orders regarding the mobilization of the Confederate Army and cavalry, reorganization of the cavalry, Munford's promotion to brigadier general, and his command and surrender; postwar financial difficulties; his cattle selling venture; and the Lynchburg Iron, Steel, and Mining Company. The bulk of the material was written after 1875 and relates to Civil War campaigns and battles, especially to the Virginia cavalry and particularly to the battle of Five Forks; Virginia Military Institute; writings on the Civil War; the flag and seal of the state of Virginia; and Virginia history. Many of the letters are annotated, although not always accurately, by Munford's nephew, Charles Talbott III. Correspondence between Munford and many former Confederate and Union officers and soldiers pertains to efforts to collect Confederate cavalry records; the history of the 2nd Virginia Cavalry as well as references to other cavalry units including the 1st, 3rd, 4th, 5th, 7th, and 8th Virginia cavalries, C.S.A., and the 6th New York Cavalry, 4th, 6th, and 16th Pennsylvania cavalries, 1st Maine Cavalry, 1st Rhode Island Cavalry, 1st Massachusetts Cavalry, and 1st Maryland Cavalry, U.S.A.; jealousy between the Virginia and South Carolina cavalries; comparisons between the cavalries of the Army of the Potomac, U.S.A., and the Army of Northern Virginia, C.S.A., and other Confederate and Union cavalries; cavalry operations, tactics, and weapons; the writing and publication of Henry B. McClellan's *The Life and Campaigns of Major-General J. E. B. Stuart* (Boston: 1885); court of inquiry review, 1879-1880, of the role of General Gouverneur Kemble Warren at the battle of Five Forks; accounts of various battles and campaigns of the Civil War, especially the battle of Five Forks, but also the battles of 1st Manassas, Gettysburg, Aldie (Virginia), Chancellorsville, Todd's Tavern (Virginia), and Appomattox, and the dispute between Munford and Rosser over the battle of Five Forks. Other correspondence concerns the history of the guns at V.M.I., including copies of letters from the Marquis de Lafayette, William Davies, Thomas Jefferson, and James Monroe; the trial of Aaron Burr, including copies of letters and documents; the early history of V. M. I.; Thomas Jonathan Jackson at V. M. I.; Munford's terms as president of the Board of Visitors at V. M. I.; 1884 and 1888; his views on discipline, insubordination, and students; dissension at Virginia Polytechnic Institute, Blacksburg, Virginia, in 1885; the Southern Historical Society and its publications; the history of secession, including letters from Douglas Southall Freeman; campaign for a Confederate memorial to be erected in Lynchburg where Munford's regiment was organized and disbanded; the Confederate Veterans Association; the United Confederate Veterans; and race riots in Indiana, 1903.

Addresses and notes concerning

Confederate cavalry fighting include a muster roll, 1863; lists of officers; a history of Munford's regiment with detailed accounts of troop movements and activities of Confederate officers, 1861-1863; maps; typed copy of a diary, 1861-1862, of a Confederate soldier describing camp life, hardships, skirmishing, picket duty, and fighting at the battles of 1st Manassas, Dranesville, and Leesburg, Virginia; material on the Maryland Campaign, 1862; typed copy of a diary, May-October, 1864, of Major James Dugué Ferguson, assistant adjutant general of Fitzhugh Lee's Cavalry Division, describing the itinerary and operations of his troops; copies of letters and articles on the Munford-Rosser feud; copy of "Spirit of the Army, Lynchburg, Va., Feb. 25, 1865," concerning the reaction of the 2nd Virginia Cavalry to the peace terms proposed by President Andrew Johnson; and a narrative of the battle of Waynesboro, Virginia, 1865, sent by Colonel Augustus Forsberg, 51st Virginia Infantry, C.S.A. Material on the battle of Five Forks consists of notes on the battle by General Munford; his unpublished manuscript on the battle; bound volume containing related letters and clippings; a short narrative (22 pp.) on the battle; extracts from the report of General George E. Pickett to General Robert E. Lee; extracts from General Rosser's reminiscences on Five Forks; "Vindication of General Anderson from the Insinuations of General Fitzhugh Lee" by C. Irvine Walker, including Richard Anderson's report to Robert E. Lee, 1866, and part of Fitzhugh Lee's report to Robert E. Lee; narratives by Confederate soldiers on the last days of the 2nd Virginia Cavalry; extracts from the report of General George Crook, U.S.A., regarding the surrender at Appomattox, Virginia; copies of correspondence between Munford and Ranald Slidell McKenzie on Munford's surrender after Appomattox; and Munford's "The Last Days of Fitz Lee's Division of Cavalry Army of Northern Virginia." Other papers relate to the activities of Confederate and Union veterans, including material on the history of the flag and seal of Virginia, and addresses to various veterans organizations and reunions; V. M. I., including material on the return of the bronze statue of George Washington taken by General David Hunter, the history of the French guns, and Thomas Jonathan Jackson, and lists of V. M. I. soldiers and officers in the C.S.A. Army; miscellaneous notes and addresses on the Constitution and the right of secession, the Society of the Cincinnati, and the Southern Historical Society; and miscellaneous poetry including "Mexican Campaign Song." Clippings generally pertain to the Civil War, including letters and accounts of the C.S.A. Army clipped from various newspapers; Confederate veterans organizations; Civil War statistics; Confederate generals and field officers of the Virginia cavalry; and the Munford-Rosser feud.

The collection contains many letters of the thirteen other children of George Wythe Munford. Correspondence of Charles Ellis Munford (1839-1862) concerns the U.S. Military Academy, war preparations and military drilling at the University of Virginia, and his recruiting duties. Other letters concern his death at Malvern Hill, Virginia, 1862. Also included are his law notebooks, 1859-1861. Personal and family letters of the daughters of George Wythe Munford contain information of the details of household economy and general conditions during the Civil War and Reconstruction. A scrapbook, 1861-1871, of Lizzie Ellis Munford contains Confederate verse and mementos, including flowers taken from the coffin of Thomas Jonathan Jackson in 1863 and from the grave of John Ewell Brown Stuart in 1864, and clippings relating to the war. There are also a number of letters from two grandsons of George Wythe Munford, Allan Talbott and Ellis Talbott, written while touring Europe and while studying at the University of Geneva and at the University of Heidelberg, 1886-1889.

Papers of the Ellis family begin with those of Charles Ellis, Sr. (1772-1840), Richmond merchant and partner of John Allan, who was the foster father of Edgar Allan Poe, and of his brother, Powhatan Ellis (1790-1863), jurist, U.S. senator, and diplomat. Letters of Charles Ellis concern business affairs and personal matters, the latter consisting largely of admonitions to his son, James, while a student at the U.S. Military Academy, West Point, New York, and of letters written from the springs of western Virginia. Letters of Margaret (Nimmo) Ellis (1790-1877), wife of Charles Ellis, Sr., are numerous from 1840 to her death and, although generally concerned with family affairs, also contain accounts of war activities and social changes resulting from the Civil War. Correspondence of Powhatan Ellis concerns national politics; party affiliation of John Tyler; the nullification debate in the Senate; Andrew Jackson's stand against South Carolina on the nullification issue; the digging of the James River Canal; his duties as minister to Mexico; Franklin Pierce's policy towards Cuba; Mississippi politics; opposition to Stephen A. Douglas; secession; the Richmond Light Blues; the formation of the Confederacy in Mississippi; legal affairs of William Allan; and family and personal matters, including visits to Berkeley Springs, Virginia.

Correspondence of Thomas Harding Ellis (1814-1898), son of Charles and Margaret (Nimmo) Ellis, merchant and businessman, relate to his education at the University of Virginia, Charlottesville, Virginia, 1831-1832; the Southern Literary Messenger; the Richmond Fayette Light Artillery; his interest in literary activities; his duties as private secretary to his uncle, Powhatan Ellis, in Mexico, 1836, and as first secretary of the legation, 1839-1841; people and events in Richmond, 1840-1860; the Civil War, including preparations in Richmond during the Peninsular Campaign; labor conditions and financial difficulties in the James River Valley after the war; his residence in Chicago, 1871-1883, with detailed accounts of the growth of the city and the great fire of 1871; the Republican National Convention of 1880; clerkships in the Departments of the Interior and the Treasury, 1887-1898; and genealogy of the Ellis family.

Letters and papers of other children of Charles and Margaret (Nimmo) Ellis are also included. Letters of James Ellis (1815-1839) in general were written from the U.S. Military Academy. One contains a reference at the time of the death of John Allan, Poe's foster father, stating that Allan had not "spent his time in a proper way" and making some reference to Allan's second wife, which has been thoroughly obliterated. Charles Ellis, Jr. (1817-189-), left many business and personal letters, the latter consisting largely of family letters and accounts of numerous visits to the springs in western Virginia, especially Warm Springs in Bath County, with minute descriptions of activities, guests, his ailments, and the young ladies whom he escorted during his long life and many sojourns at Warm Springs. Other correspondence concerns the education of James West Pegram at Clifton Academy, in Amelia County, Virginia, 1855-1856; John Brown's raid on Harpers Ferry, 1859; the railroad during the Confederacy, especially the Richmond and Petersburg Railroad during the siege of Petersburg; Ellis's efforts to remain president of the railroad after the war; and the collapse of the gallery in the courtroom of the capitol in Richmond. Correspondence of Powhatan Ellis, Jr. (1829-1906), son of Charles Ellis, Sr., major in the Confederate Army, and planter, pertains to his activities as a student at the University of Virginia, 1848-1850; as an agent to look after family lands in Kentucky; as an officer in the Confederate Army in the western theater, with particular references to the surrender of Fort Henry, the Vicksburg Campaign, and troop movements and military engagements in Mississippi and Alabama; and as a planter in Gloucester County following the Civil War.

The letters of Jane Shelton (Ellis) Tucker (1820-1901) and her husband, Nathaniel Beverley Tucker (1820-1890), relate to their wanderings and his career as a diplomat, Confederate agent in France and Canada, residence in England and political maneuverings in Washington, residence at Berkeley Springs, West Virginia, financial worries, and their frequent changes of residence. Included also are numerous letters of their children, especially of Beverley D. Tucker, later bishop of the Protestant Episcopal diocese of southern Virginia, and of Margaret Tucker. Numerous letters relative to farming operations of Richard S. Ellis (1825-1867) in Buckingham County, Virginia, are in the collection.

Letters during the Civil War and Reconstruction written by friends and relatives of the Munford and of the Ellis families discuss secession; mobilization; high prices; the blockade; difficulties in securing supplies; women making clothes for the army; the need for nurses; auctions of clothing when women went into mourning; refugees; civilian hardships; rumors; damage to salt and lead works; camp life; conscription; health conditions in the army; various battles and campaigns of the Civil War, including 1st Manassas, the West Virginia campaign against General Rosecrans, the surrender of Forts Henry and Donelson, the Peninsular Campaign, the Seven Days battles, the Vicksburg Campaign, the siege of Petersburg, and the surrender at Appomattox; trench life during the siege of Petersburg; fraternization between opposing lines; various Confederate and Union officers; cavalry regulations; the occupations of Alexandria, Virginia, by the New York Fire Zouaves; the possibility of arming Negroes; Negro celebration after the fall of Richmond; depredations by Union troops; the assassination of Abraham Lincoln; restlessness among freedmen; economic distress during Reconstruction; dispute between the Methodist Episcopal Church and the Methodist Episcopal Church, South, over property in Martinsburg, West Virginia; and the 1867 election in which U.S. troops were used to keep order while Negroes voted.

Other papers include original poems and clippings by William Munford, George Wythe Munford, and Bishop Beverley Dandridge Tucker; speeches and essays by George Wythe Munford and Charles Ellis Munford at the University of Virginia; manuscript entitled "History of William Radford's Incarceration in the Tower of London"; bills and receipts relating to household and political affairs; newspaper clippings and printed material concerning family biographies and obituaries, Confederate history, and genealogy of Virginia families; miscellaneous material relating to Virginia history; genealogical information on the Bland, Cabell, Ellis, Galt, Harrison, Jordan, Munford, Nimmo, Radford, Talbott, Tayloe, and Winston families, and a chart of the Munford, Ellis, and Tayloe families; scrapbook of the letters of Thomas Harding Ellis, published in the Richmond Standard, containing material on the Allan family; reminiscenses of Thomas Harding Ellis on the boyhood of Edgar Allan Poe; pictures; scrapbooks, 1877-1888 and 1910-1912, of Sallie (Munford) Talbott; account book, 1823-1826, and memorandum book, 1808-1809, of Charles Ellis, Sr.; account books, 1841-1853, of the administration of the estate of Charles Ellis, Sr.; letterpress copybook, 1856-1893, of Charles Ellis [Jr.?]; surveyor's notebook, 1838-1839, and commonplace book, 1835, of James Nimmo Ellis, the latter book containing records of a club formed at the United States Military Academy "for the purpose of acquiring information"; and the Ellis family Bible.

3810. MARY NOAILLES MURFREE PAPERS, 1887. 1 item. Murfreesboro (Rutherford County), Tenn.

Letter of Mary Noailles Murfree (1850-1922), novelist and short story writer who generally wrote under the name Charles Egbert Craddock, to Eliza Anna Farman Pratt, editor of Wide Awake, discussing a story she is preparing for the children's magazine.

3811. DANIEL W. MURPH PAPERS, 1861-1864. 27 items. Lincoln County, N.C.

Family correspondence of Daniel W. Murph, 10th Regiment of Artillery, N. C. Troops, C.S.A., discussing desertion in the Confederate Army, the opposition of Zebulon B. Vance to Jefferson Davis's conscription policies, and the activities of the 10th Regiment.

3812. DAVID MURPHY PAPERS, 1856-1865. 1 item and 1 vol. Cumberland County, N.C.

Papers of David Murphy, a paper manufacturer, consist of an indenture, 1865, leasing property, including land, buildings, and machinery, to William Vink for the construction of a paper mill; and a volume, 1856-1862, recording statistics on the manufacture and sale of paper, including data on the quantity, quality, and weight of the paper produced, names and locations of customers, notes on the mill business and operations, local events, and the weather, and recipes for scented oil, rosin size, black ink, medicines, and colored dyes.

3813. JAMES MADISON MURPHY PAPERS, 1864. 1 item. Calais (Washington County), Me.

Journal of James Madison Murphy, 1st Maine Veteran Infantry, U.S.A., describing shortage of rations and foraging; drills and reviews; fighting at the fourth battle of Winchester and at Cedar Creek, Virginia; Philip Henry Sheridan's scorched earth policy; guard duty; winter quarters at Strasburg and later at Winchester, Virginia; and voting in the 1st Maine Veteran Infantry Regiment in the 1864 presidential elections.

3814. E. B. MURRAY PAPERS, 1855-1865. 27 items. Walnut Hill (Franklin County), Ga.

Principally business papers of E. B. Murray and his son, W. C. Murray. Civil War letters discuss the election of a regimental commander; refugees; prices of corn and bacon; an election in Franklin County in 1864; and the death of W. C. Murray, lieutenant in 29th Georgia Regiment. Also included is a list of clothing of men in Company B, 29th Georgia Regiment; and a tax form for agricultural goods, 1865.

3815. HENRY S. MURRAY PAPERS, 1862-1864. 5 items. Goshen (Orange County), N.Y.

Civil War letters of Captain Henry S. Murray, 124th New York Regiment, U.S.A., describe his arrival in Washington, D. C.; camp life in the Washington, D. C., area; and his attempts to secure a promotion to rank of major.

3816. JOHN MURRAY, SR., AND JOHN MURRAY, JR., PAPERS, 1826, 1842. 2 items. London, England.

Letter, 1826, to the Murrays, London publishers, from Sir John Malcolm (1769-1833) sending a copy of Persia, probably his Sketches of Persia (London: 1826), for certain calculations to be made, perhaps in preparation for a new edition; and a letter from William Drysdale to the Murrays discussing attempts to erect monuments to Thomas Muir and his companions who were arrested and convicted for sedition in 1793.

3817. JOHN COBBS MURRELL PAPERS, 1822 (1852-1876) 1882. 38 items. Lynchburg (Campbell County), Va.

Correspondence of John C. Murrell (d. 1879), lawyer and Commonwealth's attorney for the county, 1865-1879, discussing personal, business, and legal affairs; personal debts; and bankruptcy.

3818. WILLIAM MURRELL PAPERS, 1793-1851. 146 items and 1 vol. Stateburg (Sumter County), S.C.

Family and business correspondence of William Murrell (d. 1830), postmaster and merchant dealing in cotton and indigo, and a letter book, 1795-1812 (314 pp.), concerning his mercantile business and association with General Thomas Sumter.

3819. BATTAILE MUSE PAPERS, 1726 (1777-1800) 1891. 6,920 items. Marsh Farm (Berkeley County, now Jefferson County), W. Va.

Correspondence and papers of Battaile Muse (d. 1803), agent for large Virginia planters and plantation owners, relating to the desertion of Tidewater farms by Virginia planters for the more fertile areas in Loudoun, Fauquier, Frederick, and Berkeley counties; the progress of the Revolutionary War; planting and the sale of indigo and other farm products; the treatment of slaves; the estate of James and John Francis Mercer, 1776-1783; the Fairfax estate; and Muse's career as rental agent for George Washington in Frederick and Fauquier counties; 1784-1792. Included also are account books and memoranda listing rent collections and other business operations. Four letters, 1847-1848, relate to a dispute in the faculty of the College of William and Mary, Williamsburg, Virginia.

3820. BENJAMIN MUSE PAPERS, 1919-1973. 747 items. Reston (Fairfax County), Va. Restricted.

The papers of Benjamin Muse (b. 1898), politician, journalist, experimental farmer, government official, and civil rights activist comprise correspondence, writings and addresses, clippings, printed material, and memoranda. The correspondence, 1937-1939 and 1941, relates chiefly to Virginia politics, Muse's resignation from the state senate in 1936, his bolt of the Democratic Party, strategy for building up the Republican Party, assistance in various political campaigns, and his gubernatorial campaign in 1941. Writings and addresses include accounts of his experiences in the British Army during World War I; speeches on Spanish and American culture, relating to his diplomatic career in Latin America; speech, 1934, praising Franklin Delano Roosevelt and the New Deal; speeches, 1936, relating to old-age assistance and transcripts of the hearings held by the joint legislative committee inquiring into the cost of such assistance to the state; addresses regarding his experiments in self-sufficient farming; speeches, 1937-1941, attacking Roosevelt's court packing scheme, advancing Republican candidates, and promoting his candidacy for governor; report, 1944, entitled "The Economic Aspect of Western Hemisphere Security," emphasizing the importance of "total" war; a chapter on the state of Virginia for Presidential Nominating Politics in 1952, edited by Paul T. David (Baltimore: 1954); speeches, 1955-1967, on the race question in the South; reports, 1962-1963, on his field trips as member of the President's Committee on Equal Opportunity in the Armed Forces; a summary of the Civil Rights Movement, 1940-1970; manuscript draft on his experiences in Mexico in 1914; and drafts, notes, and comments on his books, Tarheel Tommy Atkins (New York: 1963), Ten Years of Prelude (New York: 1964), and The American Negro Revolution (Bloomington, Ind.: 1968). Clippings relate to Muse, his family, and his gubernatorial campaign. Printed material consists of posters, broadsides, sample ballots, and campaign literature pertaining to the gubernatorial campaign. Restricted material is his reports, 1959-1964, to the Southern Regional Council on his conversations with Southern leaders on racial issues, including a summary of the conversations, his impressions, the conditions of the city, and his recommendations on how to improve race relations.

3821. JAMES W. MUSE PAPERS, 1861. 3 items. Charleston (Kanawha County), W. Va.

Letters from James W. Muse, a Confederate soldier, to his wife, commenting on the hardships of camp life and the shortage of rations.

3822. RICHARD W. MUSGROVE PAPERS, 1861-1866. 18 items. Sanbornton Bridge (Belknap County), N.H.

Personal correspondence of Richard W. Musgrove and his brother, Adam Charles Musgrove, with friends and relatives concerning personal matters, social life at a small college in New Hampshire, evangelical religion, the enlistment of A. C. Musgrove and Richard Musgrove into the army, the army hospital in Beaufort (South Carolina) during the Civil War, the capture of Richmond, and the severity of army life.

3823. JOHN B. MUSSEY PAPERS, 1855-1866. 17 items. Concord (Merrimack County), N.H.

Civil War letters of John B. Mussey, serving with the Army of the Potomac during the Peninsular Campaign, discussing personal matters, camp life, Union casualties, and the course of the war in Virginia and Louisiana.

3824. GERMAIN MUSSON PAPERS, 1815-1832. 8 items. New Orleans, La.

Accounts for freight hauled on the Mississippi River for Germain Musson, including the transportation of flour, sugar and coffee; price for a Negro; and wages for the hire of Negroes.

3825. MUTUAL RESERVE FUND LIFE ASSOCIATION PAPERS, 1898-1902. 1 vol. (301 pp.) North Carolina.

Docket of judgments rendered in cases in which the Mutual Reserve Fund Life Association of North Carolina was interested.

3826. J. C. MYERS BIOGRAPHY, 1864. 1 vol. (184 pp.) Craigsville (Augusta County), Va.

Biography of Catherine Anne Myers, sister of J. C. Myers, giving interesting insights into religious sentiment of the time. Written by J. C. Myers, the book was dedicated to "the German Baptist Church of New Hope."

3827. JOHN MYERS' SON LEDGER, 1877-1895. 1 vol. (ca. 456 pp.) Washington (Beaufort County), N.C.

Ledger of John Myers' Son, commission merchants, shipbuilders, and operators of steamboats on the Pamlico and Tar rivers, owned by Thomas Harvey Blount Myers (1827-ca. 1906). Included are accounts for the Old Dominion Steamship Company for which John Myers' Son was agent; for steamers or schooners that the company owned or dealt with, including the Cotton Plant, R. S. Myers, Washington, Beaufort, and Louisa; and for an oil mill and a cotton gin.

3828. ROSE MAE (WARREN) MYERS PAPERS, 1917-1970. 8 items. Durham, N.C.

Letters from Benjamin N. Duke to Rose Mae Warren, who married Hiram Earl Myers, a Methodist clergyman, in 1926, concerning his financing of her musical education, cash gifts to her, and his health and the places to which he traveled for diagnosis and treatment; and an obituary of Rose Mae (Warren) Myers.

3829. SAMUEL J. MYERS PAPERS, 1855.
2 items. Richmond, Va.

Correspondence between Samuel J. Myers, tobacco manufacturer, and J. Collins (perhaps actor and vocalist John Collins) concerning the booking of a theater in Richmond, for which Myers was the agent.

3830. JOHN D. MYRICK PAPERS, 1849-1873.
463 items. Norfolk, Va.

Business papers of John D. Myrick (d. 1869) cotton planter, consisting principally of tax receipts; bills for clothes, furniture, hiring of Negroes, farm supplies, liquors, books, and stationery; papers relating to the administration of his estate by John R. Kilby, a Norfolk attorney; and statements by Kilby and his associates for the suit brought by Marie E. Myrick, wife of John D. Myrick, to recover her dower rights.

3831. ROBERT ALGERNON MYRICK PAPERS, 1890-1953. 73 items and 3 vols. Littleton (Halifax County), N.C.

Papers of Robert Algernon Myrick include correspondence while Myrick attended Trinity College, Durham, North Carolina, 1888-1892, while a typing instructor at Trinity, while teaching in Halifax County, and while librarian at Trinity; correspondence concerning Myrick serving as agent for the Hickory Chair Company; letters of his cousins Martha Jenkins and Mary (Jenkins) Miles on family genealogy; letter, 1924, of Captain Wilson T. Jenkins, 14th North Carolina Regiment, C.S.A., describing the exploits of Company A during the Civil War; sections of a diary of Myrick's aunt, Mary Beckham, when teaching school in Halifax County in 1873, and in 1897, describing country life; genealogical material on the Beckham, Dandridge, and Hilliard families; and photographs of Myrick's aunt and uncle, Pattie Dandridge (Beckham) Jenkins and Newsom Edward Jenkins.

3832. JOHN QUINCY ADAMS NADENBOUSCH PAPERS, 1821-1925. 3,176 items and 8 vols. Martinsburg (Berkeley County), W. Va.

Papers of John Quincy Adams Nadenbousch, his son-in-law, Alexander Parks, Jr., and other members of his family. The collection contains material relating to the operation of flour mills by John Q. A. Nadenbousch before the Civil War; the constitution of the Berkeley Border Guards formed in Berkeley County, Virginia, in 1859, and items relating to the subsequent service of that unit in the Civil War as a company of the 2nd Virginia Regiment, including letters of General Thomas Jonathan Jackson to his officers, commissary accounts, muster rolls, provost marshal records, and a manuscript draft of a report by John Q. A. Nadenbousch as colonel of the 2nd Virginia Regiment describing the experiences of that regiment in the fight at Culp's Hill, July 2, 1863, during the battle of Gettysburg; correspondence of John Q. A. Nadenbousch as agent of the Hannis Distilling Company of Baltimore, Maryland, engaged in the operation of a distillery at Martinsburg, West Virginia; letters relating to the management of the Grand Central Hotel in Martinsburg, 1878; and letters concerning John Q. A. Nadenbousch's general financial condition after the Civil War. Papers of Alexander Parks, Jr., concern his position as local agent for Hannis Distilling Company in Martinsburg after 1874; his participation in civic affairs in Martinsburg; and his work in the Democratic Party, including his election to the state senate of West Virginia in 1890. Papers of John Nadenbousch Parks, son of Alexander Parks, Jr., include letters to his family while he was a student at Virginia Military Institute, Lexington, Virginia, 1893, and letters, 1917, to John N. Parks while he was a member of the legislature of West Virginia. Letters, 1895, of Elise Parks, daughter of Alexander Parks, Jr., concern her life as a student at Virginia Female Institute, Staunton, Virginia. Volumes in the collection include a treasurer's notebook, 1852, of a local lodge of the Independent Order of Odd Fellows; a sheriff's account book, 1825-1841, from Jefferson County, West Virginia; an account of tax levies in Jefferson County; a ledger of John Q. A. Nadenbousch, 1872-1878; and notes and accounts of the Berkeley County Agricultural and Mechanical Association.

3833. THOMAS B. NALLE PAPERS, 1805 (1848-1875) 1905. 641 items and 1 vol. "Rose Hill" (Culpeper County), Va.

Business correspondence and accounts of Thomas B. Nalle as a purser in the U.S. Navy, 1848-1875, as a member of the Virginia House of Delegates, 1875-1877, and as operator of Rose Hill farm, 1878-1887. Included are letters and copies of official printed circulars from Secretaries of the Navy James C. Dobbin, William A. Graham, George Bancroft, and Gideon Welles. Included also is an account book for Rose Hill farm.

3834. NANSEMOND AGRICULTURAL SOCIETY RECORDS, 1857-1858. 1 vol. (25 pp.) Nansemond County, Va.

Minutes, proceedings, constitution, and list of animals and articles exhibited by the Nansemond Agricultural Society.

3835. SIR CHARLES JAMES NAPIER PAPERS, 1820-1858. 25 items. Oaklands, Hampshire, England.

Papers of Sir Charles James Napier, British general, contain letters, 1820-1847, from Napier to Dr. Henry Muir discussing personal matters, Muir's work as health officer at Cephalonia and inspector general for health at Corfu, politics, Sir Frederick Adam, and the administration of the Ionian Islands. Other correspondence concerns publications of Charles James Napier, particularly letters to the <u>Naval and Military Gazette</u>; disturbances on the Isle of Man, 1840; administration in India; military affairs in India and Burma; general military matters, and politics in Britain.

3836. HENRY EDWARD NAPIER PAPERS, 1829-1859. 43 items. London, England.

Family letters of Henry Edward Napier, British naval officer, from his brother, Sir Charles James Napier, his cousin, Admiral Sir Charles Napier, and others, concerning family matters; the tariff situation, 1842; and affairs in India, 1844. Also contains a copy, 1831, of Sir George Thomas Napier's account of the death of Sir John Moore after the battle of Coruña in 1809 and a letter, 1846, to Henry Edward Napier from Ichabod Charles Wright concerning Wright's translations of Dante and Napier's <u>Florentine History</u> (London: 1846-1847).

3837. LEROY NAPIER PAPERS, 1863-1865. 5 items. Macon County, [Ala.?]

Receipts for meal, and wood received from Leroy Napier by the quartermaster department of the Confederate Army.

3838. ROBERT CORNELIS NAPIER, FIRST BARON NAPIER OF MAGDALA, PAPERS, 1868. 1 item. London, England.

Letter, 1868, from Robert Cornelis Napier, commander of the Abyssinian Expedition of 1867-1868, to James Maclagan, chief engineer at Lahore, reporting on the progress of the expedition.

3839. JOHN A. NARRON PAPERS, 1899-1912. 1 vol. Smithfield (Johnston County), N.C.

Ledger of an attorney, including records of his activities as a loan agent.

3840. ANDREW O. NASH PAPERS, 1894-1897. 1 vol. Washington, D.C.

A scrapbook of photocopies of clippings concerning the alleged co-operation between the Republican Congressional Committee and the American Protective Association in an effort to identify the Democratic Party with the sectarian interests of its Roman Catholic supporters in the congressional campaign of 1894.

3841. JAMES HEMORY NASH PAPERS, 1862-1880. 4 items. Adamsville (Fulton County), Ga.

Letters of James Hemory Nash and his brother Edward Walker Nash concern the recruitment of Confederate troops in Gwinnett County, Georgia, and James H. Nash's duties as clerk of the Confederate senate.

3842. NATIONAL DYE WORKS PAPERS, 1917-1927. 10 items and 13 vols. Burlington (Alamance County), N.C.

Financial records of the National Dye Works, which dyed, bleached, and finished seamless hosiery, include financial statements, 1924; ledger, 1917-1927; transferred ledger sheets, 1917-1925; journals, 1917-1927; cashbooks, 1917-1927; trial balances, 1917-1927; voucher registers 1923-1927; and inventories, 1918-1927.

3843. JOSIE NEAL PAPERS, 1910-1934. 163 items. Pittsboro (Chatham County), and Durham, N.C.

Personal letters to Josie Neal from friends in army camps at Mogalas (Arizona), Columbia (South Carolina), and Petersburg (Virginia), during World War I, concerning training and camp life. Also a letter, 1918, describing the influenza epidemic in Greensboro, North Carolina; printed material, including Christmas cards and advertisements from music publication companies; and a catalog of the Durham Business School, Durham, North Carolina, for the summer session, 1917.

3844. RICHARD P. NEAL PAPERS, 1826-1891. 21 items. Nashville (Davidson County), Tenn.

Correspondence and papers of the Neal family and business and professional letters written to Samuel D. Power, an attorney. Includes a bill for general merchandise purchased by Richard P. Neal in 1826 and 1827; a religious poem, 1839, by Caroline R. Neal; and bills and receipts of Samuel D. Power in the 1880s.

3845. EDWARD BAXTER NEAVE PAPERS, 1854-1884. 84 items. Salisbury (Rowan County), N.C.

Letters to Edward Baxter Neave from his wife, Ellen (Baker) Neave, and other members of his family, concerning family matters, events during Reconstruction, difficulties with postal service, and bands and concerts in Ohio and North Carolina.

3846. STERLING NEBLETT PAPERS, 1821 (1846-1867) 1871. 217 items and 1 vol. Lunenburg County, Va.

Business and personal papers and correspondence of Sterling Neblett, physician and planter. The collection concerns the buying and selling of land in Virginia, Mississippi, and Texas for himself, for friends, and as trustee of the Bank of Virginia and the Farmers' Bank of Virginia; legal difficulties involved in the selling of slaves in Mississippi and Louisiana; and his plantation and business affairs. Included also is an account book recording advancement of money by Neblett to his son, James H. Neblett.

3847. NEELD FAMILY PAPERS, 1831-1900. 26 items. Grittleton, Wiltshire, England.

Papers for the most part related to the political careers of Joseph Neeld and Sir John Neeld, concerning local elections, particularly the parliamentary election of 1831; the Reform Bill of 1832; and local administration.

3848. JOHN FRED NEEF PAPERS, 1847-1884. 735 items. Niagara (Niagara County), N.Y.

The collection contains the letters of Henry G. Delker, a farmer in Ohio, concerning farm business, commodity prices, and the presidential election of 1856; letters of John F. Neff and his brother, Michael Neff, before 1862, relating to their work as clerks in a hardware store and Michael Neff's work in a railroad shop in Chicago, Illinois; material, 1862-1871, including bills, receipts, business letters, and insurance policies, pertaining to a hardware business run by John F. Neff and Michael Neff in Niagara, New York; and letters of Elisha Whittling, comptroller of the treasury of the United States to Gilman Folsom, receiver of public moneys at Iowa City, Iowa, concerning shortages in Folsom's deposits with the Treasury Department in 1855. Also contains uncataloged letters written in German script.

3849. DAVID DUNCAN NEGLEY PAPERS, 1864-1922. 22 items. Indianapolis (Marion County), Ind.

Papers related to David Duncan Negley's command of Company C, 124th Indiana Regiment in 1864, including muster rolls, documents pertaining to Negley's promotion from first lieutenant to captain, and supply vouchers.

3850. NEGRO COLLECTION, 1757-1972. 314 items and 7 vols.

Collection of miscellaneous papers dealing with the history of the Negro in the United States, including legal and financial papers on the purchase and sale of Negro slaves and the capture of runaways; insurance policies on slaves taken out by slaveowners; legal papers concerning the status of free Negroes; and material pertaining to the activities of the National Association for the Advancement of Colored People in the 1960s. Also contains printed bibliographical information on works dealing with the Negro and events and programs related to the study of the history of the Negro. Volumes include a book of poetry and financial accounts from the early 19th century; and a bankbook kept by a freedman.

3851. GEORGE NEILSON PAPERS, 1891-1902. 12 items. Glasgow, Scotland.

Letters to George Neilson, historian and antiquary, from Frederick William Maitland, Downing Professor of the Laws of England at Cambridge University, concerning personal and professional matters; Maitland's work on various aspects of English legal history; and the development of the boroughs of England and the burghs of Scotland. There are comments on the Cambridge Modern History; the poet Huchown; Lord Acton; and Andrew Lang's History of Scotland.

3852. WILLIAM ALLAN NEILSON PAPERS, 1943-1944. 3 items. Falls Village (Litchfield County), Conn.

Material relating to William Allan Neilson's work with the "Committee of 100," acting in support of the National Association for the Advancement of Colored People.

3853. ELIZA K. NELSON PAPERS, 1823-1867. 62 items. Summit Point (Jefferson County), West Virginia

Letters to Eliza K. Nelson from her father and brothers concerning phrenology; a tour of Virginia by William Henry Harrison, just before his inauguration as president of the United States; student life at Jefferson Medical College, Philadelphia, Pennsylvania; a duel between John Hampden Pleasants and Thomas Ritchie; an outbreak of smallpox in Virginia and vaccination against the disease; and enforcement of the fugitive slave law.

3854. HUGH NELSON PAPERS, 1824-ca. 1831. 3 items. York County, Va.

Papers of Hugh Nelson, United States congressman from Virginia and ambassador to Spain, contain a subscription list for the Rivanna River Improvement Company; a letter from Nelson in Madrid, Spain; and an account of a meeting, ca. 1831, of the people of Albemarle County, Virginia, to discuss the "colored population" of the state.

3855. ROBERT EDWARD NELSON, SR., PAPERS, 1851-1887. 18 items and 1 vol. Columbia (Fluvanna County), Va.

Letters and papers of Robert Edward Nelson, Sr., concern Masonic affairs, the settlement of estates, and the Civil War, including mention of the 7th, 18th, and 44th Virginia Regiments and the Powhatan Artillery Company. Volume contains fragments of the minutes of Withers Masonic Lodge No. 212, Columbia, Virginia.

3856. THOMAS NELSON AND WILLIAM NELSON PAPERS, 1787-1829. 8 items. Yorktown (York County), and Williamsburg (James City County), Va.

Business letters of Thomas Nelson, district attorney and collector of customs at Yorktown, Virginia; property list of Colonel William Nelson, 1789; and letters concerning an expedition against the Indians in the South.

3857. W. R. NELSON REGISTERS, 1891-1926. 2 vols. Selma (Dallas County), Ala.

Records of a collector of claims.

3858. SIR EVAN NEPEAN, FIRST BARONET, PAPERS, 1793-1801. 4 items. London, England.

Papers of Sir Evan Nepean contain an undated letter concerning affairs in Bombay; extract from a letter, 1801, reporting on military operations in Egypt; letter, 1793, from Lord St. Helens concerning the problem of preventing France from buying grain in the Barbary States; and letter, 1794, from William Huskisson, discussing his status as chief clerk in the War office and his future professional plans.

3859. CHARLES TORRENCE NESBITT PAPERS, 1899-1947. 437 items and 3 vols. Wilmington (New Hanover County), N.C.

Letters and papers of Charles Torrence Nesbitt, physician and public health official, contain a typescript autobiography describing his training in medicine at the University of Pennsylvania Medical School, Philadelphia, Pennsylvania; Bellevue Hospital Medical School, New York, New York; and Baltimore Medical College, Baltimore, Maryland; Nesbitt's correspondence as public health officer of Wilmington and New Hanover County, North Carolina, 1911-1917, concerning his attempts to alert city and county officials to poor sanitary conditions and to secure effective health legislation; and miscellaneous reports and data relating to health conditions in Wilmington and New Hanover County. Three scrapbooks contain clippings, for the most part concerned with Nesbitt's public health work in North Carolina, 1911-1917.

3860. JOHN NESBITT PAPERS, 1780. 2 items. Keston Park, Kent, England.

Letters from John Robinson, secretary of the treasury, concerning the election of John Nesbitt to Parliament.

3861. ROBERT TAYLOR NESBITT PAPERS, 1861. 2 items. Marietta (Cobb County), Ga.

A letter from Robert Taylor Nesbitt (b. 1840), Confederate soldier and later Georgia commissioner of agriculture, describing his reaction to camp life in Richmond, Virginia; and a letter from his sister, mentioning the death of their mother.

3862. WILLIAM ANDREWS NESFIELD PAPERS, 1852. 1 item. London, England.

Letter of William Andrews Nesfield, British artist and landscape gardener, giving advice on the selection of plants.

3863. NEUSE MANUFACTURING COMPANY PAPERS, 1899-1941. 606 items and 20 vols. Neuse (Wake County), N.C.

Company records of a cotton textile mill, including minutes of meetings of stockholders and directors, 1899-1908; ledgers, 1912-1940; journals, 1910-1937; production records, 1912-1937; audit and other financial reports, 1915-1937; and receivership papers, 1936-1941.

3864. JOHN J. NEVITT DAYBOOK, 1845-1849. 1 vol. (478 pp.) Savannah, Ga.

Unidentified accounts.

3865. NEW BERN POST OFFICE ACCOUNTS, 1835-1837. 1 vol. (116 pp.) New Bern (Craven County), N.C.

Records of amounts paid for transportation of mail.

3866. NEW ENGLAND PROTECTIVE UNION PAPERS, 1847-1890. 929 items. Boston, Mass.

The collection contains receipts of the New England Protective Union, a federation of stores organized to provide merchandise to the laboring class at reduced cost. The receipts, for the most part, are from stores in Boston, Massachusetts, in the 1850s.

3867. VICEROYALTY OF NEW GRANADA. REAL AUDIENCIA DE SANTA FÉ DE BOGOTA. Records, 1798-1800. 1 vol. Bogotá, Colombia.

Incomplete volume containing records of a suit brought before the Audiencia of Santa Fé de Bogotá concerning a question of the rights to income from a piece of land.

3868. NEW LONDON ACADEMY MINUTES, 1826-1881. 1 vol. New London (Campbell County), Va.

Minutes of the academy board of trustees, covering elections, regulations, appointments to the faculty, and financial matters.

3869. NEW ORLEANS, LA., RECORDS, 1847-1852. 1 vol. (126 pp.) New Orleans, La.

Records of corporation licenses issued by the city of New Orleans.

3870. NEW ORLEANS, LA., REGISTER, 1857-1898. 1 vol. (150 pp.) New Orleans, La.

Volume containing name, age, date of admission, and birthplace of a number of people, probably constituting the admission book of a parish poor house.

3871. NEW YORK, N. Y., PORT PAPERS, 1853-1861. 6 items. New York, N.Y.

Letters of recommendation to the collectors of the port of New York, and a clearance paper, 1861, for the Ice Sea Witch, bound for Saint Lucia with merchandise.

3872. NEW YORK CENTRAL RAILROAD PAPERS, 1853-1892. 129 items. Albany (Albany County), and Buffalo (Erie County), N.Y.

Miscellaneous papers of the New York Central Railroad, including correspondence, legal papers, accounts, and claims.

3873. LARKIN NEWBY PAPERS, 1796 (1803-1823) 1956. 474 items and 1 vol. Fayetteville (Cumberland County), N.C.

The collection contains letters of Larkin Newby, his wife, Cecilia Newby, John Williams Walker, and Newby's friends and business associates, concerning business matters; commodity prices; policies of merchants in Natchez, Mississippi; life of Mississippi planters; duels; horse racing; politics; religion; and an attempt to incorporate the Orphan Asylum Society of Fayetteville, North Carolina. Later items concern George C. Newby, son of Larkin Newby, and other Newby descendants, and include a number of legal papers from Cumberland County, North Carolina, relating to the landholdings of the Newby-Pearce-Tillinghast families.

3874. THOMAS NEWBY DAYBOOK, 1752-1758. 1 vol. (175 pp.) Perquimans County, N.C.

Daybook of a general merchant.

3875. NEWCOMER FAMILY VOLUMES, 1811-1882. 12 vols. Washington County, Md.

Volumes of various members of the Newcomer family, including three ledgers, 1811-1827, of a milling business; an arithmetic book, ca. 1827, of William Newcomer, containing rules, problems, and computations; docket book, 1837-1839, of John Newcomer, relating to his duties as sheriff of Washington County, Maryland; docket book, 1838, for the March term of the Washington County Court kept by John Newcomer; jail docket book, 1838-1839, of John Newcomer, containing names of prisoners and brief information on their cases; ledger, 1828-1838, containing the accounts of a shoemaker; daybook and ledger, 1834-1859, containing both milling accounts and personal accounts; grain accounts, 1847-1854, from the firm of M. and J. H. Newcomer; cashbook, 1858-1860, of William Newcomer; and a ledger, 1879-1882, apparently of a milling business.

3876. CHARLES S. N. NEWELL PAPERS, 1786-1905. 300 items and 1 vol. Heidelberg (Jasper County), Miss.

Business and legal papers of Charles S. N. Newell, including deeds, wills, sales records, records of court cases, tax records, a few business letters, and a doctor's statement, 1864, that Newell was physically unfit for military service. There is a volume, 1786-1838, of accounts of Newell's farming operation.

3877. E. B. NEWELL PAPERS, 1860-1871. 9 items. Johnsonville (Williamsburg County), S.C.

Personal correspondence of E. B. Newell and his family.

3878. LEONE BURNS NEWELL PAPERS, 1913-1950. 83 items. Charlotte (Mecklenburg County), N.C.

The collection is made up for the most part of letters to Leone Burns Newell, a physician in Charlotte, North Carolina, from William deBerniere MacNider, noted pharmacologist and professor of pharmacology at the University of North Carolina, Chapel Hill, concerning personal matters, changes in the medical department of the university, and an influenza epidemic at the university, 1919.

3879. KATE NEWLIN PAPERS, 1869-1874. 4 items. Lynchburg (Campbell County), Va.

Papers of Kate Nowlin, a schoolteacher in Lynchburg, Virginia. The collection was originally cataloged as the Kate Newlin Papers.

3880. GEORGE NEWMAN PAPERS, 1861-1881. 48 items. Eden (Hancock County), Me.

Papers of George Newman contain Civil War letters from his sons, Henry H. Newman, in the 1st Maine Regiment, Heavy Artillery, and Andrew Newman, in the 8th Maine Regiment, concerning Henry Newman's attack of typhoid fever and his recovery; Andrew Newman's experiences in South Carolina and Virginia; and conditions in Richmond, Virginia, at the end of the war. Later papers concern a pension for Mary Newman.

3881. JOHN PHILIP NEWMAN PAPERS, 1865. 1 item. New Orleans, La.

Letter of John Philip Newman, a Methodist minister and later bishop of the Methodist Episcopal Church, to a fellow clergyman concerning his personal financial affairs and the prospects for the reunion of the divided Methodist Episcopal Church.

3882.  ROBERT M. NEWMAN PAPERS, 1818-1848. 11 items. Goshen (Loudoun County), Va.

Papers relating to the law practice of Robert M. Newman.

3883.  SIR JOHN NEWPORT, FIRST BARONET, PAPERS, 1792 (1807-1819) 1834. 68 items. Waterford, Ireland.

Political correspondence of Sir John Newport, a member of Parliament from Ireland, with William Wyndham Grenville, First Baron Grenville, and others, including Sir Robert Peel, Henry Grattan, and Robert Smith, First Baron Carrington, concerning the effect of an excise tax on Irish breweries, 1792; the situation in Ireland and the expedition against Copenhagen, 1807; the return of Napoleon from Elba; construction projects at harbors in Ireland; the British financial situation; the expedition against Algiers, 1816; the Catholic question in Ireland; a general discussion of Irish problems, 1818; and unrest in northern England, 1819. Also two printed speeches by Sir John Newport: "State of Ireland," 1816, and "Irish Finances," 1817.

3884.  NEWSLETTERS, 1682-1683. 3 items. London, England.

Three handwritten newsletters, predecessors of newspapers, written in London.

3885.  J. F. NEWSOM PAPERS, 1861-1863. 4 items. Jackson Hill (Davidson County), N.C.

Letters of a Confederate soldier, including a letter from Allen Newsom to General Winder concerning the use of paroled Union prisoners on his farm.

3886.  JESSE F. NEWSOM PAPERS, 1863-1865. 13 items. Halifax County, N.C.

Letters of a Confederate soldier killed in the battle of Fisher's Hill 1864, near Strasburg, Virginia.

3887.  NEWSPAPER CLIPPINGS, 1850-1897. 29 items.

Miscellaneous clippings concerning the Civil War; Reconstruction; notable Europeans, including Lord Byron, Metternich, Leopold I, and Lord Brougham; textbooks used in Southern schools, 1871-1872; and S. Parkes Cadman's memorial address for those lost in the sinking of the Titanic, 1912.

3888.  JOHN CALDWELL CALHOUN NEWTON PAPERS, 1870-1931. 3,600 items and 132 vols. Kobe, Japan.

Letters and papers of John Caldwell Calhoun Newton, a Methodist minister and missionary to Japan, concern his education at Kentucky Wesleyan College, Kentucky Military Institute, and Johns Hopkins University; his experience as a minister in Kentucky and Virginia; and his career as dean of the theological school at Kwansei Gakuin Union Mission College and Seminary in Kobe, Japan, 1888-1897, and president of that institution, 1913-1923. Papers contain family letters and correspondence with mission leaders of the church in America and missionaries of all churches in Japan. Volumes include sermon and lecture notes, some in Japanese; notebooks on courses Newton taught or had taken as a student, including 5 volumes of notes taken at Johns Hopkins University on G. Stanley Hall's lectures on philosophy, education, psychology, and psycho-physics, and one volume of notes on a history course taught by Herbert Baxter Adams; a Kwansei Gakuin classbook; a list of subscribers to the Twentieth Century Educational Fund of the Methodist Episcopal Church, South; a book of Kwansei Gakuin accounts; diaries, 1868-1869 and 1869-1879; a scrapbook; journals, 1881, 1888, and 1924; memoranda books, 1886-1888, 1889-1890, 1895-1896, 1898, and 1899-1900; pastor's books for Hillsboro, Kentucky, 1876-1877, Somerset, Kentucky, 1878-1879, Carlisle, Kentucky, 1879-1881, and Portsmouth, Virginia, 1900-1901; and notes on the scriptures and Newton's reading, including a large amount on the history of Scotland, Ireland, and Great Britain.

3889.  JOSEPH NEWTON PAPERS, 1862-1865. 13 items. New York, N.Y.

Letters of a soldier in the 19th New York Regiment, Cavalry, describing camp life and campaigning in Virginia.

3890.  WILSON CARY NICHOLAS PAPERS, 1801-1817. 5 items. Richmond, Va.

Papers of Wilson Cary Nicholas (1761-1820), Virginia soldier and statesman, containing a letter discussing political matters and the Republican (Jeffersonian) Party, and routine political and business papers.

3891.  ELIZABETH R. NICHOLLS PAPERS, 1841-1842. 6 items. Georgetown, D.C.

Personal letters concerning social life and religion.

3892.  LOUISA H. NICHOLLS PAPERS, 1838-1841. 10 items and 1 vol. [South Carolina?]

Miscellaneous poems, one signed "Marie," one "Peter Pop," and seven anonymous. Included also is a volume containing two poems by Mrs. Louisa H. Nicholls, "The Creation and the Fall of Eve" and "To Mr. --," and a number of poems, chiefly eulogies signed "J. W. F. C." and "M. C.," 1838-1841.

3893. SAMUEL JONES NICHOLLS PAPERS, 1907-1918. 5,573 items. Spartanburg (Spartanburg County), S.C. Restricted.

Papers of Samuel Jones Nicholls, attorney and United States congressman, and of his father and law partner, George W. Nicholls, concern Samuel J. Nicholls's work as secretary-treasurer of the Spartanburg County Fair Association, 1907-1908; the legal affairs of the Greenville, Spartanburg, and Anderson Railway and its parent company, the Piedmont and Northern Railway, 1912-1913; Samuel J. Nicholls's campaign for election to the U.S. Congress, 1914-1915; and the death of William Montague Nicholls, brother of Samuel J. Nicholls, in the British Royal Field Artillery, 1915. The papers of George W. Nicholls concern legal business of the Greenville, Spartanburg, and Anderson Railway, 1914-1918; and his responsibilities as city attorney of Spartanburg, South Carolina, including an attempt, 1917, to refund municipal bonds and reform the city's tax system and cases pertaining to the misconduct of troops from Camp Wadsworth, a World War I training center located near Spartanburg. Miscellaneous items include financial records from Samuel J. Nicholls's congressional campaign, election returns, and lists of voters.

3894. GEORGE T. NICHOLS NOTES, 1875-1880. 1 vol. (83 pp.) Savannah, Ga.

Notes on hunting and on dogs.

3895. JOHN GOUGH NICHOLS PAPERS, 1834. 3 items. Holmwood Park, Surrey, England.

Papers of John Gough Nichols contain a letter, 1834, concerning Wiltshire antiquities, notably Seagry Church and Bradenstoke Abbey, and notes and drawings about Bradenstoke Abbey at Seagry and the nearby site of an ancient camp.

3896. JOHN THOMAS NICHOLS PAPERS, 1860-1893. 11 items and 2 vols. Oak Grove Township (Durham County), N.C.

Papers of John Thomas Nichols include an account and memorandum book, 1860-1883, containing personal and farm accounts, 1865-1883; frequent notes and memoranda on daily farm and social activity; notes on the movements of the 30th North Carolina Regiment, 1861-1862, in eastern North Carolina on the Cape Fear River near Fort Johnston, and notes on troop movements, 1863, from Fredericksburg, Virginia, to Hagerstown, Maryland; and the constitution of the trustees of Dayton Academy, Durham County, North Carolina. Also an account book, 1887-1893, made up primarily of records of receipts and disbursements. Both volumes contain notes on church attendance and accounts of births and deaths in the Nichols family. Other items include poems and an election broadside, 1880, from the chairman of the Wake County Democratic Executive Committee.

3897. JOHN NICHOLSON PAPERS, 1793-1797. 6 items. Philadelphia, Pa.

Correspondence of John Nicholson (d. 1800), comptroller general of Pennsylvania, referring to Pennsylvania finances; speculation in Georgia lands; the selling of lots in Washington, D.C.; land sales in Pennsylvania; and a business agreement between Nicholson and William Prentiss.

3898. JOHN P. NICHOLSON PAPERS, 1879-1926. 7 items. Philadelphia, Pa.

Miscellaneous correspondence mainly between John P. Nicholson and L. L. Mackall, librarian of the De Renne Library, Wormslor, Georgia, concerning material on the history of Georgia.

3899. THOMAS A. NICHOLSON PAPERS, 1829 (1833-1863) 1905. 112 items and 1 vol. Martinsburg (Berkeley County), W. Va.

Papers of Thomas A. Nicholson concern his experiences aboard the U.S.S. Massachusetts, 1852-1855, on voyages between the eastern and western coasts of the United States and along the coast of California; service as regimental surgeon to the Oregon Mounted Volunteers during an Indian uprising in Oregon, 1855; impressions of South Africa, China, Japan, and other places on a voyage to the Far East, 1857-1860, aboard the U.S.S. Powhatan and a description of the Japanese embassy which the Powhatan brought back to the United States in 1860; and Nicholson's Civil War service, 1861-1862, with the 2nd Virginia Regiment. Letters of other members of the family concern politics and social life in Washington, D. C., 1852. Letters of Sister Mary Bernard Doll of the Monastery of the Visitation, Wilmington, Delaware, pertain to religious matters generally, but contain comments on the coal strike of 1902 and the attitude of President Theodore Roosevelt toward Roman Catholics.

3900. NICHOLSON AND COMPANY CASHBOOK AND LEDGER, 1858-1862. 1 vol. (105 pp.) Lawrenceville (Brunswick County), Va.

Cashbook, 1858-1860, and ledger, 1858-1862, of Nicholson and Company, operators of a tavern and inn, and apparently sucessors to the firm of Amos S. Drewry and Company.

3901. ALICE E. (ANDREWS) NILES PAPERS, 1859-1864. 44 items. Griffin (Spalding County), Ga.

Correspondence of the Niles family, chiefly for the Civil War period, concerning the difficulties of the four Niles brothers in the Confederate Army, the problems of people at home, and the plight of Atlanta in the summer of 1864.

3902. HEZEKIAH NILES PAPERS, 1831. Baltimore, Md.

Letter, 1831, to Hezekiah Niles, editor and publisher of Niles' Weekly Register, from William Slade, United States representative from Vermont, requesting additional copies of the address to the people of the United States by the Tariff Convention of 1831.

3903. NATHANIEL NILES PAPERS, 1846-1860. 8 items. New York, N.Y.

Letters of Henry Washington Hilliard, noted orator and congressman from Alabama, to Nathaniel Niles concerning Hilliard's re-election to Congress in 1846 and aspirations for the speakership of the House of Representatives; politics in Alabama; Hilliard's strong Union sentiments; the possibility of diplomatic posts for Hilliard, 1851, and Niles, 1857; and the difficulties of maintaining a Unionist position in Alabama in 1860.

3904. G. H. NIMMO NOTES. 1 vol. (286 pp.) Long Island (Suffolk County), N.Y.

Lecture notes in science.

3905. EUGENIUS ARISTIDES NISBET PAPERS, 1799-1934. 15,905 items and 6 vols. Macon (Bibb County), Ga.

Business correspondence of the legal firm of Eugenius A. Nisbet (1803-1871), Georgia state senator, member of U.S. Congress, supreme court of Georgia, Georgia secession convention, and Confederate Congress; and of his brother, James Alexander Nisbet, prior to the Civil War and similar records of the firm after it was joined by James Taylor Nisbet (1828-1894), lawyer, newspaper editor, and son of Eugenius A. Nisbet, just prior to and after the Civil War; and personal correspondence of the family of Junius Wingfield Nisbet (b. 1858), son of James Taylor Nisbet and Mary (Seymour) Nisbet. The legal correspondence, though voluminous, is largely routine. Other correspondence concerns Georgia politics; the La Grange Female Institute, La Grange, Georgia; purchase and sale of slaves; the offer of a professorship in law at the University of Georgia, Athens, to Eugenius A. Nisbet; Confederate trade with England; operation of the Confederate government's produce loan in Georgia; Confederate finances; sequestration of property in Georgia belonging to Northerners during the Civil War; fighting near Richmond, Virginia, 1862; Confederate impressment of slaves and commodities; financial adjustments after the Civil War; and the divorce suit of Emilie D. Branham against William H. Branham. There is material on the Presbyterian Church; many genealogical charts and letters to James Wingfield Nisbet relative to family history; letters beginning around 1900 from James Taylor Nisbet, Jr., brother of Junius Wingfield Nisbet, to the latter's wife concerning the writer's experience as a soldier in the Philippines, Cuba, and elsewhere; numerous letters concerning the education of James Wingfield Nisbet's daughters, Mary Nisbet at Lucy Cobb Institute, Athens, Georgia, and Blanch Kell Nisbet at Salem Female Academy, North Carolina, 1910-1911; invitations to Liberty, regimental, and Red Cross balls in 1918; many letters recommending Junius Wingfield Nisbet for numerous jobs, some of which he obtained; and letters, 1892, from Charles R. Nisbet to James Wingfield Nisbet, while the former was a student at the University of Georgia, Athens.

One letter, dated October 8, 1930, gives an account of Thomas Kell's friendship with Maria Clemm, aunt of Edgar Allan Poe, in Baltimore, Maryland; another, September 9, 1804, to John Nisbet near Statesville, North Carolina, describes business conditions in Fayetteville, North Carolina. Included also are the following volumes: cotton book, 1850, which also contains a list of slaves; bankbooks, 1861-1867, of James A. Nisbet; family album; Greek and Latin notebook, 1875, Athens, Georgia; legal notes of Junius A. Wingfield of Eatonton, Georgia, ca. 1868; and a diary of John W. Nisbet, 1873-1879, reflecting social life of Macon, the University of Georgia, and Nisbet's intellectual interests and family connections.

Among the correspondents are Charles L. Bartlett, Herbert Bemerton Battle, William Horn Battle, Allen D. Candler, William Crosby Dawson, Charles H. Herty, Walter B. Hill, Malcolm Johnston, Alexander R. Lawton, John M. Kell, Wilson Lumpkin, Howard E. Rondthaler, William Schley, Hoke Smith, and James M. Smith.

3906. F. M. NIVEN, JR., PAPERS, 1863. 3 items. Whitlock (Halifax County), Va.

Personal letters of F. M. Niven, Jr., and F. M. Niven, Sr., concerning the younger man's decision about where in Virginia he will go to preach; social life in Halifax County, Virginia; and events of the Civil War.

3907. FRANCIS NIXON, SR., PAPERS, 1819-1855. 46 items. Hertford (Perquimans County), N.C.

Personal letters of Francis Nixon, Sr., and business letters relating to fishing and merchandising. A letter of 1838 discusses a yellow fever epidemic in Charleston, South Carolina.

3908. THOMAS NIXON PAPERS, 1803-1884. 20 items and 1 vol. Surry County, N.C.

Miscellaneous papers of Thomas Nixon and his family, including Thomas Nixon's oath of allegiance to the United States, 1821; rules of conduct for school students, 1845; receipts; prescriptions for treatment of rheumatism and a childhood disease; account of military activity in Virginia by a regiment from Surry County, North Carolina, 1862; description of the aftermath of the battle of Chancellorsville and the desertion of a number of men in the 37th North Carolina Regiment after hearing of the death of General Thomas Jonathan Jackson, 1863; a description of Greensboro, North Carolina, during the approach of General William T. Sherman's troops in 1865; and a copy of Thomas Nixon's will, 1848. The volume contains copies of notes negotiated between Thomas Nixon and various people.

3909. LOUIS MARIE, VICOMTE DE NOAILLES PAPERS, [1795?, 1799]. 2 items. Philadelphia, Pa.

Letters written during the American business career of Louis Marie, Vicomte de Noailles (1756-1804), French soldier and man of affairs, mentioning one Bingham, his business associate.

3910. WILLIAM HENRY NOBLE PAPERS, 1807 (1861-1865) 1913. 359 items. Bridgeport (Fairfield County), Conn.

The collection contains a miscellaneous group of items, for the most part dealing with the Civil War, including a notice of a meeting of the Friends of Free Soil in Suffield, Connecticut, 1848; clippings concerning the presidential election of 1852; deeds of sale for slaves; letter concerning the presidential campaign of 1856; advertisement describing life in the coal fields at Cornplanter, Pennsylvania; invoices of medicine and hospital supplies issued to the 13th Maine Regiment in 1861, 1862, and 1864; letters from a number of Union soldiers on routine matters; scattered orders and records of various Union troops; program of a memorial day celebration by the Grand Army of the Republic, 1881, and other items dealing with veterans organizations and affairs; letter, 1883, from Washington Gladden commenting on Neal Dow; and an undated letter from Gerrit Smith to William H. Seward discussing the Whig Party, the Liberty Party, and Henry Clay. The collection also contains typed copies of letters from W. A. Willoughby, a soldier in the 10th Connecticut Regiment, concerning his service on the Sea Islands of South Carolina; New Bern, North Carolina; Saint Augustine, Florida; and Petersburg, Virginia.

3911. BAPTIST WRIOTHESLEY NOEL PAPERS, 1842. 1 item. London, England.

Letter to Baptist Wriothesley Noel from Jeffery Hale, Canadian philanthropist, discussing the state of the Church of England in the city of Quebec and the work of other Protestant denominations.

3912. NOEL EDWARD NOEL-BUXTON, FIRST BARON NOEL-BUXTON, PAPERS, 1873-1951. 1,226 items and 3 vols. London, England.

Letters and papers of Noel Edward Noel-Buxton concern family matters; religion; various elections, particularly the by-election at Whitby, 1905, and the general election of 1906; affairs in the Balkans, including the First Balkan War, 1912-1913; temperance; World War I, particularly the coming of the war and war aims; and politics in the Liberal Party and, later, the Labour Party. Clippings, mainly 1906-1941, concern politics; temperance; the Balkans; woman suffrage; the naval debate, 1914; World War I; Bulgaria; Macedonia; and slavery in Ethiopia. Also contains photographs of scenes in the Balkans and notes for speeches, 1903-1940.

3913. SUSAN C. NOLAND PAPERS, 1847-1862. 8 items. Middleburg (Loudoun County), Va.

Family letters between two sisters, Susan C. Noland and Anna C. Hoge.

3914. S. F. NORCOTT PAPERS, 1852-1854. 4 items. Murfreesboro (Hertford County), N.C.

Personal letters, one of which discusses the effects of the Crimean War on the exports of the United States.

3915. NORFLEET BROTHERS INVOICE BOOK AND INVENTORY, 1858-1876. 1 vol. (76 pp.) Suffolk (Nansemond County), Va.

Invoices of a general merchant, 1858-1861, and an inventory, 1876.

3916. HENRY NORMAN PAPERS, 1771 (1831-1836) 1837. 29 items. Granville County, N.C.

Household and plantation papers and accounts of Henry Norman, planter, and of his daughter, Ann Eliza Clark Norman; Norman's will and other papers relating to the settlement of his estate; and price lists of numerous commodities.

3917. GEORGE E. NORRIS AND JEREMIAH NORRIS LETTERS, 1861-1865. 176 items. Wenham (Essex County), Mass.

Family letters of George E. Norris, third assistant engineer on the Federal gunboat Azalia; and letters to Jeremiah Norris from friends in the Union Army, concerning life in the army and Southern girls' opinions of "Yankees."

3918. NEEDHAM NORRIS DICTIONARY, [1790?] 1 vol.

Manuscript dictionary of the English language, A-G.

3919. H. M. NORTH DIARY, 1905. 1 vol. Elizabeth City (Pasquotank County), N.C.

Diary of H. M. North, minister of City Road's Church, concerning his pastoral duties, church matters, and local events.

3920. NORTH CAROLINA PAPERS, 1788-1789. 31 items. North Carolina.

Documents concerning the ratification of the Constitution of the United States by the state of North Carolina.

3921. NORTH CAROLINA. BEAUFORT COUNTY TAX RECORDS, 1866-1869. 3 vols. Beaufort County, N.C.

Tax lists for various districts in Beaufort County.

3922. NORTH CAROLINA. BOARD OF COMMISSIONERS OF NAVIGATION AND PILOTAGE FOR THE CAPE FEAR RIVER AND BAR PAPERS, 1857-1921. 1 item and 5 vols. Wilmington (New Hanover County), N.C.

Records of the Board of Commissionners of Navigation and Pilotage for the Cape Fear River and Bar contain lists of pilots and apprentices, 1857-1895; harbor master's reports, 1865-1894; accounts of the clerk and treasurer, 1858-1869; names and classes of pilots for measuring the depth of water on bars and rips, 1865-1873, and pilots' reports, 1858-1872; lists of vessels searched and fumigated, 1858-1862; and minutes, 1912-1918.

3923. NORTH CAROLINA. CATAWBA COUNTY PUBLIC SCHOOL REGISTERS, 1885-1900. 2 vols. Catawba County, N.C.

Lists of students, showing attendance and grades.

3924. NORTH CAROLINA. CONSTITUTIONAL CONVENTION RECORDS, 1835. 1 vol. (18 pp.) Raleigh (Wake County), N.C.

List of members of the North Carolina constitutional convention of 1835, containing signatures of members signing the oath, and records of each member's expenses.

3925. NORTH CAROLINA. COURT RECORDS, 1884-1885. 1 vol. North Carolina.

Letterpress copy of statements of cases coming before the 4th Circuit, Eastern District (Federal) Court of North Carolina.

3926. NORTH CAROLINA. DAVIDSON COUNTY DOCKET BOOK, 1877-1909. 1 vol. (26 pp.) Davidson County, N.C.

Docket book of justices of the peace.

3927. NORTH CAROLINA. DURHAM COMMUNITY CHEST FEDERATION MINUTES, 1923-1926. 1 vol. (100 pp.) Durham, N.C.

3928. NORTH CAROLINA. FORSYTH COUNTY PUBLIC SCHOOL REGISTERS, 1857-1885. 2 vols. Forsyth County, N.C.

Lists of students, showing attendance and grades.

3929. NORTH CAROLINA. GENERAL ASSEMBLY MEMBERSHIP, 1808-1840. 1 vol. (182 pp.) Raleigh (Wake County), N.C.

Oath of office and signatures of members of the General Assembly of North Carolina.

3930. NORTH CAROLINA. GENERAL COURT PAPERS, 1693-1767. 18 items. Albemarle County, N.C.

Typed copies of minutes and minute dockets of the General Court of North Carolina, the originals of which are held in the North Carolina Division of Archives and History, Raleigh, North Carolina; and commentaries on various sections of the minutes. The papers of the General Court of North Carolina are published by the North Carolina Division of Archives and History in The Colonial Records of North Carolina, 2nd Series, North Carolina Higher Court Records (Raleigh: 1963-1971).

3931. NORTH CAROLINA. GUILFORD COUNTY PUBLIC SCHOOL REGISTER, 1857-1865. 1 vol. (50 pp.) Guilford County, N.C.

List of students, showing attendance and grades. Also contains general remarks pertaining to the Civil War.

3932. NORTH CAROLINA. JOHNSTON COUNTY COMMON SCHOOL DISTRICT NUMBER 4 REGISTER, 1861-1870. 1 vol. Johnston County, N.C.

Incomplete listing of students.

3933. NORTH CAROLINA. LINCOLN COUNTY SCHOOL DISTRICT MINUTE BOOK, 1852-1863. 1 vol. (62 pp.) Lincoln County, N.C.

Minutes of the school committees of school districts number 4 and number 6 of Lincoln County, North Carolina, and copies of contracts with teachers.

3934. NORTH CAROLINA. LUMBER BRIDGE LEDGER AND MINUTE BOOK, 1921-1929. 1 vol. (156 pp.) Lumber Bridge (Robeson County), N.C.

Routine town records, including financial accounts, 1921-1929, and minutes of the town board, 1921 and 1925-1929.

3935. NORTH CAROLINA. MARTIN COUNTY TAX LISTS, 1874-1881. 7 vols. Martin County, N.C.

Tax lists for Williamston, Hamilton, and Jamesville townships, Martin County, North Carolina, 1874-1876; and for Jamesville, Griffin, Williams, Williamston, Bear Grass, Cross Roads, Poplar Point, Hamilton, Robersonville, and Goose Nest townships, 1880 and 1881.

3936. NORTH CAROLINA. MARTIN COUNTY COURT OF EQUITY PAPERS, 1851-1879. 2 vols. Martin County, N.C.

Receipt book, 1851-1879, and account book, 1879, of the court of equity of Martin County, North Carolina.

3937. NORTH CAROLINA. MORGANTON CITY COMMISSIONERS MINUTES, 1865-1880. 1 vol. (218 pp.) Morganton (Burke County), N.C.

3938. NORTH CAROLINA. ORANGE COUNTY TAX LISTS, 1875. 1 vol. (204 pp.) Hillsborough (Orange County), N.C.

3939. NORTH CAROLINA. RANDOLPH COUNTY TAX LIST, 1915. 1 vol. (238 pp.) Randolph County, N.C.

3940. NORTH CAROLINA. SECRETARY OF STATE. LAND GRANT BOOK 23 AND INDEX TO LAND GRANT BOOK 20 OR 23, 1767-1771. 1 vol. (392 pp.) Raleigh (Wake County), N.C.

Volume contains manuscript copies of North Carolina land grants, 1767-1768, comprising approximately half of the land grants originally recorded in the secretary of state's record book. The index, 1767-1771, is to the whole of the original record book.

3941. NORTH CAROLINA. WAKE COUNTY COMMON SCHOOL DISTRICT NO. 1 PAPERS, 1881-1885. 2 items and 1 vol. Apex (Wake County), N.C.

Collection contains the register, 1881-1885, of a school for Negroes taught by M. W. Brown. Two items, 1885, relate to commencement exercises of that year.

3942. NORTH CAROLINA. WILKES COUNTY PUBLIC SCHOOL REGISTER, 1881-1889. 1 vol. (68 pp.) Wilkes County, N.C.

Lists of students, showing attendance and grades.

3943. NORTH CAROLINA LITERARY FUND PAPERS, 1845-1879. 28 items. Raleigh (Wake County), N.C.

Bonds and documents relating to the use of the literary fund and records of loans from the fund.

3944. NORTH CAROLINA STATE FEDERATION OF LABOR PAPERS, 1950-1951. 44 items. Salisbury (Rowan County), N.C.

The collection is made up primarily of correspondence of C. A. Fink, president of the North Carolina State Federation of Labor (AFL), and includes some letters of James F. Barrett, public relations director of the Asheville Central Labor Union. The correspondence concerns a controversy arising out of the withdrawal of an invitation from the United States Army to Dr. Ralph Brimley, superintendent of Forsyth County schools, to participate in a leadership mission to Japan in 1951, allegedly as a result of opposition to Brimley by C. A. Fink and William Green, president of the American Federation of Labor. Included also are the Proceedings of the North Carolina State Federation of Labor for 1950 and 1951.

3945. NORTH CREEK PRIMITIVE BAPTIST CHURCH MINUTES, 1790-1890. 1 vol. Beaufort County, N.C.

Minutes of the church, including lists of members and obituaries.

3946. NORTH FAMILY PAPERS, 1598-1696. 2 items. England.

Inventories of the contents of the North Family Papers, held in the Bodleian Library, Oxford University.

3947. WILLIAM J. NORTHEN PAPERS, 1891. 2 items. Atlanta, Ga.

Routine letters of William J. Northen, governor of Georgia.

3948. CHARLES STUART NORTON PAPERS, 1864-1880. 10 items. Westfield (Union County), N.J.

The collection is made up for the most part of letters to Charles Stuart Norton, United States naval officer and lighthouse inspector, from Charles Dewey, naval secretary of the Light-House Board of the United States Treasury Department, referring mainly to routine matters concerning the maintenance and construction of lighthouses and comments on various naval and governmental officers.

3949. JOHN WILLIAM NOSEWORTHY PAPERS, 1942. 1 item. Toronto, Ontario, Canada.

Photocopy of an electioneering pamphlet from John William Noseworthy's sucessful campaign for election to the House of Commons of Canada, 1942.

3950. SIR WILLIAM NOTT PAPERS, 1843. 1 item. Carmarthen, Carmarthenshire, Wales.

Letter from Sir William Nott, British general, concerning his recent campaign against the Afghans.

3951. JAMES NOURSE DIARY, 1862-1878. 1 vol. Chicago, Ill.

Copy of a diary kept by James Nourse, describing his day-to-day experiences as a Union soldier in the Chicago Board of Trade Battery Light Artillery (also called James H. Stokes' Independent Battery) and giving accounts of the battle of Stones River, December, 1862-January, 1863; the battle of Chickamauga, 1863; General William T. Sherman's advance from Tennessee to Atlanta, Georgia, and fighting around Atlanta, 1864; the battle of Nashville, 1864; and General James H. Wilson's cavalry raid through Alabama and Georgia, 1865. Also contains a list of individuals, with their death dates, probably soldiers from his unit.

3952. ANTHONY NOVITCKIE PAPERS, 1861-1862. 20 items. Sylvania (Bradford County), Pa.

Letters of Anthony Novitckie, a soldier in the 12th Pennsylvania Regiment, to his wife, describing his service in Maryland and Virginia. The letters were generally written for Novitckie by other soldiers.

3953. WILLIAM H. NUGEN PAPERS, 1862-1865. 30 items. New London (Henry County), Iowa.

Letters of William H. Nugen, a soldier in the 25th Iowa Regiment, describing his experiences in Arkansas, Mississippi, Tennessee, Alabama, and Georgia, including his participation in the siege of Vicksburg, 1863, and the battle of Atlanta, 1864.

3954. LAVALL NUGENT, COUNT NUGENT, PAPERS, 1814. 1 item. Austria.

Secret instructions from Count Nugent, an Austrian field marshal, to a subordinate, pertaining to Nugent's march on Piacenza, Italy.

3955. ROMULUS ARMISTEAD NUNN PAPERS, 1722-1960. 13,633 items and 17 vols. New Bern (Craven County), N.C.

Correspondence and papers of Romulus Armistead Nunn, lawyer and politician, mainly concerning his law practice in New Bern, North Carolina, but also reflecting his personal and political interests, especially Nunn's long association with Furnifold M. Simmons, United States senator from North Carolina. Correspondence, 1885-1959, concerns the business and legal affairs of Walter Francis Burns, particularly the erection of a statue of his ancestor, Otway Burns, a privateer in the War of 1812; local business and legal affairs of Furnifold M. Simmons; the Carolina Paper Pulp Company, for which Nunn served as a receiver; the campaigns of Furnifold M. Simmons for the United States Senate, 1906, 1912, 1918; management of the gubernatorial campaign of Locke Craig in Craven County, North Carolina, 1908; Nunn's term in the North Carolina legislature, 1911; the Democratic National Convention of 1912; community activities, including the Craven County board of education, the Firemen's Relief Fund of New Bern, Craven County Good Roads Association, the formation of the New Bern Building and Loan Association, the presidency of the Atlantic and North Carolina Railway, 1916, and the creation of the New Bern drainage district; activities in World War I, including Nunn's representation of local fishermen before the Food Administration in Washington, D. C., implementation of the selective service laws, and participation in Liberty Loan and Red Cross drives; management of the campaigns of Samuel M. Brinson for the United States Congress, 1918, 1920; duties as city attorney of New Bern, 1920, 1942-1959; legal affairs of Charles S. Bryan, 1923-1950s; tenure as North Carolina superior court judge, 1926-1930; effects of the depression on Nunn and New Bern in the 1930s; and participation in local relief programs during the depression as chairman of the central planning committee for New Bern and Craven County. Legal papers, 1791-1949, consist of deeds and land transfers; briefs for suits in which Nunn participated; and the detailed records of 22 of his major cases, dealing with bankruptcies and other legal matters. Financial papers, 1900-1942, contain bills, receipts, and financial statements, many of which deal with the government of New Bern. Clippings, 1900-1958, concern many aspects of Nunn's career, particularly his political interests. Writings and addresses contain works on North Carolina by Nunn and political speeches. Volumes include business records of the Carolina Paper Pulp Company; records of the

Mutual Aid Banking Company, 1912-1914; financial records of the Firemen's Relief Fund of New Bern; portions of a register of slaves in Muhlenburg County, Kentucky, 1839-1860; and financial records of Moses B. Lane, a general merchant of Craven County. The collection also contains photographs of the Nunn Family, group pictures of the General Assembly of North Carolina for various years, and photographs of New Bern.

3956. HALLER NUTT PAPERS, 1846 (1853-1860) 1911. 722 items and 1 vol. Natchez (Adams County), Miss.

Papers of Haller Nutt, large-scale planter of Louisiana and Mississippi, contain promissory notes, bills for goods, receipts, drafts drawn by Nutt on certain companies, accounts for cotton sales, reports for Mary and Carrie Nutt while they attended a girls' school in Philadelphia, Pennsylvania, in 1860, and items relating to the construction and furnishing of Nutt's house, "Longwood." Also included is a plantation journal, 1843-1850, containing records of planting and other work, supply lists, data on slaves, and rules for overseers.

3957. JOHN NYCUM AND JOHN Q. NYCUM PAPERS, 1825-1900. 8,998 items and 59 vols. Ray's Hill (Bedford County), Pa.

Papers of John Nycum and John Q. Nycum include the letters of Philip Weisel concerning family matters and the sale of mineral water, and the correspondence and papers of several members of the Nycum family concerning the management of general merchandise businesses; business conditions; family matters; and the Civil War, including descriptions of camp life in Pennsylvania and Louisiana and the Confederate raid on Chambersburg, Pennsylvania, 1864. The collection also contains bills, receipts, legal papers, and miscellaneous items, including advertisements, circulars, political material, and reports, 1850-1836, of several teachers in Bedford County, Pennsylvania, listing pupils and their records. Volumes include mercantile daybooks and memorandum books of John Nycum, Simon Nycum, and Philip Weisel; record books of the Evangelical Lutheran Church of Ray's Hill, Pennsylvania; account books of public schools of Bedford County; and a mercantile ledger of D. Eshleman and Company.

3958. GEORGE NYRE DAYBOOK, 1830-1840. 1 vol. (266 pp.)

Detailed accounts of a blacksmith.

3959. JOHN OAKEY PAPERS, 1838-1885. 56 items. Lynchburg (Campbell County), Va.

Miscellaneous personal and business papers of John Oakey and his family, including correspondence, bills, receipts, telegrams, and poems, concerning salt works in Virginia; diphtheria and smallpox during the Civil War; Confederate camp life and troop movements; the encounters between the C.S.S. Virginia and the U.S.S. Monitor; and comments of a Confederate soldier on eastern Tennessee.

3960. APPLETON OAKSMITH PAPERS, 1840-1949. 2,066 items and 27 vols. Hollywood (Carteret County), N.C.

Papers of Appleton Oaksmith contain family letters of his parents, Seba Smith and Elizabeth Oakes (Prince) Smith, and correspondence of Appleton Oaksmith and members of his family concerning William Walker and the Nicaraguan filibuster of 1855-1860, including Oaksmith's work as agent for Walker in the United States; Oaksmith's divorce from his first wife, Isotta Rebecchini; Oaksmith's mercantile and shipping interests; formation of William H. Frear and Company, a mercantile and contracting concern with headquarters in London, England; Oaksmith's participation in the Union League of New York City and his activity in an attempt to settle outstanding sectional differences and avoid civil war; Reconstruction and Oaksmith's activity in the state and national elections of 1876; claims of United States citizens against Nicaragua; a hurricane in Beaufort, North Carolina, 1879; and comments on Oaksmith's writings. Other papers include official papers of William Walker as president of Nicaragua; a list of emigrants from the United States to Granada, Nicaragua, 1856; legal papers; receipts; clippings concerning Oaksmith's ships; charter and minutes of the Tilden and Vance Club of Morehead City, North Carolina; and clippings of poems and articles by Oaksmith. Volumes include letter books of Appleton Oaksmith, 1874-1876 and 1874-1880; daybooks and ledgers of the mercantile firm of Mason and Company; logbook, 1871; record book, 1854-1855, of marine insurance policies; books of poetry by Appleton Oaksmith and Corinne Oaksmith; scrapbooks of clippings concerning William Walker, and art and poetry by Appleton Oaksmith; postmaster's record book; journal of Appleton Oaksmith, 1851-1852, concerning voyages to California, South America, and Africa; and a volume of Oaksmith's shipping accounts, 1853-1856.

3961. BRYANT O'BANNON PAPERS, 1839 (1844-1862) 1891. 17 items. Emmett (Wilkinson County), Ga.

Papers of Bryant O'Bannon include a report on cotton sales; personal letters; and a deposition concerning a charge of slave stealing.

3962. M. P. O'CONNOR PAPERS, 1854-1880. 2 vols. Charleston, S.C.

Ledger, 1854-1870, and letterpress book, 1877-1880, of M. P. O'Connor, an attorney.

3963. CHARLES ODOM PAPERS, 1853-1866. 14 items. Northampton County, N.C.

Civil War letters and personal letters to Charles Odom from friends and relatives living in Mississippi and Indiana.

3964. ANDERS ÖRNE PAPERS, 1881-1922. 15 items. Stockholm, Sweden.

Papers of Anders Örne, director of public relations for the Swedish Cooperative Society, include a letter emphasizing the role of Albin Johansson in the growth of the society, and photographs and postcards relating to the society and its activities.

3965. JOHANNES ADAM SIMON OERTEL PAPERS, 1857, 1872. 2 items. Vienna (Fairfax County), Va.

Papers of Johannes Adam Simon Oertel, a painter, primarily of religious subjects, consist of a letter, 1857, discussing boarding houses in Washington, D.C.; and a letter, 1872, to Oertel from William Cullen Bryant, praising his work in illustrating Bryant's poem, "Waiting at the Gate."

3966. GEORGE OGG PAPERS, 1786-1788. 13 items. Franklin (Heard County), Ga.

Papers of George Ogg concern his operations as a fur trader on the Chattahoochee River in Georgia and include mercantile accounts and references to land surveys and Indians.

3967. THADDEUS KOSCIUSZKO OGLESBY PAPERS, 1876-1918, 2,152 items and 4 vols. Georgia.

The papers of Thaddeus Kosciuszko Oglesby, journalist and book salesman, contain clippings and correspondence with many well known Southerners, for the most part concerning Oglesby's attempt to correct what he felt to be a substantial anti-Southern bias in the writing of many American historians and in accounts of the South in such reference works as the Encyclopaedia Britannica, Harper's Encyclopedia of United States History, and Appleton's Cyclopedia of American Biography. Correspondence also concerns Oglesby's work as agent for The New International Encyclopedia, his writings, national and state politics, and race relations in the South after the Civil War. Printed material in the collection includes advertisements for Oglesby's published works and for books he sold; pamphlets; and an unbound copy of Some Truths of History, written by Oglesby in response to articles on the South appearing in the 9th edition of the Encylopaedia Britannica.

3968. JAMES EDWARD OGLETHORPE PAPERS, (1738-1750) 1785. 15 items. Frederica (Glynn County), Ga.

Papers of James Edward Oglethorpe contain letters and documents relating to the acquisition of supplies for the colony of Georgia and to the defense of the colony, and a memorial supporting the appointment of Daniel Hogan to be a cadet in the Royal Regiment of Artillery at Woolwich, England.

3969. MAUDE ANNULET (ANDREWS) OHL PAPERS, 1880-ca. 1939. 8 items. Savannah, Ga.

The collection contains typescripts of poems by Maude Annulet (Andrews) Ohl, Ohl's notes on her verses, and a typescript, "Presenting Annulet Andrews--Poet," by Aubrey Harrison Starke.

3970. HYPOLITE OLADOWSKI PAPERS, 1862-1865. 18 items. Tullahoma (Coffee County), Tenn.

Papers of Hypolite Oladowski relate mainly to his service as an ordnance officer in the Confederate Army of Tennessee.

3971. "OLD TOWN CLUB" MINUTE BOOK, 1847-1850. 1 vol. (68 pp.) Baltimore, Md.

Minutes of a society organized to discount notes.

3972. EDWARD A. OLDHAM PAPERS, 1882-1945. 11 items. North Carolina.

The papers of Edward A. Oldham include a letter, 1882, from L. L. Polk on the possibility of creating a department of immigration in North Carolina; letter, 1890, from J. C. Price commenting on Oldham's article "What the Negro Most Needs"; letters of recommendation for Oldham from Thomas M. Holt; letters, 1898, from Alfred Moore Waddell concerning Waddell's revolution in Wilmington and political matters; and a letter, 1945, from Oldham to Robert Lee Flowers giving autobiographical information and discussing his career.

3973. OLIN HIGH SCHOOL PAPERS, 1859-1865. 52 items. Olin (Iredell County), N.C.

Minutes of the Philomathean Society of Olin High School, noting the subjects debated in this society, and a letter of Abram Haywood Merritt, principal of Olin High School, written on the inside pages of a printed circular advertising the school.

3974. SHELTON OLIVER ACCOUNT BOOK, 1816-1874. 1 vol. (133 pp.) Crawford (Oglethorpe County), Ga.

Accounts of a general merchant, including the accounts of the firm of E. Sims and Company.

3975. JOHN M. OLIVETT PAPERS, 1862-1865. 23 items. Pawling (Dutchess County), N.Y.

Letters of a private in the 90th New York Regiment to his sister, commenting on camp life at Key West, Florida; Louisiana; the Shenandoah Valley of Virginia; and Savannah, Georgia.

3976. CHARLES OLLIER PAPERS, 1840-1855. 12 items. London, England.

Letters from Charles Ollier (1788-1859), English publisher and author, to Sir John Philippart, concerning editorial work and the Naval and Military Gazette.

3977. EDWARD LACON OMMANNEY PAPERS, 1830-1858. 50 items. Bedford, England; and India.

Correspondence of Edward Lacon Ommanney, officer of the British Army in India, with his parents, concerning family matters, political events, the rearing and education of his children in England; and Ommanney's plans for his sons' careers. Also letters, 1858, of Edward Lacon Ommanney, son of Edward Lacon Ommanney, describing his activities during the Indian Mutiny.

3978. SIR MONTAGU FREDERICK OMMANNEY PAPERS, 1870-1906. 28 items. London, England.

Papers of Sir Montagu Frederick Ommanney, British administrator and army officer, primarily concerning Ommanney's career with Crown Agents for the Colonies and with the Colonial Office during the terms of three colonial secretaries, Joseph Chamberlain, Alfred Lyttelton, and Lord Elgin. The affairs of a number of British colonies are discussed in the correspondence, particularly South Africa.

3979. MALVERN HILL OMOHUNDRO PAPERS, 1886-1926. 14,142 items and 1 vol. Radford (Montgomery County), Va.

The papers of Malvern Hill Omohundro concern his work as attorney for the Virginia Land and Title Company and the Old Dominion Real Estate Company involving the acquisition and disposition of delinquent lands in a number of counties in Virginia and the maintenance of rental property; the consideration given to the adoption of a commission form of government by the city of Richmond, Virginia, ca. 1911; farming in Virginia; activities of the Royal Arcanum, Shockoe Council, No. 895; and Liberty Loan drives and the American Red Cross during World War I. The volume is a diary, 1912, kept by Julia Omohundro as a student at Hollins College.

3980. GEORGE WILLIAM THOMPSON OMOND PAPERS, 1877-1914. 28 items. Edinburgh, Scotland.

Papers of George William Thompson Omond, Scottish lawyer and author, are concerned for the most part with politics and the British Liberal Party, and include letters, 1885-1887, to Omond from Sir Henry Campbell-Bannerman, relating to Irish home rule, the election of 1886, and Liberal Party activities. Also letters on various political matters from George Otto Trevelyan, William E. Gladstone, Richard Burdon Haldane, and Victor Alexander Bruce.

3981. JOHN O'NEALE PAPERS, 1872-1930. 4 items. Laurens County, S.C.; and Greene County, Ind.

Papers of John O'Neale (1773-1841), Quaker leader and farmer, consist of a manuscript (164 pp.) and typescript of the "Memoirs of John O'Neale"; a letter of explanation about the manuscript; and a prospectus for its publication. The memoir describes the history of the O'Neale family in America; the Revolutionary War in South Carolina; slavery, the treatment of slaves, the slave trade, laws relating to slavery, and attitudes toward slaves; the migration of the O'Neale family to Indiana to escape the effects of slavery; agriculture; Methodists; the establishment and maintenance of Quaker churches at Bush River, South Carolina, and White River, Indiana; and Priscilla Hunt Cadwalader, a Quaker minister at White River, with a poem dedicated to her by Sidney Averile. The memoir also discusses morality, prophecy, and the evils of war, liquor, and tobacco. It concludes with a poem by the author, who apparently was John's son Cary, and an address by him to the Benjaminville School in 1871.

3982. WILLIAM O'NEALE, JR., PAPERS, 1832-1841. 3 vols. Montgomery County, Md.

The collection contains a list of free persons of color in Montgomery County, Maryland, enumerated by Sheriff William O'Neale in 1832; the ledger of a blacksmith shop, 1835-1838; and the ledger of a mercantile firm, 1832, which also contains records of lawsuits, 1840-1841.

3983. JOHN O'NEIL PAPERS, 1862. 2 items. [Massachusetts?].

Letters to John O'Neil from his sons Charles and A. F. O'Neil, both officers in the United States Navy. Charles O'Neil describes life aboard the gunboat Cincinnati and the progress of the war along the Mississippi River. A. F. O'Neil describes two weeks of service aboard the U.S.S. Tioga on a cruise to the Bermuda Islands, the Bahama Islands, and Cuba, discussing Union and Confederate sympathy in Bermuda, relations with British authorities, and the city of Havana, Cuba.

3984. ORANGE PEACE SOCIETY MINUTE BOOK, 1824-1830. 1 vol. (133 pp.) Orange County, N.C.

Volume contains a description of the founding of the Orange Peace Society, the constitution of the society, lists of members, and minutes. Also contains postal and mercantile records of Robert Woody.

3985. ORDER OF RAILROAD TELEGRAPHERS PAPERS, 1904-1949. 2 items and 6 vols. Saint Louis, Mo.

Miscellaneous printed and mimeographed material concerning the Order of Railroad Telegraphers (AFL), including agreements between the union and the Reading Company, the Central of Georgia Railway Company, and the Denver and Rio Grande Western Railroad Company; schedules of wages and rules for the Atlantic Coast Line Railroad Company and the Charleston and Western Carolina Railway Company; copy of a contract, 1949, between the Western Union Telegraph Company and the American Federation of Labor; and a pamphlet concerning laws affecting railroad telegraphers.

3986. ORDER OF RAILROAD TELEGRAPHERS, N AND W SYSTEM, DIVISION NO. 14, PAPERS, 1912-1952. 12 items and 15 vols. Portsmouth (Scioto County), Ohio.

The collection contains agreements of different types in pamphlet form, including agreements, 1912-1949, between the union and the Norfolk and Western Railway Company, detailing rates of pay and regulations for telegraphers, and similar agreements for the Atlantic Coast Line Railroad Company; the Atchison, Topeka and Santa Fe Railway Company; and the Tennessee Central Railway Company.

3987. ORIGINAL FREE WILL BAPTIST CHURCH OF NORTH CAROLINA, GENERAL CONFERENCE MINUTES AND REPORTS, 1860. 45 items. Post Oak Meeting House (Craven County), N.C.

Collection contains minutes of the sessions of the 1860 conference of the Original Free Will Baptist Church of North Carolina; a statistical report itemizing the year's record for 42 local churches; a list of delegates to the conference; and a list of ministers with their addresses.

3988. ORIGINAL FREE WILL BAPTIST CHURCH OF NORTH CAROLINA. GUM SWAMP CHURCH MEMBERSHIP LISTS, 1845, 1851. 2 items. Pitt County, N.C.

Lists of the members of Gum Swamp Church who convented in official meetings on June 21, 1845, and December 27, 1851.

3989. ORIGINS OF THE DUTCH UPRISING, 1559-1566, AND THE NEGOTIATIONS OF 1607-1608. 1 vol.

Manuscript account of the outbreak of the Eighty Years' War (1567-1648), written from the point of view of a Roman Catholic sympathizer of Philip II, King of Spain; also a manuscript giving clauses from the treaties of 1607-1608. Both documents are written in French.

3990. ROBERT PHILIPPE LOUIS EUGÉNE FERDINAND D'ORLÉANS, DUC DE CHARTRES, PAPERS, 1886. 1 item. Chartres, Eure-et Loir Department, France.

Letter from Robert Philippe Louis Eugéne Ferdinand d'Orléans to Ben W. Austin, secretary of the Northwestern Literary and Historical Society, concerning his election to honorary membership in the society.

3991. AQUILLA JOHNS ORME, SR., PAPERS, 1841 (1842-1891) 1896. 424 items. Atlanta, Ga.

Papers of Aquilla Johns Orme, Sr., include love letters from Z. E. Harmon to Apsyllab A. Calloway; letters of various members of the Orme family and their friends, for the most part dealing with family matters; Civil War letters discussing camp life in the Confederate Army and the work of the Soldier's Relief Society in Atlanta, Georgia; and letters of A. J. Orme, Jr., as a cadet at Virginia Military Institute, Lexington, Virginia.

3992. WILLIAM ORMOND JOURNALS, 1791-1803. 5 vols. Tar River Circuit (Edgecombe County), N.C.

Journals of William Ormond (1769-1803), an itinerant Methodist Episcopal minister, giving an account of his work in various localities of North Carolina and Virginia.

3993. JAMES LAWRENCE ORR PAPERS, 1852-1868. 6 items. South Carolina.

Correspondence of James Lawrence Orr (1822-1873), governor of South Carolina, including a letter, 1852, from his ward, Josephine Stephen; a letter, 1853, to President Franklin Pierce, recommending W. H. Hickman as a timber agent for the Eastern District of Florida; a letter, 1861, enclosing an order for muskets from Governor F. W. Pickens; a letter, 1866, to Governor Jonathan Worth of North Carolina referring to freedmen; and a letter, 1868, to Brigadier General Nathaniel Bradley Baker (1818-1876) in Des Moines, Iowa.

3994. JOHN M. ORR PAPERS, 1774 (1850-1870) 1911. 9,593 items and 12 vols. Leesburg (Loudoun County), Va.

Legal correspondence of John M. Orr, a Leesburg lawyer, specializing in railroad cases, and a meat supply agent for the Confederate Army. Included also are family letters; execution dockets for Loudoun County superior court, 1847-1853, and for Fauquier County superior court, 1847-1856; copies of bonds, notes, and other business records of Orr as a commission merchant; and a daybook of mercantile accounts, 1854-1855, of Orr and Arthur Lee Rogers.

3995. GEORGE OSBORN PAPERS, 1857. 1 item. Richmond, Surrey, England.

Letter to George Osborn, Methodist minister, from Henry Venn, honorary secretary of the missionary society of the church, outlining provisions for the protection of missionary activity that he and the society wanted included in a treaty with China.

3996. JOHN R. OSBORNE PAPERS, 1882-1896. 484 items. Bethany (Davidson County), N.C.

Papers of the Bethany Sub-Alliance No. 601 of the Davidson County Farmers' Alliance, kept by Osborne as secretary. The collection gives information on the activities of the Sub-Alliance and includes printed circulars, broadsides, and catalogues; correspondence with Davidson County Farmers' Alliance, the North Carolina State Farmers' Alliance, and the Sub-Alliance of Thomasville, North Carolina; a minute book, roll book, and account books of the Bethany Sub-Alliance; and a copy of the proceedings and of the constitution and bylaws of the State Alliance.

3997. THOMAS OSBORNE, FOURTH DUKE OF LEEDS, PAPERS, 1748. 1 item. London, England.

Letter to Thomas Osborne from Henry Pelham, First Lord of the Treasury, concerning Osborne's appointment as chief justice in eyre of the royal forests and parks south of the Trent River.

3998. ADELINE OSBURN PAPERS, 1834-1886. 28 items. Avondale (Carroll County), Md.

A poem, portions of sermons, and letters to Adeline Osburn and other members of her family, for the most part on personal and religious matters.

3999. FRANCES SARGENT (LOCKE) OSGOOD PAPERS, ca. 1848. 3 items. New York, N.Y.

Poem by Frances Sargent (Locke) Osgood entitled "To Little Ernest," and a letter from Osgood to Mary Pease.

4000. STEPHEN OSGOOD PAPERS, 1861-1865. 43 items. Georgetown (Essex County), Mass.

Letters to Stephen Osgood from Charles Osgood in the 14th Massachusetts Regiment and from Ward Osgood in the 15th Massachusetts Regiment concern garrison life in Virginia; the second battle of Bull Run; campaigning in Virginia; and the battle of Seven Pines, 1862. There are also scattered letters from soldiers in several other Massachusetts regiments.

4001. ARTHUR WILLIAM EDGAR O'SHAUGHNESSY PAPERS, 1859-1881. 181 items. London, England.

Papers of the poet Arthur William Edgar O'Shaughnessy contain correspondence with his publisher; with J. T. Nettleship, who illustrated some of O'Shaughnessy's poems; and with critics and other poets, including Dante Gabriel Rossetti. Other letters concern personal matters, O'Shaughnessy's work in the zoological department of the British Museum, and the possibility of O'Shaughnessy becoming English correspondent for Le Livre. The collection also contains bills, receipts, invitations, holograph drafts of some of O'Shaughnessy's poems, and transcripts by Helen Snee.

4002. JOHN MARSHALL OTEY PAPERS, 1864-1865. 37 items. Augusta (Richmond County), Ga.

The collection consists chiefly of military dispatches of John M. Otey (d. 1883), Confederate assistant adjutant general under General P. G. T. Beauregard, and is concerned with transportation difficulties. The letters from officials of the Raleigh and Gaston Railroad reveal the conditions of railroad transportation during the Civil War. Included also are letters from P. E. Hines, medical director of North Carolina general hospitals, concerning the deficiency of hospital facilities and medical supplies, and letters concerning the problems of absenteeism and desertion in the army.

4003. PETER JOHNSTON OTEY PAPERS, 1901. 2 items. Washington, D. C.

Notes on Andrew Lewis, soldier and Revolutionary patriot, written by Peter Johnston Otey, United States representative from Virginia.

4004. JOSHUA R. OTTWELL PAPERS, 1854-1880. 41 items. Mercer County, Ill.

Letters of Joshua R. Ottwell include love letters to Lucy Woods and letters written by Ottwell while a soldier in the 137th Illinois Regiment during the Civil War.

4005. SIR GORE OUSELEY, FIRST BARONET, PAPERS, 1812-1831. 4 items. Hall Barn Park, Buckinghamshire, England.

Letters of Sir Gore Ouseley, British diplomat and Oriental scholar, include letters discussing his personal affairs and scholarly interests, and letters, 1812, commenting on his relations with the Shah of Persia and his hopes of achieving peace between Persia and Russia.

4006. JULIA WHEELER (COPELAND) OUTLAND PAPERS, 1934. 1 item. Rich Square (Northampton County), N.C.

Typed copy of the memoir of Julia Wheeler (Copeland) Outland, concerning her life, relatives, and times. Contains comment on Quakers in North Carolina and their position on slavery, slavery in North Carolina, teaching, Confederate "Bushwackers," and Guilford College and New Garden Boarding School, both in Guilford County, North Carolina.

4007. JOSEPH OVERCASH PAPERS, 1846 (1860-1863) 1865. 92 items. Deep Well (Iredell County), N.C.

The collection is made up for the most part of letters to Joseph Overcash from his four sons in the Confederate Army, particularly the 6th North Carolina Regiment, concerning campaigning in Virginia, camp life, hospitals, and religion in camp.

4008. THOMAS McADORY OWEN PAPERS, 1909-ca. 1920. 4 items and 1 vol. Montgomery (Montgomery County), Ala.

A loose-leaf notebook containing a bibliography of the works and a list of the portraits of Alfred, Lord Tennyson. Items include lists of Tennyson books to be sent to dealers for price quotations.

4009. WESLEY W. PACE STAMPS, 1873-1877. 7 items. Wake County, N.C.

Printed stamps or receipts for payment of U.S. internal revenue taxes on the operation of businesses dealing in manufactured tobacco and retail liquor, near Eagle Rock and in Little River and Wakefield townships, all in Wake County.

4010. WILLIAM A. PACE PAPERS, 1862-1863. 11 items. Lynchburg (Campbell County), Va.

Letters from a Confederate soldier to his wife, written from a hospital; and three letters from officers at the hospital concerning his death, and the shipment of his effects.

4011. [ANDERSON PACK AND _____VAWTER?] DAYBOOK, 1848-1849. 1 vol. (282 pp.) Fayette County, Va.

Merchant's records.

4012. CURTIS HIDDEN PAGE PAPERS, 1895-1929. 7 items. Gilmanton (Belknap County), N.H.

Personal letters of Curtis Hidden Page (1870-1946), professor of French and English literature at Harvard University, Cambridge, Massachusetts, and at Dartmouth College, Hanover, New Hampshire; and routine letters concerning publications and speaking engagements.

4013. ELIZABETH PAGE PAPERS, 1803 (1813-1839) 1846. 34 items. Shelley (Gloucester County), Va.

Family letters of Elizabeth (Nelson) Page (b. 1770) concerning the Page and Nelson families. Included are letters from her son, Thomas Jefferson Page (b. 1808), U.S. naval explorer and Confederate naval commander, concerning his voyage on the <u>Erie</u> in the West Indies and his activities as a coastal surveyor.

4014. JAMES JELLIS PAGE PAPERS, 1843-1972. 27 items and 1 vol. Cumberland County, Va.

Papers of James Jellis Page (1822-1898), Episcopal minister, include personal correspondence, 1852-1925, including a letter, 1852, from Eleanor Parke Lewis, adopted daughter of George Washington, concerning Washington and the family; statement ordaining Page as a deacon; typescript of recollections entitled "Record of Mary Wallace Page"; letters, 1972-1973, from Page's granddaughter, Virginia N. Page, to the Manuscript Department of Duke University, Durham, North Carolina; a copy of <u>Genealogy of the Page Family of Virginia</u> (1893) by R. C. M. Page; and clippings concerning family history; John Page, founder of the family; and Rosewell, the Page family home in Virginia.

4015. JOHN PAGE PAPERS, 1777-1806. 27 items. "Rosewell" (Gloucester County), Va.

Letters from John Page (ca. 1743-1808), Virginia landowner, statesman, and member of U.S. Congress, 1789-1797, dealing with personal and family affairs, finances, troop movements, supplies for the French troops during the Revolution, and legislation. Included also are letters from Page to his young sons, written while he was attending George Washington's inauguration, 1789, and the First Congress, with brief descriptions of New York; and letters from St. George Tucker criticizing an unnamed playwright and referring to his views on religion and morality.

4016. P. A. PAGE PAPERS, 1862-1863.
2 items. Raleigh (Wake County), N.C.

Letters of P. A. Page, Confederate sergeant major in the 47th North Carolina Regiment.

4017. RICHARD LUCIAN PAGE PAPERS, 1857-1860. 1 vol. Norfolk (Norfolk County), Va.

Log of the U.S.S. Germantown, a sloop-of-war in the East Indies Squadron under the command of Richard Lucian Page (1807-1901), commander in the U.S. Navy and in the C.S.A. Navy. The log records weather and navigational information about the voyage from Norfolk, Virginia, to the Far East via Madeira Island, Cape Town (South Africa), Ceylon, Bombay (India), and Malaya; and describes stops at ports in China, the Philippine Islands, and Japan; sightings of sea life, other ships and meteors; and the maintenance of the ship and crew, desertion, and courts-martial.

4018. ROBERT NEWTON PAGE PAPERS, 1892 (1916-1920) 1930. 2,763 items and 1 vol. Biscoe (Montgomery County), N.C., and Washington, D.C.

Papers of Robert Newton Page (1859-1933), U.S. congressman, 1903-1917, include correspondence largely concerning his refusal to seek re-election to Congress because of his belief that President Woodrow Wilson was not adhering to a strictly neutral foreign policy, and relating to his gubernatorial campaign in 1920; letters, 1914, from his brother, Walter Hines Page, while ambassador to England describing the English countryside, his activities as ambassador, and his relations with the British Foreign Office; letter book, 1916, containing telegrams and letters from constituents expressing their opinions on Page's decision not to seek re-election; letters of condolence upon the death of Walter Hines Page; copy of an address, 1920, by Robert Newton Page to the students at the University of North Carolina, Chapel Hill, North Carolina; campaign literature from Page's gubernatorial race; copy of Gardner for Governor Bulletin, 1920; and literature urging the purchase of War Savings Stamps during World War I.

4019. THOMAS JEFFERSON PAGE MANUSCRIPT, ca. 1875. 17 items. Shelley (Gloucester County), Va.

Autobiography of Thomas Jefferson Page (1808-1900), commander of a United States naval expedition to South America, 1853-1860, Confederate naval commander, and plantation owner in Argentina. Page's autobiography, written in his own hand, covers the first sixty years of his life and gives an account of his family, of his early naval experiences, of his expedition to South America, of his experiences as commander of the Confederate cruiser Stonewall, and of his life in Argentina as a rancher and adviser to the Argentine Navy. Also included are fourteen pictures.

4020. THOMAS NELSON PAGE PAPERS, 1739 (1885-1920) 1926. 9,285 items and 2 vols. Richmond, Va., and Washington, D. C.

Correspondence and papers of Thomas Nelson Page (1853-1922), author, lawyer, diplomat, and civic leader. Letters prior to 1880 include personal correspondence from various members of the Page family. Letters of the 1880s refer to Page's legal practice in Richmond, Virginia, the beginning of his literary career, his marriage to Anne Seddon Bruce in 1886, and her death in 1888. Correspondence of the 1890s portrays Page's activities as a lyceum entertainer; his marriage in 1893 to Florence (Lathrop) Field, widow of Henry Field, who was a brother of Marshall Field; their removal to Washington, D. C. and Page's establishment in a literary career. The latter is revealed in extensive correspondence with the Scribner firm, with various literary personages, and with Confederate veterans. Numerous letters from the architectural firm of McKim, Meade, and White deal with construction of the Page residence in Washington. Page's leadership of the alumni campaign to raise funds for rebuilding the burned Rotunda of the University of Virginia, Charlottesville, is displayed in extensive correspondence continued into the next decade, when he led in raising the Thomas Jefferson Memorial Endowment. Letters from Moses Ezekiel concern statues, especially one of Thomas Jefferson, made by him for the university. Other letters throughout the collection reflect Page's interest in civic affairs, social reform, race relations, politics, travels in Europe, and an extended vacation in Egypt.

Of the many family and personal letters, the bulk passed between Thomas Nelson Page and his mother, Elizabeth Burwell (Nelson) Page, and brother, Rosewell Page, who lived at the ancestral estate, "Oakland," in Hanover County, Virginia. Thomas Nelson Page gave financial assistance in maintaining this home, and he owned other farms near by. His farming activities are revealed in correspondence with his tenants. Other letters show that Page gave considerable financial aid in educating various relatives, while other calls for charitable contributions were numerous.

Page's political activities are reflected in letters concerning the presidential campaigns of 1912 and 1916, and during this period he financed the Hanover Progress, a Democratic newspaper published at Ashland, Virginia. In 1913 Page was appointed ambassador to Italy. The correspondence thereafter falls into three categories; personal letters to members of the family describing new experiences in diplomatic life; routine and business correspondence; and carbon copies of diplomatic dispatches to the U.S. State Department and to President

Woodrow Wilson. The latter cover America's intervention in Mexico; the establishment of laws of warfare; intelligence reports from Gino Speranza, the embassy's political analyst; developments in Italian politics; military campaigns in the Balkans and on the Italian front; economic and military aid for Italy; Page's efforts to conciliate Italy during the Versailles Peace Conference; the Fiume question; and America's relations with the Vatican.

There are some literary manuscripts, chiefly addresses and articles, but none of Page's major literary works. Letters from Page to Robert Underwood Johnson, editor of Century Magazine, discuss Page's work as lobbyist for the American Copyright League, articles for Century Magazine, and the literary scene. Also included are numerous royalty statements from Scribner's; a prospectus of the International Association of Newspapers and Authors; memorandum, 1911, relating to the work of the American Forestry Association; photocopy of a poem written in 1892 by Rosewell Page to his nieces; and two scrapbooks containing cards and envelopes from distinguished persons, and clippings about Page's lyceum work.

4021. WALTER HINES PAGE PAPERS, 1889-1917. 23 items. New York, N.Y.

Papers of Walter Hines Page (1855-1918), editor of the Forum, Atlantic Monthly, and The World's Work, and ambassador to Great Britain, 1913-1918, relate to his editorial career. Among the papers are letters concerning the publication of articles in the various journals with which Page was associated, including three letters from James Whitcomb Riley, one of which contains portions of a poem entitled "The Sermon of the Rose"; copies of letters to Page by John Spencer Bassett and Edwin Mims pertaining to Bassett's references to Booker T. Washington in an editorial in The South Atlantic Quarterly, vol. II, no. 4 (1903); and a letter from Page asking Franklin Matthews for articles on the world cruise of the U.S. fleet, 1908.

4022. YELVERTON PEYTON PAGE PAPERS, 1844 (1851-1906) 1920. 162 items. Washington, D.C.

Papers of Yelverton Peyton Page (d. 1863), clerk in the U.S. Senate, include a letter, 1848, discussing the Negro question, Democratic politics, and the Free Soil Party and Martin Van Buren; land indenture, 1844; letters from James T. Hieskell concerning an invention to make coins entirely by machinery and opposition to the machine by mint officials at Philadelphia, Pennsylvania; Civil War letters mentioning the threat to Washington, D.C., from Confederate troops, conscription, a review of the Union Army in 1865, and Lincoln's assassination; letters, 1863, from his daughter, Bettie E. Page, while at Patapsco Institute; letter from John Cook Rives, founder of the Congressional Globe, discussing the establishment of the Government Printing Office, and his own philanthropy; letters describing the Mexican mines at Batopilas, Chihuahua, Mexico; routine letters to Page from various senators principally concerning administrative matters; and letters from his daughter who had married Gerrit S. Miller, Jr., then (1906) assistant curator of mammals at the U.S. National Museum, describing a collecting trip from southern France, Spain, and Tangier.

4023. SIR EDWARD PAGET PAPERS, 1826. 1 item. Cowes, Isle of Wight, Hampshire, England.

Letter from Lord Amherst, governor general of India, to Sir Edward Paget (1775-1849), British general and commander-in-chief in India, 1822-1825, reporting on the conclusion of the war in Burma.

4024. HENRY WILLIAM PAGET, FIRST MARQUIS OF ANGLESEY, PAPERS, 1830. 59 items. London, England.

Principally letters to Lord Anglesey (1768-1854), member of Parliament and Lord Lieutenant of Ireland, 1828-1829 and 1830-1833, discussing opposition of newspaper proprietors to stamp duties; repeal of the coal duties; the candidacies of Richard Sheil, John McClintock, John Lawless, and Edward Ayshford Sanford; political, educational, and ecclesiastical reform in Ireland; Catholic emancipation; British-French relations; patronage; death of William Huskisson; British domestic affairs; Irish politics; the repeal of the Union; the government under the Duke of Wellington; scandals and litigation surrounding the relationships of Sir Edward Smith Lees and Second Viscount Annesley with Sophia (Kelly) Connor; the application of the Tithe Composition Act; law enforcement in Ireland; and the fear of an uprising in County Westmeath. Among the correspondents are Chief Justice Bushe, Catherine Clarke, Lord Cloncurry, Frederick W. Conway, Lord Downshire, Lord Eldon, William Huskisson, Sir Joseph de Courcy Laffan, John Lawless, Sir Harcourt Lees, Edward John Littleton, John McClintock, Pierce Mahony, John M'Mullen, Lord Palmerston, Edward Ayshford Sanford, Lord Wellesley, and Lord Westmeath.

4025. THOMAS PAINE PAPERS, 1914-1930. 3 items. New York, N.Y.

Printed material relating to the New York house of Thomas Paine (1737-1809), revolutionary political pamphleteer; to the Paine Monument in New Rochelle, New York; and to the Thomas Paine Historical Association.

4026. JOHN SOMERSET PAKINGTON, FIRST
BARON HAMPTON, PAPERS, 1867.
1 item. London, England.

Letter from Baroness Herbert to John Somerset Pakington, First Baron Hampton (1799-1880), member of Parliament and governmental official, concerning the Herbert Memorial Fund and the removal of the Army Medical School to Netley after Lord Sidney Herbert's death.

4027. PALESTINE ALBUMS, ca. 1881. 2 vols.

Photographs of Palestine.

4028. SIR REGINALD FRANCIS DOUCE PALGRAVE
PAPERS, 1878, 1886. 2 items.
London, England.

Letters to Sir Reginald Francis Douce Palgrave (1829-1904), clerk in the House of Commons, concerning procedural questions--from Sir Stafford Northcote about the use of Indian revenues, and from Lord Randolph Churchill about the power of the speaker.

4029. ADELINE (OSBORNE) PALMER PAPERS,
1853-1935. 110 items. Rippon
(Jefferson County), W. Va.

Personal and family correspondence of Adeline (Osborne) Palmer concerning student life at University of Virginia, Charlottesville, Virginia, and Virginia Military Institute, Lexington, Virginia; labor conditions during Reconstruction; financial transactions of William Rainey Marshall, former governor of Minnesota; social life and customs in Washington, D. C., West Virginia, Ohio, and Missouri; and Decoration Day, 1871. Also included are several papers of Captain G. A. Flagg of the U.S. Army Quartermaster Corps in Harpers Ferry, West Virginia, 1865; land deeds, 1913, from Redondo Beach, California; and sermon notes of Henry Osborne on John Wesley.

4030. ARCHIBALD W. PALMER NOTEBOOK, 1881.
1 vol. (136 pp.) Gulf (Chatham
County), N.C.

Notebook entitled "Notes on Materia Medica and Therapeutics," containing notes on drugs, including narcotics, antispasmodic agents, diaphoretic agents, diuretics, lithontriptic agents, sialogogues, and expectorant agents.

4031. BENJAMIN MORGAN PALMER PAPERS,
1836-1860. 5 items. Columbia
(Richland County), S.C.

Letters from Benjamin M. Palmer (1818-1902), minister of the Southern Presbyterian Church and co-founder of the Southern Presbyterian Review, concerning ecclesiastical and literary matters. Included also is a letter from James Henley Thornwell.

4032. CHARLES PALMER PAPERS, 1852-1864.
35 items. Mansfield (Richland
County), Ohio.

Letter from R. Ward to Charles Palmer describing the near loss of a ship on which Jenny Lind was sailing; and Civil War letters to Palmer discussing camp life, food, the delivery of the bodies of General Zollicoffer and Colonel Payton, and the rise of the Cumberland River at Nashville, Tennessee, in December, 1862.

4033. JOHN S. PALMER PAPERS, 1861-1864.
5 items. Eutaw (Orangeburg
County), S.C.

Letters from John S. Palmer, captain in the Confederate Army, to his father concerning the mustering of troops at Charleston in 1861; fortifying Fort Ripley, Charleston Harbor, South Carolina, 1861; and general Civil War activities at Shelbyville and Chattanooga, Tennessee, 1863, and at Dalton, Georgia, 1864.

4034. JOSEPH PALMER PAPERS, 1863-1865.
4 items. Pineville (Charleston
County), S.C.

Three accounts, and a letter from Joseph Palmer on the general situation in Mississippi in 1863, with references to Generals Joseph E. Johnston and John C. Pemberton.

4035. ROBERT PALMER PAPERS, 1761-1764.
2 vols. Tarboro (Edgecombe
County), N.C.

Daybook, 1761-1762, and ledger, 1762-1764, of a mercantile firm owned by Robert Palmer.

4036. ROUNDELL PALMER, FIRST EARL OF
SELBORNE, PAPERS, 1888. 1 item.
Blackmoor, Hampshire, England.

Letter of Roundell Palmer, First Earl of Selborne (1812-1895), member of Parliament and Lord Chancellor, 1872-1874 and 1880-1885, to James S. Baily, secretary of the National Radical Union, expressing strong support for the Liberal Unionist policy. The letter was published in The Times, September 19, 1888.

4037. WILLIAM KIMBERLEY PALMER NOTEBOOKS,
1934-1937. 3 items. Chicopee
(Hampden County), Mass.

Papers of William K. Palmer, author and poet, consisting of a draft of one of his stories; and two notebooks of clippings, poems, and letters.

4038. WILLIAM P. PALMER PAPERS, 1847-1851.
5 items. Richmond, Va.

Letters to William P. Palmer, physician and editor, discussing an election in Buchanan, Virginia; Dandridge Pitts; and a cholera epidemic in New Orleans. Letters from his father, Charles Palmer, discuss personal matters and financial reverses.

4039. PALMER FAMILY PAPERS, 1841-1907. 63 items. New Hampshire.

Personal and family correspondence of the Palmer family of New Hampshire, principally concerning personal affairs and matters of local interest, but also dealing with economic conditions in Dubuque, Iowa, 1852; land speculation and railroad building in Wisconsin, 1853; how to make good cement; conditions in Goldsboro, North Carolina, in 1865; the acquisition of bounties for enlisting in the U.S. Army; the assassination of Abraham Lincoln and the rumor of the involvement of Jefferson Davis; commodity prices in New Hampshire, 1860s; life at Highland Lake Institute, East Andover, and Williams College, Williamstown, New Hampshire; and Copperheads.

4040. GEORGE F. PALMES PAPERS, 1811-1871. 39 items and 2 vols. Savannah, Ga.

Papers of George F. Palmes, financier, including letters from Daniel Baker, a student at Hampden-Sydney College, Virginia, 1811-1812; letters concerning land purchases in East Florida, 1819-1820; letters from Mary Palmes at Montpelier Female Institute, Macon, Georgia, 1848; and daybooks for the firm of Palmes & Lyon, wholesale grocers and commission merchants in Savannah, Georgia.

4041. PALMETTO GUARD MINUTES, 1877-1882. 1 vol. (300 pp.) Charleston, S.C.

Minutes of the meetings of the Palmetto Guard, also including copies of correspondence.

4042. PANAMA-PACIFIC EXPOSITION PAPERS, 1915. 1 item. Durham, N.C.

Typescript copy of a journal concerning a trip from Durham, North Carolina, to the Panama-Pacific Exposition in San Francisco, California.

4043. PANKEY FAMILY PAPERS, 1829-1899. 21 items. Campbell County, Va.

Personal and business correspondence of the Pankey family concerning commodity prices in Virginia, the weather, personal and business affairs, and C. W. Venable and the tobacco business. Civil War letters from Confederate soldiers discuss casualties, troop movements, a naval engagement during the siege of Yorktown, 1862, desertion, and a funeral in Hat Creek, Virginia. Also included is a letter, 1900, to "Ex-Governor T. D. Richardson," accusing him of slander and meddlesomeness.

4044. HENRY CLAY PARDEE PAPERS, 1853-1862. 17 items. New Bern (Craven County), N.C.

Civil War letters of Henry Clay Pardee to his father describing the battle of Roanoke Island, North Carolina; pay of privates; the opinion of General Ambrose Burnside held by his men.

4045. PARIS. BIBLIOTHÈQUE NATIONALE. DEPARTEMENT DES MANUSCRITS. PAPERS. 2 items.

Photostats, with negatives, of MS. Arabe 71 and MS. Ethiopien 146, both the Story of Zosimus.

4046. PARIS. CONVENT DE L'ANNONCIADES, MANUSCRIPT, 1777. 1 vol. (328 pp.)

"Meditations Sur Les Constitutions des Religieuses de l'Ordre de l'Anonciade C'éleste. . . . Composées par un vertueux Ecclesiastique." In French.

4047. A. J. PARKER AND BENJAMIN J. PARKER PAPERS, 1840-1895. 187 items. Woodland (Northampton County), N.C.

Principally bills and mercantile accounts of Benjamin J. Parker, cotton factor and merchant; several accounts of A. J. Parker, Methodist Episcopal minister; and letters of A. J. Parker commenting on religious matters.

4048. ALTON BROOKS PARKER PAPERS, 1904. 1 item. New York, N.Y.

Letter from James R. Gray, editor of The Atlanta (Georgia) Journal, to Alton Brooks Parker, jurist and presidential candidate of the Democratic Party in 1904, concerning Parker's campaign, the political climate in the South, and Thomas E. Watson as the nominee of the Populist Party.

4049. CALEB D. PARKER PAPERS, 1834-1922. 95 items and 4 vols. Bunker Hill (Bedford County), Va.

Papers of Caleb D. Parker, tobacco planter or merchant, and captain in a militia regiment from his county, include personal correspondence discussing a campaign for the Virginia House of Assembly in 1850; students' drunkenness and poor food at Emory and Henry College, Emory, Virginia; conditions in Washington County, Virginia, in 1855; and life in the Confederate Army. There are also a circular, 1868, advertising Sunny Side School in Bedford County; a will, 1834, of Kimball F. Prince; a book of military commands; and account books, one of which belonged to F. D. Brockman, a tailor of Charlottesville, Virginia.

4050. JOHN R. PARKER PAPERS, 1805-1842. 53 items. Boston, Mass.

Papers of John R. Parker include bills and receipts containing lists of commodity prices; two copies of a deposition; an acrostic praising Parker's patronage of the arts; and a poem concerning the salutary effects of smoking tobacco.

4051. JOHN WILLIAM PARKER PAPERS, 1849-1857. 3 items. London, England.

Two letters from John Arthur Roebuck, politician, to John William Parker (1792-1870), British publisher and printer, discussing personal matters, his History of the Whig Ministry of 1830 to the Passing of the Reform Bill (London: 1852), and his intention to defend a Nottingham paper against a libel suit from Feargus O'Connor; and a letter from George Henry Lewes presenting his proposal for a book on popular physiology.

4052. LIZZIE [NELMS?] (SMITH) PARKER PAPERS, 1854-1888. 45 items. Bladen County, N.C.

Personal and family correspondence of Lizzie [Nelms?] (Smith) Parker consists chiefly of letters from her brother, William T. Smith, concerning his activities as Confederate soldier, as a teacher at the Carolina Female College and the Anson Institute, and as a farmer in Anson County, North Carolina. Civil War letters discuss high prices; Union sentiment in Wilmington, North Carolina; the siege of Petersburg; and the activities of the 43rd Regiment, North Carolina Troops, C.S.A. Other letters describe Reconstruction in Wilmington, North Carolina, and emphasize the advantages of living in Texas.

4053. M. S. PARKER LEDGER, 1869-1880. 1 vol. (110 pp.) Richmond County, N.C.

Ledger of a saddler and harness maker.

4054. SIR HARRY SMITH PARKES PAPERS, 1853-1872. 6 items. London, England.

Papers of Sir Harry Smith Parkes (1828-1885), British diplomat and minister to Japan, 1865-1883, include two letters concerning arrangements for a tour of Bradford and other British manufacturing cities by the Iwakura embassy from Japan, and a program from a banquet in honor of the embassy; two letters to William Lockhart (1811-1896), British medical missionary, discussing the rebellion at Nanking, the situation at Canton, American diplomat Peter Parker, British success at Peking, and the imprisonment of Parkes and his entourage; and a personal letter.

4055. JOHN GIBSON PARKHURST PAPERS, 1864-1896. 8 items. Chattanooga (Hamilton County), Tenn.

Correspondence of John Gibson Parkhurst, officer in the 9th Michigan Infantry, includes personal letters; two letters from Mrs. James K. Polk concerning the sending of a trunk to her brother; and two letters from Mrs. Aaron V. Brown, a Union sympathizer living near Nashville, Tennessee, describing her activities in aiding Federal officers and refugees, and appealing for assistance.

4056. ALEXANDER PARKS, JR., PAPERS, 1870-1890. 11 vols. Martinsburg (Berkeley County), W. Va.

Ledger, 1878-1890, four daybooks, 1878-1885, and four sales books, 1870-1888, containing records of a flour mill owned by Alexander Parks, Jr.; a memorandum book kept while Parks was Worshipful Master of his lodge of Freemasons in 1875; and a receipt book with a few entries concerning a local Presbyterian church. One of the sales books also contains records, 1870-1872, of a mill owned by Henry S. Hannis and Company of Philadelphia, Pennsylvania.

4057. ENOS T. PARKS PAPERS, 1840-1855. 8 items. Tunkhannock (Wyoming County), Pa.

Family correspondence of Enos T. Parks including letters from his sisters, Lydia and Janette, of Bainbridge, Pennsylvania, concerning personal matters; and letters from his brother, Joel Parks, expressing his desire to devote full time to portrait painting and the taking of daguerreotypes.

4058. PARLIAMENTARY DIRECTORY QUESTIONNAIRE RESPONSES, 1829-1837. 150 items. England.

Principally letters from various members of Parliament containing the dates and constituencies from which they were elected. Some letters include information about events and circumstances of particular electoral contests in Great Britain and Ireland.

4059. SAMUEL SPENCER PARMELEE AND URIAH N. PARMELEE PAPERS, 1845 (1860-1865) 1911. ca. 404 items and 2 vols. Guilford (New Haven County), Conn., and Macon (Macon County), Ga.

Letters and diaries of Uriah N. Parmelee, Jr., 6th New York Cavalry, giving detailed accounts of camp life, morale, politics, rumors, and battles, raids, and skirmishes, including the Peninsular Campaign, the battles at Antietam, Fredericksburg, Chancellorsville, Gettysburg, Bristoe Station, and the Wilderness, and the Richmond Campaign;

family and official correspondence concerning the death of Uriah N. Parmelee, Jr., at the battle of Five Forks, Virginia; and correspondence of Samuel Spencer Parmelee, dealer in carriages, wagons, and leather goods in Macon (Georgia), pertaining to rents received from property in Guilford (Connecticut); the death of his father, Uriah N. Parmelee, Sr., and the settlement of the estate; the recovery in 1892 of the diary of Uriah N. Parmelee, Jr., lost near Berryville (Virginia) in 1864; and the location of Uriah's grave in the Petersburg National Cemetery in 1911.

4060. EDWARD JAMES PARRISH PAPERS, 1894-1926. 195 items and 11 vols. Durham, N.C.; and Tokyo, Japan.

Business and personal correspondence and papers of Edward James Parrish (1846-1920) and of his wife, Rosa (Bryan) Parrish. Some of the earliest papers concern the Murai Brothers Company, Ltd., a cigarette manufacturing company of Tokyo of which Parrish was first vice-president. Other papers include personal letters from Parrish written during his stay at Hot Springs, Arkansas; bills for purchases made by Rosa (Bryan) Parrish; letters from Jones Fuller, her attorney, concerning the collection of Parrish's insurance policies after his death; photographs of the Parrishes while in Japan; letterpress books, 1900-1905; notebook on tobacco trade with China and Japan, 1894-1900; a Bible owned by Parrish; a postal card album of Rosa Parrish; and two albums of Kichibei Murai containing photographs of his residences and of banks, mines, oil fields, farms and tobacco factories in which he had an interest.

4061. JOHN H. PARRISH LEDGER, 1871-1886. 1 vol. (192 pp.) Talladega (Talladega County), Ala.

Personal and professional accounts of a physician.

4062. ENOCH GREENLEAFE PARROTT PAPERS, 1831-1929. 433 items and 2 vols. Portsmouth (Rockingham County), N.H.

Personal and official papers of Enoch Greenleafe Parrott (1815-1879), officer in the U.S. Navy, include letters from Parrott to his sister, Susan Parker (Parrott) Spalding; her husband, Lyman Dyer Spalding; and their children. Topics principally concern family matters with references to places visited and Parrot's naval experiences. There is also naval correspondence dealing with an investigation surrounding punishment given Parrott by his commanding officer, Joshua Ratoon Sands; an attempt to land slaves along the Florida coast in 1858; routine orders; and Parrott's retirement. Other material includes financial papers, legal papers, lists of officers from various ships on which Parrott served, extracts from logs, ships' plans, obituaries, and two small notebooks. One notebook contains poetry written by Parrott's brother, James B. Parrott.

4063. CHARLES PARSONS BOOK, 1905. 1 vol. (2 pp.) Saint Louis, Mo.

"In Memoriam" to Charles Parsons from the State National Bank praising him for his services.

4064. MASON PARSONS PAPERS, 1812 (1815-1838) 1890. 43 items. Woodsboro (Frederick County), Md.

Family correspondence of Mason Parsons, merchant, postmaster, deputy sheriff, bank cashier, teacher, and temperance lecturer, with comments upon commodity prices, the Whig Party, Henry Clay, James K. Polk, and Stephen A. Douglas.

4065. MOSBY MONROE PARSONS PAPERS, 1861-1862. 9 items. Missouri.

Military papers of General Mosby Monroe Parsons (1822-1865), C.S.A., include two letters from Colonel John T. Hughes describing fighting at the battles of Springfield (Missouri) and Fort Scott (Kansas), Kansas Jayhawkers, rumors, casualties, prisoners, and various generals; orders concerning reorganization and staff work; circular on sentry duty; and letter from General P. G. T. Beauregard praising the military conduct of John Bordenave Villepigue at Fort Pillow.

4066. WILFRED GEORGE PARTINGTON SCRAPBOOK, ca. 1799-1809. 1 vol. (17 pp.) London, England.

Scrapbook of papers from the Anglo-Indian Collection of Wilfred George Partington (1888-ca. 1955), British author, journalist and collector, containing a broadside listing "Necessaries for a Writer to India" with Partington's notes about the item; a letter of William Robert Spencer (1769-1834), British poet and wit, seeking assistance in obtaining a writership for George Bonsall; Regulation IX of the East India Company, 1800, establishing a college at Fort William in Bengal for the training of junior civil servants; resolution of the General Court of the East India Company concerning the regulations and qualifications for the appointment of future writers and cadets; regulations for the appointment of students at the East India College who sought to become writers; and a form of a petition for nominating students to the East India College.

4067. ALDEN PARTRIDGE PAPERS, 1829. 1 item. Washington, D.C.

Letter from Horace Webster (1794-1871), professor of mathematics and natural philosophy at Geneva College, Geneva, New York, to Alden Partridge (1785-1854) discussing the college and Partridge's plan for establishing a military academy in North Carolina.

4068. BENJAMIN WARING PARTRIDGE PAPERS, 1824-1945. 111 items. Monticello (Jefferson County), Fla.

Family correspondence of Benjamin Waring Partridge (b. 1846) and his wife, Mary (Denham) Partridge; of his father, John Nathaniel Partridge, and his mother; of his parents-in-law, Andrew and Adaline Denham; and of his children. The letters principally deal with family matters, but also include comments on politics in South Carolina; attitudes in South Carolina toward tariff legislation; the activities of the 3rd Florida Volunteers, C.S.A., in South Carolina, Georgia, and Florida; life at Wofford College, Spartanburg, South Carolina; treatment and convalescence after an attack of malaria; and a convention of Confederate veterans at Houston, Texas, 1895. Also included is a short memoir written by William Waring Carroll, a grandson of John Nathaniel Partridge, about life in Monticello during Reconstruction.

4069. COVENTRY KERSEY DIGHTON PATMORE PAPERS, 1858. 1 item. London, England.

Letter from Coventry Patmore to his publisher, Ticknor and Company, Boston, Massachusetts, acknowledging receipt of a draft from the sale of "Angel in the House."

4070. SARAH A. PATRICK PAPERS, 1850. 2 items. West Buffalo (Scott County), Iowa.

Personal letters to Mrs. Sarah A. Patrick.

4071. WALTER PATRICK PAPERS, 1829-1859. 2 vols. Steuben County, N.Y.

Ledger, 1829-1859, containing accounts for goods transported, days worked, and summonses and warrants delivered; and record book, 1838-1841, with notes on various lawsuits. One case involved Patrick.

4072. PATRONS OF HUSBANDRY PAPERS, 1873-1890. 168 items and 7 vols. Raleigh (Wake County), N.C., and Richland County, S.C.

Business papers of Raleigh Grange No. 17 when R. B. Saunders and B. C. Manly served as secretaries; accounts of dues, 1873-1874; minutes, 1873-1875; a list of the subordinate Granges of North Carolina with their masters and secretaries, begun by Alonzo T. Mial as general state agent, 1875-1890; and circulars, pamphlets, and broadsides giving information on prices of commodities and farm products. Among the correspondents are N. P. Jones, Oliver Hudson Kelly, John Ott, and Thomas Stanley. Records and papers pertaining to the Cottage Grange and the Grange movement in Richland County, South Carolina, include manuals of subordinate granges, 1872-1873; proceedings of the third session of the State Grange, 1875; and minutes, 1874-1875.

4073. JEAN MAURY (COYLE) PATTEN PAPERS, 1906-1920. 15 items. Washington, D.C.

Letters to Jean Maury (Coyle) Patten, wife of John Dewhurst Patten, from John Burroughs (1837-1921), naturalist, describing personal matters; travels made by himself and his wife; the seasons and wildlife around his home in West Park, New York; a visit with President Theodore Roosevelt; his friendship with Thomas Alva Edison, Henry Ford, Dr. Clara Barrus, and Dr. Frank Baker; and a portrait of himself painted by the Hungarian Princess Elizabeth Lwoff-Parlaghy.

4074. MARY ELIZABETH PATTEN PAPERS, 1913-1943. 13 vols. Washington, D.C.

Diaries of Mary Elizabeth Patten, society leader in Washington, D.C., describing her daily activities and social functions and the people who attended them, among whom were six presidents and other national political and social figures. A scrapbook contains clippings from various newspapers, invitations, and a few letters, including one from the American ambassador to Chile, William Miller Collier, describing the political situation in Chile.

4075. JAMES PATTERSON PAPERS, 1853-1864. 14 items. Franklinville (Randolph County), N.C.

Family letters to James Patterson. Included are a letter, 1855, from a niece, Ellen Allred, discussing homesteading in Wayne County, Iowa; and letters from his son, J. A. Patterson, requesting assistance in obtaining his release from a military prison for desertion.

4076. JOHN E. PATTERSON PAPERS, 1825-1869. 118 items and 2 vols. Hamilton (Butler County), Ohio.

Mainly letters to John E. Patterson, physician, from members of his family, with references to politics and government in Ohio; Clement Laird Vallandigham; Cyrus Hall McCormick; the Presbyterian Church; and Patterson's responsibilities as a surgeon in the Union Army. A diary, 1859-1860, describes Patterson's efforts to establish a medical practice in several cities in Pennsylvania and Ohio. A diary, 1863, kept by Patterson, comments on the difficulties encountered as he tried to maintain sanitary conditions on a crowded ship, and other aspects of the Vicksburg Campaign. Also included are photographs of James R. Patterson, Charles Elliott, George Stuart Fullerton, and others, and of a building of Miami University in Ohio.

4077. ROBERT PATTERSON PAPERS, 1868. 1 item. Philadelphia, Pa.

Letter of Robert Patterson (1792-1881), U.S. Army officer, to a Mr. Woodward concerning the location of copies of orders issued by Patterson during the Civil War.

4078. ROBERT DONNELL PATTERSON PAPERS, 1951. 2 items. Durham, N.C.

Genealogical history of the Patterson family of Orange County, North Carolina, 1744-1934, with references to the related Barbee, Burroughs, Bynum, Cabe, Faucette, Rhodes, Rogers, and Yeargan families.

4079. RUFUS LENOIR PATTERSON, 1894-1898. 26 items. New York, N.Y.

Photocopies of correspondence of Rufus Lenoir Patterson (1872-1945), manufacturer of tobacco machinery, principally dealing with his early efforts to develop a machine to weigh, pack, stamp, and label smoking tobacco; patent rights to such a machine; and the tobacco industry in France, Germany, Scotland, and England. Also included are two personal letters to his wife, Margaret (Morehead) Patterson; and two newspaper clippings telling of the deaths of Patterson and of William H. Kerr.

4080. SAMUEL FINLEY PATTERSON PAPERS, 1792-1939. 2,141 items and 26 vols. Winston-Salem (Forsyth County), N.C.

Personal and business correspondence and papers of Samuel Finley Patterson (1799-1874), state legislator and president of the Raleigh and Gaston Railroad; of his son, Rufus Lenoir Patterson (1830-1879); of his granddaughter, Caroline Finley Patterson; and of Lucy Bramlette (Patterson) Patterson (1865-1942), wife of Jesse Lindsay Patterson, Samuel Finley Patterson's grandson. Early papers include the business records and daybooks of Hugh Graham concerning mercantile affairs, the purchase of land warrants, and the panic of 1819; letters of William Norwood (1767-1842) dealing with family matters and his election as a judge; letters of the Jones family, related through the wife of Samuel Finley Patterson, pertaining to family affairs; and life in 1823 at Salem Academy (Salem, North Carolina), in 1835 at the University of North Carolina, and in 1840 at Yale College; and letters from Edmund Jones Henry and James Edward Henry regarding farming in Spartanburg, South Carolina, and a temperance convention there in 1843. The papers of Samuel Finley Patterson give information of Revolutionary land claims; sale of Cherokee lands; the Raleigh and Gaston Railroad; Cincinnati (Ohio) in 1819; South Carolina politics, including nullification and support for the Van Buren administration; the Bank of the United States; Sunday customs in New Haven (Connecticut); the Whig Party in North Carolina and Virginia; Patterson's activities as a member of the North Carolina legislature; student life at the University of North Carolina in 1849 and 1867, and at the University of Virginia; Charlottesville (Virginia), in 1869; and Rufus T. Patterson's cotton and paper factories. Correspondence relating to the Civil War and Reconstruction discusses abolitionism, slavery, supplies to Confederate soldiers, refugees, prices, military affairs and leaders, the establishment of a school for Negroes, dislike of the policies of Jefferson Davis and Judah P. Benjamin, the Good Templars of Hillsborough (North Carolina), the emancipation of Louisiana from radical rule; and the threat to eliminate state funding for the support of the University of North Carolina. The papers of Lucy Bramlette (Patterson) Patterson include her diploma from Salem Female College; letters written while she was traveling in Mexico and Europe during the 1880s; letters from prominent persons in response to invitations to speak at Salem Female College; information on the Patterson Cup awarded annually for the best literary production in North Carolina; letters from a few North Carolina literary figures; correspondence regarding the location of the Daniel Boone Trail; papers relative to Mrs. Patterson's service with Kolo Serbski Sestara in caring for the orphans of Serbian soldiers; a few items relating to the visit of Queen Marie of Rumania to the United States; clippings of Lucy Bramlette (Patterson) Patterson's contributions to the Progressive Farmer, Raleigh, North Carolina; and an account of "The Groves," the home of Willie Jones.

Other papers include a list of pledges by women of Caldwell County, North Carolina, in 1862 for construction of an ironclad gunboat; broadsides advertising the Charlotte Female Institute, Charlotte (North Carolina), Gaston High School, Dallas (North Carolina), O. P. Fitzgerald's Home Newspaper and Educational Journal, Hubert H. Bancroft's History of California and the Pacific States, and a forestry conference to be held at Montreat (North Carolina); program of performances at the Opera House in Winston (North Carolina) in 1882; broadside announcing the inauguration of Governor Zebulon B. Vance in 1877; bulletin of St. Mary's School, Raleigh (North Carolina); printed speech of John K. Kuttrell entitled "Who is Responsible for Chinese Immigration"; outline of exercises for several days in a kindergarten in Chapel Hill (North Carolina); copy of the deed of trust of "The Louise Fund" established at Salem Female Academy; and the eighth annual report of the Associated Charities of Wilmington (North Carolina) for 1902.

There are several items relating to the Bolijack family, including an account book, 1855-1869, of William A. Bolijack with entries for a sawmill and for trade in barrels of lime, and an agreement, 1842, between John W. Smith and Bolijack for use of a patented sawmill on Town Fork of the Dan River in Stokes County.

4081. WILLIAM PATTERSON PAPERS, 1791-1819. 6 items. Baltimore, Md.

Papers of William Patterson (1752-1835), merchant, include financial papers relating to the settlement of an estate, a personal debt, and the indebtedness of his brother-in-law, General Samuel Smith, to the Bank of the United States; an agreement, 1793, pertaining to speculation in Georgia land; receipts for money given by Patterson as president of the Bank of Maryland; and a petition to Secretary of the Navy William Jones from a gunner who claimed he was unduly arrested.

4082. PATTERSON FAMILY PAPERS, 1744-1859. 163 items. Cross Creek (Cumberland County), N.C.

Papers relating to the business activities of three generations of the Patterson family: Duncan Patterson (d. 1793), Daniel Patterson (d. 1825), and Duncan Patterson, planters. Also included are bills, receipts, land deeds, and wills which contain genealogical information and the names of slaves.

4083. PATTERSON-CAVIN FAMILY PAPERS, 1809-1896. 211 items and 3 vols. Iredell and Alexander Counties, N.C.

Chiefly family correspondence of the related Patterson and Cavin families. Letters from family members in South Carolina, Alabama, and Tennessee concern crops, health, family events, and a political meeting at Prairieville, Alabama, at which resolutions opposing President Andrew Jackson's banking policy were passed. Civil War letters from Confederate soldiers discuss camp life, the lack of food, the siege of Petersburg, imprisonment at Point Lookout (Maryland), and illness. Also included are bills and receipts; a daybook, ca. 1820, of John Patterson; daybook, 1868-1872, of John Hilary Patterson; and an almanac.

4084. JACOB PATTISON BOOK, 1801. 1 vol. (128 pp.) Scotland.

Entitled "Familiar Letters during a Journey through the Highlands of Scotland," the volume is a transcription of letters by Pattison (ca.1759-1782), an Edinburgh medical student, giving detailed observations on his travels in 1780. The transcription was made by James Levett.

4085. FRANCES MacRAE (GRAY) PATTON PAPERS, 1942-1970. 273 items and 1 vol. Durham, N.C.

Papers of Frances MacRae (Gray) Patton, author, include a typescript of her Good Morning, Miss Dove (New York: 1954) with revisions handwritten by the author; a copy of the adaptation of the novel for a motion picture; clippings and articles about Mrs. Patton and reviews of her books; and ration books and certificates issued to the Patton family during World War II.

4086. SUE SNOWDON PATTON PAPERS, 1857-1876. 22 items. Wilkes-Barre (Luzerne County), Pa.

Letters to Sue Snowdon Patton chiefly from her husband, J. Desha Patton, and from a friend, Libbie Foster Fiske, concerning personal matters, a church revival, actor James Edward Murdock, interests in the refining of crude oil, and the effects of martial law on Wilkes-Barre during the Civil War and men going to Canada to evade the draft.

4087. CHARLES RODMAN PAUL DIARY, 1865-1866. 1 vol. (120 pp.) Belvidere (Warren County), N.J.

Brief accounts by Charles Rodman Paul, U.S. Army officer in several New Jersey regiments, of the siege of Petersburg; fighting at Hatcher's Run, Virginia, and Fort Fisher, North Carolina; marches to Appomattox Court House and Danville, Virginia; the countryside through which he traveled; duty along the Richmond and Danville Railroad; and marches in review in Petersburg, Richmond, and Washington, D.C. Also included are brief social notices.

4088. JAMES KIRKE PAULDING PAPERS, 1839. 1 item. Washington, D.C., and Hyde Park (Dutchess County), N.Y.

Routine business letter from Edward Stanly (1810-1872), U.S. congressman from North Carolina, to James Kirke Paulding (1778-1860), author and secretary of the navy, 1838-1841.

4089. JULIAN PAUNCEFOTE, FIRST BARON PAUNCEFOTE, PAPERS, 1887-1901. 3 items. London, England.

Letter from Julian Pauncefote, First Baron Pauncefote (1828-1902), British diplomat, to Townsend referring to Anglo-American relations; and two personal letters.

4090. PAW PAW LUMBER COMPANY LEDGER, 1903-1907. 1 vol. Paw Paw (Pike County), Ky.

Accounts for the lumber and mercantile operations of the Paw Paw Lumber Company.

4091. B. H. PAXSON WEIGHT BOOK, 1859. 1 vol. Washington, D.C.

Accounts listing weights of cattle.

4092. JOHN HOWARD PAYNE PAPERS, 1836. 2 items. New York, N.Y.

Letter from John Howard Payne (1791-1852) to John Ross, Cherokee leader, concerning a planned meeting of the two men; and an IOU to James Morris.

4093. JOHN WILLETT PAYNE PAPERS, 1789. 7 items. London, England.

Letters from William Ogilvie, member of the Irish House of Commons, to John Willett Payne (1752-1803), British naval officer, detailing the passage in the Irish Parliament of an address inviting the Prince of Wales to assume the regency.

4094. BOYD ELLSWORTH PAYTON PAPERS, 1929-1946. 164 items and 11 vols. Willingboro (Burlington County), N.J.

Miscellaneous papers of Boyd E. Payton (b. 1908), labor leader, include items on the poll tax in the South; pamphlets relating to labor unions and the South, the poll tax, and strikes; clippings dealing principally with the American Federation of Labor (AFL), AFL publicity, South Carolina Federation of Labor Convention, United Textile Workers of America convention, communists, and the Bessemer City strike; scrapbook, 1929, with clippings pertaining to the southern textile strike in that year; and scrapbook, 1946, containing information on the Danville (Virginia) Citizens' Committee, a group organized to fight inflation and high prices in Danville.

4095. MARY ANN PEABODY PAPERS, 1840-1892. 16 items. Petersburg (Dinwiddie County), Va.

Personal correspondence of Mary Ann Peabody, with references to Northerners who criticized slavery, George Parsons Lathrop, and traveling by stagecoach. Included are letters from Elizabeth Palmer Peabody, who introduced the kindergarten system into American education; Sophia (Peabody) Hawthorne, wife of Nathaniel Hawthorne; and Mary Tyler (Peabody) Mann, wife of Horace Mann.

4096. BERTA PEACE PAPERS, 1857-1867. 3 items. Brunswick County, Va.

Personal correspondence of the Peace family.

4097. SIR BARNES PEACOCK PAPERS, 1848-1890. 41 items. London, England.

Papers of Sir Barnes Peacock (1810-1890), British judge, include letters, 1856-1862, from Earl Canning, governor general of India, concerning the temporary replacement of Sir James Outram by Coverley Jackson, cases against Colonel Thompson and Lieutenant Gahagan, the suspension of Act 31 of 1855 on emigration, emigration to Grenada and Saint Lucia, a legislative matter in Bombay, the situation at Lucknow and Rohilkhand in 1858, the exile of the King of Delhi (Bahadur Shah II), Peacock's temporary management of the Home Department, the need for increase in the naval defense of India, the mutiny of the 5th European Regiment at Berhampore in 1859, and Peacock's work on the Penal Code Bill, 1860; letter, 1848, probably from Sir Christopher Rawlinson, commenting on Penang Island, Singapore, his salary, and work on the circuit; notes on the status of the Maharani of the Punjab, 1846-1849; letter, 1857, from Peacock giving a detailed account of the mutiny and rebellion throughout northern India; copy of the death and burial certificate of Elizabeth Mary Peacock, wife of Sir Barnes Peacock; correspondence, 1877-1883, between Sir Barnes and Emily Peacock concerning her marriage to his son, Frank, and the latter's financial situation; correspondence, 1882, between Peacock and Lord Selborne dealing with proposed legislation on the Court of Appeal in Britain and with Peacock's pension arrangements; and a printed first proof of a judgment delivered by Peacock for the Judicial Committee on the appeal of Raja Hurro Nath Roy Chowdhry Bahadoor v. Rundhir Singh and others.

4098. DRED PEACOCK BIBLIOGRAPHY. 1 vol. High Point (Guilford County), N.C.

List of newspaper and magazine articles, 1844-1873, on North Carolina history, compiled by Dred Peacock (1864-1934) and others, possibly including Charles Lee Raper. Accompanying the volume is a letter, 1939, from Peacock's son John R. Peacock to J. P. Breedlove, which comments on the authorship.

4099. JAMES B. PEAKE PAPERS, 1832-1846. 5 items. Twyman's Store (Spotsylvania County), Va.

Personal correspondence of James B. Peake, merchant, concerning employment as a schoolteacher, prices for plows, business conditions in Fredericksburg and Richmond, Virginia, and the continuation of the Chesapeake and Ohio Canal.

4100. JOHN HILLARD PEARCE PAPERS, 1792-1919. 360 items. Hoover Hill (Randolph County), N.C.

Miscellaneous papers of John Hillard Pearce (b. 1824), farmer and owner of a flour mill, include letters from relatives in Indiana and Kansas discussing personal matters, farming, and milling; land deeds; papers relating to the duties of John Hillard Pearce as clerk of the board of trustees of Tabernacle Township, with records of road maintenance and some school appointments; and a broadside, 1825, printed by John B. Troy against the State Bank of North Carolina.

4101. JOSEPHINE ANDERSON PEARSON PAPERS, 1886-1938. 192 items. Nashville (Davidson County), Tenn.

Miscellaneous papers of Josephine A. Pearson, teacher in various denominational colleges and civic leader, include clippings concerning her activities, personal correspondence, pictures, sketch of William L. Pearson, pamphlets, genealogical information on Mary Howell Bunton and the Roscoe and Pearson families, and coats of arms of those families.

4102.   SIR RICHARD PEARSON PAPERS, 1773.
        1 item.  London, England.

   Letter to Sir Richard Pearson
(1731-1806), British naval captain and
commander of the Serapis when defeated by
John Paul Jones and the Bonhomme Richard,
notifying him of his appointment as commander
of the Speedwell.

4103.   RICHMOND MUMFORD PEARSON PAPERS,
        1862-1921.  206 items and 1 vol.
        Yadkinville (Yadkin County), N.C.

   Papers of Richmond Mumford Pearson
(1805-1878), lawyer, state legislator, and
justice of the Supreme Court of North
Carolina, include petitions from men desiring
exemption from conscription during the Civil
War; papers relating to the arrests of John
Spears and M.L. Cranfield for aiding deserters
and those avoiding conscription; declarations
of various people concerning number of slaves
held; election returns from the Confederate
Army for North Carolina state officials and
officers of Yadkin County; 1864 grand jury
presentments for harboring deserters and
conscripts from the Confederate Army, for
harboring a witness from the state, and for
improper conduct toward a company of slaves;
two lists of Negroes, one for men to work on
Confederate fortifications; law notebook kept
by a student at the law school of Chief
Justice Pearson, primarily concerning property
law; and a letter, 1921, describing a riot of
Negroes and a lynching in Norlina, North
Carolina.

4104.   HENRY PEASE PAPERS, 1858.  1 item.
        Darlington, Durham, England.

   Letter from Samuel Morley to Henry
Pease (1807-1881), member of Parliament,
concerning the Parliamentary Reform Committee's plans for increased political activity.

4105.   ELIJAH WOLSEY PECK PAPERS, 1851-1879.
        27 items.  Tuscaloosa (Tuscaloosa
        County), Ala.

   Papers of Elijah Wolsey Peck, chief
justice of the Alabama Supreme Court, include
letters about the court records of his cases;
election returns from the headquarters of the
3rd Military District; letter protesting the
certification of the election of John B.
Callis as U.S. representative; and family
letters from his son, David Peck, while a
patient in the Washington Home, Chicago,
Illinois, in 1879.

4106.   MARTIN L. PECK PAPERS, 1869-1875.
        9 items.  Rainsburg (Bedford
        County), Pa.

   Letters to Martin L. Peck, schoolteacher, from friends who were also schoolteachers, discussing teachers' salaries,
curriculum, living expenses, tuition, and
other related matters.

4107.   PEDEN & KELLY PAPERS, 1835-1837.
        1 vol.  Wilkesboro (Wilkes
        County), N.C.

   Accounts of the mercantile firm of
Peden & Kelly recording items purchased
locally, including animal skins, whiskey,
grain, dairy products, cloth, tallow, and
other products.

4108.   BENJAMIN PEDRICK PAPERS, 1862-1864.
        31 items.  Fulton County, N.Y.

   Letters of William Pedrick, 115th
New York Infantry Regiment of Volunteers, to
his parents, Benjamin and Mary A. Pedrick,
and to his brother, Nelson Pedrick,
commenting on personal matters, camp life,
the presidential election of 1864, Copperheads in New York, Negroes, Generals
Ulysses S. Grant and Quincy Adams Gillmore,
and the activities of his regiment in
Virginia and Florida and on the coastal
islands of South Carolina.

4109.   JOHN C. PEDRICK PAPERS, 1863-1864.
        5 items.  New York, N.Y.

   Correspondence of John C. Pedrick
concerning speculation in cotton by treasury
and army agents, trade conditions and regulations, and the market for northern
merchandise in Tennessee and the lower
Mississippi Valley.

4110.   JOHN PEED COMMONPLACE BOOK, 1841-1847.
        1 vol.  (120 pp.)  Washington, D.C.

   Commonplace book of John Peed,
sailmaker in the U.S. Navy, containing drafts
or copies of letters, personal accounts, mess
accounts, diary entries, log entries, and
other miscellaneous records.

4111.   SALLIE SUE (ELLIS) PEEBLES PAPERS,
        1874-1926.  478 items.  Advance
        (Davie County), N.C.

   Papers of Sallie Sue (Ellis) Peebles,
music teacher and president of the county
branch of the Woman's Association for the
Betterment of Public School Houses, include
personal correspondence from friends and a
suitor, Thomas R. Wolfe; correspondence and
other papers concerning the work of the
Association; material on the Methodist
Episcopal Church, South; financial papers;
commencement and conference programs; invitations and cards; and miscellaneous printed
material.

4112.   PEEBLES FAMILY PAPERS, 1849-1908.
        12 vols.  Richmond, and Petersburg
        (Dinwiddie County), Va.

   The collection consists of John F.
Peebles's "Hoffman," an unfinished and
apparently unpublished historical novel in the
romantic tradition with the scene laid in
Virginia just prior to the American Revolution,
written in 1849; accounts as a Petersburg

physician, 1853-1855; Anne Lee Peebles's diaries, 1870 and 1878; and Helena Stockton Peebles's scrapbook, 1890, and diaries, 1901-1908.

4113. SIR ROBERT PEEL, SECOND BARONET, PAPERS, 1816-1864. 63 items. Tamworth, Staffordshire, England.

Papers of Sir Robert Peel, Second Baronet (1788-1850), member of Parliament, chief secretary for Ireland, home secretary, chancellor of the exchequer and first lord of the treasury, include personal correspondence and notes; letters to Sir William Knighton, private secretary of the King, concerning matters of importance to King George IV, including routine requests for the king's signature, the desire of General St. John for the King's sanction of a private undertaking in Brighton, the King's sponsorship of a society established in Manchester for the promotion of the fine arts, reports of the recorder at the Old Bailey and the need of the King to hold a council to receive the reports, and the petition of a school for financial aid; letter, 1826, from Peel concerning relations between England and Ireland, and British obligations towards the Irish economy; letter, 1837, from Peel to Sir James Emerson-Tennent discussing the parliamentary elections and the latter's defeat; letter, 1844, from Peel replying to a question in the House of Commons about the advance of French authority in the region of the Gabon River in French Equatorial Africa; routine correspondence dealing with requests for information and administrative matters; clippings about the birthplace and the death of Peel; and a letter from Sir Robert Peel, Third Baronet (1822-1895), commenting upon his appointment as Irish Secretary and comparing the situation in Ireland with what it was when his father held the same office.

4114. ALLEN W. PEGRAM PAPERS, 1834-1841. 2 vols. Guilford County, N.C.

Arithmetic book, 1834, and ciphering book, 1841.

4115. ARTHUR HARVEY THURSBY-PELHAM PAPERS, 1883-1886. 2 vols. Cound, Shropshire, England.

Volumes of Arthur Harvey Thursby-Pelham (b. 1874), clergyman of the Church of England, entitled "The Murray, 1883," and "The Murray, 1886," containing manuscripts written and bound together in the form of a monthly magazine. Compiled principally by Arthur Harvey Thursby-Pelham and his brother, Charles Augustus Thursby-Pelham (1871-1886), the volumes include stories, poetry, drawings, cards, two writings about the Charterhouse that Charles Thursby-Pelham attended, two watercolors, and antique cards for Christmas and the New Year.

4116. SILVIO PELLICO PAPERS. 2 items. Turin, Italy.

Poem entitled "A Dio" by Silvio Pellico (1789-1854), Italian patriot and author; and an engraving of a portrait of Pellico.

4117. SIR LEWIS PELLY PAPERS, 1875. 1 item. London, England.

Detailed, watercolor plan of the Commission Hall at Baroda, India, as it was arranged for the trial of the ruler of Baroda, Malhar Rāo, Gaekwar of Baroda, done by Dr. George Edwin Seward, Surgeon-Major of the Bombay Army, Baroda Residency Surgeon and Cantonment Magistrate at Baroda. On the reverse side of the plan is a notation and the signature of Sir Lewis Pelly (1825-1892), Indian official and then special commissioner for Baroda.

4118. LALLA PELOT PAPERS, 1852 (1857-1887) 1956. 249 items. Laurens (Laurens County), S.C.

Personal correspondence of the Pelot family and friends. Civil War letters from James Pelot and W. H. Sullivan discuss their experiences as Confederate soldiers in campaigns in northern Virginia, and at Edisto Island (South Carolina) and Kinston (North Carolina), respectively; information and rumors regarding the strength of opposing armies, tactics, and casualties; details of camp life, including food, morale, discipline, sanitary conditions, mail service, and furloughs; the shelling of Charleston, South Carolina; the devastation of the coastal plantations; and conscription and loyalty. Letters from other family members in South Carolina describe currency exchange ratios; the value of crops, especially corn; prices of land, real estate and foodstuffs; the approach of Union troops and plans to flee; and depredations by Union troops. The letters of Mrs. J. Ward Motte during the Reconstruction period discuss the prices of land, real estate and livestock; the behavior of the freedmen; the Union League; military occupation; various elections; fighting between blacks and whites during the election of 1870; and the appearance of new industry in Spartanburg, South Carolina. Scattered papers refer to education, including a record, 1863, of tuition-free scholars at Cross Hill Academy, South Carolina; and a report card, 1884, of the Newberry Female Academy, South Carolina. A letter dated only December 30 describes abolitionist activities in Laurens and Cokesbury, South Carolina.

4119. HENRY LAYFETTE PELOUZE PAPERS, 1841 (1854-1865) 1889. 171 items. Richmond, Va.

Family correspondence of Henry L. Pelouze, a Northern mechanic engaged in manufacturing type fonts and connected with the Richmond Branch Foundry. The collection includes letters from Pelouze to his wife, Jane (Tuthill) Pelouze; letters from Edward Pelouze, while manufacturing scales for weighing gold in San Francisco, California, 1850; letters referring to politics in Richmond in 1860, and business and political conditions there after the Civil War; and letters from Winfield Hanford Tuthill, written while in the Federal Army at Fortress Monroe (Virginia), Hilton Head and St. Helena's Island (South Carolina), and Fort Pulaski (Georgia).

4120. JOHN CLIFFORD PEMBERTON PAPERS, 1862. 1 item. Philadelphia, Pa.

Photocopy of a letter from Robert Chisolm to John C. Pemberton (1814-1881), officer in the U.S. Army and later the C.S.A. Army, complaining about soldiers stealing from Chisolm's island near Charleston, South Carolina. The letter was endorsed on the reverse side by Pemberton.

4121. CHARLES B. PENCE DIARY, 1899. 1 vol. (435 pp.) Quicksburg (Shenandoah County), Va.

Diary of a part-time farmer and plasterer.

4122. JACOB PENCE, JR., PAPERS, 1821-1875. 2 items and 4 vols. Shenandoah County, Va.

Mercantile records, including a fragment of an account book, 1859-1860; a ledger, 1841-1850; daybook, 1853-1860, of Jacob Pence, Jr., and John Bauserman; and a page from an account book. There is also a land deed from John Hisey and his wife, Jemima, to Jacob Pence, Jr.

4123. NETTIE PENCE DIARY, 1896. 1 vol. (240 pp.) Quicksburg (Shenandoah County), Va.

Diary of a schoolgirl.

4124. PERRY PENCE LEDGER, 1881-1892. 1 vol. (216 pp.) Edinburg (Shenandoah County), Va.

Business records of a small farm including accounts of debits and credits for hired help, milling, threshing, transportation of goods, blacksmith work, and service on roads.

4125. JOHN R. PENDELL PAPERS, 1817-1906. 1,527 items. Worcester (Worcester County), Mass.; and New York.

Personal correspondence of several generations of the family of John R. Pendell, teacher, salesman, and Baptist minister, and of the related F. D. Ingersoll and Jeduthan Stevens families, discussing family finances, social life and customs in Massachusetts and New York, the need for education for various members of the family, religion, temperance and prohibition, and the presidential elections of 1884 and 1888.

4126. DUDLEY DIGGES PENDLETON PAPERS, 1861-1865. 85 items. Jefferson County, W. Va.

Civil War letters of Dudley Diggs Pendleton (b. ca. 1841), acting adjutant general to his uncle, William Nelson Pendleton, brigadier general in the Confederate Army, written chiefly to his mother, Mrs. Hugh Nelson Pendleton, and to his brother, Robert, with comments on military activities, camp life, engagements with the enemy, death of Stonewall Jackson, family news, and sermons of William Nelson Pendleton to the soldiers.

4127. MADISON PENDLETON AND WILLIAM JAMES PENDLETON PAPERS, 1775 (1830-1890) 1932. 1,806 items. Louisa County, Va.

Family correspondence and financial papers, containing information on tobacco farming and Confederate military affairs. Included also are papers of David B. Harris and William Barret, related by marriage, and of David Bullock, William B. B. Walker, and other members of the Pendleton family.

4128. NATHANIEL PENDLETON PAPERS, 1781-1782. 3 items. Hyde Park (Dutchess County), N.Y.

Papers of Nathaniel Pendleton, farmer, jurist, and Revolutionary officer, consist of orders to troops in Georgia written by Pendleton as aide-de-camp for General Nathaniel Greene, and a letter from Joseph Clay to Pendleton concerning supplies for the Georgia troops and the seizure of British cargo ships.

4129. WILLIAM NELSON PENDLETON PAPERS, 1861-1862. 174 items. Lexington (Rockbridge County), Va.

Letters and papers of William Nelson Pendleton (1809-1883), Protestant Episcopal minister, chiefly concerning his services in the Confederate Army as a brigadier general and chief of artillery to Robert E. Lee. Included are commissions, telegrams, lists of ordnance, orders and requests for supplies, a list of captured material, special orders, contracts for supplies, a list of quartermaster's stores, and reports of officers. Among the correspondents are R. H. Chilton, Jubal A. Early, J. Gorgas, Wade Hampton, Joseph E. Johnston, Robert E. Lee, J. Letcher, and L. P. Walker.

4130. ABRAHAM PENN, SR., PAPERS, 1775-1813. 8 items. Martinsville (Henry County), Va.

Family correspondence and land indentures of Abraham Penn, Sr. (1743-1801), tobacco planter and manufacturer, and Virginia legislator.

4131. GREEN W. PENN PAPERS, 1764 (1830-1870) 1894. 180 items. Patrick County and Henry County, Va.

Personal and business correspondence of various members of the Penn family of Patrick and Henry counties, Virginia. Included is information on agricultural, commercial, and industrial aspects of tobacco; western migration and lands; life in Kentucky, Tennessee, Louisiana, and Alabama; Virginia politics and commodity prices in the 1840s; religious revivals; conflict within the Methodist Church in the 1840s over abolitionism; courts in Virginia; the defeat of General Winfield Scott in the presidential election of 1852; the hanging of several slaves; secessionist sentiment in the South; the Civil War, including discussions of the battles of First Manassas (Virginia) and Greenbrier (West Virginia), morale in the Confederate Army, sickness in the army, camp life, Confederate refugees, various Confederate officers, desertion, Jefferson Davis, supplies, the siege of Petersburg, depredations by Union troops, especially under William T. Sherman, and the prison at Point Lookout (Maryland); Radical Republicans; economic conditions during Reconstruction; freedmen; politics in New Orleans, 1874; the White League in Louisiana; the election of Rutherford B. Hayes; and other matters.

4132. JOHN PENN PAPERS, 1776-1920. 4 items. Granville County, N.C.

Copy of a letter to John Penn (1740-1788), signer of the Declaration of Independence for North Carolina, from John Adams concerning the establishment of a new government in case the colonies should declare themselves independent; a copy of Penn's will from the original in the office of the clerk of superior court of Granville County; a sketch of Penn's life by John Taylor; and a letter written to T. M. Pittman regarding John Penn from D. W. Taylor, who was descended from Penn.

4133. S. M. PENNIMAN PAPERS, 1827-1830. 12 items. New York, N.Y.

Personal letters from S. M. Penniman, New York merchant, to Mary Ann Tyler Peabody and her mother and sister, commenting on his connection with the Sunday school movement in New York.

4134. PENNSYLVANIA. PHILADELPHIA. CITY COMMISSIONERS. COUNTY AND CITY COMMISSIONERS' ELECTION RETURNS, 1843-1858. 52 items. Philadelphia, Pa.

Copies of selected pages from the County and City Commissioners' Election Returns, 1820-1858, from the Department of Records, Philadelphia, Pennsylvania, covering presidential, congressional, county, and municipal elections in the city and county of Philadelphia, 1843-1858.

4135. BENJAMIN PENNYBACKER DAYBOOK, 1812-1815. 1 vol. Pine Forge, Va.

Daybook of a general merchant and operator of Pine Forge.

4136. JOHN PEPPER PAPERS, 1847-1859. 12 items. Germanton (Stokes County), N.C.

The collection primarily consists of letters from Clarendon N. Pepper to his father, Dr. John Pepper, and concerns Clarendon's health, his experience at Emory and Henry College in Virginia, his marriage, and duty on the Stokes Circuit in the North Carolina Conference of the Methodist Episcopal Church, South. A few letters concern Dr. Pepper's services as a physician.

4137. SPENCER PERCEVAL PAPERS, 1806-1809. 7 items. London, England.

Correspondence relating to Perceval (1762-1812), British statesman and prime minister, 1809-1812, includes a letter concerning the inquiry into the conduct of Caroline Amelia Elizabeth, Princess of Wales, 1806; letters from John Morrison seeking the post of envoy to Delhi, India, and criticizing the East India Company; an invitation from Perceval to Edward Law, First Baron Ellenborough, to a formal dinner, 1807; a letter of Robert Dundas concerning the formation of Perceval's cabinet; and a letter of 1811 concerning Perceval's opinions of military events in Spain and Portugal.

4138. JUAN PÉREZ DE MONTALVÁN PAPERS. 3 items. Madrid, Spain.

Photocopies of parts 1 and 2 of a comedy, "La Puerta Macarena," by Montalván (1602-1638), poet and dramatist. The originals are in the Biblioteca Nacional, Madrid.

4139. JOHN P. PERKINS PAPERS, 1847-1851. 5 items. Brownsville (Haywood County), Tenn.

Letters to Major Robert Hairston concerning lands in the Brownsville vicinity.

4140. THOMAS PERKINS PAPERS, 1768-1790. 7 items. Kent County, Md.

The will of Thomas Perkins (d. 1768) and papers relating to the settlement of his estate.

4141. WILLIAM ROBERTSON PERKINS PAPERS, 1928-1948. 3 items. Lynchburg (Campbell County), Va., and New York, N.Y.

Papers relating to Perkins (1875-1945), counsel for James Buchanan Duke and trustee of the Duke Endowment, consisting of a copy of a letter on the relation of the university to its students, a clipping on the settlement of the Duke estate, and an article on Mary Carter Nelson, once governess in the Perkins home.

4142.   T. H. PERKINSON BANKBOOK, 1918. 1 item.   Charlottesville (Albemarle County), Va.

Savings passbook issued by the National Bank of Charlottesville.

4143.   WILLIAM H. PERKINSON PAPERS, 1882-1885.   3 vols.   Charlottesville (Albemarle County), Va.

Notes on philology relating to the work of a professor at the University of Virginia.

4144.   ABNER M. PERRIN PAPERS, 1847-1848. 2 items.   Edgefield District, S.C.

Correspondence of Perrin, a U.S. Army lieutenant concerning recruiting during the Mexican War and discharging the men afterward.

4145.   THOMAS C. PERRIN PAPERS, 1822 (1857-1895).   632 items and 2 vols.   Abbeville (Abbeville County), S.C.

Largely papers concerning Perrin's law practice in partnership with James S. Cothran, speculation in cotton, suits against the Greenville and Columbia Railroad, and affairs of the Presbyterian Church in South Carolina.   There are many letters and reports from cotton brokers and speculators in Charleston, including McGowan and Perrin, Jeffers & Cothran, George A. Trenholm and Son, and some reports from New York cotton brokers.   There is some correspondence in the 1850s with William S. Cothran, father of James S. Cothran, and president of the Rome Rail Road Company; plats of surveys of land belonging to the estate of Henry Laurens; printed matter regarding lawsuits of the Georgia, Carolina, and Northern Rail Road; and papers of L. W. Perrin, attorney for that railroad.   Several items deal with the Long Cane Presbyterian church of Abbeville County. Among other correspondents are Francis W. Dawson, Sr., William F. DeSaussure, Thomas Q. Donaldson, Alexander Cheves Haskell, Samuel McGowan, Thomas J. Robertson, William D. Simpson, Charles Henry Smith, and George A. Trenholm.

4146.   PERRONET FAMILY PAPERS, 1752-1855. 9 items and 3 vols.   Shoreham, Kent, England.

This collection consists principally of a scrapbook containing correspondence, reproductions of engravings, poetry, autographs, a pencil drawing, and an account of astrological incidents.   The correspondence is related to the Perronet family and other early leaders of the Wesleyan movement in England.   Included are letters from Vincent Perronet to his children and grandchildren stating his religious beliefs and moral principles; a letter of John Perronet, Vincent's son, defending John Locke against John Hildrop and Robert Clayton; and letters of John Wesley to Vincent Perronet's grandson-in-law, Peard Dickinson, concerning doctrinal matters and family and personal subjects.   Other authors include Charles Wesley, Sarah Wesley, Joseph Benson, Adam Clarke, James Dixon, Joseph Entwisle, John William Fletcher, Mary (Bosanquet) Fletcher, Thomas Jackson, Henry Moore, and Richard Watson.   There are engravings of John Wesley, Vincent Perronet, and Joseph Benson and a pencil drawing of William Perronet.   An account, apparently by Vincent Perronet, describes two appearances of a bright star followed by deaths in the community.   There are a printed account of the last words of Charles Wesley and a clipped obituary of Edith Thompson, great-granddaughter of Vincent Perronet.   Loose items include a discourse by Charles Perronet on man's need for religion; diaries of an unidentified young woman commenting on sermons and spiritual life; and miscellaneous letters and autographs.

4147.   ALGERNON S. PERRY AND JEREMIAH PERRY PAPERS, 1761 (1830-1850) 1891.   132 items. Franklin County, N.C.

Indentures, wills, other legal documents, and a few letters of the Perry family, large landowners and slaveholders. The most significant document is the will of Jeremiah Perry, father of Algernon Perry, 1838, leaving the property to his wife and ten children.

4148.   ALLEN C. PERRY PAPERS, 1839-1860. 11 items.   Franklinton (Franklin County), N.C.

Family correspondence of Allen C. Perry, probably a planter, including an explanation of the grading system of Midway Academy, North Carolina, in which his son was enrolled.

4149.   BENJAMIN FRANKLIN PERRY PAPERS, 1849-1867.   9 items.   Greenville (Greenville County), S.C.

Letters from Benjamin F. Perry (1805-1886), prominent South Carolina Unionist, member of U.S. Congress, 1836-1844, founder and editor of the Southern Patriot, and provisional governor of South Carolina, addressed to Armistead Burt of Abbeville, South Carolina, dealing with sequestration of property in 1863; the passage of civil rights bills; and private lawsuits.

4150. EBENEZER PERRY ACCOUNT BOOK, 1842-1844. 1 vol. [North Carolina?]

Accounts of a general merchant.

4151. JAMES PERRY PAPERS, 1812. 1 item. London, England.

A letter from James Perry (1756-1821), British journalist, asking George Hanger for a statement concerning a parliamentary investigation of funds awarded Hanger for his services during the War of the American Revolution.

4152. VESTAL W. PERRY PAPERS, 1831 (1860-1890) 1900. 1,028 items and 1 vol. High Point (Guilford County), N.C.

Letters and papers of Vestal W. Perry, planter, operator of a country store and whiskey distillery, and justice of the peace. The collection contains a few legal papers; papers from the U.S. Internal Revenue Office regarding whiskey taxes; notes concerning purchases of fertilizer by tobacco farmers; and some information on farm conditions and prices in Missouri and Indiana, 1866-1886. Included also is a ledger of mercantile accounts.

4153. WILSON PERRY AND JAMES DAVIS PAPERS, 1839-1878. 18 items. Perquimans County, N.C.

Letters and papers concerning the operation of a gristmill by Wilson Perry and James Davis near Woodville, North Carolina. One letter, 1865, written by the Federal assistant superintendent of Negro affairs, orders Davis to free some Negroes.

4154. PRESLEY CARTER PERSON PAPERS, 1767 (1829-1897) 1915. 2,500 items. Louisburg (Franklin County), N.C.

Miscellaneous bills, deeds, accounts, and correspondence of Presley C. Person (1770-1845); of his son, Thomas A. Person, and of his family; and of Willie Mangum Person (1862-1930), nephew of Thomas A. Person. The earliest papers are largely confined to deeds and copies of wills; later papers, centering around Presley C. Person, consist generally of letters and documents pertaining to the settlement of his estate with Thomas A. Person as administrator. The bulk of the collection concerns Thomas A. Person and his family, including legal papers; numerous letters in the 1840s and 1850s to Theophilus Perry from his father, Levin Perry, written from New Orleans, Louisiana, and Harrison County, Texas; letters during 1860 from Harriet (Person) Perry, wife of Theophilus Perry, in Texas, and during the war years many letters (bulk of the war correspondence) between the two; and letters from Jesse H. H. Person (d. 1863) and M. P. Person, Confederate soldiers, concerning military activities and army life. Included also are business letters and family letters filled with Civil War reminiscences; and school and college letters from various members of the family while at the following North Carolina schools: Raleigh Female Classical Institute, 1835; Wake Forest College, 1853; Warrenton Female College, 1860; and the University of North Carolina, 1860. Included also are a diary of Harriet Perry, 1869; a few business papers of W. P. Montgomery; business and personal letters of Willie Mangum Person, attorney and son of Joseph Arrington Person; and during the 1890s, a few family and personal letters of "Mrs. Joe Persons," famous for the preparation and sale of a patent medicine (only one letter concerns "Mrs. Joe Person's Remedy"). In 1904 a number of letters are addressed to Mrs. W. P. Montgomery from quacks and operators of sanatoriums concerning various remedies.

4155. PERUVIAN COLLECTION PAPERS, 1580-1892. 42 items and 21 vols, Peru.

This collection of heterogeneous material, generally relating to the colonial period of Peru, falls roughly into three groups centering around commerce and industry, literary activity, and religious and social history. Several manuscripts in the first group contain information on the mining of mercury, 1786-1787. Literary materials include the poems of Caviedes, in seventeenth century script useful for correcting errors in the copies published by Ricardo Palma; a copy of the iconoclastic and mysterious poems by Antonio de Solís; one cuaderno of the <u>Documentos históricos</u> collected by Manuel de Odriozola; and three <u>Documentos literarios</u> from contemporary publications. Among the items relating to religion and social history are a compilation of the papers of Peruvian viceroys and others, 1580-1818; an <u>expediente</u> concerning witchcraft and idolatry <u>in Peru</u>; original papers of the Provincial Council at Lima, 1772-1773, relating to the debate within the church on the modernization of learning which Charles III attempted to impose upon the empire; copy of the proceso of Tupac Amaru; and a booklet, 1794, describing the founding and development of Quito, Ecuador.

Each item and volume is listed below, with some explanation. Some of these items, formerly the property of Don Francisco Pérez de Velasco, are included in <u>Cátalogo de la Biblioteca Peruana Propriedad de Dn. Francisco Perez de Velasco</u> (Lima, 1918). For convenience in listing, the items are numbered, some singly and others in groups, according to content and author or compiler.

(1) Adios a Garcia Moreno. 26 de junio de 1866. Guayaquil. (Printed broadside.) (2) <u>El Aguila de Condorcunca</u>. 13 de febrero de 1847. Suplemento. (Article entitled "Frustrado proyecto de monarquia en Colombia. Epitome de la memoria documentada que redacta el año de 1833, el jeneral de

Colombia Jose Domingo Espinar, antiguo secretario del Libertador Simon Bolivar.") (3) Al Excelentísimo Señor Libertador de Colombia y el Perú de su apasionadisimo admirador Antonio Gonrater. 1825. Estracto del Itinerario de la Provincia de Santa Cruz de esta Republica, hasta la Provincia de San Pablo, perteneciente al Imperio del Brasil. (4) Alto Perú. Cartas Topograficas. Atlas No. 1. Quito, Ecuador. 1794. (A historical summary of the founding, peopling, and development of the city of Quito, Ecuador, prepared by Juan Ascaray, a notary of His Majesty. It contains a chronological list of bishops of Quito and is based upon documents in the archives of the city in 1794, especially a manuscript work by Dr. Miguel Sánchez Solmirón, dean of the cathedral. (5) Apuntamientos de novedades. [A unique document concerned with the succession of Charles II (1665-1700).] (6) Arequipa. Prefectura. Correspondencia. 1841. (Illuminates the political activities of Ramón Castilla and Miguel San Román.) (7) Francisco Xavier Montero, Boloños de los Reyes. Papeles que pertenecen a . . . Caracas, 1765-1770. (Petition, autos, and testimonials concerning the quality and purity of race [limpieza de sangre] of Francisco Montero Bolonos as a prerequisite for a license.) (8) Callao, Peru. Libro de la razon de salidas correspondiente a la contaduría de los efectos que registran en las embarcaciones que salen del puerto del Callao asi para los reynos de España y otros puertos de esta mar del sur en el presente año de 1774; Libro duplicado de alcaldía donde consta al entrada y salida de efectos de almacenaje á cargo de administrador del puerto del Callao, D. Manuel Lastra. 1823 (An important official document relative to the trade of Callao toward the close of the Wars of Independence.); and Estado jeneral de la matricula de los buques mercantes nacionales, su clasificacion, estade y jiro. 16 julio de 1853. (Printed broadside.) (9) Pedro Candamo, April 17, 1860, Lima, Peru. (Letter from an unidentified person to Pedro Candamo discussing the planned delivery by Candamo of a thousand ounces of gold, giving detailed instructions and threatening Candamo with death if the task is not performed.) (10) Convenio celebrado entre los generales de los ejércitos titulados nacional y del gobierno de Chile. May 3, 1814. [Signatories: Gabino Gainza (ca. 1750-1825), Juan Mackenna (1771-1814), Bernardo O'Higgins (1776-1842).] (11) Jose María Córdova y Urrutia. Restablecimiento de los archivos destruidos para formar una exacta historia del Perú. (Copy.) (12) Descripción geográfica, demonstrativa y evidente de la cuidad de Lambayeque su cituacion y extencion. Numero de pueblos y havitantes de todo su partido sur cabildos y tribunales, edificios, segun la razon estadistica que se pide, y en que abraza se enumeración el estado politico y militar, el económico civil . . . . (13) Eguidio a su amigo. Diálogo. (A hypothetical discourse between the old and the new.) (14) Esquadron de la Guarda de Honor del Excelentísimo Señor Virrey. 1 de Agosto de 1817. (A report on the Viceroy's Honor Guard, giving the number of men, horses, etc.) (15) Expediente sobre las expediciones de 1814 y 1815 por Andamarco reconocimiento de las Montañas Peruanas. (A file on the exploratory expeditions or entradas made via the town of Andamarca to the confluence of the "Pangoa and the Chanchamayo" by the Franciscan Fray Paulo Alonso Carvallo, guardian of the missionary College of Santa Rosa de Ocopa and others, in order to "restore" certain missions. Copied by Friar Julian Bovo de Revello in 1847, the manuscript consists of a letter from Carvallo to the Governor Intendent, minutes of the town council of Andamarca, and a diary of the entradas.) (16) Extracto del Viage de Mr. de la Condamine de la Academia Real de las Ciencias a su regreso de la medida del grado terrestre en Quito por el Rio de las Amazonas en el Año de 1743. (Brief account of the nearly two year journey of Carlos María de La Condamine from Quito, Ecuador, to France by way of the Marañon and Amazon rivers, containing data on latitude, longitude, velocity of rivers, width and depth of streams, and observations on altitude.) (17) Tomas Florenz. Prontuario de capellanías fundadas en el Peru. 1821. (Ecclesiastical data, generally copied from the archives of the order, covering the seventeenth and eighteenth centuries.) (18) José de Larrea de Loredo. Observación sobre el carácter de los indios. (19) Libro real del ramo de azogue de los reales almazenes de Santa Barbara de Lima al cargo del guarda de ellos e inspección del interventor que corre desde 1 de enero hasta el diziembre de 1786. Lima, 1786; and Libro manual de entrada, salida y existencia de los azogues que se hallan en los almacenes de ellos desde el 1 de enero de 1787 hasta fin de diziembre de el. Por Francisco Angel Bravo de Rueda. 1787. (Important, but restricted, sources of information on mercury production at Huancavelica and in the province of Huarochiri.) (20) Lima, Peru (Province). Concejo provincial. Paraceres que se han dado sobre los puntos pertenecientes al actual concilio provincial, celebrado en esta ciudad de los Reyes del Perú. Años de 1772 y 1773. (Copy of an invaluable collection of official opinions handed down by the Concilio provincial); and Copia de los inventarios de las alhajas de este Santa Iglesia metropolitana de los Reyes. 20 de enero de 1797. (21) Lima y San. Martín. o apuntes para la historia de la primera epoca de la Patria en Lima. 1821-1822. (A letter, dated Rio de Janeiro, August 15, 1822, in which the author [signed Un Arequipeno] charges General San Martin and Bernardo Monteagudo with tyranny, "robberies," and assassinations.) (22) Angel Luque. Memoria. Lima. (23) El Mercurio peruano. (Copy of a treatise on the origins of this celebrated periodical. Papeles varios en la Biblioteca Nacional.) (24) Antonio Álvarez Morán. Libro de cuentas correspondientes á la general que el albacea lleva con la testamentaría del finado D. Antonio Álvarez Morán, desde 4 de julio de 1820. Lima. (25) Pascual Antonio Monzon. Data de los pesos que voy pagando en vertud de decretos del superior gobierno y demas tribunales a saber. Penas de camara. Desde 1 de agosto de 1777. (26) Manuel de Odriozola (1804-1889). Colección de documentos históricos. Lima, 1860. Cuaderno 3; Colección de poesías modernas recogidas y copiadas por . . . Lima. 1837-1857. 3 cuadernos manuscritos. [Selections of poetry assembled by Odriozola consisting chiefly of sonnets, several lyrics, and some burlesque forms. Several pieces were transcribed from the initial volume of El Mercurio peruano (1791), and from El Comercio (1696, 1700). Of the six contemporary Latin American poets represented and indentified four are Peruvians: Manuel Nicolás Corpancho (1830-1863), José Joaquín Larrvia (1780-1832), Felipe Pardo y Aliaga (1806-1868), Manuel Ascencio Segura (1805-1871); one Colombian: Rafael Pombo (1833-1912); one Venezuelan: Juan Vicente Camacho (1829-1874)]; article by John M. Fein entitled "Una version desconocide de un poema de Pombo," in El Colombiano, "Supplemento" (May 3, 1953), on a poem in Colección de poesías modernas . . . ; and papeles varios de la Biblioteca Nacional. 102 pages. [Manuscript copies of originals in the Biblioteca Nacional. There are poetical works by Felipe Pardo y Aliaga (1806-1868) and Juan del Valle y Caviedes (1652-1692). Among the prose selections are: "Introducción a la historia de los Incas del Perú." (Del Mercurio peruano, 9 de setiembre de 1792); and Alvaro Navia Boloños y Moscoso, "Fundacion de la iglesia y convento de la compañia de Jesus que se arruñio en la inundación del mar en el Callao a cause del terremota del 28 de octubre de 1746."] (27) Dominique Catherine de Pérignon, 1754-1818. Memoria presentada por el embajador de Francia al excmo. señor principe de la paz. Madrid. 25 de abril de 1797. (Inquiry relative to a naval engagement between English and Spanish warships and a statement of policy by the representatives of the Directory.) (28) Peru. Balance del antiguo ramo de Jerusalem y Cautivos, conforme a las liquidaciones practicadas en el libro respectivo y ultimos datos presentados en la visita hasta 31 de diciembre de 1869. Lima. 18 de marzo de 1870. (Broadside.); Customs rates and accounts of shipments from Cuzco, 1811, 1816; Ministerio de hacienda. Cuaderno de oficios y consultas que empezó á correr el año de 1825. (Lima, 1825); Presidente (Ramón Castilla, 1845-1851), Discurso del presidente de la república, al cerrar las sesiones del congreso extraordinario de 1850; Presidente (Miguel San Román), Mensaje del presidente de la república, al congreso de 1863; Vice-presidente (Mariano H. Cevallos), Mensaje del primer vice presidente de la república, July 28, 1872. (Speech to the Peruvian congress upon his succession to the presidency); Documentos inéditos, 1580-1818. (31 original manuscript documents. Twelve are by the several viceroys of Peru, namely, Francisco Toledo, García Hurtado de Mendoza, Pedro Toledo y Leyva, Francisco Gil de Taboada de Lemos, and José Fernando de Abascal y Sousa); Viceroyalty, Testimonio de los autos seguidos contra Mariano Tupac Amaru y Andrés Mendigure sobre atribuirseles la reincidencia en la revelion, Año de 1783, Real Sala del Crimen, Escribano de camara, Don Clemente Castellanos, 1780-1783. (Typescript from the original in a volume of Manuscritos varios deposited in the Biblioteca nacional del Perú. There are six cuadernos consisting of 372 pages numbered consecutively. The half title is "Rebelion de Tupac Amaro. Tomo I.") and Documentos reservados en los autos criminales contra Mariano Tupac Amaru y Andres Mendigure sobre reincidencias y posteriores excesos cometidos de resultas de la nueva sublevacion acaesida en los altos de Marcapata Provincia de Quispicanchi. (Typescript of manuscript documents in the Biblioteca y Archivo Nacional, Lima, Peru, bound in a book entitled "Rebelion de Tupac Amaru, Tomo II"; and an incomplete typescript of the same volume.); and Viceroyalty, Expediente sobre brujerías, hechizos y maleficios de Indios en el Perú. (Original folio manuscript volume containing two cedulas signed by Charles III and IV urging the bishops not to falter in efforts to convert the Indians.) (29) Gonzalo Pizarro (1502-1548). Colección de cartas de Gonzalo Pizarro, del licenciado Gasca y de Cepeda. (30) Poesias del Colegio Maximo de San Pablo de la Compañia de Jesus. Lima, Peru, 1768. (Latin poems of the Jesuit "major college of St. Paul" in Lima on the occasion of the death of Elizabeth Farnese, the Queen.) (31) Poesías sagradas de diversos autores. Lima, Peru, 1831. (Several poems and Spanish translations of well-known religious pieces.) (32) Real Cedula de 24 diciembre del año pasado de 1788. (Decree announcing to the citizens of Peru the death of Charles III and the accession of Charles IV.) (33) Diego SaManiego. Letter book, 1587, containing the following: Copia de unas cartas del padre Diego SaManiego para el padre Julio De Atiencia provincial del Piru de la misión de Santa Cruz de la Sierra del año de 1587; copia de una del padre Francisco de Angulo que escribió de la provincia de Tacumen al padre Julio De Atiencia provincial del Piru de la Ciudad de Cordova; copia de otra del mismo padre al padre provincial en Cordova; copia de otra de Santiago del mismo padre al padre provincial; copia de una del padre Barzana de Cordova provincial de Tucuman al mismo padre provincial; and copia de otra del padre Barzana al mismo padre provincial de Santiago de Tucuman. (34) Carlos Paz Soldan. A mis conciudadanos. Lima, Peru. 1892. (Printed. An expression of views upon constitutional guarantees.) (35) Antonio de Solís. Obras liricas. (The undated original of this typescript is contained in a volume of manuscritos various at the Biblioteca nacional del Perú. There are 104 poems written in several forms including sonnets, ballads, and a few occasional poems.) (36) Spain. Sovereigns, etc., 1556-1598 (Philip II). Cédula . . . sobre los bienes de las fabricas y hospitales. 29 de enero de 1587. (Copy. Relative to Peru. Bound with this volume is a document, nuevas minas en este reyo de Nueva España . . ., 1787, a memorial on the Philippine trade entering and leaving Acapulco with data on mercury mines.) (37) Ventura

Travada. El suelo de Arequipa convertido en cielo; an el extreno del religioso monasterio de Santa Rosa de Santa Maria que fundó el illmo. S. D. D. Juan Bravo del Rivero y Correa del consejo de su magestad dignisimo obispo de Arequipa. (A copy of the original in the Biblioteca Nacional del Perú. First published in 1752, it was reprinted in Odriozola, Documentos literarios, X [Lima, 1877]. The volume is replete with details of the ecclesiastical history of the city.) (38) Juan del Valle y Caviedes (1652-1692). Colección de sus poesias, siglo XVII. (Apparently a seventeenth-century copy but more comprehensive than any published work of the Peruvian poet. According to a typed memorandum of Pérez de Velasco dated Lima, March 26, 1908, this collection is more nearly complete than those published by Ricardo Palma, and Felix Cipriano Coronel Cegarra.) (39) Viage que hizieron á Manoa los RRS. PP. Fray Manuel Gervasio Gil, Fray Valentin Arrieta y Fray Francisco de San Josef. 1767. [Manuel Gervasio Gil (1745-1807), an eminent Franciscan mathematician and physicist, was apparently the leader of this missionary expedition to the legendary country of el dorado. Information on the Indians is included.] (40) Versos dichos en Tacubaya en el convite que el Señor virrey arzobispo dió al señor diputado del Perú. El doctor Olmedo incitado por Su Excelencia Ilustrisima [1826]. (Internal evidence suggests that these lines were written at the time of the Panama Congress, the final meetings of which were held at Tacubaya.) (41) Peru (Viceroyalty). Caja Real de Lima. Razon de las Entradas diarias asi por lo que producen los Ramos de Administracion como los pertenecientes a la Contaduria, 1766-1767. (A daily record, 95 pp., of sums paid by merchants, landowners, et al. to the royal treasury in Lima.)

4156. DON PRESTON PETERS PAPERS, 1952. 2 items. Lynchburg (Campbell County), Va.

A list of the autographs and printed items collected by Don Preston Peters, a philatelist, and a clipping from the Lynchburg News, November 9, 1952, describing the acquisition of the Peters collection by Duke University Library. Manuscripts formerly owned by Peters comprise portions of two hundred and thirteen separate collections in this catalog.

4157. DON T. C. PETERS PAPERS, 1815 (1860-1872) 1881. 310 items. Lynchburg (Campbell County), Va.

Papers of a merchant and stock speculator, consisting of business letters, bills, receipts, and checks. Topics include stock speculation, zinc stocks, mercantile accounts, silverware, personal debts, banking in New York and in Lynchburg, land speculation in Iowa, and agricultural machinery. Writers of letters and other persons mentioned in the collection include Charles Minor Blackford, Sr. (1833-1903); Thomas Stanhope Flournoy (1811-1883); William Hurley; Frank G. Peters; J. M. McJimsey; John R. Garland; Paul Carrington Callaway (1815-1876); Abraham Lincoln; Ulysses S. Grant; Grenville Mellen Dodge; D. T. Williams; Oddie & St. George (firm); John Goode, Jr.; Lieutenant Coles Peters, C.S.A.; and Don T. C. Peters.

4158. REBECCA (VANSICKLES) PETERS PAPERS, 1882. 1 item. Eldora (Hardin County), Iowa.

Letter from James G. Vansickles, brother of Rebecca Peters and a farmer of Orangeville, Texas, describing his reasons for moving from Kansas to Texas, and social and economic conditions.

4159. PETERSBURG (VIRGINIA) FRANKLIN SOCIETY MINUTES, 1821-1824. 1 vol.

Minutes of a literary and debating society.

4160. ELISHA A. PETERSON PAPERS, 1862-1865. 62 items. Springdale (Hamilton County), Ohio.

Letters of a private in the 4th Ohio Volunteer Cavalry, Army of the Cumberland, and of his father, Jacob S. Peterson of Springdale, Ohio, describing army life in Tennessee, Georgia, and Alabama; the battles of Murfreesboro, 1863, and Chattanooga, 1863; respect of the soldiers for General W. S. Rosecrans; the occupation of Atlanta; Unionists in Lauderdale County, Alabama; secessionists and Copperheads in Kentucky and Ohio; punishment of a thief, a mutineer, and a deserter; the execution of spies, including a woman; and a rumored conspiracy to release the Confederate prisoners on Johnson's Island, Sandusky Bay, Ohio, November, 1863.

4161. JANE PETERSON PAPERS, 1850 (1860-1899) 1927. 163 items. Hickory (Catawba County), N.C.

Letters of John Peterson, North Carolina farmer, gunsmith, and Confederate soldier, describe to his family hardships of military life, 1864-1865; letters of his sister, Rhoda Hawn, Ironton, Missouri, and brother, Daniel, Fredericktown, Missouri, discuss domestic problems on the frontier, radical opinions, prices, and railroad and mining prospects; and letters of Jacob Peterson concern sheepherding and mining speculation in Montana during the 1880s and 1890s.

4162. PETIGRU FAMILY PAPERS, 1816-1842. 7 items. Charleston, S.C.

Legal and business papers of James Louis Petigru, an attorney and politician; and personal letters from family members to James's brother, Charles Petigru, including a description of White Sulphur Springs, West Virginia.

4163. F. D. PETIT DE VILLERS PAPERS, 1805, 1828. 2 items. Savannah, Ga.

A letter of Petit de Villers concerning consular affairs and a business letter of Major James Hamilton, Jr., of Charleston, South Carolina.

4164. C. A. PETREA COMMONPLACE BOOK, 1861-1863. 1 vol. (122 pp.) Mount Pleasant (Cabarrus County), N.C.

Addresses, diary entries, and verse concerning love, secession, peace, and Southern life.

4165. WILLIAM PETTET PAPERS, 1828. 1 item. Bellefonte (Centre County), Pa.

A letter from F. M. Ewen of Fredericksburg, Ohio, discussing the presidential campaign of 1828 in Ohio.

4166. EBENEZER PETTIGREW PAPERS, 1833-1850. 13 items. Sumterville (Sumter County), Ala.

General family correspondence among which are two letters dealing with the question of Nullification, 1833, one from Joseph H. Pettigrew, and one from R. H. Pettigrew, both of South Carolina.

4167. JAMES JOHNSTON PETTIGREW PAPERS, 1 item. Charleston, S.C.

An undated letter from Pettigrew, attorney, to his niece upon the birth of her son.

4168. THOMAS JOSEPH PETTIGREW PAPERS, 1815. 1 item. London, England.

A letter to Pettigrew (1791-1865), surgeon, from Captain Bissell Harvey, private secretary of the Duke of Kent, conveying sentiments on the death of Dr. John Coakley Lettsom.

4169. JOHN UFFOLD PETTIT PAPERS, 1824-1860. 45 items. Wabash (Wabash County), Ind.

Letters to Pettit, chiefly from his father, George C. Pettit of Albany and Fabius, New York; and from friends. Topics include party politics in New York and Indiana and the elections of 1840 in New York and of 1844 in Maine. There is also information on schools and colleges and school and college life in New York and Rhode Island, the temperance movement in Indiana, and some mention of the Oregon question.

4170. ANNIE E. PETTY PAPERS, 1847 (1860-1911). 86 items. Culpeper Court House (Culpeper County), Va.

Family letters of the Petty, Hill, and Stanton families of Virginia origin, which had divided before the Civil War, settling in Virginia, Indiana, and Alabama. Topics include postwar politics and society in Virginia and Texas; Governor Andrew Jackson Hamilton of Texas; and Texas land claimed by Mollie F. Hill of Oak Park, Virginia, and Annie E. Petty of Culpeper 1892-1893, with lengthy discussion of Texas land and inheritance laws.

4171. WILLIAM PETTY, FIRST MARQUIS OF LANSDOWNE, PAPERS, 1779-1798. 5 items. Bowood, Wiltshire, England.

Miscellaneous correspondence concerning the experience of George Cartwright as a privateer; the French fleet off the English coast, 1779; elections of 1790; personal finances; and the crisis in Ireland, 1798.

4172. WILLIAM C. PETTY AND COMPANY DAYBOOK, 1889-1890. 1 vol. (480 pp.) Archdale (Randolph County), N.C.

Daybook of a lumber, building, and contracting firm.

4173. ROBERT EDEN PEYTON PAPERS, 1827 (1843-1850) 1876. 52 items. Fauquier County, Va.

Correspondence between the families of Dr. Robert E. Peyton (1804-1872), physician of Loudoun and Fauquier counties, Virginia, and Mrs. Peyton, and the family of General Walter Jones of Washington, D.C. Many of the letters to Dr. Peyton are addressed from Reverend Joseph Packard, his brother-in-law, concerning affairs of the Protestant Episcopal Church.

4174. JOHN SMITH PHELPS PAPERS, 1850-1853. 3 items. Springfield (Greene County), Mo.

Letters to Phelps concerning Missouri politics and Thomas Hart Benton.

4175. [MURRAY?] N. PHELPS PAPERS, 1892-1894. 6 items and 1 vol. Birmingham, England.

Included is a diary of a transatlantic voyage in 1892, containing descriptions of Quebec, Montreal, Winnipeg, railroads in Canada, Great Lakes steamships, sports, Ducks Station and other places in the Canadian Rockies, ranch life and hunting trips, Vancouver during a smallpox epidemic, Victoria, and Victoria's Chinatown.

4176. WILLIAM PHELPS PAPERS, 1839, 1897. 2 items. London, England.

A letter, 1839, by Phelps (1776-1856), concerning his work on projected later volumes of his History and Antiquities of Somersetshire (London: 1836-1839); and a note from a Bristol bookseller, Walter Nield.

4177. R. JOHANNA PHILBRICK PAPERS, 1849-1890. 26 items. Savannah, Ga.

Poems, largely sentimental, by Philbrick; printed verses written by her and distributed as New Year's greetings by the Savannah *Morning News*; genealogical data on the family of Kate (Philbrick) and Daniel H. Baldwin; letters from Johanna Philbrick to her family; and a description of Charleston, South Carolina, in 1874.

4178. PHILIP II, KING OF SPAIN, PAPERS, 1571. 1 item. Madrid, Spain.

A letter to Cardinal de Granuela introducing Alexandro Buondore as Spanish representative at Rome.

4179. PHILIPPINE ISLANDS PAPERS, 1806-1886. 7 items.

Miscellaneous items including records concerning a contract between Augustin Leocadio de Landaburu and the Royal Company of the Philippines, 1806-1809; and a description of the colonization of the Island of Paragua, 1886.

4180. GEORGE SHARLANDE PHILLIPS POEMS, 1818-1880. 1 vol. [Richmond, Va.?]

A handwritten book of George S. Phillips's poems, generally concerning the South and various occasions.

4181. HENRY MYER PHILLIPS PAPERS, 1852. 1 item. Philadelphia, Pa.

A letter of Phillips, an attorney, concerning recompense for goods damaged in shipment.

4182. J. C. PHILLIPS, JOHN PHILLIPS, AND SAM L. PHILLIPS PAPERS, 1883-1927. 6 vols. Wing (Mitchell County), N.C.

Daybooks and ledgers of a general mercantile firm.

4183. JESSE PHILLIPS PAPERS, 1846-1865. 17 items. Lumberton (Robeson County), N.C.

Chiefly letters about personal affairs and the Civil War in Virginia, North Carolina, and Georgia. Correspondents include Levi L. Phillips, of the 2nd Regiment of North Carolina Infantry Volunteers, who describes the U.S. Navy blockade of Norfolk, Virginia, and Union and Confederate leadership, 1861; and Edmund M. Phillips, a Confederate soldier at Wilmington, North Carolina, who comments on military and naval actions there, 1862. Other subjects discussed include antebellum commodity prices in Georgia; wartime desertion; the Atlanta Campaign; the siege of Petersburg; the 31st Regiment of North Carolina Infantry Volunteers; camp life; casualties; food; and sickness.

4184. JOHN B. PHILLIPS PAPERS, 1845-1898. 11 items and 1 vol. Selma (Dallas County), Ala.

Included are a letter, 1873, of John Young Kilpatrick of Camden, Alabama, concerning hard times and the destitution of many Negroes; a letter of Edward C. Jones of Selma, announcing his candidacy for the office of state senator; a commonplace book recording physician's accounts, descriptions of drugs, and remedies; and several bills.

4185. SARAH ELLEN (McILWAIN) PHILLIPS PAPERS. 1 item. Selma (Dallas County), Ala.

Typescript reminiscence of Wilson's raid on Selma, 1865, describing depredations by Union troops and the loyalty of slaves to their owners.

4186. WILLIAM HORACE PHILLIPS PAPERS, 1859-1881. 123 items. Boydton (Mecklenburg County), Va.

Family correspondence and papers of William H. Phillips, the son of a plantation overseer, as a private in the Confederate Army. The letters give a general idea of army supplies and stores and of Phillips's movements from point to point in Virginia. The later material consists of copies of ballads and some original verse by Phillips.

4187. BENJAMIN PHILPOT CASH BOOK, 1841-1849. 1 vol. (180 pp.) Isle of Man.

Household accounts of Philpot, archdeacon of Sodor and Man.

4188. WILLIAM M. PIATT PAPERS, 1843 (1845-1883) 1904. 512 items. Tunkhannock (Wyoming County) and Harrisburg (Dauphin County), Pa.

Correspondence of Piatt, an attorney of Tunkhannock and a Democratic politician and member of the state legislature, relating to private legal affairs and to state legislation and politics, including bills concerning the North Branch Canal and Towanda Bridge and the price of coal; temperance and prohibition; state roads; railroads; banks; and miscellaneous acts. There is much on the Democratic Party in Pennsylvania; economic conditions; elections and appointments; Federal politics and appointments during the Civil War; patronage during Reconstruction; and mention of the effect of western railroads on land values. Correspondents include T. M. Atherton of Huntsville; George Atkinson; E. N. Baron; A. Beaumont; Charles John Biddle; William Bigler; George J. Bolton; Benjamin Harris Brewster; William Brindle; Richard Brodhead; John Brooke of Falls, Pennsylvania; Nathaniel Borrodail Browne of Philadelphia; S. W. Buck; Charles Rollin Buckalew; Simon Cameron; James Hepburn Campbell; Charles Wesley Carrigan; A. C. Case; Rev. John

Chambers; C. B. Chase; John Nesbitt Conyngham; John Creswell; Benjamin S. Dartt, Troy, Pennsylvania; M. C. Dunnier; A. Dietrick; William Elnell; Thomas S. Feron; E. Geiger; James Harding; William Muhlenberg Hiester; A. Hine of Tunkhannock; John Jessup; Francis Jordan; Allen M. Kearn; D. C. Kitchen; R. A. Lamberton of Harrisburg; Paul Leidy; John B. Linn; R. R. Little; James McClure; U. Marcus; John J. Metzger; Michael Meylert of Scranton; Les Miller; J. Morley, Jr., of Morrisville; R. W. Osterhouse; W. Patton; J. M. Quiggle of Philadelphia; Samuel J. Randall; R. W. Ross of Philadelphia; George Sanderson; H. L. Scott; Harvey Sickles; R. H. Small; Elhanan Smith; F. Smith; Chester Thomas; George Tutton; William A. Wallace; Charles F. Welles; Dr. N. Wills of Sterlingville; David Wilmot; S. S. Winchester of Wilkes-Barre; J. W. Wooding of San Francisco; and Hendrick Bradley Wright.

4189. SAMUEL THOMAS PICKARD PAPERS, 1905. 1 item. Amesbury (Essex County), Mass.

A letter from Pickard, literary executor of John Greenleaf Whittier and author of works on the poet, to [Homer?] Norris, Jr., discussing Pickard's collection of autograph letters from authors and public men. This letter was laid in a copy of Pickard's Whittier Land: A Handbook of North Boston (Boston: 1904).

4190. ADAM H. PICKEL PAPERS, 1859-1866. 78 items. Mont Clare, near Phoenixville (Chester County), Pa.

Personal correspondence of Adam and Sarah Pickel and of their son, Adam H. Pickel. The letters from Adam H. Pickel while a Federal soldier describe his travels and campaigns from Fort Lyon, West Virginia, and contain comment on saloons, conditions of the barracks and food, and lack of veracity in newspaper reports of Federal engagements. Adam Pickel's letters reflect the conditions in eastern Pennsylvania during the Civil War and comment on the abolitionists, Abraham Lincoln, and the Negro question. Sarah Pickel's letters, chiefly evangelical exhortations directed to her son, give some account of the Irish laborers of Norristown and Reading, Pennsylvania.

4191. ANDREW PICKENS PAPERS, 1781, 1803. 2 items. Pendleton (Anderson County), S.C.

A letter of 1781 concerning supplies for South Carolina troops commanded by Pickens during the American Revolution; and a letter of 1803 from Virgil Maxcy concerning personal affairs and praising the town of Beaufort, South Carolina.

4192. CORNELIUS MILLER PICKENS PAPERS, 1892-1921. 2 items and 3 vols. Charlotte (Mecklenburg County) and Morganton (Burke County), N.C.

Journal, 1921, of travel in southern Europe, the Holy Land, and northern Africa; documents concerning Pickens's career as a minister of the Methodist Episcopal Church, South; and a diary, 1892-1901, concerning personal, social, and ecclesiastical affairs in North Carolina, Virginia, and Tennessee. Prohibition is frequently discussed.

4193. FRANCIS WILKINSON PICKENS PAPERS, 1798-1900. 445 items and 1 vol. Edgefield (Edgefield County), S.C.

Political correspondence of Francis W. Pickens (1805-1869), governor of South Carolina, 1861-1863, containing information on secession and the outbreak of the Civil War. Included are acts of the South Carolina legislature during the war concerning a coast police, volunteers, and limitations of cotton acreage. The material, 1863-1900, consists of family and personal letters. Among the correspondents are P. G. T. Beauregard, M. L. Bonham, Braxton Bragg, Joseph E. Brown, Armistead Burt, Lewis Cass, W. M. Churchwell, Jefferson Davis, R. W. Gibbes, Isaac W. Hayne, J. L. Orr, F. W. Pickens, and William H. Seward. Included also is a volume of plantation records, 1839-1864.

4194. TIMOTHY PICKERING PAPERS, 1775-1795. 3 items. Salem (Essex County), Mass.

Miscellaneous items concerning Pickering, quartermaster general of the Continental Army, 1780-1783, and secretary of war, 1795.

4195. ALBERT JAMES PICKETT PAPERS, 1847. 1 item. Montgomery (Montgomery County), Ala.

A letter of Pickett (1810-1858) to William Bacon Stephens expressing gratitude at having been elected to membership in the Georgia Historical Society, and describing his research trips and his plans for writing a history of Alabama.

4196. GEORGE EDWARD PICKETT PAPERS, (1861-1864) 1896. 22 items. Richmond, Va.

Civil War material of George Edward Pickett (1825-1875), graduate of U.S. Military Academy, West Point, New York, who saw service in the Mexican War and served as brigadier general in the Confederate Army. Included are lists of casualties suffered by the 24th Virginia Regiment at Gettysburg, 1863; three letters describing the battle; and letters relating to disaffection and desertion among the troops from North Carolina and to hardships suffered by the Confederate Army around Goldsboro, North Carolina. Included also are several special orders issued from Richmond in the spring of 1864; a letter from LaSalle (Corbell) Pickett; and a letter from Charles Pickett concerning a picture and autograph of General Pickett, 1896.

4197. JOHN A. PICKETT LEDGERS, 1896-1902. 2 vols. Osceola (Guilford County), N.C.

Physician's accounts.

4198. W. S. PICKETT LEDGERS, 1853-1859. 2 vols. Leesburg (Loudoun County), Va.

A ledger pertaining to dry goods accounts, and a tailor's account book.

4199. WILLIAM J. PICKETT PAPERS, 1866. 1 item. Hampton (Calhoun County), Ark.

A letter describing Pickett's losses in slaves and cotton during the Civil War.

4200. FRANKLIN PIERCE PAPERS, 1853-1856. 9 items. Concord (Merrimack County), N.H.

Largely recommendations for office seekers, directed to Pierce as president of the United States. One item is a land grant to Washington Craft, a veteran of the Seminole War.

4201. GENEVIEVE PIERCE PAPERS, 1858-1860. 3 items. Cleveland (Cuyahoga County), Ohio.

Letters between Harriet Pierce and her daughter, Genevieve, dealing with family matters.

4202. JAMES W. PIERCE PAPERS, 1854-1879. 21 items. Westfield (Hamilton County), Ind.

Family correspondence, ca. 1860, of Pierce, of Kansas and Hamilton County, Indiana, concerning opportunities for farmers in Kansas; antislavery sentiment; rumors about abolitionist John Brown and about slave insurrections in Texas and Kentucky; and Lincoln's popularity. Later letters concern religious sects in Missouri, commodity prices, the presidential election of 1868, the political activity of Freemasons, and yellow fever in Memphis, Chattanooga, and New Orleans. Correspondents include William B. Pierce, A.G. and Cynthia Pickett, Doreas E. Cross of St. Louis, James W. Pierce, and W.R. Coggin of Warren County, Tennessee.

4203. JOHN HASSETT PIERCE PAPERS, 1861-1864. 16 items. Illinois, Mississippi, and Tennessee.

Letters to relatives by a soldier in the 11th Illinois Volunteer Cavalry, describing campaigns and movements in Illinois, Tennessee, and Mississippi; Generals Grant and Sherman; and Copperheads.

4204. OVID WILLIAMS PIERCE PAPERS, 1952-1965. 1 item and 2 vols. Weldon (Halifax County), N.C.

Drafts of Pierce's The Plantation (New York: 1953); copy of an abridgement of Pierce's "On a Lonesome Porch," printed in the Newark Sunday News (Nov. 13, 1960); and a copy of an address to the North Carolina Editorial Writers Conference, 1965, on "The Language of Revolution."

4205. WILLIAM LEIGH PIERCE PAPERS, 1785-1791. 3 items. Savannah, Ga.

Miscellaneous items relating to Pierce, a member of the Continental Congress from Georgia, relating to the boundary lines of Georgia, Pierce's debts, and the administration of his estate.

4206. FRANCIS HARRISON PIERPONT PAPERS, 1861-1866. 24 items. Wheeling (Ohio County), W. Va.

Official correspondence of Francis H. Pierpont (1814-1899), as governor of the "restored" state of Virginia. The letters concern political prisoners' pardons, information about rebels, and requests for office, and are addressed to the "Restored Government of Virginia."

4207. FRANCIS STEWART GILDEROY PIGGOTT PAPERS, 1952. 1 item. Oak Cottage, Cranleigh, Surrey, England.

A letter to General Piggott from Sir Roderick Jones commenting on his memoirs, A Life in Reuter's (London: 1951), and about one of Piggott's books on Japan.

4208. ALBERT PIKE PAPERS, 1855-1891. 7 items. Little Rock (Pulaski County), Ark.; and Washington, D.C.

Letters of Pike concerning his literary and legal work, including comment on his annotation of the Louisiana Civil Code, his vocabularies of the Creek and Comanche languages, financial arrangements, a lawsuit, and an agreement between the U.S. government and the Choctaws, 1874.

4209. GIDEON JOHNSON PILLOW PAPERS, 1861. 13 items. Columbia (Maury County), Tenn.

Largely routine items pertaining to Confederate General Pillow concerning army supplies and skirmishes around Charleston, Missouri.

4210. MATTHEW PILSON PAPERS, 1822 (1832-1849) 1882. 36 items. Augusta County, Va.

Family and business correspondence of Matthew Pilson, evidently a planter and man of some wealth and local influence, including letters asking his advice about employing a minister; letters from a niece asking him to make purchases of clothes and jewelry for her in Richmond, and quoting the prices of these articles; and personal letters with brief references to the Wallace family of Augusta County.

4211. GIFFORD PINCHOT PAPERS, 1931. 1 item. Milford (Pike County), Pa.

A letter from Pinchot, forester and governor of Pennsylvania, to Louis Edelman expressing appreciation for Edelman's remarks about Theodore Roosevelt and commenting upon his life as governor.

4212. B. GAILLARD PINCKNEY PAPERS, (1853-1854) 1863. 25 items. Charleston, S.C.

The collection is composed mainly of letters between B. Gaillard Pinckney, a young Charleston socialite and probably the son of Henry Laurens Pinckney, and his fiancée, M. Carrie Haskell, of Rantowles, South Carolina. The letters give much information concerning the manners, customs, and modes of Charleston society. Included also is a Civil War letter, 1863, from Joseph C. Haskell.

4213. CHARLES PINCKNEY PAPERS, 1796-1853. 7 items. Charleston, S.C.

Correspondence of Pinckney (1757-1824) as governor of South Carolina concerning legislation affecting the courts of the state and concerning lands; letters relating to the accounts of Pinckney as minister to Spain, 1801-1805, especially for extraordinary expenses incurred for the marriage ceremony of Ferdinand VII of Spain; and two receipts of Henry Laurens Pinckney, son of Charles, as tax collector of Charleston, 1851-1853.

4214. CHARLES COTESWORTH PINCKNEY PAPERS, 1687-1860. 1,118 items. Charleston, S.C.

The collection contains many bills, receipts, and professional and business correspondence of Pinckney (1746-1825), statesman and Revolutionary Army general, son of Charles Pinckney (d. 1758), and second cousin of Charles Pinckney (1757-1824). Topics include the siege of Savannah, 1779; the feelings of Thomas Pinckney, brother of Charles Cotesworth Pinckney, toward his mission to Spain, 1794; legislation and elections; the selection of U.S. senators; militia legislation; evaluations of political leaders; Ephraim Ramsey's opinion on the African slave trade; and Pinckney's investments in bank stock, government bonds, and Charleston real estate, 1799-1811. There are also two letters relating to Pinckney's father, Charles Pinckney (d. 1758); a few items concerning Major Alex Garden, including a steel engraved portrait and material on his essays about rattlesnakes; letters from Benjamin Stead, Charles Cotesworth Pinckney's brother-in-law; a descriptive list, 1803, of Stead's slaves; a contract, 1860, with an overseer for the management of Pinckney Island; copies of deeds 1681-1683, for Charleston land of Colonel Robert Daniell, later owned by Charles Pinckney (d. 1758), and an excerpt from Daniell's will, 1718; material relating to the settlement of the estate of Henry Middleton, father-in-law of Charles C. Pinckney, 1824; medical and other bills and receipts after 1825 of Charles C. Pinckney's daughters, Harriot and Mary, issued by Dr. M. Irvine; and legal documents concerning the settlement of the estate of Commodore Andrew Gillon (1741-1794).

4215. CHARLES COTESWORTH PINCKNEY III PAPERS, 1822-1887. 31 items and 1 vol. Charleston, S.C.

Personal and business correspondence of Pinckney (1812-1899), a Protestant Episcopal minister of South Carolina, generally addressed to Armistead Burt and relating to the settlement of the Pinckney estate and to cordial relations existing between the Pinckneys and the Burts. There are two letters of Pinckney's father; a letter of Beverley Randolph of Virginia about Potomac Bank stock; a copy of the program for re-raising the U.S. flag at Fort Sumter, 1865; papers relating to the Cincinnati Society of South Carolina; and an account book of Pinckney as agent for the board of foreign missions of the Protestant Episcopal Church.

4216. ELIZABETH (LUCAS) PINCKNEY PAPERS, 1741-1763. 28 items. Charleston, and Belmont (York County), S.C.

Papers of Elizabeth (Lucas) Pinckney, wife of Charles Pinckney (d. 1758), and promoter of indigo culture in South Carolina. Included are part of a letter book containing both personal and business letters of Mrs. Pinckney; legal papers of Charles Pinckney including a document, 1750, about early land surveys of Charleston, and an undated document concerning damages done to his property by town fortifications; and other items relating to Charles's brother William Pinckney.

4217. HENRY L. PINCKNEY PLANTATION BOOK, 1850-1867. 1 vol. Stateburg (Sumter County), S.C.

Lists of Negroes, livestock, and plantation implements; accounts of goods bought and sold, and of land under cultivation; and memoranda of rations, of time lost, etc. Entries for 1865 give accounts of "Yankee" depredations on the plantation.

4218. THOMAS PINCKNEY PAPERS, 1771-1813. 35 items. Charleston, S.C.

Correspondence of Thomas Pinckney (1750-1828), lawyer, Revolutionary figure, minister to England, and governor of South Carolina, 1787-1789. The letters concern

London gossip; construction of the Santee Canal; troops for the Creek War, 1813-1814, in Georgia; and opinion and refusal to grant extradition papers for a crime committed in Georgia. Included also are three land grants signed by Pinckney as governor; and correspondence, 1792-1795, with some material extending to 1818, relating largely to Pinckney's work as minister to Great Britain. There are letters of Alexander Hamilton, Gouverneur Morris, Joseph Anderson, William Bingham, and James Grant.

4219. RINALDO PINDELL PAPERS, 1817-1872. 4 vols. West River (Anne Arundel County), Md.

Business and family accounts, 1817-1861, 3 vols.; and a record of sermons heard, 1839-1855, 1 vol.

4220. ANDREW PINKHAM PAPERS, 1814-1880. 71 items. Clermont County, Ohio.

Family letters of Pinkham, formerly a ship captain of Nantucket, including letters of his sons Reuben and Alex during the War of 1812, a letter of 1817 from his son Thomas studying medicine at the College of William and Mary and describing taverns and bowling in Williamsburg, and letters to Thomas from V. T. West, 1839-1858, in medical practice in Union, Pike County, Indiana. Letters were written from the captured H.M.S. Queen Charlotte, 1814; the U.S.S. Hornet, 1817; U.S.S. Franklin, 1824; and U.S.S. Constellation, 1819.

4221. PINKNEY FAMILY PAPERS, 1804-1906. 12 items. Annapolis (Anne Arundel County), and Baltimore, Md.

Chiefly papers of William Pinkney (1764-1822), his brother Ninian Pinkney (1776-1825), and Ninian's son, Bishop William Pinkney (1810-1883). Included is an invitation to a dinner to honor William Pinkney upon his return from England after serving as U.S. commissioner to negotiate claims under Jay's Treaty. Material relating to Ninian Pinkney concerns his position as clerk of the executive council of Maryland and relates to expenditures for militia expenses, 1813, and to the Baltimore and Potomac Canal Survey, 1823-1824. Correspondents include Senator Robert Henry Goldsborough and William Howard. Letters to Bishop William Pinkney are from Orlando Hutton, 1844-1879, and concern Pinkney's ecclesiastical career.

4222. WILLIAM PINNELL PAPERS, 1816-1820. 14 items. Buckingham County, Va.

Largely bills and receipts of William Pinnell and of the Lilly & Pinnell merchandising firm of Lynchburg. Names mentioned include Thomas Pinnell, Lucy Pinnell, William A. Pinnell, John M. Walker, and William Duval.

4223. JAMES K. PINNIX AND COMPANY DAYBOOKS, 1851-1856. 2 vols. Stony Creek (Caswell County), N.C.

Accounts of a mercantile company.

4224. GEORGE W. PIPER PAPERS, 1898-1910. 23 items. Newburyport (Essex County), Mass.

Largely letters from Richard H. Hutton of London, England, concerning linotypes, the extraction of gold from sea water, Count James Pourtales, and other business affairs.

4225. ELIZABETH M. PIPKIN PAPERS, 1838 (1855-1864) 1880. 39 items. Harnett County, N.C.

Personal and family correspondence, including a few Civil War letters, especially from A. S. Pipkin, written from a Confederate camp at Yorktown, Virginia.

4226. WILLIAM T. PIPPEY PAPERS, 1862-1866. 138 items. Boston, Mass.

Civil War letters of William T. Pippey, lieutenant in the Federal Army, with detailed accounts of camp life and side lights on supplies for soldiers. Pippey's changing views on Negroes and abolitionists are also fully expressed.

4227. WILLIAM LEWIS PITCHER PHOTOGRAPH ALBUM, 1898. 1 vol. (24 pp.) Texas.

Photographs of Puerto Rico taken during the Spanish-American War, and one photograph of the palace of the governor-general of Cuba.

4228. PERSEY PEABODY PITKIN PAPERS, 1862-1864. 12 items. Vermont.

Papers relating to Pitkin's service as assistant quartermaster and quatermaster of U.S. Volunteers in the Army of the Potomac, including requisitions for forage for horses of the U.S. Sanitary Commission and for wagons and harness, lists of office supplies expended, and requisitions for transportation of packages of the Christian Commission.

4229. WILLIAM PITT, FIRST EARL OF CHATHAM, PAPERS, 1721-1783. 3 items. London, England.

An outline of the administrative organization, functions, and personnel of the Board of Treasury and its relations with other departments of the government of England and of Scotland, compiled from Chatham Manuscripts in the Public Record Office, London; an indenture between Lucy (Tindall) Ridgeway, Countess of Londonderry (d. 1724), and Thomas Rutly, mariner of Tormoham, Devonshire, 1721; and an undated note in which Chatham wished success for Robert Nugent, later First Earl Nugent, in an election in Bristol.

4230. WILLIAM PITT PAPERS, 1762-1884. 100 items. "Hollwood," Hayes, County Kent, England.

Correspondence largely of William Pitt (1759-1806), British statesman and prime minister, second son of William Pitt (1708-1778), First Earl of Chatham. Topics include foreign affairs; elections; tithes; studies and recreation of William Pitt and his brother John; their social activities; John's marriage; their careers in government and politics; the health of Chatham; Richard Brampton's portrait of Chatham; George Romney's portrait of Pitt; the War of the American Revolution; Richard Howe's view of Charles Middleton's naval career; international developments in the Netherlands, 1787; the illness of George III; the wars of the French Revolution; the views of Hugues Maret concerning French-English relations, 1792; parliamentary affairs; the selection of candidates for elections; a telescope ordered from Sir William Herschel by Robert Smith, First Baron Carrington; the supply of corn in England, 1795; retirements and pensions of various peers; and Arthur Philip Stanhope's collection of Pitt family papers, 1881. Letters from Pitt and members of his family are chiefly to Sir James Bland Burges, under secretary of state in the foreign department; James Grenville, brother of Lady Chatham, and Grenville's son, Baron Glastonbury; C. Jouvencal, a clerk in the privy council office and a free tenant on the estate at Hayes; George Rose, secretary of the treasury; Granville Leveson-Gower, First Marquis of Stafford, Lord Privy Seal; the Earl of Westmorland; and Edward Wilson, tutor of the Pitt children and canon at Windsor. Other authors include William Pitt (1708-1778), First Earl of Chatham; Richard Howe, First Lord of the Admiralty; John Pitt, Second Earl of Chatham; James Charles Pitt; Robert Smith, First Baron Carrington; and Arthur Philip Stanhope, Sixth Earl Stanhope.

4231. N. J. PITTMAN PAPERS, 1850-1852. 9 items. Wilmington (New Hanover County), N.C.

Professional letters to N. J. Pittman (1818-1893), a prominent physician and president of the North Carolina Medical Society, 1858, from other physicians. Pittman studied medicine in Paris, France, and was a member of the Royal Geographic Society.

4232. THOMAS MERRITT PITTMAN PAPERS, 1752-1932. 372 items and 1 vol. Henderson (Vance County), N.C.

Papers of Pittman, an attorney, relate largely to his interest in the political, social, and religious history of the state and to his connection with the North Carolina Historical Commission and the North Carolina Literary and Historical Association. There are letters from Bishop Joseph Blount Cheshire of the Protestant Episcopal Diocese of North Carolina and from Josephus Daniels discussing some of Pittman's conclusions about church history; genealogical material on the Pittman and Bennett families; material on the Torrens system of land titles proposed for adoption in the state; letters from Samuel A'Court Ashe concerning North Carolina history, particularly John Porter's role in the Cary Rebellion of the early 1700s; manuscripts collected by Pittman including material on early Baptist churches and clergymen; a letter book, 1788-1797, of John Kennedy, Jr., a Washington, North Carolina, merchant, with references to Beaufort County politics and containing letters from Thomas Blount, U.S. representative from the state; copies of Pittman's articles and addresses on biographical, political, and religious topics; minutes and program schedules of the Contemporary Club, a local scientific and literary group, 1915-1917; and addresses of Pittman's wife before the Tuesday Club.

4233. PITTSYLVANIA (VA.) MASONIC LODGE NO. 24 PAPERS, 1833-1942. 22 items. Chatham (Pittsylvania County), Va.

Miscellaneous correspondence, in part relating to Richard Jones Reid, Sr., master of the lodge.

4234. FRANCIS PLACE PAPERS, 1836, 1843. 2 items. London, England.

A letter from Place (1771-1854), British reformer, to John Fowler, secretary of the Mechanics' Institute at Sheffield, concerning labor organization, 1836, and a letter to Edwin W. Field, 1843.

4235. PLANTERS' AND MECHANICS' BANK OF SOUTH CAROLINA PAPERS, 1840-1841. 1 vol. Charleston, S.C.

Cashier's letterpress book of the Planters' and Mechanics' Bank of South Carolina chiefly concerning routine business matters. Among the correspondents are B. D. Boyd, Stephen Elliott, Franklin Elmore, Andrew A. Humphreys, William Louis, Stephen Mallory (1812-1873), Nicholas Murray, James L. Petigru, Daniel Ravenel, Robert B. Rhett, Romulus M. Saunders, and Robert Walton.

4236. CHARLES G. PLATEN MANUSCRIPT. 1 vol. (31 pp.) Savannah, Ga.

A manuscript with the title: "Oecography. The Geography of Home. Chatham County, State of Georgia: A Text-book Designed for the Use of the Grammar Schools of Savannah, Georgia."

4237. CORNELIA ANNA PLATT ALBUM, 1862-1865. 1 vol. (30 pp.) Augusta, Ga.

Autographs.

4238. PLEASANT RETREAT MALE ACADEMY RECORDS, 1868-1883. 1 vol. (13 pp.) Lincolnton (Lincoln County), N.C.

Minute book of the trustees.

4239. JAMES PLEASANTS, JR. PAPERS, 1818, 1855. 2 items. Goochland County, Va.

A letter from James Pleasants (1769-1839), member of U.S. Congress, 1803-1811, U. S. senator, 1819-1822, and governor of Virginia, 1822-1825, requesting the insertion of an advertisement in the National Intelligencer; and a letter from Benjamin Pleasants concerning a pending lawsuit against the collector of customs for the Puget Sound District.

4240. WILLIAM SWAN PLUMER PAPERS, 1859-1865. 11 items. Allegheny (Allegheny County), Pa.

Personal letters from William Swan Plumer (1802-1880), Presbyterian clergyman, founder of the Watchman of the South, and professor of theology at the Theological Seminary in Columbia, South Carolina.

4241. PLUMMER & BUDD PAPERS, 1904-1906. 1 vol. Petersburg (Dinwiddie County), Va.

A register of accounts with local investors kept by a firm serving as agents for the Southern Mutual Investment Co. of Lexington, Kentucky. The owners of Plummer & Budd were F. Harvey Plummer and William Budd.

4242. MARION TIMOTHY PLYLER PAPERS, 1912-1949. 156 items. Durham, N.C.

Manuscripts collected by Plyler, Trinity College graduate, Methodist minister, and editor of the North Carolina Christian Advocate while researching a projected biography of William Preston Few, president of Trinity College and Duke University. Included are genealogical material on the Wood, Kimball, and Harris families of North Carolina; letters; miscellaneous notes; a typescript of Few's life; and copies of Few's published articles and addresses. The collection contains notes concerning Washington Duke, Benjamin N. Duke, and James B. Duke.

4243. JOHN POAGUE PAPERS, 1857-1876. 5 items. Fancy Hill (Rockbridge County), Va.

Business letters and papers of John Poague.

4244. WILLIAM THOMAS POAGUE PAPERS, 1885-1905. 25 items. Lexington (Rockbridge County), Va.

Letters from Thomas Taylor Munford to William Thomas Poague, treasurer and military storekeeper of Virginia Military Institute, Lexington, Virginia, concerning business and personal matters and, particularly, the affairs of V. M. I.

4245. ORLANDO METCALFE POE PAPERS, 1888. 1 item. Navarre (Stark County), Ohio.

Memoir of Orlando Metcalfe Poe, engineering officer in the Union Army, entitled "Personal Recollections of the Occupation of East Tennessee and Defense of Knoxville." Poe describes the occupation of Knoxville, Tennessee, by Union forces, 1863, and their subsequent defense of the town against Confederate troops under General James Longstreet, particularly detailing the work of Union engineers in preparing fortifications. A shortened version of this narrative has been published in Battles and Leaders of the Civil War (New York: 1884-1887).

4246. GEORGE POINDEXTER PAPERS, 1804-1819. 5 items. Jackson (Hinds County), Miss.

Papers of George Poindexter (1799-1853), lawyer, attorney general of Mississippi Territory, 1803-1807, territorial representative to Congress, 1807-1813, governor, 1820-1821, and U.S. senator, 1830-1835. The collection includes a note to Colonel Thomas Rodney, 1804; comments on the possibility of a British protectorate of the Mississippi Territory; a description of a 55-day journey by boat to Natchez and comments on a yellow fever epidemic, 1810; a letter to Governor David Holmes, 1817; a letter to Joseph Gales and William W. Seaton in Washington, D.C., concerning a speech of Poindexter; and a biographical clipping written as Poindexter's eulogy.

4247. HENRY P. POINDEXTER PAPERS, 1838, 1845. 2 items. Mansfield (Louisa County), Va.

Letters to Henry P. Poindexter concerning debts.

4248. JOHN F. POINDEXTER PAPERS, 1860-1869. 32 items. Forsyth County and Germanton, (Stokes County), N.C.

Letters to John F. Poindexter concern political and economic conditions in North Carolina during the secession crisis; and campaigning in Virginia and North Carolina during the Civil War, including comments on the first battle of Manassas, camp life, the battle of Chancellorsville, the hiring of substitutes, conditions at home during the war, petitions for exemption from military service, and depredations by Union forces.

4249.   JOEL ROBERTS POINSETT PAPERS, 1825-1851. 8 items. Charleston, S.C.

Papers of Joel Roberts Poinsett, United States minister to Mexico and secretary of war under President Martin Van Buren, include a letter, 1825, on economic conditions in Mexico; a land grant, 1830, for property in Texas; a letter, 1837, from Edward B. Dudley, governor of North Carolina, complaining about the activities of troops stationed in North Carolina to supervise the removal of the Cherokee Indians; routine letters to Poinsett as secretary of war; and a letter, 1851, concerning Poinsett's personal financial affairs.

4250.   EDWARD POLAND ACCOUNT BOOKS, 1860-1862. 2 vols. Leesburg (Loudoun County), Va.

Accounts of a butcher.

4251.   POLITICAL CAMPAIGN MATERIAL, 1952-1976.

A miscellaneous collection of several thousand items containing literature and memorabilia from major, and some minor, political parties, relating to national election campaigns and political campaigns in North Carolina.

4252.   JAMES KNOX POLK PAPERS, 1831-1846. 4 items. Washington, D.C.

Papers of James Knox Polk, United States congressman and president of the United States, include a letter, 1846, from Cave Johnson about an affair involving a committee of claims, and correspondence, 1831-1832, concerning Revolutionary War claims.

4253.   LEONIDAS POLK PAPERS, 1828-1871. 13 items. Memphis (Shelby County), Tenn.

Correspondence of Leonidas Polk (1806-1864), Protestant Episcopal bishop of Louisiana and lieutenant general in the Confederate Army, including a letter, 1828, from Polk to the Reverend Charles P. McIlvaine, discussing his life, work, and preparation for the Episcopal ministry; a letter to General Gideon J. Pillow, relative to fortifications along the Mississippi and Tennessee rivers, 1861; a letter to the Reverend Benjamin Bosworth Smith, concerning the laying of a cornerstone at the University of the South, Sewanee, Tennessee; letters to Jefferson Davis, concerning routine army business and conditions of service on the Potomac River; messages relative to the condition of Confederate troops at Bethel, Tennessee, 1862; letters, 1864, concerning Confederate troop movements and organization; and a letter, 1871, from Frances (Devereux) Polk relating to a request for an autograph letter of Leonidas Polk.

4254.   SIR GEORGE POLLOCK, FIRST BARONET, PAPERS, 1854. 1 item. London, England.

Letter of British field marshal, Sir George Pollock, concerning his attack on Kabul, Afghanistan, in 1842.

4255.   CHARLES RICHARD POMEROY, JR., PAPERS, 1864. 1 vol. Pomeroy (Meigs County), Ohio.

Diary of Charles Richard Pomeroy, Jr., an officer in the 33rd Ohio Regiment in the Civil War, covers his service in the army of General William T. Sherman during the march on Atlanta, Georgia. Pomeroy describes the skirmishes in which his regiment engaged and the battles of Rocky Face Ridge and Peach Tree Creek. Diary also contains newspapers, clippings and miscellaneous notes, including a list of men killed and wounded in the 33rd Ohio Regiment and a list of arms and supplies in Company I of that regiment.

4256.   S. POMEROY AND JOHN VICKERY PAPERS, 1860-1870. 21 items. Rochester (Monroe County), N.Y.

Correspondence of the firm of Pomeroy and Vickery with cotton brokers in Memphis, Tennessee, regarding the purchase of low price cotton battings and pickings.

4257.   EDWARD POND PAPERS, 1869-1877. 6 items. Savannah, Ga.

Personal and family correspondence reflecting difficult conditions in the South after the Civil War and the tendency for ruined Southern families to seek work in other sections of the country.

4258.   JOHN WILLIAM PONSONBY, FOURTH EARL OF BESSBOROUGH, PAPERS, 1821-1833. 22 items. London, England.

Miscellaneous personal and political letters of John William Ponsonby, Fourth Earl of Bessborough, member of the House of Commons and the House of Lords, concern negotiations with Russia, 1832; changes in the poor laws; and matters relating to parliamentary debates and elections.

4259.   HUGH N. PONTON PAPERS, 1859-1864. 44 items. Nelson County, Va.

Correspondence of Hugh N. Ponton and his wife, Frances (Thompson) Ponton, during the Civil War, showing a private's reaction to the war, and the difficulties of a young wife left to manage a farm and family.

4260.  SIMEON V. POOL PAPERS, 1863-1878. 12 items. New York, N.Y.

Miscellaneous ordnance and quartermaster records of Company B, 154th New York Regiment, and a record of a judgment rendered in a legal case, 1878.

4261.  SOLOMON POOL PAPERS, 1868-1869. 5 items. Chapel Hill (Orange County), N.C.

Duplicates of monthly accounts submitted to the U.S. Internal Revenue Service by Solomon Pool, assessor of the fourth district of North Carolina, for services rendered by Pool and his staff.

4262.  W. G. POOL PAPERS, 1868-1884. 16 items. Nags Head (Dare County), N.C.

Business letters from W. G. Pool, a physician at Nags Head, North Carolina, to a certain Mathews, manager of one of Pool's farms.

4263.  EDWARD D. POOLE PAPERS, 1855-1858. 3 items. Clarksville (Mecklenburg County), Va.

Letters dealing primarily with family matters.

4264.  ERNEST POOLE PAPERS, 1923-1940. 3 items. Franconia (Grafton County), N.H.

Papers of author Ernest Poole (1880-1950) contain a draft, partly handwritten and partly typed with handwritten corrections, of his autobiographical novel, The Bridge (New York: 1940), and two typed copies of Poole's article, "Ernest Poole and His Work."

4265.  JONATHAN POOR LEDGERS, 1769-1852. 2 vols. Landaff (Grafton County), N.H.

Ledgers of Jonathan Poor, a farmer of Landaff, New Hampshire, containing accounts with local people for agricultural labor, goods, and services and a few biographical notations concerning Poor and his family.

4266.  BENJAMIN PERLEY POORE PAPERS, 1857-1884. 10 items. Washington, D.C.

Miscellaneous letters of Benjamin Perley Poore, writer and editor, concern personal matters; the new constitution of North Carolina, 1877; Poore's Political Register and Congressional Directory (Boston: 1878); and Poore's relationship with his uncle, Allen W. Dodge.

4267.  ANNIE BIDDLE POPE PAPERS, 1861-1869. 11 items. Halifax County, N.C.

Personal letters, two of which refer to relatives in the Civil War.

4268.  BENJAMIN E. POPE PAPERS, 1874. 4 items. Newsom's Depot (Southampton County), Va.

Letters concerning the indebtedness of Edward C. Robinson to Benjamin E. Pope.

4269.  POPE-CARTER FAMILY PAPERS, 1791-1967. 1,367 items and 10 vols. Giles, Maury, and Williamson Counties, Tenn.

Papers of the Pope and Carter families contain the letters, 1900-1939, of William Rivers Pope, officer in the United States Army, including a few letters dealing with his service in the Philippines, 1900-1901, and a large number of letters concerning his experiences in France in World War I from June, 1918, to June, 1919, as commander of the 113th Infantry Regiment in the Meuse-Argonne offensive and commander of the military police in the area of the American Embarcation Center, LeMans, France. World War I letters comment on the overall war effort, the peace, characteristics of soldiers, the role of the Negro soldier in the war, and the people and countryside of France. Letters, 1919-1939, deal for the most part with personal and family matters and refer to a few events of Pope's later military career, particularly his part in the stratosphere flight sponsored by the National Geographic Society and the Army Air Corps, 1934-1935.

The collection also contains letters, 1818-1821, to Dr. Benjamin Carter (1792-1865), a physician in Tennessee, from his brother John Conyers Carter (1793-1828), a lawyer in Camden, South Carolina, concerning family and professional matters, the panic of 1819 and other economic and political issues, internal improvements, and problems of the judicial system in South Carolina; and letters, 1831-1834, from his cousin John Carter, a lawyer and former congressman, pertaining to family affairs and life in Camden. Letters from members of the Clark family in Columbus, Mississippi, to members of the Pope family in Tennessee, 1827-1834, describe working on steamboats on the Mississippi and Ohio rivers, mercantile business in Columbus, and trading with the Choctaw Indians. Correspondence, 1833-1834, between Gustavus Adolphus Pope in Mississippi and his family in Tennessee concerns the agricultural situation, prices for cotton and other crops, public land policy, and attitudes on slavery and religion. Correspondence, 1836-1855, among members of the family of William Rouse Pope, including Lesey Jane (Webster) Pope and William Leonidas Pope, concerns the settling of estates, family matters, and the prospects for settling in Texas, including farming conditions, opportunities for employment, land transfers, and social and religious life. Letters, 1853-1865, of Sarah Myra (Rodes) Rivers Trotter to her daughter, Cynthia (Rivers) Carter, discuss family gossip, travels, homemaking concerns, social events, and the impact of the Civil War. Other Civil War letters include those of Benjamin Franklin Carter to his wife, Cynthia (Rivers) Carter, and the letters of William Leonidas Pope and Gustavus Adolphus Pope.

Writings include a manuscript entitled "Recollections of the [Civil] War," by Cynthia (Rivers) Carter, 1899; "History of the Military Police Corps, American Embarcation Center, A. E. F.," 1919; and "Brief History of the Twenty-Ninth Division, 1921." Legal papers, 1796-1892, pertain mainly to the Carter family and contain land grants, deeds, indentures for land, wills, court decisions, and court authorizations for the sale of slaves. Financial papers, 1791-1868, relate for the most part to the affairs of the Pope family in the 1820s and 1830s and include accounts, promissory notes, tax receipts, and receipts for purchases. Genealogical material in the collection includes Cynthia (Rivers) Carter's account of the family of her grandfather, Tyree Rodes, and a few items concerning the genealogy of slaves owned by the Carter family. Clippings, 1934-1935, pertain to the military career of William Rivers Pope, as do the newspapers and other printed material. Volumes include the notebook of Dr. Benjamin Carter, 1827, mainly concerning money owed him; two account books, 1834-1837 and 1836-1845, of William Rouse Pope, and one account book, 1851-1876, of Gustavus A. Pope; diary and memorandum book of James R. Pope, containing an account of his participation in the battle of Shiloh, 1862; anonymous notebook, 1873-1900, containing copies of legal documents; publications; and maps of various areas of France, including LeMans, the Meuse-Argonne, and Verdun.

4270. WILIE POPE PAPERS, 1838-1854. 6 items. Raleigh (Wake County), N.C.

The papers of Wilie Pope contain a copy of the will of William H. Pope, letters concerning the administration of an estate, and a letter quoting commodity prices in Clark County, Arkansas, in the spring of 1854.

4271. LOUISA BOUKNIGHT POPPENHEIM AND MARY BARNETT POPPENHEIM PAPERS, 1871-1955. 955 items and 34 vols. Charleston, S.C.

Papers of Louisa Bouknight Poppenheim and Mary Barnett Poppenheim contain correspondence relating to their education and to their leadership in women's organizations, such as the United Daughters of the Confederacy and the General Federation of Women's Clubs, including correspondence, 1884-1889, with their mother and sisters describing school life at Vassar College, Poughkeepsie, New York, and social life in Charleston, South Carolina; letters, 1909-1929, to Mary Barnett Poppenheim from neurologist Francis Arthur Scratchley, describing his many trips to Europe; and letters from James Hosmer Penniman referring to his research on George Washington and to the libraries he established at Yale University and the University of Pennsylvania. Miscellaneous items include photographs, picture postcards of various prominent structures in Europe, and printed material concerning the Protestant Episcopal Church in South Carolina. Volumes are primarily penmanship and spelling exercise books of the four Poppenheim daughters during their early education in Charleston.

4272. OCTAVIUS THEODORE PORCHER PAPERS, 1853-1869. 15 items. Willington (Abbeville County), S.C.

Letters from Octavius T. Porcher (ca. 1828-1873), Protestant Episcopal minister, to Armistead Burt. They contain comments on state and national affairs and indicate a deep concern on the part of Porcher for Burt's spiritual welfare.

4273. CHARLES W. PORTER PAPERS, 1856-1866. 204 items. Batavia (Kane County), Ill.

The collection consists chiefly of the letters of Charles W. Porter, Susan Lockwood, and their friends, concerning the courtship and eventual marriage of Porter and Lockwood.

4274. DAVID PORTER PAPERS, 1819-1823. 3 items. Boston, Mass.

A letter of David Porter, United States naval officer, concerning the finances of his father-in-law and an application, 1823, to Porter from Edward Byrne requesting a transfer from the U.S.S. Terrier to the U.S.S. Hornet. Also a brief biographical sketch of Porter's son, Theodoric Henry Porter.

4275. DAVID DIXON PORTER PAPERS, 1847-[1877?]. 14 items. Memphis (Shelby County), Tenn., and Washington, D.C.

Letters and diary of David D. Porter (1813-1891), officer in the U.S. Navy. The 337-page "Diary of Secret Service" gives an account of Porter's secret mission to Haiti as a government agent in 1847-1848. He comments in detail on the people, the geography, the mineral deposits, etc., of the island. He also discusses the government, people, and commerce of the city of Santo Domingo. Also in the collection are letters written by Porter as commander of the Mississippi Squadron, U.S. Navy, requesting commissions, and supplies for families along the Mississippi and Tennessee rivers, and issuing orders for patrolling the rivers, and a letter, 1863, to Porter from D.F. Reiley, requesting that a gunboat be assigned to Bayou Sara, Louisiana, to protect the businesses of Union men.

4276. FITZ-JOHN PORTER PAPERS, 1882-1951. 5 items. New York, N.Y., and Chicago, Ill.

Papers of Fitz-John Porter, a general in the Union Army, include a letter, 1894, from Porter, criticizing the performances of General Ambrose E. Burnside and General Jacob D. Cox in the battle of Antietam, 1862; and a letter, 1882, from John P. Jones concerning Porter's conduct at the second battle of Bull Run, 1862. The papers also contain a mimeographed report, 1951, of a "fact finding conference" which attempted to evaluate the descriptions of Porter's conduct at Second Bull Run in Kenneth Powers Williams, Lincoln Finds a General (New York: 1949-1959), and Otto Eisenschiml, The Celebrated Case of Fitz-John Porter, (Indianapolis: 1950).

4277. JOHN RICHARDSON PORTER PAPERS, 1859-1868. 2 vols. New Orleans, La.

Letter book and diary of John Richardson Porter, a Confederate soldier in the Washington (Louisiana) Artillery Battalion, describe his service in Virginia; the engagements in which he participated, including the battle of Brandy Station, 1863, the battle of Gettysburg, 1863, and the siege of Petersburg, 1865; the surrender of the Army of Northern Virginia at Appomattox; and Reconstruction in New Orleans.

4278. KATHERINE ANNE PORTER PAPERS, 1965-1966. 3 items. Washington, D.C.

Letters of Katherine Anne Porter to Gerald Ashford, a book reviewer for the San Antonio Express, discussing her childhood in Texas.

4279. WILLIAM SYDNEY PORTER PAPERS, 1905-1953. 12 items. Greensboro (Guilford County), N.C.

A letter from O. Henry, Porter's pseudonym as a writer, to George Rathborne, explaining how the name "Rathborne" happened to be chosen by O. Henry for a character in a story; and letters addressed to Henry Wysham Lanier, secretary of Doubleday, Page & Co., on matters of publication, financial and business affairs, and the author's health. [In part published by Clarence Gohdes, "Some Letters by O. Henry," South Atlantic Quarterly, XXXIII (Jan., 1939), 31-39.] Also a report on reminiscences of Porter by a Mr. Saunders.

4280. PORTSMOUTH ACADEMY. JOURNAL OF THE PROCEEDINGS OF THE TRUSTEES, 1825-1847. 1 vol. (258 pp.) Portsmouth (Norfolk County), Va.

Minutes of the board of trustees of Portsmouth Academy, Portsmouth, Virginia, providing fairly detailed information about the operation of the school. A portion of the volume was used as a scrapbook, ca. 1900.

4281. PORTSMOUTH DOCK COMPANY PAPERS, 1857. 12 items. Portsmouth (Norfolk County), Va.

Minutes, resolutions, and estimates concerning the Portsmouth Dock Company.

4282. PORTSMOUTH INSURANCE COMPANY RECORDS, 1865-1898. 1 vol. Portsmouth (Norfolk County), Va.

Minutes of annual meetings of the stockholders in the Portsmouth Insurance Company.

4283. J. R. POSEY PAPERS, 1863-1874. 3 items. Coosa County, Ala.

Letters from J. R. Posey, Confederate soldier and schoolteacher, discussing affairs in camp and at home. The last letter indicates that Posey was to teach school in Harrisville, Bell County, Texas, and gives a description of the country, living conditions, and teachers' salaries.

4284. JAMES POTEAT HOTEL REGISTER, 1883-1891. 1 vol. (103 pp.) Yanceyville (Caswell County), N.C.

Register of guests in Poteat's Hotel.

4285. ALONZO POTTER PAPERS, 1864. 1 item. Philadelphia, Pa.

Letter of Alonzo Potter, Protestant Episcopal bishop of Pennsylvania, concerning autograph letters and commenting on the distinguished service rendered by Union soldiers in the Mississippi Valley during the Civil War.

4286. ROBERT POTTER PAPERS, 1939-1944. 4 items. Marshall (Harrison County), Tex., and New Orleans, La.

Papers of Robert Potter (ca. 1800-1841), signer of the Texas Declaration of Independence and United States congressman from Texas, contain letters written 1939-1944 concerning Potter's career in the United States Navy and a typed copy of a portion of an undated autobiographical sketch by Harriet (Moore) Page Potter Ames, wife of Robert Potter, vividly describing her life in New Orleans, Louisiana; immigration to Texas and frontier life; and the killing of Robert Potter during the Regulator-Moderator War in east Texas, 1841.

4287. THOMAS POTTER PAPERS, 1832. 1 item. Manchester, England.

Letter including a resolution of thanks by a church conference to Thomas Potter for his assistance in the preparation of a model deed for the erection of chapels.

4288. WILLIAM POTTS AND WILLIAM POTTS II PAPERS, 1720 (1760-1830, 1880-1882) 1925. 404 items. Frederick (Frederick County), Md.

Papers of William Potts and William Potts II, their associates, family, and friends concern personal and family matters; opinions about the relations between Great Britain and her American colonies in the 1760s; a mercantile business in Baltimore in the 1770s; reports on sales of tobacco and cotton in London and the European tobacco market in the early nineteenth century; and the establishment of a wholesale and retail drug business in Memphis, Tennessee, after the Civil War.

4289. GEORGE POULETT LETTER BOOK, 1807-1810. 1 vol. (127 pp.) London, England.

The collection contains copies of orders received by George Poulett, British naval officer, while he commanded H.M.S. Quebec, including instructions from the lords of the admiralty and orders in council. The orders concern operations in the war against France, the blockade of France and her allies, and the handling of neutral shipping, specifically that of Russia, Prussia, Portugal, Spain, and the United States.

4290. LOUISE POUND PAPERS, 1892-1959. 24 items. Lincoln (Lancaster County), Nebr.

Willa Cather's letters, 1892-1894, to Louise Pound, athlete and scholar, concern personal and social matters. There is a manuscript of Cather's poem, "After-Glow to Edna Earlie Lindon," and a photograph of Miss Lindon. Letters from Dorothea Frances (Canfield) Fisher comment on Mrs. Fisher's writing, World War I, Roscoe Pound, Rudyard Kipling, and France. Letters, 1917-1947, from Henry Louis Mencken discuss literary and editorial affairs; his books, including The American Language; Miss Pound's writings; the United States Supreme Court; and the faculties of Johns Hopkins University and Goucher College. Letters from Louise Pound and her sister, Olivia Pound, comment on Cather and Mencken and concern the deposit of these papers at Duke University.

4291. SAMUEL POWEL III PAPERS, 1826-1865. 82 items. Rogersville (Hawkins County), Tenn.

Papers of Samuel Powel III and his family concern legal matters, including land bounties, warrants, claims, and pensions; the prices of slaves in 1850; and Democratic party politics in the presidential campaigns of 1856 and 1860 in Tennessee. There are also letters of Samuel Powel II pertaining to Democratic politics, particularly the impact of Martin Van Buren on Jacksonian patronage in 1837.

4292. CHARLES S. POWELL PAPERS, 1861-1865. 35 pp. Smithfield (Johnston County), N.C.

Typescript copy of the reminiscences of Charles S. Powell, a Confederate soldier in the 24th North Carolina Regiment and the 10th North Carolina Battalion, Heavy Artillery, describing his service in Virginia, including the battles of the Seven Days, Antietam, and Fredericksburg; the defenses of Wilmington, North Carolina; the fight against the troops of General William T. Sherman at Savannah, Georgia; and the retreat to Bentonville, North Carolina. Powell comments on Confederate deserters, the hardships and amusements of camp life, and the faithful service rendered to him by two slaves during the war.

4293. JOHN POWELL PAPERS, 1785-1822. 4 items. Linville, Ga.

The papers of John Powell contain a deed and letters concerning his finances.

4294. MARY E. V. POWELL PAPERS, 1841-1845. 7 items. Forestville (Wake County), N.C.

Personal letters of Mary Powell, and a composition written at Pleasant Grove Academy, Forestville, North Carolina, by Helen F. Powell, 1843.

4295. PAULUS POWELL PAPERS, 1850-1851. 6 items. Amherst County, Va.

Papers of Paulus Powell, a United States congressman, mainly concern politics in Virginia, including the Compromise of 1850, abolitionist resolutions in the Virginia House of Delegates, and candidates for political offices.

4296. THOMAS SPEER POWELL DIARY, 1867. 1 vol. Greenville (Greenville County), S.C.

Diary of the day-to-day life of Thomas Speer Powell, an artist and painter.

4297. WALTER POWELL PAPERS, 1664-1955. 3 items. "Apainatax," Potomac River, Va.

Copy of a letter, 1664, from Walter Powell to his brother concerning the opportunity to make a profit by investing in tobacco.

4298. WILLIAM C. POWELL PAPERS, 1883-1932. 656 items and 4 vols. Jacksonville (Duval County), Fla., and Wake Forest (Wake County), N.C.

Papers of businessman William C. Powell concern his involvement in the naval stores industry, land speculation, and mercantile business in North Carolina, Georgia, and Florida, and contain records, 1919-1932, of the W. C. Powell Company of Jacksonville, Florida, relating to land speculation and naval stores, including minutes, 1919-1932, with charter, bylaws, and some financial statements, and a ledger and journal, 1919-1932; records of Johnston, McNeill and Company of Okeechobee, Florida, 1920-1923, pertaining to naval stores, including articles of co-partnership, 1920, and financial statements, 1920-1923; records of Myakka Company, Charleston, South Carolina, 1910-1920, relating to land speculation in Florida, including a financial statement, 1912, and minutes, annual reports, financial statements, legal papers, and correspondence, 1910-1920; and records of Security Investment Company, Brunswick, Georgia, 1910-1923, dealing with speculation in Florida land, including scattered minutes, financial statements, and bylaws, 1910-1923. The collection also contains papers pertaining to the settlement of Powell's estate; a ledger, 1914-1921, containing records of investments and family accounts; a ledger, 1888-1896, for Powell's general store at Wake Forest, North Carolina; and miscellaneous letters, legal papers, and financial papers, 1883-1921, relating to Powell's various business interests.

4299. WILLIAM C. FITZHUGH POWELL PAPERS, 1831-1847. 88 items. Petersburg (Dinwiddie County), Va.

Papers of William C. Fitzhugh Powell contain letters concerning economic conditions and opportunities in Mississippi, 1835 and 1840; the estate of John W. Faulkner of Clinton, Mississippi; and the sale and transporting of slaves. Also contains bills and receipts, some of which are for slave sales, and tax receipts.

4300. WILLIAM GRATTAN TYRONE POWER PAPERS, 1840. 1 item. London, England.

Routine social letter by William Grattan Tyrone Power.

4301. ROBERTA (SMITH) POWERS PAPERS, 1847-1888. 81 items. Berryville (Clarke County), Va.

Personal and family letters of Roberta (Smith) Powers.

4302. D. THOMAS POYNOR PAPERS, 1863. 2 items. Chesterfield (Chesterfield County), Va.

Business letters addressed to Captain D. T. Poynor.

4303. MITCHELL C. PRATER PAPERS, 1861-1907. 78 items and 2 vols. Terre Haute (Vigo County), Ind.

The papers of Mitchell C. Prater, a soldier in the Union Army, contain official records of the 14th Indiana Regiment, including monthly returns of Company F, 1861-1863; quarterly abstracts of materials used by the regiment in 1863; general monthly returns; ordnance returns, camp clothing and garrison equipage returns; and monthly clothing returns. Correspondence of Prater after the war concerns his claims for a disability. The collection contains a scrapbook of poetry kept by Margaret E. (Baker) Prater and a family picture album.

4304. CALEB PRATT DAYBOOK, 1785-1789. 1 vol. Boston, Mass.

Daybook concerning the voyages of the merchant schooner Neptune from Boston, Massachusetts, to Wilmington (North Carolina), Charleston (South Carolina), and other places, giving details of navigation and cargo.

4305. HARVEY HUNTER PRATT MANUSCRIPT, ca. 1929. 461 pp. Scituate (Plymouth County), Mass.

A typed copy of "The Early Planters of Scituate, Massachusetts," by Harvey Hunter Pratt, with handwritten corrections by Pratt. This work has been published [Harvey Hunter Pratt, The Early Planters of Scituate (Scituate: 1929)].

4306. NATHANIEL A. PRATT PAPERS, 1867-1872. 8 items. Charleston, S.C.

Papers of Nathaniel A. Pratt, a geologist, contain a letter, 1868, from Francis Simmons Holmes disputing the conclusions in a forthcoming article by Pratt on geology; Pratt's reply to the criticisms; manuscript copy of an article by Pratt, 1872, on phosphate deposits and mining in South Carolina; and deeds relating to land leases and purchases in the area of Charleston, South Carolina.

4307.  WILLIAM N. PRATT PAPERS, 1857-1867. 2 vols. Prattsburg (Durham County), N.C.

Papers of William N. Pratt include a ledger, 1857-1867, containing accounts for the sale and repair of shoes, and accounts, 1863-1865, for the blacksmith business. A ledger, 1861-1865, for a blacksmith business contains an inventory, 1867, from the sale of Pratt's property by the executor of his estate.

4308.  PRATT HOSPITAL PAPERS, 1863-1864. 2 items and 1 vol. Lynchburg (Campbell County), Va.

Record book of supplies issued the wards, dining room, bake house, wash house, surgeon's office, and dispensary of Pratt Hospital. There are also several recipes.

4309.  PRESCOTT AND FLEMING DAYBOOK, 1837-1842. 1 vol. (167 pp.) Natchez (Adams County), Miss.

Records of a firm of bookbinders, blank book manufacturers, and stationers, which include titles of books, pamphlets, newspapers, and magazines bound for clients.

4310.  EBENEZER ERSKINE PRESSLY PAPERS, 1859-1919. 22 items and 5 vols. Lancaster County, S.C.; and Iredell County, N.C.

Ebenezer Erskine Pressly, minister in the Associate Reformed Presbyterian Church and later in the Presbyterian Church in the United States, served churches in South Carolina and North Carolina. His diary, 1868-1918, contains entries about the weather, crops, household occurrences, community and church happenings, and occasionally his reaction to state, national, and world affairs. There is a diary which also contains a sketch of Pressly's life; lists of sermon topics and texts, 1871-1898; records of baptisms, marriages, and funerals performed by Pressly, 1870-1886; elders and deacons he ordained, 1874-1892; accessions and dismissals in the churches which he held, 1870-1896; monies received, 1874-1883; and other financial accounts. Other items in the collection include a college theme on Samuel Adams, 1859; Pressly's license to preach, 1870; a petition relating to South Carolina's fence law of 1877; a call from the Associate Reformed Presbyterian Church at Gill's Creek, Lancaster County, South Carolina, inviting Pressly to be their pastor; and several business letters.

4311.  JOHN EBENEZER PRESSLY PAPERS, 1846-1892. 41 items. Coddle Creek (Cabarrus County), N.C.

Papers of John Ebenezer Pressly, Presbyterian minister, contain copybooks of sermons, copies of a small missionary pamphlet entitled Increase of Ministers, a scrapbook of printed sermons, and a few poems written by Pressly.

4312.  JOHN PRESTON PAPERS, 1794-1845. 11 items. Walnut Grove (Washington County), Va.

The papers of John Preston include a letter, 1830, from Walter E. Preston while he was a student at the University of Virginia, and a letter from James Wood of the Executive Council of Virginia expressing the desire of the governor that there be a majority of both houses present when the legislature next convened and discussing the appointment to the place in the United States Senate vacated by James Madison who had become minister to France.

4313.  MARGARET (JUNKIN) PRESTON PAPERS, 1864. 2 items. Lexington (Rockbridge County), Va.

Papers of Margaret (Junkin) Preston contain a signed autograph poem written by her entitled "Stonewall Jackson's Grave," and a clipping of her poem "I. H. S."

4314.  NORMAN PRESTON AND LOUISE E. PRESTON PAPERS, 1863-1879. 11 items. Worcester (Worcester County), Mass.

The collection contains a few letters concerning the fishing business and personal and family letters.

4315.  WILLIAM PRESTON AND JOHN PRESTON PAPERS, 1740 (1783-1817) 1960. 349 items. Montgomery County, Va.

Papers of William Preston (1729-1783), surveyor and justice of the peace of Botetourt County, Virginia, chiefly concern surveying and a militia expedition against the Cherokees. The bulk of the papers relate to the business and personal affairs of General John Preston, son of William, legislator and treasurer of Virginia, and surveyor of Montgomery County, Virginia, including surveying, old treaties with the Cherokees, the education of his children, legislation in the House of Delegates, stocks in the Second Bank of the United States, and other types of property. Correspondents include Richard Willing Byrd, John Floyd, Charles Clement Johnston, James Pleasants, Francis Preston, and William Radford.

4316.  WILLIAM CAMPBELL PRESTON PAPERS, 1837-1859. 10 items. Columbia (Richland County), S.C.

Personal and political letters of William Campbell Preston (1794-1860), U.S. senator, 1832-1845, and president of South Carolina College, 1845-1851, dealing with family affairs, appointments, and current politics. There is also a fragment of Preston's autobiography.

4317. AUGUSTINE PREVOST PAPERS, 1783. 2 items. New York, N.Y.

A personal letter from Augustine Prevost to Samuel Strenger and a document on the "Return of the Staff of the British American Forces Who are Desirous of Settling with Those of Other Departments."

4318. ADDIE PRICE PAPERS, 1861-1871. 11 items. Wilmington (New Hanover County), N.C.

Personal letters to Addie Price from her father, R. A. Price, while she was a student at a boarding school. There are scattered references to conditions in Wilmington, North Carolina, and a description of Savannah, Georgia, 1871.

4319. EDWIN Y. PRICE PAPERS, 1837-1876. 53 items. Appomattox County, Va.

Personal and business correspondence, bills, and receipts of Edwin Y. Price and his family in Virginia, Hopkins County, Kentucky, and elsewhere.

4320. H. H. PRICE PAPERS, 1862. 4 items. Corinth (Alcorn County), Miss.

Reports of H.H. Price, Confederate adjutant general in Daniel Ruggles's command, on the action of various Confederate units in the battle of Shiloh, April 6-7, 1862.

4321. JAMES PRICE PAPERS, 1880-1889. 36 items. Nixonton (Pasquotank County), N.C.

Personal letters written by James Price's parents to him while he attended the Bingham School, Mebanesville, North Carolina.

4322. RODMAN McCAMLEY PRICE PAPERS, 1852. 1 item. Hoboken (Hudson County), N.J.

Letter to Rodman McCamley Price from Thomas Ap Catesby Jones introducing a friend from Virginia.

4323. STERLING PRICE PAPERS, 1856. 2 items. Jefferson City (Cole County), Mo.

Two certificates of appointment for C. S. Yancey to the circuit court of Missouri signed by Sterling Price as governor of Missouri.

4324. WILLIAM B. PRICE ACCOUNT BOOKS, 1836-1859. 9 vols. Brunswick County, Va.

Physician's accounts, 1836-1853, and gristmill accounts, 1850-1859.

4325. Z. M. PRICE, THOMAS PRICE, AND JAMES PRICE PAPERS, 1861-1863. 15 items. Mississippi.

Letters of the Price brothers to their wives and parents during the Civil War, describing camp life.

4326. PRICES CURRENT BULLETINS, 1800-1903. 219 items.

Miscellaneous collection of commodity price lists mainly from cities in the United States. The reverse sides of several items have been used as stationery, and contain form business letters of Kennett and Dudley, tobacco agents at Cincinnati, Ohio.

4327. WILLIAM FRANCIS PRIDEAUX PAPERS, 1913-1914. 12 items. Hopeville, St. Peter's-in-Thanet, Kent, England.

Letters of William Francis Prideaux, British army officer and author, concern his edition of S. T. Coleridge's <u>Letters Hitherto Uncollected</u> (London: 1913).

4328. ROBERT H. PRIDGEN ACCOUNT BOOK, 1888-1891. 1 vol. (304 pp.) Warren County, N.C.

Accounts of a merchant.

4329. JOHN M. PRIM PAPERS, 1872 (1886-1894) 1935. Silver Hill (Davidson County), N.C.

The papers of John M. Prim, superintendent of the Silver Valley Mines in Davidson County, North Carolina, consist mainly of correspondence with his daughters, Mira Belle (Prim) Davis and Nannie (Prim) Johnson, concerning family, social, and religious matters.

4330. SAMUEL IRENAEUS PRIME PAPERS, 1863. 1 item. New York, N.Y.

Personal letter by Samuel Irenaeus Prime.

4331. SIR HENRY WILLIAM PRIMROSE PAPERS, 1864-1942. 259 items. London, England.

The papers of Sir Henry William Primrose, British civil servant, consist primarily of his incoming correspondence and his letters to his wife, Helen Mary (McMicking) Denman Walker Primrose. They include letters, 1864-1865, from Henry William Primrose to the principal of the school he had attended concerning his studies, and correspondence concerning William E. Gladstone's administration of 1886 and his formation of another in 1892; the question of the civil loyalty of Catholic converts, 1873; the international conference on the question of sugar bounties, 1901; the Church in Wales;

the World War in 1914-1915; and the problem of Ireland, especially the work of the committee on Irish finance, 1911-1912.

4332. JAMES REID PRINGLE PAPERS, 1847 (1863-1864) 1875. 320 items. Charleston, S.C.

Business correspondence of James Reid Pringle, a Charleston commission merchant who remained in that city transacting business for his clients during the Civil War. The material contains detailed information on economic conditions including problems of scarcity of sacks for shipping rice crops, uncertainty of rail transportation, and scarcity of horses, mules, and wagons. Among the correspondents are Benjamin Huger, F. W. Pickens, and P. C. J. Weston.

4333. SIR JOHN PRINGLE, FIRST BARONET, PAPERS, 1766. 1 item. London, England.

The papers of Sir John Pringle, a British physician, contain a letter from John Balfour, a bookseller in Edinburgh, Scotland, concerning the publication of Pringle's "Physiological Essays."

4334. ROBERT A. PRINGLE PAPERS, 1865. 1 item. Summerville (Charleston County), S.C.

Letter from Robert A. Pringle of Summerville, South Carolina, to William Ranson Johnson of Petersburg, Virginia, concerning Reconstruction in South Carolina and Virginia.

4335. DANIEL S. PRINTUP PAPERS, 1862-1865. 108 items. Union Point (Greene County), Ga.

The papers of Daniel S. Printup, an officer in the 55th Georgia Regiment during the Civil War, concern organizing and training troops in Georgia, 1862-1863; transporting supplies in Kentucky, 1863; the surrender of Printup's regiment at Cumberland Gap, Tennessee, 1863; Printup's imprisonment at Johnson's Island, Ohio, and Elmira, New York; and his exchange, 1865.

4336. W. W. PRITCHETT ACCOUNT BOOK, 1846-1860. 1 vol. (116 pp.) Blount's Creek (Beaufort County), N.C.

Accounts of the sale of property from various estates.

4337. ALEXANDRE PRIVAT D'ANGLEMONT PAPERS, 1859. 1 item. Paris, France.

Letter from Alexandre Privat d'Anglemont, French author, to Alexander Sothey.

4338. XJALMAR FREDRIK EUGEN PROCOPÉ PAPERS. 1 item. Borgå, Finland.

Facsimile of a poem by Xjalmar Fredrik Eugen Procopé (1868-1927) entitled "Boken med de sju inseglen," or "The Book with the Seven Seals."

4339. PROTESTANT EPISCOPAL CHURCH. DIOCESE OF TENNESSEE PAPERS, 1868-1923. 16 items. Sewanee (Franklin County), Tenn.

Miscellaneous personal and official letters pertaining to the Protestant Episcopal Church in Tennessee and to the University of the South, Sewanee, Tennessee. Correspondents include T. D. Bratton, Braxton Bragg, Thomas Frank Gailor, William Alexander Guerry, Chester Harding, Henry Cabot Lodge, Charles Todd Quintard, Frederick Focke Reese, and Allen Tower Treadway.

4340. ROBERT HEWSON PRUYN PAPERS, 1864. 1 item. Albany (Albany County), N.Y.

Routine official letter from R. H. Pruyn (1815-1882), U.S. minister resident in Japan, 1861-1865.

4341. ROGER ATKINSON PRYOR PAPERS, 1838-1912. 26 items. New York, N.Y.

Business letters of Roger A. Pryor (1828-1919), member of U.S. Congress, Confederate soldier, and jurist, referring principally to postwar legal matters. Included also are letters addressed to James Redpath, proprietor of the Redpath Lyceum Bureau; a letter to one Neale, a New York publisher, concerning the production and sale of Pryor's book, Essays and Addresses (New York: 1912); a letter from Pryor discussing an address that he had published; and a letter concerning Pryor's work as editor of the Richmond Enquirer.

4342. LITTLE JOHN PUGH LOGBOOK, 1858-1860. 1 vol. Elizabeth City (Pasquotank County), N.C.

Logbook containing navigator's observations and positions.

4343. CHESTER DeWITT PUGSLEY PAPERS, 1873 (1925-1938). 19,216 items. Peekskill (Westchester County), N.Y.

Correspondence, legal papers, press releases, printed material and other miscellaneous papers of Chester DeWitt Pugsley (1887-1973), New York lawyer, banker, and philanthropist. Correspondence with politicians, diplomats, educators, financiers, artists, recipients of his benefactions, and others concerns his interest in foreign affairs; the donation of bonds to Harvard Law School, Cambridge, Massachusetts, for the education of foreigners studying international law there; his desire for a position as a director of the Irving Trust Company; his trusteeship of Rollins College, Winter Park, Florida, and matters relating to that school; his efforts to establish institutes and conferences, principally on international relations, in various institutions in the United States and foreign countries; his philanthropic plans, chiefly educational; the trusteeship of the Field Library of Peekskill, New York; his donations to foreign embassies and legations for the translation into English of the addresses of their foreign ministers to their parliaments; the League to Enforce Peace; Pugsley's efforts to obtain the Democratic nomination for various local, state, and national offices, especially U.S. senator and governor of New York; his willingness to serve in the U.S. State Department and his efforts to be named under secretary of state by Franklin Delano Roosevelt in 1933; New York and national politics; the American Scenic and Historic Preservation Society; the preservation of "Lindenwald," home of Martin Van Buren (1782-1862); portrait work commissioned by Pugsley and donated to various institutions; financial requests; the Westchester (New York) County National Bank; banking; investments in stocks and in American and foreign bonds; stock analyses; real estate; insurance; the depression; railroads, especially the Seaboard All-Florida Railway Company; coal mining; business promotional schemes; financial requests from institutions and individuals, particularly during the depression; various awards given by Pugsley, such as the Pugsley Award of the National Conference of Social Work; history; Pugsley family history and genealogy; and other matters. Some letters are of a more routine nature and pertain to administrative arrangements for various institutes and conferences; and invitations to attend meetings and to join organizations. Legal papers consist chiefly of typed copies of wills, affidavits, deeds, and trusts relating to Chester DeWitt Pugsley, the Westchester County National Bank, and various institutional recipients of Pugsley's philanthropy. There are numerous press releases and clippings from news bureaus concerning Pugsley's views on foreign and domestic affairs, his benefactions, institutes and conferences held, and the activities of the American Scenic and Historical Preservation Society. Printed material includes programs of college and university commencements and institutes; notices of stockholders' meetings; advertising circulars; notices of Harvard University class reunions; and papers dealing with national and New York politics in 1916. There are also resolutions relating to world organization, the Westchester County National Bank, the Church Conference on Social Work, and the College of William and Mary, Williamsburg, Virginia; and scattered minutes of the Peekskill Field Committee, Rollins College, and the League to Enforce Peace. Miscellaneous papers include speeches on domestic and foreign topics given by Pugsley.

4344. B. G. PULLIAM AND H. T. CONNALLY PAPERS, 1801 (1875-1880). 415 items. Leasburg (Caswell County), N.C.

Business papers of a mercantile firm, containing many letters from fertilizer companies. Included also are a few papers relating to the estate of Lewis Burwell, 1802, and a few letters to A. B. Newman, a tobacco manufacturer of Leasburg. Among the correspondents are William H. Gilham, and John Ott of the Southern Fertilizing Company in Richmond, Virginia, and other fertilizer companies, including Zell's, and Allison and Addison.

4345. D. M. PULLIAM PAPERS, 1845-1858. 3 items. Richmond, Va.

Business correspondence of D. M. Pulliam, head of a Richmond slave-trading company, concerning the slave market.

4346. SARAH JANE (CLOPTON) PULLIAM ACCOUNT BOOK, 1859-1861. 1 vol. (68 pp.) [Richmond, Va.?]

Housekeeping accounts.

4347. MARY FRANCES JANE PURSLEY PAPERS, 1854-1900. 300 items. New Center (York County), S.C.

Chiefly Civil War letters to Mary Frances Jane Pursley, mainly chronicling the activities of the 18th South Carolina Volunteers, C.S.A., in which her brother, J. Warren Pursley, and other family members served. Letters describe Confederate mobilization; camp life; health conditions and hospitals; food; conditions on the South Carolina coast; guard duty; blockade running; fighting at James Island and Secessionville (South Carolina), Antietam (Maryland), Kinston and Goldsboro (North Carolina), and Bermuda Hundred (Virginia); conditions at Charleston and Sumter (South Carolina) and Richmond (Virginia); the Vicksburg Campaign; the siege of Petersburg and the decimation of the 18th South Carolina by the explosion of mines laid by Union troops; desertion; the progression of J. Warren Pursley from private to 1st lieutenant; and casualties and deaths. Other Civil War correspondence describes Confederate Army life in northern Virginia; the battle of first Manassas; the weaving of cloth for troops; and prices, crops, hogs, and local news in York County. There are also letters from relatives who migrated to Texas and Arkansas in the 1850s, and several poems.

4348. PURVIANCE FAMILY PAPERS, 1757 (1776-1920) 1932. 2,344 items and 21 vols. Baltimore, Md.

Professional and family correspondence and papers of two generations of the Purviance family and several generations of the Courtenay family, related through the marriage of Henry Courtenay and Elizabeth

Isabella Purviance in 1811. The early papers relate chiefly to Samuel Purviance (d. 1787), Baltimore merchant, and chairman of the Committee of Observation for Baltimore County, and consist of records of the interrogation of Purviance by the Council of Safety for the failure of a plan by the Committee of Observation to capture Maryland governor Robert Eden; correspondence discussing British depredations on American shipping, the extension of the Mason-Dixon line, cession of western lands, complaints against the Vandalia and Indiana Land companies, speculation in western lands, sale of lands owned by Purviance on the Chillisquaque River near Sunbury (Pennsylvania), lands owned by George Washington on the Kanawha River, and proposed development of the James River Canal; scattered letters from his wife concerning family matters; letters from his daughter, Letitia, describing her schooling in Philadelphia, Pennsylvania; and letters from his son, John Henry Purviance, regarding his supervision of his father's western lands.

The professional papers of John Henry Purviance, secretary and interpreter to the James Monroe mission, 1794-1796, and secretary of the legation in London, 1804-1810, include memoranda regarding official diplomatic transactions; accounts, 1795, of interviews between Monroe and Jean Debrie, member of the Committee of Public Safety concerning arbitration of the war between France and Great Britain, French suspicion of the Jay Treaty, and the offices of the French in negotiations pending between the United States and Algiers; an account of a conversation between Monroe and one Fulton discussing the efforts of one La Chaise to persuade France to take possession of Louisiana and Florida as a check on American expansion and as a means of luring Kentucky away from the confederation, and Monroe's attempts to strengthen the ties of western territories to the union by asking France to influence Spain to keep the Mississippi River open to American trade; memoranda, 1796, concerning the difficulties of obtaining cash for a draft sent Monroe by the U.S. Treasury; Monroe's outline of a speech to the French National Convention; rough draft of a note from Monroe to the French minister of foreign affairs, Charles Delacroix, pertaining to the Fauchet letter; several letters from Frenchmen dealing with some questionable activity in which Purviance was engaged; letter, 1801, from Fulwar Skipwith, American consul-general at Paris, regarding Pierre Louis Roederer and the ratification of the treaty of 1800 which concluded the XYZ affair; letters from the American painter John Vanderlyn dealing with business transactions; rough drafts, 1806, of articles by Monroe describing the relations between the United States, Great Britain, and France; copy of a letter from Joseph Lakanal to an unnamed royal personage urging him to assert himself as ruler of Spain; papers concerning the restoration of deserting seamen; letter, 1815, from Mr. Barnet, Skipwith's successor, mentioning the successes of Commodores Decatur and Bainbridge against the Algerian pirates, rumors among the French peasantry of the impending return of Napoleon, attitudes of the Federalist Party of the Bourbon restoration, and gossip current in diplomatic circles; document, 1815, of Bon Adrien Jeannot de Moncey, Duc de Conegliano, explaining his refusal to serve on the committee trying Marshal Ney, and making recommendations concerning France's foreign policy; letter, 1817, from the minister of Brazil to the U.S. minister containing copies of the correspondence between himself and the Russian minister dealing with a question of diplomatic protocol; and correspondence concerning Purviance's administrative duties.

Items of a more personal nature include papers relating to the financial affairs of his sister, Elizabeth Isabella Purviance, and the claims of her guardian, David Stewart, against the British government for capture of his vessels; commonplace book, 1781, containing extracts from a tour through Great Britain, excerpts from poems, and a few accounts; account book, 1801-1809, of travel expenses in the United States and Europe; commonplace book of excerpts from poems; commonplace book, 1811-1834, containing a travel diary of England and France, expenses, and a discussion of French government; a diary, 1819, of his travels including his impressions of the Bayonne-Biarritz area noted in the course of a diplomatic mission to Spain; and a memorandum book, 1818, with daily entries regarding weather, correspondence with President Monroe, and personal and financial matters.

Papers of Edward H. Courtenay (d. 1853) include correspondence with his uncle, John Henry Purviance, discussing the former's work and activities at West Point; papers dealing with the settlement of the estate of his grandfather, Hercules Courtenay (d. 1816); correspondence of Edward H. Courtenay, Jr., while attending school in Geneva, New York; personal correspondence with his brother-in-law, William Holmes McGuffey, concerning family and financial affairs; and personal correspondence with his brother, David Courtenay, regarding dealings in stocks, especially those of the Erie Railroad Company and the Aetna Life Insurance Company. Other papers of the Courtenay family include occasional records of the 1st Maryland Volunteers under Lieutenant Colonel N. T. Dushane; letters from Edward H. Courtenay, Jr., describing his work with the U.S. Coastal Survey, divided sentiment in Maryland during the Civil War, and Washington, D.C.; commissions, appointment and other military papers of Chauncey B. Reese and Henry Brewerton, husbands of Mary I. Courtenay and Sarah Courtenay, respectively, daughters of Edward H. Courtenay, Sr.; correspondence between David Courtenay and his son, William, regarding West Virginia lands which were a part of the Purviance estate, and the discovery of oil on those lands; papers relating to the administration of the estates of various members of the Courtenay family;

business papers of William C. Courtenay; financial papers, principally in stock speculation, of several members of the family; financial records of the Maryland Society of the Sons of the American Revolution and of the 5th Maryland Regiment Veteran Corps; letter, 1869, from Edward H. Courtenay, Jr., discussing efforts of Cuba to free herself from Spain and the attitude of the United States towards such efforts, and commenting upon the treatment of Chinese immigrants in the United States; and papers concerning the disappearance and probable death of David S. Courtenay, son of Edward H. Courtenay, Sr., and Virginia (Howard) Courtenay.

Volumes include a mercantile ledger, 1781-1816, of Hercules Courtenay containing accounts of food products, tar, rum, ginseng, ships and shipping ventures, and insurance; ledgers, 1764-1779, and account book for debts receivable, 1764-1776, of Dr. John Boyd, Baltimore physician, containing records of an apothecary; books of recipes and remedies; list of American vessels destroyed by the British; daybook, 1801-1804, of merchant Henry William Courtenay with accounts for flour, food, and other commodities; account books, 1824-1826 and 1835-1842, of David S. Courtenay recording money spent for postage, cash received for legal services, expenditures in lotteries, and personal expenses; address book, possibly of David S. Courtenay; anonymous account book, 1815; scrapbook, 1836, of H. W. Courtenay; diary, 1861, of a soldier including a description of his stay in a Confederate prison; and a scrapbook, 1892-1909, of clippings relating to Baltimore and to the Purviance and Courtenay families.

4349. SAMUEL HENRY PUTNAM REGIMENTAL RECORD, 1861-1864. 1 vol. (78 pp.) Worcester (Worcester County), Mass.

Regimental record of Company A, 25th Massachusetts Volunteers, written by Orderly Sergeant Samuel Henry Putnam probably early in the 1880s, describing mobilization of the company; fighting at Roanoke Island, New Bern, Beaufort, Kinston, and Plymouth (North Carolina), and at Yorktown, Bermuda Hundred, Suffolk, Port Walthal, Chesterfield Junction, Arrowfield Church, and Cold Harbor (Virginia); the siege of Petersburg; and commenting upon camp life, picket duty, casualties, social customs, and re-enlistments. The volume includes a map and notes, and forms the basis for a more detailed version published in 1886.

4350. ABNER PYLES PAPERS, 1842. 1 item and 1 vol. Newberry County, S.C.

Autobiography of Abner Pyles (b. 1772), physician and teacher, describing his education, his four marriages, and other events in his life; and a photocopy of the testimony of Dr. J. H. Davis during the lawsuit between Pyles and his fourth wife.

4351. GEORGE CLINTON QUACKENBOS PAPERS, (1806-1819) 1916. 261 items. New York, N.Y.

Bills and receipts of George Clinton Quackenbos, physician and health officer, while he was establishing his home and his practice in medicine, 1806-1819. The papers concern household furnishings, medical books and drugs, fuel, food, clothing, rent, labor hired, newspaper subscriptions, taxes, and the education of his Negro servant, John Fountain, at the African School in New York. A letter, 1897, from John Hay to Dr. John Duncan Quackenbos, grandson of George Clinton Quackenbos relates that Hay has forwarded information to the U.S. Fish Commission. There is also a social note, 1916, to Carolina Quackenbos, daughter of John Duncan Quackenbos.

4352. STEPHEN PLATT QUACKENBUSH PAPERS, 1867-1868. 2 items. Albany, N.Y.

Letters from Stephen P. Quackenbush (1823-1890), commander in the U.S. Navy, dealing with membership in the "U. N. Association."

4353. WILLIAM QUESENBURY PAPERS, 1845-1876. 29 items and 1 vol. Fort Smith (Sebastian County), Ark.

Diary, 1845-1861, contains an account of a trip to Texas, 1845-1846, describing in detail camp life, food supplies, the weather, quarrels over camping duties, hunting animals for food and for pleasure, plant and animal life, stories about local explorers, several missions and other places visited, and trading with the Caddo, Cherokee, Comanche, Kickapoo, Shawnee, and Chickasaw Indians; an account of a journey to California, 1850, giving accounts of "Mormon Town," dead animals and abandoned wagons passed, price of water, quarrels in camp, the weather, plant and animal life, details of the journey, killing buffalo, and meeting Osage, Arapahoe, and Cheyenne Indians; a long poem based on the Bible; a list of people making the trip to California for the Cherokee California Company; several short poems; a few family records; occasional entries during the 1850s; and lists of pupils in a school taught by Quesenbury in 1848 and 1849. Other papers include clippings; fragment of a letter, 1854, from John Ross concerning a speech he had delivered to the national council of the Cherokee; fragment of a letter of Albert Pike; letter, 1876, from Elias C. Boudinot, editor of Indian Progress, asking Quesenbury to take over the editorship; Quesenbury genealogy; a pamphlet, 1867, by Quesenbury containing remarks addressed to Andrew Johnson and a description of a July 4 celebration in the "Brazos Bottom" (Texas) and pictures. There are also letters from Beulah Blake to Robert H. Woody giving additional information about Quesenbury and other members of the family.

4354.   FREDERICK QUIN RECOLLECTIONS.
        1 vol. (40 pp.) New Jersey.

Personal recollections of an Irish boy's experiences in day school and boarding school, as an employee in a flower nursery, in the army stationed in Nova Scotia and later at Chamblay Barracks on the Saint Lawrence River, and as a gardener in Philadelphia, Pennsylvania.

4355.   CLIFTON QUINN DIARY, 1917-1919.
        1 vol. (179 pp.) North Carolina.

Typescript of a diary kept by Clifton Quinn while on duty on the U.S.S. Surveyor, based at Gibraltar during World War I, describing daily life on board the Surveyor; its officers; war experiences; convoy duty in the North Atlantic and the Mediterranean; liberty experiences in various ports; the progress of the war; submarines; the port of Gibraltar; U.S.S. Prometheus, Parker, Sardinia, Venetia, San Diego, Gregory, Whipple, and Shearwater; operations off the Spanish and French coasts; the sinking of the French ship Susette Fraissenette; torpedoing of H.M.S. Sculptor, Mavisbrook, and Britannia; celebration at the end of the war; the return trip across the Atlantic and demobilization in Virginia. Included also are copies of papers concerning Quinn's discharge.

4356.   JEPTHA QUINN PAPERS, 1861-1863.
        4 items. Rome (Floyd County), Ga.

Correspondence of Jeptha Quinn, farmer and Confederate soldier, giving a detailed account of picket duty and directions for making and taking a medicine composed largely of whiskey. An undated postwar letter comments on the lumber business near Savannah, Georgia.

4357.   SALLY G. QUINN PAPERS,
        1850 (1860-1864) 1927. 80 items.
        Duplin County, N.C.

Family correspondence of Sally G. Quinn, including letters from her husband, Ichabod Quinn, while serving with the Confederate Army describing camp life, health conditions, and desertion, and expressing concern about the family and crops at home; and bills and receipts, many concerning the settlement of Ichabod Quinn's estate.

4358.   CHARLES TODD QUINTARD PAPERS,
        1857-1899. 346 items. Nashville
        (Davidson County), Tenn.

Papers of Charles Todd Quintard, Confederate Army chaplain, surgeon, and aide, and bishop of the Protestant Episcopal Church of Tennessee, include correspondence from other chaplains and ministers concerning chaplains and their duties, the distribution of Bibles and religious literature to Confederate soldiers, and the Episcopal Church in Virginia, North and South Carolina, Tennessee, Georgia, Alabama, and Mississippi; requests for help in obtaining promotions, and in learning of relatives in the Army; letters seeking advice on religious matters; letters giving detailed accounts of the battles of Cheat Mountain, Perryville, Murfreesboro, and Shiloh (Tennessee), the Atlanta Campaign, and Confederate strength at Chickamauga; information on Confederate Generals Joseph E. Johnston, Leonidas Polk, John Bell Hood, Benjamin F. Cheatham, William A. Quarles, J. C. Tyler, Braxton Bragg, and John Adams; letters describing camp life, foraging for food, rumors, the capture of Yankee fortifications and prisoners, Confederate casualties, and the suffering of civilians; history of the 1st Tennessee Regiment; copy of a petition from the mayor and councilmen of Atlanta to General William T. Sherman; general and special Confederate Army orders; circulars pertaining to army regulations; receipts; circulars on the Episcopal Church; passes for Dr. Quintard; autobiographical sketch of Isham G. Harris, Tennessee congressman, governor and U.S. senator; telegrams; clippings concerning the Civil War and the activities of Quintard after the war; and a pamphlet published by the Soldiers Memorial Society, organized to preserve the memory of the soldiers of Massachusetts who had fought in the Civil War, and to give relief to the South, especially in the area of education.

4359.   WILLIAM QUYNN PAPERS,
        1750 (1817-1826) 1844. 23 items.
        Washington, D.C.

Personal correspondence of William Quynn, including a letter, 1819, describing the ordination of Jared Sparks; personal correspondence of Allen Quynn, including a letter, 1823, discussing Andrew Jackson as the favorite presidential candidate of Baltimore, Maryland, residents; and several account sheets.

4360.   LIZZIE RADFORD PAPERS, 1869-1870.
        8 items. Christiansburg
        (Montgomery County), Va.

Personal letters of Lizzie Ranford of "Arnheim" to one Captain Moore, concerning personal shopping.

4361.   WILLIAM RAFFERTY PAPERS, 1819-1829.
        4 items. Annapolis (Anne Arundel
        County), Md.

Papers of the Reverend Doctor William Rafferty, include a letter, 1829, to him from Hector Craig, Sr., a member of the United States House of Representatives from New York, discussing patronage appointments in the administration of Andrew Jackson.

4362.   SIR THOMAS STAMFORD RAFFLES PAPERS,
        1813-1829. 10 items. London,
        England.

Papers of Sir Thomas Stamford Raffles, British colonial administrator, relate to his work in the administration of Java, Bali, and Borneo, including a document, 1814, signed by Van de Wahl describing the island of Bali and its inhabitants; notes on the economic and political history of the Dutch East Indies and the economic situation of the Chinese there; a rough draft of a treaty with the sultan of Pontiana in western Borneo; and a copy of a treaty, ca. 1776, between local rulers defining the boundary between Sambas and the territory to the south.

4363.  ERMINIE (PROUTY) MOORE RAGLAND PAPERS, 1933. 1 item. Atlanta, Ga.

Typed biographical sketch of Erminie (Prouty) Moore Ragland mainly dealing with her work in various philanthropical and other organizations from about 1900 to 1933.

4364.  MAULVI RAHMAN ALI MANUSCRIPT, [1880s?] 1 vol. (60 pp.) Rewa, Vindhya Pradesh, India.

The collection contains a manuscript entitled "The Annals of Baghelkhand," which chronicles the principal events of the reigns of the Maharajas of Rewa, in Baghelkhand, from Baghdeo (549-615 A.D.) to Venkat Raman Singh in the 1880s.

4365.  ELLEN MAGEE RAIGUEL PAPERS, 1830-1950. 353 items. DeLand (Volusia County), Fla.

The papers of Ellen Magee Raiguel deal for the most part with the genealogy of the Raiguel family. There is also material on the Magee, O'Brien, Reichert, and Horter families. The collection includes pictures of Ellen Magee Raiguel and other members of the Raiguel and Horter families.

4366.  JOHN R. RAINE PAPERS, 1843 (1876-1890) 1915. 115 items. Wentworth (Rockingham County), N.C.

The papers of John R. Raine, a physician and pharmacist of Wentworth, North Carolina, contain correspondence between Raine and his brother, Charles A. Raine, a tobacconist of Danville, Virginia, commenting on the state of the tobacco manufacturing business; bills, 1877-1883, to John R. Raine for drugs and druggist's supplies; letters to Raine from patients describing their symptoms and requesting treatment; and letters, 1903-1904, from a girl attending Guilford College, Greensboro, North Carolina.

4367.  M. CAROLINE T. RAINES PAPERS, 1840-1877. 38 items. Milledgeville (Baldwin County), Ga.

Routine personal and business letters.

4368.  SAMUEL RAINEY PAPERS, 1836-1851. 12 items. York County, S.C.

Letters to Samuel Rainey, South Carolina legislator; and letters to John Bratton of Brattonsville, South Carolina, pertaining to lawsuits and the payment of bills.

4369.  MRS. CHARLES C. RAINWATER PAPERS, 1861-1865. 1 item. Saint Louis, Mo.

Typescript of the reminiscences of Mrs. Charles C. Rainwater, concerning friction between Union and Confederate sympathizers in Missouri at the beginning of the Civil War and Mrs. Rainwater's journey from Saint Louis, Missouri, to New Orleans, Louisiana, and up the Mississippi River to Missouri, to meet her husband, a wounded Confederate officer.

4370.  RALEIGH AND GASTON RAILROAD PAPERS, 1838-1871. 1 item and 2 vols. North Carolina.

The collection contains a typed copy of an apprentice's certificate, 1871; a volume, 1838-1841, showing the location of parts of the track, contractors estimates for various sections, survey data, information about supplies, and sketches of the Tar River and Cedar Creek bridges; and a volume, 1855-1858, of station agent's copies of bills for freight received at the station in Ridgeway, North Carolina.

4371.  DAVID RAMSAY PAPERS, 1789, 1810. 2 items. Charleston, S.C.

A letter, 1789, of David Ramsay, physician and historian, referring to a list of Continental officers, and a letter, 1810, from David Ramsay to the Reverend Dr. Jedidiah Morse, discussing the Reverend Dr. John Henry Livingston's sermon of 1804 about missions.

4372.  GEORGE RAMSAY, NINTH EARL OF DALHOUSIE, PAPERS, 1830. 1 item. Dalhousie Castle, Midlothian, Scotland.

Letter from George Ramsay, Ninth Earl of Dalhousie, British general and commander-in-chief in India, to Edward Foss, Jr., an attorney in London, discussing a lawsuit and an illness.

4373.  GEORGE JUNKIN RAMSEY PAPERS, 1802 (1832-1918). 4,044 items and 25 vols. Lynchburg (Campbell County), Va.

Letters and papers of George J. Ramsey (1857-1928), educator; and of his father, James B. Ramsey (d. 1871), a Presbyterian minister; and of the latter's wife, Sabra S. (Tracy) Ramsey. The letters of James B. Ramsey are concerned with his activities in 1832-1833 as a student in

Lafayette Agricultural College, Easton, Pennsylvania; his work as minister in Lynchburg; home mission work as superintendent of Spencer Academy for boys of the Choctaw nation at Doaksville, Arkansas; courtship with Sabra S. Tracy; and founding of the Lynchburg Female Academy in 1870 and its continuation by Sabra S. (Tracy) Ramsey, 1871-1885.

George J. Ramsey's papers center around his student activities at Hampden-Sydney College, Virginia, in 1872, and at the University of Virginia, Charlottesville, in 1879; and his career in education including teaching at Ogden College, Bowling Green, Kentucky, 1880-1884; presidency of Silliman Female Collegiate Institute, Clinton, Louisiana, 1884-1900; editorship of the education department of B. F. Johnson Publishing Company, Richmond, Virginia, 1900-1902; presidency of King College, Bristol, Tennessee, 1902-1904; principalship of Sayre Institute, Lexington, Kentucky, 1904-1907; professorship of education at Central University (later Centre College), Danville, Kentucky, 1907-1912; and presidency of Peace Institute, Raleigh, North Carolina, 1912-1916. Included also are many commercial broadsides and circulars relative to educational supplies and equipment and Ramsey's work with the B. F. Johnson Publishing Company; correspondence, broadsides, and circulars concerning activities of the Southern Educational Association, of which he was an officer, and of the Annual Conferences for Education in the South; and volumes consisting of account books, grade books, memoranda and notes, the most outstanding being three account books of Silliman Institute, 1885-1889, and two letterpress copybooks, 1891-1897. Among the correspondents are Nicholas Murray Butler, Charles William Dabney, Theodore Dreiser, William Goodell Frost, James Hampton Kirkland, Samuel Douglas McEnery, Condé Nast, Clarence H. Poe, Stuart H. Robinson, and Augustus E. Willson.

4374. JOHN RAMSEY AND JAMES M. RAMSEY ACCOUNT BOOKS, 1834-1884. 5 vols. Seaboard (Northampton County), N.C.

Accounts of a plantation and a general merchandise firm.

4375. DANIEL CURTIS RAND PAPERS, 1840 (1865-1878) 1893. 800 items. Pittsford (Monroe County), N.Y.

The collection contains the business correspondence of Daniel Curtis Rand, Lucia Rand, and Mortimer Wadams concerning the manufacturing of gunpowder in Middletown, Connecticut, and Pittsford, New York. Other letters of members of the Rand and Wadams families concern social life in Connecticut and describe Chicago, Illinois, after the fire of 1871. Miscellaneous items include a prospectus for The Illuminati which was to be published by the Society of the Rosy Cross, beginning in 1868.

4376. ALEXANDER RANDALL PAPERS, 1831-1851. 8 items. Annapolis (Anne Arundel County), Md.

Letters to attorney Alexander Randall mainly concerning the collection of debts and one letter, 1831, to Randall from Francis Scott Key discussing the colonization of Negroes in Africa.

4377. JAMES RYDER RANDALL PAPERS, 1874-1904. 5 items. Augusta (Richmond County), Ga.

Correspondence of James Ryder Randall (1839-1908), poet and journalist, referring to his poem, "Maryland, My Maryland," relations with publishers, and conditions during Reconstruction.

4378. DAVID RANDELL PAPERS, 1815-1837. 3 items and 1 vol. New York, N.Y.

Records of court cases of Randell, a New York attorney, indicating actions taken and financial transactions, with an index.

4379. LEE HARRIET RANDLE PAPERS, 1759-1930. 26 items. Oxford (Lafayette County), Miss.

The papers of Lee Harriet Randle are made up for the most part of letters and copies of documents dealing with the genealogy of the Griffin family of Virginia and South Carolina. Also documents relating to Randle's position as postmistress of Oxford, Mississippi.

4380. BEVERLEY RANDOLPH PAPERS, 1789-1791. 6 items. Richmond, Va.

The collection contains commissions and a land grant signed by Beverley Randolph as governor of Virginia, and a letter to Randolph from Henry Tazewell concerning a legal matter.

4381. EDMUND RANDOLPH PAPERS, 1797-1799. 6 items. Richmond, Va.

Letters of Edmund Randolph (1753-1813), attorney general in George Washington's cabinet, dealing with a lawsuit arising from the sale of slaves held in trust by James Jones and with the collection of a debt.

4382. J. F. RANDOLPH PAPERS, 1869-1876. 6 vols. Washington (Beaufort County), N.C.

Papers of J. F. Randolph, a merchant and county official of Beaufort County, North Carolina, contain five volumes pertaining to Randolph's general store, including four consecutive daybooks, 1869-1874, and an invoice book, 1876. The collection also contains a volume recording the educational expenditures of Beaufort County, 1870-1874.

4383. JOHN RANDOLPH PAPERS, 1793-1832. 29 items. Roanoke (Roanoke County), Va.

Personal letters of John Randolph of Roanoke (1773-1833), Virginia statesman and diplomat, addressed to his nephew, John St. George Randolph and to one Dr. Robinson, commenting on the relations between the new states of the South and Great Britain, and on the Napoleonic Wars, and describing a visit to England in 1822. There are also letters showing Randolph's concern over diplomatic matters and for the personal welfare of slaves, a letter from Randolph to J. M. Garnett indicating his interest in newspapers as a force for molding public opinion, and letters to Randolph from James Wilkinson concerning remarks made by Randolph about Wilkinson.

4384. THOMAS MANN RANDOLPH PAPERS, 1813-1825. 16 items. Albemarle County, Va.

Letters written by Thomas Mann Randolph (1768-1828), member of the United States Congress, 1803-1807, governor of Virginia, 1819-1822, and son-in-law of Thomas Jefferson. Most of the letters are addressed to Joseph C. Cabell and concern Randolph's desire to get the command at Norfolk during the War of 1812, his financial affairs, the Virginia Literary Fund, and schools for the poor in Virginia. There are also several letters between Craven Peyton and Cabell, relating to a misunderstanding between Randolph and Cabell, and a commission signed by Randolph as governor.

4385. WILLIAM BEVERLEY RANDOLPH PAPERS, 1828-1875. 15 items. Washington, D.C.

Letters and papers relating to the estates of J. S. G. Randolph, Richard Randolph, and William B. Randolph. Also a business letter, 1828, to Brett Randolph, brother of William Beverley Randolph.

4386. ROBERT STANLEY RANKIN PAPERS, 1957-1973. ca. 17,000 items. Durham, N.C. Restricted.

The papers of Robert Stanley Rankin, professor of political science at Duke University and member of the United States Commission on Civil Rights, concern his work on the commission, 1960-1973, and contain agendas and minutes for the monthly meetings of the commission, 1959-1973, and material on special meetings; memoranda, correspondence, statements, and news clippings dealing with the operational aspects of the commission; information on the commissioners; administrative and personnel records; budget and appropriation material, 1962-1974; material relating to the rules, regulations, administration, meetings and conferences, and publications of the state advisory committees; papers pertaining to symposiums sponsored by the Civil Rights Commission, the White House, or private sources on particular areas of concern; background studies, schedules, transcripts of proceedings, and news media clippings from the fact finding investigations of the commission, 1960-1973; and commission memoranda, correspondence, statements by both commissioners and others, transcripts of testimony before congressional committees, publications, and news clippings concerning the subject areas of scrutiny by the commission, including education, employment, political participation, housing and urban development, administration of justice, public accommodations, health and welfare, federal programs, minority groups, federal enforcement, and civil liberties and human rights.

4387. RANKIN-PARKER PAPERS, ca. 1880. 3 items. Ripley (Brown County), Ohio.

The collection contains the autobiography of the Reverend John Rankin, Presbyterian minister, describing his childhood in Kentucky, including accounts of camp meetings and denominational rivalries; his ministry in Kentucky; and his abolitionist activities, including his writings, his work as one of the founders and president of the American Reformed Tract and Book Society (later the Western Tract and Book Society), the founding of the American Anti-slavery Society, the organization of local abolition societies in various places in Ohio, and aiding fugitive slaves to escape into Canada. Also contains an account of the life of John Parker, a freeman, as he told it to Frank M. Gregg, a newspaperman of Ripley, Ohio, describing being driven from Norfolk, Virginia, to Mobile, Alabama, in a slave coffle when he was a child; Parker's purchase by a good master and his educational achievements; his escape and recapture; his purchase of freedom; and work with fugitive slaves in Ripley, Ohio. Included also is an account written by Frank M. Gregg and attributed to John Rankin of the flight of a slave woman and her child across the frozen Ohio River, which, it is claimed, formed the basis for an incident in Harriet Beecher Stowe's Uncle Tom's Cabin.

4388. JAMES L. RANSOM, THOMAS JAMES, AND WILLIAM GRAVE PAPERS, 1819-1852. 55 items. Charles Town and Shepherdstown (Jefferson County), W. Va.

Miscellaneous papers of James L. Ransom and Thomas James, farmers of Jefferson County, West Virginia; a few county papers; and accounts of William Grave, a blacksmith.

4389. JAMES M. RANSOM DAYBOOKS AND LEDGERS, 1869-1902. 14 vols. Warrenton (Warren County), N.C.

Accounts of a general merchant.

4390. MATT WHITAKER RANSOM PAPERS, 1853-1887. 6 items. Northampton County, N.C.

Letters of Matt W. Ransom (1826-1904), Confederate soldier, United States senator, 1872-1895, and minister to Mexico, concerning Bedford Brown and Ransom's family and ancestors. Also a letter, 1864, from Robert Ransom, Jr., Confederate major general, referring to captured letters concerning the conditions of troops under General Ulysses S. Grant.

4391. CHARLES LEE RAPER PAPERS, 1894-1912. 323 items and 1 vol. Chapel Hill (Orange County), N.C.

The collection contains manuscript copies of several published works by Charles Lee Raper, historian and economist, including "The Church and Private Schools of North Carolina" (1898); North Carolina: A Study in English Colonial Government (New York: 1904); Principles of Wealth and Welfare (New York: 1906); "Banking in North Carolina" (1909), with John J. Porter; and Railway Transportation (New York: 1912). There are also notes and research material collected by Raper in connection with several of the works in the collection, particularly in relation to schools and banking in North Carolina.

4392. DANIEL RAVENEL PAPERS, 1890, 1931. 2 items. Charleston, S.C.

Letter, 1890, to Daniel Ravenel from the Reverend John Stout, thanking Ravenel for assisting in the publication of a history of the Welsh Neck Baptist Church at Society Hill, South Carolina, and a letter to Ravenel from D. E. Huger Smith concerning a pamphlet by Thomas Tileston Wells entitled The Hugers of South Carolina (New York: 1931).

4393. HARRIOTT HORRY (RUTLEDGE) RAVENEL PAPERS, [1805?]-1862. 4 items. Charleston, S.C.

Miscellaneous personal letters of Harriott Horry (Rutledge) Ravenel, some of which describe life in Charleston during the Civil War.

4394. JOHN STARK RAVENSCROFT PAPERS, 1824-1829. 16 items. Raleigh (Wake County), N.C.

Personal letters of John Stark Ravenscroft (1772-1830), the first Protestant Episcopal bishop of North Carolina, addressed to Gavin Hogg, advising him on his religious duties, discussing the sale of the bishop's Negroes and personal property, and expressing his deep concern for the future of his church in "poor Raleigh."

4395. ALLEN RAWLS PAPERS, 1824-1863. 8 items. Bulloch County, Ga.

Papers concerning the purchase, sale, and transfer of slaves of the Rawls family and Ellen Rawls in particular.

4396. NEVIN RAY PAPERS, 1819 (1829-1861) 1872. 30 items. Moore County, N.C.

Personal letters to Nevin Ray, a surveyor of Moore County, from his four children, two of whom served in the Confederate Army and wrote accounts of their reactions to the Civil War.

4397. J. W. RAYNOR DIARY, 1868-1869, 1876. 1 vol. (240 pp.) Le Raysville (Bradford County), Pa.

Diary of J. W. Raynor, a Presbyterian minister, recording his pastoral activities, the texts of his sermons, and family activities. Also contains lists of books with their prices.

4398. IRA BEMAN READ PAPERS, 1864. 2 items. Ohio.

The papers of Ira Beman Read contain a letter and a reminiscence describing Read's service as an officer in the 101st Ohio Infantry involved in the Atlanta Campaign of General William T. Sherman.

4399. JACOB READ PAPERS, 1778-1821. 36 items. Charleston, S.C.

The papers of Jacob Read (1752-1816), brigadier general in the South Carolina militia, U.S. senator, 1795-1801, and Revolutionary patriot, consist of a deposition, signed by Read in 1790, concerning the ownership of a slave in possession of Richard Cureton, who refused to deliver him to Read's representative, George Dykes; commission of dower, 1794, to Ann Lord, widow of Andrew Lord; a letter from J. Alison, regarding a falsely reported uprising among the Negroes, 1797; a letter from J. Dickinson, regarding orders for the review of the brigade, 1806; a letter from Paul Hamilton, mentioning a commission for one Captain Rouark; comments on Alexander Gillon; and numerous letters concerning the business of Peter Hasenclever, Prussian iron manufacturer, who was involved in extensive litigation in the United States with Read as his attorney.

4400. JAMES READ PAPERS, 1786-1829. 1 item. Savannah, Ga.

Copy of an inventory of slaves belonging to James Read.

4401. JOHN MEREDITH READ, SR., PAPERS, 1849. 1 item. Philadelphia, Pa.

Letter to John Meredith Read from J. Pugh, concerning Pugh's attempt to secure the postmastership in San Francisco, Secretary of State James Buchanan, and the division between the South and North over the Wilmot Proviso.

4402. KEITH M. READ PAPERS, 1917-1935. 15 items. Savannah, Ga.

Papers of Keith M. Read, collector of Southern books and manuscripts, consist mainly of letters from dealers, Wailes Thomas of Atlanta, Georgia, and Harry Stone of New York, concerning the collapse of the cotton market in Atlanta, 1929-1930; the election of John Brown Gordon as United States senator from Georgia in 1873; and the acquisition of books and papers.

4403. READ, TEACKLE & COMPANY DAYBOOK, 1810-1823. 1 vol. (228 pp.) Wachapreague, Va.

Daybook of a general merchandise firm. Also contains crudely kept accounts for a firm or individual, 1864-1874.

4404. WILLIAM READ, JR., PAPERS, 1864-1865. 16 items. Boston, Mass.

Letters of William Read, Jr., concern his service in the United States Navy aboard the U.S.S. Wabash, Connecticut, and Pontoosuc. He discusses routine duties aboard ship; an attack on Fort Fisher, North Carolina, 1864; a visit to Panama, 1865; and the appearance of the Confederate ram, Stonewall, in Havana harbor, Cuba. The collection also contains an itinerary of the U.S.S. Connecticut, February 24, 1865-May 15, 1865.

4405. JOHN READMAN AND AARON HOSKINS PAPERS, 1729-1767. 13 items. St. Marys County, Md.

Two printed papers issued under the authority of the Lords Proprietors of Maryland concerning the disposition of John Readman's (d. 1736) and Aaron Hoskins's (d. 1767) estates. Included also are a copy of Readman's will, for which Hoskins was executor, and several receipts for farm products as payment of rent.

4406. S. W. REAVIES PAPERS, 1865. 1 item. Pettis County, Mo.

Letter concerning Reconstruction politics and current prices.

4407. WILLIAM W. REAVIS PAPERS, 1849-1869. 10 items and 5 vols. Henderson (Vance County), N.C.

Papers of William W. Reavis, United States postmaster at Henderson, North Carolina, contain an incomplete set of postal account books, 1849-1863, listing the non-local newspapers and periodicals received in the community, the names of persons receiving them, and the postage paid on them. There are also loose papers relating to the operations of the post office, including an inventory of local post office property, 1869.

4408. RECUEILS. AFFAIRES DIVERSES DU 18$^e$ SIÈCLE, PARTICULIEREMENT DE CELLES DE DAUPHINÉ, 18th Century. 1 vol. France.

Volume, probably written in the late 18th century, contains 32 articles relating mainly to the political, economic, social, and ecclesiastical history of the province of Dauphiné, including the boundary between Dauphiné and Sardinia; the government of Geneva in 1733; extracts from the registers of the Council of State about certain ecclesiastical matters; methods of teaching at the University of Paris; population, emigration, and the Huguenots; commerce, silk and textile production; a history of fiefs; and affairs concerning the parlement of Dauphiné.

4409. JAMES REDPATH PAPERS, 1869-1886. 9 items and 1 vol. Boston, Mass.

The papers of James Redpath contain letters to him from lecturers whose speaking engagements he booked through the Redpath Lyceum Bureau. Also a letterpress book, 1861, containing copies of letters relating to the activities of the Haitian Bureau of Emigration, Boston, Massachusetts, which Redpath headed. The letters concern the attempt to encourage free black Americans to emigrate to Haiti and include discussions of propaganda used to recruit emigrants; the appointment of local agents to arouse emigration sentiment; and personal appeals from Redpath to abolitionist friends urging them to support emigration.

4410. A. M. REED PAPERS, 1848-1900. 216 pp. Jacksonville (Duval County), Fla.

Typescript copy of the diary of A. M. Reed for the most part concerning work on his plantation near Jacksonville, Florida. Also contains comments on social events; visitors to the area; problems with slaves; local events during the Civil War; Reconstruction in Florida; and an epidemic of yellow fever in Fernandina and Jacksonville, Florida.

4411. ALONZO REED PAPERS, 1864-1866. 21 items. Spring Wells (Wayne County), Mich.

Personal letters of Alonzo Reed, a Negro soldier in the 102nd Regiment Infantry, U.S. Colored Troops, stationed in South Carolina during the latter part of the Civil War.

4412. GEORGE A. REED PAPERS, 1793-1843. 14 items. Winchester (Frederick County), Va.

Papers of George A. Reed, Methodist minister, contain sermons, hymns, texts, and miscellaneous accounts, including a journal, 1800 and 1809-1811, of religious meditations and a journal, 1820, with notes on sermons by ministers at the general conference of the Methodist Church at Philadelphia, Pennsylvania.

4413. WILLIAM BRADFORD REED PAPERS, 1853-1871. 4 items. Philadelphia, Pa.

Miscellaneous correspondence of William Bradford Reed (1806-1876), lawyer and minister to China, including a letter, 1861, referring to an unidentified incident relative to an alleged desertion to the Southern cause.

4414. WILLIAM GARRISON REED PAPERS, 1884. 38 items. Boston, Mass.

The collection contains 38 mounted photographs taken in 1884 on a trip to North Carolina made by William Garrison Reed and Charles J. McIntire to revisit the places in which they had served with the 44th Massachusetts Regiment during the Civil War. The photographs record scenes at or near New Bern, Little Washington, Kinston, Whitehall, Goldsboro battlefield, Rawle's Mill, and a road between Rawle's Mill and Little Washington. Twenty of these photographs were published to accompany Reed's description of the trip, "North Carolina Revisited," Chapter XII of the Record of the Service of the Forty-Fourth Massachusetts Volunteer Militia in North Carolina August 1862 to May 1863 (Boston: 1887).

4415. AUGUSTUS REESE PAPERS, 1861-1877. 3 items. Madison (Morgan County), Ga.

Letters of Augustus Reese, a judge of Morgan County, Georgia, and a member of the Georgia secession convention of 1861, to W. A. Hawkins inquiring about his health and offering Reese's services, 1861; to E. G. Cabaness, 1868, concerning Reese's candidacy for governor of Georgia; and to Governor A. H. Colquitt, recommending Frederick C. Foster for the office of solicitor general of the Ocmulgee circuit, 1877.

4416. E. Y. REESE PAPERS, 1858-1861. 3 items. Baltimore, Md.

Letters from E. Y. Reese, a Methodist minister of Baltimore, to the Reverend R. B. Thompson of Lynchburg, Virginia, concerning the business of the Methodist Protestant Church, hymn books, the attitude of the church on the question of slavery, the superannuate fund, and Lynchburg College.

4417. JOHN W. REESE PAPERS, 1862-1864. 28 items. Buncombe County, N.C.

Letters of John W. Reese, a soldier in the 60th North Carolina Regiment, to his wife, Cristena V. Reese, concerning his health, war weariness, and anxiety about his family. Also contains a brief description of the battle of Chattanooga, 1863.

4418. ENOS REEVES PAPERS, 1780-1781. 3 vols. Charleston, S.C.

The papers of Enos Reeves, soldier in the Revolutionary War, contain three volumes forming a portion of a journal kept in letter form. Subjects of comment in the journals include George Washington's reviewing and entertaining Indian chiefs in New Jersey; the French Army stationed at Newport, Rhode Island; the Benedict Arnold affair; the battles of King's Mountain, North Carolina, and Yorktown, Virginia; problems of discipline in the Continental Army; troop movements; social affairs; counterfeiting and the depreciation of the currency; and service in North Carolina. [This material has been published in the Pennsylvania Magazine of History and Biography, vols. 20-21 (1896-1897).]

4419. JAMES AVERY REEVES PAPERS, 1840-1919. 227 items and 1 vol. Center (Cherokee County), Ala.

The collection is made up for the most part of the papers of Reeves and Cooper, attorneys, including bills to be collected, legal briefs, subpoenas, and notes on pending litigation, and papers relating to James Avery Reeves's position as register in chancery of Cherokee County, Alabama.

4420. JOHN REEVES PAPERS, 1793. 1 item. London, England.

Statement of John Reeves, lawyer and author, concerning observations made by Lord Loughborough, the Lord Chancellor, on a plan for the police district embracing London, Middlesex, and parts of Surrey, Essex, and Kent.

4421. WILLIAM REEVES PAPERS, 1779-1823. 6 items. Wayne County, N.C.

Land deeds of William Reeves [Reaves] and his family.

4422. JAMES REEVS ARITHMETIC BOOK, 1828.

Manuscript volume of arithmetic problems and exercises.

4423. ANNIE (DEMUTH) REGENASS PAPERS, 1849-1869. 51 items. Lancaster (Lancaster County), Pa.

Letters to Annie Demuth Regenass concerning religion, particularly the Moravian Church; activities of the Moravians in North Carolina; and the early days of Salem Female Academy, Salem, North Carolina.

4424. DAVID SETTLE REID PAPERS, 1837-1881. 75 items. Wentworth (Rockingham County), N.C.

Papers of David Settle Reid, governor of North Carolina, concern slave prices, local politics, the Oregon question, and legal advice. Also a report of the activities of the North Carolina legislature of 1836 which mentions a donation for the completion of the state capitol.

4425. FRANK LEWIS REID PAPERS, 1893-1897. 14 items. Greensboro (Guilford County), N.C.

The papers of Frank Lewis Reid contain his report, 1893, as president of Greensboro Female College; letters of Solomon Lea, first president of Greensboro Female College; report, 1893, of Reid to the North Carolina Conference of the Methodist Episcopal Church, South, and report of Dred Peacock, Reid's successor as president of Greensboro Female College, to the North Carolina Conference, 1896; memoir of Mary Fleming Black; sketch of the Emerson Literary Society at Greensboro Female College; and the alumnae address of Sallie S. Cotten, 1897, on the 50th anniversary of the college.

4426. JAMES L. REID PAPERS, 1861-1862. 44 items. Madison (Morgan County), Ga.

The Civil War letters of James L. Reid of the 3rd Georgia Regiment concern Confederate fortifications on Roanoke Island, North Carolina; the capture of a Union steamer; advice to his wife on the management of their plantation; and the capture of Roanoke Island by Union forces.

4427. JOHN JAMES REID PAPERS, 1851-1919. 24 items. Edinburgh, Scotland.

The papers of John James Reid, Scottish lawyer and Liberal politician, contain letters, 1851, to Reid's father, Sir James John Reid, concerning constitutional changes affecting the supreme court of justice of the Ionian Islands; letters, 1879-1880, concerning the parliamentary election of 1880 and William E. Gladstone's campaign in Midlothian; letters, 1883, concerning the proposed local government board for Scotland; and letters, 1919, concerning the Slater murder case.

4428. WILLIAM SHIELDS REID PAPERS, 1805-1852. 1 vol. Lynchburg (Campbell County), Va.

Photocopy of the account book of William Shields Reid (1778-1853), pastor of the First Presbyterian Church in Lynchburg, recording fees received for marriages and funeral services performed, his salary for preaching, and miscellaneous sources of income, such as dividends from turnpike stock.

4429. REID FAMILY PAPERS, 1818-1891. 188 items. Sumter County, S.C.

The Reid family papers consist, for the most part, of letters to William Moultrie Reid, a Presbyterian minister, concerning the Reid family and other families of Charleston, South Carolina; Princeton University and Harvard University, 1818; Davidson College, Davidson, North Carolina, 1868; the Civil War in lower South Carolina, 1864; Christopher Gaillard and the Santee Light Artillery in the Civil War; and religious observances among Confederate troops. The collection also contains a number of William M. Reid's sermons, written mainly for funerals, and his diary, 1854-1875, which is concerned with daily routine and his ministerial duties.

4430. GEORG ANDREAS REIMER PAPERS, 1830. 1 item. Berlin, Germany.

Letter, 1830, to Georg Andreas Reimer, bookstore owner in Berlin, from Georg Wilhelm Friedrich Hegel concerning financial arrangements relative to Hegel's Enzyklopädie.

4431. GEORGE COLLIER REMEY SCRAPBOOK, 1939. 1 vol. (50 pp.) Burlington (Des Moines County), Iowa.

A scrapbook of pictures and clippings relating to the career of Rear Admiral George Collier Remey (1841-1928).

4432. CLARKE H. REMICK PAPERS, 1863-1866. 157 items.

Papers of Clarke H. Remick, officer in the Union Army, contain records of the 35th United States Infantry (Colored)--originally the 1st North Carolina Regiment (Colored)--and the 103rd United States Infantry (Colored), including monthly and quarterly inventory reports of clothing, ordnance supplies, and other items of military equipment issued to individual soldiers. Other items in the collection relate to Remick's duties as provost marshal of Savannah, Georgia.

4433. W. H. REMINGTON PAPERS, 1842-1849. 7 items. Centerville (Kent County), R.I.

Letters from W. H. Remington, acting quartermaster sergeant of the U.S. Artillery, stationed at various times in Fort Columbia (New York), Fort Brown (Texas), and Fort Johnson (North Carolina), to his brother, Thomas Remington, of Cranston, Rhode Island, and his father, Jonathan Remington, of Centerville, Rhode Island. The letters are chiefly concerned with his hopes of making enough money for a man of his station in life.

4434. WILLIAM W. RENWICK PAPERS, 1792 (1840-1927) 1948. 2,393 items and 12 vols. Newberry and Union Counties, S.C.

This collection contains the papers of several generations of the related Renwick, Rogers, Beard, Lyons, and Bothwell families of South Carolina and several other Southern states, particularly the papers of William W. Renwick, his wife, Rosannah P. (Rogers) Renwick, and his brother-in-law and sister-in-law, James Rogers and Nancy H. Rogers. The correspondence concerns family matters; a minister's views on slavery, 1821; fear of a slave insurrection in Union District, South Carolina, 1831; the presence of United States troops in Georgia to quell an Indian uprising, 1836; murder of a master by his slaves, 1842; religious instruction of slaves; temperance activity in South Carolina and Mississippi; state politics in Georgia, 1844; conditions in Ireland; and a British newspaper account of an American slave uprising as reported by an Irish relative of William W. Renwick; marketing of cotton; the Mexican War; secession in Texas; and conditions in a Confederate prison near Florence, South Carolina. Other items in the collection include financial records relating to the 1st North Carolina Regiment, the 3rd North Carolina Regiment, and the 44th Georgia Regiment in 1862; material concerning the Patrons of Husbandry; a map and history of Marion County, Florida; an ode for the dedication of the Female Academy chapel, Salem, North Carolina, 1824; and bills and receipts. Volumes include daybooks, 1874-1878 and 1880, and a notebook of James E. Renwick, a physician; commonplace book of William W. Renwick; and sawmill account book of Renwick and Rice, 1857-1859.

4435. ISAIAH RESPESS PAPERS, 1787 (1840-1870) 1887. 1,000 items. Washington (Beaufort County), N.C.

Business correspondence, accounts, and shipping bills of Isaiah Respess, a lumber and shingle manufacturer engaged in coastwise trade. He was loyal to the Union during the Civil War, and continued his shipping because of the early Federal occupation of the Washington region.

4436. RETAIL CLERKS INTERNATIONAL ASSOCIATION PAPERS, 1931-1952. 20 items and 4 vols. Lafayette (Tippecanoe County), Ind.

Papers of the Retail Clerks International Association (AFL) contain a copy of an appeal to AFL unions to patronize union clerks only, 1931; agreements; News-Let, a serial; flyers for a union movie and for organizing drives; a pamphlet giving the history of the union since 1888; and the proceedings of the twentieth convention of the association, 1947, and the twenty-first convention, 1951.

4437. REVENUE RECORDS OF THE DUCHIES OF CORNWALL AND LANCASTER, 1681-1702. 2 vols. Lancaster, England, and Cornwall, Wales.

Report of an auditor concerning crown revenues of the Duchy of Cornwall in 1688 and 1700 and a similar report on the land revenue of the crown in the Duchy of Lancaster in 1688 and 1701.

4438. DAVID P. REYNOLDS PAPERS, 1862-1864. 2 vols. East Bridgewater (Plymouth County), Mass.

The collection contains the diary of David P. Reynolds, a soldier in the 3rd Massachusetts Regiment and the 60th Massachusetts Regiment, concerning his experiences near New Bern, North Carolina, 1862-1863. Reynolds discusses camp life; troop movements; casualties; the attitudes of Southern civilians; Negroes as contraband and the Negro community of New Bern; and military engagements near New Bern. Also contains a roll book kept by Reynolds as sergeant in the 60th Massachusetts.

4439. ELMER ROBERT REYNOLDS PAPERS, 1904. 1 item. Washington, D.C.

Papers of Elmer Robert Reynolds, ethnologist and botanist, contain a letter from Arthur Jerome Eddy concerning Eddy's book, Recollections and Impressions of James A. McNeill Whistler (Philadelphia: 1904).

4440. ISAAC V. REYNOLDS PAPERS, 1862-1865. 38 items. Lebanon (Russell County), Va.

Photocopies of typescript copies of the letters of Isaac V. Reynolds, a soldier in the 16th Virginia Regiment, Cavalry, written while in training at Camp Comfort, Roanoke County, Virginia; during the Gettysburg campaign; and during the Valley Campaigns, 1864.

4441. JOHN REYNOLDS PAPERS, 1748-1756. 5 items. Savannah, Ga.

Papers of John Reynolds, British navy officer and the first colonial governor of Georgia, contain orders of Reynolds as commander of a British ship and miscellaneous papers relating to his duties as governor.

4442. LAFAYETTE P. REYNOLDS PAPERS, 1814 (1860-1879) 1914. 370 items. Jacinto (Tishomingo County), Miss.

Papers of Lafayette P. Reynolds, an attorney, concern legal matters and political affairs in Mississippi and the nation. Collection includes a letter, 1857, on the senatorial election in Mississippi; a letter concerning the Bland-Allison Act of 1878; and a memorandum concerning the position of the Farmers' Alliance in Mississippi during the late 1880s.

4443. THOMAS C. REYNOLDS PAPERS, 1861. 1 item. Jefferson City (Cole County), Mo.

Letter to Thomas C. Reynolds, an attorney in Jefferson City, Missouri, from John W. Noel, United States representative from Missouri, concerning the Wolf Island case of Missouri v. Kentucky, then before the United States Supreme Court, and a notation on the back of the letter by Reynolds giving a portion of his reply, which included an evaluation of unionist sentiment in Missouri.

4444. W. M. REYNOLDS PAPERS. 1 item. Pennsylvania.

Copy of a circular, probably written by W. M. Reynolds, Lutheran minister and educator, concerning the organization of the East Pennsylvania Synod of the Lutheran Church.

4445. ROBERT BARNWELL RHETT PAPERS, 1838-1874. 6 items and 1 vol. Charleston, S.C.

Papers of Robert Barnwell Rhett, United States senator from South Carolina and leader in the secession movement, contain routine business and political letters; letter, 1846, from Rhett to Franklin Harper Elmore concerning the elections of 1846; and a letter, 1858, from William H. Branch to R. B. Rhett, Jr., expressing the hope that the elder Rhett would be returned to the United States Senate. Also accounts, 1853-1866, from Rhett's plantation at Altamaha, Georgia.

4446. H. I. RHODES MEMORANDUM BOOK, 1845-1856. 1 vol. Leesburg (Loudoun County), Va.

Accounts of H. I. Rhodes, a general merchant. Included also are birth records of his children.

4447. HILLARY H. RHODES PAPERS, 1822-1844. 15 items and 1 vol. Leesburg (Loudoun County), Va.

A naval indent book of goods destined for marine hospital and various naval vessels, 1819-1822; Hillary H. Rhodes's commission as midshipman on the frigate Constellation; letters relative to a dispute between Rhodes and his fellow officers; orders; leaves of absence; and other miscellaneous papers.

4448. JAMES RHODES PAPERS, 1849-1866. 10 items and 1 vol. Clarke County, Ala.

Papers of James Rhodes contain a copy of a contract between Rhodes and his former slaves, 1865, and financial papers, 1863-1866. The volume contains the accounts of Rhodes and his partners, Joseph Borden and A. M. Garber, and Rhodes's personal accounts.

4449. JAMES FORD RHODES PAPERS, 1911-1919. 52 items. Boston, Mass.

Letters of James Ford Rhodes, American historian, to Thomas Sergeant Perry, give Rhodes's impressions of social conditions in England, France, Germany, and Austria during his visits to Europe in 1911, 1912, and 1914. Rhodes also comments on books he is reading, the American presidential election of 1916, negotiations between the kaiser and the czar, neutrality, the formation of the Triple Entente, British foreign policy, historical writing in France after 1870, and foreign relations of the United States.

4450. MELCHI RHODES PAPERS, 1797-1902. 2 items and 1 vol. Lincoln County, N.C.

Account book of Melchi Rhodes, farmer of Lincoln County, North Carolina, contains entries for sales of goods and services to the Quartz Gold Mining Company, Vestal's Ford, North Carolina, 1854; slave hiring, 1854-1860; money lending, 1861-1902; transactions of the postmaster of Killian's Post Office, North Carolina, 1882-1883; and general agricultural accounts, 1854-1902. Papers include Rhodes's exemption from Confederate military service, 1864.

4451. CHARLES H. RICE ACCOUNT BOOK AND SCRAPBOOK, 1859-1861. 1 vol. (280 pp.) Ridgeville (Colleton County), S.C.

A general mercantile account book of Charles H. Rice, also containing newspaper clippings. Of interest are clippings on Mother Theresa Barry of Charleston, South Carolina, and General Wade Hampton.

4452. CLARKE RICE PAPERS, 1825-1867. 28 items. Sebewa (Ionia County), Mich.

Family papers of Clarke Rice, his son, Henry Oscar Rice, and his brother, Daniel Rice, concern farm life in New York and Michigan in the 1820s, the 1850s, and the close of the Civil War; and Henry Oscar Rice's service in the 9th Michigan Regiment concerning camp life, health conditions, and new weapons, 1861-1862.

4453. JAMES HENRY RICE, JR., PAPERS, 1885 (1910-1935). 13,581 items. Wiggins (Colleton County), S.C.

The papers of James Henry Rice, Jr., naturalist, conservationist, and local historian, contain mainly correspondence reflecting his interest in natural history and the protection of wildlife; the history and contemporary politics of South Carolina; and family, business, artistic, and journalistic matters. Material pertaining to Rice's activities as a naturalist and conservationist include letters, 1910-1913, to Rice from the

Carolina Audubon Society and the National Association of Audubon Societies; correspondence, 1913-1917, with Robert Ridgway, E. H. Forbush, William Brewster, and officials of the National Museum in Washington, D.C., relating to Rice's work as inspector for the United States Biological Survey, concerning ornithology, particularly the breeding grounds, habitats, and migratory patterns of various Southeastern birds; long-term correspondence with Arthur Trezevant Wayne, author of Birds of South Carolina (Charleston: 1910); correspondence, 1927-1935, with William Chambers Coker, primarily concerning the identification of certain botanical specimens; correspondence concerning the Conservation Society of South Carolina; letters of naturalist Frank M. Chapman and explorer Carl E. Akely; correspondence with R. W. Shufeldt on natural history; letters concerning Secretary of the Interior Albert B. Fall and the Teapot Dome Scandal, 1921-1922; correspondence concerning forest lands in South Carolina with Courtlandt Braun, W. R. Mattoon of the United States Forest Service, and South Carolina state foresters, Lewis E. Staley, 1928-1931, and W. A. Smith, 1932; correspondence with W. T. Hornaday on conservation measures in the United States Congress, especially the Norbeck bill, 1929, which sought to impose hunting limits on ducks; correspondence, 1930, concerning the relationship of the National Association of Audubon Societies to the manufacturers of guns and ammunition; and letters relating to the meeting of the American Ornithologists Union in Charleston, South Carolina, 1928. Correspondence on South Carolina politics and the state's history includes letters giving the views of various candidates for state and national office and commenting on elections and other political events; letters, 1905-1918, from United States Senator Benjamin R. Tillman; correspondence with Coleman L. Blease, governor of South Carolina, on the appointment of state game wardens, 1911-1913; correspondence relating to several articles written by Rice on local history and notable South Carolinians, especially "The Paladins of South Carolina," a series appearing in the State (Columbia, South Carolina) in 1922-1923, containing material on Martin W. Gary and Reconstruction in South Carolina, and Francis Wilkinson Pickens Butler's letters about Matthew Calbraith Butler; correspondence concerning the histories of the Rice, Elliott, Stuart, Clarkson, and Smith families; letters, 1929, discussing the life and career of J. Marion Sims; and correspondence, ca. 1926, with Dudley Jones on the history of the Presbyterian Church in South Carolina. Items pertaining to business, literature, journalism and Rice's family include letters from George F. Mitchell on the development of coastal South Carolina; correspondence regarding a stock law for South Carolina, 1920-1921; correspondence with writers and academics including Marie Conway Oemler, Archibald Rutledge, Harriette Kershaw Leiding, William Peterfield Trent, Basil Lanneau Gildersleeve, and Ambrose E. Gonzales; correspondence with Dubose Heyward and John Bennett concerning the Poetry Society of South Carolina; letters from Francis Butler Simkins, Jr., 1922-1923, responding to Rice's criticism of his work; correspondence relating to Rice's work as agent for the Chee-Ha Combahee Company promoting the development of coastal lands, 1921-1922; letters concerning the development of Myrtle Beach, South Carolina, 1925; a long personal correspondence with the sculptor Frederick Wellington Ruckstull containing news of Rice's family and exchanges of opinion on politics, art, and history; letters from many of Rice's friends in the 1930s showing the effects of the Depression; and letters discussing Franklin D. Roosevelt and the New Deal. Printed matter and miscellaneous items in the collection include eulogies of Rice, several articles reflecting his interest in history and nature; report of the game warden of South Carolina, 1912; minutes of the 1932 meeting of the alumni association of the University of South Carolina; poems by Rice; and pamphlets and articles on natural history.

4454. WILLIAM RICE ACCOUNTS, 1815-1825. 3 vols. Brunswick County, Va.

Accounts of a general merchant.

4455. HENRY RICHARD PAPERS, 1858. 1 item. London, England.

A letter to Henry Richard, British political figure, from William Edward Forster, responding to Richard's pamphlet about the Indian Mutiny.

4456. ABRAHAM RICHARDS PAPERS, 1841-1846. 3 items. New York, N.Y.

Business letters to Abraham Richards, a merchant of New York, discussing cotton prices, the brigs Augusta and L. Baldwin, and building supplies.

4457. DAVIS RICHARDSON PAPERS, 1720-1885. 1,721 items and 2 vols. Frederick (Frederick County), Md.

The papers of Davis Richardson, justice of the peace of Frederick County, Maryland, and member of the House of Delegates of Maryland, are made up for the most part of bills and legal papers, including land indentures; surveyors' statements and plats; bills of sale; bonds and obligations; promissory notes; personal accounts; appraisals of estates; property evaluations; writs and summonses issued by the justices of the peace of Frederick County, Maryland; writs and warrants issued by the County and Orphans' Courts of Frederick and Baltimore counties, Maryland; copies of the court records of the Court of Oyer, Terminer and General Gaol Delivery for Baltimore County, Maryland; copies of records of the Circuit Court of the District of Columbia for Washington County, Maryland; copies of orders by and depositions made in the Orphans' Court of Frederick County and of orders issued by the Montgomery County, Maryland, Orphans' Court; and certifications by the clerks of the Baltimore County and Orphans' Courts. Also copies of decrees given by the Maryland chancellors, Alexander Contee Hanson and William Kitty; a land grant, 1812, by President James Madison; letters to Davis and William Richardson dealing with property sales, the sale of slaves, and politics in Frederick County; and two copies of the American Party ticket in Maryland, 1857, in the form of printed lists on strips of white silk. Volumes include a mill book, 1811-1814, containing the records of a flour mill; a ledger, 1825-1827, containing miscellaneous accounts; and an anonymous diary of unknown year describing travels through Pennsylvania, Ohio, and Kentucky.

4458.  ISAAC RICHARDSON PAPERS, 1856. 1 item. Cane Creek (Chatham County), N.C.

Letter to Isaac Richardson from W. M. Roberts, a master mechanic in the North Carolina Railroad Company shop, discussing a blacksmith shop for the railroad.

4459.  J. W. RICHARDSON AND COMPANY DAYBOOK, 1868-1869. 1 vol. (100 pp.) Fifesville (Goochland County), Va.

Mercantile accounts, containing also cooking recipes and household suggestions.

4460.  JAMES BURCHELL RICHARDSON PAPERS, 1803 (1822-1910). 4,110 items. Sumter District, S.C.

Family letters and business papers of James B. Richardson, plantation owner and slaveholder, and of his descendants. The letters and papers contain references to the allotment of slave labor for road and railroad construction; the impressment of slaves for work on fortifications during the Civil War; political wrangles; James B. and Richard C. Richardson's activities in the Confederate Army; social and economic conditions on South Carolina plantations before, during, and after the Civil War; the postwar depression and poverty in the South; and tenant farming during the postwar period.

4461.  VIRGINIA RICHARDSON AND BETTIE RICHARDSON PAPERS, 1845-1872. 35 items. Charlotte Court House (Charlotte County), Va.

Family and personal letters. One letter concerns the experiences of a clerk in a Richmond grocery store; another the precarious existence of the postwar schoolteacher.

4462.  WILLIAM A. B. RICHARDSON PAPERS, 1825 (1850-1860) 1869. 16 items. Johnston County, N.C.

Personal letters of William A. B. Richardson and his wife, who, together, conducted a school at Wilson, North Carolina. One letter, September, 1854, comments on patent medicines and on the proposed annexation of the Hawaiian Islands; another, July, 1860, concerns the sale of turpentine at Wilmington, North Carolina. Included also is a printed circular, 1859, concerning the Wilson schools.

4463.  J. AUGUSTUS RICHEY PAPERS, 1860-1863. 26 items. Savannah, Ga.

Miscellaneous letters of a soldier in the 8th Georgia Battalion stationed at Savannah, Georgia.

4464.  RICHMOND AND DANVILLE RAILROAD RENT BOOK, 1897-1909. 1 vol. Stem (Granville County), N.C.

Record of rents collected from tenants in houses owned by the railroad.

4465.  RICHMOND DOCK COMPANY PAPERS, 1818-1831. 7 items. Richmond, Va.

Papers relating to the condemnation of private lands to be used by the Richmond Dock Company.

4466.  RICHMOND, FREDERICKSBURG, AND POTOMAC RAILROAD COMPANY PAPERS, 1863-1864. 5 items. Richmond, Va.

Receipts of the Richmond, Fredericksburg, and Potomac Railroad and items concerning the association of that railroad with the Army of Northern Virginia during the Civil War.

4467.  ABRAHAM RICKERSON ARITHMETIC BOOK, 1803. 1 vol.

An incomplete book of arithmetic exercises and instructions.

4468.  GEORGE RICKETTS PAPERS, 1837-1892. 229 items. Elkton (Cecil County), Md.

The papers of George Ricketts, lawyer and Maryland legislator, concern family matters; Ricketts's involvement, 1852, with a bill in the Maryland legislature sanctioning the construction of a bridge across the Susquehanna River at Havre de Grace by the Philadelphia, Wilmington, and Baltimore Railroad; and land speculation in Iowa, 1856-1857. Also contains household accounts, land deeds in Maryland, a statement of Whig principles, and a subscription brochure for the Maryland Revolutionary Monument Association, 1892.

4469. JAMES A. RIDDICK PAPERS, 1851-1870. 21 items. Brunswick County, Va., and Johnson's Island (Sandusky County), Ohio.

Letters written to and by James A. Riddick, lieutenant in the Confederate Army, while imprisoned at Johnson's Island, Ohio. Included also is a clipping from the New York News concerning food supplies for the prisoners.

4470. NATHANIEL RIDDICK LEDGER, 1851-1882. 1 vol. (136 pp.) Suffolk (Nansemond County), Va.

Personal accounts.

4471. RICHARD H. RIDDICK PAPERS, 1840-1879. 408 items and 1 vol. Pantego (Beaufort County), N.C.

Business correspondence, indentures, bills, and receipts of Richard H. Riddick, a lumber dealer, including material pertaining to a runaway slave and unsuccessful attempts to recover him from Boston, Massachusetts. Also contains two copies of the Boston Commonwealth, January 31, and February 8, 1851, with editorial comments on the case written from an antislavery point of view; papers, including the articles of association, of the Albemarle Swamp Land Company; and a book of sundry accounts, 1859-1861.

4472. W. D. RIDDICK AND E. W. RIDDICK LEDGERS, 1847-1852. 2 vols. Suffolk (Nansemond County), Va.

Merchants' account books.

4473. JAMES N. RIDDLE PAPERS, 1851-1864. 38 items. Martinsburg (Berkeley County), W. Va.

Personal and family letters of James N. Riddle concerning the death of his wife and his son, tension following John Brown's raid, 1859, and family and religious matters.

4474. RIDGELEY FAMILY PAPERS, 1793-1817. 8 items. Anne Arundel County, Md.

Miscellaneous papers of several members of the Ridgeley family, including warrants issued during Charles Carnan Ridgeley's term as governor of Maryland.

4475. ROBERT RIDGWAY PAPERS, 1913. 1 item. Washington, D.C.

Letter of Robert Ridgway, American ornithologist, concerning the preparation of his book, The Birds of North and Middle America (Washington: 1901).

4476. KURT RIESS PAPERS, 1904-1933. 1 vol. Germany.

Scrapbook containing pictorial clippings from German publications concerning the German, Russian, Japanese, British, French, and United States navies; naval and land operations during the Russo-Japanese War, 1904-1905; and naval operations during World War I.

4477. PHILIP D. RIGGS PAPERS, 1862 (1863-1865) 1870. 37 items. Carthage (Athens County), Ohio.

Love letters from Philip D. Riggs, 5th Ohio Volunteer Infantry and later the 4th Ohio Volunteer Cavalry, to Celina Dobbins, with occasional references to troop movements, the hardships of camp life, infestation of camp by rats, and losses suffered by his regiment at the battle of Selma, Alabama. Two letters from relatives discuss the Dobbins and Riggs families, life in Missouri, and the suffering of civilians during the war.

4478. RIGGS FAMILY PAPERS, 1839-1933. 330 items. Washington, D.C.

Correspondence, legal papers, financial papers, pictures, and printed material of the Riggs family. Correspondence pertains to the interest of George Washington Riggs (1813-1881), founder of Riggs and Company and of the Riggs National Bank, Washington, D.C., in collecting art objects, currency, and paintings, and to his investments in Washington real estate; the investments of his daughters, Jane Riggs (1853-1930) and Alice Riggs, in various companies; the settlement of the share of the estate of Katherine Shedden (Riggs) de Geofroy (d. 1881) belonging to her sons, George de Geofroy and Antoine de Geofroy; business correspondence between Jane Riggs and the children of Cecilia (Riggs) and Henry Howard, especially George Howard; and the stranding of Jane Riggs in Germany at the outbreak of World War I. Legal papers, relating principally to the settlement of the estates of various members of the Riggs family, include estate papers of Elisha Riggs (1779-1853); will of George Washington Riggs, records of the division of the estate, and an accounting of the executor, Lawrason Riggs (1814-1888), brother of George Washington Riggs; papers pertaining to the lawsuit of Francis B. Riggs, William C. Riggs, and Mary G. Riggs, of the family of Elisha Riggs, Jr., against the remaining members of families of the children of Elisha Riggs, Sr., containing a listing of the members of the Riggs family and several wills; inventory of the estate of Thomas Lawrason Riggs, 1888; inventory of the estate of Jane Riggs, 1930-1931; guardianship papers for George de Geofroy and Antoine de Geofroy, 1893-1894; and title to a real estate lot in Washington, D.C., a legal matter involving former President Franklin Pierce. Financial papers are chiefly the statements of Alice and Jane Riggs, and a few bills of exchange relating to the commercial transactions of George Peabody and his partner, Elisha Riggs. Printed materials include pamphlets on the suit of Elisha Francis Riggs (d. 1936) against Mary McMullen, companion of Jane Riggs, for possession of family treasures; and invitations and inaugural souvenirs from the White House representing the Cleveland through the Coolidge administrations. Among the pictures are photographs of the Riggs sisters, and autographed photographs belonging to George Washington Riggs, including those of the British commissioners who settled the Alabama claims in 1871.

4479.  NICHOLAS H. RIGHTOR PAPERS, 1861. 1 item. Louisiana.

Report of Captain S. W. Fisk, of the Crescent Rifles [7th Louisiana Infantry?], C.S.A., to Major Nicholas H. Rightor, commander of the Louisiana Battalion, C.S.A., and to General John Bankhead Magruder, on a skirmish at Newport News, Virginia. [This letter is published in Official Records, Series 1, Vol. 2.]

4480.  ATLAS M. RIGSBEE ACCOUNT BOOKS, 1859-1905. 60 vols. Durham, N.C.

Ledgers, 1859-1900; cashbooks, 1878-1902; daybooks, 1888-1902; purchase and accounts payable book, 1874-1878; farm ledger, 1867-1873; and rent ledgers, 1891-1905; of Atlas M. Rigsbee (1841-1903), property owner and operator of a mercantile store handling groceries, hardware, dry goods, and, during the 1860s and early 1870s, alcoholic beverages.

4481.  JACOB AUGUST RIIS PAPERS, 1900-1910. 52 items. New York, N.Y.

Principally letters of Jacob August Riis (1849-1914), reformer, author, and journalist, to Edward William Bok, editor in chief of The Ladies' Home Journal, discussing articles Riis was writing for the magazine, his poor health, lecture tours, and his friendship with Theodore Roosevelt; to William V. Alexander, managing editor of The Ladies' Home Journal, concerning Riis's articles and his lecture tours; and to Major James Burton Pond, lecture manager, pertaining to problems with his lecture bureau. Also included are photographs of Riis from magazines, and two magazine articles giving biographical information.

4482.  MARY (ROBERTS) RINEHART PAPERS. 1 item. New York, N.Y.

Letter from Mary (Roberts) Rinehart, novelist and playwright, declining a speaking engagement for health reasons.

4483.  ELLA V. RINKER AND REUBEN E. HAMMON PAPERS, 1841-1871. 94 items. Mount Pleasant (Prince William County), Va.

Letters to Ella V. Rinker from girl friends discussing personal matters and from friends and relatives in the Confederate Army concerning skirmishes, soldiers' pay, the defeat of the Confederates at Romney (West Virginia), the review of troops at Centreville (Virginia), and troop estimates for the Centreville area; letters to Reuben E. Hammon, Confederate soldier with the Shenandoah Rangers, McDonald's Regiment [7th Virginia Cavalry?], from friends and relatives telling of rumors among civilians on the course of the war; correspondence between Ella V. Rinker and Reuben E. Hammon, who were married in 1864, concerning camp life, troop movements, picket duty, and personal matters; and two poems.

4484.  ROSWELL SABINE RIPLEY PAPERS, 1862. 2 items. Charleston, S.C.

Correspondence of Roswell Sabine Ripley (1823-1887), brigadier general in the South Carolina State Militia, with Robert Bunch, British consul at Charleston, concerning the British citizenship of Bernard Connelly, who had joined and deserted the Sarsfield Light Infantry (probably the 7th Louisiana Regiment).

4485.  WILLIAM YOUNG RIPLEY PAPERS, 1843-1933. 415 items and 4 vols. Centre Rutland (Rutland County), Vt.

Correspondence and papers of the William Young Ripley family include Civil War letters of William Young Ripley, marble dealer and banker, and of his wife to their sons, William Y. W. Ripley, captain in the 1st Vermont Infantry, and Edward Hastings Ripley, 9th Vermont Infantry, concerning personal matters, Mrs. Ripley's efforts in raising supplies for the United States Sanitary Commission, and activities in Centre Rutland to support the war effort; Civil War letters from William Y. W. Ripley describing his training in the 1st Regiment Sharpshooters, U.S. Volunteers, the part played by the regiment in the campaign against Richmond in June, 1862, his wounding at Malvern Hill, and his dispute with the regiment's commander, Hiram Berdan, whom he accused of being repeatedly absent from the battlefield; letters from Edward Hastings Ripley while a student at Union College discussing the impact of the war on college life and the problems in recruiting troops, and while fighting in Virginia; letters from Charles Ripley, son of William Young Ripley, while journeying overland to California describing travel conditions by railroad, boat, stagecoach, and horseback, Fenian raids at Buffalo (New York), and life in western mining towns; letters from Mary (Ripley) Fisher, daughter of William Young Ripley, and her husband, Cyrus M. Fisher, while living in London, 1864-1873, concerning life in London and in other European cities in which they traveled, and the details of Mary's recurrent illnesses; correspondence of William Y. W. Ripley dealing with the settlement of the estate of Cyrus M. Fisher; letters of Thomas Emerson Ripley, grandson of William Young Ripley, during the Spanish-American War commenting on war news and his efforts to obtain active military service; letters from Harry R. Dodd, great nephew of William Young Ripley, concerning life in a military camp in Georgia during the Spanish-American War and his attempts to secure an officer's commission; and letters from a soldier in Puerto Rico telling of the fighting there. Other papers include materials for a volume on the 1st United States Sharpshooters; pamphlets on the work of the United States Sanitary Commission; drafts of speeches delivered by either William Y. W. Ripley or Edward Hastings Ripley at Memorial Day celebrations or Federal veterans reunions; printed poems and stories by Julia C. R. Dorr, daughter of William Young Ripley; and genealogical information.

4486. HANSON A. RISLEY PAPERS, 1774-1908. 137 items and 1 vol. Fredonia (Chautauqua County), N.Y.

Personal correspondence of Hanson A. Risley (d. 1892 or 1893), who was employed by the U.S. Treasury Department, concerning the Republican Party, national politics, William Henry Seward, and Abraham Lincoln; numerous letters of introduction; a memoir by Risley about his relationship with William Henry Seward (1801-1872), containing Seward's comments about Horace Greeley, and discussing the struggle for patronage control between the rival factions of New York politicians in Washington; correspondence of Olive F. Risley, daughter of Hanson A. Risley, who was adopted by Seward when her father moved to Colorado at the beginning of Ulysses S. Grant's presidency, and took the name Olive Risley Seward; and papers acquired by a member of the family who collected autographs. The volume is a scrapbook containing letters and autographs. Correspondents include Comte Charles de Chambrun (French minister to the United States), Cassius Marcellus Clay, Henry Clay, Charlotte Saunders Cushman, Facundo Goñi (Spanish minister to the United States), Horace Greeley, Bret Harte, Arinori Jugoi Mori (Japanese minister to the United States), William Henry Seward, Aleksandr Georgiyevich Vlangaly (Russian minister to China), Richard Wagner, Daniel Webster, and Thurlow Weed.

4487. JAMES B. RISQUE PAPERS, 1812-1839. 4 items. Campbell County, Va.

Legal papers of James B. Risque including a document pertaining to Davidson County, Tennessee, a summons, and a letter discussing legal affairs.

4488. THE. RITSMILLER PAPERS, 1862. 2 items. McLean County, Ill.

Letters from The. Ritsmiller to his wife while on military duty in Missouri describing camp life and training routine at Benton Barracks, Saint Louis; and a march through southern Missouri.

4489. JOHN RITTER PAPERS, 1851-1895. 28 items. Moore County, N.C.

Business papers of Captain John Ritter of the North Carolina militia; tax slips; miscellaneous papers of Thomas W. Ritter; and the printed proclamation of William W. Holden, governor of North Carolina, calling a constitutional convention, May, 1865.

4490. ALFRED LANDON RIVES PAPERS, 1839-1888. 1,207 items and 5 vols. "Castle Hill" (Albemarle County), Va.

Correspondence and papers of Alfred Landon Rives (1830-1903), engineer, concerning the activities of Édouard Schwebelé as librarian at l' École des Ponts et Chaussées, Paris, France, of which Rives was a graduate; family affairs; social life and customs, including the description of a slave wedding; economic and political affairs in Virginia; the Peace Convention in Washington, D.C., February 4, 1861, at which William Cabell Rives (1793-1868), U. S. senator and minister to France, and father of Alfred Landon Rives, was a commissioner; the resignation of Alfred Landon Rives as U.S. Army engineer in 1861; his work in the Confederate Army in constructing defenses near Williamsburg, Virginia, and as chief of the Confederate Engineering Bureau; and his post-bellum career as railroad builder and architect in Richmond, Virginia. The diary and recollections of Judith Page (Walker) Rives, wife of William Cabell Rives, principally concern the stay of the family in France during her husband's service as U.S. minister, 1829-1831 and 1849-1853. The diary portion, in the form of letters to her sister, Jane Francis (Walker) Page, describes their first period in France, giving detailed accounts of a tour through western New York and New England while awaiting passage to France; the ocean voyage; household and social customs in France and the difficulties encountered; the Revolution of 1830; Versailles; a summer tour through Switzerland, Germany, Holland, and France; and her observations on the people and the countries visited. The recollections describe the return voyage to America; discussions with Samuel F. B. Morse about his theories of the telegraph; her husband's activities as U.S. senator; Jacksonian politics; a visit by Andrew Jackson to "Castle Hill"; the education of her son, Alfred Landon Rives, in France; various people met in France; a tour through Italy; and Napoléon III, his assumption of power, and his courtship of and marriage to Eugénie de Montijo. Ledgers, 1829-1855, of Francis E. Rives contain private and mercantile accounts.

4491. AMÉLIE RIVES PAPERS, 1886-1940. 22 items. Cobham (Albemarle County), Va.

Letters of Amélie Rives (1863-1945), novelist, poet and playwright, to her publishers, Richard Watson Gilder of *The Century*, David Alexander Munro of *The North American Review*, and Harper & Brothers, concerning corrections in the manuscripts of her stories and poems; handwritten draft of a poem entitled "The Butterfly's Cousins"; an extract from *Herod and Miriamne* (1893); a letter discussing her grandfather, William Cabell Rives (1793-1868); letter, 1916, to Mr. Millman about her play "The Fear Market," his reaction to it and to her books, a Canadian friend in the war, and Prince Poniatowski's praise of Canadian troops; a clipping of a letter in which she protested sentiments having been erroneously attributed to her as the author of *My Lady Tongue*; and a photograph of Rives.

4492. FRANCIS EVEROD RIVES PAPERS, 1817-1848. 18 items and 1 vol. Petersburg (Dinwiddie County), Va.

Letters of Francis Everod Rives (1792-1861), U.S. congressman from Virginia, 1837-1841, and representative of the Petersburg Railroad, concerning early railroading in North Carolina and Virginia, and the fight for the possession of the Weldon bridge over the Roanoke River and seventeen miles of track belonging to the Portsmouth and Roanoke Railroad, the sale of which Rives believed caused the dissolution of that railroad; letter to Rives from his nephew, Colonel R. B. Heath, describing his travels in Berlin and the Revolution of 1848; and a slave sales book of Rives and his partners, Peyton Mason, Sr., and Peyton Mason, Jr.

4493. GEORGE S. RIVES PAPERS, 1851-1883. 20 items. Sparta (Hancock County), Ga.

Correspondence of George S. Rives, apparently a lawyer and planter, concerning court matters, cotton sales, guano purchases, the settlement of his mother's estate, and other business affairs.

4494. JOHN COOK RIVES PAPERS, 1834-1877. 76 items. Washington, D.C.

Correspondence of John Cook Rives (1795-1864), journalist and publisher of the *Congressional Globe*, concerning subscriptions, office equipment, and a lawsuit.

4495. J. B. ROANE PAPERS, 1856-1867. 4 items. Pittsylvania County, Va.

Letter, 1856, from J. B. Roane, owner of extensive real estate holdings, to his daughter; letter, 1859, concerning the circumstances surrounding the death of Lieutenant Roane of the 4th Artillery; circular, 1863, advertising a topographical map of the battle of Gettysburg, with the positions of various Union and Confederate regiments; and a draft, 1867, of a letter or speech eulogizing a captain of the "Richmond Blues" who had just died.

4496. LETITIA LANDON ROANE DIARY, 1861-1864. 1 vol. Pittsylvania County, Va.

Diary of Letitia Landon Roane containing comments on Civil War conditions, newspaper clippings, poems, and memoranda on the cost of goods.

4497. WILLIAM HENRY ROANE PAPERS, 1838-1839. 2 items. Richmond, Va.

Letters from William Henry Roane (1787-1845), U.S. senator and grandson of Patrick Henry. One letter recommends the appointment of B. T. Archer for a midshipman's warrant in the U.S. Navy, and the other apparently concerns Roane's departure from Richmond for Washington at the opening of Congress.

4498. JEFFREY H. ROBBINS PAPERS, 1854-1869. 84 items. Randolph County, N.C.

Sermons, lecture notes, two letters, ten photographs, and a biographical sketch of Jeffrey H. Robbins (1829-1869), instructor at Trinity College (ca. 1852-1859), member of the North Carolina Conference of the Methodist Episcopal Church, South, 1859-1869, and Confederate chaplain, 1863-1865.

4499. JOHN ALBERT ROBBINS PAPERS, 1965-1974. 393 items. Bloomington, Ind.

Correspondence and working papers of John Albert Robbins, professor of English at the University of Indiana, relating to his editorship of the annual publication, *American Literary Scholarship* (1968-1972).

4500. JAMES R. ROBERSON PAPERS, 1865 (1876-1878) 1899. 55 items. Robersonville (Martin County), N.C.

Letters to James R. Roberson, an elder in the Primitive Baptist Church, from other elders and ministers.

4501. JOSIAH S. ROBERSON PAPERS, 1864-1865. 10 items. Petersburg (Dinwiddie County), Va.

Letters of a soldier in camp near Petersburg, Virginia, concerning the scarcity of food, the low value of money, dissatisfaction among the troops, and the many desertions.

4502. CHARLES BUCK ROBERTS PAPERS, 1963-1964. 2 items and 6 vols. Durham, N.C.

Two versions of a play entitled "The Dukes" written by Charles Buck Roberts; scrapbooks containing photographs of the actors and actresses who performed in "The Dukes," clippings about their performances, and the final revised stage version of the play; playbill for "The Dukes"; copies of "The Last Place" and "A Lost Day Is Hard to Find," plays written by Roberts; and an announcement, 1964, of new plays to be presented at the Triangle Coffee House, Durham, North Carolina.

4503. FREDERICK SLEIGH ROBERTS, FIRST EARL ROBERTS, PAPERS, 1874-1910. 56 items. London, England.

Letters of Frederick Sleigh Roberts, First Earl Roberts (1832-1914), British field marshal serving in India, Afghanistan, and South Africa, to publisher Richard Bentley, concerning the preparation, publication, sale, and revision of Roberts's autobiography, Forty-one Years in India, from Subaltern to Commander-in-Chief (1897); to Charles Rathbone Low, naval and military historian, pertaining to a magazine article that Low was writing about Roberts, with comments on the strengthening of defenses in the frontier region near Afghanistan; to Charles Frederic Moberly Bell, manager of The Times, dealing with matters discussed in the newspaper about the army, the strategic importance of keeping Seistan, Persia, out of Russian control, and British-Indian relations in 1877, and reporting upon eastern affairs by the newspaper's correspondent in India; and to Charles Metcalfe Macgregor explaining his failure to obtain a position in the quartermaster general's office in Simla, India.

4504. RAGLAND ROBERTS AND JOHN B. LEE PAPERS, 1816 (1844-1846) 1875. 1,755 items. Lynchburg (Campbell County), Va.

Mercantile letters, accounts, bills, receipts, and several legal papers of the merchandising firm of Roberts and Lee, with references to commodity prices in Virginia and to canal boats.

4505. S. C. ROBERTS PAPERS, 1862. 1 item. Charleston, S.C.

Letter of S. C. Roberts to his sister commenting upon the preparations for defense of Charleston harbor, the arrival of the British ship, the Economist, loaded with war material; and the Virginia's attack upon the Union fleet at Hampton Roads.

4506. WILLIAM ANDERSON ROBERTS PAPERS, 1814 (1856-1882) 1911. 1,238 items and 3 vols. Yanceyville (Caswell County), N.C.

Personal and business papers of William Anderson Roberts (1837-1900), artist, and of his wife, Mary Catherine (Watlington) Roberts (b. 1837), concerning the activities of the Methodist Church in Yanceyville, North Carolina; camp meetings and conversions; sermons; his trial and expulsion from the Methodist Church for his opposition to Methodist Church doctrine; his conversion to the Disciples of Christ, and the activities of that church in Kentucky; efforts to avoid conscription into the Confederate Army, and, after his induction, his repeated attempts to obtain a discharge by various methods; his duties as a nurse in various Confederate hospitals, as a ward master of the 1st Division General Hospital at Danville Virginia, and as clerk of the Medical Examining Board; his portrait work, including letters from his teacher, Oliver P. Copeland concerning Copeland's painting and his teaching at Oxford Female College, Oxford, North Carolina, and letters concerning the portrait Roberts painted of Alexander Campbell (1788-1866), a founder of the Disciples of Christ; his addiction to morphine and remedies to cure himself; family and personal matters; and financial affairs. Three notebooks contain lists of persons whose portraits Roberts painted and the amounts charged.

4507. ROBERTS FAMILY PAPERS, 1770-1860. 23 items. Orange County, N.C.

Business papers of the Roberts family.

4508. D. ROBERTSON ORDERLY BOOK, 1806-1816. 1 vol. Columbia, S.C.

Copies of general orders issued from brigade headquarters at Columbia, to the South Carolina Militia.

4509. DAVID ROBERTSON PAPERS, 1792-1793. 6 items. Savannah, Ga.

Business papers of David Robertson, of Johnston and Robertson, and of David Robertson & Co., dealing with rice, lumber, and promissory notes.

4510. GEORGE ROBERTSON, JR., LETTERPRESS BOOK, 1864-1865. 1 vol. (505 pp.) Savannah, Ga.

Letters from the military district of Georgia, signed by George Robertson, Jr., Confederate major of commissary subsistence.

4511. JAMES ALEXANDER ROBERTSON, SR., PAPERS, [1436?]-1939. 1,840 items. Annapolis (Anne Arundel County), Md.

Papers of James Alexander Robertson (1873-1939), librarian, government official, and historian, relating to the Philippine Islands. Correspondence, notes, and works in manuscript and typescript concern Philippine history, administrative problems and policies during the early years of American occupation, Aglipay or Independent Filipino Church, Roman Catholicism, customs, geography, book manufacturing, education, José Rizal, Freemasonry, Filipino senators, and Katipunan or Filipino Secret Society. Many letters center around James Alfred LeRoy (1875-1909), authority on the Philippine Islands. Included are letters in Spanish; and photocopies of letters written in German from Ferdinand Blumentritt, noted scholar in Far Eastern history. Other items are translations of "Memories" by Felipe G. Calderon and "Mi Ultimo Pensamiento" by José Rizal; four issues of Biblia Filipina; reproductions of early maps of the Philippines; reports of provisional governors; photographs and postcards; documents in Spanish; copies of translations of letters and documents of Filipino insurgent leaders, including Emilio Aguinaldo; general circulars, 1914, for the Department of Commerce and Police of the Philippine Islands; writing of the Mangyans; sketch of Malabang, 1911; description of Negros Province, Jimilaylan Pueblo, 1847; history and description of Mancayan township; petitions for membership in the Freemasons, 1921; typescript of a translation of a manifesto by Apolinario Mabini regarding the American occupation and the Philippine Insurrection, 1916; and minutes and proceedings of the Philippine Library Association, 1936. Papers pertaining to the Philippine Library in Manila include blueprints for the library, articles on its history, reports, bibliographies of materials concerning the Philippines and other Pacific islands, and letters of Robertson relative to the exhibition of the Philippine books at the Panama-Pacific International Exposition in San Francisco in 1915.

4512. WILLIAM ROBERTSON PAPERS, 1771-1793. 14 items. Edinburgh, Scotland.

Letters from Robertson (1721-1793), historian, to Andrew Strahan, publisher, concerning Robertson's History of the Reign of the Emperor Charles V (London: 1796) and his Historical Disquisition Concerning the Knowledge Which the Ancients Had of India (London: 1791), and revealing the problems of publication and printing in the 18th Century. There are also three engravings from a portrait of Robertson by Sir Joshua Reynolds.

4513. WILLIAM T. ROBERTSON MEMORANDUM BOOK, 1829-1875. 1 vol. (53 pp.)

Memorandum book of William T. Robertson containing home remedies, and records of births of members of the Robertson and O'Neal families.

4514. JOHN WILLIAM ROBERTSON-SCOTT PAPERS, 1895-1943. 24 items. Idbury, Oxfordshire, England.

Letters of Frederick John Dealtry Lugard, First Baron Lugard (1858-1945), British soldier, administrator, and author, who had an important role in the expansion of British authority in East Africa and Nigeria, to John William Robertson-Scott (1866-1963), British journalist and author, concerning a controversy in The Times (London) over a massacre committed by the Masai at Eldama Ravine, Kenya, in 1895; the Jameson Raid in the Transvaal; the slavery issue; a trip to Africa to exploit the British West Charterland Company's mineral concession in Ngami, Bechuanaland, with comments on the company's relationship to Joseph Chamberlain, the government, and the British South Africa Company; difficulties in crossing the Kalahari Desert because of the environment and the war in Rhodesia; famine and cattle disease in Bechuanaland; the need to occupy leased territories in the Nile Valley; the Royal Society's interest in the tsetse fly; Lugard's administration in Nigeria; the situation in South Africa, 1900; the government's education policy in its African colonies; and personal matters relating to the careers of the two men.

4515. GEORGE MAXWELL ROBESON PAPERS, 1872. 1 item. Washington, D.C.

Letter to George Maxwell Robeson (1829-1897), U.S. secretary of the navy, from an unnamed party requesting the retention of U.S. District Attorney J. P. Southworth, for failure to require the test oath of jurors in Mobile, Alabama.

4516. JAMES A. ROBESON PAPERS, 1854-1864. 7 items. [Bladen County?] N.C.

Correspondence relative to the estate of James J. McKay, for which James A. Robeson (d. 1864) was administrator, and the transportation of McKay's freed slaves to Liberia, according to the provisions of his will.

4517. BENJAMIN ROBINSON PAPERS, 1760-1912. 132 items and 1 vol. Fayetteville (Cumberland County), N.C.

Papers of Benjamin Robinson (1775-1857), physician, public health officer, and banker, include correspondence, 1804-1818, concerning family matters of the Pearce and Tillinghast families into which Robinson married; correspondence dealing with the business of the Fayetteville branch of the State Bank of North Carolina; after 1877, correspondence of Thomas Jefferson Robinson (1827-1879), son of Benjamin Robinson, and secretary of the North Carolina Board of Agriculture, and of his family; papers relating to Benjamin Robinson's service as public health officer during the smallpox epidemic in Fayetteville, 1824-1825, including expense accounts and a statistical chart for nineteen cases; financial papers concerning the business of Oliver Pearce and Nathan Pearce, rental property in Providence (Rhode Island), bills and receipts, receipts for the education of the children at academies in Fayetteville and Donaldson (North Carolina), and expenses of a trip to Virginia and Washington in 1840; deeds and indentures for land in Cumberland County, North Carolina; papers relating to the loan by Dr. Hiram Robinson to his brother, Benjamin Robinson, ca. 1824, to cover the latter's indebtedness to the State Bank of North Carolina; poetry of Polly (West) Pearce, 1783; recipes, ca. 1820; commonplace book, 1851, and a diary fragment, 1885, of Sarah Starke (Huske) Robinson (ca. 1832-1912), wife of Thomas Jefferson Robinson; genealogical information on the Huske, Tillinghast, Norwood, Hogg, and Cromartie families; portion of a ledger, 1814-1819, of the mercantile firm owned by Larkin Newby and Roderick McIntosh of Fayetteville; and a diary of Sarah Starke (Huske) Robinson, ca. 1884-1911, describing the activities of the Huske, Pearce, Tillinghast, Robinson, Hogg, and Newby families, as well as noting the development of Fayetteville in the late nineteenth and early twentieth centuries.

4518. CONWAY ROBINSON PAPERS, 1830-1833. 5 items. Richmond, Va.

Papers of Conway Robinson (1805-1884), lawyer, relating to a committee appointed in Richmond to investigate gambling in that city, including a letter from Hugh Maxwell concerning gambling laws in New York City, and a draft of the Report of the Committee of Twenty-Four, . . . for the Purpose of Devising Means to Suppress the Vice of Gambling in this City (1833).

4519. EDWIN ARLINGTON ROBINSON PAPERS, 1928. 2 items. Peterborough (Hillsborough County), N.H.

Letter from Edwin Arlington Robinson (1869-1935), poet, to Russell A. Spencer concerning the printings of Robinson's Lancelot.

4520. GEORGE FREDERICK SAMUEL ROBINSON, FIRST MARQUIS OF RIPON, PAPERS, 1855-1907. 198 items. London, England.

Political correspondence of George Frederick Samuel Robinson, First Marquis of Ripon (1827-1909), British statesman, secretary for war, 1863-1866, secretary for India, 1866, lord president of the council, 1868-1873, governor general of India, 1880-1884, first lord of the admiralty, 1886, colonial secretary, 1892-1895, and lord privy seal, 1905-1908. Included are a printed letter, 1855, from Ferdinand de Lesseps concerning the proposed Suez Canal; letters, 1856-1858, from American journalist William Henry Hurlbert commenting on Anglo-American relations, the political situation in the United States, the slave states and the slave trade, the cotton trade, Cuba, and Central America; letters, 1856, from British journalist Thornton Hunt discussing Anglo-American relations, Central America, and recruitment in the United States for the Crimean War; letters, 1858, from Lieutenant Colonel Bertie Edward Murray Gordon describing the Ionian Islands and the British administration there; letter, 1860, from Attorney General Richard Bethell returning a minute on the purchase of land for defense purposes; letter, 1862, from Colonel William F. D. Jervois commenting upon the defenses at Corfu in the Ionian Islands, and a memorandum and map, 1863, on the demolition of fortifications there; copies of letters, 1863, from Charles George Gordon regarding military operations in China during the Taiping Rebellion; correspondence, 1864, between Lord Ripon and George William Frederick Charles, Second Duke of Cambridge, discussing the fighting of Austria and Prussia with Denmark over the duchies of Schleswig and Holstein, weaknesses in the strength of the British Army and proposed reductions, the campaign in New Zealand against the Maoris and weapons considered for use against them, officer promotion procedure, disagreement between Cambridge and Sir Hugh Rose, commander in chief in India, the role of Stephen C. Denison, deputy judge advocate general, in the court martial of Colonel Crawley, and the desirability of keeping the headquarters of the North American Command at Montreal; letter, 1864, from Lord Palmerston commenting upon troop reductions and their relation to the Danish crisis; letter 1870, from Lord Dufferin pertaining to tenant-right in Ireland and the collection of arrears; letter, 1871, from Harriet Martineau objecting to the treatment of women under the Contagious Diseases Act of 1869; letter, 1873, from Lord Kimberley concerning his views on the resignations of himself and other members of the cabinet; letter, 1874, from William E. Gladstone explaining his objections to Lord Ripon's conversion to Catholicism; letter, 1892, from General George S. White reporting on conditions in Baluchistan, relations with Afghanistan, the late Sir Robert Sandeman, and Algernon Durand; letter, 1892, from the Catholic Archbishop of Westminster concerning the establishment of commercial education; letter, 1892, from Cecil Rhodes dealing with relations with the Transvaal, including the Swaziland problem; letter, 1893, from Lord Derby, governor general of Canada, relating to the prospects for tariff reform; personal letter, 1893, from exiled Empress Eugénie; letter, 1896, from Herbert Asquith discussing relations between Lord Rosebery and John Morley, and the leadership of the Liberal

Party; letter, 1906, from Lord Crewe commenting upon the Education Bill as it concerned the appointment of teachers of a particular creed; letter, 1907, from Lord Northbourne regarding his political views and the state of political parties in Britain; letters, 1907, from Winston Churchill thanking Lord Ripon for his support; and letter from James Anthony Froude appealing in behalf of inventor William Ellis Metford and his percussion rifle bullet.

4521. JAMES ROBINSON PAPERS, 1861-1864. 2 items. Wake County, N.C., and Orange Court House (Orange County), Va.

Civil War letters containing a report that England and France were fitting out ironclad ships to assist the Confederacy and were going to make a substantial loan, and references to deserters.

4522. JAMES [ROBINSON?] PAPERS, 1856-1870. 57 items. Giles County, Va.

Civil War letters of a Confederate soldier describing army life and the course of the war in Virginia. Included are several poems. The name is spelled variously Robinson, Roberson, and Robertson.

4523. JAMES T. ROBINSON AND JOHN H. ROBINSON PAPERS, 1827-1865. 11 items. Warren County, N.C.

Personal and business correspondence of James T. Robinson and John H. Robinson, brothers, concerning personal affairs, the 5th and 63rd regiments of North Carolina Cavalry Volunteers, and Confederate and Union casualties and prisoners, and mentioning the Clark, Redd, Robinson, and Sherrill families.

4524. MAGNUS L. ROBINSON PAPERS, 1888-1914. 33 items. Alexandria (Fairfax County), Va.

Correspondence of Magnus L. Robinson, journalist and editor of the National Leader, concerning the newspaper business; the 1888 meeting of the Afro-American Press Association; the political machinations and newspaper policies of T. Thomas Fortune, editor of the New York Age; fraternal affairs, including the Negro Odd Fellows and the Negro Masons; and Robinson's efforts to obtain a position as doorkeeper in the United States Congress. Correspondents include Blanche K. Bruce, T. Thomas Fortune, John Mitchell, Jr., and Morgan Treat.

4525. MANUEL ROBINSON ACCOUNT BOOK, 1860-1873. 1 vol. (98 pp.)

Personal accounts of Manuel Robinson, apparently a lawyer and plantation owner, and guardian of Joseph and Sarah Sherrill.

4526. RALPH J. ROBINSON PAPERS, 1905-1906. 54 items. Due West (Abbeville County), S.C.

Replies to Ralph Robinson's requests for information concerning the Civil War service of graduates of Erskine College. Robinson, a student of Erskine College, was on the staff of the Erskinian, the college magazine.

4527. ROBERT ROBINSON PAPERS, 1825-1901. 157 items. Chester (Chester County), S.C.

Letters, deeds, notes, and bills of Robert Robinson, principally concerned with the settlement of his estate.

4528. W. A. ROBINSON PAPERS, 1861-1862. 3 items. Raleigh (Wake County), N.C.

Civil War letters of W. A. Robinson to his brother describing the good food at Camp Carolina, near Norfolk, Virginia; hardships of army life; and the lack of supplies and clothing.

4529. W. S. ROBINSON PAPERS, 1864. 12 items. Alabama.

Personal letters of a Confederate soldier discussing the course of the war in Alabama, food, and clothing.

4530. JOHN N. ROBSON PAPERS, 1852 (1872-1873) 1923. 1,086 items. Charleston, S.C.

Business papers and correspondence of John N. Robson, a fertilizer agent whose chief product was Soluble Pacific Guano, relating to the fertilizer business, the credit system used by cotton farmers, and a guano shortage, 1873. Also included are letters referring to the Patrons of Husbandry around Lancaster County, South Carolina; and several personal letters between Robson and his son.

4531. JAMES HENRY ROCHELLE PAPERS, (1811-1898) 1907. 965 items. Courtland (formerly Jerusalem) (Southampton County), Va.

Business and personal correspondence and papers of James Rochelle (d. 1835), clerk of the superior court of Southampton County, and of his son, James Henry Rochelle (d. 1889), naval officer and member of the Hydrographic Commission of the Amazon. Letters to the elder Rochelle are from Virginia political leaders of some note, relative largely to politics, including information on public sentiment immediately preceding the War of 1812; presidential nominees and elections, 1828 and 1836; activities of the Virginia legislature; sale and hire of slaves; privateering; war in Spain and Portugal during the Napoleonic period; agricultural conditions in the United States;

commodity prices; naval activity at Fort Nelson, Virginia, March 17, 1813; the "Panama Mission," April 23, 1826; breeding of horses; and business and personal affairs. Letters of John Tyler to the widow of Rochelle concern the welfare of their children, John Tyler, Jr., and Martha Rochelle, who were married in 1838. Correspondence after 1841 is largely concerned with James Henry Rochelle, who was given a midshipman's warrant by John Tyler. Letters, 1841-1848, relate to the training period of James Henry Rochelle at the U.S. Naval Academy, Annapolis, Maryland, his popularity with other officers, and his service on the U.S. frigate Constitution. Included also are bills for his uniforms, wines, lodging, etc. Although largely routine in nature, Rochelle's letters while in the Confederate Navy as lieutenant commander and captain, contain interesting comments on activities in and around the harbor of Charleston, South Carolina, and the wrecking of the Stono, a vessel under his command. Other letters and official dispatches refer to food supplies, inspection of vessels prior to running the blockade, desertions, precautions against yellow fever, and repairs to damaged vessels. The papers, 1865-1870, are concerned with the administration of the estate of James Rochelle by William B. Shands, a nephew of James Henry Rochelle.

Beginning in 1871, the collection consists of papers relative to the functions, duties, and activities of the Hydrographic Commission of the Amazon, organized to explore and chart that part of the Amazon River lying in Peru. Rochelle, senior member of the expedition, served as acting president during the frequent absences of Admiral John Randolph Tucker. Among the records are dispatches from the Peruvian government; lists of supplies; notes on methods of finding elevations by boiling water, changing metres to inches, Fahrenheit to centigrade, etc; tables of Spanish measurements, altitude, locations, and latitude and longitude along the Yavari River; and agitations through the U.S. State Department to obtain pay from the Peruvian government for Tucker and Rochelle. There is considerable information on the history of the Rochelle family. Among the correspondents are Richard Blow, Albert Gallatin, Thomas Gholson, Edwin Gray, William Hines, B. W. Johnston, James Johnston, Samuel Kello, Stephen R. Mallory, J. Y. Mason, Richard E. Parker, Robert Taylor, and John Tyler.

4532. ROCKETT FAMILY PAPERS, 1860-1973. 9 items and 2 vols. Cline's Township (Catawba County), N.C.

Public school records, 1860-1864, from District No. 8, Catawba County, North Carolina, including names of pupils, attendance records, grades, names and occupations of parents, books used, courses, names of school officials, teachers' salaries, and remarks; Sunday school attendance records, 1871-1875; register of Public School District No. 5, Catawba County, 1897-1902; teacher's contract of Belle Rockett; and lists of students, some of which are for a Sunday school.

4533. ROCKINGHAM COUNTY PUBLIC SCHOOL REGISTER, 1894-1897. 1 vol. (66 pp.) Rockingham County, N.C.

Public school register of District 58, Rockingham County, North Carolina, containing names and ages of students, attendance records, names of parents, teachers' names and salaries, books used, and names of the members of the school committee.

4534. ROCKINGHAM PLANTATION JOURNAL, 1828-1829. 1 vol. (84 pp.) Brunson (Hampton County), S.C.

Daily record of work done by slaves on the Rockingham plantation, including mention of those who were sick and those who had run away.

4535. RAYMOND PERRY RODGERS PAPERS, 1876-1879. 2 items. Washington, D.C.

Diary (31 pp.) of Raymond Perry Rodgers (1849-1925), rear admiral in the U.S. Navy, describing the trip of the Pensacola in 1876 from the United States to join the Pacific Fleet in Panama, and the movements of the Fleet, 1877-1879. Entries are frequently routine, but there are notations concerning riots against the importation of Chinese into San Francisco, 1877; descriptions of numerous ports in Mexico, Central America and South America; discussion of a diplomatic incident between the United States and Mexico at Acapulco, 1877; report of the shipwreck of the City of San Francisco, 1877; discussion of Chilean naval operations against the Bolivian coast, 1879; and Rodgers' opinion of the Shah, flagship of Britain's Pacific Fleet. There is also a roughly drawn map of the eastern tip of Oahu Island in the Hawaiian Islands, visited by Rodgers in 1878-1879.

4536. ROBERT M. RODGERS PAPERS. 1 item. Sheridan (Grant County), Ark.

Typed copy (2 pp.) of the "Battle of Jenkins' Ferry, the Last Battle of the Famous Red River Expedition," written by Robert M. Rodgers, describing the defeat of the Union forces and mentioning Union and Confederate casualties and Negro troops.

4537. ROBERT SMITH RODGERS PAPERS, 1827-1897. 1,382 items and 7 vols. "Sion Hill," Havre de Grace (Harford County), Md.

Chiefly the Civil War military papers of Robert Smith Rodgers (b. 1811), colonel of the 2nd Maryland Eastern Shore Infantry Regiment, U.S.A., including military correspondence; telegrams; muster rolls; rosters of officers and staff; lists of deserters, recruits, reenlistments, and voluntary enlistments; reports of sick, wounded, and convalescents; inventories of personal effects of the deceased; hospital and army paroles; morning reports; ordnance returns, invoices, requisitions, issues, and transfers; quartermaster papers including records pertaining to clothing, property, and stores; monthly and quarterly returns; letter book containing routine military correspondence; and general and special orders, including an order book of the regiment, concerning camp routine, guard duty, curfew, discipline, treatment and use of contrabands, deserters, courts-martial troop movements, depredations by Union troops, seizure of property, and speculation in hay, wheat, and oats. There is also a fragmentary account of the war experiences of the 2nd Eastern Shore, written by Rodgers, concerning its actions in Maryland in 1862 and 1863, including the battle between the Monitor and the Virginia, the visit of the Prince de Joinville to the Minnesota, defenses at Cockeysville (Maryland), and skirmishing around Frederick (Maryland) and in West Virginia and Virginia in the summer of 1864, including action along the Baltimore and Ohio Railroad between Harpers Ferry and Martinsburg (West Virginia), marches to Woodstock and to New Market (Virginia), the battle of Piedmont (Virginia), and movements in Virginia, West Virginia, and Ohio, ending at Harpers Ferry.

Scattered papers relate to other members of the Rodgers family, including Commodore John Rodgers (1773-1838) and Minerva (Denison) Rodgers, parents of Robert Smith Rodgers; Sarah (Perry) Rodgers; Calbraith Perry Rodgers and Robert Slidell Rodgers, sons of Robert Smith Rodgers. Among these papers are personal correspondence; letters relating to naval matters; estate papers of John Rodgers and of Matthew Perry; bills and receipts, including specifications for a house, ca. 1840-1850; and legal papers concerning land deeds and the manumission of a slave owned by Minerva (Denison) Rodgers. Also included is a volume, ca. 1804, containing examples of mathematical computation, including navigational problems; a handmade paper compass; a navigational chart between England and the Cape Verde Islands; and a navigational logbook of the Maria, commanded by Richard M. Smith, from London to Madeira.

4538.     M. N. ROE PAPERS, 1898-1900. 21 items. Candor (Tioga County), N.Y.

Bills and accounts of a dentist, pertaining to prices and lists of dental supplies ordered from dealers and manufacturers.

4539.     COLEMAN ROGERS PAPERS, 1815-1862. 6 items. Cincinnati (Hamilton County), Ohio.

Business letters to Coleman Rogers, probably a physician, including one concerning economic conditions in Kentucky in 1820; and a letter from his nephew, William W. Wright, captain in the 112th Regiment of Illinois Volunteers, U.S.A., discussing the movement of his regiment.

4540.     C. J. & W. M. ROGERS PAPERS, 1885-1889. 7 items and 2 vols. Durham, N.C.

Records of a dealer in buggies, wagons, harnesses, guano, and general merchandise. Included are a ledger, 1887-1889; accounts receivable and payable, 1885-1889; and loose financial papers.

4541.     JAMES ROGERS PAPERS, 1760s-1790s. ca. 28,000 items. Bristol, Gloucestershire, England.

Photocopies of the business papers of James Rogers, Bristol merchant and shipowner, principally concerning trade with Africa, the West Indies, and Newfoundland Included are correspondence, chiefly incoming; lists of crew members; accounts for materials supplied various ships; receipts for advances of wages of crews; bills of lading; bills of exchange; bills and receipts; accounts of sales and purchases; information on prices of slaves, sugar, rum, fish, cotton, coffee, wood, and other products; accounts of ships, cargoes, and insurance; statements of shares in cargoes and ships; invoices; customs house papers; cargo notes; information on market conditions; litigation papers; and Rogers' bankruptcy papers, including information on how the slave trade was set up. A guide (90 pp.), containing an outline of the filing arrangment, a list of places mentioned, and a description of the voyages of each ship and the types of papers included, is available in the department. The originals are in the Public Record Office, London, England, where they are catalogued as Chancery Records, Masters' Exhibits, Senior (C. 107), Bundles 1-15.

4542.     JOHN H. ROGERS PAPERS, 1816. 1 item. Baltimore, Md.

A letter from Peter Little, U.S. representative from Maryland, concerning state politics and the method of nominating candidates.

4543.     SAMUEL ROGERS PAPERS, 1833-1847. 11 items. London, England.

Two personal letters from Samuel Rogers (1763-1855), English poet, to his sister, Sarah Rogers; letter from Rogers to Charles Mackay, poet and journalist, concerning a pension for Alfred, Lord Tennyson, Tennyson's personality, past appeals for a pension for Henry Francis Cary, and Mackay's employment and writing; several notes by Rogers; two poems by Rogers; and extracts from several letters, 1761-1793, of William Mason (1724-1797), poet, to Viscount Nuneham (later Second Earl Harcourt), copied by Rogers, concerning personal and literary matters.

4544. SION HART ROGERS PAPERS, 1846 (1853-1861) 1873. 113 items. Raleigh (Wake County), N.C.

Personal and family correspondence of Sion H. Rogers (1825-1874), member of U.S. Congress, 1853-1855 and 1871-1873, Confederate officer, and attorney general of North Carolina, 1863-1866, including letters from former schoolmates of Jane E. Haywood, who married Rogers in 1853; correspondence between Rogers and his wife while he was in Washington and she in Raleigh during 1854 concerning personal and financial matters; and Civil War letters from Rogers describing camp life, an officer's course of training, and his activities guarding the James River and the eastern coast of North Carolina. Included also are lists of jurors and an undated note from Zebulon Baird Vance.

4545. WILL ROGERS SCRAPBOOK, 1928-1933. 1 vol. (48 pp.) Beverly Hills (Los Angeles County), Calif.

Scrapbook containing newspaper clippings of "Will Rogers Says," columns written by Will Rogers (1879-1935), American humorist.

4546. WILLIAM H. ROGERS PAPERS, 1862 (1863-1865) 1911. 126 items. Stockton (Waldo County), Maine.

Military papers of William H. Rogers, 2nd lieutenant in the 6th Battery of Maine Artillery, U.S.A., including ordnance reports; letterpress copies of general orders, circulars, and telegrams; and other miscellaneous papers.

4547. ROBERT ROLINSON ACCOUNT BOOK, 1849-1878. 1 vol. (116 pp.) Hatteras (Dare County), N.C.

Accounts and receipts of Robert Rolinson relating to his various occupations as a merchant, fisherman, windmill owner, justice of the peace for Hyde County, and keeper of the Long Shoal Light Vessel.

4548. PINKNEY ROLLINS PAPERS, 1870. 17 items. Marshall (Madison County), N.C.

Letters pertaining to the duties of Pinkney Rollins as a U.S. revenue collector for the 7th North Carolina District. Most of them concern prosecution of persons who had violated the internal revenue laws, chiefly by illicit distilling operations.

4549. WILLIAM GOVETT ROMAINE PAPERS, 1857-1877, 12 items. London, England.

Nine detailed letters and memoranda, 1858-1860, from Sir Anthony Coningham Sterling, then military secretary to Colin Campbell, commander-in-chief in India, to William Govett Romaine (1815-1893), deputy judge advocate of the army in the east, 1854, second secretary to the Admiralty, 1857, and judge advocate general in India, 1869-1873, concerning the campaign in Oudh and other operations in India, appointments of army commanders, and political and military policy in general; letter, 1857, from Richard S. Dundas pertaining to arrangements for the Encounter to accompany a friend of the Pasha of Egypt to Yembo; letter, 1877, from Sir Austen Henry Layard, British ambassador to Turkey, commenting on Anglo-Turkish relations, the Russo-Turkish War, and a meeting with Sir Robert Henry Davies; and an undated letter from Alexander Milne relating to jurisdictional disputes between the Admiralty and the Board of Trade.

4550. ALFRED ROMAN PAPERS, 1864-1886. 39 items. New Orleans, La.

Correspondence of Alfred Roman (1824-1892), lawyer, sugar planter, Confederate officer, clerk of Louisiana supreme court, and judge of the criminal court of New Orleans. The letters, written in French, are concerned with reminiscences of the Civil War and Roman's book, The Military Operations of General Beauregard . . . (New York: 1883).

4551. ROMANOV FAMILY PAPERS, 1796-1852. 243 items. Saint Petersburg, Russia. Restricted.

Transcripts of letters written in French by members of the Russian imperial family. Some of the letters, translated into English, have been published in Romanov Relations, The Private Correspondence of Tsars Alexander I, Nicholas I and the Grand Dukes Constantine and Michael with Their Sister Queen Anna Pavlovna, 1817-1866, by Sydney Wayne Jackman (London: 1969). The originals are located at the Royal House Archives, The Hague, and at the Thuringian State Archives, German Democratic Republic.

4552. ROBERT J. ROMBAUER PAPERS, 1846-1916. 142 items. Saint Louis, Mo.

Miscellaneous papers of Robert J. Rombauer, Hungarian immigrant, and officer in the 1st Missouri Regiment and the 1st Missouri Reserve Corps during the Civil War, including telegrams regarding military tactics; army orders; letters from his brother, R. Guido Rombauer, concerning war activities, including mention of Negro officers; order book consisting of forms, commands and activities of the regiment; personal correspondence from family members; congratulatory letters on the 50th wedding anniversary of Rombauer and his wife; letters from Washington, D.C., regarding veterans' pensions for members of his regiment; letters from Franklin W. Smith, president of the National Galleries and Company, in which mention is made of moving the galleries from Washington, D.C., to Saint Louis; correspondence dealing with Rombauer's pamphlets written on various political questions and his book on the Union cause in Saint Louis in 1861; notes for speeches and essays on politics, economics, education, monopolies, and English poetry; description entitled "Derby Day at Clapham Common"; and a prospectus, 1902, for the Pan-American Exploring Company. There are also letters, clippings, and historical notes in a Finno-Ugric tongue of the Magyars.

4553. HENRY B. ROMMEL PAPERS, 1863-1865. 2 items. Wilmington (New Hanover County), N.C.

Letters from Henry B. Rommel, sailor in the U.S. Navy, with references to the blockade at Wilmington, North Carolina, and rumors that Sherman had taken Charleston (South Carolina), and Wilmington.

4554. HARRIETT FRANCES RONAN PAPERS, 1865. 5 items. Graham's Cross Roads, S.C.

Letters of Eugenia (Ronan) Carew, wife of Hamilton Carew, to her sister, Harriett Frances Ronan, and her mother, concerning the fate of South Carolinians at the end of the war, the exchange of her husband who was a prisoner of war, financial problems, food, rationing, high prices, illness, and family matters.

4555. ISAAC RONEY PAPERS, 1819-1871. 90 items. Petersburg (Dinwiddie County), Va.

Business and financial papers of Major Isaac Roney consisting chiefly of bills and receipts, including a physician's bill for attending a slave after childbirth. Also included are an inventory of the estate of Thomas and Rebecca Roney, 1823; and a rental contract, 1866, between Isaac Roney and a tenant.

4556. HENRY EDWARD ROOD, SR., PAPERS, 1895-1951. 90 items. New York, N.Y.

Papers of Henry Edward Rood, Sr. (1867-1954), journalist, author, and assistant editor of Harper's Magazine, including correspondence relating to his journalistic work; invitation, 1907, to a memorial performance of "Ben Hur" commemorating the eightieth birthday of General Lewis Wallace; letter, 1908, from Admiral Robert Edwin Peary (1856-1920) discussing the explorations of Frederick Albert Cook in the Arctic region, and a photocopy of a telegram from Peary announcing his discovery of the North Pole; copy of an article by General Tasker Howard Bliss entitled "The Armistices" (published in The American Journal of International Law, 16, No. 4, October, 1922); letter, 1926, from General John Joseph Pershing (1860-1948) giving a statement on preparedness; information on William H. Crook, personal bodyguard to Abraham Lincoln; letter, 1936, from Daniel Frohman, president of The Actors Fund of America, concerning several actors and actresses, and theaters; letter, 1940, from Thomas W. Lamont discussing the Zimmermann telegram of 1917 and Great Britain's war debts to J. P. Morgan and Company; invitation from Samuel L. Clemens to inspect "The Children's Educational Theater Alliance"; pamphlet, 1912, advertising a lecture to be given by Vilhjalmur Stefansson concerning his experiences in the Arctic and the discovery of the "Blond Eskimos"; the writings of Henry E. Rood, including biographical sketches of Richard H. Stoddard and Richard H. Davis, and an account of the presidential campaign of 1856 in Pennsylvania as given by Captain H. B. Jeffries, who accompanied his father in campaigning for John C. Frémont; clippings, many relating to Admiral Peary; a copy of the poem entitled "Common Noun" by John H. Finley; and an extract of a letter concerning the laying of the cornerstone of the White House.

4557. SIR GILES ROOKE PAPERS, 1774-1775. 10 items. London, England.

Correspondence of Sir Giles Rooke (1743-1808), British judge, with members of the family of his wife, Harriet Sophia (Burrard) Rooke, concerning the political struggle between the Burrards and Sir Philip Jennings for control of the governing body of the borough of Lymington, Hampshire.

4558. ANNA ELEANOR (ROOSEVELT) ROOSEVELT PAPERS, 1932-1948. 6 items. Hyde Park (Dutchess County), N.Y.

Miscellaneous papers of Anna Eleanor (Roosevelt) Roosevelt (1884-1962), reformer and wife of Franklin Delano Roosevelt, including a letter to Rose M. MacDonald thanking her for her support in Roosevelt's 1932 presidential campaign; a circular letter soliciting support for the American Association for the United Nations; and a copy of the third report of Trygve Lie, secretary-general of the United Nations.

4559. FRANKLIN DELANO ROOSEVELT PAPERS, 1933-1935. 8 items. Hyde Park (Dutchess County), N.Y.

Papers of Franklin Delano Roosevelt (1882-1945), president of the United States, consist of a letter from Roosevelt to Ray Baker Harris describing a luncheon at the U.S. embassy in London given by Walter Hines Page in honor of Roosevelt; and papers relating to the inauguration of Roosevelt in 1933, including an invitation, a program, and photographs of Roosevelt and Vice-President John Nance Garner.

4560. THEODORE ROOSEVELT PAPERS, (1901-1910) 1975. 7 items. Oyster Bay (Nassau County), N.Y.

Papers of Theodore Roosevelt (1858-1919), president of the United States, include a letter from T. M. Buffington, principal chief of the Cherokee Nation, soliciting Roosevelt's support for a bill which would provide for certain claims of the

Cherokee in the West; invitation to a reception at the White House; invitation and program of the inauguration in 1905; letter from Roosevelt to Charles J. Bonaparte congratulating him on an address; a draft of a letter to Charles Hall Davis, chairman of the executive committee of the Southern Commercial Congress, to be read at the meeting, emphasizing the role the South would play in the economic development of the nation, especially after the completion of the Panama Canal; and a clipping of an article entitled "Visit to Sagamore Hill," featuring Roosevelt's home, and an interview with his daughter, Ethel (Roosevelt) Derby (<u>National Retired Teachers Association Journal</u>, September-October, 1975).

4561. GEORGE A. ROOT PAPERS, 1863-1865. 34 items. New Haven (New Haven County), Conn.

Letters from Union soldiers to George A. Root, newspaper man, concerning camp life, scarcity and high prices of sugar and coffee; the burning of the Taylor plantation when the owner attempted to signal the Confederates; foraging, troop activities in Suffolk and Portsmouth, Virginia, and New Bern and Batchelor's Creek, North Carolina; granting of furloughs for voting purposes; burning of Washington, North Carolina; yellow fever in New Bern; the siege of Petersburg; the re-election of Lincoln; desertion; the army of occupation in Richmond, Virginia; and duty at the U.S. General Hospital, David's Island, New York.

4562. SARAH A. ROOTES PAPERS, 1822 (1858-1870) 1884. 124 items. Hickory Fork (Gloucester County), Va.

Correspondence of Sarah Rootes, consisting largely of letters from her brother, Thomas Reade Rootes (1835-1867), Confederate soldier in Company C, 4th Regiment, Texas Cavalry. The letters concern the settlement of estates, 1822-1861; the part Texas played in the Civil War; Civil War prisons, especially those in Santa Fé and New Orleans, where Rootes was imprisoned, and one in Elmira, New York, where his half brother, Henry Lamartine Hagy, was imprisoned; conditions in Houston, Texas, during Reconstruction; migration to Texas; postwar living, business, and crop conditions in Texas; cholera plagues and yellow fever epidemics in Houston, 1867; the Civil War and Reconstruction in Virginia; and postwar business conditions in Richmond, Virginia.

4563. THOMAS READE ROOTES PAPERS, 1807. 3 items. Fredericksburg (Spotsylvania County), Va.

Papers of Thomas Reade Rootes (1763-1824), lawyer and member of the Virginia House of Delegates in 1793, consisting of a claim of Rootes against Thomas Long of Liverpool; a deed for tracts of land in Harrison and Greenbrier counties, Virginia (now West Virginia); and a legal memorandum.

4564. DANIEL CALHOUN ROPER PAPERS, 1898 (1928-1938) 1941. 38,675 items and 31 vols. Washington, D.C.

Personal and political papers of Daniel Calhoun Roper (1867-1943), attorney, commissioner of internal revenue, 1917-1920, and secretary of commerce, 1933-1938. Correspondence, memoranda, and related printed materials concern national politics, especially the 1932 presidential campaign; prohibition; the Department of Commerce and Roper's duties and activities; the Business Advisory Council; the Communications Committee, 1933-1934 (forerunner of the Federal Communications Commission); the National Advisory Council; cabinet meetings; education, particularly American University (Washington, D.C.), Duke University (Durham, North Carolina), Coker College (Hartsville, South Carolina), and the District of Columbia Board of Education; agriculture, especially in the Carolinas where Roper owned farm land; the Depression; economic conditions; relief and unemployment; foreign and domestic commerce; American Peace Society; National Recovery Administration; merchant marine; railroads; China relief; fisheries; the Methodist Episcopal Church, South; and various clubs and organizations to which Roper belonged. There are also copies of memoranda from Roper as secretary of commerce to the president, of press releases, and of statements, addresses, and speeches by the secretary. Financial papers include material on the property and investments of the Roper family, brokerage statements, custodian accounts, and account books, 1928-1937. Scrapbooks, 1903-1939, contain chiefly newspaper clippings and pictures. A letter book relates to Roper's resignation from the office of commissioner of internal revenue in March, 1920. There is also a manuscript copy of Roper's book, <u>Fifty Years of Public Life</u> (Durham, North Carolina: 1941), and several papers relating to its publication by Duke University Press.

4565. ANDREW K. ROSE PAPERS, 1862 (1863-1865) 1894. 122 items and 2 vols. Dover (Cuyahoga County), Ohio.

Family letters and diaries, 1864-1865, of Andrew K. Rose (b. 1843), sergeant in the 124th Ohio Infantry, who participated in the campaigns in East Tennessee, 1863, and in the siege of Atlanta, 1864. The letters reflect the life of the common soldier, and are generally cheerful regardless of the hardships he faced. The diaries record his movements; the condition of the weather; money, clothes, and rations drawn; and routine camp life.

4566. HUGH HENRY ROSE, FIRST BARON STRATHNAIRN, PAPERS, 1867. 1 item. London, England.

Manuscript (48 pp.) entitled "Summary of the Extract from Lord Strathnairn's Report" written by Field Marshal Hugh Henry Rose, First Baron Strathnairn (1801-1885), concerning the appearance of Fenianism within the army, measures needed to combat it, and its background in the social, political, economic, and religious problems of Ireland.

4567. SIR JOHN ROSE, FIRST BARONET, PAPERS, 1870-1888. 31 items. London, England.

Correspondence of Sir John Rose, First Baronet (1820-1888), Canadian statesman, privy councillor and first minister of finance for the Dominion, 1867-1868, receiver general for the Duchy of Lancaster, 1883, and privy councillor, 1886, includes letter, 1872, from Lord Dufferin, governor general of Canada, giving his initial reactions to Canada, the disturbances in Quebec, and Prime Minister John Macdonald; letters, 1884-1888, from Francis Knollys, private secretary to the Prince of Wales, inquiring about the Women's Emigration Society, discussing his becoming a director of the Lake Copais Company, and giving his opinion of the proposed commercial department in the Imperial Institute; letter, 1886, from Rose to the Prince of Wales explaining his reservations about accepting a peerage which involved the question of home rule for Ireland; letters, 1886, from John Macdonald discussing home rule for Ireland, Canadian politics, the prospects of the Canadian Pacific Railway, economic conditions, the upcoming election, the fishery controversy with the United States, and personal matters; letter, 1887, from Donald A. Smith, Canadian financier, discussing his contribution to the Imperial Institute; letters, 1888, from Sir Herbert Jekyll, concerning the Melbourne Centennial Exhibition; and letters, 1888, from Maurice Holzmann concerning the management of the Duchy of Lancaster.

4568. SIR PHILIP ROSE, FIRST BARONET, PAPERS, 1868-1880. 10 items. London, England.

Letters to Sir Philip Rose, First Baronet (1816-1883), solicitor of the firm of Baxter, Rose, and Norton, which handled electioneering organization for the Conservative Party, 1853-1870, from Sir Edward William Watkin (1819-1901), railway promoter and Liberal politician, discussing the elections in 1880, minor political subjects, and business matters involving his railway interests; and from members of the Beckett family in Yorkshire concerning the acquisition of a peerage for the family.

4569. TOMÁS ROSIS PAPERS, 1851-1858. 30 items. Savannah, Ga.

Letters to Tomás Rosis, probably a Cuban annexationist aiding Cubans who wished to come to the United States, from a sister in Havana, Cuba, discussing family affairs, conditions in Havana, and Tomás's work in the United States; and letters from relatives and contacts concerning assistance in getting to the United States.

4570. THOMAS ROSS PAPERS, 1845. 1 item. Hastings, Sussex, England.

Letter from Thomas Ross, bookseller, stationer, and artist, reporting on the political situation at Hastings relative to the parliamentary election of 1844, the prospects in 1845, and election results for 1835 and 1837, and commenting about several members of Parliament.

4571. WILLIAM ROSS PAPERS, 1738 (1787-1833) 1875. 268 items and 3 vols. Washington (Beaufort County), N.C.

Family and business correspondence of William Ross, merchant, and of his father-in-law, John Simpson, a Scottish merchant who came to Washington, North Carolina, in the early 1780s. Simpson's letters during 1786 contain derogatory remarks about North Carolinians. There is also a daybook, 1797-1798, kept by Simpson. Ross's papers include correspondence with his children, Margaret Ross, Eleanor Ross, and John S. Ross, while in school at Warrenton and Falls of Tar River, North Carolina; a letter book, 1811-1829, containing business correspondence; and two account books which were used as scrapbooks.

4572. ROSS BAPTIST CHURCH MINUTES, 1806-1872. 3 vols. Bertie County, N.C.

Minutes and copies of the original minutes of the Ross Baptist Church.

4573. WILLIAM ROSSELLE PAPERS, 1862-1865. 5 items. Nashville (Davidson County), Tenn.

A letter to William Rosselle from James D. B. DeBow concerning a private dispute, and four passes through U.S. military lines around Memphis, Tennessee, to Rosselle, "Reporter for the House Representatives."

4574. THOMAS LAFAYETTE ROSSER PAPERS, 1861-1862. 4 items. Charlottesville (Albemarle County), Va.

Papers of Thomas Lafayette Rosser (1836-1910), Confederate general, consist of two personal letters; and memoranda concerning the case of Dr. Alonzo M. F. Eisenlard, a Union surgeon who was trying to recover his back pay.

4575. DANTE GABRIEL ROSSETTI PAPERS, [1840-1887?] 208 items. London, England.

Papers of Dante Gabriel Rossetti (1828-1882), poet and painter, include unpublished poems and sonnets, rough drafts, literary notes, fragments, and proof sheets [For a detailed description, see Paull F. Baum (ed.), *Dante Gabriel Rossetti, An Analytical List of Manuscripts in the Duke University Library with Hitherto Unpublished Verse and Prose* (Durham, North Carolina: 1931).]; letters from Rossetti to Frederic James Shields (1833-1911), painter and decorative artist, concerning personal matters, their friendship, Rossetti's painting, financial remuneration for Rossetti's works, other artists, and the state of Rossetti's mental and physical health; letter, 1870, from Rossetti to George Eliot discussing his intention for the drawing entitled "Hamlet"; personal letters of Christina Georgina Rossetti (1830-1894), poet and sister of Dante Gabriel Rossetti; other personal correspondence; photographs of Rossetti and of his death mask; and copies of some of his paintings, many of which are picture postcards.

4576. WILLIAM MICHAEL ROSSETTI PAPERS, 1850-1916. 289 items. London, England.

Correspondence of William Michael Rossetti (1829-1919), governmental official and editor, including letters to Charles Aldrich, Anne (Burrows) Gilchrist, and Herbert Harlakenden Gilchrist, concerning literature and art, with discussions of Walt Whitman, his influence in England, and his impoverishment in America; letters pertaining to the death and funeral of Rossetti's father-in-law, Ford Madox Brown (d. 1893), painter; letters relating to the death of Percy Bysshe Shelley (1792-1822); letters concerning a biography of and a memorial to Christina Georgina Rossetti (1830-1894), poet and sister of William Michael Rossetti; fragment of an article by Felix Volkhousky on efforts to bring about freedom for Russians; and other correspondence about artists and literary figures.

4577. CHARLES ROTHROCK PAPERS, 1864-1865. 8 items. Asheville (Buncombe County), N.C.

Civil War letters to Louesia Delap from her brother, Charles Rothrock, and from her husband, Valentine Delap, while stationed at Petersburg and Liberty Mills, Virginia, and in a training camp in Raleigh, North Carolina, discussing poor rations, the desertion of Confederate soldiers to the Union troops, and dissatisfaction among the soldiers.

4578. SAMUEL ROTHROCK PAPERS, 1871. 1 item. Rowan County, N.C.

Sermon of Samuel Rothrock, Lutheran minister, concerning the harmful effects of using tobacco.

4579. ROTHSCHILD BROTHERS PAPERS, 1863-1868. 63 items. Paris, France.

Correspondence and legal papers relating to the efforts of the Rothschild Brothers of Paris to secure indemnification for their tobacco which was partially destroyed in a warehouse fire in Richmond, Virginia, in 1863. The remainder was seized by the U.S. government when Richmond was occupied at the end of the Civil War.

4580. JOHN HORACE ROUND PAPERS, 1883. 2 items. Brighton, Sussex, England.

Letters to John Horace Round (1854-1928), British historian, from his mentor, William Stubbs, concerning Round's historical work, and social matters.

4581. JESSE ROUNTREE PAPERS, 1799. 1 item. Edgefield County, S.C.

Deposition of Jesse Rountree claiming that a runaway slave owned by him entered the Creek Nation.

4582. JOHN ROUTH PAPERS, 1863. 1 item. Tensas Parish, La.

Testimony of John Routh, Louisiana planter, concerning the depredations on his plantation, "Holly-Wood," by the Marine Brigade under Captain Crandel. Included is an inventory of silver, linen, supplies, books, and other personal possessions.

4583. S. S. ROUTH DAYBOOK, 1839. 1 vol. (150 pp.) Orangeburg District, S.C.

Daily accounts of goods sold by a general merchant.

4584. ROBERT ROWAND DIARY, 1846-1851. 1 vol. Charleston, S.C.

Diary of a slaveowner concerning social life and customs in Charleston, South Carolina; religion, particularly the Huguenot Church to which Rowand belonged; the weather; diseases and health conditions, including yellow fever in 1849; the Fourth of July celebrations of the Society of the Cincinnati; vital statistics; local and national politics and government; the visit to Charleston by President James K. Polk in 1849; and memorials to John C. Calhoun in 1850. There is frequent mention of members of the Bee, Buist, Drayton, Elliott, Grimke, Pinckney, Simons, Sommers, and Walker families.

4585. JAMES H. ROY, JR., NOTEBOOK, 1848-1849. 1 vol. (117 pp.) Mathews County, Va.

Legal notes taken by a student at the University of Virginia, Charlottesville, Virginia.

4586. ROYAL COTTON MILL COMPANY PAPERS, 1899-1954. 2,348 items and 37 vols. Wake Forest (Wake County), N.C.

Business papers of the Royal Cotton Mill Company and of its predecessor, the Royall Cotton Mills, including a history of the mill from 1899 into the 1940s; minutes, 1899-1931, of meetings of stockholders and of the board of directors, including the charter and bylaws, and some financial statements; audit reports, 1918-1919, 1929-1931, and 1935-1944; financial statements, 1902-1943; court files relating to the company's period in receivership, 1931-1933, and to the suit of Willis Smith (1887-1953), lawyer, U.S. senator, and an attorney and stockholder of the company, against Royal Cotton Mill Company; correspondence files of Robert E. Royall (d. 1937), an original organizer of the Royall Cotton Mills, concerning the Baptist Church and Populists in North Carolina in 1916, and the controversy over the dismissal of Professor William Turner Carstarphen from the School of Medicine at Wake Forest College, Wake Forest, North Carolina; correspondence files of Harvey Seward, who assumed control from Royall and from his father-in-law, William C. Powell; correspondence of George H. Greason, mill superintendent, and of others involved in the company; reports to the North Carolina Corporation Commission, 1909-1912, and to the North Carolina Tax Commission, 1919-1920; files on various legal, financial, and operational matters; claims against the Royall Cotton Mills, 1931-1936; ledgers, 1900-1930; journals, 1900-1919; cash journals, 1918-1932; sales invoices, 1906-1927; time books, 1903-1929; trial balances, 1922-1929; cotton purchases record, 1928-1935; general store ledgers, 1901-1913 and 1921-1924; and several clippings and printed items.

4587. THE ROYAL INSURANCE COMPANY OF LIVERPOOL DAYBOOK, 1869-1875. 1 vol. (222 pp.) Savannah, Ga.

Records of The Royal Insurance Company of Liverpool with William C. Cosens, its agent in Savannah, Georgia, including names of policy holders, and the terms, accounts, rates, and premiums of the policies.

4588. JOHN W. ROYSE PAPERS, 1862-1865. 83 items. Fredericksburg (Washington County), Ind.

Civil War correspondence of Simeon Royse, son of John W. Royse, and cousins W. H. Thompson and Simeon Garriott while serving in the 66th Indiana Infantry Volunteers, to family members in Fredericksburg, Indiana, discussing camp life, food, clothing, pay, health conditions, postal service, rumors about desertions in Grant's army, religion, belief in the Union cause, skirmishing around Corinth (Mississippi), campaigns around Atlanta and Kennesaw Mountain, Confederate raids into Indiana and on a Union picket line, Confederate attempt to blow up a train near Lafayette (Tennessee), and conditions at home.

4589. WILLIAM S. ROYSTON PAPERS, 1823-1898. 238 items. Guiney's Station (Caroline County), Va.

Business and family papers of William S. Royston, tailor, and of other members of Royston's family including summonses; fines for non-attendance of muster; receipts for docket fees; pamphlet entitled "The Tailor's Archetype," published by Allen Ward in 1823 containing patterns and a list of tailors authorized to use the "Ward system"; broadsides from Robert A. Stephens concerning fashion; bills, 1861, for the education of Royston's daughter; and correspondence concerning family matters, taxes and the cost of living, the hiring of slaves, the activities of the Locofoco Party in 1845, a proposed operation for a tumor on a Negro woman to be performed at Medical College in Richmond, meningitis epidemic in Rodney (Alabama) in 1872, social life and customs and speculation in cotton in Alabama, and the value of Virginia consol bonds, 1880-1881.

4590. ROZOY-EN-BRIE, FRANCE. EXTRAIT DES REGISTRES DE LA VALEUR DES GROS FRUITS VENDUS AU MARCHE DE LA VILLE DE ROZOY-EN-BRIE, 1596-1745. 1 vol.

Certified record of weekly price quotations of various kinds of grains, from the town market in Rozoy-en-Brie, France.

4591. ROBERT CHESTER RUARK PAPERS, 1962. 5 vols. Wilmington (New Hanover County), N.C.

Next to the final typescript of the novel Uhuru, centering on the theme of nationalism in Africa, written by Robert Chester Ruark (1915-1965), journalist and novelist.

4592. SAMUEL R. RUCKER PAPERS, 1842-1855. 14 items. Murfreesboro (Rutherford County), Tenn.

Letters from Robert Rucker, a student at the University of Virginia, Charlottesville, 1849-1851, to his father, containing comments on professors, subjects studied, and life of the students. One letter, 1850, gives an interesting account of the differences in value of money in various states.

4593. SUSAN P. RUFF PAPERS, 1835-1836. 2 items. Lexington (Rockbridge County), Va.

Personal letters to Susan P. Ruff from her brother, Dr. Samuel W. Ruff (d. 1841), U.S. Navy surgeon on the U.S.S. St. Louis, containing information on the attempts of the U.S. Navy to halt the flow of slaves into the United States via Texas; problems of supplying the navy with palatable food; sanitation and sickness aboard the ships; and the Seminole War.

4594. EDMUND RUFFIN PAPERS, 1863. 1 item. Ruthven (Prince George County), Va.

Letter of Edmund Ruffin (1794-1865), agriculturist and publisher, to Robert Reid Howison concerning the forwarding of a diary on the battles of Manassas.

4595. THOMAS RUFFIN PAPERS, 1822 (1861-1864) 1869. 21 items. Alamance County, N.C.

Family letters to Thomas Ruffin (1787-1870), chief justice of the North Carolina Supreme Court, 1833-1852, 1858, chiefly from his daughters. One letter, 1864, comments on Confederate tax collecting and the scarcity of food; another, written by Ruffin to one of his sons, strongly advises the latter not to become connected with the Ku Klux Klan.

4596. DANIEL RUGGINS PAPERS, 1845 (1861-1865) 1879. 662 items and 2 vols. Fredericksburg (Spotsylvania County), Va.

Military correspondence of Daniel Ruggles (1810-1897), captain in the U.S. Army and major general in the Confederate Army, consisting of telegrams concerned with troop movements in Louisiana and Mississippi, transportation of supplies and troops, enemy troop movements, prisoners of war, the evacuation of troops from Fort Pillow (Tennessee), railroads, especially the Southern Railroad and the Mississippi and Cincinnati Railroad in 1862, and the burning of cotton and bridges in various areas of Mississippi; and reports from officers of the day at Camp Benjamin (Louisiana) giving picket lists and conditions of supplies, equipment, hospitals, sick, and wounded. Included also are letters from civilian officials of Mississippi relative to defenses and counterfeit money; letters from Confederate women offering supplies; letter, 1859, concerning the sale of Ruggles's land in Texas, land speculation in Texas, and the administration of James Buchanan; several letters in 1847 relative to the Mexican War; and a letter from Louis Caulli, a French naturalist, asking aid of Ruggles. Included also is the diary of his sister, Lucy Ruggles, 1845-1848, containing detailed accounts of a journey in 1845, by boat, railroad, and stagecoach from Charleston, South Carolina, to Wytheville, Virginia, with comments on the backwardness of North Carolina; gossip about people in Wytheville; and her work there as a teacher. The diary also includes observations on slavery, Charleston society, contemporary literature and theology, education, and the role of women. She worked as a governess for the South Carolina aristocracy.

4597. SAMUEL BULKLEY RUGGLES PAPERS, 1839-1857. 2 items. Philadelphia, Pa.

Letter of recommendation to Samuel Bulkley Ruggles (1800-1881), lawyer and canal commissioner in New York, 1839-1858; and letter to Ruggles from Caleb Huse forwarding information.

4598. JAMES RUMSEY PAPERS, 1785-1816. 68 items. Shepherdstown (Jefferson County), W. Va.

Papers of James Rumsey (1743-1792), inventor, including letters to his brothers-in-law, Charles Morrow, merchant, and Colonel John Morrow, U.S. congressman, 1805-1809, concerning the shipment of English goods to the United States and religion; copy of minutes, 1785, of the Potomac Company which was constructing canals around the rapids in the Potomac River; legal papers concerning the financial affairs of Rumsey; papers pertaining to the settlement of Rumsey's estate; bills and receipts; and a Rumsey family tree.

4599. RICHARD RUSH PAPERS, 1812. 1 item. Philadelphia, Pa.

Letter from Richard Rush (1780-1859), comptroller of the treasury, attorney general, secretary of state, secretary of the treasury, and ambassador to France and to Great Britain, acknowledging receipt of customs accounts from Francis Page of Yorktown, Virginia.

4600. JOHN RUSKIN PAPERS, 1855-1886. 15 items. Brantwood, Lancashire, England.

Correspondence of John Ruskin (1819-1900), British author, artist, and social reformer, including letters to Harry Quilter, art critic, discussing several of Quilter's writings and current attitudes toward art; letter to Lord Leighton concerning the promotion of English art; letters to composer John Pyke Hullah dealing with the poetry of Henry Wadsworth Longfellow, Thomas Carlyle, and Henry Francis Cary's translation of Dante; personal letters of Thomas Carlyle; and a letter of Frederick Locker-Lampson discussing several of his poems and personal matters.

4601. JAMES FOWLER RUSLING PAPERS, 1864 (1880-1910) 1929. 1,100 items. Trenton (Mercer County), N.J.

Business and professional papers of James Fowler Rusling (1834-1918) relating to his activities as a pension lawyer handling the claims of Civil War veterans. Included are letters from disabled Civil War soldiers; applications for pensions; supporting documents from physicians, friends, and neighbors; affidavits; form notes and letters from the U.S. Bureau of Pensions; official certifications of births, deaths, and marriages; certificates of appeal for rejected pensions; and legal briefs from the Bureau of Pensions explaining decisions in various cases. The bulk of the papers relate to claims of New Jersey soldiers, although all states are represented. A few papers deal with claims from the Spanish-American War. There is also a printed circular, 1919, in memory of Rusling by the Military Order of the Loyal Legion of the United States, summarizing Rusling's military career.

4602.  WILLIAM C. RUSSEL PAPERS, 1856-1865. 29 items. New York, N.Y.

Correspondence of William C. Russel, lawyer, concerning the fate of his son, Cabot Jackson Russel (d. 1863), captain in the 54th Massachusetts Regiment, one of the first Negro regiments in the U.S. Army, after the Union assault on Fort Wagner, South Carolina, July 18, 1863. Letters discuss rumors of Cabot Russel's capture and death, the battle of Fort Wagner, the Negro regiment and attitudes of Southerners and Northerners toward it, George B. McClellan, and the exchange of prisoners. Also included are three letters of Cabot Jackson Russel while vacationing in New England in 1856 and 1859; and two personal letters to Cabot Russel from his aunt, Ellen Jackson.

4603.  DANIEL LINDSAY RUSSELL PAPERS, 1872-1873. 7 items. Wilmington (New Hanover County), N.C.

Letters from Daniel Lindsay Russell, planter, to his overseer concerning cotton, corn, ditching, and laborers.

4604.  EDWARD AUGUSTUS RUSSELL PAPERS, 1820-1822. 8 items. Petersburg (Dinwiddie County), Va.

Letters to Edward Augustus Russell, merchant, from business concerns in Providence, Rhode Island, and Richmond, Virginia, concerning the purchase and sale of cotton and other goods, with frequent mention of prices.

4605.  LORD JOHN RUSSELL, FIRST EARL RUSSELL, PAPERS, 1817-1874. 148 items. London, England.

Political papers, chiefly correspondence and memoranda, of Lord John Russell, First Earl Russell (1792-1878), British statesman, concerning the possibility of Charles Grey, Second Earl Grey, entering the ministry; uniting the party; abolition of slave trade, and efforts to persuade the United States to agree to the mutual right of search in shipping; church reform in Ireland; the Catholic Question; Russell's proposed duties as leader in the House of Commons; demonstrations upon the entry of Earl Mulgrave, Lord Lieutenant of Ireland, into Dublin; the replacement of the Irish Coercion Act; the Orange Society in Ireland; Mulgrave's proposed appointment of Major Stanhope; the Tithe Bill; the question of using police or troops to collect tithes; the use of church funds for education; financial support for the church, and reduction in the number of bishoprics; support and opposition to the Peel ministry; French siege of Antwerp; Reform Bill of 1832; court reform, including procedural questions, imprisonment for debt, bankruptcy cases, the Court of Chancery, and capital punishment; constitutional changes, especially in the extension of the franchise; Irish Poor Law; views of the ministers on the Irish Municipal Bill; conditions at Birmingham, including trade; Russell's loss of support in Scotland; Privilege Bill; the Corn Laws, including an article by Russell entitled "Reflexions on the Present State of the Corn Laws"; condition of the working class, and strategies to be employed to improve their condition; free trade; reform measures supported by Russell; ministry of Sir Robert Peel, Second Baronet; the shortage of labor in Jamaica; treaties among Great Britain, Spain, and Portugal on the slave trade; proposed Reform Bill of 1854; Russell's recommendations on the consolidation of statute law; intent of the Municipal Bill as viewed by Russell; various parliamentary elections; and the publication of the memoirs of Charles Cavendish Fulke Greville. Other items include a report (35 pp.) by William Whateley on the operation of provisions for voter registration, including detailed criticisms of registration procedures and specific recommendations for changes, with marginalia by Russell; speech by Russell entitled "The Obstacles Which Have Retarded Moral and Political Progress" [published in The Times, (London) November 13, 1855]; poem by Russell entitled "London in September"; clippings and an article containing biographical information; and a political cartoon satirizing the ministry of William Lamb, Second Viscount Melbourne. Correspondents include John Bright, William Cavendish, Sixth Duke of Devonshire, Earl Cottenham, Viscount Duncannon, Edward Ellice, Earl Grey, Lord Holland, Joseph Hume, Lord Lyttelton, Lord Melbourne, Earl Mulgrave, Lord Palmerston, Sir Robert Peel, Earl Spencer, Edward John Stanley, Lord Tavistock, and William Wilberforce.

4606.  JOHN F. RUSSELL PAPERS, 1808 (1876-1905) 1946. 1,078 items. New York, N.Y.

Chiefly letters to John F. Russell, physician, from his mother, Mrs. L. R. Russell, concerning life in Washington, D.C., and Greenfield, Massachusetts, where she spent the summer months; a group of Negroes stranded in Washington while en route from North Carolina to Indiana in 1879; the death of President James A. Garfield in 1881; the death and funeral of President Ulysses S. Grant in 1885; and the arrival of Coxey's Army of Peace in 1894. Also included are letters of John F. Russell to his mother containing references to his work and to a patented formula for the prevention and treatment of tuberculosis; family correspondence of Obediah Brown of Greenfield, Massachusetts, concerning family matters and life on a pioneer lumbering project in southwestern Michigan; business letters pertaining to the establishment of the western meat packing houses in the East and to the methods used to eliminate competition; and deeds for land in Michigan and Kansas.

4607. JOHN S. RUSSELL PAPERS, 1875-1915. 49 items. Winchester (Frederick County), Va.

Miscellaneous papers of John S. Russell, lieutenant in John Singleton Mosby's 43rd Battalion of Virginia Cavalry (Partisan Rangers), including letters from Mosby containing reminiscences of the war years, with references to Robert E. Lee and J. E. B. Stuart, and to Mosby's writings; letters from Marshall McCormick, attorney, concerning the trial, conviction, and subsequent pardon of Frank C. Russell, son of John S. Russell, for horse theft; and tax receipts and other financial papers.

4608. LAURAMAN HOWE RUSSELL PAPERS, 1860-1864. 30 items. Marlboro (Middlesex County), Mass.

Letters from Lauraman Howe Russell, Union Army ward-master, 13th Regiment, Massachusetts Volunteers, to his daughter, Serena Ellen Russell, describing camp life, pay, food, health conditions, desertion from the Union Army, immorality, runaway slaves, morale, prisoners, army hospitals, troop movements, the fighting at Harpers Ferry (West Virginia) and skirmishes at Williamsport (Maryland) in 1861, and Ellen Mary (Marcy) McClellan, wife of General George B. McClellan, attending soldiers at Academy Hospital, Chambersburg, Pennsylvania. A detailed daily journal, October 1, 1861-January 1, 1862, describes similar topics. Also included are sketches of the skirmish area along the Potomac River at Williamsport and of the Union Army camp site at Falmouth, Virginia; and a list of the army daily regimental calls.

4609. R. Y. RUSSELL PAPERS, 1821-1855. 12 items. York County, S.C.

Letters concerning camp meetings and educational institutions of the Independent Presbyterian Church of South Carolina, of which R. Y. Russell was a minister; calls from various churches to Russell to become pastor; and an offer of a position at Jackson College, Columbia, Tennessee. The letters show the religious feeling of the 1820s and 1830s.

4610. ROBERT E. RUSSELL PAPERS, 1798 (1835-1865) 1890. 400 items. Columbia (Richland County) and Lexington (Lexington County), S.C.

Chiefly business papers of Robert E. Russell relating to his seed and florist business. Also included are a letter, 1850, giving the price of slaves in Salem, Alabama; Civil War letters of John E. Stuart and John F. Miller from various places in Virginia, North Carolina and South Carolina; papers of Samuel J. Stuart and of the Confederate States arsenal in Charleston, South Carolina, for which Stuart was manufacturing saddle trees; voters list and tax lists for Lexington County in 1863; and withdrawal cards of the Knights of Jericho, a temperance organization.

4611. WARING RUSSELL PAPERS, 1858-1895. 10 items and 1 vol. Savannah, Ga.

Papers of the sheriff and notary public of Chatham County, Georgia; and a receipt book of the sheriff's office, containing names of many Georgia lawyers.

4612. WILLIAM RUSSELL PAPERS, (1863-1867) 1961. 5 items and 1 vol. Henrico County, Va.

Diary, 1863-1865, of William Russell, Confederate soldier, describing troop movements in South Carolina and Florida; the siege of Petersburg, including an account of the explosion of the Union mine forming the "Crater," communication between Union and Confederate lines, and ministers preaching in the trenches; engagements with the cavalry led by Philip Sheridan; and the wound he received. Also included is a newspaper article, 1867, concerning the treatment of the estate of Robert E. Lee by Union troops; note, 1864, pertaining to the loan of music books to some soldiers; and a flyer, 1961, describing the places of historic interest in Petersburg, Virginia.

4613. WILLIAM W. RUSSELL AND JOHN C. CASH PAPERS, 1852-1898. 31 items. Washington, D.C.

Papers of Majors William W. Russell and John C. Cash, paymasters of the U.S. Marine Corps during the Civil War, chiefly concerning payrolls.

4614. RUSSIAN POSTERS, 1919-1962. 52 items. Moscow and Leningrad, U.S.S.R.

Twenty-nine posters emphasizing the benefits of communism and the first "Five Year Plan" for workers, the achievements of the U.S.S.R. under communism, religion as an enemy of the people, and the struggle against and decline of capitalism; fourteen placards from the 22nd Congress of the Communist Party of the U.S.S.R. describing the strength of the country in industrial development, consumer goods, agricultural production, electrification, and the national welfare, and the collapse of the colonial system of imperialism and the problems facing capitalism; and nine facsimiles of posters.

4615. GEORGE RUST PAPERS, 1808-1879. 3,340 items and 3 vols. Baltimore, Md., and Leesburg (Loudoun County), Va.

Chiefly the business and financial papers of George Rust, Jr. (1788-1857), brigadier general of the Virginia Militia and

Virginia state legislator, 1818-1823, concerning his ventures in cattle, flour, wheat, land, guano, and various plantations. Also included are correspondence concerning Democratic politics, road construction in Virginia, salaries of state officials, appointments to various positions, and Rust's service as a presidential elector and as a delegate to the Democratic National Convention; papers relating to the business enterprises of his sons, Edgar Rust, Robert B. Rust, and Armistead Thomson Mason Rust; fragment written by T. Mason concerning the duel between John McCarthy and Armistead Thomson Mason in 1819; correspondence dealing with the financial difficulties of Alfred Rust in Arkansas, and William Rust in Texas, brothers of George Rust, Jr.; personal correspondence; land deeds; household accounts; bills and receipts, some relating to the education of Rust's children and grandchildren and to the hiring of slaves; clippings; pamphlets; and account books.

4616. JOHN RUTHERFOORD PAPERS, 1754 (1781-1865) 1931. 2,712 items and 33 vols. Richmond, Va.

Family, business, personal, and political correspondence of John Rutherfoord (1792-1866), lawyer, merchant, and governor of Virginia, 1841-1842; of his son, John Coles Rutherfoord (1825-1866), lawyer, planter, and member of the House of Delegates; of Ann Seddon (Roy) Rutherfoord (1832-1906?), wife of John Coles Rutherfoord; and of Thomas Rutherfoord (1766-1852), father of John Rutherfoord, and Richmond merchant. Early papers are those of Isaac Holmes, assistant quartermaster at Petersburg, Virginia, chiefly from Richard Claiborne concerning provisions for Revolutionary soldiers; and of James Webb, apparently a lawyer of Smithfield, Virginia, having connections with John Marshall, Spencer Roane, and John Wickham, consisting of legal correspondence and papers. The papers of Thomas Rutherfoord include a letter, 1810, expressing objections to the embargo; letters concerning family matters and Rutherfoord's ailments; correspondence dealing with business affairs, chiefly his large landholdings in Kentucky and Ohio, and the title and sale of those lands; and an article, 1812, on the necessity of a navy to protect the maritime rights of the United States.

Personal correspondence of John Rutherfoord is primarily with relatives, including his son, John Coles Rutherfoord; his brothers, Samuel Rutherfoord, William Rutherfoord, and Alexander Rutherfoord, and their families; relatives of Emily (Coles), Rutherfoord, his wife, including Tucker Coles, Isaac A. Coles, Edward Coles, Andrew Stevenson, and William Cabell Rives; his brother-in-law, Hodijah Meade; and Jane (Rutherfoord) Meade. Letters discuss family news; business matters; agriculture and the operation of their various plantations; the painting of family portraits; the marketing of wheat produced at "Rock Castle," home of John Coles Rutherfoord, during the 1840s and 1850s; visits to various springs in western Virginia; the insurance society headed by John Rutherfoord; family illnesses, including full descriptions of remedies and medicines; purchase of land; detailed accounts of the construction of a boat for use at "Rock Castle"; purchase of a buggy, including description of various types of buggies; purchase and price of guano; detailed accounts of shipping by freight boats on the James River; purchase of slaves to prevent the separation of families; sympathy for slaves; purchase of shoes and making of clothes for slaves at "Rock Castle"; details of household management, such as the making of candles and the slaughtering of sheep; Richmond social life; and current events. Also included are letters from relatives in Ireland; letters of advice from John Rutherfoord to his son, John Coles Rutherfoord, while the latter was a student at Washington College, Lexington, Virginia, and at the University of Virginia, Charlottesville, Virginia; letter, 1837, from Andrew Stevenson, U.S. minister to England, describing his and his wife's experiences in diplomatic circles in London, and papers relating to the settlement of the case of the U.S.S. Caroline, burned in 1837 by Canadian troops; a letter, 1832, from William Cabell Rives, while minister to France, concerning the instability of the French government, and Rives's conviction that slavery should be abolished; and letters discussing the activities of Thomas Ritchie (1778-1854), editor of the Richmond Enquirer, especially during 1849. Other papers relate to Rutherfoord's bank stocks, his legal practice, and mercantile affairs in Richmond, Virginia.

The political correspondence includes correspondence between Rutherfoord and John Tyler concerning national politics, 1827-1831, Andrew Jackson and his policies, Henry Clay, political intrigue, "sectional cupidity," European affairs, and Tyler's concern for the welfare of the country; correspondence with Governor William H. Seward of New York while Rutherfoord was governor of Virginia pertaining to a controversy over fugitive slaves; letters from Rutherfoord to John Coles Rutherfoord commenting extensively on the American Party or Know-Nothings in Goochland County, Virginia; letters, 1860, from C. G. Memminger regarding national politics, secession, and the possibility of war; letter, 1860, from Rutherfoord to a cousin in London discussing the election of Abraham Lincoln, national politics, and his hatred of abolitionists, and protesting that the Prince of Wales had not been mistreated in Richmond; correspondence concerning the coming of the Civil War, the scarcity of food during the war, and refugees; letter, 1861, from John Brockenbrough describing the Washington Peace Convention and commenting on the compromise plan proposed by John Jordan Crittenden; letter, written under an assumed name, to Rutherfoord from Sir William Henry Gregory, member of the British Parliament with sympathies for the Confederate States of America, regarding the possibilities of recognition of the Confederate government by England and the means of communicating with

Rutherfoord's nephew, who was attending a German university [published: Nannie M. Tilley (ed.), "England and the Confederacy," American Historical Review 44 (October, 1938), 56-60]; and papers relating to Rutherfoord's service on a committee to assess damages made by the Confederate government in erecting defenses in Richmond.

John Rutherfoord's letter book, 1825-1837, and letterpress book, 1853-1863, contain letters relating to the collection of debts; personal matters; recommendation of George Wythe Munford for clerk of the House of Delegates; political affairs; his duties as captain and later as colonel in the Richmond Fayette Light Artillery; his rank in the U.S. Army; and other matters.

The papers of John Coles Rutherfoord consist of his letters concerning literature, the activities of the Virginia House of Delegates, work on a banking bill in 1854, the Know-Nothing Party in Goochland County and their opposition to Rutherfoord's candidacy for a seat in the House of Delegates, visits to various springs in Virginia, trips to South Carolina to visit relatives, his courtship of Ann Seddon Roy, and his legal practice; correspondence regarding preparations for a European tour made by John Coles Rutherfoord and Charles Morris in 1851; letters to Rutherfoord discussing Virginia politics in the 1850s; letters from a former college mate, William M. Cooke, describing his legal practice in Saint Louis and Hannibal, Missouri, the slavery question, the growth of Saint Louis, emigrants to California and the sale of supplies to them, hunting grouse on the prairies, and the Know-Nothing Party in Missouri in 1855; letters from John D. Osborne and William Cabell Rives, Jr., containing descriptions of their travels in the North and in Europe and conditions in Paris, France; scattered letters referring to the College of William and Mary, Williamsburg, Virginia, and to the Southern Literary Messenger and John R. Thompson; and letters from William P. Munford concerning the translation of Homer's Iliad by his father, William Munford, and his own plans to have it published.

Correspondence of Ann Seddon (Roy) Rutherfoord includes letters to her husband, John Coles Rutherfoord, concerning preparations and plans for her visits to her father, William H. Roy, household matters, and their children; letters from William H. Roy to Ann Seddon (Roy) Rutherfoord; papers pertaining to the settlement of William H. Roy's estate; letters from her sister, Sue (Roy) Carter, and from her aunt, Sarah (Seddon) Bruce, describing their children, accouchements, servants, household affairs, crops, care for slaves, and, during the Civil War, refugees, the scarcity of food, family members in the Confederate Army, and crowded conditions in Richmond, Virginia; letters of James A. Seddon regarding the business affairs of Ann Seddon (Roy) Rutherfoord after the death of her husband; letters from other friends and relatives chiefly concerning personal matters; and papers relating to the operation of "Rock Castle," including scattered accounts, contracts for labor, and inventories.

Volumes consist of a notebook on rhetoric by Emily (Coles) Rutherfoord; legal notebook of John Rutherfoord containing notes on Blackstone; personal account book, 1840-1841, of John Coles Rutherfoord; autographs and clippings collected by John Coles Rutherfoord, 1836-1850; commonplace book, 1839-1842, of John Coles Rutherfoord also containing copies of several letters; "Index Rerum," 1842, kept by John Coles Rutherfoord while at the University of Virginia; notebooks of John Coles Rutherfoord while a student at Washington College, on various subjects including chemistry, mathematics, Greek history, natural and moral philosophy, political economy, Latin history, law, and the Constitution; case books, 1844-1852, and memorandum book, 1856-1862, containing records of the cases handled by John Coles Rutherfoord; memorandum book, 1846-1864, with notes on farming operations; letter book, 1857-1866, letterpress copybook, 1856-1866, and letter book and commonplace book, 1852-1858, of John Coles Rutherfoord; index, 1856-1865, of the letters received by John Coles Rutherfoord; indices to articles on politics and major events in the New York Herald, 1856-1859, and in the Richmond Examiner, 1862-1865; notebook on Rutherfoord family history; a scrapbook, 1843-1856, relating to the career of John Coles Rutherfoord in the Virginia House of Delegates; and a legal notebook, 1895-1916, of John Rutherfoord, son of John Coles Rutherfoord.

4617.  JOHN G. RUTHERFOORD PAPERS, 1922. 3 items. Richmond, Va.

Letters concerning the re-election of John Rutherfoord to the judgeship of the 9th circuit of Virginia, signed by Walter C. Berry, Governor Westmoreland Davis, and Edward Manning.

4618.  JOHN RUTHERFURD PAPERS, 1796. 1 item. Great Britain.

Letter of Captain John Rutherfurd, British officer, from Kingstown, St. Vincent, describing the character and position of a large body of insurgents.

4619.  ARCHIBALD HAMILTON RUTLEDGE PAPERS, 1939. 1 item. McClellanville (Charleston County), S.C.

Personal letter of Archibald Hamilton Rutledge (b. 1883), poet, describing his activities restoring his family home, Hampton Plantation, writing poetry, and hunting arrowheads.

4620.  BENJAMIN HUGER RUTLEDGE PAPERS, 1863. 1 item. Charleston, S.C.

Letter from Benjamin Huger Rutledge (1829-1892), lawyer, politician, and Confederate officer of the 4th Regiment, South Carolina Cavalry, describing the skirmish at Cunningham's Bluff, South Carolina, the participation of his cavalry regiment, and the defenses of the area.

4621.   EDWARD RUTLEDGE PAPERS, 1790-1820. 6 items.  Charleston, S.C.

Papers of Edward Rutledge (1749-1800), delegate to the First Continental Congress, signer of the Declaration of Independence, state legislator, and governor of South Carolina, 1798-1800, consist of a letter, 1790, to Phineas Miller, concerning his crops and the extraction of oil from cottonseeds for the purpose of lighting street lamps; letter discussing land matters, and a proposed trip by General Charles Cotesworth Pinckney to visit George Washington and to decide on the location of a fort; legal documents relating to the estates of George Evans, 1794, of Henry Middleton, and of Edward Rutledge, 1802; and a deed, 1820, of Mary Rutledge, second wife of Edward Rutledge.

4622.   HARRIOTT HORRY RUTLEDGE PAPERS, 1841. 6 items.  Charleston, S.C.

Letters from Harriott Horry Rutledge (1832-1912), author, as a nine-year-old child, to her mother, Rebecca Motte (Lowndes) Rutledge, referring to her studies, local gossip in Charleston, and Madame (Ann Manson) Talvande (d. 1850), proprietress of a boarding school in Legaré Street.  Harriott Horry Rutledge later married St. Julien Ravenel.

4623.   HUGH RUTLEDGE PAPERS, 1756, 1796. 2 items.  Charleston, S.C.

Legal document, 1756, of Sarah Hext Rutledge, widow of Dr. John Rutledge, as executrix of the estate of Andrew Rutledge concerning the ownership of a plantation; and legal document of Hugh Rutledge as judge of the Court of Equity, pertaining to the disposition of some slaves.

4624.   JOHN RUTLEDGE, SR., PAPERS, 1762-1776.  7 items. Charleston, S.C.

Chiefly legal documents, four of which relate to the case of Hetherington and Kynoch v. Lynn, and an affidavit in the case of Thompson v. Fludd.  Also included is a letter, 1776, from William Arther, Ralph Humphreys, and Jacob Richmon, the Committee of Safety for Saxe Gotha district, South Carolina, to John Rutledge, Sr. (1739-1800), Revolutionary statesman, concerning barrels of flour that Charles Cantry has offered to the public service.

4625.   JOHN RUTLEDGE, JR., PAPERS, 1760 (1788-1798) 1862.  117 items and 2 vols.  Charleston, S.C.

Correspondence and papers of John Rutledge, Jr. (1766-1819), South Carolina legislator, member of U.S. Congress, 1795-1803, brigadier general in the South Carolina Militia, and son of John Rutledge, Sr., distinguished Revolutionary statesman. The collection centers around the life and career of John Rutledge, Jr., and concerns family and business matters; the tour of Europe made by him, 1787-1789; Thomas Jefferson's interest in the adoption of the U.S. Constitution by North Carolina; political conditions in Sweden; and the marriage of John Rutledge, Jr., to Sarah Motte Smith, and the education of their children.  Included are two letters from members of the family, one relating to the Mexican War and the other to the Civil War, and a letter relative to the purchase of land.  There are also two business letters of States Rutledge; several business letters of John Rutledge, Jr., to Petit de Villers, a commission merchant of Savannah, Georgia; two letters of John Rutledge, Sr., one to Jonathan Bryan concerning the purchase of land and the other to the delegates of South Carolina in the Continental Congress, September 5, 1779, relative to the war in South Carolina; and a contract of Edward Rutledge to hire certain Negroes belonging to Charles Cotesworth Pinckney. Other letters of Edward Rutledge and John Rutledge, Sr., to John Rutledge, Jr., concerning family finances constitute a considerable portion of the collection. Among the correspondents are Charles Cadogan, Charles Drayton, Thomas Jefferson, Countess de Litta of Milan, Charles Cotesworth Pinckney, Edward Rutledge, Elizabeth (Grimké) Rutledge, John Rutledge, Sr., Benjamin Tallmadge, and Oliver Wolcott.

Included also are two journals of the travels of John Rutledge, Jr., in Europe, 1787-1788, containing not only much material of the guidebook type, the most unusual being a set of travel directions prepared for him by Thomas Jefferson in Paris [published and analyzed: Elizabeth Cometti, "Mr. Jefferson Prepares an Itinerary," Journal of Southern History, 12 (Feb. 1946), 89-106], but also information of a more valuable nature.  Young Rutledge carried letters of introduction from George Washington, and, when he left France, from Thomas Jefferson, thus meeting such people as Madame du Barry, Marie Antoinette, and Mr. and Mrs. Wilmot, the latter being a sister of General Thomas Gage.  He occasionally met Tom Paine, but, despite a letter of introduction from George Washington, was unable to see François Jean de Chastellux, the failure being attributed to the latter's extreme poverty.  Rutledge, a close observer, noted signs of the coming French Revolution; described meetings of the British Parliament; contrasted at length the French and English, including methods of getting into Paris and London society; noted much about methods of farming in Italy; and described Italian cities and inns, and traveling conveniences in France.  The journals are written with eighteenth-century frankness on personal matters and contain considerable gossip about important figures.

4626. W. A. RUYSCH PAPERS, ca. 1940s. 1 vol.

Volume entitled "Patagonia Bibliografía," attributed to W. A. Ruysch listing works about Patagonia, 1520-1949, emphasizing anthropology, ethnology, archaeology, and linguistics.

4627. JOHN PAUL RYLANDS PAPERS, 1883. 1 item. Highfields, Thelwall, Cheshire, England.

Letter of Charles Best Norcliffe, physician, to John Paul Rylands (b. 1846), barrister-at-law and member of the council of the Record Society for the Publication of Original Documents Relating to Lancashire and Cheshire, concerning personal matters and containing notes on a publication of the Society, Lancashire and Cheshire Records Preserved in the Public Record Office (London: 1882), Parts I and II.

4628. GILBERT RYLE PAPERS. 1 item. Oxford, Oxfordshire, England.

Annotated typescript of an essay by Gilbert Ryle, professor of philosophy at Oxford University, Oxford, England, reviewing Remarks on the Foundations of Mathematics by Ludwig Wittgenstein.

4629. GEORGE RYLEY PAPERS, 1715. 1 vol. England.

Photocopy of "Mr. Herbert's Temple & Church Militant Explained & Improved. A Discourse upon Each Poem. Critical & Practical" by George Ryley containing critical annotations on George Herbert's The Temple (1633). The manuscript is a copy of MS. Rawlinson D. 199 in the Bodleian Library.

4630. RALPH SADLEIR PAPERS, 1608-1618. 1 vol. Standon, Hertfordshire, England.

Manuscript volume, in Latin, containing records from the Courts of Survey held in 1608 at various manors in Gloucestershire and Worcestershire owned by Ralph Sadleir, listing the tenants of the estates with a legal description of their relationship to the manor.

4631. JAMES A. SADLER ACCOUNT BOOK, 1848-1854. 1 vol. (98 pp.) Forsyth County, N.C.

Accounts of James A. Sadler, apparently a blacksmith and whiskey dealer.

4632. SIR MICHAEL ERNEST SADLER PAPERS, 1921. 2 items. Oxford, Oxfordshire, England.

Letters to Sir Michael Ernest Sadler, vice chancellor of Leeds University, from author Walter John De La Mare, concerning arrangements for lectures at Leeds.

4633. SAINT ALBANS POLLING LIST, 1760-1761. 1 vol. (60 pp.) Saint Albans, Hertfordshire, England.

Manuscript volume listing the names of voters in the borough of Saint Albans, 1760-1761.

4634. ST. DAVID'S SOCIETY PAPERS, (1777-1811) 1854. 7 items. Society Hill (Darlington County), S.C.

Records of St. David's Society, established for the purpose of providing school facilities in Society Hill, South Carolina, giving rules, lists of members, and copies of questions asked on annual examinations.

4635. FREDERICK ST. JOHN LETTER BOOK, 1804. 1 vol. (20 pp.) Chailey, Sussex, England.

Letter book of Major General Frederick St. John (1765-1844), British army officer, who commanded the left wing of British forces under General Gerard Lake at the battle of Laswaree (1803) during the Mahratta War, containing copies of correspondence between St. John and several other officers concerning criticism of St. John's handling of his troops at Laswaree.

4636. THADDEUS ST. MARTIN PAPERS, 1936-1937. 2 items. Houma (Terre Bonne Parish), La.

Correspondence of Thaddeus St. Martin, physician and author, commenting on his novel, Madame Toussaint's Wedding Day (Boston: 1936), and local dialect.

4637. ST. MICHAEL'S PROTESTANT EPISCOPAL CHURCH MINUTES, 1782-1863. 1 vol. (193 pp.) Charleston, S.C.

Extracts from minute books.

4638. ST. PAUL'S PROTESTANT EPISCOPAL CHURCH PAPERS, 1790 (1823-1886) 1935. 1,805 items and 11 vols. Baltimore, Md.

Papers of St. Paul's Protestant Episcopal Church contain deeds and leases; certificates for burial plots; accounts of pew rents; report of part of the salary paid James Kemp, bishop of Maryland, 1823; tax receipts; expense accounts; specifications and contracts for alterations to the church, 1823; and copies of the fundamental resolutions for the government of the vestry of St. Paul's, 1851. Volumes include a sketch of the early history of St. Paul's parish and record books of the church.

4639.  JOHN SALISBURY LEDGER, 1809-1813. 1 vol. (98 pp.) Plymouth (Washington County), N.C.

Ledger of a Plymouth, North Carolina, merchant.

4640.  SALISBURY-SPENCER MINISTERIAL ASSOCIATION PAPERS, 1914-1923. 16 items and 1 vol. Rowan County, N.C.

Minutes, 1914-1923, and a few miscellaneous papers of the Salisbury-Spencer Ministerial Association, concerning interdenominational cooperation in Rowan County and the involvement of clergymen in social issues such as temperance, censorship, and Sunday legislation (blue laws).

4641.  HELEN HARRIET SALLS PAPERS, 1924-1952. 9 items. Oxford (Granville County), N.C.

Papers of Helen Harriet Salls include letters, 1924, from Frank Clyde Brown, folklorist, giving bibliographical and pedagogical hints for teaching folklore; and a letter, 1940, from Countess Alexandra L. Tolstoy concerning the publication of a work by her father, Alexander Tolstoy.

4642.  ANN LOUISA SALMOND PAPERS, 1870-1912. 17 items and 1 vol. Camden (Kershaw County), S.C.

Papers of Ann Louisa Salmond include a diary, cards, a photograph, several poems, and the constitution, membership list, and minutes of the Ladies Sewing Society of the Presbyterian Church, Camden, South Carolina, 1870-1872. Volume is _Address Delivered by Miss Mildred Lewis Rutherford, Historian-General, United Daughters of the Confederacy_ (Washington, D.C.: 1912).

4643.  SALT WORKS LETTER BOOK, 1863-1864. 1 vol. (200 pp.) Clarke County, Ala.

Business letters and accounts of the Alabama State Salt Works.

4644.  WILLIAM SALTMARSH PAPERS, 1850, 1858. 2 items. Lawrenceburg (Dearborn County), Ind.

Personal letters to William Saltmarsh.

4645.  WILLIAM SAMPLE PAPERS, 1851-1859. 5 items. Orange and Hornby (Steuben County), N.Y.

Legal documents relating to William Sample and William Sample, Jr.

4646.  J. P. N. SANDERS NOTES, 1856. 1 vol. Emory (Washington County), Va.

Notes on lectures in chemistry taken by a student at Emory and Henry College, Virginia.

4647.  JAMES R. SANDERS PAPERS, 1847-1861. 8 items. Penfield (Greene County), Ga.

Papers of James R. Sanders include correspondence concerning legal business and the treatment of a sick or an injured slave, and bills.

4648.  RICHARD W. SANDERS AND JOHN W. GREENE PAPERS AND NOTEBOOKS, 1808 (1820-1864) 1876. 225 items and 7 vols. Wytheville (Wythe County), Va.

Personal, family, and business letters, some of which deal with social life in Wytheville; others are from a relative in Missouri, praising that state; and a few give accounts of the War of 1812, the Mexican War, and the Civil War. There are seven notebooks or account books relating to the Sanders-Green Pig Iron Furnace and its connections with the Confederate government during the Civil War.

4649.  SANDERS FAMILY PAPERS, 1806-1929. 211 items and 3 vols. Walterboro (Colleton County), S.C.

The Sanford family papers are made up primarily of the papers of Derrill Burrell, Benjamin K. Sanders, and their families, concerning the management of small plantations in Colleton County, South Carolina. Correspondence contains family letters and letters from various cotton factors in Charleston, South Carolina. Financial papers include household and plantation accounts, receipts for the sale of slaves, and tax receipts. The collection also contains wills, deeds, records of lawsuits, and three volumes, including a book listing slaves and their prices and a record of days missed and wages lost by Negro workers in 1866.

4650.  WILLIAM SANDFORD PAPERS, 1833-1914. 183 items. Bath, Somersetshire, England.

Papers of William Sandford, a merchant of Manchester, England, contain correspondence relating to Sandford's interest in exiles from Hungary after the unsuccessful revolution of 1848-1849, including letters, 1846-1866, from Lajos Kossuth, John Paget, and Count László Teleki; correspondence, 1848-1863, concerning Polish affairs, with occasional mention of Italian politics; correspondence, 1860-1867, related to Sandford's work in developing the cultivation of cotton in the Ottoman Empire; and correspondence on British politics and relations with

France, Russia, Austria, and Turkey from the 1830s to the 1860s.

4651. ALEXANDER HAMILTON SANDS, JR., PAPERS, 1910-1918. 20 vols. New York, N.Y.

Papers of Alexander Hamilton Sands, Jr., executive secretary to James B. Duke and Benjamin N. Duke of the American Tobacco Company and trustee of the Duke Endowment, contain account books, 1914-1915 and 1917-1918; check stub books, 1913-1917; daybook, 1914-1915; ledger, 1914-1915; and letter books, 1910-1918, mainly concerning personal business affairs.

4652. CHARLES ADDISON SANFORD PAPERS, 1865. 2 items. Washington, D.C., and Ann Arbor (Washtenaw County), Mich.

Facsimiles of personal letters from Charles Addison Sanford to Edward Payson Goodrich, concerned primarily with the assassination of President Abraham Lincoln and public reaction to that event in Washington, D.C. [These letters have been published: Two letters on the event of April 14, 1865, William L. Clements Library Bulletin No. 47, University of Michigan: 1946.]

4653. RICHARD SANFORD PAPERS, 1801-1848. 6 items. Dartmouth (Bristol County), Mass.

Legal documents relating to landholding and to trading voyages, and personal and business letters of Richard Sanford, part owner of the sloop Washington.

4654. VINCENT SANFORD PAPERS, 1854 (1857-1859) 1865. 50 items. Greensboro (Greene County), Ga.

Official and family correspondence of Vincent Sanford, clerk of the Inferior Court of Greene County, Georgia. The official correspondence requests information concerning certain individuals of Greene County and shows efforts of land sharks and attorneys to get information which would enable them to obtain bounty lands due to men who had served in the War of 1812. In the personal correspondence are bills; receipts; letters of a Baptist minister who preached and taught school in the vicinity of Sparta, Georgia, in 1854; and an account of the region around Flemingsburg, Kentucky, by Sanford's niece, Elizabeth M. Walker, in 1858.

4655. SIR GEORGE ROSE SARTORIUS PAPERS, 1879. 1 item. Lymington, Hampshire, England.

Letter from Admiral Sir George Rose Sartorius of the British Navy reporting remarks made by General Alfred H. Horsford about tactics in the Zulu War and wars with the Kaffirs in South Africa.

4656. MANUEL SASTRON PAPERS, 1893-1900. 414 items. Manila, Philippines.

Papers of Manuel Sastron, president of the Spanish board of liquidation for the transfer of the Philippine Islands to the United States, relate to the assumption of authority in the Philippines by the government of the United States after the Spanish-American War. The collection contains letters to Sastron from various American army officers, including Charles L. McClure, J. D. Miley, Elwell Stephen Otis, and John Adley Hull; official telegrams, receipts, and communications; a portion of a report sent to the minister of the treasury in Spain, 1899; inventory of materials in a school of arts and crafts; inventory of the bureau of the mint, including an inventory of the papers of the bureau; inventory of the workshops of the office of inspector of weights and measures; confidential information on the action of the forestry engineer Cesar de Guillerna; papers concerning the fixed and movable material of the military railroad of Iligan; papers of the division of war on military matters; papers concerning public services; data on Freemasonry in the Philippines; inventory of objects and pictures delivered to the board of liquidation; abridged monthly financial reports of the board of liquidation; material on the General Tobacco Company of the Philippines; data on confidential and secret expenditures; inventory of the papers of the bureau of lotteries; inventory of the papers of the bureau of the general administration of property; material concerning an insurrection in the province of Albay; protest of the attachment of the central treasury by the United States Army; statement concerning the attachment of property by the United States Army; papers concerning the protest of the attachment of the division of communications by the United States Army; inventory of the school of navigation in Manila; inventory of the school of painting, sculpture, and engraving; inventory of the books of acts, registrations, posts, and private files of the Council of Administration; inventory of the files of the secretary-treasurer of the Council of Works of the Port of Manila; and questionnaire of the town of Tuy, province of Batangas, 1893. Partly in the Spanish language.

4657. ERIK LESLIE SATIE PAPERS, 1950. 4 items. Paris, France.

Papers of Erik Leslie Satie, French composer, contain two clippings about his life and music, a photograph, and a copy of a drawing of Satie by Picasso.

4658. FENNER B. SATTERTHWAITE PAPERS, 1824-1882. 657 items. Washington (Beaufort County), N.C.

Legal and business correspondence of Fenner B. Satterthwaite, attorney. Much of the material concerns a lawsuit over the settlement of claims to an estate which

Satterthwaite and Asa Biggs had purchased in Madison County, Alabama.

4659. JAMES R. P. SATURDAY PAPERS, 1918-1939. 47 items. Moultrie (Colquitt County), Ga.

World War I letters from Sergeant James R. P. Saturday, stationed in France, to his parents in Moultrie, Georgia, and four French student letters to Gwendolyn Saturday, Leesburg, Florida.

4660. SIR CHARLES BURSLEM SAUNDERS PAPERS, 1853-1934. 14 items. London, England.

Papers of Sir Charles Burslem Saunders, British administrator in India, contain letters, 1853-1854, from Lord Dalhousie, governor general of India, to Charles A. Saunders concerning the careers of Saunders's sons and railroad construction; letter, 1860, from Governor General Canning to Charles Burslem Saunders relating to the appointment of Saunders as judicial commissioner at Mysore; letters, 1861, 1869, and 1876, to Charles B. Saunders from John Lawrence concerning general administrative matters; and letters, 1875 and 1876, to Charles B. Saunders from Lord Northbrook concerning the visit of the Prince of Wales and other matters.

4661. FLEMING SAUNDERS II PAPERS, 1809 (1881-1883) 1884. 34 items. Franklin County, Va.

Papers of Fleming Saunders II, farmer and lawyer, contain letters dealing mainly with family matters and business, particularly land transfers in Virginia.

4662. HUBERT SAUNDERS PAPERS, 1862-1865. 75 items. Parma (Monroe County), N.Y.

The papers of Hubert Saunders, a sailor in the United States Navy during the Civil War, consist primarily of letters describing his service on the gunboat Peosta of the Mississippi squadron on the Tennessee River. Saunders describes life on board the Peosta and at the Union base in Paducah, Illinois; the defense of Paducah, 1864; the capture of Fort Pillow, 1864; operations against Confederate raiders; and contacts with local civilians.

4663. IVORY BASSETT SAUNDERS PAPERS, 1845-1876. 13 items. Wayne (Erie County), Pa.

Papers of Ivory Bassett Saunders contain letters describing camp life in the Union Army and the battle of Winchester, 1864; a letter, 1861, from a student at Oberlin College describing conditions there; and letters, 1873, of William A. Saunders describing cadet life at the United States Military Academy.

4664. J. T. SAUNDERS LEDGERS, 1896-1917. 8 vols. Lilesville (Anson County), N.C.

Ledgers of a general merchant.

4665. JOSEPH H. SAUNDERS SERMON BOOK, 1828. 1 vol. (108 pp.) Edenton (Chowan County), N.C.

Notes and sermons of an Episcopal minister.

4666. RICHARD B. SAUNDERS PAPERS, 1836-ca. 1900. 9 vols. Chapel Hill (Orange County), N.C.

General mercantile accounts, 1836-1861; accounts of Crabtree Plantation, 1868-1876; and accounts of a fertilizer agency, ca. 1880-ca. 1900.

4667. ROMULUS MITCHELL SAUNDERS PAPERS, 1833 (1846-1848) 1866. 64 items. Raleigh (Wake County), N.C.

Correspondence of Romulus M. Saunders (1791-1867), lawyer, North Carolina legislator and attorney general, member of the United States Congress, and minister to Spain, 1846-1849. The letters relate to negotiations for the purchase of Cuba, his quarrel with his secretary, Thomas Cante Reynolds, a few public questions, and family matters.

4668. W. W. SAUNDERS TOWNSHIP BOOK, 1871-1875. 1 vol. (36 pp.) Winchester (Frederick County), Va.

Minutes of meetings of the board of Greenway township, Clarke County, Virginia. Miscellaneous personal records have also been entered in this volume.

4669. WILLIAM LAURENCE SAUNDERS PAPERS, 1767-1905. 381 items and 3 vols. Raleigh (Wake County), N.C.

The collection contains the papers of William Laurence Saunders, editor and historian, his father Joseph Hubbard Saunders, Episcopal minister and educator, and other members of his family. The papers of James Saunders, grandfather of William L. Saunders, concern legal and financial matters and his estate. Papers of Joseph H. Saunders contain a letter, 1825, concerning Bishop John Stark Ravenscroft and a controversy over the purchase of slaves; letter, 1832, from Richard Benbury Creecy concerning commencement at the University of North Carolina and a new building for the Philanthropic Society at the University; letter, 1835, describing contemporary events in North Carolina, especially the election of Governor Richard Dobbs Spaight, Jr., and the appointment of David Lowry Swain as president of the University of North Carolina; letter, 1836, reporting on a quarrel between the rector and the faculty of the Episcopal School in Raleigh, North

Carolina, and plans to obtain financial backing for the Raleigh and Gaston Railroad Company; and a letter, 1838, from Joseph H. Saunders to his wife, describing a church convention in Philadelphia, Pennsylvania, and the election of Leonidas Polk as missionary bishop in Arkansas. Papers of William Laurence Saunders include a letter, 1868, from E. Graham Haywood inviting Saunders to join the "Order of Union Democracy," organized to support the Democratic Party candidates for president of the United States; letter, 1879, from Saunders to Kemp Plummer Battle, president of the University of North Carolina, concerning criticism of Saunders and Governor Thomas Jarvis by Professor George T. Winston; letter, 1889, from James Saunders, cousin of William L. Saunders, relating several stories about historical figures, including Andrew Jackson and Thomas Hart Benton; letters, 1889-1890, concerning affairs at the University of North Carolina; and items, 1890, relating to the creation of an endowed chair in history at the University of North Carolina. The collection also contains financial and genealogical papers; a scrapbook of newspaper clippings on the career of William L. Saunders; a receipt book; a recipe book; a number of sermons by Joseph H. Saunders; and a personal account book of William L. Saunders, 1856-1860.

4670. SAUNDERS & COMPANY PAPERS, 1853-1862. 2 items and 3 vols. Phoenix Mines (Cabarrus County), N.C.

Daybooks, 1853-1855, including miscellaneous accounts, 1856-1858, of a general store located in the village of Phoenix Mines. There are long accounts for B. H. Saunders and A. H. Hutchison for the purchase of goods in 1856; a reference to the estate left by one of the partners in the store; and entries for purchases by mining companies. Accompanying the volumes are two tax lists of 1862 with names and ages of slaves.

4671. JOACHIM R. SAUSSY, JR., PAPERS, 1854-1895. 14 items. Savannah, Ga.

The papers of Joachim R. Saussy, Jr., pertain for the most part to his service in the Confederate Army, including comments on camp life, Confederate officers, unidentified battles in the Shenandoah Valley in 1864, and the 7th Georgia Regiment.

4672. MINOT JUDSON SAVAGE PAPERS, 1883-1892. 3 items. Boston, Mass.

Letters to Minot J. Savage, Unitarian minister and author. One letter, 1883, from Herbert Spencer concerns a group in England interested in the development of a rational religion; one, 1892, from Lyman Abbott gives Savage permission to make use of one of his (Abbott's) letters; and the third letter, 1884, is from Phillips Brooks.

4673. SAVANNAH AND CHARLESTON RAIL ROAD COMPANY PAPERS, 1869. 1 item. Charleston, S.C.

A $500 bond issued by the Savannah and Charleston Rail Road Company.

4674. SAVANNAH AND ISLE OF HOPE RAILROAD COMPANY PAPERS, 1891-1904. 4 vols. Savannah, Ga.

Papers of the Savannah and Isle of Hope Railroad Company include ledgers, 1891-1904, and a cashbook, 1891-1900.

4675. SAVANNAH DEBATING SOCIETY PAPERS, 1869. 22 items. Savannah, Ga.

The collection contains the minutes, correspondence, and committee reports of the Debating Society of Savannah, concerning charges of misconduct against a member of the society, and the union of the debating society and the Georgia Historical Society. Includes rosters of both organizations.

4676. SAVANNAH MEDICAL CLUB MINUTES, 1889-1890. 1 vol. (162 pp.) Savannah, Ga.

Minutes of meetings of the Savannah Medical Club, at which local physicians discussed cases which they had seen and treated.

4677. SAVANNAH MUSIC CLUB SCRAPBOOKS, 1895-1903. 2 vols. Savannah, Ga.

Scrapbooks of clippings relating to the activities of the Savannah Music Club, particularly to musical programs and concerts sponsored by the club.

4678. SAVANNAH PORT PAPERS, 1754-1920. 5,591 items and 3 vols. Savannah, Ga.

Official papers of the port of Savannah, pertaining to customs, import and export trade, and shipping. The collection includes ship clearance papers, cargo lists, crew lists, crew bonds, United States Treasury Department letters, customs papers, British consular papers, salary receipts for port officials, warehouse papers, papers concerning construction and maintenance of lighthouses, lists of seamen admitted to the Savannah poor house and hospital in the 1820s and 1830s, and papers of the Savannah Port Society, a charitable organization to aid indigent seamen. Included also is a letter book, 1817-1826, of A. S. Bullock, collector of the port of Savannah, giving many references to economic conditions; a volume listing the persons who entered the port of Savannah, 1817-1818; and volumes containing lists of returns of goods on a number of ships, and inspectors' returns, 1830-1840.

4679. PHINEAS MESSENGER SAVERY PAPERS, 1828 (1840-1870) 1907. 250 items. Liberty (Clay County), Mo.

Family, business, and Civil War correspondence of Phineas M. Savery (1830-1906), lawyer and major in the Confederate Army. Included is an unpublished notebook of Savery's war record containing a list of men who served under him; a Masonic obituary notice of his death; letters to Lydia Ann (Hughes) Mitchell, mother of Savery's wife, during the early years of the collection; and letters to and from his wife, Amanda Gertrude (Mitchell) Savery, reflecting hardships occasioned by factional strife in a border state during the Civil War period.

4680. ADNA SAWYER PAPERS, 1836-1850. 14 items. Wayne (Steuben County), and Starkey (Yates County), N.Y.

Legal and business papers of Adna Sawyer made up mainly of deeds and indentures.

4681. FRANCIS A. SAWYER AND JONATHAN SAWYER PAPERS, 1841-1899. 4,147 items and 2 vols. Dover (Strafford County), N.H.

Business correspondence, bills, receipts, samples of woolen materials, and a memorandum book of a wool manufactory owned by Francis A. Sawyer and Jonathan Sawyer. Subjects discussed include prices, chemicals, dyes, and the state of the market.

4682. LEMUEL SAWYER PAPERS, 1864. 16 items. Point Lookout (St. Mary's County), Md.

Letters of Lemuel Sawyer, a Confederate soldier imprisoned at Point Lookout, Maryland.

4683. L. SAWYER PAPERS, 1824. 1 vol. Norfolk (Norfolk County), Va.

Manuscript of the text of a play entitled "Blackbeard, A Comedy in Four Acts (Founded in fact)," written by L. Sawyer.

4684. D. LEWIS SAXON PAPERS, 1838 (1850-1854) 1869. 36 items. Huntington (Laurens County), S.C.

Letters from D. Lewis Saxon while a student at Erskine College, Due West, South Carolina, and a few family letters from a relative in Wetumpka, Alabama.

4685. DANIEL SAYER PAPERS, 1864. 3 items. Brandy Station (Culpeper County), Va.

Papers relating to the clothing of Company E, 124th New York Regiment.

4686. ALFRED MOORE SCALES PAPERS, 1873-1885. 3 items. Washington, D.C.

Papers of Alfred Moore Scales (1827-1892), U.S. representative from North Carolina, 1857-1859 and 1875-1885, and governor of North Carolina, 1885-1889, including a letter, 1873, about C.S.A. General James Johnston Pettigrew; a routine letter concerning his place of residence; and an invitation to his inaugural ball in 1885.

4687. DABNEY MINOR SCALES DIARY, 1862-1863. 1 vol. (35 pp.) Savannah, Ga.

Daily entries of a passed midshipman aboard the Confederate ironclad Atlanta while stationed near Savannah, December, 1862, to April, 1863, containing comments about the weather, supplies, ship life, the Savannah River blockade, and various Confederate ships; sketches; descriptions of ordnance; and a history and description of the Atlanta. Included are pen sketches of portions of the vessel, ordnance, and other items of the ship's equipment.

4688. JOHN COLUMBIA SCANTLING PAPERS, 1881-1911. 12 items. Washington, D.C.

Chiefly letters of John Columbia Scantling, U.S. Army officer, to various congressmen discussing legislation pertaining to military affairs, particularly officer promotions, retirements and pensions; three papers relating to the attendance of his son, Philip Scantling, at Georgetown College, Washington, D.C.; and a court-martial special order.

4689. SCARBOROUGH FAMILY PAPERS, 1760-1939. 1,414 items and 23 vols. Mount Gilead (Montgomery County), N.C.

Correspondence, legal papers, financial papers, printed material, clippings, and other miscellaneous papers of the Scarborough family, chiefly farmers, of Mount Gilead, North Carolina. Correspondence with family and friends, centering around the periods 1832-1874 and 1914-1933, discusses agricultural matters, crop yields and prices, land transactions and prices, and the westward movement of agriculture; politics; nullification; slavery; religious events and opinions on religious matters; social life and customs; family matters; frontier life; Mexico during the Mexican War; the Civil War, including the home front and camp life; Reconstruction; education and student life at Davenport Female College, Lenoir, and Davidson College, Davidson, North Carolina, during the nineteenth century, and life as a professor at the U.S. Naval Academy, Annapolis, Maryland, during the 1920s; the home front during World War I; and family history. Legal papers, primarily of the nineteenth century, consist of deeds, summonses, a will, land grants, reports on local election results, sheriff's reports to the state treasurer on tax collections, and inventories of estates. Financial papers are chiefly bills and receipts relating to farming operations. There are also several accounts, stock share certificates, and lists of debts. Miscellaneous items include Republican campaign material from the 1920s and 1932; programs, including one from a national postmasters' convention in 1932; clippings, chiefly poems and articles on household hints and home remedies; genealogical information; invitations; Christmas cards; membership cards for the National Republican League in 1923; photographs; original verses and essays; notes and fragmentary writings on the history of Montgomery County; several election ballots; and a report, 1930, on North Carolina's cotton crop. Volumes consist of notes on family history compiled by Henry T. Scarborough, 1915-1922, containing genealogical material, a letter and some financial accounts regarding a deceased relative's estate; public school register of F. B. Bray of District No. 25 of Randolph County, North Carolina, 1881-1883, and District No. 62 of Chatham County, North Carolina, 1885-1887, and register of District No. 46 of Montgomery County, North Carolina, 1894-1900, containing incomplete records of pupils' names, attendance records, names of textbooks, amounts of teachers' salaries, and names of members of the local school committee; memorandum book with lists of words and several recipes; account book, 1867-1886, of S. E. Scarborough including accounts of a private school at Mount Gilead and of a farm; civil and criminal dockets, 1869-1911, for Mount Gilead Township primarily belonging to Justice of the Peace Henry T. Scarborough; accounts, 1844-1861, of Samuel Scarborough, many for blacksmithing; account books, 1887-1900 and 1909-1919, of Henry T. Scarborough, containing personal and farm accounts, payments for labor, and records of his service as supervisor for work on the public roads; ledger, 1920-1929, of Henry T. Scarborough with a few personal accounts; daybook and scrapbook, 1803-1926, containing accounts, clippings, and copies of deeds and letters; memorandum books, 1911, 1920-1921, and 1927, one of which includes extensive advertising for Columbia Fertilizers; and a ledger, 1916, including lists of voters, financial accounts, receipts, and clippings.

4690. GEORGE C. SCHEETZ PAPERS, 1862. 3 items. Northumberland (Northumberland County), Pa.

Letters of a Union soldier describing his departure from home and his journey through Harrisburg, Pennsylvania, and Washington, D.C.; camp life; rations; his impressions of Washington and northern Virginia; and a forced march in pursuit of Confederate forces near Harpers Ferry, West Virginia.

4691. H. F. SCHENCK PAPERS, 1889-1900. 13 vols. Cleveland (Rowan County), N.C.

Letter books and account books concerning the operations of Schenck's business, the Cleveland Cotton Mills on Knob Creek, six miles north of Double Shoals in Cleveland County, and perhaps relating in part to a second mill about two miles south at Lawndale. The accounts, 3 vols., include cotton purchases, cash accounts, cotton storage, and other records.

4692. JACOB R. SCHILLING PAPERS, 1865-1904. 5 vols. Darkesville (Berkeley County), W. Va.

Ledger, 1865-1867, and daybooks, 1865-1904, of a general mercantile establishment.

4693. SIR ALBERT HOUTUM-SCHINDLER PAPERS, (1889-1912) 1965. 33 items. Fenstanton, Huntingdonshire, England.

Chiefly letters from George Nathaniel Curzon, First Marquis Curzon of Kedleston (1859-1925), viceroy of India, 1899-1905, to Sir Albert Houtum-Schindler (1846-1916), engineer and authority on Persia, concerning Curzon's book Persia and the Persian Question (London: 1892); relations among Britain, Persia, and Russia; the operations of the Persian Bank Mining Rights Corporation, Limited; and various political figures in England and Persia. A draft memorandum (15 pp.) of Schindler discusses the opening of the Karun River to commerce, the Russian consular office at Meshed, the boundary problem with the Russians in northeastern Persia, and internal improvements. Also included is a letter of introduction from Pope Leo XIII to the Shah of Persia for Francesco Lesné, titular archbishop of Philippopoli and apostolic delegate; document of the king of France ordering the release of a prisoner from the Bastille; and a letter written by Lady Curzon.

4694. FRANCIS SCHNADHORST PAPERS, 1881-1887. 24 items. Woodford Green, Essex, England.

Political correspondence of Francis Schnadhorst (1840-1900), political organizer in the British Liberal Party, relating to routine political activities during the 1880s, British statesman John Bright, the electoral campaign of 1885, and the parliamentary elections of 1886.

4695. EINE SCHNELLFAHRT DURCH DEUTSCHLAND, BELGIEN, FRANKREICH UND HOLLAND IM AUGUST UND SEPTEMBER 1844. 2 vols. Germany.

Account entitled "A Quick Trip through Germany, Belgium, France and Holland in August and September, 1844."

4696. JOSHUA SCHOLEFIELD PAPERS, 1832-1841. 5 items. Birmingham, England.

Political correspondence of Joshua Scholefield (1744-1844), banker, merchant, manufacturer, and radical politician consisting of a letter, 1832, of appreciation to his supporters after he won a seat in the House of Commons; letter, 1838, inquiring about a municipal charter for Birmingham; letter, 1841, concerning the presentation of petitions against the Corn Laws, the imminent vote on Robert Peel's motion against the government, the text of his own motion on the alleviation of the condition of the manufacturing classes, and his own political future; and two letters dealing with routine political matters.

4697. MARY (HOWARD) SCHOOLCRAFT PAPERS, 1865. 1 item. Washington, D.C.

Letter from Henry Theodore Tuckerman (1813-1871) to Mary (Howard) Schoolcraft advising that circumstances were unfavorable for raising money for a memorial to her late husband, Henry Rowe Schoolcraft, explorer and ethnologist.

4698. MARY ELIZA (FLEMING) SCHOOLER PAPERS, 1810-1910. 1,081 items. Hanover County, Va.

Personal correspondence, chiefly of the Flemings, a wealthy Virginia family of educators, physicians, and soldiers. Included are school and college letters written from the viewpoints of students and teachers, with references to Hanover Academy, Taylorsville, Hanover County, Virginia; Concord Academy, Caroline County, Virginia, 1847-1849; Jefferson Medical College, Philadelphia, Pennsylvania, 1851; Worthan's Academy, Richmond, Virginia; the University of Virginia, Charlottesville, with interesting comments on Professors A. T. Bledsoe, B. L. Gildersleeve, and John B. Minor; and Edge Hill Academy, Caroline County, with which Samuel Schooler, Mary Eliza (Fleming) Schooler's husband, was at one time connected. There are also Civil War letters filled with details of hardships at home and containing excellent descriptions of the battles of Fredericksburg, Antietam, Chancellorsville, and Richmond; and letters showing living conditions and financial distress of the Reconstruction period. The later letters are those of the Schooler descendants. The collection throws much light on domestic, educational, and social conditions in Virginia, especially for the period 1840-1875. Some of the letters contain comments on John Esten Cooke, Nathaniel Hawthorne, and other literary figures.

4699. C. SCHRACK AND COMPANY PAPERS, 1862-1877. 64 items. Philadelphia, Pa.

Business correspondence of C. Schrack and Company, a firm dealing in naval stores, with frequent mention of commodity prices.

4700. JAMES M. SCHRECKHISE PAPERS, 1861-1864. 8 items. Newberry (Newberry County), S.C.

Personal letters of James M. Schreckhise, pastor, containing comments on secession sentiment in Virginia; the effects of the war on Newberry College, Newberry, South Carolina, and on civilians in the valley of Virginia; and Union Army raids in 1864.

4701. ALBERT S. SCHRIRER DIARY, 1867. 1 vol. (113 pp.) York (York County), Pa.

Diary of Albert S. Schrirer while surgeon in charge of the U.S. Naval Hospital at Norfolk, Virginia, from July 15 to November 7, 1867, containing lists of employees, accounts of repairs, copies of letters received, and a general record of his activities.

4702. EDWARD SCOFIELD, SR., PAPERS, 1840-1882. 12 items. Indiana and Illinois.

Personal correspondence of Edward Scofield, Sr., minister, including a letter, 1840, from Scofield contrasting the role of ministers and their wives in the West with their eastern counterparts; letter, 1874, from Edward Scofield, Jr., while attending Union Theological Seminary, New York; and letters, 1882, from an American traveling in Europe.

4703. SARAH P. SCOLLAY ACCOUNT BOOK AND MEMORANDUM BOOK, 1834-1878. 2 vols. Middleway (Jefferson County), W. Va.

Account book, 1834-1878, of Sarah P. Scollay containing records of wheat sales from Middleway and purchases for her daughters, Harriet L. Scollay and Mollie N. Scollay; notes on the education of her daughters; list of slaves; and records of wood loads hauled during the Civil War. A memorandum book, 1843-1860, contains household accounts, 1843-1853, and memoranda concerning household matters. There is frequent mention of Dr. Samuel Scollay, and it is probable that the early records in the account book are his.

4704. DAVID A. SCOTT ACCOUNT BOOK, 1856-1863. 1 vol. (35 pp.) Fremont (Wayne County), N.C.

Accounts of David A. Scott as administrator of the estate of Benajah Scott.

4705. G. FORRESTER SCOTT PAPERS, 1904, 1938. 2 items. Ardingly, Sussex, England.

Letter from G. Forrester Scott revealing that he had been using the pseudonym John Halsham; and personal letter from Scott's brother, J. Harold Scott.

4706. IRBY H. SCOTT PAPERS, 1845 (1861-1865) 1873. 146 items. Putnam County, Ga.

Papers of Irby H. Scott consisting primarily of letters from his son, Irby

Goodwin Scott, while serving in the 12th Georgia Regiment, C.S.A. Prior to 1861, the papers consist of family correspondence; papers relating to Irby H. Scott's services as administrator of the estates of Giles Tompkins and John Tompkins; and a letter, 1857, concerning the harboring of runaway slaves in the home of Mrs. Giles Tompkins, apparently near Eatonton, Georgia. After 1865, the collection consists chiefly of papers dealing with business matters, including a contract, 1865, with seventeen freedmen for labor on the farm of Irby H. Scott.

Letters of Irby Goodwin Scott, private and later a lieutenant of the 12th Georgia Regiment composed of men from Putnam County, record troop movements, primarily in Virginia; his yearnings for home; illness and death; rumors; his opinions of officers; love of the army; and detailed accounts of camp life, describing the construction of the quarters, the food, and methods of cooking. He complained of a letter published by his captain in the home newspaper, The Countryman, praising the brave fighting of the men from Eatonton (in Putnam County), Georgia, but failing to mention the fighting of the men from the surrounding countryside. He also ridiculed the Virginia newspapers for claiming all the credit for Virginia troops. Other papers include several letters about army life from Nicholas Ewing Scott (d. 1864) who joined his brother's regiment in 1863; and letters from Benjamin Harvey Hill concerning legal affairs.

4707. J. C. SCOTT PAPERS, 1867, 1869. 2 items. Chester (Chester County), S.C.

Letters from J. C. Scott while a student at Davidson College, Davidson, North Carolina, describing hazing for freshmen and the attitudes of upperclassmen.

4708. JACOB V. SCOTT PAPERS, 1862-1866. 20 items. Chemung (Chemung County), N.Y.

Chiefly letters of Daniel Scott (d. 1864) to his father, Jacob V. Scott, and his mother while serving in the Union Army describing camp life, food, sickness, morale, and the Atlanta campaign. Also included are a poem by Daniel Scott expressing his feelings towards his mother and towards the war; a letter from Daniel's captain telling of Daniel's death; and a form sent to the Bureau of Military Statistics, Albany, New York, by Jacob Scott recounting the war record of Daniel Scott.

4709. SIR JAMES GEORGE SCOTT SCRAPBOOKS, 1888-1897. 2 vols. London, England.

Scrapbooks of Sir James George Scott (1851-1935), British diplomat, colonial administrator, and author, relating primarily to Scott's years as chargé d'affaires at Bangkok, and as a member of the Mekong Commission, 1894-1896. The first volume consists of official correspondence while the second contains invitations, notes, drawings, some correspondence, and other items. Included are a document recording the protocols signed by France and Britain, and diplomatic correspondence concerning an investigation to establish a neutral zone between their Southeast Asian possessions of Burma and Indo-China; letters from Maurice William Ernest de Bunsen, British minister at Bangkok, discussing a dispute between the Siamese and the French over Luang Prabang (a province in Laos) and British involvement in the matter, the maintenance of Siam as a buffer state between the British and the French, and French violation of Siamese territorial rights; correspondence between G. Rolin-Jacquemyns, Belgian advisor, and King Chulalongkorn relating to extensive judicial reform in Siam; letters from R. H. Thomson reporting on the illness of King Chulalongkorn, publications in the Siam Free Press which were aiding the anti-English faction in Siam, and the carelessness of Edward Henry French, British consul at Bankok, in his dealings with Prince Devawongse, chief minister and half-brother of the king; correspondence concerning a dispute between the Siamese royal family and Robert Laurie Morant, tutor to the family; documents regarding Britain's statement of neutrality toward the belligerents in the Sino-Japanese War; letters from Alexander Michie, foreign correspondent of The Times, reporting on Chinese-Japanese relations; letters pertaining to the proposed extension of a railway in Burma to the Salween River and to Kunlon; letter from Sir William Lee-Warner, secretary in the Political and Secret Department of the India Office, discussing British relations with the warlike Wa tribes in the Burmese interior; two drawings relating to a trip made by Scott into the southern part of the Shan States; and letters in Siamese and other Southeast Asian languages.

4710. JAMES P. SCOTT PAPERS, 1828-1877. 273 items. Gordonsville (Orange County), Va.

Personal and business papers of James P. Scott, merchant, including correspondence concerning personal and business affairs, personal debts, land, crops, fertilizer, merchandise, taxes, and insurance; bills and receipts; and checks. There is occasional mention of Virginia and national politics, temperance, punishment of slaves, and student life at University of Virginia, Charlottesville, Virginia.

4711. L. J. J. SCOTT AND SALLIE W. SCOTT ESTATE BOOK, 1863-1866. 1 vol.

Estate book relating to the sale of Colonel L. J. J. Scott's and Mrs. Sallie W. Scott's property, the payment of the Confederate tax, and the hiring and selling of Negroes.

4712. OTHO SCOTT PAPERS, 1772 (1820-1859) 1910. 2,168 items and 4 vols. Belair (Harford County), Md.

Personal, legal and financial papers of Otho Scott, lawyer, including papers relating to lawsuits; circular letters concerning the strength of Andrew Jackson and of the Whigs and Henry Clay in Maryland; will of William Chesney providing for the manumission of his slaves; mortgages; bills and receipts; and fragments of almanacs, containing scattered diary entries, 1836-1847, chiefly about the weather.

4713. ROBERT G. SCOTT PAPERS, 1844-1846. 3 items. Richmond, Va.

Legal papers of Robert G. Scott, Richmond attorney.

4714. WILLIAM LAFAYETTE SCOTT PAPERS, 1811-1877. 1,017 items. Greensboro (Guilford County), N.C.

Personal and family correspondence, speeches, and papers of William L. Scott (1828-1872), schoolteacher, lawyer, and captain in the Confederate Army. The family correspondence consists of letters between Scott and his wife, Ella (Penn) Scott, before and after their marriage, letters to his family while he was a student at the University of North Carolina, Chapel Hill, and letters of Scott's brother, Levi M. Scott, Confederate receiver for the sequestration of Federal property during the Civil War. William L. Scott's letters reflect much of the atmosphere and conditions at the University of North Carolina while he was a student there, during part of that time serving as editor of the University Magazine. Other letters from Scott to his wife contain many comments on political affairs and his legal practice as well as on personal affairs. Among the papers also are comments on railroad frauds (which he investigated in 1870); accounts of his unsuccessful campaign for Congress against James M. Leach in 1870; a draft of an appeal to Negro voters dated June 6, 1870; descriptions of Ku Klux Klan activities; information on the organization and development of the Whig, the American, and the Republican parties in North Carolina; and many letters concerning Scott's numerous quarrels with fellow officers in the Confederate Army and his ultimate resignation from the army. Included also are numerous speeches and literary works of William L. Scott. Letters from Levi M. Scott discuss his activities in the North Carolina state legislature in 1856.

4715. WINFIELD SCOTT PAPERS, 1836-1846. 4 items. Dinwiddie County, Va.

Papers of Winfield Scott (1786-1866), commanding general of the U.S. Army, consisting of an order, 1836, appointing a temporary staff to muster into service men to fight the Creek Indians, and a letter, 1836, to Governor William Schley concerning the Creek War; letter, 1846, to Armistead Burt regarding awards for officers who served at Fort Brown, Texas; and copy of a report, 1846, by Scott to the secretary of war explaining his views on six months' volunteers.

4716. W. W. SCOTT PAPERS, 1880-1900. 14 items. Canal Dover (Tuscarawas County), Ohio.

Letters to W. W. Scott from various associates of William Clarke Quantrill (1837-1865), Confederate guerrilla leader in Missouri, Kansas, and Kentucky, relating to Quantrill's career and death.

4717. SCOTT HOSIERY MILLS, INC., PAPERS. 1933-1945. 2 items and 4 vols. Graham (Alamance County), N.C.

Financial papers of the Scott Hosiery Mills, Inc., manufacturers of full-fashioned silk hosiery, consisting of a ledger, 1933-1945; journal, 1940-1945; cash receipts journal, 1933-1945; cash disbursements journal, 1944-1945; a carbon copy of the statement about dissolution in 1945; and a list of items for liquidation.

4718. JAMES P. SCREVEN PAPERS, 1770-1893. 10 items. Savannah, Ga.

Miscellaneous papers of James P. Screven (d. 1859), mayor of Savannah, Georgia, and president of the Atlantic and Gulf Railroad Company, including letters of Screven relating to the rivalry between Savannah and Brunswick as the eastern terminus of the Atlantic and Gulf Railroad Company, and other matters concerning the railroad. There are also scattered papers of his son, John Screven (1827-1895?), and other members of the Screven family.

4719. GEORGE PERCIVAL SCRIVEN PAPERS, 1846-1926. 85 items and 12 vols. Washington, D.C.

Papers of George Percival Scriven (b. 1854), U.S. Army officer, consisting of family correspondence; several letters dealing with Scriven's appointment as military attaché in Rome in 1898; clippings and memorabilia of Scriven's work in Rome; diary, 1847, of Thomas Swain Scriven, captain of a packet boat, the Princess Alice, on the English Channel, containing material about shipping and passenger transport on the channel; diary, 1892, of George P. Scriven while working for the Intercontinental Railway Commission as surveyor for a railroad through El Salvador, with records of his work as well as accounts of his travels across the country; diary, 1899-1900, concerning Scriven's work with the Signal Corps on the island of Panay in the Philippines; diary, 1900, principally relating to the American occupation and pacification of the Philippine island of Bohol; diaries, 1908 and 1926, of his wife, Elizabeth McQuade, giving accounts of her tour of Spain and of an ocean voyage from Montreal, Canada, to Glasgow, Scotland;

scrapbook, 1894-1898, containing clippings, letters, and memorabilia about Scriven's service as military attaché in Mexico City and in Rome; and photograph albums, including one with pictures of Costa Rica in the 1890s, and another containing pictures of Scriven's visit to the Italian army in Albania in 1917.

4720. LANGHORNE SCRUGGS PAPERS, 1785 (1839-1900) 1941. 764 items and 1 vol. Competition (now Chatham) (Pittsylvania County), Va.

Personal and legal papers of Langhorne Scruggs, deputy clerk of the County and Circuit Court of Pittsylvania County. Correspondence discusses personal and family matters; weather and crops; conditions in Florida in 1846; iron sales in Lynchburg, Virginia, in 1846; the raising of troops for the Mexican War and celebrations in Henry County, Virginia, of the victories of General Zachary Taylor; Polk's conduct of the war; social life and customs in Virginia and Mississippi; commodity prices in Kentucky, Georgia, and Virginia; land sales in Virginia; tobacco sales and prices in Virginia; slave sales in Virginia and Georgia; cotton crops in Georgia; education in various schools, academies, and colleges in the South; the candidacy of George Coke Dromgoole (1797-1847) for U.S. representative from Virginia in 1847; Kentucky politics in 1847; the Campbellite Church or the Disciples of Christ in Kentucky and Alabama; a colonization meeting in Washington, D.C., in 1848; Zachary Taylor and the Rough and Ready Club; travel in Alabama in 1849; the presidential campaigns of 1848, 1852, and 1860; the Virginia state constitutional convention of 1850-1851, especially the issue of counting slaves in determining the ratios of legislative representation; politics in Kansas in 1856, including the issue of slave versus free states, abolitionism, the proposed constitutional convention, the pro-slavery forces, and the territorial legislature; land speculation in Kansas; Virginia banks and the panic of 1857; the Know-Nothing party in Virginia; the Virginia gubernatorial election of 1859; legislative matters in Virginia; secession in Mississippi; the Civil War; and other matters. Also included are the legal papers of Langhorne Scruggs; bills, receipts, and other financial papers relating to the tobacco business of Benjamin E. Scruggs (d. 1855): photocopies of papers pertaining to the Virginia militia; miscellaneous papers concerning social life, business, politics, and poetry; information on the Scruggs, Tunstall, and Cabell families; and a register, ca. 1853-1854, of land warrants in Virginia.

4721. RICHARD SCRUGGS PAPERS, 1804-1904. 15 items. Spartanburg (Spartanburg County), S.C.

Miscellaneous deeds and indentures of the Scruggs family of Spartanburg County, South Carolina.

4722. ROBERT J. SCRUTTON PAPERS, 1941. 20 items. London, England.

Correspondence, articles, and broadsides of the United Christian Petition Movement, founded by Robert J. Scrutton with the purpose of influencing public opinion against the war and the political and economic policies of the British government. Correspondence is chiefly between Scrutton and the Duke of Bedford. Included are two broadsides issued by the National Peace Council.

4723. JAMES WALL SCULLY PAPERS, (1861-1862) 1910. 55 items. Nashville (Davidson County), Tenn.

Correspondence and papers of James Wall Scully (1838-1918), surveyor and Federal soldier, stationed in Nashville, Tennessee, during the years covered by this correspondence. The letters concern his services as clerk to Captain Alvan Cullem Gillem under General George Henry Thomas in Kentucky; the battles of Mill Springs, Kentucky, 1862, and Shiloh, Tennessee, 1862; the siege of Corinth, Mississippi, 1862; living conditions of the times; the Germans of Pennsylvania; and the attitude of Southern women, especially those in Nashville, Tennessee, toward Federal soldiers. Included also are army commissions signed by J. M. Dickinson, Andrew Johnson, J. M. Schofield, and William Howard Taft.

4724. J. WARD SEABROOK PAPERS, 1956. 1 item. Fayetteville (Cumberland County), N.C.

Argument in favor of gradual integration presented to the Pearsall Committee, a committee appointed by North Carolina Governor Luther Hodges to study integration in the state. J. Ward Seabrook, former president of Fayetteville State Teachers College, Fayetteville, North Carolina, was a member of the Pearsall Committee.

4725. WHITEMARSH BENJAMIN SEABROOK PAPERS, 1843. 1 item. Edisto Island (Berkeley County), S.C.

Letter of Whitemarsh Benjamin Seabrook (1795-1856), planter and governor of South Carolina, 1848-1850, to Josiah E. Smith of Columbia, discussing business affairs, personal matters, and Democratic Party politics.

4726. SEAMEN'S PAPERS, 1798-1804. 11 items.

Manifests of masters of trading vessels, generally sailing from the port of Baltimore, Maryland, including John Cooper, George Foster, John H. Hill, R. Hudgins, I. B. Pearson, Thomas Taylor, and William White. Included also are coasting permits and orders to arrest the crew of one of the vessels.

4727. SEAMEN'S FRIEND SOCIETY OF WILMINGTON PAPERS, 1810-1963. 103 items and 1 vol. Wilmington (New Hanover County), N.C.

Miscellaneous papers of the Seamen's Friend Society, organized in 1853 to aid seamen in their social, moral, and religious character, include correspondence; plats; memoranda; legal papers concerning the establishment of the society, the acquisition of the property of the Wilmington Marine Hospital Association, property losses in 1865, and the extension of the charter in 1899; scattered reports of the secretary and the treasurer; minutes; agreements relating to the operation of the home and to the use of the facilities by soldiers during World War I; subscription lists of 1872 for rebuilding the home; financial papers, including miscellaneous accounts; and a ledger, 1853-1923, containing records of the society treasurer, 1853-1923, accounts for the building fund, 1872-1873, and accounts of annual dues, 1874-1875.

4728. J. F. SEAS PAPERS, 1873-1888. 6 items. Orrville (Wayne County), Ohio.

Business papers of J. F. Seas and Son concerning orders for hardware from dealers and manufacturers.

4729. JAMES ALEXANDER SEDDON, SR., PAPERS, 1862-1865. 20 items. Richmond, Va.

Correspondence of James Alexander Seddon, Sr. (1815-1880), Confederate secretary of war, include letter, 1863, from Zebulon Baird Vance requesting the return of an enlisted man for trial in North Carolina on a murder charge; correspondence with Jefferson Davis and Bradley T. Johnson relating to Governor John Pettus of Mississippi, Governor Joseph E. Brown of Georgia, and the Confederate losses at Gettysburg; letter, 1864, to Seddon stating that Amelia County, Virginia, would send its crops to the Confederate Army, with a note by Seddon commenting upon the response of the farmers along the lines open to Richmond; and letters dealing with routine office matters, such as coastal defenses, promotions, and the exchange of prisoners.

4730. ELIZABETH (BRICKEL) SEEMAN PAPERS, 1959-1961. 6 items. Erwin (Unicoi County), Tenn.

Papers of Elizabeth (Brickel) Seeman, author, consist of author's copy, printer's copy, and radio script of The Talking Dog and the Barking Man; printer's copy of In the Arms of the Mountain; letter of Elizabeth Seeman in which she comments about her treatment of local names and events in In the Arms of the Mountain; and personal letter of her husband, Ernest Seeman.

4731. JOSEPH SEGAR PAPERS, 1863. 1 item. Fortress Monroe (Elizabeth City County), Va.

Letter of Joseph Segar discussing politics.

4732. HENRY JAMES SEIBERT, SR., PAPERS, 1779 (1820-1885) 1912. 16,590 items and 68 vols. Martinsburg and Hedgesville (Berkeley County), W. Va.

Correspondence, legal and financial papers, and printed material of Henry James Seibert, Sr., Virginia state legislator, executor for numerous estates, and financial agent for emigrants to the Mid-West. Correspondence discusses personal and family matters; internal improvements in Pennsylvania during the 1820s; salt mining in Pennsylvania; commodity and land prices in Ohio during the 1820s and 1830s; Ohio politics during the 1830s and the attitude of politicians towards the Second Bank of the United States; commodity prices in Illinois during 1838 and 1840; bank failures in Ohio, 1841; wages in Ohio, 1845; care of a ward of Henry James Seibert, Sr., in an insane asylum; the National Road in Ohio; presidential elections of 1840, 1844, 1848, 1852, and 1856; the National Democratic Convention of 1844; Henry Clay and the Whig Party; the slavery question in relation to the California Territory; improvement and construction of public buildings in Washington, D.C.; coal mining in Maryland; the Compromise of 1850; cholera in New Orleans, 1850s; internal improvements in Virginia, 1850s; control and sale of liquor and distillation of whiskey; slave trade in the United States; Civil War bounty; pension claims; and other matters. Also included are bills and receipts; indentures; court summonses; account sheets; applications for pensions; prospectus, 1865, of The New Era, a newspaper to be published in Martinsburg, West Virginia; bulletin of Wellesley College, Wellesley, Massachusetts, for 1879; pamphlets containing West Virginia laws in 1887 relating to public schools; advertisements for the Maryland Lottery Company, the Kentucky State Lottery, cooking and heating stoves, women's fashions for 1884-1885, and patent medicines; Reformed Missionary Herald, 1889; almanacs; price current sheets for Baltimore, Maryland, in 1867 and 1869; premium list of the annual fair of the Ogle County (Illinois) Agricultural Board in 1881; ballots for the Greenback Party, the Democratic Party in Berkeley County (West Virginia) in 1880 and 1888, and the National Prohibition Party in 1884; pamphlet of the National Prohibition Party; form letter, 1849, explaining the stand of the Society of Friends of Great Britain and Ireland on slavery; broadsides of a U.S. pension agency; and announcement and program of the 29th annual session of the Farmers' National Congress, Raleigh, 1909. There are also financial records of the general mercantile establishments of John W. Boyd and Benjamin R. Boyd including a cash book,

1847-1855, daybooks, (1829-1855) 1888, ledgers, 1829-1865, and a memorandum book, 1849; of Hezekiah Hedges including ledgers, 1836-1847, and a daybook, 1842-1846; of Henry J. Seibert including a ledger, 1823-1840; and of William L. Seibert including daybooks, 1841-1852 and 1872-1879, and a ledger, 1854-1856.

4733. SAMUEL S. SEIG PAPERS, 1861-1866. 2 items. Monroe County, Mo.

Letter of Samuel S. Seig, Confederate soldier, giving a detailed account of the first battle of Manassas to his cousin, Mrs. Carrie Davis; and a letter of I. [or J.] F. Sieg to his brother-in-law, James, discussing Missouri politics, atrocities committed in the Border War, and the expected profits from his commission to sell E. A. Pollard's The Lost Cause (New York: 1866).

4734. B. M. SELBY PAPERS, 1849-1865. 9 items. Wilson (Wilson County), N.C.

Papers of B. M. Selby and P. W. Brown, mercantile firm of Wilson, pertaining to the sale of slaves, purchase of goods brought into Wilmington through the blockade, and sale of goods, chiefly cotton and tobacco. Included also is a pardon from Andrew Johnson, 1865, issued to Selby for participation in the Civil War.

4735. MILES C. SELDEN PAPERS, 1841-1857. 4 items. Richmond, Va.

Receipts of Miles C. Selden as administrator of the estate of Beverley Heth; and a business letter.

4736. SEMANS FAMILY PAPERS, 1809-1969. 4,676 items and 70 vols. Durham, N.C. Restricted.

Chiefly the papers of Mary Duke (Biddle) Trent Semans, city councilwoman, 1951-1955, and mayor pro tem, 1952-1955, of Durham, North Carolina, and civic leader, but also of her mother, Mary (Duke) Biddle, and of her husband, Dr. James Hustead Semans, professor at Duke University Medical Center, Durham, North Carolina. The papers of Mary (Duke) Biddle are mainly family correspondence and correspondence relating to gifts to Duke University. Correspondence, notes, writings, clippings, pamphlets, and brochures relate to the activities of Mary Duke (Biddle) Trent Semans, including her service as city councilwoman and mayor pro tem of Durham; her membership on the various civic committees including the Mayor's Committee on Human Relations; her service as first president and member of the Board of Directors of the United Fund in Durham; her membership on the Board of Trustees of Duke University and on the Board of the Duke Endowment; her service on the National Advisory Committee on Vocational Rehabilitation and as chairwoman of the Governor's Study Committee on Vocational Rehabilitation in North Carolina; her interest in art and music including the North Carolina Conservatory Committee, the Art and Music Departments of Duke University, the North Carolina Museum in Raleigh, the Museum for the Blind, and the Governor's Commission on the Fine Arts; her work in the restoration of the Executive Mansion in Raleigh; her interest in the Woman's College of Duke University, of which she was an alumna; her campaign against the discontinuance of passenger trains to Durham by the Southern Railroad Company; and other matters relating to civic needs, race relations, and the arts. Also included are notebooks and scrapbooks of her early life at Miss Hewitt's School in New York, New York, and of her marriage to Josiah Charles Trent; scrapbooks and albums containing pictures of the Duke and Biddle families; and other miscellaneous papers relating to her various interests. The papers of Dr. James Hustead Semans consist of correspondence, papers, reports, financial accounts, clippings, printed material, and pictures relating to his chairmanship of the Board of Trustees of the North Carolina School of the Arts, and their summer sessions in Siena at the Accademia Musicale Chigiana.

4737. PAUL J. SEMMES PAPERS, 1861. 2 items. Columbus (Muscogee County), Ga.

Papers of Paul J. Semmes (d. 1863), brigadier general in the Confederate Army, consisting of his acceptance of a commission and a morning report.

4738. RAPHAEL SEMMES PAPERS, 1861-1872. 9 items and 1 vol. Mobile (Mobile County), Ala.

Miscellaneous papers of Raphael Semmes (1809-1877), officer in the U.S. Navy and in the Confederate Navy, consisting of routine letters concerning his command; personal correspondence; a letter, 1872, to James R. Osgood & Co. concerning a series of articles in Atlantic Monthly on whether or not Semmes should be tried in connection with the sinking of the C.S.S. Alabama, and his desire that his own article be published; clippings relating to Semmes; and a volume containing accounts and a diary. The diary, February-May, 1865, describes his appointment as rear admiral; his duties a commander of the James River Squadron; the weather; illness; desertions; exchange of prisoners; his orders to destroy his eight ships; the withdrawal of his guns to Danville, Virginia, and the defense of the town by his naval brigade of artillery; their march to Greensboro, North Carolina, and plundering along the way; Confederate generals at the Greensboro headquarters; surrender of the Confederacy; and the march home to Alabama. [Diary published by W. Stanley Hoole (ed.), The Alabama Review, 28 (April, 1975), 129-150.]

4739.   THOMAS JENKINS SEMMES PAPERS, 1835-1890s. 35 items. New Orleans, La.

Letters to Thomas Jenkins Semmes (1824-1899), lawyer, member of the Confederate senate, 1862-1865, and a member of the law faculty of Tulane University, New Orleans, Louisiana, 1873-1879; letters to Mrs. Semmes; letters from Semmes, concerning the conduct of the Civil War, Confederate legislation, and business of the Confederate government; and a letter from Raphael Semmes concerning the powder supply for his ship, C.S.S. Sumter.

4740.   JAMES BEVERLY SENER PAPERS, 1878. 2 items. Fredericksburg (Spotsylvania County), Va.

Letters concerning the appointment of James Beverly Sener (b. 1831), editor of the Fredericksburg Ledger, to the position of chief justice of the Wyoming Territory, 1878-1884.

4741.   J. SENSENEY LEDGER, 1837-1860. 1 vol. (608 pp.) Winchester (Frederick County), Va.

Accounts of a general mercantile establishment. Many pages are blank.

4742.   HIRAM SETTLE PAPERS, 1879-1891. 22 items. Elkin (Surry County), N.C.

Chiefly minutes and other papers of the Cool Spring Baptist Church, Wilkes County, North Carolina, of which Hiram Settle was clerk.

4743.   THOMAS LEE SETTLE PAPERS, 1795 (1820-1900) 1949. 5,396 items and 245 vols. Paris (Fauquier County), Va.

Papers of Thomas Lee Settle (1836-1920), physician, and surgeon of the 11th Virginia Cavalry, C.S.A., include orders for the Virginia militia, 1797 and 1800; family letters to Texas, Missouri, and Tennessee; and correspondence concerning the education of the Settle children and friends at various schools and academies in Virginia, and at Virginia Military Institute, Lexington, Virginia. Civil War correspondence, including letters of Captain Robert H. Simpson and other Confederate soldiers, describes the battles of first Manassas, Chickahominy Swamp, and Fredericksburg, the Peninsular Campaign, crops and conditions in northern Virginia during the war, and directions for making salt. There are also records of land sales, deeds, and rent receipts; medical correspondence, prescriptions, and bills; bills and receipts for land transactions, household expenses, and apple brandy making; horse-dealing records during the Civil War; two Confederate Loan Bonds; business papers of A. H. Settle & Co., merchants of Paris, Virginia; medical diary, 1855-1858, 1861, and 1865-1866, of Thomas Lee Settle; and a diary, 1863-1864, of Thomas Lee Settle describing his activities as surgeon to the 11th Virginia Cavalry. A journal, 1863, of John S. Timberlake entitled "Trip to Florida and Salt Works, Oct. 20, 1863. With descriptions of the country and other particulars intervening on the way," contains detailed descriptions of various salt works in Georgia; "Descriptions of Florida and Health and Other Particulars (useful) as they Happen" discussing health and agricultural conditions, sugar making, and the economic conditions of Florida and Georgia plantations; and a synopsis of Adiel Sherwood's 1860 Gazetteer of Georgia. Postwar materials include Sunday school record book, 1884; letters from soldiers in the Spanish-American War discussing camp life in Florida, the Rough Riders, courts-martial, and desertion; letter, 1909, from T. C. Evans, dean of the Medical Department, University of Louisville, Louisville, Kentucky discussing his department; letters from Edgar Ackley Moore (d. 1924), physician, to his wife Pauline (Settle) Moore, daughter of Thomas Lee Settle, while serving in the U.S. Army Medical Reserve Corps during World War I, describing camp life and his experiences in America and France, the work of the Young Men's Christian Association and the American National Red Cross in France, casualties, prisoners, hospitals, and physicians; papers relating to Moore's Masonic affiliation; ledger, 1905-1907, and accounts, 1906-1912, of Edgar Ackley Moore; literary reviews; medical pamphlets; and scrapbooks and exercise books. Volumes consist of medical visiting and account books, 1855-1914, commonplace books, 1852-1867, daybook, 1901-1905, expense book, 1870-1880, ledgers, 1867-1913, and record book, 1856-1857, of Thomas Lee Settle; account book for the John Horn estate; pamphlets, including one on the San Francisco earthquake of 1906 and another on a silver mining scheme in Canada, entitled Julian Hawthorne and Company (1909); a stallion service book; and photographs. Other papers include genealogical information, original poetry, and legal documents and wills.

4744.   DANIEL SETZER PAPERS, 1858-1865. 65 items. Rowan County, N.C.

Chiefly letters of Daniel Setzer, Confederate soldier, to his wife, Susan, concerning personal matters, the welfare of his family, the scarcity of food, hardships of army life, rumors of casualties and prisoners, desertion, and other matters.

4745.   ANTONIO GABRIELE SEVEROLI PAPERS, 1816-1822. 4 items. Rome, Italy.

Letters to Cardinal Severoli (fl. ca. 1806-1830) from Maximilian Joseph, king of Bavaria; Victor Emmanuel I and Maria Terese, king and queen of Sardinia; and Annibale della Genga, vicar-general of Rome, and later Pope Leo XII.

4746. JOHN SEVIER PAPERS, 1778-1812. 7 items. Knoxville (Knox County), Tenn.

Papers of John Sevier (1745-1815), officer during the American Revolution and first governor of Tennessee, including a letter, 1787, from Richard Caswell, governor of North Carolina, concerning their land speculation in Tennessee, trials for fraud in the purchase of army supplies, opposition of the North Carolina Assembly to recent Indian treaties, and road construction in the mountains; directive, 1800, granting permission to William Lindsy and Zaduch Bowshairs to transport slaves from Tennessee to Natchez in the Mississippi Territory; a copy of a memorial sent in 1812 to the North Carolina legislature by Sevier and Isaac Shelby, first governor of Kentucky, requesting that the Assembly honor its commitment to grant the two men the sword and pistols that it had voted them for their services in the battle of King's Mountain, and the reply from John Steele; and routine papers concerning legal matters.

4747. JOSEPH W. SEWARD AND W. M. WESSON PAPERS, 1866-1884. 141 items. Gholsonville (Brunswick County), Va.

Bills, receipts, and invoices of the general mercantile firm of Seward & Wesson, dealing with Richmond and Petersburg, Virginia, wholesalers.

4748. WILLIAM HENRY SEWARD PAPERS, 1857-1899. 50 items. Auburn (Cayuga County), N.Y.

Chiefly photocopies of papers of William Henry Seward (1801-1872), governor of New York, U.S. senator, and secretary of state, relating to the period preceding the attack on Fort Sumter, concerning a speech by Seward in January, 1861, on efforts to restore the Union, attempts to avoid a civil war, secessionist prospects in Virginia and Maryland, affairs in the border states, plans for Lincoln's administration, and the decision to hold Fort Sumter. Also included are photocopies of two versions of a memorandum, April 1, 1861, entitled "Some Thoughts for the President's Consideration," and the defense of the motives and goals espoused in the memorandum written by his son, Frederick William Seward, in 1899. Among the original papers in this collection are several letters dealing with diplomatic relations with Portugal during the Civil War; letter concerning the revolt in Mexico against Maximilian; letter from Seward to artist Emanuel Leutze; and miscellaneous correspondence pertaining to routine matters. Originals of the photocopies are in the Rush Rhees Library, University of Rochester, Rochester, New York.

4749. THORNTON SEXTON PAPERS, 1862-1864. 24 items. Ashe County, N.C.

Civil War letters of a Confederate soldier principally discussing camp life in various camps around Orange, Virginia.

4750. FRANCIS CHARLES SEYMOUR, THIRD MARQUIS OF HERTFORD, PAPERS, 1831. 1 item. Ragley Hall, Warwickshire, England.

Report of Thomas Wilmot to Francis Charles Seymour, Third Marquis of Hertford (1777-1842), warden of the Stannaries, recorder of Coventry and Bodmin, and chief steward and vice admiral of the Duchy of Cornwall, concerning the revolutionary ferment and public disorder at Coventry during the crisis over the Reform Bill.

4751. HORATIO SEYMOUR PAPERS, 1836-1880. 5 items. Albany (Albany County), N.Y.

Correspondence of Horatio Seymour (1810-1886), governor of New York and presidential candidate in 1868, consists of a letter, 1836, of Seymour discussing business, politics, and the death of Samuel Meeks; letter, 1866, from Charles G. Halpine, editor of the New York Citizen, to Seymour supporting Seymour for the position of secretary of state over William Henry Seward, and supporting John T. Hoffman for mayor of New York; letter, 1868, of Seymour expressing the opinion that R. H. Gillet would be a good man to write the history of democracy; and letter, 1880, from Seymour to Stilson Hutchins of The Washington Post denying Hutchins's comments that Seymour might seek the presidential nomination, and explaining the injury that such remarks might do to the party. There is also a photocopy of a broadside, 1868, promoting the candidacy of Seymour for president of the United States among the freedmen of Alabama.

4752. THOMAS HART SEYMOUR PAPERS, 1863. 1 item. Hartford (Hartford County), Conn.

Letter of introduction for Richard R. Phelps from Thomas Hart Seymour (1807-1868), governor of Connecticut, U.S. congressman, and minister to Russia.

4753. CARLOS SFORZA PAPERS, 1933-1941. 3 items. New York, N.Y.

Letters from Count Carlos Sforza (b. 1872), Italian statesman, to William Henry Glasson, professor at Duke University, Durham, North Carolina, concerning a forthcoming lecture to be given by the Count in Durham; and a copy of the Key Reporter (1941) containing an article about Sforza and his Phi Beta Kappa key.

4754.  A. T. SHACKLEFORD PAPERS, 1862-1865. 4 items. Thomaston (Upson County), Ga.

Business letters addressed to A. T. Shackleford, clerk of the superior court of Upson County, Georgia, including one from a physician with comments on the scarcity of smallpox vaccine serum and the great demand for it.

4755.  M. E. SHACKLEFORD POEMS, 1840-1857. 1 vol. (278 pp.) Saint Louis, Mo.

Manuscript copies of sentimental and comic poems, apparently written by M. E. Shackleford.

4756.  BARTRAM A. SHAEFFER PAPERS, 1850-1860. 91 items. Harrisburg (Dauphin County), Pa.

Papers of Bartram A. Shaeffer, a member of the Pennsylvania House of Representatives, concern politics and matters before the legislature, including the French spoliation bill, 1851; granting or altering charters; development of turnpikes; fishing rights in the Susquehanna River; property rights and guardianship of orphans; the Whig Party; and requests for favors. The collection also contains financial accounts.

4757.  LUTHER M. SHARPE PAPERS. 1 item. Hillsborough (Orange County), N.C.

Genealogical chart, compiled by Stella G. Sharpe, recording the maternal line of Luther M. Sharpe.

4758.  DANIEL SHAVER PAPERS, 1864-1866. 4 items. Brownsville (Cameron County), Tex.

Letters from Daniel Shaver, a Protestant Episcopal minister and missionary from New York, New York, describing to other ministers of his denomination the conditions and hardships of their church's mission effort in Texas and Mexico.

4759.  DAVID SHAVER SERMONS AND NOTES, 1838-1895. 51 items. Atlanta, Ga.

Sermons, study notes, and one letter of David Shaver (1820-ca. 1902), Baptist minister and editor of the Christian Index.

4760.  DANIEL SHAW PAPERS, 1787-1902. 413 items. Hyde County, N.C.

Business and personal letters to Daniel Shaw, a native of England, who was naturalized in 1826 and became a successful merchant of Lake Landing, North Carolina. The business letters are from wholesale firms and commission merchants concerning the sale of corn, and from ship companies giving passenger rates to Southampton, England. Also contains bills for goods bought by Daniel Shaw from R. & W. Tannahill of Washington, D.C.; receipts; and papers relating to the estates of Willoughby Higson, Nehemiah Benson, and Andrew Shanklin.

4761.  JOHN F. SHAW PAPERS, 1812-1892. 116 items. Westville (Harnett County), N.C.

The papers of John F. Shaw relate for the most part to his position as magistrate and include a form used in the collection of the tax in kind imposed by the Confederate States in 1863; land leases; tax receipts; tax lists for Barbecue District or Barbecue Township, Harnett County, in 1869, 1870, and 1871; lists of sales; warrants; abstracts of property; wills; and advertisements for patent medicines and invalid homes.

4762.  MALCOLM SHAW LEDGER, 1852-1856. 1 vol. (562 pp.) Wadesboro (Anson County), N.C.

Merchant's account book.

4763.  JOHN BUNYAN SHEARER ACCOUNT BOOK, 1858-1889. 1 vol. (102 pp.) Chapel Hill (Orange County), N.C.

Accounts of household expenses of John Bunyan Shearer (1832-1919), president of Southwestern University, Memphis, Tennessee, 1870-1888, and of Davidson College, North Carolina, 1889-1909.

4764.  RICHARD E. SHEARIN AND ROBERT A. SHEARIN PAPERS, 1854-1885. 124 items. Macon Depot (Warren County), N.C.

Business letters, bills, and receipts of Richard E. Shearin and Bros., merchants, and letters of the Shearin family, concerning the tobacco market of Petersburg, Virginia; conditions in Mississippi County, Arkansas, 1859; Civil War camp life; and letters describing Nashville and Edgefield, Tennessee, in the 1870s. Also a daybook, 1855-1866.

4765.  JACOB SHEEK AND JONATHAN SMITH PAPERS, 1767 (1850-1869) 1939. 2,941 items. Smith Grove (Davie County), N.C.

The collection contains letters to the Sheek, Smith, and Clouse families of North Carolina from relatives who migrated to Tennessee, Kentucky, Illinois, Indiana, and Texas, concerning land and commodity prices; religion; the Mexican War; Trinity College, North Carolina; farming on the frontier; conditions in Texas, 1840-1870; secession in North Carolina; the experiences of several Confederate soldiers; and Reconstruction. The collection also contains advertisements for books and patent medicines; North Carolina ballots; circulars for girls' schools and boys' schools in Lockville and Jonesville, North Carolina; bills; receipts; and summonses from a justice of the peace.

4766. HUGH W. SHEFFEY PAPERS, 1834-1849. 7 items. Staunton (Augusta County), Va.

Routine business and political correspondence of Hugh W. Sheffey (1815-1889), Virginia lawyer, publicist, and churchman.

4767. SHEFFIELD MANOR RECORDS, 1667-1808. 4 vols. Sussex, England.

Court and survey records of Sheffield Manor contain transcripts of the proceedings of courts baron held in the manor from 1667 to 1803 and a transcript of a survey of the manor made between 1571 and 1618. Court records concern death registrations, guardianship of orphans, and numerous actions relating to the transfer of property, rent, permission to cut timber, and prosecution for unauthorized use of land. The survey shows the division of the manor into various types of holdings, lists the name of the holders, and notes the amount of tax paid each year. The survey also lists royalties, customs, and privileges of the manor.

4768. LEVI SHEFTALL AND MORDECAI SHEFTALL PAPERS, 1766-1871. 201 items and 1 vol. Savannah, Ga.

Papers of several generations of the Sheftall family of Savannah, Georgia, contain items related to the mercantile business of Levi and Mordecai Sheftall in Savannah; the work of Mordecai Sheftall as commissary general of issues for the Continental Army in Georgia; and activities of Levi Sheftall as United States agent for fortifications at Savannah, 1808. Also contains household accounts, briefs and other legal papers, receipts, and marriage settlements.

4769. HELEN L. SHELL AND MARY VIRGINIA SHELL PAPERS, 1858-1879. 80 items. Shepherdstown (Jefferson County), W. Va.

Papers of Helen L. Shell and Mary Virginia Shell deal mainly with events during the Civil War and contain letters from A. V. Stipp, a Virginia volunteer in the Union Army, describing the capture of Harpers Ferry by Confederate forces, 1862, movements of the 3rd Maryland Regiment during the battle of Gettysburg, 1863, and the subsiding of prejudice against Virginians in the Union Army; letters from J. V. Richardson of the Baltimore Light Artillery, commenting on raids and camp life; and letters from Isabella Welshaus of New Madrid, Missouri, describing guerilla raids, horse stealing, property destruction, high prices, and the strong Confederate sympathy of the region.

4770. PERCY BYSSHE SHELLEY AND MARY WOLLSTONECRAFT (GODWIN) SHELLEY PAPERS, 1814-1857. 4 vols. England. Restricted.

Typed copy of journals and letters of Percy Bysshe Shelley and Mary Wollstonecraft (Godwin) Shelley, formerly in the Ashley Library of T. J. Wise, but now in the British Museum.

The journal, containing notes of Professor Edward Dowden, opens with an account by Percy B. Shelley (1792-1822) of his flight with Mary Wollstonecraft Godwin (1797-1851) and her half sister, Claire (Clara Mary Jane) Clairmont (1798-1879), from England to the Continent. Interspersed with letters to or from friends, almost daily entries either by Shelley or Mary follow, referring, among other things, to the state of the weather; daily activities; titles of books read; financial affairs of Harriet (Westbrook) Shelley and the Godwin family; Shelley's own financial situation as it related to his father; the births and eventually the deaths of two of the children of Shelley and Mary; Claire Clairmont and Byron; literary works of Shelley; descriptions of French, Swiss, and Italian landscapes; political, social, and economic conditions in England and Scotland as shown by the letters of Fannie Imlay; Southern France and the character of the French as described by Charles Clairmont; deaths of Harriet W. Shelley and of Fannie Imlay; Mary Shelley's <u>Frankenstein</u> and its reception by the public; birth of Claire Clairmont's daughter, Allegra, and the mother's controversy with Byron over the child's custody; the Gisborne family and Henry Reveley's experiments in engineering; acquaintance of the Shelleys with Prince Alexander Mavrocordato; publishing difficulties of Shelley; activities and literary efforts of Byron, William Godwin, Thomas Jefferson Hogg, Leigh Hunt, Thomas Love Peacock, and Edward Trelawny; and of the death and burial of Edward E. Williams and Shelley as recounted by Trelawny.

Following Shelley's death and his wife's removal to England with young Percy F. Shelley, the daily entries become meager and letters by and to Mary Wollstonecraft (Godwin) Shelley predominate, with information on the settlement of the Shelley estate and the state of poverty in which Mary Wollstonecraft (Godwin) Shelley, Claire Clairmont, and young Percy Shelley lived until the death of Sir Timothy Shelley; Sir Timothy's opinion of Mary Wollstonecraft (Godwin) Shelley and her own analyses of herself and the loneliness of her life; efforts of Claire Clairmont to support herself as a governess in Russia, France, and Italy, her opinion of Byron and of his attitude toward their illegitimate daughter and toward Shelley; Byron's and Trelawny's activities in the Greek War for Independence, 1821-1829, and Byron's death; Frances Wright, including references to Robert Dale Owen and the Nashoba, Tennessee, and New Harmony, Indiana, socialistic projects in the United States through letters of Frances Wright to

Mary Wollstonecraft (Godwin) Shelley; Lord Dillon's "Eccelino" and his death; the old age and death of William Godwin; the schooling of young Percy Shelley at Harrow; the death of Sir Timothy Shelley; the publication of Trelawny's autobiography; biographies of Byron by Thomas Moore and Thomas Medwin; and projected works on Shelley by his widow, and Trelawny, and on William Godwin by Mary Wollstonecraft (Godwin) Shelley.

4771. J. B. SHELOR PAPERS, 1860-1891. 10 items. Pulaski County, Va.

Family correspondence of J. B. Shelor, Confederate soldier, and letters concerning his postwar candidacy for justice of the peace.

4772. SHENANDOAH VALLEY ASSEMBLY PAPERS, 1886-1891. 1 vol. (98 pp.) Shenandoah County, Va.

Roll of shareholders, constitution, and minutes of the Shenandoah Valley Assembly, a group which managed a religious meeting ground.

4773. JAMES BIDDLE SHEPARD PAPERS, 1780-1825. 1 vol. Raleigh (Wake County), N.C.

Papers of James Biddle Shepard, attorney and representative in the state legislature, consist of a volume containing legal briefs relating to cases argued before the Edenton District Superior Court, concerning the settlement of estates, libel, assault, and unpaid debts.

4774. ABRAHAM SHEPHERD, JR., AND JAMES H. SHEPHERD PAPERS, 1782 (1804-1878) 1880. 56 items. Shepherdstown (Jefferson County), W. Va.

Letters of Abraham Shepherd, Jr., and of his father and brothers concern the education of Abraham Shepherd, Jr., at the College of New Jersey (now Princeton University); reaction to a Baptist revival; the effect of Macon's Bill No. 2 on the price of cotton; the management of slaves; and horse breeding. The letters of Henry Shepherd, Jr., concern his business interests and comment on secession, Reconstruction, and the panic of 1873.

4775. JAMES EDWARD SHEPHERD PAPERS, 1892 (1901-1906) 1907. 155 items and 1 vol. Raleigh (Wake County), N.C.

Legal correspondence of James E. Shepherd (1847-1910), Confederate telegraph operator; judge of Beaufort County superior court, 1882-1893; chief justice of North Carolina supreme court, 1893-1897; and Raleigh lawyer.
Included in the correspondence are several letters of recommendation for Dr. Joseph J. Phillips, an applicant for a position at St. Luke's Hospital, New York City, including letters from A. C. Avery, J. B. Cheshire, and Bennett Smedes. There are also letters urging Shepherd to accept the nomination for the chief justice of North Carolina. The remainder of the collection pertains to legal matters largely involving cases bearing on a building and loan association and a lumber firm of eastern North Carolina. Included also is a commonplace book evidently kept by Shepherd while a student in Richmond, Virginia. Among the correspondents are F. H. Busbee, Angus W. McLean, and Henry A. Page.

4776. JAMES SHEPPARD PAPERS, (1830-1879) 1889. 1,537 items. Hanover County, Va.

Personal and business correspondence and business papers of James Sheppard (ca. 1816-1870), who owned large plantations in Jefferson County, Arkansas, Copiah County, Mississippi, and Hanover County, Virginia. Included are letters from New Orleans merchants and from plantation overseers with statements on prices, conditions of cotton, amounts of profit or loss of the planters, and quality and quantity of goods bought by the farmers; letters showing the relations between the New Orleans cotton market and the situation in England and Europe generally; discussions of slave problems on the farm, and social and economic conditions in Arkansas, Mississippi, and Virginia prior to the Civil War; numerous prices current; medical accounts of Dr. Joseph Sheppard; accounts of the Arkansas and Mississippi plantations; tax returns, 1859, showing James Sheppard's large land- and slave-holdings in Arkansas; and claims filed against the Federal government for large amounts of property destroyed during the Civil War. The material after James Sheppard's death consists chiefly of family letters written from Richmond, Virginia.

4777. SAMUEL SHEPPARD PAPERS, 1600s. 2 items. England.

Photocopy of the manuscript of Samuel Sheppard's "The Faerie King Fashioning Love and Honour," and a transcript of this work by Roberta Florence Brinkley.

4778. SHEPPARD BROTHERS LETTERPRESS BOOKS, 1879-1883. 3 vols. Edgefield (Edgefield County), S.C.

Letterpress books of a law firm.

4779. AUGUSTINE HENRY SHEPPERD PAPERS, ca. 1824-1850. 3 items. Surry County, N.C., and Washington, D.C.

Business letters of Augustine Henry Shepperd, member of the United States House of Representatives from North Carolina.

4780. PHILIP HENRY SHERIDAN PAPERS, 1867. 1 item.

Letter of recommendation written by General Philip Henry Sheridan as commanding general of the fifth military district.

4781. JOHN SHERMAN PAPERS, 1860-1880. 5 items. Mansfield (Richland County), Ohio.

Papers of John Sherman, United States senator from Ohio and cabinet officer, contain letters from Sherman concerning the political situation in Washington, D. C., in 1860; the conduct of the Virginia delegation to the Republican Party National Convention, 1880; and routine business of the United States Treasury Department, 1880.

4782. WILLIAM TECUMSEH SHERMAN PAPERS, 1861-1888. 21 items. New York, N.Y.

Papers of William Tecumseh Sherman, U. S. Army general, contain miscellaneous letters concerning business matters and veterans affairs, and routine military orders and papers from the Civil War, including photocopies of Sherman's telegram to President Abraham Lincoln presenting him Savannah, Georgia, as a Christmas present and Lincoln's reply, 1864; a letter, 1885, from Sherman discussing the political role of his brother, John Sherman, and a Sherman family reunion; a letter, 1886, from Sherman denying that he had ever written any poetry but expressing an interest in it; and a letter, 1888, in which Sherman defends his policies towards the South during the Civil War.

4783. E. L. SHERRILL PAPERS, 1852-1866. 7 items. Charleston, S.C.

Personal letters of E. L. Sherrill and others, containing some mention of commodity prices in South Carolina and Georgia, secession, and depredations by Union troops during the Civil War.

4784. SAMUEL P. SHERRILL ACCOUNT BOOK, 1845-1847. 1 vol. (16 pp.) Quallatown (Jackson County), N.C.

Accounts of a general merchant.

4785. JACOB SHIBLEY PAPERS, 1817-1871. 26 items. Perry County, Pa.

Deeds and other legal papers pertaining to Jacob Shibley and others, including a fragmentary legal document relating to George Ross, jurist and signer of the Declaration of Independence from Pennsylvania.

4786. GEORGE HOWELL SHIELDS PAPERS, 1868-1934. 109 items. Saint Louis, Mo.

Papers of George Howell Shields, attorney, politician, and jurist, consist of letters to Shields concerning routine political matters, lawsuits, and the attempts of his son to secure appointments in the army and diplomatic service.

4787. DANIEL SHINE PAPERS, 1793 (1809-1831). 42 items. Louisburg (Franklin County), N.C.

Personal and family letters to Daniel Shine, Methodist Episcopal minister of Franklin County, North Carolina. Many of the letters depict the religious feelings of the period among the evangelical group, conversion of sinners, camp meetings, and other religious matters.

4788. THOMAS J. SHINN PAPERS, 1837-1893. 8 items. Georgeville (Cabarrus County), N.C.

The collection includes an amnesty oath and a political pardon to Thomas J. Shinn; and letters from Shinn, a student at Trinity College, Randolph County, North Carolina, concerning college life, "Society" politics in campus elections, rumors of the possible dismissal of Dr. John Franklin Crowell, president of Trinity College, and a description of the electric light system and tobacco factories of Winston, North Carolina, in 1892.

4789. LOUIS EVAN SHIPMAN PAPERS, 1909-1926. 5 items. New York, N.Y., and New Hampshire.

Letters written to Louis Evan Shipman, playwright and editor, include a letter, 1920, from Virginia Gerson commenting on her work with Montrose J. Moses on the playwright William Clyde Fitch, and a letter, 1926, from John B. W. Gardiner concerning his professional activities and politics.

4790. J. W. SHIPP TESTIMONY, 1867-1882. 1 vol. Spartanburg (Spartanburg County), S.C.

Copies of letters and memoranda collected by A. M. Shipp, former president of Wofford College, Spartanburg, South Carolina, relating to the dismissal of his son, J. W. Shipp, from the faculty of the college in 1875.

4791. JOHN EDGAR DAWSON SHIPP DIARY, 1876. 1 vol. (116 pp.) Chattahoochee County, Ga.

Diary of John Edgar Dawson Shipp, lawyer and writer, kept while he was a student at Gordon Institute, Barnesville, Georgia, commenting on student life, the curriculum and procedure of the school, debates in the Lysian Society, and members of the faculty, especially Charles E. Lambdin, president of the school.

4792. WILLIAM DAVID SHIRER PAPERS, 1860-1893. 10 items. Berkeley County, S.C.

Family letters of William David Shirer, a Confederate soldier.

4793. JAMES SHIRLEY PAPERS, 1833-1844. 32 items. Defiance (Defiance County), Ohio.

Personal and business letters of James Shirley and others.

4794. ZACHARIAH SHIRLEY PAPERS, 1854. 2 items. Madison County, Va.

List of slaves in the estate of Thomas Shirley, giving their ages and prices.

4795. W. S. SHOCKLEY PAPERS, 1861-1864. 52 items. Jefferson (Jackson County), Ga.

Letters of W. S. Shockley, a Confederate soldier in the 18th Georgia Regiment, who served in Virginia and Tennessee, concerning rations, wages, sickness in camp, and hospital conditions.

4796. ISAAC SHOEMAKER DIARY, 1864. 1 vol. (78 pp.) Warrenton (Warren County), Miss.

Diary of Isaac Shoemaker, a Northerner who operated a cotton plantation in Mississippi, reflecting the trials of a plantation manager after slaves had been freed, and containing information on agriculture.

4797. EDWIN F. SHOENBERGER RECEIPT BOOK, 1846-1855. 1 vol. (78 pp.) Philadelphia, Pa.

Book of receipts, primarily for the sale of iron and iron products.

4798. CLEMENT KING SHORTER PAPERS, 1903-1923. 10 items. London, England.

Papers of Clement King Shorter, British journalist and author, contain letters, 1903, to William Morris Colles concerning Joseph Conrad's story "Falk," which Shorter was considering for serialization, and a letter, 1909, about copyright; copies of letters, 1916, between Shorter and H. G. Wells concerning Ireland's role in World War I and the Irish Rebellion; and three items, 1922-1923, relating to Shorter's edition of the works of George Borrow.

4799. JOHN GILL SHORTER PAPERS, 1860-1861. 3 items. Eufaula (Barbour County), Ala.

The papers of John Gill Shorter, Civil War governor of Alabama, relate to his attendance at the secession convention in Georgia in 1861, and include his commission as a representative from Alabama to the Georgia convention, a letter of instructions to Shorter from the president of the Alabama secession convention, and Shorter's letter of introduction to the president of the Georgia convention.

4800. BETTIE SHOTWELL PAPERS, 1840 (1864-1894). 39 items. Abram's Plains (Granville County), N.C.

Personal correspondence of Bettie Shotwell, including letters from her brother, J. A. Shotwell, a Confederate soldier, and from Sarah A. Skinner of Princeton, Massachusetts, concerning the temperance movement.

4801. NATHAN SHOTWELL PAPERS, 1835-1905. 26 items and 2 vols. Rogersville (Hawkins County), Tenn.

Personal and religious papers of the Reverend Nathan Shotwell. Also records of the Hawkins County Bible Society, including reports of the treasurer and the minute book, 1869-1901, of the society.

4802. WILLIAM P. SHREVE PAPERS, 1875-1894. 21 items. Boston, Mass.

Letters to William P. Shreve concerning Union veterans' organizations in which he was active, especially the Military Order of the Loyal Legion of the United States and the Third Army Corps Union.

4803. CORNELIUS SHRINER AND COMPANY ACCOUNTS, 1849-1904. 13 vols. Ceresville Mills (Frederick County), Md.

Account books, apparently of a flour mill.

4804. EDWARD A. SHRINER COPYBOOK, 1840. 1 vol. (243 pp.) Retreat School (Frederick County), Md.

Manuscript volume of mathematical rules and exercises.

4805. GEORGE ADAMS SHUFORD PAPERS, 1952-1959. ca. 38,000 items. Asheville (Buncombe County), N.C.

Papers of George Adams Shuford, U.S. congressman from North Carolina and superior court judge in North Carolina, contain correspondence, reports, speeches, and memoranda from his years in the House of Representatives, and concern agriculture, the armed services, atomic energy, elections, civil rights, civil service, commerce, the Constitution of the United States, the Democratic Party, education, electric power utilities, finance, fish and wildlife, foreign relations, highways, Indians, the House Interior and Insular Affairs Committee, irrigation and reclamation, labor, the judiciary, mines and mining, politics in

North Carolina, the post office, public lands, refugees, small business, the House Ways and Means Committee, tariffs, taxation, the Tennessee Valley authority, tobacco, veterans affairs, the Territories Subcommittee, water resources, the Blue Ridge Parkway, the Cherokee Indians, and the Hell's Canyon legislation.

4806.   WALTER H. SHUPE PAPERS, 1863-1874. 6 items. Rockland County, N.Y.

Papers of Walter H. Shupe, an attorney, are made up for the most part of personal letters to his parents concerning financial conditions in New York, the condition of the real estate market, temperance, and the Order of Good Samaritans.

4807.   JONAS SIBLEY PAPERS, 1782-1921. 180 items and 4 vols. Massachusetts.

Papers of Jonas Sibley and others contain deeds and legal papers, including patents granted to James Smalley by Germany and the United States for a cloth folding machine; correspondence concerning life in a boarding house for women, 1868, and bankruptcy proceedings against a Massachusetts firm; and miscellaneous items pertaining to personal debts, bills and accounts, and the report of a school board. Volumes include an autograph book, a book of household accounts, and a school essay book.

4808.   DANIEL EDGAR SICKLES PAPERS, 1856-1912. 23 items and 1 vol. New York, N.Y.

The papers of Daniel Edgar Sickles, Union general in the Civil War and New York businessman and politician, contain letters and telegrams concerning the Kansas-Nebraska question and the administration of President James Buchanan, the administration of courts and other civil and military matters during Sickles's term as military governor of North and South Carolina, and Sickles's defense of his actions as governor. The volume is a letterpress book, 1899-1912, containing personal and business letters by and to Sickles concerning various battles of the Civil War in which Sickles fought, especially the battle of Gettysburg; veterans' affairs and organizations; evaluations of various Union and Confederate officers, including James Longstreet, Robert E. Lee, George B. McClellan, and Joseph Hooker; Sickles's business interests; local, state and national politics, including Sickles's service on the New York City board of aldermen and his long association with the Republican Party; relations between the United States and Russia, 1904, and Sickles's recollection of James Buchanan's comment on Russo-American relations, 1854; comments by Sickles to President Theodore Roosevelt on politics, foreign relations, and the anthracite coal strike of 1904; Sickles's recollection of his negotiations with the prime minister of Spain in 1869 over the acquisition of Cuba; and the choice of a presidential nominee by the Republican Party in 1912.

4809.   JAMES BUREN SIDBURY PAPERS, 1915-1967. 64 items and 2 vols. Wilmington (New Hanover County), N.C.

The papers of James Buren Sidbury (1886-1967), pediatrician and founder of the Babies' Hospital at Wrightsville Sound, North Carolina, contain miscellaneous correspondence, reports, brochures, and clippings concerning the Babies' Hospital and its allied research center.

4810.   JOSEPH H. SIDDALL PAPERS, 1823-1826. 4 items. Philadelphia, Pa.

Papers of Joseph H. Siddall contain letters from his father, James Siddall, concerning personal and family matters and two brief manuscripts describing trips by river between Pittsburgh, Pennsylvania, and New Orleans, Louisiana.

4811.   HENRY MARLOW SIDNEY PAPERS, 1885. 1 vol. Brighton, Sussex, England.

Diary of Henry Marlow Sidney, British army officer, deals mainly with his service in the Sudan expedition of 1884-1885, and contains brief entries describing his activities and the movements of the troops with which he served.

4812.   SIDNEY KNITTING MILLS, INC., PAPERS, 1944-1948. 12 vols. Graham (Alamance County), N.C.

The papers of the Sidney Knitting Mills, Inc., a subsidiary of May McEwen Kaiser, record its operations as a manufacturer of ladies' silk hosiery from incorporation in 1944 to absorption by Burlington Industries in 1948. The collection contains a ledger, journals, a cash receipts journal, trial balances, voucher registers, and payroll summaries, all for the years 1945-1948; scattered checkbooks, 1944-1946; and a journal of invoices for sales to May McEwen Kaiser, 1945-1946.

4813.   JOHN SIEGLING, JR., PAPERS, 1845-1846. 3 items. Charleston, S.C.

Letters from John Siegling, Jr., member of a prominent Charleston family, while at Harvard Law School, Cambridge, Massachusetts. The letters describe university activities and Boston social life, and mention the Oregon question, possible war with England, and the Tirrell murder case, in which Rufus Choate won an acquittal.

4814.   MARTIN SIGMAN LEDGER, 1852-1855. 1 vol. (497 pp.) Wadesboro (Anson County), N.C.

Accounts of an inn, tavern, livery stable, and freight hauling business.

4815. LYDIA HOWARD (HUNTLEY) SIGOURNEY PAPERS, 1851. 1 item. Hartford (Hartford County), Conn.

A statement by Lydia Howard (Huntley) Sigourney concerning the death of her son from consumption.

4816. JOHN SIKES PAPERS, 1817-1893. 25 items. Bladen County, N.C.

Personal and business letters of John Sikes and others, concerning commodity prices in Tennessee, 1839; slave sales in North Carolina, 1840, 1843; politics in North Carolina; and experiences of James Hugh Malloy as a student at Davidson College, North Carolina, 1859.

4817. ALBERT SILER PAPERS, 1816 (1820-1860) 1875. 69 items. Franklin (Macon County), N.C.

Family and personal letters of two generations of the Siler family of western North Carolina, and two generations of the Chipman family in Montreal, Canada, and later of western North Carolina. The Civil War letters are those of Albert Siler, who joined the Confederate Army in 1862, and mainly concern troop movements, illnesses, and deaths of men whom he knew. The postwar letters are written from Montreal to the Chipmans in North Carolina.

4818. EDWARD E. SILL PAPERS, 1862-1864. 6 items. Flat Rock (Kershaw District), S.C.

Letters of Edward E. Sill, adjutant of the 2nd South Carolina Regiment, to his family, containing detailed descriptions of the battles of Fredericksburg, 1862, and Spotsylvania Court House, 1864, and the seige of Petersburg and Richmond, 1864.

4819. SILLIMAN COLLEGIATE INSTITUTE PAPERS, 1890-1896. 1 vol. (16 pp.) Clinton (Feliciana Parish), La.

Minutes of the faculty of Silliman Collegiate Institute.

4820. LOUISA M. (JELKS) SILLS PAPERS, 1828 (1839-1862) 1895. 35 items. Alabama, and Nash County, N.C.

Personal correspondence among various members of the Jelks and Sills families, with references to the professional duties of Louisa M. (Jelks) Sills's husband, Grey Sills, a physician. The collection includes letters from Mrs. Sills's sister written from Alabama and Mississippi concerning plantation management; letters on mercantile affairs in Alabama; a few Civil War letters commenting on economic conditions in Alabama and on politics; and letters concerning Reconstruction in Alabama.

4821. CHARLES SIMEON PAPERS, 1811, 1815. 2 items. Cambridge, Cambridgeshire, England.

Papers of Charles Simeon, British evangelical leader and author, contain a letter, 1811, to Simeon from Henry Martyn, a missionary in Persia, commenting on a translation of the Bible into Persian, financial support from the Indian government, and Martyn's relations with Moslems; and a letter, 1815, from Simeon concerning the position of chaplain to the British colony at Bencoolen, Sumatra.

4822. ARTHUR SIMKINS PAPERS, 1810-1846. 5 items. Edgefield District, S.C.

Land deeds and accounts.

4823. DAWN PEPITA (LANGLEY-HALL) SIMMONS PAPERS, 1952-1968. 407 items. Charleston, S.C. Restricted.

This collection contains the papers of author Gordon Langley Hall, made up for the most part of letters from his mother, Marjorie Hall (Ticehurst) Copper, describing her work on the household staff of Sir Harold Nicolson and his wife, Victoria Mary Sackville-West, Lady Nicolson, in Cranbrook, Kent, England. The letters concern family news and local gossip, Lady Nicolson's death, the family affairs and writings of Nigel Nicolson, and Marjorie Copper's views of events in the United States. Also a letter from Lady Nicolson to Gordon Langley Hall containing information on her background. The collection contains a number of items relating to a series of sex change treatments begun in 1967 at the Gender Identity Clinic of Johns Hopkins University, Baltimore, Maryland, at the conclusion of which Gordon Langley Hall adopted the name Dawn Pepita Langley-Hall. There are several clippings dealing with the sex change and an announcement of the forthcoming marriage of Langley-Hall and John Paul Simmons.

4824. DENNIS SIMMONS LUMBER COMPANY PAPERS, 1878-1927. 27,656 items and 82 vols. Williamston (Martin County), N.C.

Papers of the Simmons Lumber Company contain correspondence, deeds and other legal documents, pay lists, bills, receipts, letter books, and ledgers and other account books covering all aspects of the lumber business.

4825. FURNIFOLD McLENDEL SIMMONS PAPERS, 1890 (1920-1929) 1946. ca. 75,000 items. New Bern (Craven County), N.C.

Official correspondence, chiefly carbon copies, covering a large part of the public life of Furnifold M. Simmons (1854-1940), Democratic Party leader in North Carolina, and United States senator, 1901-1931. There are large gaps prior to 1918, the correspondence being approximately complete for the 1920s. There are a few comments on reform politics and the orthodox Southern position during Theodore Roosevelt's administration. Other material concerns the Underwood-Simmons Tariff, Wilsonian reforms, the financing of World War I, 1914-1918 (Simmons was chairman of the Senate Finance Committee), the Southern defection from Alfred E. Smith in 1928, and the technique of machine politics. Most of the collection, however, deals with routine political matters, such as applications and recommendations for appointments, requests for political literature, suggestions for procedure in campaigns, and aid to American veterans of World War I, 1914-1918, in securing benefits of special legislation. There are letters from many public figures of the period, including Presidents Calvin Coolidge, Herbert Clark Hoover, William Howard Taft, and Woodrow Wilson. There are also copies of the program and the major address of memorial exercises honoring Simmons, 1946.

4826. JAMES M. SIMMONS PAPERS, 1786-1794. 3 items. Savannah, Ga.

Routine legislative documents of James M. Simmons, clerk of the House of Representatives of Georgia.

4827. WILLIAM H. SIMMONS PAPERS, 1797-1881. 3 items and 6 vols. Tompkinsville (Choctaw County), Ala.

The papers of William H. Simmons contain an article on Tompkinsville, Alabama, and items relating to a grant of land in Hyde County, North Carolina, 1797. Volumes in the collection are account books of a combination saloon and general store kept by William H. Simmons, including daybooks, 1851-1857, 1861-1872; and four ledgers, 1854-1881.

4828. ROBERT NIRWANA SIMMS PAPERS, 1863-1949. 2,103 items and 3 vols. Raleigh (Wake County), N.C.

The papers of Robert Nirwana Simms, attorney and prominent Baptist layman of Raleigh, North Carolina, contain correspondence, concentrated in the years 1893-1915, concerning the campaign of Ashley Horne for the Democratic Party nomination for governor of North Carolina, 1908, including material on publicity, speaking engagements, campaign finances, and the party nominating convention; Simms's work in the church as a Baraca teacher and as an organizer and publicizer of the Baraca movement in the South; the international peace movement in North Carolina, 1908; the development of railroads in North Carolina, 1904-1908; Meredith College, Raleigh, North Carolina, 1929-1933; and prohibition in North Carolina, 1903-1920. Legal papers include material, 1904-1920, on a case involving Charles N. Hunter, a prominent advocate of education for Negroes in North Carolina, and letter books, 1900-1905, of the law firm of Douglas and Simms, concerning routine legal business.

The collection also contains material from the campaign for the 1908 gubernatorial nomination, including speeches, political advertising, and financial records, and material, 1939-1940, pertaining to Simms's work on a committee to draft a retirement insurance plan for Baptist ministers and church employees in North Carolina.

4829. WILLIAM GILMORE SIMMS PAPERS, 1838-1870. 56 items. Charleston, S.C.

Personal, literary, and political correspondence of William Gilmore Simms (1806-1870), South Carolina poet and novelist, which deals principally with the publication of his books and many projected works. Letters from Simms to Alfred Billings, Armistead Burt, Paul Hamilton Hayne [published by Jay B. Hubbell, The Last Years of Henry Timrod . . . (Durham, N.C.: 1941), and Joel Roberts Poinsett discuss literary and current political matters. Other letters comment on Abraham Lincoln, George B. McClellan, James Ryder Randall, and the nature of poetry.

4830. KEATING SIMONS PAPERS, 1854. 1 item. Charleston, S.C.

A grant of right-of-way issued in 1854 by Keating Simons to the Northeastern Railroad Company.

4831. JAMES A. SIMPSON PAPERS, 1861. 2 items. South Carolina.

Letters from James A. Simpson, Confederate private in "Hampton's Legion," describing the battle of Manassas, 1861, and commenting on camp life and an epidemic of measles.

4832. JOHN SIMPSON DAYBOOK, 1797-1798. 1 vol. Washington (Beaufort County), N.C.

Account book of a general merchant.

4833. JOHN SIMPSON PAPERS, 1833-1880. 75 items and 3 vols. Chester (Chester County), S.C.

Papers of John Simpson contain records of estates for which Simpson acted as executor, especially the estates of Rhoda Grubbs and John V. Cornwell; a contract with freedmen; and an unsigned copy of a speech, ca. 1833, on Andrew Jackson and the doctrine of states' rights. Volumes include a ledger, 1847-1864, containing accounts of a blacksmith business, charges for a studhorse, and mercantile accounts; an account book with records of the estate of John V. Cornwell; and a mercantile account book, 1844-1848, belonging to Nathan Simpson.

4834. WILLIAM DUNLAP SIMPSON PAPERS, 1798 (1852-1878) 1914. 4,076 items. Laurens (Laurens County), S.C.

Legal and personal correspondence and papers of William D. Simpson (1823-1890), governor of South Carolina, 1878-1880, and of his law partner, Henry C. Young, and of his sons who became the law partners of Henry C. Young, dealing chiefly with the Civil War and Reconstruction periods, although the subject matter is varied. Prior to 1852, the collection is confined altogether to legal papers, chiefly deeds evidently used in legal cases. The collection includes a number of letters from Congressman Daniel Wallace to F. Nance, regarding Wallace's ward, Robert Dunlop; a handwritten copy of the "Code of Honor of Duelling," written by John Lyde Wilson and published in 1858 as the Code of Honor or Rules for the Government of Principals and Seconds in Duelling; a letter from one Richardson of Asheville, North Carolina, referring to the climate, strawberry crops, slaves, Union Democrats, and the low ebb of Masonry, July, 1860; letters from W. B. Young, describing conditions and routine life in Confederate camps, mentioning the second battle of Manassas, 1862, telling of a trip to California, 1868, via the Isthmus, and describing the California climate and agricultural and labor conditions, and referring to postwar attitudes in Alabama and the attempt to rid that state of Radical rule; and a letter, 1860, from William Watson of Greenville, South Carolina, concerning the removal of Jews from the town. Among the numerous other topics discussed or mentioned in the collection are the attitude toward freedmen; suppression of papers in the North during the Civil War; secession; abolition; struggles between Conservatives and Radicals; lack of confidence in President Andrew Johnson; emigration to Missouri; a gold movement to Idaho, Montana, and Colorado; conditions in Missouri under a Radical governor and legislature; and prices for room and board, and slaves, corn, cotton, and other agricultural products in South Carolina.

4835. JOHN SINCLAIR COMMONPLACE BOOK, 1792-1801. 1 vol. (61 pp.) Edinburgh, Scotland.

Commonplace book of John Sinclair contains entries relating to his service in the 56th Regiment of the British Army in the expedition against Havana, Cuba, in 1762. Also contains a genealogy of the Sinclair family and bits of poetry and accounts.

4836. JOHN SINCLAIR SURVEY BOOK, 1833-1836. 1 vol. (104 pp.) Loudoun County, Va.

Volume containing notes and memoranda of a land surveyor.

4837. UPTON BEALL SINCLAIR, JR., PAPERS, 1908-1968. 63 items. Pasadena (Los Angeles County), Calif.

The papers of writer Upton Beall Sinclair, Jr., are made up of miscellaneous letters and notes chiefly concerning sales of Sinclair's writings; personal business; and Sinclair's interest in socialism. There is brief mention of the establishment of the Sinclair Foundation, 1931; author Gertrude Atherton; and Sinclair's book, A Captain of Industry.

4838. E. C. SINGLETON LEDGER, 1885-1890. 1 vol. (292 pp.) Charleston, S.C.

Accounts of a general merchant.

4839. RICHARD SINGLETON PAPERS, 1775 (1794-1844) 1868. 403 items. High Hills of Santee (Sumter County), S.C.

Family, business, and political correspondence and plantation accounts of Richard Singleton, captain in the Continental Army, who distinguished himself under General Francis Marion. Included are several letters from Abraham Van Buren, son of Martin Van Buren, and son-in-law of Singleton; four letters from Martin Van Buren, concerning politics and family matters; and letters of Angelica (Singleton) Van Buren, wife of Abraham Van Buren and social leader.

4840. THOMAS SINGLETON PAPERS, 1830. 1 item. Alnwick Castle, Northumberland, England.

Letter from Lord John George de la Poer Beresford, archbishop of Armagh and primate of Ireland, to Thomas Singleton, archdeacon of Northumberland, concerning the membership of a royal commission appointed to investigate the ecclesiastical courts.

4841. ROBERT SIPES DAYBOOKS, 1859-1881. 2 vols. Wesley (Verango County), Pa.

Financial records, apparently of a blacksmith.

4842. W. H. SIPLE PAPERS, 1889-1897. 2 vols. Petersburg (Grant County), W. Va.

Accounts and notebook of a physician.

4843. SKEWARKEY PRIMITIVE BAPTIST CHURCH PAPERS, 1864-1932. 1 vol. Williamston (Martin County), N.C.

Minutes, 1864-1932, and lists of members, 1867-1925, of Skewarkey Primitive Baptist Church.

4844. SKINNER FAMILY PAPERS, 1837-1875. 11 items. Prince Fredericktown (Calvert County), Md.

Letters to Anna Skinner, Sarah Skinner, and John Skinner, concerning personal and business matters.

4845. FULWAR SKIPWITH PAPERS, 1799-1818. 30 items. Philadelphia, Pa.

Papers relating to a suit against Fulwar Skipwith, American consul general to Paris, brought by William Russell, a former business partner in Paris; and a letter from John Mercer discussing business affairs and other matters.

4846. G. N. SKIPWITH ACCOUNT BOOK, 1848-1851. 1 vol. Clarksville (Mecklenburg County), Va.

Account book containing lists of items charged to the "R. & D. R. R. Co." [Richmond and Danville Railroad Company?] by G. N. Skipwith.

4847. GEORGE N. SKIPWITH DIARIES, 1868-1874. 3 vols. Richmond, Va.

Diaries concerning local happenings in Richmond, Virginia, the weather, and business affairs of George N. Skipwith (d. 1874), an employee in the office of the James River and Kanawha Canal Company at Richmond.

4848. HUMBERSTON SKIPWITH PAPERS, 1784-1853. 4 items and 1 vol. Clarksville (Mecklenburg County), Va.

Family letters, tax memoranda, and an account book of Humberston Skipwith (d. 1863), plantation owner in Mecklenburg County, Virginia.

4849. WILLIAM SLADE PAPERS, 1751-1929. 2,750 items and 31 vols. Williamston (Martin County), N.C.

Family and business correspondence and records of the Slade family, prominent in the mercantile business and in military service, including papers of General Jeremiah Slade, one of the U.S. commissioners for the Tuscarora Indians, consisting of correspondence relating to his duties as commissioner, documents signed by several Indian chiefs, accounts and notes on business transactions, guardianship accounts, and land deeds; family correspondence; letters from the University of North Carolina, Chapel Hill, North Carolina, 1820-1830; correspondence relating to the Mexican War; indentures; deeds; grants; wills; estate papers; contracts; slave lists, tax lists and receipts; tobacco warehouse receipts; wedding invitations; insurance policies; bills and receipts; letter, 1874, from Mount Airy, North Carolina, telling of the death of the Siamese twins, Eng and Chang; postcard of the Loyal Temperance Legion; photographs of Oxford, North Carolina, in 1907; letter, 1922, from Lucy Bramlette (Patterson) Patterson describing the opposition to woman suffrage from both men and women; scattered papers relating to the State Normal and Industrial School (now University of North Carolina at Greensboro), Wake Forest College (Wake Forest, North Carolina), and the Clinton Female Seminary (Clinton, Georgia); and printed material relating to the breeding of hogs and horses, guano, the cultivation and curing of bright leaf tobacco, temperance, and religion.

Of approximately three hundred letters written during the Civil War, many are from the Slade brothers, Henry, William, James, and "Bog" or J. B., who served in the Confederate Army. Included are comments on the organization of military companies; campaigns around Yorktown, Virginia, during 1861; fighting, refugees, and the enemy in eastern North Carolina; living conditions and high prices; Longstreet's Corps in Caroline County, Virginia, in 1863; and the military situation around Knoxville, Tennessee, in 1863. There are also war letters of one Eli Peal to his wife in eastern North Carolina, containing advice on farming operations; payment of taxes; accounts of skirmishes at Camp Burgwyn near Wilmington, North Carolina; difficulty of obtaining clothes; and references to guard duty. The correspondence of the Slade family also contains letters to and from the various sisters during the Civil War. Letters of "Bog" or J. B. Slade early in 1861 from Harris County, Georgia, reflect enthusiasm for the newly formed Confederacy. A few letters early in 1861 are from Henry Slade, a student at Trinity College, Randolph County, North Carolina, until he joined the army in the same year. Henry Slade mentions Braxton Craven, in whose home he boarded. Among the volumes are records of administration of the estate of Ebenezer Slade (d. 1815) with accounts of hiring slaves and rent of lands; account book, 1810-1811, and daybook, 1805-1819, of Jeremiah Slade, evidently in the lumber business; court records and receipt book, 1834-1837, kept by William Slade, apparently while serving as clerk of the court; account books, daybooks, and memorandum books of William Slade, recording supplies advanced, hogs killed, and lumber sawed; six time books, 1873-1881, of William Slade; stud books; miscellaneous account book, 1856-1869; minutes of the Trinity Baptist Church, Caswell County, North Carolina; and a record of births, marriages, and deaths in the family of William Slade.

4850. RICHARD SLATE PAPERS, 1814-1833. 4 items. Stand, Lancashire, England.

Letters of Richard Slate (1787-1867), minister of an independent church near Manchester and later in Lancashire, concerning the authenticity of an incident in Slate's biography of Oliver Heywood: a letter from a missionary in the South Sea Islands, detailing the difficulties encountered and commenting on the indolence of the natives; and a printed circular addressed to clergymen.

4851. HARRY AUGUSTUS SLATTERY PAPERS, 1901-1953. 50,844 items and 243 vols. Greenville (Greenville County), S.C., and Washington, D.C.

Correspondence, writings, speeches, official papers, and printed material, relating to the various positions held by Harry Augustus Slattery (1887-1949) during his years of public service, and reflecting his lifelong interest in conservation. The bulk of the collection relates to Slattery's positions as personal assistant to Harold L. Ickes, 1933-1938, as under secretary of the interior, 1938-1939, and as administrator of the Rural Electrification Administration, 1939-1944. Other papers concern his service as secretary to Gifford Pinchot, 1909-1912, as secretary of the National Conservation Association, 1912-1923, as special assistant to Interior Secretary Franklin K. Lane, 1917-1918, as a Washington lawyer, 1923-1933, and as counsel to the National Boulder Dam Association, 1925-1929. Also included are a typescript of Slattery's autobiography, "Behind the Scenes in Washington"; scrapbooks, 1890-1940; and albums, 1935-1941.

4852. DANIEL FRENCH SLAUGHTER PAPERS, 1787 (1830-1843) 1865. 99 items and 1 vol. Culpeper (Culpeper County), Va.

Papers of Daniel French Slaughter, attorney, state senator, 1828-1830 and 1832-1836, and state representative, 1846-1847, including papers relating to pension claims for service in the Revolutionary War, especially of Slaughter's father, Philip Slaughter (1758-1849), captain in the 11th Continental Regiment; business papers concerning personal debts, commodity prices, purchases, and slave sales; scattered legal papers and documents; correspondence discussing the Canadian expedition of American General William Hull and fighting against the British and the Indians, casualties, British prisoners, the Virginia Constitutional Convention during 1829-1830, issue of counting slaves in legislative apportionment, deportation of free Negroes, Virginia politics and various elections, Andrew Jackson and his cabinet, the Force Bill, Compromise Tariff Bill, controversy over the Second Bank of the United States, financial regulations of the U.S. Department of the Treasury, consular regulations, the Virginia militia, and matters surrounding the presidential campaign of 1860; pro-Whig presidential campaign poem for 1840; and a chart, 1850, showing facts and figures relating to the Orange and Alexandria Railroad extension.

4853. FRANK GILL SLAUGHTER PAPERS, 1964-1965. 28 items and 3 vols. Jacksonville (Duval County), Fla.

Research notes, original handwritten draft, typed revisions, galley proofs, reviewer's galleys and printed copy of Constantine: The Miracle of the Flaming Cross (1965) by Frank Gill Slaughter (b. 1908), author and physician; and Abbottempo, Book No. 4, containing Slaughter's "Lincoln's Doctor's Dog."

4854. GUILFORD H. SLAUGHTER PAPERS, 1838-1912. 226 items and 1 vol. Nashville (Davidson County), Tenn.

Personal and family correspondence and papers of Guilford H. Slaughter, planter and businessman, including itemized bills for household articles and farming equipment; a printed invitation to the funeral of Joshua W. Milton; a brief personal note written by Slaughter from a Confederate Army camp; a daybook, 1877-1882; land deeds; records, 1859-1860, of a stage mail line operated by G. H. Slaughter and Company between Nashville and Clarksville, Tennessee, and Hopkinsville, Kentucky; letter, 1873, mentioning cholera in Nashville; and papers relating to the settlement of the estate of Robert C. Bowman, father of Slaughter's wife, Amelia.

4855. MONTGOMERY SLAUGHTER PAPERS, 1862-1864. 13 items and 1 vol. Fredericksburg (Spotsylvania County), Va.

Business correspondence of Montgomery Slaughter, speculator in wheat, flour manufacturer, old-line Whig, and mayor of Fredericksburg during the Civil War. Included are papers concerning proceedings of the city council during the occupation by Federal forces; copies of many letters addressed to the U.S. commander at Fredericksburg; a few letters from Slaughter's son, William, a student at the Virginia Military Institute, Lexington; and a letter book, 1862.

4856. JOHN SLIDELL PAPERS, 1856. 2 items. New Orleans, La.

Letters of John Slidell (1793-1871), lawyer, U.S. senator, 1853-1861, and Confederate agent in France, concerning his efforts in behalf of the nomination of James Buchanan in 1856.

4857. EDWARD FEATHERSTON SMALL PAPERS, 1884-1908. 64 items. Washington (Beaufort County), N.C., and Atlanta, Ga.

Letters and papers of Edward F. Small (b. ca. 1844), Confederate flag bearer and tobacco salesman, affording much information on the sales methods of tobacco manufacturers. Included are letters of W. Duke Sons and Company, a paper on sales method of the American Tobacco Company, several literary efforts of Small, a brief account of Small's life by his daughter, B. D. Small, and newspaper clippings.

4858. JOHN HUMPHREY SMALL PAPERS, 1720 (1850-1870, 1912-1937) 1946. 9,720 items and 1 vol. Washington (Beaufort County), N.C., and Washington, D.C.

Papers of John Humphrey Small (1858-1946), attorney, planter, and U.S. congressman, 1899-1921; of his father-in-law, Colonel Rufus W. Wharton (1827-1910?) attorney and planter; and of Colonel David M. Carter (d. 1879), attorney, planter, businessman, and court official of Fairfield, North Carolina. The papers centering around Rufus W. Wharton and David M. Carter, principally legal and financial papers, include deeds and indentures; wills; inventories; estate and settlement papers; note collections; papers relating to the sale of corn by commission merchants; stock transactions; charter of the Dismal Swamp Canal Company, 1787; papers relating to the Albemarle Swamp Land Company, 1879, the Albemarle and Chesapeake Canal Company, 1881, and swamp land transactions for Carter heirs, 1879-1890; papers dealing with the administration of the estate of David M. Carter by Rufus W. Wharton, and after Wharton's death, by John Humphrey Small; correspondence concerning lumbering and farming in North Carolina during the 1890s; and personal correspondence, including letters from Frances (Carter) Schaeffer from Germany, Austria, and North Carolina.

The bulk of the papers focuses on the career of John Humphrey Small in the United States Congress, his interest in the development of rivers and harbors and the Intra-Coastal Waterway, his membership on the National Rivers and Harbors Congress, and his legal practice. Papers relating to his congressional campaign in 1898 concern North Carolina politics, especially in the 1st Congressional District, civil service abuses, the Light House Service, and the vote of Populists, Republicans, Quakers, and Negroes. Correspondence during his years in Congress discusses plans for a white grade school in Washington, North Carolina, 1903-1904; conditions of large scale farming at Edgewater, North Carolina, including descriptions of seeds, fertilizer, prices, machinery, crop conditions, and marketing, 1903-1912; problems of railroads, especially the Norfolk and Southern Railroad; the presidential campaign of 1916; coastal highway development; various rivers and harbors bills; the Inlet Waterway project; transportation via an inland waterway; the National Rivers and Harbors Congress; railroad and water transportation in relation to national defense during World War I; land acquisition and construction plans for the Intra-Coastal Waterway from Norfolk, Virginia, to Beaufort, North Carolina; problems of labor, including the movement for the eight hour day; labor shortages in eastern North Carolina during World War I; prohibition; woman suffrage; the National Guard; military service and the draft; coal shortages during the war; army camp sites; home guards; rising prices; excess profits tax; the Red Cross; various agricultural bills; national and North Carolina politics; a Congressional trip of inspection to the Far East in 1920, including Japan, Korea, and the Philippines; the Railroad Act of 1920; and routine matters such as patronage, post office appointments, appointments to West Point and Annapolis, and pensions for Spanish-American War veterans.

Correspondence after Small's retirement from Congress concerns the postwar economic depression; immigration legislation in the 1920s; the membership of the State Geological Board; the vice-presidency of the Atlantic Deeper Waterways Association; business conditions during the early 1920s and during the depression; condition of eastern North Carolina banks, 1920-1922 and 1932; Small's service as president of the National Rivers and Harbors Congress, 1920-1922; the promotion of the port of Wilmington, North Carolina, by the state; Democratic politics; the presidential campaign of 1932; the National Recovery Act; railroads in 1935; the development of airmail service; conditions during World War II; and Franklin Delano Roosevelt. Other correspondence pertains to the opening and building of his law practice in Washington, D.C.; his partnership with Angus W. McLean, governor of North Carolina, 1925-1929; and specific legal cases. Miscellaneous papers consist of the minutes of the Tri-State Aviation Corporation, photographs, invitations, and Small's speech on the inland waterway. Legal papers include the papers relating to various estates, including David M. Carter, Charles Adams, and others; papers concerning income tax; papers dealing with the development of Washington Park, North Carolina; papers pertaining to specific cases; incorporation papers of the Tri-State Aviation Company and All-American Aviation, Inc.; deeds, indentures and wills; and papers of the legal practices of David M. Carter and Rufus W. Wharton. Financial papers include bills and receipts, 1830-1940, consisting of household accounts, clothing bills, promissory notes, tax receipts, court costs, estate inventories, medical bills for family and slaves, and records of slave sales; material on Confederate taxation; papers, 1870s, of a Baltimore, Maryland, cotton factor; records, 1880s, of corn sales; tobacco warehouse receipts, 1890s, from Greenville, North Carolina; business papers dealing with Jonathan Havens, Jr., commission merchant in corn and grain in Washington, North Carolina, and founder of the Havens (cottonseed) Oil Company and receievership papers of the St. Paul (North Carolina) Cotton Mills, 1939-1941. Among the printed materials are clippings on the depression, 1930-1934; personal items; biographical material on Senator Joseph E. Ransdell of Louisiana and on Rear Admiral Colby N. Chester; copies of the Greenville (North Carolina) Daily Reflector, December 27, 1913, and the Red Triangle, Paris, April 5, 1919; seed catalogues; reprints of the House of Representatives reports and bills on immigration, 1921, and airways, 1937; broadsides of the 1920 election; plan of organization of the Democratic Party in Beaufort, North Carolina, in 1896; the "Declaration of

Principles" of the National Rivers and Harbors Congress, 1916, and its officers for 1916-1917; and a bond pamphlet for the Albemarle and Chesapeake Canal Company, 1879. The volume is the <u>Individual Voting Record By Roll Calls in the House of Representatives</u> for John H. Small during the 1st, 2nd, and 3rd sessions of the 66th Congress, 1919-1921.

4859.  WILLIAM SMALLWOOD PAPERS, 1780. 2 items. Kent County, Md.

Letters from William Smallwood (1732-1792), Revolutionary soldier, relating to the need for food and supplies for his troops, then on duty in North Carolina; and describing the strength of the Tories in western North Carolina.

4860.  RICHARD B. SMART PAPERS, 1861. 3 vols. Brighton (Suffolk County), Mass.

Letter books of Richard B. Smart, soldier in the 1st Massachusetts Volunteers, U.S.A., containing letters of Smart copied into the volumes by his sister, and describing Washington, D. C., the repulse of the 1st Massachusetts at Blackburn's Ford prior to the first battle of Manassas, camp life, drilling, picket duty, clothing, and food, with occasional references to slavery and Abraham Lincoln.

4861.  ISAIAH BUXTON SMAW PAPERS, 1851-1884. 4 items and 3 vols. Boligee (Greene County), Ala.

Ledger, 1867-1868, and daybooks, 1851-1863 and 1867-1868, of Isaiah Buxton Smaw, a retail merchant, containing mercantile and agricultural accounts, records of slave sales and estate settlements, and entries indicating amounts of cotton and meat given to freedmen working as sharecroppers; a contract; an account; an agricultural record; and a religious testimonial.

4862.  SAMUEL V. SMAW PAPERS, 1826-1867. 17 items and 1 vol. Beaufort County, N.C.

Papers of a prominent resident of Beaufort County, including a manuscript arithmetic book, 1826, which contains some fine and occasionally humorous calligraphy; a letter, 1856, from John Ellison, a student at South Lowell Academy, Durham County; a tax list, 1861, describing slaves, land, and other property; and documents relating to Smaw's service on a county committee that certified families of soldiers for relief, 1861.

4863.  GEORGE M. SMEDES NOTEBOOK. 1 vol. (284 pp.) New York, N.Y.

Notes on law lectures taken by George M. Smedes while attending Columbia University, New York, New York.

4864.  MRS. _____ SMITH JOURNAL, 1793. 1 vol. (48 pp.) Newburyport (Essex County), Mass.

Journal of Mrs. Smith describing a voyage from Boston, Massachusetts, to Savannah, Georgia; social events attended in Savannah; Negroes at work unloading vessels and on rice plantations, and at religious services; horse racing; a funeral of the son of General Nathanael Greene; religious services, including Catholic and Jewish; Charleston, South Carolina; Baltimore, Maryland; Philadelphia, Pennsylvania; seeing President and Mrs. Washington at Christ Church in Philadelphia; New York, New York; and the return home.

4865.  ALVA CARMICHAEL SMITH PAPERS, 1840-1969. 4,223 items and 2 vols. Columbus (Muscogee County), Ga.

Business papers of Alva Carmichael Smith, businessman and manager of the Southern Coal Company, chiefly relating to routine matters of purchasing, pricing, selling, and shipping. Scattered correspondence also discusses problems of the coal trade; strikes and their effects; labor-management problems; labor union activity; shortages of railroad cars, 1917 and 1919-1920; effect of an influenza epidemic on the labor force, 1920; economic distress, especially during the depression; the Southeastern Coal Merchants Association; and the Southern Appalachian Coal Operators' Association. Also included are a cashbook, 1917-1918, and an order book, 1921-1922, of the company; printed material, including advertisements from mines and dealers relating to the coal trade; financial papers; legal papers; photographs; several letters to Smith's sisters, Mary Elizabeth and Dovie; and other miscellaneous papers.

4866.  ANNA MARIA (SMITH) SMITH PAPERS, 1824-1864. 42 items. Deep Creek (Norfolk County), Va.

Personal correspondence of the Smith family. Included are letters from Anna Maria Smith and her sister, Virginia Louisa Smith, from St. Joseph's School, Baltimore, Maryland; and correspondence concerning the Civil War, Federal depredations, and runaway slaves.

4867.  ANNE P. SMITH PAPERS, 1846-1847. 3 items. Norfolk, Va.

Personal letters, two from a "bluestocking" in Troy, New York, advising Anne P. Smith how to observe Lent and what books to read; and another from a Baltimore woman praising Herman Melville's books.

4868.  AUGUSTUS JOHN SMITH PAPERS, 1862.
1 item. Tresco Island, Cornwall, England.

Letter from Augustus John Smith (1804-1872), member of Parliament, 1857-1865, discussing bills calling for the use of the ballot in municipal and parliamentary elections and mentioning how a number of members voted, and commenting on several motions on the national expenditure.

4869.  BENJAMIN BOSWORTH SMITH PAPERS, 1831-1872. 4 items. Frankfort (Franklin County), Ky.

Papers of Benjamin Bosworth Smith (1794-1884), first Protestant Episcopal bishop of Kentucky, including minutes of a meeting of the standing committee of the Episcopal Church in New Hampshire disclosing that diocese's reasons for refusing to sign testimonials prepared by the Diocese of Kentucky relevant to the elevation of Smith to the bishopric; and three letters from Smith concerning routine church affairs.

4870.  BERTRAM TAFT SMITH PAPERS. 2 items. Winston-Salem (Forsyth County), N.C.

Typescripts of two compilations entitled "Brown Men in the 'Official Records of the Union and Confederate Armies in the War of the Rebellion'" and "Brown Men in the 'Official Records of the Union and Confederate Navies,'" discussing the war records of men who attended Brown University, Providence, Rhode Island.

4871.  CHARLES HENRY SMITH PAPERS, 1888, 1894. 2 items. Lawrenceville (Gwinnett County), Ga.

Letters from Charles Henry Smith (1826-1903), humorist under pseudonym of "Bill Arp," lawyer, and Confederate soldier. One answers an inquiry about biographical material on a Judge Underwood, 1888, and the other contains a biographical sketch of A. B. Longstreet, 1894.

4872.  D. G. SMITH PAPERS, 1850-1855. 3 items. Iredell County, N.C.

A letter from D. G. Smith, concerning an influenza epidemic and "steam mills" at Tilton, Murray County, Georgia, 1852; a letter written by the Reverend Joseph Melton for J. A. Guy, concerning the hiring of a slave and a horse; and a letter from Robert A. Smith discussing crops.

4873.  EDMUND KIRBY SMITH PAPERS, 1862-1863. 5 items. Saint Augustine (Saint John's County), Fla.

Letters and a circular order from Edmund Kirby Smith (1824-1893), Confederate general and educator. One letter, June 14, 1862, to Samuel Cooper concerns General Braxton Bragg's operations between Cumberland Gap and Chattanooga, Tennessee; and another, August, 1862, to Jefferson Davis, gives a long account of the military situation in Tennessee and Kentucky.

4874.  EDWARD CHAMBERS SMITH PAPERS, 1854 (1892-1916) 1921. 368 items. Murfreesboro (Hertford County), N.C.

Papers of Edward Chambers Smith (b. 1857), prominent North Carolina lawyer and political leader, including business and legal correspondence relating to the numerous corporations for which he was attorney and stockholder; letters as a student at Davidson College, Davidson, North Carolina; and scattered political correspondence on the Populist and Democratic parties.

4875.  EDWIN SMITH PAPERS, 1810-1870. 27 items. Stokes County, N.C.

Miscellaneous papers of Edwin Smith, schoolteacher, include letter, 1841, from Smith's aunt and uncle, A. and Harriet Baker, in Indiana containing family information; letters concerning the settlement of the estate of Joseph Baker; letters from S. M. Smith describing his stay in a Confederate hospital after contracting smallpox; common school teaching contracts and certificates of Smith; letters from S. M. Smith and his brother, Tom Smith, discussing their farming operation in Georgia, the use of whites and freedmen as farm hands, and commodity prices; and a letter, 1866, from a relative in Illinois giving commodity prices.

4876.  EMMA JULIANA (GRAY) SMITH AND JOHN P. GEORGE SMITH LETTER BOOK, 1843-1845. 1 vol. Liverpool, England, and Pernambuco, Brazil.

Sixty-one letters from Emma Juliana (Gray) Smith and John P. George Smith while on an expedition in Brazil to collect various specimens of animal, insect, and plant life, giving detailed descriptions of their journey to Brazil and the difficulties in adjusting to the different climate; their life in Brazil, including housing, food, servants, family life, the English church, illness, and difficulties with laundry; dress and other customs of the various classes of Brazilians, including "the blacks," both slave and free; effects of the English attitude toward slavery in Brazil; expeditions to various parts of Brazil to collect specimens; the collection and preparation of specimens; regions visited; difficulties of transportation; cowboys; the Brazilian bush; internal affairs at the British Museum; unrest during elections in Brazil; and celebrations in honor of the birth of an heir to Pedro II of Brazil.

4877.  EVIN SMITH PAPERS, 1862-1868. 14 items. Davidson County, N.C.

Family letters of Evin Smith, private in the 28th North Carolina Regiment, C.S.A., concerning his life in the army and mentioning his participation in the battle of

Fredericksburg, war weariness, and contemplated desertion.

4878. F. R. SMITH BLOTTER, 1836-1839. 1 vol. (18 pp.) Sharpsburg (Washington County), Md.

Legal record book, listing witnesses for lawsuits.

4879. FRANCIS HENNEY SMITH PAPERS, 1834-1869. 5 items. Lexington (Rockbridge County), Va.

Correspondence of Francis Henney Smith (1812-1890), who was connected with the Virginia Military Institute as professor and superintendent, 1839-1889, concerning an order for swords, employment of a student to survey a canal route, conscripting students in 1863, obtaining a piece of sculpture, and a report of J. Williamson, a student at V. M. I.

4880. FRANCIS ORMAND JONATHAN SMITH PAPERS, 1827-1838. 11 items. Washington, D.C.

Correspondence of Francis Ormand Jonathan Smith (1806-1876), U.S. congressman from Maine, 1833-1839, discussing Martin Van Buren as Andrew Jackson's choice for presidential candidate in 1836; the interest of Henry Clay, Daniel Webster, and John McLean in the nomination; the prospects of B. W. Leigh and William C. Rives for re-election in Virginia; the impending appointment of Andrew Stevenson as minister to England; the Second Bank of the United States; and the administration of the U. S. Post Office by W. T. Barry.

4881. FRANKLIN E. SMITH PAPERS, 1818 (1835-1870) 1890. 939 items. Linwood (Delaware County), Pa.

The correspondence and papers of Franklin E. Smith (d. 1878), a Pennsylvania sea captain and lieutenant commander in the U. S. Navy, and of his family. The letters contain much information on Smith's family, his career and journeys as a sea captain, and the Civil War period. The earlier material in the collection consists of letters from Smith to his parents and to his first wife, Elizabeth, and concerns his voyages on the trading vessel Eutaw, carrying coffee and cotton between Delaware and Calcutta, India; his transfer to the brig Mary in 1831; his connection with the shipping firm of Grinnell, Minturn and Company; and the wrecking of the ship Sampson in 1841. For the period 1838-1846 the correspondence relates to Smith's second marriage, 1838, to Mary Caroline Trainer of Marcus Hook, Pennsylvania, and his settling on a farm with his wife and daughters, Sarah and Hannah. For the period 1846-1852 the collection concerns Smith's return to the sea on the brig Osceola; his service in the Mexican War; the wrecking of his ship Vera Cruz, owned by the firm Burling and Dixon; a voyage around Cape Horn, 1851; a trip to San Francisco, 1851-1852; and his sailing the Messenger for the firm Ritchie, Osgood and Company, transporting goods of Wm. Platt and Sons. The miscellaneous pre-Civil War material concerns Negro crews on sailing vessels, 1841; British negotiations for the purchase of Cuba, 1841; Genesee Farmer, 1842; Shelby County, Kentucky, 1846; the Revolution of 1848 in France; food prices, 1849; a cholera epidemic, 1849; agricultural conditions in Pennsylvania, 1851; Shanghai, China, 1851; price of cattle, 1853; the Taiping rebellion in China, 1853; Savannah, Georgia, 1855; education of young girls, 1856; relics in European churches, 1856; James Buchanan's inauguration, 1857; Stephen A. Douglas's nomination, 1860; Republican Party election in Pennsylvania, 1860; and seizure of the English vessel Patras bearing contraband. The Civil War material deals chiefly with Smith's blockading activities aboard the U.S.S. Bienville under the command of Samuel Francis Du Pont. Among the other Civil War topics mentioned or discussed are arrival of U.S.S. Bienville at Fortress Monroe, Virginia, 1861; the battle and capture of Port Royal, South Carolina, 1861; Copperhead activities in Delaware, 1861; financing of the 1st Delaware Volunteer Regiment, 1861; a recommendation by Charles I. Du Pont to William Burton that Dr. Arthur H. Grimshaw be made colonel of the 4th Delaware Regiment, 1861; activities of Federal ships off South Carolina, 1861; "Yankee" depredations, 1862; the son of James Gordon Bennett, 1862; the Democratic party, 1862; capture of Fernandina, Florida, 1862; David L. Yulee, 1862; political corruption, particularly in the Republican Party, 1862; escape of Negroes from the Confederacy to the Federal forces, 1862; propaganda, 1862; second battle of Manassas, 1862; retreat to Washington, 1862; Rebel activities around Cincinnati, Ohio, 1862; removal of George B. McClellan, 1862; attempt of ironclads to attack Charleston, South Carolina, 1863; attack on Vicksburg, Mississippi, 1863; conditions in New Orleans, 1863; Richmond campaign, 1863; arrest of C. L. Vallandigham, 1863; Confederate invasion of Pennsylvania, 1863; battle of Gettysburg, 1863; abolitionists, 1863; Lincoln-McClellan campaign, 1864; commodity prices, 1864; capture of blockade runner Annie, 1864; Sherman's activities of destruction, 1864; attack on Fort Fisher, North Carolina, 1864; and Franklin E. Smith's trial and acquittal for disobedience, 1864. The postwar letters are chiefly concerned with family affairs and include references to life in a small Pennsylvania town; Franklin E. and Mary Caroline (Trainer) Smith's attitude toward Sarah's becoming a Catholic; Sarah Smith's job as governess to Lily Apsley, daughter of a merchant in Boston, Massachusetts; gas for street lighting in Wilmington, Delaware, 1866; and conditions in Boston, 1869. Included also are anti-Republican speeches, and documents of the Southern Railroad Company. Among the correspondents are Thomas F. Bayard, Henry R. Bringhurst, John M. Clayton, Charles I. Du Pont, George P. Fisher, Arthur H. Grimshaw, and Henry H. Lockwood.

4882. FREDERICK L. SMITH COMMISSARY BOOK, 1863. 1 vol. (105 pp.) Edgefield (Edgefield County), S.C.

Commissary book of Captain Frederick L. Smith, C.S.A., containing commissary records for the officers and men of the 7th Regiment, South Carolina Volunteers.

4883. GEORGE JOHNSTON SMITH PAPERS, 1897-1935. 16 items. New Orleans, La.

Papers of George Johnston Smith concerning his service in the U.S. Army during the Spanish-American War, serving in the Philippine Islands, and the controversy over a disability pension. Included is his certificate of American citizenship, 1897.

4884. GUSTAVUS WOODSON SMITH PAPERS, 1861-1865. 5 items. Scott County, Ky.

Letters from Gustavus Woodson Smith (1822-1896), officer in the Mexican War and major general in the Confederate Army. One letter to Jefferson Davis describes the condition of the Army of the Potomac, 1861; another, to General William J. Hardee, describes the military situation in Georgia, December, 1864.

4885. H. E. SMITH AND J. P. SMITH LEDGER, 1887-1895. 1 vol. (404 pp.) Mecklenburg County, Va.

Accounts of a general store.

4886. H. TILLARD SMITH PAPERS, 1828-1885. 102 items. Baltimore, Md.

Personal and business correspondence, bills and receipts, legislative bills and petitions, and other items pertaining to H. Tillard Smith, member of the Maryland House of Delegates. Many of the letters relate to legislative subjects including a Maryland Sunday bill, business licensing, the removal of tobacco warehouses to Canton, pensions for widows of soldiers of the War of 1812, turnpike and bridge bill, the militia, merchants and agricultural shippers, Baltimore streets and alleys, an auction, mortgage tax and usury, boundary commission, education for Baltimore Negroes, the unmarked grave of General William Smallwood, and a request that laws be published in the Celtic language. Also included are a broadside concerning a Maryland bill about the Montgomery, Howard, and Carroll Railroad Company; a broadside about Maryland legislative and financial affairs; a petition against repeal of a law concerning business licenses; a poem; bills and receipts of Mary Parsons, a physician; a commencement announcement for the School of Medicine, Washington University, Saint Louis, Missouri; and correspondence relating to personal and financial affairs.

4887. HOKE SMITH PAPERS, 1880. 1 item. Atlanta, Ga.

Letter from Hoke Smith (1855-1931), lawyer, secretary of the interior, 1893-1896, governor of Georgia, 1907-1911, and U.S. senator, 1911-1921, to John W. Park concerning a mortgage.

4888. HORACE SMITH PAPERS, 1864-1867. 62 items. Williamstown (Orange County), Vt.

Letters of Willard Smith, musician in the band of the 8th Vermont Regiment, U.S.A., to his father, Horace Smith, and other members of his family, describing the journey of his regiment by ship to New Orleans, Louisiana; his stay in the Marine Hospital; an expedition up the Red River under General Nathaniel Prentiss Banks; food and guerilla fighting; the fighting in the lower Shenandoah Valley of Virginia under General Philip Sheridan; the election of 1864; John Singleton Mosby's Partisan Rangers; various Union generals; the assassination of Abraham Lincoln; and the concerts and serenades presented by the band at the end of the Civil War, ending with the Grand Review of the Union Army in Washington, D. C.

4889. JAMES SMITH PAPERS, 1860 (1861-1864) 1894. 26 items. Romeo (Macomb County), Mich.

Papers of James Smith, schoolteacher, member of the 9th Michigan Infantry Volunteers, U.S.A., and farmer, chiefly relating to his service in the Civil War. Included are an officer's commission; receipts; recommendations by doctors and officers that Smith be relieved from regular duty because of his health; commendations; a register of the hospital at West Point, Kentucky, for March, 1862; and a certificate of discharge. Other items are a teaching certificate and teaching contract with the school district of Megezee Township, Michigan, 1860; a crop report for July, 1894, that Smith compiled for the state; and a photograph of Smith, ca. 1880.

4890. JAMES STRUDWICK SMITH AND THOMAS JEFFERSON FADDIS DAYBOOK, 1819-1826. 1 vol. (334 pp.) Hillsborough (Orange County), N.C.

Daybook containing the accounts of a Hillsborough merchant, 1819-1821; and the daybook, 1824-1826, of James Strudwick Smith (1790-1859), physician and U.S. congressman, 1817-1821, and of Thomas Jefferson Faddis, physician, containing entries relating to their practice and the purchase of medicines.

4891. JOHN A. SMITH PAPERS, 1862-1865. 17 items. Mount Pleasant (Cabarrus County), N.C.

Civil War letters of a Confederate soldier discussing troops, troop movements, paroles, various Union and Confederate generals, the battles of Antietam and Drewry's Bluff, and Philip Sheridan's cavalry raid to Richmond.

4892. JOHN F. SMITH PAPERS, 1832 (1851-1859) 1863. 611 items and 3 vols. Middleway (Jefferson County), W. Va.

Papers of John F. Smith, merchant, postmaster, and constable, include business papers; summonses; papers relating to the post office; advertisements of Maryland and Delaware lotteries; monthly quotation sheets of a commercial bank; two daybooks and a memorandum book; and correspondence concerning limitations on the sale of liquor in Fremont, Ohio, in 1854, the detection and capture of runaway slaves by John H. Pope of Frederick (Maryland), and his assistants, terms on which the Illinois Central Railroad Company was prepared to sell farm lands, the Improved Order of Red Men of which Smith was a member, the Know-Nothing Party, contributions for the Washington National Monument Society, Freemasons and Odd Fellows, turnpikes in western Virginia, and personal matters including the death of Smith's wife in 1858.

4893. JOHN RUFUS SMITH ACCOUNT BOOKS, 1851-1856. 6 vols. Bunker Hill (Berkeley County), W. Va.

Daybooks of a general store containing names of purchasers, and quantity and price of each item purchased.

4894. JONATHAN KENNON THOMPSON SMITH PAPERS, 1649-1971. 181 items and 11 vols. Memphis (Shelby County), Tenn.

Miscellaneous papers of Jonathan Kennon Thompson Smith include originals and copies of letters, papers, Bible records, pictures, and printed works relating to the history of the Smith, Pearson, and Thompson families who migrated from England to Virginia, North Carolina, Tennessee, and finally to Arkansas; family correspondence of Maurice Smith (1801-1871); letters, legal papers, historical notes, genealogy, military records, cemetery records, pictures, and maps pertaining to the history of Benton County, Tennessee; copies of the Civil War letters of Stephen W. Holliday, 55th Tennessee Regiment, C.S.A., to his parents; a history of Tulip and Tulip Ridge, Arkansas, by Smith entitled The Romance of Tulip (Memphis: 1965); "On this Rock . . . the Chronicle of a Southern Family," which is a history by Smith of the family of Colonel Samuel Smith and Mary Webb Smith of Abram's Plains, North Carolina; biographies of the Captain Nicholas Martiau (1591-1657) and of Samuel Granville Smith (1794-1835); anecdotes of Confederate General Nathan Bedford Forrest; a history of the Pearson family by Smith entitled "This Valued Lineage"; history of the Thompson family by Smith entitled "These Many Hearths"; albums of the Smith family containing pictures, clippings, and copies of letters and wills dating as early as 1649; genealogy of the Melton family by Herman E. Melton entitled "Sassafras Sprouts"; an anthropological study of the Indians of Kentucky Lake, Tennessee, by C. H. McNutt and J. Bennett Graham; and a pamphlet, 1961, by Smith entitled "A Statement of Faith."

4895. JOSEPH BELKNAP SMITH PAPERS, 1802 (1845-1872). 664 items and 8 vols. Columbia Mine (Columbia County), Ga.

Business papers of Joseph Belknap Smith relating to his investments in copper mines in Michigan and Tennessee, gold mines in Georgia, the New York Bay Cemetery Company, a lumber company and a cotton and land company in England, a project to build a railroad and telegraph from Caracas to La Guaira, Venezuela, a grain mill, sawmills, and salt mines and lands in Georgia. Included are contracts; scattered financial reports; schedules of property belonging to the Columbia Mining Company containing lists of slaves and their values; contracts for hiring slaves and freedmen; land deeds; broadsides of a steamboat company in Georgia; advertisement for an apparatus of Edward N. Kent for separating gold from foreign substances; letterpress book, 1849-1855, containing copies of the correspondence of Smith and one of his partners, George Wood, about their copper mines in Tennessee; diaries, 1845-1861, 1863-1864, and 1866; daybook, 1846-1850; and a ledger, 1860-1873, containing valuations of the mine and mill properties of Smith and his partners and the amount of the Confederate soldiers' tax and war taxes for some of the Civil War years. There are also letters, 1857-1860, from Eliza Annie Dunston concerning her experiences as a teacher in Illinois and Mississippi, her travels, and her social life; scattered family correspondence; reports of the Columbia Mine post office in account with both the Federal and Confederate governments; petition of a number of Wilkes County, Georgia, citizens requesting a military exemption for Smith, miller and postmaster; circulars of Alabama Central Female College and Thomson (Georgia) High School; letters from Herschel V. Johnson and Company, agents for those who had cotton tax claims against the United States government; address of Jacob R. Davis to Negro voters of the 18th district of Georgia; and correspondence, 1860s, containing references to a ball to be given in New York City in honor of the Japanese emissaries, secession sentiment in Georgia, enlistment of volunteers, camp life and rumors in the Confederate Army, marketing of scrap iron, production of salt, raising of hogs for the Confederate government, commodity prices, the siege of Petersburg and the performance of Negro troops there, the use of buildings at Emory and Henry College (Emory, Virginia) as army hospitals, Sherman's march to the sea, the impeachment of Andrew Johnson, the difficulty of securing freedmen to work on the farms in Georgia, and elections in Georgia in 1868.

4896.   JOSIAH EDWARD SMITH PAPERS, 1753 (1793-1850) 1889. 275 items. Columbia (Richland County), S.C.

Accounts and business correspondence of the firm Smith and Darrell and of the firm Smith, De Saussure and Darrell, Charleston merchants, containing comments on commercial and shipping news in the 1790s, the inroads on American commerce in 1793, and the Jay Treaty, 1794; letters, 1842-1850, from Whitemarsh B. Seabrook to his son-in-law, Josiah E. Smith, concerning his Edisto Island plantation, crops, his work with the South Carolina Agricultural Society, and family matters; business correspondence, for the 1850s and 1860s, between Smith and J. B. Sitton of Pendleton, South Carolina; and legal correspondence of the Colcock family after 1870 (Margaret Smith married Charles Jones Colcock).

4897.   JOSIAH TOWNSEND SMITH PAPERS, 1838-1913. 652 items and 8 vols. Hertford (Perquimans County), N.C. Restricted.

Correspondence, business papers, and accounts of Josiah Townsend Smith, physician and superintendent of public instruction of Perquimans County. Letters prior to 1860 are chiefly to Smith from former classmates at Monson Academy, Monson, Massachusetts, containing information on various New England academies and colleges, including Yale College (New Haven, Connecticut), Mount Holyoke Academy (Holyoke, Massachusetts), Smith College (Northampton, Massachusetts), East Hampton Academy, and Monson Academy; New England attitudes toward slavery; abolitionism and abolitionists in New England; the Fugitive Slave Law of 1850; personal liberty laws; the Free Soil Party in Massachusetts in the 1850s; conflict over slavery in the Kansas Territory; John Brown's raid; various political figures, including Daniel Webster, Charles Sumner, and Governor Whitemarsh B. Seabrook of South Carolina; and attitudes in the North and South toward secession. Several letters from Edward F. Smith, attorney, to his brother, Josiah Townsend Smith, while the latter was attending the University of Virginia Medical College, 1845-1846, discuss North Carolina politics, the sale of land and slaves, the recruiting of volunteer troops for the Mexican War, and the Whig and Locofoco parties in North Carolina. Family correspondence of the 1880s and 1890s includes information on St. Mary's School (Raleigh, North Carolina), Peace College (Raleigh), and Chowan Baptist Female Institute (Murfreesboro, North Carolina); social life and customs; and Saint Augustine, Florida. Also included are diplomas; physician's and lawyer's licenses; pharmacist's and public school teacher's certificates; land deeds; captain's commission for Josiah Smith in the North Carolina militia; Episcopalian lay reader's license; justice of the peace warrants; memorandum books; public school registers; register for Hertford Academy, Hertford, North Carolina, 1894-1895, containing names and grades of pupils, parents' names, and tuition; religious publications; advertisements, especially for medicines; promissory notes; mortgages; ledgers and daybooks for the county school superintendent and of a drugstore; bills and receipts; clippings; a volume of poetry; and physician's account books, consisting of daybooks, 1865-1895, and ledgers, 1882-1896.

4898.   LAURA JANE SMITH PAPERS, 1887-1910. 128 items. Olive Branch (Union County), N.C.

Letters of W. Lafayette Smith (d. 1907), itinerant penmanship teacher, and his wife, Emma (Walton) Smith, to his mother, Laura Jane Smith, describing the cities in North and South Carolina in which he was teaching, horticultural matters in which his mother was interested, and life in New York, New York, where they lived after 1900. A letter, 1893, describes a meeting with Charles Henry Smith, "Bill Arp."

4899.   MORGAN LEWIS SMITH PAPERS, 1864. 1 item. Saint Louis, Mo.

Copy of a telegram from Major General Cadwallader Colden Washburn, U.S.A., commander of the Department of West Tennessee, to Brigadier General Morgan Lewis Smith, U.S.A., commander of the District of Vicksburg, warning him to be on guard against an attack by Confederate General Nathan Bedford Forrest, on retreat from his raid in middle Tennessee.

4900.   ORRA (WEVER) SMITH PAPERS, 1805-1951. 54 items. Martinsburg (Berkeley County), W. Va.

Letters, 1805-1863, from Maria Wyant of Baltimore, Maryland, to her sister, Margarete Wever, of Berkeley County, West Virginia, discussing personal and family matters; letter, 1863, from Charles G. Wever, a Confederate soldier, concerning his imprisonment by the Union Army in Washington, D. C.; address by George Wever on Sergeant Smith Prentiss (1808-1850), representative from Mississippi; letters, 1927-1951, of William Robinson Leigh, artist, and his wife, Ethel (Traphagen) Leigh, who directed The Traphagen School of Fashion, describing their travels in Africa and Central America, thanking donors for gifts to the school, and discussing exhibitions given by William Leigh; and clippings and pamphlets about William Leigh's work.

4901.  OTHO I. SMITH ACCOUNT BOOK, 1864-1873.  1 vol.  (50 pp.)

Account book of Otho I. Smith and Son.

4902.  PERSIFOR FRAZER SMITH PAPERS, 1824. 1 item.  New Orleans, La.

Letter of Persifor Frazer Smith (1798-1858), attorney and brigadier-general in the U.S. Army, to Charles S. West concerning the legal details of the lease of a plantation and thirty slaves to Francis A. Bynum, including the terms of the lease, the value of the land, problems of cotton cultivation, and Louisiana's inheritance laws.

4903.  RICHARD SMITH ACCOUNTS, 1827-1848. 1 vol.  (34 pp.) Jackson County, Fla.

Administration accounts of Richard Smith's estate and a few accounts of the Baker family.

4904.  SALLIE (GOLD) SMITH PAPERS, 1853-1885.  41 items. Gerrardstown, (Berkeley County), W. Va.

Family letters to Sallie (Gold) Smith discussing personal matters, fashions, and visiting.

4905.  SAMUEL SMITH PAPERS, 1798, 1826. 2 items.  Baltimore, Md.

Letter from Samuel Smith (1752-1839), U.S. representative, 1793-1803 and 1816-1822, and senator, 1803-1815 and 1822-1833, discussing financial matters; and a routine letter from Joseph Kent, governor of Maryland, 1826-1829, transmitting some resolutions of the Maryland General Assembly.  The resolutions are not included in the collection.

4906.  SAMUEL H. SMITH LEDGER, 1850. 1 vol.  (232 pp.) Wadesboro (Anson County), N.C.

Accounts of a blacksmith.

4907.  SIMEON SMITH PAPERS, 1768-1828. 9 items and 2 vols.  Rhode Island.

Papers of Simeon Smith, a merchant, regarding costs and profits in a fishing enterprise; bills and receipts, including one for the Pawtuxet Union Academy in 1810; account book, 1771-1774, containing accounts for the sloop *Polly*; a volume, 1781-1791, containing accounts and a scattered diary; and fragments of unidentified ships' logs in 1768.

4908.  STEPHENS CALHOUN SMITH PAPERS, 1861-1913.  21 items.  Louisville (Jefferson County), Ky.

Letters from Stephens Calhoun Smith, Confederate soldier in Hampton's Legion, discussing the capture of Fort Sumter and the battles of Leesburg, Centreville, and Kelly's Ford, Virginia, and Gettysburg; essay entitled "Personal Reminiscenses of Gettysburg"; photocopy of Smith's membership certificate in the Society of the Cincinnati; photograph of the war medals awarded to Smith for his service in the C.S.A. Army; and letters explaining the provenance of the Civil War material in the collection.

4909.  SUSANNAH MEREDITH SMITH ALBUM, 1933.  1 vol.  (13 pp.)  Leonia (Bergen County), N.J.

Photographs of Susannah Meredith Smith and other members of the Smith family, and of homes of members of the Smith family.

4910.  THOMAS M. SMITH PAPERS, 1851-1877. 352 items.  Wilmington (New Hanover County), N.C.

Correspondence of Thomas M. Smith, a general merchant at Horse Shoe, North Carolina, until 1872, a wholesale dealer in Wilmington, a Republican, and collector of U.S. Internal Revenue; of his son, Andrew Smith; and of his niece, Kate Landing.  The letters, chiefly from Kate Landing and Andrew Smith, concern student life at a preparatory school in Magnolia; Davenport Female College, Lenoir, 1871-1873; Wilson Collegiate Institute, 1874; a preparatory school at Whiteville; Wake Forest College, 1875; and the University of North Carolina, Chapel Hill, 1876-1878, all in North Carolina. There are also several short essays written by Kate Landing while at school.

4911.  WASHINGTON M. SMITH PAPERS, 1831-1916.  8,578 items.  Selma (Dallas County), Ala.

Personal, legal and financial papers of Washington M. Smith (d. 1869), lawyer, planter, and president of the Bank of Selma, relating to his law practice; his appointment as legal advisor for the Bank of Alabama in Tuscaloosa; his presidency of the Bank of Selma; the development of his plantation in Dallas County; exports of cotton and naval stores through brokers in Mobile; his real estate ventures in Selma and in Minnesota, and the inheritance by his wife, Susan (Parker) Smith, of property in Texas; the movement in the 1850s for public schools; his service on the school board of Selma, 1865-1868; his service as state representative in 1844 and in 1861-1863; his struggle after the Civil War to rebuild his estate; his efforts to establish a private banking house in Selma; his partnership with John McGinnis in a general banking and stock and gold brokerage business in New York; attempts to restore the prosperity of his plantation, including contracts with many of his former slaves; his journey to England to establish cotton markets; his despondency over economic conditions in Alabama; and his consideration of migration to California.  Included are personal correspondence between Smith and his wife while on his travels; records of slave purchases and sales; correspondence, bills, and receipts relating to the running of the plantation; scattered price current bulletins for Mobile, Alabama, 1848-1866, and for Liverpool, England, 1865-1869; Smith's petition for pardon to Andrew Johnson explaining his feelings about secession and his activities during the war; and other miscellaneous items pertaining to Smith's activities. After Smith's death in 1869, the papers chiefly relate to the education of their seven children at various schools and academies, including Virginia Military Institute (Lexington, Virginia), Moore's Business College (Atlanta, Georgia), the University of Alabama (Tuscaloosa), and Shorter College (Rome, Georgia); to the settlement and administration of the Smith estate; to a family quarrel between Susan (Parker) Smith and her children over disposal of the property in Minnesota; and to the children's efforts at various occupations. Also included are letters of Colonel Hilary A. Herbert (1834-1919), U.S. congressman from Alabama, 1877-1893, and secretary of the navy, 1893-1897, and husband of Smith's daughter, Ella, chiefly concerning family matters; letters from Leila Herbert, daughter of Hilary A. Herbert and Ella (Smith) Herbert, Washington hostess, and author of The First American, His Homes and Households (1900), discussing family matters and Washington social activities; numerous account books of Susan (Parker) Smith containing records of household expenses; course of study of the Selma Study Club, 1907-1908; catalog of the San Souci girls' school near Greenville, South Carolina, 1902-1903; the annual report of Beta Theta Pi for 1896; and other miscellaneous items.

4912. WHITEFOORD SMITH PAPERS, 1807-1893. 185 items and 8 vols. Charleston, S.C.

Letters, diaries, and miscellaneous pastoral memoranda and accounts of Whitefoord Smith (1812-1893), successively a Methodist minister of Charleston, a member of the faculty of Wofford College, Spartanburg, South Carolina, and president of the Columbia Female Seminary, South Carolina. The collection contains material on the history of the Methodist Episcopal Church in South Carolina; letters from Smith's uncle, Whitefoord Smith of Leith, Scotland, commenting on the War of 1812, the Napoleonic campaign in Spain, and current happenings in England; material pertaining to the establishment in South Carolina of a Methodist Episcopal periodical free from abolitionist control; a letter from George McDuffie, concerning Smith's desire for a professorship at South Carolina College in Columbia; a copy of a letter from John C. Calhoun, concerning the case of Bishop James O. Andrew with reference to slaveholding; copy of the resolutions drawn up by the citizens of Charleston concerning the religious instruction of slaves; Civil War material relating to gifts of the Spartanburg ladies to the soldiers, friction of the government with the press, hopes which the Confederates placed in the "ram" ships, and protests against the distillation of grain during the war; and postwar material concerning the activities of his daughter, Julia V. Smith, in the temperance movement. Included also are two diaries, 1849, 1853-1863, with brief notes relative generally to the pastoral activities of Smith; accounts and memoranda, 1844-1845; a class book, 1843; outlines of sermons, 1853; sermons; and pastoral memoranda, 1838-1849 and 1847-1870.

4913. WILLIAM SMITH PAPERS, 1785-1860. 328 items. London, England.

Papers of William Smith (1756-1835), member of Parliament, relating chiefly to the movement in England to abolish slavery, including letters from William Wilberforce discussing resolutions and plans for the abolition of slavery, the anti-slavery society, the Jamaica Law, Spanish slave trade, Spanish abolition, the punishment of criminals in Great Britain, and Wilberforce's private life and political disappointments; letters from various societies and committees concerning the abolition of slavery and approving of Smith's actions; letter from Thomas Coke explaining the different slavery laws in Jamaica; letters from various plantation owners in the British West Indies discussing their attitudes against the abolition of slavery, the purchase and hiring of slaves, attitude about the care of slaves, uses of the land, crops raised, market for produce, and shipments to England; letters from Thomas Clarkson regarding methods to be used to achieve abolition; letters describing the methods and problems involved in the abolition of slavery; parliamentary speeches and resolutions against slavery; printed statements for and against slavery; letters pertaining to the abolition of slavery in Ceylon; history of the movement for abolition; newspaper excerpts and magazine articles on slavery; petitions from the West Indies showing the difficult financial position of the planters due to high taxes, shipping costs, and low prices; lists of West Indian laws concerning slavery; papers comparing the raising of sugar cane in the West Indies and in the East Indies and India; description of a riot in Barbados in 1823 and the destruction of a Methodist chapel; and miscellaneous papers and printed material on ships involved in the slave trade, methods of obtaining slaves in Africa, conditions of Negroes in Africa, food carried on slave ships, deaths on slave ships, British exports to Africa, West Indian estates and plantations, diseases and epidemics, population, treatment of slaves, breeding of slaves versus importation, conditions of slaves in the French colonies, and a planter's plan for the emancipation of slaves over a period of thirty-four years. Other correspondence concerns the plight of Scottish peasants; various parliamentary elections; Catholic Emancipation; relations with France; parliamentary reform; the Church of England; dissenters; Indians in Canada; art in England; the case of the son of James Muir who was banished for fourteen years for joining the Society for Parliamentary Reform,

1793-1797; the death of William Wilberforce; Greek revolutionary activities; and the purchase of a life insurance policy in England by Gilbert Salton. Also included are a petition from citizens of Bombay, India, listing their grievances and requesting redress; and a letter, 1817, from John Horseman including the text of Robert Southey's poem entitled "To the Exiled Patriots," which varies from the only known published version in Samuel Taylor Coleridge's *Essays on His Own Times* (1850).

4914.   WILLIAM SMITH PAPERS, 1829.
        1 item.   York District, S.C.

Letter of William Smith (ca. 1762-1840), U. S. congressman from South Carolina, 1797-1799, and U. S. senator, 1816-1823 and 1826-1831, to John Cox, et al., the Committee of the Corporation of Georgetown, concerning the upkeep of the Chesapeake and Ohio Canal.

4915.   WILLIAM SMITH PAPERS, 1781-1920.
        37 items.   Frederick County, Va.

Bills, receipts, legal papers, and miscellaneous papers pertaining to William Smith and others, including the report card, 1849, of Sarah E. R. Ballow at the Young Ladies' Institute of Charlottesville, Virginia; several railroad passes; and a newspaper clipping discussing a Fluvanna County, Virginia, arsenal used by the Continental Army during the Revolutionary War.

4916.   WILLIAM SMITH PAPERS, 1841-1885.
        11 items.   Richmond, and "Monterosa" (Fauquier County), Va.

Papers of William Smith (1797-1887), U. S. representative, 1841-1843 and 1853-1861, governor of Virginia, 1846-1849 and 1864-1865, and Confederate general, consisting of routine letters concerning appointments to the U. S. Naval Academy, appointment of a sheriff, and exemptions from the Confederate military service; letter concerning ice for the governor's mansion; letter from Smith to Judge Treadway; and a clipping containing an autobiographical letter, 1884, written by Smith.

4917.   WILLIAM SMITH PAPERS, 1855-1869.
        5 items.   North Carolina.

Personal letters to William Smith, former resident of Guilford County, North Carolina, discussing commodity prices, local news, the location of Trinity College, and Reconstruction in North Carolina.

4918.   WILLIAM ALEXANDER SMITH PAPERS, 1765-1949.  11,573 items and 101 vols.  Ansonville (Anson County), N.C.

Correspondence, legal and financial papers, volumes, printed material and other items relating to the various activities and interests of William Alexander Smith (1843-1934), businessman and investor. Records of Smith's general mercantile business, 1866-1886, include store accounts, 1875-1886, and a purchase journal, 1875-1877, listing various expenses. Records of the operation of a store with Charles A. Smith include a ledger, an invoice book, and inventories and financial reports pertaining to the store and its failure. The management of Smith's farm on the Pee Dee River is documented by records on the cotton trade, prices, the condition of crops, and marketting, and includes agreements with tenant farmers. Records of the Yadkin Falls Manufacturing Company, Milledgeville, North Carolina, 1883-1896, of which William Smith was president, include a letter book, 1887-1888, and an account book, 1876-1887, listing the expenses for the construction of this cotton mill and an inventory of mercantile goods purchased by the company. For the Eldorado Cotton Mills, Milledgeville, 1897-1906, of which Smith also was president, there are a letter book, 1899-1902; a time book, 1898-1903; a general store ledger, 1900-1903; bank check, dividend check, and deposit books, 1898-1902; correspondence with Tucker & Carter Rope Company which Eldorado supplied with goods, 1898-1902; and records of a legal and financial controversy, 1914-1919. Other textile mills in North Carolina and South Carolina are the subject of correspondence with Francis Johnstone Murdoch, Episcopal clergyman and textile executive; with Lee Slater Overman, textile executive and U.S. senator; and with James William Cannon, operator of Cannon Mills. Correspondence with George Stephens, president of the Stephens Company, developers, and officer of the American Trust Company of Charlotte, North Carolina, concerns real estate ventures, such as the development of Myers Park residential area in Charlotte. Other records relate to investment in the Southern States Finance Company, 1922-1925. Mining of gold, copper, and mica is the subject of material on the Eagle River Mining Company in Alaska, 1905-1916, the Montana Consolidated Gold Mining Company, 1905-1918, the Monarch Mining and Smelting Company, Wickenburg, Arizona, 1906-1918, and the Spruce Pine Mica Company, Inc., Spruce Pine, North Carolina, 1924-1933. Papers concerning the insurance business comprise those of the North State Fire Insurance Company and the Dixie Fire Insurance Company, both of Greensboro, North Carolina. Relating to the railroad and the automobile industries are papers of the Edwards Railway Motor Car Company of Sanford, North Carolina, 1923-1927; the David Buick Carburetor Corporation, 1922-1932; the Fox Motor Car Company, 1922-1923; and the Winston-Salem Railway through Ansonville, 1910-1911. Other business records concern lumbering in North Carolina, 1916-1925; the Carolina Remedies Company of Union, South Carolina, 1922-1925; the W. L. Hand Medicine Company of Charlotte, North Carolina, 1923-1925; the John E. Hughes Company, Inc., tobacco processor of Danville, Virginia, 1922-1924; and the Forsyth Furniture Lines,

Inc., 1922-1923. Records of William A. Smith's activities as purchasing agent, banker, and broker include ledgers, 1873-1933; daybook, 1885-1893; letter and letterpress books, 1867-1895 and 1909-1910; and other account books. Papers relating to Smith's writings include material on the publication of his Anson Guards: Company C, Fourteenth Regiment, North Carolina Volunteers, 1861-1865 (Charlotte: 1914), including correspondence with the Stone Publishing Company, and reminiscences of several members of the Guards; papers on the causes and historiography of the Civil War, especially correspondence with Samuel A'Court Ashe, 1920s and 1930s; correspondence with Benjamin Franklin Johnson, 1915-1916, concerning a biographical sketch of Smith in Johnson's Makers of America; correspondence about Smith's pamphlet on the designing of the Confederate flag and the raising of the first flag of secession in North Carolina; and correspondence and genealogical notes used in the writing of Smith's Family Tree Book, Genealogical and Biographical (Los Angeles: 1922). There are papers concerning the United Confederate Veterans, especially while Smith was commander of the North Carolina Division during the 1920s. Correspondence, bills and receipts, ledgers, and writings concerning educational institutions relate to Carolina Female College, Ansonville, of which Smith's father, William Gaston Smith, was chairman of the board of trustees; sponsorship of the Nona Institute at Ansonville, 1906-1910, oriented toward the Episcopal Church; the University of the South, Sewanee, Tennessee, of which Smith was a trustee; Davidson College, Davidson, North Carolina, which Smith had attended before the Civil War; the education of Smith's adopted son, Bennett Dunlap Nelme, at textile schools and mills, including comment about New Bedford and Lowell textile schools in Massachusetts, 1902-1907, and about North Carolina State College, Raleigh, 1900-1903; controversy over the content of history textbooks used in the state public schools, 1921; and membership on the board of managers of the Thompson Orphanage, Charlotte, North Carolina. Correspondence with Bishop Joseph Blount Cheshire and Archdeacon Edwin A. Osborne concerns affairs of the Episcopal Church, its missions, local churches, and the diocese. Relating to the Freemasons are a history of Carolina Lodge No. 141 of Ansonville and the minutes of the lodge, 1906-1925. Scattered correspondence and other papers pertain to North Carolina elections, especially the Democratic primary of 1912; the courts; the Democratic Party; county government; the good roads movement, especially in 1916; the family life and political career of Edward Hull Crump of Memphis, Tennessee, who was the son of Smith's first cousin; and politics in Mississippi and Tennessee. Other papers include the steam mill account books, 1851-1861, of Smith & Ingram who operated a sawmill in Anson County and correspondence, 1850-1851, concerning the acquisition of the steam machinery to run the mill; diary and notebook, 1765-1789, of James Auld, farmer, clerk of the court, and operator of a store for Joseph Montfort; North Carolina Argus subscription book, 1852-1853; account books, 1840-1857, of blacksmiths; account books, 1835-1858 and 1860-1864, of grist mill operators; ledger, 1835-1845, of William Gaston Smith's mercantile business; account books, 1840s and 1850s, of Joseph Pearson Smith, brother of William Gaston Smith, and operator of a mercantile business; ledger, 1858, of Joseph Pearson Smith, and ledger, 1855-1858, of Eli Freeman, carriage repairman, containing records of the sale and repair of carriages and buggies; deeds and plats; papers relating to the administration of the estates of William Gaston Smith (1802-1879), of John Smith (1772-1854), father of William Gaston Smith, and of Mary (Bellew) Smith (1775-1872), wife of John Smith; cashbook, 1875-1902, of William Alexander Smith; an inventory of notes and accounts receivable; stock dividend ledger, 1931-1934; and the financial reports of Mary (Bennett) Smith, William Alexander Smith's wife, and Bennett Dunlap Nelme, who, after 1926, were the legal guardians of William Alexander Smith.

4919.    WILLIAM D. SMITH PAPERS, 1862-1865. 21 items. North Carolina.

Family letters of William D. Smith, Confederate soldier in the 2nd North Carolina Cavalry, concerning the hardships of war, poorly equipped soldiers, desertion, and the execution of two deserters.

4920.    WILLIAM E. SMITH PAPERS, 1861-1895. 443 items. Hartleton (Union County), Pa.

Papers of William E. Smith chiefly concerning commodity prices of goods, especially cereals and flour, which Smith furnished retail dealers in Union County. Also included are several letters, 1865, from a soldier, James B. Haslet, describing his experiences and observations during his mustering out maneuvers, including the response to a rumor about efforts to free Jefferson Davis; and a clipping, 1863, from the New York Independent containing an editorial on the New York draft riots.

4921.    WILLIAM EPHRIAM SMITH PAPERS, 1844-1882. 197 items. Albany (Doughtery County), Ga.

Personal and business papers of William Ephriam Smith (1829-1890), lawyer, planter, Confederate representative from Georgia, 1864-1865, and U. S. representative, 1875-1881, dealing chiefly with routine personal, business, and legal affairs, with scattered references to the Democratic Party, 1849, and the Whig Party, 1852, in Georgia; his travels in North Carolina, 1853; military land warrants, 1855 and 1860; a lottery in Delaware, 1855; the hiring of slaves in Georgia; the Civil War, various Confederate and Union generals, commodity prices, Confederate casualties and hospitals, and exemption from military service; Andrew Female College, 1862; the suspension of the writ of habeas corpus; Reconstruction; cotton and the cotton worm in Georgia, 1869; the Republican Party and efforts to unseat Smith; a request from a Negro committee for a contribution to a float for the inaugural parade of James A. Garfield; and requests relating to post office routes and various appointments. Also included are Smith's notes on addresses delivered in the Confederate House; and Confederate bills, acts, amendments, and resolutions concerning a peace conference with the United States, finance, currency, taxes, conscription, exemptions, a mail route, the impressment of cotton, the suspension of the writ of habeas corpus, the separation of powers in the Confederate government, the use of slaves in the Confederate Army, and matters relating to national defense.

4922. WILLIAM LOUGHTON SMITH PAPERS, 1796. 1 item. Charleston, S.C.

Letter of William Loughton Smith (1758-1812), U. S. congressman, 1789-1797, to Herman LeRoy concerning public finance and national politics.

4923. WILLIAM NATHAN HARRELL SMITH PAPERS, 1838-1886. 41 items and 1 vol. Raleigh (Wake County), N.C.

Letters from William N. H. Smith (1812-1889), lawyer, politician, member of the Confederate Congress, and chief justice of the North Carolina Supreme Court, includes a letter concerning the election of Smith to the Union Literary Society (probably of Raleigh, North Carolina); letter containing comments on Richmond in 1862, on England's disposition toward the Confederacy, and on the attitude of the Negro toward the war; two letters from John Pool opposing the reelection of Smith; twelve letters written to Smith while a member of the Confederate Congress relating to routine requests such as passports, transfers, and supplies; letters concerning conditions prevailing during the Civil War; general business and legal correspondence; and memoranda and accounts. A diary, 1846-1866, contains accounts of estates for which Smith seemed to be administrator.

4924. WILLIAM PATTERSON SMITH PAPERS, 1791-1943. 22,305 items. Gloucester County, Va.

Personal and business papers of William Patterson Smith (1796-1878), merchant and planter. The early papers generally relate to the Lewis and Sparks families of Gloucester County, whose estates were administered by Thomas Smith (1785-1841), merchant and politician, and brother of William Patterson Smith. Approximately one-half of this collection pertains to the business of William Patterson Smith and Thomas Smith in conducting their mercantile firm in Gloucester and a grain trade throughout the Chesapeake area, and consists of correspondence, bills and receipts, notes, bills of lading, orders, sales accounts, chancery court records, writs, estate papers, account books, indentures, wills, inventories, bankbooks, stock certificates, and bonds. Also included is material relating to the interests of the Smiths in land speculation in Texas, Arkansas, and West Virginia; internal improvements in Virginia and North Carolina; stocks and bonds, banks and banking; property and fire insurance; and improvements in agricultural machinery, fertilizers, and farming methods. There are abundant price data on slaves, horses, clothing, dry goods, grains, drugs, farm implements, groceries, whiskeys, cotton, tobacco, and land, 1815-1860. Another major portion of the collection is the personal correspondence of William Patterson Smith with his wife, Marion (Seddon) Smith, his brother and sisters, his children, his grandchildren, and his numerous other relatives. There is also the correspondence of the Bruce and Seddon families, related through Marion (Seddon) Smith, and of Judge Beverly Randolph Wellford, Jr., also related through the Seddon family. The collection as a whole contains information on life in tidewater Virginia, 1800-1875; social life and customs; recreations and amusements; religious life; slavery; free Negroes; the county militia system; Virginia and United States politics, 1820-1880; the Hussey and McCormick reapers; agricultural societies; the panics of 1819 and 1837; the cultivation of cotton, corn, wheat, barley, oats, and sugar cane; various academies and colleges, including Yale College (New Haven, Connecticut), the University of Virginia (Charlottesville, Virginia), the University of North Carolina (Chapel Hill, North Carolina), the College of William and Mary (Williamsburg, Virginia), Virginia Military Institute (Lexington, Virginia), and the U. S. Military Academy (West Point, New York); the Seminole War; the Mexican War; the annexation of Texas; Thomas S. Dabney in Mississippi; the California gold rush; trips to Philadelphia, New York, and the Virginia Springs; Virginia constitutional conventions of 1829 and 1850; abolition and secession; manufacture of iron, cotton, and wool; military and civilian life during the Civil War; life in Richmond, Virginia, during the Civil War; Gloucester County under Union occupation; "contrabands"; Confederate military hospitals; taxation by the Confederate government; Negro raids; confiscation of property; Union blockade of the Chesapeake Bay; the United States military prison at Newport News, Virginia; freedmen; Reconstruction; coal lands in the Kanawha Valley; and phosphate mining in Tennessee.

4925. WILLIAM R. SMITH MEMORANDUM BOOK, 1852-1855. 1 vol. Scotland Neck (Halifax County), N.C.

Accounts of William R. Smith, apparently a general merchant and a dealer in turpentine.

4926.  SIR WILLIAM SIDNEY SMITH PAPERS, 1795-1801. 2 items. London, England.

Letter of Sir William Sidney Smith (1764-1840), British admiral, proposing the transfer of the Glengary Fencibles for strategic reasons; and letter from Major General Sir Eyre Coote commending Smith's assistance in the Egyptian Campaign of 1801, and reporting military news from his camp before Alexandria, Egypt.

4927.  WILLIS SMITH, SR., PAPERS, 1919-1954. 97,809 items and 4 vols. Raleigh (Wake County), N.C. Restricted.

Personal, political, and professional papers of Willis Smith, Sr. (1887-1953), lawyer and U. S. senator, 1950-1953, including correspondence, notes and speeches, financial papers, clippings, printed material, pictures, and other miscellaneous papers. The major portion of the collection consists of personal papers; the office files from his years as U. S. senator, much of which is routine correspondence; files kept by Smith while he was president of the American Bar Association, 1945-1946; papers relating to other legal organizations, including the International Bar Association, the North Carolina State Bar Association, the Wake County Bar Association, and the International Association of Insurance Counsel; and files pertaining to his service as chairman of the board of trustees of Duke University, 1947-1953. There is also material on the Patrick Henry Memorial Foundation, the Raleigh Chamber of Commerce, the American Counsel Association, the American Judicature Society, the Attorney General's Advisory Committee on Citizenship, Louisburg College (Louisburg, North Carolina), the American Law Institute, the Presidential Memorial Commission, the Association of Life Insurance Counsel, the President's Amnesty Board, the National Probation and Parole Association, the Nuremburg trials, the Interparliamentary Union, the Smithsonian Institution, the United States Territorial Expansion Memorial Commission, and Alben W. Barkley.

4928.  ELIZABETH MOORMAN SMITHSON PAPERS, 1805 (1820-1875) 1902. 620 items. Lunenberg County, Va.

Personal correspondence of Elizabeth Moorman Smithson, including letters from former classmates and pupils; family correspondence; correspondence of William Smithson, probably her father; and several letters from Confederate soldiers, including a letter, 1861, giving a Biblical justification for slavery, and a letter, 1863, from N. M. Osborn, Jr., concerning the military outlook for the South and giving a brief secondhand account of the battle of Gettysburg.

4929.  EDGAR SMITHWICK PAPERS, 1863-1867. 30 items. Martin County, N.C.

Letters from Edgar Smithwick, a Confederate soldier serving with the 61st North Carolina Regiment, to his mother concerning financial matters and economic conditions, and describing the battlefield at Petersburg, Virginia.

4930.  HANNAH SMITHWICK PAPERS, 1836-1885. 40 items. Martin County, N.C.

Family letters to Hannah Smithwick from relatives in Athens and Courtland, Alabama, primarily concerning personal matters, with occasional references to economic conditions, diseases and epidemics, religious movements, and local customs.

4931.  SMITHWICK'S CREEK PRIMITIVE BAPTIST CHURCH RECORDS, 1803-1933. 4 vols. Martin County, N.C.

Minutes, 1803-1933; and obituaries, 1850-1928.

4932.  THOMAS ARTHUR SMOOT PAPERS, 1856-1937. 1,718 items and 7 vols. Norfolk, Va.

Principally sermons delivered by Thomas Arthur Smoot (1871-1937), Methodist clergyman, discussing the Bible, Christianity, and the Methodist Church. The volumes contain notes, accounts, clippings, and writings. Also included are an address, 1856, of "Rev. J. F. Smoot" to a Southern college discussing American writing in relation to United States politics; an article by Thomas Arthur Smoot entitled "Religious Life in the Old South"; copies and drafts of his addresses and writings; clippings; and The Hesperian Literary Society medal Smoot received as an honor graduate of the class of 1895 of Trinity College, Durham, North Carolina.

4933.  ALEXANDER SMYTH PAPERS, 1822. 1 item. Washington, D.C., and Wythe County, Va.

Letter from Alexander Smyth commenting on the adjustment of a difference of opinion between himself and John Randolph, and on the interest in the presidential election of 1824 already being expressed in Washington, D. C.

4934.  SIR JAMES CARMICHAEL-SMYTH, FIRST BARONET, PAPERS, 1785-1952. 309 items and 9 vols. Nutwood, Surry, England.

Papers of Sir James Carmichael-Smyth, First Baronet, British soldier and colonial administrator; his wife, Harriet (Morse) Carmichael-Smyth; and his son, Sir James Robert Carmichael, Second Baronet, leading figure in the company that laid the first submarine telegraph cables between England and the Continent. Correspondence contains letters, 1825, from Sir James Carmichael-Smyth to his wife while he was on a military inspection tour of Canada, dealing for the most part with personal matters; letters, 1831-1833, from Sir James Carmichael-Smyth and Harriet (Morse) Carmichael-Smyth to their son commenting on Carmichael-Smyth's duties as governor of the Bahamas and describing the resistance of local planters to the governor's attempts to protect the rights of slaves and free blacks and to prepare the colony for the abolition of slavery; and scattered family correspondence, 1840-1952, relating to the activities of Sir James Robert Carmichael, Sir James Morse Carmichael, and others. Papers, 1818-1827, pertaining to the estate of General Francis Dundas include legal documents, financial statements, and minutes of the trustees of the estate. Items relating to Sir James Robert Carmichael and his business organization, the Sub-Marine Telegraph Company between Great Britain and the Continent of Europe, 1852-1860s, the right to lay a telegraph cable from Britain to Belgium, financial matters, and contracts for the manufacture of the cable. Legal, financial, and miscellaneous papers include the marriage settlement of Robert Morse and Sophia Godwin, 1785; a baptismal certificate; an army commission and grants of honor; school compositions in Latin of Sir James Robert Carmichael, 1827-1828; and financial accounts of Sir James Robert Carmichael, 1837-1841. Printed material, 1843-1919, includes a petition, ca. 1843, concerning the legal career of David Carmichael-Smyth in India; a bill of complaint from a lawsuit involving Sir James Robert Carmichael, 1860; and a leaflet, 1861, setting out Sir James Robert Carmichael's claims against the British Foreign Office for debts incurred by his father while he was governor of British Guiana. Volumes include a memoir by Harriet (Morse) Carmichael-Smyth, for the most part concerning family matters and social events through 1810, with some information about her father, General Robert Morse; diaries of Harriet (Morse) Carmichael-Smyth, 1819-1839, 1849-1863, dealing with routine family matters, the activities of Sir James Carmichael-Smyth as governor of the Bahamas, 1829-1833, and as lieutenant governor and governor of British Guiana, 1833-1838, and the business affairs of Sir James Robert Carmichael; diary of Sir James Robert Carmichael describing his experiences as aide-de-camp to the lord lieutenant of Ireland, 1839; and account books relating to household expenses, 1819; Sir James Robert Carmichael's bank accounts, 1865-1871, 1875-1880; and a record of the sale of books in the estate of Major Robert Carmichael Smyth, 1888.

4935. THOMAS SMYTH PAPERS, 1783-1789. 2 items. Kent County, Md.

Business papers of Thomas Smyth, merchant and sheriff of Eastern Neck, Kent County, Maryland.

4936. THOMAS SMYTH PAPERS, 1830-1861. 14 vols. Charleston, S.C.

Papers of Thomas Smyth, Presbyterian clergyman and author, contain manuscript copies of sermons by Smyth on communion, death, sanctification, the nature of sin, commerce and Christianity, civil polity and Christianity, and the jubilee celebration of the Second Presbyterian Church of Charleston, South Carolina, 1861. The sermons are usually dated and often contain notes on the places they were delivered. Three of the sermons have been published [J. William Flinn, (ed.), Complete Works of Rev. Thomas Smyth, D. D. (Columbia, South Carolina: 1908-1912)].

4937. SIMON SNAVELY PAPERS, 1846-1875. 89 items. Annville (Lebanon County), Pa., and Wabash (Wabash County), Ind.

Papers of Simon Snavely, a schoolteacher in Annville, Pennsylvania, and Wabash, Indiana, concern his work as a teacher and the activities and customs of his German relatives in Pennsylvania. The collection also contains the will of John Long of Lebanon, Pennsylvania, and apprenticeship papers, 1862.

4938. THOMAS D. SNEAD PAPERS, 1856-1871. 26 items. Smithfield (Johnston County), N.C.

Papers of Thomas D. Snead, county official and state representative from Johnston County, North Carolina, contain letters commenting on the gubernatorial campaign of Zebulon B. Vance and William Johnston, 1862; military preparations at Trinity College, 1861; and the activities of the 14th and 49th North Carolina Regiments, particularly in Virginia, during the Civil War.

4939. THOMAS SNEED ACCOUNT BOOK, 1821-1829. 1 vol. (36 pp.) Person County, N.C.

Blacksmith accounts.

4940. WILLIAM DORANCE SNELL PAPERS, 1861-1862. 8 items. Massachusetts.

Letters of William Dorance Snell, a soldier in the 21st Massachusetts Regiment, concern camp life at Annapolis, Maryland, and in eastern North Carolina, and sickness in the army.

4941. ROWLAND SNELLING PAPERS, 1899-1938. 35 items. Alexandria, Egypt.

Papers of Rowland Snelling, a member of the staff of The Egyptian Gazette at Alexandria, Egypt, are made up mainly of letters to Snelling from Lord Cromer, Britain's agent and consul general in Egypt, commenting on events in Egypt and numerous aspects of British policy in the area, including railways, 1902; corruption among officials, 1903; courts of law, 1903, 1905; financial policy, 1903; mail service, 1903; the Anglo-French agreement, 1904, 1905; the trustworthiness of the Egyptian army and the question of reducing the army of occupation, 1904; self-government for Egypt, 1905; and Cromer's appraisal of Charles George Gordon, 1905.

4942. JOHN N. SNIDER PAPERS, 1861-1863. 9 items. Virginia.

Letters of John N. Snider, a Confederate soldier in the Army of Northern Virginia, concern camp life, troop movements, casualties, hardships, supplies, election of officers, prisoner exchanges, recruiting, sickness, and weather.

4943. CHARLES SNOW PAPERS, 1827-1850. 5 items. Tuscaloosa (Tuscaloosa County), Ala.

Letters of Charles Snow, a physician and druggist of Tuscaloosa, Alabama, concern his business affairs; religious and social customs, especially the celebration of Christmas and the anniversary of Andrew Jackson's victory over the British in New Orleans, Louisiana; local politics; Snow's attitude toward slavery; descriptions of Henry Clay, Vice President Millard Fillmore, and President Zachary Taylor's horse, "Old Whitey," on a trip to Washington, D. C., in 1850; and excitement in New York City in 1850 over the possibility of the secession of the southern states.

4944. JOHN SNOW PAPERS, 1863-1865. 12 items. Tuscaloosa (Tuscaloosa County), Ala.

Correspondence of John Snow (b. 1843), Confederate soldier, hardware merchant, and planter. The letters concern Civil War fighting around Chattanooga, Tennessee, 1863; the Atlanta campaign, 1864; and a visit to Massachusetts after the war.

4945. SNOW FAMILY PAPERS, 1861-1865. 1 vol. Elyria (Lorain County), Ohio.

The Snow family papers contain the letters of Horace N. Snow and Samuel W. Snow, soldiers in the Union Army during the Civil War. Letters of Horace N. Snow concern his experiences as a soldier, 1861-1862, in the 8th Ohio Regiment in Virginia; his admission to Mansion House Hospital in Arlington, Virginia, as a patient and his later work there as a clerk; and his service as a military telegraph operator in Virginia. Letters of Samuel Snow of the 25th Iowa Regiment include a description of General William T. Sherman's campaign in the Carolinas, in which Snow participated.

4946. SNOW HILL PORT PAPERS, 1808. 8 items. Snow Hill (Worcester County), Md.

Bonds of George Hall, master of the sloop Washington, and of Thomas Hall of the sloop Welcome Return, for cargoes to be transported from Philadelphia, Pennsylvania, to Snow Hill, Maryland.

4947. SOCIALIST PARTY, U.S.A., PAPERS, 1951-1976. 102 items. Milwaukee, Wis.

Papers of the Socialist Party, U.S.A., concentrate mainly in the years 1973-1975 and include press releases; policy statements; minutes of national conventions and meetings of the National Committee and the National Action Committee; material on party leaders such as Frank P. Zeidler, John Quinn Brisben, Josephine Prasser, and Arthur Redler; items relating to the socialist parties of Illinois and Wisconsin; copies of socialist publications from California, Colorado, New York, Wisconsin, and Virginia; copies of the Socialist Tribune and Hammer and Tongs; and a leaflet entitled "Program of the Socialist Party, U.S.A. for 1976."

4948. SOCIALIST PARTY OF AMERICA PAPERS, 1900-1976. 230,246 items and 177 vols. Chicago, Ill., and New York, N.Y.

Papers of the Socialist Party of America contain the files of the party's national office, 1896-1976, including correspondence of the national secretaries, supplemented by the correspondence, 1900-1910, of Carl Thompson, head of the information department; minutes; resolutions; speeches; articles; press releases; memoranda; files on socialist publications; reports of organizers; reports of state secretaries; correspondence with foreign societies; and papers of the national committee, the national action committee, and the national executive committee. Papers concern the organization of the party; the difficulties of socialists accused of violating the draft and sedition laws during World War I; the division between moderates and radicals in the party in 1919 and 1936 and ideological debates in the party during the 1930s; continuous efforts to find financial support for the party; attitude of the party toward women's rights and the rights of Negro Americans; troubles with the Ku Klux Klan and similar groups in the 1920s and concern with other right wing organizations; national election campaigns, particularly the presidential election of 1932; concern for sharecroppers and relations with the Southern Tenant Farmers' Union; development of labor colleges, including Brookwood Labor College, Katonah, New York; attitude of the Socialist Party toward the civil war in Spain, 1936-1939; opposition to the entry of the United States into World War II; civil rights; employment; international socialism; relations with labor generally and with individual unions; socialized medicine; the union of the Socialist Party and the Social Democratic Federation, 1957; and opposition to American involvement in Viet Nam. Other materials from the national office files include biographical sketches of prominent socialists and correspondence and papers related to party leaders; printed party platforms, pamphlets, broadsides, leaflets, posters, campaign material, and clippings; and financial records, such as reports on bills and dues, finance committee papers, and items relating to fund raising drives.

Papers of the Young People's Socialist League and papers related to other socialist youth groups (including the American Student Union, the Red Falcons, the International Union of Socialist Youth, Students for a Democratic Society, Frontlash, and the United States Youth Council) concern organization and membership; internal debate and dissention; work in national election campaigns; civil rights; international socialism; the peace movement; and the activities of local chapters. State and local party files contain significant material relating to the socialist parties of New York State, New Jersey, and California, and items concerning various other state socialist parties. Serials in the collection include several numbers of Hammer and Tongs, Socialist International Information, and The Socialist International, and numerous individual issues of socialist publications concerning civil rights; communism; labor; war, peace, and totalitarianism; women; youth and the Young People's Socialist League; and local, national, and international socialist concerns. Volumes in the collection include a scrapbook; proceedings of the national convention of 1919 and minutes of the national convention of 1920; letter books of William Butscher, 1900-1901, and William Mailly, 1903, national secretaries of the Socialist Party; official business, 1914-1915; records of the trial of Victor Berger for sedition, 1918; financial and membership records, 1924-1931; proceedings of the International Conference of Labor and Socialist International, 1933; financial volumes such as receipt books, check stubs, payroll books, fund drive records, and account books from the period 1957-1974; and a book of pictures of prominent socialists, 1918. The national subject file contains miscellaneous items relating to art, literature, and music; children; civil rights and civil liberties; communism; education; international socialism; labor; prohibition; public health; religion; war, peace, and totalitarianism; and women. Material concerning organizations related to the Socialist Party includes the International Solidarity Committee papers; Keep America Out of War Congress papers; League for Industrial Democracy papers; and papers of the Social Democratic Federation, 1936-1957. The collection also contains miscellaneous films, tapes, and recordings from the 1950s and 1960s, including reminiscences of Norman Thomas.

The Socialist Party papers in the Duke University Manuscript Department are separated into two chronological divisions, 1896-1969 (primarily through 1957) and 1957-1976, with a parallel arrangement of papers within these divisions. The majority of the Socialist Party papers are available on microfilm, and an extensive guide and index has been prepared.

4949. SOLOMON ISLANDS ALBUM, 1906. 1 vol.

A collection of original photographs, chiefly of large plantations and estates in the Solomon Islands.

4950. M. J. SOLOMONS SCRAPBOOK, 1861-1863. 1 vol. (483 pp.) Savannah, Ga.

The M. J. Solomons scrapbook contains clippings from a number of newspapers reporting on battles and conditions in the Confederacy during the first year and a half of the Civil War. The volume contains clippings concerning the price of food and drugs; the role of women in the Confederacy; military operations and battles, particularly in the western theater; various Georgia regiments; Southern poetry about the war; reports of arrests, depredations, and atrocities by Union troops; various Confederate leaders and generals; derogatory references to Abraham Lincoln; and the foreign relations of the Confederacy.

4951. WILLIAM D. SOMERS PAPERS, 1817 (1848-1907). 546 items. Colliersville (Shelby County), Tenn.

Family and professional correspondence of William D. Somers, a surgeon in the Confederate Army. Part of the material deals with hospitals and charities in Tennessee and other Confederate States. Many of the family letters contain accounts of poverty during Reconstruction and later.

4952. FORSTER ALEXANDER SONDLEY PAPERS. 1 item. Asheville (Buncombe County), N.C.

Manuscript of an unpublished book by Forster Alexander Sondley entitled "Christianity and the Bible."

4953. SONS OF TEMPERANCE OF NORTH AMERICA. GRAND DIVISION OF VIRGINIA. COVINGTON DIVISION NO. 244, JOURNAL, 1849-1852. 1 vol. (145 pp.) Covington (Alleghany County), Va.

Minutes of the meetings of Convington Division, No. 244, Grand Division of Virginia, Sons of Temperance of North America. Volume also contains the pledge of abstinence with the signatures of the members, a list of officers of Covington Division, some financial entries, and notes on withdrawals, violations of the pledge, and reinstatements.

4954. SONS OF TEMPERANCE OF NORTH AMERICA. GRAND DIVISION OF VIRGINIA. WORTH DIVISION, NO. 44, LEDGER AND ACCOUNT BOOK, 1853-1856. 1 vol. Port Republic (Rockingham County), Va.

Ledger and account book of Worth Division, No. 44, Grand Division of Virginia, Sons of Temperance of North America.

4955. SONS OF VETERANS, UNITED STATES OF AMERICA. CONNECTICUT. WILLIAM B. WOOSTER CAMP, NO. 25, MINUTES, 1887-1910. 1 vol. (804 pp.) Ansonia (New Haven County), Connecticut.

Routine minutes of meetings of William B. Wooster Camp, No. 25, of the Sons of Veterans, a patriotic society of descendants of Union Army veterans.

4956. CHARLES JONES SOONG PAPERS, 1884-1887. 6 items. China.

Letters from Charles J. Soong (1861-1918), a Chinese who attended Trinity College, Randolph County, North Carolina, through financial assistance of General Julian S. Carr, addressed to members of the family of James Southgate. Soong was the father of Mei-ling (Soong) Chiang (Madame Chiang Kai-shek). [See Emily Hahn, The Soong Sisters (New York: 1943).]

4957. ARMAND SOUBIE PAPERS, 1836 (1865-1876) 1889. 141 items and 26 vols. New Orleans, La.

Papers and account books of Armand Soubie, a gunsmith, and his successor, Phillippe Bouron.

4958. PIERRE SOULÉ PAPERS, 1841-1864. 45 items. New Orleans, La.

Papers of Pierre Soulé, diplomat, United States senator, and Confederate official, contain letters from Soulé to Henri Rémi, written in French, concerning legal cases, Soulé's imprisonment during the Civil War by the Union government and his exile to Cuba, the attitude of European countries toward the American Civil War, and the situation in Charleston, South Carolina, during the war. The collection also contains a number of unsigned and undated literary papers, including a series of letters describing Guadeloupe and a critical article on the poetry of Adrien Rouquette of Louisiana.

4959. ALBERT SOUNER PAPERS, 1863. 2 items. Strasburg (Shenandoah County), Va.

Personal letters of Lillie E. Souner and Albert Souner.

4960. SOUTH AFRICA PAPERS, 1943-1945. 137 items. Pretoria, South Africa.

Copies of the Commercial Newsletter and the Weekly Newsletter, two processed reports on political, social, economic, and educational matters in South Africa and the involvement of South Africa in World War II.

4961. SOUTH CAROLINA, SAINT LUKE'S PARISH. PUBLIC SCHOOLS. BOARD OF COMMISSIONERS MINUTES, 1827-1867. 1 vol. (98 pp.) Grahamville (Saint Luke's Parish), S.C.

Minutes of meetings of the board of commissioners of public schools in Saint Luke's Parish, South Carolina.

4962. SOUTH CAROLINA FEDERATION OF LABOR PAPERS, 1919-1953. 84 items and 49 vols. Charleston, S.C.

The papers of the South Carolina Federation of Labor (AFL) contain correspondence, 1931-1947, primarily drawn from the files of Aloysius Flynn, president of the South Carolina Federation of Labor from 1940 to 1942, concerning conventions, resolutions, union meetings, subscription books, and a judicial appointment. Papers also contain convention proceedings of the South Carolina Federation, 1928-1953; proceedings of the Tennessee Federation of Labor, 1950; reports, reviews, and convention yearbooks of the South Carolina Federation; a roster of officers and delegates of the Metal Trades Council of Charleston, South Carolina, 1919-1921; issues of the official organ of the South Carolina Federation, The South Carolina Federationist; and issues of The Boilermakers Journal, the official organ of the International Brotherhood of Boilermakers, Iron Ship Builders and Helpers of America.

4963. SOUTH MATTAMUSKEET PRIMITIVE BAPTIST CHURCH MINUTES, 1808-1853. 1 vol. (178 pp.) Hyde County, N.C.

Minutes of the South Mattamuskeet Primitive Baptist Church of Hyde County, North Carolina, including a copy of the church covenant, 1808, and a copy of the articles of faith.

4964. SAMUEL LEWIS SOUTHARD PAPERS, 1823-1828. 5 items. Flemington (Hunterdon County), N.J.

Letters to Samuel Lewis Southard (1787-1842), United States senator, cabinet officer, and governor of New Jersey, concerning appointments; and a letter, 1824, to Southard from Montfort Stokes of North Carolina concerning the presidential election of 1824 and a report which Stokes was preparing for the North Carolina legislature on internal improvements.

4965. SOUTHERN EXPRESS COMPANY RECEIPT BOOK, 1861-1862. 1 vol. (206 pp.) Richmond, Va.

Receipts for shipments of Confederate treasury notes to various cities in the South.

4966. SOUTHERN VULCANITE PAVING COMPANY MINUTE BOOK, 1888-1903. 1 vol. (289 pp.) Savannah, Ga.

Minutes of the board of directors of the Southern Vulcanite Paving Company.

4967. ROBERT SOUTHEY PAPERS, 1791-1840. 17 items and 2 vols. Keswick, Cumberland, England.

Papers of Robert Southey (1774-1843), British poet and author, include letters to Thomas Philips Lamb containing light verse and commenting on the French Revolution, Southey's marriage, and his literary aspirations. There are typed copies of letters to Southey's daughter and to Caroline Bowles, later his second wife [originals in the Bristol Libraries]; and other letters concerning the publication of Southey's "Joan of Arc," his daily work routine, and the study of law and foreign languages. One volume (11 leaves) contains literary notes by Southey, a letter by him referring to his History of Brazil, and one by Caroline Southey concerning her husband's health; an engraving by Nash of Southey in his study; and a small portrait. The other volume is a handwritten copy of Southey's poem, "Oliver Newman."

4968. JAMES SOUTHGATE PAPERS, 1794 (1851-1935). 1,916 items and 10 vols. Durham, N.C.

Papers of James Southgate, educator and pioneer insurance agent in North Carolina, and his family, include personal letters of Myra Ann (Muse) Southgate, mother of James Southgate; and letters of Harriet Sophia Southgate describing student life in Williamsburg, Virginia, 1817, 1836, and the panic of 1837. Papers of James Southgate and his wife, Delia Haywood (Wynne) Southgate, include letters of James Southgate as a student at the University of Virginia, 1851; letters, 1851-1855, concerning teaching duties of James Southgate at schools established by his father, James Summerville Southgate, in King and Queen County, Virginia, and Norfolk, Virginia; correspondence between James Southgate and Delia Haywood Wynne before and after their marriage, and general correspondence of the Southgate family concerning religious life, yellow fever epidemics, and the management of the Norfolk school; Civil War letters of James Southgate and Llewellyn Southgate relating to Confederate Army life in Virginia, the defeat of General Lawrence O'Bryan Branch near Ashland, Virginia, 1862, and operations of Union ironclads on the James River in Virginia; letters pertaining to James Southgate's attempts to raise money for Olin Agricultural and Mechanical College in Olin, North Carolina, including descriptions of life in New York City, 1867, and a lecture there by Charles Dickens; letters, 1871, of James Southgate on Reconstruction in North Carolina; and letters, especially after 1888, describing trips by James Southgate and members of his family to various resorts in New York State. Papers of James Haywood Southgate, son of James Southgate, concern his management of the insurance firm in Durham, North Carolina, established by his father; and his work on the board of trustees of Trinity College, Durham, North Carolina, especially in the controversy, 1898, between Walter Clark of the board of trustees and John C. Kilgo, president of Trinity College, and the controversy involving John Spencer Bassett, 1903. Papers of Mattie Logan (Southgate) Jones, daughter of James Southgate, concern genealogical studies of the Jones and Southgate families; her collection of rocks and mineral ores; and her work for civic improvement in Durham, North Carolina, including woman suffrage. Papers of Celestia Muse (Southgate) Simmons pertain to her career as a concert singer and her work at Brenau College, Gainesville, Georgia. Papers of James Southgate Jones, son of Mattie Logan (Southgate) Jones, concern his experiences as a student at Bingham School, Asheville, North Carolina, and local events in Durham, North Carolina, in the 1920s and 1930s. Volumes in the collection include "Programs and Committees of Durham Civic Association, 1915-1916," and the records of a Durham baseball club, 1891.

4969. EDWARD SOUTHWELL PAPERS, 1703-1724. 5 items. London, England.

Letters to Edward Southwell, member of the British House of Commons, concerning family matters, the debts of Edward Blackwell, and a trip made by Southwell's son.

4970. C. EUGENE SOUTHWORTH PAPERS, 1858-1866. 164 items. Hardwick (Worcester County), Mass.

Civil War letters of C. Eugene Southworth of the 31st Massachusetts Regiment, Fitzroy Southworth of the 10th Massachusetts Battery, Marcus Emmons of the 21st Massachusetts Regiment, and Martin Emmons of the 6th Connecticut Regiment concern General Benjamin F. Butler's expedition to the Gulf of Mexico and the Mississippi, 1862-1864, including action at Galveston, Texas, and Port Hudson, Louisiana; troop movements and artillery engagements in Maryland and Virginia, 1862-1865; camp life and troop movements in Burnside's division on the coast of North Carolina; duty on the South Carolina coast, 1861-1862; fighting in the peninsula of Virginia during the advance on Petersburg, Virginia, 1864; Union troop movements in Tennessee, 1864; and general comments on camp life, economic conditions, and supplies.

4971.  EMMA DOROTHEA ELIZA (NEVITTE) SOUTHWORTH PAPERS, 1849-1901. 342 items. Georgetown, D.C.

Literary correspondence of E. D. E. N. Southworth (1819-1899), popular novelist, with Robert Bonner, editor of the New York Ledger, concerning the publication of her stories, other business matters, Southworth's hatred of the Confederates, personal and family matters, and Bonner's race horses. There are also letters from Southworth to friends and relatives discussing personal and literary matters, and clippings concerning Southworth and her writing.

4972.  ELIZABETH SOWERS PAPERS, 1863. 2 items. Davidson County, N.C.

Personal letters from Elizabeth Sowers to Charles T. Pope, a Confederate soldier.

4973.  CHARLES H. SOWLE PAPERS, 1862-1866. 134 items. New Albany (Floyd County), Ind.

Civil War letters of Charles H. Sowle, a Union soldier in the 4th Kentucky Regiment, Cavalry, in Kentucky, Tennessee, and Georgia, from 1862 to 1864, concerning camp life, morale, troop movements, and skirmishes.

4974.  CLAUDE RAYMOND SOWLE PAPERS, 1858-1905. 9 items and 1 vol. Tomah (Monroe County), Wis.

Papers of Claude Raymond Sowle contain items dealing with family matters and land transactions, and material relating to Sowle's experiences in the 3rd Wisconsin Regiment during the Spanish-American War, including letters from Sowle and his diary, April-October, 1898, describing daily army life.

4975.  PLEASANT SOWELL PAPERS, ca. 1820. 1 vol.

Manuscript tune-book for sacred music written in shape-notes.

4976.  MRS. J. H. SPAFFORD PAPERS, 1913-1925. 6 items. New York, N.Y.

Letters to Mrs. J. H. Spafford from Vassar College, Poughkeepsie, New York, acknowledging the establishment of her gift scholarship; and one from Hamlin Garland, concerning the Town Hall Club.

4977.  RICHARD DOBBS SPAIGHT PAPERS, 1757 (1780-1836) 1853. 14 items. New Bern (Craven County), N.C.

Letters and papers of Richard Dobbs Spaight and of his son, establishing the claim of the elder Spaight (1758-1802), delegate to the Constitutional Convention of 1787 and governor of North Carolina, 1792-1795, 1798-1801, to a large tract of land in Craven County; and a paper endorsing a political appointment, 1785. There are also papers of his son, Richard Dobbs Spaight, Jr. (1796-1850), including a certificate of William Hill's appointment as secretary of state, 1836, and a letter from William Gaston, concerning a meeting of the trustees of a New Bern theater.

4978.  SPAIN CUSTOMS DUTIES, 1755. 1 vol. (312 pp.) Cadiz, Spain.

"Razon individual de los derechos que contribuien en la aduana de Cadiz," evidently a private record kept by a merchant of Cadiz containing an account of duties demanded by law and those actually collected in practice, and historical material on the development of customs duties, fiscal policies, and the guild merchants during the first half of the eighteenth century.

4979.  SPAIN PAPERS (POLITICAL AND MILITARY), 1427-1832. 6 items and 5 vols.

Miscellaneous legal and official documents; a volume of royal decrees (early 1700s) pertaining to the Americas and the Philippine Islands; a volume, "Indios Idolatras," by Martin de Fisner (1608), concerning the natives in New Granada (Colombia); a report on defense plans for Vera Cruz, New Spain (Mexico); a political satire, "El Siglo Illustrada," by Vera de la Ventosa, on the ministry of D. Pablo de Olavide, asistencia in Seville, 1767-1778; and a Spanish translation (1832) of a history of the Peninsular War written by an anonymous Frenchman (1808), including detailed maps of the battles of Medina de Rio Seco and Vimeiro, and the Andalucian campaign. In the Spanish language.

4980.  SPAIN PAPERS (FINANCIAL), 1624-1906. 17 items.

Papers on manufacturing, commerce, and public and private finance, including a report on the seizure by the Spanish government of a private treasure vessel from the Indies, 1544; a report concerning the debt of Castile, 1647; royal decrees on coinage, 1662, 1730; a report on the millones tax, 1747; the testimony of Francisco Solo Cado in Philadelphia concerning shipment of shellfish and production of indigo in Guatemala, 1787 [copy made in 1788]; a draft report on the real estate held by prominent Castilian families, 1797; reports to the king, 1824, 1830, on the activities of several commercial companies; an undated dissenting opinion of D. Diego de la Servio in the Council of Castile against a proposed bread tax; and a record of a license of Cebrian de Caritate of Seville for exporting slaves to Haiti. In the Spanish language.

4981. SPAIN PAPERS (MISCELLANEOUS), 1749-1862. 2 items and 2 vols.

A volume of letters and documents concerning the foundation of free primary schools in Cordoba; a narration by Juan Rojas on the history and geography of Ecuador; testimony on the nobility of the names of Corria, Tellez, and Barraona, 1776; historical notes by José Pelleza y Tovar, ca. 1639; and other unrelated items. In the Spanish language.

4982. SPAIN. MINISTRY OF FOREIGN AFFAIRS. CONSULATE. CHARLESTON, SOUTH CAROLINA. PAPERS, 1794-1898. 4,664 items and 46 vols.

Dispatches from the Madrid government, Spanish diplomatic and consular representatives in the United States, and officials in Florida, Cuba, and Puerto Rico, addressed to the Spanish consulate in Charleston, South Carolina. Prior to 1803 there are similar dispatches addressed to the Spanish vice consul at Savannah. Topics include Spanish fear of American filibustering in Florida in the 1790s, especially the activities of Samuel Hammond in 1794; the fear of English invasion of Florida, 1796, or invasion by Americans sympathetic to England; and privateering and the actions of William Augustus Bowles in seizing the fort at St. Marks (Appalachee) in 1800. Papers of the 1830s and after concern political affairs in Spain, the Carlist War, and Spanish expectations of a favorable ruling from the U. S. Supreme Court in the _Amistad_ case, 1841. Material concerning the fear of American filibustering activity in Cuba extends from the 1840s to the 1890s, and includes comment on American neutrality policy and on Northern support for and Southern opposition to filibustering after the Civil War. During the Civil War period papers relate to neutrality of the consulate; the capture of Spanish property in American vessels by Confederate privateers; the seizure of the _Nuestra Señora de Regla_ by Union forces; Beauregard's claim to have lifted the Charleston blockade, 1863; and the bombardment of Charleston. There are lists of ships entering and leaving Charleston harbor in violation of the blockade. Papers of 1865-1866 concern Spain's naval war with Chile and Peru and activity in the United States of Chilean privateers. Most of the papers in the collection are of a routine nature and concern shipping, health conditions, passports, changes of government in Spain, and legal problems encountered by Spaniards in South Carolina. Numerous papers relate to commerce between Charleston, Cuba, and Puerto Rico; and after the Civil War there are letters of the vice consul in Wilmington, North Carolina, relating to shipping at that port.

Bound volumes include letter books, shipping and passport registers, logbooks, crew lists, and an inventory of consular property. The shipping registers, 1850-1860, 1871-1896, contain information on the nature and value of cargoes entering and leaving Charleston, and on the nationality, type, origin, and destination of vessels calling at the port. Letter books relate almost entirely to such commercial affairs as the arrival and departure of Spanish ships, prices of goods, tariffs, legal problems of merchants and shippers, costs of ship repairs, and the discipline of Spanish seamen. For the Civil War period, reports of consul Francisco Muñoz Ramón de Moncada describe conditions in Charleston and news of political and military events within the Confederacy; French intrigues in Texas; the attack on Fort Sumter; Confederate policy on privateering; the capture of Fort Hatteras and other points along the coast; the ineffectiveness of the blockade; conditions in Charleston and the flight of residents; and Confederate conscription policies, especially as they concerned citizens of foreign countries. Post-Civil War letter books relate almost exclusively to routine commercial matters.

4983. SPAIN. MINISTRY OF FOREIGN AFFAIRS. VICE CONSULATE. SAVANNAH, GEORGIA. PAPERS, (1835-1897) 1935. 975 items and 4 vols.

This collection consists almost entirely of communications directed to the Spanish vice consulate in Savannah by the Madrid government, Spanish ministers, consuls, and vice consuls in the United States, and governing officials in Puerto Rico and Cuba. Most of the records concern Spain's constant concern for Cuba and the fear of filibustering expeditions from the United States; efforts of the United States government to maintain neutrality; meetings and organizations of exiles in the United States; and the sources of intelligence on such activities. Many letters deal with routine matters concerning Cuba, customs duties, shipping regulations, passports, and health certificates. There are also a number of references to political developments in Spain and to the Spanish war with Chile and Peru in 1865-1866. A few items concern Spanish neutrality during the American Civil War and the Union blockade of Confederate ports.

4984. ROBERT SPAINHOURD PAPERS, 1862. 14 items. [Rowan County, N.C.?]

Letters from Spainhourd, a Confederate soldier, to his wife, Phoebe.

4985. MRS. CHARLES SPALDING RECIPE BOOK, 1871. 1 vol. (88 pp.) Sapelo Island (McIntosh County), Ga.

Book of recipes.

4986. LYMAN GREENLEAFE SPALDING PAPERS, 1835-1889. 237 items. Portsmouth (Rockingham County), N.H.

Letters by Spalding, nephew of Admiral Enoch Greenleafe Parrott, written to members of his family and describing his service in the U. S. Navy, including the battle of Port Royal, South Carolina; the capture of blockade runners; the blockade of Charleston; life at the U.S. Naval Academy, Newport, Rhode Island; the Asiatic Squadron in the 1870s, with descriptions of people, scenery, customs, and politics in ports of China, Japan, the Middle East, and the East Indies; the naval hospital in Yokohoma, Japan; and a coastal survey around New Orleans. There are frequent references to musical events, operas, and singing groups. Also in the collection are a few financial papers, an account of Spalding's death during an experiment with torpedoes in 1881, and a portrait taken in 1876.

4987. SAMUEL P. SPALDING PAPERS, 1828. 1 vol. Springfield (Washington County), Ky.

An address, delivered at St. Mary's, a Catholic school for girls, Springfield, supporting the presidential candidacy of Andrew Jackson.

4988. THOMAS SPALDING PAPERS, 1772-1844. 8 items. Sapelo Island (McIntosh County), Ga.

Photocopies of papers relating to Spalding, planter, state legislator, and member of the 9th U.S. Congress, including a marriage settlement, 1772, between James Spalding, merchant of Frederica, St. Simon Island, Georgia, and Margery McIntosh; accounts of Thomas Spalding with Edward Swarbreck, 1804; a pamphlet by Spalding on sugar cane in South Carolina; letters of 1816 and 1844 describing the use of tabby in building construction; accounts of Oglethorpe's plantation; and land survey data by James J. Garrison.

4989. [HENRY S. SPAULDING?] PAPERS, 1862-1864. 2 items. Ohio.

A letter from a soldier in the 42nd Illinois Volunteers at Benton Barracks, Saint Louis, Missouri, evaluating the leadership of Pope, Foote, Grant, Sherman, and Hurlbut Federal hospitals in Saint Louis; and the battle of Shiloh. There is also a letter from a divinity student named "Jas.," a conscientious objector who describes work with prisoners of war.

4990. IRA SPAULDING PAPERS, 1862-1863. 7 items. Niagara Falls (Niagara County), N.Y.

Letters from Spaulding, officer in the 50th Regiment of New York Engineers and later brevet brigader general, commenting on army life and his work building pontoon bridges during the Peninsular Campaign and later across the Potomac and the Shenandoah. Most of the letters are addressed to John Dunklee, proprietor of the Clifton Hotel, Niagara Falls. The collection also contains two countersigns for April 3 and 20, 1862, of the Army of the Potomac.

4991. IKE [SPENCE?] PAPERS, 1865-1868. 4 items. Madison County, Ga.

Personal letters from Ike [Spence?] to his "Uncle Joel," commenting on local gossip, desertions in the Confederate Army, and crops.

4992. CORNELIA PHILIPPS SPENCER PAPERS, 1888-1889. 6 items. Chapel Hill (Orange County), N.C.

Two letters, with typed copies, from Spencer to R. B. Creecy describing a tragedy in the life of John De Berniere Hooper and relating her problems with her publisher over editorial changes in First Steps in North Carolina History (Raleigh: 1889).

4993. FRANK E. SPENCER PAPERS, 1862-1864. 13 items. Naugatuck (New Haven County), Conn.

Letters from friends in the Union Army, including descriptions of the occupation of New Orleans, the Atlanta campaign, 1864; and life in the 9th New York Volunteer Artillery and reflections on the Washington scene, 1864.

4994. GEORGE ELIPHAZ SPENCER PAPERS, 1872. 1 item. Decatur (Morgan County), Ala.

A letter to Spencer, U.S. senator from Alabama, written by W. W. D. Turner and concerning alleged malpractice of J. P. Southworth, district attorney in Alabama. The letter contains marginal remarks by Spencer, who forwarded it to Attorney General George Henry Williams.

4995. GEORGE TREVOR SPENCER PAPERS, 1854. 1 item. Edgemoor, Derbyshire, England.

A letter from Lord Stanley, later 15th Earl of Derby, commenting on Harriette Macdougall; the Crimean War and the British government; Lord Dalhousie; Lord Ribblesdale; relations with the United States; Jamaican politics; Lord Raglan; and Aubrey George Spencer, bishop of Jamaica. The letter was addressed to Mrs. Spencer, either Harriet Spencer, wife of George Trevor Spencer, or Eliza Spencer, wife of Aubrey George Spencer.

4996. GEORGE W. SPENCER PAPERS, 1785 (1870-1885) 1898. 97 items. Chesterfield County, S.C.

Business papers of Spencer, cotton planter of Chesterfield County, and the Meggs family of Anson County, North Carolina, largely consisting of invoices for cotton shipped to Charleston in the 1870s and 1880s; bills; receipts for general merchandise; tax receipts; and contracts with freedmen. There is also information on Reconstruction politics; the Interstate Convention of Farmers, Atlanta, 1887; cotton prices; South Carolina militia; and fighting below Richmond in

August, 1864, in which Negro troops were involved. A diary describes Spencer's daily life, especially the time he spent hunting.

4997. HERBERT SPENCER PAPERS, 1862. 1 item. London, England.

A note by Spencer (1820-1903), British philosopher, acknowledging receipt of a brochure on psychology.

4998. OLIVIA E. SPENCER PAPERS, 1840-1933. 175 items. Buckingham County, Va.

Letters to Olivia Patterson (later Mrs. Luther M. Spencer), from relatives chiefly concerning family and personal matters. The Civil War period is represented by letters from her brother, George B. Patterson, describing life in the 21st Regiment of Virginia Infantry, Patterson's fluctuating morale, and trench warfare before Petersburg. There is some genealogical data in letters of ca. 1902-1911.

4999. WILLIAM SPEROW PAPERS, 1857-1887. 67 items and 1 vol. Falling Waters (Berkeley County), W. Va.

Letters, legal papers, bills and receipts of a West Virginia farmer. In part they concern the difficulties of his life during the Civil War after he had voted for secession but subsequently openly supported the Union. There are also family letters relating to Benjamin F., John E., and Rebecca Sperow. A daybook, 1857-1885, includes parts of a war diary with accounts of Sperow's imprisonment by both Union and Confederate forces.

5000. J. L. SPERRY PAPERS, 1864-1866. 14 items. New Haven (New Haven County), Conn.

Civil War letters from Sperry to his sister, Mrs. Royal C. Nettleton, describing service with the 1st Regiment of Connecticut Cavalry in Maryland and Virginia and commenting on the battle of Winchester. In 1866 Sperry served with the 3rd United States Cavalry at Little Rock, Arkansas.

5001. WILLIAM ARNOLD SPICER PAPERS, 1865-1885. 3 vols. Providence, R.I.

This collection contains the diary, 2 vols., kept by Spicer (1845-1913) as a member of Henry Ward Beecher's Plymouth Church Excursion from New York to Charleston in 1865 for the ceremonial re-raising of the United States flag over Fort Sumter. Included are descriptions of the reaction in New York to news of Lee's surrender, conditions in Charleston at the end of the war, and the reception given to word of Lincoln's assassination. Also in the collection is a copy of Spicer's The Flag Replaced on Sumter (Providence: 1885), a paper presented before the Rhode Island Soldiers and Sailors Historical Society in 1884, based largely on the diary.

5002. ENOCH SPINKS PAPERS, 1803 (1840-1883) 1891. 49 items. Randolph County, N.C.

Family correspondence and papers of Enoch Spinks, including a deed signed by James Iredell and a letter from Trinity College, 1874.

5003. JOHN SPINKS ARITHMETIC MANUSCRIPT AND COPYBOOK, 1832. 1 vol. (38 pp.)

Arithmetic problems and rules, and pages apparently devoted to penmanship practice.

5004. ALEXANDER SPOTSWOOD PAPERS, 1732-1840. 2 items. Germanna (Spotsylvania County), Va.

A letter from Spotswood (1676-1740), lieutenant governor of Virginia, to Charles Carrol about an indentured wheelwright, Edmund Vade, and other indentured servants; and a copy of Spotswood's will.

5005. MELCHIZEDEK SPRAGINS PAPERS, 1790 (1816-1835) 1863. 210 items. Halifax County, Va.

Family correspondence of Melchizedek Spragins, including letters from Thomas S. Spragins while a student at the University of North Carolina, Chapel Hill, 1808-1809, commenting on his studies, the people whom he met, and student life there in 1809; and while assistant quartermaster at Richmond during the War of 1812, commenting on the burning of Washington and the reaction of the soldiers. Included also are a few letters from Melchizedek Spragins, Jr., a member of the Virginia House of Delegates in 1825, and from Rebecca Spragins, who married Elisha Barksdale.

5006. ROBERT STITH SPRAGINS PAPERS, 1851-1877. 12 vols. Huntsville (Madison County), Ala.

Account books, ledgers, and a daybook relating to the sale of miscellaneous merchandise, wood, meal, and salt; also accounts concerning the sale of real property. One volume, 1865-1874, contains Spragins's accounts for the estate of James Clemens. A letterpress book contains copies of letters, 1866-1869, from Tibbets and Thompson, merchants of Huntsville, to firms in Kentucky, Tennessee, Ohio, and Missouri, concerning orders and payment for foodstuffs and perhaps other merchandise. Letters in this volume between 1872 and 1875 are by Robert Stith Spragins and relate to credit, loans, insurance, and legal matters.

5007. STITH B. SPRAGINS NOTEBOOK, 1814. 1 vol. (88 pp.) Nottoway Co., Va.

Commonplace book containing copied passages on education.

5008. JOHN TITCOMB SPRAGUE PAPERS, 1863. 1 item. New York, N.Y.

A letter from General William Henry French, commander of the Third Army Corps, to General Sprague, adjutant general of the state of New York, commending Lieutenant Martindale of the 1st New York Cavalry, then commander of French's escort.

5009. WILLIAM SPRAGUE PAPERS, 1863. 2 items. Providence, R.I.

A military commission signed by Sprague (1830-1915) as governor of Rhode Island, and an order from William E. Hamlin, provost marshal, to John E. Barber regarding failure to report for military service.

5010. WILLIAM BUEL SPRAGUE PAPERS, 1843. 1 item. Albany, N.Y.

A social note by Sprague (1795-1876), clergyman and autograph collector.

5011. THOMAS SPRING-RICE, FIRST BARON MONTEAGLE OF BRANDON, PAPERS, 1831-1842. 4 items. London, England.

Miscellaneous letters of Spring-Rice, including an order to Messrs. Durand & Co., wine and brandy merchants, 1831; an evaluation of the ballot as a means of protecting the freedom of elections, 1837; and a commendation for a review of parliamentary proceedings on the Corn Laws, 1842. A letter from Sir James Stephen, undersecretary for the colonies, evaluates the prospects of missionary work in Jamaica for Monteagle's son, Aubrey Richard Spring-Rice, a Church of England clergyman, 1842.

5012. W. D. SPRUILL PAPERS, (1874-1880) 1885. 76 items. Franklinton (Franklin County), N.C.

Letters from W. D. Spruill, a local representative of a number of insurance companies.

5013. WILLIAM A. SPRUILL PAPERS, 1852-1867. 6 items. Washington County, N.C.

Business letters of William A. Spruill, farmer and Confederate soldier, concerning a deed to a tract of land in Washington County; bills and receipts; and a letter from Spruill's son attending Trinity College, Randolph County, North Carolina, concerning his expenses there.

5014. ALEXANDER SPRUNT & SON, INC., PAPERS, 1779 (1875-1953) 1960. 5,860 items and 235 vols. Wilmington (New Hanover County), N.C.

Account books, ledgers, journals, cashbooks, purchase and sales journals, inventories, and other subsidiary books, 1870s-1950s, and some office files and correspondence of a major cotton exporting firm located in Wilmington, North Carolina, and shipping goods to Great Britain, France, Germany, and elsewhere in Europe, which it purchased from the Carolinas, Georgia, Texas, and other states and processed in its compress facilities. Included are papers representing various domestic and foreign subsidiaries and branch offices, especially Champion Compress and Warehouse Company, the Wilmington Compress and Warehouse Company, Alexander Sprunt & Son, Inc. (of Delaware, a holding company), and the company's offices at New York, New York, and Le Havre, France. The letters date mostly 1904-1910 and 1919-1921, and are largely files of James Sprunt, reflecting his activities in business and his interests in secular and theological education, the Presbyterian Church in the United States, and North Carolina history. There is also material on the Laymen's Missionary Movement, and the Presbyterian mission at Kiangyin, China. Correspondents include Alexander Sprunt (1815-1884), Alexander Sprunt (1852-1937), Alexander Sprunt (b. 1898), James Sprunt (1847-1924), Kenneth Mackenzie Murchison, Francis Herman Packer, John Miller Wells, John Campbell White, and Edward Jenner Wood. There is an inventory filed with the collection.

5015. DAVID SQUIER PAPERS, 1773-1819. 11 items. Orangeburg District, S.C.

Plats of land surveyed by David Squier for the executors of the estate of Christopher Rowe, showing name of purchaser, number of acres, and purchase price.

5016. EDWARD STABLER AND WILLIAM STABLER PAPERS, 1793-1852. 47 items. Alexandria, Va.

Family and business correspondence of two pharmacists; included is information on prices of drugs, prescriptions, and the establishment of a quarterly meeting of Quakers.

5017. ABBY E. STAFFORD PAPERS, 1859-1866. 44 items. New Carlisle (Clark County), Ohio.

Civil War letters, largely by Samuel McKinney Stafford to his sister Abby Stafford, and to other members of his family. Topics include military events and army generals in Missouri and Arkansas; depredations by Union troops; Confederate guerilla activity; immorality of troops; profiteering by officers; contrabands; illness; a hospital in Keokuk, Iowa; Sherman's advance through Georgia and the capture of Fort McAllister on the Ogeechee River; the condition of former Federal prisoners at Vicksburg, including survivors of Andersonville; the wartime growth of Cairo, Illinois, and Memphis, Tennessee; and the decline of Vicksburg. Units mentioned are the 16th Ohio Independent Battery of Light Artillery and the 47th Regiment of Illinois Infantry Volunteers.

5018.  JOHN W. STALEY PAPERS, 1814-1903. 800 items and 7 vols. Randolph County, N.C., and Whitman County, Washington Terr.

The collection contains family letters of the descendants of John Staley, chiefly of his sons, John W., Eborn, and Daniel L. Staley. Topics include travel and settlement in Indiana, Kansas, Missouri, North Carolina, and Washington Territory; comparisons of prices and the scarcity of goods needed on the farms in various localities; civilian and military life during the Civil War; marches, maneuvers, and skirmishes; religious revivals in the Confederate Army; public schools of Randolph County and of Washington Territory; and the settlement of John Staley's estate after 1870 and the difficulty arising from the ownership of Confederate money. Many of the Civil War letters were written by Madison Lowes of Randolph County. Also in the collection are deeds for lands in that county.

5019.  MARMADUKE STALKARTT PAPERS, 1781. 5 items. London, England.

Five plates from Stalkartt's <u>Naval Architecture</u> (London: 1781).

5020.  ROBERT STANARD PAPERS, 1822-1849. 2 items. Richmond (Henrico County), Va.

Legal papers of Robert Stanard (1781-1846) and Robert C. Stanard, lawyers.

5021.  P. N. STANBACK PAPERS, 1802-1881. 16 items. Richmond County, N.C.

Letters of H. W. Ledbetter, Methodist circuit rider, to his brother William, 1820-1825, describing Wilkes County around Fort Defiance; a deed, 1802, for land in Richmond County, bearing the name of Thomas Stanback; and photocopies of letters of P. N. Stanback (originals in the Division of Archives and History, Raleigh) relating to local politics, 1870, in Little's Mills, Richmond County.

5022.  WALTER ALBERT STANBURY, SR., PAPERS, 1915-1954. 2,675 items and 1 vol. Asheboro (Randolph County), N.C.

Sermons delivered by the Reverend Stanbury; addresses, articles, correspondence, reports, and minutes concerning the work of the Wesley Foundation, a Methodist student organization in North Carolina colleges and universities; data on the Duke Divinity School; constitution and minutes of the North Carolina Council of Churches, 1935-1937; homecoming day address by Stanbury at Greensboro College, March 9, 1940; outlines for conferences on parental education, 1925-1934; correspondence relative to Centenary Methodist Church of Winston-Salem, 1941-1943; and correspondence with artist Irene Price about Trinity College alumni having a portrait painted of Furnifold M. Simmons. The general correspondence contains letters, 1945, about the appointment of James T. Cleland to teach homiletics in the Duke Divinity School. The collection also includes a scrapbook of newspaper clippings about the Sunday morning service at West Market Street Methodist Episcopal Church in Greensboro, North Carolina, covering Stanbury's pastorate, 1933-1937.

5023.  BENJAMIN E. STANFIELD PAPERS, 1901 (1909-1928) 1934. 676 items and 32 vols. North Carolina.

Papers concerning financial affairs of churches on circuits in the North Carolina Methodist Episcopal Conference, South, served by Benjamin E. Stanfield (1876-1935), rural minister for Grimesland, Spring Hope, Richmond County, Robeson County, Chadbourn, Jonesboro, Creedmoor, Durham Circuit, and Mount Tirzah churches. Included also are records of marriages, baptisms, and deaths of members of these churches. The volumes consist of pastor's books and sermon books.

5024.  EDWARD STANHOPE PAPERS, 1888-1889. 2 items. London, England.

This collection contains two letters received by Stanhope (1840-1893) while serving as secretary for war. A letter from Lord George Francis Hamilton, First Lord of the Admiralty, 1888, discusses strategy in the Mediterranean and on the west coast of Africa in the event of war with France; and a letter, 1889, of John Eldon Gorst, under secretary for India, concerns the military importance of keeping the headquarters of the Thames District at Chatham rather than Woolwich.

5025.  EDWARD GEORGE GEOFFREY SMITH STANLEY, FOURTEENTH EARL OF DERBY, PAPERS, 1840-1849. 4 items. Knowsley Hall, Lancashire, England.

Miscellaneous political letters by Stanley (1799-1869), secretary for war and colonies in Sir Robert Peel's second cabinet until 1845, commenting upon the Corn Laws, the Catholic question, and government abandonment of Whig principles.

5026.  EDWARD JOHN STANLEY, SECOND BARON STANLEY OF ALDERLEY, PAPERS, 1835-1864. 50 items. London, England.

Political correspondence of Stanley (1802-1869), Liberal politician, member of Parliament from North Cheshire and patronage secretary to the treasury in Lord Melbourne's second administration, chiefly relating to elections and patronage. Included are correspondence of Sir Rufane Shaw Donkin concerning his defeat in Northumberland, 1837, by William Holmes, a Tory, and Donkin's belief that Holmes had purchased votes. There are also references to voting irregularities in Denbigh, 1837; material on the organization of the Reform Club, 1836; information on Liverpool shipping investigations, 1836, and politics in the sale of crown lands, involving Lord Duncannon and Sir Edward Knatchbull, 1836; and correspondence of Lord John Russell with Henry Lascelles, Earl of Harewood, regarding the lack of magistrates in the parish of Halifax. Other correspondents include James Cappock; Thomas Drummond; John George Lambton, First Earl of Durham; John Ponsonby; John William Ponsonby, Viscount Duncannon; and Lord Palmerston.

5027. SIR HENRY MORTON STANLEY PAPERS, 1899. 1 item. Furze Hill, Surrey, England.

A letter from Stanley (1841-1904), British explorer, to R. E. Ansell agreeing to address a meeting of Liberal Unionists on the subject of the Transvaal.

5028. EDWIN McMASTERS STANTON PAPERS, 1862. 1 item. Washington, D.C.

Copy of a letter from General Ambrose Everett Burnside, commanding the Department of North Carolina, to Stanton, secretary of war recommending Ernest Staples.

5029. FRANK LEBBY STANTON MANUSCRIPT. 1 item. [Atlanta, Ga.?]

Rough draft of an unpublished poem, "A Visit from the Joy Riders," by Stanton (1857-1927).

5030. ROBERT B. STANTON LETTERPRESS BOOK, 1874-1880. 1 vol. (368 pp.) Madisonville (Hamilton County), Ohio.

Correspondence of Stanton, resident engineer for an unidentified bridge-building company.

5031. ABRAM PENN STAPLES, SR., PAPERS, 1805-1931. 639 items and 1 vol. Stuart (Patrick County), Va.

Personal and family correspondence of Abram P. Staples (1793-1856), member of the Virginia assembly, 1818-1819, and clerk of superior court in Patrick County, Virginia, 1820-1830; of his grandson, Abram Penn Staples (d. 1913), professor of law at Washington and Lee University, Lexington, Virginia; of his great granddaughter, Harris DeJarnette Staples; and a few scattered letters of other members of the family. Centering around Abram Penn Staples (1793-1856) are letters from him while a student at the University of North Carolina, Chapel Hill, 1816; letters from him while in the Virginia assembly with comments on local politics; papers connected with his services as clerk of court; and from 1838 to 1855, letters from Archibald Stuart, member of U. S. Congress from Virginia, relative to current legislative activities, business letters from Washington, C. DePauw, and one letter from Beverley Tucker relative to the progress of Staples's son, Waller, a student of law at the College of William and Mary, Williamsburg, Virginia. Beginning in 1883, there are numerous letters from Sallie Cushing Hart to her future husband, Abram Penn Staples (d. 1913). The remainder of the collection consists of letters from four ardent suitors to Harris Dejarnette Staples, daughter of Abram P. and Sallie Cushing (Hart) Staples, including a number from a titled German, Ludo von Meysenburg, and letters to her from her parents, especially from her mother, containing schemes for encouraging the suit of von Meysenburg. Included also is a single letter of Senator George W. Pepper introducing David W. Persinger, a friend of the Staples, to a lawyer in Saint Louis, Missouri; and a tax account book, 1787, kept by Samuel G. Staples, the father of Abram Penn Staples (1793-1856).

5032. JOSEPH D. STAPP PAPERS, 1856-1886. 61 items. Pickensville (Pickens County), Ala.

Correspondence of Stapp, a Confederate soldier, describing the Civil War in Mississippi, Alabama, Tennessee, and Georgia; the life of Harriet C. Stapp, Joseph's sister, at Judson Female Institute, Marion, Alabama, in 1856; student life in the Summerville Institute, Gholson, Mississippi; Stapp's duties as a surgeon's assistant with the 41st Alabama Infantry Volunteers at Tuscaloosa, 1862; Confederate leadership in the Chattanooga campaign; and legal and financial problems of Elbert Decatur Willett, Sr., in 1886. The collection also includes some literary compositions of Harriet C. Stapp; a song composed by Stapp, "The Southern Wagon: Confederate Air," dated September 1, 1861, and set to the music of "Wait for the Wagon"; and a sharecropping agreement, 1869, between Stapp and several freedmen in Pickens County.

5033. BENJAMIN STARK PAPERS, 1862. 1 item. Portland, Ore.

A letter to Stark, U. S. senator from Oregon, from William Morrow of Oakland, Sawamish County, Washington Territory, blaming Northern interference with states' rights for the coming of the Civil War and expressing fear of British seizure of the Puget Sound area.

5034. DARIUS STARR PAPERS, 1861-1864. 80 items and 1 vol. Worcester (Worcester County), Mass.

Family letters of a sergeant in the 2nd Regiment of U. S. Sharpshooters recording life in the Army of the Potomac, describing the battles of Gainesville and Fredericksburg, and remarking on emancipation, morale, newspaper reporters, and weapons. There is also a diary, 1863.

5035. STATE BANK OF COLUMBIA PAPERS, 1852-1933. 40,777 items and 100 vols. Columbia (Fluvanna County), Va.

Correspondence and records of a small-town bank and a branch bank in Cartersville, Virginia, including letters received, copies of answers, notes, and memoranda; volumes including registers of discounted bills, teller's daily balances, trial balances, note ticklers, cashbooks, accounts; and registers of checks, overdrafts, and liberty bonds. Included are requests for small loans, copies of letters to delinquent holders of notes, letters enclosing small deposits and copies of cashiers' letters protesting overdrafts and acknowledging receipts of money, numerous letters concerned with the collection of a large note of R. W. Myers, president of the Bankers Trust Company of Virginia; and, in 1922, the collection of a note of $3,000 from the Reverend James Cannon, secured by 200 shares of Freeport Texas Company. Many notes to be collected for fertilizer firms and farm machinery firms, and correspondence from Oliver J. Sands regarding taxation of bank deposits are included. There is correspondence concerning competition with the Bank of Richmond, 1906-1907; frequent warnings after 1909 from the State Corporation Commission, Banking Division, that the Bank of Columbia was ignoring careful practice regarding security and loans; and material concerning the large expansion of facilities and loans in 1921. Correspondence and records of deposits, 1922-1923, bear on the banking policy of the Tri-State Tobacco Growers' Co-operative Marketing Association for tobacco growers, including numerous letters of Oliver J. Sands as executive manager of the Association and James H. Craig, treasurer. Records include information on small business activities such as poultry farming, lumbering, fruit growing, and gold mining in Fluvanna County. Papers of 1930 and afterward concern the closing of the bank and the appointment of John Q. Rhodes of Louisa, Virginia, as receiver; and the settlement of debts, collection of loans, and disposal of bank property. There are also papers of George L. Stoneman as mayor of Columbia, mainly warrants for arrests of criminals; and six photographs of floods in Columbia.

5036. McGILVERY M. STATON PAPERS, 1807-1890. 311 items and 3 vols. Williamston (Martin County), N.C.

Personal and business papers concerning Staton, a brick dealer, farmer, and slaveholder, and other Martin County residents. One volume concerns the settlement of Staton's estate in 1861. Correspondence of Asa Biggs, William J. Bingham, Elisha Mitchell, John Spelman and David L. Swain concern the University of North Carolina, the Democratic Press and the State Journal, lotteries in North Carolina and Delaware, and the hiring of slaves.

5037. RALPH F. STAUBLY PAPERS, 1884-1913. 111 items. Martinsburg (Berkeley County), W. Va.

Routine business correspondence and other papers of an attorney, dealing with land claims, debt settlements, and other legal matters.

5038. SIR GEORGE LEONARD STAUNTON, FIRST BARONET, AND SIR GEORGE THOMAS STAUNTON, SECOND BARONET PAPERS, 1743-1885. 486 items and 8 vols. London, England.

This collection relates to Sir George Leonard Staunton (1737-1801), British diplomat, and his son, Sir George Thomas Staunton (1781-1859), politician and author of works on China. There are scattered letters of various members of the Staunton and Collins families in the late 18th century, many letters to George Leonard Staunton, fragmentary diaries, clippings, and some genealogical material. Topics of the papers of Sir George Leonard Staunton include his diplomatic career; the negotiation of a treaty with the ruler of Mysore, 1783; British rule of Madras and Calcutta, 1781-1784, and 1791; his part in the mission to China, 1792; family and personal matters; and his death.

Papers of Sir George Thomas Staunton include correspondence with his father and mother describing his education, his life at the East India Company's factory in Canton, 1798-1817, several disputes with Chinese officials, and Lord Amherst's mission to China, 1816-1817. A few letters relate to France and England in 1780-1792, Paris social life, the French National Assembly, and British attitudes toward the French Revolution. Letters from Sir George Thomas Staunton to his mother during periods of travel in England and Ireland, 1802-1819, describe his examination of various country estates there. There are also letters written while touring France, Switzerland, Italy, Germany, and Belgium. Other correspondence, including drafts of letters in Staunton's journals and letters from Henry John Temple, Third Viscount Palmerston, concern Staunton's political career in the 1830s and the reform movement. Material on elections largely concerns those of 1832 and 1835 in South Hampshire. There are also a number of travel diaries, including those of Staunton's childhood travels with his father in Europe and China. A journal, 1831-1837, records Staunton's opinions on parliamentary matters, his voting record, a list of correspondents, and other political information, especially concerning the Reform Bill of 1832.

5039. STAUNTON WOOLEN FACTORY PAPERS, 1850-1866. 2 items and 2 vols. Staunton (Augusta County), Va.

A ledger, 1850-1863, and journal, 1852-1863, recording the operations of the factory, and a letter, 1866, relating to Benjamin Crawford, manager of the mill.

5040. E. STEADMAN PAPERS, 1862-1870. 14 items. Lawrenceville (Gwinnett County), Ga.

Personal and business papers of E. Steadman including letters, receipts, and a certificate pertaining to the salt supply during the Confederacy; letter, 1865, from Bromfield Ridley discussing the disposition of tobacco they own mutually, and reporting the theft of some of the tobacco by Sherman's army; letter, 1868, concerning cotton prices and affairs in Penfield, Georgia; and a letter, 1870, discussing the Georgia State Agricultural Society.

5041. NELLIE F. STEARNS PAPERS, 1865. 1 item. New Bern (Craven County), N.C.

Letter from a Northern teacher in a Negro school describing the African church in which she is teaching and the close observation of their activities by the Southerners.

5042. HERMAN STEBBINS PAPERS, 1815-1818. 12 items. West Springfield (Hampden County), Mass.

Chiefly letters to Herman Stebbins from his brother, Charles Stebbins, and from a friend in New York, Elisa Diggins, concerning the death of Herman Stebbins' mother; relationships between men and women, especially an affair between one Moner and Miss B. Loveland; and plans for a Fourth of July celebration in 1818. A letter, 1815, from Herman Stebbins while visiting an uncle in Bryan County, Georgia, describes Bryan County and Savannah.

5043. LAURA W. STEBBINS PAPERS, 1852-1884. 800 items. Springfield (Hampden County), Mass.

Family and personal correspondence of Laura W. Stebbins, New England schoolmistress who also taught in Mississippi before and after the Civil War, and who, for a time, operated her own school in Springfield. The letters contain information on subjects taught and remuneration of teachers, allusions to the Campbellite sect, references to living conditions in Ohio, and discussion of the relative merits of Northern and Southern teachers for Southern schools. Included also are a few letters from Eugene Dow, friend of the Stebbins family, member of the 46th Massachusetts Volunteers, and connected with the Commissary of Subsistence at Norfolk, Virginia, and the Bureau of Refugees, Freedmen and Abandoned Lands, relative to the standard of living of the Negro, his education, and the status of his citizenship.

5044. EDMUND CLARENCE STEDMAN PAPERS, 1860-1905. 20 items. New York, N.Y.

Correspondence of Edmund Clarence Stedman (1833-1908), author and journalist, regarding literary matters, including letters from Virginia Wales Johnson, John James Platt, and James Brander Matthews; letter from George Cary Eggleston concerning a celebration of the birthday of Charles Dickens; letter from Margaret (Junkin) Preston discussing a forthcoming work in American literature, and a poem entitled "Sit, Jessica," in her handwriting; letter from John Russell Young concerning the publication of one of Stedman's poems; letter from Elizabeth Drew (Barstow) Stoddard, poet and novelist, discussing her literary style, and mentioning James Russell Lowell, Walt Whitman, and her husband, Richard Henry Stoddard, and Stedman's illness; letter from Stedman to Edward Payson Roe, discussing Stedman's intention to return to the writing of poetry, and the personality and literary ability of Elizabeth Drew (Barstow) Stoddard; letter from Stedman to John Q. Adams commenting on Thomas Holley Chivers; letter from Stedman to W. L. Dennett; and photocopies of letter from William Sharp concerning Sharp's activities and writing. The originals are in the Widener Memorial Collection at Harvard University, Cambridge, Massachusetts.

5045. CHARLES STEEDMAN PAPERS, 1835 (1847-1873) 1905. 170 items and 2 vols. Charleston, S.C.

Personal and professional papers of Charles Steedman (1811-1890), United States naval officer, concerning Steedman's decision to stay with the Union, and efforts of his family to persuade him to join the Confederacy; secession; naval engagements in the Chesapeake Bay area; military affairs in Charleston, South Carolina; rumors of victories and defeats; the blockading policy of the Union; the bombardment of Fort Fisher, North Carolina; orders issued to Steedman as commander of the United States naval force in Panama during the 1870s; and relations between Chile, Bolivia, and the United States during the 1880s. Also included are the personal correspondence of Steedman's father, John Steedman, concerning affairs in Charleston; a journal kept by Steedman's wife during a trip to Europe, 1878-1879; and an account book and diary, 1883-1885.

5046. JOHN STEELE PAPERS, 1797, 1825. 2 items. Salisbury (Rowan County), N.C.

Letter from William Polk, North Carolina soldier and politician, to John Steele, congressman from North Carolina and comptroller of the treasury, 1796-1802, discussing the plans of Governor William Blount for an expedition against Spanish troops in Florida and Louisiana, and politics in North Carolina and Tennessee; and a letter from Thomas Washington to John Steele, Jr., concerning a suit between Steele and Hugh Dobbins.

5047. SAMUEL STEELE PAPERS, 1790 (1798-1804) 1835. 31 items. Augusta County, Va.

Letters to Samuel Steele, largely concerning the settlement of the Mississippi Territory. Included are letters from his brother, John Steele, first secretary of the Mississippi Territory, describing his journey to Natchez by riverboat under the escort of the Cherokee Chief, Double Head, the country and the people, and his cotton plantation at Natchez; and mentioning a cotton gin and cotton prices in 1799. Included also are legal documents, 1798, 1833, 1835, in regard to land in Virginia.

5048. STEELE FAMILY PAPERS, 1901-1906. 4 vols. Turnersburg (Iredell County), and Mount Airy (Surry County), N.C.

The collection contains a time book, 1903-1906, containing employee work records from the Steele Bros. Co., a cotton mill at Mount Airy, of which Marshall K. Steele, son-in-law of Wilfred Turner of the Turnersburg Cotton Mills, was president; L. C. Steele, secretary and treasurer; and N. F. Steele, superintendent. The time book lists employees, their wages, and the amount of yarn made each day. There are also three volumes of exercise books used in the study of bookkeeping, apparently by LeRoy C. Steele (probably the same as L. C. Steele mentioned above), in Turnersburg, 1901.

5049. THADDEUS GARLAND STEM, JR., PAPERS, 1968. 1 item. Oxford (Granville County), N.C.

Typescript of A Flagstone Walk (Charlotte, N. C.: 1968), a collection of short stories by Thaddeus Garland Stem, Jr.

5050. SIR LESLIE STEPHEN PAPERS, 1861 (1866-1891) 1959. 298 items. London, England. Restricted.

Chiefly family correspondence and manuscripts of articles by Sir Leslie Stephen (1832-1904), author, philosopher, and first editor of the Dictionary of National Biography. Included are the letters of his first wife, Harriet Marian (Thackeray) Stephen, daughter of William Makepeace Thackeray, and of his second wife, Julia Prinsep (Jackson) Duckworth Stephen, whose children included Virginia Woolf and Vanessa Bell. Correspondence discusses visits to Cambridge, England, by Stephen in 1866, and 1869; almost yearly tours of Switzerland, especially the Alps, by Sir Leslie and Harriet Marian (Thackeray) Stephen after their marriage in 1867 until her death in 1875; a tour of America in 1868, where they met James Russell Lowell, Oliver Wendell Holmes, Ralph Waldo Emerson, Charles Sumner, and Elizabeth H. Putnam; meetings with George Otto Trevelyan, Henry Fawcett, Matthew Arnold, William Ernest Henley, and Alfred Tennyson; Stephen's opinion of a novel by Millicent Fawcett; and Stephen's biography of Henry Fawcett, the proceeds from his writings, and his work on the Dictionary of National Biography. Also included are a poem by Sir Henry Taylor written in 1864; report, 1895, of a committee for the establishment of a memorial to Thomas Henry Huxley; clipping, 1898, of a congratulatory letter to George Meredith on his seventieth birthday, with a note on Meredith by Stephen; report, 1900, concerning a memorial for Henry Sidgwick; several pages from the Proceedings of the Alpine Club, 1899, relating to the election of James Bryce as president; pages from The Cambridge Review, 1900, containing statements about James Porter, former master of St. Peter's College, Cambridge; proofs or printed copies of eight of Stephen's magazine articles; and twenty-one manuscripts of articles by Stephen.

5051. ALEXANDER HAMILTON STEPHENS PAPERS, 1822-1911. 3,034 items and 3 vols. Crawfordville (Taliaferro County), Va.

Correspondence and other papers of Alexander Hamilton Stephens (1812-1883), lawyer, U. S. congressman, 1843-1859 and 1873-1882, vice-president of the Confederate States of America, and governor of Georgia, 1882-1883. Much of the material relates to Stephens' law practice, to attempts to secure appointments through him as U. S. congressman and as vice-president of the Confederacy, and to requests for financial assistance. Political correspondence discusses the temperance movement in Riceboro, Georgia, 1834; Indian warfare in Georgia in the 1830s; the Force Bill; agricultural societies; law enforcement in New Orleans, Louisiana, 1841; Locofoco Whig, Free Soil, Know-Nothing and Democratic parties in Georgia and on the national level; religious fervor in Marion County, Georgia, 1846; slavery; the hiring of slaves; reinslavement of Negroes who had been emancipated; return of slaves from Liberia, 1856; the abduction of free Negroes; presidential elections, 1840, 1848, 1856, 1860 and 1876; Henry Clay; John C. Calhoun; Stephen A. Douglas; the Mexican War; the cabinet of President Zachary Taylor; the Fugitive Slave Law; the Kansas question; union versus disunion, 1850; the retreat of General Joseph E. Johnston in Georgia near the end of the Civil War; destitution in the South after the Civil War; requests for Stephens to lecture in the

North after the war; the printing of a biography of Stephens; the education of deaf and dumb children in Georgia; publication of Stephens' A Constitutional View of the Late War Between the States (Philadelphia and Chicago: 1868-1870); shipments of guano; Radicalism in Georgia; Georgia bonds; theft of public lands in Iowa; Georgia politics in the 1870s and 1880s; Robert Toombs; Ulysses S. Grant; Cuban independence; the appointment of Robert T. Clayton to the U. S. consulate at Callao, Peru; the silver question; the establishment of a National Currency Department; the Republican Party in Georgia in the 1880s; treatment of convict labor on the Marietta and North Georgia Railroad; proposed canal across Nicaragua; and other matters dealing with political, social, and economic life in Georgia and the United States. Miscellaneous items include resolutions by the State Rights Party of Milledgeville, Georgia, 1833; M'Carter's County Almanac, 1833; bulletin of the Washington Female Seminary [Washington, Georgia?;] several letters relating to student life at the University of Virginia, Charlottesville, Virginia, and at the University of Georgia, Athens, Georgia; biographical sketch of James Pleasant Waddell; broadside, 1883, relating to the building of a canal in Nicaragua; broadside advertising Tate Springs, Tennessee; bills and receipts; personal correspondence of Alexander H. Stephens with his brothers, expecially Judge Linton Stephens; and some correspondence with his niece, Mary (Stephens) Reid, relating to the settlement of the estate of her husband. Volumes are a daybook, a copybook, and a bank account book.

5052. ANN SOPHIA (WINTERBOTHAM) STEPHENS PAPERS, [1864?], 1880. 2 items. New York, N.Y.

Personal letters of Ann Sophia (Winterbotham) Stephens (1813-1886), novelist, discussing personal matters and her relations with other women writers.

5053. W. A. STEPHENS PAPERS, 1863-1864. 6 items. Wedowee (Randolph County), Ala.

Personal letters from W. A. Stephens, a Confederate private in the 37th Alabama Regiment stationed in 1863 at Vicksburg, Mississippi, and in 1864 at Florence, Alabama, concerning news of friends, the condition of crops, and the welfare of his wife.

5054. WENDELL HOLMES STEPHENSON PAPERS, 1934-1963. ca. 25,000 items. Eugene (Lane County), Ore.

Professional papers of Wendell Holmes Stephenson, historian and editor, relating to the founding and growth of the Southern Historical Association; the Journal of Southern History of which Stephenson was the first editor; his editorship of the Mississippi Valley Historical Review; his editorship with Charles W. Ramsdell and later with E. Merton Coulter of the series entitled A History of the South; his editorship with Fred C. Cole of the Southern Biography Series; affairs at the various institutions at which he taught, including the University of Kentucky, Lexington, Kentucky, Louisiana State University, Baton Rouge, Louisiana, Tulane University, New Orleans, Louisiana, and University of Oregon, Eugene, Oregon; and other institutions and organizations chiefly pertaining to the historical profession. Correspondents include historians, presidents and deans of various colleges and universities, editors, directors of university presses, and various publishing houses. Papers relating to the Journal of Southern History, filed separately as the Journal of Southern History Archives, almost exclusively deal with the writing and publication of manuscripts in the journal. Also included are a carbon copy of the final draft with corrections of his Basic History of the Old South (Princeton: 1959); original, unpublished manuscript of "Eggs that Shouldn't Have Been Laid"; copies of published articles; source material for major articles; manuscripts and some printed copies of book reviews, 1942-1962; speeches; and materials relating to history courses at Louisiana State University and University of Oregon, including outlines, syllabi, tests, and course records.

5055. JAMES C. STEPTOE PAPERS, 1811-1861. 10 items. Bedford County, Va.

Business papers of a Bedford County merchant; and a notice to James C. Steptoe and William Leftwich to sell the property of Joel Leftwich, general in the War of 1812.

5056. STERLING COTTON MILLS, INC., PAPERS, 1932-1941. 850 items. Franklinton (Franklin County), N.C.

Business papers of the Sterling Cotton Mills, Inc., manufacturers of high grade warps, skeins, tubes, and cones, relating to the company's period in receivership, including two audit reports, 1932; incoming and outgoing correspondence, 1932-1941, of Don P. Johnston, Sr., receiver from 1932 until 1936; court file, 1932-1936, from the receivership litigation, the Chase National Bank of New York et al. v. Sterling Cotton Mills; a claims file, 1932-1935; and financial statements.

5057. BENJAMIN STETSON PAPERS, 1812-1813. 2 items. Richmond, Va.

Receipt and a business letter to Benjamin Stetson, merchant, from Thomas Motley and Edward Motley, father and uncle respectively, of John Lothrop Motley (1814-1877).

5058.  JOSEPH STETSON PAPERS, 1865.
3 items.  Neponset (Bureau
County), Ill.

Letters from Joseph Stetson, a hospital steward with the 57th Illinois Troops, U.S.A., stationed at Goldsboro, North Carolina, to his mother telling of the surrender of Confederate General Joseph E. Johnston and the assassination of Abraham Lincoln.

5059.  GEORGE HUME STEUART I AND
GEORGE HUME STEUART II PAPERS,
1817 (1847-1861) 1882.  278 items.
Baltimore, Md.

Papers of General George Hume Steuart I, commander of the 1st Light Division of Maryland Volunteers, and of his son, George Hume Steuart II (1828-1903), United States Army officer, and Confederate general, concerning personal matters, U.S. Army politics; social life in Maryland; travels in Europe, 1851-1852; the Mexican War; the election of Zachary Taylor as president; Free Soilers, abolition, and "Black Republicans"; presidents Franklin Pierce and James Buchanan; the Kansas question; speculation that Maryland Whigs and Democrats were uniting against the Know-Nothings; the election of 1860; politics in the United States and in Maryland, 1860-1861; the secession question in Maryland; the Maryland Convention of 1861; the visit of Jefferson Davis to the Alabama Legislature, 1863; conscription in the Confederate Army; various Union and Confederate generals; a Quaker wedding ceremony; and railroads in Maryland, especially the Baltimore and Ohio Railroad.  Also included are several bills and receipts, army papers, and other miscellaneous papers.

5060.  [ANN STEVENS?] ARITHMETIC BOOK,
1771.  1 vol.  (210 pp.)
[Louisburg (Franklin County), N.C.?]

Samples of mathematical terms and problems.

5061.  BENJAMIN C. STEVENS PAPERS,
1861-1879.  86 items.  Tilton
(Belknap County), N.H.

Letters and clippings of Benjamin C. Stevens (b. 1839), machinist and soldier serving in the band of the 1st Regiment of Massachusetts Volunteers, discussing camp life in Maryland, Virginia, and South Carolina; the activities of the regimental band; the use of observation balloons by the Union Army; religious services; contrabands; the siege of Yorktown, and the fighting at Williamsburg, Virginia; and the siege of Charleston and the bombardment of Fort Sumter, South Carolina.

5062.  FREDERICK M. STEVENS PAPERS,
1862-1865.  9 items.  New
Orleans, La.

Chiefly the reminiscences (12 pp.) of Sara Stevens, wife of Frederick M. Stevens, schoolteacher, concerning their life during the Civil War; the siege of Vicksburg, Mississippi, and Federal occupation of the town; and the insurance provisions made by Frederick M. Stevens for his family.  Also included are Stevens' military exemption, two certified oaths of alliegance to the United States, two travel passes, a certificate of enrollment, and a paper relating to Dr. Frederick Drewry, magistrate in Ireland, who was active in suppressing the insurrections of 1798 and 1803.

5603.  THOMAS HOLDUP STEVENS PAPERS,
1823-1902.  144 items.  Middletown
(Middlesex County), Conn.

Military papers of Thomas Holdup Stevens (1819-1896), United States naval officer, relating to naval affairs, including orders, promotions, and material concerning problems in the transportation of troops and supplies and the necessity of naval support during the Peninsular campaign, 1862; the patrolling of the coast for privateers and blockade runners; the capture of the British schooner Clyde in 1863 and the British schooner Swift in 1864; and various naval officers, fleets, squadrons, and U. S. ships. Also included is a letter, 1863, from an American sailor in Calcutta, India, discussing the prospect of conscription, Sydney, Australia, Calcutta, and British pirates; a letter, 1889, relating to a Latin American tunnel deal; and a contract, 1890, for a land deed between Stevens and the American-Honduras Company concerning land in Honduras.

5064.  JOHN WHITE STEVENSON PAPERS, 1841.
1 item.  Covington (Boone
County), Ky.

Letter of John White Stevenson (1812-1886), lawyer of the firm of Phelps and Stevenson, and governor of Kentucky, 1867-1871, to the clerk of the court of Madison County, Virginia, concerning the legal affairs of Austin Bohannon.

5065.  SARAH (COLES) STEVENSON PAPERS,
1836-1841.  193 items.  Albemarle
County, Va.

Letters of Sarah (Coles) Stevenson, wife of Andrew Stevenson, U. S. minister to England, describing their years in England, places visited, people they met, and social functions they attended, with occasional references to politics and international relations.  There are also several letters of Andrew Stevenson concerning personal matters. [Portions of the Sarah (Coles) Stevenson letters have been published by William L. Royall, Century Magazine, January-March, 1909, Vol. 77.]

5066. JOHN STEWARD POEMS, 1778-1794. 1 vol. (143 pp.) Ballston (Saratoga County), N.Y.

A collection of verses, generally of a humorous character, some of which were published in the Gazette of Charleston, South Carolina.

5067. ALEXANDER PETER STEWART PAPERS, 1862-1863. 3 items. Tennessee and Kentucky.

Fragmentary letters of Alexander P. Stewart (1821-1908), major general in the Confederate Army, one of which mentions the escape of a prisoner.

5068. J. W. STEWART PAPERS, 1861. 4 items. Richmond, and Yorktown (York County), Va.

Letters from J. W. Stewart, Confederate soldier, to his uncle, describing army life and the battle of Bethel, 1861.

5069. [JOHN H. STEWART?] PAPERS, 1865-1868. 8 items. Davie County, N.C.

Letters from "J. H. S.," a seventeen-year-old Confederate cannoneer who saw service in the last campaign of Robert E. Lee's army. The letters describe army life, troop movements, skirmishes with the enemy, and Sherman's invasion of the Carolinas. This collection was formerly cataloged as the James H. S[teele] Papers.

5070. LUTHER CALDWELL STEWART PAPERS, 1955. 1 item. Hopkinsville (Christian County), Ky.

Copy of an address by Luther Caldwell Stewart (b. 1893), minister and bishop of the Colored Methodist Episcopal Church (now the Christian Methodist Episcopal Church), discussing the history and role of Methodism, and the connection between the Methodist Episcopal Church, South, and the Colored Methodist Episcopal Church, and making an appeal in behalf of the latter.

5071. ROBERT STEWART, VISCOUNT CASTLEREAGH AND SECOND MARQUIS OF LONDONDERRY, PAPERS, 1820-1825. 24 items. London, England.

Papers of Robert Stewart, Viscount Castlereagh and Second Marquis of Londonderry (1769-1822), chief secretary in Ireland, secretary of state for war and the colonies, and foreign secretary, consist of receipts for secret service funds from Sir Charles Stuart, Baron Stuart de Rothesay, and from Joseph Planta; and a letter, 1825, from Planta reporting that the accounts of Castlereagh's administration of the secret service had been settled.

5072. W. A. STEWART PAPERS, 1906. 1 item. Fayetteville (Cumberland County), N.C.

Speech of W. A. Stewart seconding the nomination of H. L. Godwin as Democratic Party candidate to the U. S. House of Representatives from North Carolina.

5073. BENJAMIN STILES ACCOUNTS, 1803-1818. 1 vol. (118 pp.) Charleston, S.C.

Accounts of the estate of Benjamin Stiles, Jr., as kept by Simeon Theus.

5074. COPELAND STILES PAPERS, 1813-1830s. 5 items. Charleston, S.C.

Miscellaneous papers of Copeland Stiles, planter, including a legal paper relating to his taking over of an estate on Johns Island, South Carolina, that had belonged to his grandmother, Mrs. Smilie; a statement of the shares of Mrs. Stiles and Miss Stiles in an estate; and a printed copy of a political poem by Governor John Lide Wilson (1784-1849) entitled "A Pasquinade of the Thirties," which analyzes prominent Charleston politicians.

5075. ROBERT A. STILES PAPERS, 1810 (1860-1872) 1897. 172 items. Richmond, Va.

Miscellaneous papers of Robert A. Stiles, including letters to Joseph Stiles, Sr., regarding the dismissal of his sons, Benjamin Stiles and Joseph Stiles, Jr., from The College of New Jersey, Princeton, New Jersey, and the requirements necessary for their admission to Yale College, New Haven, Connecticut; letters from Robert Stiles's mother concerning personal matters and religious topics; letter to Robert Stiles from Theodore W. Dwight, professor of law at Columbia University, New York, New York, listing the parts of Blackstone that he should study; several letters relating to the military service of Bradley T. Johnson; letters from Robert Stiles while serving as an officer in the Confederate Army generally dealing with introspective and religious subjects; two letters from Stephen R. Mallory to Randolph R. Stiles, Robert's brother, while serving as a Confederate soldier; and letters, 1866-1867, from the University of Virginia, Charlottesville, Virginia, by J. L. Lindsay and John B. Minor.

5076. WILLIAM H. STILES PAPERS, 1770-1838. 6 items. Savannah, Ga.

Business papers of William H. Stiles (1808-1865), lawyer, U. S. congressman, 1843-1845, chargé d'affaires to Austria, 1845-1849, and colonel in the Confederate Army. Also included is an item, 1770, relating to Captain Samuel Stiles; and an item, 1802, concerning Richard Stiles, lawyer and court official.

5077. WILLIAM RICHARD STIMSON PAPERS, 1968-1970. 15 items. New York, N.Y.

Papers of William Richard Stimson while a graduate student at Columbia University, New York, New York, consisting of mimeographed broadsides and other material relating to student activities at Columbia in 1968, the 1968 presidential election, military conscription, the nationwide boycott of grapes grown in California, and the position of Students for a Democratic Society concerning these issues.

5078. SAMUEL STIRK PAPERS, 1782-1784. 3 items. Savannah, Ga.

Papers of Samuel Stirk, attorney general for Georgia in 1782, pertaining to business and legal questions arising from the presence of Loyalists in Savannah. Included are documents dealing with the terms given British merchants by General Anthony Wayne and the Georgia assembly on the evacuation of the British forces from Savannah.

5079. W. STITH AND A. STITH ACCOUNT BOOK, 1839-1864. 1 vol. (351 pp.) [Petersburg (Dinwiddie County), Va.?]

Mercantile accounts and records of the sale of a plantation.

5080. STOCK CERTIFICATE COLLECTION, 1856-1929. 46 items.

Chiefly railroad stock certificates. There are also certificates from other companies relating to banking, insurance, construction, a stockyard, coal, a suspension bridge, refrigerator cars, and docks and terminals.

5081. CHARLES WARREN STODDARD PAPERS, 1863-1896. 13 items. San Francisco, Calif.

Photocopies of items relating to Charles Warren Stoddard (1843-1909), author and educator, including letters from Stoddard to prominent writers concerning literary matters and containing biographical information; a manuscript poem; and three poems published in San Francisco newspapers. There is also a letter, 1870, of Stoddard to William Hepworth Dixon commenting upon one of Dixon's works; and a letter, 1877, from Paul Hamilton Hayne referring to Stoddard's literary talents and his own writings.

5082. MISSOURIA H. STOKES PAPERS, 1856-1924. 182 items. Decatur (De Kalb County), Ga.

Correspondence of Missouria H. Stokes relating to personal affairs, temperance, and religion. Included is information on the national and the Georgia Woman's Christian Temperance Union (W. C. T. U.); Frances Elizabeth Caroline Willard (1839-1898), president of the national W. C. T. U., 1879-1898; temperance legislation, including a constitutional amendment; financial and other difficulties of temperance work; and the Sons of Temperance. There are letters from Mary Ann Harris Gay, author, concerning her travels over the South selling a book entitled The Pastor's Story (Nashville: 1860); letters from her sister, Mary M. Stokes, and from a nephew, T. H. Stokes; letters concerning the Harmony Male and Female Academy near Calhoun, South Carolina, Georgia Female College, Madison, Georgia, and the Sans Souci School for girls near Greenville, South Carolina; letter, 1860, describing the fraternization between white northern women teachers and Negro men in Atlanta, Georgia; a pamphlet, 1884, dealing with the plan of work of the Juvenile Department of the W. C. T. U., containing a constitution, pledge, and doxology; a pamphlet containing the 1884 address of Frances Willard urging the Republican Party to adopt the prohibition plank in their party platform; and a letter from a Confederate soldier concerning the election of Joseph Emerson Brown as governor of Georgia.

5083. WILLIAM A. STOKES PAPERS, 1833 (1836-1874) 1927. 90 items. Atlantic City (Atlantic County), N.J.

Miscellaneous papers relating to Pennsylvania railroads including accounts, 1840s, of Eli Kirk Price, lawyer, and trustee of the consolidated loan holders of the Philadelphia, Germantown, and Norristown Railroad, 1844-1848; papers concerning railroad construction and expansion in Pennsylvania in the 1850s; papers relating to various railroad companies in Pennsylvania; and papers concerning a committee of inquiry on which William A. Stokes served to make a report on the history of the Pennsylvania Railroad in 1874. Printed material consists of tickets; advertisements; and pamphlets on the Coal Run Improvement and Railroad Company, the West Chester and Philadelphia Railroad Company, the Elmira and Williamsport Railroad Company, and the New York and Middle Coalfield Railroad and Coal Company.

5084. A. J. STONE PAPERS, 1863. 3 items. Pedlar's Hill (Chatham County), N.C.

Family correspondence of A. J. Stone, Confederate soldier, and his wife, Emily Stone.

5085. EBENEZER WHITTEN STONE SCRAPBOOK, 1880. 1 vol. Roxbury (Norfolk County), Mass.

Scrapbook to commemorate the golden wedding anniversary in 1875 of Catherine L. W. Stone and Ebenezer Whitten Stone (1801-1880), adjutant general of the Massachusetts State Militia, 1851-1861. There are also obituary notices and notes concerning the funeral of Ebenezer Whitten Stone in 1880.

5086. JOHN HOSKINS STONE PAPERS, 1795-1797. 16 items. Baltimore, Md.

Business papers of John Hoskins Stone (1745-1804), governor of Maryland, 1794-1797; and two petitions.

5087. SILAS M. STONE PAPERS, 1854-1885. 1 vol. Youngsville (Franklin County), N.C.

Records of Silas M. Stone, schoolteacher and farmer, including the constitution and by-laws of the Union Academy Debating Society, and the minutes of the meetings, 1854-1855; accounts for tuition, lists of scholars, books used at Union Academy, Youngsville, North Carolina, and an agreement between Stone and the subscribers, 1858-1865; accounts, 1860-1885, for cotton crops, persons employed by Stone, and the construction of a house; home remedies; a record of horses and mules; and the plot of an orchard.

5088. WILLIAM B. STONE PAPERS, 1840-1846. 9 items. Gardner (Worcester County), Mass.

Letters address chiefly to William B. Stone, a Congregational minister, reflecting the New England attitude toward religion and reform. The letters concern the faculty and curriculum at the Andover Theological Seminary, Massachusetts, schoolteaching, a hearing in the case of a suspended minister, the New England Female Moral Reform Society of Boston, Charles C. Burleigh, the abolition lecturer, the World Abolition Convention, women's rights, and questions of doctrine.

5089. WILLIAM BRISCOE STONE PAPERS, 1774-1888. 419 items. Port Tobacco (Charles County), Md.

Chiefly the business and legal papers of William Briscoe Stone, Maryland lawyer. Deeds, wills, and similar papers make up the greater part of the collection. There are also scattered personal letters, including a letter of Michael J. Stone, a member of the U.S. First Congress, 1789-1791, announcing the establishment of the seat of government and its importance to the state of Maryland; and a letter from Alexander Matthews describing party strife in the Maryland assembly in 1840.

5090. STONE MOUNTAIN CONFEDERATE MONUMENTAL ASSOCIATION PAPERS, 1916-1927. 43 items and 1 vol. Stone Mountain (De Kalb County), and Atlanta, Georgia.

Papers of the Stone Mountain Confederate Monumental Association (S.M.C.M.A.) relating to plans for making Stone Mountain into a monument to the Confederate States of America; the controversy over the dismissal of sculptor, Gutzon Borglum, and his replacement by Augustus Lukeman; alleged mismanagement of funds by the S.M.C.M.A.; and efforts to prevent Stone Mountain from reverting to the Atlanta Chapter of the United Daughters of the Confederacy (U.D.C.); and related poems, pamphlets, and other material issued or written by D. M. Armstrong, Mildred Lewis Rutherford, Mary (Sledge) Wright, the S.M.C.M.A., and others concerning plans for the memorial and the reasons for dismissal of Borglum.

5091. LOUIS HENRY STONEMAN PAPERS, 1847-1949. 3 items. Columbia (Fluvanna County), Va.

Two carbon copies of a compilation of the history of St. John's Protestant Episcopal Church at Columbia, Rivanna Parish, Virginia, by Louis Henry Stoneman. Included are listings of the organization, vestry, ministers, confirmations, marriages, baptisms, and burials. There is also a short history of the Stoneman family compiled by Lucy J. (Stoneman) Loving.

5092. HENRY STORM PAPERS, 1872-1898. 16 items. New York, N.Y.

Correspondence of Henry Storm, evidently a historian or editor, consisting of replies from prominent individuals to whom he had written for information on their careers. Among those sending replies with biographical information were Asa Biggs, John M. Bright, C. H. Brogden, J. S. Carlile, Samuel Gibbs French, A. C. Garlington, Johnson Hagood, Joseph Johnson, John Maffitt, W. D. Porter, J. R. Tucker, and H. H. Wells.

5093. JAMES JACKSON STORROW PAPERS, 1865-1879. 40 items. Boston, Mass.

Business and legal papers of James Jackson Storrow (1837-1897), lawyer, including letters and legal documents of individual clients, including Alice L. Heard, Charles C. Jackson, G. N. Kettle, O. H. Perry, and Charlotte B. Wise; correspondence relating to several corporation cases, including the Michigan Iron Company case; and letters concerning a Federal bill for the revision of patent laws in which Storrow played a part.

5094. CORNELIA STORRS PAPERS, 1832-1838. 13 items. Richmond, Va.

Letters from Eliza S. Mosby, cousin of Cornelia Storrs, containing accounts of social life, including horse racing and betting, balls, parties, and flirtations, and matters of family interest.

5095. GEORGE STORY PAPERS, [1764?]- 1792. 8 items and 18 vols. London, England.

Papers of George Story (1738-1818), Methodist itinerant preacher and editor of the Methodist Publishing House, 1792-1807, including two letters and a fragment of another from John Wesley (1703-1791), Methodist leader, giving advice concerning Story's ministry; letter from Thomas Coke

(1747-1814), Methodist bishop, telling of an incident which occurred during a preaching mission at Newport on the Isle of Wight; a photocopy of broadside concerning Story's policy as the new editor of the Methodist Publishing House [the original is in the Rare Book Room, Perkins Library, Duke University, Durham, North Carolina]; and notebooks and records containing sermon outlines, notes on medical remedies, prescriptions, notes on medical lectures, outlines of sermons preached by John Wesley and other early Methodist ministers, membership lists for several charges served by Story, hymns, and an adaptation of Samuel Taylor's shorthand instructions.

5096. GEORGE L. STORY PAPERS, 1881-1895. 2 items and 1 vol. North Hero (Grand Isle County), Vt.

Letter and clipping from Edward W. Lambert, chief medical director of the Equitable Life Assurance Society, to George L. Story (1853-1926), Methodist minister, and a scrapbook of clippings, all concerning the harmful effects of the use of tobacco.

5097. LEONIDAS STOUT PAPERS, 1857-1928. 235 items. New Albany (Floyd County), Ind.

Miscellaneous papers of Leonidas Stout, lawyer and lieutenant colonel in the 13th Indiana Cavalry Volunteers, U.S.A., including papers relating to pension claims of Union veterans; Union recruiting lists; a broadside advertising the second reunion of the 13th Indiana Cavalry in 1889; and genealogical charts and other papers containing family history.

5098. SAMUEL HOLLINGSWORTH STOUT PAPERS, 1842 (1861-1865) 1902. 195 items. Dallas, Tex.

Chiefly the official papers of Samuel Hollingsworth Stout (1822-1903), physician, surgeon with the C.S.A. Army, and later the dean of the faculty of the medical department of the University of Dallas, Dallas, Texas, relating to his service as medical director of hospitals of the Department of Tennessee of the Confederate Army. Included are correspondence, telegrams, reports, morning reports, and other papers pertaining to transfers, receipts, transport of the wounded, supplies, inspections, relief associations, nursing, medical examining boards, the establishment of new hospitals, and vaccination for smallpox. There is a document, 1864, listing all hospitals of the Army of Tennessee, and a map, 1864, locating hospital installations between Vicksburg, Mississippi, and Montgomery, Alabama. Also included is an address, 1902, given by Dr. Stout before the Confederate Military and Surgical Association of which he was secretary, on the history of his command.

5099. HARRIET ELIZABETH (BEECHER) STOWE PAPERS, 1929-1948. 39 items. Cincinnati, Ohio.

Clippings concerning Harriet Beecher Stowe (1811-1896), author, and her work, Uncle Tom's Cabin, or Life Among the Lowly; and a social note from her.

5100. STOWE FAMILY PAPERS, 1847-1882. 12 items and 3 vols. Stowesville (Gaston County), N.C.

Business records of Larkin Stowe (d. 1857) and his sons, Jasper, William A., and E. B., who founded Stowe's textile factory on the South Fork of the Catawba River below the site of Cramerton. An account book, 1856-1874, largely relates to J. & E. B. Stowe of Charlotte, recording transactions for the factory and other businesses; mercantile accounts relating to Tom Stowe; an unsigned and undated text on the management of textile mills; and accounts apparently relating to transfer of ownership of the factory to A. R. Homesley, with many details of mill operation and plans for improvements. A mercantile ledger, 1857-1860, concerning the store at Stowesville, has entries for wages for factory hands. A ledger, 1847-1856, contains accounts for Larkin Stowe, for others of his family, and for their various businesses including the store and the operation of the mill as early as 1848. Included are accounts for workers and freedmen and women; some entries suggest that slaves may have been employed. There are also letters, 1859, concerning prices and containing illustrations of the Whitin lapper machine munufactured in Massachusetts; letters, 1876-1878, regarding the operation, production, wages, and machinery of the Mount Holly cotton mill in Gaston County; and letters and legal papers, 1878, relating to a lawsuit brought by the Stowes against the owners of Woodlawn Mills and the owners of the Lawrence Manufacturing Company over use of the waters of the South Fork of the Catawba. Among other items are a floor plan for a textile mill, 1874, and an account for purchases at a millinery shop in Charlotte, 1871.

5101. GILES LYTTON STRACHEY PAPERS, 1921-1953. 11 items. Hungerford, Berkshire, England.

Papers of Giles Lytton Strachey (1880-1932), author, including the original manuscript of Elizabeth and Essex (New York and London: 1928) and a statement by Professor Charles Richard Sanders of Duke University concerning the gift of the manuscript to the university; a letter from Strachey to Spalding, his publisher, 1921; letters, 1928, from Strachey to Crosby Gaige (1882-1949), book collector, regarding a limited edition of Elizabeth and Essex; a letter and a postcard, 1945, from Arthur Pforzheimer, antiquarian bookseller of New York, to Sanders concerning that edition and the Strachey-Gaige letters; and two letters, 1952, from

James Strachey, brother and literary executor of Lytton Strachey, to Sanders concerning the microfilming of other Strachey correspondence.

5102. SIR HENRY STRACHEY, FIRST BARONET, PAPERS, [1777?] 1 item. London, England.

Letter to Sir Henry Strachey, First Baronet (1736-1810), member of Parliament and minor governmental official, from Admiral Richard Howe, First Earl Howe, confirming plans for Strachey's visit to Philadelphia, probably as a member of the commission for restoring peace to America, of which Strachey was secretary.

5103. SIR RICHARD STRACHEY PAPERS, 1871-1905. 15 items. London, England.

Letters to Sir Richard Strachey (1817-1908), lieutenant general of the Royal Bengal Engineers, from Napoléon La Cécilia (1835-1878), professor of mathematics and general in the Paris Commune of 1871, concerning personal matters and his interest in a project for training and equipping the army of Yakub Beg (also called Atalik Ghazi), a leader of Kashgar in Chinese Turkestan who had successfully rebelled against Peking in 1864; from General Gustave Paul Cluseret (1823-1900), French military officer and high official during the Commune, outlining the project and seeking English approval; and from an Indian railway official discussing the International Railway Congress at Washington, D. C., in 1905.

5104. WILLIAM STRAHAN PAPERS, 1779. 1 item. London, England.

Personal letter to William Strahan (1715-1785), British printer and publisher, and member of the House of Commons, 1774-1784, from Sir James Pringle, Fourth Baronet.

5105. PHILIP A. STRANGE ACCOUNT BOOKS, 1856-1883. 4 vols. Fluvanna County, Va.

Accounts of a lumber mill, including a record of supplies advanced to hands.

5106. WILLIAM C. A. STRANGE PAPERS, 1791 (1813-1840) 1931. 224 items. Fluvanna County, Va.

Business papers of William C. A. Strange, and of Payton A. Strange and George P. Hodgson. Included are letters relating to contributions for the construction of a bridge across the James River at Columbia, Virginia; a folder, 1868, describing the offerings and fees at the medical and law schools of the University of Virginia, Charlottesville, Virginia; and copies of genealogical data and other records of the Strange family.

5107. PAUL STRATTON PAPERS, 1854 (1860s) 1885. 758 items. Norwood (Nelson County), Va.

Business and personal correspondence, bills, receipts, and checks of Paul Stratton, merchant and captain in the 49th Regiment Virginia Volunteers, C.S.A., concerning business affairs, personal matters, mercantile accounts, and personal debts. A number of papers relate to the Cabell family. There is also an announcement, 1869, for the summer session of the Norwood School, Norwood, Virginia.

5108. STRATTON AND JOHNSON ACCOUNT BOOK, 1853. 1 vol. Columbia (Fluvanna County), Va.

Accounts of a general mercantile firm.

5109. STRAYHORN FAMILY PAPERS, 1767-1838. 10 items. Orange County, N.C.

Land deeds of the Strayhorn family.

5110. MARY CALVERT STRIBLING PAPERS, 1835 (1920-1929) 1930. 2,515 items. Martinsburg (Berkeley County), W. Va.

Papers of Mary Calvert Stribling relating chiefly to her activities with the West Virginia chapter of the American Red Cross during World War I and through the 1920s; and to her activities as a member, treasurer in 1926, and president in 1930, of the West Virginia division of the United Daughters of the Confederacy. Other miscellaneous papers include a diploma of Mary Brown Riddle from Woodburn Female Seminary in Morgantown, West Virginia; papers relating to J. S. McClellan and Company, manufacturers of silk and cassimere hats, of which C. Stribling was a partner; letters of C. K. Stribling, commander of the U.S. receiving ship Pennsylvania, 1845-1847; business papers and reports of Ann E. Stribling relating to the estate of her husband, Cornelius Stribling, and her guardianship of their children; letters from Charles R. Stribling, son of Cornelius Stribling and Ann E. Stribling, while attending Hampden-Sydney College, Hampden-Sydney, Virginia; catalog, 1879, of Prince Edward Academy, Worsham, Virginia; business papers of Joseph A. Wishard, proprietor of a hotel in Smithsburg, Maryland; programs of a music and a travel club in Martinsburg, West Virginia; sermon notes; broadside by Carrie Chapman Catt entitled "Mrs. Catt on League of Nations and the Presidential Election"; pamphlet published by the Pro-League Independents; papers relating to the dismissal of Gutzon Borglum as the sculptor of the Stone Mountain Confederate Memorial and to attempts to raise funds for the continuation of the work on the memorial by Augustus Lukeman; materials relating to Wilson College, Chambersburg, Pennsylvania, and to Mary Baldwin College, Staunton, Virginia, of which Mary Calvert Stribling was an alumna; bulletin of the Swarthmore Chautauqua, Swarthmore, Pennsylvania; programs of services at the Presbyterian Church in Martinsburg; and map of the Winchester Presbytery.

5111. OLIVER V. STRICKLAND PAPERS, 1863-1864. 2 items. Dalton (Whitfield County), Ga.

Photocopies of letters from Oliver V. Strickland, Confederate soldier with the 43rd Georgia Regiment, to his mother, Celia Strickland, requesting money and clothes, speaking of desertion in the 52nd Georgia Regiment, and telling of his arrest for going to sleep on his post and his fear of being shot for the offense.

5112. JACOB STRICKLER PAPERS, 1731-[1889?]. 77 items. Virginia.

Letters, legal papers, bills, receipts, and miscellaneous papers relating to Jacob Strickler and other members of the Strickler family.

5113. JAMES L. STRINGFELLOW PAPERS, 1844-1850. 9 items. Stevensburgh (Culpeper County), Va.

Correspondence concerning the personal and business affairs of James L. Stringfellow and his family, with references to the settlement of estates in Virginia, and slave sales and purchases in Virginia and Alabama.

5114. CHARLES J. STROMAN PAPERS, 1842-1873. 19 items. Orangeburg (Orangeburg County), S.C.

Papers of Charles J. Stroman including a letter to Jacob Stroman concerning the sale of rice, a new variety of rice, and the state of the cotton market; letters, 1847, from Charles J. Stroman while a student at Cokesbury, South Carolina; a report on Charles Stroman while at South Carolina College, Columbia, South Carolina, in 1852; letters from D. Blanding De Saussure describing his experiences at Virginia Springs and telling of cholera in Richmond; a poetic description of various professors at South Carolina College; letter to Jacob Stroman concerning the purchase of farm commodities; certificate, 1865, claiming that Stroman's house contained arms stored there by the state government of South Carolina; and family letters.

5115. MARGERY STRONG SCRAPBOOK, 1914-1919. 1 vol. Duluth (Saint Louis County), Minn.

Scrapbook of Margery Strong, chairwoman of the English department of the Duluth State Normal School (now University of Minnesota at Duluth), Duluth, Minnesota, containing items relating largely to World War I including magazine and newspaper clippings of poems and news items, a booklet from the U.S. Food Administration, booklets from Houghton Mifflin Company, and an advertising book about the war.

5116. SANDFORD ARTHUR STRONG PAPERS, 1896-1897. 2 items. London, England.

Letters to Sandford Arthur Strong (1863-1904), British scholar, from Arthur Balfour, First Lord of the Treasury, concerning a donation from the Royal Bounty Fund and Strong's appointment as librarian to the House of Lords.

5117. JAMES P. STROTHER PAPERS, 1841. 1 item. Marion (Smyth County), Va.

Letter of James P. Strother to Charles W. Christian regarding the finances of the firm, Jamison and Williams, and Jamison's plantation and slaves.

5118. W. D. STROTHER PAPERS, 1854-1864. 6 items. Bardstown (Nelson County), Ky.

Family letters of W. D. Strother.

5119. WILLIAM SCUDDER STRYKER PAPERS, 1 item. Trenton (Mercer County), N.J.

Address of William Scudder Stryker (1838-1900), lawyer, U. S. soldier, and adjutant general of New Jersey, describing the battle of Morris Island, South Carolina, in July, 1863, and a meeting he had with Abraham Lincoln after the battle.

5120. ALEXANDER HUGH HOLMES STUART PAPERS, 1872-1876. 2 items. Staunton (Augusta County), Va.

Letter of Alexander Hugh Holmes Stuart (1807-1891), U. S. congressman, 1841-1843, and secretary of the interior, 1850-1853, discussing Stuart family genealogy; and a handbill announcing Stuart's candidacy for a seat in the Virginia House of Delegates.

5121. JAMES EWELL BROWN STUART PAPERS, 1861-1897. 23 items. Patrick County, Va.

Chiefly letters and orders of James Ewell Brown Stuart (1833-1864), Confederate general, concerning conditions prior to the first battle of Manassas, the battles of Fredericksburg and Chancellorsville, efforts to secure information about enemy troop movements, commendations for various officers and their commands, the loyalty of William Thomas Magruder, the establishment of a camp near Richmond (Virginia) for paroled Confederate cavalry prisoners, the hiring of slaves belonging to Sidney Smith Lee, and personal matters, including the death of his daughter, Flora. Included is a list of prisoners from the 30th Regiment of New York Volunteers.

5122. JEREMIAH STUART PAPERS, 1862-1865. 21 items. Massachusetts.

Letters of Jeremiah Stuart, 13th Regiment of Massachusetts Volunteers, to his parents describing camp life, rumors, shoes, the first battle of Manassas, railroads south of Washington, D. C., in 1863, Confederate deserters, and drinking, gambling, and stealing by his Northern comrades.

5123. JOHN LANE STUART PAPERS, 1852 (1861-1870) 1927. 268 items and 1 vol. Moore County, N.C.

Principally the letters of John Lane Stuart while serving in the 49th Regiment, North Carolina Infantry, describing camp life; food and clothing; marches and engagements around Richmond and Petersburg, Virginia, and in eastern North Carolina; prices of horses; and the inefficiency of administration and military leadership. Also included are letters from his step-father, John Harper, describing conditions at home and depredations by deserters and conscripts in hiding; letters from his cousin, Haywood Nall, of Indiana; school attendance records and book orders relating to Stuart's occupation as a school-teacher after the war, particularly in Montgomery County, North Carolina; and a history of Montgomery County, 1927.

5124. HARRY W. STUBBS AUTOGRAPH BOOK, 1880-1881. 1 vol. Williamston (Martin County), N.C.

Autograph album of Harry W. Stubbs while a student at the law school of Dick and Dillard, Greensboro, North Carolina.

5125. J. R. STUBBS PAPERS, 1864. 3 items. Williamston (Martin County), N.C.

Letters to J. R. Stubbs, a Confederate soldier, from his family, concerning the depredations of Federal troops in and around Tarboro, Halifax, and Williamston, North Carolina.

5126. WILLIAM C. STUBBS PAPERS, 1859-1871. 7 items. Auburn (Lee County), Ala.

Letters written by William C. Stubbs (1846-1924), agriculturist and author, as a student at the College of William and Mary, Williamsburg, Virginia, and later as professor of natural science at East Alabama College, Auburn. The early letters contain comments on secession, and the later ones describe financial difficulties of East Alabama College and the agricultural depression in the early 1870s.

5127. JOHN STUCKEY PAPERS, 1869-1870. 2 items. Atlanta (Logan County), Ill.

Family correspondence of John Stuckey.

5128. WILLIAM STUMP PAPERS, 1788 (1830-1895) 1903. 1,255 items and 3 vols. Harford County, Md.

Correspondence and business papers of the Stump family, especially of William Stump, and of the related Holloway, Harlan, Ramsay, and Reiley families, concerning family matters, social activities, and religion, including the activities of the Society of Friends. There are scattered references to the temperance and abolition movements, the presidential election of 1844, student life at Jefferson College and at Swarthmore College (Swarthmore, Pennsylvania), life on board a naval vessel in the 1840s, and fear of a Confederate raid in Pennsylvania in 1864. Business papers are largely bills and receipts. Also included are two daybooks, one belonging to a tavern keeper.

5129. JOSEPH STURGE PAPERS, 1838. 1 item. Birmingham, Warwickshire, England.

Letter from Joseph Sturge (1793-1859), British Quaker and philanthropist, to A. West of the Negro Emancipation Committee concerning arrangements for a festival to commemorate the freeing of slaves in the British colonies.

5130. SAMUEL DAVIS STURGIS, SR., PAPERS, 1846-1866. 5 items. Pennsylvania.

Letters of Samuel Davis Sturgis, Sr. (1822-1889), U.S. Army officer, describing his march into Saltillo, Mexico, with General Zachary Taylor; Los Angeles in 1849, gold deposits in California, the rush to reach the gold fields, and the extravagance of the people there; and fighting Indians in the West with Kit Carson.

5131. JOHN W. STURTEVANT PAPERS, 1863-1864. 5 items. Keene (Cheshire County), N.H.

Letters from John W. Sturtevant (1840-1892), officer in the 14th New Hampshire Infantry Volunteers, U.S.A., to his parents including four while in Washington, D. C., guarding quartermaster's supplies, concerning personal matters with occasional references to his garrison duties; and one from New York City regarding preparations to sail to New Orleans, Louisiana, and describing a Saint Patrick's Day celebration.

5132. SAMUEL STYRE PAPERS, 1862-1865. 22 items. Medina County, Ohio.

Letters of Samuel Styre serving in the 42nd Regiment and later the 96th Regiment of Ohio Volunteers describing the battle of Vicksburg; skirmishes in Mississippi, Louisiana, and Alabama; foraging missions in which Southern property was confiscated or destroyed; the presidential election of 1864; Nathaniel Prentice Banks; and Copperheads in Ohio. Also included are two letters from

Joseph Bradfield referring to the activities of the 45th Ohio Regiment.

5133. GEORGE SUCKLEY, SR., AND GEORGE SUCKLEY, JR., PAPERS, 1791 (1846-1859) 1867. 103 items. New York, N.Y.

Mainly business papers of George Suckley, Sr., merchant and shipowner, and his sons, Thomas H. Suckley, John H. Suckley (d. 1865), George Suckley, Jr. (d. 1869), physician, and Rutsen Suckley, including papers relating to the partnership of George Suckley, Sr., with Thomas Holy of Sheffield, England; letters, 1848, from Thomas H. Suckley while traveling in Italy, France, Switzerland, Holland, and England giving detailed descriptions of scenery, customs, and local politics, with occasional references to the Revolution of 1848; papers, 1850s, pertaining to the overseas trade of M. M. Freeman and Company, of which George Suckley, Jr., was a partner, including bills of sale for registered vessels and accounts of service and equipment in preparing each ship for travel; U.S. Army receipt, 1856, listing medicines, medical books, etc., relating to the service of George Suckley, Jr., as surgeon in the army; letter from George Suckley, Jr., to James Graham Cooper, physician, concerning publication of their book, The Natural History of Washington Territory . . . (New York and London: 1859); letter, 1862, from Dr. Benjamin Tappan to George Suckley, Jr., discussing U. S. Army medical personnel; several personal letters; land deeds and indentures; prices current bulletin for Maracaibo, Venezuela, 1824; legal papers; and photographs.

5134. EDWARD BURTENSHAW SUGDEN, FIRST BARON ST. LEONARDS, PAPERS, 1860. 1 item. London, England.

Letter to Edward Burtenshaw Sugden, First Baron St. Leonards (1781-1875), British jurist and politician, from John Campbell, the Lord Chancellor, discussing the Law and Equity Bill and its provisions for the common law courts.

5135. LEWIS OSBORNE SUGG PAPERS, 1829 (1860-1870) 1901. 209 items. Brower's Mill (Randolph County), N.C.

Family correspondence of Lewis Osborne Sugg, including letters from Sugg while a Confederate soldier at the Fayetteville arsenal in North Carolina; a telegram from Thomas Charles Fuller, Raleigh lawyer; references to desertions from Confederate ranks and skirmishes between them and the home guard; a letter, 1869, from Trinity College, Randolph County, North Carolina; patent medicine advertisement; and a circular, 1887, concerning a meeting to consider the question of subscription to the High Point, Randleman, Asheboro, and Southern Railroad Company.

5136. SAMUEL SUGG ACCOUNT BOOK, 1807-1825. 1 vol. Wake County, N.C.

Individual sales accounts of Samuel Sugg (1781-1827), a general merchant.

5137. SULARD AND HILLIARD LEDGER, 1839-1842. 1 vol. Saint Louis, Mo.

Accounts of a brickyard which used hired labor.

5138. COUNCIL G. SULLIVAN PAPERS, 1895-1939. 106 items. Carthage (Moore County), N.C.

Personal and business papers of Council G. Sullivan, dealer in farm equipment, machines, seeds, and other similar products, including personal and business correspondence, financial papers, advertisements and other printed material, and a mortgage deed for W. L. Sullivan.

5139. [DANIEL SULLIVAN?] LEDGER, 1777-1799. 1 vol. (121 pp.) [London, England.?]

Accounts of a merchant trading between England and the West Indies, including general accounts of merchandise sold from various ships, and accounts of freight, interest, and insurance.

5140. GEORGE SULLIVAN PAPERS, 1837. 1 item. Exeter (Rockingham County), N.H.

Personal letter from George Sullivan (1771-1838), lawyer, U. S. congressman, 1811-1813, and attorney general of New Hampshire, 1805-1806 and 1816-1835, with reference to a political pamphlet he wrote.

5141. NATHANIEL F. SULLIVAN PAPERS, 1848-1859. 6 items. Germanton (Stokes County), N.C.

Personal and business correspondence of Nathaniel F. Sullivan, including a letter, 1857, discussing cotton prices in Georgia; and a letter, 1859, concerning a split in the Democratic Party in Texas and the probable election of Samuel Houston as governor.

5142. DAVID SUMMER PAPERS, 1874-1892. 181 items. Leitersburg (Washington County), Md.

Letters to David Summer, schoolteacher, from his son, John L. Summer, Logan County, Ohio, schoolteacher, tile manufacturer, farmer, and merchant, relating to family matters, teaching, business activities, and his work in the Methodist Church, with occasional references to politics, including the presidential election of 1876, the policies of Rutherford B. Hayes and William McKinley, and the death of Jefferson Davis.

5143. JULIUS A. SUMMERS PAPERS, 1861-1864. 4 items. Iredell County, N.C.

Letters from Julius A. Summers, Confederate soldier, describing the first battle of Manassas, 1861, the defense of Richmond, and the destruction of Federal stores.

5144. SUMTER (SOUTH CAROLINA) GUARDS SCRAPBOOK, 1879-1883. 1 vol. (54 pp.) Charleston, S.C.

Scrapbook of the Sumter (South Carolina) Guards, a militia unit, containing orders, rosters, lists of absentees, and letters.

5145. SUPREME COURT. APPELLATE DIVISION-FIRST DEPARTMENT. 1 vol. (749 pp.)

Record of the case of Thorne Baker as trustee in bankruptcy of the National Drama Corporation against Thomas Dixon (1864-1946), novelist and playwright, and director and officer of the corporation, before the Appellate Division of the Supreme Court in 1923. [Published by Libman's Law Printery, New York, New York.]

5146. SURRY COUNTY AGRICULTURAL SOCIETY JOURNAL, 1819-1823. 1 vol. (55 pp.) Surry County, N.C.

Constitution, rules of order, list of subscribers and transient members, and minutes of the proceedings of the Surry County Agricultural Society.

5147. JAMES A. SUTHERLAND PAPERS, 1849-1869. 40 items. Palmyra (Fluvanna County) and Howardsville (Albemarle County), Va.

Business and family papers of James A. Sutherland, Confederate soldier in the 19th Virginia Regiment, C.S.A., and minister, concerning personal and business affairs; Confederate camp life; the Confederate Chimborazo Hospital, Richmond, Virginia, where he stayed when he had measles, 1863; drunkenness; various generals and divisions; and ministers and preaching.

5148. WILLIAM T. SUTHERLIN PAPERS, 1846-1894. 234 items. Danville (Pittsylvania County), Va.

Papers of William T. Sutherlin (1822-1893), businessman, major in the Confederate Army, president of the Virginia Agricultural Society, and manufacturer of tobacco, relating to his interests in real estate, railroad building, wheat, cotton, and especially the tobacco business during the Confederate period. Letters from Bird L. Ferrell, tobacco farmer, to his son, P. W. Ferrell, describe labor problems during and immediately following the war.

5149. LYNDON SWAIM PAPERS, 1844-1872. 32 items and 1 vol. Greensboro (Guilford County), N.C.

Papers of Lyndon Swaim, publisher, with M. S. Sherwood, of the Greensboro Patriot, 1839-1854, contain letters from his father, Moses Swaim, in Newport, Indiana, and from his brothers, Curran Swaim and Ben Swaim, in Cincinnati, Ohio, discussing wages and teachers' salaries; commodity prices; abolitionists and runaway slaves in Newport; Methodists, Quakers, and United Brethren; the rapid growth of Cincinnati and the converging of transportation routes; origins of Ohio and Indiana settlers; the population of Chillicothe, Ohio, in 1847; spiritualism; and Curran Swaim's interest and studies of art. Also included are a letter, 1846, from James F. Morehead concerning the strength of the Whigs and the Democrats in North Carolina; letter, 1847, from Calvin H. Wiley regarding the publication of his novel in Harper's; letter from Augustine H. Shepperd, U. S. congressman, discussing Zachary Taylor and Henry Clay as Whig presidential candidates in 1848, and the fight in Congress over the ratification of the Treaty of Guadalupe Hidalgo that ended the Mexican War; letter from Daniel R. Goodloe to the Patriot pertaining to the invitation to Dutch immigrants from Governor William Alexander Graham to settle in eastern North Carolina, and giving his views on free labor; letter, 1859, from Lyndon Swaim describing a speech by Edward Everett in Raleigh, North Carolina, and Swaim's visit to New Bern, North Carolina, where he saw the ruins of Governor Tryon's palace; contract, 1861, for improvements on the Methodist Church in Greensboro; copy of a bill, 1864, to incorporate Greensboro; and a letter, 1870, criticizing Governor William W. Holden. The volume is a journal of a trip made in 1852 by Curran Swaim and his brother, Henry Swaim, through western Virginia to New York describing accomodations at taverns, traveling on plank roads, religious meetings held by Negroes, Washington College and Virginia Military Institute, both in Lexington (Virginia), a Methodist camp meeting near Lexington, towns through which they passed, Washington, D.C., and Vice President William R. King and various members of Congress whom they saw.

5150. DAVID LOWRY SWAIN PAPERS, 1839-1890s. 3 items. Chapel Hill (Orange County), N.C.

Routine correspondence of David Lowry Swain (1801-1868), governor of North Carolina and president of the University of North Carolina, Chapel Hill; and a manuscript written by Dr. Richard Harrison Speight, physician, containing reminiscences of Governor Swain and of Professor W. H. Owen of the University of North Carolina.

5151. CARRIE SWANK PAPERS, 1861-1862. 2 items. Pleasant Unity (Westmoreland County), Pa.

Personal letters from Carrie Swank to her aunt, Mrs. Mary A. Roody.

5152. CLAUDE AUGUSTUS SWANSON PAPERS, 1867-1935. 64 items. Washington, D.C.

Chiefly routine correspondence of Claude Augustus Swanson (1862-1939), U. S. congressman from Virginia, 1893-1905, governor of Virginia, 1906-1910, U. S. senator, 1910-1935, and secretary of the navy in 1933, concerning post office appointments, appointments to other offices, and bids for support in his various campaigns. In a letter of May 18, 1896, Senator Thomas Staples Martin comments on the "free silver" sentiment in Virginia, and his dissatisfaction with the policies of President Grover Cleveland.

5153. JOHN SWATS PAPERS, 1857, 1865. 2 items. Burks Mill (Augusta County), Va.

A letter to John Swats from his son in Illinois advising him to move there from Virginia as farming there was lucrative; and a Civil War poem written by a North Carolinian who had joined the Federal forces.

5154. GEORGE W. SWEPSON PAPERS, 1864-1865. 3 items. Haw River (Alamance County), N.C.

Business letters of George W. Swepson, one of which concerns the purchase of cotton thread and cloth from Swepson.

5155. JAMES P. SWERINGEN PAPERS, 1833-1872. 83 items. Saint Louis, Mo.

Chiefly personal financial papers of James P. Sweringen (or Swearingen) consisting of bills, receipts, and cancelled checks relating to dry goods, hotels, riding equipment, taxes, clothing, and subscriptions to various papers and periodicals. Ten business letters deal with deeds, property, the shipment of bags, and payments of overdue notes and bills. Also included are histories, mottoes and arms of ten surnames of Celtic and Norman ancestry.

5156. HENRY BARCLAY SWETE PAPERS. 1 item. Cambridge, Cambridgeshire, England.

Letter from Henry Barclay Swete (1835-1917), author and Regius Professor of Divinity at Cambridge University, to R. L. Bensly, a Cambridge Orientalist, concerning a Syriac manuscript Swete had found at American College, Beirut, Lebanon, containing an unknown work by Theodorus, bishop of Mopsuestia (d. ca. 428), and mentioning Swete's travels in the Middle East and Heinrich Schliemann.

5157. SWIFT SHOAL MILLS DAYBOOK, 1866-1867. 1 vol. (238 pp.) Virginia.

Accounts of the Swift Shoal Mills for the milling of corn, rye, and wheat.

5158. ALGERNON CHARLES SWINBURNE PAPERS, 1866-1907. 5 items and 2 vols. London, England.

Papers of Algernon Charles Swinburne (1837-1909), author, include bound copies of manuscripts of "The Maiden Marriage" and "The Queen's Pleasance"; two personal letters to his sister, Isabel Swinburne; printed copy of his Dedicatory Epistle; personal letter from Richard G. White, editor and author; and a letter from Swinburne sending his autograph.

5159. WILLIAM SWINTON PAPERS. 1 item. New York, N.Y.

Letter from William Swinton (1833-1892), journalist and author, to Harper and Brothers requesting a review copy of a book.

5160. MARY ELIZABETH (McCLAIN) SWORD PAPERS, 1822 (1865-1896) 1905. 586 items. Williamsport (Washington County), Md.

Papers of Mary Elizabeth (McClain) Sword include papers relating to the administration of the estate of Peter Sword; letters to Mary Elizabeth (McClain) Sword and to her husband, James Monroe Sword (d. 1892), member of the Maryland House of Delegates, from friends in the Midwest discussing commodity prices in Illinois during the 1850s and 1860s, politics in Illinois, the Civil War, emigration to the Midwest from the East after the war, Clement L. Vallandigham, and Democrats in Illinois in 1869; letters from M. J. Haderman while a student at Mercersburg College (now Mercersburg Academy), Mercersburg, Pennsylvania; letters from James M. Sword to Mary Elizabeth (McClain) Sword before and after their marriage; and letters from Hattie (McClain) Gring and Ambrose Daniel Gring, missionaries to Japan during the 1880s and 1890s, describing their observations and experiences there, missionary activities, and a Chinese-Japanese-English dictionary being compiled by Ambrose Daniel Gring; and letters from other members of the Sword family.

5161. THOMAS W. SYDNOR PAPERS, 1842, 1850. 2 items. Bruington (King and Queen County), Va.

Personal letters of members of the family of Thomas W. Sydnor, minister.

5162. JOHN SYKES PAPERS, 1857-1867.
15 items. Oglethorpe County, Ga.

Business papers of John Sykes, overseer on the plantation of Henry Hull, relating to a military exemption, a furlough in 1863, oath of allegiance, taxes in kind, and a labor contract with several freedman.

5163. LEANDER DUNBAR SYME PAPERS, 1918-1919. 13 items. Kentucky.

Records and maps of World War I, possibly used by Colonel Leander Dunbar Syme while an instructor at the U. S. Military Academy, West Point, New York, including maps of the Meuse-Argonne Offensive and of the St. Mihiel Salient; typescripts of a lecture on the battle around Metz in the Franco-Prussian War, 1870, by Captain Picard, General Staff, French Army; notes on operations in the vicinity of Chateau-Thierry and the Vesle River prepared by Brigadier General Fox Conner; what appear to be training lectures or reports on postwar battlefield tours of Chateau-Thierry, St. Mihiel Operation, and the attack of the 1st Division in the Argonne Forest; an extract from the intelligence report of the 5th Army Corps; and "American Expeditionary Forces, Headquarters Services of Supply, Office of the Chief of Staff, Visitors' Bureau."

5164. ARTHUR G. SYMONDS PAPERS, 1879-1904.
36 items. London, England.

Political correspondence of Arthur G. Symonds (d. 1924), British Liberal politician, concerning the utility of local and national political associations; efforts for parliamentary reform in the 1880s; a speech of William Edward Forster at Bradford; George Otto Trevelyan's choice of a parliamentary seat for the upcoming election; a pamphlet by Symonds on the Egyptian situation; the actions of General Gordon in the Sudan; the coercive bill on Ireland and its effect on the Liberal Party; prohibition propaganda; and other political and routine matters. Among the correspondents are John Bright, Henry Campbell-Bannerman, Charles W. Dilke, William Edward Forster, Herbert Gladstone, Henry Labouchere, and Sir Wilfred Lawson.

5165. HESTER E. (VAN BIBBER) TABB PAPERS, 1816 (1820-1822). 43 items. North End (Mathews County), Va.

Letters of Virginia girls written after attending Miss Lyman's School in Philadelphia, Pennsylvania, telling something of their teachers, studies, and social life.

5166. JOHN BANISTER TABB PAPERS, 1901-1936. 16 items. Baltimore, Md.

Papers of John Banister Tabb, poet and Roman Catholic priest, contain letters relating to his poetry and a number of poems concerning the Russo-Japanese War, Harriet Beecher Stowe, John Brown, Sir Isaac Newton, the Roman Catholic Church, and Booker T. Washington's meeting with President Theodore Roosevelt in the White House.

5167. "TABLE DES DRAMES CONTENUS DANS LA COLLECTION DE LA 'FRANCE DRAMATIQUE,' DU 'MAGAZIN THÉÂTRAL' ET DU 'THÉÂTRE D'AUTREFOIS.'"
1 vol. (118 pp.) France.

Manuscript listing, in French, of plays contained in France dramatique, Magazin théâtral, and Théâtre d'autrefois.

5168. ALPHONSO TAFT PAPERS, 1884-1889.
25 items. Cincinnati, Ohio.

Papers of Alphonso Taft, judge and United States cabinet officer, contain miscellaneous personal and business letters, including a letter, 1884, from Charles H. Gray concerning national politics, politics in Ohio, and the relationship of the Republican Party in Ohio to the administration of President Chester A. Arthur; and material concerning the presidential and congressional campaigns of 1888.

5169. HARVEY F. TAFT PAPERS, (1862-1863) 1875. 75 items. Milford (Worcester County), Mass.

Letters to Harvey F. Taft from his sons in the Union Army concerning service in the Department of the Gulf, including the formation of Negro regiments and the Red River campaign of 1863; various Massachusetts regiments and batteries; United States Navy blockading operations in North Carolina and Louisiana; and pro-union sentiment in the South.

5170. ROBERT ALPHONSO TAFT PAPERS, 1949.
2 items. Washington, D.C.

Copy of a speech, 1949, by Robert A. Taft, United States senator from Ohio, entitled "The Future of the Republican Party," and a letter from Taft to Walter Neill McDonald written to accompany the speech.

5171. WILLIAM HOWARD TAFT PAPERS, 1907.
3 items. Cincinnati, Ohio.

Miscellaneous items relating to William Howard Taft, president of the United States, including a facsimile of a letter, 1907, to Taft from President Theodore Roosevelt discussing relations with Cuba.

5172. HENRY E. TAINTOR PAPERS, 1856-1864.
46 items. Hampden (Windham County), Conn.

Letters of Henry E. Taintor, a soldier in the Union Army, concern his service in the 1st Connecticut Heavy Artillery and describe camp life and daily routine; experiences in the Bermuda Line on the James River in Virginia, 1864; life in the siege line at Petersburg, Virginia, 1864; the operation of various kinds of artillery shells and guns; and visits from President

Abraham Lincoln and Senators Zachariah Chandler and William Sprague.

5173. JAMES TAIT PAPERS, 1937-1938. 8 items. Wilmslow, Cheshire, England.

Miscellaneous papers of James Tait, a professor of ancient and medieval history, include a galley proof for Tait's review of The Records of a Yorkshire Manor by Sir Thomas Selby Lawson-Tancred and Tait's notes on the book; letters from Colonel John William Robinson Parker concerning the publication of a work by the Reverend John Solloway; and two letters about Tait's investments.

5174. JAMES GOODE TAIT PAPERS, 1845-1854. 4 items. Black's Bluff (Wilcox County), Ala.

Correspondence of James Goode Tait (1833-1911), a planter in Wilcox County and, after 1849, in Colorado County, Texas; and of Robert and C. W. Tait, probably his brothers. The letters are chiefly concerned with crops and with plans for moving to Texas, although there is a description of a Fourth of July celebration in 1845.

5175. MARGARET JANE (STUART-WORTLEY) TALBOT PAPERS, 1895-1903. 11 items. London, England.

Letters to Lady Talbot from Evelyn Baring, First Earl of Cromer, concerning literary, family, and social matters.

5176. CHARLES HENRY TALBOTT II AND CHARLES HENRY TALBOTT III PAPERS, 1826 (1931-1943) 1948. 647 items and 1 vol. Richmond, Va.

Papers of Charles Henry Talbott II, Charles Henry Talbott III, and various other members of the Talbott, Munford, and Wythe families contain poems written by Charles Henry Talbott II as a student at Randolph-Macon College, Ashland, Virginia; letters, 1867, from Sallie R. Munford to Charles Henry Talbott II; correspondence between Charles Henry Talbott III and his parents while he was a student; correspondence of Charles Henry Talbott III in the 1920s and 1930s relating to the management of hotels, including material on accomodations for guests at the Yorktown Sesquicentennial, Yorktown, Virginia, 1931; correspondence of Charles Henry Talbott III with Duke University and other schools concerning the disposition of the Munford-Ellis papers; and letters pertaining to a biography of George W. Munford, written by Charles Henry Talbott III.

5177. SIR THOMAS NOON TALFOURD PAPERS, 1836. 1 item. Reading, Berkshire, England.

Letter to Sir Thomas Noon Talfourd (1795-1854), British judge and author, from Francis Jeffrey concerning a pension for an unidentified person.

5178. WILLIAM BOOTH TALIAFERRO PAPERS, 1865, 1871. 2 items. Gloucester County, Va.

A receipt for taxes, 1865, and a letter of introduction, 1871, of William B. Taliaferro, Confederate general, Virginia legislator, and judge.

5179. CHARLES MAURICE DE TALLEYRAND-PÉRIGORD, PRINCE DE BÉNÉVENT, PAPERS. 1 item. Paris, France.

A note in which Talleyrand announces his arrival at Blois by way of Tours.

5180. W. E. TALTON PAPERS, 1861. 2 items. De Kalb County, Ga.

Personal letters from W. E. Talton, Confederate private in the 7th Georgia Regiment, stationed at Winchester, Virginia, commenting on crops in Virginia and the expected short duration of the war.

5181. ROGER BROOKE TANEY PAPERS, 1809-1863. 5 items. Frederick (Frederick County), Md.

Miscellaneous business and legal papers of Roger B. Taney, chief justice of the Supreme Court of the United States.

5182. B. TANNER PAPERS, 1862, 1865. 2 items. Richmond, Va.

Personal letters of B. Tanner, a Confederate soldier.

5183. EVANS TANNER LEDGERS, 1843-1863. 4 vols. Petersburg (Dinwiddie County), Va.

Accounts of a general merchant.

5184. VINCENT TAPP PAPERS, 1786 (1808-1821) 1835. 210 items and 1 vol. Staunton (Augusta County), Va.

Business, family, and official correspondence of Vincent Tapp (b. 1757), Revolutionary soldier and clerk of Augusta County Court. Included also is information about the Tapp family; Tapp's career as a soldier; and the construction of the hall of Masonic Lodge No. 13, of which he was an active member. A volume contains records of caring for the poor in Augusta County, 1791-1822.

5185. TARBORO PRIMITIVE BAPTIST CHURCH RECORDS, 1819-1914. 30 items and 4 vols. Tarboro (Edgecombe County), N.C.

Papers of the Tarboro Primitive Baptist Church include a variety of minutes, receipts, letters, and lists, 1853-1914. Volumes include the covenant, minutes, and lists of members, 1819-1907, and treasurer's accounts, 1830-1874.

5186. WILLIAM TARRY PAPERS, 1807 (1826-1869). 323 items. Clarksville (Mecklenburg County), Va.

Family letters concerned with William Tarry; his father, Edward Tarry; and the former's five children. The letters reflect Southern social conditions in the antebellum period and the shortage of munitions during the Civil War.

5187. J. W. M. TATE DAYBOOK, 1855. 1 vol. (471 pp.) Altamont (Grundy County), Tenn.

Accounts of a general merchant.

5188. WILLIAM C. TATE PAPERS, 1780-1874. 39 items. Burke County, N.C.

Land grants; deeds; mortgages; certificates of stock in the Western North Carolina Railroad; a survey, 1874, by J. P. Beck; and a pardon, 1865, granted William C. Tate by President Andrew Johnson.

5189. JOSIAH TATTNALL, SR., PAPERS, 1766-1802. 6 items. "Bonaventure," near Savannah, Ga.

Papers of Josiah Tattnall, Sr. (1762-1803), Revolutionary soldier, United States senator, and governor of Georgia, contain letters concerning family and legal matters; letter of recommendation to Governor Tattnall from Elijah Clarke; letter of Governor Tattnall concerning a pardon; a deed, 1775; and a bond.

5190. JOSIAH TATTNALL, JR., PAPERS, 1843-1878. 39 items. Savannah, Ga.

Papers of Josiah Tattnall, Jr. (1795-1871), officer in the United States Navy and in the Confederate States Navy, contain letters, 1843-1866, pertaining to many aspects of Tattnall's career, including his service as commander of the U.S.S. Saratoga in the African squadron; the surveying of a harbor for American ships in Japan, 1859; and the conversion of the U.S.S. Merrimac into the Confederate ironclad, Virginia.

5191. OSBURN TATUM ACCOUNT BOOK, 1848-1875. 1 vol. (148 pp.)

Accounts of a physician.

5192. HENRY E. TAURMAN PAPERS, 1862. 7 items. Goochland (Goochland County), Va.

Letters of Henry E. Taurman, a soldier in the 5th Virginia Regiment, Cavalry, to his wife, describing the movements of his company.

5193. AUGUSTIN LOUIS TAVEAU PAPERS, 1741 (1830-1836) 1931. 1,858 items and 4 vols. Charleston, S.C.

Family, personal, literary, and business correspondence of Louis Augustin Thomas Taveau (1790-ca. 1857), planter; of his wife, Martha Caroline (Swinton) Ball Taveau (d. 1847); of their son, Augustin Louis Taveau (1828-1886), planter and author; of the latter's wife, Delphine (Sprague) Taveau (1832-ca. 1909); and of relatives and friends.

Papers prior to 1829 consist of a copy of the will of William Swinton made in 1741, letters between the Swinton and Girardeau families, a letter to Hugh Swinton describing the death of Josias Allston, letters in 1810 of Eliza G. Maybank to Margaret Swinton recording Charleston events, the marriage settlement of Martha Caroline (Swinton) Ball and Louis Augustin Thomas Taveau with opinions by Thomas S. Grimké and Robert Y. Hayne regarding the right to sell, loan, or mortgage any property mentioned in the settlement, and a copy of the will of Caroline Olivia (Ball) Laurens, daughter of Martha Caroline (Swinton) Ball Taveau by her first marriage.

Beginning in June, 1829, and continuing for more than a year, the collection contains letters to Martha Caroline (Swinton) Ball Taveau from her husband, Louis Augustin Thomas Taveau, while he was in France endeavoring to settle his father's estate. The burden of his letters consists of pleas for his wife to write, although he often urged her to be economical and mentioned his children and his wife's children by her first marriage.

In 1838 the papers begin to center around Augustin Louis Taveau (1828-1886), while in school at Mt. Zion Academy, Winnsboro, South Carolina. From 1838 to 1840, young Taveau received letters from his father urging economy and from his mother urging greater piety and complaining of her health and of her husband's dissipation in going to the races and theater and dining out. Included also are letters from young Taveau's half sisters. Letters from his mother show that she and the elder Taveau had separated by 1838. During the same period, there are letters from Martha Caroline (Swinton) Ball Taveau from upland South Carolina and Asheville, North Carolina, where she went for her health, and letters from the elder Taveau who was in France to supervise the return of his two daughters, Caroline Rosalie (b. 1824) and Augusta Melanie (b. 1825), who had been in school there for some time. After 1843, the elder Taveau sometimes mentions his rice planting at his plantation, "Clermont," near Charleston, but he more often urged his son to study and cease wasting money. During the same period young Taveau received letters from his friends, especially from J. A. Gadsden, while the latter attended St. Paul's College, Long Island, New York. There are numerous copies of the wills of Martha Caroline (Swinton) Ball Taveau and of Horatio Sprague around 1847 and many letters then and subsequently regarding the division of the former's personal property. From 1848 until 1854 young Taveau, usually in or near Charleston, was the central character of a correspondence centering around his need for more spending money, his desultory study of law in the office of James L. Petigru, the estrangement between his father and mother, his extensive social engagements in Charleston, his literary activities usually as a poet, and his father's complaint that his son studied too little law and wrote too many poems. In the literary correspondence of this period there are letters of William Gilmore Simms containing advice to young Taveau and letters of John R. Thompson dealing generally with the condition of the Southern Literary Messenger, which he edited. The correspondence with Thompson also deals with young Taveau's efforts to write poetry for the Messenger, one or two of his poems having been published, and with young Taveau's efforts to obtain subscribers in Charleston. Many letters of young Taveau and of his sisters, prior to 1851, are concerned with the son's efforts to get spending money from the father.

After the beginning of the elder Taveau's illness in 1851, there are numerous letters from the trustee of the elder Taveau's estate regarding spending money for the son. By June, 1852, young Taveau succeeded in getting money for a trip abroad, his tour lasting until the end of 1854. Letters and papers of that period consist of hotel bills, other papers pertaining to his travels, letters from young Taveau to his friends regarding his travels or his need for extra money, and letters from his friends and relatives in Charleston giving accounts of cholera epidemics, yellow fever epidemics, parties, trips to various springs, weddings, and general gossip. Many of these letters were from W.H. Huger and Keating L. Simons, brother-in-law of Taveau.

From 1855 until 1860, the papers contain correspondence with the publisher of Taveau's book of poems, The Magic Word and Other Poems (Boston, 1855), published under the pseudonym of "Alton," correspondence with the Sprague family in an effort to obtain the remainder of Delphine (Sprague) Taveau's patrimony, papers relative to a mortgage on Oaks Plantation held by Robert Hume, plans for Negro cabins, estimates for ditching and banking at Oaks, letters relative to the failure of Simons Brothers in Charleston in 1857 and the consequent loss of Oaks Plantation, letters of Taveau describing a trip to New Orleans (Louisiana), with his slaves and their sale, letters of Taveau to his wife describing various plantations in Mississippi and Louisiana, where he went in search of a rice plantation, and a series of letters in 1860 to and from Taveau, Ralph Elliott, and Clifford Simons regarding a supposedly slighting remark involving Taveau's credit.

Late in 1861 Taveau settled on a farm near Abbeville, South Carolina, but soon afterwards joined the Confederate Army. His career in the army continued until 1865. Letters to his wife during the war period, contain Taveau's accounts of his efforts to get on the staff of General Nathan George Evans; descriptions of Charleston during the war; accounts of his efforts and success in being transferred from any regiment ordered to the Virginia battlefields; methods for supporting his family; errands and small tasks for his wife in regard to his personal comfort; descriptions of Jackson, Mississippi, and its environs; a reference on June 20, 1863, to the artist of the London Illustrated News; descriptions of the battered condition of Fort Sumter; reference to an English gun of great range and fire power received in Charleston in 1863; reference to a torpedo boat attack on a Federal ironclad in a letter of October 8, 1863; accounts of the theft by Taveau and others of provisions and supplies sent to Fort Sumter by truce boat for Union prisoners; reference to a brief tenure in the Subsistence Department of the Army near Abbeville, South Carolina; accounts of his virtual desertion from General Thomas L. Clingman's brigade; copy of a letter evidently intended for a newspaper, protesting that gentlemen of birth and education could get no commissions in the army while sons of tinkers could; lists of supplies sent his family; accounts of high prices in Charleston; accounts of his duties as guard at the "Sub-Treasury" in Charleston; papers relating to an effort to permit Delphine (Sprague) Taveau and her three children to sail for Europe in December, 1864; and oaths of allegiance and passports issued to Taveau and his wife and children, March 3, 1865, for going to Boston, Massachusetts.

Immediately after the war, the papers contain letters and copies of letters published in the New York Tribune by Taveau under the title of "A Voice from South Carolina," stating that former Southern leaders could not be trusted and condemning them for having allowed conscription. Included also are drafts of letters from Taveau to Horace Greeley and William Aiken protesting that he, Taveau, had seen the error of his belief in slavery; letters relative to Taveau's efforts to get the position of collector of the customs at Charleston; accounts of an interview of Taveau with Greeley and with President Andrew Johnson; letter of June 25, 1865, describing conditions in Charleston and Columbia, South Carolina; a copy of a petition signed by Henry L. Benbow, A. R. Chisholm, William Gregg, and Taveau begging President Johnson to appoint a provisional governor for South Carolina; several letters to and from

William Aiken; and letters written by Taveau to his wife in the autumn of 1865 from various points in Virginia including areas near Richmond, Alexandria, and Warrenton, where he had gone in search of a farm.

Taveau and his family finally settled in 1866 on a farm near Chaptico in St. Mary's County, Maryland. From 1866 until 1881, the correspondence is concerned with efforts to obtain patents and money for developing a revolving harrow and a steam plow invented by Taveau; efforts to obtain money for meeting the annual interest on the sum owed for the farm near Chaptico; and accounts of Taveau's literary activities. Included from 1866 until 1877 are many letters of Joseph Smith, retired rear admiral of the United States Navy and old friend of Horatio Sprague, remarkable for their sympathy to Taveau, his understanding of national problems, descriptions of summer jaunts to the North, his fears that the United States was not to become a great nation, and accounts of many errands at the United States Patent Office for Taveau. There are letters and papers bearing on Taveau's efforts to interest the Ames Plow Company, as well as manufacturers of farm machinery in Dayton, Ohio, in his inventions and drawings and circulars relative to the inventions.

From 1878 until Taveau's death, his papers contain manuscripts of his poems and correspondence with many leading publishing houses regarding the publication of Montezuma (published in New York in 1883 and again in 1931). Thereafter much of his correspondence consists of letters of thanks from various relatives, friends, and well-known literary figures for copies of Montezuma sent them by Taveau; and letters to newspapers and magazines submitting his poems and usually followed by letters of rejection. During the 1880s there are many letters from T. J. Hylande-MacGrath, a genealogist of New York. There are also clippings of notices of Taveau's poem Montezuma. Included are many unpublished poems by Taveau, two volumes of poems, two volumes of "Leon de Montega; a Romance of Cadiz," a few copies of articles on agriculture, notes on genealogy, and many clippings. Included also are many letters of Augustin Louis Taveau, Jr., usually relative to the finances of the Taveau family and to his work as overseer of a farm, "Jutland," in Maryland. Throughout the collection there are many letters from the mother and sisters of Delphine (Sprague) Taveau, usually in French. Letters of her brothers, however, were generally in English.

Among the correspondents are William Aiken, Oliver Wendell Holmes, James Johnston Pettigrew, William Gilmore Simms, Joseph Smith, and John R. Thompson. [Some of Taveau's earlier literary correspondence including his letters, and replies of well-known literary figures, chiefly from John R. Thompson, have been published, although some of the biographical data concerning Taveau is incorrect; David K. Jackson (ed.) "Some Unpublished Letters of John R. Thompson and Augustin Louis Taveau," William and Mary College Quarterly, XVI (April 1936), 206-221; "Letters of Georgia Editors and a Correspondent," Georgia Historical Quarterly, XXIII (June, 1939), 170-176.]

5194.  CABELL TAVENNER AND ALEXANDER SCOTT WITHERS PAPERS, 1784 (1828-1867) 1929. 3,000 items. Wood County, W. Va.

Family and legal correspondence and papers of Cabell Tavenner (1808-1849), attorney and member of the Virginia House of Delegates, and of various members of the family of Alexander Scott Withers (1792-1865), author of Chronicles of Border Warfare . . . (Cincinnati: 1895).

The bulk of the collection is made up of legal documents, including land surveys, land grants, leases, articles of agreement, deeds of sale, trial dockets, and petitions. Personal papers of Cabell Tavenner include his compositions and an oration as a student at Jefferson College, Canonsburg, Pennsylvania, and letters, 1842, from Tavenner to his father, Thomas Tavenner, mentioning fees at the University of Virginia, types of examinations given candidates for legal degrees, student opinion on the nullification issue, and the work of Professor John A. G. Davis in promulgating Southern political views. Papers, 1833-1841, include household accounts of the Tavenner and Withers families and legal correspondence of Cabell Tavenner. Letters, 1842-1844, concern Tavenner's service in the Virginia House of Delegates, with occasional references to impeachment proceedings against Judge Scott. Also letters concerning the settlement of the estate of Cabell Tavenner.

Papers of the Withers family concern migration to Texas, ca. 1856, life in Galveston, Texas, and German settlers in Texas; agricultural prospects in Birdville, Tarrant County, Texas, 1859; life in New Orleans, Louisiana, and the state of the cotton market in that city; the division of the family between the Union and the Confederacy during the Civil War; effects of the war on life in New Orleans and Texas; postwar education of various women in the family at the Academy of Visitation (Wheeling, West Virginia), Parkersburg Female Seminary (Parkersburg, West Virginia), and Woodberry Forest School (Orange, Virginia), including frequent allusions to current fashions in women's dress; and a suit by Jennet (Withers) Tavenner and her daughter, Janet Ann Tavenner to settle a claim to a tract of land in Webster County, West Virginia.

5195.  DAVID THOMAS TAYLOE PAPERS, 1857-1882. 23 items and 8 vols. Washington (Beaufort County), N.C.

Papers of David Thomas Tayloe, a physician of Washington, North Carolina, are made up largely of statements giving charges for visits to various patients. Volumes in the collection consist of visiting lists and account books, including a ledger recording the practice of Dr. David T. Tayloe and Dr. John Kirkland Ruffin, 1859-1867; and a ledger for Tayloe's practice, 1857-1863.

5196. A. G. TAYLOR AND WILLIAM A. MILLER LEDGER, 1860-1870. 1 vol. Danville (Pittsylvania County), Va.

Accounts of a mercantile firm specializing in the sale of books and stationery.

5197. DANIEL WALTON TAYLOR PAPERS, 1842-1852. 5 items. Sherburne (Rutland County), Vt.

Letters from a student at Black River Academy, Ludlow, Vermont, concerning school life.

5198. FRANK E. TAYLOR PAPERS, 1862-1914. 87 items. Charleston, S.C.

Papers of Frank E. Taylor, businessman of Charleston, South Carolina, are made up for the most part of legal papers, including deeds, plats, a crop lien, abstracts of titles, bonds, mortgages, Taylor's will, and letters involving the settlement of his estate.

5199. GEORGE TAYLOR PAPERS, 1797-1804. 1 vol. Charlestown (Cecil County), Md.

Receipt book of George Taylor.

5200. GRIFFIN TAYLOR PAPERS, 1792 (1818-1862). 39 items. Frederick County, Va.

Papers of Griffin Taylor, probably clerk of Frederick County in 1792 and later tax collector, consisting of lists of tax assessments and rates, and few personal papers.

5201. SIR HENRY GEORGE ANDREW TAYLOR PAPERS, 1827 (1832-1837) 1893. 46 items and 3 vols. London, England.

Papers of Sir Henry George Andrew Taylor, British soldier, concern his command of the northern division of the Madras Army in India and his work in the pacification of that region under George Edward Russell, civil commissioner. Letter books for portions of 1833, 1834, 1837, and 1838, contain Taylor's private letters to Frederick Adam, governor of Madras, and letters, 1833-1837, contain Adam's portion of the correspondence. Also included are a volume containing orders to Taylor from Madras, 1832-1837; Taylor's correspondence with the quartermaster general at Madras, 1835-1837; and Taylor's orders to his subordinates, 1832-1836. A number of items in the papers of Sir Henry George Andrew Taylor have been edited by Lorenzo M. Crowell, Jr., a graduate student at Duke University and the edited copies have been added to the collection.

5202. JAMES TAYLOR PAPERS, 1831 (1843-1908) 1932. 558 items and 1 vol. Valley Town (Cherokee County), N.C.

Papers of James Taylor, who represented the Eastern or North Carolina Cherokee Indians in their dealings with the United States government, and scattered papers of William H. Thomas, a leader of the Eastern Cherokees, and David Taylor, father of James Taylor. The collection contains numerous papers relating to land transactions and business affairs among Cherokees of North Carolina; papers, 1867-1870 and 1886, concerning Eastern Cherokees who wanted to join the Cherokee Nation in Indian Territory; papers relating to the controversy between James G. Blunt and James Taylor over who was the official representative of the Eastern Cherokees; letters in the 1870s and 1880s from John Ross and Nimrod Jarrett Smith, chiefs of the Eastern Cherokees, concerning conditions among the Indians; papers pertaining to the case of the Eastern Band of Cherokee v. William H. Thomas, William Johnson, and James W. Terrell; and letters of Belva A. Lockwood, a Washington claims attorney representing the Eastern Cherokees. The volume is a copy of As I Recollect (Pocahontas Club: 1949), a book on Cherokee Indian families.

5203. JOHN TAYLOR PAPERS, 1789-1929. 12 items. Caroline County, Va.

Letters from John Taylor (1753-1824), political writer, agriculturalist, and United States senator, concerning debts of the estate of General Thomas Nelson; settlement of the estate of one Carter, evidently of West Point, Virginia; imminence of war with Great Britain in 1807; agricultural pursuits; the principles of republicanism; political theories of Albert Gallatin with reference to Thomas Jefferson; and the proposed establishment in Richmond of a newspaper to enunciate republican principles, probably to be edited by James Mercer Garnett. Included also are copies of letters and papers bearing on a pamphlet by John Adams in 1776; and the family history of John Taylor of Caroline in a letter from Taylor's grandson in 1875.

5204. JOHN B. TAYLOR LETTER BOOK, 1820-1821. 1 vol. Norfolk, Va.

Official correspondence of John B. Taylor as deputy marshal.

5205. JOHN J. TAYLOR PAPERS, 1862-1864. 10 items. Cedar Grove (Orange County), N.C.

Correspondence between John J. Taylor and his family while he was in a Confederate military camp, 1862-1864, in the western part of North Carolina. Two letters from Taylor's mother, who made the long journey from Cedar Grove to a camp near Wilmington, where her son was ill, reveal conditions in camp and the difficulties of travel.

5206. JOHN W. TAYLOR PAPERS, 1816. 2 items. Ballston Spa (Saratoga County), N.Y.

Papers of John W. Taylor, a United States congressman from New York, contain two letters written to Taylor while he was a member of the United States House of Representatives concerning the financial affairs of W. D. Cheever.

5207. JOSEPH J. TAYLOR PAPERS, 1836-1872. 5 items and 1 vol. Lockville (Chatham County), N.C.

Papers of Joseph J. Taylor contain business and political letters to Taylor, and an account book with records relating to farming, blacksmithing, and the mercantile business.

5208. RICHARD TAYLOR PAPERS, 1864-1865. 4 items. "Fashion," Saint Charles Parish, La.

Papers of Richard Taylor, general in the Confederate Army, contain general orders issued by Taylor praising his troops for stopping Union General Nathaniel P. Banks's Red River campaign, 1864; and directing the surrender of the troops of the Department of Alabama, Mississippi, and Eastern Louisiana, 1865. Also a letter, 1864, from Taylor to Colonel G. W. Brent concerning the possibility of Taylor's being stationed at Mobile, Alabama.

5209. ROSALIA E. TAYLOR PAPERS, 1852-1865. 4 items. Brunswick County, Va.

Family and social correspondence of Rosalia E. Taylor, including a comment on Petersburg, Virginia, in June, 1865.

5210. THOMAS TAYLOR PAPERS, 1862-1906. 636 items and 18 vols. Warrenton (Fauquier County), Va.

Papers of Thomas Taylor contain lecture notes, essays, and poems from his school days in Alexandria, Virginia, 1859; letters concerning his work in the War Tax Office in Montgomery, Alabama, 1863-1865; love letters to his fiancée, Annie Lawrason, 1865, which also comment on the procedure for becoming a lawyer in Louisiana; and letters, 1867, related to the management of Taylor's farm in Virginia. Letters after 1867 are those of Annie (Lawrason) Taylor and her daughter, Eliza Taylor, and deal for the most part with family matters. The collection contains a number of manuscripts of Thomas Taylor's unpublished poems, short stories, and novels, written mainly after 1872, and items relating to Taylor's invention for the improved propulsion of bicycles. Volumes include a diary, 1859, kept while Taylor was in school in Alexandria, Virginia; farm accounts, 1867; farm inventories, 1882-1892; and a scrapbook containing clippings of Taylor's published short stories.

5211. THOMAS JEROME TAYLOR PAPERS, 1787-1929. 121 items. Warrenton (Warren County), N.C.

The papers of Thomas Jerome Taylor concern his work as a Baptist minister and contain letters pertaining to his service in various churches in North Carolina and South Carolina; letters from missionaries and letters concerning the mission work of the Baptist church; and letters from other ministers and prominent Baptist laymen. Miscellaneous items include genealogical material on the Whitfield and Dargan families and several items dealing with people in Warren County, North Carolina, and vicinity.

5212. W. W. TAYLOR PAPERS, 1834-1835. 2 items.

Statement for items of jewelry and the sale of lottery tickets to W. W. Taylor by W. I. Ramsay & Co.

5213. WILLIAM TAYLOR PAPERS, 1797-1801. 3 items. Baltimore, Md.

Correspondence of William Taylor, apparently a merchant, referring to the shipping of produce and financial matters.

5214. WILLIAM TAYLOR PAPERS, 1844. 1 item. Washington, D.C.

Letter to William Taylor, member of the United States House of Representatives from Virginia, from Theodore Cuyler, dealing with legal affairs and real estate of Elliott Cresson.

5215. WILLIAM TAYLOR PAPERS, 1846-1924. 9 vols. Romney (Hampshire County), W. Va.

Volumes in this collection contain tannery records and an estate book.

5216. TAYLOR, DAVIES, AND TAYLOR PAPERS, 1811-1813. 3 items. Savannah, Ga.

Mercantile accounts, for the most part concerning lumber.

5217. LITTLETON WALLER TAZEWELL PAPERS, 1822-1829. 5 items. Norfolk, Va.

Routine correspondence of Littleton Waller Tazewell, state legislator, governor of Virginia, and United States representative and senator from Virginia, including letters to Tazewell from Robert Young Hayne concerning increasing the number of subscribers to the Southern Review and tariff legislation.

5218. ELLEN TEAGUE PAPERS, 1866-1880. 45 items. Abbott's Creek (Davidson County), N.C.

Correspondence and papers of Ellen Teague and other members of her family. Among the correspondence is a kind of family history, with information on Baptists, prepared by an older member of the family. Included also are letters from a Missouri branch of the family with comments on agricultural and economic conditions in that state during the 1870s; letters from a student at Wake Forest College, North Carolina, with an account of student life in 1876; and other family letters.

5219. JOHN TEAGUE CIPHERING BOOK, 1832. 1 vol. (104 pp.) Davidson, County, N.C.

Mathematical exercises.

5220. ISRAEL KEECH TEFFT PAPERS, 1833-1861. 8 items. Savannah, Ga.

Papers of Israel Keech Tefft concern the collecting of autographs and Tefft's work as cashier of the Bank of the State of Georgia, Savannah, Georgia.

5221. EDWARD TELFAIR PAPERS, 1764 (1771-1807) 1831. 906 items and 5 vols. Savannah, Ga.

Papers of Edward Telfair, governor of Georgia and delegate to the Continental Congress, concern various legal matters including transfer of property, settlement of estates, and recovery of property seized by the British in the Revolution; business affairs, including correspondence with James Jackson, a commission merchant in London, a contract with Jeremiah Fox of Philadelphia, 1785, to build a factory for tobacco products in Savannah, letters relating to the British market for tobacco and indigo, and correspondence with a British merchant about the marketing of rice; negotiations with various Indian tribes and relations with Indians generally, trade with Indians, and concern in the 1780s and 1790s over possible war with the Creek Indians; management of slaves, purchase and sale of slaves, runaway slaves, the mortality rate among slaves born on a plantation, difficulty of selling closely related slaves, and relations between whites and free blacks; politics and the political situation after the election of 1800; and the education of Telfair's children in the North, especially at the College of New Jersey. Volumes in the collection include a receipt book, 1764-1782; a letter book, 1769-1770, containing business correspondence with a London merchant; a daybook, 1775-1781, of Edward Telfair and Company; and a daybook, 1775-1782, and ledger, 1773-1793, of the firm of Cowper and Telfair.

5222. HENRY JOHN TEMPLE, THIRD VISCOUNT PALMERSTON, PAPERS, 1808-1865. 47 items. London, England.

Papers of Henry John Temple, Third Viscount Palmerston, British statesman, contain a letter, 1837, concerning the victory of Palmerston and his friends in recent elections; letters, 1853-1854, to the mayor of Romsey, England, relating to sanitation and the possible outbreak of cholera; memoranda, 1852-1854, from Palmerston, then serving as home secretary, to a member of his staff pertaining to administration and routine business; a note, 1834, from Palmerston to Prince Talleyrand concerning an accord which they were to sign the next day; correspondence, 1863, with Charles Ross, parliamentary reporter of The Times about proposals which England would make to Russia on the Polish situation and a controversy about the activities of Neapolitan exiles in Italy; and a report, 1848, to Palmerston from Charles Robert Gordon, secretary of the British legation at Stockholm, Sweden, on Norwegian reaction to the Schleswig-Holstein crisis.

5223. W. A. TEMPLETON PAPERS, 1861-1864. 6 items. Yorkville (York County), S.C.

Letters from W. A. Templeton, a private in the Confederate Army, most of which were written from Camp Gregg, Virginia, and discuss "Yankee" depredations in the neighborhood, rumors of peace, and the miserable condition of Virginia roads in winter.

5224. TENNESSEE COLONISATION COMPANY PAPERS, 1844-1867. 38 items. Antwerp, Belgium.

Papers of the Tennessee Colonisation Company, a European organization formed at Cologne, Germany, in 1844 to exploit about 180,000 acres of land that had been purchased in Morgan County, Tennessee, are primarily the incoming correspondence of the company, 1855-1857 and 1865-1867. The correspondence relates to controversy over the title to the property and the disposal of it, including the purchase of a large portion of the land by a group of Welsh settlers led by William Bebb, a prominent Whig politician of Ohio.

5225. PARKER G. TENNEY PAPERS, 1921-1925. 2 items and 1 vol. Massachusetts.

Typescript copy of a report for the military intelligence division of the United States general staff written by Captain Parker G. Tenney who accompanied the National Geographic Central China Expedition in 1924 as a zoological collector. The portion of the report on Indochina covers the geography, history, climate, economy, and military organizations of the region and the section on China discusses the geography, climate, population, and products of the country and gives a historical, political, and military sketch from the revolution.

5226. ALFRED TENNYSON, FIRST BARON TENNYSON, PAPERS, 1831-1909. 89 items. "Farringford," Isle of Wight, England.

Papers of Alfred, Lord Tennyson, include letters to Sophy Rawnsley concerning personal matters, the possible publication of Tennyson's poems in the United States, the value of his poetry, and the presentation of one of his volumes to Queen Victoria. Letters of Frederick Tennyson, brother of Alfred, Lord Tennyson, refer to the death of his father and the early publication of Alfred, Lord Tennyson's, poems. Letters of Hallam Tennyson, son of Alfred, Lord Tennyson, to Theodore Watts-Dunton contain allusions to his father's works.

5227. MARY VIRGINIA (HAWES) TERHUNE PAPERS, 1843 (1849-1856) 1920. 67 items. Amelia County, Va.

Letters from Mary Virginia (Hawes) Terhune (1830-1922), author, known as "Marion Harland." The letters for 1843-1857 are addressed to school friends and tell about schoolgirl affairs and her attempts to write; the remainder of the letters, 1896-1913, are to friends and contain reminiscences of her early life.

5228. ANTOINE AND BARTHELEMY TERRASSON PAPERS, 1773 (1780-1860) 1869. 1,253 items. Philadelphia, Pa.

Letters and papers of the French trading firm of Terrasson Brothers established in Philadelphia by Antoine and Barthelemy Terrasson as a branch of their father's firm, John Terrasson and Company, with headquarters in Paris and Lyons, France. Many of the letters are from John Terrasson, chiefly to Barthelemy Terrasson, who, before coming to America, had been stationed at Cadiz, to oversee the firm's trade with Lisbon, Malabar, and Macáo. While at Philadelphia, Barthelemy Terrasson also received letters from his brother, Antoine, who traveled for the firm. Many of these letters reflect the trade of the firm in grain, the furnishing of supplies to French and American armies, and the purchase of tobacco when their operations were first started at Yorktown and Alexandria (Virginia), Baltimore (Maryland), Charleston (South Carolina), and New Bern and Edenton (North Carolina). The correspondence contains frequent mention of the movement of the French fleet, forces under Rochambeau and D'Estaing, world-wide trade, rates of exchange, and evidences of speculation and trade during the Revolutionary period. Correspondence in 1784 reveals that the Terrasson brothers became involved in a quarrel with John Ross over the ownership of trading vessels which the Terrassons held jointly with Ross. Albert Gallatin carried messages to Ross for the Terrassons, and their papers also contain many drafts drawn on Stephen Girard.

The Terrassons disappear from the correspondence about 1790, and the remaining papers are concerned with Mark Prager, owner of a trading firm of Holland. Evidently some member of the Prager family married into the Terrasson family. This later correspondence concerns Prager's trade up to 1820 and the younger generations of his family, centering around Harriet Prager (d. 1864) of Philadelphia and the children of her brother, Charles Prager of Wheeling, West Virginia, during the 1850s and 1860s. These letters include comments on family affairs, slavery, Abraham Lincoln, Copperheads, and the Mason-Slidell affair. About one hundred of the letters were written during the Civil War. The collection contains very little between 1810 and 1850, and much of the early correspondence is written in a medley of French, Portuguese, and English.

5229. JOSEPH TERRY PAPERS, 1743 (1807-1827) 1874. 152 items. Halifax County, Va.

Papers of Joseph Terry contain deeds, an indenture contract, a receipt for medical treatment of slaves, business papers, and papers relating to the settlement of Joseph Terry's estate. Letters to Joseph Terry from his brother Robert Terry contain a description of Aaron Burr's entry into Lexington, North Carolina, 1808; comment on the North Carolina elections of 1808; comment on the Embargo of 1807; description of the battle of Tippecanoe and remarks on Indian fighting; and comments on earthquakes in Henderson County, North Carolina, in 1812 and 1813.

5230. WILLIAM A. TESH PAPERS, 1858-1864. 74 items. Yadkin County, N.C.

Letters from William A. Tesh, a Confederate soldier in the 28th North Carolina Regiment, concerning the raid on Hagerstown, Maryland; the battle of Gettysburg, 1863; camp life; deserters; and food prices.

5231. JESSE TETTERTON PAPERS, 1849 (1857-1861) 1884. 23 items. Bath (Beaufort County), N.C.

Personal correspondence of Jesse Tetterton, commenting on hard times and the high cost of provisions, and the apprehension of runaway slaves. Civil War letters, 1861, concern operations around Cape Hatteras, North Carolina, and Manassas Junction, Virginia.

5232. TEXAS LAND COMPANY RECORDS, 1837-1879. 1 vol. (53 pp.) Richmond, Va.

Records, including minutes of meetings of stockholders, of a company in Richmond, Virginia, which owned land in several counties in Texas.

5233. TEXTILE WORKERS UNION OF AMERICA. CHEROKEE-SPARTANBURG JOINT BOARD PAPERS, 1943-1952. 2,754 items and 5 vols. Gaffney (Cherokee County), S.C.

The papers of the Cherokee-Spartanburg Joint Board of the Textile Workers Union of America (CIO) contain the papers of Charles D. Puckett, Earl L. Smith, Paul B. Faucette, and [Wade?] Lynch, managers of the Cherokee-Spartanburg Joint Board from 1943 to 1952 including correspondence with Franz E.

Daniel, William Pollock, and Emil Rieve, and memoranda from John W. Edelman, Washington representative of the Textile Workers Union of America. There are also papers concerning Clifton Manufacturing Company and Inman Mills, including material concerning wages, contracts, negotiations, grievances, and arbitration; and records of the Cherokee-Spartanburg Joint Board including minutes, 1943-1949, correspondence, bills, reports of committees, and a roll call of delegates.

5234. TEXTILE WORKERS UNION OF AMERICA. GREENSBORO-BURLINGTON JOINT BOARD PAPERS, 1939-1951. 11,100 items and 24 vols. Greensboro (Guilford County), N.C. Restricted.

The papers of the Greensboro-Burlington Joint Board of the Textile Workers Union of America (TWUA/CIO) contain correspondence, 1931-1945, of TWUA field representatives E. W. Witt, Haywood D. "Red" Lisk, L. L. Shepherd, and Bruno Rantane concerning grievances, contracts, wages, and a union election at the Piedmont Heights Division of Burlington Mills Corporation; and the correspondence, 1945-1951, of the business managers of the Greensboro-Burlington Joint Board, Bruno Rantane and William F. Billingsley, with TWUA officials George Baldanzi, Solomon Barkin, Lewis M. Conn, William Pollock, and Emil Rieve. The main files of the Greensboro-Burlington Joint Board contain material from the national office of the TWUA, including correspondence and items concerning education and research, and an incomplete set, 1946-1950, of Memorandum from Washington; letters from Lewis M. Conn, North Carolina director of TWUA; minutes, correspondence, and treasurer's reports of the Greensboro-Burlington Joint Board; papers, 1948-1951, for Locals No. 295, No. 529, No. 700, No. 739, and No. 1113, of the TWUA, relating to work loads, seniority, rates, working conditions, and grievances; and material on various Cone Mills Corporation plants, including Proximity Mills, White Oak Mills, Tabardrey Plant, and Cone Finishing Company. Agencies and organizations represented in the collection include the American Newspaper Guild; the Retail, Wholesale, and Department Store Union; the Southern School for Workers, Inc.; Americans for Democratic Action; United Labor Political Committee; the United States Department of Labor; and the National War Labor Board. The collection also contains copies of Washington Bulletin, Shop Steward Bulletin, and C.I.O. Roundup.

5235. TEXTILE WORKERS UNION OF AMERICA. MECKLENBURG COUNTY JOINT BOARD PAPERS, 1935-1951. 4,527 items and 2 vols. Charlotte (Mecklenburg County), N.C.

The papers of the Mecklenburg County Joint Board of the Textile Workers Union of America (TWUA/CIO) contain the files 1942-1951, of James H. Fullerton, business manager of the Mecklenburg County Joint Board, including correspondence with union officials Emil Rieve, William Pollock, Solomon Barkin, Lewis M. Conn, and William J. Smith; and material pertaining to grievances, arbitration, agreements, and contracts with various textile manufacturers, including Kendall Company; Chadwick-Hoskins Company and its successor, Textron Southern, Inc.; Spatex Corporation; A. D. Julliard and Company, Inc.; and Calvine Cotton Mills, Inc. In general the papers concern benefits, wages, unemployment compensation, the Employment Security Act in North Carolina, the National Labor Relations Board, the CIO Political Action Committee, and union finances.

5236. TEXTILE WORKERS UNION OF AMERICA. SOUTH CAROLINA STATE DIRECTOR PAPERS, 1942-1952. 2,413 items and 15 vols. Greenville (Greenville County), S.C.

The collection contains the papers of Charles Edward Auslander, state director in South Carolina of the Textile Workers Union of America (TWUA), including correspondence with union leaders Emil Rieve, William Pollock, Solomon Barkin, Franz E. Daniel, and Lloyd P. Vaughan. Papers also contain letters, telegrams, financial information, records of cases before the National Labor Relations Board, grievances, reports, mimeographed fliers, lists of employees, contracts, and wage statistics relating to a number of South Carolina textile manufacturers, including Clifton Manufacturing Company, Rock Hill Printing and Finishing Company, and Woodside Mills. Other subjects covered in the papers include the cotton screen print industry, the Wage Stabilization Board, the Amalgamated Clothing Workers of America, and a strike, 1950, at Woodside Mills and subsequent relief efforts.

5237. TEXTILE WORKERS UNION OF AMERICA. SOUTHERN REGIONAL DIRECTOR'S OFFICE PAPERS, 1940-1948. 4 vols. Charlotte (Mecklenburg County), N.C.

Typed carbon, mimeographed, printed, or typed copies of contracts and agreements, including supplemental agreements and extensions of agreements, between the Textile Workers Union of America and various textile manufacturers in Alabama, Georgia, North Carolina, and South Carolina.

5238. THAILAND PAPERS, 1854-1862. 4 items.

Letters of King Mongkut (1804-1868) concerning the missionary work of Stephen Mattoon and Samuel R. House in Thailand; and the trading activities there of Samuel Gilfillan and the British Borneo Company, with descriptions of various purchases by the king, including a breech loading cannon.

5239. JONATHAN N. THATCHER PAPERS, 1889-1891. 39 items. Martinsburg (Berkeley County), W. Va.

Letters from Thomas P. Kennedy, president of the Cumberland Valley Railroad Company, concerning Thatcher's work as an agent; form letters from postal officials relating to Thatcher's work as postmaster at Inwood, West Virginia; and other items concerning Thatcher's partnership in the operation of a grain elevator.

5240. ELI THAYER PAPERS, 1888. 1 item. Worcester (Worcester County), Mass.

A letter from Thayer (1819-1899), founder of the Emigrant Aid Society, to Samuel Adams Drake concerning Thayer's desire to make Kansas a free state.

5241. JOHN THELWALL PAPERS, 1834. 2 items. England.

A letter from Thelwall (1764-1834), reformer and lecturer, to his children about his health, the sale of his writings, and his career; and a fragment of a letter from Thelwall to the Gazette mentioning Quaker approval of his lectures.

5242. RAPHAEL PROSPER THIAN PAPERS, 1819-1864. 7 items and 5 vols. Washington, D.C.

A pardon, 1819, for Isaac Parke, convicted of mutinous conduct; letters of Winfield Scott appointing Thian to a clerkship in the office of the commanding general, U.S. Army, 1853, and commending him to Edward Davis Townsend, adjutant general, 1864; a facsimile of the South Carolina ordinance of secession, 1860; a biographical sketch of Thian by his son Prosper; a portrait of Thian; a letter from Prosper Thian to R. H. Woody of Duke University Library; and five scrapbooks containing Raphael Thian's collection of antebellum and Confederate currency and bonds.

5243. DELPHINIA L. E. THINTON PAPERS, 1864-1869. 4 items. Yanceyville (Caswell County), N.C.

Personal correspondence of the Thinton and Taylor families, North Carolina farmers. Included is a manuscript copy of a song, "News from Home," copied by B. J. Thinton.

5244. DAVID THOM PAPERS, 1847-1858. 7 items. Liverpool, Lancashire, England.

Letters by Mary Howitt, author and publisher, to Thom, a Presbyterian minister, and one to Rev. George Aspinall, 1847, refusing to review Thom's Dialogues on Universal Salvation (2d ed., London: 1847) in Howitt's Journal because of the book's polemical nature. Her letters to Thom in 1849 concern her review of his new book in the Standard of Freedom. Letters of 1855 and 1858 concern the unhappy courses taken by the careers of Aspinall and of Anne Elliot Dyson, educator and reformer.

5245. A. J. K. THOMAS PAPERS, 1859-1920. 3 items and 1 vol. Iredell County, N.C.

The diary of a farmer, 1859-1861, describing weather, farm activities, local events, Presbyterian churches at Shiloh and Concord, North Carolina; and commenting upon other churches of the area, slave sales, and the formation of a temperance society.

5246. ELLA GERTRUDE (CLANTON) THOMAS DIARY, 1848-1889. 13 vols. Augusta (Richmond County), Ga. Restricted.

A diary, partly unbound, covering portions of the years 1848-1849, 1851-1852, 1855-1859, 1861-1866, 1868-1871, 1878-1889, kept by Ella Thomas (b. 1834), wife of Jefferson Thomas, a planter. The first volume, 1848-1849, is in a different hand from the bulk of the diary. Portions of the diary may be a transcript made either by Mrs. Thomas or by her daughter. The diary describes in detail Mrs. Thomas's reading, chiefly novels and literary magazines; studies at Macon Female College (now called Wesleyan College) in Macon, Georgia; class reunions; her conversion to Methodism during a series of revivals at the college; the clothing and dress of her friends, associates, and others; gossip and social life; shopping and prices; concerts, lectures, and entertainments; church services; courtship by and marriage to Jefferson Thomas; plantation life in Burke and Columbia counties; visits to a Negro church; a Negro preacher named Sam Drayton; the reading of proslavery and abolitionist literature; the institution of slavery and especially the relations between white men and Negro women; Civil War military activity, especially as it concerned Jefferson Thomas's career; Union occupation of the South; the devastation caused by Union troops; the state of Southern society after the war; a visit to New York, 1870, and interest in spiritualism; labor and servant problems; financial losses and poverty; school teaching; the earthquake of 1886. There are a few loose items, among them articles she had written for publication on Longstreet and the funeral of General Polk.

5247. FRANCIS THOMAS PAPERS, 1838, 1863. 3 items. Frederick (Frederick County), Md.

Letters by Francis Thomas (1799-1876) written while a member of the U.S. Congress and relating to congressional and state elections of 1838, reapportionment to Maryland state assembly districts in that year; and to the selection of U.S. Military Academy cadets in 1863.

5248. GEORGE HENRY THOMAS PAPERS, 1844-1865. 17 items. Southampton County, Va.

Two letters from George Henry Thomas (1816-1870) to his brother John W. Thomas concerning matrimony, farming, and real estate; thirteen telegrams sent by Thomas while a general in the Union Army at Nashville, Tennessee, 1865; and a resolution and accompanying letter concerning support in Lexington, Kentucky, for the policies of Andrew Johnson and continued occupation by United States troops.

5249. H. B. THOMAS PAPERS, 1862-1872. 9 items. Mill Hall (Clinton County), Pa.

Correspondence of H. B. Thomas and his brother William Henry Thomas while serving in the 16th Pennsylvania Cavalry during the Civil War and their father, D. P. Thomas, a wool-dyer, and other friends and relatives in Clinton County. Letters from Rebecca Heller of Blair County, Pennsylvania, 1864, describe a railroad accident, her views of the Copperheads, the reelection of Lincoln, and the marriage of a local white woman to a Negro.

5250. JAMES THOMAS PAPERS, 1860-1864. 11 items. Sparta (Hancock County), Ga.

Personal, business, and legal correspondence of Judge James Thomas, including letters commenting on slaves, Georgia courts, and the stand North Carolina took after Lincoln's election.

5251. JAMES THOMAS, JR., PAPERS, 1850 (1852-1861) 1879, 14,088 items. Richmond, Va.

This collection consists principally of the apparently complete business papers and records, 1850-1863, of James Thomas, Jr. (1806-1882), one of the largest of antebellum tobacco manufacturers. In addition to an extensive business correspondence, numerous orders for tobacco from Maine, Massachusetts, Louisiana, Georgia, the Netherlands, England, and Australia are included, as well as prices current bulletins from firms throughout the world. The collection not only gives a detailed history of Thomas's enterprises, but affords much information on the tobacco industry in general and on other phases of the economic life of Virginia in the 1850s. Some of Thomas's private correspondence is also in the collection, including an occasional letter from such men as J. L. M. Curry and George Frederick Holmes. Some information is given on Thomas's aid to Basil Manly in his work with the Virginia Baptist Seminary, Richmond, and on his financial assistance, which made it possible for the institution to remain open after the Civil War.

5252. JAMES AUGUSTUS THOMAS PAPERS, 1905 (1914-1940) 1941. 29,247 items. Shanghai, China, and White Plains (Westchester County), N.Y.

The papers of James Augustus Thomas (1862-1940), tobacco executive and philanthropist, largely consist of correspondence relating to the marketing of tobacco in the Far East; the American court in Shanghai; the British-American Tobacco Company; the Asiatic Institute; the partnership between the Standard Oil Company and the Chinese government; relations between the United States and Mexico, 1914; Willard Straight as American treaty commissioner; the work of the Navy Y.M.C.A. in China; Mustard and Co., and cigarette marketing in China; foreign troops guarding the Peking-Mukden Railroad; Fred McCormick and the China Monuments Society; Sino-Japanese relations in 1915, including the Twenty-One Demands and a proposed railroad from Chungking to Ichong; the Panama-Pacific Exposition and trade opportunities in China; the Japanese occupation of Korea; Chinese boycott of Japanese goods; the presidency of Yuan Shih-k'ai; the visit of the Chinese Trade Commission to the United States; Wellington Koo, Chinese minister to Mexico; Anson Burlingame; the changing status of women in China; production and curing of tobacco in China; purchase of indigo paste in China by the Erwin Cotton Mills of Durham, North Carolina; purchases of books from Arthur Probsthain, Oriental bookseller and publisher in London; establishment of memorials to Thomas's late wife Anna (Branson) Thomas at Duke University and to the late Willard Straight in Shanghai; the Chinese American Bank; Chinese students at Trinity College, Durham, North Carolina; the manufacture of automobiles in Rock Hill, South Carolina; the Second Consortium in China and the work of Thomas Lamont; banking and currency in China; the China Trade Act; B. N. Duke's health; missionary schools in China; the Washington Conference on the Limitation of Armaments, 1921-1922; the conflict between Chang Tso-lin and Wu P'ei-fu; the Peacock Motion Picture Corporation in China; Sun Yat-sen and his power in China; tariffs; the visit of Liang Shihi to the United States, 1924; the Dawes Plan for German currency and reparations payments; the struggle in China between Wu P'ei-fu and Feng Yu-hsiang; extraterritoriality; the death of James B. Duke; gifts to the Woman's College of Duke University; publication of Thomas's books by Duke University Press; purchase of books and manuscripts for Duke University Library; Russian influence in the Chinese Eastern Railroad in Manchuria; the gift of John D. Rockefeller, Jr., to the Tokyo American School, 1928; the education of Cheang Park Chew's children in the United States; the Council on Foreign Relations; B. N. Duke's influence on J. B. Duke's endowment of Duke University; famine and other types of relief for China; the White Plains, New York, hospital; the Chinese National Association of the Mass Education

Movement; financial assistance for the North Carolina College for Negroes; Dwight W. Morrow; the purchase of Duke Homestead by Mary (Duke) Biddle and its restoration; Yenching University in Peking; the condition of gold and silver currency in various parts of the world; books on Oriental religion and philosophy needed by Duke University Library; an attempt to assassinate T. V. Soong, 1931; Japanese aggression in Manchuria; the Kellogg-Briand Peace Pact; the Japanese attack on Shanghai; the severity of the depression in the United States; United States presidential politics and elections from the 1910s through the 1940s; the Southeastern Council; the pottery plants at Smithfield and Jugtown, North Carolina; the National Recovery Administration; a memorial to W. W. Rockhill; the assassination of Wu Ting Seng; illness and death of Mrs. B. N. Duke; the planned visit of Madame Chiang Kai-shek to the United States in 1936; H. H. Kung's trip to New York, 1937; establishment of a course in Far Eastern history at Duke University; the granting of an honorary degree by Duke to Hu Shih; Thomas's work as chairman of the Duke Memorial; the endowment of the Florence McAlister chair of medicine and medical research at Duke University; and other topics concerning relief and welfare in China, higher education in North Carolina, and Chinese-American relations.

Principal writers of letters in this collection are John J. Abbott; G. G. Allen; J. G. Anderson; Larz Anderson; Hamilton Fish Armstrong; Julean Arnold; John Earl Baker; Alice M. Baldwin; Arthur Bassett; Mary (Duke) Biddle; William K. Boyd; Harvie Branscomb; Joseph P. Breedlove; Donald M. Brodie; Florence Broesler; A. S. Brower; Edward B. Bruce; Jacques Busbee; Juliana Busbee; William M. Chadbourne; Chiang Mei-ling (Soong); Y. Chen; John B. Chevalier; Cheang Park Chew; Paul H. Clyde; Thomas Flourney Cobbs; Howard E. Cole; W. H. Donald; Henry R. Dwire; Martin Egan; W. A. Erwin; William P. Few; Fred V. Field; Louis D. Froelick; A. H. Godbey; C. E. Harber; W. R. Harris; Char. A. Herschleb; Geo. W. Hill; Stanley K. Hornbeck; Hsu Un Yuen; Albert G. Jeffress; Nelson Trusler Johnson; H. L. King; Roger A. Kingsbury; Ed Land; Alfred Landon; Robert Lansing; Henry S. Leiper; K. C. Li; Der Ling; H. K. Linn; Florence G. Lurty; William H. McAlister; Frederick McCormick; Fred A. Macnaghten; Hugh McRae; Walter H. Mallory; Justin Miller; Fred Atkins Moore; Thomas Nelson; R. C. Patterson, Jr.; C. W. Pettitt; Morris R. Poucher; John B. Powell; Arthur Probsthain; John Gilbert Reid; Frank Ritchie; Owen F. Roberts; Theodore Roosevelt, Jr.; T. A. Rustad; Alex Sands; E. A. Seeman; Ernest T. Seton; J. E. Shepard; Lorrin A. Shepard; C. C. Spalding; Fred W. Stevens; W. J. Sturgis; Gerard Swope; Alfred Saoke Sze; Henry E. Thomas; Amelie (McAlister) Upshur; C. T. Wang; William H. Wannamaker; R. L. Watt; L. R. Wilfley; C. L. L. Williams; E. T. Williams; Warwick Winston; Leo F. Wormser; Wu T'ing-fang; James Y. C. Yen; S. S. Young; and K. L. Yui.

There are also a quantity of printed material on related topics; clippings; and a transcript of an interview with Cora Deng concerning Japanese aggression in Manchuria.

5253. JOHN THOMAS PAPERS, 1859-1887. 19 items. Smith's Mills (Williamsburg County), S. C.

Personal and family letters; also a poem.

5254. JOHN THOMAS PAPERS, 1862-1866. 22 items. Georgia.

Letters by John Thomas, a workman on the Memphis and Charleston Railroad, commenting upon working and living conditions. Most of the collection consists of love letters to his wife.

5255. JOHN WESLEY THOMAS AND JOHN DRAYTON THOMAS PAPERS, 1776-1902. 64 items. England.

Letters by a number of leading Methodists, including John Wesley, to John Wesley Thomas, a clergyman, concerning speaking engagements or minor church matters. There are several letters from authors commenting on Thomas's translations of Dante. Letters of 1870 reflect on the early days of Methodism in England. The collection contains some items relating to Thomas's son, John Drayton Thomas, also a Wesleyan clergyman.

5256. REBECCA THOMAS PAPERS, 1880-1889. 48 items. Shadwell (Albemarle County), Va.

Personal letters to Rebecca Thomas from her children and friends.

5257. WILLIAM H. THOMAS PAPERS, 1840-1865. 120 items. Louisiana.

Chiefly receipts and other records of quartermasters and clerks serving under William H. Thomas, chief of subsistence in the Trans-Mississippi Department of the Confederate Army, Shreveport, Louisiana.

5258. WILLIAM HOLLAND THOMAS PAPERS, 1814-1898. 2,710 items and 79 vols. Haywood County, N.C.

Letters and papers of William H. Thomas (1805-1893), lawyer, Indian agent and trader, and colonel in the Confederate Army, concerning his life in western North Carolina, the removal of the Cherokee Indians and the status of those who remained in North Carolina, the building of roads and railroads, fighting during the Civil War in East Tennessee, postwar administration of Indian affairs, and private business of Thomas. There are also account books, daybooks, and ledgers showing a record of goods bought and sold in Thomas's five stores in Haywood and Cherokee counties. Included also are business correspondence and miscellaneous accounts,

1875-1890, of his son, William Holland Thomas, Jr., merchant and farmer of Jackson County, North Carolina. The library also holds microfilm, 2 reels, William Holland Thomas papers, 1820-1931, in the possession of James R. Thomas, Waynesville, North Carolina.

5259. THOMAS THOMASSON PAPERS, 1861-1876. 33 items. "High Bank," Haulg, Lancashire, England.

Papers relating to Thomas Thomasson (1808-1876), a textile manufacturer and political economist, contain letters from John Bright, British statesman, 1861-1874, 18 items, concerning politics, fishing trips to Scotland, personal and social affairs, the effect of the American Civil War on the cotton supply for the textile industry, and the fall of the Gladstone cabinet in 1874; letters and social notes from Bright to Emma (Thomasson) Winkworth, 1861-1876, 8 items, with reference to George Jacob Holyoake's dedication to Bright of his History of Cooperation in England (London: 1879); and letters from Thomas Henry Huxley, scientist, 1876, 3 items, concerning Thomas Thomasson's bequest to Huxley.

5260. BENJAMIN O. THOMPSON PAPERS, 1861. 1 item. Forsyth County, Ga.

A photocopy of the digest of the assessment of the Confederate war tax in the Wild Cat and Lights districts of Forsyth County by Thompson, assessor. Included is data on real estate; slaves; merchandise; bank stock; railroad and other corporation stock; money at interest; cash on hand; cattle, mules, and horses; gold watches; gold and silver plate; pianos; and pleasure carriages.

5261. HENRY J. H. THOMPSON PAPERS, 1862-1865. 258 items and 2 vols. Fair Haven, Conn.

Correspondence between Thompson (b. 1832), a soldier in the fife and drum corps of the 15th Regiment of Connecticut Volunteers, and his wife, Lucretia E. (Cooper) Thompson. Included are descriptions of the Southern countryside and comparisons of the seasons there with those of Connecticut, and descriptions of morale and camp life; peace hopes and the elections of 1864; morals of the troops; the punishment of a thief; yellow fever near New Bern, 1864; rumors; the battle of Fredericksburg and the siege of Suffolk, Virginia; the occupation of Kinston, North Carolina; and garrison duty in Washington, D. C. The volumes are diaries.

5262. HENRY YATES THOMPSON PAPERS, 1884. 1 item. London, England.

A letter to Thompson (1838-1928), proprietor of the Pall Mall Gazette, from Alfred Milner, later Lord Milner, assistant editor of the Gazette. The letter concerns William Thomas Stead, editor; the condition of the navy; and the character of the Gazette.

5263. JACOB THOMPSON PAPERS, 1859, 1861. 2 items. Washington, D.C.

Letters of Jacob Thompson (1810-1885), secretary of the interior and secret agent of the Confederate government, one, 1859, being a routine letter signed by Thompson while secretary of the interior and the other, a protest from Thompson to President Buchanan against reinforcing Fort Sumter.

5264. JAMES THOMPSON PAPERS, 1775-1793. 7 items. Eno (Orange County), N.C.

Social letters, chiefly from James Thompson to his brother, Daniel Thompson of Mill Creek Hundred, Newcastle County, Pennsylvania, are those of a Quaker family which began to migrate to North Carolina by 1775. They give genealogical data on the Chambers, Hadley, and Thompson families.

5265. JOHN A. THOMPSON PAPERS, 1846. 2 items. Jefferson County, W. Va.

Business and personal letters.

5266. JOHN H. THOMPSON PAPERS, 1908-1915. 1,500 items. Boston, Mass.

Carbon copies of letters written by a Christian Science practitioner to his patients.

5267. LELA THOMPSON PAPERS, 1896-1902. 54 items. Guilford County, N.C.

Chiefly personal letters to Lela Thompson and her relatives and friends. The writers include T. C. Amick, president of Liberty Normal College, Liberty, North Carolina, which Miss Thompson had attended; P. E. Shaw, mayor of Liberty; and S. D. McPherson II, later a prominent physician of Durham. There are also a letter, 1902, discussing student life at Baptist University, Raleigh, North Carolina; and a pamphlet, 1902, concerning the Virginia Institute for Young Ladies, Bristol, Virginia.

5268. SARAH E. THOMPSON PAPERS, 1855 (1864-1891) 1904. 137 items. Greene County, Tenn.

Correspondence of Sarah Thompson, Federal spy, who furnished General Alvan Cullem Gillem with the information which led to the attack on the command of General John H. Morgan at Greeneville, Tennessee, in which the latter was killed. The correspondence includes, in addition to an account of this incident in Mrs. Thompson's own hand, numerous testimonials of her services to the Federal government and recommendations which utimately led to very poorly paid and short-lived jobs in the Treasury Department, the Bureau of Printing and Engraving, and the Post Office Department. These letters indicate something of the poverty under which she struggled after her marriage to Orville J. Bacon, of Broome County, New York, in

January, 1866, and her belief that the government should reward her with a lucrative position in payment for her services and those of her first husband, Sylvanus H. Thompson, of Company I, 1st Regiment Tennessee Cavalry, who was captured and shot by Morgan's men as a spy. A letter of January 14, 1865, describes the work of the Refugee Relief Commission of Ohio in Cincinnati. Included also are letters of Federal soldiers to Sarah E. Thompson written to her because of her services in hospitals where she nursed wounded soldiers, and because of her lectures, after the Civil War, on her spying activities during the war.

5269. STEPHEN W. THOMPSON PAPERS, 1864. 1 item and 1 vol. Davisburg (Oakland County), Mich.

A diary of a soldier in the 5th Regiment of Michigan Cavalry Volunteers and a transcript of his military service record, which at times conflicts with statements made in the diary. The diary describes depredations by Union troops; the presidential vote in Thompson's regiment, 1864; and a number of minor battles in Virginia.

5270. THOMAS THOMPSON PAPERS, 1849-1851, 3 items. Abbeville (Abbeville County), S.C.

Personal letters written by Thomas Thompson to his wife while he was in the South Carolina senate.

5271. WADDY THOMPSON PAPERS, 1821-1851. 7 items. Greenville (Greenville County), S.C.

Papers of a Whig politician from South Carolina; state legislator; U. S. representative, 1835-1841; and ambassador to Mexico, 1842-1844. Topics include mortgage regulations in South Carolina, 1821; judicial reform in South Carolina, 1827; Federal financial assistance for a railroad in Charleston, 1830; the constitutionality of Federal treasury notes; politics; the plight of an American citizen imprisoned in Mexico and a lawsuit, 1851, of Thompson against Gilbert L. Thompson and Richard I. Coxe for failure to pay for his services as lobbyist on behalf of American citizens holding claims against Mexico, 1851. Writers of letters include David Johnson, William Ballard Preston, and Hugh Swinton Legare.

5272. WILBORN THOMPSON PAPERS (1862-1864) 1876. 48 items. Manassas (Prince William County), Va.

Personal letters of a soldier in the 56th and later the 55th Georgia regiments during the Civil War, largely consisting of directions to his wife concerning the operation of their farm. There are also comments on living conditions in the field and a few skirmishes in the area around Chattanooga, Knoxville and Lookout Mountain, Tennessee; near Vicksburg, Mississippi, in 1863; and later near Dalton, Georgia. One letter, from a friend near Richmond, Virginia, describes battles there.

5273. WILBUR THOMPSON PAPERS, 1862-1864. 2 items. Georgia.

Personal letters from Wilbur Thompson, a Confederate soldier, to his family, expressing his war weariness.

5274. WILLIAM THOMPSON RECEIPT BOOK, 1807-1811. 1 vol. (62 pp.) Charleston, S. C.

Various types of monetary receipts.

5275. WILLIAM G. THOMPSON PAPERS, 1756 (1801-1864) 1873. 92 items. Timberville (Rockingham County), Va.

The collection consists of letters and other papers of several Pennsylvania German families in the Shenandoah Valley of Virginia, including letters from George Shrader and others in Tennessee, Ohio, and Indiana. Topics include the availability of land in Indiana in the 1830s; prices of farm products near Baltimore and in Indiana; the panic of 1837; the abolition question in Woodstock, Virginia; a drought in Ohio, 1839; and the transferability of money between states. There are a few letters from Civil War soldiers. Units mentioned include the 8th Star Artillery and the 12th Virginia Cavalry. There are some miscellaneous legal papers.

5276. CHARLES THOMSON PAPERS, 1779-1788. 5 items. Philadelphia, Pa.

Miscellaneous documents signed by Charles Thomson (1729-1824), secretary of the Continental Congress. Included is an extract from the minutes of the Congress, resolutions, and other documents respecting each state's quota of money to be paid into the treasury; reorganization of the commissary department of the army; South Carolina and Georgia territorial claims; and a letter from Thomas McKean accepting an appointment to serve on a court convened to hear a question between the states of South Carolina and Georgia.

5277. CHARLES EDWARD POULETT THOMSON, FIRST BARON SYDENHAM, PAPERS, 1833-1839. 8 items. London, England.

Letters to Thomson (1799-1841), British politician, president of the Board of Trade, 1834, and governor general of Canada, 1839-1841. Letters of 1833-1835 from Edward Baines concern his and Thomson's historical writings and the need for a reduction of the tariff on olive oil imported from the Two Sicilies; a letter, 1835, from Lord Holland concerns the appointment of magistrates; letters from Sir James Stephen, under secretary for the colonies, refer to his position in the Colonial Office and to qualifications for the magistracy; a letter of Henry Labouchere relates to his negotiations and the government crisis in Paris, 1839; and a letter of Thomas Spring-Rice, chancellor of the exchequer, concerns the soap drawbacks given the textile industry.

5278. KATE THOMSON AUTOGRAPH ALBUM, 1876-1880. 1 vol. (30 pp.) "Bonnywood," Hampton County, S.C.

Autographs of friends and relatives, with verse conveying sentiments of affection; and small colored pictures of flowers and birds pasted in.

5279. SEPTIMUS SMET THORBURN PAPERS, 1897. 1 item. Bracknell, Berkshire, England.

A letter from Thorburn (1844-1924) of the India Civil Service to [Sprunt?] Reid of Aberdeen reviewing Thorburn's career, his work on a new book, and commenting on the legal, agricultural, and political situation in India as described in his recent work, His Majesty's Greatest Subject (1897).

5280. EDWARD ALSTON THORNE PAPERS, 1831 (1862-1873) 1904. 746 items. Littleton (Halifax County), N.C.

Papers of Thorne (b. 1828), including a will, 1831, of John Alston of Halifax County; antebellum letters concerning the sale of tobacco; letters of Thorne as ordnance officer in Ransom's Brigade during the Civil War, describing service at Camp Topail, near Winchester, at the battles of Fredericksburg, Kinston, Ball's Bluff, and Petersburg, and at Greeneville, Tennessee; and postwar letters concerning the production and trade in cotton, and the sale of cotton cultivators. There are also miscellaneous other business records and papers, some relating to education in North Carolina; records of the Methodist Church concerning the Roanoke Circuit, 1867-1869, and the Littleton Circuit, 1896-1897 and 1905; and a biographical sketch of Thorne. Writers of letters include J. W. Alspaugh, R. H. Anderson, J. A. Baker, P. G. T. Beauregard, G. W. Brooks, Walter Clark, Sr., Samuel Cooper, F. W. Dawson, E. C. Elmore, Josiah Gorgas, Henry Heth, D. H. Hill, B. R. Johnson, R. E. Lee, James Longstreet, B. F. Moore, J. L. Orr, Robert Ransom, Jr., J. A. Seddon, Sr., R. B. Vance, Jr., A. M. Wadden, and W. M. Wingate.

5281. JAMES W. THORNE AND ISAIAH TOWNSEND PAPERS, 1813-1837. 23 items. New York and Albany, N.Y.

Papers of Thorne, merchant of New York state, and Isaiah Townsend of Albany, a contractor for the U. S. Army during the War of 1812. The collection largely concerns the supplying of U.S. troops during that war.

5282. WILLIAM C. THORNTON PAPERS, 1805-1854. 100 items. Philadelphia, Pa.

Correspondence of the related Compton, Thornton, Treadway, and Wainwright families of London, Virginia, and Pennsylvania, centering around William C. Thornton, banker of Richmond and Philadelphia, and merchant near Prince Edward Court House, Virginia, and in New York. Letters from Townsend Compton written from London describe the fear of invasion by French troops, 1805; the depression in England and poor leadership of the government there and in Spain, 1816; and praise for the Spanish Revolution, 1820. A letter from Elizabeth Russell Norwood of Boston, 1842, concerns women's rights. One by T. T. Treadway of Prince Edward, 1842, concerns slaveholding; and a letter by Mary Treadway, 1852, comments on Uncle Tom's Cabin. Other writers of letters in the collection include Medmor Goodwin, Caroline Thornton, and Sarah H. and M. F. Thornton.

5283. WILLIAM W. THORNTON RECORD BOOK, 1860-1862. 1 vol. (102 pp.) Prince William County, Va.

Lists of names and accounts for supplies for the Prince William Cavalry Company, attached to the 36th Regiment of Virginia Militia.

5284. THOMAS THOROTON PAPERS, 1760. 1 item. London, England.

A letter from Bennet Storer, chaplain with British forces at Osnabrück, Germany, reporting on the illness of General John Manners, Marquis of Granby, British commander, and on plans for a march toward Paderborn. The letter is addressed to Thomas Thoroton (1723-1784), member of Parliament and political agent of the Duke of Rutland.

5285. BENJAMIN PETER THORP PAPERS, 1837-1889. 28 items. Granville County, N.C.

Business correspondence and accounts of the Thorp family, probably planters containing information on economic conditions in North Carolina and prices of various commodities, mainly during the 1840s.

5286. GEORGE N. THRIFT PAPERS, 1857-1860. 24 items. Greenwood (Doddridge County), Va.

Personal letters to Thrift, some of which mention the treatment of slaves and their sale in Virginia; and schools in Virginia, including Brookhill School, Albemarle County; Locust Grove Academy, Orange County; and Virginia Female Institute, Staunton.

5287. EDWARD THURLOW, FIRST BARON THURLOW, PAPERS, 1765. 1 vol. London, England.

A record of a canvass of the voters of the borough of Tamworth made prior to the by-election which brought Thurlow into Parliament; it gives the names, occupation, residences, and an evaluation of each voter's political affiliation.

5288. WILLIAM PLEASANT THURMAN NOTEBOOK, 1857-1858. 1 vol. Charlottesville, Va.

Handwritten notes taken in Latin, Greek, and mathematics classes while William P. Thurman was a student at the University of Virginia. Thurman was later a physician, settling at Fancy Grove (Bedford County), Virginia.

5289. BENJAMIN THURMOND SALE BOOK, 1848-1851. 1 vol. Buckingham County, Va.

Sale book of Benjamin Thurmond's estate.

5290. JOHN A. THURMOND PAPERS, 1825-1914. 174 items and 4 vols. Fabers Mills (Nelson County), Va.

Correspondence among Sarah (Jones) Thurmond and her sisters Mary, Eliza, and Molly Jones of Amherst County, Virginia. Sarah married John A. Thurmond, a farmer of Nelson County, and there are some of his letters referring to service in the Confederate Army. There are also several letters from Charles G. Jones in Nashville, Tennessee, to his cousin Sallie Jones, which describe cholera in 1854 and a fire in 1856. Other letters in the collection concern Civil War conditions and the militia reserves of Nelson and Amherst counties. There are also a ledger, two account books, and a memorandum book.

5291. CHARLES FRANKLIN THWING PAPERS, 1901. 1 item. Cleveland, Ohio.

A letter to Thwing from Henry M. Flagler (1830-1913) declining to participate in the creation of a memorial in Cleveland as his funds are tied up in Florida enterprises.

5292. FRANCIS ORRAY TICKNOR PAPERS, 1839-1880. 40 items. Columbus (Muscogee County), Ga.

Correspondence and thirty-seven typed copies of correspondence of Francis Orray Ticknor (1822-1874), physician, poet, musician, and horticulturist, with Paul Hamilton Hayne and William N. Nelson, containing poems and references to Ticknor's family and his activities.

5293. BARNEY TIERNAN PAPERS, 1843-1939. 15 items. Galveston (Galveston County), Tex.

Miscellaneous papers relating to Barney Tiernan and members of the Tiernan family, including a letter, 1899, concerning mining in New Mexico; a letter, 1914, discussing the transfer of a baseball team from Kewanee, Illinois, to Marshalltown, Iowa; deeds of trust; a stock certificate; and three commissions appointing M. Jeff Tiernan a notary public.

5294. FRANCES CHRISTINE (FISHER) TIERNAN PAPERS, 1872. 1 item. Salisbury (Rowan County), N.C.

Letter to an autograph collector signed by Frances Christine (Fisher) Tiernan (1846-1920), novelist, under her pseudonym of "Christian Reid."

5295. TENCH TILGHMAN PAPERS, 1781-1815. 7 items. Talbot County, Md.

Papers of Tench Tilghman (1744-1786), Revolutionary soldier, including correspondence concerning personal matters, tobacco prices, and management of tobacco interests; business papers including a bill of lading for shipping tobacco to France; and a broadside containing George Washington's eulogies on the character of Tilghman.

5296. WILLIAM TILGHMAN PAPERS, 1671 (1783-1793) 1876. 891 items and 6 vols. Chestertown (Kent County), Md., and Philadelphia, Pa.

Papers of William Tilghman (1756-1824), lawyer and chief justice of the supreme court of Pennsylvania, relate chiefly to his law practice in Maryland, 1783-1793, and to his service in the Maryland general assembly, 1788-1793, including legal papers dealing with litigation, land sales, the collection of debts, notes, the settlement of estates, and other legal matters; deeds, indentures, wills, estate records, court records, and other legal papers relating chiefly to Cecil, Kent, and Queen Anne counties; a roster, 1818-1819, of the citizens of Charles County; scattered papers pertaining to the Church of England in Maryland; occasional references to personal matters; legal and business papers concerning the family, including papers dealing with loan transactions and with the settlement of the estate of William Tilghman; scattered papers of Tilghman's father, James Tilghman, a lawyer; several bills and accounts of St. John's College, Annapolis, Maryland, and Charlotte Hall School, Charlotte Hall, Maryland; petitions and acts relating to Tilghman's career in the general assembly chiefly dealing with the settlement of local affairs, including the disposal of reserved lands, an evaluation of land in various counties, and an estimate of the cost of building a turnpike between Baltimore, Maryland, and

Washington, D. C.; and other papers dealing with legal and business matters. The volumes are a digest, 1747-1760, of cases at law in which James Tilghman was an attorney; "A System of Law concerning Estates" by Richard Tilghman IV; legal notes kept by William Tilghman as a young man; and dockets of William Tilghman in the Kent County court for the March, 1794, term.

5297.   NANNIE MAE TILLEY PAPERS, 1924-1939.
        17 items.  Durham, N.C.

Letters to Nannie Mae Tilley (b. 1899), historian and former curator of the Manuscript Department, Duke University Library, from members of the John E. Bonsack family and others relating to the Bonsack family, especially Jacob Bonsack, grandfather of John E. Bonsack and owner of a large woolen mill at Good Intent, Virginia, and James A. Bonsack, uncle of John E. Bonsack and inventor of a machine for manufacturing cigarettes. Included is an article concerning James A. Bonsack and a photocopy of his obituary from the Philadelphia (Pa.) Record, 1924.

5298.   TILLINGHAST FAMILY PAPERS, 1765-1971.
        4,861 items and 48 vols.
        Fayetteville (Cumberland
        County), N.C.

Personal, business, and legal papers of the Tillinghast family of Fayetteville, North Carolina, relating to family and business interests in New England, New York, North Carolina, and Georgia. Early correspondence is chiefly with relatives in New England discussing cotton and tobacco prices and markets, relations with France and England, the effects of the embargo on merchants in Taunton, Massachusetts, and social life and customs in North Carolina. There are also a copy of a letter, 1765, from Sir Francis Bernard, royal governor of Massachusetts, describing the turmoil in Boston and the activities of the Sons of Liberty; and a letter, 1781, from James Hogg requesting payment for supplies taken from him by the army. Papers prior to 1850 focus principally on Samuel Willard Tillinghast (d. 1860), commission merchant, and his wife, Jane (Norwood) Tillinghast, daughter of Judge William A. Norwood (1774-1842) and Robina (Hogg) Norwood, (d. 1860) whom he married in 1830, dealing with mercantile accounts and business relations with firms in New York, New York, and Providence, Rhode Island; family matters; life in Chapel Hill, Hillsborough, and Fayetteville, North Carolina; trips to New York to purchase goods for the store; the Protestant Episcopal Church; fires in 1831 and 1845 which destroyed Fayetteville; rumors in Fayetteville of slave insurrections in other parts of North Carolina; the settlement of the estate of William A. Norwood; education at the Virginia Institution for the Deaf and Dumb, Staunton, Virginia, attended by Thomas Hooper Tillinghast (b. 1833), son of Samuel Tillinghast and Jane (Norwood) Tillinghast, and at the New York Institution for the Deaf and Dumb, New York, attended by Thomas Hooper Tillinghast and his brother, David Ray Tillinghast; social life, politics, financial affairs, and cotton planting in Georgia; yellow fever in Georgia; railroad construction in North Carolina and Georgia; the building of plank roads; private schools in Hillsborough and Fayetteville; the Bingham School, Hillsborough, and later, in Mebane, North Carolina; the temperance movement, 1842; the Whigs and the Loco-Focos in North Carolina, 1840; the speeches of Louis D. Henry (1788-1846); and the growth of Fayetteville, its prospects, and need for expanded banking facilities.

Papers, 1850-1900, relate chiefly to the children of Samuel Willard Tillinghast and Jane (Norwood) Tillinghast, especially William Norwood Tillinghast, who first worked with his father, and then established Tillinghast's Crockery Store. The papers concern the Democratic and Whig conventions in 1852; the presidential election of 1852; Franklin Pierce and slavery; business, health and social life in Savannah, Georgia; studies, literary societies, and student life at Normal College (later Trinity College), Randolph County, North Carolina, 1853-1854; college life at the University of North Carolina, Chapel Hill, North Carolina, during the 1850s, and the commencements of 1852 and 1856; the Nicholas Hotel in New York, New York, 1853; life in Liberia at Monrovia as described by a former slave; commencement at the Greensboro Female College (now Greensboro College), Greensboro, North Carolina, in 1856; efforts to send Episcopal missionaries to China; the Belmont Theological Seminary, Kentucky, and the Protestant Episcopal Theological Seminary in Alexandria, Virginia; secession sentiment; the Constitution; the election of 1860; confusion in Washington, D.C., April, 1861; secessionists versus unionists in North Carolina; civilian life during the Civil War; the Emancipation Proclamation; life of a Confederate soldier, including food, casualties, blockade running, conscription, the progress of the war, preaching to troops, the battle of Gettysburg, use of observation balloons by the Union Army, and Sherman's march through Fayetteville and depredations by his troops; economic conditions after the war; conditions, conduct, and wages of freedmen; the Home Institute, Sumter, South Carolina, a school for freedmen; politics in North Carolina in 1868; Governor William W. Holden and the Radicals; Chapel Hill in 1868 after the suspension of the University; education of the deaf by Thomas Hooper Tillinghast, David Ray Tillinghast, and Sarah Ann Tillinghast; business trips to New York, New York; the movement of Davenport College, Lenoir, North Carolina, to Hickory, North Carolina, where it became Claremont College; the Spanish-American War, including mobilization, camp life, artillery school on Sullivan's Island (South Carolina), yellow fever, and camp on Tybee Island (Georgia); life in Washington, D. C., ca. 1900, including Marine Band concerts and government employment; and the visit of Queen Victoria to Dublin, Ireland.

Papers after 1900 are primarily those of Anne Troy (Wetmore) Tillinghast (d. ca. 1948), wife of John Baker Tillinghast (d. 1914), and of her daughter, Anne Wetmore Tillinghast, pertaining to public schools and education in North Carolina; various educational organizations such as the North Carolina Teachers' Assembly and the North Carolina State Primary Teachers' Association; nursing with the American Expeditionary Forces in Europe during World War I; United War Work Campaign; the Fourth Liberty Loan Drive; the Armistice celebration; the Protestant Episcopal Church, especially the 1920s through the 1940s; the Commission of Young People's Work in the Diocese of East Carolina; Young People's Conference, 1926; the Young People's Service League; St. Mary's School and Junior College, Raleigh, North Carolina; the Richmond (Virginia) Division of the College of William and Mary (now Virginia Commonwealth University); St. Paul's Girls' School, Baltimore, Maryland, where Anne Wetmore Tillinghast was recreational director; financial difficulties during the Depression; the Tar Heel Society of Maryland; the North Carolina Society of Baltimore; Anne (Wetmore) Tillinghast's membership on the Cumberland Board of Public Welfare, the board of trustees of the Fayetteville City Schools, and the Thompson Orphanage Jubilee Committee (Charlotte, North Carolina); labor and financial difficulties at the Erwin Cotton Mills, Erwin, North Carolina, and the 1934 strike; restoration of Bath, North Carolina; employment on the Works Project Administration's recreational program; the recreation department of Fayetteville; the death of Anne (Wetmore) Tillinghast; life in the U. S. Foreign Service, 1962-1966, in Saudi Arabia, the Middle East, Egypt, India, and Sweden; and other personal and family matters.

Other papers and volumes include school exercises; essays by Samuel Willard Tillinghast on education in Fayetteville, the Female High School in Fayetteville, the militia, and John C. Calhoun; bills and receipts relating to the mercantile business of Samuel Willard Tillinghast; an account book, 1783, of an "Adventuring Company" with references to voyages to Jamaica, Hamburg, and Lisbon; an account book of the Ray family; Sunday school records of St. John's Episcopal Church, Fayetteville; journal, 1804 and 1816, of Paris Jencks Tillinghast, Sr., father of Samuel Willard Tillinghast, concerning life in early Fayetteville, tobacco, river traffic and warehouses, Scottish immigration, opposition to slavery, and his shipping interests; logbook, 1804, of Daniel Jencks Tillinghast (d. 1804), son of Paris Jencks Tillinghast, Sr., regarding a voyage to the Far East for coffee and sugar; journal, 1812-1813, of William Holroyd Tillinghast (d. 1813), son of Paris Jencks Tillinghast, Sr., concerning prices, embargoes, the scarcity of goods, orations at Fayetteville Academy in 1813, and military and naval actions; letter books, 1824-1831 and 1852-1861, of Samuel Willard Tillinghast regarding his mercantile business with northern companies, including the sale of cotton, tobacco, and beeswax and his partnerships with Cyrus P. Tillinghast and, later, with D. A. Ray; a sales book, 1832-1845, from the auctioneering firms of Thomas Sanford & Co. and Samuel Willard Tillinghast at Fayetteville, containing accounts for sales of a great variety of goods, the personal effects of Henry L. Jones and of Mrs. David Smith in 1833, and of slaves in 1832; a task book, 1849-1851, for turpentine operations relating to the use of slaves and purchases of clothing for them; invoice books, 1853-1861 and 1877-1880, of Tillinghast's Crockery Store operated by William Norwood Tillinghast; the journal, 1861, of Emily Tillinghast, daughter of Samuel Willard Tillinghast, describing home life during the early months of the Confederacy; the funeral service of Edward Peet, teacher at the New York Institution for the Deaf and Dumb; the February, 1865, issue of The Fanwood Chronicle edited by David Ray Tillinghast at the New York Institution for the Deaf and Dumb; invoice books, 1866-1883, of the Fayetteville Gas Light Company of which William Norwood Tillinghast was secretary and treasurer; photocopy of a letter (56 pp.) of Sarah Ann Tillinghast describing making clothing for the Fayetteville company of the 1st North Carolina Infantry during the Civil War, and detailing the activities of the Union soldiers when Sherman captured Fayetteville; an account by Robina Tillinghast of Sherman's march through Fayetteville; statement, 1892, of the Reverend Job Turner, a missionary among the deaf; account, 1926, of the founding and history of the North Carolina Historical Commission in which Susan (Tillinghast) West took part; a family Bible; legal papers including wills, land deeds and indentures, and marriage bonds; financial papers, including receipts, profit and loss statements, and material regarding the life insurance policy of John Baker Tillinghast; papers relating to the estate of John H. Culbreth, 1930s; genealogical material; invitations; programs; funeral booklet; autograph album; records of St. John's Episcopal Church, 1930s and 1940s, of the St. John's Young People's Service League, and of the St. John's Woman's Auxiliary; writings and addresses; poetry; words to songs; religious writings, especially relating to St. John's Episcopal Church; clippings; annual celebrations of the battle of Moore's Creek; scrapbooks; notebooks; and pictures.

5299.   BENJAMIN RYAN TILLMAN, JR., PAPERS, 1894-1897. 9 items. Trenton (Edgefield County), S.C.

Papers of Benjamin Ryan Tillman, Jr. (1847-1918), farmer, governor of South Carolina, 1890-1894, and U. S. senator, 1895-1918, include correspondence discussing Tillman's senatorial campaign against Matthew Calbraith Butler, the sale of whiskey, South Carolina politics, and the election of John Gary Evans as governor; letter, and memorial to be presented by the state of South Carolina to Congress, protesting the extension of the powers of the U. S. courts; and clippings concerning an altercation in Darlington, South Carolina, between constables and private citizens over restrictions relating to alcoholic beverages.

5300. AMBROSE CRAMER TIMBERLAKE LEDGERS, 1796-1873. 6 vols. Charles Town (Jefferson County), W. Va.

Accounts of a general mercantile store, 1796-1810 and 1845-1873.

5301. JOHN W. TIMBERLAKE PAPERS, 1843-1860. 25 items. Charlottesville (Albemarle County), Va.

Correspondence relating to John W. Timberlake's business as a druggist in Charlottesville, Virginia, and to the cotton market in New Orleans, Louisiana.

5302. WALKER TIMBERLAKE PAPERS, 1814-1938. 197 items and 6 vols. Albemarle County, Va.

Chiefly business papers of Walker Timberlake, farmer, miller, and minister, concerning his various business interests, including his partnership in the James River and Staunton Plank Road Company. Also included are land deeds; personal correspondence with reference to family matters, slavery, and religion; clippings, including a sermon delivered by the Reverend Paul Whitehead on May 10, 1863, entitled "Holiness in Time of War"; account books, 1849-1880; daybooks, 1850-1868; a commonplace book, 1863-1865; and a railroad book, 1853.

5303. JOHN WESLEY TIMMONS, SR., PAPERS, 1841-1925. 93 items. Clarksville (Clinton County), Ohio.

Personal correspondence of John Wesley Timmons, Sr., and of members of the Timmons family. Civil War letters discuss the war in Kentucky and Tennessee; the battle of Stones River (Murfreesboro), Tennessee, 1862-1863; the battle of Gettysburg, Pennsylvania, 1863; camp life in the U. S. Army; casualties; prisoners; and sickness.

5304. ALEXANDER TODD PAPERS, 1902-1973. 4 items. Worthing, Sussex, England.

Letters to Alexander Todd, member of the Royal College of Veterinary Surgeons, from author William Ernest Henley concerning his Irish terrier; and an explanatory note from Todd's daughter, Mrs. John Cleland.

5305. E. BRADFORD TODD PAPERS, 1838-1875. 3 items and 1 vol. Pittsburgh, Pa.

Commonplace book of E. Bradford Todd, Pittsburgh lawyer, concerning chemistry, history, religion, politics, medicine, phrenology, the Biddle family, Egypt, and account of James Ross, senator from Pennsylvania, and other matters; an obituary and a short account of James Ross; and a letter of condolence from Melancthon Williams Jacobus concerning the death of Todd's father.

5306. WILLIAM E. TOLBERT PAPERS, 1820 (1870-1894) 1939. 1,405 items and 8 vols. Chambersburg (Franklin County), Pa.

Chiefly the business and legal papers relating to the businesses of John Huber and Robert E. Tolbert, Robert E. Tolbert and Son, and William E. Tolbert, including bills, receipts, and correspondence. Also included are letters from William E. Tolbert while serving with the chief engineer's office of the U. S. Military Railroad, Division of the Mississippi, U. S. Army; letters from Elizabeth Russell, a Methodist missionary in Nagasaki, Japan, to Emma Tolbert, describing missionary efforts, Japanese customs, reforestation in Japan, Russian refugees in Japan, and her attitude toward World War I and the Bolshevik revolution; family and personal correspondence; receipts from John Huber of the Chambersburg Beneficial Society; wedding invitations; The Pilgrim's Progress, June, 1923, official organ of the Pilgrim's Mission of India; and a broadside of the Delaware state lottery, 1860.

5307. MYRON TOLLES PAPERS, 1851-1888. 39 items and 2 vols. Rock County, Wis.

Family correspondence of Myron Tolles, farmer, concerning personal matters, Wyoming County and western New York, the election of 1864, and the assassination of Abraham Lincoln. Also included are teachers' contracts for the schools of Porter (Rock County, Wisconsin), minutes of a special meeting of the electors of the school district in January, 1862, and the district's annual report for 1864; and an insurance certificate of the Royal Templars of Temperance, 1888. The volumes are a diary of a Union soldier in Virginia and West Virginia in 1864; and a diary, 1872, of James K. Keeney concerning the routine affairs of his farm in Ohio.

5308. TOMBECKBEE ASSOCIATION OF FRENCH IMMIGRANTS PAPERS, 1817-1840. 22 items. Marengo County and Greene County, Ala.

Business correspondence, chiefly in French, between owners of land on the Tombigbee River in Alabama and a land agent concerning efforts to sell the land for a proposed French colony.

5309. CARTER BRAXTON TOMLIN PAPERS, 1906-1923. 158 items. Whitney (Dawes County), Neb., and Hanover County, Va.

Family letters from Carter Braxton Tomlin (1853-1918), salesman of farm equipment, to his daughters, Charlotte and Louise, teachers, with occasional references to the shortage of horses during World War I, and President Woodrow Wilson's peace terms. A letter by his brother, Harry B. Tomlin, describes the plight of western farmers in 1921, prices for crops, taxes, and market conditions. The volumes are an account book, 1897, for individual purchases and expenditures; and "Journal of Farm Life at 'Eocene . . . ,'" describing his daily activities and experiences, 1873-1874.

5310.   NOTLEY J. TOMLIN PAPERS, 1842-1932. 52 items. Turnersburg (Iredell County), N.C.

Chiefly legal and financial papers, including seven letters, 1847-1849, concerning the construction and equipment of the Turnersburg Cotton Mills in Iredell County, a firm of which Tomlin was co-owner. Three letters, 1856, are from the Spring Hill Forge about purchases of iron, and two are from James W. Wilson of Morganton, another of the co-founders of the Turnersburg mill. Most of the legal and financial papers, 1842-1877, date from the 1840s and 1850s, and concern the Turnersburg factory and the Eagle Mill Co., another cotton factory in Iredell County; raw and finished cotton prices; sales of slaves, 1842 and 1853; a sawmill in North Carolina, 1855; Tomlin's estate in the 1860s; expenses at Concord Female College, 1861, and Statesville Female Academy, 1853, both schools in North Carolina; and remuneration due the heirs of a soldier killed in the Mexican War. Among miscellaneous items are a statement written during the 1850s on the history of the Turnersburg factory and modern notes about that firm. Printed materials include a 1932 clipping about Southern textile mill villages.

5311.   CHARLES BROWN TOMPKINS PAPERS, 1847 (1861-1865) 1913. 462 items. Lewistown (Fulton County), Ill.

Chiefly the Civil War correspondence of Charles Brown Tompkins (1838-1913), surgeon with the 17th Regiment Illinois Infantry, with his wife, Mary (Gapen) Tompkins (1831-1873), discussing mobilization; camp life; medical and hospital conditions; the health of his regiment; various Union generals; areas passed through; skirmishes and guerrilla fighting; depredations by Union troops; the battles of Fort Donelson, Fort Henry, and Stones River (Murfreesboro), Tennessee; the battle of Iuka, Mississippi; the siege and occupation of Vicksburg; and Sherman's march from Savannah, Georgia, through the Carolinas. Mary (Gapen) Tompkins's letters describe her school for girls in Lewiston, Illinois; anti-Southern feelings; commodity prices; politics; military news; the resistance to the draft act of 1863; "Copperheads"; and civilian life during the war. Letters of Oscar Works describe life at Oberlin College, Oberlin, Ohio, in 1859. Also included are poetry; a copy of the Tompkins genealogy compiled by Charles Brown Tompkins; letters from other members of the Brown, Tompkins, and Works families; and a copy of the obituary of Charles Brown Tompkins.

5312.   DANIEL AUGUSTUS TOMPKINS PAPERS, 1774-1976. 6,401 items and 31 vols. Charlotte (Mecklenburg County), N.C.

Personal, business, legal, and financial papers of Daniel Augustus Tompkins (1851-1914), Charlotte businessman. Correspondence, 1874-1884, is principally with his fianceé, Harriet Brigham, discussing personal matters; his work and colleagues at the Bethlehem Iron Works, Bethlehem, Pennsylvania, where Tompkins was employed as a machinist, 1874-1881; economic conditions relating to Bethlehem Iron Works; life in boarding houses; social and cultural life in Bethlehem; Lehigh University, Bethlehem, Pennsylvania; his organization of a savings and loan association; John Fritz, mechanical engineer at Bethlehem Iron Works; and his work as an engineer and sales agent in Charlotte, North Carolina, for the Westinghouse Machine Company. A ledger, 1881-1886, contains accounts for public committees in Bethlehem including fire, street, lock-up, lamp, health, police, ordinance, finance, and market; and accounts, 1883-1884, for selling steam engines for the Westinghouse Machine Company. Scattered papers, 1884-1914, generally pertain to Tompkins's investments, and to his dispute over editorial policies with James Calvin Hemphill, editor of the Charlotte Observer, in which Tompkins owned a majority interest. Included are a cashbook, 1913-1914; notes and bills receivable and payable, 1889-1918; notes, 1906-1907, about gas engines; a journal, 1910-1914; and a ledger, 1907-1914. Papers, 1915-1921, consisting of correspondence, legal and financial papers, scattered minutes, and financial statements, generally relate to the settlement of the Tompkins estate and his investments in the Charlotte Observer; the Observer Printing House; the Greenville (S.C.) News; the Atherton Mills of which Tompkins was a founder; the High Shoals Company; other cotton mills in North and South Carolina, especially Parker Cotton Mills Company, Victor-Monaghan Mills, Hampton Cotton Mills and Issaqueena Mills; the Troy Oil Mill; the D. A. Tompkins Company, manufacturers, engineers, and contractors with machine and roller covering shops; the Switzerland Company, developers of the resort community of Little Switzerland, North Carolina; the Charlotte Sanatorium, a general hospital; banking investments; and the Johnson Publishing Company. There are also correspondence and other papers dealing with the writing of a biography of Daniel Augustus Tompkins by George Tayloe Winston entitled A Builder of the New South Being the Story of the Life Work of Daniel Augustus Tompkins (New York: 1920); and with bequests to Edgefield, South Carolina, for their library and for the installation of manual training and home economics in the public schools. Accounts for the estate consist of a journal, 1914-1926; cashbooks, 1914-1926; and a trial balances book, 1913-1918. There are also accounts for the D. A. Tompkins Company including a cashbook,

575

1907-1917; a ledger, 1907-1917; and a minute book, 1906-1916. Accounts for the Troy Oil Mill Company are a cashbook, 1914-1917; a general ledger, 1905-1917; and a ledger, 1914-1916. Papers after 1921 are chiefly those of Sterling Graydon (d. 1974), nephew of Daniel Augustus Tompkins, executor of the Tompkins estate, and owner of the Angus Brick Company, Ninety Six, South Carolina. Included are personal correspondence of Graydon and of his wife, Nell (Saunders) Graydon, concerning family matters, politics, economic conditions, the management of the Tompkins estate, and Graydon's ownership of the Angus Brick Company; papers relating to Graydon's stock investments, especially during the 1950s; papers dealing with Nell (Saunders) Graydon's historical writings on South Carolina; information on the Cokesbury (South Carolina) Historical Commission and the campaign to preserve the town; accounts relating to the Angus Brick Company, consisting of ledgers, 1930-1945, and cash journals, 1934-1945; a personal cash journal of Sterling Graydon, 1930-1948; and a ledger of Clint T. Graydon, 1930-1935. The collection also contains printed material and pictures.

5313. JOSEPH M. TOMPKINS PAPERS. 3 items.

Two pieces of original verse addressed to Joseph M. Tompkins by female admirers; and an item relating to prices for board and laundry.

5314. ROBERT P. TONDEE PAPERS, 1862-1868. 11 items. Richmond, Va.

Civil War letters from Robert P. Tondee and his brother, William Tondee, while serving with the 17th Georgia Regiment, C.S.A., in the Richmond area, concerning military engagements, including the second battle of Manassas; the wounds received by the two and their convalescence in hospitals; a review of Confederate troops by Generals John Bell Hood and James Ewell Brown Stuart; and a march from Lookout Mountain. Letters from B. F. Adams deal with affairs of the Tondee family.

5315. ROBERT AUGUSTUS TOOMBS PAPERS, 1846-1881. 25 items. Wilkes County, Ga.

Political correspondence of Robert Augustus Toombs (1810-1885), lawyer, U.S. congressman, 1845-1853, U.S. senator, 1853-1861, and member of the first Confederate Congress, discussing state and national politics, the Whig Party, the Kansas Question, the Free Soil Party, the Democratic nomination for president in 1856, a plan for bringing Maryland into the Confederacy, a report of Toombs's Brigade from the battle of Antietam, routine matters such as speaking engagements, and legal affairs. A clipping, 1881, describes Toomb's criticism of Jefferson Davis, the Confederate government and the army.

5316. WASHINGTON TOPHAM PAPERS, 1930. 1 item. Washington, D.C.

Letter from Washington Topham to Maud Burr Morris concerning an article written by her.

5317. TORELLO PHOLA DE PUPPIO DIARY. 1 vol. (132 pp.)

"Daily record of the acts of the most holy Ecumenical and General Council of Trent, not only of the dogmas but also of the reforms, and of other matters which transpired at Trent under Pius IV, Pontifex Maximus. Collected by the Reverend Father Torello Phola de Puppio, Jesuit Priest and Canonic. To the praise and glory of almighty God." In Latin.

5318. PETER DELLA TORRE PAPERS, 1830-1853. 7 items. Charleston, S.C.

Legal correspondence of Peter della Torre, a Charleston attorney, including quotations on fees, and a letter referring to the question of rechartering the Bank of Charleston.

5319. ALEXANDER H. TORRENCE PAPERS, 1754-1915. 559 items. Iredell County, N.C.

Family papers and correspondence of four generations of the Torrence family. The earlier papers are those of Adam Torrence (d. ca. 1780), Revolutionary soldier, and consist of plats and memoranda concerning the settlement of his estate. Most of the papers fall in the 1850s and concern the settlement of the estate of Alexander H. Torrence (d. ca. 1848), lawyer and local politician. Included are records on the hiring of slaves, 1853-1860, and on the guardianship of the children of Alexander Torrence; and lists of farm equipment and household furnishings with values.

5320. FREDERIC RIDGELY TORRENCE PAPERS, 1910. 1 item. New York, N.Y.

Letter from Frederic Ridgely Torrence (1875-1950), poet, playwright, and editor, to Edward Joseph Harrington O'Brien (1890-1941), poet and editor, concerning the publication of some of Torrence's works.

5321. JAMES TOTTEN PAPERS, 1918. 1 vol. (23 pp.) New York.

Essay by Peter Adler Alberti, Danish politician, addressed to James Totten, military attaché in the American legation in Denmark, discussing Danish neutrality in World War I, propaganda efforts by belligerent countries to influence Danish public opinion, the attitudes of Danish newspapers towards the Allied Powers, especially the United States, and how the United States could improve its image in Danish public opinion. There is also an English translation of the essay.

5322. ALBION WINEGAR TOURGÉE PAPERS, 1871-1897. 4 items. Mayville (Chautauqua County), N.Y.

Correspondence of Albion Winegar Tourgée (1838-1905), author and North Carolina superior court judge, consists of a letter to Ulysses S. Grant requesting an interview to discuss state officers for North Carolina; a letter to the Philadelphia Press regarding publication of his story, "The Dragon's Mouth"; a letter discussing a dispute over the publishing of Tourgee's writings in The Continent, a weekly magazine of which he was editor and chief contributor, 1882-1884; and a letter from Edmund Clarence Stedman sending a poem written by Tracy Robinson.

5323. TOURS (GÉNÉRALITÉ) RECORDS, 1762-1766. 1 vol. (938 pp.) Tours, France.

Tableau de la Généralité de Tours depuis 1762 jusques et compris 1766 containing a description of each province in the Généralité of Tours-Anjou, Maine, and Touraine; an estimation of the population; lists of various church dioceses and monasteries, and estimated revenues; lists of military posts; lists of noblemen and their property; an inventory of the royal domain; descriptions of the vineyards, farms and cities under the Tours jurisdiction, including the wines and crops produced, and silk and textile manufacturers; prices for grains, livestock and bread in the principal cities; outlines of the nature of the various taxes, especially the taille and the corvée; description of the assessment of taxes and the staff employed to collect them; complaints concerning the inequality and abuses of the tax system, and a plea for relief; and three maps showing the boundaries of the généralité, its subdivisions, and the rivers, roads, and post stations along the royal highways.

5324. BENJAMIN T. TOWNER PAPERS, 1817 (1841-1848) 1897. 176 items. Shepherdstown (Jefferson County), W. Va.

Business correspondence of James S. Lane and Benjamin T. Towner, Shepherdstown merchants, and personal correspondence of members of the Towner and related Schley families, discussing business affairs; family matters; the election of Benjamin Harrison and celebrations in Shepherdstown; banking conditions in Baltimore, Maryland; the need for a national bank; Henry Clay; a torchlight parade by Loco-Focos in Frederick, Maryland, 1844; sales and purchases of slaves; life in Cambridge, Massachusetts; and conditions in Frederick during the Civil War. Letters from Thomas Harris Towner while serving in the U.S. Army during the Mexican War describe mobilization and training at Fortress Monroe, Virginia; wages and uniforms; politics in Virginia; war experiences in Mexico; sickness and death among U. S. troops; his views of the Mexican people; soldiers; opinion of General Zachary Taylor; criticism of the administration for neglect of Taylor and the army; unpopularity of President James K. Polk among the troops; rumors concerning the movements of General Winfield Scott; a speech by Henry Clay on the war; and the delay in Mexico in the ratification of a treaty to end the war. Other items include passes and orders relating to exemptions during the Civil War, and an admission ticket to the impeachment trial of President Andrew Johnson.

5325. A. S. TOWNES DIARY, 1863-1865. 1 vol. (70 pp.) South Carolina.

A diary kept by A. S. Townes, a Confederate soldier in Hampton's Legion, in the back of a diary started by a Federal soldier who saw active service in western North Carolina and eastern Tennessee. Townes's entries, in pencil, concern the evacuation of Richmond and activities around Farmville in April, 1865. Entries of the Federal soldier, in ink, describe his service in western North Carolina and eastern Tennessee.

5326. GEORGE ALFRED TOWNSEND PAPERS, 1883-1888. 3 items. Gapland (Frederick County), Md.

Letters to George Alfred Townsend (1841-1914), author and journalist, requesting a biographical sketch and assistance in getting an article published; and a letter from Stewart Lyndon Woodford (1835-1913), first Union military commander of Charleston, South Carolina, and Savannah, Georgia, explaining that he had been involved in prisoner exchange during the Civil War.

5327. MEREDITH WHITE TOWNSEND PAPERS, 1856-1857. 3 items. London, England.

Letters to Meredith White Townsend (1831-1911), British journalist, consisting of two from Lord Dalhousie, governor general of India, acknowledging Townsend's support; and one from Governor General Canning commenting on an article in Townsend's Friend of India about officers of native regiments, and on the case against the 34th Regiment at Barrackpur whose actions were the first incident of the Mutiny of 1857.

5328. SYLVANUS TOWNSEND DIARY, 1863. 1 vol. Hillsboro (Caroline County), Md.

Brief diary of Sylvanus Townsend, a Methodist minister, concerning his pastoral activities and his censure by the Philadelphia Conference for refusal to vote on a resolution pledging loyalty to the U. S. government and expressing hope for the suppression of the Southern rebellion. The diary also contains lists of Townsend's expenses.

5329.  FRANCIS J. TOWNSHEND PAPERS, 1853-1895. 84 items. Prince Georges County, Md.

Chiefly family correspondence of Francis J. Townshend, apothecary serving on the U.S.S. *Gettysburg* and the U.S.S. *Enterprise*, describing personal matters and Townshend's travels. Included are letters from a student at Charlotte Hall School, Charlotte Hall, Maryland; letters of Professor William Fletcher Perrie, Austin College, Huntsville, Texas; copy of a bill passed in 1878 giving apothecaries United States Navy rank of warrant officers with equivalent pay; and a letter from a doctor giving the details of a cure for pneumonia.

5330.  GEORGE TOWNSHEND, FIRST MARQUIS TOWNSHEND, PAPERS, 1749-1801. 98 items. London, England.

Political and military correspondence of George Townshend, First Marquis Townshend (1724-1807), British army officer and lord lieutenant of Ireland, 1767-1772. Many of the letters concern military and political appointments. Other correspondence discusses the election at Tamworth and the candidacy of Lord Villiers in 1756; parliamentary elections at York in 1768; an agreement among Lord Townshend, Lord Weymouth, and Simon Luttrell whereby Luttrell was given the seat for Weobley in the House of Commons; a conversation with Theobald Taafe describing an intrigue conducted by Charles Townshend (d. 1767), Lord Townshend's brother and British statesman, for an alteration of the cabinet; the resignation of Lord Grafton as first lord of the treasury and its possible effects on the administration of Lord North; efforts to get Denham Jephson to adhere to the government party in Dublin; various matters relating to Townshend's administration in Ireland; government rejection of proposed Irish legislation on distilleries and on a bounty for coastal trade in corn; the King's approval of Townshend's administration in Ireland; staffing difficulties with generals in the Irish service; the Irish fortification policy; the activities of Lord Bute, 1771; possible changes in the cabinet, 1771; the condition of the infantry and the cavalry, 1771; Townshend's recall and the transfer of administration to Lord Harcourt; difficulties at Trinity College, 1775; investigation of the defences at Portsmouth and Plymouth, 1785; news from France, 1790; imminent dissolution of Parliament, 1790; the proposed Corn Bill, 1791; conditions of the barracks and costs involved for new ones, 1796; prospects for Irish acceptance of a union with Britain, 1800; construction problems at Sheerness wells, Kent, England; the position of Thomas Hyde Page as advisor to Lord Cornwallis on the improvement of Dublin harbor and inland navigation; and the King's commendation of measures recommended by Townshend for public security.

5331.  THOMAS TOWNSHEND, FIRST VISCOUNT SYDNEY, PAPERS, 1785-1789. 4 items. London, England.

Letters to Thomas Townshend, First Viscount Sydney (1733-1800), British statesman and home secretary, 1783-1789, from the Duke of Richmond concerning recommended changes in administrative procedures; from the Earl of Portsmouth requesting Sydney's support of the proposed canal from Andover to Redbridge; and from Lord Cornwallis in Calcutta pertaining to new orders to Captain William Monson, and relations with Hyderabad and Mysore.

5332.  JAMES FRANCIS TRACY PAPERS, 1821-1828. 29 items. Alexandria (Arlington County), Va.

Letters from James Francis Tracy from Dublin, Ireland, prior to his departure for America to take possession of property inherited from his uncle, Thomas Tracy (d. 1821); and letters from Tracy in Mount Erin, Virginia, concerning the difficulties he encountered on his new estate, troubles with his slaves, and misunderstandings with his neighbors.

5333.  LIONEL JAMES TRAFFORD PAPERS, 1884-1888. 1 vol. Hill Court, Ross, Herefordshire, England.

Memoir (35 pp. text) by Major Lionel James Trafford (1855-1900), officer in the Royal Sussex Regiment of the British Army, concerning the Sudan Expedition of 1884-1885, describing the journey of the company by boat to Korti, the overland trek with Sir Herbert Stewart's force to Gubat, the battles at Abu Klea and at Gubat, travel by steamer to relieve the siege at Khartoum, the shipwreck of the two steamers and their rescue, the leadership of Sir Charles Wilson, their arrival at Khartoum two days after the city had fallen, and their return to Egypt. Included in the memoir are twenty-nine watercolor illustrations, forty pen and ink drawings, and five maps.

5334.  WILLIAM TRAHERN AND JAMES TRAHERN ACCOUNTS, 1803-1827. 12 vols. Brunswick (Brunswick County), Va.

Merchants' accounts, including daybooks, 1803-1806, and a record of cotton storage, 1825-1827, of William Trahern; and daybooks, 1806-1822, and an index of James Trahern.

5335.  NELSON TRAVILLION PAPERS, 1846-1856. 10 items. Mocksville (Davie County), N.C.

Chiefly family letters to Nelson Travillion from his brother and nephews. One letter mentions a slave who had the privilege of finding his own employment and keeping the money received for his service. A letter, 1854, from a friend in Missouri describes the natural conditions of the state, and complains of abolitionists and teetotalers.

5336. JAMES TREAKLE PAPERS, 1861. 7 items. Alexandria (Arlington County), Va.

Family letters written to James Treakle, a Potomac riverboat pilot, imprisoned as a spy by the Confederate forces, and papers relating to his trial.

5337. SIR JOHN SALUSBURY SALUSBURY-TRELAWNY, NINTH BARONET, PAPERS, 1862. 1 item. Trelawny, Cornwall, England.

Letter from Sir John Salusbury Salusbury-Trelawny, Ninth Baronet (1816-1885), discussing the relationship of the Duchy of Cornwall to the crown and to the public.

5338. LUCIA TRENT AND RALPH CHEYNEY PAPERS, 1936. 2 items. Sierra Madre (Los Angeles County), Calif.

Two manuscript poems by Lucia Trent and Ralph Cheyney, poets and essayists.

5339. PETERFIELD TRENT SCRAPBOOK, 1858-1872. 1 vol. (208 pp.) Richmond, Va.

Scrapbook compiled by Peterfield Trent, Richmond physician, containing official records of the Sons of Temperance and other materials relating to the organization and offices held by Trent. Among the papers are clippings; a broadside, 1869, soliciting members by the Undine Temple of Honor and Temperance; manuscript of the decision of Trent in the case of Philip August, Jr., in the Shockoe Hill division, 1858; "An Appeal To The People of Virginia," in behalf of the establishment of a Virginia State Inebriates' Asylum, 1860; a broadside, 1872, entitled _An Act To Incorporate The Virginia Inebriates' Home_; a broadside, 1872, addressing the Sons of Temperance of Virginia and North Carolina in behalf of the Virginia Inebriates' Home; _Minutes of the Grand Division of the Sons of Temperance of the State of Virginia_ . . . (Richmond: 1858); reports and related correspondence of Trent to the grand division of Virginia, 1861 and 1862, including a dispute within the national division about the admission of Negro members and the reaction to the Civil War; _Journal of the Proceedings of the National Division of the Sons of Temperance of North America_ . . . (New York: 1859); _Constitutions of the Order of the Sons of Temperance of North America_ . . . (Boston: 1865), including the constitutions for the national and subordinate divisions and the code of laws; and printed minutes for the meeting of the grand division of Virginia in 1865.

5340. WILLIAM HENRY TRESCOT PAPERS, 1849-1866. 3 items. Charleston, S.C.

Letters from William Henry Trescot (1822-1898), historian and diplomat, while representing South Carolina in Washington, 1866, in the matter of adjusting difficulties arising under the Reconstruction Act. Written to James Conner, the letters concern the trial of Confederates, the South Carolina Radicals, the activities of President Andrew Johnson, and Reconstruction plans. There is also a letter concerning a pamphlet he had written.

5341. GEORGE W. TRICE PAPERS, 1836-1847. 10 items. Orange County and Wake County, N.C.

Legal papers, for the most part deeds for land in Wake and Orange counties, North Carolina, and Henderson County, Tennessee. Also papers relating to an arbitration of business claims between George W. Trice and Zachariah Trice, in Hillsborough, North Carolina.

5342. JOHN A. TRIMBLE PAPERS, 1802 (1822-1881) 1907. 2,489 items. Hillsboro (Highland County), Ohio.

Papers of John A. Trimble, a merchant of Hillsboro, Ohio, contain a letter, 1823, from a student at Transylvania College, Lexington, Kentucky, discussing the school and its president, Horace Holley; correspondence, 1816-1858, relating to Trimble's mercantile business, including comment on the panics of 1837 and 1857, the expected effect of a new tariff on the price of woolens in 1827, the tanning business of James Trimble, and John A. Trimble's quarrel with his brothers over their investment in the business; letter, 1862, giving the attitude of a Northerner toward the Civil War; letter, 1866, concerning a cholera epidemic; letter mentioning labor troubles in 1894; and letters after 1876 pertaining to John A. Trimble's insurance business.

5343. TRINITY EVANGELICAL LUTHERAN CHURCH SABBATH SCHOOL RECORD BOOK, 1845-1855. 1 vol. (284 pp.) Smithsburg (Washington County), Md.

Volume containing the weekly records of the sabbath school of Trinity Evangelical Lutheran Church, Smithsburg, Maryland, including statistics on membership and attendance, a brief statement about each Sunday's meeting, and a "Remarks" column containing comments on the general activities of the church.

5344. LYSANDER C. TRIPP PAPERS, 1864-1865. 3 items. New Bedford (Bristol County), Mass.

Business letters to Lysander C. Tripp, acting assistant paymaster in the United States Navy, concerning prize money, the Union blockade of North Carolina ports, and various ships.

5345. GEORGE MICHAEL TROUP PAPERS, 1819-1846. 5 items. Dublin (Laurens County), Ga.

Miscellaneous letters of George Michael Troup concerning a paper on rot in the cotton plant which Troup presented to an association on internal improvements in New York, 1819, and the controversy between President Andrew Jackson and Vice President John C. Calhoun in 1831.

5346. JOSEPH TROUT DAYBOOK AND LEDGER, 1818-1839. 1 vol. (350 pp.) Port Republic (Rockingham County), Va.

Financial records, probably of a saddler.

5347. JOHN W. TROUTT PAPERS, 1862-1865. 20 items. Craig County, Va.

Correspondence between John W. Troutt, a soldier in the Confederate Army, and his family and friends who lived on Sinking Creek, Craig County, including descriptions of unusual customs, such as "wool pickings" and "sugar boilings."

5348. EMMA TROXELL PAPERS, 1862-1864. 17 items. Rockford (Winnebago County), Ill.

Letters to Emma Troxell from her brother Sylvanus Troxell, a soldier in the 74th Illinois Regiment, commenting on camp life in eastern Tennessee and troop movements in General William T. Sherman's Atlanta campaign of 1864.

5349. THOMAS TRUEBLOOD PAPERS, 1866-1870. 3 items.

Correspondence of the Trueblood family, impoverished Southern farmers, including one letter, 1866, from Mary Trueblood, concerning the death of four of her children from scarlet fever.

5350. LYMAN TRUMBULL PAPERS, 1886. 1 item. Chicago, Ill.

Letter of Lyman Trumbull, United States senator, to an autograph collector.

5351. THOMAS SWAN TRUMBULL PAPERS, 1864. 6 items. Hartford (Hartford County), Conn.

Letters of Thomas Swan Trumbull, an officer in the 3rd Connecticut Artillery, describing his health, prospects for battle, and the visit of a British officer, Sir Arthur W. Mackworth.

5352. WILLIAM TRYON PAPERS, 1764-1772. 4 items. London, England.

Papers of William Tryon, British colonial administrator, contain a petition, 1767, to Tryon as colonial governor of North Carolina; a letter, 1769, from Tryon to Joseph Montfort concerning the construction of the governor's palace at New Bern, North Carolina; and a letter, 1772, of Tryon as colonial governor of New York, regarding his salary.

5353. RICHARD TUBMAN PAPERS, 1753-1858. 210 items. Augusta (Richmond County), Ga.

The earlier papers, 1753-1800, consist chiefly of deeds dealing with the transfer of land in Maryland between Peter Dent, George Tubman, and Charles Tubman. The papers for 1807-1836 are chiefly those of Richard Tubman (d. 1836) and concern his affairs in Augusta, the cotton trade, and the attitude of the farmers and merchants toward the War of 1812. There are also miscellaneous receipts and legal papers, including a list of Richard Tubman's property in Georgia, 1831. After 1836 the papers are in the name of his wife, Emily H. Tubman, who evidently continued her husband's business.

5354. CHARLES C. TUCKER PAPERS, 1866, 1870. 2 items. Washington, D.C.

Letters of Charles C. Tucker, a lawyer of Washington, D. C., concerning a cotton claim and the sale of land in Georgia, and advertising the competence of Tucker's firm to prosecute government claims.

5355. GEORGE TUCKER PAPERS, 1859. 1 item. Philadelphia, Pa.

Letter of George Tucker, political economist and author, concerning rents of Virginia tobacco property.

5356. HENRY McKEE TUCKER PAPERS, 1901-1913. 3 vols. Raleigh (Wake County), N.C.

Ledgers of Henry McKee Tucker, a physician in Raleigh, North Carolina.

5357. HENRY ST. GEORGE TUCKER PAPERS, 1796-1896. 8 items. Winchester (Frederick County), Va.

Papers of Henry St. George Tucker (1780-1848), member of the United States House of Representatives and judge in Virginia, contain a document, 1796, signed by St. George Tucker, father of Henry St. George Tucker, announcing the appointment of James Brown as the elder Tucker's lawyer; letter, 1824, of Henry St. George Tucker, concerning the hiring of a teacher for his children; personal and financial letters from Henry St. George Tucker to John Lisle; and a letter, 1896, of Henry St. George Tucker (1853-1932), grandson of Henry St. George

Tucker (1780-1848), concerning Democratic Party unity.

5358. JESSE C. TUCKER HYMNAL. 1 vol. (127 pp.)

Manuscript hymnal from the middle of the nineteenth century, probably belonging to a choirmaster or to a member of a choir.

5359. JOHN RANDOLPH TUCKER PAPERS, 1848-1879. 3 items. Winchester (Frederick County), and Lexington (Rockbridge County), Va.

Letters of John Randolph Tucker, lawyer, teacher, and United States congressman, concern his family, his law practice, the family of Edmund Randolph, and a request for help in securing a Federal job.

5360. MARY (SAMES) TUCKER PAPERS, 1936-1967. 62 items. Lexington (Rockbridge County), Va.

Papers of Mary (Sames) Tucker concern the career of Carson (Smith) McCullers, American author, who, as a girl, took piano lessons from Tucker. Letters from McCullers concern her personal life, marital problems, and poor health. Also contains letters from McCullers's mother, Marguerite Smith; a physician and close friend, Mary E. Mercer; and Margaret Sullivan, whose doctoral dissertation at Duke University was about McCullers.

5361. NATHANIEL BEVERLEY TUCKER PAPERS, 1836 (1848-1851). 56 items. Williamsburg (James City County), Va.

Typed copies of letters of Nathaniel Beverley Tucker (1784-1851), author and professor of law at the College of William and Mary, to James Henry Hammond, advocating state sovereignty and urging Hammond to take the lead in the 1850 secession movement in South Carolina. Throughout the correspondence are references to "the rights of the South," Tucker's love of Virginia, his objections to the Second Bank of the United States, his hatred of Martin Van Buren, construction of railroads, John C. Calhoun's ability, disturbances in Europe, and plans for the Nashville Convention of 1850. There are also brief references to Thomas R. Dew and George Frederick Holmes. Thirteen items are excerpts from letters of Tucker to Hammond; four letters are from Hammond to William Gilmore Simms relative to a new edition of Tucker's The Partisan Leader, the Nashville Convention, Tucker's character, and his death; one letter is from William B. Hodgson to Hammond relative to the Nashville Convention; and one original from Tucker to Henry A. Wise recommends an applicant for a position as postmaster.

5362. THOMAS TUDOR TUCKER PAPERS, 1799. 1 item. Charleston, S.C.

Letter of Thomas Tudor Tucker (1745-1828), physician, member of the Continental Congress, and treasurer of the United States, to Dr. Isaac Chanler of Charleston, South Carolina, concerning yellow fever in New York, Philadelphia, and Charleston.

5363. TILGHMAN M. TUCKER PAPERS, 1841-1843. 2 items. Jackson (Hinds County), Miss.

Letter from Tucker to Robert H. Buckner discussing a political appointment, and a document, signed by Tucker as governor of Mississippi, creating a justice of the peace.

5364. W. H. TUCKER PAPERS, 1862-1864. 13 items. Sheffield (Newton County), Ga.

Letters between W. H. Tucker and his wife Delana Tucker concern the management of their farm, and W. H. Tucker's life in the Confederate Army at Camp Gordon, Georgia, including a description of the battle of Atlanta, 1864.

5365. W. H. TUCKER PAPERS, 1861. 1 item. Richmond, Va.

A business letter of W. H. Tucker concerning personal debts.

5366. WILLIAM TUCKER PAPERS, 1841. 1 item. Amherst County, Va.

Business letter of John D. Davis and John Tankersly to William Tucker concerning personal debts and Richard I. Pryor.

5367. WILLIAM C. TUCKER PAPERS, 1844-1868. 18 items. Raleigh (Wake County), N.C.

Miscellaneous business papers, including bills, receipts, and a few items dealing with insurance.

5368. NANNIE WHITMELL TUNSTALL PAPERS, 1842 (1875-1878) 1886. 21 items. Richmond, Va.

Letters to Nannie W. Tunstall, short-story writer, from Governor James Lawson Kemper and George Washington Custis Lee, chiefly concerned with social affairs.

5369. WILLIAM TUNSTALL, JR., PAPERS, 1793-1859. 87 items. Pittsylvania Court House (Pittsylvania County), Va.

Papers of William Tunstall concern his personal business and his duties as clerk of court of Pittsylvania County, Virginia, and contain bills and receipts, including tuition bills for various girls' schools in Virginia; and correspondence, including a letter, 1823, to Tunstall from George Tucker discussing political affairs, including the protective tariff and the coming presidential election.

5370. JAMES TUPPER PAPERS, 1862-1865. 20 items. Columbia (Richland County), S.C.

Letters to James Tupper, South Carolina state auditor, and, in 1862, central secretary for a commission appointed by the South Carolina convention to enable planters to evacuate their slaves before the arrival of Federal troops. Most of the letters are from slaveowners seeking remuneration for slaves who had died while impressed by the Confederate government for defense work.

5371. MARY ELIZABETH TURLEY PAPERS, 1853-1855. 10 items. Moorefield (Hardy County), W. Va.

Personal and family correspondence of a homesick bride.

5372. A. J. TURLINGTON PAPERS, 1851-1877. 15 items. Cumberland County, N.C.

Personal and business correspondence between A. J. Turlington and his brother, W. H. Turlington, a Wilmington, North Carolina, merchant, concerning the timber and turpentine business, recreational and cultural advantages in Wilmington, and other matters. A few Civil War letters comment on yellow fever in Wilmington and conditions in the camp there.

5373. WILLIAM H. TURLINGTON PAPERS, 1859-1860. 14 items. Wilmington (New Hanover County), N.C.

Business correspondence of William H. Turlington, commission merchant of Wilmington, North Carolina, with J. H. Richardson of New York, to whom he shipped turpentine and rosin.

5374. S. C. TURNAGE DAYBOOKS AND LEDGERS, 1907-1924. 18 vols. Smithfield (Johnston County), N.C.

Accounts of S. C. Turnage, a general merchant associated with one Talton, containing agricultural prices for the period 1909-1914.

5375. A. TURNER ACCOUNT BOOK, 1822-1826. 1 vol. (132 pp.) Little River Circuit, [Va.?].

Record of books sold by an agent of the Methodist Publishing House.

5376. ANNE A. TURNER DIARY, 1821-1837. 1 vol. Fayetteville (Cumberland County), N.C.

A diary chiefly concerned with religious introspection and family matters.

5377. EDWARD C. TURNER PAPERS, 1839-1887. 140 items. "Kinloch," near The Plains (Fauquier County), Va.

Papers of Edward C. Turner concern operations at Kinloch plantation; experimentation with guano as a fertilizer; cattle and wood marketing; wool manufacturing; Turner's official connection with the Manassas Gap Railroad; and opposition to secession. There are comments on the election of 1873 in Virginia by John Singleton Mosby.

5378. GEORGE WILMER TURNER PAPERS, 1846 (1860-1876) 1896. 1,579 items. Goochland County, Va.

Family and personal correspondence and legal and business papers of George W. Turner, a Goochland County planter. The bulk of the material falls in the period after the Civil War and concerns difficulties and poverty during Reconstruction. There are letters concerning family and plantation affairs, letters pertaining to the education of Turner's six sons, letters from children in school at the College of William and Mary (Williamsburg, Virginia) and Washington and Lee University (Lexington, Virginia), and letters from his children who were teaching. The collection contains information on the beginning of public education in Virginia, Southern social life, and economic conditions during the Reconstruction period.

5379. SIR JAMES TURNER PAPERS, 17th Century. 1 vol. Craig, Ayrshire, Scotland.

A manuscript volume of essays by Sir James Turner, Scottish soldier and author, entitled "Tract's Criticall and Historicall compiled by Sir James Turner Kny't." The volume includes a criticism of George Buchanan's history of Scotland and his De Jure Regni apud Scotos; a story in which Buchanan is placed in hell; a reply to Bishop Henry Guthrie's memoirs; observations on Roderic O'Flaherty's Ogygia; an account of Mary Queen of Scots; a biography of Queen Christina of Sweden; a biography of Karl X Gustaf, king of Sweden; and several poems by Petrarch, Boccaccio, and Torquato Tasso with comment about them and Ludovico Ariosto.

5380. JESSE TURNER, SR., PAPERS, 1778-1929. 1,313 items and 3 vols. Van Buren (Crawford County), Ark.

Papers of Jesse Turner, Sr. (1805-1894), prominent Whig, lawyer, jurist, and member of the Arkansas secession convention, his wife, Rebecca (Allen) Turner (1823-1917), and his son, Jesse Turner, Jr. (1856-1919).
Papers of Jesse Turner, Sr., contain letters on Turner's political activities in the 1840s; letters on secession and descriptions of the activities and temper of the Arkansas secession convention; correspondence concerning the Little Rock and Fort Smith

Railroad; professional correspondence; copies of speeches made by Turner; and a copy of Turner's obituary and letters of condolence to his widow, 1894. Correspondence between Jesse Turner, Sr., and Rebecca Allen concern their views of home life, slavery, literature, and Christianity. Papers of Rebecca (Allen) Turner contain report cards from Steubenville Female Seminary, Steubenville, Ohio, 1838-1841; letters to her husband from Pittsburgh, Pennsylvania, during the secession crisis, describing feeling in that city and her difficulty returning to Arkansas; letters to her husband and son describing her travels, particularly to the centennial celebration in Philadelphia, 1876, and to the Columbian Exposition in Chicago, 1893; genealogical material on the Allen family; letters and journal of Edward Allen and William Hervey Allen concerning their experiences aboard steamboats on the Mississippi, Arkansas, and Ohio rivers; and letters of William Hervey Allen on the service of his son, Hervey Allen, in World War I. Papers of Jesse Turner, Jr., contain report cards from Van Buren Academy, 1867-1869; correspondence with his parents while he was a student at Kenmore University High School, Amherst County, Virginia, 1873-1875, and the University of Virginia, 1877-1879; professional correspondence as an attorney; correspondence with friends on literature; and letters to his mother in the early 1900s concerning his treatment for arthritis by Dr. Roland Jones of New York City. Other items in the collection include papers relating to Josiah Philips and a band of robbers in Norfolk and Princess Anne counties, Virginia, in the 1700s; notes and articles on the Arkansas constitution of 1836; papers relating to the political career and literary and classical studies of Judge William A. Falconer; letters written after 1871 by the family of Albert Pike, of Alexandria, Virginia, concerning financial difficulties; and later correspondence concerning Louise (Elliston) Yandell's portrait of Robert Crittenden, with information about the life of Crittenden and his duel with Henry Conway. Volumes in the collection include diaries, 1857-1859, kept by Rebecca (Allen) Turner, describing the activities of her young son, Jesse Turner, Jr.; and a scrapbook of Jesse Turner, Sr., containing material on the presidential election of 1848.

5381. JOHN TURNER ESTATE PAPERS, 1847-1862. 1 vol. [Hillsborough (Orange County), N.C.?].

Accounts of John Turner's estate as kept by John Boroughs as executor and guardian of Turner's children.

5382. JOHN R. TURNER PAPERS, 1860-1867. 153 items. Woodville (Rappahannock County), Va.

The letters of John R. Turner before the Civil War concern his activities as a merchant in Warrenton, Virginia, church meetings, and social life. Civil War letters concern his service, 1861-1862, in the 17th Virginia Regiment and, after 1862, as a commissary clerk in the division of General A. P. Hill, including a description of the battle of Fairfax Court House, camp life and army gossip, a description of the funeral of General Thomas J. Jackson, and life in Petersburg, Virginia, while it was under seige by Union forces. Letters of members of Turner's family describe life at home during the Civil War.

5383. JOSEPH TURNER PAPERS, 1864. 2 items. Fayetteville (Cumberland County), N.C.

Personal correspondence of Joseph Turner, apparently a Confederate captain, one letter concerning financial matters, and the other from a friend concerning the loss of her uncle at the battle of Cold Harbor, 1864.

5384. JOSIAH TURNER PAPERS, (1861-1865) 1880. 45 items. Hillsborough (Orange County), N.C.

Family and political letters of Josiah Turner (1821-1901), member of the Confederate Congress and editor of the Raleigh Sentinel, relating to Reconstruction and to Turner's difficulty with the family of Governor William Woods Holden.

5385. WILLIAM TURNER PAPERS, 1830-1893. 14 items. Perry County, Ala.

Personal and family letters of William Turner, some of which contain information on prices and general economic conditions in the 1830s; and a letter, 1840, to Turner from Thomas Glascock dealing with national and state politics.

5386. WILLIAM TURNER PAPERS, 1839. 2 items. Putnam County, Ga.

Letters to William Turner from Jabez Jackson relative to an appointment to the U. S. Military Academy, West Point, New York, and from Wilson Lumpkin analyzing national politics in 1839.

5387. TURNER AND TROUT INVENTORY, 1875. 1 vol. (96 pp.) Front Royal (Warren County), Va.

Inventory, apparently of a general store.

5388. WILLIAM TURPIN PAPERS, 1811. 1 item. Charleston, S.C.

Letter from William Turpin to his son, concerning disputed land on the Edisto River and the title to land near Orangeburg, South Carolina.

5389. JACK WEBB TURRENTINE PAPERS, 1835-1961. 320 items and 3 vols. Knoxville (Knox County), Tenn.

Papers consist for the most part of copies of letters relating to the genealogical researches of Jack Webb Turrentine on the Turrentine and Webb families. Also contains material pertaining to hikes on the Appalachian Trail and letters, 1907, of Samuel B. Turrentine, Jr., written shortly after he entered Trinity College, Durham, North Carolina, describing his loneliness, the school, and members of the faculty.

5390. MICHAEL H. TURRENTINE PAPERS, 1800-1868. 45 items. Hillsborough (Orange County), N.C.

Papers of Michael H. Turrentine (d. 1868), a Confederate 2nd lieutenant in the 31st North Carolina Regiment, consisting in part of letters from him while stationed at Fort Caswell or Gatling's Battery, North Carolina. The collection concerns the activities of James Turrentine as sheriff of Orange County, ca. 1838-1840, mainly relating to the land affairs of Phillips Moore and Elizabeth Moore; the gubernatorial election of 1846; social life at Kittrell Springs, North Carolina, 1860-1863; a smallpox epidemic, 1863; social conditions in eastern North Carolina, 1863; attack on the English steamer Kate by Union blockaders off Cape Fear, North Carolina, 1863; morale of Confederate soldiers, 1864; evacuation of Savannah, Georgia, 1864; and a description of Charleston, South Carolina, after a Union attack, 1864. Among the undated material are a list of slaves with prices, and diagrams and descriptions of the fortifications along the North Carolina coast during the Civil War.

5391. TUSCARORA FREIGHT BOOK, 1830-1836. 1 vol. (31 pp.) [Near Edenton (Chowan County), N.C.?].

Records of the schooner Tuscarora as kept by its master, John L. Harvey, while trading in eastern North Carolina.

5392. JAMES A. TUTT PAPERS, 1807 (1835-1858) 1908. 1,800 items and 6 vols. Calhoun (Henry County), Mo.

Papers of James A. Tutt contain business letters, receipts, promissory notes, bills, invoices, and account sheets concerning, in general, the migration of Tutt and his family from Virginia to Missouri. The papers contain comments on the hiring and selling of slaves, land speculation, and action against Mormons accused of enticing Indians to help them take over Jackson County, Missouri. There are also a ledger of Tutt's general store at Millersburg, Callaway County, Missouri, 1843-1844; a ledger kept by Matthew Arbuckle, U.S. postmaster at Calhoun, 1851-1853, showing postage paid for newspaper and periodical subscriptions by local residents; a volume containing accounts, 1873-1877, of the Calhoun Manufacturing Company, producers of wooden parts for buggies; the ledger, 1879-1883, of a sawmill owned by David H. Pigg and D. W. Pigg, with many accounts for laborers; and three incomplete volumes including a general store inventory, 1855, accounts of Tutt's wool carding operation, 1855, and mercantile accounts, 1855-1858.

5393. M. TUTWILER ACCOUNT BOOK, 1859-1865. 1 vol. Richmond, Va.

Account book of a flour mill.

5394. FRANCIS RANDLE TWEMLOW PAPERS, 1910. 1 item. Peatswood, Market Drayton, Staffordshire, England.

Letter of Francis Randle Twemlow, British army officer and author, to Mr. Boughey, a relative.

5395. JOHN TWIGGS PAPERS, 1781-1786. 5 items. Richmond County, Ga.

Papers of John Twiggs, officer in the American Revolution and Indian fighter, include a letter, 1781, to Twiggs from James Jackson concerning an attack on the British near Ogeechee, Georgia; a letter from Twigg to a merchant relating to clothing for his slaves; and a letter, 1786, to Twigg from Jared Irwin, asking for help against the Creek Indians along the Oconee River.

5396. JAMES HOGE TYLER PAPERS, 1900-1911. 3 items. Richmond, Va.

Letters from James H. Tyler (1846-1925), soldier in the Confederate Army, Virginia senator, 1877, lieutenant governor, 1889, and governor, 1898-1902. Two of the letters are addressed to General Horatio C. King, secretary of the Society of the Army of the Potomac, concerning the business of that organization, and the third is addressed to Dr. Charles E. Rice of Alliance, Ohio, in reply to an inquiry as to the letters of prominent Virginians.

5397. JOHN TYLER PAPERS, 1809-1872. 23 items. "Sherwood Forest," Charles City County, Va.

Miscellaneous public and private papers of John Tyler, president of the United States, include personal letters to his daughter, Elizabeth Tyler Waller; a letter concerning agriculture, particularly Tyler's experiments with a new variety of wheat; and a letter to his son, John Tyler, Jr., concerning William Cullen Bryant's Evening Post and Zachary Taylor. Also contains notes of introduction to members of Congress from John Tyler, Jr., and letters of Robert Tyler, son of John Tyler, including a description of Virginia politics during Reconstruction.

5398. WILLIAM TYLER PAPERS, 1799. 5 items. Augusta (Richmond County), Ga.

Correspondence of William Tyler, probably a British merchant in America, commenting on trade, transportation, and Loyalist property in Georgia.

5399. WILLIAM R. TYNER PAPERS, 1847-1849. 3 items and 2 vols. Smith Church (Northampton County), N.C.

Accounts of a general merchant and inventories of his estate.

5400. ACHILLES JAMES TYNES LEDGERS, 1882-1899. 2 vols. Tazewell County, Va.

Accounts of a general merchant.

5401. WILLIAM CORNELIUS TYREE PAPERS, 1884-1939. 344 items. Durham (Durham County), and Raleigh (Wake County), N.C.

Papers, 1884-1910, of William Cornelius Tyree, pastor of the First Baptist Church of Durham, North Carolina, and the First Baptist Church of Raleigh, North Carolina, contain letters from his wife, Lonnie (Hardaway) Tyree; personal letters from members of his congregation; business letters relating to his churches; letters from friends, including letters from other Baptist ministers concerning functions of Durham and Raleigh churches and the Southern Baptist Convention; and letters from Josiah Bailey concerning Tyree's contributions to the Biblical Recorder.

5402. BRYAN TYSON PAPERS, 1857 (1863-1886) 1903. 252 items and 2 vols. Durham, N.C., and Washington, D.C.

Letters and papers of Bryan Tyson, opponent of secession and abolitionism, government clerk, and inventor; and of his brother James Tyson. Bryan Tyson's Civil War correspondence reflects his interest in the Democratic Party and his activities in George B. McClellan's presidential campaign, 1864, but more particularly his efforts to spread Unionism among Confederate soldiers who were imprisoned in the North. Numerous letters, 1863-1865, from prisoners of war to Tyson contain requests for money, clothes, and tobacco; the bulk of these letters came from prisoners of war at Point Lookout, Maryland, although some were written from hospitals and a prison camp at Elmira, New York. These prisoners often described their indifference to the war; their intentional surrender to Union troops; their outright desertion; oaths of allegiance and the amnesty oath; their forced induction into the Confederate Army by the conscription act; the ambush and killing of men known to favor the Union; and the rounding up of deserters in North Carolina by Confederate troops, particularly in Randolph County and neighboring counties. Letters from Indiana indicate that numerous Union sympathizers fled from the same area of North Carolina during the war and settled in Indiana.

The correspondence also contains information on Tyson's business ventures, notably the sale of "McClellan's Bee Hive," and his efforts to raise money for developing an invention for removing additional gold from discarded ores. The letters also contain accounts of Tyson's travels in the interest of developing the invention. Many of Tyson's letters immediately after the war are concerned with obtaining contracts for carrying United States mail. Included also are a few family letters and two account books of James Tyson.

5403. JOHN SYMONDS UDAL PAPERS, 1921-1922. 2 items. Kenilworth, Warwickshire, England.

Letters from J. S. Udal to Macleod Yearsley concerning the publication of and reception given Udal's Dorsetshire Folk-Lore.

5404. MIGUEL DE UNAMUNO Y JUGO PAPERS, 1912-1913. 3 items. Salamanca, Spain.

Letters from Miguel de Unamuno y Jugo (1864-1936), Spanish author and scholar, to Benjamin Burges Moore (1878-1934), author and architect, discussing his conception of God, his progress on his work Del sentimiento trágica de la vida (1913), agrarian problems, a volume of poems he was preparing, and Portuguese literature.

5405. JAMES UNDERWOOD PAPERS, 1824-1831. 3 items. Cincinnati, Ohio.

Personal letters.

5406. RUTH ELIZABETH (NEWTON) UNDERWOOD PAPERS, 1926-1942. 27 items and 4 vols. Atlanta, Ga.

Papers of Ruth Elizabeth (Newton) Underwood, relating to the Southern Conference on Women and Children in Industry, of which she was chairwoman, including a report, a resolution, minutes, correspondence, financial papers, a leaflet, a pamphlet entitled The Laws of the State of Georgia, a cashbook, a notebook, and two booklets.

5407. UNION HOTEL PAPERS, 1875-1878. 2 vols. Union (Union County), S.C.

Ledger, 1875-1878, and register, 1875-1877, of the Union Hotel whose proprietors until early 1877 were Thomson and Wallace, and then were E. R. Wallace and J. H. Allen.

5408. UNION MANUFACTURING COMPANY PAPERS, (1848-1868) 1931. 1 item and 2 vols. Randleman (Randolph County), N.C.

Records of the Union Manufacturing Company whose operations included a cotton mill, a linseed oil mill, a cotton gin, carding machines, a flour mill, and a sawmill. Volumes are a daybook, 1848-1849, recording financial transactions, capital investments, and the sale of mercantile goods; and a minute book, 1848-1868, of stockholders' meetings, including reports of financial statistics. A clipping contains a biographical sketch of Samuel Hill (1857-1931), lawyer and business executive who was a grandson of Samuel Hill, the first president of the Union Manufacturing Company.

5409. UNITED ASSOCIATION OF JOURNEYMEN AND APPRENTICES OF THE PLUMBING AND PIPEFITTING INDUSTRY OF THE UNITED STATES AND CANADA, LOCAL UNION NO. 102 PAPERS, 1916-1948. 2,989 items and 5 vols. Knoxville (Knox County), Tenn.

Correspondence and papers of the United Association of Journeymen and Apprentices of the Plumbing and Pipefitting Industry of the United States and Canada, Local Union No. 102 (American Federation of Labor), chiefly for the years, 1944-1948, when E. P. Reiche was secretary. Correspondence deals with employment, labor conventions, labor legislation, and routine matters including dues, withdrawal of members, and requests for clearance cards. Several letters of 1917 pertain to a convention of the Tennessee Federation of Labor. Also included are pamphlets containing a working agreement and rules of procedure for Local 102; and minute books, 1916-1920 and 1925-1930, containing a roll call of officers, and lists of committees, members, and officers.

5410. UNITED ASSOCIATION OF JOURNEYMEN PLUMBERS, GAS FITTERS, STEAM FITTERS AND HELPERS AND SPRINKLER FITTERS OF THE UNITED STATES AND CANADA, PLUMBERS AND FITTERS LOCAL UNION NO. 227 PAPERS, 1913-1930. 27 items and 1 vol. Columbia (Richland County), S.C.

Papers of the United Association of Journeymen Plumbers, Gas Fitters, Steam Fitters and Helpers and Sprinkler Fitters of the United States and Canada, Local Union No. 227 (American Federation of Labor), consisting of minutes of meetings of Local 227, financial information, "in memoriam" resolutions, and a minute book, 1922-1930.

5411. UNITED BROTHERHOOD OF CARPENTERS AND JOINERS OF AMERICA, LOCAL UNION NO. 1778 PAPERS, 1943-1947. 245 items. Columbia (Richland County), S.C.

Chiefly correspondence of the United Brotherhood of Carpenters and Joiners of America, Local Union No. 1778 (American Federation of Labor) concerning financial matters and labor legislation. There is also some correspondence, 1945, of two officials of the South Carolina Labor News, the official organ of the South Carolina Building and Construction Trades Association.

5412. UNITED CONFEDERATE VETERANS PAPERS. 1 vol.

Songbook of the North Carolina Division of the United Confederate Veterans.

5413. UNITED DAUGHTERS OF THE CONFEDERACY PAPERS, 20th Century. 16 items.

Miscellaneous programs, calendars, yearbooks, broadsides, announcements, etc. of the United Daughters of the Confederacy.

5414. UNITED DAUGHTERS OF THE CONFEDERACY. SOUTH CAROLINA DIVISION. BLACK OAK CHAPTER MINUTE BOOK, 1910-1915. 1 vol. (108 pp.) Pinopolis (Berkeley County), S.C.

Minute book of the Black Oak Chapter of the United Daughters of the Confederacy. Included is a membership list.

5415. UNITED DAUGHTERS OF THE CONFEDERACY. SOUTH CAROLINA DIVISION. EDGEFIELD CHAPTER PAPERS, 1864-1914. 22 items and 2 vols. Edgefield (Edgefield County), S.C.

Miscellaneous papers of the Edgefield Chapter of the United Daughters of the Confederacy including lists of names of Union and Confederate soldiers buried in various places, chiefly in Georgia; reminiscences of the burning of Columbia, South Carolina, written by Mrs. E. W. Kerrison; copy of a portion of a letter of 1865 concerning depredations by Sherman's army in Bennettsville, South Carolina, and the capture and release of the writer's husband; and Nos. 19 (1913) and 20 (1914) of "Edgefield Soldiers in the War Between the States, and other Matters of Interest to the United Daughters of the Confederacy" by Agatha (Abney) Woodson, chapter historian, including a discussion of a state's right to secede, an address by Judge Milledge Lipscomb Bonham, Sr., original poems, an essay by Woodson on emancipation, copies of Confederate soldiers' letters, and a paper on education in antebellum South Carolina.

5416. UNITED SOCIETY OF BELIEVERS IN CHRIST'S SECOND APPEARING PAPERS, 1825-1910. 7 items. Pleasant Hill (Mercer County), Ky.

Typed copies of records of the Shaker community at Pleasant Hill, Kentucky, including a history of the origin and organization of the society; important events; appointments, removals, and changes in office; admission, decease and departure of members; lawsuits; covenants, declarations of trust, land titles, and other documents pertaining to the church; and a brief record of each convenant member, including birth, time of joining the community and decease.

5417. UNITED STATES. ARMY PAPERS, 1800-1945. 187 items.

Miscellaneous papers pertaining to the U. S. Army including a letter, 1813, referring to the movement of the 3rd Regiment of Infantry against the Creek Indians; letter, 1838, from Persifor Smith to Zachary Taylor concerning the Seminole Indian War; memorandum, 1839, of expenditures at Fort Brooke, Tampa Bay, Florida; letter, 1857, discussing pay accounts at Fort Davis, Texas, the routine life, Indian raids, and Robert E. Lee; letter, 1861, to the commander at Fort Pickens, Florida, urging the prevention of a seizure of forts in Pensacola Harbor; report, 1862, on the role of the 56th Regiment of Pennsylvania Volunteers in the battle of Fredericksburg; map, 1862, of the route taken in the advance to Goldsboro, North Carolina; map, 1863, of the attacking and defending forces at the siege of Washington, North Carolina; map, 1863, of the battle at Fort Butler, Donaldsonville, Louisiana; reports, 1864, of the sick and wounded of the 123rd and 160th Regiments of Ohio Volunteer Infantry; maps, 1864 or 1865, of the U.S. and C.S.A. fortifications at Petersburg, Virginia; roster, 1865, of Company E, 115th New York State Volunteers, compiled by a member of the company; broadside, 1865, of a poem composed for the 13th Pennsylvania Cavalry; U.S. Army letterheads and envelopes from the Civil War period; depositions and bail bonds of Confederate sympathizers; oaths of allegiance; passes and safe conduct certificates; letter regarding sutlers' wine; letter concerning a claim in relation to the Washington Aqueduct; statement of the seizure of the steamer Louisville; letter, 1895, pertaining to the reunion of the Third Army Corps; roster of Company E., 5th Ohio Regiment of Cavalry; report, 1943, of action against the enemy by units of the 67th Coast Artillery (anti-aircraft) Regiment in North Africa; and a copy of a citation awarding the Distinguished Flying Cross to Thomas A. McClees, ca. 1945.

5418. UNITED STATES. ARMY. EUROPEAN COMMAND. HISTORICAL DIVISION. FOREIGN MILITARY STUDIES, 1945-1954. 392 items. Washington, D.C.

Partial file of the manuscripts produced by the Foreign Military Studies Program of the Historical Division of the United States Army, European Command, consisting of historical records of World War II in Europe by former high-ranking officers of the German armed forces, including written and oral interrogations and monographs. (Many are in English.) [A copy of the Guide to Foreign Military Studies, 1945-1954, Catalog and Index (Headquarters, U.S. Army, Europe. 1954) in the collection indicates which documents are a part of the Manuscript Department's holdings.]

5419. UNITED STATES. ARMY. OFFICERS' AND SOLDIERS' MISCELLANY PAPERS, 1810-1941. 150 items.

Miscellaneous letters, notes, and documents of officers and soldiers in the U.S. Army, centering on the period of the Civil War. Letters of the Civil War discuss camp life; recruitment and conscription, health conditions, weather, food, picket duty, and fraternization with the enemy; chaplains' duties and religious services; prisoner exchanges; treatment of Federal prisoners at Libby Prison, Richmond (Virginia), and at Confederate Military Prison, Charleston (South Carolina); transportation of Confederate prisoners from Point Lookout (Maryland) to Fort Delaware on the Delaware Bay; the election of 1864; Congress and various senators; reinforcements for General Truman Seymour; areas passed through; various regiments and officers; skirmishes and raids; and various battles, including first Manassas, Cheat Mountain, Pine Mountain (Georgia), Chickamauga, Chattanooga, Petersburg, Cedar Creek (Virginia), and Atlanta. Also included are a history of the military career of Captain Henry James; a document entitled "Principal Claims of Maj. Gen. E. O. Keyes for Restoration"; a letter, 1866, of General William Babcock Hazen to General Adam Badeau disagreeing with the account of the Chattanooga campaign in Badeau's book; and a speech, 1902, in honor of Union soldiers killed during the war. Other papers include an anonymous letter to the officers of the Continental Army about an order; a letter, 1847, about the Mexican War; letter, 1854, describing life at Jefferson Barracks, Missouri, troubles with the Sioux Indians, and a projected expedition against the Sioux; letter complaining of treatment for an infraction of army regulations; letter, 1849, concerning a military escort for the shipment of supplies to Kansas; letter, 1903, regarding property owned by the Catholic Church on the Philippine Islands; several letters from soldiers in France during World War I discussing camp and trench life, immunization, pay and promotions, German reparations, American Negro soldiers, troop movements, souvenirs, commodity prices, and the adoption of French orphans by American squadrons; and a letter, 1941, of a pilot in the U.S. Army Air Corps describing his experiences, assessing the military and political situation, and stating his belief that the Japanese would not go to war.

5420. UNITED STATES. ARMY. ORDERS, 1815-1945. 17 items.

Miscellaneous orders and circulars of various organizations and divisions of the U.S. Army including orders concerning United States relations with the Cherokee, 1836; deserters from the Confederate Army; the capture and treatment of deserters of the 24th Army Corps in Virginia; the Flankers of the 24th Army Corps; the conduct of troops in the 4th Cavalry Regiment, U.S. Colored Troops, 1864; and the surrender of Germany, 1945.

5421. UNITED STATES. ARMY. PAROLED CONFEDERATES, CARE OF FREEDMEN, ETC. RECORDS, 1861-1863. 1 vol. (154 pp.) Mississippi.

Miscellaneous records, including court docket and case records of the state of Mississippi and of the U.S. government; rations for stragglers; lists of citizens and soldiers taking an oath of allegiance, occasionally including occupations; and other records.

5422. UNITED STATES. ARMY. PRISONS PAPERS, 1861. 1 vol. Fort Warren, Boston, Mass.

Autograph book of prisoners at Fort Warren, Massachusetts, with home addresses, rank in the army or position in public life, and occasionally dates and places of arrest. On several pages are drawings of women by Jesse S. Warram.

5423. UNITED STATES. ARMY. PROVOST MARSHAL LETTERPRESS BOOK, 1864-1865. 1 vol. Portsmouth, Va.

Letterpress book of the provost marshal of Portsmouth, Virginia, containing copies of letters relating to his various duties.

5424. UNITED STATES. ARMY. QUARTERMASTER'S DEPARTMENT PAPERS, 1782-1909. 52 items.

Miscellaneous papers and records of various divisions of the quartermaster's department, including lists of deserters, 1858 and 1865; commissary and ordnance reports; receipts for goods purchased by the army, 1782 and 1814; consolidated provision return of married soldiers and laundresses at Fort McIntosh, Texas, 1856; and a letter forwarding a bronze medal to a member of the 8th Army Corps in the Spanish-American War.

5425. UNITED STATES. ARMY. UNITS PAPERS, 1818-1868. 1,391 items and 12 vols.

Miscellaneous papers relating to various departments, districts, armies, corps and regiments of the U.S. Army, focusing on the Civil War period. Papers pertaining to the Department of the Cumberland, 1862-1863, 2 items, consist of a letter from General J. T. Boyle to General W. S. Rosecrans concerning troops, and an order against plundering, robbery, and straggling. Papers of the Department of the Missouri, 1862-1863, 40 items, are principally general orders, many concerned with courts-martial, and one general order of the Missouri State Militia. Papers of the Department of North Carolina, 1865, 5 items, consist of orders relating to the establishment of a military government in North Carolina and an order concerning the status of freedmen. Papers of the Department of the Tennessee, 1863-1866, 23 items, contain circulars and general and special orders dealing with local problems and courts-martial; and a letter, 1866, describing the death by hanging of seven of Andrews' Raiders in June, 1862, the remains when recovered in 1866, the death of Captain James J. Andrews, and the probable burial spot. Papers of the Department of Virginia and North Carolina, 1861-1865, 1,136 items, include records of Samuel C. Harbert, paymaster; correspondence; and records concerning the various units in the department, including discharge certificates, muster and pay rolls, pay and subsistance vouchers, and muster-out rolls.

Miscellaneous papers relating to the Second and Third Military Districts, 1863-1867, 9 items, include telegrams, a pay order, a court-martial order, an oath of allegiance, special orders, a form letter concerning a leave of absence, and an order, 1867, concerning the registration of voters for the election of members of a constitutional convention in Alabama, with lists of the number of delegates to be elected from each county. For the Fifth Military District, 1867-1868, 1 item and 1 vol., there are a letter book containing copies of letters by the commanding generals of the district and by their secretaries for civil affairs concerning the administration of Louisiana and Texas during Reconstruction, and dealing with such subjects as voter registration, the procurement of supplies, and appointments to minor posts in local governments; and a letter concerning the disposition of city funds in New Orleans.

Papers dealing with U.S. Armies consist of the Army of the Potomac, 1862-1864, 90 items, chiefly general and special orders, and directives for various divisions; and the Army of the Tennessee, 1864-1867, 8 items, including reports of the 15th Army Corps and papers concerning the 1st Regiment of Missouri Engineer Volunteers.

Pay vouchers comprise the bulk of the papers of the Army Corps of Engineers, 1818-1868, 27 items. Also included is a letter, 1827, from William Henry Chase to

Alexander Macomb reporting on a survey made to determine the improvements needed for the harbor at Pascagoula, Mississippi.

There are also papers and volumes dealing with specific regiments and companies. The volume, 1862-1865, for the 1st Connecticut Artillery (Heavy) contains a narrative of their movements, particularly those of Company B., through various towns and forts in Virginia, Maryland, and Washington, D. C., with occasional mention of promotions, and a list of deaths and wounded in Company M. Records of the 12th Connecticut Infantry Volunteers, Company D, 1861-1864, 2 vols., consist of a clothing book, 1862, and morning reports, 1861-1864, chronicling events during their service in southern Louisiana as part of the Department of the Gulf. Papers of the 9th Maine Volunteer Infantry, 1861-1863, 30 items, relate chiefly to Colonel Risworth Rich while the unit served in Fernandina, Florida, concerning routine matters of camp life, such as gambling, personal cleanliness, swearing, and proper attire. Records of the 28th Regiment of Maine Volunteers, 1862-1863, 4 vols., consist of a regimental order book, and a regimental and two company descriptive books, containing lists of soldiers, ages, complexion, color of hair and eyes, height, place of birth, occupation, details concerning their enlistment, and remarks concerning promotion, desertion, discharge, wounds received, or death. The volume, 1862-1864, for the 11th Massachusetts Infantry Volunteers, Company E, is an order book containing general and special orders relating to army regulations, courts-martial, discipline and other aspects of military life. The company descriptive book, 1861-1864, of the 17th Massachusetts Infantry Volunteers, Company K, contains lists of soldiers, ages, complexion, color of hair and eyes, height, place of birth, occupation, details concerning their enlistment, and remarks pertaining to promotion, desertion, discharge, wounds received, or death; lists of commissioned and non-commissioned officers, rank, date of appointment, and remarks about transfer, promotion, wounds received or death; a monthly summary of its activities in North Carolina; and a list of the officers and soldiers of the 5th Massachusetts Infantry, Company L, during the Spanish-American War, giving their marital status and next of kin. For the 19th Cavalry, 5th Squadron, 1st New York Dragoons, there is a mess book, 1863-1864, listing prices for food items purchased primarily by officers in the company. The papers of the 93rd Regiment of Pennsylvania Infantry Volunteers, 1862-1864, 20 items, include correspondence, orders, and circulars concerning the daily routine of the regiment such as leaves of absence, passes, preparation for troop movements, and special details for various duties. The company descriptive book, 1862, of the 155th Regiment of Pennsylvania Volunteers, Company B, contains lists of non-commissioned officers and soldiers, ages, complexion, color of hair and eyes, height, place of birth, occupation, and details concerning their enlistment, and a list of commissioned and non-commissioned officers, rank and date of appointment.

5426.    UNITED STATES. BUREAU OF THE CENSUS. CENSUS SCHEDULES, 1850-1880. 134 vols.

Original census returns as collected by the census enumerators containing abundant detailed information on the various questions covered. The following states and schedules are in the collection, either in part or in full, by counties which constitute the last item shown in the following list:

Colorado: agriculture, 1870, Arapahoe to Weld; manufacturing, 1870, Arapahoe to Weld; social statistics, 1870, Arapahoe to Weld; agriculture, 1880, Arapahoe to Weld; defective classes, 1880, Arapahoe to Weld; manufacturing, 1880, Arapahoe to Summit. District of Columbia: agriculture, manufacturing, and social statistics, 1850, 1860, 1870; agriculture, 1880; defectives, delinquents, and dependents, special manufacturing schedules, 1880; indigent and pauper, 1880. Georgia: agriculture, 1850, Appling to Putnam; social statistics, 1850, Baker to Wilkinson; agriculture, 1860, Appling to Worth; social statistics, 1860, Appling to Worth; agriculture, 1870, Appling to Worth; social statistics, 1870, Appling to Worth; agriculture, 1880, Appling to Worth; defective, delinquent, and dependent classes, 1880, Appling to Worth; manufacturing, 1880, Appling to Worth. Kentucky: agriculture, 1850, Adair to Woodford; manufacturing, 1850, Adair to Woodford; social statistics, 1850, Adair to Woodford; agriculture, 1860, Adair to Woodford; manufacturing, 1860, Adair to Woodford; social statistics, 1860, Adair to Woodford; agriculture, 1870, Adair to Woodford; agriculture (recapitulation), 1870, Allen to Woodford; manufacturing, 1870, Adair to Woodford; social statistics, 1870, Adair to Woodford; agriculture, 1880, Adair to Woodford; defective, delinquent dependent classes, 1880, Adair to Woodford; manufacturing, 1880, Adair to Woodford. Louisiana: agriculture, 1850, Ascension to Washington; social statistics, 1850, Assumption to Washington; agriculture, 1860, Ascension to Winn; social statistics, 1860, Ascension to Winn; agriculture, 1870, Ascension to Winn; agriculture (recapitulation), 1870, Ascension to Winn; social statistics, 1870, Ascension to West Feliciana; agriculture, 1880, Ascension to Winn; defective, delinquent, and dependent classes, 1880, Ascension to Winn; manufacturing, 1880, Ascension to Winn. Montana: agriculture, 1880. Nevada: agriculture, 1880. Tennessee: agriculture, 1850, Anderson to Wilson; manufacturing, 1850, Anderson to Wilson; social statistics, 1850, Anderson to Wilson; agriculture, 1860, Anderson to Wilson; manufacturing, 1860, Monroe to Wilson; social statistics, 1860, Anderson to Wilson; agriculture, 1870, Anderson to Wilson; manufacturing, 1870, Anderson to Lewis; social statistics, 1870, Anderson to Wilson; agriculture, 1880, Anderson to Wilson;

defective, dependent, and delinquent classes, 1880, Anderson to Wilson; manufacturing, 1880, Anderson to Wilson. Virginia: free inhabitants, slaves, deaths, agriculture, manufacturing, social statistics, 1860, Halifax. Wyoming: agriculture, 1880, With the exception of the Colorado material, all records are also on microfilm.

5427. UNITED STATES. CONGRESS. HOUSE OF REPRESENTATIVES. COMMITTEE OF ELECTIONS JOURNAL, 1789-1828. 1 vol. (533 pp.) Washington, D.C.

Journal of the Committee of Elections of the House of Representatives relating to contested congressional elections, resignations, deaths, and special elections to fill vacant seats; political irregularities at various levels; interpretation of state election laws; problems connected with soldiers' voting; and politics and government on the national and state levels. Included are charges submitted by challengers, and letters and affidavits of support. There is also an index to the names of all U. S. representatives and other important people mentioned in the volume.

5428. UNITED STATES. DEPARTMENT OF AGRICULTURE PAPERS, 1917. 10 items. Washington, D.C.

Posters of the War Food Administration.

5429. UNITED STATES. DEPARTMENT OF THE NAVY PAPERS, 1916-1917. 4 items. Washington, D.C.

Recruitment posters of the U.S. Navy during World War I.

5430. UNITED STATES. DEPARTMENT OF WAR. ADJUTANT AND INSPECTOR GENERAL'S OFFICE PAPERS, 1832-1900. 22 items. Washington, D.C.

Miscellaneous papers of the Adjutant and Inspector General's Office including photocopies of general orders relating to the organization of the Clothing Bureau, promotions, pay, courts-martial, the authority of the president in the commissioning of West Point cadets, supplies, deserters, the appointment of General George B. McClellan as head of Washington's defenses and troops, and articles to be sold by sutlers; letters concerning editions of the army regulations; letter, 1863, from General Lorenzo Thomas explaining a deduction of seventy-five cents per day from the pay of officers while hospitalized, which was to be credited to the U.S. Army Medical Department; and a letter, 1900, from Adjutant General H. C. Corbin pertaining to a canteen at Fort Michie, Long Island Sound.

5431. UNITED STATES. DEPARTMENT OF WAR. BUREAU OF REFUGEES, FREEDMEN, AND ABANDONED LANDS PAPERS, 1864-1866. 6 items. Natchez (Adams County), Miss.

Miscellaneous papers of the Bureau of Refugees, Freedmen, and Abandoned Lands consisting of papers concerning the enforcement of the abandoned property act; an indenture signed by Austin W. Fuller, assistant superintendent of the Freedmen's Bureau at Beaufort, North Carolina, apprenticing Esther Killingsworth; and a letter regarding the location of two Negro children separated from their mother.

5432. UNITED STATES. DEPARTMENT OF WAR. OFFICE OF THE SECRETARY OF WAR PAPERS, 1863-1865. 5 items. Washington, D.C.

Miscellaneous papers of the Office of the Secretary of War, including a pass and an order pertaining to a court-martial, both by Secretary of War Edwin M. Stanton.

5433. UNITED STATES. DEPARTMENT OF WAR. ORDNANCE OFFICE PAPERS, 1832-1871. 5 items.

Miscellaneous papers of the Ordnance Office consisting of a letter, 1832, to George Augustus Waggaman, U.S. senator from Louisiana, concerning arms for the state militia; two items, 1862, pertaining to the disposition of ordnance stores; report, 1864, of ordnance and ordnance stores received at Morris Island, South Carolina; and a letter, 1871, of Alexander Brydie Dyer, chief of ordnance, to William Buel Franklin discussing Charles Sumner, the sale of weapons to France, and the continued manufacture of arms by the U.S. government.

5434. UNITED STATES. DISTRICT AND CIRCUIT COURTS. VIRGINIA. WESTERN DISTRICT ABSTRACT, 1895-1898. 1 vol. (ca. 180 pp.) Virginia.

Records of sessions of grand, petit, and special juries for the western district of Virginia listing jurors and an account of the compensation for each.

5435. [UNITED STATES. NAVY?] LOGBOOK, 1874-1875. 1 vol. (134 pp.)

Pharmaceutical logbook, listing patients and pharmaceutical products received.

5436. UNITED STATES. NAVY PAPERS, 1818-1919. 33 items.

Miscellaneous letters, orders, receipts, and lists relating to the U.S. Navy including letter fragment, 1818, regarding merchant vessels and trade with Peru; letter, 1821, concerning pay for the crew of the Columbus; letter, 1829, discussing life aboard the U.S.S. Delaware and describing the U.S.S.

Lexington; letter, 1838, discussing the Black Hawk purchase; letter, 1857, granting land at Annapolis, Maryland, to the United States; letter, 1862, describing blockading duty off Charleston, South Carolina, and the squadron there; letter, 1863, protesting depredations committed by the crew of the U.S.S. Volunteer at the plantation of J. C. Barrow; letter, 1863, from Admiral Joseph Adams Smith describing the activities of the U.S.S. Kearsarge during its pursuit of the C.S.S. Alabama, and the Azores and its inhabitants; a list, 1864, of prizes captured by the U.S. Navy during the Civil War; poem written in honor of the U.S.S. Cumberland, sunk during the Civil War; and an order, 1919, concerning the appropriate length for sailors' hair.

5437. UNITED STATES. NAVY. U.S.S. GENERAL GRANT PAPERS, 1864. 1 vol. Alabama.

Volume concerning the activities of the U.S.S. General Grant on the Tennessee River describing other Federal gunboats encountered along the river; repairs on the General Grant; punishment of crewmen for misconduct and attempts to desert; transportation of troops; foraging; the destruction of several pontoon boats; contact with deserters; firing on Confederates along the river; and the capture of Confederate troops at Fort Deposit.

5438. UNITED STATES. POST OFFICE, LAWRENCEVILLE, GEORGIA, PAPERS, 1852-1856. 1 vol. Lawrenceville (Gwinnett County), Ga.

Accounts for the routine operations of the post office at Lawrenceville, Georgia, which functioned on a credit as well as a cash basis.

5439. UNITED STATES. POST OFFICE, SUFFOLK, VIRGINIA, PAPERS, 1804-1845. 183 items. Suffolk (Nansemond County), Va.

One hundred and one quarterly reports of Arthur Smith, postmaster, giving the financial statistics for the Suffolk post office; and receipts and orders to pay, for transactions with the office at Washington, D.C.

5440. UNITED STATES. TREASURY DEPARTMENT. DIVISION OF LOANS AND CURRENCY PAPERS, 1886-1915. 3 vols. Washington, D.C.

Volumes containing daily market price quotations on U.S. government bonds; and four tables showing prices and rates of interest realized to investors during April, 1899, for four issues of government bonds.

5441. UNITED STEELWORKERS OF AMERICA, DISTRICT 35 PAPERS, 1941-1952. 784 items and 1 vol. Atlanta, Ga.

Chiefly correspondence of William Harrison Crawford (b. 1888) and of R. E. Starnes (b. 1915), officials of the United Steelworkers of America, District 35 (Congress of Industrial Organizations), relating to support for labor unions; grievances; labor legislation; Local Union No. 2401, including correspondence, agreements, and pamphlets; the Atlantic Steel Company, Atlanta, Georgia, including material on contracts with Local Union No. 2401 and a dispute between the company and the union which came before the National War Labor Board; Atlanta Industrial Union Council, of which Starnes was vice-president; the Georgia State Industrial Union Council, of which Starnes was vice-president; National Labor Relations Board; the Regional War Labor Board in Atlanta; National War Labor Board; the Disputes Division of the National War Labor Board; the Office of Price Administration; and instructions from the United Steelworkers of America. The volume consists of specimen examples of job descriptions and classifications.

5442. UNITED TEXTILE WORKERS OF AMERICA, LOCAL UNION NO. 2598 PAPERS, 1939-1945. 28 items. Enka (Buncombe County), N.C.

Correspondence and papers of the United Textile Workers of America, Local Union No. 2598 (American Federation of Labor), including material relating to a case before the National Labor Relations Board in which the union brought charges against American Enka Corporation. Included is a detailed letter of James F. Barrett, director of publicity for the American Federation of Labor, explaining the involvement of the union in aiding persons regardless of race.

5443. J. H. UNTHANK BONDS, 1858. 7 items. Memphis (Shelby County), Tenn.

Bonds issued by J. H. Unthank covering money borrowed by him.

5444. ISHAM SIMS UPCHURCH PAPERS, 1843-1888. 35 items. Chatham County, N.C.

Letters of a Confederate soldier discussing personal affairs, commodity prices in Tennessee and Virginia, religious matters, the United States Congress, sickness, hospitals, weapons, food, the capture of a small U.S. schooner, troop movements, use of observation balloons by Union troops, the 16th Regiment of North Carolina Troops, and the writer's feelings towards Abraham Lincoln. Also included is a poem, an oath of allegiance, and a genealogical account from a family Bible.

5445. ABEL PARKER UPSHUR PAPERS, 1842-1843. 5 items. Richmond, Va.

Correspondence of Abel Parker Upshur (1791-1844), lawyer, secretary of the navy, and secretary of state under John Tyler, relating to applications for positions, recommendations, and claims.

5446. EMORY UPTON PAPERS, 1865. 1 item. Auburn (Cayuga County), N.Y.

Letter of Emory Upton (1839-1881), U.S. Army general and author, sending a photograph of himself to the addressee.

5447. SARA CARR UPTON PAPERS, 1881-1926. 36 items and 11 vols. Washington, D.C.

Letters, diaries, address books, scrapbooks, pictures, clippings, and notes of Sara Carr Upton (b. 1843), author and translator, including letters concerning the publication and review of Upton's translation of Jérôme Edouard Récéjac's Essay on the Bases of the Mystic Knowledge . . . Translated by S. C. Upton (1889); letter concerning Harriet Waters Preston, American author; and a scrapbook, 1892-1893, with photographs of the home of John Charles Frémont and clippings about the career of Italian actress Eleonora Duse.

5448. AARON VAIL PAPERS, 1793. 1 item. New York, N.Y.

Document appointing Aaron Vail commercial agent of the United States at Lorient, France.

5449. VALLEY BANK ACCOUNT BOOK, 1856-1859. 1 vol. Leesburg (Loudoun County), Va.

Ledger containing accounts of individual customers of the bank.

5450. VAMOCO MILLS COMPANY PAPERS, 1926-1942. 1,935 items. Franklinton (Franklin County), N.C.

The papers of Vamoco Mills, for the most part from the administration of Don P. Johnston, Sr., contain an operating statement, 1926-1935; financial statements, 1932-1941; court records, 1933-1938, including receivership records for Vann-Moore Mills Company, predecessor of Vamoco Mills, and papers related to the case of Virginia Trust Company, Trustee v. Vann-Moore Mills Company; correspondence of Don P. Johnston, Sr., 1932-1942; and a limited amount of material on production, stock reports, receiver's sale, and job applications.

5451. MARTIN VAN BUREN PAPERS, 1837-1891. 13 items. Kinderhook (Columbia County), N.Y.

Papers of Martin Van Buren, president of the United States, contain a personal letter, 1827, from Van Buren to Waller Tazewell, and miscellaneous items including land grants, a list of the electoral vote in 1836, and clippings.

5452. EARL VAN DORN PAPERS, 1862-1863. 4 items. Vicksburg (Warren County), Miss.

Papers of Earl Van Dorn, Confederate general, contain an appeal for volunteers to the people of Louisiana, 1862; a letter, 1862, to Van Dorn from Meriwether Jeff Thompson, reporting on the assembling of an expedition of 15,000 Union troops at Memphis, Tennessee; and a memorandum by J. R. Peacock of an interview with Irene Cheairs of Spring Hill, Tennessee, in 1951, concerning the shooting of Van Dorn by a Dr. Peters.

5453. JOHN C. VAN DUZER DIARY, 1864. 1 vol. Georgia.

Typescript copy of the diary of John C. Van Duzer, a soldier in the Union Army under General William T. Sherman, describing the movements of his unit in the advance from Atlanta to Savannah, Georgia, in 1864. Van Duzer relates Sherman's orders for the destruction of property on the line of march and describes the destruction of buildings and railroads, the burning of Howell Cobb's plantation, a brush with the 1st Alabama Regiment, Cavalry, a sham session of the Georgia legislature held by Sherman and his officers in Milledgeville, Georgia, and the capture of Savannah.

5454. PETER VAN GAASBECK PAPERS, 1794. 1 item. Kingston (Ulster County), N.Y.

Letter to Peter Van Gaasbeck, merchant, officer in the American Revolution, and member of the United States House of Representatives, from Jonathan Lawrence, concerning a pension.

5455. JOHN C. VAN HOOK PAPERS, 1879-1882. 22 items. Roxboro (Person County), N.C.

Papers of John C. Van Hook contain family letters, business papers, receipts for sale of tobacco by Van Hook and Lunsford, and a petition to the members of the North Carolina legislature for a narrow-gauge railway through Person County.

5456. GEORGE W. VAN METRE PAPERS, 1732 (1830-1910) 1943. 1,473 items and 8 vols. Martinsburg (Berkeley County), W. Va.

Papers of George W. Van Metre, a civil engineer, contain his professional notes and drawings; business papers; copies of Van Metre's weather observations; deeds for land owned by Van Metre and other members of his family to 1730; letters of Rosa (Ferrel) Van Metre and her family and friends; admission cards to lectures at the Physio-Medical College of Ohio for George Ferrel, father of Rosa (Ferrel) Van Metre; and letters, 1935-1937, of Mary J. Longfellow, a Baptist missionary to India. Volumes in the collection include business trip diaries of George W. Van Metre and his account book, 1884-1890; and daybook, 1853-1879, memorandum book, 1864-1866, and medical notes of George Ferrel.

5457. CHARLES LEONARD VAN NOPPEN PAPERS, 1881-1935. 1,137 items and 1 vol. Greensboro (Guilford County), N.C.

Papers of publisher Charles Leonard Van Noppen contain unpublished biographical sketches of prominent North Carolinians prepared for use in a projected extension of Samuel A. Ashe's Biographical History of North Carolina; portraits of many of the persons who are subjects of the sketches; printed forms returned by persons from whom biographical information had been requested; reviews of Ashe's Biographical History of North Carolina; personal letters and papers of Van Noppen; 250 brief printed summaries of the lives of prominent North Carolinians; and an album entitled Platinotypes of English Cathedrals, published in London by Eyre & Spottiswode. There are biographical sketches of Edwin Anderson Alderman, John Brevard Alexander, Sydenham Benoni Alexander, William C. Allen, Thomas Amis, Eugene Morehead Armfield, Robert Franklin Armfield, Wyatt Jackson Armfield, Charles B. Armstrong, Archibald Hunter Arrington, Thomas Atkinson, Traugott Bagge, Charles Baskerville, John Spencer Bassett, John Thomas Johnson Battle, Christopher Bechtler, Eugene Crocker Beddingfield, John Dillard Bellamy II, Risden Tyler Bennett, William Henry Bernard, Oscar William Blacknall, William Thomas Blackwell, James B. Blades, Moses Andrew Bledsoe, Jacob Weaver Bowman, James Edmund Boyd, John Luther Bridgers, Henry Alfred Brown, Peter Marshall Brown, Henry Ravenscroft Bryan, James Augustus Bryan, John Herritage Bryan, E. John Buchanan, Charles William Burkett, Robert Oswald Burton, Charles Manly Busbee, Fabius Haywood Busbee, Bion H. Butler, Joseph Caldwell, Tod R. Caldwell, John Bethune Carlyle, Samuel Price Carson, Joseph R. Chamberlain, Joseph Blount Cheshire, Henry Toole Clark, Thomas Clark, William Willis Clark, Mary Bayard Clarke, Thomas Lanier Clingman, William Henry Harrison Cobb, Charles Thaddeus Coleman, Daniel Branson Coltrane, Arthur Wayland Cooke, Charles Lee Coon, John Downey Cooper, Richard Johnson Corbitt, Lyman Atkinson Cotten, John Pickett Council, Calvin Josiah Cowles, Henry Clay Cowles, William Henry Harrison Cowles, John Martin Crenshaw, Hardy Bryan Croom, Thomas Morrow Crossan, John Franklin Crowell, John Culpeper, William Cumming, Moses Ashley Curtis, Joseph John Daniel, Robert Daniel, Adam Brevard Davidson, Joseph Jonathan Davis, Orin Datus Davis, Charles Force Deems, Christopher DeGraffenried, Moses John DeRossett, William Lord DeRosset, John Henry Dillard, James Dinwiddie, Robert Donnell, William T. Dortch, Robert Brent Drane, Edward Bishop Dudley, Charles Duffy, Francis Duffy, Rodolph Duffy, Angier Buchanan Duke, William Arrington Dunn, Thomas Eastchurch, William J. Edwards, Warren Grice Elliott, Joseph A. Engelhard, Hamilton Glover Ewart, William T. Faircloth, Garland Sevier Ferguson, Charles Fisher, Charles Frederick Fisher, Daniel G. Fowle, Robert Strange French, Adelaide Lisetta Fries, John Walker Fry, Joseph Gales, Sr., Seaton Gales, Jr., Alexander Gaston, Samuel Mallett Gattis, Donnell Gilliam, James Glasgow, William Glover, Daniel Reaves Goodloe, John Washington Graham, Joseph Graham, William A. Graham, Ralph Henry Graves, John Ruffin Green, Needham Yancey Gulley, William Anderson Guthrie, Clement Hall, Enoch Hall, James Hall, Daniel Hanmer, Charles Wilson Harris, Edward Harris, Thomas Hart, Thomas Harvey, James Hassell, Francis Lister Hawks, Raleigh Rutherford Haynes, Ernest Haywood, Dennis Heartt, Jones Tilden Hedrick, Archibald Henderson, Barbara (Bynum) Henderson, Leonard Henderson, Peter Henley, Matthew Johnston Heyer, Thomas N. Hill, John Franklin Hoke, Michael Hoke, William Alexander Hoke, Theophilus Hunter Holmes, Robert Howe, Theophilus Hunter Hill, James Iredell, Jr., Levi Silliman Ives, Thomas Neal Ivey, Fernando Godfrey James, Thomas Jarvis, Laban Linebarger Jenkins, Kate Ancrum (Burr) Johnson, Livingston Johnson, Norman H. Johnson, Milton Luther Jones, Michael Hoke Justice, John Kerr, John Kinchen, Tobias Knight, John Walter Lambeth, James Madison Leach, Emma L. Lehman, Richard Henry Lewis, Henry Armond London, Chatham Calhoun Lyon, Alexander Worth McAlister, James Rogers McConnell, Daniel McGilvary, James McKee, Jane Simpson McKimmon, Archibald Maclaine, Thomas Shelton McMullan, James Cameron MacRae, Julian Smith Mann, John Manning, Matthias M. Marshall, William Joseph Martin, William Maule, Oliver Pendleton Meares, Thomas Meredith, Robert Morrison Miller, Jr., John Haymes Mills, Thomas Miller, John Montgomery, William J. Montgomery, Hight C. Moore, George W. Mordecai, Robert Hall Morrison, William Dennis Morton, George Williams Mountcastle, Francis Johnstone Murdoch, Henry Kolloch Nash, Leonidas Lydwell Nash, James O'Kelly, Adlai Osborne, Francis Irwin Osborne, Edwin Augustus Osborne, John Palin, John Patten, Richmond Pearson, William Dorsey Pender, Samuel Field Phillips, John Pool, Solomon Pool, James Hinton Pou, George W. Pressly, Charles Price, Thomas H. Pritchard,

William Dossey Pruden, Stephen Dodson Ramseur, James Graham Ramsey, William George Randall, Charles Lee Raper, John Stark Ravenscroft, John Edwin Ray, Kenneth Rayner, William Reed, Laura Holmes Reilly, John Melanchthon Rhodes, Abel Peterson Rhyne, Daniel Efird Rhyne, Nathaniel Rice, William S. O'Brien Robinson, Kiffin Yates Rockwell, Martin Rose, William Royall, Beverly S. Royster, Hubert Ashley Royster, Alfred Moore Scales, David Schenck, Augustus Sherrill Seymour, William Sharpe, Miles Osborne Sherrill, Alonzo Craig Shuford, Nathaniel Shober Siewers, Enoch Walter Sikes, William Gaston Simmons, Charles Alphonso Smith, Egbert Watson Smith, Henry Louis Smith, Jacob Henry Smith, Samuel Macon Smith, William Smith, William Henry Snow, Samuel Spencer, Richard Stanford, Elizabeth Maxwell Steel, James C. Stevenson, Katherine Stuart, Montfort Stokes, Robert Strange (1796-1854), Robert Strange (1824-1877), Edmund Strudwick, Frederick N. Strudwick, Frederick Dallas Swindell, Cyrus Thompson, David Matt Thompson, William S. Thomson, Jacksie Daniel Thrash, Frances Christine (Fisher) Tiernan, Edward Walter Timberlake, James Walker Tufts, Leonard Tufts, Abraham Watkins Venable, Francis Preston Venable, Hugh Waddell, Samuel Wait, Alfred Augustine Watson, Edward Warren, Edward Jenner Warren, Edwin Yates Webb, Hugh Lawson White, James White, John White, Zollicoffer Wiley Whitehead, William Thornton Whitsett, Jane Renwick (Smedberg) Wilkes, Alfred Williams, Henry Horace Williams, Isham Rowland Williams, Joseph Williams, Louis Hicks Williams, Marshall McDiarmid Williams, Mary Lyde (Hicks) Williams, Virginius Faison Williams, John Gustavus Adolphus Williamson, James William Wilson, Thomas Johnston Wilson, Washington Manly Wingate, John R. Winston, Samuel Wittkowsky, Frederick A. Woodard, Thomas Jones Wooten, Dennison Worthington, Charles C. Wright, Matthew T. Yates, and Brantley York.

5458. HENRY BELL VAN RENSSELAER LEDGER, 1845-1855. 1 vol. (421 pp.) Saint Lawrence County, N.Y.

Ledger of Henry Bell Van Rensselaer, United States congressman and Union general in the Civil War, for an unidentified business.

5459. AMELIA A. VAN VLECK PAPERS, 1849 (1852-1867) 1879. 80 items. Salem (Forsyth County), N.C.

Personal letters to Amelia A. Van Vleck, apparently a music teacher at the Salem Female Academy. Included are letters from "Aggie" (probably Agnes Sophia de Schweinitz) while on a visit in Berthelsdorf, Germany, describing her travels and religious customs among the Moravians in Germany. Included also are letters from members of the Fries family of Salem.

5460. ZEBULON BAIRD VANCE PAPERS, 1857-1893. 45 items. Raleigh (Wake County), N.C.

Papers of Zebulon Baird Vance, Confederate officer, governor of North Carolina, and United States senator from North Carolina, contain miscellaneous public and private letters and documents, including a letter, 1857, from Vance to the editors of the National Intelligencer supporting the claim of Elisha Mitchell to have been the first to measure the peak in western North Carolina later called Mt. Mitchell; letter, 1858, to D. F. Caldwell on national and state politics; letter, 1863, to Vance as governor of North Carolina from Kemp P. Battle, president of the Chatham Railroad, reporting difficulties in the construction of the road and requesting changes in the railroad's charter and a loan from the state; and Vance's subsequent letter to R. S. Donnell, speaker of the House of Commons of the North Carolina legislature, requesting favorable action from the legislature in Battle's requests. Also contains a letter, 1894, from Charles N. Vance, son of Zebulon B. Vance, concerning the location of a new grave for his father; and an undated clipping from the Raleigh (North Carolina) Advocate quoting a letter from Reverend R. A. Young on Vance's religious preferences.

5461. ANN VANDER HORST PAPERS, 1875-1882. 2 vols. Charleston, S.C.

Receipt books.

5462. LAFAYETTE VANDLING PAPERS, 1861. 5 items. Northumberland (Northumberland County), Pa.

Letters from Lafayette Vandling, of the 5th Pennsylvania Regiment, in camp in northern Pennsylvania, to his cousin, Hannah C. Himes.

5463. FRANCES ANNE (HAWES) VANE, VISCOUNTESS VANE, PAPERS, 18th century. 1 item. London, England.

Undated letter of Frances Anne (Hawes) Vane, Viscountess Vane, concerning her debts and her relationship to a Mr. Craggs.

5464. SIR HENRY VANE, JR., PAPERS, 1653. 1 item. London, England.

Letter from M. Bingham to Sir Henry Vane, Jr.

5465. JOSEPHINE VARNER PAPERS, 1861-1864. 13 items. Indian Springs (Butts County), Ga.

Letters of several Confederate soldiers to Josephine Varner (1837-1928), telling of camp life and long marches in various campaigns.

5466. KATE VARNER PAPERS, 1864-1865.
7 items. Charlotte (Lee County), Iowa.

Letters to Kate Varner from James H. W. Stilley, describing the capture and burning of Columbia, South Carolina, by Union forces in 1865, and a fragmentary diary covering the march to Columbia, South Carolina.

5467. WASHINGTON VARNER PAPERS, 1870-1905.
15 items and 2 vols. Lost River (Hardy County), W. Va.

Papers of Washington Varner, a preacher for the Methodist Episcopal Church, South, in West Virginia and Virginia, contains several sermons and a notebook, 1870-1878, which includes financial accounts; lists of churches with appointments and texts of sermons; records of admissions, baptisms, marriages, funerals, and Sunday schools; and a diary, 1876-1877, dealing primarily with church work.

5468. VATICAN BASILICA OF ST. PETER RECORDS, ca. 1620-1751. 1 vol. (784 pp.) Rome, Italy.

Copies of records in Latin and Italian, including the catalogue of all archpriests of the Vatican Basilica of St. Peter from Pope Benedict (1032-1045) to Pope Paul V (1605-1621); the succession of canons in the Vatican Basilica of St. Peter; and decrees of the council for propagating the faith.

5469. JESSIE VAUGHAN PAPERS, 1822-1869.
175 items. Nottoway County, Va.

Papers of Jessie Vaughan, a tobacco and cotton farmer, contain bills, receipts, and letters from Lucy Ann (Vaughan) Freeman, concerning the settlement of her husband's estate, and from John Vaughan, describing Yalobusha County, Mississippi.

5470. ABRAHAM WATKINS VENABLE SCRAPBOOK, 1849-1851. 1 vol. Brownsville (Granville County), N.C.

Scrapbook, of Abraham Watkins Venable (1799-1876), lawyer, U.S. representative, 1847-1853, and C.S.A. congressman, containing clippings relating to slavery, the Wilmot Proviso, the Constitution and states' rights, the tariff, foreign affairs, banking, the cotton trade, President Zachary Taylor, the Whig and Democratic parties, and the death of John C. Calhoun.

5471. BERNARD VER BRYCK ARITHMETIC BOOK, 1798. 1 vol. (68 pp.)

Manuscript volume of arithmetic problems and exercises.

5472. EUGENE VERDERY, JR., AND JAMES PAUL VERDERY PAPERS, 1859-1870.
174 items. Augusta (Richmond County), Ga.

Papers of Eugene Verdery, Jr., and James Paul Verdery relate for the most part to their service in the Confederate Army. Letters from Eugene Verdery of the 63rd Georgia Regiment, concern camp life near Savannah, Georgia; a visit by General Robert E. Lee to Camp Harrison, Georgia; the C.S.S. Atlanta; a visit by Jefferson Davis to Savannah, Georgia, in 1863; and the strength of the fortifications around Savannah, 1864. Letters from James Paul Verdery of the 48th Georgia Regiment relate to religious services in camp; camp life in Virginia; fighting at Beaver Dam Station in Virginia; the Peninsular Campaign; and fighting around Petersburg, Virginia, in 1864.

5473. HARMAN VERELST PAPERS, 1741-1745.
27 items. London, England.

Routine correspondence of Harman Verelst, accountant to the trustees of the colony of Georgia and private agent of General Oglethorpe in London, to the Lords Commissioners of the Treasury and other officials, chiefly concerning the financial affairs of the colony, including the expense of maintaining a military force in the colony.

5474. RUDOLF HENRY COLE VERNER PAPERS. 1914-1918. 3 items. England.

Papers of Rudolf Henry Cole Verner, British naval officer, contain a letter, 1914, from a colleague of Verner's describing the battle of the Falkland Islands, December 8, 1914; an account of the engagement written by Verner entitled "Action off the Falklands"; and a letter, 1918, from George Trevor Collingwood to Elizabeth Mary Emily Verner, describing the death of Rudolph Henry Cole Verner.

5475. BENJAMIN H. VESTER PAPERS, 1772-1877.
134 items. Nash County, N.C.

The collection contains receipts, promissory notes, deeds, and letters relating to Benjamin H. Vester and his family including an order, 1780, to Solomon Vester, a Revolutionary soldier, instructing him to assist in the capture of deserters and delinquents in Nash County, North Carolina; letters in the 1830s commenting on land, crops, and debts in Nash County, North Carolina, and people living in Hinds County, Mississippi; and letters in the 1870s from relatives in Leake County, Mississippi, concerning various Nash County people in that area, family relations, farming conditions, prices of commodities, and the movement of people into and out of the county.

5476. PETER VIAL PAPERS, 1784-1890.
26 items. Hanover County, Va.

Miscellaneous items including legal papers; a proposal, 1831, to remove free Negroes from Virginia and to diminish the number of slaves; a letter, 1861, to Horace Greeley and the New York Tribune concerning the right of the South to secede; and a diary, 1880, recording the weather and family life.

5477. VICTORIA, AUSTRALIA. COURT OF PETTY SESSIONS RECORDS, 1849-1865. 1 vol. (310 pp.) Colac, Victoria, Australia.

Volume of records of the court of petty sessions held at Colac, Victoria, containing minutes of the sessions, 1849-1860, including the names of litigants, statements of the nature of each case, and the disposition of each by the court. After 1860 the records in the volume consist mainly of recognizances and depositions which were signed before justices of the peace. Also contains the number of voters for the local area in 1859.

5478. NICHOLAS W. VINCENT PAPERS, 1787-1822. 11 items. Charleston, S.C.

Letters to Nicholas W. Vincent, a merchant of Charleston, South Carolina, his brother, Hugh Vincent, and their mother, Martha Boscawen (Evelyn) Vincent from various attorneys and relatives in England concerning family affairs.

5479. SAMUEL VINES ARITHMETIC BOOK, 1829. 1 vol. Washington, (Beaufort County), N.C.

Manuscript volume of arithmetic problems and exercises.

5480. JOHN ROGERS VINTON PAPERS, 1814 (1837-1849) 1861. 237 items and 9 vols. Providence, R.I.

Correspondence and papers of John R. Vinton (1801-1847), a graduate of the United States Military Academy, West Point, New York, and United States Army officer stationed in New Jersey, Pennsylvania, Georgia, Florida, and North Carolina. The letters concern army and social life in Southern towns during the 1830s and 1840s, including Beaufort, North Carolina, Augusta, Georgia, and Saint Augustine and New Smyrna, Florida; the slavery controversy; Paddy Carr and the friendly Creek Indians; the character of Winfield Scott; plans for the education of Vinton's children; and the Mexican War. Included also are a copy of a speech by John Ross, the Indian leader; a diary, 1861, of Francis Laurens Vinton while on an expedition to explore the mineral resources of Honduras, giving accounts of William Walker; four letter books of John R. Vinton; and four journals including an account of a trip to Georgia and the Creek Nation and a survey of the southern and western borders of the United States.

5481. E. M. VIOLETTE PAPERS, 1911. 1 item. Adair County, Mo.

Photocopy of section three, "The Battle of Kirksville, August 6, 1862," of E. M. Violette's History of Adair County, Missouri (Kirksville, Missouri: 1911).

5482. VIRGINIA. CAMPBELL COUNTY REGISTER OF NEGROES AND FREE PEOPLE OF COLOR, 1801-1850. 1 item. Rustburg (Campbell County), Va.

Photocopy of a register kept by the clerk of the Campbell County Court from 1801 to 1850, listing the names of free Negroes in the county and giving their age, stature, complexion, and where and by whom emancipated.

5483. VIRGINIA. HALIFAX COUNTY TAX RECORDS, 1832-1833. 1 vol. (84 pp.) Banister (Halifax County), Va.

List containing the names of property owners, their place of residence, description and amount of their land holdings, distance from the courthouse, value, and the amount of tax.

5484. VIRGINIA. NELSON COUNTY SHERIFF'S BOOK, 1839-1840. 1 vol. (348 pp.) Amherst (Nelson County), Va.

Record of fees and taxes collected in Nelson County by James D. Goodwin as deputy sheriff.

5485. VIRGINIA. SHENANDOAH COUNTY RECORDS, 1828-1836. 1 vol. Shenandoah County, Va.

List of licenses issued by commissioners of revenue.

5486. VIRGINIA CITIZENS POLITICAL ACTION COMMITTEE PAPERS, 1945-1946. 683 items. Richmond, Va.

The collection contains the correspondence of Robert Allen Johnson, executive director of the Virginia Citizens Political Action Committee, a non-partisan political reform group closely associated with the Congress of Industrial Organizations. There is correspondence with Paul R. Christopher, Jack Kroll, Ernest B. Pugh, Frank Grasso, Boyd E. Payton, Moss A. Plunkett, and Clark H. Foreman. Subjects of the correspondence include the Oil Workers International Union, the Paper Workers Organizing Committee, the Virginia Federation of Telephone Workers, the Southern Conference for Human Welfare, the Committee for Georgia, the Fourth Regional Wage Stabilization Board, and the National War Labor Board.

5487. VITA DI CURZIO MARIGNOLLI, 18th century. 1 vol. (45 pp.) Florence, Italy.

Biographical sketch from the 18th century of the Florentine poet Curzio Marignolli, by an unknown author.

5488. PRESTON S. VOGEL PAPERS, 1833 (1890-1920) 1929. 1,206 items and 2 vols. Smithsburg (Washington County), Md.

Papers of Preston S. Vogel contain indentures; business papers of his wholesale fruit business; personal correspondence of Bonna G. Vogel; and a few papers concerning the Durboraw family.

5489. WILLIAM C. VOORHEES PAPERS, 1847-1850. 14 items. Ann Arbor (Washtenaw County), Mich.

Bills to William C. Voorhees for merchandise, mostly hardware.

5490. CHARLES E. WADDELL MANUSCRIPT, 1936. 1 vol. (116 pp.)

Typescript of "Fifty Years of Electrical Development in North Carolina" by Charles E. Waddell.

5491. JOHN ADDISON WADDELL PAPERS, 1829-1848. 12 items. Greenfield (Nelson County), Va.

Papers of Dr. John Addison Waddell, Whig politician, including a letter, 1838, describing the visit of Martin Van Buren to White Sulphur Springs, West Virginia an address, 1840, reviewing the administrations of Andrew Jackson and Martin Van Buren, political patronage, and the career of General William Henry Harrison; and a letter, 1848, concerning a Whig rally in New Hope precinct, Zachary Taylor, and the Baltimore Platform.

5492. EDWARD C. WADE PAPERS, 1880, 1885. 2 items. Savannah, Ga.

Business letters of Edward C. Wade, U. S. marshal at Savannah, including one on Georgia Republicans.

5493. S. C. WADE PAPERS, 1846-1868. 9 items. Virginia.

Letters, written mostly by women, depicting social life and customs, travel conditions, etc., of the antebellum period. There is some disparaging comment on a "buncombe" speech made in the U. S. Senate by Samuel Houston, and on a session of the U. S. House of Representatives which the writer of one letter witnessed.

5494. WILLIAM MORRILL WADLEY PAPERS, 1853-1922. 60 items. Savannah, Ga.

Papers of William Morrill Wadley (1813-1882), executive in the Georgia Central Railroad and the Central of Georgia Railroad, including correspondence concerning the building and extension of the Western and Atlantic Railroad in Georgia, business conditions, city and congressional elections, the use of the Western and Atlantic Railroad by Governor Herschel V. Johnson for political purposes, and other railroad matters; grocery bills, 1858; list of slaves with their appraised value in 1860; report, 1888, by the superintendent of construction for the Mexican National Railway; and cards and invitations from Mardi Gras in New Orleans, Louisiana, in 1880, and for the International Cotton Exposition in Atlanta, Georgia, in 1881.

5495. F. W. WAGENER PAPERS, 1883-1887. 25 items. Charleston, S.C.

Official correspondence of the German Artillery, Charleston, South Carolina, of which F. W. Wagener was captain, and Philip Dressel was secretary.

5496. G. W. WAGNON PAPERS, 1866. 2 items. San Saba County, Tex.

Correspondence of the Wagnon family, concerning their migration from Calcasieu, Louisiana, to San Saba County, Texas.

5497. CHARLES BOYD WAGONER PAPERS, 1890-1948. 180 items. Concord (Cabarrus County), N.C.

Papers of Charles Boyd Wagoner (1875-1945), banker, concerning his education at Trinity College (now Duke University), Durham, North Carolina, and his position as permanent secretary for the class of 1895. Included are several letters, bills, receipts, and announcements from his years at Trinity College; minutes of the 25th class reunion; letters dealing with efforts to collect a class memorial fund; a class list with addresses, 1925; references to a drive for an educational fund by churches; and references to a request for Duke centennial pledges. Other material includes a letter discussing Plato T. Durham, his feelings about injustice to Negroes, and his death; broadside material on the election of 1940, such as speeches by Irvin S. Cobb and Hiram Johnson, an attack on the appointment of Elliott Roosevelt as a captain in the army, and pro-Willkie material; a victory program of songs in 1943; pictures of students; and a bankbook with accounts for the class treasury.

5498. BENJAMIN LEONARD COVINGTON WAILES PAPERS, 1843-1862. 126 items and 29 vols. Washington County, Miss.

Correspondence and diaries of Benjamin Leonard Covington Wailes (1797-1862), agriculturist, geologist, and professor of agriculture at the University of Mississippi, Oxford, Mississippi. Correspondence is chiefly letters from other scientists concerning specimens of shells, fossils and Indian relics, and exchanges of these specimens among the various scientists. The diaries consist of Volumes V-IX, 1852-1853, and XIV-XXXVI, 1854-1862, containing detailed accounts of Wailes's farming operations and the collection of fossils, and discussing slavery, Jefferson College (Washington, Mississippi), Southern expansionism, the Know-Nothings, the panic of 1857, railroad development, natural history of Mississippi, Mississippi agricultural and historical societies, transportation on the Mississippi River, political and social events, election of 1860, secession of Mississippi, and the Civil War to November, 1862. [Partially published: Charles S. Sydnor, A Gentleman of the Old Natchez Region: Benjamin L. C. Wailes (Durham, N.C.: 1938). Eight volumes, I-IV and X-XIII, are in the Mississippi Department of Archives and History.] There is also a volume, 1850-1855, containing typed copies of correspondence and accounts of Wailes relating to a geological survey of Mississippi.

5499. PETER WAINWRIGHT, JR., PAPERS, 1767 (1801-1868) 1890. 290 items. Boston, Mass.

Correspondence and papers of Peter Wainwright, Jr., banker and churchwarden, and other members of the Wainwright family, concerning slavery, punishment of slaves, and the education of a slave who wanted to learn to read; the savings Bank of Boston; the Provident Institution of Savings; education of women in the early nineteenth century; galvanism; the Episcopal Church; the rebuilding of Petersburg after a fire in 1816; tobacco prices and tobacco manufacturing in Kentucky; the population of New Orleans, Louisiana; the Democratic Party; the administration of Franklin Pierce; Lewis Cass; and the election of 1856. Other items include an inventory and appraisement of the estate of Dr. Job Godfrey of Taunton, Massachusetts; invoices, 1816, showing import and export duties; circular letter regarding the founding of a society for the relief of needy English immigrants; an indenture; and wills.

5500. PHILIP E. WALDEN PAPERS, 1864. 42 items. St. Georges, Bermuda.

Personal letters from Philip E. Walden, an agent for a blockade-running company in England, concerning his avid support of the Confederacy; the weather, terrain and customs in Bermuda; politics; the Civil War; and his longing for his family in New Orleans.

5501. CHARLES W. WALDO PAPERS, 1846-1864. 2 vols. Keene (Cheshire County), N.H.

Daybook, 1848-1858, and ledger, 1846-1850 and 1858-1864, of a blacksmith.

5502. HARRIET WALDRON PAPERS, 1861-1865. 20 items. North Kent (Litchfield County), Conn.

Letters to Harriet Waldron from Union soldiers, especially Edwin B. Payne of the 4th New York Cavalry, concerning personal matters, the attitude of soldiers toward the war, and troop movements.

5503. LAURA WALDRON PAPERS, 1859-1883. 97 items. Charleston, S.C.

Miscellaneous papers of Laura Waldron, singer and actress, consisting of notes, calling cards, and letters from admirers; programs; a poem and two songs, "All Quiet Along the Savannah Tonight," and "Brother Come Home," by Carrie Bell Sinclair; poems by Laura Waldron; and several letters concerning Henry Farmer.

5504. EDWARD WALKER PAPERS, 1828-1853. 9 items. Frederick County, Va.

Personal letters of Edward Walker chiefly concerning family matters, with references to commodity prices in Ohio and the Society of Friends.

5505. ELBRIDGE GERRY WALKER PAPERS, 1801-1903. 1,155 items. Scottsville (Allen County) and Glasgow (Barren County), Ky.

Chiefly business papers of Elbridge Gerry Walker concerning the drug business, his partnership in the business with J. N. McKendrel, and a lawsuit against Walker brought by McKendrel. There is also correspondence relating to his father, A. S. Walker, Scottsville physician, and the practice of medicine in the antebellum South; letters and official records written by Elbridge Gerry Walker as clerk of the circuit court of Allen County; two deeds; and an essay entitled "Some Reflections on the Practice of Medicine by the System of Patent Receipts, Its Injurious Tendency, and a Method for the Remedy."

5506. GEORGE E. WALKER PAPERS, 1852-1918. 11 items. Burlington (Alamance County), N.C.

Miscellaneous personal letters, business items, poems, songs, and genealogical information on the Walker, Cates, and Lashley families.

5507. GILBERT CARLETON WALKER PAPERS, 1869-1881. 5 items. Norfolk, Va.

Letters and papers of Gilbert C. Walker (1832-1885), governor of Virginia, 1869-1874, including two documents appointing commissioners for the Commonwealth of Virginia.

5508. JAMES A. WALKER PAPERS, 1819 (1847-1857) 1877. 136 items and 1 vol. Darien (McIntosh County), Ga.

Letters of James A. Walker concerning his numerous business efforts, including a factorage and commission business, selling cotton gins, purchasing claims of Mexican War soldiers for bounty lands or scrip, cotton growing in Texas, and a lumber business; and describing the various states in which he traveled, including Indiana, Ohio, Kentucky, Louisiana, Arkansas, Texas, Connecticut and Georgia. The volume is a fragment of a pamphlet by John Livingston Hopkins regarding a challenge to a duel by McQueen McIntosh, and a later shooting incident involving McIntosh and his brother, John McIntosh, and Hopkins.

5509. [JEFFERSON WALKER?] ACCOUNT BOOK, 1834-1838. 1 vol. (122 pp.) Whitsonton (Franklin County), Ark.

Accounts of leather and hides.

5510. JOHN K. WALKER PAPERS, 1854-1876. 72 items. Alamance County, N.C.

Letters of John K. Walker, Confederate soldier with the 6th Regiment, North Carolina Troops, chiefly to relatives describing battles and engagements, and attitudes towards the war, and requesting supplies. Included is a note from his brother, William Walker, from the prison at Point Lookout, Maryland.

5511. JOHN WESLEY WALKER PAPERS, 1841 (1861-1864) 1899. 236 items. Smith Grove (Davie County), N.C.

Correspondence of Confederate soldiers serving in Virginia and North Carolina, and their friends and relatives at home discussing personal and family matters, camp life, prices, disease in the army, the Confederate prison at Salisbury, North Carolina, desertion, the use of Negroes for building fortifications in Halifax County, North Carolina, and the danger of attack on General Magruder's forces on the Peninsula, 1862.

5512. LEROY POPE WALKER PAPERS, 1861-1868. 5 items. Huntsville (Madison County), Ala.

Official letters of Leroy Pope Walker (1817-1884), lawyer, politician, and Confederate secretary of war, 1861, pertaining mainly to supplies; and a business letter.

5513. MERIWETHER LEWIS WALKER AND THOMAS L. WALKER PAPERS, 1809-1887. 818 items. Albemarle County and Campbell County, Va.

Papers of Meriwether Lewis, Thomas L. Walker, physician, and Peachy Harmer Gilmer, physician, consisting largely of bills and receipts, including several relating to Gilmer's treatment of soldiers during the Mexican War, and several for the Petersburg (Virginia) Female College and for Mrs. Mead's School, Richmond, Virginia. Correspondence makes reference to Virginia politics; the Whigs and the Democrats; the Virginia and Tennessee Railroad; abolitionism; the iron industry in Virginia; financial success of Judith Page (Walker) Rives's Christmas Eve; lack of illness in Richmond, 1867; smallpox in Lynchburg, Virginia, 1882; the building of a cotton mill in Lynchburg, 1884; the Texas legislature and governor, and the University of Texas; the curriculum at Petersburg Female College; and the impairment of health caused by tobacco factories. There are also memoranda concerning the Lynchburg water works, and railroads and investments, ca. 1874; an account and memorandum book, 1853-1879; and a sketch of the Charleston, South Carolina, defenses.

5514. MILTON WALKER AND OLIPHANT S. WALKER PAPERS, 1861-1864. 11 items. Edgefield County, S.C., and Elmira (Chemung County), N.Y.

Civil War letters written by privates in the Confederate Army. One letter, September, 1861, concerns disputes among the volunteers in camp; another, October, 1861, tells of religious services in the Confederate camp; one 1864, pertains to Milton Walker's capture at the battle of Malvern Hill, Virginia, 1862, and his imprisonment in Elmira, New York; and the remainder concern depredations at Beaufort, South Carolina, by Negroes, and contain accounts of deaths in the Walker family. Oliphant Walker was killed in the battle of Chancellorsville, Virginia, 1863.

5515. R. LEWIS WALKER DAYBOOKS AND LEDGERS, 1880-1896. 4 vols. Milton (Caswell County), N.C.

Daybooks, 1880-1882 and 1891-1896, and ledger, 1889-1896, of a drug business.

5516. ROBERT JOHN WALKER PAPERS, 1842-1855. 11 items. Natchez (Adams County), Miss. and Washington, D.C.

Letters of request and recommendation for political appointments to Robert John Walker (1801-1869), U. S. senator, 1836-1845, and secretary of the treasury, 1845-1849; a letter concerning the storage of goods in the customshouse in Savannah, Georgia; a business letter; and a receipt.

5517. WILLIAM HENRY TALBOT WALKER PAPERS, 1846-1883. 406 items. Augusta (Richmond County), Ga.

Letters from William Henry Talbot Walker (1816-1864), lieutenant colonel in the U. S. Army during the Mexican War and brigadier general in the Confederate Army, largely to his wife and primarily pertaining to personal matters. Letters referring to service in the Mexican War mention Walker's high opinion of Generals Zachary Taylor and Winfield Scott; his contempt for "Irish" Generals Robert Patterson and James Shields; other American and Mexican officers; maneuvers at Vera Cruz; and the battles of Cerro Gordo and Contreras. Other letters describe the presidential election of 1852, Walker's activities in the army recruiting service, as deputy governor of the military asylum at East Pascagoula (Mississippi), as an instructor at the U. S. Military Academy, and on frontier duty in Minnesota. Letters concerning Walker's service in the Confederate Army reveal resentment of Confederate military leaders, criticize Jefferson Davis, and describe skirmishes in northern Virginia during the autumn of 1861 and the military operations at Chattanooga. Correspondence of Walker's daughter, Molly (Walker) Schley, and her husband, Dr. Charles Schley, concerns personal matters, the presidential election of 1868, politics in Reconstruction Georgia, and postwar economic conditions.

5518. SAMUEL HOEY WALKUP JOURNAL, 1862-1865. 1 vol. Mecklenburg County, N.C.

Typed copy of the journal of Samuel Hoey Walkup (b. 1817), lawyer, and Confederate soldier in the 48th North Carolina Regiment, describing the formation of the regiment and election of field officers; the Peninsular Campaign; the battles of second Manassas, Antietam, and Fredericksburg; the siege of Petersburg; various Confederate and Union generals and units; camp life; food; pay; sickness, care of the wounded, physicians, and hospitals; Confederate bonds; commodity prices; chaplains; refugees; fraternization with the enemy; desertion; courts-martial; Walkup's arrest and release; Ulysses S. Grant; and Zebulon Baird Vance. The original is in the Southern Historical Collection, University of North Carolina, Chapel Hill, North Carolina.

5519. ELMER WILLIAM WALL PAPERS, 1940. 2 items. Durham, N.C.

Papers relating to the Salvation Army of Durham, North Carolina, and its commanding officer Elmer William Wall, consisting of a letter concerning a Christmas program, and a report of the army's activities from December 1, 1939, to November 30, 1940.

5520. GARRET DORSET WALL PAPERS, 1745-1845. 125 items. Burlington (Burlington County), N.J.

Letters chiefly to Garret Dorset Wall, attorney, and U. S. senator, 1835-1841, largely concerning legal matters and debts, with information on politics in New York and New Jersey; elections in New Jersey, 1830s; New Jersey government, 1830s; the presidential election of 1840; the Whig Party in New Jersey; land speculation in Ohio during the 1790s; and social life and customs in New York in the early 1800s. There are also copies of portions of the records of the New Jersey Supreme Court, the New Jersey Court of Chancery, and the Court of Common Pleas of Hunterdon County, New Jersey; and a subpoena.

5521. ROBERT D. WALL PAPERS, 1850-1857. Beaufort County, N.C.

Papers relating to the purchase of goods, and family letters commenting on the prices of naval stores and foodstuffs, and on politics in Beaufort County.

5522. E. R. WALLACE PAPERS, 1875-1890. 2 vols. Union (Union County), S.C.

Cashbook, 1880-1886, and receipt book, 1875-1890, of E. R. Wallace, businessman and a proprietor of the Union Hotel, Union, South Carolina, and of the mercantile firm of J. C. Hunter & Co., containing records of his personal finances and business interests.

5523. GEORGE T. WALLACE PAPERS, 1862. 4 items. Glencoe (Norfolk County), Va.

Letters from George T. Wallace, a Virginia planter near Norfolk, describing trouble with slaves because of the proximity of Federal troops.

5524. LEWIS WALLACE PAPERS, 1864-1901. 7 items. Crawfordsville (Montgomery County), Ind.

Photocopies of letters from Lew Wallace (1827-1905), author, U. S. Army officer, and U. S. minister to Turkey. The letters concern administrative matters in connection with his services during the Civil War; his visit to Palestine; and a disagreement with Robert Underwood Johnson, editor of the Century Magazine.

5525. PERCY MAXWELL WALLACE PAPERS, 1887-1922. 5 items and 16 vols. Brighton, Sussex, England.

Volumes containing copies of letters from Percy Maxwell Wallace (1863-1943), to his mother, Fanny (Gore) Wallace, while he was in India as professor of English literature at Mohammedan Anglo-Oriental College (now Aligarh Muslim University),

1887-1890, describing British social life and customs in India; teaching responsibilities at the college; his students; his conservatism and that of the college; opposition to liberalism; his management of the college cricket team; various places visited, including the site of the Mutiny of 1857 and the Khyber Pass; a pack trip overland from Simla to Mussoorie; various classes of Indians and Eurasians; and his departure. There are also two letters to Wallace from a former student at Aligarh; a letter, 1888, from Wallace; and a letter (in Persian script and a translation) from L. K. Hyder listing subscribers to a Cricket Pavilion built at Aligarh in 1901 and named in honor of Wallace.

5526. WILLIAM WALLACE PAPERS, 1831. 1 item. Edinburgh, Scotland.

Letter to William Wallace (1768-1843), mathematician and inventor of the eidograph, from Thomas Drummond discussing the eidograph and the Reform Bill.

5527. [WILLIAM WALLACE?] ACCOUNT BOOK, 1778-1780. 1 vol. (27 pp.) [Peterhead, Scotland?]

Record of expenses of a man, probably a merchant, travelling in the vicinity of Glasgow and Dumbarton.

5528. RICHARD WALLACH PAPERS, 1802-1902. 100 items. Washington, D.C.

Chiefly invitations, calling cards, and responses to invitations extended by Richard Wallach, lawyer and mayor of Washington, D. C., 1862, and other members of the Wallach family. Letters discuss personal matters, the settlement of estates, Lewis Cass, and the Whig Party.

5529. DAVID GARLAND WALLER PAPERS, 1842-1861. 55 items. Temperance (Amherst County), Va.

Personal and business correspondence, bills, receipts, orders, checks, and poems of David Garland Waller (b. 1830) and other members of the Waller family. Correspondence discusses suicide and insanity; smallpox; temperance; taxes on slaves and land in Amherst County; social life and customs; the hiring and selling of slaves in Virginia; an earthquake in Amherst County, 1852; the school at Mt. Maria [?], Virginia; Mrs. Mead's School, Richmond, Virginia; the University of Virginia, Charlottesville, Virginia; and other personal and business matters.

5530. HARCOURT EDMUND WALLER, JR., THESIS, 1943. 1 vol. (96 pp.) Princeton (Mercer County), N.J.

Senior thesis of Harcourt Edmund Waller, Jr., while a student at Princeton University, Princeton, New Jersey. Entitled "Agrarian Revolt," the thesis studies the agrarian reaction to the control of industry and commerce in post-Reconstruction South.

5531. HORATIO WALPOLE, FIRST BARON WALPOLE OF WOLTERTON, PAPERS, 1741. 1 item. "Wolterton," near Aylsham, Norfolk County, England.

Personal letter of Horatio Walpole, First Baron Walpole of Wolterton (1678-1757).

5532. SIR ROBERT WALPOLE, FIRST EARL OF ORFORD, PAPERS, 1734. 1 item. London, England.

Letter to Sir Robert Walpole, First Earl of Orford (1676-1745), British statesman, first lord of the treasury and chancellor of the exchequer, 1727-1742, from Sir Benjamin Keene, British ambassador to Spain, reporting on his talk with José Patiño, Spanish minister, about the proposed marriage of Don Carlos (later Charles III) to a relation of Emperor Charles VI and the diplomatic effects that might be expected. He also noted Germanus Bonelli.

5533. EDWARD D. WALSH PAPERS, 1863-1866. 13 items. Lenoir (Caldwell County), N.C.

Letters from Edward D. Walsh, in the 10th North Carolina Regiment, C.S.A., at Smithville (now Southport), and near Wilmington, concerning fortifications around Wilmington, the ladies of the town, etc.; and postwar love letters. One letter, 1866, from Charlotte Patrick while at Louisburg College, North Carolina, tells of "Yankee" schoolteachers coming to teach Negroes in Louisburg.

5534. JOHN WALTER PAPERS, 1868. 1 item. London, England.

Letter of John Walter (1818-1894), member of Parliament and chief proprietor of The Times, describing the details of the parliamentary election in which he was involved.

5535. WILLIAM WALTER AND COMPANY PAPERS, 1806-1814. 55 items. Boston, Mass.

Letters to William Walter and Company, a mercantile house in Boston, Massachusetts, from merchants in North Carolina and Virginia concerning the shipment of goods, including naval stores, rum, wine, lumber, corn, and barrels and staves, with references to restrictions to foreign shipping brought about by the presidential proclamation of December, 1810. Included is a bill of exchange from the United East India Company to William Walter and Company.

5536. EDWARD CARY WALTHALL PAPERS, 1880, 1897. 2 items. Grenada (Grenada County), Miss.

Letter of Edward Cary Walthall (1831-1889), lawyer, U.S. senator, and former Confederate general, to General Henry M. Cist concerning the involvement of General A. H. Colquitt in the prohibition campaign in Rhode Island and Pennsylvania, and Colquitt's interest in the Chickamauga National Park project, of which Cist was the originator; and a letter pertaining to a report by a General Cooper.

5537. GEORGE WALTON PAPERS, 1775-1814. 40 items. Augusta (Richmond County), Ga.

Miscellaneous papers of George Walton (1741-1804), lawyer, delegate to the Continental Congress, 1776-1781, governor of Georgia, 1779 and 1789, chief justice of the Georgia Supreme Court, 1783-1786 and 1793, and U. S. senator, 1795-1796. A copy of a treatise, 1781, signed by Walton, William Few, Jr., and Richard Howley, favors the maintenance of close ties between the northern colonies and South Carolina and Georgia, then controlled by the British, and emphasizes the strategic and economic importance of the southern colonies to an independent American confederation. Also included are an application, 1782, of Walton, Button Gwinnett, and Lyman Hall to the Georgia legislature for permission to import slaves from East Florida; letters, 1789, and an extract from the minutes of the executive council of Georgia concerning a request from William Few, Jr., for funds to cover debts incurred while he represented Georgia in Congress and at the Constitutional Convention; a proclamation issued by Walton requiring state officials to take the oath of allegiance to the U. S. Constitution; two letters, 1789, from George Washington, one transmitting acts for establishing the U. S. Treasury Department and the taking of a census, and one enclosing the proclamation of a general day of thanksgiving; a letter, 1789, from Henry Knox requesting information concerning veterans in Georgia eligible for government pensions; a document, 1790, listing the proceedings and practices to be followed by the superior courts in Georgia; a letter, 1790, from Thomas Jefferson sending copies of acts authorizing the first census, revising the naturalization laws, and appropriating government funds for 1790; a document, 1800, by Walton appointing Nicholas Ware guardian of a Negro woman and her three children to protect their free status; petitions concerning the settlement of estates; and legal papers pertaining to the payment of debts.

5538. WILLIAM CLAIBORNE WALTON PAPERS, 1832. 1 item. Alexandria (Arlington County), Va.

Letter of William Claiborne Walton (1793-1834), Presbyterian minister, concerning the amount of his support from the Presbyterian church should he spend half of his time preaching at revivals.

5539. HUMFREY WANLEY PAPERS, 1706. 1 item. London, England.

Letter from Humfrey Wanley (1672-1726), British antiquary and secretary of the Society for Promoting Christian Knowledge, 1702-1708, discussing books that the society was distributing, and requesting information on charity schools for the reprint of a work about them.

5540. WAR OF JENKINS' EAR PAPERS, 1739-1740. 45 items. London, England.

Pencil copies of papers of the Colonial Office from originals in the British Public Records Office, relative to the participation of North American colonies in the War of Jenkins' Ear, generally in communications with the Duke of Newcastle, secretary of the Southern Department. Included are plans of campaign; instructions for the governors and for Lord Charles Cathcart, Admiral Edward Vernon, Colonel Alexander Spotswood, Colonel William Blakeney, and other officers; plans for raising troops in North American colonies; and schedules of payment for men and officers.

5541. EDWARD H. WARD PAPERS, 1854-1921. 41 items. Riggsbee's Store (Chatham County), N.C.

Personal, legal, and business papers of Dr. Edward H. Ward, physician and agent of the North Carolina State Life Insurance Company, including several items pertaining to his medical practice and to insurance, and a letter, 1865, from a Confederate officer discussing General Joseph E. Johnston and Confederate supplies.

5542. GEORGE RAPHAEL WARD PAPERS, 1852. 1 item. England.

Letter to George Raphael Ward (1798-1878), British engraver, from Thomas Sidney Cooper, animal painter, concerning a picture painted by Ward's father, James Ward.

5543. GILES FREDERICK WARD, JR., PAPERS, 1862-1865. 163 items. Brooklyn, N.Y.

Letters of Giles Frederick Ward, Jr. (1845-1865), first lieutenant with the 92nd Infantry Regiment of New York Volunteers and aide-de-camp to General Innis Newton Palmer, to his parents and sister describing the officers under whom he served; battles and skirmishes; General Silas Casey and the battle of Seven Pines; civilian and military affairs in New Bern, North Carolina, during its occupation by Federal troops; his close relationship with General Palmer and his family; and yellow fever in New Bern. Several items, including a letter from General Palmer, describe Ward's death in a shooting accident.

5544.  HENRY WARD NOTEBOOK, 1862. 1 vol. (396 pp.) Auburn (Cayuga County), N.Y.

Notes on lectures in church history.

5545.  J. JACKSON WARD PAPERS, 1861. 2 items. Norfolk, Va.

Letters from J. Jackson Ward, describing the excitement in Norfolk pending Virginia's secession, and informing his parents of his enlistment in the Confederate Army.

5546.  JOHN D. WARD PAPERS, 1836-1863. 4 items and 1 vol. New York, N.Y.

Letter book of John D. Ward, businessman and New Jersey state legislator, chiefly dealing with routine business or personal matters. There are also letters, 1840, to Joel R. Poinsett, secretary of war, and to Charles Morris, president of the Board of Navy Commissioners, suggesting the creation of a national foundry to supply the navy with cannons, mortars, and shells, and recommending that the navy be supplied with steam vessels; letter, 1840, to Daniel Webster urging that there be strict governmental supervision of the construction of steam engines; letters, 1840-1841, to Senator Samuel Lewis Southard giving his opinion of a plan proposed by Captain Robert Field Stockton for the construction of a naval vessel and of a measure introduced by Senator John Ruggles designed to protect passengers on steam vessels; letter, 1843, to John Canfield Spencer, secretary of the treasury, suggesting that steamers built for the Treasury Department utilize the propelling machinery proposed by John Ericsson rather than that advocated by Lieutenant Hunter; letters, 1840-1844, dealing with the construction of the Croton Aqueduct and with the development of a city waterworks in New York; several letters, 1844-1863, pertaining to efforts to secure an adequate water supply for Jersey City, New Jersey; and letters, 1856, dealing with legislative matters for the state of New Jersey. Items consist of two letters, 1856, concerning legislative matters; and copies of two measures introduced in the New Jersey state legislature. Included with the collection is a descriptive calendar with a brief entry for each letter in the letter book.

5547.  JOHN ELLIOTT WARD PAPERS, 1893. 1 item. Savannah, Ga., and New York, N.Y.

Letter from John Elliott Ward (1814-1902), lawyer and U. S. minister to China, 1858-1861, stating that he was the first commander of the Irish Jasper Greens, a Georgia militia company, in 1843.

5548.  JOSHUA WARD PAPERS, 1769-1795. 53 items. Charleston, S.C.

Papers of Joshua Ward, lawyer, chiefly relating to his legal activities, especially as agent for a number of English merchants who sought to collect pre-Revolutionary debts of American citizens. There are a number of papers from the cases against Thomas Shubrick and John Gabriel Guignard. Also included are documents, 1784-1789, recording Ward's accounts with the judges and clerk of court; miscellaneous receipts; a list, 1790, of Ward's taxable property, real estate and slaves; a letter from Sarah Miles of London, England, transmitting depreciated paper dollars for redemption; and a letter, 1779, to naturalist Alexander Garden.

5549.  LEWIS WARD PAPERS, 1813 (1835-1865) 1909. 236 items. Spencer (Rowan County), N.C.

Miscellaneous papers of Lewis Ward (d. 1851), of his son, Joel Ward (d. 1854), and of other members of the Ward family, including a copy of a lease of George Kindley to Lewis Ward and Willis W. Ward on land in Randolph County, North Carolina for the purpose of gold mining; partnership agreement between Alexander Sexton and Lewis Ward to work a gold mine in Davidson County, North Carolina; papers relating to the estate of Willis Ward; letter, 1850, concerning the selection of delegates to the Nashville Convention and rumors surrounding the convention; several letters from Confederate soldiers; pamphlet entitled Ritual of the Farmers' Alliance; several political ballots of North Carolina; some information on common schools in North Carolina; and other papers.

5550.  MARY GENEVIEVE WARD THESIS, 1932. 1 vol. (201 pp.)

Master's thesis of Mary Genevieve Ward entitled "Civil War Legends of Rich Mountain and Beverly, W[est]V[irgini]a" consisting of one hundred forty-six legends chiefly preserved through oral tradition. Some were collected from newspaper clippings, scrapbooks, and diaries of Civil War veterans and their families. The emphasis of the legends is on persons and events of local interest.

5551. SHADRACH WARD PAPERS, 1854-1871. 31 items. Pleasant Grove (Alamance County), N.C.

Family correspondence of Shadrach Ward, farmer, and of his children in Missouri and North Carolina concerning agricultural conditions, "bleeding Kansas," a drought and a flood in Missouri in 1854, Thomas Hart Benton, secession, runaway Negroes in Kentucky and Missouri, and the election of 1860. Letters from Samuel B. Ward (d. 1863) and from Lemuel B. Ward describe camp life, health conditions, the possibility of a substitute, clothes, food, hospitals and medications, commodity prices, and other matters.

5552. ROBERT BRUCE WARDEN PAPERS, 1883. 1 item. Washington, D.C.

Letter from Robert Bruce Warden (1824-1888), jurist and author, regarding his biography of Salmon P. Chase.

5553. SIR THOMAS WARDLE PAPERS, (1874-1898) 1953. 248 items and 2 vols. Leek, Staffordshire, England.

Papers of Sir Thomas Wardle (1831-1909), promoter of the silk industry. Letters from William Morris (1834-1896), poet, artist, manufacturer, and socialist, discuss business matters relating to the production of dyes for silk, cotton, and wool; materials, processes, and products involved; experiments with dyes and patterns and their correct applications to cloth; the history of the use of indigo and wood as dyes; wool dyeing; the feasibility of manufacturing tapestry; the use of kermes as a dye; silk carpeting; standards and prices; the formation of the Society for the Protection of Ancient Buildings; the work of John Pearson Loughborough, architect, on churches at Truro; and personal matters. Letters from Elizabeth (Lynn) Linton (1822-1898), author, concern personal matters such as her health; her husband, from whom she was separated; her place of residence; visits to the Wardles; her publications; the unpleasant reaction to her "The New Boss" published in St. James's Budget; and the termination of her weekly articles in St. James's Budget. There are also letters from Sir William Turner Thiselton-Dyer criticizing the botanical drawings in a handbook written by Wardle, and letters from Sir George Christopher Molesworth Birdwood and from Sir Francis Philip Cunliffe-Owen supporting Wardle. A volume entitled "Absortions Spectra of Indian Dyes, 1886" records the results of the spectral analysis of dyes from plants growing in various parts of India.

Miscellaneous letters, clippings, and pictures of Frederick Darlington Wardle, son of Sir Thomas Wardle, include letters from Robert Blair Swinton concerning his work An Indian Tale or Two (1899); letters from Hugh Lloyd Parry, member of the faculty of the University College of the South West of England, pertaining to his work on a history of the Exeter Guildhall, research on the local history of Bath and Exeter, and his collection of Japanese prints; and an autograph and scrapbook, 1894-1939.

5554. CHARLES CROSSFIELD WARE PAPERS, 1953. 1 vol. Onslow County, N.C.

Papers of Charles Crossfield Ware (b. 1886), author and minister of the Disciples of Christ, consist of a typescript entitled "Concerning New River Church now Union Chapel Christian Church," containing compilations of notes on Union Chapel and its predecessors; excerpts from minutes, 1794-1881, for the Neuse, Cape Fear, Goshen, Union, and Eastern associations; miscellaneous lists, including a list of ministers, and a brief paragraph on each of the earliest Christian churches in Onslow County before 1900.

5555. JOSIAH WILLIAM WARE PAPERS, 1848-1849. 3 items. Jefferson County, W. Va.

Letters to Colonel Josiah W. Ware, concerning his business as a breeder of Cotswold sheep.

5556. WILLIAM WARE PAPERS, 1865. 2 items. Danville (Pittsylvania County), Va.

Business letters of William Ware, cashier at the branch of the Farmers Bank of Virginia, Fredericksburg, Virginia, concerning bank business.

5557. CATHERINE ANN (WARE) WARFIELD PAPERS, 1867-1868. 1 vol. "Beechmoor," Jefferson County, Ky.

Volume entitled "Southern Songs" containing poems written by Catherine Ann (Ware) Warfield (1816-1877), poet and author, telling the story of the Civil War in verse and illustrating her Southern sympathies. Some of the poems have been published.

5558. JOHN C. WARLICK PAPERS, 1901. 1 item. Lincolnton (Lincoln County), N.C.

Reminiscences of Civil War service and life in Lincoln County, North Carolina, 1865-1900, by John C. Warlick (b. 1841), 11th North Carolina Volunteers, containing information on desertion in the Confederate Army, agricultural produce and the manufacture of brooms, whiskey, and flour.

5559. CHARLES C. WARREN PAPERS, 1912-1917. 37 items. Boston, Mass.

Routine correspondence of the Boston Municipal Council, Department of Massachusetts, United Spanish War Veterans, of which Charles C. Warren was council secretary ca. 1916-1917, with references to the United Spanish War Veterans Auxiliary and the Army of the Philippines, Inc.

5560. E. WILLARD WARREN PAPERS, 1861-1867. 58 items. Glens Falls (Warren County), N.Y.

Correspondence of E. Willard Warren, lieutenant in the 3rd Pennsylvania Cavalry, U.S.A., with his wife, Sophronia (Stewart) Warren, and with his parents describing camp life, rumors, amusements, the caliber of the Union officers, and the Peninsular Campaign, including the Seven Days' battle for Richmond, 1862.

5561. FITZ-HENRY WARREN PAPERS, 1861. 1 item. Burlington (Des Moines County), Iowa.

Letter of Fitz-Henry Warren (1816-1878), journalist, politician, Union Army general, and diplomat, discussing the impending war, his support for William H. Seward for the presidency and Thurlow Weed for commissary general, and economic conditions in Iowa.

5562. G. W. WARREN LEDGERS, 1881-1883. 3 vols. Louisville (Jefferson County), Ga.

General mercantile accounts.

5563. JAMES WARREN, JR., PAPERS, 1850-1867. 157 items. New Haven (New Haven County), Conn.

Family and personal correspondence of James Warren, Jr., a marble worker and Union soldier, principally concerning personal matters and social life and customs in New England, with descriptions of torchlight parades of the Republican and Union parties in Boston, Massachusetts, in the election of 1860; mobilization in Providence, Rhode Island; departure of Rhode Island regiments; the enlistment of Massachusetts men in New York regiments; the Irish riots in Boston, 1863; and other references to the war.

5564. LEWIS WARRINGTON PAPERS, 1829-1851. 4 items. Washington, D.C.

Correspondence of Lewis Warrington (1782-1851), commodore, U.S. Navy, concerning the War of 1812, investments, and regulations about furniture and curtains at navy yards, with comments on the character of Gallagher, probably Captain John Gallagher who had died recently.

5565. GEORGE W. WARTHEN PAPERS, 1858-1893. 20 items. Sparta (Hancock County), Ga.

Letters from George W. Warthen, a captain in the Confederate Army, commenting at length on military operations around New Bern, North Carolina, Charleston, South Carolina, and Petersburg, Virginia; a petition from his soldiers asking him to resign; and two miscellaneous papers.

5566. THOMAS J. WARTHEN PAPERS, 1861-1863. 25 items. Sandersville (Washington County), Ga.

Official and personal letters of Thomas J. Warthen, colonel of the 28th Georgia Regiment, C.S.A., stationed at Manassas, Virginia, pertaining to the Civil War in Georgia and Virginia, the conscription bill, furloughs for soldiers, dissatisfaction over officers, etc. One letter, February, 1862, expresses alarm for the safety of Richmond and comments on the *Virginia*'s attempts to defend Norfolk.

5567. THOMAS WARTON PAPERS, 1768. 1 item. Oxford, Oxfordshire, England.

Letter of Thomas Warton (1728-1790), historian of English literature and poet, ordering an edition of Aristophanes by Tiberius Hemsterhuis.

5568. WARWICK & READ PAPERS, 1820-1861. 9 items. Lynchburg (Campbell County), Va.

Business papers of the merchandising firm of Warwick & Read.

5569. ALGERNON SYDNEY WASHBURN PAPERS, 1832-1884. 214 items. Boston, Mass., and Hallowell (Kennebec County), Me.

Family correspondence of Algernon Sydney Washburn concerning financial matters; the purchasing of real estate in Wisconsin; wildcat banking in Wisconsin; the discounting of bank notes; social life and customs, education, and farm life in Livermore, Maine; the panic of 1857 and its aftermath; U.S. Military Academy, West Point, New York, 1842; and troop movements and officers of the U.S. Army in the western theater during the Civil War. There are references to politics in Maine and Wisconsin, and life in Venezuela and Paris, France.

5570. AMASA C. WASHBURN PAPERS, 1831-1879. 101 items. Bloomington (McLean County), Ill.

Papers relating to the legal practice of Amasa C. Washburn including land deeds and indentures; papers concerning the administration of estates and the guardianship of minor children; and papers pertaining to his activities as a claim agent helping soldiers and their relatives secure bounties and back pay. There is also a notebook, 1861-1869, containing names of Illinois soldiers whose accounts with the U. S. government he settled.

5571. ELIHU BENJAMIN WASHBURNE PAPERS, 1863, 1867. 2 items. Galena (Jo Daviess County), Ill.

Letter of Elihu Benjamin Washburne (1816-1887) describing an expedition to Port Gibson, Mississippi, with General Ulysses S. Grant, the battle there, and the attitude of the soldiers toward Grant; and a letter concerning the re-instatement to a position for the addressee.

5572. BOOKER TALIAFERRO WASHINGTON PAPERS, 1897-1907. 4 items. Tuskegee (Macon County), Ala.

Letters of Booker T. Washington (1859-1915), educator, including one to Mrs. Dana S. Ayer appealing for financial support of Tuskegee Normal and Industrial Institute, Tuskegee, Alabama, and explaining their tuition policy, 1897; one to Marcus M. Marks, merchant, discussing a trip to the South that George Foster Peabody, banker, was taking, 1903; to Mrs. C. M. Whitney concerning the work of the Voorhees Industrial School, Denmark, South Carolina, 1906; and one to Charles E. Bigelow sending a copy of a speech made by Washington, 1907.

5573. BUSHROD WASHINGTON PAPERS, 1686-1828. 8 items. Westmoreland County, Va.

Papers of Bushrod Washington (1762-1829), nephew of George Washington and associate justice of the U. S. Supreme Court, 1798-1829, including an indenture, 1686, from Thomas Bushrod to John Clondining; letters dealing with legal matters; a letter to his mother; letters relating to financial matters, including a debt owed the estate of George Washington; and a letter concerning financial matters of the Dismal Swamp Land Company.

5574. CHARLES A[UGUSTINE?] WASHINGTON PAPERS, 1847. 1 item. "Wellington," Jefferson County, W. Va.

Letter from Charles A. Washington to his father, George Fayette Washington, concerning his plantation and the difficulty of hiring slave labor to work the land.

5575. GEORGE WASHINGTON PAPERS, 1760-1927. 41 items. Mount Vernon (Fairfax County), Va.

Miscellaneous papers of George Washington (1732-1799), commander of the Continental Army and first president of the United States, 1789-1797, include a letter, 1760, from William Digges concerning the sale of land in Virginia; copy of a lottery ticket signed by Washington in 1768; drafts of reports, 1772 and 1773, on a survey of military land on the Ohio River; facsimiles of Washington's commission as commander-in-chief of the Continental Army, 1775, and of his oath of allegiance to the United States, 1778; letter, 1778, from John Parke Custis discussing the arrival of supplies for the American forces and action taken by the Virginia assembly to recruit and equip troops; copy of a letter, 1778 [1788?], from Washington to William Thornton regarding Washington's plans for the construction of his home; letter, 1781, from Martha Washington to her housekeeper inquiring about the progress made in spinning and bleaching some cotton; facsimiles of correspondence between Washington and Charles Cornwallis, First Marquis and Second Earl Cornwallis, concerning the terms of surrender set by Washington at Yorktown, Virginia, in 1781, and a copy of the "Articles of Capitulation"; copy of a letter from Washington to Abraham Skinner pertaining to the exchange of prisoners with the British army; copy of a letter, 1783, to Baron von Steuben thanking him for his services to the American nation; list of Washington's bodyguard and the wages paid them for their services, 1783-1786; facsimile of Washington's letter accepting the presidency of the United States; letter, 1789, from Tobias Lear, Washington's private secretary, to George Augustine Washington describing President Washington's inauguration; personal letter of George Augustine Washington; letters, 1791 and 1808, discussing Washington's visit to Salem, North Carolina; facsimiles of the wills of Mary Washington, 1788, and of George Washington, 1799; business letter, 1798, of Washington, to Lear; clipping concerning the discovery of Lear's diary in which he describes Washington's final illness; clipping, of a letter, 1799, from Martha Washington thanking the addressee for his tribute to her husband; clipping announcing memorial services for Washington; table of contents listing memorial speeches and sermons delivered in Washington's honor; a plat for land belonging to John West; a letter, 1816, from Lear to Lieutenant George Haig concerning Haig's accounts with the Department of War; facsimile of a plat for land on Little Hunting Creek endorsed by Washington; legal papers, 1796-1854, concerning Thomas Law and his wife, Elizabeth Parke (Custis) Law, Edward Washington, Jr., and George W. P. Custis; a genealogical chart indicating Washington's descent from King John and twenty barons who served as sureties for the Magna Carta; and a letter regarding the appointment of a treasurer for the fund to establish the national university proposed by Washington in his will.

5576. JAMES HENRY RUSSELL WASHINGTON PAPERS, 1840-1859. 8 items. Macon (Bibb County), Ga.

Correspondence of James Henry Russell Washington (1809-1866), banker, planter, and legislator, concerning runaway slaves and overseers, the character of the Georgia legislature, and the banking and monetary agitation of the 1840s.

5577. LAWRENCE WASHINGTON PAPERS, 1857-1866. 18 items. "Campbelltown," Westmoreland County, Va.

Correspondence and clippings of Lawrence Washington (1791-1875), sheriff of Westmoreland County and state legislator, concerning the death and estate of his son, Henry Augustine Washington (ca. 1822-1858), professor at the College of William and Mary, Williamsburg, Virginia; personal letter of Cynthia B. (Tucker) Washington, wife of Henry Augustine Washington; several accounts; and two clippings concerning the deaths of other children of the Washington family.

5578. LITTLETON DENNIS QUINTON WASHINGTON PAPERS, 1856-1881. 5 items. Washington, D.C.

Correspondence of Littleton Dennis Quinton Washington, clerk in the U. S. Treasury Department, including a letter from Elisha Whittlesey, comptroller of the U. S. Treasury, concerning the presidential election of 1856 and the character of John Charles Frémont; letter, 1865, from George Washington Custis Lee commenting on the plan of Robert E. Lee to write an account of the campaigns of the Army of Northern Virginia; letter, 1876, with clipping attached from Eppa Hunton, Sr., pertaining to an article describing an alleged dispute between him and Lucius Q. C. Lamar over a clerical appointment for Washington; and a letter, 1881, from A. S. Abell, publisher of The (Baltimore) Sun, regarding an appointment.

5579. WILLIAM AUGUSTINE WASHINGTON PAPERS, 1775-1914. 15 items. "Haywood," Westmoreland County, Va.

Papers of William Augustine Washington consisting of receipts and correspondence concerning real estate transactions and other business matters; account of Dr. Thomas Thomson with Washington for medical services rendered, 1787-1793; printed letter, 1775, from Patrick Henry to John Augustine Washington, father of William Augustine Washington's wife, Jane, encouraging patrols to prevent slaves from defecting to the British; and a certificate of membership in the Royal Society for the Encouragement of Arts, Manufactures and Commerce to William De Hertburn Washington, grandson of William Augustine Washington.

5580. WASHINGTON ACADEMY MINUTES, 1784-1808. 1 vol. (160 pp.) Washington (Wilkes County), Ga.

Minutes of the board of commissioners of the Washington Academy.

5581. WASHINGTON, CINCINNATI AND ST. LOUIS RAILROAD COMPANY MINUTES, 1872-1881. 1 vol. (171 pp.) Luray (Page County), and Harrisonburg (Rockingham County), Va.

Stockholders' minute book of the Washington, Cincinnati and St. Louis Railroad Company. Many papers are blank.

5582. WASHINGTON INSTITUTE TEMPERANCE ASSOCIATION CONSTITUTION, 1857. 1 vol. (42 pp.) Harris' Depot (Cabarrus County), N.C.

Constitution and minutes of the meetings of the Washington Institute Temperance Association.

5583. WASHINGTON MINING COMPANY ACCOUNTS, 1843-1857. 2 vols. Davidson County, N.C.

Business accounts of the Washington Mining Company consisting of inventories of merchandise and records of advances of cash and merchandise sold presumably to employees.

5584. WASHINGTON NATIONAL MONUMENT SOCIETY PAPERS, 1833-1863. 29 items. Washington, D.C.

Chiefly correspondence and other papers relating to a dispute between the building committee of the Washington National Monument Society and William Easley, contractor supplying stone for the monument, over Easley's default on his contract. Included is a committee report signed by Peter Force and others recording the decision against Easley. There are also a copy of the act to incorporate the Washington National Monument Society; a facsimile containing the signatures of the officers and managers of the society in 1850; and a document, 1853, empowering John L. Browne to solicit funds at the Exhibition of Industry of All Nations in New York.

5585. [WASHINGTON PARISH AGRICULTURAL CLUB?] MINUTES, 1871. 1 vol. (62 pp.) Washington, Parish, La.

Minutes, probably of the Washington Parish Agricultural Club, discussing agricultural questions. A portion of the volume is a scrapbook, and another portion is an account book.

5586. BENJAMIN WATERS PAPERS, 1846-1887. 9 items. Bulloch County, Ga.

Land deeds and plats of surveys pertaining to the title of land sold by Benjamin Waters, Jr., to the American Freehold Land Mortgage Company of London, England.

5587. BENJAMIN WATKINS PAPERS, 1832-1843.
4 items. Pittsylvania County, Va.

Papers of Benjamin Watkins consisting of correspondence concerning the payment of debts, and documents dealing with Watkins's appointment as sheriff of Pittsylvania County.

5588. KATE M. WATKINS AUTOGRAPH ALBUMS, 1858-1870. 2 vols. New Orleans, La.

Albums containing autographs of many Confederate officers from Arkansas and Louisiana regiments.

5589. WILLIAM HENRY WATKINS LEDGER, 1866-1868. 1 vol. (255 pp.) Norwood (Stanly County), N.C.

Ledger of a country merchant.

5590. ARNOLD PETRIE WATSON PAPERS, 1892-1937. 25 items. London, England.

Papers of Arnold Petrie Watson consist chiefly of letters and printed items concerning organizations and activities at King's College, Cambridge, England, including the publication of its Register by John J. Withers. There are also three broadsides from the candidacy in 1923 of James Ramsay Montagu Butler for a parliamentary seat from Cambridge.

5591. CHARLES S. WATSON PAPERS, 1870-1887. 63 items. Leestown (Jefferson County), W. Va.

Family correspondence of Charles S. Watson concerning personal matters; the rapid sale of land and the depressed farming conditions in Jefferson County, West Virginia; the early development of Birmingham, Alabama; and the temperance movement in Leestown.

5592. D. M. WATSON LEDGER, 1872-1890. 1 vol. (228 pp.) Middleton (Hyde County), N.C.

General mercantile accounts.

5593. HENRY WATSON, JR., PAPERS. 1765 (1828-1869) 1938. 3,797 items and 18 vols. Greensboro (Hale County), Ala.

Personal and business correspondence and papers of Henry Watson, Jr. (1810-1888), lawyer and planter. Early papers relate to John Watson (d. 1824), a frequent contributor to Joel Barlow's American Mercury, and include fragments and several complete literary manuscripts; papers relating to the settlement of John Watson's estate; and several letters to Henry Watson, Sr., from Elisha Stanley. This Stanley-Watson correspondence describes Pittsburgh, Pennsylvania; Cincinnati, Ohio; and Kentucky; mercantile business and the activities of Kentuckians during the War of 1812; and the disastrous effects of peace on mercantile pursuits. The papers centering on Henry Watson, Jr., concern his education at Hartford, Connecticut, and at Harvard College, Cambridge, Massachusetts; a visit to Greensboro, Alabama, in 1831; return to his home in East Windsor, Connecticut, for the study of law with Henry Barnard; his return to Greensboro in 1834 to begin the practice of law; the establishment of a lucrative practice; the accumulation of property including a plantation and slaves; the establishment of the Planter's Insurance Company; his marriage to Sophia Peck; his efforts to dispose of two shares in the Ohio Land Company; his residence in Europe during the Civil War; and the settlement of his father's estate. Correspondence describes college life at Harvard College; life in Alabama, with accounts of the soil, settlement, and agriculture; politics in Alabama, 1834-1844; volunteers from Alabama for service in the Mexican War; westward migration; activities of Northern abolitionists in Alabama in 1836; panics of 1837 and 1857; Whig politics in the 1850s; fear in Greensboro of a slave insurrection, 1860; the presidential campaign of 1860; secession; the sale of cotton before and after the Civil War; mail service between the North and the South during the war; mobilization and preparation for war; the management of his plantation and the impressment of slaves, tools, and livestock during the war; the difficulties of Southerners in Europe during the war; inflation; railroad building in Alabama; the Union Pacific Railroad; and Reconstruction. Included are correspondence with John Erwin, Whig leader in Alabama; two land grants to Edwin Peck signed by Martin Van Buren; letters from Sophia Peck, her brother, William Peck, and her sister, Mary Eliza Peck, while in schools in Hartford, Connecticut, and New York, New York; letters from the brothers and sisters of Henry Watson, Jr., in Illinois, Iowa, and Ohio; letters from William P. Eaton, head of the Female Department of the Cahaba (Alabama) Male and Female Academy; letter of Henry Watson to an editor on the subject of fertilizers; several letters from Confederate soldiers imprisoned at Johnson's Island, Ohio; contracts of Watson with freedmen; a bulletin of the Irving Institute, Tarrytown, New York; tax lists for Greene County, Alabama; printed extracts from the diary of William Watson; bulletin of the Berlin American Female Institute; catalogs of the Cumberland University Law School, Lebanon, Tennessee, 1851-1852, and of the Greensboro (Alabama) Female Academy, 1858; letters, biographical sketch, and list of the writings of Asa Gray; biographical sketch, certificates of membership in various learned societies, and three articles of Sereno Watson (b. 1826), brother of Henry Watson, Jr., botanist, and associate editor of the Journal of Education; and letters of Henry Barnard [partially published: Bayrd Still (ed.), "Observations of Henry Barnard on the West and South of the 1840's," Journal of Southern History, VIII (May, 1942), 247-258]. A large portion of the papers are bills, receipts, and prices current. Volumes include plantation and household accounts, 1834-1866, record of Negroes, 1843-1866, bill book of the Planters' Insurance Company, 1854-1863, summaries of magazine articles and account book, 1832-1848, and diaries, 1830-1833 and 1850-1854, of Henry Watson, Jr.; and diaries, 1849-1863, and genealogical notes and records of Sereno Watson.

5594. THOMAS EDWARD WATSON PAPERS, 1902-1915. 3 items. Thomson (McDuffie County), Ga.

Letters of Thomas Edward Watson (1850-1922), author, journalist, U.S. congressman, 1891-1893, and senator, 1921-1922, and Populist leader, relating to his efforts to purchase a home near Richmond, Virginia, the sale of his books, and corrections needed in his Napoleon and the Story of France.

5595. THOMAS G. WATSON PAPERS, 1856-1866. 10 items. Lexington (Rockbridge County), Va.

Letters from Thomas G. Watson, F. B. Watson, and Wilbur Watson, brothers who attended Trinity College, Randolph County, North Carolina, concerning college life during the antebellum and Reconstruction periods; the number of students attending Trinity and an estimate of expenses for various years; war fever during 1861; and the depredations suffered by the college during the Civil War.

5596. FIELDING WATTS PAPERS, 1848-1895. 25 items. Iredell County, N.C.

Personal, legal, and business papers of Fielding Watts and other members of the Watts family. Included is a land deed, 1855; and three items, 1886, pertaining to the Due West Female College, Due West, South Carolina.

5597. GEORGE WASHINGTON WATTS PAPERS, 1881. 1 item. Durham, N.C.

Essay of George Washington Watts (1851-1921), industrialist and tobacco manufacturer, read at the Durham Lyceum. Written in the form of a letter of 1901, it is a humorous spoof on the growth of Durham and the futures of many noted residents of the city twenty years hence.

5598. ISAAC WATTS PAPERS, 1701-1788. 2 items and 8 vols. Stoke Newington, London, England.

Letter from Isaac Watts to a Mrs. Fay expressing his sympathy on her recent widowhood and extending words of spiritual comfort. The remainder of the collection is primarily written in a form of shorthand. Included are a sermon; extracts from the Bible, Genesis through Joel, and Amos through Acts; diaries of Sarah Ashurst containing spiritual reflections or discussion of theological points; and letter books of Joseph Parker, Watts's amanuensis, containing personal and business letters, and extracts from various works on topics such as faith, humility, friendship, etc.

5599. JAMES WATTS PAPERS, 1819-1868. 11 items. Iredell County, N.C.

Indentures and receipts of James Watts and Elizah Watts regarding the sale of land.

5600. W. W. WATTS LEDGER, 1860-1864. 1 vol. (Martin County), N.C.

Account book of W. W. Watts, a physician, showing services rendered and fees charged.

5601. WATTS HOSPITAL MINUTES, 1895-1896. 1 vol. (57 pp.) Durham, N.C.

Minutes recording the activities of the board of lady visitors during the early days of the hospital, containing information on early hospital facilities in Durham.

5602. THOMAS NEVILLE WAUL PAPERS, 1863-1895. 4 items. Galveston, Tex.

Correspondence of Thomas Neville Waul (1813-1903), member of the first Confederate Congress and brigadier general in the Confederate Army. One letter refers to the scarcity of food during the siege of Vicksburg, 1863.

5603. JOSEPH HOWELL WAY PAPERS, 1915. 2 items. Waynesville (Haywood County), N.C.

Biographical sketches of Joseph Howell Way (1865-1927), physician, covering his early education; his teaching in the public schools of Buncombe County, North Carolina; his studies at the Medical College of Virginia, Richmond, and Vanderbilt University, Nashville, Tennessee; his services with the North Carolina State Board of Health; and his organization in 1923 of the section of Medical Veterans of the World War and Medical Reserve Corps at Asheville, a section of the North Carolina Medical Society.

5604. ANTHONY WAYNE PAPERS, 1781-1785. 3 items. Chester County, Pa.

Correspondence of Anthony Wayne (1745-1796), general in the Continental Army, including a letter from Wayne to Joseph Reid criticizing the poor leadership of Lord Cornwallis; letter from John Habersham reporting on his mission into the interior of Georgia; and a letter from Joseph Clay of Georgia concerning a debt.

5605. HENRY CONSTANTINE WAYNE PAPERS, 1859-1864. 18 items. Milledgeville (Baldwin County), Ga.

Papers of Henry Constantine Wayne (1815-1883), U.S. Army officer during the Mexican War and adjutant and inspector general in the Confederate Army, relative to organization of the Confederate Army, commissions for officers, and ordnance supplies; and reports. Among the correspondents are Francis S. Bartow, William R. Boggs, David E. Twiggs, and William Henry Talbot Walker.

5606. JAMES MOORE WAYNE PAPERS, 1834-1842. 3 items. Savannah, Ga.

Correspondence of James Moore Wayne (ca. 1790-1867), associate justice of the U.S. Supreme Court, consisting of a letter from Wayne to Dr. Raymond Harris concerning sickness in his "negro camp," legal affairs, and states' rights; a personal letter of Wayne's nephew Clifford; and a letter from Hugh Swinton Legaré inquiring about the location of some invoices used in the case of Wood v. U. S.

5607. CARRIE WEADON PAPERS, 1899-1901. 1 vol. Hamilton (Loudoun County County), Va.

Journal of Carrie Weadon containing an autobiographical sketch, and describing her spiritual life and daily routine.

5608. ISRAEL H. WEASTON PAPERS, 1898-1899. 9 items. Washington, D.C.

Family letters of Israel H. Weaston, army paymaster clerk, concerning personal matters; his duties; his impressions of his various surroundings in Washington, D.C., Jacksonville (Florida), Chattanooga (Tennessee), and Atlanta (Georgia); and the battle of Chattanooga, 1863.

5609. FREDERIC EDWARD WEATHERLY PAPERS, 1927. 1 item. Bath, England.

Personal letter of Frederic Edward Weatherly (1848-1929) to Dr. James Young concerning an invitation.

5610. WILLIAM HARRISON WEATHERN PAPERS, 1832-1851. 22 items. Farmington (Franklin County), Me.

Personal correspondence of William Harrison Weathern, music teacher, with occasional references to Maine politics, and the Whigs, Democrats, and abolitionists in the states.

5611. GREENBURY W. WEAVER ACCOUNTS, 1851-1866. 13 vols. White Post (Clarke County), Va.

Daybooks and ledgers of a general merchant.

5612. PHILIP J. WEAVER PAPERS, 1830-1906. 887 items and 5 vols. Selma (Dallas County), Ala.

Papers of Philip J. Weaver (1797-1865), merchant and land speculator, chiefly concerning his real estate ventures primarily in Mississippi, but also in Texas, Alabama, and Tennessee. Included are tax receipts, business correspondence, lists of property holdings, land grants, deeds, and related memoranda and legal papers. There are papers pertaining to his business relationship with Henry T. Curtiss of New York, New York, and with John N. Wilie of Pontotoc, Mississippi. Papers after 1865 relate to the settlement of Weaver's estate. The volumes contain notes, lists, and descriptions of Weaver's property; and some business accounts.

5613. WILLIAM WEAVER PAPERS, 1809 (1828-1875) 1885. 3,387 items. Goshen (Rockbridge County), Va.

Business papers of William Weaver (1781-1863?), owner of the Bath Iron Works, dealing with the iron industry in Virginia, and containing information on types of items in demand; collection of debts; prices of iron, land, crops, and livestock; the hiring and use of slave labor; and diet, clothing, wages, and prices of slaves. Included are several lists of slaves, with a brief physical description and comments on their reliability as workers. Personal correspondence discusses cholera in Philadelphia, Pennsylvania, and Baltimore, Maryland, 1832; smallpox in Lexington, Virginia; typhoid in Texas, 1853; the activities and pension of a Revolutionary soldier; state and national politics, especially under Andrew Jackson; the completion of the canal from the mouth of the Brazos River to Galveston, Texas, 1853; the election of 1860; vigilance committees in Virginia; the use of substitutes; troop movements through Lynchburg and Richmond, Virginia; food prices; the death of Thomas Jonathan Jackson; and the iron industry during the war. Letters, 1861-1863, from John Letcher (1813-1884), U. S. congressman, 1851-1859, and governor of Virginia during the Civil War, discuss his message to the Virginia General Assembly concerning state and Confederate affairs in 1861; rumors; the failure of the legislature to provide replacement troops; military actions at Gordonsville and Fredericksburg, Virginia; various Confederate and Union generals; the unlikelihood of European intervention; military activity in North Carolina; and public opinion in the North.

5614. A. S. WEBB AND COMPANY ACCOUNT BOOK, 1868-1869. 1 vol. (75 pp.) Ridgeway (Warren County), N.C.

General accounts of a local merchant.

5615. MARY WEBB PAPERS, 1797-1799.
2 items. [Henry County, Ky.?]

Ballads written by or belonging to Mary Webb, including one entitled "The Wandering Young Gentlewoman; or, Cat-Skins Garland."

5616. SIDNEY JAMES WEBB, FIRST BARON PASSFIELD, PAPERS, 1905-1928.
9 items. London, England.

Correspondence of Sidney James Webb, First Baron Passfield (1859-1947), British social reformer and historian, including a letter, 1907, to Alfred Henry Miles discussing Miles's wish to retire from his connection with the Lewisham Grammar School and its relationship to the plans of municipal reformers; letter, 1907, commenting on a book by Sir John Harold Clapham, and the forthcoming publication of The Manor and The Borough; letter, 1923, asking a Mr. Sullivan to draft a habeas corpus bill for the Labour Party; letter, 1926, stating his position on the proposed reforms of the Poor Law; a letter, 1928, to Colonel Burdon, probably Conservative Unionist politician Colonel Rowland Burdon (1857-1944), concerning their different politics, his support of ratification of the new Prayer Book, his decision to retire as Seaham's member in the House of Commons, and the franchise rights of domestic servants; two letters dealing with speaking engagements; and two notes.

5617. THOMAS L. WEBB PAPERS, 1864.
4 items. Charleston, S.C.

Letters to Thomas L. Webb concerning the death of his son.

5618. WILLIAM S. WEBB PAPERS, 1829.
1 item. London, England.

Letter of William S. Webb, who in 1808 made the first survey of the high peaks of the Himalayan Mountains, explaining why he was not prepared to publish further accounts of his explorations in the Himalayas, and noting the works of James Baillie Fraser and James D. Herbert who visited the mountains after him.

5619. WILLINGTON E. WEBB PAPERS, 1842 (1870-1888) 1921. 121 items. Hanover County, Va.

Personal letters from Willington E. Webb, Protestant Episcopal minister of Virginia and New York City, with comments on church music and church architecture; and letters from Mrs. Webb, her mother, Mrs. Joseph Terry, and the Webb children.

5620. WEBB FAMILY PAPERS, 1894. 1 item. Granville County, N.C.

Photocopy of The Webb Family (Yazoo City, Miss.: 1894), compiled by Dr. Robert Dickens Webb (1824-189_).

5621. THOMAS B. WEBBER DIARY, 1861.
1 vol. (309 pp.) Byhalia (Marshall County), Miss.

Reactions of a Mississippi merchant to secession and the first days of the Civil War; and detailed information and comments on the early campaigns in the Gulf States, and Confederate efforts to take Fort Pickens, Florida.

5622. DANIEL WEBSTER PAPERS, 1837-1845.
8 items. Boston, Mass.

Miscellaneous correspondence of Daniel Webster (1782-1852), statesman and orator, U. S. congressman, senator, and secretary of state, concerning financial and personal matters. One letter from Webster to Stephen Pleasonton pertains to the release of funds designated for the relief of sailors discharged in Saint Petersburg, Russia, by the captain of the Kamschatka (Kamchatka?).

5623. E.W. WEBSTER PAPERS, (1854-1866) 1888.
135 items. Hartford County, Conn.

Papers of E. W. Webster, a carriage maker, relating chiefly to his business in Alabama, Florida, Georgia, Tennessee, Kentucky, Texas, and California where he had agencies. Correspondence during the Civil War period concerns the severing of business ties between the North and the South, the difficulty of collecting debts, and the determination of the South to resist coercion. Correspondence after the war pertains to the difficulties connected with the hiring of freedmen, poverty, and the rapid rebuilding of Atlanta, Georgia, and the depredation of a Georgia plantation by Confederate soldiers. The early correspondence consists of letters from "Sanford," also a carriage maker, to his girlfriend, Sarah M. Webster, describing Springfield, Gallatin, and Nashville, Tennessee; a slave auction he witnessed; and cholera, mosquitoes, lack of a sewerage system, steamboat accidents, the arrest of two former slaves manumitted by their white father, a printers' strike, and entertainment in Nashville.

5624. HENRY ALLEN WEDGWOOD PAPERS, 1837.
1 item. Hermitage, Woking, Surrey, England.

Letter from Henry Allen Wedgwood (1799-1885), barrister-at-law, recommending George Chilton, Jr., of London as a Liberal candidate for Newcastle.

5625. JOSIAH CLEMENT WEDGWOOD, FIRST BARON WEDGWOOD, PAPERS, 1913. 2 items. London, England.

Letter of Josiah Clement Wedgwood (1872-1943), British politician and member of the House of Commons, to S. J. Spencer Looker, discussing the situation of the ordinary members of the House, the power of the whips, and his pessimism and recommendations for parliamentary reform; and a note.

5626. THEODORE H. WEED PAPERS, 1861-1864. 21 items. Syracuse (Onondaga County), N.Y., Maryland, and Virginia.

Papers of Major Theodore H. Weed, 10th New York Cavalry, U.S.A., including letters to his sister describing the capture of a band of Confederate soldiers near Baltimore, Maryland, in 1862; troop movements around Warrington and Culpeper, Virginia, in 1863; the battle of Cold Harbor, Virginia, in 1864; and action around Petersburg following Cold Harbor. There are also muster rolls; official reports; general and special orders; and a list of prisoners captured at Morrisville, Virginia, in 1864.

5627. THURLOW WEED PAPERS, 1860-1861. 15 items. New York, N.Y.

Photocopies of letters to Thurlow Weed (1797-1882), politician and journalist, concerning efforts to avoid secession and civil war; conciliatory measures and the likelihood of their success; Horace Greeley; William Henry Seward; and the election of Ira Harris to succeed Seward as U.S. senator. The originals are located in the Rush Rhees Library, University of Rochester, Rochester, New York.

5628. A. P. WEEKS PAPERS, 1908. 26 items. Boston, Mass.

Business correspondence of A. P. Weeks, a cashier at the Merchants National Bank, Boston, Massachusetts, including correspondence inquiring about the bank accounts and safety deposit boxes of the late James Moran of Plaquemines Parish, Louisiana.

5629. J[OHN?] THOMAS WEEKS BOOKKEEPING BOOK, 1833-1834. 1 vol. Middleburg (Loudoun County), Va.

A course in single entry bookkeeping.

5630. MASON LOCKE WEEMS PAPERS, 1802-1825. 3 items. Anne Arundel County, Md.

Letters from Mason Weems (1759-1825), generally known as "Parson Weems," Protestant Episcopal clergyman, book agent, and writer, one of which is to Mathew Carey concerning business, 1802; another to James Webb introducing Weems's son and another, in the last year of his life, to Henry Charles Carey, begging the latter to help his wife, Frances (Ewell) Weems, and her children since he (Weems) was dying.

5631. DAVID ADDISON WEISIGER PAPERS, 1860-1878. 1 vol. Petersburg (Dinwiddie County), Va.

Account book of David Addison Weisiger (1818-1899), Confederate general, cashier in the Citizens Bank of Petersburg, Virginia, and businessman in Richmond, Virginia, containing notes and bills payable, 1860-1878, and notes and bills receivable, 1860-1861.

5632. JOEL ROMULUS WELBORN PAPERS, 1821-1915. 65 items and 9 vols. Deep River (Guilford County), N.C.

Family correspondence of Joel Romulus Welborn and his brother, H. Rufus Welborn, relating largely to personal affairs, but containing information on the Society of Friends, Southern refugees in Indiana, 1861-1865, and the nursery business. Among the volumes are a diary, 1869 and 1871; a minute book, 1868-1870, of the Deep River Agricultural Club; an autograph album; personal accounts, 1871-1881; and minutes, 1868, of the Deep River Council of the Union League.

5633. ELLIOTT STEPHEN WELCH PAPERS, 1862-1865. 23 items. Charleston, S.C.

Letters of Elliott Stephen Welch, Confederate cavalry officer of Hampton's Legion, and of his brother, William Hawkins Welch, Confederate soldier in the 7th South Carolina Cavalry, describing cavalry life; fighting before the battle of Antietam; hospitals; the Maryland and Virginia countryside; lack of food and clothing; skirmishing and engagements in North Carolina and in Virginia, especially in 1864 in the Richmond and Petersburg, Virginia, area; the use of Negro troops by Union forces; casualties; horse trading in the cavalry; band serenades; rumors of Sherman's march through South Carolina; and various officers, including General Martin W. Gary, General Fitzhugh Lee, and Colonel Thomas M. Logan.

5634. R. H. WELCH DIARY, 1858. 1 vol. (45 pp.)

Personal diary of R. H. Welch, a cotton planter.

5635. GEORGE WELLER PAPERS, 1833. 1 item. Vicksburg (Warren County), Miss.

Letter to George Weller (1790-1841), Episcopal clergyman, editor of the Church Register, 1826-1829, and secretary of the Tennessee Colonization Society, from James Gillespie Birney, agent of the Kentucky Colonization Society, concerning Birney's intention to visit Nashville, Tennessee, and the use of public opinion to encourage the Tennessee legislature to support financially the colonization efforts. Weller addressed the contents of the letter to the attention of the Reverend Doctor Philip Lindsley, president of the University of Nashville.

5636. GIDEON WELLES PAPERS, 1870s. 1 item. Hartford (Hartford County), Conn.

Letter to Gideon Welles (1802-1878), editor of the Hartford Times, secretary of navy, 1861-1869, and founder of the Hartford Evening Press, from Donald M. Fairfax, a naval officer, concerning the voting for delegates to the general convention, and giving his opinions on Abraham Lincoln, Andrew Johnson, and Ulysses S. Grant.

5637. ARTHUR WELLESLEY, FIRST DUKE OF WELLINGTON, PAPERS, (1819-1850) 1904. 99 items. London, England.

Papers of Arthur Wellesley, First Duke of Wellington (1769-1852), British army officer and commander-in-chief, and member of Parliament. Much of the correspondence pertains to routine social, personal, and army matters. Correspondence also discusses Wellington's acceptance of the command of the army; a conversation with Lord Anglesey, 1827, concerning political matters; his resignation of the command of the army; political sentiment in 1831; his views on the conduct of political affairs by the "middling and lower classes"; an offer to subscribe money to help the church in Ireland; his political intentions in 1836; his ideas on the construction of the defenses of Hong Kong; a plan by the Marquess of Londonderry to question the government on its policy of limiting enlistments in the army; Oxford University; his talk in the House of Lords, 1838; his policy of refusal to intervene in the policies and patronage of the army after his resignation; and his refusal to submit a petition relating to railroads. A letter, 1819, from the Duchess of Wellington concerns the murder of the Duc de Berry and her anxiety for Wellington's safety. A letter, 1832, from Wellington's brother, Henry Wellesley, First Baron Cowley, diplomat, to Neumann, probably Baron Philipp von Neumann, official in the Austrian embassy in London, discusses Wellington's report to the King that he is unable to form a government, expectations concerning the passage of the Reform Bill, and the probability that the Whigs will have to offer concessions. There are also clippings pertaining to Wellington.

5638. HENRY RICHARD CHARLES WELLESLEY, FIRST EARL COWLEY, PAPERS, 1835. 1 item. London, England.

Marriage certificate of Henry Richard Charles Wellesley, First Earl Cowley (1804-1884), British diplomat, documents Wellesley's marriage in 1833 to Olivia Cecilia FitzGerald de Ros.

5639. RICHARD COLLEY WELLESLEY, MARQUIS WELLESLEY AND SECOND EARL OF MORNINGTON, PAPERS, 1798-1820. 35 items. London, England.

Political correspondence of Richard Colley Wellesley, Marquis Wellesley and Second Earl of Mornington (1760-1842), governor general of India, includes a letter, 1798, from Rear Admiral Sir Hugh Cloberry Christian, commander-in-chief at the Cape of Good Hope, concerning naval activities at the Cape and the war with France; papers, 1799, relating to the capture of Seringapatam, capital of Mysore, including the orders of commanding General George Harris congratulating the army on its success, a report of Harris to Wellesley, and an abstract of ordnance, stores, and magazines captured at Seringapatam; letter, 1801, from Wellesley regarding the command of troops at Oudh, India; and letter, 1801, from Admiral Keith at Aboukir Bay, Egypt, pertaining to the progress of British forces against the French. A letter (113 pp.), 1802, from Wellesley to Henry Addington explains his application to resign because of conflicts with the court of directors of the East India Company, and contains information on the control of patronage; the Board of Trade; the government of Madras under Lord Clive; the army; the relationships of the directors, the governor general, and the presidency governments; and various officials such as John Bristow, John Chamier, Captain Hook, William Kirkpatrick, Lieutenant Colonel Scott, David Scott, Peter Speke, George Udney, Josiah Webbe, Arthur Wellesley, and Henry Wellesley. There are also a letter, 1804, from Edward Pellew, First Viscount Exmouth, reporting on his arrival in Asian waters; letter, 1805, from Wellesley to Sir John Coxe Hippisley, First Baronet, concerning the removal of disabilities against Roman Catholics; correspondence, 1809, between Wellesley and Martin de Garay, principal secretary of state in Spain, regarding the alliance of British forces and the Spanish Central Junta against the French, and discussing supplies, troop movements, and financial matters; letter, [1809?], pertaining to problems arising from an extension of credit to Spain; letter, 1810, from Spencer Perceval, First Lord of the Treasury and Chancellor of the Exchequer, dealing with the proposed loan and commercial treaty with Spain; letter, 1813, reporting on military movements in Spain and the situation at Majorca; letter, 1813, from William Wilberforce discussing the need for secular and religious education in India; letter, 1817, from Richard Wellesley (d. 1831), son of Lord Wellesley, to the latter's nephew, William Pole-Tylney-Long-Wellesley, inquiring as to whether he would seek reelection for the parliamentary seat from Saint Ives; an order, [1820?], from George IV regarding the enforcement of acts pertaining to the collection of taxes in Ireland; and routine letters dealing with appointments, recommendations, and social engagements.

5640. JAMES CLARKE WELLING PAPERS, 1891. 1 item. Washington, D.C.

Letter to James Clarke Welling (1825-1894), journalist, educator, and president of Columbian College (now George Washington University), Washington, D.C., from Helen Elizabeth (Ashhurst) Wharton sending a copy of her biography of her husband, Francis Wharton, and commenting on the book's publication.

5641. L. R. WELLS PAPERS, 1863-1864. 6 items. Sparta (Alleghany County), N.C.

Letters and part of a journal kept by L. R. Wells, a Confederate soldier, who took part in the invasion of Pennsylvania, 1862; and two fragments of Civil War poems.

5642. MARY ADA (BILLARD) WELLS PAPERS, 1908. 1 item. Kennett Square (Chester County), Pa.

Personal letter to Mary Ada (Billard) Wells from Emma (Taylor) Lamborn, sister of Bayard Taylor (1825-1878), poet, commenting on her brother and their family.

5643. FRANCIS CHARTERIS-WEMYSS, BARON ELCHO, PAPERS, 1804. 1 item. Gosford House, East Lothian, Scotland.

Letter from Lord Elcho to David Robertson, concerning a legal matter.

5644. JOHN WEREAT PAPERS, 1779-1798. 10 items. Savannah, Ga.

Letters of John Wereat, governor of Georgia and member of the first provincial congress of Georgia, concern the release of an imprisoned Loyalist, 1779; the ratification of the Federal Constitution by the Georgia convention in 1788; and the sale of western lands in Georgia, 1794.

5645. ARTHA BRAILSFORD WESCOAT DIARY, 1863-1864. 1 vol. (66 pp.) Edisto Island and "California," Monck's Corner (Berkeley County), S.C.

Diary of Artha Brailsford Wescoat, a fifteen-year old boy, living on a plantation in Berkeley County, South Carolina, after the threat of raids by Union troops had forced his family to leave their home on Edisto Island, South Carolina. Diary entries concern other refugee Edisto families; the coast around Edisto Island; depredations by Union troops on Edisto Island plantation houses; camp life of Confederate troops stationed near the island, including amateur theatricals and foraging for food; conditions in Charleston, South Carolina; race relations; attacks by Union forces on the defenses of Charleston, with comments on the presence of Negro troops in the Union lines; Wescoat's education; and the fight at Fort Johnson on James Island, South Carolina.

5646. JOSEPH JULIUS WESCOAT DIARY, 1863-1865. 1 vol. Charleston, S.C.

The Civil War diary of Joseph Julius Wescoat, a Confederate soldier, concerns fighting in the vicinity of Charleston, South Carolina, in 1863; battles at Drewry's Bluff, the Wilderness, and Cold Harbor, Virginia all in 1864; Wescoat's capture by Union forces in 1865; and prison life at Old Capitol Prison, Washington, D.C., and at Fort Delaware. The diary also contains genealogical material on the Wescoat family.

5647. WESLEY FAMILY PAPERS, 1726-1860. 28 items and 1 vol. England.

The papers of John Wesley, Anglican clergyman and a founder of the Methodist Church, and of his brother, Charles Wesley, an important figure in early Methodism, include a letter, 1726, from John Wesley to Charles Wesley, enclosing two of John Wesley's poems and commenting on his life as a student at Lincoln College; photocopies of sermons, 1735-1738, by Charles Wesley, many of which were preached in the American colonies; letter, 1770, from John Wesley to Joseph Benson concerning Lady Huntingdon, attendance at sermons preached by Wesley at the Tabernacle and Tottenham Court Chapel, and the estate of George Whitefield; an affidavit, 1782, endorsed by John Wesley concerning the debt on a Methodist chapel and the transferal of ownership of the chapel; letter, 1785, from Charles Wesley to Dr. Chandler describing his early career and commenting on the division between Methodists and the Anglican Church; letter, 1788, from John Wesley to Captain Richard Williams on the appointment of Methodist clergymen; letter, 1788, from John Wesley to Joseph Benson concerning theological matters; letter, 1788, from John Wesley to Samuel Bradburn on Charles Wesley's illness; and a letter, 1789, of John Wesley concerning his friend, James Kenton. Also a volume containing an inventory of the printed works owned by John Wesley at his death in 1791.

5648. JAMES J. WESSON LEDGER, 1871-1877. 1 vol. (274 pp.) Gholsonville (Brunswick County), Va.

Accounts of a general merchant.

5649. EDWIN S. WEST PAPERS, 1861-1867. 31 items.

Letters of Edwin S. West, who served in the Union Navy during the Civil War, and letters of other Union soldiers, concerning the Peninsular Campaign, 1862; West's service on the U.S.S. Hendrick Hudson in Florida waters and the U.S.S. Paul Jones in Florida and at Mobile, Alabama, 1864-1865; and Jefferson Davis.

5650. FRANCIS J. WEST PAPERS, 1854-1899. 1 vol. Cedartown (Polk County), Ga.

Scrapbook containing clippings of poems, essays, and short works of fiction.

5651. GEORGE W. WEST PAPERS, 1785 (1830-1850) 1910. 599 items. Cedartown (Polk County), Ga.

The papers of George W. West and his family contain business papers relating to the sale of farm produce and land; letters in the 1850s concerning agricultural, social and economic conditions in Texas; letters of Josephine West and her friends concerning social life in the period just before the Civil War and the difficulties of managing slaves during the Civil War; letters of John R. West, Ben West, and Buddy West, all Confederate soldiers, including a description of fighting at Arkadelphia and Camden, Arkansas, 1864; letters, 1886, from a girl studying at the State Normal College, Nashville, Tennessee; and letters concerning the legal and political career of Joseph Blance, husband of Josephine (West) Blance. Also contains patterns for weaving and newspaper clippings.

5652. JOHN SIDNEY WEST PAPERS, 1833 (1852-1860) 1861. 192 items. Gravel Hill (Buckingham County), Va.

Family and business correspondence of John Sidney West, a Virginia merchant and planter, partly concerning Buckingham Institute, a Virginia school for girls with which West was connected.

5653. THOMAS WEST ACCOUNT BOOK, 1754-1815. 1 vol. (60 pp.) Virginia.

Business accounts of Thomas West, containing records of tobacco shipped to England and sales of slaves.

5654. WEST VIRGINIA PAPERS, 1915. 1 item. (207 pp.).

Typed copy of revisions of that part of the West Virginia Code relating to the financing, location, construction, and maintenance of roads.

5655. WEST VIRGINIA. POCAHONTAS COUNTY PAPERS, 1857-1866. 1 item and 1 vol. Pocahontas County, W. Va.

Six pages from a record book of the post office at Edray, West Virginia, and a tax book for 1866.

5656. CHARLES DRAKE WESTCOTT PAPERS, 1925-1927. 5 items. Paris, France.

Clippings concerning the activities of Mrs. Charles Drake Westcott in the American Legion Auxiliary and in the Daughters of the American Revolution, and a letter of condolence, 1927, to Charles Drake Westcott on the death of his wife.

5657. WESTERN NORTH CAROLINA RAILROAD COMPANY PAPERS, 1882-1885. 1 vol. (144 pp.) Salisbury (Rowan County), N.C.

Treasurer's receipts.

5658. JOSEPH WESTMORE LEDGER, 1780-1784, 1864-1865. 1 vol. Edenton (Chowan County), N.C.

A greater portion of the ledger consists of the records of Joseph Westmore, trader and merchant, containing an inventory of the ships and cargoes at the dissolution of the firm of Joseph Westmore and William Savage in 1780; and records after 1784 of the coastwise trade from Edenton; Williamsburg and Petersburg, Virginia; and New York City, with names of brigs and schooners and mention of cargoes. In the last few pages, records were kept by an unidentified person for 1864-1865, concerning the spinning of wool and cotton.

5659. ABNER WETHINGTON PAPERS, 1867. 1 item. Jefferson County, Fla.

A contract between Wethington, owner of a plantation, and nineteen freedmen and freedwomen, stipulating the terms of labor to be performed.

5660. ELIJAH WETMORE PAPERS, 1777-1930. 524 items and 2 vols. Dansville (Livingston County), N.Y.

Miscellaneous papers, primarily of the Wetmore, Bentley, Smith, and Powers families of New York and Virginia, concerning farming and hunting in the 1860s and 1870s; affairs of W. A. Hoover and Company, manufacturers of lightning rods, New Lisbon, Ohio, 1871-1874; official business of Bethel Baptist Mariners Church of New York City, 1843-1846; copies of various orders, notices, and circular letters relating to the Confederate Army; a legal case, 1864, involving Frederick E. Sickels, inventor of a steam steering unit for ships; and genealogical research, 1923-1924, on the Lucas and Duckwall families of West Virginia. Also includes a facsimile letter, 1865, of Ulysses S. Grant thanking the citizens of Baltimore, Maryland, for the house, lot, and furnishings which they had given him, and five documents in Spanish relating to the territory of New Mexico in 1850.

5661. EDWARD MITCHELL WHALEY PAPERS, 1879-1915. 3 items. Edisto Island (Charleston County), S.C.

Papers of Edward Mitchell Whaley contain his reminiscences, including descriptions of his early schooling in Charleston, South Carolina; life as a student at the lyceum and university in Heidelberg and the University of Berlin; duels in which he engaged while he lived in Germany; a trip to Saint Petersburg while Francis W. Pickens of South Carolina was United States minister to Russia; running the Union blockade on his return trip to America after the beginning of the Civil War; service in the 1st South Carolina Regiment in the defense of Charleston, South Carolina, and in engagements at Averasboro and Bentonville, North Carolina, in 1865; guard duty at a house in or near

Greensboro, North Carolina, where Jefferson Davis and his staff lodged, 1865; and Whaley's life after the war as a cotton and rice planter. Also contains copies of obituaries of Edward Mitchell Whaley and his father, William Whaley, which appeared in the Charleston News and Courier.

5662.  RICHARD WHARTON PAPERS, 1711. 1 item. London, England.

A legal opinion about the title of Richard and Mary Wharton to property on Bishopsgate Street in London.

5663.  RICHARD WHATELY PAPERS, 1831. 1 item. Dublin, Ireland.

Letter, 1831, of Richard Whately, written shortly after he had been consecrated archbishop of Dublin, concerning his new position and the Reform Bill about which he had a proposal for the ministry in London.

5664.  LEMUEL C. WHEAT AND THOMAS C. HUNTER PAPERS, 1837 (1870-1876) 1897. 344 items. Enfield (Halifax County), N.C.

Correspondence between the Wheat and Hunter families, related through marriage. Included are correspondence of Lemuel C. Wheat, engineer of the Weldon Railroad, relating to early railroads in North Carolina, to politics, to the "unhealthy" climate of North Carolina, and to Reconstruction; letters from the Wheat girls, who attended female seminaries, concerning school life; letters from students at Davidson College, North Carolina, and Hagerstown Academy, Maryland; and a registration notice from the University of North Carolina, Chapel Hill.

5665.  PHILLIS WHEATLEY PAPERS, 1770. 1 item. Boston, Mass.

Letter of the poet Phillis Wheatley, while she was still a slave owned by the Wheatley family of Boston, Massachusetts, written for Nathaniel Wheatley, concerning a lawsuit.

5666.  ALBERT F. WHEATON DIARY, 1861. 1 vol. (147 pp.) North Branford (New Haven County), Conn.

Diary of a farmer concerning farm work, social life, and church services.

5667.  JOHN HILL WHEELER PAPERS, 1842-1852. 6 items. Beattie's Ford (Lincoln County), N.C.

Papers of author John Hill Wheeler contain letters to John Fanning Watson requesting information for Wheeler's book, Historical Sketches of North Carolina; lists of subscribers to the book; letter, 1852, from Wheeler to Benson J. Lossing concerning the Mecklenburg Declaration of Independence and the Edenton "Tea Party"; and a letter to Wheeler from Andrew Jackson, concerning the recent victory of the Democratic Party in the state and commenting on William A. Graham and Willie P. Mangum, United States senators from North Carolina.

5668.  JOSEPH WHEELER PAPERS, 1864 (1879-1899) 1903. 57 items. Wheeler (Lawrence County), Ala.

Correspondence of Joseph Wheeler (1836-1906), graduate of the United States Military Academy, West Point, New York, U. S. Army officer, lieutenant general in the Confederate Army, member of U. S. Congress, and major general in the U. S. Army during the Spanish-American War. Several letters contain correspondence concerning the Civil War, including general orders, refutation of charges that his command had impressed a citizen's mules, military telegrams, and a letter to General H. W. Halleck, May 20, 1865, telling of Wheeler's arrest and the refusal of Federal authorities to grant him a parole. Other letters contain reminiscences of the Civil War; routine communications written while a member of U. S. Congress; an article which Wheeler had promised to prepare; letters written from Manila, Philippine Islands; letters, 1888, to the editor of the Philadelphia News concerning an article about Wheeler; and one letter relative to his investments in the United States Steel Corporation.

5669.  RUSSELL WHEELER PAPERS, 1828-1843. 6 items. North Stonington (New London County), Conn.

Business letters of a merchant.

5670.  W. H. WHEELER PAPERS. 1 item. Middlesex County, Mass.

Reminiscence of the Civil War written by W. H. Wheeler, one of the five surviving officers of the 16th Massachusetts Regiment at the end of the war. Wheeler traces the career of the 16th Massachusetts from the Peninsular Campaign of 1862 through every major battle in which the Army of the Potomac was involved, except the battle of Antietam.

5671.  JOHN J. WHERRY PAPERS, 1819-1889. 321 items. New Orleans, La., and Hendersonville (Sumner County), Tenn.

Papers of John J. Wherry and his family contain letters, 1830s-1850s, to John J. Wherry concerning tobacco sales, business affairs, the Presbyterian Church in Hendersonville, Tennessee, and the severe financial difficulty of a relative; letters, 1861, from John M. Wherry, a soldier in the 1st Tennessee Regiment; and letters, in the 1880s, relating to John J. Wherry's claim for compensation for property confiscated by the Union Army during the Civil War. Papers also contain bills, notes, receipts, deeds, insurance policies, a subscription paper for the Hendersonville Presbyterian Church, and documents appointing Wheery a member of the

New Orleans and Lafayette Board of Tobacco Inspectors.

5672. F. H. WHITAKER PAPERS, 1786-1885. 53 items. Halifax County, N.C.

Papers of F. H. Whitaker and members of his family contain personal and business correspondence; legal papers and records pertaining to wills, estates, slave sales and purchases, land prices, personal debts, hunting, and personal affairs; and letters, 1864, of Lou Whitaker concerning life in the Confederate Army, effects of the war on civilians, and depredations by the Union army.

5673. JAMES WHITAKER PAPERS, 1848-1871. 8 items. Valley Town (Cherokee County), N.C.

Letters of a devout Baptist family containing some information on the spread of the denomination in western North Carolina.

5674. MATTHEW C. WHITAKER PAPERS, 1807-1830. 26 items. Halifax County, N.C.

Promissory notes, receipts, and miscellaneous papers of Matthew C. Whitaker.

5675. [SALLIE?] WHITAKER AND [ELLEN C.?] WHITAKER DIARY, ca. 1867-1868. 1 vol. Camden (Kershaw County), S.C.

Diary discusses personal, business, and agricultural affairs, particularly commodity prices, crops, and weather.

5676. ANDREW J. WHITE PAPERS, 1861-1864. 127 items. Campbellton (Campbell County, now Fulton County), Ga.

Civil War letters of Andrew J. White, a soldier in the 30th Georgia Regiment during the Civil War, concerning camp life, military hospitals, blockade runners, rumors of invasions at various places on the east coast, service at Savannah, Georgia, 1862-1863, in Mississippi, 1863, and in northern Georgia during the Atlanta Campaign.

5677. FRANK E. WHITE DIARY AND JOURNAL, 1864-1865. 2 vols. South Weymouth (Norfolk County), Mass.

Diary, 1864, of Frank E. White, lieutenant in the 4th New York Cavalry of the Union Army, beginning with accounts of camp life near City Point, Virginia, and dwelling on the winter, the flies, drawing of supplies, a trip to Winchester, Kentucky, where he was on duty for some time, and ending with an account of a trip home. The other volume, part being reminiscences and the remainder a diary, gives a long account of why he, a clerk in New York City, enlisted and what he did during the first part of his enlistment including his first experiences of combat.

5678. GEORGE MAWAMSIE WHITE PAPERS, 1875-1876. 1 vol. (8 pp.) [Salem (Taylor County), Fla?].

Volume containing watercolor sketches of Florida scenes.

5679. GILBERT CASE WHITE NOTEBOOKS, 1895-1896. 2 vols. Bethlehem (Northampton County), Pa.

Notebooks of a student at Lehigh University, Bethlehem, Pennsylvania, from courses in civil engineering and sanitary engineering.

5680. HENRY WHITE PAPERS, 1857-1863. 15 items. Baltimore, Md.

Routine business papers.

5681. HUGH LAWSON WHITE PAPERS, 1857-1863. 27 items. Knoxville (Knox County), Tenn.

Papers of Hugh Lawson White, United States senator from Tennessee, contain a letter, 1839, from White to Ephraim Hubbard Foster, concerning political issues of the day. Papers of Anne E. Peyton White relate for the most part to her autograph collection, including a letter, 1838, from J. G. Proud, Jr., enclosing a copy of his poem, "The Blind Mother"; poems by L. S. Buckingham, 1838; a letter, 1838, from John Sergeant containing an anecdote about Sir Walter Scott; and a letter, 1838, from Henry A. Wise with a story about King William IV of Great Britain. There is also a copy of an undated note from Benjamin Franklin to the Abbé de La Roche mentioning Madame Helvetius and Baron Turgot, the original of which is in the Bibliothèque Nationale.

5682. ISAIAH H. WHITE PAPERS, 1862-1865. 52 items. Richmond, Va.

The collection contains the military papers of Isaiah H. White, a physician in the Confederate Army, made up for the most part of orders and reports concerning White's work as surgeon at the military prison at Andersonville, Georgia, and as chief surgeon of hospitals attached to military prisons east of the Mississippi River.

5683. JOHN WHITE PAPERS, 1819-1828. 16 items. Baltimore, Md.

Papers of John White, cashier of the office of discount and deposit in the Baltimore branch of the Second Bank of the United States, concerning routine commerical transactions.

5684. JOHN WHITE RATION BOOK, 1778.
1 vol. (30 pp.) Georgia.

Ration book of the 4th Regiment of Continental Troops in Georgia, May-July, 1778, showing the names of the soldiers and the provisions issued to each.

5685. JOHN WHITE AND JOHN BOLLING DAYBOOKS, 1817-1848. 1 vol. Oxford (Granville County), N.C.

General mercantile accounts of the firm of White and Bolling.

5686. JOSIAH WHITE PAPERS, [1846?]. 1 vol. Philadelphia, Pa.

The collection contains a typescript copy of the autobiography of Josiah White, describing White's apprenticeship to a Philadelphia, Pennsylvania, hardware merchant; the management of White's hardware store in Philadelphia, ca. 1808; a trip to Georgia and White's opinion of slavery; the development of a waterpower site on the falls of the Schuylkill River, 1810-1819; development of the Lehigh Mine Company's anthracite coal lands, including the creation of the Lehigh Coal and Navigation Company in 1822 and the construction of the Lehigh Canal, 1827-1829; and the construction of the Delaware division of the Pennsylvania Canal, 1828-1832. Also contains a list of White's inventions.

5687. MRS. L. WHITE PAPERS, 1861. 1 item. Malone (Franklin County), N.Y.

Letter from Mrs. L. White to her children in the South commenting on Northern reaction to the Civil War and the disruption of mail service.

5688. MARY ANN WHITE PAPERS, 1820-1892. 40 items. Montpelier (Scotland County), N.C.

Papers of the White family contain letters in the 1820s from Greenock, Scotland, describing local conditions and family affairs; letters, 1865, from Canada commenting on the fate of the Confederacy and the rumors that Robert E. Lee and Jefferson Davis would flee to Canada and take prominent places in Canadian military and political life; and family letters to Mary Ann White from friends and relatives in Richmond County, North Carolina.

5689. NATHAN SMITH WHITE PAPERS, 1821-1842. 52 items. Charles Town (Jefferson County), W. Va.

Papers of Nathan Smith White, an attorney, contain letters concerning family affairs, local politics, religious revivals, economic conditions, tobacco culture, and courtship practices. There are also a report card from White's days as a student at the College of New Jersey and a rough draft of a speech.

5690. THOMAS WHITE, JR., PAPERS, 1829-1885. 223 items. Louisburg (Franklin County), N.C.

Correspondence and papers of Thomas White, Jr. (d. 1904), a general merchant, railway agent, and captain in the Confederate Army. Included are letters of application and recommendation for employment; descriptions of various resorts, including White Sulphur Springs, West Virginia, and Jones Spring, Virginia, and Shocco Springs, North Carolina; army forage requisition orders; and a few letters written while a student at the University of North Carolina, Chapel Hill, North Carolina, 1845-1858.

5691. THOMAS WILLIS WHITE PAPERS, 1835-1842. 50 items. Richmond, Va.

Letters of Thomas Willis White, founder and editor of the Southern Literary Messenger, to Lucian Minor, legal scholar, temperance advocate, and editorial advisor to the Messenger, concerning editorial policy; articles, reviews, and contributors; and the perennial financial difficulties of the periodical.

5692. W. A. WHITE PAPERS, 1859-1904. 22 items and 1 vol. Little River (Caldwell County), N.C.

Legal documents, summonses, and receipts relating to W. A. White, and a record book, 1888-1900, kept by White as justice of the peace.

5693. WALTER C. WHITE PAPERS, 1836-1857. 8 items. New Orleans, La.

Letters of Walter C. White, banking agent for Merle & Company of New Orleans, Louisiana, relating largely to his business in the Republic of Texas.

5694. WALTER STUART WHITE PAPERS, 1892. 1 item. Durham, England.

Letter of Walter Stuart White, genealogist, relating to his work, Register Book of the Christenings, Weddings, and Burials, within the Parish of Leyland, in the County of Lancaster, 1653-1710 (Manchester: 1890).

5695. WILLIAM F. WHITE PAPERS, 1862-1864. 1 vol. Mason (Effingham County County), Ill.

Diary of William F. White concerning his service in the 38th Illinois Regiment in Tennessee, 1862-1863, for the most part describing day-to-day activities in camp and on the march, including copies of a report by Lieutenant Colonel Daniel H. Gilmer and orders by Colonel William P. Carlin detailing the activities of the regiment; and White's service in the 1st Battalion of the Invalid Corps in Kentucky, Ohio, and Washington, D.C., mainly concerning guard duty at prisons.

5696. WILLIAM HENRY WHITE PAPERS, 1877-1893. 14 items. Norfolk (Norfolk County), Va.

Letters to William Henry White, an attorney, dealing with land sales, settlement of estates, the Virginia Historical Society, the Norfolk and North Carolina Canal Company, and the Democratic Party.

5697. WHITE AND BURWELL ACCOUNT BOOK, 1866-1867. 1 vol. (100 pp.) Manson (Warren County), N.C.

Records of a general mercantile firm.

5698. WHITE POST, VIRGINIA, POST OFFICE RECORD BOOK, 1849-1850. 1 vol. (140 pp.) White Post (Clarke County), Va.

Accounts of postage paid by individuals for various types of mail.

5699. GEORGE WHITEFIELD PAPERS, 1750-1759. 3 items. London, England.

Papers of George Whitefield, a leading Methodist clergyman and evangelist, contain a letter, 1750, from Whitefield discussing religious affairs in Georgia and South Carolina, the activities of James Habersham, and preaching missions to Negroes; a letter, 1759, from Whitefield to John Ryland, praising a young man for his Christian dedication; and a short commentary on an unidentified passage from the Bible.

5700. FLOYD L. WHITEHEAD PAPERS, 1814-1863. 71 items and 2 vols. Nelson County, Va.

Invoices, bills, and receipts of Floyd L. Whitehead, a slave trader, and scattered militia and tax records kept by a sheriff of Nelson County, Virginia. Volumes include an account book kept by Floyd L. Whitehead and Ralph W. Lofftus in their slave trading business, giving prices of slaves, and a volume containing newspaper clippings relating to the Whigs, Henry Clay, and the tariff.

5701. JAMES A. WHITEHEAD PAPERS, 1860-1861. 15 items. Enfield (Halifax County), N.C.

Letters from James A. Whitehead, as a student at Battleboro, North Carolina, 1860, and later as a Confederate volunteer, to his sister. The letters depict the initial enthusiasm of the soldiers at the outbreak of the Civil War, the routine of camp life, army food, and discipline.

5702. SWEPSON WHITEHEAD PAPERS, 1817-1833. 3 items. Portsmouth (Norfolk County), Va.

Business correspondence of Swepson Whitehead, apparently a lumber dealer, referring to the lumber business, land speculation, and a lawsuit to recover slaves.

5703. WILLIAMSON WHITEHEAD DIARY, 1861-1864. 1 vol. (56 pp.) Fayetteville (Cumberland County), N.C., and Virginia.

Typescript copy of the Civil War diary of Williamson Whitehead, apparently a soldier in the 1st North Carolina Regiment, concerning the capture of Fort Hatteras by Union forces; regimental elections; the regiment's welcome home, 1861; and prices in Richmond, 1864.

5704. PAMELIA (HARRISON) WHITELAW PAPERS, 1855 (1870-1880) 1923. 126 items. Madison County, Va.

Personal and family correspondence of Pamelia (Harrison) Whitelaw with friends and relatives in Mississippi, Missouri, Texas, and Virginia. There are references to social and economic affairs, 1855-1923. A few letters concern the Civil War.

5705. MOSES B. WHITENER DAYBOOK, 1853-1881. 1 vol. (136 pp.) Jacob's Fork (Catawba County), N.C.

Record book, apparently of a sawmill.

5706. JOHN W. WHITFIELD PAPERS, 1851 (1855-1863) 1901. 43 items. Nash County, N.C.

Personal and Civil War letters from John W. Whitfield, in Confederate service around Wilmington, North Carolina, and Richmond, Virginia, commenting briefly on troop movements, army health, and scarcity of food.

5707. WILLIAM WHITFIELD PAPERS, 1766-1832. 6 items. Duplin County and Halifax County, N.C.

Land deeds of William Whitfield and his son Needham.

5708. WILLIAM AIREY WHITFIELD PAPERS, 1922-1967. 191 items. Asheville (Buncombe County), N.C.

Letters concerned with sundials which William A. Whitfield made for various people, including a list of the locations of some of his sundials, photographs and drawings of his sundials, and printed articles, and advertisements about sundials.

5709. JOHN N. WHITFORD PAPERS, 1829 (1860-1904) 1921. 988 items and 23 vols. New Bern (Craven County), and Pollocksville (Jones County), N C.

Papers of John N. Whitford, commander of the 67th North Carolina Regiment during the Civil War, cotton planter, and state senator, contain contracts for the hire of slaves in the 1850s; reports of Mary E. Williamson and Caroline Williamson at school in Oxford, North Carolina; accounts of F. T. Williamson, Mary E. Williamson, and Caroline Williamson with their guardian, William Foy; fire insurance policies; papers relating to suits involving John N. Whitford; miscellaneous military papers, for the most part related to the service of John N. Whitford in the Confederate Army; contracts between Whitford and freedmen; a letter to Whitford from a former slave; miscellaneous land surveys and papers related to land transactions, household accounts, bills and receipts, and legal papers; handbills for Whitford's campaign for the state senate in 1888; papers and letters related to the breeding of horses; tax lists for the lower Black River district, New Hanover County, North Carolina; records of tax delinquents; and the wills of John N. Whitford and Mary E. (Williamson) Whitford. Volumes include a tax book for New Bern, North Carolina, 1856; account books; and memorandum books. There is printed material on the Farmers' Alliance in North Carolina and Virginia, the Knights of Honor, and the Royal Arcanum.

5710. DANIEL POWERS WHITING PAPERS, ca. 1847. 5 items. Texas and Mexico.

Lithographs of scenes from Zachary Taylor's campaign during the Mexican War which were reproduced from drawings by Daniel Powers Whiting, a captain in the 7th United States Infantry Regiment.

5711. ELLEN MARR WHITING PAPERS, 1857-1859. 1 vol. Alexandria (Arlington County), Va.

Volume contains poetry by Ellen Marr Whiting and copies of poems by many other poets.

5712. WILLIAM HENRY CHASE WHITING PAPERS, 1865. 1 item. Biloxi (Harrison County), Miss.

Letter to William Henry Chase Whiting, Confederate general, from Lieutenant John Davenport concerning the Union attack on Fort Fisher, North Carolina, with a "powder boat," in 1864. Whiting's answer appears on the verso of the note.

5713. ELIZA WHITNER PAPERS, 1858-1865. 30 items. Catawba County, N.C.

Letters to Eliza Whitner from her cousins in the Confederate Army, describing camp life in North Carolina and Virginia, and a battle near Washington, North Carolina, in 1863.

5714. ELI WHITNEY PAPERS, 1818. 1 item. New Haven (New Haven County), Conn.

Letter from Eli Whitney to William Lee, second auditor of the United States Treasury Department, concerning a remittance on Whitney's contract for manufacturing arms.

5715. HENRY B. WHITNEY DIARY, 1862-1865. 3 vols. Pulaski (Oswego County), N.Y.

The diary of Henry B. Whitney, a soldier in the 110th New York Regiment during the Civil War, concerns camp life; religion in the army; the participation of the 110th Regiment in the siege of Port Hudson, 1863; and Whitney's service as a guard at Fort Jefferson, a prison for Confederates in the Dry Tortugas, Florida, 1864, including a description of the arrival of four civilian prisoners convicted of conspiring to assassinate President Abraham Lincoln: Samuel Arnold, Dr. Samuel Mudd, Michael O'Laughlin, and Edward Spangler.

5716. NATHAN C. WHITSTONE PAPERS, 1851-1854. 3 items. Columbia (Richland County), S.C.

Letters to Nathan C. Whitstone dealing with college life, camp meetings; and the secession movement in 1851.

5717. JOHN GREENLEAF WHITTIER PAPERS, 1870-1958. 32 items. Amesbury and Danvers (Essex County), Mass.

The papers of John Greenleaf Whittier, American poet, contain a letter by Whittier identifying the "guest" in the poem "Snowbound" as Harriet Livermore; letters to Whittier from P. H. Hayne and Mary M. Hayne relating primarily to personal and literary affairs, with some mention of politics, religion, and North-South relations; and a typescript copy of a portion of John C. Hepler's introduction to his edition of Whittier's poems. Many of the items in this collection are photocopies.

5718. JAMES M. WHITTLE PAPERS, 1843-1883. 28 items. Pittsylvania County, Va.

Letters to James M. Whittle, attorney and member of the Virginia senate, dealing with legal matters, the settlement of estates, and the value and sale of slaves.

5719.  R. WHITTLESEY PAPERS, 1826. 1 item. Bedford County, Tenn.

Letter from R. Whittlesey describing business and cultural conditions in Tennessee and reporting the duel between Sam Houston and William White.

5720.  JAMES HOWARD WHITTY PAPERS, 1792-1943. 12,271 items and 4 vols. Richmond, Va.

Papers of James Howard Whitty, author and authority on the life and work of Edgar Allan Poe, contain correspondence relating to Whitty's work as organizer and first president of the Edgar Allan Poe shrine in Richmond, Virginia, and to Whitty's quarrel with the directors of the shrine in 1924; material on the history of Richmond, Virginia; business correspondence pertaining to Whitty's work on the staff of the Richmond Times; notes on and copies of correspondence of John Randolph of Roanoke, 1814-1816; notes on and copies of letters from John Charles Frémont to Joel R. Poinsett, 1838; copies of a large number of letters by Edgar Allan Poe and members of his family; documents concerning the events surrounding Poe's death; a large volume of correspondence with other Poe scholars, particularly George E. Woodberry, Mary E. Phillips, and Thomas Ollive Mabbott; and notes made by Whitty, including material for a complete Poe bibliography, and rough drafts of Whitty's writings on Poe, Virginia copyrights, the history of Richmond, and John Charles Frémont. There are also pictures, including portraits of Poe and his family, and pictures of the places where Poe lived and the museums and shrines dedicated to him; clippings, some of which are contained in scrapbooks, of articles on Poe, 1900-1935; printed material, including reviews, copies of sections of books, publication notices, and advertisements; and a volume containing the accounts of a bookseller, 1929-1936.

5721.  JOHN WICKHAM PAPERS, 1805. 1 item. [Richmond, Va.?]

Letter of John Wickham (1763-1839) concerning legal matters.

5722.  MICHAEL WIENER PAPERS, 1851-1908. 1,014 items and 14 vols. Burkittsville (Frederick County), Md.

Business correspondence, papers, and account books of Michael Wiener, proprietor of a tannery, and of his son, Henry M. Wiener, justice of the peace, consisting largely of orders, invoices, receipts, and accounts relating to the hide and leather business, and summonses to appear in court. Tannery records include account books, 1851-1888; a bark book, 1853-1871; daybooks, 1870-1887; and ledgers, 1865-1872. There is also an account book of a tavern, 1863-1865. A letter from Dr. William Osler concerns tuberculosis.

5723.  LOUIS TRESEVANT WIGFALL PAPERS, 1862. 1 item. Galveston (Galveston County), Tex.

Letter from General John Bell Hood to Louis Tresevant Wigfall (1816-1874), U. S. senator and brigadier general in the Confederate Army, concerning uniforms for Texas troops and the method of selecting company officers.

5724.  ELIZABETH S. WIGGINS PAPERS, 1860-1865. 5 items. DeKalb County, Ga.

Personal letters from Elizabeth S. Wiggins to her mother, concerning family affairs, her sons in the Confederate Army, refugees in Atlanta and the approach of Union troops, and commodity prices.

5725.  SAMUEL WILBERFORCE PAPERS, 1790-1872. 35 items. Oxford and Winchester, England.

Correspondence of Samuel Wilberforce (1805-1873), bishop of Oxford and of Winchester, relating primarily to missionary activities of the Church of England in East Africa and various British colonies. Correspondence pertaining to East Africa includes letters from John William Colenso, bishop of Natal, discussing the status of the Anglican church in Natal, his attempts to acquire financial aid, the refusal of the Society for the Propagation of the Gospel to provide aid for white residents, difficulties between the governor of Natal and his council, and injustices to the Kaffirs. A letter (17 pp.), 1860, from Christopher Palmer Rigby, British army officer, discusses economic and social conditions in Zanzibar, the slave trade there in 1859, French activities on the island, the depopulation of the adjacent African coast by slaving expeditions, British naval actions against slavers, and recent ventures into the interior. Letters, 1859-1861, from Charles Frederick Mackenzie, bishop of Central Africa, concern his preparations for his African work and his travels in England on behalf of missions, plans for a mission in the Shire River region and the selection of a site, the assistance of David Livingstone, the journey to the mission site, the freeing by Livingstone and Sir John Kirk of slaves being transported to market, the extent to which he (Mackenzie) should go in defense of Africans under his charge from the depredation of slavers and other tribes, his defense of the Manganja from the Ajawa tribesmen, and his hopes of repairing relations with the Ajawa. Contemporary copies of letters, 1859-1866, of David Livingstone describe the ascent of the Zambezi River to Tete (Mozambique), Mackenzie's destruction of a hostile village, events leading to the death of Mackenzie in 1862, the Shire country as the best strategic location for missions, and the displeasure of local Portuguese toward their government's allowance of British activity in Mozambique. A letter of

1862, describes the Shire region, the condition of the African population, the decision of Mackenzie to fight the Ajawa, the faults of Magomero as a mission site, and health conditions in that region. Correspondence of Wilberforce and Lord John Russell, foreign secretary, concern the decision to withdraw Livingstone's expedition and future help to missions from the British navy.

Other correspondence includes a letter, 1857, from Henry Labouchere, colonial secretary, concerning the lack of good clergymen in the West Indies and arrangements for three new bishoprics in New Zealand; a letter, 1860, commenting on the weak condition of the church in Tasmania; a letter, 1864, from Walter Chambers, describing mission work in Sarawak; letters, 1832 and 1833, pertaining to Wilberforce's attempts to unite the Society for the Propagation of the Gospel with the Church Missionary Society; a letter, 1790, probably from Thomas Clarkson, relating to activity in Parliament for the suppression of the slave trade; a memorandum, 1860, of Sir James Brooke, rajah of Sarawak, discussing his foreign policy toward England; and a letter, 1869, of Sir Samuel White Baker regarding his expedition on the White Nile to check the slave trade, with details of his plans to halt the slave trade, plans for a parental government in the Sudan, and lists of his forces.

5726. WILLIAM WILBERFORCE PAPERS, 1782-1833. 584 items. London, England.

Political and personal correspondence of William Wilberforce (1759-1833), member of the House of Commons. Many letters relate to his leadership in the movement for the abolition of the slave trade, discussing the evils of the slave trade; the slave trade in Dutch, English, French, Portuguese, and Spanish colonies; slavery, especially in the West Indies; the composition and distribution of pamphlets on the slave trade; the attendance of Thomas Clarkson at the Congress of Vienna against Wilberforce's advice; William Pitt's (1759-1806) support of the abolition movement; efforts to interest the Roman Catholic Church in the abolition cause; the determination as to whether abolition could be enforced; and noted English and French leaders and their position on the abolition question. Other topics discussed include the African Institute; agriculture; economic panic among farmers, 1830; the Corn Laws; American Friends; the Treaty of Amiens; the Army Training Bill; the Waterloo campaign; conditions in New South Wales, Australia; British relations with Austria, Brazil, France, Netherlands, Portugal, Spain, the United States, and the Vatican; economic conditions in Austria; Baptists; Baptist missions in India; the Church of England in England, Ireland and other British colonies; patronage and tithes of the Church of England; the Methodist Church; the Moravians; the Church Missionary Society; the Church of Scotland; Roman Catholicism in Ireland; the Roman Catholic Question and efforts to repeal disabilities against Catholics; efforts of Anglican clergymen to convert Catholics in Ireland; the Blagdon Affair; censorship of books; emigration to Canada; the Congress of Vienna; the coal trade; economic conditions in England and Scotland; education; St. David's College, South Wales; politics and government in England, France, Ireland, Jamaica, Sierra Leone, Trinidad, and Venezuela; elections; French colonies; free trade versus protection; the French Revolution; Greek Independence; Haiti; South Africa; the Society of Friends; labor; landlords and tenants; manufacturers in Scotland; the textile industry; the Royal Navy; Negro officers in the Royal Navy; parliamentary reform; prisons; need to reform the penal code; the use of capital punishment; the poor laws and poor relief; Socinianism; the New Rupture Society; personal matters including Wilberforce's failing health; and charities, especially the Bible Society. There is also a pamphlet entitled "House of Protection for the Maintenance and Instruction of Girls of Good Character."

5727. WILBERFOSS, ENGLAND, ACCOUNTS, 1799-1829. 1 vol. (244 pp.) Wilberfoss, Yorkshire, England.

Financial accounts of the administration of the poor laws in Wilberfoss, England, containing semi-annual records of the disbursements by the overseers of the poor, including the date, amount, and purpose of each expenditure and the names of each recipient; and the annual records of assessments against citizens who were taxed for poor relief including names, valuation and payments of each taxpayer. Also included are a note on the history of the volume by Gerald Robert Owst, professor of education in the University of Cambridge, Cambridge, England; and a letter and obituaries of John Bell (d. 1939), millowner and former overseer for the parish.

5728. JOHN D. WILBORN DAYBOOK, 1871-1877. 1 vol. (214 pp.) Hillsborough (Orange County), N.C.

Accounts of a general merchant.

5729. GEORGE WILBRAHAM PAPERS, 1834. 1 item. Delamere House, Cheshire, England.

Letter from George Wilbraham (1779-1852), member of Parliment, concerning interest in reform and a speaking engagement.

5730. AARON WILBUR PAPERS, 1837-1919. 152 items. Savannah, Ga.

Papers of Aaron Wilbur (1821-1869), businessman, include letters pertaining to cotton transactions during the Civil War; letters concerning Wilbur's insurance business; letters from Mrs. Wilbur describing social life and customs in Marietta, Griffin,

Americus, and Savannah (Georgia), and trips to Washington, D.C., Philadelphia (Pennsylvania), Germany and Italy; correspondence between Mrs. Wilbur and J. Ringgold McCay regarding litigation to recover commissions due Wilbur; and three notebooks containing genealogical information. Many of the papers relating to the cotton claims litigation are copies.

5731. JEREMIAH WILBUR PAPERS, 1817-1879. 1,147 items and 2 vols. New York, N.Y.

Papers of Jeremiah Wilbur, commission merchant dealing in stocks and bonds, wholesale merchandise, tobacco, coal, gold, and mercury; and speculator in land, copper, and mica mining. Correspondence concerns the founding and establishment of the Second Presbyterian Church of West Chester, New York, 1854; a comparison of the "old style" Presbyterian church with the Church of England; the use of guano for fertilizer; the impeachment proceedings against Andrew Johnson; Reconstruction politics; freedmen; Ulysses S. Grant; business and economic conditions during Reconstruction; Atlantic and California Railroad Bill No. 2, 1869; gold currency; typhoid in New York City, 1869; a trip from Charleston, South Carolina, to Savannah, Georgia, and descriptions of the two cities; the raising of a Confederate gunboat from Charleston harbor; smallpox in Philadelphia, Pennsylvania, 1872; slight business depression in England; business affairs of General Franz Sigel; the American branch of the Evangelical Alliance; United States public debt laws, 1864-1866; spinal meningitis in Saint Louis, Missouri, 1873; high wages and a rise in trade in Bristol, England, 1873; criticism of church organization; temperance; Paris, France; tobacco trade in New York; real estate in Michigan; and education, with references to Washington and Jefferson College, (Washington, Pennsylvania), Rutgers College (Brunswick, New Jersey), Yale University (New Haven, Connecticut), Checker Military Academy, Union College, and Auburn Seminary. Also included are the constitution of the Evangelical Society; records of the early church meetings of the Second Presbyterian Church; land deeds and indentures; fire insurance policies of the Home Insurance Company, 1858, and of the Dutchess County Mutual Insurance Company, 1859; bills and receipts, including some relating to the buying and selling of gold; an extract from the Royal Cornwall Gazette describing preparation of clay for china; copies of legal documents and papers pertaining to Charles Edwards (1797-1868) and his role as counsel for the British owners of the ship Hiawatha, siezed for blockade-running, in a prize case, 1862, before the United States Supreme Court; a ledger, 1855-1872; and a list of Jeremiah Wilbur's property, 1846.

5732. WALTER H. WILCOX PAPERS, 1924. 1 item. Woburn (Middlesex County), Mass.

Letter to Walter H. Wilcox from Julian S. Carr (d. 1924) concerning his recent tonsillectomy, a month before his death.

5733. JOHN WALKER WILDE ALBUM, 1824-1856. 1 vol. (41 pp.) San Francisco, Calif.

Album containing poems by John Walker Wilde.

5734. RICHARD HENRY WILDE PAPERS, 1812-1885. 26 items and 1 vol. Augusta (Richmond County), Ga.

Papers of Richard Henry Wilde (1789-1847), member of Congress, poet and literary scholar, and professor of law at the University of Louisiana (now Tulane University), New Orleans, Louisiana. Correspondence pertains to personal affairs, political concerns, including the negotiations of John Forsyth for the cession of Florida; legal matters; and American sculpture. There are also two poems by Wilde. A volume contains poems by Wilde and others, including several translations by Wilde from the Italian.

5735. BRYANT WILDER PAPERS, 1854-1907. 36 items. Franklin County, N.C.

Personal and business papers of Bryant Wilder, Confederate soldier and farmer, including items pertaining to North Carolina politics and references to Louisburg Male Academy, Louisburg, North Carolina.

5736. HENRY ARTHUR JOHN WILDER SCRAPBOOK, 1819-1929. 1 vol. (208 pp.) London, England.

Personal letters of notable people from Britain, United States, France, Germany, and elsewhere, with occasional reference to British social life and politics, Oxford and Cambridge universities, and Eton College. Included is a letter from Thomas Clarkson, stating that Lord Metcalfe, provisional governor of Canada, would assist fugitive slaves from the United States, and arguing against the flogging of British seamen and the operation of crimping houses.

5737. CALVIN HENDERSON WILEY PAPERS, 1853-1862. 11 items and 1 vol. Guilford County, N.C.

Papers of Calvin Henderson Wiley (1819-1887), lawyer, North Carolina legislator, 1850-1852, superintendent of common schools, editor of the North Carolina Journal of Education, and Presbyterian minister. Included are two questionnaires pertaining to the North Carolina public school system and teachers; a prospectus of the North Carolina

*Presbyterian*; an agreement made by Wiley to furnish nitre to the Confederate government; letters to David Settle Reid, governor of North Carolina, 1848-1852, discussing a new edition of the laws relating to common schools, a meeting with the trustees of Normal College, and textbooks; and a volume of notes, 1852-1853, on the common schools of twenty-six counties in North Carolina.

5738. ROBERT H. WILEY PAPERS, 1862-1865. 15 items. Springwater (Livingston County), N.Y.

Correspondence of Robert H. Wiley, Union officer in the 104th New York Regiment, with members of his family discussing family affairs; life in Livingston County, New York; recruiting; and Washington, D. C., during the Civil War.

5739. JOHN WILFONG PAPERS, 1809-1903. 25 items. Wilfong Mills (Lincoln County), N.C.

Miscellaneous papers relating to John Wilfong and others including land deeds; legal statement concerning the division of forty-one slaves among the heirs of Lemuel Ingram; letters and poems dealing with the death of Wilfong's daughter, Caroline (Wilfong) Bobo; several April Fool's Day poems; three sketches discussing the Wilfong genealogy; and a letter pertaining to the Shuford family. Letters from Confederate soldiers discuss several North Carolina regiments and generals, Governor Zebulon Baird Vance, the expedition of Philip Sheridan into the Shenandoah Valley, casualties, Confederate troop movements, Federal prisoners, depredations by Union troops, the fatal wounding of Milton Wilfong in the battle of Spottsylvania Courthouse, and the battles of Lynchburg, White House, and Winchester, Virginia.

5740. ARCHIBALD WILKERSON PAPERS, 1779 (1860-1910) 1933. 1,040 items and 8 vols. Maxton (Robeson County), N.C.

Papers relating to the Wilkerson (Wilkinson, Wilkison) family of North Carolina, Florida, Mississippi, and Texas. Personal correspondence includes antebellum letters discussing student life at Jefferson Medical College; several Civil War letters; letters, 1881-1901, from Duncan McMillan, Florida legislator, bookkeeper, and treasurer of Gadsden County, concerning preachers and religion, social life and customs, Florida politics, the tobacco industry in Quincy (Florida), and crimes, including murders and lynchings; letters discussing crime and tornadoes in Mississippi, and travel in the United States; and letters concerning North Carolina politics in the 20th century. Among the legal papers are land grants, a will and inventory of the estate of Samuel Brown, and a court order designating Archibald Wilkinson as road overseer. Also included are bills and receipts; account books; a scrapbook of recipes and household hints; memorandum books; a time book; and a fragment of a printed work entitled The Trial of Mrs. Ann K. Simpson.

5741. JAMES KING WILKERSON PAPERS, 1820-1929. 822 items and 74 vols. Oxford (Granville County), N.C.

Family correspondence and papers of James King Wilkerson, son of Alexander H. and Mary Ann Wilkerson, farmer, and member of Company K, 55th North Carolina Regiment, C.S.A. Included are letters from Confederate soldiers; references to the C.S.S. *Virginia*; descriptions of Confederate marches; two issues of the *Gazette* of Berea, Granville County, North Carolina, 1876; letters from James K. Wilkerson relative to crops, his Civil War services around Petersburg, Virginia, and his stay in the General Hospital at Greensboro, North Carolina; a number of almanacs which James K. Wilkerson used as diaries; two copybooks; correspondence of Lillie Wilkerson and Luther Wilkerson, children of James K. Wilkerson, discussing social life and customs, illnesses and hospitals, employment, and personal matters; and several letters from a soldier in France during World War I.

5742. EDMUND WILKINS AND WILLIAM W. WILKINS ACCOUNTS, 1824-1866. 4 vols. Northampton County, Va.

Fee book, 1824-1828, and estate book, 1843-1866, of Edmund Wilkins, lawyer, the latter containing accounts of the estates of John L. Wilkins and R. A. Broadnax, and of the trusteeship of William F. Dandridge and Susan C. Dandridge; and physician's accounts, 1829-1837, of William W. Wilkins containing records of visits to patients, medicine prescribed, and fees and payments.

5743. HENRY L. WILKINS PAPERS, 1843-1899. 14 items. Lawrenceville (Brunswick County), Va.

Correspondence and bills of Henry L. Wilkins dealing with the payment of personal debts and the sale of land.

5744. JOHN DARRAGH WILKINS PAPERS, 1858-1869. 22 items. Washington, D.C.

Letters of John Darragh Wilkins (1822-1900), U. S. Army officer, to his wife discussing living conditions on post at Albuquerque, New Mexico; camp life, the weather, and other routine concerns at Newport Barracks, Kentucky; conditions on post at Dahlonega, Georgia; deplorable conditions of the Georgia roads and of the U. S. Mint; political views of citizens of Mobile, Alabama, and economic conditions there; and officer's cottages at Fort Macon, North Carolina. A sketchbook contains drawings relating to the Civil War, including sketches of Wilkins's fellow officers, Burnside's Bridge at Antietam, a deserter at Fredericksburg, and a caricature of Horace Greeley after the 1872 election. There are also sketches of Captain Henry Wirz mistreating prisoners at Andersonville, and of escapees being chased by hounds and given refuge by a Negro woman in a log cabin.

5745. SIDNEY W. WILKINSON PAPERS, 1880-1912. 89 items and 7 vols. Edith (Catawba County), N.C.

Correspondence and legal papers of Sidney W. Wilkinson, farmer and justice of the peace. Volumes consist of a book of sermons, 1879-1893; civil and criminal dockets, 1879-1916, of cases tried before Wilkinson; a diary and account book, 1880-1886, giving an account of small farm operations; and a record, 1884-1895, of the Hopewell Church (Methodist Episcopal Church, South) of Catawba County containing Sunday school records, library lending records, and minutes of church meetings.

5746. JOHN WILKS PAPERS, 1830-1840. 7 items. London, England.

Letters to John Wilks (ca. 1765-1854), member of Parliament and honorary secretary of the Protestant Society for the Protection of Religious Freedom, consisting of a letter, 1830, from Sir Robert Peel, Second Baronet, assuring Wilks that there would be no interference with the election in Boston, Lincolnshire, in which Wilks was standing for the House of Commons; letter, 1834, from Charles Grey, Second Earl Grey, thanking Wilks for sending an address from a congregation of Independent Dissenters in York; letters, 1839-1840, from Henry Richard Vassall Fox, Third Baron Holland, concerning the responsibility for the appointment of magistrates, the likelihood of a dissolution of Commons, and the stand taken by the Protestant Society for upholding liberty of conscience advocated by John Locke; letter, 1840, from Dudley Coutts Stuart requesting a donation for relief for Polish refugees; and a letter from Edward John Stanley, Second Baron Stanley of Alderley, confirming a minor appointment.

5747. HENRY WILLARD PAPERS, 1820-1850. 14 items. Troy (Rensselaer County), N.Y.

Personal correspondence of the Willard family, concerning Mrs. Almira Barnes's distress over the early marriage of her son; Clarence Willard's journey from Troy to a school in New Haven, Connecticut; Henry Willard's student days at Dartmouth College, Hanover, New Hampshire; Laura Barnes Willard's visit to New Haven; and Eugene Bitely's journey from Troy to Paw Paw, Michigan; travel by stagecoach; internal improvements; insurance claims; Berlin, Connecticut; and personal matters.

5748. S. G. WILLARD PAPERS, 1800-1914. 490 items. Colchester (New London County), Conn.

Personal correspondence of S. G. Willard, pastor of the First Congregational Church in Colchester, and of his family, concerning family matters; church repairs; the Sunday school; women's projects; philanthropy; student life and studies at Yale College, New Haven, Connecticut, and at Smith College, Northampton, Massachusetts; education in Connecticut; and patients at the mental hospital at Middletown, Connecticut.

5749. [MARY FLORENCE WILLCOMB?] RECIPE BOOK, [1855?]. 1 vol. (6 pp.) [New York, N.Y.?]

Recipe book.

5750. FRED WILLCOX PAPERS. 1 item. Florence (Florence County), S.C.

Essay by Fred Willcox, attorney, entitled "North Carolina's Part in the French and Indian War."

5751. JAMES M. WILLCOX PAPERS, 1831-1871. 328 items. "Buckland," Charles City County, Va.

Letters and papers of the Willcox and Lamb families, united by the marriage of James M. Willcox (b. 1804) and Mary Ann S. Lamb, centering around the life of James M. Willcox, successful planter and member of the Virginia House of Delegates and affording an excellent record of farming operations and family ties during the late antebellum Civil War, and Reconstruction periods. The letters for 1831-1839 consist chiefly of correspondence of Dr. John Ferguson Lamb, a physician at Frankford, then a suburb of Philadelphia, Pennsylvania, and his daughter, Mary Ann S. (Lamb) Willcox, and concern social life in Charles City County; horse racing including the performance of William Ranson Johnson's horse, Arietta; Nat Turner's activities; the condition of Thomas Jefferson's estate, Monticello; modes of travel; and the outbreak of cholera in Norfolk, Virginia. The letters from James M. Willcox deal with his children; the operation of his two plantations, "Peace Hill" and "Buckland"; the effects of the Civil War on planting; "Yankee" plundering in eastern Virginia; and political affairs of the Radicals during Reconstruction. The Civil War letters from Walter A. Rorer, Confederate soldier in the 20th Mississippi Regiment, give detailed descriptions of camp life, campaigns, the spirit of the men, clothing, food, the defense of Vicksburg, 1863, and a battle near Kenesaw Mountain, Georgia, 1864. Letters from Eliza C. Rives, a widow, describe her efforts to support her children and aged mother by operating a tobacco farm after the war. Also included are letters from Elizabeth B. Towns, a cousin, and from Mary B. Rodney, governess at Westover plantation.

5752. JOHN WILLCOX PAPERS, 1779. 1 item. Moore County, N.C.

Letter from Joseph Morris to John Willcox, pioneer in the coal and iron industry, concerning adjustments in a debt owed Morris because of the depreciation of Continental money.

5753. W. M. WILLCOX PAPERS, 1861. 2 items. De Witt (Arkansas County), Ark.

Letter from W. M. Willcox to his brother in North Carolina discussing secession and his view that South Carolina had made a hasty decision; the Unionist views of his brother; secession sentiment in North Carolina; the presidential election of 1860; and abolitionists.

5754. HENRY WILLEY PAPERS, 1839-1961. 16 items and 12 vols. Weymouth (Norfolk County), Mass.

Papers of Henry Willey (1824-1897), teacher, lawyer, and journalist, principally relating to his avocation in the field of lichenology, including letters concerning the death of Edward Tuckerman, also a lichenologist; articles by and about Tuckerman from various journals; two letters addressed to Charles James Sprague; a reprint of the preface to the edition of Tuckerman's lichenological papers compiled by William L. Culberson; manuscript of Willey's revision of Synopsis of the Genus Arthonia and an index compiled by Culberson; manuscript drafts of books and articles by Willey; and a catalog of the works on lichens in Willey's library.

5755. WAITMAN THOMAS WILLEY PAPERS, 1870-1894. 3 items. Morgantown (Monongalia County), W. Va.

Political correspondence of Waitman Thomas Willey (1811-1900) consisting of two letters concerning the inability of Vice President Schuyler Colfax to deliver an address to some of Willey's constituents; and a letter commenting on various notable Virginians.

5756. ALBERT J. WILLIAMS LEDGERS, 1906-1935. 5 vols. Mount Olive (Wayne County), N.C.

Accounts of a store selling general merchandise, food, and gasoline.

5757. ALEXANDER WILLIAMS PAPERS, 1840-1857. 7 items. Greenville (Greene County), Tenn.

Political letters to Alexander Williams, Whig politician, consisting of letters from Wade Hampton, Jr., concerning personal affairs; a letter from W. G. ("Parson") Brownlow describing a dinner in honor of James Polk, with numerous references to intrigue and bargaining in state politics; and letters from Henry Clay discussing his defeat in 1844 and attacks made against him by his political enemies.

5758. ALFRED WILLIAMS ET AL. PAPERS, 1862-1883. 195 items. Beaufort County, S.C.

Routine papers of various sheriffs of Beaufort County, South Carolina, including W. J. Gooding, 1868; Alfred Williams, 1869-1872; George Holmes, 1872-1875; and W. M. Wilson, 1875-1883.

5759. BENJAMIN S. WILLIAMS PAPERS, 1792 (1860-1927) 1938. 859 items. Brunson (Hampton County), S.C.

Papers of Benjamin S. Williams, Confederate soldier, cotton planter, businessman and local politician, consisting of land deeds; a marriage license; several papers relating to the sale of slaves; clippings; correspondence; general orders of the South Carolina militia in 1877; and commissions of Williams for various offices. Civil War letters from Benjamin S. Williams, from his father, Gilbert W. M. Williams (d. 1863), Baptist minister and colonel in the 47th Regiment of Georgia Volunteer Infantry, and from A. D. Williams describe camp life; Colonel Williams's duties as commander of the 47th Regiment; deserters; Abraham Lincoln; military activities in Georgia from 1861 to 1862, in Mississippi in 1863, around Chattanooga (Tennessee) during 1863, and Smithfield (North Carolina) in 1865; charges against the 47th Regiment; the death of Sergeant Albert Richardson; and the disbanding of the Brunson branch of the South Carolina militia. Other correspondence discusses the destruction in South Carolina after Sherman's troops passed through; the behavior of the freedmen; articles written by Benjamin S. Williams regarding his war experiences; Tillmanism; the United Daughters of the Confederacy; affairs of the Confederate Infirmary at Columbia, South Carolina; the United Confederate Veterans; Williams's pension claim; efforts of William A. Courtenay to write a history of the battle of Honey Hill, South Carolina; the service of Dr. Abraham Dallas Williams, brother of Benjamin S. Williams, in Cuba and Puerto Rico during the Spanish-American War; the activities of the "red shirts" in South Carolina; and an investigation of the financial condition of Hampton County, South Carolina, in 1906.

5760. FRANCES AMANDA (DISMUKES) WILLIAMS PAPERS, 1847-1874. 36 items. Clopton's Mills (Putnam County), Ga.

Typed copies of letters to Frances Amanda (Dismukes) Williams from her relatives discussing personal matters, local affairs, social life and customs, temperance, religious revivals, weather and crops in Georgia, schools, sickness, mining, and the Stevens, Williams, and Dismukes families. There are also a letter from a Confederate soldier describing the hardships of camp life; and genealogical data from a Stevens family Bible.

5761. FRANCIS H. WILLIAMS PAPERS, 1835-1862. 16 items. Onslow County, N.C.

Indentures relating to the sale and purchase of land by Francis H. Williams, farmer, and members of his family.

5762. GEORGE FREDERICK WILLIAMS PAPERS, 1835 (1876-1888) 1902. 3,853 items and 2 vols. Boston, Mass.

Personal and political correspondence and papers of George Frederick Williams (1852-1932), lawyer, U.S. congressman, 1891-1893, and minister to Greece, 1913-1914, relating to his growing law business, his increasing affluence, his interest in politics, and his social life, especially in musical circles in Boston. Correspondence discusses student life at the universities of Berlin and Heidelberg, Germany; the reaction of Americans in Europe to the election of 1876; the work of the Court of Commissioners of the Alabama Claims; the rights of British subjects; Massachusetts and national politics; reform efforts in the Democratic Party; efforts to influence Republicans to vote Democratic; anti-Blaine sentiment in the Republican Party; the "Anti-Blaine Movement"; the "Committee of One Hundred"; efforts of reform Democrats in Boston to entice Carl Schurz to edit the Boston Post; disillusionment because of Grover Cleveland's failure to implement reform; division among Democrats; and Cleveland's lack of influence in the House. There are also bills and receipts; and two lesson books, one for German and one for chemistry.

5763. HENRY J. WILLIAMS PAPERS, 1839-1842. 59 items. Baltimore, Md.

Letters to Henry J. Williams from his mother requesting financial assistance; and from his brother, John S. Williams, who owned a mill, asking him to purchase supplies in Baltimore, with frequent references to his financial affairs, fluctuations in the price of wheat, and the business of his mill. One letter contains references to a lottery in Maryland.

5764. HENRY J. WILLIAMS PAPERS, 1816-1878. 25 items. Philadelphia, Pa.

Correspondence and papers of Henry J. Williams, attorney, relating to the American tour of Louis Kossuth, Hungarian patriot; his retirement as clerk of the Sessions Court, 1877; efforts of Lafayette College, Easton, Pennsylvania, to obtain Williams's library; and Howard University, Washington, D.C.

5765. INDIANA (FLETCHER) WILLIAMS PAPERS, 1804 (1846-1892) 1900. 38 items. Sweet Briar (Amherst County), Va.

Personal and business correspondence and legal papers of Indiana (Fletcher) Williams (d. 1900), founder of Sweet Briar College, Sweet Briar, Virginia; of her father, Elijah Fletcher, businessman and planter; and of her cousin and husband, Fletcher Williams, Episcopal minister, pertaining to personal and business affairs; commodity prices in Virginia; personal debts; the disposition of slaves in wills; the hiring of slaves; land prices, grants, deeds, indentures, sales, transfers, and taxes; social life and customs in Virginia; and the tract of land where Sweet Briar College is now located.

5766. JABIN S. WILLIAMS PAPERS, 1816-1861. 68 items. Becket (Berkshire County), Mass.

Papers of Jabin B. Williams, postmaster, justice of the peace, merchant, and speculator in real estate, including business correspondence, personal letters chiefly to his son, deeds, and morgages.

5767. JAMES WILLIAMS PETITION. 1 item. South Carolina.

Petition to the governor of South Carolina from members of the Little River Regiment protesting the arrest of their commanding officer, Colonel James Williams. The petition may date from the Revolutionary period.

5768. JOHN WILLIAMS PAPERS, 1775-1824. 17 items. Granville County, N.C.

Papers of John Williams, colonel in the North Carolina militia during the American Revolution, relating chiefly to the Transylvania Company and to the Revolution. Included are letters from William Johnston discussing the procurement of powder and provisions for the colonial troops in 1775, the granting of land deeds and titles in the Transylvania area, and financial affairs of the Transylvania Company; letter, 1775, from James Hogg concerning the proceedings of an assembly, possibly the assembly of the area being settled by the Louisa Company; letters, 1775, from Nathaniel Henderson requesting that Williams come to Transylvania to settle some disputes over land titles and discussing the future of the area, the interest showed by James Harrod in settling there, and the election of his brother, Richard Henderson, and Williams to represent the area at the Continental Congress; letter, 1776, from Bromfield Ridley pertaining to the raising of troops in North Carolina and the plan to prevent the Tories from joining the British governor in the state; letters from John Luttrell concerning taking new partners into the company, the choice of Abner Nash as the company's counsel in a dispute over land claimed as part of Virginia, and the selection of Williams as Granville's representative in the state assembly; letter, 1779, from Charles Bondfield asking to be among the next party to go to Transylvania; letters from Richard Henderson concerning the Transylvania

Company's dispute with Virginia, action on land titles by the North Carolina legislature, and their law partnership; letter from William Hooper urging that judges' salaries be increased, that the death penalty be abolished for horse theft, and that John Penn be publicly commended; a receipt; an indenture concerning Transylvania lands; and a letter from James Stephens to John Williams, Jr., during Williams's service as Clerk of Superior Court.

5769. JOHN WILLIAMS DIARY, 1865. 1 vol. Philadelphia, Pa.

Diary kept by a member of Company D, 95th Regiment, Pennsylvania Volunteers from April 9, 1865, until shortly after his discharge on July 22, 1865. Among other things John Williams noted comments on General Robert E. Lee's surrender as received by Federal soldiers on duty; rumors of General Joseph E. Johnston's surrender; Lincoln's assassination; a march through Halifax Court House and on to Danville, Virginia; descriptions of Confederate troops returning home; a march from Nottoway County, Virginia, to Washington, D.C.; distribution of seed to farmers of Nottoway County by "Gregg's cavalry" in May, 1865; discipline in the 95th Regiment; and personal matters.

5770. JOHN BUXTON WILLIAMS PAPERS, 1804-1870. 56 items. Warren County, N.C.

Personal and family correspondence of John Buxton Williams (1815-1877), planter, and Henry G. Williams, member of the North Carolina General Assembly in 1835, concerning farm affairs, the hiring of slaves as laborers, and personal consideration toward slaves. Included are itemized accounts from Norfolk and Richmond, Virginia, merchants.

5771. JOHN C. WILLIAMS NOTEBOOK, 1843-1872. 1 vol. Philadelphia, Pa.

Notes on medical lectures given by J. K. Mitchell, 1843; records of medical visits made by Williams as a physician in North Carolina, 1847-1850, and fees charged; a land indenture, 1869; and general accounts.

5772. JOHN J. WILLIAMS PAPERS, 1850-1868. 11 items. Washington, D.C.

Personal letters of John J. Williams, including some concerning his work as a civil engineer surveying the Tehauntepec Canal Route in Mexico, 1850.

5773. JOHN W. WILLIAMS PAPERS, 1962-1963. 10 items. Durham, N.C.

Mimeographed letters from S. Rutherfoord Harvie to Mr. and Mrs. John W. Williams discussing relatives and friends, social events, and church affairs, with occasional references to politics. Harvie quotes a letter he received from Governor Ross Barnett of Mississippi congratulating him on "defying that Kennedy bunch up in Washington."

5774. JOHN WESLEY WILLIAMS PAPERS, 1861-1863. 45 items. Haw Branch (Onslow County), N.C.

Family correspondence of John Wesley Williams (d. 1862), Confederate soldier. Williams's letters discuss camp life, food, health conditions, preaching, the weather, skirmishes, the possiblity of getting a substitute, and conditions in New Bern, North Carolina.

5775. JOSEPH S. WILLIAMS PAPERS, 1857 (1860-1865) 1882. 57 items. Pittsburgh, Pa.

Personal letters to Joseph S. Williams chiefly during the Civil War describing a murder; the suicide of a minister; Rockbridge Alum Springs, Rockbridge County, Virginia; W. DeLong's School and Pittsburgh College, Pittsburgh, Pennsylvania; John Bell and Edward Everett, candidates of the Constitutional Union Party for president and vice president in 1860; politics and government in Maryland and Pennsylvania; coal mining and iron manufacture in Pennsylvania; Francis Harrison Pierpont, first governor of West Virginia; Andrew Gregg Curtin, governor of Pennsylvania; various Union generals; the Penisular Campaign; the capture of Fort Donelson, Tennessee; the battle of Gettysburg; Union Army recruiting and casualties; rumors; violations of oaths of allegiance to the United States; the 15th and the 123rd Regiments, Pennsylvania Militia, and the 100th Pennsylvania Regiment, U.S.A.; conditions in Philadelphia, and Baltimore; and alleged vandalism in Pittsburgh by Negro soldiers in the U.S. Army.

5776. LLOYD W. WILLIAMS PAPERS, 1849-1885. 3 vols. Elizabeth City (Pasquotank County), N.C., and Baltimore, Md.

Daybooks, 1849-1861, and ledger, 1875-1885, of a lawyer, containing records of clients, fees, business handled and other matters. One volume also includes a record of goods shipped from Baltimore, Maryland, to Elizabeth City, North Carolina.

5777. NATHANIEL WILLIAMS ACCOUNT BOOK AND LETTER BOOK, 1758-1768 and 1808-1834. 1 vol. (172 pp.) Boston, Mass.

Correspondence and accounts of Nathaniel Williams, ship captain and owner, containing detailed information on the commercial transactions of a series of ships trading with Europe, the West Indies, and North America, particularly North Carolina; goods shipped; expenses of the voyages; wages to the crews; local and general business conditions; and transactions with various merchants. Five pages of the volume were used by John Wood, clerk of the court in Perquimans County, North Carolina, to register cattle marks, 1808-1834.

5778. ROBERT WILLIAMS PAPERS, 1813-1814. 2 items. Raleigh (Wake County), N.C.

Papers of Robert Williams (1773-1836), U. S. congressman, 1797-1803, governor of the Mississippi Territory, 1805-1809, and adjutant general of North Carolina, ca. 1812-1814, relating to the North Carolina militia, and to the United States Military Philosophical Society, Philadelphia, Pennsylvania.

5779. ROBERT GRAY WILLIAMS PAPERS, 1856-1946. 117 items and 6 vols. Winchester (Frederick County), Va.

Miscellaneous papers of Robert Gray Williams (1878-1946), lawyer, consists of correspondence; a mimeographed letter from the Rodney Birch Research Associates advocating a plan for world peace; papers relating to Harry Flood Byrd (1887-1966), U.S. senator, 1933-1966, including letters concerning stocks and bonds issued by H. F. Byrd and T. B. Byrd Incorporated, a receipt for charter and recording fees for the company, deeds, and a note containing the purposes and officers of the Byrd Corporation and the value of the orchards; deeds and indentures; wills; plat for "Waverly" near Winchester, Virginia; map of "Hackwood"; "Report Upon Water Supply and Purification, Winchester, Virginia"; "General Rules and Regulations Under the Trust Indenture Act of 1939"; letter and broadside relating to the campaign of Junius E. West for lieutenant governor of Virginia; broadsides concerning the Florence Railroad and Improvement Company and the Hagerstown Manufacturing, Mining and Land Improvement Company; pamphlets and leaflets containing items written by Gus W. Dyer and Remmie L. Arnold; pamphlets concerning the Baltimore and Ohio Railroad Company, the Shenandoah Valley Academy, the Curtis Publishing Company, Virginia laws, and the Home Owners' Loan Act of 1933; and a photograph of the Prince William Hotel, Manassas, Virginia.

5780. SARAH WILLIAMS PAPERS, 1862-1872. 6 items. Gettysburg (Adams County), Pa.

Papers of Mrs. Sarah Williams including four letters from her attorney, D. M. Conaughby, discussing legal affairs.

5781. STEPHEN GUION WILLIAMS PAPERS, 1882. 1 vol. (143 pp.) New York, N.Y.

Notes taken by Williams at Columbia College in the class of John William Burgess, professor of political science and constitutional law.

5782. WILLIAM WILLIAMS PAPERS, 1888. 1 vol. Waterford (Loudoun County), Va.

Memoir of William Williams, a Quaker with Union sympathies during the Civil War, describing his capture and imprisonment by Confederate soldiers as a hostage for two Confederate citizens held by Union forces; his treatment; food; living conditions; and efforts of family and friends to obtain his freedom.

5783. WILLIAM GEORGE WILLIAMS PAPERS, 1828-1875. 11 items. South Carolina.

Chiefly business papers of William George Williams (ca. 1801-1846), U. S. Army officer; a map of geographical discoveries in the Arctic region; and a map, 1828, entitled "Sketch of the Mouths and Channels of Pascagoula River."

5784. ALICE WILLIAMSON PAPERS, 1864. 1 vol. (36 pp.) Gallatin (Sumner County), Tenn.

Diary of a schoolgirl principally relating to the occupation of Gallatin, Tennessee, and the surrounding region by Union troops under General Eleazer A. Paine. She describes the occupation; atrocities attributed to the Federal troops; the presence of former slaves, projects to educate them, and their abuse by Union troops from eastern Tennessee; and the presence of Confederate troops in the area. There is occasional mention of the schoolroom and of social visits.

5785. GEORGE T. WILLIAMSON PAPERS, 1841. 2 items. Cincinnati, Ohio.

Letters dealing with the problem of land taxes in Illinois.

5786. ISABELLE (PERKINSON) WILLIAMSON PAPERS, 1885 (1909-1930). 2,520 items. Charlottesville (Albemarle County), Va.

Papers of Isabelle (Perkinson) Williamson, wife of Lee Hoomes Williamson, engineer, and of her mother, Isabelle (Holmes) Perkinson. Included are many letters to Isabelle (Holmes) Perkinson from former students of the University of Virginia who had patronized her boardinghouse in Charlottesville, Virginia; letters from Isabelle (Holmes) Perkinson to her daughter describing life in Charlottesville, and commenting on Edwin A. Alderman; and many notes and bills reflecting frequent financial difficulties. There are letters from Isabelle (Perkinson) Williamson to her mother while attending the Georgetown Visitation Convent, Washington, D.C.; while on a tour of Europe during 1909 and 1910; while visiting in Virginia and in the Panama Canal Zone; while working in the Navy Department in Washington, 1913-1917; and, after her marriage in 1917, while in Rancagua, Chile, and Puerto Rico with her husband. Also included are letters between Isabelle (Perkinson) Williamson and Lee Hoomes Williamson. Papers relating to World War I consist of letters from soldiers and war workers; food cards; and letters from

Mary Peyton, who was with a field hospital unit in France. The collection also contains information on the early moving pictures; life during the Roaring Twenties; and the beginning of the Great Depression.

5787.  JOHN WILLIAMSON PAPERS, 1772-1946. 20 items. Savannah, Ga.

Papers of Judge John Williamson (1810-1885) and of Richard R. Cuyler, whose business affairs were managed by Williamson, including papers dealing with the settlement of the estate of Teleman Cuyler; commission of Jeremiah Cuyler as judge of the District Court of the United States for Georgia; receipt for the sale of slaves; powers of attorney; license granted to a minister of the First African Church of Savannah in 1862; letters from Richard M. Cuyler and his uncle, William H. Cuyler, to Williamson containing comments on Reconstruction and on social life in New York, New York; and correspondence between Tulamon Cuyler and Mrs. Marmaduke Floyd discussing Cuyler family genealogy.

5788.  JOHN M. WILLIAMSON PAPERS, 1855-1865. 10 items. Stony Brook (Suffolk County), N.Y.

Papers of John M. Williamson pertaining to personal matters and New York politics.

5789.  LEAH H. WILLIAMSON BANKBOOK, 1917. 1 vol. (1 p.) Charlottesville (Albemarle County), Va.

Savings account passbook of Mrs. Leah H. Williamson with the National Bank of Charlottesville, Virginia.

5790.  LEE HOOMES WILLIAMSON PAPERS, 1814-1932. 495 items and 2 vols. Richmond, Va.

Chiefly business and financial papers of Lee Hoomes Williamson, vice-president of Allen J. Saville, Inc., an engineering and construction company of Richmond, Virginia. Many items concern personal debts. Legal papers include a deed; two fire insurance policies of Isabelle (Holmes) Perkinson, Williamson's mother-in-law, with the Fireman's Fund Insurance Company and with the German Alliance Insurance Association; a copy of the will of Lee H. Williamson; and Williamson's passport. There are also Christmas cards; personal and family correspondence; letters from a student at Virginia Polytechnic Institute, Blacksburg; family pictures; programs; ballots for state and county elections, 1934; and material relating to the Business and Professional Women's Club of Richmond. A letter, 1908, from John Robinson, an Englishman, to Mrs. Perkinson, describes New Year customs in the writer's home country; his interest in literature, especially Emerson; and his relief work among children of the unemployed. A Spanish-American War letter from C. S. Lancaster, U.S. Army officer, describes military maneuvers, high-ranking officers, and political influences in appointment and promotion. Included in the collection are a student's autograph book and a commonplace book.

5791.  WILLIAM WILLIAMSON PAPERS, 1921-1929. 46 items. Oacoma (Lyman County), S.D.

Chiefly constituent correspondence of William Williamson (b. 1875), U.S. congressman, 1921-1933, relating to mining interests in South Dakota and to the passage of the Smith-McNary Bill for reclamation of waste lands in the West. Included is a letter from Burton Lee French planning strategy to secure the bill's passage.

5792.  WYATT WILLIAMSON PAPERS, 1848-1918. 41 items and 2 vols. Moore County, N.C.

Papers of Wyatt Williamson and his family primarily pertaining to personal debts and personal and business affairs, consisting of receipts, correspondence, and other miscellaneous papers. Included are a letter from a Confederate soldier discussing camp life; letters from officers in the North Carolina Home Guard discussing favoritism and wealth as a factor in discharges, and the recruiting of troops for the U.S. Army in Goldsboro, North Carolina; letters discussing tobacco and an influenza epidemic in Kansas; items dealing with counterfeiting and the counterfeiter, Charles Wilson; and Williamson's account books, 1848-1849, and 1861-1878, containing information on commodity prices in North Carolina.

5793.  LEWIS KENNON WILLIE PAPERS, 1845-1848. 4 vols. Oxford (Granville County), N.C.

Diary, sermon books, and notes on the Bible of Lewis Kennon Willie, a Methodist minister.

5794.  LEWIS R. WILLIE NOTEBOOK, 1838-1839. 1 vol. (195 pp.) Prince Edward County, Va.

Lecture notes and sermons kept by Lewis R. Willie while a student at the Union Theological Seminary (Presbyterian), Prince Edward County, including notes on lectures of Dr. George A. Baxter.

5795.  MRS. E. L. WILLIS MEMORANDUM BOOKS, 1874-1875. 2 vols. Charleston, S.C.

Lists of books, pamphlets, and documents in the library of Mrs. E. L. Willis.

5796. HENRY WILLIS, JR., PAPERS, 1855-1911. 289 items. Charleston, S.C.

Bills, receipts, legal papers and business correspondence of Henry Willis, Jr. (b. ca. 1822), broker. Included are a legal document, 1855, dealing with an estate in New York and with the Vanderbilt family; papers relating to the estate of James M. Wood; and two letters, 1911, from Mexico, one of which pertains to the revolution.

5797. JAMES WILLIS PAPERS, 1799-1804. 63 items. London, England.

Papers of James Willis, chief assistant in the Examiners' Department at the East India House, consisting primarily of letters from Harford Jones (1764-1847), later Sir Harford Jones Brydges, while British resident at Baghdad concerning British relations with the Pashalik of Baghdad as well as Persia, Afghanistan, and India. The letters pertaining to Baghdad discuss the question of Jones's remaining in Baghdad or going to India; a proposed diplomatic mission to Persia; the complaint of Peter Tooke, diplomat at Constantinople, about being uninformed, especially about Egyptian affairs; the crisis in relations between the Pasha (Sulaiman, the Great), and the residency of Baghdad; the status of Jones's residency; Jones's belief in the necessity of a diplomatic post in Baghdad; vying with the French representatives for influence in the pashalik; the failure of some British diplomat to pay attention to local customs; threat of insurrection; the death of the Pasha; the questionable durability of the new government; relations with the new Pasha; Jones's assistance to Baghdad with the problem of the plague; an imperial patent for the residency in Baghdad; a dispute between Jones and Samuel Manesty, whom Jones once recommended as his successor; dispute between Manesty and the Pasha; dissension over the Pasha's rule; violations of Baghdad's borders by the Wahhabi; Russia's desire to establish an agent in Baghdad; and a dispute between the Imam of Masqat (Muscat) and the Pasha, and a request for British intercession.
Letters relating to India discuss efforts to introduce an effective cow pox vaccine; rumors that the Bombay presidency would be abolished; the dispatching of troops to join Sir Ralph Abercromby's forces in the Mediterranean; Wellesley's expected success in effecting a cession of Oudh; military efforts in Malabar and the Southern provinces; the plan of Sir Home Popham to transfer the Bombay Marines to Prince of Wales Island; Wellesley's campaign near Poona; and the anticipated war with Scindia. Letters pertaining to Persia describe the fear in Baghdad of attack from Persia; the influence of Murza Bozurg in Persia; instructions regarding relations with Tehran; concern about Russian encroachments on Turkish Armenia, in Georgia, and along the Caspian; fear of an expedition by the Shah against Russia; uprising of the Azerbaijan rebels; need for a regular British envoy at Tehran; and efforts to dissuade the Shah from a campaign against the Wahhabi. Letters dealing with Afghanistan chiefly concern the war over the throne. Also included is a document describing information obtained from an Armenian merchant who traveled from Herat, Afghanistan, to Astrakhan, Russia, containing comments on the country, populations, rulers, relations with the Russians, and conditions of travel.

5798. LARKIN WILLIS PAPERS, 1832 (1858-1873) 1884. 193 items. Richmond, and Locust Dale (Madison County), Va.

Personal and family correspondence of Larkin Willis (b. 1838), student at the University of Virginia, Charlottesville, 1854-1856, engineer in the Confederate Army, and associate principal of Locust Dale Academy, Rapidan Station, Virginia, after the Civil War, chiefly concerning personal affairs of the Willis and Turpin families. Included are nineteen Civil War letters from Mrs. Willis in Richmond describing high prices, the scarcity of food, the danger of Union success, and conditions in Richmond.

5799. NATHANIEL PARKER WILLIS PAPERS, 1854. 1 item. New York, N.Y.

A letter by Nathaniel Parker Willis (1806-1867), writer and journalist, to Maunsell B. Field discussing an article about Edgar Allan Poe that appeared in the Times.

5800. WILLIAM LEWIS WILLIS DAYBOOK, 1851-1855. 1 vol. (135 pp.) Baltimore, Md.

Pharmacy records of sales and purchases; and physician's records of patients, visits, and fees.

5801. SIR THOMAS WILLSHIRE, FIRST BARONET, PAPERS, 1806-1935. 79 items. Richings Park, Buckinghamshire, England.

Correspondence, commissions, and clippings of Sir Thomas Willshire, First Baronet (1789-1862), British Army officer, relating chiefly to his capture of Kelat, capital of Baluchistan, in 1839, with items pertaining to South Africa, 1819, Afghanistan, 1839, and Willshire's command at Chatham, 1841. Included are letters and clippings concerning military operations in Kaffraria, future boundaries, and defenses, 1819; letters of commendation; casualty returns for the 2nd or Queen's Royal Regiment at the storming of Ghaznie during the campaign in Afghanistan; letter from Sir William Macnaghten concerning defensive measures in the event of an Afghan attack; letters from Mehrab Khan, ruler of Kelat, before the battle (in Arabic script with partial translations); Willshire's report on the battle to Lord Auckland; letters pertaining to fears of Russian or Persian incursion into Afghanistan and the Kelat operation; letters and clippings dealing with efforts by Willshire and others to seek honors for the men who fought at Kelat; letters regarding Willshire's appointment as commandant at Chatham; letter of Dr. William Atkinson recounting Willshire's accidental poisoning in 1855; and commissions.

5802. WILMINGTON LYCEUM TREASURER'S BOOK, 1866. 1 vol. (39 pp.) Wilmington (New Hanover County), N.C.

Finanical records of the Wilmington Lyceum.

5803. AARON W. WILSON PAPERS, 1900-1919. 36 items. Apex (Wake County), N.C.

Papers of Aaron W. Wilson contain mercantile records and material pertaining to the United States Food Administration and the National War-Savings Committee during World War I, including a nearly complete run of the Food Administration's Official Bulletin for North Carolina between April 1, 1918, and December 1, 1918.

5804. ALEXANDER WILSON PAPERS, 1839-1840. 2 items. Greensboro (Guilford County), N.C.

Letters of Alexander Wilson, principal and teacher at Caldwell Institute, Greensboro, North Carolina, and itinerant bookseller, relating to the school and to his bookselling activities.

5805. GEORGE R. WILSON DAYBOOK, 1858-1865. 1 vol. (88 pp.) [North Carolina?]

Book of personal or household accounts.

5806. SIR GUY DOUGLAS ARTHUR FLEETWOOD WILSON PAPERS, 1887-1924. 21 items. London, England.

The papers of Sir Guy Douglas Arthur Fleetwood Wilson, British civil servant in the War Office, are made up for the most part of letters, 1892-1907, to Wilson from various secretaries of state for war, including Edward Stanhope and Lord Haldane, concerning army administration and finance, politics, and the routine business of the war office.

5807. HENDERSON WILSON DAYBOOK, 1850-1867. 1 vol. (49 pp.)

Apparently the accounts of a blacksmith. Also contains genealogical information on the Wilson family.

5808. HENRY WILSON PAPERS, 1865-1875. 4 items. Natick (Middlesex County), Mass.

Routine political correspondence of Henry Wilson (1812-1875), vice president of the United States, 1872-1875.

5809. JAMES WILSON PAPERS, 1847-1850. 22 items. London, England.

The papers of James Wilson, British politician and political economist, are made up of letters to Wilson from George William Frederick Villiers, Fourth Earl of Clarendon and Fourth Baron Hyde, written while Villiers was Lord Lieutenant of Ireland and Wilson was owner of The Economist, concerning the economic and political situation in Ireland, particularly the condition of Irish agriculture, the suppression of violence, and Villiers's opinion of the Irish people.

5810. JAMES WILSON PAPERS. 1 vol. South Carolina.

An account of the money paid, received, and due the estate of James Wilson.

5811. JAMES BRIGHT WILSON PAPERS. 5 items. Baltimore, Md.

Included in the collection is an unpublished manuscript of an edition by James B. Wilson of portions of the Old English poem, "Christ and Satan and Harrowing of Hell," with glossaries, and other literary notes.

5812. JAMES FALCONER WILSON PAPERS, 1868. 1 item. Fairfield (Jefferson County), Iowa.

Letter of James Falconer Wilson, member of the United States Congress from Iowa, concerning his autograph.

5813. JAMES GRANT WILSON PAPERS, 1894, 1912. 2 items. New York, N.Y.

Letter, 1912, of James Grant Wilson, editor, author, and soldier, concerning the disposition of the Lincoln and Thackeray collections of William Harrison Lambert, and a manuscript copy of Wilson's poem "A Serenade."

5814. JAMES L. WILSON ACCOUNT BOOKS, 1865-1881. 2 vols. Beaufort County, N.C.

Accounts of a farmer.

5815. JOHN WILSON PAPERS AND ACCOUNT BOOK, 1835-1852. 33 items and 1 vol. Milton (Caswell County), N.C.

Miscellaneous business papers of the mercantile firm of John Wilson and Richard T. Smith, including promissory notes, bills, accounts, and one account book.

5816. JOHN LEIGHTON WILSON PAPERS, 1842. 1 item. New York, N.Y.

A memorial to the American Board of Commissioners for Foreign Missions from John Leighton Wilson, Presbyterian missionary to West Africa, reporting on the emancipation of all but two of his slaves, who refused to leave him.

5817. JOHN S. WILSON PAPERS, 1837-1846. 11 items. Buchanan (Botetourt County), Va.

Letters to John S. Wilson, an attorney, relating to his law practice in Botetourt County and adjoining counties in Virginia.

5818. JOSEPH WILSON PAPERS, 1829-1853. 48 items. Bedford County, Va.

Correspondence of Joseph Wilson as clerk of Bedford County Court of Law and Chancery, containing mainly official letters, orders, summonses, legal documents, bills, and receipts.

5819. MENECE WILSON PAPERS, 1850-1881. 19 items. Orange County, N.C.

Correspondence of Menece Wilson with relatives in North Carolina, Alabama, and Arkansas, concerning the insane asylum of North Carolina at Raleigh, North Carolina; Stone Mountain, Georgia; and railroad travel in Georgia in 1850.

5820. PRISCILLA H. WILSON PAPERS, 1826-1923. 40 items. Carmel (Preston County), W. Va.

Personal letters to Priscilla H. Wilson.

5821. ROBERT WILSON PAPERS, 1853 (1866-1867) 1877. 36 items. Sartartia (Yazoo County), Miss.

Bills, accounts, promissory notes, and other business papers of Robert Wilson, a general merchant.

5822. THOMAS WILSON ACCOUNT BOOK, 1851-1852. 1 vol. (98 pp.)

Accounts of Thomas Wilson, a blacksmith, and an itemized account of money received from a sale of household articles, farm implements, and cattle.

5823. THOMAS WOODROW WILSON PAPERS, 1884-1922. 33 items. Princeton (Mercer County), N.J.

Copies of documents, correspondence, articles, bibliographies, photographs, and cartoons by or relating to Woodrow Wilson.

5824. W. A. WILSON PAPERS, 1861-1885. 5 items. [Berlin (Southampton County), Va.?]

Letters from W. A. Wilson, a Confederate soldier, describing an ocean voyage to South America, 1861, and his capture at Manassas, 1861; and three letters from members of his family dealing with personal affairs.

5825. W. LINDSAY WILSON PAPERS, 1923-1948. 30 items. Greenville (Greenville County), S.C.

Invoices for the sale of goods by the Wilson Company of Greenville, South Carolina; correspondence concerning the European situation, the Fourth Presbyterian Church of Greenville, and Muscle Shoals, Alabama; and an excerpt from one of William Bartram's books of travels. Also an unpublished article, "The Cat That Came to Clear Springs," concerning a panther in Abbeville County, South Carolina.

5826. WILLIAM WILSON PAPERS, 1813. 1 item. Fort Johnston, near Southport (Brunswick County), N.C.

A bill of lading and a receipt signed by William Wilson, an officer in the United States Army artillery corps, as commander of Fort Johnston, North Carolina.

5827. REBECCA L. (BARKSDALE) WIMBISH PAPERS, 1811-1897. 226 items and 51 vols. Halifax County, Va.

Personal correspondence of Rebecca L. (Barksdale) Wimbish and her sister Cornelia (Barksdale) Quarles, including letters from William Wimbish, who worked at an iron foundry at Union Furnace, Virginia, during the Civil War; business papers, including portions of ledgers and daybooks; and a detailed statement of the expenses of Rebecca L. Barksdale at Salem Female Academy, Salem, North Carolina, in 1849. Volumes in the collection include minutes of church meetings, 1837-1846; business records of mercantile establishments at Catawba Post Office, Peytonsburg, and Barksdale, all in Virginia, including ledgers, daybooks, and account books; a wagoner's book which was kept by John McMillian; an account book of tobacco sold in Richmond, Virginia, 1823-1826; and a child's copybook.

5828. JOHN HENRY WINDER PAPERS, 1862-1865. 5 items. Virginia.

Letters to John Henry Winder (1800-1865), brigadier general in the Confederate Army, requesting relief from field duty, permission to visit a soldier, and permission to leave a town in which the writer was paroled. One letter, 1863, concerns the exchange of a Union soldier, and a telegram, 1865, mentions the sudden death of Winder at Florence, South Carolina.

5829. LEVIN WINDER PAPERS, 1813-1815. 25 items. Baltimore, Md.

Papers of Levin Winder, Revolutionary War veteran and Federalist governor of Maryland during the War of 1812, concern his duties as governor, including a report to the General Assembly, 1813, on the state of affairs in Maryland; papers relating to the trial of free Negroes and slaves accused of plotting an insurrection in Frederick County, 1814; and recommendations for appointments.

5830. WILLIAM WINDHAM PAPERS, 1804-1806. 5 items. London, England.

Papers of William Windham, British statesman, concern military preparations in Kent and the question of war with France, 1804; Windham's instructions to General Simcoe and the Earls of Rosslyn and St. Vincent regarding the Portuguese fleet, 1806; the parliamentary election of 1806; and instructions to General William Beresford in 1806 to prepare troops from Buenos Aires for an expedition in mid-1807.

5831. JOSEPH B. WINDLEY PAPERS, 1794-1856. 22 items. Beaufort County, N.C.

Business papers, legal papers, and bills and receipts pertaining to Joseph B. Windley and his relatives and friends, including items relating to the settlement of estates, the purchase and sale of slaves, and the presidential election of 1856.

5832. MARSHALL W. WINES PAPERS, 1872-1905. 19 items. Washington, D.C.

Papers of Marshall W. Wines, who was in charge of the Miscellaneous Division of the United States Coast and Geodetic Survey.

5833. PAULINA S. WINFIELD PAPERS, 1912-1920. 8 items. Broadway (Rockingham County), Va.

Typescript short stories by Paulina S. Winfield and two letters to her by "The Editor."

5834. SIMON P. WINGARD PAPERS, 1841-1867. 103 items. Lexington (Lexington County), S.C.

Correspondence of Simon P. Wingard, a Confederate soldier in the 5th South Carolina Regiment, with his wife, Marie Wingard, and his brother, James Samuel Wingard, a soldier in the 9th South Carolina Regiment, describing life in Lexington, South Carolina; life in army camps at Grahamville, Pocataligo, and McPhersonville, South Carolina; the Peninsular Campaign in Virginia, 1862; the siege of Petersburg, Virginia, 1864-1865; desertion in the Confederate and Union armies; and Union sentiment in South Carolina, 1864. Also contains a short entry diary of Thomas F. Harrington of the 10th Massachusetts Regiment, 1862, and James S. Wingard, 1862.

5835. SIR FRANCIS REGINALD WINGATE, FIRST BARONET, PAPERS, 1884-1955. 345 items. Knockenhair, East Lothian, Scotland.

Papers of Sir Francis Reginald Wingate, First Baronet, British Army officer and colonial administrator, contain correspondence, official reports, maps, and clippings pertaining to Wingate's work as assistant adjutant general and director of military intelligence in Egypt, for the most part concerning the conflict between the British and the Mahdists in the eastern Sudan. Letters to Wingate from his superiors and subordinates in London, Cairo, southern Egypt, and the eastern Sudan, and many letterpress copies or drafts of Wingate's replies, relate to the Eastern Sudan Expeditionary Force, 1891; the military, economic, and political situation in those portions of the Sudan controlled by Britain; and estimates of conditions in the areas of the Sudan controlled by the Mahdists. Reports and memoranda include Wingate's "General Report on the Sudan, 1891" and his "Appendix"; translations of correspondence, ca. 1883, of Osman Digna, Mahdist ruler in the eastern Sudan; and indices to Mahdist letters and proclamations captured at the battle of Afafit, 1891. Printed material includes Wingate's military report on Sudan, 1890; staff diary and intelligence report from Suakin, January-March, 1891; statistics on the Egyptian Army and on the Italian Army in Africa; and newspaper clippings on Egyptian and Sudanese affairs. The collection contains several maps, dealing mainly with military operations in the Sudan.

5836. GEORGE WINGATE PAPERS, 1876-1927. 285 items. Summerhill, Godalming, Surrey, England.

Papers of George Wingate, British Army officer, contain letters and printed material concerning Wingate's duties as an assistant commissary general in India, 1876-1904, and, particularly, his work in establishing the system of grass farms used to supply forage for government animals, 1884-1892, including a petition, 1887, and supporting documents submitted by Wingate in response to criticism of his work. There are also letters relating to the scientific study of grasses; correspondence pertaining to Wingate's religious beliefs as a member of the Plymouth Brethren and the religious sentiments of many of his fellow officers; and letters concerning missionary work in Asia.

5837. JAMES A. WINGFIELD NOTEBOOK, ca. 1868. 1 vol. Eatonton (Putnam County), Ga.

Legal notes.

5838. JAMES H. WINGFIELD PAPERS, 1862. 4 items. Baton Rouge, La.

Papers of J. H. Wingfield, commander of the Western Battalion of the 1st Regiment, Partisan Rangers, C.S.A., stationed on the Amite River near Baton Rouge in 1862. Included are a description of the scouting work of these troops, and morning reports.

5839. JOHN WINN AND PHILIP JAMES WINN PAPERS, (1780-1889) 1925. 2,657 items and 27 vols. Fluvanna County, Va.

Family and business correspondence of John Winn (d. 1844); of his wife Lucy Winn; and of their numerous children, including Philip James Winn. The correspondence of John Winn, farmer, lawyer, postmaster at Winnsville, captain in the War of 1812, and agent for General John Hartwell Cocke, includes information on "Bremo," the plantation of the latter, including also a list of periodicals subscribed to by Cocke; and legal cases relative to Revolutionary bounty land. Correspondence centering around Philip James Winn includes information on the Virginia Military Institute, Lexington, and the University of Virginia, Charlottesville, both of which he attended; one letter with a description of the unusual religious services of the Dunkards; a deed for land purchased by a free Negro; records of the invention and patenting of a "New Gate Latch" by Philip J. Winn; and the interest of various members of the family in law, medicine, agriculture, mechanics, business, religion, and the operation of a stagecoach line between Richmond and Staunton, Virginia. Included also is a letter of William H. Winn containing detailed descriptions of the battles of Bethel, 1861, and Gettysburg, 1863, in which he participated as a Confederate soldier. More than half the collection consists of receipts and bills connected chiefly with John Winn's work in Revolutionary bounty lands and with Philip James Winn's invention. Twenty-seven volumes include post office accounts of John Winn and of his successor, Philip James Winn; a letter book concerning the "New Gate Latch"; accounts of the estate of Samuel Kidd; letter books; ledgers; medical notes; and records of births and deaths of slaves.

5840. ISAAC WINSLOW JOURNAL, 1824. 1 vol. (72 pp.) Boston, Mass.

Accounts of Isaac Winslow's travels by stagecoach and boat from Boston, Massachusetts, to Charleston, South Carolina, via Richmond, Virginia, and Raleigh and Wilmington, North Carolina, containing interesting comments on various localities in North Carolina.

5841. JOHN ANCRUM WINSLOW PAPERS, 1843, 1873. 2 items. Boston, Mass.

Papers of John Ancrum Winslow, United States naval officer, contain a letter, 1843, to Catharine (Winslow) Winslow concerning the beginning of John A. Winslow's voyage on the U.S.S. *Missouri*, and a voucher, 1873, from John A. Winslow to B. P. Winslow.

5842. WARREN WINSLOW PAPERS, 1859. 1 item. Fayetteville (Cumberland County), N.C.

Letter to Warren Winslow, member of the United States House of Representatives from North Carolina, from W. S. Ashe, concerning an appointment.

5843. E. D. WINSTEAD PAPERS, 1882-1924. 109 items and 9 vols. Milton (Caswell County), N.C.

The collection contains correspondence and financial papers concerning the manufacture and sale of tobacco products by E. D. Winstead & Company and the milling of flour by the Milton Roller Mill Company. Volumes in the collection include ledgers, a journal, notes and bills receivable, and a letterpress book for E. D. Winstead & Company, and daybooks for flour mills in Milton, North Carolina.

5844. WILLIAM WINSTON, JR., PAPERS, 1862-1952. 26 items and 3 vols. Rome (Floyd County), Ga.

Papers of William Winston, Jr. (1875-1952) contain a letter, 1864, of Lieutenant Colonel J. M. Crews, a Confederate cavalry officer, concerning a march from Verona, Mississippi, north to Tennessee; a letter, 1864, describing the condition of Nathan Bedford Forrest's cavalry at Tupelo, Mississippi; correspondence and scrapbooks, 1900-1901, relating to William Winston, Jr.'s service with the 40th United States Regiment during the American occupation of the Philippine Islands, including routine personal and military papers, a diary for a portion of the year 1900 describing the day-to-day life of a soldier, comments on several skirmishes and the battle at Oroquieta, Mindanao, and a number of photographs of American soldiers and the everyday activities of Filipinos.

5845. WINTERBOTTOM, RICHMAN AND COMPANY PAPERS, 1866. 4 items. Philadelphia, Pa.

Business correspondence of manufacturers of cotton yarns.

5846. ROBERT CHARLES WINTHROP PAPERS, 1885-1889. 6 items. Brookline (Norfolk County), Mass.

Miscellaneous routine letters of Robert Charles Winthrop, lawyer and member of the United States Congress, including a biographical sketch of Winthrop.

5847. WINTHROP COLLEGE PAPERS, 1954. 2 items. Rock Hill (York County), S.C.

Papers prepared by a faculty committee of Winthrop College, Rock Hill, South Carolina, concerning the censuring of the college by the American Association of University Professors.

5848. WILLIAM WIRT AND ELIZABETH WASHINGTON (GAMBLE) WIRT PAPERS, ca. 1810-1854. 34 items. Oak Grove (Westmoreland County), and Richmond, Va.

Papers of William Wirt (1772-1834), author, lawyer, and attorney general of the United States, include letters concerning his law practice; a letter relating an anecdote concerning Wirt, Henry Clay, and a General Parker; fragmentary letter, 1833, from Wirt to a law student at the University of North Carolina, Chapel Hill, North Carolina, discussing education; and a fragment of Wirt's draft of his biography of Patrick Henry. Correspondence of Elizabeth Washington (Gamble) Wirt (1784-1857), wife of William Wirt, and two sons, Dabney Carr and William C., concerns the purchase and sale of land, a debt incurred by Wirt for land he planned to develop in Florida, the widow's financial affairs, the erection of a monument to her husband, and other family matters.

5849. E. JOHN WISE PAPERS, 1801-1822. 6 items. London, England.

Letters concerning business matters.

5850. GEORGE D. WISE PAPERS, 1862. 1 item. Brooklyn, N.Y.

Letter to George D. Wise, an officer in the United States Navy, introducing the British artist Frank Vizetelly.

5851. GEORGE DOUGLAS WISE PAPERS, 1885-1888. 3 items. Richmond, Va.

Personal letters of George Douglas Wise, a member of the United States House of Representatives, concerning a job and a loan for a friend.

5852. GEORGE NEWTON WISE PAPERS, 1861-1863. 1 item and 1 vol. Alexandria (Arlington County), Va.

Diary, 1861-1863, of George Newton Wise, a Confederate soldier in the 17th Virginia Regiment, containing accounts of battles and skirmishes in Virginia at Alexandria, Manassas, Goose Creek, Leesburg, Dranesville, Williamsburg, Seven Pines, Gaines' Mill, Frazier's Farm, Malvern Hill, Fredericksburg, and Suffolk. Also a photograph of Wise in his Confederate uniform.

5853. HENRY ALEXANDER WISE PAPERS, 1833-1894. 34 items. Richmond, Va.

Papers of Henry Alexander Wise (1806-1876), member of the United States Congress, U. S. minister to Brazil, and governor of Virginia, contain correspondence, 1867-1876, with Nahum Capen, concerning a liberal government for the South, Wise's antipathy toward the Radicals, and Capen's work, "The History of Democracy"; a letter, 1859, to David Hubbard of Alabama, giving Wise's views on slavery, popular sovereignty and Kansas, and the burning of the College of William and Mary, Williamsburg, Virginia; a letter, 1853, to Wise from R. M. T. Hunter concerning their political disagreements and the selection of a cabinet by President Franklin Pierce; a letter, 1836, by Wise commenting on political corruption, particularly in the United States House of Representatives; a letter, 1856, in which Wise discusses the forthcoming presidential election; and miscellaneous official papers and personal or business letters.

5854. MICHAEL WISE LEDGERS, 1835-1853. 2 vols. Bridgewater (Rockingham County), Va.

Volumes contain the accounts of a tanner, who probably also operated as a saddler.

5855. PETER WISE AND FRANK W. WISE PAPERS, 1861-1869. 57 items. Richmond, Va.

Family correspondence of the Wise family, containing the letters of Peter Wise and his wife, Alice Wise, concerning family gossip, news of the Civil War, inflation, the scarcity of food, Union raids, and tobacco fortunes made in Richmond, Virginia. Letters of Jean (Wise) Whitwell describe the destruction of Virginia Military Institute, Lexington, and the removal of the school to Richmond, Virginia. Letters of Will, Ned, and George Wise describe life in the Confederate Army. Letters of Frank W. Wise concern his work in the Confederate Treasury Department in Richmond, Virginia, and Columbia, South Carolina; trips to Texas and Mexico for the Confederate government; and his participation in the defense of Richmond, Virginia, in 1864.

5856. THOMAS JAMES WISE PAPERS, 1896-1933. 26 items. London, England.

Copies of twenty letters between Professor Newman I. White, Eric Morrell, and T. J. Wise (1859-1937), bibliographer, dealer in rare books and manuscripts, and literary forger, regarding the purchase of books from Wise. There are also six original letters of Wise, including two to Coulson Kernahan, and one to "Percy" regarding Byron's work.

5857. WILLIAM B. WISE PAPERS, 1846-1892. 60 items and 1 vol. Murfreesboro (Hertford County), N.C.

Correspondence and accounts of William B. Wise, merchant, relating to his dry goods and naval stores business and to runaway slaves.

5858. JAMES H. WISWELL PAPERS, 1861-1867. 97 items. Hydeville (Rutland County), Vt.

Letters of James H. Wiswell, a Union soldier in 4th United States Regiment, Cavalry, concerning his training in the cavalry barracks at Carlisle, Pennsylvania, and Fort Leavenworth, Kansas; his participation in fighting in Missouri and Tennessee, including the battle of Wilson's Creek, 1861, and the Tennessee campaign at Murfreesboro, Chickamauga, and Chattanooga; cavalry life; and business speculation and economic life in Knoxville and Nashville, Tennessee, at the end of the war.

5859. JAMES WITCHER PAPERS, 1856. 2 items. Bristol (Sullivan County), Tenn.

Letters of James Witcher, an attorney, concerning the sale of slaves.

5860. WILLIAM WITHERLE PAPERS, 1826-1851. 34 items. Castine (Hancock County), Me.

Business papers of William Witherle, including letters and accounts of ships' captains, relating to the operation of the ship *Antioch*, 1826-1839, between Castine, Maine; New Orleans, Louisiana; Liverpool, England; Le Havre, France; and Philadelphia, Pennsylvania. After 1839 the papers concern another ship owned by Witherle, the *St. Cloud*, sailing in the coastal trade between New Orleans, Louisiana; New York, New York; Boston, Massachusetts; and Castine, Maine.

5861. ROBERT ENOCH WITHERS PAPERS, 1875-1894. 5 items. Wytheville (Wythe County), Va.

Letters and an autobiography of Robert Enoch Withers (1821-1907), a United States senator and consul at Hong Kong, 1885-1889.

5862. ROBERT W. WITHERS PAPERS, 1830. 1 item. Greensboro (Hale County), Ala.

Typescript copy of the presidential address of Robert W. Withers (1798-1854) delivered to the Agricultural Society of Greensboro, Alabama, criticizing the dependence of the South on cotton and advocating the restoration of soil fertility through the use of chemicals.

5863. GEORGE M. WITHERSPOON PAPERS, 1768 (1834-1872). 26 items. Lancaster County, S.C.

Business letters and papers of George M. Witherspoon as a lawyer, and personal letters outlining his career as a member of the South Carolina legislature in the 1850s, a member of the home guard, 1861, and candidate for judge, 1865. There are also a land grant, 1768, and a pardon, 1866, granted Witherspoon by President Andrew Johnson for participation in the Civil War.

5864. HENRY K. WITHERSPOON PAPERS, 1862-1863. 5 items. Camden (Kershaw County), S.C.

Personal letters of Henry K. Witherspoon, a Confederate soldier.

5865. ELVIRA WITHROW PAPERS, 1864. 2 items. Banks County, Ga.

Civil War letters of Elvira Withrow, concerning the evacuation of women from Cass Station, Georgia, to Atlanta, to Athens, and finally to Banks County, Georgia.

5866. P. A. WITMER PAPERS, 1871-1897. 14 items. Hagerstown (Washington County), Md.

Letters to P. A. Witmer from various political leaders of Maryland, concerning Witmer's appointment to the Maryland board of education; the Maryland Agricultural College; the Hagerstown, Maryland, fair of 1897; and the presidential election of 1884.

5867. JOHN WOLCOT PAPERS, 1790-1820. 352 items. Exeter, England.

Photostatic copies, with the exception of fifty-five original items from the "Pindar" works and satires on one "Crimp," of the literary and financial papers of John Wolcot (1738-1819), English physician, painter, and poet, generally known as "Peter Pindar." Included are many bills from publishers for printing and binding Wolcott's numerous literary productions as well as contracts, promissory notes, accounts from his legal advisers, papers resulting from litigation in the settlement of the estates of his uncles, and undated literary notes, many being so interlined and corrected as to be almost illegible.

5868. LAURA B. WOLCOTT PAPERS, 1840, 1844. 2 items. Salisbury (Litchfield County), Conn.

Letters to Laura B. Wolcott, a student, dealing with family affairs, the presidential campaign of 1844, and Loco-Focoism.

5869. N. S. WOLCOTT PAPERS, 1861, 1865. 2 items. Washington, D.C.

Letters of N. S. Wolcott describing Abraham Lincoln's first inauguration; Senator Louis T. Wigfall's secession speech, 1861; secession sentiment in Virginia; and the escape of a Union soldier from a Confederate military prison.

5870. OLIVER WOLCOTT PAPERS, 1795-1797. 6 items. Philadelphia, Pa.

Letters from Oliver Wolcott (1760-1833), United States secretary of the treasury, to David Henley, Indian commissioner in Tennessee, about furnishing supplies to troops sent to Tennessee in connection with Indian problems.

5871. ROGER WOLCOTT, JR., PAPERS, 1757. 1 item. Wallingford (New Haven County), Conn.

Legal document ordering that Nash Yale of Wallingford appear in the Hartford County Court.

5872. GARNET JOSEPH WOLSELEY, PAPERS, VISCOUNT WOLSELEY, PAPERS, 1873-1913. 128 items. London, England.

Papers of Garnet Joseph Wolseley, First Viscount Wolseley, British soldier and commander-in-chief of the British Army, 1895-1900, contain letters, 1873, concerning the Ashanti War; letters, 1885-1887, to Sir Alfred Edward Turner pertaining to an attempt to blackmail Turner because of his alleged involvement in a plot to murder the Mahdi of Sudan; letters, 1885-1903, to Sir Guy Douglas Fleetwood Wilson concerning the Ashanti War and Wolseley's autobiography; letters, 1891-1909, to Sir George Benjamin Wolseley relating to the Boer War, British Army commanders in South Africa, war office administration, Wolseley's relations with Lord Lansdowne, secretary of state for war, and family matters; letters, 1877, to George Bentley relating to Wolseley's part in securing publication for a novel by Maria Georgiana (Carleton) Fetherstonhaugh, and letters, 1885-1892, to Bentley, concerning Wolseley's research for and the publication of his Life of John Churchill, Duke of Marlborough (London: Bentley, 1894). Other letters in the collection concern the objectives of Charles Stewart Parnell and the Irish Party, 1886; and army administration.

5873. ALLEN WATSON WOMACK PAPERS, 1790-1870. 15 items. Pittsylvania County, Va.

The collection is made up for the most part of business papers of the Womack family, including a letter, 1864, mentioning commodity prices in Virginia during the Civil War and an appraisal list of slaves belonging to the estate of Allen Womack in 1849.

5874. JEHU J. WOMBLE PAPERS, 1850-1869. 6 items. Pittsboro (Chatham County), N.C.

Tax receipts.

5875. CHARLES WOOD, FIRST VISCOUNT HALIFAX, PAPERS, 1864. 1 item. London, England.

Letter to Charles Wood, First Viscount Halifax, British politician and administrator, commenting on a recommendation for an Indian judgeship.

5876. SIR HENRY EVELYN WOOD PAPERS, 1848-1919. 232 items. London, England.

Papers of Sir Henry Evelyn Wood, British field marshal, contain letters discussing events in the Crimean War, written as a result of the publication in 1895 of Wood's The Crimea in 1854 and in 1894; a letter, 1873, on the Ashanti War; letters, 1878-1880, pertaining to the Zulu War, particularly the death of Ronald George Elidor Campbell and the service of Piet Uys to the British cause; letters, 1880-1881, relating to the Transvaal War and the death of Sir George Colley; letters on the situation in Egypt in the 1880s and 1890s; letters, 1898-1914, from Lord Roberts on military matters; letters after 1890 concerning the administration of the army, army reform, and Wood's work in training troops; and a few letters on World War I. Other letters in the collection concern army hygiene, 1868; the efficiency of volunteer units, 1905; Australian concern about the growing power of Japan, 1895; and the disestablishment of the Church of England.

5877. JOSIAH WOOD PAPERS, 1862-1865. 81 items. New Bedford (Bristol County), Mass.

Letters of Josiah Wood, a Union soldier in the 27th Massachusetts Regiment, describe the movements of his regiments in North Carolina and Virginia; a skirmish near Petersburg, Virginia, 1863; and Wood's experiences in a Confederate prison in Richmond, Virginia.

5878. LEONARD WOOD PAPERS, 1917-1919. 3 items. Washington, D.C.

Letters of Leonard Wood, American soldier and military governor of Cuba and the Philippine Islands, concerning his interest in military preparedness.

5879. SAMUEL O. WOOD PAPERS AND ACCOUNT BOOKS, 1847 (1855-1880) 1899. 368 items. Gay's Landing (Marengo County), Ala.

Correspondence and business papers of Samuel O. Wood, plantation overseer and probably an agent for a commission merchant, including letters from James P. Tarry, owner of the plantation in Perry County, Alabama, in Wood's charge, with repeated injunctions, 1851-1854, that Wood should not whip the slaves; and information on current prices of slaves. After 1855 Wood's correspondence refers to his work in a commission house in Cahaba, Alabama, with references to prices and markets for slaves and cotton. After 1861, when Wood moved to Gay's Landing and established himself as a cotton planter and collector, his papers consist of bills, tax assessments, promissory notes, prices current, and communications from commission merchants around Mobile, Alabama.

5880. THOMAS F. WOOD, INC., PAPERS, 1913-1923. 1 vol. Wilmington (New Hanover County), N.C.

Ledger of Thomas F. Wood, Inc., wholesale and retail ship chandlers and provisioners, 1913-1923.

5881. THOMAS FANNING WOOD PAPERS, 1885. 1 item. Wilmington (New Hanover County), N.C.

Letter from Alvan Wentworth Chapman to Thomas Fanning Wood, physician and secretary of the North Carolina state board of health, concerning the Reverend Moses Ashley Curtis, botanist and minister.

5882. WILLIAM WOOD DAYBOOK, 1819-1831. 1 vol. (244 pp.) Winchester (Frederick County), Va.

Records of a general store.

5883. WILLIAM PAGE WOOD, FIRST BARON HATHERLEY, PAPERS, 1871. 1 item. London, England.

Letter to William Page Wood, First Baron Hatherley, Lord Chancellor of England, from Lord Lawrence, a recent viceroy of India, giving his opinion about appeals from courts in India to the privy council.

5884. JOHN WOODALL PAPERS, (1837-1876) 1905. 96 items. Prince Edward County, Va.

Family letters between a plantation overseer and his brother, William Woodall, a poor white farmer, throwing light on social and agricultural conditions, depicting life on a small farm in Virginia, and commenting on the migration of small farmers to the West after the Civil War. There are numerous references to the cultivation of tobacco. Included also are a few letters from Thomas T. Treadway, owner of the plantation which Woodall managed and member of the Virginia House of Delegates, regarding farming operations.

5885. ELIZABETH BOWEN WOODBERRY PAPERS, 1842-1846. 35 items. Beverly (Essex County), Mass.

Personal letters to Elizabeth Bowen Woodberry from her cousin, Isaac Story, Jr.

5886. LEVI WOODBURY PAPERS, 1830-1843. 25 items. Washington, D.C.

Papers of Levi Woodbury (1789-1851), secretary of the navy, 1831-1834, and secretary of the treasury, 1834-1841, concern the appointment of James M. Bankhead as a midshipman; the dismissal of Joseph L. Kuhn, paymaster of the marine corps; reports to Woodbury on the value of the monetary units of Brazil, England, Italy, Mexico, Puerto Rico, Venezuela, and Saint Croix; the views and directions of President Martin Van Buren on the issuance of land patents; and payments to a government revenue inspector.

5887. WOODLAWN MILLS DAYBOOK, 1874-1875. 1 vol. (329 pp.) Woodlawn Mills (Gaston County), N.C.

Records of a textile mill.

5888. WOODLAWN MILLS STORE DAYBOOK, 1879-1880. 1 vol. (237 pp.) Woodlawn Mills (Gaston County), N.C.

Records of a general store.

5889. JAMES LESLIE WOODRESS PAPERS, 1957-1976. 1,659 items. Davis (Yolo County), Calif.

Correspondence of Woodress, professor of American literature at the University of California, Davis, concerning his editorship of various works. There is correspondence between Woodress and contributors to American Literary Scholarship: an Annual, with partial manuscripts of contributions; correspondence relative to the compilation and publication of a revision of Eight American Authors (New York: 1971); correspondence between Woodress and Duke University Press concerning a revision of Dissertations in American Literature, 1891-1955, with a supplement, 1956-1961; and correspondence with Duke University Press, contributors and editors, and manuscripts of the forward, introduction, and some of the contributions for Essays Mostly on Periodical Publishing in America: A Collection in Honor of Dr. Clarence Gohdes (Durham: 1973).

5890. REBECCA WOODRING DIARY, 1872-1873. 1 item. Flint Rock (Catawba County), N.C.

Diary of Rebecca Woodring, containing information on social life, religious life, and the weather.

5891. BENJAMIN E. WOODRUFF PAPERS, 1824-1884. 454 items. Hicks Ford (Greenville County), Va.

Business papers of Benjamin E. Woodruff, containing merchants' bills and receipts, tax bills and receipts, notes for money borrowed and lent, and papers concerning the hiring of slaves. Also contains an insurance policy, licenses to preach in the Methodist Church, and a document signed by an officer of the Freedmen's Bureau establishing an apprenticeship for two orphans, 1866.

5892. ISABELLA ANN (ROBERTS) WOODRUFF PAPERS, 1857 (1860-1865) 1869. 277 items. Charleston, S.C.

Correspondence of Isabella (Roberts) Woodruff (b. 1837), a schoolteacher, giving accounts of middle-class society in Charleston, and Civil War difficulties. Included also are courtship letters of Charles F. A. Holst to Isabella (Roberts) Woodruff, beginning in 1865 and ultimately giving many details of the period during and after Sherman's march through South Carolina.

5893. JOSEPHUS WOODRUFF DIARY, 1874-1875. 1 vol. (112 pp.) Charleston, S.C.

Diary of Josephus Woodruff, Republican clerk of the South Carolina senate, for the most part concerning his business, the Republican Printing Company, which was involved in the corruption of the Reconstruction government in South Carolina, including methods of influencing legislators, divisions in the Republican Party, and Woodruff's dislike of F. W. Dawson and B. R. Riordan of the Charleston Daily News.

5894. MILFORD F. WOODRUFF PAPERS, 1858. 1 item. Lowndesboro (Lowndes County), Ala.

Personal letter of Milford F. Woodruff.

5895. ELIZABETH WOODS PAPERS, 1817-1830. 12 items. Preston, Lancaster County, England.

Attendance records of a Sunday school class for girls in the Methodist society at Preston, England, taught by Elizabeth Woods. Several of the lists also include statements of financial contributions.

5896. FRANCIS H. WOODS PAPERS, 1863-1865. 17 items. Worcester (Worcester County), Mass.

Civil War correspondence of Francis H. Woods, a Union soldier in the 137th New York Regiment, from Fortress Monroe and the siege of Petersburg, Virginia, describing his duties as cook, camp life, and prayer meetings.

5897. J. F. WOODS PAPERS, 1865. 2 items. New Bern (Craven County), and Raleigh (Wake County), N.C.

Letters of J. F. Woods, a Union soldier, describing the occupation of New Bern and Raleigh and the celebration of Union troops on hearing of Lee's surrender.

5898. JOSEPH T. WOODS PAPERS, 1833 (1862-1865) 1887. 140 items. Randolph (Portage County), Ohio.

Personal letters from Joseph T. Woods, surgeon of the 99th Ohio Regiment, to his sister "Sade." Most of the letters were written during the Civil War period and concern censorship in army camps; the battle of Port Republic, 1862; General Lew Wallace, 1862; the battle of Nashville, 1862; a battle near Chattanooga, 1863; and the attitude of Southern women toward "Yankees," 1863.

5899. LEONARD WOODS, JR., PAPERS, 1862. 1 item. Brunswick (Cumberland County), Me.

Letter of Leonard Woods, Jr., a Congregationalist clergyman and president of Bowdoin College, 1839-1866, concerning the work of his father, Leonard Woods, a noted theologian and professor at Andover Seminary.

5900. WILLIAM G. WOODS PAPERS, 1864-1865. 6 items. Johnson's Island (Erie County), Ohio, and Fort Delaware (New Castle County), Del.

Letters of William G. Woods, a Confederate prisoner of war in the Union prisons at Johnson's Island, Ohio, and Fort Delaware, Delaware, describing prison life and inquiring about friends and conditions in Caswell County, North Carolina.

5901. AGATHA (ABNEY) WOODSON PAPERS, 1896-1916. 25 items. Edgefield (Edgefield County), S.C.

Papers of Agatha (Abney) Woodson, genealogist, writer, local historian, and civic leader of Edgefield, South Carolina, contain letters, 1896-1916, pertaining to the United Daughters of the Confederacy; copies of Civil War stories by Confederate Army veterans; and poems and prose by Woodson and others on the literature of South Carolina, the Civil War, and secession.

5902. ELVIRA L. WOODSON PAPERS, 1857-1875. 21 items. Appomattox Court House (Appomattox County), Va.

Correspondence of Elvira L. Woodson with friends and relatives in Virginia and in Saline County, Missouri, describing social life, schools, and Appomattox County, Virginia, during the Civil War.

5903. WOODSTOCK INVESTMENT COMPANY RECORDS, 1891. 1 vol. (9 pp.) Roanoke (Roanoke County), Va.

Minute book of the Woodstock Company. Also contains records of antique sales, 1940-1941.

5904. JAMES L. WOODVILLE PAPERS, (1817-1847) 1871. 381 items. Fincastle (Botetourt County), Va.

Business and professional correspondence of James L. Woodville, Virginia lawyer, member of the House of Delegates, 1825, and later president of the Branch Bank of Virginia at Buchanan, Virginia.

5905. ROBERT WOODY AND NEWTON DIXON WOODY PAPERS, 1784 (1835-1887) 1939. 2,328 items and 20 vols. Chatham County and Guilford County, N.C.

Papers of Robert Woody, Newton Dixon Woody, and other members of the Woody family concern the mercantile and milling businesses of Robert Woody in Chatham County, North Carolina, and Newton Dixon Woody in Guilford County, North Carolina, in the 1850s; the decision of Newton D. Woody to leave North Carolina during the Civil War and his return in 1865; experiences of Frank H. Woody, a lawyer, in the Washington and Montana territories in the 1860s and 1870s; news from relatives living in Indiana; temperance meetings, including the General Southern Temperance Conference at Fayetteville, North Carolina, 1835; commodity prices; general economic conditions; experiences of Mary Ann Woody as a student at New Garden Boarding School, Guilford County, 1852-1853; descriptions of camp life by a soldier in the 21st North Carolina Regiment during the Civil War; experiences of Confederate soldiers in Union prisons at Johnson's Island, Ohio, and Elmira, New York, during the war; accounts of Reconstruction in Augusta, Georgia, given by a Union sympathizer, 1867-1868; and the upkeep of roads in Guilford County. Printed matter in the collection relates to the activities of Unionists in North Carolina during the Civil War and opposition to Ulysses S. Grant and the Radicals. Volumes include minutes of meetings of the Orange Peace Society, Orange County, North Carolina, 1824-1830; memorandum books; an account book kept during the construction of a Quaker church at High Falls, North Carolina, 1905-1909; minute book of meetings of the Friends of Prosperity, 1913-1914; and financial record books of Robert Woody and Newton Dixon Woody.

5906. JOHN ELLIS WOOL PAPERS, 1837-1869. 6 items. Troy (Rensselaer County), N.Y.

Papers relating to the military career of John Ellis Wool, an American soldier, including a letter, 1837, reporting on the resistance of the Cherokee Indians to efforts to remove them from North Carolina to the western United States; and a report from Buena Vista, Mexico, 1848, concerning the murder of three American soldiers.

5907. WILLIAM WOOLDRIDGE DIARY, 1855-1858. 1 vol. (244 pp.) Bridgeville (Pickens County), Ala.

Personal diary of William Wooldridge, with a few comments on a smallpox epidemic.

5908. CONSTANCE FENIMORE WOOLSON PAPERS, 1883. 1 item. Cleveland, Ohio.

Letter of author Constance Fenimore Woolson to Hamilton Wright Mabie, editor and critic associated with the Christian Union, concerning Woolson's writing, especially her novelette, For the Major; and her approval of the Christian Union.

5909. SHADRACK WOOTEN PAPERS, 1863-1894. 136 items. Clarkton (Bladen County), N.C.

Bills, receipts, indentures, warrants, and a few letters, mainly concerning the sale of land and lawsuits.

5910. WOOTEN AND TAYLOR COMPANY PAPERS, 1846-1884. 111 items. Catherine Lake (Onslow County), N.C.

Business papers of the firm of Wooten and Taylor, for the most part dealing with the purchase and sale of naval stores and general merchandise, the shipment of goods by water, and personal correspondence and legal papers of Charles Duffy and Simon B. Taylor.

5911. JOSEPH EMERSON WORCESTER PAPERS, 1830-1834. 6 items. Cambridge (Middlesex County), Mass.

Letters from Joseph Emerson Worcester (1784-1865), editor of the American Almanac, concerning material for that publication.

5912. WORTH FAMILY PAPERS, 1844-1955. 693 items and 8 vols. Wilmington (New Hanover County), N.C.

Papers of the Worth family of North Carolina contain papers of Jonathan Worth (1802-1869), lawyer and governor of North Carolina, including a few of his official papers as governor, 1865-1868; correspondence relating to his business interests and law practice; and letters of Jonathan Worth and Martitia (Daniel) Worth in the 1850s to a son at the University of North Carolina, Chapel Hill, concerning family matters and the construction of a plank road near Asheboro, North Carolina. Papers of David Gaston Worth (1831-1897) contain essays from Worth's college days; Civil War correspondence concerning financial conditions in the Confederacy and the Confederate salt works at Wilmington, North Carolina; material relating to Bingham School, Mebane, North Carolina, and the Fifth Street Methodist Church, Wilmington, North Carolina; and business papers. Papers of William Elliott Worth contain a ledger, 1906-1911, for William E. Worth and Company, dealers in ice, coal, wood, and other merchandise; and records of the Universal Oil and Fertilizer Company, including a ledger, 1903-1914, and a letter-press book, 1906-1907, concerning the manufacture and marketing of various fertilizers, cottonseed oil, and related products. Papers of Charles William Worth contain letters to his parents while he was a student at Bingham School, and at the University of North Carolina, Chapel Hill; and letters, 1912-1913, from many prominent North Carolinians attempting to have Worth appointed American consul at Shanghai, China. The collection also contains five account books, 1888-1924, of Worth & Worth and its successor, The Worth Co., a Wilmington firm of grocers and commission merchants which also traded in cotton and naval stores.

5913. FRANCIS WRANGHAM PAPERS, 1806-1836. 3 items. Yorkshire, England.

Papers of Francis Wrangham, classical scholar and miscellaneous writer, contain a copy of the poem, "Col. Thornton's Departure from York to Spy Park in Wiltshire," attributed to Martin Hawke; a poem by Wrangham entitled "Lines on Leaving Hornby Castle"; a poem eulogizing Charles James Fox, written by Wrangham; and a letter, 1836, recounting an amusing incident at the home of Walter Ramsden Hawksworth Fawkes.

5914. FLORA MAY WRENN AND LIZZIE TAYLOR WRENN PAPERS, 1906-1959. 4 items. Siler City (Chatham County), N.C.

The papers of Flora May Wrenn and Lizzie Taylor Wrenn, alumnae of Trinity College, Durham, North Carolina, include the diploma of Lizzie T. Wrenn, 1912, from Trinity College; and a letter, 1908, to Flora May Wrenn from John C. Kilgo, president of Trinity College, concerning the gymnastics course for women students.

5915. AMBROSE RANSOM WRIGHT PAPERS, 1861-1866. 23 items. Augusta (Richmond County), Ga.

Papers of Ambrose Ransom Wright, Confederate officer, Georgia legislator, and newspaper editor, contain miscellaneous letters and documents concerning Wright's service in the Confederate Army on the coast of North Carolina, 1861; the transfer of officers under Wright's command, 1863; and personal affairs and requests for assistance.

5916. BRYANT WRIGHT PAPERS, 1859-1864. 24 items. Tallapoosa County, Ala.

Correspondence of Bryant Wright, a soldier in the 29th Alabama Regiment during the Civil War, and his wife, Lydia Wright, concerning the activities of his regiment and life in Tallapoosa County, Alabama.

5917. ELIZUR WRIGHT PAPERS, 1837. 1 item. New York, N.Y.

Papers of Elizur Wright, insurance actuary, reformer, and abolitionist, contain a letter, 1837, from Ellis Gray Loring, an anti-slavery lawyer, concerning legal papers to be presented to the Massachusetts legislature dealing with jury trial for alleged fugitive slaves.

5918. GEORGE FINNEY WRIGHT PAPERS, 1864. 2 items. Baltimore, Md.

Personal letters of George Finney Wright, a Baltimore businessman originally from Accomack County, Virginia.

5919. J. D. WRIGHT AND JOSEPH WRIGHT PAPERS, 1861-1865. 38 items. Pittsylvania County, Va.

Personal correspondence of J. D. Wright and Joseph Wright, Confederate soldiers, concerning camp life, casualties and medical treatment, and the siege of Petersburg, Virginia, 1864-1865.

5920. SIR JAMES WRIGHT PAPERS, 1756-1781. 18 items. Savannah, Ga.

Papers of Sir James Wright, royal governor of Georgia, contain official papers, relating mainly to the settlement of estates. Also contains an address to Wright by loyalists in Georgia concerning the activities of Georgia patriots.

5921. JAMES M. WRIGHT PAPERS, 1861-1865. 18 items. Chamblissburg (Bedford County), Va.

Letters of James M. Wright, a Confederate soldier, showing the gradual decline of spirits among Southerners as the Civil War continued.

5922. MARCUS JOSEPH WRIGHT PAPERS, 1864-1951. 192 items. Washington, D.C.

Papers of Marcus J. Wright (1831-1922), soldier, editor of the Official Records of the War of the Rebellion, and author, contain letters relating to Wright's search for records of the Civil War and his requests for information about the war experiences of various individuals; and correspondence with W. R. Benjamin and Belmont Perry concerning the sale of papers in Wright's possession.

5923. RICHARD HARVEY WRIGHT PAPERS, 1870-1952. 232,079 items and 178 vols. Durham, N.C.

The papers of Richard Harvey Wright contain correspondence, 1873-1952; legal papers; printed matter; business papers; financial papers; and clippings relating to Wright's business interests, particularly the Wright Machinery Company of Durham, North Carolina, manufacturer of packaging for tobacco products and various other kinds of commodities. There is much information on the economic history of Durham and the development of the tobacco industry. Volumes in the collection include financial records and letterpress books for business correspondence.

5924. THOMAS S. WRIGHT PAPERS, 1845-1852. 27 items. Belford (Nash County), N.C.

Personal correspondence between Thomas S. Wright, overseer and physician, and two of his brothers who were physicians, containing information on their medical training, on Wake Forest College, North Carolina, 1845, and on medical practice in Georgia and North Carolina.

5925. WILLIAM WRIGHT PAPERS, 1827-1851. 29 items. Newark, N.J., and Washington, D.C.

Family letters of William Wright, United States senator from New Jersey, his son, Edward H. Wright, and his daughter, Kate Wright. Also contains letters, 1828-1830, to David Arnold of Rawlings, New York, from his sons, Benjamin F. Arnold and H. C. Arnold.

5926. WRIGHT FAMILY PAPERS, 1853-1882. 89 items. Cleveland County, N.C.

The Wright family papers contain the correspondence of Benjamin Wright and Elizabeth Wright with their children and other members of their families concerning personal and family matters, and letters of Noah J. Wright, Lemuel S. Wright, and Benoni C. Wright, Confederate soldiers in the 48th and 56th North Carolina Regiments, concerning the war in North Carolina and Virginia; the siege of Petersburg, Virginia, 1864; desertion among Confederate troops; and the war weariness of soldiers and civilians.

5927. WRIGHT AND CLAY CASH RECEIPTS JOURNAL, 1861-1863. 1 vol. (297 pp.) Roxboro (Person County), N.C.

Cash receipts journal of a general merchandise firm.

5928. WRIGHT-HARRIS PAPERS, 1806-1885. 200 items. Centreville (Queen Annes County), Md., and Quincy (Gadsden County), Fla.

Papers of Lydia Ann (Tilton) Wright and Isaac R. Harris contain correspondence with numerous friends and relations concerning family matters; the Mississippi Territory; the Mexican War; the Compromise of 1850; politics, business, and the construction of railroads, particularly the Pensacola and Georgia line, in Florida; travel in the United States in the 1850s; the secession crisis; and the attitude of Southerners in the period after the Civil War.

5929. J. T. WYATT PAPERS, 1860-1908. 60 items. Faith (Rowan County), and Salisbury (Rowan County), N.C.

The J. T. Wyatt papers contain business letters to E. E. Phillips and J. T. Wyatt pertaining to the quarrying and sale of granite, the Georgia state lottery, and prohibition.

5930. CHARLES CECIL WYCHE PAPERS, 1902-1924. 9,736 items. Spartanburg (Spartanburg County), S.C. Restricted.

Papers of Charles Cecil Wyche, lawyer and United States district judge for the western district of South Carolina, contain correspondence and papers concerning business and legal affairs, politics, and family matters, including Wyche's support of John Gary Evans in his campaign to be United States senator from South Carolina, 1908; descriptions of Paris, Brussels, and Berlin in letters of Isoline Wyche, 1909-1910; an attempt to prevent the granting of a pardon by Governor Cole L. Blease of South Carolina, 1911; Wyche's term in the state legislature, 1913; Wyche's legal business, particularly relating to the collection of debts and suits for damages in cases of industrial and automobile accidents; the campaign of Cole L. Blease for the governorship of South Carolina, 1916; attempts by Wyche to form a regiment of volunteers for service in Mexico or Europe; the influenza epidemic of 1920; and the national and state election of 1924, especially Wyche's support for James F. Byrnes in his race for the United States Senate against Nathaniel Barksdale Dial.

5931. WILLIAM WYLIE PAPERS, 1845-1863. 15 items. Lancaster (Lancaster County), S.C.

Letters of the Wylie family concerning politics, race relations, the Mexican War, and family matters. Civil War letters deal with the fortification of Fort Pillow, Tennessee, 1861; skirmishes of the 5th South Carolina Regiment, 1861; and the reactions of soldiers and civilians to various events during the war.

5932. RICHARD WYLLY PAPERS, 1790-1793. 3 items. Savannah, Ga.

Business papers of Richard Wylly.

5933. THOMAS K. WYLY PAPERS, 1823-1855. 22 items. Reynoldsburg (Humphreys County), Tenn., and Canton (Madison County), Miss.

Business papers of Thomas K. Wyly and John Wyly, merchants, relating to accounts in New Orleans, Baltimore, and Philadelphia, concerning cotton and tobacco markets and the Mississippi River trade.

5934. CHARLES WATKIN WILLIAMS WYNN PAPERS, 1840. 1 item. London, England.

Letter to Charles Watkin Williams Wynn, British politician, concerning information about Lord Cobham requested by John W. Croker.

5935. A. R. WYNNE PAPERS, 1818-1866. 40 items. Castalian Springs (Sumner County), Tenn.

Letters to A. R. Wynne, a prominent planter, concerning the purchase and sale of slaves; land purchases in Forsyth County, North Carolina; and the settlement of promissory notes.

5936. BENJAMIN CUDWORTH YANCEY PAPERS, 1846-1882. 102 items. Charleston, S.C.

Correspondence of Benjamin Cudworth Yancey (b. 1817), planter, lawyer, and minister to Argentina, discussing plantation affairs; the settlement of the estate of his father-in-law, Thomas Napier Hamilton; the price of slaves; difficulties in negotiating a treaty with Argentina; conditions in Atlanta, Georgia, 1861; business affairs and problems with slave labor during the Civil War; and the education of his son, Hamilton Yancey, at the University of Georgia, Athens, and at the University of Virginia, Charlottesville, and of his daughter, Mary Louise Yancey, at a school probably in Staunton, Virginia.

5937. WILLIAM LOWNDES YANCEY PAPERS, 1846. 2 items. Wetumpka (Elmore County), Ala.

Political correspondence of William Lowndes Yancey (1814-1863), lawyer, editor of the Cahaba Democrat and the Wetumpka Argus, Alabama legislator, member of U. S. Congress, 1847, and Confederate congressman.

5938. SOLOMON VANCE YANTIS PAPERS, 1863-1896. 56 items. Harpers Ferry (Jefferson County), W. Va.

Papers of Solomon Vance Yantis (1826-1899), tobacconist, secretary and part owner of a flour mill, city councilman, and postmaster, include letters concerning the work of the relief committee at Harpers Ferry in distributing aid to sufferers from a flood; letters from his son, Arnold Stevens Yantis, describing college life at Western Maryland College, Westminster, Maryland; letter from his brother-in-law in Ellensburg, Oregon, discussing the town's salmon cannery, lumbering, and the town and its citizens; bills and receipts relating to the purchase of tobacco, flour and other items; and a receipt book showing rent paid by Yantis to James McGraw.

5939. WILLIAM S. YARD PAPERS, 1861-1865. 8 items. Trenton (Mercer County), N.J.

Soldiers' letters to William S. Yard from John G. Doran, 4th Regiment of New Jersey Volunteers, U.S.A., while stationed at Camp Seminary, Virginia; from W. C. Yard, 4th Pennsylvania Cavalry, U.S.A., while stationed at Washington, D.C., concerning camp life; and from John Y. Bennett while at Fort Powhatan, Virginia, describing the heavy firing on Petersburg.

5940. FRANCIS COPE YARNALL PAPERS, 1853-1861. 4 items and 1 vol. Wynndown, Overbrook (Montgomery County), Pa.

Volume (88 pp.) entitled "Letters on Slavery, F.C.Y., 1853" of Francis Cope Yarnall (1830-1890), businessman with interests in railroads, coal operations, and slate quarries; and clippings. The work discusses the institution of slavery in the South, followed by a series of letters between Yarnall and "Professor M" in New York, New York, in which Yarnall attacks slavery and "Professor M" defends it. Topics confronted include condition and treatment of slaves; character of slaves; house servants; field hands; planters; overseers; black drivers; the agricultural system; cruelty to slaves and how it was dealt with by the legal system and in actual practice; fugitive slaves; education and religious instruction; internal slave trade; the effects of slavery on the white population and upon Southern economic development; the relation between cotton culture and slavery; effects of Northern agitation; attitudes of Southerners toward slavery and toward public opinion; effect of advances in transportation; colonization in Africa; condition of blacks in Africa; labor in the North; inequality as a condition of life; the role of an advanced race in elevating the less advanced; possible evils of abolition; the relation between Christianity and slavery; prejudice in the North and South; emancipation in Jamaica; the Fugitive Slave Law; the loss of leaders as Henry Clay, John C. Calhoun, and Daniel Webster; Southern slave laws; and the Nebraska Bill.

5941. JAMES L. YATES PAPERS, 1863-1865. 33 items. Lincoln (Logan County), Ill.

Civil War letters of Sergeant James L. Yates, Company C, 106th Regiment of Illinois Infantry, U.S.A., concerning personal matters and religious meetings in camp, with general references to the war and army life.

5942. JOSEPH M. YATES SHOP BOOK, 1827-1829. 1 vol.

Accounts of a blacksmith.

5943. LEVI SMITHWICK YATES LEDGER, 1861-1866. 1 vol. (392 pp.) Williamston (Martin County), N.C.

Physician's account book.

5944. RICHARD YATES PAPERS, 1862. 1 item. Jacksonville (Morgan County), Ill.

Letter to Richard Yates (1815-1873), then governor of Illinois, from Robert F. Stratton, surgeon with the 11th Illinois Cavalry, U.S.A., requesting a promotion.

5945. ROBERT YATES PAPERS, 1776. 1 item. Albany (Albany County), N.Y.

Facsimile of orders from Robert Yates (1738-1801), lawyer, judge, and Revolutionary patriot, to New York recruiting officers of the Continental Army.

5946. SAMUEL B. YATES PAPERS, 1860-1862. 12 items. West Milford (Harrison County), Va.

Family correspondence of Samuel B. Yates, Company F, 18th Virginia Cavalry, C.S.A., discussing sadness over the outbreak of the Civil War, division of opinion in Virginia over secession, the formation of companies on each side, food, and picket duty. There is also a list of battles in which Yates participated.

5947. LACY WALTER GILES YEA PAPERS, 1854. 1 item. Pyrland Hall, Somersetshire, England.

Letter of Lacy Walter Giles Yea (1808-1855), British army officer commanding the 7th Royal Fusiliers during the Crimean War, written from a camp before Sevastopol reporting on the lack of proper clothing and medical supplies, and losses in his regiment.

5948. JASPER YEATES PAPERS, 1778. 1 item. Lancaster (Lancaster County), Pa.

Letter to Jasper Yeates (1745-1817), lawyer, and jurist, from Samuel Johnston concerning his desire to go to England, and a lawsuit being undertaken by Yeates.

5949. JEAN CHARLOTTE WASHINGTON (LLOYD) YEATMAN PAPERS, 1826-1906. 13 items. Alexandria (Arlington County), Va.

Family correspondence of Jean Charlotte Washington (Lloyd) Yeatman, including a letter from Mary Ann Randolph (Custis) Lee concerning the death of Robert E. Lee; a letter from Fitzhugh Lee about family portraits and a revolt in Cuba in 1896; and a letter, 1904, listing the wedding party of Mary Ann Randolph (Custis) Lee and Robert E. Lee.

5950. EDWARD CLEMENTS YELLOWLEY PAPERS, 1837 (1840-1864) 1931. 84 items. Pitt County, N.C.

Official and political correspondence of Edward C. Yellowley (d. 1885), lawyer and colonel of the 68th North Carolina Regiment, C.S.A., containing routine correspondence on movement of troops and on local politics. Included also are college compositions of Yellowley and several of his speeches made while practicing law.

5951. OPHELIA YERBY PAPERS, 1862-1863. 4 items. Athens (Clarke County), Ga.

Letters to Ophelia Yerby from her cousin, N. B. Cash, Confederate soldier in Virginia, discussing camp life and army experiences.

5952. WILLIAM YERGER PAPERS, 1866. 1 item. Jackson (Hinds County), Miss.

Deposition by William Yerger relating to a bill of sale for cotton purchased by James Meagher, from Bryan Ashen in 1863.

5953. JOHN H. YERGEY PAPERS, 1871. 5 items. Philadelphia, Pa.

Copies of a bond and warrant from John H. Yergey, house carpenter, to Amos Ellis pertaining to land mortgaged for a personal loan.

5954. WILLIAM B. YONCE PAPERS, 1827 (1848-1870) 1893. 127 items. Wytheville (Wythe County), Va.

Personal and family correspondence of William B. Yonce, student at Wittenberg College, Springfield, Ohio, 1847-1851, and later a teacher at Roanoke College, Salem, Virginia; and Civil War letters, many of which were written by Yonce's sisters, showing the reactions of Southern women to the war.

5955. GEORGE W. YORK PAPERS, 1861-1863. 43 items. Standish (Cumberland County), Me.

Letters of George W. York, serving with the 25th Regiment of Maine Volunteers, U.S.A., and of Amasa Pray discussing a shipwreck in 1861; a storm off Cape Hatteras, North Carolina; the siege of Beaufort, South Carolina, 1861; the battle of Murfreesboro, 1862-1863; the naval blockade of Southern ports; commodity prices in Florida, 1862; the use of tin cans for shipping and preserving food; various United States generals and admirals; and an attack on Fort Sumter, South Carolina, 1863.

5956. YORKSHIRE, ENGLAND. EAST RIDING. COUNTY RECORD OFFICE PAPERS, 1782-1791. 878 items. Beverley, Yorkshire, England.

Photocopies of land tax returns, 1782-1783 and 1788; a freehold book, 1781; and jurors lists, 1789.

5957. _____ YOUNG NOTEBOOK, ca. 1775. 1 vol. (594 pp.)

Medical notes.

5958. CAPTAIN YOUNG DAYBOOK, 1871-1872. 1 vol. Danville (Pittsylvania County), Va.

Accounts of one Captain Young, leaf tobacco dealer, with auction warehouses.

5959. BRYANT YOUNG PAPERS, 1851-1867. 3 items. Petersburg (Dinwiddie County), Va.

Business letters of a cotton broker.

5960. JAMES H. YOUNG ACCOUNT BOOKS, 1842-1852. 2 vols. Granville County), N.C.

Business records of a general merchant.

5961. JAMES M. YOUNG PAPERS, 1822-1863. 15 items. Dallas County, Ala.

Correspondence of James M. Young, a Presbyterian minister, relating to religious matters.

5962. JAMES RICHARD YOUNG PAPERS, 1916-1938. 826 items. Raleigh (Wake County), N.C.

Papers of James Richard Young (b. 1853), insurance executive, banker, dealer in stocks and bonds, and insurance commissioner of North Carolina, 1899-1921, pertaining to the 1924 gubernatorial campaign of Angus Wilton McLean and attacks on his administration of the War Finance Corporation, 1920-1921; the work of the War Finance Corporation in North Carolina; economic conditions during the early 1920s; problems in agriculture and the cotton and tobacco trade; the Agricultural Loan Agency of War Finance Corporation; banking, especially the Merchant's National Bank, of which Young was vice president; insurance business in North Carolina, 1921-1927; the Title Insurance and Trust Company; financial affairs of Vance County, North Carolina; roads in Vance County and elsewhere in the state; the Presbyterian Church; and Peace College, Raleigh, North Carolina. Also included is correspondence and memoranda of J. Cooper Young, forest, fish, and game warden in Wake County from his superiors in the North Carolina Department of Conservation and Development.

5963. JENNIE YOUNG DIARY, 1858, 1869. 1 vol. Washington, D.C.

Diary of Jennie Young consisting chiefly of notes on a trip to England, France, and Switzerland in 1858. The later portion of the diary was written by an anonymous male.

5964. JOHN YOUNG, SR., PAPERS, (1784-1837) 1948. 8 items and 9 vols. Oxford (Granville County), and Franklin County, N.C.

Photocopies of letters, papers, and journals of John Young, Sr. (1747-1837), Methodist minister. Included are letters from other itinerant Methodist ministers discussing church matters; one item concerns a possible schism in Plank Chapel Church near Oxford, North Carolina. There are also a license as deacon signed by Bishop Francis Asbury; an appointment as an elder; and an autobiography, principally concerned with Young's conversion and church doctrine, with scattered references to biographical information. Journals, 1814-1837, contain brief entries on Young's ministerial activities, noting various homes, camps, and churches where he preached; conversions; camp meetings; Baptists; Methodists; doctrine; funerals; other ministers; reform movement in the Methodist Episcopal Church which resulted in the formation in 1830 of the Methodist Protestant Church; religious contention; the behavior of congregations; and Plank Chapel, including an attempt to burn it in 1832. There is also a clipping, 1948, referring to the Reverend E. H. Davis who wrote Historical Sketches of Franklin County.

5965. JOHN WESLEY YOUNG PAPERS, 1811-1864. 27 items. Stanton (Franklin County), N.C.

Correspondence of John Wesley Young, Methodist minister of Franklin County, North Carolina, including letters from the Reverend James E. Glenn concerning camp meetings and conversions in Abbeville District, South Carolina, where he was minister; personal letters from his nephews, William W. Young and William A. Gill; and Civil War letters from Young's sons, John W. Young, serving in the 9th North Carolina Regiment (1st North

Carolina Cavalry), and James A. Young, discussing scarcity of food, high prices, sickness, and desertion.

5966. JULIA (NASH) YOUNG JOURNAL, 1832. 1 item. Louisiana.

Journal (42 pp.) of a young wife concerning religion and social life.

5967. McCLINTOCK YOUNG PAPERS, 1835. 1 item. Washington, D.C.

Letter of McClintock Young, acting secretary of the treasury, authorizing the entry into New York of cargo carried by the ship Angelique.

5968. MATILDA YOUNG PAPERS, 1932-1933. 27 items and 1 vol. Washington, D.C.

Correspondence of Matilda Young while in France as companion to Alva Murray (Smith) Vanderbilt Belmont, with frequent reference to Mrs. Belmont, her son, Harold Stirling Vanderbilt, and her daughter, Consuelo (Vanderbilt) Spencer-Churchill Balson. The volume (173 pp.) is the memoir of Mrs. Belmont describing her youth in Mobile, Alabama, New York City, and Paris, France; her marriage to William Kissam Vanderbilt, Sr., and their subsequent divorce; social life in New York, and Newport, Rhode Island; her ideas on child rearing; the Vanderbilt homes in Newport and New York; and her involvement in the suffrage movement and other activities in behalf of women's rights.

5969. NOTLEY YOUNG PAPERS, 1827-1841. 7 items. Queen Anne (Prince Georges County), Md.

Business papers of Notley Young; and a letter, 1834, concerning the Whig victory in Maryland.

5970. PIERCE MANNING BUTLER YOUNG PAPERS, 1851-1894. 30 items. Spartanburg (Spartanburg County), S.C.

Papers of Pierce Manning Butler Young (1836-1896), major general in the Confederate Army and member of U. S. Congress, 1868-1875, including letters from his father, mother, and brother; letters from Young while in the Georgia Military Institute, Marietta, and in the Confederate Army in Florida; two letters concerning the Paris Exposition in 1878; a letter referring to the successes of the election of 1892; two letters relative to American investments in Guatemala while Young served as U. S. minister to Guatemala and Honduras, 1893-1896; lists of subscribers to speeches by Young and others; and a list of Confederate generals and their whereabouts.

5971. STARK YOUNG PAPERS, 1917-1975. 4 items. Amherst (Hampshire County), Mass.

Letters, 1917, of Stark Young (1881-1963), author, to Eleanor Fitzgibbon concerning his dislike of teaching, and other personal matters; and an issue of Precept, containing articles on Young's childhood home in Oxford, Mississippi, and on the editing of his letters.

5972. WILLIAM HENRY YOUNG PAPERS, 1827-1904. 3 items and 3 vols. Troy (Rensselaer County), N.Y.

Papers of William Henry Young (1817-1904), publisher and bookseller, consist of two clippings; a letter, 1865, containing a small fragment of the Confederate flag from Fort Fisher, North Carolina; and journals, 3 vols., of a trip to Europe on the steamer Russia, 1875.

5973. YOUNG MEN'S CHRISTIAN ASSOCIATION MINUTES, 1888-1892. 1 vol. (43 pp.) Hillsborough (Orange County), N.C.

Minutes of the Young Men's Christian Association of Hillsborough, also including records of the organizational meeting, the constitution, and the by-laws.

5974. TIMOTHY M. YOUNGLOVE PAPERS, 1847-1849. 11 items. Urbana and Hammondsport (Steuben County), N.Y.

Family correspondence of Timothy M. Younglove with occasional references to the Mexican War; the Whig Party; the candidacy of Generals Lewis Cass and William O. Butler for the presidency; the success of Millard Fillmore; Troy, New York; and medical education in Albany, New York.

5975. ISAAC B. YOUNGMAN PAPERS, 1855-1867. 16 items. Wilmot Center (Merrimack County), N.H.

Civil War letters to Isaac B. Youngman from Isaac Perkins, serving with the 15th Illinois Volunteers, and from John C. Palmer, Union soldier in Virginia, discussing the journey of the 15th Regiment through Missouri; the battle of Pittsburg Landing; scarcity of food; Perkins's work in a hospital at Tipton, Missouri; and hardships of army life; forced marches and troop movements; a Confederate raid at Holly Springs, Mississippi; the building of fortifications at Portsmouth, Virginia; the use of Negroes as laborers and teamsters; wages and prayer meetings of Negroes; resentment of whites against equipping and training Negro troops; high prices; fraternizing with Confederate soldiers; and camp at Yorktown, Virginia. There are two sketches by Perkins of the fighting of the 14th and 15th Illinois Regiments with Confederates at Hatchie River

Mississippi, and of a cemetery at Holly Springs, Mississippi. Other items are chiefly family letters.

5976. PETER L. YOUNT PAPERS, 1838-1871. 5 vols. Lincoln County, N.C.

Mercantile ledger, 1843-1845, of John Yount with family notes, 1879; two arithmetic manuscripts kept by Peter L. Yount; and physician's accounts, 1844-1871, of Peter L. Yount, with some mercantile accounts.

5977. GAVIN YUILLE PAPERS, 1841-1853. 31 items. Mobile, Ala.

Family correspondence, chiefly to Gavin Yuille from his sons, Gavin B. Yuille and William S. Yuille, while attending Nashville University (now George Peabody College for Teachers), Nashville, Tennessee, concerning their studies, their need for money, Whig strength in Nashville in 1844, and camp meetings in 1845; letters from Gavin B. Yuille while surveying the route of the Mobile and Ohio Railroad in Mississippi in 1849; and several business papers.

5978. DAVID LEVY YULEE PAPERS, 1845. 1 item. Washington, D.C.

Letter of David Levy Yulee (1810-1886), lawyer, U. S. senator, 1845-1851 and 1855-1861, and Confederate congressman, concerning the selection of a governor and members of the legislature in Florida, and listing major local and national issues that the Democratic Party should use in its campaign.

5979. EDWARD ZEA PAPERS, 1842-1903. 32 items and 22 vols. Strasburg (Shenandoah County), Va.

Papers of Edward Zea, merchant with the firm of F. M. Zea & Company and treasurer of the Winchester, Virginia, Presbytery, consisting of daybooks, 1842-1860, and a ledger, 1842-1850, of the general store in Strasburg, with a few accounts from a second store in Winchester; two other ledgers, 1868-1870 and 1879-1887; a treasurer's book, 1893, of the Winchester Presbytery recording donations made by member churches to various funds, and the disbursement of the funds for foreign and domestic missions, evangelistic work, education, relief, and church construction; a list of contributing and delinquent churches; financial papers and letters to Zea regarding Presbytery business, primarily church contributions; and two penmanship manuals.

5980. SAMUEL ZEHRING PAPERS, 1845-1848. 2 items. Mount Jackson (Shenandoah County), Va.

Personal correspondence of Samuel Zehring, a Virginia farmer, with his friends in Ohio and Indiana commenting on crops and farming operations.

5981. JACOB ZELLAR AND DAVID ZELLAR PAPERS, 1788-1895. 330 items and 1 vol. Hagerstown (Washington County), Md.

Business papers of Jacob Zellar and David Zellar consisting chiefly of bills, receipts, notes, and other papers relating to the administration of the estates of John Rench and Martin Richenbough, real estate including the sale of land in Illinois, and legal matters; and an account book.

5982. SOPHIA ZEVELY AND AUGUSTUS ZEVELY PAPERS, 1836-1860. 46 items. Forsyth County, N.C.

Correspondence of Sophia Zevely, teacher at Salem Female Academy, Salem, North Carolina, and of Augustus Zevely, her brother, a physician, including a letter from Dr. Joseph Pancoast giving professional advice; letters from another brother, Alexander Zevely, working in the Post Office Department in Washington, D.C., describing his life there and the 1839 New Year's reception at the White House; letters from a third brother, Edmund S. Zevely, concerning his activities in publishing, photography and teaching; and letters to Sophia Zevely from former students including one from a student attending Patapsco Institute, Ellicott's Mills, Maryland, describing daily life there.

5983. E. R. ZIMMERMAN COPYBOOK, 1877. 1 vol. (42 pp.)

Copybook of E. R. Zimmerman, apparently a schoolboy.

5984. JAMES C. ZIMMERMAN PAPERS, 1779-1910. 146 items. Forsyth County, N.C.

Family letters of James C. Zimmerman, Confederate soldier, to his wife, Adaline (Spease) Zimmerman, describing his experiences chiefly in Virginia. The letters comment on deserters, low morale in the Confederate Army, Zimmerman's desire for peace, his efforts to obtain a furlough, and stories from Federal soldiers regarding desertion in the Union Army. The letters also discuss the various sections through which he passed, methods of travel, exposure, marches, food, clothes, amusements, drill, accounts of the wounded and killed of the company, prices, dysentery, hatred of "Yankees," battles and skirmishes, opportunities of winning the war, the work of Federal spies, and the use of balloons by Union troops at Fredericksburg, Virginia. Included also are letters of A. J. Spease to his sister, Adaline (Spease) Zimmerman, concerning his time in the guardhouse during the war; and his life in Indiana and various other places, and his eventual settlement in Missouri, with comments on segregation in Missouri in 1868, and a grasshopper plague in Lafayette County, Missouri, in 1875.

5985. JOHN R. ZIMMERMAN PAPERS, 1863-1871. 21 items. Alexandria (Arlington County), Va.

Letters from John R. Zimmerman, Confederate soldier, while a prisoner at Point Lookout, Maryland, to Mrs. John B. Daingerfield thanking her for packages of supplies sent to the prisoners, with occasional references to life at Point Lookout; and letters, 1871, to Zimmerman concerning his work in the lumber business in Tobyhanna Mills, Pennsylvania.

5986. ERNST CHRISTIAN ZITTERAUER AND RICHARD ERNST ZITTERAUER PAPERS, 1772-1872. 179 items and 1 vol. Ebenezer (Effingham County), Ga.

Business papers of the Zitterauer family including bills, receipts, notes, and accounts of Ernst Christian Zitterauer concerning the activities of a planter dealing in flour, beef, and lumber; a deed for slaves, 1775; a land deed; a marriage settlement, 1813; inventories of estates; household accounts; papers relating to the Evangelical German Lutheran Church; business papers of Richard Ernst Zitterauer; a receipt book, 1806-1818; and several records of the Waldhour family.

5987. JOHN JOACHIM ZUBLY PAPERS, 1773-1777. 4 items. Savannah, Ga.

Papers of John Joachim Zubly (1725-1781), Presbyterian minister and Georgia Tory, include a letter from a committee concerning the uniting of the American colonies to preserve their liberties; letters dealing with legal matters; and a land indenture.

5988. JOHN C. DOUGLAS PAPERS, 1842-1847. 1 vol. (74 pp.) Chester (Chester County), S.C.

Pastoral visitation book of John C. Douglas (1809-1879), Presbyterian minister and writer, containing references to Purity Church and its elders; persons visited and other members of their households; religious affiliation and local church membership (seceders often noted); deaths; migrations; and activities at households. This volume was formerly cataloged as belonging to Abraham White.

5989. GLENNAN & O'CONNOR DAYBOOKS, 1894-1899. 2 vols. Ogdensburg (Saint Lawrence County), N.Y.

Daybooks of Glennan & O'Connor, a firm of cigar manufacturers in Ogdensburg.

5990. FRANK KING PAPERS, 1869-1884. 10 items and 28 vols. Van Buren Furnace (Shenandoah County), Va.

Business papers and records of Frank King, a physician, relating to his various business enterprises, including the Van Buren Furnace, iron ore mines, a mercantile store, a blacksmith and wagon shop, and stables. Records of the pig iron and ore mining operations of the Van Buren Furnace include a diary, 1870; time books, 1869-1882, listing workers, their work record, and their wages; production records, 1870-1871 and 1880-1882; a stock book, 1871; a cashbook, 1879-1881; a mercantile ledger, 1871-1873, containing mostly mercantile accounts with individuals, some of whom paid for goods by labor; notes describing brick kilns and iron furnaces and how they operated; a drawing of some equipment for the furnace; and a cash journal, 1879-1882, containing entries for goods and services related to the furnace. There are also daybooks, 1870-1872 and 1879-1884, 20 vols., from the mercantile store; accounts of the blacksmith and wagon shop; and a mercantile ledger, 1883-1884.

5991. WILLIAM SCHAUM PAPERS, 1862-1870. 1 item and 2 vols. Lancaster (Lancaster County), Pa.

Diary of a soldier in the 122nd Pennsylvania Volunteer Infantry and later in the 79th Pennsylvania Volunteer Infantry chiefly concerning his duties as a wagon driver with the quartermaster's department during Sherman's Carolinas campaign. The bulk of the diary is devoted to the details of camp life, an army on an extended march, the difficulties of transporting supplies, the conditions of roads, the confiscation of horses and other civilian property by forage details, and the weather. There are references to the battles of Averasboro and Bentonville, the capture of Fayetteville and Raleigh, and the surrender of Johnston's army in Durham, all in North Carolina; chaplains; medical and sanitary affairs; relations with blacks; rumors; discipline at the end of the war; and damages done to Springfield, Georgia, and Robertsville, South Carolina, by Union troops and to Fayetteville and Raleigh, North Carolina, by Confederates. Also included are several recipes for pastry, the lyrics of a song entitled "Red, White, & Blue," and an undated account of a small interracial brawl in postwar Lancaster. The item is a daguerreotype of Schaum in the uniform of a corporal of the 122nd Pennsylvania Volunteer Infantry.

# Index

## A

A. AND F. MINOR (firm): 2051
A. B. DAVIS AND CO.: 1392
A. BROUSSEAU & CO., New Orleans, Louisiana: 679
A. D. JULLIARD AND COMPANY, INC.: 5235
"A DIO" by Silvio Pellico: 4116
A. H. JONES (firm): 2888
A. H. SETTLE & CO.: 4743
A. HATTRIDGE (firm): 2933
A. S. WEBB AND COMPANY: 5614
AASEN, Denmark: 2228
ABANDONED LANDS: see CIVIL WAR--ABANDONED LANDS
ABASCAL Y SOUSA, José Fernando de: 4155
ABBAS MIRZA (1783-1833): 868
ABBEVILLE, Georgia: 3660
ABBEVILLE, South Carolina: 1971
  1700s-1800s: 3375
  1700s-1900s: 791, 842
  1800s: 2543, 3366, 4145, 4149, 5270
  1800s-1900s: 3527
  1900s: 431, 2416
  Confederate States of America:
    Army Subsistence Department: 5193
    Last meeting of Confederate cabinet: 844
    Post Office: 1181
  Law practice: 4145
  Merchants: 3319
ABBEVILLE COUNTY, South Carolina: 414, 2473, 3759, 5193
  Civil War: 607
  Panthers: 5825
  Politics and race relations: 2595
  Cities and towns:
    Abbeville: see ABBEVILLE, South Carolina
    Bordeaux: 3759
    Due West: 2473, 4526
      see also DUE WEST FEMALE COLLEGE; ERSKINE COLLEGE
    Greenwood: 2032
    Willington: 3790, 4272
ABBEVILLE MEDIUM: 1972
ABBEY, Henry: 2449
ABBOT, Caroline: 2449
ABBOT, Ezra: 3598
ABBOTT, James: 3557
ABBOTT, John Jay: 5252
ABBOTT, Joseph Carter: 3094
ABBOTT, Lyman: 4672
ABBOTT, William (Georgia): 1454
ABBOTT, William B. (Virginia): 1
ABBOTT FAMILY (Genealogy): 1792
ABBOTT AND COMPANY: 2
ABBOTTEMPO by Frank Gill Slaughter: 4583
ABBOTT'S CREEK, North Carolina: 5218
ABCARIUS, N.: 41
ABDALLAH, Sultan of the Comoro Islands: 189
ABEL, Ernest L.: 3
ABELL, Arunah Shepherdson: 5578
ABERCROMBIE, David: 3034
ABERCROMBIE, John: 2126
ABERCROMBIE, Lascelles: 4

ABERCROMBIE, T. F.: 365
ABERCROMBY, James, First Baron Dunfermline: 5
ABERCROMBY, Sir Ralph: 5797
ABERDEEN, George Hamilton Gordon, Fourth Earl of: 1755, 3472
ABERDEEN, Scotland: 3592, 5279
  Description: 1856
ABERDEEN AND TEMAIR, John Campbell Gordon, First Marquis: 2097
ABERDEENSHIRE, Scotland:
  Aberdeen: see ABERDEEN, Scotland
  Monkshill: 119
  Peterhead: 738, 5527
ABERGAVENNY, William Neville, First Marquis of: 2149
ABERNATHY, Thomas E.: 6
ABERNETHY, Daniel: 7
ABERNETHY, M. A.: 8
ABERNETHY, North Carolina: 147
ABERNETHY AND COMPANY: 9
ABERNETHY LIBRARY, Middlebury College: 10
ABILENE, Kansas: 893
ABINGDON, Virginia: 872, 1836, 2881, 3031
ABINGDON MANUFACTURING CORPORATION: 2769
ABINGTON, Pennsylvania: 270
ABNEY, Agatha: 5901
ABNEY, W.: 11
ABOLITION OF SLAVERY AND ABOLITIONIST SENTIMENT: 569, 1403, 1968, 1980, 2848, 3665, 4190, 4226, 4387, 4616, 4834, 5059, 5088, 5513, 5753, 5940
  see also SLAVE TRADE--Abolition; SLAVES--Emancipation
  Alabama: 5593
    Economic effects: 3416
  Bahama Islands: 4934
  British West Indies: 4913
  Ceylon: 4913
  Comoro Islands: 189
  Connecticut--Suffield: 3910
  France--Colonial policy: 1081
  Great Britain: 43, 280, 1913, 2149, 4913
    Colonial policy: 815, 1081, 4934, 5129, 5616
  Indiana: 245
    Newport: 5149
  Kansas: 4720
  Kentucky: 1083
  Maine: 5610
    Augusta: 83
  Maryland: 5128
  Massachusetts: 5034
    Boston: 4471
  Middle West: 1920
  Mississippi: 3415
  Missouri: 3255, 5335
  New England States: 4897
  New York: 5917
  North Carolina: 923, 2469, 4080
  Northern States: 4095
    Economic effects: 5940
  Ohio: 2678, 4387
  Pennsylvania: 421, 490
  South Carolina: 2503
    Cokesbury: 4118
    Laurens: 4118

ABOLITION OF SLAVERY AND ABOLITIONIST SENTIMENT (Continued):
  Southern States: 284, 872
  Spain: 4913
  Sudan: 67
  United States: 730, 842, 1081, 1424 1540, 1926, 2591, 2723, 2893
    Abolitionist periodicals: 1638, 5246
  Vermont: 3777
  Virginia: 1957, 4295, 4924
    Woodstock: 5275
  Washington, D.C.: 1215
ABOLITION SOCIETY OF PENNSYLVANIA: 1884
ABOLITIONISTS: see ABOLITION OF SLAVERY AND ABOLITIONIST SENTIMENT
ABORTIONS: 2591
  see also BIRTH CONTROL
ABOUKIR BAY, Egypt: 5639
ABRAHAM, A.: 1996
ABRAHAM BELL & SONS: 416
ABRAMS, Jennie Stone: 1766
ABRAM'S PLAINS, North Carolina: 4800, 4894
"ABSORBTIONS SPECTRA OF INDIAN DYES, 1886": 5553
ABSENTEEISM: see Absenteeism; Desertion; Straggling as subheadings under names of armies and navies
ABSTINENCE: see TEMPERANCE
ABSTON, James: 12
ABYSSINIAN EXPEDITION (1867-1868): 3838
ACADEMIC COSTUME: 1173
ACADEMIC FREEDOM: 1758
  North Carolina: 2705, 4968
L'ACADEMIE FRANÇAISE: 1910
ACADEMIES: see SCHOOLS
ACADEMY HOSPITAL, Chambersburg, Pennsylvania: 4608
ACADEMY OF VISITATION, Wheeling, West Virginia: 5194
ACAPULCO, Mexico: 4535
ACCADEMIA MUSICALE CHIGIANA: 4736
ACCIDENTS: 4
  see also INDUSTRIAL ACCIDENTS: RAILROADS--Accidents; TRAFFIC ACCIDENTS
ACCINELLY FAMILY: 3301
ACCOMACK COUNTY, Virginia: 152, 5918
  Belhaven: 1697
  Chincoteague: 1791
  Locust Mount: 3144
"ACCOUNT OF THE LINEAGE OF THE BROWN FAMILY" by Thomas Brown: 99
ACCOUNTING: see BOOKKEEPING
ACCOUNTS: see specific types of accounts, e.g. MERCANTILE ACCOUNTS
ACKER, Henry J.: 13
ACKERMANN, Rudolph: 1173
ACKLEN, J. A. S.: 2662
ACLAND, Sir Arthur Herbert Dyke, Thirteenth Baronet: 14, 2962
ACLAND, Sir Charles Thomas Dyke, Twelfth Baronet: 14
ACLAND, Sir Francis Dyke, Fourteenth Baronet: 2149
ACLAND, Sir Thomas Dyke, Eleventh Baronet: 14
ACT OF UNION: 535, 4024

AN ACT TO INCORPORATE THE VIRGINIA INEBRIATES' HOME: 5339
ACTING: 2073
    see also ACTORS; ACTRESSES; AMERICAN DRAMA; ENGLISH DRAMA; FRENCH DRAMA; THEATER
    Great Britain: 157, 1027
    United States: 2449
"ACTION OFF THE FALKLANDS" by Rudolf Henry Cole Verner: 5474
ACTON, Sir John Emerich Edward Dalberg, First Baron Acton: 3851
ACTORS: 3306, 3797
    North Carolina: 4502
    Pennsylvania: 4086
    United States: 4556
ACTORS FUND OF AMERICA: 4556
ACTRESS (ship): 841
ACTRESSES: 3306, 3797
    Italian: 5447
    South Carolina--Charleston: 503
    United States: 4556
THE ACTS OF SAINT PETER, A CATHEDRAL FESTIVAL PLAY by Gordon Bottomley: 583
ADAIR, James Makittrick: 15
ADAIR, Sir Robert: 16, 1164, 1875, 3183
ADAIR, William H. P.: 17
ADAIR, William P.: 18
ADAIR COUNTY, Missouri: 5481
ADAM, Sir Frederick: 3835, 5201
ADAMS, Alfred: 19
ADAMS, B. F.: 5314
ADAMS, Charles: 4858
ADAMS, Charles Francis: 706, 1364
ADAMS, Charles Francis, Jr.: 34, 103
ADAMS, Charlotte Eliza (Meriam): 3633
ADAMS, Crawford C.: 20
ADAMS, Elizabeth L.: 3633
ADAMS, G. F.: 19
ADAMS, George P.: 1097
ADAMS, Harriet: 33
ADAMS, Henry: 2849
ADAMS, Henry L.: 21
ADAMS, Herbert Baxter: 22, 3320
ADAMS, Isaac: 323
ADAMS, J. A. Stanley: 3503
ADAMS, Jane (Cockrell): 31
ADAMS, Jesse E.: 2685
ADAMS, John (1735-1826): 34, 858, 2913, 3384, 4132, 5203
    Works of: 1484
ADAMS, John (1825-1864): 4358
ADAMS, John P.: 23
ADAMS, John Q. (Georgia): 5044
ADAMS, John Quincy: 34, 1302, 1697, 2578, 3032, 3082, 3512
ADAMS, Margaret Crawford: 24
ADAMS, Myron, Jr.: 814
ADAMS, Oliver C.: 25
ADAMS, Oscar Fay: 2449
ADAMS, Samuel: 1236, 4310
ADAMS, Sarah (Eve): 26
ADAMS, Seth: 323
ADAMS, Sterling: 27
ADAMS, Thomas (Augusta County, Virginia): 28
ADAMS, Thomas (Albemarle and Fluvanna counties, Virginia): 29
ADAMS, W. G.: 30
ADAMS, Wade Hill: 31
ADAMS, William: 32
ADAMS, William C.: 33
ADAMS, William Poultney: 33
ADAMS FAMILY (Massachusetts): 34, 3633
ADAMS FAMILY (Virginia): 29
ADAMS AND SMITH (firm): 35
ADAMS COUNTY, Illinois: 3255
    Clayton: 3519
    Quincy: 715
    Schools: 2752
ADAMS COUNTY, Mississippi: 1786, 1864
    Court records: 2282
    Natchez: see NATCHEZ, Mississippi
    Washington: 2609

ADAMS COUNTY, Ohio--Manchester: 1177
ADAMS COUNTY, Pennsylvania:
    Gettysburg: see GETTYSBURG, Pennsylvania
ADAMS-ONIS TREATY: 1302
ADAMSVILLE, Georgia: 3841
ADDAMS, Jane: 3229
ADDERLEY, Charles Bowyer, First Baron Norton: 36, 1087, 3046
ADDINGTON, Henry, First Viscount Sidmouth: 2149, 2836, 5639
ADDISON, William Meade: 232
ADDISON COUNTY, Vermont--Monkton: 3665
ADDISON FERTILIZER COMPANY: see ALLISON AND ADDISON FERTILIZER COMPANY
ADDRESS AT THE FUNERAL OF MRS. ELEANOR J. W. BAKER OF DORCHESTER by Theodore T. Munger: 284
ADDRESS DELIVERED BY MISS MILDRED LEWIS RUTHERFORD, HISTORIAN-GENERAL, UNITED DAUGHTERS OF THE CONFEDERACY: 4642
ADEN: 278
ADGER (JAMES) AND COMPANY: 1388, 1891
ADGER, John: 37
ADJUTANT GENERALS: see (name of place)--Government agencies and officials--Adjutant generals
ADKINS, Apphia C.: 38
ADMIRALS: see as subheading under names of navies
ADMIRALTY COURTS: 1792
ADMISSIONS POLICIES: see as subheading under names of specific universities and colleges
ADSHEAD, George Haward: 39
ADULTERY TRIALS: 1608
ADVANCE, North Carolina: 4111
ADVERTISING: 40, 3250
    American literature: 1441
    Automobiles: 788
    Books: 2400, 4080
        North Carolina: 4765
    Coal industry: 4865
        Pennsylvania: 3910
    Convalescent homes:
        North Carolina: 4761
    Endorsements:
        Massachusetts: 3633
    False advertising: 1951
    Fertilizer: 373
    Gold milling machinery:
        Georgia: 4895
    Health resorts:
        North Carolina: 3415
        Tennessee: 5051
    House furnishings:
        Maryland: 3765
    Law practice:
        Washington, D. C.: 5354
    Lotteries--Kentucky: 4732
    Medical supplies: 1814, 4897
    Newspapers:
        Washington, D. C.: 1161
    Patent medicines: 136, 4732, 5135
        North Carolina: 4761, 4765
    Railroads:
        North Carolina: 238
    Religious literature:
        Virginia: 2485
    Schools:
        Virginia: 1894
    Subdivided by place:
        North Carolina: 2589
        United States: 40, 788, 832
ADVERTISING POLICY: see NEWSPAPERS--Advertising policy
"ADVICE FROM THE MAHARATTA CAMP 4th DEC., 1771, LEFT WITH THE NABOB BY THE GOV.": 2037
AERIAL BOMBS: see BOMBS
AERONAUTICS: see AVIATION
AESCHYLUS: 1538
AETNA LIFE INSURANCE COMPANY: 4348
AFFIRMATION BILL (Great Britain): 2324

AFGHAN WARS (1838-1919): 326, 1014, 5801
    Campaigns, battles and military actions: 3950
        Ghaznie: 5801
        Kabul: 4254
        Kelat: 5801
    Fear of Russian intervention: 5801
AFGHANISTAN:
    Foreign relations:
        Great Britain: 587, 4520, 5797
        India: 1857
    Politics and government: 3238, 5797
AFRICA: 41, 3158
    see also names of specific countries and colonies
    British colonial policy: 4514
    Description and travel: 128, 2463, 4900
        Northern: 4192
    Exploration: 306, 3158
    Missions and missionaries: 43, 2146
        Methodist: 3646
        Presbyterian: 2269
    Nationalism: 4591
    Religion: 128
    Safaris: 1424
    Slavery: 4514
    Slavery and the church: 5725
    Suppression of the slave trade by United States Navy: 3118
    Trade and commerce: 2682
        Great Britain: 4541
    Treaties (Tribal) with Great Britain: 3443
AFRICAN COLONIZATION SOCIETY: 2473
AFRICAN INSTITUTE: 5726
AFRICAN METHODIST EPISCOPAL CHURCH: 3712
AFRICAN MISSIONARY SOCIETY: 128
"THE AFRICAN RIDDLE" by Albert Bushnell Hart: 2400
AFRICAN SCHOOL, New York, New York: 4351
AFRIKA, KOLONIMAKTER OCH INFÖDDA FOLK by Karl Emil Hildebrand: 2525
AFRO-AMERICAN PRESS ASSOCIATION: 4524
"AFTER-GLOW TO EDNA EARLIE LINDON" by Willa Cather: 4290
"AFTER-MATH": 1949
AFTER SUNDOWN (periodical): 1137
AGASSIZ, Jean Louis Rodolphe: 1702, 2407
AGASSIZ, Louis: see AGASSIZ, Jean Louis Rodolphe
AGATHANASIA (Death with dignity): 2934
AGED AND AGING:
    see also GERIATRICS; RETIREMENT
    United States: 1167
    Virginia: 3820
AGENTS: see specific types of agents, e.g. INSURANCE AGENTS; and Agents as subheading under specific businesses
AGG, John: 42
AGLIONBY, Charles Yates: 43
AGLIONBY, Frances (Walker) Yates: 43
AGLIONBY, Frank K. Yates: 43
ABLIONBY, Jeannette: 43
ABLIONBY FAMILY: 43
AGLIPAY: 4511
AGNEW, J. S.: 44
AGNEW, William G.: 44
AGNOSTICISM: see FREE THOUGHT
AGOURS, Eglantine: 45
AGRARIAN REFORM: see LAND REFORM
"AGRARIAN REVOLT" by Harcourt Edmund Waller, Jr.: 5530
AGRICULTURAL ACCOUNTS: see FARM ACCOUNTS; PLANTATION ACCOUNTS
AGRICULTURAL ADJUSTMENT ACT: 592
AGRICULTURAL BANKS: see BANKS AND BANKING
AGRICULTURAL CHEMICALS: 373
    see also FERTILIZER INDUSTRY

AGRICULTURAL COLLEGES: see
  UNIVERSITIES AND COLLEGES; and
  names of specific universities and
  colleges
AGRICULTURAL CREDIT:
  see also CROP LIENS; CROP LOANS
  South Carolina: 566, 4530
AGRICULTURAL FAIRS:
  Alabama: 1031
  Maryland: 660
  South Carolina: 3893
  Virginia--Nansemond County: 3834
AGRICULTURAL IMPLEMENT WORKERS: see
  UNITED AUTOMBILE, AIRCRAFT, AND
  AGRICULTURAL IMPLEMENT WORKERS OF
  AMERICA
AGRICULTURAL IMPLEMENTS: 5309
  Prices: 5822
    South Carolina: 3801
    Tennessee: 4854
    Virginia: 4924
  Subdivided by place:
    North Carolina:
      Iredell County: 5319
    South Carolina--Stateburgh: 4217
    Virginia: 1354
      Albemarle County: 3699
AGRICULTURAL LOAN AGENCY: 5862
AGRICULTURAL MACHINERY: 1556
  see also AGRICULTURAL IMPLEMENTS;
    HARROWS; HARVESTING MACHINES;
    IRRIGATION MACHINERY; MOWING
    MACHINES; PLOWS; REAPING
    MACHINES; THRESHING MACHINES
  Improvements: 4924
  North Carolina: 4858
  Ohio--Dayton: 5193
  South Carolina: 3124
  Virginia: 4157
AGRICULTURAL MACHINERY TRADE:
  see also HARVESTING MACHINERY
    TRADE; PLOWS--Trade
  North Carolina: 3660
  West Virginia: 404
AGRICULTURAL ORGANIZATIONS:
  see also FARMERS' ALLIANCE;
    FARMERS' NATIONAL CONGRESS;
    INTERSTATE CONVENTION OF
    FARMERS; PATRONS OF HUSBANDRY;
    SOUTHERN TENANT FARMERS' UNION;
    TRI-STATE TOBACCO GROWERS'
    CO-OPERATIVE MARKETING
    ASSOCIATION
  Alabama: 5862
  Georgia: 5040
  Great Britain: 200
  Illinois: 715
  Louisiana: 5585
  Mississippi: 5498
  North Carolina: 1256, 5632
    Halifax County: 2399
    Surry County: 5146
  South Carolina: 4896
  United States: 4924, 5051
  Virginia: 3834
  West Virginia:
    Berkeley County: 3832
AGRICULTURAL PERIODICALS:
  New York: 4881
AGRICULTURAL PRACTICES:
  see also CROP ROTATION
  Improvements: 1024
    see also EXPERIMENTAL FARMING
  Italy: 4625
  Pennsylvania: 2643
  Virginia: 1354, 3560
AGRICULTURAL PRODUCTS:
  see also CROPS; FARM PRODUCE; and
    names of specific agricultural
    products
  Price fixing--Texas: 592
  Prices: 840
    see also COMMODITY PRICES
    Alabama: 647, 1602
    Great Britain: 118
    Indiana: 5275
    Kentucky: 647
    Maryland--Baltimore: 5275

AGRICULTURAL PRODUCTS:
  Prices (Continued):
    North Carolina: 165, 647, 1523,
      1602, 4689, 4858, 5374
    South Carolina: 4834
    Texas: 647
    Virginia: 3200
    West Virginia: 1784
  Transportation:
    Virginia: 404, 4124
  Subdivided by place:
    Maryland: 3254
    Mississippi Territory: 3041
    North Carolina: 4689
      Lincoln County: 5558
    Virginia: 3200
    Union of Soviet Socialist
      Republics: 4614
AGRICULTURAL PRODUCTS TRADE: 1478
  see also names of specific
    agricultural products
  Florida: 2232
  Georgia: 2232, 5651
  Maryland:
    Annapolis: 1481
    Baltimore: 5213
  Massachusetts: 3034
  Mississippi:
    Rodney: 3322
  North Carolina: 2101, 4858
  South Carolina:
    Stateburgh: 4217
  Virginia: 404, 1156, 3145
    Albemarle County: 3699
    Locust Dale: 1073
  Western States: 5309
AGRICULTURAL RESEARCH:
  see also AGRICULTURAL PRACTICES--
    Improvements; EXPERIMENTAL
    FARMING
  New York: 2616
AGRICULTURAL SOCIETIES: see
  AGRICULTURAL ORGANIZATIONS
AGRICULTURAL SOCIETY OF GREENSBORO,
  Alabama: 5862
AGRICULTURAL WORKERS:
  see also FARM ACCOUNTS; PEASANTRY
  Labor unions: see FOOD, TOBACCO,
    AGRICULTURAL AND ALLIED WORKERS
    UNION OF AMERICA
  Mexicans: 3745
  Negroes:
    see also FREEDMEN--Tenancy;
      FARM TENANCY; SHARECROPPING
    Virginia: 3719
  Wages and salaries: see WAGES AND
    SALARIES--Agricultural workers
  Subdivided by place:
    Georgia:
      Augusta: 3749
      Cherokee County: 1887
    Louisiana: 1026
    New Hampshire:
      Landaff: 4265
    North Carolina:
      New Hanover County: 4603
    Virginia:
      Edinburg: 4124
      Gloucester County: 3809
    West Virginia:
      Grant County: 767
AGRICULTURE: 5193
  see also CROP ROTATION; CROPS and
    names of specific crops; DAIRY
    FARMS; ENSILAGE; FARM ACCOUNTS;
    FARM LIFE; FARM PRODUCE; FARM
    TENANCY; FARMING; LIVESTOCK and
    names of specific types of
    livestock; PEASANTRY;
    PLANTATION ACCOUNTS; PLANTATION
    LIFE; PLANTATION MANAGEMENT;
    PLANTATIONS; RANCHING
  Study and teaching:
    Missouri: 2604
  Subdivided by place:
    Alabama: 2860, 5126, 5593
    Arkansas: 2727
    Brazil: 1289

AGRICULTURE:
  Subdivided by place (Continued):
    California: 4834
    Ceylon: 952
    China: 5225
    Colorado: 2554, 5426
    Florida: 3611, 4743
    Georgia: 245, 1229, 1231, 2727,
      2963, 3075, 5426
    Great Britain: 14, 1632, 2836,
      3498, 5726
    Illinois: 25
    India: 278, 5279
    Indiana: 245, 3981, 4152
    Ireland: 3349, 5809
    Kansas: 2554
    Kentucky: 245, 5426
    Louisiana: 1153, 5426, 5585
    Massachusetts: 3633
    Minnesota: 3524
    Mississippi: 4269, 4796
      Kemper County: 3436
    Mississippi Territory: 1038
    Missouri: 2554, 4152, 5218, 5551
    Montana: 5426
    Nevada: 5426
    New York: 1769
    North Carolina:
      1800s: 435, 484, 1323, 2161,
        2819, 5551
      1800s-1900s: 122
      1900s: 274, 325, 2188, 4564,
        5962
      Burke County: 245
      Durham County: 1256
      Guilford County: 2314
      Halifax County: 426
      Harnett County: 238
      Lee County: 238
      Montgomery County: 4689
      Orange County: 1256
    Ohio: 1177
    Pennsylvania: 4881
    South Carolina: 718, 1220, 3981,
      4564
      Camden: 5675
    Southern States: 5940
      Civil War: 608, 3648
      Dependence on cotton: 5862
    Spain: 5404
    Tennessee: 2857, 4269, 5426
    Texas: 1153, 2554, 5651
      Birdville: 5194
    United States: 122, 842
      Laws and legislation: 274,
        4805, 4858
      Statistics: 2746, 5426
    Virginia:
      1700s: 3819
      1700s-1800s: 734, 1962, 4616
      1800s: 43, 1283, 1384, 1957,
        2418, 5397, 5426
      Albemarle County: 3699
      Amherst County: 97
      Caroline County: 5203
      Fluvanna County: 5839
      Madison: 3141
      Prince Edward County: 5884
      Rappahannock: 3141
      Westover: 3141
    Washington, D.C.: 5426
    West Virginia: 43
      Berkeley Springs: 3141
      Hedgesville: 3141
    Wyoming: 5426
AGRICULTURE AND INDUSTRY: 5530
EL AGUILA DE CONDORCUNCA: 4155
AGUINALDO, Emilio: 4511
AGURS, Eglantine: 45
AICHEL, Oscar: 46
AID SOCIETIES: see AMERICAN RED
  CROSS; CIVIL WAR--AID SOCIETIES;
  ENGLISH IMMIGRANTS--Aid societies;
  FREEDMEN--Aid societies; HOSPITAL
  AID SOCIETIES; MERCHANT SEAMEN--
  Aid societies; WORLD WAR I--War
  relief

653

AID TO MINISTERS' FAMILIES: see
  CLERGY--Methodist--Aid to
  ministers' families
AID TO SOLDIERS' FAMILIES: see
  CIVIL WAR--PUBLIC WELFARE--Aid to
  soldiers' families
AIKEN, William: 5193
AIKEN, South Carolina: 1468, 3163
AIKEN COUNTY, South Carolina:
  Aiken: 1468, 3163
  Beech Island: 1220, 2291
  Graniteville: 2186
  Hamburg: 430, 669
    Race riots during
      Reconstruction: 1220
AINLEY, Henry Hinchliff: 47
AIR FORCE: see as subheading under
  names of specific countries
AIR MAIL SERVICE: see UNITED STATES--
  GOVERNMENT AGENCIES AND OFFICIALS--
  Post Office--Air mail service
"AIR--STAR SPANGLED BANNER" by
  Alexander B. Meek: 3611
AIRCRAFT COMPANIES--Maryland: 3086
AIRCRAFT WORKERS: see UNITED
  AUTOMOBILE, AIRCRAFT, AND
  AGRICULTURAL IMPLEMENT WORKERS OF
  AMERICA
AIRPORTS--North Carolina: 2379
AIRWAYS--Laws and legislation: see
  AVIATION--Laws and legislation
AIRY HILL, Virginia: 1020
AITCHISON, Sir Charles Umpherston:
  515
AIX-LA-CHAPELLE, Germany: 3029
AJAWA TRIBE (Africa): 5725
AKELY, Carl Ethan: 4453
AKERS-DOUGLAS, Aretas, First
  Viscount Chilston: 294
ALABAMA:
  see also SOUTHERN STATES
  Abolition of slavery and
    abolitionist sentiment:
    Activities of Northerners: 5593
    Economic effects: 3416
  Agricultural fairs: 1031
  Agricultural organizations: 5862
    see also ALABAMA--Patrons of
      Husbandry
  Agricultural products:
    see also ALABAMA--Crops
    Prices: 647
  Agriculture: 2860, 5126, 5593
  Authorship: 1449
  Bible societies: 1084
  Birds: 1803
  Books--Prices: 4008
  Books and reading: 3611
  Booksellers and bookselling: 3611
    Montgomery: 4008
  Bridge construction: 1181
  Canals (proposed): 2125
  Carriage trade: 5623
  Chancery Courts: see ALABAMA--
    Courts--Chancery courts
  Churches: see names of specific
    denominations under ALABAMA;
    ALABAMA--Clergy
  Civil War: see subheadings under
    CIVIL WAR; CONFEDERATE STATES OF
    AMERICA--ARMY; UNITED STATES--
    ARMY--CIVIL WAR
  Claims collections: 3857
  Clergy: 1476
    Episcopal: 1067
    Methodist: 1915
    Presbyterian: 5961
  Clerks (Retail trade): 983
  Coal industry: 897, 3188
  Coke: 642
  Commission merchants--Mobile: 5879
  Commodity prices: 1178, 2900, 5385
    Gay's Landing: 5879
    Mobile: 4911
  Commonplace books: 4184
  Community and college: 2963
  Congressional elections: 3903
  Constitutional convention: 5425

ALABAMA (Continued):
  Cotton:
    Prices: 3321
    Speculation: 3321, 4589
  Cotton growing:
    Gay's Landing: 5879
  Cotton mills:
    Huntsville (proposed): 3568
  Cotton plantations: 1084
  Cotton trade: 641, 3196, 5593,
    5879
    Mobile: 4911
  Courts:
    Chancery courts:
      Cherokee County: 4419
      Dallas County: 48
    Supreme Court: 4105
  Courtship--Selma: 3534
  Credit--Huntsville: 5006
  Crime: 1507
    see also ALABAMA--Murders
    Negroes--Mobile: 2318
  Crops: 2663, 2900, 4083
    see also ALABAMA--Agricultural
      products; and names of specific
      crops under ALABAMA
    Randolph County: 5053
    Wilcox County: 5174
  Currency: 1339
  Death: 2662
  Debating societies: 3611
  Debt collection: 4419
  Democratic Party: 1084
  Depression: 5126
    see also ALABAMA--Panic of 1837;
      ALABAMA--Panic of 1857
  Description and travel: 1490, 2822,
    3123, 3611, 4720
  Disciples of Christ: 4720
  Diseases:
    Meningitis: 4589
    Smallpox: 5907
    Typhoid fever: 1188
    Yellow fever: 1933
      Montgomery: 3290
  Economic conditions: 3415, 4911,
    5385
    see also ALABAMA--Depressions;
      ALABAMA--Poverty
    Mobile: 5744
  Education:
    see also ALABAMA--Public schools;
      ALABAMA--Schools; ALABAMA--
      Teaching
    Women: 546
      see also ALABAMA--Schools--
        Girls' schools and academies
  Elections: 1084
    see also ALABAMA--Congressional
      elections; PRESIDENTIAL
      ELECTIONS
    Policing by United States Army:
      1299
    Third Military District: 4105
  Episcopal Church--Clergy: see
    ALABAMA--Clergy--Episcopal
  Estate accounts: 5006
  Estates (Legal):
    Administration and settlement:
      478, 1084, 1497, 1986, 2040,
      4861, 5612
    Dallas County: 2979
    Madison County: 4658
  Farm Accounts: 2930, 4861
    see also ALABAMA--Plantation
      accounts
  Farm life:
    see also ALABAMA--Plantation
      life
    Greene County: 2493
  Farming: 1084
    see also ALABAMA--Plantations;
      ALABAMA--Sharecropping
    Dallas County: 223
  Fertilizer: 5862
  Finance: 4184, 5032
    see also ALABAMA--Personal
      finance

ALABAMA (Continued):
  Fourth of July celebrations: 3611,
    5174
  Fraternal societies: 1031
    see also ALABAMA--Masonry
    Dallas County: 223
  Freedmen: 2315
    Labor contracts: 1423, 4448,
      4911, 5593
    Tenancy: 4861, 5032
  Fugitive slaves: 3415
  Gold mining: 388
  Governors: see ALABAMA--Government
    agencies and officials--Governors
  Government agencies and officials:
    Governors: 1084, 4799
  Health conditions: 4083
  Hiring of slaves--Selma: 1645
  Historical studies (proposed):
    4195
  Household accounts: 5593
    Selma: 4911
  Immigration and emigration: see
    ALABAMA--Migration (from/to)
  Indians of North America--Wars:
    3415
  Insurance agents: 2013
  Insurance: 1084, 2013, 5593
    Huntsville: 5006
  Internal improvements: 1877
    see also ALABAMA--Bridge
      construction; ALABAMA--Canals;
      ALABAMA--Railroads
  Iron industry: 642, 3188
  Labor unions: 3706
  Land: 1945, 3626
    see also ALABAMA--Real estate
    Prices: 1178, 2663
    Purchases and sales: 1133
  Land agents: 5308
  Land settlement: 872, 3436, 5593
  Land speculation: 1986, 5612
  Law--Study and teaching: 976, 3611
  Law practice: 976
    Cherokee County: 4419
    Greensboro: 5593
  Lawsuits--Selma: 1645
  Legal affairs: 5032
    Huntsville: 5006
    Selma: 4911
  Legal profession:
    Associations: 3611
  Legislature: 1425, 3611
    Senate: 4184
  Literary interests: 5032
  Loans--Huntsville: 5006
  Lotteries: 1438
  Lyceums: 3611
  Masonry: 3712
  Medical practice: 1856
    Tuscaloosa: 4943
  Medical treatment: 4184
  Medicines: 4184
  Mercantile accounts: 5006
    Boligee: 4861
    Tompkinsville: 4827
  Merchants: 1915, 4820
    see also ALABAMA--Commission
      merchants
    Boligee: 4861
    Mobile: 3196
  Methodist Churches:
    Alabama Conference: 3646
    Clergy: see ALABAMA--Clergy--
      Methodist
    Negro: 249
  Migration from: 5174
  Migration to: 444, 3161
  Militia: 444, 3796
  Mining: see ALABAMA--Gold mining
  Murders: 490, 861
  National Guard: 3657
  Negroes:
    see also ALABAMA--Freedmen;
      ALABAMA--Slaves
    Religion: see ALABAMA--Methodist
      Churches--Negro
  Suffrage: 4751

ALABAMA (Continued):
　Newspapers--Carriers' addresses: 3611
　Panic of 1837: 1084, 5593
　Panic of 1857: 5593
　Patrons of Husbandry: 444
　Personal finance: 1645, 2979
　　Clarke County: 4448
　Physicians' accounts: 4061, 4184
　　Selma: 1265
　Physicians' notebooks: 1053
　Plantation accounts: 5593
　　see also ALABAMA--Farm accounts
　　Clarke County: 4448
　　Dallas County: 4911
　　Perry County: 5879
　Plantation life: 1986
　　see also ALABAMA--Farm life
　Plantation management: 4820
　　Dallas County: 4911
　　Perry County: 5879
　　Operation by women: 1084
　Plantations: 1061, 2040, 5593
　Politics and government:
　　1800s: 1084, 3415
　　1830s: 5593
　　1840s: 2662, 3903, 4911, 5593, 5937
　　1850s: 1877, 3903, 4105
　　1860s: 249, 4105, 4911, 5059
　　1870s: 4105
　　1880s: 1084
　　Mobile: 5744
　Poverty: 1084
　　Camden: 4184
　Presbyterian Churches--Clergy: see ALABAMA--Clergy--Presbyterian
　Promissory notes--Gay's Landing: 5879
　Protestant Episcopal Church: 4358
　Public schools: 4911
　Publishers and publishing:
　　Poetry: 3611
　Railroad fraud: 3188
　Railroads:
　　Construction: 5593
　　Finance: 950
　　Selma: 3101
　　Short-line: 1655
　Real estate: 5612
　　see also: ALABAMA--Land Investments--Selma: 4911
　Real estate trade: 5006
　Reconstruction: 566, 3188, 3416, 4820, 4834, 5593
　　Federal military occupation: 1299
　　Loyalty oaths: 4515
　　Mobile: 1507
　　Religion: 2663, 4861
　　Dallas County: 5961
　　Tuscaloosa: 4943
　Rice: 1803
　Riots--Montgomery: 1299
　Riverboats: 2963
　Roads: 1182
　Salt speculation: 3321
　Salt works--Clarke County: 4643
　Sawmills: 1877
　School boards--Selma: 4911
　Schools: 1877, 5593
　　see also ALABAMA--Public schools; ALABAMA--Teaching
　　Girls' schools and academies: 1476, 1947, 5032
　　see also ALABAMA--Education--Women
　　Greensboro: 5593
　Secession: 2545, 4799, 5126, 5593
　Sharecropping: 4861, 5032
　Sheriffs--Dallas County: 2979
　Slave trade: 1490, 1801, 2426, 2808, 3321, 4861, 4911, 5113, 5879
　　Mobile: 3016
　　Prices: 647, 2426, 2663, 3626, 5879
　　Salem: 4610

ALABAMA (Continued)
　Slaves: 1084, 5593
　　see also ALABAMA--Fugitive slaves; ALABAMA--Hiring of slaves
　　Behavior: 954
　　Insurrections--Greensboro (fear of): 5593
　　Loyalty--Selma: 4185
　　Recovery of--3647
　　Treatment of--Perry County: 5879
　Social conditions--Selma: 3712
　Social life and customs: 1084, 1804, 2663, 3184, 4131, 4589, 5593
　　Mobile: 3761
　Soil fertility: 5862
　Steamboat lines--Mobile: 1602
　　see also ALABAMA--Travel--Steamboats
　Suffrage: see ALABAMA--Negroes--Suffrage
　Supreme Court: see ALABAMA--Courts--Supreme Court
　Tavern accounts--Tompkinsville: 4827
　Taxation:
　　Gay's Landing: 5879
　　Greene County: 5593
　Teaching--Mobile: 3761
　Textile mills: 5237
　Theater--Mobile: 3611
　Trade and commerce:
　　Cotton: see ALABAMA--Cotton trade
　　Grain--Macon County: 3837
　　Hay--Macon County: 3837
　　Lumber: 3008
　　Meal: 5006
　　Naval stores--Mobile: 4911
　　Salt: 3321, 5006
　　Slaves: see ALABAMA--Slave trade
　　Wood: 5006
　　　Macon County: 3837
　Travel--Steamboats: 3611
　Universities and colleges: see ALABAMA CENTRAL FEMALE COLLEGE; EAST ALABAMA COLLEGE; PAYNE UNIVERSITY; TUSKEGEE INSTITUTE; UNIVERSITY OF ALABAMA
　Voter registration: 5425
　Weather: 2663
　Whig Party: 1084
　Women--Social status: 1084
ALABAMA, C.S.S.: 863, 2963, 4738, 5436
ALABAMA CENTRAL FEMALE COLLEGE: 4895
ALABAMA CLAIMS: 43, 863, 5762
ALABAMA COTTON GROWERS ASSOCIATION: 592
ALABAMA LAND COMPANY: 323
THE ALABAMA REVIEW: 4738
ALABAMA RIVER: 3123
ALABAMA STATE SALT WORKS: 4643
ALAMANCE CIRCUIT, Methodist Church: 3646
ALAMANCE COUNTY, North Carolina: 5510
　Civil War--Scarcity of food: 4595
　Ku Klux Klan: 3062
　Cities and towns:
　　Burlington: 3001, 5506
　　　Hosiery--Dyeing: 3842
　　　Hosiery mills: 1353, 3595
　　　Textile industry: 2108
　　Graham: 4812
　　Haw River: 5154
　　Pleasant Grove: 2036, 5551
ALASKA:
　Description and travel: 2084
　Field trips: 2084
　Gold mines: 4918
ALASKA COMMERCIAL COMPANY: 2881
ALASKA DREDGING AND POWER COMPANY: 1584
ALBANY, Duchess of York and: see YORK AND ALBANY, Duchess of
ALBANY, Leopold George Duncan Albert, Duke of: 2471

ALBANY, Georgia: 2533, 4921
ALBANY, New York: 3391, 3507, 3872, 4169, 4340, 4352, 4708, 4751, 5281, 5945
　Description: 33
　Law practice: 1572
　Medical education: 5974
　Social life and customs: 5010
ALBANY (warship): 636
ALBANY COUNTY, New York--Albany: see ALBANY, New York
ALBAY, Philippine Islands: 4656
ALBEA, W. W.: 3646
ALBEMARLE, North Carolina: 3530
ALBEMARLE (ram): 2617
ALBEMARLE AGRICULTURAL SOCIETY: 558
ALBEMARLE AND CHESAPEAKE CANAL COMPANY: 4858
ALBEMARLE COUNTY, North Carolina:
　General Court: 3930
ALBEMARLE COUNTY, Virginia: 29, 687, 1359, 1757, 3464, 4384, 5065, 5513
　Agriculture: 3699
　Farm accounts: 5302
　Farming: 3699
　Fences and fencing: 3699
　Grist mills: 3699
　Law practice: 523
　Mercantile accounts: 4490
　Millers' accounts: 5302
　Negroes: 3854
　Personal finance: 4384, 4490
　Plantation accounts: 3699
　Plantations: 33, 3699
　Plaster (Fertilizer): 3699
　Slaves: 523
　Tax in kind: 1181
　Tobacco culture: 3699
　Weather: 3699
　Cities and towns:
　　"Buck Island": 1957
　　"Castle Hill": 4490
　　Charlottesville: see CHARLOTTESVILLE, Virginia
　　Cobham: 958, 4491
　　Howardsville: 5147
　　Shadwell: 5256
ALBEMARLE SWAMP LAND COMPANY: 3012, 4471, 4858
ALBERT, Prince Consort of Queen Victoria: 597
ALBERT A. COBB AND COMPANY: 1119
ALBERTI, Peter Adler: 5321
ALBION TRADING COMPANY: 410
ALBRIGHT, J. J.: 1291
ALBUQUERQUE, New Mexico: 5744
ALCESTER, Frederick Beauchamp Paget Seymour, First Baron: 3744
ALCOHOLIC BEVERAGES: see LIQUOR; RUM
ALCOHOLICS--Rehabilitation: 2934
ALCOHOLICS ANONYMOUS: 2934
ALCOHOLISM: 2934
　Massachusetts: 1230
ALCORN, James Lusk: 49
ALCORN AGRICULTURAL AND MECHANICAL COLLEGE, Claiborne County, Mississippi: see OAKLAND COLLEGE
ALCORN COUNTY, Mississippi:
　Corinth: see CORINTH, Mississippi
ALDEN, Henry Mills: 2449, 2871
ALDERMAN, Edwin Anderson: 706, 5457, 5786
ALDERMAN, William: 50
ALDIE, Virginia: 1962, 3529
　see also CIVIL WAR--CAMPAIGNS, BATTLES, AND MILITARY ACTIONS--Virginia--Aldie
ALDIS AND DAVIS (firm): 70
ALDRICH, Alfred: 2449
ALDRICH, Alfred Proctor: 2449
ALDRICH, Charles: 2449, 4576
ALDRICH, Thomas Bailey: 2449
ALDRIDGE, Fred T. 2407
ALDRIDGE, S. R.: 2668
ALEXANDER, Adam Leopold: 51
ALEXANDER, Bettie: 52

ALEXANDER, Edward Porter: 53, 2871, 3262
ALEXANDER, Ethel: 54
ALEXANDER, H. F.: 60
ALEXANDER, Henry M.: 55
ALEXANDER, James H.: 56
ALEXANDER, James Webb: 1556
ALEXANDER, John: 62, 337
ALEXANDER, John Brevard: 5457
ALEXANDER, John D.: 62
ALEXANDER, John Henry: 3598
ALEXANDER, Margaret: 2120
ALEXANDER, Miller: 57
ALEXANDER, Reuben: 57
ALEXANDER, Robert: 62
ALEXANDER, Robert P.: 58
ALEXANDER, S. Caldwell: 59
ALEXANDER, Sydenham Benoni: 5457
ALEXANDER, William K.: 62
ALEXANDER, William V.: 4481
ALEXANDER, FAMILY (North Carolina): 61
ALEXANDER FAMILY (Virginia): 62, 2120
ALEXANDER AND COMPANY: see SMITH, HUIE, ALEXANDER AND COMPANY
ALEXANDER AND O'NEILL (firm): 60
ALEXANDER COUNTY, North Carolina: 399, 620, 1896, 3572, 4083
    Land deeds and indentures: 912
    Mercantile accounts: 3683
    Taylorsville: 208, 3289
ALEXANDER SPRUNT & SON, INC.: 5014
ALEXANDRE-ANGÉLIQUE, Duc de Talleyrand-Périgord: 2840
ALEXANDRIA, Egypt: 4926, 4941
    Bombardment by British (1882): 3744
    British consul in: 3471
ALEXANDRIA, Louisiana: 3275
ALEXANDRIA, Virginia:
    1600s-1900s: 1778
    1700s-1800s: 99, 3560
    1800s:
        1820s: 1827, 5332
        1830s: 5538
        1850s: 5711
        1860s: 1274, 5336, 5985
        1870s: 5985
    1800s-1900s: 4524
    Civil War:
        Confederate military activities: 5852
        Union occupation: 2648, 3809
    Commission merchants: 947
    Description: 284, 5193
    Drugs--Prices: 5016
    Medicines--Prescriptions: 5016
    Mercantile accounts: 175
    Merchants: 1920
    Personal finance: 5380
    Pharmacies: 5016
    Protestant Episcopal Theological Seminary: 5298
    Schools: 5210
    Society of Friends: 5016
    Tobacco trade: 5228
    Trade with Philadelphia: 1117
    Weddings: 5949
ALEXANDRIA COUNTY, Virginia:
    Arlington: 3157
ALEXANDRIA TURNPIKE COMPANY: see FAUQUIER AND ALEXANDRIA TURNPIKE COMPANY
ALFORD, George Benton: 63
ALFORD, Green Haywood
ALFORD, William G.: 1107
ALGER, William Rounseville: 64
ALGERIA:
    Description and travel: 2578
    Foreign relations: 2578
        Great Britain: 1599
        United States: 3041, 4348
ALGERIAN EXPEDITION: 3883
ALGIERS: see ALGERIA
ALHAIZA, Jean-Adolphe: 65
ALI, Amjad: 83
ALI, Maulvi Rahman: see RAHMAN ALI, Maulvi

ALI SAHLIB PASHA: 3183
ALIAGA, Felipe Pardo y: see PARDO Y ALIAGA, Felipe
ALIEN AND SEDITION ACTS: 1115
ALIEN PROPERTY--Seizure: 1478
    see also CIVIL WAR--ALIEN PROPERTY
ALIENS:
    Legal status:
        Carolina province: 202
        Turkey: 3183
ALIGARH MUSLIM UNIVERSITY, India: 5525
"ALINE McKENZIE" by David Howard Scanlon: 2934
ALISON, Jacob: 4399
ALL-AMERICAN AVIATION, INC: 4858
ALL HEALING SPRINGS, North Carolina: 3416
"ALL QUIET ALONG THE SAVANNAH TONIGHT" by Carrie Bell Sinclair: 5503
ALL-RUSSIAN EVANGELICAL CHRISTIAN UNION: 3633
ALL SOULS COLLEGE: see UNIVERSITY OF OXFORD--All Souls College
ALLAN, John: 1943, 3809
ALLAN, Mary: 1943
ALLAN, Thompson: 3615
ALLAN, William: 3809
ALLAN FAMILY: 3809
ALLEGANY COUNTY, Maryland:
    Cumberland: 2796, 3190, 3282, 3765
    Description: 3789
    Railroad construction: 721
ALLEGANY COUNTY, New York: 3095
ALLEGHANY COUNTY, North Carolina: 5641
ALLEGHANY COUNTY, Virginia:
    Covington: 2566, 3308
    Sons of Temperance: 4953
ALLEGHANY FORGE (Pennsylvania): 849
ALLEGHANY IRON COMPANY, Virginia: 2922
ALLEGHENY, Pennsylvania: 3789, 4240
ALLEGHENY COUNTY, Pennsylvania:
    Allegheny: 3789, 4240
    Perrysville: 2236
    Pittsburgh: see PITTSBURGH, Pennsylvania
ALLEN, Professor ____: 3588
ALLEN, A. T.: 152
ALLEN, Bennet: 3598
ALLEN, C. Tacitus: 66
ALLEN, Charles Harris: 67
ALLEN, David B.: 68
ALLEN, Dwight: 69
ALLEN, Edward: 5380
ALLEN, Ethan (1737-1789): 70
ALLEN, Ethan Alphonso: 70
ALLEN, George Garland: 1585, 5252
ALLEN, George Venable: 83
ALLEN, Sir George William: 1857
ALLEN, H.: 82
ALLEN, Hervey: see ALLEN, William Hervey, Jr.
ALLEN, J. H.: 5407
ALLEN, J. N.: 73
ALLEN, James: 71
ALLEN, James Lane: 72
ALLEN, James Walkinshaw: 73, 2792
ALLEN, John (Franklin County, North Carolina): 76
ALLEN, John (Montgomery County, North Carolina): 75
ALLEN, John (South Carolina): 82
ALLEN, John (Virginia): 74
ALLEN, John D.: 1227
ALLEN, Katherine Martin: 83
ALLEN, Maurice R.: 1197
ALLEN, Oscar H.: 77
ALLEN, R. Alfred: 78
ALLEN, Rebecca: 5380
ALLEN, Richard: 79
ALLEN, W. A.: 80
ALLEN, Weld Noble: 81
ALLEN, William (England): 1159
ALLEN, William (New York): 388

ALLEN, William C. (North Carolina): 5457
ALLEN, William C. (Tennessee): 82
ALLEN, Willis Boyd: 2449
ALLEN, William Hervey, Sr.: 5380
ALLEN, William Hervey, Jr. (1889-1949): 103, 5380
ALLEN, Zaline: 83
ALLEN FAMILY (Arkansas--Genealogy): 5380
ALLEN FAMILY (North Carolina): 83, 3727
ALLEN FAMILY (Pennsylvania--Genealogy): 5380
ALLEN FAMILY (Washington, D.C.): 83
ALLEN AND GINTER (firm): 1586
ALLEN COUNTY, Kentucky:
    Circuit courts: 5505
    Scottsville: 5505
ALLEN J. SAVILLE, INC.: 5790
ALLERTON, England: 3620
ALLEYS: see STREETS
ALLIANCE, Ohio: 5396
ALLIANCE, U.S.S.: 3403
ALLIBONE, Samuel Austin: 84
ALLISON, Elizabeth Beaty (Johnston): 85
ALLISON, John: 86
ALLISON, Martin O.: 86
ALLISON, William H.: 87
ALLISON AND ADDISON FERTILIZER COMPANY: 4344
ALLRED, Ellen: 4075
ALLRED, Joseph: 88
ALLRED, Mahlon: 88
ALLSTON, Benjamin: 89
ALLSTON, Josias: 5193
ALLSTON, Robert Francis Withers: 89
ALLSTON, Washington: 150, 2058
ALLWOOD, Philip: 90
ALMAN, Caroline: 91
ALMAN, Leonard: 91
ALMANACS: 4083, 4732
    Great Britain: 1541
    North Carolina: 5741
    United States: 5051
ALMON, John: 92
ALMOND, A. D.: 93, 523
ALMOND, A. T.: 93
ALNWICK CASTLE, England: 4840
ALPHA BOOK CLUB (North Carolina): 1128
ALPINE, Georgia: 44, 2174
ALPS--Description and travel: 5050
ALSPAUGH, John Wesley: 5280
ALSTON, J. W.: 94
ALSTON, Jane: 824
ALSTON, William: 95
ALSTON, Willis: 2458
ALTAMAHA, Georgia--Plantation accounts: 4445
ALTAMONT, Tennessee--Mercantile accounts: 5187
ALTHORP, John Charles Spencer, Viscount: 1457
"ALTON": see TAVEAU, Augustin Louis
ALTON, Illinois: 1400
ALTOONA, Pennsylvania: 1798
ALUMINUM COMPANY OF CANADA, LIMITED: 96
ALUMINUM INDUSTRY--Canada: 96
ALUMNI ASSOCIATIONS: see as subheading under names of specific universities and colleges
ALVAREZ MORAN, Antonio: 4155
ALVERSTOKE, England: 3744
AMALGAMATED CLOTHING WORKERS OF AMERICA: 1196, 1197, 1199, 1202, 5236
AMATEUR TIMES (newspaper): 1814
AMAZON INSURANCE COMPANY: 2013
AMAZON RIVER: 4155
AMBLER, Ann: 99
AMBLER, Betsy: 99
AMBLER, Beverly: 97
AMBLER, John: 97, 98
AMBLER, Lucy Johnson: 99
AMBLER, Mary Willis: 99
AMBLER, Mason Gaither: 356

AMBLER, Philip St. George: 98
AMBLER, Robert: 97
AMBLER FAMILY: 99
AMELIA COUNTY, Virginia: 205, 2034, 5227
    Crops: 4729
    Schools: 1894, 3809
AMERICAN ACADEMY OF GENERAL PRACTICE: 2934
AMERICAN ALMANAC: 5911
AMERICAN ANTIQUARIAN SOCIETY: 354, 1502
AMERICAN ANTI-SLAVERY SOCIETY: 4387
AMERICAN ARBITRATION ASSOCIATION: 1196, 1197
AMERICAN ASSOCIATION FOR THE ADVANCEMENT OF SCIENCE: 2386
AMERICAN ASSOCIATION FOR THE UNITED NATIONS: 4558
AMERICAN ASSOCIATION OF UNIVERSITY PROFESSORS: 5847
AMERICAN AUTHORS: 1097, 1385, 1771, 2449, 5889
    see also names of specific writers
    Tennessee: 3611
AMERICAN BALLADS: 5615
AMERICAN BAR ASSOCIATION: 4927
AMERICAN BOARD OF COMMISSIONERS FOR FOREIGN MISSIONS: 5816
AMERICAN CANCER SOCIETY: 1196
AMERICAN COLLEGE, Beirut, Lebanon: 5156
AMERICAN COLONIES:
    see also AMERICAN REVOLUTION and names of specific colonies; UNITED STATES for the period after July 4, 1776; GREAT BRITAIN--COLONIAL POLICY AND ADMINISTRATION--American colonies
    Governors: 5540
    Inter-colonial cooperation: 5987
    Participation in the War of Jenkins' Ear: 5540
    Politics and government: 2780
    Sermons--Methodist: 5647
    Tea trade: 1481
AMERICAN COLONIZATION SOCIETY: 100, 1778, 3012, 3038
    Opposition to: 2848
AMERICAN COMMON SCHOOL SOCIETY: 3053
AMERICAN COPYRIGHT LEAGUE: 3284, 4020
AMERICAN COUNSEL ASSOCIATION: 4927
AMERICAN COURTS IN CHINA: 5252
AMERICAN DRAMA:
    see also ACTING; STAGE ADAPTATIONS; THEATER
    1800s: 97, 872, 1424, 2449, 3797, 4683
        Massachusetts: 3108
        Washington, D. C.: 42
    1900s: 356, 1636, 3306, 3797, 4789
        North Carolina: 4502
        Reviews: 3617
"AMERICAN DRAMA VS. LITERATURE" by Walter Prichard Eaton: 1636
AMERICAN EDUCATION SOCIETY: 2607
AMERICAN ENKA CORPORATION: 5442
AMERICAN ESSAYS: 3666, 5650
AMERICAN ETHNOLOGICAL SOCIETY: 2407
AMERICAN EXPEDITIONARY FORCES: see UNITED STATES--ARMY--World War I
"AMERICAN EXPEDITIONARY FORCES, HEADQUARTERS SERVICES OF SUPPLY, OFFICE OF THE CHIEF OF STAFF VISITORS' BUREAU" by Leander Dunbar Syme: 5163
AMERICAN FARMER by John Stuart Skinner: 3699
AMERICAN FEDERATION OF HOSIERY WORKERS: 101, 1199
AMERICAN FEDERATION OF HOSIERY WORKERS (Independent): 101
AMERICAN FEDERATION OF LABOR: 224, 1883, 3066, 3558, 3985, 4094
    Legal bulletins: 3640
    Publicity: 4094
    Southern States: 2768

AMERICAN FICTION:
    1800s: 826, 5210, 5650
        Criticism: 1227, 4971, 5908
        Southern States: 3418
    1900s: 826, 958, 1398, 3418, 4037, 4204
        Film adaptations: 4085
        North Carolina: 5049
AMERICAN FORESTRY ASSOCIATION: 4020
AMERICAN FREEHOLD LAND MORTGAGE COMPANY (England): 5586
AMERICAN HISTORY LEAFLET: 2400
AMERICAN-HONDURAS COMPANY: 5063
AMERICAN INDEPENDENCE--Anniversaries: see FOURTH OF JULY CELEBRATIONS
AMERICAN INSTITUTE OF CHRISTIAN PHILOSOPHY: 1441
AMERICAN IRON MOUNTAIN COMPANY: 3703
THE AMERICAN JOURNAL OF INTERNATIONAL LAW: 4556
AMERICAN JUDICATURE SOCIETY: 4927
AMERICAN LABOR EDUCATION SERVICE, INC.: 1197
AMERICAN LABOR RESEARCH INSTITUTE, INC.: 1194
AMERICAN LAND COMPANY: 323
THE AMERICAN LANGUAGE by Henry Louis Mencken: 4290
AMERICAN LAW INSTITUTE: 4927
AMERICAN LEGION AUXILIARY: 5656
AMERICAN LEGION OF HONOR: 823
AMERICAN LITERARY SCHOLARSHIP: 4499, 5889
AMERICAN LITERARY, SCIENTIFIC AND MILITARY ACADEMY--Students' notebooks: 1168
AMERICAN LITERATURE:
    see also AMERICAN AUTHORS; AMERICAN BALLADS; AMERICAN DRAMA; AMERICAN FICTION; AMERICAN POETRY; AMERICAN SATIRE; AMERICAN WIT AND HUMOR; LAWSUITS IN LITERATURE; TREASURE-TROVE IN LITERATURE; for material on a particular state or region, see, e.g., KENTUCKY IN AMERICAN LITERATURE
    1700s-1800s: 1842
    1800s: 10, 733, 1241, 2347, 2362, 3761, 4829, 4932
    1880s-1900s: 103, 4491, 5044
    1900s: 102, 361, 985, 1636, 2062, 2689
    Advertising: 1441
    Bibliography: 102
    Civil War: see CIVIL WAR--EFFECTS ON LITERATURE
    Criticism: 102, 720, 1097, 4290, 5889
        South Carolina: 2449
    Short stories: 1608
        Criticism: 5210
        Virginia: 1878
    Translations from German:
        Georgia: 3065
    Subdivided by place:
        Connecticut: 5593
        Georgia: 924, 2374
        Kentucky: 72
        Maryland--Baltimore: 2398
        North Carolina: 1313
        South Carolina: 296, 5901
            Charleston: 1575
        Southern states: 72, 1494, 2449, 2451, 3418, 4402
        Virginia: 182, 924, 4112
        Washington, D. C.: 42
AMERICAN LITERATURE: 102, 553
AMERICAN MEDICAL ASSOCIATION: 2934
AMERICAN MERCURY: 2081, 5593
AMERICAN MISSIONS IN NORTH AFRICA: 3646
AMERICAN MISSIONARY ASSOCIATION: 3633
THE AMERICAN NEGRO REVOLUTION by Benjamin Muse: 3820
AMERICAN NEWSPAPER GUILD: 1197, 1202, 5234

AMERICAN ORNITHOLOGISTS UNION: 4453
AMERICAN PARTY: see KNOW-NOTHING PARTY
AMERICAN PEACE SOCIETY: 4564
"AN AMERICAN PHILOSOPHER IN EXILE, GEORGE SANTAYANA" by Cyril Coniston Clemens: 1097
AMERICAN POETRY:
    see also CIVIL WAR--POETRY; ENGLISH LANGUAGE--Versification; FOLK POETRY; WORLD WAR II--Poetry; and for poetry about a particular state or region, see, e.g. NORTH CAROLINA IN POETRY
    1800s: 103, 733, 783, 926, 1037, 1115, 1827, 2104, 2449, 3008, 3284, 3422, 3707, 3741, 3796, 4021, 4311, 4313, 5044, 5210, 5253, 5313, 5503, 5529, 5681, 5711, 5733, 5734
    1900s: 103, 946, 958, 1914, 2390, 2934, 3969, 4037, 4453, 4556, 5388
    Authorship: 3284, 4619
    Collections: 2640, 3700, 4689, 5650
    Criticism: 553, 1029, 3969, 4600, 4958
    Plagiarism: 1029
    Publicity: 2053
    Readings: 3259
    Translations from Italian: 425, 5734
    Subdivided by place:
        California--San Francisco: 5081
        Florida: 1653
        Georgia: 786, 991, 1029, 1841, 2894, 4177, 5029, 5292
        Indiana: 3981
        Maryland: 664, 3559, 5166, 5193
        Massachusetts: 1455, 1698
        Missouri--Saint Louis: 4755
        New York--New York: 3999
        North Carolina: 2589, 2739, 3499, 3960, 5739
        South Carolina: 2045, 3394, 3892, 5193
            Charleston: 3666
        Southern States: 1494, 2451
        Virginia:
            1700s: 604
            1800-1860: 182, 298, 732, 2248, 2713, 3809, 4180, 4743, 5176
            1861-1900: 4020, 4180, 4186, 4743
            1900s: 4743
        Washington, D. C.: 42, 1118
        West Virginia: 2342
AMERICAN POTTERY--North Carolina: 5252
AMERICAN PROTECTIVE ASSOCIATION: 3840
AMERICAN RED CROSS: 1197
    see also WORLD WAR I--War relief--American Red Cross
    Florida: 3
    North Carolina: 2188
AMERICAN REFORMED TRACT AND BOOK SOCIETY: 4387
AMERICAN RELIEF FUND: 2149
AMERICAN REVOLUTION: 99, 404, 1115, 1236, 2495, 2776, 3116, 3256, 3278, 4003, 4191, 4230, 4915, 5768
    see also CONTINENTAL ARMY; and Militia under names of specific states
    Subdivided by place:
        Bermuda: 2008
        Georgia: 2675, 2788, 4128
        New York: 2304
        North Carolina: 4418, 5768
        South Carolina: 2675, 3511, 3981, 4625
        Southern States: 2147
        Virginia: 1066, 3819
    Subdivided by subject:
        Abandoned property: 3598
        Bounty lands: 70, 3671, 3794, 5839
            Kentucky: 2842

AMERICAN REVOLUTION:
  Subdivided by subject:
    Bounty Lands (Continued):
      Virginia: 523
    British Army: 4317
      Depredations: 2931
      Evacuation from Savannah: 5078
      Officers:
        Evaluations: 5604
        Finance: 869, 1358
      Military activities--South
        Carolina: 3209, 3511
      Surrender: 3041, 5575
    British merchants in the United
      States--Georgia: 5078
    British Navy:
      Depredations on America
        shipping: 4348
      Operations: 1117
        Georgia--Savannah: 2675
    British occupation: 1890
      South Carolina--Charleston:
        2402
    British strategy: 1926, 3722
    Campaigns and battles: 2776
      Canada: 4852
      Florida: 2675
      Georgia: 1696
        Augusta: 2179
        Bryan Creek Bridge: 1664
        Ogeechee: 5395
        Savannah: 413, 2008, 2931,
          3209, 3801, 4214
      North Carolina:
        Guilford Court House: 2147
        Hillsborough: 2796
        King's Mountain: 4418
        Moore's Creek--Historical
          commemorations: 5298
      Pennsylvania--Germantown: 3041
      South Carolina:
        Charleston: 2743, 3801
        Ninety Six: 2179
      Virginia--Yorktown: 1424, 1582,
        3041, 4418
    Canadian participation: 1236
    Casualties: 4852
    Causes: 1481, 5987
    Civilian life:
      North Carolina: 2508
      Virginia: 99
    Claims: 3439, 4252
    Confiscated property:
      see also AMERICAN REVOLUTION--
        Confiscated property
      Maryland: 2605
      North Carolina: 5298
    Committees of Public Safety:
      South Carolina: 4624
      Virginia: 2633
    Confiscated property: 2780
      British merchant ships: 4128
      Loyalists: 1374
      Recovery of: 5221
      Slaves--Georgia: 3591
      Subdivided by place:
        Georgia: 3573
        Maryland: 2605
        North Carolina: 2776
          see also AMERICAN
            REVOLUTION--Claims--
            Confiscated property--
            North Carolina
        South Carolina: 3501
    Depredations by American troops:
      North Carolina: 1890
    Desertion--North Carolina: 5475
    Economic aspects: 1481
      Coinage: 2508
      Counterfeiting of currency:
        4418
      Destruction of American
        shipping: 4348
      Inflation: 2508
      North Carolina: 2508
    Foreign public opinion--France:
      1236

AMERICAN REVOLUTION:
  Subdivided by subject (Continued):
    Fortifications--South Carolina:
      1926
    French participation: 1236, 4015,
      4418
      Casualties: 1424
      Portraits of French commanders:
        1582
    Historical studies: 2881
      North Carolina: 3176
      Loyalists: 305
    Indian relations with the United
      States:
      Fighting with the British:
        4852
      New Jersey: 4418
    Land warrants: see LAND WARRANTS
    Leadership: 99
    Loyalist refugees: 3485
      Canada: 1890
    Loyalists: 1481
      Confiscated property: 1374
      Treatment of--New York: 2304
      Subdivided by place:
        Georgia: 413, 1993, 3309,
          5398, 5644, 5920, 5987
        Savannah: 5078
        North Carolina: 935, 4859,
          5768
          Historical studies: 305
        South Carolina: 1088
          King's Carolina Rangers:
            1358
        Virginia: 769
    Military activities: 2307, 3458,
      5184, 5319
      see also AMERICAN REVOLUTION--
        British Army--Military
        activities; AMERICAN
        REVOLUTION--Militia--Military
        activities
      Georgia: 5604
      North Carolina: 935
    Military supplies: 231, 2020,
      2665, 4746, 4859, 5575
      see also AMERICAN REVOLUTION--
        Militia--Military supplies
      South Carolina: 4624
      Virginia: 3560
    Militia:
      see also Militia as subheading
        under names of specific
        states
      Finance--Virginia: 3130
      Georgia: 1993
      Horses--North Carolina: 3361
      Military activities:
        Georgia: 1789
        North Carolina: 3361
        Virginia: 3130
      Military supplies--North
        Carolina: 3361
      Mobilization--North Carolina:
        3361
      Officers--Promotion: 3130
      Pay--Georgia: 3209
      Relations with the Continental
        Army: 2179
    Mobilization: 2665
      see also AMERICAN REVOLUTION--
        Militia--Mobilization
    Monuments: 4468
    Patriots--Georgia: 5920
    Peace negotiations: 2149, 5102
    Peace treaty: see TREATY OF PARIS
      (1783)
    Pensions: 2495, 2502, 3623, 4852,
      5454, 5537, 5613
      Claims: 74, 1387, 2012, 2717,
        3805
      Virginia: 523
    Politics: 2776
    Prisoner exchanges: 3389, 5575
      Martinique: 3315
      South Carolina--Charleston:
        3802

AMERICAN REVOLUTION:
  Subdivided by subject (Continued):
    Prisoners and prisons:
      American prisoners: 404
        South Carolina--Charleston:
          2019
      British prisoners: 4852
      Georgia: 1993
    Privateering: 2551
    Prize ships: 2019
    Public debt: 2059
    Public finance: 2665, 2776, 4015
    Public opinion: 2776
      North Carolina: 2508
    Reminiscences: 872
    Shipping: 2019
    Societies: see SOCIETY OF THE
      CINCINNATI
    Speculation and war profiteering:
      5228
    Spies--Execution: 2276
    Spoils: 3209
    Tories: see AMERICAN REVOLUTION--
      Loyalists
    Trade and commerce: 1481, 4348
    Treason: 2276
    Truces--Georgia: 3209
    Veterans: 1072, 5829
      Honors and awards: 4746
      Payment frauds: 105
AMERICAN SATIRE:
  District of Columbia: 42
  North Carolina--Durham: 5597
AMERICAN SCENIC AND HISTORIC
  PRESERVATION SOCIETY: 4343
AMERICAN SCULPTURE: 5374
AMERICAN SHORT LINE RAILROAD
  ASSOCIATION: 238
"AMERICAN SLAVERY AND THE IMMEDIATE
  DUTY OF SLAVEHOLDERS" by E. W.
  Caruthers: 923
AMERICAN SOCIETY FOR PSYCHICAL
  RESEARCH: 3190
AMERICAN STATE PAPERS: 1937
AMERICAN STUDENT UNION: 4948
AMERICAN STUDENTS IN EUROPE: 3029
AMERICAN STUDENTS IN GERMANY: 1407,
  3809
AMERICAN STUDENTS IN ITALY: 4736
AMERICAN STUDENTS IN SWITZERLAND:
  3809
AMERICAN STUDIES IN HONOR OF WILLIAM
  KENNETH BOYD, David K. Jackson
  (ed.): 1227, 2449
AMERICAN TEACHERS IN ARGENTINA: 3295
AMERICAN TOBACCO COMPANY: 1584, 1585,
  1914, 4857
AMERICAN TRACT SOCIETY: 1565, 2236
AMERICAN UNITARIAN ASSOCIATION: 617
AMERICAN UNIVERSITY, Washington, D.C.:
  4564
AMERICAN VETERANS COMMITTEE: 1197
AMERICAN WIT AND HUMOR: 4545
AMERICANA--Collectors and collecting:
  3734
AMERICANS FOR DEMOCRATIC ACTION: 1197,
  5234
AMERICANS IN CHINA: see CIVIL WAR--
  AMERICANS IN CHINA--Opinions of
AMERICANS IN GERMANY: 1665
AMERICANS IN GREAT BRITAIN: 43, 380,
  2058, 3809
AMERICANS IN ITALY: 2678
AMERICANS IN MEXICO--Imprisonment:
  5271
AMERICUS, Georgia: 3729
  Description: 3660
  Social life and customs: 3339, 5730
AMES, Adelbert: 961, 3022
AMES, Electa E. (Ray): 104
AMES, Elizabeth: 902
AMES, Fisher: 105
AMES, Fordyce W.: 104
AMES, Frank: 104
AMES, Harriet (Moore) Page Potter:
  4286
AMES, James Tyler: 106
AMES, Jessie (Daniel): 107

AMES, Mary (Clemmer): 2648
AMES, Winona C.: 2648
AMES, Winthrop: 3797
AMES PLOW COMPANY: 5193
AMESBURY, Massachusetts: 4189, 5717
AMHERST, William: 2147
AMHERST, William Pitt, First Earl
   Amherst: 4023, 5038
AMHERST, Massachusetts: 5971
AMHERST, Virginia: 1156, 5484
AMHERST ACADEMY, Cora, North
   Carolina: 1247
AMHERST COUNTY, Virginia: 97, 397
   2939, 4295, 5290, 5366
   Clergy: 3497
   Earthquakes: 5529
   Farming: 3788
   Medical practice: 3788
   Personal finance: 5529
   Schools: 5380
   Slaves--Taxation: 5529
   Social life and customs: 5529
   Tannery: 3788
   Tax in kind: 1181
   Taxation of property: 5529
   Cities and towns:
      Sweet Briar: 5765
   Temperance: 5529
AMICK, Jacob: 108
AMICK, John: 108
AMICK, Thomas Cicero: 5267
AMIENS, Treaty of: see TREATY OF
   AMIENS
AMIS, Thomas: 5457
AMIS DE LÉON BLOY: 555
AMISTAD CASE (1841): 4982
AMMUNITION:
   see also BOMBS; CARTRIDGE CLIPS;
      PERCUSSION RIFLE BULLET
   Manufacture: 2696
AMMUNITION BARGES--Virginia: 3741
AMNESTY: 4927
AMESTY OATHS: see CIVIL WAR--LOYALTY
   OATHS
AMORY, Thomas: 1736
AMOS, Richard: 110
AMOS FAMILY: 110
AMOS S. DREWRY AND COMPANY: 1567,
   3900
"AMOUNT EXPENSES OF A JOURNEY FROM
   CHARLESTON TO THE VIRGINIA HOT AND
   SULPHUR SPRINGS AND BACK TO
   CHARLESTON VIA PHILADELPHIA": 1891
AMOY, China: 258
AMSTERDAM, Netherlands:
   American consul in: 588
   Bondholders: 3273
   Merchants: 258
THE AMULET (periodical): 2263
AMUSEMENTS:
   see also BOWLING; CARDS; CHARADES;
      CIRCUSES; ENTERTAINING; GAMES;
      MUNICIPAL RECREATION; RIDDLES;
      TABLEAUX; WILD WEST SHOWS; and
      Amusements as subheading under
      (name of army)--Camp life--
      Amusements
   Michigan: 3221
   North Carolina: 436, 1925, 2192
   Tennessee--Nashville: 5623
   Virginia: 262
LES AMUSEMENTS DE LA COMPAGNE OR LE
   DÉFI SPIRITUEL, NOUVELLE GALANTE
   ET COMIQUE: 3119
ANACONDA, Colorado--Gold mining: 3660
"ANALYSIS AND NOTIONS AND THOUGHTS":
   2673
ANDAMAN ISLANDS: 1847
ANDAMARCA, Bolivia: 4155
ANDERS, J. D.: 103
ANDERSEN, Karl Joachim: 111
ANDERSON, A. A.: 122
ANDERSON, A. J.: 122
ANDERSON, Aden: 112
ANDERSON, Albert: 113
ANDERSON (C.) AND BROTHER (firm): 122
ANDERSON (C. AND G. J.) AND COMPANY:
   122
ANDERSON, C. J.: 122

ANDERSON, Charles (North Carolina);
   122
ANDERSON, Charles M. (Virginia): 114
ANDERSON, Charles Roberts: 2449, 3092
ANDERSON, Edward C.: 115
ANDERSON, Edwin Alexander, Jr.: 116
ANDERSON, Francis Thomas: 117
ANDERSON (G. J. AND C.) AND COMPANY:
   see ANDERSON (C. AND G. J.) AND
   COMPANY
ANDERSON (G. J.) AND COMPANY: 2749
ANDERSON, George: 118
ANDERSON, George Burgess: 832
ANDERSON, J. G.: 5252
ANDERSON, James (Scotland): 119
ANDERSON, James A.: 120
ANDERSON, James M. (Alabama): 120
ANDERSON, John: 306
ANDERSON, Joseph: 872
ANDERSON, Joseph (1757-1837): 4218
ANDERSON, Joseph Reid: 117, 2696
ANDERSON (JOSEPH REID) AND COMPANY:
   523
ANDERSON, Larz: 5252
ANDERSON, Leland: 3324
ANDERSON, Richard Heron: 121, 3809,
   5280
ANDERSON, Robert: 1299
ANDERSON, V. V.: 122
ANDERSON, William: 306
ANDERSON, Z. W.: 123
ANDERSON FAMILY (North Carolina):
   122, 3324
ANDERSON FAMILY (Virginia): 1066
ANDERSON FAMILY (West Virginia:
   Genealogy): 1946
ANDERSON, South Carolina: 534, 718
ANDERSON ACADEMY, Petersburg,
   Virginia: 858
ANDERSON AND BROTHERS (firm): 122
ANDERSON AND IJAMES (firm): 2749
ANDERSON COUNTY, South Carolina: 3546
   Anderson: 534, 718
   Pendleton: 3278, 4191, 4896
ANDERSON PACK AND _____ VAWTER
   (firm): 4011
ANDERSONVILLE, Georgia: see CIVIL
   WAR--PRISONERS AND PRISONS--Union
   prisoners--Georgia--Andersonville
ANDES MOUNTAINS--Description and
   travel: 1506
ANDOVER, England--Canals: 5331
ANDOVER, Massachusetts: 995, 1037
   see also ANDOVER THEOLOGICAL
      SEMINARY
   Social life and customs: 3034
ANDOVER THEOLOGICAL SEMINARY,
   Andover, Massachusetts: 5088, 5899
ANDRÉ, John: 2276
ANDREADES, Andreas Michael: 124
ANDREW, Benjamin: 125
ANDREW, James O.: 4912
ANDREW, John Albion: 3283
ANDREW CLOW & CO.: 1117
ANDREW FEMALE COLLEGE: 4921
ANDREWES, Gerrard: 2836
ANDREWS, Anna (Robinson): 128
ANDREWS, Benjamin Whitfield: 126
ANDREWS, Charles H.: 127
ANDREWS, Charles Wesley (d. 1875):
   128
ANDREWS, Charles Wesley II: 128
ANDREWS, Everett C.: 129
ANDREWS, George: 130
ANDREWS, James J.: 5425
ANDREWS, James O.: 131
ANDREWS, John: 2410
ANDREWS, Louis H.: 127
ANDREWS, Matthew Page I: 128
ANDREWS, Matthew Page II: 128
ANDREWS, Maude Annulet: 3969
ANDREWS, Roy Chapman: 1155
ANDREWS, Sally Page: 3325
ANDREWS, Sarah Walker (Page): 128
ANDREWS, Thomas A.: 132
ANDREWS, William (Mississippi): 130
ANDREWS, William B. G. (Virginia)
   132

ANDREWS FAMILY: 128
ANDREWS' RAIDERS: 5425
ANECDOTES: see as subheading under
   names of wars
ANESTHETICS: 1501, 3249
"ANGEL IN THE HOUSE" by Coventry
   Patmore: 4069
ANGELA, Sister: see HEATH, Laura
ANGELIQUE (ship): 5967
ANGERONA SEMINARY, Winchester,
   Virginia: 287
ANGLICANISM: see CHURCH OF ENGLAND
ANGIER, Carlotta Gilmore: 133
ANGIER, Lida (Duke): 133
ANGIER (M. A.) CO. (firm): 134
ANGIER, Malbourne A.: 134
ANGIER, Sarah Pearson: 1584, 5252
ANGIER, Sir Theodore Vivian Samuel:
   2149
ANGIER, Zaline Allen: 83
ANGIER FAMILY: 83
ANGLE, Ella: 135
ANGLE, George: 135
ANGLE, Sarah: 135
ANGLESEY, Henry William Paget, First
   Marquis of: 4024, 5637
ANGLIN, Margaret: 3797
ANGLO-FRENCH ENTENTE CORDIALE: 4941
ANGULO, Francisco de: 4155
ANGUS BRICK COMPANY: 5312
ANIMAL QUARANTINE: see LIVESTOCK
   QUARANTINE
ANIMALS: see CONFEDERATE STATES OF
   AMERICA--ARMY--Animals; UNITED
   STATES--ARMY--Civil War--Animals;
   and specific kinds of animals
   Collection of: see ZOOLOGICAL
      EXPEDITIONS
ANJOU, France: 5323
ANKENEY, Florence Winter: 136
ANKENEY, John C.: 136
ANKERWYCKE PARK, England: 2321
ANN ARBOR, Michigan: 4652, 5489
   see also UNIVERSITY OF MICHIGAN
   Clothing and dress: 3221
"THE ANNALS OF BAGHELKHAND" by
   Maulvi Rahman Ali: 4364
ANNALS OF CONGRESS: 1937
THE ANNALS OF SOUTHERN METHODISM
   by Charles Manning Force Deems:
   1441
ANNAPOLIS, Maryland:
   1700s: 1481, 3662
   1700s-1800s: 665, 2319
   1800s: 742, 1007, 4361, 4376
   1800s-1900s: 4221, 4511
   Civil War: 2602
   Land grants: 5436
   Merchants: 1386
   Universities and colleges: see
      ST. JOHN'S COLLEGE; UNITED STATES
      NAVAL ACADEMY
ANNE ARUNDEL COUNTY, Maryland: 4474,
   5630
   Annapolis: see ANNAPOLIS, Maryland
   "Cedar Park": 3627
   West River: 2267, 4219
ANNESLEY, Francis Charles, Second
   Viscount Annesley: 4024
ANNETTE ISLANDS--Description and
   travel: 2084
ANNEXATION: see UNITED STATES--
   Territorial expansion; and
   Annexation as subheading under name
   of territory to be annexed
ANNIE (blockade runner): 4881
ANNIVERSARIES: see WEDDING
   ANNIVERSARIES
   American Independence: see FOURTH
      OF JULY CELEBRATIONS
"THE ANNIVERSARY OF AMERICAN
   INDEPENDENCE, JULY 24, 1786" by
   Samuel Eusebius McCorkle: 3334
"AN ANNOTATED AND INDEXED EDITION OF
   THE LETTERS OF SHERWOOD BONNER" by
   Jean Nosser Biglane: 3363
ANNUAL CONFERENCES FOR EDUCATION IN
   THE SOUTH: 4373

659

ANNUNZIO, Gabriele d': 137, 3617
ANNVILLE, Pennsylvania: 4937
ANSELL, R. E.: 5027
ANSON, Charles V.: 189
ANSON, George (d. 1789): 190
ANSON, Sir George (1769-1849): 190
ANSON, George Edward: 1632
ANSON, Thomas, First Viscount Anson: 190
ANSON COUNTY, North Carolina: 4996
  County government: 4918
  Farming: 4952
  Public schools: 192
  Steam powered sawmills: 4918
  Taxation: 191
  Cities and towns:
    Ansonville: 4918
    Deep Creek: 2727
    Lanesboro: 409
    Lilesville: 2493, 4664
    Opossum Trot: 80
    Polkton: 1925
    Wadesboro: 2984, 3223, 4906
      Blacksmithing: 998
        Accounts: 4906
      Carriage repair: 1897
      Children of the Confederacy: 227
      Livery stables--Accounts: 4814
      Mercantile accounts: 4762
      Merchants: 222
      Taverns and inns--Accounts: 4814
ANSON GUARDS: see CONFEDERATE STATES OF AMERICA--ARMY--Regiments-- North Carolina--Infantry--14th
ANSON GUARDS: COMPANY C, FOURTEENTH REGIMENT, NORTH CAROLINA VOLUNTEERS, 1861-1865 by William Alexander Smith: 4918
ANSON INSTITUTE: 4052
ANSONIA, Connecticut--Sons of Veterans: 4955
ANSONVILLE, North Carolina: 4918
ANTHONY, Nancy: 3625
ANTHONY, Susan Brownell: 103
ANTHROPOLOGICAL STUDIES: see INDIANS OF NORTH AMERICA--Anthropological studies
ANTI-AMERICAN DEMONSTRATIONS--Mexico: 1412
"ANTI-BLAINE MOVEMENT": 5762
ANTI-CATHOLICISM: see also CATHOLIC CHURCH--Relations with Protestants
  Great Britain: 369
  United States: 20
ANTI-CORN LAW LEAGUE: 597
ANTIETAM, Maryland:
  Civil War: see CIVIL WAR--CAMPAIGNS, BATTLES, AND MILITARY ACTIONS--Maryland--Antietam
  Description: 2106
  Historic sites: 2106
ANTI-FEDERALISTS: see also FEDERALIST PARTY (Jeffersonian period)
  New England: 1333
ANTI-LABOR LEGISLATION: see LABOR LAWS AND LEGISLATION
ANTI-LYNCHING MOVEMENT--South Carolina: 300
ANTI-MASONIC PARTY: 1778
  Pennsylvania: 421
ANTIOCH (ship): 5860
ANTIPAPISM: see ANTI-CATHOLICISM
ANTIQUARIAN NOTES by George Eyre Evans: 250
ANTIQUES--Sale of: 5903
ANTIQUITIES: 128
  see also ARCHEOLOGICAL INVESTIGATIONS
  China: 1155
  Great Britain: 4176
  Greece: 345
ANTI-SALOON LEAGUE OF AMERICA: 879
ANTI-SALOON LEAGUE OF VIRGINIA: 879
ANTISEMITISM--South Carolina: 4834
ANTISLAVERY MOVEMENTS: see ABOLITION OF SLAVERY AND ABOLITIONIST SENTIMENT

ANTI-TRUST LEGISLATION--United States: 592
ANTI-UNIONISM--North Carolina: 1196, 1202
ANTONY, England: 888
ANTRIM, County, Ireland: 718
ANTWERP, Belgium: 5224
"APAINATAX," Virginia (Plantation): 4297
APALACHEE BAY, Florida: 4982
"APETHORPE HOUSE," England: 1754
APEX, North Carolina:
  Mercantile accounts: 5803
  Schools--Negro schools: 3941
APOLINARIA, Doña: 485
APOSTOLIC SUCCESSION: 5468
  see also names of specific popes
APOTHECARIES: see PHARMACISTS
APPALACHIAN MOUNTAINS--National parks and reserves: 1478
APPALACHIAN TRAIL: 5389
"AN APPEAL TO THE PEOPLE OF VIRGINIA" by Peterfield Trent: 5339
"APPENDIX" by Francis Reginald Wingate: 5835
APPERSON, Kent: 193
APPERSON, Richard: 194
APPLEBERRY, Dilmus J.: 195
APPLETON, Nathan: 196
APPLETON, W. H.: 1227
APPLETON AND CO.: 196
APPLETON'S CYCLOPEDIA OF AMERICAN BIOGRAPHY: 3967
APPOINTMENTS: see JUDGES--Appointments; POLITICS AND GOVERNMENT--Appointments; and Appointments and promotions as subheading under names of armies, e.g. UNITED STATES--ARMY--Officers--Appointments and promotions
APPOMATTOX, Virginia:
  Civil War: 1137
    see also CIVIL WAR--CAMPAIGNS, BATTLES, AND MILITARY ACTIONS--Virginia--Appomattox
APPOMATTOX COUNTY, Virginia: 1894, 4319
  Appomattox: see APPOMATTOX, Virginia
  Appomattox Court House: 5902
APPOMATTOX COURT HOUSE, Virginia: 5902
APPORTIONMENT: see Apportionment as subheading under (name of state)--Legislature
APPRENTICESHIP: 4937
  see also FREEDMEN--Apprenticeship; and Apprenticeship under names of trades and crafts
  Germany: 3808
  Great Britain--London: 3808
  New York: 782
  North Carolina: 4370
  South Carolina--Charleston: 3294
APPROPRIATIONS AND EXPENDITURES:
  see as subheading under names of countries, states, legislative bodies, and armies; PUBLIC FINANCE
APRIL FOOL'S DAY: 5739
APSLEY, Lily: 4881
AQUEDUCTS--Construction: 3145, 5546
AQUIA, Virginia: 144
ARABIC POETRY--Translations into English: 2146
ARBER, Thomas: 816
ARBITRATION: see LABOR ARBITRATION
ARBÓS, Antonio de Gimbernat y: see GIMBERNAT Y ARBÓS, Antonio de
ARBOUIN, Leslie O.: 198
ARBUCKLE, Matthew: 5392
ARBUTHNOT, Charles: 199, 2836
ARCADIA UNIVERSITY, Wolfville, Nova Scotia: 3260
ARAPAHOE INDIANS: 4353
ARCH, Joseph: 200

ARCHBISHOP OF TRIER (Prussia): 201
ARCHBISHOPS: see names of specific archbishops
ARCHDALE, John: 202
ARCHDALE FAMILY: 202
ARCHDALE, North Carolina: 4172
ARCHEOLOGICAL INVESTIGATIONS:
  see also ANTIQUITIES HISTORICAL STUDIES
  Italy: 2148
  Mississippi: 2249
  Tunisia: 3460
  Turkey--Assos: 3410
ARCHER, Allin LeRoy: 203
ARCHER, B. T.: 4497
ARCHER, Fletcher Harris: 203
ARCHER, William M.: 204
ARCHER, William Segar: 205, 872
ARCHIE BLACK'S ACADEMY, Haywood, North Carolina: 2357
ARCHITECTS--North Carolina: 465
ARCHITECTURAL DECORATION: see INTERIOR DECORATION
ARCHITECTURAL DRAWINGS--Great Britain: 3895
ARCHITECTURAL RESTORATION: see HISTORICAL RESTORATION
ARCHITECTURE:
  see also CHURCH ARCHITECTURE; DOMESTIC ARCHITECTURE; NAVAL ARCHITECTURE
  Great Britain: 1551
  Virginia: 4490
ARCHIVE OF FOLKSONG OF THE LIBRARY OF CONGRESS: 691
ARCHIVO GENERAL DE LA NACIÓN: 3649, 3650
ARCOLA, North Carolina: 1394
ARCOT, India: 2037, 2422
  Relations with East India Company: 1629
ARCTIC REGION:
  Discoveries (Geography): 5783
  Explorations: 4556
ARDELLA, A. H.: 518
ARDINGLY, England: 4705
ARDINTOUL, Scotland: 3446
ARDMORE, Oklahoma: 3248
AREHART, William H.: 207
AREHEART, J. W.: 206
AREQUIPA, Peru: 4155
"UN AREQUIPEÑO": 4155
ARGENTINA: 2271
  British consulate in: 286
  Confederate emigrants: 4019
  Currency: 1339
  Economic conditions: 2742
  Education: 3295
  Foreign exchange: 2093
  Foreign trade: 2742
  Navy--Advisors: 4019
  Politics and government: 2742
  Ranching: 4019
ARGONNE, France: 4269
ARGUS (newspaper): 5937
ARGYLE ISLAND, South Carolina: 3485
ARGYLL, George Douglas Campbell, Eighth Duke of: 294, 863, 1014, 2149
ARIETTA (race horse): 5751
ARIKARA INDIANS: 3357
ARIOSTO, Ludovico: 5379
ARISTOPHANES ed. by Tiberius Hemsterhuis: 5567
ARITHMETIC:
  Exercise books:
    1770s: 5060
    1790s: 1269, 5471
    1800s: 683, 3112, 4467
    1820s: 4422
    1830s: 2424, 3799, 5003
    1850s: 1085
  Subdivided by place:
    Georgia: 208
    Maryland: 3875
      Frederick County: 4804
    North Carolina: 208, 579, 1538, 1781, 3605, 4862
      Caswell County: 3576

ARITHMETIC:
  Exercise books:
    Subdivided by place:
      North Carolina (Continued):
        Davidson County: 5219
        Guilford County: 4114
        Hillsborough: 3677
        Lincoln County: 5976
        Surry County: 3074
        Taylorsville: 3289
        Washington: 5479
      South Carolina: 208
      United States: 1671, 1818, 2501
      Virginia: 208, 576, 2633
  Study and teaching: 3289
ARIZONA:
  see also WESTERN STATES
  Army camps--Mogalas: 3843
  Copper mines--Wickenburg: 4918
  Hydroelectric power plants: 1548
ARIZONA TERRITORY: 3760
  Description: 3552
ARKADELPHIA, Arkansas: 1154
  see also CIVIL WAR--CAMPAIGNS,
    BATTLES, AND MILITARY ACTIONS--
    Arkansas--Arkadelphia; OUACHITA
    COLLEGE
ARKANSAS:
  see also SOUTHERN STATES
  Agriculture: 2727
    see also ARKANSAS--Crops;
      ARKANSAS--Farming; ARKANSAS--
      Plantations
  Choctaw Indians: 4373
  Christianity: 5380
  Churches: see ARKANSAS--Methodist
    churches; ARKANSAS--Presbyterian
    churches
  Civil War: see subheadings under
    CIVIL WAR; CONFEDERATE STATES OF
    AMERICA; and UNITED STATES--
    ARMY--Civil War
  Commodity prices: 4776
    see also ARKANSAS--Cotton--Prices
  Clarke County: 4270
  Constitution: 5380
  Cookery: 1154
  Cotton--Prices: 1154
  Cotton growing: 4776
    Calhoun County: 4199
    Dardanelle: 3276
  Cotton land: 3053
  Cotton trade: 2856
  Crops: 837
    see also names of specific crops
      under ARKANSAS
  Currency: 1339
  Death: 5380
  Debt: 1089
  Democratic Party: 988
  Description and travel: 57, 1084,
    1361, 2727, 5508
  Dueling: 5380
  Economic conditions: 57, 836, 2727,
    2809, 4776
  Estates--Administration and
    settlement: 478, 784
  Family life: 5380
  Farm life: 1154
  Farming: 1587
    see also ARKANSAS--Agriculture;
      ARKANSAS-Plantations
    Dardanelle: 3276
  Finance: see ARKANSAS--Personal
    finance; ARKANSAS--Public finance
  Freedmen--Hampton: 4199
  Historical studies: 4894
  Land: 478
    see also ARKANSAS--Cotton land
    Speculation: 4924
  Land settlement: 872, 1438
  Law practice: 1089, 5380
  Lawsuits--Little Rock: 4208
  Literary interests: 5380
  Medicines--Prescriptions: 1154
  Methodist churches: 1361
  Migration to: 2855
  Mining: 126

ARKANSAS (Continued):
  Negroes: see ARKANSAS--Freedmen;
    ARKANSAS--Slaves
  Personal finance: 4615
    Little Rock: 4208
  Pioneer life: 2809, 4347
  Plantation accounts: 4776
  Plantations: 2517
  Politics and government: 2809, 5380
  Portraits: 5380
  Presbyterian churches: 1361
  Public finance: 1154, 2117
  Railroads: 5380
    Construction: 837
  Reconstruction: 1154
  Religion: 57, 837
    see also ARKANSAS--Christianity
  Schools:
    see also ARKANSAS--Teaching
    Girls' schools and academies:
      3142
    Mission schools: 4373
  Secession: 2184, 5380
  Slavery: 4776, 5380
  Slaves: 478
  Social conditions: 331, 1262
    Mississippi County: 4764
  Social life and customs: 1154,
    4776
  Tannery accounts--Whitsonton: 5509
  Taxation: 4776
  Teaching: 5380
    see also ARKANSAS--Schools
  Telegraph: 1154
  Temperance: 2123, 2346
  Trade and commerce:
    Cotton: see ARKANSAS--Cotton
      trade
    Hides and leather--Whitsonton:
      5509
  Universities and colleges: see
    OUACHITA COLLEGE
ARKANSAS COUNTY, Arkansas--De Witt:
  5753
"ARKANSAS FACTS"; 1361
ARKANSAS RIVER--Steamboat travel:
  5380
ARLINGTON, Virginia: 3157
"ARLINGTON," Virginia (estate):
  4612
ARLINGTON COUNTY, Virginia--
  Alexandria: see ALEXANDRIA,
  Virginia
ARLINGTON MUTUAL LIFE INSURANCE
  COMPANY: 2130
ARMAGH, Northern Ireland: 2738
ARMAGH COUNTY, Northern Ireland:
  Armagh: 2738
ARMAMENTS: see FIREARMS; ORDNANCE
ARMAMENTS INDUSTRY:
  see also DEFENSE PLANTS
  Governmental manufacture--United
    States: 5433
ARMED FORCES: see as subheading under
  names of countries
ARMENIA:
  Merchants: 5797
  Social and political reform: 1014
ARMENTROUT, J. C.: 209
ARMENTROUT, Thomas: 210
ARMFIELD, Eugene Morehead: 5457
ARMFIELD, Joseph S.: 211
ARMFIELD, Robert Franklin: 5457
ARMFIELD, Wyatt Jackson: 5457
ARMIES: see as subheading under names
  of specific countries
ARMISTEAD, Mary: 2935
ARMISTEAD, Walker Keith: 212
ARMISTEAD AND CHESSON (firm): 1015
ART AND ARTISTS: 196, 1424, 2058,
  2398, 3960, 4453, 4984
  see also ARTS; DRAWINGS; ENGRAVERS
    AND ENGRAVING; EUROPEAN ART;
    LANDSCAPE IN ART; NATURE IN ART;
    PAINTING; SCULPTURE
  Criticism--Great Britain: 4600
  Employment--United States: 2587

ART AND ARTISTS (Continued):
  Exhibitions: 4900
    Ireland: 3567
  Foreign artists:
    Employment in the United States:
      2587
  Forgeries--Great Britain: 1225
  Students' notebooks: 3325
  Study and teaching--Indiana: 5149
  Subdivided by place:
    Great Britain: 258, 1225, 4575,
      4576
      Somersetshire: 1071
    Japan: 5553
    Maryland--Baltimore: 2398
    New York: 2726
    Pennsylvania: 2728
    United States: 3965
ART AND GOVERNMENT: see GOVERNMENT
  AND ART
ART COLLECTING:
  France: 1880
  Great Britain: 1343, 5553
  India--Calcutta: 1343
  Washington, D.C.: 4478
ART GALLERIES--Berlin, Germany: 2139
"THE ARMISTICES" by Tasker Howard
  Bliss: 4556
ARMITAGE, Elkanah: 676
ARMITAGE, Frederick: 39
ARMORIES:
  see also ARSENALS
  West Virginia: 2696
ARMS LIMITATION: see WASHINGTON
  DISARMAMENT CONFERENCE
ARMS TRADE: see UNITED STATES--Arms
  trade--France
ARMSTRONG, Ann: 86
ARMSTRONG, Bennett: 215
ARMSTRONG, Charles B.: 5457
ARMSTRONG, D. M.: 5090
ARMSTRONG, David: 86
ARMSTRONG, Francis: 86
ARMSTRONG, Hamilton Fish: 5252
ARMSTRONG, J. H.: 3604
ARMSTRONG, John: 213
ARMSTRONG, Richard F.: 2963
ARMSTRONG, Thomas: 215
ARMSTRONG, Thomas T.: 214
ARMSTRONG, William G.: 215
ARMSTRONG FAMILY: 3295
ARMSTRONG GUNS: 1114
ARMY CAMPS: see Camps as subheading
  under names of armies
ARMY LIFE: see Army life as
  subheading under names of armies
ARMY MEDICAL SCHOOL (Great Britain):
  4026
ARMY OF THE PHILIPPINES, INC.: 5559
ARMY SUPPLIES: see Military supplies
  as subheading under names of armies
ARMY TRAINING BILL (Great Britain):
  5726
ARNETT, Virginia H.: 216
ARNOLD, Benedict: 2276, 4418
ARNOLD, Benjamin F.: 5925
ARNOLD, David: 5925
ARNOLD, Sir Edwin: 217, 355, 2471
ARNOLD, John: 218
ARNOLD, H. C.: 5925
ARNOLD, Julean Herbert: 5252
ARNOLD, Matthew: 5050
ARNOLD, Remmie L.: 5779
ARNOLD, Richard: 219
ARNOLD, Richard Dennis: 220
ARNOLD, Sallie E. (Umstott): 221
ARNOLD, Samuel: 5715
ARNOLD AND COOLEY (firm): 222
ARNOLD-FOSTER, Hugh: 294
ARP, Bill: see SMITH, Charles Henry
ARRIETA, Valentin: 4155
ARRINGTON, Archibald Hunter: 5457
ARROWHEADS: 4619
ARROWSMITH, Lewis G. (pseudonym):
  2081
ARSENALS:
  see also ARMORIES
  Construction: 3145

ARSENALS (Continued):
  Georgia--Augusta: 700
  Virginia--Fluvanna County: 4915
ART SOCIETIES--Great Britain: 1424
  see also ROYAL ACADEMY OF ARTS
ARTHER, William: 4624
ARTHRITIS: see DISEASES--Arthritis
ARTHUR, Andrew: 223
ARTHUR, Chester A.: 224
ARTHUR, Chester Alan (1830-1886): 5168
ARTHUR (barque): 2682
ARTHUR WILLIAM PATRICK ALBERT, First Duke of Connaught and Strathearn: 663
ARTIFICIAL LIMBS: see PROSTHESES
ARTILLERY: see as subheading under names of armies
ARTILLERY DRILL AND TACTICS: 1706
  South Carolina: 2875
ARTISANS' ORGANIZATIONS: 885
ARTISTS: see ART AND ARTISTS
ARTISTS AND PUBLISHERS--United States: 1665
ARTS:
  see also ART; PERFORMING ARTS
  Great Britain--Manchester: 4113
  North Carolina: 4736
  United States: 2398
AS I RECOLLECT by James Taylor: 5202
ASA BARNES, INC.: see WASHINGTON MADDUX AND ASA BARNES, INC.
ASBURY, Francis (1745-1816): 832, 2796, 3646, 5964
ASBURY ACADEMY, Cary, North Carolina: 2846
ASCARAY, Juan: 4155
ASCENCIO SEGURA, Manuel: 4155
ASCENSION ISLAND: 3744
ASCENSION PARISH, Louisiana: 2859
ASHANTI WAR (1873-1874): 5872, 5876
ASHANTI WAR (1900): 5872
ASHBURN, Karl Everett: 225
ASHBY, Anthony: 3512
ASHBY, Turner (1828-1862): 2792
ASHBY, Turner W.: 226
ASHBY, Miss V____: 3512
ASHE, Ann Eliza: 3673
ASHE, Corneille: 3223
ASHE, Samuel: 832
ASHE, Samuel A'Court (1840-1938): 227, 322J, 3673, 4232, 4918, 5457
ASHE, William Shepperd: 5842
ASHE, Miss Willie: 3223
ASHE FAMILY-Genealogy: 3673
ASHE COUNTY, North Carolina: 328, 4749
ASHEBORO, North Carolina: 1307, 2294, 2303, 3186, 5022
  Plank roads: 5912
ASHEN, Bryan: 5952
ASHEVILLE, North Carolina: 4952
  1800s: 1109, 1233, 3762, 4577
  1800s-1900s: 1284
  1900s: 1987, 4805, 5708
  Chamber of Commerce: 1661
  Description: 529, 1333, 5193
  Medical societies: 5603
  Schools: 661
  Slaves: 4834
  Strawberry crops: 4834
  Weather: 4834
  World War I--Medical veterans: 5603
ASHEVILLE CENTRAL LABOR UNION: 3944
ASHEVILLE DISTRICT, Methodist Church: 3646
ASHFORD, Gerald: 4278
ASHFORD, England: 367
ASHHURST, Helen Elizabeth: 5640
ASHHURST, Richard: 228
ASHLAND, Virginia: 4968
  see also RANDOLPH-MACON COLLEGE
  Newspapers--Finance: 4020
ASHLEY FAMILY (Florida): 3293
ASHLEY FAMILY (South Carolina): 3293
ASHLEY FAMILY (Virginia): 460, 3293
ASHLEY LIBRARY (Great Britain): 4770
ASHLEY RIVER (South Carolina): 202

ASHLEY-COOPER, Anthony, Seventh Earl of Shaftesbury: 229, 1632
ASHELY-COOPER, Cropley, Sixth Earl of Shaftesbury: 229
ASHLIN, Charles: 230
ASHLIN FAMILY: 230
ASHMAN, George: 231
ASHMEAD, John W.: 232
ASHMEAD, William Harris: 2084
ASHURST, Sarah: 5598
ASIA: see FAR EAST; INDOCHINA; and names of specific countries
ASIATIC INSTITUTE: 5252
ASKWITH, George Ranken, First Baron Askwith: 233
ASPINALL, George: 5244
ASPINWALL, Thomas: 2448
ASQUITH, Herbert Henry, First Earl of Oxford and Asquith: 233, 442, 663, 4520
ASSASSINATIONS:
  France (Doumer): 2398
  United States:
    James Abram Garfield: 1663, 4606
    Abraham Lincoln: 291, 689, 1084, 1505, 1510, 1938, 2223, 2361, 2405, 3207, 3809, 4022, 4039, 4652, 4888, 5001, 5058, 5307, 5715, 5769
    John Fitzgerald Kennedy: 225
ASSAULT AND BATTERY--North Carolina: 2003, 4773
ASSEMBLY, Right of: see RIGHT OF ASSEMBLY
ASSESSMENT: see TAXATION--Assessment
ASSOCIATE REFORMED PRESBYTERIAN CHURCH:
  North Carolina: 4310
  South Carolina: 2473, 4310
    Church buildings: 2880
    Relations with Methodists: 2880
ASSOCIATED CHARITIES OF WILMINGTON (North Carolina): 4080
ASSOCIATION FOR HIGHER EDUCATION: 1758
ASSOCIATION FOR THE REFORM AND CODIFICATION OF THE LAW OF NATIONS: 1792
ASSOCIATION FOR THE RELIEF OF MAIMED SOLDIERS: 2949
ASSOCIATION OF AMERICAN RAILROADS: 238
ASSOCIATION OF LIFE INSURANCE COUNSEL: 4927
ASSOS, Turkey--Archeological investigations: 3410
ASSOTEAGUE ISLAND, Virginia: 1791
ASTOR, Nancy Witcher (Langhorne) Shaw: 2955
ASTOR FAMILY: 2461
ASTRAKHAN, Russia--Description: 5797
ASTROLOGY: 4146
ASTRONOMY: 3618
ATALIK GHAZI: 5103
ATASCOSA COUNTY, Texas--Railroads: 218
ATCHISON, TOPEKA AND SANTA FE RAILWAY COMPANY: 3986
ATHEARN AND STEVENS (firm): see STEVENS AND ATHEARN
ATHENS, Alabama: 2662, 3331, 4930
ATHENS, Georgia: 349, 1121, 1434, 1458, 1887, 2326, 2783, 2789, 3297, 5865, 5951
  see also UNIVERSITY OF GEORGIA
  Civil War: 493, 1069
  Legal education: 2326
  Social life and customs: 2783
ATHENS, Greece: 124
  British embassy in: 3472
ATHENS, Ohio: see OHIO UNIVERSITY
ATHENS, Tennessee: see GRANT MEMORIAL UNIVERSITY
ATHENS COUNTY, Ohio--Carthage: 4477
ATHENS STATE NORMAL COLLEGE (Georgia): 539
ATHERTON, Gertrude Franklin (Horn): 4837

ATHERTON, T. M.: 4188
ATHERTON MILLS: 5312
ATHLETICS: see UNIVERSITIES AND COLLEGES--Athletics
ATIENCIA, Julio de: 4155
ATKINS, James: 731
ATKINS, William S.: 234
ATKINSON, Alexander S.: 235
ATKINSON, Burwell: 235
ATKINSON, George: 4188
ATKINSON, John: 1107
ATKINSON, N.: 456
ATKINSON, N. H.: 152
ATKINSON, Samuel C.: 235
ATKINSON, Thomas: 5457
ATKINSON, William: 5801
ATKINSON FAMILY: 235, 3295
ATLANTA, Georgia:
  1800s: 2545, 3991, 4759
  1860s: 3318, 5865, 5936
  1870s: 422, 670, 823, 1203, 1591, 2096, 3318
  1880s: 539, 1203, 1591, 2096, 3330, 4887
  1890s: 843, 1841, 2096
  1800s-1900s: 1573, 1727, 5029
  1900s: 1776, 3558
  1910s: 5090
  1920s: 3706, 5090, 5406
  1930s: 3706, 4363, 5406
  1940s: 3706, 5406, 5441
  1950s: 5441
  Business education: 4911
  Civil War:
    see also CIVIL WAR--CAMPAIGNS, BATTLES, AND MILITARY ACTIONS--Georgia--Atlanta
    Aid societies: 3991
    Burning of: 689
    Confederate refugees: 5724
    Union occupation: 3343, 4160, 4358
  Description: 5608
  Literary and journalistic affairs: 2374
  Medical education: see ATLANTA MEDICAL COLLEGE
  Northerners in the South: 5082
  Race relations: 5082
  Railroads: 2177
  Rebuilding after the Civil War: 5623
  Tobacco trade: 4857
  Universities and colleges: see EMORY UNIVERSITY
  World War II: 341
ATLANTA, Illinois: 5127
ATLANTA, C.S.S. (ironclad): 1798, 2223, 4687 5472
  see also CIVIL WAR--CAMPAIGNS, BATTLES, AND MILITARY ACTIONS--Naval engagements--Weehawken, U.S.S. v. Atlanta, C.S.S.
ATLANTA AND RICHMOND AIR LINE RAILWAY COMPANY: 236
ATLANTA AND ST. ANDREWS BAY RAILROAD: 1655
ATLANTA (Georgia) CONSTITUTION: 3062
ATLANTA INDUSTRIAL UNION COUNCIL: 5441
THE ATLANTA (Georgia) JOURNAL: 823 1841, 4048
ATLANTA MEDICAL COLLEGE, Atlanta, Georgia: 3390
(ATLANTA, Ga.) SUNNY SOUTH: 1887
ATLANTIC AND CALIFORNIA RAILROAD BILL NO. 2: 5731
ATLANTIC AND DANVILLE RAILROAD: 2517
ATLANTIC AND EAST CAROLINA RAILROAD: 1655
ATLANTIC AND GULF RAILROAD: 1993
ATLANTIC AND MEXICAN GULF CANAL COMPANY: 3417
ATLANTIC AND NORTH CAROLINA RAILROAD: 237, 730, 3955
ATLANTIC AND VIRGINIA FERTILIZING COMPANY: 195

ATLANTIC AND WESTERN RAILROAD: 1655
ATLANTIC AND WESTERN RAILWAY COMPANY: 238
ATLANTIC CABLE: see TRANSATLANTIC CABLE
ATLANTIC CITY, New Jersey: 5083
ATLANTIC COAST:
   Steamships: 730
   Travel--Ship: 1697
ATLANTIC COAST LINE RAILROAD: 725, 3985, 3986
ATLANTIC COUNTY, New Jersey:
   Atlantic City: 5083
ATLANTIC DEEPER WATERWAYS ASSOCIATION: 4858
ATLANTIC MONTHLY (periodical): 4021, 4738
ATLANTIC OCEAN--Travel: see TRANSATLANTIC VOYAGES; TRAVEL--Naval cruises--Atlantic Ocean
ATLANTIC STEEL COMPANY: 5441
ATLASES: 3415
ATOMIC BOMB: 1758
   Test on Bikini, Marshall Islands: 2897
ATOMIC ENERGY:
   North Carolina: 1196
   United States: 4805
ATOMIC WARFARE--France: 1424
ATTACHÉS: see Diplomatic and consular service as subheading under names of countries
"THE ATTACK OF THE 1ST DIVISION IN THE ARGONNE FOREST" by Leander Dunbar Syme: 5163
ATTICA, New York: 388
ATTLEBORO, Pennsylvania--Merchants: 3229
ATTORNEY GENERAL'S ADVISORY COMMITTEE ON CITIZENSHIP: 4927
ATTORNEYS: see LAW PRACTICE
ATTORNEYS-GENERAL: see as subheading under (STATE)--GOVERNMENT AGENCIES AND OFFICIALS--Attorney General
ATTRIBUTES OF GOD: see GOD--Attributes (Theology)
ATWATER, Martha: 239
AUBREY, G. Jean-: JEAN-AUBREY, G.
AUBURN, Alabama: 554, 5126
AUBURN, Massachusetts: 3166
AUBURN, New York: 4748, 5446, 5544
   Law practice: 388
AUBURN THEOLOGICAL SEMINARY, New York, New York: 5731
AUCKLAND, George Eden, First Earl of (1784-1849): 1640, 5801
AUCKLAND, William Eden, First Baron (1745-1814): 1641
AUCTIONS:
   see also VENDUE MASTERS
   Maryland--Baltimore: 4886
   North Carolina--Fayetteville: 5298
   Southern States--Civil War: 3809
   Virginia: 2392
      Danville: 5958
AUDEN, Wystan Hugh: 902
"AUDLEY FARM," Virginia (estate): 3200
AUGUST, Philip, Jr.: 5339
AUGUSTA, Kaiserin, consort of Wilhelm I, Emperor of Germany: 2009
AUGUSTA, Princess of Wales (d. 1772): 92
AUGUSTA, Georgia:
   1700s: 2307, 3536, 3573, 5398
   1700s-1800s: 1333, 1855, 2931, 3661, 3671, 5537
   1800s: 2827, 2937, 3024, 3339, 5246, 5517, 5734
      1820s: 2216
      1840s: 1981, 2956, 3261
      1850s: 3261
      1860s: 637, 1737, 2407, 2722, 4002, 4237, 5472, 5915
      1870s: 637, 2407
      1880s: 637
   1800s-1900s: 3065, 4377

AUGUSTA, Georgia (Continued):
   Agricultural workers: 3749
   American Revolution: 1347
      see also AMERICAN REVOLUTION--Campaigns and battles--Georgia--Augusta
   Arsenals: 700
   Business affairs: 5353
   Catholic Church: 938
   Civil War: 689, 1185
      see also CIVIL WAR--CAMPAIGNS, BATTLES, AND MILITARY ACTIONS--Georgia--Augusta
   Commission merchants: 2710
   Confederate Survivors' Association: 2388, 2894
   Cotton Trade: 497, 3583
   Courts: 2000
   Debt collection: 3672
   Freedmen's Bureau: 731
   Hay trade: 3749
   Historical studies: 2894
   Law practice: 731
   Lawsuits: 3672
   Literary interests: 2451
   Medical education: 2903
   Mercantile accounts: 138
   Personal finance: 5246
   Physicians' accounts: 168, 1581, 3672
   Plantation accounts: 3749
   Plantations: 5246
   Presbyterian Churches: 26
   Real estate: 2560
   Reconstruction: 731, 5905
   Social life and customs: 5246, 5480
   Textile industry: 1829
   United States Army--Army life: 5480
   Visit of Governor William Sprague of Rhode Island: 2545
AUGUSTA (brig): 4456
AUGUSTA ARSENAL, Augusta, Georgia: 1185, 3145
AUGUSTA CHRONICLE AND CONSTITUTION: 1972
AUGUSTA (Ga.) CONFEDERATE SURVIVORS' ASSOCIATION: 2388, 2894
AUGUSTA COUNTY, Virginia: 2887, 5047
   Business affairs: 728, 2566
   Courts--Clerks: 5184
   Land: 2986
   Plantations: 4210
   Public welfare: 5184
   Tobacco trade: 28
   Cities and towns:
      Burks Mill: 5153
      Craigsville: 3826
      Mount Solon: 1075
         Tailors' accounts: 114
      South River--Millers' accounts: 210
      Spottswood: 1591
      Staunton: see STAUNTON, Virginia
      Stuart's Draft--Mercantile accounts: 209
AUGUSTA FEMALE SEMINARY, Staunton, Virginia: 2712
AUGUSTANA COLLEGE, Rock Island, Illinois: 1768
AUGUSTANA COLLEGE AND THEOLOGICAL SEMINARY: see AUGUSTANA COLLEGE
AUGUSTIN, G. T.: 240
AUGUSTIN, W.: 240
AUGUSTIN (W. AND G. T.) (firm): 240
AUGUSTUS, James M.: 241
AULD, James: 4918
AULICK, Alberta: 242
AULICK, John H.: 242
AUMACK, Ellen: 243
AUMALE, Henri Eugène Philippe Louis d'Orleans, Duc d': 1875
AUMALE, Marie Caroline Augusta, Duchesse d': 1875
AUMALE FAMILY: 1875
"EIN AUSFLUG NACH NORDDEUTSCHLAND UND IN DIE NORDSEE IM JAHRE 1842": 244

AUSLANDER, Charles Edward: 5236
AUSTELL, Georgia: 2786
AUSTIN, Ben W.: 2371
AUSTIN, Benjamin (North Carolina): 245
AUSTIN, Charles: 3670
AUSTIN, James: 2740
AUSTIN, Joseph B.: 247
AUSTIN, Loring: 246
AUSTIN, Warren: 102
AUSTIN FAMILY: 286
AUSTIN, Texas: 1842, 2739, 3470
   see also UNIVERSITY OF TEXAS
AUSTIN COLLEGE, Huntsville, Texas: 5329
AUSTINVILLE, Virginia: 1181
AUSTRALIA: 286
   Constitution: 1792
   Court of Petty Sessions: 5477
   Courts: 1792
   Description and travel--New South Wales: 5726
   Federation of Australia: 1792
   Foreign relations--Japan: 5876
   Governors--New South Wales: 3238
   Justices of the peace: 5477
   Labor supply: 2410
   Labor unrest: 1792
   Libraries: 2282
   Separation movement: 1792
   Tobacco trade: 3179, 5251
   Voter registration: 5477
   Wool trade: 2742
AUSTRIA:
   Army:
      Artillery: 1706
      Operations: 3954
   British diplomatic and consular service in: 3472
      Vienna: 3238
   Currency: 1339
   Description and travel: 2617, 4858
   Economic conditions: 5726
   Foreign relations: 3472
      Great Britain: 2149, 3238, 4650, 5726
      Spain: 2155
      Turkey: 1164
   Historic buildings--Trieste: 2085
   Politics and government: 1755, 3238, 3472
   Social conditions: 4449
   String trio music--Scores: 1974
   Timber: 1599
   World War I: see WORLD WAR I--War relief--Austria
AUTHORS: 3797, 4576
   see also AMERICAN AUTHORS; WOMEN AUTHORS
AUTHORS AND AGENTS--United States: 1661
AUTHORS AND CRITICS: 4491, 5908
   Great Britain: 4001
AUTHORS AND EDITORS: 5889
   see also SCHOLARLY EDITING
   Great Britain: 2203
   United States: 720
AUTHORS AND PUBLISHERS: 376, 2801, 3797
   see also ARTISTS AND PUBLISHERS; PUBLISHERS AND PUBLISHING; ROYALTIES (Publishing)
   Cookbooks--United States: 2692
   Editors: 5054
   Periodicals:
      Great Britain: 2839
      United States: 3022
   Subdivided by place:
      Connecticut: 3041
      Georgia: 4377
      Great Britain:
         1700s: 4512
         1700s-1800s: 4967, 5867
         1800s: 892, 3835, 4001, 4770
            1810s: 369
            1820s: 2146
            1830s: 5241
            1840s: 4051

AUTHORS AND PUBLISHERS:
    Subdivided by place:
        Great Britain:
            1800s (Continued):
                1850s: 4051, 4069
                1870s: 5553, 5872
                1880s: 39, 5553, 5872
                1890s: 39, 4503, 5553, 5872
            1800s-1900s: 3503
            1900s: 1210, 4327, 5101, 5403
        Kentucky: 1308
        Louisiana: 1982
        Massachusetts: 4069
            Cambridge: 2400
        Mississippi: 2775
        Nebraska: 729
        New York: 1143, 4341, 4481
            New York: 5320
        North Carolina: 1521, 4918, 4992
        Pennsylvania: 848, 890, 1488
        United States:
            1800s: 305, 1227, 3586, 4829, 4971
            1820s: 2437
            1830s: 1029
            1840s: 1029
            1850s: 1029
            1860s: 1608, 2449, 2845, 5051
            1870s: 1608, 2449, 3363, 3585, 5051, 5322
            1880s: 1608, 2225, 2449, 5322, 5322, 5326
            1890s: 1449, 2225, 5322
            1800s-1900s: 72, 404, 1160, 2451, 2871, 3465, 4012, 4020, 4021, 4491, 5044, 5226
            1900s: 4837
            1900s: 1068, 4279, 5594
            1910s: 5594
            1920s: 2790
            1940s: 4641
            1950s: 985
            1960s: 985
            1970s: 902, 5889
        Virginia: 1878, 3397, 3809
AUTHORS AND READERS:
    Great Britain: 4770, 5050, 5553
    United States: 2390
AUTHORS CLUB OF NEW YORK: 3797
AUTHORS' SOCIETIES: see LITERARY SOCIETIES
AUTHORSHIP: 1097, 1241
    see also AMERICAN LITERATURE; AMERICAN POETRY--Authorship; ENGLISH LITERATURE; GHOST WRITING; PLAGIARISM
    Alabama: 1449
    Connecticut: 2046
    France: 3305
    Georgia: 924, 2747, 3969
    Great Britain: 449, 1147, 1650, 2203, 4176, 5050, 5553
    Louisiana: 4636
    Maryland: 2398, 2985
    Massachusetts: 2400, 4037
    North Carolina: 4098
    Scotland: 2736
    South Carolina: 2290
    Tennessee: 3810
    Texas: 3363
    United States: 3746, 4475, 5081, 5149
    Virginia: 924, 3320, 5227
AUTOBIOGRAPHIES: see BIOGRAPHICAL STUDIES; BIOGRAPHIES
"AUTOBIOGRAPHY" by David Dudley Field: 1792
AUTOGRAPH COLLECTING: 1424, 4285
    France: 1424
    Georgia: 5220
    Great Britain: 2126
    Illinois: 5350
    Louisiana: 2575
    Maryland: 2052
    Massachusetts: 4189
    North Carolina: 3543
    Tennessee: 5681
    United States: 1422, 2545, 5294
    Virginia: 2061, 3681, 4156

AUTOGRAPHS: 3142, 4486, 4616, 5278, 5632, 5790
    see also CIVIL WAR--Prisoners and prisons--Confederate prisoners--(place)--Autographs; CONFEDERATE STATES OF AMERICA--ARMY--Autographs
    Georgia: 2317, 4237
    Great Britain: 5158, 5553
    Iowa: 5812
    Massachusetts: 4807
        Pittsfield: 1455
        Volunteer Militia: 3562
    North Carolina: 666, 5124, 5298
        Person County: 378
    Ohio: 1040, 2862
    Scotland: 2022
    South Carolina: 3418
    Tennessee: 775
    United States Congress: 1851
    Virginia: 302, 905, 3517
        Charlottesville: 275
            University of Virginia: 3106
        Hampden-Sydney: 3740
    Washington National Monument Society (members): 5584
    West Virginia: 1946, 2301
AUTOMOBILE ACCESSORIES--Inventions: 3424
AUTOMOBILE ACCIDENTS: see TRAFFIC ACCIDENTS
AUTOMOBILE INDUSTRY:
    South Carolina--Rock Hill: 5252
    United States: 4918
AUTOMOBILE PARKING METERS: see PARKING METERS
AUTOMOBILE RACING--Georgia: 1171
AUTOMOBILE WORKERS: see UNITED AUTOMOBILE, AIRCRAFT, AND AGRICULTURAL IMPLEMENT WORKERS OF AMERICA
AUTOMOBILES--Advertising: see ADVERTISING--Automobiles
"AUXILIOS PARA BIEN GOVERNAR UNA MONARQUIA" by Melchor Rafael de Macanaz: 3312
AVA, Frederick Temple Hamilton-Temple-Blackwood, First Marquis of: see DUFFERIN AND AVA, Frederick Temple Hamilton-Temple-Blackwood, First Marquis of
AVA, Hariot Georgina (Hamilton) Hamilton-Temple-Blackwood, Marchioness of Dufferin and: see DUFFERIN AND AVA, Hariot Georgina (Hamilton) Hamilton-Temple-Blackwood, Marchioness of
AVERASBORO, North Carolina: see CIVIL WAR--CAMPAIGNS, BATTLES, AND MILITARY ACTIONS--North Carolina--Averasboro
AVERELL, William Woods: 3789
AVERETT, Thomas Hamlet: 1161
AVERILE, Sidney: 3981
AVERY, Alphonso Calhoun: 4775
AVERY, Isaac Thomas: 248
AVERY, Isaac W.: 2449
AVERY, Susan L.: 729
AVERY, Trueman G.: 249
AVERY AND STETSON: see STETSON AND AVERY
AVIATION:
    see also AIRCRAFT COMPANIES; AIRPORTS
    Italy: 137
    United States: 4858
        Laws and legislation: 4858
        Military: 3451
AVONDALE, Maryland: 3998
AWAKENING, Second: see GREAT AWAKENING (Second)
AWARDS: see HONORS AND AWARDS
AXES: 1169
AXON, Ernest: 250
AXSON, Mr. _____: 3340
AYCOCK, Charles Brantley: 1336, 1364
AYER, Mrs. Dana S.: 5572
AYER, H. G.: 251
AYLESFORD, Countess of: 3089
AYLETT, Patrick Henry: 252

AYLETT FAMILY (Genealogy): 1842
AYLOR, Albert: 253
AYLSHAM, England: 5531
AYRES, Romeyn Beck: 254
AYRESVILLE, North Carolina: 110
AYRSHIRE, Scotland--Craig: 5379
AZALIA (gunboat): 3917
AZORES--Description and travel: 1284, 5436

B

B., H. C. (North Carolina businessman): 3416
B. F. JOHNSON PUBLISHING COMPANY, Richmond, Virginia: 4373
B. M. SELBY AND P. W. BROWN (firm): 4734
B. P. DAVIS AND BROTHER: 1394
BABB, Thomas W.: 255
BABBETT, Celia: 2677
BABCOCK, Orville Elias: 256
BABER, Ambrose: 510
BABER, Marian: 510
BABIES' HOSPITAL, Wrightsville Sound, North Carolina: 4809
BABINGTON, Thomas: 867
BACCHUS (slave); 2289
BACH (FRANCIS) AND CO.: 1807
BACHELLER, Irving Addison: 103
BACHELOR (brigantine): 1088
BACHELORHOOD: 1877
  Virginia: 3809
BACHMAN, Nathan Lynn: 257
BACKUS, Electus: 259
BACKWELL, Edward: 4969
BACON, A. S.: 260
BACON, Augustus Octavius: 261
BACON, Francis Henry (1856-1940): 3410
BACON, Henry, Sr.: 3410
BACON, Herbert T.: 262
BACON, John: 1913
BACON, Orville J.: 5268
BACON, Sarah E. Thompson: 5268
BACON COUNTY, Virginia: 262
BACOT, Cyrus: 3123
BACOT FAMILY (Genealogy): 1468
BACTERIAL WARFARE: see WORLD WAR I--Bacterial warfare
BADEAU, Adam: 5419
BADGER, Frances L.: 263
BADGER, George Edmund: 263, 1363, 3483
BADGER, Mrs. George Edmund: 401
BADHAM, J. C.: 264
BADHAM, Louisa Jones: 264
BADHAM, William, Sr.: 264
BADHAM, William, Jr. (b. 1835): 264
BAGBY, Arthur Pendleton: 265
BAGBY, Bennette M.: 266
BAGBY, George William: 267, 1227
BAGBY, Louisa B. (Flippin): 266
BAGBY FAMILY (Virginia): 266
BAGFORD, John: 268
BAGGARLY, Nancy: 269
BAGGARLY, Tilmon F.: 269
BAGGE, Traugott: 5457
BAGGING--Manufacture of: 2165
BAGGS, Nicholas: 270
BAGHDAD, Iraq: 5797
BAGHDEO (549-615 A.D.) 4364
BAGLEY, Docton Warren: 271
BAGLEY, Edward F.: 272, 1123
BAGS--Shipment of: 5155
BAHADUR SHAH II, King of Delhi: 4097
BAHAMA ISLANDS:
  Abolition of slavery: 4934
  British administration: 4934
  Description and travel: 3983
BAHIA, Brazil--Description: 1644
BAIL, Lamar Q.: 3062
BAIL BONDS: 1818
  For Copperheads: 5417
BAILEY, Christopher Thomas, Jr. 274
BAILEY, Edith (Pou): 274
BAILEY, Henry: 2477
BAILEY, J. G.: 3532
BAILEY, Joseph E.: 273
BAILEY, Josiah William (1873-1946): 274, 1284, 2299, 3433, 5401
BAILEY, Letitia: 2691
BAILEY, Letitia M.: 275
BAILEY, Mary (Himbish): 274
BAILEY, Theodorus: 276
BAILEY, William Henry, Sr.: 277, 2041
BAILEY FAMILY (North Carolina): 274

BAILLIE, Charles Wallace Alexander Napier Ross Cochrane-, Second Baron Lamington: 278
BAILLIE, George: 3389
BAILLIE, Joanna: 2580
BAILLIE, Marjory Spalding: 2963
BAILLIE, Robert: 3389
BAILY, James S.: 4036
BAILY (JOSHUA L.) AND CO.: 1611
BAIN, Mollie: 279
BAIN, William T.: 279
BAINBRIDGE, William: 4348
BAINBRIDGE, Pennsylvania: 4057
BAINES, Edward (1774-1848): 1648, 5277
BAINES, Sir Edward (1800-1890): 280
BAIRD, Chambers, Sr. (b. 1811): 281
BAIRD, Chambers, Jr. (b. 1860): 281
BAIRD, James S.: 282
BAIRD, John: 2756
BAIRD, Robert: 282
BAKER, A.: 4875
BAKER, Bernard Nadal: 1747, 3229
BAKER, Charles H.: 286
BAKER, Cole: 1466
BAKER, Daniel (Virginia): 283
BAKER, Daniel (student): 4040
BAKER, Eleanor J. W.: 284
BAKER, Ellen: 3845
BAKER, Frank: 4073
BAKER, Gertrude Williamson: 356
BAKER, Gwyneth (Griffiths): 286
BAKER, H. C. (Virginia): 291
BAKER, Harriet: 4875
BAKER, Henry: 285
BAKER, Henry Dunster: 286
BAKER, (I. G.) AND COMPANY, Fort Benton, Montana Territory: 1211
BAKER, Isaac: 287
BAKER, J. A.: 5280
BAKER, James H.: 288
BAKER, James Marion: 248
BAKER, John (Georgia): 289
BAKER, John (North Carolina): 290
BAKER, John Earl: 5252
BAKER, Joseph: 4875
BAKER, L. C.: 1938
BAKER, Margaret E.: 4303
BAKER, N. C. (Virginia): 291
BAKER, Nathaniel Bradley: 3993
BAKER, Ray Stannard: 2082
BAKER, Robert Nicholson Scott: 356
BAKER, Sir Samuel White: 5725
BAKER, Thomas J.: 292
BAKER, Thorne: 5145
BAKER FAMILY (England and Australia--Genealogy): 286
BAKER FAMILY (Florida): 4903
BAKER COUNTY, Georgia--Newton: 285
BAKERIES--Georgia: 575
BAKER'S CREEK, Mississippi, Battle of: see CIVIL WAR--CAMPAIGNS, BATTLES, AND MILITARY ACTIONS--Mississippi--Baker's Creek
BALAKLAVA, U.S.S.R.: 153
BALDANZI, George: 3171, 5234
BALDWIN, Albertus Hutchinson: 2084
BALDWIN, Abraham: 2778, 2788, 3671
BALDWIN, Alice Mary: 293, 5252
BALDWIN, Daniel H.: 4177
BALDWIN, Harold Lyman: 293
BALDWIN, Kate (Philbrick): 4177
BALDWIN (MARY) COLLEGE: see MARY BALDWIN COLLEGE
BALDWIN FAMILY (Genealogy): 4177
BALDWIN COUNTY, Georgia:
  Milledgeville: see MILLEDGEVILLE, Georgia
BALDWIN UNIVERSITY, Berea, Ohio: 2693
BALFOUR, Arthur James, First Earl of Balfour: 294, 663, 1815, 2324, 5116
BALFOUR, John: 4333
BALFOUR, Lady Frances (Campbell): 233
BALFOUR OF BURLEIGH, Alexander Hugh Bruce, Sixth Baron: 1815
BALI: 4362
BALKAN STATES: 3912
  Foreign relations:
    Great Britain: 233

BALKAN WAR (1912-1913): 3912
  Public opinion--Great Britain: 233
BALL, Alwyn: 295
BALL, Mrs. Beaufort W.: 3383
BALL, Caroline Olivia: 5193
BALL, Elias Octavus: 295
BALL, Eliza Hall: 611
BALL, George H.: 611
BALL, Hugh Swinton: 295
BALL, John, Sr. (1760-1817): 295
BALL, John, Jr. (1782-1834): 295
BALL, John (South Carolina): 296
BALL, Keating Simons: 297
BALL, Martha Caroline (Swinton): 5193
BALL, Mollie: 298
BALL, Robert H.: 611
BALL, Thomas C.: 299
BALL, William Watts: 300, 2109
BALL FAMILY (South Carolina--Genealogy): 300
BALLADS:
  see also SCOTTISH BALLADS; SPANISH BALLADS
  North Carolina: 691
  Virginia: 4186
BALLARD, Emily (Childs): 806
BALLARD, F. W.: 1540
BALLARD, V. (North Carolina): 513
BALLARD'S VALLEY PLANTATION (Jamaica): 301
BALLOONS:
  see also UNITED STATES--ARMY--Civil War--Balloons
  North Carolina--Salem: 813
  United States: 4269
BALLOTS:
  see also ELECTIONS
  Great Britain: 4868, 5011
  North Carolina: 5549
BALLOWE (BALLOW), Sarah E. R.: 302, 4915
BALLS (Parties):
  see also INAUGURAL BALLS
  New York--New York: 4895
  United States: 3905
  Virginia--Richmond: 5094
  Washington, D. C.: 1728
BALL'S BLUFF, Virginia, Battle of:
  see CIVIL--CAMPAIGNS, BATTLES, AND MILITARY ACTIONS--Virginia--Ball's Bluff
BALLSTON, New York: 5066
BALLSTON SPA, New York: 5206
BALLYMONEY, Ireland: 3349
BALLYSHANNON, Ireland: 868
BALMANNO, Robert: 2632
BALSON, Consuelo (Vanderbilt) Churchill-Spencer: 5968
BALTHROPE, James M.: 303
BALTIC (ram): 907
BALTIMORE, Maryland: 5811
  1600s-1800s: 3598
  1700s: 3384, 5086, 5213
  1700s-1800s: 994, 1647, 3053, 4081, 4905
  1700s-1900s: 3145, 4348
  1800s: 260, 664, 1423, 1909, 2985, 3092, 3742, 3754, 4615, 4886, 5059, 5776
  1800s: 3728
  1810s: 3399, 3406, 3728, 4542, 5829
  1820s: 3406
  1830s: 466, 2052, 3406, 3902, 5763
  1840s: 23, 1245, 1395, 1862, 2052, 3026, 3486, 3971, 5763
  1850s: 23, 1395, 2639, 3026, 3971, 4416, 5800
  1860s: 149, 2639, 2868, 4416, 5918
  1870s: 695, 1032, 2639, 2868
  1880s: 1438, 2883
  1890s: 22, 2883
  1800s-1900s: 404, 648, 1747, 2042, 2940, 3229, 4221
  1900s: 2398, 2769, 3220, 3617, 5166
  Agricultural products:
    Prices: 5275

BALTIMORE, Maryland (Continued):
Agriculture: 660
Arts: 2398
Auctions: 4886
Banks and banking: 5324, 5683
Building construction: 2352
Business affairs: 5680, 5918
City Council: 3598
Civil War:
see also CIVIL WAR--CAMPAIGNS,
BATTLES, AND MILITARY ACTIONS--
Maryland--Baltimore
Union Army hospital: 701
Union occupation: 3264
Clergy:
Methodist: 1939
Unitarian: 4359
Commission merchants: 1355, 1442,
2819
Commodity prices: 1024, 3566, 4732
see also BALTIMORE, Maryland--
Agricultural products--Prices
Cotton factors: 4858
Debt collection: 4348
Description: 33, 284, 404, 4348,
4864
Diseases--Cholera: 5613
Elections: 3264
see also BALTIMORE, Maryland--
Presidential election of 1824
Estates (Legal):
Administration and settlement:
4348
Exchange: 3971
Financial societies: 3971
Gas lighting: 2265
Houses: 5660
Insurance: 4348
Iron and steel industry: 1169
Judaism: 2811
Legal affairs: 3754
Legal fees: 4348
Medical education: see BALTIMORE
MEDICAL COLLEGE; JOHNS HOPKINS
UNIVERSITY; UNIVERSITY OF
MARYLAND--Medical education
Mercantile accounts: 1616, 3579,
4348, 5933
Merchants: 785, 1920, 2265, 2412,
4288, 4348
see also BALTIMORE, Maryland--
Commission merchants
Finance: 5213
Negroes--Education: 4886
Optical surgery: 2830
Personal finance: 4348, 4886, 5763
Pharmacists' accounts: 4348, 5800
Physicians' accounts: 4348, 5800
Ports: 4726
Presidential election of 1824: 4359
Prisoners and prisons: 3267
Protestant Episcopal Church: 4638
Pulp and paper industry: 2265
Riots: 3264, 3598
Schools: 3607
Girls' schools and academies:
5298
Shipping: 4348
Shoemakers' accounts: 1616
Social life and customs: 1918
Streets: 4886
Textile industry: 1877
Tobacco trade: 5228
Advertising: 1586
Trade and commerce:
Agricultural products: 5213
Flour: 4348
Food: 4348
Ginseng: 4348
Liquor: 4348
Lumber: 730
Tar: 4348
Wholesale: 698, 1169, 2857
With Southern States: 1687
Turnpikes: 5296
United Daughters of the Confederacy:
2202

BALTIMORE, Maryland (Continued):
Universities and colleges: see
GOUCHER COLLEGE; JOHNS HOPKINS
UNIVERSITY; ST. MARY'S COLLEGE
Visits by Andrew Jackson and Black
Hawk: 3255
BALTIMORE AND OHIO RAILROAD: 721,
2106, 3054, 4537, 5059, 5779
BALTIMORE AND POTOMAC CANAL: 4221
BALTIMORE AND RICHMOND CHRISTIAN
ADVOCATE: 879
BALTIMORE COUNTY, Maryland: 1764,
2059, 2669
Courts: 4457
BALTIMORE MEDICAL COLLEGE, Baltimore,
Maryland: 3859
"THE BALTIMORE PLATFORM" (Democratic
Party): 5491
THE (BALTIMORE) SUN (newspaper):
149, 2105, 5578
BALUCHISTAN: 4520
BAMBERGER, Ira Leo: 304
BANCROFT, Frederic: 706, 3262
BANCROFT, George: 305, 3118, 3833
BANCROFT, Hubert Howe: 4080
BAND CONCERTS: 4888, 5633
North Carolina: 3845
Ohio: 3845
BANDINEL, James (1783-1848): 306
BANDINEL, James (1814-1893): 306
BANDINEL, James Julius Frederick: 306
BANDINEL FAMILY: 306
BANDS:
see also PUBLIC SCHOOLS--Bands;
UNITED STATES--ARMY--Bands
North Carolina and Ohio: 3845
BANGKOK, Thailand:
British embassy in: 4709
BANGOR, Maine: 1804, 2285
BANGS, John Kendrick: 2449
BANISTER, Virginia: 5483
BANK ACCOUNTS: see BANKS AND BANKING
BANK FAILURES:
Florida: 2877
New York: 2587
Ohio: 4732
United States: 3053
Virginia--Columbia: 5035
BANK-NOTES: 1339, 3191
see also BANKS AND BANKING; CURRENCY
Discounting: 5569
Virginia: 2360
Kentucky: 1309
New Jersey: 2517
North Carolina: 766
South Carolina: 881
BANK OF ALABAMA, Tuscaloosa, Alabama:
4911
BANK OF BERKELEY IN VIRGINIA: 307
BANK OF BLACKSBURG, Blacksburg,
Virginia: 308
BANK OF CAPE FEAR, Washington, North
Carolina: 215, 309, 3415
BANK OF CASWELL, Milton, North
Carolina: 310
BANK OF CHARLESTON, Charleston, South
Carolina: 5318
BANK OF CHESTER, Chester, South
Carolina: 697
BANK OF DARIEN, Darien, Georgia: 2755
BANK OF DAVIE, Mocksville, North
Carolina: 2749
BANK OF DURHAM, Durham, North
Carolina: 513, 3762
BANK OF LOUISIANA: 2755
BANK OF MARYLAND: 4081
BANK OF MECKLENBURG, Charlotte, North
Carolina: 766
BANK OF MIDDLE TENNESSEE, Lebanon,
Tennessee: 872
BANK OF RICHMOND, Richmond, Virginia:
5035
BANK OF SELMA, Selma, Alabama: 4911
BANK OF SOUTH CAROLINA: 2210
BANK OF THE STATE OF GEORGIA,
Savannah, Georgia: 311, 5220
BANK OF THE STATE OF NORTH CAROLINA:
3415

BANK OF THE UNITED STATES: 2963
BANK OF THE UNITED STATES (first):
2238
BANK OF THE UNITED STATES (second):
357, 718, 842, 1086, 1424, 1762,
1769, 3169, 3291, 3325, 3415,
4080, 4081, 4083, 4732, 4852,
4880, 5361
Baltimore, Maryland, Branch: 5683
Savannah, Georgia, Branch: 2238
Stocks: 4315
BANK OF THE VALLEY, Virginia: 2797
BANK OF THE VALLEY, Romney, West
Virginia: 312
BANK OF VIRGINIA: 3846
BANK OF YANCEYVILLE, Yanceyville,
North Carolina: 2474
BANK STOCKS: 3191, 4214, 4911, 5312
Georgia: 311
Forsyth County: 5260
Maryland: 166
United States: 5080
see also BANK OF THE UNITED
STATES (second)--Stocks
Virginia: 4215, 4616
BANKERS' ASSOCIATION, Isle of Palms,
South Carolina: 3421
BANKERS FIRE INSURANCE COMPANY OF
DURHAM, North Carolina: 2379
BANKERS TRUST COMPANY OF VIRGINIA:
5035
BANKHEAD, James M.: 5886
BANKING: see BANKS AND BANKING
"BANKING IN NORTH CAROLINA" by
Charles Lee Raper and John J.
Porter: 4391
BANKING LAW:
Great Britain: 5
Pennsylvania: 421, 4188
BANKRUPTCY:
see also BANK FAILURES; COTTON
MILLS--Bankruptcy; FINANCIAL
INSTITUTIONS--Bankruptcy
Great Britain: 2151
Bristol: 4541
Cases: 4605
Massachusetts: 4807
North Carolina: 1438, 3351
Franklinton: 5056
Mooresville: 3757
United States: 5145
Virginia: 418, 1125, 3817
Alexandria: 226
BANKRUPTCY LAWS--Georgia: 2232
BANKS, John: 313
BANKS, Nathaniel Prentiss: 314, 1253,
3770, 4888, 5132, 5208
BANKS, Robert H.: 1401
BANKS AND BANKING: 2164, 2695, 3198
see also AGRICULTURAL CREDIT; BANK-
NOTES; BILLS OF EXCHANGE;
INTERNATIONAL BANKING; NATIONAL
BANKS; WILDCAT BANKING; and
State banks as subheading under
names of specific states
Investment in:
Eastern States: 2532
Laws and legislation: see BANKING
LAW
Security--Virginia: 5035
Statistics--United States: 2746
Taxation--Virginia: 5035
Trustees--Virginia: 3846
Subdivided by place:
Alabama: 4911
China: 5252
Georgia: 1466, 3261, 3355, 5576
Macon: 823
Savannah: 311, 950, 5220
see also BANK OF THE UNITED
STATES (second)--Savannah
Branch
Great Britain: 3304
Louisiana:
New Orleans: 3274, 5693
Maryland: 389, 4081
Baltimore: 5324
Washington County: 3086

BANKS AND BANKING:
　Subdivided by place (Continued):
　　Massachusetts:
　　　Boston: 5499, 5628
　　Missouri: 4063
　　New York: 236, 559, 4157, 4343
　　　Fulton: 929
　　North Carolina: 730, 2474,
　　　2651, 3415, 3955, 4100, 4391,
　　　4858, 4918, 5962
　　　Cary: 928
　　　Charlotte: 766
　　　Durham: 513, 1041, 3762
　　　Fayetteville: 4517, 5298
　　　Milton: 310
　　　Raleigh: 2823
　　　Washington: 309
　　Pennsylvania:
　　　Blair County: 421
　　　Monongahela City: 1332
　　　Philadelphia: 2412, 5282
　　Philippine Islands: 3313
　　South Carolina: 669, 697
　　　Charleston: 1760, 4235, 5318
　　Tennessee: 872
　　　Trenton: 2371
　　Texas (Republic of): 5693
　　United States: 1016, 2723, 3053,
　　　3169, 3415, 5470
　　　see also BANK OF THE UNITED
　　　　STATES (first or second)
　　Vermont: 4485
　　Virginia: 1384, 2131, 2797,
　　　3362, 4616, 4720
　　　Blacksburg: 308
　　　Buchanan: 5904
　　　Cartersville: 5035
　　　Charlottesville: 4142
　　　Columbia: 5035
　　　Danville: 1372, 1761, 5556
　　　Fredericksburg: 5556
　　　Gloucester County: 4924
　　　Leesburg: 5449
　　　Lynchburg: 4157
　　　Richmond: 5282
　　West Virginia: 4892
　　　Martinsburg: 307
　　　Romney: 312
BANKS COUNTY, Georgia: 1994, 5865
BANNER, Joseph: 315
THE BANNER (periodical or
　newspaper): 2053
BANNERMAN, Sir Henry Campbell-:
　see CAMPBELL-BANNERMAN, Sir Henry
BANTA, William H.: 316
BAPTISM:
　Baptist Churches:
　　North Carolina: 1152
　　South Carolina: 3669
　Godparents--Great Britain: 2899
　North Carolina: 1584
　Presbyterian Churches:
　　South Carolina: 4310
BAPTISM IN A NUTSHELL by Charles
　Taylor: 1152
BAPTIST ASSOCIATIONS: see BAPTIST
　CHURCHES--Associations
BAPTIST CHURCH, Charleston, South
　Carolina: 2402
BAPTIST CHURCHES:
　see also FREE WILL BAPTIST CHURCH;
　　ORIGINAL FREE WILL BAPTIST
　　CHURCH; PRIMITIVE BAPTIST
　　CHURCH
　Associations:
　　Kentucky: 3199
　　North Carolina: 320, 484
　　Virginia: 330
　Baptism: see BAPTISM--Baptist
　　Churches
　Church buildings:
　　West Virginia: 1769
　Clergy: see CLERGY--Baptist
　Discipline--North Carolina: 1157
　Doctrine: 669
　Ethics--Georgia: 1080
　Finance:
　　North Carolina: 3538

BAPTIST CHURCHES:
　Finance:
　　North Carolina (Continued):
　　　Colerain: 1157
　　South Carolina:
　　　Greenville: 2182
　Government--Georgia: 1080
　Interchurch relations: 3494
　Liturgy and ritual: 3669
　Membership: 3669
　　Georgia: 1080
　　Kentucky: 3199
　　North Carolina:
　　　Williamston: 4843
　Missions and missionaries: see
　　MISSIONS AND MISSIONARIES--
　　Baptist
　Negroes--Canada: 176
　Newspapers: see RELIGIOUS
　　LITERATURE--Baptist
　Publications: see RELIGIOUS
　　LITERATURE--Baptist
　Revivals--West Virginia: 4774
　State conventions:
　　North Carolina: 3538
　Sunday School Conventions: see
　　SUNDAY SCHOOL CONVENTIONS--
　　Baptist
　Universities and colleges: see
　　names of specific Baptist-
　　affiliated institutions
　Subdivided by place:
　　Georgia: 1993, 2326, 2756
　　Great Britain: 5726
　　Illinois: 1806
　　Iowa: 1806
　　Louisiana: 3322
　　Mississippi: 3322
　　Missouri: 1806
　　New York--New York: 461, 5660
　　North Carolina: 274, 387, 484,
　　　2068, 4232, 4586, 5218, 5673,
　　　5964
　　　Bertie County: 2603, 4572
　　　Caswell County: 4849
　　　Colerain: 1157
　　　Durham: 5401
　　　Martin County: 4931
　　　Raleigh: 5401
　　　Robeson Union: 319
　　　Wilkes County: 4742
　　South Carolina: 561
　　　Charleston: 2402
　　　Greenville: 2182
　　　Sumterville: 3676
　　Virginia: 2685
　　　Luray: 574
　　　New Hope: 3826
BAPTIST FEMALE COLLEGE, Lexington,
　Missouri: 317
BAPTIST ORPHANAGE, Thomasville,
　North Carolina: 2874
BAPTIST SEMINARY, Richmond, Virginia:
　1402
BAPTIST UNIVERSITY, Raleigh, North
　Carolina: see MEREDITH COLLEGE,
　Raleigh, North Carolina
BAPTISTS: see BAPTIST CHURCHES
BARACA MOVEMENT:
　Southern States: 4828
BARBADOS:
　Foreign trade: 2403
　Riots: 4913
BARBARY PIRATES: 894
BARBARY STATES:
　Foreign relations: 3858
BARBE, Waitman T.W.: 2449
BARBÉ-MARBOIS, François, Marquis de:
　321, 3273
BARBECUE DISTRICT, North Carolina:
　4761
BARBECUE TOWNSHIP, North Carolina:
　4761
BARBEE FAMILY (Genealogy): 4078
BARBER, John E.: 5009
BARBOUR, James (1775-1842): 322,
　523, 1401, 3560
BARBOUR, John (Ohio): 86

BARBOUR, John Brown: 523
BARBOUR, John N. (shipper): 323
BARBOUR, John Strode, Sr.
　(1790-1855): 523
BARBOUR COUNTY, Alabama:
　Eufaula: 4799
　Freedmen--Labor contracts: 1423
BARBOURSVILLE, Kentucky: see UNION
　COLLEGE
BARCELONA, Spain: 3549
BARCLAY, John O'C: 1182
BARCLAY, Samuel M.: 324
BARDEN, Graham Arthur: 325
BARDSTOWN, Kentucky: 3755, 5118
　Civil War: 2858
BARFORD, England: 200
BARGE, Johann Heinrich Wilhelm: 111
BARGER, David: 208
BARGES: see AMMUNITION BARGES
BARHAM, Charles Middleton, First
　Baron: 4230
BARHAMVILLE, South Carolina: 3527
BARHAMVILLE SCHOOL FOR GIRLS,
　Barhamville, South Carolina: 3527
BARING, Alexander: 3273
BARING, Evelyn, First Earl of Cromer:
　67, 663, 1857, 2756, 4941, 5175
BARING (FRANCIS) AND CO.: 3273
BARING, Henry: 3315
BARING, Thomas George, First Earl of
　Northbrook: 326, 648, 1857, 4660
BARING BROTHERS AND COMPANY, London,
　England: 559
BARKER, Harley Granville Granville-:
　see GRANVILLE-BARKER, Harley
　Granville
BARKER, John (1771-1849): 3471
BARKER, John E. (Ohio): 327
BARKER, Samuel: 328
BARKER, Simeon: 329
BARKIN, Solomon: 5234, 5235, 5236
BARKLEY, Alben William: 4927
BARKSDALE, Charlotte: 331
BARKSDALE, Claiborne: 331
BARKSDALE, Cornelia: 330, 5827
BARKSDALE, Edward: 330
BARKSDALE, Elisha: 330, 5005
BARKSDALE, Grief: 331
BARKSDALE, Nancy: 331
BARKSDALE, Peter: 330
BARKSDALE, Randolph: 330
BARKSDALE, Rebecca L.: 5827
BARKSDALE, Rebecca (Spragins): 5005
BARKSDALE, Susan: 331
BARKSDALE, William: 330
BARKSDALE FAMILY (Virginia): 331
BARKSDALE, Virginia:
　Mercantile accounts: 5827
BARLEY PRODUCTION--Virginia: 4924
BARLEY TRADE: 323
BARLOW, Sir George Hilaro, First
　Baronet: 332
BARLOW, Joel: 1424, 5593
BARNARD, Henry: 5593
BARNARD, John: 333
BARNARD, John Gross: 334
BARNARDO, Thomas John: 2148
BARNBY, George: 335
BARNES, Almira: 5747
BARNES, Asa George: 3454
BARNES, John W.: 336
BARNES, Julius: 646
BARNES, Richard: 337
BARNES, William Speight: 338
BARNES, INC.: see WASHINGTON MADDUX
　AND ASA BARNES, INC.
BARNESVILLE, Georgia:
　Confederate Army camp: 18
　Description: 284
BARNET, _____ (American consul-
　general in Paris): 4348
BARNETT, Ross: 5773
BARNETT, Georgia: 2692
BARNSLEY, George: 339
BARNSLEY, Godfrey: 339
BARNSLEY, Harold: 339
BARNSLEY, Lucien: 339
BARNUM, Phineas Taylor: 1094

667

BARNUM'S (P. T.) CIRCUS: 1748
BARNWELL, Edward: 393
BARNWELL, John: 393
BARNWELL, Joseph Walker: 2449
BARNWELL, Robert E.: 1439
BARNWELL, Robert Woodward: 3485
BARNWELL COUNTY, South Carolina: 2805
BARODA, Maharaja of: see SAYAJI RAO GAEKWAR III, Maharaja of Baroda
BARODA, India: 4117
BARON, E. N.: 4188
BARONS OF THE POTOMACK AND RAPPAHANNOCK by Moncure Daniel Conway: 722
BARR, Mrs. _____ (Virginia): 661
BARR, L. A.: 340
BARRACKPUR, India: 5327
BARRANQUILLA, Colombia:
    Description: 1506
BARRAONA FAMILY (Spain): 4981
BARRE, Massachusetts: 3633
BARRELS AND BARREL STAVES TRADE:
    North Carolina: 2222, 2377, 5535
    Virginia: 5535
BARREN COUNTY, Kentucky:
    Glasgow: 2063, 5505
BARRET, William: 4127
BARRETT, Elizabeth: 2146, 2449
BARRETT, James F.: 341, 2768, 3944, 5442
BARRETT, William T.: 2363
BARRIE, Sir James Matthew: 3797
BARRIE, Robert (d. 1775): 342
BARRIE, Sir Robert (d. 1841): 342
BARRIER, N. A.: 343
BARRIER, W. A.: 344
BARRINGER, Rufus: 1925
BARRINGTON, George, Fifth Viscount Barrington: 345
BARRINGTON, George William, Seventh Viscount Barrington: 345
BARRINGTON, Henry Frederick Francis Adair: 345
BARRINGTON, Shute: 346
BARRINGTON, Sir William Augustus Curzon: 3238
BARRINGTON, New York: 2423
BARRON, Richard: 2842
BARRON, Samuel II: 347
BARROW, J. C.: 5436
BARROW, James H.: 348
BARROW, Middleton Pope: 349
BARROW, Samuel: 3118
BARROW, Thomas: 872
BARROW PLANTATION (North Carolina): 1475
BARRUS, Clara: 4073
BARRY, Alexander: 872
BARRY, Ethel (Dawson): 1424
BARRY, Herbert: 1424
BARRY, Peter Stuyvesant: 1424
BARRY, Phillip: 3797
BARRY, Mother Theresa: 4451
BARRY, William Taylor: 350, 4880
BARRYMORE, Ethel: 3797
BARSTOW, Elizabeth Drew: 2449, 5044
BARTER:
    North Carolina: 717, 2895
        Washington: 911
    Virginia: 2131, 2633
BARTHALOMEW, Joseph: 2423
BARTHOLOMEW, Edward Fry: 1768
BARTLETT, Charles L.: 3905
BARTLETT, Ellen: 351
BARTLETT, Sir Ellis Ashmead: 352
BARTLETT, Harriet F.: 353
BARTLETT, Joseph: 820
BARTLETT, Levi: 354
BARTLETT, Robert Smith: 2149
BARTLETT COMMISSION: 2936
BARTON, Benjamin Smith: 3399
BARTON, Clara: see BARTON, Clarissa Harlowe
BARTON, Clarissa Harlowe: 355, 358, 1927
BARTON, Gertrude Williamson (Baker): 356
BARTON, Jesse: 357

BARTON, Robert Thomas, Sr. (1842-1917): 356
BARTON, Robert Thomas, Jr.: 356
BARTON, Samuel R.: 358
BARTON, Seth Maxwell: 359
BARTON, Stephen: 358
BARTON FAMILY (North Carolina): 2240
BARTONSVILLE, North Carolina: 358
BARTOW, Francis S.: 5605
BARTOW, Georgia: 2860
BARTOW COUNTY, Georgia:
    Cartersville: 2365
    Cassville: 3081
BARTOW'S ARTILLERY: 1189
BARTRAM, William: 5825
BASDEN, William: 360
BASEBALL: 3797
    see also SPORTS
    New York: 3221
BASEBALL CLUBS:
    Illinois--Kewanee: 5293
    Iowa--Marshalltown: 5293
    North Carolina--Durham: 4968
BASES: see MILITARY BASES; and Military bases as subheading under names of armies
BASIC HISTORY OF THE OLD SOUTH by Wendell Holmes Stephenson: 5054
BASKERVILL, William Malone: 361
BASKERVILLE, Charles: 363, 5457
BASKERVILLE, John W.: 362
BASKERVILLE, William: 363
BASLER, Roy Prentice: 102
BASON, Frederick Thomas: 364
BASS, Frederick W.: 1921
BASS STRAITS: 286
BASSETT, Arthur: 5252
BASSETT, John Spencer: 22, 706, 960, 2705, 4021, 4968, 5457
BASSETT, Victor H.: 365
BASTARDY LAWS--Great Britain: 1775
BASTROP, Louisiana: 900
BATANGAS, Philippine Islands: 4656
BATAVIA, Illinois: 4273
BATCHELOR'S CREEK, North Carolina: 4561
BATEMAN, Sidney Frances (Cowell): 1378
BATES, Arlo: 2871
BATES, Charlotte F.: 2449
BATES, Sir Edward: 366
BATES, Herbert Ernest: 367
BATES, John A.: 368
BATES, Thomas: 369
BATES SCHOOL, Charleston, South Carolina: 1651
BATH, Thomas Thynne, First Marquis of: 5330
BATH, England: 2227, 4650, 5609
    Elections: 1753
    Historical studies: 5553
    Schools: 1753
BATH, North Carolina: 3521, 5231
    Business affairs: 705
    Historical restoration: 5298
BATH CHURCH (North Carolina): 3646
BATH CIRCUIT, Methodist Churches: 3646
BATH COUNTY, Virginia: 1094
    Hot Springs: 1094, 1891
    Warm Springs: 1094, 1718, 2878, 3809
BATH GRAMMAR SCHOOL, Bath, England: 1753
BATH IRON WORKS, Goshen, Virginia: 5613
BATHURST, Henry: 370
BATLEY & GREENWOOD (firm): see GREENWOOD & BATLEY
BATON ROUGE, Louisiana: 3775, 5838
    Civil War: 383
    Diseases: 333
    Description: 1333, 1349
    Plantation accounts: 1026
    Social life and customs: 1424
BATOPILAS, Mexico--Mining: 4022
BATTERY: see ASSAULT AND BATTERY

BATTERY WAGNER, South Carolina: 2702
BATTEY, George MaGruder: 371
BATTEY, Robert: 371
BATTEY FAMILY: 371
BATTLE, Archibald John: 1476, 2449
BATTLE, Herbert Bemerton: 3905
BATTLE, John Thomas Johnson: 5457
BATTLE, Kemp Plummer: 277, 832, 1284, 2419, 4669, 5460
BATTLE, Richard Henry: 1336
BATTLE, William Horn: 3905
"BATTLE OF JENKINS' FERRY, THE LAST BATTLE OF THE FAMOUS RED RIVER EXPEDITION" by Robert M. Rodgers: 4536
"THE BATTLE OF KIRKSVILLE, AUGUST 6, 1862" by E. M. Violette: 5481
BATTLEBORO, North Carolina: 5701
BATTLES: see Campaigns, battles, and military actions as subheading under names of specific wars
BATTLES AND LEADERS OF THE CIVIL WAR: 4245
BATTLETOWN, Virginia: 3200
BAUDET-DULARY, Alexandre-François: 65
BAUDRY DES LOZIÈRES, Louis Narcisse: 372
BAUGH & SONS COMPANY (Pennsylvania): 373
BAUGH CHEMICAL COMPANY (Maryland and Ohio): 373
BAUM, Paull Franklin: 691, 4575
BAUSERMAN, John: 374, 1920, 4122
BAUSKETT, Ann: 2961
BAUSKETT, Thomas: 2961
BAUSKETT FAMILY (South Carolina: Genealogy): 2961
BAVARIA, Germany:
    Straubinger: 2950
    Würtzburg: 174
BAXTER, George A.: 5794
BAXTER, Thomas: 375
BAXTER FAMILY (Virginia): 375
BAXTER, ROSE, AND NORTON (legal firm): 4568
BAY RIVER, North Carolina: 1871
BAYARD, Thomas Francis: 217, 4881
BAYARD FAMILY (New York--Genealogy): 2553
BAYLEY, Ada: 1113
BAYLEY, John Whitcomb: 828
BAYLOR, Frances Courtenay: 376
BAYLOR UNIVERSITY, Waco, Texas: 225
BAYNE, Charles Joseph: 2449
BAYNES, Elbert W.: 377
BAYNES, Selina E.: 378
BAYNES, Tucker: 377
BAYNTON FAMILY (Genealogy): 1424
BAYONNE, France--Description: 4348
BAYOU GENTILLY, Louisiana: see CIVIL WAR--PRISONERS AND PRISONS--Union prisoners--Louisiana--Bayou Gentilly
BAYOU SARA, Louisiana--Civil War: 4275
BEACH, Harvey R.: 379
BEACH, Henry: 379
BEACH RIDGE, New York: 3691
BEACONSFIELD, Benjamin Disraeli, First Earl of: 2148, 3236, 3722
    Portrait: 345
BEALE, Edward: 380
BEALE, Horace: 380
BEALE, James: 381
BEALE, Richard Lee Turberville: 74, 382
BEALE, William: 2725
BEALL, Frances: 3053
BEALL, Frances McCleery: 3053
BEALL, Frances Zeruiah Susanna: 3053
BEALL, John Yates: 43
BEALL, Joseph S.: 383
BEALL, Thomas: 384
BEALL, Upton: 385
BEALL, William Murdock: 3053
BEALL AND STEWART (firm): see STEWART AND BEALL

BEAMAN, George W.: 386
BEAN TRADE: 323
BEAN'S STATION, Tennessee: 3692
BEAR CREEK PRIMITIVE BAPTIST CHURCH: 387
BEAR GRASS TOWNSHIP, North Carolina: 3935
BEARD, Lizzie: 3060
BEARD FAMILY (Southern States): 4434
BEARDSLEY, Alonzo G.: 388
BEASLEY, William Fessenden: 3408
BEATTIE, Maria J.: 2642
BEATTIE'S FORD, North Carolina: 792, 5667
  Mercantile accounts: 2277
BEATTY, Lt. _____ (Great Britain): 392
BEATTY, Elie: 389
BEATTY, G. H.: 390
BEATTY FAMILY (North Carolina): 1313
BEAUCHAMP, Elizabeth H.: 391
BEAUCHAMP, Joel: 391
BEAUCHAMP, John: 391
BEAUFORT, Sir Francis: 392
BEAUFORT, North Carolina:
  Autographs: 3499
  Civil War: 494, 3166
    see also CIVIL WAR--CAMPAIGNS, BATTLES, AND MILITARY ACTIONS--North Carolina--Beaufort
  Democratic Party: 4858
  Freedmen's Bureau: 5431
  Hurricanes: 3960
  Intra-Coastal Waterway: 4858
  Social life and customs: 5480
  United States Army:
    Army life: 5480
BEAUFORT, South Carolina: 869, 1682, 1889, 1891, 1927, 2144, 4191
  see also BEAUFORT COLLEGE
  Civil War: 3264
    Depredations by Negroes: 5514
  Education--Freedmen: 2106
BEAUFORT COLLEGE, Beaufort, South Carolina: 393, 3791
BEAUFORT COUNTY, North Carolina: 911
  Business affairs: 5831
  Civil War--Aid to soldiers' families: 4862
  Courthouse: 540
  Education--Finance: 4382
  Estates--Administration and settlement: 5831
  Farm accounts: 5814
  Food prices: 5521
  Merchandise--Marketing: 5521
  Politics and government: 4232, 5521
  Primitive Baptist Church: 3945
  Schools: 394
  Slave trade: 5831
  Taxation: 3921
  Cities and towns:
    Bath: 3521, 5231
      Business affairs: 705
      Historical restoration: 5298
    Blount's Creek: 4336
    Chocowinity: 2699
    Longacre: 2222
    Pantego: 4471
      Agricultural organizations: 1323
    Washington: see WASHINGTON, North Carolina
BEAUFORT COUNTY, South Carolina: 810
  Sheriffs: 5758
  Cities and towns:
    Beaufort: 869, 1682, 1889, 1891, 1927, 2144, 4191
      see also BEAUFORT COLLEGE
      Civil War: 3264
        Depredations by Negroes: 5514
      Education--Freedmen: 2106
    Bluffton: 1572
    Grahamville: 2670
      Schools: 4961
BEAUFORT (steamship): 3827
BEAUMONT, A.: 4188

BEAUMONT, Texas--Oil fields: 1951
BEAUREGARD, Caroline (Deslonde): 805
BEAUREGARD, Pierre Gustave Toutant: 395, 484, 1186, 1468, 2363, 2364, 2449, 2792, 2818, 2944, 3184, 3501, 4002, 4065, 4193, 4982, 5280
BEAUVOIR, Mississippi: 1403
BEAVER, Pennsylvania--Weather: 3808
BEAVER COUNTY, Pennsylvania:
  Beaver--Weather: 3808
BEAVER CREEK AND BLUFF COTTON MILLS: 396
BEAVER CREEK DISTRICT, Maryland: 3329
BEAVER DAM STATION, Virginia: see CIVIL WAR--CAMPAIGNS, BATTLES, AND MILITARY ACTIONS--Virginia--Beaver Dam Station
BEBB, William: 5224
BECHTLER, Christopher: 5457
BECHUANA: see TSWANA (Bantu tribe)
BECHUANALAND: 4514
  see also SOUTH AFRICA
BECK, J. P.: 5188
BECK, James Montgomery: 3320
BECK, Jesse: 5457
BECKER, Edward C.: 3674
BECKER, George: 304
BECKET, Massachusetts: 5766
BECKETT FAMILY (Great Britain): 4568
BECKETT, England: 345
BECKHAM, John Crepps Wickliffe: 398
BECKHAM, Mary: 3831
BECKHAM, Pattie Dandridge: 3831
BECKHAM, William M.: 399
BECKHAM FAMILY (Genealogy): 3831
BECKLEY, Jno. 3130
BECKLEY, William A.: 533
BECKWITH, Sir George: 400
BECKWITH, John: 401
BECKWITH, John Watrus: 402
BECKWITH, Jonathan: 337
BEDDINGFIELD, Eugene Crocker: 5457
BEDDINGTON PARK, England: 887
BEDELL, William F.: 403
BEDFORD, Francis Russell, Seventh Duke of: 4605
BEDFORD, Hastings William Sackville Russell, Twelfth Duke of: 4722
BEDFORD, John Russell, Sixth Duke of: 1139
BEDFORD, England: 3977
BEDFORD, Pennsylvania: 324, 2275, 3784
BEDFORD, Virginia: 1140
"BEDFORD," Virginia: 1813
BEDFORD COUNTY, Pennsylvania: 231
  Bedford: 324, 2275, 3784
  Rainsburg: 4106
  Ray's Hill: 3957
BEDFORD COUNTY, Tennessee: 5719
BEDFORD COUNTY, Virginia: 753, 2136, 3731
  Business affairs: 1052
  Committee of Public Safety: 2633
  Court of Law and Chancery: 5818
  Debt collection: 3621
  Law practice: 3621
  Legal affairs: 5818
  Merchants: 5055
  Militia: 4049
    Civil War: 3788
  Real estate: 5055
  Schools: 1894
  Summonses: 5818
  Tobacco farming: 4049
  Wills: 4049
  Cities and towns:
    Bedford Court House: 2633
    Bunker Hill: 4049
    Chamblissburg: 5921
    Falling River: 2633
    Fancy Grove: 5288
    Goose Creek: 2633, 5852
    Liberty: 800, 3440
    Mount Prospect: 73
BEDFORD COURT HOUSE, Virginia: 2633

BEDFORDSHIRE, England:
  Everton: 462
BEDINGER, Caroline B. (Lawrence): 404
BEDINGER, Caroline Danske (1854-1914): 404
BEDINGER, Daniel: 404
BEDINGER, George Michael: 404
BEDINGER, George Rust: 3148
BEDINGER, Henrietta: 3148
BEDINGER, Henry (1753-1843): 404, 3721
BEDINGER, Henry (1812-1858): 404, 3710
BEDINGER, Henry (b. 1853): 404
BEDINGER, Mary: 404
BEDINGER FAMILY (West Virginia): 404
BEDMAR, Alfonso de la Cueva, Marqués de: 405
BEE, Rachel Susan: 1017
BEE FAMILY (South Carolina): 4584
BEECH ISLAND, South Carolina: 1220, 2291
BEECHER, Catharine Esther: 406, 1827
BEECHER, Harriet Elizabeth: 2503, 4387, 5099, 5166
BEECHER, Henry Ward: 407, 1608, 2552, 3029, 5001
BEECHER, Mary Louisa Amelia Boozer, Countess de Pourtalès-Gorgier: 1464
BEECHER, James Chaplin: 408
"BEECHMOOR," Kentucky: 5557
BEEF TRADE:
  Georgia--Ebenezer: 5986
  North Carolina: 2924
THE BEEHIVE: 2918
BEEKEEPING--North Carolina: 122
BEEMAN, P. T.: 409
BEERBOHM, Sir Max: 2146
BEESWAX TRADE:
  North Carolina: 2924, 5298
BEGBIE, Thomas Stirling: 410
"BEHIND THE SCENES IN WASHINGTON" by Harry Augustus Slattery: 4851
BEIDELMAN, Catherine P. (Wilmer): 411
BEIDELMAN, Daniel: 411
BEIDELMAN, Daniel, Jr.: 411
BEIDELMAN, Wilmer: 411
BEIDELMAN FAMILY (Pennsylvania): 411
BEIRUT, Lebanon: see AMERICAN COLLEGE
BEITH, Scotland: 1301
BELAIR, Maryland: 4712
BELASCO, David: 3797
BELCHER, Granville W.: 412
BELCHER, James: 413
BELCHER, William W.: 414
BELEW'S CREEK, North Carolina: 3221
BELFAST, Northern Ireland: 2403
  Foreign trade: 3230
BELFORD, North Carolina: 5924
BELFORD'S MONTHLY: 3793
BELGIAN REVOLUTION (1830):
  Battle of Antwerp: 4605
BELGIUM:
  British embassy in Brussels: 3472
  Currency: 1339
  Description and travel: 5038
  Diplomatic and consular service:
    United States: 3485
  Foreign relations:
    United States: 1787
  Independence: 280, 1775
  Submarine cables: 4934
BELGRADE INSTITUTE, Maysville, North Carolina: 3607
BELHAVEN, Virginia--Teaching: 1697
BELKNAP, William Worth: 415
BELKNAP COUNTY, New Hampshire:
  Gilmanton: 4012
  Sanbornton Bridge: 3822
  Tilton: 5061
BELL (ABRAHAM) & SONS (firm): 416
BELL, Alfred W.: 417

BELL, Charles Frederic Moberly: 2146, 4503
BELL, Christian: 423
BELL, E. J.: 418
BELL, Ebenezer: 419
BELL, Fannie: 424
BELL, George, Jr.: 1752
BELL, J. J.: 420
BELL, James C.: 416
BELL, James Martin: 421
BELL, John (1797-1869): 872, 3692, 5775
BELL, John (d. 1939): 5727
BELL, Madison: 422
BELL, Major: 423
BELL, Thomas A.: 424
BELL FAMILY (North Carolina): 417
BELL COUNTY, Texas:
  Description and travel: 4283
  Harrisville: 4283
BELL INSTITUTE, Underwood Flats, Vermont: 2544
BELLAMANN, Heinrich Hauer: 425
BELLAMANN, Henry: see BELLAMANN, Heinrich Hauer
BELLAMY, John D.: 484
BELLAMY, John Dillard: 1899, 5457
BELLAMY, Joseph: 426
BELLAMY, William: 426, 427, 1847
BELLAMY FAMILY: 426
BELLE, John: 428
A BELLE OF THE FIFTIES by Virginia Caroline (Tunstall) Clay: 1084
BELLEAU WOOD MEMORIAL ASSOCIATION: 1584
BELLEFONTE, Pennsylvania: 4165
BELLEMONT AND EAGLE FLOUR MILLS: 2165
BELLEVILLE, Louisiana: see CIVIL WAR--PRISONERS AND PRISONS--Union prisoners--Louisiana--Belleville
BELLEVUE, Michigan: 1840
BELLEVUE HOSPITAL MEDICAL SCHOOL, New York, New York: 3859
BELLEW, Mary: 4918
BELLINGER, Edward Edmund: 2612
BELLOC, Marie Adelaide: 364
BELLOWS, Henry Adams (1885-1913): 3797
BELLOWS, Henry Whitney (1814-1882): 429
BELLUNE, J. T.: 430
BELMONT, Alva Murray (Smith) Vanderbilt: 5968
BELMONT, North Carolina:
  Schools: 796
BELMONT, South Carolina: 4216
BELMONT ACADEMY, Granville County, North Carolina: 2192
BELMONT COUNTY, Ohio:
  Saint Clairsville: 357
BELMONT THEOLOGICAL SEMINARY, Kentucky: 5298
BELSHAM, Thomas: 2254
"BELVEDERE," Maryland (estate): 2669
BELVIDERE, New Jersey: 4087
"BELVOIR CASTLE," Leicestershire, England: 3498
"BEN HUR": 4556
BENBOW, Henry L.: 5193
BENCOOLEN, Sumatra: 4821
BENEDICT IX, Pope: 5468
BENEDICT, Ann: 3272
BENET, William Christie: 431
BÉNÉVENT, Charles Maurice de Talleyrand-Périgord, Prince de: 1424, 5179, 5222
BENEVOLENCE: see PHILANTHROPY
BENEVOLENT AND PROTECTIVE ORDER OF ELKS:
  North Carolina: 1669
BENEVOLENT SOCIETIES: see CHARITIES; CONFRATERNITIES; FRATERNAL SOCIETIES
BENFIELD, John: 2019
BENGAL, India:
  British military activity: 2756
  Fort William: 4066

BENGAL, India (Continued):
  Law codification: 332
  Marriage customs: 2756
BENJAMIN, Judah Philip: 395, 1181, 1364, 1403, 4080
BENJAMIN, Park: 432
BENJAMIN, W. R.: 5922
BENJAMIN BLOSSOM & SON (firm): 2940
BENJAMIN FRANKLIN KEMPER AND BROTHERS (firm): 2977
BENJAMINVILLE SCHOOL, [Indiana?]: 3981
BENNER, Edward: 433
BENNET, O.: 434
BENNETT, Belva Ann: 5202
BENNETT, Bryant: 435
BENNETT, Fannie: 1925
BENNETT, Frances N.: 436
BENNETT, James Gordon: 437, 2845, 4881
BENNETT, John (1865-1956): 4453
BENNETT, John Y.: 5939
BENNETT, Mary: 4918
BENNETT, May Friend: 3797
BENNETT, R. Nelson: 438
BENNETT, Risden Tyler: 5457
BENNETT, Thomas: 1107
BENNETT, William W.: 3646
BENNETT FAMILY (North Carolina--Genealogy): 4232
BENNETT AND HYMAN (firm): 435
BENNETT AND PRICE (firm): 435
BENNETT COLLEGE, Greensboro, North Carolina: 3581
BENNETT'S POINT, South Carolina: see CIVIL WAR--CAMPAIGNS, BATTLES, AND MILITARY ACTIONS--South Carolina--Bennett's Point
"BENNETT'S REGULATION," Kent County, Maryland: 830
BENNETTSVILLE, South Carolina: 3445
BENNETTSVILLE CIRCUIT, Methodist Church: 3646
BENNINGTON COUNTY, Vermont:
  Rupert: 2848
BENNINGTON (Vt.) JOURNAL: 2848
BENNITT, Charles: 439
BENNITT, James: 440
BENNITT FAMILY (North Carolina): 439
BENNITT HOUSE, Appomattox, Virginia: 440
BENSEL, James Berry: 2449
BENSLY, R. L.: 5156
BENSON, Catherine: 443
BENSON, Edward Frederick: 441
BENSON, Godfrey Rathbone, First Baron Charnwood: 442
BENSON, John: 443
BENSON, Joseph: 4146, 5647
BENSON, Nehemiah: 4760
BENSON, Robert B.: 162
BENSON, Thomas: 443
BENSON FAMILY (Alabama): 444
BENSON FAMILY (Pennsylvania): 443
BENT CREEK, Tennessee:
  Mercantile accounts: 2116
BENTHAM, Sir Samuel: 445
BENTINCK, Lord George: see BENTINCK, William George Frederic Cavendish (1802-1848)
BENTINCK, William Cavendish (1774-1839): 446, 868
BENTINCK, William George Frederic Cavendish (1802-1848): 446, 1110
BENTINCK, William Henry Cavendish-, Third Duke of Portland (1783-1809): 447, 2149
BENTLEY, B. G.: 448
BENTLEY, Edmund Clerihew: 449
BENTLEY, George: 5872
BENTLEY, William: 450
BENTLEY FAMILY (New York and Virginia): 5660
BENTON, Horace: 451
BENTON, Phyllis (Windsor-Clive): 1424
BENTON, Thomas Hart: 1308, 2107, 3362, 4174, 4669, 5551

BENTON BARRACKS, Saint Louis, Missouri: 4488, 4989
BENTON COUNTY, Arkansas:
  Bentonville: 2184
BENTON COUNTY, Tennessee:
  Historical studies: 4894
BENTONVILLE, Arkansas: 2184
BENTONVILLE, North Carolina: see CIVIL WAR--CAMPAIGNS, BATTLES, AND MILITARY ACTIONS--North Carolina--Bentonville
BENTONVILLE TOWNSHIP, North Carolina: 1602
BERDAN, Hiram: 4485
BEREA, North Carolina:
  Newspapers: 5741
BEREA, Ohio: 2693
BERESFORD, Lord Charles William de la Poer, First Baron Beresford: 452
BERESFORD, Lord John George de la Poer: 4840
BERESFORD, William (1797-1883): 453
BERESFORD, William Carr, First Viscount Beresford (1768-1854): 5830
BERESFORD-HOPE, Alexander James: see HOPE, Alexander James Beresford-
BERGEN COUNTY, New Jersey:
  Leonia: 4909
BERGER, Victor: 4948
BERHAMPORE, India: 4097
BERKELEY, Carter Burwell: 454
BERKELEY, Edmund: 456
BERKELEY, Sir George Cranfield: 3460
BERKELEY, Sir George Henry Frederick: 455
BERKELEY, William N.: 456
BERKELEY BORDER GUARDS (West Virginia): 3832
BERKELEY COUNTY, South Carolina: 3511, 4792
  Cherry Hill: 3367
  Comingtee: 296, 297
  Edisto Island: see EDISTO ISLAND, South Carolina
  Monck's Corner--Confederate refugees: 5645
  Pinopolis: 5414
BERKELEY COUNTY, West Virginia: 594, 1769, 2389, 4900
  Agricultural organizations: 3832
  Land: 2397, 3721
  Land claims: 5037
  Land settlement: 99
  Migration to: 3819
  Physicians: 748
  Cities and towns:
    Bunker Hill: 4893
    Darkesville: 4692
    Falling Waters: 4999
    Gerrardstown: 865, 919, 4904
    Hannisville: 2316, 4056
    Hedgesville: 159, 2342, 2478, 3174, 4732
      Agriculture: 3141
      Economic conditions: 3141
    Martinsburg: see MARTINSBURG, West Virginia
    Van Clevesville: 1257
BERKELEY COUNTY AGRICULTURAL AND MECHANICAL ASSOCIATION (West Virginia): 3832
BERKELEY SPRINGS, West Virginia: 1828
  Agriculture: 3141
  Economic conditions: 3141
  Health resorts: 3809
BERKS COUNTY, Pennsylvania:
  Reading: 2124, 4190
BERKSHIRE, England:
  Beckett: 345
  Boyne Hill: 2203
  Bracknell: 5279
  Caversham: 1320
  Hungerford: 5101
  Reading: 5177
  Wallingford:
    Social life and customs: 2759

BERKSHIRE COUNTY, Massachusetts:
　Becket: 5766
　Great Barrington: 856
　Pittsfield: 1455
　Stockbridge: 1792, 2093
BERKSHIRE STREET RAILWAY COMPANY
　(Massachusetts): 1792
BERLIN, George W.: 457
BERLIN, Margaretta C. (Van Metre):
　457
BERLIN, Connecticut: 5747
BERLIN, Germany: 2706, 4430
　British embassy in: 3238, 3472
　Churches: 2139
　Description: 781, 4492, 5930
　Libraries: 2139
　Literary affairs: 2764
　Palaces: 2139
　Persian state visit: 3722
　Universities and colleges: see
　　UNIVERSITY OF BERLIN
BERLIN, Virginia: 5824
BERLIN AMERICAN FEMALE INSTITUTE:
　5593
BERLY, Joel A.: 458
BERMUDA:
　American Revolution: 2008
　Clergy--Methodist: 2289
　Description and travel: 3983
　Land: 5500
　Public opinion:
　　American Civil War: 3983
　Social life and customs: 5500
　Trade and commerce:
　　North Carolina: 1871
　Weather: 5500
BERMUDA HUNDRED, Virginia: 2506
　see also CIVIL WAR--CAMPAIGNS,
　　BATTLES AND MILITARY ACTIONS--
　　Virginia--Bermuda Hundred
BERNARD, Bernard Lytton-: see
　LYTTON-BERNARD, Bernard
BERNARD, E. L.: 459
BERNARD, Sir Francis: 5298
BERNARD, George S.: 460
BERNARD, William Henry: 5457
BERNHARDT, Sarah: 3797
BERNSTEIN, Leonard: 902
BERRIDGE, John: 462
BERRIEN, John Fulton, Jr.: 3710
BERRIEN, John MacPherson: 463, 2326
BERRIEN, Sarah P.: 3710
BERRIEN FAMILY: 3396
BERRIEN FAMILY (Georgia): 787
BERRY, A. Moore: 1806
BERRY, Charles: 464
BERRY, Charles Ferdinand, Duc de:
　5637
BERRY, John (Maryland): 466
BERRY, John (North Carolina): 465,
　3677
BERRY, L. M.: 1806
BERRY, Thomas J. (Virginia): 461
BERRY, Thomas L. (Maryland): 466
BERRY, Wallace C.: 4617
BERRY, William: 467, 1436
BERRY, William Augustus: 3410
BERRY FAMILY: 3357
BERRY FAMILY (North Carolina--
　Genealogy): 465
BERRY FERRY, Virginia: 467
BERRY TRADE: see PERSIAN BERRY TRADE
BERRYVILLE, Virginia: 2082, 3200,
　3336, 4301
BERTHELSDORF, Germany:
　Description: 5459
BERTIE COUNTY, North Carolina:
　Baptist Churches: 2603, 4572
　Estates--Administration and
　　settlement: 2582
　Cities and towns:
　　Colerain--Baptist Church: 1157
　　Holly Grove: 1271
　　Turner's Cross Roads: 2332
BERWICKSHIRE, Scotland:
　Dryburgh: 1716
BESANCON, Henry: 468
BESANT, Sir Walter: 1113

BESORE, George: 469
BESSBOROUGH, John William Ponsonby,
　Fourth Earl of: 4258, 4605, 5026
BESSEMER CITY, North Carolina:
　Strikes: 4094
BEST, B. W.: 470
BETA THETA PI: 4911
BETHAM, Mary Matilda: 471
BETHAM, William: 471
BETHANIA, North Carolina: 2915
　Farm life: 156
BETHANIA PUBLIC SCHOOL, North
　Carolina: 813
BETHANY, Connecticut: 3778
BETHANY, North Carolina:
　Farmers' Alliance: 3996
BETHANY CHURCH (Methodist): 3646
BETHANY COLLEGE, Lancaster,
　Pennsylvania: 1785
BETHANY COLLEGE, Wellsburg, Virginia:
　3806
BETHANY SUB-ALLIANCE NO. 601: 3996
BETHEL, Connecticut: 1205
BETHEL, Georgia--Churches: 2460
BETHEL, Tennessee: 4253
BETHEL BAPTIST CHURCH, Sumterville,
　South Carolina: 3676
BETHEL BAPTIST MARINERS CHURCH,
　New York, New York: 5660
BETHEL CHURCH, Virginia: see
　CIVIL WAR--CAMPAIGNS, BATTLES, AND
　MILITARY ACTIONS--Virginia--Bethel
　Church
BETHEL PRESBYTERIAN CHURCH,
　Greenville, Virginia: 2737
BETHELL, Eleanor Margaret (Tennant):
　472
BETHELL, Richard, First Baron
　Westbury: 472, 2998, 4520
BETHESDA, Maryland: 1424
BETHESDA CHURCH, Virginia: see
　CIVIL WAR--CAMPAIGNS, BATTLES, AND
　MILITARY ACTIONS--Virginia--
　Bethesda Church
BETHLEHEM, Pennsylvania: 1536
　see also LEHIGH UNIVERSITY
　Boarding houses: 5312
　Iron industry: 5312
　Municipal services: 5312
　Schools: 3258
　　Girls' schools and academies:
　　　2828
　Social life and customs: 5312
BETHLEHEM IRON WORKS, Bethlehem,
　Pennsylvania: 5312
BETHLEHEM SEMINARY, Bethlehem,
　Pennsylvania: 3258
BETJEMAN, John: 364
BEULAH BAPTIST ASSOCIATION, North
　Carolina: 320
BEVANDAG, R. H.: 473
BEVELY, James T.: 474
BEVERIGE, Henry: 475
BEVERLEY, Carter: 2577, 3512
BEVERLEY, Lucy: 476
BEVERLEY, Robert: 476
BEVERLEY, England: 5956
BEVERLY, Massachusetts: 5885
　Shipping: 2682
BEVERLY, West Virginia:
　Civil War--Reminiscences: 5550
BEVERLY HILLS, California: 4545
BEXLEY, Nicholas Vansittart, First
　Baron: 878
BIARRITZ, France:
　Description: 4348
BIBB, Richard: 477
BIBB, Thomas: 478
BIBB, William Wyatt: 1333
BIBB COUNTY, Georgia: 3075
　Courts: 1995
　Macon: see MACON, Georgia
BIBB COUNTY ACADEMY, Macon, Georgia:
　479, 2963
BIBLE: 84, 4932, 5598
　Commentaries: 4952, 5699
　Criticism: 3666
　Study: 4828, 5793

BIBLE (Continued):
　Translation into English: 2837
　Translation into Malayalam: 739
　Translation into Persian: 4821
BIBLE SOCIETIES:
　Alabama: 1084
　Great Britain: 5726
　United States: 1565
THE BIBLE SOCIETY (Great Britain):
　5726
BIBLIA FILIPINA: 4511
BIBLIA LATINA: 84
BIBLICAL CHARACTERS: 1482
BIBLICAL QUOTATIONS: 1639
BIBLICAL RECORDER (Baptist
　publication): 274, 3538, 5401
BIBLICAL SCHOLARSHIP: 1351
　Great Britain: 2653
BIBLIOTECA NACIONAL, Madrid, Spain:
BIBLIOTHÈQUE NATIONALE: 5681
BICYCLES--Propulsion: 5210
BICYCLING: see CYCLING
BIDDLE, A. W.: 480
BIDDLE, Alexander: 480
BIDDLE, Annie: 480
BIDDLE, Anthony Joseph Drexel, Jr.:
　481
BIDDLE, Arthur: 480
BIDDLE, B. F.: 484
BIDDLE, Charles (1745-1821): 480
BIDDLE, Charles John (1819-1873):
　4188
BIDDLE, Clement (1740-1814): 2571
BIDDLE, Clement, Jr.: 480
BIDDLE, E. R.: 480
BIDDLE, George W.: 480
BIDDLE, J. Wilmer: 480
BIDDLE, James William: 480, 482,
　484
BIDDLE, Julia W.: 480
BIDDLE, L. A.: 480
BIDDLE, Lynford: 480
BIDDLE, Marion: 480
BIDDLE, Marion D.: 480
BIDDLE, Mary (North Carolina): 484
BIDDLE, Mary D. (Pennsylvania?): 480
BIDDLE, Mary (Duke): 483, 4736, 5252
BIDDLE, Mary Duke: 4736
BIDDLE, Mary L. C.: 480
BIDDLE, Rosa: 484
BIDDLE, Samuel Simpson (1811-1872):
　484
BIDDLE, Samuel Simpson, Jr.: 484
BIDDLE, Sarah: 480
BIDDLE, Thomas: 480
BIDDLE, Thomas A.: 480
BIDDLE, W. R.: 480
BIDDLE, William P.: 484
BIDDLE FAMILY: 5305
BIDDLE FAMILY (New York): 4736
BIDDLE FAMILY (North Carolina): 484,
　4736
BIDDLE FAMILY (Pennsylvania): 480
BIDDLECOMBE, Sir George: 485
BIDEFORD, England: 570
BIENVILLE, U.S.S.: 4881
BIG BETHEL, Virginia: see CIVIL WAR--
　CAMPAIGNS, BATTLES, AND MILITARY
　ACTIONS--Virginia--Big Bethel
BIG STONE GAP, Virginia: 1878
BIGELOW, Charles E.: 5572
BIGELOW, John: 2726
BIGELOW, William Frederick: 3797
BIGGE, Arthur John, First Baron
　Stamfordham: 1815
BIGGS, Asa (1811-1878): 486, 2419,
　4658, 5036, 5092
BIGGS, Della: 486
BIGGS, Henry A.: 486
BIGGS, William: 486
BIGLANE, Jean Nosser: 3363
BIGLER, William: 4188
BIKINI, Marshall Islands:
　Atomic bomb: 2897
BILBAO, Spain: 644
BILL, Annie Cecelia (Bulmer): 487
BILLARD, Mary Ada: 5642
BILLENSTEIN, J. T.: 488

BILLINGS, Alfred: 4829
BILLINGSLEY, William F.: 5234
BILLMYER, David: 489
BILLMYER, Sallie: 489
BILLMYER, William H.: 489
BILLS OF EXCHANGE: 5535
   Great Britain--Bristol: 4541
   Maryland--Baltimore: 3971
   North Carolina: 2651
   South Carolina: 810
BILLS OF LADING: 5826
   Great Britain--Bristol: 4541
BILOXI, Mississippi: 5712
BILSON-LEGGE, Henry: 736
BILTMORE, North Carolina: 1001
BINGHAM, Mr. _____ (Pennsylvania businessman): 3909
BINGHAM, M. (Great Britain): 5464
BINGHAM, Mary: 3300
BINGHAM, Robert: 3300
BINGHAM, William (1752-1804): 4218
BINGHAM, William James (North Carolina): 2940, 3176, 5036
BINGHAM SCHOOL, Asheville, North Carolina: 661, 4968
BINGHAM SCHOOL, Orange County, North Carolina: 661, 666, 675, 817, 3300, 4321, 5298, 5912
BINGHAMTON, New York: 2516
BIOGRAPHICAL HISTORY OF NORTH CAROLINA by Samuel A'Court Ashe: 5457
BIOGRAPHICAL STUDIES: 1191
   see also AMERICAN AUTHORS
   France: 3644
   Great Britain: 1070, 2146, 2953, 3022, 3684, 4770
   Italy--Florence: 5487
   Kentucky: 1308
   Massachusetts: 1792
   North Carolina: 2299
   Pennsylvania: 5686
      Philadelphia: 2790
   Scotland: 5379
   South Carolina: 1424
   Sweden: 5379
   United States: 902, 2351, 5552, 5640
   Virginia: 1778, 3269, 5176, 5607
      Criticism: 1624
BIOGRAPHIES: 4894
   see also AMERICAN AUTHORS; SOCIALISTS--Biography
   Great Britain: 2973, 3411, 5050
   North Carolina: 5457
   Peru--Lima: 3238
   South Carolina: 4350
   Tennessee: 3611, 4358
   United States: 2449, 4264, 4918, 5051
   Virginia: 2881, 4019
   Washington, D. C.: 42
BIOGRAPHY (as writing form): 1465
BIRCH, Colonel _____ (Missouri): 1620
BIRCKHEAD, Edward F.: 490
BIRCKHEAD, Millie: 490
BIRCKHEAD, Nehemiah: 490
BIRD CALLS--North Carolina: 3048
BIRDS: 4453
   North America: 4475
   North Carolina: 833
   Southern States: 1803, 4453
THE BIRDS OF NORTH AND MIDDLE AMERICA by Robert Ridgway: 4475
BIRDS OF SOUTH CAROLINA by Arthur Trezevant Wayne: 4453
BIRDVILLE, Texas: 5194
BIRDWOOD, Sir George Christopher Molesworth: 217, 5553
BIRGE, N. A.: 1186
BIRMINGHAM, Alabama:
   Early development: 5591
BIRMINGHAM, England: 582, 4175, 4696, 5129
   Exports: 480
   Politics: 491
   Trade: 4605

BIRMINGHAM POLITICAL UNION (Great Britain): 491
BIRNEY, James Gillespie: 5635
BIRTH CONTROL: 2591
   see also ABORTIONS
BIRTH OF NATION: 1521
BIRTH RECORDS: see VITAL RECORDS
BIRTHDAY COMMEMORATIONS:
   Virginia: 2955
BIRTHDAY GREETINGS:
   Great Britain: 5050
   United States: 1584
BISBY, Nellie: 388
BISCOE, North Carolina: 4018
BISHOP, Caroline (Walker): 496
BISHOP, Carrie: 496
BISHOP, Charles: 496
BISHOP, Edward: 493
BISHOP, G. Edward: 494
BISHOP, Sarah E.: 495
BISHOP, William T.: 496
BISHOPS: see as subheading under names of specific denominations, e.g. CHURCH OF ENGLAND--Bishops
BISHOPSBOURNE, England: 1210
BISHOPSGATE STREET, London, England: 5662
BISHOPVILLE, South Carolina: 1460
BISLAND, James: 492
BISLAND, Peter: 492
BISLAND, William: 492
BISMARCK, Herbert, Fürst von (1849-1904): 452
BISMARCK, Otto Edward Leopold von, Prince (1815-1898): 3472
BISSELL, Leonard: 497
BISSELL, Neddy: 498
BISSELL, Tite: 498
BISSELL, Titus: 498
BISSET, John Jarvis: 1910
BISSET, Robert: 499
BITELY, Eugene: 5747
BITTING, B. Lewis: 500
BITTING, Lewis: 279
BITTING, Mollie (Bain): 279
BITTING, William Coleman: 461
BIVEN, G. T.: 2189
BIVENS, D. T.: 501
BIVENS, John Daniel: 501
BIVENS, John Lucas: 501
BLACK, Archie: 2357
BLACK, David: 1492
BLACK, Harriet Matilda: 502
BLACK, Harvey: 503
BLACK, Hugh: 2148
BLACK, Jeremiah Sullivan (1810-1883): 1084, 1333
BLACK, Mary Fleming: 4425
BLACK, V. N.: 3183
BLACK CODES--North Carolina: 2469
BLACK CREEK TEMPERANCE SOCIETY: 1115
BLACK HAWK (Indian chief): 3255
BLACK HAWK PURCHASE: 5436
BLACK PEPPER TRADE: see PEPPER TRADE
"BLACK POINT," Georgia (estate): 1448
"BLACK REPUBLICAN": 5059
BLACK RIVER ACADEMY, Ludlow, Vermont: 5197
BLACK RIVER DISTRICT, North Carolina: 5709
"BLACKBEARD, A COMEDY IN FOUR ACTS (FOUNDED IN FACT)" by Samuel Sawyer: 4683
BLACKBURN, William Maxwell: 1210
BLACKBURNE, Francis: 504
BLACKER, Valentine: 505
BLACK-EYED PEAS TRADE:
   see also PEAS TRADE
   North Carolina: 1871
BLACKFOOT INDIANS: 1333
BLACKFORD, Charles Minor, Sr. (1833-1903): 506, 2951, 4157
BLACKHOUSE, George: 258
BLACKHOUSE, John: 258
BLACKHOUSE FAMILY (Great Britain): 258
BLACKIE, John Stuart: 507
BLACKMAIL: 5872

BLACKMON, Homer: 508
BLACKMOOR, England: 4036
BLACKMORE, Richard Doddridge: 2449
BLACKNALL, Oscar William: 5457
BLACKNALL (R.) AND SON: 509
BLACK'S (ARCHIE) ACADEMY, Haywood, North Carolina: 2357
BLACK'S BLUFF, Alabama: 5174
BLACKSBURG, Virginia: 193, 503
   see also VIRGINIA POLYTECHNIC INSTITUTE
   Banks and banking: 308
   Mercantile and rental accounts: 3039
   Merchants: 2992
   Transportation of wood and coal: 3692
BLACKSHEAR, J. William: 510
BLACKSHEAR, Marian (Baber): 510
BLACKSMITHING:
   Georgia: 245
   Indiana: 245
   Kentucky: 245
   North Carolina: 998, 1015, 1550, 4458
      Cabarrus County: 2628
      Prattsburg: 4307
   South Carolina: 2670
      Charleston: 219
   Virginia: 2633, 3045
      Chesterfield County: 2908
      Edinburg: 4124
      Pittsylvania County: 2131
BLACKSMITHS' ACCOUNTS: 3958, 5807, 5822, 5942
   Maryland:
      Montgomery County: 3982
   New Hampshire--Keene: 5501
   North Carolina: 4918, 4939
      Farmington: 2857
      Forsyth County: 4631
      Gold Hill: 3368
      Lockville: 5207
      Mount Gilead: 4689
      Prattsburg: 4307
      Wadesboro: 4906
   Pennsylvania--Wesley: 4841
   South Carolina: 2793
      Chester County: 4833
   United States: 2891
   Virginia:
      Marshall: 3582
      Van Buren Furnace: 5990
   West Virginia:
      Jefferson County: 4388
BLACKSTONE, Sir William: 4616
BLACKSTONE COLLEGE FOR GIRLS, Virginia: 879
BLACKWATER BRIDGE, Virginia:
   Civil War: 2121
BLACKWELL, Betsey: 512
BLACKWELL, Edward L.: 511
BLACKWELL, Elizabeth: 512
BLACKWELL, John: 2927
BLACKWELL, William Thomas (1839-1903): 513, 3762, 5457
BLACKWELL FAMILY (North Carolina): 2934
BLACKWELL FAMILY (Virginia): 2927
BLACKWELL'S DURHAM TOBACCO COMPANY, Durham, North Carolina: 3762
BLACKWOOD, David K.: 514
BLACKWOOD, Frederick Temple Hamilton-Temple-, First Marquis of Dufferin and Ava: 515, 2149, 4520, 4567
BLACKWOOD, Hariot Georgina (Hamilton) Hamilton-Temple-, Marchioness of Dufferin and Ava: 515
BLACKWOOD, Sir Henry, First Baronet (1770-1832): 515, 516, 2421
BLACKWOOD, Ibra C.: 2109
BLACKWOOD, J.: 514
BLACKWOOD, James J.: 514
BLACKWOOD, M. J.: 514
BLACKWOOD (WM.) & SONS (firm): 1210
BLADEN CIRCUIT, Methodist Church: 3646

BLADEN COUNTY, North Carolina:
    4052, 4516, 4816
    Land--Purchases and sales: 5909
    Land grants: 517
    Lawsuits: 5909
    Schools: 754
    Cities and towns:
        Clarkton: 2970, 5909
        Elizabethtown: 3364
        Horse Shoe Swamp: 3423
BLADENSBURG, Maryland--Clergy: 610
BLADES, James B.: 5457
BLAGDON SCHOOL (Great Britain): 5726
BLAINE, James Gillespie: 1593, 2225,
    3789, 5762
BLAIR, Mr._____(Maryland merchant):
    3006
BLAIR, Cynthia: 518
BLAIR, Francis Preston: 519, 685
BLAIR, John D.: 3809
BLAIR, Mildred: 518
BLAIR, Montgomery: 306
BLAIR, W. A.: 520
BLAIR, Walter (b. 1900): 102
BLAIR BURWELL (firm), Augusta,
    Georgia: 2360
BLAIR COUNTY, Pennsylvania:
    Creation of: 421
    Interracial marriages: 5249
    Politics: 421
    Cities and towns:
        Altoona: 1798
        Hollidaysburg: 421, 849, 1142
BLAIR DRUMMOND, Scotland: 1569
BLAKE, Beulah: 4353
BLAKE, George Charles: 2296
BLAKE, Henry Nichols: 2400
BLAKE, Lemuel: 3501
BLAKE, William: 1913
BLAKE HOUSE, East Lebanon, New
    Hampshire: 2417
BLAKELY, J. Yandell: 521
BLAKELY, Ralph Royd: 521
BLAKEMORE, N. L.: 522
BLAKENEY, William, Baron Blakeney:
    5540
BLAKEY, Angus R.: 523
BLAKEY, James: 523
BLAKEY, T. C.: 523
BLALOCK, Austin: 524
BLALOCK, Tilmon: 525
BLANC, Louis: 526
BLANCE, Joseph: 5651
BLANCE, Josephine (West): 5651
BLANCHARD, Charles W.: 527
BLANCHARD, Edward Litt Laman: 528
BLANCHE (warship): 2296
BLAND, James: 3708
BLAND, James T. (Confederate soldier):
    793
BLAND, Michael: 957
BLAND, Richard Parks: 1364
BLAND, S. O.: 646
BLAND, Theodorick, Jr.: 858
BLAND FAMILY (Virginia--Genealogy):
    3809
BLAND-ALLISON ACT: 4442
BLAND TOBACCO COMPANY: 655
BLANDING, William: 529
BLANK BOOKS INDUSTRY:
    Mississippi: 4309
BLANKS, Elizabeth J. (Holmes): 530
BLANKS, William, Jr.: 530
BLANKS FAMILY (Mississippi and North
    Carolina): 530
BLANTON, James: 531
BLANTON, James M.: 531
BLANTON, Philip Southall: 531
BLANTON, Walker B.: 531
BLATCHFORD, Samuel: 388
BLAUVELT, James L. B.: 532
BLEASE, Coleman Livingston: 501,
    2473, 4453, 5930
BLEASE MOVEMENT: see POLITICS AND
    GOVERNMENT--South Carolina--Blease
    Movement
BLECKLEY, Charles: 534
BLECKLEY, F. A.: 533
BLECKLEY, Sylvester: 534

BLEDSOE, Albert Taylor: 2449, 4698
BLEDSOE, Moses Andrew: 5457
BLEDSOE, Thomas A.: 195
"BLEEDING KANSAS": see KANSAS CONFLICT
BLESSINGTON, Marguerite (Power)
    Farmer: 3077
BLIGH, John, Fourth Earl of Darnley:
    535
BLIND:
    Education:
        New York: 3633
        Pennsylvania--Philadelphia: 3330
        South Carolina: 300
        Virginia: 872
    Rehabilitation:
        France: 3710
    Subdivided by place:
        Colorado: 5426
        Georgia: 5426
        Kentucky: 5426
        Louisiana: 5426
        North Carolina: 2188, 4736
        Tennessee: 5426
        Washington, D. C.: 5426
BLIND BABIES HOME AND KINDERGARTEN,
    New York, New York: 3633
"THE BLIND MOTHER" by J. G.
    Proud, Jr.: 5681
BLINDS: see MILLWORK INDUSTRY
BLISS, Tasker Howard: 4556
BLOCKADE: see CIVIL WAR--BLOCKADE
BLOCKADE RUNNING: see CIVIL WAR--
    BLOCKADE RUNNING
BLOIS, France: 5179
BLOMFIELD, Charles George: 536
BLOMFIELD, Charles James (1786-1857):
    537
BLOMFIELD, Dorothy Kent: 537
"BLOND ESKIMOS": 4556
BLONDEAU FAMILY (Australia and Great
    Britain--Genealogy): 286
BLOODWORTH, Timothy: 1891
BLOOMER, Amelia (Jenks): 538
BLOOMERS: 538
BLOOMFIELD, John Arthur Douglas,
    Second Baron Bloomfield: 3238
BLOOMFIELD HOUSE, Bath, England:
    2227
BLOOMINGDALE ASYLUM, White Plains,
    New York: 958
BLOOMINGTON, Illinois:
    Law practice: 5570
BLOOMINGTON, Indiana: 4499
    see also UNIVERSITY OF INDIANA
BLOSSOM (BENJAMIN) AND SON (firm):
    2940
BLOUNT, H. P.: 539
BLOUNT, John Gray: 540, 2222
BLOUNT, Nancy: 631
BLOUNT, Thomas: 4232
BLOUNT, William (1749-1800): 872,
    2486, 5046
    see also BLOUNT CONSPIRACY
BLOUNT, Willie (1768-1835): 541, 872
BLOUNT FAMILY: 542
BLOUNT CONSPIRACY: 1389, 2778, 5046
BLOUNT'S CREEK, North Carolina: 4336
BLOW, Richard: 2551, 4531
BLOY, Léon: 555
BLUDWORTH, Mary A.: 543
"THE BLUE BOY" (painting): 1225
BLUE LAWS: see SUNDAY CLOSING LAWS
BLUE RIDGE ACADEMY, Bedford County,
    Virginia: 1894
BLUE RIDGE PARKWAY: 4805
BLUE RIDGE RAIL ROAD COMPANY: 3069
BLUEFIELDS, Nicaragua: 1091
BLUEGRASS--Kentucky: 1086
BLUEGRASS AND RHODODENDRON: 1878
BLUESTOCKINGS--New York: 4867
BLUFFTON, South Carolina: 1572
BLUM, Edmund: 544
BLUM, John C.: 544
BLUMENTRITT, Ferdinand: 4511
BLUNT, Mrs._____: 3259
BLUNT, James Gillpatrick: 5202
BLUNT, William: 868
BLYTH, Elizabeth F.: 545

BOARD FOR CHRISTIAN WORK IN SANTO
    DOMINGO: 3633
BOARDING HOUSES:
    Georgia: 670
    Massachusetts: 4807
    Mississippi--Rodney: 3322
    New York: 1908
    Pennsylvania--Bethlehem: 5312
    South Carolina--Rates: 4834
    Virginia--Charlottesville: 5786
    Washington, D. C.: 588, 3965
BOARDING SCHOOLS:
    New York--Yonkers: 2553
    North Carolina: 4318
        Guilford County: 4006, 5905
BOARDMAN, Henry: 546
BOARDMAN, James Locke: 546
BOARDMAN, Margaret: 546
BOARDMAN, Volney: 546
BOARDS OF TRADE: see CHAMBERS OF
    COMMERCE
BOAT BUILDING:
    see also LIGHTERS--Construction
    Virginia: 4616
    Costs: 1492
BOATS: see CANAL BOATS; RIVERBOATS;
    STEAMBOATS
BOATWRIGHT, John L.: 3410
BOAZ, Cornelia: 2370
BOAZ, Thomas: 2756
BOBBINS: see TEXTILE MACHINERY--Parts
BOBBITT, John B.: 547
BOBO, Caroline (Wilfong): 5739
BOBROWSKI, Tadeusz: 1210
BOCCACCIO, Giovanni: 5379
BOCOCK, Thomas S. (1815-1891): 1161
BOCOCK, Willis H.: 2449
BODLEIAN LIBRARY, Oxford University:
    3946
BODYGUARDS: see Generals--Bodyguards
    as subheading under names of armies
BOER WAR (1899-1902): 5872
    British Army:
        Imperial Yeomanry: 345
    British policy: 217, 5872
    Campaigns and battles:
        Ladysmith: 1132
    Depredations: 41
BOGART, John A.: 548
BOGER, Dan P.: 91
BOGGS, William Robertson: 549, 5605
BOGGS, William Robertson, Jr.: 547
BOGGS FAMILY: 549
BOGOTA, Colombia: 3867
    Description: 1506
BOHANNON, Austin: 5064
BOILERMAKERS: see INTERNATIONAL
    BROTHERHOOD OF BOILERMAKERS, IRON
    SHIP BUILDERS AND HELPERS OF
    AMERICA
THE BOILERMAKERS JOURNAL: 4962
BOINEST, Thaddeus S.: 550
BOISSEAU, William P.: 551
BOK, Edward William: 552, 2449, 2790,
    4481
"BOKEN MED DE SJU INSEGLEN" by
    Xjalmar Fredrik Eugen Procopé: 4338
BOKER, George Henry: 553
BOLIGEE, Alabama: 4861
BOLIJACK, William: 4080
BOLIJACK FAMILY (North Carolina):
    4080
BOLIN, John A.: 554
BOLIN, Mary J.: 554
BOLÍVAR, Simón: 485, 4155
BOLIVIA:
    Description and travel: 4155
    Foreign relations:
        United States: 5045
    Mining engineering: 2473
    Missions and missionaries:
        Catholic Church: 4155
    Tin mining: 2473
BOLLERY, Joseph Claude Marie: 555
BOLLES, John N.: 323
BOLLING, A. J.: 555
BOLLING, John: 5685
BOLLING, Mary: 558
BOLLING, Richard M.: 557

BOLLING, Thomas: 558
BOLLING, William: 558
BOLLING FAMILY: 3657
BOLLING FAMILY (North Carolina): 2934
BOLLING AND WHITE (firm) see WHITE AND BOLLING
BOLOÑOS, Francisco Montero: see MONTERO BOLOÑOS, Francisco
BOLOÑOS Y MOSCOSO, Alvaro Navia: 4155
BOLTON, George J.: 4188
BOLTON, John: 559
BOLTZ, Ferdinand F.: 560
BOMAR, Edward Earle: 561
BOMAR, John E.: 561
BOMBAY, India: 866, 3858
  Description: 4017
  Grievances: 4913
  Politics and government: 4097
  United States consulate in: 286
BOMBAY (Presidency), India: see INDIA--British administration--Bombay presidency
BOMBS: 3424
  see also ATOMIC BOMB
BOMPIANI, Professor: 562
BONANZA SILVER MINE: 277
BONAPARTE, Charles Joseph: 4560
BONAPARTE, Elizabeth Patterson: 1424
BONAPARTE, Napoleon: 2266, 3273
  Burial place: 485, 2907
"BONAVENTURE," Georgia: 5189
BONAVISTA, Peru--Description: 2963
BOND, Charles: 691
BOND, Octavius: 563
BONDFIELD, Charles: 5768
BONDHOLDERS FOR LOUISIANA PURCHASE: 3273
BONDS: 1242, 4924, 5779
  see also BAIL BONDS; CONFEDERATE STATES OF AMERICA--BONDS; CORPORATION BONDS; MUNICIPAL BONDS; UNITED STATES--GOVERNMENT BONDS
  Interest rates: 5440
  Investment: 4214, 4343, 5731
  United States: 2469, 5440
  Surety and fidelity: see PUBLIC OFFICIALS--Bonding
  Subdivided by place:
    Connecticut: 2273
    Georgia: 5051, 5189
    Maryland--Frederick County: 4457
    Missouri: 3301
    New York: 1065
    North Carolina:
      North Carolina Literary Fund: 3943
      Oxford: 2455
    South Carolina:
      Charleston: 5198
    Tennessee--Memphis: 5443
    United States: 2210
    Virginia: 604, 2949, 3994
BONDURANT, Thomas M.: 564
BONE, David: 100
BONE, John Herbert A.: 103
BONE DUST (fertilizer): 3378
BONEBRAKE THEOLOGICAL SEMINARY, Dayton, Ohio: 1920
BONELLI, Germanus: 5532
BONER, John Henry: 685, 3418
BONHAM, Milledge Lipscomb, Sr.: 5415
BONHAM, Milledge Luke: 565, 1403, 4193
BONHOMME RICHARD (warship): 4102
BONMOR, Robert: 1592
BONNER, George M.: 2222
BONNER, Katherine Sherwood: 3363
BONNER, Robert: 1592, 1608, 4971
BONNER, Sherwood (pseudonym): see MACDOWELL, Katherine Sherwood Bonner
BONNEY, Charles Levett: 566
BONNEY, Eli Whitney: 566
BONNEY, Rebecca (Lee): 566

BONNEY, Usher Parsons: 566
BONNIFIELD, Lettie: 567
"BONNYWOOD," South Carolina: 5278
LES BONS AMIS (brigantine): 197
BONSACK, Jacob: 568, 5297
BONSACK, James A.: 5297
BONSACK, John: 568
BONSACK, John E.: 5297
BONSACK FAMILY (Virginia): 568
BONSACK, Virginia:
  Woolen mills: 568
BONSALL, George: 4066
BOOK AGENTS: see BOOKSELLERS AND BOOKSELLING
BOOK BUYING: 3424, 3617, 4402
  see also BOOKSELLERS AND BOOKSELLING
  Florida: 1653
  Great Britain: 2788
  Mississippi: 49
  Pennsylvania: 84
  Scotland: 1212
  South Carolina: 3162, 3801
  Virginia--Charlottesville: 3758
BOOK COLLECTING: 1778
  France: 3734
  Georgia: 4402
  Great Britain: 268, 1124, 2200, 5101
  New York: 5101
  Virginia: 1115
BOOK ILLUSTRATION: 552
  see also BOTANICAL ILLUSTRATION; ZOOLOGICAL ILLUSTRATION
  France: 555
  United States: 2062
BOOK INDUSTRY:
  Philippine Islands: 4511
BOOK PUBLISHING: see PUBLISHERS AND PUBLISHING
BOOK REVIEWS: 552, 722, 2811, 2985, 4085, 5054, 5159, 5244, 5457
  Cookery--Great Britain: 1210
  Local histories:
    North Carolina: 960
  Poetry: 2102
  Religious literature: 2485
  Subdivided by place:
    Great Britain: 5173
    Scotland: 5379
    United States: 1424, 2282, 2390, 2398
BOOK TRADE: see BOOKSELLERS AND BOOKSELLING
"THE BOOK WITH THE SEVEN SEALS" by Xjalmar Fredrik Eugen Procopé: 4338
BOOKBINDING:
  Mississippi: 1693, 4309
BOOKER, G.H.: 2449
BOOKER, George: 569
BOOKKEEPING:
  Exercise books: 5048
  Indiana: 2954
  Study and teaching: 5629
  Virginia: 1943
BOOKS: 291
  see also GIFT BOOKS
  Advertising: see ADVERTISING--Books
  Censorship: see CENSORSHIP--Books
  Prices: 4397
    Alabama: 4008
    Connecticut: 2273
    Virginia--Norfolk: 3830
  Publishing: see PUBLISHERS AND PUBLISHING
  Reviews: see BOOK REVIEWS
  Taxes: see REVENUE STAMPS
  Subdivided by place:
    North Carolina:
      Hillsborough: 1890
    United States: 3791
BOOKS AND READING: 4449, 4867
  see also AUTHORS AND READERS
  Alabama: 3611
  Georgia--Augusta: 5246
  New Jersey:
    Princeton University: 1333
"THE BOOKS OF ECLOGUES AND EULOGIES . . ." by Stefan George: 1992

BOOKSELLERS AND BOOKSELLING: 5720
  see also BOOK BUYING
  Alabama:
    Montgomery: 4008
    Tuscaloosa: 3611
  Connecticut: 2273
  Georgia: 3967
  Great Britain:
    Bristol: 4176
    London: 5252, 5856
  Mississippi: 1693
  New York--Troy: 5972
  North Carolina: 1491, 3186
    Greensboro: 5804
  Southern States: 5082
  United States: 3791, 5594
  Virginia: 2364, 5375
    Danville: 5196
BOOLE, Robert: 570
BOON, Ratliff: 571
BOONE, Hiram Cassel: 571
BOONE, Turin Bradford: 572
BOONE FAMILY: 1548
BOONE, North Carolina: 1259
BOONE COUNTY, Indiana:
  Thorntown: 328
BOONE COUNTY, Kentucky:
  Covington: 5064
BOONE TRAIL: 4080
BOOT AND SHOE INDUSTRY:
  Trade associations: 2682
  Virginia--Augusta County: 728
BOOT AND SHOE REPAIR: see SHOEMAKERS' ACCOUNTS
BOOT AND SHOE TRADE:
  see also SHOEMAKERS' ACCOUNTS
  Alabama--Montgomery: 1178
  New England: 1178
  North Carolina: 606
    Prattsburg: 4307
  Virginia: 2908
    Augusta County: 728
    Lawrenceville: 2519
BOOT- AND SHOEMAKING:
  see also SHOEMAKERS' ACCOUNTS
  Apprenticeship--Virginia: 3060
  Maryland: 3875
  New Hampshire:
    Grafton Centre: 2356
  North Carolina: 3221
  Virginia: 1666
BOOTH, Charles H.: 573
BOOTH, John D.: 2633
BOOTH, John Wilkes: 854, 2361, 3741
BOOTH, Mary Louise: 103, 2449
BOOTLEGGING--North Carolina: 1966
BOOTON, Edwin T.: 574
BOOTON, John G.: 574
BOOZER, Lemuel: 1877
BOOZER, Maria Louisa Amelia: 1464
BORCHART, Anson: 575
BORCKHOLDER, Martin: 576
BORDEAUX, South Carolina: 3759
BORDEN, Joseph: 4448
BOREMAN, Arthur: 694
BORGÅ, Finland: 4338
BORGLUM, Gutzon: 5090, 5110
BORLAND, Euclid: 577
BORLAND, Euclid, Jr.: 577
BORLAND, Thomas: 577
BORLAND FAMILY (Louisiana): 577
BORNEO--British administration: 4362
BOROUGH COURT, Winchfield, England: 2750
BOROUGHS, John: 5381
BOROUGHS--Development of: 3851
BORROW, George Henry: 578, 4798
BOSANQUET, Mary: 1317, 4146
BOSNIA-HERZEGOVINA: 3722
BOSS FAMILY (North Carolina): 1882
BOST, Jackson L.: 579
BOST, Nelson: 208, 579
BOSTON, England--Elections: 5746
BOSTON, Massachusetts: 1345
  1700s: 652, 750, 1236, 4304, 5665
  1700s-1800s: 1431, 2933, 5499, 5777
  1700s-1900s: 2983
  1800s: 284, 1694, 2417, 3266, 4050, 5569, 5762

BOSTON, Massachusetts:
  1800s (Continued):
    1800s: 5535
    1810s: 1321, 2139, 2837, 4274, 5535
    1820s: 2837, 4274, 5840
    1830s: 150, 977, 2456, 2837, 3491, 5622
    1840s: 977, 3495, 5282, 5622, 5841
    1850s: 773, 1038, 3459, 3701
    1860s: 1216, 2608, 2676, 3037, 3283, 3522, 4226, 4404, 5093
    1870s: 64, 3037, 4409, 4802, 5093 5841
    1880s: 3037, 4409, 4414, 4672, 4802
    1890s: 3108, 4672, 4802
  1800s-190us: 1074, 1219, 3228
  1900s: 487, 4449, 5559, 5628
  Abolition of slavery: 2449
  American drama: 3108
  Banks and banking: 5499, 5628
  Business affairs: 1902
  Christian Science: 5266
  Commodity prices: 2431
  Confederate prisoners: 5422
  Corporations: 5093
  Courts--Cases: 5093
  Description: 2449, 3485
  Economic conditions: 5777
  Foreign trade: 948
    With India: 2756
  Fugitive slaves: 4471
  Insurance: 1119
  Internal improvements: 1433
  Irish riots: 5563
  Land speculation: 709
  Legal affairs: 5093
  Literary affairs: 1737
  Merchants: 1736, 5777
    Imports: 1839
  Militia: 1474
  Music: 432
  Parades: 5563
  Political unrest: 5298
  Public welfare: 3561
  Real estate: 484
  Shipping: 323, 3578
    see also BOSTON, Massachusetts--
      Foreign trade; BOSTON,
      Massachusetts--Trade and
      commerce
    Coastwise shipping: 5860
  Social conditions: 4881
  Social life and customs: 4813, 5762
  Sons of Liberty: 5298
  Theater: 3108
  Tobacco trade: 1633
  Trade and commerce:
    see also BOSTON, Massachusetts--
      Foreign trade
    Forest products: 1732
    Wholesale trade: 1169
    With Virginia: 1556
  Unitarian churches: 1074
BOSTON (steamship): 150, 841
BOSTON POST (newspaper): 5762
BOSTON TEA PARTY:
  British public opinion: 2304
BOSTON VIGILANCE COMMITTEE: 580
BOTANICAL ILLUSTRATION:
  Great Britain: 5553
BOTANY:
  see also NATURAL HISTORY; PLANTS
  Great Britain: 4876
  Mexico: 2667
  Norway: 2430
BOTELER, Alexander Robinson: 581, 1227, 2180, 3516
BOTELER, Helen Macomb (Stockton): 581, 1543
BOTELER, Henry: 581
BOTETOURT COUNTY, Virginia:
  Arithmetic exercise books: 208
  Law practice: 5817
  Surveying: 4315

BOTETOURT COUNTY, Virginia (Continued):
  Cities and towns:
    Buchanan: 4038, 5817, 5904
    Fincastle: 52, 74, 117, 5904
    Pattonsburg: 2454
BOTHAM, Mary: 5244
BOTHWELL FAMILY (Southern States): 4434
BOTT, Hanah: 2146
BOTTELEY, James: 582
BOTTOMLEY, Gordon: 583
BOTTS, John Minor: 2876
BOTTS, Lawson: 584
BOUCK, William C.: 585
BOUDINOT, Annis: 730
BOUDINOT, Elias Cornelius: 4353
BOUGHEY, Mr. _____ : 5394
BOUILLON, Philippe D'Auvergne, Prince de: 1212, 2735
BOULDER DAM: 1548
BOULIGNY, Jean: 586
BOUNDARIES: see as subheading under names of countries and states
BOUNDARY DISPUTES: see (Country)--
  Foreign relations--(Country)--
  Boundaries; (State)--Boundary
  disputes--(State)
BOUNDORE, Alexandro: 4178
BOUNTIES: see CIVIL WAR--BOUNTIES;
  CORN TRADE--Bounties; UNITED
  STATES--ARMY--Civil War--Recruiting
  and enlistment--Bounties; WOLF
  SCALP BOUNTIES
BOUNTY LANDS:
  see also AMERICAN REVOLUTION--
    Bounty lands; WAR OF 1812--
    Bounty lands
  Georgia: 709, 1664, 2262
  Mississippi: 709
  Tennessee: 4291
BOURBON RESTORATION: 4348
BOURKE, Richard Southwell, Sixth Earl of Mayo: 587, 1857
BOURNE, Benjamin: 105
BOURNE, Sylvanus: 588
BOURON, Phillippe: 4957
BOUTWELL, George Sewall: 2563
BOUVERIE, John (d. 1750): 712
BOWDEN, John Malachi: 589
BOWDICH, Sarah (Wallis): 3158
BOWDITCH FAMILY (North Carolina): 1120
BOWDOIN COLLEGE, Brunswick, Maine: 5899
BOWE, Nathaniel Fleming: 590
BOWEN, Adelaide Marie: 592
BOWEN, John S.: 3703
BOWEN, Louisa: 2881
BOWEN, Morton: 591
BOWEN, Reuben Dean: 592
BOWEN FAMILY: 872
BOWER, William Horton: 593
BOWERS, George: 594
BOWERS, George Meade: 595
BOWIE, Robert: 596
BOWLES, Caroline: 4967
BOWLES, Charles: 196
BOWLES, Paul: 902
BOWLES, Thomas Gibson: 2976
BOWLES, William Augustus: 4982
BOWLING--Virginia: 4220
BOWLING GREEN, Kentucky: see OGDEN COLLEGE
BOWLING GREEN, Missouri: 1062
BOWLING GREEN, Virginia: 2637
BOWMAN, Amelia: 4854
BOWMAN, Jacob Weaver: 5457
BOWMAN, Lydia: 1443
BOWMAN, Robert C.: 4854
BOWMAN, Sarah: 1443
BOWOOD, England: 4171
BOWRING, Edgar Alfred: 597
BOWRING, Sir John: 597, 598
BOWSHAIRS, Zaduch: 4746
BOWYER, Calvert: 599
BOXBOROUGH, Massachusetts: 2456
BOXER REBELLION: 306, 2148

BOXFORD, Massachusetts: 1348
BOY SCOUT MOVEMENT: 1424
BOYCE, William Waters: 1439, 2961
BOYCE, Virginia--Law practice: 2387
BOYCOTTS:
  Chinese against Japanese goods: 5252
  Grapes from California: 5077
BOYD, Alfred: 600
BOYD, Alston: 601
BOYD, Andrew: 607
BOYD, Archibald H.: 602
BOYD, B. D.: 4235
BOYD, Benjamin R.: 4732
BOYD, Daniel: 607
BOYD, Hogmire L.: 603
BOYD, James E.: 602
BOYD, James Edmund: 5457
BOYD, Joe: 341
BOYD, John (Maryland physician): 4348
BOYD, John (Virginia broker): 604
BOYD, John T. (Confederate soldier): 607
BOYD, John W. (West Virginia merchant): 4732
BOYD, Joseph Fulton: 605
BOYD, R. P.: 607
BOYD, Robert (South Carolina): 607
BOYD, Robert (Virginia): 604
BOYD, Wier: 608
BOYD, William (South Carolina): 607
BOYD, William E. (Alabama): 609
BOYD, William Kenneth: 22, 2589, 3439, 3601, 5252
BOYD FAMILY: 761
BOYD (R. F.) AND CO.: 606
BOYDEN, Archibald Henderson: 1914
BOYDEN (NATHANIEL) AND SON: 2857
BOYDTON, Virginia: 600, 4186
  see also RANDOLPH-MACON COLLEGE
  Merchants: 362
BOYKINS DEPOT, Virginia: 1393
BOYLE, Jeremiah Tilford: 5425
BOYLE, William Kent: 610
BOYLES, Eliza Hall (Ball) Gordon: 611
BOYLES, George B.: 611
BOYLES, John R.: 611
BOYLES, Mary Ann: 612
BOYNE HILL, England: 2203
BOYS--Education: see SCHOOLS
BOYTE, Harry Chatten: 613
BOYTE FAMILY (North Carolina): 613
BOZURG, Murza: 5797
BRABY, Frederick: 2149
BRACKNELL, England: 5279
BRADBURN, J. E.: 614
BRADBURN, Samuel: 5647
BRADBURY, Samuel: 615
BRADENSTOKE ABBEY, Seagry, England: 3895
BRADFIELD, Joseph: 5132
BRADFORD, Annie (Chambers): 2449
BRADFORD, Gamaliel: 706
BRADFORD, Thomas: 616
BRADFORD, England: 4054
BRADFORD COUNTY, Pennsylvania:
  East Canton: 3083
  Le Raysville: 4397
  Sylvania: 3952
  Towanda: 3372
  Wysox: 3770
BRADLAUGH, Charles: 2149
BRADLEY, Amy Morris: 617
BRADLEY, Edward Sculley: 102
BRADLEY, Elisha: 618
BRADLEY, George Y.: 619
BRADLEY, Joseph H., Sr.: 715
BRADLEY, Stephen Row: 2138
BRADLEY FAMILY (North Carolina): 617
BRADLEY FAMILY (Virginia): 1094
BRADLEY COUNTY, Tennessee:
  Cleveland: 1917, 3766
BRADSHAW, Jonas A.: 620
BRADSHAW FAMILY (North Carolina): 620

BRADY, James: 621
BRADY, John H.: 3759
BRADY, Mary: 622
BRAGG, Braxton: 623, 805, 808, 1403, 1746, 1867, 2882, 2893, 3331, 3457, 4193, 4339, 4358, 4873
BRAGG, Thomas: 264, 624
BRAGG, William: 625
BRAGGE, Robert: 626
BRAIDWOOD, John: 558
BRAINERD, Mrs. _____ : 406
BRAMLETTE, Thomas E.: 627, 3207
BRAMPTON, Richard: 4230
BRANCH, Edward B.: 628
BRANCH, John (1782-1863): 631, 2776
BRANCH, John F.: 637
BRANCH, John P.: 629
BRANCH, Joseph: 631
BRANCH, Lawrence O'Bryan: 631, 730, 2399, 4968
BRANCH (LAWRENCE O'BRYAN) MONUMENT: 730
BRANCH, Mary Cook: 630
BRANCH, Nancy (Blount): 631
BRANCH (S.G.) AND BROTHER: 628
BRANCH, William H.: 4445
BRANCH FAMILY (North Carolina): 630
BRANCH BANK OF VIRGINIA, Buchanan, Virginia: 5904
BRANCHVILLE, South Carolina: 1749, 2213
BRANCHVILLE AND BOWMAN RAILROAD: 1480
BRAND, Mary: 1355
BRAND FAMILY: 1355
BRANDENBURG, Kentucky: 571
BRANDON, Mississippi: 2496, 2813
  Merchants: 802
BRANDON, Vermont: 2791
BRANDY--Distilling: see LIQUOR MANUFACTURING
BRANDY STATION, Virginia: 4685
  see also CIVIL WAR--CAMPAIGNS, BATTLES, AND MILITARY ACTIONS--Virginia--Brandy Station
BRANDY TRADE: see LIQUOR TRADE
BRANFORD, Connecticut:
  Vital statistics: 1205
BRANHAM, Emilie D.: 3905
BRANHAM, William H.: 3905
BRANNER, John C.: 2407
BRANSCOMB, Bennett Harvie: 5252
BRANSON, Anna: 5252
BRANSON, Eugene Cunningham: 2449
BRANSON, Rebecca: 3254
BRANSON FAMILY (Virginia): 2559
BRANT, James: 868
BRANTWOOD, England: 4600
BRASHEAR, John Alfred (1840-1920): 3618
BRASÍLIA, Brazil: 2398
BRASSEY, Thomas: 326
BRASWELL, William (b. 1907): 102
BRATHWAITE, Sir John: 3315
BRATTLEBORO, Vermont: 2104
BRATTON, John (South Carolina): 4368
BRATTON, John (1831-1898): 1825
BRATTON, T. D.: 4339
BRATTONSVILLE, South Carolina: 4368
BRAUN, Courtlandt: 4453
BRAUNE, G. M.: 632
BRAVO DEL RIVERO Y CORREA, Juan: 4155
BRAWLEY, William Huggins: 633
BRAXTON, Carter: 634
BRAY, F. B.: 4689
BRAYNE, Ann Butler: 2559
BRAZIL:
  Agriculture: 1289
  Brick manufacturing: 339
  Coffee trade--Virginia: 2363
  Confederate emigrants: 339
  Cowboys: 4876
  Currency: 5886
  Description and travel: 339, 1333, 1644, 2750, 4155, 4876
  Diamond mines: 2750
  Diplomatic and consular service:
    Russia: 4348

BRAZIL
  Diplomatic and consular service (Continued):
    United States: 4348
  Diseases--Smallpox: 1644
  Economic conditions: 339, 730
  Elections: 4876
  Electrification--Campos: 1644
  Emperor: 1644
  Floods--Campos: 1644
  Foreign relations:
    Great Britain: 1599, 5726
    United States: 1302
  Gas lighting:
    Rio Grande do Sul: 2750
  Geology: 2407
  Gold mines and mining: 339, 2750
  Historical studies: 3248
  Landslides--Campos: 1644
  Methodist Church: 1685
  Mining: see BRAZIL--Diamond mines; BRAZIL--Gold mines and mining
  Missions and missionaries:
    Presbyterian: 2269
  Natural history: 4875
  Negroes: 4876
  Pharmacies: 339
  Politics and government: 339
  Public celebrations:
    Brasília: 2398
    Campos: 1644
  Rice milling: 339
  Scientific expeditions: 2407, 4876
  Slavery: 4876
  Social life and customs: 339, 1289, 1644, 4876
  Weather: 4876
BRAZOS BOTTOM, Texas:
  Fourth of July celebrations: 4353
BRAZOS COUNTY, Texas--Bryan: 2691
BRAZOS RIVER, Texas: 5613
BREACH OF CONTRACT: 5584
BREAD PRICES--France: 5323
BREAD, CHEESE, AND KISSES by Benjamin L. Farjeon: 2146
BREAD TAX--Spain: 4980
BREADFRUIT PLANTATIONS:
  British West Indies: 1913
BREATHEDSVILLE, Maryland: 2225
BRECK, James Lloyd: 2999
BRECKINRIDGE, John Cabell: 635, 1403
BRECKINRIDGE COUNTY, Kentucky: 3199
BREEDING: see HOGS--Breeding; HORSES--Breeding; SHEEP--Cotswold sheep--Breeding
BREEDLOVE, Joseph Penn: 4098, 5252
BREESE, Samuel Livingston: 636
BREMEN, Germany: 2733
BREMER, Frederika: 2503
"BREMO," Virginia (Plantation): 5839
BREMO SEMINARY, Fluvanna County, Virginia: 558
BRENAU COLLEGE, Gainesville, Georgia: 4968
BRENT, George William: 637, 2325, 5208
BRENT, Joseph: 1825
BRENT, Richard: 638
BRETT, John: 2718
BREVARD, North Carolina: 3247
BREWER, John B.: 695
BREWERTON, Henry: 4348
BREWERTON, Sarah (Courtenay): 4348
BREWING INDUSTRY:
  see also LIQUOR MANUFACTURING
  Ireland: 3883
BREWSTER, Benjamin Harris (1816-1888): 2326, 3501, 4188
BREWSTER, William: 4453
BREWSTER-BRICK, Mrs. Joseph Keasby: 2753
BRIANT, Huldah Annie (Fain): 639
BRIANT, M. C.: 639
BRIARCLIFF MANOR, New York: 1914
BRIBERY:
  North Carolina: 2188
  South Carolina: 1424

BRICK, Mrs. Joseph Keasby Brewster: see BREWSTER-BRICK, Mrs. Joseph Keasby
BRICK TRADE:
  Maryland: 466
  North Carolina--Williamston: 5036
  South Carolina: 3123
  Virginia: 466
BRICKEL, Elizabeth: 4730
BRICKELL, Joseph: 640
BRICKMAKING: 3145
  Brazil: 339
  Louisiana: 2674
  Mississippi--Rodney: 3322
  Missouri--Saint Louis: 5137
BRICKS, North Carolina: 2753
THE BRIDGE by Ernest Poole: 4264
BRIDGE CONSTRUCTION: 421
  see also CONFEDERATE STATES OF AMERICA--ARMY--Bridge construction; PONTOON BRIDGES; UNITED STATES--ARMY--Civil War War--Bridge construction
  Alabama: 1181
  Maryland--Havre de Grace: 4468
  Missouri: 2817
  Ohio: 5030
  Virginia: 5106
BRIDGEPORT, Connecticut: 3910
BRIDGERS, Furman A.: 3270
BRIDGERS, John L.: 3626
BRIDGERS, John Luther (b. 1850): 641, 2325, 5457
BRIDGERS, Preston L.: 641
BRIDGERS, Robert R. (1819-1888): 641, 3626
BRIDGES, Charles E.: 642
BRIDGES, Robert (Maryland): 643
BRIDGES, Robert (1844-1930): 2102
BRIDGES:
  see also RAILROADS--Bridges
  Maryland:
    see also BURNSIDE'S BRIDGE
  Law and legislation: 4886
  Pennsylvania: 4188
  Philippine Islands: 3313
  South Carolina: 3044
  Tennessee (eastern): 3276
  United States: 5080
  Virginia: 253, 460
BRIDGEVILLE, Alabama:
  Diseases--Smallpox: 5907
BRIDGEWATER, Massachusetts: 2959, 4438
BRIDGEWATER, Virginia: 3215
  Saddlers' and tannery accounts: 5854
BRIDGEWATER CIRCUIT, Methodist Church: 3646
"A BRIEF EXPLICATION OF THE SHORTER CATECHISME WITH PRACTICALL INFERENCES FROM THE DOCTRINES THEREOF" by John Hutcheson: 2738
BRIEF HISTORY OF MY OPINIONS by George Santayana: 1097
"BRIEF HISTORY OF THE TWENTY-NINTH DIVISION": 4269
A BRIEF SKETCH OF THE HISTORY OF THE PROTESTANT EPISCOPAL CHURCH IN THE MISSIONARY DISTRICT OF WESTERN TEXAS: 1361
BRIGANDS AND ROBBERS:
  see also HIGHWAYMEN
  Virginia: 5380
BRIGGS, Alpheus: 645
BRIGGS, Clay Stone: 646
BRIGGS, George (Confederate soldier): 647
BRIGGS, George Nixon (1796-1861): 1474
BRIGGS, Thomas L.: 2772
BRIGHAM, Edwin H.: 3079
BRIGHAM, Harriet: 5312
BRIGHT, James Wilson: 648
BRIGHT, John (1811-1889): 515, 649, 3715, 4605, 4694, 5164, 5259
BRIGHT, John Morgan: 5092
BRIGHT, Richard (1745-1840): 650

BRIGHTWELL MANOR, Wallingford,
  England: 2759
BRIGHTON, England: 4580, 4811, 5525
  Business affairs: 4113
BRIGHTON, Massachusetts: 4860
BRIM, Kenneth Millikan: 651
BRIMLEY, Ralph: 3944
BRIMMER, Herman: 652
BRIMSTONE TRADE: 323
BRINDLE, William: 4188
BRINDLETOWN CHURCH (North Carolina):
  3646
BRINGHURST, Henry R.: 4881
BRINKLEY, Roberta Florence: 4777
BRINKLEY, Sterling G.: 3134
BRINSON, Samuel M.: 3955
BRISBANE, Albert (1809-1890): 65
BRISBANE, Arthur (1864-1936): 103,
  958
BRISBANE, William: 653
BRISBEN, John Quinn: 4947
BRISLEY, Thomas D.: 654
BRISTOE STATION, Virginia: see CIVIL
  WAR--CAMPAIGNS, BATTLES, AND
  MILITARY ACTIONS--Virginia--Bristoe
  Station
BRISTOL, England: 650
  Bankruptcy: 4541
  Booksellers and bookselling: 4176
  Commodity prices: 4541
  Elections: 4229
  Mercantile accounts: 4541
  Trade and commerce: 5731
  Wages and salaries: 5731
BRISTOL, New York: 2091
BRISTOL, Pennsylvania: see BRISTOL
  COLLEGE
BRISTOL, Tennessee: 5859
  see also KING COLLEGE
BRISTOL COLLEGE, Bristol,
  Pennsylvania:
  Students and student life: 3141
BRISTOL COUNTY, Massachusetts:
  Dartmouth: 4653
  Fall River: 1862, 2867
    Social life and customs: 2035
    Textile manufacturing: 992
  New Bedford: 368, 5344, 5877
    Textile schools: 4918
  Rehoboth: 427, 1847
BRISTOW, John: 5639
BRITANNIA, H.M.S.: 4355
BRITISH-AMERICAN TOBACCO COMPANY:
  655, 2191, 5252
BRITISH AND AMERICAN LAND AND
  EMIGRATION COMPANY: 2583
BRITISH AND FOREIGN ANTI-SLAVERY
  SOCIETY: 67
BRITISH ART: see ENGLISH ART AND
  ARTISTS
BRITISH BORNEO COMPANY: 5238
BRITISH COLUMBIA: 1792
BRITISH CRITIC: 90
BRITISH DRAMA: see ENGLISH DRAMA
BRITISH EAST AFRICA: see KENYA
BRITISH EXPEDITIONARY FORCES: see
  GREAT BRITAIN--ARMY--World War
  I--British Expeditionary Forces
BRITISH FICTION: see ENGLISH FICTION
BRITISH GUIANA:
  British administration: 4934
  Foreign exchange: 2612
BRITISH IN INDIA: 306, 2321, 3286,
  3472
  Education of children: 3977
  Personal finance: 3315
  Social life and customs: 3472, 5525
BRITISH IN MOZAMBIQUE: 5725
BRITISH IN TURKEY--Legal status:
  3183
BRITISH IN THE UNITED STATES: see
  AMERICAN REVOLUTION--British
  merchants in the United States;
  CIVIL WAR--BRITISH IN THE
  CONFEDERATE STATES OF AMERICA;
  CIVIL WAR--BRITISH IN THE UNITED
  STATES, CIVIL WAR--NEWSPAPERS--
  British correspondents in the
  Confederate States of America

BRITISH INTERVENTION: see CIVIL WAR--
  FOREIGN INTERVENTION--Great Britain
BRITISH LITERATURE: see ENGLISH
  LITERATURE
BRITISH MUSEUM, London, England:
  3385, 3598, 3715, 4876
  Zoological Department: 4001
BRITISH MUSEUM ADDITIONAL
  MANUSCRIPT 14,538: 656
BRITISH OCCUPATION: see AMERICAN
  REVOLUTION--British occupation
BRITISH POETRY: see ENGLISH POETRY
BRITISH SOUTH AFRICA COMPANY: 4514
BRITISH WEST CHARTERLAND COMPANY:
  4514
BRITISH WEST INDIES:
  see also GRENADA; WEST INDIES
  Breadfruit plantations: 1913
  Crops: 4913
  Economic conditions: 4913
  Foreign trade:
    Great Britain: 1115
    United States: 1935
  Hiring of slaves: 4913
  Plantations: 4913
  Population: 4913
    Statistics: 1913
  Schools--Negro schools: 763
  Shipping to Great Britain: 4913
  Slave trade: 1913
  Slavery:
    Laws and legislation: 4913
  Slaves: 4913
  Sugar cane: 4913
  Taxation: 4913
BRITT, Henry: 1107
BRITTON, Nathaniel Lord: 2790
BROACH, James G.: 657
BROAD BROOK, Connecticut: 351
BROAD RIVER COMPANY: 2218
BROAD STREET CHURCH (North Carolina):
  3646
BROADDUS, Andrew: 461
BROADDUS, William L.: 659
BROADFOOT, William Gilles: 658
BROADNAX, R. A.: 5742
BROADWAY, Virginia: 1827, 5833
BROCK, Thomas Leith: 96
BROCK COLLECTION, Huntington Library,
  San Marino, California: 819
BROCKENBROUGH, A.: 660
BROCKENBROUGH, John: 4616
BROCKMAN, F. D.: 4049
BROCK'S GAP, Virginia: 155
BROCKTON, Massachusetts: 3524
BROCKWELL, S. P.: 103
BRODERICK, William St. John
  Fremantle, First Earl of Midleton:
  663
BRODHEAD, Richard: 4188
BRODIE, Donald M.: 5252
BRODNAX, Joel: 662
BRODNAX, John Jr.: 661
BRODNAX, John G.: 661
BRODNAX, Mary: 661
BRODNAX, Samuel (1810-1880): 662
BRODNAX, Samuel Houston: 661
BRODNAX FAMILY (Georgia--Genealogy):
  662
BRODNAX FAMILY (North Carolina--
  Genealogy): 661
BROESLER, Florence: 5252
BROGDEN, Arthur: 664
BROGDEN, Curtis Hooks: 5092
BROGDEN, Harry: 664
BROGDEN, William: 664
BROGDEN, William, Jr.: 665
BROKEN BOW, Nebraska: 568
BROKERAGE: see names of specific
  businesses
BROMFIELD, Henry, Jr.: 313
BRONAUGH FAMILY (Virginia): 3458
BRONZE MONUMENTS: see MONUMENTS--
  Bronze
BROOK HILL INSTITUTE: 3448
BROOKE, Charleston P.: 666
BROOKE, Frances Taliaferro: 3720
BROOKE, George Guy Greville,
  Baron: 1087

BROOKE, Sir James, Rajah of Sarawak:
  2708, 5725
BROOKE, John (Pennsylvania): 4188
BROOKE, John Mercer (1826-1906):
  2724
BROOKE, John R. (United States
  general): 2991
BROOKE, John T.: 3623
BROOKE, Robert (1751-1799): 667
BROOKE, Stephens: 668
BROOKER, W. T.: 674
BROOKES, Iveson L.: 669
BROOKES FAMILY (South Carolina--
  Genealogy): 669
BROOKHILL SCHOOL, Albemarle County,
  Virginia: 5286
BROOKINGS, Robert Somers: 646
BROOKLAND FURNACE, McVeytown,
  Pennsylvania: 849
BROOKLINE, Massachusetts:
  Legal affairs: 5846
BROOKLYN, New York: 407, 2081, 2100,
  3115, 5840
  Autograph collecting: 1851
  War of 1812--Fortifications: 1908
BROOKLYN (warship): 485
BROOKLYN INDEPENDENT: 404
BROOKS, A. L.: 1336
BROOKS, Abbie M.: 670
BROOKS, Edward J.: 670
BROOKS, Francis: 672
BROOKS, George Washington: 5280
BROOKS, Phillips (1835-1893):
  3284, 4672
BROOKS, Thomas Cooke: 673
BROOKS, Ulysses R.: 674
BROOKS-SUMNER AFFAIR: see
  UNITED STATES--CONGRESS--
  Freedom of debate--Brooks-
  Sumner affair
BROOKSHIRE, Benjamin W.: 675
BROOKSHIRE, Charles E.: 675
BROOKWOOD LABOR COLLEGE, New York:
  4948
BROOM INDUSTRY:
  North Carolina: 5558
BROOME COUNTY, New York: 5268
  Binghamton: 2516
BROPHY, John: 1193
"BROTHER COME HOME" by Carrie Bell
  Sinclair: 5503
BROTHERHOOD OF LOCOMOTIVE ENGINEERS:
  3070
BROTHERHOOD OF PAINTERS, DECORATORS,
  AND PAPERHANGERS OF AMERICA: 224
BROTHERHOOD OF RAILROAD CARMEN OF
  AMERICA, No. 300: 1172
BROTHERSVILLE, Georgia: 1066
BROTHERTON, James: 677
BROTHERTON, Joseph: 676
BROTHERTON, William H.: 677
BROUGH, John (1811-1865): 801
BROUGHAM, Henry Peter, First Baron
  Brougham and Vaux: 678, 1632,
  3715, 3887
BROUGHTON, Charlotte: 3801
BROUGHTON, Joseph Melville: 2863
BROUSSEAU (A.) & CO.: 679
BROWER, Alfred: 680
BROWER, Alfred Smith: 5252
BROWER, Sarah (Goldston): 680
BROWER'S MILL, North Carolina: 5135
BROWN, Mrs. Aaron V.: 4055
BROWN, Abbie Farwell: 3797
BROWN, Adam K.: 681
BROWN, Alexander: 682
BROWN, Ann Eliza: 208, 683
BROWN, August W.: 684
BROWN, Austin: 710
BROWN, B. F.: 2440
BROWN, Bardin: 710
BROWN, Bedford (1792-1870): 685,
  4390
BROWN, Bettie R.: 686
BROWN, Charles (Virginia): 687
BROWN, Charles H. (Connecticut): 688
BROWN, Charles S. (Michigan): 689
BROWN, Charles W. (Virginia): 690

BROWN, Delphina: 518
BROWN, Duncan: 702
BROWN, Edward (British immigrant): 99
BROWN, Edward Smith (Virginia): 2951
BROWN, Edwin: 99
BROWN, Elizabeth: 99
BROWN, Ford Madox: 4576
BROWN, Frank Clyde: 691, 4641
BROWN, Sir George (1790-1865): 455
BROWN, George Hubbard (North Carolina): 692
BROWN, George M. (Virginia): 693
BROWN, George W. (West Virginia): 694
BROWN, George William (Maryland): 695
BROWN, Henry Alfred: 5457
BROWN, Herbert H.: 2449
BROWN, Hugh: 702
BROWN, J. R.: 696
BROWN, Jacob (United States general): 1515
BROWN, James (Virginia): 5357
BROWN, Jesse: 710
BROWN, John: 2693, 4202, 5166
see also JOHN BROWN'S RAID
BROWN, John A. (South Carolina): 697
BROWN, John D. (North Carolina): 544
BROWN, John R. (North Carolina merchant): 698
BROWN, John W. (Pennsylvania and North Carolina): 699
BROWN, Joseph Emerson (1821-1895): 700, 718, 1121, 1403, 2326, 2372, 2388, 4193, 4729, 5082
BROWN, Joseph P. (Pennsylvania): 870
BROWN, L. I.: 685
BROWN (LANCASTER) & CO., New York: 236
BROWN, M. W.: 3941
BROWN, Mary: 701
BROWN, Neill: 702
BROWN, Obadiah (Michigan): 703
BROWN, Obediah (Massachusetts): 4606
BROWN, P. W.: 4734
BROWN (P. W.) AND B. M. SELBY (firm): 4734
BROWN, Peter Mashall: 5457
BROWN (R. W.) AND SON: 2924
BROWN, Samuel: 5740
BROWN, Silvester: 1871
BROWN, Thomas (Florida): 99
BROWN, Thomas W., Jr. (North Carolina): 704
BROWN, Vashti: 708
BROWN, William (North Carolina): 705
BROWN, William (Virginia?): 523
BROWN, William Garrott (1868-1913): 706
BROWN, William Henry: 701
BROWN, William R. (North Carolina): 707
BROWN, William Washington: 708
BROWN FAMILY (Illinois): 5311
BROWN FAMILY (Massachusetts): 684, 4606
BROWN FAMILY (North Carolina): 685
BROWN FAMILY (Virginia): 682, 710, 1094
  Genealogy: 99
BROWN AND CLAYTON (firm): 1093
BROWN AND CO.: 990
BROWN & DE ROSSIT (firm): see DE ROSSIT AND BROWN
BROWN AND IVES (firm): 709
BROWN COUNTY, Ohio:
  Ripley: 281, 4387
BROWN COUNTY, Wisconsin:
  Green Bay: 1289
BROWN CREEK BAPTIST ASSOCIATION (North Carolina): 320
BROWN, LEFTWICH, AND CO.: 1093
BROWN UNIVERSITY, Providence, Rhode Island: 3588
  Alumni: 4870

"BROWN [UNIVERSITY] MEN IN THE 'OFFICIAL RECORDS OF THE UNION AND CONFEDERATE ARMIES IN THE WAR OF THE REBELLION'" by Bertram Taft Smith: 4870
"BROWN [UNIVERSITY] MEN IN THE 'OFFICIAL RECORDS OF THE UNION AND CONFEDERATE NAVIES'" by Bertram Taft Smith: 4870
BROWNE, Felicia Dorothea: 2146
BROWNE, G. L. P.: 711
BROWNE, G. Lathom: 2148
BROWNE, John L.: 5584
BROWNE, Nathaniel Borrodail: 4188
BROWNE, Thomas (1708?-1780): 712
BROWNE, William Hand (1828-1912): 1227, 2449, 3424
BROWNE FAMILY: 404
BROWNELL, William Crary: 103
BROWNING, Amos G.: 713
BROWNING, Elizabeth (Barrett): 2146, 2449
BROWNING, Hugh Conway: 714
BROWNING, Orville Hickman: 715, 872
BROWNING, Samuel: 602
BROWNING FAMILY (North Carolina--Genealogy): 714
BROWNLOW, William Gannaway ("Parson"): 716, 872, 5757
BROWNRIGG, Richard: 717
BROWNSBURG, Virginia: 3785
BROWNSVILLE, Georgia: 3614
BROWNSVILLE, Maryland: 2838
BROWNSVILLE, North Carolina: 5470
BROWNSVILLE, Pennsylvania: 1282
BROWNSVILLE, Tennessee:
  Girls' schools and academies: 872
  Land: 4139
BROWNSVILLE, Texas: 4758
  Memorial service: 3741
BROWNSVILLE FEMALE ACADEMY, Brownsville, Tennessee: 872
BROXBOURNE, England: 739
BROYLES, Oze Reed: 718
BRUBAKER, Benjamin: 719
BRUBAKER, Jacob: 719
BRUCCOLI, Matthew Joseph: 720
BRUCE, Alexander Hugh, Sixth Baron Balfour of Burleigh: 1815
BRUCE, Anne Seddon: 4020
BRUCE, Augusta Frederica Elizabeth: 1910
BRUCE, Blanche K.: 4524
BRUCE, Charles Key: 721
BRUCE, Edward B.: 5252
BRUCE, Henry Austin: 229
BRUCE, Philip Alexander: 722, 958
BRUCE, Sarah (Seddon): 4616
BRUCE, Victor Alexander, Ninth Earl of Elgin and Thirteenth Earl of Kincardine: 3978, 3980
BRUCE FAMILY (Virginia): 4924
BRUINGTON, Virginia: 5161
BRUN, Chevalier de: 321
BRUNDIGE, Timothy: 144
BRUNER, John Joseph: 832
BRUNS, Henry Dickson: 1494
BRUNS, Henry M.: 723
BRUNS, John: 1494
BRUNSON, South Carolina: 4534, 5759
BRUNSWICK, Georgia: 725, 787
  Land companies: 4298
  Land grants: 1374
  Railroads: 4718
BRUNSWICK, Maine: 961, 5899
BRUNSWICK Maryland: 1042
BRUNSWICK, Virginia: 5334
BRUNSWICK COUNTY, North Carolina: 2675
  Fort Johnston: 5826
BRUNSWICK COUNTY, Virginia: 2241, 2935, 4096, 4469, 5209
  Gristmills and millers' accounts: 4324
  Merchants and mercantile accounts: 4454
  Physicians' accounts: 4324

BRUNSWICK COUNTY, Virginia (Continued):
  Cities and towns:
    Brunswick: 5334
    Gholsonville:
      Merchants: 4747
      Mercantile accounts: 5648
    Lawrenceville: 240, 724, 1366, 1568, 2517, 2971, 3014, 3642, 5743
      Boot and shoe trade: 2519
      Taverns and inns: 1567, 3900
    Oak Grove: 2392
BRUNSWICK AND WESTERN RAILROAD COMPANY: 725
BRUNSWICK LAND COMPANY: 724
BRUSH, Mary E.: 726
BRUSHWOOD AND DANFORTH (firm): see DANFORTH AND BRUSHWOOD
BRUSSELS, Belgium:
  British embassy in: 3472
  Description: 5930
BRUSTER, Eleanor L.: 2650
BRUTON, D. R.: 832
BRYAN, Ann B.: 3237
BRYAN, Anna (Semmes): 2963
BRYAN, Charles S.: 730, 3955
BRYAN, Henry Ravenscroft: 730, 5457
BRYAN, J. H.: 730
BRYAN, James Augustus (1839-1923): 730, 5457
BRYAN, James L. (North Carolina): 727
BRYAN, James West (1805-1864): 730
BRYAN, John (Virginia): 3179
BRYAN, John Herritage (1798-1870): 730, 5457
BRYAN, Jonathan: 4625
BRYAN, Joseph B.: 2940
BRYAN, Mary (Shepard): 730
BRYAN, Matthew: 728
BRYAN, Rosa: 3395, 4060
BRYAN, William Jennings: 729, 1364, 2082
BRYAN, William S.: 730
BRYAN FAMILY (North Carolina--Genealogy): 730
BRYAN, Texas: 2691
BRYAN BUSINESS SCHOOL: see SADDLERS, BRYAN AND STRATTEN BUSINESS SCHOOL
BRYAN COUNTY, Georgia:
  Description and travel: 5042
BRYAN CREEK, Georgia: see AMERICAN REVOLUTION--Campaigns and battles--Georgia--Bryan Creek Bridge
BRYANT, Alice: 731
BRYANT, Emma: 731
BRYANT, John Emory: 731
BRYANT, Samuel S.: 732
BRYANT, William Cullen: 103, 733, 3965, 5397
BRYARLY, Richard: 734
BRYARLY, Rowland: 734
BRYARLY, Samuel: 734
BRYCE, James: 5050
BRYCE, James, Viscount Bryce: 735, 2419
BRYDGES, Sir Harford Jones: 5797
BRYDGES, James, Third Duke of Chandos: 736
BRYSON, Joseph Raleigh: 737
BUBB, George: see DODINGTON, George Bubb
BUBERL, Caspar: 1665
BUCHAN, David Steuart Erskine, Eleventh Earl of: 1716
BUCHAN, John, First Baron Tweedsmuir: 449
BUCHAN, Peter: 738
BUCHANAN, Andrew L.: 699
BUCHANAN, Claudius: 739
BUCHANAN, E. John: 5457
BUCHANAN, George: 5379
BUCHANAN, Hugh: 740
BUCHANAN, James (1791-1868): 685, 741, 805, 932, 1308, 1333, 2693, 3770, 4401, 5059, 5263
  Administration: 1466, 4596, 4808

BUCHANAN, James (Continued):
  Inauguration: 4881
  Nomination: 4856
BUCHANAN, John (1772-1844): 742, 743
BUCHANAN, John (19th century clergyman): 3809
BUCHANAN, Nancy: 743
BUCHANAN, Robert (1813-1866): 2918
BUCHANAN, Thomas (Maryland): 742
BUCHANAN, Thomas E. (Maryland): 743
BUCHANAN FAMILY (Maryland): 743
BUCHANAN, Virginia: 5817
  Banks and banking: 5904
  Elections: 4038
  Politics and government: 4038
BUCHANAN INVESTMENT CORPORATION: 1589
BUCHER, John Conrad: 496
BUCK, Daniel: 744
BUCK, Dudley: 3092
BUCK, S. W.: 4188
BUCK, Samuel D.: 745
"BUCK ISLAND," Virginia: 1957
BUCKALEW, Charles Rollin: 4188
BUCKHORN CIRCUIT, Methodist Chruch: 3646
BUCKHOUT, John: 746
BUCKHOUT FAMILY: 746
BUCKINGHAM, George Villiers, First Duke of: 2152
BUCKINGHAM, George Nugent-Temple-Grenville, First Marquis of: 2199
BUCKINGHAM, L. S.: 5681
BUCKINGHAM COUNTY, Virginia: 2418, 4222, 4998
  Estates--Administration and settlement: 5289
  Farming: 2378, 3809
  Mining: 3794
  Physicians' accounts: 3794
  Plantations and plantation accounts: 3794
  Schools: 5652
  Tax in kind: 1181
  Taxation assessment: 3794
  Tobacco culture: 3794
  Cities and towns:
    Diana Mills: 2370
      Tobacco planting: 2373
    Gravel Hill: 5652
    "Millbrook": 1714
    New Clanton: 1921
    "Traveller's Rest": 687
BUCKINGHAM INSTITUTE, Buckingham County, Virginia: 5652
BUCKINGHAMSHIRE, Robert Hobart, Fourth Earl of: 2565
BUCKINGHAMSHIRE, England:
  Ankerwycke Park: 2321
  Hall Barn Park: 4005
  Lilies: 2198
  Richings Park: 5801
BUCKLAND, John: 2148
BUCKLAND, William: 747
BUCKLAND, Virginia: 2728, 3532
"BUCKLAND," Virginia (estate): 5751
BUCKLES, E. G.: 748
BUCKLES, Edwin G.: 749
BUCKMINSTER, Joseph: 750
BUCKNER, Robert H.: 5363
BUCKNER, Simon B.: 637
BUCKNER, Simon Bolivar: 751
BUCKS COUNTY, Pennsylvania:
  Bristol: see BRISTOL COLLEGE
  Doylestown: 1418
BUCKSHOT WAR (1838): 421
BUCYRUS, Ohio: 3103
BUDAPEST, Hungary:
  British consulate in: 3722
  British State visit: 3722
  Literary affairs: 2764
BUDD, William: 4241
BUDD AND PLUMMER (firm): see PLUMMER AND BUDD
BUDDH GAYA (temple): 217
BUDDHIST TEMPLES:
  China: 2191
  India: 217

BUDGET: see under names of governments:
  Municipal: see MUNICIPAL BUDGETS
BUEL, David: 752
BUELL, Don Carlos: 808, 2871
BUENA VISTA, Mexico: 2137, 5906
  see also MEXICAN WAR--Campaigns and Battles--Buena Vista
BUENOS AIRES, Argentina: 5830
  American consulate in: 2271
  British consulate in: 286
  Foreign trade: 948
BUFF, Peter: 3437
BUFFALO, New York: 249, 1796, 2500, 3872
BUFFALO, Killing of: 4353
BUFFALO DISTRICT, North Carolina: 2824
BUFFALO FEMALE ACADEMY: 2407
BUFFALO PAPER MILLS: 2857
BUFFINGTON, T. M.: 4560
BUFORD, A. S. (1826-1911): 236
BUFORD, Harry (pseudonym): 3262
BUFORD, John: 753
BUGGIES: see CARRIAGES AND BUGGIES
BUGGS, John (North Carolina): 647
BUGGY TRADE: see CARRIAGE AND BUGGY TRADE
BUICK (DAVID) CARBURETOR CORPORATION: 4918
BUIE, Catherine Jane (McGeachy): 754
BUIE, Duncan A.: 754
BUIE, John: 755
BUIE, John C.: 755
BUIE, John R.: 1525
BUIE, Mary Ann S. M.: 756
BUIE FAMILY (North Carolina): 3434
A BUILDER OF THE NEW SOUTH BEING THE STORY OF THE LIFE WORK OF DANIEL AUGUSTUS TOMPKINS by George Tayloe Winston: 5312
BUILDING AND LOAN ASSOCIATIONS:
  Georgia: 2010
  North Carolina: 3410, 4775
    New Bern: 3955
    Shelby: 1951
  Pennsylvania: 5312
BUILDING CONSTRUCTION:
  Georgia: 4988
  Maryland--Baltimore: 2352
  North Carolina: 1589, 4172
    University of North Carolina: 2399
  Pennsylvania: 3557
    Philadelphia: 3569
  South Carolina: 997
  Virginia: 2550, 3557
  Washington, D. C.: 1743
  West Virginia: 2397
BUILDING FUNDS:
  North Carolina: 4727
BUILDING MATERIALS:
  see also CEMENT; TABBY (Concrete)
  Prices:
    Georgia: 339
    Tennessee: 1531
BUILDING MATERIALS INDUSTRY:
  North Carolina: 4172
BUILDING MATERIALS TRADE: 4456
  New Hampshire: 1529
BUILDING STONE TRADE:
  Washington, D. C.: 5584
BUILDINGS: see BUDDHIST TEMPLES; CHURCHES--Church buildings; HISTORIC BUILDINGS; PALACES; PUBLIC BUILDINGS; PUBLIC SCHOOL BUILDINGS
BUIST, Henry: 757
BUIST FAMILY (South Carolina): 4584
BUKOVSKY, W.: 111
BULGARIA: 3912
  Social and political reform: 1014
BULL, John: 393
BULL, Melville: 3228
BULL, William (1683-1755): 758
BULL RUN, Virginia: see CIVIL WAR--CAMPAIGNS, BATTLES, AND MILITARY ACTIONS--Virginia--Manassas
BULLER, Sir Redvers Henry: 663

BULLET, PERCUSSION RIFLE: see PERCUSSION RIFLE BULLET
THE BULLETIN (International Typographical Union): 2771
BULLOCH, Archibald: 759
BULLOCH, Archibald S.: 759
BULLOCH, Laura J.: 3310
BULLOCH COUNTY, Georgia: 5586
  Land: 3663
  Plantations: 3663
  Slave trade: 4395
BULLOCK, A. S.: 4678
BULLOCK, Barsha: 760
BULLOCK, David: 4127
BULLOCK, E. C.: 1084
BULLOCK, Harriet Bailey: 1361
BULLOCK, John: 761
BULLOCK, John II: 761
BULLOCK, Judith (Watkins): 761
BULLOCK, Leonard Henley: 795
BULLOCK, Rebecca: 761
BULLOCK, Susan M. (Cobb): 761
BULLOCK, Thomas D.: 760
BULLOCK, Walter: 761
BULLOCK, William H.: 761
BULLOCK COUNTY, Alabama:
  Midway: 983
BULMER, Annie Cecelia: 487
BULWER, Henry L.: 3183
BULWER, William Henry Lytton Earle, Baron Dalling and Bulwer: 762
BULWER-LYTTON, Edward George Earle Lytton, First Baron Lytton: 737, 2146, 3722
BULWER-LYTTON, Edward Robert, First Earl of Lytton: 3238
BULWER-LYTTON, Rosina Doyle (Wheeler), Baroness Lytton: 2146
BUNCH, Robert: 4484
BUNCOMBE COUNTY, North Carolina: 699, 4417
  Cherokee Indians: 3176
  Public schools: 5603
  Teaching: 5603
  Cities and towns:
    Asheville: see ASHEVILLE, North Carolina
    Biltmore: 1001
    Enka: 5442
    Weaverville: 833
BUNKER, Chang: see CHANG AND ENG
BUNKER, Eng: see CHANG AND ENG
BUNKER HILL, Illinois: 1670
BUNKER HILL, Virginia: 4049
BUNKER HILL, West Virginia: 4893
BUNNELL, William H.: 3196
BUNTING, Jabez: 763
BUNTON, Mary Howell: 4101
BUNTYN, Elizabeth: 764
BUNTYN, Frank: 764
BUNTYN, Morgan: 764
BUNTYN FAMILY (Genealogy): 1424
BURBRIDGE, Stephen Gano: 765
BURCH, James Kerr: 661
BURDEN FAMILY (South Carolina--Genealogy): 1468
BURDETT, Sir Francis: 3658
BURDICK, Usher Lloyd: 766
BURDON, Rowland: 5616
BUREAU COUNTY, Illinois:
  Neponset: 5058
BUREAU OF NATIONAL AFFAIRS: 1193
BUREAU OF _____ : see (name of country or state)--Government agencies and officials--Bureau of _____
BURFORD, E. S.: 1181
BURGER, Nash Kerr: 2282
BURGES, Sir James Bland: 4230
BURGESS, Hiram: 767
BURGESS, John William: 5781
BURGHCLERE OF WALDEN, Herbert Coulstoun Gardner, First Baron: 1948
BURGHS: see BOROUGHS
BURGOYNE, John (1722-1792): 92
BURGOYNE, Sir John Fox (1782-1871): 2147
BURIAL LAWS--Great Britain: 118

BURIAL PLACES: see CATACOMBS; CEMETERIES; CIVIL WAR--BURIAL GROUNDS; TOMBS
BURIALS: see FUNERALS; PREMATURE BURIAL
BURIE, O. B.: 1227
BURK, John Daly: 2815
BURKE, Billie: 3797
BURKE, Caroline: 2040
BURKE, Edmund (1729-1797): 92, 2869
BURKE, John P.: 2040
BURKE, Martha J. (Trist): 768
BURKE, Thomas (1747-1783): 769, 3116
BURKE, Thomas T.: 770
BURKE FAMILY (North Carolina): 770
BURKE COUNTY, Georgia: 1696, 3711
  Plantation life: 5246
BURKE COUNTY, North Carolina: 1247, 2698, 5188
  Agriculture: 245
  Land deeds and indentures: 61
  Politics and government: 245
  Cities and towns:
    Morganton: 248, 838, 4192, 5310
      Churches: 2111
      Mental hospitals: 2890
      Municipal government: 3937
    Quaker Meadows: 3361
BURKETT, Charles William: 5457
BURKETT, H. L.: 771
BURKHEAD, Lingurn Skidmore: 772
BURKITTSVILLE, Maryland: 5722
BURKS MILL, Virginia: 5153
BURLEIGH, Charles Calistus: 5088
BÜRLING AND DIXON (firm): 4881
BURLINGAME, Anson: 196, 773, 5252
BURLINGAME, Edward Livermore: 2449
BURLINGTON, Iowa: 4431, 5561
BURLINGTON, New Jersey: 3610
  Personal Debts: 5520
  Legal affairs: 5520
BURLINGTON, North Carolina: 3001, 5506
  Hosiery--Dyeing: 3842
  Hosiery mills: 1353, 3595
  Textile industry: 2108
BURLINGTON, Vermont: 3143
BURLINGTON COUNTY, New Jersey: 1752
  Burlington: 3610, 5520
  Willingboro: 4094
BURLINGTON (FRONT STREET) CHURCH (North Carolina): 3646
BURLINGTON CIRCUIT, Methodist Churches: 3646
BURLINGTON DYEING AND FINISHING COMPANY, INC.: 3171
BURLINGTON INDUSTRIES: 3757, 4812
BURLINGTON MILLS: 3171
  Piedmont Heights Division: 5234
BURMA:
  British administration:
    Relations with Wa tribes: 4709
  British military activities: 3224
  Colonization: 217
  Description and travel:
    Shan States: 4709
  Military affairs: 3835
  Railroad construction: 4709
BURMAN, Balthasar: 3011
BURMESE WAR: 1650
BURMESE WAR (1824-1826): 485
  Conclusion: 4023
BURN, Richard: 346
BURN, Sir Richard (1871-1947): 774
BURNELL, Rosaltha: 1406
BURNES, John Elliot: 2149
BURNETT, Frances (Hodgson): 103
BURNHAM, Annie: 775
BURNHAM, Augusta A.: 776
BURNHAM, Elethine: 776
BURNHAM, H. B.: 777
"BURNELY HALL," County Norfolk, England: 2708
BURNS, Annie Walker: 2995
BURNS, Archibald W.: 778
BURNS, Otway: 3955
BURNS, Robert (1759-1796): 3611

BURNS, Walter Francis: 3955
BURNS FAMILY (West Virginia): 865
BURNSIDE, Ambrose Everett: 334, 3778, 4044, 4276, 4970, 5028
BURNSIDE'S BRIDGE, Antietam, Maryland: 5744
BURR, Aaron: 3800, 5229
  Trial: 3809
BURR, Adeline Ellery: 2161
BURR, Frank A.: 1357
BURR, James M.: 2161
BURR, Kate Ancrum: 5457
BURR, William Henry: 779
BURRARD, Harriet Sophia: 4557
BURRELL, Derrill: 4649
BURRINGTON, George: 780
BURROUGHS, Benjamin: 781
BURROUGHS, David: 782
BURROUGHS, John (Arkansas): 784
BURROUGHS, John (1837-1921): 783, 4073
BURROUGHS, John William: 785
BURROUGHS, Richard D.: 785
BURROUGHS, Valeria G.: 786
BURROUGHS, William Berrien: 787
BURROUGHS FAMILY (Georgia): 787, 2460
BURROUGHS FAMILY (North Carolina--Genealogy): 4078
BURROW, Elizabeth: 788
BURROW, Henry: 788
BURROWS, Anne: 4576
BURROWS, Frank: 790
BURROWS, H. Lansing: 789
BURROWS, James A.: 790
BURT, Dr._____(Mississippi): 3611
BURT, Armistead: 791, 4149, 4193, 4215, 4272, 4715, 4829
BURTON, A. M.: 792
BURTON, Andrew Joyner: 796
BURTON, Columbia Y.: 793
BURTON, Horace A.: 795
BURTON, Hutchins: 795
BURTON, James H.: 794
BURTON, John: 795
BURTON, Richard Eugene: 3797
BURTON, Robert (1747-1825): 795
BURTON, Robert Oswald (1811-1891): 796, 5457
BURTON, William (1789-1866): 4881
BURTZ, Joshua: 797
BURWELL, Henry: 799
BURWELL, Lewis: 798, 4344
BURWELL, Lewis A.: 799
BURWELL, Lucy (Cole): 799
BURWELL, Mary: 799
BURWELL, Spotswood: 799
BURWELL, William: 799
BURWELL, William M. (Virginia): 800
BURWELL FAMILY (Virginia): 99
BURWELL AND WHITE (firm): see WHITE AND BURWELL
BURWELL (BLAIR) (firm): 2360
"BURWOOD PARK," England: 1775
BUS LINES: see MOTOR BUS LINES
BUSBEE, Charles Manly: 5457
BUSBEE, F. H.: 4775
BUSBEE, Fabius Haywood: 5457
BUSBEE, Jacques: 5252
BUSBEE, Juliana: 5252
BUSBEY, William H.: 801
BUSH AND LOBDELL (firm): 3235
BUSH HILL, North Carolina: 1895, 2895
BUSH RIVER, South Carolina:
  Society of Friends: 3981
BUSHE, Charles Kendal: 4024
BUSHROD, Thomas: 5573
BUSHWACKERS: see GUERRILLAS
BUSHY FORK, North Carolina: 378
BUSIC'S STORE, Brandon, Mississippi: 802
BUSINESS ACCOUNTS:
  see also accounts of specific types of businesses, e.g. MERCANTILE ACCOUNTS; TANNERY ACCOUNTS
  Georgia: 148

BUSINESS ACCOUNTS (Continued):
  Maryland--West River: 4219
  Massachusetts: 148
  North Carolina: 148
    Fairfield: 921
  South Carolina: 653
  Virginia: 148, 2051
    Petersburg and Richmond: 5631
BUSINESS ACHIEVEMENT: see SUCCESS
BUSINESS ADVISORY COUNCIL: 4564
BUSINESS AFFAIRS:
  see also FOREIGN BUSINESS ENTERPRISES; INTERNATIONAL BUSINESS AFFAIRS; WOMEN IN BUSINESS
  Canada: 1211
  Connecticut:
    New Haven: 129
    South Norwalk: 688
  Georgia: 662, 759, 823, 2096, 2179, 2740, 2901, 3231, 3318
    Augusta: 5353
    Savannah: 5076, 5932
  Great Britain: 5598
    London: 229, 922, 5849
  Illinois: 1670
  Maryland: 260
    Baltimore: 3631, 5680, 5918
    Hagerstown: 136, 1958, 2283
    Prince Fredericktown: 4844
    Sharpsburg: 979
    Upper Marlboro: 1043
  Massachusetts--Boston: 1902
  Mississippi--Pontotoc: 5612
  Missouri: 2386
  Montana: 1211
  New Hampshire: 354
  New Jersey: 1446
  New York: 416, 1211, 4751, 4808
    New York: 731, 1673, 2250, 2687, 3709, 5298, 5546, 5612
    Rochester: 2436
    Saint Lawrence County: 5458
  North Carolina: 263, 484, 631, 668, 677, 796, 832, 838, 1108, 1277, 1538, 2113, 2298, 2469, 2572, 2808, 3070, 3091, 5367, 5596
    Anson County: 409
    Beaufort County: 5831
    Burke County: 1247
    Caldwell County: 1247
    Craven County: 1871
    Cunningham's Store: 1959
    Durham: 5923
    Durham County: 1256
    Elizabeth City: 423
    Enfield: 426
    Fairfield: 921
    Fayetteville: 2354, 3905
    Lexington: 2874
    Moore County: 5792
    Mount Gilead: 2730
    Orange County: 1255, 1256
    Ridgeway: 999, 2435
    Rowan County: 1237
    Thomasville: 2906
    Williamston: 131
    Wilmington: 5912
  Ohio: 1578, 2128
    Bucyrus: 3103
    Defiance: 4793
    Logan County: 5142
    Wooster: 3103
  Oregon--Roseburg: 3518
  Pennsylvania:
    Chambersburg: 5306
    Hollidaysburg: 421
    Philadelphia: 3909
    Richmond Furnace: 2033
    Towanda: 3372
  South Carolina: 842, 1127, 3231, 4896
    Abbeville District: 414
    Charleston: 2278, 3532, 4163, 5936
    Spartanburg: 5930
    Sumter County: 3676

BUSINESS AFFAIRS (Continued):
   Southern States: 1553
   Tennessee--Hendersonville: 5671
   Texas--Laredo: 3597
   United States: 4805
   Virginia: 331, 604, 753, 1115,
      1131, 1263, 1324, 1384, 1459,
      1578, 1591, 1701, 2439, 2659,
      2887, 3068, 3084, 3556, 4243,
      4244, 4735, 4766, 5031, 5147
      Albemarle County: 687
      Bedford: 1052, 2136
      Berryville: 2082
      Charles City County: 819
      Clear Brook: 2329
      Fluvanna County: 5106, 5839
      Frederickshall: 2363
      Halifax Court House: 1250
      Lexington: 1628
      Lynchburg: 1955
      Nelson County: 682
      Patrick Springs: 1410
      Pattonsburg: 2454
      Pittsylvania County: 1261, 5873
      Richmond: 4119, 4847
      Stevensburgh: 5113
   West Virginia:
      Jefferson County: 5265
BUSINESS AND PROFESSIONAL WOMEN'S
   CLUB, Richmond, Virginia: 5790
BUSINESS CLUBS:
   South Carolina--Columbia: 3421
BUSINESS CYCLES: see DEPRESSIONS;
   PANICS
BUSINESS DEPRESSIONS: see
   DEPRESSIONS; PANICS
BUSINESS EDUCATION:
   see also BUSINESS SCHOOLS
   Georgia--Atlanta: 4911
BUSINESS ENTERPRISES:
   Florida: 5291
   Tennessee--Knoxville: 5858
BUSINESS FAILURES:
   see also BANK FAILURES;
      BANKRUPTCY
   North Carolina: 4918
   South Carolina--Charleston: 5193
BUSINESS INSURANCE: see INSURANCE--
   Business
BUSINESS LICENSING--Maryland: 4886
BUSINESS SCHOOLS:
   see also BUSINESS EDUCATION
   Maryland: 643
   North Carolina--Durham: 3843
BUSINESSWOMEN: see WOMEN IN BUSINESS
BUTCHER, ____ (British politician):
   3046
BUTCHERS' ACCOUNTS:
   North Carolina: 3410
   Virginia--Leesburg: 4250
BUTE, Marchioness of: 2421
BUTE, John Stuart, Third Earl of:
   5330
BUTLER, Anne: 3567
BUTLER, Benjamin Franklin
   (1818-1893): 323, 803, 872, 1424,
   1938, 2816, 3741, 4970
BUTLER, Bion H.: 5457
BUTLER, Charles: 804
BUTLER, Edward George Washington:
   805
BUTLER, Francis Wilkinson Pickens:
   4453
BUTLER, Harriet M. (Fuller): 808
BUTLER, Isaac: 806
BUTLER, James: 1696
BUTLER, James Ramsay Montagu: 5590
BUTLER, Josiah: 354
BUTLER, Leland W.: 806
BUTLER, Louisa: 807
BUTLER, Lucy Maria: 3567
BUTLER, Marvin Benjamin: 808
BUTLER, Matthew Calbraith
   (1836-1909): 674, 1364, 2086,
   3418, 4453, 5299
BUTLER, Nicholas Murray: 809, 2224,
   4373
BUTLER, Pierce (1744-1822): 810, 3527

BUTLER, Pierce M. (1807-1867): 791
BUTLER, R. S.: 807
BUTLER, Robert: 811
BUTLER, Thomas: 806
BUTLER, William (Georgia): 812
BUTLER, Sir William Francis: 663
BUTLER, William Orlando (1791-1880):
   1308, 3325, 5974
BUTLER FAMILY (Georgia and Florida):
   807
BUTLER FAMILY (North Carolina): 804
BUTLER FAMILY (Virginia): 806
BUTLER COUNTY, Alabama: 1304
BUTLER COUNTY, Ohio--Hamilton: 4076
BUTNER, Albert I.: 813
BUTSCHER, William: 4948
BUTTERFIELD, Daniel: 3768
"THE BUTTERFLY'S COUSINS" by Amélie
   Rives: 4491
BUTTERWORTH, Hezekiah: 2449
BUTTON, Eliza: 814
BUTTS COUNTY, Georgia: 1731
   Indian Springs: 5465
      Baptist Church: 2757
   Jackson: 622, 3575
BUXTON, Noel Edward Noel-, First
   Baron Noel-Buxton:
   see NOEL-BUXTON, Noel Edward,
      First Baron Noel-Buxton
BUXTON, Sir Thomas Fowell, First
   Baronet: 815
BUXTON, England: 250
BUXTON, Maine: 1820
BY-PATHS, A COLLECTION OF OCCASIONAL
   WRITINGS OF WILLIAMSON W.
   FULLER: 1914
BYAM FAMILY (Genealogy): 1792
BYER'S VOLUNTEERS: 1189
BYHALIA, Mississippi: 2487, 5621
BYNG, George: 3658
BYNG, George Stevens, Second Earl of
   Strafford: 816
BYNNER, Harold Witter: 103
BYNUM, Barbara: 5457
BYNUM, Benjamin Franklin, Sr.: 817
BYNUM, Benjamin Franklin, Jr.: 817
BYNUM, Francis A.: 4902
BYNUM, Hampton: 817
BYNUM, Joseph Isaac, Sr.: 2655
BYNUM, Oakley H.: 2662
BYNUM, R. S.: 817
BYNUM, William Preston I (b. 1861):
   817
BYNUM, William Preston II: 817
BYNUM FAMILY (North Carolina): 817
   Genealogy: 4078
BYRD, Anna (Munford): 3809
BYRD (H. F.) AND T. B. BYRD
   INCORPORATED: 5779
BYRD, Harry Flood (1887-1966): 224,
   818, 879, 2082, 5779
BYRD, Richard Evelyn (1888-1957):
   818, 958
BYRD, Richard Willing: 4315
BYRD, T. B.: see H. F. BYRD AND
   T. B. BYRD INCORPORATED
BYRD, Ursula Anna (Munford): 3809
BYRD, William (1674-1744): 363, 819
BYRD FAMILY (Virginia--Genealogy):
   1842
BYRD ORCHARD CORPORATION: 5779
BYRNE, Edward: 4274
BYRNES, Arthur: 2983
BYRNES, James Francis: 2109, 3451,
   5930
BYRNES, William: 820
BYROADE, Henry A.: 83
BYRON, George Gordon Noël-, Sixth
   Baron Byron: 821, 1049, 2058,
   3887, 4770, 5856
BYRON, John: 3315

## C

C., J. W. F. (poet): 3892
C., M. (poet): 3892
C. A. DAVIES AND COMPANY: 1390
C. AND G. J. ANDERSON AND COMPANY: 122
C. ANDERSON AND BROTHER: 122
C. D. HINKS & CO.: 2797
C.I.O. NEWS (periodical): 1197
C.I.O. NEWS OF NORTH CAROLINA (periodical): 1202
C.I.O. ROUND-UP (periodical): 1195, 1202, 5234
C. L. LE BARON (law firm): 3008
C. SCHRACK AND COMPANY: 4699
C. W. MAURY AND COMPANY: 3587
CABANISS, Charles H.: 822
CABANISS, Elbridge G.: 823, 4415
CABANISS, H. H.: 823
CABANISS, J. W.: 823
CABANISS, William: 822, 2680
CABANISS FAMILY (Virginia): 822, 2927
CABARRUS FAMILY (North Carolina): 2121
CABARRUS COUNTY, North Carolina: 904, 2117, 2628
  Civil War: 1331
  Gold mines: 3391
  Temperance: 5582
  Cities and towns:
    Coddle Creek: 4311
    Concord: see CONCORD, North Carolina
    Georgeville: 4788
    Harris' Depot: 5582
    Mount Pleasant: 4164, 4891
    Phoenix Mines: 4670
CABE FAMILY (North Carolina--Genealogy): 4078
CABELL, George, Jr.: 824
CABELL, Henry Coalter: 824
CABELL, James Alston: 824
CABELL, James Branch (1879-1958): 2390
CABELL, James Lawrence (1813-1889): 58, 523, 824, 1185, 1476
CABELL, Jane (Alston): 824
CABELL, Joseph Carrington (1778-1856): 872, 2815, 4384
CABELL, Julian Mayo (b. 1860): 824
CABELL, Nicholas: 824
CABELL, William Daniel: 824
CABELL, William H. (1772-1853): 824
CABELL, William Lewis (1827-1911): 824
CABELL FAMILY (Virginia): 824, 4720, 5107
  Genealogy: 3809
CABINETMAKING--Pennsylvania: 744
CABLE, Eleazar: 825
CABLE, George Washington (1844-1925): 826, 1494, 2407
CABLE, Jacob: 2719
CABLES, Ships: see SHIPS' CABLES
CABLES, Submarine: see SUBMARINE CABLES
CABLES, Transatlantic: see TRANSATLANTIC CABLE

CADAVERS: see MEDICAL EDUCATION--Cadavers; SIAMESE TWINS--Cadavers
CADDELL, Artemus S.: 827
CADDELL, W. Waithman: 2097
CADDO INDIANS--Trade with whites: 4353
CADDO PARISH, Louisiana:
  Shreveport: 3275
    Confederate Army: 5257
    Confederate Navy: 1181
CADELL, Thomas (1742-1802): 828
CADELL, Thomas (1773-1836): 828
CADET POLYTECHNIC SOCIETY OF CAROLINA MILITARY INSTITUTE: 895
CADIZ, Spain: 5228
  Customs duties: 4978
  Mercantile accounts: 4978
  Shipping: 197
CADMAN, Charles R.: 829
CADMAN, S. Parkes: 3887
CADOGAN, Charles: 4625
CADWALADER, John: 830
CADWALADER, Priscilla Hunt: 3981
CAHABA, Alabama: 609, 1947
  Commission House: 5879
  Democrat (newspaper): 5937
  Schools: 5593
CAHABA MALE AND FEMALE ACADEMY (Alabama): 5593
CAHIERS LÉON BLOY: 555
CAIN, Emma L.: 831
CAIN, John M.: 832
CAIN, Patrick H.: 832
CAIN FAMILY (North Carolina): 832
CAIRNES, Frances: 99
CAIRNS, John S.: 833
CAIRNS, William B.: 102
CAIRO, Egypt: 41, 67, 5835
CAIRO, Illinois: 5017
CALAHALN, North Carolina: 122
CALAIS, Maine: 3813
CALCASIEU, Louisiana--Migration from: 5496
CALCASIEU PARISH, Louisiana:
  Timber frauds: 20
CALCRAFT, John: 92
CALCUTTA, India: 1675, 3011, 5063
  Art collectors and collecting: 1343
  British administration: 5038
  Trade: 4881
CALDER, Robert: 834
CALDER, William: 834
CALDERON, Felipe G.: 4511
CALDERÓN DE LA BARCA, Pedro: 2058
CALDWELL, Dr. ___: 1421
CALDWELL, Charles: 1585
CALDWELL, David Frank: 835, 5460
CALDWELL, Eliza F.: 836
CALDWELL, John: 837
CALDWELL, Joseph: 5457
CALDWELL, Polly Allen: 74
CALDWELL, Tod Robinson: 838, 1336, 5457
CALDWELL, W. S.: 839
CALDWELL FAMILY (Mississippi): 836
CALDWELL COUNTY, North Carolina: 1247, 1590, 3176
  Women in the Civil War: 4080
  Cities and towns:
    Gamewell: 3324
    Lenoir: 593, 5533
      Public schools: 3177
        Bands: 3178
    Little River: 614
    Justices of the peace: 5692
CALDWELL INSTITUTE, Greensboro, North Carolina: 5804
CALEDONIA, North Carolina: 1437, 3449
CALEDONIA, Virginia: 1587
CALHOUN, Anna Maria: 1101
CALHOUN, Catherine Ann: 840
CALHOUN, J. E.: 100
CALHOUN, James Edward: 841, 1101
CALHOUN (JOHN C.) MEMORIAL ASSOCIATION: 2449

CALHOUN, John Caldwell: 357, 791, 842, 2449, 2776, 2781, 3291, 3366, 3483, 4912, 5051, 5298, 5361, 5940
  Charges of embezzlement against: 3032
  Creek Indian treaty: 1848
  Death: 5470
  Dispute with Andrew Jackson: 5345
  Honors and awards: 2399
  Memorials: 2449, 4584
  Monument: 1929
  Personal finance: 2692
CALHOUN, John Ewing: 295
CALHOUN, William Lowndes (1837-1908): 843
CALHOUN, William Patrick (b. 1851): 844
CALHOUN FAMILY (South Carolina): 842, 1101
CALHOUN, Georgia--Civil War: 696
CALHOUN, Missouri:
  Mercantile and milling accounts: 5392
CALHOUN, South Carolina--Schools: 5082
CALHOUN COUNTY, Alabama:
  Jacksonville:
    Civil War: 1853
    Medical practice: 1053
CALHOUN COUNTY, Arkansas:
  Cotton growing: 4199
  Hampton: 4199
CALHOUN COUNTY, South Carolina:
  Saint Matthews: 1371
CALHOUN COUNTY, Texas:
  Port Lavaca: 1153
CALHOUN DEBATING SOCIETY: 845
CALHOUN MANUFACTURING COMPANY, Calhoun, Missouri: 5392
CALIFORNIA: 1283
  Admission as a free state: 3317
  Agriculture: 4834
  American poetry--San Francisco: 5081
  Annexation: 3415
  Carriage and buggy trade: 5623
  Description and travel: 611, 1115, 1355, 1370, 3051, 4353, 4834
  Earthquakes--San Francisco: 4743
  Economic conditions: 1058
  Education: 1758
  Exhibitions and fairs:
    Panama-Pacific International Exposition: 4042, 4511, 5252
  Gold mining: 611, 2092, 3253, 3750
  Gold Rush: 357, 1020, 2161, 2712, 4924, 5130
  Labor: 4834
  Land deeds and indentures--Redondo Beach: 4029
  Land settlement: 693
  Lead mining: 1984
  Literary interests: 5081
    see also CALIFORNIA--American poetry
  Livestock: 3255
  Marriage prospects: 2370
  Migration to: 593, 3026, 4616, 4911
  Mining:
    see also CALIFORNIA--Gold mining; CALIFORNIA--Lead mining; CALIFORNIA--Quartz mining
    Sierra County: 25
  Natural history: 4353
  Overland mail: 1548
  Pioneer life: 2808, 4353
  Politics and government: 2299
  Quartz mining: 1984
  Race relations:
    Chinese-American: 1058
    San Francisco: 1798, 4535
  Scales--San Francisco: 4119
  Slavery:
    Extension into California: 4732
  Social conditions: 1247
  Social life and customs: 2093
  Socialist Party: 4948

CALIFORNIA (Continued):
  Universities and colleges: see
    COLLEGE OF THE PACIFIC;
    UNIVERSITY OF CALIFORNIA, DAVIS
  Water prices: 4353
  Weather: 4353
CALIFORNIA, Pennsylvania--Militia:
  2989
"CALIFORNIA," South Carolina
  (plantation): 5645
CALLAN, Nicholas: 856
CALLAO, Peru: 3459, 5051
CALLAWAY, Eliza: 847
CALLAWAY, Paul Carrington: 4157
CALLAWAY COUNTY, Missouri:
  Millersburg: 5392
CALLIGRAPHY:
  France: 555
  North Carolina: 4862
CALLIS, John B.: 4105
CALLOWAY, Apsyllab A.: 3991
CALLOWAY, James: 34
CALONNE, Charles Alexandre de: 2126
CALVERT, George Henry: 2449
CALVERT, Philip Powell: 848
CALVERT COLLEGE, New Windsor,
  Maryland: 568
CALVERT COUNTY, Maryland:
  Prince Fredericktown: 4844
CALVIN, Samuel: 849
CALVINE COTTON MILLS, INC.: 5235
CALVINISTIC THEOLOGY: 2751
CALYPSO (blockade runner): 410
CAMAK, Georgia: 3134
CAMARGO, Mexico--Mexican War: 778
CAMBRELENG, Churchill Caldom: 850
CAMBRIDGE, George William Frederick
  Charles, Second Duke of: 663,
  3067, 4520
CAMBRIDGE, Richard Owen: 3128
CAMBRIDGE, England: 3189, 4821, 5156
  see also CAMBRIDGE UNIVERSITY
  Description: 5050
  Parliamentary elections: 5590
CAMBRIDGE, Massachusetts: 706, 1230,
  1668, 2224, 2400, 2522, 2526, 2607,
  3259, 3284, 3492, 5911
  see also HARVARD UNIVERSITY
  Civil War: 963
  Social life and customs: 5324
  Swindling: 609
  United States Nautical Almanac
    Office: 2469
CAMBRIDGE, South Carolina: 2636
CAMBRIDGE (ship): 3283
CAMBRIDGE MODERN HISTORY: 3851
THE CAMBRIDGE REVIEW: 5050
CAMBRIDGE UNIVERSITY, Cambridge,
  England: 1774, 2148, 2149, 3851,
  5736
  Faculty: 5156, 5727
  King's College: 5590
CAMBRIDGESHIRE, England:
  Cambridge: see CAMBRIDGE,
    England
CAMDEN, Gideon C.: 851
CAMDEN, William S.: 852
CAMDEN, Alabama:
  Economic conditions: 4184
CAMDEN, Arkansas: see CIVIL WAR--
  CAMPAIGNS, BATTLES, AND MILITARY
  ACTIONS--Arkansas--Camden
CAMDEN, New Jersey:
  Literary affairs: 2348
CAMDEN, South Carolina: 529, 566,
  881, 1012, 2940, 3360, 5864
  Agriculture: 5675
  Commodity prices: 5675
  Cotton factors' accounts: 965
  Law practice: 4269
  Presbyterian churches: 4642
  Weather: 5675
  Women's societies and clubs: 4642
CAMDEN AND CHARLESTON STEAMBOAT
  CO.: 853
CAMDEN CIRCUIT, Methodist Church:
  3646

CAMDEN COUNTY, Georgia: 1835
  Saint Mary's: 235, 1448
  Social life and customs: 2497
CAMDEN COUNTY, New Jersey:
  Camden--Literary affairs: 2348
  Gloucester: 1076
CAMDEN COUNTY, North Carolina:
  Civil War: 1181
CAMDEN DISTRICT, Methodist Church:
  3646
CAMELS HAIR TRADE: 323
CAMENGA, Diedrich F.: 854
CAMENGA, Kate: 854
CAMERON, Duncan: 3743
CAMERON, Simon: 3557, 4188
CAMERON, Thomas Fairfax, Sixth
  Baron Fairfax of: see FAIRFAX,
  Thomas, Sixth Baron Fairfax of
  Cameron
CAMERON (WILLIAM) & BROTHER
  (tobacco firm): 655
CAMERON & CAMERON (tobacco firm):
  655
CAMERON COUNTY, Texas:
  Brownsville: 4758
  Memorial service: 3741
CAMERONIAN PRESBYTERIANS: 867
CAMMACK, C. W.: 855
CAMMACK, Robert: 855
CAMP, Josephus: 1458
CAMP, Samuel: 856
CAMP FAMILY (South Carolina): 1988
CAMP BENJAMIN, Louisiana: 1181,
  4596
CAMP BURGWYN, North Carolina: 4849
CAMP CAROLINA, Virginia: 4528
CAMP CHASE, Columbus, Ohio: 1184
CAMP COMFORT, Virginia: 4440
CAMP COOK, Virginia: 1393
CAMP COOPER, Macon, Georgia: 731
CAMP CURRITUCK CANAL, North
  Carolina: 2549
CAMP DAVIS, Lynchburg, Virginia:
  2710
CAMP EAGLE PASS, Texas: 2112
CAMP EWELL, Virginia: 2305
CAMP FAIRFIELD, Virginia: 962
CAMP FOSTER, Georgia: 44
CAMP GORDON, Georgia: 5364
CAMP GOVERNOR MOORE, Mobile,
  Alabama: 3500
CAMP GREGG, Virginia: 5223
CAMP GRIFFIN, Virginia: 1885
CAMP HAGER, Virginia: 2187
CAMP HARRISON, Georgia: 5472
CAMP HOLMES, Raleigh, North
  Carolina: 3506
CAMP JOHN SHERMAN, Washington, D.C.:
  1286
CAMP LEJEUNE MARINE BASE, North
  Carolina: 325
CAMP LEVENTHROP, North Carolina: 860
CAMP LIFE: see as subheading under
  names of armies, e.g. CONFEDERATE
  STATES OF AMERICA--ARMY--Camp life
CAMP MACON, North Carolina: 420
CAMP MANDEVELLE, Louisiana: 1772
CAMP MEETINGS: 5716
  see also EVANGELISM; RELIGIOUS
  ASSEMBLY GROUNDS
  Church of the Brethren: 221
  Methodist:
    Georgia: 1231
    North Carolina: 5964
    South Carolina: 5965
    Virginia--Lexington: 5149
  Methodist Episcopal:
    North Carolina: 3581
  Presbyterian--Kentucky: 4387
  Subdivided by place:
    Kentucky: 1356
    Mississippi: 3611
    New York: 1908
    North Carolina: 122, 1738, 1908,
      4506, 4787
      Forsyth County: 2855
    South Carolina--York County: 4609
    Tennessee: 1933, 5977

CAMP MEETINGS:
  Subdivided by place (Continued):
    Virginia:
      Halifax County: 3377
      Winchester: 2080
CAMP MITCHELL, Virginia: 1066
CAMP MORGAN, Yorktown, Virginia:
  2500
CAMP MORTON, Bardstown, Kentucky:
  2858
CAMP OGLETHORPE, Macon, Georgia:
  2124
CAMP RANDOLPH, Decatur, Georgia: 731
CAMP SEMINARY, Virginia: 5939
CAMP TOPAIL, Winchester, Virginia:
  5280
CAMP WENHAM, Massachusetts: 1349
CAMP WHITING, North Carolina: 1109
CAMPAIGN FINANCES: see ELECTIONS--
  Great Britain--Campaign finances;
  PRESIDENTIAL ELECTIONS--1928--
  Congressional investigation into
  campaign finances
CAMPAIGNS (Military): see CAMPAIGNS,
  BATTLES, AND MILITARY ACTIONS
  under names of wars
CAMPBELL, A.: 872
CAMPBELL, Alexander (1788-1866):
  917, 4506
CAMPBELL, Anna B.: 857
CAMPBELL, Arthur (1742-1811): 872
CAMPBELL, Arthur (1791-1868): 872
CAMPBELL, Charles (1807-1876): 858
CAMPBELL, Colin, First Baron Clyde:
  859, 4549
CAMPBELL, Daniel K.: 860
CAMPBELL, David (1753-1832): 872
CAMPBELL, David (1779-1859): 872
CAMPBELL, David A.: 861
CAMPBELL, Frances: 233
CAMPBELL, Lord Frederick: 862
CAMPBELL, Sir George (1824-1892):
  1014
CAMPBELL, George Douglas, Eighth
  Duke of Argyll: 294, 863, 2149
CAMPBELL, Henry L.: 857
CAMPBELL, Sir Hugh Purves-Hume-,
  Seventh Baronet: 864
CAMPBELL, J. Mason: 2999
CAMPBELL, James (1792-1850, West
  Virginia): 865
CAMPBELL, James (1794-1848,
  Tennessee): 872
CAMPBELL, James B.: 2186
CAMPBELL, James Hepburn (1820-1895):
  4188
CAMPBELL, James Lyle (1810-1875):
  865
CAMPBELL, James MacNabb: 866
CAMPBELL, James W. (ca. 1840-1910):
  865
CAMPBELL, John (1766-1840,
  Scotland): 867
CAMPBELL, John (1789-186?, Virginia):
  872
CAMPBELL, John, First Baron
  Campbell: 5134
CAMPBELL, Sir John Nicholl Robert,
  Second Baronet: 868
CAMPBELL, Juliana Rebecca (Fuller)
  Hume: 864
CAMPBELL, Killis: 102
CAMPBELL, Maria Hamilton (Campbell):
  872
CAMPBELL, Mary Owen: 872
CAMPBELL, Robert: 869
CAMPBELL, Ronald George Elidor: 5876
CAMPBELL, Thomas: 870
CAMPBELL, Thomasina M. A. E.: 355
CAMPBELL, Virginia Tabitha Jane: 872
CAMPBELL, William Bowen (1807-1867):
  872
CAMPBELL, William P. A.: 872
CAMPBELL, Zoé Jane: 871
CAMPBELL FAMILY (Virginia): 872
CAMPBELL FAMILY (West Virginia): 865
CAMPBELL AND COMPANY: see PERKINS,
  CAMPBELL AND COMPANY

683

CAMPBELL AND HOGG (firm): 2585
CAMPBELL-BANNERMAN, Sir Henry: 663, 3980, 5164
CAMPBELL COLLEGE, Buies Creek, North Carolina: 3538
CAMPBELL COUNTY, Georgia: see FULTON COUNTY, Georgia
CAMPBELL COUNTY, Virginia: 2510, 2966, 5513
  Free Negroes: 5482
  Iron foundries: 558
  Legal affairs: 4487
  Tobacco planting: 1059
  Weather: 4043
  Cities and towns:
    Lynchburg: see LYNCHBURG, Virginia
    New London:
      Farming: 2369
      Merchants: 2633
      Schools: 3868
    Rustburg: 2799
      Free Negroes: 5482
CAMPBELLITE CHURCH: see DISCIPLES OF CHRIST
CAMPBELL'S LINE (Treaty line): 2486
CAMPBELLTON, Georgia: 2671, 5676
"CAMPBELLTOWN," Virginia: 5577
CAMPILLO Y COSIO, José del: 873
CAMPING:
  Scotland: 2103
  Yellowstone National Park: 3424
CAMPOS, Brazil: 1644
CAMPS: see names of individual camps, and Camps as subheading under names of armies
CAMPS (Ancient)--Great Britain: 3895
CANAAN, Connecticut: 2039
CANADA: 1147
  Aluminum industry: 96
  American Revolution: see AMERICAN REVOLUTION
  Army--Army life: 4354
  Baptist churches--Negroes: 176
  British administration: 1260, 1632
    see also GREAT BRITAIN-- COLONIAL POLICY AND ADMINISTRATION--Canada
  Business affairs: 1211
  Church of England--Quebec: 3911
  Churches--Quebec: 3911
  Confederate emigrants: 2366
  Conservative Party: 896
  Corruption in politics: 896
  Currency: 1339
  Defense: 1599
  Description and travel: 2366, 3087, 3485, 4175, 4567
  Diseases--Smallpox: 4175
  Economic conditions: 4567
  Elections: 896, 4567
    see also CANADA--Parliamentary elections
  Electric power industry: 96
  Finance: 1941
    see also CANADA--Personal finance; CANADA--Public finance
  Folklore: 691
  Foreign trade--Jamaica: 1792
  Fugitive slaves: 3255, 4387, 5736
  Governors: 1756
  Hunting: 4175
  Hydro-electric power plants: 96
  Insurance companies: 2013
  Land purchases and sales:
    Halifax County: 3381
  Land settlement--Western Canada: 2708
  Loyalist refugees: 1890
  Migration to--From Great Britain: 5726
  Military inspection tour (1825): 4934
  Naval commission: 342

CANADA (Continued):
  Parliamentary elections: 3949
  Patent laws and legislation: 3637
  Personal finance:
    Prince Edward Island: 1756
  Politics and government: 1260, 3949, 4567
    see also CANADA--Elections
  Privy Councillor: 4567
  Public finance: 4567
  Railroads: 1211, 4567
  Ranching: 4175
  Riots--Quebec: 4567
  Silver mining: 4743
  Sports: 4175
  Territorial waters:
    Fishing rights: 4567
  Tobacco trade: 3179
  Universities and colleges: see ARCADIA UNIVERSITY
CANADAY, INC.: see CHESHIRE, SULLIVAN & CANADAY, INC.
CANADIAN PACIFIC RAILWAY: 4567
CANAL-BOATS:
  Cargo--Maryland: 1008
  Virginia: 4504
CANAL DOVER, Ohio: 4716
CANALS:
  see also INLET WATERWAY; INTRACOASTAL WATERWAY; INTEROCEANIC CANALS; and names of specific canals
  Business affairs--Maryland: 1008
  Construction: 3145
    Costs: 1007
    Delaware: 5686
    Pennsylvania: 5686
    Potomac River: 4598
    South Carolina: 4218
    Virginia: 3809
  Surveys:
    Maryland: 4221
    Mexico: 5772
    Virginia: 4879
  Subdivided by place:
    Georgia: 3417
    Great Britain: 2148
    Massachusetts: 1433
    Middle West: 2755
    New Jersey: 730
    New York: 4597
    North Carolina: 3415, 4858, 5696
      Wages of laborers: 1120
    Ohio: 2591
    Pennsylvania: 421, 849, 1433, 4188
    South Carolina: 4218
    Texas: 5613
    Virginia: 3574
      Norfolk: 5696
CANALS (Proposed):
  Alabama (Atlantic-Mississippi Canal): 2125
  Florida: 1403
  Great Britain: 5331
  Nicaragua: 5051
  Virginia: 322
CANALS AND TURNPIKE ROADS: 1930
CANADAIGUA, New York: 2193, 2250, 2587, 2690
CANAVERAL, Florida--Shore protection: 2387
CANDAMO, Pedro: 4155
CANDELABRA--Maryland: 1245
CANDLE TRADE: see TALLOW TRADE
CANDLEMAKING (Craft): 4616
CANDLER, Allen Daniel: 3905
CANDLER, Warren A.: 879
CANDLER, William Beall: 874
CANDOR, New York: 4538
CANDY, Charles: 1505
CANE CREEK, North Carolina: 875, 2618, 4458
CANE CREEK FACTORY (Cotton mill): 875
CANE REED TRADE:
  United States to Great Britain: 3230

CANFIELD, Dorothea Frances: 4290
CANNADY, Duncan S.: 876
CANNERIES: see SALMON CANNING INDUSTRY
CANNERY WORKERS: see UNITED CANNERY, AGRICULTURE, PACKING AND ALLIED WORKERS OF AMERICA
CANNING, Charles John, First Earl Canning: 877, 4097, 4660, 5327
CANNING, George (1770-1827): 258, 878, 2835, 2836
CANNING, Stratford, First Viscount Stratford de Redcliffe: 1755, 3183
CANNING AND PRESERVING: 5955
CANNON, Henry G.: 3674
CANNON, James (1864-1944): 879, 5035
CANNON, James William: 4918
CANNON, Newton: 872
CANNON MILLS COMPANY: 1195
CANON LAW: 201
CANTA, Peru: 951
CANTATAS: 3092
CANTERBURY, Archbishop of: see names of specific archbishops
CANTERBURY, Kent, England: 1765
CANTERBURY CLUB, Durham, North Carolina: 880
CANTEY, John: 881
CANTON, China: 258, 4054
  British bombardment of (1857): 2149
  East India Company: 3315
  Missions and missionaries: 1940
  Viceroy: 3315
  War (1857): 598
CANTON, Georgia: 700
CANTON, Mississippi: 5933
CANTON FALLS PLANK ROAD: see HEUVELTON AND CANTON FALLS PLANK ROAD
CANTRELL, Edward: 1357
CANTRY, Charles: 4624
CANTWELL, John Lucas: 1899
CAPE CHARLES, Virginia:
  Agriculture: 660
CAPE COLONY: 1599
  see also SOUTH AFRICA
  British administration: 3315
  Economic conditions: 345
    Statistics: 41
  Migration to: 3067
  Missions and missionaries: 41
  Politics and government: 345
  Sanitation--Cape Town: 3315
CAPE FEAR AND YADKIN VALLEY RAILWAY COMPANY: 3221
CAPE FEAR ASSOCIATION, Disciples of Christ: 5554
CAPE FEAR BAPTIST ASSOCIATION: 320
CAPE FEAR RIVER (North Carolina):
  Civil War--Attack on Fort Fisher: 81
  Intracoastal waterway: 2774
  Navigation: 3922
CAPE HATTERAS, North Carolina:
  Civil War: see CIVIL WAR-- CAMPAIGNS, BATTLES, AND MILITARY ACTIONS--North Carolina--Cape Hatteras
  Hurricanes: 3264
  Storms: 5955
CAPE HORN--Voyages around: 411, 4881
CAPE OF GOOD HOPE: see CAPE COLONY
CAPE TOWN, South Africa:
  Description: 2963, 4017
  Sanitation: 3315
CAPE VERDE ISLANDS:
  Customs duties: 3118
  Navigational charts to: 4537
CAPELL, George, Fifth Earl of Essex: 1632
CAPEN, Henry: 882
CAPEN, Nahum: 5853
CAPERS, Ellison: 883
CAPERTON, Harriette: 884
CAPITAL PUNISHMENT: 2848
  see also EXECUTIONS

CAPITAL PUNISHMENT (Continued):
  Great Britain: 649, 2198, 4605, 5726
  North Carolina: 5768
CAPITALISM: 4614
CAPITATION RATE: see POLL TAX
CAPITOLS: see UNITED STATES CAPITOL BUILDING; VIRGINIA--State Capitol Building
CAPON BRIDGE, West Virginia: 1238, 3721
  Mercantile accounts: 2652
CAPOTE, Truman: 902
CAPPOCK, James: 5026
A CAPTAIN OF INDUSTRY by Upton Beall Sinclair: 4837
CARACAS, Venezuela: 23
  Race identity: 4155
  Railroads and telegraph: 4895
CARDADOC, Sir John Francis: 2266, 2321
CARALEIGH PHOSPHATE AND FERTILIZER WORKS: 960
CARBONDALE, Illinois: 1631
CARDS: 1100, 3451
  see also GREETING CARDS; and Cards as subheadings under specific holidays
  Georgia: 1435
CARDWELL, Edward, First Viscount Cardwell: 886, 1110
CAREERS: see OCCUPATIONS
CAREW, Sir Benjamin Hallowell: 887
CAREW, Eugenia (Ronan): 4554
CAREW, Sir Reginald Pole-: 888
CAREY, Henry Charles: 889, 5630
CAREY, Mathew (1760-1839): 872, 890, 1484, 5630
CARGILL, Oscar: 102
CARGO SHIPS: see
CARHAMPTON, Simon Luttrell, First Earl: 5330
CARHART, Joseph: 648
CARIBBEAN SEA:
  British naval cruises: 2754
  Spanish seizure of vessels and cargoes: 3109
  United States naval operations: Civil War: 3983
  World War I: 116
CARICATURES: see CARTOONS AND CARTOONISTS
CARITATE, Cebrian de: 4980
CARLESBAD, Czechoslovakia: 908
CARLETON, Maria Georgiana: 5872
CARLILE, John Snyder: 5092
CARLIN, Charles C.: 879
CARLIN, William P.: 5695
CARLINGFORD, Chichester Samuel Parkinson Fortescue, First Baron: 3138
CARLISLE, George Howard, Sixth Earl of: 5, 1648
CARLISLE, James Mandeville: 891
CARLISLE, Nicholas: 957
CARLISLE, Thomas Mandeville: 263
CARLISLE, Pennsylvania: 1332
  see also DICKINSON COLLEGE
  Civil War: 1740
  Cavalry training barracks: 5858
  Description: 568
CARLIST WAR (1833-1840): 1875, 3659, 4982
  American neutrality: 4982
  British soldiers of fortune: 1504
CARLOS II, King of Spain: 4155
CARLOS III, King of Spain: 4155, 5532
CARLOS IV, King of Spain: 2055
CARLOTA, Empress of Mexico: 2085
CARLYLE, John Bethune: 5457
CARLYLE, Joseph Dacre: 2146
CARLYLE, Thomas (1795-1881): 892, 3684, 4600
CARMAN, John: 2019
CARMARTHEN, Wales: 3950
CARMARTHENSHIRE, Wales:
  Carmarthen: 3950

CARMARTHENSHIRE ANTIQUARIAN SOCIETY: 250
CARMEL, West Virginia: 5820
CARMICHAEL, Dr. _____ (Ammunition manufacturer): 2696
CARMICHAEL, Sir James Morse, Third Baronet: 4934
CARMICHAEL, Sir James Robert, Second Baronet: 4934
CARMICHAEL, Margaret Caroline (Stockton): 893
CARMICHAEL, William W.: 893
CARMICHAEL-SMYTH, David: see SMYTH, David Carmichael-
CARMICHAEL-SMYTH, Harriet (Morse): see SMYTH, Harriet (Morse) Carmichael-
CARMICHAEL-SMYTH, Sir James, First Baronet: see SMYTH, Sir James Carmichael-, First Baronet
CARMICHAEL-SMYTH, Sir Robert: see SMYTH, Sir Robert Carmichael-
CARNES, Thomas Petters: 894, 2931
CARNESVILLE, Georgia: 3782
CARNEVALI, Emanuel: 2398
CARNFORTH, England: 583
CAROLINA BROWNSTONE COMPANY, Raleigh, North Carolina: 2553
CAROLINA CIO BULLETIN (periodical): 1202
CAROLINA CITY, North Carolina:
  Civil War: 1845
CAROLINA FEMALE COLLEGE, North Carolina: 4052
  Trustees: 4918
CAROLINA LODGE NO. 141 (Masons), Ansonville, North Carolina: 4918
CAROLINA MILITARY INSTITUTE, Charlotte, North Carolina: 895
CAROLINA PAPER PULP COMPANY: 3955
CAROLINA PROVINCE:
  Church and state: 202
  Description and travel: 202
  General Court: 3930
  Germans and French in: 202
  Indians: 202
  Land and living conditions: 202
  Politics and government: 202, 780
  Trade and commerce: 780
CAROLINA REAL ESTATE TRUST COMPANY: 3447
CAROLINA REMEDIES COMPANY (South Carolina): 4918
CAROLINA TRUCKING DEVELOPMENT COMPANY (North Carolina): 3447
CAROLINE, Queen of England: 306, 650
CAROLINE AMELIA ELIZABETH, Queen, Consort of George IV, King of Great Britain: 2836, 4137
CAROLINE, U.S.S.: 4616
CAROLINE COUNTY, Maryland:
  Denton: 1329
  Hillsboro: 5328
CAROLINE COUNTY, Virginia: 806, 5203
  Civil War: 2090
  Legal affairs: 4589
  Schools and teaching: 4698
  Wills: 1022
  Cities and towns:
    Bowling Green: 2637
    Guiney's Station: 4589
    Port Royal: 940
    Ruther Glen: 3719
CARON, Sir Joseph Philippe René Adolphe: 896
CAROTHERS COAL COMPANY: 897
CAROW, Edith Kermit: 1424
CARPENTER, Esther Bernon: 2449
CARPENTER, Mary: 1087, 2148
CARPENTER FAMILY (Genealogy): 1670
CARPENTERS: see UNITED BROTHERHOOD OF CARPENTERS AND JOINERS OF AMERICA
CARPENTERS' ACCOUNTS:
  Virginia--Aldie: 3529

CARPENTRY:
  Massachusetts--Milford: 3328
CARPETBAGGERS:
  Georgia: 2407
  Virginia: 2089
CARPETS:
  Sale and distribution: Louisiana--New Orleans: 679
  Silk--Great Britain: 5553
CARR, Francis Edward Garland: 523
CARR, Julian Shakespeare: 1584, 2400, 3762, 3763, 4956, 5732
CARR, Maria: 899
CARR, Mary M.: 900
CARR, Obed William: 901
CARR, Paddy: 5480
CARR, Thomas B.: 1899
CARR, Virginia Spencer: 902
CARR CHURCH (Methodist, North Carolina): 3646
CARRAWAY, Snoad B.: 903
CARRBORO, North Carolina:
  Hosiery mills: 1612
CARRIAGE AND BUGGY MAKING:
  see also WAGONMAKING
  Connecticut: 379
  North Carolina: 3317, 3403
  Virginia--Cumberland County: 531
CARRIAGE AND BUGGY REPAIR:
  North Carolina: 4918
  Wadesboro: 1897
CARRIAGE AND BUGGY TRADE: 3572
  Alabama: 5623
  California: 5623
  Florida: 5623
  Georgia: 5623
  Kentucky: 5623
  North Carolina: 4540, 4918
  South Carolina: 3801
  Tennessee: 5623
  Texas: 5623
CARRIAGES AND BUGGIES:
  see also as subheading under TRAVEL
  Georgia--Forsyth County: 5260
  Maryland--Prices: 2217
  Virginia: 4616
CARRICK'S FORD, Virginia: see CIVIL WAR--CAMPAIGNS, BATTLES, AND MILITARY ACTIONS--Virginia--Carrick's Ford
CARRIERS' ADDRESSES: see NEWSPAPERS--Carriers' addresses
CARRIGAN, Andrew Noel: 904
CARRIGAN, Catherine: 904
CARRIGAN, Charles Wesley: 4188
CARRIGAN, Cornelia: 904
CARRIGAN, James (1788-1843): 904
CARRIGAN, John Warren: 904
CARRIGAN, Margaret Rebecca: 904
CARRIGAN, Martha Matilda: 904
CARRIGAN, Mary: 904
CARRIGAN, Nancy Elizabeth: 904
CARRIGAN, Samuel K.: 904
CARRIGAN, Sarah: 904
CARRIGAN, William Adams: 904
CARRILLO DE ALBORNOZ, José Duque de Montemar: 873
CARRINGTON, Betsy (Ambler): 99
CARRINGTON, Isaac Howell: 905
CARRINGTON, Mary Coles: 905
CARRINGTON, Robert Smith, First Baron: 3883, 4230
CARRINGTON, Seddon: 905
CARRINGTON, William A.: 906
CARRINGTON, William Fontaine: 907
CARRISON, H. G.: 2940
CARRO, Jean de: 908
CARROL, Charles: 5004
CARROL FAMILY (Georgia): 2493
CARROLL, Charles (1737-1832): 917, 3631
CARROLL, Charles (1801-1862): 909
CARROLL, Sydney: 2146
CARROLL, Thomas: 910
CARROLL, William Waring: 4068
CARROLL COUNTY, Georgia:
  Villa Rica: 874

685

CARROLL COUNTY, Maryland:
    Avondale: 3998
    Westminster: 2484, 3326, 3565
CARROLL, HOYT AND COMPANY, New
    Orleans, Louisiana: 2856
CARROLLTON, Alabama: 1145
CARROLLTON MISSION (Methodist Church,
    Georgia): 3646
CARROW, Samuel T.: 911
CARRUTH, Fred Hayden: 2449
CARSON, Alexander: 912
CARSON, Christopher: 5130
CARSON, James H.: 913, 3255
CARSON, Kit: see CARSON,
    Christopher
CARSON, R. H.: 1856
CARSON, Samuel Price (b. 1797): 5457
CARSTARPHEN, William H.: 914
CARSTARPHEN, William Turner: 4586
CARTAGENA, Colombia: 198
CARTER, _____ (Virginia man):
    5203
CARTER, Benjamin (1792-1865): 4269
CARTER, Benjamin Franklin: 4269
CARTER, Cynthia (Rivers): 4269
CARTER, David M. (d. 1879): 4858
CARTER, Farish: 2216
CARTER, Frances: 4858
CARTER, James P.: 919
CARTER, Jedediah: 915
CARTER, John Conyers: 4269
CARTER, Mary P.: 2728
CARTER, Milton: 916
CARTER, Robert (1728-1804): 917
CARTER, Robert W.: 3193
CARTER, Robert Wormeley: 918
CARTER, Sue (Roy): 4616
CARTER, Susan: 915
CARTER, Vallie Burgess: 919
CARTER, William (Ohio): 920
CARTER, William S. (North Carolina):
    921
CARTER FAMILY (North Carolina): 4269
CARTER FAMILY (Virginia): 919
CARTER COUNTY, Oklahoma:
    Ardmore: 3248
CARTER ROPE COMPANY: see TUCKER &
    CARTER ROPE COMPANY
CARTERET COUNTY, North Carolina:
    2491
    Methodist Episcopal Church, South:
    1096
    Cities and towns:
        Beaufort: see BEAUFORT, North
            Carolina
        Hollywood: 3960
CARTERSVILLE, Georgia: 2365
CARTERSVILLE, Virginia: 693
    Banks and banking: 5035
CARTHAGE, Missouri: 2384
CARTHAGE, North Carolina: 5138
CARTHAGE, Ohio: 4477
CARTHAGE, Tennessee: 872
CARTHAGE COLLEGE, Chicago, Illinois:
    1768
CARTHAGENA EXPEDITION: 1068
CARTOONS AND CARTOONISTS: 552
    see also DRAWINGS, American
    English literature: 2146
    Great Britain: 4605
    North Carolina--Duke University:
        3359
CARTRIDGE CLIPS: 3228
CARTWRIGHT, George: 4171
CARTWRIGHT, John (1740-1824): 922,
    3183
CARTWRIGHT FAMILY (Great Britain):
    922
CARUTHERS, Eli Washington: 923
CARUTHERS, William Alexander: 924
CARVALLO, Paul Alonso: 4155
CARVER, George Washington: 925
CARY, Alice: 926
CARY, Constance: 1424
CARY, Henry, Eighth Viscount
    Falkland: 2133

CARY, Henry Francis (1722-1844):
    4543, 4600
CARY, Lucia: 2133
CARY, Monimia Fairfax: 927
CARY, North Carolina: 928
CARY CIRCUIT, Methodist Church: 3646
CARY CREDIT UNION BANK, Cary, North
    Carolina: 928
CARY REBELLION: 4232
CARY SCHOOL (North Carolina): 527
CASE, A. C.: 4188
CASE, Alexander T.: 54
CASE, Samuel F.: 929
CASEY, M. B.: 930
CASEY, Silas (1807-1882): 931, 5543
CASH, John C.: 4613
CASH, N. B.: 5951
CASH FAMILY (North Carolina): 2808
CASS, Lewis (1782-1866): 581, 858,
    932, 1333, 4193, 5499, 5528, 5974
CASS STATION, Georgia: 5865
CASSARD, Paul: 933
CASSELL AND COMPANY: 3503
CASSVILLE, Georgia: 3081
CASSVILLE, Missouri: 1548
CASTALIAN SPRINGS, Tennessee:
    Plantations: 5935
CASTILE, Spain: 4980
"CASTILIANS IN THE LAND OF THE
    FLOWERS" by Benson John Lossing:
    3269
CASTILLA, Ramón: 4155
CASTINE, Maine:
    Coastwise shipping: 5860
CASTLE FAMILY (West Virginia): 968
CASTLE HAYNE VINEYARD COMPANY
    PLANTATION: 2085
"CASTLE HILL," Virginia: 4490
CASTLE PINCKNEY, Charleston, South
    Carolina: 1184
CASTLEMAN'S FERRY, Virginia: 3668
CASTLEREAGH, Robert Stewart,
    Viscount [Castlereagh] and Second
    Marquis of Londonderry: 2149,
    5071, 5637
CASTOR OIL: 2636
CASUALTIES: see AMERICAN
    REVOLUTION--Casualties; and as
    subheading under names of armies
CASWELL, Martin: 934
CASWELL, Richard (1729-1789): 935,
    1899, 4746
CASWELL CIRCUIT, Methodist Church:
    3646
CASWELL COUNTY, North Carolina: 685,
    2391, 2427
    Arithmetic exercise books: 208, 3576
    Baptist churches: 4849
    Crops: 657
    Description and travel: 2248
    Farming: 5243
    Kick and Stevens affair: 2475
    Cities and towns:
        Leasburg: 3544, 4344
        Milton: 5155, 5815, 5843
            Banks and banking: 310
            Flour mills: 5824
        Red House: 2820
        Stony Creek: 4223
        Yanceyville: 2474, 2638, 4284,
            4506, 5243
"THE CAT THAT CAME TO CLEAR SPRINGS":
    5825
CATACOMBS: 2148
CATALOGUE AND PRICE LIST OF 1885
    (Methodist Publishing House): 3646
CATAWBA, North Carolina: 2088
    Cotton mills: 3718
    Sawmills: 1658
CATAWBA COUNTY, North Carolina: 534,
    1896, 2957, 3807, 5713
    Arithmetic exercise books: 208
    Courts: 5745
    Farming: 5745
    Methodist Episcopal Church, South:
        5745
    Public schools: 4532

CATAWBA COUNTY, North Carolina
    (Continued):
    Sawmill accounts: 5705
    Schoolbook: 1085
    Sunday schools: 5745
    Teachers' records: 3923
    Cities and towns:
        Catawba: see CATAWBA, North
            Carolina
        Cline's Township: 4532
        Edith: 5745
        Flint Rock: 5890
        Hickory: 4161
            Furniture industry: 3831
            Schools: 3043
        Jacob's Fork: 5705
        Newton: 2024
            Merchants: 9, 138
        Sherrill's Ford: 1806
CATAWBA DISTRICT, Methodist Church:
    3646
CATAWBA INDIANS:
    Schools: 1923
    South Carolina: 3356
CATAWBA POST OFFICE, Virginia:
    Mercantile accounts: 5827
CATAWBA RIVER (North Carolina):
    American Revolution: 3361
    Water rights: 4100
CATAWBA SPRINGS, North Carolina:
    Description: 2636
    Iron works (Map): 529
"CÁTEDRAS Y CLAUSTROS": 3650
CATHCART, Charles, Ninth Baron
    Cathcart: 5540
CATHCART, John H.: 936
CATHEDRALS--Great Britain: 5457
CATHER, Willa Sibert: 4290
CATHERINE, Joseph S.: 1505
CATHERINE LAKE, North Carolina: 1580
    Naval stores trade: 5910
    Shipping: 5910
CATES FAMILY (North Carolina--
    Genealogy): 5506
CATHOLIC APOSTOLIC CHURCH: 3715
CATHOLIC CHURCH: 937, 5166, 5468,
    5726
    see also JANSENISM
    Apostolic succession: 5468
    Artisans' organizations: 885
    Bishops--Peru: 4155
    Church buildings--Georgia: 938
    Congregazione Dell' Immunità
        Ecclesiastica: 939
    Conversion:
        Maryland: 2692
        North Carolina--Edenton: 1376
        Pennsylvania: 4881
    Dioceses--France: 5323
    Discipline--Italy: 2015
    Doctrine: 5317
    Finance--Georgia: 938
    Liturgy and ritual: 4864
    Monasteries: see MONASTERIES
    Negroes--South Carolina: 249
    Property:
        Peru: 4155
        Philippine Islands: 5419
    Reform: 5317
    Relations with Protestants: 3899
        Great Britain: see CATHOLIC
            EMANCIPATION--Great Britain
        Ireland: 3349
            see also CATHOLIC
                EMANCIPATION--Ireland
        Netherlands: 3989
        United States: see CIVIL WAR--
            CATHOLICS
    Religious orders: see
        CONFRATERNITIES; RELIGIOUS
        ORDERS
    Societies: 1952
        see also names of specific
            societies
    Subdivided by place:
        Great Britain: 2148

CATHOLIC CHURCH:
  Subdivided by place:
    Great Britain (Continued):
      see also CHURCH AND STATE IN
        GREAT BRITAIN; GREAT
        BRITAIN--Army--Education of
        Catholic dependents;
        CATHOLIC EMANCIPATION--
        Great Britain
    Ireland: 5726
      see also CATHOLIC
        EMANCIPATION--Ireland
    Maryland: see CIVIL WAR--
      CATHOLICS--Maryland
    Pennsylvania--Sinking Valley:
      3424
    Peru: 4155
    Philippine Islands: 4511
    Virginia: 2881, 3243
CATHOLIC CHURCH AND POLITICS: 3840
CATHOLIC CHURCH OF THE HOLY TRINITY
  OF AUGUSTA, Georgia: 938
CATHOLIC EMANCIPATION: 4605
  see also POLITICAL DISABILITIES
  Great Britain: 370, 535, 1775,
    2836, 3226, 4024, 4913, 5025,
    5639, 5726
  Ireland: 1598, 3883
CATHOLIC QUESTION: see CATHOLIC
  EMANCIPATION
CATHOLIC SCHOOLS: see SCHOOLS--
  Church schools--Catholic
CATHOLICS: see CATHOLIC CHURCH
CATLETT, George Washington: 940
CATLIN, Henry: 941
CATO, Marcus Porcius, of Utica:
  2880
CATO FAMILY (Virginia--Genealogy):
  1842
CATT, Carrie (Lane) Chapman: 942,
  5110
CATTLE: 43
  see also CIVIL WAR--CONFISCATED
    PROPERTY--Cattle
  Diseases: 3176
    Bechuanaland: 4514
  Estrays:
    Illinois: 1723
    Mississippi: 1722
  Prices--Missouri: 3540
  Quarantine: see LIVESTOCK
    QUARANTINE
  Trade: see CATTLE TRADE
  Subdivided by place:
    Georgia--Forsyth County: 5260
    Kentucky: 1086
    Missouri: 865
    South Carolina: 2670
CATTLE MARKS (Register)--North
  Carolina: 5777
CATTLE RAISING: 3424
  see also COWBOYS
  Missouri: 3540
  Texas--New Washington: 3772
  Virginia: 4615
CATTLE RANCHES--Montana: 3424
CATTLE TRADE: 5822
  Florida--Milton: 3008
  Jamaica: 301
  Virginia: 3809, 5377
  Washington, D.C.: 4091
CAUDLE, Mrs. J. H.: 3223
CAUDY, James: 3721
CAUGHERTY, Ireland: 3349
CAUGHMAN, Isaiah: 1877
CAULLI, Louis: 4596
CAUSTEN, James H.: 943
CAVALLIER, Peter: 2148
CAVE SPRINGS GUARDS: 3101
CAVENDISH, Elizabeth (Harvey) Foster,
  Duchess of Devonshire: 945
CAVENDISH, Georgiana (Spencer),
  Duchess of Devonshire: 945
CAVENDISH, Henrietta Elizabeth:
  1875
CAVENDISH, Spencer Compton, Eighth
  Duke of Devonshire: 294, 944,
  1815, 2149, 2962

CAVENDISH, William, Fifth Duke of
  Devonshire: 945
CAVENDISH, William, Seventh Duke
  of Devonshire: 2149
CAVENDISH, William George Spencer,
  Sixth Duke of Devonshire: 4605
CAVENDISH-BENTINCK, William Henry:
  see BENTINCK, William Henry
  Cavendish-
CAVERSHAM, England: 1320
CAVIEDES, Juan del Valle y: see
  VALLE Y CAVIEDES, Juan del
CAVIL-CADE: 1196
CAVIN FAMILY (Southern States): 4083
CAWEIN, Madison Julius: 946
CAYUGA COUNTY, New York:
  Auburn: 4748, 5446, 5544
  Law practice: 388
CAZENOVE AND COMPANY (firm): 947
CEBALLOS, Juan Maria: 948
CECIL, Hugh Richard Heathcote, First
  Baron Quickswood: 949, 3693
CECIL, Robert Arthur Talbot
  Gascoyne-, Third Marquis of
  Salisbury: 294, 1815, 2149, 2324
CECIL COUNTY, Maryland: 2853, 5296
  Charlestown: 5199
  Elkton: 1622, 4468
  Tavern accounts: 166
CEDAR BUSH, North Carolina: 1882
CEDAR COUNTY, Iowa--West Branch:
  2644
CEDAR CREEK, Virginia: see CIVIL
  WAR--CAMPAIGNS, BATTLES, AND
  MILITARY ACTIONS--Virginia--
  Cedar Creek
CEDAR CREEK BAPTIST ASSOCIATION: 320
CEDAR FALLS STATION, Methodist
  Church: 3646
"CEDAR GROVE," Georgia: 1996
CEDAR GROVE, North Carolina: 3351,
  5205
CEDAR KEYS, Florida:
  Civil War: 700
    see also CIVIL WAR--CAMPAIGNS,
      BATTLES, AND MILITARY
      ACTIONS--Florida--Cedar Keys
CEDAR MOUNTAIN, Virginia:
  Civil War: see CIVIL WAR--
    CAMPAIGNS, BATTLES AND MILITARY
    ACTIONS--Virginia--Cedar
    Mountain
  Description: 2106
"CEDAR PARK," Maryland: 3627
CEDAR RUN, Virginia: see CIVIL
  WAR--CAMPAIGNS, BATTLES, AND
  MILITARY ACTIONS--Virginia--
  Cedar Run
CEDAR SPRING, Tennessee: 3692
CEDARTOWN, Georgia: 5650, 5651
"CÉDULA REAL SOBRE LA FUDACIÓN DEL
  ESTUDIO, SETIEMBRE, 1551": 3650
CEGARRA, Felix Cipriano Coronel:
  see CORONEL CEGARRA, Felix
  Cipriano
THE CELEBRATED CASE OF FITZ JOHN
  PORTER by Otto Eisenschiml: 4276
CELEBRATIONS: see PUBLIC
  CELEBRATIONS; VICTORY CELEBRATIONS
CEMENT: 4039
  see also BUILDING MATERIALS;
    TABBY (Concrete)
  Experiments: 3145
CEMENT STONE QUARRIES (Maryland
  and Virginia): 3145
CEMETERIES:
  see also CATACOMBS; CIVIL WAR--
    BURIAL GROUNDS; TOMBS
  Maryland--Baltimore: 4638
  Mississippi--Holly Springs: 5975
  New York: 4895
CENSORSHIP: 3617
  see also CIVIL WAR--CENSORSHIP;
    CONFEDERATE STATES OF AMERICA--
    ARMY--Censorship
  Books:
    Great Britain: 2146, 5726
    North Carolina: 2036

CENSORSHIP:
  Books (Continued):
    United States: 2390
  Moving pictures--North Carolina:
    3211
  Newspapers--Great Britain: 2918
  Subdivided by place:
    Italy: 2015
    North Carolina: 4640
    Russia: 39
CENSURES: see WINTHROP COLLEGE--
  Faculty--Discipline
CENSUS: see as subheading under
  names of countries
CENTENARY COLLEGE, Jackson,
  Louisiana:
  Students and student life: 1370
CENTENARY METHODIST CHURCH,
  Winston-Salem, North Carolina:
  5022
CENTENARY METHODIST EPISCOPAL
  CHURCH, SOUTH, Durham, North
  Carolina: 1642
THE CENTENNIAL EDITION OF THE
  WRITINGS OF SIDNEY LANIER edited
  by Charles R. Anderson: 3092
CENTENNIALS: see under name of
  event being celebrated
CENTER, Alabama: 4419
CENTER, North Carolina: 2570
CENTERVIEW, Missouri:
  Confederate emigrants: 3038
CENTERVILLE, Rhode Island: 4433
CENTERVILLE, Virginia: 2489
  see also CENTREVILLE, Virginia
  Civil War: 1137
CENTRAL AMERICA: 4520
  see also LATIN AMERICA
  British expansion in: 2836
  Description and travel: 4535, 4900
  Railroad construction: 2991
CENTRAL BANK OF GEORGIA: 1466, 3355
CENTRAL BAPTIST ASSOCIATION: 320
CENTRAL CAROLINA POWER COMPANY
  (South Carolina): 3447
CENTRAL MANUFACTURING COMPANY,
  Worthville, North Carolina: 3187
CENTRAL OF GEORGIA RAILROAD: 5494
CENTRAL OF GEORGIA RAILWAY COMPANY:
  3985
CENTRAL PLANNING COMMITTEE FOR NEW
  BERN AND CRAVEN COUNTY, North
  Carolina: 3955
THE CENTRAL PROTESTANT (periodical):
  3656
CENTRAL RAILROAD AND BANKING COMPANY
  OF GEORGIA: 950
CENTRAL SHELBY CIRCUIT, Methodist
  Church: 3646
CENTRAL UNIVERSITY: see CENTRE
  OF KENTUCKY
CENTRAL WESLEYAN COLLEGE, Warrenton,
  Missouri: 3049
CENTRE COLLEGE OF KENTUCKY,
  Danville, Kentucky: 1092, 4373
CENTRE COUNTY, Pennsylvania:
  Belefonte: 4165
CENTRE RUTLAND, Vermont: 4485
CENTREVILLE, Maryland: 5928
CENTREVILLE, Virginia: 2534
  see also CENTERVILLE, Virginia
  Civil War: 56, 1092
    see also CIVIL WAR--CAMPAIGNS,
      BATTLES, AND MILITARY ACTIONS--
      Virginia--Centreville
CENTURY MAGAZINE: 72, 1878, 2871,
  2883, 3465, 3793, 4020, 4491,
  5065, 5524
CEPHALONIA, Greece:
  Health conditions: 3835
CERESVILLE MILLS, Maryland:
  Flour mills: 4803
CEVALLOS, Mariano H.: 4155
CEYLON:
  Abolition of slavery: 4913
  Agriculture: 952
  British administration: 952
  Description and travel: 1464, 4017

CEYLON (Continued):
  Diseases:
    Inoculation against smallpox: 908
  Economic conditions: 952
  Newspapers: 952
  Trade: 952
CHACE, George Albert: 953
CHACON, Joseph Maria: 1913
CHADBOURN, North Carolina:
  Methodist Episcopal Church, South: 5023
CHADBOURNE, William Merriam: 5252
CHADBOURNE FAMILY (Maine): 3741
CHADICK, Mary Jane (Cook): 954
CHADICK, William Davidson: 954
CHADWICK, David: 955
CHADWICK-HOSKINS COMPANY, Mecklenburg County, North Carolina: 5235
CHAFFIN, Robert: 956
CHAFFIN, Washington Sandford: 956
CHAFIN'S FARM, Virginia: see CIVIL WAR--CAMPAIGNS, BATTLES, AND MILITARY ACTIONS--Virginia--Chafin's Farm
CHAILEY, England: 4635
CHAIR MANUFACTURING:
  North Carolina: 2382
  Virginia: 253
CHAIRMAKER: 788
CHAISE, Anna: 3404
CHALK, William Shove, Bishop of Chester: 1087
CHALMERS, Alexander: 957
CHALMERS, James: 2605
CHALONER, John Armstrong: 958
CHAMBERLAIN, Sir Austen (b. 1863): 233, 663
CHAMBERLAIN, Daniel Henry: 959, 1424
CHAMBERLAIN, G. Hope (Summerell): 960
CHAMBERLAIN, Joseph (b. 1836): 217, 294, 663, 2149, 3978, 4514
CHAMBERLAIN, Joseph R. (b. 1861): 5457
CHAMBERLAIN, Joshua Lawrence: 961
CHAMBERLAIN, Sir Neville Bowles: 233, 326
CHAMBERLAIN FAMILY (Genealogy): 960
CHAMBERLAYNE, William: 962
CHAMBERLIN, Alfred Otis: 963
CHAMBERLIN, G. B.: 1203
CHAMBERS, A. T.: 964
CHAMBERS, Annie: 2449
CHAMBERS, Benjamin W.: 965
CHAMBERS, Henry Alexander: 966
CHAMBERS, James S.: 967
CHAMBERS, Jennie: 968
CHAMBERS, John: 4188
CHAMBERS, Sidney C.: 969
CHAMBERS, Walter: 5725
CHAMBERS, William (1800-1883): 2146
CHAMBERS FAMILY (Great Britain): 970
CHAMBERS FAMILY (Pennsylvania and North Carolina): 5264
CHAMBERS FAMILY (West Virginia): 968
CHAMBERS OF COMMERCE:
  North Carolina: 1661
    Raleigh: 4927
  Virginia: 1198
CHAMBERSBURG, Pennsylvania:
  see also WILSON COLLEGE
  Charities: 5306
  Civil War:
    see also CIVIL WAR--CAMPAIGNS, BATTLES, AND MILITARY ACTIONS--Pennsylvania--Chambersburg
  Hospitals: 4608
CHAMBERSBURG AND BEDFORD TURNPIKE COMPANY: 971
CHAMBERSBURG BENEFICIAL SOCIETY, Chambersburg, Pennsylvania: 5306
CHAMBLAY BARRACKS, Canada: 4354
CHAMBLISS, John S.: 100
CHAMBLISSBURG, Virginia: 5921
CHAMBRUN, Charles, Comte de: 4486
CHAMBRUN FAMILY (Genealogy): 1424

CHAMIER, John: 2756, 5639
CHAMPAIGN COUNTY, Ohio: 3343
CHAMPION, Aaron: 3311
CHAMPION, Maria Sophia: 3311
CHAMPION, Matilda Montgomery: 972
CHAMPION, Sidney S.: 972
CHAMPION (warship): 2296
CHAMPION COMPRESS AND WAREHOUSE COMPANY, Wilmington, North Carolina: 5014
CHAMPION HILL, Mississippi:
  Civil War: 972
CHAMPION PAPER AND FIBER COMPANY: 1852
CHAMPLIN, Christopher: 973
CHAMPLIN, Edwin Ross: 2449
CHAMPLIN, George: 973
CHANCELLOR, I. Edgar: 974
CHANCELLORSVILLE, Virginia: see CIVIL WAR--CAMPAIGNS, BATTLES, AND MILITARY ACTIONS--Virginia--Chancellorsville
CHANCERY COURTS: see COURTS--Chancery Courts
CHANCHAMAYO RIVER (South America): 4155
CHANCY, Ransom A.: 975
CHAND, Gokul: 774
CHANDELIERS--Maryland: 1245
CHANDLER, Dr. _____ (Great Britain): 5647
CHANDLER, Allen Daniel: 1573
CHANDLER, Charles S.: 3172
CHANDLER, Daniel: 976
CHANDLER, Zachariah: 5172
CHANDOS, James Brydges, Third Duke of: 736
CHANG AND ENG: 2809, 4849
CHANG TSO-LIN: 5252
CHANGE OF SEX: see SEX CHANGE
CHANLER, Isaac: 5362
CHANLER, John Armstrong: 958
CHANNEL ISLANDS: 306
CHANNING, William Ellery: 977
CHAPEL HILL, Louisiana:
  Civil War aid societies: 3071
CHAPEL HILL, North Carolina:
  1800s: 514, 2469, 2481, 3033, 3364, 3482, 3528, 4261, 4391, 4666, 4992, 5150
  1900s: 960, 1167, 1258, 2773, 4391
  Civil War: 3247
  Effects of the suspension of the University of North Carolina on the town: 5298
  Household finance: 4763
  Kindergartens: 4080
  Social life and customs: 5298
  Universities and colleges: see UNIVERSITY OF NORTH CAROLINA AT CHAPEL HILL
CHAPEL HILL STREET, Durham, North Carolina: 969
CHAPIN, Edwin Hubbell: 978
CHAPLAINS: see as subheading under names of armies and navies
CHAPLIN, Joseph: 979
CHAPMAN, Alvan Wentworth: 5881
CHAPMAN, Carrie (Lane): 942, 5110
CHAPMAN, Elizabeth A.: 980
CHAPMAN, Frank Michler: 4453
CHAPMAN, John (Great Britain): 981
CHAPMAN, John Lee: 2446
CHAPMAN, Reuben: 2662
CHAPMAN, Robert T.: 2963
CHAPMAN, Thomas (Alabama): 983
CHAPMAN, Thomas (North Carolina): 982
CHAPMAN, William: 984
CHAPPELL, Fred Davis: 985
CHAPPELL, Leroy: 986
CHAPPELL HILL, Texas: 131
CHAPTICO, Maryland: 5193
CHARACTER EDUCATION: see MORAL EDUCATION
"CHARACTERS OF THE COURT OF GREAT BRITAIN" by John Macky: 3411

CHARADES:
  see also RIDDLES
  Vermont--Thetford: 3218
CHARCOAL FURNACES--North Carolina: 2121
CHARITABLE WORK:
  see also PHILANTHROPY
  Great Britain: 1765
  Maryland: 1862
  North Carolina: 3410
    Durham: 5519
CHARITIES:
  Children: 5790
    Great Britain: 2148
    United States: 3633
  Freedmen: see FREEDMEN--Aid societies
  Fund raising--Massachusetts: 977
  Seamen: see SEAMEN'S AID SOCIETIES
  Subdivided by place:
    Great Britain: 5726
    New Jersey: 1927
    North Carolina--Wilmington: 4080
    Pennsylvania: 2027
      Chambersburg: 5306
    United States: 480, 1197, 3633
    Virginia--Fluvanna County: 1244
CHARITON, Iowa: 3520
CHARITY ORGANIZATION SOCIETY (Great Britain): 2148
CHARITY SCHOOLS: see SCHOOLS--Charity schools
CHARLES II, King of Spain: see CARLOS II, King of Spain
CHARLES III, King of Spain: see CARLOS III, King of Spain
CHARLES IV, Emperor of Austria: 5532
CHARLES IV, King of Spain: see CARLOS IV, King of Spain
CHARLES EDWARD, The Young Pretender: 2098
CHARLES CITY COUNTY, Virginia: 819, 2383
  Social life and customs: 5751
  Cities and towns:
    Bermuda Hundred: 2506
    "Buckland": 5751
    Charles City Court House: 915, 2169
    "Sherwood Forest": 5397
CHARLES CITY COURT HOUSE, Virginia: 915, 2169
CHARLES COUNTY, Maryland: 984, 5296
  Legal affairs: 5089
  Merchants: 1487
  Cities and towns:
    Mattawoman: 3559
    Port Tobacco: 3006, 5089
CHARLES SCRIBNER'S SONS: 4020
CHARLES TOWN, West Virginia: 43, 464, 1939, 2678, 3069, 3141, 3291, 4388
  Baptist Churches: 1769
  Civil War: 1769
  Local politics: 5689
  Mercantile accounts: 5300
  Physicians: 22099
  Settlement: 99
  Social life and customs: 1918
  Surveying: 1379
  Zion Protestant Episcopal Church: 128
CHARLESTON, Missouri:
  Civil War: 42099
CHARLESTON, South Carolina: 4167
  1600s-1700s: 202
  1700s: 4621, 4623
  1740s: 4216
  1750s: 4216
  1760s: 3294, 4216, 4624
  1770s: 758, 3116, 4624
  1780s: 313, 2059, 2147, 3116, 4371, 4418, 4625
  1790s: 2059, 2875, 3116, 4625, 4922
  1700s-1800s: 295, 1682, 1891, 1926, 2218, 2613, 2696, 2780, 4218, 4399
  1700s-1900s: 1468, 2107, 2556

689

CHARLESTON, South Carolina
  (Continued):
  1800s: 1016, 1127, 2040, 2210,
    2278, 2491, 2828, 2961, 3216,
    3461, 3666, 4162, 4249, 4429,
    4445, 4829, 4912
  1810s: 4371, 5388
  1820s: 2450, 5840
  1830s: 2144, 2450, 3162, 3466
  1840s: 37, 1892, 2030, 3162,
    4813
  1850s: 37, 89, 1929, 2045, 2094,
    2695, 3620, 4783, 4830, 5340
  1860s: 89, 219, 686, 1206,
    2017, 2610, 2695, 2709, 2806,
    2818, 2864, 2944, 3340, 3420,
    3466, 3615, 3620, 3713, 4505,
    4620, 4783, 5340, 5617, 5633,
    5646
  1870s: 89, 2709, 2944, 3615,
    3713, 4041, 5795, 5893
  1880s: 2944, 4041, 5495
  1890s: 633, 2702, 3402, 4392
  1800s-1900s: 883, 987, 1424, 1575,
    2449, 4530, 5796
  1900s: 4962
  1910s: 3421, 4298
  1920s: 2414
  1930s: 4392
  1950s: 4823
  1960s: 4823
  Actresses: 5503
  American Revolution: 1088, 1926,
    2743
    Battle: see AMERICAN
      REVOLUTION--Campaigns and
      battles--South Carolina--
      Charleston
    British occupation: 2402
    Prisoner exchanges: 3802
  Banks and banking: 1760, 2755,
    4235, 5318
  Baptist churches: 2402
  Belgian consulate in: 3485
  Blacksmithing: 219
  Bonds: 5198
  British consulate in: 4484
  Business affairs: 757, 3532, 4163,
    5936
  Business failures: 5193
  Churches: 2410, 3801
    see also names of specific
      denominations under CHARLESTON
  Civil War: 395, 498, 1185, 1570,
    4118, 4347, 4393, 5645
    Battle: see CIVIL WAR--
      CAMPAIGNS, BATTLES, AND
      MILITARY ACTIONS--South
      Carolina--Charleston
    Blockade: 2831
    Confederate Army:
      Camp life: 770, 3435
      Depredations: 4120
      Mobilization: 4033
      Ordnance: 5193
    Defenses: 1017, 1189, 1606, 2610,
      4033, 5513
      Use of slave labor: 3371
    Description: 3269, 5193, 5390
    Economic conditions: 2107, 5193
    Evacuation: 1524
    Fires: 2610, 2695, 3485
    Fort Sumter: 1028
      see also CIVIL WAR--CAMPAIGNS,
        BATTLES, AND MILITARY
        ACTIONS--South Carolina--
        Fort Sumter
    Hospitals: 2124
    Prisons: 1184, 1610
    Siege: 1700
  Clergy--Universalist: 978
  Commission merchants: 3801, 4332
  Commonplace books: 723
  Cotton brokers: 4145
  Cotton factors: 566, 4649
  Cotton speculation: 4145
  Cotton trade: 1009, 1572, 2018

CHARLESTON, South Carolina
  (Continued):
  Courts: 1468
    District Court: 989
  Debating societies: 1111
  Debt collection: 5548
  Description: 249, 284, 1500, 2416,
    4177, 4864, 5731
  Diseases:
    Cholera: 5193
    Yellow fever: 3907, 4584, 5193,
      5362
  Earthquakes: 1017, 1424, 1468,
    1889, 2473
  Education: 4271, 5661
  Embargo: 3485
  Episcopal churches: 2110
  Estate accounts: 5073
  Estates: 1388
    Administration and settlement:
      4215, 5198, 5461, 5936
  Fires (1838): 2491
    see also CHARLESTON--Civil
      War--Fires
  Foreign trade: 3230
    Cuba and Puerto Rico: 4982
  Fortifications: 4216
  Fourth of July celebrations: 3532
  Free Negroes: 2564
  Freedmen: 408
  Health conditions: 477, 4584, 4982
  Huguenot churches: 4584
  Hurricanes: 2959
  Insurance: 1691
    Fire: 2448
  Labor unions: 2768
  Land deeds and indentures: 4214,
    4306, 5198
  Land prices: 1745
  Land surveys and titles: 5198
  Law--Study of: 5193
  Law practice: 3962, 5548
  Legal affairs: 5198, 5318
  Legal fees: 5318
  Lightning strikes: 2410
  Literary and Philosophical Society:
    1676
  Literature: 296
  Map: 202
  Mercantile accounts: 4838
  Merchants: 1935, 2019, 2586, 5478
    see also CHARLESTON--Commission
      merchants
  Methodist churches--Negroes: 249
  Militia: 3652, 3800, 5144
  Mining companies: 1019
  Mortgages: 5198
  Negroes: 380
    see also the following
      subheadings under CHARLESTON:
      Civil War--Defences--Use of
      slave labor; Free Negroes;
      Freedmen; Methodist churches--
      Negroes; Reconstruction--
      Military occupation--By Negro
      troops; Slave trade; Slaves--
      Insurrections
  Newspapers: 300, 1424, 2109
  Panic of 1819: 3485
  Penmanship and spelling books: 4271
  Personal finance: 5274
  Phosphate mining: 602
  Plantation life: 4584
  Plantations: 5936
  Political poetry: 5074
  Politics and government: 1562,
    2109, 4584, 5045
    Democratic National Convention:
      988, 2589, 3501
  Presbyterian churches: 4936
  Property damage: 4216
  Protestant Episcopal Church: 4637
  Railroads--Finance: 5271
  Reconstruction:
    Military occupation: 1282
      By Negro troops: 1477
  Religion: 4584

CHARLESTON, South Carolina
  (Continued):
  Salvage of Confederate gunboat:
    5731
  Schools: 1017, 4622
    Girls' schools: 1651
  Shipping: 2959
  Slave trade: 3589
    Prices: 1745
  Slaves--Insurrections: 2289
  Social life and customs:
    1800s: 686, 2449, 2451, 2959,
      3485, 4212, 4271, 4584, 4596,
      5045, 5193, 5892
    Civil War: 4393
    1900s: 300
  Spanish consulate in: 4982
  Tax collectors: 4213
  Tobacco trade: 5228
  Trade and commerce:
    Groceries: 46
    Hay and grain: 60
    Mercantile goods: 2541
    Wholesale trade: 1856
    With Philadelphia: 1117
  United States Customs Service:
    5193
  Universities and colleges: see
    THE CITADEL; COLLEGE OF
    CHARLESTON
  Visit of George Washington: 2477
  Vital statistics: 723, 4584
  Voyages to: 4304
  Wages and salaries: 3230
  Weather: 4584
  Wills: 4214, 5198
CHARLESTON, West Virginia: 331, 3821
CHARLESTON (ship): 1575
CHARLESTON AMERICAN (newspaper):
  2109
CHARLESTON AND WESTERN CAROLINA
  RAILWAY COMPANY: 3985
CHARLESTON BUILDING AND
  CONSTRUCTION TRADES COUNCIL: 2768
CHARLESTON COTTON EXCHANGE: 987
CHARLESTON COUNTY, South Carolina:
  853, 3659
  Charleston: see CHARLESTON, South
    Carolina
  Edisto Island: see EDISTO ISLAND,
    South Carolina
  Folly Island: 1430, 1845
  Fort Moultrie: 2237
  John's Island: 3164
  McClellanville: 4619
  Pineville: 4034
  Summerville: 1793, 4334
CHARLESTON (S.C.) DAILY NEWS
  (newspaper): 5893
CHARLESTON (S.C.) GAZETTE
  (newspaper): 5066
CHARLESTON (S.C.) MERCURY
  (newspaper): 267, 2094
CHARLESTON (S.C.) MILL OF THE WEST
  VIRGINIA PULP AND PAPER COMPANY:
  2768
CHARLESTON (S.C.) NEWS AND COURIER
  (newspaper): 300, 1424, 5661
CHARLESTON OBSERVATORY: 2982
CHARLESTON SHIPBUILDING AND DRYDOCK
  COMPANY: 2768
THE (Charleston) STATE (newspaper):
  300
CHARLESTON YEAR BOOK: 2402
CHARLESTOWN, Maryland: 5199
CHARLESTOWN, Massachusetts: 3057,
  3791
CHARLIER INSTITUTE FOR YOUNG
  GENTLEMEN, New York, New York: 3008
CHARLOTTE, Iowa: 5466
CHARLOTTE, North Carolina: 895,
  2041, 2476, 2480, 2529, 2897,
  3433, 3599, 3878, 4192, 5312
  Clergy: 967
  Labor Unions: 1192, 1195, 1199,
    1202, 5235, 5237
  Millinery goods trade: 5100

CHARLOTTE, North Carolina
(Continued):
  Orphanages: 4918, 5298
  Real estate investments: 4918
  Schools: 3608
    Girls' schools and academies:
      4080
    Teachers' records: 1823
  Textile industry: 5100
  Wholesale trade: 2857
CHARLOTTE AND SOUTH CAROLINA
  RAILROAD: 565
CHARLOTTE COUNTY, Virginia: 331,
  2712
  Plantations: 1922
  Cities and towns:
    Charlotte Court House: 2378,
      4461
    Cole's Ferry: 907
    Keysville: 79
    Rough Creek: 331
CHARLOTTE COURT HOUSE, Virginia:
  2378, 4461
CHARLOTTE DISTRICT, Methodist
  Church: 3646
CHARLOTTE FEMALE INSTITUTE,
  Charlotte, North Carolina: 1823
CHARLOTTE HALL, Maryland:
  Schools: 5296, 5329
CHARLOTTE HALL SCHOOL, Charlotte
  Hall, Maryland: 5296
  Students and student life: 5329
CHARLOTTE (N.C.) NEWS (newspaper):
  1202
CHARLOTTE (N.C.) OBSERVER
  (newspaper): 1202, 5312
CHARLOTTE SANATORIUM: 5312
CHARLOTTESVILLE, Virginia: 722,
  1000, 2612, 3293, 3700, 4143,
  4574, 5288
  Autographs: 275
  Banks and banking: 4142
  Boarding houses: 5786
  Business affairs: 1131
  Civil War hospitals: 824, 3350,
    1185, 2880
  Clergy--Methodist: 3758
  Debt: 974
  Description: 155
  "Monticello": 2139
  Hospitals: 3012
  Merchants: 93
  Personal finance: 4142
  Pharmacies: 5301
  Savings accounts: 4142, 5789
  Social life and customs: 5786
  Universities and colleges: see
    UNIVERSITY OF VIRGINIA
  Wool industry: 990
CHARLOTTESVILLE WOOLEN MILLS: 990
CHARLTON, Robert Millege: 991
CHARMER (steamship): 2940
CHARNWOOD, Godfrey Rathbone Benson,
  First Baron: 442
CHARTERHOUSE: 4115
CHARTERIS-WEMYSS, Francis: see
  WEMYSS, Francis Charteris-
CHARTIST MOVEMENT: 1753, 3736
CHARTRES, Robert Philippe Louis
  Eugène Ferdinand d'Orléans, Duc
  de: 3990
CHARTRES, France: 3990
CHASE, C. B.: 4188
CHASE, Harvey: 992
CHASE, Kate: 2545
CHASE, Oliver: 992
CHASE, Salmon Portland: 716, 2545,
  3628, 5552
CHASE, Samuel (Illinois): 993
CHASE, Samuel (Maryland, 1741-1811):
  994
  Impeachment: 3671
CHASE, Samuel, Jr.: 994
CHASE, Seth: 995
CHASE, William Henry: 5425
CHASE NATIONAL BANK OF NEW YORK ET
  AL. v. STERLING COTTON MILLS,
  INC.: 5056

CHASTELLUX, François Jean de: 3456
CHATEAU DE JOSSELIN: 1424
"CHATEAU-THIERRY" by Leander
  Dunbar Syme: 5163
CHATHAM, John Pitt, Second Earl of:
  4230
CHATHAM, William Pitt, First Earl
  of (1708-1778): 92, 4229, 4230
CHATHAM, England:
  British Army headquarters: 5024,
    5801
CHATHAM, Virginia: 3542, 4720
  Masonry: 4233
  Public finance: 2732
CHATHAM, H.M.S.: 3736
CHATHAM COUNTY, Georgia: 2179
  County commissioners: 996
  Courts: 1088
  Debt: 2594
  Geography of: 2107, 4236
  Militia: 1993, 2893
  Notaries: 4611
  Sheriffs: 4611
  Taxation: 3573
  Cities and towns:
    "Cedar Grove" (plantation):
      1996
    Savannah: see SAVANNAH, Georgia
CHATHAM COUNTY, North Carolina: 1096,
  1688, 3126
  Civil War: 533, 1056
  Commodity prices: 770
  Diseases--Smallpox: 770
  Medical practice: 2462, 5541
  Mercantile accounts: 5905
  Personal finance: 5905
  Tax receipts: 5874
  Cities and towns:
    Cane Creek: 875, 2618, 4458
    Gulf: 4030
    Haywood: 2357
    Lockville: 5207
    Mud Lick: 2861
    Mudlick Post Office: 1326
    Pedlar's Hill: 5084
    Pittsboro: 3843, 5874
    Riggsbee's Store: 5541
    Siler City: 1254, 2861, 5914
CHATHAM CIRCUIT, Methodist Church:
  3646
CHATHAM RAILROAD: 5460
CHATHAM TOWN COMPANY: 996
CHATTAHOOCHEE COUNTY, Georgia: 4791
CHATTAHOOCHEE RIVER (Georgia):
  Fur trade: 3966
CHATTANOOGA, Tennessee: 257, 1289,
  1452, 1593, 4055
  Civil War: 659, 689, 966
    see also CIVIL WAR--CAMPAIGNS,
      BATTLES, AND MILITARY ACTIONS--
      Tennessee--Chattanooga; CIVIL
      WAR--CAMPAIGNS, BATTLES, AND
      MILITARY ACTIONS--Tennessee--
      Sherman's March
  Description: 5608
  Diseases--Yellow fever: 4202
  Labor unions: 1197, 1200
  Methodist churches:
    Unification movement: 3646
CHATTOOGA COUNTY, Georgia:
  Alpine: 44, 2174
  Summerville: 2697
CHAUTAUQUA, New York: 2898
CHAUTAUQUA COUNTY, New York:
  Chautauqua: 2898
  Fredonia: 4486
  Mayville: 5322
CHAUTAUQUAS:
  see also LECTURES AND LECTURING;
    LYCEUMS
  Florida: 3008
  Pennsylvania--Swarthmore: 5110
CHAUVENET, William: 2552
CHAVERS, Genes V.: 998
CHEAIRS, Irene: 5452
CHEANG PANK CHEW: 5252

CHEAT MOUNTAIN, Tennessee: see
  CIVIL WAR--CAMPAIGNS, BATTLES, AND
  MILITARY ACTIONS--Tennessee--
  Cheat Mountain
CHEATHAM, Benjamin Franklin: 4358
CHEATHAM, James A.: 999
CHEATHAM, Richard: 1000
CHECKER MILITARY ACADEMY: 5731
CHEE-HA COMBAHEE COMPANY: 4453
CHEEK, John S.: 2940
CHEEK'S CREEK TOWNSHIP, North
  Carolina:
  Voter registration: 675
CHEESBOROUGH, Edmund R.: 1001
CHEESBOROUGH, John: 1001
CHEESE TRADE:
  Alabama: 3196
  New Hampshire: 1529
CHEESEBOROUGH, Essie B.: 2449
CHEESMENT-SEVERN, John: 1002
CHEEVER, William D.: 1003, 5206
CHELMSFORD, England: 1903
CHEMICAL WORKERS: see UNITED GAS,
  COKE, AND CHEMICAL WORKERS OF
  AMERICA
CHEMICALS INDUSTRY:
  see also SOAP AND COSMETICS
    MANUFACTURE
  South Carolina: 1019
CHEMISTRY: 5305
  Students' notebooks: 5762
  North Carolina:
    University of North Carolina:
      673, 1284
  Virginia: 302
    Emory and Henry College: 4646
    University of Virginia: 824
    Washington College: 4616
CHEMUNG, New York: 4708
CHEMUNG COUNTY, New York:
  Chemung: 4708
  Elmira: 408, 5514
    Civil War: 793
CHEN, Y: 5252
CHENANGO COUNTY, New York: 86
  Norwich: 2292
CHERAW, South Carolina: 2107, 2115,
  2140, 3048
  Land and development: 997
CHERAW DISTRICT, Methodist Church:
  3646
CHERAW PRESBYTERIAN CHURCH: 3371
CHEROKEE CALIFORNIA COMPANY: 4353
CHEROKEE COUNTY, Alabama: 2239
  Center: 4419
CHEROKEE COUNTY, Georgia:
  Canton: 700
  Mining: 1887
  Plantations: 797
CHEROKEE COUNTY, North Carolina:
  Mercantile accounts: 5258
  Murphy: 3025
    Civil War--Depredations: 1247
  Valley Town: 5202, 5673
CHEROKEE COUNTY, South Carolina:
  Gaffney: 5233
    see also LIMESTONE COLLEGE
  Silver mining: 2541
CHEROKEE INDIAN LAND LOTTERY: 1993
CHEROKEE INDIANS: 932, 3041, 3396,
  4805
  Agents--North Carolina: 5202
  Business affairs--North Carolina:
    5202
  Census of Eastern Band: 1036
  Claims: 4560
  Government relations: 3176, 3614,
    4560, 5202, 5420
  North Carolina: 5906
  Land:
    Land lottery: 1993
    Purchases and sales: 4080
  Land tenure: 2781
  Language: 2047
  Murder of whites--North Carolina:
    3176
  National Council: 4353

CHEROKEE INDIANS (Continued):
    Removal from North Carolina:
        5258, 5906
    Trade with whites: 4353
    Treaties: 4315
    United States: 2049
    Subdivided by place:
        Florida: 842
        Georgia: 2326
        North Carolina: 3028, 5202,
            5258
CHEROKEE - SPARTANBURG JOINT BOARD
    OF THE TEXTILE WORKERS UNION OF
    AMERICA: 5233
CHEROKEE TERRITORY: 3801
CHERRY, Lunceford R.: 1005
CHERRY, Robert Gregg: 1006, 2863
CHERRY FAMILY (North Carolina):
    1005
CHERRY HILL, Georgia: 1123
CHERRY HILL, South Carolina: 3367
CHESAPEAKE AGRICULTURAL FAIR
    ASSOCIATION: 660
CHESAPEAKE AND OHIO CANAL: 292,
    4099
    Construction and maintenance:
        3145, 4914
CHESAPEAKE AND OHIO CANAL COMPANY:
    1007, 1008
CHESAPEAKE BAY BRIDGE CO.: 2109
CHESAPEAKE BAY REGION:
    Grain trade: 4924
CHESAPEAKE CANAL COMPANY: see
    ALBEMARLE AND CHESAPEAKE CANAL
    COMPANY
CHESAPEAKE CORPORATION: 1852
CHESAPEAKE FEMALE COLLEGE,
    [Virginia?]: 1115
CHESHIRE, Joseph Blount: 4232,
    4775, 4918, 5457
CHESHIRE, England:
    Delamere House: 5729
    "Highfields": 4627
    Thelwall: 4627
    Wilmslow: 5173
CHESHIRE, SULLIVAN & CANADAY, INC.:
    1009
CHESHIRE COUNTY, New Hampshire:
    Fitzwilliam: 1865, 1983
    Keene: 5131, 5501
CHESNEY, Francis Rawdon: 1010
CHESNEY, William: 4712
CHESNUT, Alexander: 1011
CHESNUT, James, Jr. (1815-1885):
    1012, 1403
CHESNUT, John: 3501
CHESNUT FAMILY (South Carolina):
    1012
CHESSIER, James: 1013
CHESSON, Andrew: 1015
CHESSON, Frederick William: 1014
CHESSON, John B.: 1015
CHESSON, William L.: 1015
CHESSON FAMILY (North Carolina):
    1015
CHESSON AND ARMISTEAD (firm): see
    ARMISTEAD AND CHESSON
CHESSON AND HODGES (firm): see
    HODGES AND CHESSON
CHESSON AND ROSS (firm): 1015
CHESTER, Colby N.: 4858
CHESTER, William Shove Chalk,
    Bishop of: 1087
CHESTER, Pennsylvania: 3155
CHESTER, South Carolina: 4527, 4707
    Banks: 697
    Estate accounts: 4833
    Family life: 5988
    Presbyterian churches: 5988
CHESTER COUNTY, Pennsylvania: 5604
    Kennett Square: 5642
    Mont Clare: 4190
    Valley Forge: 1805
CHESTER COUNTY, South Carolina:
    Chester: see CHESTER, South
        Carolina
    Estates--Administration and
        settlement: 4833

CHESTER COUNTY, South Carolina
    (Continued):
    Mercantile accounts: 4833
    Plantation lands: 2596
CHESTER DISTRICT, South Carolina:
    1268
CHESTERFIELD, South Carolina:
    Iron works: 529
    Schools: 2855
CHESTERFIELD, Virginia: 4302
CHESTERFIELD BRIDGE (Virginia): 460
CHESTERFIELD COUNTY, South Carolina:
    Cheraw: 2107, 2115, 2140, 3048
        Land and development: 997
    Cotton plantations: 4996
    Tax receipts: 4996
CHESTERFIELD COUNTY, Virginia:
    2305, 3674
    Chesterfield: 4302
    Civil War: 1680
    Coal mining: 2908
    Manchester: 282, 1115, 3792
    Midlothian: 2908
CHESTERFIELD DISTRICT, South
    Carolina: 3371
CHESTERFIELD JUNCTION, Virginia:
    see CIVIL WAR--CAMPAIGNS,
    BATTLES, AND MILITARY ACTIONS--
    Virginia--Chesterfield Junction
CHESTERMAN, William Dallas: 2845
CHESTERTOWN, Maryland: 2605, 5296
CHETWYND-TALBOT, Charles John,
    Nineteenth Earl Shrewsbury: see
    TALBOT, Charles John Chetwynd-,
    Nineteenth Earl Shrewsbury
CHEVALIER, John B.: 1017
CHEVALIER FAMILY (France--
    Genealogy): 1424
CHEVES, John Richardson: 1017
CHEVES, Langdon: 1016, 3278, 3800
CHEVES, Rachael Susan (Bee): 1017
CHEVES FAMILY (Georgia): 1017
CHEW, Robert Smith: 1018
CHEYENNE INDIANS: 4353
CHEYNEY, Ralph: 5338
CHHATRAPATI, Sir Shahu, Maharaja of
    Kolhapur: 278
CHI PHI: 3740
CHIANG, Kai-shek: 2269
CHIANG, Kai-shek, Mme: see CHIANG,
    Mei-ling (Soong)
CHIANG, Mei-ling (Soong): 2269,
    4956, 5252
CHICAGO, Illinois:
    1800s: 247, 3240, 3335, 3641,
        3951, 4276, 5350
    1900s: 1528, 2463, 2798, 3305, 4276
    Civil War prison camp: 2681
    Columbian Exposition: 3051, 5380
    Description: 33, 403, 1768, 3809
    Fires: 2638, 2681, 3566, 3809,
        4375
    Railroad repair shops: 3848
    Socialist Party: 4948
    Textile mills: 2682
    Universities and colleges: see
        CARTHAGE COLLEGE; UNIVERSITY OF
        CHICAGO
CHICAGO, ST. LOUIS, AND TEXAS AIR
    LINE RAILWAY: 218
CHICAGO DAILY TRIBUNE: 2526
CHICHESTER, Bishop of: 2146
CHICHESTER, Thomas Pelham, Second
    Earl of: 2149
CHICKAHOMINY SWAMP, Virginia: see
    CIVIL WAR--CAMPAIGNS, BATTLES,
    AND MILITARY ACTIONS--Virginia--
    Chickahominy Swamp
CHICKAMAUGA, Tennessee:
    Civil War: 44
    see also CIVIL WAR--CAMPAIGNS,
        BATTLES, AND MILITARY
        ACTIONS--Tennessee--
        Chickamauga
CHICKAMAUGA NATIONAL PARK PROJECT:
    5536

CHICKASAW INDIANS: 2781
    Slave trade--Texas: 2117
    Trade with whites: 4353
CHICOPEE, Massachusetts: 106, 4037
CHICORA MINING AND MANUFACTURING
    COMPANY: 1019
THE CHIEF GLORY OF EVERY PEOPLE by
    Matthew Joseph Brucolli: 720
CHIGWELL, England: 3553
CHIHUAHUA, Mexico: 1939
    Mining in Batopilas: 4022
    Trade with Saint Louis, Missouri:
        2386
CHILD, Sir Smith, First Baronet:
    1087
CHILD CARE CENTERS:
    North Carolina: 1275
CHILD LABOR: see CHILDREN--
    Employment
CHILD PRODIGIES: 3567
CHILD REARING: 5968
CHILDREN:
    see also CHARITIES--Children;
        DEPENDENTS
    Diseases--Medical treatment: 3908
    see also CHILDREN'S HOSPITALS
    Employment:
        see also LABOR LAW AND
            LEGISLATION--Employment of
            women and children
        Georgia: 539
        Germany: 305
        Kentucky--Lexington: 3325
        Virginia: 1194
    Subdivided by place:
        Great Britain: 4770
        United States: 4948
        Virginia: 33, 1827
CHILDREN OF THE CONFEDERACY: 227
"THE CHILDREN'S EDUCATIONAL THEATER
    ALLIANCE": 4556
CHILDREN'S HOSPITALS:
    North Carolina: 4809
CHILDREN'S LITERATURE: 3797
    Great Britain: 4115
    United States: 3810
CHILDRESS, Nannie: 1020
CHILDRESS, Sarah: 2326, 4055
CHILDS, Emily: 806
CHILDS, George William: 1021
CHILDS, James: 806
CHILDS, Lucas S.: 3691
CHILE:
    Description and travel: 411, 3102,
        3447
    Foreign relations:
        United States: 5045
    Navy--War of the Pacific: 4535
    Politics and government: 3102,
        3447, 4074
    Social life and customs: 3447
    United States embassy in: 4074
    War with Spain: 4982, 4983
CHILES, Dabney: 1022
CHILES, Rosa Pendleton: 227
CHILLICOTHE, Ohio: 3243
    Population: 5149
CHILLISQUAQUE RIVER (Pennsylvania):
    4348
CHILSTON, Aretas Akers-Douglas,
    First Viscount: 294
CHILTON, George, Jr.: 5624
CHILTON, Robert Hall: 1023, 4129
CHILTON, Robert S., Jr.: 1024
CHIMBORAZO HOSPITAL, Richmond,
    Virginia: 348, 1185, 1886, 5147
CHINA: 2963
    Agriculture: 5225
        see also CHINA--Crops; CHINA--
            Farming; CHINA--Tobacco
            culture
    Antiquities: 1155
    Banks and banking: 5252
    Boxer Rebellion: see BOXER
        REBELLION
    British embassy in: 3315
        Peking: 3472
    Buddhist temples: 2191

CHINA (Continued):
    Crops: 2191
        see also CHINA--Agriculture
    Currency: 1339, 5252
    Description and travel:
        1790s-1800s: 5038
        1800s: 339
        1850s: 3899, 4017
        1860s: 1373, 3899, 4017
        1870s: 4986
        1900s:
            1900s: 2191
            1920s: 2463, 5225
    Diplomatic and consular service:
        Great Britain: 5038
    Domestic architecture: 2191
    East India Company: 3315
    Economic conditions: 2191
    Famine relief: 5252
    Farming: 2191
        see also CHINA--Agriculture
    Foreign relations:
        Great Britain: 597, 598, 3238,
            4054, 5038
        Japan: 83, 4709, 5252
        Russia: 5252
        United States: 5252
    Foreign trade:
        Massachusetts: 1839
        United States: 4060, 5252
    Fortifications: 1373
    Historic buildings: 2411
    Immigration and emigration:
        see also CHINESE IN (name of
            country)
        To United States: 1953, 4080
    Indigo trade: 5252
    International relief
        organizations: 3633, 4564
    Military history: 5225
    Missions and missionaries:
        1795: 3315
        1800s: 2032
        1850s: 598, 872, 2892, 3741,
            3995
        1860s: 2892
        1880s: 1382
        1933: 1940
        Baptist: 1298
        Episcopal: 5298
        Presbyterian: 2269
            Kiangyin: 5014
        History: 1298
        Teaching: 1382
            see also CHINA--Schools--
                Mission schools
    Opium War: see OPIUM WAR
    Politics and government: 4986,
        5225
    Population: 5225
    Portraits: 2411
    Press releases: 1025
    Public welfare: 5252
    Railroads: 2191, 5252
    Relations with Standard Oil
        Company: 5252
    Russo-Japanese War: see RUSSO-
        JAPANESE WAR
    Schools--Mission schools: 5252
        see also CHINA--Missions and
            missionaries--Teaching
    Sino-Japanese War: see SINO-
        JAPANESE WAR
    Social life and customs: 2191,
        4986
    Surveying: 1373
    Taiping Rebellion: see TAIPING
        REBELLION
    Tariff: 5252
    Teaching: 1382
    Tobacco culture: 2191, 5252
    Tobacco industry: 2191
    Tobacco trade: 4060
    Trade: see CHINA--Foreign trade;
        CHINA--Indigo trade; CHINA--
        Tobacco trade
    Treaties--Great Britain: 3995
    United States embassy in: 4413

CHINA (Continued):
    Universities and colleges: see
        YENCHING UNIVERSITY
    Viceroy--Canton: 3315
    Weather: 5225
    Women: 5252
CHINA (Porcelain): see PORCELAIN
CHINA FAMINE RELIEF (organization):
    3633
CHINA GROVE, North Carolina: 1428,
    2297
CHINA MONUMENTS SOCIETY: 5252
CHINA TRADE ACT: 5252
CHINATOWN: see VICTORIA, Canada--
    Chinatown
CHINCHA ISLANDS, Peru: 3459
CHINCOTEAGUE, Virginia: 1791
CHINESE AMERICAN BANK: 5252
CHINESE EASTERN RAILROAD: 5252
CHINESE IN CANADA: 4175
CHINESE IN JAMAICA: 301
CHINESE IN THE DUTCH EAST INDIES:
    4362
CHINESE IN THE UNITED STATES: 1058,
    4535
    see also CHINA--Immigration and
        emigration--To the United
        States; CHINESE STUDENTS IN THE
        UNITED STATES
    Treatment of: 4348
CHINESE-JAPANESE-ENGLISH DICTIONARY
    compiled by Ambrose Daniel Gring:
    5160
CHINESE LANGUAGE--Vocabulary: 5160
CHINESE NATIONAL ASSOCIATION OF THE
    MASS EDUCATION MOVEMENT: 5252
CHINESE NEWS SERVICE: 1025
CHINESE REVOLUTION: 5225
CHINESE STUDENTS IN THE UNITED
    STATES: 5252
CHINESE TRADE COMMISSION: 5252
CHINESE TURKESTAN:
    British strategy: 5103
CHINN, Bolling R.: 1026, 1179
CHIPMAN FAMILY (Canada): 4817
CHIPPENDALE, William Henry: 1027
CHIROL, Sir Valentine: 3286
CHISOLM, Alexander Robert: 1028,
    5193
CHISOLM, John Julian: 2830
CHISOLM, Robert: 4120
CHITTENDEN COUNTY, Vermont:
    Burlington: 3143
CHIVERS, Thomas Holley: 1029, 5044
CHLOROFORM IN SURGERY:
    Maryland: 2830
CHOATE, Joseph Hodges: 958
CHOATE, Rufus: 4813
CHOCOLATE TRADE:
    Great Britain: 369
CHOCOWINITY, North Carolina: 2699
CHOCTAW AGENCY: 3611
CHOCTAW COUNTY, Alabama:
    Tompkinsville: 4827
CHOCTAW COUNTY, Mississippi--
    Courts: 3702
CHOCTAW INDIANS: 2486, 2781
    Culture: 2249
    Government relations: 4208
        Tennessee: 2486
    Mission schools:
        Arkansas: 4373
        Mississippi: 3611
    Removal--Mississippi: 3415
    Tennessee: 2486
    Trade--Mississippi: 4269
CHOIRS:
    see also CHURCH MUSIC; SONGS AND
        MUSIC
    Great Britain: 43
CHOLERA: see DISEASES--Cholera
CHOWAN BAPTIST FEMALE INSTITUTE,
    Murfreesboro, North Carolina: 4897
CHOWAN CIRCUIT, Methodist Church:
    3646
CHOWAN COLLEGE, Murfreesboro, North
    Carolina: 274, 484, 1822
    Students and student life: 423

CHOWAN COUNTY, North Carolina:
    Edenton: see EDENTON, North
        Carolina
CHOWAN FEMALE COLLEGE: see CHOWAN
    COLLEGE
CHOWDHRY, Hurro Nath, Raja: see
    ROY CHOWDHRY, Hurro Nath, Raja
"CHRIST AND SATAN AND HARROWING OF
    HELL" edited by James Bright
    Wilson: 5811
CHRIST CHURCH, Philadelphia,
    Pennsylvania: 4864
CHRIST CHURCH COLLEGE: see
    OXFORD UNIVERSITY--Christ Church
    College
CHRIST CHURCH EPISCOPAL PARISH,
    Macon, Georgia: 2963
CHRIST PRESBYTERIAN CHURCH, Augusta,
    Georgia: 26
CHRISTIAN, B.: 1030
CHRISTIAN, Charles W.: 5117
CHRISTIAN, George: 872
CHRISTIAN, Sir Hugh Cloberry: 5639
CHRISTIAN, John Beverly: 1031
CHRISTIAN, M. E.: 1032
CHRISTIAN, Mary Ann: 1033
CHRISTIAN, S. P.: 2134
CHRISTIAN, William Walter: 1033
CHRISTIAN FAMILY (Alabama): 1031
THE CHRISTIAN ARBITRATOR AND PEACE
    RECORD: 1149
CHRISTIAN CHURCH: see DISCIPLES OF
    CHRIST
CHRISTIAN COMMISSION: 4228
CHRISTIAN COUNTY, Kentucky:
    Hopkinsville: 5070
    Postal service: 4854
THE CHRISTIAN EDUCATOR AND TRINITY
    ENDOWMENT: 547
CHRISTIAN INDEX: 1112, 3625, 4759
"THE CHRISTIAN LAWYER" (sermon): 1832
CHRISTIAN LIFE: 4936, 5699
    Great Britain: 5598
CHRISTIAN METHODIST EPISCOPAL
    CHURCH: 5070
CHRISTIAN SCIENCE:
    Massachusetts: 487
    Boston: 5266
CHRISTIAN UNION (periodical): 5908
CHRISTIANITY: 3738, 4932, 4952
    see also DEISM
    Arkansas: 5380
    Conversion--Idaho Territory: 2714
    India: 2148
    Pennsylvania: 5380
CHRISTIANITY AND COMMERCE: 4936
CHRISTIANITY AND COMMUNISM: see
    COMMUNISM AND CHRISTIANITY
CHRISTIANITY AND POLITICS: 4936
"CHRISTIANITY AND THE BIBLE" by
    Forster Alexander Sondley: 4952
CHRISTIANSBURG, Virginia: 1033, 4360
CHRISTIANSBURG & NATURAL BRIDGE
    MAIL-STAGE LINE: 1797
CHRISTINA, Queen of Sweden: 5379
CHRISTMAN FAMILY (Virginia): 2559
CHRISTMAS: 1551, 5519
    Alabama--Tuscaloosa: 4943
CHRISTMAS CARDS: 225, 3843
    Great Britain: 4115
    United States: 2656
CHRISTMAS EVE by Judith Page
    (Walker) Rives: 5513
CHRISTOPHER, Paul Revere: 1193,
    1197, 1200, 3171, 5486
CHRONICLES OF BORDER WARFARE. . . .
    by Alexander Scott Withers: 5194
"CHRONICLES OF COMINGTEE PLANTATION"
    by John Ball: 296
CHULALONGKORN, Phra Paramindr Maha,
    King of Siam: 4709
CHUNN, Willie: 1034
CHURCH AND EDUCATION: see EDUCATION
    AND THE CHURCH
CHURCH AND POLITICS: see CHRISTIANITY
    AND POLITICS; METHODIST EPISCOPAL
    CHURCH, SOUTH--Political activity

"THE CHURCH AND PRIVATE SCHOOLS OF NORTH CAROLINA" by Charles Lee Raper: 4391
CHURCH AND SLAVERY: see SLAVERY AND THE CHURCH
CHURCH AND SOCIAL PROBLEMS: 4343
   Methodist Churches: 3020
   North Carolina--Rowan County: 4640
CHURCH AND STATE IN GREAT BRITAIN: 1632, 4024, 4331, 4605
   see also CATHOLIC EMANCIPATION; DISSENTING CHURCHES; POLITICAL DISABILITIES; TITHES
CHURCH AND STATE IN THE AMERICAN COLONIES:
   Carolina Province: 202
CHURCH AND STATE IN THE UNITED STATES:
   Catholic Church: 3840
CHURCH AND WAR:
   Civil War:
      Protestant Episcopal Church: 128
   Vietnamese War:
      Methodist Churches: 3020
CHURCH ARCHITECTURE: 5619
   Great Britain--Truro: 5553
CHURCH CONFERENCE ON SOCIAL WORK: 4343
CHURCH FINANCE: see Finance as a subheading under names of specific denominations
CHURCH HISTORY: 5544
   see also Church history as subheading under names of specific denominations
   France--Dauphiné: 4408
   Great Britain--Middle Ages: 2841
   North Carolina: 1738, 4232
   Peru--Arequipa: 4155
   South Carolina: 4453
   Virginia: 872
CHURCH MISSIONARY SOCIETY: 5725, 5726
CHURCH MUSIC: 2970, 5619
   see also CHOIRS; HYMNS; SONGS AND MUSIC
   Episcopal--South Carolina: 2110
   North Carolina: 108, 1538
CHURCH OF CHRIST IN AMERICA: 1194, 1197
CHURCH OF ENGLAND: 5731
   see also OXFORD MOVEMENT; WESLEYAN MOVEMENT
   Bishops:
      see also names of specific bishops and archbishops
      Appointments: 3798
      Sierra Leone: 2149
      Conclaves--Great Britain: 2148
      Reduction in numbers: 4605
   Book of Common Prayer: 5616
   Clergy: see CLERGY--Church of England
   Diocese of Winchester: 1035
   Disestablishment: 5876
   Doctrine--Great Britain: 2953
   Finance--Great Britain: 1035, 5726
   High Church: 735
   Liturgy and ritual:
      Great Britain: 2953
   Missions and missionaries: see MISSIONS AND MISSIONARIES--Church of England
   Organization--Great Britain: 1035
   Relations with Catholic Church:
      Ireland: 5726
   Relations with Methodist churches: 2751
      Great Britain: 5647
   Schools: see SCHOOLS--Church schools--Church of England
   Sermons: see SERMONS--Church of England
   Subdivided by place:
      British colonies: 5726

CHURCH OF ENGLAND:
   Subdivided by place:
      Canada--Quebec: 3911
      Carolina Province: 202
      Great Britain: 43, 306, 346, 537, 1311, 1571, 4913, 5726
      Ireland: 5726
      Maryland: 5296
      Tasmania: 5725
      Wales: 4331
CHURCH OF GOD--Church history: 2893
CHURCH OF JESUS CHRIST OF THE LATTER DAY SAINTS: see MORMONS AND MORMONISM
CHURCH OF IRELAND:
   see also DISSENTING CHURCHES
   Archbishop of Dublin: 5663
   Disestablishment: 472, 2127
   Finance: 5637
   Reorganization: 2826
CHURCH OF SCOTLAND: 118, 306, 5726
CHURCH OF THE BRETHREN:
   Camp meetings: 221
   Virginia: 5839
CHURCH OF THE DISCIPLES:
   Massachusetts: 1074
CHURCH OFFICERS: see Deacons and Elders as subheadings under names of specific denominations
CHURCH PLATE--Great Britain: 2784
CHURCH REFORM:
   Ireland: 4605
   New England: 5088
CHURCH REGISTER (periodical): 5635
CHURCH SCHOOLS: see SCHOOLS--Church schools
CHURCH SERVICES: see CHURCHES--Liturgy and ritual; and Liturgy and ritual as subheading under names of specific denominations
CHURCH UNIVERSAL (Theology): 1892
CHURCHES:
   see also DISSENTING CHURCHES; SUNDAY SCHOOLS; and names of specific denominations [with subheadings similar to those found under CHURCHES]
   Church buildings:
      see also CATHEDRALS; CHURCH ARCHITECTURE
      Great Britain--Manchester: 4287
      North Carolina:
         African church: 5041
         Randolph County: 88
      Southern States: 1589
      Virginia: 824
         Rockingham County: 576
   Finance--North Carolina: 2347
   Fund raising: 5497
   Interchurch organizations:
      North Carolina--Rowan County: 4640
      United States: 3633
   Liturgy and ritual--Alabama: 3611
   Newspapers: see RELIGIOUS LITERATURE
   Subdivided by place:
      Canada--Quebec: 3911
      Georgia--Bethel: 2460
      Germany--Berlin: 2139
      Great Britain: 3498
         Somersetshire: 1071
      North Carolina: 1232
         Elizabeth City: 3919
         Iredell County: 5245
         Oak Grove Township: 3896
      Pennsylvania--Franklin County: 2643
      South Carolina:
         Charleston: 2107, 2410, 3801
         Edisto: 2027
      Virginia--Columbia: 5091
CHURCHILL, Frank C.: 1036
CHURCHILL, John, First Duke of Marlborough: 5872
CHURCHILL, John Wesley (Massachusetts): 1037

CHURCHILL, Lord Randolph: 294, 2324, 4028
CHURCHILL, William: 1038
CHURCHILL, Winston Leonard Spencer: 233, 4520
CHURCHILL-SPENCER, Consuelo (Vanderbilt): 5968
CHURCHMAN, John: 2812
CHURCHWELL, William Montgomery: 4193
CHURTON, Edward: 2203
CIARDI, John: 902
CID DISTRICT, North Carolina: 2041
CIGAR MANUFACTURE: see TOBACCO INDUSTRY
CIGAR TRADE:
   see also TOBACCO TRADE
   Imports from Cuba: 1442
CIGARETTE MAKING MACHINES:
   Virginia: 5297
CIGARETTE MANUFACTURING: see TOBACCO INDUSTRY
CIGARETTE SMOKING: see TOBACCO SMOKING
CIGARETTE SMOKING AND HEALTH: 83
CIGARETTE TRADE:
   see also TOBACCO TRADE
   China: 5252
CILLEY, Samuel T.: 1039
CILLEY FAMILY (Vermont): 1039
CINCINNATI, Ohio: 72, 327, 1207, 1578, 2514, 2948, 3030, 4326, 4539, 5099, 5168, 5171, 5405, 5785
   Autographs: 1040
   Civil War aid societies: 5268
   Commodity prices: 5149
   Description: 1811, 2601, 3135, 4080, 5149, 5593
   Wages and salaries: 5149
CINCINNATI (gunboat): 3983
CINCINNATI, CUMBERLAND GAP, AND CHARLESTON RAILROAD: 3692
CINCINNATI, SOCIETY OF THE: see SOCIETY OF THE CINCINNATI
CINCINNATI GAZETTE (newspaper): 2526
CINEMA: see MOVING PICTURES
CINNAMON TRADE--Great Britain: 2742
CIPHERS: see CODES
CIRCASSIA:
   Foreign relations:
      Great Britain: 258
CIRCUIT COURTS: see COURTS--Circuit courts
CIRCULAR SAWS: see SAWS
CIRCUSES: 291, 1094
   see also PERFORMING ARTS; WILD WEST SHOWS
CIST, Henry Martyn: 5536
CIST, Lewis Jacob: 1040
THE CITADEL, Charleston, South Carolina: 1424, 3451
   Commencement addresses: 3421
CITIZEN GENET AFFAIR: 3041
CITIZENS BANK, Petersburg, Virginia: 5631
CITIZENS NATIONAL BANK, Durham, North Carolina: 1041
CITIZEN'S NATIONAL BANK OF FULTON, New York: 929
CITIZENSHIP:
   see also DUAL CITIZENSHIP; NEGROES--Citizenship
   France: 372
   Qualifications:
      see also TEST OATHS
      West Virginia: 1828
   United States: 4927
      Laws and legislation: 5537
CITY CENTRAL LABOR UNION (AFL): 1172
CITY EMPLOYEES: see GOVERNMENT AND CIVIC EMPLOYEES
CITY FEDERATION OF TRADERS: 1172
CITY GOVERNMENT: see MUNICIPAL GOVERNMENT
CITY OF SAN FRANCISCO (ship): 4535

CITY POINT, Virginia:
  Civil War:
    Battle of: see CIVIL WAR--
      CAMPAIGNS, BATTLES AND MILITARY
      ACTIONS--Virginia--City Point
    Explosion of ammunition barges:
      3741
    Hospitals: 3281
    United States Army camp life:
      5677
CITY ROAD'S CHURCH, Elizabeth City,
  North Carolina: 3919
CIVIC IMPROVEMENT:
  see also URBAN DEVELOPMENT
  North Carolina--Durham: 4968
CIVIL DISORDERS: see DEMONSTRATIONS;
  RIOTS
CIVIL ENGINEERING: 3145, 3674, 5772
  Accounts: 5456
  Students' notebooks:
    Maryland: 2669
    Pennsylvania:
      Lehigh University: 5679
  Subdivided by place:
    Georgia:
      Savannah River: 89
    Great Britain: 4770
    North Carolina:
      Franklin County: 76
    Tennessee: 3069
    West Virginia: 5456
CIVIL LAW:
  see also LAWS AND LEGISLATION
  Prussia--Trier: 201
CIVIL-MILITARY RELATIONS: see as
  subheading under names of armies
CIVIL RIGHTS:
  see also CIVIL WAR--CIVIL RIGHTS;
    HABEAS CORPUS; NEGROES--
    Civil Rights
  Great Britain: 5616, 5762
  New York--New York: 2083
  South Carolina: 4149
  United States: 3020, 3066, 3820,
    4386, 4805, 4948
CIVIL SERVICE:
  Appointments: 3657
  Examinations: 1920
  Pensions:
    Great Britain: 3286
      Government and civic
        employees: 4097
  Subdivided by place:
    India: 774
    Philippine Islands: 3313
    United States: 4805, 4858

        CIVIL WAR

see also CONFEDERATE STATES OF
  AMERICA; UNITED STATES--ARMY--
  Civil War; UNITED STATES--NAVY--
  Civil War

    General references:

51, 1889, 2261, 2306, 2485, 2604,
  2865, 3092, 3327, 3587, 3906,
  3931, 4396, 4739, 4921, 5160,
  5228, 5498, 5500, 5561, 5704,
  5740, 5941
Alabama: 444, 1121, 2929, 3188, 4529,
  5032
Arizona Territory: 1181
Arkansas: 2929
Florida: 566
Georgia: 788, 1011, 1066, 1434, 2372,
  2671, 2963, 3075, 3552, 3901, 4884,
  5032, 5566
  Augusta: 1185
  Savannah: 3310
Indiana: 3698, 3963
Kentucky: 135, 2671
Louisiana: 805, 1253, 3823
  Plaquemines Parish: 375
Maryland: 4866

        CIVIL WAR

    General references:

Mississippi: 566, 1137, 1276, 2671,
  2929, 3276, 3587, 3963, 4034, 5032
Missouri: 4733
North Carolina: 19, 500, 760, 790,
  796, 1061, 1100, 1252, 1326, 1659,
  1677, 1896, 2357, 2530, 2929, 3515,
  4267, 4318, 5826, 5926
  Goldsboro: 4196
  Merryhill: 1100
  Wilmington: 1313, 3673
Ohio: 281
Pennsylvania: 4190
South Carolina: 46, 1235, 1793,
  2107, 2210, 2473, 3880, 4347,
  4429, 4834
  Charleston: 4958
Southern States: 4648
Tennessee: 135, 872, 3552, 3959,
  4269, 4723, 5032
  Knoxville: 4849
  Memphis: 4573
Texas: 2920, 4562
Virginia: 7, 19, 489, 566, 760,
  1115, 1393, 1793, 2305, 2940,
  2942, 2955, 2966, 2971, 3142, 3175,
  3823, 4562, 4938, 5566, 5751,
  5926
  Petersburg: 4577
  Richmond: 128, 2520, 3880
  Williamsburg: 3318
Washington, D.C.: 368, 931, 1058,
  4022, 5695
West Virginia: 128, 968
  Martinsburg: 4537

    Subdivided by subject:

ABANDONED LANDS: 5431
AID SOCIETIES:
  see also: CIVIL WAR--PUBLIC
    WELFARE--Aid to soldier's
    families
  Confederate: 390, 4951, 5098
  Union: 4228
  Georgia: 2372
    Atlanta: 3991
  Louisiana: 3071
  North Carolina--Raleigh: 3761
  Ohio--Cincinnati: 5268
  South Carolina: 669
    Greenville: 2183
  Tennessee: 4951
  Virginia--New Market: 2949
ALIEN PROPERTY:
  Confederate: 1365
  Union: 2792
AMERICANS IN CHINA--Opinion: 1298
ANECDOTES--Confederate: 1962
ARMISTICE (proposed): see CIVIL
  WAR--PEACE MOVEMENT
ARMY LIFE: see under names of armies
BLOCKADE: 2510, 2966, 3012, 3415,
  3809, 4881, 4982, 5955
  see also UNITED STATES--NAVY--
    Civil War--Blockade
  Effect on trade: 1181, 3440
  Chesapeake Bay: 4924
  Florida: 1610
  Georgia--Savannah: 1798
  Louisiana: 5169
  North Carolina: 1361, 5169, 5344
    Fort Fisher: 3370
    Wilmington: 1281, 2970, 3435,
      4553
  South Carolina: 5436
    Charleston: 2449, 2831, 4982
  Virginia--Norfolk: 4183
BLOCKADE RUNNING: 1187, 1301, 1403,
  1424, 2806, 3079, 3447, 4881, 4986,
  5063, 5298, 5661, 5676
  Albion Trading Company: 410
  British: 2258, 5500
  Intended: 2766

        CIVIL WAR

    Subdivided by subject:

BLOCKADE RUNNING (Continued):
  North Carolina: 565
    Fort Fisher: 3370
    Wilmington: 4734
  South Carolina: 757, 2017, 4347
    Charleston: 4531
  Sumter: 2963
BOUNTIES: 4732
  Illinois: 5570
BRITISH IN THE C.S.A.: 3606, 4484
BRITISH IN THE UNITED STATES:
  Mississippi: 3606
  Washington, D.C.: 3472
BURIAL GROUNDS: 1137, 1191, 2509
  Andrews' Raiders: 5425
  Confederate: 3378
  Spies: 2180
  Georgia: 5415
  South Carolina: 5415
  Tennessee--Franklin: 3374
  Virginia: 2305, 4059
CAMP LIFE: see CONFEDERATE STATES OF
  AMERICA--ARMY--Camp life; UNITED
  STATES--ARMY--Civil War--Camp life
CAMPAIGNS, BATTLES, AND MILITARY
  ACTIONS: 99, 546, 620, 1183, 1408,
  1948, 2469, 2579, 2791, 2960,
  3276, 3587, 3624, 4808, 4950, 5510,
  5670, 5751, 5946
  Accounts collected by DeBow: 1439
  Alabama: 2987
    Fort Deposit: 5437
    Greenville: 1186
    Huntsville: 954, 1084
    Mobile: 276, 532, 1403, 3754,
    Pollard: 1186
    Selma: 4477
    Wilson's Raid: 120, 3951, 4185
  Arkansas:
    Arkadelphia: 5651
    Camden: 5651
    Helena: 2553, 2617
    Jenkins' Ferry: 4536
    Pea Ridge: 3392
    Prairie Grove: 3392
  Florida: 662, 3127
    Cedar Keys: 700
    Fernandina: 4881
    Fort Pickens: 5621
    Jacksonville: 3264
    Pensacola: 532, 566
    Santa Rosa Island: 3647
  Georgia: 395, 972, 1276
    Atlanta: 883, 1403, 1520, 1705,
      1984, 2119, 2433, 2504, 3648,
      3729, 3901, 3951, 3953, 4183,
      4255, 4358, 4565, 4588, 4708,
      4944, 5348, 5364, 5419, 5676
      Celebration after capture: 2308
    Augusta: 2893
    Dalton: 4033
    Fort McAllister: 5017
    Fort Pulaski: 3264
    Jonesboro: 3318
    Kenesaw Mountain: 4588, 5751
    New Hope Church: 1520
    Peachtree Creek: 4255
    Pine Mountain: 5419
    Resaca: 2504
    Rocky Face Ridge: 4255
    Savannah: 560, 689, 764, 1468,
      4292, 5453
    Sherman's March: 510, 560, 689,
      1137, 1175, 1403, 2372, 2561,
      3318, 3343, 3648, 3951, 4895,
      4993, 5017, 5311, 5453
  Gulf States: 5621
  Illinois:
    Paducah: 4662
  Kansas:
    Fort Scott: 4065

CIVIL WAR

Subdivided by subject:

CAMPAIGNS, BATTLES, AND MILITARY ACTIONS (Continued):
Kentucky: 2325, 2987, 3170, 3496
  Bragg's Invasion: 755, 2893
  Mill Springs: 2092, 4723
  Morgan's raid, 1863: 765
  Perryville: 1973, 3457, 4358
Louisiana: 1763
  Fort Butler--Maps: 5417
  New Orleans: 488, 1403, 1476, 2691
  Port Hudson: 333, 1349, 2777, 5715
  Red River, 1863: 25, 383, 1253, 5169
  Red River, 1864: 2106, 4888, 5208
Maryland: 2453, 2490, 2971
  Antietam: 128, 1177, 1476, 2106, 2326, 2333, 3417, 3809, 4059, 4276, 4292, 4347, 4698, 4891, 5315, 5518, 5633
  Baltimore: 5626
  Crampton's Gap: 460
  Frederick: 4537
  Hagerstown: 5230
  Invasion of Maryland (1862): 3203
  Sharpsburg: see CIVIL WAR--CAMPAIGNS, BATTLES, AND MILITARY ACTIONS--Maryland--Antietam
  South Mountain: 1177
  Williamsport: 4608
Mississippi: 755, 1382, 1984, 2882, 2987
  Baker's Creek: 1853
  Corinth: 659, 1137, 1370, 3496, 4723
  Farmington: 1186
  Hatchie River: 5975
  Iuka: 1370, 5311
  Jackson: 3415, 3648
  Port Gibson: 5571
  Vicksburg: 336, 395, 502, 808, 972, 1137, 1268, 1403, 1853, 1984, 2490, 2561, 2829, 2881, 2898, 3276, 3357, 3392, 3520, 3555, 3788, 3809, 3953, 4076, 4347, 4881, 5132, 5751
    Naval Operations: 532
    Seige: 765, 3415, 3648, 5062, 5311
    Surrender: 1349, 2180
Mississippi River: 314, 1403, 3170
Missouri: 2987
  Island No. 10: 659
  Kirksville: 5481
  Oak Hill: 1138
  Springfield: 4065
Naval engagements: 484
  Monitor, U.S.S. v. Virginia, C.S.S.: 2091, 2777, 2829, 2963, 3959, 4537
  Virginia, C.S.S. v. Union fleet (1862): 4505
  Weehawken, U.S.S. v. Atlanta, C.S.S.: 3264
North Carolina: 316, 2257, 3037, 3434
  Averasboro: 2864, 5661, 5991
  Beaufort: 4349
  Bentonville: 689, 1364, 2864, 5661, 5991
  Cape Hatteras: 1419, 5231
  Durham: 5991
  Elizabeth City: 1327
  Fayetteville: 5991
  Fort Fisher: 81, 754, 1095, 1182, 1426, 1845, 2331, 2686, 2970, 3022, 3079, 3741, 4087, 4404, 4881, 5045, 5712
  Fort Hatteras: 4982, 5703
  Fort Macon: 494
  Goldsboro: 243, 2091, 4347
  Johnston's retreat: 2829

CIVIL WAR

Subdivided by Subject:

CAMPAIGNS, BATTLES, AND MILITARY ACTIONS:
North Carolina (Continued):
  Johnston's surrender: 123, 440, 2469, 2864, 5058, 5991
  Kinston: 1246, 2091, 3237, 3506, 4118, 4347, 4349, 5280
  New Bern: 1230, 1246, 1426, 2416, 2803, 4349
  Pamlico Sound: 1282
  Plymouth: 2617, 3095, 4349
  Raleigh: 243, 3331, 5991
  Roanoke Island: 1230, 1327, 2091, 3642, 4044, 4349, 4426
  Sherman's March: 243, 560, 689, 834, 1175, 2504, 2617, 2864, 3146, 3343, 3648, 3908, 4945, 5069, 5280, 5311, 5991
  South Mills: 3440
  Washington: 2416, 2902, 3281, 4561, 5417, 5713
  Whitehall: 2091
  Wilmington: 3201, 3741, 4553
Ohio:
  Morgan's raid: 3341
Pennsylvania: 754, 1918, 2490
  Chambersburg: 3957
  Gettysburg: 412, 820, 832, 1005, 1050, 1094, 1105, 1364, 1437, 1590, 2124, 2326, 2416, 2596, 2902, 2946, 2963, 3237, 3262, 3417, 3464, 3793, 3809, 4059, 4196, 4277, 4440, 4769, 4808, 4881, 4908, 4928, 5230, 5298, 5303, 5775, 5839
    Aftermath: 1017
    Confederate losses: 4729
    Culp's Hill: 3832
    Maps: 4495
  Invasion of (1863): 5641
South Carolina: 395, 2657, 3127
  Bennett's Point: 2997
  Bennettsville: 5415
  Charleston: 498, 883, 1403, 1426, 1476, 1845, 2107, 2124, 2223, 2449, 2596, 2695, 2702, 2805, 2806, 2818, 2944, 3624, 4881, 5645, 5646
    Bombardment: 1334, 2180
    Rumors of Sherman's taking: 4553
    Seige: 1107, 5061
  Columbia: 2893, 5415, 5466
  Cunningham's Bluff: 4620
  Edisto Island: 4118
  Fort Sumter: 24, 883, 1005, 1028, 1107, 1299, 1606, 2107, 2805, 3264, 3435, 4908, 4982, 5061, 5955
  Fort Wagner: 3264, 4602
  Fort Walker: 3264
  Honey Hill: 5759
  James Island: 4347, 5645
  Morris Island: 5119
  Port Royal: 510, 1282, 2695, 3264, 3415, 4881, 4986
  Secessionville: 4347
  Sherman's March: 560, 689, 1175, 1334, 2086, 2561, 2864, 3343, 3684, 4945, 5069, 5311, 5633, 5892, 5991
Southern States: 4982
Tennessee: 755, 1276, 2882, 2987, 3354, 3417, 3496
  Chattanooga: 883, 1017, 1403, 2831, 3122, 3648, 4033, 4160, 4417, 5032, 5419, 5608, 5858, 5898
  Cheat Mountain: 4358
  Chickamauga: 659, 1091, 1452, 2997, 3122, 3262, 3951, 4358, 5419, 5858
    Disposition of the dead: 2509
  East Tennessee: 4565, 5258

CIVIL WAR

Subdivided by Subject:

CAMPAIGNS, BATTLES, AND MILITARY ACTIONS:
Tennessee (Continued):
  Fort Donelson: 1836, 3331, 3809, 5775
  Fort Henry: 395, 3809, 5311
  Fort London: 3318
  Fort Pillow: 4065, 4596, 4662
  Franklin: 1186, 1520, 2630, 3282
  Greeneville: 5268, 5280
  Hood's campaign: 664, 972
  Johnsonville: 2681
  Knoxville: 1017, 3122, 3318, 3417, 4245
  Lookout Mountain: 2997
  Memphis: 3170
  Missionary Ridge: 1175, 1505
  Mossy Creek: 3751
  Murfreesboro: 1328, 3415, 3479, 4160, 4358, 5858, 5955
    see also CIVIL WAR--CAMPAIGNS, BATTLES, AND MILITARY ACTIONS--Tennessee--Stones River (1862)
  Nashville: 132, 135, 3282, 3951, 5898
  Pittsburg Landing: 5975
  Russellville: 3318
  Rutherford County: 104
  Sherman's March: 689, 3951
  Shiloh: 45, 395, 1186, 1984, 3457, 3496, 3566, 4269, 4320, 4358, 4723, 4989
  Stones River (1862): 808, 2235, 2858, 3457, 3951, 5303, 5311
    see also CIVIL WAR--CAMPAIGNS, BATTLES, AND MILITARY ACTIONS--Tennessee--Murfreesboro
  Wilson's Creek: 5858
Texas: 2408
  Galveston: 2777
Vermont:
  Saint Albans: 1084
Virginia: 91, 121, 122, 216, 714, 745, 905, 1058, 1384, 1425, 1501, 2068, 2257, 2320, 2370, 2396, 2547, 2681, 2691, 2966, 2971, 3354, 3434, 4007, 5269, 5578, 5984
  Aldie: 3809
  Appomattox: 2223, 3809, 4087, 4277
  Arrowfield Church: 4349
  Ball's Bluff: 2416, 5280
  Beaver Dam Station: 5472
  Bermuda Hundred: 2453, 4347, 4349, 5172
  Bethel Church: 1506, 5068, 5839
  Bethesda Church: 2038
  Big Bethel: 1801
  Brandy Station: 2416, 4277
  Bristoe Station: 2416, 4059
  Bull Run: see CIVIL WAR--CAMPAIGNS, BATTLES, AND MILITARY ACTIONS--Virginia--Manassas
  Cedar Creek: 1295, 3813, 5419
  Cedar Mountain: 251, 1505, 1740, 2106
  Cedar Run: 2490
  Centreville: 4908
  Chafin's Farm: 2453
  Chancellorsville: 460, 543, 820, 1105, 1364, 1590, 2326, 3262, 3778, 3809, 3908, 4059, 4248, 4698, 5121, 5514
  Chesterfield Junction: 4349
  Chickahominy Swamp: 4743
  City Point: 3741
  Cold Harbor: 1361, 2236, 2416, 2648, 4349, 5383, 5626, 5646
  Cross Keys: 1543
  Culpeper: 2681
  Culpeper Court House: 1564

CIVIL WAR

Subdivided by Subject:

CAMPAIGNS, BATTLES, AND MILITARY ACTIONS:
  Virginia (Continued):
    Danville: 4087
    Dranesville: 1506, 2178, 3809
    Drewry's Bluff: 343, 1680, 4891, 5646
    Fair Oaks: 1402, 2091, 3201
    Fairfax Court House: 3281, 5382
    Fisher's Hill: 3886
    Five Forks: 1272, 3809, 4059
    Fort Harrison: 66
    Fort Republic: 1543
    Franklin: 2679
    Frazier's Farm: 460, 5852
    Fredericksburg: 251, 1005, 1105, 1107, 1175, 1230, 1235, 1424, 1506, 1543, 1590, 2124, 2236, 2453, 2831, 2898, 3136, 4059, 4292, 4698, 4743, 4818, 4877, 5034, 5121, 5261, 5280, 5417, 5518, 5852
      Observation balloons: 2240
      Pictorial illustrations: 2236
      Union casualties: 3778
    French's Field: 460
    Gaines' Mill: 5852
    Gainesville: 5034
    Gordonsville: 132
    Hampton: 3318
    Hanover Court House: 2829, 3415
    Hatcher's Run: 3320, 4087
    Kelly's Ford: 1105, 4908
    Leesburg: 1506, 2305, 3809, 4908
    Lynchburg: 1177, 5739
    Malvern Hill: 460, 4485, 5514, 5852
    Manassas: 2829, 4594, 5852
    Manassas (1861): 128, 395, 565, 566, 639, 713, 832, 1105, 1145, 1204, 1506, 1601, 1788, 1826, 1865, 1947, 2092, 2305, 2510, 2654, 2831, 2882, 3318, 3357, 3809, 4131, 4248, 4347, 4733, 4743, 4831, 4860, 5122, 5143, 5231, 5419, 5824
      Map: 1444
    Manassas (1862): 251, 412, 460, 1145, 1680, 2236, 2311, 2631, 3122, 3464, 4000, 4276, 4834, 4881, 5314, 5518
    Mud March: 2898
    Nelson County: 4259
    Newport News: 2453, 4479
    Norfolk: 1403, 2453
    North Anna Creek: 1882
    Northern Virginia: 4118
    Orange Court House: 91
    Peninsular Campaign: 395, 543, 1105, 1122, 1590, 1740, 2777, 2989, 2997, 3203, 3301, 3417, 3440, 3542, 3809, 4059, 4485, 4743, 4990, 5063, 5472, 5518, 5560, 5649, 5670, 5775, 5834
    Petersburg: 395, 1175, 1361, 1426, 1845, 1882, 2223, 2236, 2243, 2297, 2416, 2493, 2744, 2777, 2803, 3133, 3142, 3181, 3469, 4083, 4087, 4347, 4561, 4929, 4970, 5209, 5280, 5419, 5472, 5877, 5939
      Crater: 334, 2416, 4612
      Siege: 78, 334, 566, 1295, 1820, 2648, 2657, 3809, 4052, 4131, 4183, 4277, 4349, 4818, 4895, 5518, 5741, 5834, 5896, 5919, 5926
      Final assault: 132
    Piedmont: 4537
    Port Republic: 5898
    Port Walthal: 4349
    Potomac River: 128, 2091
    Rappahannock Station: 820

CIVIL WAR

Subdivided by Subject:

CAMPAIGNS, BATTLES, AND MILITARY ACTIONS:
  Virginia (Continued):
    Richmond: 66, 2596, 3741, 5143
      1862: 1806, 2326, 3115, 3469, 3905
      1863: 1359, 4881, 5272
      1864: 1402, 1432, 1590, 1845, 1886, 2490, 4059, 4698, 4818, 4891, 5855
      Supply by railroad: 1183
      Surrender and burning: 1740, 1827, 3809, 3822
    Sayler's Creek: 66, 132
    Seven Days: 566, 1590, 2553, 2902, 3122, 3463, 3809, 4292, 5560
    Seven Pines: 460, 2416, 2553, 2829, 2902, 3262, 4000, 5543
    Sewell's Point: 460
    Shenandoah Valley: 1364, 3788
      1862: 314, 2396, 2971
      1864: 78, 2106, 2777, 4440, 4671
      1865: 3464, 3788, 4888, 5739
      Depredations: 1920
    Smithfield: 2121
    Spotsylvania: 1364, 1699, 1882, 2236, 2326, 4318, 4818, 5739
    Staunton: 2792
    Stuart's cavalry raids around McClellan's army (1862): 2902
    Suffolk: 132, 4349, 5261, 5852
    Todd's Tavern: 3809
    Waynesboro: 3809
    Western Virginia (1861-1862): 1836
    White House: 5739
    Wilderness: 78, 1295, 1805, 1861, 2306, 2326, 2416, 2971, 3126, 3318, 4059, 5646
    Williamsburg: 2091, 2997, 3115, 5061, 5852
    Winchester: 314, 368, 2106, 2949, 3813, 4663, 5000, 5739
    Yorktown: 2453, 3115, 4043, 4349, 4849, 5061
  Washington, D.C.: 3654
  West Virginia: 3357
    Carrick's Ford: 3339
    Cheat Mountain: 5419
    Greenbrier: 4131
    Harpers Ferry: 1436, 1590, 1680, 2648, 2792, 3532, 4608, 4769
    Laurel Hill: 3339
    Lewisburg: 1596
    Martinsburg: 2949
    Rich Mountain: 66
    Romney: 363, 4483
CATHOLICS--Maryland: 314
CAUSES: 3325
CENSORSHIP: 128, 4834
CHURCHES:
  Protestant Episcopal: 128
CIVIL RIGHTS:
  see also CIVIL WAR--MARTIAL LAW
  Suspension of Habeas corpus by Confederate government: 4921
CIVILIAN LIFE: 4358, 5018, 5672
  Care of sick and wounded: 3378
  Evacuation of women: 5865
  Farming:
    North Carolina: 2763
    Southern States: 2686
  Food prices: 5230
    North Carolina: 614
    South Carolina: 4118
  Health conditions: 1912
  Morale: 5921, 5926, 5931
    Georgia: 2882
    Massachusetts: 1537
    Mississippi: 1864
    New York: 388

CIVIL WAR

Subdivided by Subject:

CIVILIAN LIFE:
  Morale (Continued):
    North Carolina: 518, 2297
    South Carolina: 1468, 2882
    Southern States: 1836, 2939
    Tennessee: 881
    Virginia: 99, 1506, 1827
  Plantation management: 4426, 5651
  Religion: 827
  Scarcity of food: 5855
    Georgia: 1739
    North Carolina: 612, 4595
    South Carolina: 881, 2107
    Virginia: 4616, 5798
  Scarcity of horses and mules:
    South Carolina: 4332
  Scarcity of money:
    North Carolina: 2763
  Scarcity of paper:
    Southern States: 651
  Scarcity of smallpox vaccine:
    Georgia: 4754
  Scarcity of supplies: 3809, 4332
  Scarcity of textiles:
    Georgia: 1829
  Scarcity of wagons:
    South Carolina: 4332
  Subdivided by place:
    Alabama: 1084, 3331, 5053
      Tallapoosa County: 5916
    Florida--Duval County: 4410
    Georgia: 807, 1017, 1056, 2326, 3331, 3901, 5364, 5724
    Illinois: 1631, 5311
    Indiana: 808, 4588
    Kentucky: 3341
    Louisiana:
      New Orleans: 3775, 5062, 5194
    Maryland:
      Baltimore: 5775
      Frederick: 5324
    Massachusetts: 3280
    Mississippi: 530, 1180, 1370, 1382, 3276, 4596, 4769
    Missouri: 4477, 4679
    New York: 5738
    North Carolina: 269, 530, 614, 754, 827, 966, 1556, 2427, 2716, 3237, 3447, 4248, 4357, 4689, 4923, 5123, 5298
      Buncombe County: 4417
      Caswell County: 5900
      New Bern: 4438, 5543
      Randolph County: 518, 5595
    Northern States: 1352
    Pennsylvania: 5775
    South Carolina: 669, 3485, 4118, 4554, 4700
      Charleston: 1700, 2610, 4982, 5001, 5892
      Cheraw: 2107
      Florence: 2107
      Lexington: 5834
      York County: 4347
    Southern States: 43, 45, 2370, 2553, 2806, 2808, 2939, 3519, 3809
    Tennessee: 104, 3331, 3341, 4723
    Texas: 5194
    Vermont: 4485
    Virginia: 154, 375, 404, 693, 1605, 1701, 1877, 2427, 2559, 2584, 3136, 3464, 4496, 4698, 4700, 4924, 5954
      Amherst County: 5290
      Appomattox Court House: 5902
      Charlottesville: 3293
      Nelson County: 5290
      Norfolk: 2085
      Northern Neck: 3793
      Petersburg: 602, 5382
      Richmond: 566, 602, 682, 4924, 5798

## CIVIL WAR
### Subdivided by subject:

CIVILIAN LIFE:
  Subdivided by place:
    Virginia (Continued):
      Williamsburg: 2085
      Woodville: 5382
    Washington, D.C.: 2777
    West Virginia: 4999
CIVILIAN MORALE: see CIVIL WAR--
  CIVILIAN LIFE--Morale
CLAIMS: 358, 415, 1819
  see also ALABAMA CLAIMS;
    CONFEDERATE STATES OF AMERICA--
    ARMY--Casualties--Claims for
    compensation; UNITED STATES--
    ARMY--Civil War--Casualties--
    Claims for compensation
  Abandoned property: 1181
  Compensation for lost slaves:
    3442
  Compensation for military
    service: see CIVIL WAR--
    VETERANS--Union--Claims
  Confiscated property: 4579
    see also SLAVES--Recovery of
    Claims against the Confederate
      States of America: 3012, 5370
    Claims against the United
      States: 5671
    Cotton: 3479, 3606
    Georgia: 1017
    Horses: 2068
    Military use of civilian
      property:
        West Virginia: 1769
    Ships: 5731
    Virginia: 1920
  Destruction of property: 1817,
    2802, 4776
  Loss of schooner on James River:
    1938
CLOTHING AND DRESS:
  see also CONFEDERATE STATES OF
    AMERICA--ARMY--Clothing and
    dress; UNITED STATES--ARMY--
    Civil War--Clothing and dress
  Women's styles--Georgia: 510
COAST DEFENSES:
  Massachusetts: 3283
  North Carolina: 5390
  South Carolina: 2864, 4193
  Southern States: 4729
COMMODITY PRICES: 1301, 2791, 3788,
  3809, 4849, 5311, 5551, 5703,
  5975, 5984
  see also CIVIL WAR--BLOCKADE--
    Effect on trade; CIVIL WAR--
    FOOD PRICES
  Florida: 5955
  Georgia: 1397, 2365, 5724
  Louisiana: 1763
  Maryland: 3378
  Mississippi: 4769
  New York: 1763
  North Carolina: 264, 1056, 3276,
    4052, 4080, 5511
    New Bern: 1282
  Northern States: 4561
  South Carolina: 219, 4554
    Charleston: 5193
  Southern States: 523, 1183, 2240,
    3351, 4895, 4921, 5518, 5965
  Tennessee: 5444
  Virginia: 122, 363, 468, 2510,
    2939, 2966, 4496, 5444, 5511,
    5873
    Petersburg: 3730
    Richmond: 2902, 5798
CONCILIATORY EFFORTS TO AVOID WAR:
  5627
CONCLUSION OF HOSTILITIES: see
  CIVIL WAR--FINAL DAYS
CONFISCATION OF PROPERTY: 1845,
  2695, 4149, 4537, 4924, 5132

## CIVIL WAR
### Subdivided by subject:

CONFISCATION OF PROPERTY (Continued):
  see also CIVIL WAR--CLAIMS--
    Confiscated property;
    CONFEDERATE STATES OF AMERICA--
    MILITARY REQUISITIONS
  Commodities: 5991
    Georgia: 3905
  Confederate States of America:
    1969, 3012
    Army: 1154, 3044
  Cotton: 4921
    see also CIVIL WAR--CLAIMS--
      Confiscated property--Cotton
    Mississippi: 3606
    Texas: 1138
  Farm products--South Carolina: 1749
  Horses and mules: 5668, 5991
    see also CIVIL WAR--CLAIMS--
      Confiscated property--Horses
      and mules
    Georgia: 1181
  Land:
    Georgia: 3905
    Virginia: 3566
  Livestock--Alabama: 5593
  Money: 1181
  Slaves:
    see also CIVIL WAR--CONTRABANDS
    Alabama: 5593
    Georgia: 3905
  Sloop--Virginia: 3012
  Tobacco: 4579
  Tools--Alabama: 5593
  United States government property:
    1181
  Wood--Virginia: 1920
  Subdivided by place:
    Alabama: 1084
    Arkansas: 1154
    Georgia: 1993
    Louisiana: 2536
    North Carolina: 1190
    South Carolina: 566
    Southern States: 484
    Texas: 1138
    Virginia: 719
CONSCIENTIOUS OBJECTORS:
  Maryland: 3565
  Society of Friends: 2970
  Treatment of: 2555, 4989
CONSCIENTIOUS OBJECTORS IN CANADA:
  3281, 4086
CONTRABANDS: 162, 1763, 2311, 4537,
  4924, 5017, 5061
  see also CIVIL WAR--CONFISCATION
    OF PROPERTY--Slaves
  North Carolina: 3357, 4438
COTTON MILLS: see COTTON MILLS
DEPREDATIONS: 687, 689, 1181, 4727,
  5123
  see also CIVIL WAR--CLAIMS--
    Confiscated property; CIVIL
    WAR--ECONOMIC ASPECTS--
    Destruction of property;
    CONFEDERATE STATES OF AMERICA--
    ARMY--Depredations; UNITED
    STATES--ARMY--Civil War--
    Depredations
  Negroes--South Carolina: 5514
  Subdivided by place:
    Mississippi: 4769
    Virginia: 358
DISEASES: 484, 808
  see also CIVIL WAR--CIVILIAN
    LIFE--Care of the sick and
    wounded; CONFEDERATE STATES OF
    AMERICA--ARMY--Medical and
    sanitary affairs--Illness and
    disease
  Cholera: 611
  Diphtheria: 3959
  Dysentery--Virginia: 5984
  Malaria: 3264

## CIVIL WAR
### Subdivided by subject:

DISEASES (Continued):
  Measles: 607, 1806, 4831
    Confederate Army: 1731, 2510,
      5147
  Pneumonia: 607
  Smallpox: 3792, 3959, 4875
    Confederate Army: 531
    Preventive inoculation: 4754,
      5098
  Typhoid fever: 3422, 3880
  Vaccinations: 2791
  Yellow fever: 1798
    North Carolina: 3237, 3264
      New Bern: 4561, 5261, 5543
      Wilmington: 3447, 5372
    South Carolina: 3264, 4531
    Virginia--Portsmouth: 2318
  Subdivided by place:
    Georgia: 1619
    Louisiana: 333, 1619
    Mississippi: 1619
    North Carolina: 1619, 1845
    South Carolina: 1845
    Virginia: 132, 1619, 1845
DIVIDED SYMPATHIES: 2270
  District of Columbia: 4348
  Maryland: 3378, 4348
  Missouri: 4679
  West Virginia: 5194
DRAWINGS: 5744
ECONOMIC ASPECTS: 421, 3418, 3447,
  3905, 4929, 4970, 5855
  see also: GREAT BRITAIN--AMERICAN
    CIVIL WAR--Economic aspects
  Cattle raising--Texas: 465
  Destruction of property--
    Louisiana: 1424
  Finance: 3053
  Inflation--Alabama: 5593
  Rice trade--South Carolina: 3485
  Severance of business ties: 5623
  Tobacco trade: 5148
  Subdivided by place:
    Alabama: 4820
    Georgia: 510, 669, 718
    Louisiana: 4275
    Maryland: 411
    South Carolina: 82, 4332
    Southern States: 128, 266, 891,
      1403, 1912, 2553, 2744, 2966,
      3415, 5912
    Tennessee: 3524
    Virginia: 154, 411, 3809
EFFECTS ON LITERATURE: 3418
EMIGRANTS: see CONFEDERATE EMIGRANTS
EXECUTIONS: see CIVIL WAR--
  PRISONERS AND PRISONS--Union
  prisoners--Executions; CIVIL WAR--
  SPIES--Executions; CONFEDERATE
  STATES OF AMERICA--ARMY--
  Executions; UNITED STATES--ARMY--
  Civil War--Deserters--Executions
EXILES:
  see also CONFEDERATE EMIGRANTS
  Cuba: 4958
FINAL DAYS: 1403, 2617, 3809, 4738,
  5897
  see also CIVIL WAR--CAMPAIGNS,
    BATTLES, AND MILITARY ACTIONS--
    North Carolina--Johnston's
    retreat/Johnston's surrender/
    Sherman's march
  Virginia: 1295
FOOD PRICES: 605, 5230, 5613
  see also CIVIL WAR--COMMODITY
    PRICES
  Southern States: 1779, 4950
  Virginia: 1122
FOOD RATIONING: 1969, 2255
  see also UNITED STATES--ARMY--
    Civil War--Food rationing
  South Carolina: 4554
  Virginia: 1969

697

## CIVIL WAR

### Subdivided by subject:

FOREIGN INTERVENTION: 3415, 5613
  France: 4982
  Great Britain: 1889
FOREIGN PUBLIC OPINION:
  Bermuda Islands: 3983
  Canada: 5688
  Europe: 1242, 4958
  Great Britain: 43, 1021
FORTIFICATIONS: 1185
  see also CIVIL WAR--COAST DEFENSES
  Alabama: 13
  Florida: 5417
  Georgia--Savannah: 5472
  Great Lakes: 388
  North Carolina: 5390
    Halifax County--Slave labor: 5511
    Hatteras Island: 1361
    Roanoke Island: 4426
    Wilmington: 1107, 5533
    Winton: 375
  South Carolina: 484, 1189
    Charleston: 1012, 1017, 1606, 4505
      Slave labor: 3371
    Georgetown: 1107
    James Island: 2805
  Southern States--Slave labor: 1944, 4460
  Tennessee--Fort Pillow: 5931
  Virginia:
    Fortress Monroe: 4881
    Norfolk: 375
    Portsmouth: 5975
    Williamsburg: 4490
FRATERNIZATION BETWEEN UNION AND CONFEDERATE SOLDIERS: 2240, 2297, 3778, 3809, 5419, 5518, 5975
FUGITIVE SLAVES: 4608, 4881
GREAT LAKES: see CIVIL WAR--FORTIFICATIONS--Great Lakes
GUERILLAS: 2681, 4716, 4888, 5311
  Mississippi: 4769
    Natchez: 3628
  North Carolina: 4006
  Southern States: 4006
HISTORICAL CONTROVERSIES: 2400, 3809, 4918
HISTORICAL WRITINGS: 1137, 1418, 1439, 1607, 2894, 3079, 3262, 3320, 3417, 3585, 3587, 3793, 3809, 4485, 4918, 5481
  Civilian life: 3223
  Sources: 5922
  Subdivided by place:
    Arkansas: 1453
    North Carolina: 3408
    Southern States: 168, 2400
HORSE STEALING--Mississippi: 4769
HORSES:
  Prices: 1779, 5123
  Scarcity of: see CIVIL WAR--CIVILIAN LIFE--Scarcity of horses and mules
HOSPITALS: 135, 3648, 4010, 4308, 5551
  Georgia: 3555
  Kentucky--West Point: 4889
  Marine Hospital: 4888
  Maryland--Baltimore: 701
  North Carolina: 2265, 4002
    Greensboro: 375, 5741
    Inspection by Union Navy: 2265
    Raleigh: 2458
  South Carolina:
    Columbia: 5759
    Finance: 1468
  Southern States: 4875, 4921, 4951
  Tennessee: 4951
  Virginia: 19, 468, 661, 1983, 2880
    Charlottesville: 824, 3012, 3350
    City Point: 3281
    Lynchburg: 1033, 1506, 1886, 4308

## CIVIL WAR

### Subdivided by subject:

HOSPITALS:
  Virginia:
    Lynchburg (Continued):
      Commissary: 2879
    Richmond: 288, 348, 1886, 2134
    Thoroughfair Gap: 2829
  Washington, D.C.: 701, 2311
HOSPITALS, Military: see CONFEDERATE STATES OF AMERICA--ARMY--Hospitals; UNITED STATES--ARMY--Civil War--Convalescent camps; UNITED STATES--ARMY--Civil War--Hospitals
HOSTAGES--Confederate: 5782
INDIAN RELATIONS WITH THE CONFEDERATE STATES OF AMERICA: 2850
INDIAN RELATIONS WITH THE UNITED STATES--Arkansas: 2184
IRON INDUSTRY: 3447
  Virginia: 5613
IRONCLADS: see names of specific vessels and classes of vessels: e.g., MONITOR, VIRGINIA, Ellet Rams, etc.
JEWS: 639
JOURNALISM: see CIVIL WAR--NEWSPAPERS
LABOR PROBLEMS--Virginia: 5148
LADIES AID SOCIETIES: see CIVIL WAR--AID SOCIETIES
LEAD WORKS--Southern States: 3809
LEADERSHIP:
  Confederate: 1364, 2416, 3642, 4080, 4183, 4950, 5688
  Union: 1540, 4183
LOCAL DEFENSE:
  Georgia: 2317
  Virginia--Williamsburg: 4490
LOYALTY OATHS: 109, 1268, 1854, 2268, 3016, 3628, 3663, 4788, 5062, 5162, 5328, 5402, 5417, 5425, 5444
  see also PRESIDENTIAL PARDONS
  Confederate prisoners: 1184
    see also CIVIL WAR--PRISONERS AND PRISONS--Confederate prisoners--Paroles
  Violations: 5775
  Georgia: 731
  Maryland: 3378
  Mississippi: 5421
  Missouri: 1798
  North Carolina: 730, 1282, 2074, 3437
  South Carolina: 5193
  Virginia: 590, 661, 1894, 2958
MAIL SERVICE BETWEEN NORTH AND SOUTH: see CIVIL WAR--POSTAL SERVICE--Service between North and South
MARTIAL LAW:
  see also CIVIL WAR--CIVIL RIGHTS--Suspension of Habeas corpus
  Kentucky: 839, 3207
  Pennsylvania--Wilkes-Barre: 4086
MEDICAL AND SANITARY AFFAIRS: see CIVIL WAR--NURSES AND NURSING; CONFEDERATE STATES OF AMERICA--ARMY--Medical and sanitary affairs; CONFEDERATE STATES OF AMERICA--NAVY--Medical and sanitary affairs; UNITED STATES--ARMY--Civil War--Medical and sanitary affairs; UNITED STATES SANITARY COMMISSION
MEDICAL SUPPLIES: 4308
  Georgia: 1993
MEMORABILIA: see CONFEDERATE MEMORABILIA
MEMORIAL SOCIETIES--Massachusetts: 4358
MILITARY ACTIVITIES [General reference to troop movements and other activity by unidentified military forces]: 713
  Arkansas: 1154
  Georgia: 3729, 5246
  North Carolina: 1806

## CIVIL WAR

### Subdivided by subject:

MILITARY ACTIVITIES (Continued):
  South Carolina: 881, 4531
  Tennessee: 771, 1795, 3604
  Virginia: 602, 1806
  Richmond: 3436, 4996
MILITARY BURIALS: see CIVIL WAR--BURIAL GROUNDS
MILITARY GOVERNMENT: see CIVIL WAR--MARTIAL LAW; CIVIL WAR--UNION OCCUPATION
MILITARY REQUISITIONS:
  South Carolina: 1480
  Virginia: 1240
MILITARY ROADS: 5991
MORALE: see CIVIL WAR--CIVILIAN LIFE--Morale; CONFEDERATE STATES OF AMERICA--ARMY--Morale; CONFEDERATE STATES OF AMERICA--GOVERNMENT AGENCIES AND OFFICIALS--Morale; UNITED STATES--ARMY--Civil War--Morale
NAVAL ENGAGEMENTS: see CIVIL WAR--CAMPAIGNS, BATTLES, AND MILITARY ACTIONS--Naval engagements
NEWSPAPERS: 1962, 2681, 4190
  British correspondents in the Confederate States of America: 5193
  Reporters and reporting: 128, 5034
  Washington, D.C.: 2526
  Subdivided by place:
    Alabama: 1084
    Georgia: 4706
    Northern States: 56, 3755
    Virginia: 4706
NORTHERN OPINION: 4971, 5342, 5613
  New York: 5687
  Pennsylvania: 421
  Vermont: 1039
NORTHERNERS IN THE SOUTH: 2140
NURSES AND NURSING: 617, 854, 927, 2681, 2791, 2829, 3734, 3809, 4506, 5098, 5268
  see also UNITED STATES SANITARY COMMISSION
OPENING OF HOSTILITIES: 713, 2693, 2832, 3620, 3768, 4193, 4616, 4748, 5263, 5593, 5946
ORDNANCE:
  see also CONFEDERATE STATES OF AMERICA--ARMY--Ordnance; UNITED STATES--ARMY--Civil War--Ordnance
  South Carolina: 1189, 3993
  Virginia: 3480
OUTBREAK: see CIVIL WAR--OPENING OF HOSTILITIES
PATRIOTIC STATIONERY: see PATRIOTIC STATIONERY--Confederate
PEACE MOVEMENT: 533, 696, 1084, 2792
  Southern States: 264
PEACE PROCLAMATION (1865): 1980
PEACE PROSPECTS: 1432, 2745, 2629, 2966, 4748, 5261, 5984
PEACE RUMORS: 7, 5223
PEACE TERMS: 4554
  Southern Opinion: 3809
PENSIONS: 129, 281, 2106, 4601, 4732
  see also CIVIL WAR--VETERANS--Benefit legislation
  Disabled veterans: 4601
  Veterans:
    Confederate: 1154, 5759
    Union: 1619, 1819, 2106, 2547, 3027, 4552, 5097
  Widows: 659, 2808, 3282
  Subdivided by place:
    Maine: 3880
    New Jersey: 4601
    Virginia: 2645
PERSONAL NARRATIVES: see CIVIL WAR--REMINISCENCES

CIVIL WAR

Subdivided by subject:

POETRY: 122, 203, 1187, 1188, 1191, 1814, 2739, 3276, 4164, 4708, 5153, 5436, 5557, 5641, 5901
   Confederate: 1864, 3700, 4950
   Eulogies: 3320
   Union: 2124
POLITICAL PRISONERS: 1084, 1403
   see also CIVIL WAR--PRISONERS AND PRISONS
   Confederate: 1769
   Maryland: 314
   Pardons: 4206
   Virginia: 358
POSTAL SERVICE: 4588
   Georgia: 510
   Service between North and South: 5593, 5687
PRICES: see CIVIL WAR--COMMODITY PRICES; CIVIL WAR--FOOD PRICES; CIVIL WAR--HORSES--Prices
PRISONER EXCHANGES: 162, 314, 704, 2829, 4335, 4554, 4602, 4729, 4738, 4942, 5326, 5419, 5782, 5828
PRISONERS AND PRISONS: 1183, 2745, 3657, 4523, 4596, 4608, 4989
   see also CIVIL WAR--POLITICAL PRISONERS
   Confederate prison sites, South Carolina: 565
   Confederate prisoners: 607, 681, 701, 793, 820, 1184, 1191, 1505, 1590, 1820, 2791, 3095, 3502, 3520, 4958, 4999, 5303, 5415, 5668, 5824
     Aid for prisoners: 43
     Efforts to spread Unionism among prisoners: 5402
     Escaped prisoners in Canada: 1084
     Food: 4469
     Living conditions: 5900
       Scarcity of necessities: 5402
     Paroles: 2268, 5121, 5668
     Transportation: 5419
     Treatment: 3378
     Subdivided by location of capture or imprisonment:
       Delaware:
         Fort Delaware: 664, 1184, 1424, 1711, 3485, 5419, 5646, 5900
       Florida:
         Fort Jefferson: 5715
       Illinois:
         Chicago: 2681
         Rock Island: 1184
       Kentucky: 5695
       Louisiana:
         New Orleans: 4562
       Maryland: 3133
         Fort McHenry: 1184, 1889
         Point Lookout: 91, 589, 1184, 1437, 1711, 3351, 3404, 3422, 4131, 4682, 5402, 5419, 5510, 5985
       Massachusetts:
         Fort Warren: 3378, 5422
       Mississippi:
         Ship Island: 2829
       Missouri:
         Palmyra: 1184
       New Mexico:
         Santa Fé: 4562
       New York: 704
         Elmira: 871, 1483, 1602, 4335, 4562, 5402, 5905
         Fort Lafayette: 3378
         Governor's Island: 704
       North Carolina: 1845
         Fort Fisher: 2970
       Ohio: 704, 836, 1543, 5695
         Columbus--Camp Chase: 1184

CIVIL WAR

Subdivided by subject:

PRISONERS AND PRISONS:
   Confederate prisoners:
     Subdivided by location of capture or imprisonment:
       Ohio (Continued):
         Johnson's Island: 66, 704, 1116, 1184, 1682, 1718, 2161, 2829, 2902, 2941, 3775, 4160, 4335, 4469, 5593, 5900, 5905
           Autographs: 2862, 2941
           Requests for release: 1357
       Texas: 3520
       Virginia: 252, 3133
         Fort Norfolk: 915
         Fortress Monroe: 1403
         Morrisville: 5626
         Newport News: 4924
         Transport on James River: 162
       Washington, D.C.: 4900
         Guard duty: 3280, 5695
         Old Capitol Prison: 66, 1184, 1889, 3775, 5646
   Union Prisoners: 484, 1184, 1948, 2510, 2555, 4065, 4348, 4358, 4999, 5121, 5336, 5739
     Escapes and escaped prisoners: 5067, 5869
       Georgia--Andersonville: 2479
       South Carolina--Florence: 2479
     Executions: 3793, 5425
     Food: 5782
     Living conditions: 5782
     Georgia:
       Andersonville: 2479, 5017
       South Carolina--Florence: 2479
     Military hospitals attached to Confederate prisons: 5682
     Paroles: 1186, 3778, 3793
     Payment of debts: 1461
     Treatment: 5782
     Subdivided by location of capture or imprisonment:
       Georgia: 2124
         Andersonville: 1184, 1739, 3485, 5017, 5682, 5744
       Louisiana:
         Bayou Gentilly: 3342
         Belleville: 871
         New Orleans: 3342
       Mississippi:
         Vicksburg: 5017
       North Carolina: 3506, 3885
         Salisbury: 5511
           Prison hospital:
              Commissary records: 2849
              Surgeons: 2260
       South Carolina: 1461, 2124, 5193
         Charleston: 1610, 5419
         Florence: 4434
       Texas--Houston: 3342
       Virginia: 132, 677, 1105, 1601, 2124, 2490, 2989
         Richmond: 5877
           Libby Prison: 5419
PRIVATEERING: 2989
   Confederate: 3578, 4982, 5063
PRIZE SHIPS: 1190, 5344, 5436
PROFITEERING: see CIVIL WAR--SPECULATION AND WAR PROFITEERING
PUBLIC OPINION: see the following subheadings under CIVIL WAR: FOREIGN PUBLIC OPINION; NORTHERN OPINION; SOUTHERN OPINION
PUBLIC WELFARE:
   see also: CIVIL WAR--AID SOCIETIES
   Aid to soldiers' families: 3593
     Georgia: 718, 1190
     Mississippi: 4275
     North Carolina: 608, 1190
       Alexander County: 3572
       Beaufort County: 4862

CIVIL WAR

Subdivided by subject:

PUBLIC WELFARE:
   Aid to soldiers' families:
     North Carolina (Continued):
       Johnston County: 2631
     Tennessee: 4275
     Virginia: 490
RAILROADS: 4466
   see also CONFEDERATE STATES OF AMERICA--MILITARY RAILROADS; UNITED STATES--MILITARY RAILROADS
   Alabama: 3101
   Baltimore and Ohio Railroad: 2106
   Georgia--Repairs: 1181
   Mississippi: 637
   Mississippi and Cincinnati Railroad: 4596
   Ohio: 434
   South Carolina: 4332
   Southern Railroad: 4596
   Southern States: 4002
     Construction: 3101
   Virginia: 546, 1183, 3440, 3809, 4466
     Danville Railroad: 1801
RATIONING: see CIVIL WAR--FOOD RATIONING
REFUGEES: 3809, 4080, 4131, 4616, 4849, 5518
   see also CONFEDERATE EMIGRANTS; UNITED STATES--GOVERNMENT AGENCIES AND OFFICIALS--Bureau of Refugees, Freedmen, and Abandoned Lands
   Arkansas: 508
   Europe: 5593
   Georgia: 639, 3814
     Atlanta: 5724
   Indiana: 5632
   Mississippi: 1424
   North Carolina: 730, 2469, 3237
   South Carolina: 4118, 5645
   Virginia: 661, 3809
RELIEF: see CIVIL WAR--AID SOCIETIES; CIVIL WAR--CLAIMS; CIVIL WAR--PUBLIC WELFARE
RELIGIOUS LIFE: see CIVIL WAR--CIVILIAN LIFE--Religion; CONFEDERATE STATES OF AMERICA--ARMY--Religion; UNITED STATES--ARMY--Civil War--Religion
RELIGIOUS OPPOSITION: see CIVIL WAR--PEACE MOVEMENT
REMINISCENCES:
   Confederate: 674, 1191, 1403, 2416, 2553, 2829, 2849, 2944, 3159, 3783, 3793, 4269, 4550, 4607, 4679, 4918, 5668, 5759, 5901, 5922
   Union: 3095, 4245, 5670, 5677
   West Virginia: 5550
RICE TRADE--South Carolina: 1524
RUMORS: 3788, 3809, 5045, 5613, 5775
   see also CIVIL WAR--PEACE RUMORS; CONFEDERATE STATES OF AMERICA--ARMY--Rumors; UNITED STATES--ARMY--Civil War--Rumors
   Invasions of Eastern Coast of Confederate States of America: 5676
   Murder of Henry A. Wise: 2671
   North Carolina: 3237
   Sherman's capture of Charleston, South Carolina, and Wilmington, North Carolina: 4553
   Virginia: 4483
SABOTAGE BY NEGROES--North Carolina: 1419
SALT WORKS: 3447
   Georgia: 2312
   North Carolina: 1056
   Southern States: 3809

## CIVIL WAR

### Subdivided by subject:

SCARCITY OF COMMODITIES: see CIVIL WAR--CIVILIAN LIFE--Scarcity of
SHIPPING BETWEEN THE UNION AND THE CONFEDERACY: see CIVIL WAR--TRADE BETWEEN THE LINES
SLAVE REVOLTS: see SLAVES--Insurrections
SLAVES: see SLAVES--Confederate Army, Personal servants in
  Behavior: see SLAVES--Behavior
SOLDIERS' AID SOCIETIES: see CIVIL WAR--AID SOCIETIES
SONGS AND MUSIC: 3276, 4612, 5243
  see also CONFEDERATE STATES OF AMERICA--ARMY--Songs and music; UNITED STATES--ARMY--Civil War--Songs and music
  Confederate: 123, 186, 2051, 5032, 5412
SOUTHERN OPINION: 76, 1030, 2024, 2290, 5193, 5623
SOUTHERN SYMPATHIZERS: 4413, 5328, 5417, 5557
  see also COPPERHEADS
  Bail bonds: 5417
  Bermuda Islands: 5500
  Missouri: 4369
  New York: 388
SOUTHERN UNIONISTS: 1181, 3524, 3628, 5045
  see also CIVIL WAR--UNION SYMPATHIZERS
  Lecturing in the North: 716
  Murder of: 5402
  Subdivided by place:
    Alabama: 3903, 4160
    Georgia: 5905
    Kentucky: 2063
    Missouri: 4443
    North Carolina: 631, 2068, 2394, 2469, 5153, 5753, 5905
      Beaufort County: 4435
      Wilmington: 4052
    South Carolina: 4149, 5834
    Tennessee: 716, 872, 1403, 3331, 4055
      Knoxville: 2260
    Virginia: 743, 1402
    West Virginia: 4999
SPANISH NEUTRALITY: 4982, 4983
SPECULATION AND WAR PROFITEERING: 4537, 5017
  Confederate: 523, 1403, 1438
  Georgia: 3331
SPIES:
  Confederate: 5336
    Executions: 659, 4160
    Women: 2180
      Executions: 4160
  Union:
    Alabama: 13
    Executions: 5268
STATISTICS: 270, 3809
TAX IN KIND: see TAX IN KIND
TRADE BETWEEN THE LINES: 2166
  Virginia: 358
TRANSPORT OF SICK AND WOUNDED: 2134, 3642, 5098
TRANSPORTATION PASSES: 2679, 5062, 5432
  see also CONFEDERATE STATES OF AMERICA--ARMY--Transportation passes; UNITED STATES--ARMY--Civil War--Transportation passes
UNION OCCUPATION
  Alabama--Huntsville: 954
  Georgia--Atlanta: 4160
  Louisiana: 509
    New Orleans: 1403, 1424, 2777, 3613, 4993, 5062
  Maryland--Baltimore: 3264

## CIVIL WAR

### Subdivided by subject:

UNION OCCUPATION (Continued):
  Mississippi: 5421
    Corinth: 2858
    Vicksburg: 5062
  North Carolina: 5425
    Beaufort County: 4435
    Chapel Hill: 3247
    Edenton: 1376
    Kinston: 5261
    New Bern: 3037, 4438, 5543, 5897
    Raleigh: 5897
    Salem: 2829
    Washington: 2394
  South Carolina: 1418
    Beaufort: 1709
    Charleston: 1468, 2107, 3269
    Cheraw:
      Protection of Southern unionists: 2140
    Darlington: 2016
  Southern States: 5246
  Tennessee: 1477, 3409
    Gallatin: 5784
    Knoxville: 4245
  Virginia:
    Alexandria: 3809
    Fredericksburg: 4855
    Gloucester County: 4924
    Richmond: 4561
  West Virginia--Romney: 3721
UNION SYMPATHIZERS: 4577, 5169, 5782
  see also CIVIL WAR--SOUTHERN UNIONISTS
  Flight from North Carolina to Indiana: 5402
  Missouri: 4369
  North Carolina: 5298
VETERANS: 4782
  Benefit legislation: 961
    see also CIVIL WAR--PENSIONS
  Confederate: 227, 1186, 2893, 2894, 2963, 3141, 3809, 4020, 5901
    Georgia: 2388
    West Virginia: 1784
  Confederate conventions: 53, 523, 1727, 1825, 2729, 3657, 3809
    Hood's Brigade: 2691
    North Carolina: 3807
      Granville County: 1361
    Texas
      Houston: 4068
      San Marcos: 1361
    Trans-Mississippi Department: 824
  Confederate veterans' magazines: 1191
  Confederate veterans' organizations: 1424, 2096, 3587
    see also CONFEDERATE SURVIVORS' ASSOCIATION; SOCIETY OF THE ARMY OF TENNESSEE; UNITED CONFEDERATE VETERANS
    South Carolina: 543
  Union: 3809, 3910, 4808
    see also CIVIL WAR--PENSIONS
    Claims: 1461, 5570
    Maine: 2106
    Maryland: 4348
    Ohio: 78
  Union veterans' conventions: 1148, 2106, 3280, 5417
    Indiana: 3648, 5097
  Union veterans' organizations: 2106, 4808
    see also GRAND ARMY OF THE REPUBLIC
WAR BONDS--Pennsylvania: 421
WAR PROFITEERING: see CIVIL WAR--SPECULATION AND WAR PROFITEERING
WOMEN: see CIVIL WAR--NURSES AND NURSING; WOMEN IN THE CIVIL WAR

[End of entries under CIVIL WAR]

---

"CIVIL WAR LEGENDS OF RICH MOUNTAIN AND BEVERLY, W. VA.": 5550
CIVILIAN LABOR: see as subheading under names of armies and wars
CIVILIAN LIFE: see as subheading under names of wars
CLACKMORE, Richard D.: 1494
CLAGETT, Horatio: 1042
CLAGETT, Thomas: 1043
CLAIBORNE, Devereux Jarrett, Jr.: 2517
CLAIBORNE, F.: 1044
CLAIBORNE, Hamilton Cabell: 1045
CLAIBORNE, John F.: 1046
CLAIBORNE, John Francis Hamtramck: 1982
CLAIBORNE, Richard: 4616
CLAIBORNE, Thomas: 872
CLAIBORNE, William Charles Coles: 1048
CLAIBORNE AND JETER (firm): 1046
CLAIBORNE COUNTY, Mississippi: 100, 1786, 3322
  see also OAKLAND COLLEGE
  Port Gibson: 2095
  Rocky Springs: 1077
CLAIBORNE COUNTY, Tennessee:
  Cumberland Gap:
    Civil War: 18, 4335
  Treaty line with Indians: 2486
  Tazewell--Mercantile accounts: 2116
CLAIMS:
  see also ALABAMA CLAIMS; AMERICAN REVOLUTION--Claims; CIVIL WAR--CLAIMS; FRENCH SPOLIATION CLAIMS; GREAT BRITAIN--CLAIMS AGAINST; NICARAGUA--Claims against; PENSIONS; UNITED STATES--CLAIMS AGAINST
  Cotton trade: 5730
  Maryland: 3631
  North Carolina: 2553
    Against Royall Cotton Mills: 4586
    Hillsborough: 5341
  Pennsylvania--Philadelphia: 4181
  Virginia: 4563
    Richmond: 5445
  Washington, D.C.: 5417
CLAIMS COLLECTION:
  Alabama: 3857
  North Carolina: 2808
CLAIRMONT, Allegra: 1049, 4770
CLAIRMONT, Charles: 4770
CLAIRMONT, Claire: see CLAIRMONT, Clara Mary Jane
CLAIRMONT, Clara Mary Jane: 1049, 4770
"CLANDEBOYE," County Down, Northern Ireland: 515
CLANRICARDE, Ulick John DeBurgh, First Marquis of: 472
THE CLANSMAN by Thomas Dixon: 3062
  Stage adaptation: 1521
CLANTON, Ella Gertrude: 5246
CLAPHAM, Sir John Harold: 5616
CLAPP, Dexter: 429
CLARE, Ada: see McELHENEY, Jane
CLARE, William Keating: 1050
CLAREMONT COLLEGE, Hickory, North Carolina: 5298
CLARENDON, Edward Hyde, First Earl of: 2707
CLARENDON, George William Frederick Villiers, Fourth Earl of: 597, 678, 1632, 1755, 1926, 5809
CLARENDON, John Charles Villiers, Third Earl of: 1754
CLARENDON COUNTY, South Carolina:
  Unification of Methodist churches: 3646
CLARENDON PAPERS, Publication of: 2707
CLARK, Arthur Wilson: 1054
CLARK, C. P.: 1051
CLARK, Christopher Henderson: 1052

CLARK, Courtney J.: 1053
CLARK, Cynthia A. W.: 1054
CLARK, Edwin: 1055
CLARK, Eleanor: 902
CLARK, Elijah: 2307
CLARK, Enoch: 1056
CLARK, Francis: 1057
CLARK, Frederick W.: 1058
CLARK, H. W.: 355
CLARK, Harry Hayden: 102
CLARK, Henry: 1059
CLARK, Henry Selby: 1060
CLARK, Henry Toole (1808-1874): 641, 791, 1061, 2222, 5457
CLARK, Hubert Lyman: 404
CLARK, James Beauchamp: 1062
CLARK, James M.: 1063
CLARK, John (1766-1832): 3323
CLARK, Joseph D.: 1064
CLARK, Kate Upson: 2449
CLARK, M. B. T.: 1227
CLARK, Myron Holley: 1065
CLARK, Richard H.: 2449
CLARK, Samuel B.: 1066
CLARK, Theophilus: 1067
CLARK, Thomas (1741-1792): 5457
CLARK, Walter, Sr. (1846-1924): 1067, 2435, 4968, 5280
CLARK, William (1770-1838): 2301
CLARK, William Willis: 1069, 5457
CLARK FAMILY (Georgia): 1066
CLARK FAMILY (Mississippi): 4269
CLARK FAMILY (North Carolina): 2657, 4523
CLARK AND FAULKNER (firm): 1065
CLARK COUNTY, Arkansas:
  Arkadelphia: 1154
  Commodity prices: 4270
CLARK COUNTY, Ohio: 2678
  Donnelsville: 2504
  New Carlisle: 5017
CLARK THRESHING MACHINE: 2680
CLARKE, Miss____ (Civil War nurse): 3350
CLARKE, Adam (1762?-1832): 1070, 4146
CLARKE, Alfred Alexander: 1071
CLARKE, Alice (Judah): 1072
CLARKE, Sir Alured: 3315
CLARKE, Catherine: 4024
CLARKE, Elijah: 5189
CLARKE, George W.: 1073
CLARKE, Herbert Edwin: 2146
CLARKE, James Freeman: 1074, 2446
CLARKE, James T.: 1075
CLARKE, Jennie Thornley: 2449
CLARKE, Joseph E.: 1076
CLARKE, Lewis: 1077
CLARKE, Mary Bayard (Devereux): 5457
CLARKE, Mary H.: 1078
CLARKE, Robert: 1163
CLARKE, Sir Stanley De Astel Calvert: 1079
CLARKE COUNTY, Alabama:
  Personal finance: 4448
  Plantation accounts: 4448
  Salt works: 4643
CLARKE COUNTY, Georgia:
  Athens: see ATHENS, Georgia
  Militia: 1993
CLARKE COUNTY, Ohio:
  North Hampton: 1618
CLARKE COUNTY, Virginia: 1436
  Berry Ferry: 467
  Berryville: 2082, 3200, 3336, 4301
  Boyce: 2387
  Castleman's Ferry: 3668
  Greenway Township: 4668
  Millwood: 1227
  "Mountain View": 2513
  White Post: 457, 1211, 3602
    Agriculture: 734
    Mercantile accounts: 2274, 5611
    Merchants: 1436
    United States Post Office: 1436, 5698

CLARKE'S STATION BAPTIST CHURCH, Wilkes County, Georgia: 1080
CLARKSBURG, West Virginia: 851, 2395, 2447
CLARKSON, Thomas (1760-1846): 676, 1081, 1159, 4913, 5725, 5726, 5736
CLARKSON FAMILY (South Carolina): 4453
CLARKSVILLE, North Carolina: 831
CLARKSVILLE, Ohio: 5303
CLARKSVILLE, Pennsylvania: 3253
CLARKSVILLE, Tennessee: 2488
  Postal service: 4854
CLARKSVILLE, Virginia: 4263, 5186
  Railroad accounts: 4846
  Taxation: 4848
CLARKTON, North Carolina: 2970
  Indentures and warrants: 5909
CLASSICAL MYTHOLOGY:
  Translation into English: 1538
CLASSIFICATION OF ANIMALS: see ZOOLOGY--Classification
"CLAUSTRO PLENO DE ESTA REAL UNIVERSIDAD DE MEXICO, ABRIL 26 DE 1714": 3650
CLAWSON, Thomas W.: 1082
CLAY, Anna B.: 1086
CLAY, Cassius Marcellus: 519, 1083, 4486
CLAY, Clement Claiborne (1816-1882): 1084, 1877, 2662
CLAY, Clement Comer (1789-1866): 1084, 2662
CLAY, George Pinckney: 208, 1085
CLAY, Henry (1777-1852): 284, 872, 1086, 1308, 2776, 3198, 3291, 3325, 3483, 3512, 3910, 4064, 4486, 4616, 4732, 4880, 4943, 5051, 5324, 5700, 5848, 5940
  Candidacy (1848): 5149
  Defeat (1844): 5757
  Home: 3176
  Illness of: 1654
  Physical characteristics: 3727
  Political strength in Maryland: 4712
CLAY, Hugh Lawson: 1084
CLAY, John (1796-1858): 1087
CLAY, John Withers: 1084
CLAY, Joseph (1741-1805): 1088, 4128, 5604
CLAY, Joseph (1764-1811): 2788, 2931
CLAY, Susanna Claiborne (Withers): 1084
CLAY, Virginia Caroline (Tunstall): 1084
CLAY, Walter Lowe: 1087
CLAY FAMILY (Alabama): 1084
CLAY AND WRIGHT (firm): see WRIGHT AND CLAY
CLAY (Porcelain): 5731
CLAY COUNTY, Georgia:
  Civil War militia: 1189
CLAY COUNTY, Missouri--Liberty: 4679
CLAY INDUSTRIES--Georgia: 1478
CLAYPOOLE, Ann: 3607
CLAYPOOLE FAMILY (North Carolina--Genealogy): 3607
CLAYTON,____ (Kansas): 2358
CLAYTON, Augustin Smith: 3671
CLAYTON, Bruce: 706
CLAYTON, George Rootes: 1090, 2280
CLAYTON, John Middleton: 4881
CLAYTON, Martha Harper: 1091
CLAYTON, Robert: 4146
CLAYTON, Robert T.: 1091, 5051
CLAYTON, W. C.: 1092
CLAYTON, W. L.: 3525
CLAYTON FAMILY (Georgia): 1091
CLAYTON, Illinois: 3519
CLAYTON AND BROWN (firm): see BROWN AND CLAYTON
CLAYTON AND ERWIN (firm): 1089
CLAYTON AND HOGG (firm): see HOGG AND CLAYTON
CLAYTON AND LEFTWICH (firm): 1093

"CLEA": 1188
CLEAR BROOK, Virginia: 2329
CLEAR CREEK CIRCUIT, Methodist churches: 3646
CLEARSPRING, Maryland: 3004
CLEBURNE, Patrick Ronayne: 623
CLEBURNE FAMILY (Virginia--Genealogy): 1842
CLEEK, John: 1094
CLEEK FAMILY (Virginia): 1094
CLEER, James J.: 1095
CLEGG, William F.: 1096
CLEGG'S COLLEGE, Mocksville, North Carolina: 1100
CLELAND, James T.: 5022
CLELAND, Mrs. John: 5304
CLEMENS, Cyril Coniston: 1097
CLEMENS, James: 5006
CLEMENS, Jeremiah: 1098, 2662
CLEMENS, Samuel Langhorne: 720, 1099, 4556
CLEMENT, De Witt C.: 1100
CLEMENT, John Marshall: 1100
CLEMENT FAMILY (North Carolina): 1100
CLEMENT, North Carolina: 495
CLEMENTS AND POWLER (firm): see FOWLER AND CLEMENTS
CLEMM, Maria: 3905
CLEMMER, Mary: 2648
CLEMSON, Anna Maria (Calhoun): 1101
CLEMSON, Thomas Green: 791, 1101
CLEMSON, South Carolina:
  Methodist Churches: 2961
  Universities and colleges: see CLEMSON UNIVERSITY
CLEMSON COLLEGE, Clemson, South Carolina: see CLEMSON UNIVERSITY
CLEMSON UNIVERSITY, Clemson, South Carolina: 501, 1923, 3356
CLENDENIN, W. A.: 3486
CLENDENING, Andrew: 1102
CLERGY:
  see also PREACHING; SERMONS
  Education:
    see also names of specific theological seminaries
    India: 2756
  Salaries: see WAGES AND SALARIES--Clergy
  Selection and appointment:
    Virginia: 4210
  Slaveholding, Morality of:
    North Carolina: 4434
  Suicide: 5775
  Women: see WOMEN CLERGY
  Subdivided by place:
    Eastern states: 4702
    Florida: 5740
    Great Britain: 4850
    Illinois: 4702
    Indiana: 4702
    Maryland: 665, 4221
    Massachusetts--Leverett: 2407
    Montana--Helena: 2407
    New York--Florida: 86
    North Carolina: 3499
      Elizabeth City: 3919
      Rowan County: 4640
    South Carolina: 4700
    Southern States: 3277
    United States: 3809
    Virginia: 2370, 5147
      Front Royal: 1116
  Subdivided by denomination:
    Baptist:
      Alabama: 1476
      Georgia: 1476, 3625
        Sparta: 4654
      Kentucky: 3489
      Massachusetts: 4125
      North Carolina: 63, 484, 647, 4232, 5211, 5401
        Edgecombe County: 3052
        Gatesville: 2428
        Misconduct in office: 255
        Retirement income: 4828
      Rhode Island: 3055

CLERGY:
  Subdivided by denomination:
    Baptist (Continued):
      South Carolina: 669, 5211
        Charleston: 2402
      Virginia: 3489
    Catholic: 5468
      see also CATHOLIC CHURCH--
        Bishops
      France: 3644
    Christian Methodist Episcopal:
      Kentucky--Negroes: 5070
    Church of England: 5011
      Great Britain: 306, 1087,
        1765, 3798
      Isle of Man--Finance: 4187
      New Zealand: 5725
      West Indies: 5725
    Congregational: 5748, 5899
      Connecticut: 5748
      Massachusetts: 5088
        Cambridge: 2607
    Disciples of Christ:
      North Carolina: 5554
    Episcopal: 4014
      Alabama: 1067
      Florida: 1653
      Mississippi: 5635
      North Carolina: 2699
        Edenton: 1376
        Morality of slaveholding:
          4669
      South Carolina--Negroes: 2449
      Virginia: 3141, 5765
      West Virginia: 3141
    First African:
      Georgia--Savannah: 5787
    Free Will Baptist:
      North Carolina: 1107
    Independent Presbyterian:
      South Carolina: 4609
    Lutheran:
      Pennsylvania: 4444
      South Carolina: 550
      Virginia--New Market: 2485
    Methodist:
      Aid to ministers' families:
        North Carolina: 3646
      Circuit riders: 5021
        North Carolina: 956, 3473,
          3497, 5964
        Virginia: 3497, 3601
      Legal affairs--Virginia: 203
      Licensing--Virginia: 5891
      Opinion of Baptists:
        Georgia: 872
        North Carolina: 1152
      Pastoral responsibilities:
        5964
      Personal finance:
        North Carolina: 956
        Virginia: 203
      Retirement income:
        North Carolina: 3646
      Slaveholding, Morality of:
        Georgia: 872
      Trials: 3646
      Subdivided by place:
        Alabama: 1915
        Bermuda Islands: 2289
        Great Britain: 763, 1070,
          3995, 5647, 5699
        Ireland--Londonderry: 3738
        Maryland: 610, 1939, 5328
        North Carolina: 547, 796,
          1538, 1738, 1915, 2221,
          3646, 4242, 5022, 5793,
          5964, 5965
          Halifax County: 711
        Ohio: 2693
        South Carolina: 2289
        Vermont: 5096
        Virginia: 732, 3646, 4412,
          4932
            Charlottesville: 3758

CLERGY:
  Subdivided by denomination
    (Continued):
    Methodist Episcopal:
      Great Britain: 1310
      New York--New York: 3581
      North Carolina: 3992
        High Point: 3581
        Louisburg: 4787
        Woodland: 4047
      South Carolina: 4912
      Virginia: 3992
    Methodist Episcopal Church,
      South:
      Kentucky: 3888
      North Carolina: 1152, 4136,
        4192, 4498
        Chatham County: 1096
        Circuit riders: 3195
        Plymouth: 772
        Wilmington: 772
      Tennessee: 4192
      Virginia: 4192, 5467
      West Virginia: 5467
    Methodist Protestant: 3186
      Mental health--North Carolina:
        3186
      Retirement income: 4416
    Original Free Will Baptist:
      North Carolina: 3987
    Presbyterian: 3142
      Alabama: 5961
      Georgia: 5987
      Great Britain--Liverpool: 5244
      Kentucky--Lexington: 3325
      North Carolina: 702, 1547,
        1890, 3117, 3300, 4310
        Cabarrus County: 4311
        Thyatira: 3334
      Pennsylvania--Le Raysville:
        4397
      South Carolina: 2616, 4031,
        4310, 5988
        Charleston: 4936
        Columbia: 4240
        Pastoral responsibilities:
          4429, 5988
      Virginia: 1827, 2064, 2737,
        5538
        Lynchburg: 4373
          Pastoral responsibilities:
            3707
    Primitive Baptist--North
      Carolina: 4500
    Protestant Episcopal:
      Education: 4253
      Maryland: 5630
      New York: 5619
      North Carolina: 4232
        Pastoral responsibilities:
          4394
      South Carolina: 3666, 4215,
        4272
      Tennessee: 4358
      United States: 4253
      Virginia: 1565, 4173, 5619
    Unitarian:
      Maryland:
        Ordination in Baltimore: 4359
      Massachusetts--Boston: 1074
      Washington, D.C.: 1215
    United Brethren in Christ:
      Virginia: 1920
    Universalist:
      New York--New York: 978
      North Carolina: 1906
      Rhode Island: 1906
      South Carolina--Charleston:
        978
    Wesleyan Methodist:
      Great Britain: 5095, 5255,
        5647
CLERKS (Retail trade):
  Alabama--Midway: 983
  Virginia--Richmond: 4461
  Wages and salaries: see WAGES AND
    SALARIES--Clerks
CLERKS OF COURTS: see COURTS--Clerks

"CLERMONT," South Carolina
  (plantation): 5193
CLERMONT COUNTY, Ohio: 4220
CLEVELAND, Grover: see CLEVELAND,
  Stephen Grover
CLEVELAND, Stephen Grover: 1103,
  1424, 5152
  Administration: 3038, 5762
CLEVELAND, William Harry Vane, First
  Duke of (1766-1842): 868, 2149
CLEVELAND, North Carolina: 4691
CLEVELAND, Ohio: 451, 1953, 2313,
  2562, 2969, 3716, 4201, 5908
  Business affairs: 2128
  Memorials: 5291
CLEVELAND, Tennessee: 1917, 3766
CLEVELAND COTTON MILL, Lawnsdale,
  North Carolina: 1104
CLEVELAND COTTON MILLS, Knob Creek,
  North Carolina: 4691
CLEVELAND COUNTY, North Carolina:
  3437, 5926
  Cotton prices and storage: 4691
  Cotton mills: 1539, 4691
  Cotton trade: 4691
  Lawndale:
    Cotton mills: 1104, 4691
  Shelby: 1517, 1951, 2581
CLEVELAND MUSEUM OF ART: 2969
CLEVENGER, Shobal Vail: 2181
CLEWELL, Francis Christian: 2829
CLEWELL, Margaret Elizabeth: 2829
CLICK, Jacob B.: 1105
CLIFFORD, Nathan: 1106
CLIFTON, F. A.: 1107
CLIFTON, H. J.: 1107
CLIFTON, John L.: 1107
CLIFTON, JOHN L. v. FRANCIS
  WESTBROOK AND JOHN ATKINSON: 1107
CLIFTON ACADEMY, Amelia County,
  Virginia: 3809
CLIFTON HOTEL, Niagara Falls, New
  York: 4990
CLIFTON MANUFACTURING COMPANY
  (South Carolina): 5233, 5236
CLIMATE: see WEATHER
CLINCH, Duncan Lamont: 3611
CLINCH RIVER (Tennessee and
  Virginia): 2486
CLINE'S TOWNSHIP, North Carolina:
  4532
CLINGMAN, A. B.: 2808
CLINGMAN (JACOB) AND COMPANY: 1108
CLINGMAN, Thomas Lanier: 1109, 3003,
  3094, 5193, 5457
CLINGMAN FAMILY (North Carolina):
  1109, 2808
CLINTON, Dewitt: 421
CLINTON, DEWITT v. GREEN: 2172
CLINTON, George (1739-1812): 3662
CLINTON, Sir Henry (1738-1795): 2008
CLINTON, Henry Pelham Fiennes Pelham,
  Fourth Duke of Newcastle: 1110,
  2149
CLINTON, William S.: 1107
CLINTON, Alabama: 1298
CLINTON, Louisiana:
  Girls' schools and academies:
    4373, 4819
CLINTON, Maine: 2092
CLINTON, North Carolina: 1107, 1751,
  2863, 3043
CLINTON, South Carolina: 521
CLINTON COUNTY, Iowa--Comanche: 2561
CLINTON COUNTY, Missouri: 3197
CLINTON COUNTY, Ohio:
  Clarksville: 5303
  Wilmington--Civil War: 801
CLINTON COUNTY, Pennsylvania:
  Mill Hall: 5249
CLINTON FEMALE SEMINARY, Clinton,
  Georgia: 4849
CLINTONIAN DEBATING SOCIETY: 3611
CLIONIAN DEBATING SOCIETY: 1111
CLISBY, Joseph: 1112
CLIVE, Edward First Earl of Powis:
  5630

CLIVE, Ivor Miles Windsor-: see
    WINDSOR-CLIVE, Ivor Miles,
    Second Earl of Plymouth and
    Fifteenth Baron Windsor
CLIVE, Phillis Windsor-: see
    WINDSOR-CLIVE, Phillis
CLOCKS AND WATCHES:
    Georgia--Forsyth County: 5260
    Repairing and adjusting:
        North Carolina--Hillsborough:
            3300
CLODD, Edward: 1113, 2334
CLODE, Charles Mathew: 1114
CLONCLURRY, Valentine Browne
    Lawless, Second Baron: 4024
CLONDINING, John: 5573
CLOPTON, Adelaide: 1115
CLOPTON, David (1820-1892): 1084
CLOPTON, John (1756-1816): 1115
CLOPTON, John Bacon (b. 1785): 1115
CLOPTON, Joyce Wilkinson: 1115
CLOPTON, Maria (Foster): 1115
CLOPTON, Sarah Jane: 4346
CLOPTON, William Izard: 1115
CLOPTON FAMILY (Virginia): 1115
CLOPTON'S MILLS, Georgia: 5760
CLOSE, Captain _____ (British
    abolitionist): 3316
CLOSE, Sir Barry: 505
"CLOSE HALL", Wells, England: 1071
CLOTH--North Carolina: 1905
CLOTH FOLDING MACHINERY: see
    PATENTS--Cloth folding machinery
CLOTH MANUFACTURE: see COTTON MILLS;
    TEXTILE INDUSTRY; WOOLEN MILLS
CLOTH TRADE:
    Connecticut: 2410
    Great Britain: 1647, 2148
    Maryland--Baltimore: 1647
    Massachusetts: 992
    North Carolina: 35, 1611
    South Carolina: 1889
    United States: 2410
CLOTHING AND DRESS: 4589
    see also ACADEMIC COSTUME;
        BLOOMERS; SLAVES--Clothing and
        dress; and as subheading under
        names of armies
    Manufacture--Pennsylvania: 990
    Patterns: 1407, 4589
        see also SEWING
    Prices:
        North Carolina: 2819, 4858
        South Carolina: 3801
        Virginia: 4924
            Augusta County: 4210
            Norfolk: 3830
    Women's styles: 1957, 3301, 4732,
        5194
        see also CIVIL WAR--CLOTHING
            AND DRESS--Women's styles
    Subdivided by place:
        Georgia--Macon: 5246
        Jamaica: 3304
        Michigan: 3221
        Missouri--Saint Louis: 5155
        New York: 4351
        United States: 3301
        Virginia: 753, 872
            Goshen: 5613
        West Virginia: 4904
CLOTHING TRADE:
    South Carolina: 1480
    Virginia--Richmond: 4210
CLOTHING WORKERS: see AMALGAMATED
    CLOTHING WORKERS OF AMERICA;
    INTERNATIONAL LADIES' GARMENT
    WORKERS' UNION
CLOUD, Sara: 1116
CLOUD, Mary E.: 1116
CLOUGH, Hallie: 1424
CLOUGH, James: 3738
CLOVER DEPOT, Virginia: 2331
CLOVER SEED--Virginia: 2165
CLOVERDALE FURNACE, Virginia: 117
CLOVERPORT, Kentucky: 3199
CLOW, Andrew: 1117

CLOW (ANDREW) & CO.: 1117
CLOWES, Sir William Laird: 3056
CLUBS: see SOCIETIES AND CLUBS
CLUSERET, Gustave Paul: 5103
CLYDE, Colin Campbell, First Baron:
    859, 4549
CLYDE, Paul Hibbert: 5252
CLYDE (schooner): 5063
CLYMER, Mary Willing: 1118
COACHMAN, James: 758
COAD, Oral Sumner: 102
COAHOMA COUNTY, Mississippi: 49,
    1180
COAL:
    Prices:
        Great Britain: 535
        Pennsylvania: 4188
    Stocks--United States: 5080
    Transport of: see FREIGHT AND
        FREIGHTAGE--Coal
    West Virginia: 3005
COAL INDUSTRY:
    Advertising: see ADVERTISING--
        Coal industry
    Hiring of slaves--Virginia: 523
    Labor problems and unions: 4865
    Legal affairs--Georgia: 4865
    Taxation--Great Britain: 4024
    Subdivided by place:
        Alabama: 897, 3188
        Georgia--Columbus: 4865
        Pennsylvania: 5686
        Russia: 3238
COAL MINERS: see LABOR UNIONS--Coal
    Miners; MINE WORKERS; STRIKES--
    Coal miners; WAGES AND SALARIES--
    Coal miners
COAL MINING:
    Company stores--Virginia: 2908
    Georgia--Cherokee County: 1887
    Maryland: 4732
    Missouri: 2076
    Pennsylvania: 5775
        Cornplanter: 3910
    United States: 4343
    Virginia: 2922
        Chesterfield County: 2908
    West Virginia--Kanawha Valley:
        4924
COAL RUN IMPROVEMENT AND RAILROAD
    COMPANY: 5083
COAL SHORTAGES: see WORLD WAR I--
    Coal shortages
COAL TRADE:
    Great Britain: 5726
    North Carolina--Wilmington: 5912
COALING STATIONS--Hawaii: 3516
COAST AND GEODETIC SURVEY: see
    UNITED STATES--GOVERNMENT
    AGENCIES AND OFFICIALS--Coast and
    geodetic survey
COAST DEFENSES: see CIVIL WAR--
    COAST DEFENSES
COASTAL DEVELOPMENT--South Carolina:
    4453
COASTAL SURVEYING:
    Louisiana--New Orleans: 4986
    United States: see UNITED STATES--
        GOVERNMENT AGENCIES AND
        OFFICIALS--Coast and geodetic
        survey
COASTWISE SHIPPING: see SHIPPING--
    Coastwise shipping
COATS OF ARMS: 4101, 5155
COBB (ALBERT A.) AND COMPANY: 1119
COBB, COLLIER: 2699
COBB, Eaton: 1120
COBB, Howell: 637, 1121, 1333, 1434,
    2326, 5453
COBB, Irvin Shrewsbury: 5497
COBB, Job: 1122
COBB, John Nathan: 2084
COBB (LUCY) INSTITUTE, Athens,
    Georgia: 3905
COBB, Mary Ann (Lamar): 1121
COBB, Maureen: 3306
COBB, Susan M.: 761

COBB, Thomas Reade Rootes: 700, 1123,
    1422
COBB, William Henry Harrison: 5457
COBB COUNTY, Georgia:
    Austell: 2786
    Marietta: see MARIETTA, Georgia
COBBETT, Susan: 1124
COBBETT, William: 369, 1124
COBBETT'S WEEKLY POLITICAL REGISTER:
    1124
COBBS, John F.: 1125
COBBS, Thomas Flourney: 5252
COBDEN, Richard: 1126, 2149, 1632,
    3715
COBHAM, Sir Richard Temple, Viscount:
    5934
COBHAM, England: 3736
COBHAM, Virginia: 958, 4491
COBHAM HALL, Gravesend, Kent,
    England: 535
COBIA, Ann: 1127
COBIA, Henry: 3124
COBIA, Mary: 1127
COBIA, Sarah: 1127
COBLE, Albert Lucian: 1128
COBLE, Mrs. Albert Lucian: 1128
COCHRAN, A. Jackson: 1129
COCHRAN, George: 1130
COCHRAN, John Lewis: 1131
COCHRAN FAMILY (Virginia): 3687
COCHRAN FAMILY (West Virginia): 1129
COCHRANE-BAILLIE, Charles Wallace
    Alexander Napier Ross, Second
    Baron Lamington: see BAILLIE,
    Charles Wallace Alexander Napier
    Ross Cochrane-, Second Baron
    Lamington
COCKBURN, George (1856-1925): 1132
COCKBURN, Sir George (1772-1853):
    3742
COCKE, Cary Charles: 1133
COCKE, James A.: 3682
COCKE, John Hartwell: 558, 1133, 5839
COCKE, Philip St. George: 1133
COCKE, Richard Ivanhoe: 1134
COCKEFAIR, William A.: 1135
COCKEYSVILLE, Maryland:
    Civil War: 4537
COCKRELL, Francis Marion: 1136
COCKRELL, Jane: 31
COCKRELL, Mrs. Joseph E.: 31
COCKRELL, Monroe Fulkerson: 1137
COCKRELL, Sarah (Horton): 1138
COCKRUM, Mississippi: 3155
COCKS, John Somers, First Earl
    Somers: 1139
COCOA TRADE: 323
    Great Britain: 2742
CODDLE CREEK, North Carolina: 4311
"CODE OF HONOR OF DUELLING" by
    John Lyde Wilson: 4834
CODE OF HONOR OR RULES FOR THE
    GOVERNMENT OF PRINCIPALS AND
    SECONDS IN DUELLING by John Lyde
    Wilson: 4834
CODES--Confederate States of America:
    1181
CODIFICATION OF LAWS: see LAW--
    Codification
CORRINGTON, William: 326
CODY, William Frederick: 1140
CODY, Wyoming: 1140
COE FAMILY (Great Britain--
    Genealogy): 1141
COERCION ACT (Ireland): 5164
COFFEE COUNTY, Tennessee:
    Tullahoma: 1276, 2325, 3970
COFFEE GROWING--Cuba: 3808
COFFEE TRADE: 323
    Prices: 4541
    Transportation: 3824
    Subdivided by place:
        Brazil: 2363
        Delaware: 4881
        Far East: 5298
        Great Britain: 369
        India: 4881

COFFEE TRADE:
  Subdivided by place (Continued):
    North Carolina--Wilmington: 1281
    Venezuela: 23
COFFEY, T. J.: 1141
COFFIN, Lucretia: 1784
COFFIN, Robert Barry: 1143
COFFING, John: 825
COGDELL, John Stevens: 3162
COGGIN, W. R.: 4202
COGHILL, James O.: 1144
COHEN, Alonzo B.: 1145
COHEN, Solomon: 1146, 1466, 3761
COHOES, New York--Labor conditions: 3266
COINS AND COINAGE:
  see also CURRENCY; SILVER QUESTION
  Inventions: 4022
  Royal decrees--Spain: 4980
  United States: 1302
    see also AMERICAN REVOLUTION-- Economic aspects--Coinage
COIT, Daniel Wadsworth: 2046
COIT, Thomas Winthrop: 2837
COKE, Sir Edward: 2152
COKE, Thomas: 1070, 3646, 4913, 5095
COKE--Alabama: 642
COKE UPON LITTLETON: 1142
COKER, William Chambers: 4453
COKER COLLEGE, Hartsville, South Carolina: 4564
COKESBURY, South Carolina:
  Abolition of slavery: 4118
  Historic restoration: 5312
  Schools: 5114
COKESBURY (S. C.) HISTORICAL COMMISSION: 5312
COLAC, Victoria--Court of Petty Sessions: 5477
COLBORNE, John, First Baron Seaton: 1147
COLBURN, Henry (d. 1855): 103, 2146
COLBURN, Webster J.: 1148
COLBY, Robert: 1149
COLCHESTER, Connecticut:
  Congregational churches: 5748
COLCHESTER, Virginia:
  Tobacco trade: 144
COLCOCK, Charles Jones: 4896
COLCOCK, Charles Jones, Jr.: 2449
COLCOCK, Margaret (Smith): 4896
COLCOCK FAMILY: 4896
COLD HARBOR, Virginia, Battle of:
  see CIVIL WAR--CAMPAIGNS, BATTLES, AND MILITARY ACTIONS--Virginia-- Cold Harbor
COLD SPRING PLANTATION, Georgia: 781
COLD WAR: 83
COLE, Arthur Vance: 1150
COLE, Fred C.: 5054
COLE, Sir Henry: 3670
COLE, Howard Ellsworth: 5252
COLE, Jesse W.: 1151
COLE, John Nelson: 1152
COLE, Lucy: 799
COLE, Timothy: 826
COLE COUNTY, Missouri:
  Jefferson City: 2817, 4323, 4443
COLEGIO MAXIMO DE SAN PABLO DE LA COMPAÑIA DE JESUS: 4155
COLEMAN, A.: 3616
COLEMAN, Ann Mary Butler (Crittenden): 1308
COLEMAN, Ann (Raney) Thomas: 1153
COLEMAN, Chapman, Jr.: 1308
COLEMAN, Charles Thaddeus: 5457
COLEMAN, Charles Washington, Jr.: 2449
COLEMAN, H. E.: 2885
COLEMAN, Hawes H.: 1154
COLEMAN, Laurence Vail: 1155
COLEMAN, Lindsey: 1156
COLEMAN FAMILY (Arkansas): 1154

COLEMAN FAMILY (Virginia): 1156
COLEMAN FAMILY (Genealogy): 1308
COLENSO, John William: 41, 5725
COLERAIN, North Carolina: 1157
COLERAIN BAPTIST CHURCH, North Carolina: 1157
COLERIDGE, Derwent: 1473
COLERIDGE, James Duke: 1158
COLERIDGE, Sir John Taylor: 2953, 2994
COLERIDGE, Samuel Taylor: 1159, 1473, 2058, 4327, 4913
COLES, Edward: 4616
COLES, Emilie S.: 1160
COLES, Emily: 4616
COLES, Isaac A.: 872, 4616
COLES, R. T.: 1161
COLES, Sarah: 5065
COLES, Tucker: 4616
COLES, Walter: 1161
COLES CREEK COTTON GIN: 2719
COLE'S FERRY, Virginia: 907
COLE'S MILL, Orange County, North Carolina: 3337
COLEY, P. L.: 1178
COLFAX, Schuyler: 1162, 5755
COLGATE, William: 3260
COLLAPSIBLE VEHICLES--Inventions: 3424
COLLECTION OF ACCOUNTS: see DEBT COLLECTION
COLLECTIONS FOR A HISTORY OF THE . . . FAMILY OF BLAND by Nicholas Carlisle: 957
COLLECTIONS OF THE GEORGIA HISTORICAL SOCIETY, Vol. 1, 1840: 3733
COLLECTIVE BARGAINING: see LABOR ARBITRATION
COLLECTORS AND COLLECTING: see AMERICANA--Collectors and collecting; ART COLLECTING; AUTOGRAPH COLLECTING; BOOK COLLECTING; CURRENCY COLLECTING; MANUSCRIPT COLLECTING; PHILATELY
COLLEGE EDUCATION: see EDUCATION, Higher
COLLEGE LIFE: see UNIVERSITIES AND COLLEGES--College life; UNIVERSITIES AND COLLEGES-- Students and student life; and Students and student life as subheading under names of specific universities and colleges
COLLEGE OF CHARLESTON, Charleston, South Carolina: 3666
  Finance: 723
  Students' compositions: 1439
COLLEGE OF NEW JERSEY, Princeton, New Jersey: see PRINCETON UNIVERSITY
COLLEGE OF ST. JAMES, Hagerstown, Maryland: 785, 2999
COLLEGE OF THE PACIFIC, Stockton, California: 1116
COLLEGE OF WILLIAM AND MARY, Williamsburg, Virginia: 1512, 2400, 2612, 3320, 3456, 4220, 4343, 4616, 4924
  Board of Visitors: 2612
  Curriculum: 2728
  Faculty: 2728, 3819, 5577
  Fire: 5853
  Legal education: 5031
  Richmond Division: see VIRGINIA COMMONWEALTH UNIVERSITY
  Students and student life: 450, 1279, 2728, 5126, 5378
  Tuition: 2728
COLLEGE PARK, Maryland: see UNIVERSITY OF MARYLAND
COLLEGE PRESIDENTS: see UNIVERSITIES AND COLLEGES--Presidents
COLLEGE TEACHERS: see UNIVERSITIES AND COLLEGES--Faculty; and Faculty as subheading under names of specific universities and colleges

COLLEGES: see UNIVERSITIES AND COLLEGES; and names of specific universities and colleges
COLLETON COUNTY, South Carolina:
  Household and plantation accounts: 4649
  Ridgeville: 501, 4451
  Walterboro: 2828, 4649
  Wiggins: 4453
COLLES, William Morris: 4798
COLLEY, Sir George Pomeroy: 5876
COLLIDGE, T. Jefferson, Jr.: 2139
COLLIER, Julia: 2374
COLLIER, Thomas Stephens: 2449
COLLIER, William Miller: 4074
COLLIER'S (periodical): 3397
COLLIERSVILLE, Tennessee: 4951
COLLINGSWORTH INSTITUTE, Talbotton, Georgia: 3729
COLLINGWOOD, Cuthbert, First Baron Collingwood: 1164
COLLINGWOOD, George Trevor: 5474
COLLINS, Christopher: 917
COLLINS, John: 3829
COLLINS, Josiah: 1165
COLLINS, Michael: 1166
COLLINS, Thomas Hightower: 1167
COLLINS, Wilkie: 2449
COLLINS, William F.: 1168
COLLINS FAMILY (Great Britain): 5038
COLLINS FAMILY (Ohio): 770
COLLINS FAMILY (Virginia): 99
COLLINS MANUFACTURING COMPANY, Hartford, Connecticut: 1169
COLLINS TOWNSHIP, South Carolina: 501
COLOGNE, Germany: 5224
COLOMBIA: 1424
  Description and travel: 198, 1506
  Economic conditions: 1506
  Education: 1506
  Lawsuits: 3867
  Native races: 4979
  Politics and government: 1506, 4155
"COL. THORNTON'S DEPARTURE FROM YORK TO SPY PARK IN WILTSHIRE" by Martin Hawke: 5913
COLONIAL AGENTS: see as subheading under name of colony, e.g. AMERICAN COLONIES--Colonial agents in Great Britain
COLONIAL COUNCIL: see GEORGIA-- GOVERNMENT AGENCIES AND OFFICIALS-- Colonial period--Colonial Council
COLONIAL DAMES OF AMERICA:
  Virginia: 1814
COLONIAL POLICY: see as subheading under names of countries
THE COLONIAL RECORDS OF NORTH CAROLINA: 3930
COLONIAL TRADE: see as subheading under names of countries
COLONIAL WILLIAMSBURG, Virginia: 1424
COLONIZATION:
  see also NEGROES--Colonization; and Colonial policy as subheading under names of countries
  Africa: 5940
  Burma: 217
  Paragua, Island of: 4179
COLORADO:
  see also WESTERN STATES
  Agriculture: 2554, 5426
  Blind: 5426
  Dairying--Larimer County: 3199
  Deaf: 5426
  Gold mining: 2606
    see also PIKE'S PEAK GOLD RUSH
  Anaconda: 3660
  Labor conditions: 2554
  Lynching--Negroes: 2368
  Manufacturing: 5426
  Married life--Estrangement: 353
  Mentally ill: 5426

COLORADO (Continued):
    Mentally retarded: 5426
    Migration to: 3721
    Mining: 849
    Personal finance: 353
    Sheep raising: 3745
        Larimer County: 3199
    Social life and customs: 5426
COLORADO, Missouri: 1412
COLORADO COUNTY, Texas:
    Crops: 5174
    Oakland: 1741
COLORADO SPRINGS, Colorado: 353
COLORED METHODIST EPISCOPAL CHURCH:
    see CHRISTIAN METHODIST EPISCOPAL
    CHURCH
COLQUITT, Alfred Holt: 1170, 4415, 5536
COLQUITT, Walter Terry: 1170
COLQUITT, William Neyle: 1171
COLQUITT COUNTY, Georgia--Moultrie: 4659
COLTON, Calvin: 3142
COLTRANE, Daniel Branson: 5457
COLUCCI, Gio: 555
COLUCCI, Guido: 555
COLUMBIA, Maryland: 3781
COLUMBIA, Missouri: see UNIVERSITY OF MISSOURI--College of Agriculture
COLUMBIA, North Carolina--Business affairs: 215
COLUMBIA, South Carolina:
    1700s-1800s: 4896
    1700s-1900s: 2300
    1800s: 2930, 3204, 4031, 4610
        1800s: 4508
        1810s: 4508
        1820s: 1532
        1830s: 1532, 4316
        1840s: 3525, 4316
        1850s: 4316, 5716
        1860s: 1506, 2185, 5370, 5855
        1870s: 959
    1800s-1900s: 883, 3418
    1900s: 425, 720, 1172, 2086, 3421
    Army camps: 3843
    Civil War: 674, 1017, 1461
        Battle: see CIVIL WAR--
            CAMPAIGNS, BATTLES, AND
            MILITARY ACTIONS--South
            Carolina--Columbia
        Confederate infirmary: 5759
        Confederate military prison: 2124
    Description: 5193
    Girls' schools: 4912
    Governor: 565
    Labor unions: 1196, 2767, 5410, 5411
    Municipal employees: 1172
    Social life and customs: 300
    Theological education: see
        COLUMBIA THEOLOGICAL SEMINARY
    Universities and colleges: see
        SOUTH CAROLINA COLLEGE;
        UNIVERSITY OF SOUTH CAROLINA
COLUMBIA, Tennessee: 2661, 4209
    see also JACKSON COLLEGE
COLUMBIA, Virginia: 5108
    Banks and banking: 5035
    Bridge construction: 5106
    Churches: 5091
    Masonry: 3855
COLUMBIA (warship): 636
COLUMBIA CIRCUIT, Methodist Churches: 3646
COLUMBIA CITY CENTRAL LABOR UNION: 1172
COLUMBIA COUNTY, Georgia: 2006, 2449
    Columbia Mine: 4895
    Plantation life: 5246
COLUMBIA COUNTY, New York:
    Kinderhook: 5451
COLUMBIA FEMALE SEMINARY, Columbia, South Carolina: 4912
COLUMBIA FERTILIZERS: 4689
COLUMBIA FURNACE, Virginia: 160

COLUMBIA MINE, Georgia: 4895
COLUMBIA MINING AND LAND COMPANY: 2922
COLUMBIA MINING COMPANY: 4895
COLUMBIA RIVER (Washington): 140
COLUMBIA THEOLOGICAL SEMINARY, Columbia, South Carolina: 59, 4240
COLUMBIA UNIVERSITY, New York, New York: 4863, 5781
    Faculty: 369
    Legal education: 5075
    Students' notebooks: 2553, 4863
    School of Journalism: 2473
    Students and student life: 3710
    Political activity: 5077
COLUMBIAN COLLEGE, Washington, D.C.:
    see GEORGE WASHINGTON UNIVERSITY
COLUMBIAN EXPOSITION: 3051, 5380
COLUMBUS, Georgia: 1078, 1476, 1867, 2215, 2620, 4737, 5292
    Authors: 902
    Coal industry: 4865
    Description: 284, 3660
    Maps: 1182
COLUMBUS, Mississippi: 1652, 2393, 3159
    Description: 3611
    Merchants: 4269
COLUMBUS, Ohio: 230
    Civil War Prison: 1184
COLUMBUS (ship): 5436
"COLUMBUS AND THE MAYFLOWER" by Richard Monckton Milnes: 3694
COLUMBUS COUNTY, North Carolina:
    Whiteville: 3448
    Schools: 4910
COLUMBUS GUARDS: 700
COLVILLE, John, Ninth Lord Colville of Culross: 2147
COLVIN, Frances (Fetherston-Hough) Sitwell: 1210
COLVIN, Howard T.: 2772
COLVIN, Sir Sidney: 1210
COMACHO, Juan Vicente: 4155
COMAL COUNTY, Texas:
    New Braunfels: 218
    Land: 964
COMANCHE, Iowa: 2561
COMANCHE INDIANS:
    Raids in northern Mexico: 2137
    Trade with whites: 4353
COMANCHE LANGUAGE--Vocabulary: 4208
COMBE, George (1788-1858): 1087
COMBE, William (1741-1823): 1173
COMBERBATCH, A. Carlton: 3183
COMBERBATCH, Robert M.: 3183
COMER, Catherine: 1174
COMER, Nathaniel: 1174
COMER, Russell G.: 1174
COMER FAMILY: 1174
COMETTI, Elizabeth: 4625
COMFORT, Joshua: 1175
COMFORT, Merrit: 1175
COMIC OPERA--Maryland: 1862
COMINGTEE PLANTATION (South Carolina): 296, 297
COMMENCEMENT ADDRESSES: 1176
    see also UNIVERSITIES AND
        COLLEGES--Commencement
        addresses; and as subheading under
        names of specific universities
        and colleges
COMMENCEMENT EXERCISES: see also
    UNIVERSITIES AND COLLEGES--
    Commencement exercises; and as
    subheading under names of specific
    universities and colleges
    North Carolina--Wake County: 3941
COMMENTARIES ON THE LAWS OF ENGLAND by Sir William Blackstone: 4616
COMMERCE: see SHIPPING; TRADE AND COMMERCE; and specific types of commerce, e.g. COTTON TRADE; TOBACCO TRADE; etc.
COMMERCIAL ADVERTISER (New York): 42
COMMERCIAL AGENTS--United States: 5448

COMMERCIAL AND RAILROAD BANK, Vicksburg, Mississippi: 3198
COMMERCIAL CHAMBERS: see CHAMBERS OF COMMERCE
COMMERCIAL CONVENTIONS:
    Southern States: 3302
    Tennessee--Memphis: 757
COMMERCIAL COURTS: see CONSULADOS
COMMERCIAL EDUCATION--Great Britain: 4520
COMMERCIAL NEWSLETTER (South Africa): 4960
COMMERCIAL PRODUCTS:
    Marketing: 1481
    South Carolina--Greenville: 5825
    Virginia: 2165
COMMERCIAL RELATIONS: see FREE TRADE; Foreign trade as subheading under names of specific countries
COMMERCIAL TREATIES: see as subheading under names of specific countries
COMMISSARIES: see as subheading under names of armies
COMMISSARY GENERAL OF PRISONERS, Office of: see UNITED STATES--GOVERNMENT AGENCIES AND OFFICIALS--Commissary General of Prisoners
COMMISSION GOVERNMENT: see MUNICIPAL GOVERNMENT BY COMMISSION
COMMISSION HALL, Baroda, India: 4117
COMMISSION MERCHANTS:
    see also MERCHANTS
    Alabama--Mobile: 5879
    Georgia: 5508
        Augusta: 2710
        Savannah: 2232, 2280, 3696, 4040, 4625
        Waynmanville: 2272
    Great Britain--London: 5221
    Louisiana--New Orleans: 459, 872, 3322
    Maryland--Baltimore: 1355, 1442, 2819
    Massachusetts: 2933
    New York: 1107
    New York: 1355, 5731
    North Carolina: 2399, 2933, 4760, 4858, 5298
    Washington: 3827, 4858
    Wilmington: 3447, 5373, 5912
    South Carolina: 2107
        Charleston: 1891, 3124, 3801, 4332
    Virginia: 872, 2360, 2399, 2933, 3994
        Alexandria: 947
        Petersburg: 375, 1336, 2176, 3145
        Richmond: 1359
COMMISSION OF YOUNG PEOPLE'S WORK: 5298
COMMISSION ON INTERRACIAL COOPERATION: Woman's Division: 107
COMMISSIONS: see Officers--Appointments and promotions as subheading under names of armies and navies
COMMITTEE FOR CONSTITUTIONAL GOVERNMENT: 1197
COMMITTEE FOR GEORGIA: 5486
COMMITTEE OF OBSERVATION FOR BALTIMORE COUNTY, Maryland: 4348
"COMMITTEE OF 100": 3852
"COMMITTEE OF ONE HUNDRED": 5762
COMMITTEE OF PUBLIC SAFETY (Napoleonic Wars): 4348
COMMITTEE OF THE CORPORATION OF GEORGETOWN: 4914
COMMITTEE ON POLITICAL EDUCATION (Southern States): 2568
COMMITTEE ON PUBLIC INFORMATION (Foreign Department): 1424
COMMITTEES OF PUBLIC SAFETY: see AMERICAN REVOLUTION--Committees of Public Safety

COMMODITY EXCHANGES:
  Receipts: 4996
  Statistics--South Carolina: 987
COMMODITY PRICES: 4326, 5018
  see also CIVIL WAR--COMMODITY PRICES; and Prices as subheading under names of specific commodities
  Alabama: 1178, 2900, 5385
    Gay's Landing: 5879
    Mobile: 4911
  Arkansas: 4776
    Clarke County: 4270
  Confederate States of America: see CIVIL WAR--COMMODITY PRICES--Southern States
  Florida: 5955
  Georgia: 158, 377, 1251, 2232, 4183, 4720, 4783, 4875
    Augusta: 5246
    Franklin County: 1997
    Gwinnett County: 601
    Macon: 5246
    Savannah: 5494
  Great Britain: 369, 2541
    Bristol: 4541
    Liverpool: 2901, 4911
  Idaho Territory: 2714
  Illinois: 1806, 2240, 3051, 4732, 4875, 5160
  Indiana: 2240, 2294, 3051, 3540, 4152, 5149
    Hampton County: 4202
  International: 5251
  Iowa: 2294, 3333
  Kansas: 2294
  Kentucky: 4720
  Louisiana: 1242
  Maryland: 2217, 3378, 3742, 4064
    Baltimore: 1024, 3566, 4732
  Massachusetts: 2677, 4050
    Boston: 2431
  Michigan: 3221
  Mississippi: 530, 1762, 2970, 3642, 4776
    Leake County: 5475
  Missouri: 865, 3540, 4152, 4161, 4406
  New Hampshire: 4039
  New York: 1107, 1907
  North Carolina:
    1700s-1800s: 3176
    1800s: 530, 1107, 2857, 3351, 5905
    1810s: 5298
    1830s: 3916
    1840s: 5792
    1850s: 1252, 4917, 5231
    1860s: 1252, 1950, 2952, 2970, 4080, 4917, 5231, 5792
    1870s: 2548, 2952, 2970, 3415, 4072, 4080, 5792
    1880s: 2548, 2952, 4072
    1800s-1900s: 2830, 3416
    1900s: 1202
    Chatham County: 770
    Conetoe: 1362
    Elizabeth City: 423
    Granville County: 5285
    Guilford County: 2314
    Littleton: 2399
    Orange County: 3677
    Ridgeway: 999
    Washington: 652
  Ohio: 1505, 2678, 3051, 3848, 4732, 5149, 5504
    Ross County: 770
  Oregon: 3518
  Pennsylvania: 870, 3054, 4699, 4881, 4920
  South Carolina: 126, 158, 477, 566, 2831, 4783
    Camden: 5675
  Southern States: 2078, 3873
  Tennessee: 2661, 4816, 5444
  Texas: 2294
    Colorado County: 1741
    Comal County: 218

COMMODITY PRICES (Continued):
  United States: 4531, 4765, 4881
  Venezuela--Maracaibo: 5133
  Virginia:
    1700s-1800s: 1415, 3069
    1800s: 1263, 1409, 1957, 4043, 4720, 4776, 5765
    1800s: 1093
    1810s: 1093
    1820s: 1093
    1830s: 1384
    1840s: 1384, 4131, 4504
    1850s: 753, 1384, 2370
    1860s: 132, 363, 693, 2370
    1870s: 1591, 2370
    1880s: 1591
    Culpeper: 4852
    Lynchburg: 3353, 3566
    Patrick County: 1410
    Petersburg: 4604
    Richmond: 2902, 3566, 5703
  Washington, D.C.: 1024, 1920, 4760
  West Indies: 3753
  West Virginia: 2678
COMMODITY SPECULATION:
  see also AMERICAN REVOLUTION--Speculation and war profiteering; CIVIL WAR--SPECULATION AND WAR PROFITEERING; COTTON SPECULATION; SALT SPECULATION
  North Carolina: 1438
"COMMON NOUN" by John H. Finley: 4556
THE COMMONER (periodical): 729
COMMONPLACE BOOKS: 5790
  Alabama: 4184
  Georgia: 2893
  Great Britain: 1163
  Ireland: 2887
  North Carolina: 817
  South Carolina--Charleston: 723
  Virginia: 2887, 4743, 5302
  Washington, D.C.: 3373
  West Virginia: 749
COMMONWEALTH (Massachusetts): 4471
COMMUNE OF 1871: 3472
COMMUNICATIONS: see as subheading under names of armies
COMMUNICATIONS WORKERS OF AMERICA: 1196, 1199, 1202
COMMUNION: see LORD'S SUPPER
COMMUNION PLATE: see CHURCH PLATE
COMMUNISM: 1758, 4948
  France: 1424
  United States: 4094
    In labor movement: 1883
  Union of Soviet Socialist Republics: 4614, 5306
  Virginia: 1198
COMMUNISM AND CHRISTIANITY: 4614
COMMUNIST PARTY, U.S.A.: 3066
COMMUNIST PARTY OF THE U.S.S.R., 22nd Congress: 4614
COMMUNITY AND COLLEGE:
  Alabama: 2963
  New Jersey: 1395
COMMUNITY CENTERS: see SOCIAL SERVICES
COMMUNITY CHEST: 1197
  see also UNITED FUND
  North Carolina--Durham: 3927
COMMUNITY RELATIONS:
  Virginia--Mount Erin: 5332
COMORO ISLANDS:
  see also JOHANNA
  Abolition of slavery: 189
COMPAGNIA DELL ALMA CROCE DI LUCCA: 885
COMPAGNIE DES PÉNITENTS BLANCS DE NOTRE DAME DU CONFALON ET DE LA MISÉRICORDE: 2196
COMPAÑÍA ARRENDATARIA DEL MONOPOLIO DE PETROLEOS: 1424
COMPANY INSURANCE: see INSURANCE--Business
COMPANY OF THE ALMIGHTY CROSS OF LUCCA: 885

COMPANY STORES: see as subheading under names of industries, e.g. COAL MINING--Company stores
COMPANY TOWNS: see as subheading under names of industries, e.g. TEXTILE INDUSTRY--Company towns
COMPASSES: 4537
COMPETITION, Virginia: see CHATHAM, Virginia
COMPLETE WORKS OF REV. THOMAS SMYTH, D. D. edited by J. William Flinn: 4936
COMPOSERS--France: 4657
COMPOSITIONS: see STUDENTS AND STUDENT LIFE--Compositions; Students and student life--Compositions under names of specific universities and colleges
COMPROMISE OF 1850: 762, 849, 1084, 1742, 4295, 4732, 5928
COMPROMISE TARIFF BILL: 4852
COMPTON, Samuel Wilson: 1177
COMPTON, Townsend: 5282
COMPTON FAMILY (Great Britain and United States): 5282
COMSTOCK (W. S.) AND CO.: 1178
COMTE, Auguste: 2612
CONANT, Kate D.: 3218
CONAUGHBY, D.M.: 5780
CONCERTS: see BAND CONCERTS; PIANO CONCERTS; SONGS AND MUSIC--Concerts
CONCORD, Massachusetts: 2563, 2564
  Poetry: 1698
CONCORD, New Hampshire: 1634, 1902, 3823, 4200
CONCORD, North Carolina: 3003, 3465, 5497
  Labor organizations: 1195
  Presbyterian churches: 5245
CONCORD ACADEMY, Caroline County, Virginia: 4698
CONCORD FEMALE COLLEGE, Statesville, North Carolina: 893, 5310
CONCRETE: see BUILDING MATERIALS; CEMENT; TABBY (Concrete)
CONDAMINE, Carlos Maria de la: 4155
CONDEMNATION OF LAND: see EMINENT DOMAIN
CONE FINISHING COMPANY: 5234
CONE MILLS, Greensboro, North Carolina: 3171
CONE MILLS CORPORATION: 5234
CONEGLIANO, Bon-Adrien Jeannot de Moncey, Duc de: 4348
CONETOE, North Carolina: 1362
CONFEDERATE EMIGRANTS: 339, 4257
  Argentina: 4019
  Brazil: 339
  Canada: 2366
  Cuba: 3587
  France: 2210
  Great Britain: 2210, 3587
  Mexico: 2210, 3587
  Missouri: 3038
  Nicaragua: 3587
CONFEDERATE ENGINEERING BUREAU: 4490
CONFEDERATE INFIRMARY, Columbia, South Carolina: 5759
CONFEDERATE LEAGUE: 1179
CONFEDERATE MEMORABILIA: 3809
  Maryland: 2202
  Sources: 4908
CONFEDERATE MILITARY AND SURGICAL ASSOCIATION: 5098
CONFEDERATE MINING COMPANY: 3657
CONFEDERATE MUSIC: see CIVIL WAR--SONGS AND MUSIC--Confederate; CONFEDERATE STATES OF AMERICA--ARMY--Songs and Music
CONFEDERATE PEACE COMMISSIONERS: 132
CONFEDERATE REUNIONS: see CIVIL WAR--VETERANS--Confederate conventions
"THE CONFEDERATE SOLDIER IN HISTORY" (address): 66

CONFEDERATE SOLDIERS' HOME, Atlanta,
    Georgia: 843
CONFEDERATE SPIES: see CIVIL WAR--
    SPIES--Confederate

CONFEDERATE STATES OF AMERICA

AGRICULTURAL PRODUCTS TRADE: 1156
ARMY: 33, 2529, 4891, 5315, 5660
  Absenteeism: 1181, 4002
    Virginia: 1886
  Aides-de-Camp: 2980
  Alabama: 1185
  Ammunition: 1506
  Appointments: see CONFEDERATE
    STATES OF AMERICA--ARMY--
    Officers--Appointments and
    promotions
  Arkansas: 1138
  Army life: 97, 807, 832, 1186,
    1227, 1410, 1731, 1962, 2210,
    2475, 2510, 2579, 2814, 2966,
    2990, 3009, 3033, 3113, 3172,
    3318, 3339, 3440, 3457, 3642,
    3690, 3729, 3901, 4049, 4154,
    4161, 4259, 4460, 4522, 4744,
    4765, 4877, 4919, 4924, 4998,
    5018, 5069, 5121, 5290, 5672,
    5855, 5916
    see also CONFEDERATE STATES OF
      AMERICA--ARMY--Camp life
    North Carolina: 1419, 1896,
      3447
      Fort Fisher: 3370
    Tennessee:
      Bethel: 4253
    Virginia: 2205, 2297, 2396,
      3447, 4528, 4743, 4968, 5068,
      5984
      Northern: 4347
      Potomac River: 4253
  Army of Northern Virginia: 53,
    1185, 1186, 1740, 1751, 4466,
    4942, 5069, 5578
    Brigades:
      Clingman's: 1109, 5193
      Colston's: 731
      Hood's: 2691
      Toombs's: 5315
    Cavalry: 3809
    Corps:
      Fitzhugh Lee's Cavalry: 1424,
        3809
      Longstreet's (I): 121, 285,
        1424, 2990, 3357, 4849
    Divisions:
      Anderson's: 1185
      Early's: 1830
      Ewell's: 122
    Medical services: 906
    Surrender: 689, 1820, 2236,
      2416, 3281, 3809, 4277, 5001,
      5769
  Army of Tennessee: 69, 1186, 1520,
    1867
    Artillery: 1186
    Brigades:
      Crews': 1181
      Govan's: 1520
    Corps:
      Wheeler's II Cavalry: 1181
    Divisions:
      Cleburne's: 1520
      William H. Jackson's Cavalry:
        664
    Hospitals: 5098
    Morale: 69
    Ordnance: 3970
    Surrender: 123, 440, 2469,
      2829, 2864, 5058, 5991
  Army of the Cumberland:
    Corps IV: 3282
  Army of the Mississippi: 1186
    Divisions:
      Ruggles's: 1186
  Army of the West: 3308

CONFEDERATE STATES OF AMERICA

ARMY (Continued):
  Arsenals:
    North Carolina--Fayetteville:
      5135
    South Carolina--Charleston: 4610
  Artillery: 4129
  Army of the Cumberland: 3282
    Officers: 3713, 5588
  Autographs: 1187, 5422
  Battalions:
    Georgia:
      Artillery:
        22nd Siege: 1189
      Infantry:
        2nd: 1189
        2nd Sharpshooters: 1189
    Louisiana: 4479
    North Carolina:
      Artillery:
        10th: 4292
    South Carolina:
      Artillery:
        3rd (Palmetto): 2997
        7th: 1476
      Cavalry:
        19th: 2961
    Virginia:
      Artillery:
        1st: 1498
        10th: 132
  Batteries:
    Stanford's: 3457
  Bridge construction:
    Virginia: 1830
  Brigades:
    see also subheading Brigades
      under names of field armies,
      territorial districts and
      departments, and branches
      of service
    Laurel Brigade: 3141
    Virginia 5th Infantry Brigade:
      203
  Burials: see CIVIL WAR--BURIAL
    GROUNDS
  Camp life: 266, 269, 336, 484, 607,
    611, 620, 621, 647, 682, 1017,
    1116, 1138, 1183, 1268, 1560,
    1590, 1601, 1602, 1779, 1947,
    1948, 1990, 2189, 2395, 2483,
    2631, 2635, 2654, 2716, 2763,
    2808, 3038, 3040, 3059, 3123,
    3126, 3276, 3339, 3351, 3415,
    3422, 3434, 3457, 3464, 3533,
    3788, 3809, 3821, 3959, 3991,
    4007, 4083, 4118, 4126, 4131,
    4183, 4283, 4292, 4325, 4347,
    4357, 4358, 4483, 4544, 4671,
    4679, 4689, 4764, 4831, 4834,
    4849, 4854, 4895, 4942, 5123,
    5147, 5230, 5272, 5382, 5465,
    5518, 5551, 5676, 5701, 5751,
    5759, 5760, 5774, 5792, 5905, 5919
    see also CONFEDERATE STATES OF
      AMERICA--ARMY--Army life
    Amusements: 1506, 5984
      South Carolina--Edisto Island:
        5645
    Subdivided by place:
      Alabama: 204, 546, 554, 1145
      Georgia: 44, 493, 1276, 1397,
        2312
        Camp Gordon: 5364
        Dalton: 916
        Savannah: 5472
      Mississippi: 1370, 2629
      North Carolina: 264, 612,
        1005, 1255, 1259, 1271,
        1475, 2090, 2310, 2957,
        3447, 4248, 5205, 5511, 5713
        Camp Holmes: 3506
        Camp Macon: 420
        Fort Caswell: 3435, 5390
        Fort Fisher: 3432, 3435
        Gattling's Battery: 5390
        Goldsboro: 4196

CONFEDERATE STATES OF AMERICA

ARMY:
  Camp life:
    Subdivided by place:
      North Carolina (Continued):
        Martin County: 524
        Raleigh: 1523, 4577
      South Carolina: 1334
        Charleston: 770, 4347
        Edisto Island: 5645
        Fort Sumter: 4347
        Grahamville: 5834
        James Island: 2806
        McPhersonville: 5834
        Pocataligo: 5834
        South Island: 2187
      Tennessee: 44, 1259, 1276
      Virginia: 19, 204, 207, 474,
        475, 612, 677, 708, 745,
        905, 915, 1005, 1033, 1105,
        1204, 1255, 1334, 1543,
        1617, 1729, 1882, 2090,
        2187, 2310, 2335, 2534,
        2832, 2939, 2949, 2957,
        3147, 3346, 3730, 3731,
        3832, 4248, 4706, 5472, 5511,
        5713, 5951
        Camp Ewell: 2305
        Camp Gregg: 5223
        Centreville: 56
        Fredericksburg: 3464
        Liberty Mills: 4577
        Orange: 4749
        Petersburg: 4577
        Richmond: 524, 3861, 4347
        Winchester: 5280
        Yorktown: 4225
      West Virginia: 2949
  Camps:
    Georgia: 18, 731
    North Carolina: 95, 831
      Camp Leventhrop: 860
      Wilmington: 5205, 5372
    South Carolina:
      South Island: 2187
      Sullivan's Island: 2960
    Virginia: 831, 1033, 4706
      Camp Carolina: 4528
      Camp Davis, Lynchburg: 2710
      Camp Gregg: 5223
      Camp Hager: 2187
      Fredericksburg: 1500
      Freeman's Hill: 1617
      Richmond: 5121
  Casualties: 19, 612, 756, 1186,
    1384, 1410, 1476, 1705, 2490,
    2635, 2744, 2808, 2939, 3033,
    3351, 3502, 3532, 3542, 4010,
    4043, 4065, 4183, 4347, 4358,
    4523, 4612, 4817, 4921, 4942,
    5298, 5314, 5382, 5514, 5633,
    5739, 5919, 5984
    see also CONFEDERATE STATES OF
      AMERICA--ARMY--Medical and
      sanitary affairs--Care of
      wounded
  Claims for compensation: 1181
  Neglect: 3378
  Religion: 3308
  Subdivided by place:
    Arkansas: 4536
    Georgia--Atlanta campaign:
      2433
    Kentucky: 4032
    Louisiana--Camp Benjamin:
      4596
    North Carolina:
      Fort Caswell: 3435
      Fort Fisher: 3370, 3435
      North Carolina troops: 714,
        1590
    Pennsylvania:
      Gettysburg: 3464, 4196
    South Carolina--Charleston:
      3435
    Virginia: 53, 128, 132, 714,
      1886, 2949, 4706

CONFEDERATE STATES OF AMERICA
ARMY:
  Casualties:
    Subdivided by place:
      Virginia (Continued):
        Dranesville: 2178
        Malvern Hill: 3809
        West Virginia: 52
  Cattle for the Army: 3008
  Cavalry: 687, 1424, 2990
    see also CONFEDERATE STATES OF AMERICA--ARMY--Regiments--(name of state)--Cavalry
    Brigades:
      Dibrell's: 1186
      Thomas Harrison's: 1186
    Corps:
      Wheeler's: 1186
    Divisions:
      Iverson's: 1186
    Georgia: 2598
    Horse trade: 5633
    Military activities (1863): 687
    Rivalry with Union cavalry: 3809
    Surgeons: 1854
    Tactics and weapons: 3809
  Cavalry life: 5633
  Censorship: 1506
  Chaplains: 1920, 2654, 4358, 4498, 5518
  Civilian labor--Negroes: 2893
  Clothing and dress: 122, 612, 1185, 2510, 3059, 3387, 3788, 5111, 5123, 5551, 5751, 5984
    Prices of uniforms: 1506
    Texas: 5723
    Virginia: 19, 714, 1359, 3346
  Commissaries: 1185, 1701, 3792, 5382
    Accounts: 3832
    South Carolina--Seventh Regiment: 4882
  Commissary Department: 3268, 3467
  Commissions: see CONFEDERATE STATES OF AMERICA--ARMY--Officers--Appointments and promotions
  Communications: 1186, 2488, 4612
  Confiscation of property: see CIVIL WAR--CONFISCATION OF PROPERTY
  Conduct: see CONFEDERATE STATES OF AMERICA--ARMY--Discipline
  Conscientious objectors: see CONFEDERATE STATES OF AMERICA--ARMY--Recruiting and enlistment--Resistance--Conscientious objectors
  Conscription: see CONFEDERATE STATES OF AMERICA--ARMY--Recruiting and enlistment
  Convicts, Use of: 3729
  Corps: see Corps under names of field armies
  Corps of Engineers: see CONFEDERATE STATES OF AMERICA--ARMY--Engineers
  Courts-Martial: 1181, 1186, 1359, 1601, 2831, 5518
    Charges against officers: 2885
  Defenses on the Great Lakes: 388
  Department of Alabama, Mississippi, and East Louisiana:
    Surrender: 5208
  Department of Mississippi and East Louisiana:
    William W. Loring's Division: 1853
  Department of Richmond: 1186
  Department of South Carolina and Georgia: 1186
  Department of Tennessee: 5098
  Depredations: 1352, 1796, 3807
    see also CIVIL WAR--DEPREDATIONS

CONFEDERATE STATES OF AMERICA
ARMY:
  Depredations (Continued):
    Cavalry: 687
    Georgia: 5623
    North Carolina:
      Fayetteville: 5991
      Raleigh: 5991
    South Carolina: 2854
      Charleston: 4120
    Tennessee: 4588
    Virginia: 1, 359
  Desertion: 269, 336, 475, 484, 612, 677, 696, 827, 1056, 1061, 1091, 1109, 1268, 1403, 1410, 1506, 1601, 1806, 1882, 2223, 2236, 2240, 2490, 2763, 2803, 2808, 2854, 2960, 3033, 3136, 3276, 3331, 3415, 3422, 3729, 3811, 4002, 4043, 4103, 4131, 4183, 4292, 4347, 4357, 4484, 4501, 4521, 4577, 4744, 4919, 4991, 5111, 5122, 5135, 5230, 5402, 5420, 5511, 5518, 5558, 5759, 5834, 5926, 5965, 5984
    Army of Tennessee: 69
    Execution for: 2949, 4919
    North Carolina: 835, 4075, 4196, 5402
      Punishment: 2212
    South Carolina: 5193
    Virginia: 7, 1886
  Discharge pay: 1185
  Discharges: 1185, 1186, 1438, 3657
  Discipline: 122, 607, 2312, 3457, 3788, 4118, 5701
    North Carolina: 1259, 4075
    Pennsylvania: 1918
    Virginia: 905, 2396
  Diseases: see CIVIL WAR--DISEASES; CONFEDERATE STATES OF AMERICA--HEALTH CONDITIONS
  Districts:
    District of the Gulf: 1186
    District of the West: 637
  Divisions: see as subheading under names of field armies, territorial districts, departments, and cavalry
  Drill and tactics: 3382, 5984
  Drinking: 5147
  Election of officers: 132, 1947, 2189, 3814, 4942, 5518
  Elections: see CONFEDERATE STATES OF AMERICA--ARMY--Election of officers; CONFEDERATE STATES OF AMERICA--ARMY--Political elections
  Enlistment: see CONFEDERATE STATES OF AMERICA--ARMY--Recruiting and enlistment
  Engineers: 2237, 4490, 5798
    South Carolina: 2864
  Equipment: see CONFEDERATE STATES OF AMERICA--ARMY--Military supplies
  Executions: see CONFEDERATE STATES OF AMERICA--ARMY--Desertion--Execution for
  Exemptions from duty: see CONFEDERATE STATES OF AMERICA--ARMY--Medical and sanitary affairs--Exemptions from duty
  Families of soldiers: see CIVIL WAR--PUBLIC WELFARE--Aid to soldiers' families
  Family aid to soldiers:
    North Carolina: 1144
    South Carolina: 5193
  Food: 336, 502, 696, 835, 1183, 1268, 1397, 1410, 1861, 1969, 2240, 2510, 2631, 3038, 3276, 3351, 3415, 3432, 3821, 4118, 4183, 4347, 4577, 4706, 4729, 4795, 5111, 5123, 5298, 5444, 5518, 5551, 5701, 5751, 5774, 5946, 5984

CONFEDERATE STATES OF AMERICA
ARMY:
  Food (Continued):
    see also CONFEDERATE STATES OF AMERICA--ARMY--Meat supply agents; CONFEDERATE STATES OF AMERICA--ARMY--Subsistence Department
    Georgia: 4510
    Mississippi: 5602
    North Carolina: 3033, 3506
    Virginia: 7, 19, 714, 1092, 1105, 1122, 1740, 1882, 1886, 3731
  Forage: 1, 1017, 3387, 5690
  Foraging: 4358
    South Carolina: 5645
  Foreign-born soldiers: see CONFEDERATE STATES OF AMERICA--ARMY--Recruiting and enlistment--Foreign born
  Fortifications:
    see also CIVIL WAR--FORTIFICATIONS
    Slave labor: 4103
    Mississippi River: 4253
    North Carolina--Wilmington: 4292
    South Carolina--Fort Ripley: 4033
    Tennessee River: 4253
    Virginia--Petersburg--Maps: 5417
  Furloughs: see CONFEDERATE STATES OF AMERICA--ARMY--Leaves and furloughs
  Generals: 69, 132, 484, 623, 745, 1023, 1206, 1364, 1624, 1886, 2416, 2449, 2510, 3131, 3642, 4737, 4808, 4921, 4950, 5059, 5067, 5147, 5613, 5739, 5970
    see also CONFEDERATE STATES OF AMERICA--ARMY--Officers; and names of individuals
    Charges against: 3417, 3809
    Removal from command: 3262
    North Carolina--Greensboro: 4738
    Tennessee--Chattanooga: 5032
  Guard duty: 1729, 2510, 2654, 3276, 3755, 3809, 4065, 4347, 4356, 4483, 4849, 5111, 5946
    North Carolina--Greensboro: 3299, 5661
    South Carolina--Charleston: 5193
    Virginia: 359, 1359
  Guerillas: 4716, 5017
  Hatred of "Yankees": 5984
  Health conditions: 871, 1105, 1138, 1183, 1397, 1437, 1602, 2178, 2635, 2966, 2971, 3276, 3792, 3809, 4347, 4357, 4417, 4942, 5551, 5706, 5774, 5965
    see also CONFEDERATE STATES OF AMERICA--ARMY--Medical and sanitary affairs
    Alabama--Camp Governor Moore: 3500
    North Carolina: 620
    Virginia: 2949
    West Virginia: 2949
  Homesickness: see CONFEDERATE STATES OF AMERICA--ARMY--Morale
  Honors and awards: 4908
  Horses and mules: 1384, 1945, 2325
    Georgia: 1397
    Longstreet's Corps: 2990
    Theft: 700
    Virginia: 1436
  Hospitals: 122, 647, 1476, 2510, 3542, 4007, 4347, 4795, 4924, 5314, 5444, 5518, 5633, 5676, 5682
    See also CIVIL WAR--HOSPITALS; CIVIL WAR--NURSES AND NURSING; CONFEDERATE STATES OF AMERICA--ARMY--Medical and sanitary affairs

CONFEDERATE STATES OF AMERICA
ARMY:
  Hospitals (Continued):
    Alabama: 5098
    Army of Tennessee: 5098
    Florida: 2598
    Louisiana--Camp Benjamin: 4596
    Mississippi: 5098
    North Carolina: 375, 927, 1185, 2458
    South Carolina: 1185
    Virginia: 661, 1092, 1185, 2090, 2205
      Danville: 4506
      Emory: 4895
      Richmond: 5147
  Illness: see CONFEDERATE STATES OF AMERICA--ARMY--Medical and sanitary affairs--Illness and disease
  Inspections:
    Department of South Carolina and Georgia: 1186
    Virginia--Centreville: 4483
  Leaves and furloughs: 1181, 2253 2630, 2792, 3268, 3807, 4118, 5162, 5566, 5828, 5984
    Army of Mississippi: 1186
    Army of Tennessee: 1186
    North Carolina: 657
    Virginia: 1886, 2396, 3346
  Maps: 1182, 2363
  Meat supply agents: 3994
  Medical and sanitary affairs: 1186, 1854, 2069, 2305, 2458, 2966, 3038, 3422, 3673, 3761, 4007, 4010, 4083, 4118, 4131, 4795, 5098, 5444, 5919
    see also CIVIL WAR--MEDICAL SUPPLIES; CIVIL WAR--NURSES AND NURSING; and the following subheadings under CONFEDERATE STATES OF AMERICA--ARMY: Health conditions; Hospitals; Officers--Resignations for health reasons; Surgeon General's Office
    Care of the wounded: 682, 1204, 1827, 5518
      see also CONFEDERATE STATES OF AMERICA--ARMY--Casualties; CIVIL WAR--TRANSPORT OF SICK AND WOUNDED
    Exemptions from duty: 1186
    Illness and disease: 122, 269, 348, 682, 1144, 1947, 2240, 2510, 3351, 4183, 4706, 4817, 5511, 5518
      see also CIVIL WAR--DISEASES
      Georgia: 44
      Mississippi: 1370
      North Carolina: 1419
      Tennessee: 44
      Virginia: 714, 1886
      West Virginia: 52
    Medicine: 3136
      Army of Mississippi: 1186
    Services of physicians: 1017, 2510, 5518
      see also CONFEDERATE STATES OF AMERICA--ARMY--Surgeons
    Subdivided by place:
      Alabama: 5032
      Georgia: 2312
      Louisiana--Camp Benjamin: 4596
      North Carolina: 2260, 3033
        Fort Caswell: 3435
        Fort Fisher: 3370, 3435
        Wilmington: 5205
      South Carolina--Charleston: 3435
      Virginia: 475, 906, 2396, 2829
  Military activities and troop movements: 682, 1023, 1204, 1403, 1410, 1601, 1962, 2490, 2510, 2553, 2617, 2744, 2803, 2814, 3131, 3157, 3308, 3339,

CONFEDERATE STATES OF AMERICA
ARMY:
  Military activities and troop movements (Continued):
    3447, 3624, 3959, 4043, 4080, 4126, 4253, 4483, 4679, 4817, 4891, 4942, 5018, 5051, 5192, 5444, 5465, 5510, 5709, 5739, 5741, 5774, 5916, 5931, 5984
    see also CIVIL WAR--CAMPAIGNS, BATTLES, AND MILITARY ACTIONS
    Alabama: 395, 554, 3331, 3809
      Florence: 5053
      Mobile: 5208
    Florida: 4612, 5970
    Georgia: 395, 510, 1121, 1990, 2312, 2325, 3331, 5759
      Augusta: 1185
      Dalton: 5272
      Savannah: 5676
    Indiana: 4588
    Kentucky: 1268
    Louisiana: 1138, 4596
      Amite River: 5838
    Maryland: 1116, 1144, 5633
      Hagerstown: 3896
    Mississippi: 395, 637, 664, 1185, 1990, 3809, 4596, 5676, 5759, 5844
      Holly Springs: 5975
      Vicksburg: 5053, 5272
    Missouri--Charleston: 4209
    North Carolina: 271, 390, 531, 761, 1109, 1185, 1255, 1259, 1327, 2808, 4849, 5613, 5633, 5950
      Cape Fear River: 3896
      Coast: 5915
      Eastern: 3276, 4544, 5123
      Fort Johnston: 3896
      New Bern: 5565
      Smithfield: 5759
      Wilmington: 4183, 4849, 5706
    Pennsylvania: 1116, 1144
    South Carolina: 1268, 1570, 2325, 2488, 2831, 2944, 4612
      Charleston: 4347, 5045, 5565, 5661
      Eastern: 3276
      Morris Island: 2893
    Tennessee: 664, 771, 1259, 2831, 3331, 4795
      Chattanooga: 4873, 4944, 5272, 5517, 5759
      Cumberland Gap: 4873
      Eastern: 3276
      Forrest's Raid: 4899
      Gallatin: 5784
      Knoxville: 4849, 5272
      Lookout Mountain: 5272, 5314
      Shelbyville: 4033
    Texas: 1138
    Virginia: 33, 382, 390, 531, 714, 761, 1116, 1144, 1255, 1432, 2524, 2696, 2808, 2831, 2939, 2944, 2966, 3299, 3542, 3755, 3908, 4007, 4186, 4277, 4706, 4795, 4938, 5069, 5314, 5951
      Alexandria: 5852
      Culpeper Court House: 1617
      Dranesville: 5852
      Farmville: 5325
      Frazier's Farm: 5852
      Fredericksburg: 3012, 3896, 5613
      Goose Creek: 5852
      Gordonsville: 5613
      James River: 4544
      Leesburg: 5852
      Lynchburg: 5613
      Manassas: 5566
      Northern: 5517
      Peninsula: 5511
      Petersburg: 1271, 5123, 5565, 5633
      Rapidan Station: 1617

CONFEDERATE STATES OF AMERICA
ARMY:
  Military activities and troop movements:
    Virginia (Continued):
      Richmond: 3276, 5123, 5325, 5613, 5633, 5706
      Seven Pines: 5852
      Shiloh: 4320
    West Virginia: 3268
      Shepherdstown: 3012
    Western campaigns: 3457
  Military intelligence: 3157, 5121
    Kentucky: 751
  Military passes: 3382
  Military regulations: 565, 3809, 4358
  Military supplies: 122, 546, 628, 700, 1107, 1185, 1186, 1596, 1726, 1963, 2237, 2536, 2850, 2882, 3038, 3081, 3149, 3339, 3387, 3422, 4080, 4131, 4209, 4942, 5283, 5510, 5512, 5541
    Prices: 1506
    Transportation: see CONFEDERATE STATES OF AMERICA--ARMY--Transportation--Supplies
    Subdivided by place:
      Alabama: 395
      Army of Mississippi: 1186
      Army of Tennessee: 1186
      Department of South Carolina and Georgia: 1186
      Georgia: 395, 718
      Louisiana--Camp Benjamin: 4596
      Mississippi: 395, 637
      North Carolina: 3506
      South Carolina: 2185, 2670
      Virginia: 905, 1359, 1886, 1920, 4186
  Militia and Home Guards: see CONFEDERATE STATES OF AMERICA--ARMY--Units; Militia as subheading under names of states
  Miscellaneous soldiers' letters: 412, 417, 424, 546, 764, 904, 1005, 1183, 1255, 1268, 1271, 1278, 1483, 1548, 1555, 1601, 1746, 1751, 1859, 1912, 2237, 2310, 2391, 2406, 2420, 2490, 2744, 2803, 2806, 2900, 2946, 3009, 3299, 3653, 3668, 4212, 4390, 4396, 4610, 4679, 4792, 4800, 4984, 5075, 5084, 5135, 5182, 5347, 5415, 5549, 5864
    Georgia: 807
    North Carolina: 1259, 1649, 2036, 3324
    South Carolina: 1107
    Virginia: 2174
  Mobilization: 523, 2469, 3809, 4347
    Alabama: 1304
    Georgia: 4335
    Louisiana: 1424
    South Carolina--Charleston: 4033
    Tennessee: 1319
    Virginia: 1304, 1801
  Morale: 531, 710, 1183, 1271, 1285, 1506, 2554, 3059, 3339, 3354, 3415, 3457, 3469, 3788, 3792, 4118, 4131, 4417, 4501, 4577, 4877, 4928, 4998, 5180, 5273, 5390, 5402, 5510, 5514, 5565, 5566, 5701, 5751, 5921, 5926, 5931, 5984
    Homesickness: 4706
    North Carolina: 620
    Virginia: 1092, 1105, 1122, 2331
  Morals: 871
  Music: see CONFEDERATE STATES OF AMERICA--ARMY--Songs and music
  Muster rolls: 3832
  Mutiny: 2960
  Negro troops: 132, 700, 1247, 1403, 3318, 3809

CONFEDERATE STATES OF AMERICA
ARMY (Continued):
  Northerners in service: 1242
  Numbers: see CONFEDERATE STATES OF AMERICA--ARMY--Organization and troop strength
  Officers: 631, 1034, 1105, 1138, 1186, 1364, 1962, 2253, 2362, 2490, 2553, 2617, 2702, 2803, 2810, 2818, 2849, 2902, 2944, 3301, 3318, 3440, 3457, 3624, 3763, 3809, 3832, 3970, 4016, 4469, 4544, 4550, 4671, 4679, 4706, 4714, 4891, 5121, 5208, 5452, 5517, 5518, 5566, 5588, 5633, 5668, 5828
    see also CONFEDERATE STATES OF AMERICA--ARMY--Generals
    Appointments and promotions: 608, 1061, 1181, 1185, 1403, 1597, 2268, 2343, 2536, 2831, 3809, 4358, 4729, 5193, 5605, 5723
    Charges of misconduct: see CONFEDERATE STATES OF AMERICA--ARMY--Courts-Martial
    Commissions: see CONFEDERATE STATES OF AMERICA--ARMY--Officers--Appointments and promotions
    Complaints of enlisted men: 871
    Duties: 5759
    Elections: see CONFEDERATE STATES OF AMERICA--ARMY--Election of officers
    Inefficiency: 5123
    Morale: 5517
    Pay: 1107
    Portraits: 1435
    Relief from duty: 5828
    Resignations: 5565
      For health reasons: 901
    Scarcity: 2654
    Training: 4544
    Transfer: 5915
  Orders: 1901, 2268, 3657, 3807, 4358, 5208, 5668
    Defense of Savannah: 2722
    Department of South Carolina and Georgia: 1186
    Johnston's General Order No. 18: 2882
  Ordnance: 1185, 1186, 1403, 1424, 3771, 3970, 5280, 5444, 5605
    see also CIVIL WAR--ORDNANCE
    Army of Mississippi: 1186
    Army of Northern Virginia: 53
    Georgia: 2312
    South Carolina: 1606
      Charleston: 5193
  Organization and troop strength: 1185, 1186, 2400, 4253, 4849, 5605, 5946
    Kentucky: 4873
    Tennessee: 4873
      Chickamauga: 4358
  Paroles: 4891, 5828
  Pay: 871, 1123, 1185, 1438, 1947, 3422, 4483, 4795, 5518
    see also CONFEDERATE STATES OF AMERICA--ARMY--Discharge pay; CONFEDERATE STATES OF AMERICA--ARMY--Officers--Pay
    Claims: 122
    Privates: 4044
  Physicians: see CONFEDERATE STATES OF AMERICA--ARMY--Medical and sanitary affairs--Services of physicians
  Political elections: 1779, 2792, 5703
    Georgia: 1189
    North Carolina: 4103
    South Carolina: 1189
  Promotions: see CONFEDERATE STATES OF AMERICA--ARMY--Officers--Appointments and promotions

CONFEDERATE STATES OF AMERICA
ARMY (Continued):
  Provost Marshall: 905
  Quartermaster Corps: 628, 1596, 2792, 2850, 3387, 5257, 3268, 3837
  Railroads: see CONFEDERATE STATES OF AMERICA--MILITARY RAILROADS
  Reconnaissance: 5121
    Army of Mississippi: 1186
    Louisiana: 5838
    Potomac River: 19
    Tennessee River: 2944
  Recruiting and enlistment: 45, 132, 474, 700, 1056, 1181, 1185, 1242, 1947, 2808, 2966, 3415, 3690, 3788, 3807, 4118, 4942, 4982, 5059, 5298, 5402, 5545
    Exemptions: 82, 700, 1181, 1185, 1403, 1969, 4103, 4248, 4916, 4921, 5062, 5162
      Agricultural workers: 2617
      Mill workers: 2857
      Mississippi--Physicians: 3876
      North Carolina: 2068, 4450
      South Carolina: 1749
      Virginia: 2584
    Foreign-born:
      British: 700, 2150
      German: 2300
    Laws and legislation: 4921, 5566
      South Carolina: 4193
    Negroes: see CONFEDERATE STATES OF AMERICA--ARMY--Negro troops
    Resistance: 827, 1138, 2469, 2949, 3218, 3515, 3811, 4103, 4506
      Conscientious objectors: 2554, 2555
      North Carolina--Quakers: 2970
    Social effects of conscription: 122
    Substitutions: 1410, 2949, 4248, 5551, 5613, 5774
      Georgia: 1993
      North Carolina: 2631
      Virginia: 1801
    Terms of service: 3276, 3422
    Subdivided by place:
      Georgia: 718, 731, 2317, 3221, 4895
        Gwinnett County: 3841
        Wilkes County: 4895
      Louisiana: 5452
      North Carolina: 956, 2824, 3237, 3422, 3506
      South Carolina: 565, 2300
      Virginia: 1186, 2396, 3809, 4879
  Regiments: 1185, 2490
    see also the following subheadings under CONFEDERATE STATES OF AMERICA--ARMY: Units; names of field armies; and territorial departments and districts
    Alabama:
      Cavalry:
        51st: 3771
      Infantry:
        1st: 5453
        2nd: 204
        5th: 546
        7th: 3331
        13th: 204
        17th: 554
        18th: 3500
        29th: 1185, 5916
        37th: 5053
        41st: 5032
        45th: 1295
        61st: 1295
        62nd: 546
    Arkansas: 1185, 5588
      Cavalry:
        3rd: 1186

CONFEDERATE STATES OF AMERICA
ARMY:
  Regiments (Continued):
    Florida:
      Infantry:
        3rd: 4068
        8th: 1186
    Georgia: 1185, 4950
      Cavalry:
        1st: 1799
        6th: 1189
      Infantry:
        1st: 3339, 3382
        2nd: 589, 1189, 1476
        3rd: 127, 2326, 4426
        4th: 2326
        5th: 1189
        6th: 1189, 2326
        7th: 4671, 5180
        8th: 4463
        10th: 2326, 2963
        12th: 4706
        13th: 1189
        16th: 2326
        17th: 1476, 5314
        18th: 4795
        28th: 5566
        29th: 3814
        30th: 1189, 5676
        32nd: 1189
        34th: 1185
        37th: 123, 1189
        43rd: 5111
        44th: 2326, 4434
        46th: 1189, 2433
        47th: 5759
        48th: 5472
        51st: 1189
        52nd: 359, 608, 5111
        53rd: 1731
        55th: 4335, 5272
        56th: 5272
        63rd: 5472
    Kentucky: 1185
      Infantry:
        6th: 3282
    Louisiana: 1186, 5588
      Artillery:
        Washington Battalion: 4277
      Infantry:
        6th: 2691
        7th: 3775, 4479, 4484
        17th: 1186
        18th: 1186
    Maryland:
      Infantry:
        1st: 2849
    Mississippi:
      Cavalry:
        28th: 972
        Nathan Bedford Forrest's: 5844
      Infantry:
        20th: 5751
    Missouri:
      Cavalry:
        1st: 2829
    North Carolina: 5739
      Artillery:
        10th: 3811
        36th: 2970
      Cavalry:
        1st: 19
        2nd: 714, 1948, 2121, 3447, 4919
        5th: 4523
        63rd: 3237, 4523
      Infantry:
        1st: 1523, 2090, 3447, 4434, 5298, 5703
        2nd: 1186, 4183
        3rd: 4434
        4th: 1186, 2310, 3219, 3434
        5th: 760, 3126, 3447
        6th: 2554, 4007, 5510
        7th: 91, 1181, 3434, 3787
        8th: 420

CONFEDERATE STATES OF AMERICA
ARMY:
　Regiments:
　　North Carolina:
　　　Infantry (Continued):
　　　　9th: 5965
　　　　10th: 5533
　　　　11th: 1186, 3033, 5558
　　　　12th: 1186
　　　　13th: 1144, 1186, 2654
　　　　14th: 2212, 4918, 4938
　　　　　Company A: 3831
　　　　15th: 1005
　　　　16th: 5444
　　　　18th: 704
　　　　19th: 714, 2121
　　　　20th: 1331
　　　　21st: 2829, 5905
　　　　22nd: 1590
　　　　23rd: 1144, 2654
　　　　24th: 2631, 4292
　　　　25th: 1186, 3276
　　　　26th: 827, 1437
　　　　27th: 714, 1186
　　　　28th: 1419, 3038, 4877, 5230
　　　　30th: 2090, 3896
　　　　31st: 4183
　　　　33rd: 2036
　　　　35th: 524
　　　　36th: 1751
　　　　37th: 1186, 1259, 3908
　　　　40th: 1247
　　　　42nd: 2036
　　　　43rd: 2981, 4052
　　　　44th: 3126, 3727
　　　　45th: 1896, 2240
　　　　46th: 3126
　　　　47th: 4016
　　　　48th: 1882, 5518, 5926
　　　　49th: 1517, 4938, 5123
　　　　50th: 3301
　　　　52nd: 1861, 2555
　　　　55th:
　　　　　Company F: 3807
　　　　　Company K: 5741
　　　　56th: 2253, 5926
　　　　60th: 4417
　　　　61st: 4929
　　　　66th: 1186, 1255, 1256, 3038
　　　　　Company A: 3111
　　　　67th: 2631, 5709
　　　　68th: 5950
　　　　71st: 3408
　　　　87th: 3447
　　　　91st: 5390
　　　　Ransom's Brigade: 5280
　　South Carolina:
　　　Artillery:
　　　　2nd: 1017
　　　　Washington Artillery: 24
　　　Cavalry: 3809
　　　　1st: 2596
　　　　4th: 4620
　　　　5th: 1334, 2818
　　　　7th: 5633
　　　Infantry:
　　　　1st: 2185, 3340, 5661
　　　　2nd: 4818
　　　　5th: 5834, 5931
　　　　7th: 4882
　　　　9th: 1186, 5834
　　　　17th: 2596, 3293
　　　　18th: 4347
　　　　20th: 2961
　　　　　Company M: 2961
　　　　22nd: 3546
　　　　42nd: 1793
　　Tennessee: 1185
　　　Infantry:
　　　　1st: 4358, 5671
　　　　3rd: 1186
　　　　12th: 45
　　　　23rd: 2629
　　　　55th: 4894
　　Texas: 1185
　　　Cavalry:
　　　　4th--Company C.: 4562

CONFEDERATE STATES OF AMERICA
ARMY:
　Regiments
　　Texas:
　　　Cavalry (Continued):
　　　　11th: 1186
　　　　12th: 1181
　　　　17th: 1181
　　　　31st: 1138
　　Virginia: 1185
　　　Artillery:
　　　　2nd: 66
　　　　8th Star: 5275
　　　Cavalry:
　　　　1st: 2635, 3809
　　　　2nd: 3809
　　　　3rd: 3809
　　　　4th: 3809
　　　　5th: 1105, 3809, 5192
　　　　6th: 2792, 3668
　　　　7th: 155, 2792, 3809
　　　　8th: 1596, 3668
　　　　11th: 3141, 4743
　　　　12th: 207, 5275
　　　　16th: 4440
　　　　18th--Company F: 5946
　　　　36th--Prince William
　　　　　Company: 5283
　　　　43rd: 3793, 4607
　　　Infantry:
　　　　2nd: 73, 584, 2635, 2949,
　　　　　3832, 3899
　　　　3rd: 128
　　　　4th: 2635
　　　　6th: 577
　　　　7th: 3855
　　　　8th: 3668
　　　　10th: 1105
　　　　12th: 460
　　　　13th: 745, 3060
　　　　17th: 2638, 5382, 5852
　　　　18th: 531, 2902, 3855
　　　　20th: 66
　　　　21st: 2849, 2971, 3136, 4998
　　　　23rd: 2396
　　　　24th: 3587
　　　　　Casualties: 4196
　　　　25th: 475, 2949
　　　　33rd: 2597
　　　　42nd: 2949
　　　　43rd: 2413
　　　　44th: 3855
　　　　45th: 1181, 1596
　　　　48th: 2949
　　　　49th: 5107
　　　　51st: 3809
　　　　57th: 1485
　　　　61st: 348
　　　　77th: 3141
　Religion: 1204, 3276, 3528, 3563,
　　4007, 4126, 4358, 4429, 4612,
　　5075, 5298, 5444, 5472, 5514,
　　5774
　　Evangelism: 5018
　　North Carolina--Fort Fisher: 3370
　　South Carolina: 2187
　　Virginia: 1882, 2187, 3731
　　　Centreville: 56
　Reorganization: 3339, 3440, 3809,
　　4065
　Reserves--North Carolina: 2617
　Retreat: 3339
　Reviews: see CONFEDERATE STATES OF
　　AMERICA--ARMY--Inspections
　Rumors: 4118, 4358, 4706, 4744,
　　4895
　　see also CIVIL WAR--RUMORS
　　Georgia: 44
　　Tennessee: 44
　Salt agents: 1436
　Scarcity:
　　Clothing: 19, 2971, 4849, 5633
　　Food: 1268, 1779, 2331, 3809,
　　　4083, 4501, 4744, 5633, 5706,
　　　5965
　　　Mississippi--Vicksburg: 5602

CONFEDERATE STATES OF AMERICA
ARMY:
　Scarcity (Continued):
　　Military equipment: 2971, 4919
　　Munitions: 5186
　　Necessities: 2806
　　Soap: 1268
　Scouting: see CONFEDERATE STATES
　　OF AMERICA--ARMY--Reconnaissance
　Sentry duty: see CONFEDERATE
　　STATES OF AMERICA--ARMY--Guard
　　duty
　Signals: see CONFEDERATE STATES OF
　　AMERICA--ARMY--Communications
　Slaves: 3642, 4921
　　Personal servants: 1295, 4292
　Soldier suffrage: see CONFEDERATE
　　STATES OF AMERICA--ARMY--
　　Political elections
　Soldiers: 4616
　　Comparison with Union soldiers:
　　　1282
　　Personal finance: 657, 1437,
　　　5383
　Soldiers' elections: see
　　CONFEDERATE STATES OF AMERICA--
　　ARMY--Political elections
　Soldiers' letters: see
　　CONFEDERATE STATES OF AMERICA--
　　ARMY--Miscellaneous soldiers'
　　letters
　Songs and music: 123, 2510, 4612
　　see also CIVIL WAR--SONGS AND
　　　MUSIC
　Straggling:
　　Virginia: 359
　Subsistence Department:
　　see also CONFEDERATE STATES OF
　　　AMERICA--ARMY--Food
　　Georgia: 4510
　　South Carolina--Abbeville: 5193
　Supplies: see CONFEDERATE STATES
　　OF AMERICA--ARMY--Military
　　supplies
　Surgeon General's Office: 1185
　　see also CONFEDERATE STATES OF
　　　AMERICA--ARMY--Medical and
　　　sanitary affairs
　Surgeons: 1053, 1476, 2210, 2260,
　　3038, 4743, 4951, 5098
　　see also CONFEDERATE STATES OF
　　　AMERICA--ARMY--Medical and
　　　sanitary affairs--Services of
　　　physicians
　　Department of South Carolina and
　　　Georgia: 1186
　　Florida: 2598
　　Georgia--Andersonville: 5682
　Surrender:
　　see also CONFEDERATE STATES OF
　　　AMERICA--ARMY--(name of army
　　　or department)--Surrender
　　Return home of Confederate
　　　troops: 5769
　Training: 122
　　Artillery: 700
　　Cavalry--Virginia--Camp Comfort:
　　　4440
　　Infantry: 3382
　　Virginia: 2396
　　Subdivided by place:
　　　Georgia: 731, 4335
　　　North Carolina: 834, 2068,
　　　　3506
　　　Virginia: 834
　Trans-Mississippi Department:
　　1403, 2617, 5257
　Transportation: 1185, 1186, 1726,
　　3387, 3464, 4002, 4596
　　Passes: 1181, 4358
　　see also CIVIL WAR--
　　　TRANSPORTATION PASSES
　　Sick and wounded: 3157
　　Supplies: 1596, 4596
　　　Kentucky: 4335

CONFEDERATE STATES OF AMERICA
ARMY (Continued):
  Trenches and trench warfare:
    Virginia--Petersburg: 3788,
      3809, 4998
  Troop movements: see CONFEDERATE
    STATES OF AMERICA--ARMY--
    Military activities and troop
    movements
  Troop strength: see CONFEDERATE
    STATES OF AMERICA--ARMY--
    Organization and troop strength
  Uniforms: see CONFEDERATE STATES
    OF AMERICA--ARMY--Clothing and
    dress
  Units:
    see also the following
      subheadings under CONFEDERATE
      STATES OF AMERICA--ARMY:
      Battalions; Brigades;
      Divisions; Regiments; and
      names of field armies and
      territorial departments; and
      Militia as subheading under
      names of states
    Crescent Rifles: 4479
    Partisan Rangers: 1186, 4888,
      5838
    Subdivided by place:
      Georgia: 1186, 3180
        Georgia Legion: 1123
        Gray's Infantry: 1189
        Joe Thompson Artillery: 2312
      Louisiana:
        Sarsfield Light Infantry:
          see CONFEDERATE STATES OF
          AMERICA--ARMY--Regiments--
          Louisiana--Infantry: 7th
        Washington Artillery: 1186
      North Carolina:
        Manley's Battery: 486
        Martin County Volunteer
          Company: 271
      South Carolina:
        Beaufort District Cavalry
          Troop: 2670
        Governor's Horse Guards:
          2710
        Hampton Legion: 2300, 2997,
          4831, 4908, 5325, 5633
        Santee Light Artillery:
          4429
        Washington Artillery: 24
      Virginia: 1186
        Powhatan Artillery Company:
          3855
        Staunton Hill Artillery:
          2253
  Veterans: see CIVIL WAR--
    VETERANS--Confederate
  Voting: see CONFEDERATE STATES OF
    AMERICA--ARMY--Election of
    officers; CONFEDERATE STATES OF
    AMERICA--ARMY--Political
    elections
  Women soldiers: see WOMEN IN THE
    CIVIL WAR
BONDS: 1181, 1252, 1339, 2074, 2141,
  2260, 3587, 3788, 4743, 5242,
  5518
BRITISH CONSULATE IN:
  South Carolina--Charleston: 4484
BRITISH SUBJECTS IN: see CIVIL WAR--
  BRITISH IN THE CONFEDERATE STATES
  OF AMERICA
CODES: 1181
  see also CONFEDERATE STATES OF
    AMERICA--NAVY--Passwords
COMMODITY PRICES: see CIVIL WAR--
  COMMODITY PRICES--Southern States,
  or names of specific southern
  states
COMMODITY SPECULATION: see CIVIL
  WAR--SPECULATION AND WAR
  PROFITEERING

CONFEDERATE STATES OF AMERICA
CONGRESS:
  House of Representatives: 1069,
    1180, 2620, 2831, 3445, 3905,
    5315
    From Georgia: 4921
    From North Carolina: 4923, 5384
  Senate: 1084, 2860, 4739
    Clerk--Duties: 3841
CONSTITUTION: 842
  see also CONFEDERATE STATES OF
    AMERICA--FORMATION OF THE
    CONFEDERACY
COTTON AND PRODUCE LOAN: see CONFED-
  ERATE STATES OF AMERICA--PUBLIC
  FINANCE--Cotton and produce loan
COURTS: 1365
  District Courts: 1190
CURRENCY: 206, 662, 1181, 1339, 4501,
  4921, 4921, 4965, 5242
  see also CONFEDERATE STATES OF
    AMERICA--EXCHANGE
DEFENSE POLICY: 4921
ECONOMIC CONDITIONS: see CIVIL WAR--
  ECONOMIC ASPECTS; and Economic
  conditions (1860s) as subheading
  under SOUTHERN STATES or names of
  individual states
EMIGRANTS: see CONFEDERATE EMIGRANTS
EXCHANGE: 4118
FINAL DAYS: see CIVIL WAR--FINAL
  DAYS; CONFEDERATE STATES OF
  AMERICA--ARMY--Surrender
FLAG: 1191, 2691, 4918, 5972
FOREIGN AGENTS: 1181
  Bermuda: 1115
  Canada: 1084, 3809
  France: 115, 3809
  Great Britain: 115, 3556, 5500
FOREIGN RELATIONS: 2695, 4950
  France: 115, 1242, 1403, 2180,
    2449, 4521
  Great Britain: 115, 863, 1403,
    2150, 2449, 2695, 4521, 4616,
    4923
  Spain: 2180
FOREIGN TRADE: 1181
  see also CIVIL WAR--BLOCKADE--
    Effect on trade
  British West Indies: 1115
  Great Britain: 1115, 3905, 4505
FORMATION OF THE CONFEDERACY: 4921
  Mississippi: 3809
  Opinion of: 3038, 4849
GOVERNMENT AGENCIES AND OFFICIALS:
  see also CONFEDERATE STATES OF
    AMERICA--POLITICS AND GOVERNMENT
  Adjutant and Inspector General's
    Office: 1181
  Army: see CONFEDERATE STATES OF
    AMERICA--ARMY
  Attorneys-General: 624
  Bureau of Conscription: 1181
  Bureau of Ordnance: 1181
  Cabinet:
    Appointments: 1403
    Escape from Richmond: 1137
    Final meeting: 844, 2829
  Commissary Office, Kinston, North
    Carolina: 1871
  Commissioner of Taxes: 3615
  Courts: see CONFEDERATE STATES OF
    AMERICA--COURTS
  Department of Justice: 1181
  Department of State: 1181
  Engineer Bureau: 1181
  Medical Examining Board: 4506
  Navy Department: 1181
    see also CONFEDERATE STATES OF
      AMERICA--NAVY
  Navy School, Richmond, Virginia:
    2068
  Office of Inspector of General
    Field Transportation: 1181
  Post Office Department: 1146, 1181,
    1252, 4118, 4921

CONFEDERATE STATES OF AMERICA
GOVERNMENT AGENCIES AND OFFICIALS:
  Post Office Department (Continued):
    see also CIVIL WAR--MAIL SERVICE
      BETWEEN NORTH AND SOUTH
    Appointments: 1030, 1145
    Postage stamps and covers: 651
    Local offices:
      Georgia: 700, 1146, 4895
      North Carolina: 1181
      South Carolina: 1181
      Virginia: 1181
  Quartermaster General's Office:
    1181
  Secret Service: 1181, 1403
    Canada: 3148
    Virginia: 3148
  Secretary of State: 1181
  Secretary of the Navy: 3474
  Secretary of the Treasury: 1181,
    3615
  Secretary of War: 1061, 1181, 4729,
    5512
  Subsistence Department: 1181
  Tax collectors: 3416
  Tax Office: 50, 5210
  Treasury Department: 128, 1181,
    5855
    Evacuation of funds from
      Richmond: 1181
    South Carolina Branch, Columbia:
      1506
  War Department: 1181, 2553
    see also CONFEDERATE STATES OF
      AMERICA--ARMY
GOVERNMENT OFFICIALS--Morale: 1030
HOG RAISING FOR THE GOVERNMENT: 4895
LAWS AND LEGISLATION: 1180, 4739
LEADERSHIP: see CIVIL WAR--
  LEADERSHIP--Confederate
LOYALTY OATHS: see CIVIL WAR--
  LOYALTY OATHS
MEDICINES--Prices: 4950
MEMORIALS: 5090
METAL--Procurement of: 3371
MILITARY RAILROADS: 1726
  Virginia: 1137
MILITARY REQUISITIONS:
  see also CIVIL WAR--CONFISCATION
    OF PROPERTY
  Requisition of food in Virginia:
    1240
MORALE: see CIVIL WAR--CIVILIAN
  LIFE--Morale; CONFEDERATE STATES
  OF AMERICA--ARMY--Morale;
  CONFEDERATE STATES OF AMERICA--
  GOVERNMENT OFFICIALS--Morale;
  SLAVES--Morale
NAVY: 1188, 1403
  see also CONFEDERATE STATES OF
    AMERICA--GOVERNMENT AGENCIES AND
    OFFICIALS--Navy Department;
    CONFEDERATE STATES OF AMERICA--
    GOVERNMENT AGENCIES AND
    OFFICIALS--Navy School
  Commerce raiding: 1216, 1860,
    2210, 2963, 3578
    see also CIVIL WAR--PRIVATEERING
  Courts-Martial: 2724
  Crime: 1181
  Depredations--North Carolina: 4738
  Desertion: 2724, 4531, 4738
  Food: 4531
  James River Squadron: 4738
  Leaves and furloughs: 1181
  Medical and sanitary affairs: 907
    Illness and disease: 4738
  Military supplies: 2724, 4687
    4739
    Louisiana: 1181
  Mining operations:
    Georgia--Savannah: 2724
  Officers: 1399
    Admirals: 4738
  Operations: 4019, 5193

CONFEDERATE STATES OF AMERICA
  NAVY:
    Operations (Continued):
      see also CIVIL WAR--CAMPAIGNS,
        BATTLES, AND MILITARY ACTIONS;
        CONFEDERATE STATES OF AMERICA
        AMERICA--NAVY--Commerce raiding
      Carolina Coast: 2695
      Georgia: 2724
      Louisiana: 2695
      North Carolina--Wilmington: 4183
      Virginia: 2696
        James River: 4738
        Norfolk: 5566
        Yorktown: 4043
    Ordnance: 4687
    Passwords: 2724
    Rams:
      see also names of individual
        vessels
      North Carolina--Pamlico Sound:
        1282
    Sea life: 4687
    Ships: 2724, 4687, 4738
      see also names of specific
        vessels
      Alabama: 3441
      Maintenance and repair:
        Louisiana: 1181
        South Carolina--Charleston:
          4531
    Sketches: 4687
    Veterans: see CIVIL WAR--VETERANS
  PASSPORTS: 1181, 4923
    South Carolina: 5193
  POLITICAL PATRONAGE: 128, 1180,
    3615, 5051
  POLITICS AND GOVERNMENT: 132, 611,
    842, 905, 1084, 1403, 1980,
    2695, 2805, 2860, 3325, 3905,
    4820, 4982, 5500, 5315, 5512, 5613
    Appointments: 3615
    Organization of the government:
      1084
  PRIVATEERING: see CIVIL WAR--
    PRIVATEERING--Confederate
  PUBLIC DEBT: 1181
    see also CONFEDERATE STATES OF
      AMERICA--BONDS
  PUBLIC FINANCE: 700, 1181, 3615,
    3905, 4921
    see also BONDS
    Cotton and produce loan: 1439
    Georgia: 3905
  PUBLIC PROPERTY USED FOR PRIVATE
    PURPOSES: 1181
  PUBLIC WORKS: 1185
  RAILROADS: see CIVIL WAR--
    RAILROADS; CONFEDERATE STATES OF
    AMERICA--MILITARY RAILROADS;
    UNITED STATES--MILITARY RAILROADS
  RECOGNITION BY FOREIGN POWERS: see
    CONFEDERATE STATES OF AMERICA--
    FOREIGN RELATIONS
  SALT: 1384, 4895
    see also CONFEDERATE STATES OF
      AMERICA--ARMY--Salt agents
    Distribution--Virginia: 682
    Prices: 2004
  SALT TRADE: 5040
  SCRAP IRON TRADE: 4895
  SEALS: 3269
  SPECULATION: see CIVIL WAR--
    SPECULATION AND WAR PROFITEERING--
    Confederate
  TAX COLLECTORS: see CONFEDERATE
    STATES OF AMERICA--GOVERNMENT
    AGENCIES AND OFFICIALS--Tax
    collectors
  TAX IN KIND: see TAX IN KIND
  TAXATION: 1181, 1403, 1749, 3416,
    4595, 4711, 4858, 4895, 4921,
    4924
    Georgia: 5260
    North Carolina: 3043
    South Carolina: 1480
    Virginia: 1240

CONFEDERATE STATES OF AMERICA
  TEXTILE INDUSTRY:
    Governmental control: 1829
  TREASON: 484
  TREASURY CERTIFICATES: see
    CONFEDERATE STATES OF AMERICA--
    CURRENCY
  WAR PROFITEERING: see CIVIL WAR--
    SPECULATION AND WAR PROFITEERING--
    Confederate
  WOMEN: see WOMEN IN THE CIVIL WAR

[End of entries under CONFEDERATE
  STATES OF AMERICA]

CONFEDERATE SURVIVORS' ASSOCIATION:
  1825, 2096
  Georgia--Augusta: 2388, 2894
CONFEDERATE SYMPATHIZERS: see CIVIL
  WAR--SOUTHERN SYMPATHIZERS;
  COPPERHEADS
CONFEDERATE VETERAN (periodical):
  1191
CONFEDERATE VETERANS ASSOCIATION:
  843, 3809
CONFEDERATION, 1783-1789: see
  UNITED STATES--CONFEDERATION
CONFISCATED PROPERTY: see AMERICAN
  REVOLUTION--Confiscated property;
  CIVIL WAR--CONFISCATED PROPERTY;
  CIVIL WAR--MILITARY REQUISITIONS
CONFRATERNITIES--France: 2196
CONGAREE, South Carolina: 24
CONGREGATIONAL CHURCHES:
  Doctrine: 5088
  Women's work: 5748
  Connecticut--Colchester: 5748
  Massachusetts: 5088
CONGRESS (frigate): 841, 2085, 3118
CONGRESS OF INDUSTRIAL
  ORGANIZATIONS: 1883, 3066, 3171,
  3558, 5486
  Community Services Committee: 1197
  Conventions: 1194
  Department of Education and
    Research: 1197
  Industrial Union Councils:
    North Carolina: 1192
    Tennessee: 1193
    Virginia: 1194
  Organizing Committees:
    North Carolina: 1195
    South Carolina: 1196
    Tennessee: 1197
    Virginia: 1198
  Political Action Committees: 1200,
    5235
    North Carolina: 1199
    Southern States: 3558
    Tennessee: 1200
    Virginia: 1201
  Publicity Department:
    North Carolina: 1202
  War Relief Committee: 1197
CONGRESS OF VIENNA: 5726
CONGRESS PARTY (India): see INDIAN
  NATIONAL CONGRESS
CONGRESSIONAL ELECTIONS: 3190, 3840
  see also ELECTIONS
  Alabama (1846): 3903
  Georgia: 5494
  Kentucky (1839): 3199
  North Carolina:
    1860s (Confederate Congress):
      4923
    1870: 4714
    1898: 4858
    1906: 5072
    1918: 3955
    1920: 3955
    1934: 325
  Ohio (1888): 5168
  Pennsylvania:
    1840s: 4134

CONGRESSIONAL ELECTIONS:
  Pennsylvania (Continued):
    1850s: 3054, 4134
  South Carolina (1910s): 3893
  Virginia:
    1820: 3032
    1840s: 4720
    1850s-1860s: 569, 1161
  West Virginia (1890s): 2016
CONGRESSIONAL GLOBE: 4494
CONGRESSIONAL HEARINGS ON CIVIL
  RIGHTS: 4386
CONGRESSIONAL MEDAL OF HONOR: 2038
CONKLING, Roscoe: 1977
CONLEY, Benjamin: 1203
CONN, Lewis M.: 5234, 5235
CONN, W. T.: 1204
CONNALLY, H. T.: 4344
CONNALLY, Thomas Terry: 646
CONNALLY, Tom: see CONNALLY, Thomas
  Terry
CONNAUGHT AND STRATHEARN, Arthur
  William Patrick Albert, First
  Duke of: 663
CONNECTICUT:
  Abolition of slavery and
    abolitionist sentiment: 3910
  American literature: 5593
  Authors and publishers: 3041
  Authorship: 2046
  Bonds: 2273
  Books--Prices: 2273
  Booksellers and bookselling: 2273
  Carriage making: 379
  Congregational churches:
    Colchester: 5748
  Courts:
    Court of Errors: 3041
    Hartford County Court: 5871
    Superior Court: 3041
  Currency: 1339
  Cutlery industry: 1169
  Death: 4815
  Debt collection: 3041
  Democratic Party: 2684
  Description and travel: 5508
  Diseases--Consumption: 4815
  Education: 5748
    Hartford: 1827, 5593
    Women: 351
  Estates:
    Administration and settlement:
      379, 1241, 3041, 4059, 5593
  Farming:
    Hartford County: 1051
    North Branford: 5666
  Federalist Party: 3041
  Government agencies and officials:
    Bureau of Vital Statistics:
      1205
    State Attorney: 2273
    State police: 1831
  Gunpowder industry: 4375
  Historical studies: 2684
  Household finance--Hartford: 2273
  Insurance: 2273, 2684
  Law, Study of--East Windsor: 5593
  Law books: 3041
  Law practice: 2273, 3041
  Lawsuits: 3041
  Legislature: 3041
  Machine guns--Manufacture: 1979
  Mental hospitals--Middletown:
    5748
  Mercantile affairs: 1871
    North Stonington: 5669
  Merchants: 3196
    Fairfield: 1871
  Migration from: 5593
  Military schools: 295, 1168, 2870
  Militia: 2547, 3041
  Philanthropy: 5748
  Poetry--Collections: 1168
  Political patronage: 3041
  Publishers and publishing:
    Marketing: 3041
  Religion: 1402

CONNECTICUT:
  Religion (Continued):
    North Branford: 5666
  Rent: 4059
  Republican (Jeffersonian) Party: 3041
  Schools: 351, 2532
    see also CONNECTICUT--Education;
      CONNECTICUT--Military
      education
    Girls' schools and academies:
      Hartford: 1827
      New Haven: 5747
  Shipbuilding: 1549
  Slitting mills: 3041
  Social life and customs: 351, 1402, 3029, 4375
    New Haven: 4080
  Sons of Veterans, William B. Wooster Camp: 4955
  Stocks: 2273
  Students' compositions: 2745
  Sunday schools: 5748
  Teaching: 351
  Theological students: 3142
  Tobacco culture: 25
  Trade and commerce:
    Cloth: 2410
    Cutlery: 1169
    Gunpowder: 1501
    Office equipment: 2273
    Paint: 2273
    Stationery: 2273
  Turnpikes: 3041
  United States Internal Revenue collectors: 3041
  Universities and colleges: 351
    see also YALE UNIVERSITY
  Vital statistics: 1205
  Weather: 5261
  Western lands: 3041
CONNECTICUT, U.S.S.: 4404
CONNELL, John: 3287
CONNELL, John (b. 1909): see ROBERTSON, John Henry
CONNELLY, Bernard: 4484
CONNER, Fox: 5163
CONNER, James (1829-1883): 1206, 5340
CONNER, Phineas Sanborn: 1207
CONNOLLY, Eunice Louensa (Richardson): 1408
CONNOLLY, William S.: 1408
CONNOR, Henry Groves: 1284
CONNOR, Sophia (Kelly): 4024
CONRAD, Borys: 1210
CONRAD, Charles Magill: 1208
CONRAD, Elizabeth A.: 3038
CONRAD, Isaac: 1209
CONRAD, Jacob: 1209
CONRAD, Jessie (George): 1210, 1424
  Photographs: 1424
CONRAD, Joseph (1857-1924): 1210, 1424, 4798
  Photographs: 1424
CONRAD, William G.: 1211
CONRAD FAMILY: 1424
CONRAD BROTHERS, BANKERS: 1211
CONREID, Heinrich: 3797
CONSCIENTIOUS OBJECTORS: see CIVIL WAR--CONSCIENTIOUS OBJECTORS; CIVIL WAR--CONSCIENTIOUS OBJECTORS IN CANADA; CONFEDERATE STATES OF AMERICA--ARMY--Recruiting and enlistment--Resistance; UNITED STATES--ARMY--Civil War--Recruiting and enlistment--Resistance; WORLD WAR II--Conscientious objectors
CONSCRIPTION: see Recruiting and enlistment as subheading under names of armies; SELECTIVE SERVICE; UNIVERSAL MILITARY TRAINING
CONSCRIPTION ACT OF 1863: 388
CONSERVATION OF FORESTS: see FOREST CONSERVATION

CONSERVATION OF NATURAL RESOURCES: 2161, 4851
  see also FOREST CONSERVATION; WILDLIFE CONSERVATION
  Laws and legislation: 4453
    see also names of specific laws, e.g. NORBECK BILL
  United States: 4805
CONSERVATION OF WILDLIFE: see WILDLIFE CONSERVATION
CONSERVATION SOCIETY OF SOUTH CAROLINA: 4453
CONSERVATIVE AND UNIONIST: 294
CONSERVATIVE PARTY:
  Canada: 896
  Great Britain: 1311, 2324, 4568
  Scotland: 3592
CONSIDÉRANT, Victor Prosper: 65
CONSOLIDATED RAILWAYS, LIGHT AND POWER COMPANY: 3447
CONSPIRACIES:
  see also TREASON
  Great Britain: 2735
  Sudan: 41
  United States: see BLOUNT CONSPIRACY
CONSTABLE, Archibald: 1212
CONSTABLES:
  Illinois--McHenry County: 1723
  Pennsylvania: 1130
  South Carolina: 3349
    Darlington: 5299
CONSTANTINE: THE MIRACLE OF THE FLAMING CROSS by Frank Gill Slaughter: 4853
CONSTANTINOPLE, Turkey: 153
  British embassy in: 199, 3472
  Foreign trade: 3183
CONSTELLATION, U.S.S.: 4220, 4447
CONSTITUENTS: see as subheading under legislative bodies
CONSTITUTION, U.S.S.: 841, 4531
CONSTITUTION OF AGNOSTIC MORALISTS: 2225
CONSTITUTIONAL CLUB (Great Britain): 2149
CONSTITUTIONAL CONVENTIONS: see as subheading under names of states and countries
CONSTITUTIONAL HISTORY: see as subheading under names of states and countries
CONSTITUTIONAL LAW:
  Students' notebooks: 5781
  Virginia: 4616
CONSTITUTIONAL UNION GUARD: 3062
CONSTITUTIONAL UNION PARTY: 5775
  Virginia: 581
A CONSTITUTIONAL VIEW OF THE LATE WAR BETWEEN THE STATES by Alexander H. Stephens: 5051
CONSTITUTIONS:
  see also as subheading under names of countries, states, and societies and organizations
  Quotations from: 2872
CONSTITUTIONS OF THE ORDER OF THE SONS OF TEMPERANCE OF NORTH AMERICA: 5339
CONSTRUCTION:
  see also specific types of construction, e.g. BRIDGE CONSTRUCTION, ROADS--Construction
  United States: 5080
CONSTRUCTION WORKERS: see LABOR UNIONS--Construction Workers
CONSULADOS (Courts of Commerce): 586
CONSULAR SERVICE: see (name of country)--Government agencies and officials--Diplomatic and consular service
CONSUMER GOODS: see MANUFACTURED PRODUCTS; and specific types of products
CONSUMER PROTECTION: see PRODUCTION STANDARDS--Testing

CONSUMPTION: see DISEASES--Consumption
CONTAGIOUS DISEASES ACT OF 1869: 4520
CONTEMPORARY AMERICAN PHILOSOPHY, PERSONAL STATEMENTS, edited by George P. Adams and William P. Montague: 1097
CONTEMPORARY CLUB, Henderson, North Carolina: 4232
CONTESTED ELECTIONS: 415
  United States: 5427
CONTESTED WILLS: see WILLS--Contested
THE CONTINENT (periodical): 5322
CONTINENTAL ARMY:
  Army life: 3041
  Arsenals: 4915
  Civil-military relations: 2179
  Commissary General of Issues:
    see also CONTINENTAL ARMY--Military supplies
  Georgia: 4768
  Desertion--Georgia: 3536
  Discipline: 4418
  Military activities: 2495, 4015, 4418
    see also AMERICAN REVOLUTION--Campaigns and battles
    After Yorktown: 2179
    Georgia: 2931
    South Carolina: 3511
  Military supplies: 2218, 2495, 3041, 3256, 4616, 5228, 5768
    Georgia: 2179, 4128, 4768
    South Carolina: 2179
  Miscellaneous soldiers' letters: 3116
  Morale: 3041
  Officers: 3278, 4214, 4371, 4839, 5395, 5454
    Arrest of: 5767
    Orders: 5419
  Quartermaster Department: 2179, 3041, 3256, 4194, 4616
  Rations--Georgia: 5684
  Recruiting and enlistment: 2495
    New York: 5945
    Virginia: 5575
  Regiments: 4th: 5684
             11th: 4852
             Little River: 5767
  Relations with militia: 2179
  Southern Department: 3209
  Transportation: 3256
CONTINENTAL CONGRESS: 1115, 2872, 3116, 5221, 5537, 5768
  Delegates:
    Georgia: 4205
    South Carolina: 2780
  Finance: 5276
  Minutes: 5276
CONTRABAND--French West Indies: 321
CONTRABANDS: see CIVIL WAR--CONTRABANDS
CONTRACTS: 2612
  see also BREACH OF CONTRACT; FREEDMEN--Labor contracts; LABOR CONTRACTS; LABOR UNIONS--Contracts; TEACHERS' CONTRACTS
  Great Britain--Exeter: 5867
  Maryland:
    Frederick County: 4457
    Sharpsburg: 979
  North Carolina: 3415
    Martin County: 4849
  Pennsylvania--Lewistown: 2704
CONVALESCENT CAMPS: see UNITED STATES--ARMY--Civil War--Convalescent camps
CONVALESCENT HOMES:
  see also ADVERTISING--Convalescent homes
  North Carolina--Southern Pines: 3633
CONVENT DE L'ANNONCIADES (France): 4046
CONVENT OF NOTRE DAME--Maryland: 2692

CONVENTICLE ACT, Repeal of: 3120
CONVENTION OF 1800: 4348
CONVENTIONS: see COMMERCIAL
  CONVENTIONS; LABOR UNIONS--
  Conventions; Constitutional
  conventions as subheading under
  names of countries and states;
  and Conventions as subheading under
  names of political parties
CONVERSE, G.S.: 1213
CONVERSE COLLEGE, Spartanburg,
  South Carolina: 561
CONVERSION: see as subheading under
  names of denominations, e.g.
  CATHOLIC CHURCH--Conversion
CONVICT LABOR: see CONFEDERATE
  STATES OF AMERICA--ARMY--
  Convicts, Use of; PEONAGE
CONVOY DUTY: see UNITED STATES--
  NAVY--WORLD WAR I--Convoy duty
CONWAY, Francis Seymour-, First
  Marquis of Hertford: 1214
CONWAY, Frederick W.: 4024
CONWAY, Henry: 5380
CONWAY, Moncure: 1113
CONWAY, Moncure Daniel (1832-1907):
  722, 1215
CONWAY, Sir William Martin: 2148
CONWAY, South Carolina: 2854
CONYNGHAM, John Nesbitt: 4188
COO FAMILY (Great Britain--
  Genealogy): 1141
COOK, Charles E.: 1216
COOK, Ed. F.: 1217
COOK, Sir Edward Tyas: 1218
COOK, Flavius Josephus: 1219
COOK, Frederick Albert: 4556
COOK, Horatio R.: 1220
COOK, James M.: 1399
COOK, John Mason: 217
COOK, Joseph (1838-1901): see COOK,
  Flavius Josephus
COOK, Mary C.: 2407
COOK, Mary Jane (Alabama): 954
COOK, Mary Jane (California): 1221
COOK, Orchard: 1222
COOK, Sally: 1223
COOK, Thomas: 1224
COOK COUNTY, Illinois:
  Chicago: see CHICAGO, Illinois
  Evanston: 1137
COOK STOVES: see PATENTS--Cook
  stoves
COOKE, Dr. ____ : 1421
COOKE, Arthur Wayland: 5457
COOKE, Edward William: 1225
COOKE, George A.: 1226
COOKE, John Esten: 404, 1227, 2449,
  4698
COOKE, Philip Pendleton: 404, 1227
COOKE, Robert Bruce: 1228
COOKE, William M.: 4616
COOKERY: 5749, 5991
  see also MENUS
  Arkansas: 1154
  Georgia: 786, 4985
  Great Britain: 1210
  Kentucky--Lexington: 3325
  Maryland: 2692
  North Carolina: 1475, 4689, 5740
    Guilford County: 1407
  South Carolina: 60, 3552
  United States: 730
  Virginia: 1558
    Fifesville: 4459
    Lynchburg: 4308
COOKSEY, Joseph J.: 3646
COOL SPRING BAPTIST CHURCH (North
  Carolina): 4742
COOLEEMEE, North Carolina:
  Textile mills: 1719
COOLEY, Dennis: 1229
COOLEY, Henry: 1229
COOLEY AND ARNOLD (firm): see
  ARNOLD AND COOLEY
COOLIDGE, Calvin: 4825
COOLIDGE, Judson: 665
COOLIDGE, Oliver S.: 1230

COOMBE BANK, Kent, England: 862
COOMBS, James Rowe: 1231
COON, Charles Lee: 1232, 5457
COOPER, General ____ : 5536
COOPER, Albert D.: 1233
COOPER, Anthony Ashley-, Seventh
  Earl of Shaftesbury: see ASHLEY-
  COOPER, Anthony, Seventh Earl of
  Shaftesbury
COOPER, Cropley Ashley-, Sixth Earl
  of Shaftesbury: see ASHLEY-
  COOPER, Cropley, Sixth Earl of
  Shaftesbury
COOPER, Edmund: 872
COOPER, Ellen: 2854
COOPER, George P.: 1231
COOPER, James (1810-1863): 1234
COOPER, James Fenimore: 685, 720
COOPER, James Graham: 5133
COOPER, Jane: 1317
COOPER, John: 4726
COOPER, John Downey: 5457
COOPER, John Snider: 1235
COOPER, Katherine: 2146
COOPER, Lucretia E.: 5261
COOPER, Samuel (North Carolina):
  1237
COOPER, Samuel (1725-1783): 1236
COOPER, Samuel (1798-1876): 212,
  395, 581, 623, 4873, 5280
COOPER, Thomas (1759-1839): 150
COOPER, Thomas (1805-1892): 2149
COOPER, Thomas Sidney (1803-1902):
  5542
COOPER, William: 1237
COOPER FAMILY (South Carolina):
  2854, 3123
COOPER, Maine: 654
COOPER & HAINES (mercantile firm):
  1238
COOPER AND REEVES: see REEVES AND
  COOPER
COOPERATIVE BROADCASTING
  ASSOCIATION: 1196
COOPERATIVE COMMONWEALTH (Texas):
  2225
COOPERATIVE MOVEMENT:
  Great Britain: 14
COOPERATIVE SOCIETIES:
  see also TRI-STATE TOBACCO
    GROWERS' CO-OPERATIVE MARKETING
    ASSOCIATION
  Sweden-Stockholm: 3964
COOPERATIVE TRADE: see PATRONS OF
  HUSBANDRY--Georgia--Cooperative
  trade
COOSA COUNTY, Alabama: 4283
  Rockford: 930, 3500
COOSA-THATCHER-STANDARD COMPANY:
  see STANDARD-COOSA-THATCHER
  COMPANY
COOTE, Sir Eyre: 3315, 4926
COPE, Sir Arthur Stockdale: 1239
COPELAND, Julia Wheeler: 4006
COPELAND, Oliver P.: 4506
COPENHAGEN, Denmark: 111
  Description: 404
COPENHAGEN EXPEDITION: see
  NAPOLEONIC WARS--Great Britain--
  Copenhagen Expedition
COPENHAVER, Henry: 1240
COPIAH COUNTY, Mississippi:
  Gallatin: 2355
  Plantations: 4776
COPLEY, John Singleton, First Baron
  Lyndhurst: 2149
COPP, Belton A.: 1241
COPP, Daniel Denison: 1241
COPP, George A.: 1241
COPP, Mary E.: 1241
COPP FAMILY (Georgia): 1241
COPPER, Marjorie Hall Ticehurst:
  4823
COPPER--Claims: 323
COPPER MINING: 5731
  Arizona--Wickenburg: 4918
  Michigan--Investments: 4895
  North Carolina: 2121

COPPER MINING:
  North Carolina (Continued):
    Davidson County: 2041
    Payrolls: 2906
  Tennessee--Investments: 4895
COPPERHEADS: 2361, 3264, 3565,
  5228, 5249, 5311, 5417
  see also CIVIL WAR--SOUTHERN
    SYMPATHIZERS
  Delaware: 4881
  Illinois: 4203
  Kentucky: 4160
  Maine: 1787
  Maryland: 3378
  New Hampshire: 4039
  New York: 4108
  Ohio: 1505, 4160, 5132
  Vermont: 1787
COPPERPLATE ENGRAVING--North
  Carolina: 1339
COPPERSMITHING--North Carolina: 544
COPYBOOKS: see PENMANSHIP--Exercise
  books
COPYRIGHT: 3284, 4798
  Virginia: 5720
COPYRIGHT LEGISLATION:
  see also INTERNATIONAL COPYRIGHT
  Great Britain: 472
  United States: 4020
CORA, North Carolina: 1247
CORBELL, LaSalle: 4196
CORBIN, Francis Porteus: 1242
CORBIN, Henry Clark: 5430
CORBIN, Richard Washington: 1242
CORBIN FAMILY (Pennsylvania and
  Virginia): 1242
CORBITT, Richard Johnson: 5457
CORCORAN, Michael: 2989
CORCORAN, William Wilson: 1084, 1243,
  1665, 2449
CORDAGE--Virginia: 1863
CORDELE, Georgia: 2747
CÓRDOBA, Spain--Schools: 4981
CÓRDOVA Y URRUTIA, José María de:
  4155
CORFU, Ionian Islands:
  British administration: 3183
  Fortifications: 4520
  Health conditions: 3835
  Politics and government: 3183
CORINTH, Mississippi: 4320
  Civil War: 4588
  Battle: see CIVIL WAR--CAMPAIGNS,
    BATTLES, AND MILITARY ACTIONS--
    Mississippi--Corinth
  Union occupation: 2858
CORINTH BENEVOLENT SEWING SOCIETY,
  Fluvanna County, Virginia: 1244
CORK, Ireland: 2403
CORLISS, John Blaisdell: 2449
CORN:
  Prices: 3566
  New York: 2434
  South Carolina: 4834
  United States: 1587
  Western States: 3255
  Subdivided by place:
    Great Britain: 4230
    Louisiana: 3322
    Mississippi: 3322
    Missouri: 3540
    North Carolina: 2121
    South Carolina: 4118
    Virginia: 490, 2369, 3145
CORN LAWS:
  Great Britain: 5, 649, 1126, 1311,
    1632, 1775, 2149, 2836, 4605,
    4696, 5011, 5025, 5330, 5726
    Enforcement: 3050
    Repeal: 676, 2193
  Jamaica: 301
CORN PRODUCTION:
  North Carolina--Wilmington: 4603
  Virginia: 4924
    Albemarle County: 3699
CORN SHUCKING:
  South Carolina--Laurens: 3531

CORN TRADE:
    see also INDIAN CORN TRADE
    Ireland--Bounties: 5330
    North Carolina: 4760, 4858, 5535
        Wilmington: 1281
    Virginia: 5535
        Kinsley Mills: 1447
        Petersburg: 2176
CORNELIUS AND CO. (firm): 1245
CORNELIUS SHRINER AND COMPANY: 4803
CORNELL, Ezra: 2419
CORNELL, Sarah: 1246
CORNELL UNIVERSITY, Ithaca, New
    York: 2616
CORNHILL MAGAZINE: 2457
CORNHILL PLANTATION, Sumter District,
    South Carolina: 1923
CORNISH, Maine: 1106
CORNPLANTER, Pennsylvania:
    Coal mining: 3910
CORNWALL, England:
    Antony: 888
    Mounts Bay--Harbors: 3080
    Trelawney: 5337
    Treniffle: 1239
    Tresco Island: 4868
    Wick: 3236
CORNWALL, Duchy of: see DUCHY OF
    CORNWALL
CORNWALLIS, Charles, First Marquis
    and Second Earl Cornwallis: 1890,
    2149, 5330, 5575
    Criticism of: 5604
    In Calcutta, India: 5331
    Surrender at Yorktown: 3041
CORNWELL, John J. (1867-1953): 3721
CORNWELL, John V.: 4833
CORONEL CEGARRA, Felix Cipriano:
    4155
CORONERS--Virginia: 2925
CORONERS' INQUESTS--Virginia: 1383
CORPANCHO, Manuel Nicolás: 4155
CORPENING FAMILY (North Carolina):
    1247
CORPORATION ACT (Great Britain):
    3226
CORPORATION BONDS: 1339
CORPORATION COURTS: see COURTS--
    Corporation Courts
CORPORATION LAW: 2163
    North Carolina: 2553
CORPORATIONS:
    Dividends: see DIVIDENDS--
        Corporations
    Legal affairs: 4874
    Massachusetts--Boston: 5093
    Pennsylvania: 2027
CORREA, Juan Bravo del Rivero y:
    see BRAVO DEL RIVERO Y CORREA, Juan
CORRIA FAMILY (Spain): 4981
CORRUPTION IN POLITICS: 872, 3770
    Canada: 896
    Egypt: 4941
    Great Britain:
        Denbigh and Northumberland: 5026
    South Carolina: 2109, 5893
    United States: 5427
        House of Representatives: 5853
CORRUPTION IN SURVEYING: see
    SURVEYS AND SURVEYING--Corruption
CORSAIRS:
    see also PIRATES; PRIVATEERS
    British: 197
    French: 197
    Spanish: 3570
CORSICA--Description: 355
CORTINA, F. J.: 1248
CORTLAND COUNTY, New York: 2361
CORVÉE (French tax): 5323
CORWIN, Thomas: 1249
CORY, Adela Florence: 2334
CORYDON, Indiana: 1548
COSBY, Dabney, Jr.: 1250
COSENS, William C.: 1251, 4587
COSÍO, José del Campillo y: see
    CAMPILLO Y COSÍO, José del
COSMETICS MANUFACTURE: see SOAP AND
    COSMETICS MANUFACTURE

COST OF LIVING:
    North Carolina: 1202
    Pennsylvania: 4106
    Virginia: 1198, 4589
COSTA RICA:
    Pictures: 4719
    Social life and customs: 617
COSTON, Erasmus H.: 360, 1252
COTHRAN, Annie: 1424
COTHRAN, James Sproull: 4145
COTHRAN, William S.: 4145
COTHRAN & JEFFERS (firm): see
    JEFFERS & COTHRAN
COTSWOLD SHEEP: see SHEEP--Cotswold
    sheep
COTTAGE GRANGE: 4072
COTTAGE HEARTH MAGAZINE: 3363
"COTTAGE HILL," Virginia: 2955
COTTAGE HILL COLLEGE, Maryland: 2974
COTTEN, Andrew J.: 3626
COTTEN, James L.: 3626
COTTEN, Lyman Atkinson: 5457
COTTEN, Sallie (Southall): 4425
COTTENHAM, Charles Christopher
    Pepys, First Earl of: 4605
COTTLE, Edmund: 1253
COTTLE, S. H.: 2063
COTTLE, Simeon: 2063
COTTON, Sir Charles: 516
COTTON:
    Acreage allotments:
        South Carolina: 4193
    Civil War: 605
        see also CIVIL WAR--CONFISCATED
            PROPERTY--Cotton; CIVIL WAR--
            CLAIMS--Confiscated property--
            Cotton
        Destruction by Union troops: 1403
    Crops: see COTTON GROWING
    Diseases: 5345
    Marketing: see COTTON TRADE
    Prices: 4456, 4541
        Alabama: 3321
        Arkansas: 1154
        Georgia: 377, 1203, 2232, 2785,
            5141
            Penfield: 5040
            Saint Mary's: 235
        Mississippi: 3415, 4269, 5047
        North Carolina: 641, 1396, 1611,
            2399, 4918, 5298
            Cleveland County: 4691
            Iredell County: 5310
        South Carolina: 4834, 4996
        Southern States: 1460
        Tennessee: 6, 4269
            Memphis: 4256
        United States: 1587
        Virginia: 4924
    Production: see COTTON GROWING
    Sea Island Cotton: 2107, 2785, 2901
        Florida: 3611
        Great Britain (Imports): 3230
        South Carolina: 1889
    Speculation: 2785
        Alabama: 3321, 4589
        Georgia: 2232
        South Carolina: 1009, 4145
        United States government during
            the Civil War: 4109
    Storage: 1336
        North Carolina: 4691
        South Carolina: 1009
        Texas: 592
        Virginia: 5334
    Taxation: 2232
        see also COTTON MILLS--Taxation
        Claims--Georgia: 4895
        Constitutionality: 2860
        Utilization--Texas: 592
    Weaving and spinning:
        North Carolina: 5658
    Subdivided by place:
        Georgia: 662, 4921
        Great Britain: 4895
        Mississippi: 3415
        North Carolina: 2121
        South Carolina: 1572, 1745, 2210

COTTON:
    Subdivided by place (Continued):
        Southern States: 311
        Virginia: 5148
COTTON AND PRODUCE LOAN: see
    CONFEDERATE STATES OF AMERICA--
    PUBLIC FINANCE--Cotton and produce
    loan
COTTON BALING:
    Mississippi--Rodney: 3322
    Virginia--Falmouth: 2165
COTTON BROKERS: see COTTON TRADE
COTTON CULTIVATORS:
    North Carolina: 5280
    Trade: 2553
COTTON FACTORS: see COTTON TRADE
COTTON GINS:
    Instructions on use of: 1120
    Georgia: 2931
    Louisiana: 508, 840
    Mississippi: 5047
        Rodney: 3322
    North Carolina: 1660
        Beaufort County: 911
        Randleman: 5408
        Washington: 3827
    Trade: 5508
COTTON GROWING: 1980, 5634
    Alabama--Gay's Landing: 5879
    Arkansas: 4776
        Calhoun County: 4199
        Dardanelle: 3276
    Florida: 3389
    Georgia: 127, 235, 1231, 1705,
        2903, 5298
        Macon: 3905
    Louisiana: 4902
    Mississippi: 2349, 2970, 4776
        Rodney: 3322
    North Carolina: 2573, 2970, 4689,
        4918
        Halifax County: 5280
        Onslow County: 1252
        Wilmington: 4603
    South Carolina: 1877, 2267, 3123,
        3451
    Southern States: 1460, 5862
    Texas: 592, 5508
    Turkey: 4650
    Virginia: 4776, 4924
        Norfolk: 3830
        Nottoway County: 5469
COTTON GROWING AND SLAVERY: 5940
COTTON LAND:
    Arkansas: 3053
    Georgia: 106
    Louisiana: 3053
    Mississippi: 3053
COTTON MARKET: see COTTON TRADE
COTTON MARKET SPECULATION: see
    COTTON--Speculation
COTTON MILL WORKERS:
    Strikes: see STRIKES--Cotton mill
        workers
    Wages and salaries: see WAGES AND
        SALARIES--Cotton mill workers
    Work records--North Carolina: 5048
COTTON MILLS:
    see also TEXTILE INDUSTRY
    Bankruptcy:
        North Carolina: 5056
            Wake Forest: 4586
    Construction:
        Virginia: 5513
    Finance:
        North Carolina:
            Erwin: 5298
            Milledgeville: 4918
            Scotland County: 3776
            Wake County: 3863
            Wake Forest: 4586
            Worthville: 3187
    Management:
        North Carolina: 1508
    Payrolls:
        North Carolina: 3187
    Receivership--North Carolina: 4858

COTTON MILLS (Continued):
　Stocks:
　　Great Britain: 2410
　　North Carolina: 396
　Taxation--Texas: 592
　Subdivided by place:
　　Alabama--Huntsville: 3568
　　Great Britain: 43
　　North Carolina: 396, 1539, 3317,
　　　4080, 5312
　　　Cane Creek: 875
　　　Catawba: 3718
　　　Cleveland County: 4691
　　　Franklinton: 5056
　　　Iredell County: 5310
　　　Lawnsdale: 1104
　　　Milledgeville: 4918
　　　Mount Airy: 5048
　　　Mount Holly: 5100
　　　Randleman: 5408
　　　Salem: 1905
　　　Turnersburg: 2857, 5048
　　　Wake County: 3863
　　　Wake Forest: 4586
　　　Worthville: 3187
　　Pennsylvania:
　　　Philadelphia: 5845
　　South Carolina: 1480, 2961,
　　　3451, 3754, 5312
　　Southern States: 3196
　　United States: 904
　　Virginia: 4924
　　　Falmouth: 2165
COTTON PICKING--Mississippi: 2813
THE COTTON PLANT (steamship): 3827
COTTON PLANTATIONS: 5634
　Alabama: 1084
　Georgia: 2963
　Louisiana: 900, 1574
　Mississippi: 4796
　　Natchez: 5047
　　Rodney: 3322
　North Carolina: 5709
　　Franklin County: 3023
　South Carolina: 669, 5661, 5759
　　Chesterfield County: 4996
　Southern States: 284
COTTON PRESS--Patents: see PATENTS--
　Cotton press
COTTON RESEARCH: see TEXTILE
　RESEARCH
COTTON SCREEN PRINT, INDUSTRY:
　South Carolina: 5236
COTTON TRADE: 323, 1009, 1478, 5933
　Finance--South Carolina: 1009
　Regulation--United States: 1478
　Statistics--South Carolina: 987
　Subdivided by place:
　　Alabama: 641, 3196, 5593, 5879
　　　Mobile: 4911
　　Arkansas: 2856
　　Delaware: 4881
　　Europe: 592, 3689, 5014
　　Florida--Milton: 3008
　　France: 5014
　　Georgia: 235, 339, 497, 601,
　　　1090, 2232, 3303, 3961, 5353,
　　　5730
　　　Atlanta: 4402
　　　Augusta: 3583
　　　Hancock County: 4493
　　　Savannah: 1705, 2018, 2232,
　　　　3689
　　Germany: 5014
　　Great Britain: 2755, 5014
　　　London: 4288
　　India: 4881
　　Louisiana: 2856
　　　New Orleans: 4776, 5194, 5301
　　Maryland--Baltimore: 4858
　　Mississippi: 3415, 5952
　　Mississippi Valley: 1357
　　New York: 641, 903, 2172
　　North Carolina:
　　　1700s-1800s: 2530, 2889, 5298
　　　1700s-1900s: 3476
　　　1800s:
　　　　1840s: 4734, 5470

COTTON TRADE:
　Subdivided by place:
　　North Carolina:
　　　1800s (Continued):
　　　　1850s: 4734, 5470
　　　　1860s: 614, 2480, 3447,
　　　　　4734, 5087
　　　　1870s: 641, 5087
　　　　1880s: 3303, 5087
　　　1800s-1900s: 4918
　　　1900s: 5962
　　　Cleveland County: 4691
　　　Fayetteville: 1396
　　　Halifax County: 5280
　　　Person County: 1336
　　　Scotland County: 3303
　　　Wake County: 876
　　　Wilmington: 1281, 5014, 5912
　　　Woodland: 4047
　　Northern States: 3689
　　South Carolina:
　　　1700s-1800s: 1012
　　　1800s: 2940, 3203, 5114
　　　　1800s-1810s: 566, 3123
　　　　1820s: 566
　　　　1840s: 965
　　　　1850s: 965, 1388, 1889
　　　　1870s: 4996
　　　　1880s: 3303, 4996
　　　1800s-1900s: 501
　　　Charleston: 987, 1009, 1889,
　　　　1891, 2018, 2107, 4145, 4649
　　　Cheraw: 1396
　　Southern States: 565, 4434
　　Tennessee--Memphis: 4256
　　United States: 2755, 3053, 4520
　　Virginia: 435, 590, 1568, 2360,
　　　2381, 3179
　　　Petersburg: 1336, 2176, 2935,
　　　　4604, 5959
　　　Suffolk: 1838
　　West Virginia: 4774
COTTON VALLEY, Alabama: 1295
COTTON WORM--Georgia: 4921
COTTONSEED OIL:
　see also OILSEED MILLS
　North Carolina--Wilmington: 5912
　South Carolina: 4621
COUCH, Sir Arthur Thomas Quiller-:
　see QUILLER-COUCH, Sir Arthur
　Thomas
COUCH, J. W. T.: 1254
COUCH, John: 1255
COUCH, Harvey C.: 2644
COUCH, William A.: 1256
COUCH FAMILY (North Carolina): 1256
COUCHMAN, William H.: 1257
COUEISM: 1424
COULTER, E. Merton: 5054
COUNCIL, John Pickett: 5457
COUNCIL BLUFFS, Iowa: 538
COUNCIL OF CHURCHES: see NORTH
　CAROLINA COUNCIL OF CHURCHES
COUNCIL OF LABOR RELATIONS OF
　PUERTO RICO: 3066
COUNCIL OF SAFETY, Baltimore,
　Maryland: 4348
COUNCIL OF SOUTHERN UNIVERSITIES,
　INC., Chapel Hill, North Carolina:
　1258
COUNCIL OF TRENT (1545-1563): 5317
COUNCIL ON FOREIGN RELATIONS: 5252
COUNCILL, Mary A. (Horton): 1259
COUND, England: 4115
COUNSELL, H. E.: 473
COUNTERFEITING: see CURRENCY--
　Counterfeiting
COUNTING HOUSES: see BOOKKEEPING
"COUNTRY AMUSEMENTS": 3119
COUNTRY CLUBS:
　South Carolina--Charleston: 3299
COUNTRY ESTATES--Great Britain:
　5038
THE COUNTRYMAN (newspaper): 4706
COUNTY _____, Ireland: see
　under of county, e.g. ANTRIM,
　County, Ireland

COUNTY AND RURAL AREA
　SUPERINTENDENTS: 1758
COUNTY COURTS: see COURTS--County
　courts
COUNTY ELECTIONS: see LOCAL
　ELECTIONS
COUNTY GOVERNMENT:
　see also MUNICIPAL GOVERNMENT;
　POLITICS AND GOVERNMENT
　Georgia--Chatham County: 996
　Great Britain: 3847
　Maryland--Washington County: 3086
　North Carolina--Anson County: 4918
　South Carolina--Spartanburg
　　County: 3044
　Virginia--Fairfax County: 2887
COUNTY LINE, North Carolina: 1174
COUNTY ROADS--North Carolina: 2553
COUNTY TAXES: see under (name of
　place)--Taxation--County taxes
COUPER, James Hamilton: 1242, 2578
COURSE OF STUDY: see THEOLOGICAL
　SEMINARIES--Curriculum;
　UNIVERSITIES AND COLLEGES--
　Curriculum; and Curriculum as
　subheading under names of specific
　universities and colleges
"THE COURT AND KINGDOM OF ENGLAND"
　by John Macky: 3411
COURT RECORDS: see COURTS
COURT REPORTERS: see COURTS--
　Court reporters
COURTENAY, David: 4348
COURTENAY, David S.: 4348
COURTENAY, Edward: 4348
COURTENAY, Edward H.: 4348
COURTENAY, Edward H., Jr.: 4348
COURTENAY, Elizabeth Isabella
　(Purviance): 4348
COURTENAY, Henry: 4348
COURTENAY, Henry William: 4348
COURTENAY, Hercules: 4348
COURTENAY, Mary I.: 4348
COURTENAY, Sarah: 4348
COURTENAY, Virginia (Howard): 4348
COURTENAY, William: 4348
COURTENAY, William Ashmead
　(1831-1908): 723, 5759
COURTENAY, William C.: 4348
COURTENAY FAMILY: 4348
COURTHOUSES:
　North Carolina--Beaufort County:
　　540
COURTLAND, Alabama: 4930
COURTLAND, Virginia: 4531
COURTNEY, Alfred R.: 3674
COURTNEY, John Mortimer: 1260
COURTNEY, Leonard Henry, First
　Baron: 1260
COURTNEY, Louise d'Este: 1260
COURTNEY, W. L.: 706
COURTNEY, William: 1260
COURTNEY, William Prideaux: 1260
COURTNEY FAMILY (Great Britain):
　1260
COURTS:
　see also ADMIRALTY COURTS;
　AMERICAN COURTS IN CHINA;
　CORONERS' INQUISTS;
　ECCLESIASTICAL COURTS; JUDGES;
　JUDICIAL AFFAIRS; JUDICIAL
　REFORM; JURIES; JUSTICES OF
　THE PEACE; LEGAL AFFAIRS; TRIALS;
　UNITED STATES--SUPREME COURT
　Cases: 74
　　Australia: 5477
　　Maryland: 5296
　　Massachusetts: 3034
　　Boston: 5093
　　New York: 4378
　　North Carolina: 1107
　　　Davie County: 122
　　Pennsylvania: 2027
　　South Carolina: 2961
　　　Laurens District: 1001
　　Virginia:
　　　Richmond: 4616

COURTS (Continued):
　Clerks:
　　North Carolina: 4918
　　Virginia: 872
　　　Augusta County: 5184
　　　Frederick County: 5200
　　　Madison County: 5064
　　　Pittsylvania County: 5369
　Costs:
　　see also LEGAL FEES
　　North Carolina: 4858
　　South Carolina: 5548
　Court reporters:
　　North Carolina: 2776
　Judgments:
　　Georgia--Savannah: 3309
　　Maryland--Sharpsburg: 979
　　New York: 4260
　　North Carolina: 171, 3221, 3825
　　　Granville County: 68
　　Pennsylvania: 421
　　South Carolina: 2961
　　Tennessee: 4269
　Laws and legislation:
　　see also JUDICIAL REFORM
　　South Carolina: 4213
　　United States: 3041
　　Virginia: 3302
　Orders:
　　North Carolina: 3415
　Summonses:
　　see also Summonses as
　　　subheading under COURTS--
　　　(specific type of court)
　　Georgia: 2666
　　Maryland: 5722
　　　Frederick County: 4457
　　North Carolina: 832, 2354, 2833,
　　　3221, 3416, 4765, 5692
　　South Carolina: 842
　　United States: 734
　　Virginia: 117
　　　Bedford County: 5818
　　　Campbell County: 4487
　　West Virginia: 1129, 2711
　　　Jefferson County: 4892
　Subdivided by type of court:
　　Chancery Courts:
　　　Alabama:
　　　　Cherokee County: 4419
　　　　Dallas County: 48
　　　Great Britain: 4605
　　　Maryland: 2319
　　　New Jersey: 5520
　　　Virginia: 4924
　　　　Suffolk: 3012
　　Circuit Courts:
　　　District of Columbia: 4457
　　　Georgia: 2860
　　　Kentucky: 5505
　　　South Carolina: 2616
　　　Virginia: 1568, 5434
　　　　Hanover Court House: 3242
　　　　9th Circuit Court: 4617
　　County Courts:
　　　Connecticut:
　　　　Hartford County: 5871
　　　Georgia:
　　　　Hancock County: 4493
　　　　Wilkes County: 2003, 2937
　　　Maryland:
　　　　Cecil County: 5296
　　　　Frederick County: 4457
　　　　Kent County: 5296
　　　　Queen Annes County: 5296
　　　　Washington County: 3875
　　　Mississippi:
　　　　Adams County: 2282
　　　North Carolina:
　　　　Catawba County: 5745
　　　Virginia: 1568
　　　　Patrick County: 1894
　　　　Pittsylvania County: 2495
　　Corporation Courts:
　　　Virginia: 1018
　　Courts Baron:
　　　Great Britain--Sussex: 4767

COURTS:
　Subdivided by type of court
　(Continued):
　　Courts of Appeals:
　　　Great Britain: 4097
　　Courts of Common Pleas and
　　　Quarter Sessions:
　　　New Jersey:
　　　　Hunterdon County: 5520
　　　North Carolina:
　　　　Dobbs County: 934
　　Courts of Equity:
　　　North Carolina:
　　　　Forsyth County: 1209
　　　　Martin County: 3936
　　　South Carolina: 4623
　　　　Charleston: 1468
　　Courts of Errors:
　　　Connecticut: 3041
　　Courts of Law and Chancery:
　　　Virginia--Bedford County: 5818
　　Courts of Oyer and Terminer:
　　　Great Britain: 819
　　　Maryland--Baltimore County:
　　　　4457
　　Courts of Petty Sessions:
　　　Australia: 5477
　　District Courts:
　　　C.S.A.: 1190
　　　Georgia: 3330, 5787
　　　North Carolina: 1150, 1190,
　　　　1871, 3925
　　　South Carolina: 477, 989, 5930
　　　Virginia: 2700, 5434
　　General Courts:
　　　North Carolina: 3930
　　High Courts of Judicature:
　　　India: 3286
　　Inferior Courts:
　　　Georgia: 1993, 3113
　　　　Bibb County: 1995
　　　　Franklin County: 3782
　　　　Greene County: 1998, 4654
　　　　Richmond County: 2000
　　Justice Courts:
　　　Mississippi--Choctaw County:
　　　　3702
　　Juvenile Courts:
　　　North Carolina: 1275
　　Magistrates' Courts:
　　　Georgia--Greene County: 1998
　　　South Carolina--Branchville:
　　　　1749
　　Orphans' Courts:
　　　Maryland: 4457
　　Probate Courts:
　　　Mississippi: 3438
　　Sessions Courts:
　　　Pennsylvania: 5764
　　Superior Courts:
　　　Connecticut: 3041
　　　Georgia: 1993, 5537
　　　　Clerks--Upson County: 4754
　　　　Establishment of: 2923
　　　　Slave importation register:
　　　　　2002
　　　　Subdivided by place:
　　　　　Bibb County: 1995
　　　　　Greene County: 1998
　　　　　Richmond County: 2000
　　　North Carolina: 1128
　　　　Edenton District: 4773
　　　Virginia:
　　　　Campbell County: 62
　　　　Clerks--Patrick County: 5031
　　　　Fauquier County: 3994
　　　　Loudoun County: 3994
　　Superior Provost Courts:
　　　South Carolina--Darlington:
　　　　2106
　　Supreme Courts:
　　　Alabama: 4105
　　　Georgia: 3355, 3905, 5537
　　　New Jersey: 5520
　　　New York: 2172
　　　North Carolina: 1914, 2437,
　　　　2776, 3062, 4103, 4595
　　　Pennsylvania: 588, 1916

COURTS:
　Subdivided by type of court
　(Continued):
　　Survey Courts:
　　　Great Britain: 4630
　Subdivided by place:
　　Australia: 1792
　　Confederate States of America:
　　　1365
　　Connecticut--Hartford: 5871
　　Egypt: 4941
　　Georgia: 1088, 1302, 2666, 2931,
　　　3323, 3330, 5250
　　　Savannah: 2001
　　Great Britain: 504, 2836, 4113,
　　　5134
　　India: 278, 3286, 5883
　　　Bombay: 3286
　　　Madras: 3286
　　Ireland: 504
　　Jamaica: 1792
　　Louisiana: 4550
　　Massachusetts: 1222
　　Mississippi: 5421
　　Missouri: 4323
　　Nebraska Territory: 2326
　　New Jersey: 5520
　　North Carolina: 1015, 4849, 4918
　　Philippine Islands: 3313
　　South Carolina: 1424, 1468, 4269
　　Turkey: 3183
　　United States: 4805
　　Virginia: 1125, 1384, 4131
　　　Flat Creek Township: 1821
　　West Virginia: 1946, 3058, 5194
COURTS BARON: see COURTS--Courts
　Baron
COURTS-MARTIAL: see as subheading
　under names of armies and militias
COURTS OF ___: see as subheading
　under COURTS, e.g. COURTS--Courts
　of Equity
COURTSHIP: 5892
　see also LOVE LETTERS
　Alabama--Selma: 3534
　France: 4490
　Georgia: 2326, 3318
　　Augusta: 5246
　Great Britain: 380, 2227
　Illinois: 4273
　Maryland: 2217, 5160
　New York: 752, 2390
　North Carolina: 1467, 1773, 2469,
　　3290, 5312
　　Chatham County: 2861
　Pennsylvania: 2731
　South Carolina: 1424, 2960
　United States: 2714
　Virginia: 262, 4616, 5031
　West Virginia: 5689
COUSINS, F. R.: 1261
COUSINS, Frederick: 1384
COUTY, James: 3145
COVE ACADEMY, Covesville, Virginia:
　1767
COVELL, Edward N.: 523
COVENTRY, England:
　Political unrest: 4750
COVERSTONE, David: 1262
COVINGTON, John: 1263
COVINGTON, Georgia: 1268, 1434
　Land and timber: 1382
COVINGTON, Kentucky: 5064
COVINGTON, Virginia: 2566, 3308
　Sons of Temperance: 4953
COVINGTON AND MACON RAIL ROAD
　COMPANY: 1264
COWAN, James B.: 1265
COWAN, John: 1266
COWAN, Joseph: 1267
COWAN, Nancy H.: 1268
COWAN, William: 208, 1269, 1487
COWAN FAMILY (North Carolina): 1270
COWAND, Joseph J.: 1271
COWAND, Starkey: 1271
COWAND, Winifred A.: 1271
COWAND FAMILY (North Carolina): 1271
COWARD, Asbury: 2831

COWART, Robert E.: 1272
COWBOYS--Brazil: 4876
COWELL, Sidney Frances (actress): 1378
COWEN, Joseph: 1273
COWES, England: 4023
COWETA COUNTY, Georgia:
  Newnan: 740
COWLES, Calvin Josiah: 3176, 5457
COWLES, Henry Clay: 5457
COWLES, William Henry Harrison: 5457
COWLEY, Henry Richard Charles Wellesley, First Earl (1804-1884): 5638
COWLEY, Henry Wellesley, First Baron (1773-1847): 5637, 5639
COWLEY, Olivia Cecilia Fitzgerald de Ros Wellesley, Countess: 5638
COWPER, Leopold Copeland Parker: 1274
COWPER, Mary Octavine (Thompson): 1275
COWPER FAMILY: 3396
COWPER AND TELFAIR (firm): 5221
COX, Asenath Ellen: 2303
COX, E. B.: 1276
COX, Jacob Dolson: 4276
COX, James: 720
COX, John: 4914
COX, Jonathan Elwood: 1277
COX, Levi: 328
COX, Talton L. L.: 1278
COX, Thomas E.: 1279
COX, William Ruffin: 2419
COX, Zachariah: 2594
COX FAMILY (North Carolina): 1280
COX, KENDALL AND COMPANY (merchants): 1281
COXE, Richard I.: 5271
COXEY, Jacob Sechler: 4606
COXEY'S ARMY: 4606
COY, Carolina (Keith): 2959
COYLE, Jean Maury: 4073
COZZENS, Frederick Swartwout: 1143
CRAB ORCHARD, North Carolina: 3176
CRABTREE PLANTATION, Orange County, North Carolina: 4666
CRADDOCK, Charles Egbert (pseudonym): see MURFREE, Mary Noailles
CRADDOCK, Joshua: 1107
CRADOCK, Sir John Francis: see CARADOC, Sir John Francis
CRAFT, Carrie: 1282
CRAFT, David Lucius: 1282
CRAFT, H.: 57
CRAFT, Washington: 4200
CRAGGS, Mr. _____ (Great Britain): 5463
CRAIG, Alexander: 1089
CRAIG, Arthur: 1284
CRAIG, Carlyle: 1284
CRAIG, Hector, Sr.: 4361
CRAIG, James D.: 282
CRAIG, James H.: 5035
CRAIG, Sir James Henry: 2756, 3315
CRAIG, John A.: 1283
CRAIG, Locke: 1284, 3955
CRAIG, Mary E.: 1285
CRAIG, Porter: 1286
CRAIG, Scotland: 5379
CRAIG COUNTY, Virginia:
  Social life and customs: 5347
CRAIGLE, Pearl Mary Teresa (Richards): 1287
CRAIGSVILLE, Virginia: 3826
CRAIK, Dinah Maria (Mulock): 2449
CRAMERTON, North Carolina:
  Textile mills: 5100
CRAMPTON'S GAP, Maryland: see CIVIL WAR--CAMPAIGNS, BATTLES, AND MILITARY ACTIONS--Maryland--Crampton's Gap
CRANBERRY CULTURE--North Carolina: 1475
CRANBROOK, Gathorne Gathorne-Hardy, First Earl of: 1978, 2962
CRANBROOK, England: 4823

CRANCH, W. G.: 1288
CRANDALL, W. Irving: 1289
CRANE, Stephen: 720
CRANE, W. H.: 1290
CRANEY ISLAND, Virginia: 70
CRANFIELD, M. L.: 4103
CRANFORD, Tilman: 1291
CRANLEIGH, England: 4207
CRANSTON, Rhode Island: 4433
CRANWORTH, Robert Monsey Rolfe, First Baron: 2998
CRATER, Battle of: see CIVIL WAR--CAMPAIGNS, BATTLES, AND MILITARY ACTIONS--Virginia--Petersburg--Crater
CRAUFURD, Alexander Henry: 2148
CRAUFURD, Quinton: 828
CRAVEN, Bartlett Y.: 1292
CRAVEN, Braxton: 1677, 2419, 3168, 4849
CRAVEN, John A. (estate of): 621
CRAVEN, John A. (merchant): 1293
CRAVEN, Thomas Tingey: 1294
CRAVEN COUNTY, North Carolina: 982, 1871
  Civil War: 1190
  Education: 3955
  Gubernatorial elections: 3955
  Land: 730, 804
  Lumber industry: 730
  Roads: 3955
  Tax receipts: 804
  Cities and towns:
    Fort Barnwell:
      Baptist Clergy: 484
      Merchants: 482, 640
    New Bern: see NEW BERN, North Carolina
    Post Oak Meeting House:
      Original Free Will Baptist Church: 3987
CRAVEN COUNTY (N.C.) GOOD ROADS ASSOCIATION: 3955
CRAWFORD, Abel H.: 1295
CRAWFORD, Anna Harriette: 1033
CRAWFORD, Benjamin: 5039
CRAWFORD, Frances Marion: 103
CRAWFORD, George Walker: 1296
CRAWFORD, Jim (slave): 1295
CRAWFORD, John Wallace: 3008
CRAWFORD, Joel: 1297
CRAWFORD, Martha (Foster): 1298
CRAWFORD, Oswald: 2146
CRAWFORD, Samuel Wylie: 1299
CRAWFORD, Sarah Ann (Gayle): 1300
CRAWFORD, Stephen W.: 1181
CRAWFORD, Tarleton Perry: 1298
CRAWFORD, Thomas (sculptor): 2181
CRAWFORD, William (Scotland): 1301
CRAWFORD, William B. (medical student): 1300
CRAWFORD, William Harris (1772-1834): 1090, 1302, 2913, 3439, 3512
CRAWFORD, William Harrison (b. 1888): 5441
CRAWFORD FAMILY (Alabama): 1300
CRAWFORD, Georgia: 1302
  Merchants: 3974
CRAWFORD, Mississippi--Indians: 2249
CRAWFORD COUNTY, Arkansas:
  Van Buren: 2123, 3376
    Schools: 5380
    Temperance: 2346
CRAWFORD COUNTY, Georgia:
  Roberta: 2432
CRAWFORD COUNTY, Ohio:
  Bucyrus: 3103
CRAWFORDSVILLE, Indiana: 5524
CRAWFORDVILLE, Georgia: 5051
CRAWLEY, Colonel: 4520
"THE CREATION AND THE FALL OF EVE" by Louisa H. Nicholls: 3892
CREATIVE WRITING: 4619
  see also AUTHORSHIP
  Collections: 1241
CREDIT:
  Alabama--Huntsville: 5006
  Pennsylvania--Philadelphia: 228

CREDIT SYSTEM: see AGRICULTURAL CREDIT
CREECY, John Harvie: 1303
CREECY, Richard Benbury: 4669, 4992
CREEDMOOR, North Carolina:
  Methodist Episcopal Church, South: 5023
CREEK INDIANS: 2486, 2776, 3388, 4581
  see also INDIANS OF NORTH AMERICA
  Agents--Georgia: 3704
  Culture: 2249
  Finance: 3704
  Government relations: 3388, 3704
  Indian Territory: 1939
  Land tenure: 3388
  Methodist missionaries: 3646
  Raids: 2781
  Relations with whites: 2776, 5221, 5480
  Treaties--Georgia: 1848, 2778
  Subdivided by place:
    Florida: 842
    Georgia: 1789, 5395
    Tennessee: 2486
CREEK LANGUAGE--Vocabulary: 4208
CREEK WAR (1813-1814): 2781, 4218
  Alabama: 1038
CREEK WAR (1836): 1084, 2808, 3801, 4715
  Indian allies of the United States: 2842
CREEKMORE, Hubert: 2282
CREIGHTON, Johnston B.: 1352
CREIGHTON FAMILY, (Virginia--Genealogy): 1842
CRENSHAW, Edward: 1304
CRENSHAW, John Martin: 5457
CRENSHAW, Leroy: 1305
CRENSHAW (firm): 1115
CRESCENT RIFLES: see CONFEDERATE STATES OF AMERICA--ARMY--Units--Crescent Rifles; CONFEDERATE STATES OF AMERICA--ARMY--Regiments--Louisiana--Infantry--7th
CRESSON, Elliott: 5214
CRESWELL, J. Andrew Jackson: 2868
CRESWELL, John: 4188
CREWE-MILNES, Robert Offley Ashburton, First Marquis of Crewe: 4520
CREWES, James A.: 1306
CREWS, Charles C.: 1181
CREWS, J. M.: 5844
CRICKET--India: 5525
CRIME:
  see also ASSAULT AND BATTERY; BLACKMAIL; BRIGANDS AND ROBBERS; CONSPIRACIES; FRAUD; HIGHWAYMEN; HORSE STEALING; JUVENILE DELINQUENCY; KIDNAPPING; MURDERS; PENSION FRAUD; PEONAGE; POSSESSION OF STOLEN GOODS; SEDITION; SLAVE STEALING; SMUGGLING; TIMBER FRAUD; TREASON; TRESPASS; VETERANS' FRAUD
  Military services: see Crime and Depredations as subheadings under names of armies and navies
  Negroes:
    see also CIVIL WAR--SABOTAGE BY BY NEGROES; SLAVES--Trials
    Alabama--Mobile: 2318
    South Carolina--Charleston: 3012
    Virginia: 29, 3726
  Punishment:
    see also PENAL CODE; PUBLIC WHIPPINGS
    Great Britain: 4913
  Subdivided by place:
    Alabama: 1507
    Florida: 5740
    Georgia: 1993
    Great Britain: 1087, 1126, 1576
    India: 536
    Mississippi: 5740
    Ohio: 801

CRIME:
    Subdivided by place (Continued):
        Virginia--Columbia: 5035
THE CRIMEA IN 1854 AND IN 1894 by Henry Evelyn Wood: 5876
CRIMEAN WAR (1853-1856): 1632, 3472, 4995, 5876
    Americans in the British Army: 4520
    Campaigns, battles and military actions: 2168
        Sevastopol: 2168, 3472, 5947
    Economic aspects:
        Effect on United States exports: 3914
    Great Britain: 597, 649
        Army operations: 153, 2168, 3472, 5947
            Trench warfare: 2168
        Medical and sanitary affairs: 3472
        Naval operations: 153, 485, 3472
        Transport and supply: 153
    Hospitals:
        Scutari, Turkey: 2168
    Maps: 3472
CRIMINAL LAW:
    British law in India: 4097
    Reform in Georgia: 3309
CRIMINAL PROCEDURE: see INDICTMENTS
CRIMINALS: see CRIME, and specific kinds of criminals, e.g. BRIGANDS AND ROBBERS; EXTRADITION OF CRIMINALS
"CRIMP" by John Wolcot: 5867
CRIMPING: see MERCHANT SEAMEN--Recruiting
CRISCOE, Jacob: 1307
CRISP, Stephen: 1733
CRISP COUNTY, Georgia--Cordele: 2747
CRISSEY, Forrest: 2449
CRITICAL AND MISCELLANEOUS ESSAYS by Thomas Carlyle: 892
CRITICISM: see as subheading under types of literature, e.g. AMERICAN LITERATURE--Criticism
CRITIQUE OF PURE REASON by Immanuel Kant (translation): 2457
CRITTENDEN, Ann Mary Butler: 1308
CRITTENDEN, George Bibb: 3507
CRITTENDEN, John Jordan: 872, 1308, 3207, 3507, 3560, 4616
CRITTENDEN, Robert: 5380
CRITTENDEN, Thomas Theodore: 1309
CRITTENDEN FAMILY (Genealogy): 1308
CROASDILLE, D.: 2226
CROGGON, Walter: 1310
CROGHAN, William: 2842
CROKER, John Wilson: 1311, 2077, 5934
CROMARTIE FAMILY (North Carolina--Genealogy): 4517
CROMER, Evelyn Baring, First Earl of: 67, 663, 1857, 2756, 4941, 5175
CROMSON, Alice: 1312
CRONLY, Jane M.: 1313
CRONLY FAMILY (North Carolina): 1313
CRONLY AND MORRIS (firm): 1313
CRONMILLER, John: 1314
CROOK, George (1829-1890): 2991, 3809
CROOK, William Harris: 4556
CROOK, William Henry: 1315
CROOKS, R. N.: 1316
CROOM, Hardy Bryan: 5457
CROP LIENS:
    see also AGRICULTURAL CREDIT
    North Carolina: 3476
    South Carolina: 5198
CROP LOANS:
    see also AGRICULTURAL CREDIT
    Georgia: 2232
CROP ROTATION:
    Virginia:
        Albemarle County: 3699
        Nelson County: 3566

CROPS: 825
    see also AGRICULTURE; FARM PRODUCE; and names of specific kinds of crops
    Medicinal--South Carolina: 2343
    Prices:
        Mississippi: 4269
        Missouri--Pettis County: 1174
        Pennsylvania:
            Franklin County: 2643
        Southern States: 2427
        Tennessee: 4269
        Western States: 5309
    Statistics--North Carolina: 1336
    Subdivided by place:
        Alabama: 2663, 2900, 4083
            Randolph County: 5053
            Wilcox County: 5174
        Arkansas: 837
        British West Indies: 4913
        China: 2191
        Georgia: 1397, 4991, 5760
            De Kalb County: 1011
            Marietta: 3367
        Indiana: 5980
        Louisiana: 1242
        Maine--Cooper: 654
        Massachusetts: 2677
        Michigan: 4889
        Mississippi: 2663
        Missouri: 2663
            Pettis County: 1174
        New York:
            Florida: 86
            Hermon: 3296
        North Carolina: 1322, 1336, 1602, 2548, 2663, 2830, 3351, 4083, 4310, 5741
            Caswell County: 657
            Conetoe: 1362
            Guilford: 1407
            Hyde County: 419
            Iredell County: 4872
            Nash County: 5475
            Stokes County: 2800
        Ohio: 2949, 5980
            North Hampton: 1618
            Wilkes: 86
        South Carolina: 2290, 2831, 4083, 4118, 4310
            Camden: 5675
            Edisto Island: 4896
        Southern States: 2427
        Tennessee: 2661, 4083
            Wayne County: 771
        Texas: 2920, 4562
            Colorado County: 1741, 5174
        Virginia: 363, 1133, 1240, 1591, 2370, 2510, 2949, 3674, 4616, 4710, 4720, 5180, 5741, 5980
            Amelia County: 4729
            Dinwiddie County: 551
            Nelson County: 682
            Northern Virginia: 4743
            Rockbridge County: 5613
            Sperryville: 1618
CROSBY, Sarah: 1317
CROSLAND, Kate: 3390
CROSS, Dorcas E.: 4202
CROSS, George: 1319
CROSS, James F.: 1318
CROSS, Thomas: 1319
CROSS CREEK, North Carolina: 4082
CROSS HILL ACADEMY, South Carolina: 4118
CROSS KEYS, Virginia: 2978
    see also CIVIL WAR--CAMPAIGNS, BATTLES, AND MILITARY ACTIONS--Virginia--Cross Keys
CROSS ROADS TOWNSHIP, North Carolina:
    Taxation: 3935
CROSSAN, Thomas Morrow: 5457
CROSSLEY, Andrew Jackson: 615
CROSSLEY, G. R.: 3008
CROSTICK, John: 1873
CROTON AQUEDUCT: 5546
CROW INDIANS--Culture: 3424
CROWE, John Henry Verinder: 1320

CROWELL, John Franklin: 22, 1584, 2221, 4788, 5457
CROWELL, Lorenzo M., Jr.: 5201
CROWELL (THOMAS Y.) COMPANY: 3797
CROWN LANDS:
    France--Tours: 5323
    Great Britain: 5026
CROWNINSHIELD, Benjamin, III: 450
CROWNINSHIELD, Benjamin Williams (1772-1851): 1321
CROWTHER, Samuel A.: 41
CROZER SEMINARY, Chester, Pennsylvania: 3155
CROZET, Claude: 872
CRUDUP, E. A.: 1322
CRUGER, Henry: 305
CRUMP, Edward Hull: 4918
CRUMPLER, W. J.: 1323
CRUTCHFIELD, E. W.: 1324
CRUTCHFIELD, Susan Gatewood: 3587
CRYDENWISE, Henry M.: 1325
CRYSTAL PALACE (New York): 1478, 2410, 3424
CRYSTAL PALACE EXHIBITION: see GREAT EXHIBITION OF 1850
CUBA: 4520, 4667
    see also UNITED STATES--FOREIGN RELATIONS--Spain
    American occupation (1906-1909): 5878
    British occupation (1762): 4835
    Coffee growing: 3808
    Confederate emigrants: 3587
    Currency: 1339
    Customs duties: 4983
    Description and travel: 2849
        Havana: 3983
    Filibustering: 3287, 4982, 4983
    Foreign relations:
        United States: 1364, 3774, 3809, 4348, 5171
    Foreign trade:
        United States: 1442
    Health conditions: 4983
    Independence: 4348, 5051
    Insurrections: 2387, 5949
        American neutrality: 4983
        American opinion of insurrection of 1868-1878: 4348
        Refugees from insurrection of 1849-1851: 4569
    Merchants: 3808
        Havana: 3008
    Palaces (pictures): 4227
    Slave trade: 258
    Spanish administration: 4982, 4983
    Spanish-American War: see SPANISH-AMERICAN WAR
    Trade regulation: 4983
    United States consul in Havana: 3231
CUBAN REVOLUTIONARIES IN JAMAICA: 1792
CUBANS IN THE UNITED STATES (1800s): 4569, 4983
CUEVA, Alfonso de la, Marqués de Bedmar: 405
CUI BONO by Josiah Tucker: 119
CULBERSON, John: 1326
CULBERSON, Samuel J.: 1326
CULBERSON, William L.: 5754
CULBERTSON, William: 1328
CULBRETH, Thomas (1786-1843): 1329
CULLARS, Robert T.: 216
CULLEN, William: 3399
CULLODEN (ship): 176
CULLOM, Shelby Moore: 1330
CULLOMPTON, Devonshire, England: 2127
CULP, J. P.: 1331
CULPEPER, John: 202, 5457
CULPEPER, Virginia:
    Civil War:
        Battle: see CIVIL WAR--CAMPAIGNS, BATTLES, AND MILITARY ACTIONS--Virginia--Culpeper
        United States Army depredations: 3464

CULPEPER, Virginia (Continued):
    Commodity prices: 4852
    Debt: 4852
    Farming: 1931
    Legal affairs: 4852
    Slave trade: 4852
CULPEPER COUNTY, Virginia: 1263
    Estate settlement: 337
    Farming: 3141
    Cities and towns:
        Brandy Station: 4685
        Culpeper: see CULPEPER, Virginia
        Culpeper Court House: 927, 4170
            see also CIVIL WAR--CAMPAIGNS,
            BATTLES, AND MILITARY
            ACTIONS--Virginia--Culpeper
            Court House
        "Rose Hill": 3833
        Somerville: 1744, 3681
        Stevensburgh: 5113
CULPEPER COURT HOUSE, Virginia:
    927, 4170
"CULROSS," Virginia: 3560
CULTIVATING: see AGRICULTURAL
    PRACTICES; FARMING
CULTURE: see Social life and
    customs as subheading under names
    of places
CUMBER COUNTY, Kentucky:
    Marrow Bone: 57
CUMBERLAND, England:
    Keswick: 4967
    Whitehaven: 625, 1153
CUMBERLAND, Maryland: 2796, 3190,
    3282, 3765
    Description (Civil War): 3789
    Railroad construction: 721
CUMBERLAND (warship): 636, 5436
CUMBERLAND BOARD OF PUBLIC WELFARE,
    Cumberland County, North Carolina:
    5298
CUMBERLAND COUNTY, Maine:
    Brunswick: 961, 5899
    Portland: 1554, 1787, 2043, 2106,
        3551
    Standish: 5955
CUMBERLAND COUNTY, North Carolina:
    50, 756, 860, 5372
    Land deeds: 4517
    Public welfare: 5298
    Pulp and paper industry: 3812
    Weather: 3812
    Cities and towns:
        Cross Creek: 4082
        Fayetteville: see FAYETTEVILLE,
            North Carolina
CUMBERLAND COUNTY, Pennsylvania:
    Carlisle: see CARLISLE,
        Pennsylvania
    Shippensburg: 1283
CUMBERLAND COUNTY, Virginia: 531,
    4014
    Cartersville: 693, 5035
CUMBERLAND COURT HOUSE, Virginia: 38
CUMBERLAND GAP, Tennessee:
    Civil War:
        Confederate Army camp: 18
        Confederate surrender (1863):
            4335
    Treaty line with Indians: 2486
CUMBERLAND RIVER (Tennessee): 4032
CUMBERLAND UNIVERSITY LAW SCHOOL,
    Lebanon, Tennessee: 5593
CUMBERLAND VALLEY MUTUAL
    PROTECTION CO., Carlisle,
    Pennsylvania: 1332
CUMBERLAND VALLEY RAILROAD COMPANY:
    5239
"A CUMBERLAND VENDETTA": 1878
CUMBERLAND (Md.) WATER DEPARTMENT:
    3190
"THE CUMMERBUND" by Edward Lear:
    3138
CUMMING, Alfred: 1333
CUMMING, Elizabeth Wells (Randall):
    1333
CUMMING, John: 1334
CUMMING, Joseph: 1333

CUMMING, Joseph Bryan: 1203
CUMMING, Thomas: 1333
CUMMING, William (1724-1790?): 5457
CUMMING, William A.: 1899
CUMMING, William Clay: 1333
CUMMINGS, Homer Stillé: 646
CUMMINS, G. B.: 1609
CUNDIFF, Richard J.: 1335
CUNINGHAM, Alexander (d. ca. 1850):
    208, 1336
CUNINGHAM, Alexander, Jr.: 1336
CUNINGHAM, John Somerville: 1336
CUNINGHAM, John Wilson: 1336
CUNINGHAM, Richard M.: 1336
CUNINGHAM, Robert: 1336
CUNINGHAM FAMILY (North Carolina
    and Virginia): 1336
CUNLIFFE-OWEN, Sir Francis Philip:
    see OWEN, Sir Francis Philip
    Cunliffe-
CUNNINGHAM, Ann Pamela: 1337
CUNNINGHAM, Robert: 2383
CUNNINGHAM, Sumner Archibald: 2449
CUNNINGHAM, William H.: 1338
CUNNINGHAM AND WILSON (firm): see
    WILSON AND CUNNINGHAM
CUNNINGHAM'S BLUFF, South Carolina:
    Civil War:
        Battle: see CIVIL WAR--CAMPAIGNS,
            BATTLES, AND MILITARY
            ACTIONS--South Carolina--
            Cunningham's Bluff
        Defenses: 4620
CUNNINGHAM'S STORE, North Carolina:
    1336, 1959
CURETON, Richard: 4399
CURRAN, E.: 2687
CURRENCY:
    see also BANK NOTES; BILLS OF
        EXCHANGE; CIVIL WAR--CIVILIAN
        LIFE--Scarcity of money; COINS
        AND COINAGE; FOREIGN EXCHANGE;
        GREENBACKS; SILVER QUESTION;
        UNITED STATES--GOVERNMENT
        AGENCIES AND OFFICIALS--National
        Currency Department
    Counterfeiting: 5792
        see also AMERICAN REVOLUTION--
            Economic aspects--Currency--
            Counterfeiting
        Mississippi: 4596
        Texas: 2808
        United States: 2130
    Depreciation--United States: 5752
    Gold: 5252, 5731
    Silver: 5252
    Transportation of: 4965
    Subdivided by place:
        Alabama: 1339
        Argentina: 1339
        Arkansas: 1339
        Austria: 1339
        Brazil: 5886
        Canada: 1339
        Confederate States of America:
            206, 662, 1181, 1339, 4501,
            4921, 4965, 5018, 5242
        Cuba: 1339
        Delaware: 1339
        Florida: 1339
        France: 1339
        Georgia: 1339, 2933
        Germany: 1339, 5252
        Great Britain: 1339, 1775, 5886
        Haiti: 1339
        Hungary: 1339
        Indiana: 1339
        Ireland: 3349
        Italy: 1339, 5886
        Japan: 1339
        Kentucky: 1339
        Louisiana: 1339
        Maine: 1339
        Maryland: 1339
        Massachusetts: 1339
        Mexico: 1339, 5886
        Michigan: 1339
        Mississippi: 4596

CURRENCY:
    Subdivided by place (Continued):
        Missouri: 1339
        Nebraska: 1339
        New Hampshire: 1339
        New Jersey: 1339
        New York: 1339
        North Carolina: 1339
        Pennsylvania: 1339
        Philippine Islands: 1339, 3313
        Puerto Rico: 5886
        Russia: 1339
        Saint Croix: 5886
        South Carolina: 206, 1339
        Tennessee: 1339
        Texas: 1339
        United States: 849, 872, 1339,
            2164, 2881, 3415, 5576
        Venezuela: 5886
        Vermont: 1339
        Virginia: 1339
CURRENCY ACT OF 1863: 421
CURRENCY COLLECTING: 1339
    Washington, D.C.: 4478
CURRENCY CONVERTIBILITY: 5275
CURRENCY REGULATION: 2973
    Great Britain: 5
CURRICULUM: see THEOLOGICAL
    SEMINARIES--Curriculum;
    UNIVERSITIES AND COLLEGES--
    Curriculum; and Curriculum as a
    subheading under names of specific
    universities and colleges
CURRITUCK, U.S.S.: 1507
CURRITUCK CIRCUIT, Methodist churches:
    3646
CURRY, A.S.: 2371
CURRY, Jabez Lamar Monroe: 1084,
    1340, 5251
CURRY, Manly Bowie: 1340
CURRY, Manly Lamar: 1340
CURRY, Margaret: 1341
CURRY FAMILY: 1340
CURT, Louis Chevallier De: 2835
CURTIN, Andrew Gregg: 5775
CURTIS, George William: 1342
CURTIS, Joseph: 2468
CURTIS, Moses Ashley: 5457, 5881
CURTIS PUBLISHING COMPANY: 5779
CURTISS, Henry T.: 5612
CURZON, George Nathaniel, First
    Marquis Curzon of Kedleston: 67,
    278, 663, 1343, 4693
CURZON, Mary Victoria (Leiter),
    Marchioness Curzon of Kedleston:
    4693
CUSHING, Arthur D.: 41
CUSHING, Caleb: 616, 1403, 3006
CUSHING, John: 1344
CUSHING, Mary Jacobs: 1344
CUSHING, Nathaniel Grafton: 1344
CUSHING, Olive: 1344
CUSHING FAMILY (Massachusetts): 1344
CUSHMAN, Charlotte Saunders: 1345,
    4486
CUSTER, George Armstrong: 2416
CUSTER, Sallie C.: 1346
"CUSTER'S LAST CHARGE" (painting):
    1665
CUSTIS, Eleanor Parke: 805, 3560,
    4014
CUSTIS, Elizabeth Parke: 5575
CUSTIS, George Washington Parke: 5575
CUSTIS, John Parke: 5575
CUSTIS, Martha (Dandridge): 99, 4864,
    5575
CUSTIS, Mary Ann Randolph: 805, 3157,
    5949
CUSTIS FAMILY (Virginia): 128
CUSTOMS ADMINISTRATION: 4541, 4599
    see also UNITED STATES--GOVERNMENT
        AGENCIES AND OFFICIALS--Customs
        Service
    Confederate States Of America:
        3615
    Georgia--Savannah: 4678, 5516
    Spain--Cadiz: 4978

CUSTOMS DUTIES: 4978
  see also TARIFF; UNITED STATES--
    GOVERNMENT AGENCIES AND
    OFFICIALS--Customs Service
  Collection:
    Georgia:
      Irregularities at Saint Mary's:
        2497
      Savannah: 2326, 4678
    New York--New York: 548
    North Carolina: 2776
    South Carolina: 1927
    Spain--Cadiz: 4978
    Virginia: 2505
    Washington--Puget Sound: 4239
  Evasion: 2933
  Subdivided by place:
    Cape Verde Islands: 3118
    Cuba: 4983
    Great Britain: 1913
CUTHBERT, John Alexander: 393
CUTHBERT, Seth John: 1347
CUTHBERT, Georgia: 2326
  see also ANDREW FEMALE COLLEGE
  Hospitals: 3555
CUTLER, Frederick: 1348
CUTLER, Mary Salome: 1747
CUTLER, Sarah (Monroe): 1348
CUTLERY INDUSTRY AND TRADE:
  Connecticut--Hartford: 1169
CUTTACK, India: 2321
  Missions and missionaries: 2410
CUTTER, Edwin A.: 1349
CUTTS, Adele: 1190
CUXHAVEN, Germany: 2296
CUYAHOGA COUNTY, Ohio:
  Berea: 2693
  Cleveland: 451, 1953, 2313, 2562,
    2969, 3716, 4201, 5908
    Business affairs: 2128
    Memorials: 5291
  Dover: 4565
CUYLER, Jeremiah: 5787
CUYLER, Richard M.: 5787
CUYLER, Richard R. (d. 1865): 5787
CUYLER, Teleman: 5787
CUYLER, Theodore (1819-1876): 5214
CUYLER, Tulamon: 5787
CUYLER, William H.: 5787
CUYLER FAMILY (Genealogy): 5787
CYCLING--Scotland: 2103
CYCLOTRONS: 2627
CYPRESS HALL, Louisiana
  (plantation): 1026, 1179

# D

D. A. TOMPKINS COMPANY: 5312
D. &. I. MOSES (firm): 709
D. ESHLEMAN AND COMPANY: 3957
D. MacRAE (firm): see J. & D. MacRAE
D. SHELDON (firm): 2933
DABNEY, Charles William: 4373
DABNEY, Chiswell, Jr. (d. 1865): 1350
DABNEY, George William: 1350
DABNEY, Robert Lewis: 1351
DABNEY, Thomas S.: 4924
DABNEY, Virginius: 3783
DAGUERREOTYPERS:
  Pennsylvania: 4057
  Vermont: 3218
DAHLGREN, Eva: 1352
DAHLGREN, John Adolphus Bernard: 1352
DAHLGREN, Patty: 1352
DAHLONEGA, Georgia:
  Civil War: 608
    United States Army camp: 5744
  Methodist churches: 3646
DAHLONEGA METHODIST CHURCH (Georgia): 3646
DAILY & WEEKLY COURIER: 3022
DAILY GRAPHIC: 1499
THE DAILY LABORER: 2164
DAILY RICHMOND EXAMINER: 2845
DAILY TELEGRAPH: 3036
DAINESE, F.: 1466
DAINGERFIELD, Mrs. John B.: 5985
DAIRY FARMS:
  Colorado--Larimer County: 3199
  Management--Massachusetts: 2532
DAIRY TRADE:
  North Carolina: 2924
    Wilkesboro: 4107
DAISY HOSIERY MILLS, Burlington, North Carolina: 1353, 3595
DALBIAC, Sir James Charles: 1911
DALBY, B. J.: 1354
DALE, Helen Pelham: 1218
DALE, Robert William: 582
DALHOUSIE, George Ramsay, Ninth Earl of: 4372
DALHOUSIE, James Andrew Broun Ramsay, First Marquis of: 2029, 4660, 4995, 5327
DALHOUSIE CASTLE, Scotland: 4372
DALL, Mary (Brand): 1355
DALL FAMILY: 1355
DALLAM, James L.: 1356
DALLAS, Alexander James: 1714, 2963
DALLAS, George Mifflin (1792-1864): 519
DALLAS, George W.: 685
DALLAS, North Carolina--Schools: 4080
DALLAS, Texas: 1272, 5098
  see also SOUTHERN METHODIST UNIVERSITY
  Civil War: 1138
DALLAS COUNTY, Alabama: 2979, 5961
  Estates--Administration and settlement: 4911
  Plantations: 4911
  Religion: 5961
  Cities and towns:
    Cahaba: 609, 1947
      Commission House: 5879
      Democrat (newspaper): 5937
      Schools: 5593
    Orrville: 223
    Selma: see SELMA, Alabama
DALLAS COUNTY, Texas:
  Dallas: 1272, 5098
    Civil War: 1138

DALLAS CABLE RAILROAD: 1584
DALLING AND BULWER, William Henry Lytton Earle Bulwer, Baron: 762
DALRYMPLE, Sir James: 2707
DALTON, Charles Henry: 3283
DALTON, Georgia: 916, 2164, 5111
  Civil War:
    Battle: see CIVIL WAR--CAMPAIGNS, BATTLES, AND MILITARY ACTIONS--Georgia--Dalton
    Sherman's march: 689
DALY, César Dénis: 65
DAM NO. 5, Winchester, Virginia: 584
DAMAGES (Law): see LAWSUITS
DAN RIVER (North Carolina): 4080
DAN RIVER BAPTIST ASSOCIATION (Virginia): 330
DANA, Charles Anderson: 1357, 2526
DANA, Richard Henry: 2449
DANBURY, Connecticut: 2257
DANBURY, North Carolina:
  Mercantile accounts: 1919
DANDRIDGE, Adam Stephen: 404
DANDRIDGE, Caroline Danske (Bedinger): 404
DANDRIDGE, John (Great Britain): 1358
DANDRIDGE, Martha: 99, 4864, 5575
DANDRIDGE, Phillip: 743
DANDRIDGE, S. P.: 743
DANDRIDGE, Sarah: 743
DANDRIDGE, Serena Katherine: 404
DANDRIDGE, Stephen H.: 3710
DANDRIDGE, Susan C.: 5742
DANDRIDGE, William F.: 5742
DANDRIDGE FAMILY (Genealogy): 3831
DANDRIDGE FAMILY (Maryland): 743
DANDRIDGE FAMILY (Virginia): 3148
DANDRIDGE FAMILY (West Virginia): 404, 3148
DANE COUNTY, Wisconsin:
  Madison: 403, 2811
DANFORTH, John B.: 1359
DANFORTH AND BRUSHWOOD (firm): 1359
DANIEL, Anne (Leavell): 3141
DANIEL, Beverley: 1360
DANIEL, Franz E.: 1195, 1196, 5233, 5236
DANIEL, Harriet Bailey (Bullock): 1361
DANIEL, J. H.: 1362
DANIEL, Jessie: 107
DANIEL, John M.: 3141
DANIEL, John Reeves Jones: 1363
DANIEL, John Warwick: 1364, 1439, 2951
DANIEL, Joseph John: 5457
DANIEL, Lucy E.: 1361
DANIEL, Martitia: 5912
DANIEL, Mary (Fraser): 1891
DANIEL, Robert: 5457
DANIEL, Samuel Venable: 1361
DANIEL, William, Jr.: 2951
DANIEL FAMILY (Arkansas): 1361
DANIEL FAMILY (North Carolina): 1361, 1362
DANIEL FAMILY (Tennessee): 1361
DANIEL BOONE TRAIL: 4080
DANIELL, Robert: 4214
DANIELL, William C.: 1365
DANIELS, Henry: 1366
DANIELS, Josephus: 83, 879, 1367, 4232
DANIELS, Thomas Cowper: 1368
DANIELS CHURCH, Lincoln County, North Carolina: 1232
DANISH WEST INDIES:
  Sugar growing and trade: 3570
DANNER, Jacob S.: 1369
DANSVILLE, New York: 5660
DANTE ALIGHIERI (1265-1321): 425, 3836, 4600
DANTE GABRIEL ROSSETTI, AN ANALYTICAL LIST OF MANUSCRIPTS IN THE DUKE UNIVERSITY LIBRARY . . . edited by Paull F. Baum: 4575
DANTZLER, Absalom F.: 1370
DANTZLER, Lewis: 1371
DANTZLER, Susan (Millsaps): 1370
DANVERS, Massachusetts: 5717
DANVILLE, Kentucky: see CENTRE COLLEGE OF KENTUCKY

DANVILLE, Virginia: 418, 915, 1956, 2131, 5148
  Banks and banking: 1372, 1761, 5556
  Book trade: 5196
  Civil War: 5769
    Battle: see CIVIL WAR--CAMPAIGNS, BATTLES, AND MILITARY ACTIONS--Virginia--Danville
    Defense: 4738
  Courts: 1125
  Inflation: 4094
  Mercantile accounts: 1046, 2207, 2569, 5196
  Merchants: 1486, 2331
  Price regulation: 4094
  Religion: 5773
  Social life and customs: 5773
  Stationery trade: 5196
  Tobacco auctions: 5958
  Tobacco industry: 4918
DANVILLE BANK, Danville, Virginia: 1372
DANVILLE (Va.) CITIZENS' COMMITTEE: 4094
DANVILLE DISTRICT, Methodist churches: 3646
DANVILLE RAILROAD: 1801
DANYELL, Arthur Johnson: 1373
DARDANELLE, Arkansas: 3276
DARDEN, Nanny: 1107
DARE CIRCUIT, Methodist churches: 3646
DARE COUNTY, North Carolina: 1475
  Clarksville: 831
  Hatteras: 4547
  Nags Head: 4262
DARE MISSION CIRCUIT, Methodist churches: 3646
DARGAN, Clara Victoria: 3418
DARGAN FAMILY (North Carolina): 5211
DARGAN FAMILY (South Carolina--Genealogy): 3418
DARIEN, Georgia: 1779, 2647, 2963, 5508
  Land surveys: 3389
DARKESVILLE, West Virginia:
  Mercantile accounts: 4692
DARLINGTON, England: 4104
DARLINGTON, South Carolina: 1651, 1688, 1944, 3123, 3203
  Arithmetic exercise books: 208
  Constables: 5299
  Courts: 2106
  Regulation of the liquor trade: 5299
DARLINGTON COUNTY, South Carolina: 3124
  Darlington: see DARLINGTON, South Carolina
  Society Hill: 2762, 4634
DARLINGTON DISTRICT, South Carolina:
  Plantations: 1553
DARNALL, Samuel Henry: 2498
DARNALL, Thomas M.: 2498
DARNLEY, John Bligh, Fourth Earl of: 535
DARRELL AND SMITH: see SMITH AND DARRELL; SMITH, DE SAUSSURE AND DARRELL
DART, U., Sr.: 1374
DARTMOUTH, Massachusetts: 4653
DARTMOUTH COLLEGE, Hanover, New Hampshire:
  Students and student life: 2436, 5747
  Teaching: 4012
DARTT, Benjamin S.: 4188
DARWIN, Charles Robert: 582, 1219
DASHER, C.: 1375
DASHER, Christian: 1375
DASHER, Jane Elizabeth: 1375
DAUGHERTY, Beverly W.: 1376
DAUGHERTY, Helen J. (Thompson) Sawyer: 1376
DAUGHERTY, Louise: 1377
DAUGHERTY, Willie: 1376
DAUGHERTY COUNTY, Georgia:
  Albany: 2533, 4921
DAUGHTERS OF THE AMERICAN REVOLUTION: 661, 1814, 3357, 5656
  North Carolina: 2553
DAUGHTERS OF THE CONFEDERACY: see UNITED DAUGHTERS OF THE CONFEDERACY

DAUPHIN COUNTY, Pennsylvania:
   Harrisburg: see HARRISBURG,
     Pennsylvania
   Hummelstown: 496
DAUPHINE PROVINCE, France: 4408
D'AUVERGNE, Philippe, Prince de
   Bouillon: 1212, 2735
DAVENANT, William: 1163
DAVENPORT, E. C.: 1379
DAVENPORT, Fanny Elizabeth (Vining)
   Gill: 1378
DAVENPORT, Henry B.: 1379
DAVENPORT, Ira: 1380
DAVENPORT, John: 5712
DAVENPORT COLLEGE, Lenoir, North
   Carolina: 5298
DAVENPORT FEMALE COLLEGE, Lenoir,
   North Carolina: 593
   Students and student life: 4689,
     4910
DAVEY, Horace, First Baron Davey:
   1815
DAVID, Paul T.: 3820
DAVID BUICK CARBURETOR CORPORATION:
   4918
DAVID DUNLOP (tobacco firm): 655,
   1873
DAVID ROBERTSON & CO.: 4509
DAVID WATKINS & CO.: 2908
DAVIDSON, Adam Brevard: 5457
DAVIDSON, Ephraim: 1381
DAVIDSON, George F.: 1382
DAVIDSON, James: 1383
DAVIDSON, James D.: 1384
DAVIDSON, James Wood (1829-1905):
   1385, 1494, 3418
DAVIDSON, John (1797-1836): 306
DAVIDSON, John (merchant): 1386
DAVIDSON, Randall Thomas,
   Archbishop of Canterbury: 663
DAVIDSON, Samuel (1807-1898): 2653
DAVIDSON, William (1778-1857): 3094
DAVIDSON, William Lee (1746-1781):
   1387
DAVIDSON FAMILY (North Carolina):
   1382
DAVIDSON, North Carolina: see
   DAVIDSON COLLEGE
DAVIDSON COLLEGE, Davidson, North
   Carolina: 4429, 4874, 4918
   Curriculum: 1905
   Faculty: 1905
   Students and student life: 754,
     1905, 3432, 3790, 4689, 4707,
     4816, 5664
DAVIDSON COUNTY, North Carolina: 788,
   3241, 4877, 4972, 5219
   Arithmetic exercise book: 208
   Company stores: 5583
   Gold mining: 5549
   Justices of the peace: 3926
   Mercantile accounts: 138
   Mining: 2041, 5583
   Physician's accounts: 138
   Cities and towns:
     Abbott's Creek: 5218
     Bethany:
       Farmers' Alliance: 3996
     Cedar Bush: 1882
     Fair Grove: 1341
     Jackson Hill: 3885
     Lexington: 344, 2074, 2298,
       2595, 2874, 5229
       Merchants: 35
       Silver mines: 277
     Midway: 3250
     Silver Hill: 4329
     Thomasville: 788, 2906
       Barrel staves: 2377
       Farmers' Alliance: 3996
DAVIDSON COUNTY, Tennessee: 361, 4487
   see also NASHVILLE, Tennessee;
     NASHVILLE NORMAL AND COLLEGIATE
     THEOLOGICAL INSTITUTE
DAVIDSON COUNTY FARMERS' ALLIANCE:
   3996
DAVIDSON'S CREEK, North Carolina:
   1387
DAVIE, Frederick William: 1388, 1891

DAVIE, Mary (Fraser): 1388, 1891
DAVIE, Sarah (Jones): 1891
DAVIE, Victoria (Jordan): 2940
DAVIE, William Richardson: 1389,
   1891, 2256, 2776
DAVIE COUNTY, North Carolina: 391,
   2310, 2572, 5069
   Churches: 1232
   Newspapers: 122
   Politics: 122
   Public school buildings: 4111
   Cities and towns:
     Advance: 4111
     Calahaln: 122
     County Line: 1174
     Dutchman Creek: 1904
     Farmington: 2857
     Fulton: 1686
     Gold Hill:
       Blacksmith's and mercantile
         accounts: 3368
     Jamestown: 211, 2804
     Mocksville: 832, 1100, 1513,
       1936, 2749, 3343, 5335
     Settle: 832
     Smith Grove: 2021, 4765, 5511
DAVIES (C. A.) AND COMPANY: 1390
DAVIES, Emily: 1087
DAVIES, M. D.: 1391
DAVIES, Sir Robert Henry: 4549
DAVIES, William: 3809
DAVIES AND TAYLOR (firm): see
   TAYLOR, DAVIES, AND TAYLOR
DAVIS, Mr. _____ (Georgia): 3340
DAVIS (A. B.) AND CO.: 1392
DAVIS, Adeline Ellery (Burr): 2161
DAVIS, Amanda: 1393
DAVIS, Ann A.: 1556
DAVIS, Arthur Vining: 96
DAVIS (B. P.) AND BROTHER: 1394
DAIVS, Benjamin A.: 1410
DAVIS, Caleb v. Raymond Demere: 1454
DAVIS, Mrs. Carrie: 4733
DAVIS, Charles Hall: 4560
DAVIS, Charles W.: 1395
DAVIS, David: 2161
DAVIS, Dixon D.: 3451
DAVIS, Dolphin A.: 1396
DAVIS, E. A.: 1397
DAVIS, E. H. (minister): 5964
DAVIS, Frank: 1407
DAVIS, Frederic L.: 1397
DAVIS, George: 1399
DAVIS, George T. M.: 1400
DAVIS, Isaac: 1401
DAVIS, Isaac, Jr.: 1401
DAVIS, J. H.: 4350
DAVIS, James: 4153
DAVIS, Jasper: 1402
DAVIS, Jefferson: 395, 623, 805, 872,
   1084, 1364, 1403, 1505, 2180, 2449,
   2662, 4131, 4193, 4253, 4729, 4873,
   4884, 5059, 5315, 5517, 5649, 5661
   Administration: 1403, 4080
     Criticism of: 3642
   Conscription policies: 3811
   Death: 5142
   Funeral: 1403
   Imprisonment: 1403, 2562
   Military affairs (Confederate
     States of America): 2882
   Opinion of: 832
   Proposed trial of: 2545
   Relations with Joseph E. Johnston:
     2893
   Rumors surrounding: 4039, 4920,
     5688
   Visit to Georgia: 5472
   Visit to North Carolina: 3435
DAVIS, John (Virginia): 3560
DAVIS, John (1787-1854): 1404
DAVIS, John, Jr. (1770-1865): 1405
DAVIS, John A. G. (1804-1840): 5194
DAVIS, John D. (Virginia): 5366
DAVIS, John W. (missionary): 1382
DAVIS, John William: 1137
DAVIS, Joseph: 1406
DAVIS, Joseph Jonathan: 5457
DAVIS, Judith: 785

DAVIS, Julia Roxie: 1407
DAVIS, Lois (Wright) Richardson:
   1408
DAVIS, M. L.: 3272
DAVIS, Mark: 3738
DAVIS, Mary Miller: 1409
DAVIS, Mary P.: 1410
DAVIS, Matthew S., Jr. (1830-1906):
   1411
DAVIS, Mira Belle (Prim): 4329
DAVIS, Myra: 1412
DAVIS, Nancy T.: 1413
DAVIS, Noah Knowles: 1000
DAVIS, Orin Datus: 5457
DAVIS, Owen: 3797
DAVIS, Richard: 2908
DAVIS, Richard Beale: 2047
DAVIS, Richard Harding: 4556
DAVIS, Richard Hart: 650
DAVIS, Royal Jenkins: 3797
DAVIS, S. D.: 1414
DAVIS, Samuel: 1415
DAVIS, Smithson H.: 2633
DAVIS, Solomon: 1416
DAVIS, Thomas: 1401
DAVIS, Thomas v. Robert Wickliffe:
   1401
DAVIS, Varina (Howell): 1084, 1403
DAVIS, W. G.: 1417
DAVIS, Westmoreland: 4617
DAVIS, William Watts Hart: 1418
DAVIS FAMILY: 1412
DAVIS, California: 5889
   see also UNIVERSITY OF CALIFORNIA
     AT DAVIS
DAVIS AND ALDIS (firm): see ALDIS
   AND DAVIS
DAVIS MILITARY SCHOOL, Winston,
   North Carolina: 3176
DAVISBURG, Michigan: 5269
DAVISON, Mary F.: 1419
DAVISSON, E. D.: 1420
DAVISSON, Frederick Augustus: 1421
DAWES COUNTY, Nebraska: 5309
DAWES, Charles Gates: 5252
DAWLISH, Devonshire: England: 2126
   Literary affairs: 2580
DAWSON, Andrew H. H.: 1422
DAWSON, Edgar G.: 1423
DAWSON, Ethel: 1424
DAWSON, Francis Warrington
   (1840-1889): 1424, 2473, 4145,
   5280, 5893
DAWSON, Francis Warrington
   (1878-1962): 1424, 3305
DAWSON, Mary Wallace: 1426
DAWSON, Nathaniel Henry Rhodes: 1425
DAWSON, Richard William: 1426
DAWSON, Sarah Ida Fowler (Morgan):
   1424
DAWSON, Warrington: see DAWSON,
   Francis Warrington (1878-1962)
DAWSON, Sir William: 3008
DAWSON, William Crosby (1798-1856):
   1427, 2326, 3905
DAWSON, William Johnson: 2776
DAWSON, William Mercer Owens: 2634
DAY, Benjamin: 917
DAY, Mary: 361
DAY CARE CENTERS: see CHILD CARE
   CENTERS
DAYLESFORD, England: 2422
DAYTON, Alabama: 798
DAYTON, Ohio:
   Agricultural machinery: 5193
   Bonebrake Theological Seminary:
     1920
DAYTON, Virginia: 1105
   Shenandoah Seminary: 1920
DAYTON ACADEMY, Durham, North
   Carolina: 3896
DE JURE REGNI APUD SCOTOS by George
   Buchanan: 5379
"DE LA FUNDACION DE LA INSIGNE Y
   REAL UNIVERSIDAD DE MEXICO,
   NOVIEMBRE 3, 1596": 3850
DEACONS: see as subheading under
   names of religious denominations

DEAF:
  Education:
    Georgia: 5051
    New York--New York: 5298
    South Carolina: 300
    Virginia: 558, 872
      Staunton: 5298
    United States Census: 5426
DEAF AND DUMB: see DEAF
DEAF MUTES: see DEAF
DEAL, Samuel: 1428
DEAL, New Jersey: 2409
DEAN, Miles B.: 1429
DEAN, W. B.: 1430
DEANE, Charles (1813-1889): 1431
DEANE, Julia: 1432
DEARBORN, General_____: 1404
DEARBORN, Henry: 1433
DEARBORN, Henry Alexander Scammell: 1433
DEARBORN COUNTY, Indiana:
  Lawrenceburg: 4644
DEARING, Albin P.: 1434
DEARING, John J.: 1434
DEARING, St. Clair: 1435
DEARING, William: 1434
DEARMONT, Mamie: 1436
DEARMONT, Washington: 1436, 2274
DEATH: 2934, 4473, 4936
  see also AGATHANASIA; CORONERS' INQUESTS; TERMINAL CARE
  Alabama: 2662
  Arkansas: 5380
  Connecticut: 4815
  Georgia: 786, 3414
  Great Britain: 4168, 5598
  North Carolina: 1467, 3176, 5739
  Ohio--North Hampton: 1618
  Pennsylvania: 3227
  South Carolina: 2960, 3360, 5193
  United States: 2407
  Virginia: 33, 1359, 1920, 4020, 5426
    Sperryville: 1618
  West Virginia: 1770
DEATH PENALTY: see CAPITAL PUNISHMENT; DESERTION; TREASON
DEATON, Noah: 1437
DEBATES AND DEBATING:
  Georgia:
    Barnesville: 4791
    Savannah: 4675
  North Carolina--Subjects: 3973
DEBATING SOCIETIES:
  Alabama: 3611
  Georgia:
    Barnesville: 4791
    Savannah: 4675
  Louisiana: 845
  Mississippi: 3611
  North Carolina: 2357
    Olin: 3973
    Youngsville: 5087
  South Carolina: 1111
  Virginia--Petersburg: 4159
DEBERRY, David D.: 1438
DEBERRY, John: 1438
DE BÉTHUNE, Maximilien: 1424
DE BÉTHUNE FAMILY (France--Genealogy): 1424
DE BOST, Mr._____: 2351
DEBOW, James Dunwoody Brownson: 1439, 2612, 3179, 4573
DEBOW, Martha E. (Johns): 1439
DEBOW'S REVIEW: 1439
DE BRAHM, William Gerard: 1440
DEBRETIGNEY, Mr._____: 1389
DEBRIE, Jean: 4348
DE BRUYN, Mr._____: 516
DEBT:
  Imprisonment for:
    Great Britain: 4605
    Maryland: 3742
  Non-payment of:
    North Carolina: 2354
  Settlement of:
    South Carolina: 1012
    Virginia:
      Columbia: 5035

DEBT:
  Settlement of:
    South Carolina:
    Virginia (Continued):
      Pittsylvania County: 5587
    West Virginia--Martinsburg: 5037
  Subdivided by place:
    Arkansas: 1089
    Georgia: 2594, 3134, 5604
    Great Britain: 2226
    Kentucky: 1086, 1654
    Mississippi: 3415
    New York: 782, 1190
    North Carolina: 832, 1120, 1190, 1491, 2003, 4773, 5752
      Halifax County: 5672
      Montgomery County: 4689
      Moore County: 5792
      Nash County: 5475
    Pennsylvania: 213, 2594
    South Carolina: 1877
      Abbeville: 3319
    Spain--Castile: 4980
    Virginia: 974, 1384, 4247, 5848
      Alexandria: 947
      Culpeper: 4852
      Hanover County: 1824
      Richmond: 5790
      Sweet Briar: 5765
    Washington, D. C.: 1937
DEBT, National: see PUBLIC DEBT under names of countries
DEBT, Personal: see PERSONAL DEBT
DEBT, Public: see PUBLIC DEBT under names of countries
DEBT, State: see State debt under names of states
DEBT COLLECTION: 125
  Difficulty of, during the Civil War: 5623
  Lawsuits: 5730
  Subdivided by place:
    Alabama: 4419
    Connecticut: 3041
    Georgia: 5537
      Augusta: 3672
    Great Britain: 516
    Louisiana: 379
    Maryland: 4376, 5296
      Baltimore: 4348
    Mississippi: 2487
    New York: 2172
    North Carolina: 2553, 3043, 4858
    Pennsylvania: 228, 421, 496, 870, 1117, 1805
      Londonderry: 2615
    South Carolina: 5930
      Charleston: 5548
      Chester District: 1268
    Virginia: 117, 330, 574, 604, 3179, 4381, 4616, 5613
      Bedford County: 3621
      Columbia: 5035
      Petersburg: 3593
      Suffolk: 3012
    West Virginia: 1709
DE BUNSEN, Sir Maurice William Ernest, First Baronet: 4709
DE BURGH, Ulrick John, First Marquis of Clanricarde: 472
DE CAMP, J.: 369
DE CARRO, Jean: 908
DECATUR, Stephen: 4348
DECATUR, Alabama: 4994
DECATUR, Georgia: 1397, 2353, 5082
  Civil War: 731
  Orphanages: 2786
  Teaching: 2786
DECATUR, Illinois: 1346
DE CAUX, Len.: 1202
DE CHASTELLUX, François Jean: 4625
DECORATION DAY: see MEMORIAL DAY
DE CRÉQUI FAMILY (France--Genealogy): 1424
DEDHAM, Massachusetts: 105
DEDICATORY EPISTLE by Algernon C. Swinburne: 5158
DEEDS: see LAND DEEDS AND INDENTURES

DEEMS, Charles Manning Force: 1441, 2399, 2449, 3176, 5457
DEEP CREEK, North Carolina: 2727
DEEP CREEK, Virginia: 4866
DEEP RIVER, North Carolina: 1870
  Agricultural organizations: 5632
  Personal finance: 5632
DEEP RIVER (N. C.) AGRICULTURAL CLUB: 5632
DEEP RIVER (N. C.) COUNCIL OF THE UNION LEAGUE: 5632
DEEP WELL, North Carolina: 4007
DEER SKINS TRADE--Virginia: 625
DEERFIELD, Massachusetts: 333
DEFALCATION: see EMBEZZLEMENT
DEFECTIVE VISION: 72
  see also BLIND
DEFENSE: see also CIVIL WAR--COAST DEFENSES; RAILROADS IN NATIONAL DEFENSE STRATEGY; WATER TRANSPORTATION IN NATIONAL DEFENSE STRATEGY
  Canada: 1599
  Confederate States of America: 4921
  Georgia: 1993, 3968, 5473
    Richmond County: 2666
    Savannah: 2722
  Great Britain: 233, 1598
  Hong Kong: 5637
  Ireland: 3315
  Jamaica: 1792
  North Carolina--Leaksville: 3622
  Scotland: 1598
  South Carolina:
    Charleston: 5513
    Cunningham's Bluff: 4620
  United States:
    1800s: 1599, 3145
    1900s: 274, 4556, 5878
  Virginia: 2893
    Richmond: 4616
  Washington, D. C.: 3264
  World War I: 3451
A DEFENSE OF THE REVOLUTIONARY HISTORY OF THE STATE OF NORTH CAROLINA by Joseph Seawell Jones: 3176
DEFENSE PLANTS--North Carolina: 2581
DEFIANCE, Ohio: 920, 2591
  Business affairs: 4793
DEFIANCE COUNTY, Ohio:
  Defiance: 920, 2591
  Business affairs: 4793
DE FUNIAK SPRINGS, Florida: 1832
DE GARMENDIA, C. M.: 1442
DE GARMENDIA, Carlos G.: 1442
DE Gaulle, Charles-Andre-Marie-Joseph: 1424
DE GEOFROY, Antoine: 4478
DE GEOFROY, George: 4478
DE GEOFROY, Katherine Shedden (Riggs): 4478
DEGRAFFENRIED, Christopher: 5457
DE GRANUELA, Cardinal: 4178
DE HASS, Wills: 1227
DEHUFF, Henry: 1443
DEHUFF, Margaret: 1443
DEISM: see also CHRISTIANITY; FREE THOUGHT
  North Carolina: 3176
DE KALB COUNTY, Georgia: 1011, 5180
  Civil War: 5724
  Decatur: 1397, 2353, 5082
    Civil War: 731
    Orphanages: 2786
    Teaching: 2786
  Stone Mountain: 807, 5090, 5110, 5819
DELACROIX, Charles: 4348
DELAMAR, F. C.: 1444
DE LA MARE, Walter John: 364, 4632
DELAMERE HOUSE, England: 5729
DELAND, Florida: 1653, 4365
DELANE, John Thadeus: 1445, 2471
DE LANO, Fred: 1446
DE LANO, Horace Franklin: 1446
DE LANO, Martin: 1446
DELAP, Louesia: 4577

DELAP, Valentine: 4577
DELAPHANE, Patrick H.: 1447
DE LA RAMÉE, Louisa: 2146
DE LARCOHEAULION, S. C.: 1448
DELAWARE:
  Canals--Construction: 5686
  Coffee trade: 4881
  Copperheads: 4881
  Cotton trade: 4881
  Currency: 1339
  Gas lighting in Wilmington: 4881
  Lotteries: 3783, 4892, 4921, 5306
  Railroads: 3235
  Social life and customs:
    Wilmington: 3229
DELAWARE, U.S.S.: 5436
DELAWARE AND RARITAN CANAL: 730
DELAWARE BAY, Delaware:
  Civil War: 5419
DELAWARE BRANDYWINE PAPER MILLS: 2265
DELAWARE COUNTY, Indiana--Muncie: 1795
DELAWARE COUNTY, Pennsylvania: 2552
  Linwood: 4881
DE LEON, Edwin: 1910
DE LEON, Francisco: 3118
DE LEON, Thomas Cooper: 1449
DELÉRY, Edgar: 1450
DELÉRY, François Charles: 1450
DE LETTRE, M. N.: 1451
DE LETTRE, Ulric Albert: 1451
DELHI, India:
  British embassy: 4137
DE LITTA, Countess: 4625
DELKER, Henry G.: 3848
DELMAN'S SCHOOL HOUSE, Collins Township, South Carolina: 501
DE LONG, William M.: 1452
DEL SENTIMIENTO TRAGICA DE LA VIDA by Miguel de Unamuno y Jugo: 5404
DELTA BETA PHI (fraternity): 3485
DEMAGOGUES--Southern States: 872
DEMBY, J. William: 1453
DEMERARA, British Guiana:
  Social life and customs: 2612
DEMERÉ, Mary E.: 2327
DEMERE, Raymond: 1454
DEMING, Elizabeth Jane: 1455
DEMMON, E. L.: 1852
DEMOCRACY: 5853
  see also HISTORICAL STUDIES--Democracy
DEMOCRAT (newspaper, Alabama): 5937
DEMOCRATIC PARTY:
  see also REPUBLICAN (Jeffersonian) PARTY
  1800-1860: 519, 1403, 1568, 2587, 2860, 3054, 3325, 4022, 4615, 5051, 5470, 5499
  1861-1865: 519, 3778, 4615, 4881, 5402, 5499
  1866-1899: 1083, 1424, 1805, 2794, 4874, 5357, 5499
  1900s: 274, 521, 646, 1805, 2496, 4805, 4858, 4874
  Campaign issues: 5978
  Campaign literature: 4251
  Catholic influence in congressional elections of 1894: 3840
  Conventions (National):
    1844: 4732
    1848: 4615
    1852: 5298
    1860: 1084
      Baltimore, Maryland: 1544, 2860
      Charleston, South Carolina: 988, 1544, 2589, 2860, 3501
    1864: 1084
    1912: 690, 3955
    1924: 2299, 3086
    1928: 2299, 3086
    1932: 3086
    1936: 3086
    1940: 3086

DEMOCRATIC PARTY (Continued):
  Conventions (State):
    North Carolina:
      1868: 3440
      1906: 5072
      1940: 2863
  National Committee: 1198
  Patronage, Political: see POLITICAL PATRONAGE
  Platform:
    1848: 5491
    1942: 2655
  Presidential candidates: see PRESIDENTS--Nominations
  Reform: 5762
  Support for Andrew Jackson: 519
  Views of Lincoln's administration: 713
  Subdivided by place:
    Alabama: 1084
    Arkansas: 988
    Connecticut: 2684
    Florida: 988
    Georgia: 1121, 4921, 5051
    Illinois: 1400, 5160
    Kentucky: 398
    Louisiana: 988
    Maine: 5610
    Maryland: 3086, 5059
    Massachusetts: 988
    Mississippi: 988
    New York: 4343
    North Carolina:
      1800s: 1015, 1100, 1659, 5149, 5667
      1900s: 274, 4805, 4825, 4828, 4918
      Campaign literature: 4018, 4251
      Liberals (1930s): 3538
      Local politics:
        Beaufort: 4858
        Wilmington: 1313
      Union sympathizers: 4834
    Pennsylvania: 3501, 4188
    South Carolina: 988, 2300, 4725, 5759
      Campaigns of 1880 and 1892: 1480
    Southern States: 1972
    Tennessee: 4291
    Texas: 988, 5141
    Virginia:
      1800s: 1501, 5513, 5696
      1900s: 3820, 4020
      Campaign literature: 3806
      Nomination to the House of Representatives: 1161
    West Virginia: 1828
      Berkeley County: 4732
      Martinsburg: 3832
DEMOCRATIC PRESS: 5036
DEMOGRAPHIC STUDIES:
  Great Britain: 2148
DEMONSTRATIONS:
  see also RIOTS
  Anti-American in Mexico: 1412
  North Carolina:
    Durham: 2398
    Greensboro: 2050
DEMOPOLIS, Alabama:
  Civil War: 1181
  Medical practice: 1856
DEMORGAN, Augustus: 1087, 2457
DEMUTH, Annie: 4423
DENBIGH, England: 5026
DENG, Cora: 5252
DENHAM, Adaline: 4068
DENHAM, Andrew: 4068
DENHAM, Edward (1849-1925): 2449
DENHAM, Mary: 4068
DENISON, Henrietta Elizabeth Sophia: 2801
DENISON, Minerva: 4537
DENISON, Stephen C.: 4520
DENISON, William Joseph: 1456
DENMAN, Helen Mary (McMicking): 4331
DENMAN, Thomas, First Baron Denman: 1457

DENMAN, Thomas, Second Baron Denman: 1457
DENMARK, Brantley A.: 1458, 1614
DENMARK:
  Description and travel: 306, 3451
  Farming: 3451
  Foreign relations:
    Sweden: 1302
    United States: 1302
  Sermons: 2228
DENNETT, W. L.: 5044
DENNEY, Samuel B.: 1459
DENNIS, J. M.: 2376
DENNIS, John E.: 1460
DENNIS, W. H.: 1460
DENNIS SIMMONS LUMBER COMPANY: 4824
DENNISTON, Virginia: 2712
DENNY, Collins: 879
DENNY, James: 2342
DENT, Julia: 157
DENT, Peter: 5353
DENT AND CO.: see PALMER, MACKILLOP, DENT & CO.
DENTISTRY:
  Fees--Tennessee: 6
  North Carolina: 3410
  Supplies and prices: 4538
DENTISTS:
  New York--Accounts: 4538
  North Carolina: 417
DENTON, J. C.: 318
DENTON, Maryland: 1329
DENVER AND RIO GRANDE WESTERN RAILROAD COMPANY: 3985
DENVER (N. C.) SEMINARY: 2493
DE PALMA, J.: 1461
THE DEPARTMENT STORE ORGANIZER: 1195
DEPARTMENT STORE WORKERS: see RETAIL, WHOLESALE, AND DEPARTMENT STORE UNION
DEPARTMENT STORES:
  North Carolina: 3762
DEPAUW, Washington Charles: 5031
DEPENDENTS:
  see also CHILDREN; PARENTS; WIDOWS; WIVES
  North Carolina: 2188
DE PEW, Chauncy Mitchell: 3265
DE PEW, Tunis: 1462
DE PONTE, Roza Solomon: 1463
DEPREDATIONS: see as subheading under names of armies and wars
DEPRESSION (1929--France): 1424
DEPRESSION (1929--United States): 1424, 2109, 4343, 4453, 4564, 4858, 5252, 5786
  Effect on coal industry: 4865
  Emergency programs: 274
    North Carolina: 274, 3955
  Unemployment relief: 274
    North Carolina: 274
  Subdivided by place:
    Florida: 1653
    North Carolina: 5298
      New Bern: 3955
    South Carolina: 300
DEPRESSIONS:
  see also PANIC OF (date)
  Alabama--Agriculture: 5126
  Georgia: 1203
  Great Britain: 5282, 5731
  United States: 4858
DE QUINCEY, Thomas: 1465
DERBY, Edward George Geoffrey Smith Stanley, Fourteenth Earl of: 3472, 5025
DERBY, Edward Henry Stanley, Fifteenth Earl of: 2149, 2471, 3183, 3472, 4995
DERBY, Ethel Carow (Roosevelt): 4560
DERBY, Frederick Arthur Stanley, Sixteenth Earl of: 4520
"DERBY DAY AT CLAPHAM COMMON" by Robert J. Rombauer: 4552
DERBYSHIRE, England:
  Buxton: 250
  Edgemoor: 4995

DE RENNE, George Wymberley Jones: 1466
DE RENNE LIBRARY, Wormslor, Georgia: 3898
DE ROHAN, Duchess of: see ROHAN-CHABOT DE MURAT, Herminie (de la Brousse de Verteillac), Onzième Duchesse
DE ROHAN, Duke of: see ROHAN-CHABOT DE MURAT, Alain Charles Louis, Onzième Duc
DE ROSSET, Armand John (b. 1807): 1467
DEROSSET, Catherine Fullerton: 1467
DEROSSET, Elizabeth Simpson Nash: 1467
DEROSSET, Louis Henry: 1899
DEROSSET, William Lord: 1467, 5457
DEROSSETT, Moses John (1726-1767): 5457
DE ROSSIT & BROWN (firm): 2940
DE RUSSEY, Rene Edward: 2132
DERUYTER, New York: 104
DE SAUSSURE, D. Blanding: 5114
DE SAUSSURE, Daniel (1735-1798): 1889
DE SAUSSURE, Henry Alexander: 1468
DE SAUSSURE, Henry William: 1468, 1889
DE SAUSSURE, John M.: 817, 1468
DE SAUSSURE, Mary (1772-1853): 1891
DE SAUSSURE, W. H.: 3676
DE SAUSSURE, William F.: 4145
DE SAUSSURE, Wilmot Gibbes: 1468
DE SAUSSURE FAMILY:
  South Carolina: 1424
  Genealogy: 1468, 1889
DE SAUSSURE, SMITH, AND DARRELL: see SMITH, DE SAUSSURE AND DARRELL
DE SCHWEINITZ, Robert William: 1468
DESCOLLES, Arnaud: 2058
DESCRIPTION: see TRAVEL; Description as a subheading under names of cities; Description and travel as a subheading under names of countries and states
DESEGREGATION:
  see also SCHOOLS--Desegregation
  North Carolina: 4724
  United States: 3048, 4386
DESERTION: see Desertion as subheading under names of armies, navies, and wars; Absenteeism as a subheading under names of armies, navies, and wars
DESHA, Joseph: 1470
DESHA COUNTY, Arkansas:
  Napoleon--Debt: 1089
DESLONDE, Caroline: 805
DE SMET, Pierre-Jean: 1471
DES MOINES, Iowa: 3993
  Social life and customs: 3338
DES MOINES COLLEGE, West Point, Iowa: 2948
DES MOINES COUNTY, Iowa:
  Burlington: 4431, 5561
DE SOTO COUNTY, Mississippi:
  Cockrum: 3155
  Hernando: 234
  see also MISSISSIPPI FEMALE COLLEGE
D'ESTAING, Count: see ESTAING, Charles Hector, Comte d'
DESTINY IN DALLAS by Shirley Seifert: 1137
DESTITUTION: see POVERTY
DESTRUCTION OF PROPERTY: see CIVIL WAR--SABOTAGE BY NEGROES; SABOTAGE; Depredations as a subheading under names of armies and navies
DETROIT, Michigan: 259, 932
  Description: 1591, 2690
DEVAWONGSE, Prince (Thailand): 4709
DEVEAUX, Marion S.: 1472
DEVEAUX, Peter: 3704
DEVEAUX, Robert Marion: 1472
DEVEAUX, T. L.: 791
DEVEAUX, V. M.: 1472

DEVEAUX FAMILY (South Carolina): 1472
DE VERE, Aubrey Thomas: 1473
DE VERE, M. Schele: 1227, 2612
DEVEREUX, Annie Lane: 1475
DEVEREUX, Ellen: 2553
DEVEREUX, Frances: 4253
DEVEREUX, George H.: 1474
DEVEREUX, John: 1475
DEVEREUX, Margaret: 1475
DEVEREUX, Margaret Mordecai: 1475
DEVEREUX, Mary Bayard (1827-1886): 5457
DEVEREUX, Sarah Elizabeth: 1475
DEVEREUX, Thomas Pollock: 1475
DEVEREUX FAMILY:
  North Carolina: 1475
  Genealogy: 2553
DE VINGUT, Gertrude: 103
DE VIOMÉNIL, Antoine Charles du Houx, Baron: 1582
DEVONSHIRE, Elizabeth (Hervey) Foster Cavendish, Duchess of: 945
DEVONSHIRE, Georgiana (Spencer) Cavendish, Duchess of: 945
DEVONSHIRE, Spencer Compton Cavendish, Eighth Duke of: 294, 944, 1815, 2149, 2962
DEVONSHIRE, William Cavendish, Fifth Duke of: 945
DEVONSHIRE, William Cavendish, Seventh Duke of: 2149
DEVONSHIRE, William George Spencer, Sixth Duke of: 4605
DEVONSHIRE, England:
  Bideford: 570
  Cullompton: 2127
  Dawlish: 2126
    Literary affairs: 2580
  Exeter: see EXETER, England
  Larkbear: 598
  Lyneham Park: 1147
  Tavistock: 2254
  Thorverton: 1158
  Tormoham: 4229
DE VOTIE, Elizabeth Annie: 1476
DE VOTIE, Howard Jefferson: 1476
DE VOTIE, James H.: 1476
DE VOTIE, Jefferson Howard: 1476
DE VOTIE, Jewett Gindrat: 1476
DEVYVER, Frant Traver: 1195
DEW, Thomas Roderick: 2612, 5361
DEWLEY, Charles: 3948
DEWEY, John (1859-1952): 720
DEWITT, Julian F.: 1477
DEWITT FAMILY (New York): 1477
DE WITT, Arkansas: 5753
DEWITT C. FOWLER AND BROTHER (firm): 1871
DE WORMS, Henry, First Baron Pirbright: 3036
DHARMAPALA, H.: 217
DIAL, Nathaniel Barksdale: 1478, 3451, 5930
DIALECTS: see ENGLISH LANGUAGE IN THE UNITED STATES--Dialects; names of specific dialects; and Dialects as subheading under names of specific languages
DIALOGUES ON UNIVERSAL SALVATION by David Thom: 5244
DIAMOND, David Leo (b. 1915): 902
DIAMOND COTTON CHOPPER AND CULTIVATOR COMPANY, Fayetteville, North Carolina: 2553
DIAMOND JUBILEE OF QUEEN VICTORIA: 2836
DIAMOND MINES--Brazil: 2750
DIANA (barque): 2733
DIANA MILLS, Virginia: 2370
  Tobacco culture: 2373
"DIARY OF SECRET SERVICE" by David Dixon Porter: 4275
DIBBLE, Orange J.: 1479
DIBBLE, Samuel: 1424, 1480
DICK (JAMES) AND STEWART COMPANY: 1481
DICK, Robert Paine: 1482, 3763

DICK AND DILLARD LAW SCHOOL, Greensboro, North Carolina: 5124
DICKENS, Asbury: 1484
DICKENS, Charles: 2449, 3684, 4968, 5044
DICKENS, Hider D.: 1483
DICKENSON, George W.: 1485
DICKENSON, John: 1486
DICKENSON, Mahlon: 548
DICKERSONVILLE, New York: 1246
DICKEY, John: 1487, 3288
DICKINSON, Anna Elizabeth: 1487
DICKINSON, Edward B.: 1424
DICKINSON, Frances Minto: 472
DICKINSON, J.: 4399
DICKINSON, J. M.: 4723
DICKINSON, Joseph: 1489, 1490
DICKINSON, Julia Maria: 3455
DICKINSON, Matthew: 1491
DICKINSON, Peard: 4146
DICKINSON, Samuel: 1492
DICKINSON, Thomas: 1492
DICKINSON, Washington: 1490
DICKINSON, THOMPSON v.: see THOMPSON v. DICKINSON
DICKINSON AND HALL (firm): 1489
DICKINSON COLLEGE, Carlisle, Pennsylvania: 742, 3174, 3532
  Political activity among students: 3532
DICKSON, Jeannie A.: 1494
DICKSON, Joseph: 1495
DICKSON, Samuel Henry: 1494
DICKSON FAMILY (North Carolina): 1313
DICTIONARIES: 3775
  see also Dictionaries as subheading under names of specific languages, e.g. ENGLISH LANGUAGE--Dictionaries
DICTIONARY OF NATIONAL BIOGRAPHY: 5050
DICTIONARY OF THE UNITED STATES CONGRESS by Charles Lanman: 3094
DICTIONNAIRE DE SOCIOLOGIE PHALANSTÉRIENNE: GUIDE DES OEUVRES COMPLÈTES DE CHARLES FOURIER by Édouard Silberling: 65
DIDIER, Eugene Lemoine: 2449
DIES, Adolph: 1186
DIET: 1424
  Virginia--Goshen: 5613
DIETRICK, A.: 4188
DIGBY, Nova Scotia: 176
DIGBY COUNTY, Nova Scotia:
  Digby: 176
DIGGES, Anthony: 1496
DIGGES, Sir Dudley: 2152
DIGGES, William: 5575
DIGGES FAMILY: 581
DIGGINS, Elisa: 5042
DIKES: see MISSISSIPPI RIVER--Levees
DILD, Henry: 1497
DILGER, Hubert: 1498
DILKE, Sir Charles Wentworth, Second Baronet: 1499, 5164
DILLARD, James F.: 1500
DILLARD, John Henry: 5457
DILLARD, John James: 1501
DILLARD FAMILY (Virginia): 1501
DILLARD LAW SCHOOL: see DICK AND DILLARD LAW SCHOOL
DILLAWAY, Charles Knapp: 1502
DILLON, Lord    : 4770
DILLON, Frank: 1503
DILLON, Josephine: 1503
DILLON, Sir William Henry: 1504
DILTZ, Joseph Sherman: 1505
DILTZ, Mary (Milledge): 1505
DILTZ, Thomas: 1505
DIMITRY, Adelaide (Stuart): 1506
DIMITRY, Alexander: 1506, 3322
DIMITRY, John Bull Smith: 1506, 1982
DIMMOCK, Samuel E.: 2027
DIMON, Charles Augustus Ropes: 1507
DIMSDALE, Thomas, First Baron Dimsdale: 1508
DINGES, George H.: 1509
DINGES, Isaac R.: 2942

DINGES, Jacob: 2942
DINING CLUBS--Great Britain: 2759
DININNY, Ferral C., Jr.: 2922
DINNERS AND DINING:
    see also MENUS
    Virginia: 818
DINSMORE, Edgar: 1510
DINWIDDIE, James: 3762, 5457
DINWIDDIE, Robert: 1511
DINWIDDIE COUNTY, Virginia: 7, 4715
    Crops: 551
    Law practice: 2376
    Oldenplace: 3400
    Petersburg: see PETERSBURG,
        Virginia
DIPHTHERIA: see DISEASES--Diphtheria
DIPLOMACY: see Foreign relations as
    a subheading under names of
    countries
DIPLOMATIC PROTOCOL: 4348
DIPLOMATIC SERVICE: see Diplomatic
    and consular service as subheading
    under names of countries; GREAT
    BRITAIN--GOVERNMENT AGENCIES AND
    OFFICIALS--Foreign office; UNITED
    STATES--GOVERNMENT AGENCIES AND
    OFFICIALS--Department of State;
    Foreign agents as subheading under
    names of countries
DISARMAMENT: see WASHINGTON
    DISARMAMENT CONFERENCE
DISASTER RELIEF: see AMERICAN RED
    CROSS; FAMINE RELIEF; FLOOD RELIEF
DISASTERS: see EARTHQUAKES; FAMINE;
    FIRES; FLOODS; HURRICANES; LAND-
    SLIDES; TORNADOES; VOLCANIC ERUPTIONS
DISCHARGES (Military): see Discharges
    as subheading under names of
    armies and navies
DISCIPLES OF CHRIST: 3199, 5043
    Church history:
        North Carolina: 5554
    Subdivided by place:
        Alabama: 4720
        Kentucky: 4506, 4720
        North Carolina: 1523
DISCIPLINE: see as subheading under
    names of armies and navies; and as
    subheading under churches and
    denominations
"DISCORSI DE N. MACHIAVEGLI": 3385
DISCOUNT STORES:
    see also RETAIL TRADE
    New England: 3866
DISCOVRS MERVEILLEVX DE LA VIE,
ACTIONS & DÉPORTEMENS DE CATHERINE
DE MEDICIS . . . : 1721
DISCOVERIES (Geography):
    see also EXPLORATION
    Map of Arctic Region: 5783
DISCRIMINATION: 4386
    see also SEGREGATION
DISEASES:
    see also CATTLE--Diseases;
        CHILDREN--Diseases; HEART--
        Diseases; MERCHANT SEAMEN--
        Diseases; SLAVES--Diseases; and
        Diseases as subheading under
        names of armies, navies, and wars
    Treatment: see HOME REMEDIES;
        MEDICAL TREATMENT
    Subdivided by type of disease:
        Arthritis--Treatment: 5380
        Cholera: 230
            Great Britain:
                Romsey: 5222
            Louisiana: 330
                New Orleans: 4038, 4732
            Maryland:
                Baltimore: 5613
            Mauritania: 3485
            Missouri: 3255
            Ohio: 3255, 5342
            Pennsylvania: 616, 4881
                Philadelphia: 849, 3485, 5613
            South Carolina: 3278
                Charleston: 5193
            Tennessee: 330, 2080, 2661
                Nashville: 4854, 5290, 5623

DISEASES:
    Subdivided by type of disease:
        Cholera (Continued):
            Texas--Houston: 4562
            United States: 496, 3053
            Virginia: 1283
                Norfolk: 5751
                Richmond: 5114
                Suffolk: 3012
        Consumption:
            see also DISEASES--Tuberculosis
            Connecticut: 4815
        Diphtheria:
            Georgia: 1203
            Virginia: 3809
        Influenza:
            Effect on coal industry: 4865
            Kansas: 5792
            North Carolina:
                Chapel Hill: 3878
                Greensboro: 3843
            United States: 5930
        Malaria: 4068
            Control--Georgia: 365
            South Carolina: 1371
        Measles: 1731
            South Carolina: 1793
        Meningitis:
            Alabama--Rodney: 4589
            Missouri--Saint Louis: 5731
        Ophthalmia:
            Treatment in Great Britain:
                2836
        Plague:
            Baghdad: 5797
            Preventive inoculation in
                India: 278
        Pneumonia:
            Treatment: 5329
        Rheumatism:
            Home remedies--Virginia: 2633
            Treatment: 3908
        Scarlet fever: 2980
            South Carolina: 3278
            Southern States: 5349
            United States: 2225
            Washington, D. C.: 3635
        Smallpox: 5529
            Preventive inoculation: 687,
                2296, 3004, 3853
            see also CIVIL WAR--CIVILIAN
                LIVE--Scarcity of smallpox
                vaccine
            Ceylon: 908
            Georgia: 365
            India: 5797
            Vermont: 2896
        Subdivided by place:
            Alabama--Bridgeville: 5907
            Brazil--Campos: 1644
            Canada--Vancouver: 4175
            Georgia: 1203
            Louisiana: 368
            North Carolina: 608
                Chatham County: 770
                Dutchville: 1826
                Fayetteville: 4517
                Hillsborough: 5390
            Pennsylvania:
                Philadelphia: 5731
                Pittsburgh: 2678
            South Carolina: 2961, 3390
            United States: 2591
            Vermont: 2896
            Virginia: 3853
                Lexington: 5613
                Lynchburg: 5513
                Manchester: 3792
                Nelson County: 682
            West Virginia:
                Wheeling: 2678
        Tuberculosis: 5722
            see also DISEASES--Consumption
            Treatment and prevention:
                4606
            Virginia: 693
            Virginia: 33

DISEASES:
    Subdivided by type of disease:
        Typhoid fever: 72
            Alabama: 1188
            Mississippi:
                Holly Springs: 82
            New York--New York: 5731
            Texas: 5613
            Virginia: 3809
                Nelson County: 682
                Norfolk: 2857
        Typhus--Georgia: 1203
        Yellow fever:
            Alabama: 1933
                Montgomery: 3290
            Florida: 4410
            Georgia: 1203, 5298
                Savannah: 3323
            Louisiana: 266, 489
                New Orleans: 3041, 4202
            Maryland: 3399
            Mississippi: 3759
                Natchez: 1762, 4246
            New York--New York: 5362
            North Carolina: 3563, 4561
                Wilmington: 3447
            Panama: 3004
            Pennsylvania:
                Philadelphia: 2776, 5362
            South Carolina: 2094, 2695,
                3671
                Charleston: 3907, 4584, 5193,
                    5362
            Tennessee: 2080
                Chattanooga: 4202
                Memphis: 4202
            Texas--Houston: 4562
            United States: 3053
            Virginia: 330
                Nelson County: 682
                Norfolk: 3301, 4968
                Portsmouth: 3301
    Subdivided by place:
        France: 1424
        Georgia: 2460
            Clopton's Mills: 5760
        Great Britain: 1057, 2058
            see also CONTAGIOUS DISEASES
                ACT OF 1869
        Middle West: 1820
        Mississippi--Natchez: 980
        North Carolina: 329, 4930, 5741
            Stokes County: 2800
        Ohio--North Hampton: 1618
        South Carolina: 669, 1220, 4584
        Texas: 2920
        Virginia--Sperryville: 1618
DISENFRANCHISEMENT OF NEGROES: see
    NEGROES--Suffrage--
    Disenfranchisement
DISMAL SWAMP CANAL COMPANY: 4858
DISMAL SWAMP LAND COMPANY: 1512, 5573
DISMUKES, Frances Amanda: 5760
DISMUKES, R. T.: 1513
DISMUKES FAMILY (Georgia):
    5760
DISRAELI, Benjamin, First Earl of
    Beaconsfield: 2148, 3236, 3722
    Portrait: 345
DISSENTERS: see DISSENTING CHURCHES
DISSENTING CHURCHES:
    see also POLITICAL DISABILITIES
    Great Britain: 1875, 2149, 3226,
        4913
    Ireland--County Antrim: 718
DISSERTATIONS IN AMERICAN
    LITERATURE, 1891-1955 and
    supplement 1956-1961: 5889
DISTANCES--Tables, etc.: 3753
DISTILLERY WORKERS: see LABOR
    UNIONS--Distillery workers
DISTILLING INDUSTRIES: see LIQUOR
    MANUFACTURING
DISTINGUISHED FLYING CROSS: 5417
DISTRICT COURTS: see COURTS--
    District Courts
DISTRICT OF COLUMBIA: see
    WASHINGTON, D. C.

DISUNION: 5051
    see also NULLIFICATION; SECESSION;
    WAR OF 1812--New England
      disaffection
    Virginia: 2776
"DIVERSAS MATERIAS": 3650
DIVIDENDS:
    Corporation:
      United States: 4918
      Virginia--Falmouth: 2165
DIVINA COMMEDIA by Dante Alighieri:
    425, 5255
DIVINITY SCHOOLS:
    see also THEOLOGICAL SEMINARIES
    North Carolina:
      Duke University Divinity School:
        1589, 2075, 5022
DIVORCE: 5968
    see also MARITAL SEPARATION
    France: 1424
    North Carolina: 2906, 3960
    United States: 1424
DIVORCÉES: see WOMEN--Personal
    finance--Divorcées
DIX, Dorothea Lynde: 1514, 2311
DIX, John Adams: 212, 323, 1515,
    3277
DIX, John Ross: 103
DIX, Morgan: 1516
DIX, Roger Sherman: 1515
DIXIE FIRE INSURANCE COMPANY,
    North Carolina: 4918
DIXIECRATS--North Carolina: 3538
DIXON, Colonel _____ (American
    Revolution): 3361
DIXON, Archibald: 1484
DIXON, Columbus H.: 1517
DIXON, Evelyn Milus: 1518
DIXON, George: 1087
DIXON, Henry Clay: 3177
DIXON, Henry Turner: 1519
DIXON, James (1788-1871): 4146
DIXON, Madelyn (Donovan): 1521
DIXON, Mumford H.: 1520
DIXON, Thomas (1864-1946): 1521,
    5145
DIXON, William Hepworth: 5081
DIXON, William Macneile: 1522
DIXON, Winsor: 1523
DIXON, Illinois--Railroads: 3732
DIXON AND BURLING (firm): see
    BURLING AND DIXON
DOAR, S. D.: 1523
DOBBIN, James Cochran: 1525, 1848,
    3118, 3833
DOBBIN, John Moore: 1525
DOBBINS, Celina: 4477
DOBBINS, Hugh: 5046
DOBBINS FAMILY (Ohio and Missouri):
    4477
DOBBS COUNTY, North Carolina: 1523
    Courts: 934
DOBSON, Henry Austin: 1526
DOCKERY, Oliver Hart: 1527
DOCKS AND TERMINALS--Stocks: 5080
DOCKYARD COMPANIES:
    see also NAVY YARDS
    Virginia:
      Portsmouth: 4281
      Richmond: 4465
"DOCTOR ROBERT BRAGGE AND HIS LADY,
    THEIR JOURNEY TO BATH, PERFORM'D
    IN THE YEAR 1770": 626
DR. SEIDEL'S ACADEMY, Bethlehem,
    Pennsylvania: 2828
DOCTOR TOWN, Georgia: 1990
DOCTRINE: see THEOLOGY; and Doctrine
    as subheading under names of
    Christian denominations
DOCUMENTOS HISTÓRICOS, col. by
    Manuel de Odriozola: 4155
DODD, Harry R.: 4485
DODD, William Edward: 1528
DODDRIDGE COUNTY, Virginia:
    Greenwood: 5286
DODGE, Allen W.: 4266
DODGE, David: 1529
DODGE, Grenville Mellen: 4157

DODGE, Mary B.: 2449
DODGE, Mary Elizabeth (Mapes): 1530,
    2449
DODGE, Nathan P.: 523
DODGE, Ossian Euclid: 1029
DODGE AND STEVENSON MANUFACTURING
    COMPANY: 388
DODLINGTON, George Bubb, Baron
    Melcombe: 2155
DODSON, James: 1531
DOGAN, Sarah Ann Rice: 1532
DOGGEREL: 3093
    see also HUMOROUS POETRY
    Confederate Army: 1271
DOGS: 43
    see also specific breeds
    Georgia: 3894
DOHERTY, Hughes: 65
DOLL, Sister Mary Bernard: 3899
DOLLIVER, Jonathan Prentiss: 1533
DOMESTIC ARCHITECTURE: 3674
    see also INTERIOR DECORATION
    China: 2191
    Great Britain: 945
    Maryland: 4537
    Wales: 286
    Washington, D.C.: 4020
DOMESTICS: see SERVANTS
DOMINICAN REPUBLIC: 1574
    Efforts of the United States to
      acquire: 3516
    Missions and missionaries: 3633
    Sugar trade: 197
DON CARLOS: see CARLOS III, King of
    Spain
DONALD, William Henry: 5252
DONALDSON, Thomas Quint: 4145
DONALDSONVILLE, Louisiana: 2859
    Civil War:
      Battle: see CIVIL WAR--CAMPAIGNS,
        BATTLES, AND MILITARY ACTIONS--
        Louisiana--Donaldsonville
      Maps of Fort Butler: 5417
"DONATIVO DE LA REAL UNIVERSIDAD,
    OCTUBRE 27, 1704": 3650
DONEGAL, Ireland:
    Ballyshannon: 868
DONELSON, Israel: 1177
DONKIN, Sir Rufane Shaw: 5026
DONNE, William Bodham: 1534
DONNELL, John Robert: 730
DONNELL, Mary: 730
DONNELL, Richard Spaight: 5460
DONNELL, Robert: 5457
DONNELL FAMILY (North Carolina): 730
DONNELLY, Ignatius: 3524
DONNELSON, Captain _____: 3729
DONNELSVILLE, Ohio: 2504
DONOUGHMORE, John Hely-Hutchinson,
    Second Earl of: 2836
DONOVAN, Madelyn: 1521
DOOR MAKING: see MILLWORK INDUSTRY
DORAN, John G.: 5939
DORCHESTER, Massachusetts: 1766,
    1973
    Civil War: 3342
DORCHESTER COUNTY, South Carolina:
    Ravenel: 501
    Saint George: 2997
DORKING, England: 3630
DORMITORIES: see STUDENT HOUSING;
    and Student housing as subheading
    under names of specific
    universities and colleges
DORR, Julia Caroline (Ripley): 10,
    2449, 4485
D'ORSAY, Charles: 1911
DORSETSHIRE, England:
    Folklore: 5403
    Literary affairs: 2334
    Politics and government: 2149
    Shaston St. Peter: 3245
DORSETSHIRE FOLK-LORE by John Symonds
    Udal: 5403
DORSEY, Clement: 1535
DORTCH, Emeline: 714
DORTCH, Helen: 3262
DORTCH, William T.: 5457

DOSH, Mary C.: 287
DOSH FAMILY: 287
DOSS, Matthew A.: 2808
DOSS, Sally: 2808
DOSS, William: 2808
DOSTER (LEWIS) AND SONS: 1536
DOTEN, Charles C.: 1537
DOUB, Joseph C.: 1538
DOUB, Michael: 208, 1538
DOUB, Peter: 1538
DOUB, William Clark: 1538
DOUB FAMILY (North Carolina): 1538
DOUBLE CABINS, Georgia: 2614
DOUBLE HEAD (Indian chief): 5047
DOUBLE SHOALS, North Carolina:
    Cotton mills: 1539, 4691
DOUBLE SHOALS CIRCUIT, Methodist
    Church: 3646
DOUBLE SHOALS COTTON MILL: 1539
DOUBLEDAY, Abner: 1540
DOUBLEDAY, Ulyssus: 1540
DOUBLEDAY, PAGE & CO.: 4279
DOUGHERTY, Miles: 3012
DOUGHERTY COUNTY, Georgia:
    Albany: 2533, 4921
    Cotton land: 106
DOUGHOREGAN MANOR, Howard County,
    Maryland: 909
DOUGHTY FAMILY (Great Britain): 1541
DOUGLAS, Adele (Cutts): 1190
DOUGLAS, Alfred Bruce: 2146
DOUGLAS, Aretas Akers-, First Viscount
    Chilston: see AKERS-DOUGLAS, Aretas,
    First Viscount Chilston
DOUGLAS, Dunbar (Hamilton), Fourth
    Earl of Selkirk: 1716
DOUGLAS, Eleanor Hall: 1542
DOUGLAS, Elizabeth (Brown): 99
DOUGLAS, Henry Kyd: 1227, 1543
DOUGLAS, John C.: 5988
DOUGLAS, Stephen Arnold: 1084, 1544,
    3809, 4064, 5051
    Campaign of 1860: 279
    Nomination: 4881
DOUGLAS, Sylvester, First Baron
    Glenbervie: 1545
DOUGLAS AND BROTHERS (firm): 1549
DOUGLAS AND SIMMS (law firm): 4828
DOUGLAS COUNTY, Georgia:
    Villa Rica: 874
DOUGLAS COUNTY, Kansas:
    Lawrence: 2358
DOUGLAS COUNTY, Oregon:
    Roseburg: 3518
DOUGLASS, Benjamin P.: 1548
DOUGLASS, Frances Ann (Richardson)
    Taylor: 1547
DOUGLASS, Frederick: 1546, 2871
DOUGLASS, James Walter: 1547
DOUGLASS, Samuel A.: 2760
DOUGLASS, William Boone, Sr.: 1548
DOUGLASS, William Boone, Jr.: 1548
DOUGLASS FAMILY: 1548
DOUMER, Paul--Assassination of: 2398
DOUTHIT, Stephen: 1550
DOVASTON, John Freeman Edward: 1551
DOVASTON, John Freeman Milward: 1552
DOVE, James: 1553
DOVER, England--Description: 3107
DOVER, New Hampshire: 130, 2453
    Woolen mills: 4681
DOVER, Ohio: 4565
DOVER CASTLE, England: 3460
DOVER PLAINS, New York: 3269
DOW, Eugene: 5043
DOW, Moses: 1029
DOW, Neal (1804-1897): 1554, 3910
DOWD, A. J.: 1555
DOWDEN, Edward: 4770
DOWELTOWN, North Carolina:
    Mercantile accounts: 2429
DOWN, County, Northern Ireland: 515
    Mourne: 1010
DOWNEY, James: 1556
DOWNEY, Samuel Smith: 1556
DOWNEY, Thomas: 1556
DOWNING, Samuel: 1557
DOWNING FAMILY (Virginia): 1557

DOWNMAN, Robert: 1558
DOWNMAN FAMILY: 1558
DOWNS, William S.: 146, 1559, 2977
DOWNSHIRE, Arthur Blundell Sandys Trumbull Hill, Third Marquis of: 4024
DOWTIN, D. W.: 1560
DOX, Peter: 2125
DOYLE, Percy W.: 1926
DOYLESTOWN, Pennsylvania:
  Civil War: 1418
DOYNE, Susan: 3567
DRAFT ACT (1863): 5311
DRAFT EVADERS IN CANADA: see CONSCIENTIOUS OBJECTORS IN CANADA
DRAFT EVASION: see Recruiting and enlistment--Resistance under names of armies and navies
"THE DRAGON'S MOUTH" by Albion Winegar Tourgée: 5322
DRAINAGE: see LAND DRAINAGE
DRAKE, A. B.: 1602
DRAKE, Sir Francis: 1561
DRAKE, Jonathan: 758
DRAKE, Samuel Adams: 5240
DRAKE'S LANDING, Alabama: 1602
DRAMA: see AMERICAN DRAMA; ENGLISH DRAMA; FRENCH DRAMA; PLAYBILLS; SPANISH DRAMA; THEATER
DRAMA LEAGUE OF AMERICA: 3797
DRAMATISTS: 3306, 3617, 3797
  Religion and ethics: 4015
DRANE, Herbert Jackson: 646
DRANE, Robert Brent: 5457
DRANESVILLE, Virginia, Battle of: see CIVIL WAR--CAMPAIGNS, BATTLES, AND MILITARY ACTIONS--Virginia--Dranesville
DRAPER, Lyman Copeland: 832, 872
  Manuscripts: 404
DRAWBACKS: see Rebates of duties as subheading under names of products taxed
DRAWING:
  Architectural: see ARCHITECTURAL DRAWING
  Study--Germany: 1665
DRAWINGS, American: 552
  North Carolina: 691
  Women as subjects: 5422
DRAWINGS, British:
  Somersetshire: 1071
DRAYAGE: see FREIGHT AND FREIGHTAGE
DRAYTON, Carrie: 1510
DRAYTON, Charles: 4625
DRAYTON, John (1766-1822): 1562
DRAYTON, Sam: 5246
DRAYTON, Thomas Fenwick: 1466
DRAYTON, William (1776-1846): 295, 1562
DRAYTON FAMILY (South Carolina): 4584
"THE DREAM OF THE DYING PROPHET" by Alexander B. Meek: 3611
DREER, Ferdinand Julius, Sr.: 1563
DREISER, Theodore: 2390, 4373
DRENAN FAMILY (Vermont): 1564
DRESS: see CLOTHING AND DRESS; and Clothing and dress as subheading under names of armies and navies
DRESSEL, Philip: 5495
DRESSER, Charles: 1565
DREW, Thomas H.: 3232
DREW, William: 1566
DREW FAMILY (West Virginia): 1566
DREWRY (AMOS S.) AND COMPANY: 1567, 3900
DREWRY, Frederick: 5062
DREWRY'S BLUFF, Virginia, Battle of: see CIVIL WAR--CAMPAIGNS, BATTLES, AND MILITARY ACTIONS--Virginia--Drewry's Bluff
DRILL AND TACTICS: see as subheading under names of armies
DRINKER, Henry S., Jr.: 3640

DRINKING:
  see also ALCOHOLISM; and Drinking as subheading under names of armies
  Great Britain: 1087
DRINKING IN POETRY--Virginia: 182
DRINKWATER, John: 3797
DROGHEDA, Ireland--Merchants: 2884
DROMGOOLE, Edward: 1568
DROMGOOLE, George Coke: 1568, 4720
DROMGOOLE, Thomas: 1568
DROMGOOLE FAMILY (Virginia): 1568
DROP BOMBS: see BOMBS
DROUGHTS:
  see also WEATHER
  Missouri: 5551
  Ohio: 5275
  Virginia: 3485
DRUG ADDICTION: 421
DRUGS:
  Prices:
    Virginia: 4924
    Alexandria: 5016
  Retail trade--Tennessee: 4288
DRUGSTORES: see DRUGS--Retail trade; PHARMACIES
DRUM, Lavina (Morgan): 1424
DRUMMOND, Henry Home: 1569
DRUMMOND, Joseph A.: 1570
DRUMMOND, Mortimer: 103
DRUMMOND, Thomas (1797-1840): 5026, 5526
DRUNKENNESS: see ALCOHOLISM; DRINKING; and Drinking as subheading under names of armies and navies
DRURY, Thomas Wortley: 1571
DRY CREEK, South Carolina: 3404
DRY GOODS:
  Accounts:
    Virginia--Leesburg: 4198
  Prices--Virginia: 4924
  Subdivided by place:
    North Carolina: 264
    Pennsylvania:
      Hummelstown: 496
    West Virginia: 489
DRY GOODS TRADE:
  Georgia--Savannah: 2280
  Mississippi: 2888
  Missouri--Saint Louis: 5155
  North Carolina:
    Haw River: 5154
    Murfreesboro: 5857
DRY TORTUGAS, Florida:
  Civil War: 5715
DRYBURGH, Scotland: 1716
DRYSDALE, Sir William (d. 1843): 3816
DUAL CITIZENSHIP:
  Great Britain and Spain: 2155
DUANE, William: 3743
DU BARRY, Marie Jeanne Becu, Comtesse: 4625
DUBLIN, Georgia: 5345
DUBLIN, Ireland: 504, 2266, 2826, 3468, 5332, 5663
  Demonstrations: 4605
  Description: 365
  Improvement of harbors: 5330
  Painting exhibitions: 3567
  Seances: 3567
  Social life and customs: 3567
  Visit of Queen Victoria: 5298
DUBLIN DEPOT, Virginia: 1596
DUBLIN EXPOSITION (1853): 3567
DU BOIS, Egbert: 1572
DUBOIS COUNTY, Indiana: 1649
DUBOSE, Daniel: 3123
DUBOSE, Joel H.: 1573
DUBOSE, John Witherspoon: 674
DUBOSE, William I.: 3123
DUBOSE FAMILY (South Carolina): 3123
DUBREUIL, Joseph Villars: 1574
DUBUQUE, Iowa:
  Economic conditions: 4039
DUC, Henry A.: 1575

DU CANE, Sir Edmund Frederick: 1576
DUCHESS COUNTY MUTUAL INSURANCE COMPANY: 5731
DUCHY OF CORNWALL: 4437
  Relations with Crown: 5337
  Relations with public: 5337
DUCK (Textile):
  Virginia--Falmouth: 2165
"THE DUCK AND THE KANGAROO" by Edward Lear: 3138
DUCKS--Hunting limits: 4453
DUCKWALL FAMILY (West Virginia--Genealogy): 5660
DUCKWORTH, Julia Prinsep (Jackson): 5050
DUCLAUX, Agnes Mary Frances (Robinson): 2146
DU CUENNOIS, Theodore Dennis: 1198
DUDLEY, Benjamin Winslow: 1513
DUDLEY, Charles Edward: 743
DUDLEY, Edward Bishop (1789-1855): 1577, 4249, 5457
DUDLEY, Frank: 3062
DUDLEY, John W.: 1578
DUDLEY, Mildred (Smith): 99
DUDLEY, William Wade: 2446
DUDLEY AND KENNETH (firm): see KENNETH AND DUDLEY
DUDYCKINCK, E. A.: 1227
DUE WEST, South Carolina: 2473, 4526
  see also DUE WEST FEMALE COLLEGE; ERSKINE COLLEGE
DUE WEST FEMALE COLLEGE, Due West, South Carolina: 5596
  see also ERSKINE COLLEGE
DUELING:
  Arkansas: 5380
  Georgia: 220, 1090, 2963, 5508
  Germany: 5661
  Louisiana: 1424
  South Carolina: 1424, 2107
    Charleston: 2695
  Southern States: 3873
  Tennessee: 5719
  Virginia: 117, 194, 1424, 3853, 4615
DUFF, Alexander William George, First Duke of Fife: 507
DUFF GREEN, Falmouth, Virginia (firm): 2165
DUFF GREEN AND SON, Falmouth, Virginia (firm): 2165
DUFFERIN AND AVA, Frederick Temple Hamilton-Temple-Blackwood, First Marquis of: 515, 2149, 4520, 4567
DUFFERIN AND AVA, Hariot Georgina (Hamilton) Hamilton-Temple-Blackwood, Marchioness of: 515
DUFFIELD, John D.: 1579
DUFFIELD, John Thomas: 2449
DUFFIELD, Richard: 3010
DUFFIELD, William Ward: 3479
DUFFY, Charles (1808-1892): 1580, 5457, 5910
DUFFY, Charles (1838-1909): 1580
DUFFY, Francis: 5457
DUFFY, Lawrence: 1580
DUFFY, Rodolph: 5457
DUGANNE, Augustine Joseph Hickey: 103
DUGAS, Frederick A.: 1581
DUGAS, Louis Alexander: 1581
DU HOUX, Antoine Charles, Baron de Vioménil: 1582
DUIGNAN, William H.: 2626
DUKE, Angier Buchanan (1884-1923): 1583, 5457
DUKE, Benjamin Newton (1855-1929): 134, 1584, 3762, 3828, 4242, 5252
DUKE, J. E.: 1587
DUKE, James Buchanan (1856-1925): 96, 338, 1584, 1585, 1589, 1914, 3762, 4141, 4242, 5252
DUKE, Lida: 133
DUKE, Mary: 483, 4736, 5252
DUKE, Napoleon: 1587
DUKE, Richard Thomas Walker: 2612

DUKE, Sarah Pearson (Angier): 1584, 5252
DUKE (W.), SONS, AND COMPANY: 1584, 1585, 1586, 1588, 3762, 4857
DUKE, Walter Patterson: 1587
DUKE, Washington (1820-1905): 1588, 3762, 4242, 5252
DUKE, William B.: 1587
DUKE FAMILY (North Carolina and New York): 1584, 1588, 1589
    Genealogy: 1585
    Photographs: 4736
DUKE FAMILY (Virginia): 1587
DUKE CONSTRUCTION COMPANY: 1589
DUKE ENDOWMENT: 1585, 1589, 4141, 4736, 5252
DUKE ENDOWMENT SUPERANNUATE FUND: 3646
DUKE FARMS, Somerville, New Jersey: 1585, 1589
DUKE HOMESTEAD, Durham, North Carolina: 1588
    Historical restoration: 5252
DUKE MEMORIAL UNITED METHODIST CHURCH, Durham, North Carolina: 133, 3646
DUKE OF KENT (clipper): 2259
DUKE POWER COMPANY: 1589
DUKE UNIVERSITY, Durham, North Carolina: 2344, 2398, 3338, 3359, 3433, 4242, 4564, 5252
    see also NORMAL COLLEGE (1851-1859), Randolph County, North Carolina; TRINITY COLLEGE (1859-1892), Randolph County, North Carolina; TRINITY COLLEGE (1892-1924), Durham, North Carolina
    Academic Council: 2282
    American Literature: 2689
    Art Department: 4736
    Cartoons of faculty, students, and staff: 3359
    Centennial celebration: 5497
    Committee on Commonwealth Studies: 2282
    Construction: 1589
    Curriculum in Far Eastern History: 5252
    Department of Alumni Affairs: 2950
    Department of History: 2282
    Dissertations and theses: 1831, 5360
    Divinity School: 1589, 2075, 5022
    Duke Historical Publications: 2282
    Faculty: 2282
    Florence McAlister Chair of Medicine and Medical Research: 5252
    Honorary degrees: 5252
    Labor archives: 3066
    Libraries: 2282
        Acquisitions: 3244, 5101
        Manuscripts: 4156, 5176
        Manuscript Department: 4014, 4290, 5297
    Medical Center: 2934
    School of Nursing: 1946, 3338
        Alumni Association: 1946
    Music Department: 4736
    Parapsychology Laboratory: 3190
    Participation in Folklore Society: 691
    Press: see DUKE UNIVERSITY PRESS
    Student housing--Counselors: 960
    Student religious societies: 3001
    Students and student life: 613, 2747, 2950, 4141
    Trustees: 83, 4736, 4927
    University Council: 2282
    Woman's College: 4736, 5252
DUKE UNIVERSITY PRESS, Durham, North Carolina: 691, 4564, 5252, 5889
    Publication of American Literature: 102
DUKES, Alice: 1424
"THE DUKES" by Charles Buck Roberts: 4502

DULA, A. J.: 1590
DULARY, Alexandre-François Baudet-: see BAUDET-DULARY, Alexandre-François
DULL, M. M.: 1591
DULLES, John Foster: 83
DULUTH, Minnesota: 5115
DULUTH STATE NORMAL SCHOOL, Duluth, Minnesota: see UNIVERSITY OF MINNESOTA--Duluth Campus
DUMB (Deaf mutes): see DEAF
DUMBARTON, Scotland:
    Description: 5527
DUMFRIES, Virginia: 2703
    Tobacco trade: 144
DUMON, G.: 111
DUNBAR, Alexander: 1592
DUNCAN, Alexander: 805
DUNCAN, Blanton: 1593
DUNCAN, Charles B.: 1594
DUNCAN, Ennis, Jr.: 1595
DUNCAN, James: 3800
DUNCAN, Johnson Kelly (1827-1862): 1597
DUNCAN, Mary: 1597
DUNCAN, Rose: 1597
DUNCAN, William E. (Virginia): 1596
DUNCAN, William P. S. (Louisiana): 1597
DUNCANNON, John William Ponsonby, Viscount: see PONSONBY, John William, Fourth Earl of Bessborough
DUNDAS, Francis (d. 1824): 4934
DUNDAS, Henry, First Viscount Melville: 1598, 1913, 2126, 3315
DUNDAS, Sir Richard Saunders: 4549
DUNDAS, Robert Saunders, Second Viscount Melville: 1599, 2836, 4137
DUNDORE, John: 1600
DUNDORE AND EDDINS (firm): 1600
DUNFERMLINE, James Abercromby, First Baron: 5
DUNHAM, Henry Morton: 2410
DUNKARDS: see CHURCH OF THE BRETHREN
DUNKIN, Alexander: 2478
DUNKIN, Eunice (Martha): 1424
DUNKIN, Mrs. William Huger: 1424
DUNKLEE, John: 4990
DUNLAP, Mrs. D. Eli: 1923, 3356
DUNLOP, Adam L.: 1601
DUNLOP, Alexander Alfred: 3238
DUNLOP (DAVID) (tobacco firm): 655, 1873
DUNLOP, Elizabeth: 1601
DUNLOP, Robert: 4834
DUNLOP, William A.: 1601
DUNLOP (JOHN AND JAMES), London, England (firm): 3179
DUNN, J. A.: 508
DUNN, John D. (b. ca. 1827): 1602
DUNN, Robert: 1603
DUNN, S. S.: 3702
DUNN, William Arrington: 5457
DUNN FAMILY (Alabama): 1602
DUNN FAMILY (North Carolina): 1602
DUNNAGAN, Nancy: 1604
DUNNAGAN, Timothy: 1604
DUNNE, William B.: 2973
DUNNIER, M. C.: 4188
DUNNING, Mrs. Edward: 1605
DUNNING, William Archibald: 706
DUNNING FAMILY: 1605
DUNNINGTON FAMILY (Maryland): 3199
DUNNINGTON FAMILY (Virginia): 3199
DUNOVANT, Richard G. M.: 1606
DUNROBIN CASTLE, County Sutherland, Scotland: 2098
DUNSTABLE, New Hampshire: 1529
DUNSTER FAMILY (Genealogy): 286
DUNSTON, Eliza Annie: 4895
DUNTON, Walter Thomas Watts-: see WATTS-DUNTON, Walter Thomas
DUNWODY, James: 125
DUPLIN COUNTY, North Carolina: 4357
    Faison: 1107
    Land deeds and indentures: 5707
DU PONT, Charles I.: 4881
DUPONT, Henry Algernon: 2991

DU PONT, Samuel Francis: 4881
DU PONT FAMILY (Delaware): 3229
DUPREE, William B.: 1607
DUPUY, Eliza Ann: 1608
DUPUYTREN, Guillaume: 1300
DURAND, Algernon: 4520
DURAND, C.: 1609
DURAND, Sir Henry Mortimer: 2756
DURANT, Philip T.: 41
DURANTY, Walter: 958
DURBORAW FAMILY (Maryland): 5488
DURFEE, A. Y.: 1610
DURFEE, Benjamin: 1610
DURFEE, John B.: 1610
DURFEE, William H., Jr.: 1610
DURHAM, Baxter: 2749
DURHAM, Bishop of: see BARRINGTON, Shute; VAN MILDERT, William
DURHAM, Columbus: 255
DURHAM, John George Lambton, First Earl of: 1632, 5026
DURHAM, Plato Tracy: 5497
DURHAM, W. J. Hugh: 1613
DURHAM, Zachary Taylor: 1614
DURHAM, England: 346
DURHAM (County), England: 5694
    Darlington: 4104
    Durham: 346
DURHAM, North Carolina:
    1700s-1800s: 3752
    1700s-1900s: 2934
    1800s: 1588, 4480
    1840s: 133
    1850s: 5402
    1860s: 5402
    1870s: 439, 5402
    1880s: 439, 513, 1368, 4540, 5402
    1890s: 439, 880, 1368, 4060
    1800s-1900s: 286, 1584, 2604
    1900s: 83, 691, 1150, 1275, 1368, 2282, 3828, 4242
    1900s: 1588, 4060
    1910s: 2400, 3843, 4042, 4060
    1920s: 3843, 4060
    1930s: 3843
    1940s: 2650, 3214, 3748, 4085, 5519
    1950s: 4078, 4085, 4386
    1960s: 613, 4085, 4386, 4502, 5773
    1970s: 4386
    Alcoholism: 2934
    American literature: 102
    American satire: 5597
    Banks and banking: 513, 1041, 3762
    Baptist churches: 5401
    Baseball clubs: 4968
    Business affairs: 5923
    Business schools: 3843
    Child care centers: 1275
    Civic improvement: 4968
    Civil War: see CIVIL WAR--CAMPAIGNS, BATTLES, AND MILITARY ACTIONS--North Carolina--Durham
    Committee on Human Relations: 2379
    Community Chest: 3927
    Demonstrations: 2398
    Department stores: 3762
    Durham Council of Social Agencies: 1643
    Economic conditions: 5923
    Electric utility companies: 1584
    Fertilizer industry: 1584, 3762
    Fraternal organizations: 1669
        see also DURHAM--Masonry
    Grocery trade: 134
    Hosiery mills: 1612
    Hospitals: 5601
    Insurance companies: 4968
    Labor movement: 2568
    Lectures and lecturing: 4753
    Literary societies: 2251
    Lyceums: 5597
    Masonry: 1150, 3781
        see also DURHAM--Fraternal organizations
    Mercantile accounts: 4540
    Methodist churches: 1642, 3646

DURHAM, North Carolina (Continued):
　Milk industry: 1275
　Municipal budget: 2379
　Municipal government: 2379, 4736
　Newspapers: 3088
　Packaging machinery company: 5923
　Personal finance: 513
　Pharmacies: 509
　Presbyterian churches: 3762
　Railroad crossings: 969
　Railroad passenger service: 4736
　Real estate: 3762
　Schools: 3762
　　see also DURHAM--Business
　　　schools
　Tax assessment: 2379
　Textile industry: 1228, 1611, 1719
　　see also DURHAM--Hosiery mills
　Tobacco industry: 513, 1586, 5923
　　Finance: 3762
　Tobacco trade: 513
　United Fund: 4736
　Universities and colleges: see
　　DUKE UNIVERSITY; NORTH CAROLINA
　　CENTRAL UNIVERSITY; TRINITY
　　COLLEGE
　Women's societies and clubs: 5601
　Young Women's Christian
　　Association: 1584
DURHAM BUSINESS SCHOOL, Durham,
　North Carolina: 3843
DURHAM CIRCUIT, Methodist Episcopal
　Church, South: 3646, 5023
DURHAM COTTON MANUFACTURING COMPANY:
　1611
DURHAM (N. C.) COUNCIL OF SOCIAL
　AGENCIES: 1643
DURHAM (N. C.) COUNCIL ON ALCOHOLISM:
　2934
DURHAM COUNTY, North Carolina: 1256
　Farming: 440
　Maps: 3514
　Schools: 4862
　Cities and towns:
　　Durham: see DURHAM, North
　　　Carolina
　　Flat River:
　　　Mercantile accounts: 3481
　　Oak Grove Township: 3896
　　Prattsburg: 4307
　　Red Mountain: 3483
DURHAM DISTRICT, Methodist Church:
　3646
DURHAM ELECTRIC LIGHTING COMPANY:
　1584
DURHAM FERTILIZER COMPANY: 1584,
　3762
DURHAM HOSIERY COMPANY: 1612
DURHAM HOSIERY MILLS: 1612
DURHAM MASONIC LODGE NO. 352: 1150
DURHAM (N. C.) SUN (newspaper): 3088
DUSE, Eleanora: 5447
DUSHANE, Nathan T.: 4348
DUSSELDORF, Germany: 1665
DUTCH EAST INDIES: 4362
DUTCHESS COUNTY, New York:
　Dover Plains: 3269
　Hyde Park: 4088, 4128, 4558, 4559
　Pawling: 3975
　Poughkeepsie: 568, 1516, 2035
　　Social life and customs: 1908
DUTCHMAN CREEK, North Carolina: 1904
DUTCHMAN CREEK SOCIETY OF FRIENDS:
　1904
DUTCHVILLE, North Carolina: 1826
DUTILH, Etienne: 1615
DUTILH, Stephen: 1615
DUVAL, William: 4222
DUVAL COUNTY, Florida:
　Jacksonville: see JACKSONVILLE,
　　Florida
　Plantation life: 4410
DUVALL, Joseph: 1616
DUVALL, W. D. F.: 1617
DUYCKINCK, Evert Augustus: 3163
DWIGGINS, Samuel: 556
DWIGHT, Harrison Gray Otis: 3142
DWIGHT, John Sullivan: 432, 1029

DWIGHT, Theodore William: 5075
DWIRE, Henry Rudolph: 5252
DWYER, Richard M.: 1618
DYAKS: 2148
DYE, Nathan G.: 1619
DYE TRADE: 323
DYER, Alexander Brydie: 5433
DYER, Gustavus Walker: 5779
DYER, William T.: 1620
DYER, Sir William Turner Thiselton-:
　see THISELTON-DYER, Sir William
　Turner
DYES AND DYEING (Domestic): 3563
DYES AND DYEING (Industrial):
　Hosiery--North Carolina: 3842
　Prices and standards:
　　Great Britain: 5553
　Pulp and paper industry: see
　　PULP AND PAPER INDUSTRY--Dyes
　　and dyeing
　Wool industry: see WOOL INDUSTRY--
　　Dyes and dyeing
　Subdivided by place:
　　Great Britain: 5553
　　India: 5553
　　North Carolina: 1612
DYETT FAMILY (Genealogy): 1792
DYKE, F. H.: 3183
DYKE, Sir William Hart, Seventh
　Baronet: 294
DYKES, George: 4399
THE DYNASTS by Thomas Hardy: 2334
DYSON, Anne Elliot: 5244
DYSON, Jeremiah: 92

# E

E. AND J. HARDING (firm): 2331
E. B. STOWE (firm): see J. & E. B. STOWE
E. D. WINSTEAD & COMPANY, Milton, North Carolina: 5843
E. SIMS AND COMPANY, Crawford, Georgia: 3974
EAGLE MILL CO., Turnersburg, North Carolina: 2857, 5310
EAGLE RIVER MINING COMPANY, Alaska: 4918
EAGLE ROCK, North Carolina:
 Retail trade: 4009
EAGLE TAVERN, Watkinsville, Georgia: 1621
"EAGLE'S REST," Virginia: 3560
EARDLEY-WILMOT, Sir John: see WILMOT, Sir John Eardley-, First Baronet
EARLE, Edward: 1622
EARLE, Ralph E. W.: 1623
EARLE FAMILY: 718
EARLEYVILLE, Virginia: 490
EARLY, Jubal Anderson: 78, 127, 745, 1364, 1403, 1624, 3654, 4129
 Life in Canada: 2366
 Personal finance: 2593
EARLY, William L.: 523
"THE EARLY PLANTERS OF SCITUATE, MASSACHUSETTS" by Harvey Hunter Pratt: 4305
EARNHARDT, Peter C.: 1625
EARPSBOROUGH, North Carolina:
 Liquor manufacture: 2072
 Merchants: 698
EARTHQUAKES: 3618
 California--San Francisco: 4743
 Georgia (1886): 5246
 North Carolina:
  Henderson County (1812, 1813): 5229
 Philippine Islands:
  Mindanao (1902): 3789
 South Carolina:
  1812: 2636
  1886: 1424, 1468, 2512
   Charleston: 1017, 1889, 2473
 Virginia:
  Amherst County (1852): 5529
EASLEY, Ellen: 132
EASLEY, James S.: 1626
EASLEY, Pyrant: 1627
EASLEY, William: 5584
EAST, James W.: 1628
EAST: see FAR EAST; NEAR EAST
EAST AFRICA--World War I: see WORLD WAR I-- East Africa
EAST ALABAMA COLLEGE, Auburn, Alabama: 5126
EAST BEND, North Carolina: 2857
EAST BETHLEHEM, Pennsylvania: 3054
EAST CANTON, Pennsylvania: 3083
EAST DIXMONT, Maine: 1847
EAST FLORIDA: see subheadings under FLORIDA
EAST HAMPTON ACADEMY, East Hampton, Massachusetts: 4897

EAST INDIA COLLEGE, Great Britain: 3723
 Student rebellion: 2565
EAST INDIA COMPANY: 280, 332, 505, 563, 868, 1629, 4137
 China:
  Canton: 3315, 5038
  Macao: 3315
 Court of Directors: 5639
  Elections: 3315
 General Court: 4066
 Patronage: 5639
 Relations with British government: 868, 3315, 5639
 Relations with presidency governments: 868, 5639
 Training colleges--Bengal: 4066
 Widows' pensions: 2133
 Writerships and cadets: 4066
EAST INDIA CONVENTION: 1641
EAST INDIA HOUSE, London, England: 5797
EAST INDIES:
 British naval activity: 2996
 Description and travel: 4986
 Politics and government: 4986
 Social life and customs: 4986
 Sugar growing: 4913
EAST LEBANON, New Hampshire: 2417
EAST LOTHIAN, Scotland:
 Gosford House: 5643
 Knockenhair: 5835
EAST RIDING, England: 5956
EAST TENNESSEE LAND COMPANY: 1630
EAST TENNESSEE PACKING COMPANY: 1197
EAST WINDSOR, Connecticut:
 Study of law: 5593
EASTBURN, John: 3294
EASTCHURCH, Thomas (d. 1678): 5457
EASTER CARDS: 2656
EASTER REBELLION (Ireland): see SINN-FEIN REBELLION
EASTERLY, Branner: 1631
EASTERN ASSOCIATION, Disciples of Christ: 5554
EASTERN BAND OF CHEROKEE v. WILLIAM H. THOMAS, WILLIAM JOHNSON, AND JAMES W. TERRELL: 5202
EASTERN BAPTIST ASSOCIATION: 320
EASTERN LUNATIC ASYLUM, Lexington, Kentucky: 3325
EASTERN NORTH CAROLINA TRAFFIC CLUB: 238
EASTERN PUBLIC SERVICE COMPANY: 1478
EASTERN QUESTION: see GREAT BRITAIN--FOREIGN RELATIONS--Russia--Eastern Question
EASTERN STATES:
 Banks and banking: 2532
 Clergy: 4702
 Description and travel: 1355, 2983
 Meat packing industry: 4606
EASTERN SUDAN EXPEDITIONARY FORCE: 5835
EASTHOPE, Sir John, First Baronet: 1632
EASTLAKE, Lady Elizabeth (Rigby): 472
EASTMAN BUSINESS COLLEGE, Poughkeepsie, New York: 568
EASTON, Pennsylvania: see LAFAYETTE AGRICULTURAL COLLEGE; LAFAYETTE COLLEGE
EASTVILLE, Virginia: 1814
EATON, Benjamin: 1633
EATON, Charles Rust: 795
EATON, Henry James: 1634
EATON, John Henry: 872, 1635
EATON, John Rust: 1891
EATON, Walter Prichard: 1636
EATON, William (Washington, D. C.): 1637
EATON, William P. (Alabama): 5593
EATON FAMILY (Genealogy): 1634
EATON, Ohio: 1849
EATON COUNTY, Michigan:
 Bellevue: 1840

EATONTON, Georgia:
 Fugitive slaves: 4706
 Legal affairs: 3905, 5837
 Trade and commerce: 3352
EBAN, Abba: 83
EBENEZER, Georgia: 5986
EBERT, Valerius: 1638
EBORN, William Kearney: 1639
EBRINGTON, Hugh Fortescue, Viscount: 1087
EBZER, William: 917
"ECCELINO" by Lord Dillon: 4770
ECCLESIASTICAL AFFAIRS: see RELIGION
ECCLESIASTICAL COURTS:
 Great Britain: 4840
ECCLESIASTICAL FEES: see WAGES AND SALARIES--Clergy
ECCLESIASTICAL HISTORY: see CHURCH HISTORY
ECCLESTON, Sarah: 3295
ECCLESTON FAMILY: 3295
ECLIPSES, Solar: see SOLAR ECLIPSES
L'ÉCOLE DES PONTS ET CHAUSSÉES, Paris, France: 4490
"THE ECONOMIC ASPECT OF WESTERN HEMISPHERE SECURITY" by Benjamin Muse: 3820
ECONOMIC ASPECTS: see as subheading under names of wars
ECONOMIC CONDITIONS: see as subheading under names of geographic locations
ECONOMIC DEVELOPMENT: see INDUSTRIALIZATION
ECONOMIC EFFECTS: see ABOLITION OF SLAVERY AND ABOLITIONIST SENTIMENT--(place)--Economic effects
ECONOMIC POLICY: see as subheading under names of countries
ECONOMICS: 1424, 2398, 2612
 Great Britain: 1792
 Virginia:
  Students' notebooks: 1000, 4616
THE ECONOMIST (periodical): 5809
ECONOMIST (ship): 4505
ECUADOR: 4981
 Missions and missionaries:
  Presbyterian: 2269
ECUMENICAL MOVEMENT: 3020
EDDINS AND DUNDORE (firm): see DUNDORE AND EDDINS
EDDY, Arthur Jerome: 4439
EDDY, Helen M.: 3048
EDDY, Sherwood: 572
EDELMAN, John W.: 5233
EDELMAN, Louis: 4211
EDELMANN, Louise L.: 2878
EDEN, Frances: 3472
EDEN, George, First Earl of Auckland: 1640, 5801
EDEN, Robert (1741-1784): 4348
EDEN, William, First Baron Auckland: 1641
EDEN, Maine: 3880
EDENS, Lacy Thomas: 1642
EDENTON, North Carolina:
 1700s: 1736
 1700s-1800s: 2776, 2889
 1800s: 264, 1165, 1376, 1492, 2428, 2658, 4665, 5391
 Coastwise shipping: 5658
 Customs duties: 2776
 Description: 2627
 Law practice: 2467
 Mercantile accounts: 717, 5658
 Merchant ships: 5658
 Republican convention (1878): 1015
 Schools: 2776
 Tobacco trade: 5228
EDENTON ACADEMY, Edenton, North Carolina: 2776
EDENTON (N. C.) DISTRICT SUPERIOR COURT: 4773
EDENTON TEA PARTY: 5667
EDGAR, William Crowell: 3797
EDGAR ALLAN POE SHRINE, Richmond, Virginia: 5720

733

EDGE HILL, Virginia:
    Girls' schools and academies: 1409
EDGE HILL ACADEMY, Caroline County,
    Virginia: 4698
EDGE LANE HALL, Lancashire, England:
    2457
EDGECOMBE COUNTY, North Carolina:
    1005, 1120, 2646
    Methodist Episcopal clergy: 3992
    Religion: 3052
    Wills: 3626
    Cities and towns:
        Conetoe: 1362
        Earpsborough:
            Liquor manufacture: 2072
            Merchants: 698
        Tarboro: 1061, 2191, 2256, 3626
            Attorneys: 641
            Business: 2325
            Civil War: 531, 1122
            Mercantile accounts: 4035
            Primitive Baptist Church: 5185
EDGECOMBE GUARDS: see CONFEDERATE
    STATES OF AMERICA--ARMY--Regiments--
    North Carolina--Infantry--1st
EDGEFIELD, South Carolina: 844, 1972,
    4193, 4882, 5415, 5901
    Law practice: 4778
    Libraries: 5312
    Schools--Curriculum: 5312
EDGEFIELD, Tennessee:
    Description: 4764
EDGEFIELD COUNTY, South Carolina:
    4581, 5514
    Plantation accounts: 4193
    Cities and towns:
        Edgefield: see EDGEFIELD, South
            Carolina
        Trenton: 5299
        Woodlawn: 3405
            Postmaster: 1181
EDGEFIELD DISTRICT, South Carolina:
    82, 1581, 4144
    Land deeds and indentures: 4822
    Plantations: 2599
"EDGEFIELD SOLDIERS IN THE WAR
    BETWEEN THE STATES . . ." by
    Agatha (Abney) Woodson: 5415
EDGEMONT COMMUNITY CENTER, Durham,
    North Carolina: 1643
EDGEMOOR, England: 4995
EDGEWATER, North Carolina:
    Farming: 4858
EDGEWOOD, Connecticut: 3705
EDGEWORTH, Maria: 2146, 3761
EDGEWORTH DE FIRMONT, Henry Essex:
    2836
EDGEWORTH FEMALE ACADEMY, Greensboro,
    North Carolina: 1100, 2357
EDINBURG, Virginia--Farming: 4124
EDINBURGH, Scotland:
    1700s: 2707, 4512
    1700s-1800s: 867
    1800s: 507, 5526
    1800s-1900s: 3980, 4427
    Autographs: 2022
    Booksellers and bookselling: 1212,
        4333
    Personal finance: 4835
    Universities and colleges: see
        UNIVERSITY OF EDINBURGH
EDISON, Thomas Alva: 2280, 4073
EDISTO, South Carolina:
    Churches: 2027
EDISTO ISLAND, South Carolina: 2831
    Civil War: 5645
        see also CIVIL WAR--CAMPAIGNS,
            BATTLES, AND MILITARY ACTIONS--
            South Carolina--Edisto Island
    Estates--Administration and
        settlement: 3664
    Plantation life: 5661
    Plantations: 4896
    Business affairs: 4725
EDISTO RIVER, South Carolina:
    Land: 5388
EDITH, North Carolina: 5745

EDITING: see JOURNALISM--Editing;
    SCHOLARLY EDITING
EDITORIAL POLICY: see NEWSPAPERS--
    Editorial policy
EDITORS AND EDITING: see AUTHORS AND
    EDITORS; JOURNALISM; PUBLISHERS
    AND PUBLISHING
EDMOND, Kate: 1644
EDMONDS, Sterling F.: 1645
EDMOND'S SCHOOL, Charleston, South
    Carolina: 219
EDMONDSON, Henry: 1646
EDMONDSON, Isaac: 1647
EDMONDSON, Thomas (merchant): 1647
EDMONDSON, Thomas (physician): 1647
EDMONDSON, William: 1648
EDMONDSON FAMILY (Virginia): 2927
EDMONSTON, Basil B.: 1649
EDMONSTON, Benjamin: 1649
EDMONSTON, Ninian: 1649
EDMUNDS, Betsey (Blackwell): 512
EDMUNDS, Fanny: 2712
EDMUNDS, J. H.: 512
EDNEY, General         : 2050
EDNEY, Amanda E.: 1947
EDRAY, West Virginia:
    Postal service: 5655
EDUCATION: 3524, 5007, 5848
    see also KINDERGARTENS; LYCEUMS;
        PUBLIC SCHOOLS; SCHOOLS; TEACHERS'
        RECORDS; TEACHING; TEXTBOOKS;
        and names of specific subjects,
        e.g. CHEMISTRY
    Blind: see BLIND--Education
    Clergy: see CLERGY--Education;
        DIVINITY SCHOOLS; THEOLOGICAL
        SEMINARIES
    Commercial: see COMMERCIAL
        EDUCATION
    Costs--Virginia: 4589
        see also SCHOOLS--Tuition;
            UNIVERSITIES AND COLLEGES--
            Tuition
    Deaf: see DEAF--Education
    Elementary: 2815
    Federal aid: see FEDERAL AID TO
        EDUCATION
    Finance--Great Britain: 4605
    Freedmen: see FREEDMEN--Education
    Higher: 2815
        see also METHODIST CHURCHES--
            Higher Education; UNIVERSITIES
            AND COLLEGES and names of
            specific universities and
            colleges
        Georgia: 5936
        Mississippi--Rodney: 3322
        North Carolina: 5252
    Journalism: see JOURNALISM--
        Education
    Laws and legislation:
        Great Britain: 949, 2962, 4520
        North Carolina: 3538, 5737
        West Virginia: 4732
    Legal: see LAW--Study of
    Medical: see MEDICAL EDUCATION
    Minorities: see MINORITIES--
        Education
    Naval: see U.S. NAVAL ACADEMY
    Negroes: see NEGROES--Education
    Religious: see DIVINITY SCHOOLS;
        RELIGIOUS EDUCATION; SCHOOLS--
        Church schools; STUDENT RELIGIOUS
        SOCIETIES; SUNDAY SCHOOLS;
        THEOLOGICAL SEMINARIES
    Rural: see RURAL EDUCATION
    Student's notebook--Maryland: 3888
    Women: 1176, 5499
        Alabama: 546
        Catholic schools: 3424
        Connecticut: 351
        Great Britain: 3251
        Massachusetts--Brockton: 3524
        Mississippi: 3495
        North Carolina: 2032
            Louisburg: 1411
            Methodist churches: 1152

EDUCATION:
    Women (Continued):
        United States: 4881
        Virginia: 2712, 3458, 3642
            Edge Hill: 1409
        West Virginia: 4703
    Subdivided by place:
        Argentina: 3295
        California: 1758
        Colombia: 1506
        Connecticut: 5748
            Hartford: 1827, 5593
        France: 372, 4490
        Georgia: 1231, 3261
        Great Britain: 14, 258, 1087,
            1126, 1632, 1815, 2962, 3977,
            4331, 5038, 5726
            see also GREAT BRITAIN--ARMY--
                Education of Catholic
                dependents
        India: 278, 5639
            see also BRITISH IN INDIA--
                Education of children
        Ireland: 4024
        Jamaica: 1506
        Japan: 1661
        Kentucky: 3489
        Louisiana: 266
        Maine--Livermore: 5569
        Maryland: 1747
        Massachusetts: 4125
            Springfield: 5043
        Minnesota--Saint Paul: 3310
        Mississippi: 266
        Missouri: 57, 1758, 4552
        Natal: 1792
        New York: 814
            New York: 5593
        North Carolina:
            1700s-1900s: 645, 2357
            1800s: 608, 617, 813, 2192,
                2330, 2469, 2861, 5280, 5603
            1800s-1900s: 274
            1900s: 2945, 3538, 5014, 5298
            Caldwell County: 593
            Craven County: 3955
            Fayetteville: 5298
            Lenoir: 4689
        Peru: 4155
        Philippine Islands: 3313, 4511
        South Africa: 4960
        South Carolina:
            1700s: 4350
            1700s-1800s: 4625
            1800s: 1424, 1480, 2831, 2930,
                4118, 4596, 5415, 5645
            1800s-1900s: 300
            Charleston: 4271, 5661
            Laurens: 2616
        Southern States: 611, 731, 1460,
            2612, 4373, 4720
        Tennessee: 2661
        Texas: 266, 2920
        United States: 2164, 4564, 4805,
            4948, 5480
        Virginia:
            1700s-1800s: 99, 1962, 2927,
                4315
            1800s: 43, 266, 331, 404, 4615,
                4698, 4743
            1800s: 2925
            1810s: 2932
            1830s: 1351
            1840s: 824, 3495
            1850s: 5286
            1860s: 2418, 5286, 5378
            1870s: 2418, 3489, 5378
            1880s: 3307
            1890s: 3307
            1800s-1900s: 1340
        West Virginia: 404
EDUCATION ACT OF 1902
    (Great Britain): 949
EDUCATION ACT OF 1906
    (Great Britain): 4520
EDUCATION AND LABOR: see LABOR AND
    EDUCATION

EDUCATION AND THE CHURCH:
    see also DIVINITY SCHOOLS;
    RELIGIOUS EDUCATION; SCHOOLS--
    Church schools; STUDENT RELIGIOUS
    SOCIETIES; THEOLOGICAL
    SEMINARIES
  Methodist churches: see METHODIST
    CHURCHES--Higher education;
    METHODIST EPISCOPAL CHURCH,
    SOUTH--Board of Education
  Protestant Episcopal Church: 2999
EDUCATIONAL ASSOCIATIONS: 1758, 2607
  see also AMERICAN ASSOCIATION OF
    UNIVERSITY PROFESSORS; NATIONAL
    EDUCATION ASSOCIATION; SOUTHERN
    EDUCATIONAL ASSOCIATION
  North Carolina: 5298
EDUCATIONAL CONFERENCES: see ANNUAL
  CONFERENCE FOR EDUCATION IN THE
  SOUTH
EDUCATIONAL FOUNDATIONS:
  see also CHAUTAUQUAS
  Massachusetts--Boston: 776
EDUCATIONAL TELEVISION: 1758
EDUCATORS--Negroes: see NEGROES--
  Educators
EDW. S. WADDEY, Norfolk, Virginia
  (firm): 2360
EDWARD VII, King of Great Britain:
  1121, 2148, 2149, 3722, 4567,
  4616, 4660
  Accession: 1815
EDWARD AUGUSTUS, Duke of Kent and
  Strathearn: 2836
EDWARD B. JACOBS & NEWCOMEN
  (millers): 2797
EDWARD TELFAIR AND COMPANY,
  Savannah, Georgia: 5221
EDWARDS, Sir Herbert Benjamin: 1650
EDWARDS, Anna Margaret: 1926
EDWARDS, Augustus F.: 1651
EDWARDS, Charity: 1652
EDWARDS, Charles (1797-1868): 5731
EDWARDS, E. H.: 1188
EDWARDS, Frederick Commins: 1653
EDWARDS, Frederick Trevenen: 1653
EDWARDS, George T.: 1654
EDWARDS, Harry P.: 1655
EDWARDS, Harry Stilwell: 2449
EDWARDS, John, Sr.: 1656
EDWARDS, Jonathan, Jr. (1745-1801):
  3588
EDWARDS, Levi: 1657
EDWARDS, Philip Gadsden: 1926
EDWARDS, R. P.: 1658
EDWARDS, Weldon Nathaniel: 685, 1659
EDWARDS, William J. (1859-1916): 5457
EDWARDS FAMILY (Connecticut--
  Genealogy): 2553
EDWARDS RAILWAY MOTOR CAR COMPANY,
  Sanford, North Carolina: 238,
  1655, 4918
"EDWIN AND LAURA" (anonymous poem):
  182
EFFECTS OF CIVILIZATION ON THE
  PEOPLE IN EUROPEAN STATES by
  Charles Hall: 2254
EFFINGHAM COUNTY, Georgia: 1375
  Ebenezer: 5986
EFFINGHAM COUNTY, Illinois:
  Mason: 5695
EGAN, Martin: 5252
EGERTON, Colonel _____ : 2058
EGERTON, Sir Edwin Henry: 3036
EGERTON, Lady Henrietta Elizabeth
  Sophia (Denison): see GREY-EGERTON,
  Lady Henrietta Elizabeth Sophia
  (Denison)
EGERTON, William Grey: 1660
EGGLESTON, George Cary: 1227, 5044
"EGGS THAT SHOULDN'T HAVE BEEN
  LAID" by Wendell Holmes
  Stephenson: 5054
EGLESTON, Thomas (1832-1900): 2699
"EGUIDIO A SU AMIGO. DIÁLOGO": 4155
EGYPT: 5305
  American embassy in: 5298

EGYPT (Continued):
  Army: 4941
    Egyptian War (1882-1906): 5835
  British administration: 663, 2324,
    4941
  British consul in: 3472
    Alexandria: 3471
  British military activities: 3744,
    3858
  British occupation: 1499, 4941,
    5333, 5835, 5876
  Corruption in politics: 4941
  Courts: 4941
  Description and travel: 39, 2934,
    3053, 4020
  Foreign relations:
    Great Britain: 3067, 3744, 5164,
      5835
    Sudan: 5835
    Turkey: 3067
    United States: 83
  Military affairs: 1598, 3744
  Politics and government: 3744,
    4941
  Postal service: 4941
  Public finance: 4941
  Railroads: 1970, 4941
  Religion: 128
  Social life and customs: 83
  Telegraph: 2756
THE EGYPTIAN GAZETTE (periodical):
  4941
EGYPTIAN GOVERNMENT RAILWAYS: 1970
EGYPTIAN WAR (1882-1906): 4941,
  5333, 5835
EICHELBERGER, Clayton: 720
EICHELBERGER, Robert Lawrence: 1661
EIDOGRAPH: 5526
EIGHT AMERICAN AUTHORS edited by
  James L. Woodress: 5889
EIGHT-HOUR DAY:
  Massachusetts: 803
  United States: 4858
EINSTEIN, Albert: 1662
EISENHOWER, Dwight David: 83
EISENHOWER, Rudolph: 1443
EISENLARD, Alonzo M. F.: 4574
EISENSCHIML, Otto: 4276
EKIN, James Adams: 1663
ELASTIC FLUID ENGINES: 1575
ELBERT, Samuel: 1664, 2675
ELBERT COUNTY, Georgia: 3661
ELCHO, Francis Charteris-Wemyss,
  Baron: 5643
ELDAMA RAVINE, Kenya: 4514
ELDER, Betty: 518
ELDER, John Adams: 1665
ELDER, John D.: 1666
ELDER, Maggie: 1665
ELDERS (Church officers): see as
  subheading under names of specific
  denominations
ELDON, John Scott, First Earl of:
  2126, 2836, 4024
ELDORA, Iowa: 4158
EL DORADO: 4155
ELDORADO COTTON MILLS, Milledgeville,
  North Carolina: 4918
ÉLECTION DE GAP: 2195
ELECTION LAWS AND REGULATIONS:
  France: 526
  Georgia--Jefferson County: 3309
  Great Britain: 4868
  North Carolina: 1951, 2819
  United States: 5427
ELECTION REFORM:
  see also SUFFRAGE
  Georgia--Jefferson County: 3309
  Great Britain: 649
  North Carolina: 274
  United States: 2225
ELECTIONS:
  see also BALLOTS; CONFEDERATE
    STATES OF AMERICA--ARMY--Election
    of officers; CONFEDERATE STATES
    OF AMERICA--ARMY--Political
    elections; CONGRESSIONAL
    ELECTIONS; CONTESTED ELECTIONS;

ELECTIONS (Continued):
  GUBERNATORIAL ELECTIONS; JUDGES--
    Elections; LOCAL ELECTIONS;
    PRESIDENTIAL ELECTIONS; SENATORIAL
    ELECTIONS; SUFFRAGE; UNITED
    STATES--ARMY--Civil War--Election
    of officers; UNITED STATES--
    ARMY--Civil War--Political
    elections; UNITED STATES--
    CONGRESS--House of
    Representatives--Committee of
    Elections; VOTER REGISTRATION;
    VOTERS' REGISTERS; (name of
    state)--Legislature--Apportionment
  Alabama:
    1850s-1860s: 1084
    1870: 1299
    Third Military District: 4105
  Brazil (1840s): 4876
  Canada (1880s): 896, 4567
    Parliament (1942): 3949
  Georgia (1800s): 2740
    1860s: 4895
    1870s: 415, 731
    Franklin County (1864): 3814
    State legislature (1795): 2788
  Great Britain:
    1700s:
      1710s: 2071
      1730s: 2071
      1750s: 736, 5330
      1760s: 5287
      1780s: 3860
      1790s: 4171
    1700s-1800s: 535, 4230, 4913,
      5726
    1800s: 2708, 4605, 5026
      1800s: 5830
      1820s: 1124, 2149, 2836, 4258
      1830s: 816, 2149, 3847, 4024,
        4113, 4258, 4570, 4696, 5011,
        5222
      1840s: 1110, 4570
      1850s: 1158
      1860s: 4868, 5534
      1870s: 280, 3722
      1880s: 280, 1273, 3980, 4427,
        4568, 4694, 5164
      1890s: 735, 1499, 2146
    1900s:
      1900s: 3912
      1920s: 233, 5616
    Campaign finances (1833): 1456
    Laws and legislation: see ELECTION
      LAWS AND REGULATIONS
    Procedure (1884): 118
    Subdivided by place:
      Bristol (1700s): 4229
      Cambridge (1923): 5590
      Lincolnshire (1830): 5746
      Middlesex (1802): 3658
      Newcastle (1837): 5624
      Saint Ives (1817): 5639
      South Hampshire (1830s): 5038
      Whitby (1905): 3912
      York (1768): 5330
  Indiana: 1548
  Ireland: 535
    Waterford: 3468
  Maine: 4169
  Maryland:
    1800s: 5247, 5969
    1900s: 3086
    Baltimore (1861): 3264
  Mississippi (1800s): 3322
  New Jersey (1830s): 5520
  New York (1800s): 1908, 4169
  North Carolina:
    1700s-1800s: 245
    1700s-1900s: 4765
    1800s:
      1808: 5229
      1836: 1015
      1840: 1580
      1860s: 4103
      1870s: 3415, 3960
      1880s: 3896, 5709

ELECTIONS:
  North Carolina (Continued):
    1900s: 4251, 4918
    1920s: 2749, 4858
    1930s: 2299, 3538
    1950s: 4805
    Randolph County (1896): 3290
  Ohio (1874): 2291
  Pennsylvania (1800s): 4188
  South Carolina:
    1796: 2300
    1860s: 4118
    1870s: 1468, 1972, 2300, 4118
    1880s: 1480, 2512
    1890s: 1480
    1900s: 300, 4453
    Laurens (1800s): 2616
  Tennessee: 1200
  United States:
    1822: 291
    1836: 2551
    1840: 1985, 2591
    1844: 1985, 3030
    1876: 3960
      Foreign public opinion: 5762
    1888: 2794
    1892: 5970
    1900s: 4948
    1910s: 4453
    1920s: 1150, 4453, 5930
    1930s: 1150, 4453
    1940s: 1201
    1950s: 1201, 4805
  Virginia:
    1800s:
    1830s: 4852
    1840s: 581, 3255, 4852
    1860s: 581, 1955
    1870s: 1955, 5120, 5377
    1880s: 3029
    1890s: 5152
    1900s: 5152
    1930s: 5790
    1940s: 225, 1201
    1950s: 1201
    Buchanan: 4038
  West Virginia (1800s): 1828, 2016
ELECTRIC POWER INDUSTRY:
  see also HYDRO-ELECTRIC POWER
    PLANTS
  Alabama--Muscle Shoals: 1478
  Canada: 96
  North Carolina: 1584, 3447
    Winston-Salem: 4788
  South Carolina: 3447
  United States: 4805
  Virginia: 3447
ELECTRIC UTILITY COMPANIES: see
  ELECTRIC POWER INDUSTRY
ELECTRICAL CONTRACTORS:
  South Carolina--Columbia: 2767
ELECTRICAL ENGINEERING:
  North Carolina--Charlotte: 5312
ELECTRICAL WORKERS: see ELECTRICIANS;
  INTERNATIONAL BROTHERHOOD OF
  ELECTRICAL WORKERS; INTERNATIONAL
  UNION OF ELECTRICAL, RADIO, AND
  MACHINE WORKERS
ELECTRICIANS--South Carolina: 2767
ELECTRICITY: 5499
ELECTRIFICATION:
  see also GAS LIGHTING
  Brazil--Campos: 1644
ELEGY WRITTEN IN A COUNTRY
  CHURCHYARD: 3055
ELGIN, Victor Alexander Bruce, Ninth
  Earl of: 3978, 3980
ELHOLM, Augustus Christian George:
  1667
ELIAS PARKER, Petersburg, Virginia
  (firm): 2933
ELIOT, Charles William (1834-1926):
  706, 1668
ELIOT, George (pseudonym): see EVANS,
  Marian
ELIOTT, George Augustus, First Lord
  Heathfield, Baron of Gibralter:
  1913

ELIZABETH, New Jersey: 1050
ELIZABETH AND ESSEX by Giles Lytton
  Strachey: 5101
ELIZABETH CIRCUIT, Methodist
  churches: 3646
ELIZABETH CITY, North Carolina:
  423, 4342
  Civil War: 1327
    see also CIVIL WAR--CAMPAIGNS,
      BATTLES, AND MILITARY ACTIONS--
      North Carolina--Elizabeth City
  Clergy: 3919
  Embezzlement by Federal employees:
    2776
  Law practice: 5776
  School taxes assessed on freedmen:
    3012
ELIZABETH CITY CHURCH (Methodist,
  North Carolina): 3646
ELIZABETH CITY COUNTY, Virginia:
  Fortress Monroe: see FORTRESS
    MONROE, Virginia
  Hampton: 569
ELIZABETH CITY DISTRICT, Methodist
  churches: 3646
ELIZABETH FARNESE, Queen Consort of
  Spain: 4155
ELIZABETHTOWN, North Carolina: 3364
ELK FURNACE, Virginia: 1501
ELKHORN, Pennsylvania:
  Mercantile accounts: 138
ELKHORN BAPTIST CHURCH, West
  Virginia: 2129
ELKIN, North Carolina: 4742
ELKTON, Maryland:
  Household accounts: 4468
  Resident thought to be Michel Ney:
    1622
  Tavern accounts: 166
ELKVILLE, North Carolina: 2483
ELLEN GLASGOW NEWSLETTER: 2062
ELLENBOROUGH, Edward Law, First
  Baron (1750-1818): 3120
ELLENBOROUGH, Edward Law, First Earl
  of (1790-1871): 868, 3121, 3453,
  4137
ELLENSBURG, Oregon:
  Lumbering and salmon canning: 5938
ELLENWOOD, H. S.: 2940
ELLERBE, North Carolina:
  Lumber mills: 3225
ELLET, Alfred: 1670
ELLET, Alfred Washington: 1670
ELLET, Charles, Jr.: 1670
ELLET, Edward Carpenter: 1670
ELLET, Mary: 1670
ELLET, William Henry: 2612
ELLET RAMS: 1670
ELETT, William: 208, 1671
ELLICE, Edward: 4605
ELLICOTT CITY, Maryland: 50, 3424
ELLICOTT'S MILLS, Maryland:
  Schools: 3360, 4022, 5982
  Social life and customs: 3360
ELLINGTON, L. S.: 1672
ELLINGWOOD, N. Dane: 1673
ELLIOT, Gilbert, First Earl of
  Minto: 1674
ELLIOT, Sir Henry Miers: 1675
ELLIOT-MURRAY-KYNYNMOUND, Gilbert
  John, Fourth Earl of Minto: 278
ELLIOTT, Benjamin, Sr. (1787-1836):
  1676
ELLIOTT, Benjamin, Jr.: 1676
ELLIOTT, Benjamin P.: 1677
ELLIOTT, Charles: 4076
ELLIOTT, Frances Minto (Dickinson):
  472
ELLIOTT, Gladys: 3710
ELLIOTT, James B.: 779
ELLIOTT, John: 1678
ELLIOTT, Ralph: 5193
ELLIOTT, Stephen (1771-1830): 1679,
  4235
ELLIOTT, Thomas J.: 1680
ELLIOTT, Thomas P.: 1681
ELLIOTT, Thomas Rhett Smith: 1681
ELLIOTT, Warren Grice: 5457

ELLIOTT FAMILY (North Carolina): 1677
ELLIOTT FAMILY (South Carolina):
  4453, 4584
ELLIS, Charles, Sr. (1772-1840): 3809
ELLIS, Charles, Jr. (1817-189_): 3809
ELLIS, Elizabeth Throwgood: 3809
ELLIS, H.: 1683
ELLIS, Harold Milton: 102
ELLIS, Henry (1721-1806): 1684
ELLIS, Sir Henry (1777-1855): 868
ELLIS, James E.: 1685
ELLIS, James Nimmo: 3809
ELLIS, Jane Shelton: 3809
ELLIS, Jeremiah B.: 1686
ELLIS, John Willis: 1687
ELLIS, Lemuel: 1688
ELLIS, Margaret (Nimmo): 3809
ELLIS, Powhatan, Sr. (1790-1863):
  858, 3809
ELLIS, Powhatan, Jr. (1829-1906):
  3809
ELLIS, Richard S.: 3809
ELLIS, Sallie Sue: 4111
ELLIS, Thomas Harding: 3809
ELLIS FAMILY: 5176
ELLIS FAMILY (North Carolina): 1686
ELLIS FAMILY (Virginia): 3809
ELLISON, John: 4862
ELLISTON, Elizabeth (Rundall): 1689
ELLISTON, Louise: 5380
ELLISTON, Robert William: 1689
ELLS, James Nathan: 3418
ELLSWORTH, Henry Leavitt: 323, 1690
ELLSWORTH, Oliver: 2776
ELLWOOD, Thomas: 1733
ELM COTTON FACTORY, Falmouth,
  Virginia: 2165
ELMIRA, New York: 408, 5514
  Civil War: 793
    see also CIVIL WAR--PRISONERS
      AND PRISONS--Confederate
      prisoners--New York--
      Elmira
ELMIRA AND WILLIAMSPORT RAILROAD
  COMPANY: 5083
ELMORE, E. C.: 5280
ELMORE, Franklin Harper: 4235, 4445
ELMORE COUNTY, Alabama: 5937
ELMORE INSURANCE COMPANY: 1691
"ELMWOOD," Cambridge, Massachusetts:
  3284
ELNELL, William: 4188
ELOPEMENTS:
  Great Britain: 1049, 4770
EL ORO DE HIDALGO, Mexico: 1412
EL PASO, Texas--Description: 2627
EL PASO COUNTY, Colorado:
  Colorado Springs: 353
EL SALVADOR:
  Travel and railroad construction:
    4719
ELSDALE, Henry: 3056
ELSEY, George W.: 501, 1692
ELWARD, Richard: 1693
ELY, Frederick David: 1694
ELY, John: 3229
ELY, Sarah Marshall: 1927
ELY AND WALKER DRY GOODS COMPANY:
  1695
ELYRIA, Ohio: 4945
EMANCIPATION: see ABOLITION OF
  SLAVERY AND ABOLITIONIST
  SENTIMENT; EMANCIPATION
  PROCLAMATION; SLAVES--Emancipation
EMANCIPATION PROCLAMATION: 2285, 5298
EMANUEL, David: 1696
EMBARGO (Jeffersonian): 2551, 5229
  see also NONIMPORTATION
  British public opinion: 2148
  Massachusetts--Taunton: 5298
  South Carolina--Charleston: 3485
EMBARGO ACT (Jeffersonian): 1115,
  2815, 4616
EMBARGO (1812-1813): 1424
  Economic effects on North
    Carolina: 5298

EMBASSIES: see (name of country)--
    Diplomatic and consular service;
    (name of city)--Embassy in
EMBEZZLEMENT:
    North Carolina:
        By Federal employee: 2776
        From state treasury: 2458
    United States: 3032
EMBLEMS: see MOTTOES; SEALS
EMBLEMS OF LOVE by Lascelles
    Abercrombie: 4
EMBROIDERY PATTERNS: 274
EMERGENCY COMMITTEE OF ATOMIC
    SCIENTISTS: 1662
EMERSON, J. Milton: 1697
EMERSON, Ralph Waldo: 720, 1698,
    5050, 5790
EMERSON LITERARY SOCIETY: see
    GREENSBORO COLLEGE--Emerson
    Literary Society
EMERY, Edwin: 1699
EMERY, Jose R.: 1700
EMIGRANT AID SOCIETY: 5240
EMIGRATION: see IMMIGRATION AND
    EMIGRATION
EMIGRATION SOCIETIES:
    Women's Emigration Society (Great
        Britain): 4567
EMINENT DOMAIN--Virginia: 4465
EMLEN, George: 1888
EMMERSON, Arthur: 1701
EMMET, John Patton: 173
EMMETT, Georgia: 3961
EMMITTSBURG, Maryland:
    Schools: 2301
EMMONS, Martin: 4970
EMORY, Charles: 2384
EMORY, William Helmsley: 1702
EMORY, Virginia: see EMORY AND
    HENRY COLLEGE
EMORY AND HENRY COLLEGE, Emory,
    Virginia: 568, 872, 2712
    Chemistry notebook: 4646
    Civil War hospital: 4895
    Students and student life: 4049,
        4136
EMORY COLLEGE, Oxford, Georgia:
    see EMORY UNIVERSITY
EMORY UNIVERSITY, Oxford, Georgia:
    1066, 1703, 2215
EMPERORS--Germany: 3472
EMPIE, Adam: 1704
EMPIE, Susan W.: 1704
EMPIRE FURNITURE COMPANY: 1197
EMPLOYEE SENIORITY:
    Textile workers: 5234
EMPLOYEES: see specific types of
    employees, e.g. AGRICULTURAL
    WORKERS; GOVERNMENT AND CIVIC
    EMPLOYEES; etc.
EMPLOYMENT: 5851
    see also ART AND ARTISTS--Employment;
        CHILDREN--Employment; MINORITIES--
        Employment; WOMEN--Employment
    North Carolina: 5741
    Texas: 4269
    United States: 4948
    Washington, D. C.: 5298
EMPLOYMENT SECURITY ACT: 5235
ENCHANTRESS AFFAIR: 2989
ENCOUNTER (ship): 4549
ENCYCLOPAEDIA BRITANNICA: 2736, 3967
ENDOR IRON WORKS, McIver, North
    Carolina: 3447
ENDORSEMENTS: see ADVERTISING--
    Endorsements
ENDOWMENTS:
    see also MEMORIAL FUNDS
    France--Grenoble: 2197
    North Carolina: 547
        see also DUKE ENDOWMENT
    Virginia: 4020
"ENDURIN' THE WAR" compiled by
    Gertrude Jenkins: 2829
ENECKS, William R.: 1705
ENENKL, Adolph: 1706
ENERGY: see ATOMIC ENERGY

ENFIELD, Gertrude Dixon: 2661
ENFIELD, North Carolina: 426, 631,
    760, 5664, 5701
ENG AND CHANG (siamese twins): see
    CHANG AND ENG
ENGELHARD, Joseph A.: 5457
ENGINEERING: see CIVIL ENGINEERING;
    ELECTRICAL ENGINEERING; MILITARY
    ENGINEERING; MINING ENGINEERING;
    SANITARY ENGINEERING; STEAM
    ENGINES--Operators
ENGINEERS' ACCOUNTS: 3145
    see also CIVIL ENGINEERING--
        Accounts
ENGINES: see ELASTIC FLUID ENGINES;
    GAS ENGINES; MARINE ENGINES;
    STEAM ENGINES
ENGLAND, Flora D.: 1707
ENGLAND: see GREAT BRITAIN
ENGLAND (newspaper): 352
"ENGLAND AND THE CONFEDERACY" edited
    by Nannie M. Tilley: 4616
ENGLAND IN THE AGE OF THE AMERICAN
    REVOLUTION by Lewis B. Namier: 2148
ENGLE, Samuel: 1708
ENGLE, William: 303
ENGLE, William (West Virginia): 1709
ENGLEWOOD, New Jersey:
    Finance: 730
ENGLEWORTH MILLS, Worthville, North
    Carolina: 3187
ENGLISH ART AND ARTISTS: 4600, 4913,
    5850
ENGLISH CHANNEL:
    Packet boats and shipping: 4719
ENGLISH DRAMA: 47, 188, 892, 2146,
    2334, 3797
    see also THEATER
    In Georgia: 3065
    Reviews: 3617
ENGLISH FICTION: 177, 3630
ENGLISH IMMIGRANTS:
    Aid societies: 5499
ENGLISH LANGUAGE:
    Dictionaries: 2047, 3918, 5160
    Etymology: 3666
    Grammar: 2448, 2612, 2673, 3666
    Student's notebook--Virginia: 3700
    Translations from: 3478
    Translation into: 2736
    Versification: 3700
    Vocabulary: see ENGLISH LANGUAGE--
        Dictionaries
ENGLISH LANGUAGE IN THE PHILIPPINE
    ISLANDS: 3313
ENGLISH LANGUAGE IN THE UNITED STATES:
    4290
    Dialects:
        Louisiana: 4636
        North Carolina: 691, 3048
        Virginia: 2513
ENGLISH LANGUAGE NOTES: 1163
ENGLISH LAW, Study of: 3851
ENGLISH LITERATURE:
    see also AUTHORSHIP; ENGLISH DRAMA;
        ENGLISH FICTION; ENGLISH POETRY;
        ENGLISH SATIRE
    1700s: 90
    1800s: 258, 1287, 2058, 2471,
        2580, 2764
    1900s: 364, 367, 1210, 5101
    Biography: 2102, 2449, 4770
    Caricatures: 2146
    Censorship: 2146
    Criticism: 892
    Ghost writing: 2146
    Study and teaching:
        India: 5525
        New Hampshire: 4012
        North Carolina: 985
    Translations from French: 5447
    Translations from Greek: 2736, 4616
    Translations from Italian: 3836,
        5255
ENGLISH PAINTING: 5542
ENGLISH POETRY: 945, 3292
    see also VIRTUES OF WOMANHOOD IN
        POETRY; WORLD WAR I--Poetry

ENGLISH POETRY (Continued):
    1600s: 1541
    1700s-1800s: 1159, 4967
    1800s: 306, 821, 1473, 1551, 1879,
        2146, 3138, 4001, 4543, 4575,
        5050, 5913
    1800s-1900s: 4552, 5226
    Collections: 1163, 2102, 2227
    Criticism: 2058, 4600, 4629
    Old English: 5811
    Setting: 2058
ENGLISH POETS: 3808
ENGLISH SATIRE: 626, 5867
ENGLISH SILVER PLATE: 2784
THE ENGLISHMAN'S LIBRARY: 2203
ENGRAVERS AND ENGRAVING:
    see also ART AND ARTISTS;
        COPPERPLATE ENGRAVING; DRAWINGS;
        WOOD ENGRAVINGS
    Great Britain: 1071, 4967
    Italy: 4116
    Tombstones--South Carolina: 1889
    United States: 2398
ENKA, North Carolina:
    Textile workers' labor unions: 5442
ENLISTMENT: see Recruiting and
    enlistment as subheading under
    names of armies and navies
ENO, North Carolina: 5264
ENO RIVER (North Carolina): 912
ENOCH PRATT LIBRARY: 2398
ENOREE PRESBYTERY, South Carolina:
    3527
ENSILAGE: 2616
ENTERPRISE, U.S.S.: 5329
ENTERPRISE COTTON MILLS, South
    Carolina: 1480
ENTERPRISE STREET RAILROAD COMPANY,
    Savannah, Georgia: 1710
ENTERTAINING:
    see also AMUSEMENTS; BALLS
    Delaware--Wilmington: 3229
ENTLER, Joseph: 1711
ENTOMOLOGICAL NEWS: 848
ENTOMOLOGY, Nomenclature in: 848
ENTWHISTLE, Joseph: 4146
ENVELOPES (Stationery):
    Invention of double envelopes:
        3523
ENZYKLOPÄDIE by Georg Wilhelm
    Friedrich Hegel: 4430
EPIDEMICS: see DISEASES
EPISCOPAL AFFAIRS: see METHODIST
    CHURCHES--Episcopal affairs
EPISCOPAL CHURCH FEMALE MITE SOCIETY,
    Leesburg, Virginia: 1712
EPISCOPAL CHURCHES: 3141
    see also PROTESTANT EPISCOPAL CHURCH
    Bishops: 3048
    Clergy: see CLERGY--Episcopal
    Doctrine: 3141
    Interchurch relations: 3141
    Orphanages--Virginia: 2799
    Pew rent--South Carolina: 2670
    Publications: see RELIGIOUS
        LITERATURE--Episcopal
    Schools: see SCHOOLS--Church
        schools--Episcopal
    Subdivided by place:
        Massachusetts: 5499
        North Carolina: 1128, 4918
        South Carolina: 2110
        Southern States: 761
        Virginia: 3141
            Portsmouth: 1701
        West Virginia: 3141
EPISCOPAL RECORDER: 128
EPISTEMOLOGY: 2218
EPPES, Francis: 1714
EPPES, Miss J. C. R.: 1713
EPPES, John Wayles: 1714
EPPES, Maria (Jefferson): 1714
EPPS, J. D.: 1715
EPSILON PHI KAPPA DELTA: 3740
EPWORTH LEAGUE: 3646
EQUAL OPPORTUNITY: 4386
    see also UNITED STATES--ARMY--Equal
        opportunity

EQUIPMENT: see as subheading under
  names of armies, navies, and wars
EQUITABLE LIFE ASSURANCE SOCIETY:
  5096
EQUITY: see COURTS--Courts of Equity
ERICHSEN, Hugo: 2449
ERICSSON, John: 1874, 5546
ERIE (ship): 4013
ERIE CANAL:
  Appointments to collectorships:
    585
ERIE COUNTY, New York: 1479
  Buffalo: 249, 1796, 2500, 3872
ERIE COUNTY, Ohio:
  Johnson's Island: see JOHNSON'S
    ISLAND, Ohio
ERIE COUNTY, Pennsylvania:
  Wayne: 4663
ERIE RAILROAD COMPANY--Stocks: 4348
"ERIN" by Julia A. Mildred Harris:
  3611
"ERNEST POOLE AND HIS WORK": 4264
EROSION: see SOIL EROSION
"ERRYD," Wales: 286
ERSKINE, David Steuart, Eleventh
  Earl of Buchan: 1716
ERSKINE, James St. Clair, Second
  Earl of Rosslyn: 5830
ERSKINE, John (1879-1951): 3797
ERSKINE, John, Sixth Earl of Mar:
  2149
ERSKINE, Thomas, First Baron
  Erskine: 1717
ERSKINE COLLEGE, Due West, South
  Carolina: 4526
  see also DUE WEST FEMALE COLLEGE
  Students and student life: 3369,
    4684
THE ERSKINIAN: 4526
ERVIN, James R., Sr.: 1718
ERVIN FAMILY: 1916
ERWIN, Anna B. (Clay): 1086
ERWIN, Hannah: 1670
ERWIN, John: 5593
ERWIN, William Allen: 5252
ERWIN, North Carolina:
  Cotton mills and labor problems:
    5298
ERWIN, Tennessee: 4730
ERWIN AND CLAYTON (firm): see
  CLAYTON AND ERWIN
ERWIN MILLS, INC., Durham, North
  Carolina: 1584, 5252, 5298
  Cooleemee Plant: 1719
  Wage statistics: 1228
ESCALERA, Manuel Cevallos: 951
ESCAMBIA COUNTY, Florida:
  Pensacola: see PENSACOLA, Florida
ESCHEAT:
  North Carolina: 435, 3003
  Virginia--Franklin County: 2955
ESHLEMAN (D.) AND COMPANY: 3957
ESKIMOS: see BLOND ESKIMOS
ESKRIDGE, John B.: 1720
ESKRIDGE, Thomas P.: 1720
ESLAVA, Amelisse: 3611
ESPEY, Harriet N.: 85
ESPINAR, José Domingo: 4155
ESPY, James Pollard: 1728
ESSAY ON THE BASES OF THE MYSTIC
  KNOWLEDGE... by Jérôme Edouard
  Récéjac: 5447
ESSAYS: see AMERICAN ESSAYS;
  STUDENTS--Compositions
ESSAYS AND ADDRESSES by Roger
  Atkinson Pryor: 4341
ESSAYS MOSTLY ON PERIODICAL
  PUBLISHING IN AMERICA edited by
  James L. Woodress: 5889
ESSAYS ON HIS OWN TIMES by Samuel
  Taylor Coleridge: 4913
ESSENDON, England: 1508
ESSEX, George Capell, Fifth Earl
  of: 1632
ESSEX, England: 4420
  Chigwell: 3553
  Woodford Green: 4694

ESSEX COUNTY, Massachusetts:
  Amesbury: 4189, 5717
  Andover: 995, 1037
    see also ANDOVER THEOLOGICAL
      SEMINARY
    Social life and customs: 3034
  Beverly: 5885
    Shipping: 2682
  Boxford: 1348
  Danvers: 5717
  Haverhill: 2031, 3741
  Ipswich: 3015
  Newburyport: 1349, 4224, 4864
  Salem: 450, 2028, 4194
  Wenham: 3917
ESSEX COUNTY, New York:
  Ticonderoga: 1219
ESSEX COUNTY, Virginia: 476
  Civil War: 2247
  "Malvern": 347
ESTABLISHMENT: see as subheading
  under names of churches
ESTAING, Charles Hector Theodat,
  Comte d': 1236, 3209, 3444, 5228
ESTATE ACCOUNTS:
  Alabama: 5006
  Florida: 4903
  Louisiana: 2674
  North Carolina: 2833, 4336, 4704,
    5709
    Charlotte: 5312
    Hyde County: 511
    Martin County: 4849
    Raleigh: 727
    Wadesboro: 2984
  South Carolina: 2107, 3801, 5810
    Charleston: 2414, 5073
    Chester: 4833
    Saluda County: 2921
  Virginia: 28, 2949, 3104, 3809,
    4743, 5742
    Oak Grove: 2392
  Washington, D.C.: 3325
ESTATES (Landed property):
  see also COUNTRY ESTATES
  Management: 2170
    Alabama--Dallas County: 4911
    Virginia: 3104, 5332
  Surveys--Great Britain: 712
  Subdivided by place:
    Georgia: 1434
    Mississippi: 1434
    Solomon Islands: 4949
    South Carolina: 2556, 5074
    Virgin Islands: 2321
ESTATES (Legal):
  see also SLAVES--Division of
    ownership
  Administration and settlement:
    1424, 1589, 3526
    Alabama: 478, 1084, 1497, 1986,
      2040, 4861, 5612
      Dallas County: 2979
      Madison County: 4658
    Arkansas: 478, 784
    Connecticut: 379, 1241, 3041,
      4059, 5593
    Florida: 4298
      Jackson County: 4903
    France: 5193
    Georgia:
      1700s: 1664, 3573, 5920
      1700s-1800s: 2019, 2238, 2923,
        3661, 5221
      1700s-1900s: 1993
      1800s: 220, 1375, 1981, 2327,
        2670, 2740, 2827, 3396,
        3672, 4706, 4911, 5051,
        5537, 5787
      1800s-1900s: 3065
      Ebenezer: 5986
      Franklin County: 1997
      Greene County: 1998
      Hancock County: 4493
      Savannah: 3309, 3389, 3717,
        4205
    Great Britain: 2226, 2838, 3722,
      4770, 4934, 5647

ESTATES (Legal):
  Administration and settlement:
    Great Britain (Continued):
      Allerton: 3620
      Exeter: 5867
      Westmorland: 1869
    Illinois: 2080, 5570
      Loda: 806
      Macomb: 659
    Kansas: 2554
    Kentucky:
      Fayette County: 3325
    Maryland:
      1700s: 4405, 5296
      1700s-1800s: 4081, 5981
      1800s: 785, 2295, 3254
      1900s: 660
      Baltimore: 4348
      Cecil County: 5296
      Frederick County: 4457
      Harford County: 4537
      Kent County: 4140, 5296
      Queen Annes County: 5296
      Williamsport: 5160
    Massachusetts: 1344, 2468
      Boston: 323
    Mississippi: 530, 3434
      Clinton: 4299
    New York: 1390, 1585, 2407,
      3637, 5796
    New York: 4141
    North Carolina:
      1700s-1900s: 832, 1107,
        3424, 4858
      1800s: 530, 817, 1382, 1438,
        1475, 1604, 2554, 2808,
        3043, 4154, 4669, 4689,
        4760, 4849, 4875, 4918, 5549
      1800s: 1492, 4344, 5740
      1810s: 2861
      1820s: 2113
      1830s: 2113, 3916, 4270
      1840s: 2113, 2589, 2876,
        3176, 3639, 4270, 4923,
        5298
      1850s: 3301, 4270, 4923
      1860s: 1861, 2727, 3301,
        4357, 4923
      1870s: 641, 2419, 2727,
        3301
      1900s: 661, 5298
      Anson County: 2493
      Beaufort County: 5831
      Bertie County: 2582
      Bladen County: 4516
      Caldwell County: 3324
      Charlotte: 5312
      Chatham County: 2462
      Davie County: 122
      Durham County: 1256
      Edenton: 4773
      Forsyth County: 1209
      Halifax County: 5672
      Hillsborough: 5381
      Hyde County: 511
      Iredell County: 5319
      Martin County: 5036
      Mocksville: 2749
      Moore County: 3393
      Onslow County: 1252
      Person County: 3752
      Prattsburg: 4307
      Raleigh: 727
      Ramseur: 2624
      Randolph County: 621, 5018
      Richmond County: 3475
      Shelby: 1951
      Wadesboro: 2984
    Pennsylvania: 213, 421, 1536,
      1916, 2027
      Lancaster: 2492, 2497
    Peru: 4155
    South Carolina: 5810
      1700s: 4621, 4623
      1700s-1800s: 653, 842, 1472,
        2019
      1800s: 295, 1127, 1877, 2040,
        2218, 3203, 3350, 4527

ESTATES (Legal):
    Administration and settlement:
        South Carolina
            1800s (Continued):
                1810s: 1562
                1820s: 1562, 4214
                1830s: 1562, 2961
                1840s: 2961, 5193
                1850s: 1388, 1891, 3367
                1860s: 791, 1388, 3367
                1870s: 1388, 3367
                1890s: 1424, 2210
            Charleston: 2107, 4215, 5198, 5461, 5936
            Chester County: 4833
            Edgefield District: 2599
            Edisto Island: 3664
            Georgetown: 3512
            Orangeburg District: 5015
        Southern States: 1553, 4711
        Tennessee: 82, 795
            Nashville: 4854
        Texas: 4170, 4269
        United States: 480
        Vermont: 4485
        Virginia:
            1700s: 604, 3819
            1700s-1800s: 97, 2633, 2927, 4616
            1700s-1900s: 3424
            1800s: 490, 824, 1556, 1558, 1568, 1922, 2120, 3855, 4385, 4562, 5469, 5765
            1800s: 3031
            1810s: 1627, 3156
            1820s: 1627, 2190, 3560
            1830s: 1384, 2190
            1840s: 1384, 2190, 3157, 4735, 5113
            1850s: 734, 806, 1161, 1384, 3068, 4735
            1860s: 1161, 2510, 2712, 3068, 3193, 4531
            1870s: 1262, 3068, 3587, 5696
            1880s: 3401, 5696
            1890s: 3401, 5696
            1800s-1900s: 2517, 3148
            1900s: 3084, 3587
            Buckingham County: 5289
            Campbell County: 62
            Caroline County: 5203
            Charlottesville: 2612
            Culpeper County: 337
            Frederickshall: 2363
            Gloucester County: 4924
            Halifax County: 5229
            Loudoun County: 3529, 3560
            Luray: 574
            Madison County: 4794
            Nelson County: 3566
            Norfolk: 3830
            Petersburg: 1873, 4555
            Pittsylvania County: 5718
            Port Republic: 1600
            Suffolk: 3012
            Westmoreland County: 5577
            Wythe County: 872
        Washington, D.C.: 4478, 5528
        West Virginia:
            1700s-1800s: 2397
            1700s-1900s: 865, 1946
            1800s: 2389, 2711, 3010, 5194
            1800s-1900s: 2342
            Martinsburg: 5110
            Shepherdstown: 4598
    Appraisal:
        Maryland:
            Frederick County: 4457
        Massachusetts:
            Taunton: 5499
    Inventories: 418
        North Carolina:
            Smith Church: 5399
ESTES, Christopher T.: 1459
ESTIENNE, Henri: 1721
ESTIL, Benjamin: 861, 872

"THE ESTIMATION OF YIELDS FOR STATE TOBACCO TAXES": 2798
ESTONIA--Peasantry: 2139
ESTRAYS:
    Illinois:
        McHenry County: 1723
    Mississippi:
        Noxubee County: 1722
ESTRIDGE, Mary: 3020
ESTY, J. F.: 2345
ETHERIDGE, Emerson: 872
ETHERINGTON, Robert: 1088
ETHICS: 2616, 2930
    Baptist churches--Georgia: 1080
    Literary: see PLAGIARISM
    Missions and missionaries: 3248
    Subdivided by place:
        Great Britain: 4146
        United States: 1219
ETHIOPIA:
    Foreign relations:
        Great Britain: 3838
    Slavery: 3912
ETHNIC GROUPS: see MINORITIES; and specific ethnic groups
ETHNOLOGY: see AMERICAN ETHNOLOGICAL SOCIETY
ETHRIDGE, Mary Sue: 1724
ETHRIDGE FAMILY (North Carolina): 1724
ETON COLLEGE, Eton, England: 5736
    Students and student life: 2102
ETOWAH RIVER (Georgia): 1887
EUBANK, W.: 2868
EUFAULA, Alabama: 4799
EUGENE, Oregon: 5054
EUGÉNIE, Empress Consort of Napoléon III: 4490, 4520
EUGSTER, Carla Myerson: 2379
EULOGIES:
    see also CIVIL WAR--POETRY--Eulogies
    Maryland: 5295
EUPATORIA, Union of Soviet Socialist Republics: 153
EUPHRADIAN ACADEMY, Rockingham, North Carolina: 1725
EURASIANS: 5525
EURE-ET LOIR DEPARTMENT, France:
    Chartres: 3990
EUROPE:
    American students in: 3029
    Cotton trade: 592, 3689, 5014
    Description and travel:
        1700s: 960, 1884, 2869, 3396, 4625
        1700s-1800s: 5038
        1800s: 128, 573, 1798, 2407, 3008, 3284, 3761
        1810s: 2139, 2326
        1820s: 2058
        1830s: 1792
        1840s: 781, 1891
        1850s: 1109, 1792, 2521, 2985, 3053, 4616, 5059, 5193
        1860s: 1352, 2336, 2608, 3053, 4485
        1870s: 20, 139, 157, 661, 3710, 4485, 5045, 5972
        1880s: 1084, 1424, 2032, 3587, 3809, 4080, 4702
        1890s: 43, 3527, 4020
        1900s: 3306, 3424
        1900s: 4020, 4271, 5786
        1910s: 572, 4020, 4271, 4449
        1920s: 960, 4192, 4271
        1930s: 3607
    Economic conditions: 2703
    Fish culture: 3357
    Foreign relations: 92
    Hotels: 5193
    Military affairs: 92, 1499
    Pepper trade: 2682
    Political poetry: 958
    Politics and government: 43
    Sacred relics: 4881
    Social life and customs: 3710

EUROPEAN AFFAIRS: 805, 5361
EUROPEAN ART, Photographs of: 139
EUROPEAN LEADERS: 3472
EUSTIS, James Biddle: 1726
EUTAW, South Carolina: 4033
EUTAW (ship): 4881
EVANGELICAL ALLIANCE: 5731
EVANGELICAL GERMAN LUTHERAN CHURCH: 5986
EVANGELICAL KNOWLEDGE SOCIETY (West Virginia): 128
EVANGELICAL LUTHERAN CHURCH:
    Maryland--Smithsburg: 5343
    Pennsylvania--Ray's Hill: 3957
EVANGELICAL SOCIETY: 5731
EVANGELISM:
    see also CAMP MEETINGS; GREAT AWAKENING (Second); Revivals as subheading under names of specific denominations
    Presbyterian churches: 5979
    Subdivided by place:
        Georgia: 5760
            Macon: 5246
        Great Britain: 43
        North Carolina: 4787
        Pennsylvania: 4086
            Franklin County: 2643
        South Carolina: 561, 669
            Beaufort: 1891
            Conway: 2854
        Tennessee--Memphis: 3552
        United States: 872
        Virginia: 1591, 1920, 4131
        West Virginia: 5689
EVANS, Caroline (Washington): 1728
EVANS, Clement Anselm: 1727
EVANS, Edmund: 626
EVANS, George: 4621
EVANS, George DeLacy: 816
EVANS, George Eyre: 250
EVANS, George K.: 1729
EVANS, Harriet L. (Scollay): 1730
EVANS, John B.: 1731
EVANS, John Gary: 5299, 5930
EVANS, Joseph R.: 1732
EVANS, Marian: 4575
EVANS, Nathan George: 5193
EVANS, Nelson W.: 281
EVANS, Sara Margaret: 613
EVANS, Thomas (1798-1868): 1733
EVANS, Thomas Crain (b. 1860): 4743
EVANS, William E.: 2963
EVANS FAMILY (North Carolina): 1728
EVANS FAMILY (West Virginia--Genealogy): 1946
EVANSTON, Illinois: 1137
EVARTS, C. M.: 304
EVARTS, Jeremiah: 3142
EVARTS, William Maxwell: 1734
EVE, Mrs. ____ (Georgia): 1737
EVE, Oswell: 26
EVE, Sallie: 1735
EVE, Sarah: 26
EVE FAMILY (Georgia): 26
EVELYN, Martha Boscawen: 5478
EVELYN, William: 1227, 3418
EVENING CLUB AND GOLF CLUB, Savannah, Georgia: 2238
EVENING POST (newspaper): 5397
EVERARD, Richard: 1736
EVERETT, Edward: 858, 1737, 3259, 5149, 5775
EVERETT, Lillie Moore: 1738
EVERETT, Patience: 1739
EVERGLADE, C.S.S.: 2963
EVERMANN, Barton Warren: 2084
EVERSON, Ida Gertrude: 2449
EVERTON, England: 462
EVIL: see GOOD AND EVIL
EVOLUTION AND RELIGION:
    United States: 1219
EWART, Hamilton Glover: 5457
EWELL, Benjamin Stoddert: 1740, 2728
EWELL, Frances: 5630
EWELL, John S.: 1741
EWELL, Richard Stoddert: 1740

739

EWEN, F. M.: 4165
EWING, Andrew: 1742
EWING, C. L.: 163
EWING, James: 2665
EWING, Thomas (1789-1871): 1743
EWING, Thomas (1829-1896): 2517
EXCAVATIONS: see ARCHAEOLOGICAL INVESTIGATIONS
EXCESS PROFITS TAX--United States: 4858
EXCHANGE: see BILLS OF EXCHANGE; FOREIGN EXCHANGE
EXCHEQUER: see GREAT BRITAIN--GOVERNMENT AGENCIES AND OFFICIALS--Exchequer
EXCISE TAXES--Ireland: 3883
EXECUTIONS: 43
  see also CIVIL WAR--PRISONERS AND PRISONS--Union prisoners--Executions; CIVIL WAR--SPIES--Executions; CONFEDERATE STATES OF AMERICA--ARMY--Executions; HANGINGS; SPIES--Executions; UNITED STATES--ARMY--Civil War--Desertion--Executions
  North Carolina: 1577
  For murder: 2117
EXEMPTION FROM MILITARY SERVICE:
  see Recruiting and enlistment--Exemptions as subheading under names of armies and navies
EXEMPTION FROM TAXATION: see TAXATION--Exemption from
EXERCISE BOOKS: see ARITHMETIC--Exercise books
EXETER, Bishop of: see PHILLPOTTS, Henry
EXETER, England: 970, 5867
  Historical studies and historic buildings: 5553
  Legal affairs: 5867
  Literary interests: 5867
EXETER, Massachusetts:
  Social life and customs: 2410
EXETER, New Hampshire: 2044, 5140
  Social life and customs: 2043
EXETER GUILDHALL: 5553
EXHIBITION OF INDUSTRY OF ALL NATIONS (New York): 5584
EXHIBITIONS OF ART: see ART AND ARTISTS--Exhibitions; and Exhibitions as subheading under specific art medias
EXHIBITIONS AND FAIRS:
  see also AGRICULTURAL FAIRS
  International: 196
  California:
    Panama-Pacific International Exposition (1915): 4042, 4511, 5252
  France:
    Paris Exposition of 1878: 157, 5970
    Paris Exposition of 1900: 196
  Georgia:
    International Cotton Exposition (1881): 5494
    International Exposition (1895): 3376
  Great Britain:
    Great Exhibition of 1850: 597, 3424
  Illinois:
    Columbian Exposition: 3051, 5380
  New York:
    Exhibition of Industry of All Nations: 5584
  Pennsylvania:
    Philadelphia International Exhibition: 2597
  Subdivided by place:
    Australia--Melbourne: 4567
    Great Britain: 3744
    Illinois--Ogle County: 4732
    Ireland--Dublin: 3567
    Maryland--Hagerstown: 5866
    South Carolina: 2473
    Virginia--Nansemond County: 3834

EXHIBITOR'S MEDAL, Great Exhibition of 1850: 3424
EXILES: see AMERICAN REVOLUTION--Loyalist refugees; CIVIL WAR--EXILES; CIVIL WAR--REFUGEES; CONFEDERATE EMIGRANTS; HUNGARY--Uprising of 1848-1849--Exiles
EXILES FROM PARADISE by Sara Mayfield: 2398
EXMOUTH, Edward Pellew, First Viscount: 5639
"EXPEDIENTE SOBRE BRUJERÍAS, HECHIZOS Y MALEFICIOS DE INDIOS EN EL PERÚ": 4155
EXPEDITIONS: see ARCHAEOLOGICAL INVESTIGATIONS; SCIENTIFIC EXPEDITIONS; ZOOLOGICAL EXPEDITIONS
EXPERIMENT (warship): 2008
EXPERIMENTAL FARMING:
  see also AGRICULTURAL PRACTICES--Improvements; AGRICULTURAL RESEARCH
  Virginia: 3820
EXPLORATION:
  see also SCIENTIFIC EXPEDITIONS
  Africa: 306, 3158
  Florida: 3269
  South America: 2296
EXPLORATION OF SPACE: see SPACE EXPLORATION
EXPLORERS:
  Arctic regions: 4556
  Texas: 4353
EXPLOSIONS: see STEAMBOATS--Explosions
EXPORT-IMPORT COMPANIES: see FOREIGN TRADE; Foreign trade as subheading under names of countries; and specific types of trade
EXPORT LEAF TOBACCO COMPANY: 655
EXPORT TRADE PROMOTION: see FOREIGN TRADE PROMOTION
EXPORTS: see specific types of trade, e.g. COFFEE TRADE
EXPOSITION UNIVERSELLE: 157
EXPOSITIONS: see EXHIBITIONS AND FAIRS
"EXTENSIONES APROXIMIDAS DE LOS ADQUIRADOS . . . POR LAS COMPAÑIAS PETROLERAS-EXTRANJERAS. . . .": 3651
EXTERNAL DEBT:
  United States: 258
EXTRADITION OF CRIMINALS:
  Georgia: 4218
  Maryland: 3728
  North Carolina: 4729
  Pennsylvania: 3728
  South Carolina: 700, 4218
EXTRATERRITORALITY--China: 5252
EYE--Defects: see DEFECTIVE VISION
EYLES TYTHING, Savannah, Georgia: 2993
EZEKIEL, Moses Jacob: 4020

F

F., M. L.: 1744
F. & H. FRIES (millers): 1905
F. GORIN (firm): see I. AND F. GORIN
F. M. ZEA AND COMPANY, Strasburg, Virginia: 5979
FABER, John Christopher: 1745
FABERS MILLS, Virginia: 5290
FABIUS, New York: 4169
FACKLER, C. William: 1746
FACKLER FAMILY (Alabama): 1746
FACTORS:
  see also COTTON TRADE
  South Carolina--Charleston: 3801
  United States: 2432
FACTORY ACTS (Great Britain): 1648
FACULTY: see UNIVERSITIES AND COLLEGES--Faculty; and Faculty as subheading under names of specific universities and colleges
FADDIS, Thomas Jefferson: 4890
"THE FAERIE KING FASHIONING LOVE AND HONOUR" by Samuel Sheppard: 4777
FAIN, Ebenezer: 639
FAIN, Huldah Annie: 639
FAIR GROVE, North Carolina: 1341
FAIR HAVEN, Connecticut:
  Weather: 5261
FAIR LABOR STANDARDS ACT: 101, 1202
FAIR OAKS, Virginia: see CIVIL WAR--CAMPAIGNS, BATTLES, AND MILITARY ACTIONS--Virginia--Fair Oaks
FAIRCHILD, Edwin Milton: 1747
FAIRCHILD, Mary Salome (Cutler): 1747
FAIRCHILD AVIATION (firm): 3086
FAIRCLOTH, William Turner: 1748, 5457
FAIREY, Franklin William: 1749
FAIRFAX, Donald McNeill: 5636
FAIRFAX, Thomas, Sixth Baron Fairfax of Cameron: 917, 1750, 3819
FAIRFAX, Vermont: 1039, 3129
FAIRFAX COUNTY, Virginia:
  County government: 2887
  Cities and towns:
    Centreville: 2534
      Civil War: 56, 1092
      Battle: see CIVIL WAR--CAMPAIGNS, BATTLES AND MILITARY ACTIONS--Virginia--Centreville
    Fairfax Court House: see FAIRFAX COURT HOUSE, Virginia
    Mount Vernon: 5575
    Prospect Hill: 2233
    Reston: 3820
    Vienna: 3965
    "Woodlawn": 3200
FAIRFAX COURT HOUSE, Virginia:
  Civil War: 3263
    see also CIVIL WAR--CAMPAIGNS, BATTLES, AND MILITARY ACTIONS--Virginia--Fairfax Court House
FAIRFAX INSTITUTE, Alexandria, Virginia: 3141
FAIRFAX SEMINARY, Virginia: 2648

FAIRFIELD, Clarence: 2449
FAIRFIELD, Connecticut: 1871
FAIRFIELD, Iowa: 5812
FAIRFIELD, North Carolina: 921
  Merchants: 511
FAIRFIELD COUNTY, Connecticut:
  Bridgeport: 3910
  Danbury: 2257
  Fairfield: 1871
  Newtown: 162
  Norwalk: 2745
  South Norwalk: 688
FAIRFIELD COUNTY, Ohio:
  Lancaster: 1743
FAIRFIELD COUNTY, South Carolina: 2880
  Winnsboro: 936, 1385
  Schools: 5193
FAIRLIE, Robert Francis: 863
FAIRMAN, Henry Clay: 3376
FAIRS: see AGRICULTURAL FAIRS; EXHIBITIONS AND FAIRS
FAISON, Solomon Wesley: 1751
FAISON FAMILY (North Carolina): 1752
FAISON, North Carolina: 1107
FAITH, North Carolina: 5929
FALCONER, Thomas (1772-1839): 2148
FALCONER, Thomas (1805-1882): 1753
FALCONER, William Armistead: 5380
FALCONER FAMILY (Great Britain): 1753
FALCONNET, Eugene F.: 1439
"FALK" by Joseph Conrad: 4798
FALKIRK, England:
  Politics and government: 735
FALKLAND, Henry Cary, Eighth Viscount: 2133
FALKNER, William: 1771
FALKNER FEUDS: 1771
FALL, Albert Bacon: 4453
FALL RIVER, Massachusetts: 1862, 2867
  Social life and customs: 2035
  Textile industry: 992
FALLING RIVER, Virginia:
  Merchants: 2633
FALLING WATERS, West Virginia:
  Farm accounts: 4999
FALLODON, Edward Grey, First Viscount Grey of: see GREY, Edward, First Viscount Grey of Fallodon
FALLS, Pennsylvania: 4188
FALLS CREEK CHURCH, West Virginia: 2129
FALLS OF TAR RIVER, North Carolina:
  Schools: 4571
FALLS VILLAGE, Connecticut: 3852
FALMOUTH, Virginia: 1790, 2165, 3105
  United States Army camp (Civil War): 4608
FALMOUTH (ship): 2963
FALMOUTH MANUFACTURING COMPANY, Falmouth, Virginia: 2165
FALSE ADVERTISING: see ADVERTISING--False advertising
"FAMILIAR LETTERS DURING A JOURNEY THROUGH THE HIGHLANDS OF SCOTLAND" by Jacob Pattison: 4084
FAMILY LIFE:
  see also MARRIED LIFE; MOTHERS--Role in family
  Arkansas: 5380
  France: 4490
  Georgia--Butts County: 1731
  North Carolina:
    Iredell County: 4310
    Society of Friends: 1407
    Stokes County: 2800
  Pennsylvania: 5380
    Le Raysville: 4397
  South Carolina: 5193
    Chester: 5988
    Lancaster County: 4310
  Virginia: 2935, 4698, 5476
    Shenandoah County: 2975
    Staunton: 1601
    Winchester: 2974
  West Virginia: 1730
  Western States: 1601
FAMILY MEDICINE:
  Virginia: 4616

FAMILY TREE BOOK, GENEALOGICAL AND BIOGRAPHICAL by William Alexander Smith: 4918
FAMINE--Bechuanaland: 4514
FAMINE RELIEF--China: 5252
FANCY GROVE, Virginia:
  Physicians: 5288
FANCY HILL, Virginia: 4243
FANE, John, Ninth Earl of Westmorland: 4230
FANE, John, Tenth Earl of Westmorland: 1754
FANE, John, Eleventh Earl of Westmorland: 1755
FANE, Julian Henry Charles: 1755
FANKWEI by William Maxwell Wood: 2265
FANNING, Edmund: 305, 1756
THE FANWOOD CHRONICAL (newspaper for the deaf): 5298
FAR EAST: 3093
  Coffee exports: 5298
  Description and travel: 1889
  Naval (United States) cruises: 2265
  Finance: 1424
  Sugar exports: 5298
  Tobacco trade: 5252
FARISH, William P.: 1757
FARJEON, Benjamin Leopold: 2146
FARLEY, Belmont Mercer: 1758
FARLEY FAMILY (Genealogy): 1758
FARM ACCOUNTS: 1759
  see also AGRICULTURAL WORKERS; PLANTATION ACCOUNTS
  Alabama: 2930, 4861
  Georgia--Cherokee County: 1887
  Maryland: 2872, 3254
    Beaver Creek District: 3329
    Frederick County: 340
  Mississippi--Jasper County: 3876
  New Hampshire--Landaff: 4265
  North Carolina: 399, 2087
    Beaufort County: 5814
    Catawba County: 5745
    Durham County: 4480
    Fairfield: 921
    Franklin County: 5087
    Iredell County: 3787
    Lincoln County: 4450
    Lockville: 5207
    Mocksville: 2749
    Montgomery County: 4689
    Mount Gilead: 4689
    Oak Grove Township: 3896
    Raleigh: 2938
    Randolph County: 108
    Washington: 705, 911
    Washington County: 5013
  South Carolina: 501, 2961, 3405
    Branchville: 1749
  Tennessee: 3692
  Virginia:
    Albemarle County: 5302
    Clarke County: 3602
    Nelson County: 5290
    "Rose Hill": 3833
    Warrenton: 5210
  West Virginia:
    Falling Waters: 4999
    Grant County: 767
FARM COMMUNITIES, Development of:
  North Carolina--Wilmington: 3447
FARM IMPLEMENTS: see AGRICULTURAL IMPLEMENTS
FARM JOURNALS: see AGRICULTURAL PERIODICALS
FARM LAND: 4892
  Great Britain: 712
  Illinois: 247
  Virginia: 1542
FARM LIFE: 1072
  see also PLANTATION LIFE
  Promotion in moving pictures: 958
  Subdivided by place:
    Alabama--Greene County: 2493
    Arkansas: 1154

741

FARM LIFE:
  Subdivided by place (Continued):
    Connecticut:
      North Branford: 5666
    Georgia: 127, 1912
    Illinois: 1882
    Indiana: 1882
    Kansas: 1882
    Louisiana: 2493
    Maine--Livermore: 5569
    Maryland: 3254, 3378
    Michigan: 4452
    Missouri: 1882
    New Hampshire: 776
    New Jersey: 373
    New York: 4452
    North Carolina: 373, 675, 1882
      Forsyth County: 156
      Halifax County: 3831
      Oak Grove Township: 3896
    Pennsylvania: 373
      Franklin County: 2643
    Tennessee: 2493
    Virginia:
      Prince Edward County: 5884
FARM MACHINERY: see AGRICULTURAL MACHINERY
FARM MANAGEMENT: 3533
  see also PLANTATION MANAGEMENT
  Georgia: 5364
  North Carolina: 4262, 4849
  South Carolina: 1334, 2814
  Virginia: 4616, 5210
    Manassas: 5272
FARM PRODUCE PRICES:
  North Carolina:
    Halifax County: 426
  United States: 672
FARM PRODUCTS: see AGRICULTURAL PRODUCTS; and specific types of agricultural products
FARM SCHOOL, Covington, Virginia: 3308
FARM SUPPLIES:
  see also names of specific supplies, e.g. CLOVER SEED
  Scarcity of: 5018
  Subdivided by place:
    North Carolina--Carthage: 5138
    South Carolina: 2880, 5114
    Virginia:
      Albemarle County: 3699
      Falmouth: 2165
      Norfolk: 3830
FARM TENANCY: 1759
  see also FREEDMEN--Tenancy; PEASANTRY; SHARECROPPING
  Labor contracts:
    see also FREEDMEN--Labor contracts
    North Carolina:
      Richmond County: 3475
  Laws and legislation:
    North Carolina: 3447
  Subdivided by place:
    Mississippi: 1786
    North Carolina: 4918
      Beaufort County: 911
      Lumberton: 3422
    South Carolina: 4460
    Virginia: 1568, 3560
FARM WORKERS: see AGRICULTURAL WORKERS; FREEDMEN--Tenancy; PEASANTRY
FARMAN, Eliza Anna: 3810
FARMER, Henry: 5503
FARMER, Marguerite (Power): 3077
FARMERS' ALLIANCE: 5549
  Mississippi: 4442
  North Carolina: 2330, 2804, 3996, 5709
  Virginia: 5709
FARMERS' AND EXCHANGE BANK OF CHARLESTON: 1760
FARMERS BANK OF VIRGINIA, Danville, Virginia: 1761, 3846
  Fredericksburg branch: 5556

FARMERS' BUTTER AND CHEESE COMPANY, West Acton, Massachusetts: 2456
FARMERS' EDUCATIONAL AND CO-OPERATIVE UNION OF AMERICA: 592
FARMERS' FRIEND FERTILIZER: 2176
FARMERS' MUTUAL BENEFIT ASSOCIATION OF VIRGINIA: 3400
FARMERS' NATIONAL CONGRESS, Raleigh, North Carolina: 4732
FARMERS' ORGANIZATIONS: see AGRICULTURAL ORGANIZATIONS
FARMERS' STATE ALLIANCE OF NORTH CAROLINA: 1256
FARMING:
  see also AGRICULTURE; CROPS, and specific kinds of crops; DAIRY FARMS; LIVESTOCK, and specific kinds of livestock; PEASANTRY; PLANTATION MANAGEMENT; PLANTATIONS; RANCHING; SHARECROPPING
  Alabama: 1084
    Dallas County: 223
  Arkansas: 1587
    Dardanelle: 3276
  China: 2191
  Connecticut:
    Hartford County: 1051
  Denmark: 3451
  Florida: 2232, 2387
  France: 5323
  Georgia (1800s): 662, 1705, 1912, 2232, 2326, 4875
  Idaho Territory: 2714
  Illinois: 2225, 5153
    Carbondale: 1631
  Indiana: 1601, 5980
  Iowa: 1344
    Wayne County: 4075
  Kansas: 1428, 4202
  Kentucky: 1604
  Maryland: 1932, 2214, 2295
    Frederick County: 340
  Massachusetts: 427
  Middle West: 1820, 4765
  Mississippi:
    Hinds County: 3759
    Leake County: 5475
    Washington County: 5498
  Missouri: 865
  Nebraska: 1344
  New Jersey--Photographs: 1585
  New York: 1587, 5660
    Poughkeepsie: 1908
  North Carolina:
    1700s-1900s: 799, 4918
    1800s: 440, 484, 1428, 1584, 2068, 2121, 3410, 4858, 5770
    Anson County: 4052
    Caswell County: 5243
    Catawba County: 5745
    Edgewater: 4858
    Guilford County: 2330
    Hyde County: 419
    Iredell County: 5245
    Lilesville: 2493
    Martin County: 5036
    Onslow County: 1252
    Person County: 1336
    Warren County: 3307
    Whitaker's: 273
  Ohio: 1177, 3848, 5307, 5980
    Preble County: 2606
  Pennsylvania: 699
    Sinking Valley: 3424
  South Carolina: 430, 3801
    Beaufort: 1891
    Spartanburg: 4080
  Southern States: 761
  Sweden: 3451
  Tennessee: 872, 1587
    Hays County: 273
  Texas: 1587, 4269
  United States: 904
  Virginia:
    1700s: 1066

FARMING:
  Virginia (Continued):
    1700s-1800s: 558, 1262, 3560, 3671
    1700s-1900s: 4924
    1800s: 794, 1240, 1354, 1436, 1587, 2489, 4729, 5660, 5751, 5980
    1800s-1900s: 1931, 3979
    Albemarle County: 3699
    Amherst County: 3788
    Buckingham County: 2378, 3809
    Campbell County: 2369
    Culpeper County: 3141
    Cumberland County: 531
    Edinburg: 4124
    Farmville: 1729
    Gloucester County: 3809
    Hanover County: 4020
    Locust Dale: 1073
    Quicksburg: 4121
    Southampton County: 5248
    Spotsylvania County: 3141
  West Virginia: 581, 865, 1946
    Jefferson County: 4388, 5591
  Western States: 5309
  Wisconsin--Rock County: 5307
FARMING, Experimental: see EXPERIMENTAL FARMING
FARMING METHODS: see AGRICULTURAL PRACTICES; CROP ROTATION
FARMINGTON, Connecticut: 2636
FARMINGTON, Maine: 5610
FARMINGTON, Mississippi: see CIVIL WAR--CAMPAIGNS, BATTLES, AND MILITARY ACTIONS--Mississippi--Farmington
FARMINGTON, North Carolina: 2857
FARMVILLE, Virginia: 1729, 2683, 2712, 3136
  Tobacco: 531
FARNHAM, England: 332
FARNSWORTH, Isaac T.: 1762
FARNSWORTH FAMILY (Mississippi): 1762
FARR, Oren E.: 1763
FARRABOUGH, Aaron: 1764
FARRABOUGH, Jacob: 1764
FARRAGUT, David Glasgow: 276
FARRAND, William P.: 3231
FARRANT, Francis: 868
FARRAR, Cyril Lytton: 1765
FARRAR, Frederic William: 1113, 1765
FARRAR, Mary: 1766
FARRAR, Thomas J.: 1767
FARRAR FAMILY: 761
"FARRINGFORD," England: 5226
"FASHION," Louisiana: 5208
FASHION: see CLOTHING AND DRESS
FASHODA CRISIS OF 1898: 1815
FASOLD, Emma J.: 1768
FASOLD, Philip M.: 1768
FAUCETT AND COMPANY, Durham, North Carolina: 3762
FAUCETTE, Edward W.: 3177
FAUCETTE, Paul B.: 5233
FAUCETTE FAMILY (North Carolina--Genealogy): 4078
FAUCHET, Joseph: 4348
FAULKNER, Charles James (1806-1884): 581, 743, 1769
FAULKNER, Charles James (1847-1929): 1770
FAULKNER, H. D.: 1065
FAULKNER, John W.: 4299
FAULKNER, Sallie Winn: 1770
FAULKNER, William Cuthbert: 1771
FAULKNER AND CLARK (firm): see CLARK AND FAULKNER
FAUQUIER COUNTY, Virginia: 3819
  Civil War: 2829
  Land settlement: 99
  Personal finance--Women: 512
  Physicians: 4173
  Superior Court: 3994
  Cities and towns:
    Kinsley Mills: 1447
    Marshall:
      Blacksmith's accounts: 3582

FAUQUIER COUNTY, Virginia:
  Cities and towns: (Continued):
    "Monterosa": 4916
    Paris--Merchants: 4743
    The Plains: 5377
    Salem: 3125
    Somerville: 3681
    Upperville: 212, 3232
    Warrenton: see WARRENTON,
      Virginia
FAUQUIER AND ALEXANDRIA TURNPIKE
  COMPANY: 2728
FAUST by Johann Wolfgang von
  Goethe: 2058
FAVROT, Thomas P.: 1772
FAW, Enoch: 1773
FAWCETT, Edgar (1874-1904): 2449
FAWCETT, Henry (1833-1884): 1774,
  2149, 5050
FAWCETT, Millicent: 5050
FAWCETT, Sir William (1728-1804):
  499
FAWKES, Walter Ramsden Hawksworth:
  5913
FAXON (JOSIAH), Alexandria, Virginia
  (firm): 2933
FAYAL ISLAND:
  Description and travel: 1284
FAYETTE, Missouri: 1620, 2386
FAYETTE COUNTY, Georgia:
  Fayetteville: 3318
FAYETTE COUNTY, Kentucky:
  Lexington: see LEXINGTON,
    Kentucky
FAYETTE COUNTY, Pennsylvania:
  Brownsville: 1282
  Uniontown: 1426
FAYETTE COUNTY, Virginia:
  Mercantile accounts: 4011
FAYETTE COUNTY, West Virginia:
  Confederate military activities:
    3268
FAYETTEVILLE, Georgia: 3318
FAYETTEVILLE, North Carolina:
  1700s: 935, 2734
  1700s-1900s: 2161
  1800s: 530, 1525, 1547, 2354
    1800s: 3873
    1810s: 3873
    1820s: 1396, 3873, 5376
    1830s: 5376
    1850s: 1688, 2846, 5842
    1860s: 2253, 2846, 5383, 5703
    1870s: 1438
  1800s-1900s: 3403, 3447
  1900s: 4724, 5072
  Auctions: 5298
  Banks and banking: 5298
  Business affairs: 484, 3905
  Civil War:
    see also CIVIL WAR--CAMPAIGNS,
      BATTLES, AND MILITARY
      ACTIONS--North Carolina--
      Fayetteville
    Confederate depredations: 5298
    Union depredations: 956, 5298
  Cotton mills: 396
  Development and growth: 4517, 5298
  Economic conditions: 3905
  Education: 5298
  Fires: 5298
  Gas lighting: 5298
  Masonry: 1898
  Merchants: 2431
  Photographs: 2398
  Recreational programs: 5298
  Schools: 1898, 5298
  Social life and customs: 5298
  Sunday schools; 5298
  Temperance: 1556, 5905
  Universities and colleges: see
    FAYETTEVILLE STATE UNIVERSITY
  Visit of Marquis de Lafayette:
    2870
FAYETTEVILLE ACADEMY, Fayetteville,
  North Carolina: 1898, 5298
FAYETTEVILLE DISTRICT, Methodist
  Church: 3646

FAYETTEVILLE GAS LIGHT COMPANY: 5298
FAYETTEVILLE STATE TEACHERS COLLEGE,
  Fayetteville, North Carolina: see
  FAYETTEVILLE STATE UNIVERSITY
FAYETTEVILLE STATE UNIVERSITY,
  Fayetteville, North Carolina: 4724
FAZAKERLEY, John Nicholas: 1775
"THE FEAR MARKET" by Amélie Rives: 4491
FEATHERSTON, Winfield S.: 1825
FEDERAL AID TO EDUCATION: 325, 1758,
  3345
FEDERAL COMMUNICATIONS COMMISSION:
  see UNITED STATES--GOVERNMENT
  AGENCIES AND OFFICIALS--Federal
  Communications Commission
FEDERAL COUNCIL OF THE CHURCHES OF
  CHRIST IN AMERICA: 1194, 1197,
  3558, 3633
FEDERAL RESERVE BANK OF ATLANTA: 1776
FEDERAL RESERVE SYSTEM ACT: 706
FEDERALIST PARTY: 1424, 3041, 3532,
  4348
  Newspapers: 105
  Opposition to: 404
  Subdivided by place:
    Connecticut: 3041
    Virginia: 404, 3809
FEDERATION OF AUSTRALIA: see
  AUSTRALIA
FEDERATIONS--Financial (Social
  service): see COMMUNITY CHEST;
  UNITED FUND
FEIMSTER, Abner: 1777
FEIN, John M.: 4155
FELDER, John: 2815
DER FELDZUG IN NORD-VIRGINIEN IM
  AUGUST 1862 by Ferdinand Franz
  Mangold: 3480
FELICIANA PARISH, Louisiana:
  Clinton:
    Girls' schools and academies:
      4373, 4819
FELLOWS, Sir Charles: 3234
FELLOWS' LIBRARY, Winchester,
  England: 3477
FELLOWSHIP OF SOUTHERN CHURCHMEN:
  1196
FELLOWSHIPS: see SCHOLARSHIPS
FELTON, Mrs. _____ (Vermont): 3129
FELUCCA ESPERANZA (Spanish corsair):
  3570
FEMALE EDUCATIONAL SOCIETY, Liberty,
  Georgia: 2931
FEMALE SEAMEN'S FRIEND SOCIETY: 786
FENCES AND FENCING:
  Laws and legislation:
    South Carolina: 4310
    Virginia: 3642
  Virginia--Albemarle County: 3699
FENCIBLES: see Militia as subheading
  under names of places
FENDALL, Philip Ricard: 1778
FENDALL FAMILY: 1778
FENELON by Clara Victoria (Dargan)
  Maclean: 3418
FENG YU-HSIANG: 5252
FENIANISM:
  see also HOME RULE--Ireland
  Great Britain: 4566
  Raids in New York: 4485
FENNELL, E. D.: 1779
FENNER, Charles Erasmus: 1439
FENN'S BRIDGE, Georgia: 3221
FENSTANTON, England: 4693
FENTON, A. W.: 1780
FENTRISS, North Carolina: 2330
FERDINAND VII, King of Spain: 4213
FERGUSON, Anderson: 1783
FERGUSON, Betty Ann: 1783
FERGUSON, Garland Sevier, Jr.
  (b. 1843): 5457
FERGUSON, James Dugué: 3809
FERGUSON, John: 208, 1781
FERGUSON, Samuel Wragg: 1782
FERGUSON FAMILY (North Carolina): 1783
FERNANDEZ, J. O.: 3252

FERNANDINA, Florida:
  Civil War:
    see also CIVIL WAR--CAMPAIGNS,
      BATTLES AND MILITARY ACTIONS--
      Florida--Fernandina
    United States Army camp life: 5425
  Diseases--Yellow fever: 4410
FERON, Thomas S.: 4188
FERREBEE, Amanda E.: 1784
FERREBEE, Sarah Eliza: 1784
FERREL, George: 5456
FERREL, Rosa: 5456
FERREL, William (1819-1891): 1785
FERRELL, Bird L.: 5148
FERRELL, P. W.: 5148
FERRIDAY, Pendleton: 1786
FERRIDAY FAMILY (Mississippi): 1786
FERRIES:
  North Carolina--Bath: 705
FERTILIZER: 4924, 5593
  see also BONE DUST; GUANO; PLASTER
  Advertising: see ADVERTISING--
    Fertilizer
  Alabama: 5862
  North Carolina: 641, 3410, 4858
  Virginia: 195, 1587, 4710
FERTILIZER INDUSTRY: 3378
  see also AGRICULTURAL CHEMICALS
  North Carolina: 960
    Durham: 3762
  Pennsylvania--Philadelphia: 373
  South Carolina: 1019
  United States: 1115
  Virginia--Norfolk: 373
FERTILIZER TRADE:
  North Carolina: 4152, 4344, 4666
    Wilmington: 5912
  South Carolina: 4530
  Virginia--Petersburg: 2176
FESSENDEN, William Pitt: 1787
FESTERMAN, Levi A.: 1788
FESTIVALS: see PUBLIC CELEBRATIONS;
  and names of specific holidays
FETHERSTON-HOUGH, Frances: 1210
FETHERSTONHAUGH, Maria Georgiana
  (Carleton): 5872
FEUDAL COURTS: see COURTS--Courts
  baron
FEUDAL PRIVILEGES:
  Great Britain--Sussex: 4767
FEUDALISM:
  France--Dauphiné: 4408
FEW, Benjamin: 1789
FEW, Ignatius: 1789
FEW, William (1748-1828): 1789, 2788,
  5537
FEW, William Preston (1867-1940):
  706, 1584, 2075, 4242, 5252
FEW FAMILY (North Carolina--
  Genealogy): 714
FEW SOCIETY OF EMORY COLLEGE: 1703
FICKLEN, John: 1790
FIDELITY BONDS: see (name of country
  or state)--Government agencies and
  officials--Public officials--Bonding
FIEFS: see FEUDALISM
FIELD, David Dudley: 1792
FIELD, Edwin Wilkins: 4234
FIELD, Florence (Lathrop): 4020
FIELD, Frederick Vanderbilt: 5252
FIELD, Henry Martyn: 1792
FIELD, Jane Lucinda (Hopkins): 1792
FIELD, Jeanie Lucinda: 1792
FIELD, John W.: 1791
FIELD, Joseph T.: 523
FIELD (MARSHALL) AND COMPANY: 1195
FIELD, Maunsell Bradhurst: 5799
FIELD, Samuel M.: 1791
FIELD FAMILY (Massachusetts--
  Genealogy): 1792
FIELD FAMILY (Virginia): 1791
FIELD LIBRARY, Peekskill, New York:
  4343
FIELD TRIPS: see SCIENTIFIC
  EXPEDITIONS
FIELDCREST MILLS, INC.: 3187
FIELDING, William H.: 1793
FIELDS, G. S.: 2462

FIELDS, James Thomas: 103
FIELDS, John: 1791
FIELDS, Obadiah: 1794
FIELDS FAMILY (North Carolina): 2240
FIFE, Alexander William George Duff, First Duke of: 507
FIFER, John: 1795
FIFESVILLE, Virginia:
　Cookery: 4459
　Mercantile accounts: 4459
FIFTH MARYLAND REGIMENT VETERAN CORPS: 4348
FIFTH STREET METHODIST CHURCH, Wilmington, North Carolina: 3646, 5912
FIFTIETH ANNIVERSARY, CHARLESTON TYPOGRAPHICAL UNION, NO. 43: 2771
"FIFTY YEARS OF ELECTRICAL DEVELOPMENT IN NORTH CAROLINA" by Charles E. Waddell: 5490
FIFTY YEARS OF PUBLIC LIFE by Daniel Calhoun Roper: 4564
FIGHTER FOR PEACE: 3066
FILIBUSTER WAR (1855-1860): 617, 3960
FILIBUSTERS:
　see also SOLDIERS OF FORTUNE
　Cuba: 2387, 4982, 4983
　Florida: 4982
　Latin America: 2695
　Nicaragua: see FILIBUSTER WAR
FILIPINO SECRET SOCIETY: see KATIPUNAN
FILIPINOS: 5844
LA FILLE DU REGIMENT: 1862
FILLMORE, Millard: 872, 1308, 1422, 1796, 3204, 3424, 4943, 5974
　Administration: 730
FILM ADAPTATIONS: see AMERICAN FICTION--Film adaptations
FINANCE:
　see also HOUSEHOLD FINANCE; INTERNATIONAL FINANCE; PERSONAL FINANCE; PUBLIC FINANCE; and Finance as subheading under names of businesses, institutions, organizations, groups, and occupations
　Alabama: 4184, 5032
　Arkansas: 1154, 2117
　Canada: 1941
　Far East: 1424
　Georgia: 4647, 5298
　　Effingham County: 1375
　Great Britain: 369, 5173
　　Staffordshire: 190
　Louisiana: 730
　Maryland--Baltimore: 3053
　New York: 2246, 4806
　North Carolina: 1584, 2553, 3639, 3960
　　Chatham County: 1056
　　Granville County: 68, 1224
　　Lincolnton: 3317
　Ohio: 281, 2504, 3085, 3648
　Pennsylvania: 4756
　South Carolina: 718, 3552, 4034
　　Charleston: 2414, 3589
　Tennessee: 3069, 4269
　Virginia: 3788, 3809, 5357
　　Lexington: 3362
　Washington, D.C.: 3373, 4359
　West Virginia: 356
FINANCIAL AFFAIRS: see FINANCE
FINANCIAL INSTITUTIONS:
　Bankruptcy:
　　New York: 2587
　　Virginia--Columbia: 5035
　New York: 2619
　North Carolina: 4918
FINANCIAL REFORMER: 1774
FINANCIAL SOCIETIES:
　Maryland--Baltimore: 3971
FINCASTLE, Virginia: 52, 74, 117, 5904
FINCASTLE & LEWISBURG MAIL-STAGE LINE: 1797
FINDEN, William: 2148

FINDLEY, Alexander T.: 1798
FINDLEY, J. Woods: 1798
FINDLEY, James J.: 1799
FINDLEY, Joseph R.: 1798
FINDLEY, Thomas F.: 1798
FINDLEY, William M.: 1798
FINE ARTS: see ARTS
FINGAL (steamer): see ATLANTA
FINK, C. A.: 3944
FINLEY, James E. B.: 3791
FINLEY, John: 2871
FINLEY, John (1778-1865): 1800
FINLEY, John Huston (1863-1940): 4556
FINLEY, W. W.: 706
FINLEY HIGH SCHOOL, Lenoir, North Carolina: 3177
FINNEY, William A. J.: 1801
FINNO-UGRIAN LANGUAGES: 4552
FIRE EXTINGUISHERS: 2120
FIRE INSURANCE: see INSURANCE--Fire
FIRE LOSSES: see FIRES
FIRE PROTECTION:
　North Carolina--Durham: 2379
FIREARMS: see CARTRIDGE CLIPS; GATLING GUN; GUN BARRELS; MACHINE GUNS; ORDNANCE; PERCUSSION RIFLE BULLETS; UNITED STATES--ARMY-- Civil War--Firearms; and Ordnance as subheading under names of armies and navies
FIREARMS INDUSTRY:
　see also GUNSMITHING; ORDNANCE; and Ordnance as subheading under names of armies and navies
　1800s: 5714
　1900s: 4453
FIREMAN'S FUND INSURANCE COMPANY: 5790
FIREMEN'S RELIEF FUND OF NEW BERN, NORTH CAROLINA: 3955
FIRES: 291
　Florida--Jacksonville: 3264
　Great Britain:
　　Crystal Palace: 2410
　　Portsmouth: 92
　Illinois:
　　Chicago (1871): 2638, 2681, 3566, 3809, 4375
　Mississippi:
　　Natchez: 1047, 1762
　North Carolina:
　　Fayetteville: 5298
　South Carolina:
　　Charleston:
　　　1838: 2491
　　　1861: 2610, 2695, 3485
　　Columbia: 1017
　Tennessee--Nashville: 5290
　Virginia: 2678
　　Petersburg: 5499
　　Richmond (1811): 322, 872
FIRST AFRICAN CHURCH, Savannah, Georgia: 5787
THE FIRST AMERICAN, HIS HOMES AND HOUSEHOLDS by Leila Herbert: 4911
FIRST BAPTIST CHURCH, Durham, North Carolina: 5401
FIRST BAPTIST CHURCH, Raleigh, North Carolina: 5401
FIRST CONGREGATIONAL CHURCH, Colchester, Connecticut: 5748
FIRST METHODIST CHURCH, Washington, North Carolina: 3646
FIRST PRESBYTERIAN CHURCH, Durham, North Carolina: 2934, 3762
FIRST STEPS IN NORTH CAROLINA HISTORY by Cornelia Philipps Spencer: 4992
FISCAL POLICY: see PUBLIC FINANCE
FISGARD (warship): 2296
FISH, Hamilton (1808-1893): 1802
FISH, Hamilton, Jr.: 2109
FISH--Ganges River: 3577
FISH COMMISSION: see UNITED STATES-- GOVERNMENT AGENCIES AND OFFICIALS-- Bureau of Fisheries
FISH CULTURE--Europe: 3357
FISH HATCHING DEVICES: 3359

FISH TRADE: 323
　Prices: 4541
　Subdivided by place:
　　Great Britain: 2742
　　North Carolina: 2889
　　Plymouth: 1015
　　Wilmington: 1281
　　Spain: 2742
　　Virginia: 2567
FISHER, Albert Kenrick: 1803
FISHER, Amory: 1804
FISHER, Ann (Ambler): 99
FISHER, Benjamin Franklin: 1805
FISHER, Charles: 5457
FISHER, Charles Frederick: 5457
FISHER, Cyrus M.: 4485
FISHER, Dorothea Frances (Canfield): 4290
FISHER, Frances Christine: 1494, 2449, 5294, 5457
FISHER, George Park: 4881
FISHER, Jane: 1806
FISHER, John A.: 452
FISHER, Lavinia: 1806
FISHER, Leonard: 1804
FISHER, Lindley: 1807
FISHER, Mandy: 1806
FISHER, Mary (Ripley): 4485
FISHER, Walter Lowrie: 2516
FISHER AND COMPANY (shipping firm): 3578
FISHERIES: see FISHING INDUSTRY; UNITED STATES--GOVERNMENT AGENCIES AND OFFICIALS--Bureau of Fisheries
FISHER'S HILL, Virginia: see CIVIL WAR--CAMPAIGNS, BATTLES AND MILITARY ACTIONS--Virginia--Fisher's Hill
FISHING (non-commerical):
　North Carolina--Fort Fisher: 3370
　Scotland: 5259
FISHING INDUSTRY:
　see also OYSTER CULTURE
　Labrador: 636
　Massachusetts--Worcester: 4314
　Newfoundland: 636
　North Carolina: 325, 1015, 3907
　　Hatteras: 4547
　　New Bern: 3955
　Rhode Island: 4907
　United States: 3357, 4564
FISHING NETS:
　Knitting machines--Inventions: 3424
FISHING RIGHTS:
　see also TERRITORIAL WATERS--Fishing rights
　Pennsylvania:
　　Susquehanna River: 4756
FISK, Clinton Bowen: 1808
FISK, S. W.: 4479
FISK, Wilbur: 1906
FISK UNIVERSITY, Nashville, Tennessee: 2852
FISKE, Libbie Foster: 4086
FISNER, Martin de: 4979
FITCH, Clyde: see FITCH, William Clyde
FITCH, R. S.: 1809
FITCH, William Clyde: 3797, 4789
FITE, Samuel M.: 872
FITZCLARENCE, George Augustus Frederick, First Earl of Munster: 1911
FITZGERALD, Edmund B.: 1810
FITZGERALD, John (Virginia): 1811
FITZGERALD, John Forster (Scotland): 859
FITZGERALD, Oscar Penn: 4080
FITZGERALD, William: see FOSTER-VESEY- FITZGERALD, William
FITZGIBBON, Eleanor: 5971
FITZHERBERT, Alleyne, First Baron St. Helens: 3858
FITZHUGH, Anna M.: 3157
FITZHUGH, Elizabeth D.: 1812
FITZHUGH, George: 1439, 2612
FITZHUGH, Henry: 1813
FITZHUGH, Philip A.: 1814
FITZHUGH, Thomas (b. 1862): 3251

FITZHUGH, William Bullitt: 1814
FITZHUGH FAMILY (Virginia--Genealogy): 1812
FITZMAURICE, Edmond George Petty, First Baron Fitzmaurice: 1014
FITZMAURICE, Henry Charles Keith Petty-, Fifth Marquis of Lansdowne: 5872
FITZPATRICK, Benjamin: 265, 1084, 1877
FITZROY, Sir Almeric William: 1815
FITZROY, Augustus Henry, Third Duke of Grafton: 92, 5330
FITZSIMONS, Thomas: 1816
FITZWILLIAM, Charles William, Fifth Earl Fitzwilliam: 1648
FITZWILLIAM, Charles William Wentworth, Third Earl Fitzwilliam: 2149
FITZWILLIAM, W. S.: 323
FITZWILLIAM, New Hampshire: 1865, 1983
FIUME QUESTION: 4020
FIVE FORKS, Virginia, Battle of: see CIVIL WAR--CAMPAIGNS, BATTLES, AND MILITARY ACTIONS--Virginia--Five Forks
FIVE-MILE ACT, Repeal of: 3120
FIVE YEAR PLAN (Union of Soviet Socialist Republics): 4614
FLAG RAISING CEREMONIES: Fort Sumter, South Carolina: 4215, 5001
THE FLAG REPLACED ON SUMTER by William Arnold Spicer: 5001
FLAG SIGNAL INSTRUCTION COMPANY, Tuscarora, Maryland: 1442
FLAGG, George A.: 1817, 4029
FLAGG, H. O.: 208, 1818
FLAGG, Henry G.: 1819
FLAGLER, Henry Morrison: 5291
FLAGS:
　Confederate States of America: 1191, 2691, 4918
　　North Carolina:
　　　Fort Fisher: 5972
　　　Secession flag: 4918
　Virginia: 3809
A FLAGSTONE WALK by Thaddeus Garland Stem, Jr.: 5049
THE FLAMING SWORD by Thomas Dixon: 1521
FLAMMARION, Camille: 1424
FLANDERS, Benjamin Franklin: 3628
FLANDERS, Daniel J.: 1820
FLANNERY, John: 2232
FLASH, Henry Lynden: 2449
FLAT CREEK TOWNSHIP, Virginia: 1821
FLAT RIVER, North Carolina:
　Mercantile accounts: 3481
FLAT RIVER BAPTIST ASSOCIATION (North Carolina): 320
FLAT ROCK, North Carolina: 3019
FLAT ROCK, South Carolina: 4818
FLAX TRADE:
　Great Britain and Spain: 2742
FLEETWOOD, Rebecca J.: 1822
FLEISHER, Henry C.: 1202
FLEMING, Anna: 1823
FLEMING, George: 1824
FLEMING, James L.: 1825
FLEMING, M. B.: 1826
FLEMING, Mary Eliza: 4698
FLEMING, Walter Lynwood: 706
FLEMING FAMILY (North Carolina): 1826
FLEMING FAMILY (Virginia): 4698
FLEMING AND PRESCOTT (firm): see PRESCOTT AND FLEMING
FLEMING COUNTY, Kentucky: 1809
　Flemingsburg: see FLEMINGSBURG, Kentucky
FLEMINGSBURG, Kentucky:
　Description: 4654
　Literary affairs: 1608
FLEMINGTON, New Jersey: 4964
FLETCHER, Elijah: 5765
FLETCHER, John William: 4146
FLETCHER, Lucy Muse (Walton): 1827
FLETCHER, Mary (Bosanquet): 1317, 4146
FLETCHER, Patterson: 1827

FLETCHER, Robert: 1529
FLETCHER, Thomas Clement: 3703
FLETCHER FAMILY: 1827
FLETCHER, Indiana: 5765
FLETCHER AND HALL (firm): 1529
FLETCHER AND KENDALL (firm): 1529
FLICK, William Henry Harrison: 1828
FLINN, J. William: 4936
FLINN, W. H.: 1829
FLINT, Michigan: 689
FLINT ROCK, North Carolina:
　Religion and social life: 5890
FLINTSHIRE, Wales--Gyrn Castle: 366
FLIPPIN, Louisa B.: 266
FLIPPIN, Percy Scott: 2860
FLIPPIN FAMILY (Virginia): 266
FLOOD, Edward: 1830
FLOOD, Henry D.: 1364
FLOOD RELIEF:
　West Virginia--Harpers Ferry: 5938
FLOODS:
　Brazil--Campos: 1644
　Georgia: 1203
　Mississippi River: 1762, 2794
　Missouri: 5551
　Virginia:
　　Columbia (Photographs): 5035
　　Robinson's River: 253
FLORA, Anne (Putney): 1831
FLORENCE, Illinois: 2264
FLORENCE, Italy: 1464, 2181, 3385, 3836
　Biographical studies: 5487
FLORENCE, South Carolina: 2107, 5750, 5828
　Civil War prison: 4434
FLORENCE COUNTY, South Carolina:
　Florence:
FLORENCE RAILROAD AND IMPROVEMENT COMPANY: 5779
FLORENTINE HISTORY by Henry Edward Napier: 3836
FLORENZ, Tomás: 4155
FLORIDA: 4720
　see also SOUTHERN STATES
　Agriculture: 3611, 4743
　　see also FLORIDA--Farming; FLORIDA--Plantations; and names of specific crops under FLORIDA
　American poetry: 1653
　American Red Cross: 3
　American Revolution: see various subheadings under AMERICAN REVOLUTION
　Annexation (Proposed): see BLOUNT CONSPIRACY
　Bank failures: 2877
　Birds: 1803
　Book buying: 1653
　British invasion, Fear of: 4982
　Business enterprises: 5291
　Canals (Proposed): 1403
　Cession by Spain: 5734
　Chautauquas: 3008
　Civil War: see appropriate subheadings under CIVIL WAR; CONFEDERATE STATES OF AMERICA; UNITED STATES--ARMY--Civil War
　Clergy: 1653, 5740
　Commodity prices (Civil War): 5955
　Cotton--Sea Island cotton: 3611
　Cotton growing--East Florida: 3389
　Cotton trade--Milton: 3008
　Crime: 5740
　Currency: 1339
　Democratic Party: 988
　Depression (1929): 1653
　Description and travel:
　　1700s: 3173
　　1800s: 670, 1084, 1947, 4743
　Development and growth: 2417
　Diseases:
　　Yellow fever in Fernandina and Jacksonville: 4410
　Economic conditions:
　　Reconstruction: 807
　Episcopal churches: 1653
　Estate accounts: 4903

FLORIDA (Continued):
　Estates:
　　Administration and settlement: 4298
　　Jackson County: 4903
　Exploration: 3269
　Farming: 2232, 2387
　　see also FLORIDA--Agriculture; FLORIDA--Plantations; and names of specific crops under FLORIDA
　Filibusters: 4982
　Fires--Jacksonville: 3264
　Freedmen--Labor contracts: 5659
　Funeral sermons: 1832
　Government agencies and officials:
　　Governors: 5978
　Harbors--Canaveral: 2387
　Health conditions: 4743
　Historical studies: 4434
　Houses: 1584
　Hurricanes: 3
　Indians of North America:
　　Raids: 1438
　　Relations with whites: 1947
　　Social life and customs: 3173
　　Wars: see SEMINOLE WARS
　Invasions:
　　Fear of British invasion (1796): 4982
　　Proposed by Governor William Blount (1797): see BLOUNT CONSPIRACY
　　By United States Army (1818): 2781
　Labor in politics: 2568
　Labor unions: see FLORIDA--Postal unions
　Land:
　　Prices: 2387
　　Purchases and sales:
　　　East Florida: 4040
　Land claims: 3447, 3598
　Land companies: 4298
　Land deeds and indentures: 2232
　Land development: 5848
　Land settlement: 693, 1424, 3041
　Land speculation: 631, 4298
　　see also FLORIDA--Real estate investment
　Law practice: 631
　Legislature: 5978
　Lighthouses: 1440
　Lynching: 5740
　Merchants: 2232
　　Pensacola: 3008
　Military affairs: 842
　Militia--Military supplies: 1926
　Murder: 5740
　Nature essays: 1653
　Naval stores industry: 4298
　　see also FLORIDA--Turpentine industry
　New Deal--Public opinion: 1653
　Orange crops: 1575
　Overseers: 2901
　Personal finance: 1653
　Plantation life--Duval County: 4410
　Plantation management: 3447
　Plantations: 2901, 4743, 5659
　　see also FLORIDA--Agriculture; FLORIDA--Farming; and names of specific crops under FLORIDA
　Finance: 2755
　Politics and government: 5740, 5978
　　see also FLORIDA--Labor in politics
　Postal unions: 3
　Prohibition: 1248
　Railroads: 23, 2795, 4343
　　see also FLORIDA--Short-line railroads
　　Construction: 5928
　　Passengers: 2795
　Real estate investment: 2109
　　see also FLORIDA--Land speculation
　Reconstruction: 566, 4410
　　Economic conditions: 807
　　Monticello: 4068

FLORIDA (Continued):
    Relations (General) with Georgia: 2179
    Religion: 5740
        see also FLORIDA--Episcopal churches; FLORIDA--Sermons
    Rice: 1803
    Sea-walls at Canaveral: 2387
    Seminole Indians: 1438
        see also SEMINOLE WARS
    Sermons:
        see also FLORIDA--Funeral sermons
        Episcopal: 1653
    Short-line railroads: 1655
    Slave trade: 4062
    Social life and customs: 1713, 3008, 5740
        New Smyrna: 5480
        Saint Augustine: 5480
    Spiritualism: 1653
    Timber agents: 3993
    Tobacco industry--Quincy: 5740
    Trade and commerce:
        Agricultural products: 2232
        Carriages and buggies: 5623
        Cotton: see FLORIDA--Cotton trade
        Lumber--Milton: 3008
        Pine lumber--Pensacola: 3008
        Slaves: see FLORIDA--Slave trade
    Transportation: 3447
        see also FLORIDA--Canals; FLORIDA--Railroads; FLORIDA--Short-line railroads
    Turpentine industry: 2970
        see also FLORIDA--Naval stores industry
    Universities and colleges: see FLORIDA STATE UNIVERSITY; ROLLINS COLLEGE
    Watercolor sketches of Florida scenes: 5678
    Weather: 1947
    Wills: 3474
FLORIDA, East: see appropriate subheadings under FLORIDA
FLORIDA, New York: 86
FLORIDA (Confederate raider): 863
FLORIDA FEDERATION OF POST OFFICE CLERKS: 3
FLORIDA KEYS, Florida:
    Land titles: 1001
FLORIDA POSTAL GROUPS: 3
FLORIDA STATE UNIVERSITY, Tallahassee, Florida: 902
FLOUR:
    Inspection--Virginia: 2165
    Prices: 3566
        Pennsylvania: 4920
    Transportation: see FREIGHT AND FREIGHTAGE--Flour
FLOUR MILLS::
    see also GRIST MILLS
    Accounts--Maryland: 4803
    Costs--Virginia: 2165
    Subdivided by place:
        Indiana: 4100
        Kansas: 4100
        Maryland: 5763
            Frederick County: 4457
        Missouri--Saint Louis: 128
        North Carolina: 2330
            Guilford County: 5905
            Hoover Hill: 4100
            Lincoln County: 5558
            Milton: 5843
            Orange County: 3337
            Randleman: 5408
            Salem: 1905
        Virginia: 404, 558, 2229, 4615, 5157
            Falmouth: 2165
            Front Royal: 2797
            Kinsley Mills: 1447
            Richmond: 5393
            Roanoke County: 1969

FLOUR MILLS:
    Subdivided by place (Continued):
        West Virginia: 1946
            Hannisville: 2316
            Harpers Ferry: 5938
            Martinsburg: 3832
FLOUR TRADE:
    Georgia--Ebenezer: 5986
    Maryland--Baltimore: 2797, 4348
    North Carolina: 1336, 2924
    Pennsylvania: 2505
    Virginia: 490, 1336, 1556, 2165, 2600, 2797
        Petersburg: 2176
    West Virginia:
        Hannisville: 2316
FLOURNOY, E. H.: 3674
FLOURNOY, I. I.: 1458
FLOURNOY, Richard W.: 1832
FLOURNOY, Thomas Stanhope: 4157
FLOURNOY, William Walton: 1832
FLOURNOY FAMILY (Florida--Genealogy): 1832
FLOWER TRADE:
    see also NURSERIES
    South Carolina: 4610
    Washington, D.C.: 1377
FLOWERS, Humphrey: 1107
FLOWERS, Mark D.: 1833
FLOWERS, Robert Lee: 3972
FLOWERS:
    see also GARDENS AND GARDENING
    Palestine: 1834
FLOYD, Eliza Lavalette: 2612, 2881
FLOYD, George Rogers Clark: 2881
FLOYD, John (1769-1839): 1835
FLOYD, John (1783-1837): 2881, 4315
FLOYD, John Buchanan (1806-1863): 581, 1333, 1836, 2612
FLOYD, Letitia (Preston): 2881
FLOYD, Mrs. Marmaduke: 5787
FLOYD, Mary: 1911
FLOYD, Nicketti: 2881
FLOYD FAMILY (Virginia): 2881
FLOYD, Virginia: 2668
FLOYD COUNTY, Georgia:
    Rome: see ROME, Georgia
FLOYD COUNTY, Indiana:
    New Albany: 2954, 4973, 5097
FLOYD COUNTY, Virginia:
    Floyd: 2668
FLUDD, THOMPSON v.: see THOMPSON v. FLUDD
FLUSHING, New York: 3710
FLUVANNA COUNTY, Virginia: 29, 302, 1767, 1942, 3487
    Agriculture: 5839
    Arsenals: 4915
    Business affairs: 5106, 5839
    Charities: 1244
    Fruit culture: 5035
    Gold mining: 5035
    Land deeds and indentures: 5839
    Law practice: 5839
    Lumber mills and mill workers: 5105
    Lumber trade: 5035
    Medicine: 5839
    Mercantile accounts: 2834
    Plantations: 195, 1134, 5839
    Poultry farming: 5035
    Religion: 5839
    Schools: 558
    Slaves--Vital statistics: 5839
    Tax in kind: 1181
    Cities and towns:
        Columbia: 5108
            Banks and banking: 5035
            Bridge construction: 5106
            Churches: 5091
            Masonry: 3855
        Kent's Store: 1324
        Palmyra: 5147
        Union Mills:
            Grist mills: 2600
FLYING FISH (warship): 2754
FLYNN, Aloysius: 4962
FLYNN, James: 1837

FLYNN, Owen R.: 1838
FODDER: see ENSILAGE; and Forage as subheading under names of armies
FOERSTER, Norman (b. 1887): 102
FOGG BROTHERS CO.: 1839
FOLK POETRY: 1990
FOLK SONGS: see BALLADS
FOLK SPEECH: see DIALECTS
FOLKLORE:
    see also FOLK POETRY
    Bibliography--North Carolina: 691
    Study and teaching:
        North Carolina: 4641
    Subdivided by place:
        Canada: 691
        Great Britain:
            Dorsetshire: 5403
        North Carolina: 691
        United States: 691
        West Virginia: 5550
FOLKLORE SOCIETIES:
    North Carolina: 1064
FOLLETT, Edward: 1840
FOLLY ISLAND, South Carolina:
    Civil War: 1430, 1845
FOLSOM, Gilman: 3848
FOLSOM, Montgomery M.: 1841
FOND DU LAC, [Wisconsin?]:
    Law practice: 2436
FOND DU LAC COUNTY, Wisconsin: 1625
FONTAINE, Francis: 103
FONTAINE, William Winston: 1842
FONTAINE FAMILY (Virginia--Genealogy): 1842
FOOD:
    see also CIVIL WAR--CIVILIAN LIFE--Scarcity of food; CIVIL WAR--PRISONERS AND PRISONS--(Confederate or Union prisoners)--Food; COOKERY; DIET; RAILROADS--Construction--Labor--Food; SLAVES--Food; and Food as subheading under names of armies and navies
    Canning and preserving: 5955
    Prices: 5313
        see also CIVIL WAR--FOOD PRICES
        Great Britain: 535
        New York: 2225
            Volney: 2089
        North Carolina:
            Beaufort County: 5521
            Farmington: 2857
        Texas--Comal County: 218
        Virginia: 1415
    Subdivided by place:
        New York: 4351
        Texas: 4353
        Virginia: 1409
        West Virginia: 3005
FOOD AND DRUG LEGISLATION:
    United States: 592, 3410
FOOD FOR FRANCE FUND: 3710
FOOD RATIONING: see CIVIL WAR--FOOD RATIONING; UNITED STATES--ARMY--Civil War--Food rationing; WORLD WAR II--Civilian life--Rationing
FOOD, TOBACCO, AGRICULTURAL AND ALLIED WORKERS UNION OF AMERICA: 1196, 1197, 1198
FOOD TRADE:
    Georgia--Eatonton: 3352
    Kentucky: 5006
    Maryland--Baltimore: 4348
    Missouri: 5006
    North Carolina: 164
    Ohio: 5006
    Pennsylvania: 164
    Tennessee: 5006
    Virginia--White Post: 2274
FOOD WORKERS: see FOOD, TOBACCO, AGRICULTURAL AND ALLIED WORKERS UNION OF AMERICA
FOORD, James: 1843
FOOTBALL:
    see also SPORTS
    North Carolina: 3338
FOOTE, Andrew Hull: 4989

FOOTE, Henry Stuart: 1844, 2107, 3611
FOOTE, John B.: 1845
FOOTE, Mary Hallock: 2871
FOOTE, William H.: 872
FOR THE MAJOR by Constance Fenimore Woolson: 5908
FORAGE: 1803
see also ENSILAGE; HAY; and Forage as subheading under names of armies
FORBES, Alfred: 1846
FORBES, Archibald: 1424
FORBES, Edwin Fairfield: 1847
FORBES, Hastings Brudenell: 2421
FORBUSH, Edward Howe: 4453
FORCE, Peter: 1525, 1848, 2578, 5584
FORCE BILL (1833): 4852, 5051
FORD, Henry (Civil War soldier): 1850
FORD, Henry (1863-1947): 4073
FORD, Henry Allen: 2449
FORD, John M.: 1850
FORD, Thomas B.: 2449
FORD FOUNDATION: 1758
FORD MOTOR COMPANY: 788
FOREIGN AGENTS: see SPIES; and Foreign agents as subheading under names of countries
FOREIGN AID: see as subheading under name of country giving aid
FOREIGN BORN: see CONFEDERATE STATES OF AMERICA--ARMY--Recruiting and enlistment--Foreign born; IMMIGRATION AND EMIGRATION; UNITED STATES--ARMY--Civil War--Generals--Foreign born
FOREIGN BUSINESS ENTERPRISES:
see also FOREIGN INVESTMENT; INTERNATIONAL BUSINESS AFFAIRS; INTERNATIONAL FINANCE
British in the United States: 3179
Scots in the United States: 3179
FOREIGN CORRESPONDENTS: see under NEWSPAPERS, e.g. NEWSPAPERS--American correspondents in (place)
FOREIGN EXCHANGE: 5228
Rates: 323
West Indies: 3753
Subdivided by place:
Argentina: 2093
British Guiana: 2612
France: 4348
West Indies: 3753
FOREIGN INTERVENTION: see CIVIL WAR--FOREIGN INTERVENTION
FOREIGN INVESTMENT:
see also FOREIGN BUSINESS ENTERPRISES; INTERNATIONAL BUSINESS AFFAIRS; INTERNATIONAL FINANCE
Americans in Guatemala: 5970
Americans in Great Britain: 4895
Americans in the Union of Soviet Socialist Republics: 1424
Americans in Venezuela: 4895
British in Hungary: 3722
British in Russia:
Iron industry: 3238
British in the United States: 2754
Land: 3179
Louisiana Purchase bonds: 3273
Foreigners in Mexico--Land: 3651
FOREIGN LEGION SETTLERS:
Cape Colony: 3067
FOREIGN PUBLIC OPINION: see under names of wars, e.g. CIVIL WAR--FOREIGN PUBLIC OPINION
FOREIGN RELATIONS: see LEAGUE OF NATIONS; and Foreign relations as subheading under names of countries
FOREIGN REMINISCENCES by Henry Richard Vassall Fox, Third Baron Holland: 1875

FOREIGN TRADE: see FREE TRADE; Foreign trade as subheading under names of countries; and names of specific articles of commerce
FOREIGN WOMEN'S BOARD (Methodist churches): 3646
FOREMAN, Clark H.: 5486
FORENSIC PSYCHIATRY:
see also INSANITY
United States: 958
FOREST, Ohio: 3751
FOREST CONSERVATION:
see also AMERICAN FORESTRY ASSOCIATION; CONSERVATION OF NATURAL RESOURCES; CONSERVATION SOCIETY OF SOUTH CAROLINA
North Carolina: 4080
Southern States: 1852
FOREST HISTORY SOCIETY, INC.: 1852
FORESTS AND FORESTRY:
Japan: 5306
South Carolina: 4453
United States: see UNITED STATES--GOVERNMENT AGENCIES AND OFFICIALS--Forest Service
FORESTVILLE, North Carolina: 2716, 4294
FORGERIES: see ART AND ARTISTS--Forgeries; CURRENCY--Counterfeiting; LETTERS--Forgeries; LITERARY FORGERIES
FORGES--Virginia: 3098
FORMAN, Simon: 2146
FORMOSA:
Missions and missionaries:
Presbyterian: 2269
FORNEY, George Hoke: 1853
FORREST, Edwin: 1029, 3797
FORREST, Nathan Bedford: 1137, 1403, 1746, 1854, 3479, 4894, 4899, 5844
FORSBERG, Augustus: 3809
FORSTER, Fred P.: 2407
FORSTER, William (Pennsylvania): 699
FORSTER, William Edward (1818-1886): 1014, 2149, 4455, 5164
FORSYTH, Henderson: 1856
FORSYTH, John (1780-1841): 5734
FORSYTH, John (Georgia): 1855
FORSYTH, John A. (North Carolina): 1856
FORSYTH, Sir Thomas Douglas: 1857, 3238
FORSYTH, Georgia: 3314
Journalism: 2374
FORSYTH CIRCUIT, Methodist churches: 3646
FORSYTH COUNTY, Georgia:
Taxation: 5260
FORSYTH COUNTY, North Carolina: 1538, 2660, 2855, 4248, 5984
Blacksmiths' accounts: 4631
Civil War: 2763
Courts of Equity: 1209
Estates:
Administration and settlement: 1209
Schools: 813
Land--Purchases and sales: 5935
Medical practice: 5982
Teachers' records: 3928
Teaching: 5982
Cities and towns:
Belew's Creek: 3221
Bethania: 2915
Farm life: 156
Kernersville: 3000
Rural Hall: 500
Salem: see SALEM, North Carolina; WINSTON-SALEM, North Carolina
Vienna--Physicians: 1414
Winston-Salem: see WINSTON-SALEM, North Carolina
FORSYTH COUNTY (N.C.) BOARD OF EDUCATION: 813
FORSYTH COUNTY (N.C.) COURT OF EQUITY: 1209

FORSYTH FURNITURE LINES, INC.: 4918
FORSYTH MISSION TO BURMA: 1857
FORSYTH MISSION TO SINKIANG: 3238
FORSYTHE, Henderson: 1858
FORT, David: 1859
FORT, Tomlinson: 1466
FORT ANDERSON, North Carolina: 3357
FORT BARNWELL, North Carolina: 482
Baptist clergy: 484
Merchants: 640
FORT BARTOW, Georgia: 731
FORT BENTON, Montana Territory: 1121
FORT BROOKE, Florida: 5417
FORT BROWN, Texas: 3392
Mexican War: see MEXICAN WAR--CAMPAIGNS, BATTLES, AND MILITARY ACTIONS--Texas--Fort Brown
United States Army camp: 4433
FORT BUTLER, Louisiana--Maps: 5417
FORT CASWELL, North Carolina:
Civil War: 390
Confederate camp life: 3435, 5390
Visit from Jefferson Davis: 3435
FORT CLAIBORNE, Mississippi: 3123
FORT COLUMBIA, New York:
United States Army camp: 4433
FORT COLUMBUS, New York:
Civil War prison: 704
FORT DAVIS, Texas: 5417
FORT DEFIANCE, North Carolina: 5021
FORT DELAWARE, Delaware:
Civil War prison: 664, 1184, 1424, 1711, 3485, 5646, 5900
FORT DEPOSIT, Alabama:
Civil War: 5437
see also CIVIL WAR--CAMPAIGNS, BATTLES, AND MILITARY ACTIONS--Alabama--Fort Deposit
FORT DES MOINES, Iowa: 3338
FORT DODGE, Iowa: 1533
FORT DONELSON, Tennessee, Battle of: see CIVIL WAR--CAMPAIGNS, BATTLES, AND MILITARY ACTIONS--Tennessee--Fort Donelson
FORT FISHER, North Carolina:
Civil War: 390, 1419
Battle: see CIVIL WAR--CAMPAIGNS, BATTLES, AND MILITARY ACTIONS--North Carolina--Fort Fisher
Blockade: 3370
Confederate camp life: 3370, 3435
Confederate prisoners: 2970
Flags: 5972
Map: 1182
FORT GIBSON, Arkansas:
United States Army officers: 3466
FORT HARRISON, Virginia: see CIVIL WAR--CAMPAIGNS, BATTLES, AND MILITARY ACTIONS--Virginia--Fort Harrison
FORT HATTERAS, North Carolina: see CIVIL WAR--CAMPAIGNS, BATTLES, AND MILITARY ACTIONS--North Carolina--Fort Hatteras
FORT HENRY, Tennessee: 395
see also CIVIL WAR--CAMPAIGNS, BATTLES, AND MILITARY ACTIONS--Tennessee--Fort Henry
"FORT HILL," South Carolina: 1101
FORT JEFFERSON, Florida:
Civil War: 5715
FORT JOHNSON, North Carolina:
United States Army camp: 4433
FORT JOHNSON, South Carolina:
Civil War: 5645
FORT JOHNSTON, North Carolina: 5826
FORT LEAVENWORTH, Kansas:
Civil War cavalry training barracks: 5858
FORT LONDON, Tennessee: see CIVIL WAR--CAMPAIGNS, BATTLES, AND MILITARY ACTIONS--Tennessee--Fort London
FORT LYON, West Virginia: 4190

FORT McALLISTER, Georgia:
    Civil War: 3624
        see also CIVIL WAR--CAMPAIGNS,
            BATTLES, AND MILITARY ACTIONS--
            Georgia--Fort McAllister
FORT McHENRY, Maryland:
    Civil War: 3280
        Confederate prisoners: 1184,
            1889
FORT McINTOSH, Texas:
    Provision returns of married
        soldiers and laundresses (1856):
        5424
FORT MACON, North Carolina:
    Civil War: 494
        see also CIVIL WAR--CAMPAIGNS,
            BATTLES, AND MILITARY ACTIONS--
            North Carolina--Fort Macon
    Officers' quarters: 5744
FORT MARSHALL, Maryland:
    Civil War: 3280
FORT MARTIN SCOTT, Texas: 1446
FORT MASON, Texas:
    Quartermaster records: 1446
FORT MECHANIC, South Carolina: 3800
FORT MEIGS, Ohio: 443
FORT MICHIE, New York: 5430
FORT MITCHELL, Alabama: 3388
FORT MOULTRIE, South Carolina: 2237
FORT NELSON, Virginia: 4531
FORT NORFOLK, Virginia:
    Civil War: 915
FORT PICKENS, Florida: 3611
    Civil War: 5417, 5621
        see also CIVIL WAR--CAMPAIGNS,
            BATTLES, AND MILITARY
            ACTIONS--Florida--Fort Pickens
FORT PILLOW, Tennessee: 395
    Civil War:
        Battle: see CIVIL WAR--CAMPAIGNS,
            BATTLES, AND MILITARY
            ACTIONS--Tennessee--Fort
            Pillow
        Evacuation: 4596
        Fortifications: 5931
FORT POWHATAN, Virginia:
    Civil War: 5939
FORT PULASKI, Georgia:
    Civil War: 272
        Battle: see CIVIL WAR--CAMPAIGNS,
            BATTLES, AND MILITARY ACTIONS--
            Georgia--Fort Pulaski
        Map: 1182
        United States Army: 4119
FORT REPUBLIC, Virginia:
    Business affairs: 1559
    Civil War: see CIVIL WAR--
        CAMPAIGNS, BATTLES, AND MILITARY
        ACTIONS--Virginia--Fort Republic
FORT RIPLEY, South Carolina:
    Civil War fortifications: 4033
FORT SCHUYLER, New York:
    Civil War hospital: 1564
FORT SCOTT, Kansas: see CIVIL
    WAR--CAMPAIGNS, BATTLES, AND
    MILITARY ACTIONS--Kansas--Fort
    Scott
FORT SMITH, Arkansas: 4353
FORT SMITH RAILROAD: see LITTLE
    ROCK AND FORT SMITH RAILROAD
FORT SUMTER, South Carolina:
    Civil War: 4748, 5263
        see also CIVIL WAR--CAMPAIGNS,
            BATTLES, AND MILITARY ACTIONS--
            South Carolina--Fort Sumter
        Attack on (1863): 5955
        Description: 5193
        Flag raising ceremonies (1865):
            4215, 5001
FORT SUPPLY, Indian Territory: 3047
FORT TWIGGS, Georgia--Militia: 2778
FORT WAGNER, South Carolina:
    Civil War: 4602
        see also: CIVIL WAR--CAMPAIGNS,
            BATTLES, AND MILITARY ACTIONS--
            South Carolina--Fort Wagner

FORT WALKER, South Carolina: see
    CIVIL WAR--CAMPAIGNS, BATTLES, AND
    MILITARY ACTIONS--South Carolina--
    Fort Walker
FORT WARREN, Massachusetts:
    Confederate prisoners: 3378
    Autographs: 5422
FORT WASHATAW, Arkansas: 2117
FORT WAYNE AND SOUTHERN RAIL ROAD:
    2606
FORT WILLIAM, India: 4066
FORTESCUE, Chichester Samuel
    Parkinson, First Baron Carlingford:
    3138
FORTESCUE, Hugh, Third Earl
    Fortescue: 1087
FORTIFICATIONS: 1168
    see also CIVIL WAR--COAST DEFENSES;
        and Fortifications as subheading
        under names of armies and wars
    Construction: 2132, 3145
    Subdivided by place:
        China: 1373
        Georgia:
            Savannah: 2675, 4768
        Maryland: 2669
        North Carolina: 3176
        Pennsylvania:
            Philadelphia: 2489
        South Carolina--Charleston: 4216
        Texas: 1446
        Virginia--Craney Island: 70
FORTNIGHTLY REVIEW: 706, 2146
FORTRESS MONROE, Virginia: 2132,
    2696, 4731, 5896
    Civil War: 1084, 1840
        Fortifications: 4881
        Naval operations: 3281
        United States Army: 4119
        Imprisonment of Jefferson Davis:
            1403
    Mexican War: 5324
FORTUNE, T. Thomas: 4524
FORTUNES: see WEALTH
FORTY-ONE YEARS IN INDIA, FROM
    SUBALTERN TO COMMANDER-IN-CHIEF by
    Frederick Sleigh Roberts: 4503
FORTY YEARS OF AN ENGINEER'S LIFE AT
    HOME AND ABROAD . . . by Alfred
    Edward Garwood: 1970
FORUM (periodical): 4021
FOSDICK, Washington: 1860
FOSS, Edward, Jr.: 4372
FOSSILS: 5498
    Georgia: 2578
    North Carolina: 641
FOSTER, Alfred M.: 1861
FOSTER, Elizabeth (Hervey): 945
FOSTER, Ellen M.: 1862
FOSTER, Ephriam Hubbard: 330, 872,
    5681
FOSTER, Frederick C.: 4415
FOSTER, Gandy: 1863
FOSTER, George: 4726
FOSTER, Henry: 1863
FOSTER, Hugh Arnold-: see ARNOLD-
    FOSTER, Hugh
FOSTER, James (Louisiana): 1864
FOSTER, James G.: 1477
FOSTER, John (1770-1843): 2146
FOSTER, John (fl. 1795-1801,
    Virginia): 1863
FOSTER, John A. (North Carolina--
    Confederate soldier): 1861
FOSTER, Kate D.: 1864
FOSTER, Lafayette Sabine: 1865
FOSTER, Maria: 1115
FOSTER, Martha (1830-1893, Alabama):
    1298
FOSTER, Martha Lyman
    (Washington, D.C.): 1866
FOSTER (RALPH) MUSEUM, School of the
    Ozarks, Missouri: 1424
FOSTER, Susan: 1862
FOSTER, Thomas Flournoy: 1867
FOSTER, Thomas Gardner: 1867
FOSTER, William N. (Ohio): 1868
FOSTER, William Z. (1881-1961): 224

FOSTER & JENKINS (firm): see JENKINS
    & FOSTER
FOSTER-VESEY-FITZGERALD, William:
    2148
FOTHERGILL, Anthony: 1869
FOTHERGILL, William: 1869
FOTHERINGAY, Virginia: 1646
FOUCH, Annie: 2838
FOUCH, David: 2838
FOUCH FAMILY (Genealogy): 2838
FOUNDATION GRANTS: 691
FOUNDATIONS, Philanthropic: 1758,
    4927
    North Carolina: 2188
FOUNDRIES: see FORGES; IRON FOUNDRIES
FOUNTAIN, John: 4351
"FOUNTAIN ROCK," West Virginia: 581
FOURIER, Charles: see FOURIER,
    François Marie Charles
FOURIER, François Marie Charles: 65
FOURTH LIBERTY LOAN DRIVE: 5298
FOURTH OF JULY CELEBRATIONS: 2469,
    3334, 5042
    Addresses: 1676, 2932
    Society of the Cincinnati: 4584
    Southern opinion (Post-Civil War):
        1614
    Subdivided by place:
        Alabama:
            1834: 3611
            1845: 5174
        New York:
            Huntington (1840s): 726
        South Carolina:
            Charleston (1826): 3532
        Texas:
            Brazos Bottom (1867): 4353
FOURTH PRESBYTERIAN CHURCH, Greenville,
    South Carolina: 5825
FOURTH REGIONAL WAGE STABILIZATION
    BOARD: 5486
FOUST, Isaac H.: 1870
FOWLDS, Allan: 1943
FOWLE, Daniel G.: 5457
FOWLE AND LAURASON (firm): see
    LAURASON AND FOWLE
FOWLER, Charles William: 2148
FOWLER (DEWITT C.) AND BROTHER, Bay
    River, North Carolina: 1871
FOWLER, Sir John: 4234
FOWLER, Joseph S.: 1871
FOWLER, Joseph S., Jr.: 1871
FOWLER, Sir Robert Nicholas, First
    Baronet: 1872
FOWLER, Stephen: 1871
FOWLER FAMILY (Genealogy): 1424
FOWLER AND CLEMENTS (firm): 698
FOWLKES, Asa G.: 1873
FOX, Charles James: 2146, 2149
    Poetry: 5913
FOX, Daniel: 1877
FOX, Elizabeth (Vassall), Baroness
    Holland: 1875
FOX, George (1624-1691): 1733
FOX, George (Pennsylvania): 1888
FOX, Gustavus Vasa: 1874
FOX, Henry Edward, Fourth Baron
    Holland: 1875, 4605, 5277
FOX, Henry Richard Vassall, Third
    Baron Holland: 1875, 5746
FOX, Himer: 1876
FOX, Jeremiah: 5221
FOX, John (South Carolina): 1877
FOX, John William (1863-1919): 1878
FOX, Washington: 1877
FOX, William Johnson: 1879
FOX AND RICHARDSON, Richmond,
    Virginia (firm): 2360
FOX MOTOR CAR COMPANY: 4918
FOXCROFT, Frank: 2449
FOY, William: 5709
FRAME, Eliza M.: 464, 2209
FRANCE, Anatole: 1880
FRANCE:
    see also EUROPE
    Abolition of slavery:
        see also FRANCE--Slave trade--
            Abolition

FRANCE:
  Abolition of slavery (Continued):
    Colonial policy: 1081
  American Red Cross: 1792, 2553, 4743
  Arms trade with United States: 5433
  Army: 372
    American Revolution: 1236, 4418
      Casualties: 1424
      Portraits of French commanders: 1582
      Supplies: 4015
    Inspections: 2266
    Peninsular War:
      Generals: 1147
      Military activities: 1875
    Records (1800s): 372
    Supplies: 5228
  Art collectors and collecting: 1880
  Assassinations:
    Paul Doumer: 2398
  Atomic warfare: 1424
  Authorship: 3305
  Autograph collecting: 1424
  Biographical studies: 3644
  Book illustration: 555
  Bourbon restoration: 4348
  Claims against: see FRENCH SPOLIATION CLAIMS
  Clergy--Catholic: 3644
  Colonial policy and administration: 5726
    Abolition of slavery: 1081
    French Equatorial Africa: 4113
  Commercial treaties:
    United States: 1424
  Commune of 1871: 3472
  Communism: 1424
    see also FRANCE--Socialism; FRANCE--Socialists
  Composers: 4657
  Confederate emigrants: 2210
  Confraternities:
    see also FRANCE--Religious orders
    Grenoble: 2196
  Cotton trade: 5014
  Crown lands--Tours: 5323
  Currency: 1339
  Depression (1929): 1424
  Description and travel:
    1700s:
      1780s: 4625
      1790s: 2869
    1700s-1800s: 5179
    1800s: 4770, 5038
      1810s: 1049, 4348
      1820s: 1049, 2058, 2077, 4348, 4490
      1830s: 4348, 4490
      1840s: 4695, 5133, 5193
      1850s: 5963
      1860s: 2617
      1870s: 157
      1880s: 1463
    1900s:
      1900s: 4022
      1910s: 4290
      1930s: 5968
      1940s: 1275
  Diplomatic and consular service:
    Spain: 1424
    United States: 1424
      New York: 1181
  Diseases: 1424
  Economic conditions: 1424, 2742
    see also FRANCE--Depression
  Education: 372, 4490
    see also FRANCE--Medical education; FRANCE--Schools
  Election laws and regulations: 526
  Endowments--Grenoble: 2197
  Estates:
    Administration and settlement: 5193
  Exhibitions and fairs:
    Paris Exposition of 1878: 157, 5970
    Paris Exposition of 1900: 196
  Family life: 4490

FRANCE (Continued):
  Farming--Tours: 5323
  Foreign public opinion:
    United States: 1424
  Foreign relations: 1424
    Algeria: 2578
    Confederate States of America: 115, 1242, 1403, 2180, 2449, 4521
    Great Britain:
      1700s:
        1780s-1790s: 878, 2835, 3858, 4230, 5038
        Rivalry in India (1730s-1750s): 3128
        see also FRANCE--Navy--Operations--India; FRANCE--Treaties--Great Britain
      1700s-1800s: 1311, 4913, 5726, 5797
      1800s: 258, 1002, 1126, 1632, 1815, 3472, 4024, 4348, 4650
        Rivalry in Southeast Asia: 4709
      1900s: 4941
    Mexico: 2210
    Russia: 2836
    Thailand: 4709
    United States:
      1790s: 1891, 2815, 3041, 3384, 5298
      1700s-1800s: 3456, 4348
      1700s-1900s: 4486
      1800s: 1115, 1745
  Foreign trade: 2742
    Mexican War: 1424
    United States: 1424, 1935
  Franco-Prussian War: see FRANCO-PRUSSIAN WAR
  French Revolutionary Wars: see FRENCH REVOLUTIONARY WARS
  Governesses: 4770
  Grain prices:
    Rozoy-en-Brie: 4590
    Tours (Généralité): 5323
  Historic buildings: 1424, 2411
  Historic restoration: 441
  Historical studies: 4449, 5594
    French Revolution: 1982
  History--Study and teaching: 1754
  Housing interiors: 1424
  Huguenots: 2195, 3587
    Dauphiné: 4408
  Immigration and emigration:
    From Dauphiné: 4408
    To Alabama (proposed): 5308
  Intelligence Service:
    World War I: 1424
  Labor: 1424
  Literary societies: 555
  Livestock prices: 5323
  Local politics--Dauphiné: 4408
  Locomotives: 3054
  Manuscript collecting: 1424
  Medical education: 1300
  Military posts: 5323
  National Assembly: 5038
  National Convention: 4348
  Navy: 4476
    Operations: 5228
      English coast: 4171
      French Revolutionary Wars: 535
      India: 3315
  Nobility: 5323
  Oil industry: 1424
  Phrenology:
    Student's notebook: 2669
  Politics and government:
    see also FRANCE--Local politics
    1790s: 922, 3176, 5330
    1700s-1800s: 1311, 5726
    1800s: 1147, 1632, 1755, 2742, 3472
      1810s: 2840, 4348
      1820s: 1302, 4348
      1830s: 1775, 1875, 4348, 4616, 5277

FRANCE:
  Politics and government:
    1800s (Continued):
      1840s: 5133
      1870s: 3734
      1900s: 1424
  Population--Tours: 5323
  Portraits: 2411
  Privateers: 1615
  Protestants: see FRANCE--Huguenots
  Public finance: 1424, 3271
  Queens: 3271
  Railroads: 3054
  Real estate--Grenoble: 2195
  Religion: 128
  Religious orders:
    see also FRANCE--Confraternities
    Women: 2197
  Revolutions:
    July Revolution (1830): 4490
    Revolutions of 1848: 1609, 4881
  Rivers: 5323
  Roads: 5323
  Royalists: 1598, 2735
  Schools: 2963
    see also FRANCE--Education
  Sermons: 3644
  Servants: 3270
  Silk industry: 5323
  Slave trade:
    Abolition: 5726
      see also FRANCE--Abolition of slavery and abolitionist sentiment
    Colonies: 5726
  Social conditions: 4449
  Social life and customs:
    1700s: 4625
    1800s: 1049, 1424, 4490, 5133
    1900s: 1424, 3710
  Socialism: 1424
    Bibliography: 65
  Socialists--Biography: 65
  Surgery: 1300
  Taxation:
    Grenoble: 2195
    Tours: 5323
  Textile industry--Tours: 5323
  Tobacco industry: 4079
  Tobacco trade: 5295
  Travel costs: 4348
  Treaties--Great Britain: 1641
  United States ministry in: 1769
  Universities and colleges: see L'ÉCOLE DES PONTS ET CHAUSSÉES; UNIVERSITY OF PARIS
  Vineyards--Tours: 5323
  Weather: 4348
  Wool trade: 2742
  World War I: 3789
    see also WORLD WAR I
    Blind--Rehabilitation: 3710
    War relief: see FRANCE--American Red Cross; FRANCE--Young Men's Christian Association
  Young Men's Christian Association: 4743
  Zoological expeditions: 4022
FRANCE DRAMATIQUE (periodical): 5167
FRANCHISE: see SUFFRAGE
FRANCIS BACH AND CO.: 1807
FRANCIS BARING AND CO., London, England: 3273
FRANCO-PRUSSIAN WAR: 2410
  Campaigns and battles:
    France--Metz: 5163
  Economic aspects:
    Effects on British stocks: 2410
  Journalism: 43
FRANCO-PRUSSIAN WAR IN LITERATURE: 178
FRANCONIA, New Hampshire: 4264
FRANK, A. B.: 1881
FRANK, Alexander: 1882
FRANK, George W.: 1882
FRANK, Jesse M.: 1882
FRANK, Nelson: 1883
FRANK, Susanna: 1882
FRANK FAMILY (North Carolina): 1882

THE FRANK C. BROWN COLLECTION OF
  NORTH CAROLINA FOLKLORE: 691
FRANKENSTEIN by MARY W. (Godwin)
  Shelley: 4770
FRANKFORT, Germany:
  British envoy in: 3472
FRANKFORT, Kentucky: 627, 1308, 1470,
  2509, 4869
  Land titles: 1843
FRANKLIN, Bedney L.: 1887
FRANKLIN, Benjamin: 1236, 1884,
  2923, 5681
FRANKLIN, Clarence Payne: 1424
FRANKLIN, H. L.: 1885
FRANKLIN, James C.: 1886
FRANKLIN, Lucy (Haywood): 2457
FRANKLIN, Mary G.: 1887
FRANKLIN, William Buel: 5433
FRANKLIN, William Temple: 1888
FRANKLIN, Georgia:
  Mercantile accounts: 3966
FRANKLIN, North Carolina: 417, 4817
FRANKLIN, Tennessee:
  Civil War:
    Battle: see CIVIL WAR--CAMPAIGNS,
      BATTLES, AND MILITARY ACTIONS--
      Tennessee--Franklin
    Burial grounds: 3374
    78th Illinois Regiment in: 659
FRANKLIN, Virginia:
  Civil War: 1498
    see also CIVIL WAR--CAMPAIGNS,
      BATTLES, AND MILITARY ACTIONS--
      Virginia--Franklin
FRANKLIN, U.S.S.: 4220
FRANKLIN & McDONALD MINING AND
  MANUFACTURING CO.: 1887
FRANKLIN COUNTY, Arkansas:
  Ozark: 2123
  Whitsonton: 5509
FRANKLIN COUNTY, Georgia: 1993, 1997,
  2441, 2535, 3113
  Civilian protection by militia: 2307
  Cities and towns:
    Carnesville: 3782
    Walnut Hill: 3814
FRANKLIN COUNTY, Kentucky:
  Frankfort: see FRANKFORT, Kentucky
FRANKLIN COUNTY, Maine:
  Farmington: 5610
FRANKLIN COUNTY, Massachusetts:
  Deerfield: 333
  Greenfield: 3633
    Army camp life: 25
    Social life and customs: 4606
  New Salem: 2677
  Turners Falls: 3633
FRANKLIN COUNTY, Missouri: 591
FRANKLIN COUNTY, New York:
  Malone: 5687
FRANKLIN COUNTY, North Carolina: 76,
  2824, 5735, 5964
  Farm accounts: 5087
  Horses and mules: 5087
  Mercantile accounts: 2825
  Orchards: 5087
  Plantations: 1322, 4147
  Schools: 1701
  Wills: 4147
  Cities and towns:
    Franklinton: 2952
      Cotton mills: 5056
      Insurance companies: 5012
      Plantations: 4148
      Towel industry: 5450
    Louisburg:
      1700s: 5060
      1700s-1800s: 1491, 3023, 4787
      1700s-1900s: 3476
      1800s: 1411, 2873, 4154, 5690
      1800s-1900s: 3563
      Merchants: 1915
      Schools: 484, 2530, 3272
        Negro schools: 5533
    Stanton: 5965
    Youngsville: 5087

FRANKLIN COUNTY, Pennsylvania:
  Law enforcement: 1130
  World history notebook: 3412
  Cities and towns:
    Chambersburg:
      Charities: 5306
      Civil War:
        see also CIVIL WAR--CAMPAIGNS,
          BATTLES, AND MILITARY
          ACTIONS--Pennsylvania--
          Chambersburg
        Hospitals: 4608
      Universities and colleges:
        see WILSON COLLEGE
    Greencastle: 1916
    Mercersburg: 2521
    Richmond Furnace: 2033
    Waynesboro: 469
    Welsh Run: 1579
FRANKLIN COUNTY, Tennessee:
  Salem: 2369
  Sewanee: 2175, 4339
    see also UNIVERSITY OF THE SOUTH
FRANKLIN COUNTY, Vermont:
  Fairfax: 1039, 3129
FRANKLIN COUNTY, Virginia: 1335, 1490,
  3100, 4661
  Arithmetic exercise book: 208
  Escheat: 2955
  Cities and towns:
    Hale's Ford: 2593, 2633
    Sydnorsville: 474
FRANKLIN RAIL ROAD COMPANY: 1916
FRANKLINTON, North Carolina: 2952
  Cotton mills: 5056
  Insurance companies: 5012
  Lawsuits: 5056, 5450
  Plantations: 4148
  Towel industry: 5450
FRANKLINVILLE, North Carolina: 4075
  Liquor industry: 1278
FRANKLINVILLE CIRCUIT, Methodist
  churches: 3646
FRANSELLA, Albert: 111
FRANZ, Charles S.: 1443
FRASER, Alexander: 1891
FRASER, Charles (1782-1860): 1891
FRASER, Frederick: 1889
FRASER, Frederick Grimké: 1891
FRASER, Henry De Saussure: 1889
FRASER, James (Loyalist): 1890
FRASER, James, Bishop of Manchester
  (1818-1885): 2148
FRASER, James Baillie (1783-1856):
  5618
FRASER, Mary: 1891
FRASER, Mary (De Saussure)
  (1772-1853): 1891
FRASER, Mary F.: 1388, 1891
FRASER, Mary Jane (South Carolina):
  1892
FRASER, Sir Thomas (b. 1840): 2147
FRASER, Thomas Boone, Sr.: 1889
FRASER FAMILY (South Carolina): 1891
FRASER AND THOMPSON (cotton factors):
  1889
FRASER'S MAGAZINE: 2471
FRATERNAL SOCIETIES:
  see also BETA THETA PI; CHI PHI;
    DELTA BETA PHI; EPSILON PHI
    KAPPA DELTA; IMPROVED ORDER OF
    RED MEN; INDEPENDENT ORDER OF
    GOOD TEMPLARS; INDEPENDENT ORDER
    OF ODD FELLOWS; KIWANIS CLUB;
    MASONRY; ROYAL ARCANUM; SOCIETIES
    AND CLUBS
  Alabama: 1031
    Dallas County: 223
    Selma: 3712
  North Carolina: 1669, 3070
  United States: 21
FRAUD: 2497
  see also GOVERNMENT FRAUD; LAND
    FRAUD; PENSION FRAUD; RAILROAD
    FRAUD; TIMBER FRAUD; VETERANS
    FRAUD
  Massachusetts: 609
  South Carolina: 1424

FRAVEL, David: 1893
FRAVEL, Joseph: 1893
FRAVEL FAMILY (Virginia): 2559
FRAYSER, Richard Beverly: 1894
FRAYSER'S FARM, Virginia: see CIVIL
  WAR--CAMPAIGNS, BATTLES, AND
  MILITARY ACTIONS--Virginia--
  Frazier's Farm
FRAZER, Daniel F.: 2736
FRAZER, Sir James George: 2736
FRAZER, William: 3381
FRAZIER, Arthur Hugh: 1424
FRAZIER, E. W.: 1895
FRAZIER, Mary Elizabeth (Fulp): 1896
FRAZIER, Stephen: 1896
FRAZIER FAMILY (North Carolina--
  Genealogy): 1895
FRAZIER'S FARM, Virginia: see CIVIL
  WAR--CAMPAIGNS, BATTLES, AND
  MILITARY ACTIONS--Virginia--
  Frazier's Farm
FREAR (WILLIAM H.) AND COMPANY,
  London, England: 3960
FREASE, Edwin F.: 3646
FREDERICA, Georgia: 1454, 3968, 4988
  Land settlement: 3733
FREDERICK, Augustus: 1470
FREDERICK, Maryland:
  1700s-1800s: 3053, 4457
  1700s-1900s: 4288
  1800s: 1638, 5181, 5247
  1800s-1900s: 2849
  Civil War: 793
    see also CIVIL WAR--CAMPAIGNS,
      BATTLES, AND MILITARY ACTIONS--
      Maryland--Frederick
  Girls' schools and academies: 3053
  Locofoco Party: 5324
FREDERICK COUNTY, Maryland: 340
  Courts: 4457
  Estates:
    Administration and settlement:
      4457
  Free Negroes: 5829
  Justices of the peace: 4457
  Land: 112, 4457
  Legal affairs: 4457
  Missionary societies: 3804
  Politics and government: 4457
  Slave trade: 4457
  Slaves--Insurrections: 5829
  Cities and towns:
    Burkittsville: 5722
    Ceresville Mills: 4803
    Frederick: see FREDERICK, Maryland
    Gapland: 5326
    Jefferson: 3254
    Retreat School:
      Arithmetic exercise books: 4804
    Woodsboro: 4064
FREDERICK COUNTY, Virginia: 3680,
  3819, 4915, 5504
  Clergy: 2064
  Confederate Army in: 1
  Courts--Clerks: 5200
  Hay: 1
  Personal debt: 2954
  Tax collectors: 5200
  Cities and towns:
    Clear Brook: 2329
    Hayfield: 1429
    Newton: 2023
    Stephensburg: 3255
    Winchester: see WINCHESTER,
      Virginia
FREDERICK FEMALE ACADEMY, Frederick,
  Maryland: 3053
FREDERICK HUTH AND COMPANY, England:
  2742
FREDERICKSBURG, Indiana: 4588
FREDERICKSBURG, Ohio: 4165
FREDERICKSBURG, Virginia: 477, 1665,
  1812, 2051, 3242, 4563, 4596, 4740
  Banks and banking: 5556
  Boot and shoe making accounts: 1666
  Business affairs: 2165

FREDERICKSBURG, Virginia (Continued):
    Civil War: 359, 677, 1123,
      3346
      Battle: see CIVIL WAR--
        CAMPAIGNS, BATTLES, AND
        MILITARY ACTIONS--Virginia--
        Fredericksburg
      Confederate Army camps: 1500,
        3755
        Camp life: 3464
      Municipal government: 4855
      Union Army:
        Military occupation: 4855
        Use of balloons: 2240, 5984
    Corporation Court: 1018
    Description: 284
    Economic conditions: 4099
FREDERICKSBURG DISTRICT, Methodist
    churches: 3646
FREDERICKSHALL, Virginia: 2363
FREDERICKTOWN, Missouri: 4161
FREDONIA, New York: 4486
FREE NEGROES:
    see also CIVIL WAR--CONTRABANDS;
      FREEDMEN
    Arrests--Tennessee: 5623
    Colonization: see NEGROES--
      Colonization
    Deportation: 4852
    Emigration to Haiti: 4409
    "Free papers": 3276
    Guardianship:
      Georgia: 5537
      South Carolina: 758
    Insurrections (planned): 5829
    Legal status: 3850
    Personal finance: 3850
    Reinslavement--Georgia: 5051
    Relations with whites: 5221
    Religion--South Carolina: 3669
    Removal (proposed)--Virginia: 5476
    School taxes--Virginia: 3012
    Subdivided by place:
      Maryland--Montgomery County: 3982
      Virginia: 872, 4924
        Campbell County: 5482
        Census of 1860: 5426
FREE PRODUCE ASSOCIATION OF WESTERN
    VERMONT: 3665
FREE SCHOOLS:
    see also PUBLIC SCHOOLS
    North Carolina--Wilmington: 617
FREE SILVER: see SILVER QUESTION
FREE SOIL PARTY: 4022, 5051, 5059
    see also FRIENDS OF FREE SOIL
    Georgia: 5051, 5315
    Massachusetts: 4897, 5240
FREE THOUGHT: 2532
    United States: 2225
FREE TRADE: 3190
    Great Britain: 649, 1126, 1569,
      3498, 4605, 5726
    United States: 2225
FREE WILL BAPTIST CHURCH:
    see also ORIGINAL FREE WILL BAPTIST
      CHURCH
    North Carolina: 1107, 1523
FREEDLEY, H. W.: 2521
FREEDMEN: 1557, 1980, 4834, 5043,
    5731
    see also CIVIL WAR--CONTRABANDS;
      FREE NEGROES; NEGROES
    Aid societies: 3037, 3665
      see also UNITED STATES--
        GOVERNMENT AGENCIES AND
        OFFICIALS--Bureau of Refugees,
        Freedmen and Abandoned Lands
    Apprenticeship: 5891
      North Carolina: 5431
    Assistance to: 128, 3037
      see also METHODIST CHURCHES--
        Aid to freedmen; UNITED
        STATES--GOVERNMENT AGENCIES
        AND OFFICIALS--Bureau of
        Refugees, Freedmen and
        Abandoned Lands
      Mississippi: 5431
        By United States Army: 5421

FREEDMEN:
    Assistance to (Continued):
      North Carolina: 3037
      South Carolina--Charleston: 408
    Behavior: 619
      Georgia: 4895
      North Carolina: 956, 5298
      South Carolina: 4118, 5759
      Southern States: 2893, 3809
    Colonization: see NEGROES--
      Colonization
    Complaints of:
      South Carolina--Charleston: 408
    Education: 5784
      see also NEGROES--Education
      North Carolina: 2540, 3037
      South Carolina:
        Beaufort: 2106
        Sumter: 5298
      Tennessee: 1344
    Labor:
      Mississippi River dikes: 2341
      North Carolina textile mills:
        5100
    Labor contracts: 5623
      Alabama: 1423, 4448, 4911, 5593
      Florida: 5659
      Georgia: 1268, 1705, 4706,
        4895, 5162
      North Carolina: 1056, 5709
        Lumberton: 3422
        Orange County: 3315
      South Carolina: 297, 1923, 3371,
        4833, 4996
        Chester District: 1268
      Virginia: 1366, 1568, 1922, 2335
    Social status--North Carolina:
      5425
    Tenancy:
      Alabama: 4861, 5032
      North Carolina: 832
        Lumberton: 3422
    Treatment of: 5784
      South Carolina: 408, 1352,
        2695
    Wages and salaries: see WAGES
      AND SALARIES--Freedmen
    Subdivided by place:
      Alabama: 2315
      Arkansas--Hampton: 4199
      Georgia: 641, 662
      Jamaica: 301
      Mississippi: 3642
      North Carolina: 730, 754, 797,
        1376, 2469, 2720, 2808,
      South Carolina: 2473, 3405, 3993,
        4649
        Charleston: 408, 2695
      Virginia: 375, 1558, 1827, 2370,
        4131
FREEDMEN'S AID ASSOCIATION: 3665
FREEDMEN'S AND HOME RELIEF
    ASSOCIATION: 1927
FREEDMEN'S BUREAU: see UNITED
    STATES--GOVERNMENT AGENCIES AND
    OFFICIALS--Bureau of Refugees,
    Freedmen and Abandoned Lands
FREEDMEN'S LOANS--Virginia: 2380
FREEDOM OF RELIGION:
    Carolina Province: 202
    Virginia: 2887
FREEDOM OF TEACHING: see ACADEMIC
    FREEDOM
FREEHOLD: see LAND TENURE
FREEHOLD RAILROAD: 825
FREEMAN, Douglas Southall: 3809
FREEMAN, Eli: 1897, 4918
FREEMAN, Lucy Ann (Vaughan): 5469
FREEMAN, Mary Eleanor Wilkins: 103
FREEMAN FAMILY (North Carolina):
    1252
FREEMAN FAMILY (Ohio): 770
FREEMAN (M. M.) AND COMPANY: 5133
FREEMAN-THOMAS, Freeman, First
    Marquis of Willingdon: 2149
FREEMASONRY: see MASONRY
FREEPORT, Indiana--Physicians: 3221
FREEPORT ACT: 1913

FREEPORT TEXAS COMPANY: 5035
FREE-PRODUCE MOVEMENT: 3665
FREETHINKERS MAGAZINE: 2225
FREETHOUGHT: see FREE THOUGHT
FREIGHT AND FREIGHTAGE:
    see also AGRICULTURAL PRODUCTS--
      Transport of
    Coal--Virginia: 3692
    Coffee--Mississippi River: 3824
    Flour:
      Mississippi River: 3824
      Virginia: 2165
    Sugar--Mississippi River: 3824
    Wood:
      Virginia: 629, 2165, 3692
      West Virginia: 4703
    Subdivided by place:
      New York: 4071
      North Carolina:
        Wadesboro (accounts): 4814
      Pennsylvania: 480
      Virginia:
        Accounts: 2737
        James River: 4616
FREIGHT RATES: see FREIGHT
    AND FREIGHTAGE; RAILROADS--
    Freight rates
FRELIGH, Mary Hoyt: 783
FREMONT, E. Benton: 358
FRÉMONT, John Charles: 1900, 4556,
    5578, 5720
    Homes (photographs): 5447
FREMONT, North Carolina: 4704
FREMONT, Ohio: 2446
    Liquor trade: 4892
FRENCH, Alice: 10
FRENCH, Burton Lee: 5791
FRENCH, Edward Henry: 4709
FRENCH, Robert Percy: 3238
FRENCH, Robert Strange: 5457
FRENCH, S. Bassett: 581, 2792
FRENCH, Samuel Gibbs: 1901, 5092
FRENCH, Theodore: 1902
FRENCH, William Henry: 5008
THE FRENCH ACADEMY: see L'ACADÉMIE
    FRANÇAISE
FRENCH AND INDIAN WAR: 3752
    North Carolina's participation:
      5750
FRENCH BROAD RIVER (North Carolina):
    2028
FRENCH DRAMA: 5167
    Reviews: 3617
FRENCH EQUATORIAL AFRICA: 4113
FRENCH IN CAROLINA PROVINCE: 202
FRENCH IN MEXICO: 1403
FRENCH IN THE UNITED STATES: 1582,
    3903
    Georgia: 1581
    Louisiana: 1574, 3073
    South Carolina: 1581
FRENCH INDO-CHINA:
    Description and travel: 2463
FRENCH LITERATURE: 1424, 1880
    see also FRENCH DRAMA; FRENCH
      POETRY
    Influence of Edgar Allan Poe: 2764
    Student's notebook--Virginia: 1379
    Study and teaching:
      Massachusetts: 4012
    Translations into English: 3119,
      5447
    Translations into Italian: 1721
FRENCH ON ZANZIBAR: 5725
FRENCH PETROLEUM COMPANY: 1424
FRENCH POETRY: 2701, 3077
    Louisiana: 1450, 1574
FRENCH REVOLUTION: 4625
    Foreign public opinion:
      Great Britain: 1070, 5038, 5726
    Historical studies: 1982
    Royalists: 1598, 2735
FRENCH REVOLUTIONARY WARS (1789-1799):
    4230, 4967, 5639
    Campaigns, battles and military
      actions:
      Netherlands: 2266
      Saint Lucia (West Indies): 2266

FRENCH REVOLUTIONARY WARS:
  Campaigns, battles and military
    actions (Continued):
    Toulon: 1674
  Coalition against France (1793):
    1641
  Defense of Ireland: 3315
  Invasion of Great Britain
    (potential): 922
  Invasion of Ireland (planned):
    2266
  Prize ships: 3315
  Subdivided by country involved:
    France:
      Naval operations off the Irish
        coast: 535
      Great Britain: 15, 1598, 1641,
        1913, 3315
        Naval operations: 342, 887, 2836
          Irish coast: 535
FRENCH SPOLIATION CLAIMS: 850, 943,
  1424, 1475, 4756
FRENCH WEST INDIES: 1574, 1952
  see also WEST INDIES
  Contraband: 321
  Foreign trade--United States: 321
  Slavery: 4913
FRENCH'S FIELD, Virginia: see
  CIVIL WAR--CAMPAIGNS, BATTLES,
  AND MILITARY ACTIONS--Virginia--
  French's Field
FRERE, Bartholomew: 3183
FRESH AIR ART SOCIETY: 1424, 3305
FRICK, Henry Theophilus: 2871
FRIEND OF INDIA by Meredith White
  Townsend: 5327
"THE FRIENDLY ROCKS" by John
  Burroughs: 783
FRIENDS, Society of: see SOCIETY OF
  FRIENDS
FRIENDS OF FREE SOIL: 3910
FRIENDS OF PROSPERITY: 5905
FRIES, Adelaide Lisetta: 5457
FRIES (F. & H.) (firm): 1905
FRIES, Henry Elias: 1905
FRIES FAMILY (North Carolina): 5459
FRIEZE, Jacob: 1906
FROBISHER, J. J.: 2126
FROELICK, Louis D.: 5252
FROHMAN, Daniel: 2449, 3797, 4556
FROM TINDER-BOX TO THE "LARGER"
  LIGHT by Isabella Petrie-Mills: 39
FRONT ROYAL, Virginia: 464, 1116,
  2162, 2794, 2797, 5387
FRONTLASH (socialist youth group):
  4948
FRONTIER LIFE: see PIONEER LIFE
FROST, Charles S.: 1907
FROST, Daniel A.: 1908
FROST, Glen: 1907
FROST, Milton: 1909
FROST, Rebecca: 1909
FROST, Robert (1874-1963): 2689
FROST, William: 1909
FROST, William Goodell: 4373
FROTHINGHAM (brig): 21
FROUDE, James Anthony: 1910, 2471,
  4520
FRUIT CULTURE:
  see also names of specific fruits,
    e.g. ORANGE CROPS
  Mississippi--Rodney: 3322
  Virginia:
    Fluvanna County: 5035
    Nelson County: 3566
FRUIT TRADE: 323
  see also names of specific types
    of fruit trade, e.g. PERSIAN
    BERRY TRADE
  Maryland: 5488
"FRUSTRADO PROYECTO DE MONARQUIA EN
  COLOMBIA": 4155
FRY, Birkett Davenport: 637
FRY, John Walker: 5457
FRY, Rose W.: 2449
FRY, William Oswald: 523
FUGE UND FUGATO IN DER KAMMERMUSIK
  DES ROKOKO UND DER KLASSIK: 1974

FUGITIVE SLAVE LAW (1850): 1234,
  3665, 4897, 5051, 5940
  Enforcement: 3853
FUGITIVE SLAVES: 4616, 4866, 5940
  see also CIVIL WAR--CONTRABANDS;
    CIVIL WAR--FUGITIVE SLAVES;
    PERSONAL LIBERTY LAWS; SLAVES--
    Recovery of
  Capture: 4892
  Escape to Canada: 3255, 4387
  Historical studies: 2400
  Recovery of: 3850, 4471, 5231, 5702
  Trials: 3006, 5917
  Subdivided by place:
    Alabama: 3415
    Canada: 5736
    Georgia: 2460, 5576
      Eatonton: 4706
      Savannah: 3389, 5221
    Indiana--Newport: 5149
    Kentucky: 5551
    Missouri: 5551
    North Carolina: 3317, 3622,
      4471, 5857
    South Carolina: 881, 2107,
      3415, 4534, 4581
    Virginia: 2453, 2633, 5579
      Yorktown: 3741
    West Virginia: 52, 1946
FUGITIVE SLAVES by Marion Gleason
  McDougall: 2400
FULBRIGHT, William: 83
FULFORD, Absalom: 1871
FULLARTON, William: 3315
FULLER, Austin W.: 5431
FULLER, Edwin Wiley: 1915
FULLER, F. L.: 1336
FULLER, Harriet M.: 808
FULLER, Henry Middleton: 393
FULLER, Jones: 1915, 4060
FULLER, Sir Joseph: 1911
FULLER, Juliana Rebecca: 864, 1911
FULLER, Mary (Floyd): 1911
FULLER, Rebecca (Bullock): 761
FULLER, Solon L.: 1912
FULLER, Stephen: 1913, 3304
FULLER, Thomas Charles: 5135
FULLER, Williamson Whitehead: 1914
FULLER FAMILY (North Carolina): 1915
FULLERTON, Catherine: 1467
FULLERTON, David (1772-1843): 1916
FULLERTON, George Stuart: 4076
FULLERTON, James H.: 5235
FULLERTON, Joseph Scott: 1917
FULLERTON, Matthew Lind: 3213
FULLERTON, William J.: 3757
FULP, Mary Elizabeth: 1896
FULTON, ___: 4348
FULTON, Charles Carroll: 306
FULTON, Sallie M. H.: 1918
FULTON, Winston: 1919
FULTON, New York: 929
FULTON, North Carolina: 1686
FULTON COUNTY, Georgia:
  Adamsville: 3841
  Campbellton: 2671, 5676
FULTON COUNTY, Illinois:
  Lewistown: 5311
FULTON COUNTY, New York: 4108
FUND RAISING:
  Charities--Massachusetts: 977
  Churches: 5497
  Memorials: 1337, 5110
    Georgia: 1171
    New York: 5584
  Presbyterian churches:
    Virginia: 5979
  Protestant Episcopal Church:
    Virginia: 1712
  Universities and colleges: 4968
    For proposed university: 5575
    North Carolina: 547
    Virginia--Halifax County: 3377
"FUNDACION DE LA IGLESIA & CONVENTO
  DE LA COMPAÑIA DE JESUS . . ." by
  Alvaro Navia Boloños y Moscoso:
  4155

FUNDS: see MEMORIAL FUNDS; and Funds
  and scholarships under names of
  specific universities, colleges,
  and schools
FUNERAL SERMONS: 3646
  see also EULOGIES
  Florida: 1832
FUNERALS: 5964
  see also FUNERAL SERMONS
  Germany: 2009
  Louisiana: 395
  New York: 5298
  South Carolina: 4310
  Uganda: 41
  United States Capitol Building: 261
  Virginia: 1894
    Hat Creek: 4043
FUNK AND WAGNALLS CO.: 1068
FUNKHOUSER, Andrew: 1920
FUNKHOUSER, Jacob R.: 1920
FUNKHOUSER FAMILY (West Virginia):
  1920
FUQUA, Joseph: 1921
FUQUA, Samuel: 1922
FUR TRADE:
  Georgia--Chattahoochee River: 3966
  Missouri River: 3357
  Virginia: 404
FURCHES, David Moffatt: 832
FURLOUGHS: see Leaves and furloughs
  as subheading under names of armies
  and navies
FURLOW MASONIC FEMALE COLLEGE,
  [Georgia?]: 3339
FURMAN, James L.: 1923
FURMAN, John H. (d. 1902): 1923
FURMAN, McDonald: 1923, 2449
FURMAN, Richard: 3356
FURMAN FAMILY (Genealogy): 1923
FURMAN UNIVERSITY, Greenville, South
  Carolina: 1476
  Trustees: 1585
FURNACES: see CHARCOAL FURNACES;
  IRON FURNACES
FURNESS, Horace Howard: 2871
FURNISS, Henry Sanderson, First
  Baron Sanderson: 1924
FURNITURE:
  see also HOUSING--Interiors
  Prices:
    see also SCHOOL FURNITURE--
      Prices
    South Carolina: 3801
    Virginia:
      Norfolk: 3830
      Woodstock: 1893
  Subdivided by place:
    Jamaica: 3304
    New York: 4351
    Virginia: 1137, 3809
FURNITURE INDUSTRY:
  see also CHAIR MANUFACTURING;
    SCHOOL FURNITURE INDUSTRY
  North Carolina: 325, 341, 4918
    Hickory: 3831
  Virginia--Woodstock: 1893
FURNITURE TRADE:
  see also OFFICE EQUIPMENT TRADE;
    SCHOOL FURNITURE TRADE
  Georgia: 781
  North Carolina: 264
  West Virginia: 2389
FURNITURE WORKERS: see UNITED
  FURNITURE WORKERS OF AMERICA
FÜRSTENAU, Moritz: 111
FURZE HILL, England: 5027
"THE FUTURE OF THE REPUBLICAN PARTY"
  by Robert Taft (1949 speech):
  5170

## G

G. H. SLAUGHTER AND COMPANY: 4854
G. J. ANDERSON AND COMPANY, Mocksville, North Carolina: 2749
G. R. CROSSLEY, New York, New York (firm): 3008
G. T. AUGUSTIN (firm): see W. AND G. T. AUGUSTIN
GABON RIVER (Africa): 4113
GACHET FAMILY: 902
GADDY, Fannie Bennett: 1925
GADDY, Risden B.: 1925
GADDY FAMILY (Arkansas): 837
GADSDEN, J. A.: 5193
GADSDEN, James (1788-1858): 1926
GADSDEN FAMILY (Florida and South Carolina): 1926
GADSDEN COUNTY, Florida: 5740
GADSDEN PURCHASE: 1926
GAEKWAR, Sayaji Rao III, Maharaja of Baroda: see SAYAJI RAO GAEKWAR III, Maharaja of Baroda
GAEKWAR OF BARODA: see RAO, Malhar, Gaekwar of Baroda
GAFFNEY, South Carolina: 5233
see also LIMESTONE COLLEGE
GAGE, George: 1927
GAGE, Sarah Marshall (Ely): 1927
GAGE, William M.: 1928
GAGEBY, Mary: 718
GAGEBY, Neal: 718
GAHAGAN, Lieutenant _____: 4097
GAHN, Bessie W.: 2703
GAIGE, Crosby: 5101
GAILLARD, Christopher: 4429
GAILLARD, Peter Cordes: 1929
GAILLARD, Thomas: 1468
GAILLARD, W. D.: 2449
GAILOR, Thomas Frank: 4339
GAINES, Edmund Pendleton: 805, 1930, 3323
GAINES, Edwin Lewis: 1931
GAINES, J. M.: 1932
GAINES, James S.: 1933
GAINES, Letitia: 1933
GAINES, Ora B.: 1934
GAINES, Richard: 1922
GAINES' MILL, Virginia: 2143
Civil War: see CIVIL WAR--CAMPAIGNS, BATTLES, AND MILITARY ACTIONS--Virginia--Gaines' Mill
GAINESVILLE, Alabama:
Churches: 1476
Social life and customs: 489
GAINESVILLE, Georgia: 3262
see also BRENAU COLLEGE
GAINESVILLE, Virginia: see CIVIL WAR--CAMPAIGNS, BATTLES, AND MILITARY ACTIONS--Virginia--Gainesville
GAINSBOROUGH, England: 369
GAINZA, Gabino: 4155
GAIRDNER, James: 1935
GAITHER, Ella: 1936
GALENA, Illinois: 5571
GALES, Joseph (1761-1841): 2870, 3743, 5457

GALES, Joseph (1786-1860): 872, 1937, 4246
GALES, Sarah Juliana Maria: 1937
GALES, Seaton, Jr.: 5457
GALES, Weston: 2870
GALES FAMILY (North Carolina): 2870
GALES FAMILY (Virginia): 2559
GALES & SEATON (firm): 1937
GALIFFE, Jacques Augustin: 258
GALL, Franz Josef: 2669
GALLAGHER, Charles: 1938
GALLAGHER, John: 5564
GALLAHER FAMILY (Virginia and West Virginia): 1939
GALLATIN, Albert: 2913, 3273, 3805, 4531, 5203, 5228
GALLATIN, Mississippi: 2355
GALLATIN, Tennessee:
Description: 5623
Social life and customs: 5784
GALLAWAY, Mathew C.: 2662
GALLE, Ceylon--Description: 1464
GALLIMORE, Arthur R.: 1940
GALPHIN, Martha: 3671
GALSWORTHY, John: 1210
GALT, Sir Alexander Tilloch: 1941
GALT, Margaret: 1943
GALT, Robert: 1942
GALT, Thomas: 1943
GALT, William, Sr.: 1943
GALT, William, Jr.: 1943
GALT FAMILY (Virginia--Genealogy): 3809
GALVANISM: see ELECTRICITY
GALVESTON, Texas: 646, 5293, 5602, 5723
Canal to the Brazos River: 5613
Civil War: see CIVIL WAR--CAMPAIGNS, BATTLES, AND MILITARY ACTIONS--Texas--Galveston
Dry goods trade: 3534
Municipal government: 1001
Social life and customs: 3363, 5194
GALVESTON COUNTY, Texas:
Galveston: see GALVESTON, Texas
GAMBLE, Elizabeth Washington: 5848
GAMBLE, Hamilton Rowan: 3703
GAMBLE, Roger Lawson: 2647
GAMBLING: 99
see also LOTTERIES
New York: 4518
United States Army (War of 1812): 1595
Virginia: 4518
GAME LAWS: 4453
see also DUCKS--Hunting limits; and names of specific laws
GAME WARDENS:
North Carolina: 5962
South Carolina: 4453
GAMES: see AMUSEMENTS; BOWLING; CARDS; CHARADES; RIDDLES; SPORTS
GAMEWELL, North Carolina: 3324
"THE GANDER PULL OR JAMES CITY GAMES" by George Wythe Munford: 3809
GANDY FAMILY: 1944
GANGES RIVER (India): 3577
GAPEN, Mary: 5311
GAPLAND, Maryland: 5326
GARAY, Martin de: 5639
GARBER, A. M.: 4448
GARBER, James R.: 1945
GARBER FAMILY (Alabama): 1945
GARCIA MORENO, Gabriel: 4155
GARDEN, Alexander (physician): 295
GARDEN, Alexander (naturalist, 1730-1791): 5548
GARDEN, Alexander (major, 1757-1829): 4214
GARDEN SEED TRADE:
Jamaica and South Carolina: 3304
GARDENER, W. H.: 3118
GARDENS, HOUSES, AND PEOPLE (periodical): 2398

GARDENS AND GARDENING: 404, 4898
see also LANDSCAPE GARDENING; NURSERIES (Horticulture)
Maryland--Baltimore: 2398
New England: 1636
Pennsylvania--Philadelphia: 4354
GARDINER, Ann Henshaw: 1946
GARDINER, John B. W.: 4789
GARDINER FAMILY (West Virginia--Genealogy): 1946
GARDNER, Amanda E. (Edney): 1947
GARDNER, Caroline: 1948
GARDNER, Elizabeth A.: 1947
GARDNER, George: 2682
GARDNER, Herbert Coulstoun, First Baron Burghclere of Walden: 1948
GARDNER, John A.: 1947
GARDNER, John L. (North Carolina): 1950
GARDNER, Paris Cleveland: 1951
GARDNER, S. H.: 1379
GARDNER, Sarah Heath: 2468
GARDNER, Thomas J.: 1948
GARDNER, Massachusetts: 5088
GARDNER FOR GOVERNOR BULLETIN: 4018
GARDONE, Italy: 137
GARESCHÉ, Julius Peter: 1952
GARESCHÉ, Louis: 1952
GARESCHÉ FAMILY: 1952
GARFIELD, James Abram: 1953
Assassination: 1663, 4606
Inauguration: 4921
GARFIELD NATIONAL MASONIC MEMORIAL ASSOCIATION OF WASHINGTON, D.C.: 1953
GARIOTT, Simeon: 4588
GARLAND, Addison: 1954
GARLAND, Hamlin: 103, 3797, 4976
GARLAND, James (Danville, Virginia): 1956
GARLAND, James (Lynchburg, Virginia): 1955
GARLAND, James Maury: 1957
GARLAND, John R.: 4157
GARLAND, Landon Cabell: 3188
GARLAND, Lucinda Rose: 3188
GARLAND, Samuel: 1459
GARLAND, Thomas: 1957
GARLAND FAMILY (Alabama): 3188
GARLINGER, Benjamin A., Sr.: 1958
GARLINGTON, A. G.: 5092
GARLINGTON, Mississippi--Map: 1182
GARMANY (ship): 232
GARMENT MAKING: see CLOTHING AND DRESS--Manufacture
GARNER, John: 1336, 1959
GARNER, John Nance: 4559
GARNER (SAMUEL) AND CO., Winston, North Carolina: 1960
GARNER, North Carolina: 3660
GARNET, Jack H.: 1961
GARNETT, Ann: 1962
GARNETT, James Mercer (1770-1843): 1962, 4383, 5203
GARNETT, James Mercer (1840-1916): 1962
GARNETT, Muscoe Russell Hunter: 569
GARNETT, Robert Selden (1789-1840): 3512
GARNETT, Robert Selden (1819-1861): 1963, 2396
GARNETT, Theodore Stanford: 1962
GARNETT FAMILY (Genealogy): 1962
GARRARD, Israel: 2280
GARRETT, Augusta Brown: 3779
GARRETT, John Work: 2871
GARRICK, J. P.: 1964
GARRICK, James P.: 1965
GARRIS, J. P.: 1966
GARRISON, James J.: 4988
GARRISON, William A. (Indiana): 1967
GARRISON, William Lloyd: 1968, 3665
GARRISONS: see MILITARY POSTS
GARROW, Theodosia: 2146
GARST, Henry: 1969
GARST, John: 1969
GARWOOD, Alfred Edward: 1970

GARY, Eliza: 1971
GARY, Martin Witherspoon: 1424, 1971, 4453, 5633
GARYSBURG, North Carolina:
    Civil War: 834
GAS ENGINES: 5312
GAS LIGHTING:
    see also ELECTRIFICATION; STREET LIGHTING
    Brazil--Rio Grande do Sul: 2750
    Delaware--Wilmington: 4881
    Maryland--Baltimore: 2265
    North Carolina--Fayetteville: 5298
GAS WORKERS: see UNITED GAS, COKE, AND CHEMICAL WORKERS OF AMERICA
GASCOYNE-CECIL, Robert Arthur Talbot, Third Marquis of Salisbury: see CECIL, Robert Arthur Talbot Gascoyne-, Third Marquis of Salisbury
GASKELL, Elizabeth: 2843
GASKINS, W. B.: 1973
GASOLINE-POWERED RAILWAY PASSENGER CARS: 1655
GASOLINE TRADE--North Carolina: 5756
GASSMAN, Florian Leopold: 1974
GASTON, Alexander: 5457
GASTON, William: 484, 1975, 4977
GASTON CIRCUIT, Methodist churches: 3646
GASTON COUNTY, North Carolina:
    Textile mills: 5887
    Cities and towns:
        Gastonia: 1006
            Labor disputes: 3706
        Lowell: 3285
        Mount Holly--Cotton mills: 5100
        Stowesville--Textile mills: 5100
        Woodlawn Mills: 5100, 5887, 5888
GASTON HIGH SCHOOL, Dallas, North Carolina: 4080
GASTONIA, North Carolina: 1006
    Labor disputes: 3706
GASTONIA DISTRICT, Methodist churches: 3646
GATACRE, Sir William Forbes: 1976
GATE FIXTURES: see IRON GATE FIXTURES
GATE LATCHES--Inventions: 5839
GATES, Addison W.: 1977
GATES, Horatio: 872
GATES CIRCUIT, Methodist churches: 3646
GATES COUNTY, North Carolina:
    Sunbury: 1724, 2353
GATESVILLE, North Carolina: 2428
GATHORNE-HARDY, Gathorne, First Earl of Cranbrook: 1978, 2962
GATLING, Richard Jordan: 1979, 3746
GATLING GUN: 3746
GATLING'S BATTERY, North Carolina:
    Camp life: 5390
GATTI DE GAMMOND, Zoe Charlotte: 65
GATTIS, Samuel Mallett: 5457
GAULLE, Charles de: see DE GAULLE, Charles-Andre-Marie-Joseph
GAULT, Matthew: 1980
GAULT FAMILY: 1980
GAUTT, Elijah: 1877
GAY, Elbert H.: 1981
GAY, Mary Ann Harris: 5082
GAY, Sydney Howard: 2526
GAYARRÉ, Charles Étienne Arthur: 1439, 1494, 1982, 2449, 2465
GAYLE, Sarah Ann: 1300
GAYLE FAMILY (Alabama): 1300, 1707
GAYLORD, James: 1983
GAYLORD, John D.: 1983
GAYLORD, Juliette: 1983
GAYLORD, William: 1983
GAYLORD, Mrs. William L.: 1865
GAYLORD FAMILY: 1983
GAY'S LANDING, Alabama:
    Commodity prices and taxation: 5879
GAZETEER OF GEORGIA: 4743
GAZETTE (Great Britain): 5241

GAZETTE (Berea, North Carolina): 5741
GEARHART, James K.: 3640
GEBBART, Emmanuel Martin: 1984
GEBBART, Noah L., Sr.: 1984
GEDDES, Norman Bel: 3797
GEE, Charles: 1986
GEE, James T.: 1985
GEE, Joseph: 1986
GEE, Nevill: 1986
GEE, Sterling: 1986
GEE, William: 39
GEE FAMILY: 1986
GEE, HURT, & TODD (firm): see HURT, TODD, & GEE
GEIGER, E.: 4188
GEIGER, Henry C.: 1877
GELL, Sir William: 2148
GENDER IDENTITY CLINIC, Johns Hopkins University: 4823
"GENEALOGIES AND HISTORICAL RECORDER": 2994
GENEALOGY: see as subheading under specific family names
GENEALOGY OF THE PAGE FAMILY OF VIRGINIA by R. C. M. Page: 4014
GENERAL COMMITTEE ON ARMY AND NAVY CHAPLAINS: 3633
GENERAL FEATURES CORPORATION: 1167
GENERAL FEDERATION OF WOMEN'S CLUBS: 4271
GENERAL GRANT, U.S.S.: 5437
GENERAL HOSPITAL, Richmond, Virginia: 288
GENERAL HOSPITAL NO. 9, Richmond, Virginia: 2134
GENERAL MERCHANTS: see MERCHANTS
"GENERAL REPORT ON THE SUDAN, 1891" by Sir Francis Reginald Wingate: 5835
"GENERAL RULES AND REGULATIONS UNDER THE TRUST INDENTURE ACT OF 1939": 5779
GENERAL SOUTHERN TEMPERANCE CONFERENCE, Fayetteville, North Carolina: 5905
GENERAL TOBACCO COMPANY (Philippine Islands): 4656
GENERALITÉ DE GRENOBLE, France: 2195
GENERALS: see as subheading under names of armies
GENESEE COUNTY, Michigan:
    Flint: 689
GENESEE FARMER (ship): 4881
GENESEO, New York: 468
GENESIS AND GEOLOGY by Nicholas Collin Hughes: 2699
GENESIS POINT, Georgia: 3624
GENÊT, Edmond Charles: see CITIZEN GENÊT AFFAIR
GENET FAMILY (New York): 3709
GENÊT, Citizen, Affair: see CITIZEN GENÊT AFFAIR
GENEVA, New York:
    Schools: 4348
    Universities and colleges: see GENEVA COLLEGE
GENEVA, Switzerland: 258
    Description: 355, 1775
    Politics and government: 4408
    Universities and colleges: see UNIVERSITY OF GENEVA
GENEVA, Wisconsin: 69
GENEVA COLLEGE, Geneva, New York: 4067
    Finance: 1796
GENGA, Annibale della: 4745
THE GENIUS by Theodore Dreiser: 2390
GENNETT LUMBER COMPANY, Asheville, North Carolina: 1987
GENOA, Italy: 153, 323
    Description: 1775
A GENTLEMAN OF THE OLD NATCHEZ REGION: BENJAMIN L. C. WAILES by Charles S. Sydnor: 5498
GENTRY, John Joseph: 1988
GENTRY, Meredith Poindexter: 872
GENTRY FAMILY (South Carolina): 1988

GEOGRAPHY: 1989
    Student notes: 3504
GEOLOGICAL COMMISSION OF BRAZIL: 2407
GEOLOGY: 4306
    see also FOSSILS
    Brazil: 2407
    Great Britain: 747
    Mississippi: 5498
    North Carolina:
        see also NORTH CAROLINA--GOVERNMENT AGENCIES AND OFFICIALS--State Geological Board
        Study and teaching: 730
    South Carolina: 1220
GEOMETRY: 1004
GEORGE III, King of Great Britain: 1913, 1991, 2126
    Conspiracy against (1794): 2735
    Health: 4230
GEORGE IV, King of Great Britain: 4093, 4113, 5639
    Health: 2836
GEORGE V, King of Great Britain: 233, 452, 1526
    Visit to Port Said: 41
GEORGE VI, King of Great Britain: 233
GEORGE, Asa: 1990
GEORGE, David: 1990
GEORGE, Furniaful: 1990
GEORGE, George: 1990
GEORGE, Henry: 1424, 2225
GEORGE, Jessie: 1210, 1424
GEORGE, John: 1990
GEORGE, Stefan: 1992
GEORGE, Walter F.: 879
GEORGE A. TRENHOLM AND SON, Charleston, South Carolina: 4145
"GEORGE HENRY BOKER, PAUL HAMILTON HAYNE, AND CHARLES WARREN STODDARD. . . " by Jay Broadus Hubbell: 553
GEORGE LEARY (steam ship): 162
GEORGE PEABODY COLLEGE FOR TEACHERS, Nashville, Tennessee: 5635
    Medical education: 872
    Students and student life: 5977
GEORGE SANTAYANA: AN AMERICAN IN EXILE by Cyril Coniston Clemens: 1097
GEORGE WASHINGTON UNIVERSITY, Washington, D.C.: 669, 1778, 5640
    Law Department: 3587
    Students and student life: 2970, 3038
GEORGE WILLIAM FREDERICK CHARLES, Second Duke of Cambridge: 663, 3067, 4520
GEORGETOWN, District of Columbia: 384, 3891
    see also WASHINGTON, D.C.
    Literary interests: 4971
    Merchants: 785
    Surveying: 3145
GEORGETOWN, Kentucky: 3489
GEORGETOWN, South Carolina: 53, 2503, 3512
    Civil War:
        Civilian life: 1352
        Fortifications: 1107
    Rice: 545
GEORGETOWN COUNTY, South Carolina:
    Georgetown: see GEORGETOWN, South Carolina
    South Island: 2187, 2512
GEORGETOWN UNIVERISTY, Washington, D.C.: 785, 4688
GEORGETOWN VISITATION CONVENT, Washington, D.C.: 5786
GEORGEVILLE, North Carolina: 4788

GEORGIA

see also SOUTHERN STATES

GEORGIA

ADVERTISING:
 Gold milling machinery: 4895
AGRICULTURAL ORGANIZATIONS: 5040
AGRICULTURAL WORKERS:
 Augusta: 3749
 Cherokee County: 1887
AGRICULTURE: 245, 1229, 1231, 2727, 2963, 3075, 5426
 see also under GEORGIA: CROPS; FARMING; PLANTATIONS
AMERICAN LITERATURE: 924, 2374
 see also GEORGIA IN AMERICAN LITERATURE
 Translations from German: 3065
AMERICAN POETRY: 786, 991, 1029, 1841, 2894, 4177, 5029, 5292
AMERICAN REVOLUTION: see appropriate subheadings under AMERICAN REVOLUTION; CONTINENTAL ARMY
ARITHMETIC EXERCISE BOOKS: 208
ARSENALS--Augusta: 700
AUTHORS AND PUBLISHERS: 4377
AUTHORSHIP: 924, 2747, 3969
AUTOGRAPH COLLECTING--Savannah: 5220
AUTOGRAPHS: 2317, 4237
AUTOMOBILE RACING--Savannah: 1171
BAKERIES--Savannah: 575
BANK STOCKS: 311
 Forsyth County: 5260
BANKS AND BANKING: 1466, 3261, 3355, 5576
 Macon: 823
 Savannah: 311, 950, 5220
  see also BANK OF THE UNITED STATES (Second)--Savannah Branch
BAPTIST CHURCHES: 1080, 1993, 2326, 2756
 Clergy: see GEORGIA--CLERGY--Baptist
 State convention: 3625
BIRDS: 1803
BLACKSMITHING: 245
BLIND: 5426
BOARDING HOUSES: 670
BONDS: 5051, 5189
BOOK COLLECTING: 4402
BOOKS AND READING--Augusta: 5246
BOOKSELLERS AND BOOKSELLING: 3967
BOUNDARIES: 4205
BOUNDARY DISPUTES:
 South Carolina: 2666, 3671, 5276
 Western boundary: 2788
BOUNTY LANDS: 709, 1664, 2262
BUILDING AND LOAN ASSOCIATIONS: 2010
BUILDING CONSTRUCTION: 4988
BUILDING MATERIALS--Prices: 339
BUSINESS ACCOUNTS: 148
BUSINESS AFFAIRS:
 1700s: 2179
 1800s: 662, 759, 823, 2096, 2740, 2901, 3231, 3318
 Augusta: 5353
 Savannah: 5076, 5932
BUSINESS EDUCATION--Atlanta: 4911
CAMP MEETINGS--Methodist: 1231
CANALS: 3417
CARDS: 1435
CARPETBAGGERS: 2407
CARRIAGES AND BUGGIES:
 Forsyth County: 5260
CATHOLIC CHURCH: 938
CATTLE--Forsyth County: 5260
CHEROKEE INDIANS: 2326
CHILDREN--Employment: 539
CHURCHES:
 see also names of specific denominations under GEORGIA
 Bethel: 2460
CIVIL ENGINEERING:
 Savannah River: 89
CIVIL WAR: see appropriate subheadings under CIVIL WAR; CONFEDERATE STATES OF AMERICA; UNITED STATES--ARMY--Civil War

GEORGIA

CLAIMS: see GEORGIA--LAND CLAIMS
CLAY INDUSTRIES: 1478
CLERGY: 5787
 Baptist: 1476, 3625
  Sparta: 4654
 Methodist: 872
 Presbyterian: 5987
CLOCKS AND WATCHES:
 Forsyth County: 5260
CLOTHING AND DRESS--Macon: 5246
COAL INDUSTRY--Columbus: 4865
COAL MINING--Cherokee County: 1887
COMMISSION MERCHANTS: 5508
 Augusta: 2710
 Savannah: 2232, 2280, 3696, 4040, 4625
 Waynmanville: 2272
COMMODITY PRICES: 158, 377, 1397, 2232, 2365, 4183, 4720, 4783, 4875
 Augusta: 5246
 Franklin County: 1997
 Gwinnett County: 601
 Macon: 5246
 Savannah: 1251, 5494
COMMONPLACE BOOKS: 2893
CONFEDERATE SURVIVORS' ASSOCIATION:
 Augusta: 2388, 2894
CONFISCATED PROPERTY: 3573
CONGRESSIONAL ELECTIONS: 5494
CONSTITUTION (1877): 731
CONSTITUTIONAL CONVENTION (1868): 3330
COOKERY: 786, 4985
COTTON: 662, 4921
 Prices: 377, 1203, 2232, 2785, 5141
 Penfield: 5040
 Saint Mary's 235
 Speculation: 2232
 Taxation--Claims: 4895
COTTON GINS: 2931
COTTON GROWING: 127, 235, 1231, 1705, 2903, 5298
 Macon: 3905
COTTON LAND: 106
COTTON PLANTATIONS: 2963
COTTON TRADE: 235, 339, 497, 601, 1090, 2232, 3303, 3961, 5353, 5730
 Atlanta: 4402
 Augusta: 3583
 Hancock County: 4493
 Savannah: 1705, 2018, 2232, 3689
COTTON WORM: 4921
COUNTY GOVERNMENT:
 Chatham County: 996
COURTS:
 1700s: 1088, 2666
 1700s-1800s: 2931
 1800s: 1302, 3323, 3330, 5250
 Grand jury indictments: 3309
 Judgment: 3309
 Summonses: 2666
 Subdivided by type of court:
  Inferior Courts: 1993, 3113
   Bibb County: 1995
   Franklin County: 3782
   Greene County: 1998, 4654
   Richmond County: 2000
  Magistrate's Courts:
   Greene County: 1998
  Superior Courts: 1993, 5537
   Clerks--Upson County: 4754
   Establishment of: 2923
   Slave importation register: 2002
   Subdivided by place:
    Bibb County: 1995
    Greene County: 1998
    Richmond County: 2000
  Supreme Court: 3355, 3905, 5537
 Subdivided by place:
  Hancock County: 4493
  Savannah: 2001

GEORGIA

COURTS:
 Subdivided by place (Continued):
  Wilkes County: 2003, 2937
COURTSHIP: 2326, 3318
 see also GEORGIA--LOVE LETTERS
 Augusta: 5246
CREEK INDIANS: 1789, 5395
 Agents: 3704
 Treaties: 1848, 2778
CRIME: 1993
 see also GEORGIA--LAND FRAUD
CRIMINAL LAW REFORM:
 Jefferson County: 3309
CROP LOANS: 2232
CROPS: 1397, 4991, 5760
 see also specific kinds of crops under GEORGIA
 De Kalb County: 1011
 Marietta: 3667
CURRENCY: 1339, 2923
CUSTOMS ADMINISTRATION:
 Savannah: 4678, 5516
CUSTOMS DUTIES, Collection of:
 Saint Mary's: 2497
 Savannah: 2326, 4678
DEAF: 5426
 Education: 5051
DEATH: 786, 3414
DEBATING SOCIETIES: 4675, 4791
DEBT: 2594, 3134, 5604
 see also GEORGIA--PERSONAL DEBT
DEBT COLLECTION: 125, 5537
 Augusta: 3672
DEFENSE:
 see also GEORGIA--LOCAL DEFENSE
 Colonial period: 1993, 3968, 5473
DEMOCRATIC PARTY: 1121, 4921, 5051
DEPRESSIONS: 1203
 see also GEORGIA--PANIC OF 1837
DESCRIPTION AND TRAVEL (1800s):
 1800s: 5686
 1810s: 5686
 1820s: 158
 1840s: 5480, 5508
 1850s: 5508
 1860s: 1500, 2727, 4743
 1870s: 823, 2727, 5731
DISEASES: 2460, 5760
 Diphtheria: 1203
 Malaria--Control of: 365
 Smallpox: 1203
  Preventive inoculation: 365
 Typhus: 1203
 Yellow fever: 1203, 5298
  Savannah: 3323
DOGS: 3894
DUELING: 220, 1090, 2963, 5508
EARTHQUAKES (1886): 5246
ECONOMIC CONDITIONS: 311, 3355, 5051, 5494
 see also GEORGIA--DEPRESSIONS; GEORGIA--PANIC OF 1837
 Civil War: 1397
 Reconstruction: 807, 2727, 3905
EDUCATION: 1231, 3261
 see also GEORGIA--BUSINESS EDUCATION; GEORGIA--LEGAL EDUCATION; GEORGIA--MEDICAL EDUCATION
 Higher education: 5936
ELECTION LAWS AND REGULATIONS:
 Jefferson County: 3309
ELECTION REFORM:
 Jefferson County: 3309
ELECTIONS: 2740
 see also GEORGIA--CONGRESSIONAL ELECTIONS; GEORGIA--GUBERNATORIAL ELECTIONS; GEORGIA--LOCAL ELECTIONS
 1860s: 4895
 1870s: 415, 731
 Franklin County (1864): 3814
 State legislature (1795): 2788
ENGLISH DRAMA--Shakespeare: 3065
ESTATES (Landed property): 1434

755

## GEORGIA

ESTATES:
  Administration and settlement:
    1700s: 1664, 3573, 5920
    1700s-1800s: 2019, 2238, 2923, 3661, 5221
    1700s-1900s: 1993
    1800s: 220, 1375, 1981, 2327, 2670, 2740, 2827, 3396, 3672, 4706, 4911, 5051, 5537, 5787
    1800s-1900s: 3065
  Ebenezer: 5986
  Franklin County: 1997
  Greene County: 1998
  Hancock County: 4493
  Savannah: 3309, 3389, 3717, 4205
EVANGELISM: 5760
  Macon: 5246
EXHIBITIONS AND FAIRS:
  International Cotton Exposition (1881): 5494
  International Exposition (1895): 3376
FAMILY LIFE--Butts County: 1731
FARM ACCOUNTS:
  Cherokee County: 1887
FARM LIFE: 127, 1912
FARM MANAGEMENT: 5364
FARMING: 662, 1705, 1912, 2232, 2326, 4875
FINANCE: 4647, 5298
  see also GEORGIA--PERSONAL FINANCE; GEORGIA--PUBLIC FINANCE
  Effingham County: 1375
FLOODS: 1203
FOREIGN INVESTMENT IN GREAT BRITAIN AND VENEZUELA: 4895
FOREIGN TRADE: 2909
FORTIFICATIONS:
  Savannah: 2675, 4768
FOSSILS: 2578
FRAUD: see GEORGIA--LAND FRAUD
FREE NEGROES:
  Guardianship: 5537
  Reinslavement: 5051
FREE SOIL PARTY: 5051, 5315
FREEDMEN: 641, 662
  Behavior: 4895
  Labor contracts: 1268, 1705, 4706, 4895, 5162
FRENCH IN THE UNITED STATES: 1581
FUGITIVE SLAVES: 2460, 5576
  Eatonton: 4706
  Savannah: 3389, 5221
FUND RAISING: 1171
GAZETEERS: see GAZETEER OF GEORGIA
GERMAN LITERATURE:
  Translations into English: 3065
GOLD: 3555
GOLD LOTTERIES: 1887
  Meriwether County: 1999
GOLD MINES AND MINING:
  Cherokee County: 1887
  Investments: 4895
GOLD PLATE--Forsyth County: 5260
GOVERNMENT AGENCIES AND OFFICIALS:
  Attorney General: 700
  Colonial period:
    Colonial Council: 1374
    Governors: 1684, 4441, 5920
    Provision of supplies: 3968
    Trustees of the colony: 1993, 3733, 5473
  Executive Council: 1993
    Minutes: 2307
  Governors:
    Archibald Bulloch (1775-1777): 759
    George Walton (1779-1780, 1789-1790): 5537
    George Handley (1788): 2307
    Edward Telfair (1789-1793): 5221
    George Mathews (1787, 1793-1796): 3573
    Jared Irwin (1796-1797): 2778
    Josiah Tattnall, Sr. (1801-1802): 5189

## GEORGIA

GOVERNMENT AGENCIES AND OFFICIALS:
  Governors (Continued):
    John Milledge (1802-1806): 3671
    David Brydie Mitchell (1809-1813, 1815-1817): 3704
    John Clark (1819-1823): 3323
    John Forsyth (1827-1829): 1855
    Wilson Lumpkin (1831-1835): 3297
    George Rockingham Gilmer (1829-1831, 1837-1839): 2049
    Herschel Vespasian Johnson (1853-1857): 2860
    Joseph Emerson Brown (1857-1865): 700, 2388, 4729, 5082
    Charles Jones Jenkins (1865-1868): 2827
    William J. Northen (1890-1892): 3947
    Hoke Smith (1907-1911): 4887
  Public officials:
    Bonding and oaths of office: 1189
  Railroad Commission: 2280
  Receiver of Alien Property: 1365
  Sheriffs: 1375
    Chatham County: 4611
    Liberty County: 2910
    Wilkes County: 2937
  Solicitors General:
    Ocmulgee Circuit: 4415
  Tax collectors: 1375
    Savannah: 731
  Treasury: 1090, 1347, 2019
GOVERNMENT AND CIVIC EMPLOYEES: 3505
GRIST MILLS: 4895
GUANO: 4493, 5051
GUARDIANSHIP: 3711
GUBERNATORIAL ELECTIONS:
  1868: 4415
  1894: 3660
  1934: 3575
  1946: 3558
HIRING OF SLAVES: 2216, 2788, 2923, 3573, 4921, 5051
  Jasper County: 377
  Mining company: 4895
HISTORICAL SOCIETIES: see GEORGIA HISTORICAL SOCIETY
HISTORICAL STUDIES: 787, 2788, 2893, 2894, 3898
  Augusta: 2894
HOME REMEDIES: 3396, 3591
HORSE RACING--Savannah: 4864
HORSES: 2020
HOSPITALS--Cuthbert: 3555
HOUSEHOLD ACCOUNTS: 786, 2020
  Ebenezer: 5986
HOUSES--Construction: 2020
HUNTING: 3894
INDIANS OF NORTH AMERICA: 3966
  see also GEORGIA--CHEROKEE INDIANS; GEORGIA--CREEK INDIANS
  Agents--Supplies: 2432
  Government relations: 3733
  Land:
    Purchases and sales: 2020, 2666
    Raids: 2666
  Relations with whites: 2666, 2788
  Wars: 3415, 4434, 5051
INDUSTRIAL ORGANIZATION: 3706
INSURANCE: 1434, 2114, 2232
  Agents--Savannah: 4587
  Business: 5730
  Property: 127
INSURANCE COMPANIES:
  Savannah: 4587
INTERNAL IMPROVEMENTS: 1090
  see also GEORGIA--CANALS; GEORGIA--RAILROADS; GEORGIA--ROADS
JOURNALISM: 2374
  Editing: 731
JUDGES: 2372, 3113, 5787
  Circuit Courts: 2860
  Morgan County: 4415

## GEORGIA

KNOW-NOTHING PARTY: 5051
KU KLUX KLAN: 1672
LABOR CONTRACTS: 5237
LABOR GRIEVANCES:
  Steel workers: 5441
LABOR IN POLITICS: 2568
LABOR LAWS AND LEGISLATION: 5441
  Employment of women and children: 5406
LABOR UNIONS:
  Dues: 1197
  Steel workers: 5441
LAND: 311, 1203
  see also the following subheadings under GEORGIA: COTTON LAND; PUBLIC LANDS; REAL ESTATE; TIMBER LAND
  Prices--Franklin County: 1997
  Purchases and sales:
    1700s: 5644
    1700s-1800s: 2019, 2441, 3309, 3661
    1800s: 794, 1066, 1090, 2280, 3704, 5354, 5651
    Augusta: 3672
    Saint Mary's: 1448
  Subdivided by place:
    Camden County: 1835
    Covington: 1382
LAND CLAIMS: 2785
LAND COMPANIES: 3309, 4298
LAND DEEDS AND INDENTURES:
  1700s: 1664, 2666, 5189, 5987
  1700s-1800s: 2441, 5986
  1700s-1900s: 1993
  1800s: 1434, 2006, 2232, 2280, 2827, 4895, 5586
  Effingham County: 1375
  Franklin County: 1997
  Savannah: 3309, 5221
LAND FRAUD: 1090
  see also YAZOO LAND FRAUD
LAND GRANTS:
  1700s: 289, 1296, 1993, 2666, 3573
  1700s-1800s: 3671
  1800s: 1434, 2280, 2992
  Franklin County: 1997
  Great Ogeechee District: 812
LAND LAWS: 3573
LAND LOTTERIES: 1993
  Greene County: 1998
  Meriwether County: 1999
LAND SETTLEMENT: 2096, 3733
  Twiggs County: 1231
LAND SPECULATION: 3041, 3897, 4081, 4298
LAND SURVEYS: see GEORGIA--SURVEYS AND SURVEYING
LAND TITLES:
  Bulloch County: 3663
  Saint Mary's: 1448
LAND WARRANTS: 4921
LATIN NOTEBOOKS:
  University of Georgia: 3905
LAW:
  Study of: 2326
  Teaching at University of Georgia: 3905
LAW ENFORCEMENT: 422
  Savannah: 5492
LAW PRACTICE:
  1700s: 2788
  1800s: 731, 740, 2326, 2372, 2464, 2740, 4611, 5051
  Augusta: 2931
  Bartow: 2860
  Camden County: 235
  Macon: 3905
LAWSUITS: 1434, 2232, 2931
  Augusta: 3672
  Savannah: 2262
LEGAL AFFAIRS:
  1700s: 289
  1700s-1800s: 5189, 5353

GEORGIA

LEGAL AFFAIRS (Continued):
  1800s: 4647, 4706, 5606
  Eatonton: 3905, 5837
  Jasper County: 377
  Savannah: 2789, 3389, 5787, 5987
  Sparta: 5250
  Wilkes County: 5315
LEGAL EDUCATION: 2326
LEGISLATURE: 662, 2326, 2778, 5453, 5576
  see also UNITED STATES--CONGRESS--(House or Senate)--Georgia, for national legislators from Georgia
  House of Representatives: 1296
    Clerk: 4826
  Senate: 3905
    Clerk: 3081
LIQUOR--Medicinal use: 4356
LIQUOR MANUFACTURING--Illegal: 2388
LITERARY INTERESTS: 4857
LITERARY SOCIETIES: 2005
LOCAL DEFENSE:
  Civil War: see CIVIL WAR--LOCAL DEFENSE
  Richmond County: 2666
  Savannah: 2722
LOCAL ELECTIONS:
  Savannah: 2280, 5494
LOCAL POLITICS:
  Twiggs County: 1231
LOCOFOCO PARTY: 5051
LOTTERIES: 1438, 5929
  see also GEORGIA--GOLD LOTTERIES; GEORGIA--LAND LOTTERIES
LOVE LETTERS: 2326, 3991, 5254
  see also GEORGIA--COURTSHIP
LOYALISTS:
  Property: 5398
  Savannah: 5078
LOYALTY OATHS: 5537
LUMBER RAFTS: 2122
LUTHERAN CHURCHES: 1993
MANUSCRIPT COLLECTING: 4402
MANUFACTURERS' AGENTS: 2232
MANUFACTURING: 5426
MARRIAGE: 3625
MARRIAGE CONTRACTS: 4768, 4988, 5986
MASONRY: 662
MEDICAL EDUCATION:
  Atlanta: see ATLANTA MEDICAL COLLEGE
  Augusta: 2903
MEDICAL PRACTICE: 2903, 5924
  Savannah: 220
MEDICAL SOCIETIES: 364, 4676
MEDICAL TREATMENT: 2020, 2963
  see also GEORGIA--HOME REMEDIES
MEDICINE: 167
  see also GEORGIA--LIQUOR--Medicinal use
MENTAL HOSPITALS:
  Milledgeville: 127
MENTALLY ILL (census): 5426
MENTALLY RETARDED (census): 5426
MERCANTILE ACCOUNTS: 4988
  Augusta: 138, 2937
  Carroll County: 874
  Crawford: 3974
  Douglas County: 874
  Franklin: 3966
  Gwinnett County: 601
  Lincoln County: 138
  Louisville: 5562
  Middleburg: 2741
  Savannah: 1251, 5216
MERCHANT SEAMEN:
  Aid societies: 786, 4678
MERCHANTS: 1231, 1242, 1609, 1993, 2365, 4298, 4988
  see also GEORGIA--COMMISSION MERCHANTS
  Augusta: 2710
  Crawford: 3974
  Greenville: 17
  Savannah: 2019, 2232, 2497, 4768

GEORGIA

METHODIST CHURCHES: 731, 1993, 5699
  Converts: 5246
  Georgia Conference: 3646
  Liturgy and ritual: 5246
MIDWIVES: 365
MIGRATION TO: 1993
MILITARY SCHOOLS: 3729, 5970
MILITIA:
  1700s: 1667, 1696, 2788
  1800s: 1296, 2512, 3101
  American Revolution:
    Relations with the Continental Army: 2179
  Civil War: 700, 1189
  Commissaries: 1347
  Commissions: 3661
  Paymaster: 2019
  Subdivided by unit:
    Battalions:
      2nd: 1664
      4th: 843
    Regiments:
      1st Infantry (Chatham County): 1993, 2893
      7th Georgia State Guards: 3180
      Irish Jasper Greens: 5547
      see also CONFEDERATE STATES OF AMERICA--ARMY--Regiments--Georgia--Infantry--1st
  Subdivided by place:
    Clarke County: 1993
    Fort Twiggs: 2778
    Franklin County: 2307
MILL WORKERS:
  Cherokee County: 1887
    Slaves: 1887
MILLERS' ACCOUNTS:
  Cherokee County: 1887
MINE WORKERS:
  Cherokee County: 1887
    Slaves: 1887
MINES AND MINING--Clopton's Mills: 5760
MONUMENTS, etc.: 1171, 5090
MORTGAGES: 4887
MULES--Forsyth County: 5260
MUNICIPAL GOVERNMENT:
  Brunswick: 1374
  Chatham County: 996
MUSIC--Study and teaching: 2786
MUSICAL SOCIETIES: 4677
NAVAL STORES INDUSTRY: 4298
NEGRO SUFFRAGE: 662
NEGROES: 731, 2232, 2963
  see also GEORGIA--FREE NEGROES; GEORGIA--FREEDMEN; GEORGIA--SLAVES
  Voting: 4895
NEGROES IN POLITICS: 731
NEW YEAR'S GREETINGS:
  Savannah: 4177
NEWSPAPERS: 731, 1112
  Atlanta: 823
NORMAL SCHOOLS: 539
NORTHERNERS IN THE SOUTH: 2096
  Atlanta: 5082
NOTARIES--Chatham County: 4611
NULLIFICATION: 3767
NURSES AND NURSING: 365
ORPHANAGES: 2786
ORPHANS: 5426
OVERSEERS: 2020, 2903, 5576
  Oglethorpe County: 5162
PANIC OF 1837: 311
PARDONS: 5189
PATENTS--Cotton Gin: 2931
PATRONS OF HUSBANDRY: 2232
PAUPERS: 5051
PAVEMENTS--Vulcanite: 4966
PEACHES: 1397
PEONAGE: 5051
PERSONAL DEBT: 377, 1423, 5537
  Savannah: 4205
PERSONAL FINANCE: 1476, 2020, 5051
  Augusta: 5246
  Cherokee County: 1887

GEORGIA

PERSONAL FINANCE (Continued):
  Macon: 3905
  Savannah: 3311
PHARMACIES: 279
PHILANTHROPY: 4363
PHRENOLOGY: 2280
PHYSICIANS: 365, 2980
  Montgomery County: 3110
  Savannah: 4676
PHYSICIANS' ACCOUNTS: 1581
  Augusta: 168, 3672
  Lawrenceville: 167
  Savannah: 158, 339
PIANOS--Forsyth County: 5260
PLANTATION ACCOUNTS:
  Altamaha: 4445
  Augusta: 3749
  Ebenezer: 5986
PLANTATION LIFE: 2020
  Burke County: 5246
  Columbia County: 5246
PLANTATION MANAGEMENT: 1242, 5651
  By women: 2367
PLANTATIONS: 781, 1011, 1664, 4743
  see also GEORGIA--COTTON PLANTATIONS; GEORGIA--RICE PLANTATIONS
  Finance:
    Oglethorpe County: 5162
    Sparta: 4493
  Subdivided by place:
    Augusta: 5246
    Bulloch County: 3663
    Chatham County: 1996
    Cherokee County: 797
    Sapelo Island: 4988
    Savannah: 3278
POETRY: 2894
  see also GEORGIA--AMERICAN POETRY
  Collections: 1621
POLITICAL PATRONAGE: 422, 662, 731, 1203, 2497
POLITICS AND GOVERNMENT:
  see also the following subheadings under GEORGIA: COUNTY GOVERNMENT; LABOR IN POLITICS; LOCAL POLITICS; MUNICIPAL GOVERNMENT; NEGROES IN POLITICS
  1700s:
    Colonial period: 1992, 4441
    1770s: 3209
    1780s: 2262, 4826
    1790s: 4826
  1700s-1800s: 2460, 2778, 3671, 5221
  1800s: 1170, 2963, 3297, 3415, 5315
    1800s: 3704
    1810s: 3704
    1820s: 3704
    1830s: 5298
    1840s: 1121, 3081, 3355, 4434, 5298, 5385, 5576
    1850s: 1121, 1123, 1422, 3081, 3355, 5298, 5576
    1860s: 662, 700, 1121, 1123, 2388, 3081, 5517, 5915
    1870s: 1203, 2096, 5051, 5517
    1880s: 261, 1203, 2096, 5051
    1890s: 662, 2096, 3947
  1800s-1900s: 2362, 3905, 3967
  1900s: 3558
POORHOUSES--Savannah: 4678
POSTAL SERVICE: 4921
  Local offices:
    Columbia Mine: 4895
    Lawrenceville: 5438
PRESBYTERIAN CHURCHES:
  Augusta: 26
  Macon: 3905
PRICES: see GEORGIA--COMMODITY PRICES, and Prices as subheading under names of specific commodities
PRINTING: 1112

GEORGIA

PRISONERS AND PRISONS: 5426
PROHIBITION: 1248
PROMISSORY NOTES: 1434
PROPERTY LISTS: 5353
PROPERTY LOSS--Savannah: 3389
PROSTHESIS: 2280
PROTESTANT EPISCOPAL CHURCH: 4358
PUBLIC FINANCE: 2827
  Budget (1969): 3348
  Colonial period: 5473
PUBLIC HEALTH: 365
PUBLIC LANDS:
  Purchases and sales: 1296
PUBLIC SCHOOLS: 1193
RACE RELATIONS--Atlanta: 5082
RACING: see GEORGIA--AUTOMOBILE RACING; GEORGIA--HORSE RACING
RAILROADS:
  1800s: 3024, 3317
  1830s: 1297, 3767, 4718
  1840s: 4718
  1850s: 4718
  1860s: 2533
  1870s: 1933, 2177, 2533
  1880s: 1264, 2280
  1800s-1900s: 4674, 5494
  Accounts: 4674
  Construction: 1466, 2963, 5298
  Finance: 725, 950, 3508
  Labor: 5051
  Stocks: 420, 2004
    Forsyth County: 5260
  Subdivided by place:
    Marietta: 3508
    Savannah: 3629
REAL ESTATE:
  see also GEORGIA--LAND
  Investments: 3081, 4895
  Rent: 3767
  Subdivided by place:
    Augusta: 2560
    Bulloch County: 3663
    Forsyth County: 5260
    Glynn County: 2460
    Savannah: 2992, 3629
REAL ESTATE BUSINESS: 2114
RECONSTRUCTION: 51, 731, 1017, 1056, 1494, 1614, 1672, 2232, 2464, 2860, 2901, 2963, 3134, 4257, 4377, 4921, 5517
  Augusta: 5905
  Economic conditions: 377, 641, 807, 1993
  Federal military occupation: 2827
  Poverty: 2326
RELATIONS (GENERAL) WITH FLORIDA: 2179, 3733
RELATIONS (GENERAL) WITH SOUTH CAROLINA: 5537
RELIGION:
  1700s: 5699
  1800s: 786, 1413, 3625
  1800s-1900s: 2963, 5082
  Marion County: 5051
REMINISCENCES: 1231
REPUBLICAN PARTY: 731, 1091, 4921, 5051, 5492
RICE: 1803
  Prices: 2020, 2785
RICE PLANTATIONS: 1242, 2020, 2326, 2963, 4864
  "Hopeton": 1242
  Savannah: 3311
ROADS: 158, 5744
  Civil War: 1181
  Map: 1182
SALT WORKS: 4743, 4895
SAWMILL WORKERS:
  Cherokee County: 1887
    Slaves: 1887
SAWMILLS: 4895
  Cherokee County: 1887
SCHOOL BOARDS: 662

GEORGIA

SCHOOLS: 3415, 5760
  see also GEORGIA--NORMAL SCHOOLS; GEORGIA--PUBLIC SCHOOLS
  Curriculum: 2828
  Finance: 479
  Girls' schools and academies: 479
    Athens: 3905
    La Grange: 3905
    Macon: 2963
    Monroe County: 339, 2828, 2963, 4040
    Savannah: 2326
    Washington: 5051
  Negro schools: 510
  Subdivided by place:
    Macon: 479, 2963
    Talbotton: 3729
    Washington: 51, 5580
SECESSION AND SECESSIONIST SENTIMENT: 2460, 3075, 3110, 4415, 4895
SECESSION CONVENTIONS: 700, 2860, 3905, 4799
SERMONS: 991
  Baptist: 4759
SHIPPING: 2019, 2216
  Lawsuits: 1454
SILK INDUSTRY: 2238
SILVER PLATE--Forsyth County: 5260
SLATE MINING--Cherokee County: 1887
SLAVE PATROL: 1993
SLAVE STEALING: 3961
SLAVE TRADE:
  1700s: 2019, 2020, 5537
  1700s-1800s: 1993, 2778, 3671
  1800s: 781, 1090, 1434, 1466, 1789, 2002, 2280, 3661, 3905, 4720, 5787
  Prices: 4895, 5494
  Subdivided by place:
    Bulloch County: 4395
    Ebenezer: 5986
    Savannah: 1705, 5221
SLAVERY: 2460
SLAVES: 1231, 2280, 2326, 5250, 5651
  see also GEORGIA--FUGITIVE SLAVES; GEORGIA--HIRING OF SLAVES
  Clothing and dress: 5395
  Descriptions: 2002
  Diseases: 5606
    Cholera: 2578
  Disobedience: 3729
  Insurrections (Fear of): 2788
  Lists: 3905, 4400
  Marriage: 2778
  Medical treatment: 1375, 4647
  Transportation: 2778
  Treatment: 2020, 5221
  Subdivided by place:
    Cherokee County: 1887
    Forsyth County: 5260
SOCIAL CONDITIONS:
  Atlanta: 539
  Reconstruction: 2860
SOCIAL LIFE AND CUSTOMS:
  1700s-1800s: 2460
  1700s-1900s: 1993
  1800s: 1066, 1091, 5051
  1820s: 158, 832
  1830s: 5298
  1840s: 5298, 5760
  1850s: 1476, 5298, 5426, 5651, 5760
  1860s: 1476, 2860, 5426, 5760
  1870s: 5426, 5760
  Athens: 2783
  Augusta: 5480
  Macon: 5246
  Rome: 2035
  Savannah: 220, 2035, 5298
SOCIETIES AND CLUBS: 2238
  see also specific types of societies under GEORGIA, e.g. GEORGIA--MUSICAL SOCIETIES
SONGS AND MUSIC: 539
  Concerts--Savannah: 4677

GEORGIA

SOUTHERN UNIONISTS: 5905
STAGECOACH LINES: 2289
STATES' RIGHTS: 1302, 5606
STATES' RIGHTS PARTY: 5051
STEAMBOAT LINES: 4895
STEAMBOATS--Explosions: 2956
STOCKS--Forsyth County: 5260
STORAGE OF MERCHANDISE:
  Savannah: 5516
STREET-RAILROADS--Savannah: 1710
SUFFRAGE: see GEORGIA--NEGRO SUFFRAGE
SUGAR GROWING: 127
SURVEYS AND SURVEYING: 1993, 4988, 5586
  Bulloch County: 3663
  Darien: 3389
  Franklin County: 1997
  Heard County: 3966
  Saint John's Parish: 1440
  Savannah:
    Graft among surveyors: 3389
TAILORS--Greenville: 17
TANNING--Jasper County: 377
TAVERNS AND INNS:
  Greenville: 17
  Watkinsville: 1621
TAX IN KIND: 1181, 5162
  Assessments--Franklin County: 1997
TAX RECEIPTS: 1434
TAX RETURNS: 2827
TAXATION: 1121, 1189, 1993, 3814
  Assessment: 1374
  Banks County: 1994
  Chatham County: 3573
  Effingham County: 1375
  Greene County: 1998
  Richland County: 3573
TEACHERS' RECORDS:
  Watkinsville: 1621
TEACHING: 1231
  Augusta: 5246
TEMPERANCE: 662, 731, 2963, 5760
  Riceboro: 5051
TEXTILE INDUSTRY: 2272, 5237
  Augusta: 1829
TIMBER:
  Camden County: 1835
  Covington: 1382
TIMBER LAND:
  Great Ogeechee District: 812
TOBACCO--Prices: 817
TOBACCO BROKERS' FEES: 817
TOBACCO INDUSTRY:
  Construction of factories in Savannah: 5221
TOBACCO TAXES: 817
TOBACCO TRADE: 4857, 5040, 5251
  Plug tobacco: 817
  Tobacco products:
    Eatonton: 3352
TRADE AND COMMERCE:
  Agricultural products: 2232, 5651
  Beef--Ebenezer: 5986
  Carriages and buggies: 5623
  Cotton: see GEORGIA--COTTON TRADE
  Dry goods: 2280
  Flour--Ebenezer: 5986
  Food-Eatonton: 3352
  Fur--Chattahoochee River: 3966
  Furniture: 781
  Groceries--Savannah: 4040
  Hay--Augusta: 3749
  Horses: 781, 2118
  Leather: 2365
  Liquor--Eatonton: 3352
  Livestock: 781
  Lumber: 5508
    Ebenezer: 5986
    Savannah: 4356, 5216
  Millinery goods:
    Waynmanville: 2272
  Slaves: see GEORGIA--SLAVE TRADE
  Tea: 1440
  Tobacco: see GEORGIA--TOBACCO TRADE

GEORGIA:

TRADE AND COMMERCE (Continued):
  Tools: 781
  Wholesale: 1829
  Yarn: 2365
TRANSPORTATION: 3447
TRAVEL--Railroad: 5819
TREATIES--Creek Indians: 1848, 2778
TRUSTS--Railroads: 3508
TURPENTINE INDUSTRY: 2970
UNITED STATES AGENCIES AND OFFICIALS:
  Bureau of Refugees, Freedmen, and
    Abandoned Lands: 731
  Internal revenue collectors: 2280
UNITED STATES CENSUS OF 1870: 2326
UNIVERSITIES AND COLLEGES: 479, 662
  see also ANDREW FEMALE COLLEGE;
    ATHENS STATE NORMAL COLLEGE;
    BRENAU COLLEGE; EMORY UNIVERSITY;
    FURLOW MASONIC FEMALE COLLEGE;
    GEORGIA FEMALE COLLEGE; GORDON
    INSTITUTE; MERCER UNIVERSITY;
    OGLETHORPE UNIVERSITY; SHORTER
    COLLEGE; SOUTHERN MASONIC FEMALE
    COLLEGE; UNIVERSITY OF GEORGIA;
    WESLEYAN COLLEGE
  Students and student life:
    Finance: 3134
VENDUE MASTERS--Savannah: 2019
VETERANS' AFFAIRS: 2096
WAGES AND SALARIES:
  Railroad telegraphers: 3985
WAR OF 1812: see appropriate
  subheadings under WAR OF 1812
WAREHOUSES: 4678
WARRANTS (Law)--Savannah: 2262
WEATHER: 5760
  Savannah: 2785, 4687
WHIG PARTY: 1121, 4921, 5051
WILLS: 1434, 2262
  Savannah: 3309
WOMAN'S CHRISTIAN TEMPERANCE UNION:
  5082
WOMEN: 168
  Employment--Cherokee County: 1887
WOMEN IN BUSINESS: 5353

[End of entries under GEORGIA]

GEORGIA, CAROLINA, AND NORTHERN RAIL
  ROAD: 4145
GEORGIA AIRLINE RAILROAD COMPANY: 2004
GEORGIA CENTRAL RAILROAD: 402, 5494
GEORGIA FEMALE COLLEGE, Madison,
  Georgia: 5082
GEORGIA HISTORICAL QUARTERLY: 5193
GEORGIA HISTORICAL SOCIETY: 539,
  2005, 2326, 3461, 4195, 4675
GEORGIA IN AMERICAN LITERATURE: 2883
GEORGIA LAND COMPANY, Savannah,
  Georgia: 3309
GEORGIA MEDICAL SOCIETY: 364
GEORGIA MILITARY INSTITUTE, Marietta,
  Georgia: 3729, 5970
GEORGIA RAILROAD: 637, 3024
GEORGIA REPUBLICAN: 731
GEORGIA STATE AGRICULTURAL SOCIETY:
  5040
GEORGIA STATE INDUSTRIAL UNION
  COUNCIL: 5441
GERHARDT, William: 2007
GERIATRICS: 2934
  see also AGED AND AGING
GERMAIN, George Sackville, First
  Viscount Sackville: 2008
GERMAN ALLIANCE INSURANCE
  ASSOCIATION: 5790
GERMAN-AMERICAN MUTUAL LOAN AND
  BUILDING ASSOCIATION: 2010
GERMAN BAPTIST CHURCH, New Hope,
  Virginia: 3826
GERMAN DRAMA--Reviews: 3617
GERMAN LANGUAGE:
  Dictionaries: 3598
  Students' notebooks: 5762

GERMAN LITERATURE:
  Translations into English: 2058
  Georgia: 3065
GERMAN POETRY: 1992
GERMAN SOCIETY OF THE CITY OF NEW
  YORK: 2246
GERMAN VOLUNTEERS, NORTH CAROLINA
  STATE TROOPS: see CONFEDERATE STATES
  OF AMERICA--ARMY--Regiments--North
  Carolina--Infantry--18th
GERMANIC CONFEDERATION: 3472
GERMANNA, Virginia: 5004
GERMANS IN GREAT BRITAIN: 3808
GERMANS IN THE UNITED STATES: 2007,
  2010, 2949, 2950, 3808
  see also SPIES--German
  New York: 2246
  North Carolina: 1232
  Pennsylvania: 3754, 4723
    Social life and customs: 4937
  South Carolina: 46
    Civil War volunteers: 2300
  Texas: 218, 5194
GERMANTON, North Carolina: 279, 817,
  3653, 4248, 5141
  Medical services: 4136
  Postal service: 315
GERMANTOWN, Ohio: 2507
GERMANTOWN, Pennsylvania: see AMERICAN
  REVOLUTION--Campaigns and battles--
  Pennsylvania--Germantown
GERMANTOWN, U.S.S.: 4017
GERMANY:
  see also PRUSSIA
  Apprenticeship: 3808
  Armed Forces:
    High Command (1942): 2557
    Officers: 5418
  Army: 2557
    World War II--Surrender: 5420
  British embassy in: 3472
  Children--Employment: 305
  Churches--Berlin: 2139
  Cotton trade: 5014
  Currency: 1339, 5252
  Description and travel:
    1700s: 306
    1700s-1800s: 3808
    1800s: 5038
      1820s: 4490
      1830s: 4490
      1840s: 244, 4695
      1850s: 5459
      1860s: 1962, 2617, 3674, 5459
      1870s: 157, 1962, 3674
      1880s: 3674
      1890s: 1768
    1800s-1900s: 4858, 5730
  Drawing, Study of: 1665
  Dueling: 5661
  Economic conditions (1800s): 2742
  Emperors: 3472
  Foreign relations: 3472
    Great Britain: 3238
    Persia:
      State visit of the Shah: 3722
    Russia: 4449
  Foreign trade: 2742
  Franco-Prussian War: see FRANCO-
    PRUSSIAN WAR
  Funerals: 2009
  Historic buildings: 2411
  Immigration and emigration:
    see also GERMANS IN (name of
      place)
    To Carolina Province: 202
    To Great Britain: 3808
    To United States: 3808
  Imperial family: 2009
  Legal procedures: 2194
  Libraries--Berlin: 2139
  Mathematics, Study of: 632
  Medical education--Bavaria: 174
  Medical treatment: 181
  Moravian church: 5459

GERMANY (Continued):
  Music, Study of: 661
  Naturalists: 2706
  Navy: 4476
  Notaries: 2194
  Palaces--Berlin: 2139
  Patents:
    Cloth folding machinery: 4807
  Political posters (Nazi): 2011
  Politics and government:
    1800s: 2079, 2742, 3472
    1900s: 2161
  Portraits: 2411
  Posters: 2011
  Reparations: see WORLD WAR I--
    Reparations
  Social conditions: 4449
  Social life and customs: 3310
  Socialism--Bibliography: 65
  Socialists--Biography: 65
  Theater: 3617
  Theological education: 2592
  Tobacco industry: 4079
  Transatlantic voyages to: 5298
  United States consul in: 3029
  Universities and colleges: see
    UNIVERSITY OF BERLIN;
    UNIVERSITY OF HEIDELBERG
  Women--Employment: 305
  World War I: see WORLD WAR I
  World War II: see WORLD WAR II
GEROCK, Charles: 2012
GERONIMO (Apache warrior): 2991
GERRARDSTOWN, West Virginia: 865,
  919
  Social life and customs: 4904
GERSON, Virginia: 4789
GERSTMAN, Louis: 2013
GERVASIO GIL, Manuel: see GIL,
  Manuel Gervasio
GETTYSBURG, Pennsylvania:
  Civil War: 1740
    see also CIVIL WAR--CAMPAIGNS,
      BATTLES, AND MILITARY ACTIONS--
      Pennsylvania--Gettysburg
  Legal affairs: 5780
  Universities and colleges: see
    GETTYSBURG COLLEGE
GETTYSBURG, U.S.S.: 5329
GETTYSBURG COLLEGE, Gettysburg,
  Pennsylvania: 1100
GHICA, Demetrius: 3036
GHICA, Ion, Prince: 3036
GHISELIN, Henry: 3440
GHOLSON, James H.: 724
GHOLSON, Thomas: 2551, 4531
GHOLSON, Thomas S. (Virginia): 724
GHOLSON, Thomas Saunders (1808-1868):
  2014
GHOLSON, Mississippi--Students: 5032
GHOLSONVILLE, Virginia:
  Mercantile accounts: 5648
  Merchants: 4747
GHOST WRITING:
  English literature: 2146
GIANNONE, Pietro: 2015
GIANT ALCOHOL by M. W. Knapp: 2861
GIBBENS, Gordon Butcher: 2016
GIBBES, Edmund A.: 2017
GIBBES, James S.: 2018
GIBBES, Robert Wilson: 1575, 3287,
  4193
GIBBES FAMILY (Genealogy): 1424
GIBBON, Edward: 2707
GIBBONS, A. S.: 1116
GIBBONS, James, Cardinal: 2849
GIBBONS, John: 2019
GIBBONS, Joseph: 2020
GIBBONS, Sara (Cloud): 1116
GIBBONS, William, Sr. (d. ca. 1771):
  2020, 2238
GIBBONS, William, Jr. (d. ca. 1803):
  365, 2020
GIBBONS FAMILY (South Carolina):
  2019
GIBBS, William Kelly: 2021

GIBRALTER, George Augustus Eliott, First Lord Heathfield, Baron of: see ELIOTT, George Augustus, First Lord Heathfield, Baron of Gibralter
GIBRALTER: 841, 2296
  Description: 4355
  Siege by Spanish (1727): 2156
GIBSON, Christiana M.: 2022
GIBSON, Hamilton L.: 2023
GIBSON, Hugh: 1424
GIBSON, James W.: 2024
GIBSON, Randall Lee: 2025
GIBSON, Robert Atkinson, Bishop: 356
GIBSON, Thomas R.: 2449
GIBSON, William Hamilton: 3789
GIDEONITES--South Carolina: 3264
GIERLOW, John: 1029
GIFFARD, Hardinge Stanley, First Earl of Halsbury: 1815
GIFFEN, Sir Robert: 2026, 2322
GIFFORD, William: 2058
GIFT-BOOKS: 3325
GIL, Manuel Gervasio: 4155
GIL DE TABOADA DE LEMOS, Francisco: 4155
GILBERT, Henry: 2027
GILBERT, Irene E.: 1808
GILBERT, Lyman D.: 2027
GILBERT, Shepard D.: 2028
GILBERT, Sir Walter Raleigh, First Baronet: 2029
GILCHRIST, Anne (Burrows): 4576
GILCHRIST, Herbert Harlakenden: 4576
GILCHRIST, John M.: 2030
GILCHRIST & McKAY: see McKAY & GILCHRIST
GILDER, Jeannette Leonard: 2374, 2449
GILDER, Joseph B.: 2871
GILDER, Richard Watson: 72, 706, 1878, 4491
GILDERSLEEVE, Basil Lanneau: 3394, 2449, 4453, 4698
GILE, Andrew S.: 2031
GILES, J. W.: 813
GILES, Jacob: 2033
GILES, Mary Zilpha: 2032
GILES, Persis: 2032
GILES, William Branch: 2034
GILES COUNTY, Tennessee: 4269
  Pulaski: 6
GILES COUNTY, Virginia: 4522
GILFILLAN, Samuel: 5238
GILHAM, William H.: 1587, 4344
GILL, Miss _____ (Pennsylvania): 2362
GILL, Fanny Elizabeth (Vining): 1378
GILL (JOHN, JR.) AND CO.: 870
GILL, Lizzie (Ingersoll): 2035
GILL, William A.: 5965
GILL FAMILY (New York): 2035
GILL FAMILY (North Carolina): 2036
GILLEM, Alvan Cullem: 4723, 5268
GILLES, Groves: 2037
GILLESPIE, George Lewis: 2038
GILLESPIE, John: 702
GILLET, Ransom Hooker: 4751
GILLETT, Jonathan: 2039
GILLETT, Maria: 2039
GILLETT, P. W.: 2039
GILLETT, Sarah: 2039
GILLIAM, Donnell: 5457
GILLIAT (JOHN K.) AND COMPANY, London, England: 2302, 2363
GILLIG, Henry S.: 196
GILLILAND, William H.: 2040
GILLINGHAM, Alberta Bassett (Stith) Jones: 2041
GILLINGHAM FAMILY (North Carolina): 2041
GILLIS AND JANWIN (firm): see JANWIN AND GILLIS
GILLMORE, Quincy Adams: 2280, 4108
GILLON, Alexander: 4399
GILLON, Andrew: 4214
GILL'S CREEK, South Carolina: 4310

GILMAN, Arthur: 2046
GILMAN, Caroline (Howard): 103, 2045
GILMAN, Daniel Coit: 2042
GILMAN, John Taylor: 2043
GILMAN, Lawrence: 2449
GILMAN, Nathaniel: 2044
GILMAN, Samuel: 2045
GILMAN, William C.: 2046
GILMAN FAMILY (Massachusetts): 2410
GILMAN FAMILY (New Hampshire): 2044
GILMANTON, New Hampshire: 4012
GILMER, Daniel H.: 5695
GILMER, Francis Walker: 2047
GILMER, George N.: 2048
GILMER, George Rockingham: 2049
GILMER, John Adams: 3094
GILMER, Juliana (Paisley): 2050
GILMER, Peachy Harmer: 5513
GILMER, Thomas W.: 2051
GILMER FAMILY (Genealogy): 2047
GILMER COUNTY, Georgia:
  Santa Luca: 639
GILMOR, Robert: 2052
GILMORE, Marion Foster: 2053
GILPIN, Charles: 944, 2054
GILPIN, Joshua: 2265
GILPIN, Thomas: 2265
GILSON, Roy Rolfe: 2871
GIMBERNAT Y ARBOS, Antonio de: 2055
GINDRAT, Jewett: 1476
GINGER TRADE: 323
GINN AND COMPANY: 2400
GINSENG TRADE:
  Maryland--Baltimore: 4348
GINTER AND ALLEN (firm): see ALLEN AND GINTER
GIORGI, Paolo: 2056
GIRARD, Stephen: 5228
GIRARD BANK, Philadelphia, Pennsylvania: 3198
GIRARDEAU FAMILY (South Carolina): 5193
GIRARDY, Victor J. B.: 1185
GIRLS' EDUCATION: see EDUCATION--Women; SCHOOLS--Girls' schools and academies
GIRODIE, André: 2057
GIRTY, Simon: 2606
GISBORNE, Maria (James) Reveley: 2058
GISBORNE FAMILY: 4770
GISBOURN, J. Cherry: 1004
GIST, Mordecai: 2059
GIST, States Rights: 2433
GLADBERRY, J. M.: 2185
GLADDEN, Washington: 3910
GLADESBOROUGH, North Carolina:
  Liquor industry: 1278
GLADSTONE, Catherine Glynne: 2060
GLADSTONE, Herbert John, First Viscount Gladstone: 233, 2060, 2149, 5164
GLADSTONE, Steven Edward: 2060
GLADSTONE, William Ewart: 118, 233, 280, 294, 326, 1158, 1530, 2060, 2146, 2149, 3185, 3980, 4520
  Administration: 3722, 4331, 5259
  Midlothian Campaign: 4427
GLAIZE, Louisa B.: 2061
GLASCOCK, Julia: 3534
GLASCOCK, Thomas: 5385
GLASGOW, Ellen Anderson Gholson: 2062, 2689
GLASGOW, James: 5457
GLASGOW, Kentucky: 2063
  Pharmacies: 5505
GLASGOW, Scotland: 118, 859, 2703, 2736, 3851, 4719
  Description: 5527
  Textile workers: 3179
  Universities and colleges: see UNIVERSITY OF GLASGOW
GLASGOW, Virginia: 3149
GLASGOW COUNTY, North Carolina: see GREENE COUNTY, North Carolina
GLASS, Carter: 706, 879, 1364, 2082
GLASS, Elizabeth: 2065

GLASS, Joseph: 2064
GLASS, Robert Henry: 2065
GLASS: see WINDOW GLASS
GLASSON, William Henry: 2705, 4753
GLASTONBURY, James Grenville, First Baron: 4230
GLEAVES, Albert: 2066
GLEIG, George Robert: 2067
GLEN, Tyre: 2068, 2808
GLEN FALLS, New York: 5560
GLEN PARK HOTEL, Watkins, New York: 1907
GLENBERVIE, Sylvester Douglas, First Baron: 1545
GLENCOE, Virginia--Plantations: 5523
GLENELG, Charles Grant, Baron: 763, 3443
GLENGARY, Scotland--Militia: 4926
"GLENMORE," Virginia: 682
GLENN, Elizabeth F.: 2069
GLENN, James E.: 5965
GLENN, Mary (Brodnax): 661
GLENN, Richard C.: 2370
GLENN, William E.: 2370
GLENNAN & O'CONNOR, Ogdensburg, New York (firm): 5989
GLENNON, Mr. _____: 3567
GLOBE MUTUAL LIFE INSURANCE COMPANY: 974
GLOCKLER, Margaret: 2070
GLOUCESTER, William Frederick, Second Duke of: 2421
GLOUCESTER, New Jersey: 1076
GLOUCESTER, Virginia: 3494
GLOUCESTER COUNTY, New Jersey: 1901
GLOUCESTER COUNTY, Virginia: 5178
  Agricultural workers: 3809
  Banks and banking: 4924
  Estates:
    Administration and settlement: 4924
  Farming: 3809
  Mercantile affairs: 4924
  Plantations: 2776, 3809, 4015
  Wills: 4924
  Cities and towns:
    Gloucester: 3494
    Hickory Fork: 4562
    "Rosewell": 2776, 4014, 4015
    Shelley: 4013, 4019
GLOUCESTER POINT, Virginia: 2679
GLOUCESTERSHIRE, England:
  Elections: 2071
  Landlord and tenant: 4630
  Cities and towns:
    Bristol: see BRISTOL, England
    Stroud: 1976
GLOVER, George: 370
GLOVER, John Hulbert: 2457
GLOVER, Josiah: 2072
GLOVER, William: 5457
GLOVER FAMILY (Virginia): 3687
GLUCK BROTHERS, INC.: 1197
GLYN, Isabella Dallas: 2073
GLYNN, James: 3118
GLYNN, Martin Henry: 3265
GLYNN COUNTY, Georgia:
  Bethel: 2460
  Brunswick: 725, 787
    Land companies: 4268
    Land grants: 1374
    Railroads: 4718
  Frederica: 1454, 3968, 4988
    Land settlement: 3733
GLYNNE, Catherine: 2060
GOBBLE, Richmond: 2074
GOD, Attributes of: 5404
"GOD IS OUR HOME" by Costen Jordan Harrell: 2353
GODBEY, Allen Howard: 2075, 5252
GODFREY, C. O.: 2076
GODFREY, Job: 5499
GODMAN, Miss _____: 2077
GODMAN, Joseph: 2077
GODPARENTS: see BAPTISM--Godparents

GODWIN, H. L.: 5072
GODWIN, John: 2078
GODWIN, Mary Wollstonecraft: 1049, 4770
GODWIN, Parke: 65
GODWIN, Sophia: 4934
GODWIN, William: 2058, 4770
GODWIN FAMILY (Great Britain): 2058, 4770
GOERTNER, F. L.: 65
GOETHE, Johann Wolfgang von: 2058, 2079
GOHDES, Clarence Louis Frank: 102, 3694, 4279, 5889
GOLD, Daniel L.: 2080
GOLD, Daniel Lewis: 2080
GOLD, Emiline: 2080
GOLD, Louis: 2081
GOLD, Mary Washington: 2082
GOLD, Pleasant Daniel: 2419
GOLD, Sallie: 4904
GOLD, Thomas D.: 2082
GOLD:
  Extraction from ores:
    Inventions: 5402
  Extraction from sea water: 4224
  Investment:
    United States: 2469, 4911
  Prospecting: see GOLD RUSH
  Value--United States: 2360
  Subdivided by place:
    California: 5130
      see also GOLD RUSH
    Georgia: 3555
GOLD BUYING:
  New York: 5731
  United States: 2360
GOLD HILL, North Carolina:
  Blacksmith's and mercantile accounts: 3368
GOLD LOTTERIES:
  Georgia: 1887
  Meriwether County: 1999
GOLD MILLING MACHINERY: see ADVERTISING--Gold milling machinery
GOLD MINES AND MINING:
  see also MINING
  Inspection--Brazil: 2750
  Investments--Georgia: 4895
  Lawsuits--North Carolina: 2041
  Subdivided by place:
    Alabama: 388
    Alaska: 4918
    Brazil: 339
    California: 611, 1984, 2092, 3253, 3750
    Colorado: 2606
      Anaconda: 3660
    Georgia--Cherokee County: 1887
    Montana: 4918
    North Carolina: 388, 529, 1677, 2121, 2188
      Cabarrus County: 3391
      Davidson County: 2041, 5549
      Randolph County: 5549
      Vestal's Ford: 4450
    South Carolina: 529
    Virginia--Fluvanna County: 5035
GOLD PLATE--Georgia: 5260
GOLD RUSH:
  California: 357, 1020, 2161, 2712, 3253, 3750, 4924, 5130
  Colorado: see PIKE'S PEAK GOLD RUSH
  Idaho: 4834
  Montana: 4834
GOLDALMING, England: 5836
GOLDBERG, Louis P.: 9
THE GOLDEN BOUGH by Sir James George Frazer: 2736
THE GOLDEN RULE FOUNDATION: 3633
"THE GOLDEN YEARS" by Thomas Hightower Collins (newspaper column): 1167
THE GOLDEN YEARS by Thomas Hightower Collins: 1167
GOLDEN YEARS, HOW TO PREPARE TO RETIRE by Thomas Hightower Collins: 1167

GOLDSBORO, North Carolina: 547, 1432, 1728, 1748, 3237, 5058
  Civil War:
    Battle: see CIVIL WAR--CAMPAIGNS, BATTLES, AND MILITARY ACTIONS--North Carolina--Goldsboro
    Battlefield photographs (1884): 4414
    Confederate Army camp: 1896
  Social conditions: 4039
  Seymour Johnson Air Force Base: 325
GOLDSBOROUGH, Edmund Lee: 2084
GOLDSBOROUGH, Elizabeth Gamble (Wirt): 2085
GOLDSBOROUGH, Henry: 1329
GOLDSBOROUGH, Louis Malesherbes: 2085
GOLDSBOROUGH, Robert Henry: 4221
GOLDSBOROUGH FAMILY: 2085
GOLDSCHMIDT, Jenny Marie Lind-: see LIND-GOLDSCHMIDT, Jenny Marie
GOLDSMITH, Thomas: 1454
GOLDSMITHS--Great Britain: 2784
GOLDSTON, Sarah: 680
GOLDSTON, Thomas: 680
GOLDWIN, Samuel: 2146
GÓMEZ, Máximo: 2991
GOÑI, Facundo: 4486
GONRATER, Antonio: 4155
GONZALES, Ambrose Elliott: 2086, 4453
GOOCH, R. B.: 3495
GOOCHLAND, Virginia: 5192
GOOCHLAND COUNTY, Virginia: 32, 558, 2396, 4239
  Know-Nothing Party: 4616
  Plantations: 5378
  Cities and towns:
    Fifesville: 4459
    Goochland: 5192
    Hadensville: 1587
    Slabe: 2364
GOOCHLAND COURT HOUSE, Virginia: 195
GOOD AND EVIL: 3189
GOOD GOVERNMENT GROUP: 1197
GOOD INTENT, Virginia:
  Woolen mills: 568, 5297
GOOD MORNING, MISS DOVE by Frances Gray Patton: 4085
GOOD ROADS MOVEMENT:
  North Carolina: 3380, 4918
  Craven County: 3955
GOOD TEMPLARS, Independent Order of: see INDEPENDENT ORDER OF GOOD TEMPLARS
GOODE, John, Jr.: 4157
GOODE FAMILY: 761
GOODELL, Gaylord G.: 2089
GOODELL FAMILY (New York): 2089
GOODHUE AND COMPANY: 1609
GOODIN, Jesse B.: 2090
GOODING, Martha Jones: 2091
GOODING, W. J.: 5758
GOODING, Zephaniah W.: 2091
GOODING FAMILY (New York): 2091
GOODLOE, Daniel Reaves: 5149, 5457
GOODMAN, Alice H.: 3307
GOODRICH, Edward Payson: 4652
GOODRICH, Isaac E.: 2092
GOODRICH, John Zacheus: 2093
GOODWIN, James D.: 5484
GOODWIN, Mary: 1424
GOODWIN, Medmor: 5282
GOODWIN, Reuben: 1022
GOODWIN, William Archer Rutherfoord: 1424
GOODWIN FAMILY (Virginia): 2927
GOODWIN AND CO.: 1586
GOOSE CREEK, Virginia:
  Civil War: 5852
  Merchants: 2633
GOOSE NEST TOWNSHIP, North Carolina:
  Taxation: 3935
GORDON, General _____ (in Sudan): 5164
GORDON, Armistead Churchill: 958
GORDON, Bertie Edward Murray: 4520

GORDON, Cad: 2094
GORDON, Caroline Louisa: 2239
GORDON, Charles (1756-1835): 3715
GORDON, Charles George (1833-1885): 4520, 4941
GORDON, Charles Robert: 5222
GORDON, Eliza Hall (Ball): 611
GORDON, George A.: 2094
GORDON, George Hamilton, Fourth Earl of Aberdeen: 1755, 3472
GORDON, James Byron: 2239
GORDON, James H.: 2095
GORDON, John Brown: 2096, 2449, 4402
GORDON, John Campbell, First Marquis of Aberdeen and Temair: 2097
GORDON, Sir John James Hood: 888
GORDON, Lydia: 2094
GORDON, William, Seventeenth Earl of Sutherland: 2098
GORDON, William Fitzhugh: 1401
GORDON FAMILY (North Carolina--Genealogy): 2239
GORDON FAMILY (Pennsylvania): 1916
GORDON INSTITUTE, Barnesville, Georgia: 4791
GORDONSVILLE, Virginia: 154
  Civil War: 390
  see also CIVIL WAR--CAMPAIGNS, BATTLES, AND MILITARY ACTIONS--Virginia--Gordonsville
  Merchants: 4710
GORE, Charles Alexander: 2099
GORE, Fanny: 5525
GORGAS, Josiah: 4129, 5280
GORGIER, Mary Louisa Amelia Boozer Beecher, Countess of Pourtalès-: see POURTALÈS-GORGIER, Mary Louisa Amelia Boozer Beecher, Countess of
GORHAM, Henry W.: 2100
GORHAM, John C.: 2101
GORIN (I. AND F.), Philadelphia, Pennsylvania (firm): 870
GORST, Sir John Eldon: 2962, 5024
GOSCHEN, George Joachim, First Viscount: 452, 1815
"GOSFORD HOUSE," Scotland: 5643
GOSHEN, New York: 3815
GOSHEN, Virginia: 3882
  Diet: 5613
  Hiring of slaves: 5613
GOSHEN ASSOCIATION, Disciples of Christ: 5554
GOSHEN BAPTIST ASSOCIATION (Kentucky): 3199
GOSSE, Edmund William: 706, 1949, 2102, 2334
GOSSIP, James Alexander: 2103
GOSSIP, William Murray: 2103
GOSSIP FAMILY (Scotland--Genealogy): 2103
GÖTTINGEN, Germany: 2246
GOUCHER COLLEGE, Baltimore, Maryland: 4290
GOUGH, John Bartholomew: 1351
GOULD, Amelia Jenkins (Twitchell): 2106
GOULD, Charles L.: 2104
GOULD, Harrison: 2105
GOULD, John H.: 2105
GOULD, John Mead: 2106
GOULD, Louise Stedman: 2871
GOULD, Samuel McClellan: 2106
GOULD FAMILY (Maine): 2106
GOURDIN, Henry: 3666
GOURDIN, Robert Newman: 2107, 3666
GOURDIN FAMILY (South Carolina--Genealogy): 1468
GOURDIN, MATTHIESON AND COMPANY, Charleston, South Carolina: 2107
GOVERNESSES:
  France: 4770
  Italy: 4770
  Maryland: 3809
  Massachusetts: 4881
  New York--New York: 3761
  Russia: 4770
    Moscow: 1049

GOVERNESSES (Continued):
  South Carolina: 3405
  Virginia: 3809
GOVERNMENT: see POLITICS AND
  GOVERNMENT
  Theory: see POLITICAL THEORY
GOVERNMENT AND ART--United States:
  2587
GOVERNMENT AND CIVIC EMPLOYEES:
  Georgia: 3505
  Labor unions: see LABOR UNIONS--
    Government and civic employees
  Pensions--Great Britain: 4097
  Virginia: 2732
  Wages and salaries: see WAGES AND
    SALARIES--Government and civic
    employees
  Welfare funds--North Carolina:
    3955
GOVERNMENT AND THE PRESS:
  Confederate States of America:
    4912
GOVERNMENT EXPENDITURES: see
  Appropriations and expenditures
  as subheading under names of
  countries, states, and other
  governmental units
GOVERNMENT FRAUD:
  South Carolina: 1012
GOVERNMENTAL CONTROL OF RAILROADS:
  see RAILROADS--Government control
GOVERNMENTAL CONTROL OF TEXTILE
  INDUSTRY: see TEXTILE INDUSTRY--
  Government control
GOVERNMENTAL REGULATION OF WAGES
  AND SALARIES: see WAGES AND
  SALARIES--Governmental regulation
GOVERNMENTAL SALE OF ARMS: see
  UNITED STATES--ARMS TRADE--
  France
GOVERNOR MOORE (ship): 1181
GOVERNORS: see (name of state)--
  Government agencies and officials--
  Governors
GOVERNOR'S COMMISSION ON THE FINE
  ARTS (North Carolina): 4736
GOVERNOR'S ISLAND, New York:
  Civil War prison: 704
GOVERNOR'S STUDY COMMITTEE ON
  VOCATIONAL REHABILITATION IN
  NORTH CAROLINA: 4736
GOWER, Granville George Leveson-,
  Second Earl Granville: see
  LEVESON-GOWER, Granville George,
  Second Earl Granville
GOWER, Granville George Leveson-,
  First Marquis of Stafford: see
  LEVESON-GOWER, Granville George,
  First Marquis of Stafford
GOWER, Granville Leveson-, First
  Earl Granville: see LEVESON-
  GOWER, Granville, First Earl
  Granville
GOWER, Henriette Elizabeth
  (Cavendish) Leveson-, Countess
  Granville: see LEVESON-GOWER,
  Henriette Elizabeth (Cavendish),
  Countess Granville
GOWER AND CO. (shipping firm): 323
GOWRIE MINES, Chesterfield County,
  Virginia: 2908
"GOWRIE PLANTATION," Argyle Island,
  South Carolina: 3485
GRABUR SILK MILLS, INC.: 2108
GRACE, John Patrick: 2109
GRACE (W. R.) & CO.: 1091
GRACE (Theology): 937
GRACE EPISCOPAL CHURCH, Morganton,
  North Carolina: 2111
GRACE EPISCOPAL CHURCH, Charleston,
  South Carolina: 2110
GRACIE, William Benjamin: 2112
GRACY, Mercer: 2113
GRACY, Robert S.: 1856, 2113
GRACY FAMILY (North Carolina): 2113
GRADES: see TEACHERS' RECORDS

GRADING AND MARKING SYSTEMS:
  North Carolina:
    Midway Academy: 4148
GRADUATION EXERCISES: see
  COMMENCEMENT EXERCISES, and
  Commencement exercises as
  subheading under names of
  specific universities and colleges
GRADY, W. Edwin: 2114
GRAFENBURG, Germany: 3310
GRAFTON, Augustus Henry Fitzroy,
  Third Duke of: 92, 5330
GRAFTON, West Virginia: 694
GRAFTON CENTRE, New Hampshire: 2356
GRAFTON COUNTY, New Hampshire: 71
  Franconia: 4264
  Grafton Centre: 2356
  Hanover: see DARTMOUTH COLLEGE
  Landaff--Farm accounts: 4265
GRAHAM, Archibald A.: 2120
GRAHAM, Edward: 2120
GRAHAM, Edward, Jr.: 2120
GRAHAM, Emma: 2115
GRAHAM, Frank Porter: 2863
GRAHAM, George M.: 1612
GRAHAM, Hugh (North Carolina): 4080
GRAHAM, Hugh (Tennessee): 2116
GRAHAM, J. Bennett: 4894
GRAHAM, J. R.: 1192
GRAHAM, James (North Carolina): 2117
GRAHAM, Sir James Robert George,
  Second Baronet: 2149
GRAHAM, John (1718-1795, Georgia):
  2118
GRAHAM, John (1783-1885, Virginia):
  2120
GRAHAM, John A. (Virginia): 2120
GRAHAM, John Washington: 5457
GRAHAM, Joseph: 5457
GRAHAM, Margaret Alexander: 2120
GRAHAM, Maria: 899
GRAHAM, Nancy: 2120
GRAHAM, Stephen: 364
GRAHAM, Thomas, First Baron
  Lynedoch: 2147
GRAHAM, William (1746-1799): 2120
GRAHAM, William (Union soldier):
  2119
GRAHAM, William Alexander: 730, 795,
  872, 2120, 2121, 3118, 3833, 5149,
  5457, 5667
GRAHAM, William Alexander, Jr.: 2121
GRAHAM (WILLIAM) AND SIMPSON
  COMPANY: 2122
GRAHAM FAMILY (Virginia--Genealogy):
  2120
GRAHAM, North Carolina:
  Hosiery mills: 4812
GRAHAM CIRCUIT, Methodist churches:
  3646
GRAHAM'S CROSS ROADS, South
  Carolina: 4554
GRAHAMVILLE, South Carolina: 2670
  Schools: 4961
GRAIN BOATS--Maryland: 489
GRAIN ELEVATORS--West Virginia: 5239
GRAIN PRODUCTION:
  see also names of specific kinds
    of grain
  Missouri: 3540
  Virginia: 3145
GRAIN STORAGE: see GRAIN ELEVATORS
GRAIN TRADE: 323, 5228
  see also names of specific kinds
    of grain
  Law and legislation: 2581
  Prices:
    France:
      Rozoy-en-Brie: 4590
      Tours (Généralité): 5323
    Pennsylvania: 4920
    Virginia: 4924
  Subdivided by place:
    Alabama--Macon County: 3837
    Chesapeake Bay region: 4924
    Great Britain: 2193, 2755
    Maryland: 3875
      Beaver Creek District: 3329

GRAIN TRADE:
  Subdivided by place (Continued):
    North Carolina: 1871
      New Bern: 164
      Wilkesboro: 4107
    Pennsylvania: 164
      Wholesale: 2505
    South Carolina--Charleston: 60
    United States: 2193, 2755
GRAMIER, Marc-Amédée: 65
GRAMMAR: see as subheading under
  names of languages
GRANADA, Nicaragua:
  Emigrants from the United States:
    3960
GRANBERRY INSTITUTE, Rio de Janeiro,
  Brazil: 3248
GRANBY, John Manners, Marquis of:
  5284
GRAND ARMY OF THE REPUBLIC: 196,
  3910
  Michigan: 2604
  West Virginia: 1828
GRAND CAYMAN ISLAND, Cayman Islands:
  Social life and customs: 1408
GRAND CENTRAL HOTEL, Martinsburg,
  West Virginia: 3832
GRAND ISLE COUNTY, Vermont:
  North Hero: 5096
GRAND JUNCTION, Tennessee:
  Description: 155
GRAND JURY: see JURIES--Grand juries
GRAND LODGE OF NORTH CAROLINA
  (Masons): 3410
GRANGE: see PATRONS OF HUSBANDRY; and
  names of specific granges, e.g.
  COTTAGE GRANGE
GRANITE HILL, North Carolina: 3690
GRANITE QUARRIES:
  North Carolina--Rowan County: 5929
GRANITE TRADE:
  North Carolina--Rowan County: 5929
GRANITEVILLE, South Carolina: 2186
GRANT, Arthur: 2296
GRANT, Charles (1746-1823): 867, 3316
GRANT, Charles, Baron Glenelg
  (1778-1866): 763, 3443
GRANT, Daniel: 872
GRANT, George W.: 2124
GRANT, James (1720-1806): 4218
GRANT, James A.: 2124
GRANT, Julia (Dent): 157
GRANT, Mary Jane: 2124
GRANT, Sir Robert (1779-1838): 868,
  3316
GRANT, Ulysses Simpson: 157, 1084,
  1364, 2125, 4108, 4157, 4203,
  4390, 4486, 4989, 5051, 5322, 5518,
  5636, 5731
  Administration: 415
    Opposition to: 5905
  Criticism of lenient policy toward
    Lee: 3686
  Death: 4606
  Funeral: 1894, 4606
  Home (Maryland): 5660
  Inauguration: 846
  Meeting with Lincoln, April 3,
    1865: 2125
  Soldiers' opinion of: 5571
GRANT, Sir William (1752-1832): 2126
GRANT, William Charles (1817-1877):
  2127
GRANT, William G. (Ohio): 2128
GRANT COUNTY, Arkansas:
  Sheridan: 4536
GRANT COUNTY, Kansas: 1428
GRANT COUNTY, West Virginia: 767
  Petersburg: 4842
  Sunday schools: 2129
GRANT COUNTY (W. Va.) SUNDAY SCHOOL
  ASSOCIATION: 2129
GRANT MEMORIAL UNIVERSITY, Athens,
  Tennessee: 731
GRANTHAM, John William: 2130
GRANTS, Foundation: see FOUNDATION
  GRANTS

GRANTS, Land: see LAND GRANTS
GRANVILLE, Granville George
    Leveson-Gower, Second Earl: 597,
    3185, 3238
GRANVILLE, Granville Leveson-Gower,
    First Earl: 1875
GRANVILLE, Henriette Elizabeth
    (Cavendish) Leveson-Gower,
    Countess: 1875
GRANVILLE, Pennsylvania: 2345
GRANVILLE-BARKER, Harley Granville:
    3797
GRANVILLE COUNTY, North Carolina:
    1700s: 2528
    1700s-1800s: 795, 1764, 2926, 5768
    1700s-1900s: 4132
    1800s: 1556, 2339, 3484, 3727,
        5620
    Commodity prices: 5285
    Confederate reunion: 1361
    Household accounts: 3916
    Land deeds and indentures: 1224,
        2716
    Local politics: 2189
    Mercantile accounts: 3638, 5960
    Plantation accounts: 3916, 5285
    Public schools: 2833
    Schools: 2192, 2833
    Secessionist sentiment: 761
    Cities and towns:
        Abram's Plains: 4800, 4894
        Berea--Newspapers: 5741
        Brownsville: 5470
        Dutchville: 1826
        Oxford: see OXFORD, North
            Carolina
        Stem: 4464
        Stovall: 2192
        Williamsboro: 761, 2475, 2829
GRANVILLE DE VIGUE by Louisa De la
    Ramée: 2146
GRANVIN, Norway: 2430
GRASSES:
    see also BLUEGRASS
    India: 5836
GRASSHOPPERS:
    Missouri--Lafayette County: 5984
GRASSO, Frank: 5486
GRASSY CREEK PRESBYTERIAN CHURCH,
    Granville County, North Carolina:
    1556
GRASTY, Philip L.: 2131
GRASTY, William Clark: 2131
GRASTY FAMILY (Virginia): 2131
GRATIOT, Charles, Jr.: 2132
GRATTAN, Henry: 3883
GRATTAN, John: 2133
GRATTAN, Lucia (Cary): 2133
GRAVATT, John J.: 2134
GRAVE, William: 4388
GRAVE ROBBING--Pennsylvania: 531
GRAVEL HILL, Virginia:
    Mercantile affairs: 5652
    Plantations: 5652
GRAVES, James T.: 2135
GRAVES, Ralph Henry: 5457
GRAVES, Thomas (Georgia): 289
GRAVES, Thomas W. (North Carolina):
    591
GRAVES, William: 2136
GRAVES: see CATACOMBS; CEMETERIES;
    CIVIL WAR--BURIAL GROUNDS; TOMBS;
    and Burial place as subheading
    under names of prominent persons
GRAVESEND, Kent, England: 535
GRAY, Asa: 1702, 3674, 5593
GRAY, Charles H.: 5168
GRAY, D. W.: 2137
GRAY, Edward: 2141
GRAY, Edwin: 2138, 2551, 4531
GRAY, Elizabeth: 2985
GRAY, Emma Juliana: 4876
GRAY, Frances MacRae: 4085
GRAY, Francis Galley: 2139
GRAY, G. D.: 523
GRAY, G. E.: 1861
GRAY, Gordon: 3538
GRAY, Mrs. Hiram: 2140

GRAY, James R.: 4048
GRAY, James S.: 2141
GRAY, John B.: 3703
GRAY, John D.: 642
GRAY, John H.: 2006
GRAY, Richard L.: 2142
GRAY, Simon: 2148
GRAY, Thomas: 3055
GRAY FAMILY: 2141
GRAYDON, Clint T.: 5312
GRAYDON, Nell (Saunders): 5312
GRAYDON, Sterling: 5312
GRAY'S CROSS ROADS, North Carolina:
    675
GRAY'S INFANTRY: 1189
GRAYSON, John Breckenridge: 2143
GRAYSON, William (1736?-1790): 917
GRAYSON, William John: 393, 2144
GRAYSON, William John, Jr.: 2144
GRAYSON COUNTY, Texas:
    Sherman: 2850
GRAZEBROOK, Henry Sydney: 2145
GREASON, George H.: 4586
GREAT AWAKENING (Second): 872
GREAT BARRINGTON, Massachusetts: 856


GREAT BRITAIN

see also SCOTLAND
ABOLITION OF SLAVERY: 43, 280, 1913,
    2149, 4913
    see also GREAT BRITAIN--SLAVE
        TRADE--Abolition; GREAT BRITAIN--
        SLAVES--Emancipation
    Colonial policy: 815, 1081, 5129
    Bahama Islands: 4934
    Celebration of freedom: 5616
ACT OF UNION: 535, 4024
ACTING: 157, 1027
    see also ENGLISH DRAMA; GREAT
        BRITAIN--THEATER
ADMIRALTY: see GREAT BRITAIN--
    GOVERNMENT AGENCIES AND OFFICIALS--
    Admiralty
AGRICULTURAL ORGANIZATIONS:
    National Agricultural Union: 200
AGRICULTURAL PRODUCTS--Prices: 118
AGRICULTURE: 14, 1632, 2836,
    3498, 5726
    see also names of specific crops
        under GREAT BRITAIN
AIR FORCE--World War I: 3693
ALMANACS: 1541
AMERICAN CIVIL WAR:
    see also CIVIL WAR--BRITISH
        INTERVENTION; GREAT BRITAIN--
        FOREIGN RELATIONS--Confederate
        States of America; GREAT BRITAIN--
        FOREIGN RELATIONS--United States
        (1860s); GREAT BRITAIN--PUBLIC
        OPINION--American Civil War
    Economic effects on textile
        industry: 5259
AMERICAN FOREIGN INVESTMENT: 4895
AMERICAN REVOLUTION:
    see also AMERICAN REVOLUTION;
        GREAT BRITAIN--ARMY--American
        Revolution; GREAT BRITAIN--
        NAVY--Operations--American
        Revolution
    Pensions: 4151
ANTI-CATHOLICISM: 369
ANTIQUITIES--Somersetshire: 4176
APPRENTICESHIP: 3808
    see also GREAT BRITAIN--
        SHIPBUILDING--Apprenticeship
ARCHITECTURAL DRAWINGS:
    Wiltshire: 3895
ARCHITECTURE: 1551
    see also GREAT BRITAIN--CHURCH
        ARCHITECTURE; GREAT BRITAIN--
        DOMESTIC ARCHITECTURE; GREAT
        BRITAIN--NAVAL ARCHITECTURE
ARMY: 499, 1598
    see also GREAT BRITAIN--MILITIA
    Administration: 5806, 5872, 5876
    Afghan War: 3950, 5801

GREAT BRITAIN

ARMY:
    Afghan War (Continued):
        see also AFGHAN WARS
    American Revolution: 4317
        see also AMERICAN REVOLUTION--
            Campaigns and battles
        Depredations: 2931
        Evacuation from Savannah: 5078
        Generals, Evaluation of: 5604
        Military activities:
            South Carolina: 3209, 3511
        Officers:
            Financial affairs: 869, 1358
        Surrender at Yorktown: 3041,
            5575
    Appropriations: 1978
    Army life (1800s): 5637
    Army Medical School: 4026
    Barracks (1796): 5330
    Boer War: 345
        see also BOER WAR
    Cavalry (1771): 5330
    Chaplains (1760): 5284
    Courts-martial: 4520
    Crimean War: 153, 3472
        see also CRIMEAN WAR
        Army life: 3472
        Camp life: 2168
        Casualties: 5947
        Recruiting and enlistment in the
            United States: 4520
        Regiments:
            7th Royal Fusiliers: 5947
        Scarcity of clothing and medical
            supplies: 5947
        Trench warfare: 2168
    Education of Catholic dependents:
        1978
    Egypt and the Sudan:
        see also EGYPT--British military
            activity
        Egyptian War (1882-1906):
            Campaigns and battles: 5333
            Military activities: 5835
            Officers: 5333
            Reduction of occupation forces:
                4941
            Royal Sussex Regiment: 5333
        Intervention in the war between
            Egypt and the Sultan (1840):
            3447
        Military activities (1801): 4926
        Nile Expedition (1884-1885):
            3046, 4811, 5333
    Fenian infiltration: 4566
    Finance: 1756, 5806
    French Revolutionary Wars: 2836
    India: 306, 4549, 5639
        see also GREAT BRITAIN--INDIAN
            ARMY; INDIA--British military
            activities
        Forage: 5836
        Madras: 3315
        Mahratta War: 3315, 4635
        Generals: 4635
        Military activities: 4549
            Burma: 3224
            Malabar: 5797
            Poona: 5797
        Mysore War: 563
            Second (1784): 3315
            Fourth (1799): 5639
        Officers: 2266
            Appointments and promotions:
                2133, 4549
        Oudh: 5639
        Sind War: 3453
    Infantry (1771): 5330
    Medical and sanitary affairs: 5876
    Mediterranean region (1815): 1599
    Military supplies: 2147
    Mobilization--Kent: 5830
    Napoleonic Wars:
        Egypt: 5639
        Portugal: 5830
        Spain: 1147, 1875, 3446, 5639

GREAT BRITAIN

ARMY:
  Napoleonic Wars (Continued):
    Sweden: 3446
  Occupation of France (1818): 1002
  Officers: 563, 1911, 3460, 3950, 3977, 4520, 5330, 5394, 5872
    Appointments and promotions: 2029, 3073, 4520, 5330
    Financial affairs: 1358
    Hart's Army List: 2401
    Resignation of the Commander-in-chief: 5637
  Organization and troop strength (1864): 4520
  Pay (1700s): 5540
  Paymaster General: 2147
  Peninsular War: see GREAT BRITAIN--ARMY--Napoleonic Wars--(Portugal or Spain)
  Pensions: 3080
    For Widows: 2836
  Recruiting and enlistment: 1114, 1598, 5637
    American colonies: 5540
  Reform: 118, 2708, 5876
  Regiments:
    Imperial Yeomanry (Boer War): 345
    Prince Edward Island Fencibles: 1756
    Royal Regiment of Artillery: 3968
    Royal Sussex Regiment: 5333
    7th Royal Fusiliers: 5947
    19th Dragoons, in Canada: 3087
    31st Regiment of Foot, in England and Florida: 342
    31st Regiment, in China: 1373
    56th Regiment: 4835
    60th Royal Americans: 859
  Religion: 5836
  Seven Years' War: 5284
  South Africa:
    Kaffir Wars: 4655
    Military acitvities (1819): 5801
    Zulu War (1879): 5876
    Tactics: 4655
  Training: 2147, 5726
  Transportation: 2147
  Volunteer units, Efficiency of (1905): 5876
  War of 1812:
    Military activities in Canada: 3087
  World War I:
    American serving in: 3820
    British Expeditionary Force: 3710
    Recruiting and enlistment: Conscription: 3693
ART AND ARTISTS: 258, 4575, 4576
  Criticism: 4600
  Forgeries: 1225
  Painting: 1225, 2718
  Somersetshire: 1071
ART COLLECTORS AND COLLECTING: 1343, 5553
ART SOCIETIES: 1424
  see also ROYAL ACADEMY OF ARTS
ARTS--Manchester: 4113
AUTHORS: see GREAT BRITAIN--WOMEN AUTHORS
AUTHORS AND EDITORS: 2203
  see also GREAT BRITAIN--SCHOLARLY EDITING
AUTHORS AND PUBLISHERS:
  see also GREAT BRITAIN--PUBLISHERS AND PUBLISHING
  1700s: 4512
  1700s-1800s: 4967, 5867
  1800s: 892, 3835, 4001, 4770
  1810s: 369
  1820s: 2146
  1830s: 5241
  1840s: 4051
  1850s: 4051, 4069
  1870s: 5553, 5872

GREAT BRITAIN

AUTHORS AND PUBLISHERS:
  1800s (Continued):
    1880s: 39, 5553, 5872
    1890s: 39, 4503, 5553, 5872
  1800s-1900s: 3503
  1900s: 1210
  1910s: 4327
  1920s: 5101, 5403
  Periodicals: 2839
AUTHORS AND READERS: 4770, 5050, 5553
AUTHORSHIP: 449, 1147, 1650, 2203, 4176, 5050, 5553
  see also SCOTLAND--Authorship
AUTOGRAPH COLLECTING: 2126
AUTOGRAPHS: 5158, 5553
  see also SCOTLAND--Autographs
BALLOTS: 4868, 5011
BANKING LAW: 5
BANKRUPTCY: 2151
  Bristol: 4541
  Cases: 4605
BANKS AND BANKING: 3304
BAPTISM--Godparents: 2899
BAPTIST CHURCHES: 5726
BASTARDY LAWS: 1775
BIBLE SOCIETIES: 5726
BIBLICAL SCHOLARSHIP: 2653
BILLS OF EXCHANGE--Bristol: 4541
BIOGRAPHICAL STUDIES: 1070, 2146, 2953, 3022, 3684, 4770
  see also SCOTLAND--Biographical studies
BIOGRAPHIES: 2973, 3411, 5050
BIRTHDAY COMMEMORATIONS: 5050
BOOK BUYING: 2788
  see also SCOTLAND--Book buying
BOOK COLLECTING: 268, 1124, 2200, 5101
BOOK ILLUSTRATION: see GREAT BRITAIN--BOTANICAL ILLUSTRATION; GREAT BRITAIN--ZOOLOGICAL ILLUSTRATION
BOOK REVIEWS: 1210, 5173
  see also SCOTLAND--Book reviews
BOOKSELLERS AND BOOKSELLING:
  see also SCOTLAND--Booksellers and bookselling
  Bristol: 4176
  London: 5252, 5856
BOTANICAL ILLUSTRATION: 5553
BOTANY: 4876
  see also GREAT BRITAIN--PLANTS
BURIAL LAWS: 118
BUSINESS AFFAIRS: 922, 5598
  London: 229, 5849
CALVINISTIC THEOLOGY: 2751
CAMPING: see SCOTLAND--Camping
CAMPS (Ancient)--Wiltshire: 3895
CANALS:
  Andover to Redbridge (proposed): 5331
  Mersey and Irwell: 2148
CAPITAL PUNISHMENT: 649, 2198, 4605, 5726
CARPETS--Silk: 5553
CATHEDRALS: 5457
CATHOLIC CHURCH: 2148
  Schools: see GREAT BRITAIN--SCHOOLS--Church schools--Catholic
CATHOLIC EMANCIPATION: 370, 535, 1775, 2836, 3226, 4024, 4913, 5025, 5639, 5726
  see also GREAT BRITAIN--POLITICAL DISABILITIES
CATHOLICS: see GREAT BRITAIN--ARMY--Education of Catholic dependents; GREAT BRITAIN--CATHOLIC CHURCH
CENSORSHIP:
  Books: 2146, 5726
  Newspapers: 2918
CHARITABLE WORK: 1765
CHARITIES: 5726
  Children: 2148
CHILDREN: 4770

GREAT BRITAIN

CHILDREN'S LITERATURE: 4115
CHOIRS: 43
CHRISTIAN LIFE: 5598
CHRISTMAS CARDS: 4115
CHURCH ARCHITECTURE--Truro: 5553
CHURCH HISTORY: see GREAT BRITAIN--HISTORICAL STUDIES--Medieval Church
CHURCH OF ENGLAND: 43, 306, 346, 537, 1311, 1571, 4913, 5726
  see also OXFORD MOVEMENT; WESLEYAN MOVEMENT
  Bishops' conclaves: 2148
  Clergy: see GREAT BRITAIN--CLERGY--Church of England
  Doctrine: 2953
  Finance: 1035, 5726
  Liturgy and ritual: 2953
  Missions and missionaries: see GREAT BRITAIN--MISSIONS AND MISSIONARIES--Church of England
  Relations with Methodist churches: 5647
  Schools: see GREAT BRITAIN--SCHOOLS--Church schools--Church of England
  Sermons: see GREAT BRITAIN--SERMONS--Church of England
CHURCH OF ENGLAND IN WALES: 4331
CHURCH PLATE: 2784
CHURCH SCHOOLS: see GREAT BRITAIN--SCHOOLS--Church schools
CHURCHES: 3498
  see also names of specific denominations under GREAT BRITAIN; CHURCH AND STATE IN GREAT BRITAIN
  Church buildings:
    see also GREAT BRITAIN--CATHEDRALS
    Manchester: 4287
    Somersetshire: 1071
CITIZENSHIP: see DUAL CITIZENSHIP
CIVIL RIGHTS: 5762
  Legislation concerning habeas corpus: 5616
CIVIL SERVICE PENSIONS: 3286
CLAIMS AGAINST: 4348
CLERGY: 4850
  see also GREAT BRITAIN--WOMEN CLERGY
  Church of England: 306, 1087, 1765, 3798
  Methodist: 763, 1070, 3995, 5647, 5699
  Methodist Episcopal: 1310
  Presbyterian: 5244
  Wesleyan Methodist: 5095, 5255
CLUBS: see GREAT BRITAIN--SOCIETIES AND CLUBS
COAL--Prices: 535
COAL INDUSTRY--Taxation: 4024
COLONIAL AGENTS: see Colonial agents as subheading under names of specific colonies
COLONIAL POLICY AND ADMINISTRATION: 663, 1147, 1404, 2060, 2471, 2708, 3238, 3286, 3347, 3978
  see also GREAT BRITAIN--ABOLITION OF SLAVERY--Colonial policy; GREAT BRITAIN--IMPERIALISM; GREAT BRITAIN--TRANSPORTATION OF CONVICTS; British administration as subheading under names of specific colonies; Colonial agents as subheading under names of specific colonies
  Afghanistan: 326, 2756
  Africa--Education: 4514
  American colonies: 2776, 4288
    Stamp duties: 3347
  Bahama Islands: 4934
  Bali: 4362
  Borneo: 4362
  British West Indies:
    Negro schools: 763
  Burma: 217, 1857

GREAT BRITAIN

COLONIAL POLICY AND ADMINISTRATION
(Continued):
  Canada: 1632
  Carolina Province: 780
  Egypt: 1499
  India: 278, 868, 2421, 4097, 4503,
    4549, 5038
    see also GREAT BRITAIN--ARMY--
      India; GREAT BRITAIN--INDIAN
      ARMY; INDIA--British
      administration; INDIA--
      British military activity
    Bengal legal code: 332
    Madras Army mutiny: 332
    Mahratta War: 332
    Use of revenues: 4028
  Ionian Islands: 4427
  Ireland: 3185, 5639
  Java: 4362
  New Zealand: 1260
  Nigeria: 4514
  South Africa: 1910, 3978
    Boer War: 217, 5872
  Zanzibar--Slavery: 67
COLONIAL TRADE: 2322
  New England: 172
  South Carolina: 2541
  Trade regulation in Carolina
    Province: 780
  Virginia: 625
COMMERCE: see GREAT BRITAIN--TRADE
  AND COMMERCE
COMMERCIAL EDUCATION: 4520
COMMERCIAL TREATIES:
  Spain: 5639
  United States: 3041
COMMISSION MERCHANTS--London: 5221
COMMODITY PRICES: 369, 2541
  Bristol: 4541
  Liverpool: 2901, 4911
COMMONPLACE BOOKS: 1163
CONFEDERATE EMIGRANTS: 2210, 3587
CONSERVATIVE PARTY: 1311, 2324, 4568
  see also SCOTLAND--Conservative
    Party
CONSPIRACIES (1794): 2375
CONSTITUTION: 1311, 4605
CONTRACTS--Exeter: 5867
COOKERY: 1210
COOPERATIVE MOVEMENT: 14
COPYRIGHT LEGISLATION: 472
CORN: 4230
CORN LAWS: 5, 649, 1126, 1311, 1632,
  1775, 2149, 2836, 4605, 4696,
  5011, 5025, 5330, 5726
  Enforcement: 3050
  Repeal: 676, 2193
CORPORATION ACT: 3226
CORRUPTION IN POLITICS:
  Denbigh: 5026
  Northumberland: 5026
COTTON: 4895
COTTON MILLS:
  American Civil War: 43
  Stock during Franco-Prussian War:
    2410
COTTON TRADE: 2755, 5014
  London: 4288
  Sea Island cotton: 3230
COUNTRY ESTATES: 5038
COUNTY GOVERNMENT: 3847
COURTS: 504, 2836, 4113, 5134
  see also GREAT BRITAIN--VICE
    ADMIRALTY COURTS
  Appeals: 4097
  Chancery: 4605
  Courts baron--Sussex: 4767
  Oyer and Terminer: 819
  Survey: 4630
COURTSHIP: 380
  see also GREAT BRITAIN--LOVE
    LETTERS
  Poetry: 2227
CRIME: 1087, 1126, 1576
  see also specific types of crime
    and criminals under GREAT BRITAIN

GREAT BRITAIN

CRIME (Continued):
  Punishment: 4913
  see also GREAT BRITAIN--
    TRANSPORTATION OF CONVICTS
CRIMEAN WAR: see CRIMEAN WAR
CROWN LANDS: 5026
CURRENCY: 1339, 1775
  Regulation: 5
  Value: 5886
CUSTOMS DUTIES: 1913
  see also GREAT BRITAIN--TARIFF
CYCLING: see SCOTLAND--Cycling
DEATH: 4168, 5598
DEBT: 2226
  see also GREAT BRITAIN--PERSONAL
    DEBT
  Imprisonment for: 4605
DEBT COLLECTION: 516
DEFENSE: 233, 1598, 4520, 5330
  see also SCOTLAND--Defense
DEMOGRAPHIC STUDIES: 2148
DEPRESSIONS:
  1816: 5282
  1870s: 5731
DESCRIPTION AND TRAVEL:
  see also SCOTLAND--Description and
    travel
  1700s: 2776, 4348, 4969
  1800s: 43, 1115, 3179, 4348, 4911
  1800s: 5038
  1810s: 2139, 3423, 5038
  1820s: 4383
  1830s: 5065
  1840s: 5065, 5133
  1850s: 2503, 2985, 3424, 5963
  1870s: 20, 157, 1467, 3107
  1880s: 1463
  1900s: 4018
DINING CLUBS: 2759
DISEASES: 1057, 2058
  see also CONTAGIOUS DISEASES ACT
    OF 1869
  Cholera--Romsey: 5222
DISSENTING CHURCHES: 1875, 2149,
  3226, 4913
DOMESTIC ARCHITECTURE: 945
  see also GREAT BRITAIN--
    ARCHITECTURE
DRAMA: see ENGLISH DRAMA; GREAT
  BRITAIN--THEATER
DRINKING: 1087
DYES AND DYEING: 5553
ECCLESIASTICAL COURTS: 4840
ECONOMIC CONDITIONS:
  see also SCOTLAND--Economic
    conditions
  1700s: 15, 2703
  1800s: 1404, 1755, 2736, 2755,
    3883, 5726
  1900s: 2627
ECONOMICS: 1792
EDITING: see GREAT BRITAIN--
  SCHOLARLY EDITING
EDUCATION:
  see also the following subheadings
    under GREAT BRITAIN: ARMY--
    Education of Catholic
    dependents; COMMERCIAL EDUCATION;
    RELIGIOUS EDUCATION; SCHOOLS;
    TEACHING; UNIVERSITIES AND
    COLLEGES
  1700s: 5038
  1700s-1800s: 5726
  1800s: 14, 258, 1087, 1126, 1632,
    2962, 3977, 4331
  1900s: 1815
  Finance: 4605
  Laws and legislation: 2962
    Education Act of 1902: 949
    Education Act of 1906: 4520
  Women: 3251
ELECTION REFORM: 649
  see also GREAT BRITAIN--
    PARLIAMENTARY REFORM

GREAT BRITAIN

ELECTIONS:
  see also GREAT BRITAIN--LOCAL
    ELECTIONS; SCOTLAND--Elections
  1700s:
    1710s: 2071
    1730s: 2071
    1750s: 736, 5330
    1760s: 5287
    1780s: 3860
    1790s: 4171
  1700s-1800s: 535, 4230, 4913,
    5726
  1800s: 2708, 4605, 5026
    1800s: 5830
    1820s: 1124, 2149, 2836, 4258
    1830s: 816, 2149, 3847, 4024,
      4113, 4258, 4570, 4696, 5011,
      5222
    1840s: 1110, 4570
    1850s: 1158
    1860s: 4868, 5534
    1870s: 280, 3722
    1880s: 280, 1273, 3980, 4427,
      4568, 4694, 5164
    1890s: 735, 1499, 2146
  1900s:
    1900s: 3912
    1920s: 233, 5616
  Campaign finances (1833): 1456
  Laws and regulations (1862): 4868
  Procedure (1884): 118
  Subdivided by place:
    Bristol (1700s): 4229
    Cambridge (1923): 5590
    Lincolnshire (1830): 5746
    Middlesex (1802): 3658
    Newcastle (1837): 5624
    Saint Ives (1817): 5639
    South Hampshire (1830s): 5038
    Whitby (1905): 3912
    York (1768): 5330
ELOPEMENTS: 1049, 4770
ENGINEERING: 4770
ENGRAVERS AND ENGRAVING: 1071, 4967
  see also GREAT BRITAIN--WOOD
    ENGRAVING
ESTATES (Landed property):
  see also GREAT BRITAIN--COUNTRY
    ESTATES
  Surveys of estates: 712
  Value: 507
ESTATES (Legal):
  Administration and settlement:
    2226, 2838, 3722, 4770, 4934,
    5647
  Allerton: 3620
  Exeter: 5867
  Westmorland: 1869
EVANGELISM: 43
EXHIBITIONS AND FAIRS:
  Crystal Palace: see GREAT BRITAIN--
    FIRES
  Great Exhibition of 1850: 597, 3424
  Royal Naval Exhibition: 3744
FARM LAND: 712
FEUDAL PRIVILEGES--Sussex: 4767
FICTION: see ENGLISH FICTION
FINANCE: 369, 5173
  see also GREAT BRITAIN--HOUSEHOLD
    FINANCE; GREAT BRITAIN--
    PERSONAL FINANCE; GREAT
    BRITAIN--PUBLIC FINANCE; GREAT
    BRITAIN--SPECULATION
  Staffordshire: 190
FIRES:
  Crystal Palace: 2410
  Portsmouth: 92
FOLKLORE--Dorsetshire: 5403
FOOD PRICES: 535
FOREIGN AID--Spain: 5639
FOREIGN BUSINESS ENTERPRISES:
  see also SCOTLAND--Foreign business
    enterprises
  United States: 3179

## GREAT BRITAIN

FOREIGN INVESTMENT:
  Hungary: 3722
  Russia--Iron industry: 3238
  United States: 2754
    Land: 3179
    Louisiana Purchase bonds: 3273
FOREIGN RELATIONS:
  see also GREAT BRITAIN--
    GOVERNMENT AGENCIES AND
    OFFICIALS--Diplomatic and
    consular service; GREAT BRITAIN--
    GOVERNMENT AGENCIES AND
    OFFICIALS--Foreign Office;
    GREAT BRITAIN--TREATIES
  1700s: 1913
  1700s-1800s: 447, 1598, 1641, 4230
  1800s: 3472
    1830s: 1632
    1840s: 678, 1632
    1850s: 678, 2471
    1860s: 345, 2471, 3715
    1870s: 345, 472, 2471, 3036
    1880s: 345, 3036
    1890s: 3036
  1800s-1900s: 663
  1900s: 4449
  Afghanistan: 587, 4520, 5797
  Algeria: 1599, 2578
  Austria: 2149, 3238, 4650, 5726
  Balkan Peninsula: 233
  Barbary States: 3858
  Brazil: 1599, 5726
    see also GREAT BRITAIN--FOREIGN
      RELATIONS--Russia--Eastern
      Question
  Burma: 1857
  China: 597, 598, 3238, 4054, 5038
  Chinese Turkestan: 5103
  Circassia: 258
  Confederate States of America:
    115, 863, 1403, 2150, 2449,
    2695, 4521, 4616, 4923
  Egypt: 3067, 3744, 5164, 5835
  Ethiopia: 3838
  Europe: 5532
  France:
    1700s:
      1780s-1790s: 878, 2835, 3858,
        4230, 5038
      Rivalry in India (1730s-1750s):
        3128
        see also GREAT BRITAIN--
          NAVY--Operations--India;
          GREAT BRITAIN--TREATIES--
          France
    1700s-1800s: 1311, 4913, 5726,
      5797
    1800s: 258, 1002, 1126, 1632,
      1815, 3472, 4024, 4348, 4650
      Rivalry in Southeast Asia:
        4709
    1900s: 4941
  Germany: 3238
  Greece: 258, 1775
  Hungary: 3722
  India: 5797
    see also GREAT BRITAIN--
      COLONIAL POLICY AND
      ADMINISTRATION--India
    Hyderabad and Mysore: 5331
  Japan: 4054
  Latin America: 2844
  Mediterranean region: 1599
  Netherlands: 1641, 5726
  Persia: 868, 1010, 4005, 4693, 5797
  Poland: 5222
  Portugal: 118, 1599, 1775, 5726
  Russia:
    1800s: 289, 4650
      1800s: 2836
      1830s: 1632, 4258
      1860s: 345, 1857, 3238, 5222
      1870s: 345, 3238
      1880s: 345
    1800s-1900s: 4693
    Eastern Question: 1126, 1755

## GREAT BRITAIN

FOREIGN RELATIONS (Continued):
  Sarawak: 5725
  Spain: 2155, 2156, 4881, 5532,
    5639, 5726
  Teheran: 5797
  Thailand: 4709
  Transvaal: 4520
  Tunisia: 3460
  Turkey:
    1800s: 258, 3183, 4650
    1840s: 1164
    1840s: 3067
    1860s: 345
    1870s: 345, 4549
    1880s: 118, 345
  United States:
    1776-1799: 894, 2551, 2776, 2815,
      3041, 3573, 4221, 5298
    1776-1800s: 4348, 5726
    1800s: 258
      1800s: 2959
      1830s: 5065
      1840s: 5065
      1850s: 762, 4520, 4995
      1860s: 863, 3053, 3472, 3983,
        5033
        see also GREAT BRITAIN--
          FOREIGN RELATIONS--
          Confederate States of
          America
      1870s: 863
      1880s: 4089
      1890s: 217, 4089
    Peace negotiations (1813-1814):
      1302
    Oregon boundary dispute: 2193,
      4813
    Southern States (1790s-1830s):
      4383
  Vatican: 5726
FOREIGN TRADE: 1903, 2322, 2403, 2742
  Africa (1700s): 4541, 4913
  Canada (1700s): 4541
  Confederate States of America:
    1115, 3905, 4505
  Hungary (1870s): 3722
  Ireland (1700s): 2884
  Levant: 3183
  Portugal (1800s): 4289
  Prussia (1800s): 4289
  Russia:
    1700s: 535
    1800s: 535, 4289
  Spain:
    1600s: 644
    1700s: 2155
    1800s: 4289
  Sweden (1700s-1800s): 535
  United States:
    see also GREAT BRITAIN--COLONIAL
      TRADE
    1700s: 313, 1481
    1700s-1800s: 1615, 1935, 2637,
      4598
    1700s-1900s: 480
    1800s: 948, 2159, 2641, 3179,
      3230, 4289
  West Indies (1700s): 4541, 5139
FREE TRADE: 649, 1126, 1569, 3498,
  4605, 5726
FREEHOLDERS--Middlesex: 3658
FRENCH REVOLUTIONARY WARS: see
  FRENCH REVOLUTIONARY WARS;
  GREAT BRITAIN--ARMY--French
  Revolutionary Wars; GREAT
  BRITAIN--NAVY--Operations--French
  Revolutionary Wars
GEOLOGY: 747
GOLDSMITHS: 2784
GOVERNMENT: see GREAT BRITAIN--
  POLITICS AND GOVERNMENT
GOVERNMENT AGENCIES AND OFFICIALS:
  Admiralty: 326, 2200, 2836, 4549,
    5024

## GREAT BRITAIN

GOVERNMENT AGENCIES AND OFFICIALS:
  Admiralty (Continued):
    see also GREAT BRITAIN--
      GOVERNMENT AGENCIES AND
      OFFICIALS--First Lord of the
      Admiralty
  Army: see GREAT BRITAIN--ARMY
  Attorney General: 2996
  Auditor General: 2976
  Board of Trade: 597, 780, 4549,
    5277
    India: 5639
    Railroad Commission: 5
  Board of Trade and Plantations:
    2148
  Board of Treasury: 4229
    see also GREAT BRITAIN--
      GOVERNMENT AGENCIES AND
      OFFICIALS--Treasury
  Cabinet:
    1700s: 1545, 2149, 5330
    1800s: 258, 597, 1875, 2099,
      2201, 3472, 4331, 4520
    1900s: 1815
  Chancellor of the Exchequer: 2976
  Colonial Office: 3978, 5277, 5540
  Commission for Penal Servitude and
    Transportation: 2994
  Commission on the Administration
    of Roads: 2994
  Comptroller: 2976
  Comptroller of the Navy: 2296
  Consulates: see GREAT BRITAIN--
    GOVERNMENT AGENCIES AND
    OFFICIALS--Diplomatic and
    consular service
  Council of Trade: 644
  Courts: see GREAT BRITAIN--COURTS
  Crown agents for the colonies:
    3978
  Customs Office: 2836
  Diplomatic and consular service:
    1875, 3715, 4005, 4089, 5638
    see also GREAT BRITAIN--
      GOVERNMENT AGENCIES AND
      OFFICIALS--Foreign Office
    Appointments: 1755, 3238
    Claims against: 4934
    Misconduct in office: 868
    Subdivided by place:
      Argentina: 286
      Austria: 3472, 5637
        Vienna: 16, 3238
      Belgium--Brussels: 3472
      China: 3315, 5038
        Canton: 258
        Peking: 3472
      Confederate States of America:
        4484
      Egypt: 3472, 4941
        Alexandria: 3471
      France: 2149, 3472
        Paris: 1875, 5277
      Germany: 3472
        Berlin: 3238, 3472
        Munich: 3238
      Greece: 3472
      Hungary--Budapest: 3722
      India--Delhi: 4137
      Italy: 3472
      Latin America: 2844
      Manchuria: 306
      Netherlands: 3472
      Persia--Baghdad: 5797
      Portugal: 3472
      Russia: 3238, 3472
      Spain: 2155, 5532
      Thailand: 4709
      Tunis: 3460
      Turkey: 199, 3472, 4549
      United States: 3472, 4678

GREAT BRITAIN

GOVERNMENT AGENCIES AND OFFICIALS:
Diplomatic and consular service:
Subdivided by place:
United States (Continued):
see also GREAT BRITAIN--
GOVERNMENT AGENCIES AND
OFFICIALS--Diplomatic and
consular service--
Confederate States of
America
Savannah, Georgia: 2150
Washington, D.C.: 2150
Wilmington, North Carolina:
2159
Exchequer: 2199
see also GREAT BRITAIN--
GOVERNMENT AGENCIES AND
OFFICIALS--Chancellor of the
Exchequer
First Lord of the Admiralty: 1598,
1599
see also GREAT BRITAIN--
GOVERNMENT AGENCIES AND
OFFICIALS--Admiralty
First Lord of the Treasury: 3997
see also GREAT BRITAIN--
GOVERNMENT AGENCIES AND
OFFICIALS--Treasury
Foreign Office: 199, 258, 306,
3472, 4018
Letters to consuls in Savannah,
Georgia: 2150
Divided authority in India: 868
Home Department: 4097
Home Secretary: 5331
House of Commons: see GREAT
BRITAIN--PARLIAMENT--House of
Commons
House of Lords: see GREAT BRITAIN--
PARLIAMENT--House of Lords
Indian Army: see GREAT BRITAIN--
INDIAN ARMY
Inspector for Improving the Quit
Rents for North and South
Carolina: 3347
Kings of Great Britain: see
personal names of individual
monarchs (e.g. EDWARD VII, King
of Great Britain)
Lord Chancellor: 1717, 2998, 4036,
5134
Lords Commissioners of the Treasury:
5473
see also GREAT BRITAIN--
GOVERNMENT AGENCIES AND
OFFICIALS--Treasury
Magistrates: 5277, 5746
Naval Commissioner--Canada: 342
Navy: see GREAT BRITAIN--NAVY
Parliament: see GREAT BRITAIN--
PARLIAMENT
Preventive Service: 2836
Preventive Water Guard: 2836
Privy Council: 597, 4567, 5883
Privy Seal Office: 2154
Public Records Office: 3715, 4229,
5540
Royal Commission on Ecclesiastical
Discipline: 1571
Secret Service: 1598, 5071
Secretary at War: 453
Secretary of State for India: 278,
2756
Secretary of State for Ireland:
4113
Secretary of State for the Southern
Department: 2155, 2156, 3137
Secretary of State for War: 1598,
5024
Southern Department: 2155, 2156
Treasury: 2158, 2836, 5330

GREAT BRITAIN

GOVERNMENT AGENCIES AND OFFICIALS:
Treasury (Continued):
see also the following
subheadings under GREAT
BRITAIN--GOVERNMENT AGENCIES
AND OFFICIALS: Board of
Treasury; First Lord of the
Treasury; Lords Commissioners
of the Treasury
Vice Admiralty Courts: 1913
War Council: 233
War Office: 1114, 5806
Administration in South Africa:
5872
GOVERNMENT AND CIVIC EMPLOYEES:
Pensions: 4097
GRAMMAR SCHOOLS: see GREAT BRITAIN--
SCHOOLS--Grammar schools
GREETING CARDS: 4115
GUARDIANSHIP:
Children: 4770
Sussex: 4767
HERESIES AND HERETICS: 5726
HIGHWAYMEN: 3183
HISTORIC BUILDINGS: 2411
Exeter: 5553
Somersetshire: 1071
HISTORICAL RESTORATION: 5553
HISTORICAL STUDIES: 892, 957, 1910,
2282, 2471, 3715, 4512, 4580,
4628
see also GREAT BRITAIN--PUBLISHERS
AND PUBLISHING--Historical
studies; SCOTLAND--Historical
studies
Bath: 5553
Exeter: 5553
Medieval Church: 2841
Roman catacombs: 2148
Somersetshire: 4176
World War I: 1320
HOPS: 2148
HOUSEHOLD ACCOUNTS: 4934
Chigwell: 3553
ILLUSTRATION: see GREAT BRITAIN--
BOTANICAL ILLUSTRATION; GREAT
BRITAIN--ZOOLOGICAL ILLUSTRATION
IMMIGRATION AND EMIGRATION:
see also BRITISH IN (place);
SCOTLAND--Immigration and
emigration
From Great Britain:
To Canada: 5726
To the United States: 1153, 5478
To Virginia: 99
To Great Britain:
From Germany: 3808
IMPERIAL FEDERATION: 3056
IMPERIAL INSTITUTE: 4567
IMPERIALISM: 43
Central America: 2836
Mediterranean: 2836
INDENTURES: 4229
INDIAN ARMY: 278, 816, 2756
see also GREAT BRITAIN--ARMY--
India; INDIA--British military
activities
Bombay Marines: 5797
Discipline: 816
Madras: 536, 5201
Mutinies:
see also INDIAN MUTINY
Sepoy Mutiny (1806): 2321
Madras Army (1809): 332
5th European Regiment (1859):
4097
Native troops: 2321
Officers: 2321, 5327
Afghan Nepalese officers: 3286
Regiments:
1st Madras Light Cavalry: 2756
4th Native Infantry: 563
5th European: 4097
34th Regiment: 5327
INDUSTRIALIZATION: 1070, 1632

GREAT BRITAIN

INSURANCE--Maritime: 1913, 3183,
3230
INSURANCE COMPANIES: 2013, 3183
INTERIOR DECORATION:
Portraits in tile: 562
INVENTIONS--Claims for: 794
IRISH POLICY: 535, 597, 649, 678,
1139, 2149, 2471, 2626, 3693,
4024, 4113, 4331
Orange societies: 2708
IRON INDUSTRY:
Effect of Franco-Prussian War on
stocks: 2410
JACOBITES: 2149
JEFFERSONIAN EMBARGO: 2148
JOURNALISM: see GREAT BRITAIN--
NEWSPAPERS
JUDGES--Singapore: 4097
JURIES: 1541
Yorkshire: 5956
JUSTICES IN EYRE: 3997
KNIGHTHOOD: 280
LABOR: 14, 2149, 3498, 4605, 4696,
5726
see also GREAT BRITAIN--STRIKES
LABOR CONDITIONS: 5, 794, 1087
LABOR LAW AND LEGISLATION:
Woman and child labor: 1648
LABOR REFORM: 20
LABOR UNIONS--Sheffield: 4234
LABOUR PARTY: 3912, 5616
Indian policy: 2756
LAND: 507
Sussex: 4767
LAND COMPANIES: 2583, 4895
LAND REFORM: 515, 3236
LAND TENURE:
Middlesex County: 3658
Yorkshire: 5956
LAND TITLE LEGISLATION: 2998
LAND TITLES--London: 5662
LANDLORDS AND TENANTS: 5, 712, 2149,
5726
Gloucestershire: 4630
Sussex: 4767
Worcestershire: 4630
LAW--Codification: 4605
LAW PRACTICE: 1545, 1753
LAW TREATISES: 1142
LAWS AND LEGISLATION: 3046, 3715,
4605
see also names of specific acts
and subjects of legislation
LAWSUITS: 453, 3722, 4372, 4934
Bristol: 4541
Sussex--Land: 4747
LAWYERS' ACCOUNTS--Exeter: 5867
LEGAL AFFAIRS: 2198, 2322, 5478
see also SCOTLAND--Legal affairs
LEGAL PROCEDURES: 472
LIBEL TRIALS: 2836, 4051
LIBERAL PARTY:
1800s: 280, 649, 1765, 2322, 4568,
4694, 5164
1800s-1900s: 3980
1900s: 233, 3912
Candidates at Newcastle (1837):
5624
Leadership (1896): 4520
LIBERAL UNIONISTS: 4036, 5027
LIBRARIES: 1124, 4770
see also BRITISH MUSEUM
Private libraries: 2200, 5647
see also SCOTLAND--Libraries--
Private
LITERARY INTERESTS:
1700s-1800s: 2126, 4967
Exeter: 5867
1800s: 1552, 2801, 4543
1800s-1900s: 2102, 5175
1900s: 1210, 4823, 5790
LITERARY SOCIETIES: 892, 1113
LITERATURE: see ENGLISH LITERATURE;
GREAT BRITAIN--RELIGIOUS LITERATURE;
LITERATURE; LITERATURE AND STATE

## GREAT BRITAIN

LOANS: 2755, 3315
LOCAL ELECTIONS: 3847
  Bath: 1753
LOCAL POLITICS:
  Dorsetshire: 2149
  Isle of Wight: 332
  London: see LONDON, England--
    Politics and government
  Lymington: 4557
LOCOMOTIVES: 3054
LOVE LETTERS: 1552
  see also GREAT BRITAIN--COURTSHIP
LUMBER COMPANIES: 4895
MANORS: 2836
MANUFACTURERS: see SCOTLAND--
  Manufacturers
MANUSCRIPT COLLECTING: 5856
MARITAL SEPARATION: 5553
MARKETING see GREAT BRITAIN--
  PUBLISHERS AND PUBLISHING--
  Marketing
MARRIAGE CONTRACTS: 4934
MARRIAGE IN POETRY: 2227
MEDICAL NOTEBOOKS (1700s): 5095
MEDICAL TREATISES (1700s): 4333
MEDICAL TREATMENT: 1541
MEDICINES--Prescriptions: 5095
MEMORIAL FUNDS: 4026
MEMORIALS: 5050
  Joseph Conrad: 1210
MERCANTILE ACCOUNTS:
  Bristol: 4541
  London: 5139
MERCHANT SEAMEN: 5736
MERCHANTS: 258, 712, 3304
  see also AMERICAN REVOLUTION--
    British merchants in the United
    States; SCOTLAND--Merchants
  Bristol: 4541
  Collection of pre-Revolutionary
    War debts owed by United States
    citizens: 1993, 5548
  Devonshire: 570
  Liverpool: 3753
  London: 3179, 3960, 5221
METEOROLOGY: 2839
METHODIST CHURCHES: 1317, 1518,
  2751, 5726
  see also GREAT BRITAIN--WESLEYAN
    METHODIST CHURCH
  Clergy: see GREAT BRITAIN--
    CLERGY--Methodist
  Doctrine: 2751
  Finance: 5647, 5895
  Missionary societies: see GREAT
    BRITAIN--MISSIONARY SOCIETIES--
    Methodist
  Relations with the Church of
    England: 5647
  Schools: see GREAT BRITAIN--
    SCHOOLS--Church schools--
    Methodist
  Sunday schools: see GREAT BRITAIN--
    SUNDAY SCHOOLS--Methodist
  Theology: see GREAT BRITAIN--
    METHODIST CHURCHES--Doctrine
  Wesleyan Conference: 2482
METHODIST EPISCOPAL CHURCH:
  Clergy: see GREAT BRITAIN--
    CLERGY--Methodist Episcopal
MILITARY AFFAIRS:
  1700s: 3304
  1800s: 3835
  1800s-1900s: 663, 5876
MILITARY ASSISTANCE:
  Persia: 868
MILITARY INTELLIGENCE: 1598
MILITIA: 1114, 2199
MISSIONARY SOCIETIES: 5725, 5726
  Methodist: 3995
MISSIONS AND MISSIONARIES:
  Church of England--Finance: 5725
MONUMENTS: 3498, 3816
MORAVIAN CHURCH: 2751, 5726

## GREAT BRITAIN

MUNICIPAL GOVERNMENT:
  Halifax: 5026
  London: 92, 1815
  Reform: 5616
MURDERS: 4427
MUSEUMS: see BRITISH MUSEUM
MUSIC: see GREAT BRITAIN--SONGS
  AND MUSIC
NATIONAL RADICAL UNION: 4036
NAVAL ARCHITECTURE: 1599
NAVAL DEBATE OF 1914: 3912
NAVY:
  see also subheadings such as
    Admiralty, Comptroller of the
    Navy, and Naval Commissioner,
    under GREAT BRITAIN--GOVERNMENT
    AGENCIES AND OFFICIALS; TRAVEL--
    Naval cruises (Great Britain)
  1700s: 445
  1700s-1800s: 342, 4230, 5726
  1800s: 485, 1504, 1599, 5262
  1800s-1900s: 452
  1900s: 4476
  Administration: 452
  Algerian Expedition: 3883
  Appropriations and expenditures:
    1599
  Discipline: 2296
  Exploration of South America:
    2296
  Impressment: 638, 1424, 1466,
    2267, 2296
  Maneuvers: 452
  Military intelligence: 1598
  Mobilization policy: 452
  Nautical surveying: 485
  Naval cadets: 1792
  Nootke Sound controversy: 1913
  Officers: 1504, 3744, 3836, 4102,
    4441,
    Appointments: 3744
    Negroes: 5726
  Operations:
    Africa:
      Preparedness for war against
        France (1888): 5024
      Withdrawal of aid to missions:
        5725
    American Revolution: 1117
      Depredations on American
        shipping: 4348
      Savannah, Georgia: 2675
    Asia: 5638
    Cape of Good Hope: 5639
    Crimean War: 153, 485, 3472
    Egypt: 3744
    French Revolutionary Wars: 342,
      887, 2836
      Irish coast: 535
    India: 3315
    Ireland: 887, 2296
    Mediterranean: 1599, 3056, 3460,
      5024
    Napoleonic Wars: 342, 887, 1311,
      2836
      Blockade of Europe: 2296
      Morale of admirals: 1164
      Neutral shipping seizures:
        2147
      Peninsular War: 1875, 3736
      Sardinia: 1164
    Netherlands: 1599
    Philippine Islands: 3315
    Spain: 1599
    War of 1812: 1311, 2836
  Orders: 3744, 4289
  Pacific Command proposed: 1640
  Pensions: 2296
  Personnel reform: 452
  Portuguese Fleet: 5830
  Prize money: 392
  Recreation--Far East: 3744
  Religion: 3744
  Sea life: 3744
  Ship lists: 153

## GREAT BRITAIN

NAVY (Continued):
  Ships:
    see also names of specific ships
    Construction: 1599
    Drawings: 153
    Maintenance and repair: 1599
  Suppression of the slave trade:
    Madagascar: 2754
    Zanzibar: 5725
  Surgeons: 2667
  Technology: 452
NAVY YARDS: 1599
NEW YEARS CARDS: 4115
NEWSLETTERS: 3884
NEWSPAPERS: 1499, 2026, 4151
  Censorship: see GREAT BRITAIN--
    CENSORSHIP--Newspapers
  Correspondents in the Confederate
    States of America: 5193
  Correspondents in Southeast Asia:
    4709
  London: 217, 5262
  Reporters and reporting: 3036,
    4503
  Whig Party: 1632
NOBILITY: 2154, 4567, 4568
  see also SCOTLAND--Nobility
  Pensions and retirement: 4230
ORDNANCE: 1114
OXFORD MOVEMENT: 43, 306
  Political aspects: 3715
PAGAN SACRED PLACES: 2199
PARISH RATES: 3498
PARLIAMENT:
  see also GREAT BRITAIN--ELECTIONS;
    GREAT BRITAIN--PARLIAMENTARY
    INVESTIGATIONS; GREAT BRITAIN--
    PARLIAMENTARY REFORM
  1780s: 4625
  1790s: 2869, 5330
  1700s-1800s: 4230
  1800s:
    1820s: 4058, 4258
    1830s: 3121, 3715, 4058, 4258,
      5038
    1840s: 597, 4570
    1850s: 597, 3472, 4868
    1860s: 3472, 4868
    1880s: 4036
  Appropriations: 3725
  House of Commons:
    1600s: 2152
    1700s: 4969, 5330
    1800s: 2836, 3236, 4605, 5746
    Clerks: 4028
    Financial compensation for
      members: 200
    Procedures: 4028
    Speaker: 4028
    1900s: 5616, 5625
  House of Lords:
    1600s: 2152
    1800s: 345, 5637
    Librarian: 5116
    1900s: 1924
  Irish members: 3472
  Legislation: see GREAT BRITAIN--
    LAWS AND LEGISLATION; and names
    of specific acts and subjects
    of legislation
  Privileges and immunities: 4605
  Representation: 955
PARLIAMENTARY ELECTIONS: see GREAT
  BRITAIN--ELECTIONS
PARLIAMENTARY INVESTIGATIONS: 4151
PARLIAMENTARY REFORM:
  see also REFORM BILLS
  1700s: 1139
  1700s-1800s: 922, 1311, 4913,
    5726
  1800s: 4605
    1830s: 1775, 3847, 5038, 5637,
      5729
    1850s: 2149, 4104

GREAT BRITAIN

PARLIAMENTARY REFORM:
  1800s (Continued):
    1860s: 345
    1870s: 345
    1880s: 345, 5164
    1900s: 5625
PASSPORTS: 1373
PATRONAGE: see GREAT BRITAIN--
  POLITICAL PATRONAGE
PEASANTRY: see SCOTLAND--Peasantry
PENAL CODE: 5726
  see also PENAL CODE BILL
PENSIONS: 2157, 2626, 2707, 5116,
  5177
  see also GREAT BRITAIN--AMERICAN
    REVOLUTION--Pensions; GREAT
    BRITAIN--ARMY--Pensions;
    GREAT BRITAIN--CIVIL SERVICE
    PENSIONS; GREAT BRITAIN--
    NOBILITY--Pensions and
    retirement
PERCUSSION RIFLE BULLET: 4520
PERIODICALS: 2146
  see also GREAT BRITAIN--
    PUBLISHERS AND PUBLISHING--
    Periodicals
PERSONAL DEBT: 3245
  London: 5463
PERSONAL FINANCE: 15, 597, 2198,
  2626, 4097, 4171
  see also SCOTLAND--Personal
    finance
  Exeter: 5867
PHILOSOPHY: 4628
  see also GREAT BRITAIN--
    PUBLISHERS AND PUBLISHING--
    Philosophical works
PHYSIOLOGY: 4051
PLANTS: 3862
  see also GREAT BRITAIN--BOTANY
POETRY: see ENGLISH POETRY; GREAT
  BRITAIN--RELIGIOUS POETRY
POLICE: 4420
POLITICAL APPOINTMENTS: 2060, 2154
POLITICAL CARTOONS: 4605
POLITICAL CLUBS: 944, 5026
POLITICAL DISABILITIES: 2149, 3226
  see also GREAT BRITAIN--CATHOLIC
    EMANCIPATION; GREAT BRITAIN--
    DISSENTING CHURCHES; GREAT
    BRITAIN--SUFFRAGE
  Repeal of Five-mile and
    Conventicle Acts: 3120
POLITICAL PARTIES: 491
  see also names of specific
    political parties under GREAT
    BRITAIN
POLITICAL PATRONAGE: 1632, 2158,
  4024, 5330
POLITICAL REFORM: see GREAT BRITAIN--
  PARLIAMENTARY REFORM; GREAT BRITAIN--
  SOCIAL AND POLITICAL REFORM
POLITICAL UNREST--Coventry: 4750
POLITICS AND GOVERNMENT:
  see also SCOTLAND--Politics and
    government
  1700s: 4229
    1760s: 92
    1770s: 92
    1780s: 1913
    1790s: 15, 1913, 3176
  1700s-1800s: 447, 535, 922, 1598,
    2126, 4230, 5726
  1700s-1900s: 2149
  1800s: 14, 43, 258, 280, 472,
    678, 1147, 1457, 1755, 1775,
    1978, 2099, 3472, 3835, 3847,
    4605, 4650, 4912, 5038
    1800s: 1717, 4137
    1810s: 3883, 4137, 5282
    1820s: 878
    1830s: 738, 1632, 1875, 4024,
      4696, 5065, 5277, 5637
    1840s: 5, 504, 598, 1632, 2193,
      4570, 4696, 5025, 5065, 5133,
      5637

GREAT BRITAIN

POLITICS AND GOVERNMENT:
  1800s (Continued):
    1850s: 5, 598, 886, 1632, 2146,
      2471, 4104, 4455, 4995
    1860s: 345, 2471, 2756, 2918,
      3715, 4568, 5134, 5259, 5875
    1870s: 118, 345, 886, 2471,
      4568, 5259
    1880s: 118, 345, 1765, 1872,
      2736, 3693, 3744, 4036
    1890s: 2736
  1800s-1900s: 294, 452, 1014, 1079,
    1260, 1499, 1815, 2060, 3980,
    4693, 5164, 5222, 5736, 5806
  1900s: 3912
    1900s: 326, 4520
    1910s: 233, 5625
    1920s: 233
    1930s: 233
    1940s: 4722
  Appointments: see GREAT BRITAIN--
    POLITICAL APPOINTMENTS
  Governmental interference in
    Oxford (1766): 1214
  Leadership: 326
  Local government:
    see also GREAT BRITAIN--COUNTY
      GOVERNMENT; GREAT BRITAIN--
      MUNICIPAL GOVERNMENT
  Reform: see GREAT BRITAIN--
    MUNICIPAL GOVERNMENT--Reform;
    GREAT BRITAIN--PARLIAMENTARY
    REFORM; GREAT BRITAIN--SOCIAL
    AND POLITICAL REFORM; REFORM
    BILLS
  Regency crisis of George III: 1913
POLL TAX: 1978
POOR LAWS: 5, 1775, 2149, 3498,
  4258, 4605, 5616, 5726
PORTRAITS: 2411
PORTS--Mounts Bay: 3080
POVERTY: 43
PREPARATORY SCHOOLS: see GREAT
  BRITAIN--SCHOOLS--Preparatory
  schools
PRISONERS AND PRISONS: 1087, 2835,
  3809, 5726
PRIVATEERING: 4171
PROHIBITION: 5164
PROMISSORY NOTES--Exeter: 5867
PROTECTORATES:
  Mississippi Territory (proposed):
    4246
PROTESTANT DISSENTERS: see GREAT
  BRITAIN--DISSENTING CHURCHES
PUBLIC CELEBRATIONS: 5129
PUBLIC FINANCE: 1311, 2154, 2976,
  4868
  see also GREAT BRITAIN--REVENUE
  Appropriations and expenditures:
    118
  Budget: 280, 1126
  East India Company loan (1797):
    3315
  Loyalty loan (1797): 2149
PUBLIC MEETINGS, Suppression of:
  4605
PUBLIC OPINION:
  see also SCOTLAND--Morale
  American Civil War: 1021
  French Revolution: 1070
  Irish people: 5809
  Mexican War: 2193
PUBLIC WELFARE: 504, 537, 5726
  see also GREAT BRITAIN--POOR LAWS;
    GREAT BRITAIN--WORKHOUSES
  Idle: 1648
  Wilberfoss: 5727
PUBLISHERS AND PUBLISHING:
  see also GREAT BRITAIN--AUTHORS
    AND PUBLISHERS
  1700s: 4512
  1800s: 735, 738, 981, 2736, 3816
  1800s-1900s: 5590
  1900s: 5173
  Historical studies: 828

GREAT BRITAIN

PUBLISHERS AND PUBLISHING
  (Continued):
  London: 3976, 5095
  Marketing: 2148, 2736
  Periodicals: 981, 1522, 1792,
    2471, 2627, 2918
  Philosophical works: 3670
  Songs and music: 2146
  Subscription publishing: 1603
QUAKERS: see GREAT BRITAIN--SOCIETY
  OF FRIENDS
RAILROADS: 3054, 4568, 5637
RELIGION: 128, 1541, 2060, 2148,
  3912, 4146, 4672, 5598
  see also GREAT BRITAIN--CLERGY;
    GREAT BRITAIN--PAGAN SACRED
    PLACES; GREAT BRITAIN--SERMONS;
    names of specific denominations
    under GREAT BRITAIN; SCOTLAND--
    Religion
RELIGIOUS DISSENTERS: see GREAT
  BRITAIN--DISSENTING CHURCHES
RELIGIOUS EDUCATION: 2149
  see also GREAT BRITAIN--SCHOOLS--
    Church schools; GREAT BRITAIN--
    SUNDAY SCHOOLS
RELIGIOUS LIFE: 625
RELIGIOUS LITERATURE: 2203, 5539
RELIGIOUS POETRY: 5647
RELIGIOUS SOCIETIES: 5726
REVENUE STAMPS: 2708, 4024
  see also GREAT BRITAIN--COLONIAL
    POLICY AND ADMINISTRATION--
    American colonies--Stamp duties
REVENUES: 92, 4437
  see also GREAT BRITAIN--PUBLIC
    FINANCE; GREAT BRITAIN--
    TAXATION
RIOTS (1817): 2149
ROADS: 2994
ROYAL BOUNTY FUND: 5116
ROYAL FAMILY: 535, 1079
  see also names of individual
    monarchs, e.g. EDWARD VII, King
    of Great Britain
  Weddings: 3472
SACRED PLACES: see GREAT BRITAIN--
  PAGAN SACRED PLACES
SATIRE: see ENGLISH SATIRE
SCHOLARLY EDITING: 1218
SCHOOLS: 2962, 4115
  see also GREAT BRITAIN--TEACHING
  Church schools:
    Anglican: 2962
    Catholic: 2962
    Methodist: 5726
  Eton: 5736
  Students and student life: 2102
  Finance: 4113
  Grammar schools: 1753, 5616
  Harrow: 4770
  Preparatory schools: 1675
SCIENTIFIC RESEARCH: 90, 1913
SERMONS: 43, 625, 5598
  Church of England: 179, 306
  Methodist: 4146, 5647
  Wesleyan Methodist: 5095
SERVANTS: 4823
  Suffrage: 5616
SHIPBUILDING: 1164
  Apprenticeship: 2148
  By British Navy: 1599
  Ironclads for the Confederate
    States of America: 4521
SHIPPING: 3183
  see also GREAT BRITAIN--FOREIGN
    TRADE; GREAT BRITAIN--TRADE AND
    COMMERCE
  Bristol (Accounts): 4541
  English Channel: 4719
  Liverpool: 5026
  Ocean shipping: 2159
SILVERSMITHS: 2784
SLAVE TRADE: 4913
  Abolition: 3316, 4605, 5726
  Colonies: 5726

GREAT BRITAIN

SLAVE TRADE (Continued):
  Suppression: 306, 5725
  see also GREAT BRITAIN--NAVY--
    Suppression of the slave trade
SLAVES:
  see also GREAT BRITAIN--ABOLITION
    OF SLAVERY
  Emancipation: 2542
SOAP REBATES: 5277
SOCIAL AND POLITICAL REFORM:
  see also GREAT BRITAIN--LABOR
    REFORM; GREAT BRITAIN--MUNICIPAL
    GOVERNMENT--Reform; GREAT
    BRITAIN--PARLIAMENTARY REFORM;
    REFORM BILLS
  1600s: 2152
  1700s: 3347, 5331
  1800s: 597, 981, 1126, 2054, 2149,
    2708, 5026
  1900s: 1815
SOCIAL CONDITIONS (1900s): 4449
SOCIAL LIFE AND CUSTOMS:
  1700s: 4230, 4625
  1800s: 43, 306, 597, 1755, 2801,
    3251, 4230, 5065, 5133
  1800s-1900s: 5175, 5736
  1900s: 3710, 4823
SOCIALISM--Bibliography: 65
SOCIALISTS--Biography: 65
SOCIETIES AND CLUBS: 5050, 5726
  see also the following subheadings
    under GREAT BRITAIN: BIBLE
    SOCIETIES; MISSIONARY SOCIETIES;
    POLITICAL CLUBS; RELIGIOUS
    SOCIETIES; WOMEN'S SOCIETIES AND
    CLUBS
SOCIETY OF FRIENDS: 1733, 4732, 5241,
    5726
  Chelmsford: 1903
  London yearly meetings: 2555
SOCINIANISM: 5726
SOLDIERS OF FORTUNE: 700
SONGS AND MUSIC: 258, 335
  see also GREAT BRITAIN--PUBLISHERS
    AND PUBLISHING--Songs and music
SPECULATION: 2148
  see also GREAT BRITAIN--FINANCE
SPIRITUAL LIFE: 4146
STOCK EXCHANGES: 92
STRIKES:
  Coal miners: 233
  Lancashire (1853): 2149
SUBMARINE CABLES: 4934
SUFFRAGE: 280, 649, 1126, 2322, 5616
  see also the following subheadings
    under GREAT BRITAIN: ELECTIONS;
    POLITICAL DISABILITIES; VOTER
    REGISTRATION; WOMAN SUFFRAGE
SUGAR REBATES: 1913
SUNDAY SCHOOLS:
  Methodist churches--Preston: 5895
TARIFF: 280, 331, 3836, 5277
  see also GREAT BRITAIN--CUSTOMS
    DUTIES
TARIFF REFORM: 2149, 4520
TAX COLLECTION: 2158
TAX STAMPS: see GREAT BRITAIN--
    REVENUE STAMPS; GREAT BRITAIN--
    COLONIAL POLICY AND ADMINISTRATION--
    American colonies--Stamp duties
TAXATION: 676, 1774, 2200, 2708,
    3725
  see also GREAT BRITAIN--POLL TAX;
    GREAT BRITAIN--REVENUE STAMPS;
    GREAT BRITAIN--REVENUES; GREAT
    BRITAIN--TARIFF
  Wilberfoss: 5727
TAXATION OF PROPERTY: 2708
  Sussex: 4767
  Yorkshire: 5956
TEACHING: 2751
  see also GREAT BRITAIN--EDUCATION;
    GREAT BRITAIN--SCHOOLS
TEMPERANCE: 2148, 3715, 3912

GREAT BRITAIN

TEST OATHS: 3226
TEXTILE INDUSTRY: 5726
  Effects of American Civil War on:
    5259
TEXTILE WORKERS: see SCOTLAND--
    Textile workers
THEATER: 3617
THEOLOGY: 5598, 5647
  see also GREAT BRITAIN--CALVINIST
    THEOLOGY; GREAT BRITAIN--
    METHODIST CHURCHES--Doctrine
TIMBER: 712
TIMBER RIGHTS--Sussex: 4767
TITHES: 4230
  Collection: 4605
TOBACCO: 737
TOBACCO INDUSTRY: 4079
  see also SCOTLAND--Tobacco
    industry
TOBACCO TRADE:
  1700s: 456, 625, 2703
  1700s-1800s: 28, 5221, 5653
  1800s: 564, 1301, 1633, 2742, 5251
  London:
    1700s: 1813
    1800s: 4288
TRADE AND COMMERCE: 4541
  see also the following subheadings
    under GREAT BRITAIN: COLONIAL
    TRADE; FOREIGN TRADE; FREE
    TRADE; MERCHANTS; SHIPPING;
    TRADE REGULATION
  Cane reeds: 3230
  Chocolate: 369
  Cinnamon: 2742
  Cloth: 1647, 2148
  Coal: 5726
  Cocoa: 2742
  Coffee: 369
  Cotton: see GREAT BRITAIN--COTTON
    TRADE
  Fish: 2742
  Flax: 2742
  Grain: 2193, 2755
  Horses: 1991, 2637
  Iron: 535
  Iron pipe: 3230
  Liquor: 5011
  Naval stores: 3230
  Pepper: 2742
  Potatoes: see SCOTLAND--Trade and
    commerce--Potatoes
  Rice: 3230, 5221
  Salt: 3230
  Silk: 2148
  Slaves: see GREAT BRITAIN--SLAVE
    TRADE
  Staves: 3230
  Stoneware: 3230
  Sugar: 2742
  Tallow: 2742
  Tea: 369
  Tobacco: see GREAT BRITAIN--
    TOBACCO TRADE
  Wheat: 2742
  Wool: 2148, 2742
TRADE REGULATIONS: 3230
  see also GREAT BRITAIN--COLONIAL
    TRADE--Regulation in Carolina
    Province
TRANSPORTATION OF CONVICTS: 2708,
    2994
TRAVEL: see GREAT BRITAIN--
    DESCRIPTION AND TRAVEL
TRAVEL COSTS: 4348
TREATIES:
  see also GREAT BRITAIN--COMMERCIAL
    TREATIES
  African tribes: 3443
  China: 3995
  France: 1641
  Mysore: 5038
  Portugal: 4605
  Spain: 4605
  United States:
    1794: 3041

GREAT BRITAIN

TREATIES:
  United States (Continued):
    1842: (Webster-Ashburton): 1632
TRIALS:
  John Almon: 92
TUNNELS: 306
UNIONIST PARTY: see SCOTLAND--
    Unionist Party
UNITARIAN CHURCHES: 369
UNIVERSITIES AND COLLEGES: 1815,
    2201
  see also CAMBRIDGE UNIVERSITY
    (including King's College);
    EAST INDIA COLLEGE; LEEDS
    UNIVERSITY; OXFORD UNIVERSITY
    (including Lincoln College);
    ST. DAVID'S COLLEGE; UNIVERSITY
    COLLEGE OF THE SOUTH WEST OF
    ENGLAND
VALENTINES: 258
VETO--Right of local veto: 3715
VICE ADMIRALTY COURTS: 1913
VOTER REGISTRATION: 4605
  Saint Albans: 4633
WAGES AND SALARIES:
  Bristol: 5731
  Judges: 4097
  Merchant seamen: 4541
WARS: see names of specific wars as
    subheadings under GREAT BRITAIN--
    ARMY and GREAT BRITAIN--NAVY; and
    names of specific wars, e.g.
    AMERICAN REVOLUTION; CRIMEAN WAR;
    etc.
WEDDINGS: 4230
  see also GREAT BRITAIN--ROYAL
    FAMILY--Weddings
WESLEYAN METHODIST CHURCH: 1070, 5255
WHIG PARTY: 1632, 4605, 5637
WILLS: 1561
WOMAN SUFFRAGE: 3912
WOMEN: 4520
  Employment: 2149
WOMEN AUTHORS: 5553
  Anonymous: 177, 2058
WOMEN CLERGY--Methodist: 1317
WOMEN'S SOCIETIES AND CLUBS: 1903
WOOD ENGRAVING: 2146
WOOL INDUSTRY:
  Dyes and dyeing: 5553
WORKHOUSES: 1648
ZOOLOGICAL ILLUSTRATION: 3577
ZOOLOGY: 4876
  Classification: 3577

[End of entries under GREAT BRITAIN]

GREAT CACAPON, West Virginia: 1318
GREAT EASTERN (steamship): 1877
GREAT EXHIBITION OF 1850: 597, 3424
GREAT FALLS, Montana: 1211
GREAT FALLS WATER POWER MINING AND
    IRON COMPANY: 3447
GREAT LAKES:
  United States naval operations:
    636
GREAT LAKES NAVAL STATION: 829
GREAT MUTINY: see INDIAN MUTINY
GREAT OGEECHEE DISTRICT, Georgia:
    812
GREAT PLAINS: see PLAINS STATES
GREAT WALL OF CHINA: 1373
THE GREAT WESTERN INSURANCE COMPANY
    OF NEW YORK: 3620
GREECE:
  Antiquities: 345
  British embassy in Athens: 3472
  Description and travel: 39, 2934
  Economic conditions: 345
  Foreign relations:
    Great Britain: 258, 1775
    United States:
      1800s: 636, 1787
      1900s: 83

GREECE (Continued):
    Foreign trade:
        United States: 636
    Kings and rulers:
        Refusal of Leopold of Belgium
            to accept the Crown: 535
    Politics and government: 345
    Religion: 128
    Social and political reform: 1014
    War of Independence (1821-1829):
        4770, 4913, 5726
GREEK HISTORY:
    Students' notebooks:
        Washington and Lee University
            (Virginia): 4616
GREEK LANGUAGE:
    Dictionaries: 3598
    Students' notebooks:
        University of Georgia: 3905
        University of Virginia: 5288
    Study and teaching:
        University of Virginia: 2612
GREEK LITERATURE:
    Translations into English: 2736,
        3607, 4616
GREELEY, Horace: 65, 1084, 2160,
    4486, 5193, 5476, 5627, 5744
GREEN, Adeline Ellery (Burr) Davis:
    2161
GREEN, Alexander: 648
GREEN, Alice Sophia Amelia
    (Stopford): 1424
GREEN, Anna: 3711
GREEN, C.H.: 2162
GREEN, C. R.: 2163
GREEN, Charles: 339
GREEN, David: 3711
GREEN, Duff (d. ca. 1854): 2165
GREEN, Duff (1791-1875): 357, 2164
GREEN (DUFF), Falmouth, Virginia
    (firm): 2165
GREEN (DUFF) AND SON, Falmouth,
    Virginia (firm): 2165
GREEN, Duff C.: 637
GREEN, Henry: 2174
GREEN, Honor: 380
GREEN, J. H.: 2166
GREEN, James: 2167
GREEN, Jesse C.: 768
GREEN, John Ruffin: 5457
GREEN, Lucius: 2176
GREEN, McDuff: 2165
GREEN, Mark: 2168
GREEN, Moses: 2169
GREEN, Richard L.: 2170
GREEN, Thomas: 2171
GREEN, Timothy (merchant): 2172
GREEN, Timothy R. (attorney): 2172
GREEN, W. B. (Virginia): 2173
GREEN, W. T. (Georgia): 2174
GREEN, Washington: 391
GREEN, Wharton Jackson: 2161
GREEN, William (Georgia): 3711
GREEN, William (Virginia, 1806-1880):
    1873, 2531
GREEN, William (labor leader,
    1870-1952): 224, 3944
GREEN, William J. (Virginia, d. ca.
    1871): 2165
GREEN, William Mercer (Tennessee,
    1798-1887): 2175
GREEN AND LANE, Falmouth, Virginia
    (firm): 2165
GREEN AND LONGMANS: see LONGMANS,
    GREEN AND CO.
GREEN & RYLAND, Virginia (firm):
    2176
GREEN AND SCOTT, Falmouth, Virginia
    (firm): 2165
GREEN BAY, Wisconsin: 1289
GREEN COUNTY, Alabama:
    Springfield: 3017
GREEN COUNTY, New York:
    Hunter: 2311
GREEN COUNTY, North Carolina: 1523
GREEN HILL, Virginia: 2131

GREEN LINE RAIL ROAD CAR
    ASSOCIATION: 2177
GREEN PIG IRON FURNACE: see
    SANDERS-GREEN PIG IRON FURNACE
GREENBACK LABOR PARTY: 4732
    West Virginia: 1828
GREENBACKS: 2449
    Investment: 2469
GREENBRIER, West Virginia: see CIVIL
    WAR--CAMPAIGNS, BATTLES AND
    MILITARY ACTIONS--West Virginia--
    Greenbrier
GREENBRIER COUNTY, West Virginia:
    1129
    Land deeds and indentures: 4563
GREENCASTLE, Pennsylvania: 1916
GREENE, David: 2178
GREENE, George W.: 2181
GREENE, John W.: 4648
GREENE, Nathaniel: 2179, 4128, 4864
GREENE, W.: 3315
GREENE COUNTY, Alabama: 5308
    Tax lists: 5593
    Cities and towns:
        Boligee: 4861
        Clinton: 1298
GREENE COUNTY, Georgia: 1998
    Inferior Court--Clerks: 4654
    Cities and towns:
        Greensboro: see GREENSBORO,
            Georgia
        Penfield: 4647
        Union Point: 4335
GREENE COUNTY, Indiana: 3981
GREENE COUNTY, Mississippi:
    Plantations: 1553
GREENE COUNTY, Missouri:
    Springfield: 4174
GREENE COUNTY, North Carolina: 470,
    1038, 1523, 1652
    see also DOBBS COUNTY, North
        Carolina
GREENE COUNTY, Tennessee: 5268
    Cedar Spring: 3692
    Greeneville: see GREENEVILLE,
        Tennessee
GREENEVILLE, Tennessee: 5757
    see also CIVIL WAR--CAMPAIGNS,
        BATTLES, AND MILITARY ACTIONS--
        Tennessee--Greeneville
GREENFIELD, Massachusetts: 3633
    Army camp life (1863): 25
    Social life and customs: 4606
GREENFIELD, Virginia: 5491
GREENHOW, Rose (O'Neal): 2180
GREENOCK, Scotland: 5688
    Foreign trade: 3230
GREENOUGH, Horatio: 2181
GREENSBORO, Alabama: 546, 5862
    Girls' schools and academies: 5593
    Law practice: 5593
GREENSBORO, Georgia: 1091, 1427,
    2216, 2464, 4654
GREENSBORO, North Carolina:
    1800s: 602, 835, 1482, 2286, 3656,
        4714
    1800s-1900s: 661, 3029, 3763
    1900s: 985, 2231, 2299, 3171,
        4279, 5234
    Booksellers and bookselling: 5804
    Civil War: 2882
        Confederate headquarters: 4738
        Hospitals: 375, 5741
    Clergy: 2221
    Description: 3908
    Diseases--Influenza: 3843
    Insurance companies: 4918
    Leather goods trade: 606
    Legal education: 5124
    Mexican War volunteers: 2050
    Municipal government: 5149
    Newspapers: 5149
    Philately: 651
    Political demonstrations (1840):
        2050
    Publishers and publishing: 5457

GREENSBORO, North Carolina
    (Continued):
    Sunday School conventions:
        Baptist: 3415
    Tobacco industry: 556
    Universities and colleges: see
        BENNETT COLLEGE; GREENSBORO
        COLLEGE; GUILFORD COLLEGE;
        NORTH CAROLINA AGRICULTURAL AND
        TECHNICAL STATE UNIVERSITY;
        UNIVERSITY OF NORTH CAROLINA AT
        GREENSBORO
GREENSBORO COLLEGE, Greensboro,
    North Carolina: 1152, 1483, 1909,
    2539, 2857, 3307, 4425
    Commencement exercises: 5298
    Emerson Literary Society: 4425
    Homecoming: 5022
GREENSBORO COLLEGE FOR WOMEN,
    Greensboro, North Carolina: see
    GREENSBORO COLLEGE
GREENSBORO DISTRICT, Methodist
    churches: 3646
GREENSBORO FEMALE ACADEMY,
    Greensboro, Alabama: 5593
GREENSBORO FEMALE COLLEGE,
    Greensboro, North Carolina: see
    GREENSBORO COLLEGE
GREENSBORO (N.C.) PATRIOT: 5149
GREENSBURG, Pennsylvania: 213
GREENVILLE, Alabama: 1304
    see also CIVIL WAR--CAMPAIGNS,
        BATTLES, AND MILITARY ACTIONS--
        Alabama--Greenville
GREENVILLE, Georgia--Business: 17
GREENVILLE, Kentucky: 3082
GREENVILLE, Mississippi: 1782
GREENVILLE, North Carolina: 672,
    1060, 2810, 3013
    Mercantile accounts: 3739
    Merchants: 1846
    Newspapers: 4858
    Primitive Baptist Church: 318
GREENVILLE, South Carolina:
    1700s-1800s: 653
    1800s: 3510, 4296, 5271
    1800s-1900s: 3527
    1900s: 737, 3451, 4851, 5236
    Antisemitism: 4834
    Baptist churches: 2182
    Civil War: 3354
        Aid societies: 2183
    Commercial products:
        Marketing: 5825
    Lawsuits: 4149
    Newspapers: 5312
    Presbyterian churches: 5825
    Railroads: 3317
    Schools: 3405
        Military schools: 3293
    Universities and colleges: see
        FURMAN UNIVERSITY
GREENVILLE, Virginia: 2737
GREENVILLE, SPARTANBURG, AND
    ANDERSON RAILWAY: 3893
GREENVILLE COUNTY, Mississippi:
    Greenville: 1782
GREENVILLE COUNTY, South Carolina:
    444, 2625
    Greenville: see GREENVILLE, South
        Carolina
GREENVILLE COUNTY, Virginia:
    Hicks Ford: 5891
    Hiring of slaves: 5891
GREENVILLE AND COLUMBIA RAILROAD:
    4145
GREENVILLE (N.C.) DAILY REFLECTOR:
    4858
GREENVILLE DISTRICT, South Carolina:
    Baptist churches: 3669
GREENVILLE FIRST BAPTIST CHURCH,
    Greenville, South Carolina: 2182
GREENVILLE LADIES' ASSOCIATION,
    Greenville, South Carolina: 2183
GREENVILLE MILITARY ACADEMY,
    Greenville, South Carolina: 3293
GREENVILLE (S.C.) NEWS: 5312

GREENWAY TOWNSHIP, Virginia: 4668
GREENWOOD, Alfred Burton: 2184
GREENWOOD, Arkansas: 2123
GREENWOOD, South Carolina: 2032
GREENWOOD, Virginia: 5286
GREENWOOD & BATLEY (firm): 794
GREENWOOD COUNTY, South Carolina: 1560
GREENWOOD FEMALE COLLEGE, Greenwood, South Carolina: 2032
GREETING CARDS:
  see also as subheading under names of specific holidays
  Great Britain: 4115
  United States: 2656
GREGG, Frank M.: 4387
GREGG, Maxcy: 2185
GREGG, William, Jr. (1800-1867): 2186, 5193
GREGG, William L. (Confederate soldier): 2187
GREGG'S CAVALRY (1865): 5769
GREGORY, Edwin Clarke: 2188
GREGORY, Elizabeth: 2190
GREGORY, Francis H.: 3118
GREGORY, Margaret (Overman): 2188
GREGORY, Mary: 2189
GREGORY, Richard: 2190
GREGORY, Richard Henry: 2191
GREGORY, William H. (North Carolina): 2192
GREGORY, Sir William Henry: 4616
GREGORY FAMILY (Virginia): 262
GREGORY, U.S.S.: 4355
GREGSON STREET CHURCH, Durham, North Carolina: 3646
GREIG, John (1779-1858): 2193
GREIN, John Frederick: 2194
GREIN, Philip Jacob: 2194
GRENADA:
  Immigration and emigration:
    From India: 4097
  Slave trade: 973
GRENADA, Mississippi: 3457, 5536
GRENADA COUNTY, Mississippi:
  Grenada: see GRENADA, Mississippi
GRENOBLE, France: 2195
  Confraternity of White Penitents: 2196
  Monastery of Sainte Claire: 2197
GRENVILLE, Anne (Pitt): 3798
GRENVILLE, George Nugent-, Baron Nugent (1788-1850): 2198
GRENVILLE, George Nugent-Temple-, First Marquis of Buckingham (1753-1813): 2199
GRENVILLE, James (1715-1783): 4230
GRENVILLE, James, First Baron Glastonbury: 4230
GRENVILLE, Thomas: 2200
GRENVILLE, William Wyndham, First Baron Grenville: 815, 1913, 2201, 2282, 3798, 3883
GRENVILLE FAMILY (Great Britain--Genealogy): 2200
GRENVILLE-TEMPLE, Richard Temple, First Earl Temple: 92
GRESHAM, Mrs. Thomas Baxter: 2202
GRESLEY, William: 2203
GREVILLE, Charles Cavendish Fulke: 4605
GREVILLE, George Guy, Fourth Earl of Warwick: 1087
GREY, Charles, Second Earl Grey (1764-1845): 4605, 5746
GREY, Edward, First Viscount Grey of Fallodon: 663
GREY, Sir George (1799-1882): 763, 2994
GREY, Henry George, Third Earl Grey: 472, 2994, 4605
GREY-EGERTON, Lady Henrietta Elizabeth Sophia (Denison): 2801
GRIDLEY, William C.: 2204
GRIEB, C. F.: 65
GRIERSON, Mary: 3223

GRIEVANCE PROCEDURES: see LABOR DISPUTES
GRIFFIN, J. W.: 2205
GRIFFIN, John King: 3560
GRIFFIN, Sir Lepel Henry: 3238
GRIFFIN, Wingfield: 2206
GRIFFIN FAMILY (South Carolina and Virginia--Genealogy): 4379
GRIFFIN, Georgia: 1476, 1672, 2909, 3414, 3901
  Civil War: 493, 731
  Social life and customs: 5730
GRIFFIN TOWNSHIP, North Carolina:
  Taxation: 3935
GRIFFITH, A. J.: 2207
GRIFFITH, Robert Eglesfield: 2208
GRIFFITH, Samuel Walker: 1792
GRIFFITHS, Charles Ralph: 286
GRIFFITHS, Gwyneth: 286
GRIFFITHS, John (1806-1885): 472
GRIFFITHS FAMILY (Great Britain and Australia): 286
GRIGGS, Eliza M. (Frame): 464, 2209
GRIGGS, Lee: 2209
GRIGGS, Lewis: 2727
GRIGGS FAMILY: 3357
GRIGGS AND WILDE, Boston, Massachusetts (firm): 2456
GRILL, C. Franklin: 3646
GRIMBALL, Arthur: 2210
GRIMBALL, Berkley: 2210
GRIMBALL, John: 2210
GRIMBALL, John Berkley: 2210
GRIMBALL, Mrs. John Berkley: 2210
GRIMBALL, Lewis M.: 2210
GRIMBALL, William H.: 2210
GRIMBALL FAMILY (South Carolina--Genealogy): 2210
GRIMBELL, John A.: 2211
GRIMES, Bryan: 2212, 2222
GRIMES, J. B.: 1336
GRIMES, James: 2213
GRIMES, Mary: 2239
GRIMES, Sarah: 2214
GRIMES, Thomas W.: 2216
GRIMES, Thomas Wingfield, Jr. (1844-1905): 2215
GRIMES, William Henry: 2217
GRIMES FAMILY (North Carolina--Genealogy): 2239
GRIMESLAND, North Carolina: 2212
  Methodist Episcopal Church, South: 5023
GRIMKÉ, Edward Montague: 2218
GRIMKÉ, Elizabeth: 4625
GRIMKÉ, John Faucheraud: 2218, 2875
GRIMKÉ, Thomas Smith: 2218, 5193
GRIMKÉ FAMILY (South Carolina): 2218, 4584
GRIMSHAW, Arthur H.: 4881
GRINDLAY, Robert Melvill: 2219
GRINDLAY AND COMPANY: 2219
GRING, Ambrose Daniel: 5160
GRING, Hattie (McClain): 5160
GRINNELL, Fordyce, Jr.: 848
GRINNELL, MINTURN AND COMPANY: 4881
GRISSOM, Eugene: 2220
GRISSOM, Gilliam: 706
GRISSOM, William Lee: 2220
GRIST, Allen: 1493, 2222
GRIST, James Redding: 2222
GRIST, Richard: 2222
GRIST MILLS:
  see also FLOUR MILLS; MILLERS' ACCOUNTS
  Georgia: 4895
  North Carolina: 2121, 4153
  South Carolina--Branchville: 1749
  Virginia:
    Albemarle County: 3699
    Brunswick County: 4324
    Franklin County: 3100
    Kinsley Mills: 1447
GRISWOLD, C. G.: 2723
GRISWOLD, Charles: 2223
GRISWOLD, Edward: 2223
GRISWOLD, Joel: 2223

GRISWOLD, William McCrillis: 2224
GRITTLETON, England: 3847
GRIZZEL (ship): 172
GROCERY TRADE:
  see also MERCHANTS
  Accounts:
    Georgia--Savannah: 4040
    Massachusetts: 1344
  Prices--Virginia: 4924
  Subdivided by place:
    North Carolina: 134
      Charlotte: 3599
      Wilmington: 3410
    South Carolina: 46
    Virginia: 1115, 1420, 2794
      Lynchburg: 2309
      Petersburg: 2176
      Richmond: 4461
    West Virginia:
      Shepherdstown: 1711
GROESBECK, Texas: 1138
GROH, Daniel Webster: 2225
GROSE, Francis: 2226
GROSE, John: 2227
GROSSMAN, James: 720
GROTON, Connecticut: 2141
GROUSE HUNTING: 4616
GROVE, William Barry: 3384
"THE GROVES," North Carolina (plantation): 4080
GRUBBS, Rhoda: 4833
GRUNDTVIG, Nicolai Frederik Severin: 2228
GRUNDY, Felix: 872
GRUNDY COUNTY, Tennessee:
  Altamont--Mercantile accounts: 5187
GRUVER FAMILY (North Carolina): 2934
GUADALAJARA, Mexico: 1939, 3305
GUADELOUPE, West Indies:
  Description and travel: 4958
GUANAJUATO, Mexico: 1412
GUANO: 4849
  see also SOLUBLE PACIFIC GUANO
  Prices--Virginia: 4616
  Subdivided by place:
    Georgia: 4493, 5051
    New York: 5731
    North Carolina: 3447, 4540
    Peru: 641, 1423
    Southern States: 1423
    Virginia: 4615, 5377
      Albemarle County: 33
GUANO TRADE: 3459
GUARD DUTY: see as subheading under names of armies and navies
GUARDIANSHIP:
  Children:
    North Carolina: 1523, 3415, 5319
      Edenton: 1376
    Ohio: 3751
    Pennsylvania: 1443
    South Carolina: 4834
    Virginia: 2120
  Free Negroes:
    Georgia: 5537
    South Carolina: 758
  Members of royalty: see Royal family under names of countries
  Mental incompetence:
    North Carolina: 3415
    United States: 958
  Orphans:
    Great Britain--Sussex: 4767
    Illinois: 5570
    Maryland: 2295
    North Carolina: 2819, 5709
      Hillsborough: 5381
    Pennsylvania: 4756
    Virginia: 2712
  Subdivided by place: 3711
    Georgia: 3711
    Kentucky--Lexington: 3325
    North Carolina: 4849, 4918
    Virginia: 1558
GUARDS: see LABOR UNIONS--Plant guards

GUATEMALA:
　American investments: 5970
　Foreign relations:
　　Honduras: 116
　Indigo culture: 4980
　Legal affairs: 3099
　Manufacturing: 3099
　Merchants: 3099
　Missions and missionaries: 2032
　Politics and government: 116
GUBERNATORIAL ELECTIONS:
　Georgia:
　　1868: 4415
　　1894: 3660
　　1934: 3575
　　1946: 3558
　Kentucky:
　　1844-1845: 3325
　Mississippi:
　　1826: 2609
　New York:
　　1894: 1977
　North Carolina:
　　1828: 2776
　　1846: 5390
　　1850: 730
　　1860: 1602
　　1862: 4938
　　1865: 2469
　　1896: 1584
　　1908: 3955, 4828
　　1920: 4018
　　1924: 274, 5962
　　1932: 2553
　　1940: 2863
　　1944: 2863
　Ohio:
　　1863: 801, 1505
　Pennsylvania:
　　1879: 3277
　South Carolina:
　　1890s: 5299
　　1912: 844
　　1916: 5930
　Texas:
　　1859: 5141
　Virginia:
　　1859: 4720
　　1863: 3809
　　1873: 2700
　　1877: 2597
　　1921: 5779
　　1940: 1198
　　1941: 3820
　　1945: 224
　　1947: 224
　　1950s: 1198
GUBERNATORIAL IMPEACHMENTS: see
　IMPEACHMENTS--Governors
GUERNSEY, Alfred Hudson: 2845
GUERNSEY COUNTY, Ohio: 681
GUERNSEY ISLAND, Channel Islands:
　306, 1147
GUERRANT, John W.: 2229
GUERRILLAS: see as subheading under
　names of armies and wars
GUERRY, Albert Capers: 3376
GUERRY, William Alexander: 4339
GUESS, George W.: 1138
GUEST, Jacob Henry: 2230
GUEST, Romeo Holland: 2231
GUGGENHEIMER, Charles M.: 3685
GUIDE TO FOREIGN MILITARY STUDIES,
　1945-1954, CATALOG AND INDEX:
　5418
GUIGNARD, John Gabriel: 5548
GUILD, Curtis, Jr.: 3228
GUILD MERCHANTS: 4978
GUILD-O-GRAM (publication): 3020
GUILFORD, Frederick North, Second
　Earl of: 92, 5330
GUILFORD, Connecticut: 2223, 4059
GUILFORD, North Carolina:
　Merchants: 556
GUILFORD CIRCUIT, Methodist
　churches: 3646

GUILFORD COLLEGE, Greensboro, North
　Carolina: 329, 1407, 2861, 4006,
　4366, 5905
GUILFORD COUNTY, North Carolina:
　328, 2314, 2890, 3639, 4917,
　5267, 5737
　Arithmetic exercise books: 208,
　　4114
　Flour mills: 5905
　Personal finance: 5905
　Roads: 5905
　　Overseers: 2287
　Schools: 1055
　　Boarding schools: 4066, 5905
　Teachers' records: 3931
　Cities and towns:
　　Deep River: 1870 5632
　　Fentriss: 2330
　　Greensboro: see GREENSBORO,
　　　North Carolina
　　Guilford--Merchants: 556
　　Guilford Court House: 2240
　　　see also AMERICAN REVOLUTION--
　　　　Campaigns and battles--
　　　　North Carolina--Guilford
　　　　Court House
　　High Point: see HIGH POINT, North
　　　Carolina
　　Jamestown: 211
　　　Farmers' Alliance: 2804
　　Oak Ridge: 3290
　　　General store: 556
　　Osceola: 4197
　　Pleasant Garden: 2330, 2715
　　Westminster: 1407
GUILFORD COUNTY (N.C.) BAPTIST
　SUNDAY SCHOOL CONVENTION: 3415
GUILFORD COURT HOUSE, North Carolina:
　2240
　see also AMERICAN REVOLUTION--
　　Campaigns and battles--North
　　Carolina--Guilford Court House
GUILFORD MISSION, Methodist
　churches: 3646
GUILLERNA, Cesar de: 4656
GUILMARTIN (L. J.) & CO., Savannah,
　Georgia: 2232
GUILMARTIN, Lawrence J.: 2232
GUINEY'S STATION, Virginia:
　Tailoring: 4589
GUIZOT, François Pierre Guillaume:
　3630
GULF, North Carolina: 4030
GULF OF MEXICO:
　United States naval operations:
　　636
GULF SPY by Henry J. Acker: 13
GULF STATES: see CIVIL WAR--
　CAMPAIGNS, BATTLES, AND MILITARY
　ACTIONS--Gulf States
GULLEY, Needham Yancey: 5457
GUM SWAMP CHURCH (North Carolina):
　3988
GUM TRADE: 323
GUM BARRELS:
　Manufacturing processes: 794
GUNN, I. A.: 2233
GUNN, James: 3573
GUNPOWDER INDUSTRY:
　Connecticut: 4375
　New York: 4375
GUNPOWDER TRADE:
　Connecticut: 1501
GUNS:
　see also ARMSTRONG GUNS; GATLING
　　GUN; RAPID-FIRE GUNS
　Purchase during Civil War: 2610
GUNSMITHING:
　Louisiana--New Orleans: 4957
GURNEY, Anna: 284
GUTHRIDGE, Jules: 2234
GUTHRIE, John: 2788
GUTHRIE, Henry: 5379
GUTHRIE, John Brandon: 2235
GUTHRIE, Thomas: 2148
GUTHRIE, William Anderson: 5457
GUY, J. A.: 4872

GUYOT, Yves: 1424
GUYTON, Robert: 2236
GWALIOR, India: 3453
GWATHMEY (T. & R.), Lynchburg,
　Virginia (firm): 2360
GWINNETT, Button: 5537
GWINNETT COUNTY, Georgia: 3841
　Lawrenceville: 2740, 4871, 5040
　　Mercantile accounts: 601
　　Physicians' accounts: 167
　　Postal Service: 5438
GWYNN, Walter: 2237
GWYNN FAMILY (South Carolina): 3176
GYMNASTICS: see Athletics as
　subheading under names of specific
　universities and colleges
GYRN CASTLE, Flintshire, Wales: 366

## H

H. C. HAMILTON AND COMPANY, North
 Carolina (firm): 2277
H. F. BYRD AND T. B. BYRD
 INCORPORATED: 5779
HAARDT, Sara Powell: 2398
HABEAS CORPUS:
 see also CIVIL WAR--CIVIL RIGHTS--
  Suspension of habeas corpus
 Great Britain: 5616
HABERSHAM, James (1712-1775): 2238,
 5699
HABERSHAM, James, Jr.: 2238
HABERSHAM, John (1754-1799): 2238,
 2666, 2778, 3536, 5604
HABERSHAM, Joseph: 2238, 3671
HABERSHAM, Robert: 1365
HABERSHAM FAMILY (Georgia): 365,
 2238, 3396
HACKETT, Caroline Louisa (Gordon):
 2239
HACKETT, James Gordon: 2239
HACKETT, John (North or South
 Carolina): 2328
HACKETT, John C. (North Carolina):
 2240
HACKETT, Mary (Grimes): 2239
HACKETT, Sarah: 2328
HACKETT FAMILY (North Carolina):
 2240
 Genealogy: 2239
HACKLEY, Robert J.: 2241
HACKNEY (JOSEPH) AND COMPANY: 2242
HACKWOOD, England: 1343
"HACKWOOD," Virginia--Maps: 5779
HADDAM, Connecticut: 2684
HADENSVILLE, Virginia: 1587
HADERMAN, M. J.: 5160
HADERMAN, M. T.: 2243
HADLEY, Arthur Twining: 2871
HADLEY FAMILY (North Carolina and
 Pennsylvania): 5264
HADLY, Mary E.: 2244
HADOW, Sir William Henry: 2245
HAGEDORN, Hermann (1882-1964): 1424
HAGEDORN, Hermann Anton Conrad: 2246
HAGERMAND, Herbert J.: 960
HAGERSTOWN, Maryland: 136, 292,
 1958, 2283, 3212, 3378
 Aircraft companies: 3086
 Banking: 389
 Civil War: 3654
  see also CIVIL WAR--CAMPAIGNS,
   BATTLES, AND MILITARY ACTIONS--
   Maryland--Hagerstown
 Fairs and exhibitions: 5866
 Lawyers' accounts: 5981
 Mercantile accounts: 161
 Schools:
  Girls' schools and academies:
   489
  Students and student life: 5664
 Trade with Philadelphia: 1117
 Universities and colleges: see
  COLLEGE OF ST. JAMES
HAGERSTOWN ACADEMY, Hagerstown,
 Maryland:
 Students and student life: 5664

HAGERSTOWN FEMALE SEMINARY,
 Hagerstown, Maryland: 489
HAGERSTOWN MANUFACTURING, MINING
 AND LAND IMPROVEMENT COMPANY: 5779
HAGNER, Peter: 616
HAGOOD, Johnson: 1825, 2744, 5092
THE HAGUE, Netherlands: 1641
HAGUE PEACE CONFERENCE (1899): 1792
HAGY, Henry Lamartine: 4562
HAHN, Emily: 4956
HAIG, George: 5575
HAIG, H. M.: 1929
HAIG, Mary Maham: 3801
HAILE, Robert G.: 2247
HAILEY, Sir William Malcolm: 2756
HAIN AND HIESTER (firm): see
 HIESTER AND HAIN
HAINES, Hiram: 2248
HAINES FAMILY (North Carolina--
 Genealogy): 2248
HAINES & COOPER (firm): see COOPER &
 HAINES
HAIRSTON, Robert: 4139
HAITI: 1424, 5726
 see also SAINT DOMINGUE
 Currency: 1339
 Description and travel: 4275
 Immigration and emigration:
  To the United States: 4409
 Minerals: 4275
 Negroes--Colonization: 2408
 Slave trade: 4980
 United States Secret Service in:
  4275
HAITIAN BUREAU OF EMIGRATION,
 Boston, Massachusetts: 4409
HAKKAS (Chinese tribe): 1940
HALBERT, H. S.: 2249
HALBERTON, John W.: 2250
HALCYON LITERARY CLUB: 2251
HALDANE, Charles: 2871
HALDANE, Richard Burdon, First
 Viscount Haldane: 1815, 2149, 2245,
 3980, 5806
HALDERMAN, John A.: 2252
HALDON, Lawrence William Palk, Third
 Baron: 345
HALE, Edward Everett: 103
HALE, Edward Joseph: 2253
HALE, James: 103
HALE, Jeffery: 3911
HALE, Ralph Tracy: 1424
HALE, William Bayard: 2790
HALE, William Thomas: 2449
HALE COUNTY, Alabama:
 Greensboro: 546, 5862
  Girls' schools and academies:
   5593
  Law practice: 5593
HALE'S FORD, Virginia: 2633
 United States Post Office: 2593
HALFORD, Sir Henry: 2836
HALIFAX, Charles Wood, First
 Viscount: 5875
HALIFAX, England:
 Local government: 5026
HALIFAX, North Carolina: 1363, 1389,
 3256
HALIFAX, Nova Scotia: 1890
 Description: 1790
HALIFAX, Virginia: 1626
HALIFAX COUNTY, North Carolina: 1986,
 2101, 2926, 3886, 4267, 5674
 Churches: 796
 Cotton growing: 5280
 Cotton trade: 5280
 Debt: 5672
 Estates:
  Administration and settlement:
   5672
 Farm life: 3831
 Land--Prices: 5672
 Land deeds and indentures: 5707
 Promissory notes: 5674
 Slave trade: 5672
 Teaching: 3831
 Trade and commerce: 2381
 Wills: 5280, 5672

HALIFAX COUNTY, North Carolina
 (Continued):
 Cities and towns:
  Bricks--Negro schools: 2753
  Camp Leventhrop: 860
  Enfield: 426, 631, 760, 5664, 5701
  Halifax: 1363, 1389, 3256
  Littleton: 2399, 3831, 5280
  Ringwood: 711
  Scotland Neck: 4925
  Weldon: 288, 1055, 4204
HALIFAX COUNTY, Nova Scotia: 3381
HALIFAX COUNTY, Virginia:
 1700s-1800s: 330, 5005
 1800s: 1402, 2524, 2584, 2621,
  3377, 5827
 1800s-1900s: 2732
 Estates:
  Administration and settlement:
   5229
 Land deeds and indentures: 5229
 Property evaluation: 5483
 Social life and customs: 3906
 Taxation: 5483
 Tobacco trade: 2680
 Cities and towns:
  Banister: 5483
  Clover Depot: 2331
  Denniston: 2712
  Halifax: 1626
  Halifax Court House: see
   HALIFAX COURT HOUSE, Virginia
  Republican Grove: 2685
  Whitlock: 3906
HALIFAX COURT HOUSE, Virginia: 1250
 Business affairs: 822
 Civil War: 5769
 Clergy: 1565
HALL, Charles: 2254
HALL, Clement: 5457
HALL, Daniel Kirke: 2255
HALL, Dawn Pepita Langley-: 4823
HALL, Edward: 2256
HALL, Eleanor: 1542
HALL, Enoch: 5457
HALL, Fenton: 607
HALL, George: 4946
HALL, Gordon Langley: 4823
HALL, Harriet: 2267
HALL, Henry C.: 2257
HALL, J. W.: 2264
HALL, James (1744-1826): 5457
HALL, James Frederick: 2258
HALL, Jane: 2269
HALL, Jessica Dalziel: 2269
HALL, John (Great Britain): 2259
HALL, John (Maryland): 2267
HALL, Joseph W.: 2260
HALL, Libbie: 2261
HALL, Lyman: 2262, 5537
HALL, Maggie T. (Sprunt): 2269
HALL, Mary (Osborne): 2262
HALL, Samuel Carter: 2263
HALL, Susan Eliza: 2269
HALL, Thomas (Maryland): 4946
HALL, Thomas H. (North Carolina,
 1773-1853): 2256
HALL, Thomas L. (Illinois): 2264
HALL, Thomas William (Maryland): 2265
HALL, Townsend Monckton: 2266
HALL, William Henry (Maryland): 2267
HALL, William Hunt (Confederate
 soldier): 2268
HALL FAMILY (Georgia): 2372
HALL FAMILY (North Carolina): 2269
"THE HALL," Penybont, Wales: 1002
HALL AND DICKINSON (firm): see
 DICKINSON AND HALL
HALL AND FLETCHER (firm): see
 FLETCHER AND HALL
HALL BARN PARK, England: 4005
HALL COUNTY, Georgia:
 Gainesville: 3262
HALLECK, Henry Wager: 2270, 2865,
 5668
HALLETT, Benjamin Franklin: 988
HALLOCK, H. G. C.: 2449

HALLOWELL, Maine: 5569
HALPINE, Charles Graham: 4751
HALSBURY, Hardinge Stanley Giffard, First Earl of: 1815
HALSEY, John J.: 2792
HALSEY, Stephen P.: 1364
HALSEY, Thomas Lloyd: 2271
HALSHAM, John (pseudonym): see SCOTT, G. Forrester
HAMBLEN COUNTY, Tennessee: Whitesburg: 1819
HAMBURG, Germany: 5298
   Merchants: 258
HAMBURG, South Carolina: 430, 669
   Race riots during Reconstruction: 1220
HAMBURGER, Louis: 2272
HAMERSLEY, William: 2273
HAMERSLEY, William James: 2273
HAMILL, G. C.: 1436, 2274
HAMILL, George Ashman: 2275
HAMILL, William Cromwell: 2275
HAMILTON, Alexander: 2276, 3384, 4218
   Portrait: 42
HAMILTON, Andrew Jackson (1815-1875): 4170
HAMILTON, Lord Claud: 3238
HAMILTON, Sir Edward: 3715
HAMILTON, Everard: 2280
HAMILTON, Lord George Francis: 5024
HAMILTON (H. C.) AND COMPANY: 2277
HAMILTON, Hariot Georgina: 515
HAMILTON, James (South Carolina, 1786-1857): 2278, 4163
HAMILTON, James (Pennsylvania, 1819-1878): 1242
HAMILTON, John (Virginia): 2551
HAMILTON, John Andrew, First Viscount Sumner: 2279
HAMILTON, John C.: 1563
HAMILTON, John F. (Georgia): 2280
HAMILTON, John Judson: 103
HAMILTON, Joseph Grégoire de Roulhac: 2589
HAMILTON, Marmaduke: 2280
HAMILTON, Nicholas: 3715
HAMILTON, Paul (1762-1816): 2281, 4399
HAMILTON, Schuyler: 2514
HAMILTON, Thomas Napier: 5936
HAMILTON, William Baskerville: 2282
HAMILTON, William H. A.: 2283
HAMILTON FAMILY: 761
HAMILTON FAMILY (South Carolina--Genealogy): 1468
HAMILTON, New York: 701
HAMILTON, North Carolina: 435, 707
   Physicians' accounts: 5600
   Schools: 1411
HAMILTON, Ohio: 4076
HAMILTON, Virginia: 5607
HAMILTON COUNTY, Indiana: Westfield: 4202
HAMILTON COUNTY, Ohio:
   Cincinnati: see CINCINNATI, Ohio
   Madisonville: 5030
   Springdale: 4160
HAMILTON COUNTY, Tennessee:
   Chattanooga: see CHATTANOOGA, Tennessee
HAMILTON-TEMPLE-BLACKWOOD, Frederick Temple, First Marquis of Dufferin and Ava: see BLACKWOOD, Frederick Temple Hamilton-Temple-, First Marquis of Dufferin and Ava
HAMILTON-TEMPLE-BLACKWOOD, Hariot Georgina (Hamilton), Marchioness of Dufferin and Ava: see BLACKWOOD, Hariot Georgina (Hamilton) Hamilton-Temple-, Marchioness of Dufferin and Ava
HAMILTON TOWNSHIP, North Carolina:
   Tax lists: 2284, 3935
"HAMLET" (drawing): 4575
HAMLET by William Shakespeare: 103
HAMLIN, Hannibal: 2285
HAMLIN, William E.: 5009
HAMM, James S.: 490, 3611

HAMM, John Henry: 2286
HAMM FAMILY (North Carolina): 2286
HAMMER, Nathaniel A.: 2287
HAMMER AND TONGS: 4947, 4948
HAMMET, Benjamin: 2289
HAMMET, J. B. N.: 2288
HAMMET, William: 2289
HAMMON, Reuben E.: 4483
HAMMOND, Dawson V.: 2295
HAMMOND Edmund: 3183
HAMMOND, Ezra: 2294
HAMMOND, James Henry: 791, 1466, 2290, 5361
HAMMOND, M. (North Carolina): 2895
HAMMOND, Marcus Claudius Marcellus: 2290, 2291
HAMMOND, Nathan: 2295
HAMMOND, Samuel (Georgia, 1757-1842): 2293, 4982
HAMMOND, Samuel (North Carolina): 2294
HAMMOND, Thomas: 2295
HAMMOND, Vachel: 2295
HAMMOND FAMILY (Maryland): 2295
HAMMONDSPORT, New York: 5974
HAMOND, Sir Andrew Snape, First Baronet: 2296
HAMOND, Sir Graham Eden: 2296
HAMOND, Richard: 1214
HAMPDEN, Connecticut: 5172
HAMPDEN COUNTY, Massachusetts:
   Chicopee: 106, 4037
   Springfield: 5043
   West Springfield: 5042
HAMPDEN-SYDNEY, Virginia: 3740
   see also HAMPDEN-SYDNEY COLLEGE
HAMPDEN-SYDNEY COLLEGE, Hampden-Sydney, Virginia: 643, 2934, 3552, 5110
   see also HAMPDEN-SYDNEY INSTITUTE
   Students and student life: 3136, 3566, 3740, 4040, 4373
HAMPDEN-SYDNEY INSTITUTE, Farmville, Virginia: 2712
HAMPSHIRE, England:
   Church of England: 1035
   Elections (1759): 736
   Cities and towns:
      Alverstoke: 3744
      Blackmoor: 4036
      Borough Court: 2750
      Hackwood: 1343
      Hursley: 2953
      Isle of Wight: see ISLE OF WIGHT
      Lymington: 4655
         Politics and government: 4557
      Oaklands: 3835
      Portsea: 485
      Ringwood: 3286
      Winchester: 3477
HAMPSHIRE COUNTY, Massachusetts:
   Justices of the peace: 3034
   Militia: 3034
   Cities and towns:
      Amherst: 5971
      Northampton: 826, 1054, 1058
      Pelham: 3034
      Williamsburg: 2532
HAMPSHIRE COUNTY, West Virginia: 1784
   Tax lists: 3721
   Cities and towns:
      Capon Bridge: 1238, 3721
         Mercantile accounts: 2652
      Hook's Mills: 2634
      Romney: 3064, 5215
         Banks and banking: 312
         Civil War: see CIVIL WAR--CAMPAIGNS, BATTLES, AND MILITARY ACTIONS--West Virginia--Romney
HAMPSHIRE RECORD SOCIETY (Great Britain): 2148
HAMPTON, Caleb: 2297
HAMPTON, David: 2297
HAMPTON, E. D.: 2298
HAMPTON, Frank Armfield: 2299
HAMPTON, John (Confederate soldier): 2297
HAMPTON, John (South Carolina): 2300

HAMPTON, John Somerset Pakington, First Baron: 1087, 4026
HAMPTON, Mary Singleton (McDuffie): 3367
HAMPTON, Richard: 2059
HAMPTON, Wade (1752-1835): 2300, 2931
HAMPTON, Wade (1818-1902): 484, 581, 1227, 1364, 1403, 1972, 2300, 2849, 2854, 4129, 4451, 5757
   Death of: 3048
   Views on the state debt of South Carolina: 3405
HAMPTON, Arkansas--Freedmen: 4199
HAMPTON, Virginia: 569
   see also CIVIL WAR--CAMPAIGNS, BATTLES, AND MILITARY ACTIONS--Virginia--Hampton
HAMPTON COTTON MILLS: 5312
HAMPTON COUNTY, Indiana:
   Commodity prices: 4202
HAMPTON COUNTY, South Carolina:
   Land deeds and indentures: 5759
   Public finance: 5759
   Cities and towns:
      "Bonnywood": 5278
      Brunson: 4534, 5759
HAMPTON COUNTY, Virginia:
   Fortress Monroe: see FORTRESS MONROE, Virginia
HAMPTON HOSPITAL, Virginia: 1983
"HAMPTON PLANTATION," South Carolina: 4619
HAMPTON ROADS PEACE CONFERENCE: 2943
HAMPTON SOCIAL CLUB (South Carolina): 2040
HAMPTON'S LEGION: see CONFEDERATE STATES OF AMERICA--ARMY--Units--South Carolina--Hampton's Legion
HAMPTONVILLE, North Carolina: 2452, 3540
HAMTRAMCK, John Francis (d. 1803): 2301
HAMTRAMCK, John Francis (1798-1858): 1047, 2301
HAMTRAMCK, Mary R.: 2301
HAMTRAMCK, Sarah E. (Selby): 2301
HAMTRANCK: see HAMTRAMCK
HAN RIVER (China): 2191
HANCOCK, Ammon G.: 2302
HANCOCK, Asenath Ellen (Cox): 2303
HANCOCK, B. A.: 3674
HANCOCK, George: 2633
HANCOCK, John (1736-1793): 1236, 2304
HANCOCK, O. Victor: 2305
HANCOCK, R. C.: 519
HANCOCK, Torry: 2304
HANCOCK, Winfield Scott: 1346, 2306, 3789
HANCOCK FAMILY (North Carolina): 2303
HANCOCK, Maryland: 643
HANCOCK COUNTY, Georgia:
   Cotton trade: 4493
   Courts: 4493
   Estates:
      Administration and settlement: 4493
   Cities and towns:
      Sparta: 239, 686, 1297, 2367, 5565
         Clergy--Baptist: 4654
         Legal affairs: 5250
         Plantations: 4493
         Social conditions (1870): 3134
HANCOCK COUNTY, Kentucky: 3199
HANCOCK COUNTY, Maine:
   Castine: 5860
   Eden: 3880
HAND (W. L.) MEDICINE COMPANY, North Carolina: 4918
A HANDBOOK OF COOKERY FOR A SMALL HOUSE by Jessie Conrad: 1210
HANDLEY, George: 2307
HANDWRITING: see CALLIGRAPHY; PENMANSHIP
HANDY, Frank A.: 2308
HANDY (N. B.) COMPANY, Lynchburg, Virginia: 2309
HANES, Harrison H.: 2310

HANGER, George: 4151
"THE HANGING OF THE CRANE" by Henry
    Wadsworth Longfellow: 3259
HANGINGS: 689
    see also EXECUTIONS
HANKIN, Lewis: 536
HANKOW-PEKING RAILROAD, China: 2191
HANKS, Constant C.: 2311
HANLEITER, Cornelius R.: 2312
HANMER, Daniel: 5457
HANNA, Marcus Alonzo: 2313
HANNAH, Samuel: 331
HANNAH FAMILY (Virginia): 331
HANNER FAMILY (North Carolina): 2314
HANNIBAL, Jack: 2315
HANNIBAL, Missouri: 1099, 2076, 2162
    Law practice: 4616
HANNIS (HENRY S.) AND COMPANY,
    Hannisville, West Virginia: 2316,
    4056
HANNIS DISTILLING COMPANY,
    Martinsburg, West Virginia: 3832
HANNISVILLE, West Virginia: 2316,
    4056
HANOVER, Germany: 2973
HANOVER, New Hampshire: see
    DARTMOUTH COLLEGE
HANOVER ACADEMY, Taylorsville,
    Virginia: 298, 4698
HANOVER CIRCUIT, Methodist Episcopal
    Church: 3601
HANOVER COUNTY, North Carolina:
    Taxation: 5709
HANOVER COUNTY, Virginia: 456, 634,
    2495, 4698, 5309, 5476, 5619
    Debt: 1824
    Farming: 4020
    Household finance: 4020
    Land deeds and indentures: 1824
    Landlord and tenant: 4020
    Plantation: 4776
    Temperance: 1115
    Cities and towns:
        Gaines' Mill: 2143
            see also CIVIL WAR--CAMPAIGNS,
                BATTLES, AND MILITARY
                ACTIONS--Virginia--Gaines'
                Mill
        Hanover Court House: see HANOVER
            COURT HOUSE, Virginia
        Taylorsville:
            Schools: 4698
HANOVER COURT HOUSE, Virginia: 3242
    see also CIVIL WAR--CAMPAIGNS,
        BATTLES, AND MILITARY ACTIONS--
        Virginia--Hanover Court House
HANOVER PROGRESS (newspaper): 4020
HANSELL, A. J.: 1773
HANSELL, Augustin Harris: 2317
HANSELL FAMILY (Georgia): 2372
HANSELL & HARRIS (firm): 2372
HANSEN, Albert: 361
HANSFORD, William Richard: 2318
HANSON, Alexander Contee: 2319, 4457
HANWORTH, England: 1541
HAPGOOD, Norman: 706
THE HAPPINESS OF STATES by Simon
    Grey: 2148
HARALSON, W. A.: 2326
HARBER, C. E.: 5252
HARBERT, Samuel C.: 5425
HARBISON, John W.: 2320
HARBORS:
    Construction:
        Ireland: 3883
        South Carolina--Beaufort: 1927
    Improvement:
        Ireland--Dublin: 5330
        Mississippi--Pascagoula: 5425
        North Carolina: 274
        United States: 4858
    Inspections:
        Georgia--Savannah: 4678
    Laws and legislation:
        United States: 4858
    Port charges:
        North Carolina--Bath: 705

HARBORS (Continued):
    Surveys:
        Japan: 5190
    Subdivided by place:
        China: 4017
        Great Britain--Mounts Bay: 3080
        Japan: 4017
        North Carolina:
            Wilmington: 3230, 3922, 4858
        Philippine Islands: 4017
            Manila: 4656
        West Indies: 3753
HARCOURT, George Simon, Second Earl
    Harcourt: 4543
HARCOURT, George William Richard:
    2321
HARCOURT, Simon, First Earl
    Harcourt: 5330
HARCOURT, Sir William: 1815
HARCOURT, Sir William George
    Granville Venables Vernon-: 2322
HARDAWAY, James H.: 2323
HARDAWAY, Lonnie: 5401
HARDCASTLE, Edward: 2324
HARDEE, K. L.: 318
HARDEE, William Joseph (1815-1873):
    395, 1186, 2140, 2325, 4884
HARDEN, Dr. _____ (president of
    Jackson College, Tennessee): 3611
HARDEN, Ann: 2328
HARDEN, Anna: 2326
HARDEN, Edward (1784-1849): 2326
HARDEN, Edward Jenkins (Georgia):
    2327
HARDEN, Edward Randolph (1815-1884):
    2326
HARDEN, Henrietta Jane: 2326
HARDEN, John: 2328
HARDEN, Mary: 2328
HARDEN, Mary Ann Elizabeth Randolph
    (1794-1874): 2326
HARDEN, Mary Elizabeth Greenhill
    (1811-1887): 2326
HARDEN, Matilda A.: 2327
HARDEN, Sarah P.: 2328
HARDEN, William (South Carolina, fl.
    1781): 3511
HARDEN, William (Georgia, 1844-1936):
    103
HARDEN FAMILY (Georgia): 2326
HARDESTY, William G.: 2329
HARDIN, William D.: 2330
HARDIN COUNTY, Iowa:
    Eldora: 4158
HARDIN COUNTY, Ohio: 3751
HARDING, Chester: 4339
HARDING (E. AND J.) (firm): 2331
HARDING, E. Paul: 1202
HARDING, Ezekiah: 2331
HARDING, James: 4188
HARDING, Warren Gamaliel: 592
HARDINGE, Henry, First Viscount
    Hardinge: 816
HARDMAN, W. A.: 3640
HARDWARE STORES:
    Apprenticeship:
        Pennsylvania--Philadelphia: 5686
    Clerks:
        New York--Niagara: 3848
    Management:
        Pennsylvania--Philadelphia: 5686
HARDWARE TRADE:
    Michigan: 5489
    Mississippi: 2888
    New York: 1390
        Niagara: 3848
    North Carolina: 3416
    Ohio: 4728
HARDWICK, W. H.: 519
HARDWICK, Massachusetts: 4970
HARDWICKE, G. W.: 2065
HARDWICKE, Thomas: 3577
HARDY, A. J.: 2332
HARDY, Gathorne Gathorne-, First
    Earl of Cranbrook: see GATHORNE-
    HARDY, Gathorne, First Earl of
    Cranbrook
HARDY, Haywood: 2333

HARDY, Samuel: 3130
HARDY, Thomas (1840-1928): 2334
HARDY, W. D.: 2333
HARDY, William E.: 2335
HARDY COUNTY, West Virginia:
    Lost River: 5467
    Moorefield: 5371
    Civil War: 2958
    Wardensville:
        Tannery records: 146
HAREWOOD, Henry Lascelles, Second
    Earl of: 1648, 5026
HARFORD COUNTY, Maryland:
    Estates (Legal):
        Administration and settlement:
            4537
    Land deeds and indentures: 4537
    Tavern accounts: 5128
    Cities and towns:
        Belair: 4712
        Havre de Grace: 3026, 4468
        "Sion Hill": 4537
HARGADINE, Annie L.: 2336
HARGADINE, Robert W.: 2336
HARGRAVE, J. H.: 2337
HARGROVE, Elizabeth R.: 2338
HARGROVE, Israel W.: 2339
HARGROVE, Marcellus M.: 2340
HARLAN, James (1820-1899): 2341
HARLAN FAMILY (Maryland): 5128
HARLAND, Marion (pseudonym): see
    TERHUNE, Mary Virginia (Hawes)
HARLEY, Fannie Maud (Holgate): 2591
HARLEY, Thomas J.: 2342
HARLLEE, William W.: 2343
HARLOW, Virginia: 2344
HARMAN, Henry Elliott: 2449
HARMAN, Ohio: 434
HARMON, Carrie: 1033
HARMON, George W.: 2345
HARMON, Judson: 1171
HARMON, Z. E.: 3991
HARMONY, North Carolina:
    Churches: 2347
HARMONY--Rules: 108
HARMONY COUNCIL TEMPERANCE REFORM:
    2346
HARMONY HOLINESS CHURCH: 2347
HARMONY MALE AND FEMALE ACADEMY,
    South Carolina: 5082
HARMSWORTH, Alfred Charles William,
    First Viscount Northcliffe: 441,
    3265
HARNED, Thomas Biggs: 2348
HARNESS TRADE: 3572
    North Carolina: 4540
HARNETT COUNTY, North Carolina: 2357,
    4225
    Economic conditions: 238
    Taxation: 4761
    Cities and towns:
        Lillington: 238, 3206
        Westville: 4761
HARNETT TOWNSHIP, North Carolina:
    Voter registration: 3410
HARPER, Benjamin J.: 2349
HARPER, Francis: 2350
HARPER, James (1795-1869): 2351
HARPER, John: 5123
HARPER, Joseph Wesley (1801-1870):
    1227, 2449
HARPER, Julia A. (Thorne): 2351
HARPER, Mary T.: 2349
HARPER, Robert Goodloe: 2352, 2931
HARPER, William (1790-1847): 2612
HARPER AND BROTHERS (firm): 1878,
    2146, 2351, 2364, 2545, 4491,
    5159
HARPER BROS. (firm): 706
HARPER'S (1847): 5149
HARPERS FERRY, West Virginia: 968,
    1709, 2171
    Arsenal: 2696, 3771
        see also JOHN BROWN'S RAID
    Civil War: 3654, 4537
        see also CIVIL WAR--CAMPAIGNS,
            BATTLES, AND MILITARY ACTIONS--
            West Virginia--Harpers Ferry

HARPERS FERRY, West Virginia:
  Civil War (Continued):
    Hospitals: 1564
    United States Army camp: 1817
    Quartermaster Corps: 4029
  Description: 2601
  Flood relief: 5938
  Flour mills: 5938
  Merchants: 3058
  Railroad construction: 721
  Settlement: 99
  Tobacco trade: 5938
HARPERS FERRY AND WINCHESTER RAILROAD: 546
HARPER'S ENCYCLOPEDIA OF UNITED STATES HISTORY: 3967
HARPER'S MAGAZINE: 2845, 4556
HARPER'S WEEKLY: 706
HARRELL, Costen Jordan: 2353
HARRELLSVILLE, North Carolina: 1316
HARRIETT'S CHAPEL, North Carolina: 484
HARRIMAN, Tennessee: 1630
HARRINGTON, Elias B.: 2354
HARRINGTON, G. W.: 2355
HARRINGTON, Isaac: 2356
HARRINGTON, John McLean: 2357
HARRINGTON, John Stephens: 2357
HARRINGTON, Leicester Fitzgerald Charles Stanhope, Fifth Earl of: 2421
HARRINGTON, Purnell Frederick: 2066
HARRINGTON, S.C.: 2358
HARRINGTON, Thomas F.: 5834
HARRINGTON, William Stanhope, First Earl of: 2155
HARRINGTON FAMILY (North Carolina): 2357
HARRINGTON, North Carolina: 1181
HARRIS, Ada A.: 2370
HARRIS, Amanda: 872
HARRIS, Benjamin Franklin (North Carolina): 2359
HARRIS, Benjamin James (Virginia): 2360
HARRIS, Charles J. (Georgia, 1834-1892): 2362
HARRIS, Charles J. (New York): 2361
HARRIS, Charles Wilson (1771-1804): 5457
HARRIS, D. M.: 2370
HARRIS, David (Texas): 3772
HARRIS, David Bullock (Virginia, 1814-1864): 2363, 4127
HARRIS, E. H.: 637
HARRIS, Mrs. E. L.: 2364
HARRIS, E. M. (Georgia): 2365
HARRIS, Edward (d. 1813): 5457
HARRIS, Elizabeth A. F.: 2366
HARRIS, Elizabeth Baldwin (Wiley): 2367
HARRIS, Evalina M.: 2370
HARRIS, Fisher Sanford: 2368
HARRIS, Frank (1856-1931): 2146
HARRIS, Frederick (member, Virginia House of Delegates): 2363
HARRIS, Frederick A. (Campbell County, Virginia, farmer): 2369
HARRIS, George (1722-1796): 5639
HARRIS, Hannibal: 2369
HARRIS, Henry St. George: 2370
HARRIS, Ira: 5627
HARRIS, Isaac R.: 5928
HARRIS, Isham Green: 395, 2371, 4358
HARRIS, Iverson Louis: 2372
HARRIS, James (Virginia): 2373
HARRIS, James B.: 3692
HARRIS, James Edward, Second Earl of Malmesbury: 1755
HARRIS, Joel Chandler: 361, 2374
HARRIS, John D. (North Carolina): 2375
HARRIS, John Thomas: 523
HARRIS, John Y. (Virginia): 2376
HARRIS, Josiah: 2377
HARRIS, Julia A. Mildred: 3611
HARRIS, Julia C.: 2374
HARRIS, Julian LaRose: 2449
HARRIS, Levi: 2378

HARRIS, Mary C. (Wiley): 2362
HARRIS, Mary W.: 2370
HARRIS, N. W.: 2363
HARRIS, Ray Baker: 4559
HARRIS, Raymond: 5606
HARRIS, Richard: 2380
HARRIS, T. D.: 2382
HARRIS, Thomas W.: 2381
HARRIS, W. R.: 5252
HARRIS, William (Alabama): 2370
HARRIS, William (North Carolina): 131
HARRIS, William R.: 2940
HARRIS, William Torrey (1835-1909): 2224
HARRIS FAMILY (Georgia): 2372
HARRIS FAMILY (North Carolina): 2379
  Genealogy: 4242
HARRIS FAMILY (South Carolina or Tennessee): 718
HARRIS & HANSELL (firm): see HANSELL & HARRIS
HARRIS CHAIR COMPANY, Millboro, North Carolina: 2382
HARRIS COUNTY, Georgia: 4849
HARRIS COUNTY, Texas:
  New Washington: 3772
HARRIS' DEPOT, North Carolina: 5582
HARRISBURG, Pennsylvania: 2027, 2731, 2989, 3231, 3547, 3686, 4576
  Description (1862): 4690
  State legislature: 4188
HARRISBURG INSURRECTION (1838): see BUCKSHOT WAR
HARRISON, Professor _____ (University of Virginia): 267
HARRISON, Agnes: 2387
HARRISON, Benjamin (Virginia, 1726-1791): 2383
HARRISON, Benjamin (Virginia, fl. 1807-1809): 2577
HARRISON, Benjamin (1833-1901): 2384, 5324
  Inauguration: 2384
HARRISON, Burton Norvell: 1403
HARRISON, Carter Henry (1825-1893): 2449
HARRISON, Caskie: 2449
HARRISON, Charles L.: 2385
HARRISON, Constance (Cary): 1424
HARRISON, Dabney Carr: 743
HARRISON, Edwin: 2386
HARRISON, Frederic: 2471
HARRISON, George B. (Virginia): 2387
HARRISON, George Paul (Georgia): 2388
HARRISON, Georgia: 2374
HARRISON, Gessner: 2426
HARRISON, Henry (West Virginia): 2387, 2389
HARRISON, Henry Sydnor (1880-1930): 2390
HARRISON (J. & P.) (firm): 2392
HARRISON, James (Missouri, 1803-1870): 2386
HARRISON, James (West Virginia): 2397
HARRISON, James Albert (1848-1911): 2449
HARRISON, James H. (North Carolina): 2391
HARRISON, James P. (Georgia): 2374
HARRISON, James P. (Virginia): 2392
HARRISON, James Thomas (Mississippi, 1811-1879): 2393
HARRISON, Jesse: 2394
HARRISON, John W.: 2395
HARRISON, Leland: 1424
HARRISON, Louisa Virginia: 2589
HARRISON, Maria: 2387
HARRISON (P.) & CO. (firm): 2392
HARRISON, Pamelia: 5704
HARRISON, Peyton: 743
HARRISON, Robert Lewis: 103
HARRISON, Sallie (Tarry): 761
HARRISON, Samuel: 2397
HARRISON, Thomas Perrin: 706
HARRISON, William F. (Confederate soldier, Virginia): 2396
HARRISON, William Henry (1773-1841): 3366, 3853, 5491
  Death: 2678, 3631

HARRISON FAMILY: 1556
HARRISON FAMILY (Virginia--Genealogy): 2387, 3809
HARRISON FAMILY (West Virginia--Genealogy): 2397
HARRISON COUNTY, Indiana: 3199
  Corydon: 1548
HARRISON COUNTY, Mississippi:
  Beauvoir: 1403
  Biloxi: 5712
HARRISON COUNTY, Texas: 4154
HARRISON COUNTY, Virginia:
  West Milford: 5946
HARRISON COUNTY, West Virginia: 207
  Clarksburg: 851, 2395, 2447
  Land deeds and indentures: 4563
HARRISONBURG, Virginia: 899, 2498, 2911, 5581
  Courtship: 3060
HARRISS, Elias: 2399
HARRISS, I.: 2399
HARRISS, Robert Preston: 2398
HARRISS, Thomas: 2399
HARRISS, Thomas Whitmel (1795-1870): 2399
HARRISS, William H.: 2399
HARRISS FAMILY (Mississippi and Tennessee): 2399
HARRISVILLE, Texas:
  Social conditions: 4283
  Teaching: 4283
HARROD, James (1742-1793): 5768
HARROW SCHOOL, Harrow, England: 4770
HARROWBY, Dudley Ryder, Second Earl of: 1087
HARROWGATE, Tennessee: see LINCOLN UNIVERSITY
HARROWS--Maryland: 5193
"HARRY MARSHALL OF VIRGINIA" by Frederic L. Davis: 1398
HART, Albert Bushnell: 706, 2400
HART, Charles: 582
HART, Eugenia M.: 2930
HART, Henry George: 2401
HART, James David: 102
HART, Oliver: 2402
HART, Sallie Cushing: 5031
HART, Samuel: 2699
HART, Thomas: 5457
HART, William: 2403
HART FAMILY (Great Britain and Australia--Genealogy): 286
HART COUNTY, Kentucky:
  Munfordville: 751
HARTE, Bret: 4486
HARTFORD, Connecticut: 1169, 2273, 2816, 4752, 4815, 5351, 5636
  Adjutant General's office: 2547
  Education: 5593
  Manufacture of machine guns: 1979
"HARTFORD," North Carolina (Loyalist estate): 1890
HARTFORD COUNTY, Connecticut: 5623
  Courts: 5871
  Farming: 1051
  Cities and towns:
    Broad Brook: 350
    Farmington: 2636
    Hartford: see HARTFORD, Connecticut
    Thompsonville:
      Ship building: 1549
HARTFORD EVENING PRESS: 5636
HARTFORD TIMES: 5636
HARTLETON, Pennsylvania: 4920
HARTLEY, Matthew: 2404
HARTMAN, Jefferson: 2405
HARTMAN, John H.: 2406
HARTMAN, Samuel P.: 2405
HART'S ARMY LIST by Henry George Hart: 2401
HARTSOOK, D. J.: 523
HARTT, Charles Frederic: 2407
HARTT, Jessie Clark (Knight): 2407
HARTT, Lucy C. (Lynde): 2407
HARTT, Mary Bronson: 2407
HARTT, Rollin Lynde: 2407
HARTZ, Edward L.: 2408

HARVARD COLLEGE, Cambridge,
  Massachusetts: see HARVARD
  UNIVERSITY
HARVARD GUIDE TO AMERICAN HISTORY: 706
HARVARD UNIVERSITY, Cambridge,
  Massachusetts: 3598, 4429
  Class of 1841: 3701
  Curriculum: 2044
  Faculty: 3284, 4012
  Law School: 4813
    Funding for foreign students in
      in international law: 4343
    Moot Court: 2893
  Medical education: 3266
  Southern opinion of: 706
  Students and student life: 2901,
    3266, 5593
HARVESTING: see AGRICULTURAL
  PRACTICES; FARMING
HARVESTING MACHINERY TRADE: 3335
  North Carolina: 2855
HARVESTING MACHINES: 388
  see also REAPING MACHINES
HARVEY, Bissell: 4168
HARVEY, George: 1424
HARVEY, George Brinton McClellan:
  2409
HARVEY, Glen: 2410
HARVEY, James E.: 2411
HARVEY, Jonathan: 2412
HARVEY, Rosa: 2410
HARVEY, Thomas: 5457
HARVEY, William Clifton: 2413
HARVIE, Lewis E.: 1183
HARVIE, S. Rutherfoord: 5773
HARVIE FAMILY (Genealogy): 1303
HARVIN, M. A.: 2414
HARWINTON, Connecticut: 941
HARWOOD, William J.: 2415
HARWOOD MANUFACTURING CORPORATION:
  2769
HASENCLEVER, Peter: 4399
HASKELL, Alexander Cheves: 4145
HASKELL, John Cheves: 2416
HASKELL, Joseph Cheves: 1017, 4212
HASKELL, M. Carrie: 4212
HASKELL, William O.: 2417
HASKELL FAMILY (Massachusetts--
  Genealogy): 2417
HASKINS, John W.: 2418
HASKINS FAMILY (Virginia): 2418
HASLET, James B.: 4920
HASSELL, Cushing Biggs: 486, 2419
HASSELL, James: 5457
HASSELL, Sylvester: 318, 2419
HASTINGS, Eliza: 2420
HASTINGS, Francis Rawdon-, First
  Marquis of Hastings and Second
  Earl of Moira: 2421, 3446
HASTINGS, James A.: 2420
HASTINGS, Selina (Shirley), Countess
  of Huntingdon: 5647
HASTINGS, Thomas W.: 2420
HASTINGS, Warren: 2422
HASTINGS, England:
  Politics and government: 4570
HAT CREEK, Virginia--Funerals: 4043
HATCH, Philo: 2423
HATCHER, Laurence: 208, 2424
HATCHER, Orie Latham: 2425
HATCHER'S RUN, Virginia: see CIVIL
  WAR--CAMPAIGNS, BATTLES, AND
  MILITARY ACTIONS--Virginia--
  Hatcher's Run
HATCHETT, Allen Lillious: 2427
HATCHETT, William Haynie (b. 1817):
  2426
HATCHETT, William Henry
  (1860-ca. 1950): 2427
HATCHETT, William Russell
  (1794-1878): 2427
HATCHETT FAMILY (North Carolina--
  Genealogy): 2427
HATCHETT FAMILY (Virginia--
  Genealogy): 2426, 2427
HATCHIE RIVER, Mississippi: see
  CIVIL WAR--CAMPAIGNS, BATTLES, AND
  MILITARY ACTIONS--Mississippi--
  Hatchie River

HATFIELD FAMILY: 746
HATHAWAY, Thomas D.: 2428
HATHERLEY, William Page Wood, First
  Baron: 5883
HATHERTON, Edward John Littleton,
  First Baron: 3226, 4024
HATS:
  Manufacture and trade:
    West Virginia: 5110
HATTERAS, North Carolina:
  Fishing industry: 4547
  Mercantile accounts: 4547
HATTERAS CIRCUIT, Methodist churches:
  3646
HATTRIDGE, A.: 2933
HATTRIDGE (A.), Wilmington, North
  Carolina (firm): 2933
HAULG, England: 5259
HAUPTMANN, Gerhart Johann Robert:
  103, 3617
HAUSER, T. C.: 2429
HAVAAS, Johan: 2430
HAVANA, Cuba: 258, 3753
  Army camps: 77
  Confederate ships: 4404
  Description: 3983
  Expedition to: 4834
  Merchants: 3008
  Social conditions: 4569
  Trade: 948, 1442
  United States consul in: 3231
HAVEN, John A.: 2431
HAVEN, Louis Alexander Mountbatten,
  First Marquis of Milford-: see
  MILFORD-HAVEN, Louis Alexander
  Mountbatten, First Marquis of
HAVEN, Samuel Foster: 1431
HAVENS, Jonathan, Jr.: 4858
HAVENS & STRONG, New York (firm):
  see STRONG & HAVENS
HAVENS OIL COMPANY, North Carolina:
  4858
HAVERFORD, Pennsylvania: see
  HAVERFORD COLLEGE
HAVERFORD COLLEGE, Haverford,
  Pennsylvania: 1407
HAVERHILL, Massachusetts: 2031, 3741
HAVRE DE GRACE, Maryland: 3026, 4468,
  4537
HAW BRANCH, North Carolina: 5774
HAW RIVER, North Carolina:
  Dry goods trade: 5154
HAW RIVER CIRCUIT, Methodist
  churches: 3646
HAWAII:
  Annexation (proposed): 4462
  Coaling station for the United
    States: 3516
  Description and travel: 2084, 3447
    Photographs: 595
  Treaties--United States: 3516
HAWES, Frances Anne: 5463
HAWES, Mary Virginia: 5227
HAWKE, Martin Bladon, Second Baron
  Hawke: 5913
HAWKINS, Benjamin: 795, 2432, 2486
HAWKINS, Elijah T. D.: 2433
HAWKINS, John: 2434
HAWKINS, Marmaduke J.: 2435
HAWKINS, Rush Christopher: 757
HAWKINS, Tillman: 2433
HAWKINS, W. A.: 4415
HAWKINS COUNTY, Tennessee: 1531,
  1818
  Rogersville: 4291, 4801
HAWKINS COUNTY (Tenn.) BIBLE
  SOCIETY: 4801
HAWKINSTOWN, Virginia: 374, 1920
HAWKINSVILLE, Georgia: 3555
HAWKS, Byron M.: 2436
HAWKS, Francis: 2437
HAWKS, Francis Lister: 2437, 5457
HAWKS, Wells J.: 2792
HAWKS, William E.: 2438
HAWKS, William E., Jr.: 2438
HAWLEY-SMOOT TARIFF: 3190
HAWN, Rhoda: 4161
HAWTHORN FAMILY (Virginia): 2927

HAWTHORNE, Julian: 103, 2449
HAWTHORNE, Nathaniel: 720, 4095,
  4698
HAWTHORNE, Peter W.: 2439
HAWTHORNE, Sophia (Peabody): 4095
HAXALL, Mary: 1424
HAY, John: 4351
HAY, John Milton: 2440
HAY, Philip T.: 2298
HAY, William: 2441
HAY:
  see also FORAGE
  Virginia--Albemarle County: 3699
HAY TRADE:
  Alabama--Macon County: 3837
  Georgia--Augusta: 3749
  North Carolina: 2924
  South Carolina--Charleston: 60
  Virginia--Frederick County: 1
HAYDEN, Harry: 2442
HAYDEN, Horace Edwin: 2443
HAYDEN, Thomas D.: 659
HAYDEN, Mrs. W. R.: 3567
HAYES, Alexander L.: 2444
HAYES, Charles: 2148
HAYES, Elizabeth: 1424
HAYES, J. R.: 2280
HAYES, Kiffin R.: 2445
HAYES, Rutherford Birchard: 1315,
  2446
  Administration: 5142
  Appointment of Democrats: 1972
HAYES, England: 4230
HAYFIELD, Virginia: 1429
HAYLEY (ship): 2304
HAYMOND, Luther: 2447
HAYMOND, Thomas: 2447
HAYMOND, William: 2447
HAYNE, Arthur Peronneau: 791, 872,
  2448
HAYNE, Isaac W.: 4193
HAYNE, Mary Middleton (Michel):
  2449, 5717
HAYNE, Paul Hamilton, Sr.: 2449
HAYNE, Paul Hamilton (1830-1886):
  10, 553, 1494, 2374, 2449, 3418,
  3796, 4829, 5081, 5717
HAYNE, Robert Young: 2449, 2450,
  2776, 3676, 5193, 5217
HAYNE, William Hamilton: 2449, 2451
HAYNES, Frank W.: 2452
HAYNES, Joseph N.: 2453
HAYNES, Raleigh Rutherford: 5457
HAYNESVILLE, Georgia:
  Civil War: 1739
HAYS, Bertrand E.: 2454
HAYS, John Willis: 2455
HAYS, Joseph C.: 979
HAYS, Will H.: 832
HAYS COUNTY, Texas--Farming: 273
HAYTER, William G.: 3236
HAYWARD, Abraham: 2146
HAYWARD, Charles Sumner: 2456
HAYWARD, James Wood: 2456
HAYWARD FAMILY (Massachusetts): 2456
HAYWOOD, Atticus G.: 2449
HAYWOOD, E. Graham: 4669
HAYWOOD, Edmund Burke: 2458
HAYWOOD, Ernest: 5457
HAYWOOD, Francis: 2457
HAYWOOD, George W.: 2458
HAYWOOD, Jane E.: 4544
HAYWOOD, John (1755-1827): 2458
HAYWOOD, John (1762-1826): 484, 2776
HAYWOOD, Lucy: 2457
HAYWOOD, Marshall De Lancey: 3761
HAYWOOD, North Carolina: 2357
"HAYWOOD," Virginia:
  Physicians' accounts: 5579
HAYWOOD COUNTY, North Carolina:
  Livestock: 3176
  Mercantile accounts: 5258
  Cities and towns:
    Crab Orchard: 3176
    Waynesville: 1649, 2548, 5258,
      5603
      Prisoners and prisons: 641
HAYWOOD COUNTY, Tennessee: 82
  Land: 4139

HAYWOOD COUNTY, Tennessee (Continued):
    Cities and towns:
        Brownsville: 4139
            Girls' schools and academies: 872
        Stanton: 45
HAYWORTH, Clemmence G.: 2459
HAYWORTH, J. E.: 2459
HAZEL HILL, Stroud, England: 1976
HAZEN, William Babcock: 5419
HAZLEHURST, Leighton Wilson: 2460
HAZLEHURST, Mary Jane (McNish): 2460
HAZLEHURST FAMILY (Georgia): 2460
HEAD, Franklin Harvey: 2461
HEAD, William T.: 1215
HEADEN, Isaac Brooks: 2462
HEADRICKS FAMILY (North Carolina): 1882
HEALTH: see DENTISTRY; DISEASES; HEALTH CONDITIONS; HOSPITALS; MEDICAL PRACTICE; MEDICAL TREATMENT; PHYSICIANS; PHYSICIANS' ACCOUNTS; SLAVES--Health
HEALTH, Board of: see NORTH CAROLINA--GOVERNMENT AGENCIES AND OFFICIALS--Board of Health
HEALTH CONDITIONS:
    see also CIVIL WAR--CIVILIAN LIFE--Health conditions; and Medical and sanitary affairs as subheading under names of armies and navies
    Alabama: 4083
    Cuba: 4983
    Florida: 4743
    Georgia: 1090
    Greece: 3835
    Middle West: 1920
    Mozambique: 5725
    New York: 752
    North Carolina: 967, 2830, 3351, 4083
        New Hanover County: 3859
        Wilmington: 3859
    South Carolina: 477, 4083
        Charleston: 4584
    Tennessee: 4083
    Virginia: 2559
HEALTH ORGANIZATIONS:
    United States: 1197
HEALTH PROGRAMS:
    see also NATIONAL HEALTH INSURANCE
    Tennessee: 1197
HEALTH RESORTS: 3828
    Mississippi--Iuka: 3409
    New York: 1928
    North Carolina: 5690
        Halifax County: 2399
        Mooresville: 3415
    Tennessee--Tate Springs: 5051
    United States: 1084, 3053, 5193
    Virginia: 785, 3123, 3809, 4616, 4924, 5114, 5690
        Berkeley Springs: 3809
        Holston Springs: 3719
        Hot Springs: 1891
        Huguenot Springs: 3422
        In poetry: 182
        Jordan's Springs: 3135
        Sulpher Springs: 1891
        Warm Springs: 3809
    West Virginia--Sweetsprings: 1478
HEALY, Augustus: 2463
HEALY, Jeanette Reid: 2463
HEARD, Alice L.: 5093
HEARD, Columbus: 2464
HEARD COUNTY, Georgia:
    Franklin: 3966
    Land surveys: 3966
HEARN, Lafcadio: 10, 2465
HEARNE, Thomas: 268
HEARST, William Randolph: 3451
HEART--Diseases: 2934
HEARTT, Dennis: 5457
HEASLET, James B.: 2236
HEATH, George T.: 1982
HEATH, Hartwell P.: 2466
HEATH, J. H.: 2466
HEATH, John Francis: 3783

HEATH, Laura: 2467
HEATH, R. B.: 4492
HEATH, Robert R.: 2467
HEATH, Roscoe B.: 2466
HEATH, Sarah: 2468
HEATH, William (1737-1814): 2468
HEATH AND MASON (firm): 2466
HEATHCOTE WARD, Savannah, Georgia: 2992
HEATHFIELD, George Augustus Eliott, First Lord [Heathfield], Baron of Gibralter: 1913
HEATLY, Ann: 3278
HEATON, David: 3094
HEBER, Reginald: 2126
HEBREW POETRY: 1482
HEBREWS: see JEWS
HEDGES, Sir Charles (d. 1714): 3137
HEDGES, Hezekiah: 4732
HEDGES, J. H.: 1106
HEDGES, William: 720
HEDGES FAMILY (West Virginia): 2342
HEDGESVILLE, West Virginia: 159, 2342, 2478, 3174, 4732
    Agriculture: 3141
    Economic conditions: 3141
HÉDONVILLE, John de: 3424
HEDRICK, Benjamin Sherwood: 2469
HEDRICK, Charles A.: 2470
HEDRICK, Jones Tilden: 5457
HEDRICKS FAMILY (North Carolina): 1882
HEFLIN, J. Thomas: 2188
HEGEL, Georg Wilhelm Friedrich: 4430
HEIDE, Alexander: 1899
HEIDE, Rudolph E.: 1899
HEIDELBERG, Germany: see UNIVERSITY OF HEIDELBERG
HEIDELBERG, Mississippi: 3876
HEILMAN, George: 1443
HEITMAN, John Franklin: 813
HELEN TREVELYN by Sir Henry Mortimer Durand: 2756
HELENA, Arkansas: see CIVIL WAR--CAMPAIGNS, BATTLES, AND MILITARY ACTIONS--Arkansas--Helena
HELENA, Montana: 2407
HELIGOLAND: 2835
"HELL, HEAVEN, OR HOME" (projected tract): 2442
HELL-FER-SARTAIN by John William Fox, Jr.: 1878
HELLER, Rebecca: 5249
HELL'S CANYON: 4805
HELPER, Hardie Hogan: 773
HELPER, Hinton Rowan: 773, 1968, 2036, 2093
HELPS, Sir Arthur: 2471
HELSABECK, Solomon: 2471
HELSICK, Younger: 337
HELVETIUS, Madame: 5681
HELY-HUTCHINSON, John, Second Earl of Donoughmore: 2836
HEMANS, Felicia Dorothea (Browne): 2146
HEMP TRADE: 323
    Virginia: 1863
HEMPHILL, James Calvin: 2473, 5312
HEMPHILL, John: 2473
HEMPHILL, Robert Reid: 2473
HEMPHILL, William L.: 2473
HEMPHILL FAMILY (South Carolina): 2473
HEMSTERHUIS, Tiberius: 5567
HENCHENBROOK (warship): 3389
HENDAYE, France: 3270
HENDERSON, A. C.: 2473
HENDERSON, Archibald (1768-1822): 5457
HENDERSON, Archibald (1877-1963): 2790
HENDERSON, Archibald Erskine: 2475
HENDERSON, Barbara (Bynum): 5457
HENDERSON, David Henry: 2476
HENDERSON, John: 2477
HENDERSON, Leonard: 5457
HENDERSON, Mary: 2478
HENDERSON, Nathaniel: 5768

HENDERSON, Richard (1735-1785): 795, 5768
HENDERSON, Richard H. (Virginia): 3560
HENDERSON, Samuel (New York): 2479
HENDERSON, Samuel (North Carolina): 795
HENDERSON, W. F.: 2480
HENDERSON, William F.: 2481
HENDERSON, North Carolina: 95, 1144, 2087, 4232
    Postal Service accounts: 4407
HENDERSON COUNTY, North Carolina: 3276
    Earthquakes: 5229
    Flat Rock: 3019
HENDERSON COUNTY, Tennessee:
    Land deeds and indentures: 5341
HENDERSON STATION, Methodist churches: 3646
HENDERSONVILLE, Tennessee:
    Presbyterian churches: 5671
    Tobacco trade: 5671
HENDRICK, William: 3145
HENDRICK FAMILY (Virginia): 3145
HENDRICK HUDSON, U.S.S.: 5649
HENDRIX, Eugene Russell: 2482
HENDRIX, George W.: 2483
HENDRIX, Henry Leroy: 1877
HENDRIX, William: 1877
HENDRIX, William B.: 2483
HENDRIX COUNTY, Indiana:
    Economic and social conditions: 2459
HENDRY, Charles: 2484
HENING, William Waller: 2633, 3809
HENKEL, Ambrose: 2485
HENKEL, Caspar C.: 2949
HENKEL, David: 1232
HENKEL, Solomon: 2485
HENKEL FAMILY (North Carolina, Tennessee, and Virginia): 2485
HENLEY, David (1748-1823): 2486, 5870
HENLEY, Peter (d. 1758): 5457
HENLEY, Samuel: 3723
HENLEY, William Ernest: 5050, 5304
HENLEY FAMILY: 718
HENNEBES, Dr. _____ : 937
HENNEQUIN, Victor-Antoine: 65
HENRICO COUNTY, Virginia: 2713, 4612
    Land: 2415
    Magnolia: 590
    Manchester--Iron foundry: 282
HENRIETTA (revenue cutter): 437
HENRY IV, King of France: 1424, 3271
HENRY, Byron V.: 2493
HENRY, Edmund Jones: 4080
HENRY, Francis W.: 2487
HENRY, Gustavus Adolphus: 1403
HENRY, Gustavus Adolphus, Jr.: 2488
HENRY, Hugh: 2489
HENRY, Isaac: 2489
HENRY, Isom: 2493
HENRY, J. L. (Virginia); 2490
HENRY, Jacob: 2491
HENRY, James Edward (South Carolina): 4080
HENRY, James Vernor (Pennsylvania): 2492
HENRY, Jeremiah: 2493
HENRY, Joseph (1797-1878): 2148, 2494
HENRY, Louis D.: 5298
HENRY, O. (pseudonym): see PORTER, William Sydney
HENRY, Patrick (1736-1799): 858, 915, 2495, 4497, 5279, 5848
HENRY, Patrick (1843-1930): 2496
HENRY, Robert R.: 2497
HENRY, William Wirt: 523, 2495
HENRY CLAY SOCIETY, Staunton, Virginia: 2499
HENRY COUNTY, Georgia:
    Double Cabins: 2614
HENRY COUNTY, Indiana: 2328
    Middletown: 3698
HENRY COUNTY, Iowa:
    New London: 3953
HENRY COUNTY, Kentucky: 5615

HENRY COUNTY, Missouri:
  Calhoun: 5392
HENRY COUNTY, Virginia: 412, 1485,
  4131, 4720
  Martinsville: 1013, 1137, 4130
HENRY E. HUNTINGTON LIBRARY: 1236
HENRY S. HANNIS AND COMPANY: 2316,
  4056
HENSHAW, Charles: 2500
HENSHAW, Levi (1769-1843): 1946
HENSHAW, Levi (1815-1896): 1946
HENSHAW FAMILY (West Virginia): 865
  Genealogy: 1946
HENTON, Silas: 208, 2501
HEPLER, John C.: 5717
HERALDRY: see COATS OF ARMS
THE HERALDRY OF WORCESTERSHIRE by
  Henry Sydney Grazebrook: 2145
HERBERT, Catherine (Woronzow),
  Countess of Pembroke: 1911
HERBERT, Ella (Smith): 4911
HERBERT, Elizabeth (A'Court),
  Baroness Herbert of Lea: 4026
HERBERT, Francis C.: 2502
HERBERT, George: 1163, 4629
HERBERT, Hilary Abner: 3797, 4911
HERBERT, James D.: 5618
HERBERT, John: 2502
HERBERT, Leila: 4911
HERBERT, Sidney, First Baron Herbert
  of Lea: 4026
HERBERT, Thomas: 2502
HERBERT MEMORIAL FUND: 4026
"MR. HERBERT'S TEMPLE & CHURCH
  MILITANT EXPLAINED & IMPROVED. . ."
  by George Riley: 4629
HEREFORDSHIRE, England:
  Hill Court, Ross: 5333
HERESIES AND HERETICS: 656
  Great Britain: 5726
HERIOT, Edward Thomas: 2503
HERMITAGE, England: 5624
"THE HERMITAGE", Savannah, Georgia:
  2460
HERMON, New York: 3296
HERNANDO, Mississippi: 234
  see also MISSISSIPPI FEMALE
  COLLEGE
HERNDON, Ann Hull: 3587
HERNDON, Dabney M.: 3587
HERNDON FAMILY (North Carolina--
  Genealogy): 2239
HERNDON FAMILY (Virginia): 3587
HERNDON AND SMITH (firm): see SMITH
  AND HERNDON
HERNE, James A.: 3797
HEROD AND MIRIAMNE by Amélie Rives:
  4491
HEROES OF AMERICA: 500, 2469, 3062
HERR, John: 2504
HERRICK, Myron Timothy: 2871
HERRING, Fred: 1107
HERSCHEL, Sir William: 4230
HERSCHEL V. JOHNSON AND COMPANY:
  4895
HERSCHLEB, Charles A.: 5252
HERTFORD, Francis Charles Seymour,
  Third Marquis of: 4750
HERTFORD, Francis Seymour-Conway,
  First Marquis of: 1214
HERTFORD, North Carolina: 1679,
  1822, 2553, 3564
  Marketing: 3907
  Teachers' records: 4897
HERTFORD ACADEMY, Hertford, North
  Carolina: 4897
HERTFORD CHURCH, North Carolina: 3646
HERTFORD CIRCUIT, Methodist
  churches: 3646
HERTFORD COUNTY, North Carolina:
  Biographies: 3746
  Cities and towns:
    Harrellsville: 1316
    Murfreesboro: 3914, 4874, 5857
      see also CHOWAN COLLEGE
    Powellsville: 3746
HERTFORDSHIRE, England:
  Broxbourne: 739
  Essendon: 1508

HERTFORDSHIRE, England (Continued):
  Saint Albans:
    Voter registration: 4633
  Standon: 4630
  Westmill: 599
HERTY, Charles H.: 3905
HERTZLER, Edward: 2505
HERTZLER, Jacob: 2505
HERTZLER, John: 2505
HERTZLER (JOHN) AND SONS (firm):
  2505
HERTZLER FAMILY (Pennsylvania): 2505
HERVEY, Elizabeth: 945
HERVEY, Henry: 747
HERVEY, John, Baron Hervey: 747
HESPERIAN LITERARY SOCIETY: 4932
HESSE (S. F.) AND CO.: 1586
HETH, Beverly: 4735
HETH, Henry: 5280
HETH, William: 2506
HETHERINGTON AND KYNOCH v. LYNN:
  4624
HETSLER, H.: 2507
HEUVELTON AND CANTON FALLS PLANK
  ROAD: 2230
HEWES, Joseph (1730-1779): 2508
HEWITT, Fayette: 2509
HEWITT, James, Third Viscount
  Lifford: 1087
HEWITT, Richard Newton: 1955, 2510
HEWITT FAMILY: 1955
HEWLETT FAMILY (Michigan): 2604
HEXT, Sarah: 4623
HEYER (JOHN C.) AND COMPANY: 2511
HEYER, Matthew Johnston: 5457
HEYER, William A.: 2511
HEYWARD, DuBose: 10, 3394, 4453
HEYWARD, Guerard: 1682
HEYWARD, Selma: 2512
HEYWARD, T. D.: 2512
HEYWARD, William: 1682
HEYWOOD, Oliver: 4850
HIAWATHA (ship): 5731
HIBBARD, Alma: 2513
HIBERNIA, Florida--Description: 3277
HIBLER, Isaac A.: 377
HICKENLOOPER, Andrew (1837-1904): 2514
HICKERSON, Thomas Felix: 1771
HICKEY, John Joseph: 1730, 2515
HICKMAN, W. H.: 3993
HICKOK, Paul Robinson: 2516
HICKORY, North Carolina: 4161
  see also CLAREMONT COLLEGE
  Furniture industry: 3831
  Schools: 3043
HICKORY CHAIR COMPANY, Hickory, North
  Carolina: 3831
HICKORY FORK, Virginia: 4562
HICKS, David S.: 2517
HICKS, Edward Brodnax: 2517
HICKS, Sir Francis: 3260
HICKS, Granville: 902
HICKS, Mary Lyde: 5457
HICKS, Thomas (Great Britain): 2148
HICKS, Thomas (New York, 1823-1890):
  2518
HICKS, Thurston Titus: 795
HICKS, JONES & MALLORY SHOE SHOP:
  2519
HICKS FORD, Virginia:
  Mercantile accounts: 5891
  Tax receipts: 5891
HIDES AND LEATHER TRADE: 323
  see also TANNERY ACCOUNTS
  Prices--Virginia: 2520
  Subdivided by place:
    Arkansas--Whitsonton: 5509
    Georgia: 2365
    Virginia--Lawrenceville: 3014
    West Virginia--Wardensville: 146
HIDES AND SKINS:
  see also TANNING
  Georgia--Jasper County: 377
  Virginia: 625
HIDES AND SKINS TRADE:
  see also DEER SKINS TRADE
  North Carolina--Wilkesboro: 4107
  Virginia: 625

HIERHOLZER, Joseph: 2520
HIESKELL, James T.: 4022
HIESTER, Henry Muhlenberg: 2521
HIESTER, Joseph M.: 2521
HIESTER, Maria C. M.: 2521
HIESTER, William Muhlenberg: 4188
HIESTER FAMILY (Genealogy): 2521
HIESTER AND HAIN, Pennsylvania
  (firm): 2521
HIESTER AND SHIPPEN, Pennsylvania
  (firm): 2521
HIGDON FAMILY (North Carolina?): 3301
HIGGANUM, Connecticut: 2684
HIGGINS, S. W.: 323
HIGGINSON, Thomas Wentworth: 404,
  2449, 2522
HIGH, Amelia: 2819
HIGH, William H.: 2819
"HIGH BANK," Haulg, England: 5259
HIGH CHURCH: see CHURCH OF ENGLAND--
  High Church
HIGH HILLS OF SANTEE, South Carolina:
  4839
HIGH POINT, North Carolina: 1277,
  4098, 4152
  Hosiery Mills: 1612
  Labor organizations: 1195
  Schools: 3300
    Church schools: 3581
    Girls' schools and academies:
      2036
HIGH POINT, RANDLEMAN, ASHEBORO,
  AND SOUTHERN RAILROAD COMPANY: 5135
HIGH POINT FEMALE SEMINARY, High
  Point, North Carolina: 2036
HIGH SCHOOL OF CHARLESTON, South
  Carolina: 1017
HIGH SHOALS COMPANY: 5312
HIGHBY, Silas: 2523
HIGHER LAW AND THE FUGITIVE SLAVE
  BILL: 1796
"HIGHFIELDS," England: 4627
HIGHLAND COUNTY, Ohio:
  Hillsboro--Merchants: 5342
HIGHLAND LAKE INSTITUTE, East
  Andover, New Hampshire: 4039
HIGHLANDER FOLK SCHOOL: 1194, 1197,
  3558
HIGHTOWER, William A.: 2524
HIGHWAY CONSTRUCTION: see ROADS--
  Construction
HIGHWAY LAW: see ROADS--Laws and
  legislation
HIGHWAYMEN:
  see also BRIGANDS AND ROBBERS
  Great Britain: 3183
HIGHWAYS: see ROADS
HIGSON, Willoughby: 4760
HIKING:
  Appalachian Trail: 5389
  India: 5525
HILDEBRAND, Karl Emil: 2525
HILDROP, John: 4146
HILL, Ambrose Powell: 1137, 2527,
  5382
HILL, Adams Sherman: 2526
HILL, Arthur Blundel Sandys Trumbull,
  Third Marquis of Downshire: 4024
HILL, Benjamin (d. 1802): 2528
HILL, Benjamin Harvey (1823-1882):
  2326, 4706
HILL, Daniel Harvey: 395, 2529, 3262,
  5280
HILL, Daniel S.: 2530
HILL, David: 2543
HILL, David Jayne: 2871
HILL, Eugene: 3441
HILL, Francis H.: 155, 523, 2531
HILL, Frank Ernest: 2146
HILL, Frederick C.: 3607
HILL, George W.: 5252
HILL, Helen Varnum: 3325
HILL, Henrietta B.: 143
HILL, Hiram: 2532
HILL, J. A. (Georgia): 2533
HILL, J. D. (Virginia): 2534
HILL, James (Georgia minister): 2535
HILL, James Davidson (Confederate
  officer): 2536

HILL, Joel Edgar: 2537
HILL, John H.: 4726
HILL, Joseph B.: 2538
HILL, Maxwell: 2449
HILL, Mollie F.: 4170
HILL, N. (South Carolina): 2539
HILL, Nathan H.: 2540
HILL, Octavia: 2148
HILL, Otis G.: 2532
HILL, P. H. (Georgia): 3134
HILL, Richard: 2541
HILL, Rowland: 2542
HILL, Rowland, First Viscount Hill: 1911, 2147
HILL, Samuel: 5408
HILL, Samuel: (1857-1931): 5408
HILL, Theodore H.: 2851
HILL, Theophilus Hunter: 5457
HILL, Thomas N.: 5457
HILL, W. Lee: 2537
HILL, Walter Barnard: 3905
HILL, William (North Carolina): 832, 4977
HILL, William (South Carolina): 2543
HILL, William (Virginia): 2534
HILL, Wilmer W.: 2544
HILL FAMILY (Alabama): 4170
HILL FAMILY (Indiana): 4170
HILL FAMILY (Kentucky): 3325
HILL FAMILY (North Carolina--Genealogy): 3607
HILL FAMILY (Virginia): 4170
HILL COUNTY, Texas:
  Hillsboro: 3199
HILL COURT, Ross, England: 5333
"HILLERSDON HOUSE," Cullompton, England: 2127
HILLHOUSE, Harriet: 752
HILLHOUSE, William: 3041
HILLIARD, Henry Washington: 2545, 3903
HILLIARD, Joseph: 2546
HILLIARD, Paul Herman: 2547
HILLIARD FAMILY (Genealogy): 3831
HILLIARD AND SULARD (firm): see SULARD AND HILLIARD
HILLSBORO, Maryland: 5328
HILLSBORO, Ohio--Merchants: 5342
HILLSBORO, Texas: 3199
HILLSBORO DISTRICT, Methodist churches: 3646
HILLSBOROUGH, North Carolina: 4757
  1700s: 769
  1700s-1800s: 465, 2796
  1700s-1900s: 714, 3233
  1800s: 1285, 1467, 2120, 3677, 5384, 5973
  1900s: 3214
  American Revolution:
    see also AMERICAN REVOLUTION--Campaigns and battles--North Carolina--Hillsborough
    Loyalists: 1890
    Claims: 5341
  Clocks and watches: 3300
  Description: 2248
  Diseases--Smallpox: 5390
  Estates:
    Administration and settlement: 5381
  Fraternal societies: 4080
  Guardianship: 5381
  Jewelers: 3300
  Medical practice: 4890
  Mercantile accounts: 5728
  Merchants: 4890
  Militia: 440
  Physicians' accounts: 4890
  Schools: 834, 5298
  Secession: 834
  Silversmiths: 3300
  Social life and customs: 5298
  Taxation: 3938
HILLSBOROUGH, Virginia:
  Merchants: 1420
HILLSBOROUGH ACADEMY, North Carolina: 834

HILLSBOROUGH COUNTY, New Hampshire:
  Dunstable: 1529
  Manchester: 251
  Peterborough: 4519
HILTON HEAD, South Carolina:
  Civil War: 2679, 3264, 4119
  Negroes--Education: 3264
HIMALAYAN MOUNTAINS: 5618
HIMBISH, Mary: 274
HIMES, Hannah C.: 5462
HIMES, Sarah Catherine: 2548
"HINCHINGBROOK," England: 3724
HINCKLEY, Oscar B.: 2549
HINDLEY, F. A.: 2151
HINDS COUNTY, Mississippi: 5475
  Farming: 3759
  Merchants: 3759
  Cities and towns:
    Champion Hill--Civil War: 972
    Jackson: see JACKSON, Mississippi
HINDUISM:
  Relations with Europeans and Muslims in India: 278
HINE, A.: 4188
HINES, P. E.: 4002
HINES, Raymond W.: 2550
HINES, Samuel B.: 2551
HINES, William (Virginia): 2551, 4531
HINGHAM, Massachusetts: 3209
HINKS (C. D.) & CO., Baltimore, Maryland: 2797
HINKSON, John B.: 2552
HINSDALE, Anne Devereux: 2553
HINSDALE, Elizabeth Christophers: 2553
HINSDALE, Ellen (Devereux): 2553
HINSDALE, John Wetmore (1843-1921): 2553, 2617
HINSDALE, John Wetmore (1879-1971): 2553
HINSDALE FAMILY (North Carolina): 2553
HINSHAW, J. W.: 2554
HINSHAW, Mebane: 2554
HINSHAW, Thomas: 2555
HINSON, William G.: 2556
HINTON, Richard J.: 3076
HINTZE, Ernst: 2557
HIPPISLEY, Sir John Coxe, First Baronet: 5639
HIRING OF SLAVES:
  Alabama--Selma: 1645
  British West Indies: 4913
  Confederate States of America Army: 4103
  Georgia: 2216, 2788, 2923, 3573, 4921, 5051
    Jasper County: 377
    Mining company: 4895
  Mississippi: 1556
  Missouri: 5392
  North Carolina: 756, 1107, 1382, 2222, 2350, 2819, 3476, 4849, 5100, 5709, 5770
    Iredell County: 4872, 5319
    Lincoln County: 4450
    Martin County: 5036
    Mocksville: 5335
    Wage scales: 2646
  South Carolina: 1524, 4625
    Railroad construction: 4460
    Road construction: 4460
  Tennessee: 3692
  Texas--New Washington: 3772
  Virginia: 33, 330, 331, 753, 2014, 2360, 2369, 3246, 3788, 4615, 5121, 5529, 5765
    Coal industry: 523
    Iron industry: 523
    Tobacco industry: 1873
    Subdivided by place:
      Caroline County: 4589
      Goshen: 5613
      Greenville County: 5891
      Norfolk: 3830
      Patrick County: 1410

HIRING OF SLAVES (Continued):
  West Virginia: 5574
HIRST, Henry Beck: 1029, 1227
HIS MAJESTY'S GREATEST SUBJECT by S. S. Thorburn: 5279
HISEY, Jemima: 4122
HISEY, John: 4122
HISTORIA Y CONQUISTA DE TUNIZ: 2558
"HISTORIC BIT OF WASHINGTON" by Helen Collins Megrew: 3612
HISTORIC BUILDINGS: 128
  see also names of specific buildings
  China: 2411
  France: 1424, 2411
  Germany: 2411
  Great Britain: 2411
    Exeter: 5553
    Somersetshire: 1071
  Italy--Trieste: 2085
  New York--New York: 4025
  Portugal: 2411
  Russia: 2411
  United States: 2411
HISTORIC MONUMENTS: see MONUMENTS
HISTORIC SITES:
  see also MEMORIALS; MONUMENTS
  Civil War battlefields: 2106
  Virginia--Petersburg: 4612
HISTORICAL COLLECTIONS OF VIRGINIA by Henry Howe: 2673
HISTORICAL COMMEMORATIONS: see AMERICAN REVOLUTION--Campaigns and battles--North Carolina--Moore's Creek--Historical commemorations; FOURTH OF JULY CELEBRATIONS
HISTORICAL CONTROVERSIES:
  Civil War: see CIVIL WAR--HISTORICAL CONTROVERSIES
  Founding of the United States: 2400
"HISTORICAL DATA ON THE NEGRO" by Charles Spurgeon Johnson, Sr.: 2852
HISTORICAL DISQUISITION CONCERNING THE KNOWLEDGE WHICH THE ANCIENTS HAD OF INDIA by William Robertson: 4512
HISTORICAL HIGHLIGHTS OF THE EDUCATIONAL MINISTRY by Carl H. King: 3020
HISTORICAL RESEARCH: 4195
HISTORICAL RESTORATION:
  France: 441
  Great Britain: 5553
  New York: 4343
  North Carolina: 1588
    Bath: 5298
    Durham: 440
    Raleigh: 4736
  South Carolina--Cokesbury: 5312
  Virginia:
    Colonial Williamsburg: 1424
    Mount Vernon: 1737
    Stratford: 1424
HISTORICAL SKETCHES OF FRANKLIN COUNTY (N.C.) by E. H. Davis: 5964
HISTORICAL SKETCHES OF NORTH CAROLINA by John Hill Wheeler: 5667
HISTORICAL SOCIETIES:
  see also COLONIAL DAMES OF AMERICA; DAUGHTERS OF THE AMERICAN REVOLUTION; SOUTHERN HISTORICAL ASSOCIATION; SOUTHERN HISTORICAL SOCIETY; UNITED DAUGHTERS OF THE CONFEDERACY
  Georgia: see GEORGIA HISTORICAL SOCIETY
  Maryland: 3598
  Mississippi: 2282, 5498
  Missouri: 2386
  New York: 3735, 4025
  North Carolina: see NORTH CAROLINA HISTORICAL COMMISSION
  Rhode Island: 5001
  South Carolina: 2402, 5312
  United States: 3990
  Virginia: 2499, 3735

HISTORICAL STUDIES: 2973, 3746
  see also ARCHAEOLOGICAL
    INVESTIGATIONS; BIOGRAPHICAL
    STUDIES; PUBLISHERS AND
    PUBLISHING--Historical studies
  American Revolution: 2881
      North Carolina: 3176
          Loyalists: 305
  Anti-Southern bias: 3967
  Churches: see CHURCH HISTORY;
    and Church history as subheading
    under names of specific
    denominations
  Civil War: see CIVIL WAR--
    HISTORICAL WRITINGS
  Criticism--Massachusetts: 1431
  Democracy: 4751, 5853
  French Revolution: 1982
  Fugitive slaves: 2400
  Mecklenburg Declaration of
    Independence: 305
  Republican Party: 2881
  Reviews--North Carolina: 960
  Subdivided by place:
    Alabama (proposed): 4195
    Arkansas: 4894
    Connecticut: 2684
    Florida--Marion County: 4434
    France: 4449, 5594
    Georgia: 787, 2788, 2893, 2894,
      3898
        Augusta: 2894
    Great Britain: 892, 957, 1910,
      2282, 2471, 3715, 4512, 4580,
      4628
        Bath: 5553
        Exeter: 5553
        Medieval church: 2841
        Roman catacombs: 2148
        Somersetshire: 4176
        World War I: 1320
    India: 866, 4364
    Louisiana: 1923
    Massachusetts: 4305
    Mississippi Territory: 2282
    Missouri: 5481
    North Carolina: 22, 305, 960,
      1068, 1525, 1848, 1946, 2282,
      2589, 3439, 4098, 4232, 5014
    Philippine Islands: 4511
    Scotland: 5379
    South Carolina: 1923, 2788, 3356,
      4453, 5312
        Huguenots: 1468
    Southern States: 2465
    Spain: 3549
    Tennessee--Benton County: 4894
    United States: 706, 1137, 1842,
      3269
    Virginia: 858
    West Virginia:
      Berkeley County: 1946
    Western States: 3697
HISTORY:
  see also ORAL HISTORY
  Sources: 5054
  Students' notebooks:
    Maryland:
      Johns Hopkins University: 3888
    Pennsylvania:
      Franklin County: 3412
  Study and teaching: 1714, 5054
    French history: 1754
HISTORY AND ANTIQUITIES OF
  SOMERSETSHIRE by William Phelps:
  4176
HISTORY AND ANTIQUITIES OF THE
  TOWER OF LONDON: 828
HISTORY OF ADAIR COUNTY, MISSOURI
  by E. M. Violette: 5481
HISTORY OF BRAZIL by Robert Southey:
  4967
HISTORY OF CALIFORNIA AND THE
  PACIFIC STATES by Hubert H.
  Bancroft: 4080
HISTORY OF COOPERATION IN ENGLAND
  by George Jacob Holyoake: 5259

"THE HISTORY OF DEMOCRACY" by Nahum
  Capen: 5853
HISTORY OF ENGLAND FROM 1830 by
  William Nassau Molesworth: 3715
HISTORY OF FRIEDRICH II OF PRUSSIA
  CALLED FREDERICK THE GREAT by
  by Thomas Carlyle: 892
HISTORY OF GEORGIA by Charles Colcock
  Jones: 2893
HISTORY OF GREAT BRITAIN DURING THE
  REIGN OF QUEEN ANNE: 828
HISTORY OF LOUISIANA by Charles
  Étienne Arthur Gayarré: 1982
HISTORY OF MISSISSIPPI by J. F. H.
  Claiborne: 1982
HISTORY OF SCOTLAND by Andrew Lang:
  3851
HISTORY OF THE BRITISH EMPIRE IN
  INDIA by Edward Thornton: 332
"HISTORY OF THE CHURCH OF GOD" by
  Charles Colcock Jones: 2893
HISTORY OF THE EQUITABLE PIONEERS
  by George Jacob Holyoake: 3715
"THE HISTORY OF THE LAUREL BRIGADE"
  by Edward Allen Hitchcock
  McDonald: 3141
"HISTORY OF THE MILITARY POLICE
  CORPS, AMERICAN EMBARCATION CENTER,
  A. E. F.": 4269
HISTORY OF THE REIGN OF THE EMPEROR
  CHARLES V by William Robertson:
  4512
"HISTORY OF THE THIRD MISSOURI
  CAVALRY" by A. W. M. Petty: 1453
A HISTORY OF THE UNIVERSITY OF
  OXFORD, ITS COLLEGES, HALLS, AND
  PUBLIC BUILDINGS by William Combe:
  1173
HISTORY OF THE VIRGINIA DEBT
  CONTROVERSY: 2597
HISTORY OF THE WAR IN INDIA: 3128
HISTORY OF THE WAR IN THE PENINSULA
  by Sir William Francis Patrick
  Napier: 3736
HISTORY OF THE WHIG MINISTRY OF 1830
  TO THE PASSING OF THE REFORM BILL
  by John Arthur Roebuck: 4051
"HISTORY OF WILLIAM RADFORD'S
  INCARCERATION IN THE TOWER OF
  LONDON": 3809
HITE, Cornelius Baldwin, Sr.: 2559
HITE, Cornelius Baldwin, Jr.: 2559
HITE, Elizabeth Augusta (Smith):
  2559
HITE, Jacob: 175
HITLER, Adolf: 233, 2109
HITT, E. B.: 2560
HIXON, James: 3529
HOADLEY, Robert Bruce: 2561
HOAK, John T.: 2562
HOAR, Mr._____: 3284
HOAR, Ebenezer Rockwood: 2563
HOAR, Elizabeth: 2564
HOAR, George Frisbie: 1364
HOAR, Samuel: 2564
HOARE-LAVAL PACT: 233
HOBART, Marie Elizabeth Jeffries:
  356
HOBART, Robert, Fourth Earl of
  Buckinghamshire: 2565
HOBBES FAMILY (Virginia): 2566
HOBBS, James Olin, Sr.: 2566
HOBBS, James Olin, Jr.: 2566
HOBBS, Thomas: 2567
HOBHOUSE, Arthur, First Baron
  Hobhouse: 1014
HOBHOUSE, Harriet Theodora: 4995
HOBOKEN, New Jersey: 4322
HOBSON, J. A.: 2569
HOBBY, Wilbur: 2568
HOCKETT, Himelius M.: 2570
HOCKETT, Susannah: 2570
HOCKING COUNTY, Ohio:
  Logan: 135
HODGDON, Samuel: 2571
HODGE, EUGENIA M. v. WHEELING LANDS:
  3587

HODGES, J. D.: 2572
HODGES, John D.: 2573
HODGES, Luther Hartwell: 4724
HODGES AND CHESSON (firm): 1015
HODGSON, Daisy M. L.: 2575
HODGSON, Eliza S.: 2574
HODGSON, Frances: 103
HODGSON, Geroge P.: 5106
HODGSON, Minnie A. B.: 2575, 2576
HODGSON, Thomas: 2149
HODGSON, William (Virginia): 2577
HODGSON, William Brown (1801-1871):
  2290, 2578
HODNETT, John W.: 2579
HODSON, Margaret (Holford): 2580
HOEY, Clyde Roarke: 2239, 2581
HOEY FAMILY: 2581
HOFF, Joseph: 2582
HOFFMAN, David: 2583
HOFFMAN, John Thompson: 4751
"HOFFMAN" by John F. Peebles: 4112
HOGAN, Daniel: 3968
HOGE, Anna C.: 3913
HOGE, Mary C.: 2584
HOGE, Moses: 2584
HOGE, Moses Drury: 1351
HOGE, Thomas P.: 2584
HOGE, Whit: 2584
HOGG, Gavin: 4394
HOGG, James: 2734, 5298, 5768
HOGG (JAMES) AND COMPANY: see JOHN
  HUSKE AND JAMES HOGG AND COMPANY
HOGG, Robina: 5298
HOGG, Thomas Jefferson: 4770
HOGG FAMILY (North Carolina--
  Genealogy): 4517
HOGG AND CAMPBELL (firm): 2585
HOGG AND CLAYTON (firm): 2586
HOGS:
  Breeding: 4849
  Confederate States of America:
    4895
  Indiana: 1601
  Mississippi: 2813
  South Carolina: 3123
HOKE, John Franklin: 5457
HOKE, Michael: 5457
HOKE, William Alexander: 5457
HOLBERTON, John W.: 2587
HOLCOMBE, George: 2421
HOLCOMBE, Henry: 393
HOLDEN, Ann Augusta Young: 2589
HOLDEN, John (North Carolina?): 2588
HOLDEN, John A. (Louisiana): 714
HOLDEN, Kittie: 2588
HOLDEN, Laura: 2589
HOLDEN, Liberty Emery: 2969
HOLDEN, Louisa Virginia (Harrison):
  2589
HOLDEN, William H.: 2588
HOLDEN, William Woods: 484, 714,
  832, 2589, 3176, 4489, 5149, 5298,
  5384
HOLDEN FAMILY (North Carolina): 714,
  2588, 2589, 5384
  Genealogy: 714
HOLDERNESS, James: 1389
HOLDING (T. E.) & CO.: 2590
HOLFORD, Margaret: 2580
HOLGATE, Curtis: 2590
HOLGATE, Fannie Maud: 2591
HOLGATE, William C.: 2591
HOLIDAYS: see FESTIVALS; GREETING
  CARDS; PUBLIC CELEBRATIONS; and
  names of specific holidays, e.g.
  CHRISTMAS
"HOLINESS IN TIME OF WAR" by Paul
  Whitehead: 5302
HOLL,_____: 2592
HOLLAND, Asa: 2593, 2633
HOLLAND, Elizabeth (Vassall) Fox,
  Baroness: 1875
HOLLAND, Henry Edward Fox, Fourth
  Baron: 1875, 4605, 5277
HOLLAND, Henry Richard Vassall Fox,
  Third Baron: 1875, 5746
HOLLAND, John (Georgia): 2594

HOLLAND, John W. (North Carolina): 2595
HOLLAND, Peter D.: 208, 2633
HOLLAND: see THE NETHERLANDS
HOLLES, Thomas Pelham-, First Duke of Newcastle: see PELHAM-HOLLES, Thomas, First Duke of Newcastle
HOLLEY, Horace: 5342
HOLLEY, Turner W.: 2596
HOLLIDAY, Carl: 2449
HOLLIDAY, Frederick William Mackey: 2597
HOLLIDAY, John: 1523
HOLLIDAY, Stephen W.: 4894
HOLLIDAY, Thomas: 2148
HOLLIDAY FAMILY (North Carolina): 1523
HOLLIDAYSBURG, Pennsylvania: 849, 1142
  Local politics: 421
HOLLIFIELD, Horatio Nelson: 2598
HOLLINGSWORTH, Adaline A.: 2365
HOLLINGSWORTH, D. F.: 2599
HOLLINGSWORTH, John: 2599
HOLLINGSWORTH, Joseph P.: 2600
HOLLINGSWORTH, Mary: 2601
HOLLINS COLLEGE, Virginia: 3552
  Students and student life: 3979
HOLLISTER, Seth: 2602
HOLLOWAY, Emory: 102
HOLLOWAY FAMILY (Maryland): 5128
"HOLLWOOD," Hayes, England: 4230
HOLLY GROVE, North Carolina: 1271
HOLLY GROVE BAPTIST CHURCH, Bertie County, North Carolina: 2603
HOLLY SPRING CIRCUIT, Methodist churches: 3646
HOLLY SPRINGS, Mississippi: 82
  Cemeteries: 5975
  Civil War: 5975
  Description: 155
HOLLY SPRINGS, North Carolina: 63
HOLLY SPRINGS FEMALE INSTITUTE, Mississippi: 2588
HOLLY SPRINGS LAND AND IMPROVEMENT COMPANY, North Carolina: 63
"HOLLY-WOOD" PLANTATION, Louisiana: 4582
HOLLYDAY, Frederic Blackmur Mumford: 2604
HOLLYDAY, James: 2605
HOLLYWOOD, California: 300
HOLLYWOOD, North Carolina:
  Mercantile accounts: 3960
  United States Post Office: 3960
HOLMAN, Joseph: 2606
HOLMAN, Joseph George Ephriam: 2606
HOLMAN FAMILY (Ohio): 2606
HOLMES, Dr. _____ (Petersburg, Virginia): 194
HOLMES, Abiel: 2607
HOLMES, Alexander: 2608
HOLMES, Charles Frederick: 1439
HOLMES, David: 2609, 4246
HOLMES, Eliza Lavalette (Floyd): 2612, 2881
HOLMES, Elizabeth J.: 530
HOLMES, Emma Edwards: 2610
HOLMES, Francis Simmons: 4306
HOLMES, Gabriel: 2611
HOLMES, George: 5758
HOLMES, George Frederick (1820-1897): 872, 2612, 2881, 5251, 5361
HOLMES, Isaac: 4616
HOLMES, Isaac Edward (1796-1867): 2613
HOLMES, Isabelle: 5786, 5790
HOLMES, J. H.: 2608
HOLMES, John A.: 2615
HOLMES, John Bee: 2613
HOLMES, Joseph E.: 2616
HOLMES, Joseph Henry Herndon (1794-1831): 2612
HOLMES, Marcella Fayette: 2614
HOLMES, Mary Ann (Pemberton): 2612
HOLMES, Matthew: 2615
HOLMES, Nickels J.: 2616
HOLMES, Oliver Wendell: 404, 2449, 5050, 5193

HOLMES, Theopilus Hunter: 2553, 2617, 5457
HOLMES, William (Great Britain): 5026
HOLMES, William Richard: 3722
HOLMES FAMILY (North Carolina): 530
HOLMES FAMILY (Virginia): 2612
HOLMWOOD, England: 3895
HOLST, Charles F. A.: 5892
HOLSTON MANUFACTURING CORPORATION: 2769
HOLSTON SPRINGS, Virginia:
  Description: 3719
HOLT, Allen: 2618
HOLT, Hamilton (1872-1951): 706, 2449, 3797
HOLT, Hamilton Bowen (New York): 2619
HOLT, Hines: 2620
HOLT, J. (North Carolina): 2618
HOLT, James Barron: 2449
HOLT, John: 2621
HOLT (JOHN AND WILLIAM) (firm): 2621
HOLT, Michael William: 2622
HOLT, Nicholas: 2623
HOLT, Roland: 3797
HOLT, Thomas Michael: 3972
HOLT, William: 2621
HOLT, Winifred: 3710
HOLT FAMILY (Genealogy): 2623
HOLTON, A. (North Carolina physician): 2624
HOLTON, A. E.: 706
HOLTZCLAW, Ethel: 2625
HOLY, Thomas: 5133
HOLY LAND: see PALESTINE
HOLY SPIRIT (Theology): 2934
HOLYOAKE, George Jacob: 2626, 3715, 5259
HOLZMANN, Maurice: 4567
HOME, Percy J.: 2627
HOME ECONOMICS: see HOUSEHOLD MANAGEMENT
HOME FOR FREED WOMEN SLAVES, Cairo, Egypt: 67
HOME GUARDS: see Militia as subheading under names of countries and states
HOME INSTITUTE (school for freedmen in South Carolina): 5298
HOME INSURANCE COMPANY: 5731
HOME JOURNAL: 1143, 1638, 3779
HOME NEWSPAPER AND EDUCATIONAL JOURNAL: 4080
HOME OWNERS' LOAN ACT (1933): 5779
HOME REMEDIES: 4689
  see also DISEASES--Rheumatism-- Home remedies; FAMILY MEDICINE; MEDICAL TREATMENT
  Georgia: 3396, 3591
  North Carolina: 277, 3317, 3812
  South Carolina: 2670
  United States: 730, 4513
  Vermont: 3218
  Virginia: 3721, 4616
HOME RULE:
  Ireland: 649, 735, 2626, 3980, 4567
HOMEMAKING: see HOUSEHOLD MANAGEMENT
HOMEOPATHY: 2684
HOMER: 1538, 3607, 4616
HOMESICKNESS: 1049
  see also Morale as subheading under names of armies, navies and wars
  West Virginia: 5371
HOMESLEY, A. R.: 5100
HONDURAS:
  Foreign relations--Guatemala: 116
  Land deeds and indentures: 5063
  Minerals: 5480
  Politics and government: 116
  Scientific expeditions: 5480
HONEY HILL, South Carolina: see CIVIL WAR--CAMPAIGNS, BATTLES, AND MILITARY ACTIONS--South Carolina-- Honey Hill
HONEY TRADE: 323

HONEYCUTT, J. H.: 2628
HONEYMOONS: 2463
HONG KONG: 3786
  British administration: 598
  Description: 1464, 2463
  United States embassy in: 5861
HONNELL, H. L.: 2671
HONNOLL, Robert W.: 2629
HONOLULU, Hawaii--Description: 2191
HONORS AND AWARDS:
  see also AMERICAN REVOLUTION-- Veterans--Honors and awards; CONGRESSIONAL MEDAL OF HONOR; DISTINGUISHED FLYING CROSS; UNITED STATES--ARMY--Civil War-- Honors and awards; UNIVERSITIES AND COLLEGES--Honorary degrees
  Missouri: 2604
  North Carolina: 4080
  United States: 83, 3265
  Virginia: 824
HOOD, B. R.: 2631
HOOD, David W.: 2631
HOOD, George B.: 216
HOOD, John Bell: 1186, 2630, 4358, 5314, 5723
HOOD, John C.: 2631
HOOD, Thomas: 2632
HOOD FAMILY: 1558
HOOE, Gerald: 337
HOOK, Captain _____ (East India Company): 5639
HOOK, John (1745-1808): 2633
HOOK, John, Jr.: 2633
HOOK, L. C.: 2634
HOOK, Robert: 2633
HOOK, Sidney: 720
HOOK, Theodore Edward: 2077
HOOK FAMILY (Scotland and Virginia): 2633
HOOKE, Robert W.: 2635
HOOKE, William Franklin: 2635
HOOKE, William W.: 2635
HOOKER, Edward: 2636
HOOKER, John: 2636
HOOKER, Joseph (1814-1879): 4808
HOOK'S MILLS, West Virginia: 2634
HOOKSET, New Hampshire: 1980
HOOLE, William Stanley: 4738
HOOMES, John: 2637
HOOPER, Aurelia: 2638
HOOPER, J. D. (North Carolina): 2642
HOOPER, John De Berniere: 4992
HOOPER, John Walter (Maryland): 2639
HOOPER, Lucy Hamilton (Jones): 2640
HOOPER, M. S.: 2641
HOOPER, Thomas C.: 2642
HOOPER, W. A. (Massachusetts): 2641
HOOPER, William (1742-1790): 2776, 5768
HOOPER, William (fl. 1867): 2642
HOOVER, Edward: 2643
HOOVER, Herbert Clark: 879, 2644, 4825
HOOVER (W. A.) AND COMPANY, New Lisbon, Ohio: 5660
HOOVER HILL, North Carolina: 4100
HOPE, Alexander James Beresford-: 2148, 3556
HOPE, Edwin G.: 2645
HOPE, Frederick William: 2839
HOPE, Laurence: see NICOLSON, Adela Florence (Cory)
HOPE (blockade runner): 410
HOPE AND CO., Amsterdam, Netherlands: 3273
"HOPETON," Georgia: 1242
HOPEVILLE, England: 4327
HOPEWELL CHURCH, Catawba County, North Carolina: 3646
HOPEWELL CHURCH, Randolph County, North Carolina: 3646
HOPKINS, General _____: 3323
HOPKINS, Daniel C.: 2646
HOPKINS, Edward (Georgia): 2647
HOPKINS, George Washington: 872
HOPKINS, Harry (fl. 1830s): 1792
HOPKINS, Henry H.: 2648

783

HOPKINS, Jane Lucinda: 1792
HOPKINS, John Livingston: 5508
HOPKINS, Mark (1802-1887): 1792
HOPKINS, Mark III: 1792
HOPKINS, O. C.: 2649
HOPKINS, Mrs. O. K.: 2650
HOPKINS FAMILY (Genealogy): 1792
HOPKINS COUNTY, Kentucky: 4319
HOPKINSVILLE, Kentucky: 5070
   Postal service: 4854
HOPS--Great Britain: 2148
HORAH, William H.: 2651
HORN, Gertrude Franklin: 4837
HORN, John (Virginia): 4743
HORN, John (West Virginia): 2652
HORN, John, Jr. (Pennsylvania): 480
HORNADAY, William Temple: 4453
HORNBECK, Stanley Kuhl: 5252
HORNBLOWER AND MARSHALL, Lexington, Kentucky: 3325
HORNBY, Edmund: 3183
HORNBY, New York:
   Legal affairs: 4645
HORNE, Ashley: 4828
HORNE, John: 92
HORNE, Thomas Hartwell: 2653
HORNER, James H.: 2654
HORNELLSVILLE, New York: 1380
HORNET, U.S.S.: 4220, 4274
HORRY COUNTY, South Carolina:
   Conway: 2854
HORRY DISTRICT, South Carolina:
   Land: 1451
HORSE-POWERED COTTON GINS: 840
HORSE RACING: 1242, 5751
   Georgia--Savannah: 4864
   Kentucky--Louisville: 2681
   South Carolina: 2880
   Southern States: 3873
   Virginia: 2517
      Richmond: 5094
HORSE SHOE, North Carolina:
   Merchants: 4910
HORSE SHOE SWAMP, North Carolina: 3423
HORSE STEALING: 4607
   see also CIVIL WAR--HORSE STEALING; CONFEDERATE STATES OF AMERICA--ARMY--Horses and mules--Theft
HORSE TRADE: 1242
   Confederate States of America:
      Army: 5633
   Georgia: 781, 2118
   Great Britain: 1991, 2637
   North Carolina: 614, 3257
   Virginia: 1401, 2637, 4743
HORSEMAN, John: 4913
HORSES:
   see also CIVIL WAR--CONFISCATED PROPERTY--Horses and mules; and Horses and mules as subheading under names of armies
   North Carolina:
      Franklin County: 5087
   Subdivided by subject:
      Breeding: 1242, 4849
         Georgia: 2020
         Kentucky: 1086
         North Carolina: 484, 2876, 3176, 5709
         South Carolina: 2300
            Fees: 4833
         Virginia: 2637, 4531, 4743
         West Virginia: 4774
      Medicine--North Carolina: 3410
      Prices:
         New York: 2434
         South Carolina: 295, 3801
         Virginia: 4924
      Race horses: 4971
         Georgia: 2020
         New York: 1608
HORSEY, Outerbridge: 3160
HORSFORD, Alfred Hastings: 4655
HORTER FAMILY (Florida): 4365
HORTON, Gustavus: 249
HORTON, Hugh G.: 2655
HORTON, Mary A.: 1259
HORTON, Mary J.: 2656

HORTON, Sarah: 1138
HORTON, Willis: 2657
HORTON FAMILY (North Carolina): 2657
HOSHAUR, Peter: 1920
HOSIERY--Dyeing: 3842
HOSIERY INDUSTRY COMMITTEE: 101
HOSIERY MACHINERY:
   Knitting machines--Inventions: 3424
   North Carolina: 1612
HOSIERY MILLS:
   North Carolina: 1612
      Burlington: 1353, 3595
      Finance: 1612, 4717
      Graham: 4812
      Stocks: 1612, 3595
HOSIERY TRADE:
   North Carolina: 1612, 4812
HOSIERY WORKERS:
   Labor unions: see LABOR UNIONS--Hosiery workers
   North Carolina: 1612
   Wages and salaries: see WAGES AND SALARIES--Hosiery workers
HOSKINS, Aaron: 4405
HOSKINS, Edmund: 2658
HOSKINS AND THORNBURGH: see THORNBURGH AND HOSKINS
HOSKINS-CHADWICK COMPANY: see CHADWICK-HOSKINS COMPANY
HOSLER, George: 2659
HOSPITAL AID SOCIETIES:
   North Carolina--Raleigh: 2553
HOSPITALS:
   see also CHILDREN'S HOSPITALS; CONVALESCENT HOMES; MENTAL HOSPITALS; and Hospitals as subheading under names of wars, e.g. CIVIL WAR--HOSPITALS
   Military:
      see also CONFEDERATE STATES OF AMERICA--ARMY--Hospitals; UNITED STATES--ARMY--Civil War--Convalescent camps; UNITED STATES--ARMY--Civil War--Hospitals; WORLD WAR I--Field hospitals
      Mississippi-Pascagoula: 5517
      Virginia--Norfolk: 4701
   Subdivided by place:
      Georgia--Cuthbert: 3555
      Illinois--Chicago: 4105
      Iowa--Keokuk: 5017
      Maryland: 3399
      New York:
         New York: 4775
         White Plains: 5252
      North Carolina: 5741
         Durham: 2379, 5601
         Philanthropy to: 1584
         Raleigh: 2553
         Winston-Salem: 3538
      United States:
         Philanthropy to: 1589
      Virginia: 1591
HOSTAGES: see CIVIL WAR--HOSTAGES
HOT SPRINGS, Arkansas: 4060
HOT SPRINGS, Virginia: 1094, 1891
HOTELS: 5155
   see also HEALTH RESORTS
   Management:
      Maryland--Smithsburg: 5110
      South Carolina:
         Union: 5407, 5522
      Virginia: 5176
      West Virginia:
         Martinsburg: 3832
   Registers:
      North Carolina:
         Yanceyville: 4284
      Washington, D.C.: 3018
   Subdivided by place:
      Europe: 5193
      New York--New York: 5298
      Virginia--Manassas: 5779
HOUCK, W. A. v. J. J. ALBRIGHT: 1291
HOUGH, Warwick: 3703
HOUGHTON, Richard Monckton Milnes, First Baron: 2471, 3694

HOUGHTON MIFFLIN COMPANY: 5115
HOUMA, Louisiana: 4636
HOURS OF LABOR:
   see also EIGHT-HOUR DAY
   South Carolina:
      Typographical workers: 2771
   Southern States: 3558
   Virginia:
      Construction industry: 2550
      Iron industry: 5990
      Manufacturing companies: 2165
HOUSATONIC RAILROAD: 825
HOUSE, Edward Mandell: 706
HOUSE, Samuel Reynolds: 5238
HOUSE FURNISHINGS:
   see also HOUSEHOLD GOODS; HOUSING--Interiors
   Advertising: see ADVERTISING--House furnishings
   Marketing:
      Maryland--Cumberland: 3765
   North Carolina:
      Iredell County: 5319
HOUSE OF COMMONS: see GREAT BRITAIN--PARLIAMENT--House of Commons
HOUSE OF LORDS: see GREAT BRITAIN--PARLIAMENT--House of Lords
"HOUSE OF PROTECTION FOR THE MAINTENANCE AND INSTRUCTION OF GIRLS OF GOOD CHARACTER": 5726
HOUSEHOLD ACCOUNTS:
   see also PERSONAL FINANCE
   Alabama: 5593
      Selma: 4911
   Georgia: 786, 2020
      Ebenezer: 5986
   Great Britain: 4934
      Chigwell: 3553
      Isle of Man: 4187
   Maryland: 785, 2295
      Elkton: 4468
      West River: 4219
   Massachusetts: 4807
   North Carolina: 4858, 5805
      Granville County: 3916
      Jackson County: 3021
      New Bern: 5709
   Pennsylvania: 421
   South Carolina: 501, 3405
      Charleston: 1891
      Colleton County: 4649
   Virginia: 1922, 3157, 3642, 4615
      Clarke County: 3602
      Richmond: 4346
      Stafford County: 1813
   Washington, D.C.: 1937, 3325
   West Virginia: 4703
      Hedgesville: 159
      Martinsburg: 1828
      Wood County: 5194
HOUSEHOLD FINANCE:
   Connecticut--Hartford: 2273
   New York--New York: 4351
   North Carolina: 730, 3416
      Chapel Hill: 4763
   South Carolina: 1388, 3801
   Tennessee:
      Memphis: 4763
      Nashville: 4854
   Virginia: 872, 1115, 3809, 4743
      Hanover County: 4020
HOUSEHOLD GOODS: 1556, 5822
   see also HOUSE FURNISHINGS
   Louisiana--"Holly-Wood": 4582
HOUSEHOLD MANAGEMENT: 4689
   North Carolina: 1407, 2714, 5740
   South Carolina--Edgefield: 5312
   Tennessee: 4269
   Virginia: 4459, 4616
   West Virginia: 4703
HOUSER, Michael: 2660
HOUSES:
   see also SOD HOUSES
   Construction:
      see also PLASTERING
      Georgia: 2020
      Kentucky--Lexington: 3325
      Mississippi: 3956

HOUSES:
    Construction (Continued):
        North Carolina: 5087
            Charlotte: 3599
        Virginia--Mount Vernon: 5575
    Interiors--France: 1424
    Subdivided by place:
        Florida: 1584
        Maryland--Baltimore: 2398
        New York: 1584
        North Carolina: 1584, 4080
        Virginia: 1568
HOUSING: 4386
    see also Student housing as subheading under names of specific universities, colleges, and schools; and (name of country)--Diplomatic and consular service--Housing
    Tennessee: 1200
HOUSTON, Alice: 3295
HOUSTON, Christopher: 2661
HOUSTON, David Franklin: 706
HOUSTON, George Smith: 2662
HOUSTON, John W. B.: 2117
HOUSTON, Placebo: 2663
HOUSTON, Robert: 795
HOUSTON, Samuel: 872, 2664, 3176, 5141, 5493, 5719
HOUSTON, William Churchill: 2665
HOUSTON, Texas: 277, 3463
    Civil War prisoners: 3342
    Description: 377
    Development: 3772
    Diseases:
        Cholera and yellow fever: 4562
    Reconstruction: 4562
HOUSTON COUNTY, Georgia: 2727
    Perry: 3767
HOUSTONVILLE, North Carolina: 2661, 2663
HOUSTOUN, John (1744-1796): 2666, 3209, 3536
HOUSTOUN, William (1695?-1733): 2667
HOUTUM-SCHINDLER, Sir Albert: 4693
HOWARD, Caroline: 103, 2045
HOWARD, Cecilia (Riggs): 4478
HOWARD, George (Maryland): 3631
HOWARD, George (Washington, D.C.): 4478
HOWARD, George, Sixth Earl of Carlisle: 5, 1648
HOWARD, Henry (Virginia): 2668
HOWARD, Henry (Washington, D.C.): 4478
HOWARD, John Eager (1752-1827): 2669
HOWARD, John H. (South Carolina): 2670
HOWARD, Mary: 4697
HOWARD, Oliver Otis: 1439, 1607
HOWARD, Samuel: 1981
HOWARD, T. H.: 2671
HOWARD, Tazewell M.: 2671
HOWARD, Virginia: 4348
HOWARD, William (1793-1834): 2669, 4221
HOWARD COUNTY, Maryland:
    Livestock: 909
    Cities and towns:
        Columbia: 3781
        Savage: 1314
HOWARD COUNTY, Missouri:
    Fayette: 1620, 2386
HOWARD MEMORIAL LIBRARY, New Orleans, Louisiana: 3273
HOWARD RAILROAD COMPANY: see MONTGOMERY, HOWARD AND CARROLL RAILROAD COMPANY
HOWARD TULLY AND COMPANY: 642
HOWARD UNIVERSITY, Washington, D.C.: 5764
HOWARDSVILLE, Virginia: 5147
HOWE, Edward T.: 2672
HOWE, Henry: 2673
HOWE, Jedediah: 2677
HOWE, Julia (Ward): 2676
HOWE, Luther: 2674

HOWE, Mary: 2677
HOWE, Milton: 2677
HOWE, Richard, First Earl Howe: 4230, 5102
HOWE, Robert (1732-1786): 2675, 5457
HOWE, Samuel Gridley: 2676
HOWE, Solomon: 2677
HOWE, W. B. W.: 89
HOWELL, Arthur: 1614
HOWELL, Benjamin P.: 2679
HOWELL, David: 2678
HOWELL, Hannah: 2678
HOWELL, Joshua B.: 2679
HOWELL, Katherine W.: 2679
HOWELL, Varina: 1084, 1403
HOWELLS, William Dean: 720, 2449
HOWERTON, Eliza: 2680
HOWERTON, Judith: 2680
HOWERTON, Philip: 822
HOWERTON, Philip H.: 2680
HOWERTON, William Matthew: 2680
HOWISON, Robert Reid: 2612, 4594
HOWITT, Mary (Botham): 5244
HOWITT'S JOURNAL: 5244
THE HOWITZER: 1661
HOWLAND, Walter M.: 2681
HOWLEY, Richard: 5537
HOYT, Arthur: 2682
HOYT, Charles: 2682
HOYT, Henry Martyn: 3277
HOYT, Isaiah F.: 2682
HOYT, Josephine: 2682
HOYT, Thomas C.: 2682
HOYT AND COMPANY: see CARROLL, HOYT AND COMPANY
HSU UN YUEN: 5252
HU SHIH: 5252
HUAROCHIRI, Peru:
    Mercury mining: 4155
HUBARD, Edmund Wilcox: 2683
HUBBARD, Bela: 323
HUBBARD, David: 2662, 3191, 5853
HUBBARD, Epaphroditus E.: 2684
HUBBARD, Joel: 2685
HUBBARD, John F.: 2292
HUBBARD, Thaddeus: 246
HUBBARD, Wade H.: 2686
HUBBARD FAMILY (Connecticut): 2684
HUBBELL, A. (New York): 2687
HUBBELL, Horatio: 2688
HUBBELL, Jay Broadus (1885-1979): 102, 553, 1227, 2449, 2689
HUBBELL, Walter: 2690
HUBER, John: 5306
HUBERT, Ben: 2691
HUBERT, Letitia Bailey: 2691
HUBERT, Sallie Donelson: 2692
HUBERT FAMILY: 2691
HUBNER, Charles William: 2449
HUCHOWN (14th century poet): 3851
HUCKINS, George N.: 2693
HUDGINS, R.: 4726
HUDIBRASTIC VERSE: 3809
HUDLESTON, John: 3315
HUDNAL, R. H.: 648
HUDSON, Charles: 2694
HUDSON, Charles Bradford: 2084
HUDSON COUNTY, New Jersey:
    Hoboken: 4322
HUDSON WOOD & CO.: 2130
HUDSON'S BAY COMPANY: 2708
HUESTON CEMETERY, Forest, Ohio: 3751
HUGER, Alfred: 2107, 2449, 2695
HUGER, Benjamin: 2696, 4332
HUGER, Daniel: 2696
HUGER, Francis: 295
HUGER, William Harleston: 5193
HUGER FAMILY (Georgia): 3396
HUGER FAMILY (South Carolina): 2695
    Genealogy: 1468
THE HUGERS OF SOUTH CAROLINA by Thomas Tileston Wells: 4392
HUGGINS, Ossian: 2697
HUGHES, Charles Evans: 879
HUGHES, David Edward: 1113
HUGHES, Sir Edward: 3315

HUGHES, John (North Carolina, fl. 1782-1823): 2698
HUGHES, John (North Carolina, fl. ca. 1886-1893): 2699
HUGHES (JOHN E.) COMPANY, INC.: 4918
HUGHES, John T.: 4065
HUGHES, Lydia Ann: 4679
HUGHES, Nicholas Collin: 2699
HUGHES, Robert William: 2612, 2700
HUGO, Victor Marie, Viscount: 2146, 2701
HUGUENIN, Thomas Abram: 2702
HUGUENOT SPRINGS, Virginia: 3422
HUGUENOTS IN FRANCE: 2195, 3587
    Dauphiné: 4408
HUGUENOTS IN SOUTH CAROLINA: 1468
    Church in Charleston: 4584
HUIDEKOPER, Henry Shippen: 2446
HUIE AND COMPANY: see SMITH, HUIE, ALEXANDER AND COMPANY
HUIE, REID AND COMPANY, Dumfries, Virginia: 2703
HULINGS, David Watts: 2704
HULL, Charles Henry: 2705
HULL, Cordell: 879
HULL, Isaac: 3118
HULL, John Adley: 4656
HULL, William (1753-1825): 4852
HULLAH, John Pyke: 4600
HUMAN RIGHTS: see CIVIL RIGHTS
HUMANITARIAN MOVEMENTS: see SOCIAL AND POLITICAL REFORM
HUMBOLDT, Alexander Von: 2706
HUME, David: 2707
HUME, John (South Carolina): 3304
HUME, Joseph (1777-1855): 2708, 4605
HUME, Juliana Rebecca (Fuller): 864
HUME, Robert (South Carolina): 2709, 5193
HUME-CAMPBELL, Sir Hugh Purves-: see CAMPBELL, Sir Hugh Purves-Hume-
HUMMELSTOWN, Pennsylvania: 496
HUMOROUS POETRY: 5066
HUMPHREYS, Andrew Atkinson: 4235
HUMPHREYS, George W.: 103
HUMPHREYS, Ralph: 4624
HUMPHREYS COUNTY, Tennessee:
    Reynoldsburg: 5933
HUMPHRIES, E. J.: 2710
HUMRICKHOUSE, Albert: 2711
HUMRICKHOUSE, Samuel: 2711
HUNDLEY, Charles Anthony: 2712
HUNDLEY, Eddy: 2712
HUNDLEY, Elisha: 2712
HUNDLEY, Ellen: 2713
HUNDLEY, Nannie: 2712
HUNGARY:
    British consulates in: 3722
    British state visit: 3722
    Currency: 1339
    Foreign trade--Great Britain: 3722
    Politics and government: 3238, 3722
    Uprising of 1848-1849:
        Exiles: 4650
HUNGERFORD, England: 5101
HUNSUCKER'S STORE, North Carolina: 75
HUNT, Cornelius E.: 3320
HUNT, Freeman: 1439
HUNT, Gaillard: 2449
HUNT, Leigh: 2058, 4770
HUNT, Martin D.: 1138
HUNT, Nathan G.: 2714
HUNT, Pleasant: 2715
HUNT, R. F.: 2642
HUNT, Samuel G.: 2716
HUNT, Thornton Leigh: 4520
HUNT, Violet: 2146
HUNT, Washington: 2717
HUNT, William Holman: 2718
HUNT FAMILY (Genealogy): 1424
HUNT & SMITH (firm): 2719
HUNTER, Lieutenant_____ (1840s): 5546
HUNTER, Andrew: 2725

HUNTER, Andrew H. (1804-1888): 2725
HUNTER, Charles N.: 2720, 4828
HUNTER, David: 3809
HUNTER, J. C.: 2721
HUNTER (J. C.) & CO., Union, South
    Carolina: 2721, 5522
HUNTER, James (Confederate soldier):
    2722
HUNTER, James, Jr. (fl. 1778): 3256
HUNTER, Joseph: 3694
HUNTER, Robert: 306
HUNTER, Robert Mercer Taliaferro:
    569, 743, 2723, 3255, 5853
HUNTER, Thomas C.: 5664
HUNTER, William W.: 2724
HUNTER FAMILY (Great Britain--
    Genealogy): 306
HUNTER FAMILY (Pennsylvania): 2725
HUNTER, New York: 2311
HUNTER GUARDS: see CONFEDERATE STATES
    OF AMERICA--ARMY--Regiments--
    Georgia--Infantry--30th
HUNTERDON COUNTY, New Jersey:
    Court of Common Pleas: 5520
    Flemington: 4964
HUNTING: 291
    see also GROUSE HUNTING; SAFARIS;
        SPORTS
    Laws and legislation: see DUCKS--
        Hunting limits; GAME LAWS
    Subdivided by place:
        Canada: 4175
        Georgia: 3894
        India: 2756
        New York: 5660
        North Carolina: 5672
        South Carolina: 4996
        Texas: 4353
        Virginia: 5660
HUNTINGDON, Selina (Shirley)
    Hastings, Countess of: 5647
HUNTINGDON, Pennsylvania:
    Creation of a national bank: 421
HUNTINGDON COUNTY, Pennsylvania: 421
    Huntingdon: 421
    Temperance: 1798
HUNTINGDON COUNTY (Pa.) TEMPERANCE
    SOCIETY: 1798
HUNTINGDONSHIRE, England:
    Fenstanton: 4693
    "Hinchingbrook": 3724
HUNTINGTON, Daniel: 2726
HUNTINGTON (HENRY E.) LIBRARY: 1236
HUNTINGTON, New York: 726, 850
HUNTINGTON, South Carolina: 4684
HUNTLEY, Elijah: 2727
HUNTLEY, Lydia Howard: 1827, 4815
HUNTON, Charles H.: 2728
HUNTON, Eppa: 2729, 5578
HUNTON, Henry: 2728
HUNTON, Mary P. (Carter): 2728
HUNTSVILLE, Alabama: 478, 1098, 1746,
    2369, 5512
    Civil War: 954, 1084
        see also CIVIL WAR--CAMPAIGNS,
            BATTLES, AND MILITARY ACTIONS--
            Alabama--Huntsville
    Cotton mills: 3568
    Finance: 5006
    Insurance: 5006
    Legal affairs: 5006
HUNTSVILLE, North Carolina: 1108,
    2714, 2809
    Slave trade: 2113
HUNTSVILLE, Pennsylvania: 4188
HUNTSVILLE (Ala.) DEMOCRAT: 1084
HURD, Richard, Bishop of Worcester:
    2836
HURDLE MILLS, North Carolina: 647
HURLBERT, William Henry: 4520
HURLBUT, Martin Luther: 3791
HURLBUT, Stephen Augustus: 4989
HURLEY, Elias: 2730
HURLEY, William: 4157
HURON COUNTY, Ohio:
    New London: 78

HURRICANES:
    see also DISASTERS; STORMS;
        WEATHER
    Florida: 3
    North Carolina:
        Beaufort: 3960
        Cape Hatteras: 3264
    South Carolina--Charleston: 2959
HURSLEY, England: 2953
HURST, William Minor: 2731
HURT, Henry Hays: 2732
HURT, John Linn: 2732
HURT, W. B.: 2732
HURT FAMILY (Virginia): 2732
HURT, TODD, & GEE (firm): 2567
HURTADO DE MENDOZA, Garcia: 4155
HUSBAND, Hermon: 305
HUSBANDRY, Patrons of: see PATRONS
    OF HUSBANDRY
HUSE, Caleb: 4597
HUSING, Hermann: 2733
HUSKE (JOHN) AND JAMES HOGG AND
    COMPANY: 2734
HUSKE, Sarah Starke: 4517
HUSKE FAMILY (North Carolina--
    Genealogy): 4517
HUSKISSON, William: 2735, 3858,
    4024
HUSSEY REAPERS: 4924
HUSTON, John: 902
HUTCHESON, David: 2736
HUTCHESON, James: 2737
HUTCHESON, John: 2738
HUTCHINS, James Hill: 2739
HUTCHINS, Nathan Louis, Sr.
    (1799-1870): 2740
HUTCHINS, Nathan Louis, Jr.: 2740
HUTCHINS, Stilson: 2374, 4751
HUTCHINSON, John Hely-, Second Earl
    of Donoughmore: see HELY-
    HUTCHINSON, John, Second Earl of
    Donoughmore
HUTCHINSON, Julius: 516
HUTCHINSON FAMILY (South Carolina):
    3349
HUTCHISON, _____ (Georgia?
    merchant): 2741
HUTCHISON, A. H. (North Carolina):
    4670
HUTCHISON, Benjamin Franklin: 2449
HUTCHISON, Robert: 3349
HUTH (FREDERICK) AND COMPANY, Great
    Britain: 2742
HUTSON, Richard: 2743
HUTSON, Robert G.: 2744
HUTTON, Orlando: 4221
HUTTON, Richard H.: 4224
HUTTON, William B.: 3691
HUXLEY, Thomas Henry: 582, 5050,
    5259
HYATT, Gifford: 2745
HYATT, William H.: 2745
HYCO HILL STOCK FARM, Virginia: 2712
HYDE, Edward, First Earl of
    Clarendon: 2707
HYDE, Mrs. F. W.: 1865
HYDE, George William Frederick
    Villiers, Fourth Baron: 5809
HYDE, John (1848-1929): 2746
HYDE COUNTY, North Carolina: 419,
    4760
    Estates (Legal):
        Administration and settlement:
            511
    Finance: 730
    Justices of the peace: 4547
    Land grants: 4827
    Mercantile accounts: 511
    Negroes: 511
    Primitive Baptist Church: 4963
    Cities and towns:
        Fairfield: 511, 921
        Lake Comfort: 730
        Middleton:
            Mercantile accounts: 5592
HYDE PARK, New York: 4088, 4128,
    4558, 4559
HYDE PARK PLANTATION: 3053

HYDER, L. K.: 5525
HYDERABAD, India: 306
HYDERABAD SUBSIDIARY FORCE: 2266
HYDEVILLE, Vermont: 5858
HYDROELECTRIC DAMS:
    North Carolina: 2581
HYDROELECTRIC POWER PLANTS:
    see also ELECTRIC POWER INDUSTRY
    Arizona: 1548
    Canada: 96
    North Carolina: 2299
HYDROGRAPHIC COMMISSION OF THE
    AMAZON: 4531
HYDROGRAPHY: see NAUTICAL SURVEYING
HYLANDE-MacGRATH, T. J.: 5193
HYMAN, McKenzie Hooks: 2747
HYMAN AND BENNETT (firm): see
    BENNETT AND HYMAN
HYMNS: 3482, 4975, 5358
    Great Britain: 625
    Methodist churches: 3646
        Maryland: 610
        Virginia: 4412
    Methodist Protestant church: 4416
    United States: 1219
    Wesleyan Methodist church: 5095
"HYMNS, PILGRIMAGES, ALGABAL" by
    Stefan George: 1992

I

I. AND F. GORIN, Philadelphia,
 Pennsylvania (firm): 870
I. G. BAKER AND COMPANY, Fort Benton,
 Montana Territory: 1211
"I. H. S." by Margaret Junkin
 Preston: 4313
"I HAVE A RENDEZVOUS WITH DEATH":
 1766
IBERVILLE, Louisiana: 805
IBERVILLE PARISH, Louisiana:
 Iberville: 805
 Plaquemine: 845
IBSEN, Henrik: 2102, 3797
ICE SEA WITCH (ship): 3871
ICE TRADE:
 North Carolina--Wilmington: 5912
 Virginia: 4916
ICKES, Harold LeClair: 4851
IDAHO:
 Description and travel: 57
 Economic conditions: 57
 Gold rush: 4834
 Religion: 57
IDAHO TERRITORY: 2714
IDBURY, England: 4514
IDDESLEIGH, Stafford Henry
 Northcote, First Earl of: 366,
 2127, 2976, 4028
"IDEALISM" by Clifford A. Lanier:
 3092
IDLE, England: 1648
IDLER, Jacob: 2748
IDLER, William: 2748
IGUAPE, Brazil: 339
IJAMES, M. C.: 2749
IJAMES FAMILY (North Carolina): 2749
IJAMES AND ANDERSON (firm): see
 ANDERSON AND IJAMES
ILIGAN, Philippine Islands:
 Military railroads: 4656
ILLINGWORTH, Stonehewer Edward: 2750
ILLINGWORTH, Thomas: 2751
ILLINOIS:
 Agricultural organizations: 715
 Agriculture: 25
 Autograph collecting: 5350
 Baptist churches: 1806
 Baseball--Kewanee: 5293
 British foreign investment in
  land: 3179
 Business affairs: 1670
 Cattle--Estrays: 1723
 Clergy: 4702
 Commodity prices: 1806, 2240, 3051,
  4732, 4875, 5160
 Copperheads: 4203
 Courtship: 4273
 Democratic Party: 1400, 5160
 Description and travel: 33, 489,
  1177
 Economic conditions: 806
 Estates (Legal):
  Administration and settlement:
   2080, 5570
  Loda: 806
  Macomb: 659

ILLINOIS (Continued):
 Exhibitions and fairs:
  see also COLUMBIAN EXPOSITION
  Ogle County: 4732
 Farm life: 1882
 Farming: 2225, 5153
  Carbondale: 1631
 Finance: see the following sub-
  headings under ILLINOIS: Personal
  finance; Protestant Episcopal
  Church--Finance; Railroads--
  Finance; Revenue collectors
 Fires:
  Chicago: 2638, 2681, 3566, 3809,
   4375
 Government agencies and officials:
  Governors (1860s): 5944
 Guardianship--Orphans: 5570
 Insurance companies--Chicago: 2013
 Land: 247, 480, 1626
  Adams County: 3255
  Prices: 3051
  Purchases and sales: 2273, 5981
 Land deeds and indentures: 5570
 Land settlement: 25
 Land titles: 2273
 Law practice:
  Alton: 1400
  Bloomington: 5570
 Lumber trade: 3410
 Migration to:
  From Connecticut: 5593
  From North Carolina: 1649, 4765
  From Virginia: 3255
 National Road: 3054
 Newspapers:
  Editing and publishing: 2526
 Personal finance:
  Peoria: 520
 Politics and government: 3082, 5160
 Protestant Episcopal church:
  Finance: 993
 Railroads:
  Bridges: 3732
  Construction: 3410, 3732
  Finance: 3410
  Maintenance and repair: 3732
   Chicago: 3848
 Revenue collectors: 2682
 School directors: 2752
 Social life and customs: 806,
  2838, 4895
 Socialist Party: 4947
 Taxation of property: 5785
 Teaching: 351, 2225, 3051, 4895
 Textile mills: 2682
 Universities and colleges: 351
  see also AUGUSTANA COLLEGE;
   CARTHAGE COLLEGE; UNIVERSITY
   OF CHICAGO
 Wages and salaries: 1601, 2240
  Teachers: 351
 Whig Party: 1400
 Wolves--McHenry County: 1723
ILLINOIS AGRICULTURAL SOCIETY: 715
ILLINOIS CENTRAL RAILROAD: 247,
 3410, 3732, 4892
ILLITERACY: 1758
ILLNESS: see DISEASES
THE ILLUMINATI: 4375
ILLUSTRATION OF BOOKS: see BOOK
 ILLUSTRATION
ILLUSTRATION OF POETRY: 733
 United States: 3965
IMBORDEN, Thomas S.: 2753
IMLAY, Fannie: 4770
IMLAY (WILLIAM H.) AND CO.: 2360
IMMIGRANTS, English: see ENGLISH
 IMMIGRANTS
IMMIGRATION AND EMIGRATION:
 see also COLONIZATION; ENGLISH
  IMMIGRANTS; and various
  nationality groups, e.g. AMERICANS
  IN GREAT BRITAIN, IRISH IN THE
  UNITED STATES

IMMIGRATION AND EMIGRATION (Continued):
 Laws and legislation:
  see also ALIENS--Legal status
  India: 4097
  United States: 4858
 From other countries [Destination
  is the United States unless
  otherwise indicated]:
  China: 4080
  France: 5308
   Dauphiné [Destination unknown]:
    4408
  Germany: 202, 3808
  Great Britain: 99, 1153, 5478
   To Canada: 5726
  India to the West Indies: 4097
  Ireland: 3230, 3424
  Netherlands: 5149
  Scotland: 1598, 5298
  United States:
   see also AMERICAN REVOLUTION--
    Loyalist refugees;
    CONFEDERATE EMIGRANTS
   To Haiti: 4409
   To Nicaragua: 3960
  West Indies: 1016
 Internal migration:
  From Alabama: 5174
  From Connecticut: 5593
  From Eastern States: 5160
  From Kansas: 4158
  From Louisiana: 4286
   Calcasieu: 5496
  From Mississippi: 5475
  From New York: 3507
  From North Carolina: 702, 2855,
   3176, 3415, 4765, 5475
  From Pennsylvania: 5264
  From South Carolina: 444, 2616,
   3161, 3981
   Chester: 5988
  From Virginia: 558, 1920, 2369,
   2559, 3130, 3255, 5392, 5884
  From West Virginia: 5194
  To Alabama: 444, 3161
  To Arkansas: 2855
  To California: 593, 3026, 4616,
   4911
   see also CALIFORNIA--Gold rush
  To Colorado: 3721
  To Georgia: 1231
  To Illinois: 1649, 3255, 4765,
   5593
  To Indiana: 1649, 1920, 3255,
   3721, 3783, 3981, 4765, 5149
  To Iowa: 5593
  To Kentucky: 558, 3130, 3199,
   3721, 4765
  To Middle West: 5160
  To Mississippi: 130, 3161, 3415
   Leake County: 5475
  To Missouri: 1557, 1920, 3176,
   3255, 3540, 4834, 5392
  To North Carolina: 5264
  To Ohio: 1920, 3161, 3255, 5149,
   5593
  To Oregon: 593
  To Tennessee: 4765
  To Texas: 86, 593, 1980, 2855,
   4158, 4286, 4562, 4765,
   5174, 5194
   San Saba County: 5496
  To Virginia: 523
  To Western States: 128, 832,
   849, 2091, 2314, 2369, 2559,
   2595, 2616, 4131, 5593, 5884
  To Wisconsin: 1920, 3507
 To other countries:
  To Cape Colony: 3067
  To Canada: 5726
  To Great Britain: 3808
  To Haiti: 4409
  To Jamaica: 1792
  To Nicaragua: 3960
  To United States [Origin
   unknown]: 1370, 1884, 3524

787

IMMIGRATION AND EMIGRATION:
  To other countries:
    To United States [Origin
      unknown] (Continued):
      see also IMMIGRATION AND
        EMIGRATION--From other
        countries
      Georgia: 1993
      Massachusetts: 3524
      South Carolina: 550, 3405
      Public opinion: 3783
    To West Indies: 4097
IMMIGRATION SOCIETY OF NEWBERRY,
  SOUTH CAROLINA: 550
IMMORALITY: see MORALS
IMMORTAL 600: 543
IMMORTALITÉ (warship): 2754
IMPEACHMENTS:
  Governors--North Carolina: 2589
  Presidents: see PRESIDENTIAL
    IMPEACHMENTS
IMPERIAL FEDERATION: 2097
IMPERIAL NIGHT-HAWK (periodical):
  3062
IMPERIAL YEOMANRY: 345
IMPERIALISM:
  see also COLONIZATION; UNITED
    STATES--TERRITORIAL EXPANSION;
    and Annexation as subheading
    under name of territory annexed
  Collapse of: 4614
  Great Britain: 43
  United States: 2473
IMPORTS: see Foreign trade as
  subheading under names of countries;
  and specific types of trade, e.g.
  COFFEE TRADE
  Prohibition of: see EMBARGOES
IMPRESSMENT OF PROPERTY: see
  AMERICAN REVOLUTION--Confiscated
  property; CIVIL WAR--CONFISCATED
  PROPERTY
IMPRESSMENT OF SEAMEN: see GREAT
  BRITAIN--NAVY--Impressment
IMPRISONMENT: see DEBT--Imprisonment
  for; PRISONERS AND PRISONS
IMPROVED ORDER OF RED MEN: 4892
IN MEMORIAM by Richard L. Maury: 3587
IN THE ARMS OF THE MOUNTAIN by
  Elizabeth Brickel Seeman: 4730
INAUGURAL BALLS:
  Presidents:
    James A. Garfield: 1953
    Grover Cleveland: 1103
    Benjamin Harrison: 2384
INAUGURATIONS:
  Governors: see (name of state)--
    Government agencies and
    officials--Governors--
    Inaugurations
  Presidents: see Inauguration as
    subheading under names of
    specific presidents
INCE, Henry Alexander: 2755
INCOME TAX:
  United States: 1278, 4858
  Virginia: 1189
INCREASE OF MINISTERS by John
  Ebenezer Pressly: 4311
INDELIBLE DYE WORKS, Philadelphia,
  Pennsylvania: 1612
INDENTURED SERVANTS: 5004
INDENTURES: see LAND DEEDS AND
  INDENTURES
INDEPENDENCE DAY CELEBRATIONS: see
  FOURTH OF JULY CELEBRATIONS
INDEPENDENT (periodical): 2619
INDEPENDENT DISSENTERS (Great
  Britain): 5746
INDEPENDENT FILIPINO CHURCH: see
  AGLIPAY
INDEPENDENT ORDER OF GOOD TEMPLARS:
  Kentucky, Grand Lodge of: 3199
  North Carolina, Grand Lodge of:
    Health Seat Lodge, No. 40: 2087
      Hillsborough: 4080
    New Hope Lodge, No. 296: 2088

INDEPENDENT ORDER OF ODD FELLOWS:
  North Carolina:
    Farmington Lodge No. 46: 2857
  Virginia: 1402
    Bridgewater: 3215
    West Virginia: 4892
    Martinsburg: 3832
INDEPENDENT PRESBYTERIAN CHURCH:
  South Carolina: 4609
"INDEX RERUM" of John Coles
  Rutherfoord: 4616
INDEXING: 2224
INDIA: 83, 3472
  see also BRITISH IN INDIA; EAST
    INDIA COMPANY; EAST INDIA
    CONVENTION
  Agriculture: 278, 5279
  Anglo-French Rivalry: 3128
  Army: see GREAT BRITAIN--ARMY--
    India; GREAT BRITAIN--INDIAN
    ARMY
    Mutiny: see GREAT BRITAIN--
      INDIAN ARMY--Mutinies
    Mutiny of 1857: see INDIAN
      MUTINY
  Art collecting--Calcutta: 1343
  British administration:
    see also GREAT BRITAIN--
      COLONIAL POLICY AND
      ADMINISTRATION--India
    1700s-1800s: 2422, 3446
    1800s: 3835, 4097
      1800s: 2421
      1810s: 2421
      1820s: 868, 1675, 2421
      1830s: 868, 3977
      1840s: 3453, 3836, 3977
      1850s: 3977, 4549, 5327
      1860s: 4549, 5875
      1870s: 515, 4549, 5883
      1880s: 515
      1890s: 515
    1800s-1900s: 663, 4660, 5836
    1900s: 4693
    Appointments: 515
      Mysore: 4660
    Bombay Presidency: 278, 3286,
      5797
    Criminal law: 4097
    Governors Council: 3286
    Madras Presidency: 1629, 2037,
      2422, 3286, 3315, 5038, 5201,
      5639
      Civil-military relations: 3315
    Native states: 1629, 2037
      see also HYDERABAD SUBSIDIARY
        FORCE; INDIA--Native states
    Rajputana: 3645
    Sindh: 3645
  British military activities:
    see also GREAT BRITAIN--ARMY--
      India; GREAT BRITAIN--INDIAN
      ARMY
    1700s: 3315
    1700s-1800s: 505, 2756, 3446
    1800s: 455, 970, 2029, 2219,
      2321, 4549
    Madras: 536
    Mysore: 3315
    Northwest frontier: 888
  British military personnel: 455,
    2321
  Buddhist temples: 217
  Census (1886): 2756
  Christianity: 2148
  Civil Service: 774
  Clergy--Education: 2756
  Courts: 278, 5883
    High Courts of Judicature: 3286
  Cricket: 5525
  Crime: 536
  Defense: 4097
  Description and travel: 505, 563,
    2421, 2463
  Diseases:
    Plague:
      Preventive inoculation: 278

INDIA (Continued):
  Dyes and dyeing: 5553
  Education: 278, 5639
    see also BRITISH IN INDIA--
      Education of children; INDIA--
      Clergy--Education; INDIA--
      Religious education
  Finance: 326
  Fish--Ganges River: 3577
  Foreign relations:
    Afghanistan--Boundaries: 1857
    Great Britain: 5797
  Foreign trade:
    United States: 2756, 3578
  Grasses: 5836
  Government agencies and officials:
    see also INDIA--British
      Administration
    Privy Council: 3286, 5883
    Supreme Government: 868
  Hinduism:
    Relations with Europeans and
      Muslims: 278
  Historical studies: 866, 4364
  Hunting: 2756
  Immigration and emigration:
    Laws and legislation: 4097
    To West Indies: 4097
  Independence: 2756
  Industrialization: 278
  Journalism: 278
  Judges: 2324
    Appointments: 5875
  Land reform: 774
  Law codes: 863
  Legislature (proposed): 3286
  Mahratta War: see MAHRATTA WAR
  Marriage--Bengal: 2756
  Memorials: 1343
  Military affairs: 1598, 2421, 3835
  Missions and missionaries: 970,
    2032, 3011, 4821
    Baptist: 5456, 5726
    Cuttack: 2410
    Methodist: 3646
  Muslims:
    Relations with Hindus: 278
  Mutinies: see GREAT BRITAIN--
    INDIAN ARMY--Mutinies; INDIAN
    MUTINY
  Mysore War: see MYSORE WAR
  Native states:
    see also INDIA--British
      administration--Native states
    Military activities: 3315
  Political patronage: 2421
  Politics and government:
    1700s-1900s: 2756
    1800s:
      1800s: 2421, 5797
      1810s: 2421
      1820s: 2421
      1840s: 3836
      1890s: 888, 5279
    1900s: 3286
  Public buildings--Baroda: 4117
  Public finance: 278, 863, 3315
    Budget: 278
  Public health: 278
  Race riots: 3809
  Railroads: 278, 2756
    Construction: 4660
    Narrow gauge system: 863
  Relations (General) with the United
    States: 83
  Religious education: 5639
    see also INDIA--Clergy--
      Education
  Scythian Invasion: 866
  Social and political reform: 1014,
    2756
    see also INDIA--Land reform
  Social classes: 5525
  Social life and customs: 278, 505
    see also BRITISH IN INDIA--
      Social life and customs
  Sugar growing: 4913

INDIA (Continued):
 Trade and commerce: 278
  Coffee: 4881
  Foreign: see INDIA--Foreign trade
  Opium: 2756
 Transportation: 278
 Trials--Baroda: 4117
 United States embassy in: 286, 5298
 Universities and colleges: see ALIGARH MUSLIM UNIVERSITY
 Viceroyalty: 2756
 Weather: 2756
INDIAN CORN TRADE: 323
INDIAN MUTINY (1857-1858): 877, 3578, 3977, 4097, 4455, 5327
 Visit to site: 5525
INDIAN NATIONAL CONGRESS: 774, 2756, 3286
INDIAN NAVAL BRIGADE:
 Andaman Islands: 1847
INDIAN OCEAN:
 British naval cruises: 2754
INDIAN PROGRESS (newspaper): 4353
INDIAN RELATIONS: see INDIANS OF NORTH AMERICA--Government relations; INDIANS OF NORTH AMERICA--Relations with whites
INDIAN SPRINGS, Georgia: 5465
 Baptist churches: 2757
AN INDIAN TALE OR TWO by Robert Blair Swinton: 5553
INDIAN TERRITORY:
 Land: 675
 Methodist missionaries: 1939
 United States Army:
  Army life: 1282
  Physicians: 3047
INDIAN TREATIES: see INDIANS OF NORTH AMERICA--Treaties
INDIAN TREATY LINE: 2486
INDIAN UNREST by Sir Valentine Chirol: 3286
INDIAN WARS: see INDIANS OF NORTH AMERICA--Wars; and names of specific wars, e.g. CREEK WARS
INDIANA: 5905
 Abolition of slavery and abolitionist sentiment: 245, 1548
  Newport: 5149
 Agricultural products:
  Prices: 5275
 Agriculture: 245, 3981, 4152
  see also INDIANA--Crops; INDIANA--Farm life; INDIANA--Farming
 American poetry: 3981
 Art--Study and teaching: 5149
 Blacksmithing: 245
 Bookkeeping: 2954
 Clergy: 4702
  see also INDIANA--Women clergy
 Commodity prices: 2240, 2294, 3051, 3540, 4152, 5149
  Hampton County: 4202
 Crops: 5980
  see also INDIANA--Agriculture; INDIANA--Farming
 Currency: 1339
 Description and travel: 1177, 5018, 5508
 Elections: 1548
 Farm life: 1882
 Farming: 1601, 5980
  see also INDIANA--Agriculture
 Flour mills: 4100
 Fugitive slaves--Newport: 5149
 Hog raising: 1601
 Land: 480, 5275
  Prices: 3051
 Land deeds and indentures: 4100
 Land settlement: 3125, 5018
 Medical practice:
  see also INDIANA--Physicians
  Union: 4220
 Methodist churches: 3981, 5149

INDIANA (Continued):
 Migration to: 1649, 1920, 3255, 3721, 3783, 3981, 4765, 5149
 Politics and government: 4169
 Physicians:
  see also INDIANA--Medical practice
  Freeport: 3221
 Railroads--Finance: 55
 Religion: 4765
  see also names of specific denominations under INDIANA
 Republican Party: 2294
 Schools: 3981
  see also INDIANA--Teaching
 Social life and customs: 5984
 Society of Friends: 5149
  White River: 3981
 Spiritualism: 5149
 Teaching: 2954, 4937
  see also INDIANA--Schools
 Temperance: 4169
 United Brethren Churches: 5149
 United States Post Office:
  New Albany: 2954
 Universities and colleges: see UNIVERSITY OF INDIANA
 Utopian Communities:
  New Harmony: 4770
 Wages and salaries: 2240, 5149
  Teachers: 5149
 Women clergy:
  Society of Friends: 3981
INDIANA LAND COMPANY, Baltimore, Maryland: 4348
INDIANAPOLIS, Indiana: 2384, 3849
INDIANS OF NORTH AMERICA: 2661, 2893, 3524
 see also names of specific tribes, e.g. CREEK INDIANS
 Agents: 3704
  Georgia: 2432
 American Revolution: see AMERICAN REVOLUTION--Indian relations with the United States
 Anthropological studies:
  Tennessee: 4894
 Artifacts: see ARROWHEADS; INDIANS OF NORTH AMERICA--Relics
 Captives of: 2606
 Civil War: see CIVIL WAR--INDIAN RELATIONS
 Councils: 1333
 Culture:
  Florida: 3173
  Louisiana: 3173
  Mississippi: 2249
 Government relations:
  see also AMERICAN REVOLUTION--Indian relations with the United States; CIVIL WAR--INDIAN RELATIONS
  1700s: 2486, 5221, 5870
  1700s-1900s: 2893
  1800s: 322, 842, 2781, 2785, 2815, 3291, 5258
  1900s: 4805
  Laws and legislation: 1678
  North Carolina (1700s): 935
 Land:
  Purchases and sales:
   Georgia: 2020, 2666, 2785
 Land titles:
  Extinguishment in Tennessee: 3176
 Language: 3775
 Mission schools:
  Mississippi: 3611
  South Carolina: 3356
 Mounds--Mississippi: 2249
 Murder of whites: see CHEROKEE INDIANS--Murder of whites
 Raids: 3745
  Florida: 1438
  Georgia: 2666
  Plains States: 2092
  Tennessee: 5870
  Texas: 5417

INDIANS OF NORTH AMERICA:
 Raids (Continued):
  Utah: 1333
  Western Territories: 2089
 Relations with whites: 2486, 5221
  Florida: 1947
  Georgia: 2666, 2788
  North Carolina: 1736
 Relics: 3063, 5498
  see also INDIANS OF NORTH AMERICA--Mounds
 Religion: 1471
 Removal: 2842
  see also TREATY OF NEW ECHOTA; UNITED STATES--ARMY--Indian removal
  Alabama: 3291
  Tennessee: 541
 Trade: 5221
  Virginia: 625
 Trading posts--Alabama: 2486
 Treaties:
  North Carolina: 4746
  Tennessee: 2486
 Treatment of:
  Carolina Province: 202
  Tennessee: 2486
 Warfare: 5229
  Georgia: 5051
  Virginia: 404
 Wars: 1401, 2849, 5130, 5229
  see also names of specific wars, e.g. CREEK WAR
  Alabama: 3415
  Capture of Geronimo: 2991
  Georgia: 2778, 3415, 4434
  Montana:
   Little Big Horn, Battle of (painting): 1665
  Oregon: 3899
  South Carolina: 2300
  Tennessee: 2486
 Subdivided by place:
  Alabama: 2781, 3291
  Canada: 4913
  Georgia: 2785, 3966
  Middle West: 128, 1920
  Mississippi Territory: 3041
  Tennessee: 2486
  Virginia: 1511
  Western States: 1282
INDIGENT: see POORHOUSES; POVERTY
INDIGO: 5553
INDIGO CULTURE:
 Guatemala: 4980
 South Carolina: 4216
 Virginia: 3819
INDIGO TRADE: 323
 China: 5252
 Great Britain: 5221
 Virginia: 3819
INDIVIDUAL VOTING RECORD BY ROLL CALLS IN THE HOUSE OF REPRESENTATIVES: 4848
INDOCHINA: 1424, 5525
"INDIOS IDOLATRAS" by Martin de Fisner: 4979
INDUSTRIAL ACCIDENTS:
 see also WORKMEN'S COMPENSATION
 Lawsuits--South Carolina: 5930
INDUSTRIAL DEVELOPMENT: see INDUSTRIALIZATION
INDUSTRIAL MANAGEMENT:
 North Carolina: 274
 United States: 274, 325
INDUSTRIAL MEDICINE: 2934
INDUSTRIAL ORGANIZATION:
 Georgia: 3706
INDUSTRIAL PRODUCTIVITY: 3190
 Virginia:
  Falmouth: 2165
  Van Buren Furnace: 5990
INDUSTRIAL SAFETY:
 see LABOR CONDITIONS--Industrial safety
INDUSTRIAL UNION OF MARINE AND SHIPBUILDING WORKERS OF AMERICA: 1199

INDUSTRIAL WORKERS:
    Labor unions: see LABOR UNIONS--
      Industrial workers
    Wages and salaries: see WAGES AND
      SALARIES--Industrial workers
INDUSTRIALIZATION:
    Great Britain: 1070, 1632
    India: 278
    Massachusetts--Brockton: 3524
    North Carolina: 2231
    South Carolina: 300
      Spartanburg: 4118
    Virginia--Luray: 574
INDUSTRY AND AGRICULTURE: see
    AGRICULTURE AND INDUSTRY
INDUSTRY OF ALL NATIONS EXHIBITION
    (1854): 3424
INFERIOR COURTS: see COURTS--
    Inferior courts
INFLATION:
    see also AMERICAN REVOLUTION--
      Economic aspects--Inflation;
      CIVIL WAR--Economic aspects--
      Inflation; PRICE REGULATION
    Virginia--Danville: 4094
INFLUENZA: see DISEASES--Influenza
INGALLS, John James: 3022
INGALLS, Rufus: 2758
INGE, William Ralph: 2759
INGERSOLL, Charles Jared: 2760
INGERSOLL, F. D.: 4125
INGERSOLL, Lizzie: 2035
INGERSOLL, Robert Green: 2626
INGESTRE, Charles John Chetwynd-
    Talbot, Viscount: 1087
INGHAM, Samuel Delucenna: 2761
INGRAHAM, Edward Duffield: 2052
INGRAM, E. B.: 127
INGRAM, John (North Carolina): 2763
INGRAM, John H. (Great Britain):
    2763
INGRAM, Lemuel: 5739
INGRAM AND SMITH: see SMITH & INGRAM
INHERITANCE LAW:
    Louisiana: 4902
    North Carolina: 1525
    Texas: 4170
INJURIES: see ACCIDENTS; WOUNDS
INK: see PULP AND PAPER INDUSTRY--
    Ink
INLAND NAVIGATION: 4858
    see also INTRACOASTAL WATERWAY
    Improvement:
      see also RIVERS--Improvement
      Ireland: 5330
INLAND WATERWAY VESSELS: see CANAL
    BOATS; FREIGHT BOATS; RIVERBOATS
INLET WATERWAY (project): 4858
INMAN MILLS, Spartanburg, South
    Carolina: 5233
INNES, James: 2633
INNS: see TAVERNS AND INNS
INOCULATION: see as subheading under
    specific diseases, e.g. DISEASES--
    Plague--Preventive inoculation
"INQUIRING ABOUT RETIRING" by
    Thomas Hightower Collins: 1167
"AN INQUIRY CONCERNING THE PRESENT
    STATE OF THE CHURCHES IN
    HAMPSHIRE": 1035
INSANE ASYLUMS: see MENTAL HOSPITALS
INSANITY: 5529
    see also FORENSIC PSYCHIATRY;
      GUARDIANSHIP--Mental
      incompetence; MENTAL HEALTH;
      MENTAL HEALTH LAWS; SUICIDE
    Commitment and detention: 2779,
      4732
    Jurisprudence: 958
    Massachusetts: 1054
INSPECTION LAWS: 2497
INSPECTOR GENERAL OF POTASH AND
    PEARLASHES: 2497
INSTITUT DE DROIT INTERNATIONAL:
    1792
INSTITUTES OF THE LAWS OF ENGLAND:
    1142

INSTRUCTIONS FOR EXERCISING CANNON
    AND MOUNTING AND DISMOUNTING
    by John Faucheraud Grimké: 2875
INSURANCE: 4849, 5747
    Business:
      Georgia: 5730
      New York--Niagara: 3848
      North Carolina: 5962
    Fire: 5731, 5790
      North Carolina: 3416, 5709
      Pennsylvania: 2521
        Carlisle: 1332
        Monongahela City: 1332
      South Carolina: 1691
        Charleston: 2448
      Virginia: 4924
    Health: see HEALTH PROGRAMS;
      NATIONAL HEALTH INSURANCE
    Laws and legislation:
      North Carolina: 2553, 3410
    Life: 2493, 2983, 3850
      North Carolina: 3416, 3825, 4060,
        5298, 5541
      Pennsylvania:
        Monongahela City: 1332
      South Carolina: 3421
      Virginia: 974
      West Virginia: 2130
    Livestock:
      Virginia--Page County: 461
    Maritime: 162, 323, 4541, 5139
      Great Britain: 1913, 3183, 3230
      New York: 3960
      South Carolina: 1691
      United States: 1216
      Virginia: 3509
    Property: 3850
      Georgia: 127
      Louisiana--New Orleans: 679
      North Carolina: 3308
      Virginia: 461, 4924
    Rates: 3753
    Social: see WORKMEN'S COMPENSATION
    Stocks--United States: 5080
    Surety and Fidelity: see PUBLIC
      OFFICIALS--Bonding
    Unemployment: see UNEMPLOYMENT
      COMPENSATION
    Subdivided by place:
      Alabama: 1084, 2013, 5593
        Huntsville: 5006
      Connecticut: 2273, 2684
      Georgia: 1434, 2114, 2232, 4587
      Louisiana--New Orleans: 5062
      Maryland--Baltimore: 4348
      North Carolina: 1556, 3476,
        5367
        Warren County: 3307
      Ohio: 281, 5342
      Pennsylvania: 480
      United States: 1115, 1403
      Virginia: 433, 523, 2387, 2794,
        3400, 4710, 5891
        Nottoway County: 1811
INSURANCE AGENTS:
    Alabama: 2013
    Georgia--Savannah: 4587
    North Carolina--Durham: 4986
    Pennsylvania--Carlisle: 1332
    Virginia: 628
INSURANCE COMPANIES: 974, 2013,
    2983, 3308, 5096, 5731, 5790
    Lawsuits:
      New York: 3587
      North Carolina: 3825
    Subdivided by place:
      Canada: 2013
      Georgia--Savannah: 4587
      Great Britain: 2013, 3183
      Illinois--Chicago: 2013
      Massachusetts: 1119
      New York: 2983, 3620, 5731
      North Carolina: 3825, 5962
        Durham: 4968
        Franklinton: 5012
        Greensboro: 4918
      Pennsylvania:
        Cumberland County: 1332

INSURANCE COMPANIES:
    Subdivided by place (Continued):
      South Carolina:
        Charleston: 1691
      Virginia: 2387, 2493, 4616
        Alexandria: 3509
        Portsmouth: 4282
INSURANCE COMPANY OF AMERICA,
    Virginia: 523
INSURANCE WORKERS: see LABOR UNIONS--
    Insurance and allied workers
INSURRECTIONS:
    see also SLAVES--Insurrections
    Cuba: 2387
    Ireland: 5062
      see also REBELLION OF 1798
    Philippine Islands--Albay: 4656
INTEGRATION: see DESEGREGATION
INTELLECTUAL FREEDOM: see ACADEMIC
    FREEDOM
INTELLIGENCE: see MILITARY
    INTELLIGENCE
INTENDED (British brigantine): 2766
INTERCHURCH ORGANIZATIONS: see
    CHURCHES--Interchurch organizations
INTERCHURCH RELATIONS: see
    CHURCHES--Interchurch relations;
    and Interchurch relations under
    names of specific denominations
INTERCONTINENTAL RAILWAY COMMISSION:
    4719
INTEREST RATES: see BONDS--Interest
    rates; LOANS--Interest rates
INTERIOR DECORATION:
    see also CHANDELIERS; HOUSE
      FURNISHINGS; HOUSES--Interiors
    Portraits in tile: 562
INTERNAL IMPROVEMENTS:
    see also UNITED STATES--GOVERNMENT
      AGENCIES AND OFFICIALS--Works
      Progress Administration
    Alabama: 1877
    Confederate States of America:
      1185
    Georgia: 1090
    Massachusetts: 1433
    New York: 5345
      Troy: 5747
    North Carolina: 3415, 4924, 4964
    Pennsylvania: 421, 1433, 4732
    Philippine Islands: 3313
    South Carolina: 4269
    Virginia: 1075, 4732, 4924
INTERNAL MIGRATION: see IMMIGRATION
    AND EMIGRATION--Internal migration
INTERNAL REVENUE: see UNITED STATES--
    GOVERNMENT AGENCIES AND
    OFFICIALS--Internal revenue
INTERNATIONAL ASSOCIATION OF
    INSURANCE COUNSEL: 4927
INTERNATIONAL ASSOCIATION OF
    NEWSPAPERS AND AUTHORS: 4020
INTERNATIONAL BANKING: 196
    see also BANKS AND BANKING
INTERNATIONAL BAR ASSOCIATION: 4927
INTERNATIONAL BROTHERHOOD OF
    BOILERMAKERS, IRON SHIP BUILDERS
    AND HELPERS OF AMERICA: 4962
INTERNATIONAL BROTHERHOOD OF
    ELECTRICAL WORKERS:
    Conventions: 2768
    South Carolina:
      Local Union No. 382, Columbia:
        2767
      Local Union No. 776, Charleston:
        2768
INTERNATIONAL BUSINESS AFFAIRS: 196
    see also FOREIGN BUSINESS
      ENTERPRISES
INTERNATIONAL CONFERENCE OF LABOR
    AND SOCIALIST INTERNATIONAL: 4948
INTERNATIONAL CONFERENCES: 2398, 4331

INTERNATIONAL CONFERENCES (Continued):
    see also HAGUE PEACE CONFERENCE;
    INTERNATIONAL CONFERENCE OF LABOR
    AND SOCIALIST INTERNATIONAL;
    INTERNATIONAL RAILWAY CONGRESS;
    WASHINGTON DISARMAMENT CONFERENCE;
    WEST INDIES CONFERENCE
INTERNATIONAL CONGRESS OF
    FREETHINKERS: 2532
INTERNATIONAL COPYRIGHT: 1734, 1910
INTERNATIONAL COPYRIGHT TREATY: 1734
INTERNATIONAL COTTON EXPOSITION,
    Atlanta, Georgia (1881): 5494
INTERNATIONAL EXHIBITIONS AND FAIRS:
    see EXHIBITIONS AND FAIRS--
    International
INTERNATIONAL EXPOSITION, Atlanta,
    Georgia (1895): 3376
INTERNATIONAL FINANCE: 1424
    see also FOREIGN BUSINESS
    ENTERPRISES; FOREIGN INVESTMENT;
    INTERNATIONAL BUSINESS AFFAIRS
INTERNATIONAL LADIES' GARMENT
    WORKERS' UNION:
    Upper South Department: 2769
INTERNATIONAL LAW: 1792
    Study of: 4343
INTERNATIONAL MOLDERS' UNION OF
    NORTH AMERICA:
    Virginia Local Union No. 121:
    2770
INTERNATIONAL PEACE MOVEMENT: 4828
INTERNATIONAL RAILWAY CONGRESS: 5103
INTERNATIONAL RELATIONS: see
    Foreign relations as subheading
    under names of specific countries
INTERNATIONAL RELIEF ORGANIZATIONS:
    see also AMERICAN RED CROSS
    United States aid to China, Puerto
    Rico, and the Near East: 3633
INTERNATIONAL SOLIDARITY COMMITTEE:
    4948
INTERNATIONAL SUNSHINE SOCIETY:
    3633
INTERNATIONAL TRADE: see Foreign
    trade as subheading under names
    of specific countries
INTERNATIONAL TYPOGRAPHICAL UNION:
    North Carolina:
        Local Union No. 54, Raleigh:
        2772
    South Carolina:
        Local Union No. 43, Charleston:
        2771
INTERNATIONAL UNION OF ELECTRICAL,
    RADIO, AND MACHINE WORKERS: 1197,
    1198, 1201
INTERNATIONAL UNION OF MINE, MILL,
    AND SMELTER WORKERS: 1197
INTERNATIONAL UNION OF SOCIALIST
    YOUTH: 4948
INTERNATIONAL WOODWORKERS OF
    AMERICA: 1196, 1197
    Tennessee: 1197
INTERNATIONAL WORKERS OF THE WORLD:
    1951
INTEROCEANIC CANALS:
    Central America: 196
    see also PANAMA CANAL
INTERPARLIAMENTARY UNION: 4927
INTERRACIAL MARRIAGE:
    Pennsylvania--Blair County: 5249
    South Carolina: 669
    Whites and Indians of North
        America in Idaho Territory: 2714
INTERRELIGIOUS FOUNDATION FOR
    COMMUNITY ORGANIZATION: 3020
INTERSTATE COMMERCE COMMISSION: see
    UNITED STATES--GOVERNMENT AGENCIES
    AND OFFICIALS--Interstate
    Commerce Commission
INTERSTATE CONVENTION OF FARMERS,
    Atlanta, Georgia: 4996
INTERVENTION: see CIVIL WAR--
    FOREIGN INTERVENTION
INTRACOASTAL WATERWAY: 4858
    North Carolina: 2774
    South Carolina: 2774

"INTRODUCCION A LA HISTORIA DE LOS
    INCAS DEL PERÚ" : 4155
INTRODUCTION TO THE CRITICAL STUDY
    AND KNOWLEDGE OF THE HOLY
    SCRIPTURES: 2653
INVALID HOMES: see CONVALESCENT
    HOMES
INVENTIONS: 1478, 3424
    see also PATENTS
    Automobile accessories: see
        AUTOMOBILE ACCESSORIES--
        Inventions
    Bicycles: see BICYCLES--Propulsion
    Bombs: see BOMBS--Inventions
    Cigarettes: see CIGARETTE MAKING
        MACHINES--Inventions
    Collapsible vehicles: see
        COLLAPSIBLE VEHICLES--Inventions
    Coins: see COINS AND COINAGE--
        Inventions
    Engines: see ELASTIC FLUID ENGINES;
        MARINE ENGINES
    Envelopes: see ENVELOPES
        (Stationery), Double
    Fire extinguishers: see FIRE
        EXTINGUISHERS
    Fishing industry: see FISH
        HATCHING DEVICES; KNITTING
        MACHINES--Fishing nets
    Gate latches: see GATE LATCHES--
        Inventions
    Gold extraction: see GOLD--
        Extraction from ores--Inventions
    Kitchen utensils: see KITCHEN
        UTENSILS--Inventions
    Knitting machines: see HOSIERY
        MACHINERY--Knitting machines--
        Inventions; KNITTING MACHINES--
        Fishing nets
    Ordnance: see CARTRIDGE CLIPS;
        FIRING DEVICES--Inventions; GUN
        BARRELS--Manufacturing processes;
        PERCUSSION RIFLE BULLET
    Post office boxes: see POST OFFICE
        BOXES--Inventions
    Steamboats: see STEAMBOATS--
        Inventions
    Subdivided by place:
        Pennsylvania: 5686
        South Carolina: 3163
INVERNESS, Scotland:
    Social life and customs: 2103
INVESTMENT COMPANIES:
    Kentucky--Lexington: 4241
    Virginia--Petersburg: 4241
INVESTMENT TRUST COMPANY, Wilmington,
    North Carolina: 3447
INVESTMENTS: 5312, 5564, 5668
    see also FINANCE; and Investment
    in as subheading under types of
    businesses, e.g. RAILROADS--
    Investment in
    International: see FOREIGN
        INVESTMENT
    North Carolina--Wilmington: 3447
    United States: 1588
    Virginia: 5513
INWOOD, West Virginia:
    Postal service: 5239
IONIA COUNTY, Michigan:
    Sebawa: 4452
IONIAN ISLANDS: 1147
    British administration: 3835,
        4427, 4520
    Defenses on Corfu: 4520
    Politics and government: 3835
IOWA:
    Annexation: 5436
    Baptist churches: 1806
    Baseball--Marshalltown: 5293
    Commodity prices: 2294, 3333
    Description and travel: 1177
    Economic conditions: 3333, 5561
    Farming: 1344
        Wayne County: 4075
    Hospitals--Keokuk: 5017
    Land: 1626
        Prices: 849

IOWA:
    Land (Continued):
        Purchases and sales: 2273
    Land fraud: see IOWA--Public
        lands--Land fraud
    Land speculation: 4157, 4468
    Land titles: 2273
    Legislature: 415
    Migration to: 5593
    Missions and missionaries:
        Presbyterian: 1283
    Public lands--Land fraud: 5051
    Railroads--Construction: 3054
    Secret societies: 1984
    Social life and customs: 2838
    Trade and commerce:
        Dubuque: 323
    Universities and colleges: see
        DES MOINES COLLEGE
    Wheat: 1505
IOWA CITY, Iowa: 3848
IPSWICH, England: 1081
IPSWICH, Massachusetts: 3015
IRAN: 83
    see also PERSIA
IRBY, Sam: 2775
IREDELL, Hannah (Johnston): 2776
IREDELL, James (1751-1799): 2776,
    5002
IREDELL, James (1788-1853): 2776,
    5457
IREDELL FAMILY (North Carolina--
    Genealogy): 2776
IREDELL CIRCUIT, Methodist churches:
    3646
IREDELL COUNTY, North Carolina: 269,
    1428, 2113, 2905, 3600, 3787,
    4083, 5143, 5596, 5599
    Agricultural implements: 5319
    Banks and banking: 1381
    Churches: 5245
    Cotton mills: 5310
    Cotton prices: 5310
    Crops: 4872
    Estates (Legal):
        Administration and settlement:
        5319
    Family life: 4310
    Farming: 5245
    Hiring of slaves: 4872, 5319
    House furnishings: 5319
    Merchants: 1487, 3288
    Plantation accounts: 1382
    Slave trade: 5245
    Social life and customs: 4310
    Weather: 4310, 5245
    Cities and towns:
        Davidson's Creek: 1387
        Deep Well: 4007
        Granite Hill: 3690
        Harmony--Churches: 2347
        Houstonville: 2661, 2663
        Liberty: 1777
        Mooresville: 3415, 3757
        Olin: 831
            Schools: 2857, 3973
        Statesville: 893, 1966, 3219,
            3572, 3905
            Business affairs: 3688
            Churches: 1128
            Courts: 1128
            Merchants: 8, 1856, 1858
            Methodist churches: 3646
            Schools:
                Girls' schools and academies:
                5310
            Universities and colleges: see
                MITCHELL COLLEGE
        Turnersburg: 85, 2857, 5048, 5310
IRELAND, Alexander: 2149
IRELAND, Oscar Brown: 2777
IRELAND: 3883, 4434
    Agriculture: 3349, 5809
    Art exhibitions--Dublin: 3567
    Brewing industry: 3883
    British administration: 2324,
        4934, 5330

IRELAND:
  British administration (Continued):
    see also GREAT BRITAIN--
      COLONIAL POLICY AND
      ADMINISTRATION--Ireland;
      GREAT BRITAIN--IRISH POLICY
  Catholic Church: 5726
    Relations with Protestants: 3349
      see also IRELAND--Church of
        England--Relations with
        Catholics
  Catholic emancipation: 1598, 3883
  Church of England: 5726
    Relations with Catholics: 5726
      see also IRELAND--Catholic
        Church--Relations with
        Protestants
  Church of Ireland, Disestablishment
    of: 472, 2127
  Church reform: 4605
  Commonplace books: 2887
  Courts: 504
  Currency: 3349
  Defense: 3315
    see also IRELAND--Fortifications
  Description and travel:
    1700s: 2776
    1800s: 43, 2543, 5038
  Dissenting churches:
    County Antrim: 718
  Economic conditions: 1311, 3754,
    4566, 5809
  Education: 4024
  Elections: 535
    Waterford (1830): 3468
  Excise taxes: 3883
  Exhibitions and fairs:
    Dublin: 3567
  Foreign trade:
    see also IRELAND--Trade and
      commerce
    Cork: 2403
    Great Britain: 2884
    Virginia: 2884
  Fortifications: 5330
    see also IRELAND--Defense
  Government agencies and officials
    Lord Lieutenant: 4024, 5330
  Harbor construction: 3883
  Home rule: 649, 735, 2626, 3980,
    4567
  Immigration and emigration:
    To United States: 3230, 3424
      see also IRISH IN THE UNITED
        STATES
  Inland navigation: 5330
  Insurrections (1803): 5062
    see also IRELAND--Rebellion of
      1798; IRELAND--Riots
  Land: 3185
  Land laws: 3693
    see also IRISH LAND ACT
  Land reform: 649, 2149
    see also IRISH LAND ACT
  Landlord and tenant: 3238, 4520
  Law: 1311
  Law enforcement: 4024
  Liquor manufacturing:
    Proposed legislation: 5330
  Merchants: 2884
  Methodist churches:
    Londonderry: 3738
  Military affairs: 1598
  Mining--County Wicklow: 3567
  Parliament:
    see also GREAT BRITAIN--
      PARLIAMENT--Irish members
    House of Commons: 4093
  Political unrest:
    County Westmeath: 4024
  Politics and government:
    see also GREAT BRITAIN--COLONIAL
      POLICY AND ADMINISTRATION--
      Ireland; GREAT BRITAIN--IRISH
      POLICY
    1700s: 2199
    1700s-1800s: 1311, 5726
    1800s: 1775

IRELAND:
  Politics and government:
    1800s (Continued):
      1830s: 4024
      1840s: 5, 504, 678, 5809
      1850s: 5, 678, 5809
      1860s: 472, 4566
    1800s-1900s: 294
  Public finance: 4331
    see also IRELAND--Revenues
  Public welfare: 504, 1599
  Rebellion of 1798: 2266, 4171,
    5062
  Religion: 1311, 4566
  Revenues: 92
    see also IRELAND--Public finance
  Riots, Suppression: 5809
  Seances--Dublin: 3567
  Social and political reform: 4024
  Social conditions: 3754, 4566
  Social life and customs:
    Dublin: 3567
  Spiritualism--Dublin: 3567
  Suffrage: 4605
  Tax evasion: 3567
  Taxation: 3567, 5639
  Theater: 3567
  Union with Great Britain: 535,
    4024, 5330
  Trade and commerce:
    see also IRELAND--Foreign trade
    Laws and legislation: 16
    Linen exports: 2884
    Potato exports: 3230
    Wool exports: 2148
IRISH COERCION ACT: 4605
"IRISH FINANCES" by Sir John
  Newport: 3883
IRISH IN SPAIN: 2155
IRISH IN THE UNITED STATES: 43, 1050,
  3424, 3447, 3754
  Louisiana: 489
  New Jersey: 4354
  Pennsylvania:
    Norristown: 4190
    Philadelphia: 4354
    Reading: 4190
  South Carolina: 2543
IRISH JASPER GREENS: 5547
  see also CONFEDERATE STATES OF
    AMERICA--ARMY--Regiments--
    Georgia--Infantry--1st
IRISH LAND ACT: 515, 2149, 3185
IRISH MUNICIPAL BILL: 4605
IRISH PARTY--Objectives: 5872
IRISH POETRY: 3567
IRISH QUESTION: see FENIANS; HOME
  RULE
IRISH RIOTS (1863, Boston,
  Massachusetts): 5563
IRISH TERRIERS: 5304
IRON COMPANIES: see IRON INDUSTRY
IRON FOUNDRIES:
  Virginia: 282, 558
    Marion: 3513
    Union Furnace: 5827
IRON FURNACES:
  see also CHARCOAL FURNACES; SCRIP--
    Iron furnaces
  Virginia: 117, 2922
    Van Buren Furnace: 5990
    Wytheville: 4648
IRON GATE, Virginia: 2922
IRON GATE FIXTURES--Virginia: 282
IRON INDUSTRY:
  see also CIVIL WAR--Iron industry;
    COKE
  Accounts--Pennsylvania: 421
  Company stores--Virginia: 5990
  Employee work records:
    Virginia: 5990
  Hiring of slaves--Virginia: 523
  Lawsuits: 4399
  Stocks--Great Britain: 2410
  Subdivided by place:
    Alabama: 642, 3188
    Maryland--Baltimore: 1169
    New York: 1169

IRON INDUSTRY:
  Subdivided by place (Continued):
    North Carolina: 529
      Wilmington: 3447
    Pennsylvania: 5775
      Blair County: 421
      Hollidaysburg: 849
      McVeytown: 849
      Philadelphia: 1169
    Prussia: 4399
    Russia: 3238
    South Carolina: 529
    Tennessee: 1289
    United States: 3413
    Virginia: 4924, 5513, 5613
      Augusta County: 728
      Lynchburg: 3809
      Page County: 522
      Westmoreland County: 917
IRON MOUNTAIN RAILROAD, Missouri:
  2386
IRON ORE MINING:
  North Carolina: 2121
  Virginia--Van Buren Furnace: 5990
IRON PIPE TRADE: 3230
IRON PRICES: 5613
  Virginia--Page County: 522
IRON TRADE:
  see also SCRAP IRON TRADE; SHEET
    IRON TRADE
  Great Britain: 535
  Pennsylvania:
    Blair County: 421
    Philadelphia: 4797
  Virginia: 2633
    Augusta County: 728
    Lynchburg: 4720
IRON WORKERS:
  Labor unions: see INTERNATIONAL
    BROTHERHOOD OF BOILERMAKERS,
    IRON SHIP BUILDERS AND HELPERS
    OF AMERICA
  Wages: see WAGES AND SALARIES--
    Iron workers
IRONCLADS: see names of specific
  vessels and classes of vessels,
  e.g. ELLET RAMS; VIRGINIA
IRONSIDES AFFAIR: 1352
IRONTON, Missouri: 4161
IROQUOIS, U.S.S.: 3258
IRRIGATION: 4805
  see also LAND RECLAMATION
IRRIGATION MACHINERY:
  South Carolina: 1524
IRVINE, M. (physician): 4214
IRVING, Henry: 157
IRVING, Washington: 720
IRVING INSTITUTE, New York: 5593
IRVING TRUST COMPANY: 4343
IRVINGITE MOVEMENT: see CATHOLIC
  APOSTOLIC CHURCH
IRVINGTON, New York: 1584
IRWIN, Jared: 2778, 5395
IRWIN, William Henry: 3265
ISAAC A. JARRATT & SANDERFORD (firm):
  2808
ISLAND NO. 10, Missouri: see CIVIL
  WAR--CAMPAIGNS, BATTLES, AND
  MILITARY ACTIONS--Missouri--Island
  No. 10
ISLE OF MAN:
  Clergy--Church of England: 4187
  Household accounts: 4187
  Riots: 3835
ISLE OF PALMS, South Carolina: 3421
ISLE OF WIGHT, England:
  Politics and government: 332
  Cowes: 4023
  "Farringford": 5226
ISLE OF WIGHT COUNTY, Virginia:
  Smithfield: 811
  Civil War: 2121
ISRAEL, Israel: 1670
ISRAEL:
  Description and travel: 2083
ISSAQUEENA MILLS: 5312
ISTANBUL, Turkey: see CONSTANTINOPLE,
  Turkey

ISTORIA CIVILE DEL REGNO DE NAPOLI by Pietro Giannone: 2015
ITALIAN DRAMA--Reviews: 3617
ITALIAN LITERATURE:
  Translations from French: 1721
  Translations into English: 3836, 5255
ITALIAN POETRY: 2056, 4116, 5379
  Translations into English: 425, 5734
ITALY:
  see also VENICE (state)
  Agricultural practices: 4625
  Archeological investigations: 2148
  Army:
    Africa: 5835
    World War I--Albania: 4719
  Biographical studies:
    Florence: 5487
  British embassy in--Rome: 3472
  Catholic Church--Discipline: 2015
  Censorship: 2015
  Currency: 1339
    Value: 5886
  Description and travel:
    1700s:
      1780s: 4625
      1790s: 2869
    1700s-1800s: 558
    1800s: 258, 577, 4770, 5038
      1810s: 1049
      1820s: 1049, 2058
      1830s: 4490
      1840s: 5133
      1850s: 2678
      1860s: 1352
      1870s: 3694
      1880s: 39, 1424
      1890s: 39
    1800s-1900s: 5730
    1900s:
      1910s: 4020
  Economic conditions: 323
  Engravers and engravings: 4116
  Foreign relations: 3472
    Conflict between Spain and Austria: 2155
      Spanish military expedition: 873
    Triple Alliance: 2149
  Foreign trade: 323
  Governesses: 4770
  Government agencies and officials:
    Division of Aeronautics: 137
  Politics and government:
    1700s: 2155
    1800s: 3472, 4650, 5133
    1900s: 4020
  Religion: 128
  Sculptors and sculpture: 2181, 2352
  Social life and customs:
    1800s: 258, 1049, 3310, 5133
    1900s: 3710, 4020
  United States embassy in: 4020
    Rome: 4719
  United States military assistance (1910s): 4020
  War of 1860-1861: see NEAPOLITAN EXILES
  World War II: see WORLD WAR II--Italy
ITHACA, New York: 1175, 2434, 2705
  see also CORNELL UNIVERSITY
IUKA, Mississippi: see CIVIL WAR--CAMPAIGNS, BATTLES, AND MILITARY ACTIONS--Mississippi--Iuka
IVERSON, Alfred: 2779
IVES, Caleb Smith: 1067
IVES, Levi Silliman: 5457
IVES AND BROWN (firm): see BROWN AND IVES
IVEY, Thomas Neal: 5457
"IVY" (correspondent): 4
IVY PLANTING: see LANDSCAPE GARDENING
IWAKURA EMBASSY: 4054
IZARD, George: 1333, 2780

IZARD, Margaret: 3485
IZARD, Ralph: 2780, 3485

## J

J. & D. MacRAE, Wilmington, North Carolina (firm): 3447
J. & E. B. STOWE, North Carolina (firm): 5100
J. & P. HARRISON (mercantile firm): 2392
J. AND W. MOORE, Greenville, North Carolina (firm): 3739
J. C. HUNTER & CO., Union, South Carolina (firm): 2721, 5522
J. F. SEAS AND SON, Orville, Ohio (firm): 4728
J. H. NEWCOMER: see M. AND J. H. NEWCOMER
J. HARDING (firm): see E. AND J. HARDING
J. K. GILLIAT AND COMPANY, London, England (firm): 2363
J. P. MORGAN AND COMPANY: 4556
J. P. RINKER (firm): see SAMUEL M. LANTZ AND J. P. RINKER
J. S. McCLELLAN AND COMPANY, Martinsburg, West Virginia (firm): 5110
J. T. MURRAY & COMPANY, New York (firm): 530
"J. W. F. C." (poet): 3892
J. W. RICHARDSON AND COMPANY, Fifesville, Virginia: 4459
JACINTO, Mississippi: 4442
JACKMAN, Sydney Wayne: 4551
JACKSON, Andrew: 805, 1302, 1308, 1762, 2399, 2449, 2661, 2781, 3073, 3082, 3255, 3291, 4083, 4616, 4669, 4833, 4852, 4880, 4943, 4987, 5667
  Administration: 616, 850, 872, 5491, 5613
  Cherokee Indian policy: 3176
  Dispute with John C. Calhoun: 5345
  Nullification policy: 3415, 3809
  Political strength:
    In Democratic Party: 519
    Maryland: 4712
    North Carolina: 730, 2776
  Presidential campaign:
    Maryland: 4359
  Visit to Baltimore, Maryland: 3255
  Visit to "Castle Hill," Virginia: 4490
JACKSON, Asa (Virginia): 2782
JACKSON, Asa M. (Georgia): 2783
JACKSON, Asbury Hill: 2326
JACKSON, Charles C. (Massachusetts): 5093
JACKSON, Sir Charles James: 2784
JACKSON, Claiborne Fox: 3703
JACKSON, Coverley: 4097
JACKSON, David K.: 1227, 2449, 5193
JACKSON, E. E.: 2880
JACKSON, Ebenezer: 2785
JACKSON, Edward: 2794
JACKSON, Ellen: 4602
JACKSON, Evie Harden: 2786
JACKSON, Florence Barclay: 2449
JACKSON, Henry (Georgia): 3526
JACKSON, Henry Rootes (1820-1898): 2449, 2789
JACKSON, Jabez Young: 5386
JACKSON, James (London merchant): 5221
JACKSON, James (general, 1757-1806): 1090, 2788, 5395
JACKSON, James (1819-1887): 2789, 2931
JACKSON, James Streshly (1823-1862): 3207
JACKSON, John R.: 2794
JACKSON, Joseph Francis Ambrose: 2790
JACKSON, Josephus: 2791
JACKSON, Julia Prinsep: 5050
JACKSON, Martha M.: 3677
JACKSON, Mary Anna (Morrison): 2792
JACKSON, Stonewall: see JACKSON, Thomas Jonathan
JACKSON, Thomas (Great Britain, 1783-1873): 4146
JACKSON, Thomas Jonathan: 154, 314, 581, 745, 1601, 2396, 2792, 2971, 3797, 3809, 3832, 5613
  Death: 3908, 4126
  Funeral: 3624, 5382
  Portrait: 1665
JACKSON, Thomas P. (South Carolina): 2793
JACKSON, William Hicks: 664
JACKSON FAMILY (Georgia): 2326
JACKSON FAMILY (Virginia): 2794
JACKSON, Georgia: 622, 3575
JACKSON, Louisiana: see CENTENARY COLLEGE
JACKSON, Mississippi: 1506, 2211, 3606, 4246, 5363, 5952
  Civil War: 5193
    see also CIVIL WAR--CAMPAIGNS, BATTLES, AND MILITARY ACTIONS--Mississippi--Jackson
  Methodist churches:
    Unification Movement: 3646
JACKSON, Tennessee:
  Merchants: 330
JACKSON COLLEGE, Columbia, Tennessee: 4609
JACKSON COUNTY, Florida: 806
  Estates (Legal):
    Administration and settlement: 4903
JACKSON COUNTY, Georgia:
  Jefferson: 3249, 4795
JACKSON COUNTY, Illinois:
  Carbondale: 1631
JACKSON COUNTY, Iowa:
  Monmouth: 1619
JACKSON COUNTY, Mississippi:
  Moss Point: 3634
JACKSON COUNTY, Missouri:
  Kansas City: 2482
  Mormons: 5392
JACKSON COUNTY, North Carolina:
  Mercantile accounts: 5258
  Quallatown: 3021, 4784
JACKSON COUNTY, Texas: 2385
JACKSON HILL, North Carolina: 3885
JACKSONVILLE, Alabama:
  Civil War: 1853
  Medical practice: 1053
JACKSONVILLE, Florida: 4298, 4853
  Army camps: 77
  Civil War: 3264, 4410
    see also CIVIL WAR--CAMPAIGNS, BATTLES, AND MILITARY ACTIONS--Florida--Jacksonville
  Description:
    1868: 249
    1890s: 5608
    1900: 956
  Diseases--Yellow fever: 4410
  Railroads: 2795
  Social life and customs: 4410
JACKSONVILLE, Illinois: 5944
JACKSONVILLE, Tennessee: see WEST TENNESSEE COLLEGE
JACKSONVILLE, PENSACOLA & MOBILE RAILROAD COMPANY: 2795
JACOB, John Jeremiah: 2796
JACOB, Naomi: 364
JACOB CLINGMAN AND COMPANY: 1108
JACOBITE REBELLION (1740s): 2098
JACOBITES:
  Great Britain: 2149
  Spain: 2155
JACOBS (EDWARD B.) & NEWCOMEN, Front Royal, Virginia (firm): 2797
JACOB'S FORK, North Carolina: 5705
JACOBUS, Melancthon Williams, Sr.: 5305
JACOBY, Neil H.: 2798
JACQUELIN FAMILY (Virginia): 99
JACQUEMYNS, G. Rolin-: see ROLIN-JACQUEMYNS, G.
JAEGER, Mrs. _____ (Rustburg, Virginia): 2799
JAFFA, Syria--Murder: 3118
JALAPA, Mexico:
  Mexican War: 395
JAMAICA:
  British administration: 1792, 3304
  Clothing and dress: 3304
  Colonial agents: 1913
    In Great Britain: 3304
  Constitution, Suspension of: 1875
  Corn Laws: 301
  Courts: 1792
  Cuban revolutionaries in: 1792
  Defense: 1792
  Description and travel: 1506
  Economic conditions: 1506
  Education: 1506
  Foreign trade: 1913
    Canada: 1792
    United States: 1792
  Freedmen: 301
  Furniture: 3304
  Governors: 3304
  Immigration and emigration: 1792
    From China: 301
  Labor: 1792, 4605
  Laws and legislation: 1913
  Legislature: 1792
  Missions and missionaries: 5011
  Personal finance: 3304
  Plantations: 301
  Politics and government: 1506, 1913, 4995, 5726
  Rum industry: 1913
  Sculpture: 1913
  Slavery: 4913
  Slaves: 301
    Emancipation: 5940
  Smuggling: 1913
  Social life and customs: 3659
  Tariff: 1792, 1913
  Trade and commerce: 3304
    see also JAMAICA--Foreign trade
  Cattle: 301
  Garden seeds: 3304
  Rum and sugar: 301
  Voyage to: 5298
JAMAICA PLAIN, Massachusetts: 3280
  Preparatory schools: 339
JAMES, Emma: 2800
JAMES, Fernando Godfrey: 5457
JAMES, Henry (Captain): 5419
JAMES, Henry (1811-1882): 2801
JAMES, Henry (1843-1916): 1210, 2102, 2801
JAMES, Henry, First Baron James of Hereford: 1815
JAMES, John G.: 2449
JAMES, Joshua: 2802
JAMES, Maria: 2058
JAMES, Thomas: 4388
JAMES, Walter Henry, Second Baron Northbourne: 1014, 4520
JAMES, William A. (North Carolina): 2803
JAMES, Sir William Milbourne: 2756
JAMES FAMILY (North Carolina): 2800
JAMES ADGER & COMPANY, South Carolina: 1388, 1891
JAMES CITY COUNTY, Virginia: 3456
  Williamsburg: see WILLIAMSBURG, Virginia

JAMES DICK AND STEWART COMPANY, Annapolis, Maryland: 1481
JAMES DUNLOP (firm): see JOHN AND JAMES DUNLOP
JAMES HOGG AND COMPANY: see JOHN HUSKE AND JAMES HOGG AND COMPANY
JAMES ISLAND, South Carolina: 1570, 2556, 2806
  Civil War: 484
    see also CIVIL WAR--CAMPAIGNS, BATTLES, AND MILITARY ACTIONS-- South Carolina--James Island
  Fortifications: 2805
JAMES K. PINNIX AND COMPANY, Stony Creek, North Carolina: 4223
JAMES R. OSGOOD & CO.: 4738
JAMES RIVER:
  Bridge construction: 5106
  Civil War defenses: 4544
  Shipping: 4616
  Travel by packet boat: 2890
JAMES RIVER AND KANAWHA CANAL: 3574
JAMES RIVER AND KANAWHA CANAL COMPANY, Richmond, Virginia: 3574, 4847
JAMES RIVER AND STAUNTON PLANK ROAD COMPANY: 5302
JAMES RIVER CANAL:
  Construction: 3809
  Proposal: 4348
JAMES RIVER COAL CORPORATION: 2922
JAMES RIVER SQUADRON: see CONFEDERATE STATES OF AMERICA--NAVY--James River Squadron
JAMES RIVER VALLEY, Virginia: 3809
JAMESON, John Franklin: 706
JAMESON RAID (Transvaal): 4514
JAMESTOWN, North Carolina: 211
  Farmers' Alliance: 2804
JAMESVILLE TOWNSHIP, North Carolina:
  Taxation: 3935
JAMISON, David Flavel: 2449, 2612, 2805
JAMISON AND WILLIAMS (firm): 5117
JANEWAY, Jacob J.: 1351
JANSENISM: 937
JANWIN AND GILLIS (firm): 1928
JAPAN: 4207
  Art: 5553
  Currency: 1339
  Description and travel:
    1850s: 3899, 4017
    1870s: 4986
    1880s: 2532
    1890s: 217
    1905: 2191
    1920s: 2463, 4858
  Diplomatic and consular service:
    United States: 1289, 1865, 1877, 3899, 4895
  Economic conditions: 1661
  Education: 1661
  Foreign relations:
    China:
      1890s: 4709
      1915: 5252
      1932: 83
    Great Britain: 4054
    United States: 2963, 4486, 5419
  Foreign trade:
    United States: 4060
  Harbors: 5190
  Insurrections: 3744
  Methodist Episcopal Church, South:
    Higher education: 3888
  Missions and missionaries: 2241, 3888, 5160
    see also JAPAN--Schools--Mission schools
    Baptist: 561
    Methodist Episcopal Church, South: 3888
    Presbyterian: 2269
  Navy: 4476
  Politics and government: 3744, 4986, 5876
  Public celebrations:
    Okinawa: 2650

JAPAN (Continued):
  Public health: 1661
  Public welfare: 1661
  Russian refugees: 5306
  Russo-Japanese War: see RUSSO-JAPANESE WAR
  Schools--Mission schools: 2959
  Sino-Japanese War: see SINO-JAPANESE WAR
  Social life and customs:
    1800s: 4986, 5306
    1900s: 1661
  Tobacco industry: 4060
  Tobacco trade: 4060
  United States military occupation:
    see UNITED STATES--ARMY--Japanese occupation
JAPANESE LANGUAGE--Vocabulary: 5160
JAQUES, Richard E.: 2806
JAQUES, William Henry: 2807
JARRATT, Augustus: 2808
JARRATT, Isaac A.: 2113, 2419, 2808
JARRATT (ISAAC A.) & SANDERFORD (firm): 2808
JARRATT, Mary: 2808
JARRATT FAMILY (North Carolina): 2808
JARRELL, John M.: 2809
JARRELL, Juliet (Kelly): 2809
JARVIS, Charles: 1222
JARVIS, Thomas (d. 1694): 5457
JARVIS, Thomas Jordan: 2810, 4669
"JAS" (divinity school student): 4989
JASPER COUNTY, Georgia: 377
JASPER COUNTY, Mississippi: 1370
  Heidelberg: 3876
JASPER COUNTY, Missouri:
  Carthage: 2384
JASTROW, Joseph: 958, 2811
JASTROW, Rachel (Szold): 2811
JASTROW FAMILY: 2811
JAVA:
  British administration: 4362
  Description and travel: 598, 1464
  Volcanic eruptions: 1464
JAVALI MINE, Nicaragua: 3587
JAY, John (1745-1829): 34, 105, 858, 894, 2776, 2812
  see also JAY'S TREATY
JAY, John (1817-1894): 2443, 2871
JAY, Peter Augustus: 2871
JAYHAWKERS--Kansas: 4065
JAYNES, Joseph M.: 2813
JAY'S TREATY: 1115, 3041, 4221, 4896
  French opinion: 4348
JEAN-AUBREY, G.: 1210
JEFCOAT, John J.: 2814
JEFFERS & COTHRAN, Charleston, South Carolina: 4145
JEFFERSON, Joseph: 2537, 2871
JEFFERSON, Maria: 1714
JEFFERSON, Thomas: 768, 1962, 2047, 2139, 2495, 2815, 3251, 3273, 3671, 3809, 4384, 4625, 5203, 5537
  Description: 558
  Gubernatorial administration: 3130
  Interest in missionary work: 3791
  Opinion of: 3176
  Presidential administration: 3742
  Statue: 4020
  Trade in London: 28
JEFFERSON (THOMAS) MEMORIAL ENDOWMENT: 4020
JEFFERSON, Thomas George Washington: 2816
JEFFERSON, Georgia: 3249, 4795
JEFFERSON, Maryland: 3254
JEFFERSON BARRACKS, Missouri:
  Army life: 5419
JEFFERSON CIRCUIT, Methodist churches: 3646
JEFFERSON CITY, Missouri: 2817, 4323, 4443

JEFFERSON CITY BRIDGE, Jefferson City, Missouri: 2817
JEFFERSON CITY BRIDGE AND TRANSIT COMPANY, Jefferson City, Missouri: 2817
JEFFERSON COLLEGE, Canonsburg, Pennsylvania: see WASHINGTON AND JEFFERSON COLLEGE, Washington, Pennsylvania
JEFFERSON COLLEGE, Washington, Mississippi: 5498
JEFFERSON COUNTY, Arkansas: 784
  Plantations: 4776
JEFFERSON COUNTY, Florida: 5659
  Monticello: 4068
JEFFERSON COUNTY, Georgia:
  Election reform: 3309
  Cities and towns:
    Bartow: 2860
    Cherry Hill: 1123
    Louisville: 1090, 3505, 3695, 5562
JEFFERSON COUNTY, Iowa:
  Fairfield: 5812
JEFFERSON COUNTY, Kentucky:
  "Beechmoor": 5557
  Louisville: see LOUISVILLE, Kentucky
JEFFERSON COUNTY, Mississippi: 100
  Rodney: 3322
JEFFERSON COUNTY, Ohio:
  Toronto--World War I: 829
JEFFERSON COUNTY, West Virginia: 603, 909, 1566, 1708, 2515, 3010, 4126
  Blacksmiths' accounts: 4388
  Business affairs: 5265
  Courts--Summonses: 4892
  Farming: 4388, 5591
  Land--Purchases and sales: 5591
  Land settlement: 99
  Sheep--Cotswold sheep: 5555
  Sheriffs' accounts: 3832
  Cities and towns:
    Charles Town: see CHARLES TOWN, West Virginia
    Harpers Ferry: see HARPERS FERRY, West Virginia
    Leestown--Temperance: 5591
    Marsh Farm: 3819
    Middleway: 1730, 2130, 4892
      Household accounts: 4703
      Wheat trade: 4703
    Rippon: 4029
    Rose Hill: 749
    Shepherdstown: see SHEPHERDSTOWN, West Virginia
    Summit Point: 3853
    "Wellington": 5574
JEFFERSON INSURANCE COMPANY: 433, 2387
JEFFERSON MEDICAL COLLEGE, Philadelphia, Pennsylvania: 330, 531, 1476, 1613, 2530, 4698
  Students and student life: 3853, 5740
JEFFERSONVILLE, Indiana:
  Civil War Hospitals: 3007
JEFFORDS, Robert J.: 2818
JEFFRESS, Albert G.: 5252
JEFFREY, Mr. _____ (poet): 3292
JEFFREY, Francis, Lord Jeffrey: 5177
JEFFREYS, Alvarado Ovando: 2819
JEFFREYS, Amelia (High): 2819
JEFFREYS, J. Robert: 2824
JEFFREYS, Jacob H.: 2819
JEFFREYS, James G.: 2819
JEFFREYS, Mrs. James M.: 2820
JEFFREYS, John O.: 2819, 2821
JEFFREYS, Josiah R.: 2819
JEFFREYS, Leonidas: 2822
JEFFREYS, R. W.: 2823
JEFFREYS, Robert N., Sr.: 2819
JEFFREYS, Robert N., Jr.: 2819, 2822
JEFFREYS, William (d. ca. 1860): 2824
JEFFREYS, William A. (North Carolina): 2825
JEFFRIES, H. B.: 4556

JEFFRIES, Marie Elizabeth: 356
JEFFRIES, R. Walter: 2819
JEKYLL, Sir Herbert: 4567
JELKS, Louisa M.: 4820
JELKS FAMILY (North Carolina): 4820
JELLICOE, J. R.: 1210
JELLETT, John Hewitt: 2826
JENKINS, Charles Jones: 2827
JENKINS, Mrs. Christopher C.: 2828
JENKINS, Gertrude: 2829
JENKINS, J. Strickler: 2726
JENKINS, John: 1185
JENKINS, Laban Linebarger: 5457
JENKINS, Sir Leoline: 3722
JENKINS, M. I.: 2831
JENKINS, Margaret Elizabeth (Clewell): 2829
JENKINS, Martha: 3831
JENKINS, Martha I. (North Carolina): 2830
JENKINS, Mary: 3831
JENKINS, Micah: 2831
JENKINS, Newsom Edward: 3831
JENKINS, Pattie Dandridge (Beckham): 3831
JENKINS, Robert Alexander: 2829
JENKINS, Walker: 2832
JENKINS, William Horton Peace: 2833
JENKINS, Wilson T.: 3831
JENKINS FAMILY (Genealogy): 3831
JENKINS & FOSTER (firm): 2834
JENKINS' EAR, War of: see WAR OF JENKINS' EAR
JENKINS' FERRY, Arkansas: see CIVIL WAR--CAMPAIGNS, BATTLES, AND MILITARY ACTIONS--Arkansas--Jenkins' Ferry
JENKINSON, Charles, First Earl of Liverpool: 1913, 2835
JENKINSON, Robert Banks, Second Earl of Liverpool: 2836
JENKS, Amelia: 538
JENKS, William: 2837
JENNERS, William: 2838
JENNERS FAMILY (Genealogy): 2838
JENNINGS, Annie (Fouch): 2838
JENNINGS, Jonathan: 571
JENNINGS, Sir Philip: 4557
JENNINGS, Samuel: 2838
JENNINGS, Samuel II: 2838
JENNINGS FAMILY (Genealogy): 2838
JEPHSON, Denham: 5330
JERDAN, William: 2839
JERNINGHAM, Edward: 2840
JERSEY, George Bussy Villiers, Fourth Earl of: 5330
JERSEY, Channel Islands: 306
JERSEY CITY, New Jersey:
    Waterworks: 5546
JERUSALEM, Virginia: see COURTLAND, Virginia
JERVEY, Theodore Dehon: 2449
JERVIS, John, First Earl of St. Vincent: 5830
JERVOIS, William F. D.: 4520
JESSOPP, Augustus: 2841
JESSUP, John: 4188
JESUP, Thomas Sidney: 212, 2842, 3323
JETER, Samuel H.: 523
JETER, W. L.: 1046
JETER AND CLAIBORNE (firm): see CLAIBORNE AND JETER
JEUDWINE FAMILY (Great Britain): 258
JEWELERS:
    North Carolina--Hillsborough: 3300
JEWELL, Marshall: 1953
JEWELRY: 5212
    Prices--Virginia: 4210
JEWELRY TRADE:
    Virginia--Richmond: 4210
JEWETT, Milo Parker: 1476
JEWS: 1482
    see also ANTISEMITISM; HEBREW POETRY; JUDAISM; ZIONISM
    Civil War: see CIVIL WAR--JEWS
    South Carolina--Greenville: 4834

JEWSBURY, Geraldine Endsor: 2843
JIMENEZ, Don Manuel de Medina: see MEDINA Y JIMENEZ, Don Manuel de
JIMILAYLAN PUEBLO, Philippine Islands: 4511
JO DAVIESS COUNTY, Illinois:
    Galena: 5571
"JOAN OF ARC" by Robert Southey: 4967
JOANNAH (ship): 172
JOEL, Lewis: 2844
JOFFRE, Henriette: 1424
JOHANNA (Comoro Islands): 3118
JOHANSSON, Albin: 3964
JOHN, King of England: 5575
JOHN ADAMS, U.S.S.: 577, 2928
JOHN AND JAMES DUNLOP, London, England: 3179
JOHN AND WILLIAM HOLT (firm): 2621
JOHN BIRCH SOCIETY: 3020
JOHN BROWN'S RAID: 693, 1033, 2728, 2829, 3809, 4473, 4897
JOHN BRYAN, Virginia (firm): 3179
JOHN C. CALHOUN MEMORIAL ASSOCIATION: 2449
JOHN C. HEYER AND COMPANY: 2511
JOHN D. LADD, Alexandria, Virginia (firm): 2933
JOHN DUNDORE (tannery): 1600
JOHN E. HUGHES COMPANY, INC., Virginia: 4918
JOHN FLANNERY AND COMPANY, Savannah, Georgia: 2232
JOHN GILL, JR., AND CO.: 870
JOHN HERTZLER & SONS (firm): 2505
JOHN HUSKE AND JAMES HOGG AND COMPANY, North Carolina: 2734
JOHN JONES AND COMPANY, Georgia: 2909
JOHN K. GILLIAT AND COMPANY, London, England: 2302, 2363
JOHN LAIRD AND SON, Georgetown, D.C.: 3179
JOHN M. WORTH MANUFACTURING COMPANY, Worthville, North Carolina: 3187
JOHN MORGAN AND COMPANY, Shenandoah County, Virginia: 3773
JOHN MYERS' SON, Washington, North Carolina: 3827
JOHN TERRASSON AND COMPANY, Lyons and Paris, France: 5228
JOHN WILSON AND RICHARD T. SMITH (firm): 5815
JOHNS, John (1796-1876): 3141
JOHNS, John, Jr. (Virginia): 2845
JOHNS, Martha E.: 1439
JOHNS HOPKINS UNIVERSITY, Baltimore, Maryland: 3888
    Education:
        Students' notebooks: 3888
    Faculty: 648, 4290
    Gender Identity Clinic: 4823
    History--Students' notebooks: 3888
    Philosophy:
        Students' notebooks: 3888
    Psychology:
        Students' notebooks: 3888
    Psycho-physics:
        Students' notebooks: 3888
JOHN'S ISLAND, South Carolina: 3164
JOHNSON, _____: 3603
JOHNSON, A. N.: 2846
JOHNSON, Andrew (1808-1875): 581, 685, 1084, 1980, 2847, 4353, 4723, 4834, 4911, 5193, 5340, 5636, 5863
    Impeachment trial: 1787, 4895, 5324, 5731
    Pardons: 730, 3809, 5188
    Public opinion: 2225, 3129, 5248
JOHNSON, Anne Williams (Taylor): 2851
JOHNSON, Austin: 2848
JOHNSON (B. F.) PUBLISHING COMPANY, Richmond, Virginia: 4373
JOHNSON, Benjamin Franklin: 4918
JOHNSON, Bradley Tyler: 858, 2849, 5075
JOHNSON, Bushrod Rust: 5280

JOHNSON, Carter P.: 824
JOHNSON, Cave: 872, 4252
JOHNSON, Chapman: 74, 97
JOHNSON, Charles B. (Texas): 2850
JOHNSON, Charles Clement: 4315
JOHNSON, Charles Earl, Sr.: 2851
JOHNSON, Charles Earl, Jr.: 2851
JOHNSON, Charles Spurgeon: 2852
JOHNSON, Clara J.: 3789
JOHNSON, David: 5271
JOHNSON, Edward: 2853
JOHNSON, Elizabeth: 2861
JOHNSON, Ellen (Virginia): 3542
JOHNSON, Ellen (Cooper) (South Carolina): 2854
JOHNSON, Ellen L. (North Carolina): 2855
JOHNSON, Emily (Pike): 2861
JOHNSON, Francis Marion: 2857
JOHNSON, George K. (Arkansas): 2856
JOHNSON, George Wesley (North Carolina): 2857
JOHNSON, Harriet (Myers): 2858
JOHNSON, Henry (Louisiana): 2859
JOHNSON, Henry J. (Pennsylvania): 3789
JOHNSON (HERSCHEL V.) AND COMPANY: 4895
JOHNSON, Herschel Vespasian: 1403, 2860, 5494
JOHNSON, Hiram (North Carolina): 2857
JOHNSON, Hiram (1866-1945): 5497
JOHNSON, Hugh W.: 2861
JOHNSON, J. H. (North Carolina): 2857
JOHNSON, J. R. (Ohio): 2862
JOHNSON, James M.: 2857
JOHNSON, Jefferson Deems (1900-1960): 2863
JOHNSON, Jennie: 2857
JOHNSON, John (South Carolina): 2864
JOHNSON, John O. (Maine): 2865
JOHNSON, John W. (Kentucky): 3199
JOHNSON, Joseph (1785-1877): 1920, 5092
JOHNSON, Joseph Travis (1858-1919): 2866
JOHNSON, Kate Ancrum (Burr): 5457
JOHNSON, Levi: 2106
JOHNSON, Livingston: 5457
JOHNSON, Martha: 2857
JOHNSON, Martin H.: 3332
JOHNSON, Mary Frances: 3318
JOHNSON, Nadiah P.: 2867
JOHNSON, Nannie (Prim): 4329
JOHNSON, Nelson Trusler: 5252
JOHNSON, Norman H.: 5457
JOHNSON, Reverdy: 791, 1439, 2868, 3631
JOHNSON, Robert Charles (New York): 2869
JOHNSON, Robert E. (North Carolina): 2870
JOHNSON, Robert Underwood: 72, 826, 1878, 2871, 2883, 4020, 5524
JOHNSON, Thomas: 2872
JOHNSON, Virginia (Wales): 5044
JOHNSON, W. G. (North Carolina): 2857
JOHNSON, W. T. (North Carolina): 2873
JOHNSON, Will H. (North Carolina): 2874
JOHNSON, William (North Carolina): 5202
JOHNSON, William II (South Carolina): 2875
JOHNSON, William Ransom, Sr. (1782-1849): 2876, 4334, 5751
JOHNSON, William Ransom, Jr.: 2876
JOHNSON, William Samuel: 752
JOHNSON FAMILY (Connecticut--Genealogy): 2553
JOHNSON FAMILY (North Carolina): 2870
JOHNSON FAMILY (South Carolina): 2854
JOHNSON AND STRATTON (firm): see STRATTON AND JOHNSON

JOHNSON COUNTY, Missouri:
  Centerview:
    Confederate emigrants: 3038
  Warrensburg: 489, 1136
JOHNSON PUBLISHING COMPANY: 5312
JOHNSON'S ISLAND, Ohio: 836, 2862, 4469, 5900
  Civil War: 1543
  see also CIVIL WAR--PRISONERS AND PRISONS--Confederate Prisoners--Ohio--Johnson's Island
JOHNSONVILLE, South Carolina: 3877
JOHNSONVILLE, Tennessee: see CIVIL WAR--CAMPAIGNS, BATTLES, AND MILITARY ACTIONS--Tennessee--Johnsonville
JOHNSTON, Albert Sidney: 395, 1186, 1333, 2371
  Death: 251
JOHNSTON, Alexander: 103
JOHNSTON, Charles Clement: 872
JOHNSTON, Don P., Sr.: 2877, 5056, 5450
JOHNSTON, Elizabeth Beatty: 85
JOHNSTON, Eliose: 2878
JOHNSTON, Hannah: 2776
JOHNSTON, James: 4531
JOHNSTON, James A.: 2879
JOHNSTON, Jane E.: 2460
JOHNSTON, Job: 2880
JOHNSTON, John Warfield, Sr.: 2881
JOHNSTON, John Warfield, Jr. (1818-1889): 2881, 3424
JOHNSTON, Joseph Beverly: 2881
JOHNSTON, Joseph Eggleston: 127, 395, 440, 805, 1364, 1403, 1726, 1746, 1805, 2617, 2829, 2849, 2881, 2882, 4034, 4129, 4358, 5541
  Relations with Jefferson Davis: 2893
  Retreat: 5051
  Surrender: 123, 2864, 5058, 5769, 5991
JOHNSTON, Lavalette: 3424
JOHNSTON, Louisa (Bowen): 2881
JOHNSTON, Lydia (McLane): 2881
JOHNSTON, Malcolm: 3905
JOHNSTON, Mary (1870-1936): 103, 2878, 3424
JOHNSTON, Nicketti (Floyd): 2881
JOHNSTON, Olin Dewitt: 2109
JOHNSTON, Richard Malcolm: 10, 2692, 2883
JOHNSTON, Robert (Ireland): 2884
JOHNSTON, Robert D. (Confederate general): 2885
JOHNSTON, Samuel (1733-1816): 2776, 3116, 5948
JOHNSTON, Thomas: 2887
JOHNSTON, W. B.: 4531
JOHNSTON, William (1700s, Ireland and North Carolina): 2887
JOHNSTON, William (1700s, North Carolina): 5768
JOHNSTON, William (1800s, North Carolina): 565, 4938
JOHNSTON, William L. (physician): 2886
JOHNSTON, William Preston: 635
JOHNSTON, Zachariah: 2887
JOHNSTON FAMILY (South Carolina or Tennessee): 718
JOHNSTON FAMILY (Virginia): 2881
JOHNSTON, Vermont: 2544
JOHNSTON AND COMPANY: 2877
JOHNSTON AND ROBERTSON (firm): 4509
JOHNSTON COUNTY, North Carolina: 4462
  Schools: 698
  Teachers' records: 3932
  Cities and towns:
    Bentonville Township: 1602
    Earpsborough:
      Liquor manufacture: 2072
      Merchants: 698
    Princeton: 3408

JOHNSTON COUNTY, North Carolina:
  Cities and towns (Continued):
    Smithfield: 2631, 3257, 3301, 4292, 4938
      American pottery: 5252
      Lawyers' accounts: 3839
      Loans: 3839
      Mercantile accounts: 5374
JOHNSTON, McNEILL AND COMPANY, Okeechobee, Florida: 4298
JOINERS: see UNITED BROTHERHOOD OF CARPENTERS AND JOINERS OF AMERICA
JOINT COMMISSION ON METHODIST UNION: 3646
JOINT COMMITTEE ON METHODIST FEDERATION: 3646
JOINT CONVENTION OF FLORIDA POSTAL ORGANIZATIONS: 3
JOINT LABOR LEGISLATIVE BULLETIN: 1197
JOINT LABOR LEGISLATIVE COMMITTEE: 1197
JOINT LABOR LEGISLATIVE COUNCIL: 1197
JOINVILLE, François Ferdinand Philippe Louis Marie, Prince de: 4537
JONA. MEIGS, Savannah, Georgia (firm): 2360
JONES, A. H.: 2888
JONES (A. H.), Mississippi (firm): 2888
JONES, Alberta Bassett (Stith): 2041
JONES, Arthur: 2889
JONES, Benjamin (North Carolina): 2890
JONES, Benjamin Hart (South Carolina and Alabama): 2930
JONES, Calvin T.: 2891
JONES, Catherine Ella: 2892
JONES, Charles Colcock, Sr.: 2893
JONES, Charles Colcock, Jr. (1831-1893): 305, 609, 1170, 1431, 1982, 2005, 2096, 2388, 2449, 2529, 2787, 2893, 3180, 3269
JONES, Charles Edgeworth: 2894
JONES, Charles G. (Tennessee): 5290
JONES, Charles R. (North Carolina): 2895
JONES, Chester: 2896
JONES, Dudley: 4453
JONES, Edward C.: 4184
JONES, Edwin Lee: 2897
JONES, Electus W. 2898
JONES, Eliza: 5290
JONES, Ernest Charles: 2899
JONES, Eugenia M. (Hart): 2930
JONES, Eva Eve: 1423
JONES, Fletcher: 2900
JONES, Francis B.: 3193
JONES, George (1766-1838): 1466, 2006, 2901
JONES, George Noble: 2901
JONES, George W. (Confederate soldier): 2902
JONES, George Wymberley: 1466
JONES, Hamilton C.: 832
JONES, Harford: 5797
JONES, Henry (North Carolina): 2929
JONES, Henry A. (Georgia): 2903
JONES, Henry Arthur (1851-1929): 1210, 3797
JONES, Henry L. (North Carolina): 5298
JONES, Howard Mumford: 102
JONES, Iredell: 1889
JONES, Isaac Dashiell: 2904
JONES, J. F.: 2905
JONES, J. Howard: 2906
JONES, J. W.: 2907
JONES, James (d. 1801): 4381
JONES, James Southgate: 4968
JONES, Jennie Doris Arthur: 1210
JONES, Jeremiah T.: 2908
JONES, John (Liberty County, Georgia): 2910
JONES, John (Spalding County): 2909
JONES, John (Virginia): 2935

JONES (JOHN) AND COMPANY, Georgia: 2909
JONES, John Beauchamp: 1227
JONES, John F.: 127
JONES, John M.: 264
JONES, John Paul: 4102
JONES, John Percival: 4276
JONES, John Robert (Virginia): 2911
JONES, Joseph (1727-1805, Virginia): 2913
JONES, Joseph (fl. 1824, New York): 2912
JONES, Joseph (1833-1896, Georgia): 3323
JONES, Joseph S. (North Carolina): 2914
JONES, Joseph Seawell: 3176
JONES, Kate: 2915
JONES, Kimbrough: 2916
JONES, Lewis J.: 2917
JONES, Lloyd (1811-1886): 2918
JONES, Louisa: 264
JONES, Lucy Hamilton: 2640
JONES, M. (North Carolina): 2919
JONES, Martha (New York): 2091
JONES, Martha M. (Alabama): 2920
JONES, Mary: 5290
JONES, Mary (Armistead): 2935
JONES, Mary (Scanlon): 2934
JONES, Mathias: 2921
JONES, Mattie Logan (Southgate): 4968
JONES, Meriwether: 2922
JONES, Milton Luther: 5457
JONES, Molly: 5290
JONES, N. P.: 4072
JONES, Noble: 1454
JONES, Noble Wimberly: 2923
JONES, Oliver H.: 2924
JONES, Peter: 2926
JONES, Richard: 2925
JONES, Robert, Jr. (North Carolina): 2926
JONES, Robert Randolph (Virginia): 2927, 2934
JONES, Sir Roderick: 4207
JONES, Roger: 212, 2928
JONES, Roland: 5380
JONES, Rufus Henry: 2929
JONES, Sallie: 4453
JONES, Samuel Porter: 3552
JONES, Samuel T.: 2930
JONES, Sarah (North Carolina): 1891
JONES, Sarah (Virginia): 5290
JONES, Seaborn (1788-1864): 2931
JONES, Solon B.: 1089
JONES, Thomas (fl. 1700s, colonel): 917
JONES, Thomas (fl. 1816, Virginia): 2932
JONES, Thomas Ap Catesby: 3118, 4322
JONES, Thomas Catesby: 2922
JONES, Thomas K. (Massachusetts): 2933
JONES (THOMAS K.), Boston, Massachusetts (firm): 2933
JONES, Thomas Thweatt: 2934
JONES, Thomas W. (Virginia): 2935
JONES, Thomas Walter: 2936
JONES, Walter: 2936, 4173
JONES, Wesley: 1871
JONES, William (1760-1831): 1975, 4081
JONES, William (Georgia lawyer): 2937
JONES, William B. (North Carolina lawyer): 2938
JONES, William H. (Virginia): 2939
JONES, Willie (1741-1801): 1714, 2926, 4080
JONES FAMILY (Alabama): 2900
JONES FAMILY (Georgia): 3323
JONES FAMILY (New York): 2091
JONES FAMILY (North Carolina): 2934, 4080
  Genealogy: 4968
JONES FAMILY (Virginia): 2925
  Genealogy: 2934

JONES AND LISTON (firm): see LISTON, BENFIELD, AND JONES
JONES AND McKENNY, Petersburg, Virginia (firm): 3401
JONES AND NEFF (firm): see NEFF & JONES
JONES AND SMITH (firm): 2888
JONES CHAPEL STATION, Methodist churches: 3646
JONES COUNTY, Georgia:
  Civil War: 1190
JONES COUNTY, North Carolina: 3469
  Pollocksville: 5709
  Trenton: 1871
JONES SEMINARY, All Healing Springs, North Carolina: 3416
JONES SHOE SHOP: see HICKS, JONES & MALLORY SHOE SHOP
JONES SPRING, Virginia:
  Health resorts: 5690
JONESBORO, Georgia: see CIVIL WAR--CAMPAIGNS, BATTLES, AND MILITARY ACTIONS--Georgia--Jonesboro
JONESBORO, North Carolina:
  Methodist Episcopal Church, South: 5023
JONESVILLE, Virginia: 861
JORDAN, Colonel ____: 2943
JORDAN, Cora: 2940
JORDAN, Daniel W.: 2940
JORDAN, David Starr: 2084
JORDAN, Elizabeth: 2449
JORDAN, Francis: 4188
JORDAN, Henry T.: 2941
JORDAN, John (Woodstock, Virginia): 2942
JORDAN, John A. (Richmond, Virginia): 2943
JORDAN, T. A. (North Carolina): 2428
JORDAN, Thomas (1819-1895): 395, 1186, 2944
JORDAN, Valentine: 2940
JORDAN, Victoria: 2940
JORDAN FAMILY (Virginia--Genealogy): 3809
JORDAN'S SPRINGS, Virginia: 3135
JOSEPH CONRAD: LETTERS TO WILLIAM BLACKWOOD AND DAVID S. MELDRUM by W. M. Blackburn: 1210
JOSEPH CONRAD: LIFE AND LETTERS by G. Jean-Aubrey: 1210
JOSEPH CONRAD AND HIS CIRCLE by Jessie Conrad: 1210
JOSEPH CONRAD AS I KNEW HIM by Jessie Conrad: 1210
JOSEPH HACKNEY AND COMPANY: 2242
JOSEPH REID ANDERSON AND CO.: 523
JOSEPH WESTMORE AND WILLIAM SAVAGE (firm): 5658
JOSHUA L. BAILY AND CO.: 1611
JOSIAH FAXON, Alexandria, Virginia (firm): 2933
JOSLIN, Harold Vincent: 2553
"A JOURNAL AND TRAVEL OF JAMES MEACHAM, 1789-1797" by W. K. Boyd: 3601
"JOURNAL OF A CRUISE TO CALIFORNIA AND THE DIGGINS" by James M. Burr: 2161
JOURNAL OF AMERICAN FOLKLORE, 1880-1916: 691
"JOURNAL OF FARM LIFE AT 'EOCENE . . .'" by Carter Braxton Tomlin: 5309
JOURNAL OF SOUTHERN HISTORY: 1227, 5054, 5593
JOURNAL OF THE PROCEEDINGS OF THE NATIONAL DIVISION OF THE SONS OF TEMPERANCE OF NORTH AMERICA: 5339
JOURNALISM:
  see also NEWSPAPERS
  American Civil War: see CIVIL WAR--NEWSPAPERS
  Editing--Georgia: 731
  Education:
    New York: see COLUMBIA UNIVERSITY--School of Journalism
    South Carolina: 300

JOURNALISM (Continued):
  Franco-Prussian War: 43
  History--North Carolina: 2587
  Professional societies: 3538
  Yellow journalism: 2473
  Subdivided by place:
    Georgia: 2374
    Great Britain: 4151
    India: 278
    Massachusetts: 5754
    New York: 2390, 4556
    North Carolina: 1082
    United States: 2398, 2883, 4453
    Washington, D.C.: 42, 4494
JOURNALISM AND LABOR: see LABOR JOURNALISM
THE JOURNEY OF ROBERT BONGOUT AND HIS LADY, TO BATH . . . 177-: 626
JOUVENCAL, C.: 4230
JOWETT, Benjamin: 2471
JOYNER, James Yadkin: 2945
JOYNER, Joshua E.: 2946
JOYNES, Edward Southey: 267
JUDAH, Alice: 1072
JUDAISM:
  see also JEWS
  Liturgy and ritual: 4864
  Maryland--Baltimore: 2811
  Wisconsin--Madison: 2811
JUDD, Bethel T.: 1197, 1200
JUDE'S FERRY, Virginia: 2369
JUDGES:
  see also JUSTICES OF THE PEACE
  Appointments:
    India: 5875
    Missouri: 4323
    Virginia: 574, 1511
    Wyoming Territory: 4740
  Elections:
    North Carolina: 4080
    Virginia: 4617
  Subdivided by place:
    Georgia: 2372, 3113, 5787
      Circuit Courts: 2860
      Morgan County: 4415
    India: 2324
    North Carolina:
      Superior Court: 3955
    South Carolina: 5863
    Virginia: 2517
      United States District Court: 2700
JUDGMENTS: see COURTS--Judgments
JUDICIAL AFFAIRS:
  see also COURTS
  North Carolina: 274
  United States: 274
JUDICIAL REFORM:
  Great Britain: 4605
  South Carolina: 5271
  Thailand: 4709
  United States: 5299
JUDICIAL REVIEW: 2776
JUDICIARY: see COURTS
JUDICIARY ACT OF 1801 (Repeal): 3041
JUDSON FEMALE INSTITUTE, Marion, Alabama: 5032
  Students and student life: 1476
JUGTOWN, North Carolina:
  American pottery: 5252
JULIAN, Bohan: 2947
JULIAN, E. I.: 518
JULIAN, Tobias: 2947
JULIAN FAMILY (Illinois): 2080
JULIAN HAWTHORNE AND COMPANY: 4743
JULLIARD (A. D.) AND COMPANY, INC., Mecklenburg County, North Carolina: 5235
JULY 4 CELEBRATIONS: see FOURTH OF JULY CELEBRATIONS
JULY REVOLUTION (France, 1830): 4490
JUNIATA RIVER CANAL: 421
JUNIOR COLLEGES: see names of specific junior colleges
JUNIUS (pseudonym): 92
JUNKIN, Margaret: 2449, 4313, 5044

JURIES:
  Certification: 1871
  Compensation:
    Virginia: 5434
  Grand juries:
    Great Britain: 1541
  Lists:
    Great Britain:
      Yorkshire: 5956
    South Carolina: 1877
    Virginia: 5434
  Negro jurors:
    North Carolina: 3563
  Subdivided by place:
    North Carolina: 4544
    Pennsylvania: 2444
JUST, John: 1087
JUSTICE, Michael Hoke: 5457
JUSTICES IN EYRE:
  Great Britain: 3997
JUSTICES OF THE PEACE:
  Australia: 5477
  Illinois--McHenry County: 1723
  Maryland: 5722
    Frederick County: 4457
  Massachusetts: 3034
    Becket: 5766
  Mississippi: 5363
    Choctaw County: 3702
  North Carolina: 671, 1417, 1688, 3176, 3221
    Brassfield Township: 2833
    Burke County: 245
    Catawba County: 5745
    Davidson County: 3241, 3926
    Hyde County: 4547
    Little River: 5692
    Mount Gilead Township: 4689
    Wake County: 2824
    Wilkes County: 2483
  Pennsylvania: 496
  South Carolina: 169, 501, 1692
  Virginia: 33, 872, 1568
    Fotheringay: 1646
    Pulaski County: 4771
  West Virginia: 1318, 3010
JUSTIS, Horace Howard: 2948
"JUTLAND," Maryland: 5193
JUVENILE COURTS: see COURTS--Juvenile courts
JUVENILE DELINQUENCY:
  North Carolina: 1275
JUVENILES: see CHILDREN; YOUTH; YOUTH ORGANIZATIONS

## K

KACKLEY, Joseph: 3721
KAFFIR WARS: 4655
KAFFIRS:
  Natal: 5725
  South Africa: 128
KAGEY, David F.: 461, 2949
KAGEY, Henry: 2949
KAISER (MAY McEWEN) (mills): see MAY McEWEN KAISER
KALAHARI DESERT--Description: 4514
KALAMAZOO, Michigan: 573
KALAMAZOO COUNTY, Michigan:
  Kalamazoo: 573
KAMSCHATKA (ship): 5622
KANAWHA COUNTY, West Virginia:
  Charleston: 331, 3821
KANAWHA RIVER (West Virginia): 4348
  Journey by packet boat: 2890
KANAWHA VALLEY, West Virginia:
  Coal mines: 4924
KANDAHAR, Afghanistan: 2756
KANDLBINDER, Hans Karl: 2950
KANE, George Proctor: 3378
KANE COUNTY, Illinois:
  Batavia: 4273
KANSAS:
  see also MIDDLE WEST; PLAINS STATES
  Abolition of slavery: 4720
  Agriculture: 2554
    see also KANSAS--Farm life; KANSAS--Farming
  Border ruffians: 865
  Commodity prices: 2294
  Constitutional conventions (1856): 4720
  Description and travel: 5018
  Estates (Legal):
    Administration and settlement: 2554
  Farm life: 1882
  Farming: 1428, 4202
  Flour mills: 4100
  Labor conditions: 2554
  Land deeds and indentures: 4100, 4606
  Land settlement: 5018
  Land speculation: 128, 4720
  Legislature (Territorial): 4720
  Migration from: 4158
  Newspapers: 3161
  Politics and government: 4720
    see also KANSAS CONFLICT
  Sheep raising: 3745
  Social life and customs: 1428
  United States Army life: 1282
    see also subheadings under UNITED STATES--ARMY
KANSAS CITY, Missouri: 2482
KANSAS CONFLICT: 128, 2358, 2552, 3703, 5051, 5059, 5240, 5315, 5551, 5853
KANSAS FREE STATE (newspaper): 3161
KANSAS-NEBRASKA ACT: 569, 1084, 1403, 5940
KANSAS-NEBRASKA QUESTION: 1548, 4808
KARENNI STATES: 1857
KARL X GUSTAF, King of Sweden: 5379

KARLSRUHE, Germany: 2557
KARUN RIVER (Persia): 4693
KASHGAR, Chinese Turkestan: 5103
KATE (British steamer): 5390
KATIPUNAN: 4511
KATO, Takaaki: 217
KATONAH, New York: 4948
KATZENBURG COAL COMPANY: 897
KAUFMAN COUNTY, Texas--Mabank: 318
KEAN, Robert Garlick Hill: 2951
KEARN, Allen M.: 4188
KEARNEY, Henry C.: 2952
KEARSARGE, U.S.S.: 5436
KEATS, John: 2058
KEBLE, John (d. 1835): 2953
KEBLE, John (1792-1866): 2953
KEDLESTON, George Nathanial Curzon, First Marquis Curzon of: see CURZON, George Nathanial, First Marquis Curzon of Kedleston
KEECOUGHTON LITERARY SOCIETY: 1115
KEEDING, Joseph: 2954
KEELEY, Robert: 2146
KEEN, A. H.: 3199
KEEN, Elisha Ford: 2955
KEEN AND LEWIS (firm): see LEWIS AND KEEN
KEENE, Sir Benjamin: 2155, 5532
KEENE, New Hampshire: 5131
  Blacksmiths' accounts: 5501
KEENEY, James K.: 5307
KEEP AMERICA OUT OF WAR CONGRESS: 4948
KEESE, Mary: 2956
KEEVER, Alexander: 2957
KEIFER, Joseph Warren, Sr.: 2958
KEITH, Admiral _____ (Great Britain, 1801): 5639
KEITH, Carolina: 2959
KEITH, Cary: 2959
KEITH, Olive: 2959
KEITH, Sir Robert Murray: 862
KEITH, Sylvanus: 2959
KEITT, Caroline (Wadlington): 2961
KEITT, Ellison Summerfield: 2961
KEITT, J. L.: 2961
KEITT, Laurence Massillon: 2960, 2961
KEITT, Susanna (Sparks): 2960
KEITT, Thomas Ellison: 2961
KEITT, Thomas W.: 2961
KEITT FAMILY (South Carolina--Genealogy): 2961
KEKEWICH, Sir George William: 2962
KELAT, Baluchistan: 5801
KELL, Evy: 2963
KELL, John McIntosh: 127, 843, 2963, 3905
KELL, Julia Blanche (Munroe): 2963
KELL, Marjory Spalding (Baillie): 2963
KELL, Thomas: 3905
KELLER, Charlotte: 2964
KELLER, Jacob: 2964
KELLER, William: 2965
KELLEY, Amanda (Harris): 872
KELLEY, David Campbell (1832-1909): 872
KELLEY, David Campbell, Jr.: 872
KELLEY, Mary Owen (Campbell): 872
KELLEY, Thomas F.: 2966
KELLEY FAMILY: 872
KELLO, Samuel: 2967, 4531
KELLOGG, John: 2968
KELLOGG, Miner Kilbourne: 2969
KELLOGG, S. W.: 2968
KELLOGG-BRIAND PACT: 5252
KELLY, Alfred: 2971
KELLY, Ann: 2970
KELLY, Cornelia: 3219
KELLY, Hugh: 3219
KELLY, John N.: 2970
KELLY, Juliet: 2809
KELLY, Neill: 2970
KELLY, Oliver Hudson: 4072
KELLY, Rebecca A.: 2809
KELLY, Sophia: 4024
KELLY, W. D.: 2809
KELLY, Williamson: 2971
KELLY & PEDEN (firm): see PEDEN & KELLY

KELLY'S FORD, Virginia: see CIVIL WAR--CAMPAIGNS, BATTLES, AND MILITARY ACTIONS--Virginia--Kelly's Ford
KELSO, Scotland: 2839
KELTON, Robert: 2972
KELTON FAMILY (Pennsylvania): 2972
KELVIN GROVE, North Carolina: 1783
KEMBLE, Frances Anne: 1345
KEMBLE, John Mitchell: 2973
KEMP, James (1764-1827): 4638
KEMP, Laura C.: 2974
KEMP, Sarah: 2975
KEMP, William: 2975
KEMPE, Sir John Arrow: 2976
KEMPER (BENJAMIN FRANKLIN) AND BROTHERS, Port Republic, Virginia: 2977
KEMPER, Fannie V.: 2978
KEMPER, James Lawson: 523, 1243, 5368
KEMPER COUNTY, Mississippi: 3017
  Agriculture: 3436
KENAH, Colonel _____: 446
KENAN, Anna B.: 2979
KENAN, Fannie: 2979
KENAN, Michael J.: 2979
KENAN, Thomas H.: 2980
KENAN, Thomas Stephen: 2981
KENDALL, Amos: 2326, 2982
KENDALL, Edward D.: 2983
KENDALL, Seth K.: 2983
KENDALL, William P.: 2984
KENDALL AND COX (firm): see COX, KENDALL AND COMPANY
KENDALL AND FLETCHER (firm): see FLETCHER AND KENDALL
KENDALL COMPANY, Mecklenburg County, North Carolina: 5235
KENESAW INFANTRY: see GEORGIA--Militia--Regiments--7th Georgia State Guards
KENESAW MOUNTAIN, Georgia: see CIVIL WAR--CAMPAIGNS, BATTLES, AND MILITARY ACTIONS--Georgia--Kenesaw Mountain
KENILWORTH, England: 5403
KENMORE UNIVERSITY HIGH SCHOOL, Amherst County, Virginia: 5380
KENNAN, George (1845-1924): 103
KENNAN, Henry: 3801
KENNEBEC COUNTY, Maine:
  Hallowell: 5569
KENNEBEC COUNTY, New York:
  Clinton: 2092
KENNEDY, A. S.: 2987
KENNEDY, Alexander: 306
KENNEDY, Charles Rann: 3797
KENNEDY, Edith Wynne (Matthison): 3797
KENNEDY, George W.: 2989
KENNEDY, Mrs. J. G.: 1434
KENNEDY, John (North Carolina): 2222
KENNEDY, John, Jr.: 4232
KENNEDY, John Fitzgerald: 225, 5773
  Assassination: 225
KENNEDY, John Pendleton: 10, 1227, 2985, 3118
KENNEDY, John Spinks: 2662
KENNEDY, Samuel: 2986
KENNEDY, Thomas P.: 5239
KENNEDY, Will: 2987
KENNEDY FAMILY (Michigan): 2604
KENNEDY FREE LIBRARY (South Carolina): 561
KENNETT SQUARE, Pennsylvania: 5642
KENNETH AND DUDLEY, Cincinnati, Ohio (firm): 4326
KENNEY, Samuel Pierce: 2990
KENNON, Anna: 2991
KENNON, Lyman Walter Vere: 2991
KENT, Armine T.: 2146
KENT, Charles William: 2449
KENT, Edward N.: 4895
KENT, F. L.: 3694
KENT, J. L.: 523
KENT, John E.: 2992
KENT, Joseph: 4905
KENT, Richard: 2993
KENT, T. F.: 2994

KENT, William: 2457
KENT, England: 1891
    Cultivation of hops: 2148
    Police district: 4420
    Cities and towns:
        Ashford: 367
        Bishopsbourne: 1210
        Canterbury: 1765
        Coombe Bank: 862
        Cranbrook: 4823
        Gravesend: 535
        Hayes--"Hollwood": 4230
        Hopeville: 4327
        Keston Park: 3860
        Sevenoaks: 2843
        Sheerness: 5330
        Shooter's Hill: 1891
        Shoreham: 4146
KENT AND STRATHEARN, Edward Augustus, Duke of: 2836
KENT COUNTY, Maryland: 830, 4859, 4935
    Courts: 5296
    Estates (Legal):
        Administration and settlement: 4140, 5296
        Land deeds and indentures: 5296
        Wills: 4140, 5296
    Cities and towns:
        Chestertown: 2605, 5296
        Centerville: 4433
KENTON, James: 5647
KENT'S HILL, Maine: 731
KENT'S STORE, Virginia: 1324
KENTUCKY:
    see also SOUTHERN STATES
    Abolition of slavery and abolitionist sentiment: 1083
        see also KENTUCKY--Slavery--Emancipation
    Agricultural products:
        Prices: 647
    Agriculture: 245, 5426
        see also KENTUCKY--Farming; KENTUCKY--Plantations
    American literature: see KENTUCKY IN AMERICAN LITERATURE
    Authors and publishers: 1308
    Bank notes: 1309
    Baptist churches:
        Associations:
            Goshen: 3199
            North Bend: 3199
            Salem: 3199
        Clergy: see KENTUCKY--Clergy--Baptist
    Biographical studies: 1308
    Blacksmithing: 245
    Blind: 5426
    Bluegrass: 1086
    Camp meetings: 1356
        Presbyterian: 4387
    Cattle: 1086
    Children--Employment: 3325
    Civil War: see appropriate subheadings under CIVIL WAR; CONFEDERATE STATES OF AMERICA--ARMY; UNITED STATES--ARMY--Civil War
    Clergy:
        Baptist: 3489
        Christian Methodist Episcopal Church: 5070
        Methodist Episcopal Church, South: 3888
        Presbyterian: 3325
    Commodity prices: 4720
        see also KENTUCKY--Agricultural products--Prices; and Prices as subheading under KENTUCKY--(specific commodity)
    Cookery--Lexington: 3325
    Copperheads: 4160
    Courts:
        Circuit Courts: 5505
    Currency: 1339
    Deaf: 5426
    Debt: 1086, 1654

KENTUCKY (Continued):
    Democratic Party: 398
    Description and travel: 4457
        1790s: 2887
        1800s: 57, 2064
        1800s: 1843, 5593
        1820s: 3450
        1840s: 5508
        1850s: 5508
        1860s: 2063
        1870s: 1811
    Disciples of Christ: 4506, 4720
    Economic conditions: 57, 4539
        see also KENTUCKY--Poverty
        Louisville: 3141
    Education: 3489
        see also KENTUCKY--Schools
    Elections: see KENTUCKY--Gubernatorial elections
    Estates (Legal):
        Administration and settlement:
            Fayette County: 3325
    Farming: 1604
        see also KENTUCKY--Agriculture; KENTUCKY--Plantations
    Finance: see KENTUCKY--Personal finance
    Fugitive slaves: 5551
    Government agencies and officials:
        Governors:
            Thomas E. Bramlette (1863-1867): 627
            John White Stevenson (1867-1871): 5064
    Gubernatorial elections (1844-1845): 3325
    Horse racing--Louisville: 2681
    Horses--Breeding: 1086
    Houses--Construction: 3325
    Investment companies:
        Lexington: 4241
    Labor in politics: 2568
    Land: 795, 1401, 3809
        Purchases and sales: 1086, 4616
    Land deeds and indentures: 5505
        Lexington: 3325
    Land settlement: 404, 3125
    Land surveys: 2063
    Land title companies:
        Louisville: 3141
    Land titles: 1843, 4616
        Pleasant Hill: 5416
    Law practice--Lexington: 3325
    Lawsuits: 1086, 5505
        Pleasant Hill: 5416
    Loans--Interest rates: 2225
    Lotteries: 4732
    Manufacturing: 5426
    Medical education: see TRANSYLVANIA COLLEGE; UNIVERSITY OF LOUISVILLE--Medical Department
    Medical practice:
        Hancock County: 3199
    Medicine:
        Students' notebooks: 1053, 1513
    Mental hospitals--Lexington: 3325
    Mentally ill: 5426
    Mentally retarded: 5426
    Mercantile accounts--Paw Paw: 4090
    Mercantile affairs: 5593
    Merchants--Cloverport: 3199
    Methodist churches:
        Board of Trustees: 3646
        Clergy: see KENTUCKY--Clergy
        Kentucky Conference: 3646
    Migration to: 558, 3721
        From North Carolina: 4765
        From Virginia: 3130, 3199
    Militia: 3325
        Regiments:
            16th: 1595
            33rd: 1470
    Negroes in politics: 398
    Newspapers: 713
    Orphans: 5426
    Paupers: 5426
    Personal finance: 3199
        Lexington: 3325

KENTUCKY (Continued):
    Pharmacies--Glasgow: 5505
    Physicians' accounts:
        Hancock County: 3199
    Plantations: 3176
        see also KENTUCKY--Farming
    Politics and government: 20, 765, 1083, 3325, 4720
        see also KENTUCKY--Labor in politics; KENTUCKY--Negroes in politics
    Poverty: 1654
    Presbyterian churches: 4387
        Lexington: 3325
    Prisoners and prisons: 5426
    Protestant Episcopal Church:
        Bishops: 4869
    Real estate: 3325
    Religion: 57
    Schools:
        Girls' schools and academies:
            Springfield: 4987
        Lexington: 4373
    Secessionist sentiment: 4160
    Shakers--Pleasant Hill: 5416
    Slave insurrections: 4202
    Slave trade: 496
        Prices: 647
    Slavery: 3955
        Emancipation: 1086
            see also KENTUCKY--Abolition of slavery and abolitionist sentiment
    Social life and customs: 72, 1355, 4131, 5426
    Soils: 3532
    Squatters: 1843
    Streams: 3532
    Temperance: 3325
    Thanksgiving Day: 627
    Theological seminaries: 5298
    Tobacco--Prices: 2363, 5499
    Tobacco culture: 57
    Tobacco industry: 5499
    Tobacco trade: 57, 2363
    Trade and commerce:
        Carriages and buggies: 5623
        Food: 5006
        Lumber--Paw Paw: 4090
        Slaves: see KENTUCKY--Slaves
        Tobacco: see KENTUCKY--Tobacco
    Universities and colleges: 1092
        see also CENTRAL UNIVERSITY; KENTUCKY MILITARY INSTITUTE; KENTUCKY WESLEYAN COLLEGE; OGDEN COLLEGE; TRANSYLVANIA COLLEGE; UNION COLLEGE; UNIVERSITY OF KENTUCKY; UNIVERSITY OF LOUISVILLE
    Weather--Lexington: 3325
    Weddings: 571
    Wills--Lexington: 3325
    Women--Employment: 3325
    Women poets: 2053
    Wood: 3532
KENTUCKY COLONIZATION SOCIETY: 5635
KENTUCKY IN AMERICAN LITERATURE: 72, 1878
KENTUCKY LAKE, Tennessee:
    Indians of North America: 4894
KENTUCKY MILITARY INSTITUTE: 3888
KENTUCKY TRACE: 2486
KENTUCKY WESLEYAN COLLEGE: 3888
KENTUCKYIANS: 1878
KENYA:
    Description and travel: 2463
    Massacre at Eldama Ravine: 4514
KENYON, Lloyd, First Baron Kenyon: 2996
KENYON, Moses Warren: 2997
KENYON, W. A.: 2997
KEOKUK, Iowa: 3392
    Hospitals: 5017
    United States Army camp: 1076
KER, Charles Henry Bellenden: 2998
KERFOOT, John Barrett: 2999
KERMES AS A DYE: 5553
KERNAHAN, Coulson: 5856

KERNER, William G.: 3000
KERNERSVILLE, North Carolina: 3000
KERNERSVILLE ACADEMY, North Carolina: 817
KERNEY, James: 1424
KERNODLE, John Robert, Jr.: 3000
KERR, Bessie M. C.: 3002
KERR, Jane P.: 3003
KERR, John (1782-1842): 1920
KERR, John (1811-1879): 5457
KERR, William H.: 4079
KERRISON, Mrs. E. W.: 5415
KERSHAW COUNTY, South Carolina: 853
    Camden: see CAMDEN, South Carolina
KERSHAW DISTRICT, South Carolina:
    Flat Rock: 4818
KERSHNER, Edward: 3004
KESLOR, Frank B.: see KESSLER, Frank B.
KESSLER, Frank B.: 3005
KESTON PARK, England: 3860
KESWICK, England: 4967
KETCHUM, Annie (Chambers) Bradford: 2449
KETTLE, G. N.: 5093
KETTLE RIVER (Washington): 140
KEWANEE, Illinois--Baseball: 5293
KEY, David McKendree: 3523
KEY, Francis Scott: 385, 519, 3006, 3220, 4376
KEY, Philip (1750-1820): 3006
KEY, Philip Barton III (d. 1859): 3006
KEY FAMILY (Maryland): 3006
KEY REPORTER (periodical): 4753
"KEY TO MAP OF THE WESTERN NORTH CAROLINA CONFERENCE, ME[THODIST] E[PISCOPAL] CHURCH, SOUTH" by John Carlisle Kilgo: 3646
KEY WEST, Florida: 99, 386
    Civil War: 701
KEYES, E. O.: 5419
KEYES, Horace: 3007
KEYSER, Harriot (Swift): 3008
KEYSER, Nell: 3008
KEYSER (W. S.) EXPORT COMPANY, Pensacola, Florida: 3008
KEYSER, William Judah: 3008
KEYSER, William Swift: 3008
KEYSER AND COMPANY, Pensacola, Florida: 3008
KEYSER, JUDAH, AND COMPANY, Pensacola, Florida: 3008
KEYSVILLE, Virginia: 79
KEYTON, John G.: 3009
KHARTOUM, Horatio Herbert Kitchener, First Earl Kitchener of: see KITCHENER, Horatio Herbert, First Earl Kitchener of Khartoum
KHARTOUM, Sudan, Siege of: 5333
KHYBER PASS--Description: 5525
KIANGYIN, China:
    Presbyterian missionaries: 5014
KICKAPOO INDIANS:
    Trade with whites: 4353
KIDD, David: 369
KIDD, Samuel: 5839
KIDD, William (1645-1701): 2461
KIDDER FAMILY (Virginia--Genealogy): 1842
KIDNAPPED BY THE KINGFISH: 2775
KIDNAPPING--Spain: 2155
KIDWILER, Charles: 3010
KIDWILER, Jacob: 3010
KIDWILER, Michael: 3010
KIERNANDER, John Zachariah: 3011
KILBY, John Richardson: 3012, 3830
KILBY, Randolph: 3012
KILBY, Wilbur John: 3012
KILDARE (County), Ireland:
    Palmerston House: 587
KILGO, John Carlisle: 31, 1584, 3646, 4968, 5914
KILHAM, Hannah (Spurr): 2146
KILLIAN'S POST OFFICE, North Carolina: 4450
KILLINGSWORTH, Esther: 5431
KILLINGSWORTH, Mrs. M. A.: 3013

KILLION, Henry: 3014
KILNS (Brick): 5990
KILPATRICK, Franklin W.: 358
KILPATRICK, John Young: 4184
KIMBALL, D. T.: 3015
KIMBALL, Fiske: 2790
KIMBALL, Franklin G.: 3016
KIMBALL (WILLIAM S.) AND CO.: 1586
KIMBALL FAMILY (North Carolina--Genealogy): 4242
KIMBERLY, John Wodehouse, First Earl of: 2149, 2756, 4520
KIMBRAUGH, Marmaduke D.: 2714
KIMBROUGH, George H.: 3017
KIMMELL HOUSE: 3018
KINCARDINE, Victor Alexander Bruce, Thirteenth Earl of: 3978, 3980
KINCHEN, John: 5457
"KINCOCK," Virginia: 5377
KINDERGARTENS:
    Massachusetts--Boston: 3295
    Missouri--Saint Louis: 3295
    North Carolina--Chapel Hill: 4080
    United States: 4095
    Washington, D.C.: 3295
KINDERHOOK, New York: 5451
KINDLEY, George: 5549
KINE, Alson: 518
KING, Allen: 1107
KING, Bellfield: 3033
KING, Bryant: 1107
KING, Carl Howie: 3020
KING, Campbell: 3019
KING, Edward Smith: 2449
KING, Frank: 5990
KING, Grace Elizabeth: 1424
KING, H. L.: 5252
KING, H. P.: 3021
KING, Helen (Ninde): 3029
KING, Horatio (1811-1897): 3022
KING, Horatio Collins (1837-1918): 3022, 5396
KING, J. L.: 556
KING, Joel: 3023
KING, John Pendleton: 3024
KING, Johnson W.: 3025
KING, Joseph, Jr.: 3026
KING, Leander: 3027
KING, Mary (Estridge): 3020
KING, Mitchell: 2448
KING, N. J.: 3028
KING, Pendleton: 3029
KING, Rufus: 3030
KING, Rush: 3029
KING, Thomas Butler: 2963
KING, Thomas Worthington: 3030
KING, Whitfield D.: 3033
KING, William (North Carolina): 3031
KING, William B. (Virginia): 2332
KING, William Rufus Devane: 3032, 3413, 5149
KING, Willis H.: 3033
KING FAMILY: 404
KING, North Carolina: 2472
KING AND LYNN, Virginia (firm): 3031
KING AND QUEEN COUNTY, Virginia:
    Bruington: 5161
    Middlesex: 3379
    Walkerton: 3806
KING COBRA: 3062
KING COLLEGE, Bristol, Tennessee: 4373
"THE KINGDOM COME" by Stefan George: 1992
KINGMAN, Henry: 3034
KINGS AND RULERS:
    see also names of specific rulers, e.g. EDWARD VII, King of Great Britain
    Prussia: 3238
    Spain: 1340, 3549
KING'S CAROLINA RANGERS: 1358
KING'S COLLEGE, Cambridge University: see CAMBRIDGE UNIVERSITY--King's College
KINGS COUNTY, New York:
    Brooklyn: see BROOKLYN, New York

KING'S MOUNTAIN, North Carolina:
    see AMERICAN REVOLUTION--Campaigns and battles--North Carolina--King's Mountain
KING'S MOUNTAIN MILITARY SCHOOL, Yorkville, South Carolina: 2831
KING'S MOUNTAIN RAILROAD COMPANY: 3035
KINGSBURY, Roger A.: 5252
KINGSLEY, Charles: 1910
KINGSLEY, Fanny: 1910
KINGSTON, Alfred: 3715
KINGSTON, William Beatty: 3036
KINGSTON, Massachusetts:
    Civil War: 383
KINGSTON, New Hampshire: 354
KINGSTON, New York: 5454
KINGSTOWN, Saint Vincent, West Indies: 4618
KINNEIR, Sir John Macdonald: 868
KINNEY BROTHERS (firm): 1586
KINSEY, Henry: 3736
KINSLEY, Edward Wilkinson: 3037
KINSLEY MILLS, Virginia: 1447
KINSTON, North Carolina: 986, 1871, 2857
    Civil War: 714
        see also CIVIL WAR--CAMPAIGNS, BATTLES, AND MILITARY ACTIONS--North Carolina--Kinston
    Confederate Army camp: 1896
    Confederate attack on Union railroad: 1806
    Union occupation: 5261
    Photographs: 4414
    Plantations: 903
KINYOUN, Elizabeth A. (Conrad): 3038
KINYOUN, John Hendricks: 3038
KIPLING, Rudyard: 1424, 4290
KIPPS, J. H.: 3039
KIRACOFE, John H.: 3040
KIRACOFE FAMILY (Virginia): 3040
KIRBY, A. H.: 3044
KIRBY, Ephraim: 3041
KIRBY, John D. (Virginia): 724
KIRBY, John R.: 358
KIRBY, John T. (South Carolina): 3044
KIRBY, Lillian: 3043
KIRBY, Reynold Marvin: 3041
KIRBY, Samuel F.: 3042
KIRBY, William (North Carolina): 3043
KIRBY, William (Virginia): 724
KIRBY FAMILY (South Carolina): 3044
KIRBY & VERNON (firm): 3044
KIRBY & WILSON (firm): 3044
KIRK, Sir John: 5725
KIRKENDALE, Warren: 1974
KIRKLAND, James Hampton: 4373
KIRKMAN FAMILY (North Carolina): 2240
KIRKPATRICK, Thomas Jellis: 506, 2951
KIRKPATRICK, William (1754-1812): 5639
KIRKSVILLE, Missouri: see CIVIL WAR--CAMPAIGNS, BATTLES, AND MILITARY ACTIONS--Missouri--Kirksville
KISINGIRI, Zakaria Kizito: 41
KITCHEN, D. C.: 4188
KITCHEN, James B.: 3045
KITCHEN UTENSILS--Inventions: 3424
KITCHENER, Horatio Herbert, First Earl Kitchener of Khartoum: 278, 663, 3046
KITCHIN, Claude: 958
KITCHIN, George William: 2148
KITCHIN, William Walton: 1336
KITCHINER, William: 2146
KITCHING, Seymour: 3047
KITTRELL, Charlotte Wilson Powe: 3048
KITTRELL, I. W.: 2087
KITTRELL, Norman Goree: 2449
KITTRELL COLLEGE, Kittrell, North Carolina: 1584, 1588
KITTRELL SPRINGS, North Carolina:
    Social life and customs: 5390
KITTRELL'S CHURCH (North Carolina): 3646

KITTY, William: 4457
KITTY HAWK CIRCUIT, Methodist
    churches: 3646
KIVETT FAMILY (Missouri): 1948
KIWANIS CLUB:
    Alabama--Tuscaloosa: 120
KLEINSCHMIDT, William A.: 3049
KLOPFER, Henry A.: 715
KNAPP, Mr. _____ (teacher): 3567
KNAPP, G. P.: 1446
KNAPP, Martin Wells: 2861
KNATCHBULL, Sir Edward, Ninth
    Baronet: 3050, 5026
KNESEBECK, Baron _____: 1911
KNIGHT, Anna P.: 3051
KNIGHT, B. F.: 3052
KNIGHT, Frances Beall: 3053
KNIGHT, Jessie Clark: 2407
KNIGHT, John: 3053
KNIGHT, Jonathan: 3054
KNIGHT, Mary McCleery: 3053
KNIGHT, Tobias: 5457
KNIGHTHOOD:
    Great Britain: 280, 485
KNIGHTON, Sir William: 2836, 4113
KNIGHTS OF HONOR: 5709
KNIGHTS OF JERICHO:
    South Carolina: 4610
KNIGHTS OF THE GOLDEN CIRCLE: 659
    Iowa: 1984
KNITTING--Virginia: 1115
KNITTING MACHINERY:
    see also HOSIERY MACHINERY--
        Knitting machines
    Fishing nets--Inventions: 3424
    Virginia: 800
KNOCKENHAIR, Scotland: 5835
KNOLLYS, Francis, First Viscount
    Knollys: 4567
KNOTT, Charles: 3245
KNOTT, Richard Wilson: 2449
KNOTT, William: 3245
KNOW-NOTHING PARTY: 865, 2469, 2671,
    2960, 3325, 4892, 5051, 5059,
    5498
    Georgia: 5051
    Louisiana: 489
    Maryland: 4457
    Mississippi: 1370
    Missouri: 4616
    North Carolina: 4714
    South Carolina: 1877
    Virginia: 4720
        Goochland County: 4616
KNOWLES, James Davis: 3055
KNOWLES, James Sheridan (1784-1862):
    2146
KNOWLES, Sir James Thomas
    (1831-1908): 3056
KNOWSLEY HALL, England: 5025
KNOX, Alexander: 3738
KNOX, Frank: 879
KNOX, Henry: 5537
KNOX, Joseph: 3545
KNOX, Philander Chase: 1364, 3545
KNOX, Reed: 3545
KNOX, Robert: 3057
KNOX FAMILY (Ireland): 3738
KNOX COUNTY, Indiana:
    Vincennes: 1072
KNOX COUNTY, Tennessee:
    Knoxville: see KNOXVILLE,
        Tennessee
KNOXVILLE, Tennessee: 541, 4746,
    4849, 5389, 5681
    Business enterprises: 5858
    Civil War:
        see also CIVIL WAR--CAMPAIGNS,
            BATTLES, AND MILITARY ACTIONS--
            Tennessee--Knoxville
        Fortifications: 4245
        Southern Unionists: 2260
        Union occupation: 4245
    Economic conditions: 5858
    Labor unions: 1197
        Plumbers: 5409
    Land: 795
    Railroads: 3069

KNOXVILLE, Tennessee (Continued):
    Reconstruction: 716
KNOXVILLE (Tenn.) WAR HOUSING
    COMMITTEE: 1193
KOBE, Japan: 3888
KOCH, Frederick Henry: 3797
KÖHLER, Oskar: 111
KOHLHOF, Reverend Doctor _____: 739
KOLHAPUR, Maharaja of: see
    CHHATRAPATI, Sir Shahu, Maharajah
    of Kolhapur
KOLLOCK, Cornelius: 2449
KOLO SERBSKI SESTARA: 4080
KONKLE, Burton Alva: 103
KOO, Vi-Kyuin Wellington: 83, 5252
KOONCE, David: 3058
KOONCE, George: 3058
KOPMAN, Henry: 3059
KOREA:
    Description and travel: 2463, 4858
    Japanese occupation: 5252
    Presbyterian missionaries: 2269
KOSMOS CLUB, Columbia, South
    Carolina: 3421
KOSSUTH, Lajos: 4650, 5764
KOSSUTH, Louis: see KOSSUTH, Lajos
KRAKATOA (volcano): 1464
KREBS, Frank Harmon: 3060
KREBS, Henry Clay: 3060
KREBS, Isaac: 3060
KREBS, William F.: 3060
KREHBIEL, Henry Edward: 103
KROESEN, Washington: 3061
KROLL, Jack: 5486
KU KLUX KLAN: 20, 415, 546, 1191,
    3062, 4595, 4948
    Trials--South Carolina: 1889
    Subdivided by place:
        Georgia: 1672
        North Carolina: 1196, 2469,
            2589, 3062, 4714
        South Carolina: 2300, 2473, 3527
        Tennessee: 1587
            Lynchburg: 677
        Texas: 592
KUHN, Joseph L.: 5886
KUKULA, R.: 111
KUNG, H. H.: 5252
KUNKEL, John Christian: 2027
KUNLON, Burma: 4709
KUNZ, George Frederick: 3063
KUTTRELL, John K.: 4080
KUYKENDALL, A.: 3064
KUYKENDALL, James Sloan: 3721
KWAJALEIN, Marshall Islands:
    Atomic bomb test: 2897
KWANGJU, Korea: 2712
KWANSEI GAKUIN UNION MISSION
    COLLEGE AND SEMINARY, Kobe,
    Japan: 3888
KYNOCH: see HETHERINGTON AND
    KYNOCH v. LYNN
KYNYNMOUND, Gilbert John Elliot-
    Murray-, Fourth Earl of Minto: see
    ELLIOT-MURRAY-KYNYNMOUND, Gilbert
    John, Fourth Earl of Minto
KYTLE, Calvin: 3706

## L

L. BALDWIN (brigantine): 4456
L. J. GUILMARTIN & CO., Savannah, Georgia: 2232
LABICHE, Eugene: 3065
LABOR:
  see also IRISH IN THE UNITED STATES; RAILROADS--Construction--Labor; and specific types of laborers, e.g. AGRICULTURAL WORKERS
  Hours: see EIGHT-HOUR DAY; HOURS OF LABOR
  Payroll Deduction Plan: 341
  Wages: see WAGES AND SALARIES
  War Bond Campaign: 341
  Subdivided by place:
    California: 4834
    France: 1424
    Great Britain: 14, 2149, 3498, 4605, 4696, 5726
    Jamaica: 1792, 4605
    New York: 4351
    North Carolina: 3070, 5149
    Northern States: 2357, 5940
    Pennsylvania: 421
    South Carolina: 1424
    Union of Soviet Socialist Republics: 4614
    United States: 274, 325, 4805
LABOR AND EDUCATION: 3066
  see also AMERICAN LABOR EDUCATION SERVICE, INC.; HIGHLANDER FOLK SCHOOL; LABOR COLLEGES; SOUTHERN SCHOOL FOR WORKERS, INC.
LABOR AND MINORITIES:
  North Carolina: 5442
LABOR AND RELIGION:
  Southern States: 3558
  United States: 1197
  Virginia: 1194
LABOR AND SOCIALISM:
  United States: 4948
LABOR ARBITRATION:
  Textile workers:
    North Carolina: 5235
    South Carolina: 5233
  Typographical workers:
    South Carolina: 2771
  Subdivided by place:
    North Carolina: 1195
    Tennessee: 1197
    United States: 3066
LABOR COLLEGES:
  United States: 4948
LABOR CONDITIONS:
  see also CHILDREN--Employment; WOMEN--Employment
  Industrial safety:
    Virginia: 1194
  Railroads:
    Southern States: 5254
    United States: 3793
  Textile industry:
    New York: 3266
    North Carolina: 1275, 5234
  War industries:
    North Carolina: 2553

LABOR CONDITIONS (Continued):
  Subdivided by place:
    Colorado: 2554
    Great Britain: 5, 794, 1087
    Kansas: 2554
    Missouri: 2554
    North Carolina: 2548
    Texas: 2554
    Virginia: 2680, 3642, 3809
    Winchester: 283
    West Virginia: 4029
LABOR CONTRACTS:
  see also APPRENTICESHIP; FARM TENANCY--Labor contracts; FREEDMEN--Labor contracts; INDENTURED SERVANTS; LABOR UNIONS--Contracts; NEGRO SERVANTS--Labor contracts
  Alabama: 5237
  Georgia: 5237
  North Carolina: 5237
    Burlington: 5234
    Greensboro: 5234
    Mecklenburg County: 5235
  South Carolina: 5236, 5237
    Spartanburg: 5233
LABOR COSTS:
  Missouri--Saint Louis: 5137
  Virginia: 1922
LABOR DISPUTES:
  see also BOYCOTTS; CIVIL WAR--LABOR PROBLEMS; STRIKES
  Electricians--South Carolina: 2768
  Steel workers--Georgia: 5441
  Textile workers:
    North Carolina:
      Burlington: 5234
      Erwin: 5298
      Greensboro: 5234
      Mecklenburg: 5235
    South Carolina: 5236
      Spartanburg: 5233
  Subdivided by place:
    Massachusetts:
      Brockton: 3524
    North Carolina:
      Gastonia: 3706
      Marion: 3706
    Ohio: 5342
    United States: 4858
    Virginia: 1512, 5148
LABOR IN POLITICS:
  Florida: 2568
  Georgia: 2568
  Kentucky: 2568
  North Carolina: 1192, 2568
  South Carolina: 2568
  Virginia: 2568
LABOR INFORMATION BULLETIN: 1197
LABOR INSTITUTE OF AMERICA: 1197
LABOR JOURNALISM: 1883
LABOR LAWS AND LEGISLATION:
  Employment of women and children: 1478
    Georgia: 5406
  Great Britain: 1648
  North Carolina: 1275
  Subdivided by place:
    Georgia: 5441
    North Carolina: 1195, 1202
    South Carolina: 2767, 5411
    Tennessee: 1197, 1200, 5409
    United States: 325, 1197
      see also TAFT-HARTLEY ACT
    Virginia: 224, 1194
LABOR LETTER: 1194
LABOR-MANAGEMENT RELATIONS:
  Coal industry: 4865
  United States: 3066
LABOR MEDIATION: see LABOR ARBITRATION
LABOR MOVEMENT: see UNIONIZATION
LABOR NEWSPAPERS: see LABOR PUBLICATIONS
LABOR PRESS ASSOCIATED, INC.: 1196, 1202

LABOR PUBLICATIONS: 1196, 1197
  see also LABOR JOURNALISM
  North Carolina: 1195
  Southern States: 3558
  United States: 224, 1202, 2771, 3066, 3558, 3640
  Virginia: 1195
LABOR REFORM:
  see also HOURS OF LABOR; LABOR IN POLITICS
  Great Britain: 20
  United States: 1883
LABOR SHORTAGES: see WORLD WAR I--Labor shortages
LABOR SUPPLY:
  Arkansas: 1154
  Australia: 2410
  Southern States: 1101
LABOR UNIONS:
  see also ANTI-UNIONISM; UNIONIZATION
  Benefits: 5235
  Contracts:
    Electricians: 2767
    Railroad telegraphers: 3985, 3986
    Southern States: 2769
    Steel workers: 5441
    Typographical workers: 2772
  Conventions: 4436
    South Carolina: 2771, 4962
  Dues:
    Georgia: 1197
    South Carolina: 4962
      Electricians: 2767
      Typographical workers: 2771
    Tennessee: 1197
      Plumbers: 5409
  Elections:
    North Carolina:
      Burlington: 5234
      Greensboro: 3171
    Tennessee: 1200
  Finance:
    North Carolina: 1192, 1199
    South Carolina:
      Electricians: 2767
      Typographical workers: 2771
    Tennessee: 1197, 1200
    Virginia: 224
  Initiation fees:
    North Carolina: 1195
    South Carolina: 2767
  Lawsuits:
    North Carolina: 2772
    United States: 3640
  Membership: 2767
    South Carolina:
      Electricians: 2767
      Typographical workers: 2771
    Tennessee: 1197
      Plumbers: 5409
  Periodicals: see LABOR PUBLICATIONS
  Political actions: see LABOR IN POLITICS
  Public relations: see PUBLIC RELATIONS--Labor unions
  Traveling cards:
    South Carolina: 2767, 2771
  Subdivided by type of union:
    see also AMERICAN FEDERATION OF LABOR; CONGRESS OF INDUSTRIAL ORGANIZATIONS
    Agricultural implement workers: see UNITED AUTOMOBILE, AIRCRAFT, AND AGRICULTURAL IMPLEMENT WORKERS OF AMERICA
    Agricultural workers: see FOOD, TOBACCO, AGRICULTURAL AND ALLIED WORKERS UNION OF AMERICA
    Aircraft workers: see UNITED AUTOMOBILE, AIRCRAFT, AND AGRICULTURAL IMPLEMENT WORKERS OF AMERICA
    Automobile workers: see UNITED AUTOMOBILE, AIRCRAFT, AND AGRICULTURAL IMPLEMENT WORKERS OF AMERICA

LABOR UNIONS:
  Subdivided by type of union
    (Continued):
    Boilermakers: see INTERNATIONAL
      BROTHERHOOD OF BOILERMAKERS,
      IRON SHIP BUILDERS AND HELPERS
      OF AMERICA
    Cannery workers: see UNITED
      CANNERY, AGRICULTURE, PACKING,
      AND ALLIED WORKERS OF AMERICA
    Carpenters: see UNITED
      BROTHERHOOD OF CARPENTERS AND
      JOINERS OF AMERICA
    Chemical workers: see UNITED
      GAS, COKE, AND CHEMICAL WORKERS
      OF AMERICA
    Clothing workers: see
      AMALGAMATED CLOTHING WORKERS
      OF AMERICA; INTERNATIONAL
      LADIES' GARMENT WORKERS' UNION
    Communications workers: see
      COMMUNICATIONS WORKERS OF
      AMERICA; ORDER OF RAILROAD
      TELEGRAPHERS; VIRGINIA
      FEDERATION OF TELEPHONE WORKERS
    Construction workers:
      Virginia: 1198
    Department store workers: see
      RETAIL CLERKS INTERNATIONAL
      ASSOCIATION; RETAIL, WHOLESALE
      AND DEPARTMENT STORE UNION
    Distillery workers:
      Virginia: 1198
    Electrical workers: see
      INTERNATIONAL BROTHERHOOD OF
      ELECTRICAL WORKERS;
      INTERNATIONAL UNION OF
      ELECTRICAL, RADIO, AND
      MACHINE WORKERS
    Food workers: see FOOD, TOBACCO,
      AGRICULTURAL AND ALLIED WORKERS
      UNION OF AMERICA
    Furniture workers: see UNITED
      FURNITURE WORKERS OF AMERICA
    Gas workers: see UNITED GAS,
      COKE, AND CHEMICAL WORKERS OF
      AMERICA
    Government and civic employees:
      see also CITY CENTRAL LABOR
        UNION; UNITED PUBLIC WORKERS
        OF AMERICA
      South Carolina: 1172
      Tennessee: 1197
      Virginia: 1198
    Hosiery Workers: see AMERICAN
      FEDERATION OF HOSIERY WORKERS;
      AMERICAN FEDERATION OF HOSIERY
      WORKERS (INDEPENDENT)
    Industrial:
      North Carolina: 1192
      Tennessee: 1193
      Virginia: 1194
    Insurance and allied workers:
      Tennessee: 1197
      Virginia: 1198
    Iron workers: see INTERNATIONAL
      BROTHERHOOD OF BOILERMAKERS,
      IRON SHIP BUILDERS AND HELPERS
      OF AMERICA
    Joiners: see UNITED BROTHERHOOD
      OF CARPENTERS AND JOINERS OF
      AMERICA
    Metal workers: see INTERNATIONAL
      MOLDERS' UNION OF NORTH AMERICA
    Mine workers: 4865
      see also INTERNATIONAL UNION
        OF MINE, MILL, AND SMELTER
        WORKERS; UNITED MINE WORKERS
        OF AMERICA
    Municipal employees: see LABOR
      UNIONS--Government and civic
      employees
    Newspaper workers: see AMERICAN
      NEWSPAPER GUILD
    Oil workers: see OIL WORKERS
      INTERNATIONAL UNION
    Optical and instrument workers:
      Tennessee: 1197

LABOR UNIONS:
  Subdivided by type of union
    (Continued):
    Packinghouse workers: see UNITED
      CANNERY, AGRICULTURE, PACKING
      AND ALLIED WORKERS OF AMERICA;
      UNITED PACKINGHOUSE WORKERS
      OF AMERICA
    Painters: see BROTHERHOOD OF
      PAINTERS, DECORATORS AND
      PAPERHANGERS OF AMERICA
    Paper workers: 5486
      see also UNITED PAPERWORKERS
        OF AMERICA
      Tennessee: 1197
    Paperhangers: see BROTHERHOOD
      OF PAINTERS, DECORATORS AND
      PAPERHANGERS OF AMERICA
    Plant guards:
      Tennessee: 1197
    Postal workers:
      Florida: 3
      Louisiana: 3275
    Plumbers: see UNITED ASSOCIATION
      OF JOURNEYMEN AND APPRENTICES
      OF THE PLUMBING AND PIPEFITTING
      INDUSTRY OF THE UNITED STATES
      AND CANADA; UNITED ASSOCIATION
      OF JOURNEYMEN PLUMBERS, GAS
      FITTERS, STEAM FITTERS AND
      SPRINKLER FITTERS OF THE UNITED
      STATES AND CANADA
    Printers: see INTERNATIONAL
      TYPOGRAPHICAL UNION
    Radio workers: see INTERNATIONAL
      UNION OF ELECTRICAL, RADIO,
      AND MACHINE WORKERS
    Railroad carmen: see BROTHERHOOD
      OF RAILROAD CARMEN OF AMERICA
    Railroad engineers: see
      BROTHERHOOD OF LOCOMOTIVE
      ENGINEERS
    Railroad telegraphers: see ORDER
      OF RAILROAD TELEGRAPHERS
    Retail trade workers: see RETAIL
      CLERKS INTERNATIONAL
      ASSOCIATION; RETAIL, WHOLESALE
      AND DEPARTMENT STORE UNION
    Shipbuilding workers: see
      INDUSTRIAL UNION OF MARINE AND
      SHIPBUILDING WORKERS OF
      AMERICA; INTERNATIONAL
      BROTHERHOOD OF BOILERMAKERS,
      IRON SHIP BUILDERS AND HELPERS
      OF AMERICA
    Shoe workers: see UNITED SHOE
      WORKERS OF AMERICA
    Sign and pictorial painters: see
      BROTHERHOOD OF PAINTERS,
      DECORATORS, AND PAPERHANGERS
      OF AMERICA; SIGN AND PICTORIAL
      PAINTERS LOCAL UNION
    Smelter workers: see INTERNATIONAL
      UNION OF MINE, MILL, AND
      SMELTER WORKERS
    Steel workers:
      see also UNITED STEELWORKERS
        OF AMERICA
      Georgia--Atlanta: 5441
      Tennessee: 1197
      Virginia: 1198
    Stone workers: see UNITED STONE
      AND ALLIED PRODUCTS WORKERS OF
      AMERICA
    Telephone workers:
      see also COMMUNICATIONS WORKERS
        OF AMERICA; VIRGINIA
        FEDERATION OF TELEPHONE
        WORKERS
      North Carolina: 1199
      Tennessee: 1197
      Virginia: 1194, 1198
    Textile workers:
      see also TEXTILE WORKERS UNION
        OF AMERICA; UNITED TEXTILE
        WORKERS OF AMERICA
      North Carolina: 613, 1195
        Enka: 5442

LABOR UNIONS:
  Subdivided by type of union:
    Textile workers:
      North Carolina (Continued):
        Greensboro: 3171
      South Carolina: 1196
      Tennessee: 1197
    Tobacco workers:
      see also FOOD, TOBACCO,
        AGRICULTURAL AND ALLIED
        WORKERS UNION OF AMERICA;
        TOBACCO WORKERS INTERNATIONAL
        UNION
      North Carolina:
        Durham: 1150
    Transportation workers: see
      UNITED TRANSPORT SERVICE
      EMPLOYEES
    University employees:
      North Carolina: 613
    Utility workers:
      Tennessee: 1197
    Wholesale trade workers: see
      RETAIL, WHOLESALE AND
      DEPARTMENT STORE UNION
    Woodworkers: see INTERNATIONAL
      WOODWORKERS OF AMERICA
  Subdivided by place:
    Alabama: 3706
    Great Britain--Sheffield: 4234
    Massachusetts: 803
    North Carolina: 1199, 3706
    South Carolina: 300, 1424, 4962
      Columbia: 1172
    Southern States: 3558, 3706, 4094
    Tennessee: 1200
    Virginia: 1198, 1201
LABOR UNREST:
  see also BOYCOTTS; LABOR DISPUTES;
    STRIKES
  Australia: 1792
  Indiana: 2294
  Texas: 592
LABOUCHERE, Henry (1831-1912): 2026
LABOUCHERE, Henry, First Baron
  Taunton (1798-1869): 3067, 5277,
  5725
LABOUCHERE, Henry Du Pré: 5164
LABOUR PARTY (Great Britain): 3912,
  5616
  Indian policy: 2756
LABRADOR--Fishing industry: 636
LACE MAKING: 691
LACE PRICES--Massachusetts: 1839
LA CÉCILIA, Napoléon: 5103
LA CHAISE, _____: 4348
LACKAWANNA COUNTY, Pennsylvania:
  Scranton: 3227, 4188
LACKEY, Thomas: 3068
LACKEY, William A.: 3068
LACKEY FAMILY (Virginia): 3068
LACKLAND, Francis: 3069
LACKLAND, Samuel W.: 3069
LACY, Benjamin Rice: 1336, 3070
LACY, Beverly Tucker: 2120
LADD, John D.: 2933
LADD, Joseph Brown: 263
LADIES' ACADEMY OF THE VISITATION,
  Georgetown, D.C.: 2301
THE LADIES' HOME JOURNAL: 4481
LADIES' HOSPITAL AID ASSOCIATION OF
  REX HOSPITAL, Raleigh, North
  Carolina: 2553
LADIES LITERARY AND ART SOCIETY,
  Savannah, Georgia: 2005
LADIES SEWING SOCIETY (South
  Carolina): 4642
LADIES' UNION BENEVOLENT SOCIETY,
  Lexington, Kentucky: 3325
LADIES VOLUNTEER AID SOCIETY OF
  CHAPEL HILL (Louisiana): 3071
LADIES VOLUNTEER AID SOCIETY OF
  MONROE (Louisiana): 3071
LADIES VOLUNTEER AID SOCIETY OF PINE
  HILLS (Louisiana): 3071
LADOUX, Georges: 1424
LADY ASTOR DAY: 2955
LADY STIRLING (blockade runner): 410

LADYSMITH, Natal--Boer War: 1132
LAFAYETTE, Marie Joseph Paul Yves
  Roch Gilbert du Motier, Marquis de:
  1424, 3072, 3130, 3444, 3501,
  3775, 3809
  American tour: 872
  Visit to Fayetteville, North
    Carolina: 2870
LAFAYETTE, Indiana: 4436
LAFAYETTE, Tennessee:
  Civil War: 4588
LAFAYETTE AGRICULTURAL COLLEGE,
  Easton, Pennsylvania:
  Students and student life: 4373
LAFAYETTE COLLEGE, Easton,
  Pennsylvania: 5764
  Riots: 2552
  Students and student life: 2552
    Parents' letters: 2552
LAFAYETTE COUNTY, Mississippi:
  Oxford: 3076, 4379, 5971
  see also UNIVERSITY OF MISSISSIPPI
  Literary affairs: 1771
LAFAYETTE COUNTY, Missouri:
  Grasshoppers: 5984
  Lexington: 1405
    see also BAPTIST FEMALE COLLEGE
LAFFAN, Sir Joseph de Courcy: 4024
LAFFITE, Jean: 3073
LAFFOON, Mark R.: 208, 3074
LAFOURCHE PARISH, Louisiana:
  Thibodeaux: 478
LAFRANCE, Marston: 720
LAGARÉ, Hugh Swinton: 2449
LAGLEY, C. N.: 648
LA GRANGE, Georgia: 1476
  Girls' schools and academies: 3905
LA GRANGE, Indiana: 328
LAGRANGE, North Carolina: 2945
LA GRANGE, Tennessee: see LA GRANGE
  FEMALE COLLEGE
LA GRANGE FEMALE COLLEGE, La Grange,
  Tennessee: 3155
LA GRANGE FEMALE INSTITUTE, La Grange,
  Georgia: 3905
LA GUAIRA, Venezuela:
  Construction of railroads and
    telegraph: 4895
LAHORE, India:
  British administration: 3838
LAIRD (JOHN) AND SON, Georgetown,
  D.C. (firm): 3179
LAKANAL, Joseph: 4348
LAKE, Gerard, First Viscount Lake:
  4635
LAKE COMFORT, North Carolina: 730
LAKE COPAIS COMPANY: 4567
LAKE ERIE:
  Description and travel: 2690
LAKE JUNALUSKA, North Carolina: 879
LAKE LANDING, North Carolina:
  Merchants: 4760
LAKE MILLS (lumber mill): 730
LAKE ONTARIO:
  Description and travel: 2690, 3087
LAKE SUPERIOR:
  Description and travel: 3710
LAKEVILLE, Massachusetts: 953
LAMAR, Gazaway Bugg: 1365
LAMAR, John Basel: 3075
LAMAR, Lucius Quintus Cincinnatus:
  1084, 1364, 3076, 5578
LAMAR, Mary Ann: 1121
LAMAR COUNTY, Georgia:
  Barnesville:
    Confederate Army camp: 18
    Description: 284
LAMAR COUNTY, Texas:
  Paris: 155, 592, 3590
LAMARTINE, Alphonse Marie Louis de:
  3077
LAMB, Lady Caroline, Viscountess
  Melbourne: 3080
LAMB, Charles: 1024
LAMB, H. Mack: 3078
LAMB, John Ferguson: 5751
LAMB, Martha Joanna Reade (Nash):
  3022

LAMB, Mary Ann: 1024
LAMB, Mary S.: 5751
LAMB, Nancy Jane: 3078
LAMB, Thomas Philips: 4967
LAMB, William (Virginia, 1835-1909):
  3709
LAMB, William, Second Viscount
  Melbourne: 3080, 4605
LAMB FAMILY (Virginia): 5751
LAMBAYEQUE, Peru:
  Description: 4155
LAMBDIN, Charles E.: 4791
LAMBDIN, James Reid: 2728
LAMBERT, Edward W.: 5096
LAMBERT, William Harrison: 5813
LAMBERTON, R. A.: 4188
LAMBETH, Cosmo Gordon Lang, First
  Baron Lang of: see LANG, Cosmo
  Gordon, First Baron Lang of Lambeth
LAMBETH, John Walter: 5457
LAMBORN, Emma (Taylor): 5642
LAMBTON, John George, First Earl of
  Durham: 1632, 5026
LAMBUTH FAMILY: 872
LAMINGTON, Charles Wallace Alexander
  Napier Ross Cochrane-Baillie,
  Second Baron: 278
LAMINGTON, Scotland: 278
LAMOILLE COUNTY, Vermont:
  Morrisville--Civil War: 1564
LAMONT, Thomas William: 4556, 5252
LAMPSON, Frederick Locker-: see
  LOCKER-LAMPSON, Frederick
LANARKSHIRE, Scotland:
  Glasgow: see GLASGOW, Scotland
  Lamington: 278
LANCASHIRE, England:
  Strikes: 2149
  Cities and towns:
    Brantwood: 4600
    Carnforth: 583
    Edge Lane Hall: 2457
    Haulg: 5259
    Knowsley Hall: 5025
    Liverpool: see LIVERPOOL, England
    Manchester: 676, 1126, 2899
      Arts: 4113
      Church buildings: 4287
    Middleton: 1457
    Poulton: 3251
    Preston: 562, 1087, 5895
    Rochdale: 649
    Spotland: 3715
    Stand: 4850
    Swarthdale: 342
LANCASHIRE AND CHESHIRE RECORDS
  PRESERVED IN THE PUBLIC RECORD
  OFFICE: 4627
LANCASTER, C. S.: 5790
LANCASTER, Duchy of: 4437, 4567
LANCASTER, England: 4437
  Leyland Parish:
    Vital statistics: 5694
LANCASTER, Ohio: 1743
LANCASTER, Pennsylvania: 741, 2444,
  2492, 2972, 4423
  Estates: 2497
  Lawsuits: 5948
  Race relations: 5991
  Universities and colleges: see
    BETHANY COLLEGE
LANCASTER, South Carolina: 5931
LANCASTER, Virginia: 1557
LANCASTER BROWN & CO., New York, New
  York: 236
LANCASTER COUNTY, Nebraska:
  Lincoln: 729, 4290
LANCASTER COUNTY, Pennsylvania:
  Grain and flour trade: 2505
  Cities and towns:
    Lancaster: see LANCASTER,
      Pennsylvania
    Marietta: 3613
    Setez: 1881
LANCASTER COUNTY, South Carolina:
  Family life: 4310
  Legal affairs: 5863
  Social life and customs: 4310

LANCASTER COUNTY, South Carolina
  (Continued):
  Weather: 4310
  Cities and towns:
    Lancaster: 5931
LANCASTER COUNTY, Virginia:
  Lancaster: 1557
LANCELOT by Edward Arlington
  Robinson: 4519
"LANCELOT, GUINEVERE AND ARTHUR" by
  Julia Magruder: 3465
LANCKSTER FAMILY (Great Britain--
  Genealogy): 1141
LAND, Edward: 5252
LAND, Nathan P.: 3081
LAND:
  see also CIVIL WAR--ABANDONED LANDS;
    CIVIL WAR--CONFISCATION OF
    PROPERTY--Land; COTTON LAND;
    CROWN LANDS; FARM LAND; PUBLIC
    LANDS; REAL ESTATE; STATE LANDS
  Condemnation of: see EMINENT DOMAIN
  Lawsuits:
    Great Britain--Sussex: 4767
    Tennessee: 214
    Virginia: 3560
    West Virginia: 5194
    Wheeling: 3587
  Mortgages:
    Louisiana: 478
    North Carolina--Carthage: 5138
  Prices:
    Alabama: 1178, 2663, 3626
    Florida: 2387
    Georgia: 1997
    Illinois: 3051
    Indiana: 3051
    Iowa: 849
    Maryland: 3742
    Mexico: 2210
    Mississippi: 2663, 3415
    Missouri: 2663
    North Carolina: 2300, 2663, 4689
      Guilford County: 2314
      Halifax County: 5672
    Ohio: 1505, 3051, 4732
    South Carolina: 477, 4118
      Charleston: 1745
    Virginia: 4924, 5613, 5765
      Patrick County: 1410
  Purchases and sales:
    see also ESCHEAT
    Alabama: 1133
    Canada--Nova Scotia: 3381
    Carolina Province: 202, 780
    Florida, East: 4040
    Georgia:
      1700s: 5644
      1700s-1800s: 2019, 2441, 3309, 3661
      1800s: 794, 1066, 1090, 2280, 3704,
        5354, 5651
      Augusta: 3672
      Saint Mary's: 1448
    Great Britain--Sussex: 4767
    Illinois: 2273, 5981
    Iowa: 2273
    Kentucky: 1086, 4616
    Louisiana: 2674
    Maryland: 5296, 5353
    Mississippi: 57, 3846
    New York: 2172
    North Carolina:
      1700s-1800s: 3364
      1700s-1900s: 2929, 3476
      1800s: 484, 1475, 2419, 3351,
        4336, 5599
      1800s-1900s: 4689, 4897, 5709
      Clarkton: 5909
      Davie County: 122
      Forsyth County: 5935
      Halifax County: 426
      Onslow County: 5761
    Ohio: 281, 3103, 4616
    Pennsylvania: 3897
    South Carolina:
      Orangeburg District: 5015
      Sumter County: 3676
    Tennessee: 5224

LAND:
　　Purchases and sales (Continued):
　　　Texas: 724, 3772, 3846, 4269,
　　　　4596
　　　Virginia:
　　　　1700s: 1813, 5575
　　　　1700s-1800s: 4616
　　　　1700s-1900s: 4743
　　　　1800s: 74, 253, 794, 2273,
　　　　　2370, 3232, 3560, 3846,
　　　　　4661, 4720, 5696, 5743, 5765
　　　　1800s-1900s: 3979
　　　　Brunswick County: 2517
　　　　Nansemond County: 3012
　　　Washington, D.C.: 3897
　　　West Virginia: 794, 1946, 2273
　　　　Jefferson County: 5591
　　　Wisconsin: 4974
　　Rental:
　　　see also FARM TENANCY; LANDLORD
　　　　AND TENANT
　　　Great Britain--Sussex: 4767
　　　North Carolina: 4761, 4849
　　　Oklahoma: 3687
　　　South Carolina:
　　　　Charleston: 4306
　　　Virginia: 4743, 5355
　　　West Virginia: 2342
　　Subdivided by place:
　　　Alabama: 1945
　　　　Tombigee River: 5308
　　　Arkansas: 478
　　　Bermuda: 5500
　　　British West Indies: 4913
　　　Georgia: 311, 1203
　　　　Camden County: 1835
　　　　Covington: 1382
　　　Great Britain: 507
　　　Illinois: 480, 1626
　　　　Adams County: 3255
　　　Indiana: 480, 5275
　　　Iowa: 1626
　　　Ireland: 3185
　　　Kentucky: 795, 1401, 3809
　　　Louisiana: 478
　　　Maryland: 2295, 2605
　　　Massachusetts: 1344, 4653
　　　Middle West: 2208
　　　Mississippi: 2970
　　　Missouri: 480, 753
　　　Nebraska: 1849
　　　North Carolina:
　　　　1700s: 3347
　　　　1700s-1800s: 360, 730, 1764,
　　　　　3176
　　　　1800s: 391, 2298, 2970, 3003,
　　　　　3231, 4862
　　　　1800s-1900s: 675
　　　　Craven County: 730
　　　　Granville County: 1224
　　　　Indian Territory: 675
　　　　Nash County: 5475
　　　　Orange County: 5390
　　　　Pantego: 3012
　　　　Pitt County: 975
　　　　Wake County: 730
　　　Nova Scotia: 3381
　　　Ohio: 1849
　　　Pennsylvania: 480
　　　South Carolina: 1472
　　　　Edisto River: 5388
　　　　Horry District: 1451
　　　　Orangeburg: 5388
　　　Tennessee: 1001
　　　　Brownsville: 4139
　　　　Haywood County: 4139
　　　　Morgan County: 5224
　　　Texas: 964, 2662, 3657, 5232
　　　　Colorado County: 1741
　　　United States: 4765
　　　Virginia:
　　　　1700s-1800s: 1920, 2887
　　　　1800s: 523, 753, 1600, 2986,
　　　　　4710
　　　　Amherst County: 397
　　　　Henrico County: 2415
　　　　Little Hunting Creek: 5575

LAND:
　　Subdivided by place (Continued):
　　　Washington, D.C.: 849
　　　West Virginia: 4348
　　　Western States: 832, 4188
　　　Wisconsin: 3761
LAND ACQUISITION: see LAND--
　　Purchases and sales
LAND AGENTS--Alabama: 5308
LAND CLAIMS:
　　see also SQUATTERS; WESTERN LANDS
　　American Revolution: 4080
　　Florida: 3447, 3598
　　Georgia: 2785
　　Mexico: 891
　　North Carolina: 2730, 5768
　　　Craven County: 4977
　　Tennessee: 214
　　Virginia: 5768
　　　Campbell County: 62
　　West Virginia:
　　　Berkeley County: 5037
　　　Webster County: 5194
LAND COMPANIES:
　　see also LAND SPECULATION
　　Florida: 4298
　　Georgia: 3309, 4298
　　Great Britain: 2583, 4895
　　Middle West: 2712
　　New York: 2438
　　North Carolina: 4858
　　　Holly Springs: 63
　　Ohio: 5593
　　South Carolina: 4298
　　Tennessee: 1630, 2785
　　United States: 323, 2583
　　　see also DISMAL SWAMP LAND
　　　　COMPANY; LOUISA LAND COMPANY;
　　　　MERCHANTS AND MECHANICS LAND
　　　　COMPANY; TRANSYLVANIA LAND
　　　　COMPANY
　　Virginia: 1512, 3721
　　　Lawrenceville: 724
　　　Page County--Bankruptcy: 461
LAND CONFISCATION: see AMERICAN
　　REVOLUTION--Confiscated property;
　　CIVIL WAR--CONFISCATED PROPERTY--
　　Land
LAND DEEDS AND INDENTURES:
　　see also LAND TITLES
　　California:
　　　Redondo Beach: 4029
　　Florida: 2232
　　Georgia:
　　　1700s: 1664, 2666, 5189, 5987
　　　1700s-1800s: 2441, 5986
　　　1700s-1900s: 1993
　　　1800s: 1434, 2006, 2232, 2280,
　　　　2827, 4895, 5586
　　　Effingham County: 1375
　　　Franklin County: 1997
　　　Savannah: 3309, 5221
　　Honduras: 5063
　　Illinois: 5570
　　Indiana: 4100
　　Kansas: 4100, 4606
　　Kentucky: 5505
　　　Lexington: 3325
　　Maryland: 2295, 2853, 4468, 5488
　　　Cecil County: 5296
　　　Charles County: 5089
　　　Frederick County: 112, 4457
　　　Hagerstown: 1958
　　　Harford County: 4537
　　　Kent County: 5296
　　　Queen Annes County: 5296
　　　Sharpsburg: 979
　　　Washington County: 2838
　　Massachusetts: 2468, 3034, 5766
　　　Suffolk County: 1431
　　Michigan: 4606
　　Mississippi: 5612
　　Missouri--Saint Louis: 5155
　　New Jersey:
　　　Burlington County: 1752
　　New York: 782, 2172, 4680, 5133,
　　　5731
　　　Yates County: 3568

LAND DEEDS AND INDENTURES
　　(Continued):
　　North Carolina:
　　　1700s: 484
　　　1700s-1800s: 540, 1538, 2698,
　　　　3364, 4082, 4147, 5188
　　　1700s-1900s: 832, 872, 1107,
　　　　1438, 3176, 3233, 3476, 4100,
　　　　4849, 4858, 5298
　　　1800s: 817, 1556, 1656, 2294,
　　　　2660, 2776, 2824, 3763, 4689,
　　　　5002, 5596, 5599, 5771
　　　1800s-1900s: 1120, 3091, 3416,
　　　　4897, 5739
　　　Alexander County: 912
　　　Anson County: 2493
　　　Beaufort County: 692
　　　Burke County: 61, 1247
　　　Caldwell County: 1247
　　　Craven County: 804, 982
　　　Cumberland County: 4517
　　　Davie County: 122
　　　Dobbs County: 1523
　　　Duplin County: 5707
　　　Fayetteville: 2354
　　　Gamewell: 3324
　　　Glasgow County: 1523
　　　Granville County: 1224, 2339,
　　　　2716
　　　Halifax County: 3256, 5707
　　　Hillsborough: 1890
　　　Lincoln County: 61
　　　Onslow County: 1252, 5761
　　　Orange County: 912, 3752, 5109,
　　　　5341
　　　Oxford: 2455
　　　Randolph County: 88, 5018
　　　Richmond County: 5021
　　　Ridgeway: 3307
　　　Sampson County: 1752
　　　Surry County: 2419
　　　Transylvania County: 5768
　　　Tyrrell County: 215
　　　Wake County: 5341
　　　Washington County: 5013
　　　Wayne County: 4421
　　　Williamston: 4824
　　　Yadkin County: 2419
　　Ohio: 357
　　Pennsylvania--Lewistown: 2704
　　South Carolina: 1581, 1682, 2596,
　　　2744, 2961, 3366, 4822
　　　Abbeville: 3375
　　　Anderson District: 718
　　　Charleston: 2556, 4214, 4306,
　　　　5198
　　　Columbia: 3525
　　　Greenville County: 2625
　　　Hampton County: 5759
　　　Laurens County: 4834
　　　Spartanburg County: 4721
　　Tennessee: 872, 4269
　　　Henderson County: 5341
　　　Nashville: 4854
　　　Washington County: 718
　　Texas:
　　　Jackson County: 2385
　　　Liberty County: 2385
　　United States: 4022
　　Virginia:
　　　1700s-1800s: 2949, 5047
　　　1700s-1900s: 3233, 4743
　　　1800s: 3806, 4122, 4615, 5765
　　　1800s-1900s: 5302, 5779
　　　Charles City County: 819
　　　Fluvanna County: 195, 5839
　　　Halifax County: 5229
　　　Hanover County: 1824
　　　Nelson County: 3566
　　　Northern Neck: 1750
　　　Richmond: 5790
　　West Virginia: 865, 2342, 3532,
　　　5194, 5456
　　　Berkeley County: 2397
　　　Greenbrier County: 4563
　　　Harrison County: 4563
　　　Jefferson County: 2711

LAND DEEDS AND INDENTURES:
    West Virginia (Continued):
        Pocahontas County: 1837
    Western States: 3532
LAND DEVELOPMENT:
    see also COASTAL DEVELOPMENT
    Florida: 5848
    Mississippi Valley: 4348
    North Carolina: 1521
        Wilmington: 3447
    South Carolina: 1478
    Texas: 2876
    West Virginia:
        Pocahontas County: 1837
LAND DISTRIBUTION-PREEMPTION ACT: 3325
LAND DRAINAGE:
    North Carolina:
        Craven County: 3955
        New Hanover County: 4603
LAND DYAKS: see DYAKS
LAND FRAUD:
    see also PUBLIC LANDS--Land fraud
    Georgia: 1090
        see also YAZOO LAND FRAUD
    Ohio: 2120
LAND GRANTS:
    Georgia:
        1700s: 289, 1296, 1993, 2666, 3573
        1700s-1800s: 3671
        1800s: 1434, 2280, 2992
        Franklin County: 1997
        Great Ogeechee District: 812
    Maryland: 4457
        Annapolis: 5436
    Mexico: 3587
    Mississippi: 5612
    North Carolina:
        1700s: 1361, 1389, 3940
        1700s-1800s: 3364, 3386, 5188
        1700s-1900s: 832, 5740
        1800s: 1577, 4689
        Bladen County: 517
        Craven County: 804
        Durham County: 3514
        Eno River: 912
        Hyde County: 4827
        Martin County: 4849
        Wake County: 3514
    South Carolina: 2281, 3386, 3802, 4218, 5863
    Tennessee: 2664, 2847, 4269
    Texas: 4249
    United States: 34, 480, 741, 2326, 2815, 4200, 5451, 5593
    Virginia:
        1600s-1700s: 1242
        1700s: 667, 1511, 2383, 2495, 2815, 4380
        1700s-1800s: 1920
        1700s-1900s: 824
        1800s: 5765
        Charles City County: 819
    West Virginia: 5194
LAND LAWS:
    see also LAND TITLE LEGISLATION
    Georgia: 3573
    Ireland: 3693
    Mississippi: 4269
    Pennsylvania: 421
    South Carolina: 4213
    Tennessee: 4269
    Texas: 4170
LAND LOTTERIES:
    Georgia: 1993, 1998, 1999
LAND PATENTS: 5886
    Virginia: 1842
LAND RECLAMATION:
    North Carolina:
        Wilmington: 3447
    United States: 4805
    Western States: 5791
LAND REFORM:
    Great Britain: 3236
    Government loans: 515
    India: 774
    Ireland: 649, 2149
        see also IRISH LAND ACT

LAND SCRIP: see BOUNTY LANDS
LAND SETTLEMENT:
    Alabama: 872, 3436, 5593
    Arkansas: 1438
    California: 693
    Canada, Western: 2708
    Florida: 693, 1424, 3041
    Georgia: 2096, 3733
        Twiggs County: 1231
    Illinois: 25
    Indiana: 3125, 5018
    Kansas: 5018
    Kentucky: 404, 3125
    Mexico: 693
    Middle West: 128
    Mississippi: 734, 5047
    Mississippi Territory: 2609, 3041
    Missouri: 5018, 5984
    Nebraska: 1828
    North Carolina: 5018, 5768
    Ohio: 404, 734
    Old Southwest: 872
    Tennessee: 702, 734, 872
        Morgan County: 5224
    Texas: 693, 1909, 2385, 4269
    Virginia: 99
    Washington Territory: 5018
    West Virginia: 99
    Western lands: 3041
    Western States: 1601
LAND SPECULATION: 5702
    see also LAND COMPANIES
    Alabama: 1986, 5612
    Arkansas: 4924
    Florida: 4298
        Leon County: 631
    Georgia: 3041, 3897, 4081, 4298
    Iowa: 4157, 4468
    Kansas: 128, 4720
    Louisiana: 1302
    Massachusetts: 5766
    Middle West: 1920, 2447
    Mississippi: 3415, 5612
    Missouri: 5392
    New York: 3041, 5731
    North Carolina: 4298
    Ohio: 2591, 5520
    Pennsylvania: 3041
    Tennessee: 214, 4746, 5612
    Texas: 724, 2517, 4596, 4924, 5612
    Vermont: 3041
    Virginia: 2517, 3362, 4615
    West Virginia: 2447, 4924
    Western lands: 4348
    Western Reserve: 3041
    Wisconsin: 4039
LAND SURVEYS: see SURVEYS AND SURVEYING
LAND TAXES: see ESCHEAT; TAXATION OF PROPERTY
LAND TENURE:
    Great Britain:
        Middlesex: 3658
        Yorkshire: 5956
LAND TITLE COMPANIES:
    Kentucky--Louisville: 3141
LAND TITLE LEGISLATION:
    Great Britain: 2998
    North Carolina: 5768
LAND TITLES:
    see also INDIANS OF NORTH AMERICA-- Land titles; SQUATTERS
    Florida--Florida Keys: 1001
    Georgia:
        Bulloch County: 3663
        Saint Mary's: 1448
    Great Britain--London: 5662
    Illinois: 2273
    Iowa: 2273
    Kentucky: 1843, 4616
        Pleasant Hill: 5416
    North Carolina: 2776, 4232
        Transylvania County: 5768
    Ohio: 4616
    South Carolina: 1480
        Charleston: 5198
        Orangeburg: 5388
    Tennessee--Morgan County: 5224

LAND TITLES (Continued):
    Virginia: 2273, 5765
    West Virginia: 2273
        Pocahontas County: 1837
LAND WARRANTS: 1818
    Georgia: 4921
    North Carolina: 2256
        Purchases and sales: 1363, 4080
    Virginia: 3537, 4720
        Purchases and sales: 2633
THE LAND WE LOVE: 2529
LANDABURU, Augustin Leocadio de: 4179
LANDAFF, New Hampshire:
    Farm accounts: 4265
LANDES, D. C.: 3082
LANDES, John: 3082
LANDING, Kate: 4910
LANDLORD AND TENANT:
    see also FARM TENANCY; FREEDMEN-- Tenancy; LAND--Rental; LAND REFORM; REAL ESTATE--Rental; SHARECROPPING
    Contracts--Virginia: 4555
    Lawsuits--North Carolina: 1951
    Subdivided by place:
        Great Britain: 5, 712, 2149, 5726
            Gloucestershire: 4630
            Sussex: 4767
            Worcestershire: 4630
        India: 774
        Ireland: 3238, 4520
        Maryland: 2295
        North Carolina: 484, 797, 817, 2833
            Person County: 1336
            Stem: 4464
            Surry County: 2808
            Yadkin County: 2808
        Virginia--Hanover County: 4020
LANDMARK (periodical): 3787
LANDON, Alfred Mossman: 5252
LANDON, Newton: 3083
LANDON DISTRICT, South Carolina: 1181
LANDOR, Arnold Henry Savage: 2148
LANDRAM, Charles S.: 3084
LANDSCAPE GARDENING:
    University and college campuses: 3048
LANDSCAPE IN ART:
    Great Britain: 1071
LANDSEER, Sir Edwin Henry: 2148
LANDSLIDES--Brazil: 1644
LANE, Carrie: 942, 5110
LANE, Franklin Knight: 3019, 4851
LANE, James S.: 5324
LANE, John C.: 3085
LANE, Moses B.: 3955
LANE, William Preston, Jr.: 3086
LANE FAMILY (North Carolina): 1475
    Genealogy: 2553
LANE AND GREEN (firm): see GREEN AND LANE
LANE COUNTY, Oregon:
    Eugene: 5054
LANESBORO, North Carolina: 409
LANG, Andrew: 3851
LANG, Cosmo Gordon, First Baron Lang of Lambeth: 233
LANG, John: 3087
LANGDON, John: 1884
LANGENBECK, Maximilian Adolf: 174
LANGFORD, John Alfred: 2149
LANGHORNE, J. C.: 3012
LANGHORNE, Nancy Witcher: 2955
LANGLEY-HALL, Dawn Pepita: 4823
LANGSTON, John Dallas, Jr.: 3088
LANGTRY, Lillie: 3089
"THE LANGUAGE OF REVOLUTION" by Ovid Williams Pierce: 4204
LANGUAGES:
    see also DIALECTS; INDIANS OF NORTH AMERICA--Language; and names of specific languages, e.g. ENGLISH LANGUAGE
    Study and teaching: 4967
    Ancient languages:
        University of Virginia: 3251
LANGWORTHY, Edward: 2788

LANIER, Clifford Anderson: 361, 1084, 2449, 3092
LANIER, Henry Wysham: 2449, 4279
LANIER, Hosea: 3090
LANIER, Marcellus V.: 3091
LANIER, Mary (Day): 361
LANIER, Sidney: 1084, 2449, 3092
LANIER, Thomas: 795
LANIER, W. B.: 3089
LANIER FAMILY (North Carolina): 3090, 3091
"A LANIER MANUSCRIPT" by Jay B. Hubbell: 3092
LANIGAN, George Thomas: 3093
LANKESTER, Sir Edwin Ray: 1113
LANMAN, Charles: 3094
LANPHEUR, Nate: 3095
LANSDOWNE, Henry Charles Keith Petty-Fitzmaurice, Fifth Marquis of: 5872
LANSDOWNE, William Petty, First Marquis of: 92, 4171
LANSING, Robert: 3096, 5252
LANSON, Gustave: 3097
LANTZ, Samuel M.: 3098
LANZILLI, Pietro: 3099
LA PLACE, Louisiana: 714
LAPRADE, William: 3100
LAPRADE, William Thomas: 22
LAPSLEY, John Whitfield: 3101
LAREDO, Texas: 3597
LARIMER COUNTY, Colorado: 3199
LARKBEAR, England: 598
LARKIN, Henry: 892
LARNED, Josephus Nelson: 706
LARNED, Samuel: 3102
LA ROCHELLE, France: 555
LARREA DE LOREDO, José de: 4155
LARRVIA, José Joaquín: 4155
LARWILL, Joseph Hart: 3103
LASALLE COUNTY, Illinois:
    Ottawa--Churches: 993
    Utica: 3222
LASCELLES, Sir Frank: 663
LASCELLES, Henry, Earl of Harewood: 1648, 5026
LASHLEY FAMILY (North Carolina--Genealogy): 5506
LASHMAN, L. Edward, Jr.: 1202
LASKI, Harold Joseph: 2146
LASSITER, Charles Trotter: 818, 3104
LASSITER, Daniel William: 3104
LASSITER, Francis Rives: 3104
LASSITER, M. Benson: 675
"THE LAST DAYS OF FITZ LEE'S DIVISION OF CAVALRY ARMY OF NORTHERN VIRGINIA" by Thomas Taylor Munford: 3809
"THE LAST PLACE" by Charles Buck Roberts: 4502
LAST YEARS OF HENRY TIMROD by Jay B. Hubbell: 2449, 4829
THE LATE GENERAL DUNCAN, C.S.A.: 1597
LATHAM, George: 3105
LATHAM, Henry Grey: 3106
LATHROP, Daniel: 2449
LATHROP, Florence: 4020
LATHROP, George Parsons: 4095
LATHROP, Lucy: 3762
LATHROP, Minna Byrd: 3107
LATHROP, Seth: 2959
LATHROP'S STOCK COMPANY, Boston, Massachusetts: 3108
LATIMER, George: 3109
LATIMER, S. H.: 3110
LATIN:
    Dictionaries: 3598
    Students' notebooks: 2614
        Georgia:
            University of Georgia: 3905
        Virginia:
            University of Virginia: 5288
            Washington and Lee University: 4616
    Study and teaching:
        Virginia:
            University of Virginia: 2612

LATIN AMERICA:
    see also names of specific countries; SOUTH AMERICA
    Filibusters: 2695
    Spanish administration: 4979
    Tunnels (proposed): 5603
LATIN LITERATURE:
    Translations into English: 3607
LATOUCHE SCHOOL, Savannah, Georgia: 2326
LATTA, James: 3140
LATTA, Joseph W.: 3111
LATTA, Thomas: 208, 3112
LATTA AND COMPANY: see LEATHERS, LATTA AND COMPANY
LATTNER, James S.: 3113
LAUCK, Isaac: 3114
LAUCK, W. E.: 574
LAUDANUM, Addiction to: 421
LAUDERDALE COUNTY, Alabama:
    Southern Unionists: 4160
LAUGHTON, Joseph B.: 3115
LAUNCESTON, England: 1239
LAUNDRY SERVICES--Prices: 5313
LAURASON AND FOWLE, Alexandria, Virginia (firm): 2933
LAUREL GROVE, Maryland: 1535
LAUREL HILL, North Carolina: 3776
LAUREL HILL, West Virginia: see CIVIL WAR--CAMPAIGNS, BATTLES, AND MILITARY ACTIONS--West Virginia--Laurel Hill
LAURENS, Caroline Olivia (Ball): 5193
LAURENS, Henry: 3116, 4145
LAURENS, John: 3116
LAURENS FAMILY (South Carolina): 295
LAURENS, South Carolina: 1337, 1478, 2616, 3383, 3531, 4834
    Abolition of slavery: 4118
    Social life and customs: 300
LAURENS CEMETERY, Laurens, South Carolina: 3383
LAURENS COUNTY, Georgia:
    Dublin: 5345
LAURENS COUNTY, South Carolina: 1988, 3981
    Land deeds and indentures: 4834
    Legal affairs: 4834
    Cities and towns:
        Clinton: 521
        Huntington: 4684
        Laurens: see LAURENS, South Carolina
LAURENS COTTON MILLS, Laurens, South Carolina: 1478
LAURENS DISTRICT, South Carolina: 1327
    Courts--Cases: 1001
LAURENS GLASS WORKS, Laurens, South Carolina: 1478
LAURIN, Duncan W.: 3117
LAURINBURG, North Carolina: 1313, 3416, 3475
LAVALLETTE, Elie A. F.: 3118
LAVALLETTE, Mary: 3118
LAVALLETTE, Stephen Decatur: 3118
LA VIEUVILLE D'ORVILLE, Adrien de, Comte de Vignacourt: 3119
LAW, Edward, First Baron Ellenborough: 3120
LAW, Edward, First Earl of Ellenborough: 868, 3121, 3453, 4137
LAW, Elizabeth Parke (Custis): 5575
LAW, Evander McIvor: 3122
LAW, James Henry: 1825
LAW, James Robert: 3123
LAW, Julia: 3124
LAW, Thomas: 5575
LAW, William (1792-1868): 208, 3123
LAW, William Adger (1864-1936): 2086
LAW, William Augustus: 3124
LAW FAMILY (South Carolina): 3124

LAW: 2083
    see also BANKING LAW; BANKRUPTCY LAW; BASTARDY LAWS; CANON LAW; CIVIL LAW; CORPORATION LAW; ELECTION LAWS; ENGLISH LAW; INHERITANCE LAWS; INTERNATIONAL LAW; LAND LAWS; LAW PRACTICE; MARITIME LAW; and Laws and legislation as a subheading under specific subjects
    Codification:
        India: 863
        Maryland: 5296
        New York: 1792
        United States: 1792
        Virginia: 3809
    Students' notebooks: 1713, 4103
        Alabama: 1031
        Maryland: 5296
        New Jersey:
            Princeton University: 2521
        New York:
            Columbia University: 2553, 4863
        Virginia: 3809
            University of Virginia: 4585
            Washington and Lee University: 4616
    Study of: 128, 1818, 4967
        Alabama: 976, 3611
        Connecticut: 1333
            East Windsor: 5593
        Georgia: 2326
        Massachusetts: see HARVARD UNIVERSITY--Law School
        New York: 814
            New York: 4863
                see also COLUMBIA UNIVERSITY--Law School
        North Carolina: 1109, 5124, 5848
        Pennsylvania: 1142
        South Carolina:
            Charleston: 5193
        Tennessee: see CUMBERLAND UNIVERSITY--Law School
        United States: 611
        Virginia: 872
            see also COLLEGE OF WILLIAM AND MARY--Legal education; UNIVERSITY OF VIRGINIA--Legal education
        Washington, D.C.: see GEORGE WASHINGTON UNIVERSITY--Law Department
    Teaching:
        Connecticut: 1333
        Georgia:
            University of Georgia: 3905
        Great Britain:
            Cambridge University: 3851
    Subdivided by place:
        Ireland: 1311
        Virginia: 1501
LAW AND EQUITY BILL (Great Britain): 5134
LAW ASSOCIATIONS: see LEGAL ORGANIZATIONS
LAW BOOKS:
    Connecticut: 3041
    North Carolina: 3410
    South Carolina: 2880
LAW ENFORCEMENT:
    see also SHERIFFS; UNITED STATES--GOVERNMENT AGENCIES AND OFFICIALS--Deputy Marshals
    Carolina Province: 780
    Georgia: 422
        Savannah: 5492
    Ireland: 4024
    Louisiana--New Orleans: 5051
    United States: 5051
    Virginia: 3853
LAW PRACTICE: 304
    see also ADVERTISING--Law practice; LAWYERS' ACCOUNTS; LEGAL FEES
    Alabama: 976
        Cherokee County: 4419
        Greensboro: 5593

LAW PRACTICE (Continued):
　Arkansas: 1089, 5380
　British Guiana--Demerara: 2612
　Connecticut: 2273, 3041
　Florida: 631
　France: 372
　Georgia:
　　1700s: 2788
　　1800s: 731, 740, 2326, 2372,
　　　2464, 2740, 4611, 5051
　　Augusta: 2931
　　Bartow: 2860
　　Camden County: 235
　　Macon: 3905
　Great Britain: 1545
　　Bath: 1753
　Illinois: 1400
　　Bloomington: 5570
　Kentucky--Lexington: 3325
　Louisiana: 5210
　Maryland: 3539, 4712, 5296
　　Baltimore: 2985, 3598
　Massachusetts--Boston: 5762
　Minnesota--Fond du Lac: 2436
　Mississippi: 1506
　Missouri:
　　Hannibal: 4616
　　Perryville: 2515
　　Saint Louis: 4616
　New York: 388, 1572, 2210
　North Carolina:
　　1700s: 5768
　　1700s-1800s: 4773
　　1800s: 264, 277, 591, 631, 1107,
　　　2657, 2808, 3176
　　1800s-1900s: 3410, 3955
　　1900s: 2655, 4775
　　Beaufort County: 692
　　Durham: 969
　　Edenton: 2467
　　Elizabeth City: 5776
　　Goldsboro: 1748
　　Greensboro: 4714
　　Hamptonville: 2452
　　Mocksville: 1100
　　Oxford: 2455
　　Pitt County: 5950
　　Raleigh: 274, 2553, 2938
　　Shelby: 1951
　　Washington: 4858
　　Subdivided by subject:
　　　Licenses: 4897
　Ohio: 281
　　Defiance: 920
　Pennsylvania:
　　Bedford: 324
　　Harrisburg: 2027
　　Lancaster: 2444
　　Media: 2552
　　Philadelphia: 2688
　South Carolina: 561, 757, 791,
　　1480, 1651, 2961
　　Abbeville: 4145
　　Camden: 4269
　　Charleston: 3162, 3962, 5548
　　Edgefield: 4778
　Tennessee: 872
　Texas--Waxahachie: 817
　Vermont--Burlington: 3143
　Virginia:
　　1800s: 506, 872, 905, 1115, 1384,
　　　2014, 2597, 2794, 2951, 3148,
　　　3809, 3882, 4713, 5359, 5848
　　1800s-1900s: 356, 2517
　　Albemarle County: 523
　　Bedford County: 3621
　　Botetourt County: 5817
　　Boyce: 2387
　　Dinwiddie County: 2376
　　Fluvanna County: 5839
　　Lexington: 3587
　　Madison County: 523
　　Middlesex: 3379
　　Petersburg: 203, 2466, 3401
　　Richmond: 2387, 4020, 4616
　Washington, D.C.: 846, 2729, 3442,
　　3714, 4858

LAW PRACTICE (Continued):
　West Virginia: 1769
　　Jefferson County: 2515
　　Martinsburg: 5037
　Wisconsin--Fond du Lac: 2436
LAW REFORM: 1792
LAW SCHOOLS: see LAW--Study of
LAW TREATISES:
　Great Britain: 1142
　North Carolina: 3410
LAWLER, Joseph: 3125
LAWLESS, John: 4024
LAWLESS, Valentine Browne, Second
　Baron Cloncurry: 4024
LAWNDALE, North Carolina:
　Cotton mills: 1104, 4691
LAWRASON, Annie: 5210
LAWRENCE, Mrs. A. M.: 2670
LAWRENCE, Caroline B.: 404
LAWRENCE, Hannah R.: 3126
LAWRENCE, James: 3127
LAWRENCE, John: 4660
LAWRENCE, John Laird Mair, First
　Baron Lawrence: 1014, 5883
LAWRENCE, Jonathan: 5454
LAWRENCE, Luther: 3127
LAWRENCE, Mary Egerton (Thornton):
　1660
LAWRENCE, Stringer: 3128
LAWRENCE, William John: 103
LAWRENCE FAMILY: 404, 718
LAWRENCE, Kansas: 2358
LAWRENCE COUNTY, Alabama:
　Wheeler: 5668
LAWRENCE COUNTY, Illinois:
　Lawrenceville: 2080
LAWRENCE MANUFACTURING COMPANY, North
　Carolina: 5100
LAWRENCEBURG, Indiana: 4644
LAWRENCEVILLE, Georgia: 2740, 4871,
　5040
　Mercantile accounts: 601
　Physicians' accounts: 167
　Post Office: 5438
LAWRENCEVILLE, Illinois: 2080
LAWRENCEVILLE, Virginia: 1366, 1568,
　2517, 2971, 3014, 3642, 5743
　Land companies: 724
　Mercantile affairs: 240
　Shoe shop: 2519
　Taverns and inns: 1567, 3900
LAWRY, W. P.: 3129
LAWS: see LAW; ROYAL DECREES; and
　Laws and legislation as subheading
　under specific subjects
LAWS AND JOINT RESOLUTIONS OF THE
LAST SESSION OF THE CONFEDERATE
CONGRESS: 1180
THE LAWS OF THE STATE OF GEORGIA:
5406
LAWSON, America: 3130
LAWSON, B.: 3130
LAWSON, Robert (d. 1805): 3130
LAWSON, Sir Wilfrid, Second Baronet:
　3715, 5164
LAWSON-TANCRED, Sir Thomas Selby:
　5173
LAWSUITS: 3145, 5271
　see also Lawsuits as subheading
　　under specific subjects, e.g.
　　RAILROADS--Lawsuits; and names of
　　specific cases, e.g. TRINITY v.
　　BALIOL
　Alabama--Selma: 1645
　Arkansas--Little Rock: 4208
　Colombia: 3867
　Connecticut: 3041
　Georgia: 1434, 2232, 2931
　　Augusta: 3672
　　Savannah: 2262
　Great Britain: 453, 3722, 4372,
　　4934
　　Bristol: 4541
　Kentucky: 1086, 5505
　　Pleasant Hill: 5416
　Louisiana: 3160

LAWSUITS (Continued):
　Maryland:
　　Cumberland: 3190
　　Montgomery County: 3982
　Massachusetts: 5665
　Mississippi: 2012
　Missouri: 4786
　New York: 1585, 4071
　North Carolina:
　　1700s: 975
　　1700s-1800s: 5046
　　1800s: 641, 1475, 2345, 2480,
　　　2589, 5100, 5202, 5709
　　1900s: 2655, 4828
　　Bladen County: 5909
　　Franklinton: 5056, 5450
　　Wake Forest: 4586
　Ohio--Brown County: 281
　Pennsylvania: 496, 1443, 2704
　　Lancaster: 5948
　　Lewistown: 2704
　　Philadelphia: 4845
　South Carolina: 757, 3759, 4350,
　　4368, 4624, 4649
　　Abbeville: 4145
　　Charleston: 2613
　　Greenville: 4149
　Virginia: 1401, 1556, 2120, 3069,
　　4381
　　Randolph-Macon College: 879
　　Sequestration proceedings: 2633
　　Subdivided by place:
　　　Assoteague Island:
　　　　Oyster-planting rights: 1791
　　　Norfolk: 3830
　　　Portsmouth: 5702
　　　Suffolk: 3012
　Washington, D.C.: 385, 4478, 4494
　Washington:
　　Puget Sound District: 4239
LAWSUITS IN LITERATURE: 2461
LAWTON, Alexander Robert: 3131, 3905
LAWYERS: see LAW PRACTICE; and
　(name of state)--Government
　agencies and officials--Attorney
　General
LAWYERS' ACCOUNTS:
　see also LEGAL FEES
　Great Britain--Exeter: 5867
　Maryland--Hagerstown: 5981
　North Carolina:
　　Elizabeth City: 5776
　　Oxford: 2455
　　Smithfield: 3839
　　Wilmington: 3410
　South Carolina--Charleston: 3962
　Tennessee--Nashville: 3844
　Virginia: 3587
　　Danville: 1956
　　Pittsylvania County: 3708
LAY READERS: see as subheading under
　names of church denominations
LAYARD, Sir Austen Henry: 4549
LAYDEN, Charles: 3132
LAYDEN FAMILY (Great Britain): 3132
LAYDEN FAMILY (Indiana): 3132
LAYDISE, Warren E.: 3133
LAYMEN'S MISSIONARY MOVEMENT: 5014
LAYTON, Thomas: 346
LAZARUS, Rachel (Mordecai): 3761
LAZENBY, Samuel J.: 3134
LAZY HILL, North Carolina: 2508
LEA, Frances C.: 3135
LEA, Henry Charles: 103
LEA, Margaret M.: 3176
LEA, Solomon: 4425
LEACH, H. G.: 2871
LEACH, James: 3136
LEACH, James H. C.: 3136
LEACH, James Madison: 3094, 4714,
　5457
LEACH, Richard: 3136
LEACH, Sue: 3136
LEAD MINING:
　see also MINING
　California: 1984
LEAD WORKS: see CIVIL WAR--LEAD WORKS

LEADER, John Temple: 816
LEADERSHIP: see CIVIL WAR--LEADERSHIP
LEAGUE, James W.: 2130
LEAGUE FOR INDUSTRIAL DEMOCRACY: 4948
LEAGUE OF NATIONS: 2161, 2279, 5110
LEAGUE OF WOMEN VOTERS:
    North Carolina: 1275
    Virginia: 3558
LEAGUE TO ENFORCE PEACE: 1336, 2473, 4343
LEAKE, Sir John: 3137
LEAKE AND PETTIT (firm): see PETTIT AND LEAKE
LEAKE COUNTY, Mississippi: 5475
LEAKESVILLE, North Carolina:
    Defenses: 3622
    Militia: 3622
    Schools: 661
LEAR, Edward: 1225, 3138
LEAR, Tobias: 5575
LEARNED SOCIETIES: see FOLKLORE SOCIETIES; HISTORICAL SOCIETIES; LITERARY SOCIETIES; ROYAL ACADEMY OF ARTS
LEASBURG, North Carolina: 3544, 4344
LEASBURG ACADEMY, Caswell County, North Carolina: 1336
LEASBURG CHURCH (North Carolina): 3646
LEASBURG CIRCUIT, Methodist churches: 3646
LEATHER TRADE: see HIDES AND LEATHER TRADE
LEATHERS, John B.: 3140
LEATHERS, Thomas P.: 3139
LEATHERS, LATTA AND COMPANY, North Carolina: 3140
LEAVELL, Anne: 3141
LEAVELL, William Thomas: 3141
LEAVENWORTH, Abner Johnson: 3142
LEAVENWORTH, Frederick P.: 3142
LEAVENWORTH, Henry: 3143
LEAVENWORTH FAMILY (Virginia--Genealogy): 3142
LEAVES: see Leaves and furloughs as subheading under names of armies and navies
LEAVITT, Humphrey Howe: 2633
LEBANON: see AMERICAN COLLEGE, Beirut, Lebanon
LEBANON, Ohio: 1249
    Shakers: 2601
LEBANON, Pennsylvania: 1443
    Wills: 4937
LEBANON, Tennessee: 872
    see also CUMBERLAND UNIVERSITY LAW SCHOOL
LEBANON, Virginia: 4440
LEBANON COUNTY, Pennsylvania:
    Annville: 4937
    Lebanon: see LEBANON, Pennsylvania
LEBANON NORMAL SCHOOL, Ohio: 1177
LE BARON (C. L.), Pensacola, Florida (firm): 3008
LEBAS, Charles Webb: 2565
LECATO, Maggie B.: 3144
LECKIE, W. Robert: 3145
LECKIE v. JAMES COUNTY: 3145
L'ÉCOLE DES PONTS ET CHAUSSÉES, Paris, France: 4490
LE CONTE, John: 365
LECONTE, Joseph: 1702
LE CONTE FAMILY (Georgia): 365
LECTURES AND LECTURING: 2801, 3096, 3284, 3797, 4012
    see also CHAUTAUQUAS; LYCEUMS
    Southern Unionists in the North: 716
    Subdivided by place:
        Maryland: 2692
            Baltimore: 3092
        Massachusetts: 776, 4409
            Boston: 1219
            New York: 4481
        New York: 978

LECTURES AND LECTURING:
    Subdivided by place (Continued):
        North Carolina: 942, 3482
            Durham: 4753
            Raleigh: 5149
        Pennsylvania: 1488
        South Carolina: 3421
        United States: 1219, 2449, 2883, 3265, 5051, 5268
LEDBETTER, H. W.: 5021
LEDBETTER, William: 5021
LEDBETTER, William J.: 3146
LEE, Dr. ___: 3147
LEE, Arthur: 858, 1236, 2780
LEE, Cassius Francis: 3148
LEE, Charles (1731-1782): 3735
LEE, Charles (1758-1815): 2776, 3269
LEE, Charles Carter (1798-1871): 1227, 3735
LEE, Charles Henry (b. 1818): 3148
LEE, Edmund Jennings II: 3148
LEE, Edwin Grey: 3148
LEE, Fitzhugh: 1364, 1424, 3149, 3809, 5633, 5949
LEE, Francis Lightfoot: 3157
LEE, Francis S.: 566
LEE, George Washington Custis: 5368, 5578
LEE, Henrietta (Bedinger): 3148
LEE, Henry (1756-1818): 2776, 3150, 3156, 3157, 3269, 3671, 3735
LEE, Ivy Ledbetter: 2871
LEE, John (1788-1871): 3160
LEE, John B. (Virginia): 4504
LEE, John Fitzgerald: 3151
LEE, Lucy B.: 3152
LEE, Ludwell: 917
LEE, Mary Ann Randolph (Custis): 805, 3157, 5949
LEE, Philip Ludwell: 3153
LEE, R. H. (Alabama): 3154
LEE, Ranson: 3155
LEE, Rebecca (1811-1877): 566
LEE, Richard (1726-1795): 917
LEE, Richard (fl. 1797): 15
LEE, Richard Bland (1761-1827): 1778, 2913, 3156
LEE, Richard Henry (1732-1794): 769, 858, 3130, 3148, 3157
LEE, Richard Henry (1794-1865): 1778
LEE (ROBERT E.) FOUNDATION: 2188
LEE, Robert Edward: 395, 581, 805, 3157, 3357, 3560, 3687, 3792, 3807, 3809, 4129, 4607, 5280, 5417, 5578, 5949
    "Arlington" (estate): 4612
    Honors: 824
    Leadership: 1364, 4808
    Portrait: 1665
    President of Washington College: 2697
    Rumors about: 132, 5688
    Surrender: 689, 1820, 2416, 5769, 5897
    Visit to Camp Harrison, Georgia: 5472
LEE, Robert Edward III: 3157
LEE, Samuel: 3142
LEE, Samuel Adams: 3269
LEE, Sarah (Wallis) Bowdich: 3158
LEE, Sarah Juliana Maria: 1937
LEE, Sidney Smith: 2724, 5121
LEE, Stephen Dill: 843, 3159
LEE, Thomas Sim: 3160
LEE, W. H.: 1227
LEE, W. H. F.: 2732
LEE, William (1739-1795): 2304
LEE, William (fl. 1797): 15
LEE, William (fl. 1818): 5714
LEE FAMILY (Maryland): 3160
LEE FAMILY (South Carolina): 566
LEE FAMILY (Virginia): 128, 3148, 3357
    Portraits: 5949
LEE FAMILY (West Virginia): 3148
LEE AND LONGSTREET AT HIGH TIDE by Mrs. Longstreet: 3262

LEE AND McDANIEL (firm): see McDANIEL AND LEE
LEE AND ROBERTS (firm): see ROBERTS AND LEE
LEE COUNTY, Alabama:
    Auburn: 554, 5126
LEE COUNTY, Iowa:
    Charlotte: 5466
    Keokuk: 3392
        Hospitals: 5017
        United States Army camp: 1076
LEE COUNTY, North Carolina:
    Economic conditions: 238
    Sanford: 238
    Railroad motor cars: 4918
LEE COUNTY, South Carolina: 1460
LEE COUNTY, Virginia:
    Jonesville: 861
LEE-WARNER, Sir William: 4709
LEECH, David: 3161
LEEDS, Thomas Osborne, Fourth Duke of: 3997
LEEDS, Yorkshire, England: 280
    Engineers: 794
    Religion: 1317
LEEDS UNIVERSITY:
    Lectures and lecturing: 4632
LEEK, England: 5553
LEES, Sir Edward Smith: 4024
LEES, Sir Harcourt: 4024
LEES, Julia: 3567
LEESBURG, Florida: 4659
LEESBURG, Virginia: 1712, 3550, 3994, 4447, 4615
    Banks and banking: 5449
    Butchers' accounts: 4250
    Civil War: 2989, 5852
        see also CIVIL WAR--CAMPAIGNS, BATTLES, AND MILITARY ACTIONS--Virginia--Leesburg
    Dry goods accounts: 4198
    Livery accounts: 3584
    Mercantile accounts: 4446
    Saddle-making accounts: 3584
    Tailors' accounts: 4198
LEESE, Robert H.: 3118
LEESTOWN, West Virginia:
    Temperance: 5591
LEFEBVRE DE LA ROCHE, Pierre-Louis: 5681
LEFEVRE, Sir John George Shaw-: see SHAW-LEFEVRE, Sir John George
LEFTWICH, Joel: 5055
LEFTWICH, William: 5055
LEFTWICH AND CLAYTON (firm): see CLAYTON AND LEFTWICH
LEFTWICH AND CO.: see BROWN, LEFTWICH, AND CO.
LEGAL AFFAIRS:
    see also LAW PRACTICE; and Legal affairs as subheading under specific occupations or businesses
    Alabama: 5032
        Huntsville: 5006
        Selma: 4911
    Georgia: 289, 4647, 4706, 5189, 5353, 5606
        Eatonton: 3905, 5837
        Jasper County: 377
        Savannah: 2789, 3389, 5787, 5987
        Sparta: 5250
        Wilkes County: 5315
    Great Britain: 2322, 5478
        Lilies: 2198
    Guatemala: 3099
    Louisiana: 4902
        New Orleans: 4550, 4958
    Maryland: 2319, 3006, 5181
        Baltimore: 3754
        Charles County: 5089
        Frederick County: 4457
        Hagerstown: 1958, 5981
        Sharpsburg: 979
    Massachusetts: 4653
        Boston: 5093
        Brookline: 5846

LEGAL AFFAIRS (Continued):
  Mexico: 3587
  Middle West: 1820
  Mississippi--Jacinto: 4442
  Missouri: 2604
  New Jersey--Burlington: 5520
  New York: 5660
    Hornby: 4645
    New York: 5133
    Orange: 4645
    Steuben County: 4680
    Yates County: 4680
  North Carolina:
    1700s: 1389, 2256
    1700s-1900s: 2553, 2934
    1800s: 263, 624, 982, 3960,
      4923, 5596
    1800s-1900s: 2419, 5692
    1900s: 4828
    Asheboro: 2303, 3186
    Burke County: 1247
    Caldwell County: 1247
    Craven County: 1871
    Durham County: 1256
    Enfield: 426
    Fairfield: 921
    Fayetteville: 2354
    Gamewell: 3324
    Granville County: 68
    Greensboro: 3763
    Guilford County: 2330
    Harnett County: 2357
    Montgomery County: 4689
    Orange County: 1256
    Oxford: 2455
    Rowan County: 3288
    Thomasville: 2906
    Wilmington: 5912
  Ohio: 281
    Defiance: 920
  Pennsylvania: 4188
    Blair County: 421
    Gettysburg: 5780
    Lewistown: 2704
  Scotland: 5643
  South Carolina: 1127, 2670, 4162,
    4896, 5796
    Abbeville District: 414
    Beaufort County: 810
    Charleston: 2556, 2613, 2709,
      3461, 5198, 5318
    Graniteville: 2186
    Lancaster County: 5863
    Laurens County: 4834
    Spaniards in: 4982
    Spartanburg: 5930
    Sumter: 2288
  Tennessee: 4746
  Vermont--Burlington: 3143
  Virginia:
    1700s-1800s: 2887, 3560, 4616,
      5112, 5476
    1700s-1900s: 824
    1800s: 170, 195, 523, 1263, 1921,
      2173, 3068, 3809, 4563, 5214,
      5721
    1800s-1900s: 1436, 4743
    Bedford County: 5818
    Campbell County: 62, 4487
    Caroline County: 4589
    Covington: 3308
    Culpeper: 4852
    Fredericks hall: 2363
    Lynchburg: 1350
    Pittsylvania County: 3708, 5718
    Prince William County: 3532
    Richmond: 3169, 5020
    Roanoke: 5904
    Stephensburg: 3255
    Suffolk: 3012
    Sweet Briar: 5765
    Westmoreland County: 5573
  Washington, D.C.: 3714, 4851
  West Virginia: 3069
    Martinsburg: 1828
    Wood County: 5194
LEGAL EDUCATION: see LAW--Study of

LEGAL FEES:
  see also COURTS--Costs; LAWYERS'
    ACCOUNTS
  Maryland--Baltimore: 4348
  Massachusetts: 3034
  South Carolina--Charleston: 5318
  Virginia: 5742
    Staunton: 1267
LEGAL HISTORY: see ENGLISH LAW; LAW
LEGAL MALPRACTICE: see MALPRACTICE
  (Legal)
LEGAL ORGANIZATIONS:
  see also AMERICAN BAR ASSOCIATION;
    AMERICAN COUNSEL ASSOCIATION;
    AMERICAN JUDICATURE SOCIETY;
    AMERICAN LAW INSTITUTE;
    ASSOCIATION OF LIFE INSURANCE
    COUNSEL; INTERNATIONAL
    ASSOCIATION OF INSURANCE COUNSEL;
    INTERNATIONAL BAR ASSOCIATION
  Alabama: 3611
  Maryland: 3086
    Washington County: 3086
  North Carolina: see NORTH CAROLINA
    STATE BAR ASSOCIATION; WAKE
    COUNTY BAR ASSOCIATION
  United States: 3086
LEGAL PROCEDURES:
  Germany: 2194
  Great Britain: 472
  North Carolina:
    Martin County: 1639
  South Carolina: 2288
LEGARÉ, Hugh Swinton: 791, 3162,
  5271, 5606
LEGARÉ, James: 3165
LEGARÉ, James Mathewes: 3163
LEGARÉ, Kate (Walpole): 3164
LEGARÉ, Thomas: 3165
"A LEGEND OF TURKEY BUZZARD HOLLOW"
  by John Esten Cooke: 1227
LEGENDS: see FOLKLORE
LEGG, Charles A.: 3166
LEGG, Emma A.: 3166
LEGG, Luther: 3166
LEGG, William Howard: 3166
LEGGE, Henry Bilson-: see BILSON-
  LEGGE, Henry
LEGHORN, Italy: 2058
LEGISLATION: see Laws and legislation
  as subheading under specific
  subjects; JUDICIAL REVIEW;
  LOBBYING
LEGISLATURE: see (name of state)--
  Legislature; GREAT BRITAIN--
  PARLIAMENT; UNITED STATES--CONGRESS
LEGRAND, Hampton: 3167
LEGRAND, James T.: 2572, 3168
LE HAVRE, France: 5014
  Trade and commerce: 5860
LEHIGH CANAL: 5686
LEHIGH COAL AND NAVIGATION COMPANY:
  5686
LEHIGH MINE COMPANY: 5686
LEHIGH UNIVERSITY, Bethlehem,
  Pennsylvania: 5312
  Civil engineering:
    Student's notebooks: 5679
  Sanitary engineering:
    Student's notebooks: 5679
LEHMAN, Emma L.: 5457
LEICESTERSHIRE, England:
  "Belvoir Castle": 3498
LEIDING, Harriette Kershaw: 4453
LEIDY, Paul: 3686, 4188
LEIGH, Benjamin Watkins (1781-1849):
  2633, 3150, 4134, 4880
LEIGH, Benjamin Watkins (b. 1812):
  1227
LEIGH, Ethel (Traphagen): 4900
LEIGH, William Robinson: 4900
"LEIGH HUNT AS A POET" by Armine T.
  Kent: 2146
LEIGHTON, Clare: 2146
LEIGHTON, Frederick, Baron Leighton:
  4600
LEIGHTON, Henry C.: 3170
LEIGHTON, Joel B.: 1197, 3171

LEINBACH, Edward William: 3172
LEINBACH, James: 3172
LEINSTER, Roy L.: 3219
LEIPER, Henry Smith: 5252
LEIPZIG--Literary affairs: 2764
LEISY, Ernest Erwin: 102
LEITER, Mary Victoria: 4693
LEITERSBURG, Maryland: 3239, 5142
LEITH, Scotland: 4912
LEITZ, George: 2638
LEMANS, France:
  World War I: 4269
LE MARIE, François: 3173
LEMEN, William M.: 3174
LE MESURIER, Thomas: 306
LE MESURIER FAMILY (Guernsey,
  Channel Islands): 306
LEMMON FAMILY (Maryland): 664
LEMON, Eliza A.: 3175
LEMOS, Francisco Gil de Taboada de:
  see GIL DE TABOADA DE LEMOS,
  Francisco
L'ENGLE, Dr. _____ : 3474
LENINGRAD, Union of Soviet Socialist
  Republics: 4614
LENNOX, Charles, Third Duke of
  Richmond: 1913, 2149, 5331
LENNOX, George Henry: 3460
LENNOX, Lady Mary Louisa: 3460
LENOIR, Laura: 966
LENOIR, Rufus Theodore, Sr.: 3176
LENOIR, Rufus Theodore, Jr.: 3176
LENOIR, Sarah Joyce: 3176
LENOIR, Thomas: 3176
LENOIR, Thomas Isaac: 3176
LENOIR, Walter Waightstill: 3176
LENOIR, William (1751-1839): 3176
LENOIR, William Avery: 3176
LENOIR, William Ballard: 3176
LENOIR FAMILY (North Carolina--
  Genealogy): 3176
LENOIR, North Carolina: 593, 5533
  see also DAVENPORT COLLEGE
  Public schools: 3177
    Bands: 3178
LENOIR, Tennessee: 3176
LENOIR COUNTY, North Carolina:
  see also DOBBS COUNTY, North
    Carolina
  Churches: 387
  Legal papers: 670
  Cities and towns:
    Kinston: see KINSTON, North
      Carolina
    LaGrange: 2945
LENOIR (N.C.) HIGH SCHOOL: 3177
  Band: 3178
LENOX CASTLE, North Carolina: 602
LENT, Observation of: 4867
LEO XII, Pope: see GENGA, Annibale
  della
LEO XIII, Pope: 4693
LEON COUNTY, Florida:
  Land speculation: 631
  Tallahassee: 2795
"LEON DE MONTEGA: A ROMANCE OF
  CADIZ": 5193
LEONARD, Archibald: 795
LEONARD FAMILY: 1882
LEONARDTOWN, Maryland: 1406
LEONIA, New Jersey: 4909
LEONOWENS, Anna Harriette (Crawford):
  103
LEOPARD (ship): 2636
LEOPOLD I, King of the Belgians:
  535, 1787
LEOPOLD GEORGE DUNCAN ALBERT, Duke
  of Albany: 2471
LE RAYSVILLE, Pennsylvania:
  Family life: 4397
LERMAN, Leo: 902
LEROY, Herman: 4922
LESLIE, Alexander: 2147
LESLIE, Eliza: 730
LESLIE, Robert: 3179
LESLIE AND SHEPHERD, Petersburg,
  Virginia (firm): 3179

LESLIE, South Carolina:
  School for Indians: 3356
LESNÉ, Francesco, Archibishop
  of Philippopoli: 4693
LESSEPS, Ferdinand Marie de: 4520
LESTABLE, André: 3270
LESTER, George N.: 1422, 3180
LESURE, Lovell A.: 3181
LETCHER, John: 581, 1359, 1403,
  3182, 4129, 5613
LETCHER AND MAURY (firm): see MAURY
  AND LETCHER
"LETTER TO THE KING" by Junius: 92
LETTERS--Forgeries: 1953
LETTERS OF ALFRED THAYER MAHAN TO
  SAMUEL A'COURT ASHE, 1858-59 by
  Rosa Pendleton Chiles: 227
LETTERS OF GEORGE LONG ed. by
  Thomas Fitzhugh: 3251
"LETTERS OF GEORGIA EDITORS AND A
  CORRESPONDENT": 5193
"LETTERS OF NATHANIEL MACON TO JUDGE
  CHARLES TAIT" by William K. Boyd:
  3439
"LETTERS ON SLAVERY, F. C. Y., 1853"
  by Francis Cope Yarnall: 5940
LETTSOM, John Coakley: 4168
LETTSOM, W. G.: 1926
LEUTZE, Emanuel Gottlieb: 4748
LEVANT: see NEAR EAST
THE LEVANT COMPANY, London, England:
  3183
LEAVES AND DIKES: see MISSISSIPPI
  RIVER--Levees
LEVER, Charles James: 3722
LEVERETT, Massachusetts: 2407
LE VERT, Octavia (Walton): 3184
LEVESON-GOWER, Granville, First Earl
  Granville (1773-1846): 1875
LEVESON-GOWER, Granville, First
  Marquis of Stafford (1721-1803):
  4230
LEVESON-GOWER, Granville George,
  Second Earl Granville (1815-1891):
  597, 3185, 3238
LEVESON-GOWER, Henrietta Elizabeth
  (Cavendish), Countess Granville:
  1875
LEVETT, James: 4084
LEVY, Uriah Phillips: 3118
LEWALLEN, Henry: 3186
LEWARD COTTON MILLS, INC., Worthville,
  North Carolina: 3187
LEWES, George Henry: 2457, 4051
LEWIS, America (Lawson): 3130
LEWIS, Andrew: 4003
LEWIS, Burwell Boykin: 3188
LEWIS, Clive Staples: 3189
LEWIS, David John: 3190
LEWIS, Dixon Hall: 3191
LEWIS, Eleanor Parke (Custis): 805,
  3560, 4014
LEWIS, Ellis: 2444
LEWIS, Frederick B. A.: 3192
LEWIS, Frederick D.: 3199
LEWIS, George W.: 3193
LEWIS, Henry: 724
LEWIS, John C.: 3199
LEWIS, John Francis (1818-1895): 3194
LEWIS, John W. (1808-1886): 3195
LEWIS, Kate: 3199
LEWIS, Lawrence: 3200
LEWIS, Lorenzo: 3200
LEWIS, Louise: 3188
LEWIS, Lucinda Rose (Garland): 3188
LEWIS, Margaret F. C.: 523
LEWIS, Milo: 3196
LEWIS, Nicholas Meriwether: 2815
LEWIS, Richard Henry: 5457
LEWIS, Roger: 2790
LEWIS, Samuel: 3196
LEWIS, Thomas: 3196
LEWIS, Vincent: 3199
LEWIS, William: 3197
LEWIS, William Berkeley: 872
LEWIS, William David: 3198
LEWIS, William S.: 2612
LEWIS, William Winton: 3199
LEWIS FAMILY (Kentucky): 3199

LEWIS FAMILY (Virginia): 3200, 4924
  Genealogy: 1842
LEWIS AND KEEN, Cloverport, Kentucky
  (firm): 3199
LEWIS DOSTER AND SONS (firm): 1536
LEWISBURG, West Virginia: see CIVIL
  WAR--CAMPAIGNS, BATTLES, AND
  MILITARY ACTIONS--West Virginia--
  Lewisburg
LEWISHAM GRAMMAR SCHOOL, London,
  England: 5616
LEWISOHN, Ludwig: 2449
LEWISPORT, Kentucky--Masonry: 3199
LEWISTOWN, Illinois: 5311
LEWISTOWN, Pennsylvania: 2704
LEWISVILLE RIFLE COMPANY: 1268
LEXINGTON, Kentucky: 428, 635, 1083,
  1086, 1309, 1355, 3325
  Description: 1333
  Investment company: 4241
  Public support for Andrew Johnson:
    5248
  Universities and colleges: see
    TRANSYLVANIA UNIVERSITY;
    UNIVERSITY OF KENTUCKY
LEXINGTON, Massachusetts: 2694
LEXINGTON, Missouri: 1405
  see also BAPTIST FEMALE COLLEGE
LEXINGTON, North Carolina: 344, 2074,
  2298, 2595, 2874
  Merchants: 35
  Silver mines: 277
  Visit of Aaron Burr: 5229
LEXINGTON, South Carolina: 1877, 4610
  Social life and customs: 5834
LEXINGTON, Virginia:
  1700s-1800s: 2120, 3362
  1800s: 1384, 2792, 3157, 3182, 3517,
    3586, 4129, 4313, 4593, 4879,
    5359, 5595
  1800s-1900s: 924, 4244
  1900s: 5360
  Bridge construction: 1830
  Business affairs: 1628
  Camp meetings: 5149
  Diseases--Smallpox: 5613
  Law practice: 3587
  Military schools: 641
  Schools: 3202
  Universities and colleges: see
    VIRGINIA MILITARY INSTITUTE;
    WASHINGTON AND LEE UNIVERSITY
LEXINGTON (warship): 636, 5436
LEXINGTON COUNTY, South Carolina:
  Lexington: see LEXINGTON, South
    Carolina
  Tax lists: 4610
  Voter registers: 4610
LEXINGTON LIGHT INFANTRY: 3325
LEYDA, Jay: 720
LEYLAND PARISH, England:
  Vital statistics: 5694
LEYVA, Pedro Toledo y: see TOLEDO Y
  LEYVA, Pedro
LI, K. C.: 5252
LIANG SHEH-I: 5252
LIBBEY, David S.: 3201
LIBBY PRISON, Richmond, Virginia:
  2124, 2989
LIBEL AND SLANDER: 3286, 4043
  South Carolina: 1424, 5193
  United States: 958
LIBEL TRIALS:
  Great Britain: 2836, 4051
  North Carolina: 4773
LIBERAL PARTY (Great Britain): 280
  see also LIBERAL UNIONISTS
  1800s: 280, 649, 1765, 2322, 4568,
    4694, 5164
  1800s-1900s: 3980
  1900s: 233, 3912
  Candidates (1837): 5624
  Leadership (1896): 4520
LIBERAL UNIONISTS (Great Britain):
  4036, 5027
LIBERIA: 1424
  Description and travel: 3325
  Missions and missionaries: 41, 2473

LIBERIA (Continued):
  Negro colonization: 4516
  Monrovia: 5298
  Return to the United States:
    5051
  Politics and government: 3325
  Social conditions: 3012, 3325
LIBERTY, Georgia: 2931
LIBERTY, Missouri: 4679
LIBERTY, North Carolina: 1777
  see also LIBERTY NORMAL COLLEGE
LIBERTY, Virginia: 800, 3440
LIBERTY (periodical): 3397
LIBERTY, Preservation of: 5987
LIBERTY COUNTY, Georgia: 125
  Sheriff's receipts: 2910
  Sunbury: 3196
LIBERTY COUNTY, Texas:
  Tornadoes: 1557
"LIBERTY HALL," Nelson County,
  Virginia: 824
LIBERTY HALL ACADEMY, Lexington,
  Virginia: see WASHINGTON AND LEE
  UNIVERSITY
LIBERTY LOANS: see WORLD WAR I--
  Savings Bond Drives
LIBERTY MILLS, Virginia:
  Army camp: 4577
LIBERTY NORMAL COLLEGE, Liberty,
  North Carolina: 5267
LIBERTY OF CONSCIENCE: 5746
LIBERTY PARTY (United States): 3910
LIBERTYTOWN, Maryland: 2295
LIBMAN'S LAW PRINTERY, New York: 5145
LIBRARIES:
  Private:
    Great Britain: 2200, 5647
    Massachusetts: 5754
    Scotland: 1212
    South Carolina: 5795
      Charleston: 3666
    Virginia: 3809
  Subdivided by place:
    Australia: 2282
    Germany--Berlin: 2139
    Great Britain: 1124, 4770
    Massachusetts: 1747
    New York: 1747, 4343
    North Carolina: 2188
    Philippine Islands: 4511
    South Carolina: 561
    United States: 1315
LIBRARY NOTES (publication of Duke
  University): 3092
LIBRARY OF CONGRESS: 737, 1315
  Archive of Folksong: 691
  Legislative Reference Service: 3451
LICENSING:
  see also BUSINESS LICENSING
  Virginia--Shenandoah County: 5485
LICHENS: 5754
LID, Johannes: 2430
LIDDELL, Thomas Henry, First Baron
  Ravensworth: 2836
LIDE, Evan J.: 3203
LIE, Trygve: 4558
LIEBER, Francis: 2612, 3204
LIEN, Jonas H.: 77
LIEVEN, Dar'ia Khristoforovna
  (Benckendorff) Kniaginia: 3630
THE LIFE, CHARACTER, AND REMAINS OF
  THE REV. RICHARD CECIL: 3567
THE LIFE AND CAMPAIGNS OF MAJOR-
  GENERAL J. E. B. STUART by
  Henry B. McClellan: 3809
THE LIFE AND CORRESPONDENCE OF JAMES
  McHENRY by Bernard C. Steiner: 3384
"THE LIFE AND LETTERS OF CHRISTOPHER
  HOUSTON" ed. by Gertrude Dixon
  Enfield: 2661
LIFE AND LETTERS OF JOEL CHANDLER
  HARRIS: 2374
"THE LIFE AND LETTERS OF JOHN
  McINTOSH KELL" by Julia Blanche
  (Munroe) Kell: 2963
A LIFE IN REUTER'S by Sir Roderick
  Jones: 4207
LIFE INSURANCE: see INSURANCE--Life

THE LIFE OF ALGERNON CHARLES
  SWINBURNE by Sir Edmund William
  Gosse: 2102
LIFE OF JOHN CHURCHILL, DUKE OF
  MARLBOROUGH by Garnet Joseph
  Wolseley: 5872
LIFE OF JOHN J. CRITTENDEN by Ann
  Mary Butler (Crittenden) Coleman:
  1308
LIFFORD, James Hewitt, Third
  Viscount: 1087
LIGGAT, Alexander: 3205
LIGGAT, John: 3205
LIGGAT FAMILY (Genealogy): 3205
"LIGHT HORSE HARRY" LEE: see LEE,
  Henry (1756-1818)
LIGHT-SHIPS:
  North Carolina:
    Hatteras: 4547
    Neuse River: 1871
LIGHTERS (Boats)--Construction: 2132
LIGHTHOUSES:
  see also LIGHT-SHIPS
  Construction and maintenance:
    3948, 4678
  Florida: 1440
  New York--New York: 2672
  Sicily: 3118
  South Carolina: 1927
  United States: 605
LIGHTHOUSES, Bureau of: see UNITED
  STATES--GOVERNMENT AGENCIES AND
  OFFICIALS--Bureau of Lighthouses
LIGHTNER, George J.: 2165
LIGHTNING:
  see also STORMS; WEATHER
  South Carolina--Charleston: 2410
LIGHTNING RODS: 5660
LIGHTS DISTRICT, Forsyth County,
  Georgia:
    Taxation: 5260
LILESVILLE, North Carolina: 2493,
  4664
LILIES, England: 2198
LILLINGTON, North Carolina:
  Oilseed mills: 3206
  Railroads: 238
LILLINGTON OIL MILL COMPANY,
  Lillington, North Carolina: 3206
LILLY & PINNELL, Lynchburg, Virginia
  (firm): 4222
LIMA, Peru: 4155
  Biographies: 3238
LIME (chemical) INDUSTRY:
  Experiments: 3145
LIME (chemical) TRADE:
  North Carolina: 4080
LIMEHOUSE, O. B.: 2109
LIMESTONE COLLEGE, Gaffney, South
  Carolina: 561
LIMESTONE COUNTY, Alabama:
  Athens: 2662, 3331, 4930
LINCOLN, Abraham (fl. 1793,
  Massachusetts): 3208
LINCOLN, Abraham (1809-1865): 2693,
  3207, 3331, 3778, 4157, 4190,
  4486, 4556, 4616, 4782, 4829,
  4860, 5119, 5172, 5228, 5444,
  5636, 5759
  Administration: 713, 4748
    Northern opposition: 2629
  Assassination: 291, 689, 1084,
    1505, 1510, 1938, 2223, 2361,
    2405, 3207, 3809, 4022, 4039,
    4652, 4888, 5001, 5058, 5307,
    5769
    Conspiracy theory: 5715
  Election:
    1860: 805, 5250
    1864: 3280, 4561, 5249
  Funeral: 3741
  Hospital visits: 3281
  Inaugural journey: 2035
  Inauguration: 3325, 5869
  Meeting with Ulysses Simpson
    Grant (1865): 2125
  Memorabilia: see LINCOLNIANA

LINCOLN, Abraham (Continued):
  Opinion of: 832, 4202
    By Southerners: 4950
  Parentage: 2556
  Photograph of bust: 3295
  Visit to U.S.S. Minnesota: 2265
LINCOLN, Benjamin: 3209
LINCOLN, Mary (Todd): 2035
LINCOLN, Illinois: 5941
LINCOLN, Nebraska: 729, 4290
LINCOLN COLLEGE: see OXFORD
  UNIVERSITY--Lincoln College
LINCOLN COUNTY, Georgia:
  Mercantile accounts: 138
LINCOLN COUNTY, Maine:
  Union: 731
  Wiscasset: 1222
LINCOLN COUNTY, North Carolina: 677,
  2120, 3811, 4450
  Agricultural products: 5558
  Broom industry: 5558
  Churches: 1232
  Flour mills: 5558
  Land: 1656
  Land deeds and indentures: 61
  Liquor manufacturing: 5558
  Mercantile accounts: 5976
  Ministerial association: 3211
  Physicians' accounts: 5976
  Public schools: 3933
  Social life and customs: 5558
  Teachers' records: 3933
  Cities and towns:
    Beattie's Ford: 792, 5667
      Mercantile accounts: 2277
    Lincolnton: see LINCOLNTON,
      North Carolina
    Wilfong Mills: 5739
LINCOLN FINDS A GENERAL by Kenneth
  Powers Williams: 4276
LINCOLN HOSPITAL, Durham, North
  Carolina: 1584, 2379
LINCOLN UNIVERSITY, Harrowgate,
  Tennessee: 1584
LINCOLNIANA: 2285, 5813
"LINCOLN'S DOCTOR'S DOG" by Frank
  Gill Slaughter: 4853
LINCOLNSHIRE, England:
  Gainsborough: 369
LINCOLNTON, North Carolina: 2540,
  3317, 3743, 4238, 5558
  Girls' schools and academies: 3210
  Methodist churches: 3646
LINCOLNTON CIRCUIT, Methodist
  churches (North Carolina): 3646
LINCOLNTON CIRCUIT, Methodist
  churches (South Carolina): 3646
LINCOLNTON DISTRICT, Methodist
  churches: 3646
LINCOLNTON FEMALE ACADEMY,
  Lincolnton, North Carolina: 3210
LINCOLNTON FIRST CHURCH,
  Lincolnton, North Carolina: 3646
LINCOLNTON (N. C.) MINISTERIAL
  ASSOCIATION: 3211
LINCOLNTON STATION, Methodist
  churches: 3646
LIND, Hannah Smith: 3213
LIND, Jenny: see LIND-GOLDSCHMIDT,
  Jenny Marie
LIND, John: 3212, 3213
LIND, Robert C. S.: 3213
LIND-GOLDSCHMIDT, Jenny Marie: 490,
  1029, 4032
"LINDENWALD," New York: 4343
LINDON, Edna Earlie: 4290
LINDSAY, J. L.: 5075
LINDSAY, William Schaw: 36
LINDSEY, Horace B.: 3214
LINDSEY, J. W.: 127
LINDSEY, Jacob H.: 3215
LINDSEY, Stuart F.: 3215
LINDSLEY, Philip: 5635
LINDSY, William: 4746
LINEN TRADE:
  see also TEXTILE TRADE
  Ireland with the United States:
    416, 2884

LINES, Major: 3216
"LINES ON JEFFERSON DAVIS WHILE A
  PRISONER AT FORTRESS MONROE":
  1403
"LINES ON LEAVING HORNBY CASTLE"
  by Francis Wrangham: 5913
LING, Der: 5252
LINH, H. K.: 5252
LINN, John B.: 4188
LINN, Lewis Fields: 3217
LINNAEAN SOCIETY: 3577
LINOTYPE: 4224
LINSEED OIL MILLS:
  North Carolina--Randleman: 5408
LINSLEY, Kate D. (Conant): 3218
LINSTER, Cornelia (Kelly): 3219
LINSTER, Robert O.: 3219
LINTHICUM, John Charles: 3220
LINTON, Benjamin F.: 519
LINTON, Elizabeth (Lynn): 5553
LINVILLE, A. J.: 3221
LINVILLE, Aaron Y.: 3221
LINVILLE, E. Burton: 3221
LINVILLE, Georgia: 4293
LINVILLE, North Carolina: 3447
LINVILLE IMPROVEMENT COMPANY,
  Linville, North Carolina: 3447
LINWOOD, Pennsylvania: 4881
LION, Raphael: 3222
LIPPINCOTT, Margaretta: 404
LIPPINCOTT'S MAGAZINE: 72
LIPPMANN, Theo: 2398
LIPSCOMB, Andrew Adgate: 2449
LIQUOR:
  see also ALCOHOLISM; DRINKING;
  RUM; and Drinking as subheading
  under names of armies
  Evils of: 3981
  Medicinal use:
    Georgia: 4356
    North Carolina: 3410
  Prices: 4541
  Texas: 218
  Virginia: 4924
LIQUOR MANUFACTURING: 4732
  see also BREWING INDUSTRY
  Civil War: 4912
  Illegal:
    Georgia: 2388
    North Carolina: 4548
  Law and legislation:
    Ireland: 5330
  Taxation: see TAXATION--Liquor
  Subdivided by place:
    North Carolina: 122, 1278, 1861,
      2072, 2929
      Lincoln County: 5558
      Surry County: 2808
      Yadkin County: 2808
    Tennessee: 677
    Virginia: 2633, 4743
    West Virginia:
      Grant County: 767
      Hannisville: 2316
      Martinsburg: 3832
LIQUOR TRADE: 4732
  see also RUM TRADE; TAVERNS AND
  INNS; WINE TRADE
  Civil War: 2808
  Illicit: see BOOTLEGGING
  Imports from Cuba: 1442
  Regulation:
    South Carolina--Darlington: 5299
  Subdivided by place:
    Georgia--Eatonton: 3352
    Great Britain--London: 5011
    Maryland--Baltimore: 4348
    New Hampshire: 1529
    North Carolina: 122, 2808, 2924
      Forsyth County: 4631
      Rowan County: 3288
      Wake County: 4009
      Wilkesboro: 4107
      Wilmington: 1281
    Ohio--Fremont: 4892
    South Carolina: 2793, 5299
    Virginia: 1115, 1863, 2331, 2567

LIQUOR TRADE:
　　Subdivided by place (Continued):
　　　West Virginia:
　　　　Grant County: 767
　　　　Hannisville: 2316
LISBON, North Carolina:
　　Civil War: 390
LISBON, Portugal: 5298
　　Trade and commerce: 5228
LISBON (N.C.) LADIES AID SOCIETY: 390
LISBUNNY, Ireland: 3349
LISK, Haywood D.: 1192, 5234
LISLE, John: 5357
"LISTA DE LOS COLEGIOS Y SEMINARIOS DE MEXICO": 3650
LISTER, Thomas, Third Baron Ribblesdale: 4995
LISTON, BENFIELD, AND JONES, Charleston, South Carolina (firm): 2019
LISTON, Robert: 3183
LITCHFIELD, Connecticut: 406, 3041
　　Description: 1333
LITCHFIELD COUNTY, Connecticut:
　　Canaan: 2039
　　Falls Village: 3852
　　Harwinton: 941
　　Litchfield: see LITCHFIELD, Connecticut
　　North Kent: 5502
　　Salisbury: 5868
　　Washington: 2602
LITCHFIELD LAW SCHOOL, Litchfield, Connecticut: 1333
LITERARY ANTIQUITIES OF GREECE by Philip Allwood: 90
LITERARY AFFAIRS: see LITERARY INTERESTS
LITERARY AGENTS: see AUTHORS AND AGENTS
LITERARY CRITICISM: see Criticism as subheading under specific kinds of literature, e.g. AMERICAN LITERATURE--Criticism
LITERARY ETHICS: see PLAGIARISM
LITERARY FESTIVALS:
　　Mississippi: 1771
LITERARY FORGERIES: 5856
LITERARY GAZETTE: 2839
LITERARY INTERESTS:
　　Alabama: 5032
　　Arkansas: 5380
　　California: 5081
　　Georgia: 4857
　　Great Britain:
　　　1700s-1800s: 2126, 4967
　　　　Exeter: 5867
　　　1800s: 1552, 2801, 4543
　　　1800s-1900s: 2102, 5175
　　　1900s: 1210, 4823, 5790
　　Maryland: 648, 5193
　　　Baltimore: 2042
　　New York: 2351, 5044
　　North Carolina: 3433, 4080
　　Ohio: 281
　　Pennsylvania: 5380
　　South Carolina: 5193
　　United States:
　　　1800s: 2985
　　　1800s-1900s: 1215, 5717
　　　1900s: 4290
　　Virginia: 404, 1115, 3809, 4698
　　　Richmond: 4020
　　Washington, D.C.: 4020, 4971
LITERARY SOCIETIES:
　　see also STUDENT SOCIETIES
　　France: 555
　　Georgia: 2005
　　Great Britain: 892, 1113
　　North Carolina: 1128, 2251
　　　Durham: 880, 4932
　　　Henderson: 4232
　　　Raleigh: 4923
　　South Carolina: 1676, 3394, 4453
　　United States: 3990

LITERARY SOCIETIES (Continued):
　　Virginia: 4384
　　　Petersburg: 4159
LITERARY STYLE: 5044
　　Criticism: 1910
LITERARY WORLD: 3163
LITERATURE: 3472, 3617, 4576, 4596, 4616, 4948
　　see also LAWSUITS IN LITERATURE; LOCAL COLOR IN LITERATURE; PLAGIARISM; SATIRE; and specific kinds of literature, e.g. POETRY; AMERICAN LITERATURE; etc.
　　Collections: 1730, 2811
　　Students' notebooks: 2893, 3325
LITERATURE AND STATE:
　　see also POLITICS AND LITERATURE
　　Great Britain: 678
LITHOGRAPHS: 5710
LITTLE, Corneille (Ashe): 3223
LITTLE, Henry Alexander: 3224
LITTLE, Peter: 4542
LITTLE, R. R.: 4188
LITTLE, S. W.: 2749
LITTLE, BROWN, AND COMPANY: 3797
LITTLE BIG HORN RIVER, Wyoming, Battle at: 1665
LITTLE HUNTING CREEK, Virginia:
　　Land: 5575
LITTLE OSAGE, Missouri: 3703
A LITTLE PICTURE: 178
LITTLE RIVER, North Carolina: 614
　　Justices of the peace: 5692
LITTLE RIVER, South Carolina:
　　Intracoastal waterway: 2774
LITTLE RIVER CIRCUIT, Virginia: 5375
LITTLE RIVER LUMBER COMPANY, North Carolina: 3225
LITTLE RIVER TOWNSHIP, North Carolina:
　　Retail trade: 4009
LITTLE ROCK, Arkansas: 1453, 5000
　　Lawsuits: 4208
　　Personal finance: 4208
LITTLE ROCK AND FORT SMITH RAILROAD: 5380
LITTLE SWITZERLAND, North Carolina: 5312
LITTLE THEATER MOVEMENT: 3797
LITTLE'S MILLS, North Carolina:
　　Politics and government: 5021
LITTLETON, Sir Edward (1589-1645): 2152
LITTLETON, Edward John, First Baron Hatherton: 3226, 4024
LITTLETON, Massachusetts: 776
LITTLETON, North Carolina: 2399, 3831, 5280
LITTLETON CIRCUIT, Methodist churches: 3646, 5280
LIVELLY, E.: 3227
LIVELY (warship): 2296
LIVERMORE, Harriet: 5717
LIVERMORE, Thomas Leonard: 34
LIVERMORE, William Roscoe: 3228
LIVERMORE, Maine: 5569
LIVERPOOL, Charles Jenkinson, First Earl of: 1913, 2835
LIVERPOOL, Robert Banks Jenkinson: 2836
LIVERPOOL, England: 2193, 4563, 4876, 5244
　　Commodity prices: 2901, 4911
　　Cotton prices: 1609
　　Foreign trade: 331, 480, 2403, 2884, 3008, 3230
　　Merchants: 3753
　　Shipping: 5026
　　Tobacco trade: 564, 1633
　　Trade and commerce: 5860
LIVERY STABLE ACCOUNTS:
　　North Carolina--Wadesboro: 4814
　　Virginia--Leesburg: 3584
LIVESTOCK:
　　Diseases:
　　　see also CATTLE--Diseases
　　　North Carolina: 122

LIVESTOCK (Continued):
　　Prices:
　　　France--Tours: 5323
　　　Missouri: 3255
　　　Oregon: 3255
　　　South Carolina: 4118
　　　Virginia:
　　　　Rockbridge County: 5613
　　Ranging laws:
　　　South Carolina: 4453
　　Supply and demand:
　　　California: 3255
　　　Oregon: 3255
　　Subdivided by place:
　　　Mexico: 2210
　　　Middle West: 1820
　　　North Carolina:
　　　　Haywood County: 3176
　　　South Carolina:
　　　　Stateburgh: 4217
　　　United States: 909
　　　Virginia: 1240, 1354, 2712
LIVESTOCK QUARANTINE:
　　United States: 2563
LIVESTOCK TRADE:
　　Georgia: 781
　　Maryland:
　　　Beaver Creek District: 3329
　　Virginia--Hanover County: 456
LIVEZEY, Josephine E.: 3229
LIVING AUTHORS OF ENGLAND: 3163
LIVING WRITERS OF THE SOUTH: 1385
LIVINGSTON, Charles: 3230
LIVINGSTON, Edward (1764-1836): 3231
LIVINGSTON, John Henry: 4371
LIVINGSTON, Robert R.: 3273
LIVINGSTON FAMILY (New York--Genealogy): 2553
LIVINGSTON FAMILY (South Carolina or Tennessee): 718
LIVINGSTON COUNTY, New York:
　　Civil War--Civilian life: 5738
　　Cities and towns:
　　　Dansville: 5660
　　　Geneseo: 468
　　　Springwater: 5738
LIVINGSTONE, David: 5725
LE LIVRE: 4001
LLOYD, Anne: 3232
LLOYD, Jean Charlotte Washington: 5949
LLOYD, John: 3232
LLOYD, Thomas: 3214, 3233
LLOYD, William Watkiss: 3234
LLOYD FAMILY (Illinois--Genealogy): 1670
LLOYD FAMILY (North Carolina--Genealogy): 3214, 3233
LLOYD'S OF LONDON (firm): 3183
LOANS:
　　see also CROP LOANS; FREEDMEN'S LOANS; PERSONAL LOANS; USURY
　　Interest rates--Kentucky: 2225
　　Subdivided by place:
　　　Alabama--Huntsville: 5006
　　　Great Britain: 2755, 3315
　　　New York: 1065
　　　North Carolina:
　　　　Lincoln County: 4450
　　　　Literary Fund: 3943
　　　　Smithfield: 3839
　　　South Carolina--Abbeville: 3319
　　　United States: 2755
　　　Virginia: 2685, 5851
　　　　Columbia: 5035
LOBBYING: 5271
　　United Confederate Veterans: 3657
LOBDELL, George G.: 3235
LOBDELL AND BUSH (firm): see BUSH AND LOBDELL
LOBDELL CAR WHEEL COMPANY, Delaware: 3235
LOBELIA LANDS, West Virginia: 1837
LOCAL COLOR IN LITERATURE: 4730
LOCAL ELECTIONS:
　　Georgia--Savannah: 2280, 5494

LOCAL ELECTIONS (Continued):
  Great Britain: 3847
    Bath: 1753
  Maryland--Washington County: 3086
  Massachusetts--Boxborough: 2456
  New York--New York: 3221, 4751
  North Carolina: 4103
    Mount Gilead: 4689
    Randolph County: 2459
    Shelby: 1951
  Pennsylvania:
    Philadelphia: 4134
  South Carolina: 2109
  Virginia--Richmond: 5790
LOCAL GOVERNMENT: see COUNTY GOVERNMENT; MUNICIPAL GOVERNMENT; and Local government as subheading under POLITICS AND GOVERNMENT--(name of country or state)
LOCAL POLITICS: see as subheading under POLITICS AND GOVERNMENT--(name of country or state); and as subheading under local place names
LOCH, James: 5, 3236
LOCKE, Frances Sargent: 3999
LOCKE, John (1632-1704): 4146, 5746
LOCKE, Joseph L.: 3310
LOCKE, Laura J. (Bulloch): 3310
LOCKER-LAMPSON, Frederick: 4600
LOCKHART, Eleanor Anne: 714
LOCKHART, Emeline (Dortch): 714
LOCKHART, John Gibson: 2146
LOCKHART, Levi Young: 714
LOCKHART, William: 4054
LOCKHART FAMILY (North Carolina): 714
LOCKPORT, New York: 2717
  Real estate: 2755
LOCKVILLE, North Carolina:
  Accounts: 5207
LOCKWOOD, Belva Ann (Bennett): 5202
LOCKWOOD, Henry H.: 4881
LOCKWOOD, Susan: 4273
LOCKYER, Nicholas: 3073
LOCOFOCO PARTY: 3030, 5051, 5868
  Georgia: 5051
  Maryland: 2711
    Frederick: 5324
  New York: 86
  North Carolina: 4897, 5298
  Ohio--Columbus: 230
  Virginia: 4589
LOCOMOTIVES:
  see also RAILROAD MOTOR CARS; RAILROADS
  Diesel: 238
  Steam: 238
  Study of:
    France and Great Britain: 3054
LOCUST DALE, Virginia: 1073, 5798
LOCUST DALE ACADEMY, Rapidan Station, Virginia: 5798
LOCUST GROVE ACADEMY, Orange County, Virginia: 5286
"LOCUST HILL," Culpeper, Virginia: 1931
LOCUST LEVEL, North Carolina: 1312
LOCUST MOUNT, Virginia: 3144
LODA, Illinois: 806
LODGE, Henry Cabot: 103, 706, 2849, 4339
LODGING HOUSES: see BOARDING HOUSES; HOTELS; TAVERNS AND INNS
LOEB, William, Jr.: 1424
LOFFTUS, Ralph W.: 5700
LOFTIN, William F.: 3237
LOFTUS, Lord Augustus William Frederick Spencer: 3238
LOGAN, Berkely: 3239
LOGAN, H. C.: 3239
LOGAN, John Alexander: 3240, 3789
LOGAN, Samuel Frank: 1424
LOGAN, Thomas Muldrup: 5633
LOGAN, W. Turner: 2109
LOGAN, Ohio: 135

LOGAN COUNTY, Illinois:
  Atlanta: 5127
  Lincoln: 5941
LOGAN COUNTY, Kentucky:
  Russellville: 870, 1654, 3450
LOGAN COUNTY, Ohio: 5142
LOGAN'S STORE, North Carolina: 126
LOGBOOKS:
  see also TRANSATLANTIC VOYAGES; VOYAGES
  Duke of Kent: 2259
  Falmouth, U.S.S.: 2963
  Savannah, U.S.S.: 2963
  Shark, U.S.S.: 2963
  North Carolina: 4342
  Neuse River: 1871
  Rhode Island: 4907
LOGIC: 3670
  Students' notebooks:
    University of Virginia: 3148
LOHIER, John B.: 652
LOHR, Solomon B.: 3241
LOMAX, John Tayloe: 3242
LOMAX, Nannie: 3243
LOMBARDY GROVE, Virginia: 363
LOMBE, Edward: 981
LONDON, Alexander: 3244
LONDON, Anne: 3245
LONDON, Bishop of: see names of specific bishops, e.g. BLOMFIELD, Charles James
LONDON, Henry Armond: 5457
LONDON, England: 656, 945, 3089, 3292
  1600s: 1640, 2152, 3884, 5464
  1600s-1700s: 202
  1600s-1800s: 2154
  1700s: 499, 4229, 5330, 5463
  1700s: 3137, 3411, 4969, 5539
  1710s: 2155, 4969
  1720s: 780, 2155, 4969
  1730s: 780, 2155, 5532, 5540
  1740s: 3997, 5473, 5540
  1750s: 712, 736, 5699
  1760s: 92, 1214, 2151, 3304, 4333, 5287, 5352
  1770s: 92, 626, 2008, 2151, 4102, 4557, 5101, 5104, 5352
  1780s: 16, 1139, 2199, 2226, 3315, 4093, 5019
  1790s: 445, 1545, 2133, 2199, 2735, 3315, 3858
  1700s-1800s: 258, 392, 447, 878, 922, 1311, 1598, 1641, 1991, 2126, 2835, 3460, 4913, 5038, 5639, 5726
  1800s: 14, 229, 453, 472, 537, 864, 1124, 1504, 1599, 1755, 1875, 1978, 2054, 2099, 2200, 2844, 3183, 3238, 3472, 3670, 4001, 4097, 4575, 4605, 5026, 5637
  1800s: 199, 2201, 2421, 4066, 4137, 4289, 5797, 5830, 5849
  1810s: 400, 446, 516, 821, 1173, 1689, 2201, 2421, 2565, 2840, 3080, 3316, 3478, 3577, 3723, 4151, 4168, 4362, 5849
  1820s: 446, 516, 957, 1173, 1911, 2201, 2263, 2421, 2632, 2645, 3645, 3816, 4362, 5071, 5618, 5849
  1830s: 446, 1456, 1632, 1753, 1911, 2632, 2973, 3050, 3080, 3443, 3471, 3738, 3836, 4024, 4176, 4234, 4543, 5201, 5277, 5638, 5746
  1840s: 455, 597, 747, 877, 1110, 1632, 1753, 1911, 2401, 2632, 2973, 3234, 3816, 3836, 3911, 3976, 4234, 4300, 4543, 5809, 5934
  1850s: 455, 597, 877, 886, 955, 981, 1225, 1503, 1534, 1650, 1753, 2029, 2263, 2401, 2653, 2973, 3138, 3236, 3836, 3862, 3976, 4051, 4054, 4069, 4254, 4455, 4549, 5327, 1809

LONDON, England:
  1800s (Continued):
    1860s: 863, 877, 981, 1225, 1378, 1445, 1910, 2067, 2918, 3138, 3185, 3275, 3838, 4028, 4054, 4549, 4566, 4568, 4997, 5134, 5534, 5875
    1870s: 36, 863, 886, 944, 1225, 1473, 1910, 2026, 2322, 2404, 2626, 2801, 3036, 3138, 3722, 4028, 4054, 4117, 4549, 4567, 4568, 5883
    1880s: 189, 528, 735, 1872, 1910, 2145, 2322, 2626, 2801, 3036, 4028, 4089, 4567, 4709, 5024
    1890s: 67, 735, 1057, 1287, 2322, 2626, 2801, 3036, 3224, 4089, 4176, 4709, 5116
    1800s-1900s: 294, 326, 452, 678, 892, 1014, 1079, 1132, 1260, 1499, 2102, 2976, 3684, 3693, 3694, 3912, 3978, 4224, 4331, 4520, 4576, 4660, 5050, 5164, 5175, 5590, 5736, 5806, 5872, 5876
  1900s: 364, 449
    1900s: 47, 278, 442, 949, 1218, 2784, 4798, 5616, 5637
    1910s: 233, 1526, 1949, 2279, 3305, 4798, 5616, 5625
    1920s: 233, 441, 4798, 5616
    1930s: 233, 1924, 2627
    1940s: 2627, 4722
  Abolitionist sentiment: 815
  Actors: 1027
  American Civil War:
    Blockade runners: 410, 2766
  American residents: 4485
  Apprenticeship: 3808
  Art societies: 1424
  Arts: 2718
  Autographs: 5158
  Banks and banking: 559
  Bondholders: 3273
  Booksellers and bookselling: 2788, 5856
  Business affairs: 5849
  Churches: 1571
  Clergy: 763
  Commission merchants: 5221
  Cotton: 2410
  Crime: 1576
  Description:
    1780s: 4625
    1800s:
      1800s: 3808
      1820s: 2058
      1850s: 365
      1870s: 157, 3107, 3587
      1890s: 43
  Distances--Tables, etc.: 3753
  Education: 1815
  Finance: 2755
  Foreign trade: 948
  Investments in North American land (1700s): 3347
  Iron: 2410
  Land titles: 5662
  Liquor trade: 5011
  Literary interests: 1113, 3056
  Medical notebooks: 5095
  Medicines--Prescriptions: 5095
  Mercantile accounts: 5139
  Mercantile affairs: 2742
  Merchants: 3960, 5221
  Militia: 1114
  Newspapers: 352, 5262
  Personal debt: 5463
  Police: 4420
  Politics and government:
    1700s: 92, 3128
    1800s: 1857, 2060, 2994, 2998, 3067, 3120, 3121
  Publishers and publishing: 828, 1603, 1879, 3503, 5095
  Shipping companies: 323

LONDON, England (Continued):
    Slaves--Emancipation: 2542
    Social life and customs: 43, 4218
    Society of Friends: 1733
        Stoke Newington: 5598
    Tobacco trade: 28
    United States embassy in:
        1700s: 4218
        1800s: 4616
        1900s: 4018, 4559
LONDON AND LANCASHIRE FIRE INSURANCE
    COMPANY OF LIVERPOOL: 2013
LONDON AND WESTMINSTER REVIEW: 3670
LONDON DAILY TELEGRAPH: 217, 355
(LONDON) ILLUSTRATED NEWS: 5193
"LONDON IN SEPTEMBER" by Lord John
    Russell: 4605
LONDON INSTITUTE: 2154
LONDONDERRY, Robert Stewart,
    Viscount Castlereagh and Second
    Marquis of: 2149, 5071, 5637
LONDONDERRY, Northern Ireland:
    Methodist churches: 3738
LONDONDERRY, Pennsylvania: 2615
LONE JACK CIGARETTE COMPANY: 1586
LONELY HUNTER: 902
LONG, Alexander: 3246
LONG, Armistead Lindsay: 1825
LONG, Augustus White: 3247
LONG, Charles: 2836
LONG, Charles Alexander: 3248
LONG, Crawford Williamson: 3249, 3297
LONG, David: 3250
LONG, George: 3251
LONG, Huey Pierce: 2775, 3252
LONG, John (Clarksville,
    Pennsylvania): 3253
LONG, John (Lebanon, Pennsylvania):
    4937
LONG, John W. (Maryland): 3254
LONG, Joseph: 3255
LONG, Lucy Maie (York): 3248
LONG, Marianna: 85
LONG, Nicholas: 3256
LONG, Thomas: 4563
LONG (WILLIAM R.) MULE COMPANY,
    Smithfield, North Carolina: 3257
LONG FAMILY (North Carolina): 3247
LONG CANE PRESBYTERIAN CHURCH,
    Abbeville County, South Carolina:
    4145
LONG ISLAND, New York: 3904
    see also ST. PAUL'S COLLEGE
LONG SHOAL LIGHT VESSEL: 4547
LONG-WELLESLEY, William Pole-Tylney-:
    see WELLESLEY, William Pole-
    Tylney-Long-
LONGACRE, Andrew: 3258
LONGACRE, James Barton: 3261
LONGACRE, James M.: 3258
LONGACRE, Orleans: 3258
LONGACRE, North Carolina: 2222
LONGFELLOW, Henry Wadsworth: 2449,
    3259, 4600
LONGFELLOW, Mary J.: 5456
LONGFELLOW, Samuel (1819-1892): 103
LONGLEY, Ronald Stewart: 3260
LONGMANS, GREEN AND CO.: 2146
LONGSTREET, Augustus Baldwin: 791,
    3261, 4871, 5246
LONGSTREET, Helen (Dortch): 3262
LONGSTREET, James: 1403, 3261,
    3262, 3417, 3793, 4245, 4808, 5280
"LONGWOOD," Mississippi (estate):
    3956
LOOKOUT MOUNTAIN, Tennessee: see
    CIVIL WAR--CAMPAIGNS, BATTLES,
    AND MILITARY ACTIONS--Tennessee--
    Lookout Mountain
LOOMIS, Charles Battell: 2871
LOOMIS, M. D. W.: 3263
LOOMIS NATIONAL LIBRARY ASSOCIATION:
    851
LOOTING: see Depredations as
    subheading under names of armies
    and navies
LOPEZ, Carlos Antonia: 2963

LORAIN COUNTY, Ohio:
    Elyria: 4945
LORD, Andrew: 4399
LORD, Ann: 4399
LORD, Charles Phineas: 3264
LORD, Chester Sanders: 3265
LORD, George: 3266
LORD, Dr. John Chase: 1796
LORD'S SUPPER: 4936
LOREDO, José de Larrea de: see
    LARREA DE LOREDO, José de
LORIENT, France: 5448
LORIMER, Charles: 1891
LORIMER, George Horace: 3267
LORING, Ellis Gray: 5917
LORING, William Wing: 1853, 2396,
    3268
LOS ANGELES, California:
    Description: 5130
LOS ANGELES COUNTY, California:
    Beverly Hills: 4545
    Pasadena: 4837
    Sierra Madre: 5338
LOSSING, Benson John: 3269, 5667
THE LOST CAUSE by E. A. Pollard: 4733
"A LOST DAY IS HARD TO FIND" by
    Charles Buck Roberts: 4502
LOST RIVER, West Virginia: 5467
LOTI, Pierre: 3270
LOTTERIES: 5212, 5575
    see also GOLD LOTTERIES; LAND
        LOTTERIES; PHILIPPINE ISLANDS--
        Government agencies and
        officials--Bureau of Lotteries
    Alabama: 1438
    Delaware: 3783, 4892, 4921, 5036,
        5306
    Georgia: 1438, 5929
    Kentucky: 4732
    Louisiana: 2364
    Maryland: 4348, 4732, 4892, 5763
    North Carolina: 5036
        School benefit: 214
    South Carolina: 1971
LOTUS CLUB: 3265
LOUDOUN CIRCUIT, Methodist churches:
    3646
LOUDOUN COUNTY, Virginia: 638, 2782,
    3819
    Estates: 3560
    Land surveys: 4836
    Merchants: 1420
    Physicians: 4173
    Superior Court: 3994
    Cities and towns:
        Aldie: 1962, 3529
            see also CIVIL WAR--CAMPAIGNS,
                BATTLES, AND MILITARY
                ACTIONS--Virginia--Aldie
        Goshen: 3882, 5613
        Hamilton: 5607
        Hillsborough--Merchants: 1420
        Leesburg: see LEESBURG,
            Virginia
        Middleburg: 3913, 5629
            Farming: 794
            Mercantile accounts: 1369
        Philomont: 690
        Upperville: 212, 3232
        Waterford: 5782
LOUGHBOROUGH, Alexander Wedderburn,
    First Baron [Loughborough] and
    First Earl of Rosslyn: 4420
LOUGHBOROUGH, John Pearson: 5553
LOUIS XIII, King of France: 3271
LOUIS XV, King of France: 4693
LOUIS XVIII, King of France: 1002
LOUIS PHILIPPE, King of the French:
    1875
LOUIS, William: 4235
LOUISA, Virginia: 5035
LOUISA (steamship): 3827
LOUISA COUNTY, Virginia: 2645, 4127
    Mercantile accounts: 143
    Cities and towns:
        Fredericshall: 2363
        Mansfield: 4247
        Thomason's Cross Roads: 1351

LOUISA LAND COMPANY: 5768
LOUISBURG, North Carolina:
    1700s: 5060
    1700s-1800s: 1491, 3023, 4787
    1700s-1900s: 3476
    1800s: 2873, 4154, 5690
    1800s-1900s: 1411, 3563
    Merchants: 1915
    Schools: 484, 2530, 3272
        Negro schools: 5533
    Teachers' records: 3272
    Universities and colleges: see
        LOUISBURG COLLEGE
LOUISBURG ACADEMY, Louisburg, North
    Carolina: see LOUISBURG COLLEGE
LOUISBURG COLLEGE, Louisburg, North
    Carolina: 484, 1411, 1584, 1588,
    2530, 4927, 5533, 5735
    Administration: 1411
    Students and student life: 3272
    Teachers' records: 3272
    Tuition: 3272
LOUISE CAROLINE ALBERTA, Princess
    of Great Britain: 3472
"THE LOUISE FUND" (Salem Female
    Academy): 4080
LOUISIANA:
    see also SOUTHERN STATES
    Agricultural organizations: 5585
    Agricultural workers: 1026
    Agriculture: 1153, 5426, 5585
        see also the following
            subheadings under LOUISIANA:
            Cotton plantations; Crops, and
            names of specific crops;
            Plantations; Sugar plantations
    Annexation:
        1796-1797 (proposed): see BLOUNT
            CONSPIRACY
        1803: see LOUISIANA TERRITORY--
    Authors and publishers: 1982
    Authorship: 4636
    Autograph collecting: 2575
    Banks and banking:
        New Orleans: 3274, 5693
    Baptist churches: 3322
    Birds: 1803
    Blind: 5426
    Brickmaking: 2674
    Civil code: 4208
    Civil War: see appropriate
        subheadings under CIVIL WAR;
        CONFEDERATE STATES OF
        AMERICA;
        UNITED STATES--ARMY--Civil War
    Commission merchants:
        New Orleans: 459, 872, 3322
    Commodity prices: 1242
    Corn: 3322
    Cotton gins: 508, 840
    Cotton growing: 4902
    Cotton land: 3053
    Cotton plantations: 900, 1574
    Cotton trade: 2856
        New Orleans: 4776, 5194, 5301
    Courts: 4550
    Crops: 1242
    Currency: 1339
    Deaf: 5426
    Debating societies: 845
    Debt collection: 379
    Democratic Party: 988
    Description and travel:
        1717: 3173
        1840s: 622, 5508
        1850s: 622, 5193, 5508
        1860s: 622, 4369
    Diseases:
        Cholera: 330
            New Orleans: 4038, 4732
        Smallpox: 368
        Yellow fever: 266, 489
            New Orleans: 3041, 4202
    Dueling: 1424
    Education: 266
        see also LOUISIANA--Schools;
            LOUISIANA--Teaching
    English language--Dialects: 4636
    Estate accounts: 2674

LOUISIANA (Continued):
  Farm life: 2493
  Finance: 730
    see also LOUISIANA--Public
      finance
  French in America: 1574, 3073
  French poetry: 1450, 1574
  Funerals: 395
  Government agencies and officials:
    Governors: 2859, 3252
  Gunsmithing--New Orleans: 4957
  Historical studies: 1923
  Indians of North America:
    Culture: 3173
  Inheritance law: 4902
  Insurance:
    New Orleans: 5062
    Property: 679
  Know-Nothing Party: 489
  Land: 478
    see also COTTON LAND
    Mortgages: 478
    Purchases and sales: 2674
    Speculation: 1302
    Valuation: 4902
  Law enforcement:
    New Orleans: 5051
  Law practice: 5210
  Lawsuits: 3160
  Legal affairs: 4902
    New Orleans: 4550, 4958
  Legislature: 1574
  Lotteries: 2364
  Manufacturing: 5426
  Medical education: see TULANE
    UNIVERSITY--Medical education
  Mentally ill: 5426
  Mentally retarded: 5426
  Mercantile accounts:
    New Orleans: 679, 5933
  Merchants:
    see also LOUISIANA--Commission
      merchants
    New Orleans: 3008, 3358
  Migration from:
    From Calcasieu: 5496
    To Texas: 4286
  Militia: 5433
  Molasses--Storage: 679
  Orphans: 5426
  Paupers: 5426
    see also LOUISIANA--Poor houses
  Philanthropy--New Orleans: 3358
  Pirates: 3073
  Plantation accounts: 3956
    Baton Rouge: 1026
  Plantations: 508, 1179, 2802, 5193
    see also LOUISIANA--Cotton
      plantations; LOUISIANA--Sugar
      plantations
    Baton Rouge: 1026
    Leasing: 4902
    Tenas Parish: 4582
  Politics and government:
    1800-1860: 1574, 2859
    1861-1899: 395
    1900s: 2775
  Poorhouses: 3870
    see also LOUISIANA--Paupers
  Population--New Orleans: 5499
  Postal workers: 3275
  Prisoners and prisons: 5426
    see also CIVIL WAR--PRISONERS
      AND PRISONS
  Public finance:
    New Orleans: 5425
  Publishers and publishing: 1439
    Historical studies: 1982
  Railroad construction: 395, 805
  Reconstruction: 566
    see also LOUISIANA--White League
    Federal military occupation:
      5425
    New Orleans: 4277
    Redemption: 4080
  Religion: 837, 3415, 5966
  Rice: 1803
  Riots: 489

LOUISIANA (Continued):
  Schools:
    Girls' schools and academies:
      489
    Clinton: 4373, 4819
  Senatorial elections (1930): 592
  Slave trade: 1801, 2674, 3846,
    5193
    New Orleans: 2517
    Prices: 3396
  Slavery: 805, 1153
  Slaves: 478
    Behavior: 508
    Diseases: 508
    Leasing: 4902
    Treatment of: 1242
  Social life and customs: 489, 1153,
    1424, 4131, 5426, 5966
  State banks--New Orleans: 3274
  Statistics: 1439
  Sugar--Storage: 679
  Sugar growing: 1242
  Sugar plantations: 1574
    New Orleans: 4550
    Thibodeauville: 3160
  Teaching:
    see also LOUISIANA--Education;
      LOUISIANA--Schools
    New Orleans: 5062
  Theater: 489
  Timber frauds: 20
  Tobacco--Prices: 3643
  Tobacco industry:
    New Orleans: 2302
  Tobacco trade: 5251
    New Orleans: 3643
  Universities and colleges: see
    CENTENARY COLLEGE; LOUISIANA
    STATE UNIVERSITY; TULANE
    UNIVERSITY
  Voter registration: 5425
  Warehouses--New Orleans: 679
  White League: 4131
  Wholesale trade--New Orleans: 1169
  Women's societies and clubs: 3071
LOUISIANA, Missouri: 3129
LOUISIANA GUARDIAN: 2775
LOUISIANA PURCHASE: see LOUISIANA
  TERRITORY--Annexation
LOUISIANA STATE BANK, New Orleans,
  Louisiana: 3274
LOUISIANA STATE FEDERATION OF POST
  OFFICE CLERKS: 3275
LOUISIANA STATE UNIVERSITY, Baton
  Rouge, Louisiana: 5054
  History curriculum: 5054
LOUISIANA TERRITORY:
  Administration of: 3671
  Annexation: 1048, 1574, 3041, 3273
LOUISVILLE, Georgia: 1090, 3505, 3695
  Mercantile accounts: 5562
LOUISVILLE, Kentucky: 20, 398, 496,
  946, 2053, 3496, 4908
  Civil War hospitals: 3007
  Description: 1333
  Economic conditions: 3141
  Horse racing: 2681
  Land title companies: 3141
  Universities and colleges: see
    UNIVERSITY OF LOUISVILLE
LOUISVILLE (steamer): 5417
LOUISVILLE ABSTRACT AND LOAN COMPANY,
  Louisville, Kentucky: 3141
LOUISVILLE AND NASHVILLE RAILROAD:
  2096
LOUISVILLE MEDICAL INSTITUTE,
  Louisville, Kentucky: see
  UNIVERSITY OF LOUISVILLE
LOUNSBURY, Thomas Raynesford: 2871
LOUTH, County, Ireland:
  Drogheda--Merchant: 2884
LOUTIT, James: 229
LOVE, George W.: 3276
LOVE, John Wesley: 3276
LOVE, Mathew N.: 3276
LOVE, S. Ervin: 3276
LOVE: 3674
LOVE FEASTS--Pennsylvania: 2643

LOVE IN LITERATURE: 178
  see also LOVE POETRY
LOVE LETTERS:
  see also COURTSHIP
  Georgia: 2326, 3991, 5254
  Great Britain: 1552
  Illinois: 4004
  Maine--Saco: 3741
  Maryland: 3486
    Baltimore: 3742
  Massachusetts--Boston: 3491
  New York: 1961
  North Carolina: 264, 391, 1925,
    2553, 2905, 3219, 5533
    Chatham County: 2861
    Winston: 2800
  Ohio: 4477
  Pennsylvania--Philadelphia: 1226
  Southern States: 2691, 4373
  United States: 3053
  Virginia: 2553, 2949, 3060, 3542,
    5031
    Warrenton: 5210
LOVE POETRY: 2390
  North Carolina: 3677, 4164
LOVEJOY, Newell: 2449
LOVELAND, Miss B.: 5042
LOVELAND, Julia Lord (Noyes): 3277
LOVELAND FAMILY: 3277
LOVELL, Ann (Heatly) Reid: 3278
LOVELL, William S.: 3279
LOVELY, William L.: 3614
LOVING, Lucy J. (Stoneman): 5091
LOW, Charles F.: 3280
LOW, Charles Rathbone: 4503
LOW, David: 2146
LOW, James A.: 3280
LOW, Thomas: 3280
LOWDERMILK, William Harrison: 3282
LOWE, Robert, First Viscount
  Sherbrooke: 955, 2471
LOWE, Thomas G.: 711
LOWELL, Abbott Lawrence: 103
LOWELL, Anna Cabot: 3284
LOWELL, Charles Russell: 3283
LOWELL, Frances D.: 3284
LOWELL, James Russell: 3284, 5044,
  5050
LOWELL, John (1743-1802): 105
LOWELL, Joshua Adams: 1106
LOWELL, Massachusetts: 776, 803, 1408
  Textile engineering schools: 4918
LOWELL, North Carolina: 3285
LOWELL INSTITUTE, Boston,
  Massachusetts: 776
LOWELL STORE, Lowell, North Carolina:
  3285
LOWER, Thomas: 1733
LOWES, Madison: 5018
LOWNDES, Sir George Rivers: 3286
LOWNDES, Marie Adelaide (Belloc):
  364
LOWNDES, Rebecca Motte: 4622
LOWNDES, Thomas: 3287
LOWNDES, William: 3287
LOWNDES COUNTY, Alabama:
  Lowndesboro: 5894
LOWNDES COUNTY, Mississippi: 1241
  Columbus: see COLUMBUS, Mississippi
LOWNDESBORO, Alabama: 5894
LOWRANCE, Alexander: 3288
LOWRANCE, John: 3288
LOWRANCE, Miles S.: 208, 3289
LOWREY, Alice: 3290
LOWTHER, James: 1872
LOWTHER, P.: 2776
LOYAL GEORGIAN: 731
LOYAL TEMPERANCE LEGION: 4849
LOYALISTS: see AMERICAN REVOLUTION--
  Loyalist refugees; AMERICAN
  REVOLUTION--Loyalists
LOYALTY: see SLAVES--Loyalty
LOYALTY LOAN (Great Britain, 1797):
  2149
LOYALTY OATHS:
  see also CIVIL WAR--LOYALTY OATHS;
    RECONSTRUCTION--Loyalty oaths
  Georgia (1790s): 5537

LOYALTY OATHS (Continued):
  Russia Company (1804): 3753
  United States (1821): 3908
LUANG PRABANG, Laos: 4709
LUCAS, Daniel Bedinger: 3291
LUCAS, Edward: 3291
LUCAS, Edward Verrall: 3292
LUCAS, Elizabeth: 4216
LUCAS, John R.: 363
LUCAS, William (1800-1877): 743, 3291
LUCAS FAMILY (Florida): 3293
LUCAS FAMILY (South Carolina): 3293
LUCAS FAMILY (Virginia): 3148, 3293
LUCAS FAMILY (West Virginia): 3148, 5660
LUCAS COUNTY, Iowa--Chariton: 3520
LUCE, Stephen Bleecker: 2066
LUCKHARDT, Hermann: 3674
LUCKNOW, India: 4097
LUCY (PEN) SCHOOL FOR BOYS, Waverly, Maryland: 2692
LUCY COBB INSTITUTE, Athens, Georgia: 3905
LUDLOW, John Malcolm Forbes: 1087, 2918
LUDLOW, Vermont: 5197
LUFTBURROW, John: 3294
LUGARD, Frederick John Dealtry, First Baron Lugard: 4514
LUGGAGE TRADE--North Carolina: 606
LUIGGI, Alice (Houston): 3295
LUKA, Mississippi:
  Health resorts: 3409
LUKEMAN, Augustus: 5090, 5110
LUMBER:
  see also TIMBER
  Maryland--West River: 2267
  North Carolina: 238, 2824
LUMBER BRIDGE, North Carolina:
  Municipal government: 3934
LUMBER COMPANIES:
  Great Britain: 4895
LUMBER MILL WORKERS--Virginia: 5105
LUMBER MILLS:
  see also SLITTING MILLS
  Finance--North Carolina: 3225
  Maine--Toddy Pond: 3554
  Virginia--Fluvanna County: 5105
LUMBER PRODUCTS:
  North Carolina: 358
LUMBER RAFTS--Savannah River: 2122
LUMBER TRADE:
  see also SHINGLE TRADE; SHIP TIMBER; SLAVE TRADE
  Alabama: 3008
  Florida--Milton: 3008
  Georgia: 5508
    Ebenezer: 5986
    Savannah: 4356, 5216
  Illinois: 3410
  Kentucky--Paw Paw: 4090
  Martinique: 21
  Massachusetts: 1732
  Mississippi: 3008
    Rodney: 3322
  New Hampshire: 1529
  New York: 1732
  North Carolina: 21, 730, 1492, 1871, 2101, 2222, 4775, 5535
    Asheville: 1987
    Columbia: 215
    Pantego: 4471
    Williamston: 4824
  Pennsylvania: 744, 1732
    Tobyhanna Mills: 5985
  South Carolina: 1935, 2106, 3123, 4509
  Texas: 3008
  Virginia: 5535, 5702
  West Indies: 1492
  West Virginia: 1709, 2387
LUMBER YARDS--Virginia: 3574
LUMBERING:
  Michigan (southwestern): 4606
  North Carolina: 325, 1475, 4849, 4858, 4918

LUMBERING (Continued):
  Oregon--Ellensburg: 5938
  Virginia--Fluvanna County: 5035
LUMBERTON, North Carolina: 3422, 3434, 4183
  Civil War: 956
LUMBERTON (N.C.) TIMES: 3434
LUMPKIN, George: 3296
LUMPKIN, John Henry: 3297
LUMPKIN, Joseph Henry: 2326
LUMPKIN, Wilson: 3297, 3905, 5386
LUMPKIN, Georgia: 1078
LUMPKIN COUNTY, Georgia:
  Dahlonega: see DAHLONEGA, Georgia
LUNENBURG, Massachusetts: 684
LUNENBURG, Virginia: 2426
LUNENBURG COUNTY, Virginia: 66, 2439, 4928
  Physicians' accounts: 3846
  Plantations: 3846
  Cities and towns:
    Lunenburg: 2426
    Oak Forest: 3454
    Pleasant Grove: 2323
  Merchants: 2331
LUNSFORD AND VAN HOOK (firm): see VAN HOOK AND LUNSFORD
LUPTON, David P.: 3298
LUQUE, Angel: 4155
LURAY, Virginia: 461, 3084, 5581
  Baptist churches: 574
  Business expansion: 574
  Municipal government: 574
  Teaching: 2340
LURAY COLLEGE, Luray, Virginia: 461, 574
LURAY COLLEGE FOR YOUNG LADIES, Luray, Virginia: 2340
LURAY FEMALE INSTITUTE, Luray, Virginia: 461
LURTY, Florence G.: 5252
LUSHINGTON, Steven: 2836
LUTHER, Riley: 3299
LUTHERAN CHURCHES:
  see also CLERGY--Lutheran; EVANGELICAL GERMAN LUTHERAN CHURCH; EVANGELICAL LUTHERAN CHURCH; RELIGIOUS LITERATURE--Lutheran; SERMONS--Lutheran
  Georgia: 1993
  North Carolina: 1232
  Pennsylvania: 4444
    East Pennsylvania Synod: 4444
    Ray's Hill: 3957
LUTHERAN PUBLISHING HOUSE, New Market, Virginia: 2485
LUTTRELL, Henry: 92
LUTTRELL, John: 5768
LUTTRELL, Simon, First Earl Carhampton: 5330
LUZERNE COUNTY, Pennsylvania:
  Wilkes-Barre: 2443, 3277, 4086, 4188
LWOFF-PARLAGHY, Princess Elizabeth: 4073
LYCEUMS: 4020
  see also CHAUTAUQUAS; LECTURES AND LECTURING
  Alabama--Tuscaloosa: 3611
  North Carolina:
    Durham: 5597
    Wilmington: 5802
LYLE FAMILY (West Virginia): 865
LYMAN COUNTY, South Dakota:
  Oacoma: 5791
LYMAN'S (MISS) SCHOOL, Philadelphia, Pennsylvania: 5165
LYMINGTON, England: 4655
  Politics and government: 4557
LYNCH, Charles: 2211
LYNCH, Lemuel: 3300
LYNCH, Mary (Bingham): 3300
LYNCH, Patrick Neeson: 2612
LYNCH, S. Matthew: 1193
LYNCH, Thomas: 3300
LYNCH, W. B.: 3300
LYNCH, Wade: 5233

LYNCHBURG, Tennessee:
  Ku Klux Klan: 677
LYNCHBURG, Virginia: 1350
  1700s-1800s: 1350, 2925
  1700s-1900s: 3809
  1800s: 331, 2302, 3959, 4428
    1840s: 2309, 4504
    1850s: 661, 3106, 3542, 3817
    1860s: 267, 661, 1594, 1810, 2065, 3542, 3817, 4010
    1870s: 2951, 3817, 3879
  1800s-1900s: 1364, 4373
  1900s: 3685, 4141, 4156
  Banks and banking: 4157
  Civil War:
    see also CIVIL WAR--CAMPAIGNS, BATTLES AND MILITARY ACTIONS--Virginia--Lynchburg
    Confederate Army camp: 2710
    Hospitals: 1033, 2090
      Pratt Hospital: 1506, 2879, 4308
  Clergy--Presbyterian: 4373
  Commodity prices: 3566
  Cookery: 4308
  Cotton mills--Construction: 5513
  Diseases--Smallpox: 5513
  Iron industry: 3809
  Law practice: 506
  Memorials: 3809
  Mercantile accounts: 4222
  Merchants: 1093, 5568
  Municipal government: 3205
  Politics and government: 1955
  Presbyterian churches: 3707
  Schools: 1714
    Girls' schools and academies: 4373
  Slavery: 1741
  Tobacco advertising: 1586
  Trade and commerce: 3353, 2633
    Wholesale trade: 2857
  Universities and colleges: see LYNCHBURG COLLEGE
  Waterworks: 5513
LYNCHBURG COLLEGE, Lynchburg, Virginia: 4416
LYNCHBURG FEMALE ACADEMY, Lynchburg, Virginia: 4373
LYNCHBURG IRON, STEEL, AND MINING COMPANY: 3809
LYNCHBURG (Va.) NEWS: 4156
LYNCHBURG VIRGINIAN: 1810
LYNCHING:
  see also ANTI-LYNCHING MOVEMENT
  Colorado: 2368
  Florida: 5740
  North Carolina--Norlina: 4103
  South Carolina: 3390
LYNDALL, Mary A.: 3301
LYNDALL, Thomas: 3301
LYNDALL, W. B.: 3301
LYNDALL FAMILY: 3301
LYNDE, Charles R.: 2407
LYNDE, Lucy C.: 2407
LYNDHURST, John Singleton Copley, First Baron: 2149
LYNEDOCH, Thomas Graham, First Baron: 2147
LYNEHAM PARK, England: 1147
LYNN, Elizabeth: 5553
LYNN, HETHERINGTON AND KYNOCH v.: see HETHERINGTON AND KYNOCH v. LYNN
LYNN AND KING (firm): see KING AND LYNN
LYNNWOOD, Virginia: 3194
LYON, Chatham Calhoun: 5457
LYON FAMILY (North Carolina): 1523
LYON AND PALMES (firm): see PALMES AND LYON
LYON BROTHERS & COMPANY, Baltimore, Maryland: 2940
LYONS, James (b. 1801): 3302
LYONS FAMILY (Southern States): 4434
LYONS, France: 5228
LYSIAN SOCIETY, Gordon Institute, Barnesville, Georgia: 4791
LYTCH, James: 3303

LYTLE, Florence: 77
LYTTELTON, Alfred: 3978
LYTTELTON, Alfred A.: 294
LYTTELTON, George William, Fourth Baron Lyttelton: 1087
LYTTELTON, William Henry, First Baron Lyttelton: 3304, 4605
LYTTON, Edward George Earle Lytton Bulwer-, First Baron Lytton: 737, 2146, 3722
LYTTON, Edward Robert Bulwer, First Earl of Lytton: 3238
LYTTON, Rosina Doyle (Wheeler) Bulwer-, Baroness Lytton: 2146
LYTTON-BERNARD, Bernard: 1424, 3305

## M

M. A. ANGIER CO.: 134
M. AND J. H. NEWCOMER, Maryland (firm): 3875
"M. C." (poet): 3892
M. L. F. (Virginian): 1744
M. M. FREEMAN AND COMPANY: 5133
MABANK, Texas:
  Primitive Baptist Church: 318
MABBOTT, Maureen (Cobb): 3306
MABBOTT, Thomas Ollive: 102, 3306, 5720
MABIE, Hamilton Wright: 103, 706, 2449, 5908
MABINI, Apolinario: 4511
MABRY, Alice U. (Goodman): 3307
MABRY, Helen: 3307
MABRY, Robert C.: 3307
MABRY AND READ, Ridgeway, North Carolina (firm): 3307
McADOO, William Gibbs: 879, 2299
McALISTER, Alexander Worth: 5457
McALISTER, Amelie: 5252
McALISTER, Andrew: 3012
McALISTER, William H.: 5252
McALLISTER, Richard: 3309
McALLISTER, William Miller: 3308
McALLISTER, William Stephens Matthew: 3309
McALLISTER FAMILY (Georgia): 3309
McALLISTER FAMILY (Pennsylvania): 365
McALPIN, Ellen: 3310
McALPIN, Georgia: 3310
McALPIN, Henry: 3311
McALPIN, James: 3311
McALPIN, James Wallace: 3311
McALPIN, Maria Sophia (Champion): 3311
McALPIN FAMILY (Genealogy): 3311
MACANAZ, Melchor Rafael de: 3312
MACAO, China: 598
  East India Company: 3315
  Missions and missionaries: 3786
  Trade and commerce: 5228
MacARTHUR, Arthur: 3313
MacARTHUR, Douglas: 3019
MACARTHY, Charles E.: 3314
MACARTNEY, George, First Earl Macartney: 3315
MACARTNEY, Jane (Stuart): 3315
MACARTNEY, Margaret: 2776
MACARTNEY FAMILY (North Carolina--Genealogy): 2776
MACAULAY, James: 2149
MACAULAY, Thomas Babington, Baron Macaulay: 280
MACAULAY, Zachary: 867, 3316
MACAYAN TOWNSHIP, Philippine Islands: 4511
McBEE, Alexander: 3317
McBEE, Vardry Alexander: 3317
McBEE, South Carolina:
  Land development: 1478
McBRIDE, Andrew Jay: 3318
McBRIDE, B. C.: 19
McBRIDE, John: 3319
McBRIDE, Mary Frances (Johnson): 3318

McBRIDE AND POSEY, South Carolina (firm): 3319
McCABE, William Gordon: 2612, 3320
McCABE FAMILY (Virginia--Genealogy): 3320
McCAIN, Henry Pinckney: 270
McCALL, Alexander: 3321
McCALL, Dugal: 3322
McCALL, Duncan G.: 3322
McCALL, Hugh: 3323
McCALL, John: 3407
McCALL, Johnson D.: 277
McCALL, Rebecca Mariah (Oxford): 3324
McCALL, Samuel Walker: 706
McCALLA, Andrew J.: 3255
McCALLA, Helen Varnum (Hill): 3325
McCALLA, John Moore: 3325
McCALLA, John Moore, Jr.: 3325
McCANNON, William H.: 3326
McCARRAN, Patrick A.: 2109
McCARTER, George A.: 3327
McCARTER, John Gray: 3328
McCARTER FAMILY (South Carolina): 3327
M'CARTER'S COUNTRY ALMANAC (1833): 5051
McCARTHA, Thomas: 718
McCARTHY, John: 4615
McCARTHY, Justin: 2449
McCARTHY, Mary: 103
McCAULEY, William: 3329
McCAY, Henry Kent: 3330
McCAY, J. Ringgold: 5730
McCLAIN, Hattie: 5160
McCLAIN, Mary Elizabeth: 5160
McCLEARY, James Thompson: 2449
McCLEERY, Frances: 3053
McCLEERY, Mary: 3053
McCLEES, Thomas A.: 5417
McCLEISH, William: 2486
McCLELLAN, Ellen Mary (Marcy): 4608
McCLELLAN, George Brinton: 306, 2085, 2871, 2898, 3778, 4602, 4808, 4829, 4881, 5402, 5430
McCLELLAN, Henry B.: 3809
McCLELLAN (J. S.) AND COMPANY, Martinsburg, West Virginia: 5110
McCLELLAN, Robert Anderson: 3331
McCLELLAND, Robert: 3332
"McCLELLAN'S BEE HIVE": 5402
McCLELLANVILLE, South Carolina: 4619
McCLINTOCK, John (1770-1855): 4024
McCLINTOCK, John (1814-1870): 2612
McCLUNG FAMILY (Tennessee): 872
McCLURE, Charles L.: 4656
McCLURE, James: 4188
McCLURE, Samuel Sidney: 3265
McCONNELL, James Rogers: 5457
McCONNELL FAMILY (West Virginia--Genealogy): 1946
McCONNELLSBURG, Pennsylvania:
  Description: 220
McCOOK, Edward Moody: 1917
McCORD, Carrie: 1644
McCORD, Jacob: 3333
McCORD FAMILY (Virginia): 3333
McCORKLE, A. B.: 117
McCORKLE, Joseph: 1072
McCORKLE, Samuel Eusebius: 3334
McCORKLE FAMILY: 1072
McCORMICK, Cyrus Hall: 3335, 4076
McCORMICK, Frederick: 5252
McCORMICK, Marshall: 4607
McCORMICK, Mary E.: 3357
McCORMICK FAMILY: 3357
McCORMICK & PRICE, Berryville, Virginia (firm): 3336
McCORMICK REAPERS: 4924
McCOWN, Moses: 3337
McCOY, Charles: 3339
McCOY, Frances (Tutt): 3339
McCOY, Jessie Marion (Wall): 3338
McCOY, William E.: 3339
McCRACKEN COUNTY, Kentucky:
  Paducah: 1356
McCRADY, Edward, Sr.: 3340

McCRADY, Edward, Jr. (1833-1903): 1891, 3340
McCREARY, James Bennett: 3341
McCREARY, Nathaniel: 3342
McCREARY, William G.: 3343
McCUE FAMILY (West Virginia): 2342
McCULLERS, Carson (Smith): 902, 3344, 5360
McCULLERS, James Reeve: 902
McCULLERS FAMILY: 902
McCULLOCH, James M. (Virginia): 1873, 3345
McCULLOCH, James W. (Georgia): 3346
McCULLOCH AND McENERY (firm): see McENERY AND McCULLOCH
McCULLOH, Henry Eustace: 2776, 3347
McCULLOH FAMILY (North Carolina--Genealogy): 2776
McCULLOUGH, George: 3348
McCULLOUGH FAMILY (South Carolina): 3349
McCUTCHEON, William: 3350
McCUTCHEON FAMILY (South Carolina): 3350
McDADE, H. Lee: 3351
McDADE, John A.: 3351
McDADE (W. T.) AND COMPANY: 3352
McDANIEL, Henry Dickerson: 2005
McDANIEL, John R.: 641
McDANIEL AND LEE (firm): 3353
McDAVID, Peter: 3354
MacDONALD, Angus William: 3357
McDONALD, Charles James: 3355
McDONALD, Edward Allen Hitchcock: 3141
McDONALD, Furman: 3356
MACDONALD, James Ramsey: 233
MACDONALD, John Alexander: 4567
McDONALD, Marshall: 3357
MacDONALD, Rose M.: 4558
McDONALD, Walter Neill: 5170
MACDONALD FAMILY (Great Britain): 970
McDONALD FISHWAY: 3357
McDONALD MINING AND MANUFACTURING CO.: see FRANKLIN & McDONALD MINING AND MANUFACTURING COMPANY
McDONOGH, John (1779-1850): 1333, 3358, 3598
McDONOUGH, James B.: 3640
McDONOUGH FAMILY (Georgia): 2963
McDONOUGH COUNTY, Illinois:
  Macomb: 659
McDOUGALL, Angus Dougal: 3359
MACDOUGALL, Harriette: 4995
McDOUGALL, Marion Gleason: 2400
McDOWALL, Susan: 3360
McDOWALL, William Douglas: 3360
McDOWELL, Charles: 3361
McDOWELL, Irvin: 2085
McDOWELL, James I: 3362
McDOWELL, James II (1795-1851): 3362
McDOWELL, James III: 3362
MacDOWELL, Katherine Sherwood (Bonner): 3363
McDOWELL, Thomas David Smith: 3364
McDOWELL, Tremaine: 102
McDOWELL, William: 3365
McDUFFIE, George: 3366, 3367, 4912
McDUFFIE, Mary Singleton: 3367
McDUFFIE FAMILY (South Carolina--Genealogy): 3367
McDUFFIE COUNTY, Georgia:
  Thomson: 5594
  Schools: 4895
McEACHIN, D. T.: 3368
MACEDON, New York: 1977
MACEDONIA: 3912
MACEDONIAN (warship): 841
McELHENEY, Jane: 2449
McELROY, John: 270
McELWEE, S. A.: 3369
McENERY, Ruth: 2871
McENERY, Samuel Douglas: 4373
McENERY & McCULLOCH, Petersburg, Virginia (firm): 1873, 3345
McEWEN, A. D.: 3370

McEWEN, Eliza J.: 3370
McEWEN (firm): see MAY McEWEN KAISER
McEWEN KNITTING CO.: 2108
McFARLANE, Allen: 3371
McFARLANE, James: 3372
McFARLIN, Alexander: 3373
McFEE, William: 103
McGAVOCK, John: 3374
McGAVOCK CONFEDERATE CEMETERY: 3374
McGAW, John: 3375
McGAW, William: 3375
McGAW FAMILY (South Carolina): 3375
McGEACHY, Catherine Jane: 754
McGEE, Elizabeth: 518
McGEE, Lily: 3376
McGEE, William S.: 518
McGEHEE FAMILY (Virginia): 3377
MacGILL, Charles: 3378
MacGILL, James: 3378
MacGILL, General James: 3378
McGILL, John: 3179
McGILL, John D.: 3379
McGILL AND MAHONE, Virginia (firm): 3179
McGILL AND WOODWARD (firm): 3379
McGILVARY, Daniel: 5457
McGINNIS, John: 4911
McGINNIS (MARGUERITE) ET AL. v. INTERNATIONAL TYPOGRAPHICAL UNION: 2772
McGIRT, William Archibald: 3380
McGLASHAN, John: 3381
McGOWAN, James: 3382
McGOWAN, Samuel (1819-1897): 4145
McGOWAN, Samuel (1870-1934): 3383
McGOWAN AND PERRIN, Charleston, South Carolina (firm): 4145
MacGRATH, T. J. Hylande-: see HYLANDE-MacGRATH, T. J.
McGRAW, James: 5938
MACGREGOR, Charles Metcalfe: 4503
McGUFFEY, William Holmes: 4348
McHANEY, Thomas: 720
McHENRY, James: 2486, 3384
McHENRY, John Hardin: 3199
McHENRY COUNTY, Illinois:
  Estray records: 1723
MACHIAVELLI, Niccolo: 3385
MACHINE GUNS:
  Manufacture--Connecticut: 1979
MACHINE PARTS INDUSTRY: see TEXTILE MACHINERY--Parts
MACHINE WORKERS: see INTERNATIONAL UNION OF ELECTRICAL, RADIO, AND MACHINE WORKERS
MACHINERY: see AGRICULTURAL MACHINERY; HOSIERY MACHINERY; KNITTING MACHINERY; TEXTILE MACHINERY; TINWORKING MACHINERY
MACHINERY INDUSTRY: 5312
  Virginia--Marion: 3513
MACHIPONGO, Virginia: 1814
MACHODOC, Virginia:
  Tobacco trade: 144
McILVAIN, A. R.: 357
McILVAINE, Charles Pettit: 128, 4253
McILWAINE, Richard: 523
McINNIS, Alexander: 3386
McINNIS, B. L.: 3387
McINTIRE, Charles J.: 4414
McINTOSH, J. M.: 3118
McINTOSH, James Simmons: 3388
McINTOSH, John: 2931, 5508
McINTOSH, Lachlan: 3209, 3389
McINTOSH, McQueen: 5508
McINTOSH, Roderick: 4517
McINTOSH, Thomas M.: 3390
McINTOSH FAMILY (Georgia): 2963
McINTOSH COUNTY, Georgia:
  Darien: 1779, 2647, 2963, 5508
  Land survey: 3389
  Sapelo Island: 2326, 2963, 4985, 4988
McINTYRE, Archibald: 3391
McINTYRE, Benjamin Franklin: 3392
McINTYRE, D. C.: 3416

McINTYRE, H. I.: 1466
McIVER, Charles Duncan: 1336, 2833
McIVER, D. J.: 3393
McIVER, John: 3393
McJIMSEY, J. M.: 4157
McKALL, Leonard Leopold: 3394
MACKALL, Leonard Leopold: 3898
McKAY, Catherine: 3395
MACKAY, Charles (1814-1889): 4543
MACKAY, Clarence H.: 3265
MACKAY, Eliza Anne (McQueen): 3396
MacKAY, George L.: 3397
MACKAY, James (Georgia): 3706
McKAY, James J. (North Carolina): 4516
McKAY, John: 3398
McKAY AND GILCHRIST, Robeson County, North Carolina (firm): 3398
McKAY AND McLEAN, Robeson County, North Carolina (firm): 3398
MacKAYE, Percy: 3797
McKEAN, Thomas (1734-1817): 5276
McKEE, J. W.: 519
McKEE, James: 5457
McKEE, John: 2781
McKEITHAN, O. M.: 2449
McKELPESH, John H.: 3399
McKENDREL, J. N.: 5505
MACKENNA, Juan: 4155
McKENNEY, George W.: 3400
McKENNEY, Thomas Loraine: 1848
McKENNEY, William Robertson: 3401
McKENNON, Paul: 3640
McKENNY AND JONES (firm): see JONES AND McKENNY
McKENZIE, Aline: 2934
MacKENZIE, Elizabeth G.: 3402
MACKENZIE, Henry: 2126
McKENZIE, Ranald Slidell: 3809
McKEOWEN FAMILY (West Virginia): 865
MACKEREL TRADE: see FISH TRADE
McKETHAN, Alfred Augustus: 3403
McKETHAN, Alfred Augustus, Jr.: 3403
McKETHAN, Edwin Turner: 3403
MACKEY, Daniel N.: 3404
MACKEY, John T.: 3404
MACKEY, Thomas: 2300
MACKEY, Thomas J.: 609
McKIE, J. M.: 3405
McKIE, Thomas Jefferson: 3405
MACKILLOP & CO.: see PALMER, MACKILLOP, DENT & CO.
McKIM, Alexander: 3406
McKIM, Isaac: 743, 3406
McKIM, MEADE, AND WHITE, Washington, D.C. (firm): 4020
McKIMMON, Jane Simpson: 5457
McKINLEY, William: 2313, 2473, 3407
  Administration: 5142
McKINNE, David Edward: 3408
McKINNEY, D. W.: 418
McKINNEY, W. M.: 3409
McKINNON, John T.: 1438
McKOY, Mrs. F. E.: 3410
McKOY, Robert Hasell: 3410
McKOY, Thomas H., Sr.: 3410
McKOY, Thomas H., Jr.: 3410
McKOY, William Berry: 3410
MACKSBURG, West Virginia: 2470
MACKWORTH, Sir Arthur W.: 5351
MACKY, John (d. 1726): 3411
MACLAGAN, James: 3838
MACLAINE, Archibald: 2776, 5457
McLANAHAN, Isabella Craig: 3412
McLANE, Louis: 872, 3413
McLANE, Lydia: 2881
McLAUGHLIN, Andrew Cunningham: 706
McLAURIN, Anna B.: 3414
McLAURIN, Duncan: 3415
McLAURIN, Lauchlin W.: 3416
McLAURIN, Nancy: 3416
McLAURIN FAMILY (North Carolina): 530, 1313
McLAWS, Lafayette: 3417
McLEAN, Angus Wilton: 4775, 4858, 5962

MACLEAN, Clara Victoria (Dargan): 3418
McLEAN, John: 125, 2578, 4880
McLEAN, John (Scotland): 859
McLEAN (WILLIAM) HOUSE, Appomattox, Virginia: 1137
McLEAN AND McKAY: see McKAY AND McLEAN
McLEAN COUNTY, Illinois: 4488
  Bloomington: 5570
  Normal: 3051
McLENNAN, John D.: 3419
McLENNAN COUNTY, Texas:
  Waco: 1592
McLEOD, Allan: 2146
McLEOD, Thomas Gordon: 2109
McLOY, A.: 3420
McMANNEN, Archibald A.: 3646
McMASTER, Elizabeth Ann: 1791
McMASTER, Fitz Hugh: 3421
McMASTER, John Bach: 103
McMASTER, John S.: 1791
McMASTER, L. H. K.: 1791
McMASTER, William S.: 1791
McMASTER FAMILY (Virginia): 1791
McMICKING, Helen Mary: 4331
McMILLAN, Alexander: 3422
McMILLAN, Archibald: 3423
McMILLAN, Daniel: 3422
McMILLAN, David: 3422
McMILLAN, Duncan: 5740
McMILLAN, John: 5827
McMILlAN FAMILY (North Carolina): 3422
McMULLAN, Thomas Shelton: 5457
McMULLEN, Mr. _____ (Confederate emigrant): 339
McMULLEN, Benedict Dysart: 3424
M'MULLEN, John (Great Britain): 4024
McMULLEN, John (1791-1870): 3424
McMULLEN, John Francis (1830-1900): 3424
McMULLEN, John Francis II (d. 1944): 3424
McMULLEN, Joseph Benjamin: 3424
McMULLEN, Lavalette (Johnston): 3424
McMULLEN, Mary: 3424, 4478
McMULLEN, Nicketti: 3424
McMULLEN FAMILY (Ireland): 3424
McMULLEN FAMILY (Washington, D.C.): 3424
MacMURPHY FAMILY (North Carolina): 530
MacMURRAN, Joseph: 3010
MACNAGHTEN, Fred A.: 5252
MACNAGHTEN, Sir William Hay, First Baronet: 5801
McNAIR FAMILY (North Carolina): 1120
McNEELY, Robert Whitehead: 103
McNEILL, Chattie C.: 2363
McNEILL, Franklin: 3432
McNEILL, Hector H.: 3432
McNEILL, Sir John (1795-1883): 868
McNEILL, John Charles (1874-1907): 3433
McNEILL, John H. (North Carolina): 3434
McNEILL, Mary Margaret: 3435
McNEILL, Neill: 3436
McNEILL, Thomas A.: 3432
McNEILL AND COMPANY: see JOHNSTON, McNEILL AND COMPANY
McNEILLY, Robert W.: 3437
MacNIDER, William deBerniere: 3878
McNISH, Mary Jane: 2460
McNUTT, Alexander Gallatin: 3438
McNUTT, C. H.: 4894
MACOMB, Alexander: 5425
MACOMB, Illinois: 659
MACOMB COUNTY, Michigan:
  Romeo: 4889
  Washington: 1229
MACOMBER, James G.: 2898
MACON, Nathaniel: 3439
MACON, Georgia: 261, 823, 2362, 2963, 4059, 5576
  Bar association: 1121

MACON, Georgia (Continued):
    Civil War: 510, 731
        Camp Oglethorpe: 2124
    Description: 249, 284
    Law practice: 3905
    Newspapers: 1112
    Presbyterian churches: 3905
    Schools: 2828, 2963
        Girls' schools and academies: 339, 2963, 4040
    Social life and customs: 3905, 5246
    Universities and colleges: see MERCER UNIVERSITY; WESLEYAN COLLEGE
MACON, Mississippi:
    Civil War: 1424
MACON, North Carolina: 1660
MACON AND WESTERN RAILROAD: 2533
MACON COUNTY, Alabama:
    Trade with Confederate Army: 3837
    Cities and towns:
        Cotton Valley: 1295
        Tuskegee: 925
        see also TUSKEGEE INSTITUTE
MACON COUNTY, Illinois:
    Decatur: 1346
MACON COUNTY, North Carolina:
    Franklin: 417, 4817
MACON DEPOT, North Carolina: 4764
MACON FEMALE ACADEMY, Macon, Georgia: 2963
MACON FEMALE COLLEGE, Macon, Georgia: see WESLEYAN COLLEGE
MACON FREE SCHOOL, Macon, Georgia: 2963
MACON'S BILL NO. 2 (West Virginia): 4774
MACOUPIN COUNTY, Illinois:
    Bunker Hill: 1670
McPHAIL, Elizabeth: 1107
McPHEETERS, Alexander, Sr.: 3440
McPHERSON, James Birdseye: 3441
McPHERSON, John Bayard (1846-1919): 2027
McPHERSON, John D.: 3442
McPHERSON, S. D. II: 5267
McPHERSONVILLE HOSPITAL, South Carolina: 1185
McQUADE, Elizabeth: 4719
McQUEEN, Eliza Anne: 3396
McQUEEN, James: 3443
McQUEEN, John (Georgia): 3444
McQUEEN, John (South Carolina, 1804-1867): 3445
McQUEEN, M. C.: 3396
MACQUILLEN, Ephraim: 1556
MACRA, Sir John: 3446
MACRA FAMILY (Canada, India, Nepal, and Scotland): 3446
MacRAE, Alexander: 3447
MacRAE, Alexander, Jr.: 3447
MacRAE, Archibald: 3447
McRAE, Colin J.: 1181
MacRAE, Donald: 3447
MacRAE, Henry: 3447
MacRAE, Hugh: 3447, 5252
MacRAE (J. & D.), Wilmington, North Carolina (firm): 3447
McRAE, J. N. W.: 3448
MacRAE, James Cameron: 5457
McRAE, John: 1439
MacRAE, John: 3032, 3447
MacRAE, John A.: 3449
MacRAE, John Colin: 3447
MacRAE, Mary Ann G.: 3448
MacRAE, Robert Bruce: 3447
MacRAE, Roderick: 3447
MacRAE, Walter G.: 3447
MacRAE, William: 3447
McRAE FAMILY (North Carolina): 3434
McREYNOLDS, Benjamin: 3450
McREYNOLDS, Shepard S.: 3450
McREYNOLDS FAMILY (Genealogy): 3450
McSWAIN, John Jackson: 3451
McVEIGH, Townshend: 2741
"THE MAD DOG" (card game): 3452
MADAGASCAR--Slave trade: 2754

MADAM TOUSSAINT'S WEDDING DAY by Thaddeus St. Martin: 4636
MADDOCK, Sir Thomas Herbert: 3453
MADDOX, Lester G.: 3348
MADDOX, Washington: 3454
MADDUX (WASHINGTON) AND ASA BARNES, INC.: 3454
MADDUX (WILLIAM H.) AND CO.: 3454
MADDUX AND CO., Oak Forest, Va.: 3454
MADEIRA, Morocco: 4537
MADEIRA ISLANDS:
    Description and travel: 3744, 4017
    Trade with United States: 1481
MADISON, Dolly: see MADISON, Dorothea (Payne) Todd
MADISON, Dorothea (Payne) Todd: 2326, 3455, 3612
MADISON, James (1749-1812, bishop): 872, 3456
MADISON, James (1751-1836): 768, 1308, 1778, 1962, 2913, 3176, 3251, 3612, 4312, 4457
    Administration: 3742
    "Montpelier": 3455
MADISON, James (fl. 1803, South Carolina): 477
MADISON, Florida: 3293
MADISON, Georgia: 127, 4415, 4426
    see also GEORGIA FEMALE COLLEGE
    Cotton trade: 497
MADISON, Missouri: 1601
MADISON, Virginia: 2531
    Agriculture: 3141
    Economic conditions: 3141
MADISON, Wisconsin: 403
    see also UNIVERSITY OF WISCONSIN
    Judaism: 2811
MADISON COUNTY, Alabama:
    Estates--Administration and settlement: 4658
    Huntsville: see HUNTSVILLE, Alabama
MADISON COUNTY, Florida:
    Farming: 3123
    Madison: 3293
MADISON COUNTY, Georgia: 4991
MADISON COUNTY, Illinois:
    Alton: 1400
MADISON COUNTY, Kentucky:
    Land: 795
    Richmond: 3341
        Merchants: 299
MADISON COUNTY, Mississippi:
    Canton: 5933
MADISON COUNTY, New York:
    DeRuyter: 104
    Hamilton: 701
    South Brookfield: 854
MADISON COUNTY, North Carolina:
    Marshall: 4548
MADISON COUNTY, Virginia: 253, 5704
    Civil War: 523
    Courts--Clerks: 5064
    Estates--Administration and settlement: 4794
    Insurance: 523
    Law practice: 523
    Mexican War: 523
    Pensions from American Revolution: 523
    Slave trade--Prices: 4794
    Slaves: 523, 4794
    Cities and towns:
        Locust Dale: 1073, 5798
        Madison: see MADISON, Virginia
MADISON COUNTY (Ala.) BIBLE SOCIETY: 1084
MADISON PARISH, Louisiana: 1864
MADISONVILLE, Ohio: 5030
MADRAS, India: 455, 2037, 2266
    British military activity: 505, 536
    Civil-military relations: 3315
    Government agencies and officials:
        Council: 2756
        Governor: 2756
MADRAS ARMY: 536, 5201
MADRAS ARMY MUTINY: 332

MADRAS PRESIDENCY: see INDIA--British administration--Madras Presidency
MADRID, Spain: 2055, 3659, 4138, 4178
    French embassy in: 1424
    United States embassy in: 3659, 3854
MAESTRI, Robert S.: 3252
MAFFITT, John Newland: 1399, 5092
MAGAZIN THÉÂTRAL: 5167
MAGAZINE OF AMERICAN HISTORY: 1227, 3022
MAGAZINES: see PERIODICALS
MAGDALEN COLLEGE: see OXFORD UNIVERSITY--Magdalen College
MAGDALENA RIVER (Colombia): 198
MAGEE, John Euclid: 3457
MAGEE FAMILY (Florida): 4365
THE MAGIC WORD AND OTHER POEMS by Augustin Louis Taveau: 5193
MAGILL, Charles: 3458
MAGILL, Sarah: 3458
MAGISTRATES: see JUDGES; JUSTICES OF THE PEACE
MAGISTRATES' COURTS: see COURTS--Magistrates' courts
MAGNA CARTA: 5575
MAGNOLIA, Florida:
    Description: 3277
MAGNOLIA, North Carolina:
    Preparatory schools: 4910
MAGNOLIA, Virginia: 590
MAGOMERO [Mozambique?]: 5725
MAGOUN, Thatcher, Sr.: 3459
MAGOUN, Thatcher, Jr.: 3459
MAGOUN AND SON, Boston, Massachusetts (firm): 3459
MAGRA, Perkins: 3460
MAGRATH, Andrew Gordon: 3461
MAGRUDER, Allan Bowie: 3462
MAGRUDER, John Bankhead: 3417, 3463, 4479, 5511
MAGRUDER, John Bowie: 3464
MAGRUDER, Julia: 3465
MAGRUDER, William Thomas: 5121
MAGWOOD, Simon J.: 3466
MAGYARS: 4552
MAHAN, Alfred Thayer: 227
MAHAN, Dennis Hart: 2363
MAHARANI OF THE PUNJAB: 4097
MAHASKA COUNTY, Iowa:
    Oskaloosa: 3170
MAHDI OF SUDAN: 5872
MAHDISTS (Sudan): 5835
MAHONE, William: 1364, 3215, 3467
MAHONE AND McGILL: see McGILL AND MAHONE
MAHONING COUNTY, Ohio:
    Youngstown: 3085
MAHONY, Pierce: 3468, 4024
MAHRATTA STATES, India: 2037
MAHRATTA WAR (1775-1782):
    Peace settlement: 3315
MAHRATTA WAR (1803-1805): 332, 2321
    Campaigns and battles:
        Laswaree: 4635
"THE MAIDEN MARRIAGE" by Algernon C. Swinburne: 5158
MAIDES, James F.: 3469
MAIL SERVICE: see Postal service as subheading under names of countries
MAILLY, William: 4948
MAIN STREET CHURCH (Methodist, North Carolina): 3646
MAINE:
    see also NEW ENGLAND STATES
    Abolition of slavery and abolitionist sentiment: 5610
    Augusta: 83
    Copperheads: 1787
    Crops--Cooper: 654
    Currency: 1339
    Democratic Party: 5610
    Description and travel (1881): 43
    Education--Livermore: 5569
    Elections (1844): 4169
    Farm life--Livermore: 5569

MAINE (Continued):
    Love letters--Saco: 3741
    Lumber mills--Toddy Pond: 3554
    Poetry collections:
        Portland: 3551
    Politics and government: 5569, 5610
    Schools: 731
    Social life and customs: 731
        Portland: 2043
    Temperance: 1554
    Tobacco trade: 5251
    Trade and commerce: 323
        Castine: 5860
    Universities and colleges: see BOWDOIN COLLEGE
    Whig Party: 5610
MAINE (Province), France: 5323
"MAINE LAW" (1896): 1554
MAINE WESLEYAN SEMINARY, Kent's Hill, Maine: 731
MAINTENANCE OF SHIPS: see SHIPS--Maintenance and repair; and Maintenance and repair as subheading under names of navies
MAINWARING, George Boulton: 3658
MAITLAND, Frederick William: 3851
MAITLAND, Robert L.: 1475
MAJOR, James Patrick: 3470
MAJORCA:
    Peninsular War (1813): 5639
MAKEMIE, Francis: 1791
MAKERS OF AMERICA by Benjamin Franklin Johnson: 4918
MALABANG, Philippine Islands:
    Description: 4511
MALABAR, India: 536
    Trade and commerce: 5228
MALABAR (India) POLICE CORPS: 536
MALARIA: see DISEASES--Malaria
MALAYA:
    Description and travel: 4017
    Missions and missionaries: 2148
MALCOLM, John: 2263
MALCOLM, Sir John: 868, 3471, 3645, 3816
MALET, Sir Alexander, Second Baronet: 3472
MALET, Sir Edward Baldwin, Fourth Baronet: 3472
MALET, Sir Henry Charles Eden, Third Baronet: 3472
MALET, Mary Anne Dora (Spalding): 3472
MALET FAMILY (Great Britain): 3472
MALLETT, John Frederick: 3473
MALLORY, Stephen Russell: 1084, 1403, 3474, 4235, 4531, 5075
MALLORY, Walter Hampton: 5252
MALLORY SHOE SHOP: see HICKS, JONES & MALLORY SHOE SHOP
MALLOY, Charles: 3776
MALLOY, Henry W.: 3475
MALLOY, J. W.: 3432
MALLOY, James Hugh: 4816
MALLOY COTTON MILLS: see MORGAN-MALLOY COTTON MILLS
MALMESBURY, James Edward Harris, Second Earl of: 1755
MALONE, Ellis: 3476
MALONE, James Ellis: 3476
MALONE, New York: 5687
MALORY, Sir Thomas: 3477
MALPRACTICE (Legal):
    Alabama: 4994
MALTA: 153, 2296
MALVERN, Arkansas: 2809
"MALVERN," Essex County, Virginia: 347
MALVERN HILL, Virginia:
    Civil War: 3809
        see also CIVIL WAR--CAMPAIGNS, BATTLES, AND MILITARY ACTIONS--Virginia--Malvern Hill
MAMMOTH CAVE, Kentucky: 1333

MANAGEMENT: see specific kinds of management, e.g. PLANTATION MANAGEMENT; and Management as subheading under specific kinds of businesses, e.g. OILSEED MILLS--Management
MANASSAS, Georgia: 1034
MANASSAS, Virginia:
    Civil War: see CIVIL WAR--CAMPAIGNS, BATTLES, AND MILITARY ACTIONS--Virginia--Manassas
    Farm management: 5272
    Hotels: 5779
MANASSAS GAP RAILROAD: 5377
MANASSAS JUNCTION, Virginia:
    Civil War: 1137
MANBY, George William: 3478
MANCHESTER, Bishop of: see names of specific bishops, e.g. FRASER, James
MANCHESTER, William Drogo Montagu, Seventh Duke of: 2826
MANCHESTER, England: 380, 676, 1126, 2899
    Arts: 4113
    Church buildings: 4287
MANCHESTER, New Hampshire: 251
MANCHESTER, Ohio:
    Reminiscences: 1177
MANCHESTER, Pennsylvania: 496
MANCHESTER, Virginia: 1115
    Diseases--Smallpox: 3792
    Iron foundries: 282
"MANCHESTER OPHELIA" by Richard Wright Proctor: 39
MANCHURIA:
    British embassy in: 306
    Chinese Eastern Railroad: 5252
    Japanese aggression (1930s-1940s): 5252
    Russo-Japanese War: see RUSSO-JAPANESE WAR
    Sino-Japanese War: see SINO-JAPANESE WAR
MANDEVILLE, H.: 3183
MANESTY, Samuel: 5797
MANEY, Lewis M.: 3479
MANEY, Mrs. Lewis M.: 3479
MANGANJA TRIBE (Africa): 5725
MANGOLD, Ferdinand Franz: 3480
MANGUM, Addison: 3481
MANGUM, Adolphus W.: 3482
MANGUM, Adolphus Williamson: 1284
MANGUM, Willie Person: 2776, 3483, 3557, 5667
MANGUM, Wyatt: 3484
MANGUM FAMILY (North Carolina--Genealogy): 3483
MANGYANS (Philippine Islands): 4511
MANHATTAN COLLEGE, New York, New York: 3717
    Students and student life: 3717
MANHATTAN LIFE INSURANCE COMPANY: 2983
MANIGAULT, Charles Izard: 3485
MANIGAULT, Gabriel: 3485
MANIGAULT, Joseph: 3485
MANIGAULT, Louis: 3485
MANIGAULT, Margaret (Izard): 3485
MANILA, Philippine Islands: 561, 4656, 5668
    Expedition against (1797): 3315
    Military government (1900): 3313
    Ports: 4656
    School of navigation: 4656
MANKIN, Isaiah: 3486
MANKIN, Mary H.: 3486
MANLEY, H. DeHaven: 2552
MANLEY, Hezekiah: 3487
MANLY, B. C.: 4072
MANLY, Basil II (1798-1868): 2068, 5251
MANLY, Basil III (1825-1892): 3489
MANLY, Charles (North Carolina): 3488
MANLY, Charles (Virginia, 1837-1924): 3489
MANLY, Henry: 3490
MANLY, M. E.: 264

MANN, Dr. _____: 2552
MANN, Mr. _____: 3705
MANN, Adeline Susan: 3491
MANN, Ambrose Dudley: 635, 1181
MANN, Benjamin Pickman: 3492
MANN, Charles (Missouri): 3493
MANN, Charles (Virginia): 3494
MANN, Horace: 3295, 3495, 3524, 4095
MANN, John Andrew: 3496
MANN, Julian Smith: 5457
MANN, Luke: 1296
MANN, Mary Tyler (Peabody): 3295, 4095
MANN, Orrin L.: 358
MANN, Thomas: 2221, 3497
MANN, William Hodges: 879
MANN FAMILY (Michigan): 2604
MANNERS, Charles Cecil John, Sixth Duke of Rutland: 3498
MANNERS, John, Marquis of Granby: 5284
MANNERS, John James Robert, Seventh Duke of Rutland: 1110, 3498
MANNERS AND CUSTOMS: see Social life and customs as subheading under geographical names
MANNEY, Nancy L.: 3499
MANNING, Benjamin W.: 3500
MANNING, Edward: 4617
MANNING, Edward Wilson: 1899
MANNING, Henry Edward, Archbishop of Westminster: 2148, 4520
MANNING, John: 5457
MANNING, John Lawrence: 881, 3501
MANNING THE ROYAL NAVY AND MERCANTILE MARINE by William Schaw Lindsay: 36
THE MANOR AND THE BOROUGH by Sidney James Webb: 5616
MANORIAL COURTS: see COURTS--Courts baron
MANORS--Great Britain: 2836
MANSFIELD, Captain _____ (British naval officer): 1164
MANSFIELD, General _____: 3594
MANSFIELD, William Murray, First Earl of: 92, 2282
MANSFIELD, Ohio: 4032, 4781
MANSFIELD, Virginia: 4247
MANSION HOUSE HOSPITAL, Arlington, Virginia: 4945
MANSON, Edwin R.: 3502
MANSON, James Alexander: 3503
MANSON, North Carolina:
    Farm life: 799
    Mercantile accounts: 5697
MANTZ, Theresia: 1989, 3504
MANUAL TRAINING:
    South Carolina: 5312
MANUFACTURED PRODUCTS:
    Costs--Virginia: 2165
    Prices:
        see also COMMODITY PRICES
        North Carolina: 165
        Onslow County: 1252
        Union of Soviet Socialist Republics: 4614
MANUFACTURED PRODUCTS TRADE:
    Maryland: 1481
MANUFACTURERS' AGENTS:
    Georgia--Savannah: 2232
MANUFACTURING:
    see also INDUSTRIALIZATION
    Colorado: 5426
    Georgia: 5426
    Guatemala: 3099
    Kentucky: 5426
    Louisiana: 5426
    Scotland: 5726
    Tennessee: 5426
    Virginia: 5426
    Washington, D.C.: 5426
MANUMISSION OF SLAVES: see SLAVERY--Emancipation
MANUSCRIPT COLLECTING:
    France: 1424
    Georgia: 4402
    Great Britain: 5856
    North Carolina: 4156, 5252

MANUSCRIPT COLLECTING (Continued):
  Pennsylvania: 1563
  United States: 5922
MANUSCRIPTS, Syriac: 5156
MANZUTTO, Romano: 137
MAORI WAR (Second, 1860-1870): 4520
MAPES, Mary Elizabeth: 1530
MAR, John Erskine, Sixth Earl of: 2149
MARACAIBO, Venezuela:
  Commodity prices: 5133
MARAÑON RIVER (Peru): 4155
MARATANZA (ship): 1095
MARBLE, Annie (Russell): 2449
MARBLE--North Carolina: 3410
MARBLE QUARRIES--New York: 2172
MARBLE TRADE--Vermont: 4485
MARBOIS, François, Marquis de Barbé-: see BARBÉ-MARBOIS, François, Marquis de
MARBURG BROTHERS (firm): 1586
MARBURY, Horatio: 2931, 3505
MARBURY, Leonard: 1664
MARCH, Alden: 2790
MARCHBANKS, Andrew Jackson: 872
"THE MARCHINS," Chigwell, Essex, England (estate): 3553
MARCOFF, Count de: 2836
MARCOM, James Calvin: 3506
MARCONI WIRELESS TELEGRAPH COMPANY OF AMERICA: 2521
MARCUS, U.: 4188
MARCUS HOOK, Pennsylvania: 4881
MARCY, Ellen Mary: 4608
MARCY, William Learned: 3507
MARDI GRAS (1880): 5494
MARENGO COUNTY, Alabama: 5308
  Dayton: 798
  Gay's Landing: 5879
MARET, Hugues Bernard: 4230
MARIA (brig): 3570
MARIA (ship): 4537
MARIA TERESE, Queen of Sardinia: 4745
"MARIE" (poet): 3892
MARIE, Queen of Rumania: 4080
MARIE ANTOINETTE, Queen of France: 4625
MARIETTA, Georgia: 402, 3180, 3508, 3667, 3861
  see also GEORGIA MILITARY INSTITUTE
  Estates--Administration and settlement: 2670
  Social life and customs: 5730
MARIETTA, Ohio:
  Land investment: 2120
MARIETTA, Pennsylvania: 3613
MARIETTA AND CINCINNATI RAILROAD: 434, 2265
MARIETTA AND NORTH GEORGIA RAILROAD: 3508, 5051
MARIGNOLLI, Vita di Curzio: 5487
MARINE AND RIVER PHOSPHATE CO., Charleston, South Carolina: 602
MARINE ENGINEERING: see as subheading under names of navies
MARINE ENGINES: 1575
  Great Britain: 1599
MARINE INSURANCE COMPANY, Alexandria, Virginia: 3509
MARINE LIFE: 4017
MARINERS: see MERCHANT SEAMEN
MARION, Fannie M.: 3510
MARION, Francis (1732-1795): 3209, 3511, 4839
MARION, Robert: 3512
MARION, Alabama: 706, 1707
  Churches: 1476
  Girls' schools and academies: 5032
  Students and student life: 1476
  Patrons of husbandry: 444
MARION, North Carolina:
  Labor disputes: 3706
MARION, South Carolina: 2343
MARION, Virginia: 1240, 2769, 3513, 5117
MARION COUNTY, Florida: 4434

MARION COUNTY, Georgia:
  Religion: 5051
MARION COUNTY, Indiana:
  Indianapolis: 2384, 3849
  Terre Haute: 3618, 4303
MARION COUNTY, Missouri: 303
  Hannibal: 1099, 2076, 2162
    Law practice: 4616
  Palmyra: 303
    Civil War: 1683
      Prisons: 1184
MARION COUNTY, South Carolina:
  Marion: 2343
MARION DISTRICT, Methodist churches: 3646
MARION FOUNDRY AND MACHINE WORKS, Marion, Virginia: 3513
MARION MANUFACTURING CORPORATION, Marion, Virginia: 2769
MARITAL SCANDALS--Maryland: 3378
MARITAL SEPARATION:
  see also DIVORCE
  Colorado: 353
  Great Britain: 5553
  South Carolina: 5193
MARITIME INSURANCE: see INSURANCE--Maritime
MARITIME LAW: 1792
  see also RIGHT OF SEARCH; and Admiralty Courts as subheading under names of countries
MARK TWAIN QUARTERLY: 1097
MARK TWAIN'S SEVENTIETH BIRTHDAY: SOUVENIR OF ITS CELEBRATION: 1099
MARKET DRAYTON, England: 5394
MARKETING: see as subheading under types of products, e.g. COMMERCIAL PRODUCTS--Marketing, and under businesses, e.g. PUBLISHERS AND PUBLISHING--Marketing
MARKHAM, Allan Byron, Sr.: 3514
MARKHAM, Benjamin: 3515
MARKHAM, Thomas R.: 2576
MARKHAM, William, Archbishop of York: 2148
MARKLAND, A. H.: 3516
MARKLE, C. P.: 213
MARKS, Louis L.: 3517
MARKS, Marcus M.: 5572
MARKS (S.) AND COMPANY, Roseburg, Oregon: 3518
MARKS, Samuel H.: 375
MARL:
  North Carolina: 641
  South Carolina: 3123
    Mining: 1019
MARLBORO, Massachusetts: 4608
MARLBORO, South Carolina: 2664
MARLBORO COUNTY, South Carolina:
  Bennettsville: 3445
MARLBORO DISTRICT, South Carolina:
  Civil War: 565
  Slave insurrection plot: 2267
MARLBOROUGH, John Churchill, First Duke of: 5872
MARLOWE, Julia: 2537
MARQUIS, Donald Robert Perry: 2449
MARRETT, S. S.: 3519
MARRIAGE: 5747
  see also DIVORCE; ELOPEMENTS; HONEYMOONS; INTERRACIAL MARRIAGE; MARITAL SCANDALS; MARITAL SEPARATION; MARRIAGE CONTRACTS; MARRIAGE LICENSES; MARRIAGE SETTLEMENTS; MARRIED LIFE; WEDDINGS
  International: 3183
  Prospects--California: 2370
  Royalty: see Royal family under names of countries
  Subdivided by place:
    Georgia: 3625
    Great Britain: 2227
    India--Bengal: 2756
    Natal: 1792
    North Carolina: 1389, 5298
    South Carolina: 4310

MARRIAGE:
  Subdivided by place (Continued):
    United States: 1670, 5968
    Virginia: 2728, 4020, 5248
MARRIAGE CONTRACTS:
  Georgia: 4768, 4988, 5986
  Great Britain: 4934
  South Carolina: 5193
  United States: 1926
MARRIAGE LICENSES:
  North Carolina: 1107
MARRIAGE SETTLEMENTS:
  North Carolina: 2926
MARRIED LIFE:
  see also BACHELORHOOD; LOVE LETTERS; SLAVES--Married life
  Massachusetts: 1230
  New York: 5360
  South Carolina: 4350
  United States: 99
  Virginia: 1827
MARRIOTT, William: 369
MARROW BONE, Kentucky: 57
MARS (brig): 2637
MARS HILL, North Carolina: see MARS HILL COLLEGE
MARS HILL BAPTIST CHURCH (Georgia): 2326
MARS HILL COLLEGE, Mars Hill, North Carolina: 274
MARSEILLES, France:
  Description: 577
MARSH, George Perkins: 1848
MARSH, Isaac: 3520
MARSH, J. T.: 2146
MARSH, Jonathan: 3521
MARSH, Lucius B.: 3522
MARSH, Margaret (Mitchell): 103
MARSH, Othniel Charles: 641
MARSH FARM, Virginia: 3819
MARSH, TALBOT, AND WILMARTH COMPANY, Boston, Massachusetts: 3522
MARSHALL, Alexander W., Jr.: 1017
MARSHALL, Anne Eliza: 3527
MARSHALL, C. K. (minister): 1844
MARSHALL, Charles (Pennsylvania): 1733
MARSHALL, Charles Kimball (Mississippi): 3523
MARSHALL, Edward Carrington: 1589
MARSHALL, Eugene: 3524
MARSHALL, Francis: 3525
MARSHALL, John (1755-1835): 99, 1308, 2776, 3526, 4616
MARSHALL, John Warren Waldo (1820-1904): 3527
MARSHALL, Mary Willis (Ambler): 99
MARSHALL, Matthias Murray: 3528, 5457
MARSHALL, Mrs. R. H.: 3531
MARSHALL, W. L.: 3525
MARSHALL, William B. (Virginia): 3529
MARSHALL, William Rainey (1825-1896): 4029
MARSHALL FAMILY (South Carolina): 1017, 3527, 3531
MARSHALL FAMILY (Virginia): 99
MARSHALL, North Carolina: 4548
MARSHALL, Texas: 2117, 4286
MARSHALL, Virginia:
  Blacksmiths' accounts: 3582
MARSHALL AND HORNBLOWER (firm): see HORNBLOWER AND MARSHALL
MARSHALL AND PARKER, Albemarle, North Carolina (firm): 3530
MARSHALL COUNTY, Mississippi:
  Byhalia: 2487, 5621
MARSHALL COUNTY, West Virginia: 2320
MARSHALL FIELD AND COMPANY: 1195
MARSHALL ISLANDS: see BIKINI, Marshall Islands; KWAJALEIN, Marshall Islands
MARSHALLTOWN, Iowa:
  Baseball: 5293
MARSHFIELD, Massachusetts:
  Civil War: 1850
MARSTELLER, Le Claire A.: 3532
MARSTELLER, P. G.: 3532
MARSTELLER, Philip F.: 3532

MARSTELLER, Samuel Arell: 3532
MARSTON, John Westland: 1910
MARTHENKE, Harold S.: 1193
MARTIAL LAW: see CIVIL WAR--
    MARTIAL LAW
MARTIAU, Nicholas: 4894
MARTIN, Alexander: 305
MARTIN, Arthur Patchett: 39
MARTIN, Benjamin F.: 3533
MARTIN, E. Barton: 3534
MARTIN, Eunice: 1424
MARTIN, François Xavier: 2674
MARTIN, J. L.: 2662
MARTIN, James Green: 2617
MARTIN, James R.: 3535
MARTIN, Joel: 1446
MARTIN, John (Georgia): 3536
MARTIN, John K. (Virginia): 3537
MARTIN, John P.: 2696
MARTIN, John Sanford (North
    Carolina): 3538
MARTIN, Julia (Glascock): 3534
MARTIN, Luther: 3539
MARTIN, Morgan: 3540
MARTIN, Myra C.: 3541
MARTIN, Rawley White: 3542
MARTIN, Rebecca E.: 3546
MARTIN, Rowena: 3543
MARTIN, Sue A. (Richmond): 3544
MARTIN, Sir Theodore: 2471
MARTIN, Sir Thomas Byam (1773-1854):
    1599
MARTIN, Thomas Staples (1847-1919):
    5152
MARTIN, W. M.: 1691
MARTIN, Warren Frederick: 3545
MARTIN, William A. (South Carolina):
    3546
MARTIN, William E. (South Carolina):
    2612
MARTIN, William Joseph (1830-1896):
    5457
MARTIN COUNTY, North Carolina: 183,
    1639, 3089, 4929
    Baptist churches: 4931
    Civil War: 1190
    Courts of Equity: 3936
    Estate accounts: 4849
    Estates--Administration and
        settlement: 5036
    Farming: 5036
    Hiring of slaves: 5036
    Land grants: 4849
    Plantations: 5036
    Slaves--Lists: 4849
    Social life and customs: 4930
    Tax lists: 2284, 3935
    Tax receipts: 4849
    Tobacco warehouses: 4849
    Wills: 4849
    Cities and towns:
        Hamilton: 435, 707
            Physicians' accounts: 5600
            Schools: 1411
        Robersonville: 4500
        Williamston: 435, 448, 486, 914,
            2244, 2655, 5124, 5125
            Baptist churches: 4843
            Brick trade: 5036
            Civil War: 271
            Land deeds and indentures: 4824
            Lumber trade: 4824
            Mercantile affairs: 2419
            Merchants: 4849
            Physicians' accounts: 5943
MARTINDALE, Lieutenant _____: 5008
MARTINEAU, Harriet: 4520
MARTINEAU, John: 3568
MARTINIQUE:
    British conquest (1809): 400
    Prisoner exchange (1779): 3315
    Trade and commerce:
        Lumber: 21
        Naval stores: 21
MARTINSBURG, West Virginia:
    1700s-1800s: 1828
    1700s-1900s: 1946, 4732

MARTINSBURG, West Virginia
    (Continued):
    1800s: 1770, 2275, 3005, 3114,
        3556, 4056, 4473, 5239
    1800s-1900s: 595, 3899, 4900
    Banks and banking: 307
    Civil War: 2333, 3654
        see also CIVIL WAR--CAMPAIGNS,
        BATTLES, AND MILITARY ACTIONS--
        West Virginia--Martinsburg
    Debt collection: 5037
    Estates--Administration and
        settlement: 5110
    Flour mills: 3832
    Hats: 5110
    Law practice: 5037
    Liquor manufacturing: 3832
    Merchandise consignments: 3061
    Methodist churches: 3809
    Millers' accounts: 3832
    Musical societies: 5110
    Politics and government: 3832
    Teaching: 2007
    Travel clubs: 5110
    Weather: 5456
MARTINSBURG LIGHT ARTILLERY: 1770
MARTINSVILLE, Virginia: 1013, 1137,
    4130
MARTYN, Henry: 4821
MARTZ, George Jacob: 3547
MARVEL, Ik: see MITCHELL, Donald
    Grant
MARVIN, Charles Frederick: 3618
MARVIN, Lucille Wright (Murchison):
    3548
MARVIN, Reynold: 3041
MARY (brig): 4881
MARY ANN (ship): 153
MARY BALDWIN COLLEGE, Staunton,
    Virginia: 643, 5110
MARY QUEEN OF SCOTS: 5379
MARYLAND:
    Abolition of slavery and
        abolitionist sentiment: 5128
    Advertising:
        House furnishings: 3765
    Agricultural fairs: 660
    Agricultural products: 3254
    Aircraft companies:
        Washington County: 3086
    American literature:
        Baltimore: 2398
    American poetry: 664, 3559, 5166,
        5193
    American Revolution: see
        appropriate subheadings under
        AMERICAN REVOLUTION
    Arithmetic exercise books: 3875
        Frederick County: 4804
    Art--Baltimore: 2398
    Auctions--Baltimore: 4886
    Authorship: 2398, 2985
    Autograph collecting: 2052
    Bank stocks: 166
    Banks and banking: 389, 4081
        Baltimore: 5324
        Washington County: 3086
    Bills of exchange:
        Baltimore: 3971
    Blacksmiths' accounts:
        Montgomery County: 3982
    Bonds--Frederick County: 4457
    Boot and shoe making: 3875
    Boundaries: 4886
    Bridges:
        see also BURNSIDE'S BRIDGE
        Construction:
            Havre de Grace: 4468
        Law and legislation: 4886
    Building construction:
        Baltimore: 2352
    Business accounts:
        West River: 4219
    Business affairs: 260
        Baltimore: 3631, 5680, 5918
        Frederick County: 4457
        Hagerstown: 136, 1958, 2283

MARYLAND:
    Business affairs (Continued):
        Prince Fredericktown: 4844
        Sharpsburg: 979
        Upper Marlboro: 1043
    Business licensing: 4886
    Business schools: 643
    Canals:
        Business affairs: 1008
        Surveys: 4221
    Candelabra: 1245
    Carriages and buggies:
        Prices: 2217
    Catholic Church--Conversion: 2692
    Cemeteries--Baltimore: 4638
    Chandeliers: 1245
    Charter: 3598
    Chloroform in surgery: 2830
    Church of England: 5296
    Civil engineering:
        Students' notebooks: 2669
    Civil War: see appropriate
        subheadings under CIVIL WAR;
        CONFEDERATE STATES OF AMERICA--
        ARMY; UNITED STATES--ARMY--
        Civil War
    Clergy: 665, 4221
        Methodist: 610, 1939, 5328
        Unitarian--Ordination: 4359
    Coal mining: 4732
    Commission merchants:
        Baltimore: 1355, 1442, 2819
    Commodity prices: 2217, 3378,
        3742, 4064
        Baltimore: 1024, 3566, 4732
    Confederate memorabilia: 2202
    Confederate sympathizers: 3378
    Conscientious objectors: 3565
    Contracts:
        Frederick County: 4457
        Sharpsburg: 979
    Convention of 1861: 5059
    Cookery: 2692
    County government:
        Washington County: 3086
    Courts:
        Cases: 5296
        Judgments: 979
        Summonses: 5722
        Frederick County: 4457
        Subdivided by place:
            Cecil County: 5296
            Kent County: 5296
            Queen Annes County: 5296
            Washington County: 3875
        Subdivided by type of court:
            Chancery courts: 2319
            Orphans' courts: 4457
    Courtship: 2217, 5160
        see also MARYLAND--Love letters
    Currency: 1339
    Debt:
        see also MARYLAND--Personal debt
        Imprisonment for: 3742
        Owed to the State: 3539
    Debt collection: 4376, 5296
        Baltimore: 4348
    Democratic Party: 3086, 5059
    Description and travel (1800s):
        33, 3808, 5633
    Diseases:
        Cholera--Baltimore: 5613
        Yellow fever: 3399
    Domestic architecture: 4537
    Economic conditions: 5829
        Civil War: 411
    Education: 1747
        see also MARYLAND--Schools;
            MARYLAND--Teaching
        Student's notebooks: 3888
    Elections:
        1830s: 5247, 5969
        1900s: 3086
        Baltimore (1861): 3264

MARYLAND (Continued):
  Estates (Legal):
    Administration and settlement:
      1700s: 4405, 5296
      1700s-1800s: 4081, 5981
      1800s: 785, 2295, 3254
      1900s: 660
      Baltimore: 4348
      Cecil County: 5296
      Frederick County: 4457
      Harford County: 4537
      Kent County: 4140, 5296
      Queen Annes County: 5296
      Williamsport: 5160
    Appraisal:
      Frederick County: 4457
  Eulogies: 5295
  Evangelical Lutheran Church:
    Smithsburg: 5343
  Exhibitions and fairs:
    Hagerstown: 5866
  Extradition of criminals: 3728
  Farm accounts: 2872, 3254
    Beaver Creek District: 3329
    Frederick County: 340
  Farm life: 3254, 3378
  Farming: 1932, 2214, 2295
    see also MARYLAND--Plantations;
      and names of specific crops
      under MARYLAND
    Frederick County: 340
  Finance:
    see also MARYLAND--Personal
      finance; MARYLAND--Public
      finance
    Baltimore: 3053
  Financial societies:
    Baltimore: 3971
  Flour mills: 5763
    see also MARYLAND--Millers'
      accounts
    Ceresville Mills: 4803
    Frederick County: 4457
  Fortifications: 2669
  Free Negroes:
    Montgomery County: 3982
    Planned insurrection in
      Frederick County: 5829
  Fugitive slaves--Capture: 4892
  Gardens and gardening:
    Baltimore: 3298
  Gas lighting--Baltimore: 2265
  Governesses: 3809
  Government agencies and officials:
    Board of Education: 5866
    Colonial period:
      Governors:
        Horatio Sharpe (1752-1769):
          3598
      Executive Council:
        Clerks: 1329, 4221
    Governors:
      John Hoskins Stone (1794-1797):
        667, 5086
      Levin Winder (1812-1815): 5829
      Charles Carnan Ridgeley
        (1815-1818): 4474
      Joseph Kent (1826-1829): 4905
      Francis Thomas (1841-1844):
        3378
      Albert Cabell Ritchie
        (1920-1935): 3267
    Sheriffs:
      Washington County: 3875
  Grain boats: 489
  Guardianship--Orphans: 2295
  Harrows: 5193
  Historical societies: 3598
  History--Student's notebook: 3888
  Hospitals: 3399
  House furnishings:
    Cumberland: 3765
  Household accounts: 785, 2295
    Elkton: 4468
    West River: 4219
  Houses--Baltimore: 2398
  Hymns--Methodist church: 610
  Insurance--Baltimore: 4348

MARYLAND (Continued):
  Iron industry--Baltimore: 1169
  Judaism--Baltimore: 2811
  Justices of the peace: 5722
    Frederick County: 4457
  Know-Nothing Party: 4457
  Land: 2295, 2605
    see also MARYLAND--Public land
    Prices: 3742
    Purchases and sales: 5296, 5353
  Land deeds and indentures:
    1674: 2853
    1800s: 1958, 2295, 4468
    1800s-1900s: 5488
    Cecil County: 5296
    Charles County: 5089
    Frederick County: 112, 4457
    Harford County: 4537
    Kent County: 5296
    Queen Annes County: 5296
    Sharpsburg: 979
    Washington County: 2838
  Land grants: 4457
    To the United States: 5436
  Landlord and tenant: 2295
  Law:
    Codification: 5296
    Students' notebooks: 5296
  Law practice: 3539, 4712, 5296
    Baltimore: 2985, 3598
  Lawsuits:
    Cumberland: 3190
    Montgomery County: 3982
  Lawyers' accounts:
    see also MARYLAND--Legal fees
    Hagerstown: 5981
  Lectures and lecturing: 2692
    Baltimore: 3092
  Legal affairs: 2319, 3006, 5181
    Baltimore: 3754
    Charles County: 5089
    Frederick County: 4457
    Hagerstown: 1958, 5981
    Sharpsburg: 979
  Legal fees-Baltimore: 4348
  Legal organizations: 3086
    Washington County: 3086
  Legislature:
    1700s: 5296
    1800s: 2552, 4886, 4905, 5089
      Apportionment: 5247
    1900s: 3086
    House of Delegates:
      1700s-1800s: 4457
      1800s: 4886, 5160
  Literary interests: 648, 5193
    Baltimore: 2042
  Locofoco Party: 2711
    Frederick: 5324
  Lords Proprietors: 4405
  Lotteries: 4348, 4732, 4892, 5763
  Love letters: 3486
    see also MARYLAND--Courtship
    Baltimore: 3742
  Lumber--West River: 2267
  Marital scandals: 3378
  Masonry:
    Convention in Baltimore: 1438
  Medical education: 2537
    see also BALTIMORE MEDICAL
      COLLEGE; UNIVERSITY OF
      MARYLAND--Medical education
    Students' notebooks: 3399
  Medical practice: 1932, 3378
  Medical treatment: 664
  Mercantile accounts: 665
    Baltimore: 1616, 3579, 4348,
      5933
    Beaver Creek District: 3329
    Charles County: 984
    Cumberland: 3765
    Hagerstown: 136, 161
    Montgomery County: 3982
    Westminster: 3326
  Merchants: 785, 1386, 1487, 1764
    see also MARYLAND--Commission
      merchants

MARYLAND:
  Merchants (Continued):
    Baltimore: 1405, 1647, 2265,
      2412, 4288, 4348, 5213
    Charles County: 984
    Westminster: 3326
  Methodist churches:
    Baltimore Conference
      (Independent): 3646
  Militia: 1535, 2059, 4886
    Artillery: 3627
    Commissions: 3378
    Finance: 4221
    Ordnance: 3627
    1st Light Division: 5059
  Millers' accounts:
    see also MARYLAND--Flour mills
    Frederick County: 4457
    Washington County: 2838, 3875
  Missionary societies:
    Frederick County: 3804
  Mortgages: 2295, 5193
    Baltimore: 4886
  Optical surgery--Baltimore: 2830
  Orphanages: 3026
  Overseers: 2267, 5193
  Performing arts--Baltimore: 2398
  Periodicals: 2398
  Personal debt: 3742, 4081
  Personal finance: 292, 2484
    Baltimore: 4348, 4886, 5763
    Frederick County: 4457
  Pharmacists' accounts:
    Baltimore: 4348, 5800
  Philosophy--Student's notebook:
    3888
  Physicians:
    Personal finance: 1647
  Physicians' accounts:
    Baltimore: 4348, 5800
  Plantations: 743, 785, 1416
    see also MARYLAND--Farming;
      MARYLAND--Overseers; and
      specific crops under MARYLAND
  Plows, Steam powered: 5193
  Poetry: 3998
    Collections: 3559
  Poets--Women: 3559
  Political patronage: 596
    Washington County: 3086
  Politics and government:
    1700s: 2267, 5086
    1700s-1800s: 3627
    1800s: 3378, 4712, 4886
    1810s: 4542, 5829
    1840s: 5089
    1860s: 5059, 5775
    1870s: 5866
    1880s: 5866
    1890s: 5866
    1900s: 3086
    Local politics:
      Frederick County: 4457
      Washington County: 3086
  Poorhouses: 3026
  Poverty: 411
  Presidential election of 1824:
    4359
  Prisoners and prisons:
    see also CIVIL WAR--PRISONERS
      AND PRISONS
    Baltimore: 3267
    Washington County: 3875
  Promissory notes:
    Frederick County: 4457
    Sharpsburg: 979
  Property evaluation: 5296
    Frederick County: 4457
  Protestant Episcopal Church:
    Baltimore: 4638
  Psychology:
    Students' notebooks: 3888
  Psycho-physics:
    Students' notebooks: 3888
  Public celebrations:
    Baltimore: 149
  Public finance: 4886
  Public lands: 5296

MARYLAND (Continued):
  Pulp and paper industry:
    Baltimore: 2265
  Railroad law: 4886
  Railroads: 4468, 5059
    Construction--Cumberland: 721
  Religion: 1032, 1909, 3212, 3998, 5128
  Religious poetry: 5166
  Riots:
    Baltimore:
      1768: 3598
      1861: 3264
  School boards:
    Washington County: 3086
  Schools: 643, 2974
    Boys' schools and academies: 2692
    Girls' schools and academies: 489, 2301, 3053
      Baltimore: 5298
    Students and student life:
      Charlotte Hall: 5329
      Ellicott's Mills: 3360, 4022, 5982
      Hagerstown: 5664
    Students' compositions: 1747
    Students' notebooks:
      West River: 2267
    Subdivided by place:
      Baltimore: 3607, 4866
      Charlotte Hall: 5296
      Frederick County: 4804
  Secession and secessionist sentiment: 314, 1403, 4748, 5059, 5315
  Sermons: 3998
  Shipping: 4886
    Baltimore: 1442, 4348
    Coastwise shipping: 5776
  Shoemakers' accounts:
    Baltimore: 1616
  Slave trade: 2295
    Frederick County: 4457
  Slavery--Emancipation: 4712
  Slaves--Insurrections: 5829
  Snow: 3254
  Social life and customs: 743, 2838, 3809, 5059, 5128
    Baltimore: 1355
    Ellicott's Mills: 3360
  Society of Friends: 3026, 5128
  Stagecoach lines: 166
  Steel industry--Baltimore: 1169
  Storms--Baltimore: 149
  Sunday closing laws: 4886
  Sunday schools--Smithburg: 5343
  Surgery: 3378
    see also MARYLAND--Optical surgery
  Surveys and surveying: 2295
    Frederick County: 4457
    Washington County: 2838
  Tanners' accounts: 5722
  Tavern accounts: 5722
    Elkton: 166
    Harford County: 5128
  Taverns and inns: 785
  Taxation: 166, 830, 2295
  Teaching: 1920
    see also MARYLAND--Education; MARYLAND--Schools
  Temperance: 5128
  Textile industry: 1877
  Tobacco: 5295
    Prices: 5295
  Tobacco plantations:
    West River: 2267
  Tobacco trade: 5295
    Advertising: 1586
    West River: 2267
  Trade and commerce:
    Agricultural products: 5213
    Boots and shoes: 1616
    Bricks: 466
    Cloth: 1647
    Cotton: 4858
    Flour: 2797, 4348

MARYLAND:
  Trade and commerce (Continued):
    Food: 4348
    Fruit: 5488
    Ginseng: 4348
    Grain: 3875
      Beaver Creek District: 3329
    Liquor: 4348
    Livestock: 3329
    Manufactured products: 1481
    Real estate: 5981
      Frederick County: 4457
    Slaves: see MARYLAND--Slave trade
    Stoves--Cumberland: 3765
    Tar: 4348
    Tobacco: see MARYLAND--Tobacco trade
    Water pumps--Cumberland: 3765
    Wholesale trade: 1169
  Truck farming on the Eastern shore: 660
  Turnpikes: 5296
  Laws and legislation: 4886
  United Daughters of the Confederacy:
    Baltimore: 2202
  Universities and colleges: 643, 2999
    see also CALVERT COLLEGE; COLLEGE OF ST. JAMES; GOUCHER COLLEGE; JOHNS HOPKINS UNIVERSITY; ST. JOHN'S COLLEGE; ST. MARY'S COLLEGE; UNIVERSITY OF MARYLAND; WESTERN MARYLAND COLLEGE
  Wages and salaries:
    Protestant Episcopal clergy: 4638
  Warrants (Law): 4474
  Weather: 3254, 4712
    see also MARYLAND--Storms
  Wheat--West River: 2267
  Whig Party: 1329, 4064, 4712, 5059, 5969
  Wills:
    1600s: 2853
    1700s: 830, 4405
    1800s: 743
    Baltimore: 3598
    Cecil County: 5296
    Kent County: 4140, 5296
    Port Tobacco: 5089
    Queen Annes County: 5296
"MARYLAND, MY MARYLAND" by James Ryder Randall: 4377
MARYLAND AGRICULTURAL COLLEGE, College Park, Maryland: see UNIVERSITY OF MARYLAND
MARYLAND HISTORICAL SOCIETY: 3598
MARYLAND LOTTERY COMPANY: 4732
MARYLAND REVOLUTIONARY MONUMENT ASSOCIATION: 4468
MARYSVILLE, California: 1221
MASAI (African tribe): 4514
MASDEU, Juan Francisco: 3549
MASON, Armistead Thomson: 3550, 4615
MASON, Augusta S.: 3551
MASON, Benjamin F.: 3555
MASON, Bessie N.: 3552
MASON, Carry: 3560
MASON, Daniel H.: 3555
MASON, David: 2495
MASON, Eleanor Preston: 3553
MASON, Elizabeth (Price): 3560
MASON, Francis: 3560
MASON, George: 2887
MASON, Horatio: 3554
MASON, James: 3555
MASON, James Murray (1798-1871): 1403, 2085, 2180, 3556
  see also TRENT AFFAIR
MASON, Jeremiah: 3041
MASON, John Young (1799-1859): 2551, 3179, 3557, 4531
MASON, Lucy Randolph: 3171, 3558
MASON, Mary Eliza: 3559
MASON, Peyton, Sr.: 4492
MASON, Peyton, Jr.: 4492

MASON, T.: 4615
MASON, Thomson Francis (d. 1820): 3560
MASON, Thomson Francis (d. 1838): 3560
MASON, William (1724-1797): 4543
MASON FAMILY (Virginia): 3560
MASON, Illinois: 5695
MASON AND COMPANY, North Carolina (firm): 3960
MASON AND HEATH (firm): see HEATH AND MASON
MASON COUNTY, Kentucky:
  Maysville: 713
MASON-DIXON LINE: 4348
MASON HALL, North Carolina: 3300
MASON-SLIDELL AFFAIR: see TRENT AFFAIR
MASONRY (fraternal organization):
  see also FRATERNAL SOCIETIES; NEGRO MASONS
  Commissions:
    North Carolina: 2087
  Conventions:
    Maryland--Baltimore: 1438
    North Carolina: 2087
  Political activity: 4202
  Rituals: 2087, 4679
  Schools: see SCHOOLS--Masonic schools
  Subdivided by place:
    Alabama: 3712
    Georgia: 662
    Kentucky: 3199
    Mississippi: 3611
    North Carolina: 1284, 1899, 2330, 3410, 3476, 4834
      Ansonville: 4918
      Durham: 1150, 3781
      Fayetteville: 1898
      Mocksville Lodge No. 134: 2857
      Raleigh: 279
      Wilmington Lodge No. 319: 1899
    Ohio: 801
    Philippine Islands: 4511, 4656
    United States: 1899, 3041
    Virginia: 3855, 4743
      Lodge No. 13: 5184
      Albemarle County: 687
      Chatham:
        Pittsylvania Lodge No. 24: 4233
      Mecklenburg County: 1821
    West Virginia: 1828, 4892
      Berkeley County: 4056
MASSACHUSETTS:
  Abolition of slavery:
    Public opinion: 5034
  Advertising endorsements: 3633
  Agriculture: 3633
    see also the following subheadings under MASSACHUSETTS: Crops; Dairy farms; Farming; and names of specific crops
  Alcoholism: 1230
  American poetry: 1455, 1698
    see also MASSACHUSETTS--Publishers and publishing--Poetry
  American Revolution: see appropriate subheadings under AMERICAN REVOLUTION
  Authors and publishers:
    Boston: 4069
    Cambridge: 2400
  Authorship: 2400, 4037
  Autograph collecting: 4189
  Autographs: 4807
    Pittsfield: 1455
    Volunteer militia: 3562
  Bankruptcy: 4807
  Banks and banking:
    Boston: 5499, 5628
  Biographical studies: 1792
  Boarding houses: 4807
  Business accounts: 148
  Business affairs--Boston: 1902
  Canals--Boston area: 1433

827

MASSACHUSETTS (Continued):
  Carpentry--Milford: 3328
  Christian Science: 487
    Boston: 5266
  Civil War: see appropriate
    subheadings under CIVIL WAR;
    UNITED STATES--ARMY--Civil War
  Clergy:
    Baptist: 4125
    Leverett: 2407
  Coast defenses: 3283
  Commission merchants: 2933
  Commodity prices: 2677, 4050
    Boston: 2431
  Congregational churches: 5088
  Constitutional conventions (1853):
    2044
  Corporations--Boston: 5093
  Courts: 1222
    Cases: 3034
      Boston: 5093
  Crops: 2677
    see also specific kinds of crops
      under MASSACHUSETTS
  Currency: 1339
  Dairy farms--Management: 2532
  Democratic Party: 988
  Description and travel: 4944
  Economic conditions:
    see also MASSACHUSETTS--Panic
      of 1819
    Brockton: 3524
  Education: 4125
    see also MASSACHUSETTS--Schools;
      MASSACHUSETTS--Teaching
    Springfield: 5043
    Women--Brockton: 3524
  Eight-hour day: 803
  Embargo (Jeffersonian):
    Effects on Taunton merchants:
      5298
  Episcopal churches: 5499
  Estates (Legal):
    Administration and settlement:
      1344, 2468
      Boston: 323
    Appraisal--Taunton: 5499
  Farming: 427
    see also the following under
      MASSACHUSETTS: Agriculture;
      Crops, and specific kinds of
      crops; Dairy farms
  Fishing industry--Worcester: 4314
  Foreign trade: 323
    China: 1839
    Europe: 5777
    West Indies: 5777
  Fraud: 609
  Governesses: 4881
  Government agencies and officials:
    Adjutant General: 1474
    Colonial period:
      Governors:
        Sir Francis Bernard
          (1760-1769): 5298
    Governors:
      John Davis (1841-1843): 1404
      John Albion Andrew (1861-1866):
        3283
  Historical studies: 4305
    Criticism: 1431
  Household accounts: 4807
  Immigration and emigration:
    Brockton: 3524
  Industrialization--Brockton: 3524
  Insanity: 1054
  Insurance: 1119
  Internal improvements: 1433
  Justices of the peace: 3034
    Becket: 5766
  Kindergartens--Boston: 3295
  Labor disputes--Brockton: 3524
  Labor unions: 803
  Lace prices: 1839
  Land: 1344, 4653
  Land deeds and indentures: 2468,
    3034, 5766
    Suffolk County: 1431

MASSACHUSETTS (Continued):
  Land speculation: 5766
  Law practice--Boston: 5762
  Lawsuits: 5665
  Lectures and lecturing: 776, 4409
    Boston: 1219
  Legal affairs: 4653
    Boston: 5093
    Brookline: 5846
  Legal education: see HARVARD
    UNIVERSITY--Law School
  Legal fees: 3034
  Legislature: 2532
    Seating of members: 3034
  Libraries: 1747
    Private: 5754
  Local elections:
    Boxborough: 2456
  Love letters--Boston: 3491
  Married life: 1230
  Medical education:
    see also HARVARD UNIVERSITY--
      Medical education
    Brockton: 3524
  Medical practice: 856
  Medical treatment: 1344
  Medicine--Prescriptions: 856
  Mercantile affairs--Boston: 3459
  Merchandise: 3034
  Merchants: 1839
    see also MASSACHUSETTS--
      Commission merchants
    Becket: 5766
    Boston: 5777
  Militia: 1474, 5085
    Hampshire County: 3034
    Military uniforms: 3522
  Mortgages: 2417, 3633, 5766
  Murder trials: 4813
  Nativism--Brockton: 3524
  Nullification, Opinion of: 1433
  Panic of 1819: 2677
  Personal debt: 3034, 4807
  Personal finance: 1344, 4125, 4274
    Lowell: 803
  Political unrest--Boston: 5298
  Politics and government (1800s):
    1433, 3037, 5762, 5917
  Prohibition: 4125
    see also MASSACHUSETTS--Temperance
  Promissory notes: 3633
  Public welfare:
    Overseers in Boston: 3561
  Publishers and publishing:
    Poetry: 5193
  Race relations: 803
  Railroads: 2608
    Boston area: 1433
  Real estate: 484, 2468
  Religion: 1792, 4125
  Riots in Boston (1863): 5563
  School boards: 4807
  School furniture--Prices: 2417
  School furniture industry: 2417
  Schools: 743, 1423
    Curriculum--Springfield: 5043
    Preparatory schools: 339
    Students' compositions: 4807
    Textile engineering: 4918
    Subdivided by place:
      East Hampton: 4897
      Monson: 4897
      South Hadley: 4897
      Southborough: 1423
      Stockbridge: 1792
  Sermons: 977, 1236
  Shipbuilding: 1344
  Shipping: 4653
    see also MASSACHUSETTS--Foreign
      trade
    Coastwise shipping: 4304
    Boston: 3578, 5777, 5860
    Bridgewater: 2959
  Silk prices: 1839
  Slaves--Women: 5665
  Social life and customs: 4125
    Andover: 3034
    Boston: 4813

MASSACHUSETTS:
  Social life and customs
    (Continued):
    Exeter: 2410
    Fall River: 2035
    Sons of Liberty--Boston: 5298
    Southern opinion of: 706
    Storms: 3057
  Taxation: 2417
  Teaching: 1699, 5088
    see also MASSACHUSETTS--
      Education; MASSACHUSETTS--
      Schools
    South Yarmouth: 2436
  Temperance: 1344, 4125
  Textile machinery: 5100
  Textile mills--Lowell: 776
  Theological seminaries: see
    ANDOVER THEOLOGICAL SEMINARY
  Theological students: 3142
  Tolls--Bridges: 2304
  Town meetings--Boxborough: 2456
  Trade and commerce: 323
    see also MASSACHUSETTS--Foreign
      trade; MASSACHUSETTS--Shipping
    Agricultural products: 3034
    Cloth: 992
    Groceries: 1344
    Lumber: 1732
    Milk--West Acton: 2456
    School furniture: 2417
    Sugar: 1736, 2641
    Tobacco: 1633, 5251
    Turpentine: 1732
    Wholesale trade: 1169
  United States Post Office:
    Becket: 5766
  Universities and colleges: 743
    see also HARVARD UNIVERSITY;
      SMITH COLLEGE; WELLESLEY
      COLLEGE; WILLIAMS COLLEGE
  Wages and salaries--Teachers: 1344
  Water rights: 2468
  Whig Party: 743
  Wills: 706, 2468, 3034, 5499
  Women's rights: 5088
MASSACHUSETTS, U.S.S.: 3899
MASSACHUSETTS SINGLE TAX LEAGUE:
  2225
MASSACHUSETTS VOLUNTEER MILITIA:
  3562
MASSACRES--Kenya: 4514
MASSEE, Jordan: 902
MASSENBURG, Lucy C.: 3563
MASSEY, Lucius S.: 3564
MASSEY, Thomas: 3566
MASSEY, William: 3566
MASSIE, John W.: 3565
MASSIE, Thomas (d. 1834): 3566
MASSIE, William: 3566
MASSIE FAMILY (Virginia--Genealogy):
  1842, 3566
MASSY, Lucy Maria (Butler), Baroness
  Massy: 3567
MASTEN, Cornelius: 3568
MASTER BUILDERS' EXCHANGE OF
  PHILADELPHIA, Philadelphia,
  Pennsylvania: 3569
MASTS AND RIGGING: see SHIPS--Masts
  and rigging
MASTERS, Thomas: 3570
MATAMORAS, Mexico:
  Politics and government: 3392
MATANZAS, Cuba: 1442
MATCHAPUNGO ACADEMY, Belhaven,
  Virginia: 1697
MATEJKO, Aleksander: 3571
MATHEMATICS:
  see also ARITHMETIC
  Students' notebooks: 632
    New Jersey:
      Princeton University: 2521
    Virginia:
      University of Virginia: 5288
      Washington and Lee University:
        4616
  Study and teaching: 1004
    Mississippi: 1506

MATHESON, R. B.: 3572
MATHEWS, Mr._____(North Carolina): 4262
MATHEWS, Cornelius: 2612
MATHEWS, George: 2778, 3573
MATHEWS, Shailer: 706
MATHEWS, Tandy B.: 3574
MATHEWS FAMILY (Virginia): 3574
MATHEWS COUNTY, Virginia: 4585
  North End: 5165
MATHEWSON, G. H.: 3575
MATHILDA (novel): 2058
MATLOCK, John: 208, 3576
MATON, William George (Great Britain, 1774-1835): 3577
MATTON, William George (North Carolina, fl. 1859-1887): 3581
"MATTAPONI," Maryland: 596
MATTAWOMAN, Maryland: 3559
MATTHEWS, A. C.: 2662
MATTHEWS, Alexander: 5089
MATTHEWS, Franklin: 4021
MATTHEWS, George: 3578
MATTHEWS, J. M.: 764
MATTHEWS, James Brander: 103, 3797, 5044
MATTHEWS, James S.: 3579
MATTHEWS, John A.: 1396
MATTHEWS, R. S.: 3789
MATTHEWS CIRCUIT, Methodist churches: 3646
MATTHEWSON, J. B.: 3580
MATTHIESON AND COMPANY: see GOURDIN, MATTHIESON AND COMPANY
MATTHISON, Edith Wynne: 3797
MATTOON, Stephen: 5238
MATTOON, Wilbur Reed: 4453
MATTOX, James T.: 3582
MAUDE AND WRIGHT, Georgia (firm): 3583
MAULE, William: 5457
MAULSBERG, Benjamin: 3584
MAUMEE RIVER (Ohio): 443
MAUMELLE, Arkansas: 1438
MAURICE, John Frederick Denison: 2471
MAURITANIA--Cholera: 3485
MAURITIUS: 2421
MAURY, Ann Hull (Herndon): 3587
MAURY (C. W.) AND COMPANY, New York: 3587
MAURY, Dabney Herndon: 1186, 3585, 3586, 3754
MAURY, Elie: 3587
MAURY, John H.: 3587
MAURY, Lucy: 3587
MAURY, Matthew Fontaine (1806-1873): 3586, 3587
MAURY, Matthew Fontaine III (b. 1863): 3587
MAURY, Richard Launcelot: 3587
MAURY, Ruston: 3586
MAURY, Susan Gatewood (Crutchfield): 3587
MAURY FAMILY (Virginia--Genealogy): 3587
MAURY AND LETCHER, Lexington, Virginia (firm): 3587
MAURY COUNTY, Tennessee: 4269
  Columbia: 2661, 4209
    see also JACKSON COLLEGE
  Spring Hill: 5452
MAVISBROOK, H.M.S.: 4355
MAVROCORDATO, Prince Alexander: 4770
MAXCY, Jonathan: 3588
MAXCY, Virgil: 3589, 4191
MAXEY, Georgia: 3604
MAXEY, Samuel Bell: 3590
MAXIMILIAN, Emperor of Mexico: 3587
MAXIMILIAN JOSEPH, King of Bavaria: 4745
MAXSE, Leopold James: 2146
MAXTON, North Carolina: 5740
  see also SHOE HEEL, North Carolina
MAXWELL, Elizabeth: 5457
MAXWELL, Hugh: 4518
MAXWELL, James H.: 2721
MAXWELL, Sarah P.: 3591

MAXWELL, Sir William: 3592
MAY, Charles W.: 3596
MAY, David: 3593
MAY, Edward Thomas: 3596
MAY, James: 128
MAY, John Frederick: 3594
MAY HOSIERY MILLS, Burlington, North Carolina: 2108, 3595
MAY McEWEN KAISER COMPANY, INC., Burlington, North Carolina: 1353, 2108, 3595, 4812
MAYBANK, Eliza G.: 5193
MAYBERRY, W. W.: 3597
MAYBINTON, South Carolina: 2335
MAYER, Brantz: 3598
MAYER, Charles F.: 3598
MAYER, Christian: 3598
MAYER, Minor C.: 3599
MAYES, Annie Elizabeth (Stuart): 1506
MAYES, Robert Burns: 1506
MAYFIELD, Sara: 2398
MAYHEW, D. F.: 3600
MAYNARD, Edward: 2552
MAYNARD RIFLE: 2552
MAYO, Peter: 872
MAYO, Richard Southwell Bourke, Sixth Earl of: 587, 1857
MAYO MILLS: 1584
MAYOR'S COMMITTEE ON HUMAN RELATIONS, Durham, North Carolina: 4736
MAYSVILLE, Kentucky: 713
MAYSVILLE, North Carolina: 3607
MAYVILLE, New York: 5322
MAZATLAN, Mexico:
  Mexican War:
    American occupation: 3118
    Blockade: 3809
MAZZINI, Giuseppe: 1503
MAZZONI, Guido: 2056
MEACHAM, James (1763-1820): 1848
MEACHAM, James (1810-1856): 3601
MEAD, William: 1733
MEAD FAMILY (Virginia--Genealogy): 1842
MEADE, Ann Randolph: 128
MEADE, Anne: 558
MEADE, Curtis G.: 3602
MEADE, David: 558, 1512
MEADE, George (d. 1897): 3603
MEADE, George Gordon (1815-1872): 254, 820, 2270, 2306, 3603
MEADE, Hodijah: 4616
MEADE, Jane (Rutherfoord): 4616
MEADE, Mary (Randolph): 128
MEADE, R. Kidder: 724
MEADE, Richard K.: 1512
MEADE, William: 128, 2513, 3141
MEADE FAMILY (Virginia): 128, 558
MEADE (firm): see McKIM, MEADE, AND WHITE
MEADE COUNTY, Kentucky:
  Brandenburg: 571
MEADOWS, Elizabeth: 3604
MEADOWS, John: 3604
MEADOWS, Sophronia: 3604
MEADOWS, Squire: 208, 3605
MEAD'S (MRS.) SCHOOL, Richmond, Virginia: 5513, 5529
MEAGHER, James: 3606, 5952
MEAL--Virginia: 490
MEAL TRADE--Alabama: 5006
MEARES, Adelaide Savage: 3607
MEARES, Oliver Pendleton: 5457
MEARES, Walker: 3607
MEARES FAMILY (North Carolina--Genealogy): 3607
MEASLES: see CIVIL WAR--DISEASES--Measles; DISEASES--Measles
MEASUREMENT OF SHIPS: see SHIPPING--Measurement of ships
MEAT BISCUITS, Manufacture of:
  Texas: 3325
MEAT PACKING INDUSTRY:
  Eastern States: 4606
MEAT SUPPLY AGENTS: see CONFEDERATE STATES OF AMERICA--ARMY--Meat supply agents

MEBANE, North Carolina:
  Schools: 3300, 4321, 5298, 5912
MEBANESVILLE, North Carolina: see MEBANE, North Carolina
MECCA, Saudi Arabia: 118
MECHANICS' INSTITUTE, Sheffield, England: 4234
MECKLENBURG COUNTY, North Carolina: 1781, 2476, 5518
  Arithmetic exercise book: 208
  Public schools: 3608
  Textile mills: 5235
  Cities and towns:
    Charlotte: see CHARLOTTE, North Carolina
    Davidson: see DAVIDSON COLLEGE
MECKLENBURG COUNTY, Virginia: 2935, 3145
  Confederate tax in kind: 1181
  Mercantile accounts: 4885
  Merchants: 799
  Overseers: 3809
  Plantation accounts: 4848
  Cities and towns:
    Boydton: 600, 4186
      Merchants: 362
    Clarksville: 4263, 5186
      Railroad accounts: 4846
      Taxation: 4848
    Flat Creek Township: 1821
    Lombardy Grove: 363
MECKLENBURG DECLARATION OF INDEPENDENCE: 1399, 5667
  Historical studies: 305
MEDFORD, Massachusetts: 2641
MEDICAL AND CHIRURGICAL FACULTY (Maryland): 3378
MEDICAL AND SANITARY AFFAIRS: see as subheading under names of armies and navies
MEDICAL BOOKS--New York: 4351
MEDICAL COLLEGE OF SOUTH CAROLINA:
  Acids--Students' notebooks: 1371
  Dissertations: 1371
MEDICAL COLLEGE OF VIRGINIA, Richmond, Virginia: 2553, 4589, 5603
MEDICAL EDUCATION: 3297, 5924
  Admission of women to medical colleges: 3390
  Cadavers--Pennsylvania: 531
  Students' notebooks:
    see also MEDICAL NOTEBOOKS
  France: 1300
  Kentucky:
    Transylvania University: 1513
    University of Louisville: 1053
  Maryland:
    University of Maryland: 3399
  Pennsylvania: 2622, 5771
    University of Pennsylvania: 3609, 3675
  South Carolina:
    Medical College of South Carolina: 1371
  Virginia: 1509
  Subdivided by place:
    France: 1300
    Georgia:
      Atlanta: see ATLANTA MEDICAL COLLEGE
      Augusta: 2903
    Germany--Bavaria: 174
    Great Britain: see GREAT BRITAIN--ARMY--Army Medical School
    Kentucky: see TRANSYLVANIA UNIVERSITY; UNIVERSITY OF LOUISVILLE--Medical Department
    Louisiana: see TULANE UNIVERSITY--Medical education
    Maryland: 2537
      see also BALTIMORE MEDICAL COLLEGE; UNIVERSITY OF MARYLAND--Medical education

MEDICAL EDUCATION:
    Subdivided by place (Continued):
        Massachusetts:
            see also HARVARD UNIVERSITY--
                Medical education
            Brockton: 3524
        Michigan: see UNIVERSITY OF
            MICHIGAN--Medical education
        Missouri: see WASHINGTON
            UNIVERSITY--School of Medicine
        New York:
            see also BELLEVUE HOSPITAL
                MEDICAL SCHOOL
            Albany: 5974
            New York: 3221
        North Carolina: see DUKE
            UNIVERSITY--Medical Center;
            WAKE FOREST UNIVERSITY--
            School of Medicine; UNIVERSITY
            OF NORTH CAROLINA AT CHAPEL
            HILL--Medical School
        Ohio: see PHYSIO-MEDICAL COLLEGE
            OF OHIO
        Pennsylvania: 490
            Philadelphia: 872, 2935, 3788
            see also JEFFERSON MEDICAL
                COLLEGE; UNIVERSITY OF
                PENNSYLVANIA--Medical
                education
        South Carolina: see MEDICAL
            COLLEGE OF SOUTH CAROLINA
        Tennessee: see UNIVERSITY OF
            NASHVILLE--Medical education
        Virginia: 2553, 2949
            see also MEDICAL COLLEGE OF
                VIRGINIA; UNIVERSITY OF
                VIRGINIA--Medical education
        Washington, D.C.: 3788
MEDICAL NOTEBOOKS: 5456, 5957
    see also MEDICAL EDUCATION--
        Students' notebooks
    Great Britain: 5095
    North Carolina: 2481, 3410
MEDICAL PRACTICE:
    see also HOMEOPATHY; MEDICAL
        TREATMENT; PHYSICIANS;
        PHYSICIANS' ACCOUNTS
    Alabama: 1856
        Tuscaloosa: 4943
    Georgia: 2903, 5924
        Savannah: 220
    Indiana--Union: 4220
    Kentucky--Hancock County: 3199
    Maryland: 1932, 3378
    Massachusetts: 856
    New York: 1229, 2081
        New York: 4351, 4606
    North Carolina: 2462, 2537, 2714,
        4231, 5771, 5924
        Chatham County: 5541
        Durham: 2934
        Forsyth County: 5982
        Hillsborough: 4890
        Louisburg: 3476
        Nash County: 4820
        Wentworth: 4366
    Ohio: 4076
    Pennsylvania: 4076
    Southern States: 5505
    United States: 904
    Virginia: 1075, 4743
        Amherst County: 3788
    West Virginia: 748
MEDICAL RESERVE CORPS, Asheville,
    North Carolina: 5603
MEDICAL SERVICES:
    see also HEALTH PROGRAMS; HEALTH
        ORGANIZATIONS; HOSPITALS;
        PHYSICIANS' ACCOUNTS
    North Carolina: 1195
        Germanton: 4136
    South Carolina: 2709
    Virginia: 490
MEDICAL SOCIETIES: 2934
    Georgia: 364, 4676
    North Carolina: 2851
        Asheville: 5603

MEDICAL SOCIETIES (Continued):
    Virginia: 3378
MEDICAL SOCIETY OF NORTH CAROLINA:
    2851
MEDICAL SUPPLIES: 1814
    see also CIVIL WAR--MEDICAL
        SUPPLIES
    North Carolina: 3476
    South Carolina--Abbeville: 3527
    Virginia: 4308
MEDICAL TREATISES:
    Great Britain: 4333
    Virginia: 4743
MEDICAL TREATMENT:
    see also DISEASES--(name of
        disease)--Medical treatment;
        HOME REMEDIES; MEDICAL PRACTICE
    Costs: 3332, 3797
    North Carolina: 4858
    South Carolina: 4214
    Use of opium: 3246
    Subdivided by place:
        Alabama: 4184
        Georgia: 2020, 2963
        Germany: 181
        Great Britain: 1541
        Maryland: 664
        Massachusetts: 1344
        North Carolina:
            Person County: 3752
        South Carolina: 669, 1220
        Virginia: 236, 5513, 5742
MEDICAL VETERANS OF THE WORLD WAR,
    Asheville, North Carolina: 5603
MEDICI, Marie de, Queen of France:
    3271
MEDICINE:
    see also CROPS--Medicinal; FAMILY
        MEDICINE; HORSES--Medicine;
        INDUSTRIAL MEDICINE; LIQUOR--
        Medicinal use; MEDICAL SUPPLIES;
        OPIUM; PATENT MEDICINE;
        PHYSICIANS' ACCOUNTS; SOCIALIZED
        MEDICINE; and Medicine as
        subheading under names of armies
        and navies
    Prescriptions: 3325, 3529, 4348
        Rheumatism: 3908
        Arkansas: 1154
        Great Britain: 5095
        Massachusetts: 856
        North Carolina: 509, 675, 3410
        South Carolina: 1220
        United States: 3053
        Virginia: 4743
            Alexandria: 5016
    Prices: 4890
    Confederate States of America:
        4950
    Subdivided by place:
        Alabama: 4184
        Georgia--Lawrenceville: 167
        New Hampshire: 354
        New York: 1229, 4351
        North Carolina: 4030
            Charlotte: 4918
        Pennsylvania: 5305
        United States: 3524
        Virginia:
            Buckingham County: 3794
            Charlottesville: 824
            Fluvanna County: 5839
MEDICINE AND THE PRESS: 2934
MEDILL, Joseph: 2526
MEDILL, William: 1333
MEDINA COUNTY, Ohio: 5132
MEDINA Y JIMENEZ, Don Manuel de:
    3570
"MEDITATIONS HARMONIES POETIODES
    JOCELIN" by Alphonse Marie Louis
    de Lamartine: 3077
"MEDITATIONS SUR LES CONSTITUTIONS
    DES RELIGIEUSES DE L'ORDRE DE
    L'ANONCIADE CELESTE": 4046
MEDITERRANEAN REGION:
    British expansion in: 2836
    Description and travel (1910s): 572

MEDITERRANEAN SEA:
    British naval cruises (1870s):
        2754
    Description and travel:
        1801: 3570
        1838: 3447
    United States naval operations: 636
MEDIUMS: see SEANCES
MEDLEY METHODIST CHURCH, West
    Virginia: 2129
MEDLYCOTT, Elizabeth: 3567
MEDWIN, Thomas: 4770
MEECH, William W.: 3610
MEEK, Alexander Beaufort: 3611
MEEK, Alexander Black: see MEEK,
    Alexander Beaufort
MEEK, Samuel Mills: 3611
MEEKS, Samuel (d. 1836): 4751
MEETZE, Jacob: 1877
MEGEZEE TOWNSHIP, Michigan: 4889
MEGGINSON, Maria L.: 1767
MEGGS FAMILY (North Carolina): 4996
MEGREW, Helen Collins: 3612
MEHAFFEY, Calvin D.: 3613
MEHEMET ALI, Khedive of Egypt: see
    MUHAMMAD 'ALI, Khedive of Egypt
MEHRAB KHAN (ruler of Kelat): 5801
MEIGS (JONA.), Savannah, Georgia
    (firm): 2360
MEIGS, Josiah: 3671
MEIGS, Montgomery Cunningham: 1148
MEIGS, Return Jonathan (1734-1823):
    3614
MEIGS, Return Jonathan (1801-1891):
    872
MEIGS COUNTY, Ohio:
    Pomeroy: 4255
    Rutland: 1223
MEKONG COMMISSION (1890s): 4709
MELBOURNE, Lady Caroline Lamb,
    Viscountess: 3080
MELBOURNE, William Lamb, Second
    Viscount: 3080, 4605
MELBOURNE CENTENNIAL EXHIBITION:
    4567
MELCOMBE, George Bubb Dodington,
    Baron: 2155
MELDRUM, David S.: 1210
MELLICHAMP, E. H.: 2288
MELLON, Andrew William: 879
MELROSE, Virginia: 1617
MELTON, Herman E.: 4894
MELTON, Joseph: 4872
MELTON, Wightman Fletcher: 2449
MELTON FAMILY (Genealogy): 4894
MELVILLE, Henry Dundas, First
    Viscount: 1589, 1913, 2126, 3315
MELVILLE, Herman: 720, 4867
MELVILLE, Robert Saunders, Second
    Viscount: 1599, 2836, 4137
MEMBERSHIP: see as subheading under
    names of organizations and groups,
    e.g. LABOR UNIONS--Membership
MEMENTOS: see CONFEDERATE MEMORABILIA
MEMMINGER, Christopher Gustavus:
    700, 1403, 1439, 3615, 3676, 4616
A MEMOIR OF DANIEL WADSWORTH COIT
    OF NORWICH, CONNECTICUT by
    William C. Gilman: 2046
"MEMOIRS OF JOHN O'NEALE": 3981
"MEMOIRS OF SAMUEL WRAGG FERGUSON":
    1782
MEMOIRS OF THE SECRET SERVICES OF
    JOHN MACKY: 3411
MEMORABILIA: see CONFEDERATE
    MEMORABILIA
MEMORANDUM FROM WASHINGTON: 5234
"MEMORIA " by Angel Luque: 4155
MEMORIAL DAY: 4029
    Addresses: 66
    Celebration: 3910
MEMORIAL FUNDS: 5497
    Great Britain: 4026
    Washington, D.C.: 4697
MEMORIAL SERVICES:
    South Carolina: 3383
    Washington, D.C.: 1953

MEMORIAL SOCIETIES: see CIVIL WAR--
    MEMORIAL SOCIETIES
MEMORIALS: 5252
    see also HISTORIC SITES; MONUMENTS
    Confederate--Stone Mountain: 5090
    Great Britain: 5050
        To Joseph Conrad: 1210
    India: 1343
    North Carolina:
        Duke University: 5252
    Ohio--Cleveland: 5291
    United States: 4927
    Virginia--Lynchburg: 3809
"MEMORIES" by Filipe G. Calderon:
    4511
MEMPHIS, Tennessee: 775, 4253, 4275,
    4894, 4918, 5443
    Civil War: 1854, 1881, 5017
        see also CIVIL WAR--CAMPAIGNS,
            BATTLES, AND MILITARY ACTIONS--
            Tennessee--Memphis
    Commercial convention (1869): 757
    Cotton trade: 4256
    Description: 74, 3552
    Diseases:
        Cholera: 330
        Yellow fever: 4202
    Drugs:
        Wholesale and retail trade: 4288
    Economic conditions: 881
    Evangelism: 3552
    Household finance: 4763
    Merchants: 330
    Militia: 1833
    Personal debt: 5443
    Universities and colleges: see
        SOUTHWESTERN UNIVERSITY; STATE
        FEMALE COLLEGE
MEMPHIS (warship): 701
MEMPHIS AND CHARLESTON RAILROAD:
    5254
MEN AND WOMEN:
    Social relationships: 5042
MENCKEN, August: 2398
MENCKEN, Henry Louis: 103, 879, 2081,
    2390, 2398, 3617, 4290
MENCKEN, Sara Powell (Haardt): 2398
MENCKENIANA: 2398
MENDENHALL, Rachael: 518
MENDENHALL, Thomas Corwin: 3618
MENDOTA (United States gunboat): 460
MENDOZA, García Hurtado de: see
    HURTADO DE MENDOZA, García
MENEFEE, Henry L., Jr.: 3619
MENINGITIS: see DISEASES--Meningitis
MENLOVE, Edward: 3620
MENLOVE, Jane: 3620
MENLOVE, William M.: 3620
MENNIS, Calohill: 3621
MENTAL HEALTH: 2934, 3186, 3390
    see also COUEISM; FORENSIC
        PSYCHIATRY; GUARDIANSHIP--
        Mental incompetence; INSANITY;
        MENTAL HEALTH LAWS; MENTAL
        HOSPITALS; MENTALLY ILL
MENTAL HEALTH LAWS: 958
    see also FORENSIC PSYCHIATRY;
        INSANITY--Jurisprudence
MENTAL HOSPITALS:
    Commitment to: 2779, 4732
    Negroes--North Carolina: 2890
    Subdivided by place:
        Connecticut--Middletown: 5748
        Georgia--Milledgeville: 127
        Kentucky--Lexington: 3325
        New York--White Plains: 958
        North Carolina: 661, 2220
            Morganton: 2890
            Raleigh: 5819
        Virginia: 1920
MENTAL INCOMPETENCE: see
    GUARDIANSHIP--Mental incompetence
MENTAL SCIENCE:
    see also PSYCHOLOGY
    Students' notebooks: 3168

MENTALLY ILL:
    see also FORENSIC PSYCHIATRY;
        GUARDIANSHIP--Mental incompetence;
        INSANITY; MENTAL HOSPITALS
    Colorado: 5426
    Georgia: 5426
    Kentucky: 5426
    Louisiana: 5426
    Tennessee: 5426
    Washington, D.C.: 5426
MENTALLY RETARDED:
    Colorado: 5426
    Georgia: 5426
    Kentucky: 5426
    Louisiana: 5426
    Tennessee: 5426
    Washington, D.C.: 5426
MENUHIN, Yehudi: 83
MENUS: 83
    see also COOKERY
MENZIES, Robert: 3622
MERCANTILE ACCOUNTS: 11, 169, 1293
    see also BARTER
    Alabama: 5006
        Boligee: 4861
        Tompkinsville: 4827
    Georgia: 4988
        Augusta: 138, 2937
        Carroll County: 874
        Crawford: 3974
        Douglas County: 874
        Franklin: 3966
        Gwinnett County: 601
        Lincoln County: 138
        Louisville: 5562
        Middleburg: 2741
        Savannah: 1251, 5216
    Great Britain:
        Bristol: 4541
        London: 5139
    Kentucky--Paw Paw: 4090
    Louisiana:
        New Orleans: 679, 5933
    Maryland: 665
        Baltimore: 1616, 3579, 4348, 5933
        Beaver Creek District: 3329
        Charles County: 984
        Cumberland: 3765
        Hagerstown: 136, 161
        Montgomery County: 3982
        Westminster: 3326
    Mississippi: 802, 2095
        Gallatin: 2355
        Panola: 138
        Rocky Springs: 1077
        Sartartia: 5821
    Missouri:
        Calhoun: 5392
        Millersburg: 5392
    Nebraska: 568
    New Hampshire:
        Grafton County: 71
    New York--Albany: 1281
    North Carolina:
        1700s-1800s: 4080
        1800s: 399, 435, 1800, 2068, 2555,
            2857, 3176, 4047, 4152, 4374,
            4918, 5100, 5298
        1840s: 4150
        1850s: 1919, 4223, 4764
        1860s: 482, 2808, 4764
        1870s: 482, 1394, 2808
        1880s: 2895
        1800s-1900s: 4664
        Abernethy: 147
        Albemarle: 3530
        Alexander County: 3683
        Apex: 5803
        Bath: 3521
        Beattie's Ford: 2277
        Cabarrus County: 4670
        Calahaln: 122
        Caledonia: 3449
        Cane Creek: 2618
        Chapel Hill: 4666
        Chatham County: 5905
        Cherokee County: 5258

MERCANTILE ACCOUNTS:
    North Carolina (Continued):
        Craven County: 3955
        Davidson County: 138, 3241
        Durham: 4480, 4540
        Edenton: 717, 5658
        Fairfield: 511
        Fayetteville: 4517
        Flat River: 3481
        Franklin County: 2824, 2825
        Gold Hill: 3368
        Granville County: 3638, 5960
        Greenville: 1846, 3739
        Hatteras: 4547
        Haywood County: 5258
        Henderson: 95
        Hillsborough: 5728
        Hollywood: 3960
        Iredell County: 1858, 3600, 3787
        Jackson County: 5258
        Liberty: 1777
        Lincoln County: 5976
        Lockville: 5207
        Lowell: 3285
        Manson: 5697
        Middleton: 5592
        Milton: 5815
        Mocksville: 2749
        Montgomery County: 75
        Mount Olive: 5756
        Murfreesboro: 5857
        New Bern: 164, 2167
        Newton: 138
        Norwood: 5589
        Opossum Trot: 80
        Orange County: 1151, 3677
        Oxford: 5685
        Perquimans County: 165, 3874
        Plymouth: 4639
        Quallatown: 4784
        Raleigh: 2589, 2821
        Richmond County: 3167
        Ridgeway: 999, 3307, 5614
        Robeson County: 3398
        Roxboro: 5927
        Scotland Neck: 4925
        Smith Church: 5399
        Smithfield: 5374
        South Lowell: 3140
        Stokes County: 27
        Stowesville: 5100
        Tarboro: 4035
        Wadesboro: 2984, 4762
        Wake County: 1783, 3655, 5136
        Warren County: 910, 4328
        Warrenton: 4389
        Washington: 911, 3827, 4382,
            4571, 4832
        Weldon: 1055
        Wilkesboro: 4107
        Williamston: 914
        Wilmington: 3447, 5912
        Wing: 4182
        Woodlawn Mills: 5888
        Worthville: 3187
        Yadkin County: 2429, 2914
    Pennsylvania:
        Elkhorn: 138
        Philadelphia: 5933
        Warren County: 2242
    Rhode Island: 4907
    South Carolina: 501, 566, 1581,
        2213, 2793, 2961, 3203
        Charleston: 3420, 4838
        Cheraw: 2984
        Chester County: 4833
        Orangeburg District: 4583
        Pickens: 1964
        Ridgeville: 4451
        Spartanburg: 3044
        Union: 2721, 5522
        Winnsboro: 936
    Spain--Cadiz: 4978
    Tennessee: 2116, 3692
        Altamont: 5187
    United States: 3053

MERCANTILE ACCOUNTS (Continued):
  Virginia:
    1700s-1800s: 3145
    1800s: 1093, 1336, 2949, 2971, 3721
    1810s: 2360, 4135
    1820s: 12, 145
    1830s: 138, 145, 362, 3105
    1840s: 2621
    1850s: 1102, 3994
    1860s: 1102, 4157
    1870s: 2515, 4157
    1800s-1900s: 2517
    Albemarle County: 4490
    Alexandria: 175
    Amherst County: 397
    Augusta County: 209
    Barksdale: 5827
    Bedford County: 2633
    Berryville: 3336
    Blacksburg: 193, 3039
    Brunswick: 5334
    Brunswick County: 4454
    Campbell County: 2633
    Catawba Post Office: 5827
    Charlottesville: 93
    Columbia: 5108
    Danville: 1046, 2207, 2569, 5196
    Falmouth: 2165
    Fayette County: 4011
    Fifesville: 4459
    Fluvanna County: 2834
    Franklin County: 2633
    Gholsonville: 5648
    Good Intent: 568
    Harrisonburg: 2498
    Hawkinstown: 374
    Hicks Ford: 5891
    Keysville: 79
    Lawrenceville: 240
    Leesburg: 4446
    Louisa County: 143
    Lynchburg: 1594, 1955, 2309, 4222
    Martinsville: 1013
    Mecklenburg County: 799, 4885
    Middleburg: 1369
    New Market: 138
    Norfolk: 5770
    Norwood: 5107
    Oak Grove: 2392
    Petersburg: 3179, 5079, 5183
    Peytonsburg: 5827
    Pleasant Grove: 2323
    Richmond: 5770
    Shenandoah County: 160, 3678, 4122
    Sperryville: 3619
    State Mills: 3679
    Strasburg: 5979
    Stuart's Draft: 209
    Suffolk: 4472
    Tazewell County: 5400
    Van Buren Furnace: 5990
    Wachapreague: 4403
    White Post: 2274, 5611
    Winchester: 4741, 5882
    Woodville: 138
  Washington, D.C.: 384, 1937
  West Virginia: 1238, 2301, 3721
    Berkeley County: 4732
    Bunker Hill: 4893
    Capon Bridge: 2652
    Charles Town: 5300
    Darkesville: 4692
    Harpers Ferry: 3058
    Martinsburg: 1828
    Shepherdstown: 1711
MERCANTILE AFFAIRS:
  Connecticut: 1871
    North Stonington: 5669
  Kentucky: 5593
    Cloverport: 3199
  Massachusetts--Boston: 3459
  New York--New York: 2412
  North Carolina: 1871, 3984
    "Mount Tirzah": 3752
    Oxford: 2192

MERCANTILE AFFAIRS:
  North Carolina (Continued):
    Randleman: 5408
    Washington: 652
  Tennessee: 872
  Texas: 3565
  Virginia:
    Gloucester County: 4924
    Gravel Hill: 5652
    Lynchburg: 1350
    Richmond: 4616
    Shenandoah County: 3773
    Union Forge: 3098
  West Virginia:
    Middleway: 4892
MERCANTILE LIBRARY ASSOCIATION,
  New York, New York: 3259
MERCENARIES: see SOLDIERS OF FORTUNE
MERCER, Charles Fenton: 3623
MERCER, George Anderson: 3624
MERCER, James: 3819
MERCER, Jesse (Georgia, 1769-1841): 3625
MERCER, Jesse (North Carolina): 3626
MERCER, John (Virginia): 4845
MERCER, John Francis (Maryland, 1759-1821): 3627, 3819
MERCER, Mary E.: 5360
MERCER, William Newton: 3628
MERCER COUNTY, Illinois: 4004
MERCER COUNTY, Kentucky:
  Pleasant Hill: 5416
MERCER COUNTY, New Jersey:
  Princeton: see PRINCETON, New Jersey; PRINCETON UNIVERSITY
  Trenton: 1514, 2807, 4601, 5119, 5939
MERCER UNIVERSITY, Macon, Georgia: 1078, 1476
MERCERSBURG, Pennsylvania: 2521
  Schools: 5160
MERCERSBURG ACADEMY, Mercersburg, Pennsylvania: 5160
MERCHANDISE: 1950
  see also COMMERCIAL PRODUCTS
  Inventories: 2977
    Missouri--Calhoun: 5392
    Virginia:
      Front Royal: 5387
      Sperryville: 3619
  Marketing:
    Mississippi Valley: 4109
    North Carolina: 5910
      Beaufort County: 5521
      Hertford: 3907
    Tennessee: 4109
    Virginia--Lynchburg: 5568
  Prices: 3844
  Purchases and sales:
    North Carolina: 3307
      Warren County: 999
    Thailand: 5238
    Virginia--Richmond: 2633
  Storage--Louisiana: 679
  Subdivided by place:
    Massachusetts: 3034
    Virginia: 4710
MERCHANT MARINE: see UNITED STATES--MERCHANT MARINE
MERCHANT SEAMEN: 4541, 4726
  see also NEGRO SEAMEN
  Aid (Governmental): 5622
  Aid societies:
    Georgia: 786, 4678
    North Carolina: 4727
  Discipline--Spain: 4982
  Diseases--United States: 3578
  Flogging--Great Britain: 5736
  Impressment: see GREAT BRITAIN--NAVY--Impressment
  Recruiting--Great Britain: 5736
  United States: 1415, 3578
  Wages and salaries: see WAGES AND SALARIES--Merchant seamen
MERCHANTS:
  see also COMMISSION MERCHANTS; GUILDMERCHANTS

MERCHANTS (Continued):
  Apprenticeship--Virginia: 3060
  Debt collection:
    Great Britain: 1993, 5548
  Debt--Georgia: 1993
  Finance--Maryland: 5213
  Subdivided by place:
    Alabama: 1915, 4820
      Boligee: 4861
      Mobile: 3196
    Armenia: 5797
    Connecticut: 3196
      Fairfield: 1871
    Cuba: 3808
      Havanna: 3008
    Florida: 2232
      Pensacola: 3008
    Georgia:
      1700s-1800s: 1242, 4988
      1800s: 1231, 1609, 2326, 2365
      1800s-1900s: 4298
      Augusta: 2710
      Crawford: 3974
      Greenville: 17
      Savannah: 2019, 2232, 2497, 4768
    Great Britain: 258, 712, 3304
      see also AMERICAN REVOLUTION--British merchants in the United States
      Bideford: 570
      Bristol: 4541
      Liverpool: 3753
      London: 3179, 3960, 5221
    Guatemala: 3099
    Ireland: 2884
    Kentucky--Cloverport: 3199
    Louisiana:
      New Orleans: 3008, 3358
    Maryland: 785, 1386, 1487, 1764
      Baltimore: 1405, 1647, 2265, 2412, 4288, 4348, 5213
      Charles County: 984
      Westminster: 3326
    Massachusetts: 1839
      Becket: 5766
      Boston: 5777
    Mississippi:
      Columbus: 4269
      Hinds County: 3759
      Natchez: 3873
    Missouri--Saint Louis: 3012
    New Hampshire:
      Grafton County: 71
    New York: 1396, 1907, 1908, 2172, 2230, 5281, 5282
      New York: 3960, 4456, 5298
      Rochester: 4256
    North Carolina:
      1700s: 1487, 2585, 4918
      1700s-1800s: 540
      1800s: 484, 486, 556, 792, 1015, 1336, 1686, 1856, 1861, 1915, 2222, 2857, 3307, 4764, 5298
      1800s: 5535
      1810s: 5535
      1840s: 4150
      1850s: 698, 1688
      1860s: 264, 839, 1688, 2359
      1880s: 1233
      1890s: 1233
      1800s-1900s: 1660, 4298
      Anderson: 534
      Bath: 3521
      Bay River: 1871
      Bertie County: 2332
      Caledonia: 3449
      Cane Creek: 2618
      Carteret County: 2491
      Davidson County: 3241
      Edenton: 2658
      Fayetteville: 2431
      Fort Barnwell: 640
      Guilford County: 2330
      Haw River: 5154
      Hillsborough: 4890
      Horse Shoe: 4910

MERCHANTS:
  Subdivided by place:
    North Carolina (Continued):
      Montgomery County: 75
      Newton: 9
      Opossum Trot: 80
      Orange County: 1151
      Raleigh: 2819
      Richmond County: 3167
      Ridgeway: 999
      Statesville: 8
      Surry County: 2808
      Trenton: 1871
      Wadesboro: 222
      Wake County: 876, 3655
      Warren County: 4328
      Warrenton: 4389
      Washington: 911, 4382, 4571
      Williamston: 914, 2419, 4849
      Wilmington: 1908, 2511, 2586, 5372
      Yadkin County: 2808
    Ohio--Hillsboro: 5342
    Pennsylvania: 469, 1611, 2594, 3957
      Attleboro: 3229
      Harrisburg: 2027
      Philadelphia: 228, 1242
    Rhode Island: 4907
      Providence: 5298
    Scotland: 5527
    South Carolina: 566, 1242, 1396, 1480, 3123
      Abbeville: 3319
      Charleston: 2019, 2491, 2586, 3116, 3420
      Society Hill: 2762
      Stateburg: 3818
      Woodruff: 1715
    Texas--Comal County: 218
    United States: 904, 2546
    Virginia:
      1700s: 625, 1863
      1800s: 1336, 1350, 1679, 2165, 2229, 2369, 2566
      1800s: 5535
      1810s: 2360, 2633, 5535
      1820s: 2633
      1830s: 1486
      1840s: 1486, 2621
      1850s: 2331, 2992
      1860s: 418, 2331
      1870s: 1587
      1880s: 1587
      Bedford County: 5055
      Berryville: 3336
      Brunswick County: 4454
      Dinwiddie County: 2567
      Fairfax County: 2233
      Falmouth: 3105
      Fayette County: 4011
      Gholsonville: 4747
      Gordonsville: 4710
      Keysville: 79
      Leesburg: 4446
      Lynchburg: 1594, 2309, 3353
      Norfolk: 3783
      Norwood: 5107
      Oak Forest: 3454
      Paris: 4743
      Petersburg: 3179, 4604
      Pittsylvania County: 2131, 2337
      Pleasant Grove: 2323
      Powhatan County: 619
      Prince Edward Court House: 5282
      Richmond: 3454, 3758, 3809, 5057
      Sperryville: 3619
      Suffolk: 3915, 4472
      Twyman's Store: 4099
      Warrenton: 5382
      White Post: 1436
      Woodstock: 2832
    Washington, D.C.: 384, 1920, 3179
    West Indies: 1493
    West Virginia: 1238, 2130, 2711, 3061

MERCHANTS:
  Subdivided by place:
    West Virginia (Continued):
      Macksburg: 2470
      Shepherdstown: 1711, 5324
MERCHANTS AND MANUFACTURERS ASSOCIATION OF GREENSBORO, North Carolina: 602
MERCHANTS AND MECHANICS LAND COMPANY, Savannah, Georgia: 3629
MERCHANTS BANK OF NEW BERN, North Carolina: 3415
MERCHANTS NATIONAL BANK, Boston, Massachusetts: 5628
MERCHANTS NATIONAL BANK, Raleigh, North Carolina: 5962
EL MERCURIO PERUANO: 4155
MERCURY MINING:
  Mexico: 4155
  Peru: 4155
MERCURY TRADE--New York: 5731
MEREDITH, George: 1522, 3630, 5050
MEREDITH, Jonathan: 3631
MEREDITH, Thomas: 484, 5457
MEREDITH, William Morris: 3632
MEREDITH COLLEGE, Raleigh, North Carolina: 4828
  Students and student life: 5267
MERIAM, Charlotte Eliza: 3633
MERIAM, Jotham Addison: 3633
MERIAM FAMILY (Massachusetts--Genealogy): 3633
MERIDEN, England: 3047
MERION, Pennsylvania: 552
MERIWETHER, Dr. _____ (South Carolina): 3405
MERIWETHER, W. N.: 791
MERIWETHER COUNTY, Georgia: 589, 1999, 2579
  Greenville: 17
MERLE & COMPANY, Louisiana: 5693
MERRELL, Joseph W.: 3634
MERRIAM, Ruth M.: 3635
MERRIMAC (iron clad): see VIRGINIA
MERRIMACK COUNTY, New Hampshire:
  Concord: 1634, 1902, 3823, 4200
  Hookset: 1980
  Wilmot Center: 5975
MERRIMON, Augustus Summerfield: 3636
MERRITT, Abram Haywood: 3973
MERRITT, Alexander T. B.: 724
MERRITT, Benjamin H.: 3637
MERRITT, John: 3638
MERRITT, John W.: 3639
MERRITT, Lewis L.: 2774
MERRITT, Walter Gordon: 3640
MERRITT, William C.: 3639
MERRITT, William E.: 3641
MERRITT, William H. E.: 724, 3642
MERRITT FAMILY (North Carolina): 2929, 3639
MERRYHILL, North Carolina:
  Civil War: 1100
MERSEY AND IRWELL CANAL: 2148
MERTENS, John L.: 3643
MESHED, Persia:
  Russian consulate in: 4693
THE MESSENGER, Siler City, North Carolina (newspaper): 2861
MESSENGER (ship): 4881
MESSIER, Jean: 3644
MESSRS. DURAND & CO.: 5011
MESSINA, Italy: 2296
METAL: see CONFEDERATE STATES OF AMERICA--METAL--Procurement of
METAL TRADES COUNCIL, Charleston, South Carolina: 4962
METAL WORKERS: see INTERNATIONAL MOLDERS' UNION OF NORTH AMERICA
METAL WORKING: see specific types of metals worked, e.g. TINSMITHING
METCALFE, Charles Theophilus, Baron Metcalfe: 3645, 5736
METEOROLOGY: 1728, 1785
  Great Britain: 2839
METEORS: 4017
METERS--Parking: see PARKING METERS

METEYARD, Eliza: 1087
METFORD, William Ellis: 4520
THE METHODIST ADVANCE: 547
METHODIST CHURCHES: 4932
  see also METHODIST EPISCOPAL CHURCH; METHODIST EPISCOPAL CHURCH, SOUTH; METHODIST PROTESTANT CHURCH; UNITED METHODIST CHURCH
  Aid to freedmen--Tennessee: 3646
  Board of Christian Social Concerns: 3020
  Board of Hospitals: 3020
  Board of Missions: 3020, 3646
    North Carolina: 3646
  Board of Trustees:
    Kentucky: 3646
    North Carolina: 3646
  Camp meetings: see CAMP MEETINGS--Methodist
  Church buildings:
    Destruction in Barbados: 4913
    North Carolina--Greensboro: 5149
  Church history:
    North Carolina: 2221, 3646
    United States: 3646, 5070
  Circuits: 3646
    North Carolina: 3195, 5280
  Clergy: see CLERGY--Methodist
  Conferences:
    General Conference:
      Pennsylvania: 4412
      Tennessee: 33
    North Carolina: 956
    Tennessee: 3646
    United States: 3646
    Wisconsin: 3646
  Converts:
    Georgia: 5246
    North Carolina: 5964
    South Carolina: 5965
  Deacons--North Carolina: 5964
  Districts: 3646
    North Carolina: 3646
    South Carolina: 5965
  Doctrine: 1869, 4146, 5964
    Great Britain: 2751
  Education: see METHODIST CHURCHES--Higher education; SCHOOLS--Church schools--Methodist
  Elders--North Carolina: 5964
  Episcopal affairs: 2482
  Finance:
    Great Britain: 5647, 5895
    North Carolina: 2895, 3195, 3646
    South Carolina: 3646
      Clemson: 2961
  Higher education:
    North Carolina: 3020
    Proposed women's college in Raleigh: 1152
  Hymns: see HYMNS--Methodist churches
  Interchurch relations:
    Baptist churches: 3494
    Church of England: 2751, 5647
    United States: 5070
    Universalist churches: 3494
  Liturgy and ritual:
    Georgia: 5246
  Membership:
    Behavior: 5964
    North Carolina: 3195
  Missionaries: see MISSIONS AND MISSIONARIES--Methodist
  Missionary societies: see WOMEN'S MISSIONARY SOCIETY; WOMEN'S SOCIETY OF CHRISTIAN SERVICE
  Negro churches:
    Alabama: 249
    North Carolina: 1738
    South Carolina: 249
  Negroes, Ministry to: 2482
    see also METHODIST CHURCHES--Aid to freedmen
  "Plan of Union": 3646

METHODIST CHURCHES (Continued):
　Publications: see RELIGIOUS
　　LITERATURE--Methodist
　Regional School Committee: 3020
　Relations between Northern and
　　Southern Methodist churches:
　　2482
　　North Carolina: 3581
　　West Virginia--Martinsburg:
　　　3809
　Religious meditations: 4412
　Revivals: 2929
　Schisms: 2289, 2482
　　Virginia: 4131
　Sermons: see SERMONS--Methodist
　Sunday schools: see SUNDAY
　　SCHOOLS--Methodist
　Trials--North Carolina: 4506
　Unification movement: 879, 3646,
　　3881
　　South Carolina: 3646
　Subdivided by place:
　　Alabama:
　　　Alabama Conference: 3646
　　Arkansas: 1361
　　Brazil: 1685
　　Georgia: 731, 1993, 5699
　　　Georgia Conference: 3646
　　Great Britain: 1317, 1518, 2751,
　　　5726
　　　Wesleyan Conference: 2482
　　Indiana: 3981, 5149
　　Ireland--Londonderry: 3738
　　Kentucky:
　　　Kentucky Conference: 3646
　　Maryland:
　　　Baltimore Conference
　　　　(Independent): 3646
　　Mississippi: 3322
　　　Mississippi Conference: 3646
　　New York--Huntington: 726
　　North Carolina: 1316, 1538, 1738,
　　　2589, 5964, 5965
　　　Western North Carolina
　　　　Conference: 3020, 3646
　　　Wilmington: 5912
　　　Yanceyville: 4506
　　Ohio:
　　　Logan County: 5142
　　　Northern Ohio: 2693
　　Pennsylvania:
　　　Philadelphia Conference: 5328
　　Rhode Island: 1906
　　South Carolina: 3981, 5699
　　　South Carolina Conference: 3646
　　Southern States: 731
　　Tennessee:
　　　Tennessee Conference: 3646
　　United States: 1441, 2591
　　Virginia: 33
　　　Virginia Conference: 3646
　　　Winchester: 4412
　　West Virginia:
　　　West Virginia Conference: 3646
METHODIST CHURCHES AND PUBLIC
　AFFAIRS: 3020
METHODIST EPISCOPAL CHURCH:
　see also METHODIST CHURCHES;
　　METHODIST EPISCOPAL CHURCH,
　　SOUTH
　Church history:
　　South Carolina: 4912
　Circuits: 3646
　　North Carolina: 3992
　　Virginia: 3601
　Clergy: see CLERGY--Methodist
　　Episcopal
　Conferences:
　　General Conference: 426
　　North Carolina: 3581
　Deacons: 2796
　Division: 426
　Elders: 2796
　Pastoral relations: 4912
　Reform movement: 5964
　Subdivided by place:
　　North Carolina: 3581
　　Virginia: 3497

METHODIST EPISCOPAL CHURCH:
　Subdivided by place:
　　Virginia (Continued):
　　　Suffolk: 3012
　　West Virginia:
　　　Harpers Ferry: 2171
METHODIST EPISCOPAL CHURCH, SOUTH:
　2482, 4564
　Board of Education:
　　North Carolina: 3646
　　Virginia: 3646
　Board of Missions:
　　North Carolina: 3646
　Board of Temperance and Social
　　Services: 879
　Circuits: 3646
　　North Carolina: 1096, 3195, 3476,
　　　5023
　Clergy: see CLERGY--Methodist
　　Episcopal Church, South
　Conferences:
　　General Conference: 31, 879
　　North Carolina: 3646
　　Virginia: 879
　Districts:
　　North Carolina: 3646
　Finance:
　　North Carolina: 3195, 3646, 5023
　　Virginia: 5467
　　West Virginia: 5467
　Fund raising--North Carolina: 547
　Higher education--Japan: 3888
　Judicial Council: 3646
　Lake Junaluska (N.C.) assembly
　　grounds: 879
　Membership:
　　North Carolina: 3195
　　Virginia: 5467
　　West Virginia: 5467
　Missionaries: see MISSIONS AND
　　MISSIONARIES--Methodist
　　Episcopal Church, South
　Political activity:
　　North Carolina: 3176
　Reconstruction period: 2566
　Sermons: see SERMONS--Methodist
　　Episcopal Church, South
　Sunday School Board:
　　North Carolina: 3646
　Twentieth Century Educational
　　Fund: 3888
　Subdivided by place:
　　North Carolina: 1152, 1588, 4111
　　　Catawba County: 5745
　　　Durham: 133, 1642
　　　North Carolina Conference:
　　　　3646, 4136, 4425, 4498
　　　North Carolina Conference
　　　　Historical Society: 3646
　　　Western North Carolina
　　　　Conference: 3646
　　　Wilmington: 772
　　Virginia: 5467
　　West Virginia: 5467
METHODIST MEETING HOUSE (Kentucky):
　3646
METHODIST PROTESTANT CHURCH: 4416,
　5964
　Finance: 4416
　North Carolina: 3186
　　North Carolina District: 3646
METHODIST PUBLISHING HOUSE, London,
　England: 5094
METHODIST PUBLISHING HOUSE,
　Nashville, Tennessee: 3646, 5375
METHODIST STUDENT MOVEMENT:
　Duke University: 3001
METHODIST THEOLOGY: see METHODIST
　CHURCHES--Doctrine
METHODIST UNIVERSITIES AND COLLEGES:
　see names of specific universities
　and colleges affiliated with the
　Methodist church
METHODISTS: see METHODIST CHURCHES
METHUEN, Paul, First Baron Methuen:
　1632
METLAKHTLA, Annette Islands:
　Description and travel: 2084

METTAUER, John Peter: 2881
METTERNICH-WINNEBURG, Clemens Lothar
　Wenzel, Fürst von: 3630, 3887
METTS, E. S.: 3647
METZ, George P.: 3648
METZDORF, Robert F.: 2449
METZGER, John J.: 4188
MEUSE, France: 4269
MEXICAN BORDER CAMPAIGN: see UNITED
　STATES--ARMY--Mexican Border
　Campaign
"MEXICAN CAMPAIGN SONG" (poem): 3809
MEXICAN NATIONAL RAILWAY: 3597
　Construction: 5495
MEXICAN WAR (1845-1848): 203, 262,
　523, 611, 778, 842, 872, 1153,
　1174, 1424, 1468, 2117, 2301, 3325,
　3366, 3378, 3415, 3809, 4196, 4434,
　4596, 4648, 4689, 4720, 4924, 4765,
　4849, 4881, 5051, 5059, 5419, 5480,
　5906, 5928, 5931, 5974
　see also UNITED STATES--ARMY--
　　Mexican War; UNITED STATES--
　　NAVY--Mexican War
　American occupation of Mazatlan:
　　3118
　Blockade of Mazatlan: 3809
　California: 3447
　Campaigns, battles, and military
　　actions: 357
　　Pictorial works: 5710
　　Mexico:
　　　Buena Vista: 1515
　　　Cerro Gordo: 5517
　　　Contreras: 5517
　　　Monterey: 778
　　　Northeastern Mexico: 2842
　　　Saltillo: 5130
　　　Tuxpan: 2085
　　　Vera Cruz: 2842, 5517
　　Texas--Fort Brown: 4715
　Civilian life--Virginia: 4720
　Claims--Bounty lands: 5508
　Economic aspects: 1424
　Foreign public opinion:
　　Great Britain: 2193
　Medical and sanitary affairs: 5513
　Mobilization in Virginia: 4720
　Officers: 5517
　Peace treaty: see TREATY OF
　　GUADALUPE HIDALGO
　Pensions: 525
　Pictorial works: 5710
　Public opinion in the United
　　States: 2760
MEXICAN WORKERS: see AGRICULTURAL
　WORKERS--Mexicans
MEXICO: 4689
　Americans in (1914): 3820
　　see also MEXICO--Revolution
　　　(1910-1929)--American
　　　intervention
　Anti-American demonstrations
　　(1911): 1412
　Army--Mexican War: 5517
　　see also MEXICAN WAR
　Botany: 2667
　Canals--Survey: 5772
　Comanche Indian raids: 2137
　Confederate emigrants: 2210, 3587
　Currency: 1339
　　Value: 5886
　Description and travel:
　　1840s: 622, 778
　　1850s: 622
　　1860s: 622, 5855
　　1870s: 4535
　　1880s: 4080
　　1905: 1412
　Economic conditions: 4249
　European intervention:
　　Revolt against Maximilian: 4748
　Foreign investments in--Land: 3651
　Foreign relations:
　　France: 2210
　　　see also MEXICO--French
　　　intervention

MEXICO:
  Foreign relations: (Continued):
    United States:
      1840s: 2808
        see also MEXICAN WAR
      1850s: 2936
      1860s: 1249
      1870s: 4535
      1910s: 5252
  Foreign trade:
    Philippine Islands: 4155
  French intervention: 1403
  Government agencies and officials:
    Archivo General de la Nacion: 3649, 3650
    Imperial Commissioner of Colonization: 3587
  Land--Prices: 2210
  Land claims: 891
  Land grants: 3587
  Land settlement: 693
  Legal affairs: 3587
  Livestock: 2210
  Mercury mining: 4155
  Mining--Batopilas: 4022
  Missions and missionaries:
    Methodist--Teaching: 1939
    Presbyterian: 2269
    Protestant Episcopal: 4758
  Oil fields: 3651
  Political unrest (1850s): 871
  Politics and government:
    1860s: 1403, 2210
      Matamoras: 3392
    1910: 661
  Postal service between Mexico and the United States: 1249
  Railroads: 3597
    Construction: 395
  Revolution (1910-1929): 5796
    American intervention: 4020, 5930
  Shipwrecks: 2667
  Social conditions: 1926, 2217
  Social life and customs:
    1840s: 5324
    1860s: 3392, 3587
    1906: 1412
  Texas Rangers in: 2137
  United States embassy in: 3557, 3809, 4719
  Universities and colleges: see UNIVERSITY OF MEXICO
  Wars of Independence: 3649
MEXICO CITY, Mexico: 3649, 3650
  see also UNIVERSITY OF MEXICO
  United States embassy in: 4719
MEYER, Carl: 452
MEYER, Henry: 3652
MEYER, William: 3183
MEYERS, A. C.: 3653
MEYLERT, Michael: 4188
MEYSENBURG, Ludo von: 5031
MEYSENBURG, Theodore August: 3654
"MI ULTIMO PENSAMIENTO" by José Rizal: 4511
MIAL, Alonzo T.: 3655, 4072
MIAMI COUNTY, Ohio:
  Piqua: 2308
  Pleasant Hill: 3648
MIAMI UNIVERSITY, Oxford, Ohio: 4076
  Students and student life: 1177
MICA DEPOSITS:
  North Carolina: 513
MICA MINES AND MINING: 5731
  North Carolina: 4918
MICHAUX, J. L.: 3656
MICHEL, Mary Middleton: 2449, 5717
MICHEL, Middleton: 2449
MICHEL, Richard Fraser: 2449
MICHIE, Alexander: 4709
MICHIGAN:
  Amusements: 3221
  Clothing and dress: 3221
  Commodity prices (1860s): 3221
  Copper mines--Investments: 4895
  Crops: 4889
  Currency: 1339

MICHIGAN (Continued):
  Description and travel: 1177
  Farm life: 4452
  Government agencies and officials:
    Governors:
      Robert McClelland (1851-1853): 3332
  Hardware trade: 5489
  Land deeds and indentures: 4606
  Lumbering: 4606
  Medical education: see UNIVERSITY OF MICHIGAN--Medical education
  Pioneer life: 3325
  Politics and government: 2604
  Railroads: 573
  Real estate: 5731
MICHIGAN IRON COMPANY: 5093
MICKLE, William English, Sr. (1846-1920): 3657
MICKLE, William English, Jr.: 3657
MID-CENTURY WHITE HOUSE CONFERENCE ON CHILDREN AND YOUTH: 1198
MIDDLE ATLANTIC STATES:
  Description and travel: 1748, 3229
  Resorts: 3229
MIDDLE EAST: see NEAR EAST
MIDDLE GEORGIA MILITARY AND AGRICULTURAL COLLEGE: 662
MIDDLE WEST:
  see also MISSISSIPPI VALLEY; OHIO VALLEY; OLD NORTH WEST; PLAINS STATES; WESTERN STATES; and names of specific states
  Abolition of slavery and abolitionist sentiment: 1920
  Canals--Finance: 2755
  Description and travel (1800s): 128, 1681, 2366, 2983, 3524
  Diseases: 1920
  Economic conditions: 1920
  Farming: 1920
  Health conditions: 1920
  Indians of North America: 128, 1920
  Land: 2208
  Land companies: 2712
  Land settlement: 128
  Land speculation: 1920, 2447
  Legal affairs: 1920
  Livestock: 1920
  Railroads: 1920, 2606
    Finance: 2265
    Investments in: 2532
  Real estate trade: 2532
  Religion: 1920
MIDDLEBURG, Georgia:
  Mercantile accounts: 2741
MIDDLEBURG, Virginia: 3913, 5629
  Farming: 794
  Mercantile accounts: 1369
MIDDLEBURY, Vermont: see MIDDLEBURY COLLEGE
MIDDLEBURY COLLEGE, Middlebury, Vermont: 128
  Abernethy Library of American Literature Papers: 10
MIDDLESEX, England:
  Freeholders: 3658
  Police district: 4420
MIDDLESEX, Virginia: 3379
MIDDLESEX COUNTY, Connecticut:
  Haddam: 2684
  Higganum: 2684
  Middletown: see MIDDLETOWN, Connecticut
MIDDLESEX COUNTY, Massachusetts: 5670
  Boxborough: 2456
  Cambridge: see CAMBRIDGE, Massachusetts; HARVARD UNIVERSITY
  Concord: 2563, 2564
    Poetry: 1698
  Lexington: 2694
  Littleton: 776
  Lowell: see LOWELL, Massachusetts
  Marlboro: 4608
  Medford: 2641
  Natick: 5808
  Woburn: 5732

MIDDLESEX COUNTY, New Jersey:
  New Brunswick: 532
MIDDLESEX COUNTY, Virginia:
  Urbanna: 454
MIDDLETON, Arthur: 3659
MIDDLETON, Charles, First Baron Barham: 4230
MIDDLETON, Henry: 4214, 4621
MIDDLETON, James: 3660
MIDDLETON, John: 3661
MIDDLETON, Robert: 3661
MIDDLETON, England: 1457
MIDDLETON, North Carolina:
  Mercantile accounts: 5592
MIDDLETOWN, Connecticut: 636, 1168, 5063
  Manufacture of gunpowder: 4375
  Mental hospitals: 5748
  Military schools: 295, 1168, 2870
MIDDLETOWN, Indiana: 3698
MIDDLETOWN MILITARY ACADEMY, Middletown, Connecticut: 2870
MIDDLEWAY, West Virginia: 1730, 2130
  Household accounts: 4703
  Mercantile affairs: 4892
  Postal service: 4892
  Wheat trade: 4703
MIDLETON, William St. John Fremantle Broderick, First Earl of: 663
MIDLOTHIAN, Scotland: 5
  Dalhousie Castle: 4372
MIDLOTHIAN, Virginia:
  Coal mining: 2908
MID-SOUTH: 1771
MIDWAY, Alabama: 983
MIDWAY, Georgia: 1171
MIDWAY, North Carolina: 3250
MIDWAY ACADEMY, North Carolina: 4148
MIDWAY HOSPITAL, Charlottesville, Virginia: 3012
  Civil War: 3350
MIDWEST: see MIDDLE WEST
MIDWIVES--Georgia: 365
MIFFLIN, Thomas: 3662
MIFFLIN COUNTY, Pennsylvania: 699
  Lewistown: 2704
MIGRATION, Internal: see IMMIGRATION AND EMIGRATION--Internal migration
MIKELL, Wiley: 3663
MIKELL, William Joseph: 3664
MILBURN, William Henry: 2449
MILES, Alfred Henry: 5616
MILES, Henry: 3665
MILES, James Warley: 3666
MILES, Joseph A.: 3667
MILES, Mary (Jenkins): 3831
MILES, Nelson Appleton: 1084
MILES, Sarah: 5548
MILES, William Porcher: 581, 1180
MILES FAMILY (Georgia): 3667
MILEY, Amos: 3668
MILEY, Caldwell G.: 3668
MILEY, J. D.: 4656
MILEY, Thomas: 3668
MILFORD-HAVEN, Louis Alexander Mountbatten, First Marquis of: 452
MILFORD, Connecticut:
  Carriage manufacture: 379
MILFORD, Massachusetts: 3328, 5169
MILFORD, Pennsylvania: 4211
MILDFORD BAPTIST CHURCH, Greenville District, South Carolina: 3669
MILITARY ACTIVITIES: see as subheading under names of armies
MILITARY AFFAIRS: see as subheading under place names
MILITARY ART AND SCIENCE: 1168, 3116
  Officers' handbooks: 4049
  United States: 3228, 3654
MILITARY ASSISTANCE: see as subheading under names of countries
MILITARY ATTACHÉS: see (name of country)--Government agencies and officials--Diplomatic and consular service
MILITARY BASES: see MILITARY POSTS

MILITARY DISCHARGE: see Discharges
  as subheading under names of armies
MILITARY EDUCATION: see MILITARY
  SCHOOLS; and names of specific
  military schools
MILITARY ENGINEERING: 3145
MILITARY GOVERNMENT: see CIVIL WAR--
  MARTIAL LAW; CIVIL WAR--UNION
  OCCUPATION; RECONSTRUCTION--Federal
  military occupation
MILITARY INTELLIGENCE: see as
  subheading under names of armies;
  SPIES
MILITARY LAW--United States: 4688
MILITARY LIFE: see Army life and
  Camp life as subheadings under
  names of armies
MILITARY OPERATIONS OF GENERAL
  BEAUREGARD IN THE WAR BETWEEN THE
  STATES by Alfred Roman: 2364, 4550
MILITARY ORDER OF THE LOYAL LEGION
  OF THE UNITED STATES: 4601, 4802
MILITARY PARADES: see Inspections
  and reviews as subheading under
  names of armies
MILITARY PASSES: see as subheading
  under names of armies
MILITARY PENSIONS: see PENSIONS,
  Military
MILITARY POSTS:
  see also names of specific posts
    and camps
  Cherokee Indian Territory: 3614
  France--Tours: 5323
  North Carolina: 325
  Spanish in West Florida: 3041
  United States--Provision of: 3662
MILITARY PREPAREDNESS: see DEFENSE
MILITARY RAILROADS:
  Confederate States of America: 1726
    In Virginia: 1137
  Philippine Islands--Iligan: 4656
  United States: 5306
    In North Carolina: 605
MILITARY REGULATIONS: see Regulations
  as subheading under names of armies
MILITARY RELATIONS WITH CIVIL
  GOVERNMENTS: see Civil-military
  relations as subheading under
  names of armies
MILITARY ROADS: 3145
  Civil War: 5991
  Nashville to New Orleans: 2781
MILITARY SCHOOLS: 5731
  Connecticut: 295, 1168, 2870
  Georgia: 3729, 5970
  North Carolina: 895, 3176, 4067
  South Carolina: 2831, 3293
    see also THE CITADEL
  United States: see UNITED STATES
    MILITARY ACADEMY; UNITED STATES
    NAVAL ACADEMY
  Vermont: 295
  Virginia: 641
    see also VIRGINIA MILITARY
      INSTITUTE
MILITARY SOCIETIES: see UNITED
  STATES MILITARY PHILOSOPHICAL
  SOCIETY
MILITARY SUPPLIES: see as subheading
  under names of armies
MILITARY TRIALS: see Courts-martial
  as subheading under names of armies
  and navies
MILITARY UNIFORMS: see Clothing and
  dress as subheading under names of
  armies and navies
MILITIA: see AMERICAN REVOLUTION--
  Militia; CONFEDERATE STATES OF
  AMERICA--ARMY--Units; CONTINENTAL
  ARMY--Relations with militia;
  PERU--Militia; and Militia as
  subheading under names of states
MILITIA ACT OF 1852: 1114
MILK PRODUCERS ASSOC.: 592
MILK TRADE:
  Massachusetts--West Acton: 2456
  North Carolina: 1275

MILL, John Stuart: 1087, 3670
MILL CREEK HUNDRED, Pennsylvania:
  5264
MILL HALL, Pennsylvania: 5249
MILL SPRINGS, Kentucky: see CIVIL
  WAR--CAMPAIGNS, BATTLES, AND
  MILITARY ACTIONS--Kentucky--Mill
  Springs
MILL VILLAGE, New Hampshire: 1763
MILL WORKERS:
  see also HOSIERY WORKERS; SAWMILL
    WORKERS; TEXTILE WORKERS
  Georgia: 1887
    Slaves: 1887
MILLAIS, Sir John Everett, First
  Baronet: 2471
MILLAR, Andrew: 2146
MILLAR FAMILY (Virginia and West
  Virginia): 3721
MILLBORO, North Carolina: 2382
"MILLBROOK," Virginia: 1714
MILLEDGE, John: 2931, 3671, 3704
MILLEDGE, Martha (Galphin): 3671
MILLEDGE, Mary: 1505
MILLEDGE, Philip: 3573
MILLEDGE FAMILY (Georgia): 787
MILLEDGEVILLE, Georgia:
  1700s: 894
  1800s: 2980, 4367
  1800s: 1090, 3704
  1810s: 1090, 3704
  1820s: 1090, 3704
  1830s: 1296, 2049
  1840s: 1296
  1850s: 5605
  1860s: 106, 1204, 1799, 2710,
    5605
  Civil War:
    Public welfare: 3272
    Sherman's march: 689, 2372, 5453
  Courts: 2372
  Mental hospitals: 127
  States' Rights Party: 5051
  Universities and colleges: see
    OGLETHORPE UNIVERSITY
MILLEDGEVILLE, North Carolina:
  Cotton mills: 4918
MILLER, Abraham: 3687
MILLER, Andrew J.: 3672
MILLER, Andrew W.: 1424
MILLER, Ann Eliza (Ashe): 3673
MILLER, C. V.: 1424
MILLER, Cincinnatus Hiner: 3694
MILLER, Conrad: 3721
MILLER, Dudlee: 1409
MILLER, Edward C.: 3674
MILLER, Edward J.: 1920
MILLER, Elizabeth H.: 1409
MILLER, George S.: 3687
MILLER, Gerrit S., Jr.: 4022
MILLER, Mrs. Godfrey: 3687
MILLER, James (Confederate
  physician): 3673
MILLER, James E., Jr. (b. 1920): 720
MILLER, James P. (Pennsylvania):
  3675
MILLER, Joaquin: see MILLER,
  Cincinnatus Hiner
MILLER, John (Virginia): 3687
MILLER, John Blount (South Carolina,
  d. 1851): 1923, 3676
MILLER, John D. (North Carolina):
  3677
MILLER, John F. (Confederate
  soldier): 4610
MILLER, John L. (Strasburg, Virginia):
  3678
MILLER (JOHN R.) v. AMERICAN TOBACCO
  COMPANY: 1585
MILLER, John W. (State Mills,
  Virginia): 3679
MILLER, Joseph A.: 3680
MILLER, Justin: 5252
MILLER, Les: 4188
MILLER, Lewis A.: 3687
MILLER, Mabel (North Carolina and
  Virginia): 3680

MILLER, Mabel M. (Virginia): 3681
MILLER, Martha M. (Jackson): 3677
MILLER, Mary (Virginia): 1409
MILLER, Mary M. (Iowa): 518
MILLER, Matilda: 3227
MILLER, N.: 1825
MILLER, Phineas: 4621
MILLER, R. L.: 3680
MILLER, Robert Morrison, Jr.: 5457
MILLER, Shirley: 3680
MILLER, Stephen Decatur: 3682
MILLER, Thomas (North Carolina
  merchant): 3683
MILLER, Thomas (North Carolina
  deputy governor): 5457
MILLER, R. H.: 357
MILLER, St. John: 1943
MILLER, Stearne Ball: 2149
MILLER, Susan: 1923
MILLER, Warren: 2016
MILLER, William (England, b. 1869):
  3684
MILLER, William (North Carolina): 1409
MILLER, William (Virginia): 2792
MILLER, William A. (Danville,
  Virginia): 5196
MILLER, William A. (Lynchburg,
  Virginia): 3685
MILLER, William Henry (Pennsylvania,
  1829-1870): 3686
MILLER, William L. (South Carolina):
  1877
MILLER, Wirt H.: 3685
MILLER FAMILY: 3687
  Virginia: 3721
  West Virginia: 1920, 3721
MILLER LAURENCE AND COMPANY: 3688
MILLERS' ACCOUNTS:
  see also SAWMILLS--Accounts
  Georgia--Cherokee County: 1887
  Maryland:
    Frederick County: 4457
    Washington County: 2838, 3875
  Missouri--Calhoun: 5392
  North Carolina: 4918
    Milton: 5843
  Pennsylvania: 2521
  South Carolina:
    Branchville: 1749
  Virginia: 5157
    Albemarle County: 5302
    Augusta County: 210
    Brunswick County: 4324
    Franklin County: 3100
    Richmond: 5393
    Roanoke County: 1969
  West Virginia:
    Berkeley County: 4056
    Hannisville: 2316
    Martinsburg: 3832
MILLERSBURG, Missouri:
  Mercantile accounts: 5392
MILLERSVILLE, Pennsylvania: see
  MILLERSVILLE STATE COLLEGE
MILLERSVILLE STATE COLLEGE,
  Millersville, Pennsylvania: 568
MILLET, François: 1424
MILLICAN, Adam T.: 1468
MILLIKEN, Daniel L.: 3363
MILLIKEN, L. C.: 2877
MILLINERY GOODS TRADE:
  Georgia--Waynmanville: 2272
  North Carolina--Charlotte: 5100
MILLMAN, Mr. _____: 4491
"MILLMONT," Mercersburg,
  Pennsylvania: 2521
MILLMONT MILLS, Mercersburg,
  Pennsylvania: 2521
MILLS, Charles F. (Georgia): 3689
MILLS, Charles Frank (North
  Carolina): 3690
MILLS, Edgar Warner: 1889
MILLS, Mrs. Edgar Warner: 1889
MILLS, Elizabeth Amanda: 3690
MILLS, John Haymes: 5457
MILLS, Isabella Petrie: 39
MILLS, Mary S.: 3691

MILLS, Richard W.: 3690
MILLS, Robert (1781-1855): 2352
MILLS, Robert S. (Tennessee): 3692
MILLS, William Harrison: 3690
MILLS: see COTTON MILLS; FLOUR MILLS; GRIST MILLS; MILLERS' ACCOUNTS; SAWMILLS; TEXTILE INDUSTRY
MILLSAPS, Susan: 1370
MILLWOOD, Virginia: 1227
MILLWORK INDUSTRY:
    Virginia--Woodstock: 1893
MILNE, Sir Alexander, First Baronet: 4549
MILNER, Alfred, First Viscount Milner: 2149, 3693, 5262
MILNES, Richard Monckton, First Baron Houghton: 2471, 3694
MILNES, Robert Offley Ashburton Crewe-, First Marquis of Crewe: see CREWE-MILNES, Robert Offley Ashburton, First Marquis of Crewe
MILO, New York: 2912, 3568
MILROY, Robert Huston: 1967, 3788
MILTON, John (Georgia): 3695
MILTON, Joshua W.: 4854
MILTON, Florida: 3008
MILTON, Massachusetts: 1843
MILTON, New York: 86
MILTON, North Carolina:
    Banks and banking: 310
    Flour mills: 5824
    Mercantile accounts: 5815
    Millers' accounts: 5843
    Pharmacists' accounts: 5515
    Promissory notes: 5815
    Tobacco industry and trade: 5843
MILTON CIRCUIT, Methodist churches: 3646
MILTON ROLLER MILL COMPANY, Milton, North Carolina: 5843
MILWAUKEE, Wisconsin: 4947
MIMS, Edwin: 2449, 3092, 4021
MINAS GERAIS, Brazil: 2750
MINDANAO, Philippine Islands:
    Earthquakes (1902): 3789
    Spanish-American War: 5844
MINE RUN FURNACE, Virginia: 1262
MINE WORKERS:
    see also INTERNATIONAL UNION OF MINE, MILL, AND SMELTER WORKERS; UNITED MINE WORKERS OF AMERICA; and specific types of miners
    Georgia: 1887
        Slaves: 1887
        Labor disputes: 2160
MINERAL COUNTY, West Virginia: 1784
    New Creek: 221
MINERAL RIGHTS:
    Bechuanaland: 4514
    North Carolina: 3003
    Persia: 4693
MINERAL WATER TRADE:
    Pennsylvania: 3957
MINERALOGY--North Carolina: 3063
MINERALS:
    Leasing: 1937
    Mining--South Carolina: 1019
    Subdivided by place:
        Haiti: 4275
        Honduras: 5480
MINES FAMILY (Maryland): 128
MINES (Military): see CONFEDERATE STATES OF AMERICA--NAVY--Mining operations
MINES AND MINING:
    see also specific kinds of mines and mining, e.g. GOLD MINES AND MINING; DIAMOND MINES
    Arkansas: 126
    California--Sierra County: 25
    Colorado: 849
    Georgia--Clopton's Mills: 5760
    Ireland--County Wicklow: 3567
    Mexico--Batopilas: 4022
    Missouri: 669, 4161
        Saint François County: 2386
    Nevada: 1478
    New Mexico: 5293

MINES AND MINING (Continued):
    Nicaragua--Javali Mine: 3587
    Montana--Speculation: 4161
    North Carolina: 1478, 2521
    South Carolina: 1019
    South Dakota: 5791
    United States:
        Laws and legislation: 4805
        Lawsuits: 3640
    Virginia: 117
        Buckingham County: 3794
    Wisconsin: 3710
MINIMUM WAGE: see WAGES AND SALARIES--Minimum wage
MINING ENGINEERING--Bolivia: 2473
MINING STOCKS: see ZINC MINING--Stocks
MINING TOWNS--Western States: 4485
MINISTERS: see CLERGY
MINNEAPOLIS, Minnesota: 2070, 2544
MINNEQUA HISTORICAL SOCIETY: 3697
MINNESOTA:
    see also MIDDLE WEST
    Agriculture: 3524
    Description and travel: 1084, 1177, 3648
    Economic conditions: 3637
    Education--Saint Paul: 3310
    Law practice--Fond du Lac: 2436
    Personal finance: 4029
    Real estate investment: 3587, 4911
    Teaching: 2544
    Universities and colleges: see UNIVERSITY OF MINNESOTA AT DULUTH
MINNESOTA, U.S.S.: 2265, 4537
MINNICK, Andrew J.: 3698
MINNICK, Michael: 3698
MINNIGERODE, Charles: 3587
MINNIS, J. F.: 3696
MINOR (A. AND F.), Virginia (firm): 2051
MINOR, Benjamin Blake: 2612
MINOR, Hugh: 3699
MINOR, John (Virginia): 1665
MINOR, John Barbee: 1770, 4698, 5075
MINOR, Lucian: 1351, 5691
MINOR, Peter Carr: 3699
MINOR, Robert D.: 2963
MINOR, William B.: 3700
MINOR, William G.: 2612
MINORITIES:
    see also names of specific minority groups, e.g. NEGROES
    Employment: 4386
    Housing: 4386
    Political activity: 4386
MINOT, Francis: 3701
MINOTAUR, H.M.S.: 1164
MINTO, Gilbert Elliot, First Earl of (1751-1814): 1674
MINTO, Gilbert John Elliot-Murray-Kynynmound, Fourth Earl of: 278
MINTO HOUSE, Roxburghshire, Scotland: 1674
MINTURN, GRINNELL AND COMPANY: see GRINNELL, AND COMPANY
MINUTES OF THE GRAND DIVISION OF THE SONS OF TEMPERANCE OF THE STATE OF VIRGINIA . . .: 5339
MIRACLES, Doctrine of: 2695
MIRAMAR CASTLE, Trieste, Italy: 2085
MISCEGENATION: see INTERRACIAL MARRIAGE
A MISCELLANEOUS ESSAY WITH RESPECT TO OUR GREAT BOARDS, TO THE EXCHEQUER AND TO AMERICA: 3347
MISS HEWITT'S SCHOOL, New York, New York: 4736
MISS LYMAN'S SCHOOL, Philadelphia, Pennsylvania: 5165
MISSES BATES' SCHOOL, Charleston, South Carolina: 1651
MISSION SCHOOLS: see SCHOOLS--Mission schools

MISSIONARY RIDGE, Tennessee: see CIVIL WAR--CAMPAIGNS, BATTLES, AND MILITARY ACTIONS--Tennessee--Missionary Ridge
MISSIONARY SOCIETIES:
    see also AMERICAN MISSIONARY ASSOCIATION
    Methodist churches:
        see also WOMEN'S MISSIONARY SOCIETY; WOMEN'S SOCIETY OF CHRISTIAN SERVICE
        Great Britain: 3995
        United States: 3646
    Presbyterian:
        North Carolina: 2269
        United States: 2269
    Subdivided by place:
        Great Britain: 5725, 5726
        Maryland:
            Frederick County: 3804
        North Carolina: 1738
        United States: 3633
MISSIONS AND MISSIONARIES: 867, 1217
    Finance:
        Church of England:
            Great Britain: 5725
            Natal: 5725
        India: 3011
    Teaching:
        see also SCHOOLS--Mission schools
        China: 1382
        Methodist churches:
            Indian Territory: 1939
            Mexico: 1939
    Subdivided by denomination:
        Baptist: 5211
            China: 1298
            India: 5456, 5726
            Japan: 561
        Catholic Church:
            Bolivia: 4155
        Church of England:
            British Columbia: 1792
            Mozambique: 5725
            Natal: 5725
            Sarawak: 5725
        Episcopal: 4918
            China: 5298
        Methodist:
            see also CONFERENCE SCHOOLS OF CHRISTIAN MISSIONS; METHODIST CHURCHES--Board of Missions; METHODIST EPISCOPAL CHURCH, SOUTH--Board of Missions
            Africa: 3646
            Brazil: 3248
            Creek Indians: 3646
            Georgia--To Negroes: 5699
            India: 3646
            Japan--Nagasaki: 5306
            South Carolina--To Negroes: 5699
            Tunis: 3646
        Methodist Episcopal Church, South: 879
            Japan: 3888
        Presbyterian: 3142, 5979
            Africa: 2269
            Brazil: 2269
            China: 2269, 5014
            Ecuador: 2269
            Formosa: 2269
            Iowa: 1283
            Japan: 2269
            Korea: 2269
            Mexico: 2269
            West Africa: 5816
        Protestant Episcopal:
            Mexico: 4758
            Texas: 1361, 4758
    Subdivided by place:
        Africa: 43, 2146
        Cape Colony: 41
        China:
            1795: 3315
            1800s: 2032
            1850s: 598, 872, 2892, 3741, 3995

MISSIONS AND MISSIONARIES:
  Subdivided by place:
    China:
      1800s (Continued):
        1860s: 2892
        1880s: 1382
      1933-1940
      History: 1298
    Guatemala: 2032
    India: 970, 2032, 3011, 4821
      Cuttack: 2410
    Jamaica: 5011
    Japan: 2241, 3888, 5160
    Liberia: 41, 2473
    Macao: 3786
    Malaya: 2148
    Mississippi: 3001
    New Guinea: 2650
    Nigeria: 41
    North Carolina: 2111
    Palestine: 1070
    Persia: 4821
    Santo Domingo: 3633
    Shetland Islands: 1070
    Sierra Leone: 128
    South Carolina:
      Among slaves: 669
    South Sea Islands: 4850
    Tanganyika: 41
    Texas: 4353
    Thailand: 5238
    Turkey: 3008
    United States: 3791, 4371
    To deaf: 5298
MISSISSIPPI:
  see also MISSISSIPPI TERRITORY;
    SOUTHERN STATES
  Abolition of slavery and
    abolitionist sentiment: 3415
  Agricultural organizations: 5498
    see also MISSISSIPPI--Farmers'
      Alliance; MISSISSIPPI--Patrons
      of Husbandry
  Agricultural workers: see
    MISSISSIPPI--Wages and salaries--
    Agricultural workers
  Agriculture: 4269, 4796
    see also the following
      subheadings under MISSISSIPPI:
      Crops, and names of specific
      crops; Farming; Plantations;
      Sharecropping
    Kemper County: 3436
  Archeological investigations: 2249
  Authors and publishers: 2775
  Baptist churches: 3322
  Blank books industry--Natchez:
    4309
  Boarding houses--Rodney: 3322
  Book buying: 49
  Bookbinding: 1693
    Natchez: 4309
  Booksellers and bookselling: 1693
  Bounty lands: 709
  Brickmaking--Rodney: 3322
  Business affairs--Pontotoc: 5612
  Camp meetings: 3611
  Cattle--Estrays: 1722
  Cemeteries--Holly Springs: 5975
  Choctaw Indians:
    Mission schools: 3611
    Removal: 3415
    Trade: 4269
  Churches:
    see names of specific
      denominations under MISSISSIPPI
  Civil War: see appropriate
    subheadings under CIVIL WAR;
    CONFEDERATE STATES OF AMERICA;
    and UNITED STATES--ARMY--Civil
    War
  Clergy--Episcopal: 5635
  Commodity prices (1800s): 530,
    1762, 2970, 3642, 4776
    Leake County: 5475
  Corn production: 3322
  Cotton: 2349, 3415
    Prices: 3415, 4269, 5047

MISSISSIPPI (Continued):
  Cotton baling--Rodney: 3322
  Cotton gins: 5047
    Rodney: 3322
  Cotton growing: 2970, 4776
    Rodney: 3322
  Cotton land: 3053
  Cotton picking records: 2813
  Cotton plantations: 4796
    Natchez: 5047
    Rodney: 3322
  Cotton trade: 3415, 5952
  Courts: 5421
    Adams County: 2282
    Justice Court:
      Choctaw County: 3702
    Probate Courts: 3438
  Crime: 5740
  Crops: 2663
    see also the following
      subheadings under MISSISSIPPI:
      Agriculture; Farming;
      Plantations; and names of
      specific crops
    Prices: 4269
      see also MISSISSIPPI--
        Commodity prices
  Currency counterfeiting: 4596
  Debating societies: 3611
  Debt: 3415
    see also MISSISSIPPI--State debt
  Debt collection: 2487
  Defense--Civil War: 4596
  Democratic Party: 988
  Description and travel:
    1700s-1800s: 5047
    1800s: 57
    1850s: 57
    To Natchez: 3322
  Diseases:
    Natchez: 980
    Typhoid fever: 82
    Yellow fever: 3759
      Natchez: 1762, 4246
  Economic conditions:
    1700s-1900s: 3476
    1800s: 57, 530, 2591, 4776
    1820s: 1553
    1830s: 1553, 4299
    1840s: 4299
    1860s: 836, 3415
  Education: 266
    see also MISSISSIPPI--Schools;
      MISSISSIPPI--Teaching
    Higher education: 3322
    Women: 3495
  Elections: 3322
  Estates (Landed property): 1434
  Estates (Legal):
    Administration and settlement:
      530, 3434
    Clinton: 4299
  Farm accounts:
    see also MISSISSIPPI--Plantation
      accounts
    Jasper County: 3876
  Farm tenancy: 1786
  Farmers' Alliance: 4442
  Farming:
    see also the following subheadings
      under MISSISSIPPI:
      Agriculture; Crops, and names
      of specific crops; Plantations;
      Sharecropping
    Hinds County: 3759
    Leake County: 5475
    Washington County: 5498
  Fires:
    Natchez:
      1836: 1762
      1858: 1047
  Floods--Mississippi River: 1762
  Freedmen: 3642
    Assistance to: 5431
      By United States Army: 5421
  Fruit culture: 3322

MISSISSIPPI (Continued):
  Government agencies and officials:
    Department of Archives and
      History: 2282
    Governors:
      David Holmes (1826): 2609
      Tilghman M. Tucker (1842-1844):
        5363
      John Pettus (1859-1863): 4729
      Ross Barnett (1960-1964): 5773
    Secretary of State:
      John A. Grimbell: 2211
  Gubernatorial elections (1826):
    2609
  Harbor improvement:
    Pascagoula: 5425
  Health resorts--Iuka: 3409
  Hiring of slaves: 1556
  Historical societies: 2282, 5498
  Hogs: 2813
  House construction: 3956
  Indians of North America:
    see also MISSISSIPPI--Choctaw
      Indians
    Culture: 2249
    Excavations: 2249
  Justices of the peace: 5363
    Choctaw County: 3702
  Know-Nothing Party: 1370
  Land: 2970
    see also MISSISSIPPI--Cotton
      land; MISSISSIPPI--Real estate
    Prices: 2663, 3415
    Purchases and sales: 57, 3846
  Land deeds and indentures: 5612
  Land grants: 5612
  Land laws: 4269
  Land settlement: 734, 5047
  Land speculation: 3415, 5612
  Law practice: 1506
  Lawsuits: 2012
  Legal affairs--Jacinto: 4442
  Legislature: 1370
  Literary festivals: 1771
  Masonry: 3611
  Mathematics, Study of: 1506
  Mercantile accounts: 802, 2095
    Gallatin: 2355
    Panola: 138
    Rocky Springs: 1077
    Sartartia: 5821
  Merchants:
    Columbus: 4269
    Hinds County: 3759
    Natchez: 3873
  Methodist churches: 3322
    Mississippi Conference: 3646
  Migration from:
    Leake County: 5475
  Migration to: 130, 3161, 3415
    From North Carolina: 5475
  Missions and missionaries: 3001
  Natural history: 5498
  Negroes:
    see also MISSISSIPPI--Freedmen;
      MISSISSIPPI--Slaves
    Behavior--Jasper County: 1370
    Civil War: 1864
  Newspapers: 1693
  Overseers: 3956
  Patrons of Husbandry: 1506
  Plantation accounts: 3956, 4776
    see also MISSISSIPPI--Farm
      accounts
    Brandon: 2813
    Natchez: 1786
    Rodney: 3322
  Plantation life: 2349, 3393
    Rodney: 3322
  Plantation management: 4796, 4820
  Plantations: 1325, 1553, 1556,
    1670, 1762, 3628, 5193
    see also the following
      subheadings under MISSISSIPPI:
      Agriculture; Cotton
      plantations; Crops, and names
      of specific crops; Farming;
      Overseers

MISSISSIPPI:
 Plantations (Continued):
  Business affairs:
   Yazoo County: 3747
   Claiborne County: 1077
 Political patronage: 5363
 Politics and government:
  1800s: 3415
  1820s: 2211
  1830s: 2211
  1840s: 3438
  1850s: 2370, 3611, 3809, 5498
  1860s: 2370, 2970, 5498
  1870s: 2370, 2970
  1800s-1900s: 4442
  1900s: 4918
 Printing: 1693
 Promissory notes--Sartartia: 5821
 Property lists: 5612
 Prophecies: 530
 Protestant Episcopal churches: 2175, 4358
 Race relations: 2473
 Railroads: 2970, 5498
  Construction: 1556, 5977
 Reading: 3611
 Real estate: 2164
  see also MISSISSIPPI--Land
 Reconstruction: 566, 836, 1506, 2487, 2970, 3415
 Religion: 57, 530, 2663, 3415, 4269
 Sawmills--Rodney: 3322
 Schools: 3415
  see also MISSISSIPPI--Education; MISSISSIPPI--Teaching
  Girls' schools and academies: 2588
  Students and student life: 5032
 Secession and secessionist sentiment: 836, 1370, 4720, 5498, 5621
 Senatorial elections (1857): 4442
 Sharecropping: 3415
 Sheep: 2813
 Slave trade: 492, 3415, 3846, 4299
  Prices: 2663, 3642
 Slavery: 1762, 2661, 3415, 4269, 4776
 Slaves: 1382
  see also MISSISSIPPI--Hiring of slaves
  Insurrections: 2661, 3415
  Treatment: 2399
 Social life and customs:
  1700s-1800s: 2663
  1800s: 4720, 4776
   Pre-Civil War: 3873, 4895, 5498
   Post-Civil War: 836
 State debt: 3438
 Stationery industry--Natchez: 4309
 Steam engine operators: 3634
 Surveying of harbors: 5425
 Tax receipts: 5612
 Teaching: 2948, 4895, 5043
  see also MISSISSIPPI--Education; MISSISSIPPI--Schools
 Telegraph: 3415
 Temperance: 3415, 4434
 Tornadoes: 5740
  Natchez: 3415
 Trade and commerce: 1762
  Agricultural products: 3322
  Cotton: see MISSISSIPPI-- Cotton trade
  Dry goods: 2888
  Hardware: 2888
  Lumber: 3008
  Rodney: 3322
  Slaves: see MISSISSIPPI--Slave trade
  Wood--Rodney: 3322
  With Choctaw Indians: 4269
 United States Post Office: 1693
 Universities and colleges: see JEFFERSON COLLEGE; MISSISSIPPI FEMALE COLLEGE; OAKLAND COLLEGE; UNIVERSITY OF MISSISSIPPI

MISSISSIPPI (Continued):
 Wages and salaries:
  Agricultural workers: 1786
 Weather: 2663
  Rodney: 3322
 Weddings: 3076, 3611
 Whig Party: 3322
MISSISSIPPI, U.S.S.: 1610, 2733
MISSISSIPPI AND CINCINNATI RAILROAD: 4596
MISSISSIPPI CAMPAIGN OF 1863: see CIVIL WAR--CAMPAIGNS, BATTLES, AND MILITARY ACTIONS--Louisiana-- Red River, 1863
MISSISSIPPI COUNTY, Arkansas: 4764
MISSISSIPPI FEMALE COLLEGE, Hernando, Mississippi: 3155
MISSISSIPPI FREE TRADER: 1693
MISSISSIPPI HISTORICAL SOCIETY: 2282
MISSISSIPPI LAND COMPANY: 323
MISSISSIPPI RIVER:
 Civil War: 4275
  see also CIVIL WAR--CAMPAIGNS, BATTLES, AND MILITARY ACTIONS-- Mississippi River
  Confederate fortifications: 4253
 Floods: 1762, 2794
 Freight and freightage: 3824
 Levees--Maintenance: 2341
 Piracy: 3053
 Steamboats: 4269
 Trade and commerce: 2386, 4348, 5933
 Travel: 404, 4246, 4369, 4810, 5498
  Riverboat: 1556
  Steamboat: 5380
MISSISSIPPI TERRITORY: 5928
 Agricultural products: 3041
 Agriculture: 1038
 As British protectorate: 4246
 Description and travel: 3041
 Governors:
  William Charles Coles Claiborne (1801-1805): 1048
  Robert Williams (1805-1809): 5778
  David Holmes (1809-1817): 2609, 4246
 Historical studies: 2282
 Indians of North America: 3041
 Land settlement: 2609, 3041
 Legislature: 1048
 Militia: 2609
 Slavery: 4746
 Trade and commerce: 3041
  Cattle: 1038
MISSISSIPPI VALLEY:
 see also MIDDLE WEST
 Cotton trade: 1357
 Description and travel: 1060, 3524
 Land development: 4348
 Marketing of merchandise: 4109
MISSISSIPPI VALLEY HISTORICAL REVIEW: 5054
MISSISSIPPI v. N. G. NYE: 2012
MISSOURI: 4648
 see also MIDDLE WEST
 Abolition of slavery and abolitionist sentiment: 3255, 5335
 Agriculture: 2554, 4152, 5218, 5551
  see also MISSOURI--Crops, and names of specific crops; MISSOURI--Farming
  Study and teaching: 2604
 American poetry--Saint Louis: 4755
 Bags, Shipment of: 5155
 Banks and banking:
  Saint Louis: 4063
 Baptist churches: 1806
 Bonds: 3301
 Brickmaking--Saint Louis: 5137
 Bridge construction: 2817
 British foreign investment in land: 3179
 Business affairs: 2386
 Cattle: 865, 3540
  Prices: 3540

MISSOURI (Continued):
 Civil War: see appropriate subheadings under CIVIL WAR; CONFEDERATE STATES OF AMERICA; and UNITED STATES--ARMY--Civil War
 Clothing and dress:
  Saint Louis: 5155
 Coal mining: 2076
 Commodity prices: 865, 3540, 4152, 4161, 4406
 Confederate emigrants: 3038
 Corn: 3540
 Courts: 4323
 Crops: 2663
  see also the following subheadings under MISSOURI: Agriculture; Farming; and names of specific crops
  Pettis County: 1174
 Currency: 1339
 Description and travel:
  1800s: 57, 1490, 5018
  1830s: 1791
  1850s: 489, 5335
  1860s: 4369
 Diseases:
  Cholera: 3255
  Meningitis--Saint Louis: 5731
 Droughts: 5551
 Economic conditions (1800s): 57, 2264, 5218
 Education: 57, 1758, 4552
  see also MISSOURI--Teaching
 Farm life: 1882
 Farming: 865
 Floods: 5551
 Flour mills--Saint Louis: 128
 Fugitive slaves: 5551
 Government agencies and officials:
  Adjutants General: 3703
 Governors:
  Claiborne Fox Jackson (1861): 3703
  Hamilton Rowan Gamble (1861-1864): 3703
  Thomas C. Fletcher (1865-1869): 3703
 Grain: 3540
 Grasshoppers--Lafayette County: 5984
 Hiring of slaves: 5392
 Historical societies: 2386
 Historical studies: 5481
 Honors and awards: 2604
 Judicial appointments: 4323
 Kindergartens:
  Saint Louis: 3295
 Labor conditions: 2554
 Labor costs--Saint Louis: 5137
 Land: 480, 753
  Prices: 2663
 Land deeds and indentures:
  Saint Louis: 5155
 Land settlement: 5018, 5984
 Land speculation: 5392
 Landscape gardening on college campuses: 3048
 Law practice:
  Hannibal: 4616
  Perryville: 2515
  Saint Louis: 4616
 Lawsuits: 4786
 Legal affairs: 2604
 Livestock prices: 3255
 Mercantile accounts:
  Calhoun: 5392
  Millersburg: 5392
 Merchandise inventories:
  Calhoun: 5392
 Merchants--Saint Louis: 3012
 Migration to: 1557, 1920, 3176, 3255, 3540, 4834, 5392
 Militia: 3703, 5425
  Reorganization (1863): 3703
  Units:
   5th Regiment: 3703
   Southwest Battalion: 3703

MISSOURI (Continued):
  Millers' accounts--Calhoun: 5392
  Mining: 669, 4161
    Saint François County: 2386
  Mormons and mormonism: 1920
    Relations with Indians: 5392
  Newspapers: 713
  Personal finance:
    Saint Louis: 520, 5155
  Philanthropy: 2386
  Pioneer life: 4161
  Political patronage: 1620
  Politics and government:
    1800s:
      1830s: 2264
      1840s: 2264
      1850s: 2264, 4174, 4834
      1860s: 4733, 4834
      1870s: 4834
    1800s-1900s: 4786
  Railroads: 2386, 4161
  Real estate--Saint Louis: 5155
  Reconstruction: 4406
  Religion: 57, 2663
  Religious sects: 4202
  Riding equipment--Saint Louis: 5155
  Secession and secessionist sentiment: 1683
  Segregation: 5984
  Silver question: 3038
  Slave trade: 5392
    Prices: 2663, 3255
  Slavery: 3255
  Slaves: see MISSOURI--Fugitive slaves; MISSOURI--Hiring of slaves
  Social conditions: 1405, 5335
  Social life and customs:
    1700s-1800s: 2663
    1800s: 2515
    1800s-1900s: 299, 4029
  Soils: 3532
  Southern unionists: 4443, 4552
  Streams: 3532
  Taxation--Saint Louis: 5155
  Teaching: 303
    see also MISSOURI--Education
  Temperance: 3197, 5335
  Textile industry: 1695
    Federal taxation: 1695
    Finance: 1695
  Tobacco culture: 57
  Trade and commerce:
    Dry goods--Saint Louis: 5155
    Food: 5006
    Slaves: see MISSOURI--Slave trade
    Textiles: 1695
    Tobacco: 57
  Universities and colleges: see BAPTIST FEMALE COLLEGE; CENTRAL WESLEYAN COLLEGE; UNIVERSITY OF MISSOURI; WASHINGTON UNIVERSITY
  Weather: 2663
  Wood: 3532
  Wool carding--Calhoun: 5392
MISSOURI, U.S.S.: 5841
MISSOURI COMPROMISE: 1086, 2107, 2661
MISSOURI HISTORICAL SOCIETY: 2386
MISSOURI RIVER: 2817
  Fur trade: 3357
MISSOURI v. KENTUCKY: 4443
"MR. JEFFERSON PREPARES AN ITINERARY" by Elizabeth Cometti: 4625
"MR. LEE'S PLAN--MARCH 29, 1777": THE TREASON OF CHARLES LEE: 3735
"MRS. CATT ON LEAGUE OF NATIONS AND THE PRESIDENTIAL ELECTION" by Carrie Chapman Catt: 5110
"MRS. JOE PERSON'S REMEDY": 4154
MRS. MEAD'S SCHOOL, Richmond, Virginia: 5513, 5529
MITCHELL, Amanda Gertrude: 4679
MITCHELL, Sir Andrew: 3315
MITCHELL, David Brydie: 3704
MITCHELL, Donald Grant: 3705
MITCHELL, Edward Bedinger: 3710
MITCHELL, Elisha (1793-1857): 730, 5036, 5460

MITCHELL, George Frederick: 4453
MITCHELL, George Sinclair: 3706
MITCHELL, Jacob Duché: 3707
MITCHELL, James A.: 3708
MITCHELL, John, Jr. (1815-1875): 4524
MITCHELL, John A.: 3708
MITCHELL, John Fulton Berrien, Sr.: 3710
MITCHELL, John Fulton Berrien, Jr.: 3710
MITCHELL, John Kearsley (1793-1858): 5771
MITCHELL, John W. (New York): 3709
MITCHELL, Langdon Elwyn: 3797
MITCHELL, Lydia Ann (Hughes): 4679
MITCHELL, Margaret: 103
MITCHELL, Mary (Dedinger): 404
MITCHELL, Nina Cornelia: 3710
MITCHELL, Samuel: 2486
MITCHELL, Sarah P. (Berrien): 3710
MITCHELL, T.: 3802
MITCHELL, W. M.: 106
MITCHELL, William: 3711
MITCHELL FAMILY (New York--Genealogy): 3710
MITCHELL COLLEGE, Statesville, North Carolina: 3552
MITCHELL COUNTY, North Carolina:
  Wing--Mercantile accounts: 4182
MITFORD, John Freeman, First Baron Redesdale: 2836
MITTERMAIER, Professor ___: 1087
MIXON, Winfield Henri: 3712
MOBILE, Alabama:
  1800s: 976, 3016
  1840s: 3511, 5977
  1850s: 1408, 3511, 5977
  1860s: 1507, 3154, 3184, 3511, 4738
  1870s: 1507, 4738
  1800s-1900s: 1300, 3657
  American authors: 1449
  Civil War:
    see also CIVIL WAR--CAMPAIGNS, BATTLES, AND MILITARY ACTIONS-- Alabama--Mobile
    Army camp: 3500
    Fortifications: 13
  Clergy--Methodist: 1915
  Commission merchants: 5879
  Commodity prices: 4911
  Cotton trade: 4911
  Description: 249, 284, 1490
  Economic conditions: 5744
  Merchants: 1915
  Methodist churches:
    see also MOBILE--Clergy
    Negro churches: 249
  Naval stores trade: 4911
  Politics and government: 249, 5744
  Slave coffles: 4387
  Slave trade: 1801
  Social life and customs: 3761, 5968
  Spanish activities in (1780): 3209
  Spanish settlement (1800s): 3041
  Steamboat lines: 1602
  Teaching: 3761
  Test oaths: 4515
  Theater: 3611
  United States Army life: 3789
MOBILE AND OHIO RAILROAD: 5977
MOBILE BAY, Alabama: see CIVIL WAR-- CAMPAIGNS, BATTLES, AND MILITARY ACTIONS--Alabama--Mobile Bay
MOBILE COUNTY, Alabama:
  Mobile: see MOBILE, Alabama
MOBILIZATION: see AMERICAN REVOLUTION-- Mobilization; and Mobilization as subheading under names of armies
MOCKSVILLE, North Carolina: 832, 1100, 1513, 1936, 2749, 2857, 3543, 5335
  see also CLEGG'S COLLEGE
MOCKSVILLE LODGE NO. 134, Mocksville, North Carolina: 2857
MODERN LANGUAGE ASSOCIATION, American Literature Group: 102
MOFFETT, Andrew: 3713
MOFFITT, Henry M.: 3714

MOFFITT, Marshall: 1948
MOFUSSEL POLICE: 536
MOGALAS, Arizona:
  United States Army camps: 3843
MOHAMET V, Sultan of Turkey (1844-1918): 572
MOHAMMED ALI, Nabob of Arcot: 1629, 2037, 2422
MOHAMMEDAN ANGLO-ORIENTAL COLLEGE, India: see ALIGARH MUSLIM UNIVERSITY
MOHAWK (ship): 99
MOIRA, Francis Rawdon-Hastings, First Marquis of Hastings and Second Earl of: 2421, 3446
MOLASSES STORAGE:
  Louisiana--New Orleans: 679
MOLASSES TRADE:
  North Carolina: 1281
MOLDERS: see INTERNATIONAL MOLDERS' UNION OF NORTH AMERICA
MOLESWORTH, William Nassau: 3715
MOLLY (ship): 144
MOLYNEAUX, J. B.: 3716
MONAHAN, Bridget: 3717
MONAHAN, Hugh: 3717
MONARCH MINING AND SMELTING COMPANY, Arizona: 4918
"MONARQUÍA ESPAÑOLA" by Juan Francisco Masdeu: 3549
MONASTÈRE DE SAINTE CLAIRE, Grenoble, France: 2197
MONASTERIES:
  Delaware: 3899
  France--Tours: 5323
MONASTERY OF THE VISITATION, Wilmington, Delaware: 3899
MONBO COTTON MILL, Catawba, North Carolina: 3718
MONCADA, Francisco Muñoz Ramón de: 4982
MONCEY, Bon-Adrien Jeannot de, Duc de Conegliano: 4348
MONCK'S CORNER, South Carolina:
  Confederate refugees: 5645
MONCURE, Richard Cassius Lee: 2080
MONCURE, St. Leger Landon: 3719
MONER, Mr. ___: 5042
MONEY: 1339
  see also CIVIL WAR--CIVILIAN LIFE-- Scarcity of money; COINS AND COINAGE; CURRENCY; PAPER MONEY; PROMISSORY NOTES; SCRIP; SILVER QUESTION
  Transferability: see CURRENCY CONVERTIBILITY
  Value: 4592
MONEY LENDING: see LOANS; USURY
MONEY PRINTING: see COPPERPLATE ENGRAVING
MONGKUT, King of Thailand (1804-1868): 5238
MONITOR, U.S.S.: 3281
  see also CIVIL WAR--CAMPAIGNS, BATTLES, AND MILITARY ACTIONS-- Naval engagements--Monitor, U.S.S. v. Virginia, C.S.S.
MONKSHILL, Scotland: 119
MONKTON, Vermont: 3665
MONMOUTH, Iowa: 1619
MONMOUTH COUNTY, New Jersey:
  Deal: 2409
  Shrewsbury: 1446
MONMOUTHSHIRE, England:
  Newport: 1970
MONOCACY RIVER (Maryland): 3145
MONOGHAN MILLS: see VICTOR- MONOGHAN MILLS
MONONGAHELA CITY, Pennsylvania: 1332
MONONGAHELA CITY FIRE AND LIFE INSURANCE COMPANY, Monongahela City, Pennsylvania: 1332
MONONGALIA COUNTY, West Virginia:
  Morgantown: 2986, 5755
  see also WEST VIRGINIA UNIVERSITY
  Girls' schools and academies: 2794
MONOPOLIES: 4552

MONROE, Alexander: 3721
MONROE, Harriet: 2871
MONROE, J. Turner: 3721
MONROE, James (1758-1831): 70, 1308, 3251, 3273, 3720, 3809
  Minister to France: 4348
  Secretary of State: 1302, 1424
MONROE, James A.: 3721
MONROE, John: 3721
MONROE, Nathan C.: 2963
MONROE, Sarah: 1348
MONROE, Thomas: 175
MONROE, Will Seymour: 2449
MONROE, Louisiana:
  Civil War aid societies: 3071
MONROE, North Carolina: 3439
  Schools: 2573
MONROE ADVERTISER, Forsyth, Georgia (newspaper): 2374
MONROE CIRCUIT, Methodist churches: 3646
MONROE COUNTY, Alabama: 265
MONROE COUNTY, Georgia:
  Forsyth: 3314
  Journalism: 2374
MONROE COUNTY, Mississippi:
  Fort Claiborne: 3123
MONROE COUNTY, Missouri: 4733
MONROE COUNTY, New York: 2436
  Parma: 4662
  Pittsford: 4375
  Rochester:
    Business affairs: 2436
    Merchants: 4256
    Tobacco trade--Advertising: 1586
MONROE COUNTY, West Virginia:
  Civil War: 52
  Union: 884
MONROE COUNTY, Wisconsin:
  Tomah: 4974
MONROVIA, Liberia: 41
  Negro colonization: 5298
MONSON, Sir Edmund John, First Baronet: 3722
MONSON, William (1760-1807): 5331
MONSON, William John, First Viscount Oxenbridge: 3722
MONSON, Massachusetts:
  Schools: 4897
MONSON ACADEMY, Monson, Massachusetts: 4897
MONT CLARE, Pennsylvania: 4190
MONTAGU, Basil: 3723
MONTAGU, John, Fourth Earl of Sandwich: 3724
MONTAGU, Lord Robert (1825-1902): 3725
MONTAGU, William Drogo, Seventh Duke of Manchester: 2826
MONTAGUE, A. B.: 3727
MONTAGUE, Andrew Jackson: 3726
MONTAGUE, James Y.: 3727
MONTAGUE, William Pepperell: 1097
MONTAGUE FAMILY (North Carolina): 3727
MONTALEMBERT, Charles Forbes René de: 2148
MONTANA:
  see also MONTANA TERRITORY
  Agriculture: 5426
  Business affairs: 1211
  Cattle ranches: 3424
  Clergy--Helena: 2407
  Gold mines: 4918
  Gold rush: 4834
  Mining speculation: 4161
  Race relations--Helena: 2407
  Railroads: 1211
  Sheepherding: 4161
MONTANA CONSOLIDATED GOLD MINING COMPANY: 4918
"MONTANA HALL," White Post, Virginia: 1211
MONTANA TERRITORY: 5905
MONTEAGUDO, Bernardo: 4155
MONTEAGLE OF BRANDON, Thomas Spring-Rice, First Baron (1790-1866): 5011, 5277

MONTEAGLE OF BRANDON, Thomas Spring-Rice, Second Baron (b. 1849): 2149
MONTEAGLE, Tennessee:
  Highlander Folk School: 3558
MONTEITH, Walter: 3391
"MONTEROSA," Virginia: 4916
MONTEMAR, José Carrillo de Albornoz, Duque de: 873
MONTEREY, California: 1900
MONTEREY COUNTY, California:
  Monterey: 1900
MONTEREY, Mexico: 778
MONTERO BOLOÑOS, Francisco: 4155
MONTEVIDEO, Uruguay:
  Description: 2963
MONTEZUMA by Augustin Louis Taveau: 5193
MONTFORT, Joseph: 4918, 5352
MONTGOMERY, Hugh: 872
MONTGOMERY, John (d. 1744): 5457
MONTGOMERY, John, Jr. (1764-1828): 3728
MONTGOMERY, Julia: 3729
MONTGOMERY, M. I.: 910
MONTGOMERY, Matilda: 972
MONTGOMERY, Robert: 306, 2146
MONTGOMERY, Seaborn, Jr.: 3729
MONTGOMERY, W. P.: 4154
MONTGOMERY, Mrs. W. P.: 4154
MONTGOMERY, William J.: 5457
MONTGOMERY FAMILY (South Carolina or Tennessee): 718
MONTGOMERY FAMILY (Virginia): 872
MONTGOMERY, Alabama: 637, 642, 1178, 1299, 3191, 3771, 3796, 4195
  Booksellers and bookselling: 4008
  Confederate Army hospitals: 5098
  Description: 249, 284
  Diseases--Yellow fever: 3290
  Slave trade: 1801
MONTGOMERY, HOWARD, AND CARROLL RAILROAD COMPANY: 4886
MONTGOMERY CIRCUIT, Methodist churches: 3646
MONTGOMERY COUNTY, Alabama:
  Montgomery: see MONTGOMERY, Alabama
MONTGOMERY COUNTY, Georgia: 3110
MONTGOMERY COUNTY, Indiana:
  Crawfordsville: 5524
MONTGOMERY COUNTY, Maryland:
  Blacksmith's accounts: 3982
  Free Negroes: 3982
  Lawsuits: 3982
  Mercantile accounts: 3982
  Orphans' Court: 4457
  Plantations: 1416
MONTGOMERY COUNTY, North Carolina: 1438, 2113
  Agriculture: 4689
  Land: 1577
  Teachers' records: 5123
  Voter registration: 4689
  Wills: 4689
  Cities and towns:
    Biscoe: 4018
    Hunsucker's Store: 75
    Mount Gilead: 675, 2730, 4689
    Ophir: 1417
    Pekin: 675
    Star--Lumber mills: 3225
MONTGOMERY COUNTY, Ohio:
  Germantown: 2507
MONTGOMERY COUNTY, Pennsylvania: 2306
  Abington: 270
  Clarksville: 3253
  Merion: 552
  Overbrook: 5940
  Wyncote: 3267
MONTGOMERY COUNTY, Tennessee: 1319
  Clarksville: 2488
  Postal Service: 4854
MONTGOMERY COUNTY, Virginia:
  Plantations: 2633
  Surveying: 4315
  Cities and towns:
    Blacksburg: see BLACKSBURG, Virginia

MONTGOMERY COUNTY, Virginia:
  Cities and towns (Continued):
    Christiansburg: 1033, 4360
    Fotheringay: 1646
    Radford: 2770, 3979
MONTGOMERY MILLS, Pennsylvania (firm): 2521
MONTHLY REPOSITORY: 1879
MONTICELLO, Florida: 4068
MONTICELLO, Georgia: 1229
"MONTICELLO," Charlottesville, Virginia: 2139, 5751
MONTIJO, Eugénie de: see EUGÉNIE, Empress Consort of Napoléon III
MONTPELIER, North Carolina: 5688
"MONTPELIER," Virginia: 3455
MONTPELIER FEMALE INSTITUTE, Monroe County, Georgia: 339, 2828, 2963
  Students and student life: 4040
MONTREAL, Canada: 96, 4719, 4817
  Description: 3087, 4175
MONTREAT, North Carolina:
  Forest conservation: 4080
MONTROSE PLANTATION, North Carolina: 1475
MONTVILLE, Connecticut: 752
MONUMENTS: 128
  see also HISTORIC SITES; MEMORIALS; and names of specific monuments
  Georgia:
    Midway: 1171
    Stone Mountain: 5090
  Great Britain:
    To Thomas Muir: 3816
    To Robert Southey: 3498
  New York--New Rochelle: 4025
  North Carolina:
    To Otway Burns: 3955
  South Carolina:
    To John C. Calhoun: 1929
  Southern States: 3657
  United States:
    Bronze: 1665
    To George Washington: 1778, 4892, 5584
  Virginia:
    Photographs: 1424
    Virginia Military Institute: 3809
    To William Wirt: 5848
MONZON, Pascual Antonio: 4155
MOOD FAMILY (South Carolina-- Genealogy): 1468
MOODY, B. (Virginia): 3730
MOODY, Dwight Lyman: 561
MOODY, James M.: 3407
MOODY, Y. M.: 3730
MOOMAW, Jacob P.: 3731
MOORE, Captain _____: 4360
MOORE, A. (Illinois): 3732
MOORE, Allen: 3747
MOORE, Ann: 3752
MOORE, Bartholomew Figures: 5280
MOORE, Benjamin Burges: 5404
MOORE, Charles E.: 3745
MOORE, David: 3754
MOORE, Edgar Ackley: 4743
MOORE, Elizabeth: 5390
MOORE, Elizabeth S. (Stump): 3742
MOORE, F.: 3240
MOORE, Francis: 3733
MOORE, Frank: 3734
MOORE, Fred Atkins: 5252
MOORE, George (1852-1933): 2102, 2146
MOORE, George Augustus: 2146
MOORE, George Henry (1823-1892): 3269, 3734, 3735
MOORE, Sir Graham: 3736
MOORE, Harriet: 4286
MOORE, Henry (1751-1844): 3738, 4146
MOORE, Sir Henry (1713-1769): 3737
MOORE, Hight C.: 5457
MOORE, Horatio Franklin: see MOORE, Frank
MOORE (J. AND W.), Greenville, North Carolina (firm): 3739
MOORE, J. Harry: 3740
MOORE, James Otis: 3741
MOORE, John (Maryland): 3742

841

MOORE, John (North Carolina): 3743
MOORE, Sir John (1761-1809): 3736, 3836
MOORE, Sir John Samuel (1831-1916): 3744
MOORE, John T. (North Carolina): 3745
MOORE, John W.: 264
MOORE, John Wheeler, Sr. (1833-1906): 3746
MOORE, Lillie: 1738
MOORE, Marianne: 293
MOORE, Mary: 3747
MOORE, Mary Elizabeth (Ross): 3741
MOORE, Merrill: 2871, 3748
MOORE, N. B.: 3749
MOORE, Niven: 3193
MOORE, Ogle William: 1087
MOORE, Pauline (Settle): 4743
MOORE, Phillips: 3752, 5390
MOORE, R. G. (California): 3750
MOORE, R. J. (North Carolina): 999
MOORE, Sarah Elizabeth: 3741
MOORE, Sid F.: 3751
MOORE, Stephen (1733-1799): 795, 3752
MOORE, Stephen (grandson of Stephen Moore, 1733-1799): 3752
MOORE, Stephen, Second Earl Mountcashell: 2421
MOORE, T. V.: 1832, 2612
MOORE, Thomas (Cuba): 3753
MOORE, Thomas (Maryland): 3754
MOORE, Thomas (1779-1852): 821, 4770
MOORE, W. S.: 3755
MOORE, William Henry: 3756
MOORE FAMILY (Alabama): 444
MOORE FAMILY (Maine--Genealogy): 3741
MOORE FAMILY (New Hampshire-- Genealogy): 3741
MOORE FAMILY (North Carolina-- Genealogy): 3752
MOORE FAMILY (South Carolina): 1472
MOORE COUNTY, North Carolina: 3393, 4396, 4489, 5123, 5752
   Business affairs: 5792
   Civil War: 755
   Debt: 5792
   Methodist Episcopal Church, South: 1096
   Personal finance: 5792
   Schools: 827
   Cities and towns:
      Caledonia: 1437, 3449
      Carthage: 5138
MOORE MILLS CO.: see VANN-MOORE MILLS CO.
MOOREFIELD, West Virginia: 5371
   Civil War: 2958
MOORE'S BUSINESS COLLEGE, Atlanta, Georgia: 4911
MOORE'S CREEK, North Carolina: see AMERICAN REVOLUTION--Campaigns and battles--North Carolina-- Moore's Creek
MOORE'S ORDINARY, Virginia:
   Merchants: 2331
MOORESVILLE, North Carolina:
   Health resorts: 3415
   Textile mills: 3757
MOORESVILLE MILLS, Mooresville, North Carolina: 3757
MOORMAN, S. T.: 3758
MOORT, Paulus: 41
MOOSEHEART HOME AND SCHOOL: 3633
MORAGNE, Allen: 3759
MORAGNE, Isaac: 3759
MORAGNE, Peter B.: 3759
MORAGNE, Mrs. S. E.: 3759
MORAGNE FAMILY (South Carolina-- Genealogy): 3759
MORAL EDUCATION: 1747
MORAL PHILOSOPHY: see ETHICS
MORALE:
   see also CIVIL WAR--CIVILIAN LIFE-- Morale; HOMESICKNESS; and Morale as subheading under names of armies and navies
   Scotland: 15

MORALS: 3981
   see also as subheading under names of armies and navies
MORAN, Antonio Alvarez: see ÁLVAREZ MORÁN, Antonio
MORAN, George Henry Roberts: 3760
MORAN, James: 5628
MORANT, Robert Laurie: 4709
MORAVIAN CHURCH: 872
   Germany: 5459
   Great Britain: 2751, 5726
   North Carolina: 1469, 4423
   Pennsylvania: 4423
MORAVIAN WOOLEN MILLS (firm): 1536
MORDECAI, Alfred: 3761
MORDECAI, Carolina: 3761
MORDECAI, Ellen: 3761
MORDECAI, Emma: 3761
MORDECAI, George W.: 5457
MORDECAI, Isabel R.: 3761
MORDECAI, Jacob: 3761
MORDECAI, Margaret: 1475
MORDECAI, Pattie: 3761
MORDECAI, Rachel: 3761
MORDECAI, Samuel (1786-1865): 3761
MORDECAI, Samuel Fox (1852-1923): 1336
MORDECAI, Solomon: 3761
MORDECAI FAMILY (North Carolina): 1475, 3761
MORDECAI FAMILY (Virginia): 3761
MOREHEAD, Eugene: 3762
MOREHEAD, J. Turner: 3762
MOREHEAD, James F.: 5149
MOREHEAD, James Turner (1838-1919): 3763
MOREHEAD, James Turner, Jr.: 3763
MOREHEAD, John Motley (1796-1866): 2776, 3764
MOREHEAD, John Motley (1866-1923): 706, 1336
MOREHEAD, Lucy: 3762
MOREHEAD, Margaret: 4079
MOREHEAD, William: 3765
MOREHEAD BANKING COMPANY, Durham, North Carolina: 1041
MOREHEAD CITY, North Carolina:
   Political clubs: 3960
   Shipping companies: 658
MOREHOUSE PARISH, Louisiana:
   Bastrop: 900
   Point Jefferson:
      Civil War: 508
MOREL, L. D.: 1424
MORELAND, Joseph: 3766
MOREY, William: 2092
MORGAN, Arthur A.: 3767
MORGAN, Edwin Denison: 3768
MORGAN, Edwin Wright: 3769
MORGAN, George: 3775
MORGAN, Henry: 3770
MORGAN, Henry Waller (d. 1861): 1424
MORGAN, Howell: 3775
MORGAN, Irby: 3771
MORGAN (J. P.) AND COMPANY: 4556
MORGAN, James: 3772
MORGAN, James Morris: 1424
MORGAN (JOHN) AND COMPANY, Shenandoah County, Virginia: 3773
MORGAN, John Hunt (1825-1864): 1403, 3771, 5268
MORGAN, John Tyler (1824-1907): 706, 2446, 3774
MORGAN, Lavina: 1424
MORGAN, Mark: 3776
MORGAN, S. D.: 3771
MORGAN, Samuel Tate: 3762
MORGAN, Sarah Fowler: 3775
MORGAN, Sarah Ida Fowler: 1424
MORGAN, Sydney (Owenson): 2146
MORGAN, Thomas Gibbes (1799-1861): 1424, 3775
MORGAN, Thomas Gibbes (d. 1864): 3775
MORGAN, William M.: 3762
MORGAN FAMILY: 404
MORGAN FAMILY (Louisiana--Genealogy): 1424, 3775

MORGAN FAMILY (Virginia and West Virginia): 3721
MORGAN COUNTY, Alabama:
   Decatur: 4994
MORGAN COUNTY, Georgia:
   Judges: 4415
   Religion: 1413
   Cities and towns:
      Madison: 127, 4415, 4426
      Cotton trade: 497
MORGAN COUNTY, Illinois:
   Jacksonville: 5944
MORGAN COUNTY, Tennessee:
   Land and land settlement: 5224
MORGAN COUNTY, West Virginia:
   Great Cacapon: 1318
MORGAN-MALLOY COTTON MILLS, North Carolina: 3776
MORGAN'S POINT, Texas: 3772
MORGAN'S RAID: see CIVIL WAR-- CAMPAIGNS, BATTLES, AND MILITARY ACTIONS--Kentucky--Morgan's Raid
MORGANTON, North Carolina: 248, 838, 4192, 5310
   Churches: 2111
   Mental hospitals: 2890
   Municipal government: 3937
MORGANTON CIRCUIT, Methodist Churches: 3646
MORGANTOWN, West Virginia: 2986, 5755
   see also WEST VIRGINIA UNIVERSITY
   Girls' schools and academies: 2794
MORNINGTON, Richard Colley Wellesley, Marquis Wellesley and Second Earl of: 4024, 5639
MORI, Arinori Jugoi: 4486
MORIER, Isaac: 3183
MORLEY, J., Jr.: 4188
MORLEY, John: 1014, 2146, 4520
MORLEY, John, First Viscount Morley of Blackburn: 278, 663, 1815
MORLEY, Samuel: 2149, 4104
"MORMON TOWN": 4353
MORMON WAR (1857-1861): 1333
MORMONS AND MORMONISM: 1333, 1403
   Missouri: 1920
   Relations with Indians: 5392
   Utah--Political activity: 2368
THE MORNING CHRONICLE (Whig newspaper, Great Britain): 1632
MORPETH, George Howard, Viscount: 1648
MORPHINE ADDICTION:
   North Carolina: 4506
MORRELL, Eric: 5856
MORRILL, Justin Smith: 1364, 3022
MORRIS, Charles: 4616, 5546
MORRIS, Charles Jewett: 3778
MORRIS, George Pope: 3779
MORRIS, Gouverneur: 4218
MORRIS, Harrison Smith: 2449
MORRIS, James (Connecticut): 3196
MORRIS, James (New York): 4092
MORRIS, Joseph: 5752
MORRIS, Maud Burr: 5316
MORRIS, Richard I.: 674
MORRIS, Robert (1734-1806): 3780
MORRIS, Stephen Brent: 3781
MORRIS, Thomas: 3782
MORRIS, William (Great Britain, 1834-1896): 5553
MORRIS, William (North Carolina): 3738
MORRIS AND CRONLY (firm): see CRONLY AND MORRIS
MORRIS ISLAND, South Carolina:
   Civil War:
      see also CIVIL WAR--CAMPAIGNS, BATTLES, AND MILITARY ACTIONS-- South Carolina--Morris Island
   United States Army ordnance: 5433
MORRISON, Hallie N.: 3785
MORRISON, J. S.: 3784
MORRISON, James: 3785
MORRISON, John (Great Britain): 4137
MORRISON, John Robert (1814-1843): 3786

MORRISON, Mary Anna: 2792
MORRISON, Robert (1782-1834): 3786
MORRISON, Robert Hall (1798-1889): 5457
MORRISON, Thomas: 3787
MORRISON TURNING COMPANY: 1197
MORRISS, Beverly Preston: 3788
MORRISS, Jessie: 3788
MORRISS, Loula: 3788
MORRISVILLE, North Carolina: 3223
MORRISVILLE, Pennsylvania: 4188
MORRISVILLE, Vermont:
  Civil War: 1564
MORRMAN, Kate (Lewis): 3199
MORRO VELHO, Brazil--Gold mines: 2750
MORROW, Charles: 4589
MORROW, Clara J. (Johnson): 3789
MORROW, Dwight Whitney: 5252
MORROW, James (South Carolina, 1820-1865): 3790
MORROW, James Elmer (Pennsylvania): 3789
MORROW, Jay Johnson: 3789
MORROW, John: 4598
MORROW, William: 5033
MORROW COUNTY, Ohio:
  Mount Gilead: 1235
MORSE, Edward Sylvester: 2106
MORSE, Harriet: 4934
MORSE, Jedidiah: 3165, 3791, 4371
MORSE, John Torrey, Jr.: 2449
MORSE, Robert (1743-1818): 4934
MORSE, Samuel Finley Breese: 1516, 4490
MORSE, Sophia (Godwin): 4934
"LA MORTE D'ARTHURE" by Sir Thomas Malory: 3477
MORTGAGES:
  see also LAND--Mortgages
  Foreclosure:
    South Carolina: 5193
    Virginia: 3979
  Subdivided by place:
    Georgia: 4887
    Maryland: 2295, 5193
      Baltimore: 4886
    Massachusetts: 2417, 3633, 5766
    New York: 2172
    North Carolina: 832, 4897, 5188
    Pennsylvania: 421
      Philadelphia: 5953
    South Carolina: 5271
      Beaufort County: 810
      Charleston: 5198
MORTON, Harry: see LOWDERMILK, William Harrison
MORTON, Jeremiah: 523
MORTON, William Dennis: 5457
MORWITZ, Ernst: 1992
MOSBY, Eliza S.: 5094
MOSBY, Fortune: 3792
MOSBY, Frederick S.: 3792
MOSBY, John Singleton: 1364, 3793, 4607, 4888, 5377
MOSBY'S PARTISAN RANGERS: 3793, 4888
  see also CONFEDERATE STATES OF AMERICA--ARMY--Regiments-- Virginia--Cavalry--43rd
MOSBY'S WAR REMINISCENCES AND STUART'S CAVALRY CAMPAIGNS by John Singleton Mosby: 3793
MOSCOSO, Alvaro Navia Boloños y: see BOLOÑOS Y MOSCOSO, Alvaro Navia
MOSCOW, Kentucky--Description: 1811
MOSCOW, Union of Soviet Socialist Republics: 4614
MOSELEY, Arthur T.: 3794
MOSELEY, William P.: 3794
MOSES (D. & I.) (firm): 709
MOSES, Franklin J.: 3795
MOSES, Joseph Winn: 3796
MOSES, Montrose Jonas (1878-1933): 2449, 3797
MOSES, Montrose Jonas (1899-1934): 4789
MOSLEMS: see MUSLIMS

MOSQUITOES:
  Mississippi--Natchez: 1762
  Tennessee: 5623
MOSS, Charles, Bishop of Oxford: 3798
MOSS POINT, Mississippi: 3634
MOSSY CREEK, Tennessee: see CIVIL WAR--CAMPAIGNS, BATTLES, AND MILITARY ACTIONS--Tennessee-- Mossy Creek
MOTHERS--Role in family: 3567
  see also FAMILY LIFE
MOTIER, Marie Joseph Paul Roch Yves Gilbert du, Marquis de Lafayette: 872, 2870, 1424, 3072, 3130, 3444, 3501, 3775, 3809
MOTION PICTURES: see MOVING PICTURES
MOTLEY, Edward: 5057
MOTLEY, Hartwell: 208, 3799
MOTLEY, John Lothrop: 5057
MOTLEY, Thomas: 5057
MOTLEY FAMILY (Genealogy): 3799
MOTOR BUS LINES: 1478
MOTT, John R.: 879
MOTT, Lucretia (Coffin): 1784
MOTTE, A. B.: 3800
MOTTE, Abraham: 3801
MOTTE, Isaac: 3801
MOTTE, Mrs. J. Ward: 4118
MOTTE, Jacob Rhett: 3801
MOTTE, Mary: 3801
MOTTE, Mary Maham (Haig): 3801
MOTTOES: 1338
  see also PROVERBS
  Celtic: 5155
  Norman: 5155
MOULTON, Charles Wells: 2449
MOULTRIE, William: 2780, 3802
MOULTRIE, Georgia: 4659
MOUNT AIRY, North Carolina: 4849
  Cotton mills: 5048
MOUNT AIRY, Virginia: 2131
MOUNT AIRY DISTRICT, Methodist churches: 3646
MOUNT CARMEL CIRCUIT, Methodist churches: 3646
MOUNT CLIO ACADEMY, Robeson County, North Carolina: 3803
MOUNT CRAWFORD, Virginia: 1509
MOUNT DESERT, Maine:
  Description: 43
MOUNT ENERGY SCHOOL, Granville County, North Carolina: 2833
MOUNT ERIN, Virginia: 5332
MOUNT GILEAD, North Carolina: 2730
  Blacksmiths' accounts: 4689
  Farm accounts: 4689
  Local elections: 4689
  Physicians' accounts: 675
MOUNT GILEAD, Ohio: 1235
MOUNT HERMON CIRCUIT, Methodist Protestant Church: 3646
MOUNT HOLLY, North Carolina:
  Cotton mills: 5100
MOUNT HOLYOKE ACADEMY, Holyoke, Massachusetts: 4897
MOUNT JACKSON, Virginia: 1920, 5980
MOUNT MARIA, Virginia--Schools: 5529
MOUNT MITCHELL, North Carolina: 5460
  Weather station: 1001
MOUNT MITCHELL ASSOCIATION OF ARTS AND SCIENCES: 1521
MOUNT NEBO SEMINARY, Mount Nebo, Pennsylvania: 3174
MOUNT OLIVE, North Carolina:
  Gasoline trade: 5756
  Mercantile accounts: 5756
MOUNT OLIVET CHURCH (North Carolina): 3646
MOUNT PLEASANT, North Carolina: 4164, 4891
MOUNT PLEASANT, Virginia: 4483
MOUNT PLEASANT CHURCH (North Carolina): 3646
MOUNT PLEASANT MASONIC SCHOOL, Wake County, North Carolina: 1783
MOUNT PLEASANT MISSIONARY SOCIETY (Maryland): 3804

MOUNT PROSPECT, Virginia: 73
MOUNT SOLON, Virginia: 1075
  Tailors' accounts: 114
MOUNT TIRZAH, North Carolina:
  Mercantile affairs: 3752
  Methodist Episcopal Church, South: 5023
MOUNT VERNON, Ohio: 3784
MOUNT VERNON, Virginia: 99, 5575
  Preservation: 1337, 1737
MOUNT VERNON ACADEMY, Chatham County, North Carolina: 2861
MOUNT VERNON ARSENAL, Alabama:
  Army life: 3789
MOUNT VERNON LADIES ASSOCIATION OF THE UNION: 1337
THE MOUNT VERNON PAPERS: 1737
MOUNT ZION ACADEMY, Winnsboro, South Carolina: 5193
MOUNTAIN CLIMBING:
  Himalayan Mountains: 5618
MOUNTAIN GROVE, Texas: 916
"MOUNTAIN VIEW," Virginia: 2513
MOUNTAINS:
  North Carolina: 761
  Tennessee: 761
MOUNTBATTEN, Louis Alexander, First Marquis of Milford-Haven: 452
MOUNTCASHELL, Stephen Moore, Second Earl: 2421
MOUNTCASTLE, George Williams: 5457
MOUNTS BAY, England--Harbors: 3080
MOURNE, Northern Ireland: 1010
MOUZON, Edwin Dubose: 879
MOVIES: see MOVING PICTURES
MOVING PICTURES: 3306, 5786
  see also FILM ADAPTATIONS
  Censorship: see CENSORSHIP-- Moving pictures
  Promotion: 958
  Scenarios: 1521
MOWING MACHINES: 388.
MOYLAN, Stephen: 3805
MOYOCK CIRCUIT, Methodist churches: 3646
MOZAMBIQUE:
  Description and travel: 5725
  Health conditions: 5725
  Missions and missionaries: 5725
  Portuguese administration: 5725
  Race relations: 5725
MUD LICK, North Carolina: 2861
  Post Office: 1326
MUDD, Samuel A.: 5715
MUDIE, Charles Edward: 2146
MUHAMMAD 'ALI, Khedive of Egypt: 3067
MUHLENBERG, Henry Augustus: 496
MUHLENBERG, William Augustus: 2999
MUHLENBURG, John Peter Gabriel: 3130
MUHLENBERG COUNTY, Kentucky:
  Greenville: 3082
  Slave register: 3955
MUIR, Henry: 3835
MUIR, Thomas: 3816, 4913
MUIRE, Thacker: 3806
MUIRE, Thomas S. Douglas: 3806
MUIRON, Just: 65
MULATTOES:
  South Carolina: 758
  Virginia: 600
"MULBERRY GROVE," Georgia (plantation): 2179, 2326
MULE TRADE--North Carolina: 3257
MULES:
  see also CIVIL WAR--CLAIMS-- Confiscated property--Horses and mules; CIVIL WAR--CONFISCATION OF PROPERTY--Horses and mules; and Horses and mules as subheading under names of armies
  Georgia--Forsyth County: 5260
  North Carolina--Franklin County: 5087
MULGRAVE, Henry Phipps, First Earl of: 4605
MULL, Ezra: 3807
MULL, John M.: 3807
MULL, Peter M.: 3807

MÜLLER, George Henry: 3808
MÜLLER, William: 3808
MÜLLER FAMILY (Germany): 3808
MULOCK, Dinah Maria: 2449
MULTAN POTTERY: 3224
MULVANY, John R.: 357
MULVANY, P. H.: 357
MUMFORD, Frederic Blackmar: 2604
MUMFORD FAMILY (Michigan): 2604
MUNCIE, Indiana: 1795
MUNFORD, Charles Ellis: 3809
MUNFORD, Elizabeth Throwgood (Ellis): 3809
MUNFORD, George Wythe: 3809, 4616
MUNFORD, John Durburrow: 2612
MUNFORD, Lizzie Ellis: 3809
MUNFORD, Sallie Radford: 3809, 5176
MUNFORD, Thomas Taylor: 1272, 1825, 3809, 4244
MUNFORD, Ursula Anna: 3809
MUNFORD, William: 872, 3809
MUNFORD FAMILY (Virginia): 5176
  Genealogy: 3809
MUNFORDVILLE, Kentucky: 751
MUNGER, Theodore Thornton: 284
MUNICH, Germany:
  British diplomat in: 3238
MUNICIPAL BONDS: 1339
MUNICIPAL BUDGET: see as subheading under local place names
MUNICIPAL ELECTIONS: see LOCAL ELECTIONS
MUNICIPAL EMPLOYEES: see GOVERNMENT AND CIVIC EMPLOYEES
MUNICIPAL GOVERNMENT:
  see also COUNTY GOVERNMENT
  Reform: 1792
    Great Britain: 5616
  Subdivided by place:
    Georgia:
      Brunswick: 1374
      Chatham County: 996
    Great Britain:
      Halifax: 5026
      London: 92, 1815
    Louisiana--New Orleans: 1830
    New York--New York: 4808
    North Carolina:
      Durham: 4736
      Greensboro: 5149
      Lumber Bridge: 3934
      Morganton: 3937
    Virginia:
      Fredericksburg: 4855
      Greenway Township: 4668
      Luray: 574
      Richmond: 858
MUNICIPAL GOVERNMENT BY COMMISSION:
  Texas--Galveston: 1001
  Virginia--Richmond: 3979
MUNICIPAL RECREATION:
  North Carolina--Durham: 2379
MUNICIPAL SERVICES:
  Pennsylvania--Bethlehem: 5312
MUNKITTRICK, Richard Kendall: 103
MUNN, Neill: 1577
MUNRO, Mr. _____ : 1099
MUNRO, David Alexander: 706, 4491
MUNRO, John (Great Britain): 2321
MUNROE, Julia Blanche: 2963
MUNROE, Nathan Campbell: 2963
MUNROE, Tabitha Easter (Napier): 2963
MUNSEY, Frank Andrew: 3265
MUNSTER, George Augustus Frederick Fitzclarence, First Earl of: 1911
MURAI, Kichibei: 4060
MURAI BROTHERS COMPANY, LTD., Tokyo, Japan: 4060
MURAT, Achille: 3072
MURCHISON, Kenneth Mackenzie: 5014
MURCHISON, Lucille Wright: 3548
MURDER TRIALS:
  Massachusetts: 4813
  Virginia: 2794
MURDERS:
  see also ASSASSINATIONS; CHEROKEE INDIANS--Murder of whites; SLAVES--Crimes--Murder

MURDERS (Continued):
  Alabama: 490, 861
  California: 1984
  Florida: 5740
  Great Britain: 4427
  Mexico: 5906
  North Carolina: 641
  Pennsylvania: 5775
  South Carolina: 1424, 3340
  Syria: 3118
MURDOCH, Francis Johnstone: 4918, 5457
MURDOCK, James Edward: 4086
MURDOCK, Kenneth Ballard: 102
MURDOCK AND BARCLAY (firm): 324
MURFREE, Mary Noailles: 3810
MURFREESBORO, North Carolina: 3914, 4874
  see also CHOWAN COLLEGE
  Mercantile accounts: 5857
  Trade and commerce: 5857
MURFREESBORO, Tennessee: 872, 2235, 3810, 4592
  Civil War: 3479
    see also CIVIL WAR--CAMPAIGNS, BATTLES, AND MILITARY ACTIONS-- Tennessee--Murfreesboro
MURPH, Daniel W.: 3811
MURPHY, David: 3812
MURPHY, James Madison: 3813
MURPHY, John Albert: 2449
MURPHY, Patrick: 2839
MURPHY, Timothy: 825
MURPHY, North Carolina: 3025
  Civil War: 1247
MURRAY, _____ (murder victim): 641
MURRAY, E. B.: 3814
MURRAY, Henry S.: 3815
MURRAY (J. T.) & COMPANY: 530
MURRAY, James Edward: 2109
MURRAY, John, Sr. (1778-1843): 3816
MURRAY, John, Jr. (1808-1892): 3816
MURRAY, Nicholas: 4235
MURRAY, Philip: 1883
MURRAY, W. C.: 3814
MURRAY, William, First Earl of Mansfield: 92, 2282
MURRAY, William Vans (1760-1803): 3384
"THE MURRAY, 1883": 4115
"THE MURRAY, 1886": 4115
MURRAY COUNTY, Georgia:
  Tilton: 4872
MURRAY-KYNYNMOUND, Gilbert John, Elliot-, Fourth Earl of Minto: see ELLIOT-MURRAY-KYNYNMOUND, Gilbert John, Fourth Earl of Minto
MURRELL, John Cobbs: 3817
MURRELL, William: 3818
MUSCAT, Arabia: 5797
MUSCLE SHOALS, Alabama: 5825
  Hydro-electric power plant: 1478
  Trading post: 2486
MUSCOGEE COUNTY, Georgia: 2538
  Columbus: see COLUMBUS, Georgia
MUSE, Battaile: 3819
MUSE, Benjamin: 3820
MUSE, James W.: 3821
MUSE, Lucinda: 1827
MUSE, Myra Ann: 4968
MUSEUM FOR THE BLIND, Raleigh, North Carolina: 4736
MUSEUMS:
  Administration: 2494
  Great Britain: see BRITISH MUSEUM
  North Carolina--Raleigh: 4736
  United States: 4022
MUSEVILLE, Virginia: 1801
MUSGRAVE, Sir Anthony: 1792
MUSGRAVE, Dudley Field: 1792
MUSGRAVE, Jeanie Lucinda (Field): 1792
MUSGRAVE, Thomas, Archbishop of York: 2149
MUSGRAVE FAMILY (Great Britain-- Genealogy): 1792
MUSGRAVE, PULIDO v.: see PULIDO v. MUSGRAVE

MUSGROVE, Adam Charles: 3822
MUSGROVE, Richard W.: 3822
MUSIC: see SONGS AND MUSIC
MUSICAL SOCIETIES:
  Georgia--Savannah: 4677
  West Virginia--Martinsburg: 5110
MUSKINGUM COUNTY, Ohio:
  Zanesville: 357
MUSLIMS:
  Relations with Hindus in India: 278
MUSSEY, Ellen Spencer: 358
MUSSEY, John B.: 3823
MUSSOLINI, Benito: 233
MUSSON, Eliza: 4995
MUSSON, Germain: 3824
MUSSOORIE, India:
  Description: 5525
MUSTARD AND CO.: 5252
MUTES: see DEAF
MUTINIES:
  Confederate States of America: see CONFEDERATE STATES OF AMERICA-- ARMY--Mutiny
  India: see GREAT BRITAIN--INDIAN ARMY--Mutinies; INDIAN MUTINY
  On the Garmany: 232
  Pardons: 5242
MUTUAL AND BANKING COMPANY, New Bern, North Carolina: 3955
MUTUAL RESERVE FUND LIFE ASSOCIATION, North Carolina: 3825
MY LADY TONGUE by Amélie Rives: 4491
"MY NATIVE TOWN" by James Hill Hutchins: 2739
MYAKKA COMPANY, South Carolina (firm): 4298
MYERS, Catherine Anne: 3826
MYERS, Harriet: 2858
MYERS, Henry: 1098
MYERS, Hiram Earl: 3828
MYERS, J. C.: 3826
MYERS (JOHN) & SON, Washington, North Carolina: 3827
MYERS, R. W.: 5035
MYERS, Rose Mae (Warren): 3828
MYERS, Samuel J.: 3829
MYERS, T. Bailey: 276
MYERS, Thomas Harvey Blount: 3827
MYERS PARK, Charlotte, North Carolina: 4918
MYERSON, Carla: 2379
MYRICK, Frances: 680
MYRICK, John D.: 3830
MYRICK, Marie E.: 3830
MYRICK, Robert Algernon: 3831
MYRICK FAMILY (Genealogy): 3831
MYRTLE BEACH, South Carolina: 4453
MYSORE, India:
  British administration: 4660
  Treaties with Great Britain: 5038
MYSORE WAR (Second, 1780-1784):
  Peace settlement: 3315
MYSORE WAR (Fourth, 1799): 563
  Campaigns and battles:
    Seringapatam: 5639
MYSTIC (ship): 2907
MYTHOLOGY: see CLASSICAL MYTHOLOGY

# N

N. & D. TALCOTT, New York, New York (firm): 2360
N. B. HANDY COMPANY, Lynchburg, Virginia: 2309
N. I. SMITH'S SCHOOL, Leaksville, North Carolina: 661
N. M. OSBORNE & COMPANY: 388
NABOB OF ARCOT: see MOHAMMED ALI, Nabob of Arcot
NABOB OF OUDH: see VIZRI ALI, Nabob of Oudh
NABOB WALAU JAN: see WALAU JAN, Nabob
NADENBOUSCH, John Quincy Adams: 3832
NAGASAKI, Japan: 5306
NAGPUR PROVINCE, India: 2756
NAGS HEAD, North Carolina: 4262
NALL, Haywood: 5123
NALLE, Thomas B.: 3833
NAMIER, Lewis Bernstein: 2148
NANCE, F.: 4834
NANSEMOND AGRICULTURAL SOCIETY, Nansemond County, Virginia: 3834
NANSEMOND COUNTY, Virginia:
　Agricultural societies: 3834
　County government: 3012
　Suffolk: see SUFFOLK, Virginia
NANTUCKET, Massachusetts: 4220
NAPIER, Sir Charles (1786-1860): 1640, 3836
NAPIER, Sir Charles James (1782-1853): 1147, 3736, 3835, 3836
NAPIER, Francis, Tenth Baron Napier: 2756
NAPIER, Sir George Thomas: 1147, 3836
NAPIER, Henry Edward: 306, 3836
NAPIER, Leroy: 3837
NAPIER, Robert Cornelis, First Baron Napier of Magdala: 3838
NAPIER, Tabitha Easter: 2963
NAPIER, Sir William Francis Patrick: 1147, 3736
NAPIER FAMILY (Georgia): 2963
NAPIER FAMILY (Great Britain): 3836
NAPLES, Italy: 2015, 2296
　Description: 39
NAPOLEÃO, Arthur: 3567
NAPOLEON I, Emperor of the French: 872, 1302, 2266, 4348
NAPOLEON III, Emperor of the French: 43, 1755, 2180, 3472, 4490
NAPOLEON, Arkansas: 1089
NAPOLEON by Thomas Edward Watson: 5594
NAPOLEONIC WARS (1799-1815): 616, 2266, 4383
　see also PENINSULAR WAR
　Arbitration between Great Britain and France: 4348
　Blockades: 2296
　Campaigns, battles, and military actions:
　　Egypt: 2266
　　France: 4289
　　Waterloo: 2421, 5726

NAPOLEONIC WARS (Continued):
　Economic aspects:
　　Effect on commerce: 1935
　　　Cotton and tobacco trade with Virginia: 2360
　　　Great Britain: 1598, 1775, 5830
　　　see also GREAT BRITAIN--ARMY--Napoleonic Wars
　　Fear of invasion by French: 5282
　Naval operations: 342, 887, 1311, 2836
　　Copenhagen:
　　　1801: 2296
　　　1807: 3883
　　Egypt: 5639
　　Netherlands: 1599
　　Sardinia: 1164
　　Seizure of neutral ships: 2147
　　Spain: 1599
　Preparations for war: 363
　Portugal: 4531
　Spain: 4531
"A NARRATIVE OF AFFAIRS ON THE COAST OF COROMANDEL FROM 1730-1754": 3128
NARRON, John A.: 3839
NARVÁEZ, Pánfilo de: 3269
NASH, Abner: 5768
NASH, Andrew O.: 3840
NASH, Edward Walker: 3841
NASH, Elizabeth Simpson: 1467
NASH, Frank: 795
NASH, Henry Kolloch: 5457
NASH, James Hemory: 3841
NASH, Joseph: 4967
NASH, Leonidas Lydwell: 5457
NASH, Martha Joanna Reade: 3022
NASH, William: 92
NASH COUNTY, North Carolina: 5706
　American Revolution--Desertion: 5475
　Crops: 5475
　Debt: 5475
　Farming: 273
　Medical practice: 4820
　Migration from: 5475
　Cities and towns:
　　Belford: 5924
　　Whitaker's: 273
NASHOBA, Tennessee: 4770
NASHVILLE, Tennessee:
　1700s-1800s: 2781
　1800s: 2371, 4358
　1820s: 2664
　1830s: 2664
　1840s: 3321
　1850s: 3321
　1860s: 2630, 4573
　1880s: 361
　1890s: 361, 3712
　1800s-1900s: 4723
　1900s: 1217, 2852
　Amusements: 5623
　Civic activities: 4101
　Civil War: 4032
　　see also CIVIL WAR--CAMPAIGNS, BATTLES, AND MILITARY ACTIONS--Tennessee--Nashville
　　Union Army camp: 2681
　　Victory celebration after fall of Atlanta: 2308
　Description:
　　1815: 1333
　　1827: 1556
　　1833: 5635
　　1850s: 5623
　　1870s: 4764
　Diseases:
　　Cholera: 4854, 5290, 5623
　Economic conditions: 5858
　Estates--Administration and settlement: 4854
　Fires (1856): 5290
　Freedmen, Arrests of: 5623
　Labor unions: 1193, 1200
　Lawyers' accounts: 3844

NASHVILLE, Tennessee (Continued):
　Methodist churches: 33
　Newspapers: 2053
　Postal service: 4854
　Publishers and publishing: 1191
　Railroads: 218
　Religious institute (proposed): 3377
　Religious literature--Methodist: 3646
　Sewerage: 5623
　Social life and customs: 2308
　Strikes--Printers: 5623
　Theater: 872
　Universities and colleges: see FISK UNIVERSITY; GEORGE PEABODY COLLEGE FOR TEACHERS; NASHVILLE NORMAL AND COLLEGIATE THEOLOGICAL INSTITUTE; STATE NORMAL COLLEGE; VANDERBILT UNIVERSITY
NASHVILLE (blockade runner): 1424
NASHVILLE CONVENTION (1850): 5361, 5549
NASHVILLE NORMAL AND COLLEGIATE THEOLOGICAL INSTITUTE, Nashville, Tennessee: 1344
NASIR UD-DIN, Shah of Persia: 3722
NASON, Arthur Huntington: 3797
NASSAU, Bahama Islands: 1115
　Blockade running during the American Civil War: 2766
　Description (1860s): 2963
NAST, Condé: 4373
NAT TURNER INSURRECTION: 1059, 3012, 5751
NATAL:
　Boer War: 1132
　British administration: 1792, 5725
　Constitution: 1792
　Education: 1792
　Kaffirs: 5725
　Marriage: 1792
　Missions and missionaries:
　　Church of England: 5725
　　Society for the Propagation of the Gospel: 5725
NATCHEZ, Mississippi: 100, 151, 1047, 1693, 1786, 3053, 3956, 5431, 5516
　Blank books industry: 4309
　Bookbinding: 4309
　Civil War: 3628
　Cotton plantations: 5047
　Description: 3322
　Diseases: 980
　　Yellow fever: 4246
　Economic conditions (1802): 130
　Fires (1836): 1762
　Merchants: 3873
　Post-roads: 2486
　Railroad construction: 1556
　Slave trade: 492, 4746
　Social life and customs: 1762
　Stationery industry: 4309
　Tornadoes: 3415
NATHANIEL BANDS EXPEDITION (1863): see CIVIL WAR--CAMPAIGNS, BATTLES, AND MILITARY ACTIONS--Louisiana--Red River Campaign of 1863
NATHANIEL BOYDEN AND SON (firm): 2857
NATICK, Massachusetts: 5808
NATIONAL ADVISORY COMMITTEE ON VOCATIONAL REHABILITATION: 4736
NATIONAL ADVISORY COUNCIL: see UNITED STATES--GOVERNMENT AGENCIES AND OFFICIALS--National Advisory Council
NATIONAL AGRICULTURAL UNION (Great Britain): 200
NATIONAL ANTHEMS--United States: 3220
NATIONAL ANTI-CORN LAW LEAGUE: 1126
NATIONAL ARMS & AMMUNITION (firm): 794
NATIONAL ASSOCIATION FOR THE ADVANCEMENT OF COLORED PEOPLE: 2379, 3850, 3852

NATIONAL ASSOCIATION OF AUDUBON
  SOCIETIES: 4453
NATIONAL ASSOCIATION OF DEMOCRATIC
  CLUBS: 2794
NATIONAL ASSOCIATION OF HOSIERY
  MANUFACTURERS, INC.: 101
NATIONAL ASSOCIATION OF LETTER
  CARRIERS: 3
NATIONAL ASSOCIATION OF PUBLIC
  SCHOOL ADULT EDUCATORS: 1758
NATIONAL BANK OF CHARLOTTESVILLE,
  Virginia: 4142, 5789
NATIONAL BANK OF NEW YORK: 310
NATIONAL BANKS:
  see also BANK OF THE UNITED
    STATES; and National banking
    system as subheading under
    names of governments
  Pennsylvania--Huntingdon: 421
NATIONAL BOLL WEEVIL CONTROL
  ASSOCIATION: 592
NATIONAL BOULDER DAM ASSOCIATION:
  4851
NATIONAL BROADCASTING COMPANY: 3797
NATIONAL CONFERENCE OF CHRISTIANS
  AND JEWS: 1197
NATIONAL CONFERENCE OF SOCIAL WORK:
  Pugsley Award: 4343
NATIONAL CONSERVATION ASSOCIATION:
  4851
NATIONAL CONVOCATION OF METHODIST
  YOUTH: 3020
NATIONAL COOPERATIVE MILK PRODUCERS'
  FEDERATION: 592
NATIONAL COUNCIL OF CHURCHES: 3020
  Delta ministry--Mississippi: 3001
NATIONAL CURRENCY DEPARTMENT: see
  UNITED STATES--GOVERNMENT
  AGENCIES AND OFFICIALS--National
  Currency Department
NATIONAL DEBT: see Public debt as
  subheading under names of specific
  countries
NATIONAL DEFENSE: see DEFENSE
NATIONAL DRAMA CORPORATION: 5145
NATIONAL DYE WORKS, Burlington,
  North Carolina: 3842
NATIONAL EAGLE (sailing ship): 3578
NATIONAL ECONOMY LEAGUE: 3447
NATIONAL EDUCATION ASSOCIATION: 1758
  Proceedings: 2224
NATIONAL EMBLEMS: see SEALS
NATIONAL FARMERS UNION: 1193
NATIONAL FEDERATION OF POST OFFICE
  CLERKS: 3
NATIONAL GALLERIES AND COMPANY,
  Washington, D.C.: 4552
NATIONAL GEOGRAPHIC CENTRAL CHINA
  EXPEDITION: 5225
NATIONAL GEOGRAPHIC SOCIETY: 4269
NATIONAL GUARD: see as subheading
  under names of states
NATIONAL HEALTH INSURANCE:
  see also SOCIALIZED MEDICINE
  United States: 1198
NATIONAL HOME OF BEDFORD, Virginia:
  1140
NATIONAL HOUSING AGENCY: see UNITED
  STATES--GOVERNMENT AGENCIES AND
  OFFICIALS--National Housing Agency
NATIONAL INSTITUTE FOR MORAL
  EDUCATION: 1747
NATIONAL INTELLIGENCER (periodical):
  1937, 4239, 5460
NATIONAL JOURNAL (periodical): 1778
NATIONAL LABOR RELATIONS BOARD: see
  UNITED STATES--GOVERNMENT
  AGENCIES AND OFFICIALS--National
  Labor Relations Board
NATIONAL MEDIATION BOARD: see UNITED
  STATES--GOVERNMENT AGENCIES AND
  OFFICIALS--National Mediation
  Board
NATIONAL MUSEUM, Washington, D.C.:
  4453
NATIONAL NEGRO BUSINESS LEAGUE: 2379
NATIONAL PARKS AND MONUMENTS:
  Appalachian Mountains: 1478

NATIONAL PARKS AND MONUMENTS
  (Continued)
  New Mexico: 1548
  Yellowstone National Park: 3424
NATIONAL PEACE COUNCIL: 4722
NATIONAL POSTMASTERS' CONVENTION:
  4689
NATIONAL PROBATION AND PAROLE
  ASSOCIATION: 4927
NATIONAL PROHIBITION PARTY: 4732
NATIONAL RADICAL UNION (Great
  Britain): 4036
NATIONAL RECOVERY ACT: 4858
NATIONAL RECOVERY ADMINISTRATION:
  see UNITED STATES--GOVERNMENT
  AGENCIES AND OFFICIALS--National
  Recovery Administration
NATIONAL RELIGION AND LABOR
  FOUNDATION: 1196, 1197
NATIONAL RELIGIOUS AND LABOR FUND:
  3558
NATIONAL REPORTER (periodical):
  1194, 1197
NATIONAL REPUBLICAN (periodical):
  3215
NATIONAL REPUBLICAN LEAGUE: 4689
NATIONAL RETIRED TEACHERS
  ASSOCIATION JOURNAL: 4560
NATIONAL REVIEW (periodical): 2146
NATIONAL RIVERS AND HARBORS CONGRESS:
  4858
NATIONAL ROAD:
  Illinois: 3054
  Ohio: 4732
NATIONAL STUDENT CHRISTIAN
  FEDERATION:
  Duke University: 3001
NATIONAL STUDY CONFERENCE ON THE
  CHURCH AND ECONOMIC LIFE: 1194
NATIONAL UNION PARTY--Convention:
  2469
NATIONAL WAR LABOR BOARD: see UNITED
  STATES--GOVERNMENT AGENCIES AND
  OFFICIALS--National War Labor
  Board
NATIONAL WAR-SAVINGS COMMITTEE
  (World War I): 5803
NATIONALISM IN AFRICA: 4591
NATIVISM:
  see also KNOW-NOTHING PARTY; KU
    KLUX KLAN
  Massachusetts--Brockton: 3524
NATURAL BRIDGE, Virginia: see
  CHRISTIANSBURG & NATURAL BRIDGE
  MAIL-STAGE LINE
NATURAL HISTORY:
  see also BOTANY; PLANTS; ZOOLOGY
  Brazil: 4875
  California: 4353
  Germany: 2706
  Mississippi: 5498
  South Carolina: 4453
  Southern States: 2047
  Texas: 4353
  United States: 783
  Western States: 4353
THE NATURAL HISTORY OF WASHINGTON
  TERRITORY . . . by George Suckley,
  Jr., and James Graham Cooper: 5133
NATURALIZATION: see CITIZENSHIP
NATURE ESSAYS--Florida: 1653
NATURE IN ART: 4453
NAUGATUCK, Connecticut: 3196, 4993
NAUTICAL INSTRUMENTS: see COMPASSES
NAUTICAL SURVEYING:
  British Navy: 485
  United States Navy: 4013
NAVAL AND MILITARY GAZETTE: 3835,
  3976
NAVAL ARCHITECTURE--Great Britain:
  1599
NAVAL ARCHITECTURE by Marmaduke
  Stalkartt: 5019
NAVAL EDUCATION: see UNITED STATES
  NAVAL ACADEMY
NAVAL OPERATIONS: see TRAVEL--Naval
  cruises; and Naval operations as
  subheading under names of navies

NAVAL STORES INDUSTRY:
  Florida: 4298
  Georgia: 4298
  North Carolina: 753, 4298
NAVAL STORES TRADE:
  Alabama--Mobile: 4911
  Great Britain: 2296, 3230
  Martinique: 21
  New York: 5373
  North Carolina: 164, 1871, 2222,
    2586, 2924, 5372, 5373, 5535
    Catherine Lake: 5910
    Exports:
      To Great Britain: 3230
      To Martinique: 21
    Murfreesboro: 5857
    Wilmington: 2919, 5912
  Northern Europe: 2296
  Pennsylvania: 164
    Philadelphia: 4699
  South Carolina: 2586
    Charleston: 987
  Virginia: 5535
NAVAL STRATEGY IN THE AMERICAN
  REVOLUTION: 3116
NAVARRE, Ohio: 4245
NAVASSA GUANO COMPANY, Wilmington,
  North Carolina: 3447
NAVIGATION: 2815
  Aids to navigation: 4017, 4537
  Hydraulic methods: 3118
  Laws and regulations:
    see also TRADE REGULATIONS
    United States: 3041
      Potomac River: 2383
  Mathematics: 4537
  North Carolina:
    Cape Fear River: 3922
NAVIGATION ACTS (Great Britain):
  3230
NAVY YARDS:
  Great Britain: 1599
  United States: 5564
NAYLOR, Stanley: 2146
NEAL, Caroline R.: 3844
NEAL, Clementine: 2792
NEAL, James A.: 3607
NEAL, Josie: 3843
NEAL, Richard P.: 3844
NEAL FAMILY (Tennessee): 3844
NEALE, _____ (New York publisher):
  4341
NEAPOLITAN EXILES (Italy): 5222
NEAR EAST:
  see also WORLD WAR I--War relief--
    Near East
  Description and travel: 128, 572,
    4986, 5156
  Foreign trade--Great Britain: 3183
  International relief organizations:
    3633
  Politics and government: 4986
  Social life and customs: 4986
NEAR EAST RELIEF (organization):
  3633
NEAVE, Edward Baxter: 3845
NEAVE, Ellen (Baker): 3845
NEAVE FAMILY (North Carolina): 3845
NEBLETT, James H.: 3846
NEBLETT, Sterling: 3846
NEBRASKA:
  see also MIDDLE WEST; NEBRASKA
    TERRITORY; PLAINS STATES
  Authors and publishers: 729
  Currency: 1339
  Farming: 1344
  Land: 1849
  Land settlement: 1828
  Mercantile accounts: 568
  Personal finance--Whitney: 5309
  Sod houses: 1575
NEBRASKA TERRITORY:
  Courts: 2326
"NECESSARIES FOR A WRITER TO INDIA":
  4066
NEEDLEWORK: see EMBROIDERY
NEELD, Sir John, First Baronet: 3847
NEELD, Joseph: 3847

NEFF, John Fred: 3848
NEFF, Michael: 3848
NEFF & JONES, Wilmington, North
  Carolina (firm): 2924
NEGLEY, David Duncan: 3849
NEGOTIABLE INSTRUMENTS: 1339
  see also MONEY
NEGRO DRIVERS: 5940
NEGRO EDUCATORS:
  North Carolina: 2720
NEGRO EMANCIPATION COMMITTEE
  (Great Britain): 5129
NEGRO MASONS: 4524
NEGRO ODD FELLOWS: 4524
NEGRO POETRY: 3850
NEGRO REFORMATORY ASSOCIATION OF
  VIRGINIA: 3012
NEGRO SCHOOLS: see SCHOOLS--Negro
  schools
NEGRO SEAMEN: 4881
  Treatment in South Carolina:
    2564, 2695
NEGRO SERVANTS: 5940
  Behavior--Virginia: 2612
  Labor contracts:
    New York: 3637
    Virginia: 4616
NEGRO SOLDIERS: see Negro troops
  as subheading under names of
  armies
  Crime: see UNITED STATES--ARMY--
    Civil War--Negro troops--
    Depredations
NEGROES: 2311, 2852, 3524, 3850,
  4108, 4226
  see also FREE NEGROES; FREEDMEN;
    MULATTOES; SLAVES; subjects
    beginning with the word
    Negro or Negroes; and Negroes
    as subheading under occupational
    categories, e.g. PHYSICIANS--
    Negroes
  Behavior:
    Mississippi--Jasper County: 1370
  Bibliography: 3850
  Citizenship (United States): 5043
    see also UNITED STATES--
      CONSTITUTION--14th Amendment
  Civil rights (United States):
    1409, 4948
  Civil War:
    see also appropriate subheadings
      under CIVIL WAR; CONFEDERATE
      STATES OF AMERICA; and
      UNITED STATES--ARMY--Civil
      War
    Attitudes toward the war: 4923
    Depredations: 4924
    Mississippi: 1864
  Colonization: 762, 2848, 4720
    see also AFRICAN COLONIZATION
      SOCIETY; AMERICAN COLONIZATION
      SOCIETY
    Africa: 2984, 4376
    Haiti: 2408
    Liberia: 128, 2389, 3012, 3325
      From North Carolina: 4516
      Life in Monrovia: 5298
      Return from Liberia: 5051
  Contribution to American
    civilization: 2984
  Economic conditions:
    North Carolina: 2720
    United States: 2720, 3850,
      5043
  Education: 5043
    see also FREEDMEN--Education;
      SCHOOLS--Negro schools
    Maryland--Baltimore: 4886
    New York: 4351
    North Carolina: 2469, 2720,
      4828, 5041
    South Carolina--Hilton Head:
      3264
    Southern States: 3558

NEGROES (Continued):
  Lynching: see LYNCHING--Negroes
  Mental hospitals: see MENTAL
    HOSPITALS--Negroes
  Migration from North Carolina to
    Indiana: 4606
  Ministry to: see METHODIST
    CHURCHES--Aid to freedmen;
    METHODIST CHURCHES--Negroes--
    Ministry to
  Orphanages:
    Virginia--Rustburg: 2799
  Personal finance: 3850
    North Carolina: 2720
  Reconstruction: see FREEDMEN
  Religion: 5699
    see also Negroes as subheading
      under names of specific
      denominations
    Participation in white churches:
      North Carolina: 3195, 3581
      South Carolina: 249
    Prayer meetings: 5975
    Subdivided by place:
      North Carolina: 702
      Southern States: 3277
      Virginia: 5149
  Social status:
    North Carolina: 2720
    South Carolina: 1927
    Southern States: 2121
    Texas: 1138
    United States:
      1800s:
        1860s: 3392
        1880s: 4921
      1800s-1900s: 2720
      1940s: 3852
  Suffrage:
    Disenfranchisement:
      North Carolina: 2298
    Subdivided by place:
      Alabama: 4751
      Georgia: 662
      North Carolina: 2469
      South Carolina: 300, 2300,
        4118
      Southern States: 1466, 3809
      United States: 1805
      Virginia: 1787
  Taxation:
    North Carolina--Anson County: 191
  Treatment of: 5497
    British subjects in the southern
      United States: 2150
    South Carolina: 380, 2564
    United States: 2597
  Voting:
    Georgia: 4895
    North Carolina: 4858
    Subdivided by place:
      Africa: 5940
      Arkansas: 1154
      Brazil: 4876
      Georgia: 731, 2232, 2963
      North Carolina: 2048
        Hyde County: 511
      South Carolina: 566
        Camden: 2940
      Southern States: 2449, 2616,
        3277
      Virginia: 1591
        Albemarle County: 3854
      West Virginia: 748
NEGROES IN JOURNALISM: 4524
  Georgia: 731
NEGROES IN POLITICS: 693
  Members of Congress: 2517
  Georgia: 731
  Kentucky: 398
  North Carolina: 2720
  South Carolina: 1877, 1972
  United States: 2720
NEGROS PROVINCE, Philippine Islands:
  Description and travel: 4511

NEHRU, Jawaharlal: 83
NEILSON, George: 3851
NEILSON, William Allan: 3852
NELME, Bennett Dunlap: 4918
NELSON, Eliza K.: 3853
NELSON, Elizabeth (b. 1770): 4013
NELSON, Elizabeth Burwell: 4020
NELSON, Hugh: 3854
NELSON, Mary Carter: 4141
NELSON, Robert Edward, Sr.: 3855
NELSON, Thomas (1738-1789): 3130,
  3856, 5203
NELSON, Thomas (1900s): 5252
NELSON, W. R.: 3857
NELSON, William (1711-1772): 3856
NELSON FAMILY (Virginia): 4013
NELSON COUNTY, Kentucky: 3199
  Bardstown: 3755, 5118
  Civil War: 2858
NELSON COUNTY, Virginia:
  Business affairs: 1459
  Civil War:
    see also CIVIL WAR--CAMPAIGNS,
      BATTLES, AND MILITARY ACTIONS--
      Virginia--Nelson County
    Civilian life: 4259
    Tax in kind: 1181
  Crop rotation: 3566
  Estates--Administration and
    settlement: 3566
  Farm accounts: 5290
  Fruit culture: 3566
  Girls' schools and academies: 3788
  Land deeds and indentures: 3566
  Plantations: 3566
  Sheriffs: 3566, 5484, 5700
  Slave trade: 5700
  Surveys and surveying: 3566
  Taxation: 5484
  Weather: 3566
  Cities and towns:
    Amherst: 1156
      Sheriffs: 5484
      Taxation: 5484
    Elk Furnace: 1501
    Fabers Mills: 5290
    "Glenmore": 682
    Greenfield: 5491
    "Liberty Hall": 824
    Norwood:
      Merchants and mercantile
        accounts: 5107
      Schools: 824, 5107
    "Pharsalia": 3566
    Temperance: 852, 5529
    Warminster: 3574
NEPEAN, Sir Evan, First Baronet:
  2735, 3858
NEPONSET, Illinois: 5058
NEPTUNE (schooner): 4304
NESBITT, Charles Torrence: 3859
NESBITT, John: 3860
NESBITT, Robert Taylor: 3861
NESFIELD, William Andrews: 3862
NETHERLANDS:
  Bondholders--Amsterdam: 3273
  British embassy in: 3472
  Catholic Church:
    Relations with Protestants: 3989
  Description and travel:
    1820s: 4490
    1830s: 4490
    1840s: 4695, 5133
  Foreign relations: 4230
    Great Britain: 5726
    United States: 3384
  Foreign trade: 1093
  Government agencies and officials:
    Diplomatic and consular service:
      United States: 3244
    Publications acquired by Duke
      University Library: 3244
  Immigration and emigration: 5149
  Military activities--Sumatra:
    3485

NETHERLANDS (Continued):
  Naval operations in India: 3315
  Politics and government: 5133
  Shipping during World War I: 1424
  Slave trade--Colonies: 5726
  Social life and customs: 5133
  Tobacco trade: 144, 5251
  Treaties--Spain: 3989
  Wars of Independence (1556-1648): 3989
NETLEY, England:
  Army Medical School: 4026
NETTLESHIP, John Trivett: 4001
NETTLETON, Mrs. Royal C.: 5000
NEUMANN, Philipp, Freiherr von: 5637
NEUSE, North Carolina: 3863
NEUSE (Confederate gunboat): 2638
NEUSE ASSOCIATION, Disciples of Christ: 5554
NEUSE BAPTIST ASSOCIATION: 484
NEUSE DISTRICT, Methodist churches: 3646
NEUSE MANUFACTURING COMPANY: 3863
NEUSE RIVER (North Carolina):
  Land: 730
  Light-ships: 1871
NEUTRAL TRADE WITH BELLIGERANTS:
  see Economic effects--Neutral trade as subheading under names of wars
NEUTRALITY: see as subheading under names of wars, e.g. SINO-JAPANESE WAR--British neutrality
NEVADA:
  see also WESTERN STATES
  Agriculture: 5426
  Mines and mining: 1478
NEVILLE, William, First Marquis of Abergavenny: 2149
NEVITT, John J.: 3864
NEVITTE, Emma Dorothea Eliza: 4971
NEW ALBANY, Indiana: 2954, 4973, 5097
THE NEW ARIA: A TALE OF TRIAL AND TRUST by James Mathewes Legaré: 3163
NEW BANK ESTATE: 2170
NEW BEDFORD, Massachusetts: 368, 5344, 5877
  Schools--Textile engineering: 4918
NEW BERN, North Carolina:
  1700s-1800s: 484, 2167
  1800s: 263, 3473
  1810s: 1975, 2437
  1820s: 2437
  1840s: 2350
  1850s: 2350, 2394, 4044
  1860s: 2394, 3013, 3562, 4044, 5041, 5897
  1870s: 2394
  1800s-1900s: 1368, 4825
  1900s: 325, 527
  Banks and banking: 692, 730
  Civil War: 1426, 2549, 3166
    see also CIVIL WAR--CAMPAIGNS, BATTLES, AND MILITARY ACTIONS--North Carolina--New Bern
    Diseases:
      Yellow fever: 5261, 5543
    Refugees: 3237
    Union capture: 714
    Union hospital: 1845
    Union military activities: 3910
    Union occupation: 1934, 2602, 3037
  Description (1859): 5149
  Diseases--Yellow fever: 4561
  Economic growth: 730
  Fireman's Relief Fund: 3955
  Government agencies and officials:
    City attorney: 3955
  Household accounts: 5709
  Land drainage: 3955
  Mercantile accounts: 164
  Pharmacists: 1580

NEW BERN, North Carolina (Continued):
  Photographs: 3955, 4414
  Plantation accounts: 5709
  Poetry: 2739
  Postal service: 3865
  Railroads: 1655
  Schools: 263
  Social conditions: 5774
  Social life and customs: 730
  Taxation: 5709
  Theaters: 4977
  Tobacco trade: 5228
  Trade and commerce:
    Coastal trade: 1871, 1950
    Export trade: 2222
  Tryon Palace: 5352
NEW BERN ACADEMY, New Bern, North Carolina: 263
NEW BERN BUILDING AND LOAN ASSOCIATION: 3955
NEW BERN DISTRICT, Methodist churches: 3646
"THE NEW BOSS" by Elizabeth (Lynn) Linton: 5553
NEW BRAUNFELS, Texas: 218
  Land: 964
NEW BRUNSWICK, Canada: 1890
NEW BRUNSWICK, New Jersey: 532
  see also RUTGERS UNIVERSITY
NEW CARLISLE, Ohio: 5017
NEW CARTHAGE, Louisiana: 2802
NEW CASTLE COUNTY, Delaware:
  Fort Delaware: see FORT DELAWARE, Delaware
  Wilmington: see WILMINGTON, Delaware
NEW CENTER, South Carolina: 4347
NEW CLANTON, Virginia: 1921
NEW CREEK, West Virginia: 221
NEW DEAL: 1429, 3451
  Opposition to: 274
    South Carolina: 300
  Public opinion: 4453
    Florida: 1653
THE NEW EAST: 1940
NEW ENGLAND STATES:
  Anti-Federalists: 1333
  Church reform: 5088
  Description and travel:
    1800s: 339, 1827
    1820s: 4490
    1850s: 1748, 3524, 4602
    1860s: 3524
    1870s: 3229
    1880s: 3229
    1890s: 3229
  Discount stores: 3866
  Gardens and gardening: 1636
  Politics and government: 1302
  Religion: 5088
  Resorts: 3229
  Schools: 51
  Social life and customs: 5563
    In cities and towns: 3524
  Temperance: 1439
  Trade and commerce: 172
NEW ENGLAND FEMALE REFORM SOCIETY OF BOSTON: 5088
NEW ENGLAND PROTECTIVE UNION: 3866
NEW ENGLAND QUARTERLY: 2449
NEW ENGLAND SHOE AND LEATHER ASSOCIATION: 2682
THE NEW ERA (newspaper): 4732
NEW GARDEN ACADEMY (North Carolina): see GUILFORD COLLEGE
NEW GARDEN BOARDING SCHOOL (North Carolina): see GUILFORD COLLEGE
NEW GRANADA: see COLOMBIA
NEW GUINEA:
  Missions and missionaries: 2650
NEW HAMPSHIRE:
  see also NEW ENGLAND STATES
  Agricultural workers--Landaff: 4265
  Blacksmiths' accounts--Keene: 5501
  Boot- and shoemaking:
    Grafton: 2356

NEW HAMPSHIRE (Continued):
  Business affairs: 354
  Commodity prices: 4039
  Copperheads: 4039
  Currency: 1339
  Farm accounts--Landaff: 4265
  Farm life: 776
  Government agencies and officials:
    Attorney General: 5140
  Medicine: 354
  Mercantile accounts:
    Grafton County: 71
  Phrenology: 354
  Politics and government:
    1800s:
      1800s: 354, 2043
      1810s: 354
      1820s: 354
      1830s: 5140
      1860s: 1983
    1800s-1900s: 4039
  Protestant Episcopal churches: 4869
  Real estate:
    Rental in East Lebanon: 2417
  Religion: 3822
  Schools: 354, 4039
  Social life and customs--Exeter: 2043
  Theology: 354
  Trade and commerce: 323
    Building materials: 1529
    Cheese: 1529
    Liquor: 1529
    Lumber: 1529
    Real estate: 2417
    Shingles: 1529
    Tobacco: 1529
  Transatlantic slave trade: 1884
  Universities and colleges:
    see also DARTMOUTH COLLEGE; WILLIAMS COLLEGE
    Students and student life: 3822
  Wool--Prices: 4681
  Woolen mills--Dover: 4681
NEW HANOVER COUNTY, North Carolina: 2085
  Government agencies and officials:
    Board of Education: 3607
  Health conditions: 3859
  Politics and government: 3410
  Voter registration: 3410
  Wilmington: see WILMINGTON, North Carolina
NEW HANOVER RECORD & ADVERTISER: 2180
NEW HARMONY, Indiana: 4770
NEW HAVEN, Connecticut: 129, 3216, 3705, 4561, 5000, 5563, 5714
  Description (1822): 291
  Schools: 5747
  Social life and customs: 4080
  Universities and colleges: see YALE UNIVERSITY
  Vital statistics: 1205
NEW HAVEN COUNTY, Connecticut:
  Ansonia--Sons of Veterans: 4955
  Bethany: 3778
  Guilford: 2223, 4059
  Milford--Carriage manufacture: 379
  Naugatuck: 3196, 4993
  New Haven: see NEW HAVEN, Connecticut
  North Branford: 5666
  Wallingford: 5871
NEW HOPE, Virginia:
  Baptist churches: 3826
NEW HOPE CHURCH, Georgia: see CIVIL WAR--CAMPAIGNS, BATTLES, AND MILITARY ACTIONS--Georgia--New Hope Church
NEW HOPE PRECINCT, Greenfield, Virginia: 5491
THE NEW INTERNATIONAL ENCYCLOPEDIA: 3967

NEW JERSEY:
see also EASTERN STATES; MIDDLE ATLANTIC STATES; NORTHERN STATES
Bank notes: 2517
Business affairs: 1446
Canals: 730
Charities: 1927
Courts:
  Court of Chancery: 5520
  Court of Common Pleas: 5520
  Supreme Court: 5520
Currency: 1339
Elections (1830s): 5520
Farm life: 373
Farming: 1585
Government agencies and officials:
  State police: 1831
Irish in the United States: 4354
Land deeds and indentures:
  Burlington County: 1752
Law:
  Students' notebooks:
    Princeton University: 2521
  Legal affairs--Burlington: 5520
Legislature: 5546
Mathematics:
  Students' notebooks:
    Princeton University: 2521
Nurseries (horticulture): 4354
Personal debt--Burlington: 5520
Politics and government: 5520
  Appointments: 4964
Schools: 743
Social life and customs: 730
Socialist Party: 4948
Students and student life: 4354
Teaching: 1920
Universities and colleges: 743
  see also PRINCETON UNIVERSITY; RUTGERS UNIVERSITY
Waterworks--Jersey City: 5546
Whig Party: 5520
NEW MARKET, Virginia: 2485
Civil War: 475, 4537
Mercantile accounts: 138
NEW MEXICO:
see also NEW MEXICO TERRITORY; WESTERN STATES
Description and travel: 1174
Mines and mining: 5293
National parks and monuments: 1548
Sheep raising: 3745
NEW MEXICO TERRITORY: 5660
United States Army life: 3261
THE NEW MONTHLY MAGAZINE: 2146
NEW ORLEANS, Louisiana:
1700s-1900s: 1439
1800s: 395, 459, 855, 871, 1930, 3358, 4739, 5671
1810s: 404, 3073, 3824
1820s: 3824, 4810, 4902
1830s: 2456, 3824
1840s: 1597, 4154, 4958
1850s: 1597, 3274, 4154, 4856, 4958, 5588
1860s: 679, 1597, 1726, 1830, 2366, 3059, 3274, 3628, 3881, 4550, 4958, 5131, 5588
1870s: 1726, 1830, 2576, 4550
1880s: 1726, 1830, 1982, 2025, 2576, 4550
1890s: 1982, 2576
1800s-1900s: 826, 4883
1900s: 2775, 3252
Autograph collecting: 2575
Banks and banking: 5693
Civil War: 3357
  see also CIVIL WAR--CAMPAIGNS, BATTLES, AND MILITARY ACTIONS--Louisiana--New Orleans
Commodity prices: 1763
Prisoners and prisons: see CIVIL WAR--PRISONERS AND PRISONS--Confederate/Union Prisoners

NEW ORLEANS, Louisiana:
Civil War (Continued):
  Union camps: 1348
  Union occupation: 2691, 2777, 3613, 3624, 4881
Corporations: 3869
Cotton trade: 4776, 5194, 5301
Defense: 2842
Description:
  1815: 1333
  1827: 1556
  1837: 74
  1848: 284
  1850s: 489, 5193
  1860s: 155, 249, 1349, 1741, 4369
Diseases:
  Cholera: 330, 4038, 4732
  Smallpox: 368
  Yellow fever: 4202
Economic conditions: 3030
Estate accounts: 2674
Finance: 730
Gunsmithing: 4957
Insurance: 5062
Investments: 730
Land deeds and indentures: 478
Literary interests: 1494, 2465
Mercantile accounts: 5933
Merchants: 3008
Military roads: 2781
Municipal government: 1830
Poetry: 1450
Politics and government: 4131
Poorhouses: 3870
Population: 5499
Public finance: 5425
Reconstruction: 4277
Shipping:
  Coastwise shipping: 5860
Slave trade: 1801
Social life and customs: 225, 1424, 4286, 5194
Teaching: 5062
Tobacco prices: 3643
Tobacco trade: 3643
Trade and commerce: 5860
  With Saint Louis, Missouri: 2386
Universities and colleges: see TULANE UNIVERSITY; UNIVERSITY OF LOUISIANA
Visit of James G. Blaine: 1593
War of 1812: see WAR OF 1812-- Campaigns, battles, and military actions--Louisiana--New Orleans
Wholesale trade: 1169
NEW ORLEANS, JACKSON, AND MISSISSIPPI RAILWAY: 395
NEW ORLEANS AND LAFAYETTE BOARD OF TOBACCO INSPECTORS: 5671
"A NEW PHILOSOPHICAL DISCOVERY" by David C. Kelley: 872
NEW RIVER CHURCH, Disciples of Christ, North Carolina: 5554
NEW RIVER CIRCUIT, Methodist churches: 3646
NEW ROCHELLE, New York:
  Monuments: 4025
NEW RUPTURE SOCIETY (Great Britain): 5726
NEW SALEM, Massachusetts: 2677
NEW SALEM, North Carolina: 329, 1677
NEW SCHOOL PRESBYTERIAN CHURCH (Illinois): 882
NEW SMYRNA, Florida:
  Social life and customs: 5480
  United States Army life: 5480
NEW SOUTH WALES, Australia: 5726
  Governors: 3238
NEW SPAIN: see MEXICO
NEW UNION, Randolph County, North Carolina: 88
NEW WASHINGTON, Texas:
  Cattle raising: 3772
  Hiring of slaves: 3772
NEW WINDSOR, Maryland: see CALVERT COLLEGE

NEW YEAR CARDS:
  Great Britain: 4115
  United States: 2656
NEW YEAR CUSTOMS:
  Georgia--Savannah: 4177
  Great Britain: 5790
  Washington, D.C.: 5982
"NEW YEAR'S ADDRESS FOR 1850" by Julia A. Mildred Harris: 3611
NEW YORK: 2465
see also EASTERN STATES; MIDDLE ATLANTIC STATES; NEW YORK, New York; NORTHERN STATES
Abolition of slavery and abolitionist sentiment: 5917
Agricultural periodicals: 4881
Agriculture: 1769
  see also NEW YORK--Crops, and names of specific crops; NEW YORK--Farming
American Revolution: see appropriate subheadings under AMERICAN REVOLUTION; CONTINENTAL ARMY
Apprenticeship: 782
Art and artists: 2726
Author and publishers: 1143
Bank failures: 2587
Banks and banking: 236, 559, 4157, 4343
  Fulton: 929
Baseball: 3221
Blind--Education: 3633
Bluestockings--Troy: 4867
Boarding houses: 1908
Bonds: 1065
Book collecting: 5101
Booksellers and bookselling:
  Troy: 5972
Business affairs: 416, 1211, 4751, 4808
  Rochester: 2436
  Saint Lawrence County: 5458
Camp meetings: 1908
Canals: 4597
Cemeteries: 4895
Civil War: see appropriate subheadings under CIVIL WAR; UNITED STATES--ARMY--Civil War
Clergy:
  Florida: 86
  Protestant Episcopal church: 5619
Clothing and dress: 4351
Commission merchants: 1107
Commodity prices: 1107, 1907
Confederate foreign agents: 1181
Copperheads: 4108
Corn prices: 2434
Courts:
  Cases: 4378
  Judgments: 4260
  Supreme Court: 2172
Courtship: 752, 2390
  see also NEW YORK--Love letters
Crops:
  see also NEW YORK--Agriculture; NEW YORK--Farming; and names of specific crops under NEW YORK
  Florida: 86
  Hermon: 3296
Currency: 1339
Debt: 782
  Owed by Southerners: 1190
Debt collection: 2172
Democratic Party candidates: 4343
Description and travel:
  1800s: 33
  1820s: 2677, 2820, 2828
  1830s: 2677, 5298
  1840s: 5298
  1850s: 5149, 5298
  1870s: 3390
  1880s: 4968
  1890s: 4968
  1900s:
    1930s: 5252

NEW YORK:
  Description and travel (Continued):
    Saratoga Springs: 3607
    Western New York: 4490
  Economic conditions: 806
    see also NEW YORK--Panic of 1837;
      NEW YORK--Panic of 1857
    Hermon: 3296
  Education: 814
    see also the following
      subheadings under NEW YORK:
      Blind--Education; Deaf--
      Education; Negroes--Education;
      Schools
  Elections:
    see also NEW YORK--Gubernatorial
      elections
    1830s: 1908
    1840s: 4169
  Estates--Administration and
    settlement: 1390, 1585, 2407,
    3637, 5796
  Exhibitions and fairs:
    Exhibition of Industry of All
      Nations: 5584
  Farm life: 4452
  Farming: 1587, 5660
    see also NEW YORK--Agriculture;
      NEW YORK--Crops, and names of
      specific crops
    Poughkeepsie: 1908
  Fenian raids: 4485
  Finance: 2246, 4806
    see also NEW YORK--Personal
      finance
  Financial institutions: 2619
    Bankruptcy: 2587
  Food: 4351
    Prices: 2225
    Volney: 2089
  Fourth of July celebrations: 726
  Freedmen:
    Views on treatment of: 408
  Freight and freightage: 4071
  French consulate in: 1181
  Funerals: 5298
  Furniture: 4351
  Government agencies and officials:
    Bureau of Military Statistics:
      4708
    Comptroller: 2717
    Governors:
      William Tryon (1771-1776): 5352
      George Clinton (1777-1795):
        3662
      William Henry Seward
        (1839-1843): 4616
      Edwin Denison Morgan
        (1859-1863): 3768
    State Police: 1831
  Guano: 5731
  Gubernatorial elections (1894):
    1977
  Gunpowder industry: 4375
  Hardware stores--Niagara: 3848
  Health conditions: 752
  Health resorts: 1928
  Historical restoration: 4343
  Historical societies: 3735, 4025
  Horses:
    Prices: 2434
    Race horses: 1608
  Houses: 1584
  Hunting: 5660
  Insurance:
    Business--Niagara: 3848
    Maritime: 3960
  Insurance companies: 2983, 3620,
    5731
    Lawsuits: 3587
  Internal improvements: 5345
    Troy: 5747
  Iron industry: 1169
  Journalism: 2390
    see also NEW YORK--Newspapers
  Labor: 4351
  Labor conditions:
    Textile industry--Cohoes: 3266

NEW YORK (Continued):
  Land--Purchases and sales: 2172
  Land companies: 2438
  Land deeds and indentures: 782,
    2172, 4680, 5133, 5731
    Yates County: 3568
  Land speculation: 3041, 5731
  Law:
    Codification: 1792
    Students' notebooks:
      Columbia University: 2553,
        4863
    Study of: 814
      see also COLUMBIA UNIVERSITY--
        Legal education
  Law practice: 388, 1572, 2210
  Lawsuits: 1585, 4071
  Lectures and lecturing: 4481
  Legal affairs: 5660
    Hornby: 4645
    Orange: 4645
    Steuben County: 4680
    Yates County: 4680
  Libraries: 1747
    Peekskill: 4343
  Literary interests: 2351, 5044
  Loans: 1065
  Locofoco Party: 86
  Love letters: 1961
    see also NEW YORK--Courtship
  Marble quarries: 2172
  Married life: 5360
  Medical affairs: 1229
  Medical books: 4351
  Medical education:
    see also BELLEVUE HOSPITAL
      MEDICAL SCHOOL
    Albany: 5974
  Medical practice: 1229, 2081
  Medicine: 1229, 4351
  Mental hospitals: 958
  Mercantile accounts--Albany: 1281
  Merchants: 1396, 1907, 1908, 2172,
    2230, 5281, 5282
    see also NEW YORK--Commission
      merchants
    Rochester: 4256
  Methodist churches:
    Huntington: 726
  Militia--War of 1812: 1003
  Monuments--New Rochelle: 4025
  Mortgages: 2172
  Negro servants:
    Labor contracts: 3637
  Negroes:
    see also NEW YORK--Freedmen;
      NEW YORK--Race relations
    Education: 4351
      see also NEW YORK--Schools--
        Negro schools
  Newspapers: 4524
    see also NEW YORK--Journalism
    Finance: 4351
  Nurseries (horticulture): 1462
  Oats--Prices: 2434
  Painting: 2518
  Panic of 1837: 730
  Panic of 1857: 2250, 2587
  Personal finance: 481, 483, 1149,
    1583, 1589
    Ballston Spa: 5206
  Philanthropy: 2753
  Plank roads: 2230, 5149
  Political parties: 388
    see also names of specific
      political parties under NEW
      YORK
  Political patronage: 585, 1977,
    2497, 4343
  Politics and government:
    1700s-1800s: 5520
    1800s: 4169
    1830s: 4751
    1850s: 5788
    1860s: 5788
    1890s: 1907, 1977
    1800s-1900s: 4808

NEW YORK:
  Politics and government (Continued):
    1900s:
      1920s: 2299, 4343
      1930s: 4343
      1940s: 2083
      1950s: 2083
  Presbyterian churches: 1908
    West Chester: 5731
  Publishers and publishing:
    Poetry: 5193
    Troy: 5972
  Race relations: 1907
  Railroads: 1211, 3872
    Stocks: 2591
  Real estate: 1380, 2755, 5731
  Real estate business: 4806
  Religion: 752, 814, 1908
    see also NEW YORK--Camp meetings;
      and names of specific
      denominations under NEW YORK
    Hermon: 3296
  Rent: 4351
  Republican Party: 1907, 1977, 4808
  Resorts: 4968
  School life: 4169
  Schools: 480, 3008, 4169
    Boarding schools--Yonkers: 2553
    Girls' schools and academies:
      2407
    Negro schools: 4351
    Preparatory schools: 1580
    Subdivided by place:
      Geneva: 4348
      Norwich: 2292
      Tarrytown: 5593
  Ship timber: 2172
  Shipping:
    Coastwise shipping: 2959
    From North Carolina: 1950
  Social life and customs: 404, 806,
    1908, 2677, 4125, 5520
  Socialist Party: 4948
  Societies and clubs: 4806
  Steel industry: 1169
  Student societies: 3809
  Tannery accounts: 1479
  Taverns and inns: 5149
  Taxation: 1065, 4351
  Temperance: 4806
    Huntington: 726
  Theological seminaries: see
    AUBURN THEOLOGICAL SEMINARY;
    UNION THEOLOGICAL SEMINARY
  Theological students: 3142
  Tin-working machinery: 1575
  Tobacco industry:
    Machinery: 4079
    Ogdensburg: 5989
  Trade and commerce:
    Cotton: 641, 903, 2172
    Hardware: 1390
    Niagara: 3848
    Lumber: 1732
    Naval stores: 5373
    Sheet iron: 1575
    Tin: 1575
    Tobacco: 5731
      Advertising: 1586
    Turpentine: 1732
    Wholesale: 1169
    With North Carolina: 1871
    With Virginia: 1556
  Trade regulation: 4109
  Universities and colleges: 4169
    see also COLUMBIA UNIVERSITY;
      EASTMEN BUSINESS COLLEGE;
      GENEVA COLLEGE; MANHATTAN
      COLLEGE; ST. PAUL'S COLLEGE;
      UNION COLLEGE; UNITED STATES
      MILITARY ACADEMY; VASSAR
      COLLEGE
    Students and student life: 4169
  Visit of Japanese embassy: 1877
  Weather--West Park: 4073
  Wheat prices: 86
  Wholesale prices: 1907
  Wildlife--West Park: 4073

NEW YORK (Continued):
  Wills: 903, 1585, 3391
  Woolen mills--West Candor: 2204
NEW YORK, New York: 4863
  see also names of boroughs, e.g.
    BROOKLYN, New York
  1700s:
    1760s: 2812, 3737
    1780s: 2276, 2812, 4317
    1790s: 2276, 2869, 3384, 5448, 5658
  1700s-1800s: 2172
  1700s-1900s: 3797
  1800s: 305, 636, 1003, 1441, 1515, 1792, 1871, 1908, 2857, 3570, 5159
    1810s: 4378, 5281
    1820s: 4378, 5281
    1830s: 416, 3709, 4092, 4378, 5281, 5917
    1840s: 416, 429, 3709, 3903, 5816
    1850s: 55, 416, 1143, 1422, 1802, 2160, 2583, 3903, 4602, 5749, 5799
    1860s: 316, 437, 1357, 1378, 1422, 1477, 1540, 1802, 1808, 2160, 2268, 2270, 2438, 2549, 2726, 2777, 3674, 3734, 3768, 3889, 4109, 4260, 4330, 4602, 4782, 5008, 5052, 5627, 5677
    1870s: 926, 1357, 1802, 2268, 2726, 3674, 3734, 4260, 4782, 5052, 5092
    1880s: 1342, 1357, 1808, 1958, 2726, 3674, 3762, 4782, 5092, 5781
    1890s: 1961, 4079, 5092, 5547
  1800s-1900s: 1103, 1215, 2390, 2871, 3063, 4021, 4276, 4341, 4556, 5014, 5813
  1900s: 293, 3306, 4482
    1900s: 31, 809, 4048, 4789
    1910s: 31, 425, 481, 483, 1585, 2112, 3640, 4789, 5320
    1920s: 31, 425, 942, 1585, 3640, 4789
    1930s: 4753
    1940s: 1025, 3295, 4753
    1950s: 3295
  American poetry: 3999
  Authors and publishers: 4341, 4481
  Balls (parties): 4895
  Banks and banking: 236, 559
  Baptist churches: 461, 5660
  Business affairs: 731, 1065, 1609, 1673, 2246, 2250, 2687, 3709, 5298, 5546, 5612
  Civil rights: 2083
  Civil War: 2758
    Commodity prices: 1763
  Clergy:
    Methodist Episcopal: 3581
    Universalist: 978
  Commission merchants: 1355, 5731
  Cotton trade: 641, 903
  Customs duties, Collection of: 548
  Deaf--Education: 5298
  Defense: 2304
  Description:
    1700s: 4015, 4864
    1800s: 4924
    1822: 291
    1840s: 1697
    1850s: 2018
    1866: 2366
    1870: 5246
    1900s:
      1905: 2191
  Diseases:
    Arthritis--Medical treatment: 5380
    Typhoid fever: 5731
    Yellow fever: 5362
  Drama: 54
  Economic conditions (1830s): 730
  Education: 5593

NEW YORK, New York (Continued):
  Estates--Administration and settlement: 4141
  Finance: 2246
  Foreign trade: 948
  Forest products trade: 1732
  Gambling laws and legislation: 4518
  Gold buying: 5731
  Governesses: 3761
  Historic buildings: 4025
  Historical studies: 1607
  Hospitals: 4775
  Hotels: 5298
  Household finance: 4351
  Journalism: 1883
  Law--Study of: 4863
  Law practice: 388
  Lectures and lecturing: 978
  Legal affairs: 5133
  Libraries: 1236
  Lighthouses: 2672
  Literary interests: 733, 5044
  Local elections: 3221, 4751
  Local politics: 4808
  Lumber trade: 730
  Medical education: 3221
    see also BELLEVUE HOSPITAL MEDICAL SCHOOL
  Medical practice: 4351, 4606
  Mercantile affairs: 2412, 2633
  Merchants: 2924, 3960, 4456, 5298
  Mercury trade: 5731
  Municipal government: 2083, 4808
  Newspapers: 3265
    Editing and publishing: 2526
    Reporters and reporting: 2526
  Personal finance: 1583, 4651
  Philanthropy: 1589, 2753
  Ports: 3871
  Publishers and publishing:
    Periodicals: 3779, 4481
  Real estate: 2755
  Riots: 2648, 4920
  Saint Patrick's Day celebration: 5131
  Schools: 1580
    Girls' schools and academies: 4736
  Shipping: 3960
    Coastwise shipping: 5860
  Social life and customs: 871, 4898, 5787, 5968
  Socialist Party: 4948
  Stereotype foundries: 2677
  Stock brokers: 3587
  Stock exchanges: 2619
  Societies and clubs: 2246, 4976
  Street-cars: 3277
  Sunday schools: 4133
  Theological seminaries: see
    AUBURN THEOLOGICAL SEMINARY;
    UNION THEOLOGICAL SEMINARY
  Tobacco industry: 2302
  Tobacco trade: 5731
  Trade and commerce: 1093
    With North Carolina: 1950
  Union League: 3960
  Universities and colleges: see
    COLUMBIA UNIVERSITY; MANHATTAN COLLEGE
  Waterworks: 5546
  Wholesale trade: 5731
  Women poets: 3999
NEW YORK AGE: 4524
NEW YORK AND ERIE RAILROAD: 2755
NEW YORK AND MIDDLE COALFIELD RAILROAD AND COAL COMPANY: 5083
NEW YORK BAY CEMETERY COMPANY: 4895
NEW YORK CENTRAL RAILROAD: 3872
NEW YORK CITIZEN (newspaper): 4751
(NEW YORK) COMMERCIAL ADVERTISER: 42
NEW YORK COTTON EXCHANGE: 1009
NEW YORK FIRE ZOUAVES: 3809
THE (NEW YORK) HERALD: 2845, 4616
NEW YORK HISTORICAL SOCIETY: 3735
NEW YORK INDEPENDENT: 4920

NEW YORK INSTITUTION FOR THE DEAF AND DUMB: 5298
NEW YORK LEDGER: 1592, 1608, 4971
(NEW YORK) NEWS: 4469
NEW YORK NEWS WORLD-TELEGRAPH AND SUN: 1883
NEW YORK PUBLIC LIBRARY, New York, New York: 1236
(NEW YORK) SUN: 3265
NEW YORK TIMES: 5799
NEW YORK TRIBUNE: 2526, 5193, 5476
NEW YORK WORLD: 1424
NEW ZEALAND: 286
  British administration: 1260
  Clergy--Church of England: 5725
  Maori Wars: 4520
  Politics and government: 1260, 2282
NEWARK, New Jersey: 5925
NEWARK SUNDAY NEWS: 4204
NEWBERN DISTRICT, Methodist churches: 3646
NEWBERRY, South Carolina: 4700
  Girls' schools and academies: 4118
NEWBERRY COLLEGE, Newberry, South Carolina: 4700
NEWBERRY COUNTY, South Carolina: 2961, 4350, 4434, 4700
  Newberry: see NEWBERRY, South Carolina
  Pomeria: 458, 502, 550
NEWBERRY DISTRICT, South Carolina: 2290
  Maybinton: 2335
NEWBERRY FEMALE ACADEMY, Newberry, South Carolina: 4118
NEWBURYPORT, Massachusetts: 1349, 4224, 4864
NEWBY, Cecilia: 3873
NEWBY, Exum: 165
NEWBY, George C.: 3873
NEWBY, J. B.: 3495
NEWBY, Larkin: 3873, 4517
NEWBY, Thomas: 3874
NEWBY FAMILY (North Carolina): 3873, 4517
NEWCASTLE, Henry Pelham Fiennes Pelham-Clinton, Fourth Duke of: 1110, 2149
NEWCASTLE, Thomas Pelham-Holles, First Duke of: 2155, 5540
NEWCASTLE, England: 1910
  Elections: 5624
NEWCASTLE COUNTY, Pennsylvania:
  Mill Creek Hundred: 5264
NEWCASTLE-UPON-TYNE, England: 1164
  Politics and government: 1273
NEWCHWANG, Manchuria: 306
NEWCOMEN & JACOBS (firm): see
  EDWARD B. JACOBS & NEWCOMEN
NEWCOMER, John: 3875
NEWCOMER (M. AND J. H.): 3875
NEWCOMER, William 3875
NEWCOMER FAMILY (Maryland): 3875
NEWELL, Charles S. N.: 3876
NEWELL, E. B.: 3877
NEWELL, Leone Burns: 3878
NEWFOUNDLAND:
  British administration: 1792
  Fishing industry: 636
  Trade with Great Britain: 4541
NEWGATE PRISON (Great Britain): 2835
NEWINGTON GREEN, England: 1884
NEWLIN, Kate: 3879
NEWMAN, A. B.: 4344
NEWMAN, Andrew: 3880
NEWMAN, George: 917, 3880
NEWMAN, Henry H.: 3880
NEWMAN, John Philip: 3881
NEWMAN, Mary: 3880
NEWMAN, Robert M.: 3882
NEWNAN, Daniel: 872
NEWNAN FAMILY: 872
NEWNAN, Georgia: 740
NEWPORT, Sir John, First Baronet: 3883
NEWPORT, Florida--Civil War: 2598
NEWPORT, Indiana: 5149

NEWPORT, Isle of Wight: 5095
NEWPORT, Monmouthshire, England: 1970
NEWPORT, Rhode Island: 1610
    see also UNITED STATES NAVAL ACADEMY, Newport, Rhode Island
    American Revolution: 4418
    Description: 150
    Slave trade: 973
    Social life and customs: 5968
NEWPORT BARRACKS, Kentucky: 5744
NEWPORT CIRCUIT, Methodist churches: 3646
NEWPORT COUNTY, Rhode Island:
    Slave trade: 973
NEWPORT NEWS, Virginia: see CIVIL WAR--CAMPAIGNS, BATTLES, AND MILITARY ACTIONS--Virginia--Newport News
"NEWS FROM HOME" (song): 5243
NEWS-LET (periodical): 4436
NEWSLETTERS--Great Britain: 3884
NEWSOM, Allen: 3885
NEWSOM, J. F.: 3885
NEWSOM, Jesse F.: 3886
NEWSOME, James: 2819
NEWSOME, Winifred: 2819
NEWSON, E. E.: 2650
NEWSON'S DEPOT, Virginia: 4268
NEWSPAPER WORKERS: see AMERICAN NEWSPAPER GUILD
NEWSPAPERS:
    see also JOURNALISM
    Advertising policy: 461
    Advertisements of: see ADVERTISING--Newspapers
    American correspondents in France: 1424
    American correspondents in the Far East: 3093
    Associations: see AFRO-AMERICAN PRESS ASSOCIATION; INTERNATIONAL ASSOCIATION OF NEWSPAPERS AND AUTHORS
    British correspondents in France: 4001
    British correspondents in Southeast Asia: 4709
    British correspondents in the United States: see CIVIL WAR--NEWSPAPERS--British correspondents in
    Carriers' address--Alabama: 3611
    Censorship: see CENSORSHIP--Newspapers
    Church newspapers: see RELIGIOUS LITERATURE
    Civil War: see CIVIL WAR--NEWSPAPERS
    Editing and publishing: 4353
        Illinois: 2526
        New York: 2526
        North Carolina: 3538
        Ohio: 2526
        Virginia: 4341
    Editorial policy:
        North Carolina:
            Charlotte: 5312
            Durham: 3088
        South Carolina: 3682
    Federalist Party newspapers: 105, 3743
    Finance:
        South Carolina: 1424
        Virginia: 4020
            Page County: 461
    Reporters and reporting: 2845
        see also CIVIL WAR--NEWSPAPERS--Reporters and reporting
        Great Britain: 3036, 4503
        New York: 2526
        Virginia--Richmond: 5720
    Republican Party newspapers:
        Virginia (proposed): 5203
    Subscriptions:
        Mississippi: 1693
        New York: 4351
        North Carolina: 4918
            Henderson: 4407

NEWSPAPERS:
    Subscriptions (Continued):
        South Carolina: 3682
    Taxes: see REVENUE STAMPS
    Whig Party newspapers:
        Great Britain: 1632
    Subdivided by place:
        Ceylon: 952
        Denmark: 5321
        Georgia: 731, 1112
            Atlanta: 823
        Great Britain: 1499, 2026, 4151
            London: 217, 5262
        Kansas: 3161
        New York: 4524
            New York: 3265
        North Carolina: 1202
            Berea: 5741
            Calahaln: 122
            Davie County: 122
            Lumberton: 3434
            Raleigh: 4080
            Statesville: 3787
        Pennsylvania--Philadelphia: 1021
        Peru: 4155
        South Carolina: 300, 1424, 2094, 2109, 2880
            Charleston: 267
            Columbia: 2086
            Lancaster: 3682
        United States: 2449, 2815, 3022
        Virginia: 574, 682, 789, 1939, 2370
            Eastville: 1814
            Lynchburg: 1810
            Page County: 461
            Washington, D.C.: 4524
NEWSPAPERS AND PUBLIC OPINION: 4383
NEWTON, Sir Isaac: 5166
NEWTON, John Caldwell Calhoun: 3888
NEWTON, Joseph: 3889
NEWTON, Ruth Elizabeth: 5406
NEWTON, Georgia: 285
NEWTON, North Carolina: 2024
    Mercantile accounts: 138
    Merchants: 9
NEWTON, Virginia: 2023
NEWTON COUNTY, Georgia:
    Covington: 1268, 1434
    Land and timber: 1382
    Oxford: see EMORY COLLEGE
    Sheffield: 5364
NEWTOWN, Connecticut: 162
NEY, Michel (1769-1815): 1622, 4348
NGAMI, Bechuanaland: 4514
NIAGARA, New York:
    Hardware trade: 3848
    Insurance--Business: 3848
NIAGARA COUNTY, New York:
    Beach Ridge: 3691
    Dickersonville: 1246
    Lockport: 2717
    Real estate: 2755
    Niagara: 3848
    Niagara Falls: 4990
    Pekin: 3281
NIAGARA FALLS, New York: 4990
NIAGARA FALLS (New York): 180, 1591
NICARAGUA:
    Canals (proposed): 5051
    Claims against: 3960
    Confederate emigrants: 3587
    Filibuster War (1855-1860): 489, 617, 3960
    Foreign relations:
        United States: 3960
    Immigration to: 3960
    Mining--Javali Mine: 3587
    Politics and government: 1340
    Rubber prices: 1091
    Social life and customs:
        Javali Mine: 3587
NICHOLAS, Philip Norborne: 872, 2633
NICHOLAS, Wilson Cary: 2815, 3890
NICHOLAS FAMILY: 2815
NICHOLAS HOTEL, New York, New York: 5298
NICHOLLS, Edward: 3073

NICHOLLS, Elizabeth R.: 3891
NICHOLLS, George W.: 3893
NICHOLLS, Louisa H.: 3892
NICHOLLS, Samuel Jones: 3893
NICHOLS, George T.: 3894
NICHOLS, John Gough (1806-1878, Great Britain): 3895
NICHOLS, John Thomas (North Carolina): 3896
NICHOLS, Lawrence E.: 2772
NICHOLS, William Montague: 3893
NICHOLS FAMILY (North Carolina): 3896
NICHOLSON, Alfred Osborne Pope: 872
NICHOLSON, Edward: 2612
NICHOLSON, Fannie: 2539
NICHOLSON, J. P.: 3585
NICHOLSON, John (d. 1800, Pennsylvania): 3897
NICHOLSON, John (fl. 1800s, New Jersey): 411
NICHOLSON, John Page (1842-1922): 3898
NICHOLSON, Meredith: 2871
NICHOLSON, Thomas A.: 3899
NICHOLSON AND COMPANY, Lawrenceville, Virginia: 1567, 3900
NICKERSON, William M.: 2336
NICOLL, H. D.: 3715
NICOLL, Robert: 1879
NICOLSON, Adela Florence (Cory): 2334
NICOLSON, Sir Harold: 4823
NICOLSON, Nigel: 4823
NICOLSON, Victoria Mary (Sackville-West): 4823
NICOLSON FAMILY (Great Britain): 4823
NIEDERWALLUF, Germany: 2246
NIELD, Walter: 4176
NIFTY JIFFY CORPORATION: 2794
NIGER RIVER: 41
NIGERIA: 1424
    British administration: 4514
    Missions and missionaries: 41
    Slave trade: 41
NIGHTINGALE, Florence: 3472
NILE RIVER: 41
    see also WHITE NILE RIVER
NILES, Alice E. (Andrews): 3901
NILES, Hezekiah: 3902
NILES, Nathaniel: 3903
NILES FAMILY (Georgia): 3901
NILES' WEEKLY REGISTER: 3902
NIMMO, G. H.: 3904
NIMMO, Margaret: 3809
NIMMO FAMILY (Virginia--Genealogy): 3809
NIMROD (schooner): 1938
NINDE, Helen: 3029
NINETEENTH CENTURY (periodical): 3056
NINETY SIX, South Carolina: see AMERICAN REVOLUTION--Campaigns and battles--South Carolina--Ninety Six
NINEVEH, Virginia: 3680
NINONBERG, Ernest von: 3674
NISBET, Blanch Kell: 3905
NISBET, Charles Richard: 3905
NISBET, Eugenius Aristides: 3905
NISBET, James Alexander: 3905
NISBET, James Taylor: 3905
NISBET, James Taylor, Jr.: 3905
NISBET, James Wingfield: 3905
NISBET, John (North Carolina): 3905
NISBET, John W. (Georgia): 3905
NISBET, Junius Wingfield: 3905
NISBET, Mary: 3905
NISBET, Mary (Seymour): 3905
NISBET, Reuben B.: 127
NISBETT FAMILY (Georgia): 3905
NITRE: see SALTPETER
NIVEN, F. M., Sr.: 3906
NIVEN, F. M., Jr.: 3906
NIVEN, T. M.: 523
NIXON, Eccles: 3315
NIXON, Francis, Sr.: 3907

NIXON, Thomas: 3908
NIXONTON, North Carolina: 3783, 4321
"NO FATE SAVE THE VICTIM'S FAULT IS LOW" by Ralph Waldo Emerson: 1698
NO TIME FOR SERGEANTS by McKenzie Hooks Hyman: 2747
NOAILLES, Louis Marie, Vicomte de: 3909
NOBILITY: see KNIGHTHOOD; and Nobility as subheading under names of specific countries
NOBLE, William: 2006
NOBLE, William Henry: 3910
NODAWAY COUNTY, Missouri: 3540
NOEL, Baptist Wriothesley: 3911
NOEL, John W.: 4443
NOEL-BUXTON, Noel Edward, First Baron Noel-Buxton: 3912
NOEL-BYRON, George Gordon, Sixth Baron Byron: see BYRON, George Gordon Noel-, Sixth Baron Byron
NOLAND, Susan C.: 3913
NOMINATIONS FOR OFFICE:
  see also ELECTIONS, and specific types of elections, e.g. CONGRESSIONAL ELECTIONS; Conventions as subheading under names of specific parties, e.g. DEMOCRATIC PARTY--Conventions
  Methods used in Maryland: 4542
"NOMINI HALL," Virginia: 917
NONA INSTITUTE (North Carolina): 4918
NONCONFORMISTS: see DISSENTING CHURCHES
NONIMPORTATION: 1424
  see also EMBARGO
"THE NONSENSE OF IT. SHORT ANSWERS TO COMMON OBJECTIONS AGAINST WOMAN SUFFRAGE" by Thomas Wentworth Higginson: 2522
NOOTKA SOUND CONTROVERSY: 1913
NORBECK BILL (1929): 4453
NORCLIFFE, Charles Best: 4627
NORCOTT, S. F.: 3914
NORDHOFF, Charles: 959
NORFLEET BROTHERS (Virginia firm): 3915
NORFOLK, England: 2296
  Aylsham: 5531
  Hanworth: 1541
  Norwich: 370, 2841
  Politics and government: 2708
NORFOLK, Virginia:
  1800s: 486
  1800s: 1492
  1810s: 70
  1820s: 70, 4683, 5204, 5217
  1830s: 70
  1840s: 4867
  1850s: 4017
  1860s: 4017, 5507, 5545
  1870s: 2700, 5507
  1880s: 2700, 5507
  1890s: 3079
  1800s-1900s: 557, 4932
  1900s: 2773
  Books--Prices: 3830
  Canals: 5696
  Civil War: 316, 2085, 2121, 3440
    see also CIVIL WAR--CAMPAIGNS, BATTLES, AND MILITARY ACTIONS--Virginia--Norfolk
    Confederate fortifications: 375
    Prisoners and prisons: 358
    Union naval blockade: 4183
  Clothing and dress--Prices: 3830
  Cotton growing: 3830
  Cotton trade: 435
  Diseases:
    Cholera: 5751
    Typhoid: 2857
    Yellow fever: 330, 3301, 4968
  Economic conditions: 3440
  Estates--Administration and settlement: 3830
  Farm supplies: 3830
  Fertilizer industry: 373

NORFOLK, Virginia (Continued):
  Furniture--Prices: 3830
  Hiring of Negroes: 3830
  Hospitals, Military: 4701
  Intra-Coastal Waterway: 4858
  Mercantile accounts: 5770
  Merchants: 1679, 3783
  Poetry: 732
  Religion: 4968
  Schools: 4968
  Slave coffles: 4387
  Stationery--Prices: 3830
  Tax receipts: 3830
  Teaching: 4968
  United States Navy--Surgeons: 4701
  War of 1812: 2986
NORFOLK COUNTY, Massachusetts:
  Brookline: 5846
  Dedham: 105
  Dorchester: 1766, 1973
    Civil War: 3342
  Milton: 1843
  Randolph: 1253
  Roxbury: 1502, 1968, 2468, 5085
  South Weymouth: 5677
  Weymouth: 5754
NORFOLK COUNTY, Virginia:
  Brigands and robbers: 5380
  Craney Island: 70
  Deep Creek: 4866
  Glencoe: 5523
  Norfolk: see NORFOLK, Virginia
  Portsmouth: see PORTSMOUTH, Virginia
NORFOLK AND NORTH CAROLINA CANAL COMPANY: 5696
NORFOLK AND SOUTHERN RAILROAD: 4858
NORFOLK AND WESTERN RAILWAY COMPANY: 3986
NORFOLK ISLAND: 3238
NORLINA, North Carolina:
  Race riots: 4103
NORMAL, Illinois: 3051
NORMAL COLLEGE, Randolph County, North Carolina: 1773
  see also TRINITY COLLEGE, Randolph County, North Carolina; TRINITY COLLEGE, Durham, North Carolina; DUKE UNIVERSITY, Durham, North Carolina
  Trustees: 537
NORMAL SCHOOLS:
  see also SCHOOLS; UNIVERSITIES AND COLLEGES, and names of specific universities and colleges
  Georgia: 539
  North Carolina: 435, 3495
    Wilmington: 617, 3607
  Ohio: 1177
NORMAN, Felix Grundy: 2662
NORMAN, George W.: 216
NORMAN, Henry: 3916
NORMAN, Oklahoma: see UNIVERSITY OF OKLAHOMA
NORRAL, Sally Vaughn: 3761
NORRIS, A. J.: 1877
NORRIS, George E.: 3917
NORRIS, George W.: 2109
NORRIS, Homer, Jr.: 4189
NORRIS, Jeremiah: 3917
NORRIS, Needham: 3918
NORRISTOWN, Pennsylvania:
  Irish in the United States: 4190
NORTH, Frederick, Second Earl of Guilford: 92, 5330
NORTH, H. M.: 3919
NORTH, Simon Newton Dexter: 706
NORTH FAMILY (Great Britain): 3946
NORTH AMERICA:
  Birds: 4475
  Spanish administration: 4979
THE NORTH AMERICAN REVIEW: 2409, 3465, 3774, 4491
NORTH AMERICAN TRUST AND BANKING COMPANY OF NEW YORK: 2755

NORTH ANNA CREEK, Virginia: see CIVIL WAR--CAMPAIGNS, BATTLES AND MILITARY ACTIONS--Virginia--North Anna Creek
NORTH ANNA RIVER (Virginia): 460
NORTH BEND BAPTIST ASSOCIATION (Kentucky): 3199
NORTH BERWICK, Maine: 3264
NORTH BRANCH CANAL: 4188
NORTH BRANFORD, Connecticut:
  Religion: 5666
  Social life and customs: 5666
NORTH CANAAN, Connecticut: 1205

NORTH CAROLINA

see also CAROLINA PROVINCE; SOUTHERN STATES
ABOLITION OF SLAVERY AND ABOLITIONIST SENTIMENT: 923, 2469, 4080
ACADEMIC FREEDOM: 2705, 4968
ACTORS: 4502
ADVERTISING: 2589
  Books: 4765
  Convalescent homes: 4761
  Health resorts: 3415
  Patent medicines: 4761, 4765
  Railroads: 238
  Tobacco products: 1586
AGRICULTURAL IMPLEMENTS:
  Iredell County: 5319
AGRICULTURAL MACHINERY: 4858
AGRICULTURAL ORGANIZATIONS: 1256, 5632
  see also NORTH CAROLINA--FARMERS' ALLIANCE; NORTH CAROLINA--PATRONS OF HUSBANDRY
  Halifax County: 2399
  Surry County: 5146
AGRICULTURAL PRODUCTS: 4689
  Lincoln County: 5558
  Prices: 165, 647, 1523, 1602, 4689, 4858, 5374
AGRICULTURAL WORKERS:
  see also NORTH CAROLINA--WAGES AND SALARIES--Agricultural workers
  New Hanover County: 4603
AGRICULTURE:
  see also the following subheadings under NORTH CAROLINA: CROPS, and names of specific crops; FARMING, and subheadings beginning with the word FARM; PLANTATIONS, and subheadings beginning with the word PLANTATION
  1800s: 435, 484, 1323, 2161, 2819, 5551
  1800s-1900s: 122
  1900s: 274, 325, 2188, 4564, 5962
  Burke County: 245
  Durham County: 1256
  Guilford County: 2314
  Halifax County: 426
  Harnett County: 238
  Lee County: 238
  Montgomery County: 4689
  Orange County: 1256
AIRPORTS--Durham: 2379
ALMANACS: 5741
AMERICAN DRAMA: 4502
AMERICAN FICTION: 5049
AMERICAN LITERATURE: 1313
AMERICAN POETRY: 2589, 2739, 3499, 3960, 5739
AMERICAN RED CROSS: 2188
AMERICAN REVOLUTION: see AMERICAN REVOLUTION; CONTINENTAL ARMY
AMERICAN SATIRE--Durham: 5597
AMUSEMENTS: 436, 1925, 2192
ANTI-UNIONISM: 1196, 1202
APPRENTICESHIP: 4370
ARCHITECTS: 465
ARITHMETIC EXERCISE BOOKS: 208, 579, 1538, 1781, 3605, 4862
  Caswell County: 3576
  Davidson County: 5219

853

NORTH CAROLINA

ARITHMETIC EXERCISE BOOKS
 (Continued):
  Guilford County: 4114
  Hillsborough: 3677
  Lincoln County: 5976
  Surry County: 3074
  Taylorsville: 3289
  Washington: 5479
ARTS: 4736
ASSAULT AND BATTERY: 2003, 4773
ASSOCIATE REFORMED PRESBYTERIAN
 CHURCH: 4310
ATOMIC ENERGY: 1196
AUCTIONS--Fayetteville: 5298
AUTHORS AND PUBLISHERS: 1521, 4918,
 4992
 see also NORTH CAROLINA--
  PUBLISHERS AND PUBLISHING
AUTHORSHIP: 4098
AUTOGRAPH COLLECTION: 3543
AUTOGRAPHS: 666, 5124, 5298
 Person County: 378
BALLADS: 691
BALLOONS--Salem: 813
BALLOTS: 4765, 5549
 see also NORTH CAROLINA--
  ELECTIONS; and specific kinds
  of elections under NORTH
  CAROLINA
BAND CONCERTS: 3845
BANDS: 3845
 see also NORTH CAROLINA--PUBLIC
  SCHOOLS--Bands
BANK NOTES: 766
BANKRUPTCY: 1438, 3351
 Franklinton: 5056
 Mooresville: 3757
BANKS AND BANKING:
 see also NORTH CAROLINA--STATE
  BANKS
 1800s: 730, 2474, 2651, 3415, 4100
 1800s-1900s: 4391, 4918
 1900s: 4858, 5962
 Cary: 928
 Charlotte: 766
 Durham: 513, 1041, 3762
 Fayetteville: 4517, 5298
 Milton: 310
 New Bern: 3955
 Raleigh: 2823
 Washington: 309
BAPTISM: 1584
 Baptist churches: 1152
BAPTIST CHURCHES: 274, 387, 484,
 2068, 4232, 4586, 5218, 5673, 5964
 see also the following subheadings
  under NORTH CAROLINA: FREE WILL
  BAPTIST CHURCHES; ORIGINAL
  FREE WILL BAPTIST CHURCHES;
  PRIMITIVE BAPTIST CHURCHES
 Associations: 320, 484
 Clergy: see NORTH CAROLINA--
  CLERGY--Baptist
 Discipline--Colerain: 1157
 Finance: 3538
  Colerain: 1157
 Membership--Williamston: 4843
 Religious literature: see NORTH
  CAROLINA--RELIGIOUS LITERATURE--
  Baptist
 State conventions: 3538
 Subdivided by place:
  Bertie County: 2603, 4572
  Caswell County: 4849
  Colerain: 1157
  Durham: 5401
  Martin County: 4931
  Raleigh: 5401
  Robeson Union: 319
  Wilkes County: 4742
BARTER: 717, 2895
 Washington: 911
BASEBALL CLUBS--Durham: 4968
BEEKEEPING: 122
BILLS OF EXCHANGE: 2651
BIOGRAPHICAL STUDIES: 2299

NORTH CAROLINA

BIOGRAPHIES: 5457
BIRD CALLS: 3048
BIRDS: 833
BLACK CODES: 2469
BLACKSMITHING: 1015, 1550, 4458
 Cabarrus County: 2628
 Prattsburg: 4307
 Wadesboro: 998
BLACKSMITHS' ACCOUNTS: 4918, 4939
 Farmington: 2857
 Forsyth County: 4631
 Gold Hill: 3368
 Lockville: 5207
 Mount Gilead: 4689
 Prattsburg: 4307
 Wadesboro: 4906
BLIND: 2188
 Museum for: 4736
BONDS:
 see also CONFEDERATE STATES OF
  AMERICA--BONDS--North Carolina
 North Carolina Literary Fund:
  3943
 Oxford: 2455
BOOK REVIEWS: 960
BOOKS:
 see also NORTH CAROLINA--
  CENSORSHIP--Books
 Hillsborough: 1890
BOOKSELLERS AND BOOKSELLING: 1491,
 3186
 Greensboro: 5804
BOOT AND SHOE MAKING: see NORTH
 CAROLINA--SHOEMAKERS' ACCOUNTS
BOOTLEGGING: see NORTH CAROLINA--
 LIQUOR MANUFACTURE--Illegal
BOUNDARY DISPUTES--Virginia: 2893
BRIBERY: 2188
BROOM INDUSTRY--Lincoln County:
 5558
BUILDING AND LOAN ASSOCIATIONS:
 3410, 4775
 New Bern: 3955
 Shelby: 1951
BUILDING CONSTRUCTION: 1589, 4172
 University of North Carolina: 2399
BUILDING FUNDS: 4727
BUILDING MATERIALS INDUSTRY:
 Archdale: 4172
BUSINESS ACCOUNTS: 148
 Fairfield: 921
BUSINESS AFFAIRS:
 1700s: 668
 1700s-1800s: 484, 631
 1700s-1900s: 832
 1800s: 263, 838, 1538, 2469, 5596
  1810s: 1108
  1820s: 1108, 2113
  1830s: 2113
  1840s: 2113, 5367
  1850s: 2298, 5367
  1860s: 796, 2298, 5367
  1870s: 2298
  1880s: 2572
 1800s-1900s: 677, 1277, 2808,
  3070, 3091
 Anson County: 409
 Beaufort County: 5831
 Burke County: 1247
 Caldwell County: 1247
 Craven County: 1871
 Cunningham's Store: 1959
 Durham: 5923
 Durham County: 1256
 Elizabeth City: 423
 Enfield: 426
 Fairfield: 921
 Fayetteville: 2354, 3905
 Lexington: 2874
 Moore County: 5792
 Mount Gilead: 2730
 Orange County: 1255, 1256
 Ridgeway: 999, 2435
 Rowan County: 1237
 Thomasville: 2906

NORTH CAROLINA

BUSINESS AFFAIRS (Continued):
 Williamston: 131
 Wilmington: 5912
BUSINESS FAILURES: 4918
BUSINESS SCHOOLS--Durham: 3843
BUTCHERS' ACCOUNTS: 3410
CALLIGRAPHY: 4862
CAMP MEETINGS: 122, 1738, 1908,
 4506, 4787
 Forsyth County: 2855
 Methodist: 5964
 Methodist Episcopal: 3581
CANALS: 3415, 4858, 5696
 see also NORTH CAROLINA--
  INTRACOASTAL WATERWAY
CAPITAL PUNISHMENT: 5768
CARRIAGE AND BUGGY MAKING: 3317,
 3403
CARRIAGE AND BUGGY REPAIR: 4918
 Wadesboro: 1897
CARTOONS: 3359
CARY REBELLION: 4232
CATHOLIC CHURCH:
 Conversion--Edenton: 1376
CATTLE MARKS:
 Perquimans County: 5777
CENSORSHIP:
 Books: 2036
 Moving pictures: 3211
 Rowan County: 4640
CHAIR MANUFACTURING: 2382
CHAMBERS OF COMMERCE: 1661
 Raleigh: 4927
CHARCOAL FURNACES: 2121
CHARITABLE WORK: 3410
 Durham: 5519
CHARITIES:
 see also NORTH CAROLINA--
  PHILANTHROPY
 Wilmington: 4080
CHEMISTRY:
 Students' notebooks:
  University of North Carolina:
   673, 1284
CHEROKEE INDIANS: 5202, 5258
 Agents: 5202
 Business affairs: 5202
 Government relations: 5906
 Land surveys: 3028
 Murder of whites:
  Buncombe County: 3176
 Removal: 5258, 5906
CHILD CARE CENTERS: 1275
CHILDREN'S HOSPITALS:
 Wrightsville Sound: 4809
CHURCH AND SOCIAL PROBLEMS:
 Rowan County: 4640
CHURCH HISTORY: 1738, 4232
 see also NORTH CAROLINA--
  (specific denomination)--Church
  history
CHURCH MUSIC: 108, 1538
CHURCHES: 1232
 see also names of specific
  denominations under NORTH
  CAROLINA
 Church buildings: 5041
  Randolph County: 88
 Finance: 2347
 Interchurch organizations:
  Rowan County: 4640
 Subdivided by place:
  Elizabeth City: 3919
  Iredell County: 5245
  Oak Grove Township: 3896
CIVIC IMPROVEMENT--Durham: 4968
CIVIL ENGINEERING:
 Franklin County: 76
CIVIL WAR: see appropriate
 subheadings under CIVIL WAR;
 CONFEDERATE STATES OF AMERICA;
 UNITED STATES--ARMY--Civil War
CLAIMS: 2553
 Hillsborough: 5341
 Against Royall Cotton Mills: 4586

NORTH CAROLINA
  CLAIMS COLLECTION: 2808
  CLERGY: 3499
    Slaveholding, Morality of: 4434
    Subdivided by denomination:
      Baptist: 63, 484, 647, 4232,
        5211, 5401
        Edgecombe County: 3052
        Gatesville: 2428
        Misconduct in office: 255
        Retirement income: 4828
      Disciples of Christ: 5554
      Episcopal: 2699
        Edenton: 1376
        Slaveholding, Morality of:
          4669
      Methodist: 796, 1538, 1738,
        1915, 2221, 3646, 4242, 5022,
        5793, 5964, 5965
        Aid to ministers' families:
          3646
        Circuit riders: 956, 3473,
          3497, 5964
        Halifax County: 711
        Personal finance: 956
        Retirement income: 3646
      Methodist Episcopal: 3992
        High Point: 3581
        Louisburg: 4787
        Woodland: 4047
      Methodist Episcopal Church,
        South: 1152, 4136, 4192, 4498
        Chatham County: 1096
        Circuit riders: 3195
        Plymouth: 772
        Wilmington: 772
      Methodist Protestant:
        Mental health: 3186
      Original Free Will Baptist: 3987
      Presbyterian: 702, 1547, 1890,
        3117, 3300, 4310
        Coddle Creek: 4311
        Thyatira: 3334
      Primitive Baptist: 4500
      Protestant Episcopal: 4232
        Pastoral responsibilities: 4394
      Universalist: 1906
    Subdivided by place:
      Elizabeth City: 3919
      Rowan County: 4640
  CLOCKS AND WATCHES:
    Repairing and adjusting: 3300
  CLOTH--Salem: 1905
  CLOTHING AND DRESS:
    see also NORTH CAROLINA--PATTERNS;
      NORTH CAROLINA--SLAVES--
      Clothing and dress
    Prices: 2819, 4858
  COAST (Map): 202
  COMMISSION MERCHANTS: 2399, 2933,
    4760, 4858, 5298
    Washington: 3827, 4858
    Wilmington: 3447, 5373, 5912
  COMMODITY PRICES:
    see also CIVIL WAR--COMMODITY
      PRICES--North Carolina
    1700s-1800s: 3176
    1800s: 539, 1107, 2857, 3351, 5905
    1810s: 5298
    1830s: 3916
    1840s: 5792
    1850s: 1252, 4917, 5231
    1860s: 1252, 1950, 2952, 2970,
      4080, 4917, 5231, 5792
    1870s: 2548, 2952, 2970, 3415,
      4072, 4080, 5792
    1880s: 2548, 2952, 4072
    1800s-1900s: 2830, 3416
    1900s: 1202
    Chatham County: 770
    Conetoe: 1362
    Elizabeth City: 423
    Granville County: 5285
    Guilford County: 2314
    Littleton: 2399
    Orange County: 3677
    Ridgeway: 999

NORTH CAROLINA
  COMMODITY PRICES (Continued):
    Washington: 652
  COMMODITY SPECULATION: 1438
  COMMONPLACE BOOKS: 817
  COMMUNITY CHEST--Durham: 3927
  COMPANY STORES:
    Washington Mining Company: 5583
  CONGRESSIONAL ELECTIONS:
    1861-1865: 4923
    1870: 4714
    1898: 4858
    1906: 5072
    1918: 3955
    1920: 3955
    1934: 325
  CONSERVATION: see NORTH CAROLINA--
    FOREST CONSERVATION
  CONSTITUTION (1877): 2469, 4266
  CONSTITUTIONAL CONVENTIONS:
    1835: 730, 3924
    1865: 4489
    1875: 2419
  CONTRACTS: 3415
    see also NORTH CAROLINA--LABOR
      CONTRACTS
    Martin County: 4849
  CONVALESCENT HOMES:
    see also NORTH CAROLINA--
      ADVERTISING--Convalescent homes
    Southern Pines: 3633
  COOKERY: 1475, 4689, 5740
    Guilford County: 1407
  COPPER MINING: 2121
    Davidson County: 2041
    Payrolls: 2906
  COPPERPLATE ENGRAVING: 1339
  COPPERSMITHING: 544
  CORN: 2121
  CORN PRODUCTION--Wilmington: 4603
  CORPORATION LAW--Raleigh: 2553
  COST OF LIVING: 1202
  COTTON: 2121
    Prices: 641, 1396, 1611, 2399,
      4918, 5298
      Cleveland County: 4691
      Iredell County: 5310
    Storage--Cleveland County: 4691
    Weaving and spinning: 5658
  COTTON CULTIVATORS: 5280
  COTTON GINS: 1660
    Beaufort County: 911
    Randleman: 5408
    Washington: 3827
  COTTON GROWING: 2573, 2970, 4689,
    4918
    Halifax County: 5280
    Onslow County: 1252
    Wilmington: 4603
  COTTON MILL WORKERS: 5048
    see also NORTH CAROLINA--STRIKES--
      Cotton mill workers; NORTH
      CAROLINA--WAGES AND SALARIES--
      Cotton mill workers
  COTTON MILLS: 396, 1539, 3317, 4080,
    5312
    Bankruptcy: 5056
      Wake Forest: 4586
    Finance:
      Erwin: 5298
      Milledgeville: 4918
      Scotland County: 3776
      Wake County: 3863
      Wake Forest: 4586
      Worthville: 3187
    Management--Wake Forest: 4586
    Payrolls--Worthville: 3187
    Receivership: 4858
    Stocks: 396
    Subdivided by place:
      Cane Creek: 875
      Catawba: 3718
      Cleveland County: 4691
      Franklinton: 5056
      Iredell County: 5310
      Lawnsdale: 1104
      Milledgeville: 4918

NORTH CAROLINA
  COTTON MILLS:
    Subdivided by place (Continued):
      Mount Airy: 5048
      Mount Holly: 5100
      Randleman: 5408
      Salem: 1905
      Turnersburg: 2857, 5048
      Wake County: 3863
      Wake Forest: 4586
      Worthville: 3187
  COTTON PLANTATIONS: 5709
    Franklin County: 3023
  COTTON TRADE:
    1700s-1800s: 2530, 2889, 5298
    1700s-1900s: 3476
    1800s:
      1840s: 4734, 5470
      1850s: 4734, 5470
      1860s: 614, 2480, 3447, 4734,
        5087
      1870s: 641, 5087
      1880s: 3303, 5087
    1800s-1900s: 4918
    1900s: 5962
    Cleveland County: 4691
    Fayetteville: 1396
    Halifax County: 5280
    Person County: 1336
    Scotland County: 3303
    Wake County: 876
    Wilmington: 1281, 5014, 5912
    Woodland: 4047
  COTTONSEED OIL--Wilmington: 5912
  COUNTY GOVERNMENT:
    Anson County: 4918
  COUNTY ROADS: 2553
  COURTHOUSES--Beaufort County: 540
  COURTS: 1015, 4849, 4918
    see also the following subheadings
      under NORTH CAROLINA: JUDGES;
      JURIES; LAWSUITS
    Cases: 1107
      Davie County: 122
    Clerks: 4918
    Costs: 4858
    Court reporters: 2776
    Judgments: 171, 3221, 3825
      Granville County: 68
    Orders: 3415
    Summonses: 832, 2354, 2833, 3221,
      3416, 4765, 5692
    Subdivided by type of court:
      County Courts:
        Catawba County: 5745
      Courts of Equity:
        Forsyth County: 1209
        Martin County: 3936
      Courts of Common Pleas and
        Quarter Sessions:
        Dobbs County: 934
      District Courts: 1150, 1190,
        3925
        Confederate District Court:
          1190
      General Court: 3930
      Juvenile Courts: 1275
      Superior Courts: 1128
        Edenton District: 4773
      Supreme Court: 1914, 2437, 2776,
        4103, 4595
        Testimony on Ku Klux Klan
          activities: 3062
  COURTSHIP: 1467, 1773, 2469, 3290,
    5312
    see also NORTH CAROLINA--LOVE
      LETTERS
    Chatham County: 2861
  CRANBERRY CULTURE: 1475
  CRIME: see the following subheadings
    under NORTH CAROLINA: ASSAULT AND
    BATTERY; BRIBERY; EMBEZZLEMENT;
    EXTRADITION OF CRIMINALS; JUVENILE
    DELINQUENCY; MURDER; SLAVES--
    Crime; TRESPASS
  CROP LIENS: 3476

855

NORTH CAROLINA

CROPS: 1322, 1336, 1602, 2548, 2663, 2830, 3351, 4083, 4310, 5741
  see also the following subheadings under NORTH CAROLINA: AGRICULTURE; FARMING; PLANTATIONS; and names of specific crops
  Caswell County: 657
  Conetoe: 1362
  Guilford County: 1407
  Hyde County: 419
  Iredell County: 4872
  Nash County: 5475
  Stokes County: 2800
CURRENCY: 1339
CUSTOMS DUTIES--Collection: 2776
DEATH: 1467, 3176, 5739
DEBATES AND DEBATING: 3973
DEBATING SOCIETIES: 2357
  Olin: 3973
  Youngsville: 5087
DEBT: 832, 1120, 1190, 1491, 2003, 5752
  see also NORTH CAROLINA--PERSONAL DEBT; NORTH CAROLINA--PUBLIC DEBT
  Non-payment of: 2354
  Trials concerning: 4773
  Subdivided by place:
    Halifax County: 5672
    Montgomery County: 4689
    Moore County: 5792
    Nash County: 5475
DEBT COLLECTION: 2553, 3043, 4858
DEFENSE:
  see also NORTH CAROLINA--FORTIFICATIONS
  Leaksville: 3622
DEFENSE PLANTS: 2581
DEISM: 3176
DEMOCRATIC PARTY:
  1800s: 1015, 1100, 1659, 5149, 5667
  1900s: 274, 4805, 4825, 4828, 4918
  Campaign material: 4018, 4251
  Conventions:
    1868: 3440
    1906: 5072
    1940: 2863
  Liberals: 3538
  Local politics:
    Beaufort: 4858
    Wilmington: 1313
  Presidential campaign of 1928:
    Division over candidates: 3538
  Union sympathizers: 4834
DEMONSTRATIONS:
  Durham: 2398
  Greensboro: 2050
DENTISTRY: 3410
DENTISTS: 417
DEPARTMENT STORES--Durham: 3762
DEPENDENTS: 2188
DEPRESSION (1929--): 5298
  Emergency programs: 274
  Craven County: 3955
  New Bern: 3955
DESCRIPTION AND TRAVEL:
  1600s-1700s: 202
  1700s: 819
  1800s: 5018
    1810s: 3808
    1820s: 529, 5840
    1830s: 2857
    1840s: 761
    1850s: 4921
    1880s:
      Photographs: 4414
  1800s-1900s: 4898
  1900s:
    Photographs: 180
DESEGREGATION: 4724
  see also NORTH CAROLINA--SCHOOLS--Desegregation
DIALECTS: 3048
  Folk dialects: 691
DISCIPLES OF CHRIST: 1523

NORTH CAROLINA

DISCIPLES OF CHRIST (Continued):
  Church history: 5554
  Clergy: see NORTH CAROLINA--CLERGY--Disciples of Christ
DISEASES: 329, 4930, 5741
  see also NORTH CAROLINA--MEDICAL TREATMENT; NORTH CAROLINA--SLAVES--Diseases
  Influenza:
    Chapel Hill: 3878
    Greensboro: 3843
  Smallpox: 608
    Chatham County: 770
    Dutchville: 1826
    Fayetteville: 4517
    Hillsborough: 5390
  Yellow fever: 3563
    New Bern: 4561
    Wilmington: 3447
  Subdivided by place:
    Stokes County: 2800
DIVINITY SCHOOLS:
  Duke University: 1589, 2075, 5022
DIVORCE: 2906, 3960
DIXIECRATS: 3538
DRAWINGS: 691
DRY GOODS: 264
DYES AND DYEING: 1612
  Hosiery--Burlington: 3842
  Pulp and paper: see NORTH CAROLINA--PULP AND PAPER INDUSTRY--Dyes and dyeing
EARTHQUAKES--Henderson County: 5229
ECONOMIC CONDITIONS:
  see also the following subheadings under NORTH CAROLINA: DEPRESSION; PANIC OF 1819; POVERTY
  1700s-1800s: 3476
  1800s: 183, 530, 730, 3155, 4930, 5285, 5905
    1830s: 967
    1840s: 967, 1728
    1850s: 1409
    1860s: 76, 417, 1409, 1677, 2394, 4248, 5298
    1870s: 76, 1409, 1677, 2394, 5298
  1800s-1900s: 274
  1900s:
    1920s: 5962
    1930s: 3447, 3538
  Harnett County: 238
  Lee County: 238
  Ridgeway: 3307
EDUCATION:
  see also the following subheadings under NORTH CAROLINA: FREEDMEN--Education; NEGROES--Education; SCHOOLS; TEACHING
  1700s-1800s: 2357
  1700s-1900s: 645
  1800s: 608, 617, 813, 2192, 2330, 2469, 2861, 5280, 5603
  1800s-1900s: 274
  1900s: 2945, 3538, 5014, 5298
  Higher education: 5252
  Law and legislation: 5737
  Women: 2032
    Louisburg: 1411
    Methodist churches: 1152
  Subdivided by place:
    Caldwell County: 593
    Craven County: 3955
    Fayetteville: 5298
    Lenoir: 4689
EDUCATIONAL ASSOCIATIONS: 5298
ELECTION LAWS AND REGULATIONS: 1951, 2819
ELECTION REFORM: 274
ELECTIONS:
  see also the following subheadings under NORTH CAROLINA: BALLOTS; CONGRESSIONAL ELECTIONS; GUBERNATORIAL ELECTIONS; JUDGES--Elections; LABOR UNIONS--Elections; LOCAL ELECTIONS;

NORTH CAROLINA

ELECTIONS:
  see also (Continued):
    PRESIDENTIAL ELECTIONS; SENATORIAL ELECTIONS
  1700s-1800s: 245
  1800s:
    1808: 5229
    1836: 1015
    1840: 1580
    1860s: 4103
    1873: 3415
    1876: 3960
    1880: 3896
    1888: 5709
  1900s: 4251, 4918
    1920: 4858
    1924: 2749
    1930: 2299
    1936: 3538
    1950s: 4805
  Randolph County (1896): 3290
ELECTRIC POWER INDUSTRY: 1584, 3447
  Winston-Salem: 4788
EMBARGOES (1812-1813):
  Economic effects: 5298
EMBEZZLEMENT:
  By a federal employee: 2776
  From state treasury: 2458
EMPLOYMENT: 5741
ENDOWMENTS: 547
  see also DUKE ENDOWMENT; NORTH CAROLINA--FOUNDATIONS
ENGLISH LITERATURE:
  Study and teaching: 985
EPISCOPAL CHURCHES: 1128, 4918
  see also the following subheadings under NORTH CAROLINA: CLERGY--Episcopal; SCHOOLS--Church schools--Episcopal; SERMONS--Episcopal
ESCHEAT: 435, 3003
ESTATE ACCOUNTS: 2833, 4336, 4704, 5709
  Charlotte: 5312
  Hyde County: 511
  Martin County: 4849
  Raleigh: 727
  Wadesboro: 2984
ESTATES:
  Administration and settlement:
    1700s-1900s: 832, 1107, 3424, 4858
    1800s: 530, 817, 1382, 1438, 1475, 1604, 2554, 2808, 3043, 4154, 4669, 4689, 4760, 4849, 4875, 4918, 5549
      1800s: 1492, 4344, 5740
      1810s: 2861
      1820s: 2113
      1830s: 2113, 3916, 4270
      1840s: 2113, 2589, 2876, 3176, 3639, 4270, 4923, 5298
      1850s: 3301, 4270, 4923
      1860s: 1861, 2727, 3301, 4357, 4923
      1870s: 641, 2419, 2727, 3301
    1900s:
      1900s: 661
      1930s: 5298
    Anson County: 2493
    Beaufort County: 5831
    Bertie County: 2582
    Bladen County: 4516
    Caldwell County: 3324
    Charlotte: 5312
    Chatham County: 2462
    Davie County: 122
    Durham County: 1256
    Edenton: 4773
    Forsyth County: 1209
    Halifax County: 5672
    Hillsborough: 5381
    Hyde County: 511
    Iredell County: 5319
    Martin County: 5036
    Mocksville: 2749

NORTH CAROLINA
ESTATES:
  Administration and settlement:
    (Continued):
    Moore County: 3393
    Onslow County: 1252
    Person County: 3752
    Prattsburg: 4307
    Raleigh: 727
    Ramseur: 2624
    Randolph County: 621, 5018
    Richmond County: 3475
    Shelby: 1951
    Wadesboro: 2984
  Inventories:
    Smith Church: 5399
EVANGELISM: 4787
EXECUTIONS: 1577
  see also NORTH CAROLINA--CAPITAL
    PUNISHMENT
  Murder: 2117
EXTRADITION OF CRIMINALS: 4729
FAMILY LIFE:
  Iredell County: 4310
  Society of Friends: 1407
  Stokes County: 2800
FARM ACCOUNTS: 399, 2087
  Beaufort County: 5814
  Catawba County: 5745
  Durham County: 4480
  Fairfield: 921
  Franklin County: 5087
  Iredell County: 3787
  Lincoln County: 4450
  Lockville: 4207
  Mocksville: 2749
  Montgomery County: 4689
  Mount Gilead: 4689
  Oak Grove Township: 3896
  Raleigh: 2938
  Randolph County: 108
  Washington: 705, 911
  Washington County: 5013
FARM COMMUNITIES:
  Development in Wilmington: 3447
FARM LIFE: 373, 675, 1882
  Forsyth County: 156
  Halifax County: 3831
  Oak Grove Township: 3896
FARM MANAGEMENT: 4262, 4849
FARM PRODUCE:
  Prices: 426
FARM SUPPLIES:
  Carthage: 5138
FARM TENANCY: 4918
  Beaufort County: 911
  Labor contracts:
    Richmond County: 3475
  Laws and legislation: 3447
  Lumberton: 3422
FARMERS' ALLIANCE: 2330, 2804, 3996,
  5709
  Bethany: 3996
  Davidson County: 3996
  Thomasville: 3996
FARMING:
  see also the following subheadings
    under NORTH CAROLINA:
    AGRICULTURE, and subheadings
    beginning with AGRICULTURAL;
    CROPS, and names of specific
    crops; LIVESTOCK; PLANTATIONS,
    and subheadings beginning with
    PLANTATION
  1700s-1900s: 799, 4918
  1800s: 440, 484, 1428, 1584, 2068,
    2121, 3410, 4858, 5770
  Anson County: 4052
  Caswell County: 5243
  Catawba County: 5745
  Edgewater: 4858
  Guilford County: 2330
  Hyde County: 419
  Iredell County: 5245
  Lilesville: 2493
  Martin County: 5036

NORTH CAROLINA
FARMING (Continued):
  Onslow County: 1252
  Person County: 1336
  Warren County: 3307
  Whitaker's: 273
FERRIES--Bath: 705
FERTILIZER: 641, 3410, 4858
  see also NORTH CAROLINA--GUANO
FERTILIZER INDUSTRY: 960
  Durham: 3762
FINANCE: 1584, 2553, 3639, 3960
  see also the following subheadings
    under NORTH CAROLINA: HOUSEHOLD
    FINANCE; PERSONAL FINANCE;
    PUBLIC FINANCE; and Finance as
    subheading under specific
    businesses, institutions, or
    groups
  Chatham County: 1056
  Granville County: 68, 1224
  Lincolnton: 3317
  Wilmington: 3447
FIRE PROTECTION--Durham: 2379
FIRES:
  Fayetteville: 5298
FISHING--Fort Fisher: 3370
FISHING INDUSTRY: 325, 1015, 3907
  Hatteras: 4547
  New Bern: 3955
FLAGS:
  Confederate--Fort Fisher: 5972
  Secession: 4918
FLOUR MILLS: 2330
  see also NORTH CAROLINA--GRIST
    MILLS; NORTH CAROLINA--MILLERS'
    ACCOUNTS
  Guilford County: 5905
  Hoover Hill: 4100
  Lincoln County: 5558
  Milton: 5843
  Orange County: 3337
  Randleman: 5408
  Salem: 1905
FOLKLORE: 691
  Study and teaching: 4641
FOLKLORE SOCIETIES: 1064
FOOD PRICES: 614
  Beaufort County: 5521
  Farmington: 2857
FOOTBALL: 3338
FOREIGN TRADE:
  see also NORTH CAROLINA--SHIPPING;
    NORTH CAROLINA--TRADE AND
    COMMERCE
  Bermuda: 1871
  Great Britain: 3230
  West Indies: 2222
FOREST CONSERVATION: 4080
FORTIFICATIONS: 3176, 5390
  see also NORTH CAROLINA--DEFENSE
FOSSILS: 641
FOUNDATIONS: 2188
  see also NORTH CAROLINA--
    ENDOWMENTS
FRATERNAL SOCIETIES: 1669, 3070
  see also names of specific
    fraternal societies under NORTH
    CAROLINA
FREE WILL BAPTIST CHURCH: 1107, 1523
FREEDMEN: 730, 754, 797, 1376, 2469,
  2720, 2808
  Apprenticeship: 5431
  Assistance to: 3037
  Behavior: 956, 5298
  Education: 2540, 3037
  Labor contracts: 1056, 5709
    Lumberton: 3422
    Orange County: 3515
  Labor in textile mills: 5100
  Social status: 5425
  Tenancy: 832
    Lumberton: 3422
FREIGHT AND FREIGHTAGE:
  Wadesboro: 4814
FUGITIVE SLAVES: 3317, 3622, 4471,
  5857

NORTH CAROLINA
FURNITURE INDUSTRY: 325, 341, 4918
  Hickory: 3831
GAS LIGHTING--Fayetteville: 5298
GERMANS IN THE UNITED STATES: 1232
GOLD MINES AND MINING: 388, 529,
  1677, 2121, 2188
  Lawsuits--Davidson County: 2041
  Subdivided by place:
    Cabarrus County: 3391
    Davidson County: 2041, 5549
    Randolph County: 5549
    Vestal's Ford: 4450
GOOD ROADS MOVEMENT: 3380, 4918
  Craven County: 3955
GOVERNMENT AGENCIES AND OFFICIALS:
  Adjutant General: 1189, 5778
  Attorney-General: 4544
  Board of Commissioners of
    Navigation and Pilotage for the
    Cape Fear River and Bar: 3922
  Board of Education: 3538
  Board of Examiners: 2553
  Board of Health: 2553, 5603, 5881
  Colonial period:
    Governors:
      Sir Richard Everard
        (1725-1729): 1736
      William Tryon (1765-1771): 5352
    Secretary of State: 3940
  Commissioner of Labor and Printing:
    3070
  Department of Conservation and
    Development: 5962
  Division of Archives and History:
    3746, 3930
  Geological Board: 4858
  Governors:
    Thomas Burke (1781-1782): 769
    Richard Caswell (1784-1787):
      4746
    Richard Dobbs Spaight
      (1792-1795): 4977
    John Branch (1817-1820): 631
    Gabriel Holmes (1821-1824): 2611
    James Iredell, Jr. (1827-1828):
      2776
    David Lowry Swain (1832-1835):
      5150
    Edward Bishop Dudley (1836-1841):
      4249
    John Motley Morehead
      (1841-1845): 3764
    William Alexander Graham
      (1845-1849): 2121, 5149
    David Settle Reid (1851-1854):
      5737
    Thomas Bragg (1855-1859): 624
    John Willis Ellis (1859-1861):
      1687
    Henry Toole Clark (1861-1862):
      1061
    Zebulon Baird Vance (1862-1865,
      1877-1879): 5739
      Inauguration: 4080
    William Woods Holden (1865,
      1868-1870): 2589, 4489, 5149
    Jonathan Worth (1865-1868):
      3993, 5912
    Thomas Jordan Jarvis (1879-1885):
      2810
    Alfred Moore Scales (1885-1889):
      4686
      Inauguration: 4686
    Joseph Melville Broughton
      (1941-1945): 2863
    Luther Hartwell Hodges
      (1954-1961): 4724
  Highway Commission: 3380
  Pearsall Committee: 4724
  Revenue collectors: 2446
  Secretary of State: 4977
  Sheriffs:
    Beaufort County: 911
    Harnett County: 2357
    Orange County: 5390

NORTH CAROLINA
GOVERNMENT AGENCIES AND OFFICIALS:
  Sheriffs (Continued):
    Rowan County: 1291
  State Auditor: 2749
  State Treasurer: 2458, 3070
  Superintendent of Public
    Instruction: 2945
  Surgeon General: 2851
  Tax Commission: 4586
  Utilities Commission: 238
GOVERNMENT AND CIVIC EMPLOYEES: 3955
GRANITE QUARRIES--Rowan County: 5929
GRIST MILLS: 2121, 4153
  see also NORTH CAROLINA--FLOUR MILLS; NORTH CAROLINA--MILLERS' ACCOUNTS
GUANO: 3447, 4540
  see also NORTH CAROLINA--FERTILIZER
GUARDIANSHIP: 4849, 4918
  Children: 1523, 3415, 5319
  Edenton: 1376
  Mental incompetence: 3415
  Orphans: 2819, 5709
  Hillsborough: 5381
GUBERNATORIAL ELECTIONS:
  1828: 2776
  1846: 5390
  1850: 730
  1860: 1602
  1862: 4938
  1865: 2469
  1896: 1584
  1908: 3955, 4828
  1920: 4018
  1924: 274, 5962
  1932: 2553
  1940: 2863
  1944: 2863
HARBORS:
  Improvement: 274
  Port charges--Bath: 705
  Ports authority: 1661
  Wilmington: 3230, 3922, 4858
HEALTH CONDITIONS: 967, 2830, 3351, 4083
  New Hanover County: 3859
  Wilmington: 3859
HEALTH RESORTS: 5690
  Halifax County: 2399
  Mooresville: 3415
HIRING OF SLAVES: 756, 1107, 1382, 2222, 2350, 2819, 3476, 4849, 5100, 5709, 5770
  Iredell County: 4872, 5319
  Lincoln County: 4450
  Martin County: 5036
  Mocksville: 5335
  Wage scales: 2646
HISTORICAL RESTORATION: 1588
  Bath: 5298
  Bennitt House, Durham: 440
  Raleigh: 4736
HISTORICAL STUDIES: 22, 305, 1068, 1525, 1848, 2282, 2589, 3439, 4098, 4232, 5014
  American Revolution: 3176
    Loyalists: 305
  Duke University School of Nursing: 1946
  Local history: 960
  Regulators: 305
  Reviews: 960
HOME REMEDIES: 277, 3317, 3812
HONORS AND AWARDS: 4080
HORSES:
  Breeding: 484, 2876, 3176, 5709
  Franklin County: 5087
  Medicine: 3410
HOSIERY: see NORTH CAROLINA--DYES AND DYEING--Hosiery
HOSIERY MACHINERY: 1612
HOSIERY MILLS: 1612
  Finance: 4717
  Stocks: 3595

NORTH CAROLINA
HOSIERY MILLS (Continued):
  Subdivided by place:
    Burlington: 1353, 3595
    Graham: 4812
HOSIERY WORKERS: 1612
  see also NORTH CAROLINA--WAGES AND SALARIES--Hosiery workers
HOSPITAL AID SOCIETIES: 2553
HOSPITALS: 5741
  see also NORTH CAROLINA--CHILDREN'S HOSPITALS; NORTH CAROLINA--MENTAL HOSPITALS
  Civil War: see CIVIL WAR--HOSPITALS--North Carolina
  Philanthropy: 1584
  Subdivided by place:
    Durham: 2379, 5601
    Raleigh: 2553
    Winston-Salem: 3538
HOTEL REGISTERS--Yanceyville: 4284
HOUSE FURNISHINGS:
  Iredell County: 5319
HOUSEHOLD ACCOUNTS: 4858, 5805
  Granville County: 3916
  Jackson County: 3021
  New Bern: 5709
HOUSEHOLD FINANCE: 730, 3416
  Chapel Hill: 4763
HOUSEHOLD MANAGEMENT: 1407, 2714, 5740
HOUSES: 1584, 4080
  Construction:
    Charlotte: 3599
    Costs: 5087
HUNTING: 5672
HURRICANES:
  Beaufort (1879): 3960
  Cape Hatteras (1861): 3264
HYDROELECTRIC POWER PLANTS: 2299
IMPEACHMENTS:
  Governors (William Woods Holden): 2589
INDEPENDENT ORDER OF GOOD TEMPLARS:
  Health Seat Lodge, No. 40: 2087
  Hillsborough: 4080
  New Hope Lodge, No. 296: 2088
INDEPENDENT ORDER OF ODD FELLOWS:
  Farmington Lodge No. 46: 2857
INDIANS OF NORTH AMERICA: 935
  see also NORTH CAROLINA--CHEROKEE INDIANS
  Relations with whites: 1736
  Treaties: 4746
INDUSTRIAL MANAGEMENT: 274
INDUSTRIALIZATION: 2231
INHERITANCE LAWS: 1525
INSURANCE: 1556, 3476, 5367
  Business: 5962
  Fire: 3416, 5709
  Laws and legislation: 2553, 3410
  Life: 3416, 3825, 4060, 5298, 5541
  Property: 3308
  Warren County: 3307
INSURANCE AGENTS--Durham: 4968
INSURANCE COMPANIES: 5962
  Durham: 4968
  Franklinton: 5012
  Greensboro: 4918
  Lawsuits: 3825
INTERNAL IMPROVEMENTS: 3415, 4924, 4964
INTRACOASTAL WATERWAY: 2774
  Construction: 4858
IRON INDUSTRY:
  Catawba Springs: 529
  Wilmington: 3447
IRON MINING: 2121
JEWELERS--Hillsborough: 3300
JOURNALISM:
  see also NORTH CAROLINA--NEWSPAPERS
  History: 2589
JUDGES:
  see also NORTH CAROLINA--COURTS
  Elections: 4080
  Superior Court: 3955

NORTH CAROLINA
JUDGES (Continued):
  Wages: see NORTH CAROLINA--WAGES AND SALARIES--Judges
JUDICIAL AFFAIRS: 274
JURIES: 4544
  Grand juries: 4103
  Negro jurors: 3563
JUSTICES OF THE PEACE: 671, 1417, 1688, 3176, 3221
  Brassfield Township: 2833
  Burke County: 245
  Catawba County: 5745
  Davidson County: 3241, 3926
  Hyde County: 4547
  Little River: 5692
  Mount Gilead Township: 4689
  Wake County: 2824
  Wilkes County: 2483
JUVENILE DELINQUENCY: 1275
KINDERGARTENS--Chapel Hill: 4080
KNOW-NOTHING PARTY: 4714
KU KLUX KLAN: 1196, 2469, 2589, 3062, 4714
LABOR: 3070, 5149
LABOR AND MINORITIES: 5442
LABOR ARBITRATION: 1195
LABOR CONDITIONS: 2448
  Textile industry: 1275, 5234
  War industries: 2553
LABOR CONTRACTS:
  see also NORTH CAROLINA--FREEDMEN--Labor contracts; NORTH CAROLINA--TEACHERS' CONTRACTS
  Burlington: 5234
  Greensboro: 5234
  Mecklenburg County: 5235
LABOR DISPUTES:
  see also NORTH CAROLINA--STRIKES
  Textile workers:
    Burlington: 5234
    Erwin: 5298
    Greensboro: 5234
    Mecklenburg County: 5235
  Subdivided by place:
    Gastonia: 3706
    Marion: 3706
LABOR IN POLITICS: 1192, 2568
LABOR LAWS AND LEGISLATION: 1195, 1202
  Employment of women and children: 1275
LABOR PUBLICATIONS: 1195, 1202
LABOR SHORTAGES: see WORLD WAR I--Labor shortages
LABOR UNIONS: 1199, 3706
  see also AMERICAN FEDERATION OF LABOR; CONGRESS OF INDUSTRIAL ORGANIZATIONS; NORTH CAROLINA--ANTI-UNIONISM; NORTH CAROLINA--PUBLIC RELATIONS--Labor unions
  Contracts: 2772
  Elections:
    Burlington: 5234
    Greensboro: 3171
  Finance: 1192, 1199
  Initiation fees: 1195
  Lawsuits: 2772
  Subdivided by type of union:
    Industrial workers: 1192
    Telephone workers: 1199
    Textile workers: 613, 1195
      Enka: 5442
      Greensboro: 3171
    Tobacco workers:
      Durham: 1150
    University employees: 613
LAND:
  see also NORTH CAROLINA--REAL ESTATE; NORTH CAROLINA--TURPENTINE LANDS
  1700s: 3347
  1700s-1800s: 1764, 3176
  1800s: 391, 2298, 2970, 3003, 3231, 4862
  1800s-1900s: 675
  Mortgages--Carthage: 5138

NORTH CAROLINA
  LAND (Continued):
    Prices: 2300, 2663, 4689
      Guilford County: 2314
      Halifax County: 5672
    Purchases and sales:
      1700s-1800s: 3364
      1700s-1900s: 2929, 3476
      1800s: 484, 1475, 2419, 3351, 4336, 5599
      1800s-1900s: 4689, 4897, 5709
      Clarkton: 5909
      Davie County: 122
      Forsyth County: 5935
      Halifax County: 426
      Onslow County: 5761
    Rental: 4761, 4849
    Subdivided by place:
      Craven County: 730
      Granville County: 1224
      Indian Territory: 675
      Nash County: 5475
      Orange County: 5390
      Pantego: 3012
      Pitt County: 975
      Wake County: 730
  LAND CLAIMS: 2730, 5768
    Craven County: 4977
  LAND COMPANIES: 4858
    Holly Springs: 63
  LAND DEEDS AND INDENTURES:
    1700s: 484
    1700s-1800s: 360, 540, 730, 1538, 2698, 3364, 4082, 4191, 5188
    1700s-1900s: 832, 872, 1107, 1438, 3176, 3233, 3476, 4100, 4849, 4858, 5298
    1800s: 817, 1556, 1656, 2294, 2660, 2776, 2824, 3763, 4689, 5002, 5596, 5599, 5771
    1800s-1900s: 1120, 3091, 3416, 4897, 5739
    Alexander County: 912
    Anson County: 2493
    Beaufort County: 692
    Burke County: 61, 1247
    Caldwell County: 1247
    Clarkton: 5909
    Craven County: 804, 982
    Cumberland County: 4517
    Davie County: 122
    Dobbs County: 1523
    Duplin County: 5707
    Fayetteville: 2354
    Gamewell: 3324
    Glasgow County: 1523
    Granville County: 1224, 2339, 2716
    Halifax County: 3256, 5707
    Hillsborough: 1890
    Lincoln County: 61
    Onslow County: 1252, 5761
    Orange County: 912, 3752, 5109, 5341
    Oxford: 2455
    Randolph County: 88, 5018
    Richmond County: 5021
    Ridgeway: 3307
    Sampson County: 1752
    Surry County: 2419
    Transylvania County: 5768
    Tyrrell County: 215
    Wake County: 5341
    Washington County: 5013
    Wayne County: 4421
    Williamston: 4824
    Yadkin County: 2419
  LAND DEVELOPMENT: 1521
    Wilmington: 3447
  LAND DRAINAGE:
    Craven County: 3955
    New Hanover County: 4603
  LAND GRANTS:
    1700s: 1361, 1389, 3940
    1700s-1800s: 3364, 3386, 5188
    1700s-1900s: 832, 5740
    1800s: 1577, 4689
    Bladen County: 517

NORTH CAROLINA
  LAND GRANTS (Continued):
    Craven County: 804
    Durham County: 3514
    Eno River: 912
    Hyde County: 4827
    Martin County: 4849
    Wake County: 3514
  LAND RECLAMATION--Wilmington: 3447
  LAND SETTLEMENT: 5018, 5768
  LAND SPECULATION: 4298
  LAND TITLE LEGISLATION: 5768
  LAND TITLES: 2776, 4232
    Transylvania County: 5768
  LAND WARRANTS: 2256
    Purchases and sales: 1363, 4080
  LANDLORD AND TENANT: 484, 797, 817, 2833
    see also NORTH CAROLINA--FARM TENANCY
    Lawsuits: 1951
    Person County: 1336
    Stem: 4464
    Surry County: 2808
    Yadkin County: 2808
  LAW, Study of: 1109, 5124
    see also UNIVERSITY OF NORTH CAROLINA--Law School
  LAW BOOKS: 3410
  LAW PRACTICE:
    1700s: 5768
    1700s-1800s: 4773
    1800s: 264, 277, 591, 631, 1107, 2657, 2808, 3176
    1800s-1900s: 3410, 3955
    1900s: 2655, 4775
    Licenses: 4897
    Beaufort County: 692
    Durham: 969
    Edenton: 2467
    Elizabeth City: 5776
    Goldsboro: 1748
    Greensboro: 4714
    Hamptonville: 2452
    Mocksville: 1100
    Oxford: 2455
    Pitt County: 5950
    Raleigh: 274, 2553, 2938
    Shelby: 1951
    Washington: 4858
  LAW TREATISES: 3410
  LAWSUITS:
    see also Lawsuits as subheading under types of business, organizations, and subjects, e.g. NORTH CAROLINA--LABOR UNIONS--Lawsuits
    1700s: 975
    1700s-1800s: 5046
    1800s: 641, 1475, 2345, 2480, 2589, 5100, 5202, 5709
    1900s: 2655, 4828
    Bladen County: 5909
    Franklinton: 5056, 5450
    Wake Forest: 4586
  LAWYERS' ACCOUNTS:
    Elizabeth City: 5776
    Oxford: 2455
    Smithfield: 3839
    Wilmington: 3410
  LECTURES AND LECTURING: 942, 3482
    Durham: 4753
    Raleigh: 5149
  LEGAL AFFAIRS:
    1700s: 1389, 2256
    1700s-1900s: 2553, 2934
    1800s: 263, 624, 982, 3960, 4923, 5596
    1800s-1900s: 2419, 5692
    1900s: 4828
    Asheboro: 2303, 3186
    Burke County: 1247
    Caldwell County: 1247
    Craven County: 1871
    Durham County: 1256
    Enfield: 426
    Fairfield: 921

NORTH CAROLINA
  LEGAL AFFAIRS (Continued):
    Fayetteville: 2354
    Gamewell: 3324
    Granville County: 68
    Greensboro: 3763
    Guilford County: 2330
    Harnett County: 2357
    Montgomery County: 4689
    Orange County: 1256
    Oxford: 2455
    Rowan County: 3288
    Thomasville: 2906
    Wilmington: 5912
  LEGAL PROCEDURES:
    Martin County: 1639
  LEGISLATURE:
    1700s: 935
    1700s-1800s: 540, 2218, 4746
    1800s: 3929
    1830s: 1015, 3415, 4424
    1850s: 279, 1250, 4714
    1860s: 279
    1870s: 5455
    1880s: 5455
    1900s: 1195
    1950s: 1199
    Apportionment (1951): 2476
    House:
      1770s: 5768
      1850s: 264
      1860s: 5460
      1910s: 3955
      1930s: 325
    Nominations for office (1853): 2399
    Senate:
      1800s: 4080
      1900s: 2553, 2655, 2863
  LIBEL TRIALS: 4773
  LIBRARIES: 2188
  LIGHT-SHIPS:
    Hatteras: 4547
    Neuse River: 1871
  LINSEED OIL MILLS--Randleman: 5408
  LIQUOR:
    Medicinal use: 3410
  LIQUOR MANUFACTURING: 122, 1278, 1861, 2072, 2929
    Illegal:
      7th North Carolina District: 4548
      Statesville: 1966
      Lincoln County: 5558
      Surry County: 2808
      Yadkin County: 2808
  LITERARY INTERESTS: 3433, 4080
  LITERARY SOCIETIES: 1128, 2251
    Durham: 880
      Trinity College: 4932
    Henderson: 4232
    Raleigh: 4923
  LIVERY STABLES--Wadesboro: 4814
  LIVESTOCK:
    Diseases: 122
    Haywood County: 3176
  LOANS:
    see also NORTH CAROLINA--PERSONAL LOANS
    Lincoln County: 4450
    North Carolina Literary Fund: 3943
    Smithfield: 3839
  LOCAL ELECTIONS: 4103
    Mount Gilead: 4689
    Randolph County: 2459
    Shelby: 1951
  LOCAL POLITICS:
    Beaufort County: 4232, 5521
    Burke County: 245
    Davie County: 122
    Durham: 2379
    Granville County: 2189
    Little's Mills: 5021
    New Hanover County: 3410
    Pitt County: 5950
    Raleigh: 2819
    Sunbury: 1724

859

NORTH CAROLINA

LOCAL POLITICS (Continued):
  Wilmington: 3447
LOCOFOCO PARTY: 4897, 5298
LOGBOOKS: 4342
LOTTERIES: 5036
  School benefit: 214
LOVE LETTERS: 264, 391, 1925, 2553, 2905, 3219, 5533
  see also NORTH CAROLINA--COURTSHIP
  Chatham County: 2861
  Winston: 2800
LOVE POETRY: 3677, 4164
LUMBER: 238, 2824
LUMBER MILLS:
  Ellerbe and Star: 3225
LUMBER PRODUCTS: 358
LUMBERING: 325, 1475, 4849, 4858, 4918
LUTHERAN CHURCHES: 1232
  see also NORTH CAROLINA--SERMONS--Lutheran
LYCEUMS:
  Durham: 5597
  Wilmington: 5802
LYNCHING--Norlina: 4103
MANUFACTURED PRODUCTS:
  Prices: 165, 1252
MANUSCRIPT COLLECTING: 4156, 5252
MARBLE: 3410
MARL: 641
MARRIAGE: 1389, 5298
  see also NORTH CAROLINA--SLAVES--Married life; NORTH CAROLINA--WEDDINGS
MARRIAGE LICENSES: 1107
MARRIAGE SETTLEMENTS: 2926
MASONRY: 1284, 1899, 2330, 3410, 3476, 4834
  Ansonville: 4918
  Durham: 1150, 3781
  Fayetteville: 1898
  Mocksville Lodge No. 134: 2857
  Raleigh: 279
  Wilmington Lodge No. 319: 1899
MEDICAL EDUCATION: see DUKE UNIVERSITY--Medical Center; WAKE FOREST COLLEGE--School of Medicine; UNIVERSITY OF NORTH CAROLINA AT CHAPEL HILL--Medical School
MEDICAL NOTEBOOKS: 2481, 3410
MEDICAL PRACTICE: 2462, 2537, 2714, 4231, 5771, 5924
  see also NORTH CAROLINA--PHYSICIANS; NORTH CAROLINA--PHYSICIANS' ACCOUNTS
  Chatham County: 5541
  Durham: 2934
  Forsyth County: 5982
  Hillsborough: 4890
  Louisburg: 3476
  Nash County: 4820
  Wentworth: 4366
MEDICAL SERVICES: 1195
  see also NORTH CAROLINA--HOSPITALS
  Germanton: 4136
MEDICAL SOCIETIES: 2851, 2934, 4231
  Asheville: 5603
MEDICAL SUPPLIES: 3476
MEDICAL TREATMENT:
  see also the following subheadings under NORTH CAROLINA: HOME REMEDIES; HOSPITALS; LIQUOR--Medicinal use; OPTICAL SURGERY; PHYSICIANS; SLAVES--Medical treatment
  Costs: 4858
  Person County: 3752
MEDICINE: 4030
  see also NORTH CAROLINA--PATENT MEDICINE
  Manufacture in Charlotte: 4918
  Prescriptions: 509, 675, 3410
MEMORIALS:
  Duke University: 5252

NORTH CAROLINA

MENTAL HOSPITALS: 661, 2220
  For Negroes--Wilmington: 2890
  Morganton: 2890
  Raleigh: 5819
MERCANTILE ACCOUNTS:
  1700s-1800s: 4080
  1800s: 399, 435, 1800, 2068, 2555, 2857, 3176, 4047, 4152, 4374, 4918, 5100, 5298
  1840s: 4150
  1850s: 1919, 4223, 4764
  1860s: 482, 2808, 4764
  1870s: 482, 1394, 2808
  1880s: 2895
  1800s-1900s: 4664
  Abernethy: 147
  Albemarle: 3530
  Alexander County: 3683
  Apex: 5803
  Bath: 3521
  Beattie's Ford: 2277
  Cabarrus County: 4670
  Calahaln: 122
  Caledonia: 3449
  Cane Creek: 2618
  Chapel Hill: 4666
  Chatham County: 5905
  Cherokee County: 5258
  Craven County: 3955
  Davidson County: 138, 3241
  Durham: 4480, 4540
  Edenton: 717, 5658
  Fairfield: 511
  Fayetteville: 4517
  Flat River: 3481
  Franklin County: 2824, 2825
  Gold Hill: 3368
  Granville County: 3638, 5960
  Greenville: 1846, 3739
  Hatteras: 4547
  Haywood County: 5258
  Henderson: 95
  Hillsborough: 5728
  Hollywood: 3960
  Iredell County: 1858, 3600, 3787
  Jackson County: 5258
  Liberty: 1777
  Lincoln County: 5976
  Lockville: 5207
  Lowell: 3285
  Manson: 5697
  Middleton: 5592
  Milton: 5815
  Mocksville: 2749
  Montgomery County: 75
  Mount Olive: 5756
  Murfreesboro: 5857
  New Bern: 164, 2167
  Newton: 138
  Norwood: 5589
  Opossum Trot: 80
  Orange County: 1151, 3677
  Oxford: 5685
  Perquimans County: 165, 3874
  Plymouth: 4639
  Quallatown: 4784
  Raleigh: 2589, 2821
  Richmond County: 3167
  Ridgeway: 999, 3307, 5614
  Robeson County: 3398
  Roxboro: 5927
  Scotland Neck: 4925
  Smith Church: 5399
  Smithfield: 5374
  South Lowell: 3140
  Stokes County: 27
  Stowesville: 5100
  Tarboro: 4035
  Wadesboro: 2984, 4762
  Wake County: 1783, 3655, 5136
  Warren County: 910, 4328, 4389
  Washington: 911, 3827, 4382, 4571, 4832
  Weldon: 1055
  Wilkesboro: 4107

NORTH CAROLINA

MERCANTILE ACCOUNTS (Continued):
  Williamston: 914
  Wilmington: 3447, 5912
  Wing: 4182
  Woodlawn Mills: 5888
  Worthville: 3187
  Yadkin County: 2429, 2914
MERCANTILE AFFAIRS: 1871, 3984
  Mount Tirzah: 3752
  Oxford: 2192
  Randleman: 5408
  Washington: 652
MERCHANDISE:
  Marketing: 5910
  Beaufort County: 5521
  Hertford: 3907
MERCHANT SEAMEN:
  Aid societies: 4727
MERCHANTS:
  see also NORTH CAROLINA--COMMISSION MERCHANTS
  1700s: 1487, 2585, 4918
  1700s-1800s: 540
  1800s: 484, 486, 556, 792, 1015, 1336, 1686, 1856, 1861, 1915, 2222, 2857, 3307, 4764, 5298
  1800s: 5535
  1810s: 5535
  1840s: 4150
  1850s: 698, 1688
  1860s: 264, 839, 1688, 2359
  1880s: 1233
  1890s: 1233
  1800s-1900s: 1660, 4298
  Anderson: 534
  Bath: 3521
  Bay River: 1871
  Bertie County: 2332
  Caledonia: 3449
  Cane Creek: 2618
  Carteret County: 2491
  Davidson County: 3241
  Edenton: 2658
  Fayetteville: 2431
  Fort Barnwell: 640
  Guilford County: 2330
  Haw River: 5154
  Hillsborough: 4890
  Horse Shoe: 4910
  Montgomery County: 75
  Newton: 9
  Opossum Trot: 80
  Orange County: 1151
  Raleigh: 2819
  Richmond County: 3167
  Ridgeway: 999
  Statesville: 8
  Surry County: 2808
  Trenton: 1871
  Wadesboro: 222
  Wake County: 876, 3655
  Warren County: 4328
  Warrenton: 4389
  Washington: 911, 4382, 4571
  Williamston: 914, 2419, 4849
  Wilmington: 1908, 2511, 2586, 5372
  Yadkin County: 2808
METHODIST CHURCHES: 1316, 1538, 1738, 2589, 5964, 5965
  Board of Missions: 3646
  Board of Trustees: 3646
  Camp meetings: see NORTH CAROLINA--CAMP MEETINGS--Methodist
  Church buildings--Greensboro: 5149
  Church history: 2221, 3646
  Circuits: 3195, 3646, 5280
    see also names of specific circuits
  Clergy: see NORTH CAROLINA--CLERGY--Methodist
  Conferences: 956
  Converts: 5964
  Districts: 3646
    see also names of specific districts

NORTH CAROLINA

METHODIST CHURCHES (Continued):
  Finance: 2895, 3195, 3646
  Higher education: 3020
  Membership: 3195
  Negroes: 1738
  Relations between Northern and Southern churches: 3581
  Religious literature: see NORTH CAROLINA--RELIGIOUS LITERATURE--Methodist
  Revivals: 2929
  Schools: see NORTH CAROLINA--SCHOOLS--Church schools--Methodist
  Sermons: see NORTH CAROLINA--SERMONS--Methodist
  Sunday schools: see NORTH CAROLINA--SUNDAY SCHOOLS--Methodist
  Trials: 4506
  Western North Carolina Conference: 3020, 3646
  Subdivided by place:
    Wilmington: 5912
    Yanceyville: 4506
METHODIST EPISCOPAL CHURCH: 3581
  Camp meetings: see NORTH CAROLINA--CAMP MEETINGS--Methodist Episcopal
  Circuits: 3646, 3992
  Clergy: see NORTH CAROLINA--CLERGY--Methodist Episcopal
  Conferences: 3581
  Schools: see NORTH CAROLINA--SCHOOLS--Church schools--Methodist Episcopal
  Sermons: see NORTH CAROLINA--SERMONS--Methodist Episcopal
METHODIST EPISCOPAL CHURCH, SOUTH: 1152, 1588, 4111
  Board of Education: 3646
  Board of Missions: 3646
  Circuits: 1096, 3195, 3476, 3646, 5023
  Clergy: see NORTH CAROLINA--CLERGY--Methodist Episcopal Church, South
  Conferences: 3646
  Districts: 3646
  Finance: 3195, 3646, 5023
  North Carolina Conference: 3646, 4136, 4425, 4498
  North Carolina Conference Historical Society: 3646
  Political activity: 3176
  Sermons: see NORTH CAROLINA--SERMONS--Methodist Episcopal Church, South
  Sunday School Board: 3646
  Western North Carolina Conference: 3646
  Subdivided by place:
    Catawba County: 5745
    Durham: 133, 1642
    Wilmington: 772
METHODIST PROTESTANT CHURCH: 3186
  North Carolina District: 3646
MICA DEPOSITS: 513
MICA MINES--Spruce Pine: 4918
MIGRATION FROM: 702
  To Arkansas: 2855
  To Kentucky: 4765
  To Illinois: 4765
  To Indiana: 4765
  To Mississippi: 3415, 5475
  To Tennessee: 4765
  To Texas: 2855, 4765
MIGRATION TO:
  From Ireland: 3230
  From Netherlands: 5149
  From Pennsylvania: 5264
  From Scotland: 5298
MILITARY BASES: 325
MILITARY SCHOOLS: 895, 3176, 4067
MILITIA: 671, 3176, 4489, 5298, 5778

NORTH CAROLINA

MILITIA (Continued):
  American Revolution: 935, 1387, 5768
    Recruiting and enlistment: 5768
  By-laws: 2970
  Carthagena Expedition: 1068
  Civil War: 75, 5135
    Greenville Militia: 3013
    121st Regiment: 3000
  Desertion: 3622
  Discharges: 5792
  Officers: 4897
  Regiments:
    8th Regiment: 3276
    Hillsborough Regiment: 440
  Rosters: 245
MILLERS' ACCOUNTS: 4918
  see also NORTH CAROLINA--FLOUR MILLS; NORTH CAROLINA--GRIST MILLS
  Milton: 5843
MINERAL RIGHTS: 3003
MINERALOGY: 3063
MINES AND MINING: 1478, 2521
  see also specific types of mining under NORTH CAROLINA, e.g. NORTH CAROLINA--SULPHUR MINING
MISSIONARY SOCIETIES: 1738
  Presbyterian: 2269
MISSIONS AND MISSIONARIES: 2111
MONUMENTS: 3955
MORAVIAN CHURCH: 1469, 4423
MORPHINE ADDICTION: 4506
MORTGAGES: 832, 4897, 5188
  see also NORTH CAROLINA--LAND--Mortgages
MOUNTAINS: 761
MOVING PICTURES: see NORTH CAROLINA--CENSORSHIP--Moving pictures
MULES--Franklin County: 5087
MUNICIPAL GOVERNMENT:
  see also NORTH CAROLINA--COUNTY GOVERNMENT
  Durham: 4736
  Greensboro: 5149
  Lumber Bridge: 3934
  Morganton: 3937
MUNICIPAL RECREATION:
  Durham: 2379
  Fayetteville: 5298
MURDER: 641
  see also NORTH CAROLINA--SLAVES--Crime--Murder
MUSEUMS--Raleigh: 4736
MUSIC: see NORTH CAROLINA--SONGS AND MUSIC
NATIONAL GUARD: 3219
NAVAL STORES INDUSTRY: 753, 4298
NAVIGATION:
  Cape Fear River: 3922
NEGRO EDITORS: 2720
NEGRO EDUCATORS: 2720
NEGROES: 2048
  see also the following subheadings under NORTH CAROLINA: FREEDMEN; SLAVES; (specific subject or occupation), e.g. NORTH CAROLINA--METHODIST CHURCHES--Negroes
  Colonization in Liberia: 4516
  Economic conditions: 2720
  Education: 2469, 2720, 4828, 5041
    see also NORTH CAROLINA--SCHOOLS--Negro schools
  Personal finance: 2720
  Religion: 702
    Participation in white churches: 3195, 3581
  Social status: 2720
  Suffrage: 2469
    Disenfranchisement: 2298
  Taxation--Anson County: 191
  Voting: 4858
  Subdivided by place:
    Hyde County: 511
NEGROES IN POLITICS: 2720

NORTH CAROLINA

NEWSPAPERS: 4080, 4918
  see also NORTH CAROLINA--JOURNALISM
  Editing and publishing: 3538
  Editorial policy--Durham: 3088
  Subdivided by place:
    Berea: 5741
    Lumberton: 3434
    Statesville: 3787
NORTHERNERS IN THE SOUTH: 5041
NURSERIES (horticulture): 5632
OILSEED MILLS:
  see also NORTH CAROLINA--COTTONSEED OIL; NORTH CAROLINA--LINSEED OIL MILLS
  Finance: 3206, 4858
  Management: 3206
  Stocks: 3206
  Washington: 3827
OPERA--Winston-Salem: 4080
OPTICAL SURGERY: 661
ORCHARDS--Franklin County: 5087
ORIGINAL FREE WILL BAPTIST CHURCH: 3987
  Pitt County: 3988
ORPHANAGES: 2041
  Charlotte: 4918, 5298
  Fayetteville: 3873
  Thomasville: 2874
OVERSEERS: 1602, 3176
  see also NORTH CAROLINA--ROADS--Overseers
  Belford: 5924
PACKAGING MACHINERY--Durham: 5923
PALACES--New Bern: 5352
PANIC OF 1819: 4080
PARKING METERS--Durham: 2379
PATENT MEDICINES: 401, 4154
  see also NORTH CAROLINA--ADVERTISING--Patent medicines
PATRONS OF HUSBANDRY: 1323, 4072
  Lilesville: 2493
PATTERNS (clothing): 1407
PEACE SOCIETIES: 1336
  Orange County: 3984
PENMANSHIP:
  Exercise books: 2570, 2915
  Study and teaching: 3680
PEOPLE'S PARTY OF THE UNITED STATES: 4586, 4858
PERIODICALS: 2282
  see also NORTH CAROLINA--PUBLISHERS AND PUBLISHING--Periodicals
  Subscribers: 4407
PERSONAL DEBT: 3241
PERSONAL FINANCE:
  1700s-1900s: 3176
  1800s: 486, 2570, 2660, 3003
  1800s-1900s: 2934, 3424
  1900s: 1951, 3548
  Advance: 4111
  Asheboro: 2303
  Chatham County: 5905
  Craven County: 1871
  Deep River: 5632
  Durham: 513
  Gamewell: 3324
  Guilford County: 5905
  Moore County: 5792
  Mount Gilead: 4689
  Oak Grove Township: 3896
  Person County: 3752
  Raleigh: 274, 4544
  Rowan County: 1269
  Stokes County: 2800
  Warrenton: 3761
  Wilmington: 3410
PERSONAL LOANS--Surry County: 3908
PHARMACIES: 4366
PHARMACISTS' ACCOUNTS: 4897
  Milton: 5515
  Wake Forest: 2590
PHARMACISTS' CERTIFICATION: 4897
PHILANTHROPY: 1584, 1588
  see also NORTH CAROLINA--CHARITIES

NORTH CAROLINA

PHILANTHROPY (Continued):
  Durham: 133
PHILOSOPHY: 817
PHOTOGRAPHS: 691, 2028
PHYSICIANS: 1915
  Kinston: 986
  Licenses: 4897
  Nags Head: 4262
PHYSICIANS' ACCOUNTS:
  1800s: 1107, 1414, 2135, 2851, 4897, 5771
  1800s-1900s: 675
  1900s: 832
  Anson County: 409
  Davidson County: 138
  Fayetteville: 4517
  Hamilton: 5600
  Hillsborough: 4890
  Lincoln County: 5976
  Louisburg: 3476
  Mocksville: 2749
  Osceola: 4197
  Perquimans County: 4897
  Raleigh: 5356
  Ramseur: 2624
  Union County: 579
  Washington: 5195
  Williamston: 5943
PLANK ROADS:
  Asheboro: 5912
  Construction: 5298
PLANTATION ACCOUNTS: 435, 4374
  Granville County: 2528, 3916, 5285
  Iredell County: 1382
  Martin County: 4849
  New Bern: 5709
  Orange County: 4666
  Perquimans County: 290
  Person County: 1336
  Stokes County: 27
  Surry County: 2808
  Yadkin County: 2808
PLANTATION MANAGEMENT: 1602
  see also NORTH CAROLINA--OVERSEERS
  Wilmington: 4603
PLANTATIONS: 540, 730, 1061, 1475, 1556, 2808
  see also the following subheadings
    under NORTH CAROLINA:
    AGRICULTURE, and subheadings
    beginning with AGRICULTURAL;
    COTTON PLANTATIONS; CROPS, and
    names of specific crops; FARMING,
    and subheadings beginning with
    the word FARM
  Business affairs: 2824
    Person County: 1336
  Finance: 4082
  Subdivided by place:
    Franklin County: 1322, 4147
    Franklinton: 4148
    Iredell County: 1382
    Lenoir County: 903
    Martin County: 5036
    "Point Peter": 3607
PLOW HANDLES: 358
POETRY: 263, 3482, 5298
  see also the following subheadings
    under NORTH CAROLINA: AMERICAN
    POETRY; LOVE POETRY; RELIGIOUS
    POETRY
  Collections: 617, 3607, 3896, 5506
POLITICAL CLUBS:
  Morehead City: 3960
  Wilmington: 3380
POLITICAL PATRONAGE:
  1700s: 4977
  1800s: 631, 1061, 2776, 5322
  1800s-1900s: 4858
  1900s: 325
POLITICAL UNREST: 3384
POLITICS AND GOVERNMENT:
  see also the following subheadings
    under NORTH CAROLINA: COUNTY
    GOVERNMENT; ELECTIONS; LABOR IN
    POLITICS; LOCAL POLITICS; MUNICI-
    PAL GOVERNMENT; NEGROES IN POLITICS

NORTH CAROLINA

POLITICS AND GOVERNMENT (Continued):
  1700s:
    Colonial period: 4391
    1770s: 5768
    1790s: 3384, 5046
  1700s-1800s: 540, 631, 2776, 3364
  1700s-1900s: 2929, 4232
  1800s: 602, 624, 730, 835, 838, 1061, 1659, 1677, 1871, 3351, 3415, 4686, 4714, 4816, 5207, 5664
    1800s: 2491
    1820s: 2776
    1830s: 2776
    1840s: 1580, 3764
    1850s: 264, 1100, 1250, 1580, 5460
    1860s: 183, 614, 1100, 2357, 2469, 2730, 2808, 2970, 3176, 3393, 3422, 4248, 5250, 5298
    1870s: 122, 183, 593, 685, 1100, 2330, 2469, 2548, 2730, 2808, 2970, 5298
    1880s: 122, 183, 593, 2330, 2548, 2730
    1890s: 22, 122, 2330, 3972
  1800s-1900s: 274, 1284, 1336, 2435, 3410, 3763, 4103, 4310, 4874, 4897, 5735
  1900s: 1006, 1951, 2188, 2863, 3538, 4858, 5740
    1920s: 2299, 4825
    1930s: 325, 2553
    1940s: 325
    1950s: 325, 4805
  Appointments:
    1800s: 2121
    1900s: 2581
POPULIST PARTY: see NORTH CAROLINA--
  PEOPLE'S PARTY OF THE UNITED STATES
PORTRAITS: 4506
PORTS: see NORTH CAROLINA--HARBORS
POSTAL SERVICE: 754, 3845
  Local offices:
    Beattie's Ford: 792
    Calahaln: 122
    Cane Creek: 2618
    Farmington: 2857
    Henderson: 4407
    Hollywood: 3960
    Killian's Post Office: 4450
    Midway: 3250
    Murphy: 3025
    New Bern: 3865
    Orange County: 3984
    Raleigh: 2589
  Mail service: 3415
POVERTY: 1409, 3003
PRESBYTERIAN CHURCHES: 1556, 3432, 5962
  see also NORTH CAROLINA--ASSOCIATE
    REFORMED PRESBYTERIAN CHURCH
  Clergy: see NORTH CAROLINA--
    CLERGY--Presbyterian
  Doctrine: 1152
  Missionary societies: see NORTH
    CAROLINA--MISSIONARY SOCIETIES--
    Presbyterian
  Sermons: see NORTH CAROLINA--
    SERMONS--Presbyterian
  Women's work: 2269
  Subdivided by place:
    Concord: 5245
    Durham: 3762
    Fayetteville: 1438
    Shiloh: 5245
    Townsville: 1361
PRESIDENTIAL ELECTIONS:
  1812: 3176
  1928: 274
PRESIDENTIAL PARDONS: 470, 685, 2339, 4788, 5188
PRIMITIVE BAPTIST CHURCH:
  Clergy: see NORTH CAROLINA--
    CLERGY--Primitive Baptist
  Elders: 4500

NORTH CAROLINA

PRIMITIVE BAPTIST CHURCH (Continued):
  Finance--Tarboro: 5185
  Obituaries:
    Beaufort County: 3945
    Martin County: 4931
  Subdivided by place:
    Greenville: 318
    Tarboro: 5185
PRINTING: 2589
PRISONERS AND PRISONS: 641, 2821
  see also CIVIL WAR--PRISONERS AND
    PRISONS--Confederate/Union
    prisoners--North Carolina
  Raleigh: 3415
  Statesville: 1966
PROHIBITION: 2861, 2895, 3410, 4192, 4828
  see also NORTH CAROLINA--
    TEMPERANCE
  Sampson County: 2863
PROMISSORY NOTES: 4858, 4897, 5475
  Fayetteville: 2354
  Halifax County: 5674
  Milton: 5815
  Oxford: 2455
  Ridgeway: 999
PROPERTY EVALUATION:
  Randolph County: 2459
PROPERTY LISTS:
  Durham County: 1256
  Mocksville: 2749
PHOPHECIES: 530
PROTESTANT EPISCOPAL CHURCH: 4358, 5298
  Clergy: see NORTH CAROLINA--
    CLERGY--Protestant Episcopal
  Diocese of North Carolina: 4232
  Finance: 3176
  Raleigh: 4394
PROVERBS: 691
PUBLIC CELEBRATIONS:
  Townsville: 1361
PUBLIC DEBT--Repudiation: 2469
PUBLIC FINANCE:
  1700s: 2276, 2776
  1800s: 3943
PUBLIC HEALTH:
  Fayetteville: 4517
  New Hanover County: 3859
PUBLIC RELATIONS:
  Labor unions: 1201
PUBLIC SCHOOL BUILDINGS:
  Davie County: 4111
  Granville County: 2833
PUBLIC SCHOOLS: 3276, 5298, 5737
  see also NORTH CAROLINA--SCHOOLS
  Attendance:
    Catawba County: 4532
    Granville County: 2833
    Rockingham County: 4533
  Bands--Lenoir: 3178
  Commencement exercises:
    Advance: 4111
  Finance: 4897
    Granville County: 2833
  Registers: 4897
  Subdivided by place:
    Buncombe County: 5603
    Catawba County: 4532
    Fayetteville: 5298
    Granville County: 2833
    Lenoir: 3177
    Lincoln County: 3933
    New Hanover County: 3607
    Randolph County: 5018
    Rockingham County: 4533
    Wilkes County: 3942
PUBLIC SPEAKING: 2469
PUBLIC WELFARE:
  Cumberland County: 5298
PUBLISHERS AND PUBLISHING: 5252
  see also NORTH CAROLINA--
    NEWSPAPERS; NORTH CAROLINA--
    RELIGIOUS LITERATURE
  Folklore material: 691

NORTH CAROLINA

PUBLISHERS AND PUBLISHING (Continued):
  Periodicals:
    Charlotte: 2529
    Greensboro: 5457
    Oxford: 2192
PULP AND PAPER INDUSTRY: 3317, 3955, 4080
  Cumberland County: 3812
  Dyes and dyeing: 3812
  Ink: 3812
QUIT RENT: 3347
RACE RELATIONS: 274, 613, 2720, 4736, 4968
  see also the following subheadings under NORTH CAROLINA: BLACK CODES; DESEGREGATION; KU KLUX KLAN; RELIGION--Race relations; RACE RIOTS
  Durham: 2379, 2773
  Raleigh: 2773
  Wilmington: 1313
  Winston-Salem: 2773, 3538
RACE RIOTS:
  Norlina: 4103
  Wilmington: 1082, 1313, 2442, 3972
RADIO STATIONS--Licensing: 3538
RAILROAD FRAUDS: 4714
RAILROAD LAW: 2553
RAILROAD MOTOR CARS: 238
  Sanford: 4918
RAILROADS:
  1800s: 2978, 3317, 4080, 4370, 4492, 5664
    1830s: 3176
    1840s: 3176
    1850s: 3176, 4458
    1860s: 2730, 2970
    1870s: 730, 2730, 2970
    1880s: 2730, 5135
  1800s-1900s: 237, 274, 3447
  1900s: 238
    1900s: 4828
    1910s: 3955, 4918
  Bridges: 3470
  Charter: 5460
  Construction: 2189, 3221, 4370, 5258, 5298
  Crossings: 969
  Finance: 238, 1313, 4669, 5460, 5657
  Legal affairs: 1313
  Narrow gauge--Person County: 5455
  Passenger service--Durham: 4736
  Short-line: 1655
  Stocks: 237, 238, 641, 3416, 5188
  Taxation: 661
  United States military railroad: 605
RATIONING DURING WORLD WAR II: 4085
REAL ESTATE:
  see also NORTH CAROLINA--LAND; NORTH CAROLINA--PROPERTY LISTS
  Investments--Charlotte: 4918
  Laws and legislation: 4103
  Rent: 1382
  Subdivided by place:
    Chatham County: 1056
    Durham: 1584, 3762
    Hillsborough: 1890
REAL ESTATE APPRAISAL:
  Durham: 2379
REAL ESTATE BUSINESS:
  Finance: 1313
  Legal affairs: 1313
RECONSTRUCTION: 76, 754, 756, 838, 956, 1376, 1659, 1677, 2469, 2530, 2548, 2589, 2970, 3544, 3845, 3960, 4689, 4765, 4917, 4968, 5384, 5664
  Economic conditions: 2394, 5298
  Federal military occupation: 730, 2469, 4808
    Military courts: 2480
  Wilmington: 4052

NORTH CAROLINA

RELIGION:
  see also the following subheadings under NORTH CAROLINA: CHURCHES, and names of specific denominations; EVANGELISM; NEGROES--Religion
  1700s-1800s: 2663, 4787
  1700s-1900s: 4689
  1800s: 122, 530, 956, 1402, 3432, 4930
    1820s: 5376
    1830s: 967, 5376
    1840s: 967
    1850s: 436, 1362, 1773
    1870s: 817, 2330
    1880s: 817, 2330, 4329
    1890s: 2330, 4192, 4329
  1800s-1900s: 1284, 2830, 3563, 3783, 4849
  1900s:
    1930s: 2863, 5298
    1940s: 2863, 5298
  Race relations: 3581
  Subdivided by place:
    Flint Rock: 5890
    Forsyth County: 2855
    Lincoln County: 3211
    Sunbury: 1724
    Wilmington: 1313, 1908
    Woodland: 4047
RELIGIOUS LIFE: 647
  Forsyth County: 156
  Raleigh: 274
RELIGIOUS LITERATURE:
  Baptist: 274, 3538
  Methodist: 2221, 3020
  Raleigh: 3646
RELIGIOUS POETRY: 3351
RENT COLLECTION: 3043
  Stem: 4464
REPUBLICAN PARTY:
  1800s: 2357, 4714
    1860s: 5905
    1870s: 1015, 3415, 5905
    1880s: 5905
    1890s: 4858
  1800s-1900s: 1277
  1900s:
    1920s: 1128, 4689
    1930s: 4689
    1950s: 4251
    1960s: 4251
    1970s: 4251
  Conventions:
    Yadkin County: 2941
  Subdivided by place:
    Durham County: 1150
    Raleigh: 3440
RESORTS:
  see also NORTH CAROLINA--HEALTH RESORTS
  Linville: 3447
REVENUE STAMPS:
  Liquor: 4009
  Tobacco: 4009
RHYMES: 691
RIDDLES: 691
RIVERS--Transportation: 5298
ROAD TAX:
  Anson County: 191
ROADS: 274, 3415, 5962
  see also the following subheadings under NORTH CAROLINA: COUNTY ROADS; PLANK ROADS; TURNPIKES
  Construction: 3317, 5258
  Guilford County: 2287
  Improvement: see NORTH CAROLINA--GOOD ROADS MOVEMENT
  Maintenance and repair: 911
  Montgomery County: 4689
  Tabernacle Township: 4100
  Overseers: 5740
  Subdivided by place:
    Guilford County: 5905
    Vance County: 5962
ROCK COLLECTIONS: 4968

NORTH CAROLINA

ROSIN INDUSTRY: 2222
RURAL REHABILITATION:
  Wilmington: 3447
SADDLE-MAKING: 4053
SALES TAX: 3538
SALT WORKS--Wilmington: 1056, 5912
SANITATION: 3859
SAWMILLS: 1658, 2121, 5310, 4080
  Steam-powered: 3317
  Anson County: 4918
  Subdivided by place:
    Catawba County: 5705
    Randleman: 5408
    Randolph County: 1876
    Stokes County: 4080
SCHOLARSHIPS: 2819
SCHOOL BOARDS:
  Forsyth County: 813
  Granville County: 2833
SCHOOL CENSUS:
  Durham County: 1256
  Granville County: 2833
SCHOOL TAX--Anson County: 191
SCHOOLS:
  see also the following subheadings under NORTH CAROLINA: BUSINESS SCHOOLS; DIVINITY SCHOOLS; KINDERGARTENS; MILITARY SCHOOLS; PUBLIC SCHOOLS; STUDENTS AND STUDENT LIFE; TEACHERS, and subheadings beginning with the word TEACHER; TEACHING
  1800s: 817, 1701, 1871, 2714, 4148
    1830s: 3415
    1840s: 1686, 3415
    1850s: 484, 1882, 3117
    1860s: 671, 754, 1882
    1870s: 671, 1882
    1880s: 394, 661, 671, 2330
    1890s: 394, 2330
  1800s-1900s: 4391, 5549
  Boarding schools: 4318
  Guilford County: 4006, 5905
  Church schools: 1556
  Episcopal:
    Ansonville: 4918
    Raleigh: 4669
  Methodist: 1538
  Methodist Episcopal: 3581
  Commencement exercises:
    Wake County: 3941
  Curriculum: 3538
    Asheville: 566
  Desegregation: 3538
  Discipline: 3908
    Asheville: 566
  Finance: 3538
    Warrenton: 3761
  Free schools--Wilmington: 617
  Girls' schools and academies: 832, 2589, 3043
  Tuition: 1469, 2819
  Subdivided by place:
    All Healing Springs: 3416
    Charlotte: 1823, 4080
    Fayetteville: 5298
    Greensboro: 1100, 2357
    Lincolnton: 3210
    Louisburg: 3272
    Raleigh:
      Peace Institute: see PEACE COLLEGE
      Raleigh Female Classical Institute: 4154
      St. Mary's School: see ST. MARY'S COLLEGE
    Statesville: 5310
    Vernon: 2970
    Wilson: 2642
    Winston-Salem: see SALEM COLLEGE
  Laws and legislation: 3538
  Masonic schools: 1783
  Negro schools: 2753, 4080
    see also NORTH CAROLINA--TEACHING--Negro schools

NORTH CAROLINA
SCHOOLS:
  Negroes schools (Continued):
    Wake County: 3941
  Normal schools: 435, 3495
    Wilmington: 617, 3607
  Preparatory schools:
    Magnolia: 4910
  School lunch program: 3538
  Tuition:
    Granville County: 2833
    Louisburg: 3272
    Robeson County: 3803
  Subdivided by place:
    Anson County:
      Anson Institute: 4052
      District No. 23 for White
        Race: 192
    Asheville: 661, 4968
    Battleboro: 5701
    Bethania: 813
    Cary:
      Asbury Academy: 2846
      Cary School: 527
    Chatham County:
      District No. 62: 4689
      Mt. Vernon Academy: 2861
    Cora: 1247
    Dallas: 4080
    Donaldson: 4517
    Durham: 3762
      Dayton Academy: 3896
    Durham County: 1256, 4862
      High School: 2472
    Edenton: 2776
    Falls of Tar River: 4571
    Fayetteville: 4517, 5298
      Fayetteville Academy: 1898,
        5298
    Forestville: 4294
    Forsyth County: 813
    Granville County: 2833
      Belmont Academy: 2192
    Greensboro: 5804
    Haywood: 2357
    Hertford: 4897
    Hickory: 3043
    High Point: 3300
    Hillsborough: 5298
      Hillsborough Academy: 834
    Johnston County: 698
    Jonesville: 4765
    Kernersville: 817
    Leasburg: 1336
    Lincolnton: 4238
    Lockville: 4765
    Louisburg: 2530, 3272
    Maysville: 3607
    Mebane: 3300, 5298, 5912
    Monroe: 2573
    Montgomery County: 4689
    Mount Energy: 2833
    Mount Gilead: 4689
    New Bern: 263
    Oak Ridge: 1055
      Oak Ridge Institute: 3290
    Oakdale: 675
    Olin: 2857
    Orange County: 661, 666, 675,
      817, 3300, 4321, 5298, 5912
    Oxford: 5709
      Oxford Academy: 214
      Oxford Classical and Grammar
        School: 2192
    Randolph County: 4689
    Robeson County: 3803
    Rockingham: 1725
    Thyatira: 3334
    Wake County: 4294
    Warrenton: 3761, 4571
    Washington: 4858
    Wilkes County: 3942
    Wilson: 4462, 4910
    Winston-Salem: 4080
      Winston Male Academy: 817
    Youngsville: 5087

NORTH CAROLINA
SCIENCE: 817
SECESSION AND SECESSIONIST
  SENTIMENT: 761, 834, 1602, 2469,
  2530, 3237, 3422, 4248, 4765,
  5298, 5753
SEEDS: 4858
SELECTIVE SERVICE CLASSIFICATION:
  2581
SENATORIAL ELECTIONS:
  1902: 2188
  1906: 3955
  1912: 3955
  1918: 3955
  1930: 274, 2041
  1948: 2863
  1950: 2863
SERMONS: 263, 1639, 3482
  Episcopal: 4665
    Edenton: 1376
  Lutheran: 4578
  Methodist: 956
  Methodist Episcopal: 1906, 3581
  Methodist Episcopal Church, South:
    5023
    Plymouth: 772
    Wilmington: 772
  Presbyterian: 661, 923
    Coddle Creek: 4311
    Durham: 2934
    Thyatira: 3334
  Subdivided by place:
    Martin County: 1639
SHARECROPPING:
  Freedmen: 730
  Shelby: 1951
SHIP CHANDLERS' ACCOUNTS:
  Wilmington: 5880
SHIPPING: 484, 540, 2889, 5298
  Coastwise shipping: 1496, 2101,
    4304
    Edenton: 5658
    Wilmington: 1950
  Ocean shipping: 2159
  Subdivided by place:
    Catherine Lake: 5910
    Wilmington: 3447, 4982
SHIPPING COMPANIES: 658
SHIPS:
  see also NORTH CAROLINA--LIGHT-
    SHIPS; NORTH CAROLINA--
    STEAMBOATS
  Cape Fear: 3922
  Merchant ships:
    Edenton: 5658
SHIPS' PILOTS: 3922
  Apprenticeship: 3922
SHOEMAKERS' ACCOUNTS: 3221, 4307
SILVER MINING:
  Davidson County: 2041
  Lexington: 277
SILVERSMITHS:
  Hillsborough: 3300
SLAVE TRADE: 602, 730, 1107, 1252,
  1523, 1794, 2068, 2113, 2222,
  3237, 3415, 3476, 4734, 4816,
  4858, 4897, 5298, 5310
  Prices: 647, 756, 832, 2113, 2663,
    3416, 4424, 5390
  Surry County: 2808
  Yadkin County: 2808
  With Alabama: 2808
  Subdivided by place:
    Beaufort County: 5831
    Cumberland County: 50
    Davie County: 122
    Halifax County: 5672
    Iredell County: 5245
    Hillsborough: 1890
    Lumberton: 3422
    Raleigh: 4394
    Randolph County: 680
SLAVERY: 923, 3155, 3415, 4006, 4080
  Opposition to: 5298

NORTH CAROLINA
SLAVERY:
  Opposition to (Continued):
    see also NORTH CAROLINA--
      ABOLITION OF SLAVERY AND
      ABOLITIONIST SENTIMENT
SLAVES: 435, 484, 1475, 2113, 3483,
  4082, 4862
  see also NORTH CAROLINA--FUGITIVE
    SLAVES; NORTH CAROLINA--HIRING
    OF SLAVES
  Behavior: 279, 1166
  Business affairs: 1166
  Clothing and dress: 5298
  Crimes--Murder: 2117
  Diseases: 3317
  Division of ownership: 3237, 5739
  Emancipation: 1475, 4153
  Executions: 2117
  Expenses incidental to their keep:
    1322
  Health conditions: 602
  Imprisonment: 2298
  Insurrections: 423, 3390, 3415,
    5298
  Lists: 3176, 3415
    Martin County: 4849
    Yadkin County: 4103
  Married life: 1120
  Medical treatment: 2462, 2819,
    4858
  Taxation: 4670
  Treatment of: 3317, 4103, 5770
    Davie County: 122
  Vital statistics--Clarkton: 2970
  Subdivided by place:
    Asheville: 4834
SOCIAL CONDITIONS:
  1860s: 417, 1005, 5390
  1900s: 3538
SOCIAL LIFE AND CUSTOMS:
  1700s-1800s: 2663
  1700s-1900s: 799, 4232, 4689
  1800s: 730, 1402, 1428, 3155,
    5741
  1820s: 2248
  1830s: 967, 1351
  1840s: 967, 4596
  1850s: 436, 518, 1773
  1860s: 3434
  1870s: 647, 3434
  1880s: 647, 3434, 4329
  1890s: 647, 4329
  1800s-1900s: 1313, 2192, 3290,
    4897, 5298
  Beaufort: 5480
  Forsyth County: 156
  Oak Grove Township: 3896
  Randolph County: 518
  Ridgeway: 3307
  Warrenton: 3761
  Wilmington: 1313, 5372
SOCIAL SERVICES--Durham: 1643
SOCIETY OF FRIENDS: 329, 645, 2555,
  3415, 4006, 4858, 5264, 5632
  Church buildings--High Falls:
    5905
  Civil War: 2554, 2555
    Conscientious objectors: 2970
  Family life: 1407
  Subdivided by place:
    Dutchman Creek: 1904
    Yadkin County: 1904
SONGS AND MUSIC: 691, 2041, 5298
  see also NORTH CAROLINA--CHURCH
    MUSIC
  Study and teaching: 837
    Davie County: 4111
    Salem: 3172, 5459
SOUTHERN UNIONISTS: see CIVIL WAR--
  SOUTHERN UNIONISTS--North
  Carolina
SPORTS: see names of specific sports
  under NORTH CAROLINA, e.g. NORTH
  CAROLINA--FOOTBALL
STAGECOACH LINES--Fares: 1960

NORTH CAROLINA

STATE BANKS: 4100
  Fayetteville Branch: 4517
  Salisbury: 1381
STATE CAPITOL BUILDING: 4424
STATE TAXES: 191
STEAMBOAT OPERATORS' ACCOUNTS:
  Pamlico and Tar rivers: 3827
STEAMBOATS: 271
STOCKHOLDERS' MEETINGS: 5408
STOCKS: 4689
  see also NORTH CAROLINA--
    (specific type of business or
    industry)--Stocks, e.g. NORTH
    CAROLINA--RAILROADS--Stocks
  Purchases and sales: 4858
STORMS:
  see also NORTH CAROLINA--
    HURRICANES
  Cape Hatteras: 5955
STRAWBERRY CROPS--Asheville: 4834
STRIKES: 1202
  Cotton mill workers--Erwin: 5298
  Textile workers: 1195
  Subdivided by place:
    Bessemer City: 4094
STUDENT HOUSING--Counselors: 960
STUDENT LOANS: 3538
STUDENT RELIGIOUS SOCIETIES:
  Duke University: 3001
  Wesley Foundation: 5022
STUDENT SOCIETIES: 613
  Chapel Hill: 4669
  Charlotte: 895
  Greensboro: 4425
STUDENTS AND STUDENT LIFE: 3176
  Compositions: 2221, 5298
  Girls' schools and academies: 5664
  High Point: 2036
  Subdivided by place:
    Asheville: 566
    Granville County: 2192, 2833
    Hamilton: 1411
    Louisburg: 3272
    Whiteville: 4910
SUFFRAGE: see NORTH CAROLINA--
  NEGROES--Suffrage; NORTH CAROLINA--
  WOMAN SUFFRAGE
SULPHUR MINING:
  Davidson County: 2041
SUNDAY CLOSING LAWS:
  Lincoln County: 3211
  Rowan County: 4640
SUNDAY SCHOOL CONVENTIONS:
  Baptist: 3415
SUNDAY SCHOOLS: 544, 1482
  Methodist: 3646
    Catawba County: 5745
  Subdivided by place:
    Catawba County: 4532
    Fayetteville: 5298
SUPERSTITIONS: 691
SURVEYS AND SURVEYING:
  1700s: 819
  1700s-1800s: 3176, 3386
  1700s-1900s: 3476
  1800s: 1438, 1475, 2978, 5188
  1800s-1900s: 5709
  Cherokee Indian land: 3028
  Davie County: 2749
  Moore County: 4396
  Orange County: 3337
  Virginia boundary: 1687
  Wilkes County: 2483
  Wilson: 2808
TANNING--Jackson County: 3021
TAVERN ACCOUNTS:
  Louisburg: 2873
  Rowan County: 3288
  Wadesboro: 4814
TAVERNS AND INNS: 2765
  Bath: 705
TAX COLLECTION: 4689
  Beaufort County: 911
TAX EVASION--Hanover County: 5709
TAX IN KIND: 1438, 2260, 2833, 2857, 4761

NORTH CAROLINA

TAX LISTS: 4670, 4862
  Burke County: 245
  Hanover County: 5709
  Martin County: 2284, 3935
  Orange County: 3938
  Randolph County: 2459, 3939
TAX RECEIPTS: 50, 2660, 2824, 3476, 4761, 4858
  Chatham County: 5874
  Craven County: 804
  Martin County: 4849
  Wake County: 4009
TAXATION: 832, 1189, 1202, 2222, 2553, 3410
  see also CONFEDERATE STATES OF
    AMERICA--TAXATION--North
    Carolina; and the following
    subheadings under NORTH
    CAROLINA: NEGROES--Taxation;
    REVENUE STAMPS; ROAD TAX; SALES
    TAX; STATE TAX; TOBACCO TAX
  Assessment--Durham: 2379
  County taxes--Anson County: 191
  Exemption from: 1258
  Liquor: 2952
  Federal taxes: 4009, 4152
  Road work in lieu of payment of taxes: 1417
  Subdivided by place:
    Beaufort County: 3921
    Harnett County: 4761
    New Bern: 5709
    Orange County: 3515
    Wilkes County: 2483
TEACHERS:
  Certification: 122, 3276, 3538, 4897
  Selection and appointment: 2419
    Lilesville: 2493
    Tabernacle Township: 4100
    Wilson: 2642
  Wages: see NORTH CAROLINA--WAGES
    AND SALARIES--Teachers
TEACHERS' CONTRACTS: 2905
  Lincoln County: 3933
TEACHERS' INSTITUTES:
  Granville County: 2833
TEACHERS' RECORDS: 122, 264, 3434
  Bethania: 813
  Catawba County: 3923
  District 8: 4532
  Charlotte: 1823
  Forsyth County: 3928
  Granville County: 2833
  Guilford County: 3931
  Johnston County: 3932
  Louisburg: 3272
  Mecklenburg County: 3608
  Montgomery County: 5123
  Randolph County: 3596
  Wilkes County: 3942
  Youngsville: 5087
TEACHING:
  see also the following subheadings
    under NORTH CAROLINA: EDUCATION;
    SCHOOLS; (name of classroom
    subject, e.g. PENMANSHIP)--Study
    and teaching
  1800s: 1538, 4875
  1820s: 1523
  1840s: 3436
  1850s: 2357, 3436, 5737
  1860s: 76, 5737
  1870s: 76
  1880s: 76
  1800s-1900s: 1278, 4006
  Negro schools: 5041
  Subdivided by place:
    Buncombe County: 5603
    Forsyth County: 5982
    Granville County: 2833
    Guilford County: 1055
    Halifax County: 3831
    Oxford: 2654, 4506

NORTH CAROLINA

TEMPERANCE:
  1700s-1800s: 2530
  1800s: 122, 1556, 2399, 2861, 3581, 4849, 5298
  1800s-1900s: 274, 2720, 3219, 3563
  1900s: 3538
  Cabarrus County: 5582
  Greensboro: 2050
  Lincoln County: 3211
  Rowan County: 4640
TEMPERANCE SOCIETIES: 5245
TEXTBOOKS: 3538, 4918, 5737
  see also NORTH CAROLINA--
    ARITHMETIC--Exercise books; NORTH
    CAROLINA--PENMANSHIP--Exercise
    books
  Catawba County: 4532
  Granville County: 2833
  Rockingham County: 4533
TEXTILE INDUSTRY: 1195, 1584, 1588, 2359, 2877, 5237
  see also NORTH CAROLINA--COTTON
    MILLS; NORTH CAROLINA--LABOR
    CONDITIONS--Textile industry
  Company stores: 5888
  Finance: 1611
    Mooresville: 3757
  Inventories--Cooleemee: 1719
  Legal affairs: 5310
  Profits: 1611
  Silk throwing: 2108
  Stocks: 1611
    Mooresville: 3757
  Subdivided by place:
    Cramerton: 5100
    Durham: 1228, 1611, 1719
    Gaston County: 5887
    Greensboro: 3171
    Mecklenburg County: 5235
    Mooresville: 3757
    Stowesville: 5100
TEXTILE MACHINERY: 1611
  Mount Holly: 5100
  Parts: 1277
TEXTILE WORKERS:
  see also NORTH CAROLINA--STRIKES--
    Textile workers; NORTH
    CAROLINA--WAGES AND SALARIES--
    Textile workers
  Labor arbitration: 5235
THEATER:
  Durham: 4502
  New Bern: 4977
THEOLOGICAL EDUCATION: 5014
  see also NORTH CAROLINA--DIVINITY
    SCHOOLS
TOBACCO: 122, 5298
TOBACCO CULTURE: 2192, 2863, 4849
  Orange County: 3351
TOBACCO CURING: 325
TOBACCO INDUSTRY: 556, 1584, 1588
  Advertising: 1586
  Finance--Durham: 3762
  Subdivided by place:
    Durham: 513, 5923
    Milton: 5843
    Winston-Salem: 3745, 4788
TOBACCO TAX: 2952
  Wake County: 4009
TOBACCO TRADE:
  1700s: 3780
  1700s-1800s: 5298
  1800s: 1871, 4009, 4734, 5280
  1800s-1900s: 4857
  1900s: 5962
  Advertising: 1586
  Prices: 5298
    Littleton: 2399
    Winston-Salem: 3745
  Quotas: 2863
  Subdivided by place:
    Durham: 513
    Edenton: 5228
    Milton: 5843
    New Bern: 5228
    Roxboro: 5455

NORTH CAROLINA

TOBACCO TRADE:
 Subdivided by place (Continued):
  Wake County: 4009
  Winston-Salem: 3645
TOBACCO WAREHOUSES:
 Receipts:
  Greenville: 4858
  Martin County: 4849
TOBACCO WORKERS: see NORTH CAROLINA--LABOR UNIONS--Tobacco workers
TOWEL INDUSTRY--Franklinton: 5450
TRADE AND COMMERCE:
 see also NORTH CAROLINA--BARTER; NORTH CAROLINA--FOREIGN TRADE
 Agricultural machinery: 3660
 Agricultural products: 2101, 4858
 Barrels and barrel staves: 2222, 2377, 5535
 Beef: 2924
 Beeswax: 2924, 5298
 Black-eyed peas: 1871
 Boots and shoes: 606
  Prattsburg: 4307
 Bricks--Williamston: 5036
 Cane reeds: 3230
 Carriages and buggies: 4540, 4918
 Cloth: 35
  Exports: 1611
 Coal--Wilmington: 5912
 Coffee--Wilmington: 1281
 Corn: 4760, 4858, 5535
  Wilmington: 1281
 Cotton: see NORTH CAROLINA--COTTON TRADE
 Cotton cultivators: 2553
 Dairy products: 2924
  Wilkesboro: 4107
 Dry goods:
  Haw River: 5154
  Murfreesboro: 5857
 Fertilizer: 4152, 4344, 4666
  Wilmington: 5912
 Fish: 2889
  Plymouth: 1015
  Wilmington: 1281
 Flour: 1336, 2924
 Food--New Bern: 164
 Furniture: 264
 Gasoline--Mount Olive: 5756
 Grain: 1871
  New Bern: 164
  Wilkesboro: 4107
 Granite--Rowan County: 5929
 Groceries: 134
  Charlotte: 3599
  Wilmington: 3410
 Hardware: 3416
 Harness: 4540
 Harvesting machinery: 2855
 Hay: 2924
 Hides and skins:
  Wilkesboro: 4107
 Horses: 614, 3257
 Hosiery: 1612, 4812
 Ice--Wilmington: 5912
 Iron pipe--Imports: 3230
 Lime (Chemical): 4080
 Liquor: 122, 2808, 2924
  Forsyth County: 4631
  Rowan County: 3288
  Wake County: 4009
  Wilkesboro: 4107
  Wilmington: 1281
 Luggage: 606
 Lumber: 730, 1871, 2101, 2222, 4775, 5535
  Asheville: 1987
  Columbia: 215
  Pantego: 4471
  Williamston: 4824
  Exports:
   To Martinique: 21
   To West Indies: 1492
 Merchandise: 3307
  Ridgeway: 999
 Milk: 1275

NORTH CAROLINA

TRADE AND COMMERCE (Continued):
 Millinery goods--Charlotte: 5100
 Molasses--Wilmington: 1281
 Mules: 3257
 Naval stores: 164, 1871, 2222, 2586, 2924, 5372, 5373, 5535
  Catherine Lake: 5910
  Murfreesboro: 5857
  Wilmington: 2919, 5912
  Exports:
   To Great Britain: 3230
   To Martinique: 21
 Paper: 3416
 Pork: 2889, 2924
 Potatoes:
  Imports from Ireland and Scotland: 3230
 Pulp and paper: 3812
 Rice: 2924
  Exports to Great Britain: 3230
 Rum: 5535
 Salt: 35, 1336, 2889
  Imports from Great Britain: 3230
  Wilmington: 1281
 Shingles: 1492
  Beaufort County: 4435
  Columbia: 215
 Slaves: see NORTH CAROLINA--SLAVE TRADE
 Stationery: 3186, 3416
 Staves:
  Exports to Great Britain: 3230
 Stoneware:
  Imports from Great Britain: 3230
 Tallow: 4107
 Textiles: 2359
  Wilkesboro: 4107
 Timber: 3221, 3364, 5372
 Tobacco: see NORTH CAROLINA--TOBACCO TRADE
 Turpentine: 4925
  Wilmington: 4462
 Wagons: 4540
 Wholesale trade: 4760
  Wilmington: 4910
 Wine: 5535
 Wood--Wilmington: 5912
 Subdivided by place:
  Eastern North Carolina: 3591
  With New England: 172
  With New York: 1871
TREASON: 375
TRESPASS: 2003
TREATIES:
 With Indians: 4746
TRIALS: 5740
 see also NORTH CAROLINA--LIBEL TRIALS
TURNPIKES:
 Construction: 3176
TURPENTINE INDUSTRY: 2222
TURPENTINE INDUSTRY WORKERS:
 Slaves: 5298
TURPENTINE LANDS: 359
 Rental: 2350
TYPOGRAPHICAL WORKERS: see NORTH CAROLINA--WAGES AND SALARIES--Typographical workers
UNIONIZATION: 1195
 see also NORTH CAROLINA--ANTI-UNIONISM; NORTH CAROLINA--LABOR UNIONS
UNITED CONFEDERATE VETERANS: 4918, 5412
UNITED FUND--Durham: 4736
UNITED STATES CONSTITUTION:
 Formulation and ratification: 2776, 3920
UNITED STATES GOVERNMENT AGENCIES AND OFFICIALS:
 see also NORTH CAROLINA--POSTAL SERVICE
 Internal revenue collectors: 4261
UNIVERSALIST CHURCH: see NORTH CAROLINA--CLERGY--Universalist

NORTH CAROLINA

UNIVERSITIES AND COLLEGES: 484, 661, 832, 1773, 2539
 see also BENNETT COLLEGE; CAMPBELL COLLEGE; CAROLINA FEMALE COLLEGE; CHOWAN COLLEGE; CLAREMONT COLLEGE; CLEGG'S COLLEGE; CONCORD FEMALE COLLEGE; DAVENPORT COLLEGE; DAVENPORT FEMALE COLLEGE; DAVIDSON COLLEGE; DUKE UNIVERSITY; FAYETTEVILLE STATE UNIVERSITY; GREENSBORO COLLEGE; GUILFORD COLLEGE; LIBERTY NORMAL COLLEGE; LOUISBURG COLLEGE; MEREDITH COLLEGE; MITCHELL COLLEGE; NORMAL COLLEGE; NORTH CAROLINA AGRICULTURAL AND TECHNICAL STATE UNIVERSITY; NORTH CAROLINA CENTRAL UNIVERSITY; NORTH CAROLINA SCHOOL OF THE ARTS; NORTH CAROLINA STATE UNIVERSITY; OLIN AGRICULTURAL AND MECHANICAL COLLEGE; OXFORD FEMALE COLLEGE; RUTHERFORD COLLEGE; ST. MARY'S COLLEGE; SALEM COLLEGE; TRINITY COLLEGE; TRINITY COLLEGE, Durham; TRINITY COLLEGE, Randolph County; UNIVERSITY OF NORTH CAROLINA AT CHAPEL HILL; UNIVERSITY OF NORTH CAROLINA AT GREENSBORO; WAKE FOREST COLLEGE; WARRENTON FEMALE COLLEGE
 Establishment of a Methodist women's college: 1152
 Philanthropy: 1584, 1588
VITAL RECORDS:
 Warren County: 3307
VOCATIONAL REHABILITATION: 4736
VOTER REGISTRATION:
 Cheek's Creek Township: 675
 Davie County: 2749
 Fentriss: 2330
 Montgomery County: 4689
 New Hanover County: 3410
VOTING: see NORTH CAROLINA--NEGROES--Suffrage; NORTH CAROLINA--WOMAN SUFFRAGE
WAGES AND SALARIES: 1120, 1202
 Agricultural workers:
  Montgomery County: 4689
 Cotton mill workers: 5100
 Freedmen: 832, 5298
 Hosiery workers--Graham: 4812
 Judges: 5768
 Laborers: 1120
 Teachers: 3436, 3538
  Catawba County: 4532
  Granville County: 2833
  Lincolnton: 3210
  Louisburg: 3272
  Montgomery County: 4689
  Rockingham County: 4533
 Textile workers: 1611, 5100
  Burlington: 5234
  Durham: 1228
  Greensboro: 5234
  Mecklenburg County: 5235
  Mount Airy: 5048
  Worthville: 3187
 Typographical workers: 2772
WAR FINANCE CORPORATION: 5962
WAR SHIPPING ADMINISTRATION: 658
WAREHOUSES: 5298
 see also NORTH CAROLINA--TOBACCO WAREHOUSES
WARRANTS (Law): 3221, 4897
 Clarkton: 5909
 Granville County: 2833
WATER RIGHTS: 5100
WEATHER:
 1700s-1800s: 2663
 1800s: 5664
 1840s: 1871
 1850s: 1773
 1860s: 1934, 2357, 2549, 5774, 5991
 1870s: 2357
 1880s: 2357

NORTH CAROLINA
  WEATHER (Continued):
    Asheville: 4834
    Cumberland County: 3812
    Flint Rock: 5890
    Fort Fisher: 3370
    Iredell County: 4310, 5245
    Orange County: 3351
    Robeson County: 3436
  WEAVING AND SPINNING--Wool: 5658
  WEDDINGS:
    Clarksville: 4849
    Raleigh: 274
    Wilmington: 3607
  WHEAT: 2121
  WHIG PARTY: 631, 730, 1015, 1100,
    1580, 1826, 2530, 4080, 4714,
    4897, 5149, 5298
  WHITEWASH: 2905, 3410
  WILLS:
    see also NORTH CAROLINA--ESTATES--
      Administration and settlement;
      NORTH CAROLINA--INHERITANCE LAWS
    1700s-1800s: 2663, 3364, 4082
    1700s-1900s: 872, 3233, 3415, 4858,
      5298
    1800s: 730, 1107, 2339, 2970, 3416,
      3916, 4270, 4761
    1800s-1900s: 5709, 5740
    Burke County: 1247
    Caldwell County: 1247
    Durham County: 1256
    Edgecombe County: 3626
    Franklin County: 4147
    Greensboro: 3763
    Halifax County: 5280, 5672
    Martin County: 4849
    Montgomery County: 4689
    Onslow County: 1252
    Person County: 3752
    Ridgeway: 3307
    Surry County: 3908
  WINDMILLS--Hatteras: 4547
  WINDOW GLASS: 1736
  WOMAN SUFFRAGE: 274, 1275, 4968
  WOMEN:
    Employment: 5100
      see also NORTH CAROLINA--LABOR
      LAWS AND LEGISLATION--
      Employment of women and
      children
      Wilmington: 5533
  WOMEN IN THE CIVIL WAR: 5298
    Caldwell County: 4080
  WOMEN'S SOCIETIES AND CLUBS: 661,
    1128
    Durham: 5601
    Henderson: 4232
    Raleigh: 274
  WOMEN'S SOCIETY OF CHRISTIAN SERVICE:
    3020
  WOOL CARDING--Randleman: 5408
  WOOLEN MILLS:
    Winston-Salem: 1905
  WORKMEN'S COMPENSATION: 1951
  WORKS PROJECT ADMINISTRATION: 5298
  WORLD WAR I: see appropriate
    subheadings under WORLD WAR I
  WORLD WAR II: see appropriate
    subheadings under WORLD WAR II
  YOUTH ORGANIZATIONS: 5298
  ZINC MINING:
    Davidson County: 2041

  [End of entries under NORTH CAROLINA]

NORTH CAROLINA: A STUDY IN ENGLISH
  COLONIAL GOVERNMENT: 4391
NORTH CAROLINA AGRICULTURAL AND
  MECHNICAL COLLEGE FOR THE
  COLORED RACE, Greensboro, North
  Carolina: see NORTH CAROLINA
  AGRICULTURAL AND TECHNICAL STATE
  UNIVERSITY

NORTH CAROLINA AGRICULTURAL AND
  TECHNICAL STATE UNIVERSITY,
  Greensboro, North Carolina: 3410
NORTH CAROLINA ARGUS (periodical):
  4918
NORTH CAROLINA BAPTIST HOSPITAL:
  3538
NORTH CAROLINA BAPTIST MINISTERS'
  LIFE ASSOCIATION: 63
NORTH CAROLINA CENTRAL UNIVERSITY,
  Durham, North Carolina: 1584, 2379,
  5252
NORTH CAROLINA CHILDREN'S HOME
  SOCIETY: 2041
NORTH CAROLINA CHRISTIAN ADVOCATE
  (periodical): 2048, 2221, 4242
NORTH CAROLINA COLLEGE, Durham,
  North Carolina: see NORTH CAROLINA
  CENTRAL UNIVERSITY
NORTH CAROLINA COLLEGE FOR NEGROES,
  Durham, North Carolina: see NORTH
  CAROLINA CENTRAL UNIVERSITY
NORTH CAROLINA COLLEGE FOR WOMEN,
  Greensboro, North Carolina: see
  UNIVERSITY OF NORTH CAROLINA AT
  GREENSBORO
NORTH CAROLINA CONFERENCE HISTORICAL
  DIRECTORY by Joseph W. Watson and
  C. Franklin Grill: 3646
NORTH CAROLINA CONSERVATORY COMMITTEE:
  4736
NORTH CAROLINA CORPORATION COMMISSION:
  4586
NORTH CAROLINA COUNCIL OF CHURCHES:
  3020, 5022
NORTH CAROLINA EDITORIAL WRITERS
  CONFERENCE: 4204
NORTH CAROLINA FEDERATION OF WOMEN'S
  CLUBS: 1128
NORTH CAROLINA FOLKLORE SOCIETY: 691,
  1064
NORTH CAROLINA GOOD ROADS ASSOCIATION:
  3380
NORTH CAROLINA HISTORICAL COMMISSION:
  4232, 5298
NORTH CAROLINA HOSPITAL, Petersburg,
  Virginia: 661
NORTH CAROLINA IN AMERICAN LITERATURE:
  1313
NORTH CAROLINA IN AMERICAN POETRY:
  2739
NORTH CAROLINA JOURNAL OF EDUCATION:
  5737
NORTH CAROLINA LITERARY AND
  HISTORICAL ASSOCIATION: 4232
NORTH CAROLINA LITERARY FUND: 3943
NORTH CAROLINA MANUFACTURING, MINING
  AND LAND COMPANY: 3391
NORTH CAROLINA MEDICAL SOCIETY:
  2934, 4231, 5603
NORTH CAROLINA MENTAL HEALTH
  ASSOCIATION: 2934
NORTH CAROLINA MENTAL HYGIENE
  SOCIETY: 2934
NORTH CAROLINA MUSEUM: 4736
NORTH CAROLINA NEUROPSYCHIATRIC
  ASSOCIATION: 2934
NORTH CAROLINA PRESBYTERIAN
  (periodical): 5737
NORTH CAROLINA RAILROAD ASSOCIATION:
  238
NORTH CAROLINA RAILROAD COMPANY:
  1482, 4458
NORTH CAROLINA RECREATION COMMISSION:
  1199
"NORTH CAROLINA REVISITED" by
  William Garrison Reed: 4414
NORTH CAROLINA SCHOOL OF THE ARTS:
  4736
NORTH CAROLINA SEMINARY, High Point,
  North Carolina: 3851
NORTH CAROLINA SHORT LINE RAILROAD
  ASSOCIATION: 238
NORTH CAROLINA SOCIETY OF BALTIMORE:
  5298
NORTH CAROLINA STAFF BULLETIN
  (periodical): 1202

NORTH CAROLINA STATE BAR
  ASSOCIATION: 4927
NORTH CAROLINA STATE COLLEGE, Raleigh,
  North Carolina: see NORTH CAROLINA
  STATE UNIVERSITY
NORTH CAROLINA STATE FARMERS'
  ALLIANCE: 3996
NORTH CAROLINA STATE FEDERATION OF
  LABOR: 3944
NORTH CAROLINA STATE HOSPITAL FOR
  THE INSANE: 2220
NORTH CAROLINA STATE INDUSTRIAL
  UNION COUNCIL: 1192
NORTH CAROLINA STATE LIFE INSURANCE
  COMPANY: 5541
NORTH CAROLINA STATE NORMAL AND
  INDUSTRIAL COLLEGE, Greensboro,
  North Carolina: see UNIVERSITY of
  OF NORTH CAROLINA AT GREENSBORO
NORTH CAROLINA STATE PRIMARY TEACHERS'
  ASSOCIATION: 5298
NORTH CAROLINA STATE UNIVERSITY,
  Raleigh, North Carolina:
  Textile engineering: 4918
NORTH CAROLINA TEACHERS' ASSEMBLY:
  5298
"NORTH CAROLINA'S PART IN THE FRENCH
  AND INDIAN WAR": 5750
NORTH CREEK, Arkansas: 2856
NORTH CREEK PRIMITIVE BAPTIST CHURCH,
  Beaufort County, North Carolina:
  3945
NORTH DAKOTA:
  see also MIDDLE WEST; PLAINS STATES
  Governors: 766
NORTH END, Virginia: 5165
NORTH GATES CIRCUIT, Methodist
  churches: 3646
NORTH GEORGIA AGRICULTURAL SCHOOL:
  662
NORTH HAMPTON, Ohio: 1618
NORTH HERO, Vermont: 5096
NORTH KENT, Connecticut: 5502
NORTH OXFORD, Massachusetts: 358
NORTH POLE--Discovery of: 4556
NORTH SEA:
  Description and travel: 244
NORTH STATE FIRE INSURANCE COMPANY:
  4918
NORTH STONINGTON, Connecticut: 2410
  Mercantile affairs: 5669
NORTH WILKESBORO, North Carolina:
  2239
NORTH WILKESBORO DISTRICT, Methodist
  churches: 3646
NORTHAMPTON, Massachusetts: 826, 1054,
  1058
NORTHAMPTON COUNTY, North Carolina:
  1681, 3963, 4390
  Rich Square: 4006
  Seaboard: 4374
  Smith Church: 5399
  Woodland: 4047
NORTHAMPTON COUNTY, Pennsylvania:
  Bethlehem: see BETHLEHEM,
    Pennsylvania
NORTHAMPTON COUNTY, Virginia: 5742
  Cape Charles: 660
  Eastville: 1814
  Machipongo: 1814
NORTHAMPTONSHIRE, England:
  "Apethorpe House": 1754
NORTHBOURNE, Walter Henry James,
  Second Baron: 1014, 4520
NORTHBROOK, Thomas George Baring,
  First Earl of: 326, 648, 1857, 4660
NORTHCLIFFE, Alfred Charles William
  Harmsworth, First Viscount: 441,
  3265
NORTHCOTE, James Spencer: 2148
NORTHCOTE, Sir Stafford Henry, First
  Earl of Iddesleigh: 366, 2127,
  2976, 4028
NORTHEASTERN RAILROAD COMPANY: 4830
NORTHEN, William Jonathan: 3947
NORTHERN EUROPE:
  Sale of naval stores to Great
    Britain: 2296

NORTHERN IRELAND:
  Presbyterian churches: 2738
"NORTHERN LABORERS" by John McLean Harrington: 2357
NORTHERN NECK, Virginia: 1750
  Description: 3793
NORTHERN OPINION: see as subheading under specific subjects, e.g. SECESSION--Northern opinion
NORTHERN PACIFIC RAILROAD: 3637
NORTHERN STATES:
  Abolition of slavery and abolitionist sentiment: 4095
  Cotton trade: 3689
  Description and travel:
    1800s: 4616
    1820s: 2828, 3485
    1860s: 2449, 5193
    1870s: 2449, 3390, 5193
    1880s: 2449
  Labor: 5940
  Negroes--Social conditions: 3392
  Relations with Southern States: 5717
NORTHERNERS:
  Southern opinion of: 3917
    North Carolina: 5041
NORTHERNERS IN THE SOUTH:
  see also CARPETBAGGERS; SCHOOLS--Negro schools--Northern teachers
  Civil War: 2140
  Georgia: 2096
    Atlanta: 5082
  North Carolina: 5041
  South Carolina: 1572
  Virginia: 1697
    Clarke County: 2513
NORTHUMBERLAND, Hugh Percy, Second Duke of: 2126
NORTHUMBERLAND, Hugh Percy, Third Duke of: 2148
NORTHUMBERLAND, England:
  Corruption in politics: 5026
  Elections: 5026
  Cities and towns:
    Alnwick Castle: 4840
    Newcastle-upon-Tyne: 1164
      Politics and government: 1273
NORTHUMBERLAND, Pennsylvania: 4690, 5462
NORTHUMBERLAND COUNTY, Pennsylvania:
  Northumberland: see NORTHUMBERLAND, Pennsylvania
  Sunbury: 1768, 4348
NORTHUMBERLAND COUNTY, Virginia: 600
NORTHWESTERN LITERARY AND HISTORICAL SOCIETY: 3990
NORTHWESTERN NATIONAL BANK, Great Falls, Montana: 1211
NORTHWESTERN STATES: see OLD NORTH WEST; WESTERN STATES
NORTON, ____: 97
NORTON, Charles B.: 196
NORTON, Charles Bowyer Adderley, First Baron: 36, 1087, 3046
NORTON, Charles Eliot (1827-1908): 103, 706
NORTON, Charles Ledyard (1837-1909): 3022
NORTON, Charles Stuart (New Jersey): 3948
NORTON, BAXTER, AND ROSE (firm): see BAXTER, ROSE, AND NORTON
NORWALK, Connecticut: 2745
NORWAY:
  Botany: 2430
  Description and travel (1878): 157
NORWICH, Connecticut: 1865, 2046
NORWICH, England: 370, 2841
NORWICH, New York: 2292
NORWICH, Vermont: 295
NORWOOD, Elizabeth Russell: 5282
NORWOOD, Jane: 5298
NORWOOD, John (1727-1802): 3176
NORWOOD, John (fl. ca. 1809-1810): 385
NORWOOD, Robina (Hogg): 5298

NORWOOD, William (d. 1842): 4080, 5298
NORWOOD FAMILY (North Carolina--Genealogy): 4517
NORWOOD, North Carolina:
  Mercantile accounts: 5589
NORWOOD, Virginia:
  Merchants and mercantile accounts: 5107
  Schools: 824, 5107
NORWOOD HIGH SCHOOL, Norwood, Virginia: 824, 5107
NOSEWORTHY, John William: 3949
NOSTALGIA: see HOMESICKNESS
NOTARIES:
  Georgia--Chatham County: 4611
  Germany: 2194
  Texas: 5293
"NOTES ON MATERIA MEDICA AND THERAPEUTICS": 4030
NOTRE DAME, Convent of (Maryland): 2692
NOTT, Charles Cooper: 3022
NOTT, Sir William: 3950
NOTTOWAY COUNTY, Virginia: 262, 1811, 5007
  Cotton growing: 5469
  Plantation accounts: 5469
  Seed distribution: 5769
  Tobacco culture: 5469
NOURSE, James: 3951
NOVA SCOTIA, Canada:
  Army life: 4354
  Baptist churches--Negroes: 176
  Description and travel: 3381
  Government agencies and officials:
    Board of Commissioners for Auditing Public Accounts: 1756
    Governors: 1756
  Land: 3381
  Cities and towns:
    Halifax: 1890
      Description: 1790
    Pictou: 3381
    Wolfville: see ARCADIA UNIVERSITY
NOVELS: see AMERICAN FICTION; ENGLISH FICTION
NOVITCKIE, Anthony: 3952
NOXUBEE COUNTY, Mississippi: 1722, 2888
NOWLIN, Kate: 3879
NOYE, Richard D.: 2407
NOYES, E. T.: 3789
NOYES, Julia Lord: 3277
NOYES FAMILY: 3277
NUCLEAR PHYSICS: see ATOMIC ENERGY; CYCLOTRON
NUCLEAR POWER: see ATOMIC ENERGY
NUERMBERGER, G. A.: 3244
NUESTRA SEÑORA DE REGLA (ship): 4982
NUEVO SISTEMA DE GOVIERNO ECONOMICO PARA LA AMERICA .... by José del Campillo y Cosío: 873
NUGEN, William H.: 3953
NUGENT, George Nugent-Grenville, Baron: 2198
NUGENT, George Thomas John, First Marquis of Westmeath: 4024
NUGENT, Lavall, Count Nugent: 3954
NUGENT, Robert, First Earl Nugent: 4229
NUGENT-TEMPLE-GRENVILLE, George, First Marquis of Buckingham: see GRENVILLE, George Nugent-Temple-, First Marquis of Buckingham
NULLIFICATION: 357, 1086, 1424, 1769, 2449, 2776, 3048, 3291, 3413, 3415, 4689, 5194
  see also DISUNION
  Georgia: 3767
  Massachusetts--Opinion of: 1433
  South Carolina: 150, 669, 842, 2695, 3176, 3366, 4080, 4164
  Tennessee--Opinion of: 2661
  Virginia: 872
NULLIFICATION DEBATE: 3809

NUNEHAM, Viscount: see HARCOURT, George Simon, Second Earl of Harcourt
NUNN, Romulus Armistead: 3955
NUNS: see CIVIL WAR--NURSES AND NURSING; RELIGIOUS ORDERS--Women
"THE NUPTIAL FÊTE" by Alexander B. Meek: 3611
NUREMBURG TRIALS: see WAR CRIMES--Trials at Nuremburg
NURSERIES (Horticulture): 2554
  see also FLOWER TRADE; GARDENS AND GARDENING
  New Jersey: 4354
  New York: 1462
  North Carolina: 5632
  Pennsylvania: 1283
NURSERY SCHOOLS: see CHILD CARE CENTERS
NURSES AND NURSING: 3338
  see also CIVIL WAR--NURSES AND NURSING; WORLD WAR I--Nurses and nursing
  Georgia: 365
NURSING HOMES: see CONVALESCENT HOMES
NURSING TRAINING: see DUKE UNIVERSITY--Medical Center--School of Nursing
NUT BUSH PRESBYTERIAN CHURCH, Townsville, North Carolina: 1361
NUT TRADE: 323
NUTT, Carrie: 3956
NUTT, Haller: 3956
NUTT, Mary: 3956
NUTWOOD, England: 4934
NYACK, New York: 1462
  Literary affairs: 3344
NYCUM, John: 3957
NYCUM, John Q.: 3957
NYCUM, Simon: 3957
NYE, Gerald P.: 879
NYE, N. G.: 2012
NYRE, George: 3958

O

OACOMA, S. D.: 5791
OAHU, Hawaii: 4535
OAK COTTAGE, Cranleigh, England: 4207
OAK FOREST, Virginia: 3454
OAK GROVE, Brunswick County, Virginia: 2392
OAK GROVE, Westmoreland County, Virginia: 5848
OAK GROVE ACADEMY, Nottoway County, Virginia: 1811
OAK GROVE PLANTATION, Georgia: 2326
OAK GROVE TOWNSHIP, North Carolina:
  Churches: 3896
  Farm accounts: 3896
  Social life and customs: 3896
OAK HILL, Missouri: see CIVIL WAR--CAMPAIGNS, BATTLES, AND MILITARY ACTIONS--Missouri--Oak Hill
OAK PARK, Virginia: 4170
OAK RIDGE, North Carolina: 3290
  Merchants: 556
  Schools: 1055, 3290
OAK RIDGE ACADEMY, Oak Ridge, North Carolina: 1055
  Students and student life: 3290
OAK RIDGE INSTITUTE: see OAK RIDGE ACADEMY
OAKDALE, Massachusetts: 3181
OAKDALE, North Carolina:
  Schools: 675
OAKDALE ACADEMY, Oakdale, North Carolina: 675
OAKDALE CEMETERY, Wilmington, North Carolina: 2180
OAKES, George W. Ochs-: see OCHS-OAKES, George W.
OAKEY, John: 3959
OAKEY FAMILY (Virginia): 3959
OAKLAND, Texas: 1741
"OAKLAND," Halifax County, Virginia: 2680
"OAKLAND," Hanover County, Virginia: 4020
OAKLAND, Washington Territory: 5033
OAKLAND COLLEGE, Claiborne County, Mississippi: 3322
OAKLAND COUNTY, Michigan:
  Davisburg: 5269
OAKLAND FEMALE HOME SCHOOL, Nelson County, Virginia: 3788
OAKLANDS, England: 3835
OAKLEY PLANTATION, South Carolina: 1472
OAKS, North Carolina: 2940
OAKS PLANTATION, South Carolina: 5193
OAKSMITH, Appleton: 3960
OAKSMITH, Corinne: 3960
OATES, Jesse: 1107
OATHS: see LOYALTY OATHS; TEST OATHS
OATHS BILL (Great Britain, 1883): 2324
OATHS OF OFFICE: see PUBLIC OFFICIALS--Oaths of office
OATS PRICES--New York: 2434
OATS PRODUCTION:
  Virginia: 4924

OATS TRADE: 323
  Virginia: 1863
O'BANNON, Bryant: 3961
O'BANNON, John M.: 2165
OBERHOLTZER, Ellis Paxson: 2425
OBERLIN, Ohio: see OBERLIN COLLEGE
OBERLIN COLLEGE, Oberlin, Ohio:
  Students and student life: 4663, 5311
OBLIGATIONS (Law): see CONTRACTS
O'BRAN, Fred: 2838
O'BRIEN, Edward Joseph Harrington: 5320
O'BRIEN, Fitz-James: 103
O'BRIEN, W. T.: 134
O'BRIEN FAMILY (Florida): 4365
O'BRYEN, Dennis: 2146
OBSCENE MAIL: see POSTAL SERVICE--Obscene mail
"OBSERVACIÓN SOBRE EL CARÁCTER DE LOS INDIOS" by José de Larrea de Loredo: 4155
"OBSERVATIONS OF HENRY BARNARD ON THE WEST AND SOUTH OF THE 1840's": 5593
OBSERVATIONS ON A PASSAGE IN THE PREFACE TO MR. FOX'S HISTORICAL WORK, RELATING TO THE CHARACTER OF MR. SOMERVILLE AS AN HISTORIAN: 828
"OBSERVATIONS ON PERSIA AS AN ALLY, AND THE CHEAPEST AS WELL AS MOST IMPORTANT LINE OF OUR INDIAN EMPIRE": 1010
OBSERVER (Great Britain, periodical): 2146
THE OBSERVER PRINTING HOUSE: 5312
"THE OBSTACLES WHICH HAVE RETARDED MORAL AND POLITICAL PROGRESS" by Lord John Russell: 4605
OCCASIONAL VERSE: 3284
OCCUPATION (employment), Choice of: 1597, 3977
OCCUPATION OF TERRITORY: see AMERICAN REVOLUTION--British occupation; CIVIL WAR--UNION OCCUPATION; RECONSTRUCTION--Federal military occupation; and Military occupation as subheading under names of places
OCCUPATIONAL HEALTH: 2934
OCEAN SHIPPING: see SHIPPING--Ocean shipping
OCEAN VOYAGES: see TRAVEL--Ocean voyages
OCEANOGRAPHY: see NAUTICAL SURVEYING
OCHS, Adolph Simon: 3265
OCHS-OAKES, George W.: 879
OCMULGEE CIRCUIT, Georgia: 4415
OCONALUFTEE RIVER (North Carolina): 2028
OCONEE COUNTY, Georgia:
  Watkinsville: 1621
OCONEE COUNTY, South Carolina:
  Clemson: 2961
  see also CLEMSON UNIVERSITY
  "Fort Hill": 1101
OCONEE RIVER (Georgia): 5395
O'CONNELL, Daniel: 5, 535, 1632
O'CONNOR, Feargus: 4051
O'CONNOR, Michael Patrick: 3962
O'CONNOR & GLENNAN (firm): see GLENNAN & O'CONNOR
OCRACOKE CIRCUIT, Methodist churches: 3646
"THE OCTAGON" (home): 3612
ODD FELLOWS, Independent Order of: see INDEPENDENT ORDER OF ODD FELLOWS
ODD FELLOWS HALL HOSPITAL, Washington, D.C.: 701
ODDIE & ST. GEORGE (firm): 4157
"ODE TO A SKYLARK" by Percy Bysshe Shelley: 2058
ODELL, Benjamin Barker: 1907
ODES AND PSALMS OF SOLOMON: 656
ODOM, Charles: 3963

O'DONNELL, Mr. _____ (journalist): 3267
O'DONOUGHUE, Willoughby: 2604
ODRIOZOLA, Manuel de: 4155
ODYSSEY: 1538
"OECOGRAPHY. THE GEOGRAPHY OF HOME. CHATHAM COUNTY, STATE OF GEORGIA: A TEXT-BOOK DESIGNED FOR THE USE OF THE GRAMMAR SCHOOLS OF SAVANNAH, GEORGIA": 4236
OEMLER, Marie Conway: 4453
OERTEL, Johannes Adam Simon: 733, 3965
OERTEL, Julia A.: 3176
OFFICE EQUIPMENT: 4494
OFFICE EQUIPMENT TRADE:
  Connecticut: 2273
OFFICE SEEKING: see POLITICAL PATRONAGE
OFFICERS: see as subheading under names of armies and navies
OFFICIAL BULLETIN (United States Food Administration): 5803
OFFICIAL RECORDS OF THE WAR OF THE REBELLION ed. by Marcus Joseph Wright: 5922
OFFICIALS: see PUBLIC OFFICIALS
O'FLAHERTY, Roderic: 5379
OGDEN COLLEGE, Bowling Green, Kentucky: 4373
OGDENSBURG, New York:
  Hardware trade: 1390
  Merchants: 2230
  Tobacco industry: 5989
OGEECHEE, Georgia: 5395
OGEECHEE RIVER (Georgia): 5017
OGG, George: 3966
OGILBY, William: 2612
OGILVIE, William: 4093
OGLE COUNTY, Illinois:
  Agricultural fairs: 4732
OGLESBY, Thaddeus Kosciuszko: 3967
OGLETHORPE, James Edward: 1993, 3444, 3733, 3968, 4988, 5473
OGLETHORPE COUNTY, Georgia: 5162
  Plantations: 5162
  Cities and towns:
    Crawford: 1302, 3974
    Maxey: 3604
OGLETHORPE UNIVERSITY, Milledgeville, Georgia: 3092
OGYGIA by Roderic O'Flaherty: 5379
O'HARA, Charles: 2147
O'HIGGINS, Bernardo: 4155
OHIO:
  see also MIDDLE WEST; OLD NORTHWEST; WESTERN RESERVE
  Abolition of slavery and abolitionist sentiment: 2678, 4387
  Agricultural machinery:
    Dayton: 5193
  Agriculture: 1177
    see also OHIO--Crops; OHIO--Farming
  Autographs: 1040, 2862
  Band concerts: 3845
  Bank failures: 4732
  Bridge construction: 5030
  Business affairs: 1578, 2128
    Bucyrus: 3103
    Defiance: 4793
    Logan County: 5142
    Wooster: 3103
  Canals: 2591
  Clergy--Methodist: 2693
  Commodity prices: 1505, 2678, 3051, 3848, 4732, 5149, 5504
    Ross County: 770
  Congressional elections (1888): 5168
  Copperheads: 1505, 4160, 5132
  Crime: 801
  Crops: 2949, 5980
    see also OHIO--Agriculture; OHIO--Farming; and names of specific crops under OHIO

OHIO:
  Crops (Continued):
    North Hampton: 1618
    Wilkes: 86
  Currency: 1339
  Death--North Hampton: 1618
  Description and travel: 4457
    1800s: 57
    1820s: 1791
    1840s: 230, 5508
    1850s: 230, 5508
    1860s: 2601
    1870s: 1811
  Diseases:
    Cholera: 3255, 5342
    North Hampton: 1618
  Droughts: 5275
  Economic conditions: 57, 806, 2591, 3784
    see also OHIO--Panic of (date)
  Elections: 2291
    see also the following
      subheadings under OHIO:
      Congressional elections;
      Gubernatorial elections;
      Presidential election of 1828
  Farming: 1177, 3848, 5307, 5980
    see also OHIO--Crops
    Preble County: 2606
  Finance: 281, 2504, 3085, 3648
  Government agencies and officials:
    Governors:
      Allen Trimble (1822): 2611
  Gubernatorial elections:
    1863: 801, 1505
  Insurance: 281, 5342
  Labor disputes: 5342
  Land: 1849
    see also OHIO--Real estate investments
    Prices: 1505, 3051, 4732
    Purchases and sales: 281, 3103, 4616
  Land companies: 5593
  Land deeds and indentures: 357
  Land fraud: 2120
  Land settlement: 404, 734
  Land speculation: 2591, 5520
  Land titles: 4616
  Law practice: 281
    Defiance: 920
  Lawsuits--Brown County: 281
  Legal affairs: 281
    Defiance: 920
  Literary interests: 281
  Locofoco Party--Columbus: 230
  Love letters: 4477
  Masonry: 801
  Medical education: see PHYSIO-MEDICAL COLLEGE OF OHIO
  Medical practice: 4076
  Memorials--Cleveland: 5291
  Merchants--Hillsboro: 5342
  Methodist churches:
    Logan County: 5142
    Northern Ohio: 2693
  Migration to: 1920, 3161, 5149
    From Connecticut: 5593
    From Virginia: 3255
  National Road: 4732
  Newspapers: 713
    Editing and publishing: 2526
  Normal schools: 1177
  Panic of 1837: 5342
  Panic of 1857: 5342
  Physicians: 4539
  Politics and government:
    1800s: 357, 920, 4076
    1830s: 4732
    1850s: 1578
    1860s: 801, 1578
    1870s: 2291
    1880s: 5168
    1800s-1900s: 3103
  Population--Chillicothe: 5149
  Presbyterian churches: 4076
  Presidential election of 1828: 4165

OHIO (Continued):
  Race relations: 2291
  Railroads:
    Construction: 281
    Finance: 55
  Real estate investment: 2120
  Religion: 57, 451, 2949
  Republican Party: 5168
  Roads: 2591
    see also Ohio--National Road
  Schools: 2591
    see also OHIO--Normal schools;
      OHIO--Teaching
    Girls' schools and academies:
      Steubenville: 5380
  Secessionist sentiment: 4160
  Shakers: 2601
  Social life and customs: 806, 4029, 5043
  Spiritualism: 5149
  Tanning: 5342
  Teaching: 1920, 5380
    see also OHIO--Schools
    Logan County: 5142
  Theological seminaries: 1920
  Trade and commerce:
    Food: 5006
    Hardware: 4728
    Liquor regulations: 4892
  Transportation: 5149
  Union Party: 281
  Universities and colleges: see
    BALDWIN-WALLACE COLLEGE; MIAMI
    UNIVERSITY; OBERLIN COLLEGE;
    OHIO UNIVERSITY; URBANA
    UNIVERSITY; WITTENBERG COLLEGE
  Wages and salaries: 1505, 4732, 5149
    Teachers: 5149
  Weather: 2949
    see also OHIO--Droughts
    North Hampton: 1618
  Weddings--North Hampton: 1618
  Wool tariff: 5342
OHIO CANAL COMPANY: see CHESAPEAKE AND OHIO CANAL COMPANY
OHIO COUNTY, West Virginia:
  Wheeling: 4206, 5228
    Smallpox epidemic: 2678
OHIO LAND COMPANY: 5593
OHIO REFORM SCHOOL FARM: 2601
OHIO RIVER: 4387
  Description and travel: 4810
  Riverboats: 3255
  Steamboats: 4269, 5380
  Surveying: 5575
  Transportation: 3255
OHIO UNIVERSITY, Athens, Ohio: 1116
OHIO VALLEY:
  see also OLD NORTHWEST
  Description and travel: 1060
OHL, Maude Annulet (Andrews): 3969
OIL:
  Discoveries--West Virginia: 4348
  Refining--Pennsylvania: 4086
OIL FIELDS:
  Mexico: 3651
  Texas--Beaumont: 1951
OIL INDUSTRY:
  France: 1424
  Spain: 1424
OIL SPECULATION: 3687
OIL TRADE: 323
OIL WORKERS INTERNATIONAL UNION: 1194, 1198, 5486
OILSEED MILLS:
  see also COTTONSEED OIL; LINSEED OIL MILLS
  Accounts--North Carolina: 3827
  Finance:
    North Carolina: 3206, 4858
  Management--North Carolina: 3206
  Stocks--North Carolina: 3206
OKEECHOBEE, Florida: 4298
  Banking and real estate: 2877
OKEECHOBEE COUNTY, Florida:
  Okeechobee: see OKEECHOBEE, Florida
O'KELLY, James: 5457

OKINAWA, Japan: 2650
OKLAHOMA:
  Land rental: 3687
  Oil speculation: 3687
  Social conditions: 1951
  Universities and colleges: see UNIVERSITY OF OKLAHOMA
OKTIBBEHA COUNTY, Mississippi: 3611
OLADOWSKI, Hypolite: 3970
O'LAUGHLIN, Michael: 5715
OLAVIDE, Pablo de: 4979
OLD AGE: see AGED AND AGING; RETIREMENT
OLD BAILEY PRISON: 4113
OLD CAPITOL PRISON, Washington, D.C.:
  see CIVIL WAR--PRISONERS AND PRISONS--Confederate prisoners--Washington, D.C.--Old Capitol Prison
OLD COLONY AND FALL RIVER RAILROAD: 2608
OLD DOMINION REAL ESTATE COMPANY: 3979
OLD DOMINION STEAMSHIP COMPANY: 3827
OLD DOMINION TOBACCO WAREHOUSE: 2922
"OLD LETTERS FROM DUMFRIES, VA." by Bessie W. Gahn: 2703
OLD NORTHWEST:
  see also MIDDLE WEST; OHIO VALLEY
  Secession: 1084
OLD POINT COMFORT, Virginia: 2132
  see also OLD POINT COMFORT COLLEGE
OLD POINT COMFORT COLLEGE, Old Point Comfort, Virginia: 661
OLD SOUTHWEST:
  see also SOUTHERN STATES
  Land settlement: 872
"OLD TOWN CLUB," Baltimore, Maryland: 3971
OLD WARRIOR AND CLAY CLUB: 849
"OLD WHITEY" (horse): 4943
OLDENPLACE, Virginia: 3400
OLDHAM, Edward A.: 3972
OLDHAM, William P.: 1899
OLIN, North Carolina: 831, 2857, 3973
  see also OLIN AGRICULTURAL AND MECHANICAL COLLEGE
OLIN AGRICULTURAL AND MECHANICAL COLLEGE, Olin, North Carolina: 4968
OLIN HIGH SCHOOL, Olin, North Carolina: 3973
  Finance: 2857
OLIVE, Johnson: 63
OLIVE BRANCH, North Carolina: 579, 4898
  Arithmetic exercise book: 208
OLIVE BRANCH PETITION: 1991
OLIVE OIL: see TARIFFS--Olive oil
OLIVER, J. W.: 496
OLIVER, Louise d'Este (Courtney): 1260
OLIVER, Richard: 1260
OLIVER, Shelton: 3974
OLIVER FAMILY (Great Britain): 1260
"OLIVER NEWMAN" by Robert Southey: 4967
OLIVETT, John M.: 3975
OLLIER, Charles: 3976
OLMSTED, Frederick Law: 2461
OLMSTED, George T.: 730
OLNEY, Richard: 1364
OLSSON, Elis: 1852
OMAHA, Nebraska--Description: 1591
OMDURMAN, Sudan: 1976
OMMANNEY, Edward Lacon: 3977
OMMANNEY, Edward Lacon, Jr.: 3977
OMMANNEY, Sir Montagu Frederick: 3978
OMOHUNDRO, Julia: 3979
OMOHUNDRO, Malvern Hill: 3979
OMOND, George William Thompson: 3980
"ON A LONESOME PORCH" by Ovid Williams Pierce: 4204
"ON THE ROAD TO DESPOTISM" by John Esten Cooke: 1227
"ON THE WAR PATH" by George L. MacKay: 3397

"ON THIS ROCK . . . THE CHRONICLE OF A SOUTHERN FAMILY": 4894
ONASSIS, Aristotle: 83
THE ONE WOMAN by Thomas Dixon: 1521
O'NEAL, Edward Asbury: 2662
O'NEAL, Rose: 2180
O'NEALE, Cary: 3981
O'NEALE, John: 3981
O'NEALE, Margaret: 872
O'NEALE, Peggy: see O'NEALE, Margaret
O'NEALE, William: 3982
O'NEALE FAMILY: 3981
O'NEALL, John Belton: 3676
ONEIDA (ship): 81
ONEIDA COUNTY, New York: 2523
　Trenton Falls: 2518
　Utica: 1845, 2907
O'NEIL, A. F.: 3983
O'NEIL, Charles: 3983
O'NEIL, John: 3983
O'NEILL, Eugene Gladstone: 3797
O'NEILL, J. J. A.: 60
O'NEILL AND ALEXANDER (firm): see ALEXANDER AND O'NEILL
"ONLY THROUGH BOOKS AND ONLY THROUGH LIBRARIES: A SONNET FOR THE DUKE UNIVERSITY LIBRARY" by Merrill Moore: 3748
ONONDAGA COUNTY, New York:
　Syracuse: 5626
ONSLOW COUNTY, North Carolina: 1657
　Disciples of Christ: 5554
　Land: 360
　　Purchases and sales: 5761
　Land deeds and indentures: 5761
　Cities and towns:
　　Catherine Lake: 1580, 5910
　　Haw Branch: 5774
ONSLOW COUNTY, North Carolina:
　Palo Alto: 1252, 2012
ONTARIO, Canada:
　Toronto: 3949
ONTARIO COUNTY, New York:
　Bristol: 2091
　Canandaigua: 2193, 2250, 2587, 2690
　Phelps: 782
OPERA: 4986
　see also COMIC OPERA
　North Carolina:
　　Winston-Salem: 4080
OPHIR, North Carolina: 1417
OPHTHALMIA: see DISEASES--Ophthalmia
OPIUM:
　Medicinal use: 3246
　Civil War: 3741
　Use during the War of 1812: 1595
OPIUM TRADE--India: 2756
OPIUM WAR (First, 1840-1842): 2641
OPIUM WAR (Second, 1856-1860): 2265
OPPOSSUM TROT, North Carolina: 80
OPPORTUNITY AND THEODORE ROOSEVELT: 1424
OPTICAL SURGERY:
　Maryland--Baltimore: 2830
　North Carolina: 661
OPTICAL WORKERS: see LABOR UNIONS--Optical and instrument workers
ORAL HISTORY: 83
ORANGE, New York--Legal affairs: 4645
ORANGE, Virginia:
　Confederate Army camp life: 4749
ORANGE COUNTY, Indiana:
　Orleans: 2954
ORANGE COUNTY, New York:
　Goshen: 3815
　West Point: 2968
ORANGE COUNTY, North Carolina:
　1700s-1800s: 4507
　1700s-1900s: 1256, 1270, 2588, 3247, 4078
　1800s: 1604, 3515, 5819
　　1830s: 2622, 3337
　　1850s: 436, 1613
　　1860s: 1151
　　1870s: 1151

ORANGE COUNTY, North Carolina (Continued):
　Description and travel: 2248
　Farming: 440
　Land: 5390
　Land deeds and indentures: 912, 5109, 5341
　Peace societies: 3984
　Schools: 661
　Taxation: 3938
　Cities and towns:
　　Cedar Grove: 3351, 5205
　　Chapel Hill: see CHAPEL HILL, North Carolina
　　Eno: 5264
　　Hillsborough: see HILLSBOROUGH, North Carolina
　　Mason Hall: 3300
　　South Lowell:
　　　Mercantile accounts: 3140
　　　Schools: 4862
ORANGE COUNTY, Vermont:
　Strafford: 3777
　Thetford: 3218
　Williamstown: 4888
ORANGE COUNTY, Virginia: 322, 348
　Gordonsville: 154
　　Civil War: 390
　　Merchants: 4710
　"Montpelier": 3455
　Orange Court House: see ORANGE COURT HOUSE, Virginia
　Stanardsville: 1401
ORANGE AND ALEXANDRIA RAILROAD: 4852
ORANGE COURT HOUSE, Virginia: 1590, 4521
　Civil War: 677, 1859
　　see also CIVIL WAR--CAMPAIGNS, BATTLES, AND MILITARY ACTIONS--Virginia--Orange Court House
ORANGE CROPS:
　Florida: 1575
ORANGE PEACE SOCIETY, Orange County, North Carolina: 3984, 5905
ORANGE SOCIETY (Ireland): 4605
ORANGEBURG, South Carolina: 1480, 2814, 3278, 5114
　Land: 5388
　Negro policemen: 3037
　Schools: 501
ORANGEBURG COUNTY, South Carolina:
　Branchville: 1749, 2213
　Eutaw: 4033
　Orangeburg: see ORANGEBURG, South Carolina
　Orangeburg Court House: 3386
ORANGEBURG COURT HOUSE, South Carolina: 3386
ORANGEBURG DISTRICT, South Carolina: 2960, 4583
　Estates--Administration and settlement: 5015
　Land--Purchases and sales: 5015
　Mercantile accounts: 4583
ORANGEVILLE, New York:
　Description: 2677
ORANGEVILLE, Texas: 4158
ORCHARDS:
　see also FRUIT CULTURE
　North Carolina:
　　Franklin County: 5087
　　Value: 5779
ORDER OF GOOD SAMARITANS: 4806
ORDER OF RAILROAD TELEGRAPHERS: 3985
　N and W System: 3986
ORDER OF UNION DEMOCRACY: 4669
ORDERS: see COURTS--Orders; and Orders as subheading under names of armies and navies
THE ORDINANCE OF CONFESSION by William Gresley: 2203
ORDNANCE:
　see also CIVIL WAR--Ordnance; FIREARMS; GUN BARRELS; MACHINE GUNS; and Ordnance as subheading under names of armies and navies

ORDNANCE (Continued):
　Firing devices -- Inventions: 3424
　Great Britain: 1114
　South Carolina: 5114
　Thailand: 5238
ORDNANCE, Bureau of: see UNITED STATES--GOVERNMENT AGENCIES AND OFFICIALS--Bureau of Ordnance
L'ORDRE DE L'ANNONCIADE CÉLESTE: 4046
ORDWAY, Arthur: 3238
OREGON:
　see also WESTERN STATES
　Annexation: 1424, 3325
　　see also OREGON BOUNDARY DISPUTE
　Business affairs--Roseburg: 3518
　Commodity prices: 3518
　Livestock:
　　Prices: 3255
　　Supply and demand: 3255
　Lumbering--Ellensburg: 5938
　Militia: 3899
　Salmon canning industry: Ellensburg: 5938
　Universities and colleges: see UNIVERSITY OF OREGON
OREGON BOUNDARY DISPUTE: 2193, 3507, 3671, 4169, 4424, 4813
OREGON MOUNTED VOLUNTEERS:
　Medical and sanitary affairs: 3899
ORFORD, Horatio William Walpole, Fourth Earl of: 1911
ORFORD, Robert Walpole, First Earl of: 5532
ORGAN, A. M.: 2376
ORGANIZATION: see as subheading under names of armies
ORIEL COLLEGE: see OXFORD UNIVERSITY--Oriel College
ORIENT: see FAR EAST
ORIENTAL LANGUAGES AND LITERATURE: 4005
ORIGINAL FREE WILL BAPTIST CHURCH OF NORTH CAROLINA: 3987
　Pitt County: 3988
ORIGINAL SIN (Theology): 1869
ORLANDO, Florida: 1713
ORLEANISTS--Spain: 3238
ORLEANS, Henri Eugène Philippe Louis d', Duc d'Aumale: 1875
ORLEANS, Philippe Albert d', Comte de Paris: 2306
ORLÉANS, Robert Philippe Louis Eugène Ferdinand d', Duc de Chartres: 3990
ORLEANS, Indiana: 2954
ORLEANS PARISH, Louisiana:
　Tchoupetoulas: 1574
ORME, Aquilla Johns, Sr.: 3991
ORME, Aquilla Johns, Jr.: 3991
ORME, William: 2146
ORME FAMILY (Georgia): 3991
ORMOND, William: 3992
ÖRNE, Anders: 3964
ORNITHOLOGY: see BIRDS
OROQUIETA, Mindanao, Philippine Islands:
　Spanish-American War: 5844
ORPHAN ASYLUM SOCIETY OF FAYETTEVILLE, North Carolina: 3873
ORPHANAGES:
　Georgia: 2786
　Maryland: 3026
　North Carolina: 2041
　　Charlotte: 4918, 5298
　　Fayetteville: 3873
　　Thomasville: 2874
　United States: 1588
　Virginia:
　　Luray: 461, 574
　　Rustburg--For Negroes: 2799
ORPHANS:
　see also GUARDIANSHIP
　French--Adoption by United States Army squadrons: 5419
　Georgia: 5426
　Kentucky: 5426
　Louisiana: 5426

ORPHANS (Continued):
   Serbian: 4080
   Tennessee: 5426
   United States: 1589
   Virginia: 117
   Washington, D.C.: 5426
ORPHANS' COURTS: see COURTS--
   Orphans' courts
ORR, James Lawrence: 3993, 4193, 5280
ORR, John M.: 3994
ORRVILLE, Alabama: 223
ORRVILLE, Ohio: 4728
ORWIGSBURG, Pennsylvania:
   Physicians: 3754
OSAGE INDIANS: 2301, 2850, 4353
OSAGE ORANGE TREES--Virginia: 33
OSBORN, George: 3995
OSBORN, Henry Fairfield: 2871
OSBORN, N. M., Jr.: 4928
OSBORNE, Adeline (West Virginia): 4029
OSBORNE, Adlai: 5457
OSBORNE, Edwin Augustus: 4918, 5457
OSBORNE, Francis Irwin: 5457
OSBORNE, Henry: 4029
OSBORNE, John D.: 4616
OSBORNE, John R.: 3996
OSBORNE, Mary: 2262
OSBORNE (N. M.) & COMPANY: 388
OSBORNE, Lord Sydney Godolphin: 2148
OSBORNE, Thomas, Fourth Duke of
   Leeds: 3997
OSBORNE, Thomas D.: 2509
OSBURN, Adeline (Maryland): 3998
OSBURN FAMILY (Maryland): 3998
OSCEOLA, North Carolina: 4197
OSCEOLA (brig): 4881
OSGOOD, Charles: 4000
OSGOOD, Frances Sargent (Locke): 3999
OSGOOD (JAMES R.) & CO.: 4738
OSGOOD, Margaret M.: 2449
OSGOOD, Stephen: 4000
OSGOOD, Thaddeus: 3791
OSGOOD, Warren: 4000
O'SHAUGHNESSY, Arthur William
   Edgar: 4001
OSKALOOSA, Iowa: 3170
OSLER, William: 5722
OSMAN DIGNA (Ruler of Sudan): 5835
OSNABURG: 2165
OSSIPEE (warship): 636
OSTERHOUSE, R. W.: 4188
OSWEGO COUNTY, New York:
   Fulton: 929
   Pulaski: 5715
   Volney: 2089
OSWEGO STARCH COMPANY: 388
OTEY, John Marshall: 4002
OTEY, Peter Johnston: 4003
OTHO I. SMITH AND SON: 4901
OTIS, Elwell Stephen: 4656
OTSEGO COUNTY, New York: 1325
OTT, John: 4072, 4344
OTTAWA, Canada: 896
OTTAWA, Illinois--Churches: 993
"OTTER OAKS," Campbell County,
   Virginia: 2510
OTTOMAN EMPIRE--Tariff rates: 3183
OTTUMWA, Iowa: 1984
OTTWELL, Joshua R.: 4004
OUACHITA COLLEGE, Arkadelphia,
   Arkansas: 1154
OUACHITA PARISH, Louisiana:
   Chapel Hill--Civil War: 3071
OUDH, Nabob of: see VIZRI ALI, Nabob
   of Oudh
OUDH, India: 3315, 5797
   Annexation (1856): 4549
   British troops at (1801): 5639
OULD, Robert: 905
OULTON BROAD, England: 578
OUNALASKA, Alaska: 2881
OUR AMERICAN PUBLIC SCHOOLS by B. M.
   Farley: 1758
"OUR AMERICAN SCHOOLS" (radio
   programs): 1758
OURSLER, Charles Fulton: 3797

OUSELEY, Sir Gore, First Baronet: 4005
OUTER SPACE EXPLORATION: see SPACE
   EXPLORATION
OUTLAND, Julia Wheeler (Copeland): 4006
OUTRAM, Sir James: 4097
OUTTERBRIDGE, S. W.: 435
OVERALL, John: 917
OVERBROOK, Pennsylvania: 5940
OVERCASH, Joseph: 4007
OVERLAND MAIL (1858): 1548
OVERMAN, Lee Slater: 958, 1364, 2188, 4918
OVERMAN, Margaret: 2188
OVERSEERS: 5940
   see also PUBLIC WELFARE--Overseers;
   ROADS--Overseers
   Contracts:
     South Carolina: 2599, 4214
   Subdivided by place:
     Georgia: 2020, 2903, 5576
       Oglethorpe County: 5162
     Maryland: 2267, 5193
     Mississippi: 3956
     North Carolina: 1602, 3176
       Belford: 5924
     South Carolina: 2290
     Southern States: 5940
     Virginia: 3362
       Mecklenburg County: 3809
OVERTON, D. C.: 2363
OVERTON, Mary: 2363
OVERTOUN, John Campbell White, First
   Baron: 5014
OWEN, Benjamin Rush: 872
OWEN, D. B.: 2712
OWEN, Daniel W.: 2712
OWEN, F. C.: 2712
OWEN, Sir Francis Philip Cunliffe-: 5553
OWEN, John: 872
OWEN, John (1825-1889): 872
OWEN, Loulie Latimer: 2402
OWEN, Sir Richard: 747
OWEN, Robert Dale: 4770
OWEN, Thomas: 872
OWEN, Thomas McAdory: 690, 4008
OWEN, W. H.: 5150
OWEN FAMILY: 872
OWEN MEMORIAL FUND: 2712
OWENSON, Sydney: 2146
OWSLEY, William: 3325
OWST, Gerald Robert: 5727
OXENBRIDGE, William John Monson,
   First Viscount: 3722
OXFORD, A. B.: 3324
OXFORD, Bishop of: see names of
   specific bishops, e.g. MOSS,
   Charles; WILBERFORCE, Samuel
OXFORD, James: 3324
OXFORD, Rebecca Mariah: 3324
OXFORD, Sion Harrington: 3324
OXFORD, William C.: 3324
OXFORD, England: 774, 1214, 3798, 4628, 4632, 5567, 5725
   see also OXFORD UNIVERSITY
OXFORD, Georgia: 1703
   see also EMORY UNIVERSITY
OXFORD, Mississippi: 3076, 5971
   see also UNIVERSITY OF MISSISSIPPI
   Literary affairs: 1771
   Post Office: 4379
OXFORD, North Carolina:
   1700s-1800s: 5964
   1700s-1900s: 1361
   1800s: 68, 1306, 2359, 2455, 5793
   1800s-1900s: 2833, 3091, 5741
   1900s: 4641, 5049
   see also OXFORD FEMALE COLLEGE
   Description: 4849
   Mercantile accounts: 5685
   Schools: 76, 214, 5709
     Normal schools: 435
     Students and student life: 2192
   Teaching: 2654
OXFORD, Ohio: see MIAMI UNIVERSITY

OXFORD ACADEMY, Oxford, North
   Carolina: 214
OXFORD AND ASQUITH, Herbert Henry
   Asquith, First Earl of: 233, 442, 663, 4520
OXFORD CLASSICAL AND GRAMMAR SCHOOL,
   Oxford, North Carolina: 2192
OXFORD EAGLE (publication): 1771
OXFORD FEMALE COLLEGE, Oxford, North
   Carolina: 484, 4506
OXFORD HIGH SCHOOL, Oxford, North
   Carolina: 76
OXFORD IRON WORKS, Campbell County,
   Virginia: 558
OXFORD MOVEMENT:
   Great Britain: 43, 306
     Political aspects: 3715
   Influence in the United States: 128
OXFORD UNIVERSITY, Oxford, England: 43, 306, 1173, 2102, 5637, 5736
   Academic costume: 1173
   Bodleian Library: 3946
   Commencement exercises: 3798
   Effects of World War I on: 473
   Elections of chancellors: 2201, 3798
   Removal of restrictions for
     Dissenters: 2149
   Students and student life: 43, 449
   Subdivided by college:
     All Souls College: 3722
     Christ Church College: 14
     Lincoln College: 5647
     Magdalen College: 3189
     Oriel College: 2612
     Wadham College: 306
"OXFORD UNIVERSITY" by William Combe: 1173
OXFORDSHIRE, England:
   Idbury: 4514
   Oxford: see OXFORD, England
OYSTER BAY, New York: 4560
OYSTER-CULTURE:
   Virginia: 1791
OZARK, Arkansas: 2123

P

P. HARRISON & CO.: 2392
P. J. WILLIS AND BROTHERS, Galveston, Texas: 3534
P. T. BARNUM'S CIRCUS: 1748
P. W. BROWN (firm): see B. M. SELBY AND P. W. BROWN
PACE, Wesley W.: 4009
PACE, William A.: 4010
PACIFIC COAST STATES: see WESTERN STATES
PACIFIC MAIL STEAMSHIP COMPANY: 2241
PACK (ANDERSON) AND _____ VAWTER (firm): 4011
PACKAGING MACHINERY:
  North Carolina: 5923
PACKARD, Joseph: 4173
PACKER, Francis Herman: 5014
PACKET BOATS:
  see also TRAVEL--Packet boats
  English Channel: 4719
  Virginia: 33
  West Virginia--Kanawha River: 2890
PACKINGHOUSE WORKERS: see UNITED CANNERY, AGRICULTURE, PACKING AND ALLIED WORKERS OF AMERICA; UNITED PACKINGHOUSE WORKERS OF AMERICA
PACOLET, South Carolina: 2477
PADUCAH, Illinois:
  Civil War:
    see also CIVIL WAR--CAMPAIGNS, BATTLES, AND MILITARY ACTIONS--Illinois--Paducah
  Naval base: 4662
PADUCAH, Kentucky: 1356
PAGE, Ann Randolph (Meade): 128
PAGE, Anne Seddon (Bruce): 4020
PAGE, Bettie E.: 4022
PAGE, Curtis Hidden: 4012
PAGE, Elizabeth Burwell (Nelson): 4020
PAGE, Elizabeth (Nelson) (b. 1770): 4013
PAGE, Florence (Lathrop) Field: 4020
PAGE, Francis: 4599
PAGE, Harriet (Moore): 4286
PAGE, Henry A.: 4775
PAGE, James Jellis: 4014
PAGE, Jane Francis (Walker): 4490
PAGE, John (1744-1808): 581, 4014, 4015
PAGE, Mrs. John: 3809
PAGE, John M. (former slave): 128
PAGE, Leigh R.: 2517
PAGE, Matthew: 128
PAGE, P. A.: 4016
PAGE, R. C. M.: 4014
PAGE, Richard Lucian: 4017
PAGE, Robert M. (former slave): 128
PAGE, Robert Newton (1859-1933): 4018
PAGE, Rosewell: 4020
PAGE, Sarah Walker: 128
PAGE, Sir Thomas Hyde (1746-1821): 5330
PAGE, Thomas Jefferson (1808-1900): 4013, 4019

PAGE, Thomas Nelson (1853-1922): 361, 581, 2449, 3265, 4020
PAGE, Virginia N.: 4014
PAGE, Walter Hines: 706, 2400, 2449, 4018, 4021, 4559
PAGE, Yelverton Peyton: 4022
PAGE FAMILY (Virginia): 128, 2776, 4013, 4019, 4020
PAGE & CO.: see DOUBLEDAY, PAGE & CO.
PAGE COUNTY, Virginia: 2975
  Iron industry: 522
  Cities and towns:
    Luray: 461, 3084, 5581
      Baptist churches: 574
      Business expansion: 574
      Municipal government: 574
      Teaching: 2340
PAGE COURIER (newspaper): 461
PAGEOT, Alphonse J. Y.: 1424
PAGET, Lord Alfred Henry: 3238
PAGET, Sir Edward: 4023
PAGET, Henry William, First Marquis of Anglesey: 4024, 5637
PAGET, John: 4650
PAGETT FAMILY (Virginia): 2794
PAHLEVI, Mohammed Reza: 83
PAINE, Eleazer A.: 5784
PAINE, Gregory Lansing: 102
PAINE, Thomas (1737-1809): 369, 779, 4025, 4625
PAINE (THOMAS) MONUMENT: 4025
PAINT: see WHITEWASH
PAINT ROCK, Tennessee: 3692
PAINT TRADE--Connecticut: 2273
PAINTER, Franklin Verzelius Newton: 2449
PAINTERS (artists): see ART AND ARTISTS
PAINTERS (workers): see BROTHERHOOD OF PAINTERS, DECORATORS AND PAPERHANGERS OF AMERICA
PAINTINGS:
  see also ART AND ARTISTS; PORTRAITS; WATERCOLORS
  Prices: 4575
  Exhibitions--Ireland: 3567
  Restoration: 2969
  Subdivided by place:
    Great Britain: 2718, 4575
    South Carolina: 4296
    United States: 1665
PAISLEY, Juliana: 2050
PAKINGTON, John Somerset, First Baron Hampton: 1087, 4026
PALACES:
  Cuba: 4227
  Germany--Berlin: 2139
  North Carolina--New Bern: 5352
"THE PALADINS OF SOUTH CAROLINA" by James Henry Rice: 4453
PALATKA, Florida: 807
  Description: 3277
PALESTINE: 4027
  Description and travel:
    1800s: 5524
    1920s: 2934, 4192
  Flowers: 1834
  Jewish immigration: see ZIONISM
  Missions and missionaries: 1070
PALGRAVE, Sir Reginald Francis Douce: 4028
PALIN, John: 5457
PALK, Lawrence William, Third Baron Haldon: 345
PALL MALL GAZETTE (British newspaper): 5262
PALM BEACH COUNTY, Florida:
  West Palm Beach: 3
PALMA, Ricardo: 4155
PALMER, Adeline (Osborne): 4029
PALMER, Archibald W.: 4030
PALMER, Benjamin Morgan (1781-1847): 3142
PALMER, Benjamin Morgan (1818-1902): 2449, 4031
PALMER, Charles (Ohio): 4032
PALMER, Charles (Virginia): 4038

PALMER, Elizabeth: 3783
PALMER, Frederick: 1424
PALMER, Innis Newton: 5543
PALMER, John: 196
PALMER, John C. (Union soldier): 5975
PALMER, John S. (Confederate captain): 4033
PALMER, John Williamson (1825-1906): 103
PALMER, Joseph: 4034
PALMER, Robert: 4035
PALMER, Roundell, First Earl of Selborne: 4036, 4097
PALMER, William (1803-1885): 306
PALMER, William Kimberley (Massachusetts): 4037
PALMER, William P. (Virginia): 4038
PALMER FAMILY (New Hampshire): 4039
PALMER FAMILY (South Carolina or Tennessee): 718
PALMER, MACKILLOP, DENT & CO.: 2755
PALMER METHOD OF BUSINESS WRITING: 3680
PALMERSTON, Henry John Temple, Third Viscount: 1632, 1640, 1775, 2836, 3067, 3472, 4024, 4520, 4605, 5026, 5038, 5222
PALMERSTON (British transport): 153
PALMERSTON HOUSE, Ireland: 587
PALMES, George F.: 4040
PALMES, Mary: 4040
PALMES & LYON, Savannah, Georgia (firm): 4040
PALMETTO FLAG: 2449
PALMETTO GUARD (South Carolina): 4041
  Election of officers: 2610
PALMETTO HUSSARS (South Carolina): 1016
PALMETTO WOOD--Papermaking: 50
PALMYRA, Missouri: 303
  Civil War: 1683
  Prisons: 1184
PALMYRA, Virginia: 5147
PALO ALTO, North Carolina: 1252, 2012
PAMLICO BAPTIST ASSOCIATION (North Carolina): 320
PAMLICO DISTRICT, North Carolina: 1871
PAMLICO RIVER (North Carolina):
  Steamboat operators: 3827
PAMLICO SOUND, North Carolina: see CIVIL WAR--CAMPAIGNS, BATTLES, AND MILITARY ACTIONS--North Carolina--Pamlico Sound
PANACEA SPRINGS, North Carolina: 2399
PANAMA:
  Description and travel: 1115
  Diseases--Yellow fever: 3004
PANAMA CANAL: 4560
  Description and travel: 5786
PANAMA CONGRESS: 4155, 4531
PANAMA-PACIFIC INTERNATIONAL EXPOSITION, San Francisco, California: 4042, 4511, 5252
PAN-AMERICAN EXPLORING COMPANY: 4552
PANCOAST, Joseph: 5982
PANGOA RIVER (Bolivia?): 4155
PANIC OF 1819: 1086, 4924
  Massachusetts: 2677
  North Carolina: 4080
  Pennsylvania--Philadelphia: 3485
  South Carolina: 4269
    Charleston: 3485
  Virginia: 2369, 2633
PANIC OF 1837: 872, 1335, 1762, 1985, 3179, 3415, 4924, 4968, 5275
  Alabama: 1084, 5593
  Georgia: 311
  New York: 730
  Ohio: 5342
  Virginia: 1512
PANIC OF 1857: 2469, 2695, 3012, 3053, 3415, 5498, 5569
  Alabama: 5593
  New York: 2250, 2587
  Ohio: 5342
  Virginia: 4720
PANIC OF 1873--West Virginia: 4774

PANKEY FAMILY (Virginia): 4043
PANNILL, Samuel: 2131
PANOLA, Mississippi:
  Mercantile accounts: 138
PANTEGO, North Carolina:
  Agricultural organizations: 1323
  Lumber trade: 4471
PANTEGO CIRCUIT, Methodist
  churches: 3646
PANTHER CREEK, North Carolina: 2914,
  3003, 3766
PANTHERS--South Carolina: 5825
PAPER: see CIVIL WAR--CIVILIAN
  LIFE--Scarcity of paper; STATIONERY
PAPER MONEY: 1339
  see also CURRENCY; MONEY
  Redemption--United States: 5548
PAPER TRADE--North Carolina: 3416
PAPER WORKERS: see LABOR UNIONS--
  Paper workers
PAPERS WORKERS ORGANIZING COMMITTEE:
  5486
PAPERHANGERS: see BROTHERHOOD OF
  PAINTERS, DECORATORS AND
  PAPERHANGERS OF AMERICA
PAPERMAKING:
  see also PULP AND PAPER INDUSTRY
  From palmetto wood: 50
PARADES:
  Locofoco Party in Maryland: 5324
  Military: see Inspections and
    reviews as subheading under names
    of armies
PARAGUA, Island of--Colonization:
  4179
PARAMARIBO, Surinam: 2403
PARDEE, Henry Clay: 4044
PARDO Y ALIAGA, Felipe: 4155
PARDONS:
  see also AMNESTY; CIVIL WAR--
    LOYALTY OATHS; PRESIDENTIAL
    PARDONS
  Georgia: 5189
  South Carolina: 5930
PARENTS:
  see also DEPENDENTS; FAMILY LIFE;
    MOTHERS; STUDENTS AND STUDENT
    LIFE--Parents' letters
  Education: 5022
PARES, Richard: 2148
PARIS, Philippe Albert d'Orleans,
  Comte de: 2306
PARIS, France: 2701
  1600s: 3271
  1700s: 321, 3644
  1700s-1800s: 5228
  1800s: 1242, 2640, 3077, 5731
  1820s: 3072
  1830s: 5277
  1850s: 526, 4337
  1860s: 4579
  1800s-1900s: 65
  1900s: 2057, 2445, 3097, 4657,
    5656
  Americans in Paris: 1888
  Bibliothèque Nationale: 4045
  British embassy in: 1875, 2149,
    3472
  Commune of 1871: 3472
  Convent de L'Annociades: 4046
  Description:
    1780s: 4625
    1800s:
      1820s: 2077
      1850s: 365, 4616
      1890s: 3188
      1900s: 5930
    Foreign trade: 948
    German occupation: 1424
    Literary interests: 2764
    Medical education: 4231
    Newspapers:
      American correspondents: 1424
    Social life and customs:
      1700s: 5038
      1800s: 5569
      1820s: 2870
      1860s: 1424

PARIS, France:
  Social life and customs (Continued):
    1900s:
      1920s: 3710
      1930s: 5968
  United States embassy in:
    1800s: 1302, 2583, 4490
    1900s: 1424
  Universities and colleges: see
    L'ÉCOLE DES PONTS ET CHAUSSÉES;
    UNIVERSITY OF PARIS
  Visit to: 157
PARIS, Texas: 592, 3590
  Description: 155
PARIS, Virginia--Merchants: 4743
PARIS, Treaty of (1783): see TREATY
  OF PARIS
PARIS COMMUNE: see COMMUNE OF 1871
PARIS EXPOSITION OF 1878: 5970
PARIS EXPOSITION OF 1900: 196
PARISH RATES--Great Britain: 3498
PARK, Emily A.: 3262
PARK, John W.: 4887
PARK COUNTY, Wyoming--Cody: 1140
PARK HATCH, England: 2077
PARKE, Ernest: 735
PARKE, Isaac: 5242
PARKER, General _____: 5848
PARKER, A. J.: 4047
PARKER, Alton Brooks: 4048
PARKER, Benjamin J.: 4047
PARKER, Caleb D.: 4049
PARKER (ELIAS), Petersburg, Virginia
  (firm): 2933
PARKER, Frank: 300
PARKER, James: 76
PARKER, John: 4387
PARKER, John R. (Massachusetts): 4050
PARKER, John William (1792-1870): 4051
PARKER, John William Robinson: 5173
PARKER, Joseph: 5598
PARKER, Junius: 1914
PARKER, Lizzie Nelms (Smith): 4052
PARKER, M. S.: 4053
PARKER, Peter: 4054
PARKER, Richard Elliot: 4531
PARKER, Susan: 4911
PARKER, Theodore: 2449
PARKER, Thomas: 872
PARKER, U.S.S.: 4355
PARKER AND MARSHALL (firm): see
  MARSHALL AND PARKER
PARKER COTTON MILLS COMPANY: 5312
PARKERSBURG, West Virginia: 2016
  Girls' schools and academies: 5194
PARKERSBURG FEMALE SEMINARY,
  Parkersburg, West Virginia: 5194
PARKES, Sir Harry Smith: 4054
PARKHURST, John Gibson: 3479, 4054
PARKING METERS--North Carolina: 2379
PARKS, Alexander, Jr.: 2316, 3832,
  4056
PARKS, Elise: 3832
PARKS, Enos T.: 4057
PARKS, Janette: 4057
PARKS, Joel: 4057
PARKS, John Nadenbousch: 3832
PARKS, Lydia: 4057
PARKS, William: 797
PARKS: see LANDSCAPE GARDENING;
  NATIONAL PARKS AND MONUMENTS
PARLAGHY, Princess Elizabeth Lwoff-:
  see LWOFF-PARLAGHY, Princess
  Elizabeth
PARLIAMENT: see GREAT BRITAIN--
  PARLIAMENT
PARLIAMENTARY ELECTIONS: see CANADA--
  Parliamentary elections; GREAT
  BRITAIN--ELECTIONS
PARLIAMENTARY REFORM: see GREAT
  BRITAIN--PARLIAMENTARY REFORM
PARLIAMENTARY REPRESENTATION by
  David Chadwick: 955
PARMA, New York: 4662
PARMELEE, Samuel Spencer: 4059
PARMELEE, Uriah N., Sr.: 4059
PARMELEE, Uriah N., Jr.: 4059
PARNELL, Charles Stewart: 5872

PARNELL FAMILY (Ireland): 3567
PAROCHIAL SCHOOLS: see SCHOOLS--
  Church schools--Catholic
PARODIES, American: 3284
PARODIES AND IMITATIONS, OLD AND
  NEW: 3503
PAROLES: see CIVIL WAR--PRISONERS
  AND PRISONS--(Confederate or Union
  prisoners)--Paroles
PARRISH, Edward James: 4060
PARRISH, John H.: 4061
PARRISH, Rosa (Bryan): 3395, 4060
PARROTT, Enoch Greenleafe: 4062,
  4986
PARROTT, James B.: 4062
PARROTT, S. H.: 523
PARROTT, Susan Parker: 4062
PARROTT, William S.: 2662
PARRY, Hugh Lloyd: 5553
PARSLEY AND POTTER (firm): see
  POTTER & PARSLEY
"PARSON WEEMS": see WEEMS, Mason
  Locke
PARSONFIELD, Maine: 2865
PARSONS, Charles: 4063
PARSONS, George (British officer):
  3744
PARSONS, George A. (Missouri): 3703
PARSONS, Mary: 4886
PARSONS, Mason: 4064
PARSONS, Mosby Monroe: 4065
PARTIES: see ENTERTAINING
PARTINGTON, Wilfred George: 4066
THE PARTISAN LEADER by
  Nathaniel Beverley Tucker: 5361
PARTISAN RANGERS: 5838
  see also MOSBY'S PARTISAN RANGERS
PARTRIDGE, Alden: 1168, 4067
PARTRIDGE, Benjamin Waring: 4068
PARTRIDGE, John Nathaniel: 4068
PARTRIDGE, Mary (Denham): 4068
PARTRIDGE'S MILITARY ACADEMY,
  Norwich, Vermont, and Middletown,
  Connecticut: 295
PASADENA, California: 4837
PASCAGOULA, Mississippi:
  Harbor improvement: 5425
  Military hospitals: 5517
"A PASQUINADE OF THE THIRTIES" by John
  Lide Wilson: 5074
PASQUOTANK CIRCUIT, Methodist
  churches: 3646
PASQUOTANK COUNTY, North Carolina:
  1577
  Elizabeth City: see ELIZABETH CITY,
    North Carolina
  Nixonton: 3783, 4321
PASSENGER SERVICE: see as subheading
  under specific types of transport,
  e.g. RAILROADS--Passenger service
PASSENGERS: see as subheading under
  specific types of transport, e.g.
  SHIPS--Passengers
PASSFIELD, Sidney James Webb, First
  Baron: 5616
PASSPORTS:
  Confederate States of America:
    1181, 4923, 5193
  Great Britain: 1373
  Spain: 4982
  United States: 5790
PASSWORDS: see CONFEDERATE STATES
  OF AMERICA--NAVY--Passwords
PASTORAL RELATIONS: see as subheading
  under names of specific
  denominations or churches
THE PASTOR'S STORY: 5082
PATAGONIA: 4626
"PATAGONIA BIBLIOGRAFÍA" by W. A.
  Ruysch: 4626
PATAPSCO INSTITUTE, Ellicott's Mills,
  Maryland:
  Students and student life: 3360,
    4022, 5982
PATENT GRANTS--Carolina Province: 202
PATENT MEDICINES: 4462
  see also ADVERTISING--Patent
    medicines; MEDICINE

PATENT MEDICINES (Continued):
    North Carolina: 401, 4154
    Virginia: 401, 3721
PATENT OFFICE BUILDING, Washington, D.C.: 1743
PATENTS:
    Cloth folding machinery:
        Germany: 4807
        United States: 4807
    Cook stoves: 1690
    Cotton gins: 2931
    Cotton press: 3314
    Gate latches: 5839
    Harrows: 5193
    Laws and legislation:
        Canada: 3637
        United States: 5093
    Plows--Steam powered: 5193
    Portable gas generators: 3325
    Railroad car couplings: 3314
    Tobacco machinery: 4079
    United States: 643, 1548, 2172, 2469, 3228, 3314, 3424
    see also UNITED STATES--GOVERNMENT AGENCIES AND OFFICIALS--Patent Office
PATERSON, I. B.: 3183
PATILLO, Henry: 795
PATIÑO, José: 873, 5532
PATMORE, Coventry Kersey Dighton: 2718, 4069
PATRAS (British ship): 4881
PATRICK, Charlotte: 5533
PATRICK, Sarah: 4070
PATRICK, Walter: 4071
PATRICK COUNTY, Virginia: 4131, 5121
    Courts: 1894
        Superior Court clerk: 5031
    Police: 1894
    Cities and towns:
        Patrick Springs: 1410
        Stuart: 5031
PATRICK HENRY MEMORIAL FOUNDATION: 4927
PATRICK SPRINGS, Virginia: 1410
PATRIOTIC SOCIETIES:
    see also COLONIAL DAMES; DAUGHTERS OF THE AMERICAN REVOLUTION; SOCIETY OF THE ARMY OF THE POTOMAC; SOCIETY OF THE CINCINNATI; SONS OF VETERANS; UNITED DAUGHTERS OF THE CONFEDERACY
    South Carolina: 1889
PATRIOTIC STATIONERY:
    Confederate: 651, 1187
PATRIOTISM: 1434, 2863, 3280
PATRIOTS: see AMERICAN REVOLUTION--Patriots
PATROL: see SLAVE PATROL
PATRON AND PLACE-HUNTER: A STUDY OF GEORGE BUBB DODINGTON, LORD MELCOMBE by Lloyd Sanders: 2155
PATRONAGE:
    see also POLITICAL PATRONAGE; POLITICS AND GOVERNMENT--Appointments
    East India Company: 5639
    Great Britain: 2158
PATRONS OF HUSBANDRY: 531, 592
    Alabama: 444
    Georgia:
        Cooperative trade: 2232
    Mississippi: 1506
    North Carolina: 1323, 4072
        Lilesville: 2493
        Raleigh Grange No. 17: 4072
    South Carolina:
        Lancaster County: 4530
        Richland County: 4072
    Southern States: 4434
    Virginia: 1485
PATTEE, Fred Lewis: 102
PATTEN, Jean Maury (Coyle): 4073
PATTEN, John (d. 1787): 5457
PATTEN, John Wilson: 1087
PATTEN, Mary Elizabeth: 4074
PATTEN'S HOME, North Carolina: 126

PATTERNS (clothing): 4589
    see also EMBROIDERY; SEWING; TAILORING
    North Carolina: 1407
PATTERSON, Caroline Finley: 4080
PATTERSON, Daniel: 4082
PATTERSON, Duncan (d. 1793): 4082
PATTERSON, Duncan (1800s): 4082
PATTERSON, Elizabeth: 1424
PATTERSON, George (grandmaster of the Freemasons): 1899
PATTERSON, George B. (Confederate soldier): 4998
PATTERSON, Isabel: 3415
PATTERSON, J. A.: 4075
PATTERSON, James: 4075
PATTERSON, James R.: 4076
PATTERSON, Jesse Lindsay: 4080
PATTERSON, John: 4083
PATTERSON, John E. (Army physician): 4076
PATTERSON, John Hilary: 4083
PATTERSON, Lucy Bramlette (Patterson): 4080, 4849
PATTERSON, Margaret (Morehead): 4079
PATTERSON, Olivia E.: 4998
PATTERSON, Richard Cunningham, Jr. (1912-1966): 5252
PATTERSON, Robert (1792-1881): 395, 4077, 5517
PATTERSON, Robert Donnell: 4078
PATTERSON, Rufus Lenoir (1830-1879): 4080
PATTERSON, Rufus Lenoir (1872-1945): 4079
PATTERSON, Rufus T.: 4080
PATTERSON, Samuel Finley: 3176, 4080
PATTERSON, William (1752-1835): 4081
PATTERSON FAMILY: 4998
PATTERSON FAMILY (Alabama): 4083
PATTERSON FAMILY (North Carolina): 4082, 4083
    Genealogy: 4078
PATTERSON FAMILY (South Carolina): 4083
PATTERSON FAMILY (Tennessee): 4083
PATTERSON CUP (Literary award): 4080
PATTISON, Jacob: 4084
PATTON, Frances MacRae (Gray): 4085
PATTON, J. Desha: 4086
PATTON, John Mercer: 872
PATTON, Robert M.: 249
PATTON, Sue Snowdon: 4086
PATTON, W.: 4188
PATTONSBURG, Virginia: 2454
PAUL V, Pope: 5468
PAUL, Charles Rodman: 4087
PAUL, Dan M.: 2581
PAUL JONES, U.S.S.: 5649
PAULDING, Holmes Offley: 2849
PAULDING, James Kirke: 1472, 4088
PAULDING COUNTY, Georgia:
    Brownsville: 3614
PAUNCEFOTE, Julian, First Baron Pauncefote: 3022, 4089
PAUP, John W.: 2517
PAUPERS: see POOR
PAUSANIAS, King of Sparta: 2736
PAVEMENTS, Vulcanite:
    Georgia: 4966
PAW PAW, Kentucky:
    Lumber trade: 4090
PAW PAW, Michigan:
    Description: 5747
PAW PAW LUMBER COMPANY, Paw Paw, Kentucky: 4090
PAWLING, New York: 3975
PAWTUCKET, Rhode Island: 251
PAWTUXET UNION ACADEMY, Rhode Island: 4907
PAXSON, B. H.: 4091
PAY: see WAGES AND SALARIES; and Pay as subheading under names of armies and navies
PAYMASTERS: see as subheading under names of armies
PAYNE, Dorothea: 2326, 3455, 3612

PAYNE, Edwin B.: 5502
PAYNE, James E.: 1200
PAYNE, John Howard (1791-1852): 2326, 4092
PAYNE, John Willett (1752-1803): 4093
PAYNE UNIVERSITY, Selma, Alabama: 3712
PAYROLL DEDUCTION PLAN (1940s): 341
PAYROLLS: see WAGES AND SALARIES; and Payrolls as subheading under specific businesses and industries, e.g. COPPER MINING--Payrolls
PAYTON, Colonel _____ (Confederate): 4032
PAYTON, Boyd Ellsworth: 4094, 5486
PAZ SOLDAN, Carlos: 4155
PEA RIDGE, Arkansas: see CIVIL WAR--CAMPAIGNS, BATTLES, AND MILITARY ACTIONS--Arkansas--Pea Ridge
PEABODY, Elizabeth (Palmer): 3783
PEABODY, Elizabeth Palmer (1804-1894): 4095
PEABODY, George (1795-1869): 4478
PEABODY, George Foster (1852-1938): 5572
PEABODY, Herbert C.: 3196
PEABODY, Mary Ann: 4095
PEABODY, Mary Ann Tyler: 4133
PEABODY, Mary Tyler: 3295, 4095
PEABODY, Nathaniel: 3783
PEABODY, Sophia: 4095
PEACE, Berta: 4096
PEACE FAMILY (Virginia): 4096
PEACE:
    see also HAGUE PEACE CONFERENCE; HAMPTON ROADS PEACE CONFERENCE; VERSAILLES PEACE CONFERENCE
    1800s: 4164
    1900s: 83, 233, 1758, 3383, 4948, 5779
PEACE COLLEGE, Raleigh, North Carolina: 4373, 4897, 5962
PEACE CONVENTION (Washington, D.C., 1861): 4490, 4616
"PEACE HILL," Virginia (plantation): 5751
PEACE INSTITUTE, Raleigh, North Carolina: see PEACE COLLEGE
PEACE MOVEMENT: see CIVIL WAR--PEACE MOVEMENT; INTERNATIONAL PEACE MOVEMENT; VIETNAMESE WAR--Peace movement
PEACE NEGOTIATIONS: see VERSAILLES PEACE CONFERENCE; and Peace negotiations as subheading under names of wars, e.g. AMERICAN REVOLUTION--Peace negotiations
PEACE PROSPECTS:
    1812--Between Persia and Russia: 4005
    1860s: see CIVIL WAR--PEACE PROSPECTS
PEACE RUMORS: see CIVIL WAR--PEACE RUMORS; WORLD WAR II --Peace rumors
PEACE SETTLEMENT: see MAHRATTA WAR--Peace settlement; MYSORE WAR--Peace settlement
PEACE SOCIETIES:
    see also AMERICAN PEACE SOCIETY; LEAGUE OF NATIONS; LEAGUE TO ENFORCE PEACE; NATIONAL PEACE COUNCIL; UNITED CHRISTIAN PETITION MOVEMENT
    North Carolina: 1336
    Orange County: 3984
    Vermont--Rupert: 2848
PEACE SOCIETY, Rupert, Vermont: 2848
PEACE TERMS: see CIVIL WAR--PEACE TERMS
PEACE TREATIES: see names of specific peace treaties, e.g. TREATY OF GUADALUPE HIDALGO; TREATY OF PARIS; VERSAILLES TREATY
PEACHES--Georgia: 1397

PEACHTREE CREEK, Georgia: see
    CIVIL WAR--CAMPAIGNS, BATTLES,
    AND MILITARY ACTIONS--Georgia--
    Peachtree Creek
PEACOCK, Sir Barnes: 4097
PEACOCK, Dred: 4098, 4425
PEACOCK, Elizabeth Mary: 4097
PEACOCK, Emily: 4097
PEACOCK, Frank: 4097
PEACOCK, John R.: 4098, 5452
PEACOCK, Thomas Love: 4770
PEACOCK, William A.: 1432
PEACOCK MOTION PICTURE CORPORATION: 5252
PEAKE, James B.: 4099
PEAL, Eli: 4849
PEALE, Rembrandt: 581
PEARCE, John Hillard: 4100
PEARCE, John Jamison: 3770
PEARCE, Nathan: 4517
PEARCE, Oliver: 4517
PEARCE, Polly (West): 4517
PEARCE FAMILY (North Carolina): 3873, 4517
PEARL, H.M.S.: 2296, 3744
PEARL RIVER (Mississippi Territory): 3041
PEARSALL COMMITTEE (North Carolina): 4724
PEARSON, I. B.: 4726
PEARSON, Josephine Anderson: 4101
PEARSON, Sir Richard: 4102
PEARSON, Richmond (1852-1907): 5457
PEARSON, Richmond Mumford (1805-1878): 4103
PEARSON, W. S.: 2111
PEARSON, William L.: 4101
PEARSON FAMILY (Arkansas): 4894
PEARSON FAMILY (Great Britain): 4894
PEARSON FAMILY (North Carolina): 761, 4894
PEARSON FAMILY (Tennessee): 4101, 4894
PEARSON FAMILY (Virginia): 4894
PEARY, Robert Edwin: 4556
PEAS TRADE:
    see also BLACK-EYED PEAS TRADE
    Virginia--Suffolk: 1838
PEASANTRY:
    Estonia: 2139
    France: 4348
    Prussia: 2139
    Russia: 2139
    Scotland: 4913
PEASE, Henry: 4104
PEASE, Joseph A.: 67
PEASE, Mary: 3999
PEATSWOOD, England: 5394
PECK, David: 4105
PECK, Edwin: 5593
PECK, Elijah Wolsey: 4105
PECK, Martin L.: 4106
PECK, Mary Eliza: 5593
PECK, Samuel Minturn: 2449
PECK, Sophia: 5593
PECK, William: 5593
PECULATION: see EMBEZZLEMENT
PEDDLERS AND PEDDLING:
    Southern States: 3196
PEDEN & KELLY, Wilkesboro, North Carolina (firm): 4107
PEDLAR'S HILL, North Carolina: 5084
PEDRICK, Benjamin: 4108
PEDRICK, John C.: 4109
PEDRICK, Mary A.: 4108
PEDRICK, Nelson: 4108
PEDRICK, William: 4108
PEDRO II, Emperor of Brazil: 4876
PEE DEE CIRCUIT, North Carolina: 1738
PEE DEE RIVER (North Carolina): 4918
PEE DEE RIVER (South Carolina): 565
PEEBLES, Anne Lee: 4112
PEEBLES, Helena Stockton: 4112
PEEBLES, John F.: 4112
PEEBLES, Sallie Sue (Ellis): 4111
PEEBLES FAMILY (Virginia): 4112
PEED, John: 4110
PEEKSKILL, New York: 4343

PEEL, Sir Robert, Second Baronet (1788-1850): 5, 537, 1911, 2193, 2836, 3121, 3883, 4113, 4605, 4696, 5746
PEEL, Sir Robert, Third Baronet (1822-1895): 4113
PEELE, W. J.: 1284
"PEELITES" (Great Britain): 1311
PEERAGE: see Nobility as subheading under names of specific countries
PEERLESS WOOLEN MILLS: 1197
PEET, Edward: 5298
PEGGY STEWART (ship): 1481
PEGRAM, Allen W.: 208, 4114
PEGRAM, James West: 3809
PEGRAM, Robert Baker: 1424
PEGRAM HOUSE, Duke University: 960
PEKIN, New York: 3281
PEKIN, North Carolina: 675
PEKING, China:
    see also YENCHING UNIVERSITY
    British embassy in: 3472
    British in: 4054
    Description: 1373
PEKING-MUKDEN RAILROAD: 5252
PELHAM, Arthur Harvey Thursby-: 4115
PELHAM, Charles Augustus Thursby-: 4115
PELHAM, Henry: 2098, 3997
PELHAM, Thomas, Second Earl of Chichester: 2149
PELHAM, Massachusetts: 3034
PELHAM-CLINTON, Henry Pelham Fiennes, Fourth Duke of Newcastle:
    see CLINTON, Henry Pelham Fiennes Pelham-, Fourth Duke of Newcastle
PELHAM-HOLLES, Thomas, First Duke of Newcastle: 2155, 5540
PELLARIN, Charles: 65
PELLATT, Apsley: 2149
PELLEW, Edward, First Viscount Exmouth: 5639
PELLEZA Y TOVAR, José: 4981
PELLICO, Silvio: 4116
PELLY, Sir Lewis: 4117
PELOT, James: 4118
PELOT, Lalla: 4118
PELOT FAMILY (South Carolina): 4118
PELOUZE, Edward: 4119
PELOUZE, Henry Layfette: 4119
PELOUZE, Jane (Tuthill): 4119
PELTS: see HIDES AND SKINS
PEMBERTON, John Clifford: 1186, 1853, 4034, 4120
PEMBERTON, Mary Ann: 2612
PEMBERTON, Stephen: 2612
PEMBERTON FAMILY: 2612
PEMBROKE, Catherine (Woronzow) Herbert, Countess of: 1911
PEMBROKE, North Carolina: 2121
PEMBROKE (ship): 3283
PEN LUCY SCHOOL FOR BOYS, Waverly, Maryland: 2692
PENAL CODE--Great Britain: 5726
PENAL CODE BILL (1860, Great Britain): 4097
PENAL COLONIES: see TRANSPORTATION OF CONVICTS
PENAL REFORM: see PRISON REFORM
PENANG ISLAND, Singapore:
    Description: 4097
PENCE, Charles B.: 4121
PENCE, Jacob, Jr.: 4122
PENCE, Nettie: 4123
PENCE, Perry: 4124
PENDELL, John R.: 4125
PENDER, William Dorsey: 2553, 5457
PENDLETON, Dudley Digges: 581, 4126
PENDLETON, Edmund: 769
PENDLETON, Mrs. Hugh Nelson: 4126
PENDLETON, Madison: 4127
PENDLETON, Nathaniel: 4128
PENDLETON, Philip Clayton: 3556
PENDLETON, Robert: 4126
PENDLETON, William James: 4127
PENDLETON, William Nelson: 56, 581, 4126, 4189

PENDLETON FAMILY (Virginia): 581, 4127
PENDLETON FAMILY (West Virginia): 581
    Genealogy: 1946
PENDLETON, Lancashire, England: 39
PENDLETON, South Carolina: 3278, 4191, 4896
PENDLETON COUNTY, West Virginia:
    Macksburg: 2470
PENFIELD, Georgia: 4647
    see also MERCER UNIVERSITY
    Cotton prices: 5040
    Economic conditions: 5040
PENICK, Charles Clayton: 3141
PENICK, Charles Clifton (1843-1914): 2597
PENINSULAR CAMPAIGN: see CIVIL WAR--CAMPAIGNS, BATTLES, AND MILITARY ACTIONS--Virginia--Peninsular Campaign
PENINSULAR WAR (1807-1814): 1147, 3460, 3736, 4979
    see also GREAT BRITAIN--ARMY--Napoleonic Wars--(Spain or Portugal); GREAT BRITAIN--NAVY--Operations--Napoleonic Wars; NAPOLEONIC WARS
    Campaigns, battles, and military actions: 1147
    Portugal: 4137
        Vimeiro: 4979
    Spain: 4137, 4912
        Andalusia: 4979
        La Coruña: 3836
        Medina de Rio Seco: 4979
    Economic aspects: 4289
    Military activities: 1875, 5639
PENMANSHIP:
    see also CALLIGRAPHY
    Exercise books: 5003, 5979, 5983
        Alabama: 1085
        North Carolina: 2570, 2915
        South Carolina--Charleston: 4271
    Study and teaching: 4898
        North Carolina: 3680
PENN, Abraham, Sr.: 4130
PENN, Ella: 4714
PENN, Green W.: 4131
PENN, John (1740-1788): 4132, 5768
PENN, Robert L.: 1842
PENN, Thomas H.: 3704
PENN, William (1644-1718): 1733
PENN FAMILY (Pennsylvania): 4131
PENN YAN, New York: 1229, 3568
PENNIMAN, James Hosmer: 4271
PENNIMAN, S. M.: 4133
PENNSYLVANIA:
    see also MIDDLE ATLANTIC STATES; NORTHEASTERN STATES; NORTHERN STATES
    Abolition of slavery and abolitionist sentiment: 421, 490
    Actors: 4086
    Advertising:
        Coal industry: 3910
    Agricultural practices:
        Franklin County: 2643
    Agriculture: 4881
        see also the following subheadings under PENNSYLVANIA: Crops, and names of specific crops; Farming
    American Revolution: see appropriate subheadings under AMERICAN REVOLUTION
    Anti-Masonic Party: 421
    Art and artists: 2728
    Authors and publishers: 848, 1488
        see also PENNSYLVANIA--Publishers and publishing
        Philadelphia: 890
    Banking law: 421, 4188
    Banks and banking:
        Blair County: 421
        Monongahela City: 1332
        Philadelphia: 2412, 5282
    Biographical studies: 5686
        Philadelphia: 2790

PENNSYLVANIA (Continued):
 Blacksmiths' accounts--Wesley: 4841
 Blind--Education: 3330
 Boardinghouses--Bethlehem: 5312
 Bridges: 4188
 Book buying: 84
 Buckshot War: 421
 Building construction: 3557
  Philadelphia: 3569
 Business affairs:
  Chambersburg: 5306
  Hollidaysburg: 421
  Philadelphia: 3909
  Richmond Furnace: 2033
  Towanda: 3372
 Cabinetmaking: 744
 Canals: 849, 1433
  Construction: 5686
  Juniata River Canal: 421
  North Branch: 4188
 Catholic Church:
  Conversion: 4881
  Sinking Valley: 3424
 Centennial celebrations (1876): 2597, 3092, 5380
 Charities: 2027
  Chambersburg: 5306
 Chautauquas--Swarthmore: 5110
 Christianity: 5380
 Churches--Franklin County: 2643
 Civil engineering:
  Students' notebooks: 5679
 Civil War: see appropriate subheadings under CIVIL WAR; CONFEDERATE STATES OF AMERICA--ARMY; and UNITED STATES--ARMY--Civil War
 Claims--Philadelphia: 4181
 Clergy:
  Lutheran: 4444
  Presbyterian--Le Raysville: 4397
 Clothing and dress:
  Manufacture: 990
 Coal--Prices: 4188
 Coal industry: 5686
 Coal mining: 5775
  Cornplanter: 3910
 Commodity prices: 870, 3054, 4699, 4881, 4920
  see also PENNSYLVANIA--(name of specific commodity)--Prices
 Congressional elections (1854): 3054
 Constables: 1130
 Contracts--Lewistown: 2704
 Corporations: 2027
 Cotton mills--Philadelphia: 5845
 Courts:
  Cases: 2027
  Judgments: 421
  Sessions Courts: 5764
  Supreme Court: 588, 1916
 Courtship: 2731
  see also PENNSYLVANIA--Love letters
 Crops--Prices: 2643
 Currency: 1339
 Daguerreotypers: 4057
 Death: 3227
 Debt: 213, 2594
 Debt collection: 228, 421, 496, 870, 1117, 1805
  Londonderry: 2615
 Democratic Party: 3501, 4188
 Description and travel: 4457
  1700s: 1735
  1800s: 33, 872, 1891
  1820s: 2828
  1840s: 3006
  1850s: 1362, 5149
  1880s: 43

PENNSYLVANIA (Continued):
 Diseases:
  Cholera: 616, 4881
   Philadelphia: 849, 3485, 5613
  Smallpox:
   Philadelphia: 5731
   Pittsburgh: 2678
  Yellow fever:
   Philadelphia: 2776, 5362
 Economic conditions: 4188
 Elections: 4188
  see also the following subheadings under PENNSYLVANIA: Congressional elections; Local elections; Presidential election of 1856
 Estates:
  Administration and settlement: 213, 421, 1536, 1916, 2027
  Lancaster: 2492, 2497
 Evangelism: 4086
  Franklin County: 2643
 Exhibitions and fairs:
  International: 2597
 Extradition of criminals: 3728
 Family life: 5380
  Le Raysville: 4397
 Farm life: 373
  Franklin County: 2643
 Farming: 699
  see also the following subheadings under PENNSYLVANIA: Agriculture; Crops, and names of specific crops
  Sinking Valley: 3424
 Fertilizer industry:
  Philadelphia: 373
 Finance:
  see also PENNSYLVANIA--Personal finance; PENNSYLVANIA--Public finance
 Fishing rights on the Susquehanna River: 4756
 Flour--Prices: 4920
 Freight and freightage: 480
 Gardens and gardening:
  see also PENNSYLVANIA--Nurseries
  Philadelphia: 4354
 Government agencies and officials:
  Attorneys General: 2027
  Comptrollers General: 3897
  Governors:
   Andrew Gregg Curtin (1861-1867): 5775
   Gifford Pinchot (1923-1927, 1931-1935): 4211
  State Improvements System: 421
  State Police: 1831
 Grain--Prices: 4920
 Grave robbing: 531
 Guardianship: 1443, 4756
 Hardware stores:
  Apprenticeship: 5686
  Management: 5686
 History notebooks: 3412
 Insurance: 480
  Fire: 1332, 2521
  Life: 1332
 Insurance companies: 1332
 Internal improvements: 421, 1433, 4732
 Interracial marriage:
  Blair County: 5249
 Inventions: 5686
 Irish in the United States:
  Norristown: 4190
  Philadelphia: 4354
  Reading: 4190
 Iron industry: 5775
  Blair County: 421
  Hollidaysburg: 849

PENNSYLVANIA:
 Iron industry (Continued):
  McVeytown: 849
  Philadelphia: 1169
 Jurors: 2444
 Justices of the peace: 496
 Labor--Iron industry: 421
 Land: 480
  see also PENNSYLVANIA--Real estate
  Purchases and sales: 3897
 Land deeds and indentures:
  Lewistown: 2704
 Land laws: 421
 Land speculation: 3041
 Law--Study: 1142
 Law practice:
  Bedford: 324
  Harrisburg: 2027
  Lancaster: 2444
  Media: 2552
  Philadelphia: 2688
 Lawsuits: 496, 1443, 2704
  Lancaster: 5948
  Lewistown: 2704
  Philadelphia: 4845
 Lectures and lecturing: 1488
 Legal affairs: 4188
  Blair County: 421
  Gettysburg: 5780
  Lewistown: 2704
 Legislature: 4188
  House of Representatives: 4756
  Senate:
   Committee on Internal Improvements: 421
 Literary interests: 5380
 Loans: see PENNSYLVANIA--Personal loans
 Local elections--Philadelphia: 4134
 Love feasts--Franklin County: 2643
 Love letters: 1226
  see also PENNSYLVANIA--Courtship
 Lutheran churches: 4444
  East Pennsylvania Synod: 4444
  Ray's Hill: 3957
 Manuscript collecting: 1563
 Medical education: 490
  Cadavers: 531
  Students' notebooks: 2622, 5771
  University of Pennsylvania: 3609, 3675
  Subdivided by place:
   Philadelphia: 872, 2935, 3788
   see also JEFFERSON MEDICAL COLLEGE; UNIVERSITY OF PENNSYLVANIA--Medical education
 Medical practice: 4076
 Medicine: 5305
 Mercantile accounts:
  Elkhorn: 138
  Philadelphia: 5933
  Warren County: 2242
 Merchants: 469, 1611, 2594, 3957
  Attleboro: 3229
  Harrisburg: 2027
  Philadelphia: 228, 1242
 Methodist churches:
  Philadelphia Conference: 5328
 Migration from:
  see also PENNSYLVANIA GERMANS IN (place)
  To North Carolina: 5264
 Militia:
  American Revolution: 231
  Civil War: 2989
  Finance: 231
  Military supplies: 231
  Quartermaster: 2571
  Recruiting and enlistment: 231

PENNSYLVANIA:
　Militia (Continued):
　　Regiments:
　　　15th: 5775
　　　123rd: 5775
　Millers' accounts: 2521
　Moravian Church: 4423
　Mortgages: 421
　　Philadelphia: 5953
　Municipal services--Bethlehem: 5312
　Murder: 5775
　Newspapers: 1021
　Nurseries (horticulture): 1283
　　see also PENNSYLVANIA--Gardens
　　　and gardening
　Oil refining: 4086
　Personal finance: 2552
　Personal loans--Philadelphia: 5953
　Physicians: 2336
　　Personal finance: 2208
　　Bedford: 2275
　　Orwigsburg: 3754
　Physicians' accounts: 1579
　Plank roads: 5149
　Poetry: see PENNSYLVANIA--
　　Publishers and publishing--
　　Poetry
　Political patronage: 4188
　Politics and government:
　　1700s-1800s: 421
　　1800s: 324, 357, 849, 4188
　　　1830s: 685
　　　1840s: 213, 685
　　　1850s: 685, 4756
　　　1860s: 5775
　　　1870s: 2027
　　　1880s: 2027
　　　Appointments: 4188
　　1900s: 1429
　Portraits: 4057
　Presidential election of 1856: 4556
　Printing: 3490
　Prisoners and prisons: 616
　　Philadelphia: 2552
　　Religious instruction: 616
　Prohibition: 5536
　　see also PENNSYLVANIA--Temperance
　　Laws and legislation: 4188
　Protestant Episcopal Church:
　　Bishops: 4285
　Public finance: 3897
　　Specie payments: 421
　Public schools: 421
　Public welfare: 1429
　Publishers and publishing: 552
　　see also PENNSYLVANIA--Authors
　　　and publishers; PENNSYLVANIA--
　　　Printing
　　Poetry: 2640
　Race relations: 4190
　　Lancaster: 5991
　Railroad companies: 5083
　Railroads: 421, 849, 1433, 1916,
　　2027, 5083
　　Accounts: 5083
　　Laws and legislation: 4188
　Real estate--Philadelphia: 1920
　Religion: 4190
　Republican Party: 421, 4881
　Roads: 849
　　see also PENNSYLVANIA--Plank
　　　roads; PENNSYLVANIA--Turnpikes
　　Laws and legislation: 4188
　Salt mining: 4732
　Sanitary engineering:
　　Students' notebooks: 5679
　Scales:
　　Manufacture of: 1392
　　Purchases and sales: 2
　Schools: 421, 1681
　　see also the following
　　　subheading under PENNSYLVANIA:
　　　Public schools; Teachers'
　　　records; Teaching
　　Curriculum: 4106
　　Girls' schools and academies:
　　　3956

PENNSYLVANIA:
　Schools:
　　Girls' schools and academies:
　　　(Continued):
　　　Bethlehem: 2828
　　　Philadelphia: 2776, 5165
　　　Tuition: 4106
　　Subdivided by place:
　　　Bethlehem: 3258
　　　Chester: 3155
　　　Mount Nebo: 3174
　　　Philadelphia: 2362, 4348
　　　Pittsburgh: 5775
　Secession:
　　Public opinion of: 421, 5380
　Shipping: 870
　　Prices: 1615
　Shipping companies: 1615
　Slavery:
　　Public opinion of: 5380, 5686
　Social and political reform: 2027
　Social life and customs: 404
　　Mercersburg: 2521
　　Philadelphia: 3485, 5165
　Songs and music: 490
　Sons of Temperance: 496
　Steel industry: 1169
　Taverns and inns: 5149
　Teachers--Cost of living: 4106
　Teachers' records:
　　Bedford County: 3957
　Teaching: 3789, 4106, 4937
　　see also PENNSYLVANIA--Schools
　Telegraph--Blair County: 421
　Temperance:
　　see also PENNSYLVANIA--
　　　Prohibition; PENNSYLVANIA--
　　　Sons of Temperance
　　Huntingdon County: 1798
　　Laws and legislation: 4188
　Trade and commerce: 1117
　　Flour: 2505
　　Food: 164
　　Grain: 164, 2505
　　Iron:
　　　Blair County: 421
　　　Philadelphia: 4797
　　Lumber: 744, 1732
　　　Tobyhanna Mills: 5985
　　Mineral water: 3957
　　Naval stores: 164
　　　Philadelphia: 4699
　　Subdivided by place:
　　　Philadelphia: 164, 5860
　Transportation:
　　Laws and legislation: 2027
　Turnpikes: 971, 4756
　　Construction: 3041
　　Lewistown: 2704
　Universities and colleges: see
　　BETHANY COLLEGE; BRISTOL COLLEGE;
　　DICKINSON COLLEGE;
　　GETTYSBURG COLLEGE; HAVERFORD
　　COLLEGE; LAFAYETTE AGRICULTURAL
　　COLLEGE; LAFAYETTE COLLEGE;
　　LEHIGH UNIVERSITY; MERCERSBURG
　　ACADEMY; PITTSBURGH COLLEGE;
　　SWARTHMORE COLLEGE; UNIVERSITY
　　OF PENNSYLVANIA; WASHINGTON AND
　　JEFFERSON COLLEGE; WILSON COLLEGE
　Usury: 2444
　Wages and salaries--Teachers: 4106
　War bonds (1863): 421
　Warrants (Law): 5953
　Water power--Schuylkill River:
　　5686
　Western lands: 3041
　Whig Party: 421, 849, 4756
　Wills: 421
　　Contested--Lancaster: 2492
　　Lebanon: 4937
　Woolen mills: 1536
　Yarn manufacturing:
　　Philadelphia: 5845
PENNSYLVANIA CANAL:
　Delaware Division: 5686
PENNSYLVANIA GERMANS IN INDIANA: 5275

PENNSYLVANIA GERMANS IN OHIO: 5275
PENNSYLVANIA GERMANS IN TENNESSEE:
　5275
PENNSYLVANIA GERMANS IN VIRGINIA:
　5275
PENNSYLVANIA MINING COMPANY v. UNITED
　MINE WORKERS OF AMERICA: 3640
PENNSYLVANIA RAILROAD: 421, 5083
PENNY, James: 1454
PENNYBACKER, Benjamin: 4135
PENNYPACKER, Isaac R.: 3122
PENOBSCOT COUNTY, Maine:
　Bangor: 1804, 2285
　East Dixmont: 1847
　Sunkhaze: 3201
PENROSE, Boies: 1364
PENSACOLA, Florida: 3008, 3173, 3474
　Civil War: 1610
　　see also CIVIL WAR--CAMPAIGNS,
　　　BATTLES, AND MILITARY ACTIONS--
　　　Florida--Pensacola
　Spanish activities in (1780): 3209
　Warrington Navy Yard: 2963
PENSACOLA, U.S.S.: 2336, 3008, 4535
PENSACOLA AND GEORGIA RAILROAD: 5928
PENSACOLA BAY, Florida: see CIVIL
　WAR--CAMPAIGNS, BATTLES, AND
　MILITARY ACTIONS--Florida--Santa
　Rosa Island
PENSION FRAUDS: 20
PENSION PLANS: 3066
PENSIONS:
　Civil: see CIVIL SERVICE PENSIONS
　Military: 70, 322
　　see also Pensions as subheading
　　　under names of wars; Bounty
　　　lands as subheading under names
　　　of wars
　　Laws and legislation: 1478
　Widows--East India Company: 2133
　Subdivided by place:
　　Great Britain: 2157, 2626, 2707,
　　　5116, 5177
　　United States: 633, 1208, 3291,
　　　4732
PENSIONS, Bureau of: see UNITED
　STATES--GOVERNMENT AGENCIES AND
　OFFICIALS--Bureau of Pensions
PENYBONT, Wales: 1002
PEONAGE:
　Georgia: 5051
　South Carolina: 2109
"PEOPLE I HAVE KNOWN" by Lucy
　Franklin: 2457
PEOPLES BANK OF OKEECHOBEE, Florida:
　2877
PEOPLES' PARTY OF THE UNITED STATES:
　4874
　North Carolina: 4586, 4858
　Presidential candidates: 4048
PEOPLES' SAVINGS BANK OF
　MONONGAHELA CITY, Pennsylvania: 1332
PEORIA, Illinois: 221, 520
PEORIA COUNTY, Illinois:
　Peoria: 221, 520
PEOSTA, U.S.S.: 4662
PEPER HAROW PARK, Surrey, England: 663
PEPPER, Clarendon N.: 4136
PEPPER, George Wharton: 5031
PEPPER, John: 4136
PEPPER TRADE:
　Europe--Imports: 2682
　Great Britain: 2742
　Sumatra--Exports: 2682
PEPYS, Charles Christopher, First
　Earl of Cottenham: 4605
PERCEVAL, Arthur Philip: 3715
PERCEVAL, Dudley: 1158
PERCEVAL, Spencer: 2126, 2836, 4137,
　5639
PERCUSSION RIFLE BULLETS: 4520
PERCY, Hugh, Second Duke of
　Northumberland (1742-1817): 2126
PERCY, Hugh, Third Duke of
　Northumberland (1785-1847): 2148
"PERCY" (correspondent): 5856
PÉREZ DE MONTALVÁN, Juan: 4138
PÉREZ DE VELASCO, Francisco: 4155

PERFORMING ARTS:
    see also ARTS; CIRCUS; COMIC OPERA;
        OPERA; THEATER
    Maryland--Baltimore: 2398
PÉRIGNON, Dominique Catherine de:
    4155
PÉRIGORD, Alexandre-Angélique, Duc
    de Talleyrand-: see TALLEYRAND-
    PÉRIGORD, Alexandre-Angélique,
    Duc de
PÉRIGORD, Charles Maurice de
    Talleyrand-, Prince de Bénévent:
    see TALLEYRAND-PÉRIGORD, Charles
    Maurice de, Prince de Bénévent
PERIODICALS:
    Abolitionist: 1638, 5246
    Agricultural: see AGRICULTURAL
        PERIODICALS
    Labor: see LABOR PUBLICATIONS
    Publishing: see PUBLISHERS AND
        PUBLISHING--Periodicals
    Religious: see RELIGIOUS
        LITERATURE
    Reporters and reporting: 3267
    Subscribers--North Carolina: 4407
    Subdivided by place:
        Great Britain: 2146
        Maryland: 2398
        North Carolina: 2282
        South Carolina: 2449
        United States: 2449, 2871, 3793
PERKINS, Isaac: 5975
PERKINS, John P.: 4139
PERKINS, Thomas (d. 1768): 4140
PERKINS, Thomas (1800s): 323
PERKINS, William Robertson: 4141
PERKINS, CAMPBELL, AND COMPANY, New
    Orleans, Louisiana: 872
PERKINSON, Isabelle: 5786
PERKINSON, Isabelle (Holmes): 5786,
    5790
PERKINSON, T. H.: 4142
PERKINSON, William Howard: 2612, 4143
PERNAMBUCO, Brazil: 4876
PERQUIMANS CIRCUIT, Methodist
    churches: 3646
PERQUIMANS COUNTY, North Carolina:
    290, 3132, 3874, 4153
    Cattle marks: 5777
    Mercantile accounts: 165
    Cities and towns:
        Hertford: 1679, 1822, 2553, 3564
            Marketing: 3907
            Teachers' records: 4897
PERRIE, William Fletcher: 5329
PERRIN, Abner M.: 4144
PERRIN, L. W.: 4145
PERRIN, Thomas C.: 4145
PERRIN AND McGOWAN (firm): see
    McGOWAN AND PERRIN
PERRONET, Charles: 4146
PERRONET, John: 4146
PERRONET, Vincent: 4146
PERRONET, William: 4146
PERRONET FAMILY (Great Britain): 4146
PERRY, Brother_____: 3377
PERRY, Algernon S.: 4147
PERRY, Allen C.: 4148
PERRY, Belmont: 5922
PERRY, Benjamin Franklin: 1333, 2446,
    4149
PERRY, Bliss: 103, 706
PERRY, Charles C.: 1702
PERRY, Ebenezer: 4150
PERRY, Harriet (Person): 4154
PERRY, James: 4151
PERRY, Jeremiah: 4147
PERRY, John R.: 1928
PERRY, Levin: 4154
PERRY, Matthew Calbraith: 2963, 4537
PERRY, O. H. (Massachusetts): 5093
PERRY, Oliver Hazard (1785-1819):
    3742
PERRY, Sarah: 4537
PERRY, Sidney S.: 490
PERRY, Theophilus: 4154
PERRY, Thomas Sergeant: 2344, 4449
PERRY, Vestal W.: 4152

PERRY, Wilson: 4153
PERRY FAMILY (North Carolina): 4147
PERRY, Georgia: 3767
PERRY COUNTY, Alabama: 5385
    Land--Purchases and sales: 1133
    Plantations: 5879
    Slaves--Treatment of: 5879
    Cities and towns:
        Marion: see MARION, Alabama
        Uniontown: 1031, 1497, 3237
PERRY COUNTY, Illinois:
    Land settlement and crops: 25
PERRY COUNTY, Indiana: 3199
PERRY COUNTY, Missouri:
    Perryville: 2515
PERRY COUNTY, Pennsylvania: 4785
PERRYSVILLE, Pennsylvania: 2236
PERRYVILLE, Kentucky: see CIVIL WAR--
    CAMPAIGNS, BATTLES, AND MILITARY
    ACTIONS--Kentucky--Perryville
PERRYVILLE, Missouri: 2515
PERSHING, John Joseph: 2398, 4556
PERSIA: 1010
    see also IRAN
    British military assistance: 868
    Foreign relations: 572
        Baghdad: 5797
        Great Britain: 868, 1010, 4005,
            4693, 5797
        Russia--Boundaries: 4693
        Turkey: 868
    Missions and missionaries: 4821
    Peace prospects--Russia: 4005
    Photographs: 286
    Politics and government: 4693, 5797
    Public finance: 572
    Visits of state--Germany: 3722
    War with Russia (1804-1813): 5797
PERSIA AND THE PERSIAN QUESTION by
    George Nathaniel Curzon: 4693
PERSIAN BANK MINING RIGHTS
    CORPORATION, LIMITED: 4693
PERSIAN BERRY TRADE: 323
PERSINGER, David W.: 5031
PERSON, Harriet: 4154
PERSON, Jesse H. H.: 4154
PERSON, Joseph Arrington: 4154
PERSON, M. P.: 4154
PERSON, Presley Carter: 4154
PERSON, Thomas A.: 4154
PERSON, Willie Mangum: 4154
PERSON COUNTY, North Carolina:
    524, 3605, 4939
    Arithmetic exercise books: 208
    Description and travel: 2248
    Medical treatment: 3752
    Narrow gauge railroads: 5455
    Wills: 3752
    Cities and towns:
        Bushy Fork: 378
        Cunningham's Store: 1336, 1959
        Hurdle Mills: 647
        Mount Tirzah:
            Mercantile affairs: 3752
            Methodist Episcopal Church,
                South: 5023
        Roxboro: 673, 2941, 5455, 5927
PERSONAL DEBT:
    see also DEBT; DEBT COLLECTION
    Georgia: 377, 1423, 5537
        Savannah: 4205
    Great Britain:
        London: 5463
        Shaston St. Peter: 3245
    Maryland: 3742, 4081
    Massachusetts: 3034, 4807
    New Jersey--Burlington: 5520
    North Carolina:
        Davidson County: 3241
    South Carolina: 1424, 2780
    Tennessee--Memphis: 5443
    United States: 3791
    Virginia: 2370, 2633, 2668, 3817,
        4157, 4268, 4710, 5107, 5365,
        5366, 5743
        Frederick County: 2954
        Petersburg: 3593

PERSONAL FINANCE: 169, 1266
    see also HOUSEHOLD ACCOUNTS; and
        Personal finance as subheading
        under names of specific classes
        of people or occupations, e.g.
        NEGROES--Personal finance;
        PHYSICIANS--Personal finance
    Alabama: 2979
        Clarke County: 4448
        Selma: 1645
    Arkansas: 4615
        Little Rock: 4208
    British in India: 3315
    Canada--Prince Edward Island: 1756
    Colorado: 353
    Florida: 1653
    Georgia: 1476, 2020, 5051
        Augusta: 5246
        Cherokee County: 1887
        Macon: 3905
        Savannah: 3311
    Great Britain: 15, 597, 4097, 4171
        Exeter: 5867
        Lilies: 2198
        London: 2626
    Illinois--Peoria: 520
    Jamaica: 3304
    Kentucky: 3199
        Lexington: 3325
    Maryland: 292, 2484
        Baltimore: 4348, 4886, 5763
        Frederick County: 4457
    Massachusetts: 1344, 4125, 4274
        Lowell: 803
    Minnesota: 4029
    Missouri--Saint Louis: 520, 5155
    Nebraska--Whitney: 5309
    New York: 481, 483, 1149, 1583,
        1589
        Ballston Spa: 5206
        New York: 4651
    North Carolina:
        1700s-1900s: 3176
        1800s: 486, 2570, 2660, 3003
        1800s-1900s: 2934, 3424
        1900s: 1951, 3548
        Advance: 4111
        Asheboro: 2303
        Chatham County: 5905
        Craven County: 1871
        Deep River: 5632
        Durham: 513
        Gamewell: 4339
        Guilford County: 5905
        Moore County: 5792
        Mount Gilead: 4689
        Oak Grove Township: 3896
        Person County: 3752
        Raleigh: 274, 4544
        Rowan County: 1269
        Stokes County: 2800
        Warrenton: 3761
        Wilmington: 3410
    Pennsylvania: 2552
    Scotland--Edinburgh: 4835
    South Carolina: 1388, 2709, 2961,
        3366, 4249, 5193
        Charleston: 5274
        Union: 5522
        York County: 3327
    Tennessee: 5671
    Texas: 4615
        Houston: 3463
    United States: 78, 773, 4348, 5312
    Virginia:
        1600s-1800s: 5573
        1700s-1800s: 2363
        1700s-1900s: 824, 3809
        1800s: 33, 476, 858, 2612, 2685,
            3587, 4428, 4616
        Albemarle County: 4384, 4490
        Alexandria: 5380
        Amherst County: 5529
        Charlottesville: 4142, 5786
        Cobham: 958
        Mecklenburg County: 1821
        Port Royal: 940
        Portsmouth: 520

PERSONAL FINANCE:
    Virginia (Continued):
        Richmond: 4038
        Smithfield: 811
        Suffolk: 4470
        Wachapreague: 4403
        Winchester: 4607
    Washington, D.C.: 2184, 3231, 4564
    West Virginia:
        Martinsburg: 3832
        Shepherdstown: 4598
PERSONAL LIBERTY LAWS: 4897
    Vermont: 3665
PERSONAL LIBRARIES: see LIBRARIES--Private
PERSONAL LOANS:
    North Carolina--Surry County: 3908
    Pennsylvania--Philadelphia: 5953
PERSONAL RECOLLECTIONS by David Dudley Field: 1792
"PERSONAL RECOLLECTIONS OF THE OCCUPATION OF EAST TENNESSEE AND DEFENSE OF KNOXVILLE" by Orlando Metcalfe Poe: 4245
"PERSONAL REMINISCENCES OF GETTYSBURG" by Stephens Calhoun Smith: 4908
PERSONS, Mrs. Joe: 4154
PERTHSHIRE, Scotland: 1569
PERU:
    Biographies--Lima: 3238
    Catholic Church: 4155
    Church history--Arequipa: 4155
    Customs duties: 4155
    Description and travel: 4155
    Education: 4155
    Estates--Administration and settlement: 4155
    Foreign relations:
        United States: 4531
    Foreign trade: 4155
        Spain: 4155
        United States: 5436
    Guano: 641, 1423
    Mercury mining: 4155
    Militia officers: 951
    Navy:
        Surveys on the Amazon River: 4531
    Newspapers: 4155
    Poetry: 4155
    Politics and government:
        Arequipa: 4155
        Lima: 3238
    Taxation: 4155
    Trade: 4155
        see also PERU--Foreign trade
    Treaties--United States: 932
    Trials: 4155
    United States consul in:
        Callao: 5051
    Universities and colleges: see COLEGIO MAXIMO DE SAN PABLO DE LA COMPAÑIA DE JESUS
    Viceroy: 4155
    War with Spain: 4982, 4983
    Witchcraft: 4155
"PETER PINDAR": see WOLCOT, John
"PETER POP" (pseudonym): 3892
PETERBOROUGH, New Hampshire: 4519
PETERHEAD, Scotland: 738, 5527
PETERKIN, G. W.: 3141
PETERS, Dr. _____: 5452
PETERS, Coles: 4157
PETERS, Don Preston: 4156
PETERS, Don T. C.: 4157
PETERS, Frank G.: 4157
PETERS, Ralph: 480
PETERS, Rebecca (Vansickles): 4158
PETERS, Thomas R.: 616
PETERS AND REED (firm): 2377
PETERSBURG, Virginia:
    1700s: 625, 5658
    1700s-1800s: 2913
    1700s-1900s: 1336, 2927
    1800s: 194, 203, 375, 858, 1558, 2876, 4095

PETERSBURG, Virginia:
    1800s (Continued):
        1820s: 2248
        1830s: 2248, 4299
        1840s: 629, 1873, 3761, 4299
        1850s: 1873, 3761
        1860s: 628, 1873, 2413, 3467, 3761, 4334, 4501
        1870s: 3467
        1880s: 3401, 3467
        1890s: 3401
    1800s-1900s: 460, 3142, 3320
    1900s: 4241
    Arithmetic exercise books: 208
    Army camps (1910s): 3843
    Business accounts: 5631
    Civil War: 264, 486, 2335
        see also appropriate subheadings under CIVIL WAR; CONFEDERATE STATES OF AMERICA; UNITED STATES--ARMY--Civil War
        Confederate military activities: 1271
        Hospitals: 3741
        Siege and battle: see CIVIL WAR--CAMPAIGNS, BATTLES, AND MILITARY ACTIONS--Virginia--Petersburg
        Trench life: 3788
        United States Army:
            Camps: 2405
            Military activities: 3910
    Commodity prices: 4604
        see also CIVIL WAR--COMMODITY PRICES--Virginia--Petersburg
    Coroners' inquests: 1383
    Cotton trade: 4604, 5959
    Debating societies: 4159
    Debt collection: 3593
    Description: 5209
    Estates--Administration and settlement: 4555
    Historic sites: 4612
    Landlord and tenant: 4555
    Law practice: 2014, 2466
    Literary societies: 4159
    Mercantile accounts: 2176, 2567, 3179, 5079, 5183
    Merchants: 3179, 4604
    Military parades: 4087
    Militia: 2815
    Personal debt: 3593
    Physicians: 401
    Physicians' accounts: 3104, 4112
    Plantations: 5079
    Rebuilding after fire of 1816: 5499
    Rent: 4555
    Schools: 858
    Slave trade: 4492
    Taverns and inns: 3042
    Tobacco industry: 655, 3179, 3345
        Labor conditions: 3643
    Tobacco trade: 655, 3643, 4764
    Trade and commerce: 330, 2381
    Universities and colleges: see PETERSBURG FEMALE COLLEGE
    Wholesale trade: 698, 4747
PETERSBURG, West Virginia:
    Physicians' accounts: 4842
PETERSBURG (Va.) COMPANY OF RIFLEMEN: 2815
PETERSBURG FEMALE COLLEGE, Petersburg, Virginia: 5513
    Curriculum: 5513
PETERSBURG (Va.) FRANKLIN SOCIETY: 4159
PETERSBURG (Va.) NATIONAL CEMETERY: 4059
PETERSBURG RAILROAD: 4492
PETERSON, Daniel: 4161
PETERSON, Elisha A.: 4160
PETERSON, Jacob (Montana): 4161
PETERSON, Jacob S. (Ohio): 4160
PETERSON, Jane: 4161
PETERSON, John: 4161
PETERSON, T. B.: 1608
PETERSON FAMILY (New York): 388

PETIGRU, Charles: 4162
PETIGRU, James Louis: 791, 4162, 4235, 5193
PETIGRU FAMILY (South Carolina): 4162
PETIT, Charles P.: 633
PETIT DE VILLERS, F. D.: 4163, 4625
PETITION OF RIGHT (Great Britain, 1628): 2152
PETRAM, John: 3320
PETRARCH: 5379
PETREA, C. A.: 4164
PETRIE-MILLS, Isabella: 39
PETROGRAD, Russia:
    United States consulate in: 286
PETROLEUM INDUSTRY: see OIL INDUSTRY
PETTET, William: 4165
PETTIGREW, Ebenezer: 4166
PETTIGREW, James Johnston: 2553, 4167, 4686, 5193
PETTIGREW, Joseph H.: 4166
PETTIGREW, R. H.: 4166
PETTIGREW, Thomas Joseph: 4168
PETTIS COUNTY, Missouri: 1174, 4406
PETTIT, George C.: 4169
PETTIT, John Upfold: 4169
PETTIT AND LEAKE, Goochland Court House, Virginia (firm): 195
PETTIT'S BATTERY: see UNITED STATES--ARMY--Civil War--Regiments--New York--Artillery--Pettit's Battery
PETTITT, C. W.: 5252
PETTUS, John Jones: 1403, 4729
PETTY, A. W. M.: 1453
PETTY, Annie E.: 4170
PETTY, Edmond George, First Baron Fitzmaurice: 1014
PETTY, William, First Marquis of Lansdowne and Second Earl of Shelburne: 92, 4171
PETTY (WILLIAM C.) AND COMPANY, North Carolina: 4172
PETTY FAMILY (Alabama, Indiana, Virginia): 4170
PETTY-FITZMAURICE, Henry Charles Keith, Fifth Marquis of Lansdowne: see FITZMAURICE, Henry Charles Keith Petty-, Fifth Marquis of Lansdowne
PETUS AND REED (firm): 2377
PEW RENT:
    see also EPISCOPAL CHURCHES--Pew rent; PROTESTANT EPISCOPAL CHURCH--Pew rent
    Massachusetts:
        Boston: 2304
PEYTON, Balie: 872
PEYTON, Craven: 4384
PEYTON, Mary: 5786
PEYTON, Robert Eden: 4173
PEYTON, Mrs. Robert Eden: 4173
PEYTONSBURG, Virginia:
    Mercantile accounts: 5827
PFISTER'S BOOK STORE, Tuscaloosa, Alabama: 3611
PFORZHEIMER, Arthur: 5101
PHAETON, H.M.S.: 392
LA PHALANGE (periodical): 65
LE PHARE DE FRANCE: 3710
PHARMACEUTICAL EDUCATION: see UNIVERSITY OF PENNSYLVANIA--Pharmaceutical education; UNIVERSITY OF VIRGINIA--Pharmaceutical education
PHARMACIES:
    see also DRUG TRADE; MEDICINE--Prescriptions; UNITED STATES--NAVY--Medical and sanitary affairs--Pharmaceutical records
    Brazil: 339
    Georgia: 279
    Kentucky--Glasgow: 5505
    North Carolina: 4366
    Virginia:
        Alexandria: 5016
        Charlottesville: 5301
PHARMACISTS' ACCOUNTS:
    Maryland:
        Baltimore: 4348, 5800

PHARMACISTS' ACCOUNTS (Continued):
  North Carolina: 4897
    Milton: 5515
    Wake Forest: 2590
  Virginia--Staunton: 1720
PHARMACISTS' CERTIFICATION:
  North Carolina: 4897
"PHARSALIA," Nelson County,
    Virginia: 3566
PHELPS, John: 648
PHELPS, John Smith (1814-1886): 4174
PHELPS, Murray N.: 4175
PHELPS, Richard R.: 4752
PHELPS, William: 4176
PHELPS, William Lyon: 103, 958, 2871, 3797
PHELPS, New York: 782
PHELPS AND STEVENSON, Covington, Kentucky (law firm): 5064
PHILADELPHIA, Pennsylvania:
  1600s-1800s: 1242, 5296
  1700s: 1735, 3780, 3897, 5221, 5276, 5870
  1700s-1800s: 1884, 5228
  1700s-1900s: 480
  1800s: 228, 616, 1352, 2640, 2728, 3135, 4188, 5764, 5771
  1800s: 890, 1816, 1888, 3805
  1810s: 443, 3675, 4599
  1820s: 870, 2208, 3490, 4810
  1830s: 1429, 3198, 3490
  1840s: 1622, 1807, 3258, 3261, 3490, 3769, 4401, 4597, 4797
  1850s: 84, 232, 490, 3258, 4181, 4413, 4597, 4797, 5355
  1860s: 553, 889, 1021, 2336, 3258, 4077, 4120, 4285, 4413, 5769
  1870s: 889, 1226, 4056, 4413
  1880s: 1021, 3603
  1890s: 1612
  1800s-1900s: 411, 3898
  1900s: 373, 848, 3545
  American Revolution: 1117
  Banks and banking: 2412, 5282
  Blind--Education: 3330
  Building construction: 3569
  Business affairs: 1117, 3909
  Cabinetmaking: 744
  Civil War--Blockade runners: 2766
  Clothing manufacture: 990
  Cotton mills: 5845
  Debt: 2594
  Description: 291, 404, 1501, 1697, 2552, 2828, 4864, 4924, 5730
  Diseases:
    Cholera: 616, 3485, 5613
    Smallpox: 5731
    Yellow fever: 2776, 5362
  Economic conditions (1819): 3485
  Foreign trade: 1615
  Fortifications (1814): 2489
  Gardens and gardening: 4354
  Hardware stores: 5686
  Hospitals: 2336
  Irish in the United States: 4354
  Iron industry: 1169
  Labor unions: 101
  Law practice: 2688
  Lawsuits: 4845
  Literary interests: 2790
  Local elections: 4134
  Manuscript collecting: 1563
  Medical education: 2622, 3761, 3788
    see also JEFFERSON MEDICAL COLLEGE
  Mercantile accounts: 5933
  Merchants: 1611
    see also PHILADELPHIA--Trade and commerce
  Methodist churches:
    General Conference (1820): 4412
  Mexican War: 2760
  Militia: 2571
  Mortgages: 5953
  Personal loans: 5953
  Presbyterian churches: 3432
  Protestant Episcopal church: 4669

PHILADELPHIA, Pennsylvania (Continued):
  Publishers and publishing: 1487
  Real estate: 1920
  Scales:
    Manufacturing: 1392
    Marketing: 2
  Schools: 1681, 2362, 4348
    Girls' schools and academies: 2776, 5165
  Shipping: 4946
  Social life and customs: 3485, 5165
  Society of Friends: 1733
  Trade and commerce: 164, 2633, 5860
    see also PHILADELPHIA--Foreign trade; PHILADELPHIA--Shipping
    Forest products: 1732
    Iron: 4797
    Naval stores: 4699
    Wholesale trade: 2857
    With Virginia: 1556
  Travel: 33, 43, 5102
    Costs: 1891
  United States Centennial celebration: 2597, 3092, 5380
  United States Mint: 4022
  Universities and colleges: see UNIVERSITY OF PENNSYLVANIA
  World War I: 829
  Yarn manufacturing: 5845
PHILADELPHIA, U.S.S.: 3403
PHILADELPHIA, GERMANTOWN, AND NORRISTOWN RAILROAD: 5083
PHILADELPHIA, WILMINGTON, AND BALTIMORE RAILROAD: 4468
PHILADELPHIA METHODIST CHURCH, Sunbury, North Carolina: 2353
PHILADELPHIA NEWS: 5668
PHILADELPHIA PRESS, Philadelphia, Pennsylvania: 5322
PHILADELPHIA RECORD: 5297
PHILADELPHUS, North Carolina: 702
PHILANTHROPIC HALL, University of North Carolina at Chapel Hill: 2399
PHILANTHROPIC SOCIETY: see UNIVERSITY OF NORTH CAROLINA AT CHAPEL HILL--Philanthropic Society
PHILANTHROPY:
  see also CHARITABLE WORK; FOUNDATIONS--Philanthropic; RECONSTRUCTION--Southern States--Northern philanthropy
  Connecticut: 5748
  Georgia: 4363
  Louisiana--New Orleans: 3358
  Missouri: 2386
  New York: 2753
  North Carolina: 1584, 1588
    Durham: 133
  South Carolina: 2040
  Southern States: 3558
  United States: 1441, 1589, 3828, 4022, 4080, 4343
  Virginia: 4020
PHILATELY: 2810
  see also PATRIOTIC STATIONERY
  Confederate postage stamps and covers: 651
  United States: 2070
PHILBRICK, Kate: 4177
PHILBRICK, R. Johanna: 4177
PHILIP II, King of Spain: 3989, 4178
PHILIP PENDLETON COOKE by John D. Allen: 1227
PHILIPPART, Sir John: 3976
PHILIPPE SNOWDEN: L'HOMME ET SA POLITIQUE FINANCIÈRE by A. M. Andreadès: 124
PHILIPPINE INSURRECTION: 4511
  see also UNITED STATES--ARMY--Philippine military occupation
  Albay: 4656
  Bohol: 4719
PHILIPPINE ISLANDS: 1340, 4179
  Banks and banking: 3313
  Bridges: 3313
  British expedition against (1797): 3315

PHILIPPINE ISLANDS (Continued):
  Catholic Church: 4511
    Property: 5419
  Civil Service: 3313
  Courts: 3313
  Currency: 3313
  Description and travel:
    1850s: 4017
    1900s: 2463, 3552, 4858
  Earthquakes--Mindanao: 3789
  Economic conditions: 2742
  Education: 3313, 4511
  English language: 3313
  Foreign relations:
    United States: 3774
  Foreign trade: 2742
    Mexico: 4155
  Government agencies and officials:
    Auditing Department: 3313
    Bureau of the General Administration of Property: 4656
    Bureau of Lotteries: 4656
    Bureau of the Mint: 4656
    Council of Administration: 4656
    Department of Commerce and Police: 4511
    Division of War: 4656
    Forestry engineers: 4656
    Inspector of Weights and Measures: 4656
  Historical studies: 4511
  Insurrection, 1899-1901: see PHILIPPINE INSURRECTION
  Internal improvements: 3313
  Libraries--Manila: 4511
  Maps: 4511
  Masonry: 4511, 4656
  Military railroads--Iligan: 4656
  Politics and government:
    1800s: 2742
    1900s: 561, 4511
  Ports--Manila: 4656
  Public finance: 3313, 4656
  Publishers and publishing: 4511
  Religion: 4511
  Roads: 3313
  Sanitation: 3313
  Schools: 4656
  Secret societies: 4511
  Social life and customs: 3313, 4511
  Spanish administration: 4656, 4979
    Board of Liquidation: 4656
  Sugar trade: 2742
  Teaching: 1001
  Tobacco industry: 4656
  Trade and commerce: 3313
  United States acquisition: 4656
  United States occupation: 3313, 4511, 5878
    see also UNITED STATES--ARMY--Philippine military occupation
    Army Corps of Engineers: 3789
    Civil-Military relations: 3313
  World War II: see WORLD WAR II--Philippine Islands
PHILIPPINE LIBRARY, Manila, Philippine Islands: 4511
PHILIPPINE LIBRARY ASSOCIATION: 4511
PHILIPS, Josiah: 5380
PHILIPS COUNTY, Arkansas: 2856
PHILLIMORE, Joseph: 747
PHILLIPS, C. J.: 359
PHILLIPS, E. E.: 5929
PHILLIPS, Edmund M.: 4183
PHILLIPS, George Sharlande: 4180
PHILLIPS, Henry Myer: 4181
PHILLIPS, J. C.: 4182
PHILLIPS, Jesse: 4183
PHILLIPS, John (North Carolina): 4182
PHILLIPS, John B. (Alabama): 4184
PHILLIPS, John Herbert (1853-1921): 2449
PHILLIPS, Joseph J.: 4775
PHILLIPS, Levi L.: 4183
PHILLIPS, M. D.: 715
PHILLIPS, Mary Ann: 1842
PHILLIPS, Mary Elizabeth: 2790, 5720

PHILLIPS, Sam L.: 4182
PHILLIPS, Samuel Field: 5457
PHILLIPS, Sarah Ellen (McIlwain): 4185
PHILLIPS, Wendell: 2626
PHILLIPS, William Horace: 4186
PHILLPOTTS, Henry, Bishop of Exeter: 2126
PHILOLOGY NOTEBOOKS: 2612, 4143
PHILOMATHEAN SOCIETY OF OLIN HIGH SCHOOL, Olin, North Carolina: 3973
PHILOMONT, Virginia: 690
PHILOSOPHY: 1049, 2930, 3189, 3666
    see also EPISTEMOLOGY; NATURAL PHILOSOPHY
    American philosophy: 1097
    English philosophy: 2457, 2707
    French philosophy: 872
    Oriental philosophy: 5252
    Subdivided by subject:
        Notebooks: 3808
        Students' notebooks:
            Maryland:
                Johns Hopkins University: 3888
            Virginia:
                Washington and Lee University: 4616
    Subdivided by place:
        Great Britain: 4628
        North Carolina: 817
        United States: 1441, 1458
        Virginia: 872
PHILPOT, Benjamin: 4187
PHIPPS, Henry, First Earl of Mulgrave: 4605
PHOENIX LODGE NO. 8, Order of Freemasons, Fayetteville, North Carolina: 1898
PHOENIX MINES, Cabarrus County, North Carolina: 3391, 4670
PHOENIXVILLE, Pennsylvania: 4190
PHOSPHATE MINING:
    see also MINES AND MINING
    South Carolina: 1019, 1480, 4306
        Charleston: 602
    Tennessee: 4924
PHOTOGRAPHERS: see DAGUERREOTYPERS
PHOTOGRAPHY: 5982
PHRENOLOGY: 3853, 5305
    France--Student's notebook: 2669
    Georgia: 2280
    New Hampshire: 354
PHYSICAL EDUCATION AND TRAINING: 3305
PHYSICAL SURVEY OF VIRGINIA by Matthew Fontaine Maury: 3586
PHYSICALLY HANDICAPPED: see BLIND; DEAF
PHYSICIANS:
    see also MEDICAL PRACTICE
    Ethics: 3378
    General practitioners: 2934
    Licenses--North Carolina: 4897
    Negroes--Virginia: 1384
    Notebooks:
        see also MEDICAL EDUCATION-- Students' notebooks
        Alabama: 1053
    Personal finance:
        Maryland: 1647
        Pennsylvania: 2208
    Subdivided by place:
        Georgia: 365, 2980
            Montgomery County: 3110
            Savannah: 4676
        Indiana--Freeport: 3221
        North Carolina: 1915
            Kinston: 986
            Nags Head: 4262
        Ohio: 4539
        Pennsylvania: 2336
            Bedford: 2275
            Orwigsburg: 3754
        Virginia: 381, 1279, 1591, 2935
            Fancy Grove: 5288
            Richmond: 2683

PHYSICIANS:
    Subdivided by place (Continued):
        West Virginia:
            Martinsburg: 2275
PHYSICIANS' ACCOUNTS: 5191
    see also MEDICAL TREATMENT--Costs
    Alabama: 4184
        Selma: 1265
        Talladega: 4061
    Georgia: 1581
        Augusta: 168, 3672
        Lawrenceville: 167
        Savannah: 158, 339
    Kentucky--Hancock County: 3199
    Maryland:
        Baltimore: 4348, 5800
    North Carolina:
        1800s: 1107, 1414, 2135, 2851, 4897, 5771
        1800s-1900s: 675
        1900s: 832
        Anson County: 409
        Davidson County: 138
        Fayetteville: 4517
        Hamilton: 5600
        Hillsborough: 4890
        Lincoln County: 5976
        Louisburg: 3476
        Mocksville: 2749
        Osceola: 4197
        Perquimans County: 4897
        Raleigh: 5356
        Ramseur: 2624
        Union County: 579
        Washington: 5195
        Williamston: 5943
    Pennsylvania: 1579
    South Carolina: 138
        Abbeville: 3527
    United States: 2886
    Virginia:
        1790s: 456
        1800s: 30, 503, 1509, 4776, 5513, 5742
        1800s-1900s: 574, 4743
        Amherst County: 3788
        Brunswick County: 4324
        Buckingham County: 3794
        "Haywood": 5579
        Lunenburg County: 3846
        Petersburg: 3104, 4112
        Smithfield: 811
    West Virginia: 4703
        Gerrardstown: 919
        Petersburg: 4842
PHYSICIANS' FEES: see MEDICAL TREATMENT--Costs; PHYSICIANS' ACCOUNTS
PHYSICS NOTEBOOKS: 2893
"PHYSIOLOGICAL ESSAYS" by Sir John Pringle, First Baronet: 4333
PHYSIOLOGY:
    Great Britain: 4051
    Virginia:
        Student's notebook:
            University of Virginia: 58
PHYSIO-MEDICAL COLLEGE OF OHIO: 5456
PIACENZA, Italy: 3954
PIANO CONCERTS:
    Ireland--Dublin: 3567
PIANO MUSIC: 1424
PIANOS--Georgia: 5260
PIATT, John James: 2449, 5044
PIATT, William M.: 4188
PICARD, Captain _____ (French Army): 5163
PICASSO, Pablo: 4657
PICKARD, Samuel Thomas: 4189
PICKEL, Adam: 4190
PICKEL, Adam H.: 4190
PICKEL, Sarah: 4190
PICKENS, Andrew: 4191
PICKENS, Cornelius Miller: 4192
PICKENS, Francis Wilkinson: 791, 1403, 2290, 3993, 4193, 4332, 5661
PICKENS FAMILY (South Carolina): 3176
PICKENS, South Carolina: 1964

PICKENS COUNTY, Alabama:
    Freedmen--Tenancy: 5032
    Cities and towns:
        Bridgeville: 5907
        Carrollton: 1145
PICKENS COUNTY, South Carolina:
    Pickens: 1964
PICKENS DISTRICT, South Carolina: 3535
PICKENSVILLE, Alabama: 5032
PICKERING, John (1738-1805): 3671
PICKERING, Timothy (1745-1829): 872, 2776, 2913, 4194
PICKETS: see Guard duty as subheading under names of armies
PICKETT, A. G.: 4202
PICKETT, Albert James: 4195
PICKETT, Charles: 4196
PICKETT, Cynthia: 4202
PICKETT, George Edward: 1137, 3809, 4196
PICKETT, John A.: 4197
PICKETT, John F.: 3269
PICKETT, LaSalle (Corbell): 4196
PICKETT, W. S.: 4198
PICKETT, William J.: 4199
PICOT'S SCHOOL FOR YOUNG LADIES, Philadelphia, Pennsylvania: 2776
PICTOU, Canada:
    Description: 3381
PIEDMONT, Virginia:
    Civil War: 4537
PIEDMONT AND NORTHERN RAILWAY: 3893
PIEDMONT CIRCUIT, Methodist churches: 1738
PIEDMONT FEMALE ACADEMY: 490
PIEDMONT PUBLISHING COMPANY, North Carolina: 3538
PIEDMONT REAL ESTATE INSURANCE COMPANY: 3308
PIERCE, Franklin: 872, 1308, 1333, 3993, 4200, 4478, 5059, 5853
    Administration: 3809, 5499
    Election: 3032, 5298
    Views on slavery: 5298
PIERCE, Genevieve: 4201
PIERCE, Harriett: 4201
PIERCE, James W.: 4202
PIERCE, John Hassett: 4203
PIERCE, Lovick: 2224
PIERCE, Ovid Williams: 4204
PIERCE, William B.: 4202
PIERCE, William Leigh (ca. 1740-1789): 4205
PIERCE FAMILY (Ohio): 4201
PIERPONT, Francis Harrison: 4206, 5775
PIG IRON:
    Virginia--Van Buren Furnace: 5990
PIGFORD, James B.: 3043
PIGG, D. W.: 5392
PIGG, David H.: 5392
PIGGOTT, Francis Steward Gilderoy: 4207
PIGG'S POINT, Maryland: 665
PIKE, Albert: 4208, 4353, 5380
PIKE, Emily: 2861
PIKE, Moses E. D.: 2861
PIKE COUNTY, Illinois:
    Florence: 2264
PIKE COUNTY, Indiana:
    Union: 4220
PIKE COUNTY, Kentucky:
    Paw Paw: 4090
PIKE COUNTY, Missouri:
    Bowling Green: 1062
    Louisiana: 3129
PIKE COUNTY, Pennsylvania:
    Milford: 4211
PIKE'S PEAK GOLD RUSH: 3012, 4834
PILCHER FAMILY: 872
"THE PILGRIM" by William Thomas: 1910
PILGRIM'S MISSION OF INDIA: 5306
"THE PILGRIMS OF MT. VERNON" by Alexander B. Meek: 3611
THE PILGRIM'S PROGRESS (periodical): 5306

PILLAGE: see Depredations as subheading under names of armies, navies, and wars
PILLOW, Gideon Johnson: 4209, 4253
PILLSBURY, Parker: 103
PILSON, Matthew: 4210
PIMA COUNTY, Arizona:
    Tucson: 338
PIN HOOK STORE, Lowell, North Carolina: 3285
PINCHBACK, Pinckney Benton Stewart: 1546
PINCHOT, Gifford: 3229, 4211, 4851
PINCKNEY, B. Gaillard: 4212
PINCKNEY, Charles (d. 1758): 4214, 4216
PINCKNEY, Charles (1757-1824): 4213, 4214
PINCKNEY, Charles Cotesworth (1746-1825): 3501, 4214, 4621, 4625
PINCKNEY, Charles Cotesworth III (1812-1899): 4215
PINCKNEY, Cotesworth: 2612
PINCKNEY, Elizabeth (Lucas): 4216
PINCKNEY, Harriot: 4214
PINCKNEY, Henry L.: 4217
PINCKNEY, Henry Laurens (1794-1863): 4212, 4213
PINCKNEY, Mary: 4214
PINCKNEY, Thomas: 4214, 4218
PINCKNEY, William: 4216
PINCKNEY FAMILY: 3396
PINCKNEY FAMILY (South Carolina): 4584
PINCKNEY ISLAND--Management: 4214
PINCKNEY PLANTATION, South Carolina: 1472
"PINDAR" by John Wolcot: 5867
PINDELL, Rinaldo: 4219
PINDELL FAMILY (Maryland): 4219
PINE BLUFF, Arkansas:
    Description: 2727
PINE FOREST DEBATING SOCIETY: 2357
PINE FORGE, Virginia: 4135
PINE GROVE, South Carolina: 2744
PINE LAND: see TIMBER LAND
PINE LUMBER TRADE:
    see also LUMBER TRADE
    Florida--Pensacola: 3008
PINE MOUNTAIN, Georgia: see CIVIL WAR--CAMPAIGNS, BATTLES, AND MILITARY ACTIONS--Georgia--Pine Mountain
PINE TREE SUNSHINE LODGE, North Carolina: 3633
PINERO, Sir Arthur Wing: 3617
PINEVILLE, South Carolina: 4034
PINKHAM, Alex: 4220
PINKHAM, Andrew: 4220
PINKHAM, Reuben: 4220
PINKHAM, Thomas: 4220
PINKNEY, Ninian: 4221
PINKNEY, William (1764-1822): 4221
PINKNEY, William (1810-1883): 4221
PINKNEY FAMILY (Maryland): 4221
PINNELL, Lucy: 4222
PINNELL, Thomas: 4222
PINNELL, William: 4222
PINNELL, William A.: 4222
PINNELL AND LILLY (firm): see LILLY AND PINNELL
PINNIX (JAMES K.) AND COMPANY, Stony Creek, North Carolina: 4223
PINOPOLIS, South Carolina: 5414
PIONEER: 1857
PIONEER AGRICULTURAL CLUB, Halifax County, North Carolina: 2399
PIONEER LIFE: 1072, 3386, 4689, 4765
    Arkansas: 2809, 4347
    California: 2808, 4353
    Michigan: 3325
    Missouri: 4161
    Texas: 2808, 4286, 4347, 4353
    Utah: 1333
    Virginia: 404, 2881
    Western States: 4353

PIPE TRADE: see IRON PIPE TRADE
PIPEFITTERS: see UNITED ASSOCIATION OF JOURNEYMEN AND APPRENTICES OF THE PLUMBING AND PIPEFITTING INDUSTRY OF THE UNITED STATES AND CANADA; UNITED ASSOCIATION OF JOURNEYMEN PLUMBERS, GAS FITTERS, STEAM FITTERS AND HELPERS AND SPRINKLER FITTERS OF THE UNITED STATES AND CANADA
PIPER, George W.: 4224
PIPKIN, A. S.: 4225
PIPKIN, Elizabeth M.: 4225
PIPKIN, Lewis: 1107, 2819
PIPPEY, William T.: 4226
PIQUA, Ohio: 2308
PIRATES:
    see also CORSAIRS; PRIVATEERS
    Algeria: 4348
    Great Britain: 5063
    Louisiana: 3073
    Mississippi River: 3053
PIRBRIGHT, Henry De Worms, First Baron: 3036
PISANI, M. B.: 3183
PITCHER, William Lewis: 4227
PITKIN, Perley Peabody: 4228
PITMAN, John: 3255
PITT, Anne: 3798
PITT, James Charles: 4230
PITT, John, Second Earl of Chatham: 4230
PITT, William (1759-1806): 5, 499, 1641, 1913, 2126, 2149, 2835, 4230, 5726
PITT, William, First Earl of Chatham (1708-1778): 92, 4229, 4230
PITT, William Morton: 2835
PITT FAMILY: 4230
PITT COUNTY, North Carolina: 5950
    Business affairs: 668
    Land: 975
    Law practice: 5950
    Local politics: 5950
    Original Free Will Baptist Church of North Carolina: 3988
    Cities and towns:
        Greenville: see GREENVILLE, North Carolina
        Grimesland: 2212
        Methodist Episcopal Church, South: 5023
PITTMAN, N. J.: 4231
PITTMAN, Thomas Merritt: 4132, 4232
PITTMAN FAMILY (North Carolina): 4232
PITTS, Dandridge: 4038
PITTSBORO, North Carolina: 3843, 5874
PITTSBORO CIRCUIT, Methodist churches: 3646
PITTSBURG LANDING, Tennessee: see CIVIL WAR--CAMPAIGNS, BATTLES, AND MILITARY ACTIONS--Tennessee--Pittsburgh Landing
PITTSBURGH, Pennsylvania: 1663, 3213, 4810, 5305
    Description: 5593
    Diseases--Smallpox: 2678
    Secession--Public opinion: 5380
    Universities and colleges: see PITTSBURGH COLLEGE
    Vandalism: 5775
PITTSBURGH COLLEGE, Pittsburgh, Pennsylvania: 5775
PITTSFIELD, Massachusetts: 1455
PITTSFORD, New York: 4375
PITTSFORD, Vermont: 2255
PITTSYLVANIA CIRCUIT, Methodist churches: 3646
PITTSYLVANIA COUNTY, Virginia:
    1800s: 2337
    1830s: 1261, 3708
    1840s: 1261, 3708
    1850s: 1161, 3708
    1860s: 132, 1161, 1886, 5919
    1800s-1900s: 2732, 2955
    Business affairs: 5873
    Coroners' records: 2925

PITTSYLVANIA COUNTY, Virginia (Continued):
    Courts: 2495
    Clerks: 5369
    Debt, Settlement of: 5587
    Estates--Administration and settlement: 5718
    Legal affairs: 5718
    Mercantile accounts: 1046
    Sheriffs: 5587
    Slave trade: 5718
    Prices: 5873
    Trade and commerce: 2229
    Cities and towns:
        Chatham: 3542, 4720
            Masonry: 4233
            Public finance: 2732
        Competition: see Chatham
        Danville: see DANVILLE, Virginia
        Green Hill: 2131
        Mount Airy: 2131
        Museville: 1801
        Pittsylvania Court House: 5369
        Spring Garden: 2902
        Stony Hill: 2131
PITTSYLVANIA COURT HOUSE, Virginia: 5369
PITTSYLVANIA (Va.) MASONIC LODGE NO. 24: 4233
PIUS IV, Pope: 5317
PIZARRO, Gonzalo: 4155
PLACE, Francis: 4234
"PLACE OF THE AMERICAN FEDERATION OF LABOR IN THE ECONOMICS AND SOCIAL WELFARE OF THE SOUTH" by James F. Barrett: 2768
PLAGIARISM: 119
    American poetry: 1029
PLAGUE: see DISEASES--Plague
PLAINE, David H.: 568
PLAINE, Harry E.: 568
PLAINE FAMILY (Virginia): 568
THE PLAINS, Virginia: 5377
PLAINS STATES:
    see also MIDDLE WEST; WESTERN STATES
    Indian raids: 2092
"PLAN PARA EL ESTABLISIMIENTO GENERAL EN ESPAÑA DEL COMERCIO ACTIVO" by Jean Bouligny: 586
PLANK CHAPEL CHURCH, Oxford, North Carolina: 5964
PLANK ROADS:
    Construction--North Carolina: 5298
    New York: 2230, 5149
    North Carolina--Asheboro: 5912
    Pennsylvania: 5149
    Virginia: 2376, 5149
PLANT GUARDS: see LABOR UNIONS--Plant guards
PLANTA, Joseph: 5071
PLANTAGENET (warship): 2296
THE PLANTATION by Ovid Williams Pierce: 4204
PLANTATION ACCOUNTS: 2649
    see also FARM ACCOUNTS
    Alabama: 5593
        Clarke County: 4448
        Dallas County: 4911
        Perry County: 5879
    Arkansas: 4776
    Georgia:
        Altamaha: 4445
        Augusta: 3749
        Ebenezer: 5986
    Louisiana: 3956
        Baton Rouge: 1026
    Mississippi: 3956, 4776
        Brandon: 2813
        Natchez: 1786
        Rodney: 3322
    North Carolina: 435, 4374
        Granville County: 2528, 3916, 5285
        Iredell County: 1382
        Martin County: 4849
        New Bern: 5709
        Orange County: 4666

PLANTATION ACCOUNTS:
  North Carolina (Continued):
    Perquimans County: 290
    Person County: 1336
    Stokes County: 27
    Surry County: 2808
    Yadkin County: 2808
  South Carolina:
    Colleton County: 4649
    Edgefield County: 4193
    Kershaw County: 2940
    Stateburgh: 4217
  Virginia: 1354, 2925, 3642, 4615
    Albemarle County: 3699
    Buckingham County: 3794
    Fairfax County: 2233
    Hanover County: 634
    Mecklenburg County: 3145, 4848
    Nelson County: 3566
    Nottoway County: 5469
    Petersburg: 4555
    "Rock Castle": 4616
    Westmoreland County: 3153, 5577
  West Virginia: 3010
    Jefferson County: 1708
PLANTATION BUILDINGS:
  Designs and plans--Virginia: 3566
PLANTATION LIFE:
  Alabama: 1986
  Florida--Duval County: 4410
  Georgia: 2020
    Burke County: 5246
    Columbia County: 5246
  Mississippi: 2349, 3393
    Rodney: 3322
  South Carolina: 1553, 4460
    Charleston: 4584
    Chesterfield County: 4996
    Edisto Island: 5661
    Laurens: 3531
    Spartanburg: 1745
  Virginia: 743
    Richmond County: 918
    Westmoreland County: 917
PLANTATION MANAGEMENT:
  Alabama: 4820
    Dallas County: 4911
    Perry County: 5879
    Operation by women: 1084
  Florida: 3447
  Georgia: 1242, 5651
    Operation by women: 2367
  Louisiana: 1242
  Mississippi: 4796, 4820
  North Carolina: 1602
    Wilmington: 4603
  South Carolina: 1553, 3124
    Colleton County: 4649
    Stateburgh: 4217
  Southern States: 3053
  Virginia: 743, 2881, 4616
    Prince Edward County: 5884
PLANTATION RESTORATION:
  South Carolina: 4619
PLANTATION STORES (accounts):
  South Carolina:
    Richland County: 1965
  Virginia:
    Stafford County: 1813
PLANTATIONS: 1044
  see also BREADFRUIT PLANTATIONS;
    COTTON PLANTATIONS; RICE
    PLANTATIONS; TOBACCO PLANTATIONS
  Finance:
    Florida: 2755
    Georgia:
      Oglethorpe County: 5162
      Sparta: 4493
    Mississippi: 3747
    North Carolina: 2824, 4082
      Person County: 1336
    South Carolina: 1101
      Edisto Island: 4725
      Spartanburg: 1745
    Virginia: 3145
      Buckingham County: 3794
      Caroline County: 806
      Lunenburg County: 3846

PLANTATIONS (Continued):
  Leasing--Louisiana: 4902
  Sale of:
    South Carolina:
      Kershaw County: 1012
  Subdivided by place:
    Alabama: 1061, 2040, 5593
      Dallas County: 4911
      Perry County: 5879
    Arkansas: 2517
    British West Indies: 4913
    Florida: 2901, 4743, 5659
    Georgia: 781, 1011, 1664, 4743
      Augusta: 5246
      Bulloch County: 3663
      Chatham County: 1996
      Cherokee County: 797
      Sapelo Island: 4988
      Savannah: 3278
    Jamaica: 301
    Kentucky: 3176
    Louisiana: 508, 1179, 2802, 5193
      Baton Rouge: 1026
      Tensas Parish: 4582
    Maryland: 743, 785, 1416
    Mississippi: 1325, 1553, 1556,
      1670, 3628, 5193
      Claiborne County: 1077
      Natchez: 1762
    North Carolina: 540, 730, 1061,
      1475, 1556, 2808
      Franklin County: 1322, 4147
      Franklinton: 4148
      Iredell County: 1382
      Lenoir County: 903
      Martin County: 5036
      Point Peter plantation: 3607
    Solomon Islands: 4949
    South Carolina: 842, 881, 1472,
      1923, 1944, 2030, 2503, 2596,
      3801
      Barnwell County: 2805
      Charleston: 2695, 3116, 5936
      Edisto Island: 4896
      Kershaw County: 2940
      Pendleton: 3278
      Sumter District: 4460
    Southern States: 5940
    Tennessee: 1061
      Castalian Springs: 5935
      Nashville: 2308
    Texas: 1153
    Virginia: 97, 558, 734, 872, 1568,
      2633, 2935, 3362, 4615, 5377,
      5751
      Albemarle County: 3699
      Augusta County: 4210
      Battletown: 3200
      Fluvanna County: 195, 1134,
        5839
      Glencoe: 5523
      Gloucester County: 3809, 4015
      Goochland County: 32, 5378
      Gravel Hill: 5652
      Hanover County: 456
      Nelson County: 3566
      New Kent County: 1115
      Orange County: 1401
      Petersburg: 3179, 5079
      Pittsylvania County: 2131
      Prince Edward County: 5884
      Prince William County: 2489
      Richmond County: 918
      Smyth County: 5117
      Sweet Briar: 5765
    West Virginia: 128, 3010, 5574
PLANTERS' AND MECHANICS' BANK OF
  SOUTH CAROLINA, Charleston, South
  Carolina: 4235
PLANTERS BANK, New York, New York: 559
PLANTER'S INSURANCE COMPANY: 5593
PLANTING: see AGRICULTURAL PRACTICES;
  FARMING
PLANTS:
  see also BOTANY; NATURAL HISTORY
  Identification: 4453
  Great Britain: 3862
  United States: 1229

PLAQUEMINE, Louisiana: 845
PLAQUEMINES PARISH, Louisiana: 5628
  Civil War: 375
PLASTER (fertilizer):
  Virginia: 33, 490, 3560
    Albemarle County: 3699
    Falmouth: 2165
PLASTERING:
  see also HOUSES--Construction
  Virginia--Quicksburg: 4121
PLATE: see CHURCH PLATE; GOLD PLATE;
  SILVER PLATE
PLATEN, Charles G.: 4236
PLATINOTYPES OF ENGLISH CATHEDRALS:
  5457
PLATT, Cornelia Anna: 4237
PLATT, Thomas Collier: 1364, 1977
PLATT (WILLIAM) AND SONS: 4881
PLAYBILLS: 3797
"PLAYFORD HALL," Suffolk, England:
  1081
PLAYING CARDS: see CARDS
PLAYS: see AMERICAN DRAMA; ENGLISH
  DRAMA; FRENCH DRAMA; SPANISH DRAMA
PLAYWRIGHTS: see DRAMATISTS
PLEASANT GARDEN, North Carolina:
  2330, 2715
PLEASANT GARDEN CIRCUIT, Methodist
  churches: 3646
PLEASANT GARDEN (N.C.) FARMERS
  ALLIANCE: 2330
PLEASANT GROVE, North Carolina:
  2036, 5551
PLEASANT GROVE, Virginia: 2323
  Merchants: 2331
PLEASANT GROVE ACADEMY, Forestville,
  North Carolina: 4294
PLEASANT HALL, Pennsylvania: 2643
PLEASANT HILL, Kentucky:
  Lawsuits: 5416
  Shakers: 5416
PLEASANT HILL, Ohio: 3648
PLEASANT HILL SOCIETY (Methodist
  churches): 3646
PLEASANT RETREAT MALE ACADEMY,
  Lincolnton, North Carolina: 4238
PLEASANT UNITY, Pennsylvania: 5151
PLEASANTS, Benjamin: 4239
PLEASANTS, James (1769-1836): 4239,
  4315
PLEASANTS, John Hampden (1797-1846):
  117, 3853
PLEASONTON, Stephen: 5622
PLEDGER, William Anderson: 731
PLIMSOLL, Samuel: 366
PLOTS: see CONSPIRACIES
"PLOUGH-HANDS' SONG": 2374
PLOW HANDLES--North Carolina: 358
PLOWING: see AGRICULTURAL PRACTICES;
  FARMING
PLOWMAN, H.: 528
PLOWS:
  Manufacture--Virginia: 728
  Prices--Virginia: 4099
  Steam powered--Maryland: 5193
  Trade--Virginia: 728
PLUG TOBACCO TRADE: see TOBACCO
  TRADE--Plug tobacco
PLUMB, Mr. _____ (Missionary to
  China): 3315
PLUMBERS: see UNITED ASSOCIATION OF
  OF JOURNEYMEN AND APPRENTICES OF
  THE PLUMBING AND PIPEFITTING
  INDUSTRY OF THE UNITED STATES AND
  CANADA; UNITED ASSOCIATION OF
  JOURNEYMEN PLUMBERS, GAS FITTERS,
  STEAM FITTERS AND HELPERS AND
  SPRINKLER FITTERS OF THE UNITED
  STATES AND CANADA
PLUMER, William Swan: 4240
PLUMMER, F. Harvey: 4241
PLUMMER & BUDD, Petersburg, Virginia
  (firm): 4241
PLUNKETT, Achilles: 3761
PLUNKETT, Carolina (Mordecai): 3761
PLUNKETT, Moss A.: 5486
PLYLER, Marion Timothy: 4242

PLYMOUTH, Ivor Miles Windsor-Clive,
    Fifteenth Baron Windsor and
    Second Earl of: 1424
PLYMOUTH, Connecticut: 1205
PLYMOUTH, England--Defenses: 5330
PLYMOUTH, Massachusetts: 1537
PLYMOUTH, North Carolina: 435, 772,
    1015
  Civil War: see CIVIL WAR--
    CAMPAIGNS, BATTLES, AND MILITARY
    ACTIONS--North Carolina--
    Plymouth
  Clergy: 255
  Mercantile accounts: 4639
PLYMOUTH BRETHREN:
  Missions and missionaries: 5836
PLYMOUTH CHURCH, Brooklyn, New York
    (Congregational): 5001
PLYMOUTH COUNTY, Massachusetts:
  Bridgewater: 4438
    Merchants: 2959
  Hingham: 3209
  Kingston--Civil War: 383
  Lakeville: 953
  Marshfield--Civil War: 1850
  Plymouth: 1537
  Scituate: 1344, 4305
PNEUMONIA: see DISEASES--Pneumonia
POAGUE, John: 4243
POAGUE, William Thomas: 4244
POCAHONTAS COUNTY, West Virginia:
  Land deeds and titles: 1837
  Taxation: 5655
POCHMANN, Henry August: 102
POE, Clarence Hamilton: 4373
POE, Edgar Allan: 10, 1029, 1943,
    2449, 3306, 3809, 5720, 5799
  Bibliography: 5720
  Biography: 2790
  Death: 5720
  Influence on English and French
    literature: 2764
  Memorials: 5720
POE (EDGAR ALLAN) SHRINE, Richmond,
    Virginia: 5720
POE, Orlando Metcalfe: 4245
POE FAMILY (Virginia): 5720
POE, THE MAN: 2790
"POESIAS SAGRADAS DE DIVERSOS
    AUTORES" 4155
POETICAL EXTRACTS by Jane Lucinda
    (Hopkins) Field: 1792
POETRY: 1424, 2805, 2851, 3360, 4829,
    4897
  see also AMERICAN POETRY; ARABIC
    POETRY; BALLADS; DOGGEREL; ENGLISH
    POETRY; FOLK POETRY; GERMAN POETRY;
    HEBREW POETRY; HUDIBRASTIC VERSE;
    HUMOROUS POETRY; IRISH POETRY;
    ITALIAN POETRY; LOVE POETRY;
    NEWSPAPERS--Carriers' addresses;
    POLITICAL POETRY; RELIGIOUS POETRY;
    and Poetry as subheading under
    names of wars, e.g. RUSSO-
    JAPANESE WAR--Poetry
  Collections: 128, 141, 1219, 2612,
    4348, 5311
  Connecticut: 1168
  Georgia: 1621
  Maine--Portland: 3551
  Maryland: 3559
  North Carolina: 617, 3607, 3896,
    5506
  Scotland: 4835
  South Carolina: 1889
  Southern States: 3611
  Virginia: 73, 1757, 4496, 5711
  Criticism:
    Great Britain: 4629
  Publishers and publishing: see
    PUBLISHERS AND PUBLISHING--Poetry
  Women: see VIRTUES OF WOMANHOOD IN
    POETRY; WOMEN POETS
  Subdivided by place:
    Maryland: 3998
    North Carolina: 263, 3482, 5298
    Peru: 4155

POETRY:
  Subdivided by place (Continued):
    Virginia: 302, 404, 2061, 2559,
      2794
    Washington, D.C.: 42, 1118, 3373
POETRY SOCIETY OF SOUTH CAROLINA:
    3394, 4453
POGUE, J. E.: 1336
POINDEXTER, George: 4246
POINDEXTER, Henry: 4247
POINDEXTER, John F.: 4248
POINDEXTER FAMILY (North Carolina):
    2808
POINSETT, Joel Roberts: 850, 872,
    3162, 4249, 4829, 5546, 5720
POINT JEFFERSON, Louisiana:
  Civil War: 508
POINT LOOKOUT, Maryland: 4682
  see also CIVIL WAR--PRISONERS AND
    PRISONS--Confederate prisoners--
    Maryland--Point Lookout
POINT LOOKOUT, Missouri: 1424
POINT PETER PLANTATION, North
    Carolina: 3607
POINTE COUPEE PARISH, Louisiana:
    1153
POLAND, Edward: 4250
POLAND:
  Economic conditions: 3571
  Foreign relations: 92
  Photographs: 1210
  Politics and government: 4650
  Revolution of 1863-1864: see
    POLISH REVOLUTION
  Social conditions: 3571
POLE-CAREW, Sir Reginald: see CAREW,
    Sir Reginald Pole-
POLE-TYLNEY-LONG-WELLESLEY, William:
    see WELLESLEY, William Pole-Tylney-
    Long
POLICE:
  see also CONSTABLES; STATE POLICE
  Negroes:
    South Carolina--Orangeburg: 3037
    Texas: 1138
  Subdivided by place:
    Great Britain: 4420
    Virginia--Patrick County: 1894
POLISH REFUGEES--Aid to: 5746
POLISH REVOLUTION (1863-1864): 5222
POLITICAL CLUBS:
  see also AMERICAN PROTECTIVE
    ASSOCIATION; ORANGE SOCIETY;
    POLITICAL PARTIES, and names of
    specific political parties;
    SOCIETY FOR PARLIAMENTARY REFORM
  Great Britain: 944, 5026
  North Carolina:
    Morehead City: 3960
    Wilmington: 3380
  Virginia: 4720
POLITICAL CONVENTIONS: see as
  subheading under names of specific
  political parties, e.g.
  DEMOCRATIC PARTY--Conventions
POLITICAL CORRUPTION: see CORRUPTION
  IN POLITICS
POLITICAL DEMONSTRATIONS: see
  ANTI-AMERICAN DEMONSTRATIONS;
  DEMONSTRATIONS
POLITICAL DISABILITIES:
  Great Britain: 2149, 3226
    Repeal of the Five-Mile and
      Conventicle acts: 3120
POLITICAL ECONOMY: see ECONOMICS
POLITICAL PARTIES:
  see also POLITICAL CLUBS; and names
    of specific political parties
  Great Britain: 491
  New York: 388
  United States: 3096
POLITICAL PATRONAGE:
  see also POLITICS AND GOVERNMENT--
    Appointments
  Confederate States of America: 128,
    1180, 3615, 5051
  Connecticut: 3041

POLITICAL PATRONAGE (Continued):
  Georgia: 422, 662, 731, 1203, 2497
  Great Britain: 1632, 2158, 4024,
    5330
  India: 2421
  Maryland: 596, 3086
  Mississippi: 5363
  Missouri: 1620
  New York: 585, 1977, 2497, 4343
  North Carolina: 325, 631, 1061,
    2776, 4858, 4977, 5322
  Pennsylvania: 4188
  South Carolina: 521, 633, 1478,
    2278, 2613, 3451, 4316
  Tennessee: 4291
  United States:
    1800s: 388, 1086
    1820s: 4361, 4964
    1830s: 730, 741, 4361
    1840s: 741, 2326, 2760, 5051,
      5491
    1850s: 415, 741, 4200, 5051
    1860s: 415, 694
    1870s: 415, 694, 2537, 5578
    1880s: 1953, 5578
    1800s-1900s: 4858, 5152
    Army appointments (1898): 5790
    Democratic Party (1800s): 3325
    Naval appointments (1800s): 265,
      5842
  Virginia: 2700, 3215, 3302, 4206,
    5152, 5359
  Washington, D.C.: 2589, 4486
  West Virginia: 2016, 3291
POLITICAL POETRY:
  On European politics: 958
  South Carolina--Charleston: 5074
  Virginia: 3809
POLITICAL POSTERS:
  Germany (Nazi period): 2011
  United States (1900s): 4948
POLITICAL PRISONERS: see CIVIL WAR--
  POLITICAL PRISONERS
POLITICAL REFORM: see SOCIAL AND
  POLITICAL REFORM
POLITICAL REGISTER AND CONGRESSIONAL
  DIRECTORY (1878): 4266
POLITICAL SATIRE--Spain: 4979
POLITICAL SCIENCE NOTEBOOKS: 5781
  University of Virginia: 2612
POLITICAL SOCIETIES: see POLITICAL
  CLUBS
POLITICAL THEORY:
  South Carolina: 2290
  Virginia: 872
POLITICAL UNREST:
  Great Britain--Coventry: 4750
  Ireland--County Westmeath: 4024
  Massachusetts--Boston: 5298
  Mexico: 871
  North Carolina: 3384
POLITICIANS:
  see also DEMAGOGUES; POLITICS AND
    GOVERNMENT; and names of specific
    politicians
  Evaluations: 4214
  Great Britain: 4693
  North Carolina: 1006
  Persia: 4693
  Prussia: 3238
  South Carolina: 3451
  Virginia: 5755
POLITICS AND CHRISTIANITY: see
  CHRISTIANITY AND POLITICS
POLITICS AND GOVERNMENT:
  see also AMERICAN REVOLUTION--
    Politics; CHURCH AND STATE IN
    (name of place); COUNTY
    GOVERNMENT; LABOR IN POLITICS;
    MUNICIPAL GOVERNMENT; NEGROES IN
    POLITICS; POLITICAL CLUBS;
    POLITICAL PARTIES, and names of
    specific political parties;
    POLITICAL POETRY; POLITICAL
    POSTERS
  Appointments:
    see also POLITICAL PATRONAGE

POLITICS AND GOVERNMENT:
  Appointments (Continued):
    Confederate States of America: 3615
    Great Britain: 2060, 2154
    North Carolina: 2121, 2581
    Pennsylvania: 4188
    South Carolina: 1562
    United States: 2121, 2125, 2446, 4964, 5516
    Virginia: 523
  Broadsides: 122
  Bureaucracy: 872
  Theory: see POLITICAL THEORY
  Subdivided by place:
    Afghanistan: 3238, 5797
    Alabama:
      1800s: 1084, 3415
      1830s: 5593
      1840s: 2662, 3903, 4911, 5593, 5937
      1850s: 1877, 3903, 4105
      1860s: 249, 4105, 4911, 5059
      1870s: 4105
      Local politics:
        Tuscaloosa (1800s): 4943
      Views of Mobile citizens (1800s): 5744
    Argentina: 2742
    Arkansas (1800s): 2809, 5380
    Austria (1800s): 1755, 3238, 3472
    Brazil: 339
    California (1920s): 2299
    Canada:
      1800s: 4567
      1800s-1900s: 1260
      1900s: 3949
    Cape Colony: 345
    Carolina Province: 202
    Chile:
      1800s: 3102, 3447
      1900s: 4074
    China:
      1800s: 4986
      1900s: 5225
    Colombia (1800s): 1506, 4155
    Confederate States of America: 132, 611, 842, 905, 1084, 1403, 1980, 2695, 2805, 2860, 3325, 3905, 4820, 4982, 5315, 5500, 5512, 5613
    Corfu: 3183
    East Indies: 4986
    Egypt: 3744, 4941
    Europe: 43
      Poetry on: 958
    Florida (1800s): 5740, 5978
    France:
      1790s: 922, 3176, 5330
      1700s-1800s: 1311, 5726
      1800s: 1147, 1632, 1755, 2742, 3472
      1810s: 2840, 4348
      1820s: 1302, 4348
      1830s: 1775, 1875, 4348, 4616, 5277
      1840s: 5133
      1870s: 3734
      1900s: 1424
      Local politics:
        Dauphiné (1700s): 4408
    Georgia:
      1700s:
        Colonial period: 1992, 4441
        1770s: 3209
        1780s: 2262, 4826
        1790s: 4826
      1700s-1800s: 2460, 2778, 3671, 5221
      1800s: 1170, 2963, 3297, 3415, 5315
      1800s: 3704
      1810s: 3704
      1820s: 3704
      1830s: 5298
      1840s: 1121, 3081, 3355, 4434, 5298, 5385, 5576

POLITICS AND GOVERNMENT:
  Subdivided by place:
    Georgia:
      1800s (Continued):
        1850s: 1121, 1123, 1422, 3081, 3355, 5298, 5576
        1860s: 662, 700, 1121, 1123, 2388, 3081, 5517, 5915
        1870s: 1203, 2096, 5051, 5517
        1880s: 261, 1203, 2096, 5051
        1890s: 662, 2096, 3947
      1800s-1900s: 2362, 3905, 3967
      1900s: 3558
      Local politics:
        Twiggs County (1800s): 1231
    Germany:
      1800s: 2079, 2742, 3472
      1900s: 2161
    Great Britain:
      1700s: 4229
      1760s: 92
      1770s: 92
      1780s: 1913
      1790s: 15, 1913, 3176
      1700s-1800s: 447, 535, 922, 1598, 2126, 4230, 5726
      1700s-1900s: 2149
      1800s: 14, 43, 258, 280, 472, 678, 1147, 1457, 1755, 1775, 1978, 2099, 3472, 3835, 3847, 4605, 4650, 4912, 5038
      1800s: 1717, 4137
      1810s: 3883, 4137, 5282
      1820s: 878
      1830s: 738, 1632, 1875, 4024, 4696, 5065, 5277, 5637
      1840s: 5, 504, 598, 1632, 2193, 4570, 4696, 5025, 5065, 5133, 5637
      1850s: 5, 598, 886, 1632, 2146, 2471, 4104, 4455, 4995
      1860s: 345, 2471, 2756, 2918, 3715, 4568, 5134, 5259, 5875
      1870s: 118, 345, 886, 2471, 4568, 5259
      1880s: 118, 345, 1765, 1872, 2736, 3693, 3744, 4036
      1890s: 2736
      1800s-1900s: 294, 452, 1014, 1079, 1260, 1499, 1815, 2060, 3980, 5164, 5222, 5736, 5806
      1900s: 3912
      1900s: 326, 4520
      1910s: 233, 5625
      1920s: 233
      1930s: 233
      1940s: 4722
      Governmental interference in Oxford (1766): 1214
      Leadership (1900): 326
      Local government:
        Halifax (1800s): 5026
      Local politics:
        Dorsetshire: 2149
        Isle of Wight: 332
        London: see LONDON, England—Politics and government
        Lymington: 4557
      Regency crisis of George III: 1913
    Greece (1800s): 345
    Guatamala (1900s): 116
    Honduras (1900s): 116
    Hungary (1800s): 3238, 3722
    Illinois (1800s): 3082, 5160
    India:
      1700s-1900s: 2756
      1800s:
        1800s: 2421, 5797
        1810s: 2421
        1820s: 2421
        1840s: 3836
        1890s: 888, 5279
      1900s: 3286
      Bombay (mid-1800s): 4097
    Indiana (1840s): 4169
    Ionian Islands (1800s): 3835

POLITICS AND GOVERNMENT:
  Subdivided by place (Continued):
    Iran (1940s): 83
    Ireland:
      1700s: 2199
      1700s-1800s: 1311, 5726
      1800s: 1775
      1830s: 4024
      1840s: 5, 504, 678, 5809
      1850s: 5, 678, 5809
      1860s: 472, 4566
      1800s-1900s: 294
    Italy:
      1700s: 2155
      1800s: 3472, 4650, 5133
      1900s: 4020
    Jamaica:
      1700s: 1913
      1700s-1800s: 5726
      1800s: 1506, 4995
    Japan (1800s): 3744, 4986, 5876
    Kansas (1850s): 4720
    Kentucky:
      1800s: 3325
      1840s: 4720
      1850s: 1083
      1860s: 20, 765
      1870s: 20
      1880s: 20
    Liberia: 3325
    Louisiana:
      1800s: 395, 1574, 2859
      1900s: 2775
    Maine (1800s): 5569, 5610
    Maryland:
      1700s: 2267, 5086
      1700s-1800s: 3627
      1800s: 3378, 4712, 4886
      1810s: 4542, 5829
      1840s: 5089
      1860s: 5059, 5775
      1870s: 5866
      1880s: 5866
      1890s: 5866
      1900s: 3086
      Local politics:
        Frederick County (1800s): 4457
        Washington County (1900s): 3086
    Massachusetts (1800s): 1433, 3037, 5762, 5917
      Local politics:
        Boxborough: 2456
    Mexico:
      1860s: 1403, 2210
        Matamoras: 3392
      1910s: 661
    Michigan (1800s): 2604
    Mississippi:
      1800s: 3415
      1820s: 2211
      1830s: 2211
      1840s: 3438
      1850s: 2370, 3611, 3809, 5498
      1860s: 2370, 2970, 5498
      1870s: 2370, 2970
      1800s-1900s: 4442
      1900s: 4918
    Missouri:
      1800s:
        1840s: 2264
        1850s: 4174, 4834
        1860s: 4733, 4834
        1870s: 4834
      1800s-1900s: 4786
    Near East (1870s): 4986
    The Netherlands (1840s): 5133
    New England (1820s): 1302
    New Hampshire:
      1800s:
        1800s: 354, 2043
        1810s: 354
        1820s: 354
        1830s: 5140
        1860s: 1983
      1800s-1900s: 4039
    New Jersey:
      1700s-1800s: 5520

POLITICS AND GOVERNMENT:
Subdivided by place:
New Jersey (Continued):
1800s: 4964
New York:
1700s-1800s: 5520
1800s:
1830s: 4751
1840s: 4169
1850s: 5788
1860s: 5788
1890s: 1907, 1977
1800s-1900s: 4808
1900s:
1920s: 2299, 4343
1930s: 4343
1940s: 2083
1950s: 2083
Local politics:
New York: 4808
New Zealand:
1800s: 2282
1800s-1900s: 1260
North Carolina:
1700s:
Colonial period: 4391
1770s: 5768
1790s: 3384, 5046
1700s-1800s: 540, 631, 2776, 3364
1700s-1900s: 2929, 4232
1800s: 602, 624, 730, 835, 838, 1061, 1659, 1677, 1871, 3351, 3415, 4686, 4714, 4816, 5207, 5664
1800s: 2491
1820s: 2776
1830s: 2776
1840s: 1580, 3764
1850s: 264, 1100, 1250, 1580, 5460
1860s: 183, 614, 1100, 2357, 2469, 2730, 2808, 2970, 3176, 3393, 3422, 4248, 5250, 5298
1870s: 122, 183, 593, 685, 1100, 2330, 2469, 2548, 2730, 2808, 2970, 5298
1880s: 122, 183, 593, 2330, 2548, 2730
1890s: 22, 122, 2330, 3972
1800s-1900s: 274, 1284, 1336, 2435, 3410, 3763, 4103, 4310, 4874, 4897, 5735
1900s: 1006, 1951, 2188, 2863, 3538, 4858, 5740
1920s: 2299, 4825
1930s: 325, 2553
1940s: 325
1950s: 325, 4805
Local politics:
Beaufort County:
1700s: 4232
1800s: 5521
Burke County (1700s-1800s): 245
Davie County (1800s): 122
Durham (1900s): 2379
Little's Mills (1870s): 5021
New Hanover County (1800s-1900s): 3410
Pitt County (1800s-1900s): 5950
Raleigh (1800s): 2819
Sunbury (1800s): 1724
Wilmington (1850s): 3447
Ohio:
1800s: 357, 920, 4076
1830s: 4732
1850s: 1578
1860s: 801, 1578
1870s: 2291
1880s: 5168
1800s-1900s: 3103
Pennsylvania:
1700s-1800s: 421
1800s: 324, 357, 849, 4188
1830s: 685

POLITICS AND GOVERNMENT:
Subdivided by place:
Pennsylvania:
1800s (Continued):
1840s: 213, 685
1850s: 685, 4756
1860s: 5775
1870s: 2027
1880s: 2027
1900s:
1930s: 1429
Persia:
1800s: 5797
1800s-1900s: 4693
Peru:
Arequipa (1841): 4155
Lima (1800s): 3238
Philippine Islands:
1800s: 2742
1900s: 561, 4511
Poland (1800s): 4650
Portugal (1800s): 3460
Rumania (1800s): 3036
Russia:
1700s-1800s: 4551, 5797
1800s: 2836, 3036, 3472
1900s: 2161
Scotland:
1700s: 2098, 4229
1700s-1800s: 1598
1800s: 4605
1900s: 3592
Proposed board for local governments: 4427
Sierra Leone: 5726
South Africa:
1800s: 1910
1900s: 4960
South Carolina:
1700s: 3304
1700s-1800s: 842, 3287
1800s: 561, 1877, 3405, 3415, 5271
1810s: 4269
1820s: 529, 2449, 3366, 4269
1830s: 1891, 2449, 3162, 3366, 4080
1840s: 1891, 3162, 3366, 4080, 5270
1850s: 2695, 2880, 4272, 5270, 5863
1860s: 791, 1220, 1424, 2107, 2695, 2831, 3615, 4193, 4272
1870s: 669, 791, 1220, 1424, 2595, 3615, 5893
1880s: 1927
1890s: 5299
1800s-1900s: 300, 501, 566, 2473, 2866, 4068, 4460
1900s: 3048, 3451
1910s: 3383, 4453
1920s: 2109, 3383, 4453
1930s: 2109, 3383, 4453
Blease movement: 300
Local politics:
Lancaster (1830): 3682
Charleston: see CHARLESTON, South Carolina--Politics and government
Political conventions (1871): 256
Tillmanism: 300, 5759
Southern States:
1800s:
1800s: 3873
1810s: 3873
1820s: 3873
1840s: 1460
Reconstruction: 1364, 1468, 5853
1900s: 4048
Spain:
1700s: 3312
1700s-1800s: 4348
1800s: 2742, 4983
1810s: 5282
1830s: 4982

POLITICS AND GOVERNMENT:
Subdivided by place:
Spain:
1800s (Continued):
1840s: 1424
Sweden (1700s): 4625
Switzerland:
1848: 5133
Geneva (1733): 4408
Tennessee:
1700s-1800s: 5046
1800s: 330, 872, 1302, 5757
1900s: 4918
Texas:
1840s: 1980
1850s: 1980, 2370
1860s: 1980, 2370, 3719, 4170
1870s: 2370, 4170
1880s: 5513
Trinidad (1700s-1800s): 5726
United States:
1700s: 3573, 4015, 4922
1700s-1800s: 404, 842, 2460, 2776, 3069, 3362, 3456, 3671, 4348, 4839, 4905, 5427
1700s-1900s: 3325, 4486, 4689, 5203
1800s: 57, 196, 324, 421, 682, 685, 805, 849, 1170, 1424, 1433, 2290, 2578, 2742, 2881, 2963, 2985, 3196, 3378, 3415, 3483, 4686, 4710, 4924, 5051, 5271, 5305, 5315, 5613, 5734, 5928, 5970
1800s: 3287, 3455, 3512, 5221
1810s: 1943, 3287, 3439, 3455, 4599
1820s: 529, 1943, 3287, 3366, 3455, 3512, 3854, 4490, 4616, 5217, 5369
1830s: 1943, 2449, 2781, 3053, 3162, 3291, 3366, 3809, 3854, 4316, 4445, 4490, 4616, 5221, 5247, 5386, 5681
1840s: 205, 2107, 2449, 2647, 2781, 2859, 2860, 3162, 3291, 3366, 3391, 3809, 4316, 4445, 4584, 4916, 4958, 5385, 5470, 5757, 5931, 5937, 5978
1850s: 1234, 1466, 2107, 2449, 2552, 2370, 2960, 3297, 3424, 3809, 3899, 4272, 4445, 4520, 4584, 4916, 4958, 5460, 5470, 5757, 5853, 5931
1860s: 183, 314, 713, 846, 1445, 2147, 2370, 2531, 2552, 2865, 2960, 3129, 3281, 3283, 3325, 3448, 3515, 3556, 3611, 3674, 3948, 4188, 4272, 4616, 4781, 4916, 4993, 5059, 5311, 5808, 5931
1870s: 183, 959, 1203, 2273, 2370, 3254, 3674, 3948, 5142, 5755, 5808
1880s: 183, 1203, 1953, 2161, 2794, 3674, 5142, 5168, 5668, 5755
1890s: 1024, 3774, 5142, 5668, 5755
1800s-1900s: 1436, 2106, 2849, 3008, 3967, 4020, 4310, 4442, 4552, 4808, 4858, 5152, 5717, 5762
1900s: 300, 2188, 2299, 3190, 3451, 3538, 5312
1900s: 1024, 3104, 4003, 4018, 4825, 5930
1910s: 1367, 4018, 4825, 5930
1920s: 1367, 2496, 3086, 4564, 4825, 5791, 5930
1930s: 274, 325, 1367, 2398, 3086, 4564
1940s: 274, 325, 3086, 5419

POLITICS AND GOVERNMENT:
  Subdivided by place:
    United States:
      1900s (Continued):
        1950s: 325, 4927
        1960s: 5773
      Utah (1890s): 2368
      Venezuela (1700s-1800s): 5726
      Venice (state) (1620): 405
      Virginia:
        1600s-1800s: 99
        1700s: 1066
        1700s-1800s: 1401, 1962, 2363, 3362, 4312, 4315, 4616
        1800s: 330, 523, 564, 581, 1075, 1115, 1957, 2141, 2881, 3182, 3721, 3809, 4131, 4490, 4710, 4924, 5513, 5613
        1810s: 872, 3291, 3623, 4531, 4615, 5031
        1820s: 872, 3291, 4531, 4615, 4852, 4880, 5005, 5217, 5904
        1830s: 872, 1384, 3291, 3566, 4531, 4766, 4852, 4880
        1840s: 152, 1384, 3566, 4766, 4852, 4916, 5324
        1850s: 753, 1384, 2370, 3537, 4295, 4616, 4916, 5577
        1860s: 20, 905, 2370, 2531, 2559, 3537, 3674, 3719, 4170, 4206, 4731, 4916, 5397, 5577
        1870s: 20, 1801, 2370, 2559, 3537, 3674, 3833, 4170, 5397, 5507
        1880s: 20, 2794, 3674, 5507
        1890s: 2922
        1800s-1900s: 574, 1364, 1436, 2732
        1900s: 2082
        1900s: 3104
        1910s: 2712, 3104
        1930s: 1429, 3820
        1940s: 3820
      Leadership: 523
      Local politics:
        Nansemond County: 3012
        Richmond: see RICHMOND, Virginia--Politics and government
      Wales: 2245
      Washington, D.C.:
        1700s-1900s: 1946
        1800s: 1734, 2761
      West Virginia:
        1700s-1900s: 865
        1800s:
          1880s: 1769
          1890s: 2016
          1800s-1900s: 356, 404, 2634, 3832
        Local politics:
          Berkeley County: 1946
          Charles Town: 5689
          Martinsburg: 3832
        Location of state capital: 2130
      Wisconsin (1800s): 5569
      Wisconsin Territory: 2881
POLITICS AND LITERATURE:
  Great Britain: 678
  United States: 4932
POLK, Alice Morella: 3433
POLK, Frances (Devereux): 4253
POLK, James Knox: 872, 1084, 2326, 2860, 4064, 4252, 5757
  Administration: 205, 3671
  Mexican War:
    Conduct of: 4720
    Unpopularity among troops: 5324
  Visit to Charleston, South Carolina: 4584
POLK, Leonidas: 637, 805, 832, 1403, 1520, 4253, 4358, 4669, 5246
POLK, Leonidas Lafayette: 3972
POLK, Sarah (Childress): 2326, 4055
POLK, William (1758-1834): 1389, 5046

POLK, William Hawkins (1815-1862): 2860
POLK COUNTY, Georgia:
  Cedartown: 5650, 5651
POLK COUNTY, North Carolina:
  Tryon: 107, 3048
POLK COUNTY, Tennessee: 2629
POLKTON, North Carolina: 1925
POLKVILLE, North Carolina:
  Methodist churches: 3646
POLKVILLE CHURCH, Polkville, North Carolina: 3646
POLKVILLE CIRCUIT, Methodist churches: 3646
POLL BOOKS: see VOTER REGISTRATION
POLL TAX:
  Great Britain: 1978
  Southern States: 4094
  Virginia: 224, 1194
POLLARD, Edward Albert: see POLLARD, Edward Alfred
POLLARD, Edward Alfred: 4733
POLLARD, Henry Rives: 1424, 2845
POLLARD, T. H.: 3242
POLLARD, Alabama: see CIVIL WAR-- CAMPAIGNS, BATTLES, AND MILITARY ACTIONS--Alabama--Pollard
POLLOCK, Sir George, First Baronet: 4254
POLLOCK, William: 5233, 5234, 5235, 5236
POLLOCK FAMILY (North Carolina-- Genealogy): 2553
POLLOCKSVILLE, North Carolina: 5709
POLLY (sloop): 4907
POMARIA, South Carolina: 458, 502, 550
POMBO, Rafael: 4155
POMEROY, Charles Richard, Jr.: 4255
POMEROY, S.: 4256
POMEROY, Theodore Medad: 388
POMEROY, Ohio: 4255
POMEROY AND VICKERY, Rochester, New York (firm): 4256
POND, Edward: 4257
POND, James Burton: 2883, 4481
PONIATOWSKI, Prince Pierre: 4491
PONSONBY, Sir Henry Frederick: 2471
PONSONBY, John: 5026
PONSONBY, John William, Fourth Earl of Bessborough: 4258, 4605, 5026
PONTON, Frances (Thompson): 4259
PONTON, Hugh N.: 4259
PONTOON BRIDGES:
  see also BRIDGE CONSTRUCTION; and Bridge construction under names of armies
  Virginia: 4990
PONTOOSUC, U.S.S.: 4404
PONTOTOC, Mississippi:
  Business affairs: 5612
POOL, John: 3094, 4923, 5457
POOL, Simeon V.: 4260
POOL, Solomon: 4261, 5457
POOL, W. G.: 4262
POOLE, Edward D.: 4263
POOLE, Ernest: 4264
POOLE, George F.: 3691
POOLESVILLE, Maryland: 703
POONA, India: 5797
POOR, Jonathan: 4265
POOR FAMILY (New Hampshire): 4265
POOR:
  see also POVERTY; PUBLIC WELFARE; RURAL POOR
  Education--Virginia: 4384
  Georgia: 5426
  Kentucky: 5426
  Louisiana: 5426
  Tennessee: 5426
  Washington, D.C.: 5426
POOR LAWS:
  see also PUBLIC WELFARE
  Great Britain: 5, 1775, 2149, 3498, 4258, 4605, 5616, 5726
  Ireland: 4605
POOR RATES: see PARISH RATES

POOR RELIEF: see CHARITIES; PUBLIC WELFARE
POOR WHITES: see RURAL POOR
POORE, Benjamin Perley: 4266
POORHOUSES:
  see also WORKHOUSES
  Georgia--Savannah: 4678
  Louisiana--New Orleans: 3870
  Maryland: 3026
  Virginia: 2964
"POP, Peter" (pseudonym): 3892
POPE, Alexander: 828
POPE, Annie Biddle: 4267
POPE, Benjamin E.: 4268
POPE, Charles T.: 4972
POPE, Erskin: 3646
POPE, Gustavus Adolphus: 4269
POPE, James R.: 4269
POPE, John (1822-1892): 1507, 4989
POPE, John H. (Maryland): 4892
POPE, Joseph Daniel: 2449, 2612
POPE, Lesey Jane (Webster): 4269
POPE, Wilie (North Carolina): 4270
POPE, William H. (North Carolina): 4270
POPE, William Leonidas (Tennessee): 4269
POPE, William Rivers (b. 1880): 4269
POPE, William Rouse (Tennessee): 4269
POPE FAMILY (North Carolina): 4269
POPE FAMILY (Virginia and West Virginia): 581
  Genealogy: 1842
POPHAM, Sir Home Riggs: 5797
POPLAR POINT TOWNSHIP, North Carolina:
  Taxation: 3935
POPP, Wilhelm: 111
POPPENHEIM, Louisa Bouknight: 4271
POPPENHEIM, Mary Barnett: 4271
POPULATION:
  see also DEMOGRAPHIC STUDIES; VITAL STATISTICS, and Vital statistics as subheading under specific groups of people, e.g. SLAVES--Vital statistics
  British West Indies: 1913
  China: 5225
  France--Tours: 5323
  Louisiana--New Orleans: 5499
  Ohio--Chillicothe: 5149
  Shetland Islands: 229
  United States: 3145
POPULIST PARTY: see PEOPLE'S PARTY OF THE UNITED STATES
PORCELAIN: see CLAY (Porcelain)
PORCHER, Francis Peyre: 2449
PORCHER, Frederick A.: 395
PORCHER, Octavius Theodore: 4272
PORK TRADE:
  North Carolina: 2889, 2924
  Virginia--Suffolk: 1838
PORT-AU-PRINCE, Saint Domingue: 321
PORT CHARGES: see Harbors--Port charges
PORT GIBSON, Mississippi: 2095
  see also CIVIL WAR--CAMPAIGNS, BATTLES, AND MILITARY ACTIONS-- Mississippi--Port Gibson
PORT HUDSON, Louisiana: see CIVIL WAR--CAMPAIGNS, BATTLES, AND MILITARY ACTIONS--Louisiana--Port Hudson
PORT LAVACA, Texas: 1153
PORT OF ROANOKE, North Carolina: see EDENTON, North Carolina
PORT REPUBLIC, Virginia: 146, 1559, 1600, 2977
  Civil War: see CIVIL WAR--CAMPAIGNS, BATTLES, AND MILITARY ACTIONS-- Virginia--Port Republic
  Saddlers' accounts: 5346
  Sons of Temperance: 4954
PORT RICHMOND, Iowa: 243
PORT ROYAL, South Carolina:
  Civil War: see CIVIL WAR-- CAMPAIGNS, BATTLES, AND MILITARY ACTIONS--South Carolina--Port Royal

PORT ROYAL, South Carolina
  (Continued):
    Trade and commerce: 1927
PORT ROYAL, Virginia: 940
PORT SAID, Egypt: 41
PORT TOBACCO, Maryland: 3006
  Land deeds and indentures: 5089
  Wills: 5089
PORT WALTHAL, Virginia: see CIVIL
  WAR--CAMPAIGNS, BATTLES, AND
  MILITARY ACTIONS--Virginia--Port
  Walthal
PORTAGE COUNTY, Ohio:
  Randolph: 5898
PORTE, Joel: 720
PORTER, Charles W.: 4273
PORTER, David (1780-1843): 350,
  3150, 3742, 4274
PORTER, David Dixon (1813-1891):
  2536, 3192, 4275
PORTER, Fitz-John: 4276
PORTER, James: 5050
PORTER, John (New York): 388
PORTER, John (d. 1711, North
  Carolina): 4232
PORTER, John J. (North Carolina):
  4391
PORTER, John Richardson: 1087, 4277
PORTER, Katherine Anne: 1137, 4278
PORTER, Mary J.: 1160
PORTER, Noah: 3142
PORTER, Susan (Lockwood): 4273
PORTER, Theodoric Henry: 4274
PORTER, William D.: 5092
PORTER, William Sydney: 4279
PORTER, Wisconsin--Schools: 5307
PORTLAND, William Henry Cavendish-
  Bentinck, Third Duke of: 447, 2149
PORTLAND, Maine: 1554, 1787, 2106,
  3551
  Social life and customs: 2043
PORTLAND, Oregon: 5033
PORTO PRAYA, Cape Verde Islands:
  3118
PORTO RICO CHILD FEEDING COMMITTEE:
  3633
THE PORTRAIT OF MR. W. H. by Oscar
  Wilde: 2146
PORTRAITS: 4073
  see also ART AND ARTISTS; and
    Portraits as subheading under
    names of specific persons
  Arkansas: 5380
  Miniatures--Prices: 1575
  New York: 2518
  North Carolina: 4506
  Pennsylvania: 4057
  Portugal: 2411
  United Confederate Veterans: 3376
  United States: 1665, 2726, 4343
PORTRAITS IN TILE: see INTERIOR
  DECORATION--Portraits in tile
PORTS: see COALING STATIONS; HARBORS
PORTSEA, England: 485
PORTSMOUTH, John Wallop, Second Earl
  of: 5331
PORTSMOUTH, England:
  Defenses: 5330
  Fires (1771): 92
PORTSMOUTH, New Hampshire: 4062,
  4986
PORTSMOUTH, Ohio: 281
  Labor unions: 3986
PORTSMOUTH, Virginia: 1274, 1415,
  1701, 2318, 4281
  Civil War: 4561, 5423
    Fortifications: 5975
  Diseases--Yellow fever: 3301
  Insurance companies: 4282
  Lawsuits: 5702
  Personal finance: 520
  School taxes assessed on freedmen:
    3012
  Schools: 4280
PORTSMOUTH (ship): 81
PORTSMOUTH ACADEMY, Portsmouth,
  Virginia: 4280

PORTSMOUTH AND ROANOKE RAILROAD:
  624, 4492
PORTSMOUTH CIRCUIT, Methodist
  Episcopal Church: 3601
PORTSMOUTH DOCK COMPANY, Portsmouth,
  Virginia: 4281
PORTSMOUTH INSURANCE COMPANY,
  Portsmouth, Virginia: 4282
PORTUGAL:
  British embassy in: 3472
  Description and travel (1926):
    2934
  Foreign relations:
    Great Britain: 118, 1599, 1775,
      5726
    Spain: 2155
    United States: 4748
  Foreign trade:
    Great Britain: 4289
    United States: 1481
  Historic buildings: 2411
  Peninsular War: see GREAT BRITAIN--
    ARMY--Napoleonic Wars--Portugal;
    GREAT BRITAIN--NAVY--Operations--
    Napoleonic Wars--Peninsular War;
    PENINSULAR WAR
  Politics and government (1880s):
    3460
  Portraits: 2411
  Railroad construction: 1632
  Slave trade--Colonies: 5726
  Transatlantic voyages--Lisbon:
    5298
PORTUGUESE LANGUAGE: 3248
PORTUGUESE LITERATURE: 5404
POSEY, J. R.: 4283
POSEY AND McBRIDE (firm): see
  McBRIDE AND POSEY
POSSESSION OF STOLEN GOODS: 3622
POST, A. V.: 1003
POST OAK MEETING HOUSE, North
  Carolina:
  Original Free Will Baptist Church of
    North Carolina: 3987
POST CARDS: see POSTAL CARDS
POST OFFICE: see (name of country)--
  Government agencies and officials--
  Post Office; (name of state)--
  Postal service; OVERLAND MAIL;
  RAILROADS--Mail service;
  TRANSATLANTIC MAIL PACKETS
POST OFFICE BOXES, Invention of: 99
POST-ROADS: 2486
POSTAGE STAMPS: see PHILATELY
POSTAL CARDS: 3523
POSTAL SERVICE: see (name of
  country)--Government agencies and
  officials--Post Office; (name of
  state)--Postal service; CIVIL
  WAR--MAIL SERVICE BETWEEN NORTH
  AND SOUTH; OVERLAND MAIL;
  RAILROADS--Mail service;
  TRANSATLANTIC MAIL PACKETS
POSTAL WORKERS: see LABOR UNIONS--
  Postal workers
POSTMASTERS: see (name of country)--
  Government agencies and officials--
  Post Office--Local offices
POTATO TRADE:
  Exports:
    Ireland and Scotland: 3230
  Imports:
    North and South Carolina: 3230
  Prices--Rhode Island: 3580
POTEAT, James: 4284
POTOMAC, U.S.S.: 3378
POTOMAC BANK (Virginia): 4215
POTOMAC COMPANY: 4598
POTOMAC RIVER:
  Civil War: 19
    see also CIVIL WAR--CAMPAIGNS,
    BATTLES, AND MILITARY ACTIONS--
    Virginia--Potomac River
  Confederate Army life: 4253
  Navigation laws and regulations:
    2383
  Rapids: 4598
  Riverboat pilots: 5336

POTOMAC RIVER (Continued):
  Transportation: 489
POTOSI, Missouri: 669
POTSDAM CONFERENCE: 83
POTTAWATTAMIE COUNTY, Iowa:
  Council Bluffs: 538
POTTER, Alonzo: 3277, 4285
POTTER, Beatrice: 1815
POTTER, Harriet (Moore) Page: 4286
POTTER, Henry Codman: 2871
POTTER, Nathaniel: 3399
POTTER, Robert (1721-1804): 1538
POTTER, Robert (ca. 1800-1841): 4286
POTTER, Thomas: 4287
POTTER & PARSLEY, Wilmington, North
  Carolina (firm): 2924
POTTERTON, Thomas Edward: 2449
POTTERY: see AMERICAN POTTERY;
  MULTAN POTTERY
POTTERY TRADE: see STONEWARE TRADE
POTTS, John C.: 2576
POTTS, William: 4288
POTTS, William II: 4288
POTTSVILLE, Pennsylvania: 2408
POU, Edith: 274
POU, James Hinton: 5457
POU FAMILY (North Carolina): 274
POUCHER, Morris R.: 5252
POUGHKEEPSIE, New York: 568, 1516,
  2035
  see also VASSAR COLLEGE
  Social life and customs: 1908
POULETT, George: 4289
POULTON, England: 3251
POULTRY: 43
POULTRY FARMING:
  Virginia--Fluvanna County: 5035
POUND, Ezra: 2398
POUND, Louise: 4290
POUND, Olivia: 4290
POUND, Roscoe: 4290
POURTALES, James: 4224
POURTALÈS-GORGIER, Mary Louisa
  Amelia Boozer, Countess: 1464
POVERTY:
  see also POOR; and Economic
    conditions as subheading under
    names of places
  Alabama: 1084
  Camden: 4184
  Great Britain: 43
  Kentucky: 1654
  Maryland: 411
  North Carolina: 1409, 3003
  South Carolina:
    Chester District: 1268
  Southern States: 2449, 4460, 5051,
    5349, 5623
    see also RECONSTRUCTION--
    Economic conditions
  Tennessee: 4951, 5268
  Virginia: 411
    Powhatan County: 619
POWE, Charlotte Wilson: 3048
POWEL, Samuel II: 4291
POWEL, Samuel III: 4291
POWELL, Aaron Macy: 1968
POWELL, Charles S.: 4292
POWELL, Helen F.: 4294
POWELL, John (Georgia): 4293
POWELL, John (1882-1963): 1424
POWELL, John Benjamin (1886-1947):
  5252
POWELL, Mary E. V.: 4294
POWELL, Paulus: 4295
POWELL, Thomas: 3163
POWELL, Thomas Speer: 4296
POWELL (W. C.) COMPANY,
  Jacksonville, Florida: 4298
POWELL, Walter: 4297
POWELL, William C. (Florida): 4298
POWELL, William C. (North Carolina):
  4586
POWELL, William C. Fitzhugh
  (Virginia): 4299
POWELL, William Henry (1823-1879):
  2587

POWELLSVILLE, North Carolina: 3746
POWER, Marguerite: 3077
POWER, William Grattan Tyrone: 4300
POWER, Samuel D.: 3844
POWERS, Roberta (Smith): 4301
POWERS FAMILY (New York and
    Virginia): 5660
POWHATAN, U.S.S.: 3899
POWHATAN COUNTY, Virginia: 266,
    619, 2380
  Airy Hill: 1020
  Jude's Ferry: 2369
POWIS, Edward Clive, First Earl of:
    5639
POWYS, John Cowper: 364
POYNOR, D. Thomas: 4302
PRAGER, Charles: 5228
PRAGER, Harriet: 5228
PRAGER, Mark: 5228
PRAIRIE GROVE, Arkansas: see CIVIL
    WAR--CAMPAIGNS, BATTLES, AND
    MILITARY ACTIONS--Arkansas--
    Prairie Grove
PRAIRIEVILLE, Alabama: 4083
PRASCA ARBORÉ & CO.: 197
PRASSER, Josephine: 4947
PRATER, Margaret E. (Baker): 4303
PRATER, Mitchell C.: 4303
PRATT, Caleb: 4304
PRATT, Enoch: 3053
PRATT, Harvey Hunter: 4305
PRATT, Nathaniel A.: 4306
PRATT, William N.: 4307
PRATT HOSPITAL, Lynchburg, Virginia:
    Civil War: 1506, 1886, 4308
    Commissary records: 2879
PRATTSBURG, North Carolina:
    Blacksmiths' and shoemakers'
        accounts: 4307
    Estates--Administration and
        settlement: 4307
PRAY, Amasa: 5955
PRAYER by Juliana Rebecca (Fuller)
    Hume Campbell: 864
PRAYERS:
    see also PUBLIC PRAYERS
    South Carolina: 2961
"PREACHER DAN" by George L. MacKay:
    3397
PREACHING:
    see also CLERGY; SERMONS
    Negro women:
        South Carolina: 2762
    Study and teaching: 5022
    Virginia: 132
PREBLE COUNTY, Ohio: 2606
    Eaton: 1849
PRECEPT (periodical): 5971
PRE-EMPTION: see PUBLIC LANDS--
    Pre-emption
PREJUDICE: see ANTI-CATHOLICISM;
    ANTISEMITISM; SEGREGATION
"PRELUDES" by Flavius Joseph Cook:
    1219
PREMATURE BURIAL: 531
PRENTISS, Sergeant Smith: 4900
PRENTISS, William: 3897
PREPARATORY SCHOOLS: see SCHOOLS--
    Preparatory schools
PRESBYTERIAN: 37
PRESBYTERIAN CHURCHES:
    see also ASSOCIATE REFORMED
        PRESBYTERIAN CHURCH; INDEPENDENT
        PRESBYTERIAN CHURCH;
        PRESBYTERIAN CHURCH IN THE
        UNITED STATES
    Charities: 5979
    Church buildings--Construction:
        5979
    Clergy: see CLERGY--Presbyterian
    Deacons: 4310
    Doctrine:
        New Light: 3161
        North Carolina: 1152
        Northern Ireland: 2738
    Education: 5979
        see also THEOLOGICAL SEMINARIES--
            Presbyterian

PRESBYTERIAN CHURCHES:
    Education (Continued):
        South Carolina: 4609
    Elders: 4310
    Evangelism: 5979
    Finance:
        South Carolina: 4310
        Virginia: 5979
    Fund raising--Virginia: 5979
    General Assembly: 3432
    Membership: 4310
        South Carolina--Chester: 5988
    Missions: see MISSIONS AND
        MISSIONARIES--Presbyterian
    "Old style": 5731
    Revivals: 5538
    Sermons: see SERMONS--Presbyterian
    Woman's Foreign Missionary Union:
        3527
    Subdivided by place:
        Arkansas: 1361
        Georgia:
            Augusta: 26
            Macon: 3905
        Kentucky: 4387
            Lexington: 3325
        New York: 1908
            West Chester: 5731
        North Carolina: 1556, 2269, 3432,
            5962
            Concord: 5245
            Durham: 3762
            Fayetteville: 1438
            Shiloh: 5245
            Townsville: 1361
        Ohio: 4076
        Rhode Island: 1906
        South Carolina: 3123, 3371, 4031,
            4145, 4453
            Camden: 4642
            Charleston: 4936
            Enoree Presbytery: 3527
            Greenville: 5825
        Southern States: 761
        Tennessee: 2661
            Hendersonville: 5671
        United States: 2591
        Virginia: 743, 1744, 1827, 2120
            Lynchburg: 3707
            Winchester Presbytery: 5979
        West Virginia:
            Berkeley County: 4056
            Martinsburg: 5110
PRESBYTERIAN CHURCH IN THE UNITED
    STATES: 4310, 5014
    Board of World Missions: 2269
PRESBYTERIAN EYE AND EAR CHARITABLE
    HOSPITAL, Baltimore, Maryland:
    2830
PRESBYTERIAN FEMALE COLLEGIATE
    INSTITUTE, Talladega, Alabama:
    1947
PRESBYTERIAN MISSION SCHOOL, Leslie,
    South Carolina: 3356
PRESCOTT AND FLEMING, Natchez,
    Mississippi (firm): 4309
PRESCRIPTIONS: see MEDICINE--
    Prescriptions
"PRESENTING ANNULET ANDREWS--POET"
    by Aubrey Harrison Starke: 3969
PRESERVATION: see HISTORICAL
    RESTORATION
PRESIDENTIAL ELECTIONS (United
    States): 1364, 3066, 5252
    1796: 2776, 3041
    1800: 3041, 3671
    1804: 3076
    1808: 2138
    1812: 3176
    1824: 2870, 3512, 4933, 4964, 5369
        Maryland: 4359
    1828: 872, 1302, 3720, 4531, 4987
        Illinois: 3082
        Ohio: 4165
    1832: 3415
    1836: 3378, 3415, 4531, 4880, 5451

PRESIDENTIAL ELECTIONS (Continued):
    1840: 842, 1100, 1501, 1798, 2860,
        3054, 3415, 4732, 5051, 5520
    1844: 842, 1084, 1086, 1170, 2448,
        3325, 3415, 4134, 4732, 5128,
        5868
    1848: 842, 1609, 3325, 3415, 3788,
        4720, 4732, 5051, 5059, 5149,
        5380, 5974
    1852: 762, 1084, 2681, 3032, 3325,
        3910, 4131, 4720, 4732, 5298,
        5517
    1856: 1084, 1422, 1769, 3297, 3848
        3910, 4732, 5051, 5499, 5578,
        5831, 5853
        Democratic Party candidates:
            3297, 4856, 5315
        North Carolina: 2469
        Pennsylvania: 4556
        Tennessee: 4291
        Virginia: 569
    1860: 635, 1289, 2105, 2298, 2589,
        2693, 4616, 4720, 4852, 5051,
        5059, 5298, 5498, 5551, 5561,
        5563, 5593, 5613, 5753, 5775
        Tennessee: 4291
        Vice presidential candidate: 2860
    1864: 13, 635, 1282, 2223, 3280,
        4108, 4561, 4881, 4888, 5132,
        5261, 5269, 5307, 5402, 5419
        Northern States: 2966
    1868: 1865, 4202, 4751, 5517
        Alabama: 4751
    1872: 2091
    1876: 1424, 2141, 2273, 2294, 3029,
        3254, 3537, 3702, 4131, 5051,
        5142
        South Carolina: 3405
    1880: 2294, 4751
    1884: 1203, 2225, 2294, 3029, 4125,
        5866
    1888: 4125, 5168, 5324
    1896: 3407
    1904: 4048
    1912: 690, 706, 1171, 3380, 3451,
        4020, 5252
        Republican Party nomination: 4808
    1916: 2866, 3380, 3451, 4020, 4449,
        4858
    1920: 2299, 5110
    1924: 1272, 2299, 3086
    1928: 879, 2299, 3086, 3538
        Congressional investigation into
            campaign finances: 879
        North Carolina: 274
            Division over Democratic Party
                nominee: 3538
        Southern defection from
            Democratic Party: 4825
    1932: 3086, 4558, 4564, 4858, 4948
    1936: 2627, 3086, 3538
    1940: 3086, 5497
    1948: 2627
    1952: 225, 4251
    1956: 4251
    1960: 4251
    1964: 613, 4251
    1968: 4251, 5077
    1972: 4251
    1976: 4251
PRESIDENTIAL IMPEACHMENTS:
    Andrew Johnson: 1787, 4895
PRESIDENTIAL MEMORIAL COMMISSION: 4927
PRESIDENTIAL NOMINATING POLITICS IN
    1952 by Paul T. David: 3820
PRESIDENTIAL PARDONS:
    1819: 5242
    To former Confederates: 1268, 2847
        Alabama: 4911
        North Carolina: 470, 685, 2339,
            4788, 5188
        South Carolina: 5863
        Virginia: 3809
"THE PRESIDENTIAL QUESTION DISCUSSED"
    by H. V. Johnson: 2860
PRESIDENTS: see INAUGURATIONS--
    Presidents; PRESIDENTIAL ELECTIONS;
    and names of specific presidents

PRESIDENT'S AMNESTY BOARD (1950s):
    4927
PRESIDENT'S COMMITTEE ON EQUAL
    OPPORTUNITY IN THE ARMED FORCES
    (1960s): 3820
PRESNALL FAMILY (North Carolina):
    3186
PRESS AND GOVERNMENT: see GOVERNMENT
    AND THE PRESS
PRESS AND MEDICINE: see MEDICINE
    AND THE PRESS
PRESS RELEASES: 83
    see also PUBLIC RELATIONS
    China (1940s): 1025
    United States:
        Department of the Navy: 1367
PRESSLY, Ebenezer Erskine: 4310
PRESSLY, George W.: 5457
PRESSLY, John Ebenezer: 4311
PRESTON, Bowker: 2633
PRESTON, Francis (1765-1833): 4315
PRESTON, Francis Smith: 2881
PRESTON, Harriet Waters: 2449, 5447
PRESTON, John (Montgomery County,
    Virginia, general): 4315
PRESTON, John (Walnut Grove,
    Virginia): 4312
PRESTON, Letitia: 2881
PRESTON, Louise E.: 4314
PRESTON, Margaret (Junkin): 2449, 4313,
    5044
PRESTON, Norman: 4314
PRESTON, Walter E.: 4312
PRESTON, William (1729-1783): 4315
PRESTON, William Ballard
    (1805-1862): 5271
PRESTON, William Campbell
    (1794-1860): 872, 2612, 3483, 4316
PRESTON FAMILY (Massachusetts): 4314
PRESTON FAMILY (South Carolina): 4316
PRESTON FAMILY (Virginia): 2881
PRESTON, England: 562, 1087
    Methodist Sunday schools: 5895
PRESTON, Mississippi: 2349
PRESTON, Oklahoma: 3687
PRESTON COUNTY, West Virginia:
    Carmel: 5820
PRETORIA, South Africa: 4960
PREVOST, Augustine: 4317
PREWIT, James: 2815
PRICE, Addie: 4318
PRICE, Charles (1846-1905): 5457
PRICE, Edward: 2432
PRICE, Edwin Y.: 4319
PRICE, Eli Kirk: 5083
PRICE, Elizabeth: 3560
PRICE, H. H.: 4320
PRICE, Irene: 5022
PRICE, J. C.: 3972
PRICE, James (Mississippi): 4325
PRICE, James (North Carolina): 4321
PRICE, John Alton: 3752
PRICE, R. A.: 4318
PRICE, Rodman McCamley: 4322
PRICE, Sterling: 395, 4323
PRICE, Thomas: 4325
PRICE, William B.: 4324
PRICE, Z. M.: 4325
PRICE FAMILY (Kentucky and Virginia):
    4319
PRICE AND BENNETT (firm): see
    BENNETT AND PRICE
PRICE & McCORMICK (firm): see
    McCORMICK AND PRICE
PRICE FIXING: see as subheading
    under specific businesses and
    industries
PRICE REGULATION--Virginia: 4094
PRICES: see COMMODITY PRICES; and
    Prices as subheading under names
    of specific commodities and
    services, e.g. COTTON--Prices
PRICES OF SLAVES: see SLAVE TRADE--
    Prices
PRIDEAUX, William Francis: 4327
PRIDGEN, Robert H.: 4328
PRIESTLEY, Joseph: 890
PRIESTS: see CLERGY

PRIM, John M.: 4329
PRIM, Mira Belle: 4329
PRIM, Nannie: 4329
PRIM FAMILY (North Carolina): 4329
PRIME, Samuel Irenaeus: 4330
PRIMITIVE BAPTIST CHURCH:
    Clergy: see CLERGY--Primitive
        Baptist
    Doctrine: 4963
    North Carolina: 318
    Texas: 318
    Elders: 4500
    Finance:
        North Carolina--Tarboro: 5185
    Religious experiences: 318
    Subdivided by place:
        North Carolina: 4500
            Greenville: 318
            Tarboro: 5185
        Texas--Mabank: 318
PRIMROSE, Archibald Philip, Fifth
    Earl of Rosebery: 663, 1815,
    2146, 4520
PRIMROSE, Helen Mary (McMicking)
    Denman Walker: 4331
PRIMROSE, Sir Henry William: 4331
PRIMROSE, Neil, Third Earl of
    Rosebery: 306
PRINCE, Elizabeth Oakes: 3960
PRINCE, Kimball F.: 4049
PRINCE, Oliver H.: 2787
PRINCE, Richard: 1884
PRINCE DE JOINVILLE: see JOINVILLE,
    François Ferdinand Philippe Louis
    Marie, Prince de
PRINCE EDWARD ACADEMY, Worsham,
    Virginia: 5110
PRINCE EDWARD COUNTY, Virginia:
    2427, 2882, 5794
    Farm life: 5884
    Tobacco culture: 5884
    Cities and towns:
        Farmville: 1729, 2683, 2712, 3136
            Tobacco: 531
        Hampden-Sydney: 3740
            see also HAMPDEN-SYDNEY
                COLLEGE; HAMPDEN-SYDNEY
                INSTITUTE
PRINCE EDWARD COURT HOUSE, Virginia:
    Merchants: 5282
PRINCE EDWARD ISLAND, Canada: 1756
    Governors: 1756
PRINCE FREDERICKTOWN, Maryland:
    Business affairs: 4844
PRINCE GEORGE COUNTY, Virginia: 3151
    Ruthven: 4594
PRINCE GEORGES COUNTY, Maryland:
    5329
    Civil War: 664
    Cities and towns:
        Bladensburg--Clergy: 610
        "Mattaponi": 596
        Queen Anne: 5969
        Upper Marlboro: 785, 1043
PRINCE OF WALES: see GEORGE IV, King
    of Great Britain; EDWARD VII, King
    of Great Britain
PRINCE OF WALES ISLAND: 5797
PRINCE WILLIAM COUNTY, Virginia: 5283
    Tobacco trade: 144
    Cities and towns:
        Buckland: 2728, 3532
        Centerville: 2489
        Civil War: 1137
        Dumfries: 2703
            Tobacco trade: 144
        Manassas: see MANASSAS, Virginia
        Mount Pleasant: 4483
PRINCE WILLIAM HOTEL, Manassas,
    Virginia: 5779
PRINCESS ALICE (packet boat): 4719
PRINCESS ANNE COUNTY, Virginia:
    Brigands and robbers: 5380
"THE PRINCESS SONIA" by Julia
    Magruder: 3465
PRINCETON, Massachusetts: 4800
PRINCETON, New Jersey: 1662, 2665,
    3408, 3707, 5823

PRINCETON, New Jersey (Continued):
    see also PRINCETON UNIVERSITY
    Community and college: 1395
    Social life and customs: 730
PRINCETON COLLEGE, Princeton, New
    Jersey: see PRINCETON UNIVERSITY
PRINCETON UNIVERSITY, Princeton,
    New Jersey: 581, 643, 1333, 1778,
    2517, 3247, 4429, 4774, 5221
    Curriculum: 1333
    Discipline: 5075
    Law notebooks: 2521
    Mathematics notebooks: 2521
    Psychology notebooks: 2521
    Students and student life:
        1700s: 2776
        1800s: 872, 3145, 5689
        Finance: 2020
        Parents' letters: 1547
        Political activity: 1395
    Theological Seminary: 1351
    Theses: 5530
"PRINCIPAL CLAIMS OF MAJ. GEN. E. O.
    KEYES FOR RESTORATION": 5419
"PRINCIPLES OF AMERICAN POLITICAL
    PARTIES" by Robert Lansing: 3096
PRINCIPLES OF WEALTH AND WELFARE by
    Charles Lee Raper: 4391
PRINGLE, Sir James, Fourth Baronet:
    5104
PRINGLE, James Reid: 4332
PRINGLE, Sir John, First Baronet:
    4333
PRINGLE, Motte A.: 1185
PRINGLE, Robert A.: 4334
PRINGLE FAMILY (South Carolina--
    Genealogy): 1468
PRINTERS: see INTERNATIONAL
    TYPOGRAPHICAL UNION
PRINTING:
    see also LINOTYPE; STEREOTYPE
        FOUNDRIES; TYPE FOUNDRIES
    Georgia: 1112
    Mississippi: 1693
    North Carolina: 2589
    Pennsylvania: 3490
    Southern States: 3490
PRINTING PRESSES: 1884, 3022
PRINTUP, Daniel S.: 4335
PRISON ESCAPES: see CIVIL WAR--
    PRISONERS AND PRISONS--Confederate
    prisoners--Escaped prisoners in
    Canada; CIVIL WAR--PRISONERS AND
    PRISONS--Union prisoners--Escapes
    and escaped prisoners
THE PRISON NEWS (periodical): 3415
PRISON REFORM--Southern States: 3558
PRISONER EXCHANGES: see AMERICAN
    REVOLUTION--Prisoner exchanges;
    CIVIL WAR--PRISONER EXCHANGES
PRISONERS AND PRISONS:
    see also BAIL BONDS;
        TRANSPORTATION OF CONVICTS; and
        Prisoners and prisons as
        subheading under names of wars
    Debtors: see DEBT--Imprisonment
        for
    Distribution of work on slavery:
        773
    Imprisonment of slaves: see
        SLAVES--Imprisonment
    Labor: see CONFEDERATE STATES OF
        AMERICA--ARMY--Convicts, Use of;
        PEONAGE
    Religious instruction:
        Pennsylvania: 616
    Subdivided by place:
        France--Bastille: 4693
        Georgia: 5426
        Great Britain: 1087, 2835, 3809,
            5726
        Kentucky: 5426
        Louisiana: 5426
        Maryland:
            Baltimore: 3267
            Washington County: 3875
        Massachusetts--Fort Warren: 3378

PRISONERS AND PRISONS:
  Subdivided by place (Continued):
    North Carolina: 641, 2821
      Raleigh: 3415
      Statesville: 1966
    Pennsylvania: 616
      Philadelphia: 2552
    Tennessee: 5426
    Turkey: 3183
    Virginia: 872
    Washington, D.C.: 5426
PRISONERS OF WAR: see Prisoners and prisons as subheading under names of specific wars
PRITCHARD, Jeter Connelly: 1284
PRITCHARD, Thomas H.: 5457
PRITCHARD, William H.: 3355
PRITCHETT, W. W.: 4336
PRIVAT D'ANGLEMONT, Alexandre: 4337
THE PRIVATE JOURNAL OF THE MARQUESS OF HASTINGS ed. by Marchioness of Bute: 2421
PRIVATE LIBRARIES: see LIBRARIES--Private
PRIVATE SCHOOLS: see BOARDING SCHOOLS; SCHOOLS
PRIVATE USE OF PUBLIC PROPERTY: see PUBLIC PROPERTY--Private use
PRIVATEER, South Carolina: 1923, 3356
PRIVATEERING: 4982
  see also AMERICAN REVOLUTION--Privateering; CIVIL WAR--PRIVATEERING; CORSAIRS; PIRATES: WAR OF 1812--Privateering
  France: 1615
  Great Britain: 4171
  United States: 4531
PRIVILEGES AND IMMUNITIES:
  see also IMPEACHMENTS
  Great Britain: 4605
PRIVY COUNCIL: see GREAT BRITAIN--GOVERNMENT AGENCIES AND OFFICIALS--Privy Council
PRIZE MONEY: see GREAT BRITAIN--NAVY--Prize money
PRIZE SHIPS: see as subheading under names of wars, e.g. FRENCH REVOLUTIONARY WARS--Prize ships
PROBATE COURTS: see COURTS--Probate courts
PROBATION AND PAROLE:
  United States: 4927
PROBSTHAIN, Arthur: 5252
PROCEEDINGS OF THE ALPINE CLUB: 5050
PROCEEDINGS OF THE NORTH CAROLINA STATE FEDERATION OF LABOR: 3944
PROCOPÉ, Xjalmar Fredrik Eugen: 4338
PROCTER, Richard Wright: 39
PROCTOR, George: 3315
PRODUCTION AND DIRECTION: see THEATER--Production and direction
PRODUCTION COSTS--United States: 3190
PRODUCTION STANDARDS--Testing: 1951
PRODUCTIVITY, Industrial: see INDUSTRIAL PRODUCTIVITY
"PROEM! PRELUDE" by Alexander B. Meek: 3611
"PROFESSOR M": 5940
PROFESSORS: see UNIVERSITIES AND COLLEGES--Faculty; and Faculty as subheading under names of specific universities and colleges
PROFITEERING: see Speculation and war profiteering as subheading under names of wars
PROFITS: see as subheading under names of specific businesses and industries, e.g. TEXTILE INDUSTRY--Profits
"PROGRAM OF THE SOCIALIST PARTY, U.S.A., FOR 1976": 4947
"PROGRAMS AND COMMITTEES OF DURHAM [N.C.] CIVIC ASSOCIATION, 1915-1916": 4968
PROGRESSIVE CITIZENS FOR AMERICA: 1194

PROGRESSIVE FARMER (periodical): 4080
PROHIBITION:
  see also TEMPERANCE
  Enforcement: 1478
  Laws and legislation:
    Pennsylvania: 4188
  Violation:
    Florida and Georgia: 1248
  Subdivided by place:
    Great Britain: 5164
    Massachusetts: 4125
    North Carolina: 2861, 2895, 3410, 4192, 4828
      Sampson County: 2863
    Pennsylvania: 5536
    Rhode Island: 5536
    South Carolina: 300
    Texas: 592
    United States: 274, 1219, 1554, 2225, 2299, 3451, 4564, 4858, 4948, 5082, 5929
PRO-LEAGUE INDEPENDENTS: 5110
PROMETHEUS, U.S.S.: 4355
PROMETHEUS VINCTUS: 1538
PROMISSORY NOTES: 1339
  Collection of:
    see also DEBT COLLECTION
    Missouri: 5155
    Pennsylvania: 421
    Tennessee: 5935
    Virginia--Columbia: 5035
  Subdivided by place:
    Alabama--Gay's Landing: 5879
    Georgia: 1434
    Great Britain--Exeter: 5867
    Maryland:
      Frederick County: 4457
      Sharpsburg: 979
    Massachusetts: 3633
    Mississippi--Sartartia: 5821
    North Carolina: 4858, 4897, 5475
      Fayetteville: 2354
      Halifax County: 5674
      Milton: 5815
      Oxford: 2455
      Ridgeway: 999
    South Carolina: 4509
    Tennessee: 4269
    Virginia--Hicks Ford: 5891
"PRONTUARIO DE CAPELLANÍAS FUNDADAS EN EL PERÚ" by Tomas Florenz: 4155
PROPAGANDA: 83, 4614
  see also LOBBYING
PROPERTY: see LAND; REAL ESTATE
  Alien: see Alien property as subheading under wars, e.g. CIVIL WAR--ALIEN PROPERTY
PROPERTY DAMAGE:
  see also CIVIL WAR--CLAIMS--Destruction of property
  South Carolina--Charleston: 4216
PROPERTY EVALUATION:
  Maryland: 5296
    Frederick County: 4457
  North Carolina--Randolph County: 2459
  Virginia--Halifax County: 5483
PROPERTY INSURANCE: see INSURANCE--Property
PROPERTY LISTS:
  Alabama: 5612
  Georgia: 5353
  Mississippi: 5612
  North Carolina:
    Durham County: 1256
    Mocksville: 2749
  Tennessee: 5612
  Texas: 5612
  Virginia: 1242
PROPHECIES:
  Mississippi: 530
  North Carolina: 530
PROSECUTION: see INDICTMENTS
PROSPECT HILL, Virginia: 2233
PROSPECTING FOR GOLD: see GOLD RUSH
PROSTHESIS--Georgia: 2280
PROSTITUTION--South Carolina: 150

PROTECTION: see FREE TRADE; TARIFFS
PROTECTION LIFE INSURANCE COMPANY OF CHICAGO: 2013
PROTESTANT EPISCOPAL CHURCH:
  Bishops:
    Election: 4669
    Kentucky: 4869
    Mississippi: 2175
    Pennsylvania: 4285
    Virginia: 2935, 3456
  Board of Foreign Missions: 4215
  Church buildings:
    Maryland--Baltimore: 4638
  Church history:
    Maryland: 4638
    United States: 2999
  Clergy: see CLERGY--Protestant Episcopal
  Controversies: 128
  Convention (1838): 4669
  Doctrine: 128, 3666
  Effect of Civil War on: 128
  Finance:
    Illinois: 993
    Maryland--Baltimore: 4638
    North Carolina: 3176
    United States: 993
    West Virginia--Shepherdstown: 128
  Fund raising--Virginia: 1712
  Lay readers: 4897
  Missions and missionaries: see MISSIONS AND MISSIONARIES--Protestant Episcopal
  Negro members:
    South Carolina--Charleston: 89
  Pastoral relations:
    West Virginia--Shepherdstown: 128
  Pew rent:
    Maryland--Baltimore: 4638
  Sermons: see SERMONS--Protestant Episcopal
  Subdivided by place:
    Alabama: 4358
    Georgia: 4358
    Kentucky: 4869
    Maryland--Baltimore: 4638
    Mississippi: 4358
    New Hampshire: 4869
    North Carolina: 4358, 5298
      Diocese of North Carolina: 4232
      Raleigh: 4394
    South Carolina: 883, 4271, 4358
      Charleston: 4637
    Tennessee: 4339, 4358
    Texas: 1361
    Virginia: 128, 356, 4173, 4358
      Columbia: 5091
      Leesburg: 1712
    West Virginia: 128
PROTESTANT EPISCOPAL THEOLOGICAL SEMINARY (Virginia): 5298
PROTESTANT SOCIETY FOR THE PROTECTION OF RELIGIOUS FREEDOM: 5746
PROTHERO, Rowland: 1522
PROUD, J. G., Jr.: 5681
PROUTY, Erminie: 4363
PROVERBS:
  see also MOTTOES
  North Carolina: 691
PROVIDENCE, Rhode Island:
  1800s: 4517, 5480
    1800s: 3588
    1810s: 2271
    1820s: 2271, 2410, 3102, 4604
    1860s: 5001, 5009
    1870s: 5001
    1880s: 5001
  1900s: 473
  Business affairs: 3580
  Description (1831): 150
  Land speculation: 709
  Merchants: 5298
  Poetry: 3055
  United States Army recruiting: 246
  Shipping: 2959

PROVIDENCE COUNTY, Rhode Island:
    Providence: see PROVIDENCE, Rhode
        Island
PROVIDENCE TOOL COMPANY: 794
PROVIDENT INSTITUTION OF SAVINGS:
    5499
PROVINCIAL COUNCIL, Lima, Peru: 4155
PROVISIONS: see Food, and Military
    supplies, as subheadings under
    names of armies and navies
PROXIMITY MANUFACTURING COMPANY:
    5234
PROXIMITY MILLS: 5234
PRUDEN, William Dossey: 5457
PRUSSIA:
    Civil law: 201
    Foreign trade--Great Britain: 4289
    Kings and rulers: 3238
    Peasantry: 2139
    Politics and government: 3238
    Religion--Canon law: 201
PRUYN, Robert Hewson: 4340
PRYOR, Richard I.: 5366
PRYOR, Roger Atkinson: 3262, 4340
PSYCHIATRY: 2934
PSYCHIC PHENOMENA: 1006
    see also SPIRITUALISM
PSYCHOLOGY: 2811, 4997
    Students' notebooks:
        Maryland:
            Johns Hopkins University: 3888
        New Jersey:
            Princeton University: 2521
PSYCHO-PHYSICS NOTEBOOKS:
    Maryland:
        Johns Hopkins University: 3888
PUBLIC ACCOMMODATIONS, Desegregation
    of: 4386
PUBLIC BUILDINGS:
    see also UNITED STATES CAPITOL
        BUILDING; VIRGINIA--State
        Capitol Building; and names of
        other public buildings
    Construction: 3145
    Subdivided by place:
        Baroda: 4117
        Virginia--Petersburg: 279
        Washington, D.C.: 4732
PUBLIC CELEBRATIONS:
    see also FESTIVALS; HOLIDAYS; and
        names of specific celebrations,
        e.g. MEMORIAL DAY; FOURTH OF
        JULY CELEBRATIONS
    Brazil:
        Brasília: 2398
        Campos: 1644
    Ceylon: 952
    End of World War I: 4355
    End of World War II (rumors): 2650
    Great Britain:
        Abolition of slavery in the
            colonies: 5129
    Japan--Okinawa: 2650
    Maryland--Baltimore: 149
    North Carolina--Townsville: 1361
PUBLIC DEBT:
    see also AMERICAN REVOLUTION--
        Public debt
    Confederate States of America: 1181
    United States: 1714, 2776, 2959
        Laws and legislation: 5731
PUBLIC FINANCE:
    see also AMERICAN REVOLUTION--
        Public finance; CUSTOMS (Tariff);
        REVENUES; TARIFFS; WORLD WAR I--
        Savings bond drives; WORLD WAR
        II--Savings bond drives
    Confederate States of America: 700,
        1181, 3615, 3905, 4921
    Egypt: 4941
    France: 1424, 3271
    Georgia: 2827
        Colonial period: 5473
    Great Britain: 1311, 2154, 2976,
        4868
        Expenses (1883): 118
        Loan from East India Company
            (1797): 3315

PUBLIC FINANCE:
    Great Britain (Continued):
        Loyalty Loan (1797): 2149
    India: 278
        Bombay Presidency: 3286
    Ireland: 4331
    Louisiana--New Orleans: 5425
    Maryland: 4886
    North Carolina:
        1700s: 2276, 2776
        1800s: 3943
    Pennsylvania: 3897
    Persia: 572
    Philippine Islands: 3313
    South Carolina: 565
        Hampton County: 5759
    Spain: 4978, 4980, 5639
    United States:
        1700s:
            1780s: 5276
            1790s: 2276, 4922
        1700s-1800s: 4905
        1800s: 1086
            1800s: 3273
            1810s: 3623
            1820s: 564
            1830s: 564, 5622
            1840s: 5622
            1860s: 421, 2149
        1900s:
            1950s: 4805
    Virginia: 3623, 4315
        Chatham: 2732
        Mecklenburg County: 1821
PUBLIC HEALTH: 4386
    Georgia: 365
    India: 278
    Japan: 1661
    North Carolina:
        Fayetteville: 4517
        New Hanover County: 3859
    United States: 4948
PUBLIC LANDS:
    see also WESTERN LANDS
    Land fraud:
        Georgia: see YAZOO LAND FRAUD
        Iowa: 5051
    Pre-emption: 3745
    Purchases and sales--Georgia: 1296
    Subdivided by place:
        Maryland: 5296
        United States: 2776, 3291, 4805
PUBLIC LEDGER: 1021
PUBLIC MEETINGS:
    Suppression of:
        Great Britain: 4605
PUBLIC OFFICIALS:
    Bonding--Georgia: 1189
    Oaths of office--Georgia: 1189
    Office seeking: see POLITICAL
        PATRONAGE
    Turkey: 3183
PUBLIC OPINION: see as subheading
    under specific subjects, e.g.
    CIVIL WAR--FOREIGN PUBLIC OPINION;
    GREAT BRITAIN--PUBLIC OPINION--
    American Civil War
PUBLIC PRAYERS:
    see also RELIGION IN THE PUBLIC
        SCHOOLS; UNITED STATES--SUPREME
        COURT--Prayer ban decision
    Virginia: 1894
PUBLIC PROPERTY:
    Private use:
        Confederate States of America:
            1181
PUBLIC RELATIONS:
    see also LOBBYING
    Handbooks: 1758
    Labor unions:
        American Federation of Labor:
            5442
        North Carolina: 1201
        Southern States: 3558
    Radio: 1758
    Schools: 1758
    Teachers: 1758

PUBLIC SAFETY, Committees of: see
    AMERICAN REVOLUTION--Committees
    of Public Safety
PUBLIC SALES: see VENDUE MASTERS
PUBLIC SCHOOL BUILDINGS:
    North Carolina:
        Davie County: 4111
        Granville County: 2833
PUBLIC SCHOOLS:
    see also SCHOOLS
    Attendance:
        North Carolina:
            Catawba County: 4532
            Granville County: 2833
            Rockingham County: 4533
    Bands:
        North Carolina--Lenoir: 3178
    Finance:
        North Carolina: 4897
        Granville County: 2833
    Graduation exercises:
        North Carolina:
            Davie County: 4111
    Registers--North Carolina: 4897
    Subdivided by place:
        Alabama: 4911
        Georgia: 1993
        North Carolina: 3276, 5298, 5737
            Buncombe County: 5603
            Catawba County: 4532
            Fayetteville: 5298
            Granville County: 2833
            Lenoir: 3177
            Lincoln County: 3933
            New Hanover County: 3607
            Randolph County: 5018
            Rockingham County: 4533
        Pennsylvania: 421
        South Carolina:
            Saint Luke's Parish: 4961
        Texas: 2934
            El Paso: 2927
        Virginia: 2934, 5378
            Petersburg: 2927
        Washington Territory: 5018
        West Virginia: 4732
PUBLIC SECURITY--Great Britain: 5330
PUBLIC SPEAKING: 3284
    see also LECTURES AND LECTURING
    North Carolina: 2469
PUBLIC WELFARE: 4391
    see also CIVIL WAR--PUBLIC
        WELFARE--Aid to soldiers'
        families; POOR LAWS; POORHOUSES;
        SOCIAL SERVICES; UNEMPLOYMENT
        RELIEF; WORKHOUSES
    Federal programs: 4386
    Overseers:
        Great Britain--Wilberfoss: 5727
        Massachusetts--Boston: 3561
    Subdivided by place:
        China: 5252
        Great Britain: 504, 537, 5726
            Idle: 1648
            Wilberfoss: 5727
        Ireland: 504, 1599
        Japan: 1661
        North Carolina:
            Cumberland County: 5298
        Pennsylvania: 1429
        United States: 4386, 4564
        Virginia: 1429
            Augusta County: 5184
            Mecklenburg County: 1821
PUBLIC WHIPPINGS: 3622
    see also CRIME--Punishment
PUBLIC WORKS: see INTERNAL
    IMPROVEMENTS
PUBLICITY: see AMERICAN POETRY--
    Publicity; PRESS RELEASES; PUBLIC
    RELATIONS
PUBLISHERS AND PUBLISHING: 3250
    see also AUTHORS AND PUBLISHERS;
        ROYALTIES (Publishing)
    Church newspapers: see RELIGIOUS
        LITERATURE
    Educational publishing: 4373
    Finance--Washington, D.C.: 1937

PUBLISHERS AND PUBLISHING
(Continued):
  Historical studies:
    Great Britain: 828
    Louisiana: 1982
  Labor publications: see LABOR
    PUBLICATIONS
  Marketing:
    Connecticut: 3041
    Great Britain: 2148, 2736
    United States: 3981
    Virginia: 2673, 3809
      New Market: 2485
  Music: see SONGS AND MUSIC--
    Publishing
  Newspapers: see NEWSPAPERS
  Periodicals:
    Editorial policy: 848, 5691
    Finance: 5691
    Subdivided by place:
      Great Britain: 1522, 1792,
        2471, 2627, 2918
        London: 981
      New York: 3779, 4481
      North Carolina: 2529
      United States: 102, 2409, 3022,
        3793, 4021, 5193, 5691, 5899
  Philosophical works:
    Great Britain: 3670
  Poetry:
    Alabama: 3611
    Massachusetts: 5193
    New York: 5193
    Pennsylvania: 2640
  Socialist publications: see
    SOCIALIST PUBLICATIONS
  Subdivided by place:
    Great Britain:
      1700s: 4512
      1800s: 735, 738, 981, 1603,
        2736, 3816
      1800s-1900s: 5590
      1900s: 5173
      London: 3976, 5095
    Louisiana: 1439
    New York--Troy: 5972
    North Carolina: 691, 5252
      Greensboro: 5457
      Negro editors: 2720
      Oxford: 2192
    Pennsylvania: 552
    South Carolina: 1424, 2473
    United States:
      1800s: 1115, 1484, 5640, 5982
      1900s: 5054
    Washington, D.C.: 4494
PUCKETT, Charles D.: 5233
PUEBLO, Colorado: 3697
PUEBLO INDIANS: 1548
"LA PUERTA MACARENA" by Juan Pérez
  de Montalbán: 4138
PUERTO RICO:
  Currency--Value: 5886
  Description and travel:
    1898: 4227
    1910s: 5786
  Government agencies and officials:
    Council of Labor Relations:
      3066
  International relief organizations:
    Aid from the United States: 3633
  Spanish administration: 4982,
    4983
  Spanish-American War: see
    appropriate subheadings under
    SPANISH-AMERICAN WAR
PUGET SOUND:
  Fear of British seizure (1862):
    5033
PUGET SOUND DISTRICT, Washington:
  Collection of customs duties:
    4239
  Lawsuits: 4239
PUGH, Ernest Byron: 1198, 5486
PUGH, J.: 4401
PUGH, Little John: 4342
PUGH, William R.: 32
PUGSLEY, Chester Dewitt: 4343

PUGSLEY FAMILY (Genealogy): 4343
PUGSLEY AWARD: see NATIONAL
  CONFERENCE OF SOCIAL WORK--
  Pugsley Award
PULASKI, Casimir: 3209
PULASKI, New York: 5715
PULASKI, Tennessee:
  Cotton prices: 6
  Dentistry: 6
PULASKI COUNTY, Arkansas:
  Little Rock: 1453, 4208, 5000
PULASKI COUNTY, Georgia:
  Hawkinsville: 3555
PULASKI COUNTY, Virginia: 4771
  Dublin Depot: 1596
PULIDO v. MUSGRAVE: 1792
PULLIAM, B. G.: 4344
PULLIAM, D. M.: 4345
PULLIAM, Sarah Jane (Clopton): 4346
PULMAN, J. H.: 2148
PULP AND PAPER INDUSTRY:
  Dyes and dyeing:
    North Carolina: 3812
  Ink--North Carolina: 3812
  Legal affairs--Maryland: 2265
  Subdivided by place:
    Maryland--Baltimore: 2265
    North Carolina: 3317, 3955, 4080
      Cumberland County: 3812
    Southern States: 1852
PULP AND PAPER TRADE:
  North Carolina: 3812
PUMPS, Water: see WATER PUMPS
PUNCH: 1530
PUNISHMENT: see CRIME--Punishment;
  PENAL CODE; PRISONERS AND PRISONS;
  PUBLIC WHIPPINGS; and Discipline
  as subheading under names of
  universities, colleges, schools,
  armies and navies
PURCHASE OF TERRITORIES: see
  Annexation as subheading under
  name of territory annexed
"PURCHASING THE FREEDOM OF AND
  GIVING A CHRISTIAN EDUCATION TO
  NEGRO SLAVE CHILDREN": 2542
PURDON, J. H. C.: 3646
PURITY CHURCH, Chester, South
  Carolina: 5988
PURSE, Daniel Gugel: 3629
PURSLEY, J. Warren: 4347
PURSLEY, Mary Frances Jane: 4347
PURVES-HUME-CAMPBELL, Sir Hugh: see
  CAMPBELL, Sir Hugh Purves-Hume-
PURVIANCE, Elizabeth Isabella: 4348
PURVIANCE, John Henry: 4348
PURVIANCE, Letitia: 4348
PURVIANCE, Samuel: 4348
PURVIANCE FAMILY (Maryland): 4348
PURVIS, John Child: 1875
PURYEAR, Jane A.: 1109
PURYEAR, Richard Clauselle
  (d. 1867): 2808
PURYEAR, Richard Clingman (b. 1848):
  2808
PURYEAR FAMILY (North Carolina):
  2419, 2808
PUSEY, Edward Bouverie: 3715
PUTNAM, Elizabeth H.: 5050
PUTNAM, George Haven: 2871
PUTNAM, Herbert: 706
PUTNAM, Samuel Henry: 4349
PUTNAM COUNTY, Georgia: 4706, 5386
  Clopton's Mills: 5760
  Eatonton:
    Fugitive slaves: 4706
    Legal affairs: 3905, 5837
    Trade and commerce: 3352
PUTNAM COUNTY, South Carolina:
  Weather: 5760
PUTNEY, Anne: 1831
PUTNEY, Vermont: 438
PYLES, Abner: 4350
PYRENEES (ship): 153
PYRLAND HALL, England: 5947

## Q

QUACKENBOS, Carolina: 4351
QUACKENBOS, George Clinton: 4351
QUACKENBOS, John Duncan: 4351
QUACKENBUSH, Stephen Platt: 3118, 4352
QUAKER MEADOWS, North Carolina: 3361
QUAKERS: see SOCIETY OF FRIENDS
QUALLATOWN, North Carolina: 3021
  Mercantile accounts: 4784
QUANTICO, Virginia: 144
QUANTRILL, William Clarke: 4716
QUARANTINE: see LIVESTOCK QUARANTINE
QUARLES, Cornelia (Barksdale): 330, 5827
QUARLES, John W.: 330
QUARLES, William A.: 4358
QUARRIES: see specific types of quarries, e.g. MARBLE QUARRIES
QUARTERLY JOURNAL OF EDUCATION: 3251
QUARTERLY REVIEW: 1522, 2058
QUARTERMASTER CORPS: see as subheading under names of armies
QUARTZ GOLD MINING COMPANY, Vestal's Ford, North Carolina: 4450
QUARTZ MINING: see GOLD MINING
QUAY, Matthew Stanley: 1364
QUEBEC, Canada:
  Church of England: 3911
  Description:
    1810s: 3087
    1892: 4175
  Riots: 4567
  Ship chandler's accounts: 3752
QUEBEC (province), Canada:
  Hydro-electric power: 96
  Seaforth: 1941
QUEBEC, H.M.S.: 4289
QUEBEC DEVELOPMENT COMPANY, Quebec, Canada: 96
QUEEN ANNE, Maryland: 5969
QUEEN ANNES COUNTY, Maryland:
  Civil War: 664
  Courts: 5296
  Estates--Administration and settlement: 5296
  Land deeds and indentures: 5296
  Cities and towns:
    Centreville: 5928
QUEEN CHARLOTTE, H.M.S.: 4220
"THE QUEEN'S PLEASANCE" by Algernon C. Swinburne: 5158
QUEENSLAND, Australia:
  British administration: 1792
QUESENBURY, William: 4353
QUESENBURY FAMILY (Arkansas--Genealogy): 4353
THE QUESTION OF INSANITY AND ITS MEDICO-LEGAL RELATIONS by Charles Earl Johnson: 2851
QUICK FAMILY (New York): 388
"A QUICK TRIP THROUGH GERMANY, BELGIUM, FRANCE AND HOLLAND IN AUGUST AND SEPTEMBER, 1844": 4695
QUICKSBURG, Virginia: 4121, 4123
QUICKSWOOD, Hugh Richard Heathcote Cecil, First Baron: 949, 3693
QUIGGLE, J. M.: 4188
QUILLER-COUCH, Sir Arthur Thomas: 3503
QUILTER, Harry: 4600
QUILTING: 691
QUILTING PARTIES: 1407
QUIN, Frederick: 4354
QUINCY, Edmund: 1083
QUINCY, Josiah: 103
QUINCY, Florida: 5928
  Railroads: 2795
  Tobacco industry: 5740
QUINCY, Illinois: 715
QUINCY, Massachusetts: 34
QUINN, Arthur Hobson: 2790
QUINN, Clifton: 4355
QUINN, Ichabod: 4357
QUINN, Jeptha: 4356
QUINN, Sally G.: 4357
QUINTARD, Charles Todd: 2449, 4339, 4358
QUIT-RENT:
  Carolina Province: 780
  North Carolina: 3347
  South Carolina: 3347
QUITMAN, John Anthony: 872, 2211
QUITMAN, Georgia: 2326
QUITO, Ecuador: 4155
QUOTATIONS:
  see also BIBLICAL QUOTATIONS
  Collections of: 375, 1049
    see also COMMONPLACE BOOKS
  From revolutionary constitutions: 2872
  South Carolina--Charleston: 723
  Virginia:
    Virginia Military Institute: 73
QUYNN, Allen: 4359
QUYNN, William: 4359

## R

R., Edith: 1961
R. & T. GWATHMEY, Lynchburg, Virginia (firm): 2360
R. & W. TANNAHILL, Washington, D.C. (firm): 4760
R. BLACKNALL AND SON: 509
R. F. BOYD AND CO.: 606
R. J. REYNOLDS TOBACCO COMPANY: 3538
R. S. MYERS (steamship): 3827
R. W. BROWN AND SON, Wilmington, North Carolina (firm): 2924
RACE HORSES: see HORSE RACING; HORSES--Race horses
RACE IDENTITY--Caracas: 4155
RACE RELATIONS:
  see also BLACK CODES; COMMISSION ON INTERRACIAL COOPERATION; DESEGREGATION; RACE RIOTS; RELIGION--(name of place)--Race relations; SEGREGATION; SLAVE PATROL
  California:
    Chinese-American: 1058
      San Francisco: 1798, 4535
  Georgia--Atlanta: 5082
  Massachusetts: 803
  Mississippi: 2473
  Montana--Helena: 2407
  Mozambique: 5725
  New York: 1907
  North Carolina: 274, 613, 2720, 4736, 4968
    Durham: 2379
    Raleigh: 2773
    Wilmington: 1313
    Winston-Salem: 2773, 3538
  Ohio: 2291
  Pennsylvania: 4190
    Lancaster: 5991
  South Africa: 41
  South Carolina: 300, 2595, 5645
  Southern States: 2616, 3538, 3558, 3820, 3967
  United States:
    1800s: 57, 5931
    1800s-1900s: 706, 2720, 4020
    1900s: 1424, 3062, 5166
  Virginia: 2773
RACE RIOTS:
  Indiana: 3809
  North Carolina:
    Norlina: 4103
    Wilmington: 1082, 1313, 2442, 3972
  South Carolina--Hamburg: 1220
  West Virginia: 3005
RACING: see AUTOMOBILE RACING; HORSE RACING; HORSES--Race horses
RADFORD, Lizzie: 4360
RADFORD, William: 3192, 3809, 4315
RADFORD FAMILY (Virginia--Genealogy): 3809
RADFORD, Virginia: 2770, 3979
RADIO:
  Public relations: 1758
  United States: 2521
RADIO SCRIPTS: 1758, 3797

RADIO STATIONS:
  Licensing--North Carolina: 3538
RADIO WORKERS: see INTERNATIONAL UNION OF ELECTRICAL, RADIO, AND MACHINE WORKERS
RADNORSHIRE, Wales:
  Penybont: 1002
RADZIWILL, Friedrich Wilhelm Paul, Fürst: 2899
RAFFERTY, William: 4361
RAFFLES, Sir Thomas Stamford: 4362
RAG TRADE: 323
RAGAN, William Henry: 2330
RAGLAN, Lord Fitzroy James Henry Somerset, First Baron: 4995
RAGLAND, Erminie (Prouty) Moore: 4363
RAGLAND, John: 795
RAGLAND, William: 795
RAGLEY HALL, England: 4750
RAHMAN ALI, Maulvi: 4364
RAHN, William O.: 1572
RAHWAY, N. J.: 411
RAIFORD, B. B.: 3408
RAIGUEL, Ellen Magee: 4365
RAIGUEL FAMILY (Genealogy): 4365
RAILROAD BONDS--South Carolina: 4673
RAILROAD CAR COUPLINGS--Patents:
  see PATENTS--Railroad car couplings
RAILROAD CARMEN: see BROTHERHOOD OF RAILROAD CARMEN OF AMERICA
RAILROAD ENGINEERS: see BROTHERHOOD OF LOCOMOTIVE ENGINEERS
RAILROAD FRAUD:
  Alabama: 3188
  North Carolina: 4714
RAILROAD LAW:
  Maryland: 4886
  North Carolina--Raleigh: 2553
  Pennsylvania: 4188
  United States: 4858
RAILROAD MOTOR CARS:
  see also LOCOMOTIVES; RAILROADS
  North Carolina: 238
    Sanford: 4918
RAILROAD PROPERTY: 624
RAILROAD STOCKS: 707
  Confederate: 1482
  Georgia: 402, 2004
    Forsyth County: 5260
  New York: 2591
  North Carolina: 237, 238, 641, 3416, 5188
  United States: 5080
  Virginia: 236
RAILROAD SURVEYS: see RAILROADS--Construction
RAILROAD TELEGRAPHERS:
  Labor unions: see ORDER OF RAILROAD TELEGRAPHERS
  Laws and legislation: 3985
  Wages and salaries: see WAGES AND SALARIES--Railroad telegraphers
RAILROAD TIES--Virginia: 753
RAILROAD WORKERS:
  see also RAILROADS--Labor
  Unemployment: 3005
RAILROADS: 4391
  see also GASOLINE-POWERED RAILWAY PASSENGER CARS; LOCOMOTIVES; RAILROAD MOTOR CARS; TRAVEL--Railroads
  Accidents: 5249
  Advertising: see ADVERTISING--Railroads
  Agents--West Virginia: 5239
  Bridges:
    Illinois: 3732
    North Carolina: 4370
  Charter--North Carolina: 5460
  Civil War: see CIVIL WAR--RAILROADS; CONFEDERATE STATES OF AMERICA--MILITARY RAILROADS; UNITED STATES--MILITARY RAILROADS
  Coal shipments--Virginia: 2908
  Construction: 805, 2860, 5361
    Alabama: 5593

RAILROADS:
  Construction (Continued):
    Arkansas: 837
    Burma: 4709
    El Salvador: 4719
    Florida: 5928
    Georgia: 1466, 2963, 5298
    Illinois: 3410, 3732
    India: 4660
    Iowa: 3054
    Louisiana: 395, 805
    Maryland--Cumberland: 721
    Mexico: 395
    Mississippi: 1556, 5977
    North Carolina: 2189, 3221, 4370, 5258, 5298
    Ohio: 281
    Pennsylvania: 5083
    Portugal: 1632
    South Carolina: 718, 1466
    Southern States: 3101
    Spain: 1632
    Tennessee: 2814, 3069, 3692
    Venezuela: 4895
    Virginia: 753, 1624, 5148
      Richmond: 4490
    West Virginia: 721, 2396
    Wisconsin: 4039
  Crossings--North Carolina: 969
  Finance: 3637
    Alabama: 950
    Georgia: 725, 950, 3508, 4674
    Illinois: 3410
    Indiana: 55
    Middle West: 2265
    North Carolina: 238, 1313, 4669, 5460, 5657
    Ohio: 55
    Pennsylvania: 5083
    South Carolina: 3035, 4673
      Charleston: 5271
    Virginia: 236
      Clarksville: 4846
  Freight rates:
    South Carolina: 3035
    Texas: 592
  Government control: 1368
  Investment in--Middle West: 2532
  Labor:
    Food--Virginia: 753
    Georgia: 5051
    Slave labor--South Carolina: 4460
    United States: 3793, 5254
  Lawsuits: 825
    Virginia: 3994
  Legal affairs:
    North Carolina: 1313
    South Carolina: 3893
  Mail service:
    South Carolina: 3035
    United States: 263
  Maintenance and repair:
    Illinois: 3732
      Chicago: 3848
  Military railroads: see MILITARY RAILROADS
  Narrow gauge:
    India: 863
    North Carolina: 5455
  Officials: 3184
  Passenger service:
    Florida: 2795
    North Carolina--Durham: 4736
  Right of way--South Carolina: 4830
  Rolling stock and equipment: 238
  Short-line:
    Alabama: 1655
    Florida: 1655
    North Carolina: 1655
  Stockholders' meetings: 5581
  Strikes: see STRIKES--Railroads
  Taxation--North Carolina: 661
  World War I: see WORLD WAR I--Railroads
  Subdivided by place:
    Alabama--Selma: 3101
    Arkansas: 5380
    Canada: 1211, 4567

RAILROADS:
  Subdivided by place (Continued):
    Central America: 2991
    China: 2191, 5252
    Confederate States of America:
      see RAILROADS--Southern States
    Delaware: 3235
    Egypt: 1970, 4941
    Florida: 23, 2795, 4343
    France: 3054
    Georgia:
      1800s: 3024, 3317
      1830s: 1297, 3767, 4718
      1840s: 4718
      1850s: 4718
      1860s: 2533
      1870s: 1993, 2177, 2533
      1880s: 1264, 2280
      1800s-1900s: 4674, 5494
      Marietta: 3508
      Savannah: 3629
    Great Britain: 3054, 4568, 5637
    India: 278, 2756
    Maryland: 4468, 5059
    Massachusetts: 2608
      Boston: 1433
    Mexico: 3597
    Michigan: 573
    Middle West: 1920, 2606
    Mississippi: 2970, 5498
    Missouri: 2386, 4161
    Montana: 1211
    New York: 1211, 3872
    North Carolina:
      1800s: 2978, 3317, 4080, 4370, 4492, 5664
      1830s: 3176
      1840s: 3176
      1850s: 3176, 4458
      1860s: 2730, 2970
      1870s: 730, 2730, 2970
      1880s: 2730, 5135
      1800s-1900s: 237, 274, 3447
      1900s: 238
      1900s: 4828
      1910s: 3955, 4918
    Pennsylvania: 421, 849, 1433, 1916, 2027, 5083
    Russia: 1970
    South Carolina:
      1800s: 2107, 3317, 4145
      1850s: 2695
      1860s: 565, 2695, 3035, 4673
      1890s: 1480
      1800s-1900s: 2473
      Greenville: 3317
    Southern States: 1439, 4858
      Civil War: 3101, 4002, 4596, 5122
    Tennessee: 3069, 3176, 3205
    Texas: 218, 3657
    United States:
      1800s: 842, 1681, 5593
      1800s-1900s: 4858
      1900s: 4564
    Virginia:
      1800s: 4492, 5377, 5513
      1850s: 4852, 5302
      1860s: 546, 1183, 2510, 3205, 3809, 4466
      1870s: 3809
      1800s-1900s: 557, 2517
    West Virginia: 865
    Western States: 1439, 4188
RAILROADS IN NATIONAL DEFENSE STRATEGY:
  1838: 1930
  World War I: 4858
RAILWAY TRANSPORTATION by Charles Lee Raper: 4391
RAINE, Charles A.: 4366
RAINE, John R.: 4366
RAINES, M. Caroline T.: 4367
RAINEY, Joseph Hayne: 256
RAINEY, Samuel: 4368
RAINSBURG, Pennsylvania: 4106
RAINWATER, Mrs. Charles C.: 4369

RAJA HURRO NATH ROY CHOWDHRY BAHADOOR v. RUNDHIR SINGH AND OTHERS: 4097
RAJAGOPALACHARI, Chakravarti: 2756
RAJPUTANA, India: see INDIA--British administration--Rajputana
RAJPUTANA RAILWAY: 2756
RALEIGH, North Carolina:
  1700s-1800s: 4773
  1700s-1900s: 2553, 4669
  1800s: 263, 624, 1475, 2851, 3943, 4544, 5460
  1810s: 1360, 5778
  1820s: 2611, 5840
  1830s: 4270
  1840s: 113, 3028, 4270, 4667, 5367
  1850s: 113, 279, 727, 1687, 3028, 3488, 4270, 5149, 5367
  1860s: 279, 3440, 4016, 4528, 5367, 5897
  1870s: 3636, 4072
  1880s: 547, 3636, 4072
  1890s: 1068
  1800s-1900s: 227, 274, 1152, 2589, 2720, 2981, 3070, 4828
  1900s: 2863, 4927
  1900s: 1068, 4775
  1910s: 1367, 5962
  1920s: 960, 1367, 2938, 5962
  1930s: 960, 1367, 2773, 2938, 5962
  1940s: 960
  1960s: 1064
  Banks and banking: 2823
  Baptist churches: 5401
  Booksellers and bookselling: 1491
  Civil War: 1555, 3506, 4577
    see also CIVIL WAR--CAMPAIGNS, BATTLES, AND MILITARY ACTIONS--North Carolina--Raleigh
    Confederate Army:
      Camp life: 1523
      Depredations: 5991
  Constitutional convention (1835): 3924
  Description:
    1820s: 2248
    1860s: 3201
  Government agencies and officials:
    Appointments: 3507
  Historic restoration: 4736
  Labor unions: 2772
  Land: 730
  Land grants: 3940
  Lawrence O'Bryan Monument: 730
  Literary societies: 4923
  Local politics: 2819
  Maps (1847): 2553
  Mental hospitals: 2220, 5819
  Mercantile accounts: 2821
  Merchants: 2819
  Monuments: 730
  Museums: 4736
  Newspapers: 4080
  Personal finance: 4544
  Personal property, Sale of: 4394
  Physicians' accounts: 5356
  Prisoners and prisons: 3415
  Religious literature--Methodist: 3646
  Schools: 2819
    Girls' schools: 4154
  Secession: 834
  Slave trade: 4394
  Social conditions: 4394
  Social life and customs (1800s): 2870
  Universities and colleges: see MEREDITH COLLEGE; PEACE COLLEGE; NORTH CAROLINA STATE UNIVERSITY; ST. MARY'S COLLEGE
RALEIGH (N. C.) ADVOCATE: 5460
RALEIGH ADVOCATE PUBLISHING COMPANY, Raleigh, North Carolina: 3646
RALEIGH AND GASTON RAILROAD: 4002, 4080, 4370, 4669

RALEIGH BAPTIST ASSOCIATION (North Carolina): 320
RALEIGH DISTRICT, Methodist churches: 3646
RALEIGH FEMALE CLASSICAL INSTITUTE, Raleigh, North Carolina: 4154
RALEIGH (N.C.) REGISTER: 2870
RALEIGH (N.C.) SENTINEL: 5384
RALEIGH (N.C.) STANDARD: 2589
RALPH FOSTER MUSEUM, School of the Ozarks, Missouri: 1424
RALSTON, Gerard: 1433
RALSTON, Rowena: 2940
RAM, Sir Sita: 774
RAMAGE, Allene: 2357
RAMAGE, John: 3321
RAMAN SINGH, Venkat: 4364
RAMS (ships): 4912
  see also names of individual vessels, e.g. MONITOR, U.S.S.; and classes of vessels, e.g. ELLET RAMS
RAMSAY, David (1749-1815): 2788, 4371
RAMSAY, George, Ninth Earl of Dalhousie: 4372
RAMSAY, James Andrew Broun, First Marquis of Dalhousie: 2029, 4660, 4995, 5327
RAMSAY (W. I.) & CO.: 5212
RAMSAY FAMILY (Maryland): 5128
RAMSDELL, Charles William: 1180, 5054
RAMSEUR, Stephen Dodson: 5457
RAMSEUR, North Carolina: 2624
RAMSEY, David: 365
RAMSEY, Ephraim: 4214
RAMSEY, George Junkin: 4372
RAMSEY, James B. (d. 1871): 4373
RAMSEY, James Gettys McCready (1797-1884): 872
RAMSEY, James Graham (1823-1903): 5457
RAMSEY, James M. (North Carolina): 4374
RAMSEY, John: 4374
RAMSEY, N. A.: 513
RAMSEY, Sabra S. (Tracy): 4373
RANCAGUA, Chile--Description: 5786
RANCHING:
  Argentina: 4019
  Canada: 4175
RAND, Daniel Curtis: 4375
RAND, Lucia: 4375
RANDALL, Alexander: 4376
RANDALL, Elizabeth Wells: 1333
RANDALL, Henry Stephens: 1900
RANDALL, James Ryder: 2883, 4377, 4829
RANDALL, Samuel Jackson: 4188
RANDALL, William George: 5457
RANDELL, David: 4378
RANDHIR SINGH: see RUNDHIR SINGH
RANDLE, Lee Harriet: 4379
RANDLEMAN, North Carolina: 2554, 3338
  Cotton gins and cotton mills: 5408
  Flour mills: 5408
  Linseed oil mills: 5408
  Liquor industry: 1278
  Sawmills: 5408
RANDOLPH, Alfred Magill: 3141
RANDOLPH, Anne (Meade): 558
RANDOLPH, Beverly: 858, 4215, 4380
RANDOLPH, Brett: 4385
RANDOLPH, David Meade: 558
RANDOLPH, Edmund: 1920, 2633, 2887, 4381, 5359
RANDOLPH, George Wythe: 375, 1403, 1434
RANDOLPH, J. F.: 4382
RANDOLPH, John (1773-1833): 858, 2913, 3032, 3439, 4383, 4933, 5720
RANDOLPH, John St. George: 4383, 4385
RANDOLPH, Lucy (Beverley): 476

RANDOLPH, Mary: 128
RANDOLPH, Mary Ann Elizabeth: 2326
RANDOLPH, Peter: 2326
RANDOLPH, Peyton: 917
RANDOLPH, Richard: 558, 4385
RANDOLPH, Thomas Jefferson
  (1792-1875): 872, 1714
RANDOLPH, Thomas Mann (1768-1828):
  872, 3671, 4384
RANDOLPH, William Beverley: 4385
RANDOLPH FAMILY (North Carolina):
  2934
RANDOLPH FAMILY (Virginia): 558
RANDOLPH, Massachusetts: 1253
RANDOLPH, Ohio: 5898
RANDOLPH CIRCUIT, Methodist
  churches: 3646
RANDOLPH COUNTY, Alabama:
  Crops: 5053
  Cities and towns:
    Rock Mills: 3541
    Wedowee: 5053
RANDOLPH COUNTY, Indiana:
  La Grange: 328
RANDOLPH COUNTY, North Carolina:
  1800s: 88, 108, 328, 2947, 5002
  1840s: 680
  1850s: 621, 1773, 1948, 4498
  1860s: 621, 1948, 2459, 4498
  1870s: 2459
  1880s: 3078
  1800s-1900s: 2555
  Civil War: 5402
  Estates--Administration and
    settlement: 5018
  Gold mines: 5549
  Land deeds and indentures: 5018
  Liquor industry: 1278
  Public schools: 5018
  Sawmills: 1876
  Social life and customs: 518
  Taxation: 3939
  Universities and colleges: see
    TRINITY COLLEGE, Randolph
    County, North Carolina
  Cities and towns:
    Archdale:
      Building materials industry:
        4172
    Asheboro: 1307, 2294, 2303,
      3186, 5022
      Plank roads: 5912
    Brower's Mill: 5135
    Bush Hill: 1895, 2895
    Center: 2570
    Deep River: 1870
      Agriucltural organizations:
        5632
      Personal finance: 5632
    Ellerbe--Lumber mills: 3225
    Franklinville: 4075
    Gray's Cross Roads: 675
    Hoover Hill: 4100
    Millboro: 2382
    New Salem: 329, 1677
    Ramseur: 2624
    Randleman: 2554, 3338, 5408
      Liquor industry: 1278
    Reed Creek: 1870
    Science Hill: 3078
    Why not: 3299
    Worthville: 3187
RANDOLPH COUNTY, Virginia:
  Description and travel (1856): 568
RANDOLPH-MACON COLLEGE, Ashland,
  Virginia: 266, 1351, 2399
  Lawsuits against: 879
  Students and student life: 2524,
    5176
  Trustees: 3482
RAND'S MILLS, North Carolina: 3660
RANEY, Ann Thomas Coleman: 1153
RANGER'S RECORDS:
  Mississippi--Noxubee County: 1722
RANKIN, John: 4387
RANKIN, Robert Stanley: 4386
RANKIN COUNTY, Mississippi:
  Brandon: 802, 2496, 2813

RANSDELL, Joseph Eugene: 4858
RANSOM, James L. (West Virginia):
  4388
RANSOM, James M. (North Carolina):
  4389
RANSOM, Matt Whitaker: 2537, 2940,
  4390
RANSOM, Robert, Jr. (1828-1892):
  4390, 5280
RANSOM FAMILY (North Carolina--
  Genealogy): 4390
RANTANE, Bruno: 5234
RANTOWLES, South Carolina: 4212
RAO, Malhar, Gaekwar of Baroda: 4117
RAPER, Charles Lee: 4098, 4391,
  5457
RAPIDAN RIVER, Virginia: 1983
RAPID-FIRE GUNS--South Carolina:
  2610
RAPP, Wilhelm: 174
RAPPAHANNOCK COUNTY, Virginia:
  Agriculture: 3141
  Economic conditions: 3141
  Cities and towns:
    Sperryville: 1618, 3619
    Washington: 98
    Woodville: 5382
      Mercantile accounts: 138
RAPPAHANNOCK STATION, Virginia:
  see CIVIL WAR--CAMPAIGNS, BATTLES,
  AND MILITARY ACTIONS--Virginia--
  Rappahannock Station
RAT INFESTATION: see UNITED STATES--
  ARMY--Civil War--Camps--Rat
  infestation
RATHBORNE, St. George Henry: 4279
RATIONING: see CIVIL WAR--FOOD
  RATIONING; WORLD WAR II--Civilian
  life--Rationing
RATON DEL NILO (schooner): 81
RATTLESNAKES: 4214
RAVENEL, Daniel: 4235, 4392
RAVENEL, Harriott Horry (Rutledge):
  4393, 4622
RAVENEL, South Carolina: 501
RAVENSCROFT, John Stark: 2935, 4394,
  4669, 5457
RAVENSTONEDALE, England: 1869
RAVENSWORTH, Thomas Henry Liddell,
  First Baron: 2836
RAWDON-HASTINGS, Francis, First
  Marquis of Hastings: see HASTINGS,
  Francis Rawdon-, First Marquis of
  Hastings and Second Earl of Moira
RAWLE'S MILL, North Carolina: 4414
RAWLEIGH, William Thomas: 3190
RAWLEIGH TARIFF BUREAU: 3190
RAWLINGS FAMILY (West Virginia--
  Genealogy): 1946
RAWLINGS, New York: 5925
RAWLINSON, Sir Christopher: 4097
RAWLS, Allen: 4395
RAWLS, Ellen: 4395
RAWLS FAMILY: 4395
RAWNSLEY, Sophy: 5226
RAY, D. A.: 5298
RAY, Electa E.: 104
RAY, J. M.: 104
RAY, Jane C.: 104
RAY, John Edwin: 5457
RAY, Nevin: 4396
RAY FAMILY (North Carolina): 5298
RAYMOND, Allen: 103
RAYNER, Kenneth: 264, 5457
RAYNOR, C. J. N.: 1181
RAYNOR, J. W.: 4397
RAY'S HILL, Pennsylvania: 3957
RAYSVILLE, Indiana: 2809
READ, Ira Beman: 4398
READ, Jacob: 4399
READ, James: 4400
READ, John Meredith: 4401
READ, Keith M.: 4402
READ, Patty (Dahlgren): 1352
READ, William, Jr.: 4404
READ, TEACKLE & COMPANY,
  Wachapreague, Virginia: 3144, 4403
READ AND MABRY (firm): see MABRY AND
  READ

READ AND WARWICK (firm): see
  WARWICK AND READ
READE, Charles: 1494, 2449
READE, George: 264
READING, England: 5177
READING, Pennsylvania: 2124
  Irish in the United States: 4190
READING: 1049
  see also AUTHORS AND READERS
  Mississippi: 3611
READING ABILITY: 1758
READING RAILROAD: 3985
READJUSTER MOVEMENT: 3194
READMAN, John (d. 1736): 4405
REAGAN, John Henninger: 700, 1084,
  1403, 1506
REAL AUDIENCIA DE SANTA FÉ DE BOGOTÁ:
  3867
REAL ESTATE:
  see also LAND
  Inheritance--Texas: 4911
  Investments:
    Alabama--Selma: 4911
    Florida: 2109
    Georgia: 3081, 4895
    Minnesota: 3587, 4911
    North Carolina--Charlotte: 4918
    Ohio: 2120
    South Carolina: 300, 3421
      Charleston: 4214
    Washington, D.C.: 4478
    Wisconsin: 5569
  Management: 3447
  Mississippi--Vicksburg: 2164
  Rent:
    see also LANDLORD AND TENANT
    Georgia: 3767
    Kentucky--Lexington: 3325
    New Hampshire--East Lebanon: 2417
    North Carolina: 1382
    Virginia: 117, 3979
  Subdivided by place:
    France--Grenoble: 2195
    Georgia:
      Augusta: 2560
      Bulloch County: 3663
      Forsyth County: 5260
      Glynn County: 2460
      Savannah: 2992, 3629
    Kentucky: 3325
    Massachusetts: 484, 2468
    Michigan: 5731
    Mississippi: 2164
    Missouri--Saint Louis: 5155
    New York: 1380, 2755, 5731
    North Carolina:
      Chatham County: 1056
      Durham: 1584, 3762
      Hillsborough: 1890
    Pennsylvania--Philadelphia: 1920
    South Carolina: 997, 1468, 1891,
      2290, 4118, 5548
    Spain: 4980
    Virginia: 5148, 5214
      Southampton County: 5248
REAL ESTATE APPRAISAL:
  Louisiana: 4902
  North Carolina--Durham: 2379
REAL ESTATE BUSINESS:
  Finance--North Carolina: 1313
  Legal affairs--North Carolina: 1313
  Subdivided by place:
    Georgia: 2114
    New York: 4806
    South Carolina--Abbeville: 3527
    Virginia: 2794, 3979
REAL ESTATE LAW--North Carolina:
  4103
REAL ESTATE TRADE:
  Alabama: 5006
  Maryland: 5981
    Frederick County: 4457
  Middle West: 2532
  New Hampshire--East Lebanon: 2417
  United States: 2682
  Virqinia:
    Bedford County: 5055
    Petersburg: 3401

REAL ESTATE TRADE:
  Virginia (Continued):
    Richmond: 5594
    Westmoreland County: 5579
REAL PROPERTY: see LAND; REAL ESTATE
"REALES CÉDULAS": 3650
REAPING MACHINES: 388
  see also HARVESTING MACHINES; HUSSEY REAPERS; McCORMICK REAPERS
REAVIES, S. W.: 4406
REAVIS, William W.: 4407
REBATES: see SUGAR REBATES
REBECCA FURNACE COMPANY, Hollidaysburg, Pennsylvania: 849
REBECCHINI, Isotta: 3960
"REBELION OF TUPAC AMARU": 4155
REBELLION OF 1798 (Ireland): 5062
RECIPES: see COOKERY
RECOLLECTIONS AND IMPRESSIONS OF JAMES A. McNEILL WHISTLER by Arthur Jerome Eddy: 4439
"RECOLLECTIONS OF MY EARLY LIFE, WRITTEN IN THE SPRING OF 1832" by David Dudley Field: 1792
"RECOLLECTIONS OF THE [CIVIL] WAR" by Cynthia (Rivers) Carter: 4269
RECONNAISSANCE: see as subheading under names of armies
RECONSTRUCTION: 128, 872, 1466, 2553, 3008, 3129, 5731, 5787
  Corruption--South Carolina: 5893
  Economic conditions: 5731
    see also POVERTY--Southern States
    Arkansas: 1154
    Florida: 807
    Georgia: 377, 641, 1993, 2326
      De Kalb County: 807
    North Carolina: 2394, 5298
    South Carolina: 2210, 2376, 2473, 3801
    Virginia: 203, 619, 1827, 2559, 3809, 4131, 4698, 5378
  Effect on churches: 2566
  Federal military occupation:
    Alabama: 1299
    Georgia: 2827
    Louisiana: 5425
    North Carolina: 730, 2469, 4808
      Military courts: 2480
    South Carolina: 4118, 4808, 5193
    Southern States: 5248
    Texas: 5425
  Labor supply--Arkansas: 1154
  Loyalty oaths--Alabama: 4515
  Newspapers: 1424
  Northern opinion: 1631
  Redemption:
    Louisiana: 4080
    South Carolina: 1424, 2300
  Southern opinion: 1631, 2290, 5928
  Subdivided by place:
    Alabama: 566, 3188, 3416, 4820, 4834, 5593
      Mobile: 1507
    Arkansas: 1154
    Florida: 566, 4410
      Monticello: 4068
    Georgia: 51, 641, 731, 1017, 1056, 1494, 1614, 1672, 2232, 2464, 2860, 2901, 2963, 3134, 4257, 4377, 4921, 5517
      Augusta: 5905
    Louisiana: 566
      see also WHITE LEAGUE
      New Orleans: 4277
    Mississippi: 566, 836, 1506, 2487, 2970, 3415
    Missouri: 4406
    North Carolina: 76, 754, 756, 838, 956, 1376, 1659, 1677, 2469, 2530, 2548, 2589, 2970, 3544, 3845, 3960, 4689, 4765, 4917, 4968, 5384, 5664

RECONSTRUCTION:
  Subdivided by place:
    North Carolina (Continued):
      Wilmington: 4052
    South Carolina: 45, 1220, 2107, 2300, 2449, 2616, 2831, 2854, 3405, 4334, 4453, 4460, 4834, 4996, 5340, 5759
    Southern States: 266, 805, 983, 1060, 1115, 1191, 1364, 2370, 2475, 3251, 3262
      Northern philanthropy: 4358
    Texas: 566
      Houston: 4562
    Virginia: 203, 693, 1624, 1787, 2728, 3142, 3809, 4206, 4334, 4562, 4924, 5397, 5751
    West Virginia: 43, 4029, 4774
"RECORD OF MARY WALLACE PAGE": 4014
RECORD OF PROCEEDINGS IN CRIMINAL CASES: 1150
THE RECORD OF THE SERVICE OF THE FORTY-FOURTH MASSACHUSETTS VOLUNTEER MILITIA IN NORTH CAROLINA AUGUST 1862 to May 1863: 4414
RECORD SOCIETY FOR THE PUBLICATION OF ORIGINAL DOCUMENTS RELATING TO LANCASHIRE AND CHESHIRE: 4627
THE RECORDS OF A YORKSHIRE MANOR by Sir Thomas Selby Lawson-Tancred: 5173
THE RECORDS OF THE COMPANY OF THE MASSACHUSETTS BAY: 1431
RECREATIONAL PROGRAMS:
  North Carolina--Fayetteville: 5298
RECRUITING: see Recruiting and enlistment as subheading under names of armies, navies, and militias
RECUEILS, AFFAIRES DIVERSES DU 18$^e$ SIECLE, PARTICULIEREMENT DE CELLES DE DAUPHINÉ: 4408
"RED, WHITE, AND BLUE" (song): 5991
RED CROSS: see AMERICAN RED CROSS
RED EAGLE: 3611
RED FALCONS: 4948
RED HOUSE, North Carolina: 2820
RED MEN: see IMPROVED ORDER OF RED MEN
"THE RED MEN OF ALABAMA" by Alexander B. Meek: 3611
RED MOUNTAIN, North Carolina: 3483
RED RIVER:
  Carters: 3524
  Riverboat life: 2927
RED RIVER CAMPAIGN: see CIVIL WAR--CAMPAIGNS, BATTLES, AND MILITARY ACTIONS--Louisiana--Red River
"RED SHIRTS"--South Carolina: 5759
RED SPRINGS, North Carolina: 3564
RED SULPHUR SPRINGS, West Virginia: 3123
RED TRIANGLE: 4858
REDBRIDGE, England--Canals: 5331
REDD FAMILY (North Carolina): 4523
REDDING, Cyrus: 2146
REDDING, Connecticut: 1205
REDEMPTION: see RECONSTRUCTION--Redemption
REDESDALE, John Freeman Mitford, First Baron: 2836
REDFIELD, Carrie: 2527
REDGRAVE, Samuel: 1087
REDLER, Arthur: 4947
REDONDO BEACH, California:
  Land deeds (1913): 4029
REDPATH, James: 4341, 4409
REDPATH LYCEUM BUREAU, Boston, Massachusetts: 4409
REED, A. M.: 4410
REED, Alonzo: 4411
REED, Charles: 3775
REED, George A.: 4412
REED, James A.: 2109
REED, William: 5457
REED, William Bradford (1806-1876): 4413

REED, William Garrison: 4414
REED AND PETERS (firm): see PETERS AND REED
REED AND PETUS (firm): see PETUS AND REED
REED CREEK, North Carolina: 1870
REED MINE, Cabarrus County, North Carolina: 3391
REEDY RIVER POWER COMPANY: 1478
REEKS, Austin John: 1424
REEKS FAMILY (Great Britain--Genealogy): 1424
REESE, Augustus: 4415
REESE, Chauncey B.: 4348
REESE, Christina V.: 4417
REESE, E. Y.: 4416
REESE, Frederick Focke: 4339
REESE, John W.: 4417
REESE, Lizette Woodworth: 404
REESE, Mary I. (Courtenay): 4348
REESE, William N.: 1335
REESE FAMILY (South Carolina or Tennessee): 718
REEVE, Henry: 2471
REEVE, Tapping: 1333
REEVES, Enos: 4418
REEVES, James Avery: 4419
REEVES, John: 4420
REEVES, Marion Calhoun Legaré: 2449
REEVES, William: 4421
REEVES AND COOPER (Alabama): 4419
REEVS, James: 208, 4422
"REFLECTIONS ON THE PRESENT STATE OF THE CORN LAWS" by Lord John Russell: 4605
REFORESTATION: see FORESTS AND FORESTRY
REFORM: see CHURCH REFORM; JUDICIAL REFORM; LAW REFORM; PRISON REFORM; SOCIAL AND POLITICAL REFORM; and names of specific reform movements
REFORMS BILLS (Great Britain):
  see also GREAT BRITAIN--PARLIAMENTARY REFORM
  1831: 5, 1457, 3121, 5663, 5526
    Public opinion--Conventry: 4750
  1832: 1856, 3080, 3847, 4605, 5038, 5637
  1854: 4605
REFORM CLUB (Great Britain): 5026
REFORM ORGANIZATIONS--Great Britain: 1126
LA REFORME INDUSTRIELLE: 65
REFORMED MISSIONARY HERALD: 4732
REFRIGERATOR CARS: 5080
REFUGEE RELIEF COMMISSION, Cincinnati, Ohio: 5268
REFUGEES: 4805
  see also AMERICAN REVOLUTION--Loyalist refugees; CIVIL WAR--REFUGEES; RUSSIAN REVOLUTION--Refugees
REGENASS, Annie (Demuth): 4423
REGIMENTAL BALLS (parties): 3905
REGIONAL WAR LABOR BOARD, Atlanta, Georgia: 5441
REGIONALISM (United States): see SECTIONALISM (United States)
REGISTER (King's College, Cambridge University): 5590
REGISTER BOOK OF THE CHRISTENINGS, WEDDINGS, AND BURIALS, WITHIN THE PARISH OF LEYLAND, IN THE COUNTY OF LANCASTER, 1653-1710: 5694
REGISTER OF DEBATES IN CONGRESS: 1937
RÈGLEMENT POUR LA CONFRÉRIE DES PÉNITENS ÉRIGÉE EN CETTE VILLE DE GRENOBLE . . . .: 2196
REGULATOR-MODERATOR WAR (1841, Texas): 4286
REGULATORS:
  North Carolina--Historical studies: 305
REHABILITATION: see BLIND--Rehabilitation; VOCATIONAL REHABILITATION

REHOBOTH, Georgia: 216
REHOBOTH, Massachusetts: 427, 1847
REICHE, E. P.: 5409
REICHERT FAMILY (Florida): 4365
REID, Ann (Heatly): 3278
REID, Christian: see TIERNAN, Frances Christine (Fisher)
REID, David Settle: 3094, 4424, 5737
REID, Frank Lewis: 4425
REID, Henry: 245
REID, James: 144
REID, James L.: 4426
REID, Jeanette: 2463
REID, John Gilbert: 5252
REID, John James: 4427
REID, Sir John James (father of REID, John James): 4427
REID, Joseph: 5604
REID, Mary (Stephens): 5051
REID, Richard Jones, Sr.: 4233
REID, Rufus: 1382
REID, Sprunt: 5279
REID, Thomas: 1856
REID, Whitelaw: 2526
REID, William: 3278
REID, William Moultrie: 4429
REID, William Sheilds (1778-1853): 4428
REID FAMILY (South Carolina): 4429
REID AND COMPANY: see HUIE, REID AND COMPANY
REIERSON, Oscar: 523
REIFF, Daniel: see RIFE, Daniel
REILEY, D. F.: 4275
REILEY FAMILY (Maryland): 5128
REILLY, Laura Holmes: 5457
REIMER, Georg Andreas: 4430
REISE, Nathaniel: 2439
A RELATION OF MARYLAND, REPRINTED FROM THE LONDON EDITION OF 1635: 3598
"RELATIONE DELLA REPUBLICA DE VENETIA FATTA ALLA MAESTA DEL RE CATTOLOCI FILIPPO III DE SPAGNA . . . .": 405
RELAY, Maryland: 2106
RELIEF: see AMERICAN RED CROSS; CHARITIES; CHRISTIAN COMMISSION; CIVIL WAR--AID SOCIETIES; CIVIL WAR--PUBLIC WELFARE--Aid to soldiers' families; CLERGY--Aid to ministers' families; FAMINE RELIEF; FLOOD RELIEF; INTERNATIONAL RELIEF ORGANIZATIONS; PUBLIC WELFARE; UNEMPLOYMENT RELIEF; WORLD WAR I--War relief
RELIEF (U.S. storeship): 3279
RELIGION: 291, 3524
  see also BIBLE SOCIETIES; CAMP MEETINGS; CHOIRS; CHURCH AND STATE IN (name of place); CHURCH MUSIC; CHURCHES, and names of specific churches and denominations; CLERGY; DEISM; DISSENTING CHURCHES; EVANGELISM; EVOLUTION AND RELIGION; HERESIES AND HERETICS; LOVE FEASTS; MISSIONS AND MISSIONARIES; PRAYERS; PUBLIC PRAYERS; RELIGIOUS EXPERIENCES; RELIGIOUS LITERATURE; SACRED PLACES; SACRED RELICS; SERMONS; SUNDAY SCHOOLS; THEOLOGY; Religion as subheading under names of armies and navies; and names of specific religions and religious movements, e.g. CHRISTIANITY; OXFORD MOVEMENT
  Notebooks: 3808
  Oriental religion: 5252
  Race relations:
    North Carolina: 3581
    South Carolina: 669
    Southern States: 3558
  Study of: 3482
  Subdivided by place:
    Africa: 128
    Alabama: 2663, 4861

RELIGION:
  Subdivided by place:
    Alabama (Continued):
      Dallas County: 5961
      Tuscaloosa: 4943
    Arkansas: 57, 837
    Carolina Province: 202
    Connecticut: 1402, 5666
    Egypt: 128
    Florida: 5740
    France: 128
    Georgia:
      1700s: 5699
      1800s: 786, 1413, 3625
      1800s-1900s: 2963, 5082
      Marion County: 5051
    Germany--Trier: 201
    Great Britain:
      1600s: 1541
      1700s: 5598
      1700s-1800s: 4146
      1800s: 128, 4672
      1800s-1900s: 2060, 3912
      1900s:
    Greece: 128
    Idaho: 57
    Indiana: 4765
    Ireland: 1311, 4566
    Italy: 128
    Kentucky: 57
    Louisiana: 837, 3415, 5966
    Maryland: 1032, 1909, 3212, 3998, 5128
    Massachusetts: 1792, 4125
    Middle West: 1920
    Mississippi: 57, 530, 2663, 3415, 4269
    Missouri: 57, 2663
    New England: 5088
    New Hampshire: 3822
    New York: 752, 814, 1908, 3296
    North Carolina:
      1700s-1800s: 2663, 4787
      1700s-1900s: 4689
      1800s: 122, 530, 956, 1402, 3432, 4930
      1820s: 5376
      1830s: 967, 5376
      1840s: 967
      1850s: 436, 1362, 1773
      1870s: 817, 2330
      1880s: 817, 2330, 4329
      1890s: 2330, 4192, 4329
      1800s-1900s: 1284, 2830, 3563, 3783, 4849
      1900s:
        1900s: 4192
        1930s: 2863, 5298
        1940s: 2863, 5298
      Flint Rock: 5890
      Forsyth County: 2855
      Lincoln County: 3211
      Sunbury: 1724
      Wilmington: 1313, 1908
      Woodland: 4047
    Ohio: 57, 451, 2949
    Pennsylvania: 4190
    Philippine Islands: 4511
    Scotland: 5
    South Carolina:
      1700s: 5699
      1800s: 2290
      1820s: 4609
      1830s: 4609
      1850s: 4272
      1860s: 883, 4272
      1800s-1900s: 2930
      Charleston: 2695, 4584
      Chester: 5988
      Columbia: 2636
      Laurens: 2616
    Southern States: 132, 3277, 3873, 4932
    Syria: 128
    Tennessee: 2661, 4192, 4269, 4801, 4894
      Nashville: 3844
    Texas: 57, 837, 2920

RELIGION:
  Subdivided by place (Continued):
    Union of Soviet Socialist Republics: 4614
    United States:
      1700s-1800s: 4598
      1800s: 1219, 2801, 3899, 4765
      1800s-1900s: 5717
      1900s: 4948
    Utah: 57
    Virginia:
      1700s: 99, 917
      1700s-1800s: 2949
      1800s: 523, 872, 1402, 4924, 5075
      1810s: 899
      1840s: 2845
      1850s: 1359, 2370, 2845
      1860s: 1359, 2370, 2510
      1870s: 2370
      1800s-1900s: 3142, 4192, 5302
      Opinion of Northerner: 152
      Craigsville: 3826
      Danville: 5773
      Eastern Shore: 1697
      Fluvanna County: 5839
      Halifax County: 3377
      Norfolk: 4968
      Richmond: 682
      Rockbridge County: 3785
      Winchester: 2080
    Washington, D.C.: 846
    Washington Territory: 57
    West Virginia: 489, 4473
RELIGION AND EDUCATION: see EDUCATION AND THE CHURCH; RELIGIOUS EDUCATION; SCHOOLS--Church schools
RELIGION AND LABOR: see LABOR AND RELIGION
RELIGION AND SCIENCE: 1219
RELIGION AND SOCIAL PROBLEMS: see CHURCH AND SOCIAL PROBLEMS
RELIGION AND WAR: see WAR AND RELIGION
RELIGION IN THE PUBLIC SCHOOLS: 3020
RELIGIOUS AND ECCLESIASTICAL AFFAIRS: see RELIGION
RELIGIOUS ASSEMBLY GROUNDS:
  Virginia: 4772
RELIGIOUS CONFLICT: see CATHOLIC CHURCH--Relations with Protestants
RELIGIOUS EDUCATION:
  see also BARACA MOVEMENT; SCHOOLS--Church schools; SUNDAY SCHOOLS
  Great Britain: 2149
  India: 5639
RELIGIOUS EXPERIENCES:
  see also RELIGIOUS LIFE
  North Carolina: 318
  Texas: 318
RELIGIOUS FREEDOM: see FREEDOM OF RELIGION
RELIGIOUS INSTITUTE, Nashville, Tennessee: 3377
RELIGIOUS INSTRUCTION IN PRISONS: see PRISONERS AND PRISONS--Religious instruction
RELIGIOUS LIBERTY: see FREEDOM OF RELIGION
RELIGIOUS LIFE: 925, 1909
  see also RELIGIOUS EXPERIENCES
  Great Britain: 625
  North Carolina: 647
    Forsyth County: 156
    Raleigh: 274
  Texas: 4269
"RELIGIOUS LIFE IN THE OLD SOUTH" by Thomas Arthur Smoot: 4932
RELIGIOUS LITERATURE:
  Advertising: see ADVERTISING--Religious literature
  Baptist:
    North Carolina: 274, 3538
  Episcopal--South Carolina: 2670
  Lutheran: 2485
  Methodist: 4912

RELIGIOUS LITERATURE:
  Methodist (Continued):
    North Carolina: 2221, 3020
      Raleigh: 3646
    Tennessee: 3646
    Virginia: 879, 5375
  Presbyterian--South Carolina: 4031
  Protestant: 3656
  Subdivided by place:
    Great Britain: 2203, 5539
    United States: 1565, 3633
    West Virginia: 128
RELIGIOUS MEDITATIONS--Methodist: 4412
RELIGIOUS ORDERS: 3424
  see also CONFRATERNITIES
  Constitutions: 4046
  Finance--France: 2197
  Women: 1952
  France: 2197, 4046
RELIGIOUS PERIODICALS: see RELIGIOUS LITERATURE
RELIGIOUS POETRY: 4353
  Collections: 142
  Great Britain: 5647
  Maryland: 5166
  North Carolina: 3351
RELIGIOUS PUBLICATIONS: see RELIGIOUS LITERATURE
RELIGIOUS SECTS:
  see also names of specific sects
  Missouri: 4202
RELIGIOUS SOCIETIES:
  see also EVANGELICAL SOCIETY; PROTESTANT SOCIETY FOR THE PROTECTION OF RELIGIOUS FREEDOM; STUDENT RELIGIOUS SOCIETIES
  Great Britain: 5726
RELIGIOUS TERMS:
  Translation into Indian dialects of North America: 1471
REMALY, George: 213
REMARKS ON THE FOUNDATIONS OF MATHEMATICS by Ludwig Wittgenstein: 4628
REMEDIES: see HOME REMEDIES; MEDICAL TREATMENT
"REMEMBRANCES--FOR ORDER AND DECENCY TO BE KEPT, IN THE UPPER HOUSE OF PARLIAMENT, BY THE LORDS WHEN HIS MAJESTY IS NOT THERE . . .": 2152
REMEY, George Collier: 4431
RÉMI, Henri: 4958
REMICK, Clarke H.: 4432
REMINGTON, Jonathan: 4433
REMINGTON, Thomas: 4433
REMINGTON, W. H.: 4433
REMINGTON & SONS (firm): 794
REMINISCENCES: see as subheading, e.g. CIVIL WAR--REMINISCENCES
RENAUD, Hippolyte: 65
RENCH, John: 5981
RENCHER, Nicholas Harris: 2379
RENCHER FAMILY (North Carolina): 2929
RENO, Marcus Albert: 2027
RENSSELAER COUNTY, New York:
  Troy: 549, 752, 1928, 4867, 5747, 5906, 5972
RENT:
  see also LAND--Rental; LANDLORD AND TENANT; QUIT RENT; REAL ESTATE--Rent
  Connecticut: 4059
  New York: 4351
  Virginia:
    Petersburg: 4555
    Richmond: 3462
  West Virginia--Harpers Ferry: 5938
RENT COLLECTION:
  North Carolina: 3043
    Stem: 4464
  Virginia:
    Blacksburg: 3039
    Fauquier County: 3819
    Frederick County: 3819
    Luray: 574
    Smithfield: 811

RENT COLLECTION (Continued):
  West Virginia: 3005
RENWICK, Rosannah P. (Rogers): 4434
RENWICK, William W.: 4434
RENWICK FAMILY (Southern States): 4434
RENWICK AND RICE (firm, South Carolina): 4434
REPARATIONS: see WORLD WAR I--Reparations
REPORT OF THE COMMITTEE OF TWENTY-FOUR . . . FOR THE PURPOSE OF DEVISING MEANS TO SUPPRESS THE VICE OF GAMBLING IN THIS CITY (Richmond, Virginia): 4518
"REPORT UPON WATER SUPPLY AND PURIFICATION, WINCHESTER, VIRGINIA": 5779
"REPORTER FOR THE HOUSE OF REPRESENTATIVES": 4573
REPORTERS AND REPORTING: see NEWSPAPERS--Reporters and reporting; PERIODICALS--Reporters and reporting
REPORTS OF CASES ADJUDGED IN THE SUPERIOR COURT AND COURT OF ERRORS OF THE STATE OF CONNECTICUT FROM THE YEARS 1785 TO MAY, 1788 by Ephraim Kirby: 3041
REPORTS OF CASES ARGUED AND DETERMINED IN THE SUPREME COURT OF APPEALS OF VIRGINIA by William W. Hening and William Munford: 3809
REPUBLICAN CLUB, Augusta, Georgia: 731
REPUBLICAN GROVE, Virginia: 2685
REPUBLICAN (JEFFERSONIAN) PARTY: 404, 1115, 1424, 2815, 3041, 3743, 3890
  Presidential candidates (1824): 3439
  Connecticut: 3041
  Virginia: 404, 5203
REPUBLICAN PARTY:
  1800s: 1980, 4486
  1850s: 2469, 5059
  1860s: 3254, 3778, 4834, 5853
  1870s: 3254, 4834, 5762, 5853
  1880s: 5762
  1800s-1900s: 1805, 4808
  1900s: 521
    1900s: 3793
    1910s: 3793
    1940s: 5170
    1950s: 4251
    1960s: 4251
    1970s: 4251
  Caucuses (1866): 1162
  Congressional Committee (1890s): 3840
  Conventions:
    1870s: 5636
    1876: 1546
    1880: 3809
      Conduct of the Virginia delegation: 4781
    1900:
      North Carolina--Yadkin County: 2914
  Historical studies: 2881
  National Committee (1880s): 1953
  Parades (1860): 5563
  Platform (1884): 5082
  Southern views of: 279
  Subdivided by place:
    Georgia:
      1860s: 731
      1870s: 731, 4921
      1880s: 1091, 4921, 5051, 5492
      1890s: 1091
    Indiana (1876): 2294
    New York:
      1800s:
        1880s: 1977
        1890s: 1907
      1800s-1900s: 4808
    North Carolina:
      1800s: 2357, 4714
      1860s: 5905

REPUBLICAN PARTY:
  Subdivided by place:
    North Carolina:
      1800s (Continued):
        1870s: 1015, 3415, 5905
        1880s: 5905
        1890s: 4858
      1800s-1900s: 1277
      1900s:
        1920s: 1128, 4689
        1930s: 1150, 4689
        1950s: 4251
        1960s: 4251
        1970s: 4251
      Durham County: 1150
      Raleigh (1868): 3440
    Ohio (1884): 5168
    Pennsylvania:
      1850s: 421
      1860s: 4881
    South Carolina:
      1860s: 5340
      1870s: 1972, 5893
      1900s: 521
    Southern States: 706, 3262
    Virginia:
      1800s:
        1860s: 375
        1870s: 375, 3215
        1880s: 1557, 3215, 4781
        1890s: 1557
      1900s:
        1930s: 3820
      Richmond: 2105
    West Virginia: 1828, 2016
REPUBLICAN PRINTING COMPANY, Charleston, South Carolina: 5893
REQUISITIONS, Military: see CIVIL WAR--CONFISCATED PROPERTY; WORLD WAR I--Requisition of neutral property
RESACA, Georgia: see CIVIL WAR--CAMPAIGNS, BATTLES, AND MILITARY ACTIONS--Georgia--Resaca
RESEARCH TRIANGLE PARK, North Carolina: 2231
RESERVE OFFICER TRAINING CORPS:
  see as subheading under names of armies and navies
RESETTLEMENT: see WORLD WAR I--Veterans--Resettlement
RESIDENCE (Law)--France: 372
RESIN:
  see also TURPENTINE INDUSTRY
  Southern States: 605
RESISTANCE TO CONSCRIPTION: see (name of army or navy)--Recruiting and enlistment--Resistance
RESORTS:
  see also HEALTH RESORTS
  Middle Atlantic States: 3229
  New England States: 3229
  New York: 4968
  North Carolina--Linville: 3447
  Virginia: 3229
RESPASS, Thomas, Sr.: 705
RESPASS, Thomas, Jr.: 705
RESPASS, Isaiah: 4435
"RESTABLECIMIENTO DE LOS ARCHIVOS DESTRUIDOS PARA FORMAR UNA EXACTA HISTORIA DEL PERÚ" by José Maria Córdova y Urrutia: 4155
RESTON, Virginia: 3820
RESTORATION: see HISTORICAL RESTORATION
RETAIL, WHOLESALE, AND DEPARTMENT STORE UNION: 1196, 1199, 5234
RETAIL CLERKS INTERNATIONAL ASSOCIATION: 4436
RETAIL TRADE: see DISCOUNT STORES; MERCHANTS; TRADE AND COMMERCE
RETIREMENT: 1167, 2934
  see also AGED AND AGING
RETIREMENT INCOME: see CLERGY--Retirement income
RETREAT SCHOOL, Maryland:
  Arithmetic exercise books: 4804

"A RETROSPECT. HOW THE STATES OF THE FEDERAL UNION, NORTH AND SOUTH, MET THE CRISIS OF 1861": 1780
"RETURN OF THE STAFF OF THE BRITISH AMERICAN FORCES WHO ARE DESIROUS OF SETTLING WITH THOSE OF OTHER DEPARTMENTS" (1783): 4317
REUNIONS: see CIVIL WAR--VETERANS-- (Confederate or Union conventions)
REUTHER, Walter Philip: 1883
REVEL, Benjamin: 1107
REVELEY, Henry: 4770
REVELEY, Maria (James): 2058
REVELLO, Julian Bovo de: 4155
REVENEL, South Carolina:
  Justices of the peace: 1692
"REVENGE" by Julia A. Mildred Harris: 3611
THE REVENGE by Edward Young: 188
REVENUE COLLECTION: see TAX COLLECTION
REVENUE COLLECTORS: see TAX COLLECTORS
REVENUE STAMPS:
  see also GREAT BRITAIN--COLONIAL POLICY AND ADMINISTRATION-- American colonies--Stamp duties; TAXATION--Liquor; TOBACCO TAXES
  Books and papers:
    Great Britain: 2708, 4024
  Liquor--North Carolina: 4009
  Tobacco--North Carolina: 4009
REVENUES:
  see also PUBLIC FINANCE; TAXATION, and names of specific taxes, e.g. TOBACCO TAXES; CUSTOMS (Tariff)
  Great Britain: 92, 4437
  India: 863, 3315
  Ireland: 92
REVIEW, Judicial: see JUDICIAL REVIEW
REVIVALS: see EVANGELISM; and Revivals as subheading under names of specific denominations
REVOLUTIONARY WAR: see AMERICAN REVOLUTION
REVOLUTIONS OF 1848: 1126, 5133
  France: 1609, 4881
  Germany: 4492
REWA PROVINCE, India: 2756, 4364
REWARDS, PRIZES, ETC.: see HONORS AND AWARDS
REX HOSPITAL, Raleigh, North Carolina: 2553
REYNELL, James: 2147
REYNES, Marie: 1450
REYNOLDS, Charlotte Cox: 1552
REYNOLDS, D. N.: 2857
REYNOLDS, David P.: 4438
REYNOLDS, Elmer Robert: 4439
REYNOLDS, Isaac V.: 4440
REYNOLDS, John (1713-1788): 4441
REYNOLDS, John Hamilton (1796-1852): 1552
REYNOLDS, Sir Joshua: 2058, 4512
REYNOLDS, Lafayette P.: 4442
REYNOLDS (R. J.) TOBACCO COMPANY: 3538
REYNOLDS, Reuben H.: 1101
REYNOLDS, Richard Joshua: 3745
REYNOLDS, Stanley: 2370
REYNOLDS, Thomas C.: 4443
REYNOLDS, Thomas Cante: 4667
REYNOLDS, W. M.: 4444
REYNOLDSBURG, Tennessee: 5933
RHEA, John (1753-1832): 795, 2781
RHEAD, Louis: 103
RHEIMS CATHEDRAL (France): 441
RHETT, Robert Barnwell (1800-1876): 791, 3269, 4235, 4445
RHETT, Robert Barnwell (1828-1905): 267, 1084, 4445
RHEUMATISM: see DISEASES-- Rheumatism
RHINE RIVER (Germany): 1424

RHINE VALLEY:
  Description and travel: 1049
RHODE ISLAND:
  see also NEW ENGLAND STATES
  Clergy:
    Baptist: 3055
    Universalist: 1906
  Fishing industry: 4907
  Government agencies and officials:
    Governors:
      William Sprague (1860-1863): 5009
  Historical societies: 5001
  Logbooks: 4907
  Mercantile accounts: 4907
  Merchants--Providence: 5298
  Methodist churches: 1906
  Postal service:
    Local offices--Westerly: 2547
  Potato trade: 3580
  Prices: 3580
  Presbyterian churches: 1906
  Prohibition: 5536
  Schools: 4907, 4169
  Sermons--Universalist: 1906
  Shipping--Coastwise shipping: 2959
  Universities and colleges: 4169
    see also BROWN UNIVERSITY
    Students and student life: 4169
RHODE ISLAND COLLEGE, Providence, Rhode Island: see BROWN UNIVERSITY
RHODES, Cecil: 4520
RHODES, H. I.: 4446
RHODES, Hilary H.: 4447
RHODES, James (Alabama): 4448
RHODES, James Ford (1848-1927): 706, 4449
RHODES, John Melanchthon (b. 1849): 5457
RHODES, John Q. (Virginia): 5035
RHODES, Melchi: 4450
RHODES FAMILY (North Carolina-- Genealogy): 4078
RHODES FAMILY (Virginia): 4446
RHODESIA--War in (1896): 4514
RHYMES:
  North Carolina: 691
  South Carolina: 3418
RHYNE, Abel Peterson: 5457
RHYNE, Daniel Efird: 5457
RIBBLESDALE, Thomas Lister, Third Baron: 4995
RICAUD, Thomas P.: 3499
RICE, Aubrey Richard Spring-: see SPRING-RICE, Aubrey Richard
RICE, Charles E. (Ohio): 5396
RICE, Charles H. (South Carolina): 4451
RICE, Clarke: 4452
RICE, Daniel: 4452
RICE, David A.: 1480
RICE, Elmer L.: 3797
RICE, Francis W.: 196
RICE, Henry Oscar: 4452
RICE, J. W.: 3420
RICE, James Henry, Jr. (1868-1935): 2161, 4453
RICE, Nathaniel: 5457
RICE, Sarah Ann: 1532
RICE, Stephen Edward Spring-: see SPRING-RICE, Stephen Edward
RICE, Thomas Spring-: see SPRING-RICE, Thomas
RICE, William: 4454
RICE FAMILY (South Carolina): 4453
RICE AND RENWICK (firm): see RENWICK AND RICE
RICE CULTURE:
  Alabama: 1803
  Florida: 1803
  Georgia: 1803
  Louisiana: 1803
  South Carolina: 295, 1803, 5114
    Irrigation machinery: 1524
RICE MILLING--Brazil: 339

RICE PLANTATIONS:
  Labor problems--South Carolina: 3485
  Management--South Carolina: 3485
  Subdivided by place:
    Georgia: 2020, 2326, 2963, 4864
      "Hopeton": 1242
      Savannah: 3311
    South Carolina: 297, 1682, 2161, 5193, 5661
    Southern States: 284
RICE TRADE: 323
  Prices:
    Georgia: 2020, 2785
  Subdivided by place:
    Great Britain: 5221
      Imports: 3230
    North Carolina: 2924
      Exports: 3230
    South Carolina: 545, 1524, 4509, 5114
      Charleston: 2107
      Exports: 3230
    Virginia: 3179
RICEBORO, Georgia--Temperance: 5051
RICH, Risworth: 5425
RICH FORK COPPER MINE (North Carolina): 2906
RICH MOUNTAIN, West Virginia:
  Civil War:
    see also CIVIL WAR--CAMPAIGNS, BATTLES, AND MILITARY ACTIONS--West Virginia--Rich Mountain
    Reminiscences: 5550
RICH SQUARE, North Carolina: 4006
RICHARD, Henry: 4455
RICHARD E. SHEARIN AND BROS. (North Carolina): 4764
RICHARD T. SMITH (firm): see JOHN WILSON AND RICHARD T. SMITH
RICHARDS, Abraham: 4456
RICHARDS, John Gardiner: 2109
RICHARDS, Pearl Mary Teresa: 1287
RICHARDSON, ____ (North Carolina resident): 4834
RICHARDSON, Albert: 5759
RICHARDSON, Bettie: 4461
RICHARDSON, Charles Francis (1851-1913): 2449
RICHARDSON, Charles Henry (b. 1843): 1408
RICHARDSON, Christopher C.: 731
RICHARDSON, Davis: 4457
RICHARDSON, Ellen A.: 1408
RICHARDSON, Eunice Louensa: 1408
RICHARDSON, Frances Ann: 1547
RICHARDSON, Isaac: 4458
RICHARDSON, J. H.: 5373
RICHARDSON, J. V.: 4769
RICHARDSON (J. W.) AND COMPANY, Fifesville, Virginia: 4459
RICHARDSON, James Burchell: 3671, 4460
RICHARDSON, Lois (Wright): 1408
RICHARDSON, Luther: 1408
RICHARDSON, Luther L. (1841-1864): 1408
RICHARDSON, Richard C.: 4460
RICHARDSON, T. D.: 4043
RICHARDSON (THOMAS), Fayetteville, North Carolina (firm): 2360
RICHARDSON, Virginia (person): 4461
RICHARDSON, W. H.: 3183
RICHARDSON, William: 4457
RICHARDSON, William A. B.: 4462
RICHARDSON, William H.: 523, 1359
RICHARDSON FAMILY (South Carolina): 4460
RICHARDSON FAMILY (Virginia): 4461
RICHARDSON AND FOX (firm): see FOX AND RICHARDSON
RICHENBOUGH, Martin: 5981
RICHEY, J. Augustus: 4463
RICHEY, S. J.: 461
RICHINGS PARK, England: 5801
RICHLAND COUNTY, Georgia:
  Taxation: 3573

RICHLAND COUNTY, Ohio:
  Mansfield: 4032, 4781
RICHLAND COUNTY, South Carolina:
  1965, 4072
  Columbia: see COLUMBIA, South
    Carolina
  Congaree: 24
RICHMAN AND CO.: see WINTERBOTTOM,
  RICHMAN AND CO.
RICHMON, Jacob: 4624
RICHMOND, Charles Lennox, Third
  Duke of: 1913, 2149, 5331
RICHMOND, Martha A.: 3544
RICHMOND, Sue A.: 3544
RICHMOND, England: 3995
RICHMOND, Kentucky: 3341
  Merchants: 299
RICHMOND, Virginia:
  1700s: 667, 4380, 4381
  1700s-1800s: 97, 2360, 2845, 3130
  1700s-1900s: 3761, 3809, 5720
  1800s: 195, 564, 2737, 3169, 3302,
    4180, 4916, 5075, 5232, 5368,
    5688, 5798, 5848, 5853
  1800s: 1115, 3890, 5721
  1810s: 872, 962, 1115, 3623,
    3890, 5057
  1820s: 872, 4604, 5020, 5840
  1830s: 466, 2085, 2502, 2723,
    3623, 4497, 5020, 5691
  1840s: 230, 1305, 1460, 2673,
    3454, 3557, 4038, 4345, 4713,
    4735, 5020, 5691
  1850s: 87, 1409, 1704, 2520,
    2943, 3454, 3537, 4038, 4345,
    4735, 5339
  1860s: 204, 777, 1089, 1409,
    2134, 2180, 2520, 2534, 2779,
    2943, 3378, 3454, 3537, 4196,
    4466, 4965, 5068, 5182,
    5314, 5339, 5365, 5682
  1870s: 1409, 2415, 3378, 3537,
    3585, 4776, 5339
  1880s: 630, 4776, 5851
  1890s: 4196
  1800s-1900s: 252, 557, 879, 1340,
    2922, 4112, 5176
  1900s: 3397, 3558
  1900s: 3726, 5396
  1910s: 2425, 5396
  1920s: 818, 4617
  1930s: 2773
  1940s: 1303, 5486
  Architecture: 4490
  Balls (parties): 5094
  Banks and banking: 5282
  Building construction: 2550
  Business affairs: 604, 4119,
    4847, 5631
  Chamber of Commerce: 1198
  Civil War: 19, 128, 560, 677,
    834, 1092, 1115, 1122, 1183,
    1740
    see also CIVIL WAR--CAMPAIGNS,
      BATTLES, AND MILITARY ACTIONS--
      Virginia--Richmond
    Army camps: 2335
    Civilian life: 602, 1206, 1877,
      4616
    Commodity prices: 2902, 5703
    Confederate Army: 19
      Camp life: 524, 3861, 4347,
        5121
    Confederate Navy School: 2068
    Defenses: 1359, 3809, 4616,
      5143, 5566
    Hospitals: 19, 927, 2090, 2205
      Chimborazo Hospital: 348, 1185
      General Hospital: 288
      Winder Hospital: 3038
    Medical and sanitary affairs:
      906
    Military activities: 854, 3436
    Morale of officials (1862): 1030
    Prisoners and prisons:
      Libby Prison: 2124, 2989
    Reminiscences: 2416
  Claims: 5445

RICHMOND, Virginia (Continued):
  Clerks (retail trade): 4461
  Commission merchants: 1359
  Commodity prices: 3566
    see also RICHMOND--Civil War--
      Commodity prices
  Debt: 5790
  Description:
    1848: 284
    1862: 3719, 4923
    1865: 5193
    1868: 249
    In poetry (1825): 182
  Diseases:
    Cholera: 5114
    Yellow fever: 330
  Docks: 4465
  Economic conditions: 4099, 4562
  Eminent domain: 4465
  Fertilizer: 4344
  Finance: 1943
  Flour mills: 558, 5393
  Gambling: 4518
  Health conditions: 5513
  History: 99, 5720
  Hospitals: 2794
    see also RICHMOND--Civil War--
      Hospitals
  Household accounts: 4346
  Insurance business: 433
  Labor unions: 224, 1194, 1198, 1201
  Land deeds and indentures: 5790
  Law practice: 4020, 4616
  Legal affairs: 905
  Literary interests: 2062, 4020
  Local politics: 4119
  Medical education: see MEDICAL
    COLLEGE OF VIRGINIA; UNIVERSITY
    OF VIRGINIA--Medical education
  Mercantile accounts: 5770
  Mercantile affairs: 4616
  Merchants: 1556, 1863, 3758, 3809,
    5057, 5770
  Military parades: 4087
  Militia: 3809
  Millers' accounts: 5393
  Municipal government: 858
    By commission: 3979
  Newspapers: 789
    Reporters and reporting: 574,
      5720
  Personal finance: 4616
  Physicians: 381, 1279, 2683
  Publishers and publishing: 4373
  Railroads: 236
  Rent: 3462
  Schools: 4689
    Girls' schools and academies:
      2068
  Sermons: 3587
  Slave trade: 1489, 1801
  Social life and customs:
    1700s-1800s: 4616
    1800s: 3761
    1830s: 872, 5094
    1840s: 3809
    1850s: 3277, 3809
    1860s: 682, 4847
      see also RICHMOND--Civil
        War--Civilian life
    1870s: 4847
  Stagecoach lines: 5839
  Theological seminaries: see
    BAPTIST SEMINARY; UNION
    THEOLOGICAL SEMINARY
  Theater bookings: 3829
  Tobacco industry: 3179, 5251
    Advertising: 1586
  Tobacco trade: 187, 2373, 5827
    Prices: 32
  Tobacco warehouses: 4579
  Trade and commerce: 1093, 1486,
    2633
    Clothing: 4210
    Groceries: 4461
    Jewelry: 4210
    Real estate: 5594
    Slaves: see RICHMOND--Slave trade

RICHMOND, Virginia:
  Trade and commerce (Continued):
    Tobacco: see RICHMOND--Tobacco
      trade
    Wholesale trade: 2857, 4747
  Type foundries: 4119
  Universities and colleges: see
    UNIVERSITY OF RICHMOND; VIRGINIA
    COMMONWEALTH UNIVERSITY
  War of 1812: 1066
  Wealth: 5855
  Weather: 4847
RICHMOND, C.S.S.: 2963
RICHMOND, DANVILLE, AND PIEDMONT
  RAILROAD: 1183
RICHMOND, FREDERICKSBURG, AND
  POTOMAC RAILROAD: 4466
RICHMOND ACADEMY OF MEDICINE: 3378
RICHMOND AND DANVILLE RAILROAD:
  349, 4087, 4464, 4846
RICHMOND AND PETERSBURG RAILROAD:
  3809
"RICHMOND BLUES": 4495
RICHMOND BRANCH FOUNDRY: 4119
"THE RICHMOND CAVALCADE" by William
  Munford: 3809
RICHMOND CITIZENS ASSOCIATION, INC.:
  1198
RICHMOND COLLEGE, Richmond,
  Virginia: see UNIVERSITY OF
  RICHMOND
RICHMOND COUNTY, Georgia: 26, 5395
  Courts: 1993, 2000
  Local defense: 2666
  Cities and towns:
    Augusta: see AUGUSTA, Georgia
    Brothersville: 1066
RICHMOND COUNTY, North Carolina:
  1527, 3146, 3167, 3415, 4053
  Churches: 1738
  Estates--Administration and
    settlement: 3475
  Farm tenancy--Labor contracts:
    3475
  Land deeds and indentures: 5021
  Methodist Episcopal Church, South:
    5023
  Scottish Highlanders: 3386
  Cities and towns:
    Little's Mills:
      Politics and government: 5021
    Rockingham: 2572, 3756
      Religion: 1738
      Schools: 1725
    Springfield--Schools: 3117
    Stewartsville: 840
RICHMOND COUNTY, Virginia:
  Description: 2677
  Schools: 2677
  "Sabine Hall": 918
RICHMOND (Va.) DISPATCH (newspaper):
  2105, 5720
RICHMOND DOCK COMPANY, Richmond,
  Virginia: 4465
RICHMOND (Va.) ENQUIRER (newspaper):
  3587, 3809, 4341, 4616
RICHMOND (Va.) EXAMINER (newspaper):
  1424
RICHMOND FAYETTE LIGHT ARTILLERY:
  3809, 4616
"THE RICHMOND FEAST" by William
  Munford: 3809
RICHMOND FEMALE INSTITUTE, Richmond,
  Virginia: 2068
RICHMOND FURNACE, Pennsylvania: 2033
RICHMOND IN BY-GONE DAYS by
  Samuel Mordecai: 3761
RICHMOND (Va.) LEAGUE OF WOMEN
  VOTERS: 3558
RICHMOND LIGHT BLUES (militia): 3809
RICHMOND MANUFACTURING CO.,
  Providence, Rhode Island: 2410
RICHMOND (Va.) STANDARD (newspaper):
  3809
RICHMOND THEATRE FIRE (1811): 322,
  872
RICHMOND (Va.) TIMES (newspaper):
  722, 5720

RICHMOND (Va.) WHIG (newspaper): 1740, 3587
RICKERSON, Abraham: 4467
RICKERSON, William: 208
RICKETTS, George: 4468
RICKETTS FAMILY (Maryland): 4468
RICKS, W.: 1389
RICO REDUCTION AND MINING CO., Rico, Colorado: 849
RIDDICK, Anna: 3012
RIDDICK, D. E.: 255
RIDDICK, E. W.: 4472
RIDDICK, James A.: 4469
RIDDICK, Josiah: 3012
RIDDICK, Nathaniel: 4470
RIDDICK, Richard H.: 3012, 4471
RIDDICK, W. D.: 4472
RIDDICK FAMILY (Virginia): 3012
RIDDICK, Missouri: 3012
RIDDLE, James N.: 4473
RIDDLE, Mary Brown: 5110
RIDDLE FAMILY (West Virginia): 4473
RIDDLES:
    see also CHARADES
    North Carolina: 691
RIDERS BRITISH MERLIN: 1541
RIDGE SPRING, South Carolina: 2921
RIDGELEY, Charles Carnan: 4474
RIDGELEY FAMILY (Maryland): 4474
RIDGEVILLE, South Carolina: 501
    Mercantile accounts: 4451
RIDGEWAY, Lucy (Tindall), Countess of Londonderry: 4229
RIDGEWAY, North Carolina: 999, 1659, 2435, 3307
    Merchants and mercantile accounts: 910, 5614
RIDGEWAY PLANTATION, Albemarle County, Virginia: 3699
RIDGWAY, Robert: 4453, 4475
RIDING EQUIPMENT--Missouri: 5155
RIDLEY, Bromfield: 795, 5040, 5768
RIESS, Kurt: 4476
RIEVE, Emil: 3171, 5233, 5234, 5235, 5236
RIFE, Daniel: 1601
RIFE, Elizabeth (Dunlop): 1601
RIFLE BULLETS: see PERCUSSION RIFLE BULLET
RIFLES: see CARTRIDGE CLIPS; and names of specific types of rifles, e.g. MAYNARD RIFLES
RIGBY, Christopher Palmer: 5725
RIGBY, Lady Elizabeth: 472
RIGG, Ambrose: 1733
RIGG, James Harrison: 1087
RIGGING: see SHIPS--Masts and rigging
RIGGS, Alice: 4478
RIGGS, Cecilia: 4478
RIGGS, Elisha: 4478
RIGGS, Elisha, Jr.: 4478
RIGGS, Francis B.: 4478
RIGGS, George Washington: 3424, 4478
RIGGS, Jane (1853-1930): 4478
RIGGS, Jane Agnes: 3424
RIGGS, Katherine Shedden: 4478
RIGGS, Mary G.: 4478
RIGGS, Philip D.: 4477
RIGGS, Thomas Lawrason: 4478
RIGGS, William C.: 4478
RIGGS FAMILY (Genealogy): 3424
RIGGS FAMILY (Ohio and Missouri): 4477
RIGGS FAMILY (Washington, D.C.): 4478
RIGGS AND COMPANY, Washington, D.C.: 4478
RIGGS NATIONAL BANK, Washington, D.C.: 4478
RIGGSBEE, Atlas M.: 4480
RIGGSBEE'S STORE, North Carolina: 5541
RIGHT OF ASSEMBLY: see PUBLIC MEETINGS
RIGHT OF SEARCH: 4605
RIGHT TO EDUCATION: 2164
RIGHTOR, Nicholas H.: 4479
RIIS, Jacob August: 4481

RILEY, George: 4629
RILEY, James Whitcomb: 4021
RINEHART, Mary (Roberts): 4482
RINGGOLD RANGERS: 1189
RINGWOOD, England: 3286
RINGWOOD, North Carolina: 711
RINKER, Ella V.: 4483
RINKER, J. P.: 3098
RINKER (J. P.) (firm): see SAMUEL M. LANTZ AND J. P. RINKER
RIO DE JANEIRO, Brazil: 3248
    Description: 1644
RIO GRANDE DO SUL, Brazil:
    Description: 2750
RIORDAN, Bartholomew Rochefort: 5893
RIOTS:
    see also RACE RIOTS
    Alabama--Montgomery: 1299
    Barbados: 4913
    Canada--Quebec: 4567
    Great Britain (1817): 2149
    Ireland--Suppression of: 5809
    Isle of Man: 3835
    Louisiana: 489
    Maryland:
        Baltimore:
            1768: 3598
            1861: 3264
    Massachusetts--Boston: 5563
    New York:
        New York (1863): 2648, 4920
RIPLEY, Charles: 4485
RIPLEY, Edward Hastings: 4485
RIPLEY, Julia Caroline: 10, 2449, 4485
RIPLEY, Mary: 4485
RIPLEY, Robert S.: 395
RIPLEY, Roswell Sabine: 1186, 4484
RIPLEY, Thomas Emerson: 4485
RIPLEY, William Y.: 4485
RIPLEY, William Young: 4485
RIPLEY, Ohio: 281, 4387
RIPON, Frederick John Robinson, First Earl of: 2149
RIPON, George Frederick Samuel Robinson, First Marquis of: 4520
RIPPERDA, Johan Willem: 2155
RIPPON, West Virginia: 4029
RIPPY, James Fred: 2299
RISLEY, Hanson A.: 4486
RISLEY, Sir Herbert Hope: 2756
RISLEY, Olive F.: 4486
RISON, John F.: 2131
RISON FAMILY: 2131
RISQUE, James B.: 4487
RITCHIE, Albert Cabell: 3267
RITCHIE, Charles Thomson, First Baron Ritchie: 294
RITCHIE, Frank: 5252
RITCHIE, Thomas: 872, 3853, 4616
RITSMILLER, The.: 4488
RITTER, John: 4489
RITTER, Thomas W.: 4489
RITUAL: see Liturgy and ritual as subheading under specific church denominations
RITUAL OF THE FARMERS' ALLIANCE (pamphlet): 5549
RIVANNA RIVER IMPROVEMENT COMPANY (Virginia): 3854
RIVERBOATS:
    see also STEAMBOATS; TRAVEL--Riverboats
    Alabama: 2963
    Life on Red River: 2927
    Ohio River: 3255
    Potomac River--Pilots: 5336
RIVERO Y CORREA, Juan Bravo del: see BRAVO DEL RIVERO Y CORREA, Juan
RIVERS, Cynthia: 4269
RIVERS, L. Mendel: 3048
RIVERS, Sarah Myra (Rodes): 4269
RIVERS:
    see also names of specific rivers, e.g. OHIO RIVER
    Improvement--United States: 4858

RIVERS (Continued):
    Laws and legislation:
        United States: 4858
    Transportation:
        North Carolina: 5298
        Ohio River: 3255
    Subdivided by place:
        France--Tours: 5323
RIVERSIDE MILLS, INC., Randolph County, North Carolina: 3187
RIVES, Alfred Landon: 4490
RIVES, Amélie: 958, 4491
RIVES, Eliza C.: 5751
RIVES, Francis Everod: 2466, 4490, 4492
RIVES, George S.: 4493
RIVES, John Cook: 1363, 4022, 4494
RIVES, Judith Page (Walker): 4490, 5513
RIVES, William Cabell (1793-1868): 581, 850, 872, 4490, 4491, 4616, 4880
RIVES, William Cabell, Jr.: 4616
RIVES, William Cabell III: 43
RIVES FAMILY (Virginia): 4490
RIZAL, José: 4511
ROACH, Anne Simms: 2449
ROAD TAXES:
    North Carolina--Anson County: 191
ROAD VEHICLES, Steam powered:
    Texas: 3470
ROADS:
    see also COUNTY ROADS; MILITARY ROADS; PLANK ROADS; POST-ROADS; TUNNELS; TURNPIKES
    Construction: 421, 825
        North Carolina: 3317, 5258
            Guilford County: 2287
        South Carolina: 3383
            Slave labor: 4460
        Tennessee: 4746
        United States: 4858
        Virginia--Mecklenburg County: 1821
        West Virginia: 5654
    Finance--West Virginia: 5654
    Improvement:
        see also GOOD ROADS MOVEMENT
        North Carolina: 3380
    Laws and legislation:
        Pennsylvania: 4188
        West Virginia: 5654
    Maintenance and repair:
        North Carolina:
            Beaufort County: 911
            Montgomery County: 4689
            Tabernacle Township: 4100
        South Carolina: 3383
        Virginia: 4124
        West Virginia: 5654
    Overseers--North Carolina: 5740
    Subdivided by place:
        Alabama: 1182
        France--Tours: 5323
        Georgia: 158, 5744
            Civil War: 1181
                Maps: 1182
        Great Britain: 2994
        North Carolina: 274, 3415, 5962
            Guilford County: 5905
            Vance County: 5962
        Ohio: 2591
        Pennsylvania: 849
        Philippine Islands: 3313
        South Carolina: 158, 2488, 3044
        United States: 4805
            see also NATIONAL ROAD
        Virginia: 638, 2376, 5223
            Mecklenburg County: 1821
            Photographs: 253
        West Virginia: 1946, 5654
        Western States: 849
ROAKE AND VARTY (firm): 738
ROANE, Lieutenant _____: 4495
ROANE, Archibald: 872
ROANE, J. B.: 4495
ROANE, Letitia Landon: 4496
ROANE, Spencer: 872, 4616

ROANE, William Henry: 4497
ROANE COUNTY, Tennessee:
    Harriman: 1630
    Lenoir: 3176
ROANOKE, Virginia: 568, 4383, 5903
ROANOKE, Port of: see EDENTON, North Carolina
ROANOKE CIRCUIT, Methodist churches: 5280
ROANOKE CIRCUIT, Methodist Episcopal Church: 3601
ROANOKE COLLEGE, Salem, Virginia: 568
    Faculty: 5954
ROANOKE COUNTY, Virginia: 719, 1969
    Bonsack: 568
    Christiansburg: 1033, 4360
    Roanoke: see ROANOKE, Virginia
    Salem: see ROANOKE COLLEGE
ROANOKE ISLAND, North Carolina: 343
    Civil War: 1181, 1327
        see also CIVIL WAR--CAMPAIGNS, BATTLES, AND MILITARY ACTIONS--North Carolina--Roanoke Island
ROANOKE ISLAND CIRCUIT, Methodist churches: 3646
ROANOKE ISLAND STATION, Methodist churches: 3646
ROANOKE MALE ACADEMY, Hamilton, North Carolina: 1411
ROANOKE RAPIDS, North Carolina:
    Hydroelectric power: 2299
ROANOKE STEAMBOAT COMPANY: 271
ROANOKE TOBACCO COMPANY, Danville, Virginia: 3378
ROANOKE VALLEY RAILROAD: 2189
ROARING TWENTIES: 5786
ROBBERY: see BRIGANDS AND ROBBERS
ROBBINS, Jeffrey H.: 4498
ROBBINS, John Albert: 4499
ROBERDEAU, Isaac: 3145
ROBERSON, James R.: 4500
ROBERSON, Josiah S.: 4501
ROBERSONVILLE, North Carolina: 4500
ROBERSONVILLE TOWNSHIP, North Carolina:
    Taxation: 3935
ROBERT E. LEE FOUNDATION (North Carolina): 2188
ROBERT E. TOLBERT AND SON (firm): 5306
ROBERTA, Georgia: 2432
ROBERTS, Charles Buck: 4502
ROBERTS, David: 2148
ROBERTS, Frederick Sleigh, First Earl Roberts: 888, 2756, 3056, 4503, 5876
ROBERTS, Isabella Ann: 5892
ROBERTS, Joseph Jenkins (1809-1876): 3118
ROBERTS, Mary: 4482
ROBERTS, Mary Catherine (Watlington): 4506
ROBERTS, Owen F.: 5252
ROBERTS, Ragland: 4504
ROBERTS, S. C.: 4505
ROBERTS, W. M.: 4458
ROBERTS, William Anderson: 4506
ROBERTS FAMILY (North Carolina): 4507
ROBERTS AND LEE (firm): 4504
ROBERTSON, Alexander, Thirteenth Baronet: 2149
ROBERTSON, Bolling: 558
ROBERTSON, D. (South Carolina): 4508
ROBERTSON, David (Georgia): 4509
ROBERTSON, David (1795-1854, Scotland): 5643
ROBERTSON, George, Jr.: 4510
ROBERTSON, James (1742-1814): 2486
ROBERTSON, James Alexander, Sr. (1873-1939): 4511
ROBERTSON, John (1787-1873): 558
ROBERTSON, John Henry (b. 1909): 364
ROBERTSON, Reuben B.: 1852

ROBERTSON, Thomas Bolling (1779-1828): 3809
ROBERTSON, Thomas James (b. 1823): 4145
ROBERTSON, William (1721-1793): 4512
ROBERTSON, William T.: 4513
ROBERTSON, Wyndham: 872
ROBERTSON FAMILY (Virginia): 558
ROBERTSON AND JOHNSTON (firm): see JOHNSTON AND ROBERTSON
ROBERTSON-SCOTT, John William: 4514
ROBERTSVILLE, South Carolina:
    Civil War--Union depredations: 5991
ROBESON, George Maxwell: 4515
ROBESON, James A.: 4516
ROBESON COUNTY, North Carolina: 3436
    Civil War: 754, 956
    Methodist Episcopal Church, South: 5023
    Schools--Tuition: 3803
    Cities and towns:
        Lumber Bridge:
            Municipal government: 3934
        Lumberton: 3422, 3434, 4183
            Civil War: 956
        Maxton: 5740
        Philadelphus: 702
        Red Springs: 3564
        Shoe Heel: 3398
        Smith Bridge:
            Postal service: 1181
ROBESON UNION (Baptist churches): 319
ROBINSON, Dr.____: 4383
ROBINSON, Agnes Mary Frances: 2146
ROBINSON, Alexander: 581
ROBINSON, Anna: 128
ROBINSON, Benjamin: 4517
ROBINSON, Conway: 98, 4518
ROBINSON, E. R.: 318
ROBINSON, Edward D.: 4268
ROBINSON, Edwin Arlington: 4519
ROBINSON, George: 128
ROBINSON, Frederick John, First Earl of Ripon: 2149
ROBINSON, George Frederick Samuel, First Marquis of Ripon: 4520
ROBINSON, Gervais: 1494
ROBINSON, Hiram: 4517
ROBINSON, James: 4521
ROBINSON, James (Confederate soldier): 4522
ROBINSON, James T. (North Carolina): 4523
ROBINSON, John (1727-1802): 3860
ROBINSON, John (Great Britain): 5790
ROBINSON, John H. (North Carolina): 4523
ROBINSON, John M. (d. 1829): 3611
ROBINSON, Magnus L.: 4524
ROBINSON, Manuel: 4525
ROBINSON, Ralph J.: 4526
ROBINSON, Richard B.: 1568
ROBINSON, Robert: 4527
ROBINSON, Sarah Starke (Huske): 4517
ROBINSON, Stuart H.: 4373
ROBINSON, Thomas Jefferson: 4517
ROBINSON, Tracy: 5322
ROBINSON, W. A.: 4528
ROBINSON, W. S. (Alabama): 4529
ROBINSON, William S. O'Brien (b. 1852): 5457
ROBINSON FAMILY: 2085
ROBINSON FAMILY (Maryland): 128
ROBINSON FAMILY (North Carolina): 4523
ROBINSON FAMILY (West Virginia--Genealogy): 1946
ROBINSON'S RIVER, Virginia: 253
ROBSON, John N.: 4530
ROBY, Richard R.: 377
ROCAFUERTE, Vicente: 3118
ROCHAMBEAU, Jean Baptiste Donatien de Vimeur, Comte de: 5228
ROCHDALE, England: 649
ROCHELLE, James Henry: 4531
ROCHELLE, Martha: 4531

ROCHELLE FAMILY (Virginia): 4531
ROCHESTER, New York:
    Business affairs: 2436
    Merchants: 4256
    Tobacco trade--Advertising: 1586
    Universities and colleges: see UNIVERSITY OF ROCHESTER
"ROCK CASTLE," Virginia: 4616
ROCK COUNTY, Wisconsin:
    Farming: 5307
    Schools: 5307
ROCK HILL, South Carolina: 633
    Automobile industry: 5252
    Universities and colleges: see WINTHROP COLLEGE
ROCK HILL PRINTING AND FINISHING COMPANY: 5236
ROCK ISLAND, Illinois:
    Civil War prison: 1184
    Railroads--Repair: 3732
    Universities and colleges: see AUGUSTANA COLLEGE
ROCK MILLS, Alabama: 3541
ROCK SPRING CIRCUIT, Methodist churches: 3646
ROCKBRIDGE ALUM SPRINGS, Virginia: 5775
ROCKBRIDGE COUNTY, Virginia: 2887, 3068
    Crops: 5613
    Livestock prices: 5613
    Cities and towns:
        Brownsburg: 3785
        Fancy Hill: 4243
        Glasgow: 3149
        Goshen: 3882, 5613
        Lexington: see LEXINGTON, Virginia
        Rockbridge Alum Springs: 5775
ROCKEFELLER, John Davison (1839-1937): 2027
ROCKEFELLER, John Davison, Jr. (1874-1960): 5252
ROCKETT, Belle: 4532
ROCKETT FAMILY (North Carolina): 4532
ROCKFORD, Alabama: 930, 3500
ROCKFORD, Illinois: 5348
ROCKFORD, North Carolina: 1800
ROCKHILL, William Woodville: 5252
ROCKINGHAM, Charles Watson-Wentworth, Second Marquis of: 92
ROCKINGHAM, North Carolina: 2572, 3756
    Religion: 1738
    Schools: 1725
ROCKINGHAM CIRCUIT, Methodist churches (Maryland): 3646
ROCKINGHAM CIRCUIT, Methodist churches (North Carolina): 3646
ROCKINGHAM COUNTY, New Hampshire:
    Atkinson: 152
    Exeter: 2044, 5140
    Politics and social life: 2043
ROCKINGHAM COUNTY, New Hampshire:
    Kingston: 354
    Portsmouth: 4062, 4986
ROCKINGHAM COUNTY, North Carolina: 1389, 1794
    Teachers' records: 4532
    Cities and towns:
        Lenox Castle: 602
        Rockingham Court House: 3622
        Wentworth: 4366, 4424
ROCKINGHAM COUNTY, Virginia: 576, 2659, 3009, 3040
    Bridgewater: 3215, 5854
    Broadway: 1827, 5833
    Brock's Gap: 155
    Cross Keys: 2978
        see also CIVIL WAR--CAMPAIGNS, BATTLES, AND MILITARY ACTIONS--Virginia--Cross Keys
    Dayton: 1105
    Harrisonburg: 2498, 2911, 5581
        Courtship: 3060
        Reminiscences: 899
    Lynnwood: 3194
    Melrose: 1617

ROCKINGHAM COUNTY, Virginia
  (Continued):
    Mount Crawford: 1509
    Port Republic: 146, 1600, 2977
      Business affairs: 1559
      Civil War: see CIVIL WAR--
        CAMPAIGNS, BATTLES, AND
        MILITARY ACTIONS--Virginia--
        Port Republic
      Saddlers' accounts: 5346
      Sons of Temperance: 4954
    Timberville: 5275
ROCKINGHAM COURT HOUSE, North
  Carolina: 3622
ROCKINGHAM DISTRICT, Methodist
  churches (Maryland): 3646
ROCKINGHAM DISTRICT, Methodist
  churches (North Carolina): 3646
ROCKINGHAM PLANTATION, Hampton
  County, South Carolina: 4534
ROCKINGHAM STATION, Methodist
  churches: 3646
ROCKLAND COUNTY, New York: 4806
  Nyack: 1462
    Literary affairs: 3344
ROCKPORT, Arkansas: 2809
ROCKS:
  Collections--North Carolina: 4968
ROCKTOWN, Virginia: see
  HARRISONBURG, Virginia
ROCKVILLE, Maryland: 695
ROCKWELL, Kiffin Yates: 5457
ROCKY FACE RIDGE, Georgia: see
  CIVIL WAR--CAMPAIGNS, BATTLES,
  AND MILITARY ACTIONS--Georgia--
  Rocky Face Ridge
ROCKY MOUNT TURNPIKE (Virginia):
  2593
ROCKY RIVER BAPTIST ASSOCIATION
  (North Carolina): 320
ROCKY RIVER CIRCUIT, Methodist
  churches: 3646
ROCKY SPRINGS, Mississippi: 1077
RODE, Charles R.: 1029
RODES, Sarah Myra: 4269
RODES, Tyree: 4269
RODES FAMILY (Tennessee--Genealogy):
  4269
RODGERS, Calbraith Perry: 4537
RODGERS, John (1773-1838): 3742,
  4537
RODGERS, Minerva (Denison): 4537
RODGERS, Raymond Perry: 4535
RODGERS, Robert M.: 4536
RODGERS, Robert Slidell: 4537
RODGERS, Robert Smith (b. 1811):
  4537
RODGERS, Sarah (Perry): 4537
RODIN, Auguste: 1424
RODNEY, George Brydges Rodney,
  Baron: 1913
RODNEY, Mary B.: 5751
RODNEY, Thomas (1744-1811): 4246
RODNEY, Alabama:
  Diseases--Meningitis: 4589
RODNEY, Mississippi: 3322
RODNEY BIRCH RESEARCH ASSOCIATES:
  5779
ROE, Edward Payson: 2449, 5044
ROE, M. N.: 4538
"ROE DOWN," Prince George and Queen
  Annes counties, Maryland: 664
ROEBUCK, John Arthur: 4051
ROEDERER, Pierre Louis: 4348
ROGERS, Arthur Lee: 3994
ROGERS, C. J.: 4540
ROGERS, Coleman: 4539
ROGERS, Henry P.: 2871
ROGERS, James (fl. 1760s-1790s,
  Great Britain): 4541
ROGERS, James (1795-1873): 4434
ROGERS, Jane E. (Haywood): 4544
ROGERS, John H.: 4542
ROGERS, Joseph W.: 2117
ROGERS, Nancy H.: 4434
ROGERS, Rosannah P.: 4434
ROGERS, Samuel: 4543
ROGERS, Sarah: 4543

ROGERS, Sion Hart: 4544
ROGERS, W. M.: 4540
ROGERS, Will (1879-1935): 4545
ROGERS, William Allen (1854-1931):
  552
ROGERS, William H. (Maine): 4546
ROGERS FAMILY (North Carolina--
  Genealogy): 4078
ROGERS FAMILY (Southern States):
  4434
ROGERSVILLE, Tennessee: 4291, 4801
ROHAN-CHABOT DE MURAT, Alain
  Charles Louis, Onzième Duc de:
  1424
ROHAN-CHABOT DE MURAT, Herminie
  (de la Brousse de Verteillac),
  Onzième Duchesse de: 1424
ROHILKHAND, India: 4097
ROJAS, Juan: 4981
ROLFE, Robert Monsey, First Baron
  Cranworth: 2998
ROLIN-JACQUEMYNS, G.: 4709
ROLINSON, Robert: 4547
ROLLINS, Pinkney: 4548
ROLLINS FAMILY (South Carolina): 543
ROLLINS COLLEGE, Winter Park,
  Florida: 4343
ROMAINE, William Govett: 4549
ROMAN, Alfred: 2364, 4550
ROMAN CATHOLIC CHURCH: see CATHOLIC
  CHURCH
THE ROMANCE OF TULIP by Jonathan
  Kennon Thompson Smith: 4894
ROMANOV FAMILY (Russia): 4551
ROMANOV RELATIONS, THE PRIVATE
  CORRESPONDENCE OF TSARS
  ALEXANDER I, NICHOLAS I AND THE
  GRAND DUKES CONSTANTINE AND
  MICHAEL WITH THEIR SISTER QUEEN
  ANNA PAVLOVNA, 1817-1866 by
  Sydney Wayne Jackman: 4551
THE ROMANY RYE by George Henry
  Borrow: 578
ROMBAUER, R. Guido: 4552
ROMBAUER, Robert J.: 4552
ROMBAUER FAMILY (Missouri): 4552
ROME, George: 2605
ROME, Georgia: 371, 2326, 4356, 5844
  see also SHORTER COLLEGE
  Civil War: 669
  Social life and customs: 2035
ROME, Italy: 2056, 4745, 5468
  British embassy in: 3472
  Catacombs: 2148
  Description: 558
  United States embassy in: 4719
ROME RAIL ROAD COMPANY: 4145
ROMEO, Michigan: 4889
ROMILLY, John: 863
ROMMEL, Erwin J. E.: 1137
ROMMEL, Henry B.: 4553
ROMNEY, George (1734-1802): 4230
ROMNEY, West Virginia: 3064
  Banks and banking: 312
  Civil War:
    see also CIVIL WAR--CAMPAIGNS,
    BATTLES, AND MILITARY ACTIONS--
    West Virginia--Romney
  Union occupation: 3721
  Tannery accounts: 5215
ROMSEY, England:
  Diseases--Cholera: 5222
  Sanitation: 5222
RONAN, Eugenia: 4554
RONAN, Harriett Frances: 4554
RONDTHALER, Howard Edward: 3905
RONEY, Isaac: 4555
RONEY, Rebecca: 4555
RONEY, Thomas: 4555
ROOD, Henry Edward, Sr.: 4556
ROODY, Mary A.: 5151
ROOKE, Sir Giles: 4557
ROOKE, Harriet Sophia (Burrard):
  4557
ROOSEVELT, Edith Kermit (Carow):
  1424
ROOSEVELT, Anna Eleanor (Roosevelt):
  4558

ROOSEVELT, Elliott (b. 1910): 5497
ROOSEVELT, Ethel Carow: 4560
ROOSEVELT, Franklin Delano: 233,
  1528, 3451, 4453, 4858
  Administration: 3558, 4559
  Campaign support:
    1932: 4558
    1944: 2863
  Inauguration: 4559
ROOSEVELT, Nicholas: 1424
ROOSEVELT, Theodore (1858-1919):
  706, 872, 1364, 1424, 3229, 4211,
  4481, 4560, 4808, 4825, 5166,
  5171
  Administration: 1424
  African safari: 1424
  Inauguration: 4560
  Relations with Catholic Church:
    3899
  Relations with Southern States:
    3793
  Visits with Roosevelt: 4073
  Writings: 1424
ROOSEVELT, Theodore, Jr.
  (1887-1944): 5252
ROOT, Elihu: 1364
ROOT, George A.: 4561
ROOTES, Sarah A.: 4562
ROOTES, Thomas Reade (1763-1824):
  4563
ROOTES, Thomas Reade (1835-1867):
  4562
ROPER, Daniel Calhoun: 706, 4564
ROPER, Mary Smith (Grimké): 2218
ROPER, Thomas: 2218
ROPER FAMILY: 4564
ROPER HOSPITAL, Charleston, South
  Carolina: 2124
ROPES, John Codman: 3228
RORER, Walter A.: 5751
ROSCOE FAMILY (Tennessee--
  Genealogy): 4101
ROSE, Andrew K.: 4565
ROSE, George: 1913, 2149, 4230
ROSE, Hugh Henry, First Baron
  Strathnairn: 4520, 4566
ROSE, Sir John, First Baronet: 4567
ROSE, Martin: 5457
ROSE, Sir Philip, First Baronet:
  4568
ROSE, W. B.: 2415
ROSE (firm): see BAXTER, ROSE, AND
  NORTON
"ROSE HILL," Culpeper County,
  Virginia--Farm accounts: 3833
ROSE HILL, West Virginia: 749
"ROSE MORALS" by Sidney Lanier: 3092
ROSEBERY, Archibald Philip Primrose,
  Fifth Earl of: 663, 1815, 2146,
  4520
ROSEBERY, Neil Primrose, Third Earl
  of: 306
ROSEBURG, Oregon: 3518
ROSECRANS, William Starke: 2308,
  4160, 5425
ROSEWELL PLANTATION, Gloucester
  County, Virginia: 2776, 4014, 4015
ROSICRUCIANS--United States: 4375
ROSIN INDUSTRY: see TURPENTINE
  INDUSTRY
ROSIS, Tomás: 4569
ROSLIN PLANTATION, Petersburg,
  Virginia: 3179
ROSS, Charles (1800-1884): 5222
ROSS, Charles H.: 648
ROSS, Charles Hunter: 2449
ROSS, Charles W.: 1395
ROSS, David: 2633
ROSS, Eleanor: 4571
ROSS, George (1730-1779): 4785
ROSS, James (1762-1847): 5305
ROSS, John (fl. 1784): 5228
ROSS, John (1790-1866): 4092, 4353,
  5480
ROSS, John (fl. 1870s-1880s): 5202
ROSS, John S.: 4571
ROSS, Leonard Fulton: 1808
ROSS, Margaret: 4571

ROSS, Mary Elizabeth: 3741
ROSS, R. W.: 4188
ROSS, Robert (1766-1814): 3742
ROSS, Thomas: 4570
ROSS, William: 4571
ROSS AND CHESSON (firm): see CHESSON AND ROSS
ROSS AND COMARTY County, Scotland: Ardintoul: 3446
ROSS AND HOOK, New London, Virginia: 2633
ROSS BAPTIST CHURCH, Bertie County, North Carolina: 4572
ROSS COUNTY, Ohio:
  Commodity prices: 770
  Cities and towns:
    Chillicothe: 3243
      Population: 5149
ROSSELLE, William: 4573
ROSSER, Thomas Lafayette: 3793, 3809, 4574
ROSSETTI, Christina Georgia: 4575, 4576
ROSSETTI, Dante Gabriel: 2449, 4001, 4575
ROSSETTI, William Michael: 4576
ROSSLYN, Alexander Wedderburn, First Baron Loughborough and First Earl of: 4420
ROSSLYN, James St. Clair Erskine, Second Earl of: 5830
ROSTER OF NORTH CAROLINA TROOPS IN THE WAR BETWEEN THE STATES by John Wheeler Moore: 3746
ROSY CROSS, Society of the: see ROSICRUCIANS
ROTATION OF CROPS: see CROP ROTATION
ROTHESAY, Sir Charles Stuart, First Baron Stuart de: see STUART, Sir Charles, Baron Stuart de Rothesay
ROTHROCK, Charles: 4577
ROTHROCK, Samuel: 4578
ROTHSCHILD BROTHERS, Paris, France: 4579
ROUARK, Captain ___: 4399
ROUGH AND READY CLUB: 4720
ROUGH CREEK, Virginia: 331
ROUGH RIDERS: see UNITED STATES--ARMY--Spanish-American War--Regiments--United States--Cavalry--1st
ROUND, John Horace: 4580
ROUNDELL, Charles Savile: 1087
ROUNDS, Frank W., Jr.: 1589
ROUNTREE, Jesse: 4581
ROUQUETTE, Adrien Emmanuel: 4958
ROUQUETTE, François Dominique: 103
ROUSE, Adelaide Louise: 2449
ROUSSEAU, Jean Jacques: 2707
ROUTH, John: 4582
ROUTH, S. S.: 4583
ROWAN COUNTY, North Carolina:
  1700s: 3288
  1700s-1800s: 1269
  1800s: 1291, 1428, 2406
    1800s: 1237
    1810s: 1237
    1850s: 4744
    1860s: 1788, 4744, 4984
    1870s: 4578
  Churches and clergy: 4640
  Censorship: 4640
  Granite quarries: 5929
  Merchants: 1487
  Sunday closing laws: 4640
  Temperance: 4640
  Cities and towns:
    China Grove: 1428, 2297
    Cleveland: 4691
    Faith: 5929
    Salisbury: see SALISBURY, North Carolina
    Spencer: 4640, 5549
    Thyatira: 3334
ROWLAND, Robert: 4584
ROWE, Christopher: 5015

ROWE, Henry S.: 2139
ROWLETT FAMILY: 3377
ROWSE, Thomas: 3671
ROXBORO, North Carolina: 673, 2941
  Mercantile accounts: 5927
  Tobacco trade: 5455
ROXBURGHSHIRE, Scotland:
  Kelso: 2839
  Minto House: 1674
ROXBURY, Connecticut: 1205
ROXBURY, Massachusetts: 1502, 1968, 2468, 5085
ROY, Ann Seddon: 4616
ROY, James H., Jr.: 4585
ROY, Sue: 4616
ROY, William H.: 4616
ROY CHOWDHRY, Hurro Nath, Raja: 4097
ROYAL ACADEMY OF ARTS, London, England: 2718, 3138
ROYAL AIR FORCE: see GREAT BRITAIN--AIR FORCE
ROYAL ARCANUM: 5709
  Shockoe Council, No. 895: 3979
ROYAL ARCH MASONS OF THE UNITED STATES: 3041
ROYAL BOUNTY FUND (Great Britain): 5116
ROYAL CANADIAN INSURANCE COMPANY: 2013
ROYAL COLLEGE OF VETERINARY SURGEONS, England: 5304
ROYAL COMPANY OF THE PHILIPPINES: 4179
ROYAL CORNWALL GAZETTE: 5731
ROYAL COTTON MILL COMPANY, Wake Forest, North Carolina: 4586
ROYAL DOMAIN: see CROWN LANDS
ROYAL FAMILY: see as subheading under names of specific countries
ROYAL FLYING CORPS: see GREAT BRITAIN--AIR FORCE
ROYAL GEOGRAPHICAL SOCIETY: 326, 4231
ROYAL INSURANCE COMPANY OF LIVERPOOL: 2013, 4587
ROYAL NAVAL EXHIBITION: 3744
ROYAL SOCIETY (Great Britain): 4514
ROYAL SOCIETY FOR THE ENCOURAGEMENT OF ARTS, MANUFACTURES AND COMMERCE: 5579
ROYAL TEMPLARS OF TEMPERANCE: 5307
ROYALISTS: see FRENCH REVOLUTION--Royalists
ROYALL, Elizabeth: 518
ROYALL, Nancy: 518
ROYALL, Robert E.: 4586
ROYALL, William: 5457
ROYALL, William Lawrence: 252, 2597, 5065
ROYALL COTTON MILLS, Wake Forest, North Carolina: 4586
ROYALTIES (Publishing):
  see also AUTHORS AND PUBLISHERS; PUBLISHERS AND PUBLISHING
  United States: 4020
ROYSE, John W.: 4588
ROYSE, Simeon: 4588
ROYSTER, Beverly S.: 5457
ROYSTER, Hubert Ashley: 5457
ROYSTON, William S.: 4589
ROZOY-EN-BRIE, France:
  Grain prices: 4590
  Markets: 4590
RUARK, Robert Chester: 4591
RUBBER INDUSTRY: see WORLD WAR II--Rubber industry
RUBBER PRICES--Nicaragua: 1091
RUCKER, Samuel R.: 4592
RUCKSTULL, Frederick Wellington: 4453
RUDDELL, W. D.: 659
RUDOLPH, Michael: 1622
RUFF, Samuel W.: 4593
RUFF, Susan P.: 4593
RUFFIN, Edmund: 872, 1439, 2120, 2399, 4594
RUFFIN, John Kirkland: 5195
RUFFIN, Thomas: 2458, 3512, 4595
RUFFIN FAMILY: 4595
RUFFNER, William Henry: 1351

RUGGLES, Daniel: 4320, 4596
RUGGLES, John (1789-1874): 5546
RUGGLES, Lucy: 4596
RUGGLES, Samuel Bulkley: 4597
"THE RUINS," South Carolina (plantation): 1472
RUM INDUSTRY--Jamaica: 1913
RUM TRADE:
  Jamaica: 301
  North Carolina: 5535
  South Carolina: 1935
  Virginia: 5535
  West Indies: 2222
RUMANIA:
  Politics and government: 3036
RUMORS: see as subheading under names of armies, navies, and wars
RUMSEY, James (Ireland): 3567
RUMSEY, James (1743-1792): 404, 581, 4598
RUMSEY FAMILY (Genealogy): 4598
RUNAWAY SLAVES: see FUGITIVE SLAVES
RUNDALL, Elizabeth: 1689
RUNDHIR SINGH: 4097
RUNIROI PLANTATION, North Carolina: 1475
RUPERT, Vermont: 2848
RURAL EDUCATION: 1758
RURAL HALL, North Carolina: 500
RURAL LIFE: see FARM LIFE
RURAL POOR:
  North Carolina: 617
  South Carolina: 666
RUSH, Benjamin: 872, 3399, 3675, 3752
RUSH, Richard: 791, 2326, 4599
RUSH RHEES LIBRARY, University of Rochester, Rochester, New York: 4748
RUSK, Ralph Leslie: 102
RUSK, Thomas Jefferson: 2326
RUSKIN, John (1819-1900): 1218, 4600
RUSLING, James Fowler: 4601
RUSSEL, Cabot Jackson: 4602
RUSSEL, William C.: 4602
RUSSELL, Annie: 2449
RUSSELL, C. H.: 3628
RUSSELL, Daniel Lindsay: 1584, 4603
RUSSELL, Edward Augustus: 4604
RUSSELL, Elizabeth: 5306
RUSSELL, Francis, Seventh Duke of Bedford: 4605
RUSSELL, Francis Albert Rollo: 2146
RUSSELL, Frank C.: 4607
RUSSELL, George Edward: 5201
RUSSELL, Hastings William Sackville, Twelfth Duke of Bedford: 4722
RUSSELL, John: 1494
RUSSELL, Lord John, First Earl Russell: 1632, 1875, 2146, 2149, 2193, 2471, 4605, 5026, 5725
RUSSELL, John, Sixth Duke of Bedford: 1139
RUSSELL, John F. (New York): 4606
RUSSELL, John S. (Virginia): 4607
RUSSELL, Mrs. L. R.: 4606
RUSSELL, Lauraman Howe: 4608
RUSSELL, Leonard: 364
RUSSELL, Odo: 2471
RUSSELL, R. Y.: 4609
RUSSELL, Robert E.: 4610
RUSSELL, Serena Ellen: 4608
RUSSELL, Waring: 4611
RUSSELL, William (Pennsylvania): 4845
RUSSELL, William (Virginia): 4612
RUSSELL, William W. (Washington, D.C.): 4613
RUSSELL COUNTY, Alabama: 2548
  Fort Mitchell: 3388
RUSSELL COUNTY, Virginia:
  Lebanon: 4440
RUSSELL'S MAGAZINE: 2449, 3666
RUSSELLVILLE, Kentucky: 870, 1654, 3450
RUSSELLVILLE, Tennessee: see CIVIL WAR--CAMPAIGNS, BATTLES, AND MILITARY ACTIONS--Tennessee--Russellville

RUSSIA: 83, 4576
  see also UNION OF SOVIET SOCIALIST
    REPUBLICS
  British embassy in: 3472
  British foreign investment:
    Iron industry: 3238
  Censorship: 39
  Coal industry: 3238
  Currency: 1339
  Description and travel:
    1800s: 5797
    1810s: 2139
    1850s: 3053
    1860s: 3053
    1870s: 157
  Diplomatic and consular service:
    Baghdad: 5797
    Brazil: 4348
  Foreign relations: 3472
    Armenia: 5797
    France: 2836
    Georgia (Persia): 5797
    Germany: 4449
    Great Britain:
      1800s: 258, 4650
      1800s: 2836
      1830s: 1632, 4258
      1860s: 345, 1857, 3238, 5222
      1870s: 345, 3238
      1880s: 345
      1800s-1900s: 4693
      Eastern Question: 1126, 1755
      Persia--Boundaries: 4693
      Turkey: 1164, 5797
    United States: 960, 4808
  Foreign trade:
    Great Britain: 535, 4289
    United States: 1889
  Governesses: 4770
  Moscow: 1049
  Historic buildings: 2411
  Iron industry: 3238
  Navy: 4476
  Peace prospects--Persia: 4005
  Peasantry: 2139
  Politics and government:
    1700s-1800s: 4551, 5797
    1800s: 2836, 3036, 3472
    1900s: 2161
  Population: 5797
  Portraits: 2411
  Railroads: 1970
  Relations (General) with
    Yugoslavia: 83
  Revolution: see RUSSIAN
    REVOLUTION
  Rulers: 5797
  Russo-Japanese War: see RUSSO-
    JAPANESE WAR
  Russo-Turkish War: see RUSSO-
    TURKISH WAR
  Social life and customs (1800s):
    3238
  Theater: 3617
  United States embassy in:
    Petrograd: 286
    Saint Petersburg: 960
RUSSIA (steamboat): 5972
RUSSIA COMPANY: 3753
RUSSIAN POSTERS: 4614
RUSSIAN REFUGEES--Japan: 5306
RUSSIAN REVOLUTION (1917-1921): 1766
  Foreign public opinion: 5306
  Refugees: 5306
RUSSO-JAPANESE WAR: 306, 960
  Military activities: 4476
  Naval operations: 4476
  Poetry: 5166
RUSSO-TURKISH WAR: 3036, 3238, 3472,
  4549
RUST, Alfred: 4615
RUST, Armistead Thomson Mason: 4615
RUST, Edgar: 4615
RUST, George: 4615
RUST, Robert B.: 4615
RUST, William: 4615
RUST FAMILY (Virginia and West
  Virginia): 3148

RUSTAD, T. A.: 5252
RUSTBURG, Virginia: 2799
  Free Negroes: 5482
RUTGERS UNIVERSITY, New Brunswick,
  New Jersey: 5731
RUTHER GLEN, Virginia: 3719
RUTHERFOORD, Alexander: 4616
RUTHERFOORD, Ann Seddon (Roy): 4616
RUTHERFOORD, Emily (Coles): 4616
RUTHERFOORD, Jane: 4616
RUTHERFOORD, John (1792-1866): 523,
  872, 1359, 3179, 4616
RUTHERFOORD, John (fl. 1895-1916):
  4616
RUTHERFOORD, John Coles (1825-1866):
  4616
RUTHERFOORD, John G. (fl. 1922): 4617
RUTHERFOORD, Samuel: 4616
RUTHERFOORD, Thomas: 4616
RUTHERFOORD, William: 4616
RUTHERFOORD FAMILY--Portraits: 4616
RUTHERFORD, Mildred Lewis: 2400,
  4642, 5090
RUTHERFORD, S. (New York): 2210
RUTHERFORD FAMILY: 404
RUTHERFORD FAMILY (Virginia and West
  Virginia): 3148
RUTHERFORD, North Carolina: see
  RUTHERFORD COLLEGE
RUTHERFORD COLLEGE, Rutherford, North
  Carolina: 1588, 3186
RUTHERFORD COUNTY, North Carolina:
  Logan's Store: 126
  Patten's Home: 126
RUTHERFORD COUNTY, Tennessee:
  Civil War: see CIVIL WAR--
    CAMPAIGNS, BATTLES, AND MILITARY
    ACTIONS--Tennessee--Rutherford
    County
  Schools: 104
  Slaves: 104
  Cities and towns:
    Murfreesboro: 872, 2235, 3810,
      4592
      Civil War: 3479
        see also CIVIL WAR--
          CAMPAIGNS, BATTLES, AND
          MILITARY ACTIONS--
          Tennessee--Murfreesboro
RUTHERFURD, John: 4618
RUTHVEN, Virginia: 4594
RUTLAND, Charles Cecil John Manners,
  Sixth Duke of: 3498
RUTLAND, John, Third Duke of Rutland:
  5284
RUTLAND, John James Robert Manners,
  Seventh Duke of: 1110, 3498
RUTLAND, Ohio: 1223
RUTLAND COUNTY, Vermont:
  Brandon: 2791
  Centre Rutland: 4485
  Hydeville: 5858
  Pittsford: 2255
  Sherburne: 5197
  Tinmouth: 1067
RUTLEDGE, Andrew: 4623
RUTLEDGE, Archibald Hamilton: 4453,
  4619
RUTLEDGE, Benjamin Huger: 4620
RUTLEDGE, Edward: 4621, 4625
RUTLEDGE, Elizabeth (Grimké): 4625
RUTLEDGE, Harriott Horry: 4393, 4622
RUTLEDGE, Hugh: 4623
RUTLEDGE, John (South Carolina, fl.
  1756): 4623
RUTLEDGE, John (1739-1800): 3209,
  4624, 4625
RUTLEDGE, John (1766-1819): 4625
RUTLEDGE, Mary: 4621
RUTLEDGE, Rebecca Motte (Lowndes):
  4622
RUTLEDGE, Sarah (Hext): 4623
RUTLEDGE, Sarah Mote (Smith): 4625
RUTLEDGE, States: 4625
RUTLEDGE FAMILY (South Carolina): 295
RUTLEY, Thomas: 4229
RUYSCH, W. A.: 4626
RYAN, William K.: 3124

RYDER, Dudley, Second Earl of
  Harrowby: 1087
RYDER, James: 2612
RYE TRADE: 323
  Virginia: 2600
RYLAND, A. G.: 2176
RYLAND, John: 5699
RYLANDS, John Paul: 4627
RYLE, Gilbert: 4628
RYNEVELD, Willem Stephanus van: 3315

## S

S. F. HESSE AND CO.: 1586
S. G. BRANCH AND BROTHER, Petersburg, Virginia: 628
S. MARKS AND COMPANY, Roseburg, Oregon: 3518
S. T. COLERIDGE'S LETTERS HITHERTO UNCOLLECTED ed. by William Francis Prideaux: 4327
"SABINE HALL," Richmond County, Virginia: 918
SABOTAGE: see CIVIL WAR--SABOTAGE BY NEGROES
SACHSEN-WEIMAR:
  Politics and government: 2079
SACKVILLE, George Sackville Germain, First Viscount: 2008
SACKVILLE-WEST, Victoria Mary: 4823
SACO, Maine: 3741
SACRED PLACES:
  Pagan--Great Britain: 2199
SACRED RELICS--Europe: 4881
"SACRED TO THE MEMORY OF MRS. AMELISSE ESLAVA" by Julia A. Mildred Harris: 3611
SADDLE-MAKING:
  North Carolina--Richmond County: 4053
  South Carolina: 4610
  Virginia: 1559
SADDLERS, BRYAN & STRATTEN BUSINESS SCHOOL: 643
SADDLERS' ACCOUNTS:
  Virginia: 1509
    Bridgewater: 5854
    Leesburg: 3584
    Port Republic: 5346
SADDLES: 3622
SADLEIR, Michael: 364
SADLEIR, Ralph: 4630
SADLER, _____: 809
SADLER, James A.: 4631
SADLER, Sir Michael Ernest: 809, 4632
SAFARIS--Africa: 1424
SAFETY: see LABOR CONDITIONS--Industrial safety
SAFETY ADVISORY COUNCIL: 1198
SAGUENAY RIVER (Canada): 96
SAHARA DESERT--Tribes: 2578
SAILORS: see MERCHANT SEAMEN; NEGRO SEAMEN; and Navy life/Sea life as subheading under names of navies
SAILOR'S CREEK, Virginia: see CIVIL WAR--CAMPAIGNS, BATTLES, AND MILITARY ACTIONS--Virginia--Sayler's Creek
SAILS: see SHIPS--Sails
SAINT ALBANS, England:
  Voter registration: 4633
SAINT ALBANS, Vermont:
  Civil War: 1084
SAINT AUGUSTINE, Florida: 499, 4873, 4897
  Civil War--Union Army: 3910
  Description: 202, 1575, 3277
  Social life and customs: 5480
  Union Army life (1830s-1840s): 5480
SAINT BRIDE'S, Virginia: 3012
SAINT CHARLES PARISH, Louisiana: 5208

SAINT CLAIRSVILLE: Ohio: 357
ST. CLOUD (merchant ship): 5860
SAINT CROIX, Virgin Islands:
  Currency--Value: 5886
SAINT DAVID'S COLLEGE, South Wales: 5726
SAINT DAVID'S SOCIETY (South Carolina): 4634
SAINT DOMINGUE: see DOMINICAN REPUBLIC
SAINT EUSTATIUS, West Indies: 1492
SAINT FRANÇOIS COUNTY, Missouri:
  Mining: 2386
SAINT GEORGE, Bermuda: 1115, 5500
SAINT GEORGE, South Carolina: 2997
ST. GEORGE & ODDIE (firm): see ODDIE & ST. GEORGE
SAINT HELENA ISLAND, South Carolina: 485
  Civil War: 4119
  Description: 2907
SAINT HELENA PARISH, South Carolina:
  Schools: 1927
ST. HELENS, Alleyne Fitzherbert, First Baron: 3858
ST. HILDAS' HALL (school): 643
SAINT IVES, England--Elections: 5639
SAINT JAMES HALL (Maryland): see COLLEGE OF SAINT JAMES
ST. JAMES'S BUDGET (periodical): 5553
ST. JOHN, _____ (British general): 4113
ST. JOHN, Frederick: 4635
SAINT JOHN, Lake (Canada): 96
ST. JOHN DEL REY MINING COMPANY, LTD.: 2750
SAINT JOHN'S COLLEGE (Maryland): 5296
SAINT JOHN'S COUNTY, Florida:
  Saint Augustine: see SAINT AUGUSTINE, Florida
SAINT JOHN'S EPISCOPAL CHURCH, Fayetteville, North Carolina: 5298
SAINT JOHN'S ISLAND, South Carolina:
  Estates: 5074
SAINT JOHN'S PARISH, Georgia: 1440
SAINT JOHN'S PROTESTANT EPISCOPAL CHURCH, Columbia, Virginia: 5091
SAINT JOHN'S SCHOOL, Sing Sing, New York: 480
SAINT JOHN'S WOMAN'S AUXILIARY, Fayetteville, North Carolina: 5298
SAINT JOHN'S YOUNG PEOPLE'S SERVICE LEAGUE, Fayetteville, North Carolina: 5298
SAINT JOSEPH COUNTY, Indiana:
  South Bend: 1162
SAINT JOSEPH'S ACADEMY, Emmittsburg, Maryland: 2301
SAINT JOSEPH'S SCHOOL, Baltimore, Maryland: 4866
SAINT JOSEPH'S SCHOOL, Hickory, North Carolina: 3043
SAINT JOSEPH'S SEMINARY: 2467
SAINT LAWRENCE COUNTY, New York:
  Business affairs: 5458
  Hermon: 3296
  Ogdensburg: 5989
    Hardware trade: 1390
  Merchants: 2230
SAINT LAWRENCE RIVER: 4354
SAINT LAWRENCE VALLEY:
  Description and travel: 3087
ST. LEONARDS, Edward Burtenshaw Sugden, First Baron: 504, 5134
SAINT LOUIS, Missouri:
  1800s: 57, 1798
  1840s: 2264
  1860s: 2166, 4369, 4899
  1870s: 1471
  1880s: 3049
  1890s: 3049
  1800s-1900s: 1806, 4786
  1900s: 3985
  1900s: 3093, 4063, 5031
  1910s: 5031
  1920s: 5031
  American poetry: 4755
  Bags, Shipment of: 5155
  Brickmaking: 5137

SAINT LOUIS, Missouri (Continued):
  Clothing and dress: 5155
  Description: 1591
  Dry goods trade: 5155
  Finance: 2301
  Land deeds and indentures: 5155
  Law practice: 4616
  Personal finance: 520, 5155
  Real estate: 5155
  Riding equipment: 5155
  Taxation: 5155
  Textile industry and trade: 1695
  Trade and commerce:
    With Louisiana: 2386
    With Mexico: 2386
  Union sympathizers: 4552
  Universities and colleges: see WASHINGTON UNIVERSITY
SAINT LOUIS COUNTY, Minnesota:
  Duluth: 5115
  Webster Groves: 1097, 1424
SAINT LOUIS, U.S.S.: 4593
SAINT LOUIS MISSOURI FUR COMPANY: 3357
SAINT LUCIA, West Indies:
  British administration: 2403
  Foreign trade: 2403
    United States: 3871
  Immigration from India: 4097
SAINT LUKE'S HOME FOR THE SICK, Richmond, Virginia: 2794
SAINT LUKE'S HOSPITAL, New York, New York: 4775
SAINT LUKE'S PARISH, South Carolina:
  School boards: 4961
  Schools: 1927
    Public schools: 4961
SAINT MARKS, Florida: 4982
SAINT MARK'S PARISH, South Carolina: 1472
SAINT MARK'S SCHOOL, Southborough, Massachusetts: 1423
ST. MARTIN, Thaddeus: 4636
ST. MARY'S, Georgia: 235, 1448
  Social life and customs: 2497
SAINT MARY'S COLLEGE, Baltimore, Maryland: 3424
SAINT MARY'S COLLEGE, Raleigh, North Carolina: 661, 2068, 2808, 3626, 4897, 5298
  Bulletin: 4080
  Students and student life: 2680
  Tuition: 2819, 2940
SAINT MARY'S COUNTY, Maryland: 4405
  Merchants: 1487
  Cities and towns:
    Chaptico: 5193
    Laurel Grove: 1535
    Leonardtown: 1406
    Point Lookout: 4682
      see also CIVIL WAR--PRISONERS AND PRISONS--Confederate prisoners--Maryland--Point Lookout
SAINT MARY'S HOSPITAL, Philadelphia, Pennsylvania: 2336
SAINT MARY'S PARISH, Jamaica:
  Ballard's Valley Plantation: 301
SAINT MARY'S SCHOOL, Springfield, Kentucky: 4987
SAINT MARY'S SCHOOL AND JUNIOR COLLEGE, Raleigh, North Carolina: see SAINT MARY'S COLLEGE
SAINT MATTHEWS, South Carolina: 1371
SAINT MICHAEL'S EPISCOPAL CHURCH, Charleston, South Carolina: 2107, 2410
SAINT MICHAEL'S PROTESTANT EPISCOPAL CHURCH, Charleston, South Carolina: 4637
SAINT MIHIEL, France: see WORLD WAR I--Campaigns, battles, and military actions--France--Saint Mihiel
"ST. MIHIEL OPERATION" by Leander Dunbar Syme: 5163
SAINT PATRICK DAY CELEBRATIONS: 5131
SAINT PAUL, Minnesota: 3310

SAINT PAUL COTTON MILLS: 4858
SAINT PAULS, North Carolina: 2363
SAINT PAUL'S AFRICAN METHODIST
  EPISCOPAL CHURCH, Orrville,
  Alabama: 223
SAINT PAUL'S CHURCH, Richmond,
  Virginia: 3587
SAINT PAUL'S COLLEGE, Long Island,
  New York: 2999, 5193
SAINT PAUL'S GIRLS' SCHOOL,
  Baltimore, Maryland: 5298
SAINT PAUL's PARISH, South Carolina:
  2281
SAINT PAUL'S PROTESTANT EPISCOPAL
  CHURCH, Baltimore, Maryland: 4638
SAINT PETER'S-IN-THANET, England:
  4327
SAINT PETERSBURG, Russia: 4551, 5622
  American embassy in: 960
  British embassy in: 3238
  Description: 5661
SAINT PHILIP'S EPISCOPAL CHURCH,
  Charleston, South Carolina: 2107,
  3801
SAINT SIMON ISLAND, Georgia:
  Civil War: 510
  Frederica: 1454, 3968, 4988
  Land settlement: 3733
SAINT TAMMANY PARISH, Louisiana:
  Camp Mandeville: 1772
SAINT TIMOTHY'S HALL, Baltimore,
  Maryland: 3607
SAINT VALENTINE'S DAY: 2656
ST. VINCENT, John Jervis, First
  Earl of: 5830
SAINT VINCENT, West Indies:
  British administration: 1792
SAINTE CLAIRE, Monastery of,
  Grenoble, France: 2197
SALADIN (ship): 3692
SALAMANCA, Spain: 5404
SALAMANDER, H.M.S.: 3744
SALARIES: see WAGES AND SALARIES
SALE, Sir Stephen George: 2756
SALEM, Alabama:
  Slave trade--Prices: 4610
SALEM, Florida: 5678
SALEM, Iowa: 2715
SALEM, Massachusetts: 450, 2028,
  4194
SALEM, North Carolina: 315, 1469,
  1652, 1905, 3172, 3395
  see also WINSTON-SALEM, North
    Carolina
  Balloon ascension: 813
  Blacksmithing: 1550
  Civil War:
    Union occupation: 2829
  Coppersmithing: 544
  Description (1791): 5575
  Music--Study and teaching: 5459
  Universities and colleges: see
    SALEM COLLEGE
  Visit of Washington: 5575
SALEM, Tennessee: 2369
SALEM (Fauquier County), Virginia:
  3125
SALEM (Roanoke County), Virginia:
  see ROANOKE COLLEGE
SALEM ACADEMY, Winston-Salem, North
  Carolina: see SALEM COLLEGE
SALEM BAPTIST ASSOCIATION (Kentucky):
  3199
SALEM CENTER, Indiana: 808
SALEM COLLEGE, Winston-Salem, North
  Carolina: 661, 1402, 1944, 2589,
  3172, 3395, 3905, 4080, 4423,
  5459, 5982
  Chapel: 4434
  Civil War: 2829
  Expenses: 5827
  Funds and scholarships: 4080
  Tuition and board: 1469, 2819
SALEM FEMALE ACADEMY, Salem, North
  Carolina: see SALEM COLLEGE
SALEM FEMALE COLLEGE, Salem, North
  Carolina: see SALEM COLLEGE

SALES BY SAMPLE--Texas: 3534
SALES TAX: see as subheading under
  names of states
SALESMANSHIP: 2225
SALINE COUNTY, Missouri: 5902
SALISBURY, John: 4639
SALISBURY, Robert Talbot Gascoyne-
  Cecil, Third Marquis of: 294, 1815,
  2149, 2324
SALISBURY, Connecticut: 5868
  Vital statistics: 1205
SALISBURY, North Carolina:
  1700s-1800s: 5046
  1800s: 544, 3845
  1830s: 2117, 2651
  1840s: 2117, 2651
  1850s: 2260
  1860s: 2260
  1870s: 395, 5294
  1880s: 5657
  1800s-1900s: 2188, 5929
  1900s: 3020, 3944
  Banks and banking: 1381
  Church and social problems: 4640
  Civil War prison: 5511
  Methodist churches: 3646
  Wholesale trade: 2857
SALISBURY AND CHURCH STREET CHURCH
  (North Carolina): 3646
SALISBURY DISTRICT, Methodist
  churches: 3646
SALISBURY-SPENCER MINISTERIAL
  ASSOCIATION, Rowan County, North
  Carolina: 4640
"SALLIE VIC": see JORDAN, Victoria
SALLS, Helen Harriet: 4641
SALMON CANNING INDUSTRY:
  Oregon--Ellensburg: 5938
SALMOND, Ann Louisa: 4642
SALT AGENTS:
  see also CONFEDERATE STATES OF
    AMERICA--ARMY--Salt agents
  Virginia: 1436
SALT LAKE CITY, Utah: 2368
  Description: 1174
SALT MAKING:
  see also CONFEDERATE STATES OF
    AMERICA--SALT
  South Carolina: 881
  Virginia: 4743
SALT SPECULATION:
  Alabama: 3321
SALT TRADE:
  Prices--Southern States: 2004
  Subdivided by place:
    Alabama: 3321, 5006
    Great Britain--Exports: 3230
    North Carolina: 35, 1336, 2889
      Imports: 3230
      Wilmington: 1281
    South Carolina--Imports: 3230
    Southern States: 5040
    Virginia: 404, 523, 1336, 2383
    Washington, D.C.: 385
SALT WORKS:
  see also CIVIL WAR--SALT WORKS
  Alabama--Clarke County: 4643
  Georgia: 4743
    Investments in: 4895
  North Carolina:
    Wilmington: 1056, 5912
  Pennsylvania: 4732
  Virginia: 523, 2370, 3959
    Patrick County: 1410
SALTER, B.: 2431
SALTER, W. F.: 2431
SALTILLO, Mexico: 5130
SALTMARSH, William: 4644
SALTON, Gilbert: 4913
SALTPETER--Southern States: 5737
SALTUS, Francis S.: 2449
SALUDA (ship): 2959
SALUDA COUNTY, South Carolina:
  Ridge Spring: 2921
SALUSBURY-TRELAWNEY, Sir John
  Salusbury, Ninth Baronet: see
  TRELAWNEY, Sir John Salusbury
  Salusbury-, Ninth Baronet

SALVAGE (gunboats):
  South Carolina--Charleston harbor:
    5731
SALVATION ARMY: 1584
  North Carolina: 5519
SALWEEN RIVER (Burma): 4709
SAMANIEGO, Diego: 4155
SAMES, Mary: 5360
SAMPLE, William, Sr.: 4645
SAMPLE, William, Jr.: 4645
SAMPSON (ship): 4881
SAMPSON COUNTY, North Carolina: 1752,
  2078, 2617, 3043
  Clement: 495
  Clinton: 1107, 1751, 2863, 3043
  Lisbon--Civil War: 390
SAMUEL A. ASHE CHAPTER, Children of
  the Confederacy: 227
SAMUEL GARNER AND CO., Winston-Salem,
  North Carolina: 1960
SAMUEL M. LANTZ AND J. P. RINKER,
  Union Forge, Virginia: 3098
SAMUEL MORDECAI AND COMPANY,
  Petersburg, Virginia: 3761
SAN ANTONIO (Texas) EXPRESS: 4278
SAN DIEGO, U.S.S.: 4355
SAN FRANCISCO, California: 1798,
  3239, 4188, 5733
  American poetry: 5081
  Description: 1614, 2191
  Earthquakes (1906): 4743
  Exhibitions and fairs: 4042
  Manufacture of scales: 4119
  Marriage prospects: 2370
  Race riots: 4535
  Voyage to: 4881
SAN JACINTO, U.S.S.: 2265
SAN JOSEF, Francisco de: 4155
SAN JUAN, Puerto Rico: 3109
  see also SPANISH-AMERICAN WAR--
    Campaigns, battles, and military
    actions--Puerto Rico--San Juan
SAN MARCOS, Texas: 1361
SAN MARTIN, José de: 4155
SAN PABLO, Brazil: 4155
SAN PEDRO BRAZILIAN GAS COMPANY, LTD.:
  2750
SAN ROMÁN, Miguel: 4155
SAN SABA COUNTY, Texas:
  Migration to: 5496
SANBORNTON BRIDGE, New Hampshire:
  3822
SANDBURG, Carl: 2689
SANDEFUR, Earl Lafayette: 1199
SANDEMAN, Sir Robert Groves: 4520
SANDERFORD AND JARRATT (firm): see
  ISAAC A. JARRATT & SANDERFORD
SANDERS, Benjamin K.: 4649
SANDERS, Charles Richard: 5101
SANDERS, Horace T.: 358
SANDERS, J. P. N.: 4646
SANDERS, James R.: 4647
SANDERS, Lloyd: 2155
SANDERS, Richard W.: 4648
SANDERS FAMILY (South Carolina): 4649
SANDERS-GREEN PIG IRON FURNACE: 4648
SANDERSON, George: 4188
SANDERSON, Henry Sanderson Furniss,
  First Baron: 1924
SANDERSVILLE, Georgia: 2598, 5566
SANDFORD, William: 4650
SANDON, Dudley Ryder, Viscount: 1087
SANDS, Alexander Hamilton: 1227
SANDS, Alexander Hamilton, Jr.
  (1891-1960): 4651, 5252
SANDS, Joshua Ratoon: 4062
SANDS, Oliver Jackson: 5035
SANDUSKY, Ohio:
  Civil War prison: 704
SANDUSKY COUNTY, Ohio: 3441
  Fremont: 2446
    Liquor trade: 4892
  Johnson's Island: 836, 2862, 4469,
    5900
    Civil War: 1543

SANDUSKY COUNTY, Ohio:
   Johnson's Island:
     Civil War (Continued):
      see also CIVIL WAR--PRISONERS
       AND PRISONS--Confederate prisoners--Ohio--Johnson's Island
SANDWICH, John Montagu, Fourth
  Earl of: 3724
"SANDY GROVE," Bartow, Georgia: 2860
"SANFORD" (carriage maker): 5623
SANFORD, Charles Addison: 4652
SANFORD, Daniel P.: 1845
SANFORD, Edward Ayshford: 4024
SANFORD, Richard: 4653
SANFORD (THOMAS) & CO.: 5298
SANFORD, Vincent: 4654
SANFORD, Maine: 1699
SANFORD, North Carolina: 238
  Railroad motor cars: 4918
SANGAMON (ironclad): 1063
SANGAMON COUNTY, Illinois:
  Springfield: 1330, 3207
SANITARY ENGINEERING:
  Students' notebooks:
    Pennsylvania: 5679
SANITATION:
  see also Medical and sanitary
    affairs as subheading under
    names of armies, navies, and
    wars
  Cape Colony--Cape Town: 3315
  Great Britain--Romsey: 5222
  North Carolina:
    New Hanover County: 3859
    Wilmington: 3859
  Philippine Islands: 3313
  Tennessee--Nashville: 5623
SANITY: see INSANITY; MENTAL HEALTH
SANS SOUCI GIRLS' SCHOOL, Greenville,
  South Carolina: 4911, 5082
SANTA ANNA, Antonio López de: 1926
SANTA CRUZ, Bolivia: 4155
SANTA FE, New Mexico: 1174
SANTA LUCA, Georgia: 639
SANTA MARIA, Brazil: 1685
SANTA ROSA, California: 836
SANTA ROSA COUNTY, Florida:
  Milton: 3008
SANTA ROSA ISLAND, Florida: see
  CIVIL WAR--CAMPAIGNS, BATTLES,
  AND MILITARY ACTIONS--Florida--
  Santa Rosa Island
SANTAYANA, George: 1097
SANTEE CANAL (South Carolina): 4218
SANTIAGO, Chile--Description: 3102
SANTILLANA, Marqués de: 306
SANTO DOMINGO: see DOMINICAN
  REPUBLIC
SANTO DOMINGO (city), Dominican
  Republic:
  Municipal government: 4275
  Trade and commerce: 4275
SAO PAULO PROVINCE, Brazil:
  Iguape: 339
SAPELO ISLAND, Georgia: 2326, 2963,
  4985, 4988
SAPP, Sally: 2808
SARATOGA, U.S.S.: 5190
SARATOGA COUNTY, New York:
  Ballston Spa: 5066, 5206
  Saratoga Springs: see SARATOGA
    SPRINGS, New York
  Waterford: 814
SARATOGA SPRINGS, New York:
  Description: 2828, 3607
  Hotels: 1928
SARAWAK, Malaysia: 2708
  Foreign relations:
    Great Britain: 5725
  Missions and missionaries: 2148
    Church of England: 5725
SARDINIA (kingdom of): see SAVOY
SARDINIA, U.S.S.: 4355
SARDOU, Victorien: 3617
SARGENT, George Henry: 2790
SARGENT, Helen Louise: 3325
SARGENT, Jabez: 3737

SARGENT, John T.: 2801
SARMIENTO, Domingo Faustino: 3295
SARSFIELD RANGERS: see CONFEDERATE
  STATES OF AMERICA--ARMY--Regiments--
  Louisiana--Infantry--7th
SARTARTIA, Mississippi:
  Mercantile accounts: 5821
SARTORIUS, Sir George Rose: 4655
SARTWELL, Henry Parker: 1229
SASHES (wood): see MILLWORK INDUSTRY
SASS, George Herbert: 1494
"SASSAFRAS SPROUTS" by Herman E.
  Melton: 4894
SASTRON, Manuel: 4656
SATIE, Erik Leslie: 4657
SATIRE: see AMERICAN SATIRE; ENGLISH
  SATIRE; POLITICAL SATIRE
SATTERFIELD, Carlotta Gilmore
  (Angier): 133
SATTERTHWAIT, Elizabeth: 1653
SATTERTHWAITE, Fenner B.: 4658
SATURDAY, Gwendolyn: 4659
SATURDAY, James R. P.: 4659
SATURDAY EVENING POST: 1771, 2400,
  3267
SAUDI ARABIA:
  American embassy in: 5298
  Social life and customs: 83
SAUNDERS, _____ (1800s, painter of
  miniatures): 1575
SAUNDERS, _____ (1900s): 4279
SAUNDERS, B. H.: 4670
SAUNDERS, Charles A.: 4660
SAUNDERS, Sir Charles Burslem: 4660
SAUNDERS, Fleming II: 4661
SAUNDERS, Fleming A.: 1185
SAUNDERS, Hubert: 4662
SAUNDERS, Ivory Bassett: 4663
SAUNDERS, J. T.: 4664
SAUNDERS, James: 4669
SAUNDERS, James Edmund: 2662
SAUNDERS, Joseph Hubbard: 4665, 4669
SAUNDERS, Nell: 5312
SAUNDERS, Richard Benbury: 4072, 4666
SAUNDERS, Robert, Second Viscount
  Melville: 1599, 2836, 4137
SAUNDERS, Romulus Mitchell: 4235,
  4667
SAUNDERS, W. W.: 4668
SAUNDERS, William A.: 4663
SAUNDERS, William Laurence: 3437,
  4669
SAUNDERS AND COMPANY, Phoenix Mines,
  North Carolina: 4670
SAUSSY, Joachim R., Jr.: 4671
SAVAGE, John Houston: 2371
SAVAGE, Minot Judson: 4672
SAVAGE (WILLIAM) (firm): see
  JOSEPH WESTMORE AND WILLIAM SAVAGE
SAVAGE, Maryland: 1314
SAVANNAH, Georgia: 4236
  1700s: 1088, 1440, 4441, 5189, 5920
    1750s: 1684
    1760s: 289
    1770s: 289, 1664, 2118, 2666
    1780s: 289, 413, 1664, 2262,
      2293, 2666, 3444, 4826, 5644
    1790s: 2262, 2293, 2666, 4509,
      4826, 5644
  1700s-1800s: 2019, 2238, 2460,
    2901, 2923, 3309, 3389, 4400,
    4768
  1700s-1900s: 1466, 2893
  1800s: 339, 463, 781, 786, 2578,
    3278, 3310, 3311, 3381, 3417,
    4177, 4611, 4671, 5190
    1800s: 3323, 4163
    1810s: 3323
    1820s: 158, 2497, 3323, 3396,
      4163
    1830s: 2497, 3396, 5606
    1840s: 991, 1241, 2497, 3396,
      3864, 5547, 5606
    1850s: 991, 1241, 1290, 1422,
      3761, 4569, 4881
    1860s: 121, 1146, 1251, 1290,
      1365, 1422, 2312, 2388, 2789,

SAVANNAH, Georgia:
  1800s:
    1860s (Continued):
      3131, 3761, 4463, 4510, 4673,
      4950
    1870s: 1251, 1614, 2001, 2789,
      3131, 3762, 3894
    1880s: 1614, 1709, 2001, 2388,
      2512
    1890s: 1709
  1800s-1900s: 823, 924, 1017, 2232,
    3629, 3969, 4674, 4966, 5494
  1900s:
    1910s: 365, 4402
    1920s: 365, 3394, 4402
    1930s: 365, 4402
  American Revolution:
    see also AMERICAN REVOLUTION--
      Campaigns and battles--
      Georgia--Savannah
    Confiscated property--Slaves:
      3591
    Evacuation of the British: 5078
    Fortifications: 2675
    Loyalists: 5078
  Autograph collecting: 5220
  Automobile racing: 1171
  Bakeries: 575
  Banks and banking: 311, 950, 5220
    see also BANK OF THE UNITED
      STATES (second)--Savannah,
      Georgia, Branch
  British consulate in: 2150
  Building and loan associations:
    2010
  Business affairs: 1609, 2114, 5076,
    5298, 5932
  Civil War:
    see also CIVIL WAR--CAMPAIGNS,
      BATTLES, AND MILITARY ACTIONS--
      Georgia--Savannah/Sherman's
      March
    Blockade: 1798
    Defense: 2722
    Evacuation: 5390
    Fortifications: 5472
    Laying of torpedoes in harbor:
      2724
    United States provost marshal:
      4432
  Commission merchants: 4040, 4625
  Commodity prices: 5494
  Cotton trade: 1705, 2018, 3689
  Customs administration: 2326, 5516
  Debating societies: 4675
  Description:
    1793: 4864
    1815: 5042
    1848: 284
    1868: 249
    1869: 5731
    1871: 4318
  Economic conditions (1860s): 115
  Estates--Administration and
    settlement: 3717, 4205
  Finance: 2327
  Fugitive slaves: 5221
  Grocery trade: 4040
  Historical societies: 2005
  Horse racing: 4864
  Insurance agents: 4587
  Insurance companies: 4587
  Law enforcement: 5492
  Legal affairs: 5787, 5987
  Local elections: 2280, 5494
  Lumber trade: 4356, 5216
  Mercantile accounts: 3696, 5216
  Merchants: 2122
  Personal debt: 4205
  Physicians: 220, 4676
  Poorhouses: 4678
  Ports: 4678
  Railroads: 950, 4718
  Real estate: 2993
  Reconstruction: 4257
  Revenue collectors: 731

SAVANNAH, Georgia (Continued):
  Schools::
    Latouche School: 2326
    Negro schools: 510
  Slave trade: 1705, 5221
  Social life and customs:
    1790s: 4864
    1800s: 2035, 5298
    1800s-1900s: 5730
  Songs and music--Concerts: 4677
  Spanish embassy in: 4983
  Storage of merchandise: 5516
  Trade and commerce: 759, 2122
  Visit of Jefferson Davis: 5472
  Weather: 2785, 4687
SAVANNAH, C.S.S.: 2963
SAVANNAH (U.S. frigate): 2963
SAVANNAH, TYBEE, AND ATLANTIC RAILWAY CO.: 3629
SAVANNAH AND CHARLESTON RAIL ROAD COMPANY: 4673
SAVANNAH AND ISLE OF HOPE RAILROAD CO.: 3629, 4674
SAVANNAH AND WESTERN RAILROAD: 725
SAVANNAH DEBATING SOCIETY, Savannah, Georgia: 4675
SAVANNAH MEDICAL CLUB, Savannah, Georgia: 4676
SAVANNAH MUSIC CLUB, Savannah, Georgia: 4677
SAVANNAH PORT SOCIETY, Savannah, Georgia: 4678
SAVANNAH RIVER:
  Engineering: 89
  Explosion of steamboat: 2956
  Lumber rafts: 2122
SAVANNAH RIVER SWAMP, Georgia:
  Illegal liquor manufacturing: 2388
SAVANNAH VOLUNTEER GUARDS: 2512
SAVELLE, Max: 1424
SAVERY, Amanda Gertrude (Mitchell): 4679
SAVERY, Phineas Messenger: 4679
"SAVEZ": see REED, Charles
SAVILLE (ALLEN J.) INC., Richmond, Virginia: 5790
SAVINGS ACCOUNTS:
  see also BANKS AND BANKING
  Virginia:
    Charlottesville: 4142, 5789
SAVINGS ASSOCIATIONS: see BUILDING AND LOAN ASSOCIATIONS
SAVINGS BANK OF BALTIMORE, Maryland: 496
SAVINGS BANK OF BOSTON, Massachusetts: 5499
SAVINGS BOND DRIVES: see WORLD WAR I--Savings bond drives; WORLD WAR II--Savings bonds
SAVOY, France--Boundaries: 4408
SAWAMISH COUNTY, Washington Territory:
  Oakland: 5033
SAWBRIDGE, John: 92
SAWMILL ACCOUNTS:
  Georgia--Cherokee County: 1887
  North Carolina: 4080
    Catawba County: 5705
  South Carolina: 4434
  Virginia: 3679
SAWMILL WORKERS:
  Georgia:
    Cherokee County: 1887
    Slaves: 1887
SAWMILLS:
  Steam powered:
    North Carolina: 3317
      Anson County: 4918
  Subdivided by place:
    Alabama: 1877
    Georgia: 4895
    Mississippi--Rodney: 3322
    North Carolina: 1658, 2121, 5310
      Randleman: 5408
      Randolph County: 1876
      Stokes County: 4080
    South Carolina: 1927
      Branchville: 1749

SAWMILLS:
  Subdivided by place (Continued):
    Virginia: 2229
      Roanoke County: 1969
    West Virginia: 2387
SAWS--Manufacture in Virginia: 282
SAWYER, Adna: 4680
SAWYER, Francis A.: 4681
SAWYER, Helen J. (Thompson): 1376
SAWYER, Jonathan: 4681
SAWYER, L.: 4683
SAWYER, Lemuel: 4682
SAWYER, Louisa Cleveland: 1376
SAWYER, W. E.: 1877
SAXE GOTHA DISTRICT, South Carolina:
  Committee of Public Safety: 4624
SAXON, D. Lewis: 4684
THE SAXONS IN ENGLAND by John Mitchell Kemble: 2973
SAXTON, Rufus: 731
SAYAJI RAO GAEKWAR III, Maharaja of Baroda: 326
SAYER, Daniel: 4685
SAYLER'S CREEK, Virginia: see CIVIL WAR--CAMPAIGNS, BATTLES, AND MILITARY ACTIONS--Virginia--Sayler's Creek
SAYRE INSTITUTE, Lexington, Kentucky: 4373
SCALES, Alfred Moore (1827-1892): 3094, 4686
SCALES, Alfred Moore (b. 1870): 5457
SCALES, Dabney Minor: 4687
SCALES, William: 2815
SCALES (weighing instruments):
  Manufacture:
    California--San Francisco: 4119
    Pennsylvania: 1392
  Purchases and sales: 2
SCANDALS: see MARITAL SCANDALS
SCANLON, David Howard: 2934
SCANLON, Mary: 2934
SCANLON FAMILY (North Carolina): 2934
SCANTLING, John Columbia: 4688
SCANTLING, Philip: 4688
SCARBOROUGH, Henry T.: 4689
SCARBOROUGH, John C.: 671
SCARBOROUGH, S. E.: 4689
SCARBOROUGH, Samuel: 4689
SCARBOROUGH FAMILY (North Carolina--Genealogy): 4689
SCARCITY OF COMMODITIES: see as subheading under names of armies, navies, and wars
SCARLET FEVER: see DISEASES--Scarlet fever
SCENARIOS: see MOVING PICTURES--Scenarios
SCHABERG, Emma L.: 3049
SCHAEFFER, Frances (Carter): 4858
SCHAFF, Philip: 2999
SCHAFFER, _____ (German theologian): 2592
SCHAUM, William: 5991
SCHEETZ, George C.: 4690
SCHENCK, David: 5457
SCHENCK, H. F.: 4691
SCHENECTADY, New York: see UNION COLLEGE
SCHILLING, Jacob R.: 4692
SCHINDLER, Sir Albert Houtum-: see HOUTUM-SCHINDLER, Sir Albert
SCHISMS: see METHODIST CHURCHES--Schisms
SCHLESWIG-HOLSTEIN QUESTION (1848): 5222
SCHLESWIG-HOLSTEIN WAR (1864): 4520
SCHLEY, Charles: 5517
SCHLEY, Molly (Walker): 5517
SCHLEY, William: 3905, 4715
SCHLEY FAMILY (West Virginia): 5324
SCHLIEMANN, Heinrich: 5156
SCHMIDT, _____ (German theologian): 2592
SCHNADHORST, Francis: 4694

"EINE SCHNELLFAHRT DURCH DEUTSCHLAND, BELGIEN, FRANKREICH UND HOLLAND IM AUGUST UND SEPTEMBER 1844": 4695
SCHOFIELD, Edward, Sr.: 4702
SCHOFIELD, Edward, Jr.: 4702
SCHOFIELD, John McAllister: 254, 1607, 3228, 4723
SCHOFIELD, William Henry: 34, 648
SCHOHARIE COUNTY, New York: 585
SCHOLARLY EDITING:
  Periodicals: 102
  Subdivided by place:
    Great Britain: 1218
    North Carolina: 691
    United States: 720, 4290, 4499, 5054, 5971
SCHOLARSHIPS:
  see also Scholarships as subheading under names of specific universities and colleges
  North Carolina: 2819
  Southern States: 1258
SCHOLEFIELD, Joshua: 4696
SCHOOL BOARDS:
  Alabama--Selma: 4911
  Georgia: 662
  Maryland--Washington County: 3086
  Massachusetts: 4807
  North Carolina:
    Forsyth County: 813
    Granville County: 2833
  South Carolina:
    Saint Luke's Parish: 4961
SCHOOL BOOKS: see ARITHMETIC--Exercise books; PENMANSHIP--Exercise books; TEXTBOOKS
SCHOOL BUILDINGS: see PUBLIC SCHOOL BUILDINGS
SCHOOL CENSUS:
  North Carolina:
    Durham County: 1256
    Granville County: 2833
SCHOOL COMPOSITIONS: see STUDENTS AND STUDENT LIFE--Compositions
SCHOOL FURNITURE INDUSTRY AND TRADE:
  Massachusetts: 2417
SCHOOL LAW: see EDUCATION--Laws and legislation
SCHOOL LIFE: see STUDENTS AND STUDENT LIFE
SCHOOL REGISTERS: see TEACHERS' RECORDS
SCHOOL SYSTEMS:
  Analysis of eastern cities: 2930
SCHOOL TAXES:
  Virginia--Mecklenburg County: 1821
SCHOOLCRAFT, Henry Rowe: 4697
SCHOOLCRAFT, Mary (Howard): 4697
SCHOOLER, Mary Eliza (Fleming): 4698
SCHOOLER, Samuel: 4698
SCHOOLS:
  see also BUSINESS SCHOOLS; EDUCATION; KINDERGARTENS; MILITARY SCHOOLS; PUBLIC SCHOOLS; STUDENTS AND STUDENT LIFE; TEACHERS' RECORDS; TEACHING; and subheadings beginning with the words EDUCATION, EDUCATIONAL, SCHOOL, or TEACHERS
  Advertising: see ADVERTISING--Schools
  Charity schools:
    Great Britain: 5539
  Church schools:
    Anglican:
      Great Britain: 2962
    Catholic: 3424
      Great Britain: 2962
    Episcopal:
      North Carolina:
        Ansonville: 4918
        Raleigh: 4669
    Methodist:
      Great Britain: 5726
      North Carolina: 1538

SCHOOLS:
  Church schools (Continued):
    Methodist Episcopal:
      North Carolina: 3581
      Subdivided by place:
        North Carolina: 1556
  Construction: 1758
  Commencement exercises:
    North Carolina--Wake County: 3941
  Curriculum:
    Georgia: 2828
    Massachusetts--Springfield: 5043
    North Carolina: 3538
      Asheville: 566
    Pennsylvania: 4106
    South Carolina:
      Columbia: 566
      Edgefield: 5312
      Winnsboro: 566
  Desegregation:
    North Carolina: 3538
  Discipline:
    North Carolina: 3908
      Asheville: 566
    South Carolina:
      Columbia: 566
      Winnsboro: 566
  Finance:
    see also SCHOOL TAXES; SCHOOLS--
      Tuition
    Georgia: 479
    Great Britain: 4113
    North Carolina: 3538
      Warrenton: 3761
  Girls' schools and academies: 5593
    Tuition:
      Arkansas: 3142
      North Carolina: 1469, 2819
      Virginia: 5369
    Subdivided by place:
      Alabama: 1476, 1947
        Greensboro: 5593
      Connecticut--Hartford: 1827
      Georgetown, D.C.: 2301
      Georgia: 479
        Athens: 3905
        La Grange: 3905
        Macon:
          Macon Female Academy: 2963
          Montpelier Institute: 2963, 4040
        Savannah: 2326
        Washington: 5051
      Illinois--Lewistown: 5311
      Kentucky--Springfield: 4987
      Louisiana: 489
        Clinton: 4373, 4819
      Maryland: 489, 2301, 3053
        Baltimore: 5298
      Mississippi: 2588
      New York: 2407
      New York: 4736
      North Carolina: 832, 2589, 3043
        All Healing Springs: 3416
        Charlotte: 1823, 4080
        Fayetteville: 5298
        Greensboro: 1100, 2357
        Lincolnton: 3210
        Louisburg: 3272
        Raleigh:
          see also PEACE COLLEGE;
            SAINT MARY'S COLLEGE
          Raleigh Female Classical
            Institute: 4154
        Statesville: 5310
        Wilson: 2642
        Vernon: 2970
        Winston-Salem: see SALEM
          COLLEGE
      Ohio--Steubenville: 5380
      Pennsylvania: 2776, 2828, 3956, 5165
        Philadelphia: 2362
      South Carolina: 4118, 5082
        Barhamville: 3527

SCHOOLS:
  Girls' schools and academies:
    Subdivided by place:
      South Carolina (Continued):
        Charleston:
          Madame Talvande's School: 4622
          Misses Bates' School: 1651
        Greenville: 4911, 5082
        Spartanburg:
          Spartanburg Female Academy: 2854
          Spartanburg Female
            Seminary: 561
      Tennessee: 872
      United States: 2591
      Vermont--Thetford: 3218
      Virginia: 2340
        Bristol: 5267
        Buckingham County: 5652
        Charlottesville:
          Piedmont Female Academy: 490
          Young Ladies' Institute: 4915
        Edge Hill: 1409
        Luray: 461
        Lynchburg: 4373
        Nelson County: 3788
        Richmond:
          Mrs. Mead's School: 5513, 5529
          Richmond Female Institute: 2068
        Staunton: 5936
          Augusta Female Seminary: 2712
          Virginia Female
            Institute: 43, 884, 3822, 5286
        Villeboro: 3293
        Winchester: 287
      West Virginia:
        Morgantown:
          Morgantown Female
            Academy: 2794
          Woodburn Female Seminary: 5110
        Parkersburg: 5194
        Wheeling: 5194
  Masonic schools:
    North Carolina: 1783
  Mission schools:
    Methodist--Brazil: 3248
    For Indians:
      Arkansas--Choctaw: 4373
      Mississippi: 3611
      South Carolina: 3356
      Presbyterian--Catawba: 1923
    Subdivided by place:
      China: 5252
      Japan: 2959
  Negro schools:
    see also TEACHING--Negro schools
    Attendance--South Carolina: 1927
    Northern teachers:
      North Carolina: 5533
    Subdivided by place:
      British West Indies: 763
      Georgia: 510
      New York: 4351
      North Carolina: 2753, 4080
        Wake County: 3941
      South Carolina: 1477
        Beaufort: 3218
  Preparatory schools:
    Great Britain: 1675
    Massachusetts: 339
    New York: 1580
    North Carolina--Magnolia: 4910
  Primary schools--Spain: 4981
  Public relations: 1758
  School lunch program:
    North Carolina: 3538
  Textile engineering:
    Massachusetts: 4918

SCHOOLS (Continued):
  Tuition:
    North Carolina:
      Granville County: 2833
      Louisburg: 3272
      Robeson County: 3803
    Pennsylvania: 4106
    South Carolina: 4118
    Virginia: 117
  Subdivided by place:
    Alabama: 1877, 5593
    Connecticut: 351, 2532
      New Haven: 5747
    France: 2963
    Georgia: 3415
      Bibb County: 2963
      Clopton's Mills: 5760
      Talbotton: 3729
      Washington: 51
      Washington Academy: 5580
    Great Britain: 2962, 4115
      Bath: 1753
      Eton: 2102, 5736
      Harrow: 4770
      London: 5616
    Illinois: 2752
    Indiana: 3981
    Kentucky--Lexington: 4373
    Maine: 731
    Maryland: 643, 2692, 2974
      Baltimore:
        Saint Joseph's School: 4866
        Saint Timothy's Hall: 3607
      Charlotte Hall: 5296
      Frederick County: 4804
    Massachusetts: 743, 1423
      East Hampton: 4897
      Monson: 4897
      South Hadley: 4897
      Southborough: 1423
      Stockbridge: 1792
    Mississippi: 3415
    New England: 51
    New Hampshire: 354
      East Andover: 4039
    New Jersey: 743
    New York: 480, 4169
      Geneva: 4348
      New York: 3008
      Norwich: 2292
      Tarrytown: 5593
      Yonkers: 2553
    North Carolina:
      1800s: 817, 1701, 1871, 2714, 4148
      1830s: 3415
      1840s: 1686, 3415
      1850s: 484, 1882, 3117
      1860s: 671, 754, 1882
      1870s: 671, 1882
      1880s: 394, 661, 671, 2330
      1890s: 394, 2330
      1800s-1900s: 4391, 5549
      Anson County:
        Anson Institute: 4052
        District No. 23 for White
          Race: 192
      Asheville: 661, 4968
      Battleboro: 5701
      Bethania: 813
      Cary:
        Asbury Academy: 2846
        Cary School: 527
      Chatham County:
        District No. 62: 4689
        Mount Vernon Academy: 2861
      Cora: 1247
      Dallas: 4080
      Donaldson: 4517
      Durham: 3762
        Dayton Academy: 3896
        Durham County: 1256, 4862
          High school: 2472
      Edenton: 2776
      Falls of Tar River: 4571
      Fayetteville: 4517, 5298
        Fayetteville Academy: 1898, 5298
      Forestville: 4294

SCHOOLS:
  Subdivided by place:
    North Carolina (Continued):
      Forsyth County: 813
      Granville County: 2833
        Belmont Academy: 2192
      Greensboro: 5804
      Haywood: 2357
      Hertford: 4897
      Hickory: 3043
      High Point: 3300
      Hillsborough: 5298
        Hillsborough Academy: 834
      Johnston County: 698
      Jonesville: 4765
      Kernersville: 817
      Leasburg: 1336
      Lincolnton: 4238
      Lockville: 4765
      Louisburg: 2530, 3272
      Maysville: 3607
      Mebane: 3300, 5298, 5912
      Monroe: 2573
      Montgomery County: 4689
      Mount Energy: 2833
      Mount Gilead: 4689
      New Bern: 263
      Oak Ridge: 1055
        Oak Ridge Institute: 3290
      Oakdale: 675
      Olin: 2857
      Orange County: 661, 666, 675, 817, 3300, 4321, 5298, 5912
      Oxford: 5709
        Oxford Academy: 214
        Oxford Classical and Grammar School: 2192
      Randolph County: 4689
      Robeson County: 3803
      Rockingham: 1725
      Thyatira: 3334
      Wake County: 4294
      Warrenton: 3761, 4571
      Washington: 4858
      Wilkes County: 3942
      Wilmington: 617, 3607
      Wilson: 4462, 4910
      Winston-Salem: 4080
        Winston Male Academy: 817
      Youngsville: 5087
    Ohio: 2591
    Pennsylvania: 421, 1681, 3155
      Bethlehem: 3258
      Mount Nebo: 3174
      Philadelphia: 4348
    Philippine Islands: 4656
    Rhode Island: 4169, 4907
    South Carolina: 501, 4118, 1927
      Calhoun: 5082
      Charleston: 2940
        Edmond's School: 219
      Chesterfield: 2855
      Cokesbury: 5114
      Denmark: 5572
      Greenville: 3405
      Orangeburg: 501
      Society Hill: 4634
      Spartanburg: 561
      Winnsboro: 5193
    Tennessee:
      Rutherford County: 104
    Vermont--Ludlow: 5197
    Virginia:
      1800s: 330
      1820s: 4280
      1830s: 743, 872, 4280
      1840s: 743, 872, 4280
      1850s: 743, 2370, 2683
      1860s: 2370, 2559, 2648
      1870s: 2370, 3788
      Albemarle County: 5286
      Alexandria: 5210
      Amelia County: 1894, 3809
      Amherst County: 5380
      Appomattox Court House: 5902
      Bedford County: 1894
        Sunny Side School: 4049
      Belhaven: 1697

SCHOOLS:
  Subdivided by place:
    Virginia (Continued):
      Brownsburg: 3785
      Brunswick County: 2517
      Caroline County: 4698
      Covesville: 1767
      Covington: 3308
      Dayton: 1920
      Edge Hill: 4698
      Fairfax: 3141
      Farmville: 2712
      Fluvanna County: 558
      Harrisonburg: 899
      Iron Gate: 2922
      Lexington: 3202
      Mount Maria: 5529
      New London: 3868
      Norfolk: 4968
      Norwood: 824, 5107
      Nottoway County: 1811
      Orange: 5194
      Orange County: 5286
      Petersburg: 858
      Portsmouth: 4280
      Rapidan Station: 5798
      Richmond: 5194
      Richmond County: 2677
      Taylorsville: 298, 4698
      Winchester: 2559, 5779
      Worsham: 5110
    West Virginia: 1784, 1946
      Charles Town: 1379
    Wisconsin:
      Porter: 5307
      Rock County: 5307
SCHRACK (C.) AND COMPANY: 4699
SCHRECKHIRE, James M.: 4700
SCHRIRER, Albert S.: 4701
SCHROEDER, H. L.: 1424
SCHROEDER FOUNDATION: 1424
SCHURER,_____(German theologian): 2592
SCHURZ, Carl: 1468, 5762
SCHUYLER, Elizabeth: 2276
SCHUYLER COUNTY, New York:
  Watkins: 1907
SCHUYLKILL COUNTY, Pennsylvania:
  Pottsville: 2408
SCHUYLKILL RIVER--Water power: 5686
SCHWEBELE, Édouard: 4490
SCHWEINITZ, Agnes Sophia de: 5459
SCIENCE: 3904
  see also specific branches of science, e.g. CHEMISTRY; ZOOLOGY; etc.
  Experiments: 90
  North Carolina: 817
  United States: 1219
SCIENCE HILL, North Carolina: 3078
SCIENTIFIC CLASSIFICATION: see ZOOLOGY--Classification
SCIENTIFIC EXPEDITIONS:
  see also ZOOLOGICAL EXPEDITIONS
  Alaska: 2084
  Brazil: 2407, 4876
  Honduras: 5480
SCIENTIFIC RESEARCH: 1702
  Great Britain: 1913
  United States: 2120, 2578
SCIENTIFIC SOCIETIES:
  see also AMERICAN ASSOCIATION FOR THE ADVANCEMENT OF SCIENCE; LINNAEAN SOCIETY
  North Carolina: 4232
SCIOTO COUNTY, Ohio:
  Portsmouth: 281
  Labor unions: 3986
SCITUATE, Massachusetts: 1344, 4305
SCOARNEC, Pierre: 3270
SCOLLARD, Clinton: 2449
SCOLLAY, Harriet L.: 1730, 4703
SCOLLAY, Mollie N.: 4703
SCOLLAY, Samuel: 4703
SCOLLAY, Sarah P.: 4703
SCOTCH: see SCOTS IN THE UNITED STATES
SCOTCH-IRISH: see SCOTS-IRISH

SCOTCH PLAINS, New Jersey: 1160
SCOTLAND:
  Authorship: 2736
  Autographs--Edinburgh: 2022
  Biographical studies: 5379
  Book buying--Edinburgh: 1212
  Book reviews: 5379
  Booksellers and bookselling:
    Edinburgh: 4333
  Camping--Inverness: 2103
  Church of Scotland: 5726
  Conservative Party: 3592
  Cycling--Inverness: 2103
  Defense: 1598
  Description and travel:
    1770s-1780s: 4084, 5527
    1800s: 1115
    1880s: 1463
  Economic conditions: 5726
  Elections: 1598
  Fishing: 5259
  Foreign business enterprises:
    United States: 3179
  Historical studies: 5379
  Legal affairs: 5643
  Libraries--Private: 1212
  Manufacturers: 5726
  Merchants: 5527
  Migration from:
    To North Carolina: 5298
    To United States: 1598
  Nobility: 1716
  Peasantry: 4913
  Personal finance--Edinburgh: 4834
  Poetry collections: 4835
  Politics and government:
    1700s: 2098, 4229
    1700s-1800s: 1598
    1800s: 4605
    1900s: 3592
    Proposal for local government board: 4427
  Potato trade: 3230
  Religion: 5
  Textile workers--Glasgow: 3179
  Tobacco industry: 4079
  Travel costs: 5527
  Unionist Party: 3592
  Universities and colleges: see UNIVERSITY OF EDINBURGH; UNIVERSITY OF GLASGOW
SCOTLAND COUNTY, North Carolina:
  Cotton trade: 3303
  Laurel Hill: 3776
  Laurinburg: 1313, 3416, 3475
  Montpelier: 5688
SCOTLAND NECK, North Carolina:
  Mercantile accounts: 4925
SCOTS IN THE UNITED STATES: 1598
  North Carolina: 448, 3386
  Virginia: 2633
SCOTS-IRISH IN VIRGINIA: 2120
SCOTT,_____(British lieutenant colonel): 5639
SCOTT,_____(British professor): 124
SCOTT,_____(Virginia judge): 5194
SCOTT, Abram M.: 2211
SCOTT, Benajah: 4704
SCOTT, Daniel: 4708
SCOTT, David (East India Company): 5639
SCOTT, David (North Carolina): 4704
SCOTT, Ella (Penn): 4714
SCOTT, G. Forrester: 4705
SCOTT, H. L.: 4188
SCOTT, Irby Goodwin: 4706
SCOTT, Irby H.: 4706
SCOTT, J. C.: 4707
SCOTT, J. Harold: 4705
SCOTT, Jacob V.: 4708
SCOTT, James (captain): 2304
SCOTT, Sir James George (1851-1935): 4709
SCOTT, James P. (Virginia merchant): 4710
SCOTT, John, First Earl of Eldon: 2126, 2836, 4024

SCOTT, John William Robertson-: see ROBERTSON-SCOTT, John William
SCOTT, L. J. J.: 4711
SCOTT, Levi M.: 277, 4714
SCOTT, Nicholas Ewing: 4706
SCOTT, Otho: 4712
SCOTT, Robert G. (Virginia attorney): 4713
SCOTT, Robert Kingston (1826-1900): 757
SCOTT, Sallie W.: 4711
SCOTT, W. W.: 4716
SCOTT, Sir Walter: 1494, 5681
SCOTT, William Lafayette (1828-1872): 4714
SCOTT, Winfield: 220, 778, 872, 1308, 3611, 4715, 5242, 5324, 5840, 5517
SCOTT AND GREEN (firm): see GREEN AND SCOTT
SCOTT COUNTY, Iowa:
  West Buffalo: 4070
SCOTT COUNTY, Kentucky: 4884
  Georgetown: 3489
SCOTT HOSIERY MILLS, INC., Graham, North Carolina: 4717
SCOTTISH BALLADS: 738
SCOTTISH CHURCH: see CHURCH OF SCOTLAND
SCOTTISH HIGHLANDERS IN NORTH CAROLINA: 3386
SCOTTSVILLE, Kentucky: 5505
SCOUTING: see Reconnaissance as subheading under names of armies
SCRANTON, Pennsylvania: 3227, 4188
SCRAP IRON TRADE:
  Confederate States of America: 4895
SCRATCHLEY, Francis Arthur: 4271
SCREVEN, James (general): 1171
SCREVEN, James P. (d. 1859): 1466, 4718
SCREVEN, John: 1466
SCREVEN FAMILY: 3396
SCREVEN COUNTY, Georgia: 1705
SCRIBNER'S (CHARLES) SONS: 1910, 4020
SCRIP--Iron furnaces--Virginia: 2922
SCRIVEN, Elizabeth (McQuade): 4719
SCRIVEN, George Percival: 4719
SCRIVEN, Thomas Swain: 4719
SCRUGGS, Benjamin E.: 4720
SCRUGGS, Langhorne: 4720
SCRUGGS, Richard: 4721
SCRUGGS FAMILY (South Carolina): 4721
SCRUGGS FAMILY (Virginia): 4720
SCRUTTON, Robert J.: 4722
SCUDDER, Horace Elisha: 706
SCULPTOR, H.M.S.: 4355
SCULPTORS:
  Americans in Italy: 2181
  United States: 3162
SCULPTURE:
  see also AMERICAN SCULPTURE
  Italy: 2352
  Jamaica: 1913
  Virginia: 4020
SCULLY, James Wall: 4723
SCUTARI, Turkey:
  Hospitals during Crimean War: 2168
SCYTHIAN INVASION OF INDIA: 866
SEA ISLAND COTTON: see COTTON--Sea Island Cotton
SEA ISLANDS, South Carolina:
  Civil War: 1418
  Union Army activities: 3910
SEA LIFE: see as subheading under names of navies
SEA-WALLS--Florida: 2387
SEABOARD, North Carolina: 4374
SEABOARD AIRLINE RAILWAY COMPANY: 557
SEABOARD ALL-FLORIDA RAILWAY COMPANY: 4343
SEABROOK, J. Ward: 4724
SEABROOK, Whitmarsh Benjamin: 2449, 4725, 4896, 4897

SEAFORTH, Canada: 1941
SEAGRY CHURCH, Seagry, England: 3895
SEAHAM HARBOUR, England: 5616
SEALS:
  Confederate States of America: 3269
  Virginia: 3809
SEAMEN, George: 2497
SEAMEN: see MERCHANT SEAMEN; NEGRO SEAMEN
SEAMEN'S AID SOCIETIES: see MERCHANT SEAMEN--Aid societies
SEAMEN'S FRIEND SOCIETY, Wilmington, North Carolina: 4727
SEAMLESS HOSIERY INDUSTRY COMMITTEE: 101
SEANCES: 1424
  see also SPIRITUALISM
  Georgia: 339
  Ireland--Dublin: 3567
SEARCH, Right of: see RIGHT OF SEARCH
SEAS, J. F.: 4728
SEAS (J. F.) AND SON, Orville, Ohio: 4728
SEATON, John Colborne, First Baron: 1147
SEATON, William Winston: 2931, 4246
SEBASTIAN COUNTY, Arkansas:
  Fort Smith: 4353
  Greenwood: 2123
SEBAWA, Michigan: 4452
SECOND PRESBYTERIAN CHURCH, Charleston, South Carolina: 4936
SECOND PRESBYTERIAN CHURCH, Lynchburg, Virginia: 3707
SECOND PRESBYTERIAN CHURCH, West Chester, New York: 5731
SECESSION AND SECESSIONIST SENTIMENT: 45, 128, 566, 1084, 1403, 1466, 1544, 1780, 1980, 2400, 2449, 2671, 2829, 2970, 3269, 3809, 4164, 4616, 4834, 4911, 4943, 5045, 5551, 5716, 5869, 5928
  see also DISUNION
  Opposition: 5627
    see also UNION LEAGUE OF NEW YORK
    Virginia: 1894, 2728, 5377
  Public opinion: 4897
    Pennsylvania: 421, 5380
    Virginia: 5545
  Right of: 3809
  Subdivided by place:
    Alabama: 2545, 4799, 5126, 5593
    Arkansas: 2184, 5380
    Connecticut: 375
    Georgia: 2460, 3075, 3110, 4415, 4895
    Kentucky: 4160
    Maryland: 314, 1403, 4748, 5059, 5315
    Mississippi: 836, 1370, 4720, 5498, 5621
    Missouri: 1683
    North Carolina: 761, 834, 1602, 2469, 2530, 3237, 3422, 4248, 4765, 5298, 5753
    Ohio: 4160
    Old Northwest: 1084
    South Carolina: 150, 561, 791, 1468, 1877, 2210, 2300, 2695, 2805, 4193, 4445, 4783, 5242, 5361, 5415, 5753, 5901
    Southern States: 155, 3239
    Tennessee: 155, 872, 1319, 2371
    Texas: 155, 639, 3524, 4434
    Virginia: 33, 155, 375, 523, 569, 872, 907, 2531, 4700, 4748, 4924, 5476, 5869, 5946
    West Virginia: 4774
SECESSION CONVENTIONS:
  Georgia: 700, 2860, 3905, 4799
  Virginia: 523, 3721
SECESSIONVILLE, South Carolina: see CIVIL WAR--CAMPAIGNS, BATTLES, AND MILITARY ACTIONS--South Carolina--Secessionville

SECOND GREAT AWAKENING: see GREAT AWAKENING (second)
SECRET CORRESPONDENCE ILLUSTRATING THE CONDITION OF AFFAIRS IN MARYLAND: 314
SECRET HISTORY OF THE DIVIDING LINE by William Byrd of Westover: 819
SECRET SERVICE:
  Confederate States of America: 1403
  Great Britain: 1598, 5071
  United States: 4275, 4983
SECRET SOCIETIES:
  see also names of specific societies, e.g. KU KLUX KLAN; KNIGHTS OF THE GOLDEN CIRCLE; etc.
  Iowa: 1984
  Philippine Islands: 4511
SECTIONALISM IN THE UNITED STATES: 1910, 2449, 4616
  see also NORTHERNERS IN THE SOUTH; SOUTHERNERS IN THE NORTH
  Pacific coast: 3239
SECULARISM: 2626
SECURITY, Public: see PUBLIC SECURITY
SECURITY INVESTMENT COMPANY, Brunswick, Georgia: 4298
SEDDON, James Alexander (1815-1880): 623, 1403, 1969, 2630, 3157, 4616, 4729, 5280
SEDDON, Marion: 4924
SEDDON, Sarah: 4616
SEDDON FAMILY (Virginia): 4924
SEDGWICK, Ellery: 706
SEDGWICK, John: 820
SEDITION:
  see also ALIEN AND SEDITION ACTS; TREASON; WORLD WAR I--Sedition Acts
  United States: 4948
SEDLEY, Charles: 1163
SEE AMERICA FIRST LEAGUE: 2368
SEED DISTRIBUTION--Virginia: 5769
SEED PRODUCTION--South Carolina: 4610
SEEDS--North Carolina: 4858
SEEGER, Alan: 1766
SEEGERS, John Conrad: 2449
SEEMAN, Elizabeth (Brickel): 4730
SEEMAN, Ernest: 4730
SEEMAN, Ernest Albright: 5252
SEGAR, Joseph: 4731
SEGREGATION:
  see also BLACK CODES; DESEGREGATION; RACE RELATIONS
  Missouri: 5984
  South Carolina: 300
  United States: 3048
  Virginia: 1194, 1198
SEGURA, Manuel Ascencio: see ASCENCIO SEGURA, Manuel
SEIBERT, Henry James, Sr.: 4732
SEIBERT, William L.: 4732
SEIDEL'S (DR.) ACADEMY, Bethlehem, Pennsylvania: 2828
SEIFERT, Shirley: 1137
SEIG (I. or J.) F.: 4733
SEIG, Samuel S.: 4733
SEISMOSCOPES: 3618
  see also EARTHQUAKES
SEISTAN, Persia: 4503
SELBORNE, Roundell Palmer, First Earl of: 4036, 4097
SELBY, B. M.: 4734
SELBY (B. M.) AND P. W. BROWN (firm, North Carolina): 4734
SELBY, Sarah E.: 2301
SELBY, Walter: 2301
SELDEN, Miles C.: 4735
SELECTIVE SERVICE CLASSIFICATION:
  see also Recruiting and enlistment as subheading under names of armies
  North Carolina: 2581
SELIM, King of Johanna Island: 3118
SELKIRK, Dumbar (Hamilton) Douglas, Fourth Earl: 1716

SELMA, Alabama:
  1800s: 1053, 1644, 1985, 3032, 3101, 3534, 4184, 5612
  1830s: 1645
  1840s: 1645
  1860s: 163, 1945, 2205, 2325
  1870s: 1265, 2325
  1890s: 3774
  1800s-1900s: 371, 3857
  Civil War: 1425, 4185
  Coal companies: 897
  Courts: 48
  Household accounts: 4911
  Insurance: 2013
  Legal affairs: 4911
  Real estate investments: 4911
  School boards: 4911
  Social conditions: 3712
  Universities and colleges: see PAYNE UNIVERSITY
SELMA STUDY CLUB, Selma, Alabama: 4911
SELTZER, Eliza: 1443
SEMANARIO ERUDITO by Don Antonio Valladares de Sotomayor: 3312
SEMANS, James Hustead: 4736
SEMANS, Mary Duke (Biddle) Trent: 4736
SEMANS FAMILY (North Carolina): 4736
SEMINARIES: see SCHOOLS
  Theological: see names of specific theological seminaries
SEMINOLE INDIANS: 2850
  Raids: 2781
  Raids against--Florida: 1438
SEMINOLE WAR (First, 1817-1818): 2781
SEMINOLE WAR (Second, 1835-1842): 872, 1745, 2781, 3447, 3801, 4593, 4924, 5417
  Alabama troops: 3611
  Bounty lands: 4200
  Campaigns, battles, and military actions:
    Florida:
      Fort Miami: 2842
      Withacoochee River: 2842
  Military activities: 3611
  Negotiations: 2842
  Negro involvement: 2842
SEMMES, Anna: 2963
SEMMES, Paul J.: 4737
SEMMES, Raphael: 2963, 4738, 4739
SEMMES, Thomas Jenkins: 4739
SENATORIAL ELECTIONS:
  Georgia (1873): 4402
  Louisiana (1930): 592
  Maryland (1938): 3190
  Mississippi (1857): 4442
  North Carolina:
    1902: 2188
    1906: 3955
    1912: 3955
    1918: 3955
    1930: 274, 2041
    1948: 2863
    1950: 2863
  South Carolina:
    1846: 4445
    1857: 1403
    1894: 5299
    1908: 5930
    1924: 1478, 3451, 5930
    1930: 3451
  Virginia (1847): 3255
SENECA, Maryland: 3145
SENECA COUNTY, New York:
  Seneca Falls: 3133
SENECA FALLS, New York: 3133
SENER, James Beverly (b. 1831): 4740
SENIOR CITIZENS: see AGED AND AGING
"THE SENIOR FORUM" by Thomas Hightower Collins: 1167
SENNA TRADE: 323
SENSENEY, J.: 4741
SENTER, Horace: 365
SENTIMENT: see the following as subheadings under specific subjects: Foreign public opinion;

SENTIMENT (Continued): Northern opinion; Public opinion; Southern opinion
SENTINEL (gunboat): 1181
SENTINEL, Winston-Salem, North Carolina (newspaper): 3538
SEPOY ARMY: see GREAT BRITAIN--INDIAN ARMY
SEPOY MUTINY (1806): see GREAT BRITAIN--INDIAN ARMY--Mutinies--Sepoy mutiny (1806)
SEPOY MUTINY (1857-1858): see INDIAN MUTINY
SEQUESTRATION ACT: 2695
SEQUESTRATION OF PROPERTY: see Confiscated property as subheading under names of wars
SEQUESTRATION PROCEEDINGS: see LAWSUITS--Virginia--Sequestration proceedings
SERAPIS, H.M.S.: 4102
SERBIA--Aid to orphans: 4080
"A SERENADE" by James Grant Wilson: 5813
SERGEANT, John: 5681
SERGEANT FAMILY (Genealogy): 1792
SERINGAPATAM, India: 5639
"THE SERMON OF THE ROSE" by James Whitcomb Riley: 4021
SERMONS: 4029, 4219
  see also FUNERAL SERMONS
  Baptist:
    Georgia: 4759
    South Carolina: 669
  Catholic--France: 3644
  Church of England:
    Great Britain: 179, 306
  Episcopal:
    Florida: 1653
    North Carolina: 1376, 4665
    Virginia: 3141
    West Virginia: 3141
  Evangelical Lutheran:
    Denmark: 2228
  Lutheran: 2485
    North Carolina: 4578
  Methodist: 3646, 4412, 4932, 5022, 5793
    American colonies: 5647
    Great Britain: 4146
    North Carolina: 956
    Virginia: 203
  Methodist Episcopal: 1906, 4912
    North Carolina: 1906, 3581
  Methodist Episcopal Church, South: 3564, 3756, 4498, 5745
    Japan: 3888
    North Carolina: 5023
      Plymouth: 772
      Wilmington: 772
    Virginia: 5467
    West Virginia: 5467
  Presbyterian: 2934, 4310, 4397, 5794
    North Carolina: 661, 923
      Coddle Creek: 4311
      Durham: 2934
      Thyatira: 3334
    Pennsylvania--Le Raysville: 4397
    South Carolina--Charleston: 4936
    Virginia: 2051, 3142
  Protestant Episcopal: 128
    South Carolina--Charleston: 3666
  Unitarian--Massachusetts: 977
  Universalist--Rhode Island: 1906
  Wesleyan Methodist:
    Great Britain: 5095, 5647
  Subdivided by place:
    Georgia: 991
    Great Britain: 43, 179, 625, 5598
    Maryland: 3998
    Massachusetts: 977, 1236
    North Carolina: 263, 1639, 3482
      Martin County: 1639
    South Carolina: 3552
    United States: 1219
    Virginia: 630
      Richmond: 3587
SERRES, Olivia (Wilmot): 2146, 2836

SÉRURIER, Comte Louis Barbe Charles: 1424
SERVANTS:
  see also NEGRO SERVANTS
  Suffrage--Great Britain: 5616
  Wages: see WAGES AND SALARIES--Servants
  Subdivided by place:
    France: 3270
    Great Britain: 4823
    Southern States: 3048
    United States: 5246
    West Virginia: 1946
"SERVICES OF CIVIL OFFICERS AND OTHERS DURING THE MUTINY AND REBELLION": 877
SERVIO, Diego de la: 4980
SESSIONS COURTS: see COURTS--Sessions courts
SETEZ, Pennsylvania: 1881
SETON, Ernest E. Thompson: 5252
SETTLE (A. H.) & CO. (Virginia): 4743
SETTLE, Hiram: 4742
SETTLE, Pauline: 4743
SETTLE, Thomas (1831-1888): 706
SETTLE, Thomas Lee (1836-1920): 4743
SETTLE FAMILY (Missouri, Tennessee, and Texas): 4743
SETTLE, North Carolina: 832
SETTLEMENT OF LAND: see LAND SETTLEMENT
SETZER, Daniel: 4744
SETZER, Susan: 4744
SEVASTAPOL, Russia: 153
  see also CRIMEAN WAR--Campaigns, battles, and military actions--Sevastapol
SEVEN DAYS, Battle of: see CIVIL WAR--CAMPAIGNS, BATTLES, AND MILITARY ACTIONS--Virginia--Seven days
SEVEN PINES, Virginia:
  Civil War: 5852
  see also CIVIL WAR--CAMPAIGNS, BATTLES, AND MILITARY ACTIONS--Virginia--Seven Pines
SEVEN YEARS' WAR:
  see also FRENCH AND INDIAN WAR
  Campaigns and battles:
    Paderhorn, Prussia: 5284
SEVENOAKS, England: 2843
"THE SEVENTH RING" by Stefan George: 1992
SEVERN, John Cheesment: see CHEESMENT-SEVERN, John
SEVEROLI, Antonio Gabriele, Cardinal: 4745
SEVIER, John: 4746
SEVILLE, Spain: 4979
SEWANEE, Tennessee: 2175, 4339
  see also UNIVERSITY OF THE SOUTH
SEWARD, Frederick William: 4748
SEWARD, George Edwin: 4117
SEWARD, Harvey: 4586
SEWARD, Joseph W.: 4747
SEWARD, Olive Risley: 4486
SEWARD, William Henry: 581, 1308, 1505, 3910, 4193, 4486, 4616, 4748, 4751, 5561, 5627
SEWARD & WESSON (Virginia firm): 4747
SEWELL'S POINT, Virginia: see CIVIL WAR--CAMPAIGNS, BATTLES, AND MILITARY ACTIONS--Virginia--Sewell's Point
SEWERAGE SYSTEMS: see SANITATION
SEWING:
  see also CLOTHING AND DRESS--Patterns; EMBROIDERY; QUILTING PARTIES; TAILORING
  Virginia: 1244
SEX CHANGE: 4823
SEXTON, Alexander: 5549
SEXTON, Thornton: 4749
SEYMOUR, Augustus Sherrill: 5457

SEYMOUR, Edward, Twelfth Duke of
    Somerset: 326
SEYMOUR, Francis Charles, Third
    Marquis of Hertford: 4750
SEYMOUR, Frederick Beauchamp Paget,
    First Baron Alcester: 3744
SEYMOUR, Horatio: 4751
SEYMOUR, Mary: 3905
SEYMOUR, Sallie: 2217
SEYMOUR, Thomas Hart: 4752
SEYMOUR, Truman: 5419
SEYMOUR-CONWAY, Francis, First
    Marquis of Hertford: see CONWAY,
    Francis Seymour-, First Marquis
    of Hertford
SEYMOUR JOHNSON AIR FORCE BASE,
    Goldsboro, North Carolina: 325
SFORZA, Carlos: 4753
SHACKLEFORD, A. T.: 4754
SHACKLEFORD, M. E.: 4755
SHADWELL, Virginia: 5256
SHAEFFER, Bartram A.: 4756
SHAFTESBURY, Anthony Ashley-Cooper,
    Seventh Earl of: 229, 1632
SHAFTESBURY, Cropley Ashley-Cooper,
    Sixth Earl of: 229
SHADY GROVE, North Carolina: 1686
SHADY MOUNT SUNDAY SCHOOL, Forsyth
    County, North Carolina: 544
SHAH, H.M.S.: 4535
SHAH OF PERSIA: 4005
SHAKERS:
    Kentucky--Pleasant Hill: 5416
    Ohio: 2601
SHAKESPEARE, William: 735
    Hamlet: 103
    Pageants--Virginia: 2425
SHALER, Nathaniel Southgate: 1219
SHALLOW FORD, North Carolina: 3002
SHAMOKIN DAM, Pennsylvania: 2405
SHAN STATES, Burma:
    Description: 4709
SHANGHAI, China: 4881
    American courts: 5252
    American embassy: 5912
    Customs duties: 598
    Description:
        1870s: 2241
        1905: 2191
    Japanese attack on (1937): 5252
    Missions and missionaries: 1298,
        2892
    Surveying: 1373
SHANKLIN, Andrew: 4760
SHANKLIN, Margaret: 1809
SHANNON, Wilson: 3557
SHANTUNG, China:
    Tengchow--Missionaries: 1298
SHARE OUR WEALTH SOCIETY OF AMERICA:
    3252
SHARECROPPING:
    Freedmen:
        Alabama: 4861
        North Carolina: 730
    Subdivided by place:
        Alabama: 5032
        Mississippi: 3415
        North Carolina--Shelby: 1951
        United States: 4948
SHARK, U.S.S.: 2963
SHARON, Connecticut: 1205
"SHARON," Savannah, Georgia: 2020
SHARP, F. A.: 1825
SHARP, George: 1424
SHARP, Hallie: 1424
SHARP, Richard: 2148
SHARP, William: 5044
SHARPE, Horatio: 3598
SHARPE, Luther M.: 4757
SHARPE, Stella G.: 4757
SHARPE, William (1742-1818): 3116,
    5457
SHARPSBURG, Maryland: 979, 2217, 4878
    see also CIVIL WAR--CAMPAIGNS,
    BATTLES, AND MILITARY ACTIONS--
    Maryland--Sharpsburg
SHASTON ST. PETER, England: 3245
SHAVER, Daniel (fl. 1864-1866): 4758

SHAVER, David (1820-ca. 1902): 4759
SHAW, Daniel: 4760
SHAW, Elias Faison: 1752
SHAW, George Bernard: 2398, 3617
SHAW, Henry Marchmore: 3094
SHAW, John F.: 4761
SHAW, Malcolm: 4762
SHAW, Nancy Witcher (Langhorne): 2955
SHAW, P. E.: 5267
SHAW-LEFEVRE, Sir John George: 1014
SHAWN, Thomas: 3751
SHAWNEE INDIANS:
    Culture: 2249
    Trade with whites: 4353
SHEARER, John Bunyan: 4763
SHEARIN, Richard E.: 4764
SHEARIN (RICHARD E.) AND BROS.
    (North Carolina): 4764
SHEARIN, Robert A.: 4764
SHEARWATER, U.S.S.: 4355
SHEEK, Jacob: 4765
SHEEP:
    Cotswold sheep:
        Breeding--West Virginia: 5555
    Mississippi: 2813
SHEEP RAISING:
    Colorado: 3745
    Larimer County: 3199
    Kansas: 3745
    Montana: 4161
    New Mexico: 3745
SHEERNESS, England:
    Construction of wells: 5330
SHEET IRON TRADE--New York: 1575
SHEFFEY, Hugh W.: 4766
SHEFFIELD, England: 2245, 5133
    Labor unions: 4234
    Trade and commerce: 480
SHEFFIELD, Georgia: 5364
SHEFFIELD, Massachusetts: 1636
SHEFFIELD MANOR (Great Britain): 4767
SHEFTALL, Levi: 4768
SHEFTALL, Mordecai: 4768
SHEIL, Richard Lalor: 3468, 4024
SHELBURNE, William Petty, First
    Marquis of Lansdowne and Second
    Earl of: 92, 4171
SHELBY, Isaac: 4746
SHELBY, North Carolina: 1517, 1951,
    2581
SHELBY BUILDING AND LOAN ASSOCIATION,
    Shelby, North Carolina: 1951
SHELBY COUNTY, Indiana: 110
SHELBY COUNTY, Kentucky: 4881
    Shelbyville--Civil War: 839
SHELBY COUNTY, Tennessee:
    Colliersville: 4951
    Memphis: see MEMPHIS, Tennessee
SHELBY DISTRICT, Methodist churches:
    3646
SHELBY STATION CIRCUIT, Methodist
    churches: 3646
SHELBYVILLE, Kentucky:
    Civil War: 839
SHELBYVILLE, Tennessee:
    Civil War: 659
SHELDEN, John: 2152
SHELDON, Charles Monroe: 103
SHELDON, D.: 2933
SHELDON, Edward Stevens: 648
SHELL, Helen L.: 4769
SHELL, Mary Virginia: 4769
SHELL MOUND, Tennessee: 1477
SHELLAC TRADE: 323
SHELLEY, Frances (Winckley): 3080
SHELLEY, Harriet (Westbrook): 4770
SHELLEY, Mary Wollstonecraft (Godwin):
    1049, 4770
SHELLEY, Percy Bysshe: 1049, 2058,
    4576, 4770
SHELLEY, Percy Florence (1819-1889):
    4770
SHELLEY, Sir Timothy: 4770
SHELLEY, Virginia: 4013, 4019
SHELLS: 5498
SHELOR, J. B.: 4771
SHELTON, Thomas: 1877

SHELTON, Virginia Tabitha Jane
    (Campbell): 872
SHELTON, William: 872
SHENANDOAH, C.S.S.: 1860, 3320
SHENANDOAH COUNTY, Virginia: 2949,
    2964, 2975, 4772
    Commissioners of revenue: 5485
    Licensing: 5485
    Mercantile accounts: 4122
    Mercantile affairs: 3773
    Cities and towns:
        Columbia Furnace: 160
        Edinburg--Farming: 4124
        Hawkinstown: 1920
            Mercantile accounts: 374
        Mine Run Furnace: 1262
        Mount Jackson: 1920, 5980
        New Market: 2485
            Civil War: 475, 4537
            Mercantile accounts: 138
        Quicksburg: 4121, 4123
        Strasburg: 287, 3678, 3813,
            4959, 5979
        Tom's Brook: 2965
        Union Forge: 3098
        Van Buren Furnace: 5990
        Woodstock: 2942
            Abolition of slavery: 5275
            Civil War: 4537
            Furniture manufacturing: 1893
            Merchants: 2832
SHENANDOAH IRON WORKS: 522
SHENANDOAH SEMINARY, Dayton,
    Virginia: 1920
SHENANDOAH VALLEY, Virginia: 5275
    Civil War: 368
SHENANDOAH VALLEY ACADEMY, Winchester,
    Virginia: 2559, 5779
SHENANDOAH VALLEY ASSEMBLY, Mount
    Jackson, Virginia: 1920, 4772
SHENANDOAH VALLEY CAMPAIGN: see
    CIVIL WAR--CAMPAIGNS, BATTLES, AND
    MILITARY ACTIONS--Virginia--
    Shenandoah Valley
SHENK, J. E.: 574
SHEPARD, Augustine H.: 315
SHEPARD, Irwin: 2224
SHEPARD, James Biddle (1815-1871):
    4773
SHEPARD, James Edward (1875-1947):
    5252
SHEPARD, Lorrin A.: 5252
SHEPARD, Mary: 730
SHEPARD, Mary (Donnell): 730
SHEPARD, William Biddle: 730
SHEPARD FAMILY (North Carolina): 730
SHEPHERD, Abraham, Jr.: 4774
SHEPHERD, Henry, Jr.: 4774
SHEPHERD, James Edward (1847-1910):
    4775
SHEPHERD, James H. (fl. 1830): 4774
SHEPHERD, John: 2617
SHEPHERD, L. L.: 5234
SHEPHERD, Rezin Davis: 3148
SHEPHERD FAMILY: 404
SHEPHERD FAMILY (Virginia): 3148
SHEPHERD FAMILY (West Virginia): 489,
    3148
SHEPHERD AND LESLIE (firm): see
    LESLIE AND SHEPHERD
SHEPHERD COLLEGE, Shepherdstown, West
    Virginia: 3710
    Teachers' records: 3710
SHEPHERDSTOWN, West Virginia: 3325
    1700s-1800s: 2301, 4598
    1700s-1900s: 404, 3148
    1800s: 128, 581, 1711, 4388, 4769,
        4774
    1800s-1900s: 489, 3710
    1900s: 2084
    Civil War: 2792
    Merchants: 2711, 5324
    Quarries: 3145
SHEPHERDSTOWN AND WINCHESTER TURNPIKE
    COMPANY: 3148
SHEPPARD, James (ca. 1816-1870): 4776
SHEPPARD, Joseph: 4776
SHEPPARD, Samuel: 4777

SHEPPARD FAMILY (Great Britain): 258
SHEPPARD BROTHERS (law firm): 4778
SHEPPERD, Augustine Henry: 4779, 5149
SHERBROOKE, Robert Lowe, First
 Viscount: 955, 2471
SHERBURNE, Vermont: 5197
SHERIDAN, Philip Henry: 2726, 3464,
 3813, 4612, 4780, 4888, 4891, 5739
SHERIDAN, Arkansas: 4536
SHERIDAN CLASSICAL SCHOOL,
 Orangeburg, South Carolina: 501
SHERIFFS:
 Alabama--Dallas County: 2979
 Georgia:
  Commissions: 1375
  Liberty County: 2910
 North Carolina:
  Beaufort County: 911
  Harnett County: 2357
  Orange County: 5390
 South Carolina--Beaufort County:
  5758
 Virginia: 2517, 2680
  Appointments: 4916
  Halifax County: 822
  Nelson County: 3566, 5484, 5700
  Pittsylvania County: 5587
SHERIFFS' RECORDS:
 Georgia:
  Chatham County: 4611
  Wilkes County: 2937
 Maryland--Washington County: 3875
 North Carolina--Rowan County: 1291
 West Virginia:
  Jefferson County: 3832
SHERMAN, John: 2273, 2446, 4781, 4782
SHERMAN, Sidney: 3772
SHERMAN, William Tecumseh: 440, 510,
 1805, 2140, 2270, 2864, 3390,
 3524, 4203, 4358, 4398, 4782,
 4945, 5348, 5453
SHERMAN FAMILY (Ohio): 4782
SHERMAN, Texas: 2850
SHERMAN'S MARCH: see CIVIL WAR--
 CAMPAIGNS, BATTLES, AND MILITARY
 ACTIONS--Georgia/North Carolina/
 South Carolina--Sherman's march
SHERRILL, E. L.: 4783
SHERRILL, J. E.: 3757
SHERRILL, Joseph: 4525
SHERRILL, Miles Osborne: 5457
SHERRILL, Samuel P.: 4784
SHERRILL, Sarah: 4525
SHERRILL FAMILY (North Carolina):
 4523
SHERRILL'S FORD, North Carolina: 1806
SHERWOOD, Adiel: 4743
SHERWOOD, M. S.: 5149
SHERWOOD, Robert E.: 103
"SHERWOOD FOREST," Charles City
 County, Virginia: 5397
SHETLAND ISLANDS:
 Economic conditions: 229
 Missions and missionaries: 1070
 Population: 229
SHIBLEY, Jacob: 4785
SHIELDS, Frederic James: 4575
SHIELDS, George Howell: 4786
SHIELDS, James: 5517
SHIELDS FAMILY (North Carolina):
 1255
SHIH CHAO-CHI: see SZE, Sao-ke Alfred
SHILOH, North Carolina:
 Presbyterian churches: 5245
SHILOH, Tennessee: see CIVIL WAR--
 CAMPAIGNS, BATTLES, AND MILITARY
 ACTIONS--Tennessee--Shiloh
SHILOH SABBATH SCHOOL (North
 Carolina): 1556
SHINE, Daniel: 4787
SHINGLE TRADE:
 see also LUMBER TRADE
 New Hampshire: 1529
 North Carolina: 1492
  Beaufort County: 4435

SHINGLE TRADE:
 North Carolina (Continued):
  Columbia: 215
 Virginia: 1512
SHINN, Thomas J.: 4788
SHIP CHANDLERS' ACCOUNTS:
 North Carolina--Wilmington: 5880
 Quebec: 3752
SHIP ISLAND, Mississippi: see CIVIL
 WAR--PRISONERS AND PRISONS--
 Confederate prisoners--Mississippi--
 Ship Island
SHIP TIMBER:
 New York: 2172
 Virginia: 1701
SHIPBUILDING:
 see also BOAT BUILDING; NAVAL
  ARCHITECTURE; SHIP TIMBER;
  STEAMBOATS--Construction; WORLD
  WAR II--Shipbuilding industry
 Accounts: 3827
 Apprenticeship:
  Great Britain: 2148
 Connecticut: 1549
 Great Britain: 1164
  By the Navy: 1599
  Ironclads for the Confederate
   States of America: 4521
 Massachusetts: 1344
 South Carolina--Charleston: 3294
SHIPBUILDING WORKERS: see INDUSTRIAL
 UNION OF MARINE AND SHIPBUILDING
 WORKERS OF AMERICA; INTERNATIONAL
 BROTHERHOOD OF BOILERMAKERS, IRON
 SHIP BUILDERS, AND HELPERS OF
 AMERICA
SHIPMAN, Louis Evan: 4789
SHIPP, Albert Micajah: 4790
SHIPP, J. W.: 4790
SHIPP, John Edgar: 4791
SHIPPEN AND HIESTER (firm): see
 HIESTER AND SHIPPEN
SHIPPENSBURG, Pennsylvania: 1283
SHIPPING: 291, 2933
 see also HARBORS; INLAND WATER
  TRANSPORTATION; INSURANCE--
  Marine; RIGHT OF SEARCH; STEAMBOAT
  LINES; STEAMBOATS; TRADE AND
  COMMERCE; and Foreign trade as
  subheading under names of specific
  countries
 Cargo: 4541, 5139, 5776, 5777, 5967
  Prices: 4982
  Records: 5391
 Coastwise shipping: 4726
  Louisiana--New Orleans: 5860
  Maine--Castine: 5860
  Maryland:
   Baltimore: 5776
   Snow Hill: 4946
  Massachusetts: 4304
   Boston: 3578, 5777, 5860
   Bridgewater: 2959
  New York: 2959
   New York: 1950, 5860
  North Carolina: 1496, 2101, 4304,
   5777
   Edenton: 5658
   Elizabeth City: 5776
   New Bern: 1950
  Pennsylvania--Philadelphia: 4946
  Rhode Island--Providence: 2959
  South Carolina: 4304
   Charleston: 2959
  United States: 3578
 Finance: 5777
 Food: 5955
 Lawsuits: 3570
  Georgia: 1454
  United States: 1615
 Measurement of ships: 1495
 Ocean shipping: 2259, 5133
  British West Indies to Great
   Britain: 4913
  Great Britain to North Carolina:
   2159

SHIPPING (Continued):
 Prices:
  British West Indies: 4913
  Pennsylvania: 1615
 River shipping: 382
  James River (Virginia): 4616
 Subdivided by place:
  Georgia: 2019, 2216
   Savannah Port: 4678
  Great Britain: 3183
   Bristol: 4541
   English Channel: 4719
   Liverpool: 5026
  Maryland: 4886
   Baltimore: 1442, 4348
  Massachusetts: 4653, 5777
  Netherlands: 1424
  New York--New York: 3960
  North Carolina: 484, 540, 2889,
   5298
   Catherine Lake: 5910
   Wilmington: 3447, 4982
  Pennsylvania: 870
  South Carolina: 2019
  Spain: 4982
  United States: 4896
SHIPPING COMPANIES:
 see also STEAMBOAT LINES
 North Carolina: 658
 Pennsylvania: 1615
 United States: 4881
SHIPS:
 see also TRANSATLANTIC MAIL
  PACKETS; and names of individual
  vessels and specific types of
  vessels
 Construction: see SHIPBUILDING
 Maintenance and repair:
  see also Ships--Maintenance and
   repair as subheading under
   names of navies
  Great Britain: 1599
  Spanish ships in Charleston,
   South Carolina: 4982
  United States: 3578
 Masts and rigging: 2259
 Measurement: see SHIPPING--
  Measurement of ships
 Passenger service: 2259, 4760
  see also PACKET BOATS;
   STEAMBOATS--Passengers
 Prize ships: see CIVIL WAR--PRIZE
  SHIPS
 Purchase and registration: 5133
 Sails: 3406
  Making of: 4110
 Steering gear--Inventions: 5660
 Subdivided by place:
  North Carolina: 3922
   Edenton: 5658
  United States: 323
  Virginia: 2913
SHIPS' CABLES--Virginia: 1863
SHIPS' PILOTS:
 Apprenticeship: 3922
 North Carolina: 3922
SHIPWRECKS:
 1820: 2058
 1858: 3183
 1861: 5955
 Subdivided by ship:
  City of San Francisco: 4535
  Diana: 2733
  Frothingham: 21
  Mississippi, U.S.S.: 2733
  Sampson, U.S.S.: 4881
  Snow Assiento: 2667
 Subdivided by place:
  Nile River: 5333
  South Carolina: 3808
SHIRE RIVER (Africa): 5725
SHIRER, William David: 4792
SHIRER FAMILY (South Carolina): 4792
SHIRLEY, James: 4793
SHIRLEY, John M.: 870
SHIRLEY, Selina: 5647
SHIRLEY, Thomas: 4794

SHIRLEY, Zachariah: 4794
SHOBER, Francis Edwin: 3094
SHOCCO SPRINGS, North Carolina:
    Health resorts: 5690
SHOCKLEY, W. S.: 4795
SHOE HEEL, North Carolina: 3398
SHOE INDUSTRY: see BOOT AND SHOE
    INDUSTRY; SHOEMAKERS' ACCOUNTS
SHOE TRADE: see BOOT AND SHOE TRADE
SHOE WORKERS: see UNITED SHOE
    WORKERS OF AMERICA
SHOEMAKER, Isaac: 4796
SHOEMAKER, William Lukens: 103
SHOEMAKERS' ACCOUNTS:
    Maryland--Baltimore: 1616
    North Carolina--Prattsburg: 4307
SHOENBERGER, Edwin F.: 4797
SHOOTER'S HILL, Kent, England: 1891
SHOP STEWARD BULLETIN: 5234
SHOREHAM, England: 4146
SHORE PROTECTION:
    Florida--Canaveral: 2387
SHORT, _____ (instructor at
    Transylvania College): 1421
SHORT LINE RAILROAD ASSOCIATION
    OF NORTH CAROLINA: 238
SHORT-LINE RAILROADS: see RAILROADS--
    Short-line
SHORT STORIES: see AMERICAN
    LITERATURE--Short stories
SHORTER, Clement: 1113
SHORTER, Clement King: 4798
SHORTER, E. S.: 1084
SHORTER, John Gill: 4799
SHORTER COLLEGE, Rome, Georgia: 4911
SHORTHAND:
    Study of--Great Britain: 5095
SHOTWELL, Bettie: 4800
SHOTWELL, J. A.: 4800
SHOTWELL, James Thomson: 706
SHOTWELL, Nathan: 4801
"SHOULD THE U.S. GOVERNMENT CONTROL
    THE RAILROADS?" by Thomas
    Cowper Daniels: 1368
SHRADER, George: 5275
SHREVE, William P.: 4802
SHREVEPORT, Louisiana: 3275
    Civil War:
        Confederate Army: 5257
        Confederate Navy: 1181
SHREWSBURY, Charles John Chetwynd-
    Talbot, Nineteenth Earl: 1087
SHREWSBURY, New Jersey: 1446
SHRINER (CORNELIUS) AND COMPANY,
    Ceresville Mills, Maryland: 4803
SHRINER, Edward A.: 4804
SHROPSHIRE, England:
    Cound: 4115
    West Felton: 1551, 1552
SHUBRICK, Richard: 2029
SHUBRICK, Thomas: 5548
SHUBRICK, William Branford: 3118
SHUFELDT, Robert Wilson: 4453
SHUFORD, Alonzo Craig: 5457
SHUFORD, George Adams: 4805
SHUFORD FAMILY (North Carolina):
    5739
SHUGBOROUGH HALL, Staffordshire,
    England: 190
SHULLS MILLS, North Carolina: 3176
SHUPE, Walter H.: 4806
SHURTLEFF, Harold: 1424
SHUSTER, William Morgan: 572
SHUTTLES: see TEXTILE MACHINERY--
    Parts
SHUTTLEWORTH, Philip Nicholas: 2146
SIAM: see THAILAND
SIAM FREE PRESS: 4709
SIAMESE TWINS:
    Cadavers: 2809
    Death: 4849
SIBERIAN EXPEDITION: see UNITED
    STATES--ARMY--Siberian Expedition
SIBLEY, Jonas: 4807
SICILY--Lighthouses: 3118
SICK, Transport of: see Transport of
    sick and wounded as subheading
    under names of wars

SICK SOLDIERS RELIEF SOCIETY, Raleigh,
    North Carolina: 3761
SICKELS, Frederick Ellsworth: 5660
SICKLES, Daniel Edgar: 254, 4808
SICKLES, Harvey: 4188
SICKNESS: see DISEASES
SIDBURY, James Buren: 4809
SIDDALL, Joseph H.: 4810
SIDGWICK, Henry: 5050
SIDLE, Jacob: 1443
SIDMOUTH, Henry Addington, First
    Viscount: 2149, 2836, 5639
SIDNEY, Henry Marlow: 4811
SIDNEY KNITTING MILLS, INC. (North
    Carolina): 4812
SIEGE OF SAVANNAH by Charles Jones,
    Jr.: 2787
SIEGLING, John, Jr.: 4813
SIENA, Italy: 4736
SIERRA COUNTY, California:
    Mining: 25
SIERRA LEONE:
    Church of England: 2149
    Missions and missionaries: 128
    Politics and government: 5726
    Social and political reform: 1014
    Trade policy: 1913
SIERRA LEONE STUDENTS IN GREAT
    BRITAIN: 867
SIERRA MADRE, California: 5338
SIEWERS, Nathaniel Shober: 5457
SIGEL, Franz: 3654, 5731
"EL SIGLO ILLUSTRADA" by Vera de la
    Ventosa: 4979
SIGMAN, Martin: 4814
SIGN AND PICTORIAL PAINTERS LOCAL
    UNION: 224
SIGNAL CORPS: see as subheading
    under names of armies
SIGNAL OFFICE: see UNITED STATES--
    GOVERNMENT AGENCIES AND OFFICIALS--
    Signal Office
SIGNALS (military): see Communications
    as subheading under names of armies
SIGOURNEY, Lydia Howard (Huntley):
    1827, 4815
SIKES, Enoch Walter: 5457
SIKES, John: 4816
SILBERLING, Édouard: 65
SILER, Albert: 4817
SILER FAMILY (North Carolina): 4817
SILER CITY, North Carolina: 1254,
    5914
    Newspapers: 2861
SILK: see CARPETS--Silk
"SILK HOPE," Savannah, Georgia: 2326
SILK INDUSTRY:
    France--Tours: 5323
    Georgia: 2238
SILK THREAD AND YARN: see TEXTILE
    INDUSTRY--Silk throwing
SILK TRADE: 323
    Great Britain: 2148
    Prices--Massachusetts: 1839
SILKWORM CULTURE--Southern States:
    761
SILL, Edward E.: 4818
SILLIMAN, Benjamin: 1468
SILLIMAN COLLEGIATE INSTITUTE,
    Clinton, Louisiana: 4373
    Faculty: 4819
SILLS, Grey: 4820
SILLS, Louisa M. (Jelks): 4820
SILLS FAMILY (North Carolina): 4820
SILOS--New York: 2616
SILSDEN, England: 2751
SILVER HILL, North Carolina: 4329
SILVER MINES AND MINING:
    see also MINES AND MINING
    Company stores--North Carolina:
        5583
    Subdivided by place:
        Canada: 4743
        North Carolina:
            Davidson County: 2041
            Lexington: 277
        South Carolina: 2541

SILVER PLATE:
    see also ENGLISH SILVER PLATE
    Georgia: 5260
SILVER QUESTION: 3415, 4442, 5051
    Missouri: 3038
    South Carolina: 2473
    Virginia: 5152
SILVER VALLEY MINES, Davidson
    County, North Carolina: 4329
SILVERSMITHS:
    Great Britain: 2784
    North Carolina--Hillsborough: 3300
    Virginia: 4157
SIMCOE, John Graves: 5830
SIMEON, Charles: 4821
SIMKINS, Arthur: 4822
SIMKINS, Francis Butler, Jr.: 4453
SIMLA, India: 4503
    Description: 5525
SIMMONS, Celestia Muse (Southgate):
    4968
SIMMONS, Dawn Pepita Langley-Hall:
    4823
SIMMONS (DENNIS) LUMBER COMPANY,
    Williamston, North Carolina: 4824
SIMMONS, Furnifold McLendel: 1336,
    2041, 2299, 2435, 3955, 4825
    Memorials: 4825
    Portraits: 5022
SIMMONS, J. F.: 2449
SIMMONS, James M.: 4826
SIMMONS, John Paul: 4823
SIMMONS, William Gaston: 5457
SIMMONS, William H.: 4827
SIMMS, Philip: 1424
SIMMS, Robert Nirwana: 4828
SIMMS, William Elliott: 635
SIMMS, William Gilmore: 10, 720,
    1227, 1439, 1494, 2449, 2612,
    2851, 4829, 5193, 5361
SIMMS AND DOUGLAS (firm): see
    DOUGLAS AND SIMMS
SIMONS, Clifford: 5193
SIMONS, Katherine Drayton Mayrant:
    103
SIMONS, Keating: 4830
SIMONS, Keating Lewis: 5193
SIMONS FAMILY (South Carolina): 4584
SIMONS BROTHERS, Charleston, South
    Carolina (firm): 5193
SIMONTON, Charles Henry: 24
SIMPSON, Ann K.: 5740
SIMPSON, James A.: 4831
SIMPSON, John (1728-1788, New Bern,
    North Carolina): 484
SIMPSON, John (fl. 1780s-1790s,
    Washington, North Carolina):
    4571, 4832
SIMPSON, John (fl. 1800s, South
    Carolina): 4833
SIMPSON, Nathan: 4833
SIMPSON, R. H.: 1920
SIMPSON, Robert H.: 4743
SIMPSON, Samuel: 484
SIMPSON, William Dunlap: 4145, 4834
SIMPSON, William P.: 357
SIMPSON FAMILY (North Carolina): 484
SIMPSON CO.: see WILLIAM GRAHAM AND
    SIMPSON CO.
SIMS (E.) AND COMPANY, Crawford,
    Georgia: 3974
SIMS, James Marion: 2449, 4453
SIN (theology): 4936
SINCLAIR, Arthur: 2963
SINCLAIR, Carrie Bell: 5503
SINCLAIR, John (Scotland): 4835
SINCLAIR, John (Virginia): 4836
SINCLAIR, Upton Beall, Jr.: 4837
SINCLAIR FAMILY (genealogy): 4835
SINCLAIR FOUNDATION: 4837
SIND:
    see also INDIA--British
        administration
    Annexation to India: 3453
SIND WAR: 3453
SING SING, New York: 480
SINGAPORE--Description: 2463
SINGERS: 4986
    Georgia: 4968

SINGH, Rundhir: see RUNDHIR SINGH
SINGH, Venkat Raman: see RAMAN SINGH, Venkat
SINGLE TAX--United States: 2225
SINGLETARY CHURCH (North Carolina): 3646
SINGLETON, Angelica: 4839
SINGLETON, E. C.: 4838
SINGLETON, Mathew: 1472
SINGLETON, R. W.: 2612
SINGLETON, Richard: 1472, 4839
SINGLETON, Thomas: 4840
SINGLETON FAMILY (South Carolina): 1472, 4839
SINKING CREEK (Virginia): 5347
SINKING VALLEY, Pennsylvania:
  Farming: 3424
SINN-FEIN REBELLION (1916): 4798
SINO-JAPANESE WAR: 306
  British neutrality: 4709
  Campaigns and battles--Shanghai: 5252
THE SINS OF THE FATHERS by Thomas Dixon: 1521
"SION HILL," Havre de Grace, Maryland: 4537
SIOUSSAT, St. George Leakin: 737
SIOUX INDIANS: 932, 3357
  Government relations: 5419
  Raids: 5419
  Treaties--United States: 3162
  Wars:
    1854: 5419
    1862-1865: 3524
    1876: 2849
SIPES, Robert: 4841
SIPLE, W. H.: 4842
SISSIBOO BAPTIST CHURCH, Digby, Nova Scotia: 176
"SIT, JESSICA" by Margaret Junkin Preston: 5044
SITTON, J. B.: 4896
"LA SITUATION" by Louis Blanc: 526
SITWELL, Frances (Fetherston-Hough): 1210
SIX-POWER CONSORTIUM: 5252
65 VALIANTS by Alice Houston Luiggi: 3295
"SKETCH OF THE MOUTHS AND CHANNELS OF PASCAGOULA RIVER": 5783
SKETCHES OF PERSIA by Sir John Malcolm: 3816
SKEWARKEY PRIMITIVE BAPTIST CHURCH, Williamston, North Carolina: 4843
SKINNER, Abraham: 5575
SKINNER, Anna: 4844
SKINNER, John: 4844
SKINNER, John Stuart: 3742
SKINNER, Sarah (Maryland): 4844
SKINNER, Sarah A. (Massachusetts): 4800
SKINNER FAMILY (Maryland): 4844
SKINS: see HIDES AND SKINS
SKIPWITH, Fulwar: 4348, 4845
SKIPWITH, George N.: 4846, 4847
SKIPWITH, Humberston: 4848
SKIPWORTH, George C.: 519
SKIRVING, William: 1682
SLABE, Virginia: 2364
SLADE, Daniel Denison: 3266
SLADE, Ebenezer: 4849
SLADE, Henry: 4849
SLADE, J. B. "Bog": 4849
SLADE, James: 4849
SLADE, Jeremiah: 4849
SLADE, William (North Carolina): 4849
SLADE, William (Vermont): 3902
SLADE FAMILY (North Carolina): 4849
SLANDER: see LIBEL AND SLANDER
SLANEY, Robert A.: 1087
SLATE, Richard: 4850
SLATE DEPOSITS--Virginia: 2908
SLATE MINES AND MINING:
  Georgia--Cherokee County: 1887
SLATER, John: 295
SLATER MURDER CASE (Great Britain): 4427
SLATTERY, Harry Augustus: 4851

SLAUGHTER, Amelia (Bowman): 4854
SLAUGHTER, Daniel French: 4852
SLAUGHTER, Frank Gill: 4853
SLAUGHTER (G. H.) AND COMPANY: 4854
SLAUGHTER, Guilford H.: 4854
SLAUGHTER, James E.: 395
SLAUGHTER, Montgomery: 4855
SLAUGHTER, Philip: 4852
SLAUGHTER, Sally A.: 1790
SLAUGHTER, W. S.: 855
SLAUGHTER, William: 4855
SLAVE COFFLE: 4387
SLAVE PATROL:
  Georgia: 1933
  Virginia: 33, 5579
SLAVE STEALING--Georgia: 3961
SLAVE TRADE: 1014
  Abolition of:
    see also ABOLITION OF SLAVERY AND ABOLITIONIST SENTIMENT
    France: 5726
    Great Britain: 3316, 4605, 5726
  Accounts:
    Virginia: 2363
      Nelson County: 5700
  History of: 4541
  Lawsuits: 4381
  Prices: 3824, 4541
    Alabama: 647, 2426, 2663, 3626, 5879
      Salem: 4610
    Georgia: 4895, 5494
    Kentucky: 647
    Louisiana: 3396
    Mississippi: 2663, 3642
    Missouri: 2663, 3255
    North Carolina: 647, 756, 832, 2113, 2663, 3416, 4424, 5390
      Surry County: 2808
      Yadkin County: 2808
    South Carolina: 2290, 3709, 4649, 4834, 5936
      Charleston: 1745
    Southern States: 1460
    Tennessee: 4291
    Texas: 647
    United States: 3255
    Virginia: 523, 3642, 3708, 4924, 5613, 5700
      Madison County: 4794
      Pittsylvania County: 5873
  Regulation:
    United States: 2776
  Suppression:
    Great Britain: 306, 5725
    Madagascar: 2754
    Sudan: 5725
    United States: 99, 2907, 3325, 3557
      see also UNITED STATES--NAVY--Suppression of the slave trade
  Transatlantic: 1884, 4214
    Conditions on slave ships: 99, 4913
    To South Carolina: 2094
  Treaties among Great Britain, Spain and Portugal: 4605
  Subdivided by place:
    Alabama: 1490, 1801, 2426, 2808, 3321, 4861, 4911, 5113, 5879
      Mobile: 3016
    British colonies: 5726
    British West Indies: 1913
    Cuba: 258
    Dutch colonies: 5726
    Florida: 4062
    French colonies: 5726
    Georgia:
      1700s: 2019, 2020, 5537
      1700s-1800s: 1993, 2778, 3671
      1800s: 781, 1090, 1434, 1466, 1789, 2002, 2280, 3661, 3905, 4720, 5787
      Bulloch County: 4395
      Ebenezer: 5986
      Savannah: 1705, 5221
    Great Britain: 4913

SLAVE TRADE:
  Subdivided by place (Continued):
    Grenada: 973
    Haiti: 4980
    Kentucky: 496
    Louisiana: 1801, 2674, 3846, 5193
      New Orleans: 2517
    Maryland: 2295
      Frederick County: 4457
    Mississippi: 492, 3415, 3846, 4299
    Missouri: 5392
    Nigeria: 41
    North Carolina:
      1700s-1800s: 1107, 3476
      1800s: 730, 1523, 2222, 3415, 4858, 4897
      1820s: 1794, 2113
      1830s: 2068, 2113, 2808, 3237, 5298
      1840s: 602, 2068, 2113, 4734, 4816, 5310
      1850s: 602, 1252, 4734, 5310
      1860s: 602, 1252, 4734
      Beaufort County: 5831
      Cumberland County: 50
      Davie County: 122
      Halifax County: 5672
      Hillsborough: 1890
      Iredell County: 5245
      Lumberton: 3422
      Raleigh: 4394
      Randolph County: 680
    Portuguese colonies: 5726
    South Carolina:
      1700s: 2019
      1700s-1800s: 2300, 3981
      1800s: 1877, 2290, 2961, 4649, 5759
      1800s: 2636
      1810s: 2636
      1840s: 2670, 3801
      1850s: 2670, 3801
      1860s: 2670, 3371, 3801
      Charleston: 2017, 3589
      Edgefield District: 2599
      Sumter: 3676, 3795
    Southern States: 5940
    Spain: 4913, 4980
    Spanish colonies: 5726
    Tennessee: 1933, 3692, 4269, 5623, 5859, 5935
    Texas: 2117
    United States: 1856, 3053, 3293, 3850, 3910, 4250, 4732
    Virginia:
      1700s: 330
      1700s-1800s: 3069, 4616, 5653
      1800s: 523, 2014, 3200, 3642
      1800s: 1093
      1810s: 29, 1093, 2967
      1820s: 1093
      1830s: 590, 3708, 4299
      1840s: 590, 1489, 2363, 4299, 4345, 4720, 5113, 5529
      1850s: 117, 590, 661, 1489, 1801, 2363, 2943, 4345, 4720, 5286, 5529
      1860s: 661, 2363, 2955, 2971, 5529
      Culpeper: 4852
      Patrick County: 1410
      Petersburg: 4492
      Pittsylvania County: 5718
    West Virginia: 2389, 5324
    Zanzibar: 5725
SLAVERY: 1014, 1335, 1403, 2311, 2693, 2848, 2970, 3445, 4022, 4689, 5228, 5470, 5480, 5498, 5499, 5853
  Biblical justification: 4928
  Economic effects: 5940
  Extension to U.S. territories: 1234, 1424
    see also WILMOT PROVISO
    California: 4732

SLAVERY:
  Extension to U.S territories
      (Continued):
    Kansas: 4897
  Laws and legislation:
    British West Indies: 4913
    Jamaica: 4913
    South Carolina: 3981
    Southern States: 5940
  Northern opinion of: 566, 5940
    Indiana: 4202
    Massachusetts: 977
    New England States: 4897
    Pennsylvania: 5380, 5686
  Opposition to:
    see also ABOLITION OF SLAVERY
      AND ABOLITIONIST SENTIMENT
    North Carolina: 5298
  Proslavery literature: 5246
  Quaker opinion: 4006, 4732
  Social effects: 5940
  Southern opinion: 5940
    Alabama: 4943
    Arkansas: 5380
    Mississippi: 4269
    South Carolina: 5193
    Tennessee: 4269
  Subdivided by place:
    Africa: 4514
    Arkansas: 4776
    Brazil: 4876
    British West Indies: 4913
    Ethiopia: 3912
    French West Indies: 4913
    Georgia: 2460
    Jamaica: 4913
    Kentucky: 3955
    Louisiana: 805, 1153
    Mississippi: 1762, 2661, 3415,
      4776
    Mississippi Territory: 4746
    Missouri: 3255
    North Carolina: 923, 3155, 3415,
      4006, 4080
    South Carolina: 150, 561, 718,
      2210, 2473, 2503, 2940, 3801,
      3981
      Charleston: 2695
    Southern States: 284, 1460,
      2616, 3390, 4596, 5940
    Tennessee: 771
    Texas: 1153
    United States: 743, 762, 773,
      842, 849, 1072, 3054, 3783,
      4860, 5051, 5298, 5940
    Virginia: 152, 693, 872, 1059,
      1605, 1957, 2633, 2967, 3179,
      4776, 4924, 5282, 5302, 5476
      Clarke County: 2513
      Westmoreland County: 917
    West Indies: 5726
    West Virginia: 1769
    Zanzibar: 67
SLAVERY AND THE CHURCH: 5940
  Africa: 5725
  South Carolina: 4912
  Subdivided by denomination:
    Catholic church: 5726
    Methodist Episcopal church:
      Virginia: 3601
    Methodist Protestant church: 4416
SLAVES:
  see also AMERICAN REVOLUTION--
    Confiscated property--Slaves;
    FUGITIVE SLAVES; HIRING OF
    SLAVES; and Slaves as subheading
    under specific industries and
    types of workers, e.g. MILL
    WORKERS--Slaves
  Behavior:
    Civil War: 5936
      Alabama: 954
      Georgia: 3729
      South Carolina: 3485
      Virginia: 2370, 5523
    Subdivided by place:
      Florida--Duval County: 4410

SLAVES:
  Behavior:
    Subdivided by place (Continued):
      Louisiana: 508
      North Carolina: 279, 1166
      South Carolina: 1877
      Virginia: 375
  Breeding versus importation: 4913
  Business affairs:
    North Carolina: 1166
  Children--Mortality: 5221
  Civil War: 5936
    see also CIVIL WAR--CONFISCATION
      OF PROPERTY--Slaves; CIVIL
      WAR--FORTIFICATIONS--South
      Carolina--Charleston--Slave
      labor; CONFEDERATE STATES OF
      AMERICA--ARMY--Negro troops;
      CONFEDERATE STATES OF AMERICA--
      ARMY--Slaves--Personal servants;
      SLAVES--Behavior--Civil War
    Georgia: 5651
    Morale in Alabama: 1084
  Clothing and dress:
    Georgia: 5395
    North Carolina: 5298
    South Carolina: 1891, 1923
    Virginia: 4616
  Crimes:
    see also SLAVES--Trials
    Murder:
      North Carolina: 2117
      Southern States: 4434
      Virginia: 3687, 4131
  Descriptions--Georgia: 2002
  Diseases:
    Cholera--Georgia: 2578
    Subdivided by place:
      British West Indies: 4913
      Georgia: 5606
      Louisiana: 508
      North Carolina: 3317
  Division of ownership:
    North Carolina: 3237, 5739
    South Carolina--Edisto Island:
      3644
    Tennessee: 82
    Virginia: 1627, 5765
      Petersburg: 1873
  Duties:
    Mississippi--Rodney: 3322
    South Carolina: 3531, 3801
      Hampton County: 4534
  Education: 4387, 5499, 5940
  Emancipation:
    see also ABOLITION OF SLAVERY
      AND ABOLITIONIST SENTIMENT
    Northern opinion: 1798
    Southern opinion: 5415
    Subdivided by place:
      British West Indies: 4913
      Great Britain: 2542
      Indiana: 1548
      Jamaica: 1875, 5940
      Kentucky: 1086
      Maryland: 4712
      North Carolina: 1475, 4153
      South Carolina: 758
      Virginia: 5482
        Nansemond County: 3012
        Westmoreland County: 917
      United States: 3495, 4537,
        5816
        see also UNITED STATES--
          CONSTITUTION--Amendments--
          13th Amendment
      West Virginia: 128, 2389
  Executions:
    North Carolina: 2117
    Virginia: 3720, 4131
  Expenses incidental to their keep:
    North Carolina: 1322
    South Carolina--Greenville: 653
  Food:
    South Carolina: 297, 1923
  Health:
    North Carolina: 602

SLAVES:
  Health (Continued):
    South Carolina: 4534
    Tennessee: 3692
    Virginia: 1133, 2925
  Illness: see SLAVES--Diseases
  Imprisonment--North Carolina: 2298
  Insurrections: 4399
    Alabama--Greensboro: 5593
    Georgia: 2788
    Kentucky: 4202
    Maryland--Frederick County: 5829
    Mississippi: 2661, 3415
    North Carolina: 423, 3390, 3415,
      5298
    South Carolina: 2210, 2449
      Camden: 1012
      Charleston: 2289
      Marlboro District: 2267
      Union District: 4434
    Spanish West Indies: 1913
    Texas: 4202
    United States: 743
    Virginia: 1059, 1115, 2370, 3720
  Lawsuits over ownership:
    South Carolina: 4399, 4623
    Virginia: 2633
  Leasing--Louisiana: 4902
  Lists:
    Georgia: 3905, 4400
    Mississippi--Rodney: 3322
    North Carolina: 3176, 3415
      Martin County: 4849
      Yadkin County: 4103
    South Carolina: 2670, 4214, 5548
      Charleston: 295
      Stateburg: 4217
    Virginia: 5613, 5873
      Madison County: 4794
      Nansemond County: 3012
    West Virginia: 4703
  Loyalty:
    Alabama--Selma: 4185
    South Carolina: 1793
  Marriages:
    see also SLAVES--Weddings
    Georgia: 2778
  Married life--North Carolina: 1120
  Medical treatment:
    Georgia: 1375, 4647
    North Carolina: 2462, 2819,
      4858
    South Carolina: 3485
    United States: 3053
    Virginia: 5229
  Missionaries to:
    South Carolina: 669
  Prices: see SLAVE TRADE--Prices
  Punishment: 5499
    Virginia: 4710
  Purchase of freedom: 4387
    Virginia: 3642
  Purchases and sales: see SLAVE
    TRADE
  Quarters--South Carolina: 5193
  Recovery of: 4387
    Alabama: 3647
  Relations with masters:
    see also SLAVES--Women--
      Relations with masters
    South Carolina: 3531
    Virginia: 5332
      Norfolk: 5523
  Religion: 4864, 5940
    South Carolina:
      Charleston: 4912
      Greenville District: 3669
    Southern States: 4434
  Seizure by Spanish: 3109
  Supplies:
    Mississippi--Rodney: 3322
    South Carolina: 297, 1891
  Taxation:
    North Carolina: 4670
    Virginia--Amherst County: 5529
  Transportation--Georgia: 2778

SLAVES (Continued):
  Treatment of: 1602, 4383, 4387, 5940
    Alabama--Perry County: 5879
    British West Indies: 4913
    Georgia: 2020, 5221
    Louisiana: 1242
    Mississippi: 2399
    North Carolina: 3317, 4103, 5770
      Davie County: 122
    South Carolina: 2670, 2695, 3981
    Tennessee: 104
    United States: 3053
    Virginia: 1697, 1813, 3819, 4616, 5286
    West Virginia: 128, 4774
  Trials--Virginia: 1511
  Vital statistics:
    North Carolina--Clarkton: 2970
    South Carolina: 1923, 3801
    Virginia--Fluvanna County: 5839
  Weddings--Virginia: 4490
  Women: 132
    Massachusetts: 5665
    Relations with masters: 5246
    Subdivided by place:
      Alabama: 1084, 5593
      Arkansas: 478
      Georgia: 1231, 2280, 2326, 5250
        Cherokee County: 1887
        Forsyth County: 5260
      Jamaica: 301
      Louisiana: 478
      Mississippi: 1382
      North Carolina: 435, 484, 1475, 2113, 3483, 4082, 4862
        Asheville: 4834
      South Carolina: 2503, 2880, 3123
      Tennessee: 1319, 4269
      Texas: 1741
      Virginia: 33, 43, 558, 1354, 1558, 1568, 1741, 2131, 2369, 2510, 3068, 5426
        Amherst County: 397
        Smyth County: 5117
      West Virginia: 43, 1946
SLEDGE, Mary: 5090
SLIDELL, John: 805, 1181, 1242, 2085, 4856
SLITTING MILLS--Connecticut: 3041
SLOGANS: 3248
SLUDER, James: 328
SMALL, B. D.: 4857
SMALL, Edward Featherston: 4857
SMALL, John Humphrey: 692, 4858
SMALL, Peter: 282
SMALL, R. H.: 4188
SMALLEY, James: 4807
SMALLPOX: see DISEASES--Smallpox
SMALLWOOD, William: 4859, 4886
SMART, Richard B.: 4860
SMAW, Isaiah Buxton: 4861
SMAW, Samuel V.: 208, 705, 4862
SMAW, Thomas D.: 705
SMEDBERG, Jane Renwick: 5457
SMEDES, Aldert: 2940
SMEDES, Bennett: 4775
SMEDES, George M.: 4863
SMELTER WORKERS: see INTERNATIONAL UNION OF MINE, MILL, AND SMELTER WORKERS
SMILES, Samuel: 2146, 2471
SMILIE, Mrs. _____ (South Carolina): 5074
SMIRKE, Sir Robert: 1911
SMITH, Mrs. _____ (Massachusetts): 4864
SMITH, Alexander: 872
SMITH, Alfred Emmanuel: 2299, 2496, 3538, 4825
SMITH, Alva Carmichael: 4865
SMITH, Alva Murray: 5968
SMITH, Andrew: 4910
SMITH, Anna Maria (Smith): 4866
SMITH, Anne P.: 4867
SMITH, Arthur: 5439

SMITH, Augustus John: 4868
SMITH, Benjamin Bosworth: 4253, 4869
SMITH, Bertram Taft: 4870
SMITH, Carson: 902, 3344, 5360
SMITH, Charles A. (North Carolina merchant): 4918
SMITH, Charles Alphonso (1864-1924): 5457
SMITH, Charles Henry (1826-1903): 4145, 4871, 4898
SMITH, D. E. Huger: 4392
SMITH, D. G.: 4872
SMITH, Mrs. David: 5298
SMITH, Donald Alexander, First Baron Strathcona: 4567
SMITH, Dovie: 4865
SMITH, Earl L.: 5233
SMITH, Edmund Kirby: 1403, 4873
SMITH, Edward Chambers: 4874
SMITH, Edward F.: 4897
SMITH, Edwin: 4875
SMITH, Egbert Watson: 5457
SMITH, Elhanan: 4188
SMITH, Elizabeth: 4881
SMITH, Elizabeth Augusta: 2559
SMITH, Elizabeth Oakes (Prince): 3960
SMITH, Ella: 4911
SMITH, Ellison DuRant: 592, 2109, 3451
SMITH, Emma Juliana (Gray): 4876
SMITH, Emma (Walton): 4898
SMITH, Enoch: 1401
SMITH, Evin: 4877
SMITH, F. (Pennsylvania): 4188
SMITH, F. R.: 4778
SMITH, Francis Henney (1812-1890): 4879
SMITH, Francis Hopkinson (1838-1915): 103
SMITH, Francis Ormand Jonathan (1806-1876): 4880
SMITH, Franklin E. (d. 1878): 4881
SMITH, Franklin W.: 4552
SMITH, Frederick L.: 4882
SMITH, George D. (Confederate soldier): 510
SMITH, George E.: 1424
SMITH, George Johnston (Louisiana): 4883
SMITH, Gerald L. K.: 3252
SMITH, Gerrit: 3910
SMITH, Gustavus Woodson: 395, 4884
SMITH, H. E.: 4885
SMITH, H. Tillard: 4886
SMITH, Hannah: 4881
SMITH, Harry: 735
SMITH, Henry A. M.: 1424
SMITH, Henry Louis: 5457
SMITH, Hiram Moore: 3179
SMITH, Hoke: 1573, 3905, 4887
SMITH, Horace: 4888
SMITH, Horatio: 2146
SMITH, J. Ambler: 2141
SMITH, J. P.: 4885
SMITH, Jacob Henry: 5457
SMITH, James (Maryland): 2059
SMITH, James (Michigan): 4889
SMITH, James McCune (1813-1865): 1029, 3905
SMITH, James Strudwick (1790-1859): 4890
SMITH, Jessica Randolph: 2161
SMITH, John (1579/80-1631): 858
SMITH, John (1772-1854): 4918
SMITH, John A. (North Carolina): 4891
SMITH, John Augustine (1782-1865): 3156
SMITH, John Benjamin (Great Britain): 676
SMITH, John F. (West Virginia): 4892
SMITH, John Granville (1800s): 1556
SMITH, John P. George: 4876
SMITH, John R. (Virginia): 1137
SMITH, John Rufus (West Virginia): 4893
SMITH, John W. (North Carolina): 4080
SMITH, Jonathan (North Carolina): 4765

SMITH, Jonathan Kennon Thompson (Tennessee): 4894
SMITH, Joseph (1790-1877): 5193
SMITH, Joseph Adams (1837-1907): 5436
SMITH, Joseph Belknap (Georgia): 4895
SMITH, Joseph Pearson (North Carolina): 4918
SMITH, Josiah Edward (South Carolina): 4725, 4896
SMITH, Josiah Townsend (North Carolina): 4897
SMITH, Julia V.: 4912
SMITH, Kate Douglas: 3797
SMITH, Larkin: 236
SMITH, Laura Jane: 4898
SMITH, Lizzie Nelms: 4052
SMITH, Margaret: 4896
SMITH, Marguerite (Waters): 902, 5360
SMITH, Marion (Seddon): 4924
SMITH, Mary (Bellew) (1775-1872): 4918
SMITH, Mary (Bennett): 4918
SMITH, Mary Caroline (Trainer): 4881
SMITH, Mary Elizabeth: 4865
SMITH, Mary Webb: 4894
SMITH, Maurice: 4894
SMITH, Mildred: 99
SMITH, Morgan Lewis: 4899
SMITH, Nimrod Jarrett: 5202
SMITH, Norman B.: 2325
SMITH, Orlando Jay: 2449
SMITH, Orra (Wever): 4900
SMITH, Otho I.: 4901
SMITH, Persifor Frazer: 4902, 5417
SMITH, Preston: 3729
SMITH, Reed: 648
SMITH, Richard (Florida): 4903
SMITH, Richard M. (ship's captain): 4537
SMITH, Richard T. (North Carolina): 5815
SMITH, Robert (North Carolina): 1492
SMITH, Robert (Virginia): 3012
SMITH, Robert, First Baron Carrington: 3883, 4230
SMITH, Robert A. (North Carolina): 4872
SMITH, Roberta: 4301
SMITH, S. M.: 4875
SMITH, Sallie (Gold): 4904
SMITH, Samuel (1752-1839, Maryland): 4081, 4905
SMITH, Samuel (North Carolina): 4894
SMITH, Samuel A. (Kentucky): 2063
SMITH, Samuel Granville (1794-1835): 4894
SMITH, Samuel H. (North Carolina): 4906
SMITH, Samuel Macon (1851-1910): 5457
SMITH, Sarah (b. ca. 1830): 4881
SMITH, Sarah Motte: 4625
SMITH, Seba (1792-1868): 3960
SMITH, Simeon: 4907
SMITH, Spencer: 3183
SMITH, Stephen Catterson: 3567
SMITH, Stephens Calhoun: 4908
SMITH, Susan (Parker): 4911
SMITH, Susannah Meredith: 4909
SMITH, Thomas (1785-1841): 4924
SMITH, Thomas M. (North Carolina): 4910
SMITH, Tom (Georgia): 4875
SMITH, Virginia Louisa: 4866
SMITH, W. Lafayette (d. 1907): 4898
SMITH, W. Scott: 1083
SMITH, Washington M. (d. 1869): 4911
SMITH, Whitefoord (Leith, Scotland): 4912
SMITH, Whitefoord (Charleston, South Carolina, 1812-1893): 4912
SMITH, Willard (Union soldier): 4888
SMITH, William (Frederick County, Virginia): 4915
SMITH, William (Shenandoah County? Virginia): 2949
SMITH, William (d. 1743, North Carolina): 5457

SMITH, William (1756-1835, Great Britain): 4913
SMITH, William (ca. 1762-1840, South Carolina): 4914
SMITH, William (1796-1887, Virginia governor): 1401, 1403, 3255, 4916
SMITH, William (fl. 1855-1869, North Carolina): 4917
SMITH, William Alexander (1843-1934): 4918
SMITH, William Allan: 4453
SMITH, William D. (North Carolina): 4919
SMITH, William E. (Pennsylvania): 4920
SMITH, William Ephraim (1829-1890): 4921
SMITH, William Gaston (North Carolina): 4918
SMITH, William J. (b. 1902): 1195, 5235
SMITH, William Loughton (1758-1812): 4922
SMITH, William Nathan Harrell: 3746, 4923
SMITH, William Oliver: 3179
SMITH, William Patterson (1796-1878): 4924
SMITH, William R. (North Carolina): 4925
SMITH, Sir William Sidney (1764-1840): 4926
SMITH, William T. (North Carolina): 4052
SMITH, Willis (1887-1953): 4586, 4927
SMITH FAMILY: 902
  Genealogy: 4918
SMITH FAMILY (Arkansas): 4894
SMITH FAMILY (Great Britain): 4894
SMITH FAMILY (New Jersey): 4909
SMITH FAMILY (New York): 5660
SMITH FAMILY (North Carolina): 4894
SMITH FAMILY (South Carolina): 4453
SMITH FAMILY (Tennessee): 4894
SMITH FAMILY (Virginia): 3458, 4894, 5660
SMITH, DE SAUSSURE AND DARRELL, Charleston, South Carolina (firm): 4896
SMITH, HUIE, ALEXANDER AND COMPANY: 144, 2703
SMITH AND ADAMS (firm): see ADAMS AND SMITH
SMITH AND DARRELL, Charleston, South Carolina (firm): 4896
SMITH AND HERNDON, Eutaw, Alabama (law firm): 2173
SMITH AND HUNT (firm): see HUNT AND SMITH
SMITH & INGRAM, Anson County, North Carolina (sawmill): 4918
SMITH AND JONES (firm): see JONES AND SMITH
SMITH AND WILSON (firm): see JOHN WILSON AND RICHARD T. SMITH
SMITH BILL (1918--United States): 3545
SMITH BRIDGE, North Carolina:
  Civil War: 1181
SMITH CHURCH, North Carolina:
  Estates and mercantile accounts: 5399
SMITH COLLEGE, Northampton, Massachusetts: 4897
  Students and student life: 5748
SMITH GROVE, North Carolina: 2021, 4765, 5511
SMITH ISLAND, Cape Fear River, North Carolina: 264
SMITH-McNARY BILL (1920s--United States): 5791
SMITHEY, James W.: 1873
SMITHFIELD, North Carolina: 2631, 3257, 3301, 4292, 4938
  see also SOUTHPORT, North Carolina
  American pottery: 5252
  Lawyers' accounts: 3839

SMITHFIELD, North Carolina (Continued):
  Loans: 3839
  Mercantile accounts: 5
SMITHFIELD, Virginia:
  Civil War: 2121
  see also CIV
    BATTLES,
    Virginia--
SMITH'S MILLS, Sou
SMITH'S (N. I.) SCH
  North Carolina: 661
SMITHSBURG, Maryland:
  Evangelical Lutheran c 5343
  Hotel management: 5110
  Sunday schools: 5343
SMITHSON, Elizabeth Moorman:
SMITHSON, William: 4928
SMITHSON FAMILY (Virginia): 4928
SMITHSON FUNDS: 566
SMITHSONIAN INSTITUTION, Washington, D.C.: 2494, 3281, 4927
SMITHVILLE, North Carolina: 5533
SMITHWICK, Edgar: 4929
SMITHWICK, Hannah: 4930
SMITHWICK'S CREEK PRIMITIVE BAPTIST CHURCH, Martin County, North Carolina: 4931
SMOKING: see CIGARETTE SMOKING; TOBACCO SMOKING
SMOOT, J. F.: 4932
SMOOT, Thomas Arthur (1871-1937): 4932
SMUGGLING:
  Jamaica: 1913
  United States: 20
SMUTS, Jan Christian: 1320
SMYTH, Alexander: 4933
SMYTH, Sir David Carmichael-: 4934
SMYTH, Harriet (Morse) Carmichael-: 4934
SMYTH, J. Jones: 3117
SMYTH, Sir James Carmichael-, First Baronet: 4934
SMYTH, Sir Robert Carmichael-: 4934
SMYTH, Thomas (Maryland): 4935
SMYTH, Thomas (1808-1873, South Carolina): 4936
SMYTH COUNTY, Texas:
  Mountain Grove: 916
SMYTH COUNTY, Virginia:
  Marion: 1240, 2769, 3513, 5117
  Plantations and slaves: 5117
SMYTHE, A.: 2285
SNAPP, G. H.: 1920
SNAVELY, Simon: 4937
SNEAD, Thomas D. (North Carolina): 4938
SNEAD, Thomas Lowndes (1828-1890): 1422
SNEAD, Thomas T. L. (Virginia): 2728
SNEE, Helen: 4001
SNEED, Thomas (North Carolina blacksmith): 4939
SNELL, William Dorance: 4940
SNELLING, Rowland: 4941
SNIDER, John N.: 4942
SNIVELY FAMILY: 1916
SNODGRASS, Robert Verdier: 1946
SNODGRASS FAMILY (West Virginia--Genealogy): 1946
SNOW, Charles: 4943
SNOW, Horace N.: 4945
SNOW, John: 4944
SNOW, Samuel W.: 4945
SNOW, William Henry: 5457
SNOW FAMILY (Ohio): 4945
SNOW--Maryland: 3254
SNOW ASSIENTO (ship): 2667
SNOW HILL, Maryland:
  Ports: 4946
"SNOWBOUND" by John Greenleaf Whittier: 5717
SNOWDEN, M. A.: 2449
SNOWDEN, Yates: 2449
SNYDER, John: 1614

...REFORM
  1628: 2152
  1700s: 3347, 5331
  1800s: 597, 981, 1126, 2054, 2149, 2708, 5026
  1900s: 1815
  Greece: 1014
  India: 1014, 2756
  Ireland: 4024
  Pennsylvania: 2027
  Sierra Leone: 1014
  South Africa: 1014
  Turkey: 1014
  United States: 196, 4020, 4825
  Virginia: 5486
SOCIAL CLASSES--India: 5525
SOCIAL CONDITIONS: see as subheading under names of specific places
SOCIAL DEMOCRACY: see SOCIALISM
SOCIAL DEMOCRATIC FEDERATION: 2083, 4948
SOCIAL LIFE AND CUSTOMS: see as subheading under names of specific places
SOCIAL SERVICES:
  North Carolina--Durham: 1643
SOCIALISM: 2083, 4837
  see also COMMUNISM
  Bibliography:
    France: 65
    Germany: 65
    Great Britain: 65
    United States: 65
  Subdivided by place:
    France: 1424
    United States: 2083, 4948
SOCIALISM AND LABOR: see LABOR AND SOCIALISM
THE SOCIALIST INTERNATIONAL: 4948
SOCIALIST INTERNATIONAL INFORMATION: 4948
SOCIALIST PARTY, U.S.A.: 4947
  Illinois: 4947
  Wisconsin: 4947
SOCIALIST PARTY OF AMERICA: 4948
  California: 4948
  New Jersey: 4948
  New York: 4948
SOCIALIST PUBLICATIONS: 4947, 4948
SOCIALIST TRIBUNE: 4947
SOCIALISTS:
  Biography: 4948
  France: 65
  Germany: 65
  Great Britain: 65
  United States: 65
SOCIALIZED MEDICINE:
  see also HEALTH PROGRAMS; NATIONAL HEALTH INSURANCE
  United States: 4948
SOCIETIES AND CLUBS: 3305
  see also ART SOCIETIES; BIBLE SOCIETIES; BOY SCOUT MOVEMENT; BUSINESS CLUBS; CHURCHES--Interchurch organizations; CIVIL WAR--MEMORIAL SOCIETIES; COUNTRY CLUBS; DEBATING SOCIETIES; DINING CLUBS; FINANCIAL SOCIETIES; FRATERNAL SOCIETIES; HISTORICAL SOCIETIES; LITERARY SOCIETIES; MISSIONARY SOCIETIES; PATRIOTIC

SOCIETIES AND CLUBS (Continued):
SOCIETIES; POLITICAL CLUBS;
SCIENTIFIC SOCIETIES; SECRET
SOCIETIES; STUDENT RELIGIOUS
SOCIETIES; STUDENT SOCIETIES;
TEMPERANCE SOCIETIES; WOMEN'S
SOCIETIES AND CLUBS; YOUTH
ORGANIZATIONS
  Georgia: 2238
  Great Britain: 5050, 5726
  New York: 4806
    New York: 2246, 4976
  South Carolina:
    Charleston: 2040
    Society Hill: 4634
  United States: 3265, 5593
SOCIETY FOR PARLIAMENTARY REFORM:
  4913
SOCIETY FOR PROMOTING CHRISTIAN
  KNOWLEDGE: 5539
SOCIETY FOR PSYCHICAL RESEARCH,
  London, England: 3190
SOCIETY FOR THE PROPAGATION OF THE
  GOSPEL: 5725
  Natal: 5725
SOCIETY FOR THE PROTECTION OF ANCIENT
  BUILDINGS (Great Britain): 5553
SOCIETY HILL, South Carolina: 2762
  Schools: 4634
  Societies and clubs: 4634
SOCIETY HILL UNION FACTORY: 3754
SOCIETY OF AMERICAN AUTHORS: 72
SOCIETY OF AUTHORS: 113
SOCIETY OF FRIENDS: 1407, 3665
  Church buildings:
    North Carolina--High Falls: 5905
  Civil War:
    Conscientious objectors:
      North Carolina: 2970
        Treatment of: 2554, 2555
  Family life--North Carolina: 1407
  Subdivided by place:
    Great Britain: 1733, 4732, 5241,
      5726
      Chelmsford: 1903
      London: 2555
    Indiana: 5149
      White River: 3981
    Ireland: 4732
    Maryland: 3026, 5128
    North Carolina: 329, 645, 2555,
      3415, 4006, 4858, 5264, 5632
      Dutchman Creek: 1904
      Yadkin County: 1904
    South Carolina--Bush River: 3981
    United States: 3054, 5726
    Virginia: 5504
      Alexandria: 5016
SOCIETY OF FRIENDS CHURCH, High Falls,
  North Carolina: 5905
SOCIETY OF SAINT VINCENT DE PAUL:
  1952
SOCIETY OF THE ARMY OF TENNESSEE:
  2514
SOCIETY OF THE ARMY OF THE POTOMAC:
  5396
SOCIETY OF THE CINCINNATI: 3809,
  4908
  South Carolina: 4215
    Charleston: 4584
SOCIETY OF THE ROSY CROSS: see
  ROSICRUCIANS
SOCINIANISM--Great Britain: 5726
SOD HOUSES--Nebraska: 1575
SODA SPRINGS LAND AND CATTLE COMPANY:
  2438
SOFER, Cyril: 41
SOIL EROSION--Virginia: 3642
SOIL FERTILITY--Alabama: 5862
SOILS:
  Kentucky and Missouri: 3532
SOLAR ECLIPSES (1860): 1785
SOLDAN, Carlos Paz: see PAZ SOLDAN,
  Carlos
"A SOLDIER AND MR. LINCOLN" by
  Alexander T. Case: 54

SOLDIER SUFFRAGE: see Election of
  officers and Political elections
  as subheadings under names of
  armies
SOLDIERS AND SAILORS HISTORICAL
  SOCIETY (Rhode Island): 5001
SOLDIERS MEMORIAL SOCIETY
  (Massachusetts?): 4358
SOLDIERS' MEMORIAL SOCIETY, Wilmington,
  North Carolina: 617
SOLDIERS' BONUS: see PENSIONS,
  Military
SOLDIERS OF FORTUNE:
  Carlist War: 1504
  Great Britain: 700
SOLDIERS' RELIEF SOCIETY (Georgia?):
  3991
SOLIS, Antonio de: 4155
SOLLOWAY, John: 5173
SOLMIRON, Miguel Sánchez: 4155
SOLO CADO, Francisco: 4980
SOLOMON, Roza: 1463
SOLOMON, Odes and Psalms of: see
  ODES AND PSALMS OF SOLOMON
SOLOMON ISLANDS:
  Estates and plantations: 4949
SOLOMON RIVER HYDRAULIC MINING
  COMPANY: 1584
SOLOMONS, M. J.: 4950
SOLUBLE PACIFIC GUANO: 4530
"SOME LETTERS BY O. HENRY" ed. by
  Clarence Gohdes: 4279
"SOME NEW LETTERS OF CONSTANCE
  FENIMORE WOOLSON": 2449
"SOME OF MY EXPERIENCES AS A
  CONFEDERATE SOLDIER, IN THE CAMP
  AND ON THE BATTLEFIELD, IN THE
  ARMY OF NORTHERN VIRGINIA" by
  John Malachi Bowden: 589
"SOME REFLECTIONS ON THE PRACTICE OF
  MEDICINE BY THE SYSTEM OF PATENT
  RECEIPTS, ITS INJURIOUS TENDENCY,
  AND A METHOD FOR THE REMEDY": 5505
"SOME REMINISENCES OF THE PAST,
  1900" by Robert Banks Jenkinson,
  Second Earl of Liverpool: 2836
"SOME THOUGHTS FOR THE PRESIDENT'S
  CONSIDERATION" by William Henry
  Seward: 4748
SOME TRUTHS OF HISTORY by Thaddeus
  Kosciuszko Oglesby: 3967
"SOME UNPUBLISHED LETTERS OF JOHN R.
  THOMPSON AND AUGUSTIN LOUIS TAVEAU"
  by David K. Jackson: 5193
SOMERS, John Somers Cocks, First
  Earl: 1139
SOMERS, William D.: 4951
SOMERS, New York: 3637
SOMERSET, Edward Seymour, Twelfth
  Duke of: 326
SOMERSET, Fitzroy James Henry, First
  Baron Raglan: 4995
SOMERSETSHIRE, England:
  Antiquities: 4176
  Art and artists: 1071
  Drawings and engravings: 1071
  Historical studies: 4176
  Cities and towns:
    Bath: 2227, 4650, 5609
      Elections: 1753
      Historical studies: 5553
      Schools: 1753
    Pyrland Hall: 5947
    Wells: 1071
SOMERVILLE, Thomas: 828
SOMERVILLE, New Jersey: 1585
SOMERVILLE, Virginia: 1744, 3681
SOMERVILLE, West Virginia:
  Union Army camp: 1452
"SOMETHING DOING IN THE ORIENT" by
  George T. Lanigan: 3093
SOMMERS FAMILY (South Carolina):
  4584
SOMMERVILLE, John: 2118
SONDLEY, Forster Alexander: 4952
SONDLEY, Harriet: 2961

SONGS AND MUSIC: 111, 4948
  see also CANTATAS; CHOIRS; CHURCH
    MUSIC; CIVIL WAR--SONGS AND MUSIC;
    COMPOSERS; HYMNS; NATIONAL
    ANTHEMS; OPERA; PIANO MUSIC;
    STRING TRIO MUSIC
  Concerts:
    Georgia:
      Augusta: 5246
      Macon: 5246
      Savannah: 4677
    West Virginia: 1770
  Notebooks--Virginia: 1045
  Political--United States: 5497
  Publishing: 3843
    Great Britain: 2146
  Scores--North Carolina: 691
  Study and teaching: 3828
    see also HARMONY--Rules
    Georgia: 2786
    Germany: 661
    North Carolina: 837
      Davie County: 4111
      Winston-Salem: 3172, 5459
  Tune-books: 4975
  Subdivided by place:
    Georgia: 539
    Great Britain: 258, 335
    North Carolina: 691, 2041, 5298
    Pennsylvania: 490
    South Carolina: 5503
    United States: 432, 2407, 3633
    Virginia: 2559
SONGS AND POEMS OF THE SOUTH: 3611
SONOMA COUNTY, California:
  Santa Rosa: 836
SONS OF LIBERTY:
  Massachusetts--Boston: 5298
SONS OF TEMPERANCE: 330, 2593, 5082,
  5339
  Negro members: 5339
  North Carolina:
    Davie County: 2857
  Pennsylvania: 496
  Virginia:
    Covington Division No. 244: 4953
    Grand Division: 5339
    Shockoe Hill Division: 5339
    Worth Division No. 44: 4954
SONS OF THE AMERICAN REVOLUTION: 3357
  Maryland Society: 4348
SONS OF VETERANS, UNITED STATES OF
  AMERICA:
  Connecticut: 4955
SOONG, Charles Jones: 4956
SOONG, Mei-ling: 4956
SOONG, Tse-Ven: 5252
THE SOONG SISTERS by Emily Hahn: 4956
SOPER, Henry Marlin: 2449
SOPHIA FREDERICA MATHILDA, Queen of
  the Netherlands: 3472
SOPWITH, Thomas: 1225
SOTHEY, Alexander: 4337
SOTOMAYOR, Antonio Valladares de:
  see VALLADARES DE SOTOMAYOR,
  Antonio
SOUBIE, Armand: 4957
SOULÉ, Pierre: 858, 1403, 4958
SOUNER, Albert: 4959
SOUNER, Lillie E.: 4959
SOURIS, Cardinal de: 3271
SOUSA, José Fernando de Abascal y:
  see ABASCAL Y SOUSA, José Fernando de
SOUTH, Robert: 47
THE SOUTH: see SOUTHERN STATES
SOUTH AFRICA: 41, 1147, 4514, 5726,
  5801
  see also BECHUANALAND; CAPE COLONY;
    GREAT BRITAIN--ARMY--South Africa
  Boer War: see BOER WAR
  British administration: 1910, 2324,
    3978, 5872
    Policy toward Boers: 3693
  Description and travel (1850s): 3899
  Economic conditions: 4960
  Education: 4960

SOUTH AFRICA (Continued):
  Politics and government: 1910, 4960
  Race relations: 41
  Social and political reform: 1014
  Social conditions: 4960
SOUTH AMERICA:
  see also LATIN AMERICA; and names of specific countries
  Description and travel (1800s): 1506, 4535, 5824
  Exploration (1845): 2296
  Foreign trade: 323
    United States: 3578
  Spanish administration: 4979
  Travel--Ocean voyages: 3960
  United States naval operations: 841, 3118, 4019
SOUTH ATLANTIC QUARTERLY: 2282, 3092, 4021
SOUTH AUSTRALIA: 1147
  British administration: 1792
SOUTH BEND, Indiana: 1162
SOUTH BROOKFIELD, New York: 854
SOUTH CAMDEN CIRCUIT, Methodist churches: 3646

SOUTH CAROLINA

see also CAROLINA PROVINCE; SOUTHERN STATES
ABOLITION OF SLAVERY AND ABOLITIONIST SENTIMENT: 2503
  Cokesbury: 4118
  Laurens: 4118
ACTRESSES--Charleston: 5503
AGRICULTURAL CREDIT: 566, 4530
AGRICULTURAL FAIRS:
  Spartanburg County: 3893
AGRICULTURAL IMPLEMENTS:
  Prices: 3801
  Stateburg: 4217
AGRICULTURAL MACHINERY: 3124
AGRICULTURAL ORGANIZATIONS: 4896
  see also SOUTH CAROLINA--PATRONS OF HUSBANDRY
AGRICULTURAL PRODUCTS--Prices: 4834
AGRICULTURAL WORKERS: see SOUTH CAROLINA--WAGES AND SALARIES--Agricultural workers
AGRICULTURE: 718, 1220, 3981, 4564
  see also the following subheadings under SOUTH CAROLINA: CROPS, and names of specific crops; FARMING, and subheadings beginning with the word FARM; PLANTATIONS, and subheadings beginning with the word PLANTATION
  Camden: 5675
AMERICAN LITERATURE: 296, 5901
  Charleston: 1575
  Criticism: 2449
AMERICAN POETRY: 2045, 3394, 3892, 5193
  Charleston: 3666
AMERICAN REVOLUTION: see appropriate subheadings under AMERICAN REVOLUTION; CONTINENTAL ARMY
ANTI-LYNCHING MOVEMENT: 300
APPRENTICESHIP:
  Shipbuilding industry: 3294
ARITHMETIC EXERCISE BOOKS: 208
ARMY CAMPS--Columbia (1910s): 3843
ARTILLERY DRILL AND TACTICS: 2875
ASSOCIATE REFORMED PRESBYTERIAN CHURCH: 2473, 4310
  Church buildings: 2880
  Relations with Methodists: 2880
AUTHORSHIP: 2290
AUTOGRAPHS: 3418
AUTOMOBILE INDUSTRY:
  Rock Hill: 5252
BANK-NOTES: 881
BANKS AND BANKING: 669, 697
  Charleston: 1760, 4235, 5318
BAPTISM:
  Baptist churches: 3669
  Presbyterian Churches: 4310

SOUTH CAROLINA

BAPTIST CHURCHES: 561
  Baptism: see SOUTH CAROLINA--BAPTISM--Baptist churches
  Clergy: see SOUTH CAROLINA--CLERGY--Baptist
  Finance--Greenville: 2182
  Sermons: see SOUTH CAROLINA--SERMONS--Baptist
  Subdivided by place:
    Charleston: 2402
    Greenville: 2182
    Sumter: 3676
BILLS OF EXCHANGE: 810
BIOGRAPHICAL STUDIES: 1424, 4453
BIOGRAPHIES: 4350
BIRDS: 1803
BLACKSMITHING: 2670
  Charleston: 219
BLACKSMITH'S ACCOUNTS: 2793
  Chester County: 4833
BLIND--Education: 300
BOARDING HOUSES--Rates: 4834
BONDS--Charleston: 5198
BOOK BUYING: 3801
  Charleston: 3162
BOUNDARY DISPUTES:
  With Georgia: 2666, 3671, 5276
BRIBERY: 1424
BRIDGES: 3044
BUILDING CONSTRUCTION: 997
BUSINESS ACCOUNTS: 653
BUSINESS AFFAIRS: 842, 1127, 3231, 4896
  Abbeville District: 414
  Charleston: 2278, 3532, 4163, 5936
  Spartanburg: 5930
  Sumter County: 3676
BUSINESS CLUBS--Columbia: 3421
BUSINESS FAILURES--Charleston: 5193
CAMP MEETINGS:
  Methodist: 5965
  York County: 4609
CANALS: 4218
  see also SOUTH CAROLINA--INTRACOASTAL WATERWAY
  Construction: 4218
CARRIAGES AND BUGGIES--Prices: 3801
CATAWBA INDIANS: 3356
CATHOLIC CHURCHES:
  Negro members: 249
CATTLE: 2670
CHEMICALS INDUSTRY: 1019
CHILDREN: see SOUTH CAROLINA--GUARDIANSHIP--Children
CHURCH HISTORY: 4453
CHURCH MUSIC--Episcopal: 2110
CHURCHES:
  see also names of specific denominations under SOUTH CAROLINA
  Charleston: 2107, 2410, 3801
  Edisto: 2027
CIVIL RIGHTS: 4149
CIVIL WAR: see appropriate subheadings under CIVIL WAR; CONFEDERATE STATES OF AMERICA; UNITED STATES--ARMY--Civil War
CLERGY: 4700
  see also SOUTH CAROLINA--PREACHING; SOUTH CAROLINA--WAGES AND SALARIES--Clergy
  Baptist: 669, 5211
    Charleston: 2402
  Episcopal--Negroes: 2449
  Independent Presbyterian: 4609
  Lutheran: 550
  Methodist: 2289
  Methodist Episcopal: 4912
  Presbyterian: 2616, 4031, 4310, 5988
    Charleston: 4936
    Columbia: 4240
    Pastoral responsibilities: 4429
  Protestant Episcopal: 3666, 4215, 4272
  Universalist--Charleston: 978

SOUTH CAROLINA

CLOTHING AND DRESS--Prices: 3801
COASTAL DEVELOPMENT: 4453
COLONIAL AFFAIRS: 2780
COMMERCIAL PRODUCTS:
  Marketing--Greenville: 5825
COMMISSION MERCHANTS: 2107
  Charleston: 1891, 3124, 3801, 4332
COMMODITY PRICES:
  see also CIVIL WAR--COMMODITY PRICES--South Carolina
  1800s:
    1800s: 477
    1820s: 158
    1850s: 4783
    1860s: 2831, 4783
    1880s: 126
    1800s-1900s: 566
    Camden: 5675
COMMONPLACE BOOKS:
  Charleston: 723
CONGRESSIONAL ELECTIONS (1914): 3893
CONSTABLES: 3349
  Darlington: 5299
COOKERY: 60, 3552
CORN: 4118
  Prices: 4834
CORN SHUCKING: 3531
CORRUPTION IN POLITICS: 2109, 5893
COTTON: 1572, 1745, 2210
  Acreage allotments: 4193
  Prices: 4834, 4996
  Sea Island cotton: 1889
  Speculation: 1009, 4145
  Storage: 1009
COTTON GROWING: 1877, 2267, 3123, 3451
COTTON MILLS: 1480, 2961, 3451, 3754, 5312
COTTON PLANTATIONS: 669, 5661, 5759
  Chesterfield County: 4996
COTTON SCREEN PRINT INDUSTRY: 5236
COTTON TRADE:
  1700s-1800s: 1012
  1800s: 2940, 3203, 5114
    1800s: 566, 3123
    1810s: 566, 3123
    1820s: 566
    1840s: 965
    1850s: 965, 1388, 1889
    1870s: 4996
    1880s: 3303, 4996
  1800s-1900s: 501
  Charleston: 987, 1009, 1889, 1891, 2018, 2107, 4145, 4649
  Cheraw: 1396
  Sea Island cotton: 3230
  Charleston: 2107
COTTONSEED OIL: 4621
COUNTRY CLUBS--Charleston: 3299
COUNTY GOVERNMENT:
  Spartanburg County: 3044
COURTS: 1424, 1468, 4269
  see also SOUTH CAROLINA--JUDGES; SOUTH CAROLINA--JURIES
  Cases: 2961
    Laurens District: 1001
  Costs: 5548
  Judgment: 2961
  Laws and legislation: 4213
  Summonses: 842
  Subdivided by type of court:
    Circuit courts: 2616
    Courts of Equity: 4623
      Charleston: 1468
    District Courts: 989
      Clerks: 477
    Magistrates' Courts:
      Branchville: 1749
    Superior Provost Courts:
      Darlington: 2106
    United States federal courts:
      Opinion on power of: 431
COURTSHIP: 1424, 2960

925

SOUTH CAROLINA

CRIME: see the following subheadings under SOUTH CAROLINA: BRIBERY; EXTRADITION OF CRIMINALS; FRAUD; GOVERNMENT FRAUD; LIBEL AND SLANDER; MURDER
CROP LIENS: 5198
CROPS: 2290, 2831, 4083, 4118, 4310, 5760
   Camden: 5675
   Edisto Island: 4896
   Medicinal: 2343
CURRENCY: 1339
   Value: 206
CUSTOMS DUTIES--Collection: 1927
CUSTOMS SERVICE--Charleston: 5193
DEAF--Education: 300
DEATH: 2960, 3360, 5193
   see also SOUTH CAROLINA--FUNERALS
DEBATING SOCIETIES: 1111
DEBT: 1877
   see also SOUTH CAROLINA--PERSONAL DEBT; SOUTH CAROLINA--STATE DEBT
   Abbeville: 3319
   Settlement: 1012
DEBT COLLECTION: 5930
   Charleston: 5548
   Chester District: 1268
DEFENSES: 5114
   see also SOUTH CAROLINA--FORTIFICATIONS
   Charleston: 5513
   Cunningham's Bluff: 4620
DEMOCRATIC PARTY: 988, 2300, 4725, 5759
   see also DEMOCRATIC PARTY--Conventions (National)--Charleston, South Carolina
DEPRESSION (1929- ): 300
DESCRIPTION AND TRAVEL:
   1800s: 1891, 3754
   1800s: 2636
   1810s: 2636, 3808
   1820s: 529, 2664
   1830s: 2664, 2822
   1850s: 4616
   1860s: 1500, 1927
   1870s: 5731
   1800s-1900s: 4898
   Accommodation (1820): 158
DISEASES: 669, 1220, 4584
   see also SOUTH CAROLINA--MEDICAL TREATMENT; SOUTH CAROLINA--PHYSICIANS
   Cholera: 3278
   Charleston: 5193
   Malaria: 1371
   Measles: 1793
   Scarlet fever: 3278
   Smallpox: 2961, 3390
   Yellow fever: 2094, 2695, 3671
      Charleston: 3907, 4584, 5193, 5362
DUELING: 1424, 2107
   Charleston: 2695
EARTHQUAKES:
   1812: 2636
   1886: 1424, 1468, 2512
   Charleston: 1017, 1889, 2473
ECONOMIC CONDITIONS:
   see also the following subheadings under SOUTH CAROLINA: DEPRESSION (1929- ); PANIC OF 1819; POVERTY
   1700s-1800s: 3476
   1800s:
      1860s: 791, 2210, 2376, 2473, 3801, 4554
      1870s: 791, 2210, 2376, 2473, 3801
   1800s-1900s: 4460
   1900s: 4453
   Spartanburg: 1745
EDUCATION:
   see also the following subheadings under SOUTH CAROLINA: BLIND--Education; DEAF--Education; FREEDMEN--Education; JOURNALISM--

SOUTH CAROLINA

EDUCATION:
   see also (Continued):
      Education; NEGROES--Education; PRESBYTERIAN CHURCHES--Education; SCHOOLS and subheadings beginning with the word SCHOOL; TEACHING, and subheadings beginning with the word TEACHERS
   1700s: 4350
   1700s-1800s: 4625
   1800s: 1424, 1480, 2831, 2930, 4118, 4596, 5415, 5645
   1800s-1900s: 300
   Charleston: 4271, 5661
   Laurens: 2616
ELECTIONS:
   see also the following subheadings under SOUTH CAROLINA: CONGRESSIONAL ELECTIONS; GUBERNATORIAL ELECTIONS; LOCAL ELECTIONS; PRESIDENTIAL ELECTION OF 1876; SENATORIAL ELECTIONS
   1796: 2300
   1800s:
      1860s: 4118
      1870s: 1468, 1972, 2300, 4118
      1880s: 1480, 2512
      1890s: 1480
   1900s: 300, 4453
   Laurens: 2616
ELECTRIC POWER INDUSTRY: 3447
ELECTRICAL CONTRACTORS--Columbia: 2767
ELECTRICIANS: 2767
EMBARGO (Jeffersonian): 3485
ENGRAVINGS--Tombstones: 1889
EPISCOPAL CHURCHES:
   Clergy: see SOUTH CAROLINA--CLERGY--Episcopal
   Music: 2110
   Pew rent: 2670
   Religious literature: see SOUTH CAROLINA--Religious literature--Episcopal
ESTATE ACCOUNTS: 2107, 3801, 5810
   Charleston: 2414, 5073
   Chester: 4833
   Saluda County: 2921
ESTATES (landed property): 2556, 5074
ESTATES (legal):
   Administration and settlement: 5810
   see also SOUTH CAROLINA--WILLS
   1700s: 4621, 4623
   1700s-1800s: 653, 842, 1472, 2019
   1800s: 295, 1127, 1877, 2040, 2218, 3203, 3350, 4527
      1810s: 1562
      1820s: 1562, 4214
      1830s: 1562, 2961
      1840s: 2961, 5194
      1850s: 1388, 1891, 3367
      1860s: 791, 1388, 3367
      1870s: 1388, 3367
      1890s: 1424, 2210
   Charleston: 2107, 4215, 5198, 5461, 5936
   Chester County: 4833
   Edgefield District: 2599
   Edisto Island: 3664
   Georgetown: 3512
   Orangeburg District: 5015
EVANGELISM: 561, 669
   Beaufort: 1891
   Conway: 2854
EXHIBITIONS AND FAIRS: 2473
   see also SOUTH CAROLINA--AGRICULTURAL FAIRS
EXTRADITION OF CRIMINALS: 700, 4218
FACTORS--Charleston: 3801
FAMILY LIFE: 5193
   Chester: 5988
   Lancaster County: 4310

SOUTH CAROLINA

FARM ACCOUNTS: 501, 2961, 3405
   Branchville: 1749
FARM MANAGEMENT: 1334, 2814
FARM SUPPLIES: 5114, 2880
FARM TENANCY: 4460
FARMING: 430, 3801
   see also the following subheadings under SOUTH CAROLINA: AGRICULTURE, and subheadings beginning with the word AGRICULTURAL; CROPS, and names of specific crops; LIVESTOCK, and names of specific kinds of livestock; PLANTATIONS, and subheadings beginning with the word PLANTATION
   Beaufort: 1891
   Spartanburg: 4080
FERTILIZER INDUSTRY: 1019
FINANCE: 718, 3552, 4034
   see also the following subheadings under SOUTH CAROLINA: HOUSEHOLD FINANCE; PERSONAL FINANCE; PUBLIC FINANCE
   Charleston: 2414, 3589
FIRES:
   Charleston:
      1838: 2491
      1861: 2610, 2695, 3485
   Columbia: 1017
FOREIGN TRADE: 1935, 2909
   British West Indies: 2541
   Great Britain: 2541, 3230
FORESTS AND FORESTRY: 4453
FORTIFICATIONS:
   see also SOUTH CAROLINA--DEFENSES
   Charleston: 4216
FOURTH OF JULY CELEBRATIONS:
   Charleston (1826): 3532
FRAUD: 1424
   see also SOUTH CAROLINA--GOVERNMENT FRAUD
FREE NEGROES: see SOUTH CAROLINA--GUARDIANSHIP--Free Negroes
FREEDMEN: 2473, 3405, 3993, 4649
   Assistance to--Charleston: 408
   Behavior: 4118, 5759
   Complaint of--Charleston: 408
   Education:
      Beaufort: 2106
      Sumter: 5298
   Labor contracts: 297, 1923, 3371, 4833, 4996
      Chester District: 1268
   Treatment: 408, 1352, 2695
   Wages: see SOUTH CAROLINA--WAGES AND SALARIES--Freedmen
   Subdivided by place:
      Charleston: 408, 2695
FRENCH IN SOUTH CAROLINA: 1581
FUGITIVE SLAVES: 881, 2107, 3415, 4534, 4581
FUNERALS--Lancaster County: 4310
FURNITURE PRICES: 3801
GEOLOGY: 1220
GERMANS IN SOUTH CAROLINA: 46
   Civil War volunteers: 2300
GIDEONITES--Hilton Head: 3264
GOLD MINES AND MINING:
   Description: 529
GOVERNESSES: 3405
GOVERNMENT AGENCIES AND OFFICIALS:
   Executive Council (Civil War): 565
   Game wardens: 4453
   Governors:
      Thomas Pinckney (1787-1789): 4218
      Charles Pinckney (1806-1808): 4213
      Francis Wilkinson Pickens (1860-1862): 4193
      James L. Orr (1865-1868): 3993
      Daniel H. Chamberlain (1874-1876): 1424
      William Dunlap Simpson (1878-1880): 4834

SOUTH CAROLINA

GOVERNMENT AGENCIES AND OFFICIALS:
  Governors (Continued):
    Coleman Livingston Blease
      (1911-1915): 4453
  Highway Commission: 3383
  Ordnance Office (Civil War): 1189
  Secretary of War (Civil War): 2805
  Sheriffs--Beaufort County: 5758
  Treasury Department: 1189
GOVERNMENT FRAUD: 1012
GRIST MILLS--Branchville: 1749
GUARDIANSHIP:
  Children: 4834
  Free Negroes: 758
GUBERNATORIAL ELECTIONS:
  1894: 5299
  1912: 844
  1916: 5930
HARBORS:
  Federal aid to Beaufort: 1927
HEALTH CONDITIONS: 477, 4083
  Charleston: 4584
HIRING OF SLAVES: 1524, 4460, 4625
HISTORICAL RESTORATION:
  Cokesbury: 4312
HISTORICAL SOCIETIES: 2402, 5312
HISTORICAL STUDIES: 1923, 2788,
  3356, 4453, 5312
  Huguenot settlement: 1468
HOGS: 3123
HOME REMEDIES: 2670
HORSE RACING: 2880
HORSES:
  Breeding: 2300
    Fees--Chester County: 4833
  Prices: 295, 3801
HOTEL MANAGEMENT:
  Union: 5407, 5522
HOURS OF LABOR:
  Typographical workers: 2771
HOUSEHOLD ACCOUNTS: 501, 3405
  Charleston: 1891
  Colleton County: 4649
HOUSEHOLD FINANCE: 1388, 3801
HUGUENOTS IN SOUTH CAROLINA: 1468
  Church in Charleston: 4584
HUNTING: 4996
HURRICANES--Charleston: 2959
IMMIGRATION SOCIETIES: 550
INDIANS OF NORTH AMERICA:
  see also SOUTH CAROLINA--CATAWBA
    INDIANS
  Wars: 2300
INDIGO CULTURE: 4216
INDUSTRIAL ACCIDENTS--Lawsuits: 5930
INDUSTRIALIZATION: 300
  Spartanburg: 4118
INSURANCE:
  Fire: 1691
    Charleston: 2448
  Life: 3421
  Maritime: 1691
INSURANCE COMPANIES--Charleston:
  1691
INTERNAL IMPROVEMENTS: 4269
INTERRACIAL MARRIAGE: 669
INTRACOASTAL WATERWAY: 2774
INVENTIONS: 3163
IRON INDUSTRY: 529
IRRIGATION MACHINERY--Rice: 1524
JOURNALISM--Education: 300
JUDGES: 5863, 5930
  see also SOUTH CAROLINA--COURTS;
    SOUTH CAROLINA--JURIES
JUDICIAL REFORM: 5271
JURIES: 1877
JUSTICES OF THE PEACE: 501, 1692
KNOW-NOTHING PARTY: 1877
KU KLUX KLAN: 2300, 2473, 3527
  Trials: 1889
LABOR: 1424
LABOR ARBITRATION: 2771
LABOR CONTRACTS: 5236, 5237

SOUTH CAROLINA

LABOR CONTRACTS (Continued):
  see also the following subheadings
    under SOUTH CAROLINA: FREEDMEN--
    Labor contracts; LABOR UNIONS--
    Contracts; OVERSEERS--Contracts
  Spartanburg: 5233
LABOR DISPUTES:
  Electricians: 2768
  Textile workers: 5236
  Spartanburg: 5233
LABOR IN POLITICS: 2568
LABOR LAWS AND LEGISLATION: 2767,
  5411
LABOR UNIONS: 300, 1424, 4962
  see also SOUTH CAROLINA--
    UNIONIZATION
  Contracts: 2767
  Conventions: 4962
    Typographical union: 2771
  Dues: 4962
    Electricians: 2767
    Typographical union: 2771
  Finance:
    Electricians: 2767
    Typographical union: 2771
  Initiation fees:
    Electricians: 2767
  Membership:
    Typographical union: 2771
  Textile workers: 1196
  Traveling cards: 2767, 2771
  Subdivided by place:
    Columbia: 1172
LAND: 1472
  Prices: 477, 4118
    Charleston: 1745
  Purchases and sales:
    Orangeburg District: 5015
    Sumter County: 3676
  Rental--Charleston: 4306
  Subdivided by place:
    Edisto River: 5388
    Horry District: 1451
    Orangeburg: 5388
LAND COMPANIES: 4298
LAND DEEDS AND INDENTURES: 1581,
  1682, 2596, 2744, 2961, 3366, 4822
  Abbeville: 3375
  Anderson District: 718
  Charleston: 2556, 4214, 4306, 5198
  Columbia: 3525
  Greenville County: 2625
  Hampton County: 5759
  Laurens County: 4834
  Spartanburg County: 4721
LAND DEVELOPMENT: 1478
LAND GRANTS: 2281, 3386, 3802, 4218,
  5863
LAND LAWS AND LEGISLATION: 4213
LAND TITLES: 1480
  Charleston: 5198
  Orangeburg: 5388
LAW, Study of:
  Charleston: 5193
LAW BOOKS: 2880
LAW PRACTICE: 561, 757, 791, 1480,
  1651, 2961
  Abbeville: 4145
  Camden: 4269
  Charleston: 3162, 3962, 5548
  Edgefield: 4778
LAWSUITS: 757, 3759, 4350, 4368,
  4624, 4649
  see also Lawsuits as subheading
    under specific subjects, e.g.
    SOUTH CAROLINA--SLAVES--Lawsuits
    over ownership
  Abbeville: 4145
  Charleston: 2613
  Greenville: 4149
LAWYERS' ACCOUNTS:
  Charleston: 3962
LECTURES AND LECTURING: 3421

SOUTH CAROLINA

LEGAL AFFAIRS: 1127, 2670, 4162,
  4896, 5796
  Abbeville District: 414
  Beaufort County: 810
  Charleston: 2556, 2613, 2709, 3461,
    5198, 5318
  Graniteville: 2186
  Lancaster County: 5863
  Laurens County: 4834
  Spartanburg: 5930
  Sumter County: 2288
  With Spain: 4982
LEGAL FEES--Charleston: 5318
LEGAL PROCEDURES: 2288
LEGISLATURE:
  1770s-1780s: 2780
  1850s: 5863
  1910s: 5930
  Appropriations and expenditures:
    2696
  Senate: 5270
LIBEL AND SLANDER: 1424, 5193
LIBRARIES: 561
  Private: 5795
    Charleston: 3666
LIGHTHOUSES: 1927
LIGHTNING--Charleston: 2410
LITERARY INTERESTS: 5193
LITERARY SOCIETIES: 1676, 3394,
  4453
LIVESTOCK:
  see also the following subheadings
    under SOUTH CAROLINA: CATTLE;
    HOGS; HORSES
  Prices: 4118
  Ranging laws: 4453
  Stateburg: 4217
LOANS--Abbeville: 3319
LOCAL ELECTIONS (1910s): 2109
LOCAL POLITICS: 3682
LOTTERIES: 1971
LUTHERAN CHURCHES: see SOUTH
  CAROLINA--CLERGY--Lutheran
LYNCHING: 3390
  see also SOUTH CAROLINA--ANTI-
    LYNCHING MOVEMENT
MANUAL TRAINING: 5312
MARITAL SEPARATION: 5193
MARL: 3123
  Mining: 1019
MARRIAGE: see SOUTH CAROLINA--
  INTERRACIAL MARRIAGE; SOUTH
  CAROLINA--Weddings
MARRIAGE CONTRACTS: 5193
MARRIED LIFE: 4350
MEDICAL EDUCATION: see MEDICAL
  COLLEGE OF SOUTH CAROLINA
MEDICAL SERVICES: 2709
MEDICAL SUPPLIES--Abbeville: 3527
MEDICAL TREATMENT: 669, 1220
  see also SOUTH CAROLINA--HOME
    REMEDIES; SOUTH CAROLINA--
    PHYSICIANS
  Costs: 4214
MEDICINES:
  see also SOUTH CAROLINA--CROPS--
    Medicinal
  Prescriptions: 1220
MEMORIAL SERVICES: 3383
MERCANTILE ACCOUNTS: 501, 566, 1581,
  2213, 2793, 2961, 3123
  Charleston: 3420, 4838
  Cheraw: 2984
  Chester County: 4833
  Orangeburg District: 4583
  Pickens: 1964
  Ridgeville: 4451
  Spartanburg: 3044
  Union: 2721, 5522
  Winnsboro: 936
MERCHANTS: 566, 1242, 1396, 1480,
  3123
  see also SOUTH CAROLINA--
    COMMISSION MERCHANTS
  Abbeville: 3319

SOUTH CAROLINA

MERCHANTS (Continued):
  Charleston: 2019, 2491, 2586, 3116, 3420
  Society Hill: 2762
  Stateburg: 3818
  Woodruff: 1715
METHODIST CHURCHES: 3981, 5699
  Camp meetings: see SOUTH CAROLINA--CAMP MEETINGS--Methodist
  Clergy: see SOUTH CAROLINA--CLERGY--Methodist
  Finance: 3646
  Clemson: 2961
  Negro churches: 249
  South Carolina Conference: 3646
  Unification movement: 3646
METHODIST EPISCOPAL CHURCHES:
  Church history: 4912
  Clergy: see SOUTH CAROLINA--CLERGY--Methodist Episcopal
MIGRATION FROM: 2616, 3161
  To Alabama: 444
  To Indiana: 3981
MIGRATION TO: 3405
  From Ireland: 3230
MILITARY SCHOOLS: 2831, 3293
  see also THE CITADEL
MILITIA: 758, 1877, 4508, 4996, 5144
  American Revolution:
    Little River Regiment: 5767
    Relations with Continental Army: 2179
    Supplies: 4191
  Artillery:
    Charleston: 3800
    German Artillery: 3652
  Civil War: 1186, 5863
  Courts-martial--Charleston: 3800
  Inspections and reviews: 4399
  Law and legislation: 4214
  Officers: 4399
  Orders: 5759
  Units:
    Black Creek militia: 3123
    Brunson Branch: 5759
    Lewisville Rifle Company: 1268
    Palmetto Hussars: 1016
MILLERS' ACCOUNTS:
  Branchville: 1749
MINERALS--Mining: 1019
MINES AND MINING: 1019
  see also the following subheadings under SOUTH CAROLINA: GOLD MINES AND MINING; PHOSPHATE MINES AND MINING; SILVER MINES AND MINING
MISSION SCHOOLS: see SOUTH CAROLINA--SCHOOLS--Mission schools
MISSIONS AND MISSIONARIES:
  Among slaves: 669
MONUMENTS: 1929
MORTGAGES:
  Foreclosure: 5193
  Payment: 810
  Regulations: 5271
  Subdivided by place:
    Charleston: 5198
MULATTOES: 758
MURDERS: 1424, 3340
NATURAL HISTORY: 4453
NAVAL STORES--Prices: 987
NEGRO SEAMEN:
  Treatment: 2564, 2695
NEGRO SOLDIERS--Crime: 3012
NEGROES: 566
  see also the following subheadings under SOUTH CAROLINA: FREEDMEN; MULATTOES; SLAVES; and Negroes as subheading under names of specific subjects, e.g. SOUTH CAROLINA--CATHOLIC CHURCH--Negro members
  Education:
    see also SOUTH CAROLINA--SCHOOLS--Negro schools
    Hilton Head: 3264

SOUTH CAROLINA

NEGROES (Continued):
  Religion:
    see also SOUTH CAROLINA--CLERGY--Episcopal--Negroes
    Participation in white churches: 249
  Social status: 1927
  Suffrage: 300, 2300, 4118
  Treatment: 380, 2564
  Subdivided by place:
    Camden: 2940
NEGROES IN POLITICS: 1877, 1972
NEW DEAL--Opposition to: 300
NEWSPAPERS: 300, 1424, 2094, 2109, 2880
  Editorial policy: 3682
  Finance: 1424
  Subscriptions: 3682
  Subdivided by place:
    Charleston: 267
    Columbia: 2086
    Lancaster: 3682
NORTHERNERS IN THE SOUTH: 1572
NULLIFICATION: 150, 669, 842, 2695, 3176, 3366, 4080, 4164
OVERSEERS: 2290
  Contracts: 2599, 4214
PAINTING: 4296
PANIC OF 1819: 4269
  Charleston: 3485
PANTHERS--Abbeville County: 5825
PARDONS: 5930
  see also SOUTH CAROLINA--PRESIDENTIAL PARDONS
PATRIOTIC SOCIETIES: 1889
PATRONS OF HUSBANDRY:
  Lancaster County: 4530
  Richland County: 4072
PENMANSHIP EXERCISE BOOKS: 4271
PEONAGE: 2109
PERIODICALS: 2449
PERSONAL DEBT: 1424, 2780
PERSONAL FINANCE: 1388, 2709, 2961, 3366, 4249, 5193
  see also SOUTH CAROLINA--WOMEN--Personal finance
  Charleston: 5274
  Union: 5522
  York County: 3327
PHILANTHROPY: 2040
PHOSPHATE MINES AND MINING: 602, 1019, 1480, 4306
PHYSICIANS' ACCOUNTS: 138
  Abbeville: 4527
PLANTATION ACCOUNTS:
  Colleton County: 4649
  Edgefield County: 4193
  Kershaw County: 2940
  Stateburg: 4217
PLANTATION LIFE: 1553, 4460
  Charleston: 4584
  Chesterfield County: 4996
  Edisto Island: 5661
  Laurens: 3531
  Spartanburg: 1745
PLANTATION MANAGEMENT: 1553, 3124
  see also SOUTH CAROLINA--OVERSEERS
  Colleton County: 4649
  Stateburg: 4217
PLANTATION RESTORATION: 4619
PLANTATION STORE ACCOUNTS:
  Richland County: 1965
PLANTATIONS: 842, 881, 1472, 1923, 1944, 2030, 2503, 2596, 3801
  see also the following subheadings under SOUTH CAROLINA: AGRICULTURE, and subheadings beginning with the word AGRICULTURAL; COTTON PLANTATIONS; CROPS, and names of specific crops; FARMING, and subheadings beginning with the word FARM; RICE PLANTATIONS
  Business affairs:
    Edisto Island: 4725
    Spartanburg: 1745

SOUTH CAROLINA

PLANTATIONS (Continued):
  Finance: 1101
  Sale of: 1012
  Subdivided by place:
    Barnwell County: 2805
    Charleston: 2695, 3116, 5936
    Edisto Island: 4896
    Kershaw County: 2940
    Pendleton: 3278
    Sumter District: 4460
POETRY: 2045
  see also SOUTH CAROLINA--POLITICAL POETRY
  Collections: 1889
POLICE:
  see also SOUTH CAROLINA--CONSTABLES
  Negroes--Orangeburg: 3037
POLITICAL PATRONAGE: 521, 633, 1478, 2278, 2613, 3451, 4316
POLITICAL POETRY--Charleston: 5074
POLITICAL THEORY: 2290
POLITICS AND GOVERNMENT:
  see also the following subheadings under SOUTH CAROLINA: CORRUPTION IN POLITICS; COUNTY GOVERNMENT; LABOR IN POLITICS; LOCAL POLITICS; NEGROES IN POLITICS; SOCIAL AND POLITICAL REFORM
  1700s: 3304
  1700s-1800s: 842, 3287
  1800s: 561, 1877, 3405, 3415, 5271
  1810s: 4269
  1820s: 529, 2449, 3366, 4269
  1830s: 1891, 2449, 3162, 3366, 4080
  1840s: 1891, 3162, 3366, 4080, 5270
  1850s: 2695, 2880, 4272, 5270, 5863
  1860s: 791, 1220, 1424, 2107, 2695, 2831, 3615, 4193, 4272
  1870s: 300, 669, 791, 1220, 1424, 2595, 3615, 5893
  1880s: 300, 1927
  1890s: 300, 5299
  1800s-1900s: 501, 566, 2473, 2866, 4068, 4460
  1900s: 3048, 3451
  1910s: 3383, 4453
  1920s: 2109, 3383, 4453
  1930s: 2109, 3383, 4453
  Appointments: 1562
  Blease movement: 300
  Tillmanism: 300, 5759
POSTAL SERVICE:
  see also SOUTH CAROLINA--RAILROADS--Mail service
  Confederate post offices: 1181
  Obscene mail: 2109
POVERTY:
  see also SOUTH CAROLINA--RURAL POOR
  Chester District: 1268
PRAYERS: 2961
PREACHING--Negro women: 2762
PRESBYTERIAN CHURCHES: 3123, 3371, 4031, 4145, 4453
  Baptism: see SOUTH CAROLINA--BAPTISM--Presbyterian churches
  Clergy: see SOUTH CAROLINA--CLERGY--Independent Presbyterian/Presbyterian
  Education: 4609
    see also SOUTH CAROLINA--SCHOOLS--Mission schools--Presbyterian
  Membership--Chester: 5988
  Religious literature: see SOUTH CAROLINA--RELIGIOUS LITERATURE--Presbyterian
  Sermons: see SOUTH CAROLINA--SERMONS--Presbyterian
  Subdivided by place:
    Camden: 4642
    Charleston: 4936
    Enoree Presbytery: 3527
    Greenville: 5825

SOUTH CAROLINA

PRESIDENTIAL ELECTION OF 1876: 3405
PRESIDENTIAL PARDONS: 5863
PROHIBITION: 300
   see also SOUTH CAROLINA--TEMPERANCE
PROMISSORY NOTES: 4509
PROPERTY DAMAGE--Charleston: 4216
PROSTITUTION: 150
PROTESTANT EPISCOPAL CHURCHES: 883, 4271, 4358
   Charleston: 4637
   Clergy: see SOUTH CAROLINA--
     CLERGY--Protestant Episcopal
   Doctrine: 3666
   Negro members: 89
   Sermons: see SOUTH CAROLINA--
     SERMONS--Protestant Episcopal
PUBLIC FINANCE: 565
   Hampton County: 5759
PUBLIC SCHOOLS:
   Saint Luke's Parish: 4961
PUBLISHERS AND PUBLISHING: 1424, 2473
QUIT RENT: 3347
RACE RELATIONS: 300, 2595, 5645
   see also the following subheadings
     under SOUTH CAROLINA: CIVIL
     RIGHTS; KU KLUX KLAN; RACE
     RIOTS; RELIGION--Race relations;
     SEGREGATION
RACE RIOTS--Hamburg: 1220
RAILROAD BONDS: 4673
RAILROAD TELEGRAPHERS: see SOUTH
   CAROLINA--WAGES AND SALARIES--
   Railroad telegraphers
RAILROADS:
   see also SOUTH CAROLINA--TRAVEL--
     Railroads
   1800s: 2107, 3317, 4145
   1850s: 2695
   1860s: 565, 2695, 3035, 4673
   1890s: 1480
   1800s-1900s: 2473
   Construction: 718, 1466
     Slave labor: 4460
   Finance: 3035, 4673
     Charleston: 5271
   Freight rates: 3035
   Legal affairs: 3893
   Mail service: 3035
   Right of way: 4830
   Subdivided by place:
     Greenville: 3317
REAL ESTATE: 997, 1468, 1891, 2290, 4118, 5548
   Investments: 300, 3421
     Charleston: 4214
REAL ESTATE BUSINESS:
   Abbeville: 3527
RECONSTRUCTION: 45, 1220, 2107, 2300, 2376, 2449, 2616, 2831, 2854, 3405, 4334, 4453, 4460, 4834, 4996, 5340, 5759
   Corruption: 5893
   Economic conditions: 791, 2210, 2376, 2473, 3801
   Federal military occupation: 1282, 4118, 4808, 5193
   Journalism: 1424
   Redemption: 1424, 2300
"RED SHIRTS": 5759
RELATIONS (general) WITH GEORGIA: 5537
RELIGION:
   see also the following subheadings
     under SOUTH CAROLINA:
     EVANGELISM; NEGROES--Religion;
     SLAVES--Religion; and names of
     specific denominations
   1750s: 5699
   1800s: 2290, 2930
   1820s: 4609
   1830s: 4609
   1850s: 4272
   1860s: 883, 4272
   Race relations: 669

SOUTH CAROLINA

RELIGION (Continued):
   Subdivided by place:
     Charleston: 2695, 4584
     Chester: 5988
     Columbia: 2636
     Laurens: 2616
RELIGIOUS LITERATURE:
   Episcopal: 2670
   Presbyterian: 4031
REPUBLICAN PARTY:
   1860s: 5340
   1870s: 1972, 5893
   1900s: 521
RHYMES: 3418
RICE: 295, 1803, 5114
   Irrigation machinery: 1524
RICE PLANTATIONS: 297, 1682, 2161, 5193, 5661
   Labor problems: 3485
   Management: 3485
ROADS: 158, 2488, 3044
   Construction: 3383
     Slave labor: 4460
   Maintenance and repair: 3383
RURAL POOR: 666
SALT WORKS: 881
SAWMILL ACCOUNTS: 1749, 4434
SAWMILLS: 1927
   Branchville: 1749
SCHOOL BOARDS:
   Saint Luke's Parish: 4961
SCHOOL LIFE: 300
SCHOOLS: 501, 4118
   see also the following subheadings
     under SOUTH CAROLINA: EDUCATION;
     MILITARY SCHOOLS; PUBLIC SCHOOLS;
     STUDENTS AND STUDENT LIFE;
     TEACHERS' RECORDS; TEACHING
   Attendance: 1927
   Curriculum:
     Columbia: 566
     Edgefield: 5312
     Winnsboro: 566
   Discipline:
     Columbia: 566
     Winnsboro: 566
   Girls' schools and academies: 4118, 5082
     Barhamville: 3527
     Charleston:
       Madame Talvande's School: 4622
       Misses Bates' School: 1651
     Greenville: 4911, 5082
     Spartanburg:
       Spartanburg Female Academy: 2854
       Spartanburg Female Seminary: 561
   Mission schools:
     Catawba Indians: 3356
     Presbyterian: 1923
   Negro schools:
     see also SOUTH CAROLINA--TEACHING--
       Negro schools
     Attendance: 1927
     Beaufort: 3218
     Civil War: 1477
   Tuition: 4118
   Subdivided by place:
     Calhoun: 5082
     Charleston: 2940
       Edmond's School: 219
     Chesterfield: 2855
     Cokesbury: 5114
     Denmark: 5572
     Greenville: 3405
     Orangeburg: 501
     Society Hill: 4634
     Spartanburg: 561
     Winnsboro: 5193
SECESSION AND SECESSIONIST SENTIMENT: 150, 561, 791, 1468, 1877, 2210, 2300, 2695, 2805, 4193, 4445, 4783, 5242, 5361, 5415, 5753, 5901
SEED PRODUCTION: 4610
SEGREGATION: 300

SOUTH CAROLINA

SENATORIAL ELECTIONS:
   1846: 4445
   1857: 1403
   1894: 5299
   1908: 5930
   1924: 1478, 3451, 5930
   1930: 3451
SERMONS: 3552
   Baptist: 669
   Presbyterian: 4936
   Protestant Episcopal: 3666
SHIPPING:
   American Revolution: 2019
   Coastwise shipping: 4304
   Charleston: 2959
SHIPWRECKS: 3808
SILVER MINES AND MINING: 2541
SILVER QUESTION: 2473
SLAVE TRADE:
   1700s: 2019
   1700s-1800s: 2300, 3981
   1800s: 1877, 2290, 2961, 4649, 5759
   1800s: 2636
   1810s: 2636
   1840s: 2670, 3801
   1850s: 2670, 3801
   1860s: 2670, 3371, 3801
   Prices: 2290, 3709, 4649, 4834, 5936
   Charleston: 1745
   Transatlantic: 2094
   Subdivided by place:
     Charleston: 2017, 3589
     Edgefield District: 2599
     Sumter: 3676, 3795
SLAVERY: 150, 561, 718, 2210, 2473, 2503, 2940, 3801, 3981
   Laws and legislation: 3981
   Southern opinion: 5193
   Subdivided by place:
     Charleston: 2695
SLAVERY AND THE CHURCH: 4912
SLAVES: 2503, 2880, 3123
   see also SOUTH CAROLINA--
     FUGITIVE SLAVES; SOUTH CAROLINA--
     HIRING OF SLAVES
   Behavior: 1877, 3485
   Clothing and dress: 1891, 1923
   Division of ownership:
     Edisto Island: 3664
   Duties: 3801
     Hampton County: 4534
     Laurens: 3531
   Emancipation: 758
   Expenses incidental to their keep:
     Greenville: 653
   Food: 297, 1923
   Health: 4534
   Insurrections: 2210, 2449
     Camden: 1012
     Charleston: 2289
     Marlboro District: 2267
     Union District: 4434
   Lawsuits over ownership: 4399, 4623
   Lists: 2670, 4214, 5548
     Charleston: 295
     Stateburg: 4217
   Loyalty: 1793
   Medical treatment: 3485
   Missionaries to: 669
   Quarters: 5193
   Relations with masters: 3531
   Religion:
     Charleston: 4912
     Greenville District: 3669
   Supplies: 297, 1891
   Treatment: 2670, 2695, 3981
   Vital statistics: 1923, 3801
SOAP AND COSMETICS MANUFACTURE:
   Union: 4918
SOCIAL CONDITIONS: 3012

SOUTH CAROLINA

SOCIAL LIFE AND CUSTOMS:
   1700s-1800s: 4839
   1700s-1900s: 842
   1800s: 1889, 2115, 2210
      1820s: 158
      1850s: 2094
      1860s: 1927
      1870s: 300
      1880s: 300
      1890s: 300
   1800s-1900s: 543
   1900s: 2161
   Charleston:
      1800s: 2959, 3485
      1810s: 2959, 3485
      1820s: 2959, 3485
      1840s: 4596
      1860s: 686
      1880s: 4271
   Spartanburg: 1745
   "Up-country": 3485
   Walterboro: 2828
SOCIETIES AND CLUBS:
   see also the following subheadings under SOUTH CAROLINA: BUSINESS CLUBS; COUNTRY CLUBS; DEBATING SOCIETIES; HISTORICAL SOCIETIES; IMMIGRATION SOCIETIES; LITERARY SOCIETIES; PATRIOTIC SOCIETIES; TEMPERANCE SOCIETIES; WOMEN'S SOCIETIES AND CLUBS
   Charleston: 2040
   Society Hill: 4634
SOCIETY OF FRIENDS:
   Bush River: 3981
SOCIETY OF THE CINCINNATI: 4215
   Charleston: 4584
SONGS AND MUSIC: 5503
   see also SOUTH CAROLINA--CHURCH MUSIC
SOUTHERN UNIONISTS: see CIVIL WAR--SOUTHERN UNIONISTS
SPELLING EXERCISE BOOKS:
   Charleston: 4271
STAGECOACH LINES: 2289
   Service: 2696
STATE DEBT: 3405
STATES' RIGHTS: 300, 3366, 5361
STEAMBOAT LINES: 853
STORMS:
   see also SOUTH CAROLINA--HURRICANES
   John's Island: 3164
STRIKES:
   Textile workers:
      Woodside Mills: 5236
   Typographical workers: 2771
STUDENTS AND STUDENT LIFE: 1472, 1480
   see also SOUTH CAROLINA--SCHOOLS
   Accounts: 2930
   Compositions: 3801
   Parents' letters: 3790, 5193
      Charleston: 2144
      Columbia: 566
      Winnsboro: 566
SUFFRAGE: 2695
   see also SOUTH CAROLINA--NEGROES--Suffrage; SOUTH CAROLINA--WOMAN SUFFRAGE
SUGAR GROWING: 4988
SURVEYS AND SURVEYING: 1480, 3386, 3802, 4145
   Charleston: 4216, 5198
   Orangeburg District: 5015
TARIFF--Public opinion: 150
TAX COLLECTORS--Charleston: 4213
TAX IN KIND: 3044, 3801
TAX LISTS: 5548
   Lexington County: 4610
TAX RECEIPTS: 2709, 4649
   Chesterfield County: 4996
TAXATION: 1877
   see also SOUTH CAROLINA--TOBACCO TAX
TEACHERS' RECORDS: 4118
   Charleston: 1017

SOUTH CAROLINA

TEACHING: 2032
   see also the following subheadings under SOUTH CAROLINA: EDUCATION; GOVERNESSES; SCHOOLS; WAGES AND SALARIES--Teachers
   Negro schools: 1927
      see also SOUTH CAROLINA--SCHOOLS--Negro schools
   Beaufort: 3218
TEMPERANCE: 543, 2473, 3123, 4434
   see also SOUTH CAROLINA--PROHIBITION
   Spartanburg: 4080
TEMPERANCE SOCIETIES: 4610
TEXTILE INDUSTRY: 300, 4918, 5236, 5237
   Stocks: 300
   Subdivided by place:
      Charleston: 1009
      Spartanburg: 5233
TEXTILE WORKERS:
   see also the following subheadings under SOUTH CAROLINA: LABOR DISPUTES; LABOR UNIONS--Textile workers; STRIKES--Textile workers; WAGES AND SALARIES--Textile workers
   Labor arbitration: 5233
THEOLOGICAL SEMINARIES: see COLUMBIA THEOLOGICAL SEMINARY
TINSMITHING: 1575
TOBACCO PRICES: 817
TOBACCO TAX: 817
TRADE AND COMMERCE:
   see also SOUTH CAROLINA--FOREIGN TRADE; SOUTH CAROLINA--SHIPPING
   Agricultural products: 4217
   Bricks: 3123
   Cane reeds: 3230
   Cloth: 1889
   Clothing: 1480
   Cotton: see SOUTH CAROLINA--COTTON TRADE
   Fertilizer: 4530
   Garden seeds: 3304
   Grain: 60
   Groceries: 46
   Hay: 60
   Iron pipe: 3230
   Liquor: 2793, 5299
      Regulation: 5299
   Lumber: 1935, 2106, 3123, 4509
   Naval stores: 2586
      Charleston: 987
   Potatoes: 3230
   Rice: 545, 1524, 4509, 5114
      Charleston: 2107
      Exports to Great Britain: 3230
   Rum: 1935
   Salt: 3230
   Slaves: see SOUTH CAROLINA--SLAVE TRADE
   Staves: 3230
   Stoneware: 3230
   Tar: 1935
   Tobacco: 500, 817
      Charleston: 5228
   Turpentine: 3123
   Wine: 1935
      Charleston: 2107
   Wood: 430
TRAFFIC ACCIDENTS:
   Lawsuits: 5930
TRANSPORTATION: 669, 3447
TRAVEL--Railroads: 2503
TURPENTINE INDUSTRY--Camden: 2940
TYPOGRAPHICAL WORKERS:
   Labor arbitration: 2771
UNION LEAGUE: 4118
UNIONIZATION: 1196
   see also SOUTH CAROLINA--LABOR UNIONS
UNITED STATES BUREAU OF REFUGEES, FREEDMEN AND ABANDONED LANDS: 3405
UNIVERSALIST CHURCHES: see SOUTH CAROLINA--CLERGY--Universalist

SOUTH CAROLINA

UNIVERSITIES AND COLLEGES: 300, 561, 1424, 1877
   see also BEAUFORT COLLEGE; THE CITADEL; CLEMSON UNIVERSITY; COKER COLLEGE; COLLEGE OF CHARLESTON; CONVERSE COLLEGE; ERSKINE COLLEGE; FURMAN UNIVERSITY; GREENWOOD FEMALE COLLEGE; LIMESTONE COLLEGE; NEWBERRY COLLEGE; SPARTANBURG FEMALE COLLEGE; UNIVERSITY OF SOUTH CAROLINA; WINTHROP COLLEGE; WOFFORD COLLEGE
   Commencement addresses: 2880
   Students and student life:
      Finance: 3044
      Lists: 1480
   Subdivided by place:
      Cambridge: 2636
VENDUE MASTERS--Charleston: 2019
VITAL STATISTICS: 4310
   see also SOUTH CAROLINA--SLAVES--Vital statistics
   Charleston: 4584
VOTING REGISTERS:
   Lexington County: 4610
WAGES AND SALARIES:
   Agricultural workers: 2961
   Clergy: 150
   Electricians--Columbia: 2767
   Freedmen: 4649
   Railroad telegraphers: 3985
   Teachers: 1927
   Textile workers: 5236
      Spartanburg: 5233
   Typographical workers: 2771
   Subdivided by place:
      Charleston: 3230
WEATHER: 1923, 5991
   Camden: 5675
   Charleston: 4584
   Lancaster County: 4310
   Society Hill: 2762
WEAVING AND SPINNING: 4347
WEDDINGS: 4823, 5193
   Charleston: 686
WHIG PARTY: 5271
WILDLIFE CONSERVATION: 4453
WILLS:
   see also SOUTH CAROLINA--ESTATES--Administration and settlement
   1700s: 758
   1700s-1800s: 842, 5193
   1700s-1900s: 2961
   1800s: 3801
   1800s-1900s: 4649
   Charleston: 2556, 4214, 5198
WOMAN SUFFRAGE: 300, 2473
WOMAN'S CHRISTIAN TEMPERANCE UNION: 2473
WOMEN:
   Personal finance--Charleston: 1891
WOMEN IN THE CIVIL WAR: 2473
   Spartanburg: 4912
WOMEN POETS: 2045
WOMEN'S SOCIETIES AND CLUBS: 4642
WOOLEN MILLS: 3754

[End of entries under SOUTH CAROLINA]

SOUTH CAROLINA AGRICULTURAL SOCIETY: 4896
SOUTH CAROLINA AUDUBON SOCIETY: 4453
SOUTH CAROLINA BAPTIST HISTORICAL SOCIETY: 2402
SOUTH CAROLINA BUILDING AND CONSTRUCTION TRADES ASSOCIATION: 5411
SOUTH CAROLINA FEDERATION OF LABOR: 4962
   Conventions: 4094
THE SOUTH CAROLINA FEDERATIONIST: 4962
SOUTH CAROLINA FREE SCHOOL FUND: 1927

SOUTH CAROLINA IN AMERICAN
    LITERATURE: 5901
SOUTH CAROLINA INTER-STATE AND WEST
    INDIAN EXPOSITION: 2473
SOUTH CAROLINA LABOR NEWS: 5411
SOUTH CAROLINA LAND COMMISSION: 1480
SOUTH CAROLINA MEDICAL ASSOCIATION:
    3405
SOUTH CAROLINA POWER COMPANY: 2768
SOUTH CAROLINA SCHOOL FOR THE DEAF,
    DUMB, AND BLIND: 300
SOUTH DAKOTA:
    see also MIDDLE WEST; PLAINS
        STATES
    Mines and mining: 5791
    Social life and customs: 2838
SOUTH GUILFORD CIRCUIT, Methodist
    churches: 3646
SOUTH HAMPSHIRE, England:
    Elections: 5038
SOUTH ISLAND, South Carolina: 2512
    Confederate Army camp: 2187
SOUTH LONDONDERRY, Vermont: 857
SOUTH LOWELL, North Carolina:
    Mercantile accounts: 3140
SOUTH LOWELL ACADEMY, Durham County,
    North Carolina: 4862
SOUTH MATTAMUSKEET PRIMITIVE BAPTIST
    CHURCH, Hyde County, North
    Carolina: 4963
SOUTH MILL CREEK BAPTIST CHURCH
    (West Virginia): 2129
SOUTH MILLS, North Carolina: see
    CIVIL WAR--CAMPAIGNS, BATTLES,
    AND MILITARY ACTIONS--North
    Carolina--South Mills
SOUTH MOUNTAIN, Maryland: see CIVIL
    WAR--CAMPAIGNS, BATTLES, AND
    MILITARY ACTIONS--Maryland
    South Mountain
SOUTH NORWALK, Connecticut: 688
SOUTH RIVER, Virginia:
    Miller's accounts: 210
SOUTH SEA ISLANDS:
    Missions and missionaries: 4850
    Social life and customs: 4850
SOUTH TEXAS COTTON GROWERS ASSOC.:
    592
SOUTH WEYMOUTH, Massachusetts: 5677
SOUTH YARMOUTH, Massachusetts:
    Teaching: 2436
SOUTHALL, Sallie: 4425
SOUTHAMPTON, England: 4760
SOUTHAMPTON COUNTY, Virginia: 2946,
    2967
    Farming: 5248
    Real estate: 5248
    Cities and towns:
        Berlin: 5824
        Boykins Depot: 1393
        Courtland: 4531
        Franklin:
            Civil War: 1498
                see also CIVIL WAR--CAMPAIGNS,
                    BATTLES, AND MILITARY
                    ACTIONS--Virginia--Franklin
        Newson's Depot: 4268
SOUTHARD, Samuel Lewis: 4964, 5546
SOUTHBOROUGH, Massachusetts:
    Schools: 1423
SOUTHBRIDGE, Massachusetts: 1699
SOUTHEAST ASIA: see FRENCH INDOCHINA;
    GREAT BRITAIN--FOREIGN RELATIONS--
    France--Rivalry in Southeast Asia;
    INDOCHINA
SOUTHEASTERN COAL MERCHANTS
    ASSOCIATION: 4865
SOUTHEASTERN COUNCIL: 5252
SOUTHEASTERN FOREST EXPERIMENT
    STATION: 1852
SOUTHEASTERN UNITED STATES: see
    SOUTHERN STATES
SOUTHERN APPALACHIAN COAL OPERATORS'
    ASSOCIATION: 4865
SOUTHERN BAPTIST CONVENTION: 1476,
    5401

SOUTHERN BAPTIST CONVENTION
    (Continued):
    Foreign Mission Board: 561
    South China Mission: 1940
SOUTHERN BIOGRAPHY SERIES: 5054
SOUTHERN CHURCHMAN: 1565
SOUTHERN COAL COMPANY: 4865
SOUTHERN COMMERCIAL CONGRESS: 4560
SOUTHERN COMMERCIAL CONVENTION: 3302
SOUTHERN CONFERENCE EDUCATIONAL
    FUND: 1197, 3558
SOUTHERN CONFERENCE FOR HUMAN
    WELFARE: 1196, 5486
SOUTHERN CONFERENCE ON WOMEN AND
    CHILDREN IN INDUSTRY: 5406
SOUTHERN DEMOCRATIC PARTY (1930s): 300
SOUTHERN ECONOMIC COUNCIL: 3447
SOUTHERN EDUCATIONAL ASSOCIATION:
    3473
SOUTHERN EXPRESS COMPANY, Richmond,
    Virginia: 4965
SOUTHERN FELLOWSHIPS FUND: 1258
SOUTHERN FERTILIZER COMPANY,
    Richmond, Virginia: 1587, 4344
SOUTHERN HISTORICAL ASSOCIATION:
    5054
SOUTHERN HISTORICAL SOCIETY: 1624,
    3809
SOUTHERN INDEX: 1677
SOUTHERN LITERARY FESTIVAL: 1771
SOUTHERN LITERARY MESSENGER: 3163,
    3809, 4616, 5193, 5691
SOUTHERN MASONIC FEMALE COLLEGE: 1434
SOUTHERN METHODIST RECORDER: 879
SOUTHERN METHODIST UNIVERSITY,
    Dallas, Texas: 31
SOUTHERN MUTUAL INVESTMENT CO.,
    Lexington, Kentucky: 4241
SOUTHERN OPINION: see as subheading
    under specific subjects
SOUTHERN PACIFIC RAILROAD: 707, 3793
SOUTHERN PATRIOT (periodical): 4149
SOUTHERN PINES, North Carolina:
    Convalescent homes: 3633
SOUTHERN PRESBYTERIAN REVIEW
    (newspaper): 4031
SOUTHERN QUARTERLY (periodical): 3659
"SOUTHERN QUESTION" by Charles E. A.
    Gayarre: 2465
SOUTHERN RAILROAD COMPANY: 163, 4596,
    4736, 4881
SOUTHERN REGIONAL COUNCIL, INC.: 1198,
    1202, 3558
SOUTHERN REVIEW (periodical): 2449,
    5217
SOUTHERN SCHOOL FOR WORKERS, INC.:
    1194, 1197, 1198, 3558, 5234
SOUTHERN SHORT LINE RAILROAD
    CONFERENCE: 238
"SOUTHERN SONGS" by Catherine Ann
    (Ware) Warfield: 5557
SOUTHERN STATES: 1170, 2616, 4520
    see also names of specific
        southern states
    Abolition of slavery and
        abolitionist sentiment: 284, 872
    Agriculture: 608, 1423
        Dependence on cotton: 5862
    Agriculture and industry: 5530
    American literature: 72, 1494,
        2449, 2451, 3418, 4402
    American poetry: 1494, 2451
    Attitudes toward Northerners: 284
    Auctions: 3809
    Baraca movement: 4828
    Birds: 4453
    Booksellers and bookselling: 5082
    Business affairs: 1553
    Church buildings: 1589
    Clergy: 3277
    Commercial conventions: 3302
    Commodity prices: 2078, 3873
        see also CIVIL WAR--COMMODITY
            PRICES--Southern States
    Cotton: 311, 605
        Prices: 1460
    Cotton growing: 1460, 5862

SOUTHERN STATES (Continued):
    Cotton mills: 3196
    Cotton plantations: 284
    Cotton trade: 565, 4434
    Crops: 2427
        Prices: 2427
    Demagogues: 872
    Democratic Party: 1972
    Description and travel:
        1800s: 1115
        1810s: 2047
        1820s: 2047
        1830s: 3490
        1840s: 284, 3490, 3570, 4596
        1850s: 1748, 3277
        1860s: 155, 3424, 5082, 5261
        1900s:
            1900s: 5572
            1950s: 1137
    Diseases--Scarlet fever: 5349
    Dueling: 3873
    Economic conditions:
        1800s:
            1850s: 5940
            1860s: 266, 1523, 3251, 5940
            1870s: 3251
        1900s:
            1900s: 4560
            1930s: 2768
            1940s: 2768
            1950s: 2768
    Economic importance to the
        Confederation: 5537
    Education: 611, 731, 1460, 2612,
        4373, 4720
    Episcopal churches: 761
    Estates:
        Administration and settlement:
            1553, 4711
    Farming: 761
    Fiction: 3418
    Foreign relations:
        Great Britain: 4383
    Foreign trade: 1687
    Forest conservation: 1852
    Freedmen:
        Behavior: 2893, 3809
    Guano: 1423
    Historical studies: 2465
    Horse racing: 3873
    Hours of labor: 3558
    Labor and religion: 3558
    Labor conditions: 3558
    Labor publication: 3558
    Labor supply: 1101
    Labor unions: 3558, 3706, 4094
        see also AMERICAN FEDERATION OF
            LABOR; CONGRESS OF INDUSTRIAL
            ORGANIZATIONS
    Contracts: 2769
    Love letters: 2691, 4373
    Medical practice: 5505
    Methodist churches: 731
    Monuments: 3657
    Natural history: 2047
    Negroes: 2449, 2616, 3277
        Education: 3558
        Religion: 3277
        Social status: 2121
        Suffrage: 1466, 3809
    Northern opinion of: 1408, 2677,
        3308, 5311
    Overseers: 5940
    Patrons of husbandry: 4434
    Peddlers and peddling: 3196
    Philanthropy: 3558
    Plantation management: 3053
    Plantations: 5940
    Poetry:
        see also SOUTHERN STATES IN POETRY
        Collections: 3611
    Politics and government:
        1800s:
            1800s: 3873
            1810s: 3873
            1820s: 3873

SOUTHERN STATES:
  Politics and government:
    1800s (Continued):
      1840s: 1460
      1860s: 1364, 1468, 5853
      1870s: 1364, 1468, 5853
    1900s:
      1900s: 4048
  Poll tax: 4094
  Postal service: 3415
  Poverty: 2449, 4460, 5051, 5349, 5623
  Presbyterian churches: 761
  Printing: 3490
  Prison reform: 3558
  Public relations:
    Labor unions: 3558
  Pulp and paper industry: 1852
  Race relations: 2616, 3538, 3558, 3820, 3967
  Railroads: 1439, 4858
    Civil War: 3101, 4002, 4596, 5122
  Reconstruction: 266, 805, 983, 1060, 1115, 1191, 1364, 2370, 2475, 3251, 3262
    Northern philanthropy: 4358
  Relations with Northern States: 5717
  Religion: 132, 3277, 3873, 4932
    Race relations: 3558
  Republican Party: 706, 3262
  Resin: 605
  Rice plantations: 284
  Scholarships: 1258
  Secession and secessionist sentiment: 155, 3239
  Servants: 3048
  Silkworm culture: 761
  Slave trade: 5940
    Prices: 1460
  Slavery: 284, 1460, 2616, 3390, 4596
    Laws and legislation: 5940
  Slaves:
    Crime--Murder: 4434
    Religion: 4434
  Social conditions:
    1860s: 2361
    1870s: 3251
    1900s: 2768
  Social life and customs:
    1800s: 805
      Antebellum: 404, 1947
      Civil War: 4164
      Post-war: 5246
  States' rights: 1403
  Strikes: 3558
    Textile workers: 4094
  Surveys and surveying: 5480
  Teaching: 5043
  Telegraph: 1021
  Territorial expansion: 5498
  Textbooks: 3887
  Textile industry: 1612
    Company towns: 5310
  Tobacco: 1460
  Travel by railroad, stagecoach, and steamboat: 249, 284
  Unionization: 1202, 3066
  Unitarian churches: 429
  Universities and colleges: 2449, 4720
    Funds and scholarships: 1258
  Wages and salaries:
    Industrial workers: 3558
  Weather: 941, 1183, 2427, 3648, 4565, 5261
  Wills: 1556
SOUTHERN STATES FINANCE COMPANY: 4918
SOUTHERN STATES IN POETRY: 4180
SOUTHERN STUDENT ORGANIZING COMMITTEE: 613
SOUTHERN TEMPERANCE CONVENTION, Fayetteville, North Carolina: 1556
SOUTHERN TENANT FARMERS' UNION: 4948
SOUTHERN UNIONISTS: see CIVIL WAR--SOUTHERN UNIONISTS
SOUTHERN VULCANITE PAVING COMPANY, Savannah, Georgia: 4966

"THE SOUTHERN WAGON: CONFEDERATE AIR": 5032
SOUTHERNERS: see SOUTHERN STATES
SOUTHERNERS IN THE NORTH: 2469
SOUTHEY, Carolina (Bowles): 4967
SOUTHEY, Robert: 678, 4913, 4967
  Monuments: 3498
  Parodies: 3284
SOUTHGATE, Celestia Muse: 4968
SOUTHGATE, Delia Haywood (Wynne): 4968
SOUTHGATE, Harriet Sophia: 4968
SOUTHGATE, James: 4956, 4968
SOUTHGATE, James Haywood: 4968
SOUTHGATE, James Summerville: 4968
SOUTHGATE, Llewellyn: 4968
SOUTHGATE, Mattie Logan: 4968
SOUTHGATE, Myra Ann (Muse): 4968
SOUTHGATE FAMILY (North Carolina and Virginia--Genealogy): 4968
SOUTHPORT, North Carolina: 5826
  see also SMITHVILLE, North Carolina
SOUTHWELL, Edward: 4969
SOUTHWELL FAMILY (Great Britain): 4969
SOUTHWEST VIRGINIA INSTITUTE, Glade Springs, Virginia: 3788
SOUTHWESTERN STATES:
  see also WESTERN STATES
  Wells: 3248
SOUTHWESTERN UNIVERSITY, Memphis, Tennessee:
  Presidents: 4763
SOUTHWORTH, C. Eugene: 4970
SOUTHWORTH, Emma Dorothea Eliza (Nevitte): 4971
SOUTHWORTH, Fitzroy: 4970
SOUTHWORTH, J. P.: 4515, 4994
SOVEREIGNTY: 3096
  see also STATES' RIGHTS
SOWELL, Pleasant: 4975
SOWERS, Elizabeth: 4972
SOWLE, Charles H. (Indiana): 4973
SOWLE, Claude Raymond (Wisconsin): 4974
SOWLE FAMILY (Wisconsin): 4974
SPACE EXPLORATION: 83
SPAFFORD, Mrs. J. H.: 4976
SPAIGHT, Richard Dobbs (1758-1802): 730, 2776, 4977
SPAIGHT, Richard Dobbs (1796-1850): 730, 4669, 4977
SPAIN:
  see also entries beginning with the word SPANISH
  Agriculture: 5404
  Army:
    Peninsular War:
      Military activities: 1875, 5639
      Military supplies: 5639
  Belligerency in the West Indies: 92
  British embassy in: 2155
  Carlist War (1833-1840): see CARLIST WAR
  Citizenship: see DUAL CITIZENSHIP
  Civil War (1936-1939):
    Foreign public opinion: 4948
  Coins and coinage: 4980
  Colonial policy and administration:
    Latin America: 4979
    North America: 4979
    Philippine Islands: 4979
    West Florida: 3041
  Commercial treaties:
    Great Britain: 5639
  Confiscation of property:
    Slaves: 3109
    West Indies: 4980
  Customs duties:
    Collection in Cadiz: 4978
  Description and travel: 2811
    1800s: 1775
      1800s: 1875
      1880s: 1340
    1900s:
      1900s: 4022, 4719
      1920s: 2934
  Economic conditions: 2742
  Foreign aid to: see GREAT BRITAIN--FOREIGN AID--Spain

SPAIN (Continued):
  Foreign relations:
    Austria: 2155
    Great Britain:
      1700s:
        1710s: 2155
        1720s: 2155
        1730s: 2155, 2156, 5532
      1700s-1800s: 5726
      1800s:
        1800s: 5639
        1840s: 4881
    Portugal: 2155
    United States:
      1700s-1800s: 4982
      1700s-1900s: 4486
      1800s:
        1800s: 3041
        1820s: 3854
        1830s: 3854
        1840s: 4667
        1860s: 4808
      1800s-1900s: 1364, 4983
  Foreign trade: 2742
    Great Britain: 644, 2155, 4289
    Peru: 4155
    United States: 1481
  Gibraltar, Siege of: 2156
  Government agencies and officials:
    Diplomatic and consular service:
      United States: 4982
        Georgia: 4982, 4983
      Vatican: 4178
  Historical studies: 3549
  Immigration and emigration: see SPANISH IN FLORIDA
  Kidnapping: 2155
  Kings and rulers: 1340, 3549
    see also names of specific kings and rulers
  Legal affairs in South Carolina: 4982
  Literature: see SPANISH DRAMA; SPANISH LITERATURE; SPANISH POETRY
  Mercantile accounts--Cadiz: 4978
  Merchant seamen: 4982
  Military activities: 2155
  Military expeditions in Italy: 873
  Military posts--West Florida: 3041
  Monarchical government: 3312
  Nobility: 2055, 4981
  Oil industry: 1424
  Orleanists: 3238
  Passports: 4982
  Political satire: 4979
  Politics and government:
    1700s: 3312
    1800s: 2742, 4348, 4983
    1810s: 5282
    1830s: 4982
    1840s: 1424
  Public finance: 4978, 4980, 5639
  Railroad construction: 1632
  Real estate: 4980
  Revolution (1820): 5282
  Royal family:
    Guardianship and marriage of the Queen (1840s): 1424
    Weddings: 4213
  Schools:
    Primary schools in Cordoba: 4981
  Shipping: 4982
  Slave trade: 4913
    With colonies: 5726
    With Haiti: 4980
  Social life and customs (1880s): 1340
  Spanish-American War: see SPANISH-AMERICAN WAR
  Taxation: 4980
  Trade and commerce: 4980
    see also SPAIN--Shipping
    Fish: 2742
    Flax: 2742
    Slaves: see SPAIN--Slave trade
    Sugar: 197
    Tallow: 2742
    Tobacco: 2742
    Wheat: 2742
    Wool: 2742

SPAIN (Continued):
　Trade regulation: 586
　Treaties:
　　see also SPAIN--Commercial
　　　treaties
　　Netherlands: 3989
　War with Chile: 4982, 4983
　War with Peru: 4982, 4983
　Zoological expeditions: 4022
SPAINHOURD, Phoebe: 4984
SPAINHOURD, Robert: 4984
SPAINHOWER, S. B.: 1960
SPALDING, _____ (British publisher):
　5101
SPALDING, C. C.: 5252
SPALDING, Charles: 2963
SPALDING, Mrs. Charles: 4985
SPALDING, Evy (Kell): 2963
SPALDING, James: 4988
SPALDING, Lyman Dyer: 4062
SPALDING, Lyman Greenleafe (New
　Hampshire): 4986
SPALDING, Mary Anne Dora: 3472
SPALDING, Randolph: 2963
SPALDING, Samuel P.: 4987
SPALDING, Susan Parker (Parrott): 4062
SPALDING, Thomas (1774-1851): 2326,
　2963, 4988
SPALDING, Volney: 731
SPALDING FAMILY (Georgia): 2963
SPALDING AND THOMPSON (firm): see
　THOMPSON AND SPALDING
SPALDING COUNTY, Georgia:
　Civil War--Militia: 1189
　Cities and towns:
　　Griffin: 1476, 1672, 2909, 3414,
　　　3901
　　　Civil War: 493, 731
　　　Social life and customs: 5730
SPALDING GRAYS: 1189
SPANGLER, Edward: 5715
SPANISH-AMERICAN WAR (1898): 761,
　1054, 1128, 1364, 2849, 3008, 3149,
　3447, 3596, 3657, 3774
　see also UNITED STATES--ARMY--
　　Spanish-American War
　Campaigns, battles, and military
　　actions:
　　Cuba: 2991
　　　San Juan: 3552
　　　Santiago: 3552
　　Philippine Islands:
　　　Mindanao: 5844
　　Puerto Rico: 4485
　Civilian life:
　　Vermont: 4485
　Medical and sanitary affairs: 5759
　Pictorial works: 4227
　Reporters and reporting: 2849
　United States military assistance
　　to Cuba: 2991
　Veterans: 5559
　　Benefits: 325
　　Pensions: 4601, 4858, 4883
SPANISH DRAMA: 4138
SPANISH IN FLORIDA: 3733
SPANISH LITERATURE:
　Students' notebooks:
　　University of Virginia: 1379
SPANISH POETRY: 5404
SPANISH PRIVATEERS IN THE UNITED
　STATES: 4982
SPANISH WEST INDIES:
　Slave insurrections: 1913
SPARKS, Jared: 4359
SPARKS, Susanna: 2960
SPARKS FAMILY (Virginia): 4924
SPARROW, William: 128
SPARTA, Georgia: 239, 686, 1297, 2367,
　5565
　Clergy--Baptist: 4654
　Legal affairs: 5250
　Plantations: 4493
　Social conditions: 3134
SPARTA, North Carolina: 5641
SPARTANBURG, South Carolina: 561,
　1745, 1988, 2866, 3044, 4721, 4790,
　5970

SPARTANBURG, South Carolina
　(Continued):
　Business affairs: 5930
　Farming: 4080
　Industrialization: 4118
　Labor unions: 1196
　Legal affairs: 5930
　Public finance: 3893
　Schools:
　　Boys' schools and academies: 561
　　Girls' schools and academies:
　　　Spartanburg Female Academy:
　　　　2854
　　　Spartanburg Female Seminary:
　　　　561
　Temperance: 4080
　Textile mills: 5233
　Universities and colleges: see
　　CONVERSE COLLEGE; SPARTANBURG
　　FEMALE COLLEGE; WOFFORD COLLEGE
SPARTANBURG COUNTY, South Carolina:
　444
　County commissioners: 3044
　Exhibitions and fairs: 3893
　Land deeds and indentures: 4721
　Cities and towns:
　　Pacolet: 2477
　　Spartanburg: see SPARTANBURG,
　　　South Carolina
　　Woodruff: 1715
SPARTANBURG COUNTY (S.C.) FAIR
　ASSOCIATION: 3893
SPARTANBURG DISTRICT, Methodist
　churches: 3646
SPARTANBURG FEMALE ACADEMY,
　Spartanburg, South Carolina: 2854
SPARTANBURG FEMALE COLLEGE,
　Spartanburg, South Carolina: 219
　Student accounts: 3044
SPARTANBURG FEMALE SEMINARY,
　Spartanburg, South Carolina: 561
SPARTANBURG MALE ACADEMY,
　Spartanburg, South Carolina: 561
SPATEX CORPORATION, Mecklenburg
　County, North Carolina: 5235
SPAULDING, H. A.: 256
SPAULDING, Henry S.: 4989
SPAULDING, Ira: 4990
SPEAKING ENGAGEMENTS: see LECTURES
　AND LECTURING
SPEARS, John: 4103
SPEASE, A. J.: 5984
SPEASE, Adaline: 5984
SPECIE PAYMENTS:
　see also CURRENCY; and Public
　　finance as subheading under names
　　of governments
　Pennsylvania: 421
　Suspension of payments in North
　　Carolina: 3422
SPECK FAMILY (West Virginia): 2342
SPECULATION:
　see also AMERICAN REVOLUTION--
　　Speculation and war profiteering;
　　CIVIL WAR--SPECULATION AND WAR
　　PROFITEERING; COMMODITY
　　SPECULATION; COTTON--Speculation;
　　LAND SPECULATION; SALT
　　SPECULATION; STOCKS--Speculation
　Georgia: 3331
　Great Britain: 2148
　Southern States: 523
SPEEDWELL (British warship): 4102
SPEIGHT, Richard Harrison: 5150
SPEIR FAMILY (Great Britain and
　Australia): 286
SPEKE, Peter: 5639
SPELLING EXERCISE BOOKS:
　South Carolina--Charleston: 4271
SPELMAN, John: 5036
SPENCE, Ike: 4991
SPENCER, Aubrey George, Bishop of
　Jamaica: 4995
SPENCER, Cornelia (Philipps): 4992
SPENCER, Earl: 445
SPENCER, Eliza (Musson): 4995
SPENCER, Frank E.: 4993

SPENCER, George Eliphaz (1836-1893):
　4994
SPENCER, George Trevor (1799-1866):
　4995
SPENCER, George W. (South Carolina):
　4996
SPENCER, Georgiana: 945
SPENCER, Harriet Theodora (Hobhouse):
　4995
SPENCER, Herbert (1820-1903): 1603,
　2471, 4672, 4997
SPENCER, John Canfield (1788-1855):
　5546
SPENCER, John Charles, Third Earl
　Spencer: 1457, 4605
SPENCER, Jones: 511
SPENCER, Luther M.: 4998
SPENCER, Olivia E. (Patterson): 4998
SPENCER, Russell A.: 4519
SPENCER, Samuel: 5457
SPENCER, Virginia: 902
SPENCER, William Robert: 4066
SPENCER FAMILY: 4998
SPENCER, North Carolina: 5549
　Church and social problems: 4640
SPENCER ACADEMY, Doaksville, Arkansas:
　4373
SPERANZA, Gino: 4020
SPEROW, Benjamin F.: 4999
SPEROW, John E.: 4999
SPEROW, Rebecca: 4999
SPEROW, William: 4999
SPERRY, J. L.: 5000
SPERRYVILLE, Virginia: 1618
　Mercantile accounts: 3619
THE SPHERE (periodical): 2627
SPICE AND EXTRACT TRADE: 3190
　see also CINNAMON TRADE
SPICER, William Arnold: 5001
SPIES:
　see also AMERICAN REVOLUTION--
　　Spies; CIVIL WAR--SPIES; Foreign
　　agents as subheading under names
　　of specific countries
　Executions:
　　United States: 2276
　　Germans in the United States: 2188
　Women:
　　Confederate: 2180
　　　Executions: 4160
　　Union: 5268
　　Venezuela: 485
SPILLER, Robert Ernest: 102
SPINDLE, Emiline (Gold): 2080
SPINDLES:
　Manufacture in Virginia: 282
SPINKS, Enoch: 5002
SPINKS, John: 208, 5003
SPINKS FAMILY (North Carolina): 5002
SPINNING: see WEAVING AND SPINNING
"SPIRIT OF THE ARMY, LYNCHBURG, VA.,
　FEB. 25, 1865": 3809
SPIRITUAL LIFE:
　Great Britain: 4146
　Virginia: 5607
　　Catholicism: 3243
SPIRITUALISM: 3190, 5246
　see also SEANCES
　Florida: 1653
　Georgia: 339
　Indiana: 5149
　Ireland--Dublin: 3567
　Ohio: 5149
　Virginia: 958
SPOILS: see AMERICAN REVOLUTION--
　Spoils
SPORTS:
　see also BASEBALL; BOWLING; FOOTBALL;
　　GAMES; HUNTING
　Canada: 4175
SPOTLAND, England: 3715
SPOTSWOOD, Alexander: 5004, 5540
SPOTSWOOD, Ann Butler (Brayne): 2559
SPOTSYLVANIA COUNTY, Virginia:
　Civil War: see CIVIL WAR--CAMPAIGNS,
　　BATTLES, AND MILITARY ACTIONS--
　　Virginia--Spotsylvania County

933

SPOTSYLVANIA COUNTY, Virginia
    (Continued):
  Farming: 3141
  Wills: 5004
  Cities and towns:
    Fredericksburg: see FREDERICKSBURG,
      Virginia
    Germanna: 5004
    Twyman's Store: 4099
SPOTSYLVANIA COURT HOUSE, Virginia:
    see CIVIL WAR--CAMPAIGNS, BATTLES,
    AND MILITARY ACTIONS--Virginia--
    Spotsylvania Court House
SPOTTSWOOD, Virginia: 1591
SPRAGINS, Melchizedek: 5005
SPRAGINS, Melchizedek, Jr.: 5005
SPRAGINS, Rebecca: 5005
SPRAGINS, Robert Stith: 5006
SPRAGINS, Stith B.: 5007
SPRAGINS, Thomas S.: 5005
SPRAGUE, Charles James: 5754
SPRAGUE, Delphine: 5193
SPRAGUE, Horatio: 5193
SPRAGUE, John Titcomb: 1299, 5008
SPRAGUE, Kate (Chase): 2545
SPRAGUE, William (1830-1915): 2545,
    5009, 5172
SPRAGUE, William Buell (1795-1876):
    616, 872, 5010
SPRAGUE, Connecticut:
  Vital statistics: 1205
SPRAY WATER POWER AND LAND COMPANY:
    1584
SPRIGG, Samuel: 3728
SPRIGHT'S BRIGADE: 1138
"SPRING BROOK," New York: 2035
SPRING GARDEN, Pennsylvania: 744
SPRING GARDEN, Virginia: 2902
SPRING HILL, Tennessee: 5452
SPRING HILL FORGE: 5310
SPRING HOPE, North Carolina:
  Methodist Episcopal Church, South:
    5023
SPRING-RICE, Aubrey Richard: 5011
SPRING-RICE, Stephen Edward: 326
SPRING-RICE, Thomas, First Baron
    Monteagle of Brandon: 5011, 5277
SPRING-RICE, Thomas, Second Baron
    Monteagle of Brandon: 2149
SPRING WELLS, Michigan: 4411
SPRINGDALE, Ohio: 4160
SPRINGER, Nelson: 2627
SPRINGFIELD, Alabama: 3017
SPRINGFIELD, Georgia:
  Union Army depredations: 5991
SPRINGFIELD, Illinois: 1330, 3207
SPRINGFIELD, Kentucky: 4987
SPRINGFIELD, Massachusetts:
  Education: 5043
SPRINGFIELD, Missouri: 4174
  see also CIVIL WAR--CAMPAIGNS,
    BATTLES, AND MILITARY ACTIONS--
    Missouri--Springfield
SPRINGFIELD, North Carolina:
  Schools: 3117
SPRINGFIELD, Ohio: see WITTENBERG
    COLLEGE
SPRINGFIELD, Tennessee:
  Description: 5623
SPRINGS: see HEALTH RESORTS
SPRINGWATER, New York: 5738
SPRUCE PINE, North Carolina:
  Mica mining: 4918
SPRUCE PINE MICA COMPANY, INC.,
    Spruce Pine, North Carolina: 4918
SPRUILL, W. D.: 5012
SPRUILL, William A.: 5013
SPRUNT, Alexander (1815-1884): 2159,
    5014
SPRUNT, Alexander (1852-1937): 5014
SPRUNT, Alexander (b. 1898): 5014
SPRUNT (ALEXANDER) & SON, INC.: 2159,
    5014
SPRUNT, James (1847-1924): 2159, 5014
SPRUNT, Maggie T.: 2269
SPURR, Hannah: 2146
SQUATTERS--Kentucky: 1843
SQUIER, David: 5015

STABLER, Edward: 5016
STABLER, William: 5016
STABLES: see LIVERY STABLES
STACY, Walter P.: 1935
STAFFORD, Abby E.: 5017
STAFFORD, Granville Leveson-Gower,
    First Marquis: 4230
STAFFORD, Samuel McKinney: 5017
STAFFORD COUNTY, Virginia:
  Bedford: 1813
  Falmouth: 1790, 2165, 3105
    Union Army camp: 4608
STAFFORDSHIRE, England:
  Leek: 5553
  Peatswood: 5394
  Shugborough Hall: 190
  Tamworth: 4113
    Elections: 5330
  Teddesley Park: 3226
STAGE ADAPTATIONS:
  see also AMERICAN DRAMA; ENGLISH
    DRAMA; FRENCH DRAMA; SPANISH
    DRAMA; THEATER
  The Clansman by Thomas Dixon: 1521
STAGE MAIL SERVICE:
  Kentucky and Tennessee: 4854
STAGECOACH LINES:
  Business operations:
    Virginia: 1797
    West Virginia: 1797
  Fares--North Carolina: 1960
  Service--South Carolina: 2696
  Subdivided by place:
    Georgia: 2289
    Maryland: 166
    South Carolina: 2289
    Virginia: 5839
    West Virginia: 1797
STAGECOACHES: see STAGECOACH LINES;
    TRAVEL--Stagecoach
STAGG, James T.: 134
STALEY, Daniel L.: 5018
STALEY, Eborn: 5018
STALEY, John W.: 5018
STALEY, Lewis E.: 4453
STALKARTT, Marmaduke: 5019
STAMFORDHAM, Arthur John Bigge, First
    Baron: 1815
STAMP COLLECTING: see PHILATELY
STAMP DUTIES: see GREAT BRITAIN--
    COLONIAL POLICY AND ADMINISTRATION--
    American Colonies--Stamp duties;
    REVENUE STAMPS
STAMPS: see PHILATELY
STANARD, Robert: 5020
STANARD, Robert C.: 98, 5020
STANARDSVILLE, Virginia: 1401
STANBACK, P. N.: 5021
STANBACK, Thomas: 5021
STANBURY, Walter Albert (1884-1954):
    5022
STAND, England: 4850
STANDARD-COOSA-THATCHER COMPANY,
    Chattanooga, Tennessee: 1197
STANDARD OF FREEDOM (periodical):
    5244
STANDARD OIL COMPANY:
  Relations with China: 5252
STANDARDS, Bureau of: see UNITED
    STATES--GOVERNMENT AGENCIES AND
    OFFICIALS--National Bureau of
    Standards
STANDISH, Maine: 5955
STANDON, England: 4630
STANFIELD, Benjamin E.: 5023
STANFORD, Richard: 5457
STANFORD, Kentucky:
  Merchants: 299
STANHOPE, Arthur Philip, Sixth Earl
    Stanhope: 4230
STANHOPE, Edward (1840-1893): 2149,
    5024, 5806
STANHOPE, Leicester Fitzgerald
    Charles, Fifth Earl of Harrington:
    2421
STANHOPE, Lovell: 3304
STANHOPE, Philip Henry, Fourth Earl
    Stanhope: 1002, 4605

STANHOPE, William, First Earl of
    Harrington: 2155
STANISLAUS RIVER, California: 3750
STANLEY, Arthur Penrhyn: 306, 1910
STANLEY, Augusta Frederica Elizabeth
    (Bruce): 1910
STANLEY, Caroline Abbot: 2449
STANLEY, Edward George Geoffrey
    Smith, Fourteenth Earl of Derby:
    3472, 5025
STANLEY, Edward Henry, Fifteenth Earl
    of Derby: 2149, 2471, 3183, 3472,
    4995
STANLEY, Edward John, Second Baron
    Stanley of Alderley: 1632, 4605,
    5026, 5746
STANLEY, Elisha: 5593
STANLEY, Frederick Arthur, Sixteenth
    Earl of Derby: 4520
STANLEY, Sir Henry Morton: 5027
STANLEY, Thomas: 4072
STANLEY CREEK CIRCUIT, Methodist
    churches: 3646
STANLY, Alex C.: 692
STANLY, Edward: 4088
STANLY, John: 484
STANLY COUNTY, North Carolina:
  Albemarle: 3530
  Locust Level: 1312
  Norwood: 5589
STANSFIELD, William Rookes Crompton:
    1648
STANTON, Edwin McMasters: 2085, 5028,
    5432
STANTON, Frank Lebby: 2449, 5029
STANTON, Robert B.: 5030
STANTON FAMILY (Alabama, Indiana,
    Virginia): 4170
STANTON, North Carolina: 5965
STANTON, Tennessee: 45
STANTONSBURG, North Carolina: 2135
STAPLES, Abram Penn (1793-1856): 5031
STAPLES, Abram Penn (d. 1913): 5031
STAPLES, Ernest: 5028
STAPLES, Harris DeJarnett: 5031
STAPLES, Sallie Cushing (Hart): 5031
STAPLES, Samuel G.: 5031
STAPLES, Waller Redd: 5031
STAPP, Harriet C.: 5032
STAPP, Joseph D.: 5032
STAR, North Carolina:
  Lumber mills: 3225
"THE STAR OF THE COVENANT" by Stefan
    George: 1992
"THE STAR SPANGLED BANNER": 3220
STARBUCK, Samuel: 2542
STARK, Benjamin: 5033
STARK, Nathan: 2300
STARK COUNTY, Ohio:
  Navarre: 4245
STARKE, Aubrey Harrison: 3969
STARKE, Georgia (Harrison): 2374
STARKE, Nora-Belle: 2374
STARKE, William Pinckney: 2291
STARKEY, New York: 4680
STARK'S VOLUNTEERS (Civil War): 1189
STARKVILLE, Mississippi:
  Political rallies: 3611
STARNES, R. E.: 5441
STARR, Darius: 5034
THE STATE (South Carolina newspaper):
    2086
STATE ATTORNEYS: see as subheading
    under names of individual states
STATE BANK OF COLUMBIA, Virginia:
    5035
STATE BANK OF NORTH CAROLINA: 4100
  Fayetteville: 4517
  Salisbury: 1381
STATE BANKS: 2164
  see also BANKS AND BANKING
  Louisiana--New Orleans: 3274
  North Carolina: 4100
    Fayetteville: 4517
    Salisbury: 1381
STATE BAPTIST CONVENTIONS: see
    BAPTIST CHURCHES--State conventions

STATE BONDS--Virginia: 4589
STATE CORPORATION COMMISSION: 5035
STATE DEBT: see as subheading under
    names of individual states
    Federal assumption: see UNITED
       STATES--STATE DEBTS--Funding
STATE JOURNAL (North Carolina): 5036
STATE LANDS: see LAND
STATE LAWS, Compilation of: 667
STATE MILLS, Virginia: 3679
STATE NATIONAL BANK, Saint Louis,
    Missouri: 4063
STATE NATIONAL BANK, Raleigh, North
    Carolina: 2823
STATE NORMAL COLLEGE, Nashville,
    Tennessee: 5651
"STATE OF IRELAND" by Sir John
    Newport: 3883
STATE PAPERS AND CORRESPONDENCE
    ILLUSTRATIVE OF THE SOCIAL AND
    POLITICAL STATE OF EUROPE by
    John Mitchell Kemble: 2973
STATE POLICE:
    Connecticut: 1831
    New Jersey: 1831
    New York: 1831
    Pennsylvania: 1831
STATE RIGHTS PARTY:
    Georgia--Milledgeville: 5051
STATE TAXES: see Taxation as
    subheading under names of
    individual states
STATE VISITS: see as subheading under
    specific countries and locations
STATEBURG, South Carolina: 1472,
    3682, 3818
    Plantations: 4217
    Slaves: 4217
"A STATEMENT OF FAITH" by J. K. T.
    Smith: 4894
STATES' RIGHTS: 842, 4833, 5470
    Georgia: 1302, 5606
    South Carolina: 300, 3366, 5361
    Southern States: 1403
    Virginia: 569, 872, 5361
    Washington Territory: 5033
STATESMEN: see POLITICIANS
STATESVILLE, North Carolina: 893,
    1966, 3219, 3572, 3905
    Business affairs: 3688
    Churches: 1128
    Courts: 1128
    Girls' schools and academies: 5310
    Mercantile accounts: 1858
    Merchants: 8, 1856
    Methodist churches: 3646
    Universities and colleges: see
       CONCORD FEMALE COLLEGE;
       MITCHELL COLLEGE
STATESVILLE DISTRICT, Methodist
    churches: 3646
STATESVILLE FEMALE ACADEMY,
    Statesville, North Carolina: 5310
STATIONERY:
    see also PATRIOTIC STATIONERY
    Prices--Virginia: 3830
STATIONERY INDUSTRY:
    Mississippi--Natchez: 4309
STATIONERY TRADE:
    Connecticut: 2273
    North Carolina: 3186, 3416
    Virginia--Danville: 5196
STATISTICS: see Statistics and
    Vital statistics as subheadings
    under specific subjects
STATON, McGilvery M.: 5036
STATUS: see NEGROES--Social status;
    WOMEN--Social status
STATUTE OF LIMITATIONS: 2163
STAUBLY, Ralph F.: 5037
STAUNTON, Sir George Leonard, First
    Baronet: 3315, 5038
STAUNTON, Sir George Thomas, Second
    Baronet: 5038
STAUNTON FAMILY (Great Britain): 5038
STAUNTON, Virginia:
    1700s-1800s: 5184

STAUNTON, Virginia (Continued):
    1800s: 1542, 1601
    1810s: 1267
    1830s: 4766
    1840s: 2499, 4766
    1850s: 1720
    1860s: 1720
    1870s: 3489, 5120
    Circus: 1094
    Civil War: 1830
       see also CIVIL WAR--CAMPAIGNS,
          BATTLES, AND MILITARY ACTIONS--
          Virginia--Staunton
    Deaf--Education: 5298
    Girls' schools and academies: 5936
       Augusta Female Seminary: 2712
       Floral School: 2978
       Virginia Female Institute: 43,
          884, 5286
          Students and student life: 3832
    Poll book: 3215
    Stagecoach lines: 5839
    Universities and colleges: see
       MARY BALDWIN COLLEGE
    Woolen mills: 5039
STAUNTON WOOLEN FACTORY, Staunton,
    Virginia: 5039
STAVE TRADE:
    see also BARRELS AND BARREL STAVE
       TRADE; LUMBER TRADE
    Exports from North and South
       Carolina to Great Britain: 3230
    Virginia: 1512
STAVES: see BARRELS AND BARREL STAVES
STEAD, Benjamin: 4214
STEAD, William Thomas: 2146, 5262
STEADMAN, E.: 5040
STEAM ENGINES:
    Construction: 5546
    Marine: see MARINE ENGINES
    Operators--Mississippi: 3634
STEAM ENGINES TRADE:
    Pennsylvania: 5312
STEAM POWERED MACHINERY:
    Georgia: 4872
STEAM POWERED PLOWS: see PLOWS--
    Steam powered
STEAM POWERED ROAD VEHICLES: see
    ROAD VEHICLES--Steam powered
STEAM POWERED SAWMILLS: see SAWMILLS--
    Steam powered
STEAMBOAT LINES:
    Accounts: 3827
    Alabama: 1602
    Passengers:
       Legislation for protection of:
          5546
       Lists--Alabama River: 1602
    Subdivided by place:
       Georgia: 4895
       South Carolina: 853
STEAMBOAT OPERATORS' ACCOUNTS:
    North Carolina:
       Pamlico and Tar rivers: 3827
STEAMBOATS:
    see also RIVERBOATS; TRAVEL--
       Steamboats
    Accidents: 5623
    Construction: 3139, 5546
       see also SHIPBUILDING
    Explosions--Georgia: 2956
    Invention and development: 404, 581
    Subdivided by place:
       Alabama: 1602
       Atlantic Coast: 730
       Mississippi River: 4269
       North Carolina: 271
       Ohio River: 4269
STEAMSHIPS: see STEAMBOATS
STEARNS, Nellie F.: 5041
STEARNS FAMILY: 3295
STEBBINS, Charles: 5042
STEBBINS, Herman: 5042
STEBBINS, Laura W.: 5043
STEDLER, Peter: 1664
STEDMAN, Arthur: 103, 2449
STEDMAN, Edmund Clarence: 404, 2449,
    5044, 5322

STEDMAN, Thomas Lathrop: 2871
STEEDMAN, Charles: 5045
STEEDMAN, John: 5045
STEEL, Elizabeth (Maxwell) Gillespie:
    5457
STEEL, Robert E.: 111
STEEL INDUSTRY:
    see also IRON INDUSTRY
    Maryland--Baltimore: 1169
    New York: 1169
    Pennsylvania--Philadelphia: 1169
    United States: 3413
STEEL TRADE: 323
STEEL WORKERS: see LABOR UNIONS--
    Steel workers
STEELE, James H.: 5069
STEELE, John (1764-1815): 4746, 5046,
    5047
STEELE, John, Jr.: 5046
STEELE, LeRoy C.: 5048
STEELE, Marshall K.: 5048
STEELE, N. F.: 5048
STEELE, Samuel: 5047
STEELE FAMILY (North Carolina): 5048
STEELE BROS. CO., Mount Airy, North
    Carolina: 5048
STEFANSSON, Vilhjalmur: 4556
STEIN, Robert: 648
STEINER, Bernard Christian: 3384
STEM, Thaddeus Garland, Jr.: 5049
STEM, North Carolina:
    Landlord and tenant: 4464
STEPHEN, Harriet Marian (Thackeray):
    5050
STEPHEN, Sir James: 5011, 5277
STEPHEN, Josephine: 3993
STEPHEN, Julia Prinsep (Jackson)
    Duckworth: 5050
STEPHEN, Sir Leslie: 5050
STEPHENS, Alexander Hamilton: 1308,
    1333, 1422, 2280, 2449, 2860, 5051
STEPHENS, Ann Sophia (Winterbotham):
    5052
STEPHENS, George: 4918
STEPHENS, James: 5768
STEPHENS, Linton: 5051
STEPHENS, Mary: 5051
STEPHENS, Robert A.: 4589
STEPHENS, W. A.: 5053
STEPHENS, William Bacon: 4195
STEPHENSBURG, Virginia: 3255
STEPHENSON, Ann: 641
STEPHENSON, Wendell Holmes: 5054
STEPTOE, James C.: 5055
STEREOTYPE FOUNDRIES:
    see also TYPE FOUNDRIES
    New York--New York: 2677
STERLING, Ada: 1084
STERLING, Sir Anthony Coningham: 4549
STERLING COTTON MILLS, INC.,
    Franklinton, North Carolina: 5056
STERLINGVILLE, Pennsylvania: 4188
STETSON, Benjamin: 5057
STETSON, Joseph: 5058
STETSON & AVERY, New Orleans,
    Louisiana: 2456
STEUART, George Hume, Sr.: 5059
STEUART, George Hume, Jr. (1828-1903):
    5059
STEUBEN, Friedrich Wilhelm Ludolf
    Gerhard Augustin, Baron von: 3130,
    5575
STEUBEN COUNTY, Indiana:
    Salem Center: 808
STEUBEN COUNTY, New York: 2261, 4071
    Hammondsport: 5974
    Hornby--Legal affairs: 4645
    Hornellsville: 1380
    Orange--Legal affairs: 4645
    Urbanna: 5974
    Wayne: 4680
STEUBENVILLE, Ohio:
    Girls' schools and academies: 5380
STEUBENVILLE AND INDIANA RAIL ROAD:
    55
STEUBENVILLE FEMALE SEMINARY,
    Steubenville, Ohio: 5380
STEVENS, Ann: 208, 5060

STEVENS, Benjamin C.: 5061
STEVENS, Frank Lincoln: 2449
STEVENS, Frederick M.: 5062
STEVENS, Frederick Waeir: 5252
STEVENS, Jeduthan: 4125
STEVENS, Josiah B.: 1107
STEVENS, Needham: 1107
STEVENS, Sara: 5062
STEVENS, Thomas Holdup: 5063
STEVENS FAMILY (Georgia): 5760
STEVENS & ATHEARN, Boston, Massachusetts (firm): 2360
STEVENSBURGH, Virginia:
  Business affairs: 5113
STEVENSON, A. (Virginia): 2169
STEVENSON, Adlai Ewing: 1364
STEVENSON, Andrew: 872, 1359, 4616, 4880, 5065
STEVENSON, James C.: 5457
STEVENSON, John White: 5064
STEVENSON, Sarah (Coles): 5065
STEVENSON AND DODGE (firm): see DODGE AND STEVENSON MANUFACTURING COMPANY
STEVENSON AND PHELPS (firm): see PHELPS AND STEVENSON
STEWARD, John: 5066
STEWART, Alexander Peter: 1607, 5067
STEWART, Andrew Donaldson: 567
STEWART, Daniel: 1171
STEWART, David: 4348
STEWART, Sir Herbert: 5333
STEWART, J. W.: 5068
STEWART, John H.: 5069
STEWART, Luther Caldwell: 5070
STEWART, Robert, Viscount Castlereagh and Second Marquis of Londonderry: 2149, 5071, 5637
STEWART, Sophronia: 5560
STEWART, W. A.: 5072
STEWART FAMILY (Georgia): 787
STEWART AND BEALL (firm): 385
STEWART AND DICK (firm): see JAMES DICK AND STEWART COMPANY
STEWARTSVILLE, North Carolina: 840
STILES, Miss _____ (South Carolina): 5074
STILES, Mrs. _____ (South Carolina): 5074
STILES, Benjamin (Virginia): 5075
STILES, Benjamin, Jr. (South Carolina): 5073
STILES, Copeland: 5074
STILES, Joseph, Sr.: 5075
STILES, Joseph, Jr.: 5075
STILES, Mary Ann: 3396
STILES, Randolph R.: 5075
STILES, Richard: 5076
STILES, Robert A.: 5075
STILES, Samuel: 5076
STILES, William Henry: 2326, 5076
STILES FAMILY: 3396
STILL, Bayrd: 1843, 5593
STILLEY, James H. W.: 5466
STILLMAN, William James: 2871
STIMSON, Henry Lewis: 706
STIMSON, John Ward: 2871
STIMSON, William Richard: 5077
STIPP, A. V.: 4769
STIRK, Samuel: 5078
STITH, A. (Virginia): 5079
STITH, Alberta Bassett: 2041
STITH, Fred H.: 277, 2041
STITH, W. (Virginia): 5079
STITH, William: 3695
STITH FAMILY (North Carolina): 2041
STOCK BROKERS:
  New York: 3587
  New York: 5731
STOCK EXCHANGES:
  see also STOCKS
  Great Britain: 92
  New York: 2619
STOCK MARKET: see STOCK EXCHANGES
STOCKARD, Henry Jerome: 2449
STOCKBRIDGE, Massachusetts: 1792, 2093

STOCKBRIDGE ACADEMY, Stockbridge, Massachusetts: 1792
STOCKHOLM, Sweden: 2525
  British embassy: 5222
  Cooperative societies: 3964
STOCKS:
  see also BANK STOCKS; BONDS; DIVIDENDS--Corporations; RAILROAD STOCKS; and Stocks as subheading under specific industries and businesses, e.g. COTTON MILLS--Stocks
  Investments: 1242, 4348, 4924, 5312, 5779
    Virginia: 2712
  Purchases and sales:
    North Carolina: 4858
  Speculation: 4348
    Virginia: 4157
  Subdivided by place:
    Connecticut: 2273
    Georgia: 5260
    North Carolina: 4689
    Texas: 5293
    United States: 2210, 5080
      Purchased in England: 3423
STOCKTON, Annis (Boudinot): 730
STOCKTON, Ebenezer S.: 581
STOCKTON, Helen Macomb: 581
STOCKTON, John M.: 323
STOCKTON, Margaret Caroline: 893
STOCKTON, Robert: 581
STOCKTON, Robert Field: 730, 5546
STOCKTON, California: see COLLEGE OF THE PACIFIC
STOCKTON, Maine: 4546
STOCKYARDS--United States: 5080
STODDARD, Charles Warren: 553, 5081
STODDARD, Elizabeth Drew (Barstow): 2449, 5044
STODDARD, Richard Henry: 2449, 4556, 5044
STODDART, Joseph Marshall: 72, 376
STOKE NEWINGTON, England: 5598
STOKES, Frederick Abbott: 2449
STOKES, Henry: 2426
STOKES, Mary M.: 5082
STOKES, Missouria H.: 5082
STOKES, Montfort: 4964, 5457
STOKES, Peter: 2426
STOKES, T. H.: 5082
STOKES, William A.: 5083
STOKES, William Brickly (1814-1897): 872
STOKES CIRCUIT, Methodist Episcopal Church, South: 4136
STOKES COUNTY, North Carolina: 214, 813, 1538, 2537, 2660, 4875
  Arithmetic exercise books: 208
  Civil War: 612
  Mercantile accounts: 27
  Plantation accounts: 27
  Sawmills: 4080
  Cities and towns:
    Ayresville: 110
    Danbury:
      Mercantile accounts: 1919
    Germanton: 279, 315, 817, 3653, 4136, 4248, 5141
    King: 2472
    Walnut Cove: 2800
STOKESBURG CHURCH (North Carolina): 3646
STONE, A. J.: 5084
STONE, Catherine L. W.: 5085
STONE, Ebenezer Whitten: 5085
STONE, Eleazar W.: 1474
STONE, Emily: 5084
STONE, Hamilton J.: 1185
STONE, Harry: 4402
STONE, Jennie: 1766
STONE, John Hoskins: 667, 5086
STONE, John Seeley (1795-1882): 128
STONE, Michael Jenifer: 5089
STONE, Silas M.: 5087
STONE, William B. (Massachusetts): 5088

STONE, William Briscoe (Maryland): 5089
STONE MOUNTAIN, Georgia: 807, 5819
  Monuments: 5090, 5110
STONE MOUNTAIN CONFEDERATE MEMORIAL: 5110
STONE MOUNTAIN CONFEDERATE MONUMENTAL ASSOCIATION: 5090
STONE PUBLISHING COMPANY, Charlotte, North Carolina: 4918
STONE WORKERS: see UNITED STONE AND ALLIED PRODUCTS WORKERS OF AMERICA
STONEMAN, George L.: 5035
STONEMAN, Louis Henry: 5091
STONEMAN, Lucy J.: 5091
STONEMAN FAMILY (Virginia): 5091
STONE'S RIVER, Tennessee: see CIVIL WAR--CAMPAIGNS, BATTLES, AND MILITARY ACTIONS--Tennessee--Stone's River
STONEWALL, C.S.S.: 4019, 4404
"STONEWALL JACKSON'S GRAVE" by Margaret Junkin Preston: 4313
STONEWARE TRADE:
  From Great Britain to North and South Carolina: 3230
STONINGTON, Connecticut: 2547
  Vital statistics: 1205
STONO, C.S.S.: 4531
STONY BROOK, New York: 5788
STONY CREEK, North Carolina: 4223
STONY HILL, Virginia: 2131
STOPFORD, Alice Sophia Amelia: 1424
STORAGE OF MERCHANDISE:
  see also WAREHOUSES
  Georgia--Savannah: 5516
  Louisiana--New Orleans: 679
  Virginia: 2737
STORER, Bennet: 5284
STOREY, Moorfield: 706
STORM, Henry: 5092
STORMS:
  see also DISASTERS; HURRICANES; LIGHTNING; WEATHER
  Maryland--Baltimore (1867): 149
  Massachusetts (1836): 3057
  North Carolina:
    Cape Hatteras (1861): 5955
  South Carolina:
    John's Island (1800s): 3164
STORROW, James Jackson: 5093
STORRS, Cornelia: 5094
STORRS FAMILY (Alabama): 1031
STORY, George (1738-1818): 5095
STORY, George (1853-1926): 5096
STORY, Isaac, Jr.: 5885
STORY, John Patten: 3228
STORY OF FRANCE by Thomas Edward Watson: 5594
THE STORY OF THE MAKING OF BUCHANAN STREET by Daniel Frazer: 2736
"THE STORY OF THE WILMINGTON REBELLION": 2442
STOUGHTON, John: 3728
STOUT, John: 4392
STOUT, Leonidas: 5097
STOUT, Samuel Hollingsworth: 5098
STOUT FAMILY (Indiana--Genealogy): 5097
STOVALL, North Carolina: 2192
STOVES: 4732
  Marketing--Maryland: 3765
  Patents: see PATENTS--Cook stoves
STOWE, E. B.: 5100
STOWE, Harriet Elizabeth (Beecher): 2503, 4387, 5099, 5166
STOWE (J. & E. B.), Charlotte, North Carolina: 5100
STOWE, Jasper: 5100
STOWE, Larkin: 5100
STOWE, Tom: 5100
STOWE, William A.: 5100
STOWE FAMILY (North Carolina): 5100
STOWESVILLE, North Carolina:
  Mercantile accounts: 5100
  Textile mills: 5100
STRACHEY, George: 3238

STRACHEY, Giles Lytton: 5101
STRACHEY, Sir Henry, First Baronet: 5102
STRACHEY, James: 5101
STRACHEY, Sir Richard: 5103
STRAFFORD, George Stevens Byng, Second Earl of: 816
STRAFFORD, Vermont: 3777
STRAFFORD COUNTY, New Hampshire:
    Dover: 130, 2453, 4681
STRAGGLING: see as subheading under names of armies; Absenteeism as subheading under names of armies
STRAHAN, Andrew: 828, 4512
STRAHAN, William: 5104
STRAIGHT, Willard Dickerman: 5252
STRAIN, Isaac G.: 3118
STRANGE, Payton A.: 5106
STRANGE, Philip A.: 5105
STRANGE, Robert (1796-1854): 5457
STRANGE, Robert (1824-1877): 5457
STRANGE, T. W.: 641
STRANGE, William C. A.: 5106
STRANGE FAMILY (Virginia--Genealogy): 5106
STRASBURG, Virginia: 287, 3678, 4959
    Civil War: 3813
    Mercantile accounts: 5979
STRASBURG LAND AND IMPROVEMENT COMPANY: 3721
STRATFORD DE REDCLIFFE, Stratford Canning, First Viscount: 1755, 3183
"STRATFORD," Virginia: 1424
STRATHCONA, Donald Alexander Smith, First Baron: 4567
STRATHEARN, Arthur William Patrick Albert, Duke of Connaught and: see CONNAUGHT AND STRATHEARN, Arthur William Patrick Albert, Duke of
STRATHEARN, Edward Augustus, Duke of Kent and: see KENT AND STRATHEARN, Edward Augustus, Duke of
STRATHNAIRN, Hugh Henry Rose, First Baron: 4520, 4566
STRATTEN, BRYAN, AND SADDLERS BUSINESS SCHOOL: see SADDLERS, BRYAN AND STRATTEN BUSINESS SCHOOL
STRATTON, Paul: 5107
STRATTON, Robert F.: 5944
STRATTON AND JOHNSON, Columbia, Virginia (firm): 5108
STRAUBINGER, Germany: 2950
STRAUS, Nathan: 3265
STRAUS, Philip G.: 1367
STRAWBERRY CROPS:
    North Carolina--Asheville: 4834
STRAYHORN, W. E.: 1285
STRAYHORN FAMILY (North Carolina): 5109
STREAMS:
    Kentucky and Missouri: 3532
STREET, James (Georgia): 3604
STREET, Sarah: 3604
STREET-CARS--New York: 3277
STREET LIGHTING: see GAS LIGHTING
STREET-RAILROADS:
    Georgia--Savannah: 1710
    North Carolina--Wilmington: 3447
STREETS:
    Maryland--Baltimore: 4886
    Washington, D.C.: 3281
STRENGER, Samuel: 4317
STRENGTH: see Organization and troop strength as subheading under names of armies
STRETTON, Hesba: 1113
STRIBLING, Ann E.: 5110
STRIBLING, C. K.: 5110
STRIBLING, Charles R.: 5110
STRIBLING, Cornelius: 5110
STRIBLING, Mary Calvert: 5110
STRICKLAND, Celia: 5111
STRICKLAND, Joseph: 1107
STRICKLAND, Oliver V.: 5111

STRICKLER, Jacob: 5112
STRICKLER FAMILY (Virginia): 5112
STRIKES:
    see also BOYCOTTS; LABOR DISPUTES
    Coal miners: 2225, 3899
    Great Britain: 233
    United States: 4808
        Effects on economy: 4865
    Cotton mill workers:
        North Carolina--Erwin: 5298
    Printers:
        Tennessee--Nashville: 5623
    Railroads:
        Indiana--Hendrix County: 2459
    Steel workers:
        United States: 1883
    Teachers: 1758
    Telephone workers:
        Virginia: 1198
    Textile workers:
        North Carolina: 1195
        South Carolina: 5236
        Southern States: 4094
    Typographical workers:
        South Carolina: 2771
    Subdivided by place:
        Great Britain--Lancashire: 2149
        North Carolina: 1202
            Bessemer City: 4094
        Southern States: 3558
        Tennessee: 1197
        United States: 3066
STRING TRIO MUSIC--Scores: 1974
STRINGFELLOW, James L.: 5113
STRODE, Samuel: 3721
STRODE, William: 1163
STROMAN, Charles J.: 5114
STROMAN FAMILY (South Carolina): 5114
STRONG, Margery: 5115
STRONG, Sandford Arthur: 5116
STRONG & HAVENS, New York, New York: 2360
STROTHER, David Hunter: 1227
STROTHER, James P.: 5117
STROTHER, John A.: 2341
STROTHER, W. D.: 5118
STROTHER, W. P.: 523
STROTHER FAMILY (Kentucky): 5118
STROTHER FAMILY (South Carolina--Genealogy): 3418
STROUD, England: 1976
STRUDWICK, Edmund: 5457
STRUDWICK, Frederick N.: 5457
THE STRUGGLES, PERILS AND HOPES OF THE NEGROES IN THE UNITED STATES by C. Clifton Penick: 2597
STRYKER, William Scudder: 5119
STUART, Adelaide: 5120
STUART, Alexander Hugh Holmes: 872, 5120
STUART, Annie Elizabeth: 1506
STUART, Archibald: 5031
STUART, Charles (West Virginia): 2986
STUART, Sir Charles, First Baron Stuart de Rothesay: 5071
STUART, Charles Edward: see CHARLES EDWARD, The Young Pretender
STUART, Dudley Coutts: 5746
STUART, Flora: 5121
STUART, James Ewell Brown: 581, 3793, 3809, 4607, 5121, 5314
STUART, Jane: 3315
STUART, Jeremiah: 5122
STUART, John (Virginia): 2577
STUART, John, Third Earl of Bute: 5330
STUART, John Allen (South Carolina): 393
STUART, John E.: 4610
STUART, John Lane: 5123
STUART, Katherine: 5457
STUART, Louisa: 2146
STUART, Oscar J. E.: 1506
STUART, Ruth (McEnery): 2871
STUART, Samuel J.: 4610
STUART, Sir Simeon, Third Baronet: 736
STUART FAMILY (Mississippi): 1506

STUART FAMILY (South Carolina): 4453
STUART FAMILY (Virginia--Genealogy): 5120
STUART, Iowa: 3078
STUART, Virginia: 5031
STUART DE ROTHESAY, Sir Charles Stuart, First Baron: 5071
STUART-WORTLEY, Margaret Jane: 5175
STUART'S DRAFT, Virginia:
    Merchants: 209
STUBBS, Harry W.: 5124
STUBBS, J. R.: 5125
STUBBS, William (1825-1901): 2841, 4580
STUBBS, William Carter (1846-1924): 5126
STUCKEY, John: 5127
STUCKEY FAMILY (Illinois): 5127
STUD BOOKS: see HORSES--Breeding
STUDENT HOUSING:
    see also as subheading under names of specific schools, colleges, and universities
    Connecticut--Litchfield: 1333
    Counselors--North Carolina: 960
STUDENT LOANS:
    see also STUDENTS AND STUDENT LIFE--Finance
    North Carolina: 3538
STUDENT PUBLICATIONS: see UNIVERSITIES AND COLLEGES--Student publications; and names of specific student publications
STUDENT RELIGIOUS SOCIETIES:
    North Carolina:
        Duke University: 3001
        Wesley Foundation: 5022
STUDENT SOCIETIES:
    see also LITERARY SOCIETIES; STUDENT RELIGIOUS SOCIETIES; and names of specific student societies
    New York: 3809
    North Carolina: 613
        Chapel Hill: 4669
        Charlotte: 895
        Greensboro: 4425
    United States: 5077
    Virginia: 1115
STUDENTS AND STUDENT LIFE:
    see also UNIVERSITIES AND COLLEGES--College life; UNIVERSITIES AND COLLEGES--Students and student life; and Students and student life as subheading under names of specific schools, universities and colleges
    Compositions: 5950
    Connecticut: 2745
    Maryland--Baltimore: 1747
    Massachusetts: 4807
    North Carolina: 2221, 5298
    South Carolina: 3801
    Virginia: 1436
    Foreign: see students by nationality, e.g. AMERICAN STUDENTS IN EUROPE
    Girls' schools and academies:
        Alabama: 5032
        Maryland: 2974
        North Carolina: 5664
            High Point: 2036
    Notebooks:
        see also Notebooks as subheading under specific subjects
        Maryland--West River: 2267
    Parents' letters: 3418
    North Carolina: 4321
    South Carolina: 3790, 5193
        Charleston: 2144
    Virginia: 2728, 2974, 3560, 4616, 5176
        Lynchburg: 1714
        Richmond: 87
    West Virginia: 3174
    Subdivided by place:
        Alabama--Tuskegee: 925
        Arkansas: 4353
        Georgia: 2828

STUDENTS AND STUDENT LIFE:
  Subdivided by place (Continued):
    Great Britain: 2102
    Maryland:
      Ellicott's Mills: 3360, 4022, 5982
    Mississippi: 5032
      Rodney: 3322
    New Jersey: 4354
    New York: 4169
    North Carolina: 3176
      Asheville: 566
      Granville County: 2192, 2833
      Hamilton: 1411
      Louisburg: 3272
      Whiteville: 4910
    Rhode Island: 4169
    South Carolina: 300, 1472, 1480
      Columbia: 566
      Winnsboro: 566
    Virginia: 4123, 5227
      Caroline County: 4698
      Richmond: 4698
    Washington, D.C.: 669
STUDENTS FOR A DEMOCRATIC SOCIETY: 613, 4948, 5077
STUDIES IN EARLY AMERICAN HISTORY: A NOTABLE LAWSUIT: 2461
STUDY: 97
  see also Study and teaching as subheading under names of specific subjects, e.g. SONGS AND MUSIC--Study and teaching
"A STUDY OF SCRIPTURE TEACHING AS TO THE HOLY SPIRIT" by John Blackwell: 2934
STUMP, Elizabeth S.: 3742
STUMP, William: 5128
STUMP FAMILY (Maryland): 5128
STURGE, Joseph: 5129
STURGIS, Appleton: 2777
STURGIS, Samuel Davis, Sr. (1822-1889): 5130
STURGIS, W. J.: 5252
STURTEVANT, John W.: 5131
STYRE, Samuel: 5132
SUAKIN, Sudan: 5835
SUBKE, Walter Carl: 3383
SUBLETT, Martha: 2966
SUBLETT, Samuel M.: 2966
SUBMARINE CABLE COMPANIES:
  Great Britain: 4934
SUBMARINE CABLES:
  see also TRANSATLANTIC CABLES
  Belgium: 4934
  Great Britain: 4934
SUB-MARINE TELEGRAPH COMPANY: 4934
SUBMARINE WARFARE:
  see also WORLD WAR I--Submarine warfare
  Logistics and battle tactics: 116
"SUBSTITUCIONES DE CÁTEDRAS Y LUGARES DESDE EL AÑO DE 1724 HASTA 1830": 3650
SUBSTITUTIONS: see Recruiting and enlistment--Substitutions as subheading under names of armies
SUBTREASURIES: 872
SUB-TREASURY BILL: 718
SUCCESS: 1551
SUCKLEY, George, Sr.: 5133
SUCKLEY, George, Jr. (d. 1869): 5133
SUCKLEY, John H.: 5133
SUCKLEY, Rutsen: 5133
SUCKLEY, Thomas H.: 5133
SUDAN:
  Abolition of slavery: 67
  British administration: 5725
  British Army:
    Military activities: 5164, 5835
    Nile Expedition (1884-1885): 3046, 4811, 5333
  British conquest: 1976
  Conspiracies: 41
  Economic conditions: 5835
  Foreign relations--Egypt: 5835
  Politics and government: 5835

SUDAN (Continued):
  Slave trade, Suppression of: 5725
  Tombs: 1974
SUDAN EXPEDITION (1884-1885): see SUDAN--British Army--Nile Expedition
SUER DE SANG by Léon Bloy: 555
SUEZ CANAL: 4520
SUFFIELD, Connecticut:
  Abolition of slavery and abolitionist sentiment: 3910
SUFFOLK, England: 1141
  Ipswich: 1081
SUFFOLK, Virginia: 1838, 3012
  Civil War: 1845
    see also CIVIL WAR--CAMPAIGNS, BATTLES, AND MILITARY ACTIONS--Virginia--Suffolk
  Union military activities: 4561
  Mercantile accounts: 4472
  Merchants: 3915
  Personal finance: 4470
  Postal service--Finance: 5439
SUFFOLK COUNTY, Massachusetts:
  Land deeds and indentures: 1431
  Cities and towns:
    Brighton: 4860
    Charlestown: 3057, 3791
    Dorchester: 1766, 1973
      Civil War: 3342
    Jamaica Plain: 3280
      Preparatory schools: 339
    Roxbury: 1502, 1968, 2468, 5085
SUFFOLK COUNTY, New York:
  Huntington: 726, 850
  Long Island: 3904
    see also SAINT PAUL'S COLLEGE
  Stony Brook: 5788
SUFFOLK DISTRICT, Methodist churches: 3646
SUFFRAGE:
  see also NEGROES--Suffrage; WOMAN SUFFRAGE
  Great Britain: 280, 649, 1126, 2322, 5616
  Ireland: 4605
  South Carolina: 2695
  United States: 5
SUFISM: 3710
SUGAR:
  Storage--Louisiana: 679
  Tariff: see TARIFF--Sugar
  Transportation by river: 3824
"SUGAR BOILING"--Virginia: 5347
SUGAR CANE: see SUGAR GROWING
SUGAR GROVE, North Carolina: 19
SUGAR GROWING:
  British West Indies: 4913
  Danish West Indies: 3570
  East Indies: 4913
  Georgia: 127
  India: 4913
  Louisiana: 1242
  South Carolina: 4988
  Virginia: 4924
SUGAR INDUSTRY: see WORLD WAR II--Sugar industry
SUGAR PLANTATIONS:
  Louisiana: 1242, 1574
  New Orleans: 4550
  Thibodeauville: 3160
SUGAR REBATES:
  Great Britain: 1913
SUGAR TRADE: 323
  Prices: 4541
  Subdivided by place:
    Danish West Indies: 3570
    Far East: 5298
    Great Britain: 2472
    Jamaica: 301
    Massachusetts: 1736, 2641
    North Carolina: 1736
    Philippine Islands: 2742
    Saint Domingue: 197
    Spain--Cadiz: 197
SUGDEN, Edward Burtenshaw, First Baron St. Leonards: 504, 5134

SUGG, Lewis Osborne: 5135
SUGG, Samuel: 5136
SUGG FAMILY (North Carolina): 5135
SUICIDE: 3674, 5529
  see also CLERGY--Suicide
SULAIMAN, THE GREAT, Pasha of Baghdad: 5797
SULARD AND HILLIARD, Saint Louis, Missouri (firm): 5137
SULLIVAN, Mr. ____: 5616
SULLIVAN, Council G.: 5138
SULLIVAN, Daniel: 5139
SULLIVAN, George: 5140
SULLIVAN, John W.: 323
SULLIVAN, Margaret: 5360
SULLIVAN, Nathaniel F.: 5141
SULLIVAN, W. H. (South Carolina): 4118
SULLIVAN, W. L. (North Carolina): 5138
SULLIVAN, CHESHIRE AND CANADAY (firm):
  see CHESHIRE, SULLIVAN & CANADAY, INC.
SULLIVAN COUNTY, New Hampshire:
  Mill Village: 1763
SULLIVAN COUNTY, Tennessee: 1933
  Bristol: 5859
    see also KING COLLEGE
SULLIVAN POWER COMPANY (South Carolina): 1478
SULLIVAN'S ISLAND, South Carolina: 1186, 1793
  American Revolution: 2743
  Civil War: 1477
  Spanish-American War:
    Artillery training: 5298
SULLY, Maximilien de Béthune, Duc de: 1424
SULPHUR MINING:
  North Carolina:
    Davidson County: 2041
SULPHUR SPRINGS, Virginia: 1891
  Civil War: 2681
SULPHUR TRADE: see BRIMSTONE TRADE
SULTANA (ship): 162
SULZER, William: 3265
SUMATRA:
  British chaplains: 4821
  Dutch military expedition (1821): 3485
  Pepper trade: 2682
"SUMMARY OF THE EXTRACT FROM LORD STRATHNAIRN'S REPORT" by Hugh Henry Rose, First Baron Strathnairn: 4566
SUMMER, A. G.: 2612
SUMMER, David: 5142
SUMMER, Henry: 2880
SUMMER, John L.: 5142
SUMMERELL, G. Hope: 960
SUMMERHILL, England: 5836
SUMMERS, Julius A.: 5143
"SUMMERSEAT," Laurel Grove, Maryland: 1535
SUMMERVILLE, Georgia: 2697
SUMMERVILLE, South Carolina: 1793, 4334
SUMMERVILLE INSTITUTE, Gholson, Mississippi: 5032
SUMMIT POINT, West Virginia: 3853
SUMMONSES: see COURTS--Summonses
SUMNER, Charles (1811-1874): 863, 3062, 4897, 5050, 5433
SUMNER, George: 103
SUMNER, John Andrew Hamilton, First Viscount: 2279
SUMNER COUNTY, Tennessee:
  Castalian Springs: 5935
  Gallatin: 5623, 5784
  Hendersonville: 5671
SUMTER, Thomas: 3676, 3818
SUMTER, South Carolina: 3501
  Freedmen--Education: 5298
  Slave trade: 3795
SUMTER, C.S.S.: 2963, 3258, 4739
SUMTER COUNTY, Alabama:
  Sumterville: 4164
SUMTER COUNTY, South Carolina: 2288, 4429
  Business affairs: 3676

SUMTER COUNTY, South Carolina
  (Continued):
  Land--Purchases and sales: 3676
  Privateering: 3356
  Cities and towns:
    High Hills of Santee: 4839
    Stateburg: 1472, 3682, 3818, 4217
    Sumter: see SUMTER, South
      Carolina
    Sumterville: 3676
SUMTER DISTRICT, South Carolina: 3350
  Farming: 3123
  Plantations: 4460
  Privateering: 1923
SUMTER GUARDS (South Carolina
  militia): 5144
SUMTERVILLE, Alabama: 4166
SUMTERVILLE, South Carolina:
  Baptist churches: 3676
  Slave trade: 3676
THE SUN (Louisville, Kentucky?): 946
SUN, Eclipses of: see SOLAR ECLIPSES
THE SUN VIRGIN by Thomas Dixon: 1521
SUN YAT-SEN: 5252
SUNBURY, Georgia: 3196
SUNBURY, North Carolina: 1724, 2353
SUNBURY, Pennsylvania: 1768, 4348
SUNDAY CLOSING LAWS:
  Maryland: 4886
  North Carolina:
    Lincoln County: 3211
    Rowan County: 4640
SUNDAY SCHOOL CONVENTIONS:
  Baptist--North Carolina: 3415
SUNDAY SCHOOLS:
  Baptist--West Virginia: 2129
  Congregational--Connecticut: 5748
  Methodist:
    Great Britain--Preston: 5895
    North Carolina:
      Catawba County: 5745
    United States: 3646
    West Virginia: 2129
  Methodist Episcopal Church, South:
    see also METHODIST EPISCOPAL
    CHURCH, SOUTH--Sunday School
    Board
    Virginia: 5467
    West Virginia: 5467
  Subdivided by place:
    Maryland--Smithsburg: 5343
    New York--New York: 4133
    North Carolina: 544, 1482, 3646
      Catawba County: 4532
      Fayetteville: 5298
    United States: 2838
    Virginia: 3719, 4743
SUNDIALS: 5708
SUNG, Mei-ling: 2269
SUNKHAZE, Maine: 3201
SUNNY SIDE SCHOOL, Bedford County,
  Virginia: 4049
SUPERIOR COURTS: see COURTS--Superior
  Courts
SUPERIOR PROVOST COURTS: see COURTS--
  Superior Provost Courts
SUPERSTITIONS--North Carolina: 691
SUPPLIES: see FARM SUPPLIES; INDIANS
  OF NORTH AMERICA--Agents--Supplies;
  SLAVES--Supplies; and Military
  supplies as subheading under names
  of armies
SUPREME COURT: see UNITED STATES--
  SUPREME COURT
SUPREME COURTS: see COURTS--Supreme
  Courts
SURGERY:
  see also CHLOROFORM IN SURGERY;
  OPTICAL SURGERY; SEX CHANGE;
  TONSILLECTOMY
  Student's notebook:
    University of Virginia: 58
  Subdivided by place:
    France: 1300
    Maryland: 3378
SURETY BONDS: see PUBLIC OFFICIALS--
  Bonding

SURINAM:
  British administration: 2403
  Foreign trade: 2403
SURRENDER: see as subheading under
  names of armies and navies, e.g.
  CONFEDERATE STATES OF AMERICA--
  ARMY--Army of Northern Virginia--
  Surrender
SURREY, England: 4420
  Beddington Park: 887
  "Burwood Park": 1775
  Cobham: 3736
  Cranleigh: 4207
  Dorking: 3630
  Farnham: 332
  Furze Hill: 5027
  Goldalming: 5836
  Holmwood: 3895
  Nutwood: 4934
  Park Hatch: 2077
  Peper Harow Park: 663
  Richmond: 3995
  Wandsworth: 90
  Woking: 5624
SURRY COUNTY, North Carolina: 288,
  2068, 2808, 4779
  Agricultural organizations: 5146
  Arithmetic exercise books: 208,
    3074
  Civil War: 3908
  Land deeds and indentures: 2419
  Personal loans: 3908
  Wills: 3908
  Cities and towns:
    Elkin: 4742
    Huntsville: 1108, 2714, 2809
      Slave trade: 2113
    Mount Airy: 4849, 5048
    Rockford: 1800
SURRY COUNTY, Virginia:
  Plantations: 1133
SURRY COUNTY (N. C.) AGRICULTURAL
  SOCIETY: 5146
SURRY OF EAGLE'S NEST by John Esten
  Cooke: 1227
SURVEYOR, U.S.S.: 4355
SURVEYS AND SURVEYING: 1004
  see also CANALS--Surveying;
  COASTAL SURVEYING; ESTATES--
  Surveys; NAUTICAL SURVEYING
  Notebooks: 1818
  Virginia: 3809
  Student's notebook:
    West Virginia: 1379
  Subdivided by place:
    China: 1373
    District of Columbia: 3145
    Georgia: 1440, 1993, 4988, 5586
      Bulloch County: 3663
      Darien: 3389
      Franklin County: 1997
      Heard County: 3966
      Savannah--Corruption: 3389
    Kentucky: 2063
    Maryland: 2295
      Frederick County: 4457
      Washington County: 2838
    Mississippi:
      Harbor at Pascagoula: 5425
    North Carolina: 819, 1438, 1475,
      2978, 3176, 3386, 3476, 5188,
      5709
      Cherokee Indian land: 3028
      Davie County: 2749
      Moore County: 4396
      North Carolina-Virginia
        border: 1687
      Orange County: 3337
      Wilkes County: 2483
      Wilson: 2808
    Ohio River: 5575
    South Carolina: 1480, 3386, 3802,
      4145
      Charleston: 4216, 5198
      Orangeburg District: 5015
    Southern States: 5480
    Tennessee: 3069

SURVEYS AND SURVEYING:
  Subdivided by place (Continued):
    United States: 1548, 3587
    Virginia: 819, 1485, 4315
      Loudoun County: 2782, 4836
      Montgomery County: 4315
      Nelson County: 3566
    West Virginia:
      Wood County: 5194
    Western States: 5480
SUSETTE FRAISSENETTE (ship): 4355
SUSQUEHANNA RIVER (Maryland): 4468
SUSSEX, England:
  Courts baron: 4767
  Cities and towns:
    Ardingly: 4705
    Brighton: 4580, 4811, 5525
      Business affairs: 4113
    Chailey: 4635
    Hastings: 4570
    Worthing: 1522, 5304
SUSSEX COUNTY, Virginia:
  Blacksmithing: 3045
SUTHERLAND, James A.: 5147
SUTHERLAND, William Gordon,
  Seventeenth Earl: 2098
SUTHERLAND COUNTY, Scotland: 2098
SUTHERLIN, William T.: 5148
SUTTON, Mary: 2410
SWAIM, Ben: 5149
SWAIM, Curran: 5149
SWAIM, Henry: 5149
SWAIM, Lyndon: 5149
SWAIM, Moses: 5149
SWAIN, David Lowry: 305, 1525, 1848,
  3176, 4669, 5036, 5150
SWAIN FAMILY (North Carolina): 2240
SWANK, Carrie: 5151
SWANN, Don: 2398
SWANSON, Claude Augustus: 879, 1336,
  5152
SWANVILLE TOWNSHIP, Maine:
  Toddy Pond--Lumber mills: 3554
SWARBRECK, Edward: 4988
SWARTHDALE, England: 342
SWARTHMORE, Pennsylvania:
  see also SWARTHMORE COLLEGE
  Chautauquas: 5110
SWARTHMORE CHAUTAUQUA, Swarthmore,
  Pennsylvania: 5110
SWARTHMORE COLLEGE, Swarthmore,
  Pennsylvania:
  Students and student life: 5128
SWATS, John: 5153
SWAZILAND: 4520
SWEARINGEN, James P.: see SWERINGEN,
  James P.
SWEARINGEN FAMILY: 404
SWEDEN:
  American embassy in: 404, 5298
  Biographical studies: 5379
  Cooperative societies:
    Stockholm: 3964
  Description and travel:
    1794: 306
    1878: 157
    1900s: 3451
  Farming: 3451
  Foreign relations--Denmark: 1302
  Foreign trade--Great Britain: 535
  Politics and government: 4625
  Treaties--United States: 404
SWEDENBORGIAN CHURCH: 404
SWEDISH COOPERATIVE SOCIETY: 3964
SWEET BRIAR, Virginia:
  Legal affairs and wills: 5765
SWEET BRIAR COLLEGE, Sweet Briar,
  Virginia: 5765
SWEETSPRINGS, West Virginia:
  Health resorts: 1478
SWEPSON, George W.: 5154
SWERINGEN, James P.: 5155
SWETE, Henry Barclay: 5156
SWIFT, George P.: 2272
SWIFT, Harriot: 3008
SWIFT, Joseph Gardner: 1433
SWIFT, Joshua: 1015

SWIFT (British schooner): 5063
SWIFT SHOAL MILLS (Virginia): 5157
"THE SWIFTNESS OF TIME" by Julia A.
    Mildred Harris: 3611
SWIM, Allan L.: 1202
SWINBURNE, Algernon Charles: 2102,
    2449, 5158
SWINBURNE, Isabel: 5158
SWINDELL, Frederick Dallas: 5457
SWINDLING: see FRAUD
SWINTON, George: 868
SWINTON, Hugh: 5193
SWINTON, Margaret: 5193
SWINTON, Martha Caroline: 5193
SWINTON, Robert Blair: 5553
SWINTON, William (South Carolina):
    5193
SWINTON, William (1833-1892, New
    York): 5159
SWINTON FAMILY (South Carolina--
    Genealogy): 1468, 5193
SWISHER, Charles: 2634
SWITZERLAND:
    Description and travel:
        1800s: 4770, 5038
        1810s: 1049
        1820s: 1049, 4490
        1830s: 4490
        1840s: 5133
        1850s: 558, 5963
        1860s: 5050
        1870s: 5050
        1880s: 1463
        Geneva: 1775
    Politics and government: 5133
        Geneva: 4408
    Social life and customs:
        1810s: 1049
        1820s: 1049
        1840s: 5133
    Universities and colleges: see
        UNIVERSITY OF GENEVA
THE SWITZERLAND COMPANY: 5312
SWOPE, Gerard: 5252
SWORD, James Monroe: 5160
SWORD, Mary Elizabeth (McClain): 5160
SWORD, Peter: 5160
SWORD FAMILY (Maryland): 5160
SYDENHAM, Charles Edward Poulett
    Thomson, First Baron of: 3050,
    5277
SYDNEY, Thomas Townshend, First
    Viscount: 5331
SYDNEY, Australia: 5063
SYDNOR, Charles Sackett: 5498
SYDNOR, Epas.: 3550
SYDNOR, Thomas W.: 5161
SYDNOR FAMILY (Virginia): 5161
SYDNORSVILLE, Virginia: 474
SYKES, John: 5162
SYLVANIA, Pennsylvania: 3952
SYME, Miss L. A.: 2806
SYME, Leander Dunbar: 5163
SYMINGTON, Andrew James: 2146
SYMONDS, Alfred R.: 306
SYMONDS, Arthur G.: 5164
SYNOPSIS OF THE GENUS ARTHONIA: 5754
SYRACUSE, New York: 5626
SYRIA:
    see also NEAR EAST
    Murder--Jaffa affair: 3118
    Religion: 128
"A SYSTEM OF LAW CONCERNING ESTATES"
    by Richard Tilghman IV: 5296
A SYSTEM OF PHILOSOPHY by Herbert
    Spencer: 1603
SZE, Sao-ke Alfred: 5252
SZOLD, Rachel: 2811
SZOLD FAMILY: 2811

T

T. R. GWATHMEY, Lynchburg, Virginia: 2360
T. C. WILLIAMS COMPANY, Petersburg, Virginia: 655
T. E. HOLDING AND COMPANY: 2590
T. FISHER UNWIN (firm): 1210
TAAFE, Theobald: 5330
TABARDREY PLANT (Cone Mills Corporation): 5234
TABB, Hester E. (Van Bibber): 5165
TABB, John Bannister: 3424, 5166
TABB FAMILY (West Virginia): 865
TABBY (Concrete): 4988
  see also BUILDING MATERIALS; CEMENT
TABER FAMILY (Virginia or West Virginia): 3721
TABER & CO.: 1860
TABERNACLE (Great Britain): 5647
TABERNACLE CHURCH (North Carolina): 3646
TABERNACLE TOWNSHIP, North Carolina:
  Municipal government: 4100
THE TABLE (periodical): 1143
TABLEAU DE LA GÉNÉRALITÉ DE TOURS DEPUIS 1762 JUSQUES ET COMPRIS 1766: 5323
TABLEAUX:
  United Confederate Veterans: 3376
TABOADA DE LEMOS, Francisco Gil de:
  see GIL DE TABOADA DE LEMOS, Francisco
TACUBAYA, Mexico: 4155
TAFFANEL, Paul: 111
TAFT, Alphonso: 5168
TAFT, Harvey F.: 5169
TAFT, Robert (fl. 1202): 542
TAFT, Robert Alphonso (1889-1953): 5170
TAFT, William Howard: 2516, 3229, 4723, 4825, 5171
  Administration: 1424
  Member of Philippine Commission: 3313
TAFT-HARTLEY ACT: 1199, 1201
TAGORE, Sir Rabindranath: 3797
TAILLE (French tax): 5323
TAILORING:
  see also SEWING
  Georgia--Greenville: 17
  Virginia: 330
    Guiney's Station: 4589
    Mount Solon: 114
TAILORS' ACCOUNTS:
  Virginia:
    Charlottesville: 4049
    Leesburg: 4198
"THE TAILOR'S ARCHETYPE" by Allen Ward: 4589
TAINTOR, Henry E.: 5172
TAIPING REBELLION (1850-1864): 1298, 4520, 4881
TAIT, C. W. (Alabama): 5174
TAIT, Charles (1768-1835): 3439
TAIT, James (British professor, fl. 1937-1938): 5173
TAIT, James Goode (Southern planter, 1833-1911): 5174

TAIT, Robert: 5174
"TAKE CARE OF YOURSELF" (card game): 3452
TAKU FORTS, China: 598
  Description (1862): 1373
TALBOT, Charles Chetwynd, Second Earl of Talbot of Hensol: 2149
TALBOT, Charles John Chetwynd-, Nineteenth Earl Shrewsbury: 1087
TALBOT, Margaret Jane (Stuart-Wortley): 5175
TALBOT, Tom: 3284
TALBOT AND WILMARTH COMPANY: see MARSH, TALBOT, AND WILMARTH COMPANY
TALBOT COUNTY, Georgia:
  Talbotton: 2178
    Schools: 3729
TALBOT COUNTY, Maryland: 5295
TALBOTT, Allan: 3809
TALBOTT, Charles III: 3809
TALBOTT, Charles Henry II: 5176
TALBOTT, Charles Henry III: 5176
TALBOTT, Ellis: 3809
TALBOTT, Sallie Radford (Munford): 3809, 5176
TALBOTT FAMILY (Virginia): 5176
  Genealogy: 3809
TALBOTTON, Georgia: 2178
  Schools: 3729
TALCOTT, Andrew: 2132
TALCOTT (N. & D.), New York, New York (firm): 2360
THE TALES OF MOTHER GOOSE annotated by Montrose Moses: 3797
TALFOURD, Sir Thomas Noon: 5177
TALIAFERRO, William Booth: 5178
TALIAFERRO COUNTY, Georgia:
  Crawfordville: 5051
TALISMAN (Civil War blockade runner): 410
THE TALKING DOG AND THE BARKING MAN by Elizabeth Brickel Seeman: 4730
TALLADEGA, Alabama: 4061
  Description (1891): 3759
  Presbyterian Female Collegiate Institute: 1947
TALLADEGA COUNTY, Alabama:
  Talladega: see TALLADEGA, Alabama
TALLAHASSEE, Florida:
  see also FLORIDA STATE UNIVERSITY
TALLAPOOSA COUNTY, Alabama: 5916
TALLEYRAND-PÉRIGORD, Alexandre-Angélique, Duc de: 2840
TALLEYRAND-PÉRIGORD, Charles Maurice de, Prince de Bénévent: 1424, 5179, 5222
TALLMADGE, Benjamin: 4625
TALLMERS, W. B.: 3691
TALLOW TRADE:
  Great Britain: 2742
  North Carolina--Wilkesboro: 4107
  Spain: 2742
TALMADGE, Eugene: 2109, 3575
TALMAGE, Thomas DeWitt: 3029
TALTON, ____ (North Carolina merchant): 5374
TALTON, W. E.: 5180
TALVANDE, Ann Manson: 4622
TAMPA BAY, Florida: 5417
TAMPICO, Mexico: 948
TAMWORTH, England: 4113
  Elections: 5330
TAMWORTH BOROUGH, England:
  Voting registers: 5287
TANCRED, Sir Thomas Selby Lawson-:
  see LAWSON-TANCRED, Sir Thomas Selby
TANEY, Roger Brooke: 3053, 5181
TANGANYIKA:
  Missions and missionaries: 41
TANGIER:
  Bombardment: 636
  Description and travel: 4022
  Zoological expeditions: 4022
TANJORE: India: 2037
TANKERSLY, John: 5366

TANNAHILL (R. & W.), Washington, D.C. (firm): 4760
TANNER, B.: 5182
TANNER, Evans: 5183
TANNERY ACCOUNTS:
  Arkansas--Whitsonton: 5509
  Maryland: 5722
  New York: 1479
  Virginia: 146, 1600, 2942
    Bridgewater: 5854
    Lawrenceville: 3014
    Port Republic: 2977
  West Virginia:
    Romney: 5215
    Wardensville: 146
TANNING:
  Georgia--Jasper County: 377
  North Carolina:
    Jackson County: 3021
  Ohio: 5342
  Virginia: 1559, 2942
    Amherst County: 3788
  West Virginia: 3064
TAPESTRY MANUFACTURE: 5553
"THE TAPESTRY OF LIFE AND THE SONGS OF DREAM AND OF DEATH WITH A PRELUDE" by Stefan George: 1992
TAPP, Vincent: 5184
TAPP FAMILY (Virginia): 5184
TAPPAN, Benjamin (1773-1857): 357
TAPPAN, Benjamin (fl. 1862): 5133
TAPPAN, Lewis: 3445
THE HEEL EDITOR by Josephus Daniels: 83
TAR HEEL SOCIETY OF MARYLAND: 5298
TAR RIVER, North Carolina:
  Steamboat operators' accounts: 3827
TAR RIVER BAPTIST ASSOCIATION (North Carolina): 320
TAR RIVER CIRCUIT, Methodist churches: 3646
TAR RIVER CIRCUIT, Methodist Episcopal Church: 3992
TAR RIVER CIRCUIT, Methodist Episcopal Church, South: 3476
TAR TRADE:
  Maryland--Baltimore: 4348
  South Carolina--Exports: 1935
TARBORO, North Carolina: 1061, 2191, 2256, 3626
  Business affairs: 2325
  Civil War: 531, 1122
  Law practice: 641
  Mercantile accounts: 4035
  Primitive Baptist Church: 5185
TARBORO PRIMITIVE BAPTIST CHURCH, Tarboro, North Carolina: 5185
TARHEEL TOMMY ATKINS by Benjamin Muse: 3820
TARIFF:
  see also CUSTOMS (Tariff); PUBLIC FINANCE; TAXATION
  Laws and legislation (United States):
    1820s: 3406, 5217, 5369
    1840s: 2904
  Public opinion (1831): 150
  see also NULLIFICATION
  Rates:
    Great Britain: 5277
    Ottoman Empire: 3183
    United States:
      1816: 5499
      1900s: 3190
  Subdivided by product:
    Agricultural: see CORN LAWS
    Olive oil--Great Britain: 5277
    Soap--Great Britain: 5277
    Sugar (1901): 4331
    Wool: 5342
  Subdivided by place:
    China: 5252
    Great Britain:
      1820s: 331
      1842: 3836
      1860: 280

TARIFF:
   Subdivided by place (Continued):
     Jamaica:
       1790s: 1913
       1870s-1880s: 1792
     United States:
       1700s-1800s: 669
       1800s: 842, 849
         1810s: 2449
         1820s: 2449, 3366
         1830s: 1302, 3366, 3902, 5700
         1840s: 1302, 3325, 3366, 3727, 5470, 5700
         1850s: 5470, 5700
       1900s: 3190
       1950s: 4805
TARIFF COMMISSION: see UNITED STATES--GOVERNMENT AGENCIES AND OFFICIALS--Tariff Commission
TARIFF CONVENTION OF 1831: 3902
TARIFF NUT SHELL: 2225
TARIFF REFORM:
   Great Britain: 2149, 4520
TARLTON, Elisha Warfield: 3207
TARPON SPRINGS, Florida:
   Description: 2627
TARRANT COUNTY, Texas:
   Birdville: 5194
TARRY, Edward: 5186
TARRY, James P.: 5879
TARRY, Sallie: 761
TARRY, William: 5186
TARRYTOWN, New York: 2258
   Schools: 5593
TARTT, Thomas: 3012
TASMANIA:
   Church of England: 5725
   United States consulate in: 286
TASSO, Torquato: 5379
TATE, Allen John Orley: 2689
TATE, J. W. M.: 5187
TATE, William C.: 5188
TATE SPRINGS, Tennessee:
   Health resorts: 5051
TATTNALL, Josiah (fl. 1785, Georgia Loyalist): 3309
TATTNALL, Josiah, Sr. (1762-1803): 5189
TATTNALL, Josiah, Jr. (1795-1871): 2696, 5190
TATTNALL FAMILY: 3396
TATTNALL COUNTY, Georgia:
   Manassas: 1034
TATUM, Osburn: 5191
TAUNTON, Henry Labouchere, First Baron: 3067, 5277, 5725
TAUNTON, Massachusetts:
   Embargo (Jeffersonian): 5298
   Estates--Appraisal: 5499
TAURMAN, Henry E.: 5192
TAUSSIG, Charles William: 3797
TAUSSIG, Frank William: 706
TAVEAU, Augusta Melaine: 5193
TAVEAU, Augustin Louis, Sr. (1828-1886): 5193
TAVEAU, Augustin Louis, Jr.: 5193
TAVEAU, Caroline Rosalie: 5193
TAVEAU, Delphine (Sprague): 5193
TAVEAU, Louis Augustin Thomas: 5193
TAVEAU, Martha Caroline (Swinton) Ball: 5193
TAVEAU FAMILY (South Carolina): 295
TAVENNER, Cabell: 5194
TAVENNER, Janet Ann: 5194
TAVENNER, Jennet Scott (Withers): 5194
TAVENNER, Thomas: 5194
TAVERN ACCOUNTS:
   Alabama--Tompkinsville: 4827
   Maryland: 5722
     Elkton: 166
     Harford County: 5128
   North Carolina:
     Louisburg: 2873
     Rowan County: 3288
   Virginia: 3365
     Lawrenceville: 3900

TAVERNS AND INNS:
   Georgia:
     Greenville: 17
     Watkinsville: 1621
   Maryland: 785
   New York: 5149
   North Carolina: 2765
     Bath: 705
     Wadesboro: 4814
   Pennsylvania: 5149
   Virginia: 1567, 3042, 3900, 5149
     Mount Airy: 2131
     Williamsburg: 4220
TAVISTOCK, Francis Russell, Marquis of: 4605
TAVISTOCK, England: 2254
TAX COLLECTION: 5886
   Enforcement laws: 4852, 5051
   Confederate States of America: 4595
   Great Britain: 2158
   Ireland: 5639
   North Carolina: 4689
     Beaufort County: 911
TAX COLLECTORS:
   see also UNITED STATES--GOVERNMENT AGENCIES AND OFFICIALS--Internal revenue collectors
   Confederate States of America: 3416
   Georgia: 731, 1375
   Illinois: 2682
   North Carolina: 2446
   South Carolina--Charleston: 4213
   Virginia: 3721
     Frederick County: 5200
TAX EVASION:
   Ireland: 3567
   North Carolina--Hanover County: 5709
TAX EXEMPTION: see TAXATION--Exemption from
TAX IN KIND:
   Georgia: 1181, 5162
     Franklin County: 1997
   North Carolina: 1438, 2260, 2833, 2857, 4761
   South Carolina: 3044, 3801
   Virginia: 1181, 1920, 1969
TAX LISTS:
   Alabama--Greene County: 5593
   North Carolina: 4670, 4862
     Burke County: 245
     Hanover County: 5709
     Martin County: 2284, 3935
     Orange County: 3938
     Randolph County: 2459, 3939
   South Carolina: 5548
     Lexington County: 4610
TAX RECEIPTS:
   Confederate States of America:
     North Carolina: 50
   Georgia: 1434
   Massachusetts--Boston: 2304
   Mississippi: 5612
   North Carolina: 2660, 2824, 3476, 4761, 4858
     Chatham County: 5874
     Craven County: 804
     Martin County: 4849
     Wake County: 4009
   South Carolina: 2709, 4649
     Chesterfield County: 4996
   Tennessee: 4269
   Virginia: 5178
     Buckingham County: 3794
     Goochland County: 32
     Hicks Ford: 5891
     Norfolk: 3830
TAX RETURNS--Georgia: 2827
TAX STAMPS: see GREAT BRITAIN--COLONIAL POLICY AND ADMINISTRATION--American Colonies--Stamp duties; REVENUE STAMPS

TAXATION: 825
   see also CUSTOMS (Tariff); EXCESS PROFITS TAX; EXCISE TAXES; INCOME TAX; POLL TAX; PUBLIC FINANCE; REVENUES; SINGLE TAX; TARIFF; UNITED STATES--GOVERNMENT AGENCIES AND OFFICIALS--Internal revenue collectors; taxes on specific products, e.g. TOBACCO TAXES; and Taxation as subheading under names of specific businesses and industries, e.g. COAL INDUSTRY--Taxation
   Assessment:
     Georgia: 1374
     North Carolina--Durham: 2379
     Virginia:
       Buckingham County: 3794
       Frederick County: 5200
     West Virginia:
       Jefferson County: 3832
   Exemption from:
     North Carolina: 1258
   Laws and legislation:
     Confederate States of America: 4921
     United States: 2581, 2863
   Liquor: 2808
     North Carolina: 2952
     United States: 2469
       In North Carolina: 4009, 4152
   Local taxes: see PARISH RATES
   Negroes:
     North Carolina--Anson County: 191
   Sales tax: see as subheading under names of specific states
   Stamp duties: see GREAT BRITAIN--COLONIAL POLICY AND ADMINISTRATION--American Colonies--Stamp duties; REVENUE STAMPS
   Subdivided by place:
     Alabama--Gay's Landing: 5879
     Arkansas: 4776
     British West Indies: 4913
     Confederate States of America: 1181, 1403, 1749, 4711, 4858, 4895, 4924
       see also TAX IN KIND
       Georgia: 5260
       North Carolina: 3043
       South Carolina: 1480
       Virginia: 1240
     France:
       Grenoble: 2195
       Tours: 5323
     Georgia: 1121, 1189, 1993, 3814
       Banks County: 1994
       Chatham County: 3573
       Effingham County: 1375
       Greene County: 1998
       Richland County: 3573
     Great Britain: 676, 1774, 2200, 2708, 3725
       Wilberfoss: 5727
     Ireland: 3567, 5639
     Maryland: 166, 830, 2295
     Massachusetts: 2417
     Missouri--Saint Louis: 5155
     New York: 1065, 4351
     North Carolina: 832, 1189, 1202, 2222, 2553, 3410
       Road work in lieu of payment of taxes: 1417
       Beaufort County: 3921
       Harnett County: 4761
       New Bern: 5709
       Orange County: 3515
       Wilkes County: 2483
     Peru: 4155
     South Carolina: 1877
     Spain: 4980
     United States:
       1790s: 3041
       1800s:
         1840s: 3727
         1890s: 2922

TAXATION:
  Subdivided by place:
    United States (Continued):
      1900s: 3066
      1950s: 4805
    Virginia:
      1780s: 2495, 5031
      1800s: 1920, 4589, 4710
      1860s: 1410
      1890s: 2922
      Clarksville: 4848
      Halifax County: 5483
      Mecklenburg County: 1821
      Nelson County: 5484
    West Virginia: 3058
      Pocahontas County: 5655
    Western States: 5309
TAXATION OF PROPERTY:
  see also ESCHEAT; PARISH RATES
  Great Britain: 2708
    Sussex: 4767
    Yorkshire: 5956
  Illinois: 5785
  Virginia: 33, 1920, 5765
    Amherst County: 5529
TAXES: see TAXATION
TAXIDERMY--Ireland: 3567
TAYLOE, David Thomas: 5195
TAYLOE, John: 3612
TAYLOE, Julia Maria (Dickinson): 3455
TAYLOE FAMILY (Virginia--Genealogy): 3809
TAYLOR, Dr. _____ : 380
TAYLOR, A. G.: 5196
TAYLOR, Anne Williams: 2851
TAYLOR, Annie (Lawrason): 5210
TAYLOR, Bayard: 2449, 5642
TAYLOR, Benjamin: 1308
TAYLOR, D. W.: 4132
TAYLOR, Daniel Walton: 5197
TAYLOR, David: 5202
TAYLOR, Eliza: 5210
TAYLOR, Emma: 5642
TAYLOR, Frances Ann (Richardson): 1547
TAYLOR, Frank E.: 5198
TAYLOR, George: 5199
TAYLOR, Griffin: 5200
TAYLOR, Henry (Maryland?): 743
TAYLOR, Sir Henry (1800-1886): 2471, 5050
TAYLOR, Sir Henry George Andrew: 5201
TAYLOR, Henry P. (North Carolina): 1547
TAYLOR, James (North Carolina, 1791): 2276
TAYLOR, James (North Carolina, 1800s): 5202
TAYLOR, John (1753-1824): 872, 4132, 5203
TAYLOR, John B. (Virginia): 5204
TAYLOR, John J. (North Carolina): 5205
TAYLOR, John W. (1784-1854): 523, 5206
TAYLOR, Johnston: 872
TAYLOR, Joseph J.: 5207
TAYLOR, Lewis: 2517
TAYLOR, Richard (1826-1879): 5208
TAYLOR, Rosalia E.: 5209
TAYLOR, S.: 2857
TAYLOR, Samuel (1749-1811): 5095
TAYLOR, Simon B.: 5910
TAYLOR, Thomas (Maryland): 4726
TAYLOR, Thomas (Virginia): 5210
TAYLOR, Thomas Jerome (North Carolina): 5211
TAYLOR, Tom (1817-1880): 2471
TAYLOR, W. W.: 5212
TAYLOR, Walter Herron: 2212
TAYLOR, William (Baltimore merchant): 5213
TAYLOR, William (congressman from Virginia): 5214
TAYLOR, William (West Virginia tanner): 5215

TAYLOR, William Cooke: 1087
TAYLOR, Zachary: 872, 1296, 1308, 2776, 4720, 4943, 5059, 5130, 5397, 5417, 5470, 5491, 5517, 5710
  Administration: 3321
    Cabinet: 5051
  Election as president: 263, 5149
  Mexican War: 778, 2301
    Soldiers' opinion of: 5324
TAYLOR FAMILY (North Carolina): 761, 5243
TAYLOR FAMILY (Pennsylvania): 5642
TAYLOR FAMILY (Virginia): 761, 5203, 5209
TAYLOR, DAVIES, AND TAYLOR, Savannah, Georgia (firm): 5216
TAYLOR AND WOOTEN CO.: see WOOTEN AND TAYLOR CO.
TAYLOR COUNTY, Florida:
  Salem: 5678
TAYLOR COUNTY, West Virginia:
  Grafton: 694
TAYLORSVILLE, North Carolina: 3289
  Arithmetic exercise books: 208
TAYLORSVILLE, Virginia:
  Schools: 4698
TAZEWELL, Henry: 3456, 4380
TAZEWELL, Littleton Waller: 5217, 5451
TAZEWELL, Tennessee:
  Mercantile accounts: 2116
TAZEWELL COUNTY, Virginia:
  Mercantile accounts: 5400
TCHOUPETOULAS, Louisiana: 1574
TEA:
  Destruction of: 1481
  see also BOSTON TEA PARTY; EDENTON TEA PARTY
TEA GROWING--United States: 2847
TEA TAX--American Colonies: 1481
TEA TRADE:
  American Colonies: 1481
  Georgia: 1440
  Great Britain: 369
TEACHER ASSOCIATIONS: see EDUCATIONAL ASSOCIATIONS
TEACHERS:
  see also TEACHING
  Certification:
    Michigan: 4889
    North Carolina: 122, 3276, 3538, 4897
  Cost of living--Pennsylvania: 4106
  Foreign: see AMERICAN TEACHERS IN ARGENTINA; MISSIONS AND MISSIONARIES
  Personal finance--Virginia: 806
  Private:
    Virginia: 2513, 5357
  Public relations: 1758
  Selection and appointment:
    North Carolina: 2419
      Lilesville: 2493
      Tabernacle Township: 4100
      Wilson: 2642
    Virginia: 4099
  Social and economic status:
    Virginia: 4461
  Strikes: see STRIKES--Teachers
  Wages and salaries: see WAGES AND SALARIES--Teachers
TEACHERS' CONTRACTS:
  North Carolina: 2905
    Lincoln County: 3933
    Moore County: 827
  Wisconsin--Porter: 5307
TEACHERS' INSTITUTES:
  North Carolina: 2833
TEACHERS' RECORDS:
  see also EDUCATION; SCHOOLS; STUDENTS AND STUDENT LIFE; TEACHING
  Georgia--Watkinsville: 1621
  North Carolina: 122, 264, 3434
    Bethania: 813
    Catawba County: 3923, 4532
    Charlotte: 1823

TEACHERS' RECORDS:
  North Carolina (Continued):
    Forsyth County: 3928
    Granville County: 2833
    Guilford County: 3931
    Johnston County: 3932
    Louisburg: 3272
    Mecklenburg County: 3608
    Montgomery County: 5123
    Randolph County: 3596
    Wilkes County: 3942
    Youngsville: 5087
  Pennsylvania:
    Bedford County: 3957
  South Carolina: 4118
    Charleston: 1017
  Virginia: 2559, 2794, 3587
    Charlottesville: 4915
    Elizabeth City County: 1115
    Luray: 461
  West Virginia:
    Shepherdstown: 3710
TEACHING:
  see also EDUCATION; GOVERNESSES; SCHOOLS; STUDENTS AND STUDENT LIFE; TEACHERS' RECORDS; UNIVERSITIES AND COLLEGES--Faculty; and Study and teaching as subheading under names of specific subjects, e.g. ART--Study and teaching
  Blind: see BLIND--Education
  Deaf: see DEAF--Education
  Freedom of: see ACADEMIC FREEDOM
  Negro schools:
    see also NEGROES--Education
    North Carolina: 5041
    South Carolina: 1927
      Beaufort: 3218
  Subdivided by place:
    Alabama--Mobile: 3761
    Arkansas: 5380
    China: 1382
    Connecticut: 351
    France: 4408
    Georgia: 1231
      Augusta: 5246
    Great Britain: 2751
    Illinois: 351, 2225, 3051, 4895
    India: 5525
    Indiana: 2954, 4937
    Louisiana--New Orleans: 5062
    Maryland: 1920
    Massachusetts: 1699, 5088
      South Yarmouth: 2436
    Minnesota: 2544
    Mississippi: 2948, 4895, 5043
    Missouri: 303
    New Jersey: 1920
    North Carolina: 76, 1278, 1523, 1538, 2357, 3436, 4006, 4875, 5737
      Buncombe County: 5603
      Forsyth County: 5982
      Granville County: 2833
      Guilford County: 1055
      Halifax County: 3831
      Oxford: 2654, 4506
    Ohio: 1920, 5380
      Logan County: 5142
    Pennsylvania: 3789, 4106, 4937
    Philippine Islands: 1001
    South Carolina: 2032
    Southern States: 5043
    Tennessee: 983
      Rutherford County: 104
    Texas--Harrisville: 4283
    United States: 904, 2091, 3789
    Vermont: 2544
    Virginia: 117, 152, 1920, 2340, 2370, 2925, 3783, 3788, 5378
      Caroline County: 4698
      King and Queen County: 4968
      Louisa County: 3307
      Lynchburg: 3879
      Norfolk: 4968
      Taylorsville: 4698
      Wytheville: 4596

TEACHING:
   Subdivided by place (Continued):
      West Virginia: 1784, 2007
      Wisconsin: 2896
TEACKLE AND CO.: see READ, TEACKLE & COMPANY
TEAGUE, Ellen: 5218
TEAGUE, John: 208, 5219
TEAGUE FAMILY (North Carolina): 5218
TEAPOT DOME SCANDAL: 4453
TEDDESLEY PARK, England: 3226
TEFFT, Israel Keech: 1466, 2326, 5220
TEHUANTEPEC CANAL (Mexico): 5772
TELEGRAPH: 2982, 4490
   see also SUBMARINE CABLES; TRANSATLANTIC TELEGRAPH
   Construction--Venezuela: 4895
   Military--Virginia: 4945
   Subdivided by place:
      Arkansas: 1154
      Egypt: 2756
      Mississippi: 3415
      Pennsylvania--Blair County: 421
      Southern States: 1021
TELEKI, László: 4650
TELEPHONE WORKERS: see LABOR UNIONS--Telephone workers
TELESCOPES: 4230
TELEVISION: see EDUCATIONAL TELEVISION
TELFAIR, Edward: 5221
TELFAIR (EDWARD) AND COMPANY, Savannah, Georgia: 5221
TELFAIR FAMILY (Virginia--Genealogy): 1842
TELFAIR AND COWPER (firm): see COWPER AND TELFAIR
TELLEZ FAMILY (Spain): 4981
TELLICHERRY, India: 536
TEMAIR, John Campbell Gordon, First Marquis Aberdeen and: see ABERDEEN AND TEMAIR, John Campbell Gordon, First Marquis
TEMPERANCE, Virginia: 852, 5529
TEMPERANCE: 421, 1402, 1482, 1728, 2449, 2493, 4800, 4912, 5529, 5731, 5905
   see also PROHIBITION; TEMPERANCE SOCIETIES
   Laws and legislation:
      Georgia: 5082
      Pennsylvania: 4188
      United States: 1554, 5082
   Subdivided by place:
      Arkansas: 2123, 2346
      Georgia: 662, 731, 2963
         Clopton's Mills: 5760
         Riceboro: 5051
      Great Britain: 2148, 3715, 3912
      Indiana: 4169
      Kentucky: 3325
      Maine: 1554
      Maryland: 5128
      Massachusetts: 4125
      Mississippi: 3415, 4434
      Missouri: 5335
      New England: 1439
      New York: 4806
         Huntington: 726
      North Carolina:
         1700s-1800s: 2530
         1800s: 122, 1556, 2399, 2861, 3581, 4849, 5298
         1800s-1900s: 274, 2720, 3219, 3563
         1900s: 3538
         Cabarrus County: 5582
         Greensboro: 2050
         Lincoln County: 3211
         Rowan County: 4640
      Pennsylvania:
         Huntingdon County: 1798
      South Carolina: 543, 2473, 3123, 4434
         Spartanburg: 4080
      United States:
         1800s: 731, 1219, 1351, 2591
         1800s-1900s: 3029
         1900s: 879

TEMPERANCE:
   Subdivided by place (Continued):
      Virginia:
         1800s: 523, 693, 1115, 2566, 4710, 5339
         1900s: 879
      Washington, D.C.: 701
      West Virginia: 489, 2711
         Leestown: 5591
TEMPERANCE AND RELIGION:
   United Brethren Church: 1920
TEMPERANCE SOCIETIES:
   see also LOYAL TEMPERANCE LEGION; ROYAL TEMPLARS OF TEMPERANCE; SONS OF TEMPERANCE; UNDINE TEMPLE OF HONOR AND TEMPERANCE; WASHINGTON INSTITUTE TEMPERANCE ASSOCIATION
   International organizations: 879
   Massachusetts: 1344
   Missouri: 3197
   North Carolina: 5245
   South Carolina: 4610
   West Virginia--Shepherdstown: 2711
TEMPERANCE SOCIETY OF THE FORK, Clinton County, Missouri: 3197
TEMPLE, Major    : 2096
TEMPLE, Anne: 3806
TEMPLE, Daniel E.: 2360
TEMPLE, Eliza: 2360
TEMPLE, Frederick, Archbishop of Canterbury: 1815
TEMPLE, Henry John, Third Viscount Palmerston: 1632, 1640, 1755, 2836, 3067, 3472, 4024, 4520, 4605, 5026, 5038, 5222
TEMPLE, Maurice: 2360
TEMPLE, R. B.: 263
TEMPLE, Richard, Viscount Cobham: 5934
TEMPLE, Richard Temple Grenville-Temple, First Earl: 92
THE TEMPLE by George Herbert: 4629
TEMPLE-BLACKWOOD, Frederick Temple Hamilton-, First Marquis of Dufferin and Ava: see BLACKWOOD, Frederick Temple Hamilton-Temple-, First Marquis of Dufferin and Ava
TEMPLE-BLACKWOOD, Hariot Georgina (Hamilton) Hamilton-, Marchioness of Dufferin and Ava: see BLACKWOOD, Hariot Georgina (Hamilton) Hamilton-Temple-, Marchioness of Dufferin and Ava
TEMPLE-GRENVILLE, George Nugent-, First Marquis of Buckingham: see GRENVILLE, George Nugent-Temple-, First Marquis of Buckingham
TEMPLEMAN FAMILY (Virginia): 99
TEMPLES: see BUDDHIST TEMPLES
TEMPLETON, J. M.: 527
TEMPLETON, Margaret C.: 2920
TEMPLETON, W. A.: 5223
TEMPLETON, Massachusetts: 3152
TEN YEARS OF PRELUDE by Benjamin Muse: 3820
TENANCY ACTS (India): 774
TENANT FARMING: see FARM TENANCY
TENANTS: see LANDLORD AND TENANT
TENGCHOW, China: 1298
TENNANT, Eleanor Margaret: 472
TENNANT, Thomas: 3631
TENNENT, Sir James Emerson (1804-1869): 2263, 4113
TENNESSEE:
   see also SOUTHERN STATES
   Agricultural implements:
      Prices: 4854
   Agriculture: 2857, 4269, 5426
      see also the following subheadings under TENNESSEE: Crops, and names of specific crops; Farming; Plantations
   Amusements--Nashville: 5623
   Authorship: 3810
   Autograph collecting: 5681
   Autographs--Memphis: 775

TENNESSEE (Continued):
   Banks and banking:
      Lebanon: 872
      Trenton: 2371
   Biographies: 3611, 4358
   Blind: 5426
   Bonds--Memphis: 5443
   Bounty lands: 4291
   Bridges: 3276
   Building materials--Prices: 1531
   Business affairs:
      Hendersonville: 5671
   Business enterprises:
      Knoxville: 5858
   Camp meetings: 1933, 5977
   Choctaw Indians: 2486
   Civil engineering: 3069
   Civil War: see appropriate subheadings under CIVIL WAR; CONFEDERATE STATES OF AMERICA; UNITED STATES--ARMY--Civil War
   Clergy:
      Methodist Episcopal Church, South: 4192
      Protestant Episcopal: 4358
   Commercial conventions:
      Memphis: 757
   Commodity prices: 2661, 4816, 5444
   Copper mines--Investments: 4895
   Cotton:
      Prices: 6, 4269
      Memphis: 4256
   Cotton trade--Memphis: 4256
   Courts--Judgments: 4269
   Creek Indians: 2486
   Crops: 2661, 4083
      Prices: 4269
      Wayne County: 771
   Currency: 1339
   Deaf: 5426
   Democratic Party: 4291
   Dentistry--Fees: 6
   Description and travel:
      1830s: 2822, 2857, 3090
      1840s: 761, 3090
      1850s: 3524
      1860s: 3524
   Diseases:
      Cholera: 330, 2080, 2661
         Nashville: 4854, 5290, 5623
      Yellow fever: 2080
         Chattanooga: 4202
         Memphis: 4202
   Dueling: 5719
   Economic conditions: 2857, 3476
      Knoxville: 5858
      Nashville: 5858
   Education: 2661
      see also TENNESSEE--Schools; TENNESSEE--Teaching
   Elections (1900s): 1200
      see also TENNESSEE--Presidential elections
   Estates--Administration and settlement: 82, 795, 4854
   Evangelism--Memphis: 3552
   Farm accounts: 3692
   Farm life: 2493
   Farming: 872, 1587
      see also the following subheadings under TENNESSEE: Agriculture; Crops, and names of specific crops; Plantations
   Finance: 3069, 4269
      see also TENNESSEE--Household finance; TENNESSEE--Personal finance
   Fires--Nashville (1856): 5290
   Free Negroes--Arrests: 5623
   Freedmen--Education: 1344
   Government agencies and officials:
      Department of Employment Security: 1197
      Department of Labor: 1197
      Department of Public Welfare: 1197

TENNESSEE:
  Government agencies and officials
      (Continued):
    Governors:
      John Sevier (1785-1788): 4746
      Samuel Houston (1827-1829): 2664
      Andrew Johnson (1862-1865):
          2847
  Health conditions: 4083
  Health programs: 1197
  Health resorts:
    Tate Springs: 5051
  Hiring of slaves: 3692
  Historical studies:
    Benton County: 4894
  Household finance:
    Memphis: 4763
    Nashville: 4854
  Household management: 4269
  Housing: 1200
  Indians of North America:
    see also names of specific
        tribes under TENNESSEE
    Anthropological studies: 4894
    Government relations: 2486
    Land titles--Extinguishment:
        3176
    Removal: 541
    Treatment of: 2486
    Wars: 2486
  Iron industry: 1289
  Ku Klux Klan: 1587
    Lynchburg: 677
  Labor arbitration: 1197
  Labor laws and legislation: 1197,
      1200, 5409
  Labor unions: 1200
    see also CONGRESS OF INDUSTRIAL
        ORGANIZATIONS
    Dues: 1197
    Elections: 1200
    Finance: 1197, 1200
    Government and civic employees:
        1197
    Industrial: 1193
    Insurance and allied workers:
        1197
    Membership: 1197
    Optical and instrument workers:
        1197
    Paper workers: 1197
    Plant guards: 1197
    Plumbers: 5409
    Steel workers: 1197
    Telephone workers: 1197
    Textile workers: 1197
    Utility workers: 1197
  Land: 1001
    Lawsuits: 214
    Purchases and sales: 5224
    Subdivided by place:
      Brownsville: 4139
      Haywood County: 4139
      Morgan County: 5224
  Land claims: 214
  Land companies: 1630
  Land deeds and indentures: 872,
      4269
    Henderson County: 5341
    Nashville: 4854
    Washington County: 718
  Land grants: 2664, 2847, 4269
  Land laws: 4269
  Land settlement: 702, 734, 872
    Morgan County: 5224
  Land speculation: 214, 4746, 5612
  Land titles--Morgan County: 5224
  Law practice: 872
  Lawyers' accounts--Nashville: 3844
  Legal affairs: 4746
  Legal education: see CUMBERLAND
      UNIVERSITY LAW SCHOOL
  Legislature: 872, 1197, 5635
  Liquor manufacturing: 677
  Manufacturing: 5426
  Mentally ill: 5426
  Mentally retarded: 5426

TENNESSEE (Continued):
  Mercantile accounts: 2116, 3692
    Altamont: 5187
  Mercantile affairs: 872
  Methodist churches:
    Conferences: 3646
    General Conference: 33
    Tennessee Conference: 3646
  Migration to:
    From North Carolina: 4765
  Militia:
    1st Brigade, Enrolled Militia,
        District of Memphis: 1833
  Mosquitoes: 5623
  Mountains: 761
  Negroes: see the following
      subheadings under TENNESSEE:
      Free Negroes; Freedmen; Slaves
  Orphans: 5426
  Personal debt--Memphis: 5443
  Personal finance: 5671
  Phosphate mining: 4924
  Plantations: 1061
    see also the following
        subheadings under TENNESSEE:
        Agriculture; Crops, and names
        of specific crops; Farming
    Castalian Springs: 5935
    Nashville: 2308
  Political patronage:
    Democratic Party: 4291
  Politics and government:
    1790s: 5046
    1800s: 330, 872
    1820s: 1302, 5046
    1840s: 5757
    1850s: 5757
    1900s: 4918
  Poor: 5426
  Poverty: 4951, 5268
  Presbyterian churches: 2661
    Hendersonville: 5671
  Presidential elections:
    1804: 3076
    1856: 4291
    1860: 4291
  Prisoners and prisons: 5426
  Promissory notes: 4269
    Collection of: 5935
  Property lists: 5612
  Protestant Episcopal churches:
      4339, 4358
  Railroads: 3069, 3176, 3205
    Construction: 2814, 3069, 3692
  Religion: 2661, 4192, 4269, 4801,
      4894
    Nashville: 3844
  Religious literature:
    Methodist: 3646
  Road construction: 4746
  Schools:
    see also TENNESSEE--Education;
        TENNESSEE--Teaching
    Girls' schools and academies: 872
    Rutherford County: 104
  Secession and secessionist
      sentiment: 155, 872, 1319, 2371
  Slave trade: 1933, 3692, 4269,
      5623, 5859, 5935
    Prices: 4291
  Slavery: 771, 4269
  Slaves: 1319, 4269
    Division of ownership: 82
    Health: 3692
    Treatment of: 104
  Social conditions: 5719
  Social life and customs: 3766,
      4131, 4269, 5426
  Southern Unionists: 716, 1403,
      3331
    Knoxville: 2260
  Strikes: 1197
    Printers--Nashville: 5623
  Surveying: 3069
  Tax receipts: 4269
  Teaching: 983
    Rutherford County: 104
  Theater: 872

TENNESSEE (Continued):
  Tobacco trade--Hendersonville: 5671
  Trade and commerce: 4109
    Carriages and buggies: 5623
    Drugs--Memphis: 4288
    Food: 5006
  Universities and colleges: 731
    see also FISK UNIVERSITY; GEORGE
        PEABODY COLLEGE FOR TEACHERS;
        GRANT MEMORIAL UNIVERSITY;
        JACKSON COLLEGE; KING COLLEGE;
        LA GRANGE FEMALE COLLEGE;
        NASHVILLE NORMAL AND
        COLLEGIATE THEOLOGICAL
        INSTITUTE; SOUTHWESTERN
        UNIVERSITY; STATE NORMAL
        COLLEGE; TENNESSEE STATE
        FEMALE COLLEGE; UNION
        UNIVERSITY; UNIVERSITY OF THE
        SOUTH; VANDERBILT UNIVERSITY;
        WEST TENNESSEE COLLEGE
    Philanthropy: 1584
    Students and student life:
      Greenville: 872
  Utopian communities: 4770
  Voter registration: 1200
  Wages and salaries: 1200
  Wagoners: 2814
  Weather: 2661
    Wayne County: 771
  Whig Party: 872
  Wills: 872, 4269
  Women authors: 3810
  Workmen's compensation: 1197
TENNESSEE AND PACIFIC RAILROAD: 1439
TENNESSEE CENTRAL RAILWAY COMPANY:
    3986
TENNESSEE COLONISATION COMPANY,
    Antwerp, Belgium: 5224
TENNESSEE COLONIZATION SOCIETY: 5635
TENNESSEE COMMITTEE FOR JUSTICE IN
    COLUMBIA: 1197
TENNESSEE FEDERATION OF LABOR: 4962
  Convention (1917): 5409
TENNESSEE FURNITURE INDUSTRIES, INC.:
    1197
TENNESSEE INDUSTRIAL PLANNING
    NEWSLETTER: 1197
TENNESSEE LAND COMPANY: 2785
TENNESSEE RIVER: 2944
  Civil War: 4275
    Confederate fortifications: 4253
    Union naval operations: 5437
TENNESSEE STATE FEMALE COLLEGE,
    Memphis, Tennessee: 775, 2588
TENNESSEE STATE INDUSTRIAL UNION
    COUNCIL: 1193
TENNESSEE STATE PLANNING COMMISSION:
    1197
TENNESSEE VALLEY AUTHORITY: 4805
TENNEY, Parker G.: 5225
TENNYSON, Alfred, First Baron
    Tennyson: 2449, 4543, 5050, 5226
  Bibliography: 4008
  Portraits: 4008
TENNYSON, Frederick: 5226
TENNYSON, Hallam: 5226
TENSAS PARISH, Louisiana: 3322
  New Carthage: 2802
  Plantations: 4582
TERHUNE, Mary Virginia (Hawes): 5227
TERMINAL CARE: 2934
TERRASSON, Antoine: 5228
TERRASSON, Barthelemy: 5228
TERRASSON (JOHN) AND COMPANY, Paris
    and Lyons, France: 5228
TERRASSON BROTHERS, Philadelphia,
    Pennsylvania: 5228
TERRE BONNE PARISH, Louisiana:
  Houma: 4636
TERRE HAUTE, Indiana: 3618, 4303
TERRELL, James W.: 5202
TERRIER, U.S.S.: 4274
TERRITORIAL EXPANSION: see
    Annexation as subheading under
    names of territories annexed

945

TERRITORIAL WATERS:
  Fishing rights:
    see also FISHING RIGHTS
    Canada: 4567
TERRY, Alfred Howe: 1418, 2679, 2991
TERRY, Joseph: 5229
TERRY, Mrs. Joseph: 5619
TERRY, Robert: 5229
TESH, William A.: 5230
TEST ACT (Great Britain, 1827): 3226
TEST OATHS:
  see also LOYALTY OATHS
  Abolition of:
    Great Britain: 3226
    West Virginia: 1828
    North Carolina: 2469
TETE, Mozambique:
  Description: 5725
TETTERTON, Jesse: 5231
TEXAS:
  see also SOUTHERN STATES
  Agricultural products:
    Prices: 647
      Price fixing: 592
  Agriculture: 1153, 2554, 5651
    see also the following
      subheadings under TEXAS: Crops,
      and names of specific crops;
      Farming; Plantations
    Birdville: 5194
  American poetry: see TEXAS IN
    POETRY
  Annexation by the United States:
    1086, 1424, 3325, 4924
    Effect on foreign affairs: 3325
  Authorship: 3363
  Banks and banking:
    Republic of Texas: 5693
  Business affairs--Laredo: 3597
  Canals: 5613
  Cattle raising:
    New Washington: 3772
  Civil War: see appropriate
    subheadings under CIVIL WAR;
    CONFEDERATE STATES OF AMERICA;
    UNITED STATES--ARMY--Civil War
  Commodity prices: 2294
    Colorado County: 1741
    Comal County: 218
  Cotton--Storage: 592
  Cotton growing: 592, 5508
  Cotton mills--Taxation: 592
  Crops: 2920, 4562
    see also names of specific crops
      under TEXAS
    Colorado County: 1741, 5174
  Currency: 1339
  Currency counterfeiting: 2808
  Democratic Party: 988, 5141
  Description and travel:
    1800s: 57, 1355, 4052
    1840s: 510, 622, 4353, 5508
    1850s: 510, 622, 5508
    1860s: 155, 510, 622, 1592,
      5855
    1870s: 1614, 2559
    Bell County (1874): 4283
  Diseases: 2920
    Cholera--Houston: 4562
    Typhoid fever: 5613
    Yellow fever--Houston: 4562
  Economic conditions:
    1800s: 57
    1850s: 5651
    1860s: 4562
    1880s: 4158
  Education: 266, 2920
  Employment prospects: 4269
  Estates--Administration and
    settlement: 4170, 4269
  Explorers: 4353
  Farming: 1587, 4269
    see also the following
      subheadings under TEXAS:
      Agriculture; Crops, and names
      of specific crops;
      Plantations
    Hays County: 273

TEXAS (Continued):
  Food: 4353
    Prices--Comal County: 218
  Fortifications: 1446
  Fourth of July celebrations:
    Brazos Bottom: 4353
  Government agencies and officials:
    Farm Bureau: 592
    Governors:
      A. J. Hamilton: 4170
  Gubernatorial elections: 5141
  Hiring of slaves:
    New Washington: 3772
  Hunting: 4353
  Independence from Mexico: 2089,
    4286
  Inheritance laws: 4170
  Ku Klux Klan: 592
  Labor conditions: 2554
  Labor unrest: 592
  Land: 964, 2662, 3657, 5232
    Colorado County: 1741
    Purchases and sales: 724, 3772,
      3846, 4269, 4569
  Land deeds and indentures:
    Jackson County: 2385
    Liberty County: 2385
  Land development: 2876
  Land grants: 4249
  Land laws and legislation: 4170
  Land settlement: 693, 1909, 2385,
    4269
  Land speculation: 724, 2517, 4596,
    4924, 5612
  Law practice--Waxahachie: 817
  Liquor prices: 218
  Mercantile affairs: 3565
  Merchants--Comal County: 218
  Migration to: 86, 593, 1980, 2855,
    4562, 5194
    From Alabama: 5174
    From Kansas: 4158
    From Louisiana: 4286
    From North Carolina: 4765
  Missions and missionaries: 4353
    Protestant Episcopal: 1361, 4758
  Municipal government by
    commission:
      Galveston: 1001
  Natural history: 4353
  Negroes:
    see also TEXAS--Hiring of slaves;
      TEXAS--Slaves
    Social status: 1138
  Notaries: 5293
  Oil fields--Beaumont: 1951
  Personal finance: 4615
    Houston: 3463
  Pioneer life: 2808, 4286, 4347,
    4353
  Plantations: 1153
    see also the following
      subheadings under TEXAS:
      Agriculture; Crops, and names
      of specific crops; Farming
  Police--Negroes: 1138
  Politics and government:
    1840s: 1980
    1850s: 1980, 2370
    1860s: 1980, 2370, 3719, 4170
    1870s: 2370, 4170
    1880s: 5513
  Primitive Baptist Church:
    Mabank: 318
  Prohibition: 592
  Property lists: 5612
  Protestant Episcopal Church: 1361
  Public schools: 2934
    El Paso: 2927
  Railroads: 218, 3657
    Freight rates: 592
  Reconstruction: 566
    Federal military occupation: 5425
    Houston: 4562
  Religion: 57, 837, 2920
  Religious life: 4269
  Road vehicles--Steam powered: 3470

TEXAS (Continued):
  Secession and secessionist
    sentiment: 155, 639, 3524, 4434
  Slave trade: 2117
    Prices: 647
    Suppression by United States
      Navy: 4593
  Slaves: 1741
    see also TEXAS--Hiring of slaves
    Rumors about insurrections: 4202
  Social conditions: 1262, 1909,
    4765, 5651
    Harrisville: 4283
  Social life and customs:
    1800s: 1153, 2920
    1830s: 4269
    1840s: 4269
    1850s: 4269
    1860s: 3392, 4170
    1870s: 4170
    1880s: 299
    1890s: 299
    1900s: 3657
    Galveston (1877): 3363
    Orangeville (1882): 4158
  Stocks: 5293
  Teaching--Harrisville: 4283
  Tornadoes: 1557
  Trade and commerce:
    Carriages and buggies: 5623
    Lumber: 3008
    Slaves: see TEXAS--Slave trade
  Traveling salesmen: 3534
  Universities and colleges: see
    AUSTIN COLLEGE; BAYLOR
    UNIVERSITY; UNIVERSITY OF TEXAS
  Voter registration: 5425
  Weather: 4353
  Woolen mills--Taxation: 592
TEXAS COUNTY, Missouri: 1949
TEXAS DECLARATION OF INDEPENDENCE:
  4286
TEXAS GRAIN DEALERS ASSOCIATION: 592
TEXAS IN POETRY: 2739
TEXAS LAND COMPANY, Richmond,
  Virginia: 5232
TEXAS RANGERS: 2137, 3520
TEXAS REVOLUTION: 2089
THE TEXT OF THE OLD TESTAMENT
  CONSIDERED by Samuel Davidson: 2653
TEXTBOOKS: 1758
  North Carolina: 3538, 4918, 5737
    Catawba County: 4532
    Granville County: 2833
    Rockingham County: 4533
  Southern States: 3887
  United States Constitution: 3501
TEXTILE BULLETIN: 1195
TEXTILE ENGINEERING: see SCHOOLS--
  Textile engineering; and Textile
  engineering as subheading under
  names of specific universities and
  colleges
TEXTILE INDUSTRY:
  see also COTTON MILLS; HOSIERY
    MILLS; SILK INDUSTRY; TAPESTRY
    MANUFACTURE; WEAVING AND
    SPINNING; WOOLEN MILLS
  Company stores:
    North Carolina: 5888
  Company towns:
    Southern States: 5310
  Employee seniority:
    North Carolina: 5234
  Federal taxation--Missouri: 1695
  Finance:
    Missouri: 1695
    North Carolina: 1611
      Mooresville: 3757
  Government control:
    Confederate States of America:
      1829
  Inventories:
    North Carolina--Cooleemee: 1719
  Labor conditions: see LABOR
    CONDITIONS--Textile industry
  Legal affairs--North Carolina: 5310

TEXTILE INDUSTRY (Continued):
　Management: 5100
　Profits--North Carolina: 1611
　Rebates of duties on soap:
　　Great Britain: 5277
　Silk throwing--North Carolina: 2108
　Stocks:
　　North Carolina: 1611
　　　Mooresville: 3757
　　South Carolina: 300
　Subdivided by place:
　　Alabama: 5237
　　France:
　　　Dauphiné: 4408
　　　Tours: 5323
　　Georgia: 5237
　　　Augusta: 1829
　　　Waynmanville: 2272
　　Great Britain: 5259, 5726
　　Illinois: 2682
　　Maryland: 1877
　　Massachusetts--Lowell: 776
　　Missouri: 1695
　　North Carolina: 1195, 1584, 1588, 2359, 2877, 5237
　　　Cramerton: 5100
　　　Durham: 1228, 1611, 1719
　　　Gaston County: 5887
　　　Greensboro: 3171
　　　Mecklenburg County: 5235
　　　Mooresville: 3757
　　South Carolina: 300, 4918, 5236, 5237
　　　Charleston: 1009
　　　Spartanburg: 5233
　　Southern States: 1612
　　Virginia--Falmouth: 2165
TEXTILE MACHINERY:
　see also HOSIERY MACHINERY; KNITTING MACHINERY
　Parts--North Carolina: 1277
　Subdivided by place:
　　Massachusetts: 5100
　　North Carolina: 1611
　　　Mount Holly: 5100
TEXTILE RESEARCH: 5234
TEXTILE TRADE:
　see also DRY GOODS TRADE; HOSIERY TRADE; MILLINERY GOODS TRADE
　Importation of Irish linen: 416
　Missouri: 1695
　North Carolina: 2359
　　Wilkesboro: 4107
　Virginia: 2165
TEXTILE WORKERS:
　Education: 5234
　Labor unions: see LABOR UNIONS--Textile workers
　Scotland--Glasgow: 3179
　Wages and salaries: see WAGES AND SALARIES--Textile workers
TEXTILE WORKERS UNION OF AMERICA: 1195, 1196, 1197, 1198, 1199, 1202, 5233
　Convention (1941): 3171
　Finance: 5235
　Local unions: 5234
　North Carolina:
　　Greensboro-Burlington Joint Board: 5234
　　Mecklenburg County Joint Board: 5235
　South Carolina:
　　Cherokee-Spartanburg Joint Board: 5233
　　South Carolina State Director: 5236
　Southern Regional Director: 5237
TEXTILE WORKERS VOICE: 3066
TEXTRON SOUTHERN, INC., Mecklenburg County, North Carolina: 5235
TEXTILES: see CIVIL WAR--CIVILIAN LIFE--Scarcity of textiles; DRY GOODS; and names of specific kinds of textile goods, e.g. DUCK (Textile)
THACKERAY, Harriet Marian: 5050

THACKERAY, William Makepeace: 3684, 5813
THAILAND:
　British embassy in: 4709
　Description and travel: 2463
　Foreign relations--France: 4709
　Judicial reform: 4709
　Kings and rulers: 5238
　Missions and missionaries: 5238
　Public opinion:
　　Opposition to British: 4709
　Royal family: 4709
THAMES DISTRICT (Great Britain): 5024
THAMES TUNNEL: 306
THANET, Octave: see FRENCH, Alice
THANKSGIVING DAY:
　1789: 5537
　1863: 627
THARP, Mary (Van Metre): 457
THATCHER, Jonathan N.: 5239
THATCHER COMPANY: see STANDARD-COOSA-THATCHER COMPANY
THAYER, Abbott Handerson: 826
THAYER, Eli: 5240
THAYER, Sylvanus: 2363
THAYER, William Roscoe: 706
THEATER:
　see also ACTING; AMERICAN DRAMA; DRAMATISTS; ENGLISH DRAMA; FRENCH DRAMA; LITTLE THEATER MOVEMENT; PERFORMING ARTS; SPANISH DRAMA
　Production and direction:
　　Finance: 1521
　　Massachusetts--Boston: 3108
　　United States: 54
　Reviews: 3617
　Subdivided by place:
　　Alabama--Mobile: 3611
　　Germany: 3617
　　Great Britain: 3617
　　Ireland: 3617
　　Louisiana: 489
　　North Carolina--Durham: 4502
　　Russia: 3617
　　Tennessee: 872
　　United States: 3029, 3617
THEATER BOOKINGS:
　Virginia--Richmond: 3829
THEATER PROGRAMS: 3797
　Massachusetts--Boston: 3108
THEATERS (buildings):
　North Carolina--New Bern: 4977
　United States: 4556
　Virginia: see RICHMOND THEATRE FIRE
THÉÂTRE D'AUTREFOIS: 5167
THELWALL, John: 5241
THELWALL, England: 4627
THEODAT, Charles Hector, Comte d'Estaing: 1236, 3209, 3444, 5228
THEODORUS, Bishop of Mopsuestia: 5156
THEOLOGICAL SEMINARIES:
　Baptist: see VIRGINIA BAPTIST SEMINARY
　Congregational: see ANDOVER THEOLOGICAL SEMINARY
　New York: see UNION THEOLOGICAL SEMINARY
　Presbyterian: see AUBURN THEOLOGICAL SEMINARY; COLUMBIA (S.C.) THEOLOGICAL SEMINARY; PRINCETON THEOLOGICAL SEMINARY; UNION THEOLOGICAL SEMINARY (Virginia)
　Protestant Episcopal: see BELMONT THEOLOGICAL SEMINARY; PROTESTANT EPISCOPAL THEOLOGICAL SEMINARY
　United Brethren in Christ: see BONEBRAKE THEOLOGICAL SEMINARY
THEOLOGICAL STUDENTS:
　see also Students and student life as subheading under names of specific theological seminaries
　Connecticut: 3142
　Massachusetts: 3142
　New York: 3142

THEOLOGY: 656, 4596
　see also BIBLICAL SCHOLARSHIP; CALVINISTIC THEOLOGY; CHURCH UNIVERSAL; DEISM; GOD, Attributes of; GOOD AND EVIL; GRACE; HOLY SPIRIT (Theology); MIRACLES, Doctrine of; ORIGINAL SIN; SOCINIANISM; and Doctrine as subheading under names of specific denominations
　Study and teaching: 5899
　　Germany: 2592
　　North Carolina: 5014
　Subdivided by place:
　　Great Britain: 5598, 5647
　　New Hampshire: 354
　　United States: 1219
　　Virginia: 917
THERAPEUTIC SPRINGS: see HEALTH RESORTS
"THESE MANY HEARTHS" by J. K. T. Smith: 4984
THESES: see as subheading under names of specific universities and colleges
THETFORD, Vermont: 3218
THEUS, Simeon: 5073
THIAN, Prosper: 5242
THIAN, Raphael Prosper: 5242
THIBODEAUX, Louisiana: 478
　Sugar plantations: 3160
THIBODEAUX PARISH, Louisiana: 623
THIERS, Louis Adolphe: 3734
THIESEN, Frederick: 2271
THIGPEN FAMILY (North Carolina): 1120
THINTON, B. J.: 5243
THINTON, Delphinia L. E.: 5243
THINTON FAMILY (North Carolina): 5243
THIRD ARMY CORPS UNION (Union veterans organization): 4802
"THIS VALUED LINEAGE" by J. K. T. Smith: 4894
THISELTON-DYER, Sir William Turner: 5553
THISTLE, Taylor Z.: 1344
THOM, David: 5244
THOMAS, A. J. K.: 5245
THOMAS, Alisha: 2276
THOMAS, Anna (Branson): 5252
THOMAS, Augustus: 3797
THOMAS, Chester: 4188
THOMAS, D. P.: 5249
THOMAS, Edith Matilda: 2871
THOMAS, Edward: 2027
THOMAS, Ella Gertrude (Clanton): 5246
THOMAS, Francis: 3378, 5247
THOMAS, Freeman Freeman-, First Marquis of Willingdon: see FREEMAN-THOMAS, Freeman, First Marquis of Willingdon
THOMAS, George Henry: 4723, 5248
THOMAS, H. B.: 5249
THOMAS, Henry E.: 5252
THOMAS, Howard: 1913
THOMAS, James (Georgia judge): 5250
THOMAS, James, Jr. (1806-1882, Virginia): 5251
THOMAS, James Augustus (1862-1940): 5252
THOMAS, James R. (North Carolina): 5258
THOMAS, Jefferson: 5246
THOMAS, Jesse Burgess: 2301
THOMAS, John (Georgia): 5254
THOMAS, John (South Carolina): 5253
THOMAS, John Drayton (Great Britain): 5255
THOMAS, John W. (Virginia): 5248
THOMAS, John Wesley (1798-1872, Great Britain): 5255
THOMAS, Lorenzo (1804-1875): 5430
THOMAS, Nannie D.: 743
THOMAS, Norman Mattoon: 4948
THOMAS, Rebecca: 5256
THOMAS, Wailes: 4402
THOMAS, William (d. 1554): 1910

THOMAS, William George (North
    Carolina): 1915
THOMAS, William Henry
    (Pennsylvania): 5249
THOMAS, William Holland (1805-1893):
    3025, 5202, 5257, 5258
THOMAS, William Holland, Jr.: 5258
THOMAS FAMILY (Maryland): 743
THOMAS FAMILY (North Carolina): 1915
THOMAS FAMILY (South Carolina): 5253
THOMAS COUNTY, Georgia:
    Thomasville: 2317, 3390
        Social life and customs: 2493
THOMAS F. WOOD, INC., Wilmington,
    North Carolina: 5880
THOMAS JEFFERSON IN 1814 ed. by
    Henry S. Rowe and T. Jefferson
    Collidge, Jr.: 2139
THOMAS JEFFERSON MEMORIAL
    ENDOWMENT: 4020
THOMAS K. JONES, Boston,
    Massachusetts (firm): 2933
THOMAS PAINE HISTORICAL ASSOCIATION:
    4025
THOMAS RICHARDSON, Fayetteville,
    North Carolina (firm): 2360
THOMAS SANFORD & CO. (North
    Carolina): 5298
THOMAS Y. CROWELL COMPANY: 3797
THOMASON, James: 3453
THOMASON'S CROSS ROADS: 1351
THOMASSON, Emma: 5259
THOMASSON, Thomas: 5259
THOMASTON, Connecticut: 1205
THOMASTON, Georgia: 4754
THOMASVILLE, Georgia: 2317, 3390
    Social life and customs: 2493
THOMASVILLE, North Carolina: 788,
    2906
    Barrel staves: 2377
    Farmers' Alliance: 3996
THOMASVILLE (N.C.) SUB-ALLIANCE:
    3996
THOMPKINS, Henry B.: 1458
THOMPSON, Colonel _____ : 4097
THOMPSON, Anna Boynton: 2400
THOMPSON, Benjamin O.: 5260
THOMPSON, Carl: 4948
THOMPSON, Cyrus: 5457
THOMPSON, Daniel: 5264
THOMPSON, David Matt: 5457
THOMPSON, Edith: 4146
THOMPSON, Frances: 4259
THOMPSON, Gilbert L.: 5271
THOMPSON, Helen J.: 1376
THOMPSON, Henry J. H. (b. 1832): 5261
THOMPSON, Henry Yates (1838-1928):
    5262
THOMPSON, Hugh Smith: 1424
THOMPSON, Jacob: 581, 5263
THOMPSON, James (fl. 1717, New Jersey):
    1752
THOMPSON, James (fl. 1775-1793, North
    Carolina): 5264
THOMPSON, James Maurice (1844-1901):
    2449
THOMPSON, John A. (West Virginia):
    5265
THOMPSON, John Edgar: 421
THOMPSON, John H.: 5266
THOMPSON, John Reuben (1823-1873):
    103, 581, 1494, 2449, 2612, 3163,
    4616, 5193
THOMPSON, Lela: 5267
THOMPSON, Lucretia E. (Cooper): 5261
THOMPSON, Mary Ellen: 2469
THOMPSON, Mary Octavine: 1275
THOMPSON, Meriwether Jefferson: 5452
THOMPSON, R. B. (Virginia): 4416
THOMPSON, Sarah E.: 5268
THOMPSON, Stephen W.: 5269
THOMPSON, Sylvanus H.: 5268
THOMPSON, Thomas: 5270
THOMPSON, Vance Charles: 1424
THOMPSON, W. H. (Indiana): 4588
THOMPSON, Waddy (1798-1868): 791,
    872, 5271

THOMPSON, Waddy (1867-1939): 2449
THOMPSON, Wilborn: 5272
THOMPSON, Wilbur: 5273
THOMPSON, William (fl. 1775-1813,
    North Carolina): 1752
THOMPSON, William (South Carolina):
    5274
THOMPSON, William G. (Virginia):
    5275
THOMPSON, William H. (North
    Carolina): 2446
THOMPSON FAMILY (Alabama): 444
THOMPSON FAMILY (Arkansas): 4894
THOMPSON FAMILY (Great Britain):
    4894
THOMPSON FAMILY (North Carolina):
    4894, 5264
THOMPSON FAMILY (Pennsylvania):
    5264
THOMPSON FAMILY (Tennessee): 4894
THOMPSON FAMILY (Virginia): 4894
THOMPSON AND FRASER: see FRASER
    AND THOMPSON
THOMPSON AND SPALDING (firm): 785
THOMPSON AND TIBBETS: see TIBBETS
    AND THOMPSON
THOMPSON ORPHANAGE, Charlotte, North
    Carolina: 4918
THOMPSON ORPHANAGE JUBILEE
    COMMITTEE: 5298
THOMPSON v. DICKINSON: 3242
THOMPSON v. FLUDD: 4624
THOMPSON'S CROSS ROADS, Virginia:
    1351
THOMPSONVILLE, Connecticut:
    Shipbuilding: 1549
THOMSON, _____ (South Carolina hotel
    owner): 5407
THOMSON, Catherine: 448
THOMSON, Charles (1729-1824): 5276
THOMSON, Charles Edward Poulett,
    First Baron Sydenham: 3050, 5277
THOMSON, Kate: 5278
THOMSON, R. H.: 4709
THOMSON, William S. (b. 1866): 5457
THOMSON, Georgia: 5594
    Schools: 4895
THOMSON (Ga.) HIGH SCHOOL: 4895
THORBURN, Septimus Smet: 5279
THOREAU, Henry David: 720, 1636
THORN SPRINGS, Virginia: 3424
THORNBURGH AND HOSKINS (firm): 3692
THORNE, Edward Alston: 5280
THORNE, James W.: 5281
THORNE, Jennie Doris Arthur (Jones):
    1210
THORNE, John: 1637
THORNE, Julia A.: 2351
THORNTON, Caroline: 5282
THORNTON, Edward (1799-1885): 332
THORNTON, Sir Edward (1817-1906):
    3238
THORNTON, Henry: 867
THORNTON, M. F.: 5282
THORNTON, Mary Egerton: 1660
THORNTON, Sarah H.: 5282
THORNTON, Thomas (d. 1814): 3183
THORNTON, William (1759-1828): 5575
THORNTON, William C. (Pennsylvania):
    5282
THORNTON, William W. (Virginia): 5283
THORNTON FAMILY (Great Britain,
    Virginia and Pennsylvania): 5282
THORNTOWN, Indiana: 328
THORNWELL, James Henley: 2612, 4031
THOROTON, Thomas: 5284
THOROUGHFAIR GAP, Virginia:
    Civil War hospital: 2829
THORP, Benjamin Peter: 5285
THORVERTON, England: 1158
THRASH, Jacksie Daniel: 5457
THREE RIVERS, Canada:
    Description: 3087
THRESHING MACHINES:
    Virginia: 1591, 2680
THRIFT, George N.: 5286
THROOP, Enos Thompson: 2497

THURBER, George: 3674
THURLOW, Edward, First Baron
    Thurlow: 5287
THURMAN, William Pleasant: 5288
THURMOND, Benjamin: 5289
THURMOND, John A.: 5290
THURMOND, Sarah (Jones): 5290
THURMOND, Strom: 3048
THURSBY-PELHAM, Arthur Harvey: see
    PELHAM, Arthur Harvey Thursby-
THURSBY-PELHAM, Charles Augustus:
    see PELHAM, Charles Augustus
    Thursby-
THWING, Charles Franklin: 5291
THYATIRA, North Carolina: 3334
THYNNE, Thomas, Third Viscount
    Weymouth and First Marquis of
    Bath: 5330
TIBBETS AND THOMPSON, Huntsville,
    Alabama (firm): 5006
TICEHURST, Marjorie Hall: 4823
TICHBORNE CLAIMANT (Great Britain):
    3722
TICKNOR, Francis Orray: 5292
TICKNOR FAMILY (Georgia): 5292
TICKNOR AND COMPANY, Boston,
    Massachusetts: 4069
TICONDEROGA, New York: 1219
TIDEWATER CIO POLITICAL ACTION
    COMMITTEE: 1201
TIDEWATER POWER COMPANY (Virginia):
    3447
TIENTSIN, China--Description: 1373
TIERNAN, Barney: 5293
TIERNAN, Frances Christine (Fisher):
    1494, 2449, 5294, 5457
TIERNAN, M. Jeff: 5293
TIERNAN FAMILY (Texas): 5293
TIERNEY, George: 2149
TILDEN, Samuel Jones: 2273, 2726
TILDEN AND VANCE CLUB, Morehead
    City, North Carolina: 3960
TILES--Portraits in tile: see
    INTERIOR DECORATION--Portraits in
    tile
TILESTON NORMAL SCHOOL, Wilmington,
    North Carolina: 617, 3607
TILGHMAN, Alexander: 3647
TILGHMAN, James: 5296
TILGHMAN, Richard IV: 5296
TILGHMAN, Susan: 3647
TILGHMAN, Tench: 5295
TILGHMAN, William: 5296
TILLETT, Wilbur Fisk: 799
TILLEY, Nannie Mae: 2449, 5297
TILLINGHAST, Anne Troy (Wetmore):
    5298
TILLINGHAST, Anne Wetmore: 5298
TILLINGHAST, Cyrus P.: 5298
TILLINGHAST, Daniel Jencks: 5298
TILLINGHAST, David Ray: 5298
TILLINGHAST, Emily: 5298
TILLINGHAST, Jane (Norwood): 5298
TILLINGHAST, John Baker: 5298
TILLINGHAST, Paris Jencks, Sr.: 5298
TILLINGHAST, Samuel Willard: 5298
TILLINGHAST, Sarah Ann: 5298
TILLINGHAST, Susan: 5298
TILLINGHAST, Thomas Hooper: 5298
TILLINGHAST, William Holroyd: 5298
TILLINGHAST, William Norwood: 5298
TILLINGHAST FAMILY (North Carolina):
    3873, 4517, 5298
TILLINGHAST'S CROCKERY STORE (North
    Carolina): 5298
TILLMAN, Benjamin Ryan: 592, 1364,
    1424, 2473, 3405, 4453, 5299
TILLMAN, James A.: 1107
TILLMANISM: see POLITICS AND
    GOVERNMENT--South Carolina--
    Tillmanism
TILLSON, Ida: 2959
TILTON, Eleanor: 720
TILTON, George S.: 2681
TILTON, Lydia Ann: 5928
TILTON, Georgia:
    Steam powered machinery: 4872

TILTON, New Hampshire: 5061
TIMBER:
  see also SHIP TIMBER
  Austria: 1599
  Georgia:
    Camden County: 1835
    Covington: 1382
  Great Britain: 712
TIMBER AGENTS--Florida: 3993
TIMBER FRAUDS--Louisiana: 20
TIMBER LAND:
  Georgia--Great Ogeechee District: 812
TIMBER RIGHTS:
  Great Britain--Sussex: 4767
TIMBER TRADE:
  North Carolina: 3221, 3364, 5372
TIMBERLAKE, Ambrose Cramer: 5300
TIMBERLAKE, Edward Walter: 5457
TIMBERLAKE, Henry: 3806
TIMBERLAKE, John S.: 4743
TIMBERLAKE, John W. (Virginia): 5301
TIMBERLAKE, Walker: 5302
TIMBERVILLE, Virginia: 5275
TIMEPIECES: see CLOCKS AND WATCHES
THE TIMES (London): 4036, 4503, 4709, 5534
THE TIMES (North Carolina): 2357
THE TIMES OF CEYLON (newspaper): 952
TIMMONS, John Wesley, Sr.: 5303
TIMMONS FAMILY (Ohio): 5303
TIMROD, Henry: 2449, 3418
TIN CANS (food containers): 5955
TIN MINING:
  see also MINING
  Bolivia: 2473
TIN TRADE--New York: 1575
TINSMITHING--South Carolina: 1575
TINWORKING MACHINERY--New York: 1575
TINDALL, Lucy: 4229
TINMOUTH, Vermont: 1067
TINSLEY, William: 2146
TIOGA, U.S.S.: 3983
TIOGA COUNTY, New York:
  Candor: 4538
  West Candor: 2204
TIPPAH COUNTY, Mississippi:
  Civil War: 755
TIPPECANOE, Battle of (1811): 5229
TIPPECANOE CLUB, Howard County, Missouri: 1620
TIPPECANOE COUNTY, Indiana:
  Lafayette: 4436
TIPTON, John: 571
TIPTON, Missouri--Hospitals: 5975
TIPU SULTAN: 3315
TIRRELL MURDER TRIAL: 4813
TIRZAH CIRCUIT, Methodist churches: 3646
TISHOMINGO COUNTY, Mississippi:
  Jacinto: 4442
TITANIC (sinking of): 3887
TITCHFIELD, Scott: 2146
TITHE BILL (1830s, Great Britain): 4605
TITHE COMPOSITION ACT (1830, Great Britain): 4024
TITHERINGTON, Richard Handfield: 2449
TITHES:
  Great Britain: 4230
    see also CHURCH AND STATE IN GREAT BRITAIN
  Collection: 4605
TITLE INSURANCE AND TRUST COMPANY: 5962
TITO, Josip Broz: 83
TITUS ("Southern ruffian"): 2358
"TO EGERIA" by Alexander B. Meek: 3611
"TO LITTLE ERNEST" by Frances Sargent (Locke) Osgood: 3999
"TO MISS S. WARING, ON HER SEEING ME PAINT THE HEARTH IN MY HUSBAND'S STUDY" by Caroline (Howard) Gilman: 2045

"TO MR._____" by Louisa H. Nicholls: 3892
"TO NORA BELLE": 2374
"TO THE EXILED PATRIOTS" by Robert Southey: 4913
"TO THE HUMBLE-BEE": 1698
"TO THE SAMPSON COUNTY VOLUNTEERS" by S. W. Faison: 1751
TOBACCO: 3981, 5792
  Civil War: see CIVIL WAR--CONFISCATION OF PROPERTY--Tobacco
  Physiological effect: 4578, 5096, 5513
    see also CIGARETTE SMOKING AND HEALTH
  Storage:
    Virginia--Richmond: 4579
  Subdivided by place:
    Great Britain: 737
    Maryland: 5295
    North Carolina: 122, 5298
    Southern States: 1460
    United States: 4805
    Virginia: 331, 490, 2369, 5355
      Richmond: 187
TOBACCO BROKERS: see TOBACCO TRADE
TOBACCO CULTURE:
  China: 2191, 5252
  Connecticut: 25
  Kentucky: 57
  Maryland--West River: 2267
  Missouri: 57
  North Carolina: 2192, 2863, 4849
    Orange County: 3351
  Virginia: 99, 2712, 4127, 5751
    Albemarle County: 3699
    Bedford County: 4049
    Buckingham County: 3794
    Halifax County: 330
    Henry County: 4131
    Nottoway County: 5469
    Patrick County: 4131
    Prince Edward County: 5884
    Spring Garden: 2902
    Westmoreland County: 917
  West Virginia: 5689
TOBACCO CURING:
  North Carolina: 325
TOBACCO FACTORS: see TOBACCO TRADE
TOBACCO FARMING: see TOBACCO CULTURE
TOBACCO INDUSTRY: 83
  Accounts:
    North Carolina--Milton: 5843
    Virginia--Petersburg: 1873
  Advertising: 1586
  Chewing tobacco:
    Virginia: 2337
      Petersburg: 3345
  Construction of factories:
    Georgia--Savannah: 5221
  Finance:
    North Carolina--Durham: 3762
  Machinery:
    see also PATENTS--Tobacco machinery
    Cigarette making machines: 5297
    New York: 4079
    Packaging machinery: 5923
    Virginia--Danville: 3378
  Stocks--Virginia: 655
  Taxation: see TOBACCO TAXES
  Subdivided by place:
    China: 2191
    Florida--Quincy: 5740
    France: 4079
    Germany: 4079
    Great Britain: 4079
    Japan: 4060
    Kentucky: 5499
    Louisiana--New Orleans: 2302
    New York:
      New York: 2302
      Ogdensburg: 5989
    North Carolina: 556, 1584, 1588
      Durham: 513, 5923
      Milton: 5843

TOBACCO INDUSTRY:
  Subdivided by place:
    North Carolina (Continued):
      Winston-Salem: 3745, 4788
    Philippine Islands: 4656
    Scotland: 4079
    Virginia: 4043, 4131, 4366
      Danville: 3378, 4918
      Petersburg: 655, 2302, 3179
      Richmond: 2302, 3179, 5251
      Spring Garden: 2902
      Stafford County: 1813
      Winchester: 2142
TOBACCO INDUSTRY AND HEALTH: 5513
TOBACCO INSTITUTE: 83
TOBBACO MACHINERY: see PATENTS--Tobacco machinery; TOBACCO INDUSTRY--Machinery
TOBACCO MANUFACTURE: see TOBACCO INDUSTRY
TOBACCO MARKETING: see TOBACCO TRADE
TOBACCO PLANTATIONS:
  Maryland--West River: 2267
  Virginia:
    Campbell County: 1059
TOBACCO PLANTING: see TOBACCO CULTURE
TOBACCO SMOKING: 4050
  see also CIGARETTE SMOKING AND HEALTH
TOBACCO TAXES: 2798
  Georgia: 817
  North Carolina: 2952
    Wake County: 4009
  South Carolina: 817
  United States: 2876
  Virginia: 1568
TOBACCO TRADE:
  see also CIGAR TRADE; CIGARETTE TRADE
  Finance--Virginia: 454
  Plug tobacco prices:
    Georgia and South Carolina: 817
  Prices: 2703, 3566
    Kentucky: 2363, 5499
    Louisiana--New Orleans: 3643
    Maryland: 5295
    North Carolina: 5298
      Littleton: 2399
      Winston-Salem: 3745
    Virginia: 558, 1957, 2363, 4924
      Danville: 3378
      Petersburg: 3643
      Richmond: 32, 2305, 2373
  Quotas--North Carolina: 2863
  Tobacco products:
    Georgia--Eatonton: 3352
  Subdivided by place:
    Australia: 3179, 5251
    Brazil: 2363
    Canada: 3179
    China: 4060, 5252
    Europe: 2703, 4288
    Far East: 5252
    France: 5295
    Georgia: 817, 4857, 5040, 5251
    Great Britain:
      1700s: 456, 625, 2703
      1700s-1800s: 28, 5221, 5653
      1800s: 564, 1301, 1633, 2742, 5251
      London:
        1700s: 1813
        1800s: 4288
    Japan: 4060
    Kentucky: 57, 2363
    Louisiana: 5251
      New Orleans: 3643, 5933
    Maine: 5251
    Maryland: 5295
      Baltimore: 5228, 5933
      West River: 2267
    Massachusetts: 1633, 5251
    Missouri: 57
    Netherlands: 144, 5251
    New Hampshire: 1529
    New York: 5731

TOBACCO TRADE:
　　Subdivided by place (Continued):
　　　North Carolina
　　　　1700s: 3780
　　　　1700s-1800s: 5298
　　　　1800s: 1871, 4734, 5280
　　　　1800s-1900s: 4857
　　　　1900s: 5962
　　　　Advertising: 1586
　　　　Durham: 513
　　　　Edenton: 5228
　　　　Milton: 5843
　　　　New Bern: 5228
　　　　Roxboro: 5455
　　　　Wake County: 4009
　　　　Winston-Salem: 3745
　　　Ohio--Cincinnati: 4326
　　　South Carolina: 500, 817
　　　　Charleston: 5228
　　　Spain: 2742
　　　Tennessee--Hendersonville: 5671
　　　United States: 2742, 5933
　　　Virginia:
　　　　1600s: 4297
　　　　1700s: 144, 456, 625, 1556
　　　　1700s-1800s: 28, 1863, 2363, 2633, 2637, 3179, 5653
　　　　1800s: 138, 564, 1093, 2360, 2381, 2567, 2680, 4720, 5148
　　　　1900s: 2922
　　　　Alexandria: 5228
　　　　Danville: 5958
　　　　Halifax County: 822
　　　　Henry County: 4131
　　　　Lynchburg: 2302
　　　　Middlesex County: 454
　　　　Nottoway County: 1811
　　　　Patrick County: 4131
　　　　Petersburg: 655, 1336, 2176, 2302, 3643, 4764
　　　　Pittsylvania County: 1161
　　　　Richmond: 2302, 2373, 5827
　　　　Stafford County: 1813
　　　　Yorktown: 5228
　　　West Virginia:
　　　　Harpers Ferry: 5938
TOBACCO WAREHOUSES:
　　Maryland: 4886
　　Receipts: 5958
　　North Carolina:
　　　Greenville: 4858
　　　Martin County: 4849
TOBACCO WORKERS: see LABOR UNIONS--Tobacco workers; WAGES AND SALARIES--Tobacco workers
TOBACCO WORKERS INTERNATIONAL UNION: 1150
TOBACCOLAND KIWANIS CLUB: 83
TOBYHANNA MILLS, Pennsylvania:
　　Lumber trade: 5985
TOD, James: 3645
TODD, Alexander: 5304
TODD, Charles Burr: 72
TODD, Dorothea (Payne): 2326, 3455, 3612
TODD, E. Bradford: 5305
TODD, Mary: 2035
TODD & GEE: see HURT, TODD & GEE
TODD'S TAVERN, Virginia: see CIVIL WAR--CAMPAIGNS, BATTLES, AND MILITARY ACTIONS--Virginia--Todd's Tavern
TODDY POND, Maine:
　　Lumber mill accounts: 3554
TOKYO, Japan: 4060
TOKYO AMERICAN SCHOOL, Tokyo, Japan: 5252
TOLBERT, Emma: 5306
TOLBERT, Robert E.: 5306
TOLBERT (ROBERT E.) AND SON: 5306
TOLBERT, William E.: 5306
TOLEDO, Francisco: 4155
TOLEDO Y LEYVA, Pedro: 4155
TOLLES, Myron: 5307
TOLLS:
　　Bridges--Massachusetts: 2304
　　Roads--Virginia: 2728

TOLSTAIA, Aleksandra L'vovna, grafinīa: 4641
TOLSTOI, Alekseĭ Nikolaevich, graf: 4641
TOLSTOY, Alexandra Leo: see TOLSTAIA, Aleksandra L'vovna, grafinīa
TOLSTOY, Alexander: see TOLSTOI, Alekseĭ Nikolaevich, graf
"TOM SAWYER AND DON QUIXOTE" by George Santayana: 1097
TOMAH, Wisconsin: 4974
TOMATOES: 291
TOMBECKBEE ASSOCIATION OF FRENCH IMMIGRANTS (Alabama): 5308
TOMBIGEE RIVER, Alabama:
　　Land: 5308
TOMBS--Sudan: 1974
TOMBSTONES: see ENGRAVINGS--Tombstones
TOMKINS, John: 1733
TOMLIN, Carter Braxton: 5309
TOMLIN, Charlotte: 5309
TOMLIN, Louise: 5309
TOMLIN, Notely J.: 5310
TOMLINSON, R. R.: 518
TOMPKINS, Charles Brown: 5311
TOMPKINS (D. A.) COMPANY: 5312
TOMPKINS, Daniel Augustus: 5312
TOMPKINS, Giles: 4706
TOMPKINS, Mrs. Giles: 4706
TOMPKINS, John: 4706
TOMPKINS, Joseph M.: 5313
TOMPKINS, Mary (Gapen): 5311
TOMPKINS FAMILY (Genealogy): 5311
TOMPKINS COUNTY, New York:
　　Ithaca: 1175, 2434, 2705
　　see also CORNELL UNIVERSITY
TOMPKINSVILLE, Alabama:
　　Mercantile accounts: 4827
　　Tavern accounts: 4827
TOM'S BROOK, Virginia: 2965
TONDEE, Robert P.: 5314
TONDEE, William: 5314
TONDEE FAMILY (Virginia): 5314
TONNAGE AND POUNDAGE (Great Britain): 2152
TONSILLECTOMY: 5732
TOOKE, Peter: 5797
TOOKER, Lewis Frank: 2871
TOOLE, J. Henry: 633
TOOLS:
　　Trade--Georgia
TOOMBS, Robert Augustus: 1121, 1422, 3671, 5051, 5315
TOPHAM, Washington (person): 5316
TOPOGRAPHY:
　　United States: 3145
　　Venice (state): 405
TORELLO PHOLA DE PUPPIO: 5317
TORIES (American Revolution): see AMERICAN REVOLUTION--Loyalists
TORMOHAM, England: 4229
TORNADOES:
　　Mississippi: 5740
　　　Natchez: 3415
　　Texas: 1557
TORONTO, Canada: 3949
TORONTO, Ohio:
　　World War I: 829
TORPEDOES:
　　see also CONFEDERATE STATES OF AMERICA--NAVY--Mining operations
　　Experiments: 4986
TORRE, Peter della: 5318
TORRENCE, Adam: 5319
TORRENCE, Alexander H.: 5319
TORRENCE, Frederic Ridgely: 2871, 5320
TORRENS SYSTEM (land title registration): 4232
TOTAL ABSTINENCE SOCIETY, Shepherdstown, West Virginia: 2711
TOTTEN, James: 5321
TOTTEN, Silas: 2728
TOTTENHAM COURT CHAPEL (Great Britain): 5647

TOUCEY, Isaac: 3118
TOULON, France:
　　French Revolutionary Wars: 1674
TOURAINE (Province), France: 5323
TOURGEE, Albion Winegar: 2540, 5322
TOURISM: see TRAVEL
TOURIST TRADE--Western States: 2368
TOURS (Généralité), France: 5323
TOURS, France: 5179, 5323
TOVAR, José Pelleza Y: see PELLEZA Y TOVAR, José
TOWANDA, Pennsylvania: 3372
TOWANDA BRIDGE (Pennsylvania): 4188
TOWEL INDUSTRY:
　　North Carolina--Franklinton: 5450
TOWER OF LONDON: 3809
TOWN AND GOWN: see COMMUNITY AND COLLEGE
TOWN FORK CREEK (North Carolina): 4080
TOWN HALL CLUB, New York, New York: 4976
TOWN MEETINGS:
　　Massachusetts--Boxborough: 2456
TOWNE, Charles Hanson: 3394
TOWNER, Benjamin T.: 5324
TOWNER, Thomas Harris: 5324
TOWNER FAMILY (West Virginia): 5324
TOWNES, A. S.: 5325
TOWNS, Elizabeth B.: 5751
TOWNSEND, _____: 4089
TOWNSEND, Edward Davis (1817-1893): 5242
TOWNSEND, Edward Waterman (1855-1942): 2871
TOWNSEND, Frederick: 3311
TOWNSEND, George Alfred: 5326
TOWNSEND, Isaiah: 5281
TOWNSEND, Meredith White: 5327
TOWNSEND, Sylvanus: 5328
TOWNSHEND, Charles (1725-1767): 5330
TOWNSHEND, Francis J.: 5329
TOWNSHEND, George, First Marquis Townshend: 92, 5330
TOWNSHEND, Thomas, First Viscount Sydney: 5331
TOWNSVILLE, North Carolina: 2338
　　Presbyterian Church: 1361
TOWSON, Nathan: 1926
TRACTS, Religious: see RELIGIOUS LITERATURE
"TRACT'S CRITICALL AND HISTORICAL COMPILED BY SIR JAMES TURNER KYN'T": 5379
TRACY, Frank Basil: 706
TRACY, James Francis: 5332
TRACY, Sabra S.: 4373
TRACY, Thomas (d. 1821): 5332
TRADE ACTS (Great Britain, 1822): 3230
TRADE AND CHRISTIANITY: see CHRISTIANITY AND TRADE
TRADE AND COMMERCE: 2933
　　see also AMERICAN REVOLUTION--Trade and commerce; BARTER; MERCHANTS; PEDDLERS AND PEDDLING; SHIPPING; Foreign trade as subheading under names of specific countries and states; and specific kinds of trade, e.g. COTTON TRADE; TOBACCO TRADE
　　Coastal trade:
　　　New Bern to New York: 1871
　　Africa: 2682, 4913
　　Carolina Province: 780
　　Ceylon: 952
　　China: 5252
　　France:
　　　Dauphiné (Province): 4408
　　　Le Havre: 5860
　　Germany--Ulm: 3598
　　Great Britain: 4541
　　　Bristol: 5731
　　　Liverpool: 5860
　　India: 278
　　Iowa--Dubuque: 323
　　Louisiana--New Orleans: 5860

TRADE AND COMMERCE (Continued):
    Maine: 323
        Castine: 5860
    Massachusetts: 323
    Middle West: 1920
    Mississippi: 1762
    Mississippi River: 2386, 5933
    Mississippi Territory: 3041
    New England: 172
    New Hampshire: 323
    North Carolina: 172, 5391
        Hertford: 3907
    Pennsylvania: 1117
        Philadelphia: 164, 5860
    Peru: 4155
    Philippine Islands: 3313
    Portugal--Lisbon: 5228
    Spain: 4980
    United States: 274, 4564, 4678,
        4805, 4896, 5398
    Virginia: 1066
        Suffolk: 1838
    West Indies: 172
TRADE AND NAVIGATION LAWS: see
    NAVIGATION--Laws and legislation;
    TRADE REGULATION
TRADE ASSOCIATIONS: see BOOT AND
    SHOE INDUSTRY--Trade associations
TRADE REGULATION:
    Cuba: 4983
    Great Britain: 3230
        In Carolina Province: 780
    Ireland: 16
    New York: 4109
    Spain: 586
    United States: 3041
TRADE UNIONS: see LABOR UNIONS
TRADING POSTS: see INDIANS OF NORTH
    AMERICA--Trading posts
TRAFFIC ACCIDENTS:
    Lawsuits--South Carolina: 5930
TRAFFORD, Lionel James: 5333
TRAHERN, James: 1336, 5334
TRAHERN, William: 1336, 5334
TRAINER, Mary Caroline: 4881
TRAINING, Military: see UNIVERSITY
    OF VIRGINIA--Military training;
    and Training as subheading under
    names of armies
TRAITORS: see TREASON
TRANQUILITY PLANTATION (North
    Carolina): 1361
TRANSATLANTIC CABLES: 1792
TRANSATLANTIC MAIL PACKETS: 3053
TRANSATLANTIC SLAVE TRADE: see
    SLAVE TRADE--Transatlantic
TRANSATLANTIC TELEGRAPH: 2688, 2712
TRANSATLANTIC VOYAGES:
    see also TRAVEL--Ocean voyages
    1700s:
        1740s: 2541
        1750s: 197
        1760s: 197
        1780s: 5298
    1800s: 43
        1800s: 2570
        1820s: 99, 841, 4490
        1840s: 2682, 4876
        1850s: 2503, 3960
        1890s: 4175
    1900s: 180
        1920s: 4719
        1940s: 300
TRANSLATIONS: see Translations from/
    into as subheading under specific
    forms of literature, e.g. ITALIAN
    POETRY--Translations into English;
    BIBLE--Translations into
TRANSPACIFIC VOYAGES (1870s): 2241
    see also TRAVEL--Ocean voyages
TRANSPORT OF AGRICULTURAL PRODUCTS:
    see AGRICULTURAL PRODUCTS--
    Transport of
TRANSPORT OF SICK AND WOUNDED: see
    CIVIL WAR--TRANSPORT OF SICK AND
    WOUNDED

TRANSPORTATION:
    see also Transportation as
    subheading under names of armies;
    and specific means of
    transportation, e.g. CANALS;
    RAILROADS; SHIPPING; STEAMBOAT
    LINES
    Effect of advancements on slavery:
        5940
    Laws and legislation:
        Pennsylvania: 2027
    Rates:
        Confederate States of America:
            4965
        Virginia: 2520
    Subdivided by place:
        Brazil: 4876
        Confederate States of America:
            1726
        Florida: 3447
        Georgia: 3447
        India: 278
        Mississippi River: 5498
        Ohio: 5149
        South Carolina: 669, 3447
        United States: 5398
        Virginia: 1486, 1512, 3440, 3447
TRANSPORTATION OF CONVICTS:
    Great Britain: 2708, 2994
TRANSPORTATION OF CURRENCY: see
    CURRENCY--Transportation of
TRANSPORTATION OF FREIGHT: see
    FREIGHT AND FREIGHTAGE
TRANSPORTATION PASSES: see CIVIL
    WAR--TRANSPORTATION PASSES; and
    Transportation passes as subheading
    under names of armies
TRANSPORTATION WORKERS: see UNITED
    TRANSPORT SERVICE EMPLOYEES
TRANSSEXUALISM: see SEX CHANGE
TRANSVAAL: 1792, 2322, 5027
    Foreign relations:
        Great Britain: 4520
    Jameson Raid: 4514
TRANSVAAL WAR (1880-1881): 5876
TRANSYLVANIA COLLEGE, Lexington,
    Kentucky: see TRANSYLVANIA
    UNIVERSITY
TRANSYLVANIA COMPANY: 795, 1843, 5768
TRANSYLVANIA COUNTY, North Carolina:
    Brevard: 3247
    Land deeds and indentures: 5768
TRANSYLVANIA UNIVERSITY, Lexington,
    Kentucky: 5342
    Medical education: 1421, 3199
    Students' notebooks: 1513
TRAPHAGEN, Ethel: 4900
THE TRAPHAGEN SCHOOL OF FASHION: 4900
TRAPPSCHUH, Bernhard: see LYTTON-
    BERNARD, Bernard
"TRATTATO DE' RIMEDJ CONTRO LE
    SCOMMUNICHE INVALIDE . . . LUGLIO
    1723" by Pietro Giannone: 2015
TRAVADA, Ventura: 4155
TRAVEL:
    1800s: 281, 372, 733, 983, 3325,
        4269, 5205, 5751
    1900s: 2398, 4073
    Boat:
        Massachusetts to South Carolina:
            5840
        Mississippi River: 404
        South Carolina to Virginia: 4596
    Carriage:
        New York: 33
        Virginia: 33
    Horseback:
        New York to California: 4485
    Naval cruises (Great Britain):
        Atlantic Ocean: 2754
        Australia: 3744
        Caribbean Sea: 2754
        Far East: 3744
        Indian Ocean: 2754
        Madeira Islands: 3744
        Mediterranean Sea: 2754

TRAVEL (Continued):
    Naval cruises (United States):
        2963, 5329, 5841
        Azores: 3447
        Caribbean Sea: 3983
        China: 4986
        East coast to west coast: 3899
        East Indies: 4986
        Hawaii: 3447
        Japan: 4986
        Mediterranean Sea: 3447
        Near East: 4986
        Pacific Ocean: 2870
        South America: 841, 3118, 4019
        West Indies: 841, 4013
        To Chile: 3447
        To Far East: 2265, 3899, 4017
    Ocean voyages: 5298
        see also TRANSATLANTIC VOYAGES;
        TRANSPACIFIC VOYAGES
        Around Cape Horn: 411, 4881
        Indian Ocean: 2682
        South America: 1506, 3960
        To California: 2893, 3960, 4881
            Via Isthmus of Panama: 4834
        To India:
            From Great Britain: 2421
            From United States: 4881
        To Pacific coast:
            From Great Britain: 2259
        To South America: 5824
    Packet boats:
        James and Kanawha rivers: 2890
    Railroad: 221, 3415
        Canada: 4175
        Georgia: 5819
        Kentucky: 1811
        Ohio: 1811
        South Carolina: 2503
            To Virginia: 4596
        Southern States: 249, 284
        Texas: 218
        United States: 1697
            New York to California: 4485
        Virginia: 1811
    Riverboat:
        Colombia: 198
        Mississippi--Natchez: 5047
        Mississippi River: 1556, 4246
        Ohio River: 3255
        United States:
            New York to California: 4485
    Ship: 4032
        Atlantic Coast: 618, 1697
        North Sea: 244
        Spain to Great Britain: 1875
        To New Orleans: 4888
    Stagecoach: 4095, 5747
        New England States: 150
        Southern States: 249, 284
        United States:
            New York to California: 4485
        Virginia: 330
        To South Carolina:
            From Baltimore: 3808
            From Boston: 5840
        To Virginia:
            From South Carolina: 4596
    Steamboat:
        Arkansas River: 5380
        Atlantic Coast: 618
        Canada--Great Lakes: 4175
        Mississippi River: 5380
        Ohio River: 4269, 5380
        Passenger accommodations:
            Long Island Sound: 150
        Red River: 155
        Southern States: 249, 284
        Virginia: 330
        Natchez to Houston: 151
        Tuscaloosa to Tampa Bay: 3611
        To Europe: 5972
        To India: 3471
    Wagon:
        Kentucky: 2064
        Virginia: 2064

TRAVEL (Continued):
  Subdivided by place:
    Afghanistan: 5797
    Africa:
      1800s: 128
      1900s: 2463, 4900
      Northern: 4192
    Alabama (1800s): 1490, 2822,
      3611, 4720
    Andes Mountains: 1506
    Arctic region: 4556
    Arkansas:
      1800s: 57, 1084, 5508
      1900s: 1361
    Austria: 2617, 4858
    Azores: 1284
    Belgium (1800s): 4695, 5038
    Bolivia (1847): 4155
    Brazil:
      1810s: 1333
      1840s: 4876
      1870s: 2750
      1880s: 1644
    Burma--Shan States: 4709
    California: 611, 1115, 1355,
      1370, 3051, 4353
    Canada:
      1810s: 3087
      1820s: 3485
      1860s: 2366
    Central America (1900s): 4900
    Ceylon (1800s): 1464
    Chile (1825): 3102
    China:
      1700s-1800s: 5038
      1800s: 339
      1860s: 1373
      1900s:
        1900s: 2191
        1920s: 2463
    Colombia (1800s): 1506
    Connecticut (1840s-1850s): 5508
    Cuba: 2849
    Denmark:
      1790s: 306
      1900s: 3451
    Eastern States: 1355, 2983
    Egypt:
      1800s:
        1850s: 3053
        1860s: 3053
        1880s: 39
        1890s: 39
      1800s-1900s: 4020
      1900s:
        1920s: 2934
    El Salvador (1892): 4719
    Europe:
      1700s:
        1780s: 1884, 4625
        1790s: 960, 2869, 3396
      1700s-1800s: 5038
      1800s: 128, 573, 1798, 2407,
        3008, 3284, 3761
        1810s: 2139, 2326
        1820s: 2058
        1830s: 1792
        1840s: 781, 1891
        1850s: 1109, 1792, 2521,
          2985, 3053, 4616, 5059,
          5193
        1860s: 1352, 2336, 2608,
          3053, 4485
        1870s: 20, 157, 661, 3710,
          4485, 5045
        1880s: 661, 1084, 1424, 2032,
          3587, 3809, 4080, 4702
        1890s: 43, 3527
      1800s-1900s: 4020
      1900s: 3306, 3424
        1900s: 4271, 5786
        1910s: 572, 4271, 4449, 5786
        1920s: 960, 4192, 4271
        1930s: 3607
    Far East (1800s): 1889
    Fayal Island: 1284
    Florida:
      1800s: 1947

TRAVEL:
  Subdivided by place:
    Florida:
      1800s (Continued):
        1850s: 1084
        1860s: 4743
        1870s: 670
    France:
      1700s:
        1780s: 4625
        1790s: 2869
      1700s-1800s: 5179
      1800s: 4770, 5038
        1810s: 1049, 4348
        1820s: 1049, 2058, 2077,
          4348, 4490
        1830s: 4348, 4490
        1840s: 4695, 5133, 5193
        1850s: 5963
        1860s: 2617
        1870s: 157
        1880s: 1463
      1900s:
        1900s: 4022
        1930s: 5968
        1940s: 1275
    French Indo-China (1920s): 2463
    Georgia:
      1800s:
        1800s: 5686
        1810s: 5686
        1820s: 158
        1840s: 5480, 5508
        1850s: 5508
        1860s: 1500, 4743
        1870s: 5731
    Germany:
      1794: 306
      1800s: 5038
        1820s: 4490
        1830s: 4490
        1840s: 244, 4695
        1850s: 5459
        1860s: 1962, 2617, 3674, 5459
        1870s: 157, 1962, 3674
        1880s: 3674
        1890s: 1768
      1800s-1900s: 4858, 5730
      Berlin: 4492
    Great Britain:
      1700s:
        1720s: 4969
        1770s: 2776
        1780s: 4348
      1800s: 43, 1115, 3179, 4911
        1800s: 5038
        1810s: 2139, 3423, 4348, 5038
        1820s: 4348, 4383
        1830s: 4348
        1840s: 5133
        1850s: 2503, 2985, 3424, 5963
        1870s: 20, 157, 1467, 3107
        1880s: 1463
    Greece:
      1880s-1890s: 39
      1920s: 2934
    Hawaii: 2084
    Hong Kong:
      1800s: 1464
      1920s: 2463
    Idaho (1800s): 57
    Illinois: 33, 489, 1177
    India:
      1800s: 563, 2421
      1900s: 2463
    Indiana: 1177, 5018, 5508
    Iowa: 1177
    Ireland:
      1770s: 2776
      1800s: 43, 2543, 5038
    Italy:
      1700s:
        1780s: 4625
        1790s: 2869
      1700s-1800s: 558
      1800s: 577, 4770, 5038
        1810s: 1049
        1820s: 1049, 2058

TRAVEL:
  Subdivided by place:
    Italy:
      1800s (Continued):
        1830s: 4490
        1840s: 5133
        1850s: 2678
        1860s: 1352
        1880s: 39, 1424
        1890s: 39
      1800s-1900s: 5730
      1900s: 4020
      Genoa: 1775
      Naples: 39
    Jamaica (1800s): 1506
    Japan:
      1887: 2532
      1893: 217
      1905: 2191
      1920s: 2463, 4858
    Java (1800s): 598, 1464
    Kalahari Desert: 4514
    Kansas: 5018
    Kentucky: 4457
      1794: 2887
      1800s: 57
        1800s: 1843
        1820s: 3450
        1840s: 5508
        1850s: 5508
    Kenya (1920s): 2463
    Khyber Pass (1880s): 5525
    Korea (1920s): 2463, 4858
    Lake Erie (1838): 2690
    Lake Ontario (1838): 2690
    Lake Superior (1860): 3710
    Liberia: 3325
    Louisiana:
      1840s: 622, 5508
      1850s: 622, 5193, 5508
      1860s: 622, 4369
    Maine (1881): 43
    Maryland (1800s): 33, 4944
    Mexico:
      1840s: 622, 778
      1850s: 622
      1860s: 622, 5855
      1880s: 4080
    Michigan: 1177
    Middle Atlantic States: 1748,
      3229
    Middle West: 128, 1601, 1681,
      2366, 2983
    Minnesota: 1084, 1177
    Mississippi:
      1700s-1800s: 5047
      1800s: 57, 3611
      Natchez: 3322
    Mississippi River: 404, 4246,
      4369, 4810
    Mississippi Territory: 3041
    Mississippi Valley: 1060, 3524
    Missouri:
      1800s: 57, 1490, 5018
      1850s: 489
      1860s: 4369
    Mozambique: 5725
    Near East: 5156
      1800s: 128
      1900s: 572
    Netherlands:
      1820s: 4490
      1830s: 4490
      1840s: 4695, 5133
    New England States:
      1800s: 339, 1827
      1820s: 4490
      1850s: 1748, 4602
      1870s-1890s: 3229
    New Mexico--Santa Fe: 1174
    New York:
      1800s: 33
      1820s: 2677, 2820, 2828
      1830s: 2677, 5298
      1840s: 5298
      1850s: 5149, 5298
      1870s: 3390
      1880s: 4968

TRAVEL:
  Subdivided by place:
    New York:
      1800s (Continued):
        1890s: 4968
      1900s:
        1930s: 5252
      New York City: 2366, 5246
      Saratoga Springs: 3607
      Western New York: 4490
    North Carolina:
      1700s: 819
      1800s: 5018
      1810s: 3808
      1820s: 529
      1830s: 2857
      1840s: 761
      1850s: 4921
      Photographs:
        1884: 4414
        1900s: 180
      Winston-Salem: 5575
    Northern States:
      1800s: 4616
      1820s: 2828, 3485
      1860s: 2449, 5193
      1870s: 2449, 3390, 5193
      1880s: 2449
    Norway (1878): 157
    Ohio: 4457
      1800s: 57
      1840s: 230, 5508
      1850s: 230, 5508
      1860s: 2601
    Ohio River (1820s): 4810
    Ohio Valley (1842): 1060
    Palestine:
      1800s: 5524
      1900s: 2934, 4192
    Panama (1800s): 1115
    Panama Canal Zone (1900s): 5786
    Pennsylvania: 4457
      1770s: 1735
      1800s: 33
      1810s: 872
      1820s: 872, 2828
      1830s: 872
      1840s: 3006
      1850s: 1362, 5149
      1880s: 43
      Philadelphia: 4924, 5730
    Peru (1743): 4155
    Philippine Islands (1920s): 2463, 4858
    Portugal (1920s): 2934
    Rhine Valley (1800s): 1049
    Russia:
      1800s: 5797
      1810s: 2139
      1850s: 3053
      1860s: 3053
      1870s: 157
      Saint Petersburg: 5661
    Tangier (1906): 4022
    Scotland :
      1700s:
      1770s: 5527
      1780s: 4084, 5527
      1800s: 1115
      1880s: 1463
    South Carolina:
      1800s: 3754, 4616
      1800s: 2636
      1810s: 2636, 3808
      1820s: 529, 2664
      1830s: 2664, 2822
      1860s: 1500
      1870s: 5731
      Accommodations (1820): 158
    Southern States:
      1800s: 1115
      1810s: 2047
      1820s: 2047
      1830s: 3490
      1840s: 284, 3490, 3570, 4596
      1850s: 1748, 3277
      1860s: 155, 3424, 5082, 5261

TRAVEL:
  Subdivided by place:
    Southern States (Continued):
      1900s:
        1900s: 5572
        1950s: 1137
    Spain: 2811
      1800s: 1775
      1900s:
        1900s: 4022, 4719
        1920s: 2934
    Sweden:
      1794: 306
      1878: 157
      1900s: 3451
    Switzerland:
      1800s: 4770, 5038
      1810s: 1049
      1820s: 1049, 4490
      1830s: 4490
      1840s: 5133
      1850s: 558, 5963
      1860s: 5050
      1870s: 5050
      1880s: 1463
      Geneva: 1775
    Tennessee:
      1800s:
      1830s: 2822, 2857
      1840s: 761
    Texas:
      1800s: 57, 1355
      1840s: 510, 622, 4353, 5508
      1850s: 510, 622, 5508
      1860s: 155, 510, 622, 1592, 5855
      1870s: 1614, 2559
    Thailand (1920s): 2463
    Turkey:
      1800s: 3053
      1900s: 2934
    United States:
      1780s: 1582
      1800s:
      1840s: 5493
      1850s: 5493, 5928
      1860s: 5050, 5493
      1880s: 2626
      1800s-1900s: 5740
      1900s: 3424
    Uruguay (1816): 1333
    Utah (1800s): 57
      Salt Lake City: 1174
    Virginia:
      1700s: 819
      1800s: 43, 3560
      1810s: 872, 2677, 3808
      1820s: 872, 2677, 3450
      1830s: 872, 2822
      1840s: 230, 1697, 1790, 3853
      1850s: 568, 5149
      1860s: 155, 5193
      1870s: 3229
      1880s: 3229
      1890s: 3229
      Photographs (1900s): 180
      "Monticello": 2139
      Williamsburg: 630
    Washington, D.C.:
      1800s: 33
      1820s: 2216, 2820
      1830s: 2216
      1850s: 4943
      1800s-1900s: 5730
      Expenses (1840): 4517
    Washington Territory (1800s): 57, 5018
    West Virginia (1800s): 43
    Western States:
      1800s: 1798
      1850s: 406, 4353
      1860s: 1282
      1870s: 1282, 1614
    Wisconsin: 568, 1177
  Subdivided by destination:
    To California:
      From New York: 2191
      From North Carolina: 4042

TRAVEL:
  Subdivided by destination (Continued):
    To Connecticut:
      From New York: 5747
    To Georgia:
      From Massachusetts: 4864
    To Louisiana:
      From New York: 1333
    To Michigan:
      From New York: 5747
    To Missouri:
      From Maryland: 1405
    To Utah: 1333
TRAVEL CLUBS:
  West Virginia--Martinsburg: 5110
TRAVEL EXPENSES:
  Europe: 4348
  France: 4348
  Great Britain: 4348
  Pennsylvania: 1891
  Scotland: 5527
  South Carolina: 1891
  United States: 4348
  Virginia: 1891, 4517
TRAVELING SALESMEN: 2554
  Texas: 3534
TRAVELLERS' REST, South Carolina: 2792
"TRAVELLER'S REST," Virginia: 687
TRAVILLION, Nelson: 5335
TRAVIS COUNTY, Texas:
  Austin: 1842, 2739, 3470
  see also UNIVERSITY OF TEXAS
TREADWAY, Judge _____ : 4916
TREADWAY, Mary: 5282
TREADWAY, Thomas T.: 5282, 5884
TREADWAY FAMILY (London, Pennsylvania, Virginia): 5282
TREAKLE, James: 5336
TREASON:
  see also AMERICAN REVOLUTION--Treason; CONFEDERATE STATES OF AMERICA--TREASON; SEDITION
  North Carolina: 375
  Trials: 3809
TREASURE-TROVE IN LITERATURE: 2461
TREASURY: see as subheading under names of governments
TREAT, Morgan: 4524
TREATIES: see as subheading under names of countries; INDIANS OF NORTH AMERICA--Treaties
"TREATISE AGAINST HERESIES, AND OTHER THEOLOGICAL WORKS": 656
TREATY-MAKING POWER:
  United States Senate: 3190
TREATY OF AMIENS: 5726
TREATY OF GUADALUPE HIDALGO: 5149
  Ratification--Mexico: 5324
TREATY OF NEW ECHOTA: 2049
TREATY OF PARIS: 2776, 3315
TREDEGAR IRON WORKS, Richmond, Virginia: 117
"A TREE. A ROCK. A CLOUD.": 3344
TREES: see FORESTS AND FORESTRY; NURSERIES (Horticulture)
TRELAWNY, Edward John: 4770
TRELAWNY, Sir John Salusbury Salusbury-, Ninth Baronet: 5337
TRELAWNY, England: 5337
TREMONT TEMPLE, Boston, Massachusetts: 1219
TRENCH WARFARE: see Trenches and trench warfare as subheading under names of armies
TRENHOLM (GEORGE A.) AND SON, Charleston, South Carolina: 4145
TRENHOLM, George Alfred (1807-1876): 1439, 3461, 4145
TRENHOLM FAMILY: 1424
TRENIFFLE, England: 1239
TRENT, Josiah Charles: 4736
TRENT, Lucia: 5338
TRENT, Mary Duke (Biddle): 4736
TRENT, Peterfield: 5339
TRENT, William Peterfield: 2449, 4453
TRENT: 3442

TRENT, Council of: see COUNCIL OF TRENT
TRENT AFFAIR: 2085, 3203, 5228
TRENT CIRCUIT, Methodist churches: 3646
TRENT RIVER (Great Britain): 3997
TRENT RIVER (North Carolina): 730
TRENTANOVE, Raimondo: 2352
TRENTON, New Jersey: 1514, 2807, 4601, 5119, 5939
TRENTON, North Carolina:
    Merchants: 1871
TRENTON, South Carolina: 5299
TRENTON, Tennessee:
    Banks and banking: 2371
TRENTON FALLS, New York: 2518
TRESCO ISLAND, England: 4868
TRESCOTT, William Henry: 5340
TRESPASS:
    North Carolina: 2003
    Virginia: 1512
TREVELYAN, Sir Charles Edward: 863
TREVELYAN, George Macaulay (1876-1962): 2146
TREVELYAN, George Otto, Second Baronet (1838-1928): 3980, 5050, 5164
TREVETT, Russell: 2999
THE TRIAL OF MRS. ANN K. SIMPSON: 5740
TRIALS:
    see also ADULTERY TRIALS; CLERGY--Methodist--Trials; COURTS; FUGITIVE SLAVES--Trials; KU KLUX KLAN--Trials; LIBEL TRIALS; MURDER TRIALS; TREASON--Trials
    Great Britain: 92
    India--Baroda: 4117
    North Carolina: 5740
    Peru: 4155
    United States: 2545
TRIANGLE COFFEE HOUSE, Durham, North Carolina: 4502
TRICE, George W.: 5341
TRICE, Zachariah: 5341
TRIER, Germany: 201, 2194
TRIESTE, Italy: 323
    Miramar Castle: 2085
TRIGG, William: 3031
TRIMBLE, Allen: 2611
TRIMBLE, James: 5342
TRIMBLE, John A.: 5342
TRINIDAD:
    Photographs: 286
    Politics and government: 5726
    United States consulate in: 286
TRINITY BAPTIST CHURCH, Caswell County, North Carolina: 4849
TRINITY CHURCH, Edisto, South Carolina: 2027
TRINITY COLLEGE, Dublin, Ireland: 5330
TRINITY COLLEGE, Durham, North Carolina: 22, 338, 1585, 1588, 2705, 2861, 3247, 3831, 4242
    see also DUKE UNIVERSITY; TRINITY COLLEGE, Randolph County, North Carolina
    Alumni: 5022, 5914
        Class of 1895: 5497
    Athletics: 1368
    Commencement addresses (1909): 1533
    Construction of: 1584
    Faculty: 5389
    Gymnastics for women: 5914
    Honor graduates: 4932
    Librarians: 3831
    Students and student life: 5389, 5497
        Students' compositions: 3020
    Trustees: 4968
TRINITY COLLEGE, Randolph County, North Carolina: 817, 901, 1252, 1411, 1588, 2427, 2572, 3168, 3596, 4765, 4917, 4956, 5002, 5135
    see also DUKE UNIVERSITY; TRINITY COLLEGE, Durham, North Carolina

TRINITY COLLEGE, Randolph County, North Carolina (Continued):
    Commencement exercises (1882): 3596
    Curriculum: 5298
    Effects of the Civil War on: 5595
    Endowments: 547
    Faculty: 4498
        Greek professors: 901
    Finance: 547, 901
    Founding: 1677
    Literary societies: 5298
    Mental Science: 3168
    Military preparations: 4938
    Students and student life: 754, 832, 4788, 4849, 5298, 5595
        Finance: 5013, 5595
        Political activity: 4788
        Notebooks: 2021
    Teachers' records: 3596
    Theses: 1368
    Trustees: 5737
    Tuition: 2032
    Women: 2032
TRINITY COLLEGE CIRCUIT, Methodist churches: 3646
TRINITY COLLEGE DISTRICT, Methodist churches: 3646
TRINITY COLLEGE ENDOWMENT FUND: 547
TRINITY COLLEGE HISTORICAL SOCIETY: 22
TRINITY EPISCOPAL CHURCH, Portsmouth, Virginia: 1701
TRINITY EVANGELICAL LUTHERAN CHURCH, Smithsburg, Maryland: 5343
TRINITY PARK HIGH SCHOOL, Durham, North Carolina: 2472
TRINITY v. BALIOL: 5
"TRIP TO FLORIDA AND SALT WORKS, OCT. 20, 1863": 4743
"A TRIP TO NORTH GERMANY AND IN THE NORTH SEA, 1842": 244
TRIPLE ALLIANCE: 2149
TRIPLE ENTENTE: 4449
TRIPLETT, Simon: 917
TRIPP, Lysander C.: 5344
TRIST, Martha J.: 768
TRIST FAMILY: 768
TRI-STATE AVIATION CORPORATION: 4858
TRI-STATE TOBACCO GROWERS' CO-OPERATIVE MARKETING ASSOCIATION: 5035
TROLLOPE, Theodosia (Garrow): 2146
TROOP MOVEMENTS: see Military activities and troop movements as subheading under names of armies
TROTH, Henry: 2062
TROTTER, Sarah Myra (Rodes) Rivers: 4269
TROUBETZKOY, Amélie (Rives) Chanler: 958, 4491
TROUBETZKOY, Pierre: 958
TROUP, George Michael: 1333, 2326, 5345
TROUP, Henry: 136
TROUP, Samuel: 136
TROUP COUNTY, Georgia: 1170, 3419
TROUT, Joseph: 5346
TROUT, Wilbur A.: 2794
TROUT, William Fitzgerald: 2794
TROUT FAMILY (Virginia): 2794
TROUT AND TURNER (firm): see TURNER AND TROUT
TROUTT, John W.: 5347
TROWBRIDGE, John Townsend: 1037
TROXELL, Emma: 5348
TROXELL, Sylvanus: 5348
TROY, Alexander (b. 1853): 2449
TROY, John B.: 4100
TROY, New York: 549, 752, 5906
    Bluestockings: 4867
    Booksellers and bookselling: 5972
    Hotels: 1928
    Internal improvements: 5747
    Publishers and publishing: 5972
TROY, Pennsylvania: 4188
TROY COTTON AND WOOL MANUFACTORY: 992

TROY HOUSE, Troy, New York: 1928
THE TROY OIL MILL COMPANY: 5312
TRUCES: see AMERICAN REVOLUTION--Truces
TRUCK FARMING:
    Maryland--Eastern Shore: 660
TRUEBLOOD, Mary: 5349
TRUEBLOOD, Thomas: 5349
TRUMAN, Harry S.: 3538
    Administration: 3558
TRUMBULL, Henry Clay: 2449
TRUMBULL, John: 1582
TRUMBULL, Lyman: 5350
TRUMBULL, Thomas Swan: 5351
TRUMBULL FAMILY (Connecticut): 3277
TRUNKS: see LUGGAGE
TRURO, England:
    Church architecture: 5553
TRUSTEES: see METHODIST CHURCHES--Board of Trustees; and Trustees as subheading under names of specific universities and colleges
TRUSTEESHIP:
    Virginia: 5742
    Suffolk: 3012
TRUSTS:
    see also ANTI-TRUST LEGISLATION
    Georgia--Railroads: 3508
TRUTH (British newspaper): 2026
TRYON, William: 305, 5149, 5352
TRYON, North Carolina: 107, 3048
TSETSE FLIES: 4514
TSWANA (Bantu tribe): 128
TUBERCULOSIS: see DISEASES--Tuberculosis
TUBMAN, Charles: 5353
TUBMAN, Emily H.: 5353
TUBMAN, George: 5353
TUBMAN, Richard: 5353
TUCKER, Benjamin Q.: 1871
TUCKER, Beverley Dandridge (1846-1930): 3809
TUCKER, Charles C.: 5354
TUCKER, Cynthia B.: 5577
TUCKER, Delana: 5364
TUCKER, George (1775-1861): 2426, 5355, 5369
TUCKER, H. C.: 3248
TUCKER, Henry B.: 318
TUCKER, Henry McKee: 5356
TUCKER, Henry St. George (1780-1848): 743, 872, 1962, 5357
TUCKER, Jane Shelton (Ellis): 3809
TUCKER, Jesse C.: 5358
TUCKER, John Randolph (1812-1883): 4531, 5092
TUCKER, John Randolph (1823-1897): 5359
TUCKER, Josiah: 119
TUCKER, Margaret: 3809
TUCKER, Mary (Sames): 5360
TUCKER, Nathaniel Beverley (1784-1851): 5031, 5361
TUCKER, Nathaniel Beverley (1820-1890): 404, 743, 1227, 3809
TUCKER, St. George (1752-1827): 858, 3809, 4015, 5357
TUCKER, Thomas Tudor: 5362
TUCKER, Tilghman Mayfield: 5363
TUCKER, W. H. (Georgia): 5364
TUCKER, W. H. (Virginia): 5365
TUCKER, William (Virginia): 97, 5366
TUCKER, William C. (North Carolina): 5367
TUCKER & CARTER ROPE COMPANY: 4918
TUCKERMAN, Edward: 5754
TUCKERMAN, Frederick: 103
TUCKERMAN, Henry Theodore: 103, 4697
TUCSON, Arizona: 338
TUESDAY CLUB, Henderson, North Carolina: 4232
TUFTS, James Walker: 5457
TUFTS, Leonard: 5457
TUITION: see SCHOOLS--Tuition; and Tuition as subheading under names of specific universities and colleges

TULANE UNIVERSITY, New Orleans,
    Louisiana: 5054
    Faculty: 5734
    Medical education: 444, 1476
TULIP, Arkansas:
    Historical studies: 4894
TULIP RIDGE, Arkansas:
    Historical studies: 4894
TULLAHOMA, Tennessee: 3970
    Civil War: 1276, 2325
TULLY, Eleanor: 2449
TULLY (HOWARD) AND COMPANY: 642
TULLY, Richard Walton: 2449
TUMORS--Surgery: 4589
TUNISIA: 2558
    Antiquities--Zaghouan: 3460
    British consulate in: 3460
    Description and travel: 3460
    Foreign relations:
        Great Britain: 3460
    Methodist missionaries: 3646
TUNKHANNOCK, Pennsylvania: 4057, 4188
TUNNELS:
    Great Britain: 306
    Latin America: 5063
TUNSTALL, Nannie Whitmell: 1243, 5368
TUNSTALL, Virginia Caroline: 1084
TUNSTALL, William, Jr.: 5369
TUNSTALL FAMILY (Virginia): 4720
TUPAC AMARO, Mariano: 4155
TUPELO, Mississippi: 5844
TUPPER, James: 5370
TUPPER, Martin Farquhar: 1765, 2471, 2985
TURBERVILLE, George Lee: 917
TURBERVILLE, John: 917
TURGOT, Anne Robert Jaques, Baron de L'Aulne: 5681
TURIN, Italy: 4116
TURKEY:
    Aliens--Legal status: 3183
    Archaeological investigations:
        Assos: 3410
    British embassy in:
        Constantinople: 3472
    Cotton growing: 4650
    Courts: 3183
    Description and travel:
        1800s: 3053
        1900s: 2934
    Foreign relations:
        Austria: 1164
        Egypt: 3067
        Great Britain:
            1800s: 258, 3183, 4650
            1800s: 1164
            1840s: 3067
            1860s: 345
            1870s: 345, 4549
            1880s: 118, 345
        Persia: 868
        Russia: 1164
        see also RUSSO-TURKISH WAR
        United States (1800s): 636, 1787
    Foreign trade:
        United States: 636
    Government agencies and officials:
        Officials' behavior: 3183
    Missions and missionaries: 3008
    Prisoners and prisons: 3183
    Russo-Turkish War: see RUSSO-
        TURKISH WAR
    Social and political reform: 1014
    Social conditions: 92
TURLEY, Mary Elizabeth: 5371
TURLINGTON, A. J.: 5372
TURLINGTON, William H.: 5372, 5373
TURNAGE, S. C.: 5374
TURNER, A. (Virginia): 5375
TURNER, Adine: 872
TURNER, Sir Alfred Edward: 5872
TURNER, Anne A.: 5376
TURNER, Arlin: 102, 720, 1771
TURNER, Edward C.: 5377
TURNER, George Wilmer: 5378
TURNER, Henry McNeal: 731
TURNER, Sir James (1615-1686?): 5379

TURNER, James N.: 2978
TURNER, Jesse, Sr. (1805-1894): 5380
TURNER, Jesse, Jr. (1856-1919): 5380
TURNER, Job: 5298
TURNER, John (North Carolina): 5381
TURNER, John R. (Virginia): 5382
TURNER, Joseph: 5383
TURNER, Joseph Mallord William: 2148
TURNER, Josiah: 2589, 5384
TURNER, Nat: 1059, 3012, 5751
TURNER, Rebecca (Allen): 5380
TURNER, Robert H.: 523
TURNER, W.: 2857
TURNER, W. W. D.: 4994
TURNER, Wilfred: 5048
TURNER, William (Alabama): 5385
TURNER, William (Georgia): 5386
TURNER FAMILY (West Virginia--
    Genealogy): 1946
TURNER AND TROUT, Front Royal,
    Virginia (general store): 5387
TURNER'S CROSS ROADS, North
    Carolina: 2332
TURNERS FALLS, Massachusetts: 3633
TURNERSBURG, North Carolina: 85, 5310
    Cotton mills: 2857, 5048, 5310
TURNERSBURG COTTON MILLS,
    Turnersburg, North Carolina:
    2857, 5048, 5310
TURNPIKES:
    Construction:
        Connecticut: 3041
        North Carolina: 3176
        Pennsylvania: 3041
    Laws and legislation:
        Maryland: 4886
    Lawsuits--Pennsylvania: 2704
    Stocks--Virginia: 4428
    Subdivided by place:
        Maryland: 5296
        Pennsylvania: 971, 4756
        Virginia: 2593, 2728, 3148, 3860, 4892
TURPENTINE INDUSTRY:
    see also NAVAL STORES INDUSTRY
    Florida: 2970
    Georgia: 2222
    North Carolina: 2222
    South Carolina--Camden: 2940
TURPENTINE INDUSTRY WORKERS:
    Slaves--North Carolina: 5298
TURPENTINE LANDS:
    North Carolina: 359
    Rental of: 2350
TURPENTINE TRADE:
    see also NAVAL STORES TRADE
    Massachusetts: 1732
    New York: 1732
    North Carolina: 4925
        Wilmington: 4462
    South Carolina: 3123
TURPIN, William: 5388
TURPIN FAMILY (Virginia): 5798
TURRENTINE, Jack Webb: 5389
TURRENTINE, Michael H.: 5390
TURRENTINE, Samuel Bryant, Jr.: 5389
TURRENTINE FAMILY (Genealogy): 5389
TUSCALOOSA, Alabama: 120, 1804, 2315, 3188, 4105, 4944
    Booksellers and bookselling: 3611
    Civil War: 5032
    Local politics: 4943
    Lyceum: 3611
    Map: 1182
    Medical practice: 4943
    Religion: 4943
    Social life and customs: 4943
    Universities and colleges: see
        UNIVERSITY OF ALABAMA
TUSCALOOSA COUNTY, Alabama: 2920
    Tuscaloosa: see TUSCALOOSA, Alabama
TUSCALOOSA MOOT COURT, Tuscaloosa,
    Alabama: 3611
TUSCARAWAS COUNTY, Ohio:
    Canal Dover: 4716

TUSCARORA, Maryland: 1442
TUSCARORA (schooner): 2101, 5391
TUSCARORA INDIANS:
    Government relations: 4849
TUSCARORA STEAM AND GRIST MILLS: 730
TUSKASEGEE RIVER (North Carolina): 2028
TUSKEGEE, Alabama: 925, 5572
TUSKEGEE INSTITUTE, Tuskegee,
    Alabama: 925
    Finance: 5572
    Students and student life: 925
    Tuition: 5572
TUSKEGEE NORMAL AND INDUSTRIAL
    INSTITUTE, Tuskegee, Alabama:
    see TUSKEGEE INSTITUTE
TUSPAN, Mexico: 636
TUTHILL, Jane: 4119
TUTHILL, Winfield Hanford: 4119
TUTORS: see TEACHERS--Private
TUTT, Frances: 3339
TUTT, James A.: 5392
TUTT, Tom: 3339
TUTTLE, John C.: 2940
TUTTLE, William A.: 2940
TUTTON, George: 4188
TUTWILER, Henry: 3251
TUTWILER, M.: 5393
TUY, Philippine Islands: 4656
TWAIN, Mark: see CLEMENS, Samuel Langhorne
TWEED, William Marcy: 460
TWEEDSMUIR, John Buchan, First Baron: 449
TWEMLOW, Francis Randle: 5394
TWENTIETH CENTURY EDUCATIONAL FUND:
    see METHODIST EPISCOPAL CHURCH,
    SOUTH--Twentieth Century
    Educational Fund
22ND SESSION, THE VIRGINIA-CAROLINAS
    TYPOGRAPHICAL CONFERENCE: 2771
TWIGG, David Emanuel: 5605
TWIGGS, Hanford Dade Duncan: 2449
TWIGGS, John: 5395
TWIGGS COUNTY, Georgia: 1231
TWITCHELL, Adelthia: 2106
TWITCHELL, Amelia Jenkins: 2106
TWO LETTERS ON THE EVENT OF APRIL 14, 1865: 4652
THE TWO PARSONS by George Wythe Munford: 3809
TWO YEARS ON THE ALABAMA by Arthur Sinclair: 2963
TWYMAN'S STORE, Virginia:
    Plows--Prices: 4099
TYBEE ISLAND, Georgia:
    Spanish-American War:
        Army camps: 5298
TYDINGS, Millard E.: 2109
TYLER, Bailey: 3560
TYLER, Elizabeth: 5397
TYLER, J. C.: 4358
TYLER, James Hoge: 5396
TYLER, John (1747-1813): 2913
TYLER, John (1790-1862): 1308, 1351, 1697, 2776, 3607, 3809, 4531, 4616, 5397, 5445
TYLER, John Jr. (1819-1896): 4531, 5397
TYLER, Lyon Gardiner: 2400
TYLER, Martha (Rochelle): 4531
TYLER, Moses Coit: 2449
TYLER, Robert: 5397
TYLER, Samuel: 2612
TYLER, William (Georgia): 5398
TYLNEY-LONG-WELLESLEY, William
    Pole--see WELLESLEY, William
    Pole-Tylney-Long-
TYNDALL, John: 582
TYNER, William R.: 5399
TYNES, Achilles James: 5400
TYPE FOUNDRIES:
    see also STEREOTYPE FOUNDRIES
    Virginia--Richmond: 4119
TYPHOID FEVER: see DISEASES--Typhoid fever
TYPHUS: see DISEASES--Typhus

TYPING:
    Study and teaching: 3831
TYPOGRAPHICAL WORKERS: see
    INTERNATIONAL TYPOGRAPHICAL UNION
TYREE, Lonnie (Hardaway): 5401
TYREE, William Cornelius: 5401
TYRRELL COUNTY, North Carolina:
    Columbia--Business affairs: 215
    Land deeds and indentures: 215
TYSON, Bryan: 5402
TYSON, James: 5402

U

U.D.A. CONGRESSIONAL NEWSLETTER: 1196
"U.N. ASSOCIATION": 4352
UPA ADVERTISER: 1196
UPA ADVISOR: 1198
UDAL, John Symonds: 5403
UDNEY, George: 5639
UGANDA:
  Funerals: 41
UHURU by Robert Chester Ruark: 4591
ULM, Germany:
  Trade and commerce: 3598
ULSTER COUNTY, New York:
  Kingston: 5454
  West Park: 783
    Weather: 4073
    Wildlife: 4073
UMSTOTT, Sallie E.: 221
UNALASKA: see OUNALASKA
UNAMUNO Y JUGO, Miguel de: 5404
UNCLE TOM'S CABIN by Harriet Beecher Stowe: 4387, 5099, 5282
UNDERWOOD, James: 5405
UNDERWOOD, John Curtiss: 4871
UNDERWOOD, Oscar Wilder: 690, 706, 1171
UNDERWOOD, Ruth Elizabeth (Newton): 5406
UNDERWOOD FLATS, Vermont: 2544
UNDERWOOD NATIONAL CAMPAIGN COMMITTEE: 690
UNDERWOOD-SIMMONS TARIFF: 4825
UNDINE TEMPLE OF HONOR AND TEMPERANCE: 5339
UNEMPLOYMENT:
  see also as subheading under kinds of workers, e.g. RAILROAD WORKERS--Unemployment
  United States: 4564
  West Virginia: 3005
UNEMPLOYMENT COMPENSATION:
  North Carolina:
    Mecklenburg County: 5235
UNEMPLOYMENT RELIEF: see DEPRESSION; PUBLIC WELFARE
UNGER, Richard: 111
UNICOI COUNTY, Tennessee:
  Erwin: 4730
UNIFORMS: see Clothing and dress as subheading under names of armies and navies
UNION, Indiana:
  Medical practice: 4220
UNION, Maine: 731
UNION, South Carolina:
  Hotel management: 5407, 5522
  Mercantile accounts: 2721, 5522
  Personal finance: 5522
  Soap and cosmetics manufacture: 4918
UNION, West Virginia: 884
UNION, Act of: see ACT OF UNION
UNION, U.S.S.: 386, 701
UNION ACADEMY, Youngsville, North Carolina: 5087
UNION ACADEMY DEBATING SOCIETY, Youngsville, North Carolina: 5087

UNION ARMY: see UNITED STATES--ARMY--Civil War
UNION ASSOCIATION, Disciples of Christ: 5554
UNION BANK OF FLORIDA, Tallahassee, Florida: 2755
UNION CHAPEL CHRISTIAN CHURCH (North Carolina): 5554
UNION CHURCH (North Carolina): 3646
UNION COLLEGE, Barbourville, Kentucky: 5731
UNION COLLEGE, Schenectady, New York: 3588
  Students and student life: 4485
UNION CORNER CHURCH (West Virginia): 2129
UNION COUNTY, Kentucky: 1604
UNION COUNTY, New Jersey:
  Elizabeth: 1050
  Scotch Plains: 1160
  Westfield: 3948
UNION COUNTY, North Carolina: 2069
  Monroe: 3439
    Schools: 2573
  Olive Branch: 579, 4898
    Arithmetic exercise book: 208
UNION COUNTY, Pennsylvania:
  Hartleton: 4920
UNION COUNTY, South Carolina: 4434
  Pine Grove: 2744
  Union: see UNION, South Carolina
UNION COURTHOUSE, South Carolina: 477
UNION DISTRICT, South Carolina: 4434
UNION FLAX MILLS, Chicago, Illinois: 2682
UNION FOR DEMOCRATIC ACTION: 1196
UNION FORGE, Virginia: 3098
UNION FURNACE, Virginia:
  Iron foundries: 5827
THE UNION GOSPEL NEWS: 3633
UNION HOTEL, Union, South Carolina: 5407, 5522
UNION LEAGUE (South Carolina): 4118
UNION LEAGUE OF AMERICA: 3062
UNION LEAGUE OF NEW YORK CITY: 3960
UNION LITERARY SOCIETY (North Carolina): 4923
UNION MANUFACTURING COMPANY, Randleman, North Carolina: 5408
UNION MILLS, North Carolina: 3237
UNION MILLS, Virginia:
  Grist mills: 2600
UNION OF SOVIET SOCIALIST REPUBLICS: 1424
  see also RUSSIA
  Agricultural products: 4614
  Communism: 4614
  Economic conditions: 4614
  Electrification: 4614
  Foreign relations:
    China: 5252
    United States: 3538
  Industrialization: 4614
  Labor: 4614
  Religion: 4614
  Social conditions: 4614
UNION PACIFIC RAILROAD: 2076, 5593
UNION PARTY: 3767
  Massachusetts--Boston: 5563
  Ohio: 281
UNION POINT, Georgia: 4335
UNION SEMINARY, Norwich, New York: 2292
UNION SYMPATHIZERS: see CIVIL WAR--UNION SYMPATHIZERS
UNION THEOLOGICAL SEMINARY, New York, New York: 4702
UNION THEOLOGICAL SEMINARY, Richmond, Virginia: 3415, 3740, 5794
  Faculty: 2051
UNION UNIVERSITY, Murfreesboro, Tennessee: 872
UNIONIST PARTY (Scotland): 3592
UNIONIZATION:
  see also LABOR IN POLITICS; LABOR UNIONS
  North Carolina: 1195

UNIONIZATION (Continued):
  South Carolina: 300, 1196
  Southern States: 1202, 3066
  United States: 4436
UNIONTOWN, Alabama: 1031, 1497, 3237
UNIONTOWN, Pennsylvania: 1426
UNITARIAN CHURCHES: 1792
  Great Britain: 369
  Massachusetts: 1074
  Southern States: 429
UNITAS FRATRUM: see MORAVIAN CHURCH
UNITED ASSOCIATION OF JOURNEYMEN AND APPRENTICES OF THE PLUMBING AND PIPEFITTING INDUSTRY OF THE UNITED STATES AND CANADA:
  Local Union No. 102: 5409
  Plumbers and Fitters Local Union No. 227: 5410
UNITED AUTOMOBILE, AIRCRAFT, AND AGRICULTURAL IMPLEMENT WORKERS OF AMERICA: 1197, 1198
  Virginia: 1198
UNITED BRETHREN CHURCHES:
  Indiana: 5149
UNITED BROTHERHOOD OF CARPENTERS AND JOINERS OF AMERICA: 341
  Local Union No. 1778: 1172, 5411
UNITED CAMPUS CHRISTIAN FELLOWSHIP: 3001
UNITED CANNERY, AGRICULTURE, PACKING AND ALLIED WORKERS OF AMERICA: 1197, 1198
UNITED CHRISTIAN PETITION MOVEMENT (Great Britain): 4722
UNITED CONFEDERATE VETERANS: 1480, 1727, 3657, 3809, 5759
  Conventions: 3376
  Political activity: 3657
  Reunions: 824, 1727, 3657
  Subdivided by place:
    North Carolina: 4918, 5412
    Trans-Mississippi Department: 824
UNITED DAUGHTERS OF THE CONFEDERACY: 661, 2161, 4271, 4642, 5413, 5759, 5901
  Poetry: 66
  Subdivided by place:
    Georgia: 5090
    Maryland--Baltimore: 2202
    North Carolina--Raleigh: 2553
    South Carolina:
      Black Oak Chapter: 5414
      Edgefield Chapter: 5415
    West Virginia: 1784, 5110
UNITED EAST INDIA COMPANY: 5535
UNITED ELECTRICAL, RADIO, AND MACHINE WORKERS OF AMERICA: 1198
UNITED FUND:
  see also COMMUNITY CHEST
  North Carolina--Durham: 4736
UNITED FURNITURE WORKERS OF AMERICA: 1193, 1196, 1197, 1202
  North Carolina: 1195
UNITED GAS, COKE, AND CHEMICAL WORKERS OF AMERICA: 1197, 1198
UNITED LABOR CONFERENCE: 1197
UNITED LABOR LEGISLATIVE COMMITTEE: 1198
UNITED LABOR POLITICAL COMMITTEE: 5234
UNITED LABOR POLITICAL COMMITTEE FOR NORTH CAROLINA: 1199
UNITED MERCHANTS AND MANUFACTURERS, INC.: 1202
UNITED METHODIST CHURCHES:
  see also METHODIST CHURCHES
  General Conference: 3020
UNITED METHODIST DEVELOPMENT FUND: 3020
UNITED MINE WORKERS OF AMERICA: 1197, 1198, 3640
UNITED NATIONS: 4558
  Relations with the United States: 3538
UNITED NATIONS EDUCATIONAL, SCIENTIFIC AND CULTURAL ORGANIZATION: 83
UNITED PACKINGHOUSE WORKERS OF AMERICA:
  Tennessee: 1197

UNITED PAPERWORKERS OF AMERICA:
  1196, 1198
UNITED PRESS ASSOCIATIONS OF
  AMERICA: 1424
UNITED PUBLIC WORKERS OF AMERICA:
  1194
UNITED SHOE WORKERS OF AMERICA: 1198
UNITED SOCIETY OF BELIEVERS IN
  CHRIST'S SECOND APPEARING: see
  SHAKERS
UNITED SPANISH WAR VETERANS:
  Massachusetts: 5559
UNITED SPANISH WAR VETERANS
  AUXILIARY: 5559

### UNITED STATES

see also AMERICAN COLONIES for
  subjects prior to July 4, 1776;
  and names of specific states
ABOLITION OF SLAVERY AND
  ABOLITIONIST SENTIMENT: 730, 842,
  1081, 1424, 1540, 1926, 2591, 2723,
  2893
  see also ABOLITION OF SLAVERY AND
    ABOLITIONIST SENTIMENT
  Abolitionist periodicals: 1683,
    5246
ACTING: 2449
ACTORS AND ACTRESSES: 4556
ADVERTISING: see ADVERTISING
AGED AND AGING: 1167
AGRICULTURAL ORGANIZATIONS: see
  AGRICULTURAL ORGANIZATIONS
AGRICULTURAL PRACTICES:
  Improvements: 1024
AGRICULTURE: 122, 842
  Laws and legislation: 274, 4805,
    4858
  Statistics: 2746, 5426
ALMANACS: 5051
AMERICAN REVOLUTION: see AMERICAN
  REVOLUTION; CONTINENTAL ARMY
ANNIVERSARIES: see FOURTH OF JULY
  CELEBRATIONS; UNITED STATES--
  CENTENNIAL CELEBRATION
ANTI-CATHOLICISM: 20
ANTI-TRUST LEGISLATION: 592
ARITHMETIC EXERCISE BOOKS: 1671,
  1818, 2501
ARMED FORCES:
  1780s: 3627
  1900s: 1758, 4805
    World War I: 3451
ARMS INDUSTRY:
  Governmental manufacture: 5433
ARMS TRADE--France: 5433
ARMY: 842, 5417, 5906

#### Subdivided by place:

Alabama: 415
Florida: 842
Kansas: 1782
South Carolina--Charleston: 1282
Utah: 1782
Western States: 1282

#### Subdivided by subject:

Adjutant General: 2928
Air Corps: 4269
Army life: 3228, 5059
  see also UNITED STATES--ARMY--
    Camp life
  Alabama:
    Mobile: 3789
    Mount Vernon Arsenal: 3789
  Colorado: 2831
  Florida:
    New Smyrna: 5480
    Saint Augustine: 5480
  Georgia--Augusta: 5480
  Indian Territory: 1282
  Kansas: 1282
  Missouri--Jefferson Barracks:
    5419

### UNITED STATES

ARMY:

#### Subdivided by subject:

Army life (Continued):
  New Mexico Territory: 3261
  North Carolina--Beaufort: 5480
  Texas--Fort McIntosh: 5424
Army of Tennessee: 5425
Artillery: 4433
  North Carolina
    Fort Johnston: 5826
Bands: 5298
Bases: see MILITARY BASES; and
  names of specific military bases
Battalions:
  2nd Artillery: 70
Camp life: 29
  see also UNITED STATES--ARMY--
    Army life
  New Mexico--Albuquerque: 5744
  New York--Fort Michie: 5430
  Texas--Fort Davis: 5417
Camps:
  New York--Fort Columbia: 4433
  North Carolina:
    Fort Johnston: 4433
  Texas--Fort Brown: 4433
Chaplains: 3633
Civil-military relations: 3388
  Louisiana: 5425
  Texas: 5425
Civilian labor--Texas: 5424
Clothing and dress: 990, 5430
Commissaries: 5424
  Georgia--Savannah: 3323
  Reorganization of the department:
    5276
Corps--15th Army: 5425
Courts-martial: 212, 4688, 5425,
  5430
Courts of Inquiry:
  Battle of Five Forks: 3809
Desertion: 246, 5424, 5430
Department of the South: 2781
Discipline: 5419
Division of Mississippi:
  Military railroad: 5306
Engineers: 3789, 4490
  Pay: 5425
  Philippine Islands: 3789
Equal opportunity: 3820
Escort Guard Service: 5419
European Command:
  Historical Division: 5418
Fifth Military District: 5425
Food: 5430
  Texas--Fort Mason: 1446
Frontier duty: 5517
Garrisons: 3614
Generals: 132
  see also UNITED STATES--ARMY--
    Officers
German Artillery: 5495
Indian removal: 2842, 3801
  see also INDIANS OF NORTH
    AMERICAN--Removal
  North Carolina: 4249
Laws and legislation:
  Army Bill (1879): 1424
  Retirement: 1663
Leaves and furloughs: 5425
Medical and sanitary affairs: 3760,
  3801, 5133
  Indian Territory: 3047
  Texas--Fort Martin Scott: 1446
Mexican Border Campaign (1916):
  356, 2112
Military affairs: 805
Military intelligence:
  Philippine Islands: 1661
Military regulations: 5430
Military supplies: 212, 246, 5424,
  5430
  Kansas: 5419

### UNITED STATES

ARMY:

#### Subdivided by subject:

Military supplies (Continued):
  Louisiana: 5425
  Tennessee: 5870
  Texas: 5425
  Fort Mason: 1446
Negro troops--Texas: 1138
Northern Division: 1515
Office of the Commanding General:
  5242
Officers: 246, 549, 1446, 1661,
  1782, 3019, 4616, 5059, 5419,
  5783
  see also UNITED STATES--ARMY--
    Generals
  Appointments and promotions:
    4688, 4786, 5430
  Arkansas--Fort Gibson: 3466
  Discharges: 803
  Discipline: 3507
  Orders: 1901, 5420, 5430
  Ordnance: 5424
  Pay: 4433, 5425, 5430
  Paymasters: 5608
  Payrolls: 2842
  Pensions: 3417, 4688
Philippine Insurrection: see
  PHILIPPINE INSURRECTION
Philippine Islands:
  Civil-military relations: 3313
  Philippine military occupation:
    2991, 4269, 4656, 5844
  Panay: 4719
Political elections: 5427
Quartermaster Department: 428,
  3323, 5424
  Texas--Fort Mason: 1446
Reconstruction:
  Political elections, Monitoring
    of: 1299, 3809
Recruiting and enlistment: 70, 212,
  246, 5517
Resistance: 613
Regiments:
  Artillery:
    3rd: 212
    4th: 4495
  Cavalry:
    3rd: 5000
  Infantry:
    4th: 3388
    8th: 246
    86th (Colored): 1507
    Hugh McCall's Company: 3323
Retirements: 4688
Second Military District: 5425
Siberian Expedition: 1661
Signal Corps:
  Panay, Philippine Islands: 4719
Soldiers: 5419
Surgeons: 3760, 3801, 5133
Third Military District: 5425
Veterans: 3789
  see also Veterans as subheading
    under names of wars

#### American Revolution:

see CONTINENTAL ARMY

#### War of 1812:

see also Militia as subheading
  under names of states
Adjutant General's Office: 1772
Army life: 2967, 2975
  see also UNITED STATES--ARMY--
    War of 1812--Camp life
Brigades:
  Chamberlayne's Brigade: 962
Camp life: 1066, 1595
  see also UNITED STATES--ARMY--
    War of 1812--Army life

UNITED STATES

ARMY:

### War of 1812 (Continued):

Courts-martial: 872
Crime: 1595
Desertion: 1595
Discharges: 29
Discipline: 1333, 1595
Diseases: 29
Drinking: 1595
Food: 2169
Gambling: 1595
Medical and sanitary affairs: 1595
Military activities and troop
  movements: 3041
    Florida: 2781
    Georgia: 2781
Military supplies: 1003, 2169,
  5281
    New York: 1003
Miscellaneous soldiers' letters:
  4220
Morale: 872
Officers: 872, 1333, 1595, 3529
  Appointments and promotions:
    4384
Opium: 1595
Orders: 2169
Organization: 872
Quartermaster Corps: 5005
Recruiting and enlistment:
  Substitutions: 29
Regiments:
  Artillery:
    3rd: 3041
  Infantry:
    Kentucky:
      16th: 1595
      Lexington Light Infantry:
        3325
      Infantry Volunteer Militia:
        3325
Training: 1595

### Creek War (1813-1814):

Recruiting and enlistment:
  Georgia: 4218
Regiments:
  Infantry:
    3rd: 5417

### Creek War (1836):

Military activities and troop
  movements: 2842

### Seminole War (1817-1818):

Military activities and troop
  movements:
    Florida: 2781

### Seminole War (1835-1842):

Florida: 2842
Foraging--Florida: 3611
Military activities and troop
  movements: 2781
Regiments:
  Alabama Regiment of Volunteers:
    3611

### Mexican War (1846-1848):

395, 3325, 5324
Army life--Camargo, Mexico: 778
Casualties: 5324
  Claims for compensation: 5310
Clothing and dress: 5324
Courts-martial: 3325
Discharges: 4144
Health conditions: 5324
Honors and awards: 4715

UNITED STATES

ARMY:

### Mexican War (Continued):

Military activities and troop
  movements: 805
    Mexico: 5324
      Eastern Mexico: 2842
Military passes: 5324
Military reports: 525
Military supplies: 525, 1901, 2143
Militia rosters: 3325
Miscellaneous soldiers' letters:
  1038
Mobilization:
  Alabama: 5593
  North Carolina: 2050
  Virginia--Fortress Monroe: 5324
Officers: 5130
  Appointments and promotions: 2760
Orders: 1901, 2301
Pay: 1901, 5324
Quartermaster Department: 2842
Recruiting and enlistment: 4144,
  4897
  Exemptions: 5324
Regiments:
  Infantry:
    7th: 5710

### Civil War (1861-1865):

General references subdivided by
  place:

Alabama: 1135
Florida: 1325, 2223, 2361
Georgia--Savannah: 5326
Kentucky: 1135, 1840
Maryland: 1564
Mississippi: 1135
North Carolina: 1840, 3152
Ohio: 1840
South Carolina: 731, 1325, 1430,
  2223, 2361
  Charleston: 5326
Tennessee: 801, 1135, 1840
Virginia: 383, 1135, 1564, 1840,
  1850, 2223, 2361, 3152
Washington, D.C.: 251, 1564, 1840,
  1850
West Virginia: 968

### Subdivided by subject:

Animals--West Virginia: 1817
Army life: 196, 1230, 1344, 1625,
  1980, 2257, 2405, 2507, 3166,
  3201, 3281, 3613, 3917, 4390,
  4565, 4990, 4993, 5034, 5941,
  5975
  see also UNITED STATES--ARMY--
    Civil War--Camp life
  Alabama: 4160
  Georgia: 4160
    Fort Pulaski: 4119
  Louisiana: 1408
    New Orleans: 1348
  Maryland: 1983
  North Carolina: 1934, 2549
  South Carolina:
    Hilton Head: 4119
    Saint Helena's Island: 4119
  Tennessee: 243, 1328, 3181, 4160
  Virginia: 1408, 1967, 1983, 2500
    Fortress Monroe: 4119
    Petersburg: 2405
  Washington, D.C.: 2898
Army of the Cumberland: 1148, 1328,
  4160
Army of the Ohio:
  Quartermaster Corps: 605
  2nd Division: 605
  23rd Corps: 605

UNITED STATES

ARMY:

### Civil War:

Subdivided by subject (Continued):

Army of the Potomac: 700, 2989,
  3115, 3823, 5034, 5425, 5670
  Cavalry:
    Rivalry with Confederate
      cavalry: 3809
  Countersigns: 4990
  Depredations: 1889
  XI Corps: 3263
  Engineers: 615
  Quartermaster Department: 1817,
    2758, 4228
Army of the Tennessee: 5425
Balloons: 565, 5061, 5298, 5444
  Virginia:
    Fredericksburg: 2240, 5984
Bands: 5061
Battalions:
  Massachusetts:
    Infantry:
      3rd: 3166
  New York:
    Artillery:
      4th: 1540
Batteries:
  Illinois:
    Light Artillery:
      Chicago Board of Trade
        Battery: 3951
      James H. Stokes' Independent
        Battery: 3951
Bridge construction:
  Potomac and Shenandoah rivers:
    4990
Brigades:
  Marine Brigade--Depredations: 4582
Camp life: 69, 135, 615, 681, 701,
  765, 941, 1050, 1175, 1235, 1253,
  1505, 1564, 1699, 1809, 1820,
  1845, 1881, 2031, 2092, 2100,
  2124, 2223, 2311, 2453, 2681,
  2777, 2791, 2867, 2987, 3007,
  3127, 3502, 3519, 3520, 3823,
  4032, 4059, 4108, 4226, 4349,
  4452, 4477, 4537, 4561, 4565,
  4588, 4608, 4663, 4690, 4708,
  4723, 4769, 4860, 4970, 4973,
  5122, 5172, 5261, 5303, 5311,
  5419, 5560, 5715, 5896, 5898,
  5991
  see also UNITED STATES--ARMY--
    Civil War--Army life
  Amusements: 5560
  District of Columbia: 3815
  Florida:
    Fernandina: 5425
    Key West: 3975
  Georgia: 1619
    Dahlonega: 5744
    Savannah: 3975
  Illinois: 659
  Iowa--Keokuk: 1076
  Kentucky: 403, 808
    Camp Morton, Bardstown: 2858
    Newport Barracks: 5744
  Louisiana: 1349, 1619, 1763,
    3957, 3975
  Maryland: 3133, 5061
    Annapolis: 4940
  Massachusetts: 25
    Camp Wenham: 1349
  Mississippi: 1619
  Missouri: 659, 4488
  North Carolina: 963, 1619, 1845,
    2602, 4940
    Fort Macon: 5744
    New Bern: 3281, 4438
  Pennsylvania: 820, 1050, 1798
    3957, 5462
  Potomac Ri--

UNITED STATES

ARMY:

Civil War:

Subdivided by subject:

Camp life (Continued):
  South Carolina: 1798, 5061
  Tennessee: 808, 3409, 5348, 5695
  Texas:
    Fort Brown, Brownsville: 3392
  Virginia: 251, 403, 820, 963,
    1619, 2091, 2602, 3133, 3409,
    3889, 4000, 5061
    Camp Seminary: 5939
    City Point: 5677
    Fort Powhatan: 5939
    Petersburg: 2243
    Shenandoah Valley: 3975
    Winchester: 1868
    Yorktown: 5975
  Washington, D.C.: 494, 1058
Camps:
  Missouri:
    Benton Barracks, Saint Louis:
      4989
    Rat infestation: 4477
  Tennessee: 2681
    Clarksville: 1286
  Virginia--Falmouth: 4608
  Washington, D.C.: 1286
  West Virginia:
    Fort Lyon: 4190
    Somerville: 1452
Care of freedmen--Mississippi: 5421
Casualties: 69, 135, 388, 701, 1207,
  2106, 2490, 2679, 2791, 3007,
  3610, 3641, 3823, 4349, 4523,
  4537, 4708, 5303, 5425, 5775
  Claims for compensation: 4303
  Memorials: 5419
  Personal effects of deceased:
    4537
  Transportation: 162
  Subdivided by place:
    Arkansas: 4536
    Maryland: 3133
    North Carolina--New Bern: 4438
    Ohio: 4255
    Pennsylvania: 820
    Tennessee--Murfreesboro: 3479
    Virginia: 820, 3133
Cavalry: 1186, 1881, 3524
  Cavalry life: 5858
  Military activities and troop
    movements: 4612
  Rivalry with Confederate cavalry:
    3809
Censorship: 5898
Chaplains: 2311, 5419, 5991
  Methodist churches: 2311
  Virginia:
    Alexandria: 2648
    Newport News: 3610
Civil-military relations: 2258
Civilian labor: 605
  Maryland: 1817
  Negroes: 1817, 5975
  West Virginia: 1817
Clothing and dress: 1418, 1820,
  3283, 4303, 4537, 4565, 4588,
  4685, 4860, 5425, 5991
  Florida: 5425
  Shoes: 5122
  Tennessee: 1819
Colored troops: see UNITED STATES--
  ARMY--Civil War--Negro troops
Commissaries: 3328
Commissary of Subsistence:
  Virginia--Norfolk: 5043
Commodity prices--Georgia: 2504
Communications with Confederate
  Army: 4612
Confiscation of property: see
  CIVIL WAR--CONFISCATION OF
  PROPERTY

UNITED STATES

ARMY:

Civil War:

Subdivided by subject (Continued):

Convalescent camps:
  Virginia: 2648
Cooks: 5896
Corps:
  3rd Army Corps: 5008
    Reunions: 5417
  4th Army Corps: 1917
  15th Army Corps: 5425
  18th Army Corps: 3741
  24th Army Corps: 5420
  Artillery:
    13th Artillery Corps:
      10th Division: 765
  Invalid Corps:
    1st Battalion:
      Veteran Reserve Corps: 5695
Corps of Engineers: see UNITED
  STATES--ARMY--Civil War--
  Engineers
Courts-martial: 281, 605, 1519,
  1791, 4276, 4537, 5425, 5432
Curfews: 4537
Department of Annapolis: 314
Department of Mississippi and
  Eastern Louisiana: 3357
Department of North Carolina: 5425
Department of the Cumberland: 5425
Department of the Gulf: 5169, 5425
  Ordnance Office: 2777
Department of the Mississippi:
  3493
  Finance: 1357
Department of the Missouri: 5425
Department of the South: 2258
Department of the Tennessee: 5425
Department of Virginia and North
  Carolina: 5425
Department of West Tennessee: 4899
Depredations: 689, 1334, 1352,
  1410, 1820, 1889, 1984, 2802,
  3301, 3378, 3648, 3809, 4537,
  4561, 4866, 4881, 4950, 5017,
  5040, 5122, 5132, 5223, 5246,
  5269, 5311, 5425, 5453, 5672,
  5739, 5855
  see also CIVIL WAR--DEPREDATIONS
  Alabama--Selma: 4185
  Georgia: 510, 669
    Springfield: 5991
  Mississippi: 1403, 4596
    Brandon: 3293
    Jackson: 3293
  North Carolina: 3237, 4248
    Fayetteville: 956, 5298
    Halifax: 5125
    Lumberton: 956
    Murphy: 1247
    Tarboro: 5125
    Williamston: 5125
  South Carolina: 4118, 4783, 5759
    Bennettsville: 5415
    Columbia: 5415
    Edisto Island: 5645
    Robertsville: 5991
    Stateburg: 4217
  Tennessee--Gallatin: 5784
  Virginia: 99, 358, 2958, 3136
    Culpeper: 3464
    Eastern Virginia: 5751
    Sulphur Springs: 2681
  West Virginia: 581
    Middleway: 1730
Desertion: 1175, 1505, 1806, 1845,
  1984, 2236, 2490, 2865, 3778,
  4160, 4537, 4561, 4608, 5424,
  5425, 5834, 5984
  Executions--Virginia: 2547
  Pennsylvania: 820
  Rumors: 4588
  Virginia: 820

UNITED STATES

ARMY:

Civil War:

Subdivided by subject (Continued):

Discharges: 688, 1230, 1868, 2106,
  4920, 5425
  Medical: 808, 4537, 4889
  Michigan: 2604
Discipline: 69, 1418, 2408, 4160,
  4537, 5261, 5425, 5769, 5991
  Pennsylvania: 820
  Virginia: 820, 2958
Diseases: see CIVIL WAR--DISEASES
District of Harpers Ferry: 3654
District of Vicksburg: 4899
Divisions:
  Casey's Division: 931
  Coast Division--Signal Corps: 1282
  Milroy's Division: 2958
  Drinking: 3281, 4190, 5122, 5417
  South Carolina: 1418
Election of officers: 3264
Engineers: 1235
  Maryland: 1235
  Tennessee--Knoxville: 4245
  Virginia: 1235
Equipment: 2257, 3127, 3283, 3710
  Missouri: 3703
Family aid to soldiers: 1885
Finance: 2106
Food: 854, 1505, 1820, 1973, 2223,
  2236, 2453, 2987, 3264, 3283,
  3502, 3648, 3778, 3813, 4032,
  4190, 4565, 4588, 4608, 4690,
  4708, 4860, 4888, 5419
  Georgia: 1619
  Louisiana: 1619
  Maryland: 3133
  Mississippi: 1619, 5421
  North Carolina: 1619, 1934
  Virginia: 1619, 2958, 3133
    Western Virginia: 1967
Food prices: see CIVIL WAR--FOOD
  PRICES
Forage: 605, 4228, 4537
Foraging: 2816, 3519, 3641, 4561,
  5132, 5991
  Pennsylvania: 820
  Virginia: 820, 3813
Fortifications:
  Tennessee--Knoxville: 4245
  Virginia:
    Petersburg: 2243
    Maps: 5417
Furloughs: see UNITED STATES--ARMY--
  Civil War--Leaves and furloughs
Gambling: 5122
  Florida--Fernandina: 5425
Generals: 69, 2449, 2510, 4808,
  4921, 5017, 5059, 5311, 5613,
  5775, 5955
  see also UNITED STATES--ARMY--
    Civil War--Officers
  Bodyguards: 1230
  Evaluations: 659
  Foreign born: 2893
Guard duty: 135, 2453, 2681, 3007,
  3264, 4349, 4537, 4588, 4860,
  5419
  Florida--Fort Jefferson: 5715
  Kentucky: 5695
  Maryland:
    Relay--Railroads: 2106
  Ohio: 5695
    Railroads: 434
  Pennsylvania: 820
  Virginia: 820, 3813, 4087
    Petersburg: 2243
    Western Virginia: 1967
  Washington, D.C.: 5131, 5261,
    5695
Health conditions: 941, 1763, 1845,
  3127, 3281, 4452, 4588, 4608,
  5303, 5351, 5419, 5677

UNITED STATES

ARMY:

### Civil War:

Subdivided by subject:

Health conditions (Continued):
  Florida: 5425
  Virginia: 3778
Historical writings: see CIVIL
  WAR--HISTORICAL WRITINGS
Homesickness: see UNITED STATES--
  ARMY--Civil War--Morale
Honors and awards: 2958
Horses and mules: 4228
  Mississippi: 3493
Hospitals: 135, 1505, 1564, 1820,
  2681, 2791, 3741, 4608, 5311
  3rd Division: 3741
  Indiana--Jeffersonville: 3007
  Kentucky--Louisville: 3007
  Maryland:
    Baltimore: 701
    Point Lookout: 854
  Missouri--Saint Louis: 4989
  North Carolina:
    Goldsboro: 5058
    New Bern: 1845
    Wilmington: 1845
  South Carolina:
    Beaufort: 3822
    Charleston: 2867
  Virginia: 468
    Arlington: 4945
    Newport News: 3610
  Washington, D.C.: 701, 1840, 2311
  West Virginia: 1769
    Harpers Ferry: 2867
    Martinsburg: 2867
Illness: see UNITED STATES--ARMY--
  Civil War--Medical and sanitary
  affairs--Illness and disease
Indian troops: 2311
Inspections and reviews: 1881, 4022,
  4087, 4888
Leaves and furloughs: 135, 1175,
  1230, 1845, 2106, 2124, 2681,
  3328, 4561, 5425
Medical and sanitary affairs: 78,
  135, 1207, 1820, 2311, 2791,
  2816, 3281, 3283, 3594, 3648,
  3741, 3910, 4537, 4889, 4940,
  5017, 5133, 5311, 5975, 5991
  see also CIVIL WAR--MEDICAL
    SUPPLIES; UNITED STATES
    SANITARY COMMISSION
  Army Medical Department: 5430
  Illness and disease: 2681, 3502,
    4708
  Medicine: 3910
Military activities and troop
  movements: 654, 765, 1235, 1408,
  2031, 2258, 2816, 2867, 3007,
  3115, 3127, 3392, 4537, 4539,
  4552, 4565, 4596, 4608, 5311,
  5351, 5419, 5502, 5975, 5991
  Alabama: 1505, 3524, 5132
    Wilson's Raid: 120
  Arkansas: 3519, 5017
  Florida: 3502, 4108
    Saint Augustine: 3910
  Georgia: 1619, 4973, 5453, 5724
  Gulf of Mexico: 4970
  Illinois: 4203
  Kentucky: 659, 808, 3524, 3751,
    4973, 5303
    Winchester: 5677
  Louisiana: 1253, 1619, 3502,
    3519, 3522, 5132, 5425
    Port Hudson: 4970
  Maryland: 1505, 4537, 4970, 5000,
    5425
    Annapolis: 1282
    Williamsport: 4608

UNITED STATES

ARMY:

### Civil War:

Subdivided by subject:

Military activities and troop
  movements (Continued):
  Mississippi: 1619, 3519, 3520,
    4203, 4899, 5132
    Corinth: 4588
  Mississippi River: 4970
  Mississippi Valley: 1357, 4285
  Missouri: 3519, 5017, 5858, 5975
    Southern Missouri: 4488
  Missouri River Valley: 3524
  North Carolina: 953, 1282, 1619,
    4849, 4970, 5425, 5877
    Batchelor's Creek: 4561
    Goldsboro--Maps: 5417
    New Bern: 3910, 4438, 5543
    Western North Carolina: 5325
    Wilmington: 3201
  Ohio: 3751, 4537
  South Carolina: 2325, 4411, 4700,
    4970
    Beaufort: 3264
    Coastal Islands: 4108
    Hilton Head: 3264
    Port Royal: 3264
    Sea Islands: 3910
  Tennessee: 659, 771, 808, 1505,
    3524, 3751, 4032, 4203, 4970,
    4973, 5303, 5695, 5858
    Eastern Tennessee: 5325
    Memphis: 5452
    Nashville: 5248
  Texas--Galveston: 4970
  Virginia: 1505, 1619, 3502, 4000,
    4108, 4537, 4945, 4970, 5000,
    5307, 5425, 5677, 5877, 5975
    Culpeper: 5626
    Danville: 5769
    Fort Monroe: 5896
    Halifax Court House: 5769
    James River: 162
    New Market: 4537
    Petersburg: 3910, 5626
    Portsmouth: 4561
    Shenandoah Valley: 3654
    Suffolk: 4561
    Warrington: 5626
    Woodstock: 4537
    Yorktown: 2657
  Washington, D.C.: 1282, 3283, 5425
  West Virginia: 52, 4537, 5307
    Harpers Ferry: 4537, 4690
    Martinsburg: 4537
  Western Theater: 5569
Military art and science: see
  UNITED STATES--MILITARY ART AND
  SCIENCE
Military government: see CIVIL WAR--
  MILITARY GOVERNMENT
Military intelligence: 3441, 5984
Military passes: 2255, 4573, 5417
Military regulations: 1418, 5425
  Quartermaster Department: 1817
Military supplies: 135, 605, 2106,
  2255, 2257, 2842, 3264, 3710,
  3849, 4226, 4228, 4255, 4303,
  4432, 4537, 4970, 5991
  Captured: 605
  Destruction: 5143
  Prices: 3751
  Subdivided by place:
    Maryland: 1817
    Tennessee: 2408
    Virginia: 5677
    West Virginia: 1817
Military trials--Tennessee: 2847
Miscellaneous soldiers' letters:
  703, 1548, 2104, 3910
Mobilization: 5311
  Authorization for state regiments:
    3283

UNITED STATES

ARMY:

### Civil War:

Subdivided by subject:

Mobilization (Continued):
  Massachusetts: 4349
  Pennsylvania: 421
  Rhode Island--Providence: 5563
Morale: 1505, 1845, 1885, 2777,
  3181, 4059, 4588, 4608, 4708,
  4973, 5034, 5261, 5502
Morals: 1699, 1845, 1853, 3281,
  4608, 5017, 5261
  Florida: 5425
Muster rolls: 3849, 4537, 5626
Negro officers: 4552
Negro troops: 605, 615, 854, 1348,
  1468, 1510, 1845, 1984, 2257,
  2311, 2469, 2816, 3264, 3281,
  3392, 4602, 5169, 5633
  see also UNITED STATES--ARMY--
    Civil War--Regiments--United
    States
  Depredations: 3012, 5775
  Equal pay: 3036
  North Carolina:
    1st Infantry (Colored): 4432
  Public opinion: 1798, 4602, 5975
  Subdivided by place:
    Arkansas: 4536
    Maryland: 1175
    South Carolina: 1477
      Charleston: 5645
    Virginia: 1827, 4996
      Petersburg: 4895
Occupation of Confederate territory:
  see CIVIL WAR--UNION OCCUPATION
Officers: 415, 1105, 1138, 1352,
  2490, 3392, 3493, 3522, 3613,
  3849, 4087, 4398, 4537, 4539,
  4546, 4888, 4889, 4891, 5248,
  5419, 5446, 5518, 5524, 5543,
  5560, 5744
  see also UNITED STATES--ARMY--
    Civil War--Generals
  Appointments and promotions: 388,
    1540, 1798, 1805, 2124, 2306,
    2679, 3264, 3493, 3815, 4881,
    5425, 5944
  Charges against: 4276
  Courts-martial: 4881
  Elections: see UNITED STATES--
    ARMY--Civil War--Election of
    officers
  Evaluations: 659, 3741
  Pay: 2867
  Orders: 129, 931, 2255, 2280, 3391,
    4077, 4537, 4546, 4552, 5425,
    5626
  South Carolina:
    Georgetown: 1352
    Hilton Head: 2679
  Virginia: 2270
    Gloucester Point: 2679
    Winchester: 2958
  West Virginia--Moorefield: 2958
Ordnance: 115, 383, 3357, 3710,
  4260, 4452, 4537, 4546, 5034,
  5172, 5433
  South Carolina: 2679
    Morris Island: 5433
  Tennessee: 1819
  Virginia: 2679
Organization and troop strength:
  196, 2893, 3493
Pay: 605, 1175, 1230, 1344, 2124,
  4565, 4608, 5425, 5430
  Claims: 2682
    Prisoners of war: 1461
  North Carolina: 1845
  Tennessee: 1819
Paymaster General: 1519
Paymasters: 281, 616

UNITED STATES

ARMY:

*Civil War:*

Subdivided by subject (Continued):

Pensions: see CIVIL WAR--PENSIONS
Political elections: 2504, 3813, 5269
Promotions: see UNITED STATES--ARMY--Civil War--Officers--Appointments and promotions
Property damage--Remuneration: see CIVIL WAR--CLAIMS--Destruction of property
Provost marshal:
  Virginia--Portsmouth: 5423
Quartermaster Corps: 1663, 2681, 5991
  West Virginia--Harpers Ferry: 4029
Quartermaster Department: 3328, 4260, 4537
  Army of the Potomac: 1817
  South Carolina: 2679
  Tennessee--Chattanooga: 2408
  Virginia: 2679, 3263
  Washington, D.C.: 5131
Rations: see UNITED STATES--ARMY--Civil War--Food
Reconnaissance: 3519
Recruiting and enlistment: 388, 856, 941, 1175, 1918, 2257, 2842, 3280, 3648, 3769, 4022, 4349, 4485, 4537, 5097, 5419, 5677, 5738, 5775
  Bounties: 4039
    Ohio: 281
  Negroes: see UNITED STATES--ARMY--Civil War--Negro troops
  Resistance: 3281, 3565, 3641, 4948, 5009, 5311
  Substitutions: 856, 2223, 2896
    New York: 1477
  Subdivided by place:
    Maine: 5425
    Massachusetts: 5425
    Michigan: 2604
    Missouri: 3703
    New Hampshire: 3822
    New York: 5563
    North Carolina--Goldsboro: 5792
    Ohio: 281
    Pennsylvania: 5425
Regimental calls: 4608
Regiments: 2490, 5419
  Connecticut:
    Artillery:
      1st Heavy Artillery: 5172
        Company B: 5425
      3rd: 5351
    Cavalry:
      1st: 1983, 5000
      21st: 1983
    Infantry:
      6th: 4970
      8th: 2257, 2602
      10th: 3910
      12th:
        Company D: 5425
      15th:
        Fife and drum corps: 5261
      19th: 941
      21st: 2547
      25th: 2816
      27th: 3778
  Delaware:
    Infantry:
      1st: 4881
      4th: 4881
  Illinois:
    Artillery:
      1st: 3641
    Cavalry:
      3rd: 3519
      11th: 4203, 5944

UNITED STATES

ARMY:

*Civil War:*

Subdivided by subject:

Regiments:
  Illinois (Continued):
    Infantry:
      14th: 5975
      15th: 5975
      16th: 659
      17th: 5311
      38th: 5695
      42nd: 4989
      47th: 5017
      53rd: 2119
      57th: 5058
      74th: 5348
      78th: 659
      106th:
        Company C: 5941
      112th: 4539
      137th: 4004
  Indiana:
    Cavalry:
      13th: 5097
    Infantry:
      14th: 4303
      15th: 1135, 3409
      44th: 808
      52nd: 2987
      66th: 4588
      70th: 2384
      84th: 1795
      88th: 560
      99th: 3648
      124th:
        Company C: 3849
  Iowa:
    Infantry:
      2nd: 243
      15th: 1984
      19th: 3392
      24th: 1619
      25th: 3953, 4945
      26th: 2561
      33rd: 3170
      34th: 3520
  Kentucky:
    Cavalry:
      4th: 4973
    Infantry:
      1st: 801, 2235
  Louisiana:
    Infantry:
      4th (Colored): 1348
  Maine:
    Artillery:
      1st: 3280, 3880
      6th Battery: 4546
    Cavalry:
      1st: 3809
      2nd: 3502
    Infantry:
      1st: 2106
      6th: 654
      8th: 731, 3201, 3880
      9th: 5425
      10th: 2106
      11th: 605, 3127
      12th: 731
      13th: 3910
      25th: 5955
      28th: 5425
      29th: 2106
    Veteran Infantry:
      1st: 3813
  Maryland:
    Artillery:
      Baltimore Light Artillery: 4769
    Cavalry:
      1st: 3809

UNITED STATES

ARMY:

*Civil War:*

Subdivided by subject:

Regiments:
  Maryland (Continued):
    Infantry:
      1st: 4348
      2nd Eastern Shore: 4537
      3rd: 4769
  Massachusetts: 5169
    Cavalry:
      1st: 2681, 3166, 3809
      3rd: 368
    Infantry:
      1st: 4860, 5061
      2nd: 368
      3rd: 953, 1537, 4438
      4th: 1253
      6th: 3264, 3280
      8th: 3264
      10th: 1058, 4970, 5834
      11th:
        Company E: 5425
      13th: 4608, 5122
      14th: 4000
      15th: 4000
      16th: 5670
        Company B: 3280
      17th:
        Company K: 5425
      21st: 4940
      23rd: 963
      24th: 1230
      25th: 3328
        Company A: 4349
      26th: 1408
      27th: 5877
      31st: 4970
      32nd: 2682
      35th: 2031
      36th: 3181
      37th: 1850
      42nd: 3342
      44th: 3562, 4414
      46th: 1934, 5043
      47th: 1348, 3522
      48th: 1349
      51st: 3166
      54th (Colored): 1510, 3037, 4602
      55th (Colored): 3037
      60th: 4438
  Michigan:
    Cavalry:
      5th: 5269
      9th: 3479
    Engineers:
      1st: 2604
    Infantry:
      9th: 4452, 4889
      21st: 689
      23rd: 2858
      25th: 3007
      28th: 1840
  Missouri:
    see also MISSOURI--Militia
    Cavalry:
      3rd: 1453
    Engineers:
      1st: 5425
    Infantry:
      1st: 4552
      1st Reserve Corps: 4552
  New Hampshire:
    Artillery:
      6th Heavy Artillery: 1820
    Cavalry:
      1st: 251
    Infantry:
      10th: 2453
      14th: 5131
      16th: 1763

UNITED STATES

ARMY:

### Civil War:

#### Subdivided by subject:

Regiments (Continued):
  New Jersey: 4087
    Infantry:
      4th: 5939
  New York:
    Artillery:
      7th Battery: 854
      8th Heavy Artillery: 3691
      9th: 3133, 4993
      14th Heavy Artillery: 2479
      23rd Independent Battery: 3281
      Pettit's Battery: 2360
      Rocket Battalion: 3281
    Cavalry:
      1st: 5008
      3rd: 358
      4th: 5502, 5677
      5th: 3691
      6th: 3809, 4059
      10th: 5626
      19th: 3889, 5425
      22nd: 78
    Engineers:
      1st: 2258
      15th: 3083
      50th: 4990
    Infantry:
      2nd: 1003, 3710
      5th: 388
      9th: 1050
      12th: 3768
      13th: 2100
      20th: 2311
      23rd: 1246
      30th: 5121
      38th: 3115
      47th: 605
      56th: 605
      61st: 701
      85th: 2091, 3095
      90th: 1325, 3975
      92nd: 5543
      100th: 605, 2500
      104th: 468, 5738
      110th: 929, 5715
      11th: 388
      115th: 4108
        Company E: 5417
      117th: 1845
      120th: 2648, 2898
      124th: 3815
        Company E: 4685
      137th: 5896
      138th: 388
      147th: 929
      150th: 3269
      154th: 2898
        Company B: 4260
      184th: 929
    Fire Zouaves: 3809
    New York State Volunteers: 1175
  North Carolina:
    Infantry:
      1st: see UNITED STATES--ARMY--Civil War--Regiments--United States--Infantry--35th (Colored)
      2nd: see UNITED STATES--ARMY--Civil War--Regiments--United States--Infantry--36th (Colored)
  Ohio:
    Artillery:
      16th Independent Battery: 5017
    Cavalry:
      4th: 4160, 4477

---

UNITED STATES

ARMY:

### Civil War:

#### Subdivided by subject:

Regiments:
  Ohio:
    Cavalry (Continued):
      5th:
        Company E: 5417
      7th: 2280
    Infantry:
      5th: 4477
      7th: 1235, 3280, 3716
      8th: 4945
      8th (Colored): 1235
      10th: 2829
      12th: 1177
      25th: 567
      33rd: 4255
        Company I: 4255
      38th: 1328
      42nd: 5132
      45th: 5132
      66th: 1505
      80th:
        Company I: 681
      90th: 135
      94th: 2504
        Company C: 2308
      96th: 5132
      99th: 5898
      101st: 4398
      107th: 1235
      110th: 1868, 2958
      118th: 3751
      122nd: 2958
      123rd--Casualties: 5417
      124th: 4565
      160th--Casualties: 5417
  Pennsylvania:
    Cavalry:
      3rd: 5560
      4th: 3809, 5939
      6th: 3809
      13th--Poetry: 5417
      16th: 3809, 5249
    Infantry:
      1st: 616
      5th: 5462
      12th: 3952
      19th: 411
      49th: 2405
      52nd: 605
      56th: 2306, 5417
      71st: 2989
      79th: 5991
      85th: 1426, 2679
      88th: 2124
      93rd: 5425
      95th: 820, 5769
      100th: 5775
      104th: 605, 1418
      122nd: 5991
      139th: 2236
      155th:
        Company B: 5425
  Rhode Island: 5563
    Cavalry:
      1st: 3809
    Infantry:
      4th: 394
      5th: 1610
      9th: 1610
  Tennessee:
    Cavalry:
      1st: 1819
        Company I: 5268
    Infantry:
      4th: 1819
  United States:
    Artillery:
      2nd: 3769

---

UNITED STATES

ARMY:

### Civil War:

#### Subdivided by subject:

Regiments:
  United States (Continued):
    Cavalry:
      4th: 5858
      4th (Colored): 5420
      5th: 2125
    Infantry:
      1st: 2842
      1st (Colored): 3741
      3rd: 2521
      22nd (Colored): 3741
      35th (Colored): 3037, 4432
      36th (Colored): 3037
      90th (Colored): 1325
      102nd (Colored): 4411
      103rd (Colored): 4432
    Sharpshooters:
      1st: 4485
      2nd: 857, 5034
  Vermont:
    Infantry:
      1st: 4485
      8th: 4888
      9th: 4485
      12th: 2255, 2791
  West Virginia:
    Infantry:
      12th: 2320
  Wisconsin:
    Infantry:
      3rd: 1625
      55th: 13
Relations with Negroes: 5991
Religion: 1699, 2236, 2311, 2681, 3181, 3648, 4588, 5061, 5419, 5715, 5941
  Prayer meetings: 5896
  Virginia: 2648
Reorganization: 654
Resignations: 272
Rumors: 1845, 2236, 2270, 2988, 3007, 3281, 3648, 4160, 4920, 5122, 5261, 5560, 5991
  Georgia: 1619
  Louisiana: 1619
  Mississippi: 1619
  North Carolina: 1619
  Virginia: 1619
Scarcity of coffee: 4561
Scarcity of food: 5975
Scarcity of sugar: 4561
Signal Corps: 814, 1282, 1805, 2777
Soldiers:
  Claims: 5570
  Comparison with Confederate soldiers: 1282
  Distinguished service: 4285
  Personal finance: 929
  Vital statistics:
    Maine: 5425
    Massachusetts: 5425
Songs and music: 494
  see also CIVIL WAR--SONGS AND MUSIC
Southern opinion: 4723
Southerners in: 4769
Stationery: 5417
Straggling: 5425
  Mississippi: 5421
Subsistence Department: 2255
Surgeons: 2124, 4076, 5898, 5944
  Appointments: 3283
  Pay: 4574
Target-practice: 3281
Training: 2989
  Artillery: 3493
  Infantry: 2031, 2958, 4485, 4860
  Maryland: 2602

963

UNITED STATES

ARMY:

### Civil War:

#### Subdivided by subject:

Training (Continued):
  Missouri:
    Saint Louis--Benton Barracks:
      4488
  Washington, D.C.: 1845
Transportation: 605, 1845, 5991
  Maryland: 1817
  Tennessee: 2408
  West Virginia: 1817
Transportation to:
  Louisiana:
    New Orleans: 4888
      From New York: 5131
  North Carolina: 3281
Transportation passes: 2255
Trenches and trench warfare: see
  CIVIL WAR--CAMPAIGNS, BATTLES,
  AND MILITARY ACTIONS--Virginia--
  Petersburg--Siege
Troop movements: see UNITED STATES--
  ARMY--Civil War--Military
  activities and troop movements
Units: see UNITED STATES--ARMY--
  Civil War--Regiments
Wagoners: 5991

#### Spanish-American War (1898):

Army life: 4974
  see also UNITED STATES--ARMY--
    Spanish-American War--Camp life
Cuba: 3905
Philippine Islands: 3905, 5844
Camp life: 5298
  see also UNITED STATES--ARMY--
    Spanish-American War--Army life
  Florida: 4743
  Georgia: 4485
Camps:
  Cuba--Havana: 77
  Florida--Jacksonville: 77
  Georgia--Tybee Island: 5298
Corps:
  8th Army Corps: 5424
Courts-martial: 4743
Desertion: 4743
Diseases--Yellow fever: 5298
Honors and awards: 5424
Military activities and troop
  movements: 5790
  Cuba: 5759
  Philippine Islands: 4883, 5844
  Puerto Rico: 5759
Mobilization: 5298
  Florida: 2991
Officers: 5668, 5790
  Appointments and promotions: 4485
Regiments:
  Alabama:
    Infantry:
      2nd: 3657
  Massachusetts: 185
    Infantry:
      2nd: 185
      5th:
        Company L: 5425
  Nebraska:
    Infantry:
      3rd: 77
  North Carolina:
    Infantry:
      1st: 3219
      2nd: 1313
        Company K: 3447
  South Dakota:
    Infantry:
      1st: 77
  United States:
    Cavalry:
      1st (Rough Riders): 4743

UNITED STATES

ARMY:

### Spanish-American War:

Regiments:
  United States (Continued):
    Infantry:
      40th: 5844
  Wisconsin:
    Infantry:
      3rd: 4974
Training:
  Artillery:
    South Carolina:
      Sullivan's Island: 5298

### World War I:

Army life: 5380
  see also UNITED STATES--ARMY--
    World War I--Camp life
Camp life: 1275, 3843
  see also UNITED STATES--ARMY--
    World War I--Army life
  France: 4743, 5419
  Photographs: 3797
  United States: 4743
Camps:
  Arizona--Nogales: 3843
  South Carolina--Columbia: 3843
  United States: 4858
  Virginia--Petersburg: 3843
Casualties--France: 4743
Civil-military relations: 3893
Corps:
  5th Army Corps: 5163
Corps of Engineers: see UNITED
  STATES--ARMY--World War I--
  Engineers
Discharges--Temporary: 2970
Divisions:
  Cavalry:
    2nd: 3019
  Infantry:
    1st: 3019
    29th: 4269
Engineers--France: 3789
France: 4269
Hospitals:
  Field hospitals: 5786
  France: 4743
Immunization: 5419
Medical and sanitary affairs:
  Medical Reserve Corps: 4743
  Services of physicians: 4743
Military activities and troop
  movements: 5419
Military police:
  France--LeMans: 4269
Military supplies: 3451
Miscellaneous soldiers' letters:
  4659, 5741, 5786
Negro troops: 4269, 5419
Officers:
  Appointments and promotions: 3545,
    5419
Orders: 94
Pay: 5419
Physicians: see UNITED STATES--
  ARMY--World War I--Medical and
  sanitary affairs--Services of
  physicians
Prisoners and prisons--France: 4743
Recreation: 3797
Recruiting and enlistment: 5930
  Selective Service: 3955
Regiments:
  Infantry:
    113th: 4269
Training: 1275
  Infantry: 3843
Trench life:
  France: 5419

UNITED STATES

ARMY (Continued):

### World War II:

Air Corps:
  Military operations: 5419
  Pilots: 5419
Camp life: 3338
  Iowa--Fort Des Moines: 3338
Divisions:
  Infantry:
    32nd: 1661
    77th: 1661
  Americal Division: 1661
Eighth Army: 1661
Medical and sanitary affairs:
  Services of physicians: 2934
Military activities and troop
  movements: 5417
Physicians: see UNITED STATES--
  ARMY--World War II--Medical and
  sanitary affairs--Services of
  physicians
Regiments:
  Artillery:
    67th Coast Artillery: 5417
Training: 1661, 3338
United States occupation of Japan:
  1661
Women soldiers: 3338
Women's Army Auxiliary Corps: 3338

### Vietnam War:

Recruiting and enlistment:
  Resistance: 5077

ART AND ARTISTS: 3965
  Employment: 2587
ARTICLES OF CONFEDERATION: 3041
ARTS: 2398
ASSASSINATIONS: see ASSASSINATIONS
ATOMIC BOMB: 2897
ATOMIC ENERGY: 4805
AUTHORS: see AMERICAN AUTHORS
AUTHORS AND EDITORS: 720
AUTHORS AND PUBLISHERS:
  1800s: 305, 1227, 3586, 4829, 4971
  1820s: 2437
  1830s: 1029
  1840s: 1029
  1850s: 1029
  1860s: 1608, 2449, 2845, 5051
  1870s: 1608, 2449, 3363, 3585,
    5051, 5322
  1880s: 1608, 2225, 2449, 5322,
    5326
  1890s: 1449, 2225, 5322
  1800s-1900s: 72, 404, 1160, 2451,
    2871, 3465, 4012, 4020, 4021,
    4491, 5044, 5226
  1900s: 4837
  1900s: 1068, 4279, 5594
  1910s: 5594
  1920s: 2790
  1940s: 4641
  1950s: 985
  1960s: 985
  1970s: 902, 5889
  Cookbooks: 985
  Periodicals: 3022
AUTHORS AND READERS: 2390
AUTHORSHIP: 3746, 4475, 5081, 5149
AUTOGRAPH COLLECTING: 1422, 2545,
  5294
AUTOMOBILE INDUSTRY: 4918
AVIATION: 4858
  Laws and legislation: 4858
  Military aviation: 3451
BALLADS: see AMERICAN BALLADS
BALLOONS: 4269
  see also UNITED STATES--ARMY--
    Civil War--Balloons
BALLS: 3905
  see also INAUGURAL BALLS
BANK FAILURES: 3053

UNITED STATES

BANK STOCKS: 5080
  see also BANK OF THE UNITED STATES
    (second)--Stocks
BANKRUPTCY: 5145
BANKS AND BANKING: 1016, 2723, 3053,
    3169, 3415, 5470
  see also BANK OF THE UNITED STATES
  Statistics: 2746
BIBLE SOCIETIES: 1565
BIOGRAPHICAL STUDIES: 902, 2351,
    5552, 5640
BIOGRAPHIES: 2449, 4264, 4918, 5051
BONDS: 2210
  see also UNITED STATES--GOVERNMENT
    BONDS
  Investments: 2469, 5440
BOOK ILLUSTRATION: 2062
BOOK REVIEWS: 1424, 2282, 2390, 2398
BOOKSELLERS AND BOOKSELLING: 3791,
    5594
BOYCOTTS: 5077
BRIDGES: 5080
BRITISH BUSINESS ENTERPRISES: 3179
CENSORSHIP--Books: 2390
CENSUS: 1484
  see also UNITED STATES--GOVERNMENT
    AGENCIES AND OFFICIALS--Bureau
    of the Census
  1st (1790): 5537
  7th (1850): 5426
  8th (1860): 5426
  9th (1870): 5426
    Georgia: 2326
  10th (1880): 3215, 5426
    Georgia: 1993
    Instructions: 122
    West Virginia: 1828
  11th (1890): 122
    Cherokee Indians: 1036
CENTENNIAL CELEBRATION (1876): 5380
CHARITIES: 480, 1197, 3633
  Children: 3633
CHILDREN: 4948
CHILDREN'S LITERATURE: 3810
CHRISTMAS CARDS: 2656
CHURCHES: see CHURCHES, and names of
    specific denominations
CITIZENSHIP: 4927
  see also NEGROES--Citizenship
  Laws and legislation: 5537
CIVIL RIGHTS: 3020, 3066, 3820, 4386,
    4805, 4948
  see also NEGROES--Civil rights
CIVIL SERVICE: 4805, 4858
CIVIL WAR: see CIVIL WAR; CONFEDERATE
    STATES OF AMERICA; UNITED STATES--
    ARMY--Civil War; UNITED STATES--
    NAVY--Civil War
CLAIMS AGAINST: 571, 3325, 5354
  Inventions: 794
CLERGY: see CLERGY
CLOTHING AND DRESS: 3301
COAL MINES AND MINING: 4343
  Stocks: 5080
COALING STATIONS--Hawaii: 3516
COLONIAL POLICY AND ADMINISTRATION:
  Philippine Islands: 4511
COINS AND COINAGE: 1302
COMMERCIAL AGENTS IN FRANCE: 5448
COMMERCIAL TREATIES:
  France: 1424
  Great Britain: 3041
COMMODITY PRICES: see COMMODITY PRICES
COMMUNISM: 4094
  In labor movement: 1883
CONFEDERATION PERIOD: 3662
  Public finance: 5276
  Strategic importance of Southern
    States: 5537
CONGRESS:
  see also CONTINENTAL CONGRESS
  1700s:
    1780s: 4015
    1790s: 2815, 4015
  1800s: 1480
    1800s: 1222

UNITED STATES

CONGRESS:
  1800s (Continued):
    1820s: 3191
    1830s: 42, 3191
    1840s: 3325
    1850s: 3325, 3770, 5149
    1860s: 872, 2125, 3281, 5419,
      5444
    1870s: 2125, 3254, 4266
  Appointments: 4524
  Autographs: 1851
  Conflict of interest: 3191
  Freedom of debate:
    Brooks-Sumner affair: 3054
  Negro members: 2517
  Power to nominate president and
    vice-president proposed: 2138
  Private legislation: 3004
  Recognition of national anthem:
    3220
  Tariff debates (1824): 3406

  Subdivided by legislative body:

  House of Representatives:
    1800s: 1866, 3556, 5031, 5493
    Alabama: 5668, 5937
    Georgia:
      1700s: 3573
      1700s-1800s: 3671
      1800s: 1121, 4921, 5315
    Maryland: 3190, 5247
    Massachusetts: 5762
    Missouri: 1062, 4443
    North Carolina:
      1800s: 1527, 3094
      1800s-1900s: 4858
      1900s: 325, 4018, 4805
    South Carolina:
      1800s: 633, 1480, 2613, 3366,
        3445, 5271, 5970
      1900s: 3451
    Virginia:
      1700s: 4015
      1800s: 404, 1714, 3291, 4916,
        5853
      1800s-1900s: 5152
      1900s: 3104
    Subdivided by subject:
      Committee on Education and
        Labor: 325
      Committee on Elections: 5427
      Committee on Interior and
        Insular Affairs: 4805
      Committee on Ways and Means:
        4805
      Constituent relations:
        North Carolina: 631, 4018
        South Dakota: 5791
      Seating of members: 2393
      Speaker (1846): 3903
      Territories Subcommittee: 4805
  Senate: 1352, 5419, 5493
    Alabama: 3774, 4994
    Georgia:
      1700s: 5537
      1800s: 2860, 3671, 5315
    Illinois: 2161
    Louisiana:
      1800s: 4958
      1900s: 3252
    Mississippi: 1403, 5516
    Missouri: 1136
    North Carolina:
      1800s: 631, 3094, 3636
      1900s: 274, 2581, 4825, 4927
    Pennsylvania: 1234
    South Carolina:
      1700s: 2780
      1700s-1800s: 4399
      1800s: 3366, 4445
      1900s: 1478
    Texas: 3590
    Virginia:
      1800s: 1714, 2881, 3169, 3424,
        4490, 4497, 5217, 5861

UNITED STATES

CONGRESS:

  Subdivided by legislative body:

  Senate:
    Virginia (Continued):
      1900s: 5152
    West Virginia: 694
    Subdivided by subject:
      Appointments--Virginia: 4312
      Clerks: 4022
      Constituent relations: 1478
      Debates: see NULLIFICATION
        DEBATE; WEBSTER-HAYNE DEBATE
      Ratification of the Treaty of
        Guadalupe Hidalgo: 5149
      Treaty-making power: 3190
CONSTITUTION: 3809, 4805, 5298, 5470
  Amendments: 2776, 3022, 3671
    13th Amendment: 1805
    14th Amendment: 716, 2469
    18th Amendment: see PROHIBITION
    19th Amendment: see WOMAN SUFFRAGE
    21st Amendment: see PROHIBITION
  Formulation and ratification: 3041
    Georgia: 5644
    North Carolina: 2776, 3920, 4625
  Textbooks on: 3501
CONSTITUTIONAL CONVENTION (1787):
  4977
CONSERVATION OF NATURAL RESOURCES:
  4805
  see also UNITED STATES--WILDLIFE
    CONSERVATION
CONTESTED ELECTIONS: 5427
COPYRIGHT LEGISLATION: 4020
CORRUPTION IN POLITICS: 5427
  House of Representatives: 5853
COTTON: see COTTON, and subjects
    beginning with the word COTTON
COURTS:
  Circuit Courts: see COURTS--Circuit
    Courts
  District Courts: see COURTS--
    District Courts:
  Federal Courts:
    Southern opinion on the power of:
      431
  Laws and legislation: 3041
  Supreme Court: 2776, 2812, 2872,
    4290, 5573
    Appellate Division: 5145
    Cases: 3442, 4443, 5606
    Decisions: 958, 3176
    Prayer ban decision: 3020
    Dispute of 1937: 3820
    Justices: see names of specific
      justices
COURTSHIP: 2714
CURRENCY: 849, 872, 1339, 2164, 2881,
  3415, 5576
  see also UNITED STATES--COINS AND
    COINAGE
  Counterfeiting: 2130
  Depreciation: 5752
DEATH: 2407
DEFENSE:
  1800s: 1599, 3145
  1900s: 274, 4556, 5878
DEMOCRATIC PARTY: see DEMOCRATIC
  PARTY
DESCRIPTION AND TRAVEL:
  1700s: 1582
  1800s:
    1840s: 5493
    1850s: 5493, 5928
    1860s: 5050, 5493
    1880s: 2626
  1800s-1900s: 5740
  1900s:
    1900s: 2191, 3424
    1910s: 3424, 4042
DESEGREGATION: 3048, 4386
DISEASES:
  Cholera: 496, 3053
  Influenza: 5930

UNITED STATES

DISEASES (Continued):
  Scarlet fever: 2225
  Smallpox: 2591
  Yellow fever: 3053
DIVORCE: 1424
DRAMA: see AMERICAN DRAMA
DRAWINGS: see DRAWINGS, American
ECONOMIC CONDITIONS:
  see also DEPRESSION (1929--United States); DEPRESSIONS; PANIC OF (date)
  1700s: 1481, 2703
  1800s: 2742
    1810s: 4678
    1820s: 4678
    1830s: 323, 1335
    1840s: 1728, 2755, 3391
    1850s: 3012, 5231
    1860s: 183, 421, 2147, 5231, 5517
    1870s: 183, 882, 5517
    1880s: 183, 5517
  1800s-1900s: 4552
  1900s: 4865
    1900s: 4560
    1920s: 4564
    1930s: 274, 4564
    1940s: 274, 2627
    1950s: 5312
EDUCATION: 2164, 4564, 4805, 4948, 5480
  see also AMERICAN STUDENTS IN (name of country); AMERICAN TEACHERS IN (name of country); EDUCATION, and subjects beginning word EDUCATION or EDUCATIONAL; FEDERAL AID TO EDUCATION; SCHOOLS; TEACHING; UNIVERSITIES AND COLLEGES
  Women: 4881
EIGHT-HOUR DAY: 4858
ELECTION LAWS AND REGULATIONS: 5427
ELECTION REFORM: 2225
ELECTIONS:
  see also BALLOTS; CONGRESSIONAL ELECTIONS; GUBERNATORIAL ELECTIONS; JUDGES--Elections; LOCAL ELECTIONS; PRESIDENTIAL ELECTIONS; SENATORIAL ELECTIONS; and the following subheadings under UNITED STATES: ARMY--Civil War--Election of officers/ Political elections; CONTESTED ELECTIONS; VOTER REGISTRATION
  1800s:
    1822: 291
    1836: 2551
    1840: 1985, 2591
    1844: 1985, 3030
    1876: 3960
      Foreign public opinion: 5762
    1888: 2794
    1892: 5790
  1900s: 4453, 4948
    1920s: 1150, 5930
    1930s: 1150
    1940s: 1201
    1950s: 1201, 4805
ELECTRIC POWER INDUSTRY: 4805
EMBARGO: see EMBARGO; EMBARGO ACT
EMBEZZLEMENT: 3032
  By Federal employee in North Carolina: 2776
EMPLOYMENT: 4948
ENGRAVERS AND ENGRAVINGS: 2398
ETHICS: 1219
EVANGELISM: 872
EVOLUTION AND RELIGION: 1219
EXTERNAL DEBTS:
  Revolutionary War era debts owed to Great Britain: 258
FARMING: see FARMING and subheadings beginning with the word FARM
FEDERALIST PARTY: see FEDERALIST PARTY
FERTILIZER INDUSTRY: 1115
FICTION: see AMERICAN FICTION
FISHING INDUSTRY: 3357, 4564

UNITED STATES

FOLKLORE: 691
FOOD AND DRUG LEGISLATION: 592, 3410
FOREIGN INVESTMENTS:
  In Great Britain: 4895
  In Guatemala: 5970
  In the Union of Soviet Socialist Republics: 1424
  In Venezuela: 4895
FOREIGN RELATIONS: 83, 1962
  see also UNITED STATES--GOVERNMENT AGENCIES AND OFFICIALS--Diplomatic and Consular Service
  1700s-1800s: 4383
  1800s: 196, 1222, 2578, 3325, 3455, 5470
  1800s-1900s: 1024, 4310
  1900s: 274, 3190, 3538, 4343, 4449, 4805
  Algeria: 3041, 4348
  Belgium: 1787
  Bolivia: 5045
  Brazil: 1302
  Chile: 5045
  China: 5252
  Cuba: 1364, 3774, 3809, 4348, 5171
  Denmark: 1302
  Egypt: 83
  Europe: 588, 894, 4616
  France:
    1700s: 2468
    1790s: 1891, 2506, 2815, 3041, 3384, 5298
    1700s-1800s: 3456, 4348
    1700s-1900s: 4486
    1800s: 1115, 1745
    1900s: 1424
  Germany: 592
  Great Britain:
    1776-1799: 894, 2551, 2776, 2815, 3041, 3573, 4221, 5298
    1776-1800s: 4348, 5726
    1800s: 258
      1800s: 2959
      1830s: 5065
      1840s: 5065
      1850s: 762, 4520, 4995
      1860s: 863, 3053, 3472, 3983, 5033
      see also GREAT BRITAIN--FOREIGN RELATIONS--Confederate States of America
      1870s: 863
      1880s: 4089
      1890s: 217, 4089
    Oregon boundary dispute: 2193, 4813
    Peace negotiations (1813-1814): 1302
    Southern States: 4383
  Greece:
    1800s: 636, 1787
    1900s: 83
  Iran: 83
  Japan: 2963, 4486, 5419
  Mexico:
    see also MEXICO--American intervention
    1800s:
      1840s: 2808
      see also MEXICAN WAR
      1850s: 2936
      1860s: 1249
      1870s: 4535
    1900s: 5252
  The Netherlands: 3384
  Nicaragua: 3960
  Peru: 4531, 5436
  Philippine Islands: 3774
  Portugal: 4748
  Russia: 286, 960, 4808
  Spain:
    1700s: 5046
    1700s-1800s: 4982
    1700s-1900s: 4486
    1800s: 3041, 3854, 4667, 4808
    1800s-1900s: 1364, 4983

UNITED STATES

FOREIGN RELATIONS (Continued):
  Turkey: 636, 1787
  Union of Soviet Socialist Republics: 286, 3538
  United Nations: 3538
  The Vatican: 4020
FOREIGN TRADE:
  see also UNITED STATES--SHIPPING
  1700s-1800s: 5228
  1800s: 196, 2742
    1810s: 2403, 3485
    1830s: 323
    1850s: 5133
    1890s: 1024
  1800s-1900s: 3008
  1900s:
    1930s: 274, 4564
    1940s: 274
  Argentina: 948
  China: 4060, 5252
  Cuba: 948, 1442
  Europe: 1615
  Far East: 2641
  France: 948, 1424, 1615, 1935
  Great Britain:
    1700s: 313, 1481
    1700s-1800s: 1615, 2637, 4598
    1700s-1900s: 480
    1800s: 948, 2641, 3179, 4289
  Greece: 636
  India: 2756, 3578
  Jamaica: 1792
  Japan: 4060
  Madeira Islands: 1481
  Mexico: 948
  Portugal: 1481
  Russia: 1889
  Saint Lucia: 3871
  South America: 3578
  Spain: 1481
  Turkey: 636
  Union of Soviet Socialist Republics: 286
  West Indies: 1481, 1615
FORENSIC PSYCHIATRY: 958
FREE THOUGHT: 2225
FREE TRADE: 2225
GOLD: see GOLD; GOLD BUYING
GOVERNMENT AGENCIES AND OFFICIALS:
  Army: see UNITED STATES--ARMY
  Biological Survey: 4453
  Bureau of Fisheries: 2084, 4351
  Bureau of Lighthouses: 4858
  Bureau of Ordnance: 2085
  Bureau of Pensions: 4601
  Bureau of Printing and Engraving: 5268
  Bureau of Refugees, Freedmen and Abandoned Lands: 605, 1015, 1980, 2449, 5043, 5891
    Farming operations in Virginia: 1366
    Georgia: 731
    North Carolina: 2469
      Beaufort: 5431
      Robeson County: 956
    South Carolina: 1927, 3405
    Virginia: 1366
  Bureau of the Census:
    see also UNITED STATES--CENSUS
    Clerks: 3809
    Statistics: 1439
  Cabinet:
    1810s: 1086
    1820s: 4852
    1830s: 4852
    1840s: 2647
    1850s: 5853
    1930s: 4564
  Coast and Geodetic Survey: 1785, 4013, 4348
    Miscellaneous Division: 5832
  Commission of Indian Affairs: 2486
    Indian agents: 2301
  Commission on Civil Rights: 4386
  Commissioner of Fish and Fisheries: 3357

UNITED STATES

GOVERNMENT AGENCIES AND OFFICIALS (Continued):
  Commissioner of Indian Affairs: 2326, 4849
    Tennessee: 5870
  Commissioner of Internal Revenue: 4564
  Communications Committee: 4564
  Comptroller of the Treasury: 5046
  Consular Bureau: 1024
  Customs Service:
    Georgia: 2497
    Massachusetts: 3209
    Missouri: 2166
    New York: 3871
    North Carolina: 2437
    South Carolina: 5193
  Department of Agriculture: 1278, 2746, 5428
    Bureau of Crop Estimates: 1336
  Department of Commerce: 4564
  Department of Immigration: 3972
  Department of Justice: 3793
  Department of Labor: 1194, 1197, 1198, 1202, 5234
  Department of State: 4020
    Preservation of records: 2696
  Department of the Interior: 3332, 4851
    Administration: 715
    Clerks: 3809
    Investigations: 20
  Department of the Navy: 1367, 5429, 5786
    Press releases: 1367
  Department of the Treasury: 70, 1197, 2913, 3413, 3805, 4486, 4781, 5546, 5578, 5714
    Appointments: 5268
    Auditor: 3325
    Clerks: 3809
    Division of Loans and Currency: 5440
    Establishment: 5537
    Investigations: 20
    Light-House Board: 3948
    Regulations: 4852
    Revenue collection--Iowa: 3848
  Department of War: 2486, 5431, 5575
    Appointments: 1635, 3384
    Adjutant and Inspector General's Office: 5430
    Clothing Bureau: 5430
    Ordnance Office: 5433
  Diplomatic and consular service:
    1700s-1800s: 4383
    1800s: 2252
      1800s: 4163
      1840s: 3809
      1850s: 3809
      1880s: 1308
      1890s: 1024, 1308
    1900s: 83
    Appointments:
      1800s: 2578
        1820s: 4880
        1830s: 4880
        1850s: 3903
        1860s: 1109
        1890s: 1024
      1800s-1900s: 4786
    Housing: 1024
    Political interference: 1024
    Regulations: 4852
    Salaries: 588, 1024
    Social life:
      Denmark: 404
      Iran: 83
    <u>Subdivided by place</u>:
      Algeria: 2578
      Argentina: 2271, 5936
      Belgium: 1101
      Brazil: 2810, 4348
      Chile: 3102, 4074
      China: 4413, 5861, 5912
      Cuba: 3231

UNITED STATES

GOVERNMENT AGENCIES AND OFFICIALS:
  Diplomatic and consular service:
    <u>Subdivided by place</u> (Continued):
      Denmark: 5321
      Egypt: 5298
      France:
        <u>1790s</u>: 4348
        <u>1800s</u>: 4490
          <u>1800s</u>: 4845
          <u>1810s</u>: 1302, 4845
          <u>1830s</u>: 4616
          <u>1850s</u>: 1769, 2583
          <u>1860s</u>: 1769
        <u>1900s</u>: 1424
      Germany: 3029
      Great Britain:
        <u>1790s</u>: 4218
        <u>1800s</u>: 1910
          <u>1800s</u>: 4348
          <u>1830s</u>: 4616, 5065
          <u>1840s</u>: 5065
        <u>1900s</u>: 4018, 4559
      Greece: 5762
      Guatemala: 5970
      India: 286, 5298
      Iran: 83
      Italy: 2871, 4020, 4719
      Mexico: 3557, 3809, 4390, 4719, 5271
      The Netherlands: 588, 3384
      Peru: 5051
      Russia: 286, 960, 2139
      Saudi Arabia: 5298
      Spain:
        <u>1700s</u>: 4214
        <u>1800s</u>: 3659
          <u>1800s</u>: 4213
          <u>1810s</u>: 1855, 4348
          <u>1820s</u>: 1855, 3854
          <u>1830s</u>: 3854
          <u>1880s</u>: 1340
        <u>1800s-1900s</u>: 4983
      Sweden: 404, 5298
      Tasmania: 286
      Trinidad: 286
      Turkey: 5524
  District attorneys:
    Maryland: 232
    North Carolina: 602
    Pennsylvania: 232
  Federal Communications Commission: 1195, 4564
  Federal Emergency Relief Administration: 365
  Federal Power Commission: 2299
  Federal Trade Commission: 1951
  Fish Commission: <u>see</u> UNITED STATES--GOVERNMENT AGENCIES AND OFFICIALS--Bureau of Fisheries
  Food Administration: 3955, 5115, 5803
  Forest Service: 4453
    Southeastern Forest Experiment Station: 1852
  Government Printing Office: 4022
  Government Weather Station: 1001
  Information Agency: 83
  Internal revenue collectors:
    Connecticut: 3041
    Georgia: 2280
    North Carolina: 4261, 4548, 4910
  Internal Revenue Service:
    North Carolina: 1278, 4152
  Interstate Commerce Commission: 238
  Marshals:
    Appointments: 422
    Georgia: 2326, 5492
    Kentucky: 3325
  Mint: 4022
    Georgia: 5744
  National Advisory Council: 4564
  National Bureau of Standards: 1951
  National Currency Department: 5051
  National Housing Agency: 1197

UNITED STATES

GOVERNMENT AGENCIES AND OFFICIALS (Continued):
  National Labor Relations Board: 1195, 1197, 1199, 5235, 5441
    Cases: 5442
    Textile workers: 5236
  National Mediation Board: 3190
  National Museum of Natural History: 4022
  National Recovery Administration: 5252
  National War Labor Board: 341, 1197, 5234, 5486
    Disputes Division: 5441
  Nautical Almanac Office: 2469
  Office for Emergency Management: 1193
  Office of Price Administration: 1194, 1197, 5441
  Office of Price Stabilization: 1202
  Office of the Commissary General of Prisoners: 1360
  Patent Office: 2469, 2530, 2847, 3343, 5193
    <u>see also</u> PATENTS
  Pension Office: 3770
  Post Office: 1252, 3041, 3523, 4348, 4805, 5982
    <u>see also</u> POST OFFICE BOXES; POSTAL UNIONS
    Administration of: 4880
    Appointments: 4858, 5152, 5268, 5361
    Local offices:
      California--San Francisco: 4401
      Georgia:
        Columbia Mine: 4895
        Lawrenceville: 5438
      Indiana: 2954
      Massachusetts--Becket: 5766
      Mississippi:
        Natchez: 1693
        Oxford: 4379
      Missouri--Calhoun: 5392
      North Carolina:
        Beattie's Ford: 792
        Calahaln: 122
        Cane Creek: 2618
        Farmington: 2857
        Henderson: 4407
        Hollywood: 3960
        Killian's Post Office: 4450
        Midway: 3250
        Murphy: 3025
        New Bern: 3865
        Orange County: 3984
        Raleigh: 2589
      Rhode Island--Westerly: 2547
      South Carolina--Charleston: 2696
      Virginia:
        Hales Ford: 2593
        Mount Airy: 2131
        State Mills: 3679
        Suffolk: 5439
        White Post: 1436, 5698
        Winnsville: 5839
      West Virginia:
        Edray: 5655
        Inwood: 5239
        Middleway: 4892
        Shepherdstown: 2711
    Mail service: 5402
      <u>see also</u> CIVIL WAR--MAIL SERVICE BETWEEN NORTH AND SOUTH
      North Carolina: 315, 3415
      Southern States: 3415
      To Mexico: 1249
    Obscene mail--South Carolina: 2109
    Postal Guide: 350
    Railroad mail service: 263
    <u>Subdivided by place</u>:
      Georgia: 4921, 5438
      North Carolina: 754, 3845
      South Carolina: 2696

UNITED STATES

GOVERNMENT AGENCIES AND OFFICIALS:
 Post Office:
  Subdivided by place (Continued):
   Vermont: 3218
   West Virginia: 1946
 Postmaster General: 3614
 Presidents: see names of specific
  presidents
 President's Commission on Health
  Needs of the Nation: 1202
 Railroad Administration: 238
 Revenue Service: 437
  Appointments: 694
 Rural Electrification Administration:
  4851
 Secret Service: 605
  In Haiti: 4275
 Secretary of Commerce:
  Daniel Calhoun Roper (1933-1938):
   4564
 Secretary of State:
  James Monroe (1811-1817): 1424
  Edward Livingston (1831-1833):
   3231
  John Forsyth (1834-1841): 1855
  Daniel Webster (1841-1843,
   1850-1852): 5622
  Abel Parker Upshur (1843): 5445
  William Maxwell Evarts
   (1877-1881): 1734
  Robert Lansing (1915-1920): 3096
  Selection of (1866): 4751
 Secretary of War:
  Timothy Pickering (1795): 4194
  James McHenry (1796-1800): 3384
  John C. Calhoun (1817-1825): 842
  Joel Roberts Poinsett (1837-1841):
   4249
  Jefferson Davis (1853-1857): 1403
  Edwin M. Stanton (1862-1868):
   5432
  William Worth Belknap (1869-1876):
   415
 Secretary of the Interior:
  Jacob Thompson (1857-1861): 5263
  James Harlan (1865-1866): 2341
  Hoke Smith (1893-1896): 4887
 Secretary of the Navy:
  William Jones (1813-1814): 4081
  John Branch (1829-1831): 631
  Levi Woodbury (1831-1834): 5886
  James Kirke Paulding (1838-1841):
   4088
  Abel Parker Upshur (1843): 5445
  John Young Mason (1844-1849):
   3557
  William Alexander Graham
   (1850-1852): 2121
  James Cochran Dobbin (1853-1857):
   1525, 1848
  Gideon Welles (1861-1869): 5636
  Hilary A. Herbert (1893-1897):
   4911
  Claude Augustus Swanson (1933):
   5152
 Secretary of the Treasury:
  Oliver Wolcott (1795-1800): 5870
  Samuel Ingham (1829-1831): 2761
  McClintock Young (1834): 5967
  Levi Woodbury (1834-1841): 5886
  Robert John Walker (1845-1849):
   5516
  Howell Cobb (1857-1860): 1121
  George S. Boutwell (1869-1873):
   2563
  John Serman (1877-1881): 2273
 Signal Office: 1785
 Tariff Commission: 581, 3190
 Wage Stabilization Board: 1194,
  1197, 1198, 2768, 5236
 War Finance Corporation: 5962
  Agricultural Loan Agency: 5962
 War Food Administration: 5428
 War Savings Staff: 341
 War Shipping Administration:
  North Carolina: 658

UNITED STATES

GOVERNMENT AGENCIES AND OFFICIALS
(Continued):
 Works Progress Administration:
  Malaria control experiments: 365
 Works Project Administration:
  North Carolina: 5298
GOVERNMENT AND ART: 2587
GOVERNMENT BONDS: 5440
GOVERNMENT PUBLICATIONS: 3598
GOVERNMENTAL CONTROL OF INDUSTRY: see
 RAILROADS--Governmental control;
 TEXTILE INDUSTRY--Governmental
 control
GOVERNMENTAL REGULATION OF WAGES AND
 SALARIES: see WAGES AND SALARIES--
 Government regulation/Minimum wage
GUARDIANSHIP:
 Mental incompetence: 958
HARBOR IMPROVEMENTS:
 Laws and legislation: 4858
HEALTH ORGANIZATIONS: 1197
HEALTH RESORTS: 1084, 3053, 5193
HISTORIC BUILDINGS: 2411
HISTORICAL CONTROVERSIES:
 Civil War: see CIVIL WAR--HISTORICAL
  CONTROVERSIES
 Founding of the United States: 2400
HISTORICAL SOCIETIES: 3990
HISTORICAL STUDIES: see HISTORICAL
 STUDIES
HONORS AND AWARDS: see HONORS AND
 AWARDS
HOSPITALS, Military: see UNITED
 STATES--ARMY--Civil War--
 Convalescent camps/Hospitals
HYMNS: 1219
IMMIGRATION AND EMIGRATION: see
 AMERICANS IN (name of country);
 IMMIGRATION AND EMIGRATION;
 (nationality) IN THE UNITED STATES,
 e.g. GERMANS IN THE UNITED STATES
IMPERIALISM: 2473
 see also UNITED STATES--TERRITORIAL
  EXPANSION; and Annexation as
  subheading under names of
  territories annexed
INAUGURATION OF PRESIDENTS: see
 INAUGURAL BALLS; and Inauguration as
 subheading under names of specific
 presidents
INCOME TAX: 1278, 4858
INDIAN AFFAIRS: see INDIANS OF NORTH
 AMERICA; UNITED STATES--GOVERNMENT
 AGENCIES AND OFFICIALS--Commission
 of Indian Affairs/Commissioner of
 Indian Affairs
INDUSTRIAL MANAGEMENT: 274, 325
INSANITY--Jurisprudence: 958
INSURANCE: see INSURANCE
INTERNAL REVENUE LAW: 4548
INTERNATIONAL BANKING: 196
INTERNATIONAL RELIEF:
 China: 4564
INTERNATIONAL RELIEF ORGANIZATIONS:
 3633
IRON INDUSTRY: 3413
JOURNALISM: see JOURNALISM; NEWSPAPERS
JUDICIAL AFFAIRS: 274
JUDICIAL REFORM: 5299
KINDERGARTENS: 4095
KNOW-NOTHING PARTY: see KNOW-NOTHING
 PARTY
LABOR: 274, 325, 4805
 see also LABOR, and subjects
  beginning with the word LABOR
LABOR LAWS AND LEGISLATION: 325, 1197
 see also names of specific laws
LAND: see LAND, and subjects
 beginning with the word LAND;
 UNITED STATES--PUBLIC LANDS;
 WESTERN LANDS
LAWS AND LEGISLATION:
 see also UNITED STATES--CONGRESS;
  and names of specific laws
 Codification: 1792
LECTURES AND LECTURING: 1219, 2449,
 2883, 3265, 5051, 5268

UNITED STATES

LEGAL ORGANIZATIONS: 3086
 see also AMERICAN BAR ASSOCIATION;
  AMERICAN COUNSEL ASSOCIATION;
  AMERICAN JUDICATURE SOCIETY;
  AMERICAN LAW INSTITUTE;
  ASSOCIATION OF LIFE INSURANCE
  COUNSEL
LIBEL AND SLANDER: 958
LIBRARIES: see LIBRARY OF CONGRESS
LITERARY INTERESTS:
 1800s: 2985
 1800s-1900s: 1215, 5717
 1900s: 4290
LITERARY SOCIETIES: 3990
LITERATURE: see AMERICAN LITERATURE
LOYALISTS: see AMERICAN REVOLUTION--
 Loyalist refugees/Loyalists
LOYALTY OATHS:
 see also CIVIL WAR--LOYALTY OATHS;
  RECONSTRUCTION--Loyalty oaths
 1778: 5575
 1821: 3908
MANUSCRIPT COLLECTING: 5922
MARINE CORPS:
 Civil War: 4613
 Military supplies: 2928
 Nicaragua: 1340
 Officers: 2928
  Appointments and promotions: 1954
 Payrolls: 2928
MARRIAGE: 1670, 5968
MARRIAGE CONTRACTS: 1926
MARRIED LIFE: 99
MASONRY: 1899, 3041
MEMORIALS: 4927
MENTAL HEALTH LAWS: 958
MERCHANT MARINE: 4564
MERCHANT SEAMEN: 1415, 3578
METHODIST CHURCHES: see METHODIST
 CHURCHES
MEXICAN WAR: see MEXICAN WAR; UNITED
 STATES--ARMY--Mexican War; UNITED
 STATES--NAVY--Mexican War
MILITARY ACADEMY: see UNITED STATES
 MILITARY ACADEMY
MILITARY AFFAIRS: 274, 3451, 4688,
 5419
MILITARY ART AND SCIENCE: 3228, 3654
MILITARY ASSISTANCE:
 Cuba: 2991
 Italy: 4020
MILITARY LAW: 4688
MILITARY POLICE: 777
MILITARY POSTS:
 see also names of specific military
  posts
 Provision of: 3662
MILITARY RAILROADS: 5306
 Civil War--North Carolina: 605
MINES AND MINING:
 Laws and legislation: 4805
 Lawsuits: 3640
MISSIONARIES: see MISSIONARY SOCIETIES;
 MISSIONS AND MISSIONARIES
MONUMENTS:
 Bronze: 1665
 To George Washington: 1778, 4892,
  5584
NATIONAL ANTHEM: 3220
NATIONAL BANKING SYSTEM: 646, 718,
 2164, 5324
 see also BANK OF THE UNITED STATES
NATIONAL CAPITAL:
 see also WASHINGTON, D.C.
 Location of: 1789, 5089
NATIONAL GUARD: 4858
NATIONAL PARKS: see NATIONAL PARKS
 AND MONUMENTS
NATURAL HISTORY: 783
NAVAL ACADEMY: see UNITED STATES
 NAVAL ACADEMY
NAVAL LYCEUM: 1954
NAVIGATION:
 Laws and regulations: 3041
 Potomac River: 2383

UNITED STATES

NAVY:
see also UNITED STATES--GOVERNMENT
AGENCIES AND OFFICIALS--
Department of the Navy/
Secretary of the Navy
1800s: 227, 2085, 2870, 3948, 4286,
4537
1900s: 1367, 4476
Appointments and promotions: 1098,
2281, 4497
Chaplains: 3633
Courts-martial: 3004, 3150, 4017
Cruises:
see also TRAVEL--Naval cruises
(United States)
Expedition to the Southern
Hemisphere: 3447
World cruise of 1908: 4021
Desertion: 4017, 4348
Discipline: 4081
Fleets:
Mediterranean Fleet: 3118
Pacific Fleet: 4535
Food: 2085, 4110, 4593
Health conditions: 3004, 4593
Hospitals--Supplies: 4447
Leaves and furloughs: 4447
Life ashore:
Florida: 2963
Hawaii: 3403
Logs: 4062, 4110
see also LOGBOOKS
Marine engineering: 2085
Medical and sanitary affairs: 577,
2265, 2489, 3118, 4593
Illness and disease: 3004
Pharmaceutical records: 5435
Nautical surveying: 4013
Naval regulations: 5436
Naval Reserve: 2807
Officers: 227, 2066, 2085, 2963,
3118, 3403, 3447, 3948, 4013,
4017, 4274, 4431, 4531, 4535,
5841
Appointments and promotions:
265, 305, 1321, 3557, 3728
Disputes: 4447
Punishment: 4062
Warrant officers: 5329
Operations:
see also TRAVEL--Naval cruises
(United States)
Atlantic Ocean: 3279
Azores: 3447
Far East: 4017
Great Lakes: 636
Gulf of Mexico: 2085
Hawaii: 3447
Mediterranean Sea: 636, 3447
Pacific Ocean: 4535
Panama: 4404, 5045
South America: 4019
West Indies: 4013
Orders: 4447, 5436
Ordnance: 5546
Pay: 5436
Personal finance: 4110
Pharmacists: 5329
Protection of maritime rights: 4616
Punishment: 3118
Pursers' accounts: 3833
Sailing instructions: 2085
Sea life: 81, 356, 1115, 2963,
3899, 4019, 5128, 5436
Ships: 2265, 5436
see also names of specific ships
Construction: 5546
Ship timber: 1701
Itinerary: 2085
Maintenance and repair: 4017
Sails: 4110
Steamships: 5546
Storeships: 3279
Squadrons:
African Squadron: 5190
Asiatic Squadron: 4986

UNITED STATES

NAVY:
Squadrons (Continued):
East Indies Squadron: 4017
European Squadron: 2085
Supplies: 3118, 3279, 4447
Suppression of the slave trade:
3557, 4593
Africa: 3118
Surgeons: 2336, 2489, 3004, 4593
Virginia--Norfolk: 4701
Young Men's Christian Association:
5252

War of 1812:

Officers: 5564

Mexican War:

636
Naval operations: 2842
Vera Cruz: 3378

Civil War:

2085
Bases--Illinois: 4662
Blockades: 2312, 4983, 5045
see also CIVIL WAR--BLOCKADES
North Carolina: 5390
Savannah River: 4687
South Carolina--Charleston: 4986
Civil-military relations:
Louisiana--Bayou Sara: 4275
Coast patrols: 5063
Courts-martial: 81
Depredations: 2802, 5436
Desertion: 5437
Discipline: 5437
Foraging: 5437
Medical and sanitary affairs: 2265
Mississippi--Vicksburg: 4076
New York--New York: 3192
Pennsylvania--Philadelphia: 3192
Portugal: 3192
Officers: 3192, 5045, 5063, 5850,
5955
Appointments and promotions: 5063
Operations: 1507, 3917, 4986, 5063,
5436
see also CIVIL WAR--CAMPAIGNS,
BATTLES, AND MILITARY ACTIONS--
Naval engagements
Alabama--Mobile: 5649
Caribbean Sea: 3983
Chesapeake Bay: 5045
Florida: 5649
Georgia--Genesis Point: 3524
Martinique: 3258
Mississippi River: 3983
North Carolina:
Cape Fear: 5390
Fort Fisher: 5045
Wilmington: 4553
South Carolina:
Charleston: 1874
Coast: 4881
Tennessee River: 4662, 5437
Virgin Islands: 3258
Virginia--James River: 4968
West Indies: 3258
Orders: 5063
Mississippi River: 4275
Potomac River Flotilla: 1294
Recruiting and enlistment:
Conscription: 5063
Resignations to join the
Confederate Navy: 2963
Sea life: 3983, 4404
Ships: 1063, 5344
see also names of specific ships
James River: 2085
Maintenance and repair: 5437
Tennessee River: 5437
Squadrons:
Mississippi Squadron: 4275, 4662

UNITED STATES

NAVY:

Civil War:

Squadrons (Continued):
Western Gulf Blockading Squadron:
81
Transportation: 5063
Tennessee River: 5437

World War I:

829
Caribbean Sea: 116
Convoy duty:
Mediterranean Sea: 4355
North Atlantic Ocean: 4355
Demobilization--Virginia: 4355
Discharges: 4355
Leaves and furloughs: 4355
Navy Bureau of Supplies and
Accounts: 3383
Officers: 4355
Operations: 4476
French coast: 4355
Gibraltar: 4355
Spanish coast: 4355
Pay: 3383
Recruiting and enlistment: 5429
Sea life: 4355
NAVY YARDS: 5564
NEGROES: see NEGROES
NEGROES IN POLITICS: 2720
NEWSPAPERS: see JOURNALISM; NEWSPAPERS
PAPER MONEY:
see also MONEY; UNITED STATES--
CURRENCY
Redemption: 5548
PASSPORTS: 5790
PATENTS: see PATENTS; UNITED STATES--
GOVERNMENT AGENCIES AND OFFICIALS--
Patent Office
PATRIOTISM: 1434, 2863, 3280
PENSIONS: 663, 1208, 3291, 4732
see also CIVIL SERVICE PENSIONS
Military: see Pensions as subheading
under names of wars; Bounty lands
as subheading under names of wars
PERIODICALS: 2449, 2871, 3793
see also UNITED STATES--PUBLISHERS
AND PUBLISHING--Periodicals
Reporters and reporting: 3267
PHILANTHROPY: 1441, 1589, 3828, 4022,
4080, 4343
PHILOSOPHY: 1441, 1458
PLANTS: 1229
POETRY: see AMERICAN POETRY
POLITICAL PARTIES: 3096
see also names of specific
political parties
POLITICAL PATRONAGE:
1800s: 388, 1086
1820s: 4361, 4964
1830s: 730, 741, 4361
1840s: 741, 2326, 2760, 5051,
5491
1850s: 415, 741, 4200, 5051
1860s: 415, 694
1870s: 415, 694, 2537, 5578
1880s: 1953, 5578
1800s-1900s: 4858, 5152
Army appointments (1898): 5790
Democratic Party (1800s): 3325
Naval appointments (1800s): 265,
5842
POLITICAL POSTERS: 4948
POLITICS AND GOVERNMENT:
1700s: 3573, 4015, 4922
1700s-1800s: 404, 842, 2460, 2776,
3069, 3362, 3456, 3671, 4348,
4839, 4905, 5427
1700s-1900s: 3325, 4486, 4689,
5203
1800s: 57, 196, 324, 421, 682,
685, 805, 849, 1170, 1424, 1433,

969

UNITED STATES
POLITICS AND GOVERNMENT:
  1800s (Continued): 2290, 2578,
    2742, 2881, 2963, 2985, 3196,
    3378, 3415, 3483, 4686, 4710,
    4924, 5051, 5271, 5305, 5315,
    5613, 5734, 5928, 5970
  1800s: 3287, 3455, 3512, 5221
  1810s: 1943, 3287, 3439, 3455,
    4599
  1820s: 529, 1943, 3287, 3366,
    3455, 3512, 3854, 4490, 4616,
    5217, 5369
  1830s: 1943, 2449, 2781, 3053,
    3162, 3291, 3366, 3809, 3854,
    4316, 4445, 4490, 4616, 5221,
    5247, 5386, 5681
  1840s: 205, 2107, 2449, 2647,
    2781, 2859, 2860, 3162, 3291,
    3366, 3391, 3809, 4316, 4445,
    4584, 4916, 4958, 5385, 5470,
    5757, 5931, 5937, 5978
  1850s: 1234, 1466, 2107, 2370,
    2449, 2552, 2960, 3297, 3424,
    3809, 3899, 4272, 4445, 4520,
    4584, 4916, 4958, 5460, 5470,
    5757, 5853, 5931
  1860s: 183, 314, 713, 846, 1445,
    2147, 2370, 2531, 2552, 2865,
    2960, 3129, 3281, 3283, 3325,
    3448, 3515, 3556, 3611, 3674,
    3948, 4188, 4272, 4616, 4781,
    4916, 4993, 5059, 5311, 5808,
    5931
  1870s: 183, 959, 1203, 2273,
    2370, 3254, 3674, 3948, 5142,
    5755, 5808
  1880s: 183, 1203, 1953, 2161,
    2794, 3674, 5142, 5168, 5668,
    5755
  1890s: 1024, 3774, 5142, 5668,
    5755
  1800s-1900s: 1436, 2106, 2849,
    3008, 3967, 4020, 4310, 4442,
    4552, 4808, 4858, 5152, 5717,
    5762
  1900s: 300, 2188, 2299, 3190,
    3451, 3538, 5312
  1900s: 1024, 3104, 4003, 4018,
    4825, 5930
  1910s: 1367, 4018, 4825, 5930
  1920s: 1367, 2496, 3086, 4564,
    4825, 5791, 5930
  1930s: 274, 325, 1367, 2398,
    3086, 4564
  1940s: 274, 325, 3086, 5419
  1950s: 325, 4927
  1960s: 5773
  Appointments: 4964
  Bureaucracy: 872
POLITICS AND LITERATURE: 4932
POPULATION: 3145
PORTRAITS: 1665, 2411, 2726, 4343
PRIVATEERING:
  see also AMERICAN REVOLUTION--
    Privateering; CIVIL WAR--
    PRIVATEERING
  Against Spain: 2771
PROBATION AND PAROLE: 4927
PROHIBITION: see PROHIBITION
PUBLIC DEBT: 1714, 2776, 2959
  Laws and legislation: 5731
PUBLIC FINANCE:
  1700s:
    1780s: 5276
    1790s: 2276, 4922
  1700s-1800s: 4905
  1800s: 1086
    1800s: 3273
    1810s: 3623
    1820s: 564
    1830s: 564, 5622
    1840s: 5622
    1860s: 421, 2149
  1900s:
    1950s: 4805

UNITED STATES
PUBLIC FINANCE (Continued):
  Appropriations and expenditures:
    1478, 5537
    For North Carolina: 2581
  Budget: 646
PUBLIC HEALTH: 4948
PUBLIC LANDS: 2776, 3291, 4805
  see also WESTERN LANDS
PUBLIC OPINION OF FRANCE: 1424
PUBLIC WELFARE: 4386, 4564
PUBLISHERS AND PUBLISHING:
  1800s: 1115, 1484, 5640, 5982
  1900s: 5054
  Marketing: 3981
  Periodicals: 102, 2409, 3022,
    3793, 4021, 5193, 5691, 5889
RACE RELATIONS: see RACE RELATIONS
RADIO: 2521
RAILROAD LAW: 4858
RAILROADS:
  see also RAILROADS IN NATIONAL
    DEFENSE STRATEGY; UNITED STATES--
    MILITARY RAILROAD
  1800s: 842, 1681, 5593
  1800s-1900s: 4858
  1900s: 4564
  Government control: 1368
  Labor conditions: 3793, 5254
RELATIONS (GENERAL) WITH BRITISH
  COLONIES: 3238
RELATIONS (GENERAL) WITH EGYPT: 83
RELATIONS (GENERAL) WITH INDIA: 83
RELATIONS WITH INDIANS: see INDIANS
  OF NORTH AMERICA--Government
  relations
RELIGION:
  see also RELIGIOUS LITERATURE
  1700s-1800s: 4598
  1800s: 1219, 2801, 3899, 4765
  1800s-1900s: 5717
  1900s: 4948
RELIGION AND SCIENCE: 1219
REPUBLICAN PARTY: see REPUBLICAN
  PARTY
RETIREMENT: 1167, 2934
ROADS:
  see also NATIONAL ROAD
  Construction: 4805, 4858
SATIRE: see AMERICAN SATIRE
SCHOLARLY EDITING: 720, 4290, 4499,
  5054, 5971
  Periodicals: 102
SCIENCE: 1219
SCIENTIFIC RESEARCH: 2120, 2578
SCOTS BUSINESS ENTERPRISES: 3179
SCULPTORS: 3162
  Americans in Italy: 2181
SCULPTURE: see AMERICAN SCULPTURE
SECESSION: see SECESSION AND
  SECESSIONIST SENTIMENT
SECTIONALISM: 1910, 2449, 4616
  see also NORTHERNERS IN THE SOUTH;
    SOUTHERNERS IN THE NORTH
  Pacific coast: 3239
SEDITION: 4948
  see also UNITED STATES--TREASON
SEGREGATION: 3048
SERMONS: 1219
SERVANTS: 5246
SHIPPING: 4896
  see also SHIPPING; UNITED STATES--
    FOREIGN TRADE
  Lawsuits: 1615
SHIPPING COMPANIES: 4881
SHIPS: 323
  see also UNITED STATES--NAVY; and
    names of specific vessels
  Maintenance and repair: 3578
SLAVE TRADE: 1856, 3053, 3293, 3850,
  3910, 4520, 4732
  Prices: 3255
  Regulation: 2776
  Suppression: 99, 2907, 3325, 3557
    see also UNITED STATES--NAVY--
      Suppression of the slave
      trade

UNITED STATES
SLAVERY: see SLAVERY
SLAVES:
  see also SLAVES
  Emancipation: 3495, 4537, 5816
    see also UNITED STATES--
      CONSTITUTION--Amendments--
      13th Amendment
SOCIAL AND POLITICAL REFORM: 196,
  4020, 4825
SOCIAL CONDITIONS: 2801
SOCIAL LIFE AND CUSTOMS:
  1800s: 3251
  1900s: 2398, 3710, 5786
SOCIALISM: 2083, 4948
  Bibliography: 65
SOCIALISTS--Biography: 65
SOCIETIES AND CLUBS: see SOCIETIES
  AND CLUBS
SONGS AND MUSIC: 432, 2407, 3633
  see also CIVIL WAR--SONGS AND
    MUSIC; UNITED STATES--HYMNS
  Political: 5497
SPIES: see SPIES
STATE DEBTS--Funding: 2776
STEEL INDUSTRY: 3413
STRIKES: see STRIKES
SUFFRAGE: 5
  see also NEGROES--Suffrage;
    UNITED STATES--WOMAN SUFFRAGE
TARIFF:
  see also UNITED STATES--GOVERNMENT
    AGENCIES AND OFFICIALS--Tariff
    Commission
  1700s-1800s: 669
  1800s: 842, 849
    1810s: 2449
    1820s: 2449, 3366
    1830s: 1302, 3366, 3902, 5700
    1840s: 1302, 3325, 3366, 3727,
      5470, 5700
    1850s: 5470, 5700
  1900s: 3190
    1950s: 4805
  Laws and legislation: 2904, 3406,
    5217, 5369
  Rates:
    1800s: 5499
    1900s: 3190
TAXATION:
  see also UNITED STATES--INCOME
    TAX; UNITED STATES--GOVERNMENT
    AGENCIES AND OFFICIALS--Internal
    Revenue Service
  1790s: 3041
  1800s:
    1840s: 3727
    1890s: 2922
  1900s: 3066
    1950s: 4805
  Laws and legislation: 2581, 2863
  Liquor tax: 2469
  North Carolina: 2914, 4009, 4152
TEA GROWING: 2847
TEACHING: 904, 2091, 3789
TEMPERANCE:
  see also UNITED STATES--PROHIBITION
  1800s: 731, 1219, 1351, 2591
  1800s-1900s: 3029
  1900s: 879
  Laws and legislation: 1554, 5082
TERRITORIAL EXPANSION: 1364, 4348,
  4927
  see also Annexation as subheading
    under territories annexed
TERRITORIAL WATERS:
  Fishing rights: 4567
THEATER: 3029, 3617
  Production and direction: 54
THEATERS: 4556
THEOLOGY: 1219
TOPOGRAPHY: 3145
TRADE AND COMMERCE: 274, 4564,
  4678, 4805, 4896, 5398
  see also AMERICAN REVOLUTION--
    Trade and commerce; UNITED
    STATES--FOREIGN TRADE;

UNITED STATES
TRADE AND COMMERCE (Continued):
  UNITED STATES--SHIPPING; and
   United States as subheading
   under specific kinds of trade,
   e.g. GRAIN TRADE--United
   States
  Indians of North America: 2432
TRADE REGULATION: 3041
  Grain exports to India: 2581
TRANSPORTATION: 5398
TREASON:
  see also AMERICAN REVOLUTION--
   Treason; UNITED STATES--
   SEDITION
  Trials: 3809
TREASURY NOTES:
  Constitutionality: 5271
TREATIES:
  see also names of specific treaties
  Argentina: 5936
  Cherokee Indians: 2049
  Great Britain:
   see also JAY'S TREATY
   1794: 3041
   1840s: 1632
  Hawaii: 3516
  Peru: 932
  Sioux Indians: 3162
  Spain: 4214
  Sweden: 404
UNEMPLOYMENT: 4564
UNIVERSAL MILITARY TRAINING: 4858
  Laws and legislation: 2581
VETERANS' AFFAIRS: 4805
  see also Veterans as subheading
   under names of specific wars
  Benefits: 325
VOCATIONAL REHABILITATION: 4736
WAGES:
  see also WAGES AND SALARIES
  Minimum wage legislation: 325
WAR OF 1812: see UNITED STATES--
  ARMY--War of 1812; UNITED STATES--
  NAVY--War of 1812; WAR OF 1812
WATERWAYS: 4858
WHIG PARTY: see WHIG PARTY
WILDLIFE CONSERVATION: 4805
WIT AND HUMOR: see AMERICAN WIT
  AND HUMOR
WOMAN SUFFRAGE: 404, 3617, 4849,
  4858, 5968
  Amendment to the Constitution:
   1946
WOMEN: 4948
  see also UNITED STATES--ARMY--
   World War II--Women's Army
   Auxiliary Corps; WOMEN IN THE
   CIVIL WAR
  Employment: 3066
  Social status: 731
WOMEN AUTHORS: 5052
WOMEN'S RIGHTS: 2469, 3029, 5282,
  5968
WOMEN'S SOCIETY OF CHRISTIAN
  SERVICE: 3020, 3646
WORLD WAR I: see UNITED STATES--
  ARMY--World War I; UNITED STATES--
  NAVY--World War I; WORLD WAR I
WORLD WAR II: see UNITED STATES--
  ARMY--World War II; UNITED
  STATES--NAVY--World War II;
  WORLD WAR II
YOUTH ORGANIZATIONS: 4948

[End of entries under UNITED STATES]

UNITED STATES CAPITOL BUILDING,
  Washington, D.C.: 3343
  Funerals: 261
UNITED STATES FEDERAL RESERVE
  SYSTEM: see FEDERAL RESERVE
  SYSTEM ACT
UNITED STATES GAZETTE: 42
UNITED STATES GENERAL HOSPITAL,
  David's Island, New York: 4561

UNITED STATES HOTEL, Saratoga
  Springs, New York: 1928
UNITED STATES MILITARY ACADEMY,
  West Point, New York: 4924
  1800s: 4348, 5517
   1810s: 1302, 3761
   1820s: 2363, 3761
   1830s: 2363
   1840s: 5569
   1850s: 1782, 3809
   1860s: 5668
   1890s: 3789
  1900s: 5163
  Appointments: 415, 1086, 2776, 4858,
   5247, 5386, 5430
  Student societies: 3809
  Students and student life:
   1800s:
    1830s: 3809
    1840s: 2968
    1870s: 4663
   1900s:
    1905: 1661
  Parents' letters: 3809
UNITED STATES MILITARY PHILOSOPHICAL
  SOCIETY, Philadelphia,
  Pennsylvania: 5778
UNITED STATES NAVAL ACADEMY,
  Annapolis, Maryland: 227, 356,
  1284, 1363, 2085
  Appointments: 81, 242, 2776, 4858,
   4916
  Faculty: 4689
  Students and student life: 1575,
   2552, 4531
UNITED STATES NAVAL ACADEMY, Newport,
  Rhode Island: 3192, 4986
UNITED STATES NAVAL HOSPITAL,
  Norfolk, Virginia: 4701
UNITED STATES NAVAL WAR COLLEGE: 116
UNITED STATES SANITARY COMMISSION:
  617, 2236, 2311, 4228, 4485
  New England Women's Auxiliary
   Association: 1983
UNITED STATES STEEL CORPORATION: 5668
UNITED STATES TERRITORIAL EXPANSION
  MEMORIAL COMMISSION: 4927
UNITED STATES YOUTH COUNCIL: 4948
UNITED STEELWORKERS OF AMERICA: 1197,
  1198, 1199, 1202
  District 35 (Georgia): 5441
  Local Union No. 2401: 5441
  Strikes: 1883
UNITED STONE AND ALLIED PRODUCTS
  WORKERS OF AMERICA: 1202
UNITED TEXTILE WORKERS OF AMERICA:
  4094
  Local Union No. 2598: 5442
UNITED TRANSPORT SERVICE EMPLOYEES:
  1202
UNITED WAR WORK CAMPAIGN: 5298
UNIVERSAL LIFE INSURANCE COMPANY OF
  NEW YORK: 3587
UNIVERSAL MILITARY TRAINING:
  United States: 4858
  Laws and legislation: 2581
UNIVERSAL OIL AND FERTILIZER COMPANY,
  Wilmington, North Carolina: 5912
UNIVERSALIST CHURCHES:
  Clergy: see CLERGY--Universalist
  Interchurch relations:
   With Baptist churches and
    Methodist churches: 3493
UNIVERSALIST MAGAZINE: 4714
UNIVERSITIES AND COLLEGES:
  see also COMMUNITY AND COLLEGE;
   DIVINITY SCHOOLS; LABOR COLLEGES;
   NORMAL SCHOOLS
  College life: 5716
   North Carolina: 76
   South Carolina: 300
  Commencement addresses:
   South Carolina: 2880
  Faculty: 523, 4101
   see also AMERICAN ASSOCIATION OF
    UNIVERSITY PROFESSORS
  Finance--North Carolina: 547

UNIVERSITIES AND COLLEGES (Continued):
  Funds and scholarships:
   Southern States: 1258
  Honorary degrees:
   Great Britain: 2201
  Housing: see STUDENT HOUSING
  Laws and legislation:
   North Carolina: 1361
  Lectures and lecturing: 1219
  Literary societies--Virginia: 461
  Philanthropy:
   North Carolina: 1584, 1588
   Tennessee: 1584
  Presidents--Virginia: 3456
  Student organizations: see STUDENT
   RELIGIOUS SOCIETIES; STUDENT
   SOCIETIES
  Student publications: 4753
  Students and student life:
   Personal finance--Georgia: 3134
   Subdivided by place:
    New York: 4169
    North Carolina: 1361
    Rhode Island: 4169
    South Carolina: 1480
    Tennessee--Greenville: 872
  Teaching: 5971
  Theses: 5550
  Town and gown: see COMMUNITY AND
   COLLEGE
  Trustees:
   Mississippi--Rodney: 3322
  Tuition--Virginia: 1814
  Women's colleges:
   Methodist church affiliated:
    1152
   Personal finance of students:
    3044
  Subdivided by place:
   Alabama: see ALABAMA CENTRAL
    FEMALE COLLEGE; EAST ALABAMA
    COLLEGE; PAYNE UNIVERSITY;
    TUSKEGEE INSTITUTE; UNIVERSITY
    OF ALABAMA
   Arkansas: see OUACHITA COLLEGE
   California: see COLLEGE OF THE
    PACIFIC; UNIVERSITY OF
    CALIFORNIA, Davis
   Canada: see ARCADIA UNIVERSITY
   China: see YENCHING UNIVERSITY
   Connecticut: 351
    see also YALE UNIVERSITY
   Florida: see FLORIDA STATE
    UNIVERSITY; ROLLINS COLLEGE
   France: see L'ÉCOLE DES PONTS ET
    CHAUSSÉES; UNIVERSITY OF PARIS
   Georgia: 479, 662
    see also ANDREW FEMALE COLLEGE;
    ATHENS STATE NORMAL COLLEGE;
    BRENAU COLLEGE; EMORY
    UNIVERSITY; FURLOW MASONIC
    FEMALE COLLEGE; GEORGIA
    FEMALE COLLEGE; GORDON
    INSTITUTE; MERCER UNIVERSITY;
    OGLETHORPE UNIVERSITY;
    SOUTHERN MASONIC FEMALE
    COLLEGE; SHORTER COLLEGE;
    UNIVERSITY OF GEORGIA;
    WESLEYAN COLLEGE
   Germany: see UNIVERSITY OF BERLIN;
    UNIVERSITY OF HEIDELBERG
   Great Britain: 1815, 2201
    see also CAMBRIDGE UNIVERSITY
     (including King's College);
     EAST INDIA COLLEGE; LEEDS
     UNIVERSITY; OXFORD UNIVERSITY
     (including Lincoln College);
     SAINT DAVID'S COLLEGE;
     UNIVERSITY COLLEGE OF THE
     SOUTH WEST OF ENGLAND
   Illinois: 351
    see also AUGUSTANA COLLEGE;
     CARTHAGE COLLEGE; UNIVERSITY
     OF CHICAGO
   India: see ALIGARH MUSLIM
    UNIVERSITY
   Indiana: see UNIVERSITY OF INDIANA

UNIVERSITIES AND COLLEGES:
  Subdivided by place (Continued):
  Iowa: see DES MOINES COLLEGE
  Kentucky: 1092
    see also CENTRAL UNIVERSITY;
      KENTUCKY MILITARY INSTITUTE;
      KENTUCKY WESLEYAN COLLEGE;
      OGDEN COLLEGE; TRANSYLVANIA
      COLLEGE; UNION COLLEGE;
      UNIVERSITY OF KENTUCKY;
      UNIVERSITY OF LOUISVILLE
  Lebanon: see AMERICAN COLLEGE
  Louisiana: see CENTENARY COLLEGE;
    LOUISIANA STATE UNIVERSITY;
    TULANE UNIVERSITY
  Maine: see BOWDOIN COLLEGE
  Maryland: 643, 2999
    see also CALVERT COLLEGE;
      COLLEGE OF SAINT JAMES;
      GOUCHER COLLEGE; JOHNS HOPKINS
      UNIVERSITY; SAINT JOHN'S
      COLLEGE; SAINT MARY'S COLLEGE;
      UNIVERSITY OF MARYLAND;
      WESTERN MARYLAND COLLEGE
  Massachusetts: 743
    see also HARVARD UNIVERSITY;
      SMITH COLLEGE; WELLESLEY
      COLLEGE; WILLIAMS COLLEGE
  Mexico: see UNIVERSITY OF MEXICO
  Michigan: see UNIVERSITY OF
    MICHIGAN
  Minnesota: see UNIVERSITY OF
    MINNESOTA
  Mississippi: see JEFFERSON COLLEGE;
    MISSISSIPPI FEMALE COLLEGE;
    OAKLAND COLLEGE; UNIVERSITY
    OF MISSISSIPPI
  Missouri: see BAPTIST FEMALE
    COLLEGE; CENTRAL WESLEYAN
    COLLEGE; UNIVERSITY OF MISSOURI;
    WASHINGTON UNIVERSITY
  New Hampshire: 3822
    see also DARTMOUTH COLLEGE;
      WILLIAMS COLLEGE
  New Jersey: 743
    see also PRINCETON UNIVERSITY;
      RUTGERS UNIVERSITY
  New York: 4169
    see also COLUMBIA UNIVERSITY;
      EASTMAN BUSINESS COLLEGE;
      GENEVA COLLEGE; MANHATTAN
      COLLEGE; SAINT PAUL'S
      COLLEGE; UNION COLLEGE;
      UNITED STATES MILITARY
      ACADEMY; VASSAR COLLEGE
  North Carolina: 484, 661, 832,
    1773, 2539
    see also BENNETT COLLEGE;
      CAMPBELL COLLEGE; CAROLINA
      FEMALE COLLEGE; CHOWAN
      COLLEGE; CLAREMONT COLLEGE;
      CLEGG'S COLLEGE; CONCORD
      FEMALE COLLEGE; DAVENPORT
      COLLEGE; DAVENPORT FEMALE
      COLLEGE; DAVIDSON COLLEGE;
      DUKE UNIVERSITY; FAYETTEVILLE
      STATE UNIVERSITY; GREENSBORO
      COLLEGE; GUILFORD COLLEGE;
      LIBERTY NORMAL COLLEGE;
      LOUISBURG COLLEGE; MEREDITH
      COLLEGE; MITCHELL COLLEGE;
      NORMAL COLLEGE; NORTH CAROLINA
      AGRICULTURAL AND TECHNICAL
      STATE UNIVERSITY; NORTH
      CAROLINA CENTRAL UNIVERSITY;
      NORTH CAROLINA SCHOOL OF THE
      ARTS; NORTH CAROLINA STATE
      UNIVERSITY; OLIN AGRICULTURAL
      AND MECHANICAL COLLEGE; OXFORD
      FEMALE COLLEGE; RUTHERFORD
      COLLEGE; SAINT MARY'S COLLEGE;
      SALEM COLLEGE; TRINITY COLLEGE,
      Durham; TRINITY COLLEGE,
      Randolph County; UNIVERSITY OF
      NORTH CAROLINA AT CHAPEL HILL;
      UNIVERSITY OF NORTH CAROLINA
      AT GREENSBORO; WAKE FOREST
      COLLEGE; WARRENTON FEMALE
      COLLEGE

UNIVERSITIES AND COLLEGES:
  Subdivided by place (Continued):
  Ohio: see BALDWIN-WALLACE COLLEGE;
    MIAMI UNIVERSITY; OBERLIN
    COLLEGE; OHIO UNIVERSITY;
    URBANA UNIVERSITY; WITTENBERG
    COLLEGE
  Oklahoma: see UNIVERSITY OF
    OKLAHOMA
  Oregon: see UNIVERSITY OF OREGON
  Pennsylvania: see BETHANY COLLEGE;
    BRISTOL COLLEGE; DICKINSON
    COLLEGE; GETTYSBURG COLLEGE;
    HAVERFORD COLLEGE; LAFAYETTE
    AGRICULTURAL COLLEGE; LAFAYETTE
    COLLEGE; LEHIGH UNIVERSITY;
    MERCERSBURG ACADEMY; PITTSBURGH
    COLLEGE; SWARTHMORE COLLEGE;
    UNIVERSITY OF PENNSYLVANIA;
    WASHINGTON AND JEFFERSON
    COLLEGE; WILSON COLLEGE
  Peru: see COLEGIO MAXIMO DE SAN
    PABLO DE LA COMPAÑIA DE JESUS
  Rhode Island: 4169
    see also BROWN UNIVERSITY;
      RHODE ISLAND COLLEGE
  Scotland: see UNIVERSITY OF
    EDINBURGH; UNIVERSITY OF
    GLASGOW
  South Carolina: 300, 561, 1424,
    1877
    see also BEAUFORT COLLEGE; THE
      CITADEL; CLEMSON UNIVERSITY;
      COKER COLLEGE; COLLEGE OF
      CHARLESTON; CONVERSE COLLEGE;
      ERSKINE COLLEGE; FURMAN
      UNIVERSITY; GREENWOOD FEMALE
      COLLEGE; LIMESTONE COLLEGE;
      NEWBERRY COLLEGE; SPARTANBURG
      FEMALE COLLEGE; UNIVERSITY
      OF SOUTH CAROLINA; WINTHROP
      COLLEGE; WOFFORD COLLEGE
    Cambridge: 2636
  Southern States: 2449, 4720
  Switzerland: see UNIVERSITY OF
    GENEVA
  Tennessee: 731
    see also FISK UNIVERSITY;
      GEORGE PEABODY COLLEGE FOR
      TEACHERS; GRANT MEMORIAL
      UNIVERSITY; JACKSON COLLEGE;
      KING COLLEGE; LA GRANGE
      FEMALE COLLEGE; NASHVILLE
      NORMAL AND COLLEGIATE
      THEOLOGICAL INSTITUTE;
      SOUTHWESTERN UNIVERSITY; STATE
      NORMAL COLLEGE; TENNESSEE
      STATE FEMALE COLLEGE; UNION
      UNIVERSITY; UNIVERSITY OF THE
      SOUTH; VANDERBILT UNIVERSITY;
      WEST TENNESSEE COLLEGE
  Texas: see AUSTIN COLLEGE; BAYLOR
    UNIVERSITY; UNIVERSITY OF TEXAS
  United States (proposed): 5575
  Vermont: see MIDDLEBURY COLLEGE
  Virginia: 661, 743, 1115
    see also BETHANY COLLEGE;
      BLACKSTONE COLLEGE FOR GIRLS;
      COLLEGE OF WILLIAM AND MARY;
      EMORY AND HENRY COLLEGE;
      HAMPDEN-SYDNEY COLLEGE;
      HOLLINS COLLEGE; LURAY COLLEGE;
      LYNCHBURG COLLEGE; OLD POINT
      COMFORT COLLEGE; PETERSBURG
      FEMALE COLLEGE; RANDOLPH-MACON
      COLLEGE; ROANOKE COLLEGE;
      SWEET BRIAR COLLEGE; UNIVERSITY
      OF RICHMOND; UNIVERSITY OF
      VIRGINIA; VIRGINIA COMMONWEALTH
      UNIVERSITY; VIRGINIA MILITARY
      INSTITUTE; VIRGINIA POLYTECHNIC
      INSTITUTE; WASHINGTON AND LEE
      UNIVERSITY
  Washington, D.C.: see AMERICAN
    UNIVERSITY; GEORGE WASHINGTON
    UNIVERSITY; GEORGETOWN COLLEGE;
    HOWARD UNIVERSITY

UNIVERSITIES AND COLLEGES:
  Subdivided by place (Continued):
  West Virginia: 489
    see also SHEPHERD COLLEGE;
      WEST VIRGINIA UNIVERSITY
  Wisconsin: see UNIVERSITY OF
    WISCONSIN
UNIVERSITY, Mississippi: see
  UNIVERSITY OF MISSISSIPPI
UNIVERSITY CHRISTIAN MOVEMENT: 3001
UNIVERSITY COLLEGE OF THE SOUTH WEST
  OF ENGLAND: 5553
UNIVERSITY EMPLOYEES: see LABOR
  UNIONS--University employees
UNIVERSITY OF ALABAMA, Tuscaloosa,
  Alabama: 1084, 2940, 3188, 4911
  Community relations: 2963
  Law--Students' notebooks: 1031
UNIVERSITY OF BERLIN, Berlin,
  Germany:
  Students and student life: 5661,
    5762
UNIVERSITY OF CALIFORNIA, Davis,
  California: 5889
UNIVERSITY OF CHICAGO, Chicago,
  Illinois:
  Social Science Research Committee:
    2798
UNIVERSITY OF EDINBURGH, Edinburgh,
  Scotland: 363, 2616
UNIVERSITY OF GENEVA, Geneva,
  Switzerland:
  Students and student life: 3809
UNIVERSITY OF GEORGIA, Athens,
  Georgia: 662, 1090, 2006, 2215,
    3905, 5936
  Land grants to: 3695
  Students and student life: 3905,
    5051
    Parents' letters: 2326
UNIVERSITY OF GLASGOW, Glasgow,
  Scotland: 306
  Honorary degrees: 3715
UNIVERSITY OF HEIDELBERG, Heidelberg,
  Germany:
  American students: 3809
  Students and student life: 5661,
    5762
UNIVERSITY OF INDIANA, Bloomington,
  Indiana:
  Faculty: 4499
UNIVERSITY OF KENTUCKY, Lexington,
  Kentucky: 5054
UNIVERSITY OF LOUISIANA: see TULANE
  UNIVERSITY
UNIVERSITY OF LOUISVILLE, Louisville,
  Kentucky:
  Medical Department: 4743
    Students' notebooks: 1053
UNIVERSITY OF MARYLAND, College Park,
  Maryland: 5866
  Medical education: 3136
  Students' notebooks: 3399
UNIVERSITY OF MEXICO, Mexico City,
  Mexico: 3650
UNIVERSITY OF MICHIGAN, Ann Arbor,
  Michigan:
  Medical education: 3221
UNIVERSITY OF MINNESOTA, Duluth
  Campus, Duluth, Minnesota: 5115
UNIVERSITY OF MISSISSIPPI, Oxford,
  Mississippi: 2282, 2612, 5498
  Southern Literary Festival: 1771
  Students and student life: 1506
UNIVERSITY OF MISSOURI, Columbia,
  Missouri:
  College of Agriculture: 2604
UNIVERSITY OF NORTH CAROLINA AT
  CHAPEL HILL, Chapel Hill, North
  Carolina: 1252, 4924
  1800s: 1361, 2399, 3364, 5036,
    5150, 5664
  1820s: 4849
  1830s: 4080
  1840s: 484, 1336
  1850s: 2553, 2808, 2857, 5912
  1860s: 2553, 4154
  1880s: 4669

UNIVERSITY OF NORTH CAROLINA AT
  CHAPEL HILL:
  1800s (Continued):
    1890s: 4669
  1900s:
    1930s: 3247
    1960s: 3571
  Addresses: 4018
  Admissions policies: 1816
  Chemistry:
    Students' notebooks: 673, 1284
  Commencement exercises: 4669, 5298
  Curriculum: 5005
  Establishment: 2776
  Faculty:
    Appointments: 2572
    Disputes with students: 1858
  Finance: 3415, 4080
  Geology instruction: 730
  History Department: 4669
  Influenza epidemic: 3878
  Land holdings containing mica: 513
  Law School: 5848
  Medical education: 3878
  Philanthropic Society: 4669
  Reorganization: 2419
  School of Science: 2469
  Students and student life:
    1800s: 1568, 2338, 2680, 3176
      1800s: 5005
      1810s: 5031
      1840s: 4080, 4714, 5690
      1850s: 2978, 5298
      1860s: 796, 1361, 4080
      1870s: 832, 4910
      1880s: 2861
    1800s-1900s: 3626
    Parents' letters: 5912
  Suspension of the university: 5298
  Trustees: 3334
  University Magazine: 1068, 4714
UNIVERSITY OF NORTH CAROLINA AT
  GREENSBORO, Greensboro, North
  Carolina: 942, 985, 4849
  Commencement exercises: 2833
  Department of English: 985
UNIVERSITY OF OKLAHOMA, Norman,
  Oklahoma: 3248
UNIVERSITY OF OREGON, Eugene, Oregon:
  5054
  Curriculum: 5054
UNIVERSITY OF OXFORD: see OXFORD
  UNIVERSITY
UNIVERSITY OF PARIS, Paris, France:
  4408
UNIVERSITY OF PENNSYLVANIA,
  Philadelphia, Pennsylvania: 3675
  Admissions policies: 1816
  Chemistry instruction: 1942
  Libraries: 4271
  Medical education: 365, 1942, 2336,
    3859
    Students and student life: 2714,
      2851
    Students' notebooks: 3609
  Pharmaceutical education: 173
UNIVERSITY OF RICHMOND, Richmond,
  Virginia: 2612
UNIVERSITY OF ROCHESTER, Rochester,
  New York:
  Rush Rees Library: 2449
UNIVERSITY OF SOUTH CAROLINA,
  Columbia, South Carolina:
  1800s: 1468, 1877, 2636, 3485,
    4316, 5114
  1800s-1900s: 300, 1385, 2473
  1900s: 3451
  Alumni Association: 4453
  Commencement addresses: 2880
  Faculty: 4912, 5114
  Students' accounts: 2930
  Students and student life: 2930,
    3790
UNIVERSITY OF TEXAS, Austin, Texas:
  5513

UNIVERSITY OF THE SOUTH, Sewanee,
  Tennessee: 2175, 4339
  Laying of the cornerstone: 4253
  Trustees: 4918
UNIVERSITY OF VIRGINIA,
  Charlottesville, Virginia: 4924
  1800s: 51, 558, 1084, 1133, 1877,
    2612, 5839, 5936
    1820s: 3251
    1830s: 3251
    1840s: 4616, 5529
    1850s: 2192, 3106, 5529
    1860s: 2192, 5075, 5529
    1870s: 1000
  1900s: 5786
  Administration: 2612
  Alumni: 4020
  Autographs: 3106
  Chemistry:
    Students' notebooks: 824
  Civil War: 3642
  Class rosters: 1000
  Curriculum: 2612, 3291, 4592
  Examination questions: 2612
  Faculty: 523, 2426, 3291, 4143,
    4592, 4698
    Biography: 267
  Finance: 5194
  French literature:
    Students' notebooks: 1379
  Legal education: 1770, 4585, 5106,
    5194
    Students' notebooks: 2206
  Libraries: 3251
  Logic--Students' notebooks: 3148
  Medical education: 58, 5106
  Military training: 3809
  Pharmaceutical education: 173
  Poetry: 182
  Social life: 2510
  Spanish literature:
    Students' notebooks: 1379
  Students and student life:
    1800s: 330, 4698, 4710, 5051
      1830s: 2426, 3809, 4312
      1840s: 2597, 2822, 4592
      1850s: 1250, 3291, 3464, 4592,
        4968, 5798
      1860s: 4080
      1870s: 4373, 5380
      1880s: 3587
    1800s-1900s: 4029
    Compositions: 3809
    Parents' letters: 1714
    Students' notebooks: 3700
UNIVERSITY OF VIRGINIA MEDICAL
  COLLEGE, Richmond, Virginia: 4897
UNIVERSITY OF WISCONSIN, Madison,
  Wisconsin: 2811
UNIVERSITY STATION, North Carolina:
  1584
UNSELD, Henry E.: 489
UNTERMEYER, Louis: 103, 902
UNTHANK, J. H.: 5443
UNWIN (T. FISHER) (firm): 1210
UPCHURCH, Isham Sims: 5444
UPCHURCH FAMILY (North Carolina--
  Genealogy): 5444
UPPER MARLBORO, Maryland: 785, 1043
UPPER ROCKINGHAM CIRCUIT, Methodist
  churches: 3646
UPPERVILLE, Virginia: 212, 3232
UPSHUR, Abel Parker: 5445
UPSHUR, Amelie (McAlister): 5252
UPSON, Columbus: 1181
UPSON COUNTY, Georgia:
  Civil War:
    Preventive inoculation against
      smallpox: 4754
    Tax in kind: 1181
  Superior Courts: 4754
  Cities and towns:
    Thomaston: 4754
    Waynmanville: 2272
UPTON, Clarence Horace: 355

UPTON, Emory: 5446
UPTON, Sara Carr: 5447
UPWARD, Mr. _____ (contractor):
  2750
URBAN DEVELOPMENT: 4386
  see also CIVIL IMPROVEMENT
URBANA, New York: 5974
URBANA, Ohio: see URBANA UNIVERSITY
URBANA UNIVERSITY, Urbana, Ohio:
  2291
URBANNA, Virginia: 454
URNER, Milton G.: 3789
URRUTIA, José María Córdova y: see
  CÓRDOVA Y URRUTIA, José María
URUGUAY:
  Description and travel: 1333
USURY--Pennsylvania: 2444
UTAH:
  see also WESTERN STATES
  Currency: 1339
  Description and travel: 57
    Salt Lake City: 1174
  Economic conditions: 57
  Mormon churches: 2368
  Pioneer life: 1333
  Politics and government: 2368
  Religion: 57
UTAH TERRITORY:
  Governors: 1333
UTICA, Illinois: 3222
UTICA, New York: 1845, 2907
UTILITY WORKERS: see LABOR UNIONS--
  Utility workers
UTOPIAN COMMUNITIES:
  Indiana: 4770
  Tennessee: 4770
UYS, Piet: 5876

## V

VACCINATION: see DISEASES--Smallpox--Preventive inoculation
VADE, Edmund: 5004
VAIL, Aaron: 5448
VAIL, Robert William Glenrole: 1424
VALENTINES--Great Britain: 258
VALERIE AYLMER by Frances Christine (Fisher) Tiernan: 1494
VALETTA, Malta: 2296
VALHOPE, Carol North: 1992
VALLADARES DE SOTOMAYOR, Antonio: 3312
VALLANDIGHAM, Clement Laird: 801, 1505, 4076, 4881, 5160
VALLE Y CAVIEDES, Juan del: 4155
VALLEY BANK, Leesburg, Virginia: 5449
VALLEY CAMPAIGN: see CIVIL WAR--CAMPAIGNS, BATTLES, AND MILITARY ACTIONS--Virginia--Shenandoah Valley
VALLEY FORGE, Pennsylvania: 1805
VALLEY FORGE IRON WORKS, Saint Francis County, Missouri: 3703
VALLEY LAND AND IMPROVEMENT CO. (Virginia): 461
VALLEY MUTUAL LIFE ASSOCIATION OF VIRGINIA: 2493
VALLEY TOWN, North Carolina: 5202, 5673
VALLEY TURNPIKE COMPANY (Virginia): 3680
VÁMBÉRY, Ámin: 3722
VAMOCO MILLS COMPANY, Franklinton, North Carolina: 5450
VAN ALLEN, Peter L.: 1090
VANAMEE, William: 783
VAN BIBBER, Hester E.: 5165
VAN BOKKELEN, Libertus: 2999
VAN BUREN, Abraham: 1472, 4839
VAN BUREN, Angelica (Singleton): 4839
VAN BUREN, Martin: 685, 805, 872, 2497, 2860, 3366, 3378, 4022, 4839, 4880, 5451, 5593, 5886
 Administration: 4080, 5491
 Preservation of home: 4343
 Public opinion of: 5361
  West Virginia: 2515
 Visit to White Sulphur Springs, Virginia: 5491
VAN BUREN, Arkansas: 2123, 3376
 Schools: 5380
  Girls' schools and academies: 3142
 Temperance: 2346
VAN BUREN ACADEMY, Van Buren, Arkansas: 5380
VAN BUREN COUNTY, Michigan: 703
VAN BUREN FEMALE SEMINARY, Van Buren, Arkansas: 3142
VAN BUREN FURNACE, Virginia: 5990
VANCE, Charles N.: 5460
VANCE, Harriet N. (Espey): 85
VANCE, Robert B., Jr.: 5280

VANCE, Zebulon Baird: 85, 484, 832, 1403, 1590, 1948, 2537, 3811, 4080, 4544, 4938, 4729, 5460, 5518, 5739
VANCE FAMILY (North Carolina): 85
VANCE COUNTY, North Carolina:
 Finance: 5962
 Roads: 5962
 Cities and towns:
  Henderson: 95, 1144, 2087, 4232
   Postal Service accounts: 4407
  Townsville: 2338
   Presbyterian churches: 1361
  Williamsboro: 761, 2475, 2829
VAN CLEVESVILLE, West Virginia: 1257
VANCOUVER EXPEDITION (British Navy): 342
VANCOUVER ISLAND, Canada: 2708
 Description and travel: 3744
VANDALIA, Illinois: 1649
VANDALIA LAND COMPANY: 4348
VANDALISM:
 Pennsylvania--Pittsburgh: 5775
VAN DEN BERGH, Max: 1101
VANDERBILT, Alva Murray (Smith): 5968
VANDERBILT, Consuelo: 5968
VANDERBILT, Cornelius: 1441, 3265
VANDERBILT, Harold Sterling: 5968
VANDERBILT, William Kissam, Sr.: 5968
VANDERBILT FAMILY (New York): 5796, 5968
VANDERBILT FAMILY (Rhode Island): 5968
VANDERBILT UNIVERSITY, Nashville, Tennessee: 5603
 Faculty: 361
VANDER HORST, Ann: 5461
VANDERHORST, Mrs. Elias: 2210
VANDERHORST FAMILY (South Carolina): 2210
VAN DERLIP, G. W.: 2518
VANDERLYN, John: 4348
VAN DE WAHL: 4362
VANDLING, Lafayette: 5462
VAN DOREN, Carl Clinton: 3797
VAN DORN, Earl: 1403, 5452
VAN DORN FAMILY (New York): 388
VAN DUZER, John C.: 5453
VANE, Frances Anne (Hawes), Viscountess Vane: 5463
VANE, Sir Henry, Jr.: 5464
VANE, William Harry, First Duke of Cleveland: 868, 2149
VAN GAASBECK, Peter: 5454
VAN HOOK, John C.: 5455
VAN HOOK AND LUNSFORD, Roxboro, North Carolina: 5455
VAN METRE, George W.: 5456
VAN METRE, Margaretta C.: 457
VAN METRE, Mary: 457
VAN METRE, Rosa (Ferrel): 5456
VAN MILDERT, William, Bishop of Durham: 2126
VANN, Henry: 3995
VANN, R. T.: 255
VANN-MOORE MILLS COMPANY: 5450
VAN NOPPEN, Charles Leonard: 5457
VAN RENSSELAER, Cornelius: 3709
VAN RENSSELAER, Henry Bell: 5458
VAN REYPEN, William Knickerbocker: 3192
VAN SCHAACK, Henry Cruger: 305
VANSICKLES, James G.: 4158
VANSICKLES, Rebecca: 4158
VANSITTART, Nicholas, First Baron Bexley: 878
VAN VLECK, Amelia A.: 5459
VAN VLECK, Carter: 659
VAN ZANDT COUNTY, Texas: 1861
"VARIOUS LEGAL DOCUMENTS WHICH COULD BE USEFUL NOT ONLY TO AN APOSTOLIC NOTARY BUT ALSO TO AN IMPERIAL NOTARY": 2194
VARNA, Bulgaria: 153
VARNER, Hendley: 2963

VARNER, Josephine: 5465
VARNER, Kate: 5466
VARNER, Washington: 5467
VARNER FAMILY (Georgia): 2963
VARNUM, Joseph Bradley, Jr.: 3325
VARNUM FAMILY (Kentucky): 3325
VARRENTRAPP, Georg: 1087
VARTY AND ROAKE (firm): see ROAKE AND VARTY
VASSALL, Elizabeth: 1875
VASSAR COLLEGE, Poughkeepsie, New York: 4976
 Funds and scholarships: 4976
 Students and student life: 4271
VATICAN BASILICA OF ST. PETER: 5468
VATICAN CITY: 937, 939
 Foreign relations:
  Great Britain: 5726
  United States: 4020
 Spanish embassy in: 4178
VATICAN COUNCIL--Decrees: 5468
VAUGHAN, Jessie: 5469
VAUGHAN, John: 5469
VAUGHAN, Lloyd P.: 1196, 5236
VAUGHAN, Lucy Ann: 5469
VAWTER AND PACK: see ANDERSON PACK AND VAWTER (firm)
VELAQUES, Loreta Janeta: 3262
VELASCO, Francisco Pérez de: see PÉREZ DE VELASCO, Francisco
VELLORE, India: 2321
VENABLE, Abraham Watkins: 5457, 5470
VENABLE, C. W.: 4043
VENABLE, Charles Scott: 523
VENABLE, Francis Preston: 5457
VENABLE, James R.: 3062
VENDUE MASTERS:
 Georgia and South Carolina: 2019
VENETIA, U.S.S.: 4355
VENEZUELA:
 American foreign investment: 4895
 Carthagena Expedition: 1068
 Claims against: 2748
 Coffee trade: 23
 Commodity prices--Maracaibo: 5133
 Currency--Value: 5886
 Politics and government: 5726
 Railroad construction: 4895
 Social life and customs: 5569
 Spies--Women: 485
 Telegraph construction: 4895
VENICE (state): 405
VENICE, Italy:
 Social life and customs: 3310
VENTOSA, Vera de la: 4979
VERA CRUZ, Mexico:
 Defense (1700s): 4979
 Mexican War: 636
  see also MEXICAN WAR--Campaigns, battles, and military actions--Mexico--Vera Cruz
 Shipwrecks: 2667
VERA CRUZ (shipwreck of): 4881
VERANGO COUNTY, Pennsylvania:
 Wesley: 4841
VER BRYCK, Bernard: 5471
VERDERY, Eugene, Jr.: 5472
VERDERY, James Paul: 5472
VERDIER FAMILY (West Virginia--Genealogy): 1946
VERDUN, France: 4269
VERELST, Harman: 5473
VERMONT:
 see also NEW ENGLAND STATES
 Abolition of slavery and abolitionist sentiment: 3777
 Banks and banking: 4485
 Charades: 3218
 Clergy--Methodist: 5096
 Copperheads: 1787
 Currency: 1339
 Daguerreotypers: 3218
 Diseases:
  Smallpox: 2896
  Preventive inoculation: 2896
 Estates--Administration and settlement: 4485

VERMONT (Continued):
  Free-produce movement: 3665
  Home remedies: 3218
  Land speculation: 3041
  Law practice--Burlington: 3143
  Legal affairs--Burlington: 3143
  Marble trade: 4485
  Peace societies--Rupert: 2848
  Personal liberty laws: 3665
  Personal service: 3218
  Schools: 5197
    Girls' schools and academies: 3218
    Military schools: 295
  Teaching: 2544
  Universities and colleges: see MIDDLEBURY COLLEGE
VERNER, Elizabeth Mary Emily: 5474
VERNER, Rudolf Henry Cole: 5474
VERNET, Horace: 2587
VERNON, Edward: 5540
VERNON FAMILY (New York): 3709
VERNON, North Carolina: 2970
VERNON & KIRBY (firm): see KIRBY & VERNON
VERNON FEMALE ACADEMY, Vernon, North Carolina: 2970
VERNON-HARCOURT, Sir William George Granville Venables: see HARCOURT, Sir William George Granville Venables Vernon-
VERNOR, Benjamin: 2492, 2497
VERNOR FAMILY (Pennsylvania): 2497
VERONA, Mississippi: 5844
VERSAILLES, France: 1424, 1582, 3305
  Description: 4490
  Housing--Interiors: 1424
VERSAILLES PEACE CONFERENCE: 3096, 4020
VERSAILLES TREATY: 4269
"UNA VERSION DESCONOCIDE DE UN POEMA DE POMBO" by John M. Fein: 4155
VESEY-FITZGERALD, William: see FOSTER-VESEY-FITZGERALD, William
VESTAL'S FORD, North Carolina: 4450
VESTER, Benjamin H.: 5475
VESTER, Solomon: 5475
VETERANS: see as subheading under names of wars, e.g. CIVIL WAR--VETERANS
VETERANS' AFFAIRS:
  United States: 4805
    Benefits: 325
      see also PENSIONS--Military
VETERANS' FRAUD:
  American Revolution: 105
VETERANS' ORGANIZATIONS: see AMERICAN LEGION AUXILIARY; ARMY OF THE PHILIPPINES, INC.; CONFEDERATE SURVIVORS' ASSOCIATION; GRAND ARMY OF THE REPUBLIC; MILITARY ORDER OF THE LOYAL LEGION OF THE UNITED STATES; SOCIETY OF THE ARMY OF TENNESSEE; SOCIETY OF THE CINCINNATI; THIRD ARMY CORPS UNION; UNITED CONFEDERATE VETERANS; UNITED SPANISH WAR VETERANS
VETERINARY QUARANTINE: see LIVESTOCK QUARANTINE
VETO:
  Right of local veto in Great Britain: 3715
VIAL, Peter: 5476
VIAUD, Louis Marie Julien: see LOTI, Pierre
VICE PRESIDENTS:
  Elections: see PRESIDENTIAL ELECTIONS
  Nominations by Congress: 2138
VICK, Bushrod W.: 1109
VICKERY, John: 4256
VICKERY & POMEROY: see POMEROY AND VICKERY
VICKSBURG, Mississippi: 1520, 2166, 3438, 3523, 5452, 5635
  Civil War: 3357, 5017

VICKSBURG, Mississippi:
  Civil War (Continued):
    see also CIVIL WAR--CAMPAIGNS, BATTLES, AND MILITARY ACTIONS--Mississippi--Vicksburg
    Confederate Army hospitals: 5098
  Plantations: 1325
  Real estate: 2164
VICTOR EMMANUEL I, King of Sardinia: 4745
VICTOR-MONAGHAN MILLS: 5312
VICTORIA, Queen of Great Britain: 1057, 5226
  Biographical study of: 3022
  Diamond Jubilee: 2836
  Visit to Dublin, Ireland: 5298
VICTORIA, Crown Princess of Prussia: 2471
VICTORIA, Canada:
  Chinatown: 4175
  Description: 4175
VICTORIA MEMORIAL HALL, Calcutta, India: 1343
VICTORY CELEBRATIONS:
  see also PUBLIC CELEBRATIONS
  Tennessee--Nashville (1864): 2308
VIDAL, Francisco: 3118
VIENNA, Austria:
  British embassy in: 16, 3238
  Musical scores: 1974
VIENNA, North Carolina:
  Physicians: 1414
VIENNA, Virginia: 3965
VIENNA, Congress of: see CONGRESS OF VIENNA
VIETNAMESE WAR: 613
  Opposition in the United States: 4948
  Peace movement: 4948
  Relation of the Methodist Church to: 3020
VIGILANCE COMMITTEES--Virginia: 5613
VIGNACOURT, Adrien de La Vieuville, Comte de: 3119
VIGO COUNTY, Indiana:
  Terre Haute: 3618, 4303
VIGOUREUX, Clarisse: 65
VILLA, Francisco: 2112
VILLA RICA, Georgia: 874
VILLARD, Henry: 2526
VILLEBORO FEMALE SEMINARY (Virginia): 3293
VILLEPIGUE, John Bordenave: 4065
VILLIERS, Charles Pelham: 2149
VILLIERS, George, First Duke of Buckingham: 2152
VILLIERS, George Bussy, Fourth Earl of Jersey: 5330
VILLIERS, George William Frederick, Fourth Earl of Clarendon and Fourth Baron Hyde: 597, 678, 1632, 1755, 1926, 5809
VILLIERS, John Charles, Third Earl of Clarendon: 1754
VIMEUR, Jean Baptiste Donatien de, Comte de Rochambeau: 5228
VIMSLYKE, Delavern: 3691
VINAVER, Eugene: 3477
VINCENNES, Indiana: 1072
VINCENT, Hugh: 5478
VINCENT, John Martin: 22
VINCENT, Martha Boscawen (Evelyn): 5478
VINCENT, Nicholas W.: 5478
VINCENT FAMILY (Texas--Genealogy): 465
VINDHYA PRADESH, India:
  Rewa: 4364
"VINDICATION OF GENERAL ANDERSON FROM THE INSINUATIONS OF GENERAL FITZ HUGH LEE" by General C. Irvine Walker: 3809
VINES, Samuel: 208, 5479
VINEYARDS--France: 5323
VINING, Fanny Elizabeth: 1378
VINK, William 50, 3812
VINTON, Francis Laurens: 5480

VINTON, John Rogers: 5480
VIOLETTE, E. M.: 5481
VIRGIL: 3607
"THE VIRGIN AND CHILD" (painting): 2969
VIRGIN ISLANDS:
  see also DANISH WEST INDIES
  Estates: 2321

VIRGINIA

see also SOUTHERN STATES
ABOLITION OF SLAVERY AND ABOLITIONIST SENTIMENT: 1957, 4295, 4924
  Woodstock: 5275
ADVERTISING:
  Religious literature: 2485
  Schools and academies: 1894
AGED AND AGING, Assistance to: 3820
AGRICULTURAL FAIRS:
  Nansemond County: 3834
AGRICULTURAL IMPLEMENTS: 1354
  Albemarle County: 3699
  Prices: 4924
AGRICULTURAL MACHINERY: 4157
AGRICULTURAL ORGANIZATIONS: 3834
  see also names of specific organizations under VIRGINIA
AGRICULTURAL PRACTICES: 1354, 3560
  see also VIRGINIA--CROP ROTATION; VIRGINIA--EXPERIMENTAL FARMING
AGRICULTURAL PRODUCTS: 3200
  Prices: 3200
  Transportation of: 404, 4124
AGRICULTURAL WORKERS:
  Edinburg: 4124
  Gloucester County: 3809
  Negroes: 3719
AGRICULTURE:
  see also the following subheadings under VIRGINIA: CROPS, and names of specific crops; FARMING; LIVESTOCK; PLANTATIONS
  1700s: 3819
  1700s-1800s: 734, 1962, 4616
  1800s: 43, 1283, 1384, 1957, 2418, 5397, 5426
  Albemarle County: 3699
  Amherst County: 97
  Caroline County: 5203
  Fluvanna County: 5839
  Madison: 3141
  Prince Edward County: 5884
  Rappahannock: 3141
  Westover: 3141
AMERICAN LITERATURE: 182, 924, 4112
  see also VIRGINIA IN AMERICAN LITERATURE
  Short stories: 1878
AMERICAN POETRY:
  1700s: 604
  1800s: 4180, 5176
  1800s: 3809
  1810s: 3809
  1820s: 182, 2248, 3809
  1830s: 732, 2248
  1850s: 298, 2713
  1860s: 4186
  1870s: 4186
  1880s: 4186
  1890s: 4020
  1800s-1900s: 4743
AMERICAN REVOLUTION: see appropriate subheadings under AMERICAN REVOLUTION; CONTINENTAL ARMY
AMUSEMENTS: 262
ARCHITECTURE--Richmond: 4490
ARITHMETIC EXERCISE BOOKS: 208, 576, 2633
ARMY CAMPS:
  Civil War: see CONFEDERATE STATES OF AMERICA--ARMY--Camps--Virginia
  World War I: 3843
ARSENALS--Fluvanna County: 4915
AUCTIONS:
  Oak Grove: 2392
  Tobacco--Danville: 5958

VIRGINIA

AUTHORS AND PUBLISHERS: 1878, 3397, 3809
　see also VIRGINIA--PUBLISHERS AND PUBLISHING
AUTHORSHIP: 924, 3320, 5227
AUTOGRAPH COLLECTION: 2061, 3681, 4156
AUTOGRAPHS: 302, 905, 3517
　Charlottesville: 275
　　University of Virginia: 3106
　Hampden-Sydney: 3740
BACHELORHOOD: 3809
BALLADS: 4186
BALLS (Parties)--Richmond: 5094
BANK FAILURES--Columbia: 5035
BANK STOCKS: 4215, 4616
BANKRUPTCY: 418, 1125, 3817
　Alexandria: 226
BANKS AND BANKING: 1384, 2131, 2797, 3362, 4616, 4720
　Taxation: 5035
　Trustees: 3846
　Subdivided by place:
　　Blacksburg: 308
　　Buchanan: 5904
　　Cartersville: 5035
　　Charlottesville: 4142
　　Columbia: 5035
　　Danville: 1372, 1761, 5556
　　Fredericksburg: 5556
　　Gloucester County: 4924
　　Leesburg: 5449
　　Lynchburg: 4157
　　Richmond: 5282
BAPTIST CHURCHES: 2685
　Associations: 330
　Clergy: see VIRGINIA--CLERGY--Baptist
　Luray: 574
　New Hope: 3826
BARLEY PRODUCTION: 4924
BARTER: 2131, 2633
BIOGRAPHICAL STUDIES: 1778, 3269, 5176, 5607
　Criticism: 1624
BIOGRAPHIES: 2881, 3809, 4019
BIRTHDAY COMMEMORATIONS: 2955
BLACKSMITHING: 2633, 3045
　Chesterfield County: 2908
　Edinburg: 4124
　Pittsylvania County: 2131
BLACKSMITHS' ACCOUNTS:
　Marshall: 3582
　Van Buren Furnace: 5990
BLIND--Education: 872
BOARDING HOUSES:
　Charlottesville: 5786
BOAT BUILDING: 4616
　Costs: 1492
BONDS: 604, 2949, 3994, 4589
BOOK BUYING--Charlottesville: 3758
BOOK COLLECTING: 1115
BOOKKEEPING: 1943
BOOKS:
　Prices--Norfolk: 3830
BOOKSELLERS AND BOOKSELLING: 2364, 5375
　Danville: 5196
BOOT AND SHOE INDUSTRY: 1666
　Apprenticeship: 3060
　Augusta County: 728
BOUNDARY DISPUTES:
　North Carolina: 2893
BOWLING--Williamsburg: 4220
BRIDGES: 253, 460
　Construction: 5106
BRIGANDS AND ROBBERS:
　Norfolk County: 5380
　Princess Anne County: 5380
BRITISH FOREIGN INVESTMENT:
　Land: 3179
BUILDING CONSTRUCTION: 2550, 3557
BUSINESS ACCOUNTS: 148, 2051
　Petersburg: 5631
　Richmond: 5631

VIRGINIA

BUSINESS AFFAIRS:
　1700s: 604, 2887
　1800s: 331, 1263, 3556
　1820s: 2794
　1830s: 1384, 1459, 4766, 5031
　1840s: 1384, 1459, 2439, 2659, 4735, 4766, 5031, 5147
　1850s: 753, 1384, 1578, 2439, 2659, 3068, 4243, 4735, 5031, 5147
　1860s: 1115, 1131, 1578, 1701, 2439, 3068, 4243, 5147
　1870s: 1578, 1591, 3068, 4243
　1880s: 1324, 1591
　1800s-1900s: 4244
　1900s: 3084
　Albemarle County: 687
　Bedford County: 1052, 2136
　Berryville: 2082
　Charles City County: 819
　Clear Brook: 2329
　Fluvanna County: 5106, 5839
　Frederickshall: 2363
　Halifax Court House: 1250
　Lexington: 1628
　Lynchburg: 1955
　Nelson County: 682
　Patrick Springs: 1410
　Pattonsburg: 2454
　Pittsylvania County: 1261, 5873
　Richmond: 4119, 4847
　Stevensburgh: 5113
BUTCHERS' ACCOUNTS:
　Leesburg: 4250
CAMP MEETINGS:
　Methodist--Lexington: 5149
　Halifax County: 3377
　Winchester: 2080
CANAL-BOATS: 4504
CANALS: 3574
　Construction: 3809, 4879
　Norfolk: 5696
　Proposed: 322
CARPENTERS' ACCOUNTS--Aldie: 3529
CARPETBAGGERS: 2089
CARRIAGE AND BUGGY MAKING:
　Cumberland County: 531
CARRIAGES AND BUGGIES: 4616
CATHOLIC CHURCH: 2881, 3243
CATTLE RAISING: 4615
CHAIR MANUFACTURING: 253
CHAMBERS OF COMMERCE: 1198
CHARITIES:
　see also VIRGINIA--PHILANTHROPY
　Fluvanna County: 1244
CHEMISTRY:
　Students' notebooks: 302
　　Emory and Henry College: 4646
　　University of Virginia: 824
　　Washington and Lee University: 4616
CHILDREN: 33, 1827
　see also VIRGINIA--GUARDIANSHIP--Children
　Employment: 1194
CHURCH HISTORY: 872
CHURCH OF THE BRETHREN: 5839
CHURCHES:
　see also names of specific denominations under VIRGINIA
　Church buildings: 824
　　Rockingham County: 576
　　Columbia: 5091
CIGARETTE MAKING MACHINES: 5297
CIVIL WAR: see appropriate subheadings under CIVIL WAR; CONFEDERATE STATES OF AMERICA; UNITED STATES--ARMY--Civil War
CLAIMS: 4563
　Richmond: 5445
CLERGY: 2370, 5147
　Baptist: 3489
　Episcopal: 3141, 5765
　Lutheran: 2485
　Methodist: 732, 3646, 4412, 4932

VIRGINIA

CLERGY:
　Methodist (Continued):
　　Charlottesville: 3758
　　Circuit riders: 3497, 3601
　　Legal affairs: 203
　　Licensing: 5891
　　Personal finance: 203
　Methodist Episcopal: 3992
　Methodist Episcopal Church, South: 4192, 5467
　Presbyterian: 1827, 2064, 2737, 5538
　　Lynchburg: 3707, 4373
　Protestant Episcopal: 1565, 4173, 5619
　United Brethren in Christ: 1920
　Subdivided by place:
　　Front Royal: 1116
　Subdivided by subject:
　　Selection and appointment: 4210
　　Wages and salaries: see VIRGINIA--WAGES AND SALARIES--Clergy
CLERKS (retail trade):
　Richmond: 4461
CLOTHING AND DRESS: 753, 872
　Prices: 4924
　　Augusta County: 4210
　　Norfolk: 3830
　Goshen: 5613
COAL MINERS: see VIRGINIA--WAGES AND SALARIES--Coal miners
COAL MINING: 2922
　Chesterfield County: 2908
　Company stores: 2908
　Hiring of slaves: 523
COLONIAL AGENTS IN GREAT BRITAIN: 819
COLONIAL DAMES OF AMERICA: 1814
COMMERCIAL PRODUCTS--Marketing: 2165
COMMISSION MERCHANTS: 872, 2360, 2399, 2933, 3994
　Alexandria: 947
　Petersburg: 375, 1336, 2176, 3145
　Richmond: 1359
COMMODITY PRICES:
　1700s-1800s: 1415, 3069
　1800s: 1263, 1409, 1957, 4043, 4720, 4776, 5765
　1800s: 1093
　1810s: 1093
　1820s: 1093
　1830s: 1384
　1840s: 1384, 4131, 4504
　1850s: 753, 1384, 2370
　1860s: 132, 363, 693, 2370
　　see also CIVIL WAR--COMMODITY PRICES--Virginia
　1870s: 1591, 2370
　1880s: 1591
　Culpeper: 4852
　Lynchburg: 3353, 3566
　Nelson County: 682
　Patrick County: 1410
　Petersburg: 4604
　Richmond: 3566, 5703
COMMONPLACE BOOKS: 2887, 4743, 5302
COMMUNISM: 1198
COMMUNITY RELATIONS:
　Mount Erin: 5332
CONGRESSIONAL ELECTIONS:
　1820s: 3032
　1840s: 4720
　1850s-1860s: 569, 1161
CONSTITUTION:
　1868: 1787
　1928: 818
CONSTITUTIONAL CONVENTIONS:
　1829: 872, 4852, 4924
　1850: 3291, 4720, 4924
CONSTITUTIONAL UNION PARTY: 581
CONSTITUTIONAL LAW:
　Student's notebook:
　　Washington and Lee University: 4616
COOKERY: 1558
　see also VIRGINIA--DIET; VIRGINIA--FOOD

VIRGINIA

COOKERY (Continued):
  Fifesville: 4459
  Lynchburg: 4308
COPYRIGHTS: 5720
CORDAGE FOR SHIPS: 1863
CORN: 490, 2369
CORN PRODUCTION: 3145, 4924
  Albemarle County: 3699
CORONERS' INQUESTS:
  see also VIRGINIA--GOVERNMENT
    AGENCIES AND OFFICIALS--
    Coroners
  Petersburg: 1383
COST OF LIVING: 1198, 4589
COTTON: 5148
  Prices: 4924
  Storage--Brunswick: 5334
COTTON BALING--Falmouth: 2165
COTTON GROWING: 4776, 4924
  Norfolk: 3830
  Nottoway County: 5469
COTTON MILLS: 4924
  Construction--Lynchburg: 5513
  Falmouth: 2165
COTTON TRADE: 435, 590, 1568, 2360, 2381, 3179
  Petersburg: 1336, 2176, 2935, 4604, 5959
  Suffolk: 1838
COUNTY GOVERNMENT:
  Fairfax County: 2887
COURTS: 1125, 1384, 4131
  Cases--Richmond: 4616
  Clerks: 872
    Augusta County: 5184
    Frederick County: 5200
    Madison County: 5064
    Pittsylvania County: 5369
  Laws and legislation: 3302
  Summonses: 117
    Bedford County: 5818
    Campbell County: 4487
  Subdivided by type of court:
    Chancery courts: 4924
      Suffolk: 3012
    Circuit courts: 1568
      Hanover Court House: 3242
      Ninth Circuit Court: 4617
    County Courts: 1568
      Patrick County: 1894
      Pittsylvania County: 2495
    Court of Law and Chancery:
      Bedford County: 5818
    Local courts:
      Flat Creek Township: 1821
    Superior Courts:
      Clerks--Patrick County: 5031
      Campbell County: 62
      Fauquier County: 3994
      Loudoun County: 3994
    United States District Courts: 2700, 5434
COURTSHIP: 262, 4616, 5031
  see also VIRGINIA--LOVE LETTERS
CRIME:
  see also specific kinds of crime under VIRGINIA
  Columbia: 5035
  Negroes: 29, 3726
    see also VIRGINIA--SLAVES--Crime
CROP ROTATION:
  Albemarle County: 3699
  Nelson County: 3566
CROPS:
  see also the following subheadings under VIRGINIA: AGRICULTURE; FARMING; and names of specific crops
  1700s-1800s: 2949
  1800s: 1133, 4710, 4720, 5741
  1800s: 363
  1810s: 363
  1840s: 5980
  1850s: 2370, 4616

VIRGINIA

CROPS:
  1800s (Continued):
  1860s: 1240, 2370, 2510, 3674, 4616, 5180
  1870s: 1591, 2370, 3674
  1880s: 1591, 3674
  Amelia County: 4729
  Nelson County: 682
  Northern Virginia: 4743
  Rockbridge County: 5613
  Sperryville: 1618
CURRENCY: 1339
CUSTOMS DUTIES--Collection: 2505
DEAF:
  Education: 558, 872
  Staunton: 5298
DEATH: 33, 1359, 1920, 4020, 5426,
  Sperryville: 1618
DEBATING SOCIETIES:
  Petersburg: 4159
DEBT: 974, 1384, 4247, 5848
  see also VIRGINIA--PERSONAL DEBT; VIRGINIA--STATE DEBT
  Alexandria: 947
  Culpeper: 4852
  Hanover County: 1824
  Richmond: 5790
  Sweet Briar: 5765
DEBT COLLECTION: 117, 330, 604, 3179, 4381, 4616, 5613
  Bedford County: 3621
  Columbia: 5035
  Luray: 574
  Petersburg: 3593
  Pittsylvania County: 5587
  Suffolk: 3012
DEFENSE: 2893
  see also VIRGINIA--FORTIFICATIONS
  Richmond: 4616
DEMOCRATIC PARTY:
  1800s: 1501, 5513, 5696
  1900s: 3820, 4020
  Campaign literature (1885): 3806
  Nominations to House of Representatives: 1161
DESCRIPTION AND TRAVEL:
  see also VIRGINIA--TRAVEL
  1700s: 819
  1800s: 43, 330, 3560
  1810s: 872, 2677, 3808
  1820s: 872, 2677, 3450
  1830s: 872, 2822
  1840s: 152, 230, 1697, 1790, 3853
  1850s: 568, 5149
  1860s: 155, 4087, 4690, 5193, 5633
  1870s: 1811, 2890, 3229
  1880s: 3229
  1890s: 3229
  1900s: 5786
  Photographs: 180
DIET:
  see also VIRGINIA--COOKERY; VIRGINIA--FOOD
  Goshen: 5613
DINNERS AND DINING: 818
DISEASES:
  Cholera: 1283
    Norfolk: 5751
    Richmond: 5114
    Suffolk: 3012
  Diphtheria: 3809
  Rheumatism--Home remedies: 2633
  Smallpox: 3853
    Lexington: 5613
    Lynchburg: 5513
    Manchester: 3792
    Nelson County: 682
  Tuberculosis: 33
    Treatment: 693
  Typhoid fever: 3809
    Nelson County: 682
    Norfolk: 2857
  Yellow fever: 330
    Nelson County: 682

VIRGINIA

DISEASES:
  Yellow fever (Continued):
    Norfolk: 3301, 4968
    Portsmouth: 3301
    Sperryville: 1618
DISUNION: 2776
DIVIDENDS--Corporations: 2165
DOCKYARD COMPANIES:
  Portsmouth: 4281
  Richmond: 4465
DROUGHTS: 3485
DRUGS:
  Prices: 4924
  Alexandria: 5016
DRY GOODS:
  Accounts--Leesburg: 4198
  Prices: 4924
DUCK (textile)--Falmouth: 2165
DUELING: 117, 194, 1424, 3853, 4615
EARTHQUAKES--Amherst County: 5529
ECONOMIC CONDITIONS:
  see also the following subheadings under VIRGINIA: COST OF LIVING; INFLATION; PANIC OF (date); POVERTY
  1700s: 2703
  1700s-1800s: 1542
  1800s: 3566, 4490, 4776
  1850s: 5251
  1860s: 203, 411, 619, 1827, 2559, 3440, 3809, 4131, 4698, 5378
  1870s: 203, 253, 619, 1827, 2559, 3809, 4131, 4698, 5378
  1800s-1900s: 5704
  Madison: 3141
  Rappahannock: 3141
  Richmond: 4562
  Western Virginia: 2566
  Westover: 3141
ECONOMICS:
  Students' notebooks:
    University of Virginia: 1000
    Washington and Lee University: 4616
EDUCATION:
  see also the following subheadings under VIRGINIA: BLIND--Education; DEAF--Education; POOR--Education; SCHOOLS; TEACHING
  1700s: 99, 1962
  1700s-1800s: 2927, 4315
  1800s: 43, 266, 331, 404, 4615, 4698, 4743
  1800s: 2925
  1810s: 2932
  1830s: 1351
  1840s: 824, 3495
  1850s: 5286
  1860s: 2418, 5286, 5378
  1870s: 2418, 3489, 5378
  1880s: 3307
  1890s: 3307
  1800s-1900s: 1340
  Costs: 4589
  Women: 2712, 3458, 3642
  Edge Hill: 1409
ELECTIONS:
  see also the following subheadings under VIRGINIA: CONGRESSIONAL ELECTIONS; GUBERNATORIAL ELECTIONS; LOCAL ELECTIONS; PRESIDENTIAL ELECTIONS; SENATORIAL ELECTIONS
  1800s:
  1830s: 4852
  1840s: 581, 3255, 4852
  1860s: 581, 1955
  1870s: 1955, 5120, 5377
  1880s: 3029
  1800s-1900s: 5152
  1900s:
  1930s: 5790
  1940s: 225, 1201
  1950s: 1201
  Buchanan: 4038
ELECTRIC POWER INDUSTRY: 3447
EMINENT DOMAIN--Richmond: 4465

VIRGINIA

ENDOWMENTS: 4020
EPISCOPAL CHURCHES: 3141
   Clergy: see VIRGINIA--CLERGY--
      Episcopal
   Orphanages--Rustburg: 2799
   Portsmouth: 1701
   Sermons: see VIRGINIA--SERMONS--
      Episcopal
ESCHEAT--Franklin County: 2955
ESTATE ACCOUNTS: 28, 2949, 3104,
   3809, 4743, 5742
   Oak Grove: 2392
ESTATES (landed property):
   Management: 3104, 5332
ESTATES (legal):
   Administration and settlement:
      1700s: 604, 3819
      1700s-1800s: 2633, 2927, 4616
      1700s-1900s: 3424
      1800s: 490, 824, 1556, 1558,
         1568, 1922, 2120, 3855, 4385,
         4562, 5469, 5765
      1800s: 97, 3031
      1810s: 1627, 3156
      1820s: 1627, 2190, 3560
      1830s: 1384, 2190
      1840s: 1384, 2190, 3157, 4735,
         5113
      1850s: 734, 806, 1161, 1384,
         3068, 4735
      1860s: 1161, 2510, 2712, 3068,
         3193, 4531
      1870s: 1262, 3068, 3587, 5696
      1880s: 3401, 5696
      1890s: 3401, 5696
      1800s-1900s: 2517, 3148
      1900s: 3084
      1900s: 3587
   Buckingham County: 5289
   Campbell County: 62
   Caroline County: 5203
   Charlottesville: 2612
   Culpeper County: 337
   Frederickshall: 2363
   Gloucester County: 4924
   Halifax County: 5229
   Loudoun County: 3529, 3560
   Luray: 574
   Madison County: 4794
   Nelson County: 3566
   Norfolk: 3830
   Petersburg: 1873, 4555
   Pittsylvania County: 5718
   Port Republic: 1600
   Suffolk: 3012
   Westmoreland County: 5577
   Wythe County: 872
EVANGELISM: 1591, 1920, 4131
EXHIBITIONS AND FAIRS:
   Nansemond County: 3834
EXPERIMENTAL FARMING: 3820
FAMILY LIFE: 2935, 4698, 5476
   Shenandoah County: 2975
   Staunton: 1601
   Winchester: 2974
FAMILY MEDICINE: 4616
FARM ACCOUNTS:
   Albemarle County: 5302
   Clarke County: 3602
   Nelson County: 5290
   "Rose Hill": 3833
   Warrenton: 5210
FARM LAND: 1542
FARM LIFE:
   Prince Edward County: 5884
FARM MANAGEMENT: 4616, 5210
   Manassas: 5272
FARM SUPPLIES:
   Albemarle County: 3699
   Falmouth: 2165
   Norfolk: 3830
FARM TENANCY: 1568, 3560
FARMERS' ALLIANCE: 5709

VIRGINIA

FARMING:
   see also the following subheadings
      under VIRGINIA: AGRICULTURE;
      CROPS, and names of specific
      crops; EXPERIMENTAL FARMING;
      LIVESTOCK; PLANTATIONS; POULTRY
      FARMING
   1700s: 1066
   1700s-1800s: 558, 1262, 3560, 3671
   1700s-1900s: 4924
   1800s: 1436, 1587, 5751
   1810s: 2489
   1820s: 2489
   1840s: 2489, 5980
   1850s: 1354
   1860s: 1240, 4729, 5660
   1870s: 794, 5660
   1880s: 794
   1890s: 794
   1800s-1900s: 3979
   1900s: 1931
   Albemarle County: 3699
   Amherst County: 3788
   Buckingham County: 2378, 3809
   Campbell County: 2369
   Culpeper County: 3141
   Cumberland County: 531
   Edinburg: 4124
   Farmville: 1729
   Gloucester County: 3809
   Hanover County: 4020
   Locust Dale: 1073
   Quicksburg: 4121
   Southampton County: 5248
   Spotsylvania County: 3141
FEDERALIST PARTY: 3809
   Opposition to: 404
FENCES AND FENCING:
   Albemarle County: 3699
   Laws and legislation: 3642
FERTILIZER: 195, 1587, 4710
   see also VIRGINIA--GUANO;
      VIRGINIA--PLASTER (fertilizer)
FERTILIZER INDUSTRY--Norfolk: 373
FINANCE: 3788, 3809, 5357
   see also the following subheadings
      under VIRGINIA: HOUSEHOLD
      FINANCE; PERSONAL FINANCE; PUBLIC
      FINANCE
   Lexington: 3362
FIRES: 2678
   Petersburg: 5499
   Richmond Theatre (1811): 322, 872
FLAGS: 3809
FLOODS:
   Columbia: 5035
   Robinson's River: 253
FLOUR MILLS: 404, 558, 2229, 4615,
   5157
   Falmouth: 2165
   Front Royal: 2797
   Kinsley Mills: 1447
   Richmond: 5393
   Roanoke County: 1969
FOOD:
   see also VIRGINIA--COOKERY;
      VIRGINIA--DIET
   Prices: 1415
FOREIGN TRADE:
   Great Britain: 625
   Ireland: 2884
FORGES--Union Forge: 3098
FORTIFICATIONS:
   see also VIRGINIA--DEFENSE
   Craney Island: 70
FOURTH OF JULY ORATIONS: 2932
FREE NEGROES: 872, 1558, 4924
   Campbell County: 5482
   Census of 1860: 5426
   Proposed removal of: 5476
   School taxes: 3012
FREEDMEN: 375, 1827, 2370, 4131
   Labor contracts: 1366, 1568, 1922,
      2335
FREEDMEN'S LOANS: 2380
FREEDOM OF RELIGION: 2887

VIRGINIA

FREIGHT AND FREIGHTAGE: 2737
   Coal: 3692
   Dry goods: 2165
   Flour: 2165
   Wood: 629, 2165, 3692
   On the James River: 4616
FRENCH LITERATURE:
   Students' notebooks:
      University of Virginia: 1379
FRUIT CULTURE:
   Fluvanna County: 5035
   Nelson County: 3566
FUGITIVE SLAVES: 2453, 2633, 5579
   Yorktown: 3741
FUND RAISING--Halifax County: 3377
FUNERALS: 1894
   Hat Creek: 4043
FURNITURE: 1137, 3809
   Prices:
      Norfolk: 3830
      Woodstock: 1893
FURNITURE INDUSTRY:
   Woodstock: 1893
GAMBLING: 4518
GOLD MINING--Fluvanna County: 5035
GOVERNESSES: 3809
GOVERNMENT AGENCIES AND OFFICIALS:
   Agriculture Commissioner: 531
   Commissioners--Appointments: 5507
   Coroners:
      Pittsylvania County: 2925
   Department of Labor and Industry:
      1198
   Governors:
      Thomas Jefferson (1779-1781):
         3130
      Benjamin Harrison (1781-1784):
         2383
      Robert Brooke (1794-1796): 667
      William H. Cabell (1805-1808):
         824
      Thomas Mann Randolph (1819-1822):
         4384
      William Branch Giles
         (1827-1830): 2034
      John Rutherfoord (1841-1842):
         4616
      William Smith (1846-1849,
         1864-1865): 1401, 4916
      Henry Alexander Wise (1856-1860):
         3809, 5853
      John Letcher (1860-1864): 3182,
         5613
      Francis Harrison Pierpont
         (1865-1867): 4206
      Gilbert Carleton Walker
         (1870-1874): 5507
      Frederick William Mackey Holliday
         (1878-1882): 2597
      James Hoge Tyler (1898-1902):
         5396
      Claude Augustus Swanson
         (1906-1910): 5152
   Governor's Council: 3809
   Sheriffs: 2517, 2680
      Appointments: 4916
      Halifax County: 822
      Nelson County: 3566, 5484, 5700
      Pittsylvania County: 5587
   Wages and salaries: see VIRGINIA--
      WAGES AND SALARIES--State
      officials
GOVERNMENT AND CIVIC EMPLOYEES: 2732
GRAIN PRICES: 4924
GRAIN PRODUCTION: 3145
GREEK HISTORY:
   Students' notebooks:
      Washington and Lee University:
         4616
GREEK LANGUAGE:
   Students' notebooks:
      University of Virginia: 5288
   Study and teaching:
      University of Virginia: 2612

## VIRGINIA

GRIST MILLS:
  see also VIRGINIA--FLOUR MILLS;
    VIRGINIA--MILLERS' ACCOUNTS
  Albemarle County: 3699
  Brunswick County: 4324
  Franklin County: 3100
  Kinsley Mills: 1447
GROCERIES--Prices: 4924
GUANO: 4615, 5377
  Albemarle County: 33
GUARDIANSHIP: 1558
  Children: 2120
  Orphans: 2712
GUBERNATORIAL ELECTIONS:
  1859: 4720
  1863: 3809
  1873: 2700
  1877: 2597
  1921: 5779
  1940s: 1198
  1941: 3820
  1945: 224
  1947: 224
HAY--Albemarle County: 3699
HEALTH CONDITIONS: 2559
HEALTH RESORTS: 785, 3123, 3809,
    4616, 4924, 5114, 5690
  Berkeley Springs: 3809
  Holston Springs: 3719
  Hot Springs: 1891
  Huguenot Springs: 3422
  In poetry: 182
  Jordan's Springs: 3135
  Sulphur Springs: 1891
  Warm Springs: 3809
HIDES AND LEATHER--Prices: 2520
HIDES AND SKINS:
  Lawrenceville: 3014
HIRING OF SLAVES: 33, 330, 331,
    753, 2014, 2360, 2369, 3246,
    3788, 4615, 5121, 5529, 5765
  Coal industry: 523, 2908
  Iron industry: 523
  Tobacco industry: 1873
  Subdivided by place:
    Caroline County: 4589
    Goshen: 5613
    Greenville County: 5891
    Norfolk: 3830
    Patrick County: 1410
HISTORIC SITES:
  Petersburg: 4612
HISTORICAL RESTORATION:
  Colonial Williamsburg: 1424
  Mount Vernon: 1737
  Stratford: 1424
HISTORICAL SOCIETIES: 2499, 3735,
    5696
HISTORICAL STUDIES: 858
  see also VIRGINIA--CHURCH HISTORY
HOME REMEDIES: 3721, 4616
  see also VIRGINIA--DISEASES--
    Rheumatism--Home remedies
HONORS AND AWARDS: 824
HORSE RACING: 2517
  Richmond: 5094
HORSES:
  Breeding: 2637, 4531, 4743
  Prices: 4924
HOSPITALS: 1591
  see also CIVIL WAR--HOSPITALS
  Military--Norfolk: 4701
HOTELS:
  Management: 5176
  Manassas: 5779
HOURS OF LABOR:
  Construction industry: 2550
  Iron industry: 5990
  Manufacturing companies: 2165
HOUSEHOLD ACCOUNTS: 1922, 3157,
    3642, 4615
  Clarke County: 3602
  Richmond: 4346
  Stafford County: 1813
HOUSEHOLD FINANCE: 872, 1115, 3809,
    4743

## VIRGINIA

HOUSEHOLD FINANCE (Continued):
  Hanover County: 4020
HOUSEHOLD MANAGEMENT: 4459, 4616
HOUSES: 1568
  Construction--Mount Vernon: 5575
HUNTING: 5660
HYMNS--Methodist: 4412
INCOME TAXES: 1189
INDEPENDENT ORDER OF ODD FELLOWS:
    1402
  Bridgewater: 3215
INDIANS OF NORTH AMERICA: 1511
  Warfare: 404
INDIGO CULTURE: 3819
INDUSTRIAL PRODUCTIVITY:
  Falmouth: 2165
  Van Buren Furnace: 5990
INDUSTRIALIZATION--Luray: 574
INFLATION--Danville: 4094
INSANITY--Jurisprudence: 958
INSURANCE: 433, 523, 2387, 2794,
    3400, 4710, 5891
  Nottoway County: 1811
  Fire: 4924
  Life: 974
  Livestock: 461
  Maritime: 3509
  Property: 4924
  Page County: 461
INSURANCE AGENTS: 628
INSURANCE COMPANIES: 2387, 2493,
    4616
  Alexandria: 3509
  Portsmouth: 4281
INTERNAL IMPROVEMENTS: 1075, 4732,
    4924
INVESTMENT COMPANIES:
  Petersburg: 4241
INVESTMENTS: 5513
IRON FOUNDRIES: 282, 558
  Marion: 3513
  Union Furnace: 5827
IRON FURNACES: 117, 2922
  Van Buren Furnace: 5990
  Wytheville: 4648
IRON GATE FIXTURES: 282
IRON INDUSTRY: 4924, 5513, 5613
  Employee work records:
    Van Buren Furnace: 5990
  Hiring of slaves: 523
  Hours of labor: 5990
  Subdivided by place:
    Augusta County: 728
    Lynchburg: 3809
    Page County: 522
    Westmoreland County: 917
IRON ORE MINING:
  Van Buren Furnace: 5990
IRON PRICES--Page County: 522
JUDGES:
  Appointments: 1511
  Page County: 574
  Brunswick County: 2517
  Elections: 4617
  United States District Court: 2700
JURIES: 5434
JUSTICES OF THE PEACE: 33, 872, 1568
  Fotheringay: 1646
  Pulaski County: 4771
KNITTING: 1115
KNITTING MACHINERY: 800
KNOW-NOTHING PARTY: 4720
  Goochland County: 4616
LABOR AND RELIGION: 1194
LABOR CONDITIONS: 2680, 3642
  Industrial safety: 1194
  James River Valley: 3809
  Winchester: 283
LABOR COSTS: 1922
LABOR DISPUTES: 1512, 5148
LABOR IN POLITICS: 2568
LABOR LAWS AND LEGISLATION: 224, 1194
LABOR PUBLICATIONS: 1195
LABOR UNIONS: 1198, 1201
  see also CONGRESS OF INDUSTRIAL
    ORGANIZATIONS

## VIRGINIA

LABOR UNIONS (Continued):
  Finance: 224
  Construction workers: 1198
  Distillery workers: 1198
  Government and civic employees:
    1198
  Industrial: 1194
  Insurance and allied workers: 1198
  Steel workers: 1198
  Telephone workers: 1194, 1198
LAND:
  see also VIRGINIA--FARM LAND;
    VIRGINIA--REAL ESTATE
  1700s-1800s: 1920, 2887
  1800s: 523, 753, 1600, 2986, 4710
  Lawsuits: 3560
  Prices: 4924, 5613, 5765
  Patrick County: 1410
  Purchases and sales:
    1700s: 1813, 5575
    1700s-1800s: 4616
    1700s-1900s: 4743
    1800s: 74, 253, 794, 2273, 2370,
      3232, 3560, 3846, 4661, 4720,
      5696, 5743, 5765
    1800s-1900s: 3979
  Brunswick County: 2517
  Nansemond County: 3012
  Rental: 4743, 5355
  Subdivided by place:
    Amherst County: 397
    Henrico County: 2415
    Little Hunting Creek: 5575
LAND CLAIMS: 5768
  Campbell County: 62
LAND COMPANIES: 1512, 3721
  Bankruptcy--Page County: 461
  Lawrenceville: 724
LAND DEEDS AND INDENTURES:
  1700s-1800s: 2949, 5047
  1700s-1900s: 3233, 4743
  1800s: 3806, 4122, 4615, 5765
  1800s-1900s: 5302, 5779
  Charles City County: 819
  Fluvanna County: 195, 5839
  Halifax County: 5229
  Hanover County: 1824
  Nelson County: 3566
  Northern Neck: 1750
  Richmond: 5790
LAND GRANTS:
  1600s-1700s: 1242
  1700s: 667, 1511, 2383, 2495,
    2815, 4380
  1700s-1800s: 1920
  1700s-1900s: 824
  1800s: 5765
  Charles City County: 819
LAND PATENTS: 1842
LAND SETTLEMENT: 99
LAND SPECULATION: 2517, 3362, 4615
LAND TITLES: 2273
  Transfer: 5765
LAND WARRANTS: 3537, 4720
  Purchases and sales: 2633
LANDLORD AND TENANT:
  see also the following subheadings
    under VIRGINIA: FARM TENANCY;
    LAND--Rental; REAL ESTATE--Rent;
    RENT
  Contracts--Petersburg: 4555
  Hanover County: 4020
LANGUAGES:
  Ancient languages:
    Study and teaching: 3251
LATIN:
  Students' notebooks:
    University of Virginia: 5288
    Washington and Lee University:
      4616
  Study and teaching:
    University of Virginia: 2612
LAW: 1501
  Codification: 3809
  Notebooks: 3809

VIRGINIA

LAW (Continued):
  Students' notebooks:
    University of Virginia: 4585
    Washington and Lee University: 4616
  Study of: 872
    see also COLLEGE OF WILLIAM AND MARY--Legal education; UNIVERSITY OF VIRGINIA--Legal education
LAW ENFORCEMENT: 3853
LAW PRACTICE:
  1800s: 506, 872, 1115, 1384, 2014, 2597, 2794, 2951, 3148, 3809, 3882, 4713, 5359, 5848
  1800s-1900s: 356, 2517
  Albemarle County: 523
  Bedford County: 3621
  Botetourt County: 5817
  Boyce: 2387
  Dinwiddie County: 2376
  Fluvanna County: 5839
  Lexington: 3587
  Madison County: 523
  Middlesex: 3379
  Petersburg: 203, 2466, 3401
  Richmond: 2387, 4020, 4616
LAWSUITS: 1401, 1556, 2120, 3069, 4381
  see also as subheading under VIRGINIA--(subject)--Lawsuits
  Assoteague Island:
    Oyster-planting rights: 1791
  Randolph-Macon College: 879
  Sequestration proceedings: 2633
  Subdivided by place:
    Norfolk: 3830
    Portsmouth: 5702
    Suffolk: 3012
LAWYERS' ACCOUNTS: 3587
  Danville: 1956
  Pittsylvania County: 3708
LEAGUE OF WOMEN VOTERS: 3558
LEGAL AFFAIRS:
  1700s-1800s: 2887, 3560, 4616, 5112, 5476
  1700s-1900s: 824
  1800s: 170, 195, 523, 1263, 1921, 2173, 3068, 3809, 4563, 5214, 5721
  1800s-1900s: 1436, 4743
  Bedford County: 5818
  Campbell County: 62, 4487
  Caroline County: 4589
  Covington: 3308
  Culpeper: 4852
  Fredericshall: 2363
  Lynchburg: 1350
  Pittsylvania County: 3708, 5718
  Prince William County: 3532
  Richmond: 3169, 5020
  Roanoke: 5904
  Stephensburg: 3255
  Suffolk: 3012
  Sweet Briar: 5765
  Westmoreland County: 5573
LEGAL FEES: 5742
  Staunton: 1267
LEGISLATURE:
  1780s: 2887
  1790s: 4312
  1800s: 4270
    1810s: 4531, 4615
    1820s: 872, 4531, 4615
    1830s: 4531
  1800s-1900s: 5779
  1900s: 1198
  Apportionment:
    Counting of slaves: 4720, 4852
  Clerks: 3809
  House of Delegates:
    1700s-1800s: 1401, 2363, 4315
    1800s: 4616, 5751, 5884
      1800s: 1714
      1810s: 3291, 5031
      1820s: 3291, 5005, 5904

VIRGINIA

LEGISLATURE:
  House of Delegates:
    1800s (Continued):
      1830s: 3291, 3566
      1840s: 3566, 5194
      1850s: 4049
      1870s: 3833, 5120
    1900s: 3104
    Abolitionist resolutions (1850s): 4295
    Discussion of slavery (1831): 1059
    In poetry: 182
    Railroad appropriations: 753
  Senate:
    1800s: 5718
    1900s: 3104, 3820
LIBRARIES--Private: 3809
LICENSING--Shenandoah County: 5485
LIQUOR MANUFACTURING: 2633
  Apple brandy: 4743
  Prices: 4924
LITERARY INTERESTS: 404, 1115, 3809, 4698
  Richmond: 4020
LITERARY SOCIETIES: 4384
  Petersburg: 4159
LIVERY ACCOUNTS--Leesburg: 3584
LIVESTOCK: 1240, 1354, 2712
  see also VIRGINIA--CATTLE RAISING; VIRGINIA--INSURANCE--Livestock
  Prices--Rockbridge County: 5613
LOANS: 2685, 5851
  Columbia: 5035
LOCAL ELECTIONS--Richmond: 5790
LOCAL POLITICS:
  Nansemond County: 3012
  Richmond: 4119
LOCOFOCO PARTY: 4589
LOVE LETTERS: 2553, 2949, 3060, 3542, 5031
  see also VIRGINIA--COURTSHIP
  Warrenton: 5210
LUMBER MILL WORKERS:
  Fluvanna County: 5105
LUMBER MILLS:
  Fluvanna County: 5105
LUMBER YARDS--Warminster: 3574
LUMBERING--Fluvanna County: 5035
LUTHERAN CHURCHES: see VIRGINIA--CLERGY--Lutheran; VIRGINIA--RELIGIOUS LITERATURE--Lutheran
MACHINERY INDUSTRY--Marion: 3513
MANUFACTURED PRODUCTS--Costs: 2165
MANUFACTURING: 5426
MARRIAGE: 132, 2728, 4020, 5248
  see also VIRGINIA--WEDDINGS
MARRIED LIFE: 1827
MASONRY: 3855, 4743
  Albemarle County: 687
  Chatham:
    Pittsylvania Lodge No. 24: 4233
  Lodge No. 13: 5184
  Mecklenburg County: 1821
MEAL: 490
MEDICAL EDUCATION: 2553, 2949
  see also MEDICAL COLLEGE OF VIRGINIA; UNIVERSITY OF VIRGINIA--Medical education
  Students' notebooks: 1509
MEDICAL PRACTICE: 1075, 4743
  Amherst County: 3788
MEDICAL SERVICES: 490
MEDICAL SOCIETIES: 3378
MEDICAL SUPPLIES: 4308
MEDICAL TREATISES: 4743
MEDICAL TREATMENT: 236, 5513, 5742
  see also VIRGINIA--HOME REMEDIES; VIRGINIA--SLAVES--Medical treatment
MEDICINE:
  see also VIRGINIA--FAMILY MEDICINE; VIRGINIA--PATENT MEDICINE
  Buckingham County: 3794
  Charlottesville: 824
  Fluvanna County: 5839

VIRGINIA

MEDICINE (Continued):
  Prescriptions: 4743
  Alexandria: 5016
MEMORIALS--Lynchburg: 3809
MENTAL HOSPITALS: 1920
MERCANTILE ACCOUNTS:
  1700s-1800s: 3145
  1800s: 1336, 2949, 2971, 3721
    1800s: 1093
    1810s: 1093, 2360, 4135
    1820s: 12, 145, 1093
    1830s: 138, 145, 362, 3105
    1840s: 2621
    1850s: 1102, 3994
    1860s: 1102, 4157
    1870s: 2515, 4157
  1800s-1900s: 2517
  Albemarle County: 4490
  Alexandria: 175
  Amherst County: 397
  Augusta County: 209
  Barksdale: 5827
  Bedford County: 2633
  Berryville: 3336
  Blacksburg: 193, 3039
  Brunswick: 5334
  Brunswick County: 4454
  Campbell County: 2633
  Catawba Post Office: 5827
  Charlottesville: 93
  Columbia: 5108
  Danville: 1046, 2207, 2569, 5196
  Falmouth: 2165
  Fayette County: 4011
  Fifesville: 4459
  Fluvanna County: 2834
  Franklin County: 2633
  Gholsonville: 5648
  Good Intent: 568
  Harrisonburg: 2498
  Hawkinstown: 374
  Hicks Ford: 5891
  Keysville: 79
  Lawrenceville: 240
  Leesburg: 4446
  Louisa County: 143
  Lynchburg: 1594, 1955, 2309, 4222
  Martinsville: 1013
  Mecklenburg County: 799, 4885
  Middleburg: 1369
  New Market: 138
  Norfolk: 5770
  Norwood: 5107
  Oak Grove: 2392
  Petersburg: 3179, 5079, 5183
  Peytonsburg: 5827
  Pleasant Grove: 2323
  Richmond: 5770
  Shenandoah County: 160, 3678, 4122
  Sperryville: 3619
  State Mills: 3679
  Strasburg: 5979
  Stuart's Draft: 209
  Suffolk: 4472
  Tazewell County: 5400
  Van Buren Furnace: 5990
  Wachapreague: 4403
  White Post: 2274, 5611
  Winchester: 4741, 5882
  Woodville: 138
MERCANTILE AFFAIRS:
  Gloucester County: 4924
  Gravel Hill: 5652
  Lynchburg: 1350
  Richmond: 4616
  Shenandoah County: 3773
  Union Forge: 3098
MERCHANDISE: 4710
  Inventories:
    Front Royal: 5387
    Sperryville: 3619
  Marketing--Lynchburg: 5568
  Purchases and sales:
    Richmond: 2633

VIRGINIA

MERCHANTS:
  see also VIRGINIA--COMMISSION
    MERCHANTS
  1700s: 625, 1863
  1800s: 1336, 1350, 1679, 2165,
    2229, 2369
  1800s: 5535
  1810s: 2360, 2633, 5535
  1820s: 2633
  1830s: 1486
  1840s: 1486, 2621
  1850s: 2331, 2992
  1860s: 418, 2331
  1870s: 1587
  1880s: 1587
  Apprenticeship: 3060
  Bedford County: 5055
  Berryville: 3336
  Brunswick County: 4454
  Dinwiddie County: 2567
  Fairfax County: 2233
  Falmouth: 3105
  Fayette County: 4011
  Gholsonville: 4747
  Gordonsville: 4710
  Keysville: 79
  Leesburg: 4446
  Lynchburg: 1594, 2309, 3353
  Norfolk: 3783
  Norwood: 5107
  Oak Forest: 3454
  Paris: 4743
  Petersburg: 3179, 4604
  Pittsylvania County: 2131, 2337
  Pleasant Grove: 2323
  Powhatan County: 619
  Prince Edward Court House: 5282
  Richmond: 3454, 3758, 3809, 5057
  Sperryville: 3619
  Suffolk: 3915, 4472
  Twyman's Store: 4099
  Warrenton: 5382
  White Post: 1436
  Woodstock: 2832
METHODIST CHURCHES: 33
  Camp meetings: see VIRGINIA--CAMP
    MEETINGS--Methodist
  Clergy: see VIRGINIA--CLERGY--
    Methodist
  Religious literature: see
    VIRGINIA--RELIGIOUS LITERATURE--
    Methodist
  Schisms: 4131
  Sermons: see VIRGINIA--SERMONS--
    Methodist
  Virginia Conference: 3646
  Winchester: 4412
METHODIST EPISCOPAL CHURCH: 3497
  Circuits: 3601
  Clergy: see VIRGINIA--CLERGY--
    Methodist Episcopal
  Slavery: 3601
  Suffolk: 3012
METHODIST EPISCOPAL CHURCH, SOUTH:
  5467
  Board of Education: 3646
  Clergy: see VIRGINIA--CLERGY--
    Methodist Episcopal Church, South
  Quarterly conferences: 879
  Sermons: see VIRGINIA--SERMONS--
    Methodist Episcopal Church, South
  Sunday schools: see VIRGINIA--
    SUNDAY SCHOOLS--Methodist
    Episcopal Church, South
MIGRATION FROM: 1920, 2369, 2559
  To Illinois: 3255
  To Kentucky: 558, 3130
  To Missouri: 5392
  To Western States: 5884
MIGRATION TO: 523
  From England: 99
MILITARY SCHOOLS: see VIRGINIA--
  SCHOOLS--Military schools
MILITIA:
  1700s-1800s: 2913, 3362, 4924
  1800s: 872, 4615, 4720, 4852, 5700

VIRGINIA

MILITIA (Continued):
  American Revolution: 3130
  Brigades--16th: 913
  Civil War:
    1st Virginia Militia: 1359
    Amherst County: 5290
    Bedford County: 3788
    Nelson County: 5290
  Commissions (1804): 2986
  Orders: 913, 4743
  Regiments:
    Artillery:
      2nd Elite Corps: 2169
      Monongalia Artillery: 2986
    Cavalry: 330
    Infantry:
      1st: 3255
      5th: 3550
      114th: 3721
  War of 1812: 99
  Subdivided by place:
    Bedford County: 4049
    Petersburg: 2815
    Richmond: 3809
MILLERS' ACCOUNTS: 5157
  Albemarle County: 5302
  Augusta County: 210
  Brunswick County: 4324
  Franklin County: 3100
  Richmond: 5393
  Roanoke County: 1969
MILLWORK INDUSTRY--Woodstock: 1893
MINES AND MINING: 117
  Buckingham County: 3794
MONUMENTS: 5848
  Lexington: 3809
  Photographs: 1424
MORTGAGES--Foreclosure: 3979
MULATTOES:
  Northumberland County: 600
MUNICIPAL GOVERNMENT:
  Fredericksburg: 4855
  Greenway Township: 4668
  Luray: 574
  Richmond: 858
MUNICIPAL GOVERNMENT BY COMMISSION:
  3979
MURDER: see VIRGINIA--SLAVES--Crime--
  Murder
MURDER TRIALS: 2794
NATIONAL GUARD:
  Mexican Border Campaign: 356
NEGRO SERVANTS:
  Behavior: 2612
  Labor contracts: 4616
NEGROES: 1591
  see also the following
    subheadings under VIRGINIA: FREE
    NEGROES; FREEDMEN; MULATTOES;
    SLAVES
  Albemarle County: 3854
  Crime: see VIRGINIA--CRIME--
    Negroes
  Orphanages--Rustburg: 2799
  Religion: 5149
  Suffrage: 1787
NEWSPAPERS: 574, 682, 789, 1939,
  2370
  Editing and publishing: 4341
  Finance: 4020
  Reporters and reporting:
    Richmond: 5720
  Subdivided by place:
    Eastville: 1814
    Lynchburg: 1810
    Page County: 461
    Richmond: 5203
NORTHERNERS IN THE SOUTH: 1697
  Clarke County: 2513
OATS PRODUCTION: 4924
ORPHANAGES:
  see also VIRGINIA--NEGROES--
    Orphanages
  Whosoever Farm: 461, 574

VIRGINIA

ORPHANS: 117
  see also VIRGINIA--GUARDIANSHIP--
    Orphans
OSAGE ORANGE TREES: 33
OVERSEERS: 3362
  Mecklenburg County: 3809
OYSTER-CULTURE:
  Assoteague Island: 1791
PACKET BOATS: 33
PAGEANTS: 2425
PANIC OF 1819: 2369, 2633
PANIC OF 1837: 1512
PANIC OF 1857: 4720
PATENT MEDICINES: 401, 3721
PATRONS OF HUSBANDRY: 1485
PERSONAL DEBT: 2370, 2633, 2668,
  3817, 4157, 4268, 4710, 5107,
  5365, 5366, 5743
  Frederick County: 2954
  Petersburg: 3593
PERSONAL FINANCE:
  see also Personal finance as
    subheading under VIRGINIA--
    (subject), e.g. VIRGINIA--
    WOMEN--Personal finance
  1600s-1800s: 5573
  1700s-1800s: 2363
  1700s-1900s: 824, 3809
  1800s: 33, 476, 858, 2612, 2685,
    3587, 4428, 4616
  Albemarle County: 4384, 4490
  Alexandria: 5380
  Amherst County: 5529
  Charlottesville: 4142, 5786
  Cobham: 958
  Mecklenburg County: 1821
  Port Royal: 940
  Portsmouth: 520
  Richmond: 4038
  Smithfield: 811
  Suffolk: 4470
  Wachapreague: 4403
  Winchester: 4607
PHARMACIES:
  Alexandria: 5016
  Charlottesville: 5301
PHARMACISTS' ACCOUNTS:
  Staunton: 1720
PHILANTHROPY: 4020
  see also VIRGINIA--CHARITIES
PHILOSOPHY: 872
PHYSICIANS: 381, 1279, 1591, 2935
  Negroes: 1384
  Fancy Grove: 5288
  Richmond: 2683
PHYSICIANS' ACCOUNTS:
  1700s: 456
  1800s: 30, 503, 1509, 4776, 5513,
    5742
  1800s-1900s: 574, 4743
  Amherst County: 3788
  Brunswick County: 4324
  Buckingham County: 3794
  "Haywood": 5579
  Lunenburg County: 3846
  Petersburg: 3104, 4112
  Smithfield: 811
PHYSIOLOGY:
  Students' notebooks:
    University of Virginia: 58
PIG IRON--Van Buren Furnace: 5990
PIONEER LIFE: 404, 2881
PLANK ROADS: 2376, 5149
PLANTATION ACCOUNTS: 1354, 2925,
  3642, 4615
  Albemarle County: 3699
  Buckingham County: 3794
  Fairfax County: 2233
  Hanover County: 634
  Mecklenburg County: 3145, 4848
  Nelson County: 3566
  Nottoway County: 5469
  Petersburg: 4555
  "Rock Castle": 4616
  Westmoreland County: 3153, 5577

## VIRGINIA

PLANTATION BUILDINGS:
  Designs and plans: 3566
PLANTATION LIFE: 743
  "Sabine Hall": 918
  Westmoreland County: 917
PLANTATION MANAGEMENT: 743, 2881, 4616
  Prince Edward County: 5884
PLANTATION STORE ACCOUNTS:
  Stafford County: 1813
PLANTATIONS:
  see also the following subheadings under VIRGINIA: AGRICULTURE; CROPS, and names of specific crops; FARMING; TOBACCO PLANTATIONS
  1700s-1800s: 97, 558, 1568, 2633
  1800s: 734, 872, 2935, 3362, 4615, 5377, 5751
  Business affairs: 3145
    Buckingham County: 3794
    Caroline County: 806
    Lunenburg County: 3846
  Subdivided by place:
    Albemarle County: 3699
    Augusta County: 4210
    Battletown: 3200
    Fluvanna County: 195, 1134, 5839
    Glencoe: 5523
    Gloucester County: 3809, 4015
    Goochland County: 32, 5378
    Gravel Hill: 5652
    Hanover County: 456
    Nelson County: 3566
    New Kent County: 1115
    Orange County: 1401
    Petersburg: 3179, 5079
    Pittsylvania County: 2131
    Prince Edward County: 5884
    Prince William County: 2489
    Richmond County: 918
    Smyth County: 5117
    Sweet Briar: 5765
PLASTER (fertilizer): 33, 490, 3560
  Albemarle County: 3699
  Falmouth: 2165
PLASTERING--Quicksburg: 4121
PLOWS:
  Manufacture of:
    Augusta County: 728
  Prices:
    Twyman's Store: 4099
POETRY: 302, 404, 2061, 2559, 2794
  see also VIRGINIA--AMERICAN POETRY; VIRGINIA--POLITICAL POETRY
  Collections: 73, 1757, 4496, 5711
POLICE--Patrick County: 1894
POLITICAL CLUBS: 4720
POLITICAL PATRONAGE: 2700, 3215, 3302, 4206, 5152, 5359
POLITICAL POETRY: 3809
POLITICAL THEORY: 872
POLITICIANS: 5755
POLITICS AND GOVERNMENT:
  see also the following subheadings under VIRGINIA: COUNTY GOVERNMENT; LABOR IN POLITICS; LOCAL ELECTIONS; MUNICIPAL GOVERNMENT
  1600s-1800s: 99
  1700s: 1066
  1700s-1800s: 1401, 1962, 2363, 3362, 4312, 4315, 4616
  1800s: 330, 523, 564, 581, 1075, 1115, 1957, 2141, 2881, 3182, 3721, 3809, 4131, 4490, 4710, 4924, 5513, 5613
  1810s: 872, 3291, 3623, 4531, 4615, 5031
  1820s: 872, 3291, 4531, 4615, 4852, 4880, 5005, 5217, 5904
  1830s: 872, 1384, 3291, 3566, 4531, 4766, 4852, 4880
  1840s: 152, 1384, 3566, 4766, 4852, 4916, 5324

## VIRGINIA

POLITICS AND GOVERNMENT:
  1800s (Continued):
    1850s: 753, 1384, 2370, 3537, 4295, 4616, 4916, 5577
    1860s: 20, 905, 2370, 2531, 2559, 3537, 3674, 3719, 4170, 4206, 4731, 4916, 5397, 5577
    1870s: 20, 1801, 2370, 2559, 3537, 3674, 3833, 4170, 5397, 5507
    1880s: 20, 2794, 3674, 5507
    1890s: 2922
  1800s-1900s: 574, 1364, 1436, 2732
  1900s: 2082
  1910s: 2712, 3104
  1930s: 1429, 3820
  1940s: 3820
  Appointments: 523
  Leadership: 523
POLL TAX: 224, 1194
PONTOON BRIDGES: 4990
POOR:
  see also VIRGINIA--POVERTY
  Education: 4384
POORHOUSES: 2964
POSTAL SERVICE:
  Local offices: 2131
    Hales Ford: 2593
    Suffolk: 5439
    White Post: 1436
POULTRY FARMING:
  Fluvanna County: 5035
POVERTY:
  Northern Virginia: 411
  Powhatan County: 619
PRESBYTERIAN CHURCHES: 743, 1744, 1827, 2120
  Clergy: see VIRGINIA--CLERGY--Presbyterian
  Finance: 5979
  Fund raising: 5979
  Sermons: see VIRGINIA--SERMONS--Presbyterian
  Subdivided by place:
    Lynchburg: 3707
    Winchester: 5979
PRESIDENTIAL ELECTIONS (1856): 569
PRESIDENTIAL PARDONS: 3809
PRICE REGULATION:
  Danville: 4094
PRISONERS AND PRISONS: 872
  see also CIVIL WAR--PRISONERS AND PRISONS
PROMISSORY NOTES:
  Hicks Ford: 5891
PROPERTY EVALUATION:
  Halifax County: 5483
PROPERTY LISTS: 1242
PROTESTANT EPISCOPAL CHURCH: 128, 356, 4173, 4358
  Bishops: 2935, 3456
  Clergy: see VIRGINIA--CLERGY--Protestant Episcopal
  Columbia: 5091
  Fund raising--Leesburg: 1712
PUBLIC BUILDINGS:
  Petersburg: 279
PUBLIC FINANCE: 3623, 4315
  see also VIRGINIA--STATE DEBT
  Chatham: 2732
  Mecklenburg County: 1821
PUBLIC PRAYERS: 1894
PUBLIC SCHOOLS: 2683, 2934, 5378
  Petersburg: 2927
PUBLIC WELFARE: 1429
  Augusta County: 5184
  Mecklenburg County: 1821
PUBLISHERS AND PUBLISHING:
  see also VIRGINIA--AUTHORS AND PUBLISHERS
  Educational materials: 4373
  Marketing: 2673, 3809
  New Market: 2485
RACE RELATIONS: 2773
  see also VIRGINIA--SEGREGATION; VIRGINIA--SLAVE PATROL

## VIRGINIA

RAILROAD STOCKS: 236
RAILROAD TIES: 753
RAILROADS:
  1800s: 4492, 5377, 5513
  1850s: 4852, 5302
  1860s: 546, 1183, 2510, 3205, 3809, 4466
  1870s: 3809
  1800s-1900s: 557, 2517
  Coal shipments: 2908
  Construction: 753, 1624, 5148
    Labor--Food: 753
    Richmond: 4490
  Finance: 236
    Clarksville: 4846
  Lawsuits: 3994
  Stockholders' meetings: 5581
REAL ESTATE: 5148, 5214
  Rent: 117, 3979
  Southampton County: 5248
REAL ESTATE BUSINESS: 2794, 3979
RECONSTRUCTION: 203, 693, 1624, 1787, 3142, 3809, 4206, 4334, 4562, 4924, 5397, 5751
  Economic conditions: 203, 619, 1827, 2559, 3809, 4131, 4698, 5378
  Family life: 2728
RELIGION:
  see also the following subheadings under VIRGINIA: CAMP MEETINGS; CHURCHES, and names of specific denominations; EVANGELISM; LABOR AND RELIGION; NEGROES--Religion; SERMONS; SUNDAY SCHOOLS
  1700s: 99, 917
  1700s-1800s: 2949
  1800s: 523, 872, 1402, 4924, 5075
  1810s: 899
  1820s: 899
  1840s: 152, 2845
  1850s: 1359, 2370, 2845
  1860s: 1359, 2370, 2510
  1870s: 2370
  1890s: 4192
  1800s-1900s: 3142, 5302
  Craigsville: 3826
  Danville: 5773
  Eastern Shore: 1697
  Fluvanna County: 5839
  Halifax County: 3377
  Norfolk: 4968
  Richmond: 682
  Rockbridge County: 3785
  Winchester: 2080
RELIGIOUS ASSEMBLY GROUNDS: 4772
RELIGIOUS LITERATURE:
  Lutheran--New Market: 2485
  Methodist: 879, 5375
RENT:
  see also the following subheadings under VIRGINIA: LANDLORD AND TENANT; LAND--Rental; REAL ESTATE--Rent
  Petersburg: 4555
  Richmond: 3462
RENT COLLECTION:
  Blacksburg: 3039
  Fauquier County: 3819
  Frederick County: 3819
  Luray: 574
  Smithfield: 811
REPUBLICAN (JEFFERSONIAN) PARTY: 404, 5203
REPUBLICAN PARTY:
  1800s:
    1860s: 375
    1870s: 375, 3215
    1880s: 1557, 3215, 4781
    1890s: 1557
  1900s:
    1930s: 3820
  Richmond: 2105
RESORTS: 3229
  see also VIRGINIA--HEALTH RESORTS

VIRGINIA

ROADS: 638, 2376, 5223
  see also the following subheadings
    under VIRGINIA: PLANK ROADS;
    TOLLS--Roads; TURNPIKES
  Construction:
    Mecklenburg County: 1821
  Maintenance and repair: 4124
  Mecklenburg County: 1821
  Photographs: 253
SADDLEMAKING: 1559
SADDLERS' ACCOUNTS: 1509
  Bridgewater: 5854
  Leesburg: 3584
  Port Republic: 5346
SALT AGENTS: 1436
SALT WORKS: 523, 2370, 3959, 4743
  Patrick County: 1410
SAVINGS ACCOUNTS:
  Charlottesville: 4142, 5789
SAWMILLS: 2229
  Roanoke County: 1969
  State Mills: 3679
SAWS--Manufacture: 282
SCHOOL TAXES:
  see also VIRGINIA--FREE NEGROES--
    School taxes
  Mecklenburg County: 1821
SCHOOLS: 330, 743, 872, 2370, 2559,
  2648, 3788
  see also the following subheadings
    under VIRGINIA: EDUCATION;
    PUBLIC SCHOOLS; STUDENTS AND
    STUDENT LIFE; TEACHING
  Girls' schools and academies: 2340
    Bristol: 5267
    Buckingham County: 5652
    Charlottesville:
      Piedmont Female Academy: 490
      Young Ladies' Institute: 4915
    Edge Hill: 1409
    Luray: 461
    Lynchburg: 4373
    Nelson County: 3788
    Richmond:
      Mrs. Mead's School: 5513, 5529
      Richmond Female Institute:
        2068
    Staunton: 5936
      Augusta Female Seminary: 2712
      Virginia Female Institute: 43,
        884, 3832, 5286
    Villeboro: 3293
    Winchester: 287
  Military schools: 641
    see also VIRGINIA MILITARY
      INSTITUTE
  Management and organization: 4280
  Norfolk: 4968
  Tuition: 117
    Girls' schools and academies:
      5369
  Subdivided by place:
    Albemarle County: 5286
    Alexandria: 5210
    Amelia County:
      Clifton Academy: 3809
      Washington Academy: 1894
    Amherst County: 5380
    Appomattox Court House: 5902
    Bedford County:
      Blue Ridge Academy: 1894
      Sunny Side School: 4049
    Belhaven: 1697
    Brownsburg: 3785
    Brunswick County: 2517
    Caroline County: 4698
    Covesville: 1767
    Covington: 3308
    Dayton: 1920
    Edge Hill: 4698
    Fairfax County: 3141
    Farmville: 2712
    Fluvanna County: 558
    Harrisonburg: 899
    Iron Gate: 2922
    Lexington: 3202

VIRGINIA

SCHOOLS:
  Subdivided by place (Continued):
    Mount Maria: 5529
    New London: 3868
    Norwood: 824, 5107
    Nottoway County: 1811
    Orange: 5194
    Orange County: 5286
    Petersburg: 858
    Portsmouth: 4280
    Rapidan Station: 5798
    Richmond: 4698
    Richmond County: 2677
    Taylorsville: 298, 4698
    Winchester: 2559, 5779
    Worsham: 5110
SCOTS: 2633
SCOTS-IRISH: 2120
SCRIP--Iron Furnaces: 2922
SCULPTURE: 4020
SEALS: 3809
SECESSION AND SECESSIONIST
  SENTIMENT: 33, 155, 375, 523, 569,
  872, 907, 2531, 4700, 4748, 4924,
  5476, 5545, 5869, 5946
  Opposition to: 1894, 2728, 5377
SECESSION CONVENTION OF 1861: 523,
  3721
SEED DISTRIBUTION:
  Nottoway County: 5769
SEGREGATION: 1194, 1198
SENATORIAL ELECTIONS (1847): 3255
SERMONS: 630
  Episcopal: 3141
  Methodist: 203, 4412
  Methodist Episcopal Church, South:
    5467
  Presbyterian: 2051, 3142
  Richmond: 3587
SEWING SOCIETIES: 1244
SHIP TIMBER: 1701
SHIPS: 2913
SHIPS' CABLES: 1863
SILVER QUESTION: 5152
SILVERWARE: 4157
SLATE DEPOSITS: 2908
SLAVE PATROL: 33, 5579
SLAVE TRADE:
  1700s: 330
  1700s-1800s: 3069, 4616, 5653
  1800s: 523, 2014, 3200, 3642
  1800s: 1093
  1810s: 29, 1093, 2967
  1820s: 1093
  1830s: 590, 3708
  1840s: 590, 1489, 2363, 4345,
    4720, 5113, 5529
  1850s: 117, 590, 661, 1489, 1801,
    2363, 2943, 4345, 4720, 5286,
    5529
  1860s: 661, 2363, 2955, 2971,
    5529
  Accounts: 2363
    Nelson County: 5700
  Prices: 523, 3642, 3708, 4924,
    5613, 5700
    Madison County: 4794
    Pittsylvania County: 5873
  Subdivided by place:
    Culpeper: 4852
    Patrick County: 1410
    Petersburg: 4492
    Pittsylvania County: 5718
SLAVERY: 152, 693, 872, 1059, 1605,
  1957, 2633, 2967, 3179, 4776, 4924,
  5282, 5302, 5476
  Clarke County: 2513
  Westmoreland County: 917
SLAVES: 33, 43, 558, 1354, 1558, 1568,
  1741, 2131, 2369, 2510, 3068, 5426
  Behavior: 2370, 5523
  Clothing and dress: 4616
  Crime--Murder: 3687, 4131
  Division of ownership: 1627, 1873,
    5765
  Emancipation: 5482

VIRGINIA

SLAVES:
  Emancipation (Continued):
    Westmoreland County: 917
  Executions: 3720, 4131
  Health: 1133, 2925
  Insurrections: 1059, 1115, 2370,
    3720
  Lawsuits over ownership: 2633
  Lists: 5613, 5873
    Madison County: 4794
    Nansemond County: 3012
  Medical treatment: 5229
  Punishment: 4710
  Purchase of freedom: 3642
  Relations with masters: 5332
    Norfolk: 5523
  Taxation--Amherst County: 5529
  Treatment of: 1697, 1813, 3819,
    4616, 5286
  Trials: 1511
  Vital statistics:
    Fluvanna County: 5839
  Weddings: 4490
  Subdivided by place:
    Amherst County: 397
    Smyth County: 5117
SOCIAL AND POLITICAL REFORM: 5486
SOCIAL CONDITIONS: 1005
  Louisa County: 3307
SOCIAL LIFE AND CUSTOMS:
  1600s-1800s: 99
  1700s: 1066, 1813
  1700s-1800s: 1542
  1800s: 128, 404, 806, 1402, 2935,
    3809, 4490, 4698, 4720, 4776,
    5186, 5368, 5493, 5765
  1800s: 1093, 2776
  1810s: 899, 1093, 1943, 2776
  1820s: 1093, 1943
  1830s: 743, 1827, 1943
  1840s: 743, 1605, 1827
  1850s: 743, 1605, 1827, 2370
  1860s: 1605, 2370, 2728, 4170,
    5378, 5426
  1870s: 1591, 2370, 2559, 2728,
    3008, 4170, 5378
  1880s: 1591
  1890s: 1591
  1800s-1900s: 5704
  In poetry (1825): 182
  In small towns: 1137
  Subdivided by place:
    Appomattox Court House: 5902
    Clarke County: 2513
    Craig County: 5347
    Eastern shore: 1697
    Richmond: 682, 872, 3761
    Tidewater: 4924
    Wytheville: 4648
SOCIETY OF FRIENDS: 5504
  Alexandria: 5016
SOIL EROSION: 3642
SONGS AND MUSIC: 2559
  Notebooks: 1045
SONS OF TEMPERANCE:
  Covington Division No. 244: 4953
  Grand Division of Virginia: 5339
  Shockoe Hill Division: 5339
  Worth Division No. 44: 4954
SOUTHERN UNIONISTS: 1402
SPANISH LITERATURE:
  Students' notebooks:
    University of Virginia: 1379
SPINDLES--Manufacture: 282
SPIRITUAL LIFE: 5607
  Catholicism: 3243
SPIRITUALISM: 958
STAGECOACH LINES:
  Business operations: 1797
  Richmond to Staunton: 5839
STATE ASYLUM FOR THE DEAF, DUMB,
  AND BLIND: 872
STATE BONDS--Value: 4589
STATE CAPITOL BUILDING: 3809
STATE DEBT: 693, 2597, 3194
  see also READJUSTER MOVEMENT

983

VIRGINIA

STATES' RIGHTS: 569, 872, 5361
STATIONERY PRICES--Norfolk: 3830
STOCKHOLDERS' MEETINGS:
  Marion: 3513
  Portsmouth Insurance Company: 4282
STOCKS:
  Investments: 2712
  Speculation: 4157
STORAGE OF MERCHANDISE: 2737
STRIKES:
  Telephone workers: 1198
STUDENT SOCIETIES: 1115
STUDENTS AND STUDENT LIFE: 4123, 5227
  see also VIRGINIA--SCHOOLS
  Compositions: 1436
  Parents' letters: 2728, 2974,
    3560, 4616, 5176
  Lynchburg: 1714
  Richmond: 87
  Subdivided by place:
    Caroline County: 4698
    Richmond: 4698
SUFFRAGE: see VIRGINIA--NEGROES--
  Suffrage; VIRGINIA--VOTER
  REGISTRATION
"SUGAR BOILING": 5347
SUGAR GROWING: 4924
SUNDAY SCHOOLS: 3719, 4743
  Methodist Episcopal Church, South:
    5467
SURVEYING: 819, 1485, 4315
  Loudoun County: 2782, 4836
  Montgomery County: 4315
  Nelson County: 3566
  North Carolina boundary: 1687
  Notebooks: 3809
TAILORING: 330
  Guiney's Station: 4589
  Mount Solon: 114
TAILORS' ACCOUNTS:
  Charlottesville: 4049
  Leesburg: 4198
TANNERY ACCOUNTS: 146, 1600, 2942
  Bridgewater: 5854
  Lawrenceville: 3014
  Port Republic: 2977
TANNING: 1559, 2942
  Amherst County: 3788
TAVERN ACCOUNTS: 3365
  Lawrenceville: 3900
TAVERNS AND INNS: 1567, 3042, 3900,
  5149
  Mount Airy: 2131
  Williamsburg: 4220
TAX COLLECTORS: 3721
  Frederick County: 5200
TAX IN KIND: 1181, 1920, 1969
TAX RECEIPTS: 5178
  Buckingham County: 3794
  Goochland County: 32
  Hicks Ford: 5891
  Norfolk: 3830
TAXATION:
  see also the following subheadings
    under VIRGINIA: INCOME TAXES;
    POLL TAX; SCHOOL TAXES;
    SLAVES--Taxation; TOBACCO TAXES
  1700s: 2495, 5031
  1800s: 1920, 4589, 4710
  1860s: 1410
  1890s: 2922
  Assessment:
    Buckingham County: 3794
    Frederick County: 5200
  County taxes: 5700
  Subdivided by place:
    Clarksville: 4848
    Halifax County: 5483
    Mecklenburg County: 1821
    Nelson County: 5484
TAXATION OF PROPERTY: 33, 1920, 5765
  Amherst County: 5529
TEACHERS:
  see also VIRGINIA--GOVERNESSES
  Personal finance: 806
  Private: 2513, 5357

VIRGINIA

TEACHERS (Continued):
  Selection and appointment: 4099
  Social and economic status: 4461
TEACHERS' RECORDS: 2559, 2794, 3587
  Charlottesville: 4915
  Elizabeth City County: 1115
  Luray: 461
TEACHING:
  see also the following subheadings
    under VIRGINIA: EDUCATION;
    GOVERNESSES; SCHOOLS; STUDENTS
    AND STUDENT LIFE
  1700s-1800s: 2925
  1800s:
    1840s: 152
    1850s: 117, 2370
    1860s: 2370
    1870s: 2370, 5378
    1880s: 1920, 3788
    1890s: 3788
  1800s-1900s: 2340, 3783
  Caroline County: 4698
  King and Queen County: 4968
  Louisa County: 3307
  Lynchburg: 3879
  Norfolk: 4968
  Taylorsville: 4698
  Wytheville: 4596
TEMPERANCE: 523, 693, 879, 1115,
  2566, 4710, 5339
  see also VIRGINIA--SONS OF
    TEMPERANCE
TEXTILE INDUSTRY:
  Falmouth: 2165
THEATER BOOKINGS--Richmond: 3829
THEOLOGY: 917
THRESHING MACHINES: 1591, 2680
TOBACCO: 331, 490, 2369, 5355
  Richmond: 187
TOBACCO CULTURE: 99, 2712, 4127,
  5751
  Albemarle County: 3699
  Bedford County: 4049
  Buckingham County: 3794
  Halifax County: 330
  Henry County: 4131
  Nottoway County: 5469
  Patrick County: 4131
  Prince Edward County: 5884
  Spring Garden: 2902
  Westmoreland County: 917
TOBACCO CURING: 363
TOBACCO INDUSTRY: 4043, 4131, 4366
  Advertising: 1586
  Chewing tobacco: 2337
    Petersburg: 3345
  Stocks: 655
  Subdivided by place:
    Danville: 3378, 4918
    Petersburg: 655, 1873, 3179
    Richmond: 2302, 3179, 5251
    Spring Garden: 2902
    Stafford County: 1813
    Winchester: 2142
TOBACCO PLANTATIONS:
  Campbell County: 1059
TOBACCO TAXES: 1568
TOBACCO TRADE:
  1600s: 4297
  1700s: 144, 456, 625, 1556
  1700s-1800s: 28, 1863, 2363, 2633,
    2637, 3179, 5653
  1800s: 138, 564, 1093, 2360, 2381,
    2567, 2680, 4720, 5148
  1900s: 2922
  Finance: 454
  Prices: 558, 1957, 2363, 4924
    Danville: 3378
    Petersburg: 3643
    Richmond: 32, 2305, 2373
  With Brazil: 2363
  Subdivided by place:
    Alexandria: 5228
    Danville: 5958
    Halifax County: 822
    Henry County: 4131

VIRGINIA

TOBACCO TRADE:
  Subdivided by place (Continued):
    Lynchburg: 2302
    Middlesex County: 454
    Nottoway County: 1811
    Patrick County: 4131
    Petersburg: 655, 1336, 2176,
      2302, 3643, 4764
    Pittsylvania County: 1161
    Richmond: 2302, 2373, 5827
    Stafford County: 1813
    Yorktown: 5228
TOBACCO WORKERS: see VIRGINIA--
  WAGES AND SALARIES--Tobacco
  workers
TOLLS--Roads: 2728
TRADE AND COMMERCE: 1066
  see also VIRGINIA--FOREIGN TRADE;
    VIRGINIA--MERCHANTS
  Suffolk: 1838
  With Indians: 625
  Subdivided by product:
    Agricultural products: 404,
      1156, 3145
    Albemarle County: 3699
    Locust Dale: 1073
    Barrels and barrel staves: 5535
    Boots and shoes: 2908
      Augusta County: 728
      Lawrenceville: 2519
    Bricks: 466
    Cattle: 3809, 5377
    Clothing--Richmond: 4210
    Corn:
      Kinsley Mills: 1447
      Petersburg: 2176
    Deer skins: 625
    Fertilizer--Petersburg: 2176
    Fish: 2567
    Flour: 490, 1336, 1556, 2165,
      2600, 2797
      Petersburg: 2176
    Food--White Post: 2274
    Fur: 404
    Groceries: 1115, 1420, 2794
      Lynchburg: 2309
      Petersburg: 2176
      Richmond: 4461
    Hay--Frederick County: 1
    Hemp: 1863
    Hides and leather:
      Lawrenceville: 3014
    Hides and skins: 625
    Horses: 1401, 2637, 4743
    Ice: 4916
    Indigo: 3819
    Iron: 2633
      Augusta County: 728
      Lynchburg: 4720
    Jewelry--Richmond: 4210
    Liquor: 1115, 1863, 2331, 2567
    Livestock--Hanover County: 456
    Lumber: 5535, 5702
    Machinery: 3513
    Naval stores: 5535
    Peas--Suffolk: 1838
    Oats: 1863
    Plows--Augusta County: 728
    Pork--Suffolk: 1838
    Real estate:
      Bedford County: 5055
      Petersburg: 3401
      Richmond: 5594
      Westmoreland County: 5579
    Rice: 3179
    Rum: 5535
    Rye: 2600
    Salt: 404, 523, 1336, 2383
    Shingles: 1512
    Slaves: see VIRGINIA--SLAVE
      TRADE
    Stationery--Danville: 5196
    Staves: 1512
    Textiles: 2165
    Tobacco: see VIRGINIA--TOBACCO
      TRADE

VIRGINIA

TRADE AND COMMERCE:
  Subdivided by product (Continued):
    Wheat: 2165, 2381, 2600, 4616
      Kinsley Mills: 1447
      Petersburg: 2176
    Wholesale:
      Petersburg: 4747
      Richmond: 4747
    Wine: 5535
    Wood: 629, 5377
TRANSPORTATION: 1486, 1512, 3440, 3447
  see also specific modes of transportation under VIRGINIA
  Rates: 2520
TRAVEL:
  see also VIRGINIA--DESCRIPTION AND TRAVEL
  By carriage: 33
  By railroad: 1811
TRAVEL EXPENSES: 1891, 4517
TRESPASS: 1512
TRUSTEESHIP: 5742
  Suffolk: 3012
TURNPIKES: 2593, 2728, 3148, 3680
  Stocks: 4428
  Western Virginia: 4892
TYPE FOUNDRIES--Richmond: 4119
UNITED STATES BUREAU OF REFUGEES, FREEDMEN, AND ABANDONED LANDS: 1366
UNIVERSITIES AND COLLEGES: 661, 743, 1115
  see also BETHANY COLLEGE; BLACKSTONE COLLEGE FOR GIRLS; COLLEGE OF WILLIAM AND MARY; EMORY AND HENRY COLLEGE; HAMPDEN-SYDNEY COLLEGE; HOLLINS COLLEGE; LURAY COLLEGE; LYNCHBURG COLLEGE; OLD POINT COMFORT COLLEGE; PETERSBURG FEMALE COLLEGE; RANDOLPH-MACON COLLEGE; ROANOKE COLLEGE; SWEET BRIAR COLLEGE; UNIVERSITY OF RICHMOND; UNIVERSITY OF VIRGINIA; VIRGINIA COMMONWEALTH UNIVERSITY; VIRGINIA MILITARY INSTITUTE; VIRGINIA POLYTECHNIC INSTITUTE; WASHINGTON AND LEE UNIVERSITY
  Tuition: 1814
VIGILANCE COMMITTEES: 5613
VOTER REGISTRATION: 2566
WAGES AND SALARIES: 244
  Clergy: 117, 5538
    Episcopal: 3141
    Presbyterian: 4428
  Coal miners: 2908, 2922
  In Falmouth: 2165
  Iron workers:
    Van Buren Furnace: 5990
  State officials: 4615
  Tobacco workers: 655
WAGON MAKING:
  Newton: 2023
  Shenandoah County: 2965
  Van Buren Furnace: 5990
WAGONERS' ACCOUNTS: 5827
WAGONS:
  Prices--Newton: 2023
WAR OF 1812: see VIRGINIA--MILITIA--War of 1812; WAR OF 1812
WARRANTS--Columbia: 5035
WATERWAYS--Construction: 4858
WATERWHEELS--Manufacture: 282
WEALTH--Richmond: 5855
WEATHER: 1092, 1133, 1591, 2510, 2949, 4720, 4942, 5476, 5677
  Albemarle County: 3699
  Campbell County: 4043
  Dinwiddie County: 551
  Nelson County: 682, 3566
  Richmond: 4847
  Sperryville: 1618
WEAVING AND SPINNING: 1542
  Cotton: 5575

VIRGINIA

WEDDINGS: 33
  see also VIRGINIA--SLAVES--Weddings
  Alexandria: 5949
  Northern Neck: 3793
  Sperryville: 1618
WESTERN LANDS: 2887
WHEAT: 490, 2369, 5148
  Powhatan County: 2380
  Prices: 363, 558
  Transportation: 2165
WHEAT HARVESTING:
  Albemarle County: 1757
WHEAT PRODUCTION: 33, 4615, 4924
  Albemarle County: 1757, 3699
WHIG PARTY: 4080, 5513
  Greenfield: 5491
WIDOWS: 117
  Personal finance: 5848
WILLS:
  1700s: 2383, 5575
  1700s-1800s: 2949
  1700s-1900s: 3233, 4743
  1800s: 1133, 1624, 1943, 2887, 3806
  1800s-1900s: 3587, 5779
  Bedford County: 4049
  Caroline County: 1022
  Gloucester County: 4924
  Lynchburg: 1350
  Nansemond County: 3012
  Richmond: 5790
  Spotsylvania County: 5004
  Suffolk: 3012
  Sweet Briar: 5765
WOMEN:
  see also VIRGINIA--WIDOWS
  Personal finance: 512
WOMEN IN THE CIVIL WAR:
  Managing a farm: 4259
  Nursing: 2829, 2880
WOOL CARDING: 2165
"WOOL PICKING": 5347
WOOLEN MILLS: 990, 4924, 5377
  Bonsack: 568
  Good Intent: 568, 5297
  Staunton: 5039
YOUNG MEN'S CHRISTIAN ASSOCIATION: 574
ZINC MINING--Stocks: 4157

[End of entries under VIRGINIA]

VIRGINIA (ironclad): 316, 1066, 2085, 5190, 5566, 5741
  see also CIVIL WAR--CAMPAIGNS, BATTLES, AND MILITARY ACTIONS--Naval engagements--Monitor, U.S.S. v. Virginia, C.S.S.
VIRGINIA (no. 2, ironclad): 1181
VIRGINIA: A TRAGEDY AND OTHER POEMS by Marion Foster Gilmore: 2053
VIRGINIA AND TENNESSEE RAILROAD: 3205, 5513
VIRGINIA BAPTIST SEMINARY, Richmond, Virginia: 5251
VIRGINIA BIBLE SOCIETY: 1565
VIRGINIA CHILD LABOR COMMITTEE: 1194
VIRGINIA CITIZENS POLITICAL ACTION COMMITTEE: 5486
VIRGINIA COMMONWEALTH UNIVERSITY, Richmond, Virginia: 5298
VIRGINIA COUNCIL OF CHURCHES: 1194
VIRGINIA COUNCIL OF STATE: 819
"THE VIRGINIA DECLARATION OF INDEPENDENCE" by John Esten Cooke: 1227
VIRGINIA ELECTRIC COMPANY: 2299
VIRGINIA FEDERATION OF TELEPHONE WORKERS: 5486
VIRGINIA FEMALE INSTITUTE, Staunton, Virginia: 43, 884, 5286
  Students and student life: 3832
VIRGINIA FIRST by Lyon Gardiner Tyler: 2400
VIRGINIA FREE PRESS: 1939
VIRGINIA HISTORICAL SOCIETY: 3735, 5696
VIRGINIA IN AMERICAN LITERATURE: 4112

VIRGINIA INSTITUTE FOR YOUNG LADIES, Bristol, Virginia: 5267
VIRGINIA INSTITUTION FOR THE DEAF AND DUMB, Staunton, Virginia: 5298
VIRGINIA JOURNAL OF SCIENCE: 2047
VIRGINIA LAND AND TITLE COMPANY: 3979
VIRGINIA LITERARY FUND: 4384
VIRGINIA MAGAZINE OF HISTORY AND BIOGRAPHY: 722
VIRGINIA-MARYLAND BRIDGE COMPANY: 3148
VIRGINIA MILITARY INSTITUTE, Lexington, Virginia:
  1800s: 4743, 4879, 4924
  1830s: 5839
  1840s: 3809, 5839
  1850s: 3308, 5149
  1860s: 375, 3357, 3440, 3532
  1870s: 3357, 4911
  1800s-1900s: 4244
  Alumni: 2922
  Board of Visitors: 3809
  Faculty: 3586
  Founding: 872
  Relocation to Richmond: 5855
  Students and student life:
    1800s: 3145, 3991
    1850s: 1718
    1860s: 4855
    1870s: 1568
    1880s: 3809
    1890s: 3832
    1800s-1900s: 4029
    Students' notebooks (1840s): 73
    Student's scrapbook (1847-1851): 2911
VIRGINIA POLYTECHNIC INSTITUTE, Blacksburg, Virginia: 3809
  Students and student life: 5790
VIRGINIA SPRINGS, Virginia: 566
VIRGINIA STATE CHAMBER OF COMMERCE: 1198
VIRGINIA STATE INEBRIATES' ASYLUM: 5339
VIRGINIA STATE INDUSTRIAL UNION COUNCIL: 1194
VIRGINIA TRUST COMPANY, TRUSTEE v. VANN-MOORE MILLS COMPANY: 5450
VIRGINIA UNITED LABOR COMMITTEE: 1198
VIRTUES OF WOMANHOOD IN POETRY: 2227
"A VISIT FROM THE JOY RIDERS" by Frank Lebby Stanton: 5029
"VISIT TO SAGAMORE HILL": 4560
VITAL RECORDS:
  Disabled Civil War veterans: 4601
  North Carolina:
    Primitive Baptist church:
      Beaufort County: 3945
    Martin County: 4931
    Ridgeway: 3307
  South Carolina:
    Charleston: 4584
    Presbyterian churches: 4310
VIZETELLY, Frank: 2180, 5850
VIZRI ALI, Nabob of Oudh: 3315
VLANGALY, Aleksandr Georgiyevich: 4486
VOCALISTS: see SINGERS
VOCATION: see OCCUPATION, Choice of
VOCATIONAL REHABILITATION:
  North Carolina: 4736
  United States: 4736
VOGEL, Bonna G.: 5488
VOGEL, Preston S.: 5488
VOICE by Ellen Glasgow: 2062
"A VOICE FROM SOUTH CAROLINA": 5193
VOIGT, Christian Gottlab von: 2079
VOLCANIC ERUPTIONS--Java: 1464
VOLKHOUSKY, Felix: 4576
VOLNEY, New York: 2089
VOLUNTEER, U.S.S.: 5436
VOLUNTOWN, Connecticut: 1205
VOLUSIA COUNTY, Florida:
  Deland: 1653, 4365
VOORHEES, Daniel Wolsey: 1364
VOORHEES, William C.: 5489

VOORHEES INDUSTRIAL SCHOOL,
  Denmark, South Carolina: 5572
VOTER REGISTRATION:
  see also SUFFRAGE; TEST OATHS
  Alabama: 5425
  Australia: 5477
  Great Britain: 4605
    Saint Albans: 4633
  Louisiana: 5425
  North Carolina:
    Cheek's Creek Township: 675
    Fentriss: 2330
    Harnett Township: 3410
    Montgomery County: 4689
    North Calahaln Township: 2749
  Tennessee: 1200
  Texas: 5425
  Virginia: 2566
"A VOYAGE TO GEORGIA, BEGUN THE 15TH
  OF OCTOBER, 1735" by Francis
  Moore: 3733
VOYAGES: see TRANSATLANTIC VOYAGES;
  TRANSPACIFIC VOYAGES; TRAVEL--
  Naval cruises; TRAVEL--Ocean
  voyages
VULCANITE PAVEMENTS: see PAVEMENTS--
  Vulcanite

W

W. A. HOOVER AND COMPANY, New
  Lisbon, Ohio: 5660
W. AND G. T. AUGUSTIN, Lawrenceville,
  Virginia (firm): 240
W. C. POWELL COMPANY, Jacksonville,
  Florida: 4298
W. DELONG'S SCHOOL, Pittsburgh,
  Pennsylvania: 5775
W. DUKE, SONS, AND COMPANY, Durham,
  North Carolina: 1584, 1585, 1586,
  1588, 3762, 4857
W. I. RAMSAY & CO.: 5212
W. J. BINGHAM & SONS' SELECT SCHOOL,
  Oaks, North Carolina: 2940
W. L. HAND MEDICINE COMPANY,
  Charlotte, North Carolina: 4918
W. MOORE (firm): see J. AND W. MOORE
W. R. GRACE AND CO. (New York): 1091
W. S. KEYSER EXPORT COMPANY,
  Pensacola, Florida: 3008
W. T. McDADE AND COMPANY, Eatonton,
  Georgia: 3352
W. TANNAHILL (firm): see R. & W.
  TANNAHILL
WA TRIBE (Burma): 4709
WABASH, Indiana: 4169, 4937
WABASH COUNTY, Indiana:
  Wabash: see WABASH, Indiana
WABASH, U.S.S.: 4404
WACHAPREAGUE, Virginia: 3144
  Mercantile accounts: 4403
WACHSMUTH, John Gottfried: 1615
WACO, Texas: 1592
  see also BAYLOR UNIVERSITY
WADAMS, Mortimer: 4375
WADDEL, Moses: 2006
WADDELL, Alfred Moore: 3972
WADDELL, Charles Edward: 5490
WADDELL, Hugh: 5457
WADDELL, James Pleasant: 5051
WADDELL, John Addison: 5491
WADDELL'S REVOLUTION: see RACE
  RIOTS--North Carolina--Wilmington
WADDEN, A. M.: 5280
WADDEY (EDW. S.), Norfolk, Virginia
  (firm): 2360
WADDY, J. R.: 637
WADDY THOMPSON v. GILBERT
  THOMPSON AND RICHARD I. COXE: 5271
WADE, Edward C.: 5492
WADE, S. C.: 5493
WADESBORO, North Carolina: 1313,
  2984, 3223
  Blacksmithing: 998
  Blacksmiths' accounts: 4906
  Carriage and buggy repair: 1897
  Children of the Confederacy: 227
  Freight and freightage: 4814
  Livery stables: 4814
  Merchants and mercantile accounts:
    222, 4762
  Taverns and inns: 4814
WADESBORO CIRCUIT, Methodist
  churches: 3646
WADHAM COLLEGE: see OXFORD
  UNIVERSITY--Wadham College
WADKINS FAMILY: see WATKINS FAMILY

WADLEY, Thomas Proctor: 2145
WADLEY, William Morrill: 5494
WADLINGTON, Ann (Bauskett): 2961
WADLINGTON, Caroline: 2961
WADLINGTON, Harriet (Sondley): 2961
WADLINGTON, James: 2961
WADLINGTON, Thomas: 2961
WADLINGTON, Thomas, Sr.: 2961
WADLINGTON FAMILY (South Carolina--
  Genealogy): 2961
WADSWORTH, William Henry: 3207
WAGE STABILIZATION BOARD: see UNITED
  STATES--GOVERNMENT AGENCIES AND
  OFFICIALS--Wage Stabilization
  Board
WAGENER, F. W.: 5495
WAGES AND SALARIES:
  Advances: 1759
  Agricultural workers:
    Maryland: 340
    Mississippi: 1786
    North Carolina:
      Montgomery County: 4689
    South Carolina: 2961
  Aides: 3116
  Clergy:
    Baptist--Kentucky: 3199
    Episcopal:
      Virginia: 3141
      West Virginia: 3141
    Presbyterian--Virginia: 4428
    Protestant Episcopal:
      Maryland: 4638
      Subdivided by place:
        South Carolina: 150
        Virginia: 117, 5538
  Clerks--Alabama: 3626
  Coal miners:
    Virginia: 2908, 2922
  Cotton mill workers:
    North Carolina: 5100
  Electricians:
    South Carolina--Columbia: 2767
  Freedmen:
    North Carolina: 832, 5298
    South Carolina: 4649
  Government and civic employees:
    1302
    Washington, D.C.: 2725
  Governmental regulation: 5486
  Hosiery workers: 101
    North Carolina: 4812
  Industrial workers:
    Southern States: 3558
  Iron workers:
    Slaves: 5613
    Virginia--Van Buren Furnace:
      5990
  Judges:
    Great Britain: 4097
    North Carolina: 5768
  Labor: 2170
  Merchant seamen:
    Alabama: 1602
    Great Britain: 4541
  Minimum wage: 325
  Negroes: 2170, 3824, 5975
  Port workers: 4678
  Railroad telegraphers: 3986
    Georgia: 3985
    South Carolina: 3985
  Railroad workers: 3793
  Servants--United States: 2210
  Soldiers: see Pay as subheading
    under names of armies
  State officials--Virginia: 4615
  Teachers: 5043
    Alabama: 3626
    Connecticut: 351
    Illinois: 351
    Indiana: 5149
    Massachusetts: 1344
    North Carolina: 3436, 3538
      Catawba County: 4532
      Granville County: 2833
      Lincolnton: 3210
      Louisburg: 3272

WAGES AND SALARIES:
  Teachers:
    North Carolina (Continued):
      Montgomery County: 4689
      Rockingham County: 4533
    Ohio: 5149
    Pennsylvania: 4106
    South Carolina: 1927
    Texas--Harrisville: 4283
  Textile workers:
    North Carolina: 1611, 5100
      Burlington: 5234
      Durham: 1228
      Greensboro: 5234
      Mecklenburg County: 5235
      Mount Airy: 5048
      Worthville: 3187
    South Carolina: 5236
      Spartanburg: 5233
  Tobacco workers--Virginia: 655
  Typographical workers:
    North Carolina: 2772
    South Carolina: 2771
  World War II: see WORLD WAR II--
    Wages and salaries
  Subdivided by place:
    Great Britain--Bristol: 5731
    Illinois: 1601, 2240
    Indiana: 2240, 5149
    North Carolina: 1120, 1202
    Ohio: 1505, 4732, 5149
    South Carolina--Charleston: 3230
    Tennessee: 1200
    United States: 3066
    Virginia: 224
      Falmouth: 2165
WAGGAMAN, George Augustus: 5433
WAGNALLS CO.: see FUNK AND WAGNALLS
  CO.
WAGNER, Richard: 4486
WAGNER, Robert Ferdinand: 879
WAGNON, G. W.: 5496
WAGNON FAMILY (Louisiana and Texas):
  5496
WAGON MAKING:
  Virginia:
    Newton: 2023
    Shenandoah County: 2965
    Van Buren Furnace: 5990
WAGON TENTS:
  Manufacture in Virginia: 2165
WAGONER, Charles Boyd: 5497
WAGONERS AND WAGONERS' ACCOUNTS:
  Mississippi: 234
  Tennessee: 2814
  Virginia: 5827
WAGONS:
  see also CIVIL WAR--CIVILIAN LIFE--
    Scarcity of wagons
  Prices--Virginia: 2023
  Trade--North Carolina: 4540
WAHHABIS: 5797
WAI CHOW, China: see WAIYEUNG, China
WAILES, Benjamin Leonard Covington:
  5498
WAINWRIGHT, Peter: 1633
WAINWRIGHT, Peter, Jr.: 5499
WAINWRIGHT FAMILY (Great Britain,
  Pennsylvania, Virginia): 5282
WAIT, Samuel: 5457
"WAIT FOR THE WAGON" (song): 5032
"WAITING" (poem): 783
"WAITING AT THE GATE" by William
  Cullen Bryant: 3965
WAIYEUNG, China: 1940
WAKE COUNTY, North Carolina: 1783,
  2090, 2657, 2822, 2916, 2929, 4521
  Democratic Party: 3896
  Justices of the Peace: 2824
  Land: 730
  Land deeds and indentures: 5341
  Legal organizations: 4927
  Maps: 3514
  Mercantile accounts: 3655, 5136
  Revenue stamps: 4009
  Tax receipts: 4009

WAKE COUNTY, North Carolina
(Continued):
  Cities and towns:
    Apex:
      Mercantile accounts: 5803
      Negro schools: 3941
    Cary: 928
    Forestville: 2716, 4294
    Garner: 3660
    Holly Springs: 63
    Neuse: 3863
    New Light: 876
    Raleigh: see RALEIGH, North
      Carolina
    Wake Forest: see WAKE FOREST,
      North Carolina
WAKE COUNTY (N.C.) BAR ASSOCIATION:
  4927
WAKE COUNTY (N.C.) DEMOCRATIC
  EXECUTIVE COMMITTEE: 3896
WAKE FOREST, North Carolina: 2493,
  4298, 4586
  Cotton mills: 4586
  Pharmacies: 2590
  Textile mills: 2877
  Universities and colleges: see
    WAKE FOREST COLLEGE
WAKE FOREST COLLEGE, Wake Forest,
  North Carolina:
  1800s: 484
  1830s: 3415
  1840s: 3727, 5924
  1850s: 1748, 1751, 2857, 4154
  1870s: 2493, 4849
  1800s-1900s: 274
  Relocation to Winston-Salem: 3538
  School of Medicine: 1166
  Students and student life: 1166,
    2338, 2493, 4910, 5218
  Finance: 1166
  Students' notebooks: 1748
WAKE FOREST INSTITUTE, Wake Forest,
  North Carolina: see WAKE FOREST
  COLLEGE
WAKE FOREST UNIVERSITY, Winston-
  Salem, North Carolina: see WAKE
  FOREST COLLEGE--Relocation to
  Winston-Salem
WAKEFIELD TOWNSHIP, North Carolina:
  Retail trade: 4009
WALAU JAU, Nabob: 1629
WALDEN, Herbert Coulstoun Gardner,
  First Baron Burghclere of: see
  BURGHCLERE OF WALDEN, Herbert
  Coulstoun Gardner, First Baron
WALDEN, Philip E.: 5500
WALDEN FAMILY (Louisiana): 5500
WALDHOUR FAMILY: 5986
WALDO, Charles W.: 5501
WALDO COUNTY, Maine:
  Stockton: 4546
  Toddy Pond--Lumber mills: 3554
WALDRON, Harriet: 5502
WALDRON, James Albert: 2449
WALDRON, Laura: 5503
WALES, Virginia: 5044
WALES:
  see also GREAT BRITAIN
  Domestic architecture: 286
  Immigration and emigration: see
    WELSH IN TENNESSEE
  Politics and government: 2245
WALHALLA, South Carolina: 2410
WALKER, _____ (South Carolina
  minister): 1891
WALKER, A. S.: 5505
WALKER, C. Irvine: 3809
WALKER, Caroline: 496
WALKER, Daniel P.: 2814
WALKER, Edward: 5504
WALKER, Elbridge Gerry: 5505
WALKER, Elizabeth M.: 4654
WALKER, Frances: 43
WALKER, George E.: 5506
WALKER, Gilbert Carleton: 5507
WALKER, Helen Mary (McMicking)
  Denman: 4331

WALKER, James A. (Georgia): 5508
WALKER, James W.: 523
WALKER, Jane Francis: 4490
WALKER, Jefferson: 5509
WALKER, John K.: 5510
WALKER, John M. (Virginia?): 4222
WALKER, John Wesley (North
  Carolina): 5511
WALKER, Judith Page: 4490, 5513
WALKER, Leroy Pope: 1084, 4129, 5512
WALKER, Meriwether Lewis: 5513
WALKER, Milton: 5514
WALKER, Molly: 5517
WALKER, Oliphant S.: 5514
WALKER, R. Lewis: 5515
WALKER, Robert John: 2448, 2802,
  5516
WALKER, Sears Cook: 2982
WALKER, Slater T.: 496
WALKER, Thomas (1715-1794): 1512
WALKER, Thomas J. (North Carolina):
  134
WALKER, Thomas L. (Virginia): 5513
WALKER, W. H. C.: 1821
WALKER, William (1824-1860): 617,
  3960, 5480
WALKER, William (Confederate
  soldier): 5510
WALKER, William B. B.: 4127
WALKER, William Henry Talbot: 2433,
  2980, 5517, 5605
WALKER FAMILY (North Carolina--
  Genealogy): 5506
WALKER FAMILY (South Carolina):
  4584, 5514
WALKER FAMILY (Virginia): 5504
WALKER AND ELY (firm): see ELY AND
  WALKER DRY GOODS COMPANY
WALKERTON, Virginia: 3806
WALKUP, Samuel Hoey: 5518
WALL, Elmer William: 5519
WALL, Garret Dorset: 5520
WALL, H. C.: 1186
WALL, Jessie Marion: 3338
WALL, Marion A.: 3338
WALL, Robert D.: 5521
WALLACE, Charles Montriou: 1115
WALLACE, Daniel (1801-1859): 561,
  4834
WALLACE, E. R.: 2721, 5407, 5522
WALLACE, Fanny (Gore): 5525
WALLACE, George T.: 5523
WALLACE, H. N.: 523
WALLACE, Henry Agard: 3558
WALLACE, Jefferson (1823-1864): 1115
WALLACE, Jefferson (b. 1864): 1115
WALLACE, Joyce Wilkinson (Clopton):
  1115
WALLACE, Lewis: 4556, 5524, 5898
WALLACE, Percy Maxwell: 5525
WALLACE, William (fl. 1778-1780):
  5527
WALLACE, William (1768-1843): 5526
WALLACE (WILLIAM) & SONS: 1115
WALLACE, William Andrew: 4188
WALLACE, William Manson, Jr.: 1115
WALLACE FAMILY (Great Britain): 1115
WALLACE FAMILY (Virginia): 1115, 4210
WALLACH, Richard: 5528
WALLACH FAMILY (Washington, D.C.): 5528
WALLER, David Garland: 5529
WALLER, Elizabeth (Tyler): 5397
WALLER, Harcourt Edmund, Jr.: 5530
WALLER FAMILY (Genealogy): 1424
WALLING, Jesse: 2537
WALLINGFORD, Connecticut: 5871
WALLINGFORD, England:
  Social life and customs: 2759
WALLIS, Sarah: 3158
WALLOP, John, Second Earl of
  Portsmouth: 5331
WALNUT COVE, North Carolina: 2800
WALNUT GROVE, Georgia:
  School board: 662
WALNUT GROVE, Virginia: 4312
WALNUT HILL, Arkansas:
  Civil War: 508

WALNUT HILL, Georgia: 3814
WALPOLE, Horatio, First Baron
  Walpole of Wolterton: 5531
WALPOLE, Horatio William, Fourth
  Earl of Orford: 1911
WALPOLE, Kate: 3164
WALPOLE, Robert, First Earl of
  Orford: 5532
WALSH, Edward D.: 5533
WALSH, Nicholas: 1943
WALSH, Robert: 2583
WALSH, Thomas: 2149
WALTER, Eugene: 3797
WALTER, John: 5534
WALTER (WILLIAM) AND COMPANY, Boston,
  Massachusetts: 2933, 5535
WALTERBORO, South Carolina: 4649
  Social life and customs: 2828
WALTHALL, Edward Cary: 5536
WALTON, Edward: 1869
WALTON, Emma: 4898
WALTON, George: 2931, 5537
WALTON, Lucinda (Muse): 1827
WALTON, Lucy Muse (1822-1908): 1827
WALTON, Octavia: 3184
WALTON, Robert: 4235
WALTON, William Claiborne: 1827,
  5538
WALTON FAMILY (Virginia): 1827
WALTON, WHANN AND COMPANY,
  Wilmington, Delaware: 2833
WALTON COUNTY, Florida:
  De Funiak Springs: 1832
WALTON COUNTY, Georgia:
  Walnut Grove: 662
WALWORTH COUNTY, Wisconsin:
  Geneva: 69
"THE WANDERING YOUNG GENTLEWOMAN;
  OR, CAT-SKINS GARLAND": 5615
WANDSWORTH, Surrey, England: 90
WANG, Chengting T.: 5252
WANLEY, Humfrey: 5539
WANNAMAKER, William Hane: 5252
WAPELLA, Illinois: 3732
WAPELLO COUNTY, Iowa:
  Ottumwa: 1984
  Port Richmond: 243
WAR: 1758, 3981, 4020, 4948
  Prevention: 3383
WAR AND RELIGION: see CHURCH AND WAR
WAR BONDS: see CIVIL WAR--WAR BONDS;
  WORLD WAR II--War bonds; and
  Public finance as subheading under
  names of wars
WAR CLAIMS: see Claims as subheading
  under names of armies, navies, and
  wars
WAR CRIMES:
  Trials at Nuremburg: 4927
WAR DEBTS: see WORLD WAR I--War debts
"THE WAR IN ARKANSAS" by J. William
  Demby: 1453
WAR OF 1812: 369, 752, 1401, 1424,
  1637, 2517, 2661, 2808, 2967, 3176,
  3529, 4648, 4912, 5281, 5564, 5839
  see also Militia as subheading
    under names of states; UNITED
    STATES--ARMY--War of 1812;
    UNITED STATES--NAVY--War of 1812
  Bounty lands: 2326
  Georgia: 4654
  Campaigns, battles, and military
    actions: 5298
    Alabama--Mobile: 2781
    Canada:
      Chippewa: 3087
      Lundy's Lane: 3087
      Upper Canada: 1595
    Florida: 1333
    Louisiana:
      New Orleans: 3073
        Anniversaries: 4943
    Maryland:
      Baltimore: 3742
      Chesapeake Bay: 3742
      Fort McHenry: 3742
    Michigan--River Raisin: 3325

WAR OF 1812:
  Campaigns, battles, and military
    actions (Continued):
    New York: 1333
    Ohio--Fort Meigs: 443
    Virginia:
      Alexandria: 1066
      Norfolk: 3169
    Washington, D.C.: 5005
  Causes: 5203
  Economic aspects: 1889
    Kentucky: 5593
    Maryland: 3728
    Virginia: 99
      Cotton and tobacco trade:
        2360
  Fortifications:
    New York--Brooklyn: 1908
    Pennsylvania--Philadelphia:
      2489
  French participation: 1595
  Indian participation: 1595
  Military activities--Virginia:
    2986
  New England disaffection: 2551
  Pensions: 2326
    Widows: 4886
  Poetry: 3325
  Prisoners and prisons: 1360
  Privateers: 2658
  Public opinion: 4531, 5353
    South Carolina: 2636
  General references arranged by
    place:
    Canada: 1599
    Georgia: 1993, 2785
    Michigan: 259
    Virginia: 29, 454, 558, 962
      Norfolk: 4384
    West Virginia: 128
WAR OF JENKINS' EAR: 2155, 5540
  Military strategy: 5540
WAR OF INDEPENDENCE: see AMERICAN
  REVOLUTION; and War of
  Independence as subheading under
  names of countries, e.g.
  GREECE--War of Independence
WAR OF THE PACIFIC:
  Naval operations: 4535
WAR OF THE SPANISH SUCCESSION:
  Naval operations: 3137
WAR PROFITEERING: see Speculation
  and war profiteering as subheading
  under names of wars
WAR RELIEF: see CIVIL WAR--PUBLIC
  WELFARE; WORLD WAR I--War relief
WAR TALKS OF CONFEDERATE VETERANS
  by George S. Bernard: 460
WARBURTON, John: 2148
WARD, Aaron: 685
WARD, Anna Lydia: 2449
WARD, Edward H.: 5541
WARD, Frederick Oldfield: 2632
WARD, George Raphael: 5542
WARD, Giles Frederick, Jr.
  (1845-1865): 5543
WARD, Henry: 5544
WARD, Henry D. A.: 1468
WARD, J. Jackson: 5545
WARD, James: 5542
WARD, Joel: 5549
WARD, John D.: 5546
WARD, John Elliott (1814-1902): 5547
WARD, Joshua: 5548
WARD, Julia: 2676
WARD, Lemuel B.: 5551
WARD, Lewis (d. 1851): 5549
WARD, Mary Genevieve: 5550
WARD, R.: 4032
WARD, Robert De Courcy: 2409
WARD, Samuel B.: 5551
WARD, Shadrach: 5551
WARD, William Hayes: 404, 2449
WARD, Willis W.: 5549
WARD FAMILY (Missouri): 5551
WARD FAMILY (North Carolina): 5549,
  5551

WARD GOLD MINE, Davidson County,
  North Carolina: 2041
WARD SYSTEM OF TAILORING: 4589
WARDELL, Thomas: 2076
WARDEN, Robert Bruce: 5552
WARDENSVILLE, West Virginia: 146
WARDLAW, Andrew Bowie: 1385
WARDLE, Frederick Darlington: 5553
WARDLE, Sir Thomas: 5553
WARD'S STATION, Georgia:
  Civil War: 1276
WARE, Catherine Ann: 5557
WARE, Charles Crossfield: 5554
WARE, Josiah William: 909, 5555
WARE, Nicholas: 5537
WARE, William: 5556
WAREHOUSES:
  Georgia: 4678
  Louisiana--New Orleans: 679
  North Carolina: 5298
WARFARE: see ATOMIC WARFARE;
  BACTERIAL WARFARE; INDIANS OF
  NORTH AMERICA--Warfare; SUBMARINE
  WARFARE
WARFIELD, Catherine Ann (Ware): 5557
WARFORD, A. B.: 3118
WARING, J. J.: 365
WARING, Joseph Fred: 365
WARING, Miss S.: 2045
WARLICK, John C.: 5558
WARM SPRINGS, Virginia: 1094, 1718,
  2878
  Health resorts: 3809
WARMINSTER, Virginia:
  Lumber yards: 3574
WARNER, Charles Dudley: 2449, 2871
WARNER, Sir William Lee-: see
  LEE-WARNER, Sir William
WARRAM, Jesse S.: 5422
WARRANTS (Law):
  Georgia--Savannah: 2262
  Maryland: 4474
  North Carolina: 3221, 4897
    Clarkton: 5909
    Granville County: 2833
  Pennsylvania: 5953
  Virginia--Columbia: 5035
WARREN, Charles C.: 5559
WARREN, E. Willard: 5560
WARREN, Edward (b. 1828): 2458, 5457
WARREN, Edward Jenner (1826-1876):
  5457
WARREN, Eleanor (Clark): 902
WARREN, Fitz-Henry: 5561
WARREN, G. W.: 5562
WARREN, Gouverneur Kemble: 3809
WARREN, James, Jr.: 5563
WARREN, Jane W. (Ray): 104
WARREN, Jared W.: 104
WARREN, John Collins: 365
WARREN, Rose Mae: 3828
WARREN, Sophronia (Stewart): 5560
WARREN COUNTY, Georgia:
  Barnett: 2692
  Camak: 3134
WARREN COUNTY, Mississippi:
  Warrenton: 4796
WARREN COUNTY, New Jersey:
  Belvidere: 4087
WARREN COUNTY, New York:
  Glen Falls: 5560
WARREN COUNTY, North Carolina: 4523,
  5770
  Civil War: 1190
  Mercantile accounts: 4328
  Cities and towns:
    Arcola: 1394
    Macon: 1660
    Macon Depot: 4764
    Manson:
      Farm life: 799
      Mercantile accounts: 5697
    Monroe: 3439
    Ridgeway: 999, 1659, 2435, 3307
      Merchants and mercantile
        accounts: 910, 5614

WARREN COUNTY, North Carolina:
  Cities and towns (Continued):
    Warrenton: see WARRENTON, North
      Carolina
WARREN COUNTY, Ohio:
  Lebanon: 1249
  Shakers: 2601
WARREN COUNTY, Pennsylvania:
  Merchants: 2242
WARREN COUNTY, Virginia:
  Front Royal: 464, 1116, 2162,
    2794, 2797, 5387
  Nineveh: 3680
WARREN, U.S.S.: 3809
WARRENSBURG, Missouri: 1136
  Description: 489
WARRENTON, Mississippi: 4796
WARRENTON, Missouri: see CENTRAL
  WESLEYAN COLLEGE
WARRENTON, North Carolina: 623,
  1166, 2830, 2870, 5211
  Mercantile accounts: 4389
  Schools: 484, 3761, 4571
  Social life and customs: 3761
  Temperance: 2399
  Universities and colleges: see
    WARRENTON FEMALE COLLEGE
WARRENTON, Virginia: 512, 2729,
  3793
  Description: 5193
  Farm accounts: 5210
  Merchants: 5382
  Social life and customs: 5382
WARRENTON DISTRICT, Methodist
  churches: 3646
WARRENTON FEMALE COLLEGE,
  Warrenton, North Carolina: 4154
WARRENTON TEMPERANCE ASSOCIATION,
  Warrenton, North Carolina: 2399
WARRINGTON, Lewis: 99, 3118, 5564
WARRINGTON NAVY YARD, Pensacola,
  Florida: 2963
WARS OF THE VENDÉE (1793-1796): 1598
WARSAW, Poland: 3571
WARTHEN, George W.: 5565
WARTHEN, Thomas J.: 5566
WARTON, Joseph: 828
WARTON, Thomas: 5567
WARWICK, George Guy Greville, Fourth
  Earl of: 1087
WARWICK, William B.: 2792
WARWICK & READ, Lynchburg, Virginia:
  5568
WARWICKSHIRE, England:
  Barford: 200
  Birmingham: see BIRMINGHAM, England
  Kenilworth: 5403
  Ragley Hall: 4750
WASHBURN, Algernon Sydney: 5569
WASHBURN, Amasa C.: 5570
WASHBURN, Cadwallader Colden: 1881,
  4899
WASHBURN, Elizabeth: 2409
WASHBURNE, Elihu Benjamin: 5571
WASHINGTON, Booker Taliaferro: 706,
  4021, 5166, 5572
WASHINGTON, Bushrod: 2577, 2678, 5573
WASHINGTON, Caroline: 1728
WASHINGTON, Charles Augustine: 5574
WASHINGTON, Cynthia B. (Tucker): 5577
WASHINGTON, Edward, Jr.: 5575
WASHINGTON, George (1732-1799): 99,
  175, 1337, 1511, 1512, 3384, 3501,
  3612, 3775, 4014, 4271, 4348,
  4418, 4621, 4864, 5295, 5537,
  5575
  Administration: 2468
  Biographies: 2351
  Bust by Raimondo Trentanvoe: 2352
  Death: 5575
  Estate: 5573
  Inauguration: 4015, 5575
    Centennial celebration: 2096
  Lawsuits: 3069
  Memorials: 5575
  Monuments: 1178, 5584
  Personal finance: 3819

WASHINGTON, George (Continued):
  Statues: 3809
  Visit to North Carolina: 5575
  Visit to South Carolina: 2477
  Will: 5575
WASHINGTON, George Augustine: 5575
WASHINGTON, George Fayette: 5574
WASHINGTON, Henry Augustine: 5577
WASHINGTON, James Henry Russell: 5576
WASHINGTON, Jane (Washington): 5579
WASHINGTON, John Augustine: 5579
WASHINGTON, Lawrence: 5577
WASHINGTON, Littleton Dennis Quinton: 5578
WASHINGTON, Martha (Dandridge) Custis: 99, 4864, 5575
WASHINGTON, Mary: 5575
WASHINGTON, Thomas: 5046
WASHINGTON, Walter E.: 3348
WASHINGTON, William Augustine: 5579
WASHINGTON, William De Hertburn: 5579
WASHINGTON FAMILY: 4014
  Genealogy: 5575
WASHINGTON FAMILY (North Carolina--Genealogy): 730
WASHINGTON FAMILY (Virginia): 99, 404, 3148, 5577
WASHINGTON FAMILY (West Virginia): 3148
WASHINGTON:
  see also WASHINGTON TERRITORY
  Photographs of the Columbia and Kettle rivers: 140
WASHINGTON, Connecticut: 2602
WASHINGTON, D. C.:
  see also UNITED STATES--NATIONAL CAPITAL
  1790s: 2486, 4832
  1700s-1800s: 3150, 5427
  1700s-1900s: 1758, 3424
  1800s: 99, 519, 891, 943, 1243, 1785, 1954, 2085, 2141, 2411, 3022, 3094, 3357, 3612, 4173, 4208, 4266, 4275, 4385, 4613, 5242, 5564, 5578, 5584, 5925
  1800s: 2138, 3455
  1810s: 1360, 3156, 3455, 4246, 4359
  1820s: 350, 1635, 3231, 3455, 4067, 4359, 4779, 4880, 4933
  1830s: 350, 1484, 1635, 1637, 3217, 3231, 3413, 4088, 4252, 4779, 4880, 5886, 5967
  1840s: 1106, 1208, 1484, 1544, 1702, 2904, 2982, 4110, 4252, 4720, 4779, 5214, 5516, 5886, 5978
  1850s: 415, 1208, 1234, 1484, 1544, 1702, 1802, 2527, 2892, 3632, 4091, 5263, 5516, 5744, 5772, 5963
  1860s: 276, 334, 355, 415, 1445, 1519, 1544, 1802, 1874, 1866, 2106, 2125, 2892, 3151, 3283, 3594, 4697, 5028, 5263, 5432, 5744, 5769, 5772, 5869, 5963
  1870s: 256, 355, 415, 1802, 1844, 2125, 4515, 4535, 4686
  1880s: 355, 1803, 2736, 3516, 4686, 5552
  1890s: 779, 2736, 2746, 3840
  1800s-1900s: 83, 1805, 1952, 2847, 2866, 3526, 4018, 4022, 4552, 4564, 4688, 4719, 5152, 5402, 5440, 5447, 5832, 5922
  1900s: 879, 2299
    1900s: 1036, 2234, 2440, 4003, 4073, 4439, 5103
    1910s: 572, 1367, 3096, 3545, 4073, 4475, 5428, 5429, 5878
    1920s: 1155, 1367, 3545
    1930s: 257, 766, 1367, 5316, 5968
    1940s: 371, 2581, 3244, 5170, 5418
    1950s: 2581, 5418
    1960s: 4278

WASHINGTON, D.C. (Continued):
  Advertising:
    Law practice: 5354
    Newspapers: 1161
  Agriculture: 5426
  American Colonization Society: 3038
  Art collecting: 4478
  Balls (Parties): 1728
  Biographies: 42
  Blind: 5426
  Board of Education: 4564
  Boarding houses: 588, 3965
  British embassy in: 3472
  Building stone trade: 5584
  Civil War: 5298
    see also appropriate subheadings under CIVIL WAR; CONFEDERATE STATES OF AMERICA--ARMY; and UNITED STATES--ARMY--Civil War
    Defense: 3264, 5430
    Fortifications: 3778
  Commodity prices: 1024, 4760
  Commonplace books: 3373
  Currency: 1339
  Currency collecting: 4478
  Deaf: 5426
  Debt: 1937
  Description:
    1800s: 404
    1800s: 3041, 3512
    1820s: 2216, 2820
    1830s: 42, 1827, 2216
    1840s: 284, 1697, 1827
    1850s: 486, 1827, 4943, 5149
    1860s: 249, 2308, 4690, 4860, 5738
    1880s: 3221
    1890s: 5608
    1800s-1900s: 5730
    1900s: 3789
    Photographs: 180
  Diseases--Scarlet fever: 3635
  Domestic architecture: 4020
  Drama: 42
  Employment: 5298
  Estate accounts: 3325
  Estates--Administration and settlement: 4478, 5528
  Finance: 3373, 4359
    see also WASHINGTON, D.C.--Personal finance
  Flower trade: 1377
  French embassy in: 1424
  Gossip: 2326
  Hotel registers: 3018
  Household accounts: 1937, 3325
  Journalism: 42
  Kindergartens: 3295
  Land: 849
    Purchases and sales: 3897
  Law practice: 846, 2729, 3442, 3714, 4858
  Lawsuits: 385, 4478, 4494
  Legal affairs: 3714, 4851
  Legal education: see GEORGE WASHINGTON UNIVERSITY--Law Department
  Literary interests: 4020, 4971
  Literature: 42
  Manufacturing: 5426
  Marine Band concerts: 5298
  Medical education: 3788
  Memorial services for President Garfield: 1953
  Mentally ill: 5426
  Mentally retarded: 5426
  Mercantile accounts: 384, 1937
  Merchants: 384, 1920, 3179
  Military parades: 4087
    Grand Review of the Union Army: 4888
  Militia: 846
  Museums: 2494
  Negroes: 1546
  Newspapers: 4524
  Orphans: 5426
  Patent Office: 3343

WASHINGTON, D.C. (Continued):
  Patents: 1690
  Paupers: 5426
  Personal finance: 2184, 3231, 4564
  Poetry: 42, 1118, 3373
  Political patronage: 2589
  Politics and government:
    1700s-1900s: 1946
    1800s: 1734, 2761
    Historical studies: 1848
  Prisoners and prisons: 5426
    Old Capitol Prison: 5646
  Public buildings: 1743, 4732
  Public opinion:
    Assassination of Lincoln: 4652
  Publishers and publishing: 1937, 4494
  Real estate investments: 4478
  Religion: 846
  Satire: 42
  Schools:
    see also WASHINGTON, D.C.--Board of Education
    Girls' schools and academies: 2301
  Social life and customs:
    1800s: 404, 871, 1084
    1810s: 872
    1820s: 872, 1061, 1623
    1830s: 872, 1061, 1623, 5982
    1840s: 1086, 1728, 2326
    1850s: 2960, 3899, 5426
    1860s: 1121, 2960, 3325, 5426, 5528
    1870s: 5426
    1880s: 2161, 3809
    1890s: 3809
    1800s-1900s: 4029, 4606
    1900s: 1424, 4074
    1900s: 2234, 4911, 5298
  Streets: 3281
  Surveying: 3145
  Turnpikes: 5296
  Unitarian churches: 1215
  Universities and colleges: see AMERICAN UNIVERSITY; GEORGE WASHINGTON UNIVERSITY; GEORGETOWN UNIVERSITY; HOWARD UNIVERSITY
  Wages and salaries:
    Government and civic employees: 2725
  Walls: 3145
  Weather: 846
WASHINGTON, Georgia: 51, 844, 1029, 1500, 1667, 3625
  County courts: 2003
  Schools: 5580
    Girls' schools and academies: 5051
  Social life and customs: 1137
WASHINGTON, Michigan: 1229
WASHINGTON, Mississippi: 2609
  see also JEFFERSON COLLEGE
WASHINGTON, North Carolina:
  1700s: 4232
  1700s-1800s: 540
  1800s: 2745, 2902, 3596, 4435, 4658, 4857
  Arithmetic exercise books: 208, 5479
  Banks and banking: 309
  Civil War: see CIVIL WAR--CAMPAIGNS, BATTLES, AND MILITARY ACTIONS--North Carolina--Washington
  Commission merchants: 3827, 4858
  Cotton gins: 3827
  Farming: 705
  Law practice: 692, 4858
  Lumber trade: 2222
  Maritime affairs: 1496
  Mercantile affairs: 652
  Merchants and mercantile accounts: 911, 1493, 3827, 4382, 4571, 4832
  Methodist churches: 3646
  Naval stores trade: 2222

WASHINGTON, North Carolina
  (Continued):
    Oilseed mills: 3827
    Photographs: 4414
    Physicians' accounts: 5195
    Schools: 4858
WASHINGTON, Pennsylvania: see
  WASHINGTON AND JEFFERSON COLLEGE
WASHINGTON, Virginia: 98
WASHINGTON (sloop): 4653, 4946
WASHINGTON (steamship): 3827
WASHINGTON, CINCINNATI AND ST.
  LOUIS RAILROAD: 5581
WASHINGTON ACADEMY, Washington,
  Georgia: 5580
WASHINGTON ACADEMY, Amelia County,
  Virginia: 1894
WASHINGTON AND JEFFERSON COLLEGE,
  Washington, Pennsylvania: 5731
    Students and student life: 5128,
      5194
WASHINGTON AND LEE UNIVERSITY,
  Lexington, Virginia: 2120, 2400,
  3202, 4616, 5149
    Curriculum: 2697
    Students and student life: 1055,
      1250, 3136, 5378
WASHINGTON AQUEDUCT BRIDGE: 5417
WASHINGTON ARMAMENT CONFERENCE:
  5252
WASHINGTON BULLETIN: 5234
WASHINGTON COLLEGE, Lexington,
  Virginia: see WASHINGTON AND
  LEE UNIVERSITY
WASHINGTON COUNTY, Georgia: 2778
  Sandersville: 2598, 5566
WASHINGTON COUNTY, Indiana:
  Fredericksburg: 4588
WASHINGTON COUNTY, Kentucky:
  Springfield: 4987
WASHINGTON COUNTY, Maine:
  Calais: 3813
  Cooper: 654
WASHINGTON COUNTY, Maryland: 1543,
  1932, 3875
    Aircraft companies: 3086
    Banks and banking: 3086
    Circuit courts: 4457
    County government: 3086
    Farming: 2214
    School boards: 3086
    Cities and towns:
      Beaver Creek District: 3329
      Breathedsville: 2225
      Brownsville: 2838
      Brunswick: 1042
      Clearspring: 3004
      Hagerstown: see HAGERSTOWN,
        Maryland
      Hancock: 643
      Leitersburg: 3239, 5142
      Saint James Hall: see COLLEGE
        OF SAINT JAMES
      Sharpsburg: 979, 2217, 4878
      Smithsburg: 5110, 5488
        Evangelical Lutheran Church:
          5343
      Williamsport: 743, 1008, 5160
WASHINGTON COUNTY, Mississippi:
  Farming: 5498
WASHINGTON COUNTY, North Carolina:
  1004, 1015
    Farm accounts: 5013
    Land deeds and indentures: 5013
    Cities and towns:
      Plymouth: 435, 772, 1015
        Civil War: see CIVIL WAR--
          CAMPAIGNS, BATTLES, AND
          MILITARY ACTIONS--North
          Carolina--Plymouth
        Clergy: 255
        Mercantile accounts: 4639
WASHINGTON COUNTY, Ohio:
  Harman: 434
WASHINGTON COUNTY, Pennsylvania:
  East Bethlehem: 3054
WASHINGTON COUNTY, Tennessee:
  Land deeds and indentures: 718

WASHINGTON COUNTY, Texas:
  Chappell Hill: 131
WASHINGTON COUNTY, Virginia:
  Social conditions: 4049
    Cities and towns:
      Abingdon: 872, 1836, 2881, 3031
      Walnut Grove: 4312
WASHINGTON DISTRICT, Methodist
  churches: 3646
WASHINGTON FEMALE SEMINARY,
  Washington, Georgia: 5051
WASHINGTON HOME, Chicago, Illinois
  (hospital): 4105
WASHINGTON INSTITUTE TEMPERANCE
  ASSOCIATION, Harris' Depot, North
  Carolina: 5582
WASHINGTON MADDUX AND ASA GEORGE
  BARNES, INC.(firm): 3454
WASHINGTON MINING COMPANY, Davidson
  County, North Carolina: 5583
WASHINGTON NATIONAL MONUMENT
  SOCIETY, Washington, D.C.: 1778,
  5584
    Contributions: 4892
WASHINGTON PARK, North Carolina:
  4858
WASHINGTON PARISH, Louisiana: 5585
WASHINGTON PARISH (La.) AGRICULTURAL
  CLUB: 5585
WASHINGTON (D.C.) POST: 958, 4751
WASHINGTON (Ga.) POST: 2374
WASHINGTON REPUBLICAN: 42
WASHINGTON STATION, Methodist
  churches: 3646
WASHINGTON TERRITORY: 5905
  see also WASHINGTON
  Description and travel: 57, 5018
  Economic conditions: 57
  Land settlement: 5018
  Public schools: 5018
  Religion: 57
  States' rights (opinion): 5033
WASHINGTON TOWNSHIP, Pennsylvania:
  Law enforcement: 1130
WASHINGTON UNIVERSITY, Saint Louis,
  Missouri: 2386
    School of Medicine: 4886
WASHTENAW COUNTY, Michigan:
  Ann Arbor: 4652, 5489
  see also UNIVERSITY OF MICHIGAN
  Clothing and dress: 3221
WATAUGA COUNTY, North Carolina:
  Boone: 1259
  Shulls Mills: 3176
  Sugar Grove: 19
WATCHES: see CLOCKS AND WATCHES
WATCHWORDS: see CONFEDERATE STATES
  OF AMERICA--NAVY--Passwords
WATCHMAN OF THE SOUTH (periodical):
  4240
WATER POWER:
  Development on the Schuylkill
    River: 5686
WATER PRICES:
  Western States: 4353
WATER PUMPS:
  Marketing in Maryland: 3765
WATER RIGHTS:
  Massachusetts: 2468
  North Carolina: 5100
WATER TRANSPORTATION IN NATIONAL
  DEFENSE STRATEGY:
    World War I: 4858
WATERCOLORS--Florida: 5678
WATERFORD, Connecticut: 1205
WATERFORD, Ireland: 3883
  Elections: 3468
WATERFORD, New York: 814
WATERFORD, Virginia: 5782
WATERING PLACES: see HEALTH RESORTS
WATERLOO MILLS, Virginia: 12
WATERS, Benjamin, Jr.: 5586
WATERS, Marguerite: 902, 5360
WATERS FAMILY: 902
WATERSTRAAT, F.: 111
WATERTOWN, New York: 3192
WATERWAYS:
  see also CANALS; RIVERS

WATERWAYS (Continued):
  Construction:
    North Carolina: 4858
    Virginia: 4858
  Military: 3145
  United States: 4858
WATERWHEELS:
  Manufacture in Virginia: 282
WATERWORKS:
  New Jersey--Jersey City: 5546
  New York--New York: 5546
  Virginia--Lynchburg: 5513
WATKIN, Sir Edward William: 4568
WATKINS, Benjamin: 5587
WATKINS, David: 2908
WATKINS, Howell D.: 2908
WATKINS, Judith: 761
WATKINS, Kate M.: 5588
WATKINS, William Henry: 5589
WATKINS FAMILY: 1752
WATKINS, New York: 1907
WATKINSVILLE, Georgia: 1621
WATLINGTON, Mary Catherine: 4506
WATSON, Alfred Augustine: 5457
WATSON, Arnold Petrie: 5590
WATSON, Charles S.: 5591
WATSON, D. M.: 5592
WATSON, F. B.: 5595
WATSON, G. B.: 3301
WATSON, Henry, Sr.: 5593
WATSON, Henry, Jr. (1810-1888): 5593
WATSON, Henry Brereton Marriott:
  2146
WATSON, John (d. 1824): 5593
WATSON, John Fanning (1779-1860):
  5667
WATSON, John William Clark: 872
WATSON, Joseph W.: 3646
WATSON, Richard: 4146
WATSON, Robert L.: 3179
WATSON, Robert Spence: 1910
WATSON, Sereno: 5593
WATSON, Sophia (Peck): 5593
WATSON, Thomas Edward (1856-1922):
  2449, 4048, 5594
WATSON, Thomas G. (Virginia): 5595
WATSON, Wilbur: 5595
WATSON, William: 5593
WATSON, William (South Carolina):
  4834
WATSON-WENTWORTH, Charles, Second
  Marquis of Rockingham: 92
WATSON FAMILY: 3301
  Genealogy: 5593
WATT, R. L.: 5252
WATTERSON, Henry: 1364
WATTS, Charles: 3788
WATTS, Elizah: 5599
WATTS, Fielding: 5596
WATTS, George Washington: 3762, 5597
WATTS, Gerard: 3762
WATTS, Isaac (1674-1748): 5598
WATTS, Isaac Harrison: 1998
WATTS, James: 5599
WATTS, Thomas Hill: 1403
WATTS, W. W.: 5600
WATTS FAMILY (North Carolina): 5596
WATTS FAMILY (South Carolina--
  Genealogy): 300
WATTS-DUNTON, Walter Theodore: 5226
WATTS HOSPITAL, Durham, North
  Carolina: 2934, 5601
WAUCHOPE, George Armstrong: 1385,
  2449
WAUGH, William P.: 1800
WAUL, Thomas Neville: 5602
"WAVERLY," Frederick County,
  Virginia: 5779
WAX TRADE: 323
WAXAHACHIE, Texas:
  Law practice: 817
WAY, Joseph Howell: 5603
WAY-BILLS--Maryland: 1008
WAYNE, Anthony (1745-1796): 413,
  3536, 5078, 5604
WAYNE, Arthur Trezevant: 4453
WAYNE, Clifford: 5606
WAYNE, Henrietta Jane (Harden): 2326

WAYNE, Henry Constantine: 5605
WAYNE, James Moore: 2326, 5606
WAYNE, New York: 4680
WAYNE, Pennsylvania: 4663
WAYNE COUNTY, Georgia:
   Doctor Town: 1990
WAYNE COUNTY, Iowa--Farming: 4075
WAYNE COUNTY, Michigan:
   Spring Wells: 4411
WAYNE COUNTY, New York:
   Macedon: 1977
WAYNE COUNTY, North Carolina: 1280
   Land deeds and indentures: 4421
   <u>Cities</u> <u>and</u> <u>towns</u>:
      Fremont: 4704
      Goldsboro: <u>see</u> GOLDSBORO, North
         Carolina
      Mount Olive: 5756
      Union Mills: 3237
WAYNE COUNTY, Ohio: 3027
   Orrville: 4728
   Wooster: 3103
WAYNE COUNTY, Tennessee:
   Waynesboro: 771
WAYNESBORO, Pennsylvania: 469
WAYNESBORO, Tennessee: 771
WAYNESBORO, Virginia: <u>see</u> CIVIL
   WAR--CAMPAIGNS, BATTLES, AND
   MILITARY ACTIONS--Virginia--
   Waynesboro
WAYNESVILLE, North Carolina: 1649,
   2548, 5258, 5603
   Prisoners and prisons: 641
WAYNMANVILLE, Georgia: 2272
WEADON, Carrie: 5607
WEALTH: 4391
   Virginia--Richmond: 5855
WEAPONS TRADE BETWEEN FOREIGN
   POWERS: <u>see</u> UNITED STATES--
   ARMS TRADE--France
WEASON, G.: 3130
WEASTON, Israel H.: 5608
WEATHER:
   <u>see also</u> DROUGHTS; HURRICANES;
     LIGHTNING; SNOW; STORMS
   Alabama: 2663
   Bermuda Islands: 5500
   Brazil: 4876
   California: 4353
   China: 5225
   Connecticut: 5261
   Florida: 1947
   France: 4348
   Georgia:
      Putnam County: 5760
      Savannah: 2785, 4687
   India: 2756
   Indochina: 5225
   Kentucky--Lexington: 3325
   Maryland: 3254, 4712
   Mississippi: 2663
      Rodney: 3322
   Missouri: 2663
   New York--West Park: 4073
   North Carolina: 1773, 1871, 1934,
     2357, 2549, 2663, 3436, 5664,
     5774, 5991
      Asheville: 4834
      Cumberland County: 3812
      Flint Rock: 5890
      Fort Fisher: 3370
      Iredell County: 4310, 5245
      Orange County: 3351
   Oceanic: 2259, 4017
   Ohio: 2949
      North Hampton: 1618
   South Carolina: 1923, 5991
      Camden: 5675
      Charleston: 4584
      Lancaster County: 4310
      Society Hill: 2762
   Southern States: 941, 1183, 2427,
     3648, 4565, 5261
   Tennessee: 2661
      Wayne County: 771
   Texas: 4353
   Virginia: 1092, 1133, 1591, 2510,
     2949, 4720, 4942, 5476, 5677

WEATHER:
   Virginia (Continued):
      Albemarle County: 3699
      Campbell County: 4043
      Dinwiddie County: 551
      Nelson County: 682, 3566
      Richmond: 4847
      Sperryville: 1618
      Washington, D.C.: 846
   West Virginia:
      Martinsburg: 5456
   Western States: 4353
WEATHER STATIONS:
   North Carolina--Mount Mitchell:
     1001
WEATHERLY, Frederic Edward: 5609
WEATHERN, William Harrison: 5610
WEAVER, George: 1436
WEAVER, Greenbury W.: 1436, 5611
WEAVER, Philip J.: 5612
WEAVER, William: 5613
WEAVERVILLE, North Carolina: 833
WEAVING AND SPINNING:
   Cotton--Virginia: 5575
   Patterns: 5651
   South Carolina: 4347
   Virginia: 1542
   Wool--North Carolina: 5658
WEBB (A. S.) AND COMPANY, Ridgeway,
   North Carolina: 5614
WEBB, Beatrice (Potter): 1815
WEBB, D. C.: 5617
WEBB, Edwin Yates: 5457
WEBB, James (Virginia attorney):
   4616, 5630
WEBB, James W. (English professor):
   1771
WEBB, John F.: 2778
WEBB, Mary: 5615
WEBB, Robert Dickens: 5620
WEBB, Sidney James, First Baron
   Passfield: 5616
WEBB, Thomas L.: 5617
WEBB, William S.: 5618
WEBB, Willington E.: 5619
WEBB, Mrs. Willington E.: 5619
WEBB FAMILY (Genealogy): 5389
WEBB FAMILY (North Carolina): 5620
THE WEBB FAMILY compiled by Dr.
   Robert Dickens Webb: 5620
WEBB COUNTY, Texas:
   Laredo: 3597
WEBBE, Josiah: 5639
WEBBER, Charles C.: 1194, 1201
WEBBER, Thomas B.: 5621
WEBER, John Langdon: 2449
WEBER, William Lander: 2449
WEBSTER, Daniel: 566, 872, 1308,
   3118, 3483, 4486, 4880, 4897,
   5546, 5622, 5940
   Speeches: 284, 3191
   Visit to Savannah: 2460
WEBSTER, E. W.: 5623
WEBSTER, Horace: 1796, 4067
WEBSTER, James Claude: 2148
WEBSTER, Lesey Jane: 4269
WEBSTER, Sarah M.: 5623
WEBSTER COUNTY, Iowa:
   Fort Dodge: 1533
WEBSTER COUNTY, Kentucky: 1604
WEBSTER COUNTY, West Virginia: 5194
WEBSTER GROVES, Missouri: 1097, 1424
WEBSTER-ASHBURTON TREATY: 1632
WEBSTER-HAYNE DEBATE: 730
WEDDERBURN, Alexander, First Baron
   Loughborough and First Earl of
   Rosslyn: 4420
WEDDING ANNIVERSARIES--Golden: 5085
WEDDINGS:
   <u>see also</u> ELOPEMENTS; HONEYMOONS;
     SLAVES--Weddings; and Royal
     family--Weddings as subheading
     under names of specific countries
   Great Britain: 4230
   Kentucky: 571
   Maryland--Baltimore: 1747
   Mississippi: 3076, 3611

WEDDINGS (Continued):
   North Carolina:
      Clarksville: 4849
      Raleigh: 274
      Wilmington: 3607
   Ohio--North Hampton: 1618
   Quaker ceremony: 5059
   South Carolina: 4823, 5193
      Charleston: 686
   Virginia: 33
      Alexandria: 5949
      Northern Neck: 3793
      Sperryville: 1618
WEDGWOOD, Henry Allen: 5624
WEDGWOOD, Josiah Clement, First
   Baron Wedgwood: 5625
WEDOWEE, Alabama: 5053
WEED, Theodore H.: 5626
WEED, Thurlow: 4486, 5561, 5627
WEEDON, George: 3627
WEEHAWKEN, U.S.S.: <u>see</u> CIVIL WAR--
   CAMPAIGNS, BATTLES, AND MILITARY
   ACTIONS--Naval engagements--
   Weehawken, U.S.S. v. Atlanta,
   C.S.S.
WEEKLY HERALD, Richmond, Virginia:
   789
WEEKLY INFORMATION BULLETINS: 238
WEEKLY NEWS: 2357
WEEKLY NEWSLETTER, Pretoria, South
   Africa: 4960
WEEKLY WASHINGTON (D.C.) UNION: 1161
WEEKS, A. P.: 5628
WEEKS, John Thomas: 5629
WEEKS, Stephen Beauregard: 22
WEEMS, Frances (Ewell): 5630
WEEMS, Mason Locke: 5630
WEIGHTS AND MEASURES:
   <u>see also</u> SCALES
   French: 2973
   Latin: 2973
   Tables: 3753
WEIS, John: 2711
WEISEL, Philip: 3957
WEISIGER, David Addison: 5631
WEISS, _____ (German theologian):
   2592
WEISS, William W.: 1202
WEIZÄCKER, _____ (German theologian):
   2592
WELBORN, H. Rufus: 5632
WELBORN, Joel Romulus: 5632
WELBORNE, J. W.: 1014
WELCH, Amanda E. (Ferrebee): 1784
WELCH, Elliott Stephen: 5633
WELCH, R. H.: 5634
WELCH, William Hawkins: 5633
WELCOME RETURN (sloop): 4946
WELDON, North Carolina: 288, 4204
   Mercantile accounts: 1055
WELDON BRIDGE (Roanoke River): 4492
WELDON RAILROAD (North Carolina):
   5664
WELLER, George: 5635
WELLES, Charles F.: 4188
WELLES, Gideon: 872, 2085, 3192,
   3833, 5636
WELLESLEY, Arthur, First Duke of
   Wellington: 1911, 2836, 3598,
   4024, 5637, 5639, 5797
WELLESLEY, Henry, First Baron Cowley:
   5637, 5639
WELLESLEY, Henry, Richard Charles,
   First Earl Cowley: 5638
WELLESLEY, Henry Robert Edward: 2756
WELLESLEY, Magdalen Montagu, Duchess
   of Wellington: 5637
WELLESLEY, Olivia Cecilia
   Fitzgerald de Ros, Countess
   Cowley: 5638
WELLESLEY, Richard: 5639
WELLESLEY, Richard Colley, First
   Marquis Wellesley and Second Earl
   of Mornington: 4024, 5639
WELLESLEY, William Pole-Tylney-Long:
   5639

WELLESLEY, Massachusetts: see
    WELLESLEY COLLEGE
WELLESLEY COLLEGE, Wellesley,
    Massachusetts: 2269, 4732
    Students and student life: 2269,
        3741
WELLFORD, Beverly Randolph, Jr.:
    4924
WELLING, James Clarke: 5640
WELLINGTON, Arthur Wellesley, First
    Duke of: 1911, 2836, 3598, 4024,
    5637, 5639, 5797
WELLINGTON, Magdalen Montagu
    Wellesley, Duchess of: 5637
"WELLINGTON," Jefferson County, West
    Virginia: 5574
WELLS, Carolyn: 103
WELLS, Henry Horatio: 5092
WELLS, Herbert George: 4798
WELLS, John Miller: 5014
WELLS, L. R.: 5641
WELLS, Mary Ada (Billard): 5642
WELLS, Thomas Tileston: 4392
WELLS, Somersetshire, England: 1071
WELLS:
    Construction:
        Great Britain--Kent: 5330
        Southwest United States: 3248
WELLSBURG, Virginia: see BETHANY
    COLLEGE
WELSH IN TENNESSEE: 5224
WELSH NECK BAPTIST CHURCH, Society
    Hill, South Carolina: 4392
WELSH RUN, Pennsylvania: 1579
WELSHAUS, Isabella: 4769
WELTY, Eudora: 902, 2282
WEMBLE, G. S.: 2983
WEMYSS, Francis Charteris-, Baron
    Elcho: 5643
WENHAM, Massachusetts: 3917
WENTWORTH, Charles Watson-, Second
    Marquis of Rockingham: see
    WATSON-WENTWORTH, Charles, Second
    Marquis of Rockingham
WENTWORTH, North Carolina: 4366,
    4424
WENZEL, Clemens Lothar, Fürst von
    Metternich-Winneburg: 3630, 3887
WEOBLEY, England: 5330
WEREAT, John: 3209, 5644
WESCOAT, Artha Brailsford: 5645
WESCOAT, Joseph Julius: 5646
WESCOAT FAMILY (South Carolina--
    Genealogy): 5646
WESLEY, Charles: 3646, 4146, 5647
WESLEY, John: 1070, 1317, 1738,
    3738, 4029, 4146, 5095, 5255,
    5647
WESLEY, Sarah: 4146
WESLEY FAMILY (Great Britain): 5647
WESLEY, Pennsylvania:
    Blacksmiths' accounts: 4841
WESLEY FOUNDATION, Methodist
    churches: 5022
WESLEYAN COLLEGE, Macon, Georgia:
    5246
    Teachers' records: 2272
WESLEYAN FEMALE COLLEGE, Macon,
    Georgia: see WESLEYAN COLLEGE
WESLEYAN METHODIST CHURCHES:
    see also CLERGY--Wesleyan
        Methodist; SERMONS--Wesleyan
        Methodist
    Great Britain: 1070, 5255
WESLEYAN MISSIONARY SOCIETY: 763
WESLEYAN MOVEMENT: 4146
WESSON, James J.: 5648
WESSON, W. M.: 4747
WESSON (firm): see SEWARD & WESSON
WEST, A.: 5129
WEST, Ben: 5651
WEST, Buddy: 5651
WEST, Charles S.: 4902
WEST, Edwin S.: 5649
WEST, Francis J.: 5650
WEST, George W.: 5651
WEST, H. R.: 3495
WEST, John: 5575

WEST, John R.: 5651
WEST, John Sidney: 5652
WEST, Josephine: 5651
WEST, Junius Edgar: 5779
WEST, Polly: 4517
WEST, Susan (Tillinghast): 5298
WEST, Thomas: 5653
WEST, V. T.: 4220
WEST, Victoria Mary Sackville-: see
    SACKVILLE-WEST, Victoria Mary
WEST, William H.: 3784
WEST FAMILY (Virginia--Genealogy):
    1842
THE WEST: see WESTERN STATES
WEST ACTON, Massachusetts: 2456
WEST BATON ROUGE, Louisiana: 1179
WEST BRANCH, Iowa: 2644
WEST BUFFALO, Iowa: 4070
WEST CANDOR, New York: 2204
WEST CHESTER AND PHILADELPHIA
    RAILROAD COMPANY: 5083
WEST DAVIE CIRCUIT, Methodist
    churches: 3646
WEST END LIBERAL CLUB, London,
    England: 944
WEST FELTON, England: 1551, 1552
WEST INDIES:
    see also BRITISH WEST INDIES;
        FRENCH WEST INDIES
    British administration: 4618
    Clergy--Church of England: 5725
    Commodity prices: 3753
    Description and travel: 4013
    Foreign trade: 2403
        Great Britain: 4541, 5139
        New England: 172
        North Carolina: 2222
        United States: 1481
    Harbors: 3753
    Insurrections: 4618
    Lumber trade: 1492
    Maps: 3753
    Merchants: 1493
    Rum trade: 2222
    Slavery: 5726
    Spanish activities in: 92
    United States naval operations:
        841
WEST INDIES CONFERENCE (1944): 2398
WEST MARKET STREET METHODIST
    EPISCOPAL CHURCH, Greensboro,
    North Carolina: 5022
WEST MILFORD, Virginia: 5946
WEST PALM BEACH, Florida:
    Postal unions: 3
WEST PARK, New York: 783
    Weather: 4073
    Wildlife: 4073
WEST POINT, Iowa: see DES MOINES
    COLLEGE
WEST POINT, New York: see UNITED
    STATES MILITARY ACADEMY
WEST POINT, Virginia:
    Pulp and paper industry: 1852
WEST RIVER, Maryland: 2267
    Business and household accounts:
        4219
WEST SPRINGFIELD, Massachusetts:
    5042
WEST TENNESSEE COLLEGE, Jacksonville,
    Tennessee: 872
WEST VIRGINIA:
    see also MIDDLE ATLANTIC STATES;
        SOUTHERN STATES; VIRGINIA
    Agricultural organizations:
        Berkeley County: 3832
    Agricultural products--Prices:
        1784
    Agricultural workers:
        Grant County: 767
    Agriculture: 43
        see also the following
            subheadings under WEST
            VIRGINIA: Farming; Plantations;
            and names of specific crops
        Berkeley Springs: 3141
        Hedgesville: 3141
    American poetry: 2342

WEST VIRGINIA (Continued):
    Armories--Harpers Ferry: 2696
    Autographs: 1946, 2301
    Banks and banking: 4892
        Martinsburg: 307
        Romney: 312
    Baptist churches:
        Church buildings: 1769
        Revivals: 4774
        Sunday schools: see WEST
            VIRGINIA--Sunday schools--
            Baptist
    Blacksmiths' accounts:
        Jefferson County: 4388
    Building construction: 2397
    Business affairs:
        Jefferson County: 5265
    Citizenship qualifications: 1828
    Civil engineering: 5456
    Civil War: see appropriate
        subheadings under CIVIL WAR;
        CONFEDERATE STATES OF AMERICA;
        and UNITED STATES--ARMY--Civil
        War
    Clergy:
        Episcopal: 3141
        Methodist Episcopal Church,
            South: 5467
    Clothing and dress: 4904
    Coal: 3005
    Coal mines--Kanawha Valley: 4924
    Commodity prices: 2678
    Congressional elections (1894):
        2016
    Constitutional Convention of 1872:
        1769
    Courts: 1946, 3058, 5194
        Summonses: 1129, 2711
        Jefferson County: 4892
    Courtship: 5689
    Death: 1770
    Debt, Settlement of:
        Martinsburg: 5037
    Democratic Party: 1828
        Berkeley County: 4732
        Martinsburg: 3832
    Description and travel: 43
        Packet boat on the Kanawha
            River: 2890
    Diseases:
        Smallpox:
            Wheeling: 2678
    Dry goods: 489
    Economic conditions: 5689
        see also WEST VIRGINIA--Panic
            of 1873
        Berkeley Springs: 3141
        Hedgesville: 3141
    Education: 404
        see also the following
            subheadings under WEST
            VIRGINIA: Public schools;
            Schools; Teaching
        Laws and legislation: 4732
        Women: 4703
    Elections (1800s): 1828, 2016
        see also WEST VIRGINIA--
            Congressional elections
    Episcopal churches: 3141
    Estates:
        Administration and settlement:
            1700s-1800s: 2397
            1700s-1900s: 865, 1946
            1800s: 2389, 2711, 3010, 5194
            1800s-1900s: 2342
            Martinsburg: 5110
            Shepherdstown: 4598
    Evangelism: 5689
        see also WEST VIRGINIA--Baptist
            churches--Revivals
    Family life:
        Meddleway: 1730
    Farm accounts:
        Falling Waters: 4999
        Grant County: 767
    Farming: 581, 865, 1946

WEST VIRGINIA:
  Farming (Continued):
    see also the following
      subheadings under WEST
      VIRGINIA: Agriculture;
      Plantations; and names of
      specific crops
    Jefferson County: 4388, 5591
  Finance: 356
    see also WEST VIRGINIA--Personal
      finance
  Flood relief--Harpers Ferry: 5938
  Flour mills: 1946
    see also WEST VIRGINIA--Millers'
      accounts
    Hannisville: 2316
    Harpers Ferry: 5938
    Martinsburg: 3832
  Folklore: 5550
  Freight and freightage: 4703
  Fugitive slaves: 52, 1946
  Government agencies and officials:
    District attorneys: 1828
    Governors:
      Francis Harrison Pierpont
        (1861-1868): 5775
    Sheriffs:
      Jefferson County: 3832
  Grain elevators: 5239
  Grand Army of the Republic: 1828
  Greenback Labor Party: 1828
  Hats:
    Manufacture in Martinsburg: 5110
  Health resorts: 1478
  Hiring of slaves: 5574
  Historical studies:
    Berkeley County: 1946
  Homesickness: 5371
  Horses--Breeding: 4774
  Hotel management:
    Martinsburg: 3832
  Household accounts: 4703
    Hedgesville: 159
    Martinsburg: 1828
    Wood County: 5194
  Household management: 4703
  Independent Order of Odd Fellows:
    4892
  Insurance--Life: 2130
  Justices of the peace: 1318, 3010
  Labor conditions: 4029
  Land: 4348
    Lawsuits: 5194
      Wheeling: 3587
    Purchases and sales: 794, 1946,
      2273
      Jefferson County: 5591
    Rental: 2342
  Land claims:
    Berkeley County: 5037
    Webster County: 5194
  Land deeds and indentures: 865,
    2342, 3532, 5194, 5456
    Berkeley County: 2397
    Greenbrier County: 4563
    Harrison County: 4563
    Jefferson County: 2711
    Pocahontas County: 1837
  Land development:
    Pocahontas County: 1837
  Land grants: 5194
  Land settlement: 99
  Land speculation: 2447, 4924
  Land titles: 2273
    Pocahontas County: 1837
  Law practice: 1769
    Jefferson County: 2515
    Martinsburg: 5037
  Legal affairs: 3069
    Martinsburg: 1828
    Wood County: 5194
  Legislature: 404, 489, 2130
    Senate: 3832
  Liquor manufacturing:
    Grant County: 767
    Hannisville: 2316
    Martinsburg: 3832

WEST VIRGINIA (Continued):
  Local politics:
    Berkeley County: 1946
    Charles Town: 5689
    Martinsburg: 3832
  Masonry: 1828, 4892
    Berkeley County: 4056
  Medical practice: 748
  Mercantile accounts: 1238, 2301,
    3721
    Berkeley County: 4732
    Bunker Hill: 4893
    Capon Bridge: 2652
    Charles Town: 5300
    Darkesville: 4692
    Harpers Ferry: 3058
    Martinsburg: 1828
    Shepherdstown: 1711
  Mercantile affairs:
    Middleway: 4892
  Merchants: 1238, 2130, 2711, 3061
    Macksburg: 2470
    Shepherdstown: 1711, 5324
  Methodist churches:
    Relations between Northern
      and Southern churches: 3809
    Sunday schools: see WEST
      VIRGINIA--Sunday schools--
      Methodist
    West Virginia Conference: 3646
  Methodist Episcopal Church:
    Harpers Ferry: 2171
  Methodist Episcopal Church, South:
    5467
  Militia: 1709, 1770, 1946
  Millers' accounts:
    Berkeley County: 4056
    Hannisville: 2316
    Martinsburg: 3832
  Musical societies:
    Martinsburg: 5110
  Negroes: 748
    see also WEST VIRGINIA--Slaves
  Oil discoveries: 4348
  Panic of 1873: 4774
  Personal finance:
    Martinsburg: 3832
    Shepherdstown: 4598
  Physicians--Martinsburg: 2275
  Physicians' accounts: 4703
    Gerrardstown: 919
    Petersburg: 4842
  Plantation accounts: 3010
    Jefferson County: 1708
  Plantations: 128, 3010, 5574
    see also the following
      subheadings under WEST
      VIRGINIA: Agriculture;
      Farming; and names of specific
      crops
  Political patronage: 2016, 3291
    see also WEST VIRGINIA--
      Politics and government--
      Appointments
  Politics and government:
    see also WEST VIRGINIA--Local
      politics
    1700s-1900s: 865
    1800s: 1769, 2016
    1800s-1900s: 356, 404, 2634, 3832
    Appointments: 3291
      see also WEST VIRGINIA--
        Political patronage
  Postal service: 1946
    Local offices:
      Edray: 5655
      Inwood: 5239
      Middleway: 4892
      Shepherdstown: 2711
  Presbyterian churches:
    Berkeley County: 4056
    Martinsburg: 5110
    Winchester Presbytery: 5110
  Protestant Episcopal Church: 128
  Public schools: 4732
  Race riots: 3005
  Railroad workers--Unemployment:
    3005

WEST VIRGINIA (Continued):
  Railroads: 865
    Agents: 5239
    Construction: 721, 2396
    Reconstruction: 43, 4029, 4774
    Religion: 489, 4473
    Religious literature: 128
    Rent--Harpers Ferry: 5938
    Rent collection: 3005
    Republican Party: 1828, 2016
  Roads: 1946
    Construction: 5654
    Laws and legislation: 5654
  Sawmills: 2387
  Schools: 1784, 1946
    see also the following
      subheadings under WEST
      VIRGINIA: Education;
      Public schools;
      Teaching
    Charles Town: 1379
    Girls' schools and academies:
      Morgantown:
        Morgantown Female Academy:
          2794
        Woodburn Female Seminary:
          5110
    Parkersburg: 5194
    Wheeling: 5194
  Secession: 4774
  Sermons--Episcopal: 3141
  Servants: 1946
  Sheep:
    Breeding of Cotswold sheep: 5555
  Slave trade: 2389, 5324
  Slavery: 1769
  Slaves: 43, 1946
    see also WEST VIRGINIA--Fugitive
      slaves; WEST VIRGINIA--Hiring
      of slaves
    Emancipation: 128, 2389
    Lists: 4703
    Treatment of: 128, 4774
  Social life and customs: 128, 404,
    968, 4029
    Jefferson County: 2515
  Songs and music:
    Concerts: 1770
  Stagecoach lines: 1797
  State capital: 489
    Location: 2130
  Sunday schools:
    Baptist: 2129
    Methodist: 2129
  Surveys and surveying:
    Student's notebook: 1379
    Wood County: 5194
  Tannery accounts:
    Romney: 5215
    Wardensville: 146
  Tanning: 3064
  Taxation: 3058
    Assessment--Jefferson County:
      3832
    Pocahontas County: 5655
  Teachers' records:
    Shepherdstown: 3710
  Teaching: 1784, 2007
    see also the following
      subheadings under WEST
      VIRGINIA: Education; Public
      schools; Schools
  Temperance: 489, 2711
    Leestown: 5591
  Temperance societies:
    Shepherdstown: 2711
  Test oaths, Abolition of: 1828
  Tobacco culture: 5689
  Trade and commerce:
    Agricultural machinery: 404
    Cotton: 4774
    Flour: 2316
    Groceries--Shepherdstown: 1711
    Hats: 5110
    Liquor:
      Grant County: 767
      Hannisville: 2316
    Lumber: 1709, 2387

WEST VIRGINIA:
    Trade and commerce (Continued):
        Slaves: see WEST VIRGINIA--
            Slave trade
        Tobacco--Harpers Ferry: 5938
        Wheat--Middleway: 4703
    Travel clubs--Martinsburg: 5110
    Unemployment--Railroad workers:
        3005
    United Daughters of the
        Confederacy: 1784, 5110
    Universities and colleges: see
        SHEPHERD COLLEGE; WEST VIRGINIA
        UNIVERSITY
    Wages and salaries:
        Episcopal clergy: 3141
    Weather--Martinsburg: 5456
    Wills: 2342
WEST VIRGINIA AGRICULTURAL COLLEGE,
    Morgantown, West Virginia: see
    WEST VIRGINIA UNIVERSITY
WEST VIRGINIA PULP AND PAPER COMPANY,
    Charleston, South Carolina,
    branch: 2768
WEST VIRGINIA UNIVERSITY,
    Morgantown, West Virginia: 489
WESTBROOK, Francis: 1107
WESTBROOK, Harriet: 4770
WESTBURY, Eleanor Margaret
    (Tennant), Baroness: 472
WESTBURY, Richard Bethell, First
    Baron: 472, 2998
WESTCHESTER, New York:
    Presbyterian churches: 5731
WESTCHESTER COUNTY, New York:
    Briarcliff Manor: 1914
    Peekskill: 4343
    Somers: 3637
    Tarrytown: 2258
    White Plains: 958, 5252
    Yonkers: 2066
        Boarding schools: 2553
WESTCHESTER COUNTY NATIONAL BANK
    (New York): 4343
WESTCOTT, Charles Drake: 5656
WESTCOTT, Mrs. Charles Drake: 5656
WESTERLY, Rhode Island: 2547
WESTERN AND ATLANTIC RAILROAD:
    1297, 5495
WESTERN CAROLINA MALE ACADEMY: 2007
WESTERN LANDS: 2776, 3384
    Land settlement: 3041
    Purchases and sales: 3179
    Subdivided by place:
        Connecticut: 3041
        Pennsylvania: 3041
        Virginia: 2887
WESTERN MARYLAND COLLEGE,
    Westminster, Maryland: 5938
WESTERN NORTH CAROLINA MINING AND
    IMPROVEMENT COMPANY: 2521
WESTERN NORTH CAROLINA RAILROAD:
    2978, 5188, 5657
WESTERN NORTH CAROLINA STAGE COACH
    COMPANY: 3447
WESTERN RESERVE:
    see also WESTERN LANDS
    Land speculation: 3041
WESTERN STATES: 2240
    see also MIDDLE WEST; PLAINS
        STATES; SOUTHWESTERN STATES
    Agricultural products: 5309
    Agricultural workers:
        Mexicans: 3745
    Buffalo: 4353
    Corn--Prices: 3255
    Crops--Prices: 5309
    Description and travel:
        1800s: 1601, 1798
        1850s: 406, 4353
        1860s: 1282
        1870s: 1282, 1614
    Economic conditions (1920s): 5309
    Farming: 5309
    Historical studies: 3697
    Indians of North America:
        Raids: 2089

WESTERN STATES (Continued):
    Land: 832, 4188
    Land reclamation: 5791
    Land settlement: 1601
    Migration to: 128, 832, 849, 2091,
        2314, 2369, 2595, 2616, 4131,
        5593
        From Virginia: 2559, 5884
    Natural history: 4353
    Pioneer life: 4353
    Railroads: 1439, 4188
    Roads: 849
    Sheep ranching: 3745
    Surveying: 5480
    Taxation: 5309
    Tourist trade: 2368
    United States Army in: 1282
    Water--Prices: 4353
    Weather: 4353
    Wheat--Prices: 3255
WESTERN TRACT AND BOOK SOCIETY:
    4387
WESTERN UNION TELEGRAPH COMPANY:
    3985
WESTFIELD, Indiana: 4202
WESTFIELD, New Jersey: 3948
WESTINGHOUSE MACHINE COMPANY,
    Charlotte, North Carolina: 5312
WESTMEATH, George Thomas John
    Nugent, First Marquis of: 4024
WESTMEATH, County, Ireland: 4024
WESTMILL, England: 599
WESTMINSTER, Archbishop of: see
    names of specific archbishops,
    e.g. MANNING, Henry Edward
WESTMINSTER, Maryland: 2484, 3326,
    3565
    see also WESTERN MARYLAND COLLEGE
WESTMINSTER, North Carolina: 1407
WESTMINSTER REVIEW: 981, 1792
WESTMINSTER REVIEW COMPANY: 1792
WESTMINSTER SCHOOL (Great Britain):
    747
WESTMORE, Joseph: 5658
WESTMORE (JOSEPH) AND WILLIAM
    SAVAGE (firm): 5658
WESTMORELAND COUNTY, Pennsylvania:
    Greensburg: 213
    Pleasant Unity: 5151
WESTMORELAND COUNTY, Virginia: 382,
    1023, 2728, 3153, 5573
    Estates--Administration and
        settlement: 5577
    Land settlement: 99
    Plantation accounts: 5577
    Real estate trade: 5579
    Cities and towns:
        "Campbelltown": 5577
        "Haywood": 5579
        "Nomini Hall": 917
    Oak Grove: 5848
WESTMORLAND, John Fane, Ninth Earl
    of: 4230
WESTMORLAND, John Fane, Tenth Earl
    of: 1753
WESTMORLAND, John Fane, Eleventh
    Earl of: 1755
WESTMORLAND, England: 471
    Ravenstonedale: 1869
WESTON, Plowden C. J.: 4332
WESTOVER, Virginia:
    Agricultural and economic
        conditions: 3141
"WESTOVER," Virginia (plantation):
    363, 5751
WESTTOWN SCHOOL, Westtown,
    Pennsylvania: 1681
WESTVILLE, North Carolina: 4761
WESTVILLE CIRCUIT, Methodist
    churches: 3646
WETHERELL, Sir Charles: 2149
WETHINGTON, Abner: 5659
WETMORE, Anne Troy: 5298
WETMORE, Elijah: 5660
WETMORE FAMILY (New York and
    Virginia): 5660
WETUMPKA, Alabama: 4684, 5937

WETUMPKA (Ala.) ARGUS (newspaper):
    5937
WEVER, Charles G.: 4900
WEVER, George: 4900
WEVER, Margarete: 4900
WEVER, Maria: 4900
WEVER, Orra: 4900
WEYMOUTH, Thomas Thynne, Third
    Viscount: 5330
WEYMOUTH, Massachusetts: 5754
WHALEY, Edward Mitchell: 5661
WHALEY, William: 5661
WHALING: 1860
WHANN AND CO.: see WALTON, WHANN
    AND CO.
WHARTON, Francis: 5640
WHARTON, Helen Elizabeth (Ashhurst):
    5640
WHARTON, Henry Marvin: 461
WHARTON, Mary: 5662
WHARTON, Richard: 5662
WHARTON, Rufus W.: 4858
"WHAT THE NEGRO MOST NEEDS" by
    Edward A. Oldham: 3972
WHATELEY, William: 4605
WHATELY, Richard: 5663
WHEAT, Lemuel C.: 5664
WHEAT:
    Experimentation with new variety:
        5397
    Prices: 3566, 5763
        New York: 86
        Virginia: 363, 558
        Western States: 3255
    Transportation of:
        Virginia--Falmouth: 2165
    Subdivided by place:
        Maryland--West River: 2267
        North Carolina: 2121
        Virginia: 490, 2369, 5148
            Powhatan County: 2380
WHEAT HARVESTING:
    Virginia--Albemarle County: 1757
WHEAT PRODUCTION:
    Iowa: 1505
    Virginia: 4615, 4924
        Albemarle County: 33, 1757, 3699
WHEAT TRADE: 323
    Great Britain: 2742
    Spain: 2742
    Virginia: 2165, 2381, 2600, 4616
        Kinsley Mills: 1447
        Petersburg: 2176
    West Virginia:
        Middleway: 4703
WHEATLEY, Nathaniel: 5665
WHEATLEY, Phillis: 5665
WHEATLEY FAMILY (Massachusetts):
    5665
WHEATON, Albert F.: 5666
WHEELER, Edward B.: 2868
WHEELER, Ella: 103
WHEELER, John Hill: 3746, 5667
WHEELER, Joseph: 700, 2049, 2325,
    2630, 5668
WHEELER, Rosina Doyle: 2146
WHEELER, Russell: 2410, 5669
WHEELER, Mrs. T. M.: 3284
WHEELER, W. H.: 5670
WHEELER, Alabama: 5668
WHEELING, West Virginia: 4206, 5228
    Diseases--Smallpox: 2678
    Lawsuits: see HODGE, EUGENIA M. v.
        WHEELING LANDS
WHEELOCK, John Hall: 2689
WHEELWRIGHTS: 5004
WHERRY, John J.: 5671
WHERRY FAMILY: 872
WHEWELL, William: 2457
WHIG PARTY (Great Britain): 1632,
    4605, 5637
WHIG PARTY (United States): 872,
    1086, 1208, 1403, 1778, 3012,
    3054, 3276, 3325, 3366, 3396,
    3483, 3910, 4468, 4732, 4852, 5051
    5315, 5470, 5491, 5528, 5593,
    5700, 5757, 5974
    Conventions (1852): 5298

WHIG PARTY (United States)
    (Continued):
    Alabama: 1084
    Georgia: 1121, 4921, 5051
    Illinois: 1400
    Maine: 5610
    Maryland: 1329, 4064, 4712, 5059, 5969
    Massachusetts: 743
    Mississippi: 3322
    New Jersey: 5520
    North Carolina: 631, 730, 1015, 1100, 1580, 1826, 2530, 4080, 4714, 4897, 5149, 5298
    Pennsylvania: 421, 849, 4756
    South Carolina: 5271
    Tennessee: 872
        Nashville: 5977
    Virginia: 4080, 5513
        Greenfield: 5491
WHILDEN, Joseph: 1691
WHIPPINGS: see PUBLIC WHIPPINGS; PUNISHMENT
WHIPPLE, Edwin Percy: 2449
WHIPPLE, U.S.S.: 4355
WHISKEY--Distilling: see LIQUOR MANUFACTURING
WHISKEY REBELLION: 2571, 2776, 3041
WHISKEY TRADE: see LIQUOR TRADE
WHISPER (sloop): 3012
WHITAKER, Daniel Kimball: 2612
WHITAKER, Ellen C.: 5675
WHITAKER, F. H.: 5672
WHITAKER, James: 5673
WHITAKER, Lou: 5672
WHITAKER, Matthew C.: 5674
WHITAKER, Sallie: 5675
WHITAKER'S, North Carolina: 273
WHITBREAD, Samuel: 3478
WHITBY, England:
    Elections (1905): 3912
WHITE, Andrew J.: 5676
WHITE, Ann E. Peyton: 5681
WHITE, Bernard C.: 3503
WHITE, Frank E.: 5677
WHITE, George Mawamsie: 5678
WHITE, Sir George Stuart: 452, 888, 3224, 4520
WHITE, Gilbert Case: 5679
WHITE, Henry (fl. 1857-1863): 5680
WHITE, Henry (1850-1927): 2871
WHITE, Horace: 2526
WHITE, Hugh Lawson: 872, 5457, 5681
WHITE, Isaiah H.: 5682
WHITE, J. W.: 3032
WHITE, James: 5457
WHITE, John (fl. 1585-1593): 5457
WHITE, John (fl. 1778, Georgia): 5684
WHITE, John (fl. 1819-1828, Maryland): 5683
WHITE, John (fl. 1817-1848, North Carolina): 5685
WHITE, Joseph R.: 1197
WHITE, Josiah: 5686
WHITE, Mrs. L. (New York): 5687
WHITE, Mary Ann: 5688
WHITE, Maunsell: 1439
WHITE, Nathan Smith: 5689
WHITE, Newman Ivey: 691, 5856
WHITE, Philo: 685
WHITE, Robert G.: 5158
WHITE, Thomas, Jr. (d. 1904): 5690
WHITE, Thomas Willis (1788-1843): 10, 404, 3809, 5691
WHITE, W. A.: 5692
WHITE, Walter C.: 5693
WHITE, Walter Stuart: 5694
WHITE, William (fl. 1798-1804): 4726
WHITE, William (fl. 1826): 5719
WHITE, William Allen (1868-1944): 1137
WHITE, William F.: 5695
WHITE, William Henry (1847-1920): 5696
WHITE, William Pinkney: 3598
WHITE FAMILY (Pennsylvania): 365

WHITE (firm): see McKIM, MEADE, AND WHITE
WHITE AND BOLLING, Oxford, North Carolina: 5685
WHITE AND BURWELL, Manson, North Carolina: 799, 5697
WHITE BROTHERHOOD: 3062
WHITE HOUSE, Virginia: see CIVIL WAR--CAMPAIGNS, BATTLES, AND MILITARY ACTIONS--Virginia--White House
WHITE HOUSE (Washington, D.C.):
    Laying of the cornerstone: 4556
    Menus: 83
    New Year reception (1839): 5982
    Party for the Prince of Wales (1860): 1121
WHITE LEAGUE (Louisiana): 4131
WHITE NILE RIVER (expedition in 1869): 5725
WHITE OAK MILLS: 5234
WHITE PENITENTS, Confraternity of: 2196
WHITE PLAIN ACADEMY, Chesterfield, South Carolina: 2855
WHITE PLAINS, New York: 5252
    Mental hospitals: 958
WHITE POST, Virginia: 457, 1211, 3602
    Agriculture: 734
    Mercantile accounts: 2274, 5611
    Merchants: 1436
    Postal service: 1436, 5698
WHITE RIVER, Indiana:
    Society of Friends: 3981
WHITE SAND CIRCUIT, Methodist churches: 3646
WHITE SULPHUR SPRINGS, West Virginia: 1402, 5491
    Description: 3330, 4162
    Health resorts: 5690
WHITEFIELD, George: 1070, 2751, 5647, 5699
WHITEHALL, North Carolina: 4414
    see also CIVIL WAR--CAMPAIGNS, BATTLES, AND MILITARY ACTIONS-- North Carolina--Whitehall
WHITEHAVEN, England: 625, 1153
WHITEHEAD, Floyd L.: 5700
WHITEHEAD, George: 1733
WHITEHEAD, Harriett: 3012
WHITEHEAD, James A.: 5701
WHITEHEAD, Paul: 5302
WHITEHEAD, Swepson: 5702
WHITEHEAD, William B.: 3012
WHITEHEAD, Williamson: 5703
WHITEHEAD, Zollicoffer Wiley: 5457
WHITELAW, Pamelia (Harrison): 5704
WHITEN LAPPER MACHINE: 5100
WHITENER, Moses B.: 5705
WHITESBURG, Tennessee: 1819
WHITEVILLE, North Carolina: 3448
    Students and student life: 4910
WHITEWASH:
    North Carolina: 2905, 3410
WHITFIELD, H. D.: 2496
WHITFIELD, John W.: 5706
WHITFIELD, William: 5707
WHITFIELD, William Airey: 5708
WHITFIELD FAMILY (North Carolina): 5211
WHITFIELD COUNTY, Georgia:
    Dalton: 916, 2164, 5111
    Civil War: 689
        see also CIVIL WAR--CAMPAIGNS, BATTLES, AND MILITARY ACTIONS--Georgia--Dalton
WHITFORD, John N.: 5709
WHITFORD, Mary E. (Williamson): 5709
WHITING, Daniel Powers: 5710
WHITING, Ellen Marr: 5711
WHITING, William Henry Chase: 5712
WHITINSVILLE, Massachusetts: 1699
WHITLOCK, Louise Clark: 2449
WHITLOCK, Virginia: 3906
WHITMAN, Walt: 720, 2348, 4576, 5044
    Criticism: 2449

WHITMAN COUNTY, Washington Territory: 5018
WHITNER, Eliza: 5713
WHITNEY, Mrs. C. M.: 5572
WHITNEY, Eli: 2931, 5714
WHITNEY, Giddings: 1424
WHITNEY, Henry B.: 5715
WHITNEY, Reuben M.: 3198
WHITNEY, Nebraska:
    Personal finance: 5309
WHITSETT, William Thornton: 5457
WHITSETT FAMILY (Texas): 218
WHITSONTON, Arkansas:
    Tannery accounts: 5509
WHITSTONE, Nathan C.: 5716
WHITTIER, John Greenleaf: 404, 2449, 4189, 5717
WHITTIER LAND: A HANDBOOK OF NORTH BOSTON: 4189
WHITTLE, James M.: 5718
WHITTLE, William C.: 3320
WHITTLESEY, Elisha: 3006, 5578
WHITTLESEY, R.: 5719
WHITTLING, Elisha: 3848
WHITTY, James Howard: 2790, 5720
WHITWELL, Jean (Wise): 5855
"WHO IS RESPONSIBLE FOR CHINESE IMMIGRATION" by John K. Kuttrell: 4080
WHOLESALE TRADE:
    see also specific kinds of trade
    Georgia: 1829
    Louisiana--New Orleans: 1169
    Maryland--Baltimore: 1169
    Massachusetts--Boston: 1169
    New York: 1169
        New York: 5731
        Prices: 1907
    North Carolina: 1169
        Wilmington: 4910
    Pennsylvania--Philadelphia: 228
    Virginia:
        Petersburg: 4747
        Richmond: 4747
WHOLESALE TRADE WORKERS: see RETAIL, WHOLESALE AND DEPARTMENT STORE UNION
"WHO'S LOONEY NOW?": 958
WHOSOEVER FARM, Luray, Virginia (orphanage): 461, 574
WHY NOT, North Carolina: 3299
WHY NOT? (serial): 1202
WIATT FAMILY (Illinois): 2080
WICHITA INDIANS: 2850
WICK, England: 3236
WICKENBURG, Arizona:
    Copper mines: 4918
WICKHAM, John (1763-1839): 4616, 5721
WICKHAM, Nina Cornelia (Mitchell): 3710
WICKHAM, William: 3798
WICKLIFFE, Robert: 1401
WICKLOW, County, Ireland:
    Mining: 3567
WIDE AWAKE (children's magazine): 3810
WIDENER MEMORIAL COLLECTION, Harvard University: 5044
WIDOWS:
    see also CIVIL WAR--PENSIONS-- Widows; DEPENDENTS
    Virginia: 117
        Personal finance: 5848
WIENER, Henry M.: 5722
WIENER, Michael: 5722
WIERT, Marie: 2409
WIFFEN, Benjamin: 2149
WIGFALL, Louis Trezevant: 791, 1084, 5723, 5869
WIGGIN, Kate Douglas (Smith): 3797
WIGGINS, Elizabeth S.: 5724
WIGGINS, South Carolina: 4453
WILBERFORCE, Samuel: 5725
WILBERFORCE, William: 815, 867, 4605, 4913, 5639, 5726

WILBERFOSS, England:
    Public welfare: 5727
    Taxation: 5727
WILBORN, John D.: 5728
WILBRAHAM, George: 5729
WILBRAHAM ACADEMY (New England?): 2532
WILBUR, Aaron: 5730
WILBUR, Jeremiah: 5731
WILBUR FAMILY (Georgia--Genealogy): 5730
WILCOCKS, Miss H. M.: 2210
WILCOX, Ella (Wheeler): 103
WILCOX, Walter H.: 5732
WILCOX COUNTY, Alabama: 1877, 1986, 2040
    Black's Bluff: 5174
    Crops: 5174
WILD CAT DISTRICT, Forsyth County, Georgia:
    Taxation: 5260
WILD WEST SHOWS: 1140
WILDCAT BANKING:
    Wisconsin: 5569
WILDE, John Walker: 5733
WILDE, Oscar: 2146
WILDE, Percival: 3797
WILDE, R. H.: 2290
WILDE, Richard Henry: 305, 5734
WILDE, Sir Thomas: 1632
WILDE AND GRIGGS (firm): see GRIGGS AND WILDE
WILDEN, William: 3350
WILDER, Bryant: 5735
WILDER, Henry Arthur John: 5736
WILDERNESS CAMPAIGN: see CIVIL WAR--CAMPAIGNS, BATTLES, AND MILITARY ACTIONS--Virginia--Wilderness
"WILDFLOWER GARDENS OF OLD NEW ENGLAND" by Walter Prichard: 1636
WILDLIFE:
    Colombia: 198
    New York--West Park: 4073
WILDLIFE CONSERVATION:
    see also AMERICAN FORESTRY ASSOCIATION
    South Carolina: 4453
    United States: 4805
WILEY, Calvin Henderson: 5149, 5737
WILEY, Elizabeth Baldwin: 2367
WILEY, Louis: 3265
WILEY, Mary C.: 2362
WILEY, Robert H.: 5738
WILFLEY, Lebbeus Redman: 2409, 5252
WILFONG, Caroline: 5739
WILFONG, John: 5739
WILFONG FAMILY (North Carolina--Genealogy): 5739
WILFONG MILLS, North Carolina: 5739
WILHELM I, Emperor of Germany: 2009
WILHELM II, Emperor of Germany: 452, 809
WILIE, John N.: 5612
WILKERSON, Alexander H.: 5741
WILKERSON, Archibald: 5740
WILKERSON, James King: 5741
WILKERSON, Lillie: 5741
WILKERSON, Luther: 5741
WILKERSON, Mary Ann: 5741
WILKERSON, William P.: 490
WILKERSON FAMILY: 5740
WILKES, Jane Renwick (Smedberg): 5457
WILKES, John (1727-1797): 92
WILKES, Ohio: 86
WILKES-BARRE, Pennsylvania: 2443, 3277, 4086, 4188
WILKES COUNTY, Georgia: 123, 5315
    Baptist churches: 1080
    Civil War: 4895
    Courts: 2937
    Legal affairs: 5315
    Cities and towns:
        Rehoboth: 216
        Washington: see WASHINGTON, Georgia

WILKES COUNTY, North Carolina: 1861
    Baptist churches: 4742
    Description and travel: 5021
    Teachers' records: 3942
    Cities and towns:
        Elkville: 2483
        North Wilkesboro: 2239
        Wilkesboro: 1800, 4107
WILKESBORO, North Carolina: 1800, 4107
WILKINS, Edmund: 5742
WILKINS, Henry L.: 5743
WILKINS, John Darragh: 5744
WILKINS, John L.: 5742
WILKINS, William W.: 5742
WILKINSON, James: 4383
WILKINSON, Sidney W.: 5745
WILKINSON FAMILY: 5740
WILKINSON COUNTY, Georgia:
    Emmett: 3961
WILKISON FAMILY: 5740
WILKS, John (ca. 1765-1854): 5746
"WILL ROGERS SAYS" (newspaper column): 4545
WILLARD, Clarence: 5747
WILLARD, Frances Elizabeth Caroline: 2449, 5082
WILLARD, Henry: 5747
WILLARD, Laura Barnes: 5747
WILLARD, S. G.: 5748
WILLCOMB, Mary Florence: 5749
WILLCOX, Fred: 5750
WILLCOX, James M.: 5751
WILLCOX, John: 5752
WILLCOX, Mark: 480
WILLCOX, Mary S. (Lamb): 5751
WILLCOX, W. M.: 5753
WILLCOX FAMILY (Virginia): 5751
WILLET S. ROBBINS (schooner): 1181
WILLETT, Elbert Decatur, Sr.: 5032
WILLETT, New York: 2361
WILLEY, Henry: 5754
WILLEY, Waitman Thomas: 5755
WILLIAM III, King of Great Britain: 3715
WILLIAM IV, King of Great Britain: 2149, 5681
WILLIAM AND MARY COLLEGE, Williamsburg, Virginia: see COLLEGE OF WILLIAM AND MARY
WILLIAM AND MARY COLLEGE QUARTERLY: 5193
WILLIAM B. WOOSTER CAMP, No. 25, Sons of Veterans: 4955
WM. BLACKWOOD & SONS: 1210
WILLIAM C. PETTY AND COMPANY (North Carolina): 4172
WILLIAM CAMERON & BROTHER: 655
WILLIAM E. WORTH AND COMPANY: 5912
WILLIAM FREDERICK, Second Duke of Gloucester: 2421
WILLIAM GRAHAM AND SIMPSON COMPANY: 2122
WILLIAM H. FREAR AND COMPANY, London, England: 3960
WM. H. IMLAY & CO., Hartford, Connecticut: 2360
WILLIAM H. MADDUX AND CO., Oak Forest, Virginia: 3454
WILLIAM HOLT (firm): see JOHN AND WILLIAM HOLT
WILLIAM L. CLEMENTS LIBRARY BULLETIN: 4652
WILLIAM McLEAN HOUSE, Appomattox, Virginia: 1137
WM. PLATT AND SONS: 4881
WILLIAM R. LONG MULE COMPANY, Smithfield, North Carolina: 3257
WILLIAM S. KIMBALL AND CO.: 1586
WILLIAM SAVAGE (firm): see JOSEPH WESTMORE AND WILLIAM SAVAGE
WILLIAM WALLACE & SONS: 1115
WILLIAM WALTER & COMPANY, Boston, Massachusetts: 2933, 5535
WILLIAMS, A. Maria: 1552
WILLIAMS, Abraham Dallas: 5759
WILLIAMS, Albert J.: 5756

WILLIAMS, Alexander: 5757
WILLIAMS, Alfred (1805-1896, North Carolina): 5457
WILLIAMS, Alfred (fl. 1869-1872, South Carolina): 5758
WILLIAMS, Benjamin (1751-1814): 1816
WILLIAMS, Benjamin S. (South Carolina): 5759
WILLIAMS, C. L. L.: 5252
WILLIAMS, D. T.: 4157
WILLIAMS, Edward Ellerker (1793-1822): 4770
WILLIAMS, Edward Thomas (1854-1944): 5252
WILLIAMS, Fletcher: 5765
WILLIAMS, Floyd W.: 660
WILLIAMS, Frances Amanda (Dismukes): 5760
WILLIAMS, Francis H.: 5761
WILLIAMS, George Frederick (1852-1932): 5762
WILLIAMS, George Henry (1820-1910): 4994
WILLIAMS, George W. (Confederate officer): 3624
WILLIAMS, Gilbert W. M.: 5759
WILLIAMS, H. C.: 3648
WILLIAMS, Henry G. (North Carolina): 5770
WILLIAMS, Henry Horace (1858-1940): 5457
WILLIAMS, Henry J. (Maryland): 5763
WILLIAMS, Henry J. (Pennsylvania): 5764
WILLIAMS, Herbert S.: 1197
WILLIAMS, Indiana (Fletcher): 5765
WILLIAMS, Isham Rowland: 5457
WILLIAMS, Jabin B.: 5766
WILLIAMS, James (North Carolina): 2846
WILLIAMS, James (South Carolina): 5767
WILLIAMS, Jared: 3721
WILLIAMS, John (North Carolina): 795, 5768
WILLIAMS, John (Pennsylvania): 5769
WILLIAMS, John, Jr. (North Carolina): 5768
WILLIAMS, John Buxton (1815-1877): 5770
WILLIAMS, John C. (Pennsylvania): 5771
WILLIAMS, John J. (Washington, D.C.): 5772
WILLIAMS, John S. (Maryland?): 5763
WILLIAMS, John Sharp: 2496, 2619
WILLIAMS, John Skelton (1865-1926): 646
WILLIAMS, John W. (North Carolina): 5773
WILLIAMS, John Wesley (d. 1862, North Carolina): 5774
WILLIAMS, Joseph (1748-1827): 5457
WILLIAMS, Joseph (fl. 1882, Anglican missionary): 41
WILLIAMS, Joseph S. (Pennsylvania): 5775
WILLIAMS, Kenneth Powers: 4276
WILLIAMS, Lewis: 795, 2326, 3176
WILLIAMS, Lloyd W.: 5776
WILLIAMS, Louis Hicks: 5457
WILLIAMS, Marshall McDiarmid: 5457
WILLIAMS, Mary Lyde (Hicks): 5457
WILLIAMS, Nathaniel: 5777
WILLIAMS, Nicklas: 3766
WILLIAMS, Otho Holland: 3130
WILLIAMS, Richard: 5647
WILLIAMS, Robert (1773-1836): 5778
WILLIAMS, Sir Robert, First Baronet: 2976
WILLIAMS, Robert Gray (1878-1946): 5779
WILLIAMS, Sarah: 5780
WILLIAMS, Stanley Thomas: 102
WILLIAMS, Stephen Guion: 5781
WILLIAMS (T. C.) COMPANY, Petersburg, Virginia: 655

WILLIAMS, Tennessee: 902
WILLIAMS, Thomas: 3738
WILLIAMS, Virginius Faison: 5457
WILLIAMS, Walter: 2449
WILLIAMS, William (1787-1850): 3323
WILLIAMS, William (fl. 1888, Virginia): 5782
WILLIAMS, William George (ca. 1801-1846): 5783
WILLIAMS FAMILY (South Carolina): 718, 5760
WILLIAMS FAMILY (Tennessee): 718
WILLIAMS AND JAMISON (firm): see JAMISON AND WILLIAMS
WILLIAMS COLLEGE, Williamstown, New Hampshire:
  Students and student life: 1792, 2407, 4039
WILLIAMS TOWNSHIP, North Carolina:
  Taxation: 3935
WILLIAMSBORO, North Carolina: 761, 2475, 2829
WILLIAMSBURG, Massachusetts: 2532
WILLIAMSBURG, Virginia: 1511, 3456, 4343, 5361, 5658
  see also COLONIAL WILLIAMSBURG
  Bowling: 4220
  Civil War: 2085, 3318
    see also CIVIL WAR--CAMPAIGNS, BATTLES, AND MILITARY ACTIONS--Virginia--Williamsburg
  Defenses: 4490
  Description: 630, 1605
  History: 99
  Students and student life: 4968
  Taverns and inns: 4220
  Universities and colleges: see COLLEGE OF WILLIAM AND MARY
WILLIAMSBURG COUNTY, South Carolina:
  Johnsonville: 3877
  Smith's Mills: 5253
WILLIAMSON, Alice: 5784
WILLIAMSON, Andrew: 3209
WILLIAMSON, Caroline: 5709
WILLIAMSON, D. D.: 3470
WILLIAMSON, F. T.: 5709
WILLIAMSON, George T.: 5785
WILLIAMSON, Hugh: 484, 2776
WILLIAMSON, Isabelle (Perkinson): 5786
WILLIAMSON, J.: 4879
WILLIAMSON, John (1810-1885, Georgia): 5787
WILLIAMSON, John Gustavus Adolphus: 5457
WILLIAMSON, John M. (New York): 5788
WILLIAMSON, Leah H.: 5789
WILLIAMSON, Lee Hoomes: 5786, 5790
WILLIAMSON, Mary (Maryland?): 2301
WILLIAMSON, Mary E. (North Carolina): 5709
WILLIAMSON, Robert H.: 1743
WILLIAMSON, William (b. 1875): 5791
WILLIAMSON, Wyatt: 5792
WILLIAMSON FAMILY: 5790
WILLIAMSON COUNTY, Tennessee: 4269
  Franklin:
    Civil War:
      see also CIVIL WAR--CAMPAIGNS, BATTLES, AND MILITARY ACTIONS--Tennessee--Franklin
    Burial grounds: 3374
    78th Illinois Regiment in: 659
WILLIAMSPORT, Maryland: 743, 1008
  Civil War: see CIVIL WAR--CAMPAIGNS, BATTLES, AND MILITARY ACTIONS--Maryland--Williamsport
  Estates--Administration and settlement: 5160
WILLIAMSTON, North Carolina: 435, 448, 486, 914, 2244, 2655, 5124, 5125
  Baptist churches: 4843
  Brick trade: 5036
  Civil War: 271
  Land deeds and indentures: 4824
  Lumber trade: 4824

WILLIAMSTON, North Carolina (Continued):
  Merchants: 2419, 4849
  Physicians' accounts: 5943
WILLIAMSTON TOWNSHIP, North Carolina:
  Taxation: 3935
WILLIAMSTOWN, New Hampshire: see WILLIAMS COLLEGE
WILLIAMSTOWN, Vermont: 4888
WILLIE, Lewis Kennon: 5793
WILLIE, Lewis R.: 5794
WILLINGBORO, New Jersey: 4094
WILLINGDON, Freeman Freeman-Thomas, First Marquis of: 2149
WILLINGHAM, William W.: 1626
WILLINGTON, South Carolina: 3790, 4272
WILLIS, Mrs. E. L.: 5795
WILLIS, Henry, Jr.: 5796
WILLIS, James: 5797
WILLIS, John W.: 466
WILLIS, Larkin: 5798
WILLIS, Nathaniel Parker: 5799
WILLIS (P. J.) AND BROTHERS, Galveston, Texas: 3534
WILLIS, William Lewis: 5800
WILLIS FAMILY (Great Britain and Australia): 286
WILLIS FAMILY (Virginia): 5798
WILLKIE, Wendell Lewis: 5497
WILLOCK, George: 868
WILLOCK, Sir Henry: 868
WILLOUGHBY, W. A.: 3910
WILLS, Mary Ann (Phillips): 1842
WILLS, N.: 4188
WILLS: 4894
  see also ESTATES--Administration and settlement
  Contested--Pennsylvania: 2492
  British Guiana: 2612
  Florida: 3474
  Georgia: 1434, 2262
    Savannah: 3309
  Great Britain: 1561
  Kentucky--Lexington: 3325
  Maryland:
    1600s: 2853
    1700s: 830, 4405
    1800s: 743
    Baltimore: 3598
    Cecil County: 5296
    Kent County: 4140, 5296
    Port Tobacco: 5089
    Queen Annes County: 5296
  Massachusetts: 706, 2468, 3034, 5499
  New York: 903, 1585, 3391
  North Carolina:
    1700s-1800s: 2663, 3364, 4082
    1700s-1900s: 872, 3233, 3415, 4858, 5298
    1800s: 730, 1107, 2339, 2970, 3416, 3916, 4270, 4761
    1800s-1900s: 5709, 5740
    Burke County: 1247
    Caldwell County: 1247
    Durham County: 1256
    Edgecombe County: 3626
    Franklin County: 4147
    Greensboro: 3763
    Halifax County: 5280, 5672
    Martin County: 4849
    Montgomery County: 4689
    Onslow County: 1252
    Person County: 3752
    Ridgeway: 3307
    Surry County: 3908
  Pennsylvania: 421
    Lebanon: 4937
  South Carolina:
    1700s: 758
    1700s-1800s: 842, 5193
    1700s-1900s: 2961
    1800s: 3801
    1800s-1900s: 4649
    Charleston: 2556, 4214, 5198
  Southern States: 1556
  Tennessee: 872, 4269

WILLS (Continued):
  Virginia:
    1700s: 2383, 5575
    1700s-1800s: 2949, 3233, 4743
    1800s: 1133, 1624, 1943, 2887, 3806
    1800s-1900s: 3587, 5779
    Bedford County: 4049
    Caroline County: 1022
    Gloucester County: 4924
    Lynchburg: 1350
    Nansemond County: 3012
    Richmond: 5790
    Spotsylvania County: 5004
    Suffolk: 3012
    Sweet Briar: 5765
  West Virginia: 2342
WILLSHIRE, Sir Thomas, First Baronet: 5801
WILMARTH COMPANY: see MARSH, TALBOT, AND WILMARTH COMPANY
WILMER, Catherine P.: 411
WILMER, John: 411
WILMER, Mary: 411
WILMER, Richard Hooker: 2449
WILMER FAMILY (Pennsylvania): 411
WILMINGTON, Delaware: 2833, 3235
  Entertaining: 3229
  Street lighting: 4881
WILMINGTON, North Carolina:
  1700s: 2147
  1700s-1900s: 3607
  1800s: 1467, 2924
  1830s: 1577
  1840s: 1577
  1850s: 1399, 2919, 4231
  1860s: 2919, 3268, 3673, 4553
  1870s: 1399, 4603
  1880s: 5881
  1800s-1900s: 617, 1313, 1915, 2269, 3410
  1900s: 3548, 4809
  1910s: 116, 3380
  1920s: 3380
  1930s: 3380
  1960s: 4591
  British consulate in: 2159
  Burial place of Confederate spy: 2180
  Business affairs: 5912
  Charities: 4080
  Civil War: 486, 704, 834, 1095, 1419, 4183
    see also CIVIL WAR--CAMPAIGNS, BATTLES, AND MILITARY ACTIONS--North Carolina--Wilmington
    Blockade: 2970, 3435
    Blockade running: 4734
    Confederate Army camp: 2686, 5372
    Cotton trade: 565
    Fortifications: 1107
    Union Army hospital: 1845
    Union occupation: 3447
  Coal trade: 5912
  Commission merchants: 5373, 5912
  Cotton trade: 5014, 5912
  Cottonseed oil: 5912
  Description:
    1780s: 4304
    1840s: 248
    1850s: 3258
    1860s: 249
  Diseases--Yellow fever: 5372
  Fertilizer trade: 5912
  Foreign trade: 21, 3230
  Health conditions: 3859
  Ice trade: 5912
  Legal affairs: 5912
  Lumbering: 2222
  Lyceums: 5802
  Maps: 1182
  Masonry: 1899
  Mental hospitals for Negroes: 2890
  Mercantile accounts: 5912
  Mercantile affairs: 2511, 2585

WILMINGTON, North Carolina
(Continued):
Merchants: 1281, 1908, 2586, 5372
see also WILMINGTON--Commission merchants
Methodist churches: 3646, 5912
Methodist Episcopal Church, South: 772
Naval stores trade: 5912
Politics and government: 3447
Ports: 3230, 3922, 4858
Race relations: 1082
Race riots: 1313, 2442, 3972
Reconstruction: 4052
Salt works: 1056, 5912
Seamen's Friend Society: 4727
Ship chandlers' accounts: 5880
Shipping: 21, 658, 4982
Social conditions: 4318
Social life and customs: 1908, 5372, 5533
Turpentine industry: 2222
Turpentine trade: 4462
Wholesale trade: 2857, 4910
Women: 5533
Wood trade: 5912
WILMINGTON, Ohio:
Civil War: 801
WILMINGTON, CHARLOTTE, AND RUTHERFORD RAILROAD COMPANY: 1313
WILMINGTON AND MANCHESTER RAILROAD: 3447
WILMINGTON AND WELDON RAILROAD: 641
WILMINGTON CHURCH, Wilmington, North Carolina (Methodist): 3646
WILMINGTON COMPRESS AND WAREHOUSE COMPANY, Wilmington, North Carolina: 5014
WILMINGTON DISTRICT, Methodist churches: 3646
WILMINGTON HIBERNIAN SOCIETY, Wilmington, North Carolina: 3447
WILMINGTON LYCEUM, Wilmington, North Carolina: 5802
WILMINGTON MARINE HOSPITAL ASSOCIATION, Wilmington, North Carolina: 4727
WILMINGTON (N.C.) MESSENGER (newspaper): 1082
WILMINGTON MISSION, Wilmington, North Carolina: 617
WILMINGTON (N.C.) STAR: 1082
WILMINGTON STREET RAILROAD COMPANY, Wilmington, North Carolina: 3447
WILMOT, Mr. ___: 4625
WILMOT, Mrs. ___: 4625
WILMOT, David: 4188
WILMOT, Sir John Eardley Eardley-, First Baronet: 1087
WILMOT, Olivia: 2146, 2836
WILMOT, Thomas: 4750
WILMOT CENTER, New Hampshire: 5975
WILMOT PROVISO: 718, 4401, 5470
WILMSLOW, England: 5173
WILSON, Aaron W.: 5803
WILSON, Alexander: 5804
WILSON, Alpheus Waters: 1939
WILSON, Augusta Virginia: 1939
WILSON, Augustus E.: 4373
WILSON, Benjamin H.: 1424
WILSON, Charles: 5792
WILSON, Sir Charles William: 5333
WILSON, David Alec: 892
WILSON, Edward: 4230
WILSON, George F.: 1209, 2429
WILSON, George R.: 5805
WILSON, Gilbert Lord: 2449
WILSON, Sir Guy Douglas Arthur Fleetwood: 1499, 5806, 5872
WILSON, Henderson: 5807
WILSON, Henry: 5808
WILSON, James (1805-1860): 5809
WILSON, James (South Carolina): 5810
WILSON, James Bright (Maryland): 5811

WILSON, James Falconer (1828-1895): 5812
WILSON, James Grant (1832-1914): 5813
WILSON, James Harrison (1837-1925): 120, 3951, 4185
WILSON, James L. (North Carolina): 5814
WILSON, James W. (North Carolina): 5310
WILSON, James William (b. 1832): 5457
WILSON, John (North Carolina): 5815
WILSON (JOHN) AND RICHARD T. SMITH (firm): 5815
WILSON, John Leighton (1809-1886): 41, 5816
WILSON, John Lyde (1784-1849): 4834, 5074
WILSON, John Moulder (1837-1919): 3228
WILSON, John S. (Virginia): 5817
WILSON, Joseph: 5818
WILSON, Menece: 5819
WILSON, Norval: 2080
WILSON, Priscilla H.: 5820
WILSON, Robert (Great Britain): 2193
WILSON, Robert (Mississippi): 5821
WILSON, Robert (South Carolina): 3535
WILSON, Thomas (1663-1755): 2953
WILSON, Thomas (fl. 1850s, blacksmith): 5822
WILSON, Thomas Johnston (1815-1900): 5457
WILSON, Thomas Woodrow: see WILSON, Woodrow
WILSON, W. A. (Virginia): 5824
WILSON, W. Lindsay: 5825
WILSON, W. M. (South Carolina): 5758
WILSON, William (North Carolina): 5826
WILSON, Woodrow: 706, 879, 1284, 4020, 4825, 5823
Authorship: 2351
Foreign policy: 4018
Illness: 1424
Peace terms: 5309
Photographs: 1424
Presidential elections: 3380
WILSON FAMILY (Genealogy): 5807
WILSON FAMILY (Virginia): 1939, 5824
WILSON FAMILY (West Virginia): 1939
WILSON, North Carolina: 1232
Merchants: 4734
Schools: 4462
Girls' schools and academies: 2642
Students and student life: 4910
Surveys and surveying: 2808
WILSON & CUNNINGHAM, Norfolk, Virginia: 2933
WILSON AND KIRBY (firm): see KIRBY AND WILSON
WILSON COLLEGE, Chambersburg, Pennsylvania: 253, 5110
Students and student life: 1828
WILSON COLLEGIATE INSTITUTE, Wilson, North Carolina: 4910
WILSON COMPANY, Greenville, South Carolina: 5825
WILSON COUNTY, North Carolina:
Stantonsburg: 2135
Wilson: see WILSON, North Carolina
WILSON DISTRICT, Methodist churches: 3646
WILSON FEMALE SEMINARY, Wilson, North Carolina: 2642
WILSON-PATTEN, John: see PATTEN, John Wilson-
WILSON'S CREEK, Tennessee: see CIVIL WAR--CAMPAIGNS, BATTLES, AND MILITARY ACTIONS--Tennessee--Wilson's Creek
WILTSHIRE FAMILY: 1828
WILTSHIRE, England:
Antiquities: 3895
Architectural drawings: 3895

WILTSHIRE, England (Continued):
Cities and towns:
Bowood: 4171
Grittleton: 3847
WIMBISH, Cornelia (Barksdale): 330
WIMBISH, Rebecca L. (Barksdale): 5827
WIMBISH, William: 5827
WINCHESTER, James Ridout: 2449
WINCHESTER, S. S.: 4188
WINCHESTER, England: 3477, 5725
WINCHESTER, Kentucky:
Civil War: 5677
WINCHESTER, Virginia:
1700s-1800s: 5357
1700s-1900s: 3687
1800s: 242, 2559, 2597, 3556, 5359
1820s: 291
1840s: 283, 287, 3333
1850s: 283, 287, 1102, 2142, 3333
1860s: 584, 913, 1102, 1868, 2601, 2635, 2974, 3060, 3193, 3333
1870s: 2635, 4668
1890s: 376, 3298
1800s-1900s: 356, 3458, 5779
Business affairs: 3680
Civil War: 745
see also CIVIL WAR--CAMPAIGNS, BATTLES, AND MILITARY ACTIONS--Virginia--Winchester
Confederate Army camp: 5180
Union Army camp: 2958, 3813
Legal education: 872
Merchants and mercantile accounts: 1920, 4741, 5882
Methodist churches: 4412
Personal finance: 4607
Schools: 287
WINCHESTER COLLEGE, England: 3477
WINCHESTER REPEATING ARMS COMPANY: 794
WINCHESTER SCHOOL (England): 1675
WINCHESTER WAR MEMORIAL COMMITTEE (England): 3286
WINCHFIELD, England: 2750
WINCKLEY, Frances: 3080
WINDER, John Henry: 3885, 5828
WINDER, Levin: 5829
WINDER HOSPITAL, Richmond, Virginia: 19, 3038
WINDHAM, William (1750-1810): 2149, 5830
WINDHAM COUNTY, Connecticut:
Hampden: 5172
WINDHAM COUNTY, Vermont:
Brattleboro: 2104
Putney: 438
South Londonderry: 857
WINDLEY, Joseph B.: 5831
WINDMILLS--North Carolina: 4547
WINDOW GLASS--North Carolina: 1736
WINDSOR-CLIVE, Ivor Miles, Second Earl of Plymouth and Fifteenth Baron Windsor: 1424
WINDSOR-CLIVE, Phillis: 1424
WINDSOR SHADES, Virginia: 298
WINDWARD ISLANDS: see GRENADA
WINE TRADE:
see also LIQUOR TRADE
Cuba: 1442
North Carolina: 5535
South Carolina: 1935
Charleston: 2107
Virginia: 5535
WINES, Marshall W.: 5832
WINFIELD, Paulina S.: 5833
WINFREE, Jack Metauer: 2553
WING, North Carolina:
Mercantile accounts: 4182
WINGARD, James Samuel: 5834
WINGARD, Marie: 5834
WINGARD, Simon P.: 5834
WINGATE, Francis Reginald, First Baronet: 5835
WINGATE, George: 5836

WINGATE, W. M.: 5280
WINGATE, Washington Manly: 5457
WINGFIELD, James A. (Georgia): 5837
WINGFIELD, James H. (Louisiana): 5838
WINGFIELD, Junius A.: 3905
WINGFIELD, Samuel Griffin: 552
WINGFIELD, Susan: 3528
WINKLER, Theodor: 111
WINKWORTH, Emma (Thomasson): 5259
WINN, John: 5839
WINN, Lucy: 5839
WINN, Philip James: 5839
WINN, Sallie: 1770
WINN, William H.: 5839
WINNEBAGO COUNTY, Illinois:
    Rockford: 5348
WINNEBAGO INDIANS--Removal: 3801
WINNEBURG, Clemens Lothar Wenzel,
    Fürst von Metternich-: see
    METTERNICH-WINNEBURG, Clemens
    Lothar Wenzel, Fürst von
WINNIPEG, Canada--Description: 4175
WINNSBORO, South Carolina: 936, 1385
    Schools: 5193
WINNSVILLE, Virginia: 5839
WINSLOW, B. P.: 5841
WINSLOW, Catharine (Winslow): 5841
WINSLOW, Isaac: 5840
WINSLOW, John Ancrum: 5841
WINSLOW, Warren: 3094, 5842
WINSOR, Justin: 64
WINSTEAD (E. D.) & COMPANY, Milton,
    North Carolina: 5843
WINSTEAD, Edward D.: 5843
WINSTON, Francis Donnell: 1284
WINSTON, George Tayloe: 1284, 4669, 5312
WINSTON, John A.: 490
WINSTON, John R. (1839-1888): 5457
WINSTON, Patrick Henry: 3783
WINSTON, Warwick: 5252
WINSTON, William, Jr.: 5844
WINSTON FAMILY (Virginia--Genealogy): 3809
WINSTON, North Carolina: see WINSTON-SALEM, North Carolina
WINSTON CIRCUIT, Methodist
    Protestant church: 3646
WINSTON MALE ACADEMY (Winston-Salem, North Carolina?): 817
WINSTON-SALEM, North Carolina: 1960, 2773, 2829, 2857, 4870
    see also NORTH CAROLINA SCHOOL OF THE ARTS; SALEM COLLEGE
    Electric power industry: 4788
    Military schools: 3176
    Newspapers: 3538
    Opera: 4080
    Race relations: 3538
    Tobacco industry: 3745, 4788
    Tobacco trade: 3745
WINSTON-SALEM (N.C.) JOURNAL: 3538
WINSTON-SALEM RAILWAY: 4918
WINTER, William: 2449
WINTER PARK, Florida: see ROLLINS COLLEGE
WINTERBOTHAM, Ann Sophia: 5052
WINTERBOTTOM, RICHMAN AND COMPANY,
    Philadelphia, Pennsylvania: 5845
WINTHROP, Joseph August: 1889
WINTHROP, Robert Charles: 5846
WINTHROP COLLEGE, Rock Hill, South
    Carolina:
    Faculty--Discipline: 5847
WINTHROP GUARD: see UNITED STATES--ARMY--Civil War--Regiments--Massachusetts--Infantry--16th--Company B
WINTON, North Carolina:
    Confederate fortifications: 375
WIRT, Catherine: 2085
WIRT, Dabney Carr: 581, 5848
WIRT, Elizabeth Gamble: 2085
WIRT, Elizabeth Washington (Gamble): 5848
WIRT, William (1772-1834): 2085, 5848

WIRT, William C.: 5848
WIRZ, Henry: 5744
WISCASSET, Maine: 1222
WISCONSIN: 13
    see also WISCONSIN TERRITORY
    Description and travel: 568, 1177
    Farming--Rock County: 5307
    Judaism--Madison: 2811
    Land: 3761
        Purchases and sales: 4974
    Land speculation: 4039
    Law practice: 2436
    Methodist churches:
        Conferences: 3646
    Migration to: 1920, 3507
    Mines: 3710
    Politics and government: 5569
    Railroad construction: 4039
    Real estate investments: 5569
    Schools--Porter: 5307
    Socialist Party: 4947
    Teachers' contracts--Porter: 5307
    Teaching: 2896
    Universities and colleges: see UNIVERSITY OF WISCONSIN
    Wildcat banking: 5569
WISCONSIN TERRITORY:
    Politics and government: 2881
WISE, Alice: 5855
WISE, Charlotte B.: 5093
WISE, E. John: 5849
WISE, Frank W.: 5855
WISE, George (Virginia): 5855
WISE, George D. (New York): 5850
WISE, George Douglas (Virginia): 5851
WISE, George Newton (Virginia): 5852
WISE, Henry Alexander: 152, 523, 569, 2671, 3809, 5361, 5681, 5853
WISE, Jean: 5855
WISE, Michael: 5854
WISE, Ned: 5855
WISE, Peter: 5855
WISE, Thomas James: 4770, 5856
WISE, Will: 5855
WISE, William B.: 5857
WISE FAMILY (Virginia): 5855
WISE COUNTY, Virginia:
    Big Stone Gap: 1878
WISEMAN, Nicholas Patrick Stephen,
    Cardinal: 2180
WISHARD, Joseph A.: 5110
WISTER, Owen: 2449
WISWELL, James H.: 5858
WIT AND HUMOR: see AMERICAN WIT AND HUMOR
WITCHCRAFT--Peru: 4155
WITCHER, James: 5859
WITHERLE, William: 5860
WITHERS, Alexander Scott: 5194
WITHERS, Jennet Scott: 5194
WITHERS, John: 1181
WITHERS, John James: 5590
WITHERS, Robert Enoch (1821-1907): 5861
WITHERS, Robert W. (1798-1854): 5862
WITHERS, Susanna Claiborne: 1084
WITHERS MASONIC LODGE NO. 212,
    Columbia, Virginia: 3855
WITHERSPOON, George M.: 5863
WITHERSPOON, Henry K.: 5864
WITHROW, Elvira: 5865
WITMER, P. A.: 5866
WITNESSES:
    see also TRIALS
    Protection of: 4103
WITT, E. W.: 5234
WITTENBERG COLLEGE, Springfield,
    Ohio:
    Students and student life: 5954
WITTGENSTEIN, Ludwig Adolf Peter,
    Count: 4628
WITTKOWSKY, Samuel: 5457
WOBURN, Massachusetts: 5732
WODEHOUSE, John, First Earl of
    Kimberley: 2149, 2756, 4520
WOFFORD, B. E.: 2487
WOFFORD, J. Frank: 2487

WOFFORD COLLEGE, Spartanburg, South
    Carolina: 1584, 4068
    Faculty: 4912
        Dismissal: 4790
    Students and student life: 754
WOKING, England:
    Hermitage: 5624
WOLCOT, John: 5867
WOLCOTT, Laura B.: 5868
WOLCOTT, N. S.: 5869
WOLCOTT, Oliver: 3041, 4625, 5070
WOLCOTT, Roger (1679-1767): 5871
WOLCOTT FAMILY (Connecticut): 5868
WOLCOTT, Connecticut: 1205
WOLF ISLAND, Missouri: 4443
WOLF SCALP BOUNTIES:
    Illinois--McHenry County: 1723
WOLFE, Thomas R.: 4111
WOLFVILLE, Nova Scotia, Canada:
    see ARCADIA UNIVERSITY
WOLSELEY, Garnet Joseph, First
    Viscount Wolseley: 452, 663, 5872
WOLSELEY, Sir George Benjamin: 5872
WOLTERTON, Horatio Walpole, First
    Baron Walpole of: see WALPOLE,
    Horatio, First Baron Walpole of
    Wolterton
"WOLTERTON," Aylsham, England: 5531
WOMACK, Allen Watson: 5873
WOMACK FAMILY (Virginia): 5873
WOMAN SUFFRAGE:
    Amendment to the United States
        Constitution: 1946
    Great Britain: 3912
    North Carolina: 274, 1275, 4968
    South Carolina: 300, 2473
    United States: 404, 3617, 4849, 4858, 5968
WOMAN SUFFRAGE ORGANIZATIONS: see
    LEAGUE OF WOMEN VOTERS
WOMANHOOD: see VIRTUES OF WOMANHOOD
    IN POETRY
WOMAN'S ASSOCIATION FOR THE
    BETTERMENT OF PUBLIC SCHOOL
    HOUSES: 4111
WOMAN'S CHRISTIAN TEMPERANCE UNION:
    Georgia: 5082
    North Carolina: 3219
    South Carolina: 2473
    United States: 5082
WOMAN'S FOREIGN MISSIONARY UNION
    (Presbyterian churches): 3527
WOMBLE, Jehu J.: 5874
WOMEN: 3524, 4596
    see also MOTHERS; WIDOWS
    Drawings of: see DRAWINGS,
        American--Women
    Education: see EDUCATION--Women;
        SCHOOLS--Girls' schools & academies
    Employment: 3524
        see also LABOR LAWS AND
            LEGISLATION--Employment of
            women and children
        Georgia--Cherokee County: 1887
        Germany: 305
        Great Britain: 2149
        Kentucky--Lexington: 3325
        North Carolina: 5100
        United States: 3066
    Equal rights: see WOMEN'S RIGHTS
    Personal finance: 184, 617
        Divorcées: 349, 1153
        South Carolina--Charleston: 1891
        Virginia--Fauquier County: 512
    Psychology: 2934
    Relationship with men: see MEN AND
        WOMEN--Social relationships
    Religious orders: see RELIGIOUS ORDERS
    Social status:
        Alabama: 1084
        China: 5252
        United States: 731
    Spies: see SPIES--Women
    Subdivided by place:
        Georgia: 168
        Great Britain: 4520
        North Carolina--Wilmington: 5533

WOMEN:
　Subdivided by place (Continued):
　　United States: 4948
WOMEN AUTHORS: 2160
　see also names of specific women
　　authors
　Anonymous:
　　Great Britain: 177, 2058
　Great Britain: 5553
　Tennessee: 3810
　United States: 5052
WOMEN CLERGY:
　Methodist--Great Britain: 1317
　Society of Friends--Indiana: 3981
WOMEN IN BUSINESS:
　Georgia: 5353
WOMEN IN MEDICINE: 3390
WOMEN IN THE CIVIL WAR: 1191, 2617,
　2806, 3809
　see also CIVIL WAR--CIVILIAN
　　LIFE--Evacuation of women;
　　CIVIL WAR--NURSES AND NURSING
　Confederate soldiers: 3262
　North Carolina: 5298
　　Caldwell County: 4080
　Northern States: 3734
　South Carolina: 2473
　　Spartanburg: 4912
　Southern States: 4950, 5954
　Virginia: 2880
　　Nelson County: 4259
WOMEN OF THE WAR by Frank Moore:
　3734
WOMEN POETS: 2934, 5665
　see also names of specific women
　　poets
　Kentucky: 2053
　Maryland: 3559
　New York--New York: 3999
　South Carolina: 2045
WOMEN SOLDIERS: see UNITED STATES--
　ARMY--World War II--Women's Army
　Auxiliary Corps; WOMEN IN THE
　CIVIL WAR--Confederate soldiers
WOMEN'S CLOTHING: see CIVIL WAR--
　CLOTHING AND DRESS--Women's
　styles; CLOTHING AND DRESS--
　Women's styles
WOMEN'S CLUBS: see WOMEN'S SOCIETIES
　AND CLUBS
WOMEN'S EMIGRATION SOCIETY: 4567
WOMEN'S FOREIGN MISSIONARY SOCIETY
　(Presbyterian churches): 2269
WOMEN'S MISSIONARY COUNCIL
　(Methodist churches): 3646
WOMEN'S MISSIONARY SOCIETY
　(Methodist churches): 1738, 3646
WOMEN'S RIGHTS:
　Massachusetts: 5088
　United States: 2469, 3029, 5282,
　　5968
WOMEN'S SOCIETIES AND CLUBS:
　see also BUSINESS AND PROFESSIONAL
　　WOMEN'S CLUB; COLONIAL DAMES
　　OF AMERICA; DAUGHTERS OF THE
　　AMERICAN REVOLUTION; GENERAL
　　FEDERATION OF WOMEN'S CLUBS;
　　LADIES' HOSPITAL AID ASSOCIATION
　　OF REX HOSPITAL; MISSIONARY
　　SOCIETIES; UNITED DAUGHTERS OF
　　THE CONFEDERACY; YOUNG WOMEN'S
　　CHRISTIAN ASSOCIATION; and names
　　of organizations beginning with
　　WOMAN'S or WOMEN'S
　Great Britain--Chelmsford: 1903
WOMEN'S SOCIETIES AND CLUBS:
　Louisiana: 3071
　North Carolina: 661, 1128
　　Davie County: 4111
　　Durham: 5601
　　Henderson: 4232
　　Raleigh: 274
　South Carolina--Camden: 4642
　United States: 1337
WOMEN'S SOCIETY OF CHRISTIAN SERVICE
　(Methodist churches):
　North Carolina: 3020
　United States: 3020, 3646

WOOD, Alexander: 3200
WOOD, Charles, First Viscount
　Halifax: 5875
WOOD, Edward Jenner: 5014
WOOD, George: 4895
WOOD, George Bacon (1797-1879): 173
WOOD, Sir Henry Evelyn: 5876
WOOD (HUDSON) & CO.: 2130
WOOD, James (Virginia): 4312
WOOD, James M.: 5796
WOOD, John (d. 1856, Great Britain):
　2149
WOOD, John (Maryland): 2265
WOOD, John (North Carolina): 5777
WOOD, Josiah: 5877
WOOD, Leonard: 5878
WOOD, Samuel O.: 5879
WOOD, Sterling Martin: 395
WOOD (THOMAS F.) INC., Wilmington,
　North Carolina (firm): 5880
WOOD, Thomas Fanning: 5881
WOOD, William (Virginia): 5882
WOOD, William Maxwell (navy
　physician): 2265
WOOD, William Page, First Baron
　Hatherley: 5883
WOOD FAMILY (North Carolina--
　Genealogy): 4242
WOOD:
　see also LUMBER; TIMBER
　Kentucky and Missouri: 3532
　Transportation: see FREIGHT AND
　　FREIGHTAGE--Wood; WOOD TRADE
WOOD ARTICLES: see MILLWORK INDUSTRY
WOOD AS A DYE: 5553
WOOD COUNTY, West Virginia:
　Household accounts: 5194
　Legal affairs: 5194
　Cities and towns:
　　Parkersburg: 2016
　　　Girls' schools and academies:
　　　　5194
WOOD-ENGRAVINGS: 2263
　Great Britain: 2146
WOOD PULP: see PULP AND PAPER
　INDUSTRY
WOOD TRADE: 323, 3616
　see also LUMBER TRADE
　Prices: 4541
　Subdivided by place:
　　Alabama: 5006
　　　Macon County: 3837
　　Mississippi--Rodney: 3322
　　North Carolina--Wilmington: 5912
　　South Carolina: 430
　　Virginia: 629, 5377
WOOD v. UNITED STATES: 5606
WOODALL, John: 5884
WOODALL, William: 5884
WOODARD, Frederick A.: 5457
WOODBERRY, Elizabeth Bowen: 5885
WOODBERRY, George Edward: 5720
WOODBERRY FOREST SCHOOL, Orange,
　Virginia: 5194
WOODBRIDGE, Connecticut: 1205
WOODBURN FEMALE SEMINARY,
　Morgantown, West Virginia: 5110
WOODBURY, Levi: 685, 3118, 5886
WOODBURY, New Jersey: 1901
WOODEN MACHINE PARTS INDUSTRY: see
　TEXTILE MACHINERY--Parts
WOODFORD, Stewart Lyndon: 5326
WOODFORD GREEN, England: 4694
WOODIN, William R.: 3269
WOODING, J. W.: 4188
WOODLAND, North Carolina:
　Cotton trade: 4047
　Religion: 4047
"WOODLAWN," Georgia: 1302
WOODLAWN, South Carolina: 3405
　Postal service: 1181
"WOODLAWN," Fairfax County,
　Virginia: 3200
WOODLAWN MILLS, North Carolina: 5887
　Mercantile accounts: 5888
WOODLAWN MILLS (North Carolina firm):
　3285, 5100, 5887

WOODLAWN MILLS STORE, Woodlawn Mills,
　North Carolina: 5888
"WOODLEY," Ellicott, Maryland: 3424
WOODRESS, James Leslie: 5889
WOODRING, Rebecca: 5890
WOODROOF, Alfred: 1501
WOODROW WILSON CLUB, Wilmington,
　North Carolina: 3380
WOODRUFF, Benjamin E.: 5891
WOODRUFF, Isabella Ann (Roberts):
　5892
WOODRUFF, Josephus: 5893
WOODRUFF, Milford F.: 5894
WOODRUFF, South Carolina:
　Social life and customs: 1715
WOODS, Elizabeth: 5895
WOODS, Francis H.: 5896
WOODS, J. F.: 5897
WOODS, Joseph T.: 5898
WOODS, Leonard, Sr.: 5899
WOODS, Leonard, Jr.: 5899
WOODS, Lucy: 4004
WOODS, "Sade": 5898
WOODS, William G.: 5900
WOODSBORO, Maryland: 4064
WOODSDALE CIRCUIT, Methodist
　churches: 3646
WOODSIDE MILLS (South Carolina):
　5236
WOODSON, Agatha (Abney): 5901
WOODSON, Elvira L.: 5902
WOODSON FAMILY (Virginia--
　Genealogy): 1842
WOODSTOCK, Virginia: 2942
　Abolition of slavery: 5275
　Civil War: 4537
　Furniture industry: 1893
　Merchants: 2832
WOODSTOCK INVESTMENT COMPANY,
　Roanoke, Virginia: 5903
WOODVILLE, James L.: 5904
WOODVILLE, North Carolina:
　Grist mills: 4153
WOODVILLE, Virginia: 5382
　Mercantile accounts: 138
WOODWARD, Mr.　　: 4077
WOODWARD, Delia White: 3247
WOODWARD, Rufus: 3701
WOODWARD AND McGILL (firm): see
　McGILL AND WOODWARD
WOODWORKERS: see INTERNATIONAL
　WOODWORKERS OF AMERICA
WOODY, Frank H.: 5905
WOODY, Mary Ann: 5905
WOODY, Newton Dixon: 5905
WOODY, Robert: 3984, 5905
WOODY, Robert Hilliard: 4353, 5242
WOODY FAMILY (North Carolina and
　Indiana): 328
WOOL, John Ellis: 2301, 5906
WOOL: see TARIFF--Wool; WEAVING AND
　SPINNING--Wool
WOOL CARDING:
　Missouri--Calhoun: 5392
　North Carolina--Randleman: 5408
　Virginia--Falmouth: 2165
WOOL INDUSTRY: see WOOLEN MILLS
"WOOL PICKING"--Virginia: 5347
WOOL RESEARCH: see TEXTILE RESEARCH
WOOL TRADE: 323
　Prices--New Hampshire: 4681
　Subdivided by place:
　　Australia: 2742
　　France: 2742
　　Great Britain: 2148, 2742
　　Spain: 2742
WOOLDRIDGE, William: 5907
WOOLEN MILLS:
　Dyes and dyeing: 4681
　Great Britain: 5553
　Pennsylvania: 5249
　Taxation--Texas: 592
　Subdivided by place:
　　New Hampshire--Dover: 4681
　　New York--West Candor: 2204
　　North Carolina:
　　　Winston-Salem: 1905
　　Pennsylvania: 1536

1001

WOOLEN MILLS:
   Subdivided by place (Continued):
     South Carolina: 3754
     Virginia: 990, 4924, 5377
       Bonsack: 568
       Good Intent: 568, 5297
       Staunton: 5039
WOOLSEY, M. B.: 3118
WOOLSON, Constance Fenimore: 2449, 5908
WOOLWICH, England: 3968
   Military headquarters: 5024
WOOSTER (WILLIAM B.) CAMP, No. 25, Sons of Veterans: 4955
WOOSTER, Ohio: 3103
WOOTEN, Shadrack: 5909
WOOTEN, Thomas Jones: 5457
WOOTEN AND TAYLOR COMPANY, Catherine Lake, North Carolina: 5910
WORCESTER, Joseph Emerson: 393, 5911
WORCESTER, England: 1358
WORCESTER, Massachusetts:
   1790s: 3208
   1800s:
     1800s: 3208
     1840s: 1404
     1850s: 3701
     1860s: 4314, 4349, 5034
     1870s: 4314
     1880s: 5240
     1890s: 185
   1800s-1900s: 4125
WORCESTER COUNTY, Maryland:
   Snow Hill: 4946
WORCESTER COUNTY, Massachusetts:
   Auburn: 3166
   Barre: 3633
   Gardner: 5088
   Hardwick: 4970
   Lunenburg: 684
   Milford: 3328, 5169
   North Oxford: 358
   Oakdale: 3181
   Southbridge: 1699
   Templeton: 3152
   Whitinsville: 1699
   Worcester: see WORCESTER, Massachusetts
WORCESTER v. GEORGIA: 3176
WORCESTERSHIRE, England:
   Daylesford: 2422
   Landlord and tenant: 4630
   Worcester: 1358
WORDSWORTH, William: 2058
WORKHOUSES:
   see also POORHOUSES
   Great Britain--Idle: 1648
WORKMEN'S COMPENSATION:
   North Carolina: 1951
   Tennessee: 1197
WORKMEN'S COMPENSATION LAW: 1951
WORKS, Oscar: 5311
WORKS FAMILY (Illinois): 5311
WORKS OF ALEXANDER POPE: 828
WORKS OF ALL NATIONS EXHIBITION (Great Exhibition of 1850): 3424
THE WORKS OF LORD BRYON: 821
THE WORKS OF SIR THOMAS MALORY by Eugene Vinaver: 3477
WORKS PROJECTS ADMINISTRATION: see UNITED STATES--GOVERNMENT AGENCIES AND OFFICIALS--Works Projects Administration
THE WORLD ABOLITION CONVENTION: 5088
WORLD COUNCIL OF CHURCHES: 3020
WORLD LEAGUE AGAINST ALCOHOLISM: 879
WORLD POLITICS: 2161, 3096
   see also LEAGUE OF NATIONS; and Foreign relations as subheading under names of specific countries
"THE WORLD-SICK MAN" by Julia A. Mildred Harris: 3611
WORLD WAR I: 300, 1128, 1653, 2103, 2334, 2553, 3451, 3912, 4290, 4355, 5115, 5876
   see also World War I as subheading under names of armies and navies

WORLD WAR I (Continued):
   Alien property--United States: 3545
   Allied Supreme War Council: 1424
   American preparedness: see LEAGUE TO ENFORCE PEACE
   American volunteer troops: 5930
   Americans in Germany: 4478
   Americans in the British Army: 3893
   Armistice: 5298
   Bacterial warfare: 1424
   Bombs--Inventions: 3424
   Campaigns, battles, and military actions:
     Balkans: 4020
     East Africa: 1320
     Falkland Islands: 5474
     France: 2712
       Château-Thierry: 5163
       Meuse-Argonne: 4269, 5163
       St. Mihiel: 3019, 5163
       The Somme: 473
       Vesle River: 5163
     Italy: 4020
   Canadian participation: 4491
   Central Powers: 1424
   Civilian life:
     France: 3710
     Great Britain: 3710
       Effects on Oxford University: 473
     Italy: 3710
     United States: 3710, 4689
       Georgia--Atlanta: 1776
       Scarcity of horses: 5309
   Commodity prices: 5419
   Conservation of resources: 5428
   Diseases--France: 1424
   Economic aspects:
     Cotton trade in Europe: 592
     Rising prices: 4858
   Governmental regulation of food distribution: 5786, 5803
   Intervention of the United States: 2109
   Labor conditions:
     North Carolina:
       Shortages: 4858
       War industries: 2553
   Liberty balls: 3905
   Liberty loans: see WORLD WAR I--Savings bond drives--Liberty loans
   Maps: 5163
   Medical and sanitary affairs: 2081
     see also WORLD WAR I--Nurses and nursing
   Military intelligence: 5163
   Military use of civilian property: 4727
   Neutrality:
     Of Denmark: 5321
     Of the United States: 2109, 4018, 4449
   Nurses and nursing: 5298
   Peace negotiations: see VERSAILLES PEACE CONFERENCE
   Peace proposals of Woodrow Wilson: 5309
   Peace prospects: 473
   Peace treaty: see VERSAILLES TREATY
   Pensions: 521
   Poetry: 1949
   Propaganda--Denmark: 5321
   Public finance:
     United States: 4825
       see also WORLD WAR I--Savings bond drives
   Public opinion: 1766, 5306
     Denmark: 5321
   Public welfare: see WORLD WAR I--War relief
   Railroads:
     North Carolina: 238
     United States: 4858
   Reparations:
     Germany: 1424, 5252, 5419

WORLD WAR I (Continued):
   Requisition of neutral property: 1424
   Savings bond drives: 1776, 4018
     Liberty loans: 3979, 5298
     North Carolina: 3955
   Sedition Acts--United States: 4948
   Spies: see SPIES--German
   Submarine warfare: 4355
   Transportation: 1424
   Veterans' benefits (United States): 325, 4825
     Resettlement: 3019
   Veterans' organizations:
     Medical veterans in North Carolina: 5603
   War debts: 4556
     France: 1424
   War relief: 3710, 5298
     Aid to women and children: 2712
     American Red Cross: 1766, 3424, 3979, 4858
     Balls: 3905
     Drives: 3955
     Europe: 3424
     France: 1792, 2553, 4743
     West Virginia chapter: 5110
     Subdivided by place:
       Austria: 1424
       France: 3710, 4743
       Near East: 1424
   War work: 5786
   Women's work: 3710
   Young Men's Christian Association: 1424
     In France: 4743
   General references by place:
     France: 1210, 1424, 4269
     Great Britain: 4331
     Ireland: 4798
     United States: 592, 2473, 3096
WORLD WAR II: 300, 1320
   Americans in Europe: 2239
   Anti-war sentiments: 4722
   Campaigns, battles, and military actions:
     Europe: 5418
     Japan (planned invasion): 1661
     New Guinea: 1661
     Philippine Islands: 1661
   Civilian life:
     Rationing: 4085
     Food: 1776
     Subdivided by place:
       Georgia: 1776
       Great Britain: 3190
       North Carolina: 3538
       United States: 4858
       Wales: 3190
   Conscientious objectors:
     Great Britain: 4722
   Entry into the war:
     Opposition in the United States: 3538, 4948
   German occupation of France: 1424
   Peace rumors: 2650
   Poetry: 2445
   Railroads--North Carolina: 238
   Rubber industry: 1776
   Savings bonds: 341, 1776
   Shipbuilding industry: 1776
   Sugar industry: 1776
   Transatlantic voyages: 300
   Troop entertainment: 3338
   Veterans' benefits: 325
   Wages and salaries:
     United States: 1776
   War bond campaigns: 341
   General references subdivided by place:
     Europe: 2011
     Great Britain: 300, 3190
     Italy: 300
     Philippine Islands: 1661
     South Africa: 4960
THE WORLD'S WORK: 4021
WORMSER, Leo F.: 5252
WORMSLOR, Georgia: 3898

WORONTZOV, Alexandre Romanovitch, Second Count Worontzov: 2836
WORONTZOV, Mikhail Séméonovitch, Fourth Count and Prince Worontzov: 2836
WORONTZOV, Séméon Romanovitch, Third Count Worontzov: 2836
WORONZOW, Catherine: 1911
WORTH, Charles William: 5912
WORTH, David Gaston: 5912
WORTH (JOHN M.) MANUFACTURING COMPANY, Worthville, North Carolina: 3187
WORTH, Jonathan: 832, 3993, 5912
WORTH, Martitia (Daniel): 5912
WORTH, William Elliott: 5912
WORTH FAMILY (North Carolina): 5912
WORTH AND WORTH, Wilmington, North Carolina (firm): 5912
THE WORTH COMPANY, Wilmington, North Carolina: 5912
WORTH DIVISION NO. 44, Sons of Temperance: 4954
WORTH MANUFACTURING COMPANY, Worthville, North Carolina: 2382, 3187
WORTH MANUFACTURING COMPANY STORE: 3187
WORTHAN'S ACADEMY, Richmond, Virginia: 4698
WORTHING, England: 1522, 5304
WORTHINGTON, Dennison: 5457
WORTHINGTON FAMILY: 404
WORTHVILLE, North Carolina: 3187
WORTHVILLE STORE COMPANY: 3187
WORTLEY, Margaret Jane Stuart-: see STUART-WORTLEY, Margaret Jane
WOUNDED: see Casualties as subheading under names of armies and navies
WRANGHAM, Francis: 5913
WREN, Sir Christopher: 1551
WRENN, Flora May: 5914
WRENN, Lizzie Taylor: 5914
WRIGHT, Ambrose Ransom: 5915
WRIGHT, B.: 369
WRIGHT, Benjamin: 5926
WRIGHT, Benoni C.: 5926
WRIGHT, Bryant: 5916
WRIGHT, Charles C.: 5457
WRIGHT, Edward H.: 5925
WRIGHT, Elizabeth (North Carolina): 5926
WRIGHT, Elizabeth (Washburn): 2409
WRIGHT, Elizur: 5917
WRIGHT, Frances: 4770
WRIGHT, George Finney: 5918
WRIGHT, Hendrick Bradley: 4188
WRIGHT, Horatio Gouverneur: 820
WRIGHT, Ichabod Charles: 3836
WRIGHT, J. D.: 5919
WRIGHT, Sir James (1716-1785): 2780, 5920
WRIGHT, James M. (Virginia): 5921
WRIGHT, John: 599
WRIGHT, Joseph (Virginia): 5919
WRIGHT, Joseph Hill: 3607
WRIGHT, Kate: 5925
WRIGHT, Lemuel S.: 5926
WRIGHT, Lois: 1408
WRIGHT, Lydia (Alabama): 5916
WRIGHT, Lydia Ann (Tilton) (Maryland): 5928
WRIGHT, Marcus Joseph: 5922
WRIGHT, Mary (Sledge): 5090
WRIGHT, Noah J.: 5926
WRIGHT, Richard Harvey: 5923
WRIGHT, Thomas S.: 5924
WRIGHT, William (1794-1866): 5925
WRIGHT, William W.: 4539
WRIGHT FAMILY (Florida and Maryland): 5928
WRIGHT FAMILY (North Carolina): 5926
WRIGHT AND CLAY, Roxboro, North Carolina (firm): 5927
WRIGHT AND MAUDE (firm): see MAUDE AND WRIGHT

WRIGHT MACHINERY COMPANY, Durham, North Carolina: 5923
WRIGHTSVILLE SOUND, North Carolina: Children's hospitals: 4809
WRITERS: see AMERICAN AUTHORS; WOMEN AUTHORS
WRITING: see AUTHORSHIP; CREATIVE WRITING
WU P'EI'FU: 5252
WU TING-FANG: 5252
WU TING SENG: 5252
WUNDER, Henry S.: 2942
WÜRTZBURG, Germany: 174
WYANT, Maria (Wever): 4900
WYATT, J. T.: 5929
WYATT, William Edward: 2999
WYBURD, W. H.: 868
WYCHE, Charles Cecil: 5930
WYCHE, Isoline: 5930
WYETH, Joseph: 1733
WYLIE, William: 5931
WYLLY, Richard: 5932
WYLY, John: 5933
WYLY, Thomas K.: 5933
WYNCOTE, Pennsylvania: 3267
WYNDHAM, George: 294
WYNN, Charles Watkin Williams: 5934
WYNNDOWN, Pennsylvania: 5940
WYNNE, A. R.: 5935
WYNNE, Delia Haywood: 4968
WYOMING:
see also WESTERN STATES; WYOMING TERRITORY
Agriculture: 5426
WYOMING COUNTY, New York: 5307
WYOMING COUNTY, Pennsylvania: Tunkhannock: 4057, 4188
WYOMING TERRITORY:
Judicial appointments: 4740
WYSOX, Pennsylvania: 3770
WYTHE, George: 917
WYTHE FAMILY (Virginia): 5176
WYTHE COUNTY, Virginia: 4933
Income tax: 1189
Cities and towns:
Austinville: 1181
Wytheville: see WYTHEVILLE
WYTHEVILLE, Virginia: 3424, 5861, 5954
Social life and customs: 4596, 4648

## XYZ

XYZ AFFAIR: 4348
XANTHIAN MARBLES by William Watkiss Lloyd: 3234
YADKIN BAPTIST ASSOCIATION (North Carolina): 320
YADKIN COUNTY, North Carolina: 2808, 2809, 3038, 5230
  Elections: 4103
  Land deeds and indentures: 2419
  Republican Party convention (1900): 2914
  Slaves: 4103
  Society of Friends: 1904
  Subdivided by place:
    Doweltown: 2429
    East Bend: 2857
    Hamptonville: 2452, 3540
    Huntsville: 1108, 2714, 2809
      Slave trade: 2113
    Panther Creek: 2914, 3003, 3766
    Shallow Ford: 3002
    Yadkinville: 2429, 4103
YADKIN DISTRICT, Methodist churches: 3646
YADKIN FALLS MANUFACTURING COMPANY (North Carolina): 4918
YADKIN MANUFACTURING COMPANY (North Carolina): 1438
YADKINVILLE, North Carolina: 4103
  Mercantile accounts: 2429
YAKUB BEG: 5103
YALE, Nash: 5871
YALE COLLEGE, New Haven, Connecticut: see YALE UNIVERSITY
YALE UNIVERSITY, New Haven, Connecticut:
  1800s: 51, 1402, 4897, 4924, 5731
  1810s: 3165
  1830s: 2292
  1840s: 3485, 4080
  1900s: 4271
  1920s: 3020
  Admissions policies: 5075
  Museum: 641
  Students and student life: 1213, 2597, 3396, 5748
YALOBUSHA COUNTY, Mississippi: 5469
"YAMASSEE," Savannah, Georgia: 2460
YANCEY, Benjamin Cudworth: 5936
YANCEY, C.S.: 4323
YANCEY, Hamilton: 5936
YANCEY, Mary Louise: 5936
YANCEY, William Lowndes: 1084, 5937
YANCEY COUNTY, North Carolina: 525
YANCEYVILLE, North Carolina: 2638, 5243
  Banks and banking: 2474
  Hotel registers: 4284
  Methodist churches: 4506
YANCEYVILLE CIRCUIT, Methodist churches: 3646
YANDELL, Louise (Elliston): 5380
"YANKEE STADIUM AFFAIR": 2083
"YANKEE TOM" (New Englander): 3109
YANTIS, Arnold Stevens: 5938
YANTIS, Solomon Vance: 5938
YARD, W. C.: 5939

YARD, William S.: 5939
YARN MANUFACTURING:
  Pennsylvania--Philadelphia: 5845
YARN TRADE--Georgia: 2365
YARNALL, Francis Cope: 5940
YATES, Charles: 43
YATES, Frances (Walker): 43
YATES, James L.: 5941
YATES, Joseph M.: 5942
YATES, Levi Smithwick: 5943
YATES, Matthew Tyson: 5457
YATES, Richard: 5944
YATES, Robert: 5945
YATES, Samuel B.: 5946
YATES FAMILY (West Virginia): 43
YATES COUNTY, New York: 2912
  Land deeds and indentures: 3568
  Cities and towns:
    Barrington: 2423
    Milo: 2912, 3568
    Penn Yan: 1229, 3568
    Starkey: 4680
YAVARI RIVER (Peru): 4531
YAZOO COUNTY, Mississippi:
  Plantations: 3747
  Sartartia: 5821
YAZOO DEPOSIT: 1090
YAZOO LAND FRAUD: 1993, 2788, 3041, 3704, 3780
YEA, Lacy Walter Giles: 5947
YEADON, England: 2751
"THE YEAR OF THE SOUL" by Stefan George: 1992
A YEAR ON THE PUNJAB FRONTIER by Sir Herbert Benjamin Edwardes: 1650
YEARGAN FAMILY (North Carolina--Genealogy): 4078
YEARSLEY, Macleod: 5403
YEATES, Jasper: 5948
YEATMAN, James: 128
YEATMAN, Jean Charlotte Washington (Lloyd): 5949
YELLOW FEVER: see CIVIL WAR--DISEASES--Yellow fever; DISEASES--Yellow fever
YELLOW JOURNALISM: see JOURNALISM--Yellow journalism
YELLOWLEY, Edward Clements: 5950
YELLOWSTONE NATIONAL PARK: 3424
YEMBO, Arabia: 4549
YEN, James Y. C.: 5252
YEN YANG-CHU: see YEN, James Y. C.
YENCHING UNIVERSITY, Peking, China: 5252
YERBY, Ophelia: 1887, 5951
YERGER, Jacob Shall (or Shaul): 872
YERGER, William: 5952
YERGEY, John H.: 5953
YOKOHAMA, Japan:
  Description: 2241
  Hospitals: 4986
YOLO COUNTY, California:
  Davis: 5889
YONCE, William B.: 5954
YONKERS, New York: 2066
  Boarding schools: 2553
YORK, Archbishop of: see names of specific archbishops, e.g. MUSGRAVE, Thomas
YORK, Brantley: 5457
YORK, Davidson Victor: 3248
YORK, George W.: 5955
YORK, Lucy Maie: 3248
YORK, Pennsylvania: 4701
  Social life and customs: 1918
YORK, South Carolina: 543, 3122, 3552, 5223
  Business affairs: 697
  Railroads: 3035
YORK AND ALBANY, Frederica Charlotte Ulrica Catherina, Duchess of: 2149
YORK AND ALBANY, Frederick Augustus, Duke of: 499
YORK COUNTY, Maine:
  Buxton: 1820
  Cornish: 1106

YORK COUNTY, Maine (Continued):
  North Berwick: 3264
  Parsonfield: 2865
  Saco: 3741
  Sanford: 1699
YORK COUNTY, Pennsylvania:
  Spring Garden: 744
  York: 4701
YORK COUNTY, South Carolina: 2539, 3327, 4368, 4609
  Indian mission schools: 1923
  Cities and towns:
    Belmont: 4216
    New Center: 4347
    Rock Hill: 633
      Automobile industry: 5252
      Universities and colleges: see WINTHROP COLLEGE
    York: see YORK, South Carolina
YORK COUNTY, Virginia: 3854
  Yorktown: see YORKTOWN, Virginia
YORK DISTRICT, South Carolina: 3161, 4914
YORKE, John: 2151
YORKSHIRE, England: 5913
  Juries: 5956
  Land tenure: 5956
  Taxation of property: 5956
  Cities and towns:
    Allerton: 3620
    Beverley: 5956
    East Riding: 5956
    Idle: 1648
    Leeds: 280
      Engineers: 794
      Religion: 1317
    Sheffield: 2245, 5133
      Labor unions: 4234
      Trade and commerce: 480
    Silsden: 2751
    Wilberfoss:
      Public welfare: 5727
      Taxation: 5727
    Yeadon: 2751
YORKTOWN, Virginia: 3856, 4225, 5068
  American Revolution: see AMERICAN REVOLUTION--Campaigns and battles--Virginia--Yorktown
  Civil War: 1122
    see also CIVIL WAR--CAMPAIGNS, BATTLES, AND MILITARY ACTIONS--Virginia--Yorktown
    Confederate Army camp: 2174
    Union Army camp: 2500
      Camp life: 5975
  Customs house: 4599
  Fugitive slaves: 3741
  History of: 99
  Hotels: 5176
  Social life and customs: 2776
  Tobacco trade: 5228
YORKTOWN (Va.) SESQUICENTENNIAL (1931): 5176
YORKVILLE, South Carolina: see YORK, South Carolina
YOUNG, _____ (1775): 5957
YOUNG, Captain _____ (Virginia): 5958
YOUNG, A.: 3802
YOUNG, Ann Augusta: 2589
YOUNG, Brigham: 1333
YOUNG, Bryant: 5959
YOUNG, Edward (1693-1765): 188
YOUNG, Edward (fl. 1834): 3491
YOUNG, Francis Brett: 364
YOUNG, Henry C.: 4834
YOUNG, J. Cooper: 5962
YOUNG, James (Great Britain): 5609
YOUNG, James A. (North Carolina): 5965
YOUNG, James H. (North Carolina): 5960
YOUNG, James M. (Alabama): 5961
YOUNG, James Richard (North Carolina): 5962
YOUNG, Jennie: 5963

YOUNG, John (1747-1837, North Carolina): 5964
YOUNG, John (fl. 1787, South Carolina): 2613
YOUNG, John Russell (1840-1899): 5044
YOUNG, John W.: 5965
YOUNG, John Wesley (North Carolina): 5965
YOUNG, Julia Nash: 5966
YOUNG, Louis Gourdin: 3666
YOUNG, McClintock: 5967
YOUNG, Matilda: 5968
YOUNG, Moses: 3116
YOUNG, Notley: 5969
YOUNG, Pierce Manning Butler: 5970
YOUNG, Robert Anderson: 5460
YOUNG, S. S.: 5252
YOUNG, Stark: 3797, 5971
YOUNG, Thomas John: 3666
YOUNG, Mrs. Thomas John: 3666
YOUNG, W. B.: 4834
YOUNG, William Henry (1817-1904): 5972
YOUNG, William W.: 5965
YOUNG, William Wesley (b. 1868): 2790
YOUNG LADIES' INSTITUTE, Charlottesville, Virginia: 4915
YOUNG MEN'S CHRISTIAN ASSOCIATION:
  North Carolina--Hillsborough: 5973
  Virginia--Luray: 574
  World War I: 1424
    France: 4743
YOUNG PEOPLE'S CONFERENCE: 5298
YOUNG PEOPLE'S SERVICE LEAGUE (North Carolina): 5298
YOUNG PEOPLE'S SOCIALIST LEAGUE: 4948
YOUNG WOMEN FRIENDS' CHRISTIAN UNION (Great Britain): 1903
YOUNG WOMEN'S CHRISTIAN ASSOCIATION: 1361
YOUNGLOVE, Timothy M.: 5974
YOUNGMAN, Isaac B.: 5975
YOUNGSTOWN, Ohio: 3085
YOUNGSVILLE, North Carolina: 5087
YOUNT, John: 5976
YOUNT, Peter L.: 5976
YOUNT FAMILY (North Carolina): 5976
YOUTH--Social activities: 2616
YOUTH ORGANIZATIONS:
  see also BOY SCOUT MOVEMENT; YOUNG MEN'S CHRISTIAN ASSOCIATION; YOUNG WOMEN'S CHRISTIAN ASSOCIATION
  North Carolina: 5298
  United States: 4948
YOUTH'S COMPANION: 706
YUAN SHI-K'AI: 5252
YUBA COUNTY, California:
  Marysville: 1221
YUGOSLAVIA:
  Relations with Russia: 83
YUI, K. L.: 5252
YUILLE, Gavin: 5977
YUILLE, Gavin B.: 5977
YUILLE, William S.: 5977
YULEE, David Levy: 1403, 4881, 5978
YURKA, Blanche: 3306
YURKA, Rose: 3306
ZAGHOUAN, Tunisia:
  Antiquities: 3460
ZAGHWAN, Tunisia: see ZAGHOUAN, Tunisia
ZAMBEZI RIVER:
  Description and travel: 5725
ZANESVILLE, Ohio: 357
ZANGA: 188
ZANZIBAR:
  Economic conditions: 5725
  French activities: 5725
  Slave trade: 5725
  Slavery: 67
  Social life and customs: 5725
ZEA, Edward: 5979

ZEA (F. M.) AND COMPANY, Strasburg, Virginia: 5979
ZEHRING, Samuel: 5980
ZEIDLER, Frank P.: 4947
ZELL FERTILIZER COMPANY: 4344
ZELLAR, David: 5981
ZELLAR, Jacob: 5981
ZELLER, Alice (Bryant): 731
ZEMAUN SHAH: 3315
ZEVELY, Alexander: 5982
ZEVELY, Augustus: 5982
ZEVELY, Edmund S.: 5982
ZEVELY, Sophia: 5982
ZIMMERMAN, Adaline (Spease): 5984
ZIMMERMAN, E. R.: 5983
ZIMMERMAN, James C.: 5984
ZIMMERMAN, John R.: 5985
ZIMMERMAN, Joseph: 3751
ZIMMERMAN, Joshua S.: 3721
ZIMMERMAN, Laura: 3124
ZIMMERMANN, Arthur: 4556
ZIMMERMANN TELEGRAM (1917): 4556
ZINC MINING:
  North Carolina:
    Davidson County: 2041
  Stocks--Virginia: 4157
ZION-PARNASSUS, Thyatira, North Carolina: 3334
ZION PROTESTANT EPISCOPAL CHURCH, Charles Town, West Virginia: 128
ZIONISM: 1766, 2811
ZION'S CHURCH (North Carolina): 1232
ZITTERAUER, Ernst Christian: 5986
ZITTERAUER, Richard Ernst: 5986
ZOLLICOFFER, Felix Kirk: 872, 4032
ZOLLICOFFER, Jerome B.: 1363
ZOOLOGICAL EXPEDITIONS:
  Brazil: 4876
  China: 5225
  France: 4022
  Spain: 4022
  Tangier: 4022
ZOOLOGICAL ILLUSTRATION:
  Great Britain: 3577
  United States: 404
ZOOLOGY: 2106
  see also NATURAL HISTORY
  Classification--Great Britain: 3577
ZOSIMUS (Saint): 4045
ZUBLY, John Joachim: 5987
ZULU WAR: see GREAT BRITAIN--ARMY--South Africa--Zulu War
ZULUS: 1792